The Bill James Handbook 2018

Baseball Info Solutions

www.baseballinfosolutions.com

Published by ACTA Sports

A Division of ACTA Publications

Cover Design by Tom A. Wright
Front Cover Photo by Gary A. Vasquez, USA TODAY Sports
Back Cover Photo by Adam Hunger, USA TODAY Sports

First Edition: November 2017

Published by:
ACTA Sports, a division of ACTA Publications
4848 North Clark Street
Chicago, IL 60640
(800) 397-2282
www.actasports.com www.actapublications.com

ISBN: 978-0-87946-590-2
ISSN: 1940-8668

Printed in the United States of America by McNaughton & Gunn

Dedication

This book is dedicated to the 2013 Windsor Lancers baseball team for setting world records for most candy and corn nuts consumed by a single bullpen, and making the pursuit of a club team championship better than winning the World Series itself.

I also want to extend my thanks to all the video scouts for their tireless work of logging every possible data point under the sun of the entire 2017 major and minor league seasons. If it were easy, everyone would do it. My job wouldn't exist without you.

Finally, acknowledgements are due to any developer out there who has created a robust, well-documented code library that I have been able to slam my code into in order to look a lot smarter and more capable than I actually am. So far, no one seems to be the wiser.

Ben Stanczak

Table of Contents

Introduction

Stop. You have the wrong book.

If you're looking for a book by the mystery author Bill James, you've got the wrong guy. If you're looking for the psychologist William James, you've got the wrong century, though I suppose his books are still floating around in certain college libraries. If you're looking for the true crime author Bill James, you have the right guy (!) and the correct publication year (!), but you're in the wrong section. You're looking for *The Man From the Train*. Turn around, make a left and go down four aisles towards the checkout counter, just before you get to the SAT prep section. You can't miss it.

But, if you saw the baseball player on the cover and still opened this 600+ page behemoth, congratulations! You're in the right place. Welcome to the 29th edition of The Bill James Handbook!

If you're a rookie Handbook reader, we're thrilled to have you. If you've been with us for at least one of the previous 28 books, welcome back! We hope you like the injuries article, the Hard Hit Balls data, and Bill's new Hall of Fame Monitor section. After all, he did literally write the book on the statistical standards for admission to Cooperstown.

Whether you're new to baseball or a life-long fan, the 2017 Major League season was fun to watch. We saw more home runs, more 22-game winning streaks, and more baseball than ever before in just about every way you can count it. We saw more pitches than ever before and more pitchers than ever before, which might have something to do with the aforementioned home run record. We set a league swinging strikes record for the seventh consecutive year. We saw four home runs in a game by the same player, twice. We saw records broken related to rookie home runs (thanks to front and back cover players Cody Bellinger and Aaron Judge), pinch-hit at bats in a season (Ichiro Suzuki, Pinch Hitting on page 449), career doubles plays grounded into (Albert Pujols, Register on page 85), and times reached on catcher's interference in a career (Jacoby Ellsbury, Register on page 85).

Don't you just love it?

Ben Jedlovec
October 13, 2017

The New Hall of Fame Monitor

Bill James

In last year's version of this book, I promised that I would revise and update the Hall of Fame Monitor. There were some problems with it, the largest of which had to do with relievers. When I originally invented the system in the early 1980s, late 1970s, whenever it was, modern relief pitching was in its adolescence. The only reliever in the Hall of Fame at that time was Hoyt Wilhelm. It was impossible to say what the standards would be for a Hall of Fame reliever. It's a general problem. We think about Hall of Famers significantly differently now than we did in the 1970s. It's a different world. Although the system always "worked" at a certain level, I felt it was time to take a fresh look at the issue.

The Hall of Fame monitor is not intended to tell you who SHOULD be in the Hall of Fame. Who should be in the Hall of Fame is a question for Hall of Fame voters. This is not a value system; it is a tracking system.

There are certain accomplishments that are vastly more common among Hall of Fame players than among non-Hall of Famers. Between 1920 and 1980 there were 5,434 seasons in which a player had 500 plate appearances—1,117 by players now in the Hall of Fame, and 4,317 by players not now in the Hall of Fame. The Hall of Famers had 200 hits in 15% of their seasons (164 of 1,117). The non-Hall of Famers had 200 hits in 3.5% of their seasons (151 of 4,317). A 200-hit season was more than four times as common in the Hall of Fame population as in the non-Hall of Fame population.

We can thus say that when a player gets 200 hits in a season, he has done something characteristic of a Hall of Fame career. If a player drives in 100 runs in a season, that's characteristic of a Hall of Fame career. If he hits .300 as a regular, if he hits 30 home runs, if he leads the league in batting average or stolen bases, all of these things are characteristic of a Hall of Fame career at different levels.

It is not about my opinion, you understand. While both were great players, it is my own conclusion that Dwight Evans was a greater player than Jim Rice—but the fact is that Rice did far more things that are characteristic of a Hall of Fame career than did Evans. Rice had 135 points on the Hall of Fame monitor; Evans had 75, and Rice was the one selected for immortality. Catfish Hunter and Luis Tiant had careers which were in many respects closely parallel, with essentially the same numbers of starts, innings, wins and the same ERA, in the same leagues in the same years. I believe that Tiant, on close study, had a better career than Catfish—but the fact is that Hunter did more things that were characteristic of a Hall of Fame career. Catfish leads 128 to 98 on the Hall of Fame monitor, and Catfish in fact is in the Hall of Fame, while Tiant is not. I think that Buddy Bell was a heck of a player, that he could reasonably be in the Hall of Fame—but he has only 48 points on the Hall of Fame Monitor, and was dropped from the Hall of Fame ballot after a few years.

We are simply trying to track the progress that each player is making toward the Hall of Fame. In this system (as in the old one) the range of 70 to 130 is a gray area. In general, if a player has more than 100 points in the Hall of Fame monitor by the end of his career, he probably will be selected to the Hall of Fame. If he has less than 100 points, he probably will not be. However, some players in the range of 70 to 99 points are selected for Cooperstown, while some players with 100 to 130 points are not selected, and we are not in any way arguing about that. We're not trying to say who SHOULD be in the Hall of Fame. We are just noting that it is a minor anomaly in the voting, which is probably best explained as a flaw in our system.

We will start our charts with catchers, and we will include 1) any Hall of Famer who started his career in 1961 or later, 2) any player not in the Hall of Fame who had 70 or more points in the Hall of Fame monitor, 3) anyone recently retired with 50 or more points, and 4) those active players who are above a certain age/score standard. There are 13 catchers who meet one of these standards:

AGE	Johnny Bench	Ivan Rodriguez	Mike Piazza	Gary Carter	Carlton Fisk	Joe Mauer	Ted Simmons	Thurman Munson	Yadier Molina	Buster Posey	Bill Freehan	Jorge Posada	Salvador Perez
18							0						
19	0	0					0				0		
20	8	4		0			0				0		
21	20	12		1	0	0	4		0		0		0
22	52	20		1	0	1	10	0	1	0	5		0
23	61	30	0	8	0	10	15	6	5	8	9	0	5
24	92	45	14	11	9	11	19	8	5	8	17	0	15
25	104	57	22	15	15	25	28	9	11	34	27	0	27
26	125	72	32	25	15	50	31	18	19	37	41	3	35
27	144	98	44	33	16	66	39	26	27	48	49	7	37
28	156	106	64	47	18	66	50	41	38	59	54	15	
29	171	118	80	53	34	73	55	60	48	70	62	18	
30	175	121	97	66	43	81	63	73	62	74	67	26	
31	179	127	109	75	43	83	64	79	66		68	35	
32	184	140	123	87	51	84	68	81	70		70	38	
33	184	142	130	93	55	85	81		74		72	41	
34	184	154	130	99	60	89	82		76		72	43	
35	185	162	135	99	66		83					51	
36		165	140	99	67		83					51	
37		167	144	100	79		83					56	
38		168	144	100	80		83					58	
39		168			83							58	
40					83								
41					85								
42					87								
43					89								
44					89								
45					89								
						Active			Active	Active			Active
Final	185	168	144	100	89		83	81			72	58	

As you can see, if that chart makes sense to you:

1) Johnny Bench, an MVP at age 22 and again at age 24, had pretty much locked up a Cooperstown plaque by the time he was in his mid-twenties,

2) No active catcher seems likely to meet the standard of Bench or Ivan Rodriguez,

3) Joe Mauer was doing extremely well through age 30, but has not done much to help himself the last four years. Mauer and Yadi Molina are about the

same age.   Mauer at one point was far ahead of Molina as a Hall of Fame candidate, leading him 66 to 27 through age 27 (2010), but Molina has largely caught up.

4) Four active catchers could be described as viable Hall of Fame candidates at this point: Mauer, Molina, Posey and Salvador Perez.   Of those four, Buster Posey is probably the strongest candidate.

5) Among recently retired catchers Jorge Posada is the strongest Hall of Fame candidate.   However, Posada almost certainly fell short of a Hall of Fame standard, unless those standards change in the future.

Career values for other players not listed here: Lance Parrish, 55; Bob Boone, 44; Benito Santiago, 43; Jason Kendall, 42; A. J. Pierzynski, 33; Darrell Porter, 33; Jim Sundberg, 33; Javier Lopez, 32; Brian McCann, 31; Jason Varitek, 29; Russell Martin, 24.   Victor Martinez, we will discuss as a Designated Hitter.

At first base we have a larger field of candidates.   Whereas at catcher the two big dogs—Bench and Pudge—are players who are already retired and in the Hall of Fame, at first base the two best players of the expansion era, Pujols and Cabrera, are both still active.   At this time, Pujols and Cabrera rank as the 16th and 26th highest-scoring Hall of Fame candidates of all time, at any position. First let us chart the players who probably ARE Hall-of-Fame Qualified at the present time:

Age	Albert Pujols	Miguel Cabrera	Mark McGwire	Todd Helton	Steve Garvey	Jeff Bagwell	Dick Allen	Rafael Palmeiro	Eddie Murray	Don Mattingly	Jim Thome
33	214	188	87	119	114	111	118	68	91	102	90
34	222	189	109	119	115	114	118	85	98	103	90
35	230		131	124	121	120	118	95	101		97
36	234		132	124	126	122		103	104		102
37	237		132	126	129	122		111	107		104
38				126	129			117	107		104
39				128				118	115		104
40								123	118		104
41									118		104
	Active	Active									
Final			132	128	129	122	118	123	118	103	104

Mark McGwire's candidacy has been much discussed. A reader could look at the number I have for him—132 points—and say that history has proven this to be a wrong evaluation of how the voters will think about Mark McGwire, since we have him just ABOVE the gray area. But here's the thing: History is still happening. Johnny Mize, with a score of 166, was not elected until 28 years after his retirement. Chuck Klein, with a score of 138, was not elected until 36 years after his retirement. Goose Goslin, with a score of 143, was not elected until 30 years after his retirement. The system was wrong until it was right. I try to manage the system so that it is right at the end of the day.

People get hung up on what the Hall of Fame's eligibility rules are and what their election practices are and where a player is NOW in that structure, but (a) I wrote 25 years ago that the Hall of Fame changes its rules more often than a hooker changes her underwear, and (b) the election system has been thoroughly re-invented several times since I wrote that. The Hall of Fame revises its rules constantly due to pressure from its various constituency groups—fans, players, sportswriters, the commissioner's office. The pressures are much more durable than the rules.

This is what I think will happen. Over time, the argument about McG-wire will focus on two issues: (1) was he doing anything that a lot of other players were not doing, and (2) was he really a bad guy? But he not only was not a bad guy, he was a great guy, and he wasn't doing anything that a hundred other players were not also doing. Those issues will be resolved in his favor, and the sports-writers who were 10-year-old boys in 1998 will soon be the 45-year-old leaders of the sports writing industry. When those things happen, he's going to be elected.

In designing this new system, I adjusted downward the batting stats of the steroid era, counting a 40-homer season as a 30-homer season and a .900 OPS as an .800 OPS, etc. I think it is clear that those adjustments have to be made, and history has not yet given us a full picture of how much the voters will discount the steroid era numbers, over time. I could be over-adjusting; I could be adjusting not enough. We'll see. In another 40 years I will be 108, so it will be somebody else's problem.

Todd Helton is not yet on the ballot. Helton's numbers are inflated both by the era and by playing in the greatest hitter's park of the last hundred years. It is my opinion that, even when you let all of the air out of his numbers, he remains a Hall of Fame caliber player.   But we'll see how the voters feel about it.

I think that it is a safe statement to say that, while he was active, Steve Garvey was regarded as a Hall of Fame player.   I never liked Garvey, as a player; I always felt, and I wrote every year, that he was not all he was cranked up to be. After he retired he had some personal conduct/public relations issues which changed him from a player with a positive public image to an ex-player with a negative public image.   He started at 42% in the voting—far higher than most Hall of Fame members start—but went steadily downward.

But while I never liked Garvey and would not advocate for his selection, he did have the skills that the Hall of Fame has usually preferred—and he was a good player.   In my opinion, he was right on the edge of being a deserving Hall of Famer.   Garvey and Dave Parker, to me, are the Hall of Fame's chalk line.   They are the guys who are right on the line.   There are a lot of players who have been selected who were less deserving.

Dick Allen had Hall of Fame skills but personal conduct issues which damaged his teams; I wouldn't vote for him but I acknowledge that his numbers do meet the standard.   Palmeiro was a steroid case without the overpowering numbers of a Barry Bonds or the public impact of Mark McGwire.   Time is on his side.   Memories rot; statistics endure.   Don Mattingly is like Joe Torre: it's a little hard to figure why he wasn't elected just as a player, but perhaps his post-playing career will get him elected.

There have been a large number of first baseman in the Expansion era who have taken a run at a Hall of Fame career but pulled up short.   By my count there are at least 11 of those:

Mark Teixeira	97	Ryan Howard	84
Jason Giambi	90	Will Clark	83
Fred McGriff	90	Andres Galarraga	82
Carlos Delgado	88	Cecil Cooper	76
Keith Hernandez	87	Cecil Fielder	56
Lance Berkman	87		

In addition to Pujols and Cabrera, who have booked their reservations for Cooperstown, there are seven active first basemen who have some chance to push their credentials up to a Hall of Fame level: Adrian Gonzalez, Joey Votto, Paul Goldschmidt, Chris Davis, Anthony Rizzo, Freddie Freeman and Eric Hosmer.

Age	Tony Perez	Adrian Gonzalez	Joey Votto	Paul Goldschmidt	Chris Davis	Anthony Rizzo	Freddie Freeman	Eric Hosmer
27	15	19	37	43	25	44	33	32
29	35	48	56	58	39			
30	38	54	57		41			
31	47	58	64		43			
32	51	68	72					
33	59	71	84					
35	65	74						
44	75							
Final	75	Active	Active	Active	Active	Active	Active	Active

None of those active players is a Hall of Famer now; they all have work to do. Mostly they have a LOT of work to do.   But they're in the hunt. These totals printed above, by the way, do not include the credit the player may earn for helping his team win the World Series in 2017.   We go to press in mid-October.   We don't yet know who will win the World Series, although you will know that when you read this.   Whoever wins, that helps the Hall of Fame case of their biggest stars.   Also, post-season awards help a player's Hall of Fame case; it is easy to demonstrate that winning those awards has an impact on future voting.   We have to write the book under the handicap of not officially knowing that Aaron Judge will be the American League Rookie of the Year, and of actually not knowing whether Judge or Altuve will win the MVP Award.

No disrespect to Tony Perez, but he really does not have the batting record one usually expects of a Hall of Fame first baseman.   Perez' career OPS, .804, is very low for a Hall of Fame first baseman.   It is lower than Bill White (.806), Kevin Millar (.810), Bob Watson (.811), Sean Casey (.814), Tino Martinez (.815), Keith Hernandez (.821), Joe Adcock (.822), Boog Powell (.822), Mark Grace (.825), Cecil Fielder (.827), Roy Sievers (.829), Gil Hodges (.846), Kent Hrbek (.848), Ted Kluszewski (.850), Derrek Lee (.859), Norm Cash (.862), or John Olerud (.863), and none of them are in the Hall of Fame.   The eleven first basemen in the Mark Teixeira/Prince Fielder chart above all have higher OPS than Perez except Cecil Cooper, who is one point below him.   Perez hit .300 only twice as a regular, and hit 30 home runs only twice—as opposed to Ted Kluszewski, who hit .300 with 35 homers four straight seasons, or Cecil Cooper, who hit .300 seven times and also hit 30 homers twice.

Several good things happened for Tony Perez. He was a key member of a great team, which helped his visibility. He had a long career. He was very well liked. And then there is this: Nature abhors a vacuum. There were three Hall of Fame first basemen who came along almost at the same time in the late 1950s—McCovey, Cepeda, Killebrew. After them, there is not another obvious Hall of Fame first baseman until Eddie Murray in the late 1970s Nature abhors a vacuum. When the field gets crowded, somebody gets pushed out; when the field is empty, somebody gets pushed in. He has marginal Hall of Fame credentials.

Hall of Fame Monitor scores for other notable first basemen of the last 50 years: Mo Vaughn, 75; Boog Powell, 66: John Olerud, 62; Mark Grace, 57; Paul Konerko, 57; Cecil Fielder, 56; Pedro Guerrero, 55; George Scott, 52; Derrek Lee, 52; Tino Martinez, 51; Dave Kingman, 46; Bill Buckner, 50; Bob Watson, 42; Lee May, 41; Wally Joyner, 40; Justin Morneau, 39. Jose Abreu has 35 points in just four seasons, although since he started late, he does not meet the age/progress standard to be included in the charts above.

There are five Hall of Fame second basemen who have come to the majors since 1961: Rod Carew, Roberto Alomar, Ryne Sandberg, Joe Morgan and Craig Biggio. Robinson Cano will be the sixth:

Age	Rod Carew	Roberto Alomar	Ryne Sandberg	Joe Morgan	Craig Biggio	Robinson Cano
25	30	60	51	11	4	12
30	104	110	118	62	46	103
34	157	164	156	140	90	130
36	168	165	159	143	96	
39	186			147	107	
40				149	108	
41					114	
						Active
Final	186	165	159	149	114	

Carew actually played a few more games at first base than at second. For what it is worth, I would emphasize that I believe that Joe Morgan was the greatest player of these six. The Hall of Fame monitor is more impressed with others, because the Hall of Fame monitor mimics group thinking, and group thinking tends to miss some fine points. But there is no doubt that all six of these are legitimate Hall of Famers.

In addition to Cano, there are five active second basemen who plausibly could be Hall of Famers based on their records to this point in their careers: Dustin Pedroia, Chase Utley, Jose Altuve, Dee Gordon and Jose Ramirez:

Age	Dustin Pedroia	Chase Utley	Jose Altuve	Dee Gordon	Jose Ramirez
25	41	0	39		16
27	53	25	77	23	
29	70	55		34	
33	85	70			
38		79			

Altuve and Pedroia are the strongest Hall of Fame candidates in the group. In addition to those, there have been eleven second basemen in the expansion era who have taken a run at a Hall of Fame career, but who ultimately fell short, or probably fell short.

Jeff Kent	94	Davey Lopes	54
Michael Young	88	Bobby Grich	54
Lou Whitaker	65	Willie Randolph. . .	54
Chuck Knoblauch . .	64	Steve Sax	53
Bret Boone	61	Frank White	48
Luis Castillo	55		

Bobby Grich, like Dwight Evans, was a great player who just did not do the things that a Hall of Fame voter likes to see. Third base. There are three Hall of Fame third basemen who have come to the major leagues since 1961: Mike Schmidt, George Brett and Wade Boggs. Chipper Jones will probably join them in 2018, we believe, and Adrian Beltre, still active, appears to be Hall-of-Fame validated. There are three active third basemen in mid-career who have played at a Hall of Fame level during portions of their careers and who have some chance to make the cut (David Wright, Donaldson and Longoria), and there are three young third basemen who have shown Hall of Fame promise:

Age	Mike Schmidt	George Brett	Wade Boggs	Chipper Jones	Adrian Beltre	David Wright	Josh Donaldson	Evan Longoria	Nolan Arenado	Kris Bryant	Manny Machado
24	11	38	0	24	5	33		26	23	29	27
25	19	45	13	35	21	45	0	30	41	35	
26	32	67	22	55	23	52	0	30	54		
31	116	118	107	97	42	78	46	44			
33	149	141	126	100	74	79					
38	216	168	168	129	110						
39	216	174	168	129							
41			173								
					Active	Active	Active	Active	Active		Active
Total	216	176	173	129		Active		Active		Active	

Through the age of 30 (2009) Adrian Beltre had only 32 points on the Hall of Fame meter, while the previous four Hall of Fame third basemen (Schmidt, Brett, Boggs and Chipper) had 92, 114, 91 and 95 at the same age. Beltre trailed them all by at least 91 to 32—but he has had a Hall of Fame career in his thirties. Other third basemen who have made a good run since 1961:

Scott Rolen	82	Darrell Evans	51
Aramis Ramirez	67	Graig Nettles	51
Bobby Bonilla	64	Terry Pendleton	50
Matt Williams	60	Buddy Bell	48
Vinny Castilla	54	Bill Madlock	47

There are four shortstops who have come to the majors since 1961 and who are now in the Hall of Fame (Yount, Ozzie Smith, Ripken and Barry Larkin) and there are two recent retirees who have what would appear to be overwhelming credentials for Hall of Fame selection, those being Derek Jeter and Alex Rodriguez:

Age	Alex Rodriguez	Cal Ripken	Derek Jeter	Robin Yount	Ozzie Smith	Barry Larkin
25	109	70	45	16	8	3
30	213	130	91	78	44	31
35	273	169	163	114	97	81
37	274	179	180	122	116	88
40	283	195	197		121	89
41					121	
Total	283	195	197	122	121	89

A-Rod, like Trout, Pujols and Bench, had his Hall of Fame position pretty well nailed down by his mid-twenties. Ripken was Hall-of-Fame good by about age 29, Jeter by about age 31, Robin Yount by 33 and Ozzie Smith not until age 36. Larkin was never a Hall of Fame lock; he was on the bubble and he made it, which I am not in any way criticizing or second-guessing; I assume the voters are smarter than my statistical imitation of how they think.

There are at least nine shortstops who played in 2016 or 2017 and who have some chance to have Hall of Fame credentials. Three of those are veteran players—Jimmy Rollins, Jose Reyes and Troy Tulowitzki—but the bulk of them are players who are too young to be regarded as serious Hall of Fame candidates (Xander Bogaerts, Jean Segura, Corey Seager, Francisco Lindor, Addison Russell, Carlos Correa.) We have to remember: most Hall of Fame candidates will fall short, and this is particularly true at shortstop, where players come up young because defensive skills peak much earlier than offensive skills. In their time Zoilo Versalles, Jim Fregosi, Edgar Renteria and Garry Templeton looked like the sky was the limit for them.

Age	Jimmy Rollins	Jose Reyes	Troy Tulowitzki	Xander Bogaerts	Jean Segura	Corey Seager	Francisco Lindor	Addison Russell	Carlos Correa
23	14	19	4	17	3	16	20	10	11
24	17	32	11	19	4				
27	35	47	42		22				
30	77	63	59						
32	79	66	60						
34	87	68							
37	89								

Among retired players who may have fallen short, Miguel Tejada and Nomar Garciaparra may have been the strongest candidates:

Miguel Tejada	93	Edgar Renteria	65
Nomar Garciaparra	83	Julio Franco	59
Omar Vizquel	72	Tony Fernandez	53
Alan Trammell	70	Jay Bell	44
Bert Campaneris	68	Larry Bowa	44
Dave Concepcion	65	Rafael Furcal	40

I would not be shocked if Tejada or Vizquel beat the system and was elected. People like to say "If Ozzie Smith makes the Hall of Fame, why doesn't Omar Vizquel?", and then they will say that the two players are just the same. Well. . . Ozzie won thirteen Gold Gloves; Omar won eleven. Ozzie was the starting shortstop in the All Star game eleven times; Omar never was. Ozzie played in 21 World Series games; Omar, in 13. Ozzie was the starting shortstop on a World Championship team (1982); Omar was not. Ozzie stole 50 bases in a season twice, and 580 in his career; Omar stole a lot of bases, but never 50 in a season, and 404 in his career. You're welcome to see it the way you see it, but if you don't have big hitting numbers those are the things that put you in the Hall of Fame.

There are six Hall of Fame left fielders who came to the majors since 1961. They break down as three American Leaguers, three National Leaguers, three power hitters, three leadoff men, three players who came up in the early sixties, and three players who debuted in the seventies.

Age	Carl Yastrzemski			Jim Rice	Rickey Henderson	
	Lou Brock					Tim Raines
		Willie Stargell				
25	25	16	10	60	48	55
30	108	60	34	107	119	84
35	132	108	95	135	164	95
36	137	118	95	135	166	95
40	162	130	110		180	99
43	163				186	
44					186	
Total	163	130	110	135	186	99

And now we get into some interesting and borderline screwy cases. There appear to be only two active left fielders who have a big chance at a Hall of Fame ceremony.   Both are veterans; both are career .300 hitters with 300+ home runs, and they score by the formula at 97 and 92 points, meaning that both of them are close to 50/50 shots for the Hall of Fame: Ryan Braun and Matt Holliday.

But Braun, of course, has an issue that may trouble the voters. Holliday had some big numbers in Coors Field at the tag end of the steroid era, but still, he proved his merit after leaving Colorado and after the numbers went back to historic norms, so I'll buy the idea that he is. . .not a strong Hall of Fame candidate, but a reasonable one.   Braun, I'm skeptical.

Then we get into the recently retired candidates, where the numbers continue to be screwy.

Ryan Braun	97		
Matt Holliday	92		
Barry Bonds	267	Greg Luzinski	68
Manny Ramirez	169	Carl Crawford	56
George Foster	100	Garrett Anderson . .	55
Albert Belle	93	Vince Coleman	52
Alfonso Soriano . . .	87	Moises Alou	51
Luis Gonzalez	73		

(1) Bonds, of course, is the defining test case in a long-running debate. The Hall of Fame monitor only states what is obvious anyway, which is that he is a highly qualified Hall of Fame player based strictly on his statistics.

(2) Manny Ramirez is an even harder case than Bonds.   He opened the ballot at 24% despite driving in about the same number of runs in his career as Carl Yastrzemski and Ted Williams.   I don't have any idea how the special issues regarding Manny will sort themselves out over the years, and I am not trying to tell Hall of Fame voters how they should think about exceptional cases.   I am glad it isn't my problem.

(3) George Foster. . .well, that IS my problem in a sense.   I think there should be some way to write the formulas so that George Foster doesn't show up as a Hall of Fame tossup, but if there is such a way I haven't found it yet.

In some respects, George Foster is a close parallel to Don Mattingly, who also shows up in the Hall of Fame monitor as a player who COULD have been elected. Both Foster and Mattingly were quite certainly Hall of Fame caliber players for a period of four years, Foster from 1976 to 1979 and Mattingly from 1984 to 1987. Both were RBI men—the best RBI men in baseball in their prime years. Foster in his four-year run finished 2nd, 1st, 6th and 12th in the MVP voting; Mattingly finished 5th, 1st, 2nd and 7th. However, both Foster and Mattingly had shorter-than-normal periods as dominant players, and both then played on for several years as average or below-average players. Both retired short of 2,000 career games played, and short of the statistical markers which would have guaranteed their enshrinement.

Foster in the second half of his career became an unpopular player. He signed a big-money contract with the Mets, didn't earn his money and didn't seem to many fans to be trying to earn his money. A good defensive outfielder early in his career, he became an absolutely awful defensive outfielder with the Mets, and—like Jay Bruce—he just wasn't accepted by the Mets' fans. He never got to 10% in Hall of Fame voting.

Mattingly, a very well-liked player, always enjoyed a good reputation even after he could no longer play well. He started at 28% in the voting but went steadily backward until his vote totals were similar to Foster's. Neither player got close to selection.

But I wouldn't bet a lot of money that they won't eventually be picked up by a committee. Players who are dominant for a short period of time, historically, have often been decisively rejected by the BBWAA voters, but then elected by a committee many years later. That happened to Chuck Klein, Hack Wilson, Hal Newhouser, Jim Bottomley, Earle Combs, and others.

In center field, I think we can put all of our main players in one chart. We have, in center field:

(a) Three Hall of Famers who have come along since 1961,

(b) One player who appears to have Hall of Fame credentials but who for some reason has not been selected,

(c) One active player who appears to have completed his Hall of Fame assignments, and

(d) Four active players who have some sort of Hall of Fame resume that they are working on, but who still have work to do.

Age	Ken Griffey Jr.	Kirby Puckett	Andre Dawson	Dale Murphy	Carlos Beltran	Mike Trout	Andrew McCutchen	Adam Jones	Curtis Granderson
25	72	3	16	6	17	95	16	5	2
30	163	72	56	99	60		54	39	39
31	163	100	59	112	69			41	53
34	166	126	99	115	80				58
36	172		119	117	97				63
37	179		122	117	97				
40	180		124		108				
41			124						
						Active	Active		Active
Total	180	126	124	117	Active			Active	

Jacoby Ellsbury and Matt Kemp were over the line where we would consider them Hall of Fame candidates until they were about 30, but have dropped below the line now. Adam Jones could have been considered a candidate a couple of years ago, but probably not now. Charlie Blackmon picked up a bunch of points last year, ignoring the whole Coors Field problem, but is 31 years old and had almost nothing before last year, so he's not really a candidate. Marcell Ozuna is like that, too; he had a big year in 2017, but is not at this time on a Hall of Fame schedule.

Dale Murphy was a little like Mattingly and Foster, in that his greatness left him in mid-career and he played on for several years as just another player. Carlos Beltran isn't an overwhelmingly qualified Hall of Famer, but does appear to me to be above the line, probably. Carlos plays on into 2017 as a relic of 20th century baseball. The Kansas Royals in 1999-2000 had an outfield of Johnny Damon, Carlos Beltran and Jermaine Dye. Damon was then 25 and 26, Beltran was 22 and 23, Jermaine Dye was 24 and 25. It's actually the best young outfield in baseball history. No one else has ever had three young outfielders with careers ahead of them as good as those three, although there is an argument for the Red Sox of the mid-seventies.

Kenny Lofton and Bernie Williams are the best of the players who took a run at a Hall of Fame career but ultimately fell short, probably. . .I have sixteen of those:

Kenny Lofton	95	Juan Pierre	62
Bernie Williams	94	Reggie Smith	61
Fred Lynn	86	Willie McGee	60
Al Oliver	78	Andruw Jones	57
Jim Edmonds	77	Cesar Cedeno	56
Johnny Damon	70	Marquis Grissom	52
Josh Hamilton	69	Jimmy Wynn	52
Willie Wilson	64	Bobby Murcer	50

Some of these are players that I personally would support for Hall of Fame selection, but that's another book; I'll get to THAT book in a couple of years if I stay healthy. Andruw Jones will be new on the Hall of Fame ballot this year, and I know that there are people who think he has a Hall of Fame case. I don't see it, myself, but then, that's up to the voters.

Jim Edmonds dropped off the ballot after one year. That's a part of the process that still needs to be fixed, or needs to be fixed again. A player as good as Edmonds should not drop off the ballot after one vote. There is a Hall of Fame case to be made for Edmonds. He shouldn't slip through the cracks because there is ONE vote when not enough voters focus on what he has accomplished. There should be a "re-nomination" process in which a committee can say "David Eckstein has dropped off the ballot, that's OK, but we think the voters should be given a few more chances to consider Jim Edmonds."

In right field we have, again, three Hall of Famers (Reggie, Gwynn and Dave Winfield) who have come to the majors since 1961, which seems like the usual number, and one active player who is a FQHOF (Fully Qualified Hall of Famer). Then we have four active players who have done enough that the Hall of Fame would be following their flight paths, those four being Jose Bautista, Bryce Harper, Giancarlo Stanton and Mookie Betts:

Age	Reggie Jackson	Tony Gwynn	Dave Winfield	Ichiro Suzuki	Jose Bautista	Bryce Harper	Giancarlo Stanton	Mookie Betts
24	19	17	3		0	43	26	32
27	59	57	30	28	1		42	
30	89	85	48	68	33			
35	140	127	106	134	71			
36	154	133	119	147	72			
40	166	164	134	153				
41	166	164	140	153				
43			140	158				
				Active		Active		Active
Total	166	164	140		Active		Active	

Ordinarily we start out with a good number of candidates, but as they age they mostly disappear. Nelson Cruz is an odd case of a player who didn't emerge as a star until he was well past thirty, but who may yet become a Hall of Fame candidate. Cruz is actually older than Jose Bautista (above), and whereas Bautista has 72 points, Cruz has only 62, but whereas Bautista appears to be done, Cruz is still putting up markers every year. In right field we have SIX retired players who are not in the Hall of Fame although they have what are traditionally Hall of Fame numbers, far more than at any other position. Those are:

Vladimir Guerrero . .	156	Dave Parker	117
Sammy Sosa	134	Juan Gonzalez	110
Larry Walker	118	Gary Sheffield	103

Five of those six players who have been passed over for the Hall of Fame (so far) are steroid-era players. They'll sort themselves out over time. Vladimir, I would think, will be elected in a year or two. I marked the steroid era in my data as 1994 to 2009, based on the number of runs scored per game in those years. I know that steroids were banned in 2005, but steroids build muscle. Muscles don't disappear when you stop using the steroids. The number of runs scored per game remained above historic norms until 2009.

We're dealing with a complex phenomenon here—too complicated to be perfectly sorted out by my simple Hall of Fame prediction system. There were other things, other than steroids, that caused a lot of runs to be scored in that era. Sportswriters are, on the one hand (1) discounting the numbers for the fact that the statistics are outside of historical norms, and (2) punishing the steroid users for violating the rules, or what sportswriters imagine to have been the rightful rules. I know that some of these players were accused of using steroids, but I don't actually know which ones; I can never keep track of all of that. Some of these players eventually will be elected to the Hall of Fame; some won't.

Dave Parker is not from the steroid era, but he has similar issues. In my view, it is not wrong for sportswriters to make selections based on off-field considerations. The Hall of Fame is an honor; it is not a paycheck. It's based on respect and admiration for the player as well as on-field accomplishments. If a player didn't respect the game, maybe he is not entitled to respect, I don't know. I am trying to predict as best I can how the process will view each player, but the process is more complicated than the best mathematical model of it that I can build. I hope everybody understands that I'm not trying to pass judgment on the decisions of others.

Beyond that there are two issues with these six players. When there are a large group of qualified players at a position, it takes time for the Hall of Fame to honor all of those who should be honored. In essence, they have to line up and wait their turn. Second, the balancing of hitting and fielding value has been complicated by the rapid evolution of fielding metrics. It is my opinion that the people who are creating WAR numbers by combining hitting and fielding statistics don't quite know what they are doing, and don't really have the proportions right. Over time these evaluations may change as a better understanding develops. We'll see.

In addition to these players, there are fifteen other right fielders coming to the majors since 1961 who made a good run at the Hall of Fame, but probably fell short. Those fifteen are:

Tony Oliva	88	Dante Bichette	65
Jose Canseco	83	Paul O'Neill	64
Bobby Bonds	82	David Justice	58
Joe Carter	77	Ken Singleton	55
Bobby Abreu	76	Rusty Staub	54
Dwight Evans	75	Ruben Sierra	53
Magglio Ordonez	74	Brian Giles	52
Darryl Strawberry	69		

I'll include players with no clear position along with the Designated Hitters. There are two players that I would consider Designated Hitters in the Hall of Fame, Frank Thomas and Paul Molitor. Edgar Martinez has not yet been able to gain election, but appears to be at least marginally qualified for Hall of Fame status. David Ortiz, although starting late, seems to have passed all three of those in terms of traditional Hall of Fame qualifications.

In addition to those four, there are three active Designated Hitters who have some chance to wind up with Hall of Fame numbers: Hanley Ramirez, Victor Martinez and Edwin Encarnacion.

Age	David Ortiz	Frank Thomas	Paul Molitor	Edgar Martinez	Hanley Ramirez	Victor Martinez	Edwin Encarnacion
25	0	42	28	0	53	3	2
30	56	104	43	19	67	28	22
33	76	122	59	47	76	42	48
34	85	123	76	59		45	57
38	128	135	110	99		59	
40	155	138	129	105			
41			130	107			
					Active		Active
Total	155	138	130	107	Active	Active	

The Big Papi had NO Hall of Fame points in his six seasons with the Twins, but began to accumulate them as soon as he came to Boston. But with apologies to those of you who are certain to conclude that I am in some manner favoring the Red Sox, the most interesting name here is Hanley Ramirez.

Playing shortstop, third base, left field, first base and DH, Hanley has been collecting Hall of Fame markers like a squirrel collecting nuts. He was Rookie of the Year in 2006, which is a Hall of Fame marker. He stole 50 bases in a season twice. He has hit 40 doubles three times. He drove in a hundred runs in 2009, and again in 2016. He scored a hundred runs four times. He has hit .300 as a regular four times. He hit 30 homers in 2008, and again in 2016. He won a batting championship in 2009. He was the starting shortstop for the National League in the 2008 and 2010 All Star games. He still has work to do to reach the Hall of Fame standard, but he is even with or ahead of any of these other players at the same age, except Frank Thomas. I don't think people think of Hanley as a great player, but he has some numbers.

In addition to those there are six players who should be mentioned.

Pete Rose 215	Hal McRae 52
Harold Baines 54	Chili Davis 41
Don Baylor 52	Tony Phillips 29

Baines, Baylor, McRae and Chili Davis had very good careers, although they seem to have been stopped somewhere about Oneonta or Chenango Forks. You all know the story of Pete Rose; he has no clear position, having made the All Star team at second base, third base, first base, left field, right field, and Hialeah. Tony Phillips, although not a Hall of Famer, was a unique player who was outstanding defensively at many different positions.

Turning our attention now to pitchers. . .right handed starting pitchers, left-handed starting pitchers, and closers.   There are 18 right-handed starting pitchers who started their careers in 1961 or later and who have Hall of Fame Monitor scores of 100 or greater.   Twelve of those eighteen are in the Hall of Fame: Tom Seaver, Greg Maddux, Nolan Ryan, Jim Palmer, Gaylord Perry, Phil Niekro, Don Sutton, Ferguson Jenkins, Pedro Martinez, John Smoltz, Bert Blyleven and Catfish Hunter:

Age	Seaver	Maddux	Ryan	Palmer	Perry	Niekro	Sutton	Jenkins	Martinez	Smoltz	Blyleven	Hunter
20		0	0	8			6		0		10	1
25	62	23	21	48	5	0	32	44	31	27	56	30
30	149	130	93	127	46	26	82	109	116	78	81	120
35	190	178	135	165	115	62	115	134	144	96	113	
40	218	210	162		159	115	149			135	136	
Final	219	213	204	175	171	152	150	146	146	138	136	128

There is NO right-handed starting pitchers of the expansion era who has made the Hall of Fame with a monitor score of less than 100—or, for that matter, less than 128.   Monitor score of 100 or more: 12 for 18; monitor score less than 100, zero for a couple of thousand.

The six pitchers who score at 100 or more but have not yet been selected are Roger Clemens, Curt Schilling, Jack Morris, Justin Verlander, David Cone and Roy Halladay:

Age	Clemens	Schilling	Verlander	Morris	Cone	Halladay
25	63	8	16	8	11	9
30	129	35	95	53	53	42
34	176	77	118	74	76	98
35	204	90		81	89	99
36	210	91		97	96	100
39	241	118		112	101	
40	252	122			101	
44	279					
Final	279	122	Active	112	101	100

A brief comment about each of the six:

1) When working on the system, I score its accuracy by measuring the "anomalies". If a player has more than 100 points and is eligible for the Hall of Fame but has not been elected, that's an anomaly, with the size of the anomaly being his monitor score minus 100. If a player has less than 100 points and IS in the Hall of Fame, that's an anomaly, with the size of the anomaly being 100 minus his score.

Roger Clemens has an anomaly score of 179. This is more than 60% of the total anomaly score for all pitchers in history—not just pitchers since 1961, but all pitchers, ever. There are starting pitchers prior to 1961 who made the Hall of Fame with scores under 100, but the only other anomaly in the voting which is comparable to Clemens is Barry Bonds.

2) Curt Schilling is conducting a personal campaign to keep himself out of the Hall of Fame.

3) I assume Verlander is in, although it will help him if he coasts past 200 career wins.

4) Jack Morris, of course, is one of the most controversial Hall of Fame omissions of the last 40 years. I do not advocate Morris' selection, but his record is consistent with Hall of Fame selections from before 1970.

5) I think Roy Halladay will probably skate in because (1) he is deserving, and (2) players sometimes do well if they retire quickly after they lose it, like Catfish Hunter.

6) Although no one talks about David Cone as a Hall of Fame candidate, he may be the most interesting name on the list. He dropped off the ballot after one vote, and no one has put up a big squawk about that.

David Cone had a remarkable career. A lot of people dismissed Cone as a Hall of Fame candidate because he retired short of 200 career wins, with a record of 194-126. But historically, many starting pitchers with won-lost records like that have been selected to the Hall of Fame (Jack Chesbro, 198-132; Ed Walsh, 195-126; Dazzy Vance, 197-140; Rube Waddell, 193-143; Lefty Gomez, 189-102.) Those guys were not better pitchers than David Cone.

In the last 50 years, Hall of Fame thinking has been dominated by career totals. This started when 3000 hits and 300 wins became huge events, which happened in the 1957-1963 era, about 1960. Once 300 wins was an automatic qualification for the Hall of Fame, then people figured, well, if 300 wins is an automatic Hall of Famer, then you have to get close to 300 wins to be considered.

But I don't think that's a perfect way to think about the issue. Not bragging, I hope, but our field—sabermetrics—has more influence on how others think through these issues now than we did years ago. I think it is the consensus conclusion of people in sabermetrics that, while career longevity is a relevant and valid issue, sometimes pitchers with 180 wins have actually contributed more to their teams' success than pitchers with 260 or 270 wins—or even pitchers with 300 wins.

I think of David Cone as a great pitcher. Over time, the evaluation of pitchers will rest more on WAR and less on wins. We have to get better estimates of WAR, I think, and we have to wait for old ways of thinking to pass away and for new ones to permeate the culture. When those things happen, I think David Cone may get the recognition he deserves as an all-time great.

OK, two boxes left to check here: active right-handed starting pitchers (other than Justin Verlander) who look like they could be Hall of Famers, and other right-handed starters of the expansion era who made a run at the Hall of

Fame but fell short.   There are, I think, at least nine active right-handed starting pitchers who have some chance to be considered.   Those are Max Scherzer, Felix Hernandez, Zack Greinke, Adam Wainwright, John Lackey, James Shields, Johnny Cueto, Corey Kluber and Carlos Martinez.   Carlos Martinez and Corey Kluber are too young to be taken seriously in this context, and speculation about James Shields reviving his career and making a run at the Hall of Fame, at this point, probably involves a knuckleball.   The serious candidates are Scherzer, Hernandez and Greinke:

Age	Scherzer	Felix	Greinke	Wainwright	Lackey	Cueto	Shields	Kluber	Martinez
25	3	45	25	13	11	4	4	0	16
26	5	52	28	13	15	13	12	0	
27	10	58	32	28	19	13	15	0	
28	30	72	38	39	30	30	19	21	
29	43	77	42	39	31	37	29	25	
30	54	79	51	41	33	46	34	42	
31	81	79	66	58	37	47	41	61	
32	95		69	69	39		48		
33			75	69	46		54		
34				71	46		55		
35				72	49		55		
36					55				
37					59				
38					59				

Corey Kluber's total will increase from 61 to 66 if he is voted the Cy Young Award. By my count, 42 right-handed starting pitchers of the expansion era have made it at least half of the way to Cooperstown:

Luis Tiant 98	Rick Reuschel 68	Burt Hooton 58
Kevin Brown 97	Bret Saberhagen 68	Roy Oswalt 58
Orel Hershiser 92	Tim Hudson 68	J.R. Richard 58
Mike Mussina 92	Mel Stottlemyre 67	Mike Boddicker . . . 57
Dwight Gooden . . . 88	Joe Niekro 66	Jim Lonborg 57
Bartolo Colon 76	Dave Stieb 65	Dennis Leonard . . . 55
Denny McLain 74	Jake Peavy 63	Kevin Appier 54
Bob Welch 74	Chris Carpenter 63	Jered Weaver 54
Tim Lincecum 73	Mike Scott 63	Jack Billingham . . . 53
Dennis Martinez . . 73	Rick Sutcliffe 63	Rick Wise 53
Dave Stewart 73	Mike Moore 62	Doug Drabek 52
Derek Lowe 71	Livan Hernandez . . . 61	A.J. Burnett 51
Charlie Hough 69	Andy Messersmith . . 60	Kevin Millwood . . . 50
Dean Chance 68	Mike Torrez 59	Javier Vazquez 50

There have been six left-handed starters beginning their careers since 1961 who have Hall of Fame monitor scores over 100. Three of those six (Randy Johnson, Steve Carlton and Tom Glavine) are in the Hall of Fame. One is still active (Kershaw) and one reaches the ballot for the first time this year (Andy Pettitte). The only one who has been passed over by Hall of Fame voters is Mickey Lolich.

Age	Big Unit / Carlton / Glavine			Kershaw / Lolich / Pettite		
25	1	23	29	73	16	26
29	34	83	75	132	53	52
35	121	166	135		113	85
37	185	200	145		113	101
40	234	221	154			104
42	247	222	163			
43	247	222				
45	253					
	Active					
Total	253	222	163		113	104

I hope I don't accidentally get Pettitte elected by saying that he is over the line. He is just barely over the line, and I don't care one way or the other whether he gets elected; I just don't want to be accidentally influencing the vote.

As is true among right-handed starters, no left-handed starter coming to the majors since 1961 has made the Hall of Fame with a monitor score less than 100, although there were several older lefties who did. Kershaw is far ahead of any other lefty of the last 50 years at the same age, even Carlton and Randy, which may not mean as much you might assume. Often the late bloomers among pitchers are the ones who have staying power. Other than Kershaw, six active left-handers would appear to be working on Hall of Fame resumes: CC Sabathia, David Price, Jon Lester, Madison Bumgarner, Cole Hamels and Chris Sale:

Age	Sabathia	Price	Lester	Bumgarner	Hamels	Sale
25	14	16	15	51	13	12
27	43	41	23	62	23	28
28	54	53	26		31	44
31	80	76	52		46	
32	87		67		51	
33	87		70		51	
36	91					

Sale and Sabathia are the only ones in that group who had good seasons in 2017. I count 26 left-handed starters of the expansion era who had at least a half of a Hall of Fame career:

Tommy John	98	Cliff Lee	75
Vida Blue	96	David Wells	73
Ron Guidry	93	Mark Langston	71
Johan Santana	93	Ken Holtzman	70
Sam McDowell	88	Jerry Reuss	70
Jerry Koosman	87	Jamie Moyer	67
Dave McNally	87	Mike Flanagan	62
Frank Tanana	87	Kenny Rogers	62
Frank Viola	85	Chuck Finley	60
Wilbur Wood	82	Barry Zito	60
Fernando Valenzuela	77	Bruce Hurst	51
Mark Buehrle	76	Jon Matlack	50
Jimmy Key	75	Bob Veale	50

The only two starting pitchers of the expansion era who score at "98"— JUST short of a Hall of Fame career—are Tommy John and Luis Tiant. John and Tiant were minor league teammates in 1964, and came out of the Cleveland Indians system at about the same time.   The Indians also had Sam McDowell—Hall of Fame score of 88—who was in the majors earlier, but who was actually younger than either John or Tiant, and they also had Sonny Siebert, also a rookie in 1964, who would win 140 major league games with a Hall of Fame score of 38, and they had Mudcat Grant, who would win 21 games for the Twins in 1965. They had Gary Bell, then 27 years old; he would win 121 games.   The previous year they had traded away Jim Perry, who had 163 wins left at the time they traded him away.   In the minors they had Steve Hargan, who in 1966 somebody in The Sporting News would say was the best pitcher in the American League, not to mention Mike Hedlund, who in 1971 would go 15-8 for a third-year expansion team.   It is hard to understand how a team with so much young pitching talent could do so little with it.

OK, relievers.   I revamped the Hall of Fame Monitor basically to deal with relievers, more than any other one issue, and frankly, relievers remain a challenge.   There are five relievers debuting post-1961 who have scores of 100 or more, but only two of those (Rollie Fingers and Dennis Eckersley) are actually in the Hall of Fame.   The record isn't that bleak; two of the others are Mariano Rivera, who will be as close to an automatic selection when he becomes eligible as God ever made, and Trevor Hoffman, who got 74% of the vote in last year's election, so really, it's four out of five.   The only actual outlier is Dan Quisenberry, rejected by the Hall of Fame despite a score of 101.

But there are two relievers SHORT of 100 points who HAVE been elected: Bruce Sutter and Goose Gossage.   Believe me, I tried every way that I could think of to jimmy the system so that Sutter and Gossage would be over 100 points, but I couldn't find any way to do it that didn't cause more problems than it solved.   I could increase the weight given to leading the league in Saves, for example, but that pushes Lee Smith over the Hall of Fame line before it does Sutter, and it pushes up Quisenberry—who is already on the wrong side of the line—faster than it does Gossage, who we are trying to help.   Here's a chart of those seven—the five relievers (post-1961) who have scores over 100, plus the two who were selected although their scores are a little bit short of 100:

Age	Rivera	Eckersley	Fingers	Hoffman	Quisienberry	Sutter	Goose
25	0	28	21	2		14	29
30	69	39	82	43	56	66	70
35	142	78	118	68	98	87	86
37	154	107	119	79	101		87
38	166	111	119	89			87
39	188	111		97			87
40	194	114		99			87
41	211	118		102			87
42	211	126		113			92
43	219	127					
Total	219	127	119	113	101	87	92

No active reliever, in my judgment, has nailed down a spot in the Hall of Fame, and that gives us a final count of active players who appear to have Hall-of-Fame-Qualified records: eight. Albert Pujols, Miguel Cabrera, Robinson Cano, Adrian Beltre, Carlos Beltran, Ichiro Suzuki, Justin Verlander and Clayton Kershaw. The active relievers who have some chance to make the Hall of Fame, however, are numerous. I think I have eight of them, granted that three of those are just kids who haven't hit a bump in the road yet:

Age	Fernando Rodney	Francisco Rodriguez	Craig Kimbrel	Aroldis Chapman	Kenley Jansen	Cody Allen	Kelvin Herrera	Roberto Osuna
22		12	0	0	0		2	14
25		41	53	16	11	7	19	
27		64	71	27	20	24	26	
28		66	74	40	32	29		
29	6	71	85	43	51			
35	29	89						
40	54							

OK, my last chart is relievers of the expansion era who took a run at a Hall of Fame career, but fell short of 100 points and have not been elected, at least so far. There are 26 of those:

Lee Smith	88	Mike Stanton	61
John Franco	85	Ron Perranoski	61
Mike Marshall	85	Jonathan Papelbon	59
Joe Nathan	84	Roberto Hernandez	58
Jose Mesa	83	Armando Benitez	57
Robb Nen	81	Dave Righetti	55
Billy Wagner	81	Eric Gagne	55
John Wetteland	76	Clay Carroll	54
Kent Tekulve	70	Rick Aguilera	54
Randy Myers	64	Duane Ward	53
Jeff Reardon	64	Jose Valverde	50
Sparky Lyle	64	Tom Henke	50
Todd Worrell	64	Ugueth Urbina	50

I will explain all the points in the new Hall of Fame Monitor in some other article somewhere; this is already by far the longest article in the almost thirty-year history of this book.   I appreciate your staying with me.

Hard Hit Balls

Bill James

In baseball it helps to hit the ball hard; we're planning to hire Captain Obvious to advertise this point for us. Hal McRae used to say that in order to hit .300, a batter had to hit the ball hard 7 times out of 10 at bats.   This was back in the 1980s, before we had a lot of the data we have now; whatever was said by some veteran ballplayer who seemed to know what he was talking about was good enough, because nobody really knew.

Obviously it helps to hit the ball hard, but how much does it really help? You don't have to hit the ball hard 7 times in 10 to hit .300, and this is a good thing because nobody actually hits the ball hard 7 times out of 10.   Baseball Info Solutions tracks hard hit balls, using exit velocity but also several other parameters. If you hit the ball 110 miles an hour straight up in the air so the catcher can catch it when gravity wins, that's not what is meant by a Hard Hit Ball.

The best hitters hit the ball hard a little bit less than one-third of the time. Nick Castellanos was the major league leader in 2017, hitting the ball hard in 31.1% of his plate appearances.   David Ortiz in 2016 was at 33.2%, which was the highest percentage we have on record.

Out of 100 major league plate appearances in modern baseball:

1 will result in a hit batsmen,

8 will result in a walk,

20 will result in a strikeout,

And 70 to 71 will result in a ball put in play (including home runs as balls put into play).

Obviously these numbers change over time; in 2017 the numbers of strikeouts and walks were up a little.

Of the balls in play, you'll have about 22 Hard Hit Balls, 13 will be dribblers or weakly-hit balls, soft hit balls, and about 36 will be tweeners, neither hard hit nor softly hit.

The average hitter will hit .538 on a hard hit ball, .268 on a medium-hit ball, and .158 on soft-hit balls. But these numbers are not universal. In 2016 the major league leader in batting average on soft-hit balls (20 or more plays) was Austin Jackson, who hit .400 on soft-hit balls (8 for 20). In 2017 the leader in that category was Austin Jackson, who hit .360 on soft-hit balls (9 for 25). Obviously Jackson has a relevant skill there other than hitting the ball hard. He's very fast, and if the ball comes off the end of his bat, he's got a good shot to beat it out. Adam Lind, on the other hand, is 5-for-155 on soft-hit balls over the last three years. Kris Bryant has hit .286 on soft-hit balls over the last three years (55 for 196); Kendrys Morales has hit .084.

You can see, then, that the ability to beat out a hit on a soft-hit ball is a real variable among hitters. The standard deviation of batting average on hard hit balls (among players with 100 hard hit balls over the last three years) is .047. On soft-hit balls among the same players, it's about the same, .044. Giancarlo Stanton and Miguel Sano will hit about .660 when they hit the ball hard, because when those guys hit the ball hard, it goes to places where it is very difficult for anyone to make a play on the ball. Victor Martinez, on the other hand, hits relatively poorly on hard hit balls (.409 in 2017, .446 over the last three years) because 1) Martinez hits scorching line drives, which can be caught, rather than hard-hit fly balls, which are often homers, and 2) Martinez doesn't run well, which enables infielders to play deep against him.

The question I am trying to get to is, what role does hitting the ball hard actually play in the success of a hitter? Obviously you do much better when you hit the ball hard than when you don't, but how large is this factor in the overall success of the hitter? That really is what I want to know.

There are two measures of how often a batter hits the ball hard—how often he hits the ball hard as a percentage of plate appearances, and how often he hits the ball hard as a percentage of balls in play. As a percentage of plate appearances, the players who hit the ball hard most often were Nick Castellanos, J. D. Martinez, Yoenis Cespedes, Jose Abreu and Victor Martinez. But as a percentage of balls in play, the top five were J. D. Martinez, Alex Avila, Colby Rasmus, Joey Gallo and Rhys Hoskins.

The part of this that I didn't understand is, to what extent is it true that players who hit the ball hard tend to strike out more? Do players who hit the ball hard do so because they are, in the archaic expression of my childhood, swinging from the heels?

No, they don't. If you sort the players by how often they hit the ball hard relative to plate appearances, then those who hit the ball hardest don't strike out more than those who don't; they strike out less. That being the case, those players obviously are far better hitters, on average, then those who strike out more and hit the ball hard less often.

Over the last three years there have been 1,318 hitters (not including pitchers) who have had 100 or more plate appearances. Of these 1,318 hitters, there were 230 who hit the ball hard 25% of the time or more, 466 who hit the ball hard less than 20% of the time, and 622 whose hard-hit-ball percentage was between 20.000 and 25.000. Those who hit the ball hard (the top 230) have an average OPS of .828. Those who hit the ball hard least often have an average OPS of .654. That's just a huge, huge difference. It's basically the difference between Ernie Banks and Zoilo Versalles.

If you sort them the other way, by hard hit balls as a percentage of balls in play, then the hard hitters group does strike out more than the soft contract group, but even so, their strikeout to walk ratio is about the same. Even sorted in the less advantageous way, those who hit the ball hard most often are the best hitters.

OK, in the chart below the categories are Plate Appearances (PA) and Balls in Play (In Play), then for each quality of contact there is the number of balls that were hit (#), the number of Hits (Hits), and the number of Total Bases (TB). To the far right of the table, there is the percent of plate appearances ending with a Hard Hit Ball (Hard Pct) and the OPS of the Player (OPS). These are the top 50 hitters in the major leagues, 2017, in terms of how often they hit the ball hard:

Hard Hit Balls
Top 50 Batters in Hard Pct with 100+ PA

Player	Total PA	In Play	Hard #	Hard Hits	Hard TB	Medium #	Medium Hits	Medium TB	Soft #	Soft Hits	Soft TB	Hard Pct	OPS
Castellanos, Nick	665	477	207	101	215	215	56	74	55	10	12	31.1%	0.811
Martinez, J.D.	489	308	151	97	259	114	30	35	43	4	4	30.9%	1.066
Cespedes, Yoenis	321	232	98	53	119	86	26	32	48	6	6	30.5%	0.892
Abreu, Jose	675	506	205	118	261	221	57	67	80	14	15	30.4%	0.906
Martinez, Victor	435	331	132	54	96	158	43	47	41	3	3	30.3%	0.697
Machado, Manny	690	524	207	106	232	220	47	55	97	10	10	30.0%	0.782
Lind, Adam	301	226	89	49	102	106	30	33	31	2	2	29.6%	0.875
Seager, Corey	613	411	181	106	201	177	48	51	53	5	6	29.5%	0.854
Gurriel, Yulieski	564	473	166	98	187	232	51	60	75	9	10	29.4%	0.817
Molina, Yadier	543	437	159	66	138	206	62	73	72	9	9	29.3%	0.751
Turner, Justin	543	409	159	74	155	210	67	80	40	6	7	29.3%	0.945
Cabrera, Miguel	529	362	154	69	136	172	42	45	36	6	6	29.1%	0.728
Perez, Salvador	499	381	145	81	179	173	37	46	63	8	8	29.1%	0.792
Cano, Robinson	648	510	188	93	182	257	67	80	65	6	6	29.0%	0.791
Zimmerman, Ryan	576	403	163	97	231	183	50	57	57	12	12	28.3%	0.930
Braun, Ryan	425	308	120	69	149	129	25	28	59	8	8	28.2%	0.823
Flores, Wilmer	362	288	102	50	115	139	34	42	47	7	7	28.2%	0.795
Kinsler, Ian	613	465	172	75	167	206	46	50	87	9	10	28.1%	0.725
Rasmus, Colby	129	77	36	24	59	29	9	10	12	1	1	27.9%	0.896
Pujols, Albert	636	504	177	78	157	247	57	64	80	8	8	27.8%	0.672
Betts, Mookie	712	554	198	95	197	255	58	78	101	13	13	27.8%	0.803
Blackmon, Charlie	725	515	201	113	267	226	81	99	88	19	21	27.7%	1.000
Goldschmidt, Paul	665	415	184	109	249	184	51	59	47	6	6	27.7%	0.966
Murphy, Daniel	593	460	164	89	184	219	69	92	77	14	14	27.7%	0.928
Hechavarria, Adeiny	348	267	96	50	93	124	29	33	47	7	8	27.6%	0.695
Lindor, Francisco	723	566	199	111	248	286	57	71	81	10	10	27.5%	0.842
Correa, Carlos	481	334	132	82	171	152	40	50	50	11	11	27.4%	0.941
Ramirez, Jose	645	521	177	98	222	257	78	107	87	10	12	27.4%	0.957
Voit, Luke	124	83	34	19	39	43	8	9	6	1	1	27.4%	0.736
Cabrera, Asdrubal	540	402	148	80	145	185	49	58	69	5	5	27.4%	0.785
Bruce, Jay	617	419	169	83	214	201	51	60	49	7	8	27.4%	0.832
Hoskins, Rhys	212	126	58	35	95	52	8	9	16	1	1	27.4%	1.014
Arenado, Nolan	680	507	186	100	252	232	68	82	89	19	21	27.4%	0.959
Aguilar, Jesus	311	188	85	46	107	74	27	33	29	1	1	27.3%	0.837
Parra, Gerardo	425	334	116	59	107	170	51	58	48	11	12	27.3%	0.793
Beltre, Adrian	389	294	106	61	130	137	37	43	51	8	8	27.2%	0.915
Tomas, Yasmany	180	117	49	28	64	50	10	11	18	2	2	27.2%	0.758
Mahtook, Mikie	379	271	103	53	111	126	28	33	42	15	15	27.2%	0.787
Mauer, Joe	597	445	162	88	132	226	70	82	57	5	5	27.1%	0.801
Ozuna, Marcell	679	471	184	118	260	201	58	60	86	15	16	27.1%	0.924
Smoak, Justin	637	434	171	96	234	206	47	54	57	8	8	26.8%	0.883
Cruz, Nelson	645	423	172	109	250	189	45	49	62	6	6	26.7%	0.924
Morales, Kendrys	608	428	162	89	190	201	48	56	65	2	2	26.6%	0.753
Pollock, A.J.	466	354	124	65	140	160	40	51	70	8	9	26.6%	0.801
Moreland, Mitch	576	393	153	75	167	187	44	51	53	6	7	26.6%	0.769
Bellinger, Cody	548	337	145	80	219	145	43	55	47	5	5	26.5%	0.933
Brantley, Michael	375	292	99	54	98	152	42	47	41	5	5	26.4%	0.801
Utley, Chase	353	255	93	44	90	120	24	30	42	5	5	26.3%	0.728
Castillo, Welington	365	246	96	51	116	120	40	46	30	5	5	26.3%	0.813
Schebler, Scott	531	353	139	76	192	146	27	30	68	7	7	26.2%	0.791

Injury Information

Joe Rosales

Historically, analysts have been frustrated by the lack of comprehensive data when studying the impact of injuries on major league baseball players. Disabled list (DL) information is available, but that data is limited. Players often sit out a handful of games as a result of minor injuries that don't result in a DL stint, leaving no record of those injuries ever occurring.

To address this data deficiency, Baseball Info Solutions (BIS) began collecting detailed injury information at the beginning of the 2015 Major League Baseball season. The idea was to create a comprehensive database that would catalog all events that could potentially have an effect on the physical health of a player, no matter how severe. That means not only keeping track of obvious injuries, but also documenting smaller events like a player fouling a ball off of his foot. Even if a player shows no visible pain as the result of an event, we have a record of anything that could potentially impact a player's performance.

In order to be truly comprehensive, BIS keeps track of both on-field and off-field injuries, and we document any updated information that becomes available in the days, weeks, and months following the initial injury event. These updates are crucial to the dataset because it is not always clear what the exact injury is when it first occurs, and sometimes players have setbacks that alter the initial prognosis for a return to health (or at least a return to the playing field).

As a brief synopsis, we collect as many of the following pieces of information as are available for a given event:

- Type of Injury
- General Region of the Body
- Specific Body Part
- Severity Rating
- Whether the Player had to Leave the Game
- Diagnosis
- Prognosis
- Treatment

The type of injury is a categorization of how the injury occurred. Examples include Collision with Wall, Foul Off Body, and Throwing a Pitch, among others.

The severity rating for an injury event is rated on a 1 to 5 scale. At the low end, 1's are assigned to plays that result in no visible pain for the player at all. At the high end, 5's represent the most severe injuries that result in the player experiencing extreme pain and possibly being immobile, bleeding, or needing to be helped off the field.

By maintaining a comprehensive record of each potential injury event that takes place, from its initial occurrence all the way through the treatment and ultimate return of the player, there are many ways in which one can explore the results.

For instance, the table below shows all of the injuries from 2015-17 broken down by Injury Type.

Injury Events by Type, 2015-17

Injury Type	Total
Struck by Batted Ball/Bat	4479
Hit By Pitch	4027
Foul off Body	3741
Fielding a Batted/Thrown Ball	469
Running the Bases	391
Collision with Player	308
On a Swing	294
Other	275
Collision with Wall	270
Throwing a Pitch	262
Sliding into a Base	256
Throwing (non-pitch)	36

These results show that an overwhelming majority of potential injury events happen around home plate as a result of the pitch. Either the batter fouls the ball off of himself, or he fouls it off the catcher, or the batter simply gets hit by the pitch.

However, despite the batter and catcher being the most exposed to potential injuries, their risk of having to leave the game because of an injury is actually quite low, as the next table shows.

Percent of Injury Events Where the Player had to Leave the Game (by Type), 2015-17

Injury Type	Pct
Throwing a Pitch	51.1%
Throwing (non-Pitch)	36.1%
Running the Bases	32.2%
On a Swing	19.4%
Other	15.6%
Fielding a Batted/Thrown Ball	15.6%
Sliding into a Base	13.3%
Collision with a Player	12.0%
Collision with Wall	9.3%
Hit by Pitch	2.2%
Struck by Batted Ball/Bat	2.1%
Foul Off Body	0.4%

Throwing requires many different parts of the body and a lot of exertion, so it is not that much of a surprise to see that those types of injuries most often lead to players being removed from the game, especially pitchers for whom throwing is their livelihood.

Another way to look at injuries is to see which areas of the body are most affected. The following table shows a breakdown of how many events occurred to each region of the body.

Injury Events by Region, 2015-17

Region of the Body	Total
Ankle/Foot/Toes	4063
Head	2449
Lower Legs/Knee	2394
Arm/Elbow	1992
Wrist/Hand/Finger	1650
Chest/Back/Spine	1303
Upper Legs/Thighs	1102
Shoulder	1068
Pelvis/Hips	767
Other	453
Neck	141
Internal Organs	40

At the top of the list, two of the three most affected regions of the body involve the lower extremities, which is not that much of a surprise given how often batters foul the ball off themselves. However, second on that list are events affecting the head. Given the greater understanding that medical professionals are gaining regarding the effects of concussions and repeated head trauma on people in general and athletes in particular, this type of data could help illuminate which players may be at greater risk than others.

In fact, when we put together a list of the individual players that were involved in the most injury events since the start of the 2015 season, 30 of the top 32 players on the list are catchers.

The following chart shows how many injury events occurred to players when they were playing the field broken down by defensive position.

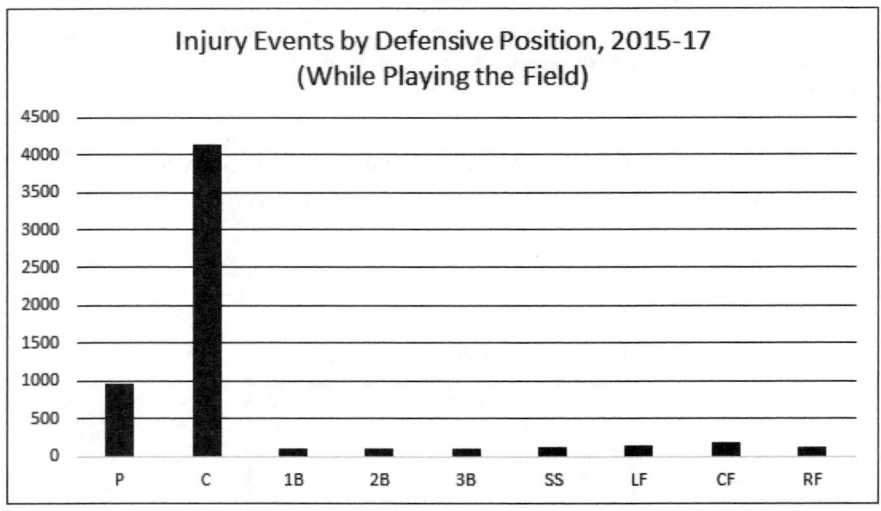

Catchers were involved in the most potential injury events by far. If we break those injury events down by type of injury, we see the following:

Catcher Injury Events by Type, 2015-17

Injury Type	Total
Struck by Batted Ball/Bat	3844
Fielding a Batted/Thrown Ball	120
Other	72
Collision with Player	64
Throwing	7

The clichéd phrase that catchers take a beating behind the plate clearly has firm grounding in reality. Being struck by a foul ball or a batter's swing represents 93 percent of the events that affect catchers.

So where on the body are catchers getting hit?

Catchers Struck by Batted Ball/Bat by Region of the Body, 2015-17

Region of the Body	Total
Head	1934
Wrist/Hand/Finger	391
Lower Legs/Knee	310
Ankle/Foot/Toes	268
Shoulder	256
Chest/Back/Spine	189
Upper Legs/Thighs	174
Arm/Elbow	134
Pelvis/Hips	122
Other	51
Neck	15

The head accounts for 50 percent of events when catchers take a foul ball or batter's backswing off their body, and is impacted far more often than any other part of the body.

Here are the five catchers that were hit in the head most often since the start of 2015.

Most Hits in the Head—Catchers, 2015-17

Player	Total
Salvador Perez	60
Cameron Rupp	55
Matt Wieters	53
Russell Martin	53
Yasmani Grandal	52

The data included in this book only begins to scratch the surface of the possible research that could be done with BIS's comprehensive injury database. One could study how leg injuries affect a player's speed, how wrist injuries affect a player's power, how arm injuries affect a pitcher's velocity, etc. Or one could look at injury recurrence and what aspects of those injuries make it more likely for recurrence to take place. The possibilities for further study are extensive, and with the larger sample sizes that come with more years of data collection, the more likely those studies are to return substantive results.

Starting Pitcher Rankings

Ben Jedlovec

Who is the best starting pitcher in baseball, right now? No, not who had the best season, or who should win the Cy Young Awards. If you could pick any pitcher to start a game for you tonight, based on their track record and recent performance, who would it be? Go ahead, think about it for a moment. I'll wait... Ready? Ok, great.

Clayton Kershaw used to be the obvious answer, and some of you no doubt stuck with him. You have a great case. After the Dodgers' ace first claimed the title in May 2013 from Justin Verlander, he's held the top spot at the end of every season through 2016. On top of that, in 2017 he led the National League in ERA and Strikeout-to-Walk Ratio (and Wins, if you go for that sort of thing). But, after years of utter dominance, the 29-year-old has begun to show signs of mortality. His ERA "rose" to 2.31, his worst mark since 2012. He also spent some time on the DL due to a back injury for the second straight year. After all, the 10-year veteran has logged over 2,000 innings (including the postseason) on his still-young arm.

Others of you might have jumped to Max Scherzer, who has a strong argument as well. The 2016 NL Cy Young Award winner finished with a 2.51 ERA and struck out a career high 12.0 batters per nine innings, though that somehow didn't lead the league (see Ray, Robbie, who jumped from the 67th-ranked pitcher to the 15th-ranked pitcher). In recent seasons, Scherzer has been the only one to challenge Kershaw's reign. Scherzer has taken the top spot from Kershaw briefly on five occasions: for 35 days in the first half of 2014, for 5 days in early July 2015, for another 35 days from mid-June to mid-July 2017, again for 5 days in late July, and for 34 days in late 2017.

The thing about Scherzer, though, is that he's never been able to put any distance between himself and the rest of the pack the way Kershaw has. Scherzer has never been able to get more than 25 points ahead of Kershaw, while Kershaw had opened up an 85-point lead over Scherzer a month before he hit the DL in 2016. Kershaw's score reached 640 at his peak before his 2016 back injury; Scherzer has never topped 615.

The Red Sox fans in the audience no doubt put Chris Sale at the top of their list.

Freshly motivated by his offseason trade to Boston, Sale wasted no time impressing his new fan base with eight consecutive starts with double-digit strikeouts across April and May. He would go on to lead all of MLB in innings, strikeouts, and FIP (Fielding-Independent Pitching). Also of significance is his durability. Despite concerns about his mechanics out of college, Sale has proven to be one of the more durable starters in baseball, not missing a start since 2014 (well, not missing a start due to injury, anyway), unlike the three pitchers ranked ahead of him in our list.

By our methodology, Corey Kluber has the strongest claim to the title as the best pitcher in baseball, and by a comfortable margin. For starters, his 2017 stats are strong: MLB-bests in ERA (2.25), complete games (five), shutouts (three), and strikeout-to-walk ratio (7.36). He did miss some time early in the year with a back injury, but he showed no sign of lingering issues over the final four months of the year. He was the best pitcher on perhaps the greatest pitching staff in MLB history, even if it took a 22-game winning streak to start receiving some overdue attention.

Kluber took the title on September 7 with a 13-strikeout, two-run victory over the last-place White Sox, and then he took off. In the start after taking the top spot, Kluber recorded his third shutout of the season, a five-hit affair with eight strikeouts to boot. He followed that with seven shutout innings in his next start, then 10 strikeouts and two unearned runs in the start after that, and five light innings with one earned run in his last outing of the year to stay fresh for the playoffs. In other words, Kluber only allowed one earned run in four starts after taking the top spot.

Will Kluber immediately yield the title in 2018 to Kershaw, Scherzer, or Sale? Or will he make a multi-year run, similar to Kershaw's? You'd think that Sale's and Kershaw's relative youth (28 and 29 years old, respectively) gives them the best chances at sticking around for a while, but it's not as though Kluber (31) or Scherzer (33) are on the decline either. In any case, we are witnessing a historic group of elite pitchers.

The Starting Pitcher Rankings are based on park-adjusted Game Scores. Each pitcher starts his career at a score of 300, and for every game he starts, 30 percent of his Game Score is added to 97 percent of his previous Starting Pitcher Ranking Score. If he pitches well, his score goes up, but if he pitches worse or doesn't start a game for an extended period, his score goes down. Be sure to check out BillJamesOnline.com for a full explanation of the system and the daily updates throughout the year, including the playoffs.

Starting Pitcher Rankings

Player	April 1 Score	Rank	May 1 Score	Rank	June 1 Score	Rank	July 1 Score	Rank	Aug 1 Score	Rank	Sept 1 Score	Rank	Oct 2 Score	Rank
Kluber, Corey	538.8	3	543.5	4	537.5	4	568.8	4	582.6	4	607.6	2	625.5	1
Scherzer, Max	550.8	2	557.0	2	580.8	2	605.8	1	608.8	2	613.8	1	606.1	2
Kershaw, Clayton	564.6	1	573.9	1	582.3	1	597.8	2	609.4	1	605.8	3	591.1	3
Sale, Chris	513.9	8	548.7	3	557.0	3	578.9	3	587.3	3	594.5	4	590.0	4
Verlander, Justin	520.3	6	518.3	7	519.3	8	518.2	8	522.0	8	551.4	6	578.2	5
Greinke, Zack	481.4	15	499.7	11	530.7	6	540.2	5	553.0	5	552.9	5	553.1	6
Strasburg, Stephen	461.0	23	479.0	19	499.6	15	505.7	12	513.8	11	528.1	10	552.1	7
Carrasco, Carlos	449.1	25	481.7	18	494.8	16	499.4	14	497.7	16	518.3	13	539.7	8
Bumgarner, Madison	533.7	5	540.3	5	532.5	5	525.0	7	528.5	7	539.4	8	533.2	9
Arrieta, Jake	515.0	7	512.7	8	510.2	10	504.1	13	519.7	9	539.8	7	527.2	10
deGrom, Jacob	444.7	29	463.2	28	470.9	23	494.4	17	513.7	12	520.5	12	521.6	11
Hendricks, Kyle	496.8	11	499.1	12	506.3	11	496.7	15	491.9	20	506.8	17	521.5	12
Quintana, Jose	472.7	17	473.4	25	472.8	22	495.3	16	508.3	14	503.0	18	519.5	13
Santana, Ervin	435.3	33	477.5	21	505.5	12	493.2	18	493.8	19	511.4	15	519.1	14
Ray, Robbie	401.1	67	425.4	50	465.2	30	485.3	21	491.3	21	498.6	20	516.6	15
Gonzalez, Gio	422.7	43	449.2	31	456.2	35	488.7	20	510.1	13	521.2	11	515.8	16
Martinez, Carlos	448.1	26	456.1	29	492.8	17	515.5	9	502.0	15	507.7	16	511.7	17
Lester, Jon	534.1	4	528.3	6	527.7	7	535.3	6	529.6	6	514.9	14	510.5	18
Archer, Chris	470.7	18	484.8	16	503.7	13	507.3	11	514.1	10	529.3	9	510.2	19
Tanaka, Masahiro	465.8	21	474.9	24	457.8	32	471.1	30	490.9	22	500.7	19	506.3	20
Happ, J.A.	470.7	19	472.5	26	466.0	28	479.2	23	474.0	31	485.8	27	502.7	21
Hamels, Cole	481.9	14	492.7	14	485.2	20	476.2	26	487.8	23	496.9	21	500.8	22
Samardzija, Jeff	444.5	30	448.8	32	469.0	25	478.8	25	480.1	26	491.8	23	500.5	23
Lackey, John	478.4	16	478.0	20	476.1	21	475.4	27	480.5	25	488.0	25	495.6	24
Keuchel, Dallas	440.8	31	476.7	22	488.3	19	489.7	19	479.5	29	480.7	31	494.8	25
Teheran, Julio	465.5	22	468.2	27	467.6	27	462.7	35	469.3	34	487.2	26	494.6	26
Bauer, Trevor	416.7	47	417.1	61	436.4	48	452.0	41	453.2	48	475.7	36	491.7	27
Pomeranz, Drew	404.8	60	420.0	59	437.1	44	450.4	42	468.9	35	483.0	28	491.3	28
Severino, Luis	300.0	158	340.6	131	377.4	105	408.3	81	442.5	56	459.7	50	490.5	29
Stroman, Marcus	405.7	58	428.3	47	443.2	40	460.0	37	475.0	30	482.0	30	490.2	30
Hill, Rich	393.8	79	395.1	85	399.2	86	424.2	67	448.0	54	461.7	48	489.9	31
Porcello, Rick	488.4	12	492.7	13	491.9	18	479.0	24	495.8	18	496.1	22	489.0	32
Estrada, Marco	482.0	13	501.8	10	502.5	14	485.2	22	479.7	28	477.4	34	488.8	33
Cueto, Johnny	508.1	9	507.1	9	514.3	9	509.3	10	496.5	17	489.8	24	487.1	34
Anderson, Chase	397.2	73	422.5	51	436.4	47	465.4	32	458.4	41	465.1	43	486.4	35
Cole, Gerrit	406.0	56	430.4	46	443.7	38	444.1	46	467.6	36	479.6	32	484.7	36
Darvish, Yu	370.1	103	412.5	65	436.7	46	465.5	31	461.5	39	472.7	38	484.6	37
Odorizzi, Jake	445.8	27	454.3	30	470.7	24	464.8	33	463.1	38	454.8	54	482.2	38
Dickey, R.A.	430.2	38	431.6	45	430.8	54	455.3	40	471.5	32	483.0	29	478.5	39
Nelson, Jimmy	377.6	92	385.3	95	413.9	72	447.5	45	471.4	33	477.7	33	478.4	40
Gausman, Kevin	414.7	48	406.6	73	414.7	68	414.7	74	440.8	58	464.2	44	477.8	41
Roark, Tanner	432.3	37	445.5	33	456.4	34	436.7	53	449.9	52	473.4	37	475.9	42
Sabathia, CC	409.7	54	420.0	58	437.7	43	448.2	44	452.6	50	464.2	45	473.2	43
Walker, Taijuan	384.7	89	410.5	66	422.1	60	428.5	63	450.2	51	466.1	42	471.6	44
Gray, Sonny	394.3	78	375.6	104	395.6	92	421.9	69	443.8	55	466.2	41	470.5	45
Price, David	502.3	10	490.3	15	465.0	31	473.7	29	485.1	24	477.4	35	469.9	46
Kennedy, Ian	457.4	24	481.9	17	465.8	29	475.1	28	479.9	27	460.1	49	463.3	47
Gray, Jon	399.3	70	404.6	75	396.9	90	397.1	94	403.5	97	430.9	74	463.1	48
Duffy, Danny	411.2	52	432.1	44	442.8	41	435.8	54	457.9	42	461.8	47	461.7	49
Straily, Dan	405.3	59	422.4	53	443.5	39	458.9	38	457.7	43	470.6	39	461.2	50
Fulmer, Michael	396.7	75	422.5	52	445.9	37	458.4	39	466.0	37	467.7	40	461.0	51
Paxton, James	354.0	114	396.8	84	403.8	82	405.0	86	452.7	49	456.8	53	460.3	52
Maeda, Kenta	400.0	68	408.1	69	418.9	63	435.8	55	449.9	53	459.5	51	460.2	53
Davies, Zach	374.7	97	380.7	98	394.7	93	410.0	79	432.6	69	457.3	52	459.1	54
Cashner, Andrew	378.6	91	390.2	90	412.9	75	409.1	80	430.3	71	450.9	57	458.3	55
Leake, Mike	402.0	66	432.9	43	457.2	33	463.2	34	453.6	46	441.1	62	457.3	56
Chacin, Jhoulys	322.4	137	344.8	124	358.8	122	390.7	102	425.3	75	434.9	68	453.9	57
Salazar, Danny	417.9	46	433.9	41	432.1	53	424.9	66	438.7	62	451.1	56	453.5	58
Hernandez, Felix	445.1	28	443.2	36	435.4	51	435.0	57	454.3	44	447.8	58	452.1	59
Wacha, Michael	375.1	96	398.7	82	404.8	81	414.9	73	439.6	60	434.7	69	449.5	60
Godley, Zack	300.0	158	308.6	181	352.0	133	387.3	104	407.8	91	430.4	75	448.9	61
Nola, Aaron	300.0	158	312.6	169	322.5	173	361.2	133	409.9	88	429.1	80	448.4	62
Gibson, Kyle	386.3	88	383.1	97	379.7	100	395.3	96	402.6	99	418.7	90	446.9	63
Hammel, Jason	423.0	42	420.8	54	422.0	61	440.0	52	453.9	45	462.5	46	446.6	64
Lynn, Lance	300.0	158	339.0	133	372.6	111	391.1	101	426.3	73	443.0	61	446.2	65
Syndergaard, Noah	467.4	20	475.0	23	468.5	26	461.0	36	453.3	47	445.5	59	446.1	66
Corbin, Patrick	300.0	158	347.1	120	349.8	138	372.8	119	390.0	109	435.7	67	443.7	67
Chatwood, Tyler	382.2	90	401.6	78	421.6	62	443.4	47	437.2	65	427.2	81	442.7	68
Nova, Ivan	368.9	106	409.0	68	423.4	59	439.4	51	438.7	61	436.8	66	442.6	69
Gonzalez, Miguel	398.1	72	414.0	62	417.5	65	404.0	87	412.7	86	437.3	65	442.4	70
Rodriguez, Eduardo	361.5	111	386.6	93	413.7	70	407.7	84	405.8	92	421.7	85	441.9	71

Starting Pitcher Rankings

Player	April 1 Score	Rank	May 1 Score	Rank	June 1 Score	Rank	July 1 Score	Rank	Aug 1 Score	Rank	Sept 1 Score	Rank	Oct 2 Score	Rank
Wood, Alex	300.0	158	319.8	162	365.6	114	397.9	93	410.2	87	429.3	79	441.5	72
Bundy, Dylan	326.8	132	375.8	103	396.2	91	403.5	88	415.0	83	444.3	60	440.1	73
Hellickson, Jeremy	418.5	45	443.3	35	433.2	52	441.4	49	442.3	57	440.9	63	438.7	74
Tomlin, Josh	391.2	81	387.3	92	413.1	73	407.8	83	432.8	68	426.1	82	438.3	75
Manaea, Sean	376.3	93	394.6	86	418.6	64	431.6	60	440.1	59	429.9	78	438.3	76
Nolasco, Ricky	394.9	76	407.5	71	413.6	71	435.2	56	432.9	67	431.2	73	437.9	77
Garcia, Jaime	376.3	94	392.0	88	417.4	66	420.7	70	432.5	70	432.7	72	436.9	78
Montgomery, Jordan			323.2	156	349.4	140	388.0	103	398.1	101	411.2	98	433.5	79
Eickhoff, Jerad	412.2	51	428.0	48	425.4	58	427.0	64	438.0	63	439.7	64	433.2	80
Perez, Martin	374.3	100	388.3	91	407.2	78	405.9	85	404.2	95	423.2	84	433.0	81
Fiers, Mike	406.0	57	407.0	72	416.8	67	442.4	48	459.2	40	453.3	55	433.0	82
Cobb, Alex	300.0	158	321.1	158	363.9	116	385.8	105	408.9	90	420.3	87	432.5	83
Moore, Matt	409.5	55	420.4	57	426.4	57	419.0	71	420.0	79	433.0	71	430.8	84
Shields, James	396.8	74	412.9	63	405.2	80	401.1	91	389.7	111	408.7	101	430.1	85
Morton, Charlie	300.0	158	324.1	155	350.9	135	343.4	158	378.9	119	401.8	109	428.5	86
Kuhl, Chad	318.2	140	331.5	145	350.5	137	373.9	117	393.9	103	415.1	95	427.6	87
Berrios, Jose	300.0	158	300.0	197	340.8	150	376.0	114	392.5	105	417.1	93	427.1	88
Marquez, German	300.0	158	308.6	180	350.8	136	366.9	126	404.6	94	423.5	83	427.0	89
Clevinger, Mike	300.0	158	300.0	197	338.9	153	362.9	132	381.3	117	409.9	100	426.5	90
Snell, Blake	332.8	124	353.8	117	354.2	130	348.1	149	366.1	139	402.4	108	424.5	91
Miley, Wade	404.2	62	433.7	42	440.8	42	425.0	65	415.3	82	434.4	70	423.9	92
Foltynewicz, Mike	348.5	115	371.0	106	377.8	103	414.0	75	422.4	78	421.3	86	423.4	93
Peacock, Brad	300.0	158	300.0	197	315.8	185	347.3	150	375.8	124	394.7	117	423.2	94
Liriano, Francisco	433.1	36	443.4	34	428.6	56	437.0	52	437.1	66	430.1	76	422.6	95
Pineda, Michael	413.5	49	435.4	38	453.3	36	450.0	43	437.8	64	430.0	77	422.5	96
Miranda, Ariel	318.5	139	344.6	125	374.8	108	410.8	77	416.7	81	418.9	89	418.6	97
Urena, Jose	300.0	158	300.0	197	328.9	167	358.7	135	385.2	114	399.9	111	418.1	98
Colon, Bartolo	423.6	41	427.0	49	407.4	77	391.7	100	389.8	110	414.7	97	418.0	99
Graveman, Kendall	375.9	95	398.9	81	403.2	83	395.7	95	388.0	112	396.0	115	416.7	100
Williams, Trevor	300.0	158	300.0	197	326.1	170	353.0	142	372.6	127	396.9	114	416.7	101
Vargas, Jason	300.0	158	344.1	126	369.9	113	408.3	82	405.3	93	405.8	104	416.1	102
Freeland, Kyle			336.5	138	370.1	112	382.8	109	402.1	100	417.3	92	414.4	103
Shoemaker, Matt	410.5	53	419.3	60	436.3	49	434.8	59	427.1	72	419.3	88	411.8	104
Volquez, Edinson	390.8	82	398.5	83	409.7	76	434.9	58	426.2	74	418.5	91	411.0	105
Lamet, Dinelson					316.9	183	344.2	156	357.9	148	398.8	112	410.1	106
Castillo, Luis							314.1	202	361.1	146	400.9	110	408.7	107
Santiago, Hector	412.9	50	436.8	37	436.8	45	431.3	61	423.6	76	415.8	94	408.3	108
Zimmermann, Jordan	392.6	80	393.5	87	392.1	94	413.8	76	413.8	85	408.3	102	408.2	109
Perdomo, Luis	330.1	129	338.7	134	364.4	115	381.4	110	381.8	116	397.0	113	408.1	110
Wainwright, Adam	374.5	98	377.7	100	412.9	74	410.2	78	422.6	77	414.9	96	405.4	111
Richard, Clayton	304.9	151	331.2	144	357.1	124	366.0	127	364.5	141	390.9	119	405.2	112
Jimenez, Ubaldo	404.4	61	402.9	77	397.6	89	402.7	89	409.0	89	402.5	107	404.8	113
Sanchez, Aaron	429.8	39	434.0	40	436.3	50	428.8	62	418.2	80	410.5	99	403.0	114
Ryu, Hyun-Jin	300.0	158	329.9	147	336.9	155	356.9	136	367.5	135	391.4	118	401.8	115
Boyd, Matt	332.0	126	356.4	115	356.5	125	350.2	146	363.9	143	368.9	141	400.6	116
Anderson, Tyler	369.9	104	375.5	105	402.0	84	394.0	99	386.3	113	378.5	131	400.4	117
Iwakuma, Hisashi	429.8	40	435.1	39	430.0	55	422.5	68	414.7	84	407.0	103	399.5	118
Bridwell, Parker					306.2	202	317.2	191	354.3	150	374.0	135	398.1	119
McHugh, Collin	437.1	32	420.6	56	389.6	96	359.6	134	351.8	152	383.6	124	397.7	120
Gallardo, Yovani	390.2	84	399.3	80	397.7	88	402.1	90	403.7	96	402.8	105	397.4	121
McCullers, Lance	332.7	125	358.6	112	400.3	85	418.5	72	402.7	98	395.9	116	396.6	122
Ramirez, JC			330.3	146	360.8	118	370.0	121	392.1	106	402.7	106	395.2	123
Newcomb, Sean							338.0	165	349.4	155	374.5	134	390.7	124
Taillon, Jameson	300.0	158	338.6	135	332.7	162	355.4	138	350.6	153	368.4	142	390.7	125
Tillman, Chris	434.9	35	420.7	55	414.0	69	395.0	98	396.3	102	386.8	120	383.7	126
Rodon, Carlos	402.2	65	385.0	96	354.0	131	334.0	170	352.7	151	384.0	123	383.2	127
Guerra, Junior	370.1	102	369.0	108	378.4	102	384.5	107	393.0	104	386.0	121	380.6	128
Mejia, Adalberto			312.3	172	330.8	163	353.1	141	377.7	122	373.3	137	379.5	129
Ramirez, Erasmo	300.0	158	308.5	183	317.5	180	322.7	187	320.1	192	352.4	160	377.4	130
Conley, Adam	356.4	113	363.6	110	355.9	126	348.4	148	367.3	137	385.3	122	377.1	131
Chen, Wei-Yin	399.2	71	412.5	64	406.3	79	398.8	92	391.0	107	383.3	125	375.8	132
Koehler, Tom	403.5	63	407.7	70	397.9	87	383.4	108	383.2	115	383.1	126	375.6	133
Faria, Jake							347.1	151	370.9	131	380.7	128	375.5	134
Blach, Ty	300.0	158	317.4	164	339.0	151	350.6	144	368.6	134	378.9	130	375.3	135
Feldman, Scott	300.0	158	334.3	141	359.9	119	395.1	97	390.4	108	381.7	127	374.2	136
Junis, Jakob					304.5	205	319.9	190	313.1	203	349.3	164	374.2	137
Romano, Sal			301.4	196	300.0	220	300.0	228	322.8	184	350.3	162	374.1	138
Lugo, Seth	306.7	148	300.0	197	300.0	220	323.0	185	338.7	166	347.1	167	372.4	139
Senzatela, Antonio			343.9	128	377.5	104	379.6	112	377.9	121	379.2	129	372.2	140
Cotton, Jharel	300.0	158	317.8	163	334.8	157	352.5	143	347.3	157	364.1	147	371.7	141
Fister, Doug	364.2	109	345.4	123	314.4	187	311.7	205	317.6	195	358.6	153	371.4	142
Griffin, A.J.	335.9	122	353.4	118	362.4	117	354.9	139	347.1	158	369.2	140	370.1	143
Montgomery, Mike	300.0	158	300.0	197	300.0	220	331.2	174	337.1	171	351.8	161	370.1	144
Velasquez, Vince	348.1	116	360.7	111	373.4	109	366.9	125	376.9	123	377.1	133	369.6	145

Starting Pitcher Rankings

Player	April 1 Score	April 1 Rank	May 1 Score	May 1 Rank	June 1 Score	June 1 Rank	July 1 Score	July 1 Rank	Aug 1 Score	Aug 1 Rank	Sept 1 Score	Sept 1 Rank	Oct 2 Score	Oct 2 Rank
Garza, Matt	322.5	136	321.7	157	347.4	141	363.0	130	379.4	118	377.3	132	369.4	146
Montero, Rafael	300.0	158	300.0	197	301.7	213	308.3	213	324.2	182	360.7	151	369.0	147
Suter, Brent	300.0	158	300.0	197	300.0	220	300.6	226	343.9	162	344.8	168	368.9	148
Andriese, Matt	322.2	138	346.7	121	380.8	99	377.7	113	369.9	132	362.2	149	367.9	149
Lively, Ben							333.8	171	331.2	176	340.4	171	366.4	150
Adleman, Tim	309.4	145	313.4	166	343.8	146	369.0	123	375.7	125	373.8	136	366.3	151
Sanchez, Anibal	369.8	105	346.5	122	315.5	186	324.9	180	345.2	161	337.5	176	365.5	152
Stephenson, Robert	300.0	158	300.0	197	300.0	220	300.0	228	303.8	222	334.1	179	365.1	153
Finnegan, Brandon	387.4	87	399.3	79	391.6	95	385.5	106	378.0	120	370.2	138	362.7	154
Hoffman, Jeff	300.0	158	300.0	197	318.4	178	346.9	152	360.2	147	369.5	139	362.0	155
Bailey, Homer	300.0	158	300.0	197	300.0	220	292.7	421	321.1	191	334.0	180	361.5	156
Holland, Derek	315.5	142	348.6	119	377.2	107	373.7	118	363.8	144	366.4	144	359.9	157
Norris, Daniel	323.8	134	344.0	127	359.5	121	372.4	120	364.0	142	356.3	155	359.7	158
Meyer, Alex	300.0	158	304.2	190	328.2	168	364.4	129	374.6	126	366.8	143	359.3	159
Gsellman, Robert	304.1	153	311.6	174	325.9	171	332.8	173	325.5	181	333.5	181	359.3	160
Giolito, Lucas	300.0	158	300.0	197	300.0	220	300.0	228	300.0	235	317.8	206	359.2	161
Chavez, Jesse	300.0	158	329.1	148	355.7	127	367.0	124	372.2	129	365.5	145	358.0	162
Skaggs, Tyler	305.8	150	337.8	136	330.8	164	323.3	183	315.5	199	333.0	183	357.9	163
Stratton, Chris									300.0	235	335.5	178	357.8	164
Weaver, Jered	390.6	83	406.2	74	387.8	97	380.3	111	372.5	128	364.8	146	357.3	165
McCarthy, Brandon	300.0	158	334.3	142	354.5	128	375.7	115	371.1	130	363.3	148	355.8	166
Martinez, Nick	300.0	158	320.0	161	334.7	158	350.4	145	340.1	165	352.4	159	355.1	167
Weaver, Luke	300.0	158	300.0	197	300.0	220	300.0	228	303.9	221	330.5	187	354.9	168
Mengden, Daniel	300.0	158	300.0	197	299.1	412	300.0	228	300.0	235	300.0	244	354.6	169
Jackson, Edwin	303.7	154	300.0	197	300.0	220	300.0	228	322.8	185	352.9	157	353.8	170
Ross, Joe	330.5	128	334.4	140	338.2	154	365.4	128	369.0	133	361.2	150	353.7	171
Biagini, Joe			329.7	165	346.4	153	337.5	170	341.7	170	353.4	172
Cain, Matt	300.0	158	337.1	137	343.1	147	341.4	163	348.7	156	350.1	160	353.2	173
Miller, Shelby	374.4	99	390.2	89	382.5	98	375.0	116	367.2	138	359.5	152	352.0	174
Peralta, Wily	367.7	107	380.2	99	377.3	106	369.8	122	362.1	145	354.3	156	346.8	175
Bettis, Chad	402.6	64	385.4	94	354.4	129	324.4	182	300.0	235	324.4	195	346.2	176
Gaviglio, Sam					316.6	184	353.6	140	346.7	159	339.0	173	345.6	177
Blackburn, Paul							311.0	207	340.2	164	352.5	158	345.0	178
Leiter, Mark							315.5	198	316.9	197	331.0	185	340.7	179
Cahill, Trevor	300.0	158	324.9	154	346.8	142	339.3	164	349.8	154	347.6	165	340.1	180
Despaigne, Odrisamer	300.0	158	300.0	197	300.0	220	300.0	228	300.0	235	311.6	216	339.7	181
Pelfrey, Mike	317.3	141	305.9	188	342.6	149	356.7	137	365.0	140	357.9	154	339.5	182
Thompson, Jake	300.0	158	300.0	197	300.0	220	300.0	228	308.9	207	305.4	238	338.5	183
Lopez, Reynaldo	300.0	158	300.0	197	300.0	220	300.0	228	300.0	235	315.0	209	338.2	184
Pivetta, Nick			303.8	192	313.6	188	337.3	166	367.5	136	310.6	219	338.0	185
Woodruff, Brandon											321.2	198	337.4	186
Sims, Luke									306.8	212	333.5	182	337.3	187
Richards, Garrett	300.0	158	304.1	191	300.0	220	300.0	228	300.0	235	300.0	244	337.1	188
Cole, A.J.	300.0	158	300.0	197	301.7	214	300.0	228	300.0	235	320.7	199	335.4	189
Harvey, Matt	322.9	135	342.7	129	357.3	123	362.9	131	355.2	149	347.4	166	333.9	190
Fulmer, Carson											300.0	244	333.5	191
Anderson, Brett	300.0	158	312.5	170	303.4	209	300.0	228	300.0	235	307.8	230	332.2	192
Matz, Steven	331.6	127	301.4	194	300.0	220	333.3	172	337.9	169	339.3	172	331.8	193
Pruitt, Austin			308.5	182	300.8	217	300.0	228	304.4	217	338.6	174	331.6	194
Albers, Andrew	300.0	158	300.0	197	300.0	220	300.0	228	300.0	235	309.6	223	331.0	195
Butler, Eddie	300.0	158	300.0	197	319.4	176	346.0	155	346.0	160	338.3	175	330.8	196
Moore, Andrew							307.5	214	326.7	179	319.0	204	330.5	197
Gohara, Luiz											329.2	198
Wood, Travis	300.0	158	300.0	197	300.0	220	300.0	228	312.5	204	336.6	177	328.6	199
Farmer, Buck	300.0	158	300.0	197	313.4	189	316.2	196	308.4	210	309.2	225	327.8	200
Peters, Dillon											313.4	212	327.3	201
Wheeler, Zack			68.1	412	333.9	159	334.9	168	340.4	163	332.6	184	325.1	202
Karns, Nathan	300.0	158	320.0	160	353.7	132	346.2	154	338.5	167	330.7	186	323.2	203
Musgrove, Joe	307.8	147	325.2	153	342.9	148	336.0	167	338.1	168	330.3	188	322.8	204
Mahle, Tyler											306.0	237	322.8	205
Alcantara, Raul	300.0	158	300.0	197	300.0	220	300.0	228	300.0	235	300.0	244	322.7	206
Norris, Bud	301.3	156	300.0	197	300.0	220	300.0	228	300.0	235	300.0	244	320.6	207
Wright, Steven	363.1	110	357.7	113	350.9	134	343.4	157	335.7	172	327.9	189	320.4	208
Triggs, Andrew	300.0	158	339.2	132	359.6	120	343.3	160	335.5	173	327.8	190	320.3	209
Ynoa, Gabriel	300.0	158	300.0	197	300.0	220	300.0	228	300.0	235	300.0	244	320.2	210
Hahn, Jesse	300.0	158	334.8	139	344.2	145	342.2	161	335.2	174	327.5	191	320.0	211
Buchholz, Clay	367.6	108	357.2	114	349.5	139	342.0	162	334.2	175	326.5	193	319.0	212
Brault, Steven	300.0	158	300.0	197	300.0	220	300.0	228	300.0	235	300.0	244	318.8	213
Garrett, Amir			332.4	143	332.8	160	331.0	175	323.2	183	315.5	208	317.8	214
Flaherty, Jack											299.9	419	317.7	215
Ross, Tyson	300.0	158	300.0	197	300.0	220	317.1	192	322.1	188	324.8	194	317.3	216
Smith, Chris									322.7	186	326.7	192	317.2	217
Covey, Dylan			307.2	186	313.2	191	305.7	217	300.0	235	300.0	244	316.0	218
Heaney, Andrew	300.0	158	300.0	197	300.0	220	300.0	228	300.0	235	316.3	207	315.7	219

Starting Pitcher Rankings

Player	April 1 Score	Rank	May 1 Score	Rank	June 1 Score	Rank	July 1 Score	Rank	Aug 1 Score	Rank	Sept 1 Score	Rank	Oct 2 Score	Rank
Stephens, Jackson							306.5	215	300.2	233	300.0	244	315.2	220
O'Grady, Chris									321.3	189	322.4	196	314.9	221
Flexen, Chris									300.8	231	319.1	203	314.8	222
Gonzales, Marco	300.0	158	300.0	197	300.0	220	300.0	228	300.0	235	309.3	224	314.1	223
Merritt, Ryan	300.0	158	300.0	197	300.0	220	302.0	223	300.0	235	320.4	200	313.9	224
Wilkerson, Aaron													313.4	225
Scribner, Troy											319.9	201	313.2	226
Gossett, Daniel							315.4	199	330.2	177	342.5	169	311.9	227
Delgado, Randall	300.0	158	300.0	197	317.3	181	334.7	169	327.0	178	319.2	202	311.7	228
Bibens-Dirkx, Austin					303.9	208	329.2	177	325.8	180	318.8	205	311.3	229
McGuire, Deck													310.7	230
Worley, Vance	300.0	158	300.0	197	309.5	196	305.3	219	303.4	224	321.8	197	310.5	231
Slegers, Aaron											308.2	228	309.9	232
Stripling, Ross	300.0	158	300.0	197	300.0	220	300.0	228	300.0	235	308.9	226	309.8	233
Fried, Max													309.7	234
Velazquez, Hector					300.0	220	305.4	218	300.0	235	300.0	244	308.5	235
Bergman, Christian	300.0	158	300.0	197	318.5	177	329.9	176	322.2	187	314.4	210	306.9	236
Gant, John	300.0	158	300.0	197	300.0	220	300.0	228	300.0	235	300.0	244	306.5	237
Gee, Dillon	300.0	158	300.0	197	300.0	220	300.0	228	300.0	235	312.1	214	306.1	238
Eflin, Zach	300.0	158	327.1	150	321.4	174	314.4	201	306.6	214	313.5	211	306.0	239
Lyles, Jordan	300.0	158	300.0	197	300.0	220	300.0	228	300.0	235	300.0	244	305.8	240
Bell, Chad													304.6	241
Rowley, Chris											312.1	215	304.6	242
Holmberg, David	300.0	158	300.0	197	304.1	207	328.6	178	321.1	190	313.4	213	304.5	243
Stewart, Brock	300.0	158	300.0	197	300.0	220	300.0	228	303.3	225	302.8	240	304.0	244
Shipley, Braden	304.1	152	300.0	197	300.0	220	300.0	228	300.0	235	300.0	244	303.8	245
Banda, Anthony									304.2	220	311.2	217	303.3	246
Cessa, Luis	309.0	146	300.0	197	300.0	220	312.8	203	311.2	206	310.8	218	303.3	247
Martes, Francis							324.6	181	318.3	194	310.6	220	303.1	248
Tepesch, Nick	300.0	158	300.0	197	300.0	220	300.0	228	300.0	235	310.1	221	302.6	249
Urias, Julio	324.6	133	325.4	152	332.7	161	325.2	179	317.5	196	309.7	222	302.2	250
Castro, Miguel													302.0	251
Milone, Tommy	300.0	158	311.7	173	310.0	195	302.5	221	300.0	235	308.1	229	300.9	252
Paulino, David	300.0	158	300.0	197	307.2	198	323.0	186	316.0	198	308.2	227	300.7	253
Jeffress, Jeremy													300.5	254
All Others													300	255

Team Statistics

Lindsay Zeck

Three teams—the Dodgers, Indians, and Astros—finished the season with over 100 wins in 2017 for the first time since the Yankees, Braves, and Astros achieved this feat nearly twenty years ago in 1998. Each of the three teams dominated baseball at a different point in the season. The Astros had the best record in baseball in April and May (38-16), the Dodgers did in June and July (41-10), and the Indians did in August, September, and October (45-13). The Indians dominance during this time gave us one of the top stories of the season as they won 22 games in a row between August 24th and September 14th, breaking the American League winning-streak record.

The Indians may have finished with the second-best record in baseball, but they won only 6 of 20 games against their National League opponents, which was tied for the third-worst record in interleague play. The two teams with a worse interleague record, winning 5 of 20, were the Phillies and Reds, two of the three worst teams in the NL.

The Indians and Astros tied for the best record in away games winning 53 of 81. They were two of the only four teams to have a better record away than at home. The best team at home was the Dodgers. They won 57 of their 81 games at Dodger Stadium. Amazingly, up until their slide at the end of August into September when they lost 17 of 18 games, they had won 52 of 66 games at home.

The only division that was won by fewer than six games was the AL East, with the Yankees finishing two games behind the Red Sox. Despite the exciting race to the finish, the Red Sox had led the division since their win against the Indians on July 31st. All the division leaders from this point on went on to win their divisions.

Over the next several pages, we can find out things like:
- The Astros' offense led all of baseball in hits, doubles, total bases, runs, and RBI. They also had the lowest number of strikeouts.
- The eight teams with the lowest ERAs among starters all made the playoffs.
- The Mets had the worst defense this season. Their fielders combined to cost the team 72 runs despite being one of only six teams to save runs at each of the three outfield positions

2017 American League Standings

Overall

EAST	W-L	Pct	GB	D1	LD1	LLd
Boston Red Sox	93-69	.574	0.0	97	10/1	5.5
New York Yankees	91-71	.562	2.0	59	7/31	4.0
Tampa Bay Rays	80-82	.494	13.0	2	4/3	1.0
Toronto Blue Jays	76-86	.469	17.0	0	-	0.0
Baltimore Orioles	75-87	.463	18.0	33	5/20	2.0

CENTRAL	W-L	Pct	GB	D1	LD1	LLd
Cleveland Indians	102-60	.630	0.0	125	10/1	17.0
Minnesota Twins	85-77	.525	17.0	49	6/25	3.0
Kansas City Royals	80-82	.494	22.0	0	-	0.0
Chicago White Sox	67-95	.414	35.0	5	5/4	0.5
Detroit Tigers	64-98	.395	38.0	14	4/26	1.5

WEST	W-L	Pct	GB	D1	LD1	LLd
Houston Astros	101-61	.623	0.0	177	10/1	21.0
Los Angeles Angels	80-82	.494	21.0	7	4/13	1.5
Texas Rangers	78-84	.481	23.0	0	-	0.0
Seattle Mariners	78-84	.481	23.0	0	-	0.0
Oakland Athletics	75-87	.463	26.0	1	4/3	0.0

Wild Card Clinch Dates: New York 9/26, Minnesota 9/27. Division Clinch Dates:Cleveland 9/16, Houston 9/16, Boston 9/30.
D1 = Number of days a team had at least a share of first place of their division; LD1 = Last date the team had at least a share of first place; LLd = The largest number of games that a team led their division by.

East Division

Tm	AT Home	AT Road	VERSUS East	VERSUS Cent	VERSUS West	VERSUS NL	LHS	RHS	Day	Night	Grass	Turf	1-Rn	5+Rn	XInn	April	May	June	July	Aug	Sept	Pre	Post
Bos	48-33	45-36	41-35	20-14	16-16	16-4	18-19	75-50	25-23	68-46	80-64	13-5	22-19	29-19	15-3	13-11	16-12	16-12	13-14	18-9	17-11	50-39	43-30
NYY	51-30	40-41	44-32	18-15	14-19	15-5	24-23	67-48	34-26	57-45	85-61	6-10	18-26	37-13	5-6	15-8	15-12	13-15	14-12	14-15	20-9	47-43	44-28
TB	42-39	38-43	35-41	18-15	16-17	11-9	19-29	61-53	27-28	53-54	36-39	44-43	21-24	18-24	8-6	12-14	17-13	13-13	12-13	13-15	13-14	47-43	33-39
Tor	42-39	34-47	33-43	13-18	21-14	9-11	18-24	58-62	31-29	45-57	30-41	46-45	26-27	16-27	5-14	8-17	18-10	11-15	12-15	13-15	14-14	41-47	35-39
Bal	46-35	29-52	37-39	13-21	17-15	8-12	26-24	49-63	23-26	52-61	66-77	9-10	21-20	20-30	12-4	15-8	12-16	12-16	12-14	17-12	7-21	42-46	33-41

Central Division

Tm	AT Home	AT Road	VERSUS East	VERSUS Cent	VERSUS West	VERSUS NL	LHS	RHS	Day	Night	Grass	Turf	1-Rn	5+Rn	XInn	April	May	June	July	Aug	Sept	Pre	Post
Cle	49-32	53-28	22-12	50-26	24-8	6-14	36-24	66-36	39-17	63-43	98-57	4-3	20-15	38-11	4-2	14-10	13-14	15-12	15-11	19-9	26-4	47-40	55-20
Min	41-40	44-37	15-18	41-35	16-17	13-7	26-23	59-54	28-33	57-44	82-74	3-3	15-18	29-27	3-1	12-11	14-12	14-15	10-15	20-10	15-14	45-43	40-34
KC	43-38	37-44	17-15	35-41	19-15	9-11	18-23	62-59	26-27	54-55	75-80	5-2	25-16	22-32	4-7	7-16	15-14	17-9	16-10	15-15	10-18	44-43	36-39
CWS	39-42	28-53	13-20	33-43	15-18	6-14	20-26	47-69	25-29	42-66	64-92	3-3	21-23	22-31	5-5	13-10	11-18	11-16	6-18	11-18	15-15	38-49	29-46
Det	34-47	30-51	16-17	31-45	9-24	8-12	21-22	43-76	27-30	37-68	63-93	1-5	17-23	18-34	1-4	12-12	13-16	10-15	12-14	11-17	6-24	39-48	25-50

West Division

Tm	AT Home	AT Road	VERSUS East	VERSUS Cent	VERSUS West	VERSUS NL	LHS	RHS	Day	Night	Grass	Turf	1-Rn	5+Rn	XInn	April	May	June	July	Aug	Sept	Pre	Post
Hou	48-33	53-28	21-13	15-17	50-26	15-5	24-24	77-37	32-16	69-45	96-56	5-5	19-13	35-19	4-4	16-9	22-7	16-11	15-9	11-17	21-8	60-29	41-32
LAA	43-38	37-44	19-13	11-23	39-37	11-9	24-24	56-58	19-23	61-59	76-79	4-3	27-22	19-14	8-7	14-13	14-15	14-14	9-13	18-10	11-17	45-47	35-35
Tex	41-40	37-44	12-20	18-16	34-42	14-6	22-18	56-66	20-23	58-61	72-81	6-3	13-24	28-28	5-5	11-14	15-14	13-13	11-14	16-12	12-17	43-45	35-39
Sea	40-41	38-43	13-19	18-16	35-41	12-8	22-23	56-61	22-31	56-53	76-79	2-5	26-15	28-20	7-5	11-15	14-14	15-12	14-12	12-15	12-16	43-47	35-37
Oak	46-35	29-52	16-19	20-11	32-44	7-13	19-26	56-61	34-27	41-60	74-80	1-7	21-21	20-28	4-9	11-14	12-15	12-16	12-14	11-16	17-12	39-50	36-37

Team vs. Team Breakdown

	EAST Bos	NYY	TB	Tor	Bal	CENTRAL Cle	Min	KC	CWS	Det	WEST Hou	LAA	Tex	Sea	Oak
Boston Red Sox	-	8	11	13	9	4	5	2	6	3	3	2	5	3	3
New York Yankees	11	-	12	9	12	2	4	5	4	3	2	2	3	5	2
Tampa Bay Rays	8	7	-	9	11	3	4	3	3	5	4	4	2	1	5
Toronto Blue Jays	6	10	10	-	7	2	3	2	3	3	3	3	4	6	5
Baltimore Orioles	10	7	8	12	-	1	2	3	4	3	1	2	6	4	4
Cleveland Indians	3	5	4	4	6	-	12	12	13	13	5	6	6	4	3
Minnesota Twins	2	2	4	4	5	7	-	11	12	11	1	5	4	3	3
Kansas City Royals	4	2	4	4	3	7	8	-	9	11	4	6	1	5	3
Chicago White Sox	1	3	3	3	3	6	7	10	-	10	4	3	4	3	1
Detroit Tigers	4	3	2	3	4	6	8	8	9	-	3	3	1	1	1
Houston Astros	4	5	3	4	5	1	5	3	2	4	-	12	12	14	12
Los Angeles Angels	4	4	3	4	4	0	2	1	4	4	7	-	8	12	12
Texas Rangers	1	3	4	3	1	1	3	6	3	5	7	11	-	8	8
Seattle Mariners	3	2	5	1	2	2	4	2	4	6	5	7	11	-	12
Oakland Athletics	4	2	2	3	4	4	3	3	5	5	7	7	11	7	-

2017 National League Standings

Overall

EAST Team	W-L	Pct	GB	D1	LD1	LLd	CENTRAL Team	W-L	Pct	GB	D1	LD1	LLd	WEST Team	W-L	Pct	GB	D1	LD1	LLd
Washington Nationals	97-65	.599	0.0	178	10/1	21.0	Chicago Cubs	92-70	.568	0.0	95	10/1	7.0	Los Angeles Dodgers	104-58	.642	0.0	112	10/1	21.0
Miami Marlins	77-85	.475	20.0	3	4/16	0.0	Milwaukee Brewers	86-76	.531	6.0	65	7/25	5.5	Arizona Diamondbacks	93-69	.574	11.0	18	6/1	1.0
Atlanta Braves	72-90	.444	25.0	0	-	0.0	St Louis Cardinals	83-79	.512	9.0	13	5/16	1.5	Colorado Rockies	87-75	.537	17.0	65	6/20	2.5
New York Mets	70-92	.432	27.0	10	4/15	1.5	Pittsburgh Pirates	75-87	.463	17.0	0	-	0.0	San Diego Padres	71-91	.438	33.0	0	-	0.0
Philadelphia Phillies	66-96	.407	31.0	3	4/9	0.0	Cincinnati Reds	68-94	.420	24.0	18	5/7	1.5	San Francisco Giants	64-98	.395	40.0	0	-	0.0

Wild Card Clinch Dates: Arizona 9/24, Colorado 9/30. Division Clinch Dates:Washington 9/10, Los Angeles 9/22, Chicago 9/25.
D1 = Number of days a team had at least a share of first place of their division; LD1 = Last date the team had at least a share of first place; LLd = The largest number of games that a team led their division

East Division

Tm	Home	Road	East	Cent	West	AL	LHS	RHS	Day	Night	Grass	Turf	1-Rn	5+Rn	XInn	April	May	June	July	Aug	Sept	Pre	Post
Was	47-34	50-31	47-29	19-15	21-11	10-10	22-15	75-50	27-29	70-36	97-65	0-0	30-21	32-16	7-4	17-8	16-11	14-14	16-8	18-11	16-13	52-36	45-29
Mia	42-36	35-49	34-42	15-19	19-13	9-11	13-21	64-64	23-25	54-60	76-84	1-1	18-22	25-32	6-5	11-12	10-18	14-13	14-12	17-12	11-18	41-46	36-39
Atl	37-44	35-46	33-43	11-21	19-15	9-11	15-15	57-75	22-27	50-63	70-90	2-0	19-24	19-31	6-8	10-13	12-16	16-12	10-15	11-17	13-17	42-45	30-45
NYM	37-44	33-48	37-39	14-19	12-21	7-13	15-23	55-69	14-33	56-59	70-92	0-0	21-24	23-35	3-8	10-14	13-14	14-14	11-13	10-20	12-17	39-47	31-45
Phi	39-42	27-54	39-37	11-21	11-23	5-15	24-21	42-75	26-30	40-66	66-96	0-0	21-36	19-24	7-10	11-12	6-22	9-18	13-12	11-19	16-13	29-58	37-38

Central Division

Tm	Home	Road	East	Cent	West	AL	LHS	RHS	Day	Night	Grass	Turf	1-Rn	5+Rn	XInn	April	May	June	July	Aug	Sept	Pre	Post
ChC	48-33	44-37	21-13	46-30	13-19	12-8	21-14	71-56	37-36	55-34	91-69	1-1	26-17	31-20	7-3	13-11	12-16	15-13	16-8	17-12	19-10	43-45	49-25
Mil	46-38	40-38	18-14	40-36	17-17	11-9	17-17	69-59	32-29	54-47	82-75	4-1	25-22	19-18	5-11	13-13	15-12	15-14	12-13	15-12	16-12	50-41	36-35
StL	44-37	39-42	22-10	34-42	19-15	8-12	19-16	64-63	26-27	57-52	83-79	0-0	24-29	28-17	5-9	12-12	13-13	13-16	14-12	15-13	16-13	43-45	40-34
Pit	44-37	31-50	21-13	33-43	11-21	10-10	17-24	58-63	28-22	47-65	74-85	1-2	20-24	21-28	8-9	11-13	13-17	13-13	14-11	12-17	12-16	42-47	33-40
Cin	39-42	29-52	13-20	37-39	13-20	5-15	9-29	59-65	25-36	43-58	67-89	1-5	13-22	22-34	3-7	11-13	13-15	10-17	8-18	15-14	11-17	39-49	29-45

West Division

Tm	Home	Road	East	Cent	West	AL	LHS	RHS	Day	Night	Grass	Turf	1-Rn	5+Rn	XInn	April	May	June	July	Aug	Sept	Pre	Post
LAD	57-24	47-34	24-10	23-9	41-35	12-8	33-15	71-43	30-14	74-44	104-58	0-0	25-19	30-13	8-4	14-12	19-9	21-7	20-3	17-10	13-17	61-29	43-29
Ari	52-29	41-40	19-14	17-16	45-31	12-8	25-17	68-52	28-21	65-48	93-69	0-0	29-23	30-18	9-3	16-11	17-11	17-9	10-14	16-13	17-11	53-36	40-33
Col	46-35	41-40	17-16	18-15	42-34	10-10	28-20	59-55	35-23	52-52	87-75	0-0	21-14	28-26	2-3	16-10	17-12	15-12	12-12	12-15	15-14	52-39	35-36
SD	43-38	28-53	14-19	16-17	33-43	8-12	19-27	52-64	19-31	52-60	71-91	0-0	19-19	9-36	4-7	11-16	11-17	11-14	14-11	12-16	12-17	38-50	33-41
SF	38-43	26-55	9-23	18-16	29-47	8-12	18-30	46-68	22-35	42-63	64-98	0-0	23-24	18-28	12-7	9-17	13-16	9-18	9-16	13-16	11-15	34-56	30-42

Team vs. Team Breakdown

	Was	Mia	Atl	NYM	Phi	ChC	Mil	StL	Pit	Cin	LAD	Ari	Col	SD	SF
Washington Nationals	-	13	10	13	11	4	3	3	3	6	3	4	4	5	5
Miami Marlins	6	-	8	12	8	3	2	2	3	5	1	4	4	5	5
Atlanta Braves	9	11	-	7	6	1	4	1	2	3	3	4	3	5	4
New York Mets	6	7	12	-	12	2	2	3	3	4	0	1	3	3	5
Philadelphia Phillies	8	11	13	7	-	3	3	1	2	2	3	1	2	1	4
Chicago Cubs	3	4	6	4	4	-	10	14	10	12	2	3	2	2	4
Milwaukee Brewers	4	4	2	5	3	9	-	11	9	11	3	3	3	5	3
St Louis Cardinals	3	5	5	4	5	5	8	-	11	10	3	4	4	4	4
Pittsburgh Pirates	4	4	5	3	5	9	10	8	-	6	1	3	3	3	1
Cincinnati Reds	1	2	3	3	4	7	8	9	13	-	0	3	3	3	4
Los Angeles Dodgers	3	6	4	7	4	4	3	4	6	6	-	8	9	13	11
Arizona Diamondbacks	2	3	2	6	6	3	4	3	4	3	11	-	11	11	12
Colorado Rockies	3	2	4	3	5	5	4	2	3	4	10	8	-	12	12
San Diego Padres	2	1	2	4	5	4	2	3	3	4	6	8	7	-	12
San Francisco Giants	1	1	3	1	3	3	4	3	5	3	8	7	7	7	-

American League Batting

Tm	G	AB	H	2B	3B	HR	(Hm	Rd)	TB	R	RBI	TBB	IBB	SO	HBP	SH	SF	ShO	SB	CS	SB%	GDP	LOB	Avg	OBP	Slg
Hou	162	5611	1581	346	20	238	(115	123)	2681	896	854	509	27	1087	70	11	61	6	98	42	.70	139	1686	.282	.346	.478
NYY	162	5594	1463	266	23	241	(140	101)	2498	858	821	616	22	1386	64	18	56	3	90	22	.80	119	1732	.262	.339	.447
Cle	162	5511	1449	333	29	212	(95	117)	2476	818	780	604	30	1153	50	23	45	6	88	23	.79	125	1779	.263	.339	.449
Min	162	5557	1443	286	31	206	(110	96)	2409	815	781	593	26	1342	46	26	39	2	95	28	.77	105	1704	.260	.334	.434
Tex	162	5430	1326	255	21	237	(125	112)	2334	799	756	544	18	1493	81	27	39	6	113	44	.72	110	1533	.244	.320	.430
Bos	162	5669	1461	302	19	168	(73	95)	2305	785	735	571	48	1224	53	9	36	10	106	31	.77	141	1727	.258	.329	.407
Sea	162	5551	1436	281	17	200	(97	103)	2351	750	714	487	31	1267	78	14	35	11	89	35	.72	131	1628	.259	.325	.424
Bal	162	5650	1469	269	12	232	(135	97)	2458	743	713	392	12	1412	50	10	37	12	32	13	.71	138	1549	.260	.312	.435
Oak	162	5464	1344	305	15	234	(129	105)	2381	739	708	565	15	1491	43	13	40	6	57	22	.72	129	1599	.246	.319	.436
Det	162	5556	1435	289	35	187	(109	78)	2355	735	699	503	21	1313	52	11	27	12	65	34	.66	128	1640	.258	.324	.424
LAA	162	5415	1314	251	14	186	(97	89)	2151	710	678	523	30	1198	70	17	46	12	136	44	.76	141	1578	.243	.315	.397
CWS	162	5513	1412	256	18	186	(99	87)	2300	706	670	401	17	1397	76	35	33	8	71	31	.70	124	1586	.256	.314	.417
KC	162	5536	1436	260	24	193	(88	105)	2323	702	660	390	19	1166	45	17	37	15	91	31	.75	160	1578	.259	.311	.420
TB	162	5478	1340	226	32	228	(106	122)	2314	694	671	545	33	1538	55	16	48	11	88	34	.72	115	1623	.245	.317	.422
Tor	162	5499	1320	269	5	222	(105	117)	2265	693	661	542	12	1327	51	25	35	9	53	24	.69	153	1614	.240	.312	.412
AL	1215	83034	21229	4194	334	3170	(1623	1547)	35601	11443	10901	7785	361	19794	884	272	614	129	1272	458	.74	1958	24556	.256	.324	.429

American League Pitching

Tm	G	CG	Rel	IP	BFP	H	R	ER	HR	SH	SF	HB	TBB	IBB	SO	WP	Bk	W	L	Pct.	ShO	Sv-Op	Hld	OAvg	OOBP	OSlg	ERA
Cle	162	7	497	1440.2	5866	1267	564	529	163	16	20	45	406	15	1614	48	1	102	60	.630	19	37-47	87	.236	.294	.380	3.30
NYY	162	2	477	1448.2	6078	1248	660	599	192	18	31	53	504	18	1560	83	4	91	71	.562	7	36-59	70	.228	.298	.382	3.72
Bos	162	5	515	1482.1	6217	1384	648	610	195	16	40	49	465	18	1580	43	3	93	69	.574	11	39-57	83	.245	.306	.406	3.70
Hou	162	1	519	1446.0	6111	1314	700	662	192	17	20	70	522	17	1593	86	4	101	61	.623	9	45-66	91	.240	.313	.407	4.12
TB	162	0	511	1445.0	6099	1324	704	638	193	26	38	48	503	37	1352	83	4	80	82	.494	9	53-75	93	.242	.309	.403	3.97
LAA	162	1	543	1440.2	6030	1373	709	672	224	24	30	44	470	25	1312	57	6	80	82	.494	10	43-64	77	.251	.314	.429	4.20
Sea	162	1	527	1440.1	6132	1399	772	713	237	24	60	53	490	28	1244	73	7	78	84	.481	9	39-65	93	.254	.318	.435	4.46
Tor	162	2	578	1465.0	6316	1460	784	720	203	14	38	48	549	25	1372	53	4	76	86	.469	6	45-71	79	.258	.326	.429	4.42
Min	162	6	520	1436.0	6205	1487	788	732	224	23	42	69	483	37	1166	52	8	85	77	.525	11	42-62	82	.266	.330	.446	4.59
KC	162	1	538	1437.2	6218	1480	791	737	196	21	46	52	519	24	1216	48	6	80	82	.494	6	39-60	94	.265	.331	.434	4.61
Tex	162	2	464	1434.1	6211	1443	816	742	214	11	40	74	559	22	1107	63	7	78	84	.481	6	29-50	66	.261	.335	.434	4.66
CWS	162	0	520	1421.2	6200	1384	820	755	242	14	39	68	632	36	1193	67	5	67	95	.414	3	25-40	55	.254	.337	.450	4.72
Oak	162	1	525	1431.0	6167	1444	826	743	210	17	46	61	502	17	1202	84	3	75	87	.463	9	35-60	95	.261	.327	.439	4.67
Bal	162	1	492	1441.0	6293	1505	841	795	242	17	48	60	579	21	1233	53	6	75	87	.463	10	35-52	58	.269	.342	.458	4.97
Det	162	2	510	1420.1	6298	1586	894	846	218	15	62	61	538	42	1202	53	4	64	98	.395	4	32-55	75	.282	.348	.463	5.36
AL	1215	32	7736	21630.2	92441	21098	11337	10493	3145	273	600	855	7721	382	19946	946	72	1225	1205	.504	126	574-883	1198	.254	.322	.426	4.37

American League Fielding

Team	G	Inn	PO	Ast	OFAst	E	(Throw	Field)	TC	DP	GDP	SB	CS	SB%	CPkof	PPkof	PB	UER	UERA	FPct
Cleveland	162	1440.2	4322	1446	32	76	38	38	5844	167	139	50	37	.57	2	1	9	35	0.22	.987
Minnesota	162	1436.0	4308	1476	22	78	31	47	5862	143	126	75	29	.72	0	1	16	56	0.35	.987
Kansas City	162	1437.2	4313	1524	24	79	33	46	5916	145	127	87	30	.74	1	3	11	54	0.34	.987
Los Angeles	162	1440.2	4322	1463	28	80	36	44	5865	135	114	71	43	.62	3	5	10	37	0.23	.986
Detroit	162	1420.1	4261	1389	19	85	39	46	5735	146	129	85	37	.70	0	4	14	48	0.30	.985
Toronto	162	1465.0	4395	1570	28	92	42	50	6057	145	128	119	26	.82	0	1	8	64	0.39	.985
Baltimore	162	1441.0	4323	1609	28	94	45	49	6026	175	150	77	34	.69	2	2	8	46	0.29	.984
New York	162	1448.2	4346	1467	21	95	38	57	5908	102	85	65	26	.71	2	1	21	61	0.38	.984
Houston	162	1446.0	4338	1526	25	99	46	53	5963	153	133	102	14	.88	0	7	16	38	0.24	.983
Tampa Bay	162	1445.0	4335	1433	25	100	44	56	5868	129	113	83	22	.79	4	5	15	66	0.41	.983
Seattle	162	1440.1	4321	1422	34	103	35	68	5846	147	125	80	26	.75	2	2	15	59	0.37	.982
Texas	162	1434.1	4303	1616	35	108	45	63	6027	173	156	87	28	.76	1	6	8	74	0.46	.982
Boston	162	1482.1	4447	1390	28	107	62	45	5944	126	116	61	39	.61	2	1	19	58	0.35	.982
Chicago	162	1421.2	4265	1541	40	114	35	79	5920	157	139	120	26	.82	0	7	11	65	0.41	.981
Oakland	162	1431.0	4293	1597	22	121	49	72	6011	162	126	111	42	.73	0	4	16	83	0.52	.980
American League	1215	21630.2	64892	22469	411	1431	618	813	88792	2205	1906	1273	459	.73	19	50	197	844	0.35	.984

National League Batting

	BATTING																		BASERUNNING					PERCENTAGES		
Tm	G	AB	H	2B	3B	HR	(Hm	Rd)	TB	R	RBI	TBB	IBB	SO	HBP	SH	SF	ShO	SB	CS	SB%	GDP	LOB	Avg	OBP	Slg
Col	162	5534	1510	293	38	192	(110	82)	2455	824	793	519	46	1408	44	62	41	11	59	34	.63	143	1601	.273	.338	.444
ChC	162	5496	1402	274	29	223	(116	107)	2403	822	785	622	54	1401	82	48	32	10	62	31	.67	134	1711	.255	.338	.437
Was	162	5553	1477	311	31	215	(107	108)	2495	819	796	542	56	1327	31	43	45	7	108	30	.78	116	1651	.266	.332	.449
Ari	162	5525	1405	314	39	220	(122	98)	2457	812	776	578	44	1456	54	39	27	6	103	30	.77	106	1650	.254	.329	.445
Mia	162	5602	1497	271	31	194	(95	99)	2412	778	743	486	48	1282	67	50	41	8	91	30	.75	119	1681	.267	.331	.431
LAD	162	5408	1347	312	20	221	(115	106)	2362	770	730	649	41	1380	64	31	38	8	77	28	.73	119	1694	.249	.334	.437
StL	162	5470	1402	284	28	196	(90	106)	2330	761	728	593	36	1348	65	47	44	6	81	31	.72	139	1682	.256	.334	.426
Cin	162	5484	1390	249	38	219	(117	102)	2372	753	715	565	41	1329	72	50	42	8	120	39	.75	116	1689	.253	.329	.433
NYM	162	5510	1379	286	28	224	(101	123)	2393	735	713	529	31	1291	57	36	37	7	58	23	.72	118	1662	.250	.328	.434
Atl	162	5584	1467	289	26	165	(77	88)	2303	732	706	474	57	1184	66	59	32	10	77	31	.71	137	1731	.263	.326	.412
Mil	162	5467	1363	267	22	224	(120	104)	2346	732	695	547	34	1571	53	42	26	8	128	41	.76	116	1600	.249	.322	.429
Phi	162	5535	1382	287	36	174	(104	70)	2263	690	654	494	25	1417	47	21	36	10	59	25	.70	128	1606	.250	.315	.409
Pit	162	5458	1331	249	36	151	(73	78)	2105	668	635	519	39	1213	88	42	28	10	67	36	.65	120	1692	.244	.318	.386
SF	162	5551	1382	290	28	128	(48	80)	2112	639	612	467	37	1204	36	31	52	11	76	34	.69	136	1683	.249	.309	.380
SD	162	5356	1251	227	31	189	(89	100)	2107	604	576	460	20	1499	53	52	33	12	89	33	.73	99	1579	.234	.299	.393
NL	1215	82533	20985	4203	461	2935	(1484	1451)	34915	11139	10657	8044	609	20310	879	653	554	132	1255	476	.73	1846	24912	.254	.325	.423

National League Pitching

	HOW MUCH THEY PITCHED					WHAT THEY GAVE UP												THE RESULTS									
Tm	G	CG	Rel	IP	BFP	H	R	ER	HR	SH	SF	HB	TBB	IBB	SO	WP	Bk	W	L	Pct.	ShO	Sv-Op	Hld	OAvg	OOBP	OSlg	ERA
LAD	162	2	536	1444.2	5925	1226	580	543	184	39	22	40	442	33	1549	40	10	104	58	.642	16	51-67	97	.228	.290	.380	3.38
Ari	162	2	513	1441.0	6072	1309	659	586	171	36	37	38	516	45	1482	82	5	93	69	.574	11	43-62	92	.240	.309	.398	3.66
Was	162	3	487	1446.2	6068	1300	672	623	189	35	31	60	495	39	1457	44	5	97	65	.599	5	46-63	88	.239	.308	.396	3.88
ChC	162	2	531	1447.1	6108	1294	695	636	194	28	29	66	554	29	1439	73	4	92	70	.568	8	38-57	90	.238	.315	.398	3.95
Mil	162	1	550	1445.2	6164	1381	697	642	185	39	29	64	553	45	1346	50	2	86	76	.531	12	54-79	101	.252	.326	.414	4.00
StL	162	3	546	1450.1	6153	1393	705	646	183	40	45	67	493	50	1351	38	0	83	79	.512	12	43-60	90	.253	.320	.411	4.01
Pit	162	2	502	1440.2	6208	1464	731	676	182	53	29	58	511	32	1262	58	2	75	87	.463	12	36-57	82	.264	.330	.431	4.22
Col	162	1	549	1437.2	6177	1453	757	721	190	49	44	50	532	20	1270	69	10	87	75	.537	9	47-61	111	.264	.332	.439	4.51
SF	162	3	502	1452.0	6287	1515	776	726	182	51	39	50	496	42	1234	55	3	64	98	.395	5	32-54	66	.268	.331	.438	4.50
Phi	162	1	506	1441.0	6235	1471	782	729	221	37	47	63	527	39	1309	50	11	66	96	.407	7	33-57	73	.265	.333	.447	4.55
SD	162	2	517	1430.2	6169	1417	816	742	226	32	35	75	554	28	1325	73	11	71	91	.438	12	45-62	81	.259	.333	.441	4.67
Atl	162	0	530	1441.1	6306	1463	821	766	192	53	36	70	584	39	1258	58	5	72	90	.444	6	36-59	81	.263	.339	.438	4.72
Mia	162	1	580	1442.2	6318	1450	822	772	193	59	34	75	627	59	1202	57	3	77	85	.475	7	34-60	98	.263	.344	.432	4.82
NYM	162	2	568	1434.2	6378	1538	863	799	220	49	53	55	593	51	1374	55	5	70	92	.432	5	34-54	73	.273	.345	.448	5.01
Cin	162	2	504	1430.0	6286	1442	869	821	248	52	49	77	631	37	1300	62	7	68	94	.420	8	33-47	57	.263	.345	.465	5.17
NL	1215	27	7921	21626.1	92854	21116	11245	10418	2960	652	568	908	8108	588	20158	864	83	1205	1225	.496	135	605-899	1280	.256	.327	.425	4.34

National League Fielding

	Fielding																			
Team	G	Inn	PO	Ast	OFAst	E	(Throw	Field)	TC	DP	GDP	SB	CS	SB%	CPkof	PPkof	PB	UER	UERA	FPct
Miami	162	1442.2	4328	1554	21	73	(33	40)	5955	156	132	67	30	.69	5	2	12	50	0.31	.988
Colorado	162	1437.2	4313	1730	18	77	(41	36)	6120	168	143	67	27	.71	2	7	18	36	0.23	.987
Cincinnati	162	1430.0	4290	1623	40	81	(35	46)	5994	132	107	79	42	.65	3	5	9	48	0.30	.986
Philadelphia	162	1441.0	4323	1497	30	82	(40	42)	5902	145	119	91	30	.75	0	8	17	53	0.33	.986
San Francisco	162	1452.0	4356	1522	20	87	(37	50)	5965	127	116	73	37	.66	2	5	6	50	0.31	.985
Washington	162	1446.2	4340	1434	31	86	(39	47)	5860	139	119	94	29	.76	0	1	10	49	0.30	.985
Los Angeles	162	1444.2	4334	1367	19	88	(47	41)	5789	131	109	68	28	.71	3	3	19	37	0.23	.985
St Louis	162	1450.1	4351	1595	23	94	(51	43)	6040	164	145	54	32	.63	4	4	7	59	0.37	.984
Chicago	162	1447.1	4342	1656	24	95	(52	43)	6093	139	119	121	35	.78	6	14	13	59	0.37	.984
New York	162	1434.2	4304	1456	26	92	(45	47)	5852	125	112	102	29	.78	1	2	7	64	0.40	.984
Atlanta	162	1441.1	4324	1578	19	97	(45	52)	5999	137	118	99	30	.77	1	9	20	65	0.41	.984
Pittsburgh	162	1440.2	4322	1662	33	99	(37	62)	6083	156	133	95	28	.77	4	3	15	55	0.34	.984
Arizona	162	1441.0	4323	1604	20	108	(40	68)	6035	140	125	69	32	.68	1	7	12	73	0.46	.982
San Diego	162	1430.2	4292	1623	31	113	(60	53)	6028	177	156	76	34	.69	0	4	8	74	0.47	.981
Milwaukee	162	1445.2	4337	1624	29	115	(46	69)	6076	164	145	99	32	.76	7	12	11	55	0.34	.981
National League	1215	21626.1	64879	23525	384	1387	(648	739)	89791	2200	1898	1254	475	.73	39	86	184	827	0.34	.985

Team Pitching Staff Summary

Team	Starters				Bullpen					
	IP	ERA	ERA Rank	W-L	IP	ERA	ERA Rank	W-L	Sv-Opp	Sv Pct
Arizona Diamondbacks	941.1	3.61	3	66-51	499.2	3.78	5	27-18	43-62	69%
Atlanta Braves	914.1	4.80	21	46-72	527.0	4.58	26	26-18	36-59	61%
Baltimore Orioles	846.0	5.70	30	45-69	595.0	3.93	12	30-18	35-52	67%
Boston Red Sox	951.1	4.06	8	64-54	531.0	3.15	2	29-15	39-57	68%
Chicago Cubs	888.1	4.05	7	64-47	559.0	3.80	6	28-23	38-57	67%
Chicago White Sox	873.1	5.09	25	38-75	548.1	4.28	18	29-20	25-40	63%
Cincinnati Reds	820.0	5.55	29	44-73	610.0	4.65	27	24-21	33-47	70%
Cleveland Indians	951.1	3.52	2	81-38	489.1	2.89	1	21-22	37-47	79%
Colorado Rockies	887.0	4.59	16	63-56	550.2	4.40	20	24-19	47-61	77%
Detroit Tigers	891.2	5.20	28	47-70	528.2	5.63	30	17-28	32-55	58%
Houston Astros	899.2	4.03	6	71-39	546.1	4.27	17	30-22	45-66	68%
Kansas City Royals	867.1	4.89	24	52-58	570.1	4.24	16	28-24	39-60	65%
Los Angeles Angels	871.2	4.38	12	44-58	569.0	3.92	11	36-24	43-64	67%
Los Angeles Dodgers	885.0	3.39	1	72-39	559.2	3.38	4	32-19	51-67	76%
Miami Marlins	830.2	5.12	26	47-55	612.0	4.40	20	30-30	34-60	57%
Milwaukee Brewers	873.0	4.10	10	59-40	572.2	3.83	8	27-36	54-79	68%
Minnesota Twins	869.2	4.73	19	61-57	566.1	4.40	20	24-20	42-62	68%
New York Mets	865.2	5.14	27	49-64	569.0	4.82	29	21-28	34-54	63%
New York Yankees	910.1	3.98	5	62-47	538.1	3.34	3	29-24	36-59	61%
Oakland Athletics	877.2	4.74	20	52-61	553.1	4.57	25	23-26	35-60	58%
Philadelphia Phillies	890.1	4.80	21	43-62	550.2	4.18	14	23-34	33-57	58%
Pittsburgh Pirates	894.2	4.47	13	48-59	546.0	3.84	10	27-28	36-57	63%
San Diego Padres	879.1	4.83	23	45-62	551.1	4.49	24	26-29	45-62	73%
San Francisco Giants	958.2	4.58	15	42-73	493.1	4.34	19	22-25	32-54	59%
Seattle Mariners	870.2	4.70	18	47-53	569.2	4.08	13	31-31	39-65	60%
St Louis Cardinals	919.1	4.13	11	61-50	531.0	3.81	7	22-29	43-60	72%
Tampa Bay Rays	899.1	4.08	9	52-51	545.2	3.83	8	28-31	53-75	71%
Texas Rangers	918.1	4.66	17	56-59	516.0	4.76	28	22-25	29-50	58%
Toronto Blue Jays	868.1	4.57	14	47-60	596.2	4.21	15	29-26	45-71	63%
Washington Nationals	973.0	3.63	4	72-47	473.2	4.41	23	25-18	46-63	73%

Team Defense
Defensive Runs Saved by Position and Team

Team	P	C	1B	2B	3B	SS	LF	CF	RF	Shifts	Total
Tampa Bay Rays	-2	-1	3	-6	10	8	8	26	12	30	88
Boston Red Sox	2	27	8	-2	-3	-11	5	10	33	6	75
Los Angeles Dodgers	-4	21	1	9	9	16	8	-13	19	8	74
Cleveland Indians	3	13	7	6	0	6	0	3	-5	24	57
Los Angeles Angels	-5	27	-1	-1	-12	33	-12	-1	2	16	46
Milwaukee Brewers	7	7	-4	7	3	8	0	-4	-2	23	45
Chicago Cubs	-3	-7	11	3	-2	17	-9	1	11	16	38
Cincinnati Reds	6	0	11	-7	7	-2	9	10	-7	8	35
St Louis Cardinals	13	10	1	0	16	-10	9	-14	7	3	35
Minnesota Twins	-5	8	9	-5	-9	-2	-3	27	0	8	28
New York Yankees	3	-2	-4	-6	-3	-3	15	9	9	5	23
Arizona Diamondbacks	-2	6	11	4	-12	-1	-8	6	8	11	23
Pittsburgh Pirates	6	-8	5	10	12	-3	17	-17	-16	10	16
Seattle Mariners	-9	-2	-1	0	-3	-1	3	9	9	10	15
Texas Rangers	5	-10	2	3	2	4	4	-1	-10	14	13
Miami Marlins	-2	-9	0	3	-2	9	11	-9	10	-2	9
Colorado Rockies	12	-13	-5	8	19	7	-6	-7	-8	0	7
Houston Astros	2	-9	-8	3	-7	-1	7	4	-2	18	7
Chicago White Sox	-3	-13	-1	20	9	-9	-18	0	0	17	2
San Diego Padres	3	7	0	-6	-14	-4	1	9	4	-2	-2
Toronto Blue Jays	-10	10	3	4	-3	-8	-16	13	-11	13	-5
Baltimore Orioles	4	0	-9	1	3	-5	-1	-13	-1	10	-11
Atlanta Braves	7	15	-1	-7	-2	-10	-22	2	-5	6	-17
Kansas City Royals	-8	-12	-8	5	-9	-6	6	8	-18	1	-41
Washington Nationals	-22	-8	-10	-20	8	11	-2	-5	4	3	-41
San Francisco Giants	4	-3	7	-10	-2	5	-5	-32	-8	1	-43
Oakland Athletics	-4	-8	-4	-3	20	-17	-14	-14	-4	0	-48
Philadelphia Phillies	-5	-23	-9	1	3	-5	-1	-2	-16	7	-50
Detroit Tigers	-13	-12	-8	-3	-22	-1	11	0	-21	8	-61
New York Mets	-15	-6	-10	-17	-17	-24	1	3	10	3	-72

Batting By Position

Pos	AB	H	2B	3B	HR	(Hm	Rd)	TB	R	RBI	TBB	IBB	SO	HBP	SH	SF	SB	CS	SB%	GDP	LOB	Avg	OBP	Slg
P	4580	570	77	7	26	(15	11)	739	239	268	159	0	2011	16	469	10	4	1	.80	61	1930	.124	.156	.161
C	17295	4262	867	35	633	(318	315)	7098	2022	2257	1545	97	4224	245	66	118	71	31	.70	488	5560	.246	.315	.410
1B	18290	4849	1023	73	962	(480	482)	8904	2687	2913	2162	171	4555	195	6	145	137	61	.69	486	5667	.265	.347	.487
2B	18804	5052	994	105	558	(279	279)	7930	2624	2251	1648	98	3836	219	76	140	389	143	.73	399	5172	.269	.332	.422
3B	18322	4718	973	79	770	(385	385)	8159	2532	2613	1866	112	4175	211	29	162	197	87	.69	468	5403	.258	.330	.445
SS	18616	4910	995	118	534	(261	273)	7743	2447	2192	1429	115	3842	125	71	120	365	128	.74	401	5351	.264	.319	.416
LF	18462	4724	938	90	679	(323	356)	7879	2558	2374	1844	89	4499	179	51	136	363	123	.75	397	5202	.256	.327	.427
CF	18618	4919	947	157	616	(288	328)	8028	2815	2093	1740	93	4496	237	84	104	625	205	.75	316	4938	.264	.333	.431
RF	18558	4897	967	96	817	(406	411)	8507	2762	2644	1999	118	4556	182	32	127	237	103	.70	417	5317	.264	.339	.458
DH	9171	2231	409	14	393	(198	195)	3847	1147	1306	934	47	2388	87	10	64	38	19	.67	248	3073	.243	.317	.419
PH	4838	1078	206	21	116	(49	67)	1674	545	641	502	30	1518	67	31	42	52	14	.79	123	1837	.223	.302	.346
PR	9	4	1	0	1	(1	0)	8	204	6	1	0	0	0	0	0	49	19	.72	0	18	.444	.500	.889

Fielding By Position

Pos	Inn	PO	Ast	E	(Throw	Field)	TC	DP	GDP	FPct
P	43257.0	2381	4821	348	263	85	7550	375	264	.954
C	43257.0	40412	2549	311	223	74	43272	270	15	.993
1B	43257.0	39383	2867	266	67	183	42516	4029	231	.994
2B	43257.0	8395	12662	381	129	251	21438	3237	1045	.982
3B	43257.0	3172	9037	522	232	284	12731	1001	709	.959
SS	43257.0	6563	13263	531	234	296	20357	2958	1348	.974
LF	43257.0	8709	296	145	30	114	9150	45	1	.984
CF	43257.0	11437	235	150	34	116	11822	53		.987
RF	43257.0	9319	264	164	54	109	9747	58		.983

Team Efficiency Summary

Lindsay Zeck

The most exciting divisional race of the 2017 season was between the Boston Red Sox and the New York Yankees, who were battling for the top spot in the American League East. It came down to the last two days of the season, when the Red Sox defeated the Houston Astros 6-3 to claim their second consecutive division title. This is the first time they have won the division in consecutive seasons since the AL East was created in 1969.

The Yankees finished two games behind the Red Sox with 91 wins. However, in evaluating their efficiency, we see that they were the least efficient team in the league, and based on Efficiency Wins—determined using the expected number of runs scored and allowed using various components of production (singles, doubles, home runs, etc.)—they were actually expected to win 102 games! The Yankees were expected to score 846 runs, the second most in Major League Baseball after the Astros and 97 more than the Red Sox, and allow 646 runs—the third fewest in baseball behind the Indians and Dodgers. The Yankees also had the third-highest expected run differential (+200) behind the two AL 100-plus game winners, the Indians and Astros, who were expected to outscore their opponents by 262 and 208 runs, respectively.

The other exciting race at the end of the season was a battle between the Colorado Rockies, the Milwaukee Brewers, and the St. Louis Cardinals for the National League's second Wild-Card spot. The Cardinals were eliminated by the Cubs with four games left to play in the season, and the Brewers, who were trailing the Rockies by two games, were slated to play the Cards at Busch Stadium for their final series. After the Brewers and Rockies both won the first game of their respective series, it came down to the last two games. The Brewers needed to win both and the Rockies needed to lose both for the Brew Crew to force a play-in game at Coors Field.

The Brewers started strong and, in the third inning, took a 6-0 lead over the Cardinals. They couldn't hold on, however, as the Cards answered with four runs in the bottom of the frame and then piled on three more in the bottom of the eighth to take a 7-6 lead. They were able to hold on to the lead and eliminate the Brewers from playoff contention. The Brewers would go on to end the season just one win behind the Rockies.

It is the Cardinals, however, that, like the Yankees, were inefficient. They were tied with the Reds as the least efficient team in the National League. If we look at their Efficiency Wins, they were expected to win 89 games, seven more than the Brewers and three more than the Rockies.

The tables in this section contain four different efficiency numbers:

1. Offensive efficiency (Hit Eff): Comparison of the expected number of runs scored using components of production to the actual number of runs scored by each team.
2. Defensive efficiency (Pit Eff): Comparison of the expected number of runs allowed using components of production to the actual number of runs allowed by each team.
3. Runs efficiency (Runs Eff): Comparison of the expected number of wins based on actual runs scored and runs allowed by each team to the actual number of wins.
4. Overall efficiency (Overall Eff): Comparison of the expected number of wins based on expected runs scored and allowed to the actual number of wins.

2017 American League Team Efficiency Summary

	RC	Runs	Hit Eff	Exp RA	RA	Pit Eff	Exp Wins	Wins	Runs Eff	Eff Wins	Wins	Overall Eff
Kansas City Royals	685	702	103	766	791	97	71	80	112	72	80	111
Baltimore Orioles	728	743	102	851	841	101	71	75	106	68	75	110
Toronto Blue Jays	676	693	103	767	784	98	71	76	107	71	76	107
Los Angeles Angels	665	710	107	716	709	101	81	80	99	75	80	107
Boston Red Sox	749	785	105	695	668	104	94	93	99	87	93	107
Texas Rangers	733	799	109	797	816	98	79	78	98	74	78	105
Minnesota Twins	804	815	101	791	788	100	84	85	102	82	85	103
Chicago White Sox	697	706	101	827	820	101	69	67	97	67	67	100
Oakland Athletics	732	739	101	783	826	95	72	75	104	76	75	99
Houston Astros	895	896	100	687	700	98	101	101	100	102	101	99
Seattle Mariners	744	750	101	762	772	99	79	78	99	79	78	99
Detroit Tigers	738	735	100	873	894	98	65	64	98	68	64	95
Tampa Bay Rays	720	694	96	683	704	97	80	80	100	85	80	94
Cleveland Indians	827	818	99	565	564	100	110	102	93	110	102	92
New York Yankees	846	858	101	646	660	98	102	91	89	102	91	89

2017 National League Team Efficiency Summary

	RC	Runs	Hit Eff	Exp RA	RA	Pit Eff	Exp Wins	Wins	Runs Eff	Eff Wins	Wins	Overall Eff
San Diego Padres	618	604	98	796	816	98	57	71	124	61	71	117
Pittsburgh Pirates	663	668	101	751	731	103	74	75	102	71	75	106
Milwaukee Brewers	738	732	99	727	697	104	85	86	101	82	86	105
Colorado Rockies	798	824	103	750	757	99	88	87	99	86	87	101
New York Mets	746	735	99	863	863	100	68	70	103	69	70	101
Los Angeles Dodgers	778	770	99	583	580	101	103	104	101	104	104	100
Chicago Cubs	794	822	103	687	695	99	94	92	97	93	92	99
Washington Nationals	812	819	101	648	672	96	97	97	100	99	97	98
San Francisco Giants	634	639	101	768	776	99	65	64	98	66	64	97
Arizona Diamondbacks	794	812	102	657	659	100	98	93	95	96	93	97
Atlanta Braves	730	732	100	796	821	97	72	72	100	74	72	97
Miami Marlins	787	778	99	784	822	95	77	77	101	81	77	95
Philadelphia Phillies	689	690	100	794	782	102	71	66	93	70	66	95
Cincinnati Reds	775	753	97	856	869	99	69	68	98	73	68	93
St Louis Cardinals	764	761	100	690	705	98	87	83	95	89	83	93

Paul Goldschmidt   Brett Gardner
DJ LeMahieu   Byron Buxton
Nolan Arenado   Mookie Betts
Andrelton Simmons   Martin Maldonado
Javier Baez   Dallas Keuchel

THE FIELDING BIBLE AWARDS 2017

The Fielding Bible Awards 2017

John Dewan

We have two new panelists on our panel this year, Ben Lindbergh and Travis Sawchik. Welcome, Ben and Travis!

They are now part of our 12-person expert voting panel which selects the winners of the annual Fielding Bible Awards, now in its 12th year. They are the ones who stand up and say "This is the best fielder at this position in the major leagues last season." The panel awards ten winners each year, one at each position plus an additional award that goes to the best defensive multi-position player.

The name Andrelton Simmons is synonymous with the word Defense. With his 2017 Fielding Bible Award as a shortstop, that makes five years in a row. A first in Fielding Bible Award history.

There are six other repeat award winners this year. Dallas Keuchel (P) wins his fourth award, all in a row. Nolan Arenado (3B) has now won three in a row. Paul Goldschmidt (1B) also has three, but he does it every other year. Brett Gardner

(LF) gets his third, but the last one was six years ago. Mookie Betts (RF) and Javy Baez (Multi-Pos) repeat from last year. The three first-time winners are DJ LeMahieu (2B), Byron Buxton (CF) and Martin Maldonado (C).

Here's a short refresher course on how the awards are determined: we ask our panel of twelve experts to rank 10 players at each position on a scale from one to ten. We then use the same scoring technique as the Major League Baseball MVP voting. A first place vote gets 10 points, second place 9 points, third place 8 points, etc. Total up the points for each player and the player with the most points wins the award. A perfect score is 120.

Here are the Fielding Bible Awards for the 2017 season:

First Base – Paul Goldschmidt, Arizona Diamondbacks

Goldschmidt has tremendous range at first base, affording him opportunities to make plays that no other fielders even have a chance at. He often fields the ball 30+ feet away from the bag, diving or sliding to his right and throwing to the pitcher or racing to the bag to get the out. He's great at fielding throws, as evidenced by his MLB-leading Scoop Runs Saved, but that skill is also on display on hard-hit grounders, where he's able to snag balls that would likely eat up other first basemen.

Previous Winners:

2016	Anthony Rizzo	2011	Albert Pujols
2015	Paul Goldschmidt	2010	Daric Barton
2014	Adrian Gonzalez	2009	Albert Pujols
2013	Paul Goldschmidt	2008	Albert Pujols
2012	Mark Teixeira	2007	Albert Pujols

Second Base – DJ LeMahieu, Colorado Rockies

Being the tallest second baseman in the league at 6'4" might cost him some fluidity and quick-twitch ability compared to the Jose Altuves of the world, but LeMahieu makes up for it with his ability to dive to his sides or leap to get line drives over his head. He makes most of his bones on plays up the middle, particularly with that range and by making throws across his body on the move. But he still passes the eye test on plays to his left, doing an excellent job sliding and turning around to make the throw from the ground. He led second baseman in Good Fielding Plays this season with 50, and has not finished outside the top three at the position in GFPs in the last four seasons.

Previous Winners:

2016	Dustin Pedroia	2011	Dustin Pedroia
2015	Ian Kinsler	2010	Chase Utley
2014	Dustin Pedroia	2009	Aaron Hill
2013	Dustin Pedroia	2008	Brandon Phillips
2012	Darwin Barney	2007	Aaron Hill

Third Base – Nolan Arenado, Colorado Rockies

Arenado is essentially a shortstop who plays third base. Arenado is the only infielder to make at least six plays above average on both batted balls to his left and to his right in each of the past two seasons. This outstanding range applies to not only groundballs, but also to pop flies as Arenado is an expert at navigating foul territory on the third base side. Additionally, Arenado thrives on making the barehanded play on dribblers up the third base line. Arenado has led all third baseman in Good Fielding Plays (GFP) in each of the past three seasons, with 57 GFPs during the 2017 season.

Previous Winners:

2016	Nolan Arenado	2011	Adrian Beltre
2015	Nolan Arenado	2010	Evan Longoria
2014	Josh Donaldson	2009	Ryan Zimmerman
2013	Manny Machado	2008	Adrian Beltre
2012	Adrian Beltre	2007	Pedro Feliz

Shortstop – Andrelton Simmons, Los Angeles Angels

There isn't a more deserving player than Andrelton Simmons to be the first to win five Fielding Bible Awards in a row. Everything he does out on the field looks effortless, from diving to make a stop on the right side of second base to making a throw from deep in the third base/shortstop hole. Not only are his physical traits among the elite at the position, but he's also one of the most intelligent players on the field at all times, seemingly always making the play to the correct base.

Previous Winners:

2016	Andrelton Simmons	2011	Troy Tulowitzki
2015	Andrelton Simmons	2010	Troy Tulowitzki
2014	Andrelton Simmons	2009	Jack Wilson
2013	Andrelton Simmons	2008	Jimmy Rollins
2012	Brendan Ryan	2007	Troy Tulowitzki

Left Field – Brett Gardner, New York Yankees

It's been six years since Gardner won his last Fielding Bible Award, but he looked just as good out there in 2017 as he did in 2011. He still possesses outstanding speed, allowing him to get to flyballs that others can't reach. He's also adept at tracking back toward the wall, as he made more than a few jumping catches near the wall that saved extra-base hits. Lest you think he only excels at fielding flyballs, he also had 10 outfield Kills (direct throws to a base to nab a runner) this season, tied for second most.

Previous Winners:

2016	Starling Marte	2011	Brett Gardner
2015	Starling Marte	2010	Brett Gardner
2014	Alex Gordon	2009	Carl Crawford
2013	Alex Gordon	2008	Carl Crawford
2012	Alex Gordon	2007	Eric Byrnes

Center Field – Byron Buxton, Minnesota Twins

With the exception of Billy Hamilton, Buxton is perhaps the fastest current major league regular. Even those rare times when he doesn't get the best initial read on a flyball, Buxton is able to use his sprinter speed and long strides to cover even the largest of outfields with ease. In 2017 Buxton was the only outfielder to make at least nine plays above average on both shallow and deeply batted balls. Buxton is fearless when he goes after flyballs. Even though he possesses excellent anticipation of where the outfield wall is and just how much real estate he has to work with, he won't hesitate to crash into the wall and give up his body if it means the out will be recorded, just like he did during the 2017 American League Wild Card game. Buxton's closing speed and ability to use the proper angles to cut off balls also frequently deters base runners from taking the extra base on batted balls that he is unable to run down.

Previous Winners:

2016	Kevin Pillar	2011	Austin Jackson
2015	Kevin Kiermaier	2010	Michael Bourn
2014	Juan Lagares	2009	Franklin Gutierrez
2013	Carlos Gomez	2008	Carlos Beltran
2012	Mike Trout	2007	Andruw Jones

Right Field – Mookie Betts, Boston Red Sox

Betts makes it look easy. Even as he's tracking a ball, he doesn't necessarily run like a gazelle. You rarely see him laying out for a catch. But he always gets there. He just extends his arm or jumps just enough to make the catch. His body control at the point of the catch is excellent, leading to several beautiful leaping grabs or late mid-air adjustments to the ball. He tends to shade himself towards center field a bit more because of his flexibility to his left, and he is unafraid of making catches at or near the wall. Playing in Fenway Park with its deep right-center field and short wall down the right field line, Betts' center fielder range and his agility at the wall are especially impactful.

Previous Winners:

2016	Mookie Betts	2011	Justin Upton
2015	Jason Heyward	2010	Ichiro Suzuki
2014	Jason Heyward	2009	Ichiro Suzuki
2013	Gerardo Parra	2008	Franklin Gutierrez
2012	Jason Heyward	2007	Alex Rios

Catcher – Martin Maldonado, Los Angeles Angels

In his first full season behind the plate, Maldonado has proven himself to be one of the best defensive catchers in the game. In fact, *the* best, according to the Fielding Bible Award panel. He was above average in all five components of catcher Defensive Runs Saved, but he was particularly good at framing, where he saved 12 runs for the Angels, fourth-most in baseball. In terms of fielding balls in front of the plate, he is able to get out in front of the plate extremely quickly and throw out runners at first with his strong throwing arm (which he also used to save three runs in preventing potential stolen bases).

Previous Winners:

2016	Buster Posey	2011	Matt Wieters
2015	Buster Posey	2010	Yadier Molina
2014	Jonathan Lucroy	2009	Yadier Molina
2013	Yadier Molina	2008	Yadier Molina
2012	Yadier Molina	2007	Yadier Molina

Pitcher – Dallas Keuchel, Houston Astros

Keuchel only made 23 starts this year and still led all pitchers in Defensive Runs Saved. He saved nine runs, tied with voting runner-up Tyler Chatwood. Keuchel's release and follow-through are controlled in such a way that he keeps his hips squared to the plate, making it easier for him to get a quick jump on dribblers or get his eyes on a hard grounder that's hit right back to him. His ability to thwart the running game is legendary; he has only allowed 11 stolen bases total over the last four years.

Previous Winners:

2016	Dallas Keuchel	2011	Mark Buehrle
2015	Dallas Keuchel	2010	Mark Buehrle
2014	Dallas Keuchel	2009	Mark Buehrle
2013	R.A. Dickey	2008	Kenny Rogers
2012	Mark Buehrle	2007	Johan Santana

Multi-Position – Javier Baez, Chicago Cubs

Baez possesses arm strength that is above average when he plays on the left side of the diamond, and becomes downright ridiculous when he is playing second base. Baez believes he can make every throw on the diamond, and the vast majority of the time he is correct. Whether he is positioned at second base or shortstop, Baez is incredibly adept at ranging to his right, setting his feet, and getting off a strong accurate throw all in one fluid motion. He is also excellent as a relay man, using his aforementioned arm strength to cut down runners who attempt to take an extra base. No matter what position he is playing, Baez loves to position himself incredibly deep on the infield prior to the pitch to allow himself ample time and the opportunity of having every angle available to him as he chases down groundballs. Finally, Baez' ability to make quick tags directly upon receiving the ball has aided in making base runners extra wary when attempting to swipe second base.

Previous Winners:

2016	Javier Baez	2014	Lorenzo Cain
2015	Ender Inciarte		

Background of the Fielding Bible Awards

While *The Fielding Bible, The Fielding Bible—Volume II, The Fielding Bible—Volume III, and The Fielding Bible—Volume IV* put a lot of emphasis on the numbers, especially Defensive Runs Saved, we feel that visual observation and subjective judgment are still very important parts of determining the best defensive players. Also, we believe people have a right to know who is voting and all the players they are voting for. Therefore, in setting up the Fielding Bible Awards, we took the following steps:

1. *We appointed a panel of experts to vote.* We have a panel of 12 experts plus three "tie-breaker" ballots. (See below.)

2. *We rate everybody in one group.* The Gold Glove vote is divided into National League and American League. We make ours different by putting everybody together. Besides, is playing shortstop in the American League one thing and playing shortstop in the National League a different thing, or are they really very much the same thing? A few years back we had a great example of this decision. Without the Fielding Bible Award, Jack Wilson wins *nada*, because he switched leagues in mid-year. According to our panelists (and unlike the Gold Glove

voters), Jack was the best fielding shortstop in baseball in 2009. Period. He deserved to be recognized for that.

3. *We use a 10-man ballot and a 10-point scale.* We use a 10-man ballot. We give 10 points for first place, 9 points for second place, etc, down to 1 point for tenth place. We feel strongly that a 10-man ballot with weighted positions leads to more accurate outcomes.

4. *We defined the list of candidates.* Only players who actually were regulars at the position are candidates. This eliminates the possibility of a vote going to somebody who wasn't really playing the position.

5. *We are publishing the balloting.* We summarize the voting at each position, clearly identifying whom everybody voted for. Publishing the actual vote totals encourages the voters to take their votes more seriously. Also, we feel the public will have more respect for the voting if they have more insight into the process.

A perfect score is 120 points. If all 12 voters place one player first on their ballot, he scores 120. Only one player had a perfect score of 120 this year: Mookie Betts.

Here are the tie-breaker rules (which came into play in our very first year (2010) and in 2013). They are applied one at a time until we have a winner:

1. Most first-place votes wins.
2. Count the tie-breaker ballots, highest point tally wins.
3. Award goes to player with the higher plus/minus rating.

Ballots were due four days after the end of the regular season. Here is this year's panel:

Ben Lindbergh is a staff writer for *The Ringer,* where he hosts two podcasts, *Achievement Oriented* and *The Ringer MLB Show*. He also hosts the *Effectively Wild* podcast for *FanGraphs*. He is a former staff writer for *FiveThirtyEight* and *Grantland*, a former editor-in-chief of *Baseball Prospectus*, and the *New York Times* bestselling co-author of *The Only Rule Is It Has to Work: Our Wild Experiment Building a New Kind of Baseball Team*. He lives in New York City.

Since you have this book, you probably know **Bill James**, a baseball writer and analyst published for more than thirty years. Bill is the Senior Baseball Operations Advisor for the Boston Red Sox and the author of *The Man from the Train: The Solving of a Century-Old Serial Killer Mystery* (published in September 2017), which he co-wrote with his daughter, Rachel.

The **BIS Video Scouts** at Baseball Info Solutions (BIS) study every game of the season, multiple times, charting a huge list of valuable game details.

As the MLB Network on-air host of *MLB Now* and *MLB Tonight*, **Brian Kenny** brings an analytical perspective on the game of baseball to a national television audience. He also won a 2003 Sports Emmy Award as host of ESPN's *Baseball Tonight*.

The man who created Strat-O-Matic Baseball, **Hal Richman**, continues to lead his company's annual in-depth analysis of each player's season. Hal cautions SOM players that his voting on this ballot may or may not reflect the eventual fielding ratings for players in his game. Ballots were due prior to the completion of his annual research effort to evaluate player defense.

Named the best sports columnist in America in 2012 by the National Sportswriters and Sportscasters Hall of Fame, **Joe Posnanski** was formerly the National Columnist at NBC Sports and is now the Executive Columnist for MLB Advanced Media.

For over twenty-five years, BIS owner **John Dewan** has collected, analyzed, and published in-depth baseball statistics and analysis. He has authored or co-authored four volumes of *The Fielding Bible*.

Mark Simon has been a researcher for ESPN Stats & Information since 2002. He is a regular contributor on baseball (often writing on defense) for ESPN.com, and is the author of *Numbers Don't Lie: The Biggest Numbers in Yankees History* (published by Triumph Books in June 2016).

Peter Gammons serves as an on-air and online analyst for MLB Network, MLB.com and NESN (New England Sports Network). He is the 56th recipient of the J. G. Taylor Spink Award for outstanding baseball writing given by the BBWAA (Baseball Writers Association of America).

Rob Neyer has been a working writer for 25 years, and most recently has contributed to *The New York Times*, Vice Sports, and Complex. When he's not writing, he's thinking about not writing. Rob will live in Portland, Oregon for as long as they let him.

The **Tom Tango Fan Poll** represents the results of a poll taken at Fangraphs.com. Besides hosting the website Tango on Baseball (www.tangotiger.net), Tom is the Senior Data Architect - Stats at MLBAM and is the co-author of *The Book: Playing the Percentages in Baseball.*

Travis Sawchik is a staff writer for *FanGraphs* and a contributor for *The Athletic*. He is the author of the *New York Times* best-selling book *Big Data Baseball: Math, Miracles, and the End of a 20-Year Losing Streak*. He previously covered the Pittsburgh Pirates for the *Pittsburgh Tribune-Review*.

Our three tie-breakers are **Ben Jedlovec**, President of Baseball Info Solutions and co-author of *The Fielding Bible-Volume III* and *The Fielding Bible-Volume IV*, **Dan Casey**, veteran Video Scout and Senior Operations Analyst at BIS, and **Hans Van Slooten**, who runs Baseball-Reference.com.

Fielding Bible Awards Voting

Below we show the final point tally for The Fielding Bible Awards in the 2017 season. We asked a panel of experts to complete a 12-man ballot ranking players from 1 to 10 based on their defensive abilities. We show the ranks in the tables below. We then awarded points in the same way as Major League Baseball's MVP voting: 10 points for a first place vote, 9 for second, etc., down to 1 point for 10th place. We cover all nine positions, looking at only their fielding work for the 2015 season. Position players are eligible if they played at least 600 innings while catchers require a minimum of 500 innings. Either can qualify with 10 Runs Saved, as well. Pitchers require a minimum of 120 innings pitched or 5 Runs Saved.

In 2014, we introduced a Multi-Position Award for fielders who are excellent defensive players but do not call any one position their home. For a player to qualify for the Multi-Position Award, he must have played at least 600 innings across all positions and played no more than 70 percent of those innings at any one position

First Basemen

First Basemen	Ben	Bill	BIS Video Scouts	Brian	Hal	Joe	John	Mark	Peter	Rob	Tango Fan Poll	Travis	Total Points
Paul Goldschmidt	6	1	1	1	1	1	1	3	2	3	1	1	110
Brandon Belt	2	2	4	2	2	4	4	1	1	2	4		93
Anthony Rizzo	3	3	3	5	4	2	2	6	6	1	5	3	89
Joey Votto	1	6	2	3	8	3	3	2	3	4	7	2	88
Mitch Moreland	7	4	7	7	3		5	7	5	5		4	56
Joe Mauer	5	8	5	4	5	6	6	5	10		9	5	53
Carlos Santana	4	10	6	6	10	7	7	4	4	6	10	6	52
Freddie Freeman			8		7	5	9				3		23
Josh Bell	8	9		8		9		8	9			7	19
Eric Hosmer		5	9						7		6		17
Others receiving points: Wil Myers 11, Cody Bellinger 10, C.J. Cron 9, Justin Smoak 9, Chris Davis 7, Danny Valencia 5, Yulieski Gurriel 3, Logan Morrison 3, Matt Carpenter 2, Mark Reynolds 1													

Second Basemen

Second Basemen	Ben	Bill	BIS Video Scouts	Brian	Hal	Joe	John	Mark	Peter	Rob	Tango Fan Poll	Travis	Total Points
DJ LeMahieu	1	7	1	2	2	1	2	3	1	1	2	1	108
Ian Kinsler	2	2	2	1	1	4	1	1	3	4	9	5	97
Yolmer Sanchez	3		5	4	5	3	4	2	2	3		4	75
Dee Gordon	7	4	4	3	7	2	9	6	7	6	10	2	65
Jonathan Schoop	10	1	10	5	4	6	5		5	7	5		52
Josh Harrison	4		9	8		5	3	8	6	5		3	48
Whit Merrifield	5	6	6	7		7	8	9	4	9		7	42
Jose Altuve		3	3		8	10		5			1	6	41
Dustin Pedroia		8	7	6	3		6		8	10	8		32
Logan Forsythe	6				10		9	7		2			21
Others receiving points: Robinson Cano 18, Brian Dozier 16, Brandon Drury 16, Cesar Hernandez 9, Joe Panik 5, Kolten Wong 4, Ben Zobrist 4, Jose Peraza 3, Darwin Barney 2, Jed Lowrie 1, Rougned Odor 1													

Third Basemen

Third Basemen	Ben	Bill	BIS Video Scouts	Brian	Hal	Joe	John	Mark	Peter	Rob	Tango Fan Poll	Travis	Total Points
Nolan Arenado	1	1	1	1	1	1	1	2	2	1	1	1	118
Matt Chapman	3	8	3	2	5	4	2	1	1	3	3	2	95
Manny Machado	6	6	2	3	2	3	5	4	3	8	2	5	83
Anthony Rendon	2	5	4	8	3	2	6	6	7	6	4	3	76
Evan Longoria	7	7	5	4	4	5	3	5	4	4	10	4	70
Jedd Gyorko	4	9	7	5	9		4	3	5	2			51
Todd Frazier	5		10	9		6		7	6	5		6	34
Justin Turner	9	2	6		8	10	10	8	9			9	28
Kyle Seager			8		6		8			7	5		21
David Freese	8			10		7	7	9		9		7	20

Others receiving points: Josh Donaldson 16, Eugenio Suarez 15, Jose Ramirez 14, Kris Bryant 10, Joey Gallo 3, Travis Shaw 3, Mike Moustakas 2, Alex Bregman 1

Shortstops

Shortstops	Ben	Bill	BIS Video Scouts	Brian	Hal	Joe	John	Mark	Peter	Rob	Tango Fan Poll	Travis	Total Points
Andrelton Simmons	1	1	1	1	1	1	1	1	1	1	3	1	118
Addison Russell	2	3	2	2	4	3	2	3	2	2		2	94
Brandon Crawford	3	5	4	3	2	2	3		3	3	4	5	84
Francisco Lindor	8	4	3	7	3	4	5	7	6	6	1	7	71
Trevor Story	7	9	5	4		7	4	5	5		9	4	51
Corey Seager	4		6				6	4	4	7		3	43
Adeiny Hechavarria	6	2		5	8			6	8	4			38
Jose Iglesias	9	6	7	8	7	5					5	6	35
Orlando Arcia	5					8	8	9	7	5			24
Javier Baez			9		9	9					2		15

Others receiving points: Didi Gregorius 15, Zack Cozart 13, Elvis Andrus 11, Carlos Correa 10, Wilmer Difo 10, Freddy Galvis 10, Alcides Escobar 7, Jean Segura 5, J.J. Hardy 4, Chris Owings 1, Miguel Rojas 1

Left Fielders

Left Fielders	Ben	Bill	BIS Video Scouts	Brian	Hal	Joe	John	Mark	Peter	Rob	Tango Fan Poll	Travis	Total Points
Brett Gardner	1	1	1	1	1	2	1	1	1	1	3	1	117
Alex Gordon	2	6	2	2	2	3	4	4	6	4	1	2	94
Marcell Ozuna	5	2	3	3	8	4	6	3	2	2	10	3	81
Tommy Pham	3	5	4	4	6	5	5	2	7	5	7	4	75
Starling Marte	7	8	9		3	1	2	5	3	3			58
Andrew Benintendi	8	3	5	5	4	9	8	8	4	10	4	7	57
Adam Duvall	4	7	6	6	9	6	3	7	8	7	9	6	54
Justin Upton	6	4	7			7	7	6	5	6			40
Gerrado Parra	10		8	10		8		9		9	5	5	24
Guillermo Heredia					10						2		10

Others receiving points: Eddie Rosario 10, Delino DeShields 8, Ben Revere 6, Nori Aoki 5, Chris Taylor 5, Yoenis Cespedes 4, Michael Brantley 3, Corey Dickerson 3, Ben Gamel 3, Adam Frazier 2, Khris Davis 1

Center Fielders

Center Fielders	Ben	Bill	BIS Video Scouts	Brian	Hal	Joe	John	Mark	Peter	Rob	Tango Fan Poll	Travis	Total Points
Byron Buxton	1	1	1	1	1	1	1	2	1	1	1	1	119
Kevin Kiermaier	3	2	2	2	5	2	2	1	2	3	2	2	104
Kevin Pillar		5	3	4	2	3	5	4	4	5	6	3	77
Billy Hamilton	6	8	5	7	6	4	3	9		7	4	4	58
Jackie Bradley Jr.	5	4	4	5	3	8	8	7	8		5	8	56
Juan Lagares			7	3	9	5	4	3	5	6			46
Jarrod Dyson	8	6	10	8	7	10	7	6	9	2	8	5	46
Ender Inciarte	2		6		4	7	9		3	9	3		45
Lorenzo Cain	4	9			6	6			10	8	7	10	28
Michael Taylor	9	9				9	10		4			6	19

Others receiving points: A.J. Pollock 17, Aaron Hicks 14, Manuel Margot 12, Mike Trout 6, Adam Engel 5, Odubel Herrera 4, Bradley Zimmer 4

Right Fielders

Right Fielders	Ben	Bill	BIS Video Scouts	Brian	Hal	Joe	John	Mark	Peter	Rob	Tango Fan Poll	Travis	Total Points
Mookie Betts	1	1	1	1	1	1	1	1	1	1	1	1	120
Jason Heyward	2	2	3	2	2	2	2	2	3	2	4	3	103
Yasiel Puig	3		2	5	3	3	3	3	2	3	2	2	90
Aaron Judge	4	7	5	4	9	6	4	7	6	5	6	5	64
Giancarlo Stanton	5	8	4	3	10	4	6		4	4	10	4	59
Mitch Haniger	7		8		5	7	8	4	7			6	36
Steven Souza Jr.	6		6	7		8	9	6	10		8	8	31
Bryce Harper		4	7			10		10			3	7	25
Josh Reddick	9		10	8	6		5	9	9	10		9	24
Stephen Piscotty	10	5	9	9			7	5				10	22

Others receiving points: Kole Calhoun 21, Max Kepler 18, David Peralta 15, Jay Bruce 12, Joey Rickard 5, Jose Bautista 4, Carlos Gonzalez 4, Gregory Polanco 3, Avisail Garcia 2, Nick Markakis 2

Catchers

Catchers	Ben	Bill	BIS Video Scouts	Brian	Hal	Joe	John	Mark	Peter	Rob	Tango Fan Poll	Travis	Total Points
Martin Maldonado	4	1	1	1	1	1	1	2	1	2		4	102
Austin Hedges	2	10	2	2	9	7	3	3	2	1	2	1	88
Yasmani Grandal	3		4	5	8	2	2	1	3	3		2	77
Tyler Flowers	1	4	9	3		5	6	5		4		3	59
Yadier Molina		3	5	8	5	3		10	9		4	9	43
Tucker Barnhart		5	3	4	4	6		6	7				42
Christian Vazquez	5	9	7		6	10			4	6	5	6	41
Buster Posey		2			3	4	10		10	10	1	10	38
Sandy Leon	7			10	7		9	4	6	5			29
Salvador Perez		7	6		2	8					3		29

Others receiving points: Caleb Joseph 25, Roberto Perez 22, Manny Pina 22, Jason Castro 18, Yan Gomes 8, Mike Zunino 7, Willson Contreras 5, Gary Sanchez 4, J.T. Realmuto 1

Pitchers

Pitchers	Ben L.	Bill	BIS Video Scouts	Brian	Hal	Joe	John	Mark	Peter	Rob	Ben J.	Travis	Total Points
Dallas Keuchel	1	3	1	1	1	1	1	1	1	1	8	2	110
Tyler Chatwood	4	5	4	3	8	3	2	2	6	4	1	1	89
Mike Leake	2	9	2	2	2	4	4	3	3	5	9	3	84
Zack Greinke	3	2	7		3	2	3		2	7	2	10	69
R.A. Dickey	5		3	6	4	5	5	5		2		4	60
Marcus Stroman		1	5	4		8	7		4	3	3		53
Jhoulys Chacin	6		6	7		7	6		7	6		8	35
Zach Davies	9		8	9				9	8		10	6	18
Ivan Nova		8				9		6		9		7	16
Luis Severino	8	6									8	6	16

Others receiving points: Patrick Corbin 15, Alex Cobb 13, Julio Teheran 12, Kyle Gibson 11, Jeremy Hellickson 10, Wade Miley 9, Jose Quintana 8, Gerrit Cole 7, Josh Tomlin 7, Aaron Nola 6, Jeff Samardzija 6, Masahiro Tanaka 4, Jacob deGrom 1, Chris Sale 1

Multi-Position

Players	Ben	Bill	BIS Video Scouts	Brian	Hal	Joe	John	Mark	Peter	Rob	Tango Fan Poll	Travis	Total Points
Javier Baez	1	4	1	6	1	1	4	3	1		1	1	97
Jose Ramirez		2	3	2	2	2	9	8			4	2	65
Yolmer Sanchez	2		4		3		1	1				4	51
Josh Harrison	6		6	3	7	8	6	5				3	44
Chris Taylor	3		7	1				7	4	4			40
Cody Bellinger	4		8		5	7	7		2			5	39
Hernan Perez				4			2	6		2			30
Wilmer Difo	9		5	10			10	2		1			29
Aaron Hicks	8		2	7	8		5					9	27
Logan Forsythe	5					3	8	4					24

Others receiving points: Marwin Gonzalez 23, Ben Zobrist 22, Kike Hernandez 17, Chris Owings 17, Guillermo Heredia 16, Adam Frazier 14, Ryan Goins 12, Delino DeShields 11, David Peralta 9, Daniel Descalso 8, Yangervis Solarte 8, George Springer 8, Randal Grichuk 7, Austin Jackson 7, Eduardo Nunez 7, Andrew Romine 7, Aaron Altherr 5, Joey Gallo 5, Taylor Motter 5, Jon Jay 4, Ian Happ 1, Jose Reyes 1

Defensive Runs Saved Leaders

Lindsay Zeck

This season's Defensive Runs Saved champion is no stranger to the title. Shortstop Andrelton Simmons of the Los Angeles Angels topped the leader board for the third time in the past five seasons. He just barely scraped by last year's crown-winner Mookie Betts with 32 DRS to Betts' 31. Simmons and Betts led their teams to the most infield and outfield DRS, respectively. Simmons did so even though his teammates cost the Angels runs at the three other infield positions. Betts didn't have to work alone, however, as both Andrew Benintendi and Jackie Bradley Jr. made the leaderboard for their respective positions, saving the Red Sox 9 and 10 runs, respectively.

The second-best defensive infield of 2017 was the Colorado Rockies. They were led by the best defensive third baseman in the game for the third season in a row, Nolan Arenado, who saved his team 20 runs. He, like Betts, didn't have to work alone. The Rockies saw great defense at three of the four infield positions. Along with Arenado's stellar defense, DJ LeMahieu finished tied with Yolmer Sanchez with the most runs saved for a second baseman with eight, and Trevor Story finished with 11 runs saved—the third most for a qualified shortstop behind Simmons and Addison Russell.

Arenado had a new competitor this season. The rookie Matt Chapman of the Oakland Athletics saved just one fewer run than Arenado, despite playing over 600 fewer innings. His 19 runs saved in 727 innings was the second highest rate of DRS per innings played of any fielder to play at least 600 innings at a given position. The highest rate was none other than Kevin Kiermaier, the player who has saved 89 runs in center field over the past three seasons—the most of any player at any one position. He finished the 2017 season saving just 10 runs fewer (22) than Simmons in 540 fewer innings.

This season's worst defender was Denard Span, who cost the San Francisco Giants 27 runs in center field. These cost runs greatly contributed to the Giants having the worst defensive outfield in baseball. While Span hurt the Giants the most, of their 13 players to play at least 50 innings in the outfield, the only one to save any runs was Jarrett Parker. He saved four in left field and two in right.

The second-worst defender this season isn't as obvious when looking at the 2017 trailers. Jose Reyes of the New York Mets cost his team 26 runs, just one shy of Span. While he does appear on the following pages as the worst defensive short-stop costing 15 runs at his primary position, he also managed to cost the Mets another 11 runs between three other positions. He cost five runs at both second and third base, and one in left field.

In this section you will find Defensive Runs Saved leaders and trailers for each defensive position, both for the 2017 season alone and for the last three seasons combined.

Infield Runs Saved Leaders

First Basemen 3-Year Leaders		Second Basemen 3-Year Leaders		Third Basemen 3-Year Leaders		Shortstops 3-Year Leaders	
Goldschmidt, Paul	32	Kinsler, Ian	37	Arenado, Nolan	58	Simmons, Andrelton	75
Rizzo, Anthony	30	Gordon, Dee	17	Beltre, Adrian	39	Crawford, Brandon	49
Belt, Brandon	28	Sanchez, Yolmer	17	Machado, Manny	33	Russell, Addison	44
Moreland, Mitch	19	Harrison, Josh	16	Chapman, Matt	19	Ahmed, Nick	35
Mauer, Joe	13	Baez, Javier	16	Turner, Justin	18	Lindor, Francisco	32
Gonzalez, Adrian	11	LeMahieu, DJ	14	Gyorko, Jedd	18	Hechavarria, Adeiny	23
Freeman, Freddie	10	Forsythe, Logan	14	Donaldson, Josh	16	Cozart, Zack	17
Myers, Wil	9	Merrifield, Whit	10	Prado, Martin	15	Tulowitzki, Troy	15
Davis, Chris	7	Sogard, Eric	10	Rendon, Anthony	15	Story, Trevor	15
Adams, Matt	7	Wong, Kolten	9	Seager, Kyle	14	Seager, Corey	11

First Basemen 3-Year Trailers		Second Basemen 3-Year Trailers		Third Basemen 3-Year Trailers		Shortstops 3-Year Trailers	
Joseph, Tommy	-16	Murphy, Daniel	-30	Castellanos, Nicholas	-34	Reyes, Jose	-25
Alvarez, Pedro	-13	Kendrick, Howie	-15	Escobar, Yunel	-31	Cabrera, Asdrubal	-23
Carter, Chris	-13	Giavotella, Johnny	-15	Valencia, Danny	-21	Bogaerts, Xander	-22
Hosmer, Eric	-12	Odor, Rougned	-13	Sandoval, Pablo	-18	Tejada, Ruben	-15
Zimmerman, Ryan	-11	Castro, Starlin	-12	Franco, Maikel	-18	Diaz, Aledmys	-14
Morrison, Logan	-10	Lowrie, Jed	-10	Flores, Wilmer	-17	Suarez, Eugenio	-12

First Basemen 2017 Leaders		Second Basemen 2017 Leaders		Third Basemen 2017 Leaders		Shortstops 2017 Leaders	
Votto, Joey	11	LeMahieu, DJ	8	Arenado, Nolan	20	Simmons, Andrelton	32
Belt, Brandon	11	Sanchez, Yolmer	8	Chapman, Matt	19	Russell, Addison	15
Santana, Carlos	10	Kinsler, Ian	6	Gyorko, Jedd	16	Story, Trevor	11
Goldschmidt, Paul	10	Harrison, Josh	6	Longoria, Evan	11	Seager, Corey	10
Moreland, Mitch	10	Merrifield, Whit	5	Frazier, Todd	10	Crawford, Brandon	9
Rizzo, Anthony	9	Drury, Brandon	5	Freese, David	8	Riddle, J.T.	7
Mauer, Joe	7	Zobrist, Ben	5	Rendon, Anthony	7	Arcia, Orlando	6
Bell, Josh	6	Ramirez, Jose	5	Machado, Manny	6	Lindor, Francisco	5
Cron, C.J.	3	Forsythe, Logan	5	Turner, Justin	6	Hechavarria, Adeiny	5
Valencia, Danny	2	Baez, Javier	5	Beltre, Adrian	6	Iglesias, Jose	4

First Basemen 2017 Trailers		Second Basemen 2017 Trailers		Third Basemen 2017 Trailers		Shortstops 2017 Trailers	
Joseph, Tommy	-10	Murphy, Daniel	-15	Spangenberg, Cory	-14	Reyes, Jose	-15
Alonso, Yonder	-9	Panik, Joe	-11	Castellanos, Nicholas	-14	Bogaerts, Xander	-11
Cabrera, Miguel	-8	Gennett, Scooter	-8	Lamb, Jake	-13	Diaz, Aledmys	-10
Zimmerman, Ryan	-8	Phillips, Brandon	-7	Escobar, Yunel	-9	Semien, Marcus	-9
Smith, Dominic	-7	Castro, Starlin	-6	Flores, Wilmer	-8	Anderson, Tim	-8
Hosmer, Eric	-7	Walker, Neil	-5	Moustakas, Mike	-8	Swanson, Dansby	-7

Outfield Runs Saved Leaders

Left Fielders 3-Year Leaders		Center Fielders 3-Year Leaders		Right Fielders 3-Year Leaders	
Marte, Starling	52	Kiermaier, Kevin	89	Betts, Mookie	64
Gardner, Brett	30	Pillar, Kevin	50	Heyward, Jason	54
Duvall, Adam	23	Hamilton, Billy	32	Puig, Yasiel	25
Cespedes, Yoenis	21	Cain, Lorenzo	31	Stanton, Giancarlo	23
Gordon, Alex	20	Buxton, Byron	31	Eaton, Adam	22
Upton, Justin	17	Pollock, A.J.	25	Granderson, Curtis	20
Rasmus, Colby	17	Lagares, Juan	25	Polanco, Gregory	19
Van Slyke, Scott	13	Dyson, Jarrod	25	Chisenhall, Lonnie	13
Ozuna, Marcell	12	Bradley Jr., Jackie	24	Reddick, Josh	12
Conforto, Michael	9	Inciarte, Ender	22	Piscotty, Stephen	12

Left Fielders 3-Year Trailers		Center Fielders 3-Year Trailers		Right Fielders 3-Year Trailers	
Kemp, Matt	-29	McCutchen, Andrew	-52	Martinez, J.D.	-23
Grossman, Robbie	-22	Span, Denard	-44	Choo, Shin-Soo	-21
Werth, Jayson	-21	Fowler, Dexter	-29	Beltran, Carlos	-20
Davis, Khris	-20	Maybin, Cameron	-26	Bautista, Jose	-19
Kim, Hyun Soo	-18	Eaton, Adam	-22	Trumbo, Mark	-17
Cabrera, Melky	-17	Jones, Adam	-18	Santana, Domingo	-14

Left Fielders 2017 Leaders		Center Fielders 2017 Leaders		Right Fielders 2017 Leaders	
Gardner, Brett	17	Buxton, Byron	24	Betts, Mookie	31
Ozuna, Marcell	11	Kiermaier, Kevin	22	Puig, Yasiel	18
Pham, Tommy	10	Pillar, Kevin	15	Heyward, Jason	18
Gordon, Alex	9	Lagares, Juan	15	Stanton, Giancarlo	10
Benintendi, Andrew	9	Hicks, Aaron	12	Judge, Aaron	9
Marte, Starling	9	Bradley Jr., Jackie	10	Haniger, Mitch	8
Upton, Justin	8	Dyson, Jarrod	10	Piscotty, Stephen	8
Duvall, Adam	8	Hamilton, Billy	9	Souza Jr., Steven	7
Aoki, Nori	6	Margot, Manuel	8	Bruce, Jay	6
DeShields, Delino	5	Taylor, Michael A.	8	Reddick, Josh	5

Left Fielders 2017 Trailers		Center Fielders 2017 Trailers		Right Fielders 2017 Trailers	
Kemp, Matt	-17	Span, Denard	-27	Cabrera, Melky	-10
Davis, Khris	-13	Fowler, Dexter	-18	Williams, Nick	-9
Cabrera, Melky	-10	McCutchen, Andrew	-16	Joyce, Matt	-8
Schwarber, Kyle	-9	Pederson, Joc	-12	Bautista, Jose	-8
Carrera, Ezequiel	-8	Jones, Adam	-12	Springer, George	-7
Revere, Ben	-7	Broxton, Keon	-7	Smith, Seth	-6

Pitcher/Catcher Runs Saved Leaders

Pitchers 3-Year Leaders		Catchers 3-Year Leaders	
Keuchel, Dallas	29	Posey, Buster	42
Greinke, Zack	20	Maldonado, Martin	38
Leake, Mike	18	Grandal, Yasmani	36
Dickey, R.A.	15	Perez, Roberto	29
Tanaka, Masahiro	14	Flowers, Tyler	27
Cole, Gerrit	12	Castro, Jason	25
Chatwood, Tyler	12	Hedges, Austin	25
Miley, Wade	12	Joseph, Caleb	24
Chacin, Jhoulys	11	Norris, Derek	22
Severino, Luis	11	Zunino, Mike	20

Pitchers 3-Year Trailers		Catchers 3-Year Trailers	
Nelson, Jimmy	-17	Hundley, Nick	-32
Volquez, Edinson	-13	Vogt, Stephen	-19
Jimenez, Ubaldo	-12		
Lackey, John	-11		
Syndergaard, Noah	-10		
Betances, Dellin	-9		

Pitchers 2017 Leaders		Catchers 2017 Leaders	
Keuchel, Dallas	9	Maldonado, Martin	22
Chatwood, Tyler	9	Hedges, Austin	20
Leake, Mike	8	Grandal, Yasmani	17
Dickey, R.A.	7	Leon, Sandy	15
Chacin, Jhoulys	7	Pina, Manny	14
Davies, Zach	6	Vazquez, Christian	12
Cobb, Alex	6	Barnhart, Tucker	11
Hellickson, Jeremy	6	Flowers, Tyler	11
Stroman, Marcus	5	Castro, Jason	10
Nova, Ivan	5	Joseph, Caleb	10

Pitchers 2017 Trailers		Catchers 2017 Trailers	
Montero, Rafael	-7	Lucroy, Jonathan	-15
Sanchez, Anibal	-6	Rupp, Cameron	-10
Hammel, Jason	-5	Castillo, Welington	-9
Biagini, Joe	-5	McCann, Brian	-8
Skaggs, Tyler	-4		
Pruitt, Austin	-4		

Shift Update

John Dewan

After five straight years of an increasing number of shifts, Major League Baseball teams have leveled off in their frequency of shifting in 2017. You can see from the chart below that in 2016 teams shifted more than 10 times as often as they did in 2011. While they are still shifting more than 10 times as often in 2017 as well, the number of shifts dropped from 28,130 in 2016 to 26,705 in 2017.

MLB Shifts By Season

Season	Shifts
2011	2,350
2012	4,577
2013	6,882
2014	13,299
2015	17,826
2016	28,130
2017	26,705

* Note: The shift count is based on the number of times a ball was hit into play while a shift was on.

But the shift remains effective. There are some who speculate that the decreasing number of shifts is evidence that the shift is less effective than it was a few years ago. However, the numbers in the following chart suggest that the shift remains as effective as ever. The shift needs to be employed against the appropriate batters and in the right situations, of course, but overall teams are saving about 1.3 runs for every 100 shifts they use. Other than a fluctuation in 2013 and 2014 as teams experimented with different types of shifts, the rate has remained steady since the first year of uptick in 2012.

MLB Runs Saved per 100 Shifts

Season	Shifts	Shift Runs Saved	Runs/100
2010	2,463	25	1.02
2011	2,350	28	1.19
2012	4,577	62	1.35
2013	6,882	117	1.70
2014	13,299	144	1.08
2015	17,826	238	1.34
2016	28,130	378	1.34
2017	26,705	346	1.30

One thing we want to point out. Baseball Info Solutions has changed their method of measuring Shift Runs Saved. In previous years Shift Runs Saved measured how many runs were saved shifting compared to the average MLB defense. In the earlier seasons, shifting didn't make up much of the "average MLB defense." But now that there are many more shifts overall as part of the average MLB defense, it is better to measure the value of shifting against not shifting at all.

You may notice that Shift Runs Saved numbers shown here have changed from previous editions of the Handbook and compared to other sources. The new technique now measures the value of shifting compared to not shifting at all, a better method now that we are in the days of frequent shifting.

Here is a team-by-team look at how often they are shifting.

American League

Team	2016	2017	Change
Astros	1869	1522	-347
Rays	1588	1515	-73
White Sox	783	1490	707
Mariners	1482	1479	-3
Yankees	1380	1242	-138
Angels	1479	1018	-461
Orioles	787	938	151
Twins	835	906	71
Blue Jays	875	877	2
Rangers	834	833	-1
Indians	788	716	-72
Athletics	841	714	-127
Red Sox	696	677	-19
Royals	460	657	197
Tigers	545	478	-67
Total	15242	15062	-180
Average	1016	1004	-12

National League

Team	2016	2017	Change
Brewers	1489	1578	89
Pirates	1489	1386	-103
Reds	877	1018	141
Marlins	452	901	449
Dodgers	681	859	178
Diamondbacks	821	749	-72
Nationals	765	726	-39
Braves	1026	692	-334
Giants	858	682	-176
Rockies	1355	671	-684
Padres	826	660	-166
Phillies	502	610	108
Mets	536	465	-71
Cardinals	812	344	-468
Cubs	399	302	-97
Total	12888	11643	-1245
Average	859	776	-83

*All totals reflect Shifts on Balls In Play

The White Sox increased their shifting the most, nearly doubling what they did in 2016 and consequently saving an extra seven runs (22 in 2017 compared to 15 in 2016). The only other team to shift at least 200 more times than last year is the Marlins, who also nearly doubled their 2016 total but still remain outside the top 10 in terms of total shifts.

On the other side of things, the Rockies were the biggest decliner in terms of total number of shifts. They were originally one of the late adopters, shifting the least frequently in MLB as late as 2014, but it seemed they had made the decision to change that the past couple years when they were one of just three teams to shift over 1,000 times in both 2015 and 2016. Now they're back near the bottom, and it's reflected in their runs saved total, as shifting saved them just 3 runs in 2017 after saving them 22 in 2016.

Hits Lost and Gained to the Shift

Alex Vigderman

At Baseball Info Solutions, we can judge how effective shifts are against individual players by comparing hits lost and gained when the shift is on. This season, Mitch Moreland and Anthony Rizzo suffered most at the hands of the shift. Taking the difference between their hits lost and gained, they each had a net of 22 hits lost. The fourth most victimized hitter was Albert Pujols (19 net hits lost), whose inclusion at the top of this list is notable because he hits right-handed, which makes shifting a risky proposition against all but the slowest hitters.

To that point, we can look at Brian Dozier, another right-handed batter with a pull-heavy power stroke. He lost 21 hits to the shift this season, even more than Pujols. He also gained 24 hits when shifted, giving him a net of three hits gained (tied for third place among all hitters). With teams costing themselves more than they save by shifting Dozier, perhaps they need to reconsider their understanding of his batted ball tendencies.

How do we determine how many hits were lost or gained due to the shift? From the data collected at BIS, we know the likelihood of an out being made on every ball in play based on where and how hard it was hit. From that, we can objectively determine how many hits were lost or gained, depending on the outcome. For example, for a groundball that goes for a hit 60 percent of the time, if that ball happens to make it through the infield against a shifted defense, then the hitter gained 0.4 hits on that play (1 actual hit minus 0.6 expected hits). If, instead, the shifted defense converted that ball into an out, the hitter would have lost 0.6 hits (0 actual hits minus 0.6 expected hits). We sum up these partial gains and losses to arrive at a player's Hits Lost or Hits Gained, rounded to the nearest integer.

In the section that follows, you will find a table split into two halves. The first shows data for 2017 only and the second shows aggregated data since 2010 (when BIS began collecting shift data). In both cases, you will find listed the number of shifts on balls in play that a player saw, how many hits he lost, how many hits he gained, and the net of his hits lost and gained.

Hits Lost and Gained to the Shift

Player	2017 Season				Career Since 2010			
	Shifts	Lost	Gained	Net	Shifts	Lost	Gained	Net
Moreland, Mitch	338	39	17	22	1075	102	66	36
Rizzo, Anthony	370	38	16	22	1395	119	66	53
Smoak, Justin	303	31	10	21	823	83	40	43
Pujols, Albert	246	28	9	19	1132	128	71	57
Morrison, Logan	285	26	8	18	818	86	32	54
Duda, Lucas	240	24	8	16	940	85	35	50
Odor, Rougned	335	32	16	16	592	51	29	22
Morales, Kendrys	304	33	18	15	1133	119	69	50
Davis, Chris	233	27	13	14	1367	125	81	44
Bruce, Jay	338	28	14	14	1358	113	76	37
Calhoun, Kole	288	31	19	12	747	75	51	24
Lamb, Jake	236	25	13	12	542	55	35	20
Belt, Brandon	220	18	7	11	824	58	38	20
Joyce, Matt	245	22	11	11	780	72	42	30
McCann, Brian	240	24	13	11	1577	136	77	59
Votto, Joey	187	17	7	10	673	61	50	11
Valbuena, Luis	182	17	7	10	473	39	25	14
Gordon, Alex	245	22	12	10	725	61	42	19
Encarnacion, Edwin	212	21	11	10	979	88	48	40
Seager, Kyle	369	28	18	10	1241	95	72	23
Schwarber, Kyle	208	23	13	10	293	30	24	6
Franco, Maikel	97	13	4	9	260	28	14	14
Walker, Neil	125	13	5	8	371	32	24	8
Martinez, Victor	228	24	16	8	962	92	61	31
Moss, Brandon	185	15	7	8	1063	82	50	32
Moustakas, Mike	342	25	17	8	960	72	52	20
Stanton, Giancarlo	219	26	19	7	513	55	41	14
Wieters, Matt	179	16	9	7	582	50	31	19
Avila, Alex	148	16	9	7	460	52	27	25
Carpenter, Matt	276	19	12	7	556	36	23	13
Duvall, Adam	165	15	9	6	307	26	16	10
Bautista, Jose	165	15	9	6	696	66	43	23
Santana, Carlos	309	25	19	6	1170	101	63	38
Alonso, Yonder	237	19	13	6	608	54	38	16
Gallo, Joey	196	17	11	6	230	19	12	7
Conforto, Michael	179	17	12	5	371	34	20	14
Mazara, Nomar	257	23	18	5	443	39	40	-1
Jones, Ryder	40	6	1	5	40	6	1	5
Miller, Brad	78	9	4	5	222	23	19	4
Pederson, Joc	139	13	8	5	467	40	28	12
Shaw, Travis	199	18	13	5	495	41	29	12
Kepler, Max	164	14	9	5	256	21	15	6
Cabrera, Asdrubal	109	10	5	5	404	32	21	11
Kemp, Matt	88	7	2	5	506	47	24	23
Grandal, Yasmani	156	14	9	5	416	39	23	16
Castro, Jason	99	10	5	5	390	42	23	19
Longoria, Evan	97	10	6	4	468	41	33	8
Jaso, John	94	6	2	4	435	43	27	16
Sanchez, Gary	116	14	10	4	160	20	14	6
Ozuna, Marcell	74	6	2	4	118	8	8	0
Mesoraco, Devin	35	4	0	4	136	17	9	8
Souza Jr., Steven	70	8	4	4	109	11	8	3
Mauer, Joe	108	13	9	4	334	34	26	8
Utley, Chase	82	9	5	4	572	50	37	13
Young, Chris	86	7	3	4	319	25	15	10
Machado, Manny	90	9	5	4	148	15	10	5
Castellanos, Nick	96	9	5	4	185	15	13	2
Schebler, Scott	218	20	16	4	343	33	27	6
Betts, Mookie	39	6	2	4	95	9	8	1
Cespedes, Yoenis	75	8	4	4	464	40	38	2
Bell, Josh	107	11	7	4	137	15	8	7
Smith, Dominic	72	9	6	3	72	9	6	3
Tulowitzki, Troy	62	8	5	3	264	28	17	11
Frazier, Todd	112	8	5	3	273	19	15	4
Napoli, Mike	68	6	3	3	306	27	19	8
Cruz, Nelson	85	7	4	3	360	32	27	5
Grossman, Robbie	76	7	4	3	112	10	5	5
Leon, Sandy	79	7	4	3	178	12	15	-3
Heyward, Jason	118	9	6	3	506	44	35	9
Martin, Russell	44	4	1	3	112	11	4	7
Headley, Chase	167	15	12	3	675	58	43	15
Murphy, Daniel	153	12	9	3	317	28	21	7
Dickerson, Corey	178	17	14	3	362	23	25	-2

Hits Lost and Gained to the Shift

Player	2017 Season				Career Since 2010			
	Shifts	Lost	Gained	Net	Shifts	Lost	Gained	Net
McCutchen, Andrew	146	14	11	3	494	47	41	6
Bour, Justin	203	18	15	3	499	50	34	16
Kipnis, Jason	71	7	4	3	191	20	12	8
Saunders, Michael	96	9	6	3	316	29	22	7
Davidson, Matt	27	4	1	3	27	4	1	3
Herrmann, Chris	75	8	5	3	143	13	13	0
Harrison, Josh	45	4	1	3	61	5	2	3
Lind, Adam	159	15	12	3	791	76	55	21
Ramirez, Hanley	59	5	3	2	127	14	10	4
Chisenhall, Lonnie	54	6	4	2	151	10	8	2
Reynolds, Mark	63	6	4	2	361	29	31	-2
Arenado, Nolan	58	5	3	2	224	18	16	2
Espinosa, Danny	52	3	1	2	168	14	8	6
Goins, Ryan	42	5	3	2	61	6	3	3
Joseph, Tommy	53	5	3	2	81	8	5	3
Pearce, Steve	99	8	6	2	313	26	20	6
Lowrie, Jed	174	9	7	2	345	25	21	4
Castro, Starlin	29	3	1	2	72	7	4	3
Vogt, Stephen	149	12	10	2	663	46	41	5
Hicks, Aaron	33	3	1	2	75	7	7	0
Nava, Daniel	54	4	2	2	162	19	8	11
Beltre, Adrian	48	4	2	2	180	13	13	0
Cabrera, Miguel	29	2	0	2	172	19	14	5
Lobaton, Jose	29	3	1	2	60	8	3	5
Abreu, Jose	45	4	2	2	169	15	12	3
Renfroe, Hunter	55	4	2	2	58	5	2	3
Polanco, Jorge	53	4	2	2	78	6	4	2
Mahtook, Mikie	27	3	1	2	39	4	1	3
Haniger, Mitch	64	6	4	2	87	8	6	2
Pillar, Kevin	29	4	2	2	66	7	7	0
Lindor, Francisco	57	7	5	2	108	11	7	4
Springer, George	61	5	3	2	126	14	8	6
McCann, James	27	3	1	2	47	4	3	1
Parker, Jarrett	65	7	5	2	92	9	6	3
Gamel, Ben	52	6	4	2	55	7	4	3
Sano, Miguel	76	6	5	1	169	11	13	-2
Rosario, Eddie	77	6	5	1	155	13	10	3
Bradley Jr., Jackie	213	20	19	1	461	46	38	8
Stassi, Brock	27	2	1	1	27	2	1	1
Story, Trevor	35	3	2	1	85	10	5	5
Olson, Matt	81	7	6	1	91	8	7	1
Narvaez, Omar	30	3	2	1	35	4	2	2
Diaz, Aledmys	27	2	1	1	43	2	3	-1
Devers, Rafael	60	5	4	1	60	5	4	1
Fowler, Dexter	69	6	5	1	192	14	12	2
Castillo, Welington	72	6	5	1	174	13	16	-3
Escobar, Eduardo	37	2	1	1	103	6	6	0
Donaldson, Josh	97	7	6	1	363	33	25	8
Turner, Justin	31	3	2	1	67	5	5	0
Hoying, Jared	29	3	2	1	48	4	4	0
Gattis, Evan	40	3	2	1	171	17	11	6
Gennett, Scooter	61	4	3	1	127	10	7	3
Gomes, Yan	47	4	3	1	143	14	8	6
Franklin, Nick	26	2	1	1	78	5	4	1
Barnhart, Tucker	63	6	5	1	136	11	9	2
Rasmus, Colby	56	3	2	1	649	47	26	21
Perez, Salvador	79	5	4	1	176	11	12	-1
Smith, Seth	209	18	17	1	889	81	64	17
Zobrist, Ben	71	3	2	1	342	31	20	11
Parra, Gerardo	49	4	3	1	81	6	6	0
Davis, Khris	104	7	6	1	277	28	17	11
Adams, Matt	166	13	13	0	717	58	52	6
Gillaspie, Conor	30	3	3	0	178	17	13	4
Plouffe, Trevor	45	2	2	0	144	14	10	4
Gonzalez, Carlos	264	25	25	0	964	91	88	3
Gregorius, Didi	46	2	2	0	109	8	8	0
Carter, Chris	50	3	3	0	474	32	23	9
Myers, Wil	48	4	4	0	197	17	21	-4
Dietrich, Derek	67	5	5	0	181	13	13	0
Gyorko, Jedd	40	2	2	0	94	8	4	4
Granderson, Curtis	259	18	18	0	1128	97	55	42
Martinez, J.D.	61	5	5	0	189	14	21	-7
Kinsler, Ian	55	3	3	0	190	13	14	-1
Valencia, Danny	56	5	5	0	245	24	23	1
Sandoval, Pablo	26	3	3	0	98	11	6	5
Brantley, Michael	66	7	7	0	131	12	15	-3

Hits Lost and Gained to the Shift

Player	2017 Season				Career Since 2010			
	Shifts	Lost	Gained	Net	Shifts	Lost	Gained	Net
Drew, Stephen	44	2	2	0	350	26	19	7
Gonzalez, Adrian	119	8	8	0	1340	118	76	42
Beltran, Carlos	231	16	16	0	934	80	67	13
Kim, Hyun Soo	34	3	3	0	138	11	17	-6
Delmonico, Nick	29	2	2	0	29	2	2	0
Bird, Gregory	71	4	4	0	111	7	7	0
Seager, Corey	161	11	11	0	329	25	22	3
Maxwell, Bruce	48	4	4	0	78	7	6	1
Russell, Addison	35	2	2	0	82	6	3	3
Cron, C.J.	29	2	2	0	91	5	5	0
Drury, Brandon	26	4	4	0	55	7	7	0
Rupp, Cameron	26	1	2	-1	71	8	6	2
Contreras, Willson	33	2	3	-1	58	5	7	-2
Vargas, Kennys	87	8	9	-1	197	17	16	1
Panik, Joe	41	3	4	-1	91	8	8	0
Suarez, Eugenio	79	5	6	-1	181	15	12	3
Collins, Tyler	34	2	3	-1	73	4	6	-2
Wong, Kolten	59	6	7	-1	154	15	12	3
Puig, Yasiel	42	4	5	-1	107	8	9	-1
Zunino, Mike	70	4	5	-1	167	11	9	2
Bellinger, Cody	232	18	19	-1	232	18	19	-1
Zimmer, Bradley	42	2	3	-1	42	2	3	-1
Asuaje, Carlos	32	2	3	-1	32	2	3	-1
Peralta, David	117	13	14	-1	336	34	35	-1
Montero, Miguel	73	4	5	-1	326	28	25	3
Hosmer, Eric	237	24	25	-1	724	74	74	0
Freeman, Freddie	244	16	17	-1	995	83	64	19
Gonzalez, Marwin	111	6	7	-1	192	11	18	-7
Crawford, Brandon	62	5	6	-1	220	17	21	-4
Garcia, Avisail	35	4	5	-1	56	7	8	-1
Ellsbury, Jacoby	27	1	2	-1	84	5	8	-3
Sanchez, Hector	49	3	4	-1	96	9	5	4
Herrera, Odubel	31	2	3	-1	57	5	5	0
Yelich, Christian	40	4	5	-1	81	8	9	-1
Trout, Mike	49	2	3	-1	210	11	21	-10
Rosales, Adam	28	1	2	-1	57	4	3	1
Blackmon, Charlie	104	8	9	-1	185	13	13	0
Markakis, Nick	65	5	6	-1	170	18	11	7
Descalso, Daniel	30	1	2	-1	88	5	7	-2
Cain, Lorenzo	37	2	4	-2	55	4	5	-1
Goldschmidt, Paul	55	4	6	-2	137	10	14	-4
Galvis, Freddy	28	2	4	-2	51	4	4	0
Grichuk, Randal	64	3	5	-2	162	10	13	-3
Schimpf, Ryan	67	3	5	-2	142	6	7	-1
Upton, Justin	64	4	6	-2	144	10	11	-1
Thames, Eric	173	9	11	-2	178	9	12	-3
Cabrera, Melky	67	6	8	-2	129	10	11	-1
Cozart, Zack	30	2	4	-2	75	7	9	-2
Choo, Shin-Soo	255	21	23	-2	538	51	45	6
Healy, Ryon	123	11	13	-2	157	13	17	-4
Benintendi, Andrew	176	11	13	-2	194	12	14	-2
Ramirez, Jose	75	3	5	-2	99	5	8	-3
Polanco, Gregory	102	7	9	-2	258	20	15	5
Harper, Bryce	157	12	14	-2	520	49	37	12
Schoop, Jonathan	52	4	6	-2	125	14	13	1
Baez, Javier	67	4	7	-3	205	15	16	-1
Happ, Ian	51	3	6	-3	51	3	6	-3
Gurriel, Yulieski	39	3	6	-3	49	4	7	-3
Judge, Aaron	109	6	9	-3	126	7	11	-4
Zimmerman, Ryan	27	3	6	-3	47	4	9	-5
Cano, Robinson	190	14	17	-3	680	62	57	5
Jones, Adam	84	5	8	-3	223	16	20	-4
Solarte, Yangervis	117	7	10	-3	300	28	25	3
Dozier, Brian	225	21	24	-3	540	49	46	3
Kiermaier, Kevin	71	6	9	-3	203	17	20	-3
Trumbo, Mark	115	6	9	-3	233	14	18	-4
Bryant, Kris	207	13	17	-4	499	37	40	-3
Reddick, Josh	198	9	14	-5	723	53	52	1

2017 Career Register

Ben Jedlovec

Welcome to the book's meat and potatoes, the Career Register. The statistics you find here are complete through the end of the 2017 regular season.

The 2017 season may go down as the year of the home run, perhaps best exemplified by rookie sluggers Cody Bellinger (39 home runs) and Aaron Judge (52). The remarkable fact about Bellinger's and Judge's seasons wasn't the number of home runs that they hit—we wouldn't have been shocked to see Nelson Cruz or Chris Davis put up such numbers—but how they came out of seemingly nowhere. Even if you prorate their minor league averages (as outlined in these pages), you'd have expected Bellinger to hit 22 home runs in his 480 MLB at-bats in 2017 and Judge to hit 23 (in 542 AB).

On the other hand, take a look at Giancarlo Stanton's career (page 312). On the surface, you see that his league-leading 59 homers (league-leading totals are indicated in **boldface** throughout the section) tops his previous career high (37) by 60 percent. Under slightly closer examination, however, we note that Stanton also stayed healthy for the first time in his career. In fact, if you apply Stanton's pre-2017 rate of 208 homers in 2980 at-bats to his 2017 at-bats, he'd have set a career high with 42 home runs just because he stayed healthy. (Of course, he still exceeded that by 17, so let's not take anything away from the leap he took.)

Let's take one more moment to reflect on a couple of the game's elder statesmen. Adrian Beltre surpassed 3,000 hits in 2017, one of those arbitrary thresholds that shouldn't change how we think of him, but it will almost certainly net him the recognition that is long overdue given his accomplishments (Register on page 106, HOF Monitor on page 12, and certainly don't miss his Runs Saved Multi-Year Summary on page 362). Immediately in front of him in this section, Carlos Beltran is also winding down a 20-year, well-rounded, Cooperstown-worthy career. Oddly enough, Beltran has never led his lead in any category except one (he played all 162 games as a spry 25-year-old Royal in 2002), and he currently finds himself just short of many noteworthy counting stat thresholds such as 3,000 hits and 500 home runs.

Speaking of career milestones, Albert Pujols surpassed 600 home runs this year. His Register on page 273 reads like two different players' careers accidentally merged together. Since he signed with the Angels after the 2011 season, he's been an entirely different player. His best season in LA has fallen short of even his worst season in St. Louis in nearly every department: Hits, Total Bases, Runs, Runs Created, Total Bases on Balls, Batting Average, OBP, SLG, and OPS. He's only led the league in one category since arriving on the West Coast: Grounding Into Double Plays, for which he now holds the career record.

In addition to the statistics cited above, we've included select minor league statistics and pronunciations where we thought they might be helpful. We've also included key biographical information for every player, including the player's age as of June 30, 2018. We've also worked in the impressive Japanese statistics of Shohei Otani, who may be making his stateside debut before the next edition of the Handbook.

Fernando Abad

Pitches: L Bats: L Pos: RP-48   ah-BAHD   Ht: 6'1" Wt: 220 Born: 12/17/1985 Age: 32

Year	Team	Lg	G	GS	CG	GF	IP	BFP	H	R	ER	HR	SH	SF	HB	TBB	IBB	SO	WP	Bk	W	L	Pct	Sh	Sv-Op	Hld	ERC	ERA
							HOW MUCH HE PITCHED				**WHAT HE GAVE UP**													**THE RESULTS**					
2010	Hou	NL	22	0	0	6	19.0	76	14	6	6	3	0	1	0	5	0	12	0	0	0	1	.000	0	0-0	6	2.49	2.84
2011	Hou	NL	29	0	0	1	19.2	99	28	18	16	5	1	2	1	9	0	15	0	0	1	4	.200	0	0-2	7	8.06	7.32
2012	Hou	NL	37	6	0	8	46.0	208	57	27	26	6	2	1	3	19	1	38	4	0	0	6	.000	0	0-0	3	6.13	5.09
2013	Was	NL	39	0	0	17	37.2	166	42	14	14	3	0	0	1	10	0	32	0	0	0	3	.000	0	0-1	2	4.05	3.35
2014	Oak	AL	69	0	0	17	57.1	216	34	11	10	4	1	2	4	15	3	51	0	0	2	4	.333	0	0-2	9	1.64	1.57
2015	Oak	AL	62	0	0	17	47.2	205	45	23	22	11	3	3	1	19	3	45	4	0	2	2	.500	0	0-3	5	4.63	4.15
2016	2 Tms	AL	57	0	0	15	46.2	198	40	20	19	4	0	1	1	22	2	41	1	1	1	6	.143	0	1-5	8	3.50	3.66
2017	Bos	AL	48	0	0	15	43.2	182	40	18	16	4	0	2	1	14	1	37	0	1	2	1	.667	0	1-2	2	3.32	3.30
16	Min	AL	39	0	0	8	34.0	138	27	11	10	2	0	1	0	14	2	29	0	1	1	4	.200	0	1-2	6	2.72	2.65
16	Bos	AL	18	0	0	7	12.2	60	13	9	9	2	0	0	1	8	0	12	1	0	0	2	.000	0	0-3	2	5.81	6.39
	Postseason		1	0	0	0	0.1	1	0	0	0	0	0	0	0	0	0	0	0	0	0	0	-	0	0-0	0	0.00	0.00
	8 ML YEARS		363	6	0	96	317.2	1350	300	137	129	40	7	12	12	113	10	271	9	2	8	27	.229	0	2-15	38	3.87	3.65

Jose Abreu

Bats: R Throws: R Pos: 1B-139;DH-18   uh-BRAY-you   Ht: 6'3" Wt: 255 Born: 1/29/1987 Age: 31

Year	Team	Lg	G	AB	H	2B	3B	HR	(Hm	Rd)	TB	R	RBI	RC	TBB	IBB	SO	HBP	SH	SF	SB	CS	GDP	Avg	OBP	Slg	OPS
						BATTING															**RUNNING**			**AVERAGES**			
2014	CWS	AL	145	556	176	35	2	36	(15	21)	323	80	107	113	51	15	131	11	0	4	3	1	14	.317	.383	**.581**	.964
2015	CWS	AL	154	613	178	34	3	30	(16	14)	308	88	101	105	39	11	140	15	0	1	0	6	16	.290	.347	.502	.850
2016	CWS	AL	159	624	183	32	1	25	(15	10)	292	67	100	92	47	7	125	15	0	9	0	2	21	.293	.353	.468	.820
2017	CWS	AL	156	621	189	43	6	33	(16	17)	**343**	95	102	116	35	6	119	15	0	4	3	0	21	.304	.354	.552	.906
	4 ML YEARS		614	2414	726	144	12	124	(62	62)	1266	330	410	426	172	39	515	56	0	18	6	3	72	.301	.359	.524	.883

Cristhian Adames

Bats: B Throws: R Pos: PH-10;1B-1;2B-1;SS-1   kris-tee-YAHN ah-DAHM-ess   Ht: 6'0" Wt: 185 Born: 7/26/1991 Age: 26

Year	Team	Lg	G	AB	H	2B	3B	HR	(Hm	Rd)	TB	R	RBI	RC	TBB	IBB	SO	HBP	SH	SF	SB	CS	GDP	Avg	OBP	Slg	OPS
						BATTING															**RUNNING**			**AVERAGES**			
2017	Albq*	AAA	89	323	85	19	6	11	(-	-)	149	47	52	48	29	0	68	0	2	8	3	4	6	.263	.317	.461	.778
2014	Col	NL	7	15	1	0	0	0	(0	0)	1	1	0	0	0	0	5	0	0	0	0	0	1	.067	.067	.067	.133
2015	Col	NL	26	53	13	1	1	0	(0	0)	16	4	3	4	3	1	11	1	1	0	0	1	0	.245	.298	.302	.600
2016	Col	NL	121	225	49	7	3	2	(0	2)	68	25	17	17	24	0	47	4	3	0	2	3	5	.218	.304	.302	.607
2017	Col	NL	12	13	0	0	0	0	(0	0)	0	1	0	0	1	0	6	0	0	0	0	0	0	.000	.071	.000	.071
	4 ML YEARS		166	306	63	8	4	2	(0	2)	85	31	20	21	28	1	69	5	4	0	2	4	6	.206	.283	.278	.561

Austin Adams

Pitches: R Bats: R Pos: RP-6   Ht: 6'2" Wt: 225 Born: 5/5/1991 Age: 27

Year	Team	Lg	G	GS	CG	GF	IP	BFP	H	R	ER	HR	SH	SF	HB	TBB	IBB	SO	WP	Bk	W	L	Pct	Sh	Sv-Op	Hld	ERC	ERA
							HOW MUCH HE PITCHED				**WHAT HE GAVE UP**													**THE RESULTS**					
2013	Burlgtn	A	27	0	0	9	31.2	136	25	17	14	0	0	0	1	17	0	36	14	0	2	1	.667	0	1--	-	2.86	3.98
2014	InldEm	A+	42	0	0	10	59.1	261	27	28	25	3	5	2	10	53	0	80	14	2	3	2	.600	0	1--	-	3.25	3.79
2015	InldEm	A+	9	0	0	2	14.2	62	10	5	4	0	0	0	2	7	0	21	3	0	2	1	.667	0	0--	-	2.49	2.45
2015	Ark	AA	27	0	0	7	36.2	156	22	13	12	0	0	3	2	31	0	49	8	1	1	1	.500	0	1--	-	3.17	2.95
2016	Ark	AA	32	0	0	14	41.1	174	29	14	14	2	0	1	3	24	0	61	4	0	0	1	.000	0	4--	-	3.11	3.05
2017	Syrcse	AAA	44	0	0	16	59.0	265	44	21	14	2	0	3	4	37	3	91	9	0	6	2	.750	0	5--	-	3.12	2.14
2017	Was	NL	6	0	0	3	5.0	29	4	4	2	0	0	1	1	8	0	10	1	0	0	0	-	0	0-0	0	7.11	3.60

Lane Adams

Bats: R Throws: R Pos: PH-51;LF-27;CF-11;PR-9;RF-7   Ht: 6'3" Wt: 220 Born: 11/13/1989 Age: 28

Year	Team	Lg	G	AB	H	2B	3B	HR	(Hm	Rd)	TB	R	RBI	RC	TBB	IBB	SO	HBP	SH	SF	SB	CS	GDP	Avg	OBP	Slg	OPS
						BATTING															**RUNNING**			**AVERAGES**			
2013	Wilmg	A+	87	323	89	23	2	7	(-	-)	137	56	39	54	43	2	66	2	0	2	23	6	6	.276	.362	.424	.786
2013	NWArk	AA	44	156	38	7	1	5	(-	-)	62	30	26	24	18	0	45	3	0	0	15	0	2	.244	.333	.397	.731
2014	NWArk	AA	105	405	109	25	3	11	(-	-)	173	66	36	68	45	2	86	9	2	4	38	9	5	.269	.352	.427	.779
2015	NWArk	AA	97	373	111	21	3	12	(-	-)	174	58	49	67	36	0	98	2	0	3	29	6	7	.298	.360	.466	.826
2015	Omha	AAA	37	115	26	5	0	4	(-	-)	43	14	13	14	13	0	21	1	1	2	2	1	5	.226	.305	.374	.679
2016	Trntn	AA	84	289	73	12	1	6	(-	-)	105	49	32	43	36	0	84	5	0	2	31	5	3	.253	.343	.363	.707
2016	Tenn	AA	22	83	27	6	0	3	(-	-)	42	12	19	17	5	0	20	2	1	0	9	0	0	.325	.378	.506	.884
2017	Gwnntt	AAA	48	178	47	10	2	7	(-	-)	82	21	30	28	15	0	60	0	0	1	15	3	4	.264	.320	.461	.780
2014	KC	AL	6	3	0	0	0	0	(0	0)	0	1	0	0	0	0	2	0	0	0	0	0	0	.000	.000	.000	.000
2017	Atl	NL	85	109	30	4	1	5	(2	3)	51	19	20	18	10	0	37	1	1	1	10	0	3	.275	.339	.468	.807
	2 ML YEARS		91	112	30	4	1	5	(2	3)	51	20	20	18	10	0	39	1	1	1	10	0	3	.268	.331	.455	.786

Matt Adams

Bats: L Throws: R Pos: 1B-62;PH-51;LF-19;DH-2   Ht: 6'3" Wt: 260 Born: 8/31/1988 Age: 29

Year	Team	Lg	G	AB	H	2B	3B	HR	(Hm	Rd)	TB	R	RBI	RC	TBB	IBB	SO	HBP	SH	SF	SB	CS	GDP	Avg	OBP	Slg	OPS
						BATTING															**RUNNING**			**AVERAGES**			
2012	StL	NL	27	86	21	6	0	2	(1	1)	33	8	13	9	5	0	24	0	0	0	0	0	3	.244	.286	.384	.669
2013	StL	NL	108	296	84	14	0	17	(10	7)	149	46	51	49	23	0	80	0	0	0	0	1	9	.284	.335	.503	.839
2014	StL	NL	142	527	152	34	5	15	(8	7)	241	55	68	65	26	5	114	3	0	7	3	2	9	.288	.321	.457	.779
2015	StL	NL	60	175	42	9	0	5	(1	4)	66	14	24	16	10	1	41	0	0	1	1	0	1	.240	.280	.377	.657
2016	StL	NL	118	297	74	18	0	16	(11	5)	140	37	54	46	25	1	81	2	0	3	0	1	5	.249	.309	.471	.780
2017	2 Tms	NL	131	339	93	22	1	20	(12	8)	177	46	65	55	23	5	88	1	0	4	0	0	5	.274	.319	.522	.841

						BATTING															RUNNING			AVERAGES			
Year Team	Lg	G	AB	H	2B	3B	HR	(Hm	Rd)	TB	R	RBI	RC	TBB	IBB	SO	HBP	SH	SF	SB	CS	GDP	Avg	OBP	Slg	OPS
17 StL	NL	31	48	14	2	0	1	(0	1)	19	4	7	6	4	0	17	0	0	1	0	0	0	.292	.340	.396	.735
17 Atl	NL	100	291	79	20	1	19	(12	7)	158	42	58	49	19	5	71	1	0	3	0	0	5	.271	.315	.543	.858
Postseason		26	93	21	3	0	4	(3	1)	36	10	11	12	8	2	24	1	0	0	0	0	2	.226	.294	.387	.681
6 ML YEARS		586	1720	466	103	6	75	(43	32)	806	206	275	240	112	12	428	6	0	15	4	4	32	.271	.315	.469	.784

Jim Adduci

ah-DOO-see

Bats: L Throws: L Pos: RF-26;PR-3;DH-2;PH-2   **Ht: 6'2" Wt: 210 Born: 5/15/1985 Age: 33**

						BATTING															RUNNING			AVERAGES			
Year Team	Lg	G	AB	H	2B	3B	HR	(Hm	Rd)	TB	R	RBI	RC	TBB	IBB	SO	HBP	SH	SF	SB	CS	GDP	Avg	OBP	Slg	OPS
2017 Toledo*	AAA	55	215	62	13	1	4	(-	-)	89	32	27	32	20	1	59	0	0	4	10	3	2	.288	.343	.414	.757
2013 Tex	AL	17	31	8	1	0	0	(0	0)	9	2	0	3	3	0	9	0	0	0	2	0	0	.258	.324	.290	.614
2014 Tex	AL	44	101	17	3	0	1	(0	1)	23	13	8	6	10	0	27	0	1	2	3	1	2	.168	.239	.228	.467
2017 Det	AL	29	83	20	6	2	1	(0	1)	33	14	10	11	10	0	27	0	0	0	1	1	1	.241	.323	.398	.720
3 ML YEARS		90	215	45	10	2	2	(0	2)	65	29	18	20	23	0	63	0	1	2	6	2	3	.209	.283	.302	.586

Tim Adleman

Pitches: R Bats: R Pos: SP-20; RP-10   **Ht: 6'5" Wt: 225 Born: 11/13/1987 Age: 30**

		HOW MUCH HE PITCHED						WHAT HE GAVE UP												THE RESULTS							
Year Team	Lg	G	GS	CG	GF	IP	BFP	H	R	ER	HR	SH	SF	HB	TBB	IBB	SO	WP	Bk	W	L	Pct	Sh	Sv-Op	Hld	ERC	ERA
2014 Bkrsfld	A+	8	0	0	2	8.0	49	18	13	11	3	0	0	0	7	0	8	0	0	0	1	.000		0- -	-	17.44	12.38
2014 Pnscla	AA	30	6	0	11	79.0	314	70	28	25	7	3	0	2	20	1	70	2	0	3	8	.273		0- -	-	3.01	2.85
2015 Pnscla	AA	27	26	0	0	150.0	611	134	52	44	7	6	0	2	49	2	113	6	0	9	10	.474		0- -	-	2.97	2.64
2016 Lsvlle	AAA	10	10	0	0	56.2	227	52	18	15	4	1	0	2	10	0	38	2	0	3	1	.750		0- -	-	2.78	2.38
2016 Cin	NL	13	13	0	0	69.2	287	64	32	31	13	6	1	5	20	1	47	0	0	4	4	.500	0	0-0	0	4.11	4.00
2017 Cin	NL	30	20	0	4	122.1	531	124	79	75	29	1	4	6	51	1	108	1	1	5	11	.313	0	0-0	2	5.48	5.52
2 ML YEARS		43	33	0	4	192.0	818	188	111	106	42	7	5	11	71	2	155	1	1	9	15	.375	0	0-0	2	4.97	4.97

Ehire Adrianza

eh-EE-ray ah-dree-AHN-zah

Bats: B Throws: R Pos: SS-29;LF-17;PH-14;2B-9;3B-9;PR-6;1B-4;DH-1   **Ht: 6'1" Wt: 170 Born: 8/21/1989 Age: 28**

						BATTING															RUNNING			AVERAGES			
Year Team	Lg	G	AB	H	2B	3B	HR	(Hm	Rd)	TB	R	RBI	RC	TBB	IBB	SO	HBP	SH	SF	SB	CS	GDP	Avg	OBP	Slg	OPS
2017 Roch*	AAA	10	37	8	0	0	0	(-	-)	8	1	3	2	6	0	11	0	1	0	0	1	1	.216	.326	.216	.542
2013 SF	NL	9	18	4	1	0	1	(0	1)	8	3	3	1	1	0	5	0	1	0	0	0	1	.222	.263	.444	.708
2014 SF	NL	53	97	23	6	0	0	(0	0)	29	10	5	6	5	1	22	1	2	1	1	1	2	.237	.279	.299	.578
2015 SF	NL	52	113	21	7	1	0	(0	0)	30	11	11	12	15	0	20	4	2	0	3	2	2	.186	.303	.265	.569
2016 SF	NL	40	63	16	2	0	2	(1	1)	24	3	7	6	2	0	13	2	4	0	0	1	0	.254	.299	.381	.679
2017 Min	AL	70	162	43	9	2	2	(0	2)	62	30	24	24	16	1	25	1	1	6	8	1	0	.265	.324	.383	.707
5 ML YEARS		224	453	107	25	3	5	(1	4)	153	57	50	49	39	2	85	8	10	7	12	5	5	.236	.304	.338	.641

Jesus Aguilar

AGG-you-lahr

Bats: R Throws: R Pos: 1B-77;PH-66;DH-3;3B-1   **Ht: 6'3" Wt: 250 Born: 6/30/1990 Age: 28**

						BATTING															RUNNING			AVERAGES			
Year Team	Lg	G	AB	H	2B	3B	HR	(Hm	Rd)	TB	R	RBI	RC	TBB	IBB	SO	HBP	SH	SF	SB	CS	GDP	Avg	OBP	Slg	OPS
2014 Cle	AL	19	33	4	0	0	0	(0	0)	4	2	3	4	4	0	13	0	0	1	0	0	1	.121	.211	.121	.332
2015 Cle	AL	7	19	6	1	0	0	(0	0)	7	0	2	4	0	0	7	1	0	0	0	0	0	.316	.350	.368	.718
2016 Cle	AL	9	6	0	0	0	0	(0	0)	0	0	0	0	0	0	4	0	0	0	0	0	0	.000	.000	.000	.000
2017 Mil	NL	133	279	74	15	2	16	(4	12)	141	40	52	47	25	1	94	4	0	3	0	0	8	.265	.331	.505	.837
4 ML YEARS		168	337	84	16	2	16	(4	12)	152	42	57	51	29	1	115	5	0	4	0	0	9	.249	.315	.451	.766

Nick Ahmed

Bats: R Throws: R Pos: SS-48;PH-7   **Ht: 6'2" Wt: 195 Born: 3/15/1990 Age: 28**

						BATTING															RUNNING			AVERAGES			
Year Team	Lg	G	AB	H	2B	3B	HR	(Hm	Rd)	TB	R	RBI	RC	TBB	IBB	SO	HBP	SH	SF	SB	CS	GDP	Avg	OBP	Slg	OPS
2014 Ari	NL	25	70	14	2	0	1	(1	0)	19	9	4	3	3	0	10	0	2	0	0	1	2	.200	.233	.271	.504
2015 Ari	NL	134	421	95	17	6	9	(4	5)	151	49	34	38	29	1	81	1	5	3	4	5	4	.226	.275	.359	.634
2016 Ari	NL	90	284	62	9	1	4	(1	3)	85	26	20	18	15	3	58	4	2	3	5	2	9	.218	.265	.299	.564
2017 Ari	NL	53	167	42	8	1	6	(3	3)	70	24	21	18	10	3	39	1	0	0	3	4	6	.251	.298	.419	.717
4 ML YEARS		302	942	213	36	8	20	(9	11)	325	108	79	77	57	7	188	6	9	6	12	12	21	.226	.273	.345	.618

Andrew Albers

Pitches: L Bats: R Pos: SP-6; RP-3   **Ht: 6'1" Wt: 200 Born: 10/6/1985 Age: 32**

		HOW MUCH HE PITCHED						WHAT HE GAVE UP												THE RESULTS							
Year Team	Lg	G	GS	CG	GF	IP	BFP	H	R	ER	HR	SH	SF	HB	TBB	IBB	SO	WP	Bk	W	L	Pct	Sh	Sv-Op	Hld	ERC	ERA
2017 Gwnntt*	AAA	26	17	0	1	120.2	490	120	38	35	6	3	8	1	19	0	115	3	1	12	3	.800	0	0- -	-	2.85	2.61
2013 Min	AL	10	10	1	0	60.0	249	64	34	27	6	2	2	1	7	0	25	0	1	2	5	.286	1	0-0	0	3.45	4.05
2015 Tor	AL	1	0	0	0	2.2	11	1	1	1	1	0	0	0	2	0	1	0	0	0	0	-	0	0-0	0	3.75	3.38
2016 Min	AL	6	2	0	0	17.0	85	16	11	11	5	0	0	0	6	0	16	1	0	0	0	-	0	0-0	0	8.84	5.82
2017 Sea	AL	9	6	0	2	41.0	178	43	22	16	6	0	1	2	10	0	37	1	0	5	1	.833	0	1-1	0	4.15	3.51
4 ML YEARS		26	18	1	5	120.2	523	135	73	55	18	2	3	4	25	0	79	2	1	7	6	.538	1	1-1	0	4.37	4.10

Matt Albers

Pitches: R **Bats:** L **Pos:** RP-63 **Ht:** 6'1" **Wt:** 225 **Born:** 1/20/1983 **Age:** 35

Year Team	Lg	HOW MUCH HE PITCHED						WHAT HE GAVE UP												THE RESULTS							
		G	GS	CG	GF	IP	BFP	H	R	ER	HR	SH	SF	HB	TBB	IBB	SO	WP	Bk	W	L	Pct	Sh	Sv-Op	Hld	ERC	ERA
2006 Hou	NL	4	2	0	0	15.0	66	17	10	10	1	2	0	0	7	0	11	0	0	0	2	.000	0	0-0	0	4.97	6.00
2007 Hou	NL	31	18	0	2	110.2	508	127	77	72	18	6	8	7	50	6	71	7	0	4	11	.267	0	0-0	0	5.76	5.86
2008 Bal	AL	28	3	0	5	49.0	208	43	21	19	4	1	3	2	22	1	26	1	0	3	3	.500	0	0-2	6	3.62	3.49
2009 Bal	AL	56	0	0	13	67.0	309	80	43	41	3	5	2	2	36	3	49	3	0	3	6	.333	0	0-4	10	5.41	5.51
2010 Bal	AL	62	0	0	19	75.2	329	78	41	38	6	3	0	2	34	5	49	2	0	5	3	.625	0	0-2	7	4.35	4.52
2011 Bos	AL	56	0	0	10	64.2	289	62	35	34	7	4	2	5	31	1	68	2	0	4	4	.500	0	0-3	10	4.44	4.73
2012 2 Tms		63	0	0	12	60.1	241	46	21	16	9	1	2	2	22	3	44	1	0	3	1	.750	0	0-6	9	3.13	2.39
2013 Cle	AL	56	0	0	21	63.0	262	57	25	22	2	2	0	1	23	3	35	6	0	3	1	.750	0	0-0	1	2.99	3.14
2014 Hou	AL	8	0	0	1	10.0	42	10	1	1	0	0	0	1	3	0	8	0	0	0	0	-	0	0-1	3	3.46	0.90
2015 CWS	AL	30	0	0	5	37.1	149	31	6	5	3	0	3	1	9	2	28	0	0	2	0	1.000	0	0-0	6	2.52	1.21
2016 CWS	AL	58	1	0	11	51.1	237	67	44	36	10	3	2	3	19	1	30	4	0	2	6	.250	0	0-4	13	6.75	6.31
2017 Was	NL	63	0	0	23	61.0	233	35	12	11	6	0	1	4	17	0	63	0	0	7	2	.778	0	2-5	14	1.76	1.62
12 Bos	AL	40	0	0	8	39.1	157	30	14	10	6	0	2	1	15	3	25	0	0	2	0	1.000	0	0-4	7	3.16	2.29
12 Ari	NL	23	0	0	4	21.0	84	16	7	6	3	1	0	1	7	0	19	1	0	1	1	.500	0	0-2	2	3.07	2.57
12 ML YEARS		515	24	0	122	665.0	2873	653	336	305	69	27	23	30	273	25	482	26	0	36	39	.480	0	2-27	79	4.18	4.13

Ozzie Albies

Bats: B **Throws:** R **Pos:** 2B-57 **Ht:** 5'9" **Wt:** 160 **Born:** 1/7/1997 **Age:** 21

Year Team	Lg	BATTING																			RUNNING			AVERAGES			
		G	AB	H	2B	3B	HR	(Hm	Rd)	TB	R	RBI	RC	TBB	IBB	SO	HBP	SH	SF	SB	CS	GDP	Avg	OBP	Slg	OPS
2014 2 Tms	Low	57	198	72	7	3	1	(-	-)	88	41	19	44	28	1	23	4	6	3	22	5	2	.364	.446	.444	.891
2015 Rome	A	98	394	122	21	8	0	(-	-)	159	64	37	64	36	0	56	2	4	3	29	8	4	.310	.368	.404	.771
2016 Missi	AA	82	330	106	22	7	4	(-	-)	154	56	33	62	33	3	57	6	0	2	21	9	3	.321	.391	.467	.858
2016 Gwnntt	AAA	56	222	55	11	3	2	(-	-)	78	27	20	25	19	0	39	1	3	2	9	4	0	.248	.307	.351	.659
2017 Gwnntt	AAA	97	411	117	21	8	9	(-	-)	181	67	41	64	28	1	90	2	3	4	21	2	2	.285	.330	.440	.771
2017 Atl	NL	57	217	62	9	5	6	(1	5)	99	34	28	36	21	0	36	3	1	2	8	1	3	.286	.354	.456	.810

Al Alburquerque

Pitches: R **Bats:** R **Pos:** RP-21 AL-buh-kur-kee **Ht:** 6'0" **Wt:** 195 **Born:** 6/10/1986 **Age:** 32

Year Team	Lg	HOW MUCH HE PITCHED						WHAT HE GAVE UP												THE RESULTS							
		G	GS	CG	GF	IP	BFP	H	R	ER	HR	SH	SF	HB	TBB	IBB	SO	WP	Bk	W	L	Pct	Sh	Sv-Op	Hld	ERC	ERA
2017 Omha*	AAA	22	0	0	0	26.0	108	21	11	6	0	1	2	0	5	1	28	2	0	2	1	.667	0	3- -		1.61	2.08
2017 Charllt*	AAA	10	0	0	4	11.2	48	10	6	6	3	0	0	0	5	0	15	1	0	0	0	-	0	2- -		4.57	4.63
2011 Det	AL	41	0	0	11	43.1	182	21	9	9	0	2	1	2	29	4	67	4	0	6	1	.857	0	0-0	6	1.73	1.87
2012 Det	AL	8	0	0	0	13.1	53	6	1	1	0	0	0	0	8	0	18	0	1	0	0	-	0	0-0	1	1.50	0.68
2013 Det	AL	53	0	0	12	49.0	220	39	25	25	5	0	1	2	34	5	70	9	1	4	3	.571	0	0-0	10	4.02	4.59
2014 Det	AL	72	0	0	15	57.1	236	46	16	16	7	0	2	3	21	1	63	2	2	3	1	.750	0	1-1	17	3.23	2.51
2015 Det	AL	67	0	0	12	62.0	271	63	29	29	4	1	2	1	33	3	58	5	4	4	1	.800	0	0-1	7	4.51	4.21
2016 LAA	AL	2	0	0	1	2.0	12	2	3	1	1	0	0	0	2	0	1	0	0	0	0	-	0	0-0	0	8.14	4.50
2017 2 Tms	AL	21	0	0	7	18.0	71	10	5	5	0	0	0	0	8	0	14	0	0	0	2	.000	0	0-0	3	1.49	2.50
17 KC	AL	11	0	0	5	10.0	42	7	4	4	0	0	0	0	6	0	9	0	0	0	1	.000	0	0-0	1	2.55	3.60
17 CWS	AL	10	0	0	2	8.0	29	3	1	1	0	0	0	0	2	0	5	0	0	0	1	.000	0	0-0	2	0.65	1.13
Postseason		14	0	0	5	10.0	43	7	6	6	2	1	0	0	6	2	14	1	1	1	1	.500	0	0-0	3	3.51	5.40
7 ML YEARS		264	0	0	58	245.0	1045	187	88	86	17	3	6	8	135	13	291	20	8	17	8	.680	0	1-2	44	3.19	3.16

Arismendy Alcantara

Bats: B **Throws:** R **Pos:** PH-37;2B-10;CF-7;RF-7;SS-6;3B-4;PR-4;LF-3 ahr-ees-MEN-dee_ahl-KAHN-tar-ah **Ht:** 5'10" **Wt:** 170 **Born:** 10/29/1991 **Age:** 26

Year Team	Lg	BATTING																			RUNNING			AVERAGES			
		G	AB	H	2B	3B	HR	(Hm	Rd)	TB	R	RBI	RC	TBB	IBB	SO	HBP	SH	SF	SB	CS	GDP	Avg	OBP	Slg	OPS
2017 Pnscla*	AA	17	61	10	3	3	0	(-	-)	19	9	8	4	7	0	19	0	0	0	0	1	1	.164	.250	.311	.561
2014 ChC	NL	70	278	57	11	2	10	(5	5)	102	31	29	23	17	0	93	2	1	2	8	5	3	.205	.254	.367	.621
2015 ChC	NL	11	26	2	0	0	0	(0	0)	2	5	1	1	5	0	11	0	1	0	1	0	0	.077	.226	.077	.303
2016 Oak	AL	16	19	4	1	0	0	(0	0)	5	2	2	0	0	0	8	0	0	0	3	3	1	.211	.211	.263	.474
2017 Cin	NL	70	105	18	3	1	1	(1	0)	26	13	7	6	2	0	38	0	1	0	2	0	2	.171	.187	.248	.435
4 ML YEARS		167	428	81	15	3	11	(6	5)	135	51	39	30	24	0	150	2	3	2	14	8	6	.189	.235	.315	.550

Raul Alcantara

Pitches: R **Bats:** R **Pos:** SP-4; RP-4 ahl-KAHN-tar-ah **Ht:** 6'4" **Wt:** 220 **Born:** 12/4/1992 **Age:** 25

Year Team	Lg	HOW MUCH HE PITCHED						WHAT HE GAVE UP												THE RESULTS							
		G	GS	CG	GF	IP	BFP	H	R	ER	HR	SH	SF	HB	TBB	IBB	SO	WP	Bk	W	L	Pct	Sh	Sv-Op	Hld	ERC	ERA
2013 2 Tms	Low	27	27	1	0	156.1	649	157	74	54	11	5	3	8	24	0	124	8	1	12	6	.667	1	0- -	-	3.13	3.11
2015 Stcktn	A+	15	15	0	0	48.2	202	54	24	21	3	4	2	2	8	0	29	1	1	2	6	.250	0	0- -	-	3.73	3.88
2016 Mdlnd	AA	17	17	0	0	90.0	390	100	52	48	11	5	3	3	27	1	73	6	0	5	6	.455	0	0- -	-	4.60	4.80
2016 Nashv	AAA	8	8	0	0	45.2	172	38	7	6	1	3	0	0	3	0	32	0	0	4	0	1.000	0	0- -	-	1.64	1.18
2017 Nashv	AAA	18	3	0	7	33.2	141	36	10	10	0	0	2	0	7	0	22	1	0	1	2	.333	0	4- -	-	3.04	2.67
2016 Oak	AL	5	5	0	0	22.1	103	31	18	18	9	0	2	4	4	0	14	1	1	1	3	.250	0	0-0	-	8.76	7.25
2017 Oak	AL	8	4	0	2	24.0	108	22	21	19	5	0	1	3	12	1	12	0	1	1	2	.333	0	0-0	-	5.17	7.13
2 ML YEARS		13	9	0	2	46.1	211	53	39	37	14	0	3	7	16	1	26	1	2	2	5	.286	0	0-0	-	6.84	7.19

Sandy Alcantara

ahl-KAHN-tar-ah   Ht: 6'4" Wt: 170 Born: 9/7/1995 Age: 22

				HOW MUCH HE PITCHED						WHAT HE GAVE UP										THE RESULTS						
Year	Team	Lg	G	GS	CG	GF	IP	BFP	H	R	ER	HR	SH	SF	HB	TBB	IBB	SO	WP	Bk	W	L	Pct	Sh	Sv-Op	Hld	ERC	ERA
2015	Cards	R	12	12	0	0	64.1	267	59	30	23	3	0	0	5	20	0	51	10	1	4	4	.500	0	0- -	-	3.28	3.22
2016	2 Tms	Low	23	23	1	0	122.2	533	103	62	54	4	2	4	10	59	0	153	14	3	5	11	.313	0	0- -	-	3.31	3.96
2017	Sprgfld	AA	25	22	0	2	125.1	555	125	64	60	13	2	6	15	54	0	106	20	1	7	5	.583	0	0- -	-	4.71	4.31
2017	StL	NL	8	0	0	3	8.1	39	9	6	4	2	0	0	0	6	0	10	0	0	0	0	-	0	0-0	0	7.04	4.32

Victor Alcantara

ahl-KAHN-tar-ah   Ht: 6'2" Wt: 190 Born: 4/3/1993 Age: 25

				HOW MUCH HE PITCHED						WHAT HE GAVE UP										THE RESULTS						
Year	Team	Lg	G	GS	CG	GF	IP	BFP	H	R	ER	HR	SH	SF	HB	TBB	IBB	SO	WP	Bk	W	L	Pct	Sh	Sv-Op	Hld	ERC	ERA
2013	Orem	R+	17	12	0	2	59.0	280	73	59	49	10	2	1	2	35	0	48	14	1	2	5	.286	0	0- -	-	7.03	7.47
2014	Burlgtn	A	27	20	0	3	125.1	519	98	57	53	6	4	3	4	60	0	117	18	1	7	6	.538	0	1- -	-	3.03	3.81
2015	InldEm	A+	27	27	0	0	136.0	614	152	98	85	10	1	7	9	58	0	125	20	1	7	12	.368	0	0- -	-	4.91	5.63
2016	Ark	AA	29	20	0	4	111.0	486	106	62	53	9	5	3	5	57	0	79	7	0	3	7	.300	0	0- -	-	4.35	4.30
2017	Erie	AA	30	2	0	4	54.2	237	46	26	21	1	2	1	1	34	1	57	3	1	1	2	.333	0	1- -	-	3.54	3.46
2017	Toledo	AAA	9	1	0	2	20.0	96	22	13	9	0	0	1	3	12	0	16	3	0	0	1	.000	0	0- -	-	5.16	4.05
2017	Det	AL	6	0	0	2	7.1	39	12	7	7	1	0	1	2	4	0	5	1	0	0	0	-	0	0-0	0	10.32	8.59

Scott Alexander

Ht: 6'2" Wt: 190 Born: 7/10/1989 Age: 28

				HOW MUCH HE PITCHED						WHAT HE GAVE UP										THE RESULTS						
Year	Team	Lg	G	GS	CG	GF	IP	BFP	H	R	ER	HR	SH	SF	HB	TBB	IBB	SO	WP	Bk	W	L	Pct	Sh	Sv-Op	Hld	ERC	ERA
2017	Omha*	AAA	7	0	0	1	7.2	34	9	4	4	1	0	0	0	3	0	4	0	0	1	0	1.000	0	0- -	-	5.31	4.70
2015	KC	AL	4	0	0	3	6.0	25	5	3	3	0	0	0	1	3	0	3	1	0	0	0	-	0	0-0	0	3.67	4.50
2016	KC	AL	17	0	0	4	19.0	84	24	7	7	1	0	1	0	7	0	16	0	0	0	0	-	0	0-1	0	5.24	3.32
2017	KC	AL	58	0	0	9	69.0	283	62	23	19	3	1	2	0	28	0	59	3	0	5	4	.556	0	4-6	9	3.27	2.48
	3 ML YEARS		79	0	0	16	94.0	392	91	33	29	4	1	3	1	38	0	78	4	0	5	4	.556	0	4-7	9	3.67	2.78

Jorge Alfaro

Ht: 6'2" Wt: 225 Born: 6/11/1993 Age: 25

							BATTING															RUNNING			AVERAGES			
Year	Team	Lg	G	AB	H	2B	3B	HR	(Hm	Rd)	TB	R	RBI	RC	TBB	IBB	SO	HBP	SH	SF	SB	CS	GDP	Avg	OBP	Slg	OPS
2013	3 Tms		113	404	107	24	1	18	(-	-)	187	72	61	68	32	0	122	20	0	3	18	3	10	.265	.346	.463	.809
2014	MrtlBh	A+	100	398	104	22	5	13	(-	-)	175	63	73	56	23	0	100	12	0	4	6	5	6	.261	.318	.440	.758
2014	Frisco	AA	21	88	23	4	0	4	(-	-)	39	12	14	13	6	1	23	5	0	0	0	0	4	.261	.343	.443	.787
2015	Frisco	AA	49	190	48	15	2	5	(-	-)	82	22	21	26	9	0	61	8	0	0	2	1	3	.253	.314	.432	.746
2016	Rdng	AA	97	404	115	22	2	15	(-	-)	186	68	67	61	22	0	105	4	1	4	3	2	9	.285	.325	.460	.785
2017	LV	AAA	84	324	78	13	2	7	(-	-)	116	34	43	34	16	1	113	8	0	2	1	1	12	.241	.291	.358	.649
2016	Phi	NL	6	16	2	0	0	0	(0	0)	2	0	0	0	1	1	8	0	0	0	0	0	0	.125	.176	.125	.301
2017	Phi	NL	29	107	34	6	0	5	(3	2)	55	12	14	20	3	1	33	4	0	0	0	0	2	.318	.360	.514	.874
	2 ML YEARS		35	123	36	6	0	5	(3	2)	57	12	14	20	4	2	41	4	0	0	0	0	2	.293	.336	.463	.799

Anthony Alford

Ht: 6'1" Wt: 215 Born: 7/20/1994 Age: 23

							BATTING															RUNNING			AVERAGES			
Year	Team	Lg	G	AB	H	2B	3B	HR	(Hm	Rd)	TB	R	RBI	RC	TBB	IBB	SO	HBP	SH	SF	SB	CS	GDP	Avg	OBP	Slg	OPS
2014	2 Tms	Low	14	54	14	1	0	2	(-	-)	21	8	5	7	5	0	21	1	0	0	5	0	0	.259	.333	.389	.722
2015	2 Tms	Low	107	413	123	25	7	4	(-	-)	174	91	35	77	67	1	109	4	0	3	27	7	5	.298	.398	.421	.820
2016	Dnedin	A+	92	339	80	17	2	9	(-	-)	128	53	44	49	53	0	117	5	0	4	18	6	3	.236	.344	.378	.722
2017	Nham	AA	68	245	76	14	0	5	(-	-)	105	41	24	48	35	2	45	6	1	2	18	3	4	.310	.406	.429	.835
2017	Tor	AL	4	8	1	1	0	0	(0	0)	2	0	0	0	0	0	3	0	0	0	0	0	0	.125	.125	.250	.375

Cody Allen

Ht: 6'1" Wt: 210 Born: 11/20/1988 Age: 29

				HOW MUCH HE PITCHED						WHAT HE GAVE UP										THE RESULTS						
Year	Team	Lg	G	GS	CG	GF	IP	BFP	H	R	ER	HR	SH	SF	HB	TBB	IBB	SO	WP	Bk	W	L	Pct	Sh	Sv-Op	Hld	ERC	ERA
2012	Cle	AL	27	0	0	9	29.0	126	29	12	12	2	1	1	0	15	0	27	0	0	0	1	.000	0	0-1	1	4.39	3.72
2013	Cle	AL	77	0	0	12	70.1	301	62	22	19	7	4	4	1	26	2	88	9	0	6	1	.857	0	2-4	11	3.24	2.43
2014	Cle	AL	76	0	0	44	69.2	279	48	21	16	7	2	2	1	26	5	91	4	0	6	4	.600	0	24-28	9	2.32	2.07
2015	Cle	AL	70	0	0	58	69.1	286	56	26	23	2	1	2	2	25	2	99	9	0	2	5	.286	0	34-38	5	2.51	2.99
2016	Cle	AL	67	0	0	55	68.0	264	41	23	19	8	3	2	0	27	2	87	3	0	3	5	.375	0	32-35	0	2.14	2.51
2017	Cle	AL	69	0	0	55	67.1	282	57	24	22	9	1	0	2	21	0	92	9	0	3	7	.300	0	30-34	4	3.18	2.94
	Postseason		11	0	0	8	14.0	57	9	1	0	0	0	0	1	5	1	25	0	0	0	0	-	0	6-6	1	1.63	0.00
	6 ML YEARS		386	0	0	233	373.2	1538	293	128	111	35	12	11	6	140	11	484	34	0	20	23	.465	0	122-140	25	2.80	2.67

Greg Allen

Bats: B **Throws:** R **Pos:** CF-21;PR-6;LF-5;PH-1   **Ht:** 6'0" **Wt:** 175 **Born:** 3/15/1993 **Age:** 25

Year	Team	Lg	G	AB	H	2B	3B	HR	(Hm	Rd)	TB	R	RBI	RC	TBB	IBB	SO	HBP	SH	SF	SB	CS	GDP	Avg	OBP	Slg	OPS
									BATTING												RUNNING			AVERAGES			
2014	MhVlly	A-	57	225	55	8	2	0	(-	-)	67	46	19	33	27	1	26	15	1	2	30	5	1	.244	.361	.298	.658
2015	2 Tms	Low	126	492	133	28	2	7	(-	-)	186	85	45	77	55	1	60	21	10	2	46	16	6	.270	.367	.378	.745
2016	Lynbrg	A+	92	346	103	16	4	4	(-	-)	139	93	31	71	58	0	51	19	7	2	38	7	2	.298	.424	.402	.825
2016	Akron	AA	37	145	42	7	3	3	(-	-)	64	26	13	26	19	1	27	8	1	1	7	6	0	.290	.399	.441	.840
2017	Akron	AA	71	258	68	16	1	2	(-	-)	92	37	34	38	22	0	55	13	4	6	21	2	1	.264	.344	.357	.701
2017	Cle	AL	25	35	8	1	0	1	(0	1)	12	7	6	4	2	0	8	1	0	1	1	0	0	.229	.282	.343	.625

Abraham Almonte

Bats: B **Throws:** R **Pos:** RF-32;LF-20;CF-8;PH-7;PR-7;DH-4   **Ht:** 5'9" **Wt:** 210 **Born:** 6/27/1989 **Age:** 29

Year	Team	Lg	G	AB	H	2B	3B	HR	(Hm	Rd)	TB	R	RBI	RC	TBB	IBB	SO	HBP	SH	SF	SB	CS	GDP	Avg	OBP	Slg	OPS
									BATTING												RUNNING			AVERAGES			
2017	Clmbs*	AAA	23	77	20	6	1	2	(-	-)	34	11	6	14	15	4	13	0	0	0	3	1	4	.260	.380	.442	.822
2013	Sea	AL	25	72	19	4	0	2	(1	1)	29	10	9	9	6	0	21	0	2	2	1	0	2	.264	.313	.403	.715
2014	2 Tms		59	204	47	10	1	3	(2	1)	68	19	15	18	12	0	60	1	2	1	4	3	5	.230	.275	.333	.609
2015	2 Tms		82	232	58	12	5	5	(4	1)	95	36	24	28	21	0	52	0	3	2	7	1	5	.250	.310	.409	.719
2016	Cle	AL	67	182	48	20	1	1	(1	0)	73	24	22	20	8	1	42	1	0	3	8	0	5	.264	.294	.401	.695
2017	Cle	AL	69	172	40	8	3	3	(2	1)	63	26	14	19	20	0	46	1	1	1	2	1	2	.233	.314	.366	.681
14	Sea	AL	27	106	21	5	1	1	(0	1)	31	10	8	10	6	0	40	1	0	0	3	1	1	.198	.248	.292	.540
14	SD	NL	32	98	26	5	0	2	(2	0)	37	9	7	8	6	0	20	0	2	1	1	2	4	.265	.305	.378	.682
15	SD	NL	31	54	11	3	0	0	(0	0)	14	6	4	3	5	0	19	0	3	0	1	1	1	.204	.271	.259	.530
15	Cle	AL	51	178	47	9	5	5	(4	1)	81	30	20	25	16	0	33	0	0	2	6	0	4	.264	.321	.455	.776
	5 ML YEARS		302	862	212	54	10	14	(10	4)	328	115	84	94	67	1	221	3	8	9	22	5	19	.246	.300	.381	.680

Miguel Almonte

Pitches: R **Bats:** R **Pos:** RP-2   **Ht:** 6'2" **Wt:** 210 **Born:** 4/4/1993 **Age:** 25

Year	Team	Lg	G	GS	CG	GF	IP	BFP	H	R	ER	HR	SH	SF	HB	TBB	IBB	SO	WP	Bk	W	L	Pct	Sh	Sv-Op	Hld	ERC	ERA
			HOW MUCH HE PITCHED						WHAT HE GAVE UP												THE RESULTS							
2013	Lxngtn	A	25	25	1	0	130.2	535	115	53	45	6	2	5	7	36	0	132	10	2	6	9	.400	0	0- -		2.84	3.10
2014	Wilmg	A+	23	22	0	0	110.0	463	107	60	55	9	3	4	11	32	1	101	8	6	6	8	.429	0	0- -		3.81	4.50
2015	NWArk	AA	17	17	0	0	67.0	293	65	31	30	4	2	1	8	27	0	55	4	0	4	4	.500	0	0- -		4.12	4.03
2015	Omha	AAA	11	6	0	0	36.2	155	33	24	22	3	0	2	3	15	0	41	1	2	2	2	.500	0	0- -		3.82	5.40
2016	Omha	AAA	21	12	0	4	60.0	280	63	43	36	5	2	3	3	42	1	57	5	2	3	7	.300	0	0- -		5.64	5.40
2016	NWArk	AA	11	0	0	4	16.0	73	24	13	13	4	0	0	0	4	0	15	1	0	2	1	.667	0	0- -		7.82	7.31
2017	NWArk	AA	7	6	0	0	29.0	113	22	7	6	2	0	0	2	6	0	35	1	0	1	0	1.000	0	0- -		2.24	1.86
2017	Omha	AAA	9	3	0	1	18.0	75	20	3	3	1	0	0	1	7	0	17	0	0	1	0	.000	0	0- -		4.90	1.50
2015	KC	AL	9	0	0	3	8.2	41	7	6	6	4	0	0	1	7	0	10	0	0	0	2	.000	0	0-0	0	7.83	6.23
2017	KC	AL	2	0	0	0	2.0	12	5	3	3	0	0	0	0	2	0	0	0	0	0	0	-	0	0-0	0	17.04	13.50
	2 ML YEARS		11	0	0	3	10.2	53	12	9	9	4	0	1	1	9	0	10	0	0	0	2	.000	0	0-0	0	9.52	7.59

Albert Almora Jr.

Bats: R **Throws:** R **Pos:** CF-104;PH-43;LF-1;RF-1   **Ht:** 6'2" **Wt:** 190 **Born:** 4/16/1994 **Age:** 24

Year	Team	Lg	G	AB	H	2B	3B	HR	(Hm	Rd)	TB	R	RBI	RC	TBB	IBB	SO	HBP	SH	SF	SB	CS	GDP	Avg	OBP	Slg	OPS
									BATTING												RUNNING			AVERAGES			
2013	Kane	A	61	249	82	17	4	3	(-	-)	116	39	23	43	17	1	30	3	1	2	4	4	7	.329	.376	.466	.842
2014	Dytona	A+	89	367	104	20	2	7	(-	-)	149	55	50	46	12	1	46	2	0	4	6	3	15	.283	.306	.406	.712
2014	Tenn	AA	36	142	33	7	2	2	(-	-)	50	20	10	11	2	0	22	1	0	0	1	1	6	.232	.248	.352	.600
2015	Tenn	AA	106	405	110	26	4	6	(-	-)	162	69	46	56	32	1	47	4	4	6	9	4	10	.272	.327	.400	.727
2016	Iowa	AAA	80	320	97	18	3	4	(-	-)	133	46	43	43	9	0	44	0	2	5	10	3	7	.303	.317	.416	.733
2016	ChC	NL	47	112	31	9	1	3	(1	2)	51	14	14	16	5	0	20	0	0	0	0	0	5	.277	.308	.455	.763
2017	ChC	NL	132	299	89	18	1	8	(4	4)	133	39	46	44	19	1	53	0	3	2	1	0	8	.298	.338	.445	.782
	Postseason		9	10	0	0	0	0	(0	0)	0	1	0	0	0	0	2	0	1	0	0	0	1	.000	.000	.000	.000
	2 ML YEARS		179	411	120	27	2	11	(5	6)	184	53	60	60	24	1	73	0	3	2	1	0	13	.292	.330	.448	.777

Yonder Alonso

Bats: L **Throws:** R **Pos:** 1B-135;PH-13;DH-1   YONN-dur ah-LONN-zo   **Ht:** 6'1" **Wt:** 230 **Born:** 4/8/1987 **Age:** 31

Year	Team	Lg	G	AB	H	2B	3B	HR	(Hm	Rd)	TB	R	RBI	RC	TBB	IBB	SO	HBP	SH	SF	SB	CS	GDP	Avg	OBP	Slg	OPS
									BATTING												RUNNING			AVERAGES			
2010	Cin	NL	22	29	6	2	0	0	(0	0)	8	2	3	0	0	0	10	0	0	0	0	0	1	.207	.207	.276	.483
2011	Cin	NL	47	88	29	4	0	5	(2	3)	48	9	15	16	10	0	21	0	0	0	0	0	2	.330	.398	.545	.943
2012	SD	NL	155	549	150	39	0	9	(3	6)	216	47	62	71	62	9	101	3	1	4	3	0	14	.273	.348	.393	.741
2013	SD	NL	97	334	94	11	0	6	(4	2)	123	34	45	46	32	5	47	2	0	7	6	0	9	.281	.341	.368	.710
2014	SD	NL	84	267	64	19	1	7	(3	4)	106	27	27	26	17	1	36	1	0	3	6	1	8	.240	.285	.397	.682
2015	SD	NL	103	354	100	18	1	5	(3	2)	135	50	31	40	42	3	48	3	0	3	2	5	13	.282	.361	.381	.742
2016	Oak	AL	156	482	122	34	0	7	(3	4)	177	52	56	58	45	1	74	1	0	4	3	1	15	.253	.316	.367	.683
2017	2 Tms	AL	142	451	120	22	0	28	(17	11)	226	72	67	79	68	6	118	2	0	0	2	0	9	.266	.365	.501	.866
17	Oak	AL	100	319	85	17	0	22	(15	7)	168	52	49	59	50	6	88	2	0	0	1	0	6	.266	.369	.527	.896
17	Sea	AL	42	132	35	5	0	6	(2	4)	58	20	18	20	18	0	30	0	0	0	1	0	3	.265	.353	.439	.793
	8 ML YEARS		806	2554	685	149	2	67	(35	32)	1039	293	306	336	276	25	455	12	1	21	22	7	71	.268	.340	.407	.747

Dan Altavilla

Pitches: R Bats: R Pos: RP-41 | all-ta-VILL-ah | Ht: 5'11" Wt: 200 Born: 9/8/1992 Age: 25

Year	Team		HOW MUCH HE PITCHED						WHAT HE GAVE UP											THE RESULTS						
			G	GS	CG	GF	IP	BFP	H	R	ER	HR	SH	SF	HB	TBB	IBB	SO	WP	Bk	W	L	Pct	Sh	Sv-Op	Hld	ERC	ERA
2014	Everett	A-	14	14	0	0	66.0	293	74	36	32	7	0	0	4	32	0	66	4	0	5	3	.625	0	0- -	-	5.58	4.36
2015	Bkrsfld	A+	28	28	1	0	148.1	628	138	82	67	11	1	7	7	53	0	134	13	2	6	12	.333	1	0- -	-	3.55	4.07
2016	Jacksn	AA	43	0	0	35	56.2	235	40	15	12	3	5	1	3	22	1	65	2	0	7	3	.700	0	16- -	-	2.32	1.91
2017	Tacom	AAA	20	0	0	15	23.1	100	17	4	4	1	0	1	1	15	2	36	2	0	2	0	1.000	0	6- -	-	3.17	1.54
2016	Sea	AL	15	0	0	7	12.1	48	11	1	1	0	0	1	1	1	0	10	1	0	0	0	-	0	0-1	1	2.09	0.73
2017	Sea	AL	41	0	0	13	46.2	203	43	27	22	9	0	4	1	20	1	52	9	0	1	1	.500	0	0-4	2	4.38	4.24
	2 ML YEARS		56	0	0	20	59.0	251	54	28	23	9	0	5	2	21	1	62	10	0	1	1	.500	0	0-5	3	3.87	3.51

Aaron Altherr

Bats: R Throws: R Pos: LF-52;RF-50;CF-19;PH-7 | ALL-tair | Ht: 6'5" Wt: 215 Born: 1/14/1991 Age: 27

Year	Team	Lg				BATTING															RUNNING			AVERAGES			
			G	AB	H	2B	3B	HR	(Hm	Rd)	TB	R	RBI	RC	TBB	IBB	SO	HBP	SH	SF	SB	CS	GDP	Avg	OBP	Slg	OPS
2014	Phi	NL	2	5	0	0	0	0	(0	0)	0	0	0	0	0	0	2	0	0	0	0	0	0	.000	.000	.000	.000
2015	Phi	NL	39	137	33	11	4	5	(2	3)	67	25	22	23	16	0	41	5	1	2	6	2	3	.241	.338	.489	.827
2016	Phi	NL	57	198	39	6	0	4	(2	2)	57	23	22	20	23	2	69	6	0	0	7	2	4	.197	.300	.288	.587
2017	Phi	NL	107	372	101	24	5	19	(14	5)	192	58	65	55	32	2	104	7	0	1	5	4	12	.272	.340	.516	.856
	4 ML YEARS		205	712	173	41	9	28	(18	10)	316	106	109	98	71	4	216	18	1	3	18	8	19	.243	.326	.444	.770

Jose Altuve

Bats: R Throws: R Pos: 2B-149;DH-3;PH-1;PR-1 | al-TOO-vay | Ht: 5'6" Wt: 165 Born: 5/6/1990 Age: 28

Year	Team	Lg				BATTING															RUNNING			AVERAGES			
			G	AB	H	2B	3B	HR	(Hm	Rd)	TB	R	RBI	RC	TBB	IBB	SO	HBP	SH	SF	SB	CS	GDP	Avg	OBP	Slg	OPS
2011	Hou	NL	57	221	61	10	1	2	(2	0)	79	26	12	18	5	0	29	2	5	1	7	3	5	.276	.297	.357	.654
2012	Hou	NL	147	576	167	34	4	7	(4	3)	230	80	37	76	40	0	74	6	4	4	33	11	8	.290	.340	.399	.740
2013	Hou	AL	152	626	177	31	2	5	(4	1)	227	64	52	67	32	5	85	2	4	8	35	13	24	.283	.316	.363	.678
2014	Hou	AL	158	660	225	47	3	7	(4	3)	299	85	59	106	36	7	53	5	1	5	56	9	20	.341	.377	.453	.830
2015	Hou	AL	154	638	200	40	4	15	(9	6)	293	86	66	98	33	8	67	9	3	6	38	13	17	.313	.353	.459	.812
2016	Hou	AL	161	640	216	42	5	24	(15	9)	340	108	96	132	60	11	70	7	3	7	30	10	15	.338	.396	.531	.928
2017	Hou	AL	153	590	204	39	4	24	(9	15)	323	112	81	118	58	3	84	9	1	4	32	6	19	.346	.410	.547	.957
	Postseason		6	26	4	0	0	0	(0	0)	4	2	2	1	1	0	3	0	0	0	1	1	1	.154	.185	.154	.339
	7 ML YEARS		982	3951	1250	243	23	84	(47	37)	1791	561	403	615	264	34	462	40	21	35	231	65	108	.316	.362	.453	.816

Jose Alvarado

Pitches: L Bats: L Pos: RP-35 | Ht: 6'2" Wt: 245 Born: 5/21/1995 Age: 23

Year	Team	Lg		HOW MUCH HE PITCHED						WHAT HE GAVE UP											THE RESULTS						
			G	GS	CG	GF	IP	BFP	H	R	ER	HR	SH	SF	HB	TBB	IBB	SO	WP	Bk	W	L	Pct	Sh	Sv-Op	Hld	ERC	ERA
2014	Rays	R	12	11	0	0	40.1	178	28	28	17	1	0	0	2	29	0	46	7	1	5	1	.167	0	0- -	-	3.22	3.79
2015	Prnctn	R+	5	5	0	0	17.0	81	18	19	18	1	3	0	5	13	0	18	0	0	0	2	.000	0	0- -	-	7.12	9.53
2016	2 Tms	Low	37	0	0	17	70.2	312	50	32	24	1	4	1	1	55	1	85	14	1	4	1	.800	0	2- -	-	3.29	3.06
2017	Mont	AA	9	0	0	2	11.1	42	4	3	3	1	0	1	0	5	0	14	1	0	2	1	.667	0	0- -	-	1.24	2.38
2017	Drham	AAA	16	0	0	4	18.1	81	11	8	8	1	0	0	0	13	1	26	3	0	0	2	.000	0	1- -	-	2.56	3.93
2017	TB	AL	35	0	0	6	29.2	123	24	12	12	1	2	1	0	9	1	29	2	0	0	3	.000	0	0-0	7	2.19	3.64

Dario Alvarez

Pitches: L Bats: L Pos: RP-20 | Ht: 6'1" Wt: 170 Born: 1/17/1989 Age: 29

Year	Team	Lg		HOW MUCH HE PITCHED						WHAT HE GAVE UP											THE RESULTS						
			G	GS	CG	GF	IP	BFP	H	R	ER	HR	SH	SF	HB	TBB	IBB	SO	WP	Bk	W	L	Pct	Sh	Sv-Op	Hld	ERC	ERA
2017	RdRck*	AAA	18	1	0	8	27.0	115	24	7	7	3	0	1	4	10	0	36	3	0	2	0	1.000	0	0- -	-	4.06	2.33
2014	NYM	NL	4	0	0	0	1.1	8	4	2	2	1	0	0	0	0	0	1	0	0	0	0	-	0	0-1	1	22.76	13.50
2015	NYM	NL	6	0	0	0	3.2	19	5	5	5	2	1	0	2	1	0	2	0	1	1	0	1.000	0	0-0	1	12.00	12.27
2016	2 Tms		26	0	0	9	26.2	113	28	16	15	6	0	1	3	7	2	41	5	0	3	1	.750	0	0-0	1	5.16	5.06
2017	Tex	AL	20	0	0	3	16.1	82	19	8	5	1	0	2	1	14	0	17	2	1	2	0	1.000	0	0-0	3	6.77	2.76
16	Atl	NL	16	0	0	4	15.0	61	11	5	5	3	0	0	1	5	2	28	4	0	3	1	.750	0	0-0	1	3.09	3.00
16	Tex	AL	10	0	0	5	11.2	52	17	11	10	3	0	1	2	2	0	13	1	0	0	0	-	0	0-0	0	8.34	7.71
	4 ML YEARS		56	0	0	12	48.0	222	56	31	27	10	1	3	6	22	2	61	7	2	6	1	.857	0	0-1	6	6.64	5.06

Henderson Alvarez

Pitches: R Bats: R Pos: SP-3 | Ht: 6'0" Wt: 205 Born: 4/18/1990 Age: 28

Year	Team	Lg		HOW MUCH HE PITCHED						WHAT HE GAVE UP											THE RESULTS						
			G	GS	CG	GF	IP	BFP	H	R	ER	HR	SH	SF	HB	TBB	IBB	SO	WP	Bk	W	L	Pct	Sh	Sv-Op	Hld	ERC	ERA
2011	Tor	AL	10	10	0	0	63.2	259	64	26	25	8	1	2	4	8	0	40	2	0	1	3	.250	0	0-0	0	3.49	3.53
2012	Tor	AL	31	31	1	0	187.1	807	216	110	101	29	2	4	3	54	2	79	3	1	9	14	.391	1	0-0	0	5.01	4.85
2013	Mia	NL	17	17	1	0	102.2	418	90	42	41	2	0	4	2	27	1	57	4	1	5	6	.455	1	0-0	0	2.66	3.59
2014	Mia	NL	30	30	3	0	187.0	772	198	65	55	14	7	4	8	33	3	111	4	0	12	7	.632	3	0-0	0	3.56	2.65
2015	Mia	NL	4	4	0	0	22.1	102	28	18	16	1	4	1	0	7	1	9	3	1	0	4	.000	0	0-0	0	4.57	6.45
2017	Phi	NL	3	3	0	0	14.2	67	14	7	7	2	0	0	1	11	1	6	0	1	0	1	.000	0	0-0	0	5.42	4.30
	6 ML YEARS		95	95	5	0	577.2	2425	610	268	245	56	14	15	22	140	8	302	16	4	27	35	.435	5	0-0	0	3.93	3.82

Jose Alvarez

Pitches: L Bats: L Pos: RP-64

Ht: 5'11" Wt: 190 Born: 5/6/1989 Age: 29

Year	Team	Lg	G	GS	CG	GF	IP	BFP	H	R	ER	HR	SH	SF	HB	TBB	IBB	SO	WP	Bk	W	L	Pct	Sh	Sv-Op	Hld	ERC	ERA
2017	Salt Lk*	AAA	9	0	0	2	11.2	46	10	3	3	0	0	0	0	2	0	10	1	0	0	0	-	0	0--	-	1.91	2.31
2013	Det	AL	14	6	0	0	38.2	172	42	26	25	7	2	2	2	16	1	31	0	1	1	5	.167	0	0-0	2	5.41	5.82
2014	LAA	AL	2	0	0	1	0.2	3	1	0	0	0	0	0	0	0	0	1	0	0	0	0	-	0	-	0	4.47	0.00
2015	LAA	AL	64	0	0	18	67.0	283	58	29	26	5	0	1	5	23	4	59	1	0	4	3	.571	0	0-1	7	3.13	3.49
2016	LAA	AL	64	0	0	12	57.1	256	71	29	22	4	1	1	1	15	4	51	2	0	1	3	.250	0	0-1	11	4.55	3.45
2017	LAA	AL	64	0	0	12	48.2	203	50	23	21	7	1	0	0	12	5	45	1	0	0	3	.000	0	1-3	13	3.78	3.88
	Postseason		1	0	0	0	3.0	10	0	0	0	0	0	0	0	1	0	3	0	0	0	0	-	0	0-0	1	0.13	0.00
	5 ML YEARS		208	6	0	43	212.1	917	222	107	94	23	4	4	8	66	14	187	4	1	6	14	.300	0	1-5	33	4.06	3.98

Pedro Alvarez

Bats: L Throws: R Pos: DH-7;PH-6;1B-2

Ht: 6'3" Wt: 250 Born: 2/6/1987 Age: 31

Year	Team	Lg	G	AB	H	2B	3B	HR	(Hm	Rd)	TB	R	RBI	RC	TBB	IBB	SO	HBP	SH	SF	SB	CS	GDP	Avg	OBP	Slg	OPS
2017	Norfolk*		138	547	131	30	1	26	(-	-)	241	60	89	73	42	2	137	2	0	4	1	0	16	.239	.294	.441	.735
2010	Pit	NL	95	347	89	21	1	16	(12	4)	160	42	64	50	37	1	119	0	0	2	0	0	8	.256	.326	.461	.788
2011	Pit	NL	74	235	45	9	1	4	(0	4)	68	18	19	14	24	1	80	2	1	0	1	0	11	.191	.272	.289	.561
2012	Pit	NL	149	525	128	25	1	30	(12	18)	245	64	85	77	57	6	180	1	0	3	1	0	10	.244	.317	.467	.784
2013	Pit	NL	152	558	130	22	2	36	(16	20)	264	70	100	66	48	7	186	4	0	4	2	0	16	.233	.296	.473	.770
2014	Pit	NL	122	398	92	13	1	18	(8	10)	161	46	56	42	45	6	113	2	0	0	8	3	12	.231	.312	.405	.717
2015	Pit	NL	150	437	106	18	0	27	(14	13)	205	60	77	52	48	9	131	2	0	4	2	0	6	.243	.318	.469	.787
2016	Bal	AL	109	337	84	20	0	22	(14	8)	170	43	49	46	37	1	97	0	0	2	1	0	6	.249	.322	.504	.826
2017	Bal	AL	14	32	10	1	0	1	(1	0)	14	4	4	5	2	0	10	0	0	0	0	0	0	.313	.353	.438	.790
	Postseason		7	23	6	1	0	3	(1	2)	16	4	7	5	2	1	10	0	0	1	0	0	0	.261	.308	.696	1.003
	8 ML YEARS		865	2869	684	129	6	154	(77	77)	1287	347	454	352	298	31	916	11	1	15	15	3	69	.238	.311	.449	.760

Alexi Amarista

ah-mah-REE-stah

Bats: L Throws: R Pos: PH-52;2B-19;SS-18;CF-9;RF-9;LF-5;PR-3;3B-1

Ht: 5'6" Wt: 160 Born: 4/6/1989 Age: 29

Year	Team	Lg	G	AB	H	2B	3B	HR	(Hm	Rd)	TB	R	RBI	RC	TBB	IBB	SO	HBP	SH	SF	SB	CS	GDP	Avg	OBP	Slg	OPS
2011	LAA	AL	23	52	8	3	1	0	(0	0)	13	2	5	1	2	0	8	0	1	0	0	0	1	.154	.182	.250	.432
2012	2 Tms		106	275	66	15	5	5	(0	5)	106	36	32	31	17	1	42	0	6	2	8	4	2	.240	.282	.385	.668
2013	SD	NL	146	368	87	14	4	5	(1	4)	124	35	32	40	22	1	57	2	3	1	4	2	7	.236	.282	.337	.619
2014	SD	NL	148	423	101	13	2	5	(3	2)	133	39	40	43	29	5	69	1	8	5	12	1	6	.239	.286	.314	.600
2015	SD	NL	118	324	66	10	4	3	(1	2)	93	28	30	28	24	4	55	1	3	5	5	1	6	.204	.257	.287	.544
2016	SD	NL	65	140	36	2	0	0	(0	0)	38	9	11	14	8	2	26	0	1	1	9	2	5	.257	.295	.271	.567
2017	Col	NL	96	168	40	10	0	3	(0	3)	59	22	19	17	7	0	38	0	1	0	1	0	5	.238	.269	.351	.620
12	LAA	AL	1	0	0	0	0	0	(0	0)	0	1	0	0	0	0	0	0	0	0	0	0	0	-	-	-	-
12	SD	NL	105	275	66	15	5	5	(0	5)	106	35	32	31	17	1	42	0	6	2	8	4	2	.240	.282	.385	.668
	7 ML YEARS		702	1750	404	67	16	21	(5	16)	566	171	169	174	109	13	295	4	23	15	39	10	32	.231	.275	.323	.599

Brett Anderson

Pitches: L Bats: L Pos: SP-13

Ht: 6'3" Wt: 230 Born: 2/1/1988 Age: 30

Year	Team	Lg	G	GS	CG	GF	IP	BFP	H	R	ER	HR	SH	SF	HB	TBB	IBB	SO	WP	Bk	W	L	Pct	Sh	Sv-Op	Hld	ERC	ERA
2017	Tenn*	AA	6	5	0	0	27.1	119	34	17	14	2	1	2	1	9	0	15	3	0	2	2	.500	0	0--	-	5.34	4.61
2009	Oak	AL	30	30	1	0	175.1	735	180	94	79	20	4	4	3	45	1	150	0	1	11	11	.500	1	0-0	0	3.84	4.06
2010	Oak	AL	19	19	0	0	112.1	470	112	41	35	6	3	2	7	22	2	75	4	2	7	6	.538	0	0-0	0	3.16	2.80
2011	Oak	AL	13	13	1	0	83.1	356	86	40	37	8	4	1	7	25	1	61	0	1	3	6	.333	0	0-0	0	4.20	4.00
2012	Oak	AL	6	6	0	0	35.0	137	29	11	10	1	0	0	1	7	1	25	1	0	4	2	.667	0	0-0	0	2.13	2.57
2013	Oak	AL	16	5	0	4	44.2	200	51	32	30	5	1	0	0	21	1	46	0	0	1	4	.200	0	3-3	1	5.27	6.04
2014	Col	NL	8	8	0	0	43.1	180	44	18	14	1	1	1	0	13	3	29	0	1	1	3	.250	0	0-0	0	3.20	2.91
2015	LAD	NL	31	31	1	0	180.1	750	194	82	74	18	3	2	2	46	2	116	4	2	10	9	.526	0	0-0	0	4.05	3.69
2016	LAD	NL	4	3	0	0	11.1	62	25	15	15	4	1	1	0	4	0	5	2	0	1	2	.333	0	0-0	0	14.27	11.91
2017	2 Tms		13	13	0	0	55.1	251	73	41	39	5	0	3	0	21	0	38	2	0	4	4	.500	0	0-0	0	5.87	6.34
17	ChC	NL	6	6	0	0	22.0	111	34	22	20	2	0	1	0	12	0	16	1	0	2	2	.500	0	0-0	0	7.85	8.18
17	Tor	AL	7	7	0	0	33.1	140	39	19	19	3	0	2	0	9	0	22	1	0	2	2	.500	0	0-0	0	4.62	5.13
	Postseason		3	2	0	1	9.1	40	10	7	7	1	0	0	0	3	0	10	1	0	1	1	.500	0	0-0	0	4.23	6.75
	9 ML YEARS		140	128	3	4	741.0	3141	794	374	333	68	17	14	20	204	11	545	13	6	42	47	.472	1	3-3	1	4.05	4.04

Brian Anderson

Bats: R Throws: R Pos: 3B-25;PH-3

Ht: 6'3" Wt: 185 Born: 5/19/1993 Age: 25

Year	Team	Lg	G	AB	H	2B	3B	HR	(Hm	Rd)	TB	R	RBI	RC	TBB	IBB	SO	HBP	SH	SF	SB	CS	GDP	Avg	OBP	Slg	OPS
2014	2 Tms	Low	59	230	69	10	1	11	(-	-)	114	38	49	41	19	1	39	5	1	2	1	1	2	.300	.363	.496	.859
2015	Jupiter	A+	132	477	112	22	2	8	(-	-)	162	50	62	52	40	0	109	9	1	3	2	2	10	.235	.304	.340	.644
2016	Jupiter	A+	49	182	55	12	2	3	(-	-)	80	27	25	32	22	0	38	1	0	2	3	0	6	.302	.377	.440	.816
2016	Jaxnvl	AA	86	301	73	9	1	8	(-	-)	108	38	40	39	36	0	59	5	0	3	0	0	6	.243	.330	.359	.689
2017	Jaxnvl	AA	87	311	78	14	3	14	(-	-)	140	53	55	50	36	0	71	9	0	5	1	1	10	.251	.341	.450	.791
2017	NewOr	AAA	33	118	40	7	0	8	(-	-)	71	21	26	28	12	1	27	5	0	2	0	1	4	.339	.416	.602	1.018
2017	Mia	NL	25	84	22	7	1	0	(0	0)	31	11	8	11	10	0	28	0	0	1	0	0	1	.262	.337	.369	.706

93

Chase Anderson

Pitches: R Bats: R Pos: SP-25   Ht: 6'1" Wt: 200 Born: 11/30/1987 Age: 30

		HOW MUCH HE PITCHED						WHAT HE GAVE UP											THE RESULTS						
Year	Team	Lg	G	GS	CG	GF	IP	BFP	H	R	ER	HR	SH	SF	HB	TBB	IBB	SO	WP	Bk	W	L	Pct	Sh	Sv-Op	Hld	ERC	ERA
2014	Ari	NL	21	21	0	0	114.1	486	117	56	51	16	4	4	2	40	2	105	4	0	9	7	.563	0	0-0	0	4.39	4.01
2015	Ari	NL	27	27	0	0	152.2	640	158	75	73	18	3	9	7	40	2	111	3	0	6	6	.500	0	0-0	0	4.08	4.30
2016	Mil	NL	31	30	0	1	151.2	647	155	83	74	28	4	3	4	53	0	120	4	0	9	11	.450	0	0-0	0	4.76	4.39
2017	Mil	NL	25	25	0	0	141.1	569	113	47	43	14	5	2	7	41	1	133	0	0	12	4	.750	0	0-0	0	2.80	2.74
4 ML YEARS			104	103	0	1	560.0	2342	543	261	241	76	16	18	20	174	5	469	11	0	36	28	.563	0	0-0	0	3.98	3.87

Drew Anderson

Pitches: R Bats: R Pos: RP-2   Ht: 6'3" Wt: 185 Born: 3/22/1994 Age: 24

		HOW MUCH HE PITCHED						WHAT HE GAVE UP											THE RESULTS						
Year	Team	Lg	G	GS	CG	GF	IP	BFP	H	R	ER	HR	SH	SF	HB	TBB	IBB	SO	WP	Bk	W	L	Pct	Sh	Sv-Op	Hld	ERC	ERA
2013	Wmspt	A-	15	15	0	0	76.1	294	58	21	17	5	1	0	2	20	1	54	1	0	6	3	.667	0	0- --	-	2.29	2.00
2014	2 Tms	Low	11	10	0	0	49.2	218	51	23	20	2	1	0	5	18	0	52	4	0	5	5	.500	0	0- --	-	4.04	3.62
2016	2 Tms	Low	15	15	0	0	70.0	279	55	26	21	3	0	3	2	22	0	78	2	0	3	4	.429	0	0- --	-	2.43	2.70
2017	Rdng	AA	21	21	0	0	107.2	446	81	49	43	13	3	4	8	40	0	86	4	2	9	4	.692	0	0- --	-	3.05	3.59
2017	Phi	NL	2	0	0	1	2.1	14	6	7	6	0	0	1	0	1	0	2	0	0	0	0	-	0	0-0	0	13.44	23.14

Tim Anderson

Bats: R Throws: R Pos: SS-145;PR-1   Ht: 6'1" Wt: 185 Born: 6/23/1993 Age: 25

					BATTING															RUNNING			AVERAGES			
Year	Team	Lg	G	AB	H	2B	3B	HR	(Hm	Rd)	TB	R	RBI	RC	TBB	IBB	SO	HBP	SH	SF	SB	CS	GDP	Avg	OBP	Slg	OPS
2013	Knapol	A	68	267	74	10	5	1	(-	-)	97	45	21	39	23	0	78	7	2	2	24	4	5	.277	.348	.363	.711
2014	2 Tms	Low	74	303	89	18	7	8	(-	-)	145	50	33	46	9	0	73	5	0	2	10	4	4	.294	.323	.479	.801
2014	Brham	AA	10	44	16	3	0	1	(-	-)	22	7	7	7	0	0	9	0	1	0	1	0	0	.364	.364	.500	.864
2015	Brham	AA	125	513	160	21	12	5	(-	-)	220	79	46	82	24	0	114	7	4	2	49	13	6	.312	.350	.429	.779
2016	Charltt	AAA	55	247	75	10	2	4	(-	-)	101	39	20	33	8	0	58	0	1	0	11	4	5	.304	.325	.409	.734
2016	CWS	AL	99	410	116	22	6	9	(5	4)	188	57	30	45	13	0	117	1	6	1	10	2	15	.283	.306	.432	.738
2017	CWS	AL	146	587	151	26	4	17	(7	10)	236	72	56	59	13	0	162	3	2	1	15	1	13	.257	.276	.402	.679
2 ML YEARS			245	997	267	48	10	26	(12	14)	413	129	86	104	26	0	279	4	8	2	25	3	28	.268	.289	.414	.703

Tyler Anderson

Pitches: L Bats: L Pos: SP-15; RP-2   Ht: 6'4" Wt: 210 Born: 12/30/1989 Age: 28

		HOW MUCH HE PITCHED						WHAT HE GAVE UP											THE RESULTS						
Year	Team	Lg	G	GS	CG	GF	IP	BFP	H	R	ER	HR	SH	SF	HB	TBB	IBB	SO	WP	Bk	W	L	Pct	Sh	Sv-Op	Hld	ERC	ERA
2013	2 Tms	Low	16	16	0	0	89.2	367	71	40	28	10	3	3	2	27	0	76	5	0	4	3	.571	0	0- --	-	2.72	2.81
2014	Tulsa	AA	23	23	0	0	118.1	474	90	37	26	3	6	3	4	40	0	106	8	3	7	4	.636	0	0- --	-	2.29	1.98
2016	Col	NL	19	19	0	0	114.1	478	119	50	45	12	6	3	3	28	2	99	4	3	5	6	.455	0	0-0	0	3.85	3.54
2017	Col	NL	17	15	0	1	86.0	362	88	48	46	16	5	2	2	26	0	81	6	2	6	6	.500	0	0-0	0	4.57	4.81
2 ML YEARS			36	34	0	1	200.1	840	207	98	91	28	11	5	5	54	2	180	10	5	11	12	.478	0	0-0	0	4.16	4.09

Matt Andriese

Pitches: R Bats: R Pos: SP-17; RP-1   ANN-dreese   Ht: 6'2" Wt: 225 Born: 8/28/1989 Age: 28

		HOW MUCH HE PITCHED						WHAT HE GAVE UP											THE RESULTS						
Year	Team	Lg	G	GS	CG	GF	IP	BFP	H	R	ER	HR	SH	SF	HB	TBB	IBB	SO	WP	Bk	W	L	Pct	Sh	Sv-Op	Hld	ERC	ERA
2015	TB	AL	25	8	0	8	65.2	282	69	32	30	8	1	3	2	18	1	49	2	2	3	5	.375	0	2-2	0	4.08	4.11
2016	TB	AL	29	19	1	3	127.2	527	131	64	62	17	0	6	1	25	1	109	3	4	8	8	.500	1	1-1	4	3.68	4.37
2017	TB	AL	18	17	0	1	86.0	374	90	48	43	16	0	1	4	28	1	76	3	2	5	5	.500	0	1-1	0	4.80	4.50
3 ML YEARS			72	44	1	12	279.1	1183	290	144	135	41	1	10	7	71	3	234	8	8	16	18	.471	1	4-4	4	4.11	4.35

Elvis Andrus

Bats: R Throws: R Pos: SS-157;DH-1   AHN-droos   Ht: 6'0" Wt: 200 Born: 8/26/1988 Age: 29

					BATTING															RUNNING			AVERAGES			
Year	Team	Lg	G	AB	H	2B	3B	HR	(Hm	Rd)	TB	R	RBI	RC	TBB	IBB	SO	HBP	SH	SF	SB	CS	GDP	Avg	OBP	Slg	OPS
2009	Tex	AL	145	480	128	17	8	6	(3	3)	179	72	40	65	40	0	77	6	12	3	33	6	4	.267	.329	.373	.702
2010	Tex	AL	148	588	156	15	3	0	(0	0)	177	88	35	79	64	0	96	5	17	5	32	15	6	.265	.342	.301	.643
2011	Tex	AL	150	587	164	27	3	5	(2	3)	212	96	60	76	56	0	74	5	16	1	37	12	17	.279	.347	.361	.708
2012	Tex	AL	158	629	180	31	9	3	(1	2)	238	85	62	92	57	0	96	5	17	3	21	10	15	.286	.349	.378	.727
2013	Tex	AL	156	620	168	17	4	4	(0	4)	205	91	67	72	52	1	97	4	16	6	42	8	19	.271	.328	.331	.659
2014	Tex	AL	157	619	163	35	1	2	(1	1)	206	72	41	59	46	0	96	3	9	7	27	15	21	.263	.314	.333	.647
2015	Tex	AL	160	596	154	34	2	7	(4	3)	213	69	62	68	46	1	78	2	8	9	25	9	14	.258	.309	.357	.667
2016	Tex	AL	147	506	153	31	7	8	(5	3)	222	75	69	87	47	2	70	4	4	7	24	8	18	.302	.362	.439	.800
2017	Tex	AL	158	643	191	44	4	20	(7	13)	303	100	88	104	38	0	101	3	1	4	25	10	18	.297	.337	.471	.808
Postseason			42	173	46	4	1	1	(0	1)	55	21	7	15	12	0	24	1	4	1	9	5	6	.266	.316	.318	.633
9 ML YEARS			1379	5268	1457	251	41	55	(21	34)	1955	748	524	702	446	4	785	37	100	40	266	93	132	.277	.335	.371	.706

Miguel Andujar

Bats: R **Throws:** R **Pos:** 3B-3;DH-2;PH-1　　AN-doo-har　　**Ht:** 6'0" **Wt:** 215 **Born:** 3/2/1995 **Age:** 23

Year	Team	Lg	G	AB	H	2B	3B	HR	(Hm	Rd)	TB	R	RBI	RC	TBB	IBB	SO	HBP	SH	SF	SB	CS	GDP	Avg	OBP	Slg	OPS
2013	Yanks2	R	34	133	43	11	0	4	(-	-)	66	18	25	24	7	1	21	3	0	1	4	1	5	.323	.368	.496	.864
2014	CtnSC	A	127	484	129	25	4	10	(-	-)	192	75	70	64	35	1	83	3	2	3	5	1	15	.267	.318	.397	.715
2015	Tampa	A+	130	485	118	24	5	8	(-	-)	176	54	57	54	29	0	90	3	0	3	12	1	10	.243	.288	.363	.651
2016	Tampa	A+	58	230	65	10	2	10	(-	-)	109	34	41	37	18	0	30	3	0	0	1	3	6	.283	.343	.474	.817
2016	Trntn	AA	72	282	75	16	2	2	(-	-)	101	28	42	36	21	0	42	7	0	9	2	1	3	.266	.323	.358	.681
2017	Trntn	AA	67	254	79	23	1	7	(-	-)	125	30	52	42	12	0	39	2	0	5	2	3	7	.311	.341	.492	.833
2017	S-WB	AAA	58	227	72	13	1	9	(-	-)	114	36	30	42	17	1	33	2	0	6	3	0	6	.317	.364	.502	.866
2017	NYY	AL	5	7	4	2	0	0	(0	0)	6	0	4	4	1	0	0	0	0	0	1	0	0	.571	.625	.857	1.482

Nori Aoki

Bats: L **Throws:** R **Pos:** LF-64;RF-47;PH-10;CF-2;DH-1;PR-1 AH-oh-kee　　**Ht:** 5'9" **Wt:** 180 **Born:** 1/5/1982 **Age:** 36

Year	Team	Lg	G	AB	H	2B	3B	HR	(Hm	Rd)	TB	R	RBI	RC	TBB	IBB	SO	HBP	SH	SF	SB	CS	GDP	Avg	OBP	Slg	OPS
2012	Mil	NL	151	520	150	37	4	10	(4	6)	225	81	50	80	43	1	55	13	7	5	30	8	6	.288	.355	.433	.787
2013	Mil	NL	155	597	171	20	3	8	(5	3)	221	80	37	80	55	1	40	11	8	3	20	12	9	.286	.356	.370	.726
2014	KC	AL	132	491	140	22	6	1	(0	1)	177	63	43	69	43	0	49	6	8	1	17	8	5	.285	.349	.360	.710
2015	SF	NL	93	355	102	12	3	5	(2	3)	135	42	26	49	30	0	25	6	1	4	14	5	8	.287	.353	.380	.733
2016	Sea	AL	118	417	118	24	4	4	(2	2)	162	63	28	51	34	0	45	9	5	1	7	9	9	.283	.349	.388	.738
2017	3 Tms		110	336	93	20	2	5	(1	4)	132	48	35	42	29	1	44	3	1	5	10	2	12	.277	.335	.393	.728
17	Hou	AL	71	202	55	12	1	2	(0	2)	75	28	19	22	15	1	29	2	1	4	5	2	11	.272	.323	.371	.694
17	Tor	AL	12	32	9	1	0	3	(1	2)	19	4	8	5	1	0	5	0	0	0	0	0	0	.281	.294	.594	.888
17	NYM	AL	27	102	29	7	1	0	(0	0)	38	16	8	15	13	0	10	1	0	1	5	0	1	.284	.371	.373	.743
	Postseason		14	41	8	0	0	0	(0	0)	8	7	3	5	5	0	3	1	0	1	2	1	0	.195	.292	.195	.487
	6 ML YEARS		759	2716	774	135	22	33	(14	19)	1052	377	219	371	234	3	258	48	30	15	98	44	49	.285	.350	.387	.738

Jayson Aquino

Pitches: L **Bats:** L **Pos:** SP-2; RP-2　　a-KEE-no　　**Ht:** 6'1" **Wt:** 225 **Born:** 11/22/1992 **Age:** 25

Year	Team	Lg	G	GS	CG	GF	IP	BFP	H	R	ER	HR	SH	SF	HB	TBB	IBB	SO	WP	Bk	W	L	Pct	Sh	Sv-Op	Hld	ERC	ERA
2013	2 Tms	Low	15	14	0	0	87.0	365	87	48	42	5	4	4	5	26	0	73	2	1	0	10	.000	0	0- -	-	3.68	4.34
2014	Mdest	A+	16	16	1	0	95.0	423	113	66	57	7	3	7	12	30	0	74	9	2	5	10	.333	0	0- -	-	5.23	5.40
2015	3 Tms	Low	24	24	0	0	137.1	572	135	58	50	8	2	6	5	30	0	86	6	4	5	11	.313	0	0- -	-	3.14	3.28
2016	Bowie	AA	20	19	1	1	115.1	501	130	55	50	7	5	4	5	33	0	77	6	2	5	10	.333	1	0- -	-	4.24	3.90
2016	Norfolk	AAA	5	0	0	0	13.0	51	12	3	3	0	0	0	0	3	0	12	0	0	2	0	1.000	0	0- -	-	2.51	2.08
2017	Norfolk	AAA	21	21	0	0	114.2	505	125	63	54	11	4	3	5	41	0	89	6	1	3	10	.231	0	0- -	-	4.55	4.24
2016	Bal	AL	3	0	0	2	2.1	8	1	0	0	0	0	0	0	0	0	3	0	0	0	0	-	0	0-0	0	0.40	0.00
2017	Bal	AL	4	2	0	1	13.1	62	15	12	11	4	0	0	0	6	0	13	1	0	1	2	.333	0	0-0	0	6.27	7.43
	2 ML YEARS		7	2	0	3	15.2	70	16	12	11	4	0	0	0	6	0	16	1	0	1	2	.333	0	0-0	0	5.04	6.32

Victor Arano

Pitches: R **Bats:** R **Pos:** RP-10　　**Ht:** 6'2" **Wt:** 200 **Born:** 2/7/1995 **Age:** 23

Year	Team	Lg	G	GS	CG	GF	IP	BFP	H	R	ER	HR	SH	SF	HB	TBB	IBB	SO	WP	Bk	W	L	Pct	Sh	Sv-Op	Hld	ERC	ERA
2013	Ddgrs	R	13	8	0	1	49.1	218	52	34	23	4	0	1	0	13	0	49	9	0	3	2	.600	0	0- -	-	3.53	4.20
2014	Gt Lks	A	22	15	0	4	86.0	363	88	42	39	11	2	2	0	20	0	83	7	1	4	7	.364	0	3- -	-	3.69	4.08
2015	Clrwtr	A+	24	22	1	0	124.0	516	131	69	65	7	1	4	11	26	1	69	11	1	4	12	.250	1	0- -	-	3.78	4.72
2016	Clrwtr	A+	35	0	0	13	63.0	253	52	21	16	4	1	2	1	15	0	71	2	0	4	1	.800	0	4- -	-	2.39	2.29
2016	Rdng	AA	11	0	0	3	16.2	66	11	6	4	2	0	0	0	4	1	24	1	0	1	1	.500	0	1- -	-	1.75	2.16
2017	Rdng	AA	32	0	0	24	38.2	165	39	20	18	7	2	3	1	11	0	38	7	0	1	2	.333	0	9- -	-	4.29	4.19
2017	Phi	NL	10	0	0	2	10.2	42	6	2	2	0	0	0	0	4	0	13	0	0	1	0	1.000	0	0-0	2	1.35	1.69

Chris Archer

Pitches: R **Bats:** R **Pos:** SP-34　　**Ht:** 6'2" **Wt:** 195 **Born:** 9/26/1988 **Age:** 29

Year	Team	Lg	G	GS	CG	GF	IP	BFP	H	R	ER	HR	SH	SF	HB	TBB	IBB	SO	WP	Bk	W	L	Pct	Sh	Sv-Op	Hld	ERC	ERA
2012	TB	AL	6	4	0	1	29.1	122	23	17	15	3	1	0	1	13	0	36	2	0	1	3	.250	0	0-0	0	3.24	4.60
2013	TB	AL	23	23	2	0	128.2	525	107	49	46	15	1	5	8	38	2	101	7	0	9	7	.563	2	0-0	0	3.13	3.22
2014	TB	AL	32	32	0	0	194.2	822	177	85	72	12	4	9	8	72	1	173	8	0	10	9	.526	0	0-0	0	3.36	3.33
2015	TB	AL	34	34	1	0	212.0	868	175	85	76	19	2	2	3	66	0	252	13	0	12	13	.480	1	0-0	0	2.79	3.23
2016	TB	AL	33	33	0	0	201.1	850	183	100	90	30	6	4	3	67	0	233	11	0	9	19	.321	0	0-0	0	3.66	4.02
2017	TB	AL	34	34	0	0	201.0	852	193	101	91	27	1	2	5	60	0	249	15	0	10	12	.455	0	0-0	0	3.75	4.07
	Postseason		2	0	0	0	1.2	6	1	0	0	0	0	1	0	0	0	2	0	0	0	0	-	0	0-0	0	0.75	0.00
	6 ML YEARS		162	160	3	1	967.0	4039	858	437	390	106	15	22	28	316	3	1044	56	0	51	63	.447	3	0-0	0	3.34	3.63

Orlando Arcia

Bats: R **Throws:** R **Pos:** SS-152;PH-7;PR-1　　ARR-see-ya　　**Ht:** 6'0" **Wt:** 165 **Born:** 8/4/1994 **Age:** 23

Year	Team	Lg	G	AB	H	2B	3B	HR	(Hm	Rd)	TB	R	RBI	RC	TBB	IBB	SO	HBP	SH	SF	SB	CS	GDP	Avg	OBP	Slg	OPS
2013	Wisc	A	120	442	111	14	5	4	(-	-)	147	67	39	49	35	2	40	6	2	1	20	9	15	.251	.314	.333	.647
2014	BrvdCt	A+	127	498	144	29	5	4	(-	-)	195	65	50	72	42	0	65	2	3	1	31	11	17	.289	.346	.392	.738
2015	Biloxi	AA	129	512	157	37	7	8	(-	-)	232	74	69	83	30	1	73	3	4	3	25	8	17	.307	.347	.453	.800

Year Team	Lg	G	AB	H	2B	3B	HR	(Hm	Rd)	TB	R	RBI	RC	TBB	IBB	SO	HBP	SH	SF	SB	CS	GDP	Avg	OBP	Slg	OPS
2016 ColSpr	AAA	100	404	108	19	6	8	(-	-)	163	59	53	53	29	2	77	3	2	2	15	8	18	.267	.320	.403	.723
2016 Mil	NL	55	201	44	10	3	4	(2	2)	72	21	17	20	15	0	47	0	0	0	8	0	6	.219	.273	.358	.631
2017 Mil	NL	153	506	140	17	2	15	(8	7)	206	56	53	63	36	9	100	1	2	3	14	7	10	.277	.324	.407	.731
2 ML YEARS		208	707	184	27	5	19	(10	9)	278	77	70	83	51	9	147	1	2	3	22	7	16	.260	.310	.393	.703

Nolan Arenado

Bats: R Throws: R Pos: 3B-157;PH-3   ahr-eh-NOD-oh   **Ht:** 6'2" **Wt:** 205 **Born:** 4/16/1991 **Age:** 27

Year Team	Lg	G	AB	H	2B	3B	HR	(Hm	Rd)	TB	R	RBI	RC	TBB	IBB	SO	HBP	SH	SF	SB	CS	GDP	Avg	OBP	Slg	OPS
2013 Col	NL	133	486	130	29	4	10	(5	5)	197	49	52	48	23	1	72	1	2	2	2	0	16	.267	.301	.405	.706
2014 Col	NL	111	432	124	34	2	18	(16	2)	216	58	61	60	25	1	58	4	1	5	2	1	13	.287	.328	.500	.828
2015 Col	NL	157	616	177	43	4	42	(20	22)	354	97	130	116	34	13	110	4	0	11	2	5	17	.287	.323	.575	.898
2016 Col	NL	160	618	182	35	6	41	(25	16)	352	116	133	128	68	10	103	2	0	8	2	3	17	.294	.362	.570	.932
2017 Col	NL	159	606	187	43	7	37	(19	18)	355	100	130	130	62	9	106	4	1	6	3	2	21	.309	.373	.586	.959
5 ML YEARS		720	2758	800	184	23	148	(85	63)	1474	420	506	482	212	34	449	15	4	32	11	11	84	.290	.340	.534	.875

Shawn Armstrong

Pitches: R Bats: R Pos: RP-21   **Ht:** 6'2" **Wt:** 225 **Born:** 9/11/1990 **Age:** 27

		HOW MUCH HE PITCHED						WHAT HE GAVE UP										THE RESULTS							
Year Team	Lg	G	GS	CG	GF	IP	BFP	H	R	ER	HR	SH	SF	HB	TBB	IBB	SO	WP	Bk	W	L	Pct	Sh	Sv-Op	Hld	ERC	ERA
2017 Clmbs*	AAA	28	0	0	14	29.1	126	27	10	10	3	1	0	2	11	0	36	3	0	1	1	.500	0	10- -	-	3.80	3.07
2015 Cle	AL	8	0	0	5	8.0	30	5	2	2	1	0	0	0	2	0	11	0	0	0	0	-	0	0-0	0	1.84	2.25
2016 Cle	AL	10	0	0	2	10.2	44	9	3	3	1	1	0	0	5	2	7	1	0	0	0	-	0	0-0	0	3.25	2.53
2017 Cle	AL	21	0	0	14	24.2	108	23	12	12	5	0	0	1	10	0	20	1	0	1	0	1.000	0	0-0	0	4.50	4.38
3 ML YEARS		39	0	0	21	43.1	182	37	17	17	7	1	0	1	17	2	38	2	0	1	0	1.000	0	0-0	0	3.67	3.53

Jake Arrieta

Pitches: R Bats: R Pos: SP-30   air-ee-ETT-uh   **Ht:** 6'4" **Wt:** 225 **Born:** 3/6/1986 **Age:** 32

		HOW MUCH HE PITCHED						WHAT HE GAVE UP										THE RESULTS							
Year Team	Lg	G	GS	CG	GF	IP	BFP	H	R	ER	HR	SH	SF	HB	TBB	IBB	SO	WP	Bk	W	L	Pct	Sh	Sv-Op	Hld	ERC	ERA
2010 Bal	AL	18	18	0	0	100.1	449	106	57	52	9	4	2	4	48	3	52	5	0	6	6	.500	0	0-0	0	4.74	4.66
2011 Bal	AL	22	22	0	0	119.1	523	115	70	67	21	3	2	4	59	2	93	0	0	10	8	.556	0	0-0	0	4.93	5.05
2012 Bal	AL	24	18	0	1	114.2	496	122	82	79	16	3	4	5	35	3	109	4	0	3	9	.250	0	0-0	1	4.47	6.20
2013 2 Tms		14	14	0	0	75.1	324	59	41	40	9	2	3	5	41	1	60	1	0	5	4	.556	0	0-0	0	3.82	4.78
2014 ChC	NL	25	25	1	0	156.2	614	114	46	44	5	5	3	4	41	2	167	8	0	10	5	.667	1	0-0	0	1.85	2.53
2015 ChC	NL	33	33	4	0	229.0	870	150	52	45	10	4	1	6	48	2	236	6	0	22	6	.786	3	0-0	0	1.53	1.77
2016 ChC	NL	31	31	1	0	197.1	795	138	72	68	16	2	1	6	76	1	190	16	0	18	8	.692	1	0-0	0	2.45	3.10
2017 ChC	NL	30	30	0	0	168.1	707	150	82	66	23	1	4	10	55	3	163	14	0	14	10	.583	0	0-0	0	3.64	3.53
13 Bal	AL	5	5	0	0	23.2	111	25	19	19	2	0	3	2	17	1	23	1	0	1	2	.333	0	0-0	0	5.91	7.23
13 ChC	NL	9	9	0	0	51.2	213	34	22	21	7	2	0	3	24	0	37	0	0	4	2	.667	0	0-0	0	2.94	3.66
Postseason		7	7	1	0	42.0	170	31	17	17	5	0	1	4	11	1	53	1	0	4	2	.667	1	0-0	0	2.61	3.64
8 ML YEARS		197	191	6	1	1161.0	4778	954	502	461	109	24	20	43	403	17	1070	54	0	88	56	.611	5	0-0	1	3.01	3.57

Bronson Arroyo

Pitches: R Bats: R Pos: SP-14   uh-ROY-oh   **Ht:** 6'4" **Wt:** 190 **Born:** 2/24/1977 **Age:** 41

		HOW MUCH HE PITCHED						WHAT HE GAVE UP										THE RESULTS							
Year Team	Lg	G	GS	CG	GF	IP	BFP	H	R	ER	HR	SH	SF	HB	TBB	IBB	SO	WP	Bk	W	L	Pct	Sh	Sv-Op	Hld	ERC	ERA
2000 Pit	NL	20	12	0	1	71.2	338	88	61	51	10	5	2	4	36	6	50	3	1	2	6	.250	0	0-0	0	6.18	6.40
2001 Pit	NL	24	13	1	1	88.1	390	99	54	50	12	4	6	4	34	6	39	4	1	5	7	.417	0	0-0	2	5.09	5.09
2002 Pit	NL	9	4	0	1	27.0	123	30	14	12	1	1	1	0	15	3	22	0	0	2	1	.667	0	0-0	1	4.64	4.00
2003 Bos	AL	6	0	0	2	17.1	66	10	5	4	0	0	0	1	4	2	14	0	0	0	0	-	0	1-1	0	1.14	2.08
2004 Bos	AL	32	29	0	0	178.2	764	171	99	80	17	5	4	6	47	3	142	5	0	10	9	.526	0	0-0	0	3.65	4.03
2005 Bos	AL	35	32	0	1	205.1	878	213	116	103	22	4	4	14	54	3	100	5	1	14	10	.583	0	0-0	0	4.04	4.51
2006 Cin	NL	35	35	3	0	240.2	992	222	98	88	31	9	2	5	64	7	184	6	0	14	11	.560	1	0-0	0	3.37	3.29
2007 Cin	NL	34	34	1	0	210.2	921	232	109	99	28	10	7	13	63	6	156	4	0	9	15	.375	0	0-0	0	4.68	4.23
2008 Cin	NL	34	34	1	0	200.0	871	219	116	106	29	13	6	6	68	2	163	6	0	15	11	.577	0	0-0	0	4.83	4.77
2009 Cin	NL	33	33	3	0	220.1	923	214	101	94	31	9	5	9	65	6	127	1	0	15	13	.536	2	0-0	0	3.94	3.84
2010 Cin	NL	33	33	2	0	215.2	880	188	95	93	29	6	6	6	59	5	121	1	1	17	10	.630	0	0-0	0	3.21	3.88
2011 Cin	NL	32	32	1	0	199.0	855	227	119	112	46	6	5	6	45	5	108	1	0	9	12	.429	1	0-0	0	5.20	5.07
2012 Cin	NL	32	32	1	0	202.0	835	209	86	84	26	7	6	5	35	1	129	3	0	12	10	.545	1	0-0	0	3.68	3.74
2013 Cin	NL	32	32	2	0	202.0	823	199	88	85	32	4	7	7	34	2	124	1	2	14	12	.538	1	0-0	0	3.63	3.79
2014 Ari	NL	14	14	1	0	86.0	357	92	40	39	10	3	2	3	19	1	47	2	0	7	4	.636	0	0-0	0	4.08	4.08
2017 Cin	NL	14	14	0	0	71.0	322	94	59	58	23	5	2	2	19	2	45	1	0	3	6	.333	0	0-0	0	7.22	7.35
Postseason		12	4	0	3	29.1	127	24	17	15	5	0	0	2	13	0	26	0	0	1	0	1.000	0	0-0	2	3.91	4.60
16 ML YEARS		419	383	16	6	2435.2	10338	2507	1260	1158	347	91	64	105	661	60	1571	42	6	148	137	.519	6	1-1	3	4.17	4.28

Christian Arroyo

Bats: R Throws: R Pos: 3B-22;SS-10;2B-2;PH-1   **Ht:** 6'1" **Wt:** 180 **Born:** 5/30/1995 **Age:** 23

Year Team	Lg	G	AB	H	2B	3B	HR	(Hm	Rd)	TB	R	RBI	RC	TBB	IBB	SO	HBP	SH	SF	SB	CS	GDP	Avg	OBP	Slg	OPS
2013 Giants	R	45	184	60	18	5	2	(-	-)	94	47	39	36	19	1	32	2	0	4	3	2	1	.326	.388	.511	.898
2014 2 Tms	Low	89	361	105	17	3	6	(-	-)	146	49	62	50	22	1	53	2	1	6	7	3	5	.291	.330	.404	.734

Year	Team	Lg	G	AB	H	2B	3B	HR	(Hm	Rd)	TB	R	RBI	RC	TBB	IBB	SO	HBP	SH	SF	SB	CS	GDP	Avg	OBP	Slg	OPS
2015	SnJos	A+	90	381	116	28	2	9	(-	-)	175	48	42	60	19	1	73	5	2	2	5	3	11	.304	.344	.459	.803
2016	Rchmd	AA	119	474	130	36	1	3	(-	-)	177	57	49	58	29	2	72	3	4	7	1	1	17	.274	.316	.373	.689
2017	Scrmto	AAA	25	91	36	7	0	4	(-	-)	55	18	16	24	6	1	12	5	0	0	2	0	1	.396	.461	.604	1.065
2017	SF	NL	34	125	24	5	0	3	(2	1)	38	9	14	7	8	1	32	1	0	1	1	2	4	.192	.244	.304	.548

Cody Asche

Bats: L Throws: R Pos: DH-14;PH-3;1B-2;3B-1;LF-1   ASH-ee   Ht: 6'1" Wt: 205 Born: 6/30/1990 Age: 28

Year	Team	Lg	G	AB	H	2B	3B	HR	(Hm	Rd)	TB	R	RBI	RC	TBB	IBB	SO	HBP	SH	SF	SB	CS	GDP	Avg	OBP	Slg	OPS
2017	Charllt*	AAA	87	291	85	15	1	14	(-	-)	144	42	57	59	49	1	75	2	0	5	4	1	1	.292	.392	.495	.887
2013	Phi	NL	50	162	38	8	1	5	(4	1)	63	18	22	18	15	3	43	1	0	1	1	0	1	.235	.302	.389	.691
2014	Phi	NL	121	397	100	25	0	10	(6	4)	155	43	46	44	33	4	102	0	3	1	0	1	7	.252	.309	.390	.699
2015	Phi	NL	129	425	104	22	3	12	(5	7)	168	41	39	47	26	3	111	4	0	1	1	2	4	.245	.294	.395	.689
2016	Phi	NL	71	197	42	15	0	4	(3	1)	69	22	18	17	18	0	54	2	0	1	3	1	1	.213	.284	.350	.635
2017	CWS	AL	19	57	6	1	0	1	(0	1)	10	5	4	0	3	1	21	2	0	0	0	0	1	.105	.177	.175	.353
	5 ML YEARS		390	1238	290	71	4	32	(18	14)	465	129	129	126	95	11	331	9	3	4	5	4	14	.234	.293	.376	.668

Alec Asher

Pitches: R Bats: R Pos: RP-18; SP-6   Ht: 6'4" Wt: 230 Born: 10/4/1991 Age: 26

			HOW MUCH HE PITCHED						WHAT HE GAVE UP											THE RESULTS						
Year	Team	Lg	G	GS	CG	GF	IP	BFP	H	R	ER	HR	SH	SF	HB	TBB	IBB	SO	WP	Bk	W	L	Pct	Sh	Sv-Op	Hld	ERC	ERA
2017	Norfolk*	AAA	10	10	0	0	50.1	224	62	26	26	6	2	0	1	15	1	36	2	0	3	3	.500	0	0- -	-	5.19	4.65
2015	Phi	NL	7	7	0	0	29.0	138	42	30	30	8	2	1	1	10	0	16	2	2	0	6	.000	0	0-0	0	8.10	9.31
2016	Phi	NL	5	5	0	0	27.2	111	22	11	7	1	2	1	2	4	0	13	0	0	2	1	.667	0	0-0	0	1.93	2.28
2017	Bal	AL	24	6	0	6	60.0	265	61	36	35	10	1	2	7	23	2	47	4	0	2	5	.286	0	0-0	0	5.02	5.25
	3 ML YEARS		36	18	0	6	116.2	514	125	77	72	19	5	4	10	37	2	76	6	2	4	12	.250	0	0-0	0	4.89	5.55

Barrett Astin

Pitches: R Bats: R Pos: RP-6   Ht: 6'1" Wt: 225 Born: 10/22/1991 Age: 26

			HOW MUCH HE PITCHED						WHAT HE GAVE UP											THE RESULTS						
Year	Team	Lg	G	GS	CG	GF	IP	BFP	H	R	ER	HR	SH	SF	HB	TBB	IBB	SO	WP	Bk	W	L	Pct	Sh	Sv-Op	Hld	ERC	ERA
2013	Helena	R+	12	8	0	0	37.2	167	41	25	18	6	0	1	1	11	0	31	2	0	1	1	.500	0	0- -	-	4.53	4.30
2014	Wisc	A	27	18	0	8	121.2	525	132	76	67	12	3	5	5	36	0	81	9	0	8	7	.533	0	4- -	-	4.31	4.96
2015	Dytona	A+	16	11	1	0	74.2	305	62	28	19	0	4	3	1	18	0	61	2	0	4	3	.571	0	0- -	-	2.00	2.29
2015	Pnscla	AA	14	14	0	0	76.2	337	85	50	48	9	2	1	2	39	0	61	3	0	4	6	.400	0	0- -	-	5.58	5.63
2016	Pnscla	AA	37	11	0	5	103.1	403	74	31	26	8	2	2	6	25	1	96	5	0	9	3	.750	0	0- -	-	2.14	2.26
2017	Lsvlle	AAA	26	3	0	3	48.2	233	71	38	33	4	1	2	0	22	1	44	2	1	3	4	.429	0	0- -	-	6.88	6.10
2017	Cin	NL	6	0	0	1	8.0	41	9	6	6	2	0	1	2	7	0	2	0	0	0	0	-	0	0-0	0	9.31	6.75

Carlos Asuaje

Bats: L Throws: R Pos: 2B-84;PH-9;1B-1   a-SWAH-hay   Ht: 5'9" Wt: 158 Born: 11/2/1991 Age: 26

Year	Team	Lg	G	AB	H	2B	3B	HR	(Hm	Rd)	TB	R	RBI	RC	TBB	IBB	SO	HBP	SH	SF	SB	CS	GDP	Avg	OBP	Slg	OPS
2013	Lowell	A-	52	171	46	12	1	1	(-	-)	63	19	20	25	27	0	33	1	2	3	4	3	3	.269	.366	.368	.735
2014	2 Tms	Low	129	480	149	38	12	15	(-	-)	256	86	101	100	59	0	90	11	2	7	8	5	8	.310	.393	.533	.927
2015	PortInd	AA	131	495	123	23	7	8	(-	-)	184	60	61	65	56	1	88	7	10	2	9	6	8	.248	.332	.372	.704
2016	ElPaso	AAA	134	535	172	32	11	9	(-	-)	253	98	69	97	49	0	82	3	5	5	10	5	10	.321	.378	.473	.851
2017	ElPaso	AAA	62	228	57	9	5	3	(-	-)	85	44	35	35	40	0	33	4	3	2	1	1	2	.250	.369	.373	.741
2016	SD	NL	7	24	5	2	0	0	(0	0)	7	2	2	3	1	0	4	0	0	0	0	0	0	.208	.240	.292	.532
2017	SD	NL	89	307	83	14	1	4	(1	3)	111	28	21	38	28	0	76	2	5	1	0	1	6	.270	.334	.362	.696
	2 ML YEARS		96	331	88	16	1	4	(1	3)	118	30	23	41	29	0	80	2	5	1	0	1	6	.266	.328	.356	.684

Tyler Austin

Bats: R Throws: R Pos: 1B-8;RF-7;DH-6;PH-3   Ht: 6'2" Wt: 220 Born: 9/6/1991 Age: 26

Year	Team	Lg	G	AB	H	2B	3B	HR	(Hm	Rd)	TB	R	RBI	RC	TBB	IBB	SO	HBP	SH	SF	SB	CS	GDP	Avg	OBP	Slg	OPS
2013	Trntn	AA	83	319	82	17	1	6	(-	-)	119	43	40	45	41	0	79	3	0	3	4	0	12	.257	.344	.373	.717
2014	Trntn	AA	105	396	109	20	5	9	(-	-)	166	56	47	58	36	0	80	2	0	3	6	3	8	.275	.336	.419	.756
2015	S-WB	AAA	73	264	62	8	0	4	(-	-)	82	33	27	28	26	0	81	4	1	4	8	1	15	.235	.309	.311	.619
2015	Trntn	AA	21	77	20	5	2	2	(-	-)	35	8	8	12	8	0	16	1	0	0	3	2	4	.260	.337	.455	.792
2016	Trntn	AA	50	177	46	10	1	4	(-	-)	70	22	29	28	30	0	46	1	0	2	1	1	5	.260	.367	.395	.762
2016	S-WB	AAA	57	201	65	24	0	13	(-	-)	128	39	49	51	32	0	59	0	0	1	5	0	9	.323	.415	.637	1.051
2017	S-WB	AAA	47	171	47	14	1	10	(-	-)	93	29	32	31	18	1	52	0	0	1	0	0	4	.275	.342	.544	.886
2016	NYY	AL	31	83	20	3	0	5	(5	0)	38	7	12	12	7	0	36	0	0	0	1	0	1	.241	.300	.458	.758
2017	NYY	AL	20	40	9	2	0	2	(0	2)	17	4	8	6	4	0	17	0	0	2	0	0	1	.225	.283	.425	.708
	2 ML YEARS		51	123	29	5	0	7	(5	2)	55	11	20	18	11	0	53	0	0	2	1	0	2	.236	.294	.447	.741

Alex Avila

Bats: L Throws: R Pos: C-78;PH-22;1B-19;DH-8;PR-1   ah-VEE-lah   Ht: 5'11" Wt: 210 Born: 1/29/1987 Age: 31

								BATTING											RUNNING			AVERAGES			
Year Team	Lg	G	AB	H	2B	3B	HR	(Hm Rd)	TB	R	RBI	RC	TBB	IBB	SO	HBP	SH	SF	SB	CS	GDP	Avg	OBP	Slg	OPS
2009 Det	AL	29	61	17	4	0	5	(4 1)	36	9	14	12	10	0	18	0	0	1	0	0	0	.279	.375	.590	.965
2010 Det	AL	104	294	67	12	0	7	(4 3)	100	28	31	26	36	0	71	2	1	0	2	2	12	.228	.316	.340	.656
2011 Det	AL	141	464	137	33	4	19	(10 9)	235	63	82	86	73	9	131	3	3	8	3	1	8	.295	.389	.506	.895
2012 Det	AL	116	367	89	21	2	9	(7 2)	141	42	48	53	61	2	104	2	2	2	2	0	12	.243	.352	.384	.736
2013 Det	AL	102	330	75	14	1	11	(7 4)	124	39	47	37	44	0	112	1	1	3	0	0	10	.227	.317	.376	.693
2014 Det	AL	124	390	85	22	0	11	(3 8)	140	44	47	48	61	1	151	3	1	2	0	3	6	.218	.327	.359	.686
2015 Det	AL	67	178	34	5	0	4	(2 2)	51	21	13	20	40	0	66	0	1	0	0	1	4	.191	.339	.287	.626
2016 CWS	AL	57	169	36	6	0	7	(5 2)	63	19	11	17	38	0	78	1	0	1	0	0	3	.213	.359	.373	.732
2017 2 Tms	AL	112	311	82	13	1	14	(8 6)	139	41	49	55	62	2	120	1	1	1	0	1	10	.264	.387	.447	.834
17 Det	AL	77	219	60	11	0	11	(6 5)	104	30	32	37	43	2	80	1	0	1	0	1	6	.274	.394	.475	.869
17 ChC	NL	35	92	22	2	1	3	(2 1)	35	11	17	18	19	0	40	0	1	0	0	0	4	.239	.369	.380	.750
Postseason		34	110	16	2	0	3	(2 1)	27	6	7	4	11	0	43	1	1	0	0	0	1	.145	.230	.245	.475
9 ML YEARS		852	2564	622	130	8	87	(50 37)	1029	306	342	354	425	14	851	13	10	18	7	8	65	.243	.351	.401	.752

Luis Avilan

Pitches: L Bats: L Pos: RP-61   ah-VEE-lan   Ht: 6'2" Wt: 225 Born: 7/19/1989 Age: 28

		HOW MUCH HE PITCHED						WHAT HE GAVE UP												THE RESULTS							
Year Team	Lg	G	GS	CG	GF	IP	BFP	H	R	ER	HR	SH	SF	HB	TBB	IBB	SO	WP	Bk	W	L	Pct	Sh	Sv-Op	Hld	ERC	ERA
2012 Atl	NL	31	0	0	2	36.0	142	27	9	8	1	3	0	1	10	1	33	3	1	1	0	1.000	0	0-0	5	2.00	2.00
2013 Atl	NL	75	0	0	7	65.0	256	40	12	11	1	1	1	4	22	2	38	3	1	5	0	1.000	0	0-2	27	1.62	1.52
2014 Atl	NL	62	0	0	14	43.1	193	47	22	22	2	3	2	3	21	7	25	5	0	4	1	.800	0	0-2	8	4.55	4.57
2015 2 Tms	NL	73	0	0	9	53.1	220	48	24	24	6	1	2	1	15	2	49	2	1	2	5	.286	0	0-3	17	3.18	4.05
2016 LAD	NL	27	0	0	3	19.2	82	12	8	7	0	2	0	2	10	4	28	1	0	3	0	1.000	0	0-1	9	1.84	3.20
2017 LAD	NL	61	0	0	5	46.0	194	42	16	15	2	0	0	1	23	3	52	1	0	2	3	.400	0	0-2	13	3.57	2.93
15 Atl	NL	50	0	0	7	37.2	154	35	15	15	4	0	1	0	10	2	31	1	1	2	4	.333	0	0-3	11	3.16	3.58
15 LAD	NL	23	0	0	2	15.2	66	13	9	9	2	1	1	1	5	0	18	1	0	0	1	.000	0	0-0	6	3.21	5.17
Postseason		11	0	0	2	7.2	31	7	0	0	0	0	1	0	2	1	6	1	0	0	0	-	0	0-1	2	2.30	0.00
6 ML YEARS		329	0	0	40	263.1	1087	216	91	87	12	10	5	12	100	19	225	15	3	17	9	.654	0	0-10	73	2.77	2.97

Mike Aviles

Bats: R Throws: R Pos: SS-15;PH-13;2B-6;3B-6;1B-2;RF-1   uh-VEE-less   Ht: 5'10" Wt: 205 Born: 3/13/1981 Age: 37

								BATTING											RUNNING			AVERAGES			
Year Team	Lg	G	AB	H	2B	3B	HR	(Hm Rd)	TB	R	RBI	RC	TBB	IBB	SO	HBP	SH	SF	SB	CS	GDP	Avg	OBP	Slg	OPS
2017 NewOr*	AAA	55	178	52	8	2	1	(- -)	67	22	24	22	10	0	24	1	3	4	1	2	2	.292	.326	.376	.703
2008 KC	AL	102	419	136	27	4	10	(4 6)	201	68	51	62	18	4	58	2	0	2	8	3	12	.325	.354	.480	.833
2009 KC	AL	36	120	22	3	1	1	(1 0)	30	10	8	4	4	0	26	0	2	1	1	0	3	.183	.208	.250	.458
2010 KC	AL	110	424	129	16	3	8	(4 4)	175	63	32	47	20	0	49	1	0	3	14	5	13	.304	.335	.413	.748
2011 2 Tms	AL	91	286	73	17	3	7	(4 3)	117	31	39	31	13	0	44	2	4	4	14	4	8	.255	.289	.409	.698
2012 Bos	AL	136	512	128	28	0	13	(7 6)	195	57	60	57	23	0	77	2	3	6	14	6	6	.250	.282	.381	.650
2013 Cle	AL	124	361	91	15	0	9	(3 6)	133	54	46	35	15	0	41	3	7	8	14	5	11	.252	.282	.368	.650
2014 Cle	AL	113	344	85	16	1	5	(2 3)	118	38	39	27	13	0	49	1	11	5	14	5	10	.247	.273	.343	.616
2015 Cle	AL	98	290	67	10	0	5	(1 4)	92	37	17	19	20	0	38	1	5	1	3	1	18	.231	.282	.317	.599
2016 Det	AL	68	167	35	5	1	1	(1 0)	45	17	6	9	9	0	27	2	3	0	2	2	5	.210	.258	.269	.528
2017 Mia	NL	37	86	20	2	0	1	(1 0)	25	5	8	9	6	2	15	2	3	0	0	0	3	.233	.298	.291	.589
11 KC	AL	53	185	41	11	3	5	(2 3)	73	14	31	18	9	0	27	2	3	3	10	2	5	.222	.261	.395	.656
11 Bos	AL	38	101	32	6	0	2	(2 0)	44	17	8	13	4	0	17	0	1	1	4	2	3	.317	.340	.436	.775
10 ML YEARS		915	3009	786	139	13	60	(28 32)	1131	380	306	300	141	6	424	16	38	30	78	31	89	.261	.295	.376	.671

John Axford

Pitches: R Bats: R Pos: RP-22   Ht: 6'5" Wt: 220 Born: 4/1/1983 Age: 35

		HOW MUCH HE PITCHED						WHAT HE GAVE UP												THE RESULTS							
Year Team	Lg	G	GS	CG	GF	IP	BFP	H	R	ER	HR	SH	SF	HB	TBB	IBB	SO	WP	Bk	W	L	Pct	Sh	Sv-Op	Hld	ERC	ERA
2009 Mil	NL	7	0	0	6	7.2	34	5	3	3	0	0	0	0	6	1	9	1	0	0	0	-	0	1-1	0	2.62	3.52
2010 Mil	NL	50	0	0	43	58.0	238	42	17	16	1	2	2	2	27	3	76	4	0	8	2	.800	0	24-27	3	2.33	2.48
2011 Mil	NL	74	0	0	63	73.2	305	59	19	16	4	1	1	0	25	1	86	8	0	2	2	.500	0	46-48	0	2.44	1.95
2012 Mil	NL	75	0	0	54	69.1	310	61	42	36	10	1	2	2	39	2	93	10	0	5	8	.385	0	35-44	3	4.33	4.67
2013 2 Tms	NL	75	0	0	16	65.0	289	73	32	29	10	4	1	2	26	3	65	5	0	7	7	.500	0	0-7	19	5.25	4.02
2014 2 Tms		62	0	0	28	54.2	243	43	26	24	6	3	4	2	36	3	63	5	0	2	4	.333	0	10-13	2	3.96	3.95
2015 Col	NL	60	0	0	43	55.2	250	56	27	26	4	0	2	0	32	4	62	1	0	4	5	.444	0	25-31	2	4.45	4.20
2016 Oak	AL	68	0	0	13	65.2	289	65	30	29	6	2	2	3	30	1	60	4	0	6	4	.600	0	3-10	15	4.33	3.97
2017 Oak	AL	22	0	0	5	21.0	109	27	16	15	3	1	2	2	17	0	21	1	0	0	1	.000	0	0-1	1	8.14	6.43
13 Mil	NL	62	0	0	13	54.2	245	62	29	27	10	3	1	1	23	3	54	5	0	6	7	.462	0	0-6	19	5.53	4.45
13 StL	NL	13	0	0	3	10.1	44	11	3	2	0	1	0	1	3	0	11	0	0	1	0	1.000	0	0-1	0	3.75	1.74
14 Cle	AL	49	0	0	24	43.2	196	34	21	19	6	3	3	1	30	3	51	4	0	2	3	.400	0	10-13	2	4.11	3.92
14 Pit	NL	13	0	0	4	11.0	47	9	5	5	0	0	1	1	6	0	12	1	0	0	0	1.000	0	0-0	0	3.33	4.09
Postseason		12	0	0	8	12.2	51	7	2	2	1	0	0	0	6	0	18	0	0	1	0	1.000	0	3-4	0	1.91	1.42
9 ML YEARS		493	0	0	274	470.2	2067	431	212	194	44	14	16	12	238	18	535	39	0	34	33	.507	0	144-182	45	3.97	3.71

Erick Aybar

Bats: B **Throws:** R **Pos:** SS-99;PH-12 EYE-barr **Ht:** 5'10" **Wt:** 195 **Born:** 1/14/1984 **Age:** 34

Year	Team	Lg	G	AB	H	2B	3B	HR	(Hm	Rd)	TB	R	RBI	RC	TBB	IBB	SO	HBP	SH	SF	SB	CS	GDP	Avg	OBP	Slg	OPS
2006	LAA	AL	34	40	10	1	1	0	(0	0)	13	5	2	4	0	0	8	0	0	0	1	0	1	.250	.250	.325	.575
2007	LAA	AL	79	194	46	5	1	1	(0	1)	56	18	19	16	10	0	32	2	3	2	4	4	8	.237	.279	.289	.568
2008	LAA	AL	98	346	96	18	5	3	(2	1)	133	53	39	49	14	0	45	5	9	1	7	2	2	.277	.314	.384	.699
2009	LAA	AL	137	504	157	23	9	5	(2	3)	213	70	58	73	30	1	54	5	12	5	14	7	9	.312	.353	.423	.776
2010	LAA	AL	138	534	135	18	4	5	(3	2)	176	69	29	51	35	1	81	7	11	2	22	8	7	.253	.306	.330	.636
2011	LAA	AL	143	556	155	33	8	10	(2	8)	234	71	59	72	31	1	68	6	9	3	30	6	13	.279	.322	.421	.743
2012	LAA	AL	141	517	150	31	5	8	(4	4)	215	67	45	63	22	1	61	5	7	2	20	4	11	.290	.324	.416	.740
2013	LAA	AL	138	550	149	33	5	6	(4	2)	210	68	54	61	23	1	59	3	8	5	12	7	14	.271	.301	.382	.683
2014	LAA	AL	156	589	164	30	4	7	(2	5)	223	77	68	74	36	4	62	5	3	8	16	9	10	.278	.321	.379	.700
2015	LAA	AL	156	597	161	30	1	3	(1	2)	202	74	44	60	25	1	73	4	7	5	15	6	12	.270	.301	.338	.639
2016	2 Tms		126	415	101	19	2	3	(0	3)	133	34	34	37	31	6	70	6	3	4	3	5	15	.243	.303	.320	.623
2017	SD	NL	108	333	78	15	1	7	(4	3)	116	37	22	33	28	2	57	4	3	2	11	4	5	.234	.300	.348	.648
16	Atl	NL	97	335	81	14	2	2	(0	2)	105	27	26	26	20	5	59	6	3	4	3	5	14	.242	.293	.313	.607
16	Det	AL	29	80	20	5	0	1	(0	1)	28	7	8	11	11	1	11	0	0	0	0	0	1	.250	.341	.350	.691
	Postseason		17	61	16	3	1	0	(0	0)	21	4	4	7	1	0	5	0	4	0	4	0	2	.262	.274	.344	.618
	12 ML YEARS		1454	5175	1402	256	46	58	(24	34)	1924	643	473	593	285	18	670	52	75	39	155	62	107	.271	.313	.372	.685

Harrison Bader

Bats: R **Throws:** R **Pos:** CF-20;LF-7;PH-6;RF-3;PR-3 **Ht:** 6'0" **Wt:** 195 **Born:** 6/3/1994 **Age:** 24

Year	Team	Lg	G	AB	H	2B	3B	HR	(Hm	Rd)	TB	R	RBI	RC	TBB	IBB	SO	HBP	SH	SF	SB	CS	GDP	Avg	OBP	Slg	OPS
2015	2 Tms	Low	61	235	73	13	2	11	(-	-)	123	40	32	46	15	0	49	7	0	1	17	6	5	.311	.368	.523	.892
2016	Sprgfld	AA	82	318	90	12	4	16	(-	-)	158	48	41	54	25	0	93	10	0	3	11	10	2	.283	.351	.497	.848
2016	Memp	AAA	49	147	34	7	1	3	(-	-)	52	22	17	15	11	0	38	3	0	0	2	3	0	.231	.298	.354	.652
2017	Memp	AAA	123	431	122	18	1	20	(-	-)	202	74	55	71	34	0	118	10	1	3	15	9	3	.283	.347	.469	.816
2017	StL	NL	32	85	20	3	0	3	(0	3)	32	10	10	10	5	1	24	1	0	1	2	1	1	.235	.283	.376	.659

Javier Baez

Bats: R **Throws:** R **Pos:** 2B-80;SS-73;3B-8;PH-8;1B-4;RF-1 BYE-ezz **Ht:** 6'0" **Wt:** 190 **Born:** 12/1/1992 **Age:** 25

Year	Team	Lg	G	AB	H	2B	3B	HR	(Hm	Rd)	TB	R	RBI	RC	TBB	IBB	SO	HBP	SH	SF	SB	CS	GDP	Avg	OBP	Slg	OPS
2014	ChC	NL	52	213	36	6	0	9	(3	6)	69	25	20	12	15	0	95	1	0	0	5	1	5	.169	.227	.324	.551
2015	ChC	NL	28	76	22	6	0	1	(1	0)	31	4	4	5	4	1	24	0	0	0	1	2	0	.289	.325	.408	.733
2016	ChC	NL	142	421	115	19	1	14	(8	6)	178	50	59	53	15	3	108	11	1	2	12	3	8	.273	.314	.423	.737
2017	ChC	NL	145	469	128	24	2	23	(13	10)	225	75	75	69	30	15	144	1	6	2	10	3	10	.273	.317	.480	.796
	Postseason		23	83	23	4	0	3	(2	1)	36	9	11	10	2	0	25	0	0	1	4	0	1	.277	.291	.434	.724
	4 ML YEARS		367	1179	301	55	3	47	(25	22)	503	154	158	139	64	19	371	13	7	4	28	9	23	.255	.300	.427	.727

Pedro Baez

Pitches: R **Bats:** R **Pos:** RP-66 BYE-ezz **Ht:** 6'0" **Wt:** 230 **Born:** 3/11/1988 **Age:** 30

Year	Team	Lg	G	GS	CG	GF	IP	BFP	H	R	ER	HR	SH	SF	HB	TBB	IBB	SO	WP	Bk	W	L	Pct	Sh	Sv-Op	Hld	ERC	ERA
2014	LAD	NL	20	0	0	8	24.0	92	16	7	7	3	1	1	0	5	1	18	0	0	0	0	0-	0	0-0	5	1.79	2.63
2015	LAD	NL	52	0	0	8	51.0	208	47	22	19	4	3	3	1	11	1	60	1	1	4	2	.667	0	0-3	11	2.87	3.35
2016	LAD	NL	73	0	0	10	74.0	295	52	27	25	11	1	2	2	22	0	83	3	2	3	2	.600	0	0-2	23	2.52	3.04
2017	LAD	NL	66	0	0	6	64.0	280	56	24	21	9	0	0	2	29	2	64	1	1	3	6	.333	0	0-3	23	3.84	2.95
	Postseason		11	0	0	0	9.2	46	9	11	7	2	1	0	2	7	0	8	0	0	0	0	-	0	0-0	1	6.72	6.52
	4 ML YEARS		211	0	0	32	213.0	875	171	80	72	27	5	6	5	67	4	225	5	4	10	10	.500	0	0-8	62	2.90	3.04

Andrew Bailey

Pitches: R **Bats:** R **Pos:** RP-4 **Ht:** 6'3" **Wt:** 240 **Born:** 5/31/1984 **Age:** 34

Year	Team	Lg	G	GS	CG	GF	IP	BFP	H	R	ER	HR	SH	SF	HB	TBB	IBB	SO	WP	Bk	W	L	Pct	Sh	Sv-Op	Hld	ERC	ERA
2017	Salt Lk*	AAA	7	0	0	0	6.2	30	9	9	6	3	0	0	0	1	0	4	0	0	0	2	.000	0	0--	-	7.51	8.10
2009	Oak	AL	68	0	0	54	83.1	323	49	17	17	5	3	2	0	24	3	91	6	0	6	3	.667	0	26-30	1	1.44	1.84
2010	Oak	AL	47	0	0	42	49.0	189	34	8	8	3	2	3	0	13	1	42	0	0	1	3	.250	0	25-28	0	1.82	1.47
2011	Oak	AL	42	0	0	37	41.2	170	34	18	15	3	1	1	0	12	2	41	0	0	0	4	.000	0	24-26	1	2.42	3.24
2012	Bos	AL	19	0	0	13	15.1	74	21	12	12	2	0	0	0	8	2	14	0	1	1	1	.500	0	6-9	0	6.73	7.04
2013	Bos	AL	30	0	0	17	28.2	116	23	12	12	7	1	0	0	12	0	39	0	0	3	1	.750	0	8-13	8	4.13	3.77
2015	NYY	AL	10	0	0	3	8.2	41	9	8	5	2	0	2	0	5	1	6	0	0	1	0	1.000	0	0-0	0	6.39	5.19
2016	2 Tms		45	0	0	14	43.2	190	41	26	26	7	3	3	2	17	0	41	3	1	3	1	.750	0	6-7	4	4.23	5.36
2017	LAA	AL	4	0	0	2	4.0	13	1	0	0	0	0	0	0	0	0	2	0	0	2	0	1.000	0	0-0	0	0.14	0.00
16	Phi	NL	33	0	0	4	32.1	144	32	23	23	6	3	2	1	15	0	33	2	1	3	1	.750	0	0-1	4	4.95	6.40
16	LAA	AL	12	0	0	10	11.1	46	9	3	3	1	0	1	1	2	0	8	1	0	0	0	-	0	6-6	0	2.38	2.38
	8 ML YEARS		265	0	0	182	274.1	1116	212	101	95	29	10	11	2	91	9	276	9	2	16	14	.533	0	95-113	16	2.64	3.12

Homer Bailey

Pitches: R **Bats:** R **Pos:** SP-18
Ht: 6'4" **Wt:** 223 **Born:** 5/3/1986 **Age:** 32

		HOW MUCH HE PITCHED						WHAT HE GAVE UP												THE RESULTS						
Year Team	Lg	G	GS	CG	GF	IP	BFP	H	R	ER	HR	SH	SF	HB	TBB	IBB	SO	WP	Bk	W	L	Pct	Sh	Sv-Op	Hld	ERC	ERA
2007 Cin	NL	9	9	0	0	45.1	205	43	32	29	3	1	6	3	28	1	28	1	1	4	2	.667	0	0-0	0	4.61	5.76
2008 Cin	NL	8	8	0	0	36.1	180	59	36	32	8	5	2	0	17	1	18	4	1	0	6	.000	0	0-0	0	9.31	7.93
2009 Cin	NL	20	20	0	0	113.1	496	115	61	57	12	4	4	3	52	1	86	6	0	8	5	.615	0	0-0	0	4.56	4.53
2010 Cin	NL	19	19	1	0	109.0	465	109	55	54	11	2	1	3	40	6	100	3	1	4	3	.571	1	0-0	0	4.01	4.46
2011 Cin	NL	22	22	0	0	132.0	561	136	68	65	18	4	4	5	33	2	106	4	0	9	7	.563	0	0-0	0	4.01	4.43
2012 Cin	NL	33	33	2	0	208.0	874	206	97	85	26	5	5	8	52	3	168	3	0	13	10	.565	1	0-0	0	3.73	3.68
2013 Cin	NL	32	32	2	0	209.0	849	181	85	81	20	8	4	10	54	2	199	5	2	11	12	.478	1	0-0	0	2.99	3.49
2014 Cin	NL	23	23	1	0	145.2	604	134	60	60	16	5	4	7	45	1	124	5	1	9	5	.643	1	0-0	0	3.57	3.71
2015 Cin	NL	2	2	0	0	11.1	51	16	7	7	3	0	0	0	4	2	3	0	0	0	1	.000	0	0-0	0	7.64	5.56
2016 Cin	NL	6	6	0	0	23.0	111	35	19	17	2	0	2	2	7	0	27	1	0	2	3	.400	0	0-0	0	7.04	6.65
2017 Cin	NL	18	18	0	0	91.0	420	112	67	65	11	5	2	8	42	2	67	4	0	6	9	.400	0	0-0	0	6.26	6.43
Postseason		2	1	0	0	9.0	32	3	1	1	0	1	1	1	1	0	12	0	0	0	0	-	0	0-0	0	0.52	1.00
11 ML YEARS		192	192	6	0	1124.0	4816	1146	587	552	130	39	34	49	374	21	926	36	6	66	63	.512	4	0-0	0	4.19	4.42

Anthony Banda

Pitches: L **Bats:** L **Pos:** SP-4; RP-4
Ht: 6'2" **Wt:** 190 **Born:** 8/10/1993 **Age:** 24

		HOW MUCH HE PITCHED						WHAT HE GAVE UP												THE RESULTS						
Year Team	Lg	G	GS	CG	GF	IP	BFP	H	R	ER	HR	SH	SF	HB	TBB	IBB	SO	WP	Bk	W	L	Pct	Sh	Sv-Op	Hld	ERC	ERA
2013 Helena	R+	14	14	0	0	60.2	263	64	40	30	7	3	0	1	25	0	45	8	2	3	4	.429	0	0- -	-	4.68	4.45
2014 2 Tms	Low	26	20	0	5	118.2	505	116	47	40	6	4	0	2	45	0	117	16	2	9	6	.600	0	2- -	-	3.61	3.03
2015 Visalia	A+	28	27	1	0	151.2	626	150	67	56	8	3	4	4	39	0	152	12	3	8	8	.500	1	0- -	-	3.30	3.32
2016 Mobile	AA	13	13	0	0	76.1	325	70	23	18	4	5	0	1	28	0	84	6	0	6	2	.750	0	0- -	-	3.18	2.12
2016 Reno	AAA	13	13	0	0	73.2	317	73	36	30	6	3	1	2	27	1	68	6	0	4	4	.500	0	0- -	-	3.84	3.67
2017 Reno	AAA	22	22	0	0	122.0	531	125	76	73	15	5	3	2	51	0	116	12	0	8	7	.533	0	0- -	-	4.53	5.39
2017 Ari	NL	8	4	0	1	25.2	115	26	17	17	1	0	0	3	10	1	25	2	0	2	3	.400	0	0-0	0	3.98	5.96

Jett Bandy

Bats: R **Throws:** R **Pos:** C-50;PH-10;PR-1
Ht: 6'4" **Wt:** 235 **Born:** 3/26/1990 **Age:** 28

		BATTING																	RUNNING			AVERAGES			
Year Team	Lg	G	AB	H	2B	3B	HR	(Hm	Rd)	TB	R	RBI	RC	TBB	IBB	SO	HBP	SH	SF	SB	CS	GDP	Avg	OBP	Slg	OPS
2017 ColSpr*	AAA	12	42	13	2	0	2	(-	-)	21	7	14	8	5	1	5	3	0	1	0	1	1	.310	.412	.500	.912
2015 LAA	AL	2	2	1	0	0	1	(0	1)	4	1	1	1	0	0	0	0	0	0	0	0	0	.500	.500	2.000	2.500
2016 LAA	AL	70	209	49	9	0	8	(6	2)	82	23	25	20	11	0	38	4	3	4	1	0	5	.234	.281	.392	.673
2017 Mil	NL	60	169	35	6	0	6	(4	2)	59	14	18	14	15	0	51	4	0	0	1	0	5	.207	.287	.349	.636
3 ML YEARS		132	380	85	15	0	15	(10	5)	145	38	44	35	26	0	89	8	3	4	2	0	10	.224	.285	.382	.666

Johnny Barbato

Pitches: R **Bats:** R **Pos:** RP-24
Ht: 6'1" **Wt:** 235 **Born:** 7/11/1992 **Age:** 25

		HOW MUCH HE PITCHED						WHAT HE GAVE UP												THE RESULTS						
Year Team	Lg	G	GS	CG	GF	IP	BFP	H	R	ER	HR	SH	SF	HB	TBB	IBB	SO	WP	Bk	W	L	Pct	Sh	Sv-Op	Hld	ERC	ERA
2013 Lk Els	A+	49	7	0	26	88.0	381	90	54	49	8	5	3	6	33	0	89	1	0	3	6	.333	0	14- -	-	4.35	5.01
2014 SnAnt	AA	27	0	0	22	31.1	129	26	12	10	3	3	0	1	10	0	33	3	0	2	2	.500	0	16- -	-	2.94	2.87
2015 Trntn	AA	26	0	0	2	42.1	180	42	19	19	4	1	3	3	14	1	44	1	0	2	2	.500	0	0- -	-	4.01	4.04
2015 S-WB	AAA	14	0	0	5	25.0	95	13	1	1	1	2	0	0	11	1	26	1	0	4	0	1.000	0	3- -	-	1.54	0.36
2016 S-WB	AAA	31	1	0	13	48.1	203	38	17	14	3	0	1	1	23	0	49	1	0	3	2	.600	0	3- -	-	3.04	2.61
2017 Indy	AAA	26	2	0	13	35.1	144	28	12	12	7	0	0	1	11	0	36	0	0	1	0	1.000	0	4- -	-	3.34	3.06
2016 NYY	AL	13	0	0	5	13.0	57	13	11	11	2	0	0	2	5	0	15	0	0	1	2	.333	0	0-0	0	5.11	7.62
2017 Pit	NL	24	0	0	7	28.2	130	25	13	13	4	0	0	0	18	0	23	1	0	0	1	.000	0	0-0	0	4.75	4.08
2 ML YEARS		37	0	0	12	41.2	187	38	24	24	6	0	0	4	23	0	38	1	0	1	3	.250	0	0-0	0	4.86	5.18

Austin Barnes

Bats: R **Throws:** R **Pos:** C-55;PH-34;2B-21;3B-1;DH-1
Ht: 5'10" **Wt:** 190 **Born:** 12/28/1989 **Age:** 28

		BATTING																	RUNNING			AVERAGES			
Year Team	Lg	G	AB	H	2B	3B	HR	(Hm	Rd)	TB	R	RBI	RC	TBB	IBB	SO	HBP	SH	SF	SB	CS	GDP	Avg	OBP	Slg	OPS
2015 LAD	NL	20	29	6	2	0	0	(0	0)	8	4	1	3	6	0	6	1	1	0	1	0	2	.207	.361	.276	.637
2016 LAD	NL	21	32	5	1	0	0	(0	0)	6	3	2	3	5	0	9	0	0	0	0	0	0	.156	.270	.188	.458
2017 LAD	NL	102	218	63	15	2	8	(6	2)	106	35	38	46	39	1	43	5	0	0	4	1	6	.289	.408	.486	.895
Postseason		2	1	0	0	0	0	(0	0)	0	1	0	0	0	0	1	0	0	0	0	0	0	.000	.000	.000	.000
3 ML YEARS		143	279	74	18	2	8	(6	2)	120	42	41	52	50	1	58	6	1	0	5	1	8	.265	.388	.430	.818

Danny Barnes

Pitches: R **Bats:** L **Pos:** RP-60
Ht: 6'1" **Wt:** 195 **Born:** 10/21/1989 **Age:** 28

		HOW MUCH HE PITCHED						WHAT HE GAVE UP												THE RESULTS						
Year Team	Lg	G	GS	CG	GF	IP	BFP	H	R	ER	HR	SH	SF	HB	TBB	IBB	SO	WP	Bk	W	L	Pct	Sh	Sv-Op	Hld	ERC	ERA
2014 Dnedin	A+	36	0	0	19	38.2	164	36	20	18	4	1	3	1	12	0	49	1	0	0	5	.000	0	7- -	-	3.42	4.19
2015 Nham	AA	40	1	0	17	60.2	262	64	24	20	5	2	3	1	19	2	74	0	0	3	2	.600	0	4- -	-	3.90	2.97
2016 Nham	AA	24	0	0	11	35.2	126	17	5	4	3	0	0	0	4	0	40	0	0	2	1	.667	0	1- -	-	0.90	1.01
2016 Buffalo	AAA	17	0	0	9	25.2	88	6	1	1	0	0	0	2	2	0	37	0	0	1	0	1.000	0	5- -	-	0.27	0.35
2016 Tor	AL	19	0	0	4	13.2	58	14	6	6	0	0	2	0	5	0	14	1	0	0	0	-	0	0-0	1	3.42	3.95
2017 Tor	AL	60	0	0	13	66.0	265	48	26	26	11	0	0	2	24	1	62	1	0	3	6	.333	0	0-4	11	2.97	3.55
2 ML YEARS		72	0	0	17	79.2	323	62	32	32	11	0	2	2	29	1	76	2	0	3	6	.333	0	0-4	12	3.06	3.62

Jacob Barnes

Pitches: R Bats: R Pos: RP-73 **Ht: 6'2" Wt: 220 Born: 4/14/1990 Age: 28**

Year	Team	Lg	G	GS	CG	GF	IP	BFP	H	R	ER	HR	SH	SF	HB	TBB	IBB	SO	WP	Bk	W	L	Pct	Sh	Sv-Op	Hld	ERC	ERA
2013	BrvdCt	A+	21	14	1	2	105.1	442	98	43	36	6	6	5	3	36	0	66	3	1	9	6	.600	0	0--	-	3.31	3.08
2014	Hntsvl	AA	23	21	0	0	105.2	442	94	57	50	9	4	5	10	38	0	75	6	1	2	6	.250	0	0--	-	3.65	4.26
2015	Biloxi	AA	39	6	0	8	75.0	317	74	32	28	2	2	1	2	30	1	84	7	0	4	5	.444	0	0--	-	3.65	3.36
2016	ColSpr	AAA	17	0	0	8	22.1	84	14	3	3	1	1	0	0	7	0	23	3	0	2	1	.667	0	1--	-	1.66	1.21
2016	Mil	NL	27	0	0	7	26.2	106	24	9	8	1	1	1	0	6	1	26	2	0	0	1	.000	0	1-1	0	2.50	2.70
2017	Mil	NL	73	0	0	8	72.0	304	57	35	32	8	0	3	3	33	4	80	6	0	3	4	.429	0	2-7	24	3.31	4.00
2 ML YEARS			100	0	0	15	98.2	410	81	44	40	9	1	4	3	39	5	106	8	0	3	5	.375	0	3-8	24	3.08	3.65

Matt Barnes

Pitches: R Bats: R Pos: RP-70 **Ht: 6'4" Wt: 210 Born: 6/17/1990 Age: 28**

Year	Team	Lg	G	GS	CG	GF	IP	BFP	H	R	ER	HR	SH	SF	HB	TBB	IBB	SO	WP	Bk	W	L	Pct	Sh	Sv-Op	Hld	ERC	ERA
2014	Bos	AL	5	0	0	3	9.0	39	11	4	4	1	0	1	0	2	0	8	0	0	0	0	-	0	0-0	0	4.72	4.00
2015	Bos	AL	32	2	0	7	43.0	199	56	28	26	9	2	0	2	15	0	39	4	0	3	4	.429	0	0-0	3	6.66	5.44
2016	Bos	AL	62	0	0	13	66.2	287	62	32	30	6	2	1	3	31	1	71	4	0	4	3	.571	0	1-2	16	4.06	4.05
2017	Bos	AL	70	0	0	15	69.2	287	57	31	30	7	1	3	1	28	0	83	3	0	7	3	.700	0	1-3	21	3.20	3.88
Postseason			1	0	0	0	1.2	7	3	1	0	0	0	0	0	0	0	1	0	0	0	0	-	0	0-0	0	7.19	0.00
4 ML YEARS			169	2	0	38	188.1	812	186	95	90	23	5	5	6	76	1	201	11	0	14	10	.583	0	2-5	40	4.32	4.30

Tony Barnette

Pitches: R Bats: R Pos: RP-50 **Ht: 6'1" Wt: 190 Born: 11/9/1983 Age: 34**

Year	Team	Lg	G	GS	CG	GF	IP	BFP	H	R	ER	HR	SH	SF	HB	TBB	IBB	SO	WP	Bk	W	L	Pct	Sh	Sv-Op	Hld	ERC	ERA
2016	Tex	AL	53	0	0	9	60.1	246	54	16	14	4	1	2	4	16	1	49	6	0	7	3	.700	0	0-1	15	3.06	2.09
2017	Tex	AL	50	0	0	7	57.1	252	64	36	35	7	0	6	2	22	4	57	4	0	2	1	.667	0	2-6	4	4.91	5.49
Postseason			3	0	0	0	4.0	15	3	0	0	0	0	0	0	0	0	1	0	0	0	0	-	0	0-0	0	1.13	0.00
2 ML YEARS			103	0	0	16	117.2	498	118	52	49	11	1	8	6	38	5	106	10	0	9	4	.692	0	2-7	19	3.93	3.75

Darwin Barney

Bats: R Throws: R Pos: 2B-73;3B-44;PH-18;SS-10;PR-5;LF-4;DH-2 **Ht: 5'10" Wt: 180 Born: 11/8/1985 Age: 32**

Year	Team	Lg	G	AB	H	2B	3B	HR	(Hm	Rd)	TB	R	RBI	RC	TBB	IBB	SO	HBP	SH	SF	SB	CS	GDP	Avg	OBP	Slg	OPS
2010	ChC	NL	30	79	19	4	0	0	(0	0)	23	12	2	6	6	0	12	0	0	0	0	0	0	.241	.294	.291	.585
2011	ChC	NL	143	529	146	23	6	2	(2	0)	187	66	43	60	22	2	67	8	7	4	9	2	14	.276	.313	.353	.666
2012	ChC	NL	156	548	139	26	4	7	(7	0)	194	73	44	60	33	1	58	3	3	1	6	1	11	.254	.299	.354	.653
2013	ChC	NL	141	501	104	25	1	7	(4	3)	152	49	41	30	36	5	64	6	4	6	4	2	22	.208	.266	.303	.569
2014	2 Tms	NL	94	237	57	11	2	3	(2	1)	81	24	23	27	17	2	34	4	2	2	1	0	1	.241	.300	.342	.642
2015	2 Tms		17	27	7	1	0	2	(0	0)	14	4	4	4	1	0	2	0	2	0	0	0	0	.259	.286	.519	.804
2016	Tor	AL	104	279	75	13	2	4	(2	2)	104	35	19	27	22	1	48	1	2	2	2	2	8	.269	.322	.373	.695
2017	Tor	AL	129	336	78	14	0	6	(2	4)	110	34	25	27	18	0	64	2	5	1	7	2	13	.232	.275	.327	.602
14	ChC	NL	72	204	47	10	2	2	(2	0)	67	18	16	19	9	2	31	1	2	1	1	0	1	.230	.265	.328	.594
14	LAD	NL	22	33	10	1	0	1	(0	1)	14	6	7	8	8	0	3	3	0	1	0	0	0	.303	.467	.424	.891
15	LAD	NL	2	4	0	0	0	0	(0	0)	0	0	0	0	0	0	0	0	0	0	0	0	0	.000	.000	.000	.000
15	Tor	AL	15	23	7	1	0	2	(0	2)	14	4	4	4	1	0	2	0	2	0	0	0	0	.304	.333	.609	.942
Postseason			7	15	1	0	0	0	(0	0)	1	1	0	0	0	0	3	1	1	0	0	0	1	.067	.125	.067	.192
8 ML YEARS			814	2536	625	117	15	31	(19	12)	865	297	201	241	155	11	349	24	25	16	29	9	69	.246	.294	.341	.635

Tucker Barnhart

Bats: B Throws: R Pos: C-110;PH-12;PR-1 **Ht: 5'11" Wt: 192 Born: 1/7/1991 Age: 27**

Year	Team	Lg	G	AB	H	2B	3B	HR	(Hm	Rd)	TB	R	RBI	RC	TBB	IBB	SO	HBP	SH	SF	SB	CS	GDP	Avg	OBP	Slg	OPS
2014	Cin	NL	21	54	10	0	0	1	(1	0)	13	3	1	2	4	1	10	0	2	0	0	0	0	.185	.241	.241	.482
2015	Cin	NL	81	242	61	9	0	3	(2	1)	79	23	18	22	25	5	45	2	2	3	0	1	10	.252	.324	.326	.650
2016	Cin	NL	115	377	97	23	1	7	(6	1)	143	34	51	51	36	8	72	2	2	3	1	0	12	.257	.323	.379	.702
2017	Cin	NL	121	370	100	24	2	7	(2	5)	149	26	44	50	42	11	68	3	5	3	4	0	12	.270	.347	.403	.750
4 ML YEARS			338	1043	268	56	3	18	(11	7)	384	86	114	125	107	25	195	7	11	9	5	1	34	.257	.328	.368	.696

Kyle Barraclough

Pitches: R Bats: R Pos: RP-66 BAIR-ah-claw **Ht: 6'3" Wt: 225 Born: 5/23/1990 Age: 28**

Year	Team	Lg	G	GS	CG	GF	IP	BFP	H	R	ER	HR	SH	SF	HB	TBB	IBB	SO	WP	Bk	W	L	Pct	Sh	Sv-Op	Hld	ERC	ERA
2015	Mia	NL	25	0	0	5	24.1	98	12	8	7	1	0	2	0	18	2	30	1	0	2	1	.667	0	0-1	6	2.25	2.59
2016	Mia	NL	75	0	0	6	72.2	306	45	24	23	1	2	2	2	44	2	113	9	1	6	3	.667	0	0-4	29	2.81	2.85
2017	Mia	NL	66	0	0	12	66.0	286	53	25	22	5	3	4	2	38	3	76	6	1	6	2	.750	0	1-5	22	3.53	3.00
3 ML YEARS			166	0	0	23	163.0	690	110	57	52	7	5	8	4	100	6	219	15	1	14	6	.700	0	1-10	57	2.78	2.87

Franklin Barreto

Bats: R Throws: R Pos: SS-11;2B-10;PH-3;PR-3;DH-2   Ht: 5'10" Wt: 190 Born: 2/27/1996 Age: 22

								BATTING													RUNNING			AVERAGES			
Year	Team	Lg	G	AB	H	2B	3B	HR	(Hm	Rd)	TB	R	RBI	RC	TBB	IBB	SO	HBP	SH	SF	SB	CS	GDP	Avg	OBP	Slg	OPS
2013	2 Tms	Low	59	228	63	21	7	4	(-	-)	110	34	26	37	15	0	56	8	1	0	10	6	3	.276	.343	.482	.825
2014	Vancvr	A-	73	289	90	23	4	6	(-	-)	139	65	61	58	26	1	64	10	0	3	29	5	5	.311	.384	.481	.865
2015	Stcktn	A+	90	338	102	22	3	13	(-	-)	169	50	47	57	15	0	67	4	1	6	8	3	6	.302	.333	.500	.833
2016	Mdlnd	AA	119	462	130	25	3	10	(-	-)	191	63	50	67	36	1	91	6	1	2	30	15	10	.281	.340	.413	.753
2017	Nashv	AAA	111	469	136	19	7	15	(-	-)	214	63	54	73	27	3	141	9	3	2	15	8	8	.290	.339	.456	.796
2017	Oak	AL	25	71	14	1	2	2	(1	1)	25	10	6	5	5	0	33	0	0	0	2	0	1	.197	.250	.352	.602

Jake Barrett

Pitches: R Bats: R Pos: RP-28   Ht: 6'2" Wt: 240 Born: 7/22/1991 Age: 26

			HOW MUCH HE PITCHED						WHAT HE GAVE UP										THE RESULTS							
Year	Team	Lg	G	GS	CG	GF	IP	BFP	H	R	ER	HR	SH	SF	HB	TBB	IBB	SO	WP	Bk	W	L	Pct	Sh	Sv-Op	Hld	ERC	ERA
2013	Visalia	A+	28	0	0	27	27.1	118	21	7	6	2	0	0	3	9	0	37	4	0	2	1	.667	0	15- -	-	2.67	1.98
2013	Mobile	AA	24	0	0	20	24.2	96	18	4	1	2	0	1	0	3	1	22	2	0	1	1	.500	0	14- -	-	1.56	0.36
2014	Mobile	AA	25	0	0	17	26.1	110	25	7	7	0	1	1	0	12	3	24	2	0	1	2	.333	0	12- -	-	3.23	2.39
2014	Reno	AAA	30	0	0	25	29.0	119	22	13	12	3	1	2	1	15	1	23	4	0	1	0	1.000	0	16- -	-	3.43	3.72
2015	Reno	AAA	22	0	0	21	23.0	104	27	15	13	1	2	1	0	12	0	21	0	0	1	3	.250	0	11- -	-	5.21	5.09
2015	Mobile	AA	25	0	0	10	30.0	131	34	14	14	2	1	3	0	11	0	30	2	0	3	0	1.000	0	4- -	-	4.49	4.20
2017	Reno	AAA	20	0	0	6	22.0	92	18	12	12	2	0	1	0	11	0	19	5	0	2	0	1.000	0	3- -	-	3.46	4.91
2016	Ari	NL	68	0	0	12	59.1	250	47	25	23	6	0	3	3	28	4	56	4	0	1	2	.333	0	4-9	8	3.33	3.49
2017	Ari	NL	28	0	0	5	27.0	121	27	18	15	7	0	2	0	15	2	26	1	0	1	1	.500	0	0-1	2	5.75	5.00
	2 ML YEARS		96	0	0	17	86.1	371	74	43	38	13	0	5	3	43	6	82	5	0	2	3	.400	0	4-10	10	4.05	3.96

Anthony Bass

Pitches: R Bats: R Pos: RP-2   Ht: 6'2" Wt: 200 Born: 11/1/1987 Age: 30

			HOW MUCH HE PITCHED						WHAT HE GAVE UP										THE RESULTS							
Year	Team	Lg	G	GS	CG	GF	IP	BFP	H	R	ER	HR	SH	SF	HB	TBB	IBB	SO	WP	Bk	W	L	Pct	Sh	Sv-Op	Hld	ERC	ERA
2017	RdRck*	AAA	18	12	0	2	75.1	324	79	43	35	7	2	1	1	28	0	87	9	0	3	4	.429	0	0- -	-	4.28	4.18
2011	SD	NL	27	3	0	6	48.1	198	41	9	9	3	2	0	1	21	1	24	1	0	2	0	1.000	0	0-0	4	3.28	1.68
2012	SD	NL	24	15	1	3	97.0	411	89	59	51	10	2	2	1	39	3	80	5	1	2	8	.200	0	1-1	1	3.65	4.73
2013	SD	NL	24	0	0	8	42.0	193	51	26	25	4	1	0	0	20	4	31	5	0	0	0	-	0	0-0	-	5.41	5.36
2014	Hou	AL	21	0	0	8	27.0	119	32	20	19	6	0	1	2	7	1	7	2	0	1	1	.500	0	2-4	4	5.74	6.33
2015	Tex	AL	33	0	0	7	64.0	272	66	33	32	5	3	3	1	20	1	45	1	0	0	0	-	0	0-1	0	3.81	4.50
2017	Tex	AL	2	0	0	1	5.2	31	14	9	9	1	0	1	0	4	0	1	1	0	0	0	-	0	0-0	0	12.41	14.29
	6 ML YEARS		131	18	1	36	284.0	1224	293	156	145	29	8	7	5	107	10	188	15	1	5	9	.357	0	3-6	9	4.21	4.60

Antonio Bastardo

Pitches: L Bats: R Pos: RP-9   bah-STAHR-doh   Ht: 5'11" Wt: 202 Born: 9/21/1985 Age: 32

			HOW MUCH HE PITCHED						WHAT HE GAVE UP										THE RESULTS							
Year	Team	Lg	G	GS	CG	GF	IP	BFP	H	R	ER	HR	SH	SF	HB	TBB	IBB	SO	WP	Bk	W	L	Pct	Sh	Sv-Op	Hld	ERC	ERA
2017	Indy*	AAA	12	1	0	0	11.1	54	11	5	4	2	0	0	1	8	0	9	0	0	2	0	1.000	0	0- -	-	5.97	3.18
2009	Phi	NL	6	5	0	0	23.2	106	26	18	17	4	0	0	2	9	0	19	0	0	2	3	.400	0	0-0	0	5.41	6.46
2010	Phi	NL	25	0	0	2	18.2	86	19	9	9	1	0	0	2	9	0	26	0	0	2	0	1.000	0	0-1	3	4.46	4.34
2011	Phi	NL	64	0	0	15	58.0	225	28	17	17	6	2	2	0	26	0	70	4	0	6	1	.857	0	8-9	17	1.69	2.64
2012	Phi	NL	65	0	0	10	52.0	224	40	26	25	7	1	2	2	26	3	81	5	0	2	5	.286	0	1-5	26	3.42	4.33
2013	Phi	NL	48	0	0	15	42.2	179	33	12	11	4	1	1	1	21	1	47	4	0	3	2	.600	0	2-5	14	2.91	2.32
2014	Phi	NL	67	0	0	17	64.0	271	43	31	28	4	3	3	2	34	4	81	5	0	5	7	.417	0	0-2	12	2.54	3.94
2015	Pit	NL	66	0	0	18	57.1	239	39	19	19	4	2	0	3	26	2	64	8	0	4	1	.800	0	1-2	9	2.50	2.98
2016	2 Tms	NL	69	0	0	11	67.2	297	60	37	34	11	2	3	4	32	3	74	6	4	3	0	1.000	0	0-2	15	4.27	4.52
2017	Pit	NL	9	0	0	5	9.0	52	16	15	15	5	0	0	0	9	0	8	2	0	1	0	1.000	0	0-0	0	16.33	15.00
	16 NYM	NL	41	0	0	11	43.2	195	41	24	23	8	2	1	3	21	2	46	1	2	0	0	-	0	0-1	7	4.78	4.74
	16 Pit	NL	28	0	0	0	24.0	102	19	13	11	3	0	2	1	11	1	28	5	2	3	0	1.000	0	0-1	8	3.40	4.13
	Postseason		6	0	0	0	2.2	11	2	0	0	0	1	0	0	1	0	4	0	0	0	0	-	0	0-0	1	2.01	0.00
	9 ML YEARS		419	5	0	93	393.0	1679	304	184	175	44	14	11	16	192	13	470	34	4	27	20	.574	0	12-26	95	3.32	4.01

Trevor Bauer

Pitches: R Bats: R Pos: SP-31; RP-1   Ht: 6'1" Wt: 190 Born: 1/17/1991 Age: 27

			HOW MUCH HE PITCHED						WHAT HE GAVE UP										THE RESULTS							
Year	Team	Lg	G	GS	CG	GF	IP	BFP	H	R	ER	HR	SH	SF	HB	TBB	IBB	SO	WP	Bk	W	L	Pct	Sh	Sv-Op	Hld	ERC	ERA
2012	Ari	NL	4	4	0	0	16.1	77	14	13	11	2	1	1	1	13	0	17	2	0	1	2	.333	0	0-0	0	5.12	6.06
2013	Cle	AL	4	4	0	0	17.0	81	15	11	10	3	0	1	1	16	0	11	1	0	1	2	.333	0	0-0	0	6.47	5.29
2014	Cle	AL	26	26	0	0	153.0	663	151	76	71	16	1	8	11	60	4	143	6	0	5	8	.385	0	0-0	0	4.27	4.18
2015	Cle	AL	31	30	1	1	176.0	744	152	90	89	23	4	1	5	79	1	170	7	1	11	12	.478	0	0-0	0	3.86	4.55
2016	Cle	AL	35	28	1	3	190.0	811	179	96	90	20	4	7	9	70	1	168	3	0	12	8	.600	0	0-0	0	3.85	4.26
2017	Cle	AL	32	31	0	0	176.1	749	181	84	82	25	1	3	5	60	0	196	3	1	17	9	.654	0	0-0	0	4.46	4.19
	Postseason		5	4	0	1	13.2	61	18	8	8	3	0	1	0	4	0	17	0	0	0	2	.000	0	0-0	0	6.49	5.27
	6 ML YEARS		132	123	2	5	728.2	3125	692	370	353	89	11	21	32	298	6	705	22	2	47	41	.534	0	0-0	0	4.17	4.36

Buddy Baumann

Pitches: L Bats: L Pos: RP-23   Ht: 5'11" Wt: 198 Born: 12/9/1987 Age: 30

Year	Team	Lg	G	GS	CG	GF	IP	BFP	H	R	ER	HR	SH	SF	HB	TBB	IBB	SO	WP	Bk	W	L	Pct	Sh	Sv-Op	Hld	ERC	ERA
2013	Omha	AAA	30	0	0	11	49.0	219	49	15	15	5	2	2	1	23	2	66	2	0	3	0	1.000	0	1- -	-	4.29	2.76
2014	Omha	AAA	40	1	0	13	90.1	378	85	35	32	6	2	6	2	31	1	68	0	1	2	4	.333	0	2- -	-	3.41	3.19
2015	Omha	AAA	34	6	0	9	77.0	328	65	29	26	5	3	2	8	25	2	84	5	0	3	4	.429	0	3- -	-	3.01	3.04
2016	ElPaso	AAA	24	0	0	7	28.2	117	22	10	10	3	1	0	1	12	0	31	2	0	1	1	.500	0	2- -	-	3.12	3.14
2016	SD	NL	11	0	0	2	9.2	40	7	4	4	0	0	0	1	4	0	10	0	0	1	0	1.000	0	0-0	2	2.41	3.72
2017	SD	NL	23	0	0	2	17.2	72	11	5	5	4	0	0	3	7	2	21	0	0	2	1	.667	0	0-1	4	3.38	2.55
	2 ML YEARS		34	0	0	4	27.1	112	18	9	9	4	0	0	4	11	2	31	0	0	3	1	.750	0	0-1	6	3.04	2.96

Jose Bautista

Bats: R Throws: R Pos: RF-143;DH-11;3B-8;PH-2;1B-1   bah-TEE-stah   Ht: 6'0" Wt: 205 Born: 10/19/1980 Age: 37

Year	Team	Lg	G	AB	H	2B	3B	HR	(Hm	Rd)	TB	R	RBI	RC	TBB	IBB	SO	HBP	SH	SF	SB	CS	GDP	Avg	OBP	Slg	OPS
2004	4 Tms		64	88	18	3	0	0	(0	0)	21	6	2	2	7	0	40	0	1	0	0	1	1	.205	.263	.239	.502
2005	Pit	NL	11	28	4	1	0	0	(0	0)	5	3	1	0	3	0	7	0	0	0	1	0	2	.143	.226	.179	.404
2006	Pit	NL	117	400	94	20	3	16	(11	5)	168	58	51	55	46	2	110	16	3	4	2	4	12	.235	.335	.420	.755
2007	Pit	NL	142	532	135	36	2	15	(8	7)	220	75	63	71	68	1	101	4	4	6	6	3	16	.254	.339	.414	.753
2008	2 Tms		128	370	88	17	0	15	(5	10)	150	45	54	43	40	5	91	2	4	1	1	1	12	.238	.313	.405	.718
2009	Tor	AL	113	336	79	13	3	13	(5	8)	137	54	40	42	56	1	85	4	6	2	4	0	9	.235	.349	.408	.757
2010	Tor	AL	161	569	148	35	3	54	(33	21)	351	109	124	132	100	2	116	10	0	4	9	2	10	.260	.378	.617	.995
2011	Tor	AL	149	513	155	24	2	43	(20	23)	312	105	103	133	132	24	111	6	0	4	9	5	8	.302	.447	.608	1.056
2012	Tor	AL	92	332	80	14	0	27	(11	16)	175	64	65	58	59	2	63	4	0	4	5	2	11	.241	.358	.527	.886
2013	Tor	AL	118	452	117	24	0	28	(14	14)	225	82	73	81	69	2	84	3	0	4	7	2	13	.259	.358	.498	.856
2014	Tor	AL	155	553	158	27	0	35	(18	17)	290	101	103	112	104	11	96	9	1	6	6	2	19	.286	.403	.524	.928
2015	Tor	AL	153	543	136	29	3	40	(23	17)	291	108	114	113	110	2	106	5	0	8	8	2	19	.250	.377	.536	.913
2016	Tor	AL	116	423	99	24	1	22	(10	12)	191	68	69	75	87	1	103	3	0	4	2	2	21	.234	.366	.452	.817
2017	Tor	AL	157	587	119	27	0	23	(10	13)	215	92	65	69	84	3	170	8	0	7	6	3	16	.203	.308	.366	.674
04	Bal	AL	16	11	3	0	0	0	(0	0)	3	3	0	1	1	0	3	0	0	0	0	0	0	.273	.333	.273	.606
04	TB	AL	12	12	2	0	0	0	(0	0)	2	1	1	0	3	0	7	0	0	0	0	1	0	.167	.333	.167	.500
04	KC	AL	13	25	5	1	0	0	(0	0)	6	1	1	0	1	0	12	0	0	0	0	0	0	.200	.231	.240	.471
04	Pit	NL	23	40	8	2	0	0	(0	0)	10	1	0	1	2	0	18	0	1	0	0	0	1	.200	.238	.250	.488
08	Pit	NL	107	314	76	15	0	12	(3	9)	127	38	44	39	38	4	77	2	6	3	1	1	10	.242	.325	.404	.729
08	Tor	AL	21	56	12	2	0	3	(2	1)	23	7	10	4	2	1	14	0	2	1	0	0	2	.214	.237	.411	.648
	Postseason		20	74	18	4	0	6	(3	3)	40	12	16	17	14	0	19	0	0	0	0	0	1	.243	.364	.541	.904
	14 ML YEARS		1676	5726	1430	294	17	331	(168	163)	2751	970	927	986	965	56	1283	74	23	57	66	29	168	.250	.362	.480	.842

Rafael Bautista

Bats: R Throws: R Pos: RF-11;PH-6;PR-2;LF-1;CF-1   bow-TEE-stah   Ht: 6'2" Wt: 165 Born: 3/8/1993 Age: 25

Year	Team	Lg	G	AB	H	2B	3B	HR	(Hm	Rd)	TB	R	RBI	RC	TBB	IBB	SO	HBP	SH	SF	SB	CS	GDP	Avg	OBP	Slg	OPS
2013	Nats	R	52	202	65	7	2	1	(-	-)	79	44	27	36	18	0	34	9	5	1	26	7	2	.322	.400	.391	.791
2014	Hgrstn	A	134	487	141	20	5	5	(-	-)	186	97	54	74	33	0	72	8	10	5	69	15	4	.290	.341	.382	.723
2015	3 Tms	Low	66	255	70	10	2	1	(-	-)	87	32	14	31	12	0	30	4	3	2	26	4	3	.275	.315	.341	.656
2016	Hrsbrg	AA	136	543	153	12	4	4	(-	-)	185	77	39	75	45	0	94	8	8	3	56	10	5	.282	.344	.341	.685
2017	Syrcse	AAA	43	176	44	9	1	0	(-	-)	55	23	11	16	9	0	26	1	2	0	7	4	2	.250	.290	.313	.603
2017	Nats	R	13	44	13	2	1	0	(-	-)	17	7	3	7	5	0	5	3	0	0	2	1	0	.295	.404	.386	.790
2017	Was	NL	17	25	4	0	0	0	(0	0)	4	2	1	2	0	5	0	0	1	.160	.222	.160	.382

Pedro Beato

Pitches: R Bats: R Pos: RP-1   bay-AH-toh   Ht: 6'6" Wt: 230 Born: 10/27/1986 Age: 31

Year	Team	Lg	G	GS	CG	GF	IP	BFP	H	R	ER	HR	SH	SF	HB	TBB	IBB	SO	WP	Bk	W	L	Pct	Sh	Sv-Op	Hld	ERC	ERA
2017	LV*	AAA	52	0	0	48	55.2	228	41	17	17	4	0	2	3	20	1	42	5	0	1	3	.250	0	33- -	-	2.52	2.75
2011	NYM	NL	60	0	0	7	67.0	283	59	41	32	5	2	4	4	27	3	39	1	0	2	1	.667	0	0-1	11	3.45	4.30
2012	2 Tms		11	0	0	2	12.0	51	11	9	9	1	0	0	1	5	0	12	1	0	1	0	1.000	0	0-0	1	3.96	6.75
2013	Bos	AL	10	0	0	5	10.0	46	12	5	4	1	0	0	1	2	0	5	0	0	1	1	.500	0	0-0	-	4.58	3.60
2014	Atl	NL	3	0	0	1	4.1	19	3	0	0	0	0	0	0	3	0	3	0	0	0	0	-	0	0-0	0	2.74	0.00
2017	Phi	NL	1	0	0	0	0.2	2	0	0	0	0	0	0	0	0	0	1	0	0	0	0	-	0	0-0	0	0.00	0.00
12	NYM	NL	7	0	0	2	4.1	20	5	5	5	1	0	0	0	2	0	5	1	0	0	0	-	0	0-0	1	6.09	10.38
12	Bos	AL	4	0	0	0	7.2	31	6	4	4	0	0	0	1	3	0	7	0	0	1	0	1.000	0	0-0	0	2.83	4.70
	5 ML YEARS		85	0	0	15	94.0	401	85	55	45	7	2	4	6	37	3	60	2	0	4	2	.667	0	0-1	12	3.55	4.31

Chris Beck

Pitches: R Bats: R Pos: RP-57   Ht: 6'3" Wt: 225 Born: 9/4/1990 Age: 27

Year	Team	Lg	G	GS	CG	GF	IP	BFP	H	R	ER	HR	SH	SF	HB	TBB	IBB	SO	WP	Bk	W	L	Pct	Sh	Sv-Op	Hld	ERC	ERA
2017	Charllt*	AAA	5	0	0	2	8.0	33	6	2	2	1	0	0	4	1	6	1	0	1	0	1.000	0	1- -	-	3.13	2.25
2015	CWS	AL	1	1	0	0	6.0	31	10	5	4	0	1	0	0	4	0	3	0	0	0	1	.000	0	0-0	0	8.52	6.00
2016	CWS	AL	25	0	0	4	25.1	123	31	18	18	3	0	1	2	17	1	20	0	0	2	2	.500	0	0-1	5	6.95	6.39
2017	CWS	AL	57	0	0	12	64.2	294	73	48	46	16	1	3	4	34	3	42	1	0	2	1	.667	0	0-1	3	6.81	6.40
	3 ML YEARS		83	1	0	16	96.0	448	114	71	68	19	2	4	6	55	4	65	1	0	4	4	.500	0	0-2	8	6.97	6.38

Gordon Beckham

Bats: R **Throws:** R **Pos:** 2B-5;SS-4;PR-2;3B-1;PH-1   **Ht:** 6'0" **Wt:** 190 **Born:** 9/16/1986 **Age:** 31

Year	Team	Lg	G	AB	H	2B	3B	HR	(Hm	Rd)	TB	R	RBI	RC	TBB	IBB	SO	HBP	SH	SF	SB	CS	GDP	Avg	OBP	Slg	OPS
2017	Tacom*	AAA	83	328	86	16	0	9	(-	-)	129	37	45	41	20	1	58	5	0	2	3	2	9	.262	.313	.393	.706
2009	CWS	AL	103	378	102	28	1	14	(4	10)	174	58	63	61	41	0	65	6	1	4	7	4	10	.270	.347	.460	.808
2010	CWS	AL	131	444	112	25	2	9	(7	2)	168	58	49	52	37	0	92	7	6	4	4	6	9	.252	.317	.378	.695
2011	CWS	AL	150	499	115	23	0	10	(7	3)	168	60	44	48	35	0	111	13	7	3	5	3	6	.230	.296	.337	.633
2012	CWS	AL	151	525	123	24	0	16	(12	4)	195	62	60	58	40	0	89	7	8	2	5	4	10	.234	.296	.371	.668
2013	CWS	AL	103	371	99	22	1	5	(3	2)	138	46	24	36	28	2	56	4	1	4	5	1	10	.267	.322	.372	.694
2014	2 Tms	AL	127	446	101	27	0	9	(4	5)	155	53	44	32	22	2	81	7	3	5	3	0	17	.226	.271	.348	.618
2015	CWS	AL	100	211	44	8	0	6	(3	3)	70	24	20	17	19	1	43	2	1	4	0	1	6	.209	.275	.332	.607
2016	2 Tms	NL	88	245	52	16	1	5	(2	3)	85	25	31	22	26	1	52	4	0	4	1	0	12	.212	.294	.347	.641
2017	Sea	AL	11	17	3	0	0	0	(0	0)	3	2	0	0	1	0	2	0	0	0	1	0	2	.176	.222	.176	.399
14	CWS	AL	101	390	86	24	0	7	(3	4)	131	43	36	28	19	1	70	5	3	5	3	0	12	.221	.263	.336	.598
14	LAA	AL	26	56	15	3	0	2	(1	1)	24	10	8	4	3	1	11	2	0	0	0	0	5	.268	.328	.429	.756
16	Atl	NL	85	240	52	16	1	5	(2	3)	85	25	30	22	26	1	50	4	0	3	1	0	12	.217	.300	.354	.655
16	SF	NL	3	5	0	0	0	0	(0	0)	0	0	1	0	0	0	2	0	0	1	0	0	0	.000	.000	.000	.000
	Postseason		2	1	0	0	0	0	(0	0)	0	0	0	0	0	0	1	1	0	0	0	0	0	.000	.500	.000	.500
	9 ML YEARS		964	3136	751	173	5	74	(42	32)	1156	388	335	326	249	6	591	50	27	30	31	19	82	.239	.303	.369	.672

Tim Beckham

Bats: R **Throws:** R **Pos:** SS-119;2B-17;3B-1;DH-1;PH-1   **Ht:** 6'1" **Wt:** 205 **Born:** 1/27/1990 **Age:** 28

Year	Team	Lg	G	AB	H	2B	3B	HR	(Hm	Rd)	TB	R	RBI	RC	TBB	IBB	SO	HBP	SH	SF	SB	CS	GDP	Avg	OBP	Slg	OPS
2013	TB	AL	5	7	3	0	0	0	(0	0)	3	1	1	1	0	0	0	0	0	1	0	0	0	.429	.375	.429	.804
2015	TB	AL	83	203	45	7	4	9	(3	6)	87	24	37	26	13	0	69	3	0	4	3	1	3	.222	.274	.429	.702
2016	TB	AL	64	198	49	12	5	5	(1	4)	86	25	16	23	14	0	67	1	2	0	2	1	3	.247	.300	.434	.735
2017	2 Tms	AL	137	533	148	18	5	22	(9	13)	242	67	62	81	36	0	167	4	1	1	6	5	10	.278	.328	.454	.782
17	TB	AL	87	317	82	5	3	12	(5	7)	129	31	36	39	24	0	110	2	1	1	5	4	8	.259	.314	.407	.721
17	Bal	AL	50	216	66	13	2	10	(4	6)	113	36	26	42	12	0	57	2	0	0	1	1	2	.306	.348	.523	.871
	4 ML YEARS		289	941	245	37	14	36	(13	23)	418	117	116	131	63	0	303	8	3	6	11	7	16	.260	.310	.444	.755

Cam Bedrosian

Pitches: R **Bats:** R **Pos:** RP-48   beh-DROH-zhee-ann   **Ht:** 6'0" **Wt:** 230 **Born:** 10/2/1991 **Age:** 26

Year	Team	Lg	G	GS	CG	GF	IP	BFP	H	R	ER	HR	SH	SF	HB	TBB	IBB	SO	WP	Bk	W	L	Pct	Sh	Sv-Op	Hld	ERC	ERA
2014	LAA	AL	17	0	0	4	19.1	93	23	17	14	2	0	1	0	12	1	20	1	1	0	1	.000	0	0-1	1	5.88	6.52
2015	LAA	AL	34	0	0	10	33.1	156	40	21	20	3	1	2	2	19	2	34	2	0	1	0	1.000	0	0-0	1	6.05	5.40
2016	LAA	AL	45	0	0	9	40.1	162	30	7	5	1	0	1	2	14	1	51	3	0	2	0	1.000	0	1-2	7	2.25	1.12
2017	LAA	AL	48	0	0	13	44.2	190	41	26	22	5	1	1	0	17	1	53	7	0	6	5	.545	0	6-11	10	3.56	4.43
	4 ML YEARS		144	0	0	36	137.2	601	134	71	61	11	2	5	4	62	5	158	13	1	9	6	.600	0	7-14	19	4.02	3.99

Matt Belisle

Pitches: R **Bats:** R **Pos:** RP-62   bell-EYE-el   **Ht:** 6'3" **Wt:** 230 **Born:** 6/6/1980 **Age:** 38

Year	Team	Lg	G	GS	CG	GF	IP	BFP	H	R	ER	HR	SH	SF	HB	TBB	IBB	SO	WP	Bk	W	L	Pct	Sh	Sv-Op	Hld	ERC	ERA
2003	Cin	NL	6	0	0	2	8.2	39	10	5	5	1	2	1	1	2	0	6	0	0	1	1	.500	0	0-1	0	4.73	5.19
2005	Cin	NL	60	5	0	17	85.2	382	101	49	42	11	4	2	6	26	6	59	3	0	4	8	.333	0	1-4	8	5.08	4.41
2006	Cin	NL	30	2	0	5	40.0	180	43	18	16	5	1	2	3	19	1	26	3	0	2	0	1.000	0	0-1	0	5.29	3.60
2007	Cin	NL	30	30	1	0	177.2	771	212	111	105	26	7	9	7	43	4	125	6	1	8	9	.471	0	0-0	0	5.05	5.32
2008	Cin	NL	6	6	0	0	29.2	142	47	27	24	4	1	2	0	6	0	14	2	0	1	4	.200	0	0-0	0	6.87	7.28
2009	Col	NL	24	0	0	6	31.0	133	35	21	19	6	0	2	1	5	1	22	1	0	3	1	.750	0	0-0	1	4.50	5.52
2010	Col	NL	76	0	0	11	92.0	365	84	34	30	7	4	2	2	16	5	91	3	1	7	5	.583	0	1-2	21	2.67	2.93
2011	Col	NL	74	0	0	10	72.0	301	77	33	26	5	4	0	4	14	3	58	2	0	10	4	.714	0	0-7	14	3.65	3.25
2012	Col	NL	80	0	0	14	80.0	348	91	36	33	5	4	0	3	18	6	69	1	1	3	8	.273	0	3-10	26	3.87	3.71
2013	Col	NL	72	0	0	16	73.0	301	76	37	35	6	1	2	1	15	2	62	3	0	5	7	.417	0	0-5	24	3.42	4.32
2014	Col	NL	66	1	0	13	64.2	282	74	35	35	4	4	5	1	19	2	43	3	0	4	7	.364	0	0-2	6	4.31	4.87
2015	StL	NL	34	0	0	10	33.2	149	34	10	10	1	2	1	3	15	2	25	0	0	1	1	.500	0	0-1	7	4.05	2.67
2016	Was	NL	40	0	0	6	46.0	186	43	13	9	2	1	1	1	7	3	32	2	0	0	0	—	0	0-0	4	2.43	1.76
2017	Min	NL	62	0	0	20	60.1	247	48	31	27	7	2	1	2	22	6	54	2	1	2	2	.500	0	9-14	17	2.95	4.03
	Postseason		2	0	0	0	2.0	7	0	0	0	0	0	0	0	1	0	2	0	0	0	0	—	0	0-0	1	0.27	0.00
	14 ML YEARS		660	44	1	130	894.1	3826	975	460	416	91	38	29	34	227	41	686	31	4	51	57	.472	0	14-47	128	4.10	4.19

Jeff Beliveau

Pitches: L **Bats:** L **Pos:** RP-19   BELL-iv-oh   **Ht:** 6'1" **Wt:** 190 **Born:** 1/17/1987 **Age:** 31

Year	Team	Lg	G	GS	CG	GF	IP	BFP	H	R	ER	HR	SH	SF	HB	TBB	IBB	SO	WP	Bk	W	L	Pct	Sh	Sv-Op	Hld	ERC	ERA
2017	Buffalo*	AAA	29	1	0	4	50.1	207	34	18	17	5	1	2	2	26	1	60	1	0	4	1	.800	0	2- -	—	2.94	3.04
2012	ChC	NL	22	0	0	4	17.2	86	21	9	9	5	1	0	1	12	1	17	1	1	1	0	1.000	0	0-0	1	7.98	4.58
2013	TB	AL	1	0	0	0	0.2	4	1	0	0	0	0	0	0	1	0	0	0	0	0	0	—	0	0-0	0	10.76	0.00
2014	TB	AL	30	0	0	6	24.0	100	19	7	7	1	1	2	7	1	28	1	1	0	0	—	0	1-1	6	2.40	2.63
2015	TB	AL	5	0	0	0	2.2	15	6	4	4	1	0	0	1	0	2	0	0	0	0	—	0	0-0	1	14.72	13.50
2017	Tor	AL	19	0	0	6	15.2	70	17	14	13	4	1	2	1	6	1	17	0	0	1	1	.500	0	0-0	1	5.77	7.47
	5 ML YEARS		77	0	0	16	60.2	275	64	34	33	11	3	3	4	27	3	64	2	2	2	1	.667	0	1-1	10	5.28	4.90

Chad Bell

Pitches: L Bats: R Pos: RP-24; SP-4 　　　　Ht: 6'3" Wt: 200 Born: 2/28/1989 Age: 29

		HOW MUCH HE PITCHED					WHAT HE GAVE UP													THE RESULTS							
Year Team	Lg	G	GS	CG	GF	IP	BFP	H	R	ER	HR	SH	SF	HB	TBB	IBB	SO	WP	Bk	W	L	Pct	Sh	Sv-Op	Hld	ERC	ERA
2014 2 Tms	Low	19	19	1	0	87.2	376	97	38	36	9	3	3	2	27	0	50	0	0	8	3	.727	0	0--	-	4.48	3.70
2015 Frisco	AA	27	23	0	1	141.1	608	154	83	72	11	2	4	5	42	1	118	3	2	7	13	.350	0	0--	-	4.17	4.58
2016 RdRck	AAA	5	2	0	0	18.0	67	12	4	3	0	0	0	0	5	0	19	1	0	1	0	1.000	0	0--	-	1.54	1.50
2016 Toledo	AAA	28	10	0	4	80.1	346	79	34	33	4	2	0	1	38	5	69	3	0	10	4	.714	0	0--	-	3.91	3.70
2017 Toledo	AAA	7	7	0	0	34.1	141	34	15	13	3	0	1	1	10	0	31	1	0	2	4	.333	0	0--	-	3.75	3.41
2017 Det	AL	28	4	0	6	62.1	293	81	49	48	12	0	0	3	31	3	57	1	0	0	3	.000	0	0-0	1	7.21	6.93

Josh Bell

Bats: B Throws: R Pos: 1B-147;PH-17;DH-2 　　　　Ht: 6'2" Wt: 230 Born: 8/14/1992 Age: 25

								BATTING												RUNNING			AVERAGES			
Year Team	Lg	G	AB	H	2B	3B	HR	(Hm	Rd)	TB	R	RBI	RC	TBB	IBB	SO	HBP	SH	SF	SB	CS	GDP	Avg	OBP	Slg	OPS
2013 WV	A	119	459	128	37	2	13	(-	-)	208	75	76	76	52	1	90	3	0	5	1	2	10	.279	.353	.453	.806
2014 Bradtn	A+	84	331	111	20	4	9	(-	-)	166	45	53	62	25	1	43	2	4	1	5	4	11	.335	.384	.502	.886
2014 Altna	AA	24	94	27	2	0	0	(-	-)	29	13	7	11	8	0	12	0	0	0	4	1	1	.287	.343	.309	.652
2015 Altna	AA	96	368	113	17	6	5	(-	-)	157	47	60	63	44	4	50	2	3	9	7	4	11	.307	.376	.427	.803
2015 Indy	AAA	35	121	42	7	3	2	(-	-)	61	20	18	28	21	2	15	1	0	2	2	0	4	.347	.441	.504	.946
2016 Indy	AAA	114	421	124	23	4	14	(-	-)	197	57	60	76	57	8	74	4	0	2	3	7	17	.295	.382	.468	.850
2016 Pit	NL	45	128	35	8	0	3	(2	1)	52	18	19	18	21	0	19	0	0	3	0	1	4	.273	.368	.406	.775
2017 Pit	NL	159	549	140	26	6	26	(11	15)	256	75	90	86	66	4	117	1	0	4	2	4	15	.255	.334	.466	.800
2 ML YEARS		204	677	175	34	6	29	(13	16)	308	93	109	104	87	4	136	1	0	7	2	5	19	.258	.341	.455	.796

Cody Bellinger

Bats: L Throws: L Pos: 1B-93;LF-39;RF-5;CF-4;PH-4;DH-1 　　　　Ht: 6'4" Wt: 210 Born: 7/13/1995 Age: 22

								BATTING												RUNNING			AVERAGES			
Year Team	Lg	G	AB	H	2B	3B	HR	(Hm	Rd)	TB	R	RBI	RC	TBB	IBB	SO	HBP	SH	SF	SB	CS	GDP	Avg	OBP	Slg	OPS
2013 Ddgrs	R	47	162	34	9	6	1	(-	-)	58	25	30	21	31	0	46	1	1	0	3	3	0	.210	.340	.358	.698
2014 2 Tms	Low	51	215	67	14	6	3	(-	-)	102	51	34	37	15	0	40	0	0	3	8	0	6	.312	.352	.474	.826
2015 Rcuca	A+	128	478	126	33	4	30	(-	-)	257	97	103	89	52	1	150	4	2	8	10	2	7	.264	.336	.538	.873
2016 Tulsa	AA	114	399	105	17	1	23	(-	-)	193	61	65	73	59	2	94	3	0	4	8	2	2	.263	.359	.484	.843
2017 OkCity	AAA	18	67	23	4	0	5	(-	-)	42	15	15	18	9	1	22	1	0	0	7	0	0	.343	.429	.627	1.055
2017 LAD	NL	132	480	128	26	4	39	(19	20)	279	87	97	94	64	13	146	1	0	3	10	3	5	.267	.352	.581	.933

Brandon Belt

Bats: L Throws: L Pos: 1B-98;LF-15;PH-3;RF-1 　　　　Ht: 6'5" Wt: 220 Born: 4/20/1988 Age: 30

								BATTING												RUNNING			AVERAGES			
Year Team	Lg	G	AB	H	2B	3B	HR	(Hm	Rd)	TB	R	RBI	RC	TBB	IBB	SO	HBP	SH	SF	SB	CS	GDP	Avg	OBP	Slg	OPS
2011 SF	NL	63	187	42	6	1	9	(2	7)	77	21	18	20	20	1	57	2	0	0	3	2	3	.225	.306	.412	.718
2012 SF	NL	145	411	113	27	6	7	(5	2)	173	47	56	63	54	5	106	3	0	4	12	2	3	.275	.360	.421	.781
2013 SF	NL	150	509	147	39	4	17	(6	11)	245	76	67	82	52	4	125	6	1	3	5	3	4	.289	.360	.481	.841
2014 SF	NL	61	214	52	8	0	12	(2	10)	96	30	27	24	18	2	64	2	0	1	3	1	4	.243	.306	.449	.755
2015 SF	NL	137	492	138	33	5	18	(5	13)	235	73	68	78	56	2	147	4	0	4	9	3	3	.280	.356	.478	.834
2016 SF	NL	156	542	149	41	8	17	(6	11)	257	77	82	105	104	4	148	5	0	4	0	4	7	.275	.394	.474	.868
2017 SF	NL	104	382	92	27	3	18	(8	10)	179	63	51	60	66	2	104	2	0	1	3	2	5	.241	.355	.469	.823
Postseason		37	127	29	2	2	2	(1	1)	41	14	13	16	21	1	40	0	0	3	1	2	0	.228	.331	.323	.654
7 ML YEARS		816	2737	733	181	27	98	(34	64)	1262	387	369	432	370	20	751	24	1	17	35	16	29	.268	.358	.461	.819

Carlos Beltran

Bats: B Throws: R Pos: DH-107;LF-13;PH-11;RF-1 　　BELL-trahn　　Ht: 6'1" Wt: 215 Born: 4/24/1977 Age: 41

								BATTING												RUNNING			AVERAGES			
Year Team	Lg	G	AB	H	2B	3B	HR	(Hm	Rd)	TB	R	RBI	RC	TBB	IBB	SO	HBP	SH	SF	SB	CS	GDP	Avg	OBP	Slg	OPS
1998 KC	AL	14	58	16	5	3	0	(0	0)	27	12	7	9	3	0	12	1	0	1	3	0	2	.276	.317	.466	.783
1999 KC	AL	156	663	194	27	7	22	(12	10)	301	112	108	100	46	2	123	4	0	10	27	8	17	.293	.337	.454	.791
2000 KC	AL	98	372	92	15	4	7	(4	3)	136	49	44	43	35	2	69	0	2	4	13	0	12	.247	.309	.366	.675
2001 KC	AL	155	617	189	32	12	24	(7	17)	317	106	101	118	52	2	120	5	1	5	31	1	7	.306	.362	.514	.876
2002 KC	AL	162	637	174	44	7	29	(19	10)	319	114	105	117	71	1	135	4	3	7	35	7	12	.273	.346	.501	.847
2003 KC	AL	141	521	160	14	10	26	(10	16)	272	102	100	117	72	4	81	2	0	7	41	4	8	.307	.389	.522	.911
2004 2 Tms		159	599	160	36	9	38	(15	23)	328	121	104	124	92	10	101	7	3	7	42	3	8	.267	.367	.548	.915
2005 NYM	NL	151	582	155	34	2	16	(6	10)	241	83	78	88	56	5	96	2	4	6	17	6	9	.266	.330	.414	.744
2006 NYM	NL	140	510	140	38	1	41	(15	26)	303	127	116	121	95	6	99	4	1	7	18	3	6	.275	.388	.594	.982
2007 NYM	NL	144	554	153	33	3	33	(11	22)	291	93	112	97	69	10	111	2	1	10	23	2	6	.276	.353	.525	.878
2008 NYM	NL	161	606	172	40	5	27	(14	13)	303	116	112	116	92	13	96	1	1	6	25	3	11	.284	.376	.500	.876
2009 NYM	NL	81	308	100	22	1	10	(3	7)	154	50	48	54	47	10	43	1	0	1	11	1	9	.325	.415	.500	.915
2010 NYM	NL	64	220	56	11	3	7	(3	4)	94	21	27	31	30	5	39	1	0	4	3	1	4	.255	.341	.427	.768
2011 2 Tms	NL	142	520	156	39	6	22	(14	8)	273	78	84	96	71	7	88	3	0	4	4	2	18	.300	.385	.525	.910
2012 StL	NL	151	547	147	26	1	32	(20	12)	271	83	97	87	65	15	124	2	1	4	13	6	9	.269	.346	.495	.842
2013 StL	NL	145	554	164	30	3	24	(12	12)	272	79	84	91	38	1	90	1	1	2	2	1	12	.296	.339	.491	.830
2014 NYY	AL	109	403	94	23	0	15	(11	4)	162	46	49	44	37	2	80	4	0	5	3	1	11	.233	.301	.402	.703
2015 NYY	AL	133	478	132	34	1	19	(10	9)	245	57	67	69	45	2	85	2	0	6	0	0	12	.276	.337	.471	.808
2016 2 Tms	AL	151	552	163	33	0	29	(19	10)	283	73	93	84	35	4	101	2	0	4	1	0	19	.295	.337	.513	.850
2017 Hou	AL	129	467	108	29	0	14	(8	6)	179	60	51	43	33	3	102	3	0	6	0	0	9	.231	.283	.383	.666
04 KC	AL	69	266	74	19	2	15	(8	7)	142	51	51	57	37	7	44	2	1	3	14	3	4	.278	.367	.534	.901
04 Hou	NL	90	333	86	17	7	23	(7	16)	186	70	53	67	55	3	57	5	2	4	28	0	4	.258	.368	.559	.926
11 NYM	NL	98	353	102	30	2	15	(9	6)	181	61	66	72	60	6	61	2	0	4	3	0	9	.289	.391	.513	.904
11 SF	NL	44	167	54	9	4	7	(5	2)	92	17	18	24	11	1	27	1	0	0	1	2	9	.323	.369	.551	.920

		BATTING															RUNNING			AVERAGES			
Year Team	Lg	G	AB	H	2B	3B	HR	(Hm Rd)	TB	R	RBI	RC	TBB	IBB	SO	HBP	SH	SF	SB	CS	GDP	Avg	OBP	Slg	OPS
16 NYY	AL	99	359	109	42	9	0	7	(14 8)	196	50	64	55	22	3	70	2	0	4	0	0	13	.304	.344	.546	.890
16 Tex	AL	52	193	54	12	0	7	(5 2)	87	23	29	29	13	1	31	0	0	0	1	0	6	.280	.325	.451	.776
Postseason		55	195	63	13	1	16	(7 9)	126	45	41	53	36	2	27	2	1	1	11	0	3	.323	.432	.646	1.078
20 ML YEARS		2586	9768	2725	565	78	435	(213 222)	4751	1582	1587	1649	1084	104	1795	51	18	110	312	49	203	.279	.350	.486	.837

Adrian Beltre

Bats: R **Throws:** R **Pos:** 3B-65;DH-28;PH-1 **Ht:** 5'11" **Wt:** 220 **Born:** 4/7/1979 **Age:** 39

		BATTING															RUNNING			AVERAGES			
Year Team	Lg	G	AB	H	2B	3B	HR	(Hm Rd)	TB	R	RBI	RC	TBB	IBB	SO	HBP	SH	SF	SB	CS	GDP	Avg	OBP	Slg	OPS
1998 LAD	NL	77	195	42	9	0	7	(5 2)	72	18	22	20	14	0	37	3	2	0	3	1	4	.215	.278	.369	.648
1999 LAD	NL	152	538	148	27	5	15	(6 9)	230	84	67	84	61	12	105	6	4	5	18	7	4	.275	.352	.428	.780
2000 LAD	NL	138	510	148	30	2	20	(7 13)	242	71	85	85	56	2	80	2	3	4	12	5	13	.290	.360	.475	.835
2001 LAD	NL	126	475	126	22	4	13	(4 9)	195	59	60	60	28	1	82	5	2	5	13	4	9	.265	.310	.411	.720
2002 LAD	NL	159	587	151	26	5	21	(7 14)	250	70	75	74	37	4	96	4	1	6	7	5	17	.257	.303	.426	.729
2003 LAD	NL	158	559	134	30	2	23	(13 10)	237	50	80	66	37	4	103	5	1	6	2	2	13	.240	.290	.424	.714
2004 LAD	NL	156	598	200	32	0	48	(23 25)	376	104	121	120	53	9	87	2	0	4	7	2	15	.334	.388	.629	1.017
2005 Sea	AL	156	603	154	36	1	19	(7 12)	249	69	87	75	38	6	108	5	0	4	3	1	15	.255	.303	.413	.716
2006 Sea	AL	156	620	166	39	4	25	(16 9)	288	88	89	85	47	4	118	10	1	3	11	5	15	.268	.328	.465	.792
2007 Sea	AL	149	595	164	41	2	26	(11 15)	287	87	99	79	38	2	104	2	0	4	14	2	18	.276	.319	.482	.802
2008 Sea	AL	143	556	148	29	1	25	(10 15)	254	74	77	71	50	10	90	2	0	4	8	2	11	.266	.327	.457	.784
2009 Sea	AL	111	449	119	27	0	8	(4 4)	170	54	44	47	19	1	74	7	0	2	13	2	19	.265	.304	.379	.683
2010 Bos	AL	154	589	189	49	2	28	(13 15)	326	84	102	103	40	10	82	5	0	7	2	1	25	.321	.365	.553	.919
2011 Tex	AL	124	487	144	33	0	32	(23 9)	273	82	105	80	25	0	53	5	0	8	1	1	13	.296	.331	.561	.892
2012 Tex	AL	156	604	194	33	2	36	(20 16)	339	95	102	109	36	8	82	5	0	9	1	0	8	.321	.359	.561	.921
2013 Tex	AL	161	631	199	32	0	30	(15 15)	321	88	92	97	50	12	78	7	0	2	1	0	15	.315	.371	.509	.880
2014 Tex	AL	148	549	178	33	1	19	(11 8)	270	79	77	99	57	13	74	3	0	5	1	1	15	.324	.388	.492	.879
2015 Tex	AL	143	567	163	32	4	18	(13 5)	257	83	83	83	41	4	65	3	0	8	1	0	18	.287	.334	.453	.788
2016 Tex	AL	153	583	175	31	1	32	(14 18)	304	89	104	108	48	6	66	6	0	3	1	1	10	.300	.358	.521	.879
2017 Tex	AL	94	340	106	22	1	17	(7 10)	181	47	71	71	39	2	52	4	0	6	1	0	7	.312	.383	.532	.915
Postseason		28	111	29	6	0	5	(1 4)	50	16	11	11	4	1	25	2	0	1	0	0	2	.261	.297	.450	.747
20 ML YEARS		2814	10635	3048	613	37	462	(229 233)	5121	1475	1642	1616	814	110	1636	91	14	95	120	42	266	.287	.340	.482	.821

Andrew Benintendi

Bats: L **Throws:** L **Pos:** LF-123;CF-30;PH-8 **Ht:** 5'10" **Wt:** 170 **Born:** 7/6/1994 **Age:** 23

		BATTING															RUNNING			AVERAGES			
Year Team	Lg	G	AB	H	2B	3B	HR	(Hm Rd)	TB	R	RBI	RC	TBB	IBB	SO	HBP	SH	SF	SB	CS	GDP	Avg	OBP	Slg	OPS
2015 2 Tms	Low	54	198	62	7	4	11	(- -)	110	36	31	46	35	2	24	2	1	3	10	3	4	.313	.416	.556	.972
2016 Salem	A+	34	135	46	13	7	1	(- -)	76	30	32	31	15	2	9	3	0	2	8	2	3	.341	.413	.563	.976
2016 Portlnd	AA	63	237	70	18	5	8	(- -)	122	40	44	43	24	2	30	0	0	2	8	7	2	.295	.357	.515	.872
2016 Bos	AL	34	105	31	11	1	2	(0 2)	50	16	14	20	10	0	25	1	1	1	1	0	0	.295	.359	.476	.835
2017 Bos	AL	151	573	155	26	1	20	(7 13)	243	84	90	96	70	7	112	6	1	8	20	5	16	.271	.352	.424	.776
Postseason		3	9	3	1	0	1	(0 1)	7	1	2	1	0	0	1	0	0	0	0	0	1	.333	.333	.778	1.111
2 ML YEARS		185	678	186	37	2	22	(7 15)	293	100	104	116	80	7	137	7	2	9	21	5	16	.274	.353	.432	.785

Joaquin Benoit

Pitches: R **Bats:** R **Pos:** RP-52 ben-WAH **Ht:** 6'4" **Wt:** 250 **Born:** 7/26/1977 **Age:** 40

		HOW MUCH HE PITCHED						WHAT HE GAVE UP											THE RESULTS							
Year Team	Lg	G	GS	CG	GF	IP	BFP	H	R	ER	HR	SH	SF	HB	TBB	IBB	SO	WP	Bk	W	L	Pct	Sh	Sv-Op	Hld	ERC	ERA
2001 Tex	AL	1	1	0	0	5.0	26	8	6	6	3	0	1	0	3	0	4	0	0	0	0	-	0	0-0	0	13.11	10.80
2002 Tex	AL	17	13	0	2	84.2	405	91	51	50	6	4	3	5	58	2	59	7	0	4	5	.444	0	1-1	0	5.52	5.31
2003 Tex	AL	25	17	0	1	105.0	462	99	67	64	23	1	4	3	51	0	87	3	1	8	5	.615	0	0-0	0	5.03	5.49
2004 Tex	AL	28	15	0	2	103.0	456	113	67	65	19	2	10	8	31	0	95	3	0	3	5	.375	0	0-0	0	5.10	5.68
2005 Tex	AL	32	9	0	6	87.0	369	69	39	36	9	2	1	2	38	0	78	1	0	4	4	.500	0	0-0	5	3.15	3.72
2006 Tex	AL	56	0	0	7	79.2	347	68	49	43	5	0	3	3	38	4	85	3	0	1	1	.500	0	0-2	7	3.30	4.86
2007 Tex	AL	70	0	0	22	82.0	337	68	28	26	6	3	2	2	28	2	87	3	0	7	4	.636	0	6-13	19	2.83	2.85
2008 Tex	AL	44	0	0	8	45.0	209	40	28	25	6	2	0	0	35	2	43	3	0	3	2	.600	0	1-4	13	5.02	5.00
2010 TB	AL	63	0	0	16	60.1	217	30	10	9	6	0	2	0	11	1	75	1	0	1	2	.333	0	1-4	25	1.14	1.34
2011 Det	AL	66	0	0	13	61.0	241	47	22	20	5	1	5	2	17	1	63	3	0	4	3	.571	0	2-7	29	2.46	2.95
2012 Det	AL	73	0	0	18	71.0	288	59	31	29	14	3	3	1	22	2	84	2	0	5	3	.625	0	2-6	30	3.48	3.68
2013 Det	AL	66	0	0	43	67.0	265	47	15	15	5	4	0	1	22	2	73	2	0	4	1	.800	0	24-26	9	2.15	2.01
2014 SD	NL	53	0	0	17	54.1	205	28	10	9	3	2	2	1	14	2	64	3	1	4	2	.667	0	11-12	16	1.20	1.49
2015 SD	NL	67	0	0	11	65.1	254	36	17	17	7	2	1	2	23	1	63	2	0	6	5	.545	0	2-6	28	1.78	2.34
2016 2 Tms	AL	51	0	0	6	48.0	204	37	17	15	5	1	2	1	24	1	52	1	0	3	1	.750	0	1-4	18	3.26	2.81
2017 2 Tms	NL	52	0	0	13	50.1	213	43	28	26	7	0	1	1	22	1	46	1	0	1	6	.143	0	2-6	13	3.73	4.65
16 Sea	AL	26	0	0	2	24.1	111	20	16	14	4	1	1	1	15	1	28	1	0	1	1	.500	0	0-2	8	4.30	5.18
16 Tor	AL	25	0	0	4	23.2	93	17	1	1	1	0	1	0	9	0	24	0	0	2	0	1.000	0	1-2	10	2.25	0.38
17 Phi	NL	44	0	0	12	42.0	171	32	19	19	5	0	0	0	16	1	43	0	0	1	4	.200	0	2-5	13	2.83	4.07
17 Pit	NL	8	0	0	1	8.1	42	11	9	7	2	0	1	1	6	0	3	1	0	0	2	.000	0	0-1	0	9.20	7.56
Postseason		20	0	0	5	22.1	88	17	7	7	3	0	0	1	5	0	27	2	0	1	0	1.000	0	3-5	5	2.57	2.82
16 ML YEARS		764	55	0	185	1068.2	4498	883	485	455	129	27	40	32	437	21	1058	38	2	58	49	.542	0	53-91	212	3.37	3.83

Christian Bergman

Pitches: R Bats: R Pos: SP-8; RP-5   Ht: 6'1" Wt: 195 Born: 5/4/1988 Age: 30

Year	Team	Lg	G	GS	CG	GF	IP	BFP	H	R	ER	HR	SH	SF	HB	TBB	IBB	SO	WP	Bk	W	L	Pct	Sh	Sv-Op	Hld	ERC	ERA
2017	Tacom*	AAA	16	16	1	0	86.0	377	102	53	51	7	1	2	1	18	0	63	1	0	9	4	.692	1	0- -	-	4.26	5.34
2014	Col	NL	10	10	0	0	54.2	249	75	37	36	9	1	1	1	10	2	31	0	0	3	5	.375	0	0-0	0	5.74	5.93
2015	Col	NL	30	4	0	6	68.1	286	82	36	36	8	2	1	0	15	1	37	4	0	3	1	.750	0	0-0	0	4.75	4.74
2016	Col	NL	15	1	0	5	24.2	119	39	24	23	7	2	1	0	6	0	22	0	0	1	3	.250	0	0-1	0	8.27	8.39
2017	Sea	AL	13	8	0	2	54.0	230	61	31	30	12	4	1	3	15	1	33	0	0	4	5	.444	0	0-0	0	5.56	5.00
4 ML YEARS			68	23	0	13	201.2	884	257	128	125	36	9	4	4	46	4	123	4	0	11	14	.440	0	0-1	0	5.65	5.58

Jose Berrios

Pitches: R Bats: R Pos: SP-25; RP-1   beh-REE-ohs   Ht: 6'0" Wt: 185 Born: 5/27/1994 Age: 24

Year	Team	Lg	G	GS	CG	GF	IP	BFP	H	R	ER	HR	SH	SF	HB	TBB	IBB	SO	WP	Bk	W	L	Pct	Sh	Sv-Op	Hld	ERC	ERA
2013	Crpds	A	19	19	0	0	103.2	455	105	58	46	6	2	3	9	40	0	100	13	1	7	7	.500	0	0- -	-	4.12	3.99
2014	FtMyrs	A+	16	16	1	0	96.0	389	78	29	21	4	2	2	4	23	0	109	5	3	9	3	.750	1	0- -	-	2.27	1.97
2014	NwBrit	AA	8	8	1	0	40.2	163	33	17	16	2	1	2	2	12	0	28	1	1	3	4	.429	0	0- -	-	2.60	3.54
2015	Chatt	AA	15	15	1	0	90.2	367	77	32	31	6	3	3	5	24	0	92	0	0	8	3	.727	1	0- -	-	2.79	3.08
2015	Roch	AAA	12	12	0	0	75.2	300	59	24	22	6	0	2	6	14	0	83	4	1	6	2	.750	0	0- -	-	2.31	2.62
2016	Roch	AAA	17	17	1	0	111.1	432	74	39	31	8	3	3	3	36	0	125	3	0	10	5	.667	0	0- -	-	2.06	2.51
2017	Roch	AAA	6	6	0	0	39.2	152	24	8	5	2	0	2	0	8	0	39	0	0	3	0	1.000	0	0- -	-	1.30	1.13
2016	Min	AL	14	14	0	0	58.1	281	74	56	52	12	2	0	5	35	0	49	1	0	3	7	.300	0	0-0	0	7.85	8.02
2017	Min	AL	26	25	0	0	145.2	616	131	71	63	15	3	4	13	48	0	139	7	1	14	8	.636	0	0-0	0	3.62	3.89
2 ML YEARS			40	39	0	0	204.0	897	205	127	115	27	5	4	18	83	0	188	8	1	17	15	.531	0	0-0	0	4.73	5.07

Quintin Berry

Bats: L Throws: L Pos: PR-5;LF-2;CF-1;PH-1   Ht: 6'1" Wt: 195 Born: 11/21/1984 Age: 33

Year	Team	Lg	G	AB	H	2B	3B	HR	(Hm	Rd)	TB	R	RBI	RC	TBB	IBB	SO	HBP	SH	SF	SB	CS	GDP	Avg	OBP	Slg	OPS
2017	Roch*	AAA	14	36	7	1	1	0	(-	-)	10	5	0	2	4	0	11	0	0	0	1	2	0	.194	.275	.278	.553
2017	ColSpr*	AAA	10	14	12	1	0	2	(-	-)	19	9	3	7	5	0	9	1	0	0	2	0	1	.286	.375	.452	.827
2012	Det	AL	94	291	75	10	6	2	(1	1)	103	44	29	44	25	0	80	7	6	1	21	0	4	.258	.330	.354	.684
2013	Bos	AL	13	8	5	0	0	1	(0	1)	8	5	4	5	1	0	2	0	0	0	3	0	0	.625	.667	1.000	1.667
2014	Bal	AL	10	2	0	0	0	0	(0	0)	0	3	0	0	0	0	1	0	0	0	1	0	0	.000	.000	.000	.000
2015	ChC	NL	8	1	0	0	0	0	(0	0)	0	1	0	0	0	0	1	0	0	0	2	1	0	.000	.000	.000	.000
2017	Mil	NL	7	3	0	0	0	0	(0	0)	0	0	0	0	0	0	2	0	0	0	2	1	0	.000	.000	.000	.000
Postseason			14	26	5	2	0	0	(0	0)	7	3	0	3	2	0	6	0	1	0	5	0	1	.192	.250	.269	.519
5 ML YEARS			132	305	80	10	6	3	(1	2)	111	53	33	49	26	0	86	7	6	1	29	2	4	.262	.333	.364	.697

Dellin Betances

Pitches: R Bats: R Pos: RP-66   DELL-inn buh-TAN-siss   Ht: 6'8" Wt: 265 Born: 3/23/1988 Age: 30

Year	Team	Lg	G	GS	CG	GF	IP	BFP	H	R	ER	HR	SH	SF	HB	TBB	IBB	SO	WP	Bk	W	L	Pct	Sh	Sv-Op	Hld	ERC	ERA
2011	NYY	AL	2	1	0	0	2.2	16	1	2	2	0	0	1	0	6	0	2	0	0	0	0	-	0	0-0	0	7.94	6.75
2013	NYY	AL	6	0	0	3	5.0	26	9	6	6	1	0	0	0	2	0	10	0	0	0	0	-	0	0-0	0	9.81	10.80
2014	NYY	AL	70	0	0	8	90.0	341	46	15	14	4	2	3	4	24	1	135	2	1	5	0	1.000	0	1-5	22	1.24	1.40
2015	NYY	AL	74	0	0	17	84.0	332	45	17	14	6	1	1	3	40	2	131	9	0	6	4	.600	0	9-13	28	1.94	1.50
2016	NYY	AL	73	0	0	20	73.0	299	54	31	25	5	1	1	1	28	0	126	6	0	3	6	.333	0	12-17	28	2.48	3.08
2017	NYY	AL	66	0	0	21	59.2	261	29	20	19	3	1	0	11	44	0	100	5	1	3	6	.333	0	10-13	19	2.86	2.87
Postseason			1	0	0	0	1.2	7	1	1	1	0	0	0	0	1	0	4	0	0	0	0	-	0	0-0	0	2.03	5.40
6 ML YEARS			291	1	0	69	314.1	1275	184	91	80	19	5	6	20	144	3	504	22	2	17	16	.515	0	32-48	97	2.11	2.29

Christian Bethancourt

Pitches: R Bats: R Pos: RP-4   BETH-an-court   Ht: 6'2" Wt: 213 Born: 9/2/1991 Age: 26

Year	Team	Lg	G	GS	CG	GF	IP	BFP	H	R	ER	HR	SH	SF	HB	TBB	IBB	SO	WP	Bk	W	L	Pct	Sh	Sv-Op	Hld	ERC	ERA
2017	ElPaso	AAA	34	1	0	10	41.2	210	50	40	38	8	1	2	5	33	0	23	2	0	3	2	.600	0	0- -	-	8.19	8.21
2016	SD	NL	2	0	0	1	1.2	10	1	0	0	0	0	0	0	3	0	1	0	0	0	0	-	0	0-0	0	8.50	0.00
2017	SD	NL	4	0	0	1	3.2	25	6	9	6	1	0	0	0	8	0	2	2	0	0	0	-	0	0-0	0	18.17	14.73
2 ML YEARS			6	0	0	2	5.1	35	7	9	6	1	0	0	0	11	0	3	2	0	0	0	-	0	0-0	0	15.00	10.13

Chad Bettis

Pitches: R Bats: R Pos: SP-9   Ht: 6'1" Wt: 200 Born: 4/26/1989 Age: 29

Year	Team	Lg	G	GS	CG	GF	IP	BFP	H	R	ER	HR	SH	SF	HB	TBB	IBB	SO	WP	Bk	W	L	Pct	Sh	Sv-Op	Hld	ERC	ERA
2013	Col	NL	16	8	0	0	44.2	208	55	34	28	6	3	1	2	20	2	30	2	1	1	3	.250	0	0-1	3	5.95	5.64
2014	Col	NL	21	0	0	9	24.2	127	42	26	25	4	5	0	1	10	2	13	5	0	0	2	.000	0	0-1	0	8.84	9.12
2015	Col	NL	20	20	0	0	115.0	502	120	56	54	11	7	2	3	42	2	98	6	0	8	6	.571	0	0-0	0	4.20	4.23
2016	Col	NL	32	32	1	0	186.0	814	204	107	99	22	10	3	7	59	5	138	4	0	14	8	.636	1	0-0	0	4.51	4.79
2017	Col	NL	9	9	0	0	46.1	200	52	27	26	8	5	1	1	11	0	30	3	0	2	4	.333	0	0-0	0	4.68	5.05
5 ML YEARS			98	69	1	9	416.2	1851	473	250	232	51	30	7	14	142	11	309	20	1	25	23	.521	1	0-2	4	4.83	5.01

Mookie Betts

Bats: R Throws: R Pos: RF-153

Ht: 5'9" Wt: 180 Born: 10/7/1992 Age: 25

Year	Team	Lg	G	AB	H	2B	3B	HR	(Hm	Rd)	TB	R	RBI	RC	TBB	IBB	SO	HBP	SH	SF	SB	CS	GDP	Avg	OBP	Slg	OPS
2014	Bos	AL	52	189	55	12	1	5	(1	4)	84	34	18	30	21	0	31	2	1	0	7	3	2	.291	.368	.444	.812
2015	Bos	AL	145	597	174	42	8	18	(9	9)	286	92	77	100	46	1	82	2	3	6	21	6	2	.291	.341	.479	.820
2016	Bos	AL	158	672	214	42	5	31	(17	14)	359	122	113	130	49	1	80	2	0	7	26	4	12	.318	.363	.534	.897
2017	Bos	AL	153	628	166	46	2	24	(8	16)	288	101	102	115	77	9	79	2	0	5	26	3	9	.264	.344	.459	.803
	Postseason		3	10	2	1	0	0	(0	0)	3	1	0	0	2	0	1	0	0	0	0	0	1	.200	.333	.300	.633
	4 ML YEARS		508	2086	609	142	16	78	(35	43)	1017	349	310	375	193	11	272	8	4	18	80	16	25	.292	.351	.488	.839

Joe Biagini

Pitches: R Bats: R Pos: RP-26; SP-18

bee-ah-gee-nee

Ht: 6'5" Wt: 240 Born: 5/29/1990 Age: 28

Year	Team	Lg	G	GS	CG	GF	IP	BFP	H	R	ER	HR	SH	SF	HB	TBB	IBB	SO	WP	Bk	W	L	Pct	Sh	Sv-Op	Hld	ERC	ERA
2013	Augsta	A	20	20	0	0	96.2	430	102	63	54	5	1	1	4	42	0	79	6	0	7	6	.538	0	0- -	-	4.31	5.03
2014	SnJos	A+	23	23	0	0	128.0	541	133	58	57	5	3	3	6	46	0	103	10	0	10	9	.526	0	0- -	-	4.01	4.01
2015	Rchmd	AA	23	22	0	0	130.1	533	112	45	35	5	4	0	4	34	0	84	7	0	10	7	.588	0	0- -	-	2.52	2.42
2016	Tor	AL	60	0	0	12	67.2	295	69	28	23	3	2	3	5	19	1	62	3	0	4	3	.571	0	1-3	8	3.52	3.06
2017	Tor	AL	44	18	0	3	119.2	517	125	78	71	15	0	2	2	42	0	97	6	0	3	13	.188	0	1-3	9	4.38	5.34
	Postseason		6	0	0	0	7.1	26	3	0	0	0	0	0	1	0	6	1	0	0	0	-	0	0-1	0	0.55	0.00
	2 ML YEARS		104	18	0	15	187.1	812	194	106	94	18	2	5	7	61	1	159	9	0	7	16	.304	0	2-6	17	4.06	4.52

Austin Bibens-Dirkx

Pitches: R Bats: R Pos: RP-18; SP-6

Ht: 6'1" Wt: 210 Born: 4/29/1985 Age: 33

Year	Team	Lg	G	GS	CG	GF	IP	BFP	H	R	ER	HR	SH	SF	HB	TBB	IBB	SO	WP	Bk	W	L	Pct	Sh	Sv-Op	Hld	ERC	ERA
2013	Nham	AA	12	10	0	0	65.2	267	47	19	14	3	1	3	5	17	0	57	2	0	3	4	.429	0	0- -	-	2.00	1.92
2013	Dnedin	A+	17	13	0	1	101.0	414	84	43	32	6	1	2	4	26	0	98	5	0	9	5	.643	0	0- -	-	2.51	2.85
2014	Nham	AA	17	12	0	2	74.0	295	67	30	26	11	1	3	0	12	0	57	3	0	6	4	.600	0	1- -	-	2.97	3.16
2014	Buffalo	AAA	17	4	0	4	39.1	166	40	18	17	4	1	0	1	11	0	35	2	0	2	2	.500	0	0- -	-	3.82	3.89
2015	Buffalo	AAA	5	3	0	0	17.1	74	20	9	9	1	1	0	0	4	0	18	1	0	0	1	.000	0	0- -	-	3.99	4.67
2015	Nham	AA	20	18	0	0	97.0	417	100	51	44	11	3	1	3	28	0	86	6	0	7	8	.467	0	0- -	-	3.98	4.08
2016	RdRck	AAA	17	13	0	0	85.0	365	85	42	41	11	2	1	5	25	0	62	1	0	3	2	.600	0	0- -	-	4.06	4.34
2016	RdRck	AAA	6	3	0	0	23.2	97	22	9	8	3	1	0	0	7	1	20	2	0	5	2	.000	0	0- -	-	3.45	3.04
2017	Tex	AL	24	6	0	6	69.1	299	74	36	36	14	0	2	3	20	0	38	3	0	5	2	.714	0	0-0	-	4.90	4.67

Greg Bird

Bats: L Throws: R Pos: 1B-46;PH-6;DH-2

Ht: 6'4" Wt: 220 Born: 11/9/1992 Age: 25

Year	Team	Lg	G	AB	H	2B	3B	HR	(Hm	Rd)	TB	R	RBI	RC	TBB	IBB	SO	HBP	SH	SF	SB	CS	GDP	Avg	OBP	Slg	OPS
2013	CtnSC	A	130	458	132	36	3	20	(-	-)	234	84	84	105	107	4	132	6	0	2	1	1	9	.288	.428	.511	.938
2014	Tampa	A+	75	274	76	22	1	7	(-	-)	121	36	32	49	45	3	70	1	0	5	1	0	5	.277	.375	.442	.817
2014	Trntn	AA	27	95	24	8	0	7	(-	-)	53	16	11	20	18	0	27	2	0	1	0	0	0	.253	.379	.558	.937
2015	Trntn	AA	49	182	47	16	0	6	(-	-)	81	29	29	30	24	1	30	5	0	1	1	1	4	.258	.358	.445	.804
2015	S-WB	AAA	34	136	41	7	1	6	(-	-)	68	15	23	24	11	0	27	1	0	2	0	0	1	.301	.353	.500	.853
2017	S-WB	AAA	15	47	14	4	0	3	(-	-)	27	12	7	11	11	0	9	0	0	1	0	0	2	.298	.424	.574	.998
2015	NYY	AL	46	157	41	9	0	11	(5	6)	83	26	31	30	19	0	53	1	0	1	0	0	1	.261	.343	.529	.871
2017	NYY	AL	48	147	28	7	0	9	(8	1)	62	20	28	26	19	0	42	0	2	2	0	0	2	.190	.288	.422	.710
	Postseason		1	3	1	0	0	0	(0	0)	1	0	0	0	0	0	1	0	0	0	0	0	0	.333	.333	.333	.667
	2 ML YEARS		94	304	69	16	0	20	(13	7)	145	46	59	56	38	0	95	3	0	3	0	0	3	.227	.316	.477	.793

Ty Blach

Pitches: L Bats: R Pos: SP-24; RP-10

block

Ht: 6'2" Wt: 200 Born: 10/20/1990 Age: 27

Year	Team	Lg	G	GS	CG	GF	IP	BFP	H	R	ER	HR	SH	SF	HB	TBB	IBB	SO	WP	Bk	W	L	Pct	Sh	Sv-Op	Hld	ERC	ERA
2013	SnJos	A+	22	20	0	1	130.1	526	124	46	42	8	4	1	2	18	0	117	8	1	12	4	.750	0	0- -	-	2.64	2.90
2014	Rchmd	AA	25	25	1	0	141.0	596	142	53	49	8	7	3	3	39	2	91	5	0	8	8	.500	0	0- -	-	3.39	3.13
2015	Scrmto	AAA	27	27	2	0	165.1	699	189	92	82	16	9	5	2	31	0	95	6	0	11	12	.478	2	0- -	-	4.08	4.46
2016	Scrmto	AAA	26	26	3	0	162.2	655	147	65	62	9	5	7	2	38	0	113	6	1	14	7	.667	2	0- -	-	2.73	3.43
2016	SF	NL	4	2	0	2	17.0	62	8	2	2	1	1	0	0	5	0	10	0	1	1	0	1.000	0	0-0	0	1.18	1.06
2017	SF	NL	34	24	1	3	163.2	692	179	91	87	17	10	5	1	43	2	73	3	0	8	12	.400	1	0-0	0	4.14	4.78
	Postseason		2	0	0	1	3.1	11	2	0	0	0	0	0	0	0	0	3	0	0	1	0	1.000	0	0-0	0	0.82	0.00
	2 ML YEARS		38	26	1	5	180.2	754	187	93	89	18	11	5	1	48	2	83	3	1	9	12	.429	1	0-0	0	3.79	4.43

Paul Blackburn

Pitches: R Bats: R Pos: SP-10

Ht: 6'1" Wt: 195 Born: 12/4/1993 Age: 24

Year	Team	Lg	G	GS	CG	GF	IP	BFP	H	R	ER	HR	SH	SF	HB	TBB	IBB	SO	WP	Bk	W	L	Pct	Sh	Sv-Op	Hld	ERC	ERA
2013	Boise	A-	13	12	0	0	46.0	203	41	26	17	3	1	1	1	29	0	38	3	0	2	3	.400	0	0- -	-	4.22	3.33
2014	Kane	A	24	24	0	0	117.0	484	108	48	42	6	3	5	7	31	0	75	6	0	9	4	.692	0	0- -	-	3.07	3.23
2015	MrtlBh	A+	18	18	0	0	89.2	371	89	36	31	3	3	3	6	22	0	63	6	0	7	5	.583	0	0- -	-	3.31	3.11
2016	Tenn	AA	18	18	0	0	102.1	421	96	47	36	6	6	5	1	26	0	72	4	0	6	4	.600	0	0- -	-	2.96	3.17
2016	Jacksn	AA	8	7	0	0	40.2	166	42	16	16	2	0	6	0	9	0	27	1	0	3	1	.750	0	0- -	-	3.30	3.54
2017	Nashv	AAA	15	14	0	0	79.2	328	69	34	27	6	0	1	4	26	0	56	1	0	5	6	.455	0	0- -	-	3.03	3.05
2017	Oak	AL	10	10	0	0	58.2	238	58	22	21	7	5	0	1	16	0	22	1	0	3	1	.750	0	0-0	0	3.62	3.22

Charlie Blackmon

Bats: L **Throws:** L **Pos:** CF-158;PH-1 **Ht:** 6'3" **Wt:** 210 **Born:** 7/1/1986 **Age:** 31

Year	Team	Lg	G	AB	H	2B	3B	HR	(Hm	Rd)	TB	R	RBI	RC	TBB	IBB	SO	HBP	SH	SF	SB	CS	GDP	Avg	OBP	Slg	OPS
2011	Col	NL	27	98	25	1	0	1	(1	0)	29	9	8	10	3	1	8	0	1	0	5	1	2	.255	.277	.296	.573
2012	Col	NL	42	113	32	8	0	2	(1	1)	46	15	9	11	4	0	17	3	1	0	1	2	4	.283	.325	.407	.732
2013	Col	NL	82	246	76	17	2	6	(3	3)	115	35	22	35	7	0	49	3	2	0	7	0	1	.309	.336	.467	.803
2014	Col	NL	154	593	171	27	3	19	(13	6)	261	82	72	87	31	5	96	13	6	5	28	10	3	.288	.335	.440	.775
2015	Col	NL	157	614	176	31	9	17	(7	10)	276	93	58	95	46	2	112	13	5	4	43	13	4	.287	.347	.450	.797
2016	Col	NL	143	578	187	35	5	29	(12	17)	319	111	82	110	43	4	102	13	3	4	17	9	2	.324	.381	.552	.933
2017	Col	NL	159	644	**213**	35	**14**	37	(24	13)	**387**	**137**	104	**151**	65	9	135	10	3	3	14	10	4	**.331**	.399	.601	1.000
	7 ML YEARS		764	2886	880	154	33	111	(61	50)	1433	482	355	499	199	21	519	55	21	16	115	45	20	.305	.359	.497	.856

Aaron Blair

Pitches: R **Bats:** R **Pos:** SP-1 **Ht:** 6'4" **Wt:** 250 **Born:** 5/26/1992 **Age:** 26

Year	Team	Lg	G	GS	CG	GF	IP	BFP	H	R	ER	HR	SH	SF	HB	TBB	IBB	SO	WP	Bk	W	L	Pct	Sh	Sv-Op	Hld	ERC	ERA
2013	2 Tms	Low	11	11	0	0	48.2	203	44	20	17	2	1	3	3	17	0	41	1	1	1	3	.250	0	0- -	-	3.24	3.14
2014	2 Tms	Low	19	19	1	0	107.2	463	95	56	51	8	1	4	11	35	0	125	9	0	5	4	.556	0	0- -	-	3.29	4.26
2014	Mobile	AA	8	8	0	0	46.1	182	30	11	10	4	2	0	2	16	0	46	3	0	4	1	.800	0	0- -	-	2.17	1.94
2015	Mobile	AA	13	13	1	0	83.1	332	70	28	25	8	2	1	3	23	0	64	8	0	6	3	.667	0	0- -	-	2.95	2.70
2015	Reno	AAA	13	12	0	0	77.0	316	67	31	27	5	2	2	1	27	1	56	2	0	7	2	.778	0	0- -	-	3.03	3.16
2016	Gwnntt	AAA	13	13	0	0	71.2	314	77	38	37	4	2	0	3	32	1	71	6	0	5	4	.556	0	0- -	-	4.58	4.65
2017	Gwnntt	AAA	25	25	2	0	127.1	575	135	72	71	10	3	7	8	56	0	104	11	0	7	9	.438	0	0- -	-	4.60	5.02
2016	Atl	NL	15	15	0	0	70.0	324	82	61	59	14	3	7	6	34	4	46	0	0	2	7	.222	0	0-0	0	6.51	7.59
2017	Atl	NL	1	1	0	0	3.0	19	5	5	5	1	1	1	0	5	0	3	1	0	0	1	.000	0	0-0	0	16.54	15.00
	2 ML YEARS		16	16	0	0	73.0	343	87	66	64	15	4	8	6	39	4	49	1	0	2	8	.200	0	0-0	0	6.88	7.89

Andres Blanco

Bats: B **Throws:** R **Pos:** PH-35;3B-16;2B-15;1B-11;SS-4;DH-1 **Ht:** 5'10" **Wt:** 195 **Born:** 4/11/1984 **Age:** 34

Year	Team	Lg	G	AB	H	2B	3B	HR	(Hm	Rd)	TB	R	RBI	RC	TBB	IBB	SO	HBP	SH	SF	SB	CS	GDP	Avg	OBP	Slg	OPS
2004	KC	AL	19	60	19	2	2	0	(0	0)	25	9	5	12	5	0	6	1	1	0	1	2	0	.317	.379	.417	.795
2005	KC	AL	26	79	17	0	1	0	(0	0)	19	6	5	3	0	0	5	1	4	2	0	1	3	.215	.220	.241	.460
2006	KC	AL	33	87	21	4	1	0	(0	0)	27	9	9	9	5	0	14	1	3	0	0	1	2	.241	.290	.310	.601
2009	ChC	NL	53	123	31	8	0	1	(1	0)	42	15	9	9	8	3	14	1	6	0	0	2	4	.252	.303	.341	.644
2010	Tex	AL	68	166	46	10	1	0	(0	0)	58	17	13	19	11	1	24	3	3	2	0	2	0	.277	.330	.349	.679
2011	Tex	AL	36	76	17	3	0	2	(2	0)	26	9	3	4	4	0	14	0	2	0	0	1	1	.224	.263	.342	.605
2014	Phi	NL	25	47	13	5	0	1	(1	0)	21	4	3	6	2	1	6	0	4	0	0	0	4	.277	.306	.447	.753
2015	Phi	NL	106	233	68	22	3	7	(4	3)	117	32	25	34	21	0	44	4	3	0	1	1	11	.292	.360	.502	.863
2016	Phi	NL	90	190	48	15	1	4	(1	3)	77	26	21	26	11	0	41	7	0	1	2	3	7	.253	.316	.405	.721
2017	Phi	NL	80	130	25	4	0	3	(3	0)	38	10	13	11	12	0	34	0	0	2	1	0	1	.192	.257	.292	.549
	10 ML YEARS		536	1191	305	73	9	18	(12	6)	450	137	109	133	79	5	202	18	26	7	5	13	33	.256	.310	.378	.688

Gregor Blanco

Bats: L **Throws:** L **Pos:** LF-44;CF-35;PH-17;RF-6;PR-6 **Ht:** 5'11" **Wt:** 175 **Born:** 12/24/1983 **Age:** 34

Year	Team	Lg	G	AB	H	2B	3B	HR	(Hm	Rd)	TB	R	RBI	RC	TBB	IBB	SO	HBP	SH	SF	SB	CS	GDP	Avg	OBP	Slg	OPS
2008	Atl	NL	144	430	108	19	4	1	(0	1)	138	52	38	60	74	2	99	6	6	3	13	5	3	.251	.366	.309	.676
2009	Atl	NL	24	43	8	0	1	0	(0	0)	10	5	1	2	4	0	9	0	1	0	2	0	1	.186	.255	.233	.488
2010	2 Tms		85	237	67	9	4	1	(1	0)	87	31	14	30	29	1	50	0	2	1	11	4	5	.283	.360	.367	.727
2012	SF	NL	141	393	96	14	5	5	(2	3)	135	56	34	50	51	2	104	2	5	2	26	6	0	.244	.333	.344	.676
2013	SF	NL	141	452	120	17	6	3	(0	3)	158	50	41	54	52	4	95	1	3	3	14	9	10	.265	.341	.350	.690
2014	SF	NL	146	393	102	18	6	5	(2	3)	147	51	38	53	41	1	77	3	6	1	16	5	4	.260	.333	.374	.707
2015	SF	NL	115	327	95	19	3	5	(0	5)	135	59	26	41	40	7	59	2	0	3	13	5	3	.291	.368	.413	.781
2016	SF	NL	106	241	54	10	4	1	(1	0)	75	28	18	22	29	4	51	1	1	1	6	3	5	.224	.309	.311	.620
2017	Ari	NL	90	224	55	10	3	3	(0	3)	80	43	13	28	31	0	59	0	1	0	15	1	2	.246	.337	.357	.694
	10 Atl	NL	36	58	18	1	1	0	(0	0)	21	9	3	8	8	1	15	0	0	0	1	2	2	.310	.394	.362	.756
	10 KC	AL	49	179	49	8	3	1	(1	0)	66	22	11	22	21	0	35	0	2	1	10	2	3	.274	.348	.369	.717
	Postseason		37	131	24	4	2	2	(0	2)	38	21	11	14	18	0	24	1	3	0	2	0	1	.183	.287	.290	.577
	9 ML YEARS		992	2740	705	111	36	24	(6	18)	960	375	223	340	351	21	603	15	25	14	116	38	33	.257	.343	.350	.694

Joe Blanton

Pitches: R **Bats:** R **Pos:** RP-51 **Ht:** 6'3" **Wt:** 225 **Born:** 12/11/1980 **Age:** 37

Year	Team	Lg	G	GS	CG	GF	IP	BFP	H	R	ER	HR	SH	SF	HB	TBB	IBB	SO	WP	Bk	W	L	Pct	Sh	Sv-Op	Hld	ERC	ERA
2004	Oak	AL	3	0	0	1	8.0	30	6	5	5	1	0	0	0	2	0	6	0	0	0	0	-	0	0-0	0	2.52	5.63
2005	Oak	AL	33	33	2	0	201.1	835	178	86	79	23	2	7	5	67	3	116	4	2	12	12	.500	0	0-0	0	3.37	3.53
2006	Oak	AL	32	31	1	0	194.1	856	241	111	104	17	3	9	5	58	4	107	3	0	16	12	.571	1	0-0	0	5.09	4.82
2007	Oak	AL	34	**34**	3	0	230.0	950	**240**	106	101	16	5	8	4	40	4	140	3	1	14	10	.583	1	0-0	0	3.30	3.95
2008	2 Tms		33	33	0	0	197.2	855	211	110	103	22	2	4	4	66	3	111	2	0	9	12	.429	0	0-0	0	4.33	4.69
2009	Phi	NL	31	31	0	0	195.1	837	198	89	88	30	11	4	8	59	4	163	7	0	12	8	.600	0	0-0	0	4.25	4.05
2010	Phi	NL	29	28	0	0	175.2	765	206	104	94	27	5	7	3	43	6	134	2	0	9	6	.600	0	0-0	0	4.81	4.82
2011	Phi	NL	11	8	0	1	41.1	180	52	23	23	5	5	2	1	9	0	35	0	0	1	2	.333	0	0-0	0	5.13	5.01
2012	2 Tms		31	30	2	1	191.0	806	207	106	100	29	8	4	3	34	5	166	5	0	10	13	.435	1	0-0	0	4.00	4.71
2013	LAA	AL	28	20	0	7	132.2	611	180	96	89	29	1	5	4	34	4	108	9	0	2	14	.125	0	0-0	0	6.48	6.04
2015	2 Tms		36	4	0	13	76.0	309	69	26	24	7	1	3	1	16	5	79	2	0	7	2	.778	0	2-2	0	2.77	2.84
2016	LAD	NL	75	0	0	15	80.0	315	55	23	22	7	0	3	2	26	4	80	3	0	7	2	.778	0	0-1	28	2.17	2.48

Year	Team	Lg	G	GS	CG	GF	IP	BFP	H	R	ER	HR	SH	SF	HB	TBB	IBB	SO	WP	Bk	W	L	Pct	Sh	Sv-Op	Hld	ERC	ERA
2017	Was	NL	51	0	0	13	44.1	195	53	29	28	10	1	1	1	13	2	39	1	0	2	4	.333	0	0-0	7	5.74	5.68
08	Oak	AL	20	20	0	0	127.0	550	145	74	70	12	1	2	1	35	3	62	1	0	5	12	.294	0	0-0	0	4.33	4.96
08	Phi	NL	13	13	0	0	70.2	305	66	36	33	10	1	2	3	31	0	49	1	0	4	0	1.000	0	0-0	0	4.33	4.20
12	Phi	NL	21	20	2	1	133.1	560	141	74	68	22	6	3	3	18	2	115	4	0	8	9	.471	1	0-0	0	3.77	4.59
12	LAD	NL	10	10	0	0	57.2	246	66	32	32	7	2	1	0	16	3	51	1	0	2	4	.333	0	0-0	0	4.54	4.99
15	KC	AL	15	4	0	6	41.2	172	43	19	18	6	1	2	0	7	1	40	0	0	2	2	.500	0	2-2	0	3.59	3.89
15	Pit	NL	21	0	0	7	34.1	137	26	7	6	1	0	1	1	9	4	39	2	0	5	0	1.000	0	0-0	0	1.84	1.57
	Postseason		17	6	0	1	48.1	207	44	26	25	8	1		3	16	4	41	2	0	3	2	.600	0	0-0	1	3.81	4.66
	13 ML YEARS		427	252	8	51	1767.2	7544	1896	914	860	223	44	57	41	467	44	1284	41	3	101	97	.510	3	2-3	35	4.18	4.38

Jabari Blash

Bats: R Throws: R Pos: RF-33;LF-18;PH-12   Ht: 6'5" Wt: 235 Born: 7/4/1989 Age: 28

Year	Team	Lg	G	AB	H	2B	3B	HR	(Hm	Rd)	TB	R	RBI	RC	TBB	IBB	SO	HBP	SH	SF	SB	CS	GDP	Avg	OBP	Slg	OPS
2013	Hi Dsrt	A+	80	283	73	16	3	16	(-	-)	143	42	53	52	40	0	85	6	0	3	14	8	9	.258	.358	.505	.864
2013	Jacksn	AA	29	97	30	3	0	9	(-	-)	60	13	21	25	20	1	28	3	0	1	1	1	1	.309	.442	.619	1.060
2014	Jacksn	AA	37	127	30	7	1	6	(-	-)	57	27	22	25	28	2	35	5	0	3	4	1	3	.236	.387	.449	.835
2014	Tacom	AAA	45	162	34	8	0	12	(-	-)	78	23	37	25	17	0	57	8	0	2	2	2	2	.210	.312	.481	.794
2015	Tacom	AAA	56	197	52	8	0	22	(-	-)	126	41	47	44	28	0	63	1	0	2	3	1	3	.264	.355	.640	.995
2015	Jacksn	AA	60	209	58	16	2	10	(-	-)	108	38	34	43	31	0	60	6	0	2	5	0	7	.278	.383	.517	.900
2016	ElPaso	AAA	62	177	46	12	0	11	(-	-)	91	30	34	40	41	1	66	8	0	3	1	2	3	.260	.415	.514	.929
2017	ElPaso	AAA	72	235	67	16	1	20	(-	-)	145	53	62	60	48	0	88	7	0	1	3	2	5	.285	.419	.617	1.036
2016	SD	NL	38	71	12	2	0	3	(1	2)	23	7	5	5	11	0	34	2	0	0	1	0	3	.169	.298	.324	.622
2017	SD	NL	61	164	35	6	0	5	(2	3)	56	24	16	18	28	0	66	2	0	1	1	2	5	.213	.333	.341	.675
	2 ML YEARS		99	235	47	8	0	8	(3	5)	79	31	21	23	39	0	100	4	0	1	2	2	8	.200	.323	.336	.659

Michael Blazek

Pitches: R Bats: R Pos: RP-4; SP-1   BLAY-zek   Ht: 6'0" Wt: 205 Born: 3/16/1989 Age: 29

Year	Team	Lg	G	GS	CG	GF	IP	BFP	H	R	ER	HR	SH	SF	HB	TBB	IBB	SO	WP	Bk	W	L	Pct	Sh	Sv-Op	Hld	ERC	ERA
2017	ColSpr*	AAA	26	13	0	7	85.0	363	87	36	35	5	2	4	1	33	0	66	4	0	3	4	.429	0	2- -	-	3.97	3.71
2013	2 Tms	NL	18	0	0	7	17.1	84	16	12	11	3	1	1	1	13	0	14	0	0	0	1	.000	0	0-0	0	5.57	5.71
2015	Mil	NL	45	0	0	17	55.2	222	40	17	15	3	1	2	1	18	1	47	3	0	5	3	.625	0	0-0	4	2.11	2.43
2016	Mil	NL	41	0	0	7	41.1	201	52	31	26	7	1	4	2	27	3	36	2	0	3	1	.750	0	0-1	9	7.31	5.66
2017	Mil	NL	5	1	0	2	8.2	37	12	9	8	6	1	0	0	1	0	7	0	0	0	1	.000	0	0-0	0	9.88	8.31
13	StL	NL	11	0	0	3	10.1	52	10	8	8	2	0	0	1	10	0	10	0	0	0	0	-	0	0-0	0	7.25	6.97
13	Mil	NL	7	0	0	4	7.0	32	6	4	3	1	1	1	0	3	0	4	0	0	0	1	.000	0	0-0	0	3.35	3.86
	4 ML YEARS		109	1	0	33	123.0	544	120	69	60	19	4	7	4	59	4	104	5	0	8	6	.571	0	0-1	13	4.69	4.39

Richard Bleier

Pitches: L Bats: L Pos: RP-57   BLY-er   Ht: 6'3" Wt: 215 Born: 4/16/1987 Age: 31

Year	Team	Lg	G	GS	CG	GF	IP	BFP	H	R	ER	HR	SH	SF	HB	TBB	IBB	SO	WP	Bk	W	L	Pct	Sh	Sv-Op	Hld	ERC	ERA
2013	RdRck	AAA	8	2	0	0	19.0	83	23	9	8	1	2	1	0	7	1	8	0	0	1	1	.500	0	0- -	-	4.83	3.79
2013	Frisco	AA	34	2	0	6	62.1	256	61	27	22	5	0	2	1	13	1	41	4	0	5	5	.500	0	4- -	-	3.15	3.18
2014	Nham	AA	34	5	0	8	84.2	359	100	47	37	13	1	1	3	11	1	43	5	2	6	5	.545	0	1- -	-	4.53	3.93
2015	Hrsbrg	AA	16	15	0	0	103.0	404	95	32	28	6	4	1	5	9	1	40	0	0	8	3	.727	0	0- -	-	2.46	2.45
2015	Syrcse	AAA	12	11	1	0	68.2	278	75	24	21	0	1	1	2	7	0	25	2	0	6	2	.750	1	0- -	-	2.96	2.75
2016	S-WB	AAA	12	10	0	2	58.0	240	66	25	24	2	2	0	1	11	0	25	2	1	2	3	.400	0	1- -	-	3.74	3.72
2017	Norfolk	AAA	8	0	0	1	14.2	52	9	3	1	0	0	0	0	0	0	15	0	0	0	0	-	0	1- -	-	0.80	0.61
2016	NYY	AL	23	0	0	8	23.0	92	20	6	5	0	0	1	1	4	0	13	0	0	0	0	-	0	0-0	2	2.11	1.96
2017	Bal	AL	57	0	0	14	63.1	265	62	23	14	6	3	4	4	13	3	26	5	0	2	1	.667	0	0-0	3	3.33	1.99
	2 ML YEARS		80	0	0	22	86.1	357	82	29	19	6	3	5	5	17	3	39	5	0	2	1	.667	0	0-0	5	2.99	1.98

Jerry Blevins

Pitches: L Bats: L Pos: RP-75   Ht: 6'6" Wt: 190 Born: 9/6/1983 Age: 34

Year	Team	Lg	G	GS	CG	GF	IP	BFP	H	R	ER	HR	SH	SF	HB	TBB	IBB	SO	WP	Bk	W	L	Pct	Sh	Sv-Op	Hld	ERC	ERA
2007	Oak	AL	6	0	0	1	4.2	25	8	6	5	1	0	0	0	2	0	3	0	0	0	1	.000	0	0-0	0	9.08	9.64
2008	Oak	AL	36	0	0	8	37.2	156	32	14	13	2	0	1	3	13	2	35	0	0	1	3	.250	0	0-1	5	3.00	3.11
2009	Oak	AL	20	0	0	5	22.1	90	19	12	12	2	0	1	0	6	1	23	0	0	0	0	-	0	0-0	0	2.68	4.84
2010	Oak	AL	63	0	0	9	48.2	220	54	20	20	7	3	1	0	18	1	46	0	0	2	1	.667	0	1-2	11	4.81	3.70
2011	Oak	AL	26	0	0	11	28.1	122	24	14	9	2	2	3	1	14	1	26	0	0	0	0	-	0	0-0	0	3.45	2.86
2012	Oak	AL	63	0	0	17	65.1	261	45	20	18	7	5	2	5	25	5	54	2	0	5	1	.833	0	1-1	14	2.66	2.48
2013	Oak	AL	67	0	0	14	60.0	245	47	23	21	7	3	5	4	17	2	52	2	0	5	0	1.000	0	0-4	4	2.78	3.15
2014	Was	NL	64	0	0	25	57.1	240	48	31	31	3	3	3	1	23	6	66	2	0	2	3	.400	0	0-0	9	2.78	4.87
2015	NYM	NL	7	0	0	1	5.0	19	0	0	0	0	0	0	0	0	0	4	0	0	0	0	-	0	0-1	5	0.00	0.00
2016	NYM	NL	73	0	0	8	42.0	178	36	14	13	4	2	3	1	15	3	52	1	0	4	2	.667	0	2-3	16	3.02	2.79
2017	NYM	NL	75	0	0	5	49.0	217	43	16	16	4	0	1	4	24	2	69	2	0	6	0	1.000	0	1-8	19	3.79	2.94
	Postseason		6	0	0	1	7.0	22	1	0	0	0	0	0	0	1	0	2	0	0	0	0	-	0	0-0	0	0.05	0.00
	11 ML YEARS		500	0	0	104	420.1	1769	356	170	158	39	18	20	20	157	23	430	9	0	26	11	.703	0	5-20	83	3.18	3.38

Xander Bogaerts

Bats: R Throws: R Pos: SS-146;PR-2   ZAN-derr BO-garts   Ht: 6'1" Wt: 210 Born: 10/1/1992 Age: 25

Year	Team	Lg	G	AB	H	2B	3B	HR	(Hm	Rd)	TB	R	RBI	RC	TBB	IBB	SO	HBP	SH	SF	SB	CS	GDP	Avg	OBP	Slg	OPS
2013	Bos	AL	18	44	11	2	0	1	(0	1)	16	7	5	4	5	0	13	0	0	1	1	0	1	.250	.320	.364	.684
2014	Bos	AL	144	538	129	28	1	12	(7	5)	195	60	46	43	39	1	138	8	2	7	2	3	11	.240	.297	.362	.660
2015	Bos	AL	156	613	196	35	3	7	(5	2)	258	84	81	88	32	1	101	3	3	3	10	2	16	.320	.355	.421	.776
2016	Bos	AL	157	652	192	34	1	21	(11	10)	291	115	89	98	58	0	123	6	0	3	13	4	14	.294	.356	.446	.802
2017	Bos	AL	148	571	156	32	6	10	(4	6)	230	94	62	81	56	6	116	6	0	2	15	1	17	.273	.343	.403	.746
	Postseason		15	39	11	3	1	0	(0	0)	16	10	2	5	6	0	13	0	0	1	0	0	1	.282	.370	.410	.780
	5 ML YEARS		623	2418	684	131	11	51	(27	24)	990	360	283	314	190	8	491	23	5	16	41	10	59	.283	.339	.409	.748

Mike Bolsinger

Pitches: R Bats: R Pos: RP-6; SP-5   BOWL-sing-er   Ht: 6'1" Wt: 215 Born: 1/29/1988 Age: 30

Year	Team	Lg	G	GS	CG	GF	IP	BFP	H	R	ER	HR	SH	SF	HB	TBB	IBB	SO	WP	Bk	W	L	Pct	Sh	Sv-Op	Hld	ERC	ERA
2017	Buffalo*	AAA	16	5	0	4	47.2	180	42	9	9	2	1	0	0	8	0	42	2	1	4	2	.667	0	1- -	-	2.39	1.70
2014	Ari	NL	10	9	0	0	52.1	238	66	36	32	7	3	4	0	17	1	48	0	1	1	6	.143	0	0-0	0	5.42	5.50
2015	LAD	NL	21	21	0	0	109.1	466	104	49	44	11	3	2	1	45	3	98	6	1	6	6	.500	0	0-0	0	3.87	3.62
2016	LAD	NL	6	6	0	0	27.2	122	33	21	21	7	2	0	2	9	1	25	0	0	1	4	.200	0	0-0	0	6.43	6.83
2017	Tor	AL	11	5	0	2	41.1	196	48	32	29	9	0	5	3	27	0	39	3	0	0	3	.000	0	0-0	0	7.45	6.31
	4 ML YEARS		48	41	0	2	230.2	1022	251	138	126	34	8	11	6	98	5	210	9	2	8	19	.296	0	0-0	0	5.12	4.92

Emilio Bonifacio

Bats: B Throws: R Pos: PH-30;LF-8;PR-3;RF-2;CF-1   boh-nee-FAH-see-oh   Ht: 5'10" Wt: 210 Born: 4/23/1985 Age: 33

Year	Team	Lg	G	AB	H	2B	3B	HR	(Hm	Rd)	TB	R	RBI	RC	TBB	IBB	SO	HBP	SH	SF	SB	CS	GDP	Avg	OBP	Slg	OPS
2017	Jacksn*	AA	24	91	26	5	2	1	(-	-)	38	15	5	11	4	0	15	0	4	1	5	4	2	.286	.313	.418	.730
2007	Ari	NL	11	23	5	1	0	0	(0	0)	6	2	2	4	4	0	3	0	0	0	0	1	0	.217	.333	.261	.594
2008	2 Tms	NL	49	169	41	6	5	0	(0	0)	57	29	14	16	14	0	46	0	0	3	7	4	3	.243	.296	.337	.633
2009	Fla	NL	127	461	116	11	6	1	(1	0)	142	72	27	41	34	0	95	2	8	4	21	9	5	.252	.303	.308	.611
2010	Fla	NL	73	180	47	6	3	0	(0	0)	59	30	10	24	17	0	42	0	1	3	12	0	1	.261	.320	.328	.648
2011	Fla	NL	152	565	167	26	7	5	(1	4)	222	78	36	83	59	1	129	1	11	5	40	11	4	.296	.360	.393	.753
2012	Mia	NL	64	244	63	3	4	1	(1	0)	77	30	14	30	25	1	52	1	4	0	30	3	3	.258	.330	.316	.645
2013	2 Tms	AL	136	420	102	22	3	3	(1	2)	139	54	31	39	30	0	103	2	6	3	28	8	4	.243	.295	.331	.625
2014	2 Tms	NL	110	394	102	17	4	3	(2	1)	136	47	24	46	26	2	85	0	6	0	26	8	2	.259	.305	.345	.650
2015	CWS	AL	47	78	13	2	0	0	(0	0)	15	5	4	7	1	2	27	1	1	0	1	4	1	.167	.198	.192	.390
2016	Atl	NL	24	38	8	0	0	0	(0	0)	8	6	3	3	3	0	12	0	2	0	1	0	0	.211	.268	.211	.479
2017	Atl	NL	38	38	5	1	1	0	(0	0)	8	2	3	0	1	0	9	0	4	1	0	0	1	.132	.150	.211	.361
08	Ari	NL	8	12	2	1	0	0	(0	0)	3	3	2	1	0	0	5	0	0	0	1	0	0	.167	.167	.250	.417
08	Was	NL	41	157	39	5	5	0	(0	0)	54	26	12	15	14	0	41	0	0	3	6	4	2	.248	.305	.344	.649
13	Tor	AL	94	262	57	16	1	3	(1	2)	84	33	20	19	13	0	66	2	3	2	12	6	3	.218	.258	.321	.579
13	KC	AL	42	158	45	6	2	0	(0	0)	55	21	11	20	17	0	37	0	3	1	16	2	1	.285	.352	.348	.700
14	ChC	NL	69	276	77	14	3	2	(2	0)	103	35	18	37	16	2	49	0	6	0	14	6	1	.279	.318	.373	.692
14	Atl	NL	41	118	25	3	1	1	(0	1)	33	12	6	9	10	0	36	0	0	0	12	2	1	.212	.273	.280	.553
	11 ML YEARS		831	2610	669	95	33	13	(6	7)	869	355	165	287	215	4	603	7	43	19	166	48	23	.256	.313	.333	.645

Jorge Bonifacio

boh-nee-FAH-see-oh

Bats: R Throws: R Pos: RF-92;LF-9;DH-8;PH-7;PR-3;CF-1   Ht: 6'1" Wt: 195 Born: 6/4/1993 Age: 25

Year	Team	Lg	G	AB	H	2B	3B	HR	(Hm	Rd)	TB	R	RBI	RC	TBB	IBB	SO	HBP	SH	SF	SB	CS	GDP	Avg	OBP	Slg	OPS
2013	2 Tms	Low	63	236	70	14	5	2	(-	-)	100	36	35	38	27	0	46	3	0	3	1	2	3	.297	.372	.424	.795
2013	NWArk	AA	25	93	28	7	0	2	(-	-)	41	15	19	15	11	1	23	0	0	1	2	1	1	.301	.371	.441	.812
2014	NWArk	AA	132	505	116	20	4	4	(-	-)	156	49	51	51	50	0	127	5	0	6	8	3	14	.230	.302	.309	.611
2015	NWArk	AA	125	483	116	30	2	17	(-	-)	201	60	64	64	42	0	126	5	1	5	3	2	8	.240	.305	.416	.721
2016	Omha	AAA	134	495	137	22	6	19	(-	-)	228	82	86	83	51	1	130	7	3	2	6	2	9	.277	.351	.461	.812
2017	Omha	AAA	13	51	16	2	2	3	(-	-)	31	6	12	11	6	0	8	0	0	0	0	0	1	.314	.386	.608	.994
2017	KC	AL	113	384	98	15	1	17	(8	9)	166	55	40	51	35	0	118	2	0	1	1	1	8	.255	.320	.432	.752

Lisalverto Bonilla

Pitches: R Bats: B Pos: RP-6; SP-4   leez-al-VEHR-toe boh-NEE-ya   Ht: 6'0" Wt: 225 Born: 6/18/1990 Age: 28

Year	Team	Lg	G	GS	CG	GF	IP	BFP	H	R	ER	HR	SH	SF	HB	TBB	IBB	SO	WP	Bk	W	L	Pct	Sh	Sv-Op	Hld	ERC	ERA
2013	RdRck	AAA	26	2	0	8	43.0	206	52	42	38	8	6	1	1	24	3	56	2	0	5	5	.500	0	0- -	-	6.48	7.95
2013	Frisco	AA	21	0	0	16	30.1	117	16	1	1	0	1	0	2	9	0	50	0	0	2	0	1.000	0	6- -	-	1.23	0.30
2014	RdRck	AAA	39	6	0	15	74.2	317	73	36	34	9	0	2	1	25	1	92	7	1	4	2	.667	0	1- -	-	3.86	4.10
2016	OkCity	AAA	24	6	1	2	73.2	319	76	39	35	4	2	1	1	27	1	79	3	2	4	5	.444	0	2- -	-	3.81	4.28
2016	Tulsa	AA	7	7	0	0	37.1	156	33	15	14	2	1	2	1	13	0	39	2	0	1	2	.333	0	0- -	-	3.04	3.38
2017	Lsvlle	AAA	18	8	0	2	62.2	267	61	31	25	6	2	2	0	23	0	59	7	0	3	4	.429	0	2- -	-	3.76	3.59
2014	Tex	AL	5	3	0	0	20.2	83	13	8	7	2	0	0	1	12	1	17	1	0	3	0	1.000	0	0-0	0	3.00	3.05
2017	Cin	NL	10	4	1	0	36.2	172	42	33	33	8	2	2	2	22	0	28	3	0	1	3	.250	0	0-0	0	6.97	8.10
	2 ML YEARS		15	7	1	0	57.1	255	55	41	40	10	2	2	3	34	1	45	4	0	4	3	.571	0	0-0	0	5.44	6.28

John Bormann

Bats: R Throws: R Pos: PH-1   Ht: 6'0" Wt: 205 Born: 4/4/1993 Age: 25

								BATTING											RUNNING			AVERAGES			
Year	Team	Lg	G	AB	H	2B	3B	HR	(Hm | Rd)	TB	R	RBI	RC	TBB	IBB	SO	HBP	SH	SF	SB	CS	GDP	Avg	OBP	Slg	OPS
2015	Brstol	R+	25	98	23	5	0	0	(- | -)	28	10	11	7	3	0	12	4	0	0	0	1	1	.235	.286	.286	.571
2016	WV	A	52	177	43	9	1	2	(- | -)	60	22	20	17	11	0	20	1	4	3	0	0	3	.243	.286	.339	.625
2017	Bradtn	A+	39	120	22	6	0	0	(- | -)	28	11	10	7	15	0	26	2	3	2	0	3	1	.183	.281	.233	.514
2017	Pit	NL	1	1	0	0	0	0	(0 | 0)	0	0	0	0	0	0	1	0	0	0	0	0	0	.000	.000	.000	.000

Buddy Boshers

Pitches: L Bats: L Pos: RP-38   bo-SHEERS   Ht: 6'3" Wt: 205 Born: 5/9/1988 Age: 30

			HOW MUCH HE PITCHED					WHAT HE GAVE UP										THE RESULTS						
Year	Team	Lg	G	GS	CG	GF	IP	BFP	H	R	ER	HR	SH	SF	HB	TBB	IBB	SO	WP	Bk	W	L	Pct	Sh	Sv-Op	Hld	ERC	ERA
2017	Roch*	AAA	18	0	0	3	14.2	65	16	6	6	1	0	0	0	8	0	15	2	0	0	0	-	0	0--	-	5.06	3.68
2013	LAA	AL	25	0	0	1	15.1	63	13	8	8	0	0	0	1	8	1	13	0	0	0	0	-	0	0-0	6	3.33	4.70
2016	Min	AL	37	0	0	9	36.0	152	35	21	17	3	0	3	1	7	1	37	1	0	2	0	1.000	0	0-0	5	3.00	4.25
2017	Min	AL	38	0	0	1	35.0	153	37	20	19	7	1	2	2	10	1	28	2	0	1	0	1.000	0	0-0	3	4.76	4.89
	3 ML YEARS		100	0	0	11	86.1	368	85	49	44	10	1	5	4	25	3	78	3	0	3	0	1.000	0	0-0	11	3.77	4.59

Chris Bostick

Bats: R Throws: R Pos: PH-13;2B-3;LF-3;PR-2   Ht: 5'10" Wt: 190 Born: 3/24/1993 Age: 25

								BATTING											RUNNING			AVERAGES			
Year	Team	Lg	G	AB	H	2B	3B	HR	(Hm	Rd)	TB	R	RBI	RC	TBB	IBB	SO	HBP	SH	SF	SB	CS	GDP	Avg	OBP	Slg	OPS
2013	Beloit	A	129	489	138	25	8	14	(-	-)	221	75	89	83	51	0	122	6	4	5	25	8	7	.282	.354	.452	.806
2014	MrtlBh	A+	130	495	124	31	8	11	(-	-)	204	81	62	70	47	1	116	7	3	4	24	11	8	.251	.322	.412	.734
2015	Ptomc	A+	62	234	64	10	3	4	(-	-)	92	23	18	35	19	0	44	7	2	2	15	3	4	.274	.344	.393	.737
2015	Hrsbrg	AA	75	296	73	12	5	8	(-	-)	119	34	40	36	12	0	56	5	2	2	16	5	7	.247	.286	.402	.688
2016	Hrsbrg	AA	71	262	76	11	8	6	(-	-)	121	34	33	43	25	0	58	4	2	4	8	8	3	.290	.356	.462	.818
2016	Syrcse	AAA	64	222	45	11	2	2	(-	-)	66	27	18	17	16	1	67	2	1	1	3	2	4	.203	.261	.297	.559
2017	Indy	AAA	126	486	143	33	3	7	(-	-)	203	75	57	75	45	1	97	8	7	3	8	9	8	.294	.362	.418	.779
2017	Pit	NL	20	27	8	2	0	0	(0	0)	10	6	1	4	4	0	9	1	0	0	0	1	0	.296	.406	.370	.777

Justin Bour

Bats: L Throws: R Pos: 1B-102;PH-6;DH-1;PR-1   BOOR   Ht: 6'3" Wt: 265 Born: 5/28/1988 Age: 30

								BATTING											RUNNING			AVERAGES			
Year	Team	Lg	G	AB	H	2B	3B	HR	(Hm	Rd)	TB	R	RBI	RC	TBB	IBB	SO	HBP	SH	SF	SB	CS	GDP	Avg	OBP	Slg	OPS
2014	Mia	NL	39	74	21	3	0	1	(1	0)	27	10	11	13	9	1	19	0	0	0	0	0	0	.284	.361	.365	.726
2015	Mia	NL	129	409	107	20	0	23	(10	13)	196	42	73	58	34	3	101	2	0	1	0	0	19	.262	.321	.479	.800
2016	Mia	NL	90	280	74	12	1	15	(9	6)	133	35	51	44	38	9	56	0	0	3	0	0	6	.264	.349	.475	.824
2017	Mia	NL	108	377	109	18	0	25	(14	11)	202	52	83	71	47	7	95	1	0	4	1	0	10	.289	.366	.536	.902
	4 ML YEARS		366	1140	311	53	1	64	(34	30)	558	139	218	186	128	20	271	3	0	8	1	0	37	.273	.346	.489	.835

Peter Bourjos

Bats: R Throws: R Pos: LF-41;CF-37;RF-14;PR-14;PH-10;DH-2   BORE-juss   Ht: 6'1" Wt: 175 Born: 3/31/1987 Age: 31

								BATTING											RUNNING			AVERAGES			
Year	Team	Lg	G	AB	H	2B	3B	HR	(Hm	Rd)	TB	R	RBI	RC	TBB	IBB	SO	HBP	SH	SF	SB	CS	GDP	Avg	OBP	Slg	OPS
2010	LAA	AL	51	181	37	6	4	6	(1	5)	69	19	15	13	6	0	40	2	3	1	10	3	2	.204	.237	.381	.618
2011	LAA	AL	147	502	136	26	11	12	(7	5)	220	72	43	66	32	0	124	10	7	1	22	9	7	.271	.327	.438	.765
2012	LAA	AL	101	168	37	7	0	3	(1	2)	53	27	19	18	15	0	44	3	6	3	3	1	2	.220	.291	.315	.606
2013	LAA	AL	55	175	48	3	3	3	(1	2)	66	26	12	19	10	0	43	6	4	1	6	0	8	.274	.333	.377	.710
2014	StL	NL	119	264	61	9	5	4	(2	2)	92	32	24	27	20	1	78	4	5	1	9	3	5	.231	.294	.348	.643
2015	StL	NL	117	195	39	8	3	4	(2	2)	65	32	13	14	19	4	59	6	4	1	5	8	2	.200	.290	.333	.623
2016	Phi	NL	123	355	89	20	7	5	(1	4)	138	40	23	33	17	2	91	4	6	1	6	4	6	.251	.292	.389	.681
2017	TB	AL	100	188	42	9	3	5	(2	3)	72	27	15	16	12	0	53	1	1	1	5	4	2	.223	.278	.383	.655
	Postseason		5	2	0	0	0	0	(0	0)	0	0	0	0	0	0	1	0	0	0	0	0	0	.000	.000	.000	.000
	8 ML YEARS		813	2028	489	88	36	42	(17	25)	775	275	164	206	131	7	532	36	36	10	66	32	34	.241	.298	.382	.680

Matt Bowman

Pitches: R Bats: R Pos: RP-75   Ht: 6'0" Wt: 175 Born: 5/31/1991 Age: 27

			HOW MUCH HE PITCHED					WHAT HE GAVE UP										THE RESULTS						
Year	Team	Lg	G	GS	CG	GF	IP	BFP	H	R	ER	HR	SH	SF	HB	TBB	IBB	SO	WP	Bk	W	L	Pct	Sh	Sv-Op	Hld	ERC	ERA
2013	2 Tms	Low	21	21	0	0	127.0	522	111	45	43	8	1	5	5	35	0	116	15	1	10	4	.714	0	0--	-	2.84	3.05
2014	Bnghtn	AA	17	17	0	0	98.1	417	102	45	34	7	0	4	7	27	1	92	3	0	7	6	.538	0	0--	-	3.76	3.11
2014	LsVgs	AAA	7	6	0	0	36.1	153	38	15	14	1	2	0	0	9	0	32	0	0	3	2	.600	0	0--	-	3.24	3.47
2015	LsVgs	AAA	28	26	2	1	140.0	643	184	97	86	15	8	5	2	51	1	77	8	1	7	16	.304	1	0--	-	5.87	5.53
2016	StL	NL	59	0	0	12	67.2	281	59	31	26	4	1	1	1	20	2	52	0	0	2	5	.286	0	0-1	13	2.71	3.46
2017	StL	NL	75	0	0	10	58.2	247	52	29	26	4	2	4	5	18	2	46	1	0	3	6	.333	0	2-5	23	3.15	3.99
	2 ML YEARS		134	0	0	22	126.1	528	111	60	52	8	3	5	6	38	4	98	1	0	5	11	.313	0	2-6	36	2.91	3.70

Brad Boxberger

Pitches: R Bats: R Pos: RP-30
Ht: 6'2" Wt: 205 Born: 5/27/1988 Age: 30

Year	Team	Lg	G	GS	CG	GF	IP	BFP	H	R	ER	HR	SH	SF	HB	TBB	IBB	SO	WP	Bk	W	L	Pct	Sh	Sv-Op	Hld	ERC	ERA
2012	SD	NL	24	0	0	4	27.2	120	22	12	8	3	0	1	2	18	1	33	0	0	0	0	-	0	0-0	1	4.28	2.60
2013	SD	NL	18	0	0	6	22.0	94	19	9	7	3	3	2	0	13	0	24	0	0	0	1	.000	0	1-1	0	4.43	2.86
2014	TB	AL	63	0	0	10	64.2	247	34	17	17	9	2	2	4	20	0	104	3	2	5	2	.714	0	2-5	18	1.84	2.37
2015	TB	AL	69	0	0	53	63.0	271	54	29	26	9	2	1	2	32	5	74	5	1	4	10	.286	0	**41-47**	2	4.01	3.71
2016	TB	AL	27	0	0	3	24.1	114	23	13	13	3	0	1	2	19	1	22	0	0	4	3	.571	0	0-3	7	5.75	4.81
2017	TB	AL	30	0	0	10	29.1	121	23	11	11	4	1	1	1	11	3	40	1	0	4	4	.500	0	0-2	5	3.03	3.38
	6 ML YEARS		231	0	0	86	231.0	967	175	91	82	31	8	8	11	113	10	297	9	3	17	20	.459	0	44-58	33	3.48	3.19

Matt Boyd

Pitches: L Bats: L Pos: SP-25; RP-1
Ht: 6'3" Wt: 215 Born: 2/2/1991 Age: 27

Year	Team	Lg	G	GS	CG	GF	IP	BFP	H	R	ER	HR	SH	SF	HB	TBB	IBB	SO	WP	Bk	W	L	Pct	Sh	Sv-Op	Hld	ERC	ERA
2017	Toledo*	AAA	8	8	1	0	51.0	199	35	16	16	7	2	0	1	13	0	53	1	0	3	3	.500	0	0- -	-	2.22	2.82
2015	2 Tms	AL	13	12	0	0	57.1	252	71	50	48	17	1	3	1	20	0	43	4	0	1	6	.143	0	0-0	0	7.04	7.53
2016	Det	AL	20	18	0	1	97.1	412	97	51	49	17	0	3	4	29	0	82	1	0	6	5	.545	0	0-0	0	4.35	4.53
2017	Det	AL	26	25	1	0	135.0	605	157	84	79	18	3	6	3	53	3	110	2	0	6	11	.353	1	0-0	0	5.28	5.27
15	Tor	AL	2	2	0	0	6.2	36	15	11	11	5	0	1	0	1	0	7	2	0	0	2	.000	0	0-0	0	17.16	14.85
15	Det	AL	11	10	0	0	50.2	216	56	39	37	12	1	2	1	19	0	36	2	0	1	4	.200	0	0-0	0	5.88	6.57
	3 ML YEARS		59	55	1	1	289.2	1269	325	185	176	52	4	12	8	102	3	235	7	0	13	22	.371	1	0-0	0	5.30	5.47

Blaine Boyer

Pitches: R Bats: R Pos: RP-32
Ht: 6'3" Wt: 225 Born: 7/11/1981 Age: 36

Year	Team	Lg	G	GS	CG	GF	IP	BFP	H	R	ER	HR	SH	SF	HB	TBB	IBB	SO	WP	Bk	W	L	Pct	Sh	Sv-Op	Hld	ERC	ERA
2017	Pwtckt*	AAA	11	0	0	5	15.1	64	13	5	5	0	2	1	0	7	0	12	0	0	0	2	.000	0	2- -	-	2.82	2.93
2005	Atl	NL	43	0	0	5	37.2	158	32	13	13	1	1	1	2	17	0	33	2	0	4	2	.667	0	0-2	9	3.21	3.11
2006	Atl	NL	2	0	0	0	0.2	7	4	3	3	0	0	0	0	1	0	0	0	0	0	0	-	0	0-0	1	47.92	40.50
2007	Atl	NL	5	0	0	2	5.1	26	10	3	2	0	1	0	0	1	1	3	2	0	0	0	-	0	0-0	1	7.41	3.38
2008	Atl	NL	76	0	0	18	72.0	313	73	51	47	10	3	4	2	25	4	67	2	0	2	6	.250	0	1-5	14	4.19	5.88
2009	3 Tms	NL	48	0	0	21	54.2	241	56	36	25	1	4	1	5	20	0	29	2	0	0	2	.000	0	0-0	4	3.81	4.12
2010	Ari	NL	54	0	0	11	57.0	251	59	32	27	3	3	2	1	29	1	29	2	0	3	2	.600	0	0-4	5	4.45	4.26
2011	NYM	NL	5	0	0	3	6.2	33	13	8	8	2	1	0	1	1	0	1	0	0	0	2	.000	0	1-1	0	12.04	10.80
2014	SD	NL	32	0	0	11	40.1	160	34	16	16	2	2	1	0	8	0	29	1	0	0	1	.000	0	0-0	5	2.21	3.57
2015	Min	AL	68	0	0	12	65.0	268	62	24	18	5	3	2	0	19	4	33	5	0	3	6	.333	0	1-3	19	3.20	2.49
2016	Mil	AL	61	0	0	17	66.0	282	80	30	29	4	0	2	1	17	3	26	0	0	2	4	.333	0	1-3	5	4.54	3.95
2017	Bos	AL	32	0	0	11	41.1	178	50	20	20	3	1	1	1	14	3	33	1	0	1	1	.500	0	0-1	2	5.00	4.35
09	Atl	NL	3	0	0	1	1.1	11	3	6	6	0	0	0	1	3	0	2	0	0	0	1	.000	0	0-0	0	23.46	40.50
09	StL	NL	15	0	0	4	16.1	70	14	10	8	1	3	0	1	5	0	9	0	0	0	0	-	0	0-0	2	2.82	4.41
09	Ari	NL	30	0	0	16	37.0	160	39	20	11	0	1	1	3	12	0	18	2	0	0	1	.000	0	0-0	2	3.71	2.68
	11 ML YEARS		426	0	0	111	446.2	1917	473	236	208	31	19	14	13	152	16	283	17	0	15	26	.366	0	4-19	65	4.05	4.19

Brad Brach

Pitches: R Bats: R Pos: RP-67
BROCK
Ht: 6'6" Wt: 215 Born: 4/12/1986 Age: 32

Year	Team	Lg	G	GS	CG	GF	IP	BFP	H	R	ER	HR	SH	SF	HB	TBB	IBB	SO	WP	Bk	W	L	Pct	Sh	Sv-Op	Hld	ERC	ERA
2011	SD	NL	9	0	0	4	7.0	38	9	5	4	0	0	0	1	7	4	11	1	0	0	2	.000	0	0-0	0	6.51	5.14
2012	SD	NL	67	0	0	13	66.2	280	50	28	28	11	1	3	2	33	7	75	4	0	2	4	.333	0	0-1	15	3.47	3.78
2013	SD	NL	33	0	0	6	31.0	141	36	15	11	3	0	3	0	19	0	31	4	0	1	0	1.000	0	0-0	2	6.03	3.19
2014	Bal	AL	46	0	0	8	62.1	254	48	24	22	6	2	4	1	25	1	54	2	0	7	1	.875	0	0-0	8	2.90	3.18
2015	Bal	AL	62	0	0	12	79.1	324	57	25	24	7	3	2	0	38	3	89	1	0	5	3	.625	0	1-2	14	2.78	2.72
2016	Bal	AL	71	0	0	16	79.0	311	57	23	18	7	0	3	0	25	1	92	4	1	10	4	.714	0	2-7	24	2.27	2.05
2017	Bal	AL	67	0	0	36	68.0	275	51	27	24	7	1	3	0	26	1	70	4	1	4	5	.444	0	18-24	9	2.70	3.18
	Postseason		3	0	0	0	3.2	16	3	0	0	0	0	0	0	3	1	3	0	0	1	0	1.000	0	0-0	0	3.56	0.00
	7 ML YEARS		355	0	0	95	393.1	1623	308	147	131	41	7	18	4	173	17	422	20	2	29	19	.604	0	21-34	72	3.09	3.00

Silvino Bracho

Pitches: R Bats: R Pos: RP-21
BRAH-cho
Ht: 5'10" Wt: 190 Born: 7/17/1992 Age: 25

Year	Team	Lg	G	GS	CG	GF	IP	BFP	H	R	ER	HR	SH	SF	HB	TBB	IBB	SO	WP	Bk	W	L	Pct	Sh	Sv-Op	Hld	ERC	ERA
2017	Reno*	AAA	33	0	0	14	35.1	145	25	17	16	8	0	0	1	17	1	48	1	0	3	2	.600	0	8- -	-	3.74	4.08
2015	Ari	NL	13	0	0	3	12.1	50	9	2	2	2	0	0	1	4	1	17	1	0	0	0	-	0	1-1	0	2.95	1.46
2016	Ari	NL	26	0	0	11	24.2	119	31	22	20	7	0	1	3	10	1	17	3	0	0	2	.000	0	0-0	0	7.32	7.30
2017	Ari	NL	21	0	0	10	20.2	87	18	14	13	5	0	0	0	7	0	25	1	0	0	0	-	0	0-0	0	3.98	5.66
	3 ML YEARS		60	0	0	24	57.2	256	58	38	35	14	0	1	4	21	2	59	5	0	0	2	.000	0	1-1	0	5.10	5.46

Chasen Bradford

Pitches: R **Bats:** R **Pos:** RP-28   **Ht:** 6'1" **Wt:** 229 **Born:** 8/5/1989 **Age:** 28

Year Team	Lg	G	GS	CG	GF	IP	BFP	H	R	ER	HR	SH	SF	HB	TBB	IBB	SO	WP	Bk	W	L	Pct	Sh	Sv-Op	Hld	ERC	ERA
2013 Stluci	A+	30	0	0	13	43.2	185	45	18	18	3	0	1	0	9	0	43	1	0	6	2	.750	0	3- -	-	3.21	3.71
2013 Bnghtn	AA	20	0	0	7	25.1	102	19	6	2	1	4	0	0	8	2	18	1	0	3	1	.750	0	1- -	-	1.98	0.71
2014 Bnghtn	AA	23	0	0	21	26.2	113	26	8	6	0	0	1	0	6	0	25	2	0	1	2	.333	0	11- -	-	2.54	2.03
2014 LsVgs	AAA	34	0	0	15	46.0	193	54	21	18	6	1	2	0	4	0	41	4	0	3	2	.600	0	5- -	-	3.98	3.52
2015 LsVgs	AAA	53	0	0	28	63.2	287	86	35	29	3	1	1	4	14	3	46	2	0	5	4	.556	0	7- -	-	5.17	4.10
2016 LsVgs	AAA	56	0	0	15	65.2	292	85	39	36	5	5	3	1	13	1	54	3	0	5	3	.625	0	5- -	-	4.76	4.93
2017 LsVgs	AAA	33	0	0	26	35.2	160	47	20	16	3	1	2	0	7	1	28	4	0	1	1	.500	0	11- -	-	4.82	4.04
2017 NYM	NL	28	0	0	7	33.2	143	30	17	14	3	0	1	0	13	1	27	1	0	2	0	1.000	0	0-0	3	3.26	3.74

Archie Bradley

Pitches: R **Bats:** R **Pos:** RP-63   **Ht:** 6'4" **Wt:** 225 **Born:** 8/10/1992 **Age:** 25

Year Team	Lg	G	GS	CG	GF	IP	BFP	H	R	ER	HR	SH	SF	HB	TBB	IBB	SO	WP	Bk	W	L	Pct	Sh	Sv-Op	Hld	ERC	ERA
2015 Ari	NL	8	8	0	0	35.2	161	36	23	23	3	1	1	2	22	1	23	0	0	2	3	.400	0	0-0	0	5.12	5.80
2016 Ari	NL	26	26	0	0	141.2	638	154	84	79	16	2	7	4	67	8	143	7	2	8	9	.471	0	0-0	0	4.96	5.02
2017 Ari	NL	63	0	0	13	73.0	290	55	14	14	4	1	1	1	21	2	79	0	1	3	3	.500	0	1-7	25	2.14	1.73
3 ML YEARS		97	34	0	13	250.1	1089	245	121	116	23	4	9	7	110	11	245	7	3	13	15	.464	0	1-7	25	4.09	4.17

Jackie Bradley Jr.

Bats: L **Throws:** R **Pos:** CF-132;PH-2   **Ht:** 5'10" **Wt:** 200 **Born:** 4/19/1990 **Age:** 28

Year Team	Lg	G	AB	H	2B	3B	HR	(Hm	Rd)	TB	R	RBI	RC	TBB	IBB	SO	HBP	SH	SF	SB	CS	GDP	Avg	OBP	Slg	OPS
2013 Bos	AL	37	95	18	5	0	3	(2	1)	32	18	10	8	10	0	31	2	0	0	2	0	1	.189	.280	.337	.617
2014 Bos	AL	127	384	76	19	2	1	(1	0)	102	45	30	27	31	1	121	5	1	2	8	0	10	.198	.265	.266	.531
2015 Bos	AL	74	221	55	17	4	10	(5	5)	110	43	43	41	27	0	69	3	1	3	3	0	5	.249	.335	.498	.832
2016 Bos	AL	156	558	149	30	7	26	(12	14)	271	94	87	86	63	5	143	10	0	5	9	2	10	.267	.349	.486	.835
2017 Bos	AL	133	482	118	19	3	17	(6	11)	194	58	63	70	48	4	124	9	0	2	8	3	8	.245	.323	.402	.726
Postseason		3	10	1	0	0	0	(0	0)	1	0	0	0	0	0	7	1	0	0	0	0	0	.100	.182	.100	.282
5 ML YEARS		527	1740	416	90	16	57	(26	31)	709	258	233	232	179	10	488	29	2	12	30	5	34	.239	.318	.407	.726

Michael Brady

Pitches: R **Bats:** R **Pos:** RP-16   **Ht:** 6'0" **Wt:** 195 **Born:** 3/21/1987 **Age:** 31

Year Team	Lg	G	GS	CG	GF	IP	BFP	H	R	ER	HR	SH	SF	HB	TBB	IBB	SO	WP	Bk	W	L	Pct	Sh	Sv-Op	Hld	ERC	ERA
2013 Jaxnvl	AA	49	0	0	44	53.0	214	42	12	9	2	6	2	3	9	2	55	0	0	2	2	.500	0	23- -	-	1.90	1.53
2014 Ark	AA	28	2	0	12	42.1	175	41	16	14	3	3	2	0	10	0	42	2	0	1	4	.200	0	2- -	-	3.08	2.98
2014 Salt Lk	AAA	17	1	0	5	25.2	119	30	21	20	1	1	3	0	13	0	21	2	0	0	2	.000	0	2- -	-	4.92	7.01
2015 Ark	AA	32	19	0	2	119.1	484	124	55	50	10	2	3	3	12	1	113	2	0	7	7	.500	0	0- -	-	3.14	3.77
2016 Hrsbrg	AA	17	11	1	2	74.0	294	68	28	25	6	4	3	1	13	3	64	0	2	3	6	.333	0	0- -	-	2.72	3.04
2017 Nashv	AAA	17	8	0	3	53.1	211	45	22	19	5	1	1	0	6	0	51	0	1	3	1	.750	0	0- -	-	2.13	3.21
2017 Oak	AL	16	0	0	12	31.2	136	33	22	20	7	1	2	5	6	2	24	1	0	0	0	-	0	0-0	0	4.87	5.68

Michael Brantley

Bats: L **Throws:** L **Pos:** LF-87;PH-3;DH-2   **Ht:** 6'2" **Wt:** 200 **Born:** 5/15/1987 **Age:** 31

Year Team	Lg	G	AB	H	2B	3B	HR	(Hm	Rd)	TB	R	RBI	RC	TBB	IBB	SO	HBP	SH	SF	SB	CS	GDP	Avg	OBP	Slg	OPS
2009 Cle	AL	28	112	35	4	0	0	(0	0)	39	10	11	16	8	0	19	0	1	0	4	4	3	.313	.358	.348	.707
2010 Cle	AL	72	297	73	9	3	3	(2	1)	97	38	22	32	22	0	38	0	4	2	10	2	6	.246	.296	.327	.623
2011 Cle	AL	114	451	120	24	4	7	(4	3)	173	63	46	56	34	2	76	3	3	5	13	5	11	.266	.318	.384	.702
2012 Cle	AL	149	552	159	37	4	6	(3	3)	222	63	60	76	53	12	56	0	4	7	12	9	7	.288	.348	.402	.750
2013 Cle	AL	151	556	158	26	3	10	(9	1)	220	66	73	86	40	1	67	4	3	8	17	4	11	.284	.332	.396	.728
2014 Cle	AL	156	611	200	45	2	20	(11	9)	309	94	97	114	52	4	56	8	0	5	23	1	16	.327	.385	.506	.890
2015 Cle	AL	137	529	164	45	0	15	(9	6)	254	68	84	94	60	8	51	2	0	5	15	1	14	.310	.379	.480	.859
2016 Cle	AL	11	39	9	2	0	0	(0	0)	11	5	7	5	3	1	6	0	0	1	1	0	1	.231	.279	.282	.561
2017 Cle	AL	90	338	101	20	1	9	(6	3)	150	47	52	51	31	3	50	2	0	4	11	1	8	.299	.357	.444	.801
Postseason		1	4	1	0	0	0	(0	0)	1	0	0	0	0	0	0	0	0	0	0	0	0	.250	.250	.250	.500
9 ML YEARS		908	3485	1019	212	17	70	(44	26)	1475	454	452	530	303	31	419	19	11	34	106	27	77	.292	.349	.423	.772

Rob Brantly

Bats: L **Throws:** R **Pos:** C-6;DH-4;PH-3   **Ht:** 6'1" **Wt:** 195 **Born:** 7/14/1989 **Age:** 28

Year Team	Lg	G	AB	H	2B	3B	HR	(Hm	Rd)	TB	R	RBI	RC	TBB	IBB	SO	HBP	SH	SF	SB	CS	GDP	Avg	OBP	Slg	OPS
2017 Lsvlle*	AAA	46	168	50	6	1	5	(-	-)	73	21	16	24	9	0	25	1	0	1	3	2	5	.298	.335	.435	.770
2017 Charllt*	AAA	37	119	34	5	0	5	(-	-)	54	18	30	21	11	0	14	8	0	4	0	1	3	.286	.373	.454	.827
2012 Mia	NL	31	100	29	8	0	3	(1	2)	46	14	8	14	13	2	16	0	0	0	1	1	1	.290	.372	.460	.832
2013 Mia	NL	67	223	47	9	0	1	(1	0)	59	11	18	14	15	1	53	2	0	3	0	0	8	.211	.263	.265	.528
2015 CWS	AL	14	33	4	1	0	1	(1	0)	8	3	6	1	2	0	8	0	0	1	0	0	1	.121	.167	.242	.409
2017 CWS	AL	14	31	9	1	0	2	(1	1)	16	4	5	7	3	0	14	2	0	0	0	0	0	.290	.389	.516	.905
4 ML YEARS		126	387	89	19	0	7	(4	3)	129	32	37	36	33	3	91	4	0	4	1	1	10	.230	.294	.333	.628

Steven Brault

Pitches: L Bats: L Pos: RP-7; SP-4   Ht: 6'0" Wt: 200 Born: 4/29/1992 Age: 26

Year	Team	Lg	G	GS	CG	GF	IP	BFP	H	R	ER	HR	SH	SF	HB	TBB	IBB	SO	WP	Bk	W	L	Pct	Sh	Sv-Op	Hld	ERC	ERA
2013	Abrdn	A-	12	12	0	0	43.0	169	35	14	10	1	0	1	2	12	0	38	1	0	1	2	.333	0	0--	-	2.44	2.09
2014	2 Tms	Low	25	24	2	0	146.1	574	114	48	45	4	4	3	10	30	0	124	10	0	11	8	.579	0	0--	-	2.07	2.77
2015	Bradtn	A+	13	13	0	0	65.2	273	62	28	22	3	4	0	2	21	0	45	3	0	4	1	.800	0	0--	-	3.26	3.01
2015	Altna	AA	15	15	0	0	90.0	363	72	22	20	1	2	0	3	19	0	80	0	0	9	3	.750	0	0--	-	1.90	2.00
2016	Indy	AAA	16	15	0	1	71.1	314	66	35	31	8	3	0	3	35	0	81	2	1	2	7	.222	0	0--	-	4.02	3.91
2017	Indy	AAA	21	20	0	0	120.1	481	85	26	26	5	0	4	5	44	0	109	3	0	10	5	.667	0	0--	-	2.24	1.94
2016	Pit	NL	8	7	0	0	33.1	166	45	26	18	5	3	0	2	17	1	29	1	0	0	3	.000	0	0-0	0	6.99	4.86
2017	Pit	NL	11	4	0	2	34.2	162	41	21	18	3	2	1	2	14	1	23	0	0	1	0	1.000	0	1-1	0	5.06	4.67
	2 ML YEARS		19	11	0	2	68.0	328	86	47	36	8	5	1	4	31	2	52	1	0	1	3	.250	0	1-1	0	5.99	4.76

Ryan Braun

Bats: R Throws: R Pos: LF-95;PH-5;DH-4   Ht: 6'2" Wt: 205 Born: 11/17/1983 Age: 34

Year	Team	Lg	G	AB	H	2B	3B	HR	(Hm	Rd)	TB	R	RBI	RC	TBB	IBB	SO	HBP	SH	SF	SB	CS	GDP	Avg	OBP	Slg	OPS
2007	Mil	NL	113	451	146	26	6	34	(17	17)	286	91	97	94	29	1	112	7	0	5	15	5	13	.324	.370	.634	1.004
2008	Mil	NL	151	611	174	39	7	37	(23	14)	338	92	106	100	42	4	129	6	0	4	14	4	13	.285	.335	.553	.888
2009	Mil	NL	158	635	203	39	6	32	(15	17)	350	113	114	133	57	1	121	13	0	3	20	6	7	.320	.386	.551	.937
2010	Mil	NL	157	619	188	45	1	25	(13	12)	310	101	103	104	56	1	105	4	0	3	14	3	17	.304	.365	.501	.866
2011	Mil	NL	150	563	187	38	6	33	(16	17)	336	109	111	124	58	2	93	5	0	3	33	6	9	.332	.397	.597	.994
2012	Mil	NL	154	598	191	36	3	41	(24	17)	356	108	112	125	63	15	128	11	0	5	30	7	12	.319	.391	.595	.987
2013	Mil	NL	61	225	67	14	2	9	(5	4)	112	30	38	39	27	7	56	0	0	1	4	5	8	.298	.372	.498	.869
2014	Mil	NL	135	530	141	30	6	19	(8	11)	240	68	81	74	41	3	113	6	0	3	11	5	17	.266	.324	.453	.777
2015	Mil	NL	140	506	144	27	3	25	(8	17)	252	87	84	91	54	4	115	4	0	3	24	4	20	.285	.356	.498	.854
2016	Mil	NL	135	511	156	23	3	30	(15	15)	275	80	91	93	46	10	98	4	0	3	16	5	20	.305	.365	.538	.903
2017	Mil	NL	104	380	102	28	2	17	(7	10)	185	58	52	53	38	2	76	3	0	4	12	4	15	.268	.336	.487	.823
	Postseason		15	58	22	9	0	2	(2	0)	37	7	12	13	4	0	13	1	0	1	1	0	0	.379	.422	.638	1.060
	11 ML YEARS		1458	5629	1699	345	45	302	(151	151)	3040	937	989	1030	511	50	1146	65	0	37	193	54	151	.302	.364	.540	.905

John Brebbia

Pitches: R Bats: L Pos: RP-50   Ht: 6'1" Wt: 185 Born: 5/30/1990 Age: 28

Year	Team	Lg	G	GS	CG	GF	IP	BFP	H	R	ER	HR	SH	SF	HB	TBB	IBB	SO	WP	Bk	W	L	Pct	Sh	Sv-Op	Hld	ERC	ERA
2013	2 Tms	Low	34	0	0	12	68.2	298	73	35	31	4	2	2	3	16	1	49	1	0	0	5	.000	0	1--	-	3.54	4.06
2016	Sprgfld	AA	24	0	0	6	37.2	161	41	17	17	6	0	2	3	6	0	38	1	0	3	2	.600	0	2--	-	4.30	4.06
2016	Memp	AAA	19	0	0	6	30.1	146	41	22	21	3	1	1	4	13	0	30	1	0	2	3	.400	0	0--	-	6.82	6.23
2017	Memp	AAA	15	1	0	5	26.2	101	16	5	5	2	1	1	1	5	0	29	1	0	1	1	.500	0	3--	-	1.44	1.69
2017	StL	NL	50	0	0	13	51.2	209	37	15	14	8	1	0	5	11	3	51	2	0	0	0	-	0	0-1	5	2.45	2.44

Alex Bregman

Bats: R Throws: R Pos: 3B-132;SS-30;2B-4;DH-2;PH-2;PR-2   Ht: 6'0" Wt: 180 Born: 3/30/1994 Age: 24

Year	Team	Lg	G	AB	H	2B	3B	HR	(Hm	Rd)	TB	R	RBI	RC	TBB	IBB	SO	HBP	SH	SF	SB	CS	GDP	Avg	OBP	Slg	OPS
2015	2 Tms	Low	66	272	80	13	4	4	(-	-)	113	37	34	44	29	2	30	4	2	4	13	6	7	.294	.366	.415	.781
2016	CpChr	AA	62	236	70	16	2	14	(-	-)	132	54	46	55	42	3	26	6	1	0	5	3	5	.297	.415	.559	.975
2016	Fresno	AAA	18	78	26	6	0	6	(-	-)	50	17	15	17	5	0	12	0	0	0	2	1	2	.333	.373	.641	1.015
2016	Hou	AL	49	201	53	13	3	8	(3	5)	96	31	34	37	15	0	52	0	0	1	2	0	1	.264	.313	.478	.791
2017	Hou	AL	155	556	158	39	5	19	(9	10)	264	88	71	87	55	2	97	7	1	7	17	5	15	.284	.352	.475	.827
	2 ML YEARS		204	757	211	52	8	27	(12	15)	360	119	105	124	70	2	149	7	1	8	19	5	16	.279	.342	.476	.818

Craig Breslow

Pitches: L Bats: L Pos: RP-37
BREHZ-loh   Ht: 6'0" Wt: 190 Born: 8/8/1980 Age: 37

Year	Team	Lg	G	GS	CG	GF	IP	BFP	H	R	ER	HR	SH	SF	HB	TBB	IBB	SO	WP	Bk	W	L	Pct	Sh	Sv-Op	Hld	ERC	ERA
2017	Clmbs*	AAA	7	0	0	1	4.2	21	5	2	2	0	0	0	1	2	1	4	0	0	0	0	-	0	0--	-	4.37	3.86
2005	SD	NL	14	0	0	3	16.1	78	15	6	4	1	0	1	1	13	0	14	1	0	0	0	-	0	0-0	1	4.98	2.20
2006	Bos	AL	13	0	0	3	12.0	55	12	5	5	0	0	2	1	6	1	12	2	1	0	0	-	0	0-0	3	3.78	3.75
2008	2 Tms	AL	49	0	0	13	47.0	189	34	12	10	1	2	0	0	19	2	39	4	1	0	2	.000	0	1-2	5	2.12	1.91
2009	2 Tms	AL	77	0	0	9	69.2	281	48	31	26	8	4	1	3	29	0	55	3	1	8	7	.533	0	0-2	15	2.79	3.36
2010	Oak	AL	75	0	0	23	74.2	304	53	26	25	9	2	0	0	29	4	71	0	1	4	4	.500	0	5-7	16	2.53	3.01
2011	Oak	AL	67	0	0	10	59.1	261	69	29	25	4	3	2	2	21	1	44	3	0	0	3	.000	0	0-3	8	4.74	3.79
2012	2 Tms		63	0	0	16	63.1	261	52	22	19	5	3	3	2	22	2	61	2	0	3	0	1.000	0	0-1	9	2.86	2.70
2013	Bos	AL	61	0	0	13	59.2	237	49	16	12	3	0	2	2	18	0	33	2	0	5	2	.714	0	0-1	13	2.66	1.81
2014	Bos	AL	60	0	0	16	54.1	260	73	40	36	8	1	0	2	26	0	36	2	0	2	4	.333	0	1-2	2	7.14	5.96
2015	Bos	AL	45	2	0	18	65.0	280	69	33	30	12	3	5	2	23	5	46	2	0	0	4	.000	0	1-4	15	4.91	4.15
2016	Mia	NL	15	0	0	4	14.0	63	21	9	7	1	4	2	0	4	0	7	2	0	0	2	.000	0	0-1	2	6.62	4.50
2017	2 Tms	AL	37	0	0	9	35.1	159	41	21	20	4	1	4	2	14	2	23	1	0	1	1	.500	0	0-1	1	5.23	5.09
08	Cle	AL	7	0	0	3	8.1	40	10	3	3	1	0	0	0	5	0	7	0	0	0	0	-	0	0-0	0	6.09	3.24
08	Min	AL	42	0	0	10	38.2	149	24	9	7	0	2	0	0	14	2	32	4	1	0	2	.000	0	1-2	5	1.49	1.63
09	Min	AL	17	0	0	5	14.1	64	11	11	10	3	2	0	1	11	0	11	3	0	1	2	.333	0	0-2	2	5.38	6.28
09	Oak	AL	60	0	0	4	55.1	217	37	20	16	5	2	1	2	18	0	44	0	1	7	5	.583	0	0-2	13	2.21	2.60
12	Ari	NL	40	0	0	12	43.1	180	38	15	13	5	2	1	1	13	0	42	1	0	2	0	1.000	0	0-0	4	3.19	2.70
12	Bos	AL	23	0	0	4	20.0	81	14	7	6	0	1	2	1	9	2	19	1	0	1	0	1.000	0	0-1	5	2.12	2.70

Year Team	Lg	HOW MUCH HE PITCHED						WHAT HE GAVE UP												THE RESULTS							
		G	GS	CG	GF	IP	BFP	H	R	ER	HR	SH	SF	HB	TBB	IBB	SO	WP	Bk	W	L	Pct	Sh	Sv-Op	Hld	ERC	ERA
17 Min	AL	30	0	0	8	31.0	143	38	19	18	4	1	4	2	12	2	18	1	0	1	1	.500	0	0-1	0	5.66	5.23
17 Cle	AL	7	0	0	1	4.1	16	3	2	2	0	0	0	0	2	0	5	0	0	0	0	-	0	0-0	1	2.34	4.15
Postseason		10	0	0	0	7.1	36	6	3	2	0	0	1	2	7	1	6	0	0	1	0	1.000	0	0-1	4	5.16	2.45
12 ML YEARS		576	2	0	137	570.2	2428	536	250	219	56	20	20	17	226	18	442	25	5	23	30	.434	0	8-24	76	3.80	3.45

Austin Brice

Pitches: R Bats: R Pos: RP-22   Ht: 6'4" Wt: 235 Born: 6/19/1992 Age: 26

Year Team	Lg	HOW MUCH HE PITCHED						WHAT HE GAVE UP												THE RESULTS							
		G	GS	CG	GF	IP	BFP	H	R	ER	HR	SH	SF	HB	TBB	IBB	SO	WP	Bk	W	L	Pct	Sh	Sv-Op	Hld	ERC	ERA
2013 Grnsbr	A	26	23	0	0	113.0	541	118	84	72	11	2	2	14	82	0	111	7	0	8	11	.421	0	0--	-	6.13	5.73
2014 Jupiter	A+	25	24	0	0	127.1	552	114	66	51	5	5	5	13	55	0	109	17	1	8	9	.471	0	0--	-	3.58	3.60
2015 Jaxnvl	AA	25	25	0	0	125.1	556	114	74	65	11	3	5	12	69	0	127	10	0	6	9	.400	0	0--	-	4.47	4.67
2016 Jaxnvl	AA	27	13	0	4	93.1	384	79	39	30	5	3	3	7	29	0	79	6	1	4	7	.364	0	2--	-	2.92	2.89
2016 NewOr	AAA	5	0	0	3	8.2	28	3	1	1	1	0	0	0	1	0	10	0	0	0	0	-	0	2--	-	0.71	1.04
2017 Lsvlle	AAA	15	0	0	5	21.1	94	23	10	9	0	0	1	1	9	2	21	0	0	1	2	.333	0	1--	-	3.91	3.80
2016 Mia	NL	15	0	0	2	14.0	59	9	12	11	2	0	0	2	5	1	14	0	0	0	1	.000	0	0-0	1	2.63	7.07
2017 Cin	NL	22	0	0	4	32.2	137	33	18	18	6	1	1	3	7	0	26	0	0	0	0	-	0	0-0	1	4.38	4.96
2 ML YEARS		37	0	0	6	46.2	196	42	30	29	8	1	1	5	12	1	40	0	0	0	1	.000	0	0-0	2	3.82	5.59

Parker Bridwell

Pitches: R Bats: R Pos: SP-20; RP-1   Ht: 6'4" Wt: 185 Born: 8/2/1991 Age: 26

Year Team	Lg	HOW MUCH HE PITCHED						WHAT HE GAVE UP												THE RESULTS							
		G	GS	CG	GF	IP	BFP	H	R	ER	HR	SH	SF	HB	TBB	IBB	SO	WP	Bk	W	L	Pct	Sh	Sv-Op	Hld	ERC	ERA
2013 Dlmrva	A	26	26	0	0	142.2	631	141	86	75	9	3	6	9	59	0	144	8	0	8	9	.471	0	0--	-	3.99	4.73
2014 Frdrck	A+	26	26	1	0	141.1	607	123	75	70	11	1	1	9	70	0	142	6	2	7	10	.412	0	0--	-	3.86	4.46
2015 Bowie	AA	18	18	1	0	97.0	418	96	48	43	7	2	2	2	38	0	93	5	0	4	5	.444	0	0--	-	3.87	3.99
2016 Bowie	AA	18	7	0	2	55.2	249	56	33	28	7	0	1	3	28	0	38	1	0	1	1	.500	0	1--	-	4.92	4.53
2016 2 Tms	Low	5	0	0	0	11.0	41	5	3	3	1	0	0	1	3	0	11	0	0	3	1	.750	0	0--	-	1.38	2.45
2017 Salt Lk	AAA	6	5	0	0	27.1	115	26	16	13	2	0	1	1	8	0	24	1	0	2	3	.400	0	0--	-	3.34	4.28
2016 Bal	AL	2	0	0	1	3.1	15	5	5	5	2	0	0	0	1	0	3	0	0	0	0	-	0	0-0	0	11.35	13.50
2017 LAA	AL	21	20	0	0	121.0	492	115	52	49	19	0	2	4	30	0	73	4	0	10	3	.769	0	0-0	0	3.81	3.64
2 ML YEARS		23	20	0	1	124.1	507	120	57	54	21	0	2	4	31	0	76	4	0	10	3	.769	0	0-0	0	3.98	3.91

Lewis Brinson

Bats: R Throws: R Pos: LF-8;CF-8;PH-6   Ht: 6'3" Wt: 195 Born: 5/8/1994 Age: 24

Year Team	Lg	BATTING																	RUNNING			AVERAGES			
		G	AB	H	2B	3B	HR	(Hm	Rd)	TB	R	RBI	RC	TBB	IBB	SO	HBP	SH	SF	SB	CS	GDP	Avg	OBP	Slg	OPS
2013 Hkry	A	122	447	106	18	2	21	(-	-)	191	64	52	65	48	0	191	8	0	5	24	7	5	.237	.322	.427	.749
2014 2 Tms	Low	89	347	100	16	2	13	(-	-)	159	53	50	56	33	0	96	3	1	1	12	9	5	.288	.354	.458	.812
2015 Hi Dsrt	A+	64	258	87	22	7	13	(-	-)	162	51	42	64	31	0	64	6	0	3	13	6	5	.337	.416	.628	1.044
2015 Frisco	AA	28	110	32	8	1	6	(-	-)	60	14	23	19	6	0	28	1	1	2	1	1	1	.291	.328	.545	.873
2016 Frisco	AA	77	304	72	14	6	11	(-	-)	131	46	40	38	17	0	64	2	1	2	11	4	8	.237	.280	.431	.711
2016 ColSpr	AAA	23	89	34	9	0	4	(-	-)	55	14	20	19	2	0	21	0	0	2	4	2	5	.382	.387	.618	1.005
2017 ColSpr	AAA	76	299	99	22	4	13	(-	-)	168	66	48	66	32	3	62	5	0	4	11	5	5	.331	.400	.562	.962
2017 Mil	NL	21	47	5	0	1	2	(0	2)	13	2	3	4	7	1	17	1	0	0	0	0	0	.106	.236	.277	.513

Zach Britton

Pitches: L Bats: L Pos: RP-38   Ht: 6'3" Wt: 195 Born: 12/22/1987 Age: 30

Year Team	Lg	HOW MUCH HE PITCHED						WHAT HE GAVE UP												THE RESULTS							
		G	GS	CG	GF	IP	BFP	H	R	ER	HR	SH	SF	HB	TBB	IBB	SO	WP	Bk	W	L	Pct	Sh	Sv-Op	Hld	ERC	ERA
2017 3 Tms*	Low	5	2	0	2	5.0	18	2	0	0	0	0	0	0	3	0	5	0	0	0	0	-	0	0--	-	1.47	0.00
2011 Bal	AL	28	28	0	0	154.1	666	162	93	79	12	8	7	1	62	3	97	7	0	11	11	.500	0	0-0	0	4.24	4.61
2012 Bal	AL	12	11	0	0	60.1	270	61	37	34	6	0	1	2	32	3	53	4	0	5	3	.625	0	0-0	0	4.70	5.07
2013 Bal	AL	8	7	0	0	40.0	182	52	23	22	4	1	1	1	17	1	18	1	0	2	3	.400	0	0-0	0	6.14	4.95
2014 Bal	AL	71	0	0	49	76.1	285	46	17	14	4	3	0	1	23	0	62	0	0	3	2	.600	0	37-41	7	1.62	1.65
2015 Bal	AL	64	0	0	58	65.2	253	51	16	14	3	0	0	1	14	1	79	5	0	4	1	.800	0	36-40	0	2.02	1.92
2016 Bal	AL	69	0	0	63	67.0	254	38	7	4	1	1	0	0	18	3	74	10	0	2	1	.667	0	47-47	0	1.18	0.54
2017 Bal	AL	38	0	0	30	37.1	161	39	12	12	1	1	1	0	18	1	29	4	0	2	1	.667	0	15-17	0	4.18	2.89
Postseason		6	0	0	4	4.2	24	5	2	2	0	1	0	0	5	2	5	0	0	0	0	-	0	2-2	1	5.28	3.86
7 ML YEARS		290	46	0	200	501.0	2071	449	205	179	31	14	10	6	184	12	412	31	0	29	22	.569	0	135-145	7	3.19	3.22

Rex Brothers

Pitches: L Bats: L Pos: RP-27   Ht: 6'0" Wt: 210 Born: 12/18/1987 Age: 30

Year Team	Lg	HOW MUCH HE PITCHED						WHAT HE GAVE UP												THE RESULTS							
		G	GS	CG	GF	IP	BFP	H	R	ER	HR	SH	SF	HB	TBB	IBB	SO	WP	Bk	W	L	Pct	Sh	Sv-Op	Hld	ERC	ERA
2017 Missi*	AA	10	0	0	4	9.2	41	7	4	3	0	0	0	0	5	0	18	4	0	0	0	-	0	1--	-	2.33	2.79
2017 Gwnntt†	AAA	7	0	0	3	7.0	25	4	2	2	0	0	0	0	1	0	8	2	1	0	0	-	0	1--	-	0.97	2.57
2011 Col	NL	48	0	0	6	40.2	172	33	14	13	4	0	0	0	20	2	59	2	0	1	2	.333	0	1-3	16	3.31	2.88
2012 Col	NL	75	0	0	10	67.2	295	63	33	29	5	3	3	1	37	7	83	5	1	8	2	.800	0	0-5	18	3.99	3.86
2013 Col	NL	72	0	0	40	67.1	281	51	16	13	5	1	0	0	36	2	76	3	3	2	1	.667	0	19-21	12	3.09	1.74
2014 Col	NL	74	0	0	15	56.1	273	65	38	35	7	1	4	2	39	0	55	5	1	4	6	.400	0	0-6	15	6.43	5.59
2015 Col	NL	17	0	0	1	10.1	46	9	2	2	0	0	1	0	8	0	5	1	0	1	0	1.000	0	0-0	0	4.12	1.74
2017 Atl	NL	27	0	0	8	23.2	105	23	19	19	3	0	0	1	12	3	33	2	0	4	3	.571	0	0-0	2	4.48	7.23
6 ML YEARS		313	0	0	80	266.0	1172	244	122	111	24	5	8	4	152	14	311	18	5	20	14	.588	0	20-35	63	4.18	3.76

Jonathan Broxton

Pitches: R Bats: R Pos: RP-20   Ht: 6'4" Wt: 285 Born: 6/16/1984 Age: 34

Year	Team	Lg	G	GS	CG	GF	IP	BFP	H	R	ER	HR	SH	SF	HB	TBB	IBB	SO	WP	Bk	W	L	Pct	Sh	Sv-Op	Hld	ERC	ERA
2005	LAD	NL	14	0	0	5	13.2	68	13	11	9	0	0	2	1	12	2	22	2	0	1	0	1.000	0	0-1	1	4.65	5.93
2006	LAD	NL	68	0	0	20	76.1	320	61	25	22	7	3	1	1	33	6	97	7	0	4	1	.800	0	3-7	12	2.97	2.59
2007	LAD	NL	83	0	0	18	82.0	334	69	30	26	6	0	1	1	25	3	99	4	0	4	4	.500	0	2-8	32	2.71	2.85
2008	LAD	NL	70	0	0	32	69.0	285	54	29	24	2	3	3	3	27	5	88	3	0	3	5	.375	0	14-22	13	2.48	3.13
2009	LAD	NL	73	0	0	58	76.0	300	44	24	22	4	0	3	1	29	1	114	2	0	7	2	.778	0	36-42	1	1.65	2.61
2010	LAD	NL	64	0	0	46	62.1	271	64	30	28	4	3	1	2	28	5	73	1	0	5	6	.455	0	22-29	3	4.21	4.04
2011	LAD	NL	14	0	0	12	12.2	62	15	10	8	2	0	0	0	9	2	10	0	0	1	2	.333	0	7-8	0	6.47	5.68
2012	2 Tms		60	0	0	39	58.0	238	56	18	16	2	2	1	3	17	0	45	0	0	4	5	.444	0	27-33	10	3.34	2.48
2013	Cin	NL	34	0	0	8	30.2	133	27	17	14	4	1	2	4	12	2	25	0	0	2	2	.500	0	0-3	13	3.97	4.11
2014	2 Tms	NL	62	0	0	18	58.2	231	41	15	15	4	2	1	1	19	0	49	0	0	4	3	.571	0	7-15	23	2.14	2.30
2015	2 Tms	NL	66	0	0	15	60.1	257	61	32	31	7	5	1	0	22	1	63	0	0	4	5	.444	0	0-3	17	4.11	4.62
2016	StL	NL	66	0	0	14	60.2	259	52	32	29	7	2	3	3	24	5	57	1	0	4	2	.667	0	0-3	12	3.40	4.30
2017	StL	NL	20	0	0	8	15.2	78	23	12	12	2	3	2	0	11	2	16	1	0	0	1	.000	0	0-0	1	8.36	6.89
12	KC	AL	35	0	0	32	35.2	151	36	11	9	1	2	1	2	14	0	25	0	0	1	2	.333	0	23-27	0	3.93	2.27
12	Cin	NL	25	0	0	7	22.1	87	20	7	7	1	0	0	1	3	0	20	0	0	3	3	.500	0	4-6	10	2.44	2.82
14	Cin	NL	51	0	0	16	48.1	189	32	10	10	3	2	1	1	17	0	37	0	0	4	2	.667	0	7-13	21	2.06	1.86
14	Mil	NL	11	0	0	2	10.1	42	9	5	5	1	0	0	0	2	0	12	0	0	0	1	1.000	0	0-2	2	2.55	4.35
15	Mil	NL	40	0	0	10	36.2	156	41	24	24	5	2	1	0	10	1	37	0	0	1	2	.333	0	0-1	11	4.50	5.89
15	StL	NL	26	0	0	5	23.2	101	20	8	7	2	3	0	0	12	0	26	0	0	3	3	.500	0	0-2	6	3.53	2.66
	Postseason		19	0	0	13	19.2	89	20	9	8	2	0	0	1	9	0	22	0	0	0	3	.000	0	3-5	1	4.50	3.66
	13 ML YEARS		694	0	0	293	676.0	2836	580	285	256	51	24	21	20	268	34	758	21	0	43	38	.531	0	118-174	137	3.17	3.41

Keon Broxton

Bats: R Throws: R Pos: CF-139;PH-15;PR-3   Ht: 6'3" Wt: 195 Born: 5/7/1990 Age: 28

Year	Team	Lg	G	AB	H	2B	3B	HR	(Hm	Rd)	TB	R	RBI	RC	TBB	IBB	SO	HBP	SH	SF	SB	CS	GDP	Avg	OBP	Slg	OPS
2015	Pit	NL	7	2	0	0	0	0	(0	0)	0	3	0	0	0	0	1	0	0	0	1	1	0	.000	.000	.000	.000
2016	Mil	NL	75	207	50	10	4	9	(2	7)	89	28	19	32	36	0	88	0	1	0	23	4	2	.242	.354	.430	.784
2017	Mil	NL	143	414	91	15	4	20	(10	10)	174	66	49	46	40	1	175	7	1	1	21	7	3	.220	.299	.420	.719
	3 ML YEARS		225	623	141	25	5	29	(12	17)	263	97	68	78	76	1	264	7	2	1	45	12	5	.226	.317	.422	.739

Jay Bruce

Bats: L Throws: L Pos: RF-133;1B-12;DH-3;PH-2   Ht: 6'3" Wt: 225 Born: 4/3/1987 Age: 31

Year	Team	Lg	G	AB	H	2B	3B	HR	(Hm	Rd)	TB	R	RBI	RC	TBB	IBB	SO	HBP	SH	SF	SB	CS	GDP	Avg	OBP	Slg	OPS
2008	Cin	NL	108	413	105	17	1	21	(13	8)	187	63	52	49	33	1	110	4	0	2	4	6	8	.254	.314	.453	.767
2009	Cin	NL	101	345	77	15	2	22	(13	9)	162	47	58	47	38	2	75	2	1	1	3	3	5	.223	.303	.470	.773
2010	Cin	NL	148	509	143	23	5	25	(19	6)	251	80	70	71	58	5	136	1	0	5	5	4	12	.281	.353	.493	.846
2011	Cin	NL	157	585	150	27	2	32	(16	16)	277	84	97	96	71	14	158	5	1	2	8	7	8	.256	.341	.474	.814
2012	Cin	NL	155	560	144	35	4	34	(21	13)	288	89	99	85	62	11	155	4	0	7	9	3	5	.252	.327	.514	.841
2013	Cin	NL	160	626	164	43	1	30	(16	14)	299	89	109	88	63	13	185	2	0	5	7	3	9	.262	.329	.478	.807
2014	Cin	NL	137	493	107	21	1	18	(10	8)	184	71	66	54	44	5	149	2	1	5	12	3	8	.217	.281	.373	.654
2015	Cin	NL	157	580	131	35	4	26	(13	13)	252	72	87	61	58	8	145	2	0	9	9	5	10	.226	.294	.434	.729
2016	2 Tms	NL	147	539	135	27	6	33	(17	16)	273	74	99	87	44	7	126	3	0	3	4	2	14	.250	.309	.506	.815
2017	2 Tms	NL	146	555	141	29	2	36	(15	21)	282	82	101	94	57	0	139	2	0	3	1	1	11	.254	.324	.508	.832
16	Cin	NL	97	370	98	22	6	25	(14	11)	207	60	80	67	27	3	83	2	0	3	4	2	11	.265	.316	.559	.875
16	NYM	NL	50	169	37	5	0	8	(3	5)	66	14	19	20	17	4	43	1	0	0	0	0	3	.219	.294	.391	.685
17	NYM	NL	103	406	104	20	0	29	(11	18)	211	61	75	68	39	0	102	1	0	2	0	1	9	.256	.321	.520	.841
17	Cle	AL	43	149	37	9	2	7	(4	3)	71	21	26	26	18	0	37	1	0	1	1	0	2	.248	.331	.477	.808
	Postseason		10	34	8	2	0	2	(0	2)	16	3	6	4	4	0	5	1	0	0	0	1	0	.235	.333	.471	.804
	10 ML YEARS		1416	5205	1294	272	29	277	(153	124)	2455	751	838	732	528	66	1378	27	3	42	62	37	90	.249	.319	.472	.790

Jaycob Brugman

Bats: L Throws: L Pos: CF-40;PH-6;LF-4;RF-1;PR-1   Ht: 6'0" Wt: 195 Born: 1/18/1992 Age: 26

Year	Team	Lg	G	AB	H	2B	3B	HR	(Hm	Rd)	TB	R	RBI	RC	TBB	IBB	SO	HBP	SH	SF	SB	CS	GDP	Avg	OBP	Slg	OPS
2013	Vrmnt	A-	49	165	43	9	4	1	(-	-)	63	13	23	20	7	0	48	3	0	1	7	0	4	.261	.301	.382	.683
2014	2 Tms	Low	120	443	124	25	6	21	(-	-)	224	67	72	80	51	1	115	2	1	4	8	5	6	.280	.354	.506	.860
2015	Mdlnd	AA	132	500	130	27	8	6	(-	-)	191	61	63	69	62	0	89	2	0	2	11	7	14	.260	.343	.382	.725
2016	Mdlnd	AA	38	157	41	7	3	5	(-	-)	69	27	20	23	16	0	33	2	0	1	2	3	3	.261	.335	.439	.775
2016	Nashv	AAA	94	386	114	26	4	7	(-	-)	169	50	67	62	36	2	88	2	1	8	5	3	3	.295	.352	.438	.790
2017	Nashv	AAA	38	153	42	5	1	1	(-	-)	52	17	9	20	19	1	28	0	0	0	3	1	2	.275	.355	.340	.695
2017	Oak	AL	48	143	38	2	0	3	(2	1)	49	12	12	18	18	1	38	0	0	1	1	2	1	.266	.346	.343	.688

Kris Bryant

Bats: R Throws: R Pos: 3B-144;RF-7;1B-2;LF-2;CF-2;PH-1   Ht: 6'5" Wt: 230 Born: 1/4/1992 Age: 26

Year	Team	Lg	G	AB	H	2B	3B	HR	(Hm	Rd)	TB	R	RBI	RC	TBB	IBB	SO	HBP	SH	SF	SB	CS	GDP	Avg	OBP	Slg	OPS
2015	ChC	NL	151	559	154	31	5	26	(21	5)	273	87	99	104	77	0	199	9	0	5	13	4	7	.275	.369	.488	.858
2016	ChC	NL	155	603	176	35	3	39	(17	22)	334	121	102	120	75	5	154	18	0	3	8	5	3	.292	.385	.554	.939
2017	ChC	NL	151	549	162	38	4	29	(18	11)	295	111	73	113	95	5	128	15	0	6	7	5	8	.295	.409	.537	.946
	Postseason		26	99	26	6	1	5	(3	2)	49	13	13	17	12	0	33	1	0	0	1	0	3	.263	.348	.495	.843
	3 ML YEARS		457	1711	492	104	12	94	(56	38)	902	319	274	337	247	10	481	42	0	14	28	14	18	.288	.388	.527	.915

Jake Buchanan

Pitches: R Bats: R Pos: RP-5   **Ht:** 6'0" **Wt:** 235 **Born:** 9/24/1989 **Age:** 28

Year	Team	Lg		HOW MUCH HE PITCHED							WHAT HE GAVE UP										THE RESULTS						
			G	GS	CG	GF	IP	BFP	H	R	ER	HR	SH	SF	HB	TBB	IBB	SO	WP	Bk	W	L	Pct	Sh	Sv-Op	Hld	ERC	ERA
2017	Iowa*	AAA	8	8	0	0	41.2	191	49	26	22	5	2	1	2	19	2	29	1	0	2	2	.500	0	0- -	-	5.58	4.75
2017	Reno*	AAA	11	11	0	0	61.1	253	61	29	29	2	1	1	2	9	0	38	3	0	5	0	1.000	0	0- -	-	2.75	4.26
2014	Hou	AL	17	2	0	9	35.1	154	41	19	18	4	3	0	1	12	1	20	2	0	1	3	.250	0	0-0	0	5.00	4.58
2015	Hou	AL	5	0	0	1	9.0	37	5	2	2	1	1	0	1	4	0	5	2	0	0	0	-	0	0-0	0	2.37	2.00
2016	ChC	NL	2	1	0	1	6.0	21	3	1	1	1	0	0	0	1	0	4	0	0	1	0	1.000	0	0-0	0	1.36	1.50
2017	Cin	NL	5	0	0	3	14.1	77	24	13	13	1	2	1	3	7	2	4	0	0	0	0	-	0	0-0	0	8.79	8.16
	4 ML YEARS		29	3	0	14	64.2	289	73	35	34	7	6	1	5	24	3	33	4	0	2	3	.400	0	0-0	0	5.00	4.73

Clay Buchholz

Pitches: R Bats: L Pos: SP-2   BUCK-holtz   **Ht:** 6'3" **Wt:** 190 **Born:** 8/14/1984 **Age:** 33

Year	Team	Lg		HOW MUCH HE PITCHED							WHAT HE GAVE UP										THE RESULTS						
			G	GS	CG	GF	IP	BFP	H	R	ER	HR	SH	SF	HB	TBB	IBB	SO	WP	Bk	W	L	Pct	Sh	Sv-Op	Hld	ERC	ERA
2007	Bos	AL	4	3	1	0	22.2	88	14	6	4	0	0	1	1	10	0	22	0	0	3	1	.750	1	0-0	0	1.90	1.59
2008	Bos	AL	16	15	1	0	76.0	357	93	63	57	11	0	3	2	41	1	72	2	1	2	9	.182	0	0-0	0	6.40	6.75
2009	Bos	AL	16	16	0	0	92.0	399	91	44	43	13	2	3	2	36	1	68	1	0	7	4	.636	0	0-0	0	4.31	4.21
2010	Bos	AL	28	28	1	0	173.2	711	142	55	45	9	5	5	5	67	1	120	7	1	17	7	.708	1	0-0	0	2.88	2.33
2011	Bos	AL	14	14	0	0	82.2	353	76	34	32	10	1	4	2	31	1	60	3	0	6	3	.667	0	0-0	0	3.72	3.48
2012	Bos	AL	29	29	2	0	189.1	802	187	104	96	25	5	9	12	64	2	129	2	2	11	8	.579	1	0-0	0	4.29	4.56
2013	Bos	AL	16	16	1	0	108.1	416	75	23	21	4	1	2	1	36	0	96	1	0	12	1	.923	1	0-0	0	2.00	1.74
2014	Bos	AL	28	28	2	0	170.1	737	182	108	101	17	3	4	10	54	2	132	8	0	8	11	.421	2	0-0	0	4.37	5.34
2015	Bos	AL	18	18	1	0	113.1	469	114	48	41	6	1	2	5	23	0	107	3	0	7	7	.500	0	0-0	0	3.23	3.26
2016	Bos	AL	37	21	0	7	139.1	588	130	80	74	21	2	6	5	55	1	93	1	0	8	10	.444	0	0-0	0	4.23	4.78
2017	Phi	NL	2	2	0	0	7.1	40	16	10	10	1	0	2	0	3	0	5	0	0	1	1	.000	0	0-0	0	12.26	12.27
	Postseason		6	6	0	0	29.2	133	34	15	14	4	1	0	2	10	1	24	2	1	0	1	.000	0	0-0	0	5.10	4.25
	11 ML YEARS		208	190	9	7	1175.0	4960	1120	575	524	117	20	41	45	420	9	904	28	4	81	62	.566	6	0-0	2	3.83	4.01

Ryan Buchter

Pitches: L Bats: L Pos: RP-71   BOOK-ter   **Ht:** 6'4" **Wt:** 258 **Born:** 2/13/1987 **Age:** 31

Year	Team	Lg		HOW MUCH HE PITCHED							WHAT HE GAVE UP										THE RESULTS						
			G	GS	CG	GF	IP	BFP	H	R	ER	HR	SH	SF	HB	TBB	IBB	SO	WP	Bk	W	L	Pct	Sh	Sv-Op	Hld	ERC	ERA
2014	Atl	NL	1	0	0	0	1.0	3	0	0	0	0	0	0	0	1	0	1	0	0	0	1	.000	0	0-0	0	1.26	0.00
2016	SD	NL	67	0	0	10	63.0	247	34	20	20	4	0	2	2	31	3	78	3	0	3	0	1.000	0	1-2	20	1.94	2.86
2017	2 Tms		71	0	0	12	65.1	268	44	25	21	10	0	3	4	26	1	65	0	1	4	3	.571	0	1-3	20	2.86	2.89
17	SD	NL	42	0	0	5	38.1	161	28	15	13	7	0	1	1	18	0	47	0	1	3	3	.500	0	1-3	15	3.48	3.05
17	KC	AL	29	0	0	7	27.0	107	16	10	8	3	0	2	3	8	1	18	0	0	1	0	1.000	0	0-0	5	2.03	2.67
	3 ML YEARS		139	0	0	22	129.1	518	78	45	41	14	0	5	6	58	4	144	3	1	8	3	.727	0	2-5	40	2.40	2.85

Walker Buehler

Pitches: R Bats: R Pos: RP-8   **Ht:** 6'2" **Wt:** 175 **Born:** 7/28/1994 **Age:** 23

Year	Team	Lg		HOW MUCH HE PITCHED							WHAT HE GAVE UP										THE RESULTS						
			G	GS	CG	GF	IP	BFP	H	R	ER	HR	SH	SF	HB	TBB	IBB	SO	WP	Bk	W	L	Pct	Sh	Sv-Op	Hld	ERC	ERA
2017	Rcuca	A+	5	5	0	0	16.1	63	8	3	2	0	1	0	1	5	0	27	0	0	0	0	-	0	0- -	-	1.13	1.10
2017	Tulsa	AA	11	11	0	0	49.0	195	40	19	19	5	0	2	0	15	0	64	1	0	2	2	.500	0	0- -	-	2.82	3.49
2017	OkCity	AAA	12	3	0	3	23.1	100	19	12	12	1	1	0	0	11	0	34	3	1	1	1	.500	0	1- -	-	2.89	4.63
2017	LAD	NL	8	0	0	2	9.1	44	11	8	8	2	0	0	0	8	1	12	1	0	1	0	1.000	0	0-0	1	8.22	7.71

Madison Bumgarner

Pitches: L Bats: R Pos: SP-17   **Ht:** 6'5" **Wt:** 250 **Born:** 8/1/1989 **Age:** 28

Year	Team	Lg		HOW MUCH HE PITCHED							WHAT HE GAVE UP										THE RESULTS						
			G	GS	CG	GF	IP	BFP	H	R	ER	HR	SH	SF	HB	TBB	IBB	SO	WP	Bk	W	L	Pct	Sh	Sv-Op	Hld	ERC	ERA
2009	SF	NL	4	4	1	0	10.0	40	8	2	2	2	1	1	0	3	1	10	0	0	0	0	-	0	0-0	0	3.14	1.80
2010	SF	NL	18	18	0	0	111.0	472	119	40	37	11	0	4	5	26	2	86	1	1	7	6	.538	0	0-0	0	3.98	3.00
2011	SF	NL	33	33	0	0	204.2	844	202	82	73	12	12	4	5	46	5	191	0	1	13	13	.500	0	0-0	0	3.14	3.21
2012	SF	NL	32	32	2	0	208.1	849	183	87	78	23	7	4	7	49	6	191	3	2	16	11	.593	1	0-0	0	2.95	3.37
2013	SF	NL	31	31	0	0	201.1	803	146	68	62	15	10	4	6	62	6	199	6	0	13	9	.591	0	0-0	0	2.23	2.77
2014	SF	NL	33	33	4	0	217.1	873	194	81	72	21	9	5	6	43	3	219	4	1	18	10	.643	2	0-0	0	2.83	2.98
2015	SF	NL	32	32	4	0	218.1	869	181	73	71	21	5	4	7	39	2	234	1	0	18	9	.667	2	0-0	0	2.43	2.93
2016	SF	NL	34	34	4	0	226.2	912	179	79	69	26	3	6	8	54	0	251	4	1	15	9	.625	1	0-0	0	2.57	2.74
2017	SF	NL	17	17	1	0	111.0	450	101	41	41	17	2	1	3	20	3	101	0	0	4	9	.308	0	0-0	0	3.14	3.32
	Postseason		16	14	3	1	102.1	398	74	25	24	8	6	1	5	18	2	87	0	0	8	3	.727	3	1-1	0	1.88	2.11
	9 ML YEARS		234	231	15	1	1508.2	6112	1313	553	505	148	49	33	47	342	28	1482	19	6	104	76	.578	6	0-0	0	2.81	3.01

Aaron Bummer

Pitches: L Bats: L Pos: RP-30   **Ht:** 6'3" **Wt:** 200 **Born:** 9/21/1993 **Age:** 24

Year	Team	Lg		HOW MUCH HE PITCHED							WHAT HE GAVE UP										THE RESULTS						
			G	GS	CG	GF	IP	BFP	H	R	ER	HR	SH	SF	HB	TBB	IBB	SO	WP	Bk	W	L	Pct	Sh	Sv-Op	Hld	ERC	ERA
2014	Gr Falls	R+	16	0	0	3	22.0	89	18	7	6	1	0	0	2	6	0	28	3	0	0	0	-	0	1- -	-	2.67	2.45
2016	3 Tms	Low	15	0	0	3	16.2	75	16	10	9	0	0	2	0	7	0	18	4	0	1	2	.333	0	0- -	-	3.05	4.86
2017	WinSa	A+	11	0	0	2	11.0	47	10	6	6	2	0	0	0	3	0	15	1	0	0	2	.000	0	2- -	-	3.45	4.91
2017	Brham	AA	17	1	0	10	33.0	137	29	11	11	2	2	1	0	16	3	34	2	0	1	3	.250	0	3- -	-	3.43	3.00
2017	CWS	AL	30	0	0	3	22.0	91	13	11	11	4	1	1	1	15	1	17	1	0	1	3	.250	0	0-1	7	3.70	4.50

Dylan Bundy

Pitches: R Bats: B Pos: SP-28 Ht: 6'1" Wt: 200 Born: 11/15/1992 Age: 25

Year Team	Lg	G	GS	CG	GF	IP	BFP	H	R	ER	HR	SH	SF	HB	TBB	IBB	SO	WP	Bk	W	L	Pct	Sh	Sv-Op	Hld	ERC	ERA
2012 Bal	AL	2	0	0	2	1.2	6	1	0	0	0	0	0	0	0	0	0	0	0	0	0	-	0	0-0	0	2.46	0.00
2016 Bal	AL	36	14	0	6	109.2	474	109	52	49	18	1	1	6	42	4	104	0	0	10	6	.625	0	0-0	3	4.61	4.02
2017 Bal	AL	28	28	1	0	169.2	698	152	82	80	26	0	7	7	51	0	152	0	0	13	9	.591	1	0-0	0	3.68	4.24
3 ML YEARS		66	42	1	8	281.0	1178	262	134	129	44	1	8	13	94	4	256	0	0	23	15	.605	1	0-0	3	4.03	4.13

Billy Burns

Bats: B Throws: R Pos: CF-4;PR-2;RF-1;PH-1 Ht: 5'9" Wt: 170 Born: 8/30/1989 Age: 28

								BATTING													RUNNING			AVERAGES			
Year Team	Lg	G	AB	H	2B	3B	HR	(Hm	Rd)	TB	R	RBI	RC	TBB	IBB	SO	HBP	SH	SF	SB	CS	GDP	Avg	OBP	Slg	OPS
2017 Omha*	AAA	99	354	101	7	4	0	(-	-)	116	50	22	49	44	1	60	4	9	2	24	11	4	.285	.369	.328	.696
2014 Oak	AL	13	6	1	0	0	0	(0	0)	1	4	0	0	0	0	0	0	0	0	3	1	0	.167	.167	.167	.333
2015 Oak	AL	125	520	153	18	9	5	(3	2)	204	70	42	72	26	1	81	6	1	2	26	8	5	.294	.334	.392	.726
2016 2 Tms	AL	97	311	73	11	4	0	(0	0)	92	39	13	23	10	2	37	6	3	2	17	5	3	.235	.271	.296	.566
2017 KC	AL	7	6	1	0	0	0	(0	0)	1	1	0	0	0	0	1	0	0	0	0	1	0	.167	.167	.167	.333
16 Oak	AL	73	274	64	11	4	0	(0	0)	83	32	12	22	10	2	30	4	3	1	14	3	3	.234	.270	.303	.573
16 KC	AL	24	37	9	0	0	0	(0	0)	9	7	1	1	0	0	7	2	0	1	3	2	0	.243	.275	.243	.518
4 ML YEARS		242	843	228	29	13	5	(3	2)	298	114	55	95	36	3	119	12	4	4	46	15	8	.270	.308	.353	.662

Alan Busenitz

Pitches: R Bats: R Pos: RP-28 Ht: 6'1" Wt: 180 Born: 8/22/1990 Age: 27

Year Team	Lg	G	GS	CG	GF	IP	BFP	H	R	ER	HR	SH	SF	HB	TBB	IBB	SO	WP	Bk	W	L	Pct	Sh	Sv-Op	Hld	ERC	ERA
2013 Orem	R+	21	0	0	9	38.2	152	37	13	10	3	1	0	1	4	0	27	2	0	5	2	.714	0	1--	-	2.75	2.33
2014 Burlgtn	A	49	0	0	34	69.2	281	55	18	15	7	4	2	1	21	3	62	8	2	4	5	.444	0	17--	-	2.16	1.94
2015 Ark	AA	16	8	1	2	53.1	247	80	43	40	7	4	2	1	16	0	38	7	0	1	5	.167	0	0--	-	7.13	6.75
2015 InldEm	A+	21	0	0	10	46.1	199	49	17	17	2	1	2	4	16	0	44	6	0	0	2	.000	0	2--	-	4.21	3.30
2016 Ark	AA	24	0	0	12	32.2	126	28	7	7	2	0	0	2	5	0	32	1	0	1	0	1.000	0	2--	-	2.51	1.93
2016 Salt Lk	AAA	10	0	0	3	13.0	62	16	13	11	1	1	1	2	5	0	13	1	0	0	1	.000	0	3--	-	5.66	7.62
2016 Chatt	AA	5	0	0	0	7.2	32	9	3	3	0	0	0	2	1	0	5	0	0	0	0	-	0	0--	-	4.60	3.52
2016 Roch	AAA	6	0	0	3	7.2	35	8	3	3	0	0	1	0	4	2	5	0	0	2	0	1.000	0	1--	-	3.49	3.52
2017 Roch	AAA	24	0	0	7	35.1	132	19	7	7	0	1	1	2	10	0	39	6	0	3	0	1.000	0	2--	-	1.25	1.78
2017 Min	AL	28	0	0	10	31.2	121	22	9	7	4	0	5	0	9	0	23	2	0	1	1	.500	0	0-1	2	2.31	1.99

Matt Bush

Pitches: R Bats: R Pos: RP-57 Ht: 5'9" Wt: 180 Born: 2/8/1986 Age: 32

Year Team	Lg	G	GS	CG	GF	IP	BFP	H	R	ER	HR	SH	SF	HB	TBB	IBB	SO	WP	Bk	W	L	Pct	Sh	Sv-Op	Hld	ERC	ERA
2016 Frisco	AA	12	0	0	9	17.0	63	9	5	5	2	0	1	1	4	0	18	2	0	0	2	.000	0	5--	-	1.57	2.65
2016 Tex	AL	58	0	0	15	61.2	243	44	18	17	4	1	3	1	14	0	61	2	0	7	2	.778	0	1-4	22	1.83	2.48
2017 Tex	AL	57	0	0	22	52.1	240	57	30	22	7	0	1	4	19	0	58	2	0	3	4	.429	0	10-15	10	4.81	3.78
Postseason		2	0	0	1	3.2	14	1	1	0	0	0	0	0	2	1	6	0	0	1	0	1.000	0	0-0	0	0.66	0.00
2 ML YEARS		115	0	0	37	114.0	483	101	48	39	11	1	4	5	33	0	119	4	0	10	6	.625	0	11-19	32	3.10	3.08

Drew Butera

Bats: R Throws: R Pos: C-74;1B-4;PH-2;PR-1 bue-TARE-ah Ht: 6'1" Wt: 200 Born: 8/9/1983 Age: 34

								BATTING													RUNNING			AVERAGES			
Year Team	Lg	G	AB	H	2B	3B	HR	(Hm	Rd)	TB	R	RBI	RC	TBB	IBB	SO	HBP	SH	SF	SB	CS	GDP	Avg	OBP	Slg	OPS
2010 Min	AL	49	142	28	6	1	2	(0	2)	42	12	13	7	4	0	25	4	3	2	0	0	5	.197	.237	.296	.533
2011 Min	AL	93	234	39	9	1	2	(1	1)	56	19	23	11	11	0	42	2	6	1	0	0	7	.167	.210	.239	.449
2012 Min	AL	42	111	22	6	0	1	(1	0)	31	7	5	6	9	0	26	2	0	0	0	0	5	.198	.270	.279	.550
2013 2 Tms		6	10	1	0	0	0	(0	0)	1	0	0	0	0	0	5	0	0	0	0	0	0	.100	.100	.100	.200
2014 LAD	NL	61	170	32	6	1	3	(0	3)	49	16	14	10	17	1	41	2	1	2	0	0	1	.188	.267	.288	.555
2015 2 Tms	AL	55	107	21	3	0	1	(0	1)	27	9	5	6	6	0	26	2	5	0	0	1	0	.196	.252	.252	.505
2016 KC	AL	56	123	35	10	1	4	(0	4)	59	18	16	15	8	0	36	0	2	0	0	0	2	.285	.328	.480	.808
2017 KC	AL	75	163	37	4	1	3	(1	2)	52	18	14	18	12	0	41	1	1	0	0	0	0	.227	.284	.319	.603
13 Min	AL	2	3	0	0	0	0	(0	0)	0	0	0	0	0	0	1	0	0	0	0	0	0	.000	.000	.000	.000
13 LAD	NL	4	7	1	0	0	0	(0	0)	1	0	0	0	0	0	4	0	0	0	0	0	0	.143	.143	.143	.286
15 LAA	AL	10	21	4	0	0	0	(0	0)	4	3	0	0	0	0	2	0	0	0	0	1	0	.190	.190	.190	.381
15 KC	AL	45	86	17	3	0	1	(0	1)	23	6	5	6	6	0	24	2	5	0	0	0	0	.198	.266	.267	.533
Postseason		3	1	0	0	0	0	(0	0)	0	0	0	0	1	0	0	0	0	0	0	0	0	.000	.500	.000	.500
8 ML YEARS		437	1060	215	44	5	16	(3	13)	317	99	90	73	67	1	242	13	18	5	0	1	18	.203	.258	.299	.557

Eddie Butler

Pitches: R Bats: R Pos: SP-11; RP-2 Ht: 6'2" Wt: 180 Born: 3/13/1991 Age: 27

Year Team	Lg	G	GS	CG	GF	IP	BFP	H	R	ER	HR	SH	SF	HB	TBB	IBB	SO	WP	Bk	W	L	Pct	Sh	Sv-Op	Hld	ERC	ERA
2017 Iowa*	AAA	8	8	0	0	45.2	191	49	12	11	1	0	1	2	12	0	30	1	0	2	0	1.000	0	0--	-	3.67	2.17
2014 Col	NL	3	3	0	0	16.0	76	23	12	12	2	2	0	0	7	1	3	0	0	1	1	.500	0	0-0	0	6.98	6.75
2015 Col	NL	16	16	1	0	79.1	370	102	57	52	13	6	1	4	42	4	44	0	0	3	10	.231	0	0-0	0	7.12	5.90
2016 Col	NL	17	9	0	0	64.0	293	87	57	51	13	2	3	3	21	1	47	1	0	2	5	.286	0	0-0	0	7.00	7.17
2017 ChC	NL	13	11	0	2	54.2	237	50	24	24	4	1	1	2	28	2	30	3	0	4	3	.571	0	0-0	0	3.96	3.95
4 ML YEARS		49	39	1	2	214.0	976	262	150	139	32	11	4	9	98	8	124	4	0	10	19	.345	0	0-0	0	6.22	5.85

Byron Buxton

Bats: R Throws: R Pos: CF-137;PR-5   Ht: 6'2" Wt: 190 Born: 12/18/1993 Age: 24

Year Team	Lg	G	AB	H	2B	3B	HR	Hm	Rd	TB	R	RBI	RC	TBB	IBB	SO	HBP	SH	SF	SB	CS	GDP	Avg	OBP	Slg	OPS
2015 Min	AL	46	129	27	7	1	2	(0	2)	42	16	6	10	6	0	44	1	2	0	2	2	1	.209	.250	.326	.576
2016 Min	AL	92	298	67	19	6	10	(6	4)	128	44	38	33	23	0	118	3	4	3	10	2	2	.225	.284	.430	.714
2017 Min	AL	140	462	117	14	6	16	(8	8)	191	69	51	63	38	2	150	4	5	2	29	1	1	.253	.314	.413	.728
3 ML YEARS		278	889	211	40	13	28	(14	14)	361	129	95	106	67	2	312	8	11	5	41	5	4	.237	.295	.406	.701

Asdrubal Cabrera

Bats: B Throws: R Pos: SS-45;3B-44;2B-32;PH-16;DH-1;PR-1azz-DRUE-bull   Ht: 6'0" Wt: 205 Born: 11/13/1985 Age: 32

Year Team	Lg	G	AB	H	2B	3B	HR	Hm	Rd	TB	R	RBI	RC	TBB	IBB	SO	HBP	SH	SF	SB	CS	GDP	Avg	OBP	Slg	OPS
2007 Cle	AL	45	159	45	9	2	3	(1	2)	67	30	22	27	17	0	29	2	5	3	0	0	7	.283	.354	.421	.775
2008 Cle	AL	114	352	91	20	0	6	(5	1)	129	48	47	48	46	2	77	4	11	5	4	4	8	.259	.346	.366	.713
2009 Cle	AL	131	523	161	42	4	6	(4	2)	229	81	68	81	44	1	89	1	10	3	17	4	13	.308	.361	.438	.799
2010 Cle	AL	97	381	105	16	1	3	(2	1)	132	39	29	46	25	0	60	5	11	3	6	4	10	.276	.326	.346	.673
2011 Cle	AL	151	604	165	32	3	25	(13	12)	278	87	92	100	44	5	119	11	4	4	17	5	10	.273	.332	.460	.792
2012 Cle	AL	143	555	150	35	1	16	(10	6)	235	70	68	74	52	3	99	6	1	2	9	4	18	.270	.338	.423	.762
2013 Cle	AL	136	508	123	35	2	14	(8	6)	204	66	64	51	35	1	114	8	6	5	9	3	10	.242	.299	.402	.700
2014 2 Tms		146	553	133	31	4	14	(6	8)	214	74	61	57	49	2	108	7	1	6	10	2	15	.241	.307	.387	.694
2015 TB	AL	143	505	134	28	5	15	(7	8)	217	66	58	53	36	4	107	3	1	6	6	3	14	.265	.315	.430	.744
2016 NYM	NL	141	521	146	30	1	23	(18	5)	247	65	62	76	38	3	103	7	0	2	5	1	14	.280	.336	.474	.810
2017 NYM	NL	135	479	134	32	0	14	(5	9)	208	66	59	70	50	1	83	5	1	5	3	2	19	.280	.351	.434	.785
14 Cle	AL	97	378	93	22	2	9	(5	4)	146	54	40	36	27	1	79	7	0	4	7	2	11	.246	.305	.386	.692
14 Was	NL	49	175	40	9	2	5	(1	4)	68	20	21	21	22	1	29	0	1	2	3	0	4	.229	.312	.389	.700
Postseason		17	68	14	1	0	2	(2	0)	21	7	8	6	3	0	18	0	3	1	0	0	3	.206	.236	.309	.545
11 ML YEARS		1382	5140	1387	310	23	139	(79	60)	2160	692	630	683	436	22	988	59	51	44	86	32	138	.270	.331	.420	.752

Melky Cabrera

Bats: B Throws: L Pos: LF-104;RF-46;DH-9;PH-1   Ht: 5'10" Wt: 210 Born: 8/11/1984 Age: 33

Year Team	Lg	G	AB	H	2B	3B	HR	Hm	Rd	TB	R	RBI	RC	TBB	IBB	SO	HBP	SH	SF	SB	CS	GDP	Avg	OBP	Slg	OPS
2005 NYY	AL	6	19	4	0	0	0	(0	0)	4	1	0	0	0	0	2	0	0	0	0	0	0	.211	.211	.211	.421
2006 NYY	AL	130	460	129	26	2	7	(3	4)	180	75	50	68	56	3	59	2	5	1	12	5	9	.280	.360	.391	.752
2007 NYY	AL	150	545	149	24	8	8	(4	4)	213	66	73	70	43	0	68	5	10	9	13	5	14	.273	.327	.391	.718
2008 NYY	AL	129	414	103	12	1	8	(4	4)	141	42	37	37	29	5	58	3	4	3	9	2	11	.249	.301	.341	.641
2009 NYY	AL	154	485	133	28	1	13	(9	4)	202	66	68	69	43	4	59	4	4	4	10	2	15	.274	.336	.416	.752
2010 Atl	NL	147	458	117	27	3	4	(1	3)	162	50	42	45	42	11	64	1	5	3	7	1	8	.255	.317	.354	.671
2011 KC	AL	155	658	201	44	5	18	(6	12)	309	102	87	92	35	3	94	1	7	5	20	10	13	.305	.339	.470	.809
2012 SF	NL	113	459	159	25	10	11	(2	9)	237	84	60	83	36	4	63	0	1	5	13	5	8	.346	.390	.516	.906
2013 Tor	AL	88	344	96	15	2	3	(3	0)	124	39	30	39	23	0	47	0	2	3	2	2	7	.279	.322	.360	.682
2014 Tor	AL	139	568	171	35	3	16	(7	9)	260	81	73	84	43	3	67	3	2	5	6	2	19	.301	.351	.458	.808
2015 CWS	AL	158	629	172	36	2	12	(6	6)	248	70	77	81	40	2	88	2	2	10	3	0	18	.273	.314	.394	.709
2016 CWS	AL	151	591	175	42	5	14	(6	8)	269	70	86	89	47	2	69	0	3	5	0	0	17	.296	.345	.455	.800
2017 2 Tms	AL	156	620	177	30	2	17	(9	8)	262	79	85	84	36	1	74	2	2	6	1	2	19	.285	.324	.423	.746
17 CWS	AL	98	397	117	17	0	13	(8	5)	173	54	56	59	25	1	52	1	2	3	0	0	7	.295	.336	.436	.771
17 KC	AL	58	223	60	13	2	4	(1	3)	89	24	29	24	11	0	22	1	0	3	1	2	12	.269	.303	.399	.702
Postseason		22	75	16	2	0	1	(0	1)	21	8	7	5	3	0	16	0	2	0	0	0	0	.213	.244	.280	.524
13 ML YEARS		1676	6250	1786	344	44	131	(60	71)	2611	824	768	840	473	38	812	23	47	59	98	36	158	.286	.335	.418	.753

Miguel Cabrera

Bats: R Throws: R Pos: 1B-115;DH-14;PH-1   Ht: 6'4" Wt: 240 Born: 4/18/1983 Age: 35

Year Team	Lg	G	AB	H	2B	3B	HR	Hm	Rd	TB	R	RBI	RC	TBB	IBB	SO	HBP	SH	SF	SB	CS	GDP	Avg	OBP	Slg	OPS
2003 Fla	NL	87	314	84	21	3	12	(7	5)	147	39	62	51	25	3	84	2	4	1	0	2	12	.268	.325	.468	.793
2004 Fla	NL	160	603	177	31	1	33	(14	19)	309	101	112	92	68	5	148	6	0	8	5	2	20	.294	.366	.512	.879
2005 Fla	NL	158	613	198	43	2	33	(11	22)	344	106	116	108	64	12	125	2	0	6	1	0	20	.323	.385	.561	.947
2006 Fla	NL	158	576	195	50	2	26	(15	11)	327	112	114	132	86	27	108	10	0	4	9	6	18	.339	.430	.568	.998
2007 Fla	NL	157	588	188	38	2	34	(19	15)	332	91	119	122	79	23	127	5	1	7	2	1	17	.320	.401	.565	.965
2008 Det	AL	160	616	180	36	2	37	(19	18)	331	85	127	109	56	6	126	3	0	9	1	0	16	.292	.349	.537	.887
2009 Det	AL	160	611	198	34	0	34	(19	15)	334	96	103	114	68	14	107	5	0	1	6	2	22	.324	.396	.547	.942
2010 Det	AL	150	548	180	45	1	38	(17	21)	341	111	126	122	89	32	95	3	0	8	3	3	17	.328	.420	.622	1.042
2011 Det	AL	161	572	197	48	0	30	(15	15)	335	111	105	141	108	22	89	3	0	5	2	1	24	.344	.448	.586	1.033
2012 Det	AL	161	622	205	40	0	44	(28	16)	377	109	139	123	66	17	98	3	0	6	4	1	28	.330	.393	.606	.999
2013 Det	AL	148	555	193	26	1	44	(17	27)	353	103	137	146	90	19	94	5	0	2	3	0	19	.348	.442	.636	1.078
2014 Det	AL	159	611	191	52	1	25	(13	12)	320	101	109	110	60	10	117	3	0	11	1	1	21	.313	.371	.524	.895
2015 Det	AL	119	429	145	28	1	18	(7	11)	229	64	76	93	77	15	82	3	0	2	1	1	19	.338	.440	.534	.974
2016 Det	AL	158	595	188	31	1	38	(20	18)	335	92	108	106	75	15	116	4	0	5	0	0	26	.316	.393	.563	.956
2017 Det	AL	130	469	117	22	0	16	(11	5)	187	50	60	65	54	6	110	3	0	3	0	1	15	.249	.329	.399	.728
Postseason		55	205	57	10	0	13	(4	9)	106	29	38	34	27	7	48	2	1	0	3	0	7	.278	.368	.517	.885
15 ML YEARS		2226	8322	2636	545	17	462	(232	230)	4601	1371	1613	1624	1065	226	1626	60	5	78	38	21	294	.317	.395	.553	.948

Trevor Cahill

Pitches: R Bats: R Pos: SP-14; RP-7   KAY-hill   Ht: 6'4" Wt: 240 Born: 3/1/1988 Age: 30

Year Team	Lg	G	GS	CG	GF	IP	BFP	H	R	ER	HR	SH	SF	HB	TBB	IBB	SO	WP	Bk	W	L	Pct	Sh	Sv-Op	Hld	ERC	ERA
2009 Oak	AL	32	32	0	0	178.2	773	185	99	92	27	4	7	4	72	1	90	5	0	10	13	.435	0	0-0	0	4.79	4.63
2010 Oak	AL	30	30	1	0	196.2	783	155	73	65	19	3	6	6	63	1	118	2	2	18	8	.692	1	0-0	0	2.81	2.97
2011 Oak	AL	34	34	0	0	207.2	901	214	102	96	19	8	6	8	82	1	147	15	0	12	14	.462	0	0-0	0	4.34	4.16
2012 Ari	NL	32	32	2	0	200.0	839	184	93	84	16	12	6	11	74	0	156	10	2	13	12	.520	1	0-0	0	3.66	3.78
2013 Ari	NL	26	25	0	1	146.2	636	143	70	65	13	9	9	6	65	2	102	17	0	8	10	.444	0	0-0	0	4.19	3.99
2014 Ari	NL	32	17	0	8	110.2	499	123	76	69	9	6	3	4	55	2	105	5	0	3	12	.200	0	0-0	0	5.11	5.61
2015 2 Tms	NL	26	3	0	6	43.1	187	44	27	26	4	3	1	2	16	1	36	2	0	1	3	.250	0	1-2	0	4.15	5.40
2016 ChC	NL	50	1	0	16	65.2	284	49	22	20	7	0	0	5	35	3	66	3	0	4	4	.500	0	0-1	4	3.42	2.74
2017 2 Tms		21	14	0	1	84.0	381	91	50	46	16	2	0	3	45	1	87	16	0	4	3	.571	0	0-0	1	5.97	4.93
15 Atl	NL	15	3	0	6	26.1	124	36	23	22	2	2	1	1	11	1	14	1	0	0	3	.000	0	0-0	0	6.22	7.52
15 ChC	NL	11	0	0	0	17.0	63	8	4	4	2	1	0	1	5	0	22	1	0	0	1	1.000	0	0-0	2	1.52	2.12
17 SD	NL	11	11	0	0	61.0	263	58	29	25	6	1	0	3	24	1	72	14	0	4	3	.571	0	0-0	0	3.92	3.69
17 KC	AL	10	3	0	1	23.0	118	33	21	21	10	1	0	0	21	0	15	2	0	0	0	-	0	0-0	1	12.52	8.22
Postseason		6	0	0	1	5.1	24	7	2	2	0	1	0	0	0	0	8	1	0	1	1	.500	0	0-1	2	3.29	3.38
9 ML YEARS		283	188	3	32	1233.1	5283	1188	612	563	130	47	38	49	507	12	907	75	4	73	79	.480	2	1-3	7	4.14	4.11

Lorenzo Cain

Bats: R Throws: R Pos: CF-151;DH-3;PR-1   Ht: 6'2" Wt: 205 Born: 4/13/1986 Age: 32

Year Team	Lg	G	AB	H	2B	3B	HR	Hm	Rd	TB	R	RBI	RC	TBB	IBB	SO	HBP	SH	SF	SB	CS	GDP	Avg	OBP	Slg	OPS
2010 Mil	NL	43	147	45	11	1	1	(1	0)	61	17	13	23	9	0	28	1	0	1	7	1	1	.306	.348	.415	.763
2011 KC	AL	6	22	6	1	0	0	(0	0)	7	4	1	2	1	0	4	0	0	0	0	0	0	.273	.304	.318	.623
2012 KC	AL	61	222	59	9	2	7	(3	4)	93	27	31	32	15	0	56	3	0	4	10	0	4	.266	.316	.419	.734
2013 KC	AL	115	399	100	21	3	4	(3	1)	139	54	46	46	33	2	90	4	0	6	14	6	10	.251	.310	.348	.658
2014 KC	AL	133	471	142	29	4	5	(3	2)	194	55	53	67	24	2	108	4	0	3	28	5	9	.301	.339	.412	.751
2015 KC	AL	140	551	169	34	6	16	(9	7)	263	101	72	90	37	4	98	12	0	4	28	6	16	.307	.361	.477	.838
2016 KC	AL	103	397	114	19	1	9	(3	6)	162	56	56	53	31	3	84	2	0	4	14	5	15	.287	.339	.408	.747
2017 KC	AL	155	584	175	27	5	15	(3	12)	257	86	49	90	54	1	100	5	0	2	26	2	20	.300	.363	.440	.803
Postseason		31	122	36	7	0	1	(0	1)	46	24	19	26	16	3	23	1	1	2	8	1	1	.295	.376	.377	.753
8 ML YEARS		756	2793	810	151	22	57	(25	32)	1176	400	321	403	204	12	568	31	0	24	127	25	75	.290	.342	.421	.763

Matt Cain

Pitches: R Bats: R Pos: SP-23; RP-4   Ht: 6'3" Wt: 230 Born: 10/1/1984 Age: 33

Year Team	Lg	G	GS	CG	GF	IP	BFP	H	R	ER	HR	SH	SF	HB	TBB	IBB	SO	WP	Bk	W	L	Pct	Sh	Sv-Op	Hld	ERC	ERA
2005 SF	NL	7	7	1	0	46.1	181	24	12	12	4	2	1	0	19	1	30	1	0	2	1	.667	0	0-0	0	1.61	2.33
2006 SF	NL	32	31	1	1	190.2	818	157	93	88	18	11	6	6	87	1	179	9	2	13	12	.520	1	0-0	0	3.35	4.15
2007 SF	NL	32	32	1	0	200.0	832	173	84	81	14	8	5	5	79	3	163	12	0	7	16	.304	0	0-0	0	3.23	3.65
2008 SF	NL	34	34	1	0	217.2	933	206	95	91	19	7	7	7	91	9	186	7	2	8	14	.364	1	0-0	0	3.84	3.76
2009 SF	NL	33	33	4	0	217.2	886	184	73	70	22	10	6	3	73	6	171	9	0	14	8	.636	0	0-0	0	3.06	2.89
2010 SF	NL	33	33	4	0	223.1	896	181	84	78	22	6	7	4	61	4	177	8	0	13	11	.542	2	0-0	0	2.65	3.14
2011 SF	NL	33	33	1	0	221.2	907	177	82	71	9	11	6	9	63	5	179	4	0	12	11	.522	2	0-0	0	2.31	2.88
2012 SF	NL	32	32	2	0	219.1	876	177	73	68	21	11	9	9	51	1	193	8	0	16	5	.762	2	0-0	0	2.57	2.79
2013 SF	NL	30	30	0	0	184.1	760	158	85	82	23	6	2	5	55	3	158	1	0	8	10	.444	0	0-0	0	3.15	4.00
2014 SF	NL	15	15	0	0	90.1	371	81	47	42	13	3	2	2	32	2	70	2	0	2	7	.222	0	0-0	0	3.73	4.18
2015 SF	NL	13	11	0	0	60.2	271	71	39	39	12	1	4	4	20	0	41	1	0	2	4	.333	0	0-0	0	5.79	5.79
2016 SF	NL	21	17	0	2	89.1	397	103	58	56	16	8	6	6	32	1	72	5	0	4	8	.333	0	0-0	0	5.70	5.64
2017 SF	NL	27	23	0	1	124.1	568	157	85	75	18	3	6	2	49	6	75	3	0	3	11	.214	0	0-0	1	5.92	5.43
Postseason		8	8	0	0	51.1	210	40	13	12	6	1	0	6	14	2	33	1	0	4	2	.667	0	0-0	0	2.92	2.10
13 ML YEARS		342	331	15	4	2085.2	8699	1849	910	853	211	87	67	62	712	42	1694	70	4	104	118	.468	6	0-0	1	3.33	3.68

Kole Calhoun

Bats: L Throws: L Pos: RF-154;PH-2   Ht: 5'10" Wt: 205 Born: 10/14/1987 Age: 30

Year Team	Lg	G	AB	H	2B	3B	HR	Hm	Rd	TB	R	RBI	RC	TBB	IBB	SO	HBP	SH	SF	SB	CS	GDP	Avg	OBP	Slg	OPS
2012 LAA	AL	21	23	4	1	0	0	(0	0)	5	2	1	0	2	1	6	0	0	0	1	0	0	.174	.240	.217	.457
2013 LAA	AL	58	195	55	7	2	8	(5	3)	90	29	32	33	21	0	41	1	0	5	2	2	6	.282	.347	.462	.808
2014 LAA	AL	127	493	134	31	3	17	(7	10)	222	90	58	75	38	0	104	2	2	5	5	3	5	.272	.325	.450	.776
2015 LAA	AL	159	630	161	23	2	26	(16	10)	266	78	83	85	45	1	164	5	2	4	4	1	6	.256	.308	.422	.731
2016 LAA	AL	157	594	161	35	5	18	(7	11)	260	91	75	93	67	0	118	6	0	5	2	3	10	.271	.348	.438	.786
2017 LAA	AL	155	569	139	23	2	19	(8	11)	223	77	71	85	71	4	134	8	0	6	5	1	10	.244	.333	.392	.725
Postseason		3	15	5	0	0	0	(0	0)	5	1	0	1	0	0	1	0	0	0	0	0	0	.333	.333	.333	.667
6 ML YEARS		677	2504	654	120	14	88	(43	45)	1066	367	320	371	244	6	567	22	4	22	19	10	37	.261	.330	.426	.755

Willie Calhoun

Bats: L Throws: R Pos: LF-11;DH-1;PH-1   Ht: 5'8" Wt: 187 Born: 11/4/1994 Age: 23

Year Team	Lg	G	AB	H	2B	3B	HR	Hm	Rd	TB	R	RBI	RC	TBB	IBB	SO	HBP	SH	SF	SB	CS	GDP	Avg	OBP	Slg	OPS
2015 3 Tms	Low	73	285	90	23	1	11	(-	-)	148	48	48	56	35	0	38	1	0	2	2	1	6	.316	.390	.519	.909
2016 Tulsa	AA	133	503	128	25	1	27	(-	-)	236	75	88	79	46	4	65	5	1	6	0	0	15	.254	.320	.469	.789
2017 OkCity	AAA	99	373	111	24	5	23	(-	-)	214	64	67	76	36	3	49	1	0	4	3	2	7	.298	.357	.574	.931
2017 RdRck	AAA	29	113	35	3	1	8	(-	-)	64	16	26	21	6	1	12	0	1	0	0	0	3	.310	.345	.566	.911
2017 Tex	AL	13	34	9	0	0	1	(1	0)	12	3	4	6	2	0	7	1	0	0	0	0	0	.265	.324	.353	.677

Orlando Calixte

ka-LEEKS-tay

Bats: R **Throws:** R **Pos:** LF-9;PH-7;3B-5;SS-4;PR-4;RF-3;CF-2;DH-1 **Ht:** 5'11" **Wt:** 180 **Born:** 2/3/1992 **Age:** 26

								BATTING										RUNNING			AVERAGES			
Year	Team	Lg	G	AB	H	2B	3B	HR	(Hm | Rd)	TB	R	RBI	RC	TBB	IBB	SO	HBP	SH	SF	SB	CS	GDP	Avg	OBP	Slg	OPS
2013	NWArk	AA	123	484	121	25	4	8	(- | -)	178	59	36	56	42	2	131	3	4	3	14	11	15	.250	.312	.368	.680
2014	NWArk	AA	96	374	89	15	1	11	(- | -)	139	43	37	41	27	0	92	0	6	5	9	5	7	.238	.286	.372	.657
2015	Omha	AAA	107	354	81	11	2	8	(- | -)	120	38	27	38	27	2	84	2	11	0	22	3	8	.229	.287	.339	.626
2016	NWArk	AA	38	139	41	9	0	2	(- | -)	56	26	14	20	9	0	31	0	2	2	14	3	4	.295	.333	.403	.736
2016	Omha	AAA	88	332	88	17	5	9	(- | -)	142	48	29	45	28	1	68	0	5	2	5	6	2	.265	.320	.428	.748
2017	Scrmto	AAA	97	378	92	15	5	14	(- | -)	159	48	43	47	21	0	83	0	2	0	19	4	9	.243	.283	.421	.704
2015	KC	AL	2	3	0	0	0	0	(0 | 0)	0	1	0	0	0	0	0	0	0	0	0	0	0	.000	.000	.000	.000
2017	SF	NL	29	49	7	1	0	0	(0 | 0)	8	5	6	2	3	0	16	0	1	2	1	0	1	.143	.185	.163	.348
	2 ML YEARS		31	52	7	1	0	0	(0 | 0)	8	6	6	2	3	0	16	0	1	2	1	0	1	.135	.175	.154	.329

Jamie Callahan

Pitches: R **Bats:** R **Pos:** RP-9 **Ht:** 6'2" **Wt:** 230 **Born:** 8/24/1994 **Age:** 23

			HOW MUCH HE PITCHED						WHAT HE GAVE UP												THE RESULTS						
Year	Team	Lg	G	GS	CG	GF	IP	BFP	H	R	ER	HR	SH	SF	HB	TBB	IBB	SO	WP	Bk	W	L	Pct	Sh	Sv-Op	Hld	ERC	ERA
2013	Lowell	A-	13	12	0	0	59.2	239	48	27	26	4	0	3	2	17	0	54	3	1	5	1	.833	0	0- --		2.57	3.92
2014	Grnvlle	A	25	25	0	0	108.2	520	137	95	84	12	0	6	5	66	0	89	10	1	3	13	.188	0	0- --		6.80	6.96
2015	Grnvlle	A	31	6	0	10	89.1	397	94	52	45	4	2	2	3	33	0	94	6	0	7	6	.538	0	3- --		3.89	4.53
2016	Salem	A+	36	0	0	18	65.2	287	53	30	24	1	1	1	4	38	1	63	4	0	5	3	.625	0	7- --		3.28	3.29
2017	Portlnd	AA	10	0	0	9	13.0	47	8	2	2	0	0	0	0	0	0	20	1	0	4	1	.800	0	2- --		0.79	1.38
2017	Pwtckt	AAA	22	0	0	14	29.0	126	28	14	13	2	0	1	0	13	0	36	1	0	1	1	.500	0	4- --		3.83	4.03
2017	LsVgs	AAA	9	0	0	8	10.0	45	12	5	2	2	0	0	0	4	0	10	0	0	1	1	.500	0	1- --		6.01	1.80
2017	NYM	NL	9	0	0	5	6.2	30	7	4	3	0	0	1	0	1	0	5	0	0	0	0	-	0	0-1	1	2.46	4.05

Johan Camargo

Bats: B **Throws:** R **Pos:** 3B-43;SS-27;PH-14;2B-9;PR-3;LF-1 **Ht:** 6'0" **Wt:** 160 **Born:** 12/13/1993 **Age:** 24

								BATTING										RUNNING			AVERAGES			
Year	Team	Lg	G	AB	H	2B	3B	HR	(Hm | Rd)	TB	R	RBI	RC	TBB	IBB	SO	HBP	SH	SF	SB	CS	GDP	Avg	OBP	Slg	OPS
2013	Danvle	R+	57	228	67	7	4	0	(- | -)	82	28	14	31	18	0	31	5	5	0	3	3	5	.294	.359	.360	.718
2014	2 Tms	Low	132	478	127	18	4	1	(- | -)	156	60	46	52	35	0	63	2	16	9	7	6	8	.266	.313	.326	.639
2015	Carlina	A+	130	391	101	15	6	1	(- | -)	131	50	32	44	30	0	54	4	20	4	4	2	9	.258	.315	.335	.650
2016	Missi	AA	126	446	119	26	6	4	(- | -)	169	46	43	52	24	0	82	1	17	3	1	1	10	.267	.304	.379	.683
2017	Gwnntt	AAA	33	129	38	9	1	4	(- | -)	61	17	20	21	8	1	22	2	1	2	1	0	4	.295	.340	.473	.813
2017	Atl	NL	82	241	72	21	2	4	(2 | 2)	109	30	27	32	12	2	51	0	2	1	0	0	5	.299	.331	.452	.783

Leonel Campos

Pitches: R **Bats:** R **Pos:** RP-13

LEE-oh-nel KAM-pohs **Ht:** 6'2" **Wt:** 215 **Born:** 7/17/1987 **Age:** 30

			HOW MUCH HE PITCHED						WHAT HE GAVE UP												THE RESULTS						
Year	Team	Lg	G	GS	CG	GF	IP	BFP	H	R	ER	HR	SH	SF	HB	TBB	IBB	SO	WP	Bk	W	L	Pct	Sh	Sv-Op	Hld	ERC	ERA
2017	Buffalo*	AAA	26	0	0	18	32.2	132	20	6	6	2	1	0	0	14	0	39	2	0	3	0	1.000	0	9- --		1.93	1.65
2014	SD	NL	6	0	0	1	7.0	33	9	5	4	0	0	0	0	4	0	9	2	0	0	0	-	0	0-0	0	5.67	5.14
2015	SD	NL	1	0	0	0	1.0	5	1	1	1	0	0	0	0	1	0	1	0	0	0	0	-	0	0-0	0	5.48	9.00
2016	SD	NL	18	0	0	10	22.0	98	18	16	14	3	1	1	1	14	2	24	1	0	1	0	1.000	0	0-0	0	4.22	5.73
2017	Tor	AL	13	0	0	6	13.2	60	11	6	4	2	0	0	1	8	0	15	1	0	0	0	-	0	0-0	0	4.32	2.63
	4 ML YEARS		38	0	0	17	43.2	196	39	28	23	5	1	1	2	27	2	49	4	0	1	0	1.000	0	0-0	0	4.51	4.74

Jeimer Candelario

Bats: B **Throws:** R **Pos:** 3B-36;PH-4;1B-1

JAY-mer can-duh-LAIR-ee-oh **Ht:** 6'1" **Wt:** 210 **Born:** 11/24/1993 **Age:** 24

								BATTING										RUNNING			AVERAGES			
Year	Team	Lg	G	AB	H	2B	3B	HR	(Hm | Rd)	TB	R	RBI	RC	TBB	IBB	SO	HBP	SH	SF	SB	CS	GDP	Avg	OBP	Slg	OPS
2013	Kane	A	130	500	128	35	1	11	(- | -)	198	71	57	74	68	1	88	2	0	2	1	0	18	.256	.346	.396	.742
2014	2 Tms	Low	125	462	103	25	5	11	(- | -)	175	56	63	47	41	1	89	2	0	2	0	4	9	.223	.288	.379	.667
2015	MrtlBh	A+	82	318	86	25	3	5	(- | -)	132	42	39	42	20	0	62	3	0	2	0	1	5	.270	.318	.415	.733
2015	Tenn	AA	46	158	46	10	1	5	(- | -)	73	21	25	29	22	1	21	1	0	1	0	0	7	.291	.379	.462	.841
2016	Tenn	AA	56	210	46	17	1	4	(- | -)	77	30	23	27	32	0	46	1	0	1	0	0	5	.219	.324	.367	.690
2016	Iowa	AAA	76	264	88	22	3	9	(- | -)	143	44	54	59	38	2	53	3	0	4	0	2	7	.333	.417	.542	.959
2017	Iowa	AAA	81	286	76	27	3	12	(- | -)	145	39	52	53	41	1	72	2	0	1	0	0	4	.266	.361	.507	.868
2017	Toledo	AAA	29	121	32	9	1	3	(- | -)	52	13	19	15	5	0	32	1	0	1	1	0	1	.264	.297	.430	.727
2016	ChC	NL	5	11	1	0	0	0	(0 | 0)	1	0	0	0	2	1	5	1	0	0	0	0	0	.091	.286	.091	.377
2017	2 Tms		38	127	36	9	0	3	(2 | 1)	54	18	16	19	13	0	30	2	0	0	0	0	3	.283	.359	.425	.784
17	ChC	NL	11	33	5	2	0	1	(0 | 1)	10	2	3	1	1	0	12	2	0	0	0	0	1	.152	.222	.303	.525
17	Det	AL	27	94	31	7	0	2	(2 | 0)	44	16	13	18	12	0	18	0	0	0	0	0	2	.330	.406	.468	.874
	2 ML YEARS		43	138	37	9	0	3	(2 | 1)	55	18	16	19	15	1	35	3	0	0	0	0	3	.268	.353	.399	.751

Mark Canha

Bats: R **Throws:** R **Pos:** RF-22;LF-20;CF-19;PH-8;1B-3;DH-2 CAN-uh **Ht:** 6'2" **Wt:** 210 **Born:** 2/15/1989 **Age:** 29

								BATTING										RUNNING			AVERAGES			
Year	Team	Lg	G	AB	H	2B	3B	HR	(Hm | Rd)	TB	R	RBI	RC	TBB	IBB	SO	HBP	SH	SF	SB	CS	GDP	Avg	OBP	Slg	OPS
2017	Nashv*	AAA	75	272	77	25	3	12	(- | -)	144	52	50	55	34	0	62	7	1	3	4	0	4	.283	.373	.529	.903
2015	Oak	AL	124	441	112	22	3	16	(8 | 8)	188	61	70	62	33	0	96	8	0	3	7	2	9	.254	.315	.426	.742
2016	Oak	AL	16	41	5	0	0	3	(1 | 2)	14	4	6	0	0	0	20	1	0	1	0	1	1	.122	.140	.341	.481
2017	Oak	AL	57	173	36	13	1	5	(3 | 2)	66	16	14	13	7	0	56	6	0	1	2	0	5	.208	.262	.382	.644
	3 ML YEARS		197	655	153	35	4	24	(12 | 12)	268	81	90	75	40	0	172	15	1	5	9	3	15	.234	.291	.409	.700

Robinson Cano

Bats: L Throws: R Pos: 2B-150;PH-2   kuh-NOE   Ht: 6'0" Wt: 210 Born: 10/22/1982 Age: 35

Year Team	Lg	G	AB	H	2B	3B	HR	(Hm	Rd)	TB	R	RBI	RC	TBB	IBB	SO	HBP	SH	SF	SB	CS	GDP	Avg	OBP	Slg	OPS
2005 NYY	AL	132	522	155	34	4	14	(5	9)	239	78	62	59	16	1	68	3	7	3	1	3	16	.297	.320	.458	.778
2006 NYY	AL	122	482	165	41	1	15	(9	6)	253	62	78	74	18	3	54	2	1	5	5	2	19	.342	.365	.525	.890
2007 NYY	AL	160	617	189	41	7	19	(10	9)	301	93	97	94	39	5	85	8	1	4	4	5	19	.306	.353	.488	.841
2008 NYY	AL	159	597	162	35	3	14	(7	7)	245	70	72	64	26	3	65	5	1	5	2	4	18	.271	.305	.410	.715
2009 NYY	AL	161	637	204	48	2	25	(14	11)	331	103	85	79	30	2	63	3	0	4	5	7	22	.320	.352	.520	.871
2010 NYY	AL	160	626	200	41	3	29	(16	13)	334	103	109	118	57	14	77	8	0	5	3	2	19	.319	.381	.534	.914
2011 NYY	AL	159	623	188	46	7	28	(16	12)	332	104	118	111	38	11	96	12	0	8	8	2	18	.302	.349	.533	.882
2012 NYY	AL	161	627	196	48	1	33	(22	11)	345	105	94	110	61	10	96	7	0	2	3	2	22	.313	.379	.550	.929
2013 NYY	AL	160	605	190	41	0	27	(11	16)	312	81	107	120	65	16	85	6	0	5	7	1	18	.314	.383	.516	.899
2014 Sea	AL	157	595	187	37	2	14	(9	5)	270	77	82	106	61	20	68	6	0	3	10	3	19	.314	.382	.454	.836
2015 Sea	AL	156	624	179	34	1	21	(11	10)	278	82	79	84	43	5	107	3	0	4	2	6	26	.287	.334	.446	.779
2016 Sea	AL	161	655	195	33	2	39	(17	22)	349	107	103	100	47	8	100	8	0	5	0	1	18	.298	.350	.533	.882
2017 Sea	AL	150	592	166	33	0	23	(11	12)	268	79	97	96	49	8	85	4	0	3	1	0	18	.280	.338	.453	.791
Postseason		51	203	45	10	3	8	(5	3)	85	22	33	23	11	3	28	2	0	1	0	2	7	.222	.267	.419	.686
13 ML YEARS		1998	7802	2376	512	33	301	(158	143)	3857	1144	1183	1215	550	106	1049	75	10	56	51	38	252	.305	.354	.494	.848

Carter Capps

Pitches: R Bats: R Pos: RP-11   Ht: 6'5" Wt: 230 Born: 8/7/1990 Age: 27

	HOW MUCH HE PITCHED						WHAT HE GAVE UP											THE RESULTS							
Year Team	Lg	G	GS	CG	GF	IP	BFP	H	R	ER	HR	SH	SF	HB	TBB	IBB	SO	WP	Bk	W	L	Pct	Sh	Sv-Op	Hld	ERC	ERA
2017 ElPaso*	AAA	24	0	0	6	25.2	105	18	15	8	1	0	0	0	9	0	28	1	0	1	1	.500	0	2--	-	1.93	2.81
2012 Sea	AL	18	0	0	2	25.0	109	25	11	11	0	1	1	0	11	0	28	1	0	0	0	-	0	0-0	2	3.49	3.96
2013 Sea	AL	53	0	0	11	59.0	270	73	37	36	12	2	1	2	23	4	66	5	0	3	3	.500	0	0-2	9	6.23	5.49
2014 Mia	NL	17	0	0	5	20.1	86	19	9	9	1	0	1	2	5	0	25	2	0	0	0	-	0	0-0	1	3.13	3.98
2015 Mia	NL	30	0	0	8	31.0	118	18	5	4	2	1	1	2	7	0	58	2	0	1	0	1.000	0	0-2	11	1.50	1.16
2017 SD	NL	11	0	0	6	12.1	49	12	9	9	2	0	1	0	2	0	7	1	0	0	0	-	0	0-0	1	3.49	6.57
5 ML YEARS		129	0	0	32	147.2	632	147	71	69	17	4	5	6	48	4	184	11	0	4	3	.571	0	0-4	24	3.97	4.21

Victor Caratini

Bats: B Throws: R Pos: PH-15;C-12;1B-8;LF-1;RF-1   Ht: 6'1" Wt: 215 Born: 8/17/1993 Age: 24

Year Team	Lg	G	AB	H	2B	3B	HR	(Hm	Rd)	TB	R	RBI	RC	TBB	IBB	SO	HBP	SH	SF	SB	CS	GDP	Avg	OBP	Slg	OPS
2013 Danvle	R+	58	200	58	23	1	1	(-	-)	86	29	25	38	39	1	49	5	0	2	0	2	6	.290	.415	.430	.845
2014 2 Tms	Low	101	376	104	22	5	5	(-	-)	151	49	55	54	38	2	69	4	1	4	1	1	15	.277	.346	.402	.748
2015 MrtlBh	A+	112	393	101	31	1	4	(-	-)	146	39	53	55	49	1	75	5	0	6	0	0	22	.257	.342	.372	.714
2016 Tenn	AA	115	412	120	25	2	6	(-	-)	167	57	47	68	54	1	80	6	0	8	2	1	15	.291	.375	.405	.780
2017 Iowa	AAA	83	292	100	27	3	10	(-	-)	163	50	61	63	27	3	48	1	0	6	1	0	12	.342	.393	.558	.951
2017 ChC	NL	31	59	15	3	0	1	(0	1)	21	6	2	3	4	1	13	3	0	0	0	0	3	.254	.333	.356	.689

Stephen Cardullo

Bats: R Throws: R Pos: PH-8;LF-6;RF-2   Ht: 6'0" Wt: 215 Born: 8/31/1987 Age: 30

Year Team	Lg	G	AB	H	2B	3B	HR	(Hm	Rd)	TB	R	RBI	RC	TBB	IBB	SO	HBP	SH	SF	SB	CS	GDP	Avg	OBP	Slg	OPS
2016 Albq	AAA	115	406	125	26	5	17	(-	-)	212	71	72	78	37	2	58	4	0	5	6	3	9	.308	.367	.522	.889
2017 Hrtfrd	AA	41	128	25	5	1	4	(-	-)	44	17	17	15	22	2	22	1	0	0	1	0	4	.195	.318	.344	.662
2016 Col	NL	27	56	12	3	1	2	(2	0)	23	5	6	5	3	0	12	0	0	0	0	0	2	.214	.254	.411	.665
2017 Col	NL	15	28	4	0	0	0	(0	0)	4	2	3	2	3	0	7	1	0	0	0	0	0	.143	.250	.143	.393
2 ML YEARS		42	84	16	3	1	2	(2	0)	27	7	9	7	6	0	19	1	0	0	0	0	2	.190	.253	.321	.574

Shane Carle

Pitches: R Bats: R Pos: RP-3   Ht: 6'4" Wt: 185 Born: 8/30/1991 Age: 26

	HOW MUCH HE PITCHED						WHAT HE GAVE UP											THE RESULTS							
Year Team	Lg	G	GS	CG	GF	IP	BFP	H	R	ER	HR	SH	SF	HB	TBB	IBB	SO	WP	Bk	W	L	Pct	Sh	Sv-Op	Hld	ERC	ERA
2013 Jmstwn	A-	14	4	0	2	50.1	202	47	18	12	3	4	0	2	6	0	43	1	1	1	0	1.000	0	1--	-	2.57	2.15
2014 2 Tms	Low	27	23	0	0	137.0	586	151	72	56	12	2	5	13	22	0	83	4	2	4	8	.333	0	0--	-	3.98	3.68
2015 NwBrit	AA	26	26	3	0	160.1	672	167	71	62	12	7	4	5	31	0	100	5	1	14	7	.667	2	0--	-	3.44	3.48
2016 Albq	AAA	27	19	0	1	111.1	502	147	75	67	9	5	6	5	32	0	88	2	0	5	8	.385	0	0--	-	5.57	5.42
2017 Albq	AAA	36	3	0	6	62.0	272	74	38	37	8	2	1	0	22	1	50	3	0	3	5	.375	0	1--	-	5.28	5.37
2017 Col	NL	3	0	0	3	4.0	19	6	3	3	1	0	0	0	0	0	4	1	0	0	0	-	0	0-0	0	5.94	6.75

Matt Carpenter

Bats: L Throws: R Pos: 1B-120;3B-16;2B-13;PH-3;DH-2   Ht: 6'3" Wt: 205 Born: 11/26/1985 Age: 32

Year Team	Lg	G	AB	H	2B	3B	HR	(Hm	Rd)	TB	R	RBI	RC	TBB	IBB	SO	HBP	SH	SF	SB	CS	GDP	Avg	OBP	Slg	OPS
2011 StL	NL	7	15	1	1	0	0	(0	0)	2	0	0	0	4	0	4	0	0	0	0	0	0	.067	.263	.133	.396
2012 StL	NL	114	296	87	22	5	6	(3	3)	137	44	46	46	34	2	63	3	0	7	1	1	10	.294	.365	.463	.828
2013 StL	NL	157	626	199	55	7	11	(6	5)	301	126	78	119	72	1	98	9	3	7	3	3	4	.318	.392	.481	.873
2014 StL	NL	158	595	162	33	2	8	(4	4)	223	99	59	93	95	2	111	8	2	9	5	3	3	.272	.375	.375	.750
2015 StL	NL	154	574	156	44	3	28	(13	15)	290	101	84	108	81	5	151	6	0	4	4	3	5	.272	.365	.505	.871

Year Team	Lg	G	AB	H	2B	3B	HR	(Hm	Rd)	TB	R	RBI	RC	TBB	IBB	SO	HBP	SH	SF	SB	CS	GDP	Avg	OBP	Slg	OPS
2016 StL	NL	129	473	128	36	6	21	(9	12)	239	81	68	87	81	6	108	1	1	0	1	0	4	.271	.380	.505	.885
2017 StL	NL	145	497	120	31	2	23	(9	14)	224	91	69	94	109	4	125	5	3	4	0	4	4	.241	.384	.451	.835
Postseason		39	136	33	8	1	6	(4	2)	61	20	16	19	11	0	39	9	2	5	2	1	5	.243	.300	.449	.749
7 ML YEARS		864	3076	853	222	25	97	(44	53)	1416	542	404	547	476	20	660	40	10	36	15	15	31	.277	.377	.460	.838

Carlos Carrasco

Pitches: R **Bats:** R **Pos:** SP-32   **Ht:** 6'3" **Wt:** 212 **Born:** 3/21/1987 **Age:** 31

		HOW MUCH HE PITCHED						WHAT HE GAVE UP										THE RESULTS						
Year Team	Lg	G	GS	CG	GF	IP	BFP	H	R	ER	HR	SH	SF	HB	TBB	IBB	SO	WP	Bk	W	L	Pct	Sh	Sv-Op	Hld	ERC	ERA
2009 Cle	AL	5	5	0	0	22.1	112	40	23	22	6	0	1	1	11	1	11	0	1	0	4	.000	0	0-0	0	11.36	8.87
2010 Cle	AL	7	7	1	0	44.2	188	47	20	19	6	2	1	1	14	1	38	1	0	2	2	.500	0	0-0	0	4.42	3.83
2011 Cle	AL	21	21	1	0	124.2	536	130	68	64	15	3	7	4	40	3	85	3	0	8	9	.471	0	0-0	0	4.24	4.62
2013 Cle	AL	15	7	0	5	46.2	218	64	36	35	4	2	3	3	18	2	30	2	1	1	4	.200	0	0-0	0	6.11	6.75
2014 Cle	AL	40	14	1	12	134.0	529	103	40	38	7	2	3	3	29	1	140	4	0	8	7	.533	1	1-1	0	2.00	2.55
2015 Cle	AL	30	30	3	0	183.2	730	154	75	74	18	1	6	5	43	2	216	5	0	14	12	.538	1	0-0	0	2.72	3.63
2016 Cle	AL	25	25	1	0	146.1	599	134	64	54	21	1	3	4	34	2	150	4	1	11	8	.579	1	0-0	0	3.31	3.32
2017 Cle	AL	32	32	1	0	200.0	798	173	73	73	21	1	6	10	46	2	226	10	0	18	6	.750	0	0-0	0	2.99	3.29
8 ML YEARS		175	141	8	17	902.1	3710	845	399	379	98	12	30	27	235	14	896	29	2	62	52	.544	3	1-1	0	3.37	3.78

Ezequiel Carrera

ee-ZEEK-ee-ull

Bats: L **Throws:** L **Pos:** LF-91;RF-27;PH-17;PR-17;CF-10;DH-1   **Ht:** 5'11" **Wt:** 185 **Born:** 6/11/1987 **Age:** 31

							BATTING												RUNNING			AVERAGES			
Year Team	Lg	G	AB	H	2B	3B	HR	(Hm	Rd)	TB	R	RBI	RC	TBB	IBB	SO	HBP	SH	SF	SB	CS	GDP	Avg	OBP	Slg	OPS
2011 Cle	AL	68	202	49	8	3	0	(0	0)	63	27	14	25	16	0	35	1	7	0	10	5	4	.243	.301	.312	.613
2012 Cle	AL	48	147	40	6	3	2	(0	2)	58	20	11	17	8	1	35	1	1	1	8	1	3	.272	.312	.395	.707
2013 2 Tms		15	17	3	0	0	0	(0	0)	3	3	1	1	1	0	5	2	1	0	0	0	1	.176	.300	.176	.476
2014 Det	AL	45	69	18	4	1	0	(0	0)	24	12	2	6	3	1	14	1	0	0	7	1	0	.261	.301	.348	.649
2015 Tor	AL	91	172	47	8	0	3	(1	2)	64	27	26	26	11	0	45	2	5	2	2	1	1	.273	.321	.372	.693
2016 Tor	AL	110	270	67	9	1	6	(5	1)	96	47	23	34	27	0	70	4	7	2	7	4	8	.248	.323	.356	.679
2017 Tor	AL	131	287	81	10	1	8	(6	2)	117	38	20	40	30	0	75	3	5	0	10	1	4	.282	.356	.408	.764
13 Phi	NL	13	13	1	0	0	0	(0	0)	1	2	0	0	1	0	4	2	0	0	0	0	0	.077	.250	.077	.327
13 Cle	AL	2	4	2	0	0	0	(0	0)	2	1	1	1	0	0	1	0	1	0	0	0	1	.500	.500	.500	1.000
Postseason		14	36	10	0	2	1	(0	1)	17	6	3	5	3	0	8	0	0	0	2	0	0	.278	.333	.472	.806
7 ML YEARS		508	1164	305	45	9	19	(12	7)	425	174	97	149	96	2	279	14	26	5	44	13	23	.262	.324	.365	.690

Chris Carter

Bats: R **Throws:** R **Pos:** 1B-56;PH-6;RF-2;DH-1   **Ht:** 6'4" **Wt:** 245 **Born:** 12/18/1986 **Age:** 31

							BATTING												RUNNING			AVERAGES			
Year Team	Lg	G	AB	H	2B	3B	HR	(Hm	Rd)	TB	R	RBI	RC	TBB	IBB	SO	HBP	SH	SF	SB	CS	GDP	Avg	OBP	Slg	OPS
2017 Nashv*	AAA	36	131	33	5	1	9	(-	-)	67	21	22	24	19	0	49	3	0	1	0	0	4	.252	.357	.511	.869
2010 Oak	AL	24	70	13	1	0	3	(1	2)	23	8	7	5	7	0	21	0	0	1	1	0	3	.186	.256	.329	.585
2011 Oak	AL	15	44	6	0	0	0	(0	0)	6	2	0	0	2	0	20	0	0	0	0	0	1	.136	.174	.136	.310
2012 Oak	AL	67	218	52	12	0	16	(5	11)	112	38	39	36	39	1	83	0	0	3	0	0	4	.239	.350	.514	.864
2013 Hou	AL	148	506	113	24	2	29	(10	19)	228	64	82	74	70	1	212	4	0	5	2	0	8	.223	.320	.451	.770
2014 Hou	AL	145	507	115	21	1	37	(21	16)	249	68	88	74	56	6	182	5	0	4	5	2	12	.227	.308	.491	.799
2015 Hou	AL	129	391	78	17	0	24	(17	7)	167	50	64	55	57	1	151	6	0	5	1	2	5	.199	.307	.427	.734
2016 Mil	NL	160	549	122	27	1	41	(24	17)	274	84	94	73	76	1	206	9	0	10	3	1	18	.222	.321	.499	.821
2017 NYY	AL	62	184	37	5	1	8	(4	4)	68	20	26	17	20	0	76	2	0	2	0	0	5	.201	.284	.370	.653
Postseason		6	17	5	1	0	1	(1	0)	9	3	1	3	3	0	7	0	0	0	0	0	0	.294	.400	.529	.929
8 ML YEARS		750	2469	536	107	5	158	(82	76)	1127	334	400	334	327	10	951	26	0	30	12	5	56	.217	.312	.456	.768

Curt Casali

Bats: R **Throws:** R **Pos:** C-8;PH-3   **Ht:** 6'3" **Wt:** 235 **Born:** 11/9/1988 **Age:** 29

cuh-SAL-ee

							BATTING												RUNNING			AVERAGES			
Year Team	Lg	G	AB	H	2B	3B	HR	(Hm	Rd)	TB	R	RBI	RC	TBB	IBB	SO	HBP	SH	SF	SB	CS	GDP	Avg	OBP	Slg	OPS
2017 Drham*	AAA	85	300	79	10	0	5	(-	-)	104	36	48	40	37	2	65	4	1	1	0	0	9	.263	.351	.347	.698
2014 TB	AL	30	72	12	3	0	0	(0	0)	15	10	3	3	8	0	23	2	2	0	0	0	2	.167	.268	.208	.477
2015 TB	AL	38	101	24	6	0	10	(7	3)	60	13	18	14	8	0	34	2	1	1	0	0	2	.238	.304	.594	.898
2016 TB	AL	84	226	42	10	0	8	(3	5)	76	23	25	18	25	1	82	2	3	0	0	0	2	.186	.273	.336	.609
2017 TB	AL	9	9	3	0	0	1	(1	0)	6	2	3	2	3	0	3	0	0	0	0	0	0	.333	.462	.667	1.128
4 ML YEARS		161	408	81	19	0	19	(11	8)	157	48	49	37	44	1	142	6	6	2	0	0	6	.199	.285	.385	.670

Andrew Cashner

Pitches: R **Bats:** R **Pos:** SP-28   **Ht:** 6'6" **Wt:** 235 **Born:** 9/11/1986 **Age:** 31

		HOW MUCH HE PITCHED						WHAT HE GAVE UP										THE RESULTS						
Year Team	Lg	G	GS	CG	GF	IP	BFP	H	R	ER	HR	SH	SF	HB	TBB	IBB	SO	WP	Bk	W	L	Pct	Sh	Sv-Op	Hld	ERC	ERA
2010 ChC	NL	53	0	0	9	54.1	248	55	31	29	8	6	2	4	30	5	50	4	1	2	6	.250	0	0-1	16	5.22	4.80
2011 ChC	NL	7	1	0	0	10.2	39	3	2	2	1	0	0	0	4	0	8	0	0	0	0	-	0	0-0	1	0.91	1.69
2012 SD	NL	33	5	0	5	46.1	196	42	23	22	5	3	1	1	19	1	52	2	0	3	4	.429	0	0-4	6	3.73	4.27
2013 SD	NL	31	26	1	2	175.0	707	151	68	60	12	6	3	4	47	3	128	5	0	10	9	.526	1	0-0	1	2.74	3.09
2014 SD	NL	19	19	2	0	123.1	506	110	42	35	7	3	4	1	29	3	93	2	0	5	7	.417	2	0-0	0	2.57	2.55
2015 SD	NL	31	31	0	0	184.2	804	200	111	89	19	8	6	6	66	3	165	3	0	6	16	.273	0	0-0	0	4.53	4.34
2016 2 Tms	NL	28	27	0	1	132.0	588	142	83	77	19	6	5	7	60	3	112	3	0	5	11	.313	0	0-0	0	5.28	5.25

Year Team	Lg	G	GS	CG	GF	IP	BFP	H	R	ER	HR	SH	SF	HB	TBB	IBB	SO	WP	Bk	W	L	Pct	Sh	Sv-Op	Hld	ERC	ERA
		HOW MUCH HE PITCHED						**WHAT HE GAVE UP**												**THE RESULTS**							
2017 Tex	AL	28	28	0	0	166.2	704	156	75	63	15	2	5	9	64	0	86	10	1	11	11	.500	0	0-0	0	3.86	3.40
16 SD	NL	16	16	0	0	79.1	347	80	47	42	13	4	3	6	30	0	67	1	0	4	7	.364	0	0-0	0	4.80	4.76
16 Mia	NL	12	11	0	1	52.2	241	62	36	35	6	2	2	1	30	3	45	2	0	1	4	.200	0	0-0	0	6.01	5.98
8 ML YEARS		230	137	3	17	893.0	3792	859	435	377	86	34	26	32	319	17	694	29	2	42	64	.396	3	0-5	24	3.80	3.80

Santiago Casilla

cuh-SEE-ya

Pitches: R Bats: R Pos: RP-63   Ht: 6'0" Wt: 210 Born: 7/25/1980 Age: 37

Year Team	Lg	G	GS	CG	GF	IP	BFP	H	R	ER	HR	SH	SF	HB	TBB	IBB	SO	WP	Bk	W	L	Pct	Sh	Sv-Op	Hld	ERC	ERA
		HOW MUCH HE PITCHED						**WHAT HE GAVE UP**												**THE RESULTS**							
2004 Oak	AL	4	0	0	2	5.2	32	5	8	8	3	0	0	1	9	0	5	0	0	0	0	-	0	0-0	0	13.22	12.71
2005 Oak	AL	3	0	0	3	3.0	12	2	1	1	0	0	0	0	1	0	1	1	0	0	0	-	0	0-0	0	1.57	3.00
2006 Oak	AL	2	0	0	1	2.1	10	2	3	3	0	0	0	0	2	0	2	0	0	0	0	-	0	0-0	0	4.61	11.57
2007 Oak	AL	46	0	0	10	50.2	219	43	25	25	6	0	3	1	23	6	52	5	0	3	1	.750	0	2-5	12	3.39	4.44
2008 Oak	AL	51	0	0	9	50.1	229	60	22	22	5	3	2	3	20	2	43	6	0	2	1	.667	0	2-3	7	5.34	3.93
2009 Oak	AL	46	0	0	15	48.1	233	61	36	32	6	1	3	3	25	3	35	5	0	1	2	.333	0	0-0	5	6.32	5.96
2010 SF	NL	52	0	0	13	55.1	225	40	14	12	2	2	1	4	26	4	56	10	0	7	2	.778	0	2-3	11	2.68	1.95
2011 SF	NL	49	0	0	20	51.2	211	33	11	10	1	4	0	2	25	1	45	5	0	2	2	.500	0	6-7	6	2.11	1.74
2012 SF	NL	73	0	0	37	63.1	272	55	24	20	8	2	1	2	22	4	55	1	0	7	6	.538	0	25-31	12	3.24	2.84
2013 SF	NL	57	0	0	12	50.0	208	39	14	12	2	2	3	2	25	6	38	8	0	7	2	.778	0	2-3	22	2.88	2.16
2014 SF	NL	54	0	0	31	58.1	218	35	13	11	3	2	0	3	15	2	45	3	1	3	3	.500	0	19-23	10	1.56	1.70
2015 SF	NL	67	0	0	55	58.0	244	51	19	18	6	2	1	2	23	2	62	1	0	4	2	.667	0	38-44	3	3.52	2.79
2016 SF	NL	62	0	0	44	58.0	241	50	23	23	8	3	1	5	19	2	65	4	2	2	5	.286	0	31-40	3	3.62	3.57
2017 Oak	AL	63	0	0	33	59.0	259	58	29	28	8	1	6	6	22	1	57	3	0	4	5	.444	0	16-23	4	4.48	4.27
Postseason		25	0	0	8	19.2	82	15	3	2	0	0	0	2	5	1	20	3	0	1	0	1.000	0	4-4	4	1.91	0.92
14 ML YEARS		629	0	0	285	614.0	2613	534	242	225	58	22	21	34	257	33	561	52	3	42	31	.575	0	143-182	92	3.52	3.30

Nicholas Castellanos

cahs-teh-YAHN-ohs

Bats: R Throws: R Pos: 3B-129;RF-21;DH-7;PH-2   Ht: 6'4" Wt: 210 Born: 3/4/1992 Age: 26

Year Team	Lg	G	AB	H	2B	3B	HR	(Hm	Rd)	TB	R	RBI	RC	TBB	IBB	SO	HBP	SH	SF	SB	CS	GDP	Avg	OBP	Slg	OPS
		BATTING																		**RUNNING**			**AVERAGES**			
2013 Det	AL	11	18	5	0	0	0	(0	0)	5	1	0	1	0	0	5	0	0	0	0	0	0	.278	.278	.278	.556
2014 Det	AL	148	533	138	31	4	11	(6	5)	210	50	66	63	36	3	140	3	0	7	2	2	7	.259	.306	.394	.700
2015 Det	AL	154	549	140	33	6	15	(6	9)	230	42	73	66	39	1	152	1	0	6	0	3	21	.255	.303	.419	.721
2016 Det	AL	110	411	117	25	4	18	(5	13)	204	54	58	67	28	1	111	3	0	5	1	1	4	.285	.331	.496	.827
2017 Det	AL	157	614	167	36	10	26	(14	12)	301	73	101	97	41	0	142	5	0	5	4	5	12	.272	.320	.490	.811
Postseason		3	10	1	0	0	1	(0	1)	4	1	1	0	2	1	1	0	0	0	0	0	0	.100	.250	.400	.650
5 ML YEARS		580	2125	567	125	24	70	(31	39)	950	220	298	294	144	5	546	12	0	23	7	11	44	.267	.314	.447	.761

Fabio Castillo

Pitches: R Bats: R Pos: RP-2   Ht: 6'1" Wt: 235 Born: 2/19/1989 Age: 29

Year Team	Lg	G	GS	CG	GF	IP	BFP	H	R	ER	HR	SH	SF	HB	TBB	IBB	SO	WP	Bk	W	L	Pct	Sh	Sv-Op	Hld	ERC	ERA
		HOW MUCH HE PITCHED						**WHAT HE GAVE UP**												**THE RESULTS**							
2013 Rchmd	AA	14	2	0	3	32.1	142	25	15	12	1	1	2	0	17	1	44	4	1	2	2	.500	0	0- -	-	2.68	3.34
2013 Fresno	AAA	23	5	0	2	57.0	269	75	44	41	6	2	5	2	26	0	51	3	0	4	5	.444	0	0- -	-	6.34	6.47
2014 Bowie	AA	18	0	0	8	28.0	133	30	22	16	3	1	1	1	20	0	22	3	0	0	1	.000	0	0- -	-	5.92	5.14
2014 Pnscla	AA	7	0	0	3	7.2	35	10	5	2	2	0	1	0	3	0	5	0	0	0	0	-	0	0- -	-	7.17	2.35
2014 Lsvlle	AAA	15	0	0	5	23.0	96	17	8	7	0	0	0	1	12	0	15	0	0	2	1	.667	0	1- -	-	2.65	2.74
2016 SnAnt	AA	7	7	0	0	39.0	163	35	21	19	6	1	0	2	16	1	40	6	0	3	4	.429	0	0- -	-	4.19	4.38
2016 ElPaso	AAA	7	6	0	0	38.2	172	46	21	20	3	5	1	0	17	0	26	0	0	0	3	.000	0	0- -	-	5.26	4.66
2017 OkCity	AAA	22	16	0	1	84.1	358	77	40	40	9	3	5	5	31	1	85	5	0	4	8	.333	0	1- -	-	3.74	4.27
2017 LAD	NL	2	0	0	0	1.1	8	3	2	2	0	0	0	0	1	0	2	1	0	0	0	-	0	0-0	0	12.64	13.50

Luis Castillo

Pitches: R Bats: R Pos: SP-15   Ht: 6'2" Wt: 190 Born: 12/12/1992 Age: 25

Year Team	Lg	G	GS	CG	GF	IP	BFP	H	R	ER	HR	SH	SF	HB	TBB	IBB	SO	WP	Bk	W	L	Pct	Sh	Sv-Op	Hld	ERC	ERA
		HOW MUCH HE PITCHED						**WHAT HE GAVE UP**												**THE RESULTS**							
2014 Augsta	A	48	0	0	31	58.2	256	56	23	20	6	1	2	1	25	3	66	3	0	2	2	.500	0	10- -	-	3.87	3.07
2015 2 Tms	Low	35	16	0	12	107.0	446	103	42	38	4	1	1	4	33	0	94	5	0	6	6	.500	0	4- -	-	3.28	3.20
2016 Jupiter	A+	23	21	1	0	117.2	457	95	29	27	2	1	2	3	18	0	91	3	0	8	4	.667	0	0- -	-	1.82	2.07
2017 Pnscla	AA	14	14	1	0	80.1	317	68	24	23	5	6	3	3	13	0	81	3	1	4	4	.500	0	0- -	-	2.32	2.58
2017 Cin	NL	15	15	0	0	89.1	359	64	32	31	11	4	3	3	32	1	98	2	1	3	7	.300	0	0-0	0	2.70	3.12

Welington Castillo

WELL-ing-tunn

Bats: R Throws: R Pos: C-88;DH-6;PH-3   Ht: 5'10" Wt: 220 Born: 4/24/1987 Age: 31

Year Team	Lg	G	AB	H	2B	3B	HR	(Hm	Rd)	TB	R	RBI	RC	TBB	IBB	SO	HBP	SH	SF	SB	CS	GDP	Avg	OBP	Slg	OPS
		BATTING																		**RUNNING**			**AVERAGES**			
2010 ChC	NL	7	20	6	4	0	1	(0	1)	13	3	5	3	1	0	7	0	0	0	0	0	0	.300	.333	.650	.983
2011 ChC	NL	4	13	2	0	0	0	(0	0)	2	0	0	0	0	0	4	0	0	0	0	0	1	.154	.154	.154	.308
2012 ChC	NL	52	170	45	11	0	5	(4	1)	71	16	22	22	17	2	51	2	0	1	0	0	4	.265	.337	.418	.754
2013 ChC	NL	113	380	104	23	0	8	(1	7)	151	41	32	44	34	3	97	11	1	2	2	0	13	.274	.349	.397	.746
2014 ChC	NL	110	380	90	19	0	13	(6	7)	148	28	46	44	26	0	102	7	2	2	0	0	7	.237	.296	.389	.686
2015 3 Tms		110	342	81	15	1	19	(7	12)	155	42	57	41	25	1	92	6	0	5	0	0	12	.237	.296	.453	.750
2016 Ari	NL	113	416	110	24	0	14	(8	6)	176	41	68	58	33	3	121	4	0	4	2	0	5	.264	.322	.423	.745
2017 Bal	AL	96	341	96	11	0	20	(13	7)	167	44	53	52	22	0	97	0	0	2	0	0	10	.282	.323	.490	.813

Year	Team	Lg	G	AB	H	2B	3B	HR	(Hm	Rd)	TB	R	RBI	RC	TBB	IBB	SO	HBP	SH	SF	SB	CS	GDP	Avg	OBP	Slg	OPS
15	ChC	NL	24	43	7	2	0	2	(1	1)	15	5	5	2	3	1	12	1	0	0	0	0	0	.163	.234	.349	.583
15	Sea	AL	6	25	4	0	0	0	(0	0)	4	3	2	0	1	0	5	0	0	2	0	0	0	.160	.179	.160	.339
15	Ari	NL	80	274	70	13	1	17	(6	11)	136	34	50	39	21	0	75	5	0	3	0	0	10	.255	.317	.496	.813
8 ML YEARS			605	2062	534	107	1	80	(40	40)	883	215	283	264	158	9	571	30	3	16	4	0	52	.259	.319	.428	.747

Jason Castro

Bats: L **Throws:** R **Pos:** C-108;PH-3   **Ht:** 6'3" **Wt:** 215 **Born:** 6/18/1987 **Age:** 31

Year	Team	Lg	G	AB	H	2B	3B	HR	(Hm	Rd)	TB	R	RBI	RC	TBB	IBB	SO	HBP	SH	SF	SB	CS	GDP	Avg	OBP	Slg	OPS
2010	Hou	NL	67	195	40	8	1	2	(1	1)	56	26	8	12	22	2	41	0	0	0	0	0	4	.205	.286	.287	.573
2012	Hou	NL	87	257	66	15	2	6	(3	3)	103	29	29	33	31	2	61	1	2	4	0	0	8	.257	.334	.401	.735
2013	Hou	AL	120	435	120	35	1	18	(13	5)	211	63	56	76	50	3	130	2	0	4	2	1	4	.276	.350	.485	.835
2014	Hou	AL	126	465	103	21	2	14	(10	4)	170	43	56	45	34	1	151	9	1	3	1	0	11	.222	.286	.366	.651
2015	Hou	AL	104	337	71	19	0	11	(8	3)	123	38	31	29	33	1	115	2	0	3	0	0	5	.211	.283	.365	.648
2016	Hou	AL	113	329	69	16	3	11	(5	6)	124	41	32	34	45	0	123	1	1	0	2	1	8	.210	.307	.377	.684
2017	Min	AL	110	356	86	22	0	10	(6	4)	138	49	47	45	45	1	108	4	1	1	0	0	10	.242	.333	.388	.720
Postseason			6	16	1	0	0	0	(0	0)	1	1	2	0	2	0	8	0	0	0	0	0	2	.063	.167	.063	.229
7 ML YEARS			727	2374	555	136	9	72	(46	26)	925	289	259	274	260	10	729	19	5	15	5	2	51	.234	.313	.390	.702

Miguel Castro

Pitches: R **Bats:** R **Pos:** RP-38; SP-1   **Ht:** 6'7" **Wt:** 205 **Born:** 12/24/1994 **Age:** 23

			HOW MUCH HE PITCHED						WHAT HE GAVE UP									THE RESULTS							
Year	Team	Lg	G	GS	CG	GF	IP	BFP	H	R	ER	HR	SH	SF	HB	TBB	IBB	SO	WP	Bk	W	L	Pct	Sh	Sv-Op	Hld	ERC	ERA
2017	Bowie*	AA	6	0	0	2	24.1	98	23	13	12	1	1	2	0	6	0	11	1	1	3	0	1.000	0	0- -	-	2.89	4.44
2015	2 Tms		18	0	0	12	17.2	83	21	13	12	4	0	2	0	10	2	18	2	1	0	3	.000	0	4-6	1	6.61	6.11
2016	Col	NL	14	0	0	2	14.2	67	18	10	10	3	1	0	1	5	0	12	0	0	0	0	-	0	0-1	7	6.21	6.14
2017	Bal	AL	39	1	0	8	66.1	274	53	29	26	8	3	4	2	28	4	38	2	0	3	3	.500	0	0-0	1	3.27	3.53
15	Tor	AL	13	0	0	9	12.1	57	15	7	6	2	0	2	0	6	2	12	2	1	0	2	.000	0	4-6	1	5.86	4.38
15	Col	NL	5	0	0	3	5.1	26	6	6	6	2	0	0	0	4	0	6	0	0	0	1	.000	0	0-0	0	8.41	10.13
3 ML YEARS			76	1	0	24	98.2	424	92	52	48	15	4	6	3	43	6	68	4	1	3	6	.333	0	4-7	9	4.24	4.38

Simon Castro

Pitches: R **Bats:** R **Pos:** RP-26   SEE-moan   **Ht:** 6'5" **Wt:** 230 **Born:** 4/9/1988 **Age:** 30

			HOW MUCH HE PITCHED						WHAT HE GAVE UP									THE RESULTS							
Year	Team	Lg	G	GS	CG	GF	IP	BFP	H	R	ER	HR	SH	SF	HB	TBB	IBB	SO	WP	Bk	W	L	Pct	Sh	Sv-Op	Hld	ERC	ERA
2017	Nashv*	AAA	33	0	0	25	38.0	167	24	21	14	3	3	1	6	21	3	63	9	0	3	5	.375	0	4- -	-	2.88	3.32
2013	CWS	AL	4	0	0	4	6.2	28	5	2	2	1	1	0	1	3	0	6	0	0	0	1	.000	0	0-0	0	3.90	2.70
2015	Col	NL	11	0	0	2	10.1	47	11	7	7	0	2	0	1	5	0	9	0	0	2	0	1.000	0	0-0	0	4.37	6.10
2017	Oak	AL	26	0	0	7	37.0	153	32	20	18	7	0	1	2	14	0	35	1	0	1	3	.250	0	0-1	0	4.16	4.38
3 ML YEARS			41	0	0	13	54.0	228	48	29	27	8	3	1	4	22	0	50	1	0	3	4	.429	0	0-1	0	4.18	4.50

Starlin Castro

Bats: R **Throws:** R **Pos:** 2B-109;DH-2;PH-2   STARR-linn   **Ht:** 6'2" **Wt:** 230 **Born:** 3/24/1990 **Age:** 28

Year	Team	Lg	G	AB	H	2B	3B	HR	(Hm	Rd)	TB	R	RBI	RC	TBB	IBB	SO	HBP	SH	SF	SB	CS	GDP	Avg	OBP	Slg	OPS
2010	ChC	NL	125	463	139	31	5	3	(1	2)	189	53	41	56	29	7	71	6	4	4	10	8	14	.300	.347	.408	.755
2011	ChC	NL	158	**674**	**207**	36	9	10	(4	6)	291	91	66	93	35	2	96	2	0	4	22	9	20	.307	.341	.432	.773
2012	ChC	NL	**162**	**646**	183	29	12	14	(7	7)	278	78	78	91	36	5	100	4	0	5	25	**13**	15	.283	.323	.430	.753
2013	ChC	NL	161	**666**	163	34	2	10	(9	1)	231	59	44	55	30	0	129	7	1	1	9	6	21	.245	.284	.347	.631
2014	ChC	NL	134	528	154	33	1	14	(3	11)	231	58	65	72	35	4	100	4	0	2	4	4	18	.292	.339	.438	.777
2015	ChC	NL	151	547	145	23	2	11	(3	8)	205	52	69	54	21	6	91	5	1	4	5	5	15	.265	.296	.375	.671
2016	NYY	AL	151	577	156	29	1	21	(15	6)	250	63	70	69	24	1	118	3	1	5	4	0	15	.270	.300	.433	.734
2017	NYY	AL	112	443	133	18	1	16	(10	6)	201	66	63	69	23	1	93	4	0	3	2	0	9	.300	.338	.454	.792
Postseason			9	34	6	1	0	1	(1	0)	10	2	2	2	1	1	1	0	0	0	0	0	0	.176	.200	.294	.494
8 ML YEARS			1154	4544	1280	233	33	99	(52	47)	1876	520	496	559	233	26	798	35	7	28	81	45	130	.282	.320	.413	.733

Gavin Cecchini

Bats: R **Throws:** R **Pos:** 2B-20;PH-12   chick-KEE-nee   **Ht:** 6'2" **Wt:** 196 **Born:** 12/22/1993 **Age:** 24

Year	Team	Lg	G	AB	H	2B	3B	HR	(Hm	Rd)	TB	R	RBI	RC	TBB	IBB	SO	HBP	SH	SF	SB	CS	GDP	Avg	OBP	Slg	OPS
2013	Bklyn	A-	51	194	53	8	0	0	(-	-)	61	18	14	20	14	0	30	0	2	2	2	3	1	.273	.319	.314	.633
2014	2 Tms	Low	125	461	114	27	5	8	(-	-)	175	78	56	63	57	1	81	3	1	8	10	4	9	.247	.329	.380	.709
2015	Bnghtn	AA	109	439	139	26	4	7	(-	-)	194	64	51	74	42	0	55	2	0	2	3	4	8	.317	.377	.442	.819
2016	LsVgs	AAA	117	446	145	27	2	8	(-	-)	200	71	55	80	48	0	55	0	4	1	4	1	16	.325	.390	.448	.838
2017	LsVgs	AAA	110	453	121	27	3	6	(-	-)	172	68	39	59	40	1	61	2	2	0	5	4	16	.267	.329	.380	.709
2016	NYM	NL	4	6	2	2	0	0	(0	0)	4	2	2	2	0	0	2	1	0	0	0	0	0	.333	.429	.667	1.095
2017	NYM	NL	32	77	16	2	0	1	(0	1)	21	4	7	4	4	1	19	1	0	0	0	1	3	.208	.256	.273	.529
2 ML YEARS			36	83	18	4	0	1	(0	1)	25	6	9	6	4	1	21	2	0	0	0	1	3	.217	.270	.301	.571

Brett Cecil

Pitches: L **Bats:** R **Pos:** RP-73   SEE-sill   **Ht:** 6'3" **Wt:** 235 **Born:** 7/2/1986 **Age:** 31

		HOW MUCH HE PITCHED						WHAT HE GAVE UP										THE RESULTS							
Year	Team	Lg	G	GS	CG	GF	IP	BFP	H	R	ER	HR	SH	SF	HB	TBB	IBB	SO	WP	Bk	W	L	Pct	Sh	Sv-Op	Hld	ERC	ERA
2009	Tor	AL	18	17	0	1	93.1	422	116	59	55	17	0	2	5	38	0	69	0	0	7	4	.636	0	0-0	0	6.53	5.30
2010	Tor	AL	28	28	0	0	172.2	726	175	87	81	18	1	6	1	54	2	117	7	1	15	7	.682	0	0-0	0	3.88	4.22
2011	Tor	AL	20	20	2	0	123.2	532	122	68	65	22	3	5	6	42	1	87	1	0	4	11	.267	1	0-0	0	4.47	4.73
2012	Tor	AL	21	9	0	2	61.1	270	70	40	39	11	3	3	3	23	0	51	0	0	2	4	.333	0	0-0	1	5.68	5.72
2013	Tor	AL	60	0	0	12	60.2	250	44	20	19	4	3	2	3	23	3	70	5	1	5	1	.833	0	1-3	11	2.42	2.82
2014	Tor	AL	66	0	0	17	53.1	234	46	16	16	2	0	3	1	27	4	76	1	0	2	3	.400	0	5-7	24	3.16	2.70
2015	Tor	AL	63	0	0	24	54.1	214	39	17	15	4	1	0	2	13	3	70	4	0	5	5	.500	0	5-8	9	1.95	2.48
2016	Tor	AL	54	0	0	8	36.2	157	39	17	16	6	1	1	2	8	0	45	0	0	1	7	.125	0	0-4	9	4.33	3.93
2017	StL	NL	73	0	0	12	67.1	277	67	31	29	7	0	5	0	16	3	66	3	0	2	4	.333	0	1-7	13	3.41	3.88
	Postseason		8	0	0	0	6.0	21	1	0	0	0	1	0	0	4	0	6	0	0	0	0	-	0	0-1	1	0.90	0.00
	9 ML YEARS		403	74	2	76	723.1	3082	718	355	335	91	12	27	23	244	16	651	21	2	43	46	.483	1	12-29	67	4.07	4.17

Darrell Ceciliani

Bats: L **Throws:** L **Pos:** LF-1;CF-1;DH-1;PH-1;PR-1   ses-see-lee-AH-nee   **Ht:** 6'1" **Wt:** 220 **Born:** 6/22/1990 **Age:** 28

							BATTING												RUNNING			AVERAGES			
Year	Team	Lg	G	AB	H	2B	3B	HR	(Hm | Rd)	TB	R	RBI	RC	TBB	IBB	SO	HBP	SH	SF	SB	CS	GDP	Avg	OBP	Slg	OPS
2017	Buffalo*	AAA	22	77	12	1	0	0	(- | -)	13	5	3	1	3	0	21	1	0	0	1	0	1	.156	.198	.169	.366
2015	NYM	NL	39	68	14	2	0	1	(1 | 0)	19	5	3	6	4	0	25	2	0	0	5	1	0	.206	.270	.279	.550
2016	Tor	AL	13	27	3	2	0	0	(0 | 0)	5	2	1	0	1	0	14	1	0	0	0	0	0	.111	.172	.185	.358
2017	Tor	AL	3	5	2	1	0	1	(0 | 1)	6	2	3	3	0	0	0	0	0	0	0	0	0	.400	.400	1.200	1.600
	3 ML YEARS		55	100	19	5	0	2	(1 | 1)	30	9	7	9	5	0	39	3	0	0	5	1	0	.190	.250	.300	.550

Xavier Cedeno

Pitches: L **Bats:** L **Pos:** RP-9   seh-DAYN-yo   **Ht:** 5'11" **Wt:** 210 **Born:** 8/26/1986 **Age:** 31

				HOW MUCH HE PITCHED							WHAT HE GAVE UP									THE RESULTS						
Year	Team	Lg	G	GS	CG	GF	IP	BFP	H	R	ER	HR	SH	SF	HB	TBB	IBB	SO	WP	Bk	W	L	Pct	Sh	Sv-Op	Hld	ERC	ERA
2011	Hou	NL	3	0	0	0	1.2	11	7	5	5	2	0	0	0	0	0	0	0	0	0	0	-	0	0-0	0	43.10	27.00
2012	Hou	NL	44	0	0	12	31.0	138	30	15	13	3	2	3	1	14	1	36	3	0	0	1	.000	0	1-3	6	4.05	3.77
2013	2 Tms		16	0	0	3	12.1	60	15	12	9	1	0	1	2	8	0	9	0	0	0	0	-	0	0-0	2	6.24	6.57
2014	Was	NL	9	0	0	4	7.0	30	10	4	3	1	0	0	0	5	0	5	0	0	0	0	-	0	0-0	0	5.27	3.86
2015	2 Tms		66	0	0	10	46.0	189	40	13	12	4	0	0	2	14	2	47	6	0	4	1	.800	0	1-3	19	3.05	2.35
2016	TB	AL	54	0	0	7	41.1	174	36	17	17	2	1	2	0	13	1	43	3	0	3	4	.429	0	0-5	19	2.62	3.70
2017	TB	AL	9	0	0	0	3.0	21	7	5	4	3	1	0	0	4	1	0	0	0	1	1	.500	0	0-3	0	25.88	12.00
13	Hou	AL	5	0	0	0	6.1	37	10	11	8	0	1	0	2	7	0	3	0	0	0	0	-	0	0-0	0	11.27	11.37
13	Was	NL	11	0	0	3	6.0	23	5	1	1	1	0	1	0	1	0	6	0	0	0	0	-	0	0-0	2	1.84	1.50
15	Was	NL	5	0	0	1	3.0	15	3	2	2	1	0	0	1	2	0	4	2	0	0	0	-	0	0-2	0	8.41	6.00
15	TB	AL	61	0	0	9	43.0	174	37	11	10	3	0	0	1	12	2	43	4	0	4	1	.800	0	1-1	19	2.74	2.09
	7 ML YEARS		201	0	0	36	142.1	623	145	71	63	15	5	5	5	53	5	140	12	0	8	7	.533	0	2-14	46	4.14	3.98

Juan Centeno

Bats: L **Throws:** R **Pos:** C-22;PH-1   sen-TAIN-no   **Ht:** 5'9" **Wt:** 195 **Born:** 11/16/1989 **Age:** 28

							BATTING												RUNNING			AVERAGES			
Year	Team	Lg	G	AB	H	2B	3B	HR	(Hm | Rd)	TB	R	RBI	RC	TBB	IBB	SO	HBP	SH	SF	SB	CS	GDP	Avg	OBP	Slg	OPS
2017	Fresno*	AAA	65	235	73	12	1	1	(- | -)	90	25	33	33	16	0	37	1	3	2	0	1	7	.311	.354	.383	.737
2013	NYM	NL	4	10	3	0	0	0	(0 | 0)	3	0	1	1	0	0	1	0	0	0	0	0	0	.300	.300	.300	.600
2014	NYM	NL	10	30	6	0	0	0	(0 | 0)	6	1	2	2	3	0	5	0	0	0	0	0	2	.200	.273	.200	.473
2015	Mil	NL	10	21	1	1	0	0	(0 | 0)	2	0	0	0	2	0	7	0	0	0	0	0	0	.048	.130	.095	.226
2016	Min	AL	52	176	46	12	1	3	(1 | 2)	69	16	25	20	12	0	38	1	3	0	0	0	8	.261	.312	.392	.704
2017	Hou	AL	25	52	12	0	0	2	(2 | 0)	18	5	4	4	4	1	12	0	1	0	0	0	2	.231	.286	.346	.632
	5 ML YEARS		101	289	68	13	1	5	(3 | 2)	98	22	32	27	21	1	63	1	4	0	0	0	12	.235	.289	.339	.628

Francisco Cervelli

Bats: R **Throws:** R **Pos:** C-78;PH-5   sir-VEL-lee   **Ht:** 6'1" **Wt:** 210 **Born:** 3/6/1986 **Age:** 32

							BATTING												RUNNING			AVERAGES			
Year	Team	Lg	G	AB	H	2B	3B	HR	(Hm | Rd)	TB	R	RBI	RC	TBB	IBB	SO	HBP	SH	SF	SB	CS	GDP	Avg	OBP	Slg	OPS
2008	NYY	AL	3	5	0	0	0	0	(0 | 0)	0	0	0	0	0	0	3	0	0	0	0	0	1	.000	.000	.000	.000
2009	NYY	AL	42	94	28	4	0	1	(0 | 1)	35	13	11	11	2	0	11	0	4	1	0	3	1	.298	.309	.372	.682
2010	NYY	AL	93	266	72	11	3	0	(0 | 0)	89	27	38	40	33	1	42	6	8	4	1	1	7	.271	.359	.335	.694
2011	NYY	AL	43	124	33	4	0	4	(2 | 2)	49	17	22	17	9	0	29	2	1	1	4	1	4	.266	.324	.395	.719
2012	NYY	AL	3	1	0	0	0	0	(0 | 0)	0	1	0	0	1	0	0	0	0	0	0	0	0	.000	.000	.000	.500
2013	NYY	AL	17	52	14	3	0	3	(3 | 0)	26	12	8	9	8	0	9	1	0	0	0	0	1	.269	.377	.500	.877
2014	NYY	AL	49	146	44	11	1	2	(1 | 1)	63	18	13	19	11	0	41	5	0	0	1	0	5	.301	.370	.432	.802
2015	Pit	NL	130	451	133	17	5	7	(6 | 1)	181	56	43	46	46	1	94	8	4	1	1	0	12	.295	.370	.401	.771
2016	Pit	NL	101	326	86	14	1	1	(0 | 1)	105	42	33	40	56	1	72	6	0	5	6	2	14	.264	.377	.322	.699
2017	Pit	NL	81	265	66	13	2	5	(2 | 3)	98	31	31	30	32	0	65	6	0	1	0	2	7	.249	.342	.370	.712
	Postseason		4	6	1	0	0	0	(0 | 0)	1	0	0	0	0	0	2	1	0	0	0	0	0	.167	.286	.167	.452
	10 ML YEARS		562	1730	476	77	12	23	(14 | 9)	646	217	199	228	198	3	366	34	17	13	13	10	52	.275	.358	.373	.732

Hunter Cervenka

Pitches: L **Bats:** L **Pos:** RP-5   sir-VEN-kuh   **Ht:** 6'1" **Wt:** 245 **Born:** 1/3/1990 **Age:** 28

Year	Team	Lg	G	GS	CG	GF	IP	BFP	H	R	ER	HR	SH	SF	HB	TBB	IBB	SO	WP	Bk	W	L	Pct	Sh	Sv-Op	Hld	ERC	ERA
2013	Dytona	A+	11	0	0	7	21.2	94	13	8	7	0	1	0	1	15	0	21	3	0	1	0	1.000	0	5--	-	2.63	2.91
2013	Tenn	AA	30	0	0	11	38.1	163	29	14	13	1	5	0	1	20	1	33	3	1	5	1	.833	0	1--	-	2.76	3.05
2014	Tenn	AA	48	0	0	6	61.2	256	44	28	26	1	2	1	4	31	0	65	5	0	4	4	.500	0	1--	-	2.65	3.79
2015	Iowa	AAA	12	0	0	5	13.0	79	21	16	16	2	1	0	0	15	2	20	2	1	0	1	.000	0	0--	-	10.68	11.08
2015	Gwnntt	AAA	14	0	0	3	16.2	71	13	1	0	0	1	0	2	8	0	23	4	0	1	0	1.000	0	0--	-	2.96	0.00
2017	NewOr	AAA	44	0	0	16	39.1	182	38	23	20	7	2	3	3	26	0	39	3	0	1	4	.200	0	0--	-	5.82	4.58
2016	2 Tms	NL	68	0	0	11	43.1	182	31	19	17	3	1	0	1	28	5	42	6	0	1	0	1.000	0	0-0	11	3.23	3.53
2017	Mia		5	0	0	0	4.2	24	1	8	8	0	1	0	2	8	0	6	1	0	0	0	-	0	0-0	0	5.38	15.43
16	Atl	NL	50	0	0	8	34.0	139	20	14	12	2	1	0	1	23	5	35	6	0	1	0	1.000	0	0-0	9	2.61	3.18
16	Mia	NL	18	0	0	3	9.1	43	11	5	5	1	0	0	0	5	0	7	0	0	0	0	-	0	0-0	2	5.73	4.82
	2 ML YEARS		73	0	0	11	48.0	206	32	27	25	3	2	1	3	36	5	48	7	0	1	0	1.000	0	0-0	11	3.45	4.69

Yoenis Cespedes

Bats: R **Throws:** R **Pos:** LF-74;PH-5;DH-1   yo-EHN-ess SESS-peh-des   **Ht:** 5'10" **Wt:** 220 **Born:** 10/18/1985 **Age:** 32

Year	Team	Lg	G	AB	H	2B	3B	HR	(Hm	Rd)	TB	R	RBI	RC	TBB	IBB	SO	HBP	SH	SF	SB	CS	GDP	Avg	OBP	Slg	OPS
2012	Oak	AL	129	487	142	25	5	23	(11	12)	246	70	82	90	43	5	102	7	0	3	16	4	9	.292	.356	.505	.861
2013	Oak	AL	135	529	127	21	4	26	(14	12)	234	74	80	65	37	5	137	5	0	3	7	7	8	.240	.294	.442	.737
2014	2 Tms	AL	152	600	156	36	6	22	(13	9)	270	89	100	85	35	3	128	3	0	7	7	2	13	.260	.301	.450	.751
2015	2 Tms		159	633	184	42	6	35	(10	25)	343	101	105	103	33	5	141	5	0	5	7	5	14	.291	.328	.542	.870
2016	NYM	NL	132	479	134	25	1	31	(14	17)	254	72	86	83	51	8	108	7	0	6	3	1	14	.280	.354	.530	.884
2017	NYM	NL	81	291	85	17	2	17	(5	12)	157	46	42	44	26	5	61	2	0	2	0	1	7	.292	.352	.540	.892
14	Oak	AL	101	399	102	26	3	17	(11	6)	185	62	67	55	28	3	80	1	0	4	3	2	8	.256	.303	.464	.767
14	Bos		51	201	54	10	3	5	(2	3)	85	27	33	30	7	0	48	2	0	3	4	0	5	.269	.296	.423	.719
15	Det	AL	102	403	118	28	2	18	(5	13)	204	62	61	58	19	2	87	1	0	4	3	4	9	.293	.323	.506	.829
15	NYM	NL	57	230	66	14	4	17	(5	12)	139	39	44	45	14	3	54	4	0	1	4	1	5	.287	.337	.604	.942
	Postseason		25	98	26	3	1	3	(2	1)	40	11	14	14	3	0	25	1	0	1	3	0	1	.265	.291	.408	.699
	6 ML YEARS		788	3019	828	166	24	154	(67	87)	1504	452	495	470	225	31	677	29	0	26	40	20	65	.274	.328	.498	.826

Luis Cessa

Pitches: R **Bats:** R **Pos:** SP-5; RP-5   SESS-uh   **Ht:** 6'0" **Wt:** 205 **Born:** 4/25/1992 **Age:** 26

Year	Team	Lg	G	GS	CG	GF	IP	BFP	H	R	ER	HR	SH	SF	HB	TBB	IBB	SO	WP	Bk	W	L	Pct	Sh	Sv-Op	Hld	ERC	ERA
2013	Savann	A	21	21	1	0	130.0	537	136	53	45	11	8	2	0	19	0	124	4	1	8	4	.667	0	0--	-	3.23	3.12
2014	Stluci	A+	20	20	1	0	114.2	472	110	54	51	7	3	5	3	27	0	83	6	0	7	8	.467	0	0--	-	3.09	4.00
2015	Bnghtn	AA	13	13	0	0	77.1	318	77	25	22	2	5	1	0	17	1	61	4	0	7	4	.636	0	0--	-	2.88	2.56
2015	LsVgs	AAA	5	5	0	0	24.1	119	40	25	23	3	1	0	1	4	0	24	0	0	0	3	.000	0	0--	-	7.11	8.51
2015	Toledo	AAA	7	7	0	0	37.2	170	46	27	25	2	0	3	2	15	0	34	1	1	1	3	.250	0	0--	-	5.27	5.97
2016	S-WB	AAA	15	14	1	0	77.1	309	66	33	26	8	2	3	0	23	0	69	3	0	6	3	.667	1	0--	-	3.00	3.03
2017	S-WB	AAA	14	13	0	1	78.1	326	75	37	30	7	0	1	2	26	0	67	0	0	4	6	.400	0	0--	-	3.67	3.45
2016	NYY	AL	17	9	0	5	70.1	285	64	36	34	16	1	1	3	14	0	46	2	0	4	4	.500	0	0-0	0	3.81	4.35
2017	NYY	AL	10	5	0	2	36.0	160	36	21	19	7	0	0	3	17	0	30	2	0	0	3	.000	0	0-0	0	5.43	4.75
	2 ML YEARS		27	14	0	7	106.1	445	100	57	53	23	1	1	6	31	0	76	4	0	4	7	.364	0	0-0	0	4.35	4.49

Alejandro Chacin

Pitches: R **Bats:** R **Pos:** RP-6   cha-SEEN   **Ht:** 6'0" **Wt:** 204 **Born:** 6/24/1993 **Age:** 25

Year	Team	Lg	G	GS	CG	GF	IP	BFP	H	R	ER	HR	SH	SF	HB	TBB	IBB	SO	WP	Bk	W	L	Pct	Sh	Sv-Op	Hld	ERC	ERA
2013	Dayton	A	44	0	0	23	65.0	277	42	27	21	4	2	4	6	33	0	72	14	0	4	3	.571	0	9--	-	2.62	2.91
2014	Dayton	A	48	0	0	31	65.0	281	52	23	17	2	4	1	7	28	3	84	7	0	4	4	.500	0	20--	-	2.91	2.35
2015	2 Tms		39	0	0	25	51.1	211	39	21	19	3	4	1	4	15	0	72	1	0	3	0	1.000	0	11--	-	2.41	3.33
2016	Pnscla	AA	52	0	0	46	60.2	258	51	12	12	2	2	4	3	26	3	75	3	0	5	2	.714	0	30--	-	2.95	1.78
2017	Lsvlle	AAA	44	0	0	15	69.1	303	63	26	20	4	5	5	7	27	0	63	7	1	0	3	.000	0	1--	-	3.56	2.60
2017	Cin	NL	6	0	0	3	6.0	32	11	7	7	2	0	0	0	4	0	6	0	0	0	0	-	0	0-0	0	13.09	10.50

Jhoulys Chacin

Pitches: R **Bats:** R **Pos:** SP-32   yoo-LEES cha-SEEN   **Ht:** 6'3" **Wt:** 215 **Born:** 1/7/1988 **Age:** 30

Year	Team	Lg	G	GS	CG	GF	IP	BFP	H	R	ER	HR	SH	SF	HB	TBB	IBB	SO	WP	Bk	W	L	Pct	Sh	Sv-Op	Hld	ERC	ERA
2009	Col	NL	9	1	0	3	11.0	48	6	6	6	1	1	0	0	11	0	13	2	0	0	1	.000	0	0-0	0	3.87	4.91
2010	Col	NL	28	21	0	2	137.1	583	114	64	50	10	6	5	9	61	5	138	4	0	9	11	.450	0	0-0	0	3.33	3.28
2011	Col	NL	31	31	2	0	194.0	827	168	87	78	20	5	3	4	87	1	150	7	0	11	14	.440	1	0-0	0	3.61	3.62
2012	Col	NL	14	14	0	0	69.0	314	80	35	34	10	1	1	2	32	0	45	3	0	3	5	.375	0	0-0	0	5.73	4.43
2013	Col	NL	31	31	0	0	197.1	816	188	82	76	11	3	7	3	61	3	126	5	1	14	10	.583	0	0-0	0	3.26	3.47
2014	Col	NL	11	11	0	0	63.1	272	63	38	38	8	2	3	1	28	1	42	4	0	1	7	.125	0	0-0	0	4.52	5.40
2015	Ari	NL	5	4	0	0	26.2	111	24	11	10	4	1	0	0	10	0	21	0	0	2	1	.667	0	0-0	0	3.80	3.38
2016	2 Tms	NL	34	22	1	5	144.0	632	153	81	77	14	4	6	5	55	4	119	8	1	6	8	.429	0	0-0	0	4.42	4.81
2017	SD	NL	32	32	0	0	180.1	765	157	82	78	19	6	6	14	72	5	153	7	1	13	10	.565	0	0-0	0	3.67	3.89
16	Atl	NL	5	5	0	0	26.2	117	29	17	16	4	2	1	1	8	0	27	0	0	1	2	.333	0	0-0	0	4.42	5.40
16	LAA	AL	29	17	1	5	117.1	515	124	64	61	10	2	5	4	47	4	92	8	1	5	6	.455	0	0-0	0	4.42	4.68
	9 ML YEARS		195	167	3	10	1023.0	4368	953	486	447	97	29	31	38	417	19	807	40	3	59	67	.468	1	0-0	0	3.82	3.93

Andrew Chafin

Pitches: L Bats: R Pos: RP-71   Ht: 6'2" Wt: 225 Born: 6/17/1990 Age: 28

		HOW MUCH HE PITCHED					WHAT HE GAVE UP										THE RESULTS						
Year Team	Lg	G	GS	CG	GF	IP	BFP	H	R	ER	HR	SH	SF	HB	TBB	IBB	SO	WP	Bk	W	L	Pct	Sh	Sv-Op	Hld	ERC	ERA
2014 Ari	NL	3	3	0	0	14.0	60	13	6	6	0	2	0	1	8	1	10	2	0	0	1	.000	0	0-1	4	3.92	3.86
2015 Ari	NL	66	0	0	6	75.0	306	56	23	23	3	3	2	1	30	6	58	2	0	5	1	.833	0	2-2	16	2.30	2.76
2016 Ari	NL	32	0	0	1	22.2	98	22	18	17	1	1	0	1	11	1	28	2	0	0	1	.000	0	0-1	6	4.01	6.75
2017 Ari	NL	71	0	0	12	51.1	221	48	21	20	5	2	1	2	21	3	61	1	1	1	0	1.000	0	0-0	17	3.78	3.51
4 ML YEARS		172	3	0	19	163.0	685	139	68	66	9	8	3	5	70	11	157	7	1	6	3	.667	0	2-3	39	3.12	3.64

Aroldis Chapman

Pitches: L Bats: L Pos: RP-52   ah-ROLL-diss   Ht: 6'4" Wt: 212 Born: 2/28/1988 Age: 30

		HOW MUCH HE PITCHED					WHAT HE GAVE UP										THE RESULTS						
Year Team	Lg	G	GS	CG	GF	IP	BFP	H	R	ER	HR	SH	SF	HB	TBB	IBB	SO	WP	Bk	W	L	Pct	Sh	Sv-Op	Hld	ERC	ERA
2010 Cin	NL	15	0	0	3	13.1	51	9	4	3	0	0	0	0	5	0	19	2	0	2	2	.500	0	1-3	13	1.82	2.03
2011 Cin	NL	54	0	0	13	50.0	207	24	21	20	2	1	0	2	41	0	71	4	0	4	1	.800	0	1-3	13	2.69	3.60
2012 Cin	NL	68	0	0	52	71.2	276	35	13	12	4	0	1	4	23	0	122	4	0	5	5	.500	0	38-43	6	1.35	1.51
2013 Cin	NL	68	0	0	55	63.2	258	37	18	12	8	1	0	3	29	0	112	6	0	4	5	.444	0	38-43	0	2.33	2.54
2014 Cin	NL	54	0	0	44	54.0	202	21	12	12	1	1	1	2	24	0	106	4	0	0	3	.000	0	36-38	0	1.18	2.00
2015 Cin	NL	65	0	0	54	66.1	278	43	13	12	3	0	2	5	33	1	116	7	0	4	4	.500	0	33-36	0	2.45	1.63
2016 2 Tms		59	0	0	52	58.0	222	32	12	10	2	0	1	0	18	0	90	8	1	4	1	.800	0	36-39	0	1.33	1.55
2017 NYY	AL	52	0	0	42	50.1	210	37	20	18	3	0	1	2	20	2	69	5	0	4	3	.571	0	22-26	1	2.53	3.22
16 NYY	AL	31	0	0	29	31.1	120	20	8	7	2	0	0	0	8	0	44	2	1	3	0	1.000	0	20-21	0	1.59	2.01
16 ChC	NL	28	0	0	23	26.2	102	12	4	3	0	0	1	0	10	0	46	6	0	1	1	.500	0	16-18	0	1.04	1.01
Postseason		18	0	0	12	20.1	86	16	10	7	1	1	1	2	8	0	25	2	0	2	1	.667	0	4-8	0	2.91	3.10
8 ML YEARS		435	0	0	315	427.1	1704	238	113	105	22	3	6	19	193	3	705	40	1	27	24	.529	0	204-229	24	1.87	2.21

Matt Chapman

Bats: R Throws: R Pos: 3B-84   Ht: 6'0" Wt: 210 Born: 4/28/1993 Age: 25

		BATTING																RUNNING			AVERAGES			
Year Team	Lg	G	AB	H	2B	3B	HR	(Hm | Rd)	TB	R	RBI	RC	TBB	IBB	SO	HBP	SH	SF	SB	CS	GDP	Avg	OBP	Slg	OPS
2014 2 Tms	Low	53	204	51	9	4	5	(- | -)	83	23	20	24	8	0	47	5	0		2	1	5	.250	.295	.407	.702
2015 Stckton	A+	80	304	76	21	3	23	(- | -)	172	60	57	60	39	0	79	5	0	4	4	1	5	.250	.341	.566	.907
2016 Mdlnd	AA	117	438	107	26	4	29	(- | -)	228	78	83	78	59	5	147	3	0	4	7	4	7	.244	.335	.521	.856
2016 Nashv	AAA	18	76	15	1	1	7	(- | -)	39	14	13	11	9	1	26	0	0	0	0	0	2	.197	.282	.513	.796
2017 Nashv	AAA	49	175	45	6	2	16	(- | -)	103	30	30	35	25	1	63	1	0	3	5	4	2	.257	.348	.589	.937
2017 Oak	AL	84	290	68	23	2	14	(8 | 6)	137	39	40	42	32	0	92	2	0	2	0	3	2	.234	.313	.472	.785

Tyler Chatwood

Pitches: R Bats: R Pos: SP-25; RP-8   Ht: 6'0" Wt: 185 Born: 12/16/1989 Age: 28

		HOW MUCH HE PITCHED					WHAT HE GAVE UP										THE RESULTS						
Year Team	Lg	G	GS	CG	GF	IP	BFP	H	R	ER	HR	SH	SF	HB	TBB	IBB	SO	WP	Bk	W	L	Pct	Sh	Sv-Op	Hld	ERC	ERA
2011 LAA	AL	27	25	0	0	142.0	633	166	81	75	14	6	3	6	71	4	74	3	1	6	11	.353	0	0-0	0	5.78	4.75
2012 Col	NL	19	12	0	3	64.2	294	74	43	39	9	4	2	0	33	2	41	4	0	5	6	.455	0	1-1	0	5.62	5.43
2013 Col	NL	20	20	1	0	111.1	476	118	44	39	5	2	4	4	41	5	66	10	0	8	5	.615	0	0-0	0	4.05	3.15
2014 Col	NL	4	4	0	0	24.0	101	21	13	12	4	0	2	2	8	0	20	2	0	1	0	1.000	0	0-0	0	3.91	4.50
2016 Col	NL	27	27	0	0	158.0	669	147	75	68	15	2	3	5	70	2	117	7	0	12	9	.571	0	0-0	0	4.01	3.87
2017 Col	NL	33	25	1	3	147.2	631	136	79	77	20	4	3	4	77	2	120	12	2	8	15	.348	1	1-1	0	4.58	4.69
6 ML YEARS		130	113	2	6	647.2	2804	662	335	310	67	18	17	21	300	15	438	38	3	40	46	.465	1	2-2	0	4.67	4.31

Jesse Chavez

Pitches: R Bats: R Pos: SP-21; RP-17   CHAH-vezz   Ht: 6'2" Wt: 175 Born: 8/21/1983 Age: 34

		HOW MUCH HE PITCHED					WHAT HE GAVE UP										THE RESULTS						
Year Team	Lg	G	GS	CG	GF	IP	BFP	H	R	ER	HR	SH	SF	HB	TBB	IBB	SO	WP	Bk	W	L	Pct	Sh	Sv-Op	Hld	ERC	ERA
2008 Pit	NL	15	0	0	6	15.0	74	20	11	11	2	3	1	0	9	2	16	2	0	0	1	.000	0	0-2	0	6.76	6.60
2009 Pit	NL	73	0	0	24	67.1	286	69	33	30	11	1	1	1	22	3	47	5	0	1	4	.200	0	0-4	15	4.39	4.01
2010 2 Tms		51	0	0	26	62.2	280	69	44	41	11	5	3	1	23	7	45	2	0	5	5	.500	0	0-1	6	4.85	5.89
2011 KC	AL	4	0	0	3	7.2	39	12	9	9	3	0	0	0	5	0	8	0	0	0	0	-	0	0-0	0	11.48	10.57
2012 2 Tms	AL	13	2	0	3	24.2	123	34	29	27	7	0	1	3	11	1	30	1	0	1	1	.500	0	0-0	0	8.32	9.85
2013 Oak	AL	35	0	0	16	57.1	248	50	27	25	3	6	2	3	20	4	55	5	0	2	4	.333	0	1-2	1	2.85	3.92
2014 Oak	AL	32	21	0	5	146.0	621	142	64	56	17	1	4	5	49	3	136	7	0	8	8	.500	0	0-0	0	3.89	3.45
2015 Oak	AL	30	26	0	3	157.0	672	164	78	73	18	4	6	2	48	2	136	3	0	7	15	.318	0	1-1	0	4.08	4.18
2016 2 Tms	AL	62	0	0	9	67.0	282	71	36	33	12	0	1	2	18	3	63	1	0	2	2	.500	0	0-3	10	4.56	4.43
2017 LAA	AL	38	21	0	6	138.0	586	148	83	82	28	0	2	2	45	2	119	1	0	7	11	.389	0	0-1	1	5.06	5.35
10 Atl	NL	28	0	0	16	36.2	162	40	24	24	6	3	2	1	12	3	29	0	0	3	2	.600	0	0-0	0	4.65	5.89
10 KC	AL	23	0	0	10	26.0	118	29	20	17	5	2	1	0	11	4	16	2	0	2	3	.400	0	0-1	6	5.13	5.88
12 Tor	AL	9	2	0	2	21.1	102	25	22	20	6	0	1	2	10	1	27	0	0	1	1	.500	0	0-0	0	6.90	8.44
12 Oak	AL	4	0	0	1	3.1	21	9	7	7	1	0	0	1	1	0	3	1	0	0	0	-	0	0-0	0	18.70	18.90
16 Tor	AL	39	0	0	6	41.1	173	43	22	21	9	0	1	2	10	0	42	1	0	1	2	.333	0	0-2	7	4.75	4.57
16 LAD	NL	23	0	0	3	25.2	109	28	14	12	3	0	0	0	8	3	21	0	0	1	0	1.000	0	0-1	3	4.24	4.21
10 ML YEARS		353	70	0	101	742.2	3211	779	414	387	112	20	21	19	250	27	655	27	0	33	51	.393	0	2-14	33	4.50	4.69

Wei-Yin Chen

Pitches: L Bats: R Pos: SP-5; RP-4   way-yin   Ht: 6'0" Wt: 200 Born: 7/21/1985 Age: 32

			HOW MUCH HE PITCHED						WHAT HE GAVE UP											THE RESULTS							
Year	Team	Lg	G	GS	CG	GF	IP	BFP	H	R	ER	HR	SH	SF	HB	TBB	IBB	SO	WP	Bk	W	L	Pct	Sh	Sv-Op	Hld	ERC	ERA
2012	Bal	AL	32	32	0	0	192.2	818	186	97	86	29	5	8	5	57	0	154	2	1	12	11	.522	0	0-0	0	3.88	4.02
2013	Bal	AL	23	23	0	0	137.0	572	142	62	62	17	2	6	2	39	2	104	3	0	7	7	.500	0	0-0	0	4.11	4.07
2014	Bal	AL	31	31	0	0	185.2	772	193	77	73	23	5	4	3	35	2	136	2	0	16	6	.727	0	0-0	0	3.67	3.54
2015	Bal	AL	31	31	0	0	191.1	792	192	78	71	28	5	8	5	41	0	153	3	0	11	8	.579	0	0-0	0	3.80	3.34
2016	Mia	NL	22	22	0	0	123.1	520	134	69	68	22	3	4	3	24	0	100	1	0	5	5	.500	0	0-0	0	4.38	4.96
2017	Mia	NL	9	5	0	1	33.0	132	25	14	14	3	0	1	1	9	0	25	1	0	2	1	.667	0	0-0	0	2.39	3.82
	Postseason		3	3	0	0	15.1	69	22	9	8	2	0	0	0	2	0	10	0	0	1	1	.500	0	0-0	0	5.68	4.70
	6 ML YEARS		148	144	0	1	863.0	3606	872	397	374	122	20	31	19	205	4	672	12	1	53	38	.582	0	0-0	0	3.86	3.90

Robinson Chirinos

Bats: R Throws: R Pos: C-85; DH-2; PH-1   chee-REE-nos   Ht: 6'1" Wt: 210 Born: 6/5/1984 Age: 34

			BATTING																		RUNNING			AVERAGES			
Year	Team	Lg	G	AB	H	2B	3B	HR	(Hm	Rd)	TB	R	RBI	RC	TBB	IBB	SO	HBP	SH	SF	SB	CS	GDP	Avg	OBP	Slg	OPS
2011	TB	AL	20	55	12	2	0	1	(1	0)	17	4	7	5	5	0	13	0	0	0	0	0	1	.218	.283	.309	.592
2013	Tex	AL	13	28	5	3	0	0	(0	0)	8	3	0	0	2	0	6	0	0	0	0	0	1	.179	.233	.286	.519
2014	Tex	AL	93	306	73	15	0	13	(6	7)	127	36	40	38	17	1	71	7	4	4	0	1	4	.239	.290	.415	.705
2015	Tex	AL	78	233	54	16	1	10	(4	6)	102	33	34	28	28	0	62	5	5	2	0	0	4	.232	.325	.438	.762
2016	Tex	AL	57	147	33	11	0	9	(1	8)	71	21	20	21	15	0	44	5	1	2	0	1	4	.224	.314	.483	.797
2017	Tex	AL	88	263	67	13	1	17	(10	7)	133	46	38	44	34	0	79	10	1	1	1	0	5	.255	.360	.506	.866
	Postseason		4	11	3	0	0	1	(0	1)	6	1	3	3	1	0	2	0	0	0	0	0	0	.273	.333	.545	.879
	6 ML YEARS		349	1032	244	60	2	50	(22	28)	458	143	139	136	101	1	275	27	11	9	1	2	18	.236	.318	.444	.762

Lonnie Chisenhall

Bats: L Throws: R Pos: RF-45; CF-19; PH-18; LF-11; 1B-7   CHIZ-en-hall   Ht: 6'2" Wt: 190 Born: 10/4/1988 Age: 29

			BATTING																		RUNNING			AVERAGES			
Year	Team	Lg	G	AB	H	2B	3B	HR	(Hm	Rd)	TB	R	RBI	RC	TBB	IBB	SO	HBP	SH	SF	SB	CS	GDP	Avg	OBP	Slg	OPS
2011	Cle	AL	66	212	54	13	0	7	(2	5)	88	27	22	24	8	1	49	1	1	1	0	0	3	.255	.284	.415	.699
2012	Cle	AL	43	142	38	6	1	5	(4	1)	61	16	16	18	8	0	27	1	0	0	2	1	2	.268	.311	.430	.741
2013	Cle	AL	94	289	65	17	0	11	(4	7)	115	30	36	31	16	0	56	2	1	0	1	0	8	.225	.270	.398	.668
2014	Cle	AL	142	478	134	29	1	13	(6	7)	204	62	59	69	39	3	99	8	4	3	3	1	8	.280	.343	.427	.770
2015	Cle	AL	106	333	82	19	1	7	(3	4)	124	38	44	39	23	3	69	1	2	3	4	1	0	.246	.294	.372	.667
2016	Cle	AL	126	385	110	25	5	8	(4	4)	169	43	57	61	23	2	70	3	3	6	6	0	4	.286	.328	.439	.767
2017	Cle	AL	82	236	68	17	1	12	(6	6)	123	34	53	46	25	2	55	3	3	3	2	2	6	.288	.360	.521	.881
	Postseason		15	46	12	0	0	1	(1	0)	15	4	5	4	2	0	14	1	1	1	0	0	1	.261	.300	.326	.626
	7 ML YEARS		659	2075	551	126	9	63	(29	34)	884	250	287	288	142	11	425	19	14	14	19	5	31	.266	.316	.426	.742

Ji-Man Choi

Bats: L Throws: R Pos: 1B-6; PH-2   gee-man choy   Ht: 6'1" Wt: 230 Born: 5/19/1991 Age: 27

			BATTING																		RUNNING			AVERAGES			
Year	Team	Lg	G	AB	H	2B	3B	HR	(Hm	Rd)	TB	R	RBI	RC	TBB	IBB	SO	HBP	SH	SF	SB	CS	GDP	Avg	OBP	Slg	OPS
2013	Hi Dsrt	A+	48	181	61	24	3	7	(-	-)	112	34	40	45	27	1	33	2	0	1	0	1	5	.337	.427	.619	1.045
2013	Jacksn	AA	61	198	53	10	3	9	(-	-)	96	21	39	38	32	2	28	4	0	2	2	2	5	.268	.377	.485	.862
2013	Tacom	AAA	13	45	11	2	0	2	(-	-)	19	9	6	6	4	0	7	2	1	0	0	0	2	.244	.333	.422	.756
2014	Tacom	AAA	70	237	67	7	2	5	(-	-)	93	41	30	38	36	0	42	3	3	2	2	2	10	.283	.381	.392	.774
2015	Tacom	AAA	18	57	17	4	0	1	(-	-)	24	8	16	10	10	1	14	0	0	1	0	1	2	.298	.403	.421	.824
2016	Salt Lk	AAA	53	188	65	18	1	5	(-	-)	100	31	31	44	31	1	34	2	1	5	4	3	4	.346	.434	.532	.966
2017	S-WB	AAA	87	288	83	25	1	15	(-	-)	155	42	69	59	39	3	86	4	0	7	3	1	2	.288	.373	.538	.911
2016	LAA	AL	54	112	19	4	0	5	(3	2)	38	9	12	8	16	1	27	0	0	1	2	4	2	.170	.271	.339	.611
2017	NYY	AL	6	15	4	1	0	2	(2	0)	11	2	5	3	2	0	5	0	0	0	0	0	1	.267	.333	.733	1.067
	2 ML YEARS		60	127	23	5	0	7	(5	2)	49	11	17	11	18	1	32	0	0	2	2	4	3	.181	.279	.386	.665

Shin-Soo Choo

Bats: L Throws: L Pos: RF-77; DH-65; PH-8   SHIN-sue CHEW   Ht: 5'11" Wt: 210 Born: 7/13/1982 Age: 35

			BATTING																		RUNNING			AVERAGES			
Year	Team	Lg	G	AB	H	2B	3B	HR	(Hm	Rd)	TB	R	RBI	RC	TBB	IBB	SO	HBP	SH	SF	SB	CS	GDP	Avg	OBP	Slg	OPS
2005	Sea	AL	10	18	1	0	0	0	(0	0)	1	1	1	0	3	0	4	0	0	0	0	0	0	.056	.190	.056	.246
2006	2 Tms	AL	49	157	44	12	3	3	(2	1)	71	23	22	24	18	2	50	2	1	1	5	3	3	.280	.360	.452	.812
2007	Cle	AL	6	17	5	0	0	0	(0	0)	5	5	5	3	2	1	5	0	0	1	0	1	0	.294	.350	.294	.644
2008	Cle	AL	94	317	98	28	3	14	(10	4)	174	68	66	72	44	4	78	5	0	4	4	3	5	.309	.397	.549	.946
2009	Cle	AL	156	583	175	38	6	20	(11	9)	285	87	86	111	78	5	151	17	0	7	21	2	9	.300	.394	.489	.883
2010	Cle	AL	144	550	165	31	2	22	(8	14)	266	81	90	106	83	11	118	11	0	2	22	7	11	.300	.401	.484	.885
2011	Cle	AL	85	313	81	11	3	8	(7	1)	122	37	36	38	36	3	78	6	0	3	12	5	7	.259	.344	.390	.733
2012	Cle	AL	155	598	169	43	2	16	(8	8)	264	88	67	96	73	0	150	14	0	1	21	7	11	.283	.373	.441	.815
2013	Cin	NL	154	569	162	34	2	21	(10	11)	263	107	54	111	112	5	133	26	3	2	20	11	3	.285	.423	.462	.885
2014	Tex	AL	123	455	110	19	4	13	(5	8)	176	58	40	54	58	3	131	12	0	4	3	4	9	.242	.340	.374	.714
2015	Tex	AL	149	555	153	32	3	22	(12	10)	257	94	82	99	76	1	147	15	2	5	4	2	7	.276	.375	.463	.838
2016	Tex	AL	48	178	43	7	0	7	(2	5)	71	27	17	25	25	1	60	6	3	1	6	3	1	.242	.357	.399	.756
2017	Tex	AL	149	544	142	20	1	22	(9	13)	230	96	78	97	77	3	134	7	3	5	12	3	18	.261	.357	.423	.780
06	Sea	AL	4	11	1	1	0	0	(0	0)	2	0	0	0	0	0	4	1	0	0	0	0	1	.091	.167	.182	.348
06	Cle	AL	45	146	43	11	3	3	(2	1)	69	23	22	24	18	2	46	1	1	1	5	3	2	.295	.373	.473	.846
	Postseason		7	27	6	0	0	2	(0	2)	12	6	4	3	1	0	9	1	1	0	0	0	1	.222	.276	.444	.720
	13 ML YEARS		1322	4854	1348	275	26	168	(84	84)	2179	772	644	836	685	37	1225	122	9	35	130	51	84	.278	.378	.449	.827

Tony Cingrani

Pitches: L Bats: L Pos: RP-47   sin-GRAHN-ee   Ht: 6'4" Wt: 214 Born: 7/5/1989 Age: 28

Year	Team	Lg	HOW MUCH HE PITCHED						WHAT HE GAVE UP										THE RESULTS						
			G	GS	CG	GF	IP	BFP	H	R	ER	HR	SH	SF	HB	TBB	IBB	SO	WP	Bk	W	L	Pct	Sh	Sv-Op	Hld	ERC	ERA
2012	Cin	NL	3	0	0	1	5.0	22	4	1	1	1	0	0	0	2	0	9	0	0	0	0	-	0	0-0	0	3.38	1.80
2013	Cin	NL	23	18	0	0	104.2	420	72	37	34	14	4	4	2	43	1	120	4	0	7	4	.636	0	0-0	1	2.78	2.92
2014	Cin	NL	13	11	0	2	63.1	280	62	33	32	12	2	2	1	35	2	61	1	2	2	8	.200	0	0-0	0	5.29	4.55
2015	Cin	NL	35	1	0	7	33.1	155	31	21	21	3	1	2	3	25	3	39	2	1	0	3	.000	0	0-2	9	5.19	5.67
2016	Cin	NL	65	0	0	34	63.0	271	54	30	29	5	1	1	3	37	1	49	3	1	2	5	.286	0	17-23	8	4.12	4.14
2017	2 Tms	NL	47	0	0	15	42.2	176	40	22	20	10	1	0	1	12	0	52	4	0	0	0	-	0	0-1	9	4.29	4.22
17	Cin	NL	25	0	0	7	23.1	99	25	14	14	9	0	0	1	6	0	24	1	0	0	0	-	0	0-1	4	6.15	5.40
17	LAD	NL	22	0	0	8	19.1	77	15	8	6	1	1	0	0	6	0	28	3	0	0	0	-	0	0-0	5	2.30	2.79
	6 ML YEARS		186	30	0	59	312.0	1324	263	144	137	45	9	9	10	154	7	330	14	4	11	20	.355	0	17-26	27	4.01	3.95

Steve Cishek

Pitches: R Bats: R Pos: RP-49   SEE-sheck   Ht: 6'6" Wt: 215 Born: 6/18/1986 Age: 32

Year	Team	Lg	HOW MUCH HE PITCHED						WHAT HE GAVE UP										THE RESULTS						
			G	GS	CG	GF	IP	BFP	H	R	ER	HR	SH	SF	HB	TBB	IBB	SO	WP	Bk	W	L	Pct	Sh	Sv-Op	Hld	ERC	ERA
2010	Fla	NL	3	0	0	2	4.1	15	1	0	0	0	0	0	0	1	0	3	0	0	0	0	-	0	0-0	0	0.35	0.00
2011	Fla	NL	45	0	0	21	54.2	229	45	18	16	1	3	0	3	19	7	55	5	0	2	1	.667	0	3-3	2	2.38	2.63
2012	Mia	NL	68	0	0	36	63.2	275	54	26	19	3	3	2	6	29	6	61	1	1	5	2	.714	0	15-19	13	3.28	2.69
2013	Mia	NL	69	0	0	62	69.2	281	53	19	18	3	3	3	2	22	6	74	1	0	4	6	.400	0	34-36	1	2.15	2.33
2014	Mia	NL	67	0	0	55	65.1	275	58	26	23	3	5	3	1	21	2	84	1	0	4	5	.444	0	39-43	0	2.78	3.17
2015	2 Tms	NL	59	0	0	23	55.1	243	55	26	22	4	1	2	1	27	3	48	1	0	2	6	.250	0	4-9	6	4.17	3.58
2016	Sea	AL	62	0	0	40	64.0	258	44	21	20	8	1	0	4	21	2	76	4	0	4	6	.400	0	25-32	5	2.51	2.81
2017	2 Tms	AL	49	0	0	11	44.2	174	26	10	10	3	0	1	3	14	1	41	3	1	3	2	.600	0	1-4	15	1.70	2.01
15	Mia	NL	32	0	0	15	32.0	144	37	19	16	2	1	2	0	14	3	28	0	0	2	6	.250	0	3-7	3	4.66	4.50
15	StL	NL	27	0	0	8	23.1	99	18	7	6	2	0	0	1	13	0	20	1	0	0	0	-	0	1-2	3	3.53	2.31
17	Sea	AL	23	0	0	8	20.0	80	13	7	7	3	0	1	1	7	1	15	1	1	1	1	.500	0	1-4	6	2.48	3.15
17	TB	AL	26	0	0	3	24.2	94	13	3	3	0	0	0	2	7	0	26	2	0	2	1	.667	0	0-0	9	1.25	1.09
	8 ML YEARS		422	0	0	250	421.2	1750	336	146	128	25	16	11	20	154	27	449	16	2	24	28	.462	0	121-146	46	2.67	2.73

Preston Claiborne

Pitches: R Bats: R Pos: RP-1   Ht: 6'2" Wt: 225 Born: 1/21/1988 Age: 30

Year	Team	Lg	HOW MUCH HE PITCHED						WHAT HE GAVE UP										THE RESULTS						
			G	GS	CG	GF	IP	BFP	H	R	ER	HR	SH	SF	HB	TBB	IBB	SO	WP	Bk	W	L	Pct	Sh	Sv-Op	Hld	ERC	ERA
2017	RdRck*	AAA	38	0	0	32	38.0	162	37	9	8	2	1	2	1	15	0	42	1	0	3	1	.750	0	16- -	-	3.72	1.89
2013	NYY	AL	44	0	0	12	50.1	214	51	23	23	7	2	0	2	14	4	42	2	0	0	2	.000	0	0-0	4	3.96	4.11
2014	NYY	AL	18	0	0	9	21.0	96	24	9	7	1	0	2	0	10	3	16	0	0	3	0	1.000	0	0-1	0	4.47	3.00
2017	Tex	AL	1	0	0	1	2.0	10	5	3	3	0	0	0	0	0	0	2	0	0	0	0	-	0	0-0	0	12.01	13.50
	3 ML YEARS		63	0	0	22	73.1	320	80	35	33	8	2	2	2	24	7	60	2	0	3	2	.600	0	0-1	4	4.30	4.05

Alex Claudio

Pitches: L Bats: L Pos: RP-69; SP-1   Ht: 6'3" Wt: 180 Born: 1/31/1992 Age: 26

Year	Team	Lg	HOW MUCH HE PITCHED						WHAT HE GAVE UP										THE RESULTS						
			G	GS	CG	GF	IP	BFP	H	R	ER	HR	SH	SF	HB	TBB	IBB	SO	WP	Bk	W	L	Pct	Sh	Sv-Op	Hld	ERC	ERA
2014	Tex	AL	15	0	0	5	12.1	54	14	4	4	0	0	0	0	4	0	14	0	1	0	0	-	0	0-0	0	3.79	2.92
2015	Tex	AL	18	0	0	6	15.2	66	12	6	5	4	0	2	1	6	2	13	1	0	1	1	.500	0	0-1	3	3.74	2.87
2016	Tex	AL	39	0	0	15	51.2	217	55	19	16	2	0	2	1	10	0	34	0	0	4	1	.800	0	0-0	2	3.28	2.79
2017	Tex	AL	70	1	0	38	82.2	323	71	26	23	5	1	3	2	15	4	56	0	3	4	2	.667	0	11-15	7	2.37	2.50
	Postseason		2	0	0	0	5.0	18	3	0	0	0	0	0	0	3	0	0	0	0	0	0	-	0	0-0	0	2.46	0.00
	4 ML YEARS		142	1	0	64	162.1	660	152	55	48	11	1	7	4	35	6	117	1	4	9	4	.692	0	11-16	12	2.89	2.66

Mike Clevinger

Pitches: R Bats: R Pos: SP-21; RP-6   Ht: 6'4" Wt: 210 Born: 12/21/1990 Age: 27

Year	Team	Lg	HOW MUCH HE PITCHED						WHAT HE GAVE UP										THE RESULTS						
			G	GS	CG	GF	IP	BFP	H	R	ER	HR	SH	SF	HB	TBB	IBB	SO	WP	Bk	W	L	Pct	Sh	Sv-Op	Hld	ERC	ERA
2014	3 Tms	Low	23	22	0	1	99.2	428	94	58	49	11	3	2	7	43	0	100	8	1	4	4	.500	0	0- -	-	4.30	4.42
2015	Akron	AA	27	26	0	1	158.0	639	127	53	48	8	4	6	9	40	0	145	11	1	9	8	.529	0	0- -	-	2.40	2.73
2016	Clmbs	AAA	17	17	1	0	93.0	380	78	32	31	8	0	3	1	35	0	97	8	0	11	1	.917	0	0- -	-	3.12	3.00
2017	Clmbs	AAA	7	7	0	0	34.0	140	28	10	10	3	1	1	1	14	0	38	2	0	3	2	.600	0	0- -	-	3.26	2.65
2016	Cle	AL	17	10	0	3	53.0	233	50	31	31	8	0	1	0	29	0	50	2	0	3	3	.500	0	0-0	0	4.72	5.26
2017	Cle	AL	27	21	0	1	121.2	502	92	46	42	13	1	0	3	60	2	137	3	0	12	6	.667	0	0-0	0	3.29	3.11
	Postseason		4	0	0	3	5.2	24	3	3	3	1	0	0	0	5	0	5	3	1	0	0	-	0	0-0	0	3.99	4.76
	2 ML YEARS		44	31	0	4	174.2	735	142	77	73	21	1	1	3	89	2	187	5	0	15	9	.625	0	0-0	0	3.71	3.76

Tyler Clippard

Pitches: R Bats: R Pos: RP-67   Ht: 6'3" Wt: 200 Born: 2/14/1985 Age: 33

Year	Team	Lg	HOW MUCH HE PITCHED						WHAT HE GAVE UP										THE RESULTS						
			G	GS	CG	GF	IP	BFP	H	R	ER	HR	SH	SF	HB	TBB	IBB	SO	WP	Bk	W	L	Pct	Sh	Sv-Op	Hld	ERC	ERA
2007	NYY	AL	6	6	0	0	27.0	124	29	19	19	6	0	0	0	17	1	18	2	1	3	1	.750	0	0-0	0	6.37	6.33
2008	Was	NL	2	2	0	0	10.1	48	12	5	5	2	0	0	0	7	1	8	1	0	1	1	.500	0	0-0	0	6.90	4.35
2009	Was	NL	41	0	0	8	60.1	246	36	20	18	9	3	1	1	32	1	67	1	1	4	2	.667	0	0-1	3	2.79	2.69
2010	Was	NL	78	0	0	18	91.0	378	69	33	31	8	3	7	2	41	4	112	1	1	11	8	.579	0	1-11	23	2.91	3.07
2011	Was	NL	72	0	0	8	88.1	329	48	18	18	11	4	3	0	26	2	104	1	0	3	0	1.000	0	0-7	38	1.61	1.83
2012	Was	NL	74	0	0	42	72.2	307	55	32	30	7	3	4	2	29	2	84	5	0	2	6	.250	0	32-37	13	2.73	3.72

Year	Team	Lg	HOW MUCH HE PITCHED						WHAT HE GAVE UP												THE RESULTS							
			G	GS	CG	GF	IP	BFP	H	R	ER	HR	SH	SF	HB	TBB	IBB	SO	WP	Bk	W	L	Pct	Sh	Sv-Op	Hld	ERC	ERA
2013	Was	NL	72	0	0	6	71.0	275	37	19	19	9	2	1	4	24	1	73	2	0	6	3	.667	0	0-3	33	1.79	2.41
2014	Was	NL	75	0	0	6	70.1	278	47	22	17	5	2	2	4	23	1	82	0	0	7	4	.636	0	1-7	40	1.98	2.18
2015	2 Tms	NL	69	0	0	36	71.0	301	49	25	23	8	1	2	4	31	2	64	6	0	5	4	.556	0	19-25	8	2.72	2.92
2016	2 Tms		69	0	0	17	63.0	262	54	27	25	10	1	0	1	26	2	72	5	3	4	6	.400	0	3-6	25	3.80	3.57
2017	3 Tms	AL	67	0	0	23	60.1	264	47	33	32	10	3	3	2	31	1	72	11	0	2	8	.200	0	5-11	9	3.73	4.77
15	Oak		37	0	0	30	38.2	167	25	12	12	3	0	1	2	21	1	38	1	0	1	3	.250	0	17-21	0	2.62	2.79
15	NYM	NL	32	0	0	6	32.1	134	24	13	11	5	1	1	2	10	1	26	5	0	4	1	.800	0	2-4	8	2.82	3.06
16	Ari	NL	40	0	0	10	37.2	155	34	18	18	7	1	0	0	15	0	46	1	3	2	3	.400	0	1-3	13	4.23	4.30
16	NYM	NL	29	0	0	7	25.1	107	20	9	7	3	0	0	1	11	2	26	4	0	2	3	.400	0	2-3	12	3.19	2.49
17	NYY	AL	40	0	0	7	36.1	158	28	21	20	7	3	1	1	19	1	42	5	0	1	5	.167	0	1-6	8	3.88	4.95
17	CWS	AL	11	0	0	7	10.0	44	8	2	2	0	0	1	0	5	0	12	3	0	1	1	.500	0	2-2	0	2.56	1.80
17	Hou	AL	16	0	0	9	14.0	62	11	10	10	3	0	1	1	7	0	18	3	0	0	2	.000	0	2-3	1	4.19	6.43
	Postseason		14	0	0	1	12.2	53	9	6	6	2	1	0	0	5	0	11	1	0	0	1	.000	0	0-0	8	2.77	4.26
	11 ML YEARS		625	8	0	164	685.1	2812	483	253	237	85	22	23	17	287	18	756	35	6	48	43	.527	0	61-108	192	2.77	3.11

Tyler Cloyd

CLOID

Pitches: R Bats: R Pos: RP-1   Ht: 6'3" Wt: 210 Born: 5/16/1987 Age: 31

Year	Team	Lg	HOW MUCH HE PITCHED						WHAT HE GAVE UP												THE RESULTS							
			G	GS	CG	GF	IP	BFP	H	R	ER	HR	SH	SF	HB	TBB	IBB	SO	WP	Bk	W	L	Pct	Sh	Sv-Op	Hld	ERC	ERA
2017	Tacom*	AAA	19	14	0	3	60.1	264	64	41	38	8	2	1	1	17	0	48	1	0	1	1	.500	0	1- -	-	4.12	5.67
2012	Phi	NL	6	6	0	0	33.0	138	33	18	18	8	2	0	2	7	0	30	0	0	2	2	.500	0	0-0	0	4.54	4.91
2013	Phi	NL	13	11	0	1	60.1	282	83	45	44	7	2	1	1	25	2	41	3	0	2	7	.222	0	0-0	0	6.55	6.56
2017	Sea	AL	1	0	0	0	1.0	4	2	0	0	0	0	0	0	0	0	1	0	0	1	0	1.000	0	0-0	0	9.49	0.00
	3 ML YEARS		20	17	0	1	94.1	424	118	63	62	15	4	1	3	32	2	72	3	0	5	9	.357	0	0-0	0	5.88	5.92

Alex Cobb

Pitches: R Bats: R Pos: SP-29   Ht: 6'3" Wt: 205 Born: 10/7/1987 Age: 30

Year	Team	Lg	HOW MUCH HE PITCHED						WHAT HE GAVE UP												THE RESULTS							
			G	GS	CG	GF	IP	BFP	H	R	ER	HR	SH	SF	HB	TBB	IBB	SO	WP	Bk	W	L	Pct	Sh	Sv-Op	Hld	ERC	ERA
2011	TB	AL	9	9	0	0	52.2	224	49	21	20	3	0	1	1	21	1	37	2	0	3	2	.600	0	0-0	0	3.44	3.42
2012	TB	AL	23	23	2	0	136.1	569	130	67	61	11	3	6	9	40	2	106	8	1	11	9	.550	1	0-0	0	3.56	4.03
2013	TB	AL	22	22	1	0	143.1	578	120	46	44	13	1	2	3	45	4	134	5	1	11	3	.786	0	0-0	0	2.92	2.76
2014	TB	AL	27	27	0	0	166.1	681	142	56	53	11	4	4	10	47	1	149	8	0	10	9	.526	0	0-0	0	2.87	2.87
2016	TB	AL	5	5	0	0	22.0	104	32	22	21	5	1	1	0	7	0	16	0	0	1	2	.333	0	0-0	0	7.40	8.59
2017	TB	AL	29	29	0	0	179.1	742	175	78	73	22	2	1	6	44	2	128	8	1	12	10	.545	0	0-0	0	3.64	3.66
	Postseason		2	2	0	0	11.2	51	13	3	2	0	0	1	0	3	0	10	1	0	1	0	1.000	0	0-0	0	3.75	1.54
	6 ML YEARS		115	115	3	0	700.0	2898	648	290	272	65	11	15	29	204	10	570	31	3	48	35	.578	1	0-0	0	3.38	3.50

Chris Coghlan

KAHG-lin

Bats: L Throws: R Pos: 3B-18;PH-10;LF-8;2B-3;DH-1;PR-1   Ht: 6'0" Wt: 195 Born: 6/18/1985 Age: 33

Year	Team	Lg	BATTING																	RUNNING			AVERAGES			
			G	AB	H	2B	3B	HR	(Hm	Rd)	TB	R	RBI	RC	TBB	IBB	SO	HBP	SH	SF	SB	CS	GDP	Avg	OBP	Slg	OPS
2009	Fla	NL	128	504	162	31	6	9	(5	4)	232	84	47	91	53	2	77	4	1	3	8	5	3	.321	.390	.460	.850
2010	Fla	NL	91	358	96	20	3	5	(5	0)	137	60	28	43	33	1	84	4	3	2	10	3	3	.268	.335	.383	.718
2011	Fla	NL	65	269	62	20	1	5	(4	1)	99	33	22	23	22	3	49	4	1	2	7	6	3	.230	.296	.368	.664
2012	Mia	NL	39	93	13	1	0	1	(1	0)	17	10	10	2	9	1	12	0	1	2	0	2	4	.140	.212	.183	.394
2013	Mia	NL	70	195	50	10	3	1	(0	1)	69	10	10	20	17	1	43	1	0	1	2	0	1	.256	.318	.354	.672
2014	ChC	NL	125	385	109	28	5	9	(5	4)	174	50	41	59	39	2	81	3	3	2	7	4	5	.283	.352	.452	.804
2015	ChC	NL	148	440	110	25	6	16	(6	10)	195	64	41	63	58	6	94	3	1	1	11	2	8	.250	.341	.443	.784
2016	2 Tms		99	261	49	12	2	6	(1	5)	83	35	30	30	35	3	73	3	0	1	2	1	4	.188	.290	.318	.608
2017	Tor	AL	36	75	15	2	0	1	(0	1)	20	7	5	7	9	0	22	1	1	1	0	0	2	.200	.299	.267	.566
16	Oak	AL	51	158	23	5	0	5	(0	5)	43	14	14	10	13	1	47	1	0	0	1	1	2	.146	.215	.272	.487
16	ChC	NL	48	103	26	7	2	1	(1	0)	40	21	16	20	22	2	26	2	0	1	1	0	2	.252	.391	.388	.779
	Postseason		15	19	1	0	0	0	(0	0)	1	2	0	0	1	1	7	0	0	0	0	0	0	.053	.100	.053	.153
	9 ML YEARS		801	2580	666	149	26	53	(27	26)	1026	353	234	338	275	19	535	24	13	13	47	23	34	.258	.334	.398	.731

A.J. Cole

Pitches: R Bats: R Pos: SP-8; RP-3   Ht: 6'5" Wt: 215 Born: 1/5/1992 Age: 26

Year	Team	Lg	HOW MUCH HE PITCHED						WHAT HE GAVE UP												THE RESULTS							
			G	GS	CG	GF	IP	BFP	H	R	ER	HR	SH	SF	HB	TBB	IBB	SO	WP	Bk	W	L	Pct	Sh	Sv-Op	Hld	ERC	ERA
2017	Syrcse*	AAA	18	18	0	0	93.1	433	127	65	61	7	3	6	3	36	3	80	3	0	4	5	.444	0	0- -	-	6.06	5.88
2015	Was	NL	3	1	0	1	9.1	44	14	11	6	1	1	1	0	1	1	9	1	0	0	0	-	0	1-1	0	5.38	5.79
2016	Was	NL	8	8	0	0	38.1	168	37	24	22	7	0	3	2	14	1	39	1	0	1	2	.333	0	0-0	0	4.39	5.17
2017	Was	NL	11	8	0	0	52.0	229	51	23	22	8	3	1	3	27	0	44	2	1	3	5	.375	0	0-0	0	5.15	3.81
	3 ML YEARS		22	17	0	1	99.2	441	102	58	50	16	4	5	5	42	2	92	4	1	4	7	.364	0	1-1	0	4.88	4.52

Gerrit Cole

Pitches: R Bats: R Pos: SP-33   Ht: 6'4" Wt: 225 Born: 9/8/1990 Age: 27

Year	Team	Lg	HOW MUCH HE PITCHED						WHAT HE GAVE UP												THE RESULTS							
			G	GS	CG	GF	IP	BFP	H	R	ER	HR	SH	SF	HB	TBB	IBB	SO	WP	Bk	W	L	Pct	Sh	Sv-Op	Hld	ERC	ERA
2013	Pit	NL	19	19	0	0	117.1	469	109	43	42	7	5	2	3	28	0	100	4	0	10	7	.588	0	0-0	0	3.02	3.22
2014	Pit	NL	22	22	0	0	138.0	571	127	58	56	11	10	0	9	40	1	138	9	1	11	5	.688	0	0-0	0	3.37	3.65
2015	Pit	NL	32	32	0	0	208.0	832	183	71	60	11	7	6	0	44	1	202	7	0	19	8	.704	0	0-0	0	2.66	2.60

Year	Team	Lg	G	GS	CG	GF	IP	BFP	H	R	ER	HR	SH	SF	HB	TBB	IBB	SO	WP	Bk	W	L	Pct	Sh	Sv-Op	Hld	ERC	ERA
2016	Pit	NL	21	21	1	0	116.0	506	131	57	50	7	4	6	6	36	3	98	5	1	7	10	.412	0	0-0	0	4.35	3.88
2017	Pit	NL	33	33	0	0	203.0	849	199	98	96	31	5	1	4	55	1	196	7	0	12	12	.500	0	0-0	0	3.89	4.26
	Postseason		3	3	0	0	16.0	61	11	7	7	4	0	0	2	3	0	14	0	0	1	2	.333	0	0-0	0	2.50	3.94
	5 ML YEARS		127	127	1	0	782.1	3227	749	327	304	67	31	15	32	203	6	734	32	2	59	42	.584	0	0-0	0	3.40	3.50

Taylor Cole

Pitches: R **Bats:** R **Pos:** RP-1   **Ht:** 6'1" **Wt:** 200 **Born:** 8/20/1989 **Age:** 28

Year	Team	Lg	G	GS	CG	GF	IP	BFP	H	R	ER	HR	SH	SF	HB	TBB	IBB	SO	WP	Bk	W	L	Pct	Sh	Sv-Op	Hld	ERC	ERA
2013	2 Tms	Low	27	27	0	0	137.0	618	147	77	60	5	6	3	12	61	0	103	17	1	7	12	.368	0	0--	-	4.52	3.94
2014	Dnedin	A+	24	23	0	0	132.0	541	114	55	45	4	0	3	6	39	0	171	17	1	8	9	.471	0	0--	-	2.69	3.07
2015	Nham	AA	28	28	1	0	164.0	690	174	80	74	18	6	3	7	55	0	128	12	1	7	10	.412	1	0--	-	4.57	4.06
2016	Nham	AA	12	11	0	0	61.2	259	70	32	26	6	0	4	0	17	0	54	1	0	3	4	.429	0	0--	-	4.46	3.79
2017	2 Tms	Low	5	4	0	0	7.0	29	6	0	0	0	0	0	1	1	0	9	0	0	0	0	-	0	0--	-	1.69	0.00
2017	Tor	AL	1	0	0	0	1.0	10	6	4	4	0	0	0	1	1	0	1	0	0	0	0	-	0	0-0	0	55.76	36.00

Dusty Coleman

Bats: R **Throws:** R **Pos:** SS-27;PH-1   **Ht:** 6'2" **Wt:** 205 **Born:** 4/20/1987 **Age:** 31

Year	Team	Lg	G	AB	H	2B	3B	HR	(Hm	Rd)	TB	R	RBI	RC	TBB	IBB	SO	HBP	SH	SF	SB	CS	GDP	Avg	OBP	Slg	OPS
2013	Mdlnd	AA	130	484	126	34	10	3	(-	-)	189	65	61	68	57	1	155	6	5	2	17	10	7	.260	.344	.390	.735
2014	Mdlnd	AA	135	489	109	27	2	18	(-	-)	194	79	81	62	47	0	202	9	4	5	16	5	10	.223	.300	.397	.697
2015	NWArk	AA	26	92	32	9	0	2	(-	-)	47	12	18	22	14	0	23	7	0	1	4	4	1	.348	.465	.511	.976
2015	Omha	AAA	73	251	69	11	2	7	(-	-)	105	31	27	35	14	1	70	4	7	0	8	2	3	.275	.323	.418	.742
2016	Omha	AAA	56	188	45	11	2	5	(-	-)	75	26	21	22	12	0	58	3	4	0	6	3	3	.239	.296	.399	.695
2017	ElPaso	AAA	94	327	68	17	6	15	(-	-)	142	43	48	42	32	1	125	2	1	8	11	3	11	.208	.276	.434	.711
2015	KC	AL	4	5	0	0	0	0	(0	0)	0	0	0	0	0	0	3	0	0	0	0	0	0	.000	.000	.000	.000
2017	SD	NL	27	66	15	3	0	4	(3	1)	30	6	9	7	2	0	33	2	0	1	1	0	1	.227	.268	.455	.722
	2 ML YEARS		31	71	15	3	0	4	(3	1)	30	6	9	7	2	0	36	2	0	1	1	0	1	.211	.250	.423	.673

Tyler Collins

Bats: L **Throws:** L **Pos:** CF-26;RF-17;PH-7;LF-4;PR-1   **Ht:** 5'11" **Wt:** 215 **Born:** 6/6/1990 **Age:** 28

Year	Team	Lg	G	AB	H	2B	3B	HR	(Hm	Rd)	TB	R	RBI	RC	TBB	IBB	SO	HBP	SH	SF	SB	CS	GDP	Avg	OBP	Slg	OPS
2017	Toledo*	AAA	74	260	75	14	2	9	(-	-)	120	29	46	46	29	0	72	2	0	5	11	2	2	.288	.358	.462	.820
2014	Det	AL	18	24	6	0	0	1	(0	1)	9	3	4	3	1	0	4	0	0	0	0	0	1	.250	.280	.375	.655
2015	Det	AL	60	192	51	11	9	4	(2	2)	80	18	25	27	13	0	43	1	1	0	2	1	2	.266	.316	.417	.732
2016	Det	AL	56	136	32	2	3	4	(2	2)	52	14	15	19	13	0	38	1	0	1	1	1	1	.235	.305	.382	.687
2017	Det	AL	49	150	29	4	1	5	(4	1)	50	18	14	10	18	0	55	0	0	1	0	4	2	.193	.278	.333	.611
	4 ML YEARS		183	502	118	17	7	14	(8	6)	191	53	58	59	45	0	140	2	1	2	3	6	6	.235	.299	.380	.680

Josh Collmenter

Pitches: R **Bats:** R **Pos:** RP-11   COLE-men-ter   **Ht:** 6'3" **Wt:** 240 **Born:** 2/7/1986 **Age:** 32

Year	Team	Lg	G	GS	CG	GF	IP	BFP	H	R	ER	HR	SH	SF	HB	TBB	IBB	SO	WP	Bk	W	L	Pct	Sh	Sv-Op	Hld	ERC	ERA
2017	Gwnntt*	AAA	5	4	0	1	20.0	84	20	8	8	3	1	0	0	5	0	21	0	0	1	1	.500	0	0--	-	3.79	3.60
2011	Ari	NL	31	24	0	3	154.1	621	137	61	58	17	9	2	5	28	2	100	1	1	10	10	.500	0	0-0	0	2.82	3.38
2012	Ari	NL	28	11	0	7	90.1	375	92	39	37	13	5	0	0	22	2	80	1	0	5	3	.625	0	0-0	0	3.85	3.69
2013	Ari	NL	49	0	0	10	92.0	384	79	34	32	8	8	0	2	33	8	85	3	0	5	5	.500	0	0-1	5	3.01	3.13
2014	Ari	NL	33	28	1	2	179.1	719	163	75	69	18	8	5	4	39	2	115	2	0	11	9	.550	1	1-1	0	3.02	3.46
2015	Ari	NL	44	12	1	19	121.0	499	129	53	51	18	2	6	1	24	2	63	1	0	4	6	.400	1	1-1	1	4.05	3.79
2016	2 Tms	NL	18	3	0	10	41.1	173	36	17	17	7	3	0	3	16	1	33	0	0	3	0	1.000	0	0-0	0	4.11	3.70
2017	Atl	NL	11	0	0	5	17.0	87	29	19	17	7	2	1	0	6	2	18	1	0	0	2	.000	0	0-0	0	10.46	9.00
16	Ari	NL	15	0	0	10	22.1	97	21	12	12	4	1	0	2	11	1	17	0	0	1	0	1.000	0	0-0	0	5.08	4.84
16	Atl	NL	3	3	0	0	19.0	76	15	5	5	3	2	0	1	5	0	16	0	0	2	0	1.000	0	0-0	0	3.03	2.37
	Postseason		1	1	0	0	7.0	26	2	1	1	1	0	0	1	2	0	6	0	0	1	0	1.000	0	0-0	0	1.18	1.29
	7 ML YEARS		214	78	2	56	695.1	2858	665	298	281	88	37	14	15	168	19	494	9	1	38	35	.521	2	2-3	6	3.47	3.64

Alex Colome

Pitches: R **Bats:** R **Pos:** RP-65   COHL-oh-may   **Ht:** 6'1" **Wt:** 220 **Born:** 12/31/1988 **Age:** 29

Year	Team	Lg	G	GS	CG	GF	IP	BFP	H	R	ER	HR	SH	SF	HB	TBB	IBB	SO	WP	Bk	W	L	Pct	Sh	Sv-Op	Hld	ERC	ERA
2013	TB	AL	3	3	0	0	16.0	71	14	8	4	2	0	0	1	9	0	12	1	0	1	1	.500	0	0-0	0	4.41	2.25
2014	TB	AL	5	3	0	1	23.2	97	19	7	7	1	0	1	0	10	0	13	3	0	2	0	1.000	0	0-0	0	2.77	2.66
2015	TB	AL	43	13	0	5	109.2	457	112	50	48	9	2	7	4	31	4	88	8	0	8	5	.615	0	0-5	8	3.78	3.94
2016	TB	AL	57	0	0	48	56.2	226	43	12	12	6	0	0	2	15	1	71	1	0	2	4	.333	0	37-40	1	2.46	1.91
2017	TB	AL	65	0	0	53	66.2	281	57	27	24	4	3	6	3	23	7	58	4	0	2	3	.400	0	47-53	1	2.79	3.24
	5 ML YEARS		173	19	0	107	272.2	1132	245	104	95	22	5	14	10	88	12	242	17	0	15	13	.536	0	84-98	10	3.20	3.14

133

Bartolo Colon

Pitches: R **Bats:** R **Pos:** SP-28   co-LONE   **Ht:** 5'11" **Wt:** 285 **Born:** 5/24/1973 **Age:** 45

			HOW MUCH HE PITCHED					WHAT HE GAVE UP												THE RESULTS						
Year	Team	Lg	G	GS	CG	GF	IP	BFP	H	R	ER	HR	SH	SF	HB	TBB	IBB	SO	WP	Bk	W	L	Pct	Sh	Sv-Op	Hld	ERC	ERA
1997	Cle	AL	19	17	1	0	94.0	427	107	66	59	12	4	1	3	45	1	66	5	0	4	7	.364	0	0-0	0	5.53	5.65
1998	Cle	AL	31	31	6	0	204.0	883	205	91	84	15	10	2	3	79	5	158	4	0	14	9	.609	2	0-0	0	3.87	3.71
1999	Cle	AL	32	32	1	0	205.0	858	185	97	90	24	5	4	7	76	5	161	4	0	18	5	.783	1	0-0	0	3.68	3.95
2000	Cle	AL	30	30	2	0	188.0	807	163	86	81	21	2	3	4	98	4	212	4	0	15	8	.652	1	0-0	0	3.97	3.88
2001	Cle	AL	34	34	1	0	222.1	947	220	106	101	26	8	4	2	90	2	201	4	1	14	12	.538	0	0-0	0	4.24	4.09
2002	2 Tms		33	33	8	0	233.1	966	219	85	76	20	19	6	2	70	5	149	4	0	20	8	.714	3	0-0	0	3.29	2.93
2003	CWS	AL	34	34	9	0	242.0	984	223	107	104	30	5	8	5	67	3	173	8	3	15	13	.536	0	0-0	0	3.47	3.87
2004	LAA	AL	34	34	0	0	208.1	897	215	122	116	38	5	8	3	71	1	158	1	0	18	12	.600	0	0-0	0	4.64	5.01
2005	LAA	AL	33	33	2	0	222.2	906	215	93	86	26	9	4	3	43	0	157	2	1	21	8	.724	0	0-0	0	3.28	3.48
2006	LAA	AL	10	10	1	0	56.1	251	71	39	32	11	4	1	3	11	0	31	1	0	1	5	.167	1	0-0	0	5.61	5.11
2007	LAA	AL	19	18	0	0	99.1	453	132	74	70	15	4	3	5	29	1	76	1	0	6	8	.429	0	0-0	1	6.17	6.34
2008	Bos	AL	7	7	0	0	39.0	173	44	23	17	5	3	2	2	10	0	27	0	0	4	2	.667	0	0-0	0	4.53	3.92
2009	CWS	AL	12	12	0	0	62.1	276	69	42	29	13	4	3	2	21	3	38	1	0	3	6	.333	0	0-0	0	5.22	4.19
2011	NYY	AL	29	26	1	0	164.1	694	172	85	73	21	2	6	3	40	1	135	0	0	8	10	.444	1	0-0	0	3.95	4.00
2012	Oak	AL	24	24	0	0	152.1	636	161	62	58	17	3	4	1	23	3	91	0	0	10	9	.526	0	0-0	0	3.45	3.43
2013	Oak	AL	30	30	3	0	190.1	769	193	60	56	14	3	6	0	29	0	117	1	0	18	6	.750	3	0-0	0	3.07	2.65
2014	NYM	NL	31	31	0	0	202.1	846	218	97	92	22	8	4	5	30	3	151	2	0	15	13	.536	0	0-0	0	3.63	4.09
2015	NYM	NL	33	31	1	1	194.2	815	217	94	90	25	9	7	4	24	5	136	0	0	14	13	.519	1	0-0	0	3.84	4.16
2016	NYM	NL	34	33	0	0	191.2	791	200	81	73	24	7	4	3	32	2	128	0	0	15	8	.652	0	0-0	0	3.63	3.43
2017	2 Tms		28	28	1	0	143.0	648	192	112	103	28	6	3	1	35	0	89	1	1	7	14	.333	0	0-0	0	6.15	6.48
02	Cle	AL	16	16	4	0	116.1	467	104	37	33	11	6	3	2	31	1	75	3	0	10	4	.714	2	0-0	0	3.09	2.55
02	Mon	NL	17	17	4	0	117.0	499	115	48	43	9	13	3	0	39	4	74	1	0	10	4	.714	1	0-0	0	3.48	3.31
17	Atl	NL	13	13	0	0	63.0	299	92	66	57	11	4	2	1	20	0	42	1	0	2	8	.200	0	0-0	0	7.07	8.14
17	Min	NL	15	15	1	0	80.0	349	100	46	46	17	2	1	0	15	0	47	0	1	5	6	.455	0	0-0	0	5.43	5.18
	Postseason		17	10	1	2	67.0	278	66	27	26	6	2	2	2	26	4	52	0	0	3	5	.375	0	0-1	0	4.06	3.49
	20 ML YEARS		537	528	37	1	3315.1	14027	3421	1622	1490	407	120	83	61	923	46	2454	43	6	240	176	.577	13	0-0	1	3.99	4.04

Christian Colon

Bats: R **Throws:** R **Pos:** 2B-10;3B-10;PH-2;PR-2   co-LONE   **Ht:** 5'10" **Wt:** 185 **Born:** 5/14/1989 **Age:** 29

						BATTING																RUNNING			AVERAGES			
Year	Team	Lg	G	AB	H	2B	3B	HR	(Hm	Rd)	TB	R	RBI	RC	TBB	IBB	SO	HBP	SH	SF	SB	CS	GDP	Avg	OBP	Slg	OPS
2017	NewOr*	AAA	49	149	45	8	0	1	(-	-)	56	17	13	23	16	3	26	3	8	1	6	3	1	.302	.379	.376	.755
2014	KC	AL	21	45	15	5	1	0	(0	0)	22	8	6	9	3	0	4	0	1	0	2	0	1	.333	.375	.489	.864
2015	KC	AL	43	107	31	5	0	0	(0	0)	36	8	6	12	11	0	17	0	1	0	3	2	2	.290	.356	.336	.692
2016	KC	AL	54	147	34	6	0	1	(1	0)	43	13	13	13	11	0	31	2	1	0	0	1	4	.231	.294	.293	.586
2017	2 Tms		24	50	8	1	0	0	(0	0)	9	4	0	0	5	1	10	0	2	0	0	0	4	.160	.236	.180	.416
17	KC	AL	7	17	3	0	0	0	(0	0)	3	1	0	0	1	0	3	0	1	0	0	0	2	.176	.222	.176	.399
17	Mia	NL	17	33	5	1	0	0	(0	0)	6	3	0	0	4	1	7	0	1	0	0	0	2	.152	.243	.182	.425
	Postseason		3	2	2	0	0	0	(0	0)	2	2	2	2	0	0	0	0	1	0	1	0	0	1.000	1.000	1.000	2.000
	4 ML YEARS		142	349	88	17	1	1	(1	0)	110	33	25	34	30	1	62	2	5	0	5	3	11	.252	.315	.315	.630

Michael Conforto

Bats: L **Throws:** R **Pos:** LF-52;CF-43;PH-13;RF-11;DH-1   **Ht:** 6'1" **Wt:** 215 **Born:** 3/1/1993 **Age:** 25

						BATTING																RUNNING			AVERAGES			
Year	Team	Lg	G	AB	H	2B	3B	HR	(Hm	Rd)	TB	R	RBI	RC	TBB	IBB	SO	HBP	SH	SF	SB	CS	GDP	Avg	OBP	Slg	OPS
2015	NYM	NL	56	174	47	14	0	9	(4	5)	88	30	26	29	17	0	39	1	0	2	0	1	4	.270	.335	.506	.841
2016	NYM	NL	109	304	67	21	1	12	(7	5)	126	38	42	35	36	2	89	5	0	3	2	1	6	.220	.310	.414	.725
2017	NYM	NL	109	373	104	20	1	27	(16	11)	207	72	68	77	57	5	113	8	0	2	2	0	3	.279	.384	.555	.939
	Postseason		12	30	6	0	0	3	(2	1)	15	3	6	5	1	0	8	1	0	2	0	0	0	.200	.235	.500	.735
	3 ML YEARS		274	851	218	55	2	48	(27	21)	421	140	136	141	110	7	241	14	0	7	4	2	13	.256	.348	.495	.843

Adam Conley

Pitches: L **Bats:** L **Pos:** SP-20; RP-2   **Ht:** 6'3" **Wt:** 200 **Born:** 5/24/1990 **Age:** 28

						HOW MUCH HE PITCHED						WHAT HE GAVE UP											THE RESULTS						
Year	Team	Lg	G	GS	CG	GF	IP	BFP	H	R	ER	HR	SH	SF	HB	TBB	IBB	SO	WP	Bk	W	L	Pct	Sh	Sv-Op	Hld	ERC	ERA
2017	NewOr*	AAA	12	12	0	0	62.1	275	69	41	38	7	4	5	2	25	0	41	10	0	3	3	.500	0	0--	-	4.95	5.49
2015	Mia	NL	15	11	0	1	67.0	281	65	28	28	7	1	4	3	21	1	59	0	0	4	1	.800	0	0-0	0	3.80	3.76
2016	Mia	NL	25	25	0	0	133.1	584	125	59	57	13	7	3	11	62	7	124	9	0	8	6	.571	0	0-0	0	4.21	3.85
2017	Mia	NL	22	20	0	1	102.2	463	114	74	70	19	8	2	8	42	4	72	5	0	8	8	.500	0	0-0	0	5.63	6.14
	3 ML YEARS		62	56	0	2	303.0	1328	304	161	155	39	16	9	22	125	12	255	14	0	20	15	.571	0	0-0	0	4.59	4.60

Willson Contreras

Bats: R **Throws:** R **Pos:** C-108;PH-15;1B-5;LF-4;RF-2;3B-1   **Ht:** 6'1" **Wt:** 210 **Born:** 5/13/1992 **Age:** 26

						BATTING																RUNNING			AVERAGES			
Year	Team	Lg	G	AB	H	2B	3B	HR	(Hm	Rd)	TB	R	RBI	RC	TBB	IBB	SO	HBP	SH	SF	SB	CS	GDP	Avg	OBP	Slg	OPS
2013	Kane	A	86	310	77	11	5	11	(-	-)	131	46	46	44	26	0	66	7	1	1	8	3	11	.248	.320	.423	.742
2014	Dytona	A+	80	281	68	14	2	5	(-	-)	101	40	37	33	28	0	66	5	1	2	5	5	6	.242	.320	.359	.679
2015	Tenn	AA	126	454	151	34	4	8	(-	-)	217	71	75	91	57	0	62	7	0	3	4	4	22	.333	.413	.478	.891
2016	Iowa	AAA	55	204	72	16	3	9	(-	-)	121	40	43	51	28	1	32	6	0	2	4	4	6	.353	.442	.593	1.035
2016	ChC	NL	76	252	71	14	1	12	(8	4)	123	33	35	41	26	0	67	4	0	1	2	2	7	.282	.357	.488	.845
2017	ChC	NL	117	377	104	21	0	21	(10	11)	188	50	74	76	45	2	98	3	1	2	5	4	13	.276	.356	.499	.855
	Postseason		17	39	10	2	0	1	(1	0)	15	4	5	6	4	0	10	0	0	0	0	0	0	.256	.326	.385	.710
	2 ML YEARS		193	629	175	35	1	33	(18	15)	311	83	109	117	71	2	165	7	1	3	7	6	20	.278	.356	.494	.851

Garrett Cooper

Bats: R **Throws:** R **Pos:** 1B-13   **Ht:** 6'6" **Wt:** 230 **Born:** 12/25/1990 **Age:** 27

Year Team	Lg	G	AB	H	2B	3B	HR	(Hm	Rd)	TB	R	RBI	RC	TBB	IBB	SO	HBP	SH	SF	SB	CS	GDP	Avg	OBP	Slg	OPS
2013 2 Tms	Low	48	184	52	10	3	6	(-	-)	86	26	30	29	17	0	51	2	0	0	0	0	9	.283	.350	.467	.817
2014 3 Tms	Low	67	210	55	15	0	4	(-	-)	82	28	27	29	21	0	58	7	0	1	1	0	8	.262	.347	.390	.738
2015 BrvdCt	A+	119	422	124	32	2	8	(-	-)	184	55	54	67	35	0	88	8	1	4	1	1	11	.294	.356	.436	.792
2016 Biloxi	AA	92	301	90	22	1	4	(-	-)	126	27	49	45	20	0	55	5	0	3	3	3	9	.299	.350	.419	.768
2016 ColSpr	AAA	36	127	35	5	0	5	(-	-)	55	17	20	18	10	1	20	1	0	1	0	0	8	.276	.331	.433	.764
2017 ColSpr	AAA	75	279	102	29	0	17	(-	-)	182	64	82	73	33	4	48	2	0	6	0	0	10	.366	.428	.652	1.080
2017 NYY	AL	13	43	14	5	1	0	(0	0)	21	3	6	6	1	0	12	0	0	1	0	0	0	.326	.333	.488	.822

Patrick Corbin

Pitches: L **Bats:** L **Pos:** SP-32; RP-1   **Ht:** 6'3" **Wt:** 210 **Born:** 7/19/1989 **Age:** 28

Year Team	Lg	G	GS	CG	GF	IP	BFP	H	R	ER	HR	SH	SF	HB	TBB	IBB	SO	WP	Bk	W	L	Pct	Sh	Sv-Op	Hld	ERC	ERA
2012 Ari	NL	22	17	0	3	107.0	454	117	56	54	14	2	5	4	25	2	86	1	0	6	8	.429	0	1-1	0	4.31	4.54
2013 Ari	NL	32	32	3	0	208.1	860	189	81	79	19	8	1	9	54	1	178	13	0	14	8	.636	0	0-0	0	3.14	3.41
2015 Ari	NL	16	16	0	0	85.0	357	91	34	34	9	2	1	2	17	0	78	4	0	6	5	.545	0	0-0	0	3.82	3.60
2016 Ari	NL	36	24	0	6	155.2	701	177	**109**	89	24	6	5	5	66	2	131	9	0	5	13	.278	0	1-1	2	5.47	5.15
2017 Ari	NL	33	32	0	0	189.2	826	208	97	85	26	4	5	3	61	8	178	10	0	14	13	.519	0	0-0	0	4.55	4.03
5 ML YEARS		139	121	3	9	745.2	3198	782	377	341	92	22	17	23	223	13	651	37	0	45	47	.489	0	2-2	2	4.21	4.12

Franchy Cordero

Bats: L **Throws:** R **Pos:** CF-25;PH-7;LF-1   **Ht:** 6'3" **Wt:** 175 **Born:** 9/2/1994 **Age:** 23

Year Team	Lg	G	AB	H	2B	3B	HR	(Hm	Rd)	TB	R	RBI	RC	TBB	IBB	SO	HBP	SH	SF	SB	CS	GDP	Avg	OBP	Slg	OPS
2013 Padres	R	35	141	47	4	6	3	(-	-)	72	23	17	29	10	0	33	2	2	2	11	0	0	.333	.381	.511	.891
2014 2 Tms	Low	83	325	83	10	5	9	(-	-)	130	45	44	40	18	2	111	6	2	2	16	8	7	.255	.305	.400	.705
2015 FtWyn	A	126	481	117	13	1	5	(-	-)	147	59	34	44	31	2	121	4	5	3	22	11	5	.243	.293	.306	.598
2016 Lk Els	A+	74	297	85	16	8	5	(-	-)	132	47	35	44	19	1	83	5	0	1	11	8	7	.286	.339	.444	.783
2016 SnAnt	AA	59	245	75	8	8	6	(-	-)	117	31	19	41	17	4	67	2	0	0	12	6	2	.306	.356	.478	.834
2017 ElPaso	AAA	93	390	127	21	18	17	(-	-)	235	68	64	84	23	1	118	4	2	0	15	4	1	.326	.369	.603	.972
2017 SD	NL	30	92	21	3	3	3	(3	0)	39	15	9	9	6	0	44	0	1	0	1	1	0	.228	.276	.424	.699

Allen Cordoba

Bats: R **Throws:** R **Pos:** LF-43;PH-29;SS-28;CF-7;PR-4;3B-3;RF-3;2B-1   **Ht:** 6'1" **Wt:** 175 **Born:** 12/6/1995 **Age:** 22

Year Team	Lg	G	AB	H	2B	3B	HR	(Hm	Rd)	TB	R	RBI	RC	TBB	IBB	SO	HBP	SH	SF	SB	CS	GDP	Avg	OBP	Slg	OPS
2015 Cards	R	53	202	69	6	2	2	(-	-)	85	40	20	37	15	0	20	7	2	3	11	3	4	.342	.401	.421	.822
2016 Jhscty	R+	50	196	71	16	5	0	(-	-)	97	49	18	44	21	0	19	2	0	1	22	4	3	.362	.427	.495	.922
2017 SD	NL	100	202	42	2	2	4	(1	3)	60	17	15	16	18	1	54	4	0	3	2	2	.208	.282	.297	.579

Carlos Correa

Bats: R **Throws:** R **Pos:** SS-108;DH-1   coh-RAY-uh   **Ht:** 6'4" **Wt:** 215 **Born:** 9/22/1994 **Age:** 23

Year Team	Lg	G	AB	H	2B	3B	HR	(Hm	Rd)	TB	R	RBI	RC	TBB	IBB	SO	HBP	SH	SF	SB	CS	GDP	Avg	OBP	Slg	OPS
2015 Hou	AL	99	387	108	22	1	22	(12	10)	198	52	68	68	40	2	78	1	0	4	14	4	10	.279	.345	.512	.857
2016 Hou	AL	153	577	158	36	3	20	(8	12)	260	76	96	93	75	5	150	5	0	3	13	3	12	.274	.361	.451	.811
2017 Hou	AL	109	422	133	25	1	24	(11	13)	232	82	84	86	53	5	92	2	0	4	2	1	12	.315	.391	.550	.941
Postseason		6	24	7	1	0	2	(2	0)	14	2	4	4	0	0	6	1	0	0	0	0	1	.292	.320	.583	.903
3 ML YEARS		361	1386	399	83	5	66	(31	35)	690	210	248	247	168	12	309	8	0	11	29	8	34	.288	.366	.498	.863

Jarred Cosart

Pitches: R **Bats:** R **Pos:** SP-6; RP-1   KOH-zart   **Ht:** 6'3" **Wt:** 206 **Born:** 5/25/1990 **Age:** 28

Year Team	Lg	G	GS	CG	GF	IP	BFP	H	R	ER	HR	SH	SF	HB	TBB	IBB	SO	WP	Bk	W	L	Pct	Sh	Sv-Op	Hld	ERC	ERA
2013 Hou	AL	10	10	0	0	60.0	246	46	15	13	3	0	2	0	35	0	33	3	0	1	1	.500	0	0-0	0	3.31	1.95
2014 2 Tms		30	30	0	0	180.1	766	173	80	74	9	3	8	3	73	1	115	7	0	13	11	.542	0	0-0	0	3.61	3.69
2015 Mia	NL	14	13	0	0	69.2	296	63	35	35	10	2	1	1	33	1	47	7	0	2	5	.286	0	0-0	0	4.24	4.52
2016 2 Tms	NL	13	13	0	0	57.0	268	61	41	38	4	1	1	2	39	2	38	3	0	0	4	.000	0	0-0	0	6.00	6.00
2017 SD	NL	7	6	0	0	24.0	114	26	15	13	0	1	0	2	19	0	15	1	1	0	2	.000	0	0-0	0	5.75	4.88
14 Hou	AL	20	20	0	0	116.1	507	119	61	57	7	2	6	3	51	1	75	7	0	9	7	.563	0	0-0	0	4.18	4.41
14 Mia	NL	10	10	0	0	64.0	259	54	19	17	2	1	2	0	22	0	40	0	0	4	4	.500	0	0-0	0	2.64	2.39
16 Mia	NL	4	4	0	0	19.2	92	19	14	13	0	1	1	0	16	2	11	2	0	0	1	.000	0	0-0	0	4.50	5.95
16 SD	NL	9	9	0	0	37.1	176	42	27	25	4	0	0	2	23	0	27	1	0	0	3	.000	0	0-0	0	5.93	6.03
5 ML YEARS		74	72	0	0	391.0	1690	369	186	173	26	7	12	8	199	4	248	21	1	16	23	.410	0	0-0	0	4.06	3.98

Jharel Cotton

Pitches: R Bats: R Pos: SP-24

juh-REL

Ht: 5'11" Wt: 195 Born: 1/19/1992 Age: 26

Year	Team	Lg	G	GS	CG	GF	IP	BFP	H	R	ER	HR	SH	SF	HB	TBB	IBB	SO	WP	Bk	W	L	Pct	Sh	Sv-Op	Hld	ERC	ERA
2013 2 Tms		Low	13	11	1	1	64.0	254	46	24	24	4	2	0	1	20	1	61	4	0	2	5	.286	1	0- -	-	2.12	3.38
2013 Chatt		AA	8	0	0	3	10.0	48	15	12	9	0	0	1	0	3	0	11	1	0	0	2	.000	0	0- -	-	5.66	8.10
2014 Rcuca		A+	25	20	1	4	126.2	519	113	70	57	18	5	6	1	34	0	138	5	0	6	10	.375	1	0- -	-	3.29	4.05
2015 2 Tms		Low	5	3	0	0	25.2	100	18	6	6	1	0	1	0	8	0	34	2	0	1	0	1.000	0	0- -	-	1.90	2.10
2015 Tulsa		AA	11	8	0	0	62.2	248	49	18	16	4	4	1	0	21	0	71	3	0	5	2	.714	0	0- -	-	2.53	2.30
2015 OkCity		AAA	5	0	0	0	7.1	32	9	4	4	0	0	2	0	2	0	9	3	0	0	0	-	0	0- -	-	4.15	4.91
2016 OkCity		AAA	22	16	1	2	97.1	403	80	59	53	17	4	2	0	32	0	119	10	0	8	5	.615	1	0- -	-	3.26	4.90
2016 Nashv		AAA	6	6	1	0	38.1	147	28	12	12	3	1	0	0	7	1	36	2	0	3	1	.750	1	0- -	-	1.79	2.82
2016 Oak		AL	5	5	0	0	29.1	112	20	10	7	4	0	0	0	4	0	23	1	0	2	0	1.000	0	0-0	0	1.70	2.15
2017 Oak		AL	24	24	0	0	129.0	566	133	91	80	28	4	5	4	53	1	105	9	2	9	10	.474	0	0-0	0	5.26	5.58
2 ML YEARS			29	29	0	0	158.1	678	153	101	87	32	4	5	4	57	1	128	10	2	11	10	.524	0	0-0	0	4.51	4.95

Daniel Coulombe

Pitches: L Bats: L Pos: RP-72

KOO-lohm

Ht: 5'10" Wt: 190 Born: 10/26/1989 Age: 28

Year	Team	Lg	G	GS	CG	GF	IP	BFP	H	R	ER	HR	SH	SF	HB	TBB	IBB	SO	WP	Bk	W	L	Pct	Sh	Sv-Op	Hld	ERC	ERA
2014 LAD		NL	5	0	0	0	4.1	22	5	3	2	1	0	0	0	2	0	4	2	0	0	0	-	0	0-0	0	5.49	4.15
2015 2 Tms			14	0	0	4	16.0	72	17	10	10	0	0	0	0	9	0	11	2	0	0	0	-	0	0-1	0	4.32	5.63
2016 Oak		AL	35	0	0	11	47.2	193	37	24	24	6	2	3	0	17	2	54	3	0	3	1	.750	0	0-1	2	2.84	4.53
2017 Oak		AL	72	0	0	10	51.2	219	46	22	20	4	0	1	4	22	1	39	5	0	2	2	.500	0	0-1	13	3.74	3.48
15 LAD		NL	5	0	0	3	8.1	40	9	7	7	0	0	0	0	6	0	7	1	0	0	0	-	0	0-0	0	4.87	7.56
15 Oak		AL	9	0	0	1	7.2	32	8	3	3	0	0	0	0	3	0	4	1	0	0	0	-	0	0-1	0	3.72	3.52
4 ML YEARS			126	0	0	25	119.2	506	105	59	56	11	2	4	4	50	3	108	12	0	5	3	.625	0	0-3	15	3.52	4.21

Dylan Covey

Pitches: R Bats: R Pos: SP-12; RP-6

Ht: 6'2" Wt: 195 Born: 8/14/1991 Age: 26

Year	Team	Lg	G	GS	CG	GF	IP	BFP	H	R	ER	HR	SH	SF	HB	TBB	IBB	SO	WP	Bk	W	L	Pct	Sh	Sv-Op	Hld	ERC	ERA
2013 2 Tms		Low	14	14	0	0	59.1	259	73	29	25	4	0	0	1	18	0	46	7	0	1	1	.500	0	0- -	-	4.93	3.79
2014 2 Tms		Low	26	25	2	0	140.0	596	148	90	85	5	1	2	10	41	0	92	7	0	7	14	.333	0	0- -	-	3.86	5.46
2015 Stcktn		A+	26	26	0	0	140.1	595	135	65	56	13	2	3	6	43	0	100	7	0	8	9	.471	0	0- -	-	3.60	3.59
2016 Mdlnd		AA	6	6	0	0	29.1	123	21	14	6	2	0	0	1	17	0	26	3	0	2	1	.667	0	0- -	-	3.18	1.84
2017 CWS		AL	18	12	0	4	70.0	309	83	60	60	20	1	1	1	34	1	41	6	1	0	7	.000	0	0-0	0	7.33	7.71

Kaleb Cowart

Bats: B Throws: R Pos: 2B-30;3B-24;PH-5;PR-5

Ht: 6'3" Wt: 225 Born: 6/2/1992 Age: 26

Year	Team	Lg	G	AB	H	2B	3B	HR	(Hm	Rd)	TB	R	RBI	RC	TBB	IBB	SO	HBP	SH	SF	SB	CS	GDP	Avg	OBP	Slg	OPS
2017 Salt Lk*		AAA	90	367	114	25	1	12	(-	-)	177	65	57	70	44	0	73	0	0	2	19	5	4	.311	.383	.482	.865
2015 LAA		AL	34	46	8	2	0	1	(1	0)	13	8	4	3	5	0	19	0	1	0	1	1	1	.174	.255	.283	.538
2016 LAA		AL	31	85	15	4	0	1	(0	1)	22	8	8	3	0	0	23	1	0	1	0	0	1	.176	.184	.259	.443
2017 LAA		AL	50	102	23	5	1	3	(2	1)	39	18	11	11	10	1	28	3	2	0	4	2	4	.225	.313	.382	.695
3 ML YEARS			115	233	46	11	1	5	(3	2)	74	34	23	17	15	1	70	4	3	1	5	3	6	.197	.257	.318	.575

Zack Cozart

Bats: R Throws: R Pos: SS-112;PH-9;DH-1

COE-zart

Ht: 6'0" Wt: 204 Born: 8/12/1985 Age: 32

Year	Team	Lg	G	AB	H	2B	3B	HR	(Hm	Rd)	TB	R	RBI	RC	TBB	IBB	SO	HBP	SH	SF	SB	CS	GDP	Avg	OBP	Slg	OPS
2011 Cin		NL	11	37	12	0	0	2	(2	0)	18	6	3	3	0	0	6	0	1	0	0	0	0	.324	.324	.486	.811
2012 Cin		NL	138	561	138	33	4	15	(6	9)	224	72	35	51	31	0	113	3	2	3	4	0	11	.246	.288	.399	.687
2013 Cin		NL	151	567	144	30	3	12	(5	7)	216	74	63	56	26	2	102	2	13	10	0	0	18	.254	.284	.381	.665
2014 Cin		NL	147	506	112	18	5	4	(1	3)	152	48	38	36	25	3	79	7	5	0	7	0	13	.221	.268	.300	.568
2015 Cin		NL	53	194	50	10	1	9	(4	5)	89	28	28	23	14	1	29	2	1	3	3	3	4	.258	.310	.459	.769
2016 Cin		NL	121	464	117	28	2	16	(7	9)	197	67	50	53	37	3	84	2	1	4	4	1	9	.252	.308	.425	.732
2017 Cin		NL	122	438	130	24	7	24	(12	12)	240	80	63	87	62	0	78	3	0	4	3	0	5	.297	.385	.548	.933
Postseason			6	24	5	0	0	0	(0	0)	5	2	0	1	3	0	5	1	0	0	0	0	0	.208	.321	.208	.530
7 ML YEARS			743	2767	703	143	22	82	(39	43)	1136	375	280	309	195	9	491	19	23	24	21	4	62	.254	.305	.411	.716

Brandon Crawford

Bats: L Throws: R Pos: SS-138;PH-8

Ht: 6'2" Wt: 215 Born: 1/21/1987 Age: 31

Year	Team	Lg	G	AB	H	2B	3B	HR	(Hm	Rd)	TB	R	RBI	RC	TBB	IBB	SO	HBP	SH	SF	SB	CS	GDP	Avg	OBP	Slg	OPS
2011 SF		NL	66	196	40	5	2	3	(0	3)	58	22	21	20	23	1	31	0	1	0	1	3	4	.204	.288	.296	.584
2012 SF		NL	143	435	108	26	3	4	(1	3)	152	44	45	40	33	6	95	3	2	3	1	4	4	.248	.304	.349	.653
2013 SF		NL	149	499	124	24	9	9	(2	7)	181	52	43	42	42	6	96	5	1	3	1	2	10	.248	.311	.363	.674
2014 SF		NL	153	491	121	20	10	10	(4	6)	191	54	69	72	59	10	129	2	2	10	5	3	4	.246	.324	.389	.713
2015 SF		NL	143	507	130	33	4	21	(8	13)	234	65	84	69	39	9	119	11	0	4	6	4	18	.256	.321	.462	.782
2016 SF		NL	155	553	152	28	11	12	(4	8)	238	67	84	82	57	10	115	4	0	9	7	0	13	.275	.342	.430	.772
2017 SF		NL	144	518	131	34	4	14	(6	8)	209	58	77	61	42	3	113	1	0	9	3	5	18	.253	.305	.403	.709
Postseason			38	127	30	6	1	1	(0	1)	41	13	17	14	15	2	32	0	1	2	2	0	2	.236	.313	.323	.635
7 ML YEARS			953	3199	806	170	34	73	(25	48)	1263	362	423	386	295	45	698	26	6	38	24	21	71	.252	.317	.395	.712

J.P. Crawford

Bats: L **Throws:** R **Pos:** 3B-13;SS-6;2B-4;PH-2   **Ht:** 6'2" **Wt:** 180 **Born:** 1/11/1995 **Age:** 23

Year	Team	Lg	G	AB	H	2B	3B	HR	(Hm	Rd)	TB	R	RBI	RC	TBB	IBB	SO	HBP	SH	SF	SB	CS	GDP	Avg	OBP	Slg	OPS
2013	2 Tms	Low	53	195	60	9	3	1	(-	-)	78	34	21	34	32	0	35	0	1	0	14	6	2	.308	.405	.400	.805
2014	2 Tms	Low	123	463	132	23	0	11	(-	-)	188	69	48	74	65	0	74	4	2	4	24	14	5	.285	.375	.406	.781
2015	Clrwtr	A+	21	79	31	1	0	1	(-	-)	35	15	8	18	14	0	9	1	1	0	5	2	0	.392	.489	.443	.932
2015	Rdng	AA	86	351	93	21	7	5	(-	-)	143	53	34	55	49	2	45	1	1	3	7	2	8	.265	.354	.407	.761
2016	Rdng	AA	36	136	36	8	0	3	(-	-)	53	23	13	23	30	0	21	0	0	0	5	3	2	.265	.398	.390	.787
2016	LV	AAA	87	336	82	11	1	4	(-	-)	107	40	30	38	42	0	59	1	4	2	7	4	5	.244	.328	.318	.647
2017	LV	AAA	127	474	115	20	6	15	(-	-)	192	75	63	72	79	1	97	1	1	1	5	4	10	.243	.351	.405	.756
2017	Phi	NL	23	70	15	4	1	0	(0	0)	21	8	6	9	16	0	22	0	0	1	1	0	1	.214	.356	.300	.656

Stefan Crichton

Pitches: R **Bats:** R **Pos:** RP-8   CRY-ton   **Ht:** 6'3" **Wt:** 200 **Born:** 2/29/1992 **Age:** 26

Year	Team	Lg	G	GS	CG	GF	IP	BFP	H	R	ER	HR	SH	SF	HB	TBB	IBB	SO	WP	Bk	W	L	Pct	Sh	Sv-Op	Hld	ERC	ERA
2013	Orioles	R	6	4	0	0	23.0	86	13	5	5	1	0	1	1	3	0	21	1	0	3	1	.750	0	0--	-	1.11	1.96
2014	Abrdn	A-	20	1	0	10	44.1	195	56	26	22	2	2	2	4	7	1	40	5	1	2	5	.286	0	1--	-	4.53	4.47
2015	2 Tms	Low	35	1	0	13	79.1	329	78	40	30	1	4	3	5	13	0	68	2	0	4	4	.500	0	6--	-	2.74	3.40
2016	Bowie	AA	48	4	0	23	72.1	316	73	35	30	4	4	3	4	26	1	61	4	1	2	6	.250	0	1--	-	3.80	3.73
2017	Norfolk	AAA	29	0	0	15	47.2	205	47	16	16	2	1	1	2	11	0	50	4	1	7	2	.778	0	2--	-	3.01	3.02
2017	Bal	AL	8	0	0	1	12.1	62	26	11	11	2	0	1	0	4	0	8	2	1	0	0	-	0	0-0	1	12.21	8.03

Kyle Crick

Pitches: R **Bats:** L **Pos:** RP-30   **Ht:** 6'4" **Wt:** 220 **Born:** 11/30/1992 **Age:** 25

Year	Team	Lg	G	GS	CG	GF	IP	BFP	H	R	ER	HR	SH	SF	HB	TBB	IBB	SO	WP	Bk	W	L	Pct	Sh	Sv-Op	Hld	ERC	ERA
2013	SnJos	A+	14	14	0	0	68.2	281	48	20	12	1	1	1	1	39	0	95	8	0	3	1	.750	0	0--	-	2.66	1.57
2014	Rchmd	AA	23	22	0	0	90.1	398	78	42	38	7	2	0	1	61	0	111	12	0	6	7	.462	0	0--	-	4.31	3.79
2015	Rchmd	AA	36	11	0	5	63.0	302	47	26	23	2	0	3	7	66	1	73	6	0	3	4	.429	0	0--	-	4.99	3.29
2016	Rchmd	AA	23	23	0	0	109.0	499	110	72	61	8	5	4	10	67	0	86	9	0	4	11	.267	0	0--	-	5.18	5.04
2017	Scrmto	AAA	24	0	0	13	29.1	124	24	9	9	1	0	1	1	13	1	39	0	0	1	2	.333	0	6--	-	2.87	2.76
2017	SF	NL	30	0	0	14	32.1	134	22	13	11	2	1	0	1	17	1	28	6	0	0	0	-	0	0-0	1	2.68	3.06

Kyle Crockett

Pitches: L **Bats:** L **Pos:** RP-4   **Ht:** 6'2" **Wt:** 175 **Born:** 12/15/1991 **Age:** 26

Year	Team	Lg	G	GS	CG	GF	IP	BFP	H	R	ER	HR	SH	SF	HB	TBB	IBB	SO	WP	Bk	W	L	Pct	Sh	Sv-Op	Hld	ERC	ERA
2017	Clmbs*	AAA	51	0	0	15	48.0	198	42	23	18	2	1	2	5	11	0	49	1	1	5	5	.500	0	4--	-	2.78	3.38
2014	Cle	AL	43	0	0	7	30.0	122	26	6	6	2	2	0	3	8	2	28	0	1	4	1	.800	0	0-0	5	2.99	1.80
2015	Cle	AL	31	0	0	4	17.2	74	17	9	8	1	0	2	1	7	0	15	0	0	0	0	-	0	0-0	3	3.90	4.08
2016	Cle	AL	29	0	0	4	16.0	70	16	9	9	0	0	1	0	7	2	17	1	1	0	0	-	0	0-0	3	3.26	5.06
2017	Cle	AL	4	0	0	0	1.2	11	4	2	2	0	0	0	1	1	0	2	0	0	0	0	-	0	0-0	0	15.90	10.80
4 ML YEARS			107	0	0	15	65.1	277	63	26	25	3	2	3	5	23	4	62	1	2	4	1	.800	0	0-0	11	3.56	3.44

C.J. Cron

Bats: R **Throws:** R **Pos:** 1B-98;PH-5   CROHN   **Ht:** 6'4" **Wt:** 235 **Born:** 1/5/1990 **Age:** 28

Year	Team	Lg	G	AB	H	2B	3B	HR	(Hm	Rd)	TB	R	RBI	RC	TBB	IBB	SO	HBP	SH	SF	SB	CS	GDP	Avg	OBP	Slg	OPS
2017	Salt Lk*	AAA	22	82	22	6	0	4	(-	-)	40	14	23	14	7	0	15	4	0	3	1	0	2	.268	.344	.488	.832
2014	LAA	AL	79	242	62	12	1	11	(5	6)	109	28	37	35	10	0	61	1	0	0	0	0	10	.256	.289	.450	.739
2015	LAA	AL	113	378	99	17	1	16	(11	5)	166	37	51	46	17	1	82	5	0	3	3	1	9	.262	.300	.439	.739
2016	LAA	AL	116	407	113	25	2	16	(9	7)	190	51	69	66	24	1	75	7	0	5	2	3	9	.278	.325	.467	.792
2017	LAA	AL	100	339	84	14	1	16	(8	8)	148	39	56	51	22	0	96	7	0	3	3	2	5	.248	.305	.437	.741
	Postseason		3	9	1	1	0	0	(0	0)	2	0	0	0	2	0	4	0	0	0	0	0	0	.111	.273	.222	.495
4 ML YEARS			408	1366	358	68	5	59	(31	28)	613	155	213	198	73	2	314	20	0	11	8	6	33	.262	.307	.449	.756

Nelson Cruz

Bats: R **Throws:** R **Pos:** DH-147;RF-5;PH-4   **Ht:** 6'2" **Wt:** 230 **Born:** 7/1/1980 **Age:** 37

Year	Team	Lg	G	AB	H	2B	3B	HR	(Hm	Rd)	TB	R	RBI	RC	TBB	IBB	SO	HBP	SH	SF	SB	CS	GDP	Avg	OBP	Slg	OPS
2005	Mil	NL	8	5	1	1	0	0	(0	0)	2	1	0	1	2	0	0	0	0	0	0	0	0	.200	.429	.400	.829
2006	Tex	AL	41	130	29	3	0	6	(3	3)	50	15	22	18	7	0	32	0	0	1	1	0	1	.223	.261	.385	.645
2007	Tex	AL	96	307	72	14	0	9	(4	5)	118	35	34	32	21	1	87	2	1	1	2	4	5	.235	.287	.384	.671
2008	Tex	AL	31	115	38	9	1	7	(4	3)	70	19	26	30	17	2	28	1	0	0	3	1	1	.330	.421	.609	1.030
2009	Tex	AL	128	462	120	21	1	33	(18	15)	242	75	76	72	49	6	118	2	0	2	20	4	9	.260	.332	.524	.856
2010	Tex	AL	108	399	127	31	3	22	(13	9)	230	60	78	77	38	5	81	1	1	6	17	4	12	.318	.374	.576	.950
2011	Tex	AL	124	475	125	28	1	29	(19	10)	242	64	87	79	33	1	116	2	0	3	9	5	8	.263	.312	.509	.821
2012	Tex	AL	159	585	152	45	0	24	(18	6)	269	86	90	80	48	2	140	4	0	4	8	4	7	.260	.319	.460	.779
2013	Tex	AL	109	413	110	18	0	27	(13	14)	209	49	76	69	35	2	109	4	0	4	5	1	14	.266	.327	.506	.833
2014	Bal	AL	159	613	166	32	2	40	(15	25)	322	87	108	93	55	8	140	5	0	5	4	5	17	.271	.333	.525	.859
2015	Sea	AL	152	590	178	22	1	44	(17	27)	334	90	93	108	59	9	164	5	0	1	3	2	6	.302	.369	.566	.936

Year	Team	Lg	G	AB	H	2B	3B	HR	(Hm	Rd)	TB	R	RBI	RC	TBB	IBB	SO	HBP	SH	SF	SB	CS	GDP	Avg	OBP	Slg	OPS
2016	Sea	AL	155	589	169	27	1	43	(17	26)	327	96	105	101	62	5	159	9	0	7	2	0	15	.287	.360	.555	.915
2017	Sea	AL	155	556	160	28	0	39	(19	20)	305	94	119	112	70	7	140	12	0	7	1	1	15	.288	.375	.549	.924
	Postseason		41	154	45	10	0	16	(10	6)	103	31	34	35	12	2	36	1	0	0	1	1	4	.292	.347	.669	1.016
	13 ML YEARS		1425	5239	1447	280	12	323	(160	163)	2720	768	914	872	496	48	1314	48	2	41	75	31	110	.276	.342	.519	.861

Johnny Cueto

Pitches: R **Bats:** R **Pos:** SP-25   KWAY-toe   **Ht:** 5'11" **Wt:** 220 **Born:** 2/15/1986 **Age:** 32

Year	Team	Lg	G	GS	CG	GF	IP	BFP	H	R	ER	HR	SH	SF	HB	TBB	IBB	SO	WP	Bk	W	L	Pct	Sh	Sv-Op	Hld	ERC	ERA
2008	Cin	NL	31	31	0	0	174.0	769	178	101	93	29	9	5	14	68	1	158	6	1	9	14	.391	0	0-0	0	4.95	4.81
2009	Cin	NL	30	30	0	0	171.1	740	172	90	84	24	5	3	14	61	0	132	4	0	11	11	.500	0	0-0	0	4.57	4.41
2010	Cin	NL	31	31	1	0	185.2	780	181	79	75	19	9	3	9	56	5	138	5	2	12	7	.632	1	0-0	0	3.75	3.64
2011	Cin	NL	24	24	3	0	156.0	631	123	51	40	8	10	4	10	47	0	104	5	1	9	5	.643	1	0-0	0	2.55	2.31
2012	Cin	NL	33	33	2	0	217.0	888	205	73	67	15	6	6	12	49	5	170	1	3	19	9	.679	0	0-0	0	3.13	2.78
2013	Cin	NL	11	11	0	0	60.2	242	46	20	19	7	2	1	1	18	1	51	1	0	5	2	.714	0	0-0	0	2.57	2.82
2014	Cin	NL	34	34	4	0	243.2	961	169	69	61	22	7	1	15	65	2	242	1	1	20	9	.690	2	0-0	0	2.18	2.25
2015	2 Tms		32	32	2	0	212.0	866	194	87	81	21	5	4	8	46	1	176	0	4	11	13	.458	2	0-0	0	3.06	3.44
2016	SF	NL	32	32	5	0	219.2	881	195	71	68	15	7	3	8	45	0	198	3	1	18	5	.783	2	0-0	0	2.71	2.79
2017	SF	NL	25	25	0	0	147.1	648	160	77	74	22	7	3	8	53	2	136	4	1	8	8	.500	0	0-0	0	4.97	4.52
15	Cin	NL	19	19	1	0	130.2	516	93	42	38	11	4	3	6	29	1	120	0	4	7	6	.538	1	0-0	0	2.00	2.62
15	KC	AL	13	13	1	0	81.1	350	101	45	43	10	1	1	2	17	0	56	0	0	4	7	.364	1	0-0	0	5.05	4.76
	Postseason		8	8	2	0	41.2	170	33	22	21	7	1	1	1	12	0	32	0	0	2	4	.333	0	0-0	0	3.02	4.54
	10 ML YEARS		283	283	17	0	1787.1	7406	1623	718	662	182	67	33	99	508	18	1505	30	14	122	83	.595	8	0-0	0	3.36	3.33

William Cuevas

Pitches: R **Bats:** B **Pos:** RP-1   KWAY-vahs   **Ht:** 6'2" **Wt:** 215 **Born:** 10/14/1990 **Age:** 27

Year	Team	Lg	G	GS	CG	GF	IP	BFP	H	R	ER	HR	SH	SF	HB	TBB	IBB	SO	WP	Bk	W	L	Pct	Sh	Sv-Op	Hld	ERC	ERA
2013	Salem	A+	26	26	1	0	135.1	573	139	82	76	13	5	5	4	40	0	109	12	1	8	9	.471	0	0- -	-	3.94	5.05
2014	Salem	A+	24	10	0	8	95.2	415	92	57	50	7	1	9	9	32	0	80	9	1	2	6	.250	0	1- -	-	3.75	4.70
2015	Portlnd	AA	19	19	0	0	95.1	410	84	43	36	4	1	4	3	41	0	91	9	0	8	5	.615	0	0- -	-	3.22	3.40
2015	Pwtckt	AAA	7	7	0	0	41.0	165	29	12	12	3	0	1	1	14	0	37	1	0	3	2	.600	0	0- -	-	2.26	2.63
2016	Pwtckt	AAA	25	18	1	2	131.0	567	134	71	61	18	6	4	5	45	0	85	4	0	6	8	.429	0	0- -	-	4.38	4.19
2017	Toledo	AAA	9	9	0	0	44.1	197	50	26	20	5	0	0	2	12	0	34	1	0	2	4	.333	0	0- -	-	4.45	4.06
2017	NewOr	AAA	15	11	0	1	59.2	254	48	36	36	6	3	4	2	31	1	47	0	0	2	7	.222	0	0- -	-	3.59	5.43
2016	Bos	AL	3	0	0	2	5.0	24	5	2	2	0	1	0	0	6	0	3	0	0	0	1	.000	0	0-0	0	6.82	3.60
2017	Det	AL	1	0	0	0	0.1	5	3	4	4	0	0	0	1	0	0	1	0	0	0	0	-	0	0-0	0	83.91	108.0
	2 ML YEARS		4	0	0	2	5.1	29	8	6	6	0	1	0	1	6	0	4	0	0	0	1	.000	0	0-0	0	10.66	10.13

Charlie Culberson

Bats: R **Throws:** R **Pos:** SS-11;2B-2;PH-2;3B-1   **Ht:** 6'0" **Wt:** 200 **Born:** 4/10/1989 **Age:** 29

Year	Team	Lg	G	AB	H	2B	3B	HR	(Hm	Rd)	TB	R	RBI	RC	TBB	IBB	SO	HBP	SH	SF	SB	CS	GDP	Avg	OBP	Slg	OPS
2017	OkCity*	AAA	108	384	96	13	4	4	(-	-)	129	37	32	40	26	2	68	1	2	1	7	3	11	.250	.299	.336	.634
2012	SF	NL	6	22	3	0	0	0	(0	0)	3	0	1	0	0	0	7	0	1	0	0	0	0	.136	.136	.136	.273
2013	Col	NL	47	99	29	5	1	2	(0	2)	40	12	12	13	4	1	23	0	0	1	5	1	5	.293	.317	.404	.721
2014	Col	NL	95	210	41	7	2	3	(2	1)	61	17	24	14	12	2	62	5	4	2	2	2	6	.195	.253	.290	.544
2016	LAD	NL	34	67	20	3	0	1	(1	0)	26	6	7	9	1	0	13	0	0	0	1	0	2	.299	.309	.388	.697
2017	LAD	NL	15	13	2	1	0	0	(0	0)	3	0	1	0	2	0	4	0	0	0	0	0	0	.154	.267	.231	.497
	Postseason		4	7	0	0	0	0	(0	0)	0	0	0	0	0	0	2	0	0	0	0	0	0	.000	.000	.000	.000
	5 ML YEARS		197	411	95	16	2	6	(3	3)	133	35	45	36	19	3	109	5	5	3	8	3	15	.231	.272	.324	.595

Zac Curtis

Pitches: L **Bats:** L **Pos:** RP-6   **Ht:** 5'9" **Wt:** 190 **Born:** 7/4/1992 **Age:** 25

Year	Team	Lg	G	GS	CG	GF	IP	BFP	H	R	ER	HR	SH	SF	HB	TBB	IBB	SO	WP	Bk	W	L	Pct	Sh	Sv-Op	Hld	ERC	ERA
2014	Hlsbro	A-	24	0	0	22	27.0	109	18	5	3	0	1	0	0	12	0	42	1	0	2	1	.667	0	14- -	-	1.90	1.00
2015	Kane	A	53	0	0	45	54.0	206	33	9	8	2	4	1	1	12	0	75	5	0	4	4	.500	0	33- -	-	1.37	1.33
2016	Visalia	A+	8	0	0	3	10.1	49	12	8	6	0	0	0	1	5	0	22	3	0	1	0	1.000	0	2- -	-	4.80	5.23
2016	Mobile	AA	19	0	0	11	19.2	82	17	7	7	3	1	0	0	6	0	30	0	0	1	0	1.000	0	4- -	-	3.25	3.20
2017	Ark	AA	41	0	0	37	51.1	220	43	21	20	3	1	4	6	19	0	60	6	0	1	2	.333	0	13- -	-	3.20	3.51
2016	Ari	NL	21	0	0	2	13.1	67	13	10	10	2	0	0	3	13	1	10	0	0	0	1	.000	0	0-1	1	7.56	6.75
2017	2 Tms		6	0	0	3	8.1	36	6	4	1	1	1	0	2	3	0	6	2	0	0	0	-	0	0-0	0	3.38	1.08
17	Sea	AL	3	0	0	2	4.2	21	3	3	1	0	0	0	2	1	0	2	1	0	0	0	-	0	0-0	0	3.56	0.00
17	Phi	NL	3	0	0	1	3.2	15	3	1	1	0	1	0	0	2	0	4	0	0	0	0	-	0	0-0	0	3.10	2.45
	2 ML YEARS		27	0	0	5	21.2	103	19	14	11	2	1	0	5	16	1	16	2	0	0	1	.000	0	0-1	1	5.85	4.57

John Curtiss

Pitches: R **Bats:** R **Pos:** RP-9   **Ht:** 6'4" **Wt:** 200 **Born:** 4/5/1993 **Age:** 25

Year	Team	Lg	G	GS	CG	GF	IP	BFP	H	R	ER	HR	SH	SF	HB	TBB	IBB	SO	WP	Bk	W	L	Pct	Sh	Sv-Op	Hld	ERC	ERA
2014	Elizab	R+	9	6	0	1	31.1	129	33	8	8	1	1	0	0	7	0	41	3	0	2	1	.667	0	0- -	-	3.29	2.30
2015	2 Tms	Low	21	7	0	9	54.0	242	69	35	32	10	0	2	4	14	0	51	4	0	4	3	.571	0	2- -	-	6.13	5.33

138

Year Team	Lg	G	GS	CG	GF	IP	BFP	H	R	ER	HR	SH	SF	HB	TBB	IBB	SO	WP	Bk	W	L	Pct	Sh	Sv-Op	Hld	ERC	ERA
2016 2 Tms	Low	44	0	0	20	61.0	251	44	20	18	0	2	4	3	25	1	85	7	0	0	2	.000	0	5--	-	2.16	2.66
2017 Chatt	AA	21	0	0	19	25.0	99	12	3	2	0	1	0	0	12	0	35	3	0	2	0	1.000	0	13--	-	1.32	0.72
2017 Roch	AAA	18	0	0	13	24.1	95	11	5	5	0	0	1	0	10	0	33	3	0	0	0	-	0	6--	-	1.10	1.85
2017 Min	AL	9	0	0	4	8.2	38	9	8	8	2	0	0	1	2	0	10	2	0	0	0	-	0	0-0	0	4.89	8.31

Cheslor Cuthbert

Bats: R **Throws:** R **Pos:** 3B-44;1B-6;DH-5;2B-3;PH-3;PR-1 CHESS-lohr **Ht:** 6'1" **Wt:** 190 **Born:** 11/16/1992 **Age:** 25

Year Team	Lg	G	AB	H	2B	3B	HR	(Hm	Rd)	TB	R	RBI	RC	TBB	IBB	SO	HBP	SH	SF	SB	CS	GDP	Avg	OBP	Slg	OPS
2017 Omha*	AAA	15	59	16	3	1	4	(-	-)	33	10	9	11	7	0	11	1	0	1	0	0	2	.271	.353	.559	.912
2015 KC	AL	19	46	10	2	1	1	(1	0)	17	6	8	6	4	0	9	0	0	0	0	0	0	.217	.280	.370	.650
2016 KC	AL	128	475	130	28	1	12	(4	8)	196	49	46	57	32	0	96	0	1	2	2	0	14	.274	.318	.413	.731
2017 KC	AL	58	143	33	7	0	2	(1	1)	46	10	18	11	9	0	39	0	0	1	0	0	2	.231	.275	.322	.596
3 ML YEARS		205	664	173	37	2	15	(6	9)	259	65	72	74	45	0	144	0	1	3	2	0	16	.261	.306	.390	.696

Tyler Danish

Pitches: R **Bats:** R **Pos:** SP-1 **Ht:** 6'0" **Wt:** 200 **Born:** 9/12/1994 **Age:** 23

Year Team	Lg	G	GS	CG	GF	IP	BFP	H	R	ER	HR	SH	SF	HB	TBB	IBB	SO	WP	Bk	W	L	Pct	Sh	Sv-Op	Hld	ERC	ERA
2013 2 Tms	Low	15	1	0	0	30.0	111	17	6	4	1	0	1	0	5	0	28	0	0	1	0	1.000	0	0--	-	1.08	1.20
2014 2 Tms	Low	25	25	0	0	129.2	524	115	43	30	7	1	1	4	33	0	103	3	1	8	3	.727	0	0--	-	2.79	2.08
2015 Brham	AA	26	26	2	0	142.0	635	175	82	71	13	2	5	5	60	0	90	3	0	8	12	.400	0	0--	-	5.76	4.50
2016 Brham	AA	12	12	1	0	75.1	308	71	38	37	3	2	1	0	16	0	47	2	0	3	7	.300	1	0--	-	2.67	4.42
2016 Charllt	AAA	7	5	0	0	29.1	134	39	21	19	0	0	1	1	10	0	21	2	0	1	3	.250	0	0--	-	5.13	5.83
2017 Charllt	AAA	26	25	1	0	138.1	634	175	107	84	18	2	6	5	47	0	71	7	0	4	14	.222	0	0--	-	5.70	5.47
2016 CWS	AL	3	0	0	2	1.2	12	6	2	2	0	0	0	0	3	1	0	0	0	0	0	-	0	0-0	0	31.12	10.80
2017 CWS	AL	1	1	0	0	5.0	23	3	0	0	0	0	0	0	6	0	6	0	0	1	0	1.000	0	0-0	0	4.17	0.00
2 ML YEARS		4	1	0	2	6.2	35	9	2	2	0	0	0	0	9	1	6	0	0	1	0	1.000	0	0-0	0	9.53	2.70

Chase d'Arnaud

dar-NO

Bats: R **Throws:** R **Pos:** PH-13;SS-10;PR-7;2B-4;LF-4;3B-3;1B-1;RF-1 **Ht:** 6'2" **Wt:** 205 **Born:** 1/21/1987 **Age:** 31

Year Team	Lg	G	AB	H	2B	3B	HR	(Hm	Rd)	TB	R	RBI	RC	TBB	IBB	SO	HBP	SH	SF	SB	CS	GDP	Avg	OBP	Slg	OPS
2017 ElPaso*	AAA	46	173	51	8	1	4	(-	-)	73	39	19	29	17	0	33	2	1	2	12	1	2	.295	.361	.422	.783
2011 Pit	NL	48	143	31	6	2	0	(0	0)	41	17	6	8	4	0	36	1	2	1	12	2	3	.217	.242	.287	.528
2012 Pit	NL	8	6	0	0	0	0	(0	0)	0	2	1	0	0	0	2	0	0	0	1	0	0	.000	.000	.000	.000
2014 Pit	NL	8	0	0	0	0	0	(0	0)	0	2	0	0	0	0	0	0	0	0	0	2	0	-	-	-	-
2015 Phi	NL	11	17	3	0	1	0	(0	0)	5	2	0	1	1	0	7	0	0	0	0	1	0	.176	.222	.294	.516
2016 Atl	NL	84	233	57	14	2	1	(1	0)	78	24	21	25	23	1	50	3	0	3	9	3	5	.245	.317	.335	.652
2017 3 Tms		35	58	11	2	0	1	(0	1)	16	12	3	3	4	1	20	0	0	0	5	1	0	.190	.242	.276	.518
17 Atl	NL	11	8	3	0	0	0	(0	0)	3	5	0	1	2	0	3	0	0	0	0	0	0	.375	.500	.375	.875
17 Bos	AL	2	1	1	0	0	0	(0	0)	1	2	0	1	0	0	0	0	0	0	0	0	0	1.00	1.000	1.000	2.000
17 SD	NL	22	49	7	2	0	1	(0	1)	12	5	3	1	2	1	17	0	0	0	5	1	0	.143	.176	.245	.421
6 ML YEARS		194	457	102	22	5	2	(1	1)	140	59	31	37	32	2	115	4	2	4	27	9	8	.223	.278	.306	.584

Travis d'Arnaud

dar-NO

Bats: R **Throws:** R **Pos:** C-93;PH-18;2B-1;3B-1;DH-1;PR-1 **Ht:** 6'2" **Wt:** 210 **Born:** 2/10/1989 **Age:** 29

Year Team	Lg	G	AB	H	2B	3B	HR	(Hm	Rd)	TB	R	RBI	RC	TBB	IBB	SO	HBP	SH	SF	SB	CS	GDP	Avg	OBP	Slg	OPS
2013 NYM	NL	31	99	20	3	0	1	(1	0)	26	4	5	6	12	0	21	0	0	1	0	0	3	.202	.286	.263	.548
2014 NYM	NL	108	385	93	22	3	13	(5	8)	160	48	41	39	32	5	64	2	1	1	1	0	15	.242	.302	.416	.718
2015 NYM	NL	67	239	64	14	1	12	(6	6)	116	31	41	36	23	0	49	4	0	2	0	0	7	.268	.340	.485	.825
2016 NYM	NL	75	251	62	7	0	4	(4	0)	81	27	15	17	19	1	50	3	2	1	0	0	7	.247	.307	.323	.629
2017 NYM	NL	112	348	85	19	1	16	(5	11)	154	39	57	41	23	3	59	2	0	3	0	0	12	.244	.293	.443	.735
Postseason		14	55	10	1	0	3	(2	1)	20	5	7	3	0	0	17	1	0	1	0	0	2	.182	.193	.364	.557
5 ML YEARS		393	1322	324	65	5	46	(21	25)	537	149	159	139	109	9	243	11	3	8	1	0	44	.245	.306	.406	.712

Yu Darvish

YOO DARR-vish

Pitches: R **Bats:** R **Pos:** SP-31 **Ht:** 6'5" **Wt:** 220 **Born:** 8/16/1986 **Age:** 31

Year Team	Lg	G	GS	CG	GF	IP	BFP	H	R	ER	HR	SH	SF	HB	TBB	IBB	SO	WP	Bk	W	L	Pct	Sh	Sv-Op	Hld	ERC	ERA
2012 Tex	AL	29	29	0	0	191.1	816	156	89	83	14	2	7	10	89	1	221	8	0	16	9	.640	0	0-0	0	3.31	3.90
2013 Tex	AL	32	32	0	0	209.2	841	145	68	66	26	0	5	8	80	1	277	7	1	13	9	.591	0	0-0	0	2.70	2.83
2014 Tex	AL	22	22	2	0	144.1	605	133	54	49	13	1	2	2	49	1	182	14	1	10	7	.588	1	0-0	0	3.39	3.06
2016 Tex	AL	17	17	0	0	100.1	416	81	43	38	12	0	4	3	31	0	132	6	0	7	5	.583	0	0-0	0	2.87	3.41
2017 2 Tms		31	31	0	0	186.2	766	159	83	80	27	2	3	6	58	1	209	12	1	10	12	.455	0	0-0	0	3.35	3.86
17 Tex	AL	22	22	0	0	137.0	564	115	63	61	20	1	3	5	45	0	148	9	1	6	9	.400	0	0-0	0	3.39	4.01
17 LAD	NL	9	9	0	0	49.2	202	44	20	19	7	1	0	1	13	1	61	3	0	4	3	.571	0	0-0	0	3.27	3.44
Postseason		2	2	0	0	11.2	49	10	8	7	4	1	1	2	1	0	11	0	0	0	2	.000	0	0-0	0	4.07	5.40
5 ML YEARS		131	131	2	0	832.1	3444	674	337	316	92	5	21	29	307	5	1021	47	3	56	42	.571	1	0-0	0	3.13	3.42

Matt Davidson

Bats: R Throws: R Pos: DH-60;3B-34;1B-19;PH-10 **Ht:** 6'3" **Wt:** 230 **Born:** 3/26/1991 **Age:** 27

								BATTING														RUNNING			AVERAGES			
Year	Team	Lg	G	AB	H	2B	3B	HR	(Hm	Rd)	TB	R	RBI	RC	TBB	IBB	SO	HBP	SH	SF	SB	CS	GDP	Avg	OBP	Slg	OPS
2013	Ari	NL	31	76	18	6	0	3	(1	2)	33	8	12	12	10	1	24	1	0	0	0	1	1	.237	.333	.434	.768
2016	CWS	AL	1	2	1	0	0	0	(0	0)	1	1	1	0	0	0	1	0	0	0	0	0	0	.500	.500	.500	1.000
2017	CWS	AL	118	414	91	16	1	26	(15	11)	187	43	68	48	19	0	165	5	0	5	0	1	12	.220	.260	.452	.711
	3 ML YEARS		150	492	110	22	1	29	(16	13)	221	52	81	60	29	1	190	6	0	5	0	2	13	.224	.273	.449	.722

Zach Davies

Pitches: R Bats: R Pos: SP-33 **Ht:** 6'0" **Wt:** 155 **Born:** 2/7/1993 **Age:** 25

			HOW MUCH HE PITCHED						WHAT HE GAVE UP											THE RESULTS						
Year	Team	Lg	G	GS	CG	GF	IP	BFP	H	R	ER	HR	SH	SF	HB	TBB	IBB	SO	WP	Bk	W	L	Pct	Sh	Sv-Op	Hld	ERC	ERA
2015	Mil	NL	6	6	0	0	34.0	139	26	14	14	2	1	0	0	15	0	24	0	0	3	2	.600	0	0-0	0	2.74	3.71
2016	Mil	NL	28	28	0	0	163.1	682	166	79	72	20	3	4	6	38	0	135	3	0	11	7	.611	0	0-0	0	3.83	3.97
2017	Mil	NL	33	33	0	0	191.1	817	204	90	83	20	7	5	9	55	3	124	2	0	17	9	.654	0	0-0	0	4.24	3.90
	3 ML YEARS		67	67	0	0	388.2	1638	396	183	169	42	11	9	15	108	3	283	5	0	31	18	.633	0	0-0	0	3.93	3.91

Chris Davis

Bats: L Throws: R Pos: 1B-125;3B-2;DH-2 **Ht:** 6'3" **Wt:** 230 **Born:** 3/17/1986 **Age:** 32

								BATTING														RUNNING			AVERAGES			
Year	Team	Lg	G	AB	H	2B	3B	HR	(Hm	Rd)	TB	R	RBI	RC	TBB	IBB	SO	HBP	SH	SF	SB	CS	GDP	Avg	OBP	Slg	OPS
2008	Tex	AL	80	295	84	23	2	17	(8	9)	162	51	55	44	20	1	88	1	0	1	1	2	5	.285	.331	.549	.880
2009	Tex	AL	113	391	93	15	1	21	(11	10)	173	48	59	50	24	2	150	2	0	2	0	0	6	.238	.284	.442	.726
2010	Tex	AL	45	120	23	9	0	1	(0	1)	35	7	4	5	15	3	40	0	0	1	3	0	3	.192	.279	.292	.571
2011	2 Tms	AL	59	199	53	12	0	5	(2	3)	80	25	19	23	11	1	63	0	0	0	1	0	4	.266	.305	.402	.707
2012	Bal	AL	139	515	139	20	0	33	(22	11)	258	75	85	85	37	6	169	7	0	3	2	3	8	.270	.326	.501	.827
2013	Bal	AL	160	584	167	42	1	53	(28	25)	370	103	138	134	72	12	199	10	0	7	4	1	4	.286	.370	.634	1.004
2014	Bal	AL	127	450	88	16	0	26	(13	13)	182	65	72	58	60	9	173	9	1	5	2	1	2	.196	.300	.404	.704
2015	Bal	AL	160	573	150	31	0	47	(29	18)	322	100	117	117	84	6	208	8	0	5	2	3	6	.262	.361	.562	.923
2016	Bal	AL	157	566	125	21	0	38	(17	21)	260	99	84	82	88	3	219	6	0	3	1	0	6	.221	.332	.459	.792
2017	Bal	AL	128	456	98	15	1	26	(15	11)	193	65	61	55	61	4	195	3	0	4	1	1	7	.215	.309	.423	.732
11	Tex	AL	28	76	19	3	0	3	(1	2)	31	9	6	7	5	0	24	0	0	0	0	0	2	.250	.296	.408	.704
11	Bal	AL	31	123	34	9	0	2	(1	1)	49	16	13	16	6	1	39	0	0	0	1	0	2	.276	.310	.398	.708
	Postseason		7	27	5	0	0	0	(0	0)	5	1	2	1	2	0	11	1	0	0	0	0	0	.185	.267	.185	.452
	10 ML YEARS		1168	4149	1020	204	5	267	(145	122)	2035	638	694	653	472	47	1504	48	1	31	17	11	51	.246	.328	.490	.818

J.D. Davis

Bats: R Throws: R Pos: 3B-22;PH-5;1B-2 **Ht:** 6'3" **Wt:** 225 **Born:** 4/27/1993 **Age:** 25

								BATTING														RUNNING			AVERAGES			
Year	Team	Lg	G	AB	H	2B	3B	HR	(Hm	Rd)	TB	R	RBI	RC	TBB	IBB	SO	HBP	SH	SF	SB	CS	GDP	Avg	OBP	Slg	OPS
2014	2 Tms	Low	73	266	78	16	1	13	(-	-)	135	38	52	51	28	0	66	6	0	2	5	0	6	.293	.371	.508	.878
2015	Lancst	A+	120	485	140	28	3	26	(-	-)	252	93	101	94	54	0	157	10	0	3	5	2	12	.289	.370	.520	.889
2016	CpChr	AA	126	485	130	34	1	23	(-	-)	235	61	81	79	45	0	143	5	0	4	1	3	8	.268	.334	.485	.818
2017	CpChr	AA	87	351	98	18	0	21	(-	-)	179	49	60	61	31	1	90	3	0	3	5	2	8	.279	.340	.510	.850
2017	Fresno	AAA	16	61	18	5	0	5	(-	-)	38	10	18	14	9	1	18	0	0	0	0	0	0	.295	.370	.623	.993
2017	Hou	AL	25	62	14	4	0	4	(2	2)	30	8	7	4	4	0	20	1	0	1	1	1	3	.226	.279	.484	.763

Khris Davis

Bats: R Throws: R Pos: LF-116;DH-37;PH-1 **Ht:** 5'10" **Wt:** 195 **Born:** 12/21/1987 **Age:** 30

								BATTING														RUNNING			AVERAGES			
Year	Team	Lg	G	AB	H	2B	3B	HR	(Hm	Rd)	TB	R	RBI	RC	TBB	IBB	SO	HBP	SH	SF	SB	CS	GDP	Avg	OBP	Slg	OPS
2013	Mil	NL	56	136	38	10	0	11	(5	6)	81	27	27	25	11	0	34	5	0	1	3	0	4	.279	.353	.596	.949
2014	Mil	NL	144	501	122	37	2	22	(12	10)	229	70	69	58	32	0	122	10	0	6	4	1	13	.244	.299	.457	.756
2015	Mil	NL	121	392	97	16	2	27	(16	11)	198	54	66	57	44	1	122	1	0	3	6	2	9	.247	.323	.505	.828
2016	Oak	AL	150	555	137	24	2	42	(19	23)	291	85	102	77	42	0	166	8	0	5	1	2	19	.247	.307	.524	.831
2017	Oak	AL	153	566	140	28	1	43	(26	17)	299	91	110	98	73	1	195	6	0	7	4	0	20	.247	.336	.528	.864
	5 ML YEARS		624	2150	534	115	7	145	(78	67)	1098	327	374	315	202	2	639	30	0	22	18	5	65	.248	.319	.511	.829

Rajai Davis

Bats: R Throws: R Pos: CF-83;LF-25;PH-16;RF-7;PR-5;DH-2 RAH-jay **Ht:** 5'10" **Wt:** 195 **Born:** 10/19/1980 **Age:** 37

								BATTING														RUNNING			AVERAGES			
Year	Team	Lg	G	AB	H	2B	3B	HR	(Hm	Rd)	TB	R	RBI	RC	TBB	IBB	SO	HBP	SH	SF	SB	CS	GDP	Avg	OBP	Slg	OPS
2006	Pit	NL	20	14	2	1	0	0	(0	0)	3	1	0	0	2	0	3	0	1	0	1	3	0	.143	.250	.214	.464
2007	2 Tms	NL	75	190	53	11	2	1	(0	1)	71	32	9	26	21	1	28	4	3	1	22	6	1	.279	.361	.374	.735
2008	2 Tms		113	214	52	5	4	3	(0	3)	74	30	19	24	8	0	40	1	2	1	29	6	1	.243	.272	.346	.618
2009	Oak	AL	125	390	119	27	5	3	(1	2)	165	65	48	63	29	0	70	7	2	4	41	12	12	.305	.360	.423	.784
2010	Oak	AL	143	525	149	28	3	5	(5	0)	198	66	52	62	26	0	78	4	1	5	50	11	10	.284	.320	.377	.697
2011	Tor	AL	95	320	76	21	6	1	(1	0)	112	44	29	32	15	0	63	1	1	1	34	11	4	.238	.273	.350	.623
2012	Tor	AL	142	447	115	24	3	8	(5	3)	169	64	43	59	29	3	102	6	1	4	46	13	8	.257	.309	.378	.687
2013	Tor	AL	108	331	86	16	2	6	(3	3)	124	49	24	36	21	0	67	5	1	2	45	6	8	.260	.312	.375	.687
2014	Det	AL	134	461	130	27	2	8	(4	4)	185	64	51	62	22	0	75	5	3	3	36	11	7	.282	.320	.401	.721
2015	Det	AL	112	341	88	16	11	6	(6	2)	150	55	30	37	22	0	76	3	1	3	18	6	5	.258	.306	.440	.746
2016	Cle	AL	134	454	133	23	12	12	(3	9)	176	74	48	62	33	0	106	5	1	2	43	6	9	.249	.306	.388	.693
2017	Oak	AL	117	336	79	19	2	5	(3	2)	117	56	20	29	27	1	83	1	1	1	29	7	12	.235	.293	.348	.641
07	Pit	NL	24	48	13	2	1	0	(0	0)	17	6	2	6	7	0	3	0	1	1	5	2	1	.271	.357	.354	.711

Year	Team	Lg	G	AB	H	2B	3B	HR	(Hm	Rd)	TB	R	RBI	RC	TBB	IBB	SO	HBP	SH	SF	SB	CS	GDP	Avg	OBP	Slg	OPS
07	SF	NL	51	142	40	9	1	1	(0	1)	54	26	7	20	14	1	25	4	2	0	17	4	0	.282	.363	.380	.743
08	SF	NL	12	18	1	0	0	0	(0	0)	1	2	0	0	1	0	6	0	0	0	4	0	0	.056	.105	.056	.161
08	Oak	AL	101	196	51	5	4	3	(0	3)	73	28	19	24	7	0	34	1	2	1	25	6	1	.260	.288	.372	.660
17	Oak	AL	100	300	70	17	2	5	(3	2)	106	49	18	26	26	1	70	0	1	1	26	6	0	.233	.294	.353	.647
17	Bos	AL	17	36	9	2	0	0	(0	0)	11	7	2	3	1	0	13	1	0	0	3	1	2	.250	.289	.306	.595
Postseason			18	40	7	1	0	1	(1	0)	11	4	4	5	1	0	9	1	0	1	4	0	1	.175	.209	.275	.484
12 ML YEARS			1318	4023	1062	218	42	60	(31	29)	1544	600	373	492	255	5	791	42	18	27	394	100	77	.264	.313	.384	.696

Rookie Davis

Pitches: R Bats: R Pos: SP-6; RP-1   Ht: 6'5" Wt: 255 Born: 4/29/1993 Age: 25

Year	Team	Lg	G	GS	CG	GF	IP	BFP	H	R	ER	HR	SH	SF	HB	TBB	IBB	SO	WP	Bk	W	L	Pct	Sh	Sv-Op	Hld	ERC	ERA
2013	2 Tms	Low	13	13	0	0	52.0	229	55	19	11	1	1	1	4	13	0	47	6	0	2	4	.333	0	0--	-	3.43	1.90
2014	CtnSC	A	27	25	0	1	126.0	554	134	73	69	7	2	8	7	42	0	106	7	0	7	8	.467	0	0--	-	4.02	4.93
2015	Tampa	A+	19	19	0	0	97.1	406	94	48	40	4	2	6	4	18	1	105	3	0	6	6	.500	0	0--	-	2.78	3.70
2015	Trntn	AA	6	5	0	0	33.1	144	38	19	16	1	2	1	3	8	0	24	1	0	2	1	.667	0	0--	-	4.13	4.32
2016	Pnscla	AA	19	19	0	0	101.0	414	88	37	33	10	4	4	5	30	0	62	6	0	10	3	.769	0	0--	-	3.21	2.94
2016	Lsvlle	AAA	5	4	0	0	24.0	115	38	21	20	3	0	1	0	7	0	15	0	1	0	2	.000	0	0--	-	7.32	7.50
2017	Lsvlle	AAA	11	11	1	0	60.1	259	68	34	32	10	2	2	1	13	0	54	3	0	4	4	.500	0	0--	-	4.55	4.77
2017	Cin	NL	7	6	0	0	24.0	123	38	25	23	7	2	1	1	14	0	20	3	0	1	3	.250	0	0-0	0	10.42	8.63

Taylor Davis

Bats: R Throws: R Pos: PH-3;1B-2;3B-2;C-1   Ht: 5'10" Wt: 200 Born: 11/28/1989 Age: 28

Year	Team	Lg	G	AB	H	2B	3B	HR	(Hm	Rd)	TB	R	RBI	RC	TBB	IBB	SO	HBP	SH	SF	SB	CS	GDP	Avg	OBP	Slg	OPS
2013	Dytona	A+	28	83	18	2	0	2	(-	-)	26	9	8	7	9	0	15	0	0	0	0	1	2	.217	.293	.313	.607
2014	Tenn	AA	53	138	44	11	1	4	(-	-)	69	19	29	26	12	2	14	1	0	1	0	0	3	.319	.375	.500	.875
2015	Iowa	AAA	83	259	80	19	2	4	(-	-)	115	29	29	41	21	0	37	0	2	0	0	1	14	.309	.361	.444	.805
2015	Tenn	AA	21	72	23	7	0	5	(-	-)	45	11	14	15	5	0	11	0	1	0	0	0	1	.319	.364	.625	.989
2016	Tenn	AA	15	56	19	3	1	0	(-	-)	24	7	10	9	4	0	6	0	0	3	0	0	4	.339	.365	.429	.794
2016	Iowa	AAA	67	223	56	13	1	2	(-	-)	77	24	20	29	30	0	28	1	3	1	2	0	12	.251	.341	.345	.686
2017	Iowa	AAA	102	357	106	27	1	6	(-	-)	153	41	62	57	37	0	45	1	3	8	0	3	14	.297	.357	.429	.786
2017	ChC	NL	8	13	3	1	0	0	(0	0)	4	1	1	2	0	0	4	0	0	0	0	0	0	.231	.231	.308	.538

Wade Davis

Pitches: R Bats: R Pos: RP-59   Ht: 6'5" Wt: 225 Born: 9/7/1985 Age: 32

Year	Team	Lg	G	GS	CG	GF	IP	BFP	H	R	ER	HR	SH	SF	HB	TBB	IBB	SO	WP	Bk	W	L	Pct	Sh	Sv-Op	Hld	ERC	ERA
2009	TB	AL	6	6	1	0	36.1	150	33	19	15	2	0	0	0	13	1	36	1	0	2	2	.500	1	0-0	0	3.12	3.72
2010	TB	AL	29	29	0	0	168.0	722	165	77	76	24	3	6	5	62	2	113	4	0	12	10	.545	0	0-0	0	4.25	4.07
2011	TB	AL	29	29	1	0	184.0	795	190	96	91	23	5	7	8	63	1	105	6	0	11	10	.524	0	0-0	0	4.38	4.45
2012	TB	AL	54	0	0	15	70.1	284	48	20	19	5	0	1	0	29	1	87	2	0	3	0	1.000	0	0-1	6	2.25	2.43
2013	KC	AL	31	24	0	2	135.1	618	169	89	80	15	1	5	4	58	2	114	7	0	8	11	.421	0	0-0	0	5.88	5.32
2014	KC	AL	71	0	0	11	72.0	279	38	8	8	0	1	3	3	23	0	109	1	0	9	2	.818	0	3-6	33	1.23	1.00
2015	KC	AL	69	0	0	24	67.1	251	33	8	7	3	0	2	0	20	1	78	1	0	8	1	.889	0	17-18	18	1.16	0.94
2016	KC	AL	45	0	0	40	43.1	176	33	9	9	0	0	0	3	16	0	47	4	0	2	1	.667	0	27-30	0	2.35	1.87
2017	ChC	NL	59	0	0	56	58.2	242	39	16	15	6	1	0	3	28	1	79	7	0	4	2	.667	0	32-33	0	2.77	2.30
Postseason			23	1	0	10	32.1	124	22	4	3	1	0	0	0	9	0	46	2	0	4	0	1.000	0	4-4	3	1.67	0.84
9 ML YEARS			393	88	2	148	835.1	3517	748	342	320	78	10	22	26	312	10	768	33	0	59	39	.602	1	79-88	57	3.46	3.45

Grant Dayton

Pitches: L Bats: L Pos: RP-29   Ht: 6'2" Wt: 215 Born: 11/25/1987 Age: 30

Year	Team	Lg	G	GS	CG	GF	IP	BFP	H	R	ER	HR	SH	SF	HB	TBB	IBB	SO	WP	Bk	W	L	Pct	Sh	Sv-Op	Hld	ERC	ERA
2013	Jaxnvl	AA	30	0	0	11	38.0	160	33	10	10	4	1	0	1	12	0	56	2	0	4	4	.500	0	1--	-	3.11	2.37
2014	Jaxnvl	AA	11	0	0	4	16.1	71	17	2	2	0	2	0	0	4	0	18	0	0	0	1	.000	0	3--	-	2.90	1.10
2014	NewOr	AAA	39	0	0	11	55.2	238	53	24	23	10	1	1	1	22	3	61	1	0	2	2	.500	0	1--	-	4.34	3.72
2015	NewOr	AAA	25	0	0	8	35.0	131	25	11	11	1	2	2	1	5	1	35	4	0	2	1	.667	0	0--	-	1.51	2.83
2015	OkCity	AAA	9	0	0	3	11.2	53	16	12	12	1	0	0	1	3	0	13	2	0	1	1	.500	0	0--	-	6.01	9.26
2015	Tulsa	AA	8	0	0	2	10.2	47	9	3	3	0	1	0	0	7	2	17	2	0	0	2	.000	0	1--	-	3.13	2.53
2016	OkCity	AAA	26	0	0	11	36.1	140	22	12	10	2	1	0	1	8	1	63	0	0	2	2	.500	0	4--	-	1.40	2.48
2016	Tulsa	AA	12	0	0	5	15.2	58	8	6	4	0	0	0	1	3	0	28	0	0	3	0	1.000	0	1--	-	1.00	2.30
2017	OkCity	AAA	5	0	0	1	4.2	24	9	4	4	1	0	0	0	1	0	7	0	0	0	1	.000	0	1--	-	9.93	7.71
2016	LAD	NL	25	0	0	8	26.1	101	14	7	6	4	0	0	1	6	0	39	0	0	1	0	1.000	0	0-2	6	1.56	2.05
2017	LAD	NL	29	0	0	6	23.2	102	19	13	13	5	1	3	0	12	1	20	0	0	1	1	.500	0	0-1	4	4.02	4.94
Postseason			7	0	0	1	3.1	18	6	3	3	1	0	0	0	2	0	6	0	0	0	0	-	0	0-0	1	11.76	8.10
2 ML YEARS			54	0	0	6	50.0	203	33	20	19	9	1	3	1	18	1	59	0	0	1	2	.333	0	0-3	10	2.62	3.42

Alejandro De Aza

Bats: L **Throws:** L **Pos:** RF-14;LF-13;PH-8;PR-2;CF-1   day-AH-zah   **Ht:** 6'0" **Wt:** 195 **Born:** 4/11/1984 **Age:** 34

								BATTING											RUNNING			AVERAGES			
Year	Team	Lg	G	AB	H	2B	3B	HR	(Hm Rd)	TB	R	RBI	RC	TBB	IBB	SO	HBP	SH	SF	SB	CS	GDP	Avg	OBP	Slg	OPS
2017	Syrcse*	AAA	56	186	52	11	0	4	(- -)	75	30	19	29	25	1	30	1	0	0	2	0	3	.280	.368	.403	.771
2007	Fla	NL	45	144	33	8	2	0	(0 0)	45	14	8	11	6	1	37	1	5	2	2	0	2	.229	.261	.313	.574
2009	Fla	NL	22	20	5	1	0	0	(0 0)	6	6	3	4	5	0	5	0	1	1	0	0	0	.250	.385	.300	.685
2010	CWS	AL	19	30	9	3	0	0	(0 0)	12	7	2	4	1	0	4	0	1	0	2	1	0	.300	.323	.400	.723
2011	CWS	AL	54	152	50	11	3	4	(2 2)	79	29	23	34	17	1	34	1	1	0	12	5	2	.329	.400	.520	.920
2012	CWS	AL	131	524	147	29	6	9	(2 7)	215	81	50	79	47	3	109	9	4	1	26	12	1	.281	.349	.410	.760
2013	CWS	AL	153	607	160	27	4	17	(4 13)	246	84	62	82	50	1	147	6	6	6	20	8	8	.264	.323	.405	.728
2014	2 Tms	AL	142	477	120	24	8	8	(4 4)	184	56	41	58	39	2	119	6	3	3	17	10	7	.252	.314	.386	.700
2015	3 Tms		114	325	85	17	7	7	(3 4)	137	51	35	47	31	3	84	5	2	2	7	5	6	.262	.333	.422	.755
2016	NYM	NL	130	234	48	9	0	6	(2 4)	75	31	25	23	26	1	67	5	1	1	4	3	5	.205	.297	.321	.618
2017	Was	NL	28	62	12	2	3	0	(0 0)	20	8	9	6	3	1	16	0	3	2	1	0	1	.194	.224	.323	.546
14	CWS	AL	122	395	96	19	5	5	(4 1)	140	45	31	45	33	2	100	6	2	3	15	7	6	.243	.309	.354	.663
14	Bal	AL	20	82	24	5	3	3	(0 3)	44	11	10	13	6	0	19	0	1	0	2	3	1	.293	.341	.537	.877
15	Bal	AL	30	103	22	4	1	3	(1 2)	37	16	7	10	7	2	34	2	0	0	2	2	1	.214	.277	.359	.636
15	Bos	AL	60	161	47	9	5	4	(2 2)	78	23	25	30	12	1	36	2	2	1	3	1	2	.292	.347	.484	.831
15	SF	NL	24	61	16	4	1	0	(0 0)	22	12	3	7	12	0	14	1	0	1	2	2	3	.262	.387	.361	.747
	Postseason		6	21	7	3	0	0	(0 0)	10	4	3	4	1	0	1	1	0	0	0	0	0	.333	.391	.476	.867
	10 ML YEARS		838	2575	669	131	33	51	(17 34)	1019	367	258	348	225	13	622	33	27	18	91	44	32	.260	.325	.396	.721

Chase De Jong

Pitches: R **Bats:** L **Pos:** SP-4; RP-3   **Ht:** 6'4" **Wt:** 205 **Born:** 12/29/1993 **Age:** 24

			HOW MUCH HE PITCHED						WHAT HE GAVE UP											THE RESULTS						
Year	Team	Lg	G	GS	CG	GF	IP	BFP	H	R	ER	HR	SH	SF	HB	TBB	IBB	SO	WP	Bk	W	L	Pct	Sh	Sv-Op	Hld	ERC	ERA
2013	Bluefld	R+	13	10	1	0	56.0	235	58	21	19	2	1	1	1	10	0	66	0	0	2	3	.400	0	0- -	-	3.02	3.05
2014	Lnsng	A	23	21	0	0	97.0	425	113	59	52	12	3	3	7	22	0	73	6	0	1	6	.143	0	0- -	-	4.77	4.82
2015	2 Tms	Low	25	24	1	0	136.1	562	119	63	52	15	3	4	4	33	1	129	4	0	11	7	.611	0	0- -	-	2.92	3.43
2016	Tulsa	AA	25	25	2	0	141.2	564	106	51	45	15	5	5	3	39	0	125	9	0	14	5	.737	1	0- -	-	2.42	2.86
2017	Tacom	AAA	15	15	0	0	84.0	379	99	61	56	18	1	7	4	27	0	61	5	0	3	6	.333	0	0- -	-	5.76	6.00
2017	Ark	AA	5	5	0	0	28.2	127	32	20	19	3	1	2	3	10	0	18	2	0	1	3	.250	0	0- -	-	5.04	5.97
2017	Sea	AL	7	4	0	2	28.1	125	31	20	20	5	1	1	0	13	0	13	0	0	0	3	.000	0	0-1	-	5.49	6.35

Jorge De La Rosa

Pitches: L **Bats:** L **Pos:** RP-65   **Ht:** 6'1" **Wt:** 215 **Born:** 4/5/1981 **Age:** 37

			HOW MUCH HE PITCHED						WHAT HE GAVE UP											THE RESULTS						
Year	Team	Lg	G	GS	CG	GF	IP	BFP	H	R	ER	HR	SH	SF	HB	TBB	IBB	SO	WP	Bk	W	L	Pct	Sh	Sv-Op	Hld	ERC	ERA
2004	Mil	NL	5	5	0	0	22.2	113	29	20	16	1	1	3	1	14	0	5	3	0	0	3	.000	0	0-0	0	6.12	6.35
2005	Mil	NL	38	0	0	13	42.1	208	48	23	21	1	2	2	0	38	4	42	6	0	2	2	.500	0	0-2	5	6.04	4.46
2006	2 Tms		28	13	0	4	79.0	367	81	59	57	14	2	4	2	54	1	67	6	1	5	6	.455	0	0-0	1	6.05	6.49
2007	KC	AL	26	23	0	1	130.0	589	160	88	84	20	2	4	3	53	6	82	4	1	8	12	.400	0	0-0	0	5.93	5.82
2008	KC	NL	28	23	0	0	130.0	571	128	77	71	13	6	7	7	62	3	128	14	1	10	8	.556	0	0-0	0	4.50	4.92
2009	Col	NL	33	32	0	0	185.0	799	172	95	90	20	11	6	9	83	3	193	12	1	16	9	.640	0	0-0	0	4.11	4.38
2010	Col	NL	20	20	0	0	121.2	512	105	62	57	15	3	3	5	55	4	113	9	1	8	7	.533	0	0-0	0	3.86	4.22
2011	Col	NL	10	10	1	0	59.0	245	48	25	23	4	4	1	2	22	0	52	6	1	5	2	.714	0	0-0	0	2.88	3.51
2012	Col	NL	3	3	0	0	10.2	53	17	14	11	5	1	0	0	2	0	6	2	0	0	2	.000	0	0-0	0	9.22	9.28
2013	Col	NL	30	30	0	0	167.2	714	170	70	65	11	11	5	5	62	5	112	5	0	16	6	.727	0	0-0	0	3.92	3.49
2014	Col	NL	32	32	0	0	184.1	768	161	90	84	21	9	5	9	67	2	139	9	0	14	11	.560	0	0-0	0	3.55	4.10
2015	Col	NL	26	26	1	0	149.0	635	137	73	69	17	4	8	3	65	3	134	6	2	9	7	.563	0	0-0	0	3.94	4.17
2016	Col	NL	27	24	0	0	134.0	614	157	93	82	23	4	3	8	63	3	108	7	1	8	9	.471	0	0-0	0	6.16	5.51
2017	Ari	NL	65	0	0	8	51.1	219	46	24	24	7	2	1	3	21	4	45	5	0	3	1	.750	0	0-1	17	3.91	4.21
06	Mil	NL	18	3	0	4	30.1	146	32	30	29	4	1	3	1	22	1	31	4	0	2	2	.500	0	0-0	0	5.90	8.60
06	KC	NL	10	10	0	0	48.2	221	49	29	28	10	1	1	1	32	0	36	2	1	3	4	.429	0	0-0	0	6.14	5.18
	14 ML YEARS		371	241	2	26	1466.2	6407	1459	813	754	172	62	52	57	661	38	1226	94	9	104	85	.550	0	0-3	23	4.51	4.63

Rubby De La Rosa

Pitches: R **Bats:** R **Pos:** RP-9   ROO-bee   **Ht:** 6'0" **Wt:** 210 **Born:** 3/4/1989 **Age:** 29

			HOW MUCH HE PITCHED						WHAT HE GAVE UP											THE RESULTS						
Year	Team	Lg	G	GS	CG	GF	IP	BFP	H	R	ER	HR	SH	SF	HB	TBB	IBB	SO	WP	Bk	W	L	Pct	Sh	Sv-Op	Hld	ERC	ERA
2017	Reno*	AAA	19	0	0	3	20.1	90	17	8	7	3	1	0	4	9	0	28	2	0	1	2	.333	0	0- -	-	4.40	3.10
2011	LAD	NL	13	10	0	2	60.2	254	54	26	25	6	2	0	0	31	3	60	3	0	4	5	.444	-	0-1	1	3.94	3.71
2012	LAD	NL	1	0	0	0	0.2	4	0	2	2	0	0	0	0	0	0	0	0	0	0	0	-	0	0-0	0	7.00	27.00
2013	Bos	AL	11	0	0	7	11.1	53	15	7	7	2	0	0	3	2	0	6	1	0	0	2	.000	0	0-0	0	6.76	5.56
2014	Ari	NL	19	18	0	1	101.2	441	116	51	50	12	3	5	2	50	0	74	3	1	4	8	.333	0	0-0	0	4.96	4.43
2015	Ari	NL	32	32	0	0	188.2	809	193	103	98	32	8	5	4	63	3	150	2	2	14	9	.609	0	0-0	0	4.49	4.68
2016	Ari	NL	13	10	0	1	50.2	222	43	26	24	8	1	1	4	20	1	54	2	1	4	5	.444	0	0-0	0	3.75	4.26
2017	Ari	NL	9	0	0	1	7.2	34	7	4	4	2	0	0	0	4	1	12	0	1	0	1	.000	0	0-1	2	4.90	4.70
	7 ML YEARS		98	70	0	12	421.1	1817	428	219	210	62	14	11	13	157	8	356	11	5	26	30	.464	0	0-2	3	4.50	4.49

Jose De Leon

Pitches: R **Bats:** R **Pos:** RP-1

Ht: 6'1" **Wt:** 220 **Born:** 8/7/1992 **Age:** 25

Year Team	Lg	G	GS	CG	GF	IP	BFP	H	R	ER	HR	SH	SF	HB	TBB	IBB	SO	WP	Bk	W	L	Pct	Sh	Sv-Op	Hld	ERC	ERA
2013 2 Tms	Low	14	13	0	0	53.0	250	67	48	41	6	0	2	9	21	0	53	9	0	3	5	.375	0	0--	-	6.44	6.96
2014 2 Tms	Low	14	12	0	0	77.0	314	58	29	19	3	3	1	4	21	0	119	7	2	7	0	1.000	0	0--	-	2.10	2.22
2015 Rcuca	A+	7	7	0	0	37.2	148	26	9	7	1	1	0	4	8	0	58	1	0	4	1	.800	0	0--	-	1.78	1.67
2015 Tulsa	AA	16	16	1	0	76.2	317	61	35	31	11	2	1	2	29	1	105	2	0	2	6	.250	1	0--	-	3.25	3.64
2016 OkCity	AAA	16	16	0	0	86.1	342	62	29	28	9	3	4	1	20	0	111	4	0	7	1	.875	0	0--	-	2.05	2.92
2017 2 Tms	Low	7	5	0	0	26.1	101	15	4	4	1	0	0	1	10	0	30	1	0	2	0	1.000	0	0--	-	1.67	1.37
2016 LAD	NL	4	4	0	0	17.0	80	19	17	12	5	3	1	3	7	1	15	0	0	2	0	1.000	0	0-0	0	6.82	6.35
2017 TB	AL	1	0	0	0	2.2	15	4	3	3	1	0	0	0	3	0	2	2	0	0	0	1.000	0	0-0	0	12.97	10.13
2 ML YEARS		5	4	0	0	19.2	95	23	20	15	6	3	1	3	10	1	17	2	0	3	0	1.000	0	0-0	0	7.60	6.86

Jaff Decker

Bats: L **Throws:** L **Pos:** CF-12;RF-4;PH-2;LF-1

JEFF

Ht: 5'9" **Wt:** 190 **Born:** 2/23/1990 **Age:** 28

Year Team	Lg	G	AB	H	2B	3B	HR	(Hm	Rd)	TB	R	RBI	RC	TBB	IBB	SO	HBP	SH	SF	SB	CS	GDP	Avg	OBP	Slg	OPS
2017 Nashv*	AAA	93	351	96	13	1	6	(-	-)	129	41	36	48	38	2	93	1	3	5	15	5	7	.274	.342	.368	.709
2013 SD	NL	13	26	4	0	0	1	(0	1)	7	3	2	0	3	0	4	0	1	1	0	1	0	.154	.233	.269	.503
2014 Pit	NL	5	5	0	0	0	0	(0	0)	0	0	0	0	0	0	3	0	0	0	0	0	0	.000	.000	.000	.000
2015 Pit	NL	23	28	6	1	1	0	(0	0)	9	8	1	4	7	0	9	0	1	0	1	0	1	.214	.371	.321	.693
2016 TB	AL	19	52	8	1	0	0	(0	0)	9	5	4	4	4	0	14	0	0	1	1	0	1	.154	.211	.173	.384
2017 Oak	AL	17	50	10	1	1	0	(0	0)	13	4	1	4	8	0	17	1	3	0	1	1	1	.200	.322	.260	.582
5 ML YEARS		77	161	28	3	2	1	(0	1)	38	16	5	8	22	0	47	1	5	2	2	2	2	.174	.274	.236	.510

Jacob deGrom

Pitches: R **Bats:** L **Pos:** SP-31

duh-GRAHM

Ht: 6'4" **Wt:** 180 **Born:** 6/19/1988 **Age:** 30

Year Team	Lg	G	GS	CG	GF	IP	BFP	H	R	ER	HR	SH	SF	HB	TBB	IBB	SO	WP	Bk	W	L	Pct	Sh	Sv-Op	Hld	ERC	ERA
2014 NYM	NL	22	22	0	0	140.1	565	117	44	42	7	5	3	1	43	2	144	1	0	9	6	.600	0	0-0	0	2.57	2.69
2015 NYM	NL	30	30	0	0	191.0	751	149	59	54	16	10	7	2	38	2	205	6	0	14	8	.636	0	0-0	0	2.13	2.54
2016 NYM	NL	24	24	1	0	148.0	604	142	53	50	15	5	3	3	36	0	143	4	0	7	8	.467	1	0-0	0	3.40	3.04
2017 NYM	NL	31	31	1	0	201.1	827	180	87	79	28	3	5	2	59	5	239	7	0	15	10	.600	0	0-0	0	3.36	3.53
Postseason		4	4	0	0	25.0	105	21	8	8	2	2	0	0	8	1	29	0	0	3	1	.750	0	0-0	0	2.65	2.88
4 ML YEARS		107	107	2	0	680.2	2747	588	243	225	66	23	18	8	176	9	731	18	0	45	32	.584	1	0-0	0	2.84	2.98

Paul DeJong

Bats: R **Throws:** R **Pos:** SS-86;2B-20;PH-4

Ht: 6'1" **Wt:** 195 **Born:** 8/2/1993 **Age:** 24

Year Team	Lg	G	AB	H	2B	3B	HR	(Hm	Rd)	TB	R	RBI	RC	TBB	IBB	SO	HBP	SH	SF	SB	CS	GDP	Avg	OBP	Slg	OPS
2015 2 Tms	Low	66	256	81	18	3	9	(-	-)	132	42	41	53	29	0	52	5	0	2	13	4	6	.316	.394	.516	.909
2016 Sprgfld	AA	132	496	129	29	2	22	(-	-)	228	62	73	76	40	2	144	10	0	6	3	2	5	.260	.324	.460	.784
2017 Memp	AAA	48	177	53	9	0	13	(-	-)	101	27	34	32	9	0	46	2	1	1	0	2	3	.299	.339	.571	.909
2017 StL	NL	108	417	119	26	1	25	(11	14)	222	55	65	57	21	1	124	4	0	1	1	0	8	.285	.325	.532	.857

Randall Delgado

Pitches: R **Bats:** R **Pos:** RP-21; SP-5

Ht: 6'4" **Wt:** 220 **Born:** 2/9/1990 **Age:** 28

Year Team	Lg	G	GS	CG	GF	IP	BFP	H	R	ER	HR	SH	SF	HB	TBB	IBB	SO	WP	Bk	W	L	Pct	Sh	Sv-Op	Hld	ERC	ERA
2011 Atl	NL	7	7	0	0	35.0	147	29	12	11	5	0	0	1	14	1	18	2	0	1	1	.500	0	0-0	0	3.48	2.83
2012 Atl	NL	18	17	0	0	92.2	401	89	48	45	8	5	3	4	42	4	76	5	1	4	9	.308	0	0-0	0	4.10	4.37
2013 Ari	NL	20	19	1	0	116.1	473	116	59	55	24	5	5	1	23	2	79	3	1	5	7	.417	1	0-0	0	4.03	4.26
2014 Ari	NL	47	4	0	6	77.2	339	71	44	42	6	2	2	3	35	2	86	5	0	4	4	.500	0	0-0	2	3.69	4.87
2015 Ari	NL	64	1	0	13	72.0	308	63	28	26	7	2	2	1	33	2	73	7	0	8	4	.667	0	1-3	12	3.59	3.25
2016 Ari	NL	79	0	0	14	75.0	337	77	39	37	8	3	5	2	36	3	68	7	0	5	2	.714	0	0-3	7	4.56	4.44
2017 Ari	NL	26	5	0	5	62.2	259	60	31	25	6	4	2	0	14	0	60	1	0	1	2	.333	0	1-2	2	3.11	3.59
7 ML YEARS		261	53	1	38	531.1	2264	505	261	241	64	21	19	12	197	14	460	30	2	28	29	.491	1	2-8	23	3.87	4.08

Nick Delmonico

Bats: L **Throws:** R **Pos:** LF-27;DH-11;1B-4;PH-3;PR-1

Ht: 6'2" **Wt:** 230 **Born:** 7/12/1992 **Age:** 25

Year Team	Lg	G	AB	H	2B	3B	HR	(Hm	Rd)	TB	R	RBI	RC	TBB	IBB	SO	HBP	SH	SF	SB	CS	GDP	Avg	OBP	Slg	OPS
2013 2 Tms	Low	82	298	69	16	1	13	(-	-)	126	41	39	46	48	2	80	4	0	0	7	2	7	.232	.346	.423	.769
2014 BrvdCt	A+	37	141	37	8	0	4	(-	-)	57	11	15	17	7	0	34	1	0	1	2	2	0	.262	.300	.404	.704
2015 Brham	AA	62	223	53	24	0	3	(-	-)	86	26	26	28	25	0	52	1	1	3	2	1	5	.238	.313	.386	.699
2016 Brham	AA	38	142	48	14	2	10	(-	-)	96	25	31	35	13	0	33	1	3	0	1	0	2	.338	.397	.676	1.073
2016 Charlt	AAA	72	260	64	16	0	7	(-	-)	101	32	30	34	29	0	74	1	1	4	2	0	3	.246	.320	.388	.708
2017 Charlt	AAA	99	378	99	18	3	12	(-	-)	159	55	45	58	46	3	73	4	0	1	4	2	6	.262	.347	.421	.768
2017 CWS	AL	43	141	37	4	0	9	(3	6)	68	25	23	23	23	0	31	2	0	0	2	0	5	.262	.373	.482	.856

Matt den Dekker

Bats: L **Throws:** L **Pos:** RF-2;LF-1;PH-1;PR-1   **Ht:** 6'2" **Wt:** 210 **Born:** 8/10/1987 **Age:** 30

								BATTING												RUNNING			AVERAGES			
Year Team	Lg	G	AB	H	2B	3B	HR	(Hm Rd)	TB	R	RBI	RC	TBB	IBB	SO	HBP	SH	SF	SB	CS	GDP	Avg	OBP	Slg	OPS
2017 NewOr*	AAA	20	77	19	7	1	3	(- -)	37	9	13	10	3	1	20	1	0	1	2	1	1	.247	.280	.481	.761
2017 Toledo*	AAA	59	179	45	10	3	5	(- -)	76	28	16	26	24	1	50	0	2	1	8	5	1	.251	.338	.425	.763
2013 NYM	NL	27	58	12	1	0	1	(0 1)	16	7	6	5	4	0	23	1	0	0	4	1	0	.207	.270	.276	.546
2014 NYM	NL	53	152	38	11	0	0	(0 0)	49	23	7	17	21	0	34	1	0	0	7	4	1	.250	.315	.322	.667
2015 Was	NL	55	99	25	6	1	5	(3 2)	48	12	12	12	9	0	20	0	2	0	0	1	0	.253	.315	.485	.800
2016 Was	NL	19	34	6	1	0	1	(1 0)	10	3	4	5	4	0	10	1	0	0	1	0	0	.176	.282	.294	.576
2017 Det	AL	4	7	1	0	0	0	(0 0)	1	1	0	0	1	0	4	0	0	0	0	0	0	.143	.250	.143	.393
5 ML YEARS		158	350	82	19	1	7	(4 3)	124	46	29	39	39	0	91	3	2	0	12	6	1	.234	.316	.354	.671

Matt Dermody

Pitches: L **Bats:** R **Pos:** RP-23   DER-mud-ee   **Ht:** 6'5" **Wt:** 190 **Born:** 7/4/1990 **Age:** 27

		HOW MUCH HE PITCHED						WHAT HE GAVE UP												THE RESULTS							
Year Team	Lg	G	GS	CG	GF	IP	BFP	H	R	ER	HR	SH	SF	HB	TBB	IBB	SO	WP	Bk	W	L	Pct	Sh	Sv-Op	Hld	ERC	ERA
2013 2 Tms	Low	16	3	0	1	43.1	178	46	12	8	0	2	0	1	4	0	51	1	0	5	1	.833	0	0- -	-	2.66	1.66
2014 Lnsng	A	27	12	0	2	96.0	429	113	62	50	5	5	1	3	36	0	65	8	0	4	6	.400	0	0- -	-	4.76	4.69
2015 Dnedin	A+	35	1	0	8	77.0	340	98	46	36	2	1	5	3	13	0	62	1	0	4	1	.800	0	1- -	-	4.27	4.21
2016 Dnedin	A+	16	0	0	10	18.1	74	21	4	4	0	0	2	0	1	0	20	0	0	1	1	.500	0	3- -	-	2.95	1.96
2016 Nham	AA	16	0	0	5	19.2	72	12	3	2	1	0	1	0	2	0	21	1	0	2	0	1.000	0	0- -	-	1.13	0.92
2016 Buffalo	AAA	15	0	0	5	16.1	75	22	9	5	0	1	1	0	5	0	6	0	0	0	0	-	0	0- -	-	4.87	2.76
2017 Buffalo	AAA	33	1	0	10	43.0	186	48	21	17	6	0	1	1	11	1	39	2	0	5	1	.833	0	1- -	-	4.47	3.56
2016 Tor	AL	5	0	0	1	3.0	16	6	4	4	1	0	0	0	0	0	5	1	0	0	0	-	0	0-0	0	12.18	12.00
2017 Tor	AL	23	0	0	3	22.1	95	23	13	11	6	0	1	2	5	1	15	1	0	2	0	1.000	0	0-0	1	5.00	4.43
2 ML YEARS		28	0	0	4	25.1	111	29	17	15	7	0	1	2	5	1	20	2	0	2	0	1.000	0	0-0	1	5.77	5.33

Daniel Descalso

Bats: L **Throws:** R **Pos:** 2B-45;LF-36;PH-35;1B-19;3B-15;SS-1;DH-1   dess-CAL-so   **Ht:** 5'10" **Wt:** 190 **Born:** 10/19/1986 **Age:** 31

								BATTING												RUNNING			AVERAGES			
Year Team	Lg	G	AB	H	2B	3B	HR	(Hm Rd)	TB	R	RBI	RC	TBB	IBB	SO	HBP	SH	SF	SB	CS	GDP	Avg	OBP	Slg	OPS
2010 StL	NL	11	34	9	2	0	0	(0 0)	11	6	4	5	2	0	6	1	0	0	1	0	0	.265	.324	.324	.648
2011 StL	NL	148	326	86	20	3	1	(1 0)	115	35	28	40	33	9	65	3	10	3	2	2	3	.264	.334	.353	.687
2012 StL	NL	143	374	85	10	7	4	(0 4)	121	41	26	29	37	3	83	5	7	3	6	3	5	.227	.303	.324	.627
2013 StL	NL	123	328	78	25	1	5	(1 4)	120	43	43	40	22	5	56	3	3	2	6	3	7	.238	.290	.366	.656
2014 StL	NL	104	161	39	11	0	0	(0 0)	50	20	10	15	20	0	33	2	1	0	1	3	2	.242	.333	.311	.644
2015 Col	NL	101	185	38	3	2	5	(1 4)	60	22	14	14	20	6	45	0	4	0	1	2	3	.205	.283	.324	.607
2016 Col	NL	99	250	66	12	2	8	(3 5)	106	38	38	45	34	3	56	1	0	4	3	0	6	.264	.349	.424	.773
2017 Ari	NL	131	344	80	16	5	10	(7 3)	136	47	51	49	48	4	89	4	0	2	4	0	6	.233	.332	.395	.727
Postseason		44	84	18	2	0	2	(1 1)	26	16	6	5	4	2	19	0	5	1	2	0	2	.214	.247	.310	.557
8 ML YEARS		860	2002	481	99	20	33	(13 20)	719	252	222	237	216	26	433	19	25	14	24	13	28	.240	.318	.359	.677

Anthony DeSclafani

Pitches: R **Bats:** R **Pos:** P   DEE-skla-fa-nee   **Ht:** 6'1" **Wt:** 195 **Born:** 4/18/1990 **Age:** 28

		HOW MUCH HE PITCHED						WHAT HE GAVE UP												THE RESULTS							
Year Team	Lg	G	GS	CG	GF	IP	BFP	H	R	ER	HR	SH	SF	HB	TBB	IBB	SO	WP	Bk	W	L	Pct	Sh	Sv-Op	Hld	ERC	ERA
2014 Mia	NL	13	5	0	4	33.0	146	40	23	23	4	4	3	2	5	0	26	2	0	2	2	.500	0	0-0	-	4.56	6.27
2015 Cin	NL	31	31	0	0	184.2	785	194	93	83	17	10	5	5	55	5	151	6	0	9	13	.409	0	0-0	0	4.00	4.05
2016 Cin	NL	20	20	1	0	123.1	507	120	51	45	16	7	3	4	30	2	105	6	1	9	5	.643	1	0-0	0	3.67	3.28
3 ML YEARS		64	56	1	4	341.0	1438	354	167	151	37	21	11	11	90	7	282	14	1	20	20	.500	1	0-0	0	3.94	3.99

Delino DeShields

Bats: R **Throws:** R **Pos:** LF-60;CF-51;PR-11;DH-8;PH-3   **Ht:** 5'9" **Wt:** 200 **Born:** 8/16/1992 **Age:** 25

								BATTING												RUNNING			AVERAGES			
Year Team	Lg	G	AB	H	2B	3B	HR	(Hm Rd)	TB	R	RBI	RC	TBB	IBB	SO	HBP	SH	SF	SB	CS	GDP	Avg	OBP	Slg	OPS
2015 Tex	AL	121	425	111	22	10	2	(2 0)	159	83	37	66	53	1	101	3	7	4	25	8	1	.261	.344	.374	.718
2016 Tex	AL	74	182	38	7	0	4	(0 4)	57	36	13	16	15	0	54	2	3	1	8	3	1	.209	.275	.313	.588
2017 Tex	AL	120	376	101	15	2	6	(5 1)	138	75	22	54	44	0	109	3	13	4	29	8	2	.269	.347	.367	.714
Postseason		5	24	7	3	0	0	(0 0)	10	4	2	4	0	0	2	0	0	0	1	0	0	.292	.292	.417	.708
3 ML YEARS		315	983	250	44	12	12	(7 5)	354	194	72	136	112	1	264	8	23	9	62	19	4	.254	.333	.360	.693

Ian Desmond

Bats: R **Throws:** R **Pos:** LF-66;1B-27;PH-5;SS-1;CF-1   **Ht:** 6'3" **Wt:** 215 **Born:** 9/20/1985 **Age:** 32

								BATTING												RUNNING			AVERAGES			
Year Team	Lg	G	AB	H	2B	3B	HR	(Hm Rd)	TB	R	RBI	RC	TBB	IBB	SO	HBP	SH	SF	SB	CS	GDP	Avg	OBP	Slg	OPS
2009 Was	NL	21	82	23	7	2	4	(2 2)	46	9	12	10	5	0	14	0	1	1	1	0	2	.280	.318	.561	.879
2010 Was	NL	154	525	141	27	4	10	(8 2)	206	59	65	58	28	3	109	5	9	7	17	5	9	.269	.308	.392	.700
2011 Was	NL	154	584	148	27	5	8	(7 1)	209	65	49	65	35	2	139	4	11	5	25	10	9	.253	.298	.358	.656
2012 Was	NL	130	513	150	33	2	25	(10 15)	262	72	73	73	30	1	113	3	0	1	21	6	17	.292	.335	.511	.845
2013 Was	NL	158	600	168	38	3	20	(10 10)	272	77	80	81	43	3	145	5	2	5	21	6	16	.280	.331	.453	.784
2014 Was	NL	154	593	151	26	3	24	(12 12)	255	73	91	78	46	0	183	6	0	3	24	5	17	.255	.313	.430	.743
2015 Was	NL	156	583	136	27	2	19	(11 8)	224	69	62	59	45	0	187	3	6	4	13	5	9	.233	.290	.384	.674

Year	Team	Lg	G	AB	H	2B	3B	HR	(Hm	Rd)	TB	R	RBI	RC	TBB	IBB	SO	HBP	SH	SF	SB	CS	GDP	Avg	OBP	Slg	OPS
									BATTING												**RUNNING**			**AVERAGES**			
2016	Tex	AL	156	625	178	29	3	22	(10	12)	279	107	86	92	44	2	160	5	0	3	21	6	11	.285	.335	.446	.782
2017	Col	NL	95	339	93	11	1	7	(2	5)	127	47	40	47	24	1	87	4	2	4	15	4	13	.274	.326	.375	.701
	Postseason		12	51	13	2	0	0	(0	0)	15	4	2	3	1	0	12	0	0	0	1	0	0	.255	.269	.294	.563
	9 ML YEARS		1178	4444	1188	225	25	139	(78	61)	1880	578	558	563	300	12	1137	35	31	33	158	47	103	.267	.317	.423	.740

Odrisamer Despaigne

Pitches: R **Bats:** R **Pos:** RP-10; SP-8

oh-DREE-sa-mehr des-PAHN-yay

Ht: 6'0" **Wt:** 200 **Born:** 4/4/1987 **Age:** 31

Year	Team	Lg	G	GS	CG	GF	IP	BFP	H	R	ER	HR	SH	SF	HB	TBB	IBB	SO	WP	Bk	W	L	Pct	Sh	Sv-Op	Hld	ERC	ERA
				HOW MUCH HE PITCHED							**WHAT HE GAVE UP**											**THE RESULTS**					
2017	NewOr*	AAA	20	10	0	5	70.0	288	62	25	24	6	4	3	2	24	1	49	2	0	2	4	.333	0	2- -	-	3.29	3.09
2014	SD	NL	16	16	0	0	96.1	404	85	44	36	6	8	1	5	32	0	65	0	0	4	7	.364	0	0-0	0	3.12	3.36
2015	SD	NL	34	18	0	5	125.2	547	142	82	81	17	8	3	9	32	3	69	7	0	5	9	.357	0	0-0	0	4.75	5.80
2016	2 Tms		19	0	0	5	30.1	135	36	21	20	3	0	2	1	16	1	17	0	1	0	2	.000	0	0-2	1	6.02	5.93
2017	Mia	NL	18	8	0	5	58.1	254	57	31	26	3	2	2	3	24	1	31	1	0	2	3	.400	0	1-1	1	3.81	4.01
16	Bal	AL	16	0	0	5	27.1	122	32	18	17	3	0	1	1	15	1	17	0	1	0	2	.000	0	0-2	1	6.11	5.60
16	Mia	NL	3	0	0	3	3.0	13	4	3	3	0	0	1	0	1	0	0	0	0	0	0	-	0	0-0	0	5.24	9.00
	4 ML YEARS		87	42	0	18	310.2	1340	320	178	163	29	18	8	18	104	5	182	8	1	11	21	.344	0	1-3	2	4.16	4.72

Chris Devenski

Pitches: R **Bats:** R **Pos:** RP-62

Ht: 6'3" **Wt:** 210 **Born:** 11/13/1990 **Age:** 27

Year	Team	Lg	G	GS	CG	GF	IP	BFP	H	R	ER	HR	SH	SF	HB	TBB	IBB	SO	WP	Bk	W	L	Pct	Sh	Sv-Op	Hld	ERC	ERA
				HOW MUCH HE PITCHED							**WHAT HE GAVE UP**											**THE RESULTS**					
2013	2 Tms	Low	29	18	0	3	118.2	551	166	91	87	16	6	4	8	40	0	97	5	1	8	5	.615	0	1- -	-	6.84	6.60
2014	Lancst	A+	17	11	0	2	76.2	319	70	42	35	8	2	1	3	12	0	77	1	0	5	5	.500	0	2- -	-	2.76	4.11
2014	CpChr	AA	10	5	0	1	41.1	174	33	21	18	7	0	1	0	18	0	37	2	0	5	3	.625	0	0- -	-	3.53	3.92
2015	CpChr	AA	24	17	0	5	119.2	501	117	43	40	12	1	3	2	33	0	104	4	0	7	4	.636	0	2- -	-	3.54	3.01
2016	Hou	AL	48	5	0	16	108.1	408	79	26	26	4	1	1	3	20	0	104	2	0	4	4	.500	0	1-1	5	1.74	2.16
2017	Hou	AL	62	0	0	10	80.2	316	50	26	24	11	0	1	2	26	3	100	2	0	8	5	.615	0	4-10	24	2.10	2.68
	2 ML YEARS		110	5	0	26	189.0	724	129	52	50	15	1	2	5	46	3	204	4	0	12	9	.571	0	5-11	29	1.90	2.38

Rafael Devers

Bats: L **Throws:** R **Pos:** 3B-56;PH-2;DH-1

Ht: 6'0" **Wt:** 195 **Born:** 10/24/1996 **Age:** 21

Year	Team	Lg	G	AB	H	2B	3B	HR	(Hm	Rd)	TB	R	RBI	RC	TBB	IBB	SO	HBP	SH	SF	SB	CS	GDP	Avg	OBP	Slg	OPS
									BATTING												**RUNNING**			**AVERAGES**			
2014	RedSx	R	42	157	49	11	2	4	(-	-)	76	21	36	28	14	0	30	2	0	1	1	0	3	.312	.374	.484	.858
2015	Grnvlle	A	115	469	135	38	1	11	(-	-)	208	71	79	70	24	0	84	8	1	6	3	2	12	.288	.329	.443	.773
2016	Salem	A+	128	503	142	32	8	11	(-	-)	223	64	71	77	40	2	94	1	0	2	18	6	5	.282	.335	.443	.779
2017	Portlnd	AA	77	287	86	19	3	18	(-	-)	165	48	56	58	31	4	55	1	0	1	0	3	8	.300	.369	.575	.944
2017	Bos	AL	58	222	63	14	0	10	(6	4)	107	34	30	34	18	3	57	0	0	0	3	1	5	.284	.338	.482	.819

Aledmys Diaz

Bats: R **Throws:** R **Pos:** SS-68;PH-8;3B-4;LF-3;2B-1;PR-1

ah-LED-mees

Ht: 6'1" **Wt:** 195 **Born:** 8/1/1990 **Age:** 27

Year	Team	Lg	G	AB	H	2B	3B	HR	(Hm	Rd)	TB	R	RBI	RC	TBB	IBB	SO	HBP	SH	SF	SB	CS	GDP	Avg	OBP	Slg	OPS
									BATTING												**RUNNING**			**AVERAGES**			
2014	Sprgfld	AA	34	117	34	8	1	3	(-	-)	53	15	18	17	2	0	24	2	3	1	6	2	2	.291	.311	.453	.764
2014	PlmBh	A+	13	44	10	2	0	2	(-	-)	18	5	6	7	7	0	10	2	0	1	1	0	1	.227	.352	.409	.761
2015	Sprgfld	AA	102	375	99	26	2	10	(-	-)	159	47	46	52	29	0	62	4	1	0	6	5	10	.264	.324	.424	.748
2015	Memp	AAA	14	50	19	3	0	3	(-	-)	31	12	6	12	6	1	5	1	0	1	0	1	2	.380	.448	.620	1.068
2017	Memp	AAA	46	170	43	9	1	4	(-	-)	66	19	26	20	10	0	30	4	0	3	3	3	2	.253	.305	.388	.693
2016	StL	NL	111	404	121	28	3	17	(7	10)	206	71	65	75	41	6	60	7	2	6	4	4	10	.300	.369	.510	.879
2017	StL	NL	79	286	74	17	0	7	(5	2)	112	31	20	27	13	1	42	0	1	1	4	1	9	.259	.290	.392	.682
	2 ML YEARS		190	690	195	45	3	24	(12	12)	318	102	85	102	54	7	102	7	3	7	8	5	19	.283	.338	.461	.799

Dayan Diaz

Pitches: R **Bats:** R **Pos:** RP-9; SP-1

DIE-yahn

Ht: 5'10" **Wt:** 195 **Born:** 2/10/1989 **Age:** 29

Year	Team	Lg	G	GS	CG	GF	IP	BFP	H	R	ER	HR	SH	SF	HB	TBB	IBB	SO	WP	Bk	W	L	Pct	Sh	Sv-Op	Hld	ERC	ERA
				HOW MUCH HE PITCHED							**WHAT HE GAVE UP**											**THE RESULTS**					
2013	2 Tms		8	1	0	4	14.0	61	11	3	2	2	0	0	1	6	0	19	3	0	0	1	.000	0	1- -	-	3.44	1.93
2013	Tenn	AA	5	0	0	1	7.0	31	5	4	4	1	1	0	1	3	0	10	2	0	0	0	-	0	0- -	-	3.27	5.14
2014	Salem	A+	24	0	0	22	33.2	135	21	8	5	1	0	3	1	14	0	40	4	2	0	1	.000	0	6- -	-	1.89	1.34
2014	Portlnd	AA	11	0	0	5	16.1	72	16	5	5	0	1	0	1	7	0	16	0	0	2	1	.667	0	1- -	-	3.55	2.76
2015	Portlnd	AA	9	0	0	6	15.2	56	7	2	2	0	0	1	0	2	0	17	1	1	0	0	-	0	2- -	-	0.62	1.15
2015	Pwtckt	AAA	28	0	0	12	57.0	247	47	16	12	3	4	0	2	28	1	49	3	0	2	1	.667	0	4- -	-	3.18	1.89
2016	Lsvlle	AAA	40	1	0	13	56.0	230	52	20	19	2	1	0	0	16	1	46	1	0	7	1	.875	0	1- -	-	2.83	3.05
2017	Fresno	AAA	35	0	0	19	48.0	204	47	22	22	3	1	2	0	18	0	52	4	0	4	3	.571	0	2- -	-	3.62	4.13
2016	Cin	NL	6	0	0	0	6.2	36	10	9	7	2	1	1	0	7	0	3	0	0	0	0	-	0	0-0	0	12.17	9.45
2017	Hou	AL	10	1	0	4	13.0	58	17	14	13	3	0	0	0	4	0	20	4	0	1	1	.500	0	0-0	0	6.60	9.00
	2 ML YEARS		16	1	0	4	19.2	94	27	23	20	5	1	1	0	11	0	23	4	0	1	1	.500	0	0-0	0	8.42	9.15

Edwin Diaz

Pitches: R Bats: R Pos: RP-66
Ht: 6'3" Wt: 165 Born: 3/22/1994 Age: 24

		HOW MUCH HE PITCHED						WHAT HE GAVE UP												THE RESULTS							
Year Team	Lg	G	GS	CG	GF	IP	BFP	H	R	ER	HR	SH	SF	HB	TBB	IBB	SO	WP	Bk	W	L	Pct	Sh	Sv-Op	Hld	ERC	ERA
2013 Pulski	R+	13	13	0	0	69.0	260	45	14	11	5	2	5	5	18	0	79	2	0	5	2	.714	0	0--	-	1.95	1.43
2014 Clinton	A	24	24	1	0	116.0	483	96	50	43	5	3	4	10	42	0	111	5	2	6	8	.429	1	0--	-	2.97	3.34
2015 Bkrsfld	A+	7	7	0	0	37.0	141	21	7	7	3	1	1	4	9	0	42	2	0	2	0	1.000	0	0--	-	1.67	1.70
2015 Jacksn	AA	20	20	0	0	104.1	443	102	56	53	5	2	3	7	37	0	103	2	1	5	10	.333	0	0--	-	3.73	4.57
2016 Jacksn	AA	16	6	0	4	40.2	162	32	13	10	3	1	1	2	7	0	54	2	1	3	3	.500	0	1--	-	2.13	2.21
2016 Sea	AL	49	0	0	23	51.2	217	45	16	16	5	0	0	3	15	2	88	6	1	0	4	.000	0	18-21	13	3.05	2.79
2017 Sea	AL	66	0	0	52	66.0	278	44	28	24	10	1	2	3	32	2	89	3	1	4	6	.400	0	34-39	7	3.01	3.27
2 ML YEARS		115	0	0	75	117.2	495	89	44	40	15	1	2	6	47	4	177	9	2	4	10	.286	0	52-60	15	3.03	3.06

Elias Diaz

Bats: R Throws: R Pos: C-55;PH-15
Eh-lee-ahs
Ht: 6'1" Wt: 215 Born: 11/17/1990 Age: 27

		BATTING																		RUNNING			AVERAGES			
Year Team	Lg	G	AB	H	2B	3B	HR	(Hm	Rd)	TB	R	RBI	RC	TBB	IBB	SO	HBP	SH	SF	SB	CS	GDP	Avg	OBP	Slg	OPS
2017 Indy*	AAA	57	218	58	10	0	2	(-	-)	74	19	27	23	10	0	36	0	1	0	3	0	6	.266	.298	.339	.638
2015 Pit	NL	2	2	0	0	0	0	(0	0)	0	0	0	0	0	0	1	0	0	0	0	0	0	.000	.000	.000	.000
2016 Pit	NL	1	4	0	0	0	0	(0	0)	0	0	1	0	0	0	0	0	0	0	0	0	0	.000	.000	.000	.000
2017 Pit	NL	64	188	42	14	0	1	(0	1)	59	18	19	15	11	0	38	0	0	1	1	0	8	.223	.265	.314	.579
3 ML YEARS		67	194	42	14	0	1	(0	1)	59	18	20	15	11	0	40	0	0	1	1	0	8	.216	.257	.304	.561

Jairo Diaz

Pitches: R Bats: R Pos: RP-4
HIGH-row
Ht: 6'0" Wt: 200 Born: 5/27/1991 Age: 27

		HOW MUCH HE PITCHED						WHAT HE GAVE UP												THE RESULTS							
Year Team	Lg	G	GS	CG	GF	IP	BFP	H	R	ER	HR	SH	SF	HB	TBB	IBB	SO	WP	Bk	W	L	Pct	Sh	Sv-Op	Hld	ERC	ERA
2017 Albq*	AAA	20	0	0	8	18.0	74	16	10	10	1	1	0	0	7	0	17	0	0	0	1	.000	0	3--	-	3.21	5.00
2014 LAA	AL	5	0	0	2	5.2	24	4	2	2	0	0	1	0	3	0	8	0	0	0	0	-	0	0-0	0	2.29	3.18
2015 Col	NL	21	0	0	5	19.0	78	16	6	5	2	0	0	0	6	0	18	0	0	0	1	.000	0	0-1	7	2.93	2.37
2017 Col	NL	4	0	0	3	5.0	30	12	6	5	0	0	0	1	5	0	2	0	0	0	0	-	0	0-0	0	17.54	9.00
3 ML YEARS		30	0	0	10	29.2	132	32	14	12	2	0	1	1	14	0	28	0	0	0	1	.000	0	0-1	7	4.74	3.64

Jumbo Diaz

Pitches: R Bats: R Pos: RP-31
Ht: 6'4" Wt: 315 Born: 2/27/1984 Age: 34

		HOW MUCH HE PITCHED						WHAT HE GAVE UP												THE RESULTS							
Year Team	Lg	G	GS	CG	GF	IP	BFP	H	R	ER	HR	SH	SF	HB	TBB	IBB	SO	WP	Bk	W	L	Pct	Sh	Sv-Op	Hld	ERC	ERA
2017 Fresno*	AAA	12	0	0	8	12.1	52	11	4	4	1	0	0	0	5	0	11	1	0	1	0	1.000	0	3--	-	3.38	2.92
2014 Cin	NL	36	0	0	12	34.2	142	29	13	13	3	0	2	0	14	4	37	1	0	1	1	.000	0	0-1	8	3.00	3.38
2015 Cin	NL	61	0	0	16	60.1	255	58	29	28	9	3	2	3	18	3	70	5	1	2	1	.667	0	1-5	7	3.92	4.18
2016 Cin	NL	45	0	0	11	43.0	182	36	20	15	8	1	0	1	19	1	37	5	0	1	1	.500	0	0-1	4	3.97	3.14
2017 TB	AL	31	0	0	5	30.0	136	32	20	19	4	1	2	0	15	2	28	4	0	1	4	.200	0	0-3	6	4.91	5.70
4 ML YEARS		173	0	0	44	168.0	715	155	82	75	24	5	6	4	66	10	172	15	1	4	7	.364	0	1-10	25	3.91	4.02

Miguel Diaz

Pitches: R Bats: R Pos: RP-28; SP-3
Ht: 6'1" Wt: 175 Born: 11/28/1994 Age: 23

		HOW MUCH HE PITCHED						WHAT HE GAVE UP												THE RESULTS							
Year Team	Lg	G	GS	CG	GF	IP	BFP	H	R	ER	HR	SH	SF	HB	TBB	IBB	SO	WP	Bk	W	L	Pct	Sh	Sv-Op	Hld	ERC	ERA
2014 Brewrs	R	13	5	0	0	47.0	206	42	24	22	3	1	1	3	20	0	53	5	1	4	2	.667	0	0--	-	3.50	4.21
2015 Brewrs	R	7	5	0	1	20.1	81	20	12	5	1	1	4	1	5	0	23	1	0	0	3	.000	0	0--	-	3.21	2.21
2016 Wisc	A	26	15	0	8	94.2	404	83	49	39	7	1	1	5	29	1	91	12	3	1	8	.111	0	3--	-	2.97	3.71
2017 SD	NL	31	3	0	8	41.2	192	44	35	34	11	2	2	3	25	0	33	5	1	1	1	.500	0	0-0	0	6.87	7.34

Yandy Diaz

Bats: R Throws: R Pos: 3B-40;DH-6;LF-3;PH-3
Ht: 6'2" Wt: 185 Born: 8/8/1991 Age: 26

		BATTING																		RUNNING			AVERAGES			
Year Team	Lg	G	AB	H	2B	3B	HR	(Hm	Rd)	TB	R	RBI	RC	TBB	IBB	SO	HBP	SH	SF	SB	CS	GDP	Avg	OBP	Slg	OPS
2014 Carlina	A+	76	283	81	7	5	2	(-	-)	104	42	37	46	49	1	35	3	2	1	3	3	4	.286	.396	.367	.763
2015 Akron	AA	132	476	150	13	5	7	(-	-)	194	61	55	86	78	0	65	3	3	4	9	7	15	.315	.412	.408	.819
2016 Akron	AA	26	84	24	0	1	2	(-	-)	32	13	14	17	24	0	16	1	0	1	6	2	0	.286	.445	.381	.826
2016 Clmbs	AAA	95	360	117	22	3	7	(-	-)	166	53	44	69	47	1	70	1	2	6	5	1	7	.325	.399	.461	.860
2017 Clmbs	AAA	85	309	108	17	1	5	(-	-)	142	56	33	60	60	1	56	1	2	2	1	2	11	.350	.454	.460	.914
2017 Cle	AL	49	156	41	8	1	0	(0	0)	51	25	13	18	21	0	35	1	0	1	2	0	5	.263	.352	.327	.679

Alex Dickerson

Bats: L Throws: L Pos: LF
Ht: 6'3" Wt: 235 Born: 5/26/1990 Age: 28

		BATTING																		RUNNING			AVERAGES			
Year Team	Lg	G	AB	H	2B	3B	HR	(Hm	Rd)	TB	R	RBI	RC	TBB	IBB	SO	HBP	SH	SF	SB	CS	GDP	Avg	OBP	Slg	OPS
2013 Altna	AA	126	451	130	36	3	17	(-	-)	223	61	68	75	27	4	89	8	2	3	10	7	14	.288	.337	.494	.832
2014 SnAnt	AA	34	137	44	11	2	3	(-	-)	68	20	24	24	9	1	28	1	0	0	0	1	2	.321	.367	.496	.864
2015 ElPaso	AAA	125	459	141	36	9	12	(-	-)	231	82	71	88	45	2	96	8	0	7	4	0	10	.307	.374	.503	.877
2016 ElPaso	AAA	62	217	83	16	3	10	(-	-)	135	50	51	54	14	6	27	5	0	4	0	0	7	.382	.425	.622	1.047
2015 SD	NL	11	8	2	0	0	0	(0	0)	2	0	0	0	0	0	3	0	0	0	0	0	1	.250	.250	.250	.500
2016 SD	NL	84	253	65	16	2	10	(5	5)	115	39	37	40	26	2	44	4	0	2	5	1	5	.257	.333	.455	.788
2 ML YEARS		95	261	67	16	2	10	(5	5)	117	39	37	40	26	2	47	4	0	2	5	1	6	.257	.331	.448	.779

Corey Dickerson

Bats: L **Throws:** R **Pos:** LF-93;DH-55;PH-11   **Ht:** 6'1" **Wt:** 200 **Born:** 5/22/1989 **Age:** 29

Year	Team	Lg	G	AB	H	2B	3B	HR	(Hm	Rd)	TB	R	RBI	RC	TBB	IBB	SO	HBP	SH	SF	SB	CS	GDP	Avg	OBP	Slg	OPS
2013	Col	NL	69	194	51	13	5	5	(4	1)	89	32	17	23	16	0	41	0	1	2	2	2	1	.263	.316	.459	.775
2014	Col	NL	131	436	136	27	6	24	(15	9)	247	74	76	79	37	6	101	1	0	4	8	7	6	.312	.364	.567	.931
2015	Col	NL	65	224	68	18	2	10	(5	5)	120	30	31	39	10	0	56	0	0	0	0	1	3	.304	.333	.536	.869
2016	TB	AL	148	510	125	36	3	24	(7	17)	239	57	70	59	33	6	134	2	0	2	0	2	12	.245	.293	.469	.761
2017	TB	AL	150	588	166	33	4	27	(14	13)	288	84	62	87	35	6	152	3	0	2	4	3	11	.282	.325	.490	.815
	5 ML YEARS		563	1952	546	127	20	90	(45	45)	983	277	256	287	131	18	484	6	1	10	14	15	33	.280	.325	.504	.829

R.A. Dickey

Pitches: R **Bats:** R **Pos:** SP-31   **Ht:** 6'3" **Wt:** 215 **Born:** 10/29/1974 **Age:** 43

Year	Team	Lg	G	GS	CG	GF	IP	BFP	H	R	ER	HR	SH	SF	HB	TBB	IBB	SO	WP	Bk	W	L	Pct	Sh	Sv-Op	Hld	ERC	ERA
2001	Tex	AL	4	0	0	1	12.0	53	13	9	9	3	0	0	0	7	1	4	1	0	0	1	.000	0	0-0	0	6.57	6.75
2003	Tex	AL	38	13	1	6	116.2	513	135	68	66	16	4	3	5	38	5	94	5	2	9	8	.529	1	1-1	3	5.09	5.09
2004	Tex	AL	25	15	0	2	104.1	480	136	77	65	17	3	3	4	33	1	57	5	1	6	7	.462	0	1-1	0	6.08	5.61
2005	Tex	AL	9	4	0	2	29.2	134	29	23	22	4	0	1	2	17	0	15	2	0	1	2	.333	0	0-0	1	5.18	6.67
2006	Tex	AL	1	1	0	0	3.1	18	8	7	7	6	0	0	0	1	0	1	0	0	0	1	.000	0	0-0	0	32.05	18.90
2008	Sea	AL	32	14	0	9	112.1	500	124	65	65	15	4	6	2	51	4	58	11	1	5	8	.385	0	0-0	0	5.19	5.21
2009	Min	AL	35	1	0	13	64.1	293	74	34	33	8	2	2	4	30	1	42	4	0	1	1	.500	0	0-0	1	5.66	4.62
2010	NYM	NL	27	26	2	0	174.1	713	165	62	55	13	7	3	4	42	3	104	11	0	11	9	.550	1	0-0	1	3.11	2.84
2011	NYM	NL	33	32	1	0	208.2	876	202	85	76	18	16	7	9	54	2	134	9	1	8	13	.381	0	0-0	1	3.40	3.28
2012	NYM	NL	34	33	5	1	233.2	927	192	78	71	24	9	7	9	54	2	230	4	1	20	6	.769	3	0-0	0	2.70	2.73
2013	Tor	AL	34	34	3	0	224.2	943	207	113	105	35	2	6	6	71	0	177	7	1	14	13	.519	1	0-0	0	3.87	4.21
2014	Tor	AL	34	34	1	0	215.2	914	191	101	89	26	2	4	14	74	2	173	5	0	14	13	.519	0	0-0	0	3.58	3.71
2015	Tor	AL	33	33	2	0	214.1	884	195	97	93	25	3	11	11	61	1	126	9	2	11	11	.500	0	0-0	0	3.48	3.91
2016	Tor	AL	30	29	0	1	169.2	728	169	97	84	28	1	3	6	63	0	126	5	1	10	15	.400	0	0-0	0	4.57	4.46
2017	Atl	NL	31	31	0	0	190.0	815	193	99	90	26	7	5	10	67	3	136	13	2	10	10	.500	0	0-0	0	4.47	4.26
	Postseason		2	2	0	0	6.1	31	9	6	5	2	0	1	1	2	0	4	1	0	0	1	.000	0	0-0	0	8.58	7.11
	15 ML YEARS		400	300	15	35	2073.2	8791	2033	1015	930	264	60	61	90	663	25	1477	91	12	120	118	.504	6	2-2	6	4.01	4.04

O'Koyea Dickson

Bats: R **Throws:** R **Pos:** LF-5;PH-5   **Ht:** 5'11" **Wt:** 220 **Born:** 2/9/1990 **Age:** 28

Year	Team	Lg	G	AB	H	2B	3B	HR	(Hm	Rd)	TB	R	RBI	RC	TBB	IBB	SO	HBP	SH	SF	SB	CS	GDP	Avg	OBP	Slg	OPS
2013	Rcuca	A+	122	468	131	32	3	15	(-	-)	214	68	88	75	29	0	68	17	0	9	4	2	12	.280	.338	.457	.796
2014	Chatt	AA	126	461	124	36	3	17	(-	-)	217	71	73	75	38	2	67	14	2	5	5	6	7	.269	.340	.471	.810
2015	OkCity	AAA	117	386	101	27	0	13	(-	-)	167	48	50	53	21	1	63	6	1	6	2	0	10	.262	.305	.433	.738
2016	OkCity	AAA	101	329	108	28	3	18	(-	-)	196	63	64	74	36	1	64	6	0	6	1	5	6	.328	.398	.596	.994
2017	OkCity	AAA	116	403	99	22	1	24	(-	-)	195	70	76	67	44	1	97	7	0	4	4	1	11	.246	.328	.484	.811
2017	LAD	NL	7	7	1	0	0	0	(0	0)	1	0	0	0	2	1	2	0	0	0	0	0	0	.143	.333	.143	.476

Jake Diekman

Pitches: L **Bats:** L **Pos:** RP-11   DEEK-man   **Ht:** 6'4" **Wt:** 200 **Born:** 1/21/1987 **Age:** 31

Year	Team	Lg	G	GS	CG	GF	IP	BFP	H	R	ER	HR	SH	SF	HB	TBB	IBB	SO	WP	Bk	W	L	Pct	Sh	Sv-Op	Hld	ERC	ERA
2017	Frisco*	AA	5	1	0	0	5.0	18	3	1	1	0	0	1	0	0	0	6	0	0	1	0	1.000	0	0- -	1	0.75	1.80
2012	Phi	NL	32	0	0	7	27.1	131	25	17	12	1	1	0	3	20	3	35	1	0	1	1	.500	0	0-1	4	4.45	3.95
2013	Phi	NL	45	0	0	11	38.1	164	34	15	11	1	2	1	0	16	2	41	2	1	1	4	.200	0	0-1	11	2.89	2.58
2014	Phi	NL	73	0	0	19	71.0	313	66	36	30	4	2	7	3	35	5	100	7	0	5	5	.500	0	0-4	18	3.73	3.80
2015	2 Tms		67	0	0	7	58.1	260	53	28	26	5	0	0	3	31	0	69	2	0	2	1	.667	0	0-3	16	4.11	4.01
2016	Tex	AL	66	0	0	14	53.0	221	36	22	20	4	0	2	3	26	1	59	3	0	4	2	.667	0	4-5	26	2.72	3.40
2017	Tex	AL	11	0	0	2	10.2	45	4	3	3	1	0	2	0	10	1	13	0	0	0	0	-	0	1-1	5	2.58	2.53
	15 Phi	NL	41	0	0	6	36.2	175	40	23	21	3	0	0	2	24	0	49	1	0	2	1	.667	0	0-2	6	5.60	5.15
	15 Tex	AL	26	0	0	1	21.2	85	13	5	5	2	0	0	1	7	0	20	1	0	0	0	-	0	0-1	10	1.89	2.08
	Postseason		6	0	0	2	7.0	29	7	4	4	1	0	0	0	2	1	6	0	0	0	0	-	0	0-0	1	3.76	5.14
	6 ML YEARS		294	0	0	60	258.2	1134	218	121	102	16	5	12	12	138	12	317	15	1	13	13	.500	0	5-15	80	3.50	3.55

Derek Dietrich

Bats: L **Throws:** R **Pos:** 3B-103;PH-19;1B-10;2B-10;LF-5   DEE-trick   **Ht:** 6'0" **Wt:** 205 **Born:** 7/18/1989 **Age:** 28

Year	Team	Lg	G	AB	H	2B	3B	HR	(Hm	Rd)	TB	R	RBI	RC	TBB	IBB	SO	HBP	SH	SF	SB	CS	GDP	Avg	OBP	Slg	OPS
2013	Mia	NL	57	215	46	10	2	9	(3	6)	87	32	23	24	11	1	56	7	0	0	1	0	1	.214	.275	.405	.679
2014	Mia	NL	49	158	36	6	2	5	(1	4)	61	31	17	22	13	0	38	10	2	0	1	0	1	.228	.386	.712
2015	Mia	NL	90	250	64	14	3	10	(3	7)	114	38	24	32	23	2	65	13	0	3	0	2	4	.256	.346	.456	.802
2016	Mia	NL	128	351	98	25	4	7	(3	4)	149	39	42	57	32	2	84	24	0	5	1	0	6	.279	.374	.425	.798
2017	Mia	NL	135	406	101	22	5	13	(7	6)	172	56	53	59	36	5	98	18	0	4	0	1	4	.249	.334	.424	.758
	5 ML YEARS		459	1380	345	72	17	44	(17	27)	583	196	159	194	115	10	341	72	2	12	3	3	16	.250	.337	.422	.759

Wilmer Difo

DEE-fo

Bats: B **Throws:** R **Pos:** SS-57;PH-31;2B-25;PR-7;3B-6;RF-3;LF-2;CF-1 **Ht:** 5'11" **Wt:** 200 **Born:** 4/2/1992 **Age:** 26

				BATTING																RUNNING			AVERAGES			
Year Team	Lg	G	AB	H	2B	3B	HR	(Hm Rd)	TB	R	RBI	RC	TBB	IBB	SO	HBP	SH	SF	SB	CS	GDP	Avg	OBP	Slg	OPS
2017 Syrcse*	AAA	10	40	7	2	0	0	(- -)	9	5	1	2	5	0	6	0	0	0	0	0	2	.175	.267	.225	.492
2015 Was	NL	15	11	2	0	0	0	(0 0)	2	1	0	0	0	0	2	0	0	0	0	0	0	.182	.182	.182	.364
2016 Was	NL	31	58	16	3	0	1	(1 0)	22	14	7	9	8	1	12	0	0	0	3	0	0	.276	.364	.379	.743
2017 Was	NL	124	332	90	10	4	5	(3 2)	123	47	21	34	24	6	74	1	5	3	10	1	7	.271	.319	.370	.690
Postseason		2	2	0	0	0	0	(0 0)	0	0	0	0	0	0	1	0	0	0	0	0	0	.000	.000	.000	.000
3 ML YEARS		170	401	108	13	4	6	(4 2)	147	62	28	43	32	7	88	1	5	3	13	1	7	.269	.323	.367	.689

Josh Donaldson

Bats: R **Throws:** R **Pos:** 3B-105;DH-7;SS-4;PH-1 **Ht:** 6'1" **Wt:** 210 **Born:** 12/8/1985 **Age:** 32

				BATTING																RUNNING			AVERAGES			
Year Team	Lg	G	AB	H	2B	3B	HR	(Hm Rd)	TB	R	RBI	RC	TBB	IBB	SO	HBP	SH	SF	SB	CS	GDP	Avg	OBP	Slg	OPS
2010 Oak	AL	14	32	5	1	0	1	(0 1)	9	1	4	3	2	0	12	0	0	0	0	0	0	.156	.206	.281	.487
2012 Oak	AL	75	274	66	16	0	9	(3 6)	109	34	33	33	14	0	61	5	0	1	4	1	6	.241	.289	.398	.687
2013 Oak	AL	158	579	174	37	3	24	(13 11)	289	89	93	112	76	2	110	6	1	6	5	2	15	.301	.384	.499	.883
2014 Oak	AL	158	608	155	31	2	29	(11 18)	277	93	98	105	76	5	130	7	0	4	8	0	16	.255	.342	.456	.798
2015 Tor	AL	158	620	184	41	2	41	(24 17)	352	122	123	131	73	0	133	6	2	10	6	0	16	.297	.371	.568	.939
2016 Tor	AL	155	577	164	32	5	37	(21 16)	352	122	99	121	109	6	119	9	2	3	7	1	16	.284	.404	.549	.953
2017 Tor	AL	113	415	112	21	0	33	(14 19)	232	65	78	98	76	1	111	3	0	2	2	2	5	.270	.385	.559	.944
Postseason		31	120	35	10	0	4	(3 1)	57	17	13	21	12	1	31	1	0	0	1	0	2	.292	.361	.475	.836
7 ML YEARS		831	3105	860	179	12	174	(86 88)	1585	526	528	603	426	14	676	36	5	26	32	6	74	.277	.368	.510	.878

Sean Doolittle

Pitches: L **Bats:** L **Pos:** RP-53 **Ht:** 6'2" **Wt:** 210 **Born:** 9/26/1986 **Age:** 31

		HOW MUCH HE PITCHED						WHAT HE GAVE UP												THE RESULTS						
Year Team	Lg	G	GS	CG	GF	IP	BFP	H	R	ER	HR	SH	SF	HB	TBB	IBB	SO	WP	Bk	W	L	Pct	Sh	Sv-Op	Hld	ERC	ERA
2012 Oak	AL	44	0	0	7	47.1	191	40	18	16	3	2	2	0	11	1	60	0	0	2	1	.667	0	1-2	18	2.36	3.04
2013 Oak	AL	70	0	0	11	69.0	266	53	24	24	4	3	0	2	13	1	60	2	0	5	5	.500	0	2-7	26	2.00	3.13
2014 Oak	AL	61	0	0	40	62.2	236	38	19	19	5	2	1	0	8	1	89	0	0	2	4	.333	0	22-26	5	1.23	2.73
2015 Oak	AL	12	0	0	7	13.2	57	12	6	6	1	0	1	0	5	0	15	0	0	1	0	1.000	0	4-5	1	3.10	3.95
2016 Oak	AL	44	0	0	13	39.0	155	33	14	14	6	4	0	0	8	2	45	1	0	2	3	.400	0	4-6	10	2.79	3.23
2017 2 Tms		53	0	0	34	51.1	197	34	18	16	5	0	3	0	10	1	62	3	0	2	0	1.000	0	24-26	19	1.62	2.81
17 Oak	AL	23	0	0	6	21.1	79	12	8	8	3	0	1	0	2	0	31	1	0	1	0	1.000	0	3-4	8	1.23	3.38
17 Was	NL	30	0	0	28	30.0	118	22	10	8	2	0	2	0	8	1	31	2	0	1	0	1.000	0	21-22	1	1.99	2.40
Postseason		8	0	0	1	9.0	41	10	6	4	1	3	1	0	2	0	11	0	0	0	1	.000	0	0-3	7	3.75	4.00
6 ML YEARS		284	0	0	112	283.0	1102	210	99	95	24	11	7	2	55	6	331	6	0	14	13	.519	0	57-72	69	1.92	3.02

Brian Dozier

DOE-zhur

Bats: R **Throws:** R **Pos:** 2B-152;PH-1 **Ht:** 5'11" **Wt:** 200 **Born:** 5/15/1987 **Age:** 31

				BATTING																RUNNING			AVERAGES			
Year Team	Lg	G	AB	H	2B	3B	HR	(Hm Rd)	TB	R	RBI	RC	TBB	IBB	SO	HBP	SH	SF	SB	CS	GDP	Avg	OBP	Slg	OPS
2012 Min	AL	84	316	74	11	1	6	(4 2)	105	33	33	24	16	0	58	1	4	3	9	2	10	.234	.271	.332	.603
2013 Min	AL	147	558	136	33	4	18	(8 10)	231	72	66	74	51	0	120	6	3	4	14	7	14	.244	.312	.414	.726
2014 Min	AL	156	598	145	33	1	23	(11 12)	249	112	71	87	89	1	129	9	3	6	21	7	8	.242	.345	.416	.762
2015 Min	AL	157	628	148	39	4	28	(13 15)	279	101	77	87	61	2	148	7	0	8	12	4	10	.236	.307	.444	.751
2016 Min	AL	155	615	165	35	5	42	(21 21)	336	104	99	102	61	6	138	8	2	5	18	2	12	.268	.340	.546	.886
2017 Min	AL	152	617	166	30	4	34	(18 16)	306	106	93	106	78	6	141	8	0	2	16	7	11	.269	.357	.496	.853
6 ML YEARS		851	3332	834	181	19	151	(75 76)	1506	528	439	480	356	15	734	39	12	30	90	29	65	.250	.327	.452	.779

Oliver Drake

Pitches: R **Bats:** R **Pos:** RP-64 **Ht:** 6'4" **Wt:** 215 **Born:** 1/13/1987 **Age:** 31

		HOW MUCH HE PITCHED						WHAT HE GAVE UP												THE RESULTS						
Year Team	Lg	G	GS	CG	GF	IP	BFP	H	R	ER	HR	SH	SF	HB	TBB	IBB	SO	WP	Bk	W	L	Pct	Sh	Sv-Op	Hld	ERC	ERA
2015 Bal	AL	13	0	0	5	15.2	72	16	7	5	1	0	2	0	9	0	17	3	0	0	0	-	0	0-0	2	4.50	2.87
2016 Bal	AL	14	0	0	5	18.0	74	11	11	8	2	1	0	0	7	0	21	1	0	1	0	1.000	0	0-1	5	2.01	4.00
2017 2 Tms		64	0	0	15	56.0	251	63	31	29	6	3	0	0	25	2	62	3	1	3	5	.375	0	1-4	5	4.96	4.66
17 Bal	AL	3	0	0	1	3.1	18	6	3	3	0	0	0	0	3	0	3	1	0	0	0	-	0	0-0	0	10.76	8.10
17 Mil	NL	61	0	0	14	52.2	233	57	28	26	6	3	0	0	22	2	59	2	1	3	5	.375	0	1-4	5	4.63	4.44
3 ML YEARS		91	0	0	25	89.2	397	90	49	42	9	4	2	0	41	2	100	7	1	4	5	.444	0	1-5	7	4.22	4.22

Stephen Drew

Bats: L **Throws:** R **Pos:** PH-24;SS-13;3B-11;2B-2 **Ht:** 6'0" **Wt:** 200 **Born:** 3/16/1983 **Age:** 35

				BATTING																RUNNING			AVERAGES			
Year Team	Lg	G	AB	H	2B	3B	HR	(Hm Rd)	TB	R	RBI	RC	TBB	IBB	SO	HBP	SH	SF	SB	CS	GDP	Avg	OBP	Slg	OPS
2006 Ari	NL	59	209	66	13	7	5	(3 2)	108	27	23	31	14	4	50	0	2	1	2	0	1	.316	.357	.517	.874
2007 Ari	NL	150	543	129	28	4	12	(6 6)	201	60	60	71	60	5	100	3	5	8	9	0	4	.238	.313	.370	.683
2008 Ari	NL	152	611	178	44	11	21	(9 12)	307	91	67	97	41	3	109	1	3	6	3	3	5	.291	.333	.502	.836
2009 Ari	NL	135	533	139	29	12	12	(4 8)	228	71	65	76	49	7	87	1	5	7	5	1	5	.261	.320	.428	.748
2010 Ari	NL	151	565	157	33	12	15	(5 10)	259	83	61	84	62	2	108	3	2	7	10	5	8	.278	.352	.458	.810
2011 Ari	NL	86	321	81	21	5	5	(3 2)	127	44	45	41	30	2	74	1	1	1	4	4	3	.252	.317	.396	.713
2012 2 Tms		79	287	64	13	1	7	(4 3)	100	38	28	30	37	2	76	0	0	3	1	2	2	.223	.309	.348	.657
2013 Bos	AL	124	442	112	29	8	13	(6 7)	196	57	67	63	54	3	124	1	0	4	6	0	9	.253	.333	.443	.777

Year Team	Lg	G	AB	H	2B	3B	HR	(Hm	Rd)	TB	R	RBI	RC	TBB	IBB	SO	HBP	SH	SF	SB	CS	GDP	Avg	OBP	Slg	OPS
								BATTING												**RUNNING**			**AVERAGES**			
2014 2 Tms	AL	85	271	44	14	1	7	(4	3)	81	18	26	19	27	3	75	0	0	2	1	1	1	.162	.237	.299	.536
2015 NYY	AL	131	383	77	16	1	17	(9	8)	146	43	44	40	37	1	71	1	4	3	0	2	7	.201	.271	.381	.652
2016 Was	NL	70	143	38	11	1	8	(6	2)	75	24	21	22	16	0	31	2	0	4	0	1	3	.266	.339	.524	.864
2017 Was	NL	46	95	24	7	0	1	(1	0)	34	9	17	13	8	0	21	0	0	3	0	0	2	.253	.302	.358	.660
12 Ari	NL	40	135	26	8	1	2	(0	2)	42	17	12	12	19	1	35	0	0	1	0	1	1	.193	.290	.311	.601
12 Oak	AL	39	152	38	5	0	5	(4	1)	58	21	16	18	18	1	41	0	0	2	1	1	1	.250	.326	.382	.707
14 Bos	AL	39	131	23	6	1	4	(2	2)	43	11	11	12	14	2	39	0	0	0	1	1	1	.176	.255	.328	.583
14 NYY	AL	46	140	21	8	0	3	(2	1)	38	7	15	7	13	1	36	0	0	2	0	0	0	.150	.219	.271	.491
Postseason		32	108	22	3	2	3	(2	1)	38	10	9	8	6	0	36	0	0	1	1	0	1	.204	.243	.352	.595
12 ML YEARS		1268	4403	1109	258	63	123	(60	63)	1862	565	524	587	435	33	926	13	22	44	41	19	50	.252	.318	.423	.741

Brandon Drury

Bats: R **Throws:** R **Pos:** 2B-114;PH-20;DH-3;3B-1   DROO-ree   **Ht:** 6'2" **Wt:** 210 **Born:** 8/21/1992 **Age:** 25

Year Team	Lg	G	AB	H	2B	3B	HR	(Hm	Rd)	TB	R	RBI	RC	TBB	IBB	SO	HBP	SH	SF	SB	CS	GDP	Avg	OBP	Slg	OPS
								BATTING												**RUNNING**			**AVERAGES**			
2015 Ari	NL	20	56	12	3	0	2	(0	2)	21	3	8	4	2	0	8	1	0	0	0	0	5	.214	.254	.375	.629
2016 Ari	NL	134	461	130	31	1	16	(12	4)	211	59	53	59	31	2	100	3	0	4	1	1	14	.282	.329	.458	.786
2017 Ari	NL	135	445	119	37	2	13	(7	6)	199	41	63	62	28	1	103	5	0	2	1	1	9	.267	.317	.447	.764
3 ML YEARS		289	962	261	71	3	31	(19	12)	431	103	124	125	61	3	211	9	0	6	2	2	28	.271	.319	.448	.767

Lucas Duda

Bats: L **Throws:** R **Pos:** 1B-93;DH-24;PH-11   DOO-duh   **Ht:** 6'4" **Wt:** 255 **Born:** 2/3/1986 **Age:** 32

Year Team	Lg	G	AB	H	2B	3B	HR	(Hm	Rd)	TB	R	RBI	RC	TBB	IBB	SO	HBP	SH	SF	SB	CS	GDP	Avg	OBP	Slg	OPS
								BATTING												**RUNNING**			**AVERAGES**			
2010 NYM	NL	29	84	17	6	0	4	(3	1)	35	11	13	5	6	0	22	1	0	1	0	0	2	.202	.261	.417	.678
2011 NYM	NL	100	301	88	21	3	10	(2	8)	145	38	50	44	33	3	57	7	1	5	1	0	5	.292	.370	.482	.852
2012 NYM	NL	121	401	96	15	0	15	(9	6)	156	43	57	58	51	0	120	4	0	3	1	0	5	.239	.329	.389	.718
2013 NYM	NL	100	318	71	16	0	15	(9	6)	132	42	33	38	55	4	102	9	0	2	0	3	1	.223	.352	.415	.767
2014 NYM	NL	153	514	130	27	0	30	(14	16)	247	74	92	91	69	8	135	9	0	4	3	2	9	.253	.349	.481	.830
2015 NYM	NL	135	471	115	33	4	27	(19	8)	229	67	73	69	66	7	138	14	0	3	0	2	12	.244	.352	.486	.838
2016 NYM	NL	47	153	35	7	0	7	(4	3)	63	20	23	18	15	2	36	2	0	2	0	0	1	.229	.302	.412	.714
2017 2 Tms		127	423	92	28	0	30	(15	15)	210	50	64	57	60	6	135	6	0	2	0	0	9	.217	.322	.496	.818
17 NYM	NL	75	252	62	21	0	17	(11	6)	134	30	37	37	37	4	73	2	0	0	0	0	6	.246	.347	.532	.879
17 TB	AL	52	171	30	7	0	13	(4	9)	76	20	27	20	23	2	62	4	0	2	0	0	3	.175	.285	.444	.729
Postseason		14	47	11	2	0	1	(0	1)	16	3	8	7	5	0	20	0	1	1	0	0	0	.234	.302	.340	.642
8 ML YEARS		812	2665	644	153	3	138	(75	63)	1217	345	405	380	355	30	745	52	1	22	5	7	44	.242	.340	.457	.796

Brian Duensing

Pitches: L **Bats:** L **Pos:** RP-68   DUNN-sing   **Ht:** 6'0" **Wt:** 200 **Born:** 2/22/1983 **Age:** 35

Year Team	Lg	G	GS	CG	GF	IP	BFP	H	R	ER	HR	SH	SF	HB	TBB	IBB	SO	WP	Bk	W	L	Pct	Sh	Sv-Op	Hld	ERC	ERA
			HOW MUCH HE PITCHED							**WHAT HE GAVE UP**												**THE RESULTS**				
2009 Min	AL	24	9	0	3	84.0	359	84	37	34	7	3	2	3	31	1	53	1	0	5	2	.714	0	0-0	1	4.00	3.64
2010 Min	AL	53	13	1	11	130.2	535	122	42	38	11	4	0	3	35	5	78	1	0	10	3	.769	1	0-0	9	3.18	2.62
2011 Min	AL	32	28	1	0	161.2	711	193	102	94	21	7	6	1	52	3	115	3	0	9	14	.391	1	0-0	0	5.12	5.23
2012 Min	AL	55	11	0	8	109.0	472	126	71	62	10	2	3	2	27	3	69	5	0	4	12	.250	0	0-1	7	4.31	5.12
2013 Min	AL	73	0	0	9	61.0	268	68	28	27	4	2	2	2	22	4	56	6	0	6	2	.750	0	1-4	15	4.35	3.98
2014 Min	AL	62	0	0	10	54.1	229	52	20	20	6	1	1	4	20	2	33	2	0	3	3	.500	0	0-4	7	3.84	3.31
2015 Min	AL	55	0	0	9	48.2	209	46	24	23	5	2	1	4	21	4	24	3	0	4	1	.800	0	1-2	6	4.17	4.25
2016 Bal	AL	14	0	0	4	13.1	55	13	6	6	2	0	0	0	3	1	10	1	0	1	0	1.000	0	0-0	0	3.47	4.05
2017 ChC	NL	68	0	0	12	62.1	257	58	19	19	6	1	0	2	18	1	61	2	0	1	1	.500	0	0-1	13	3.39	2.74
Postseason		3	2	0	0	8.1	40	14	10	10	2	0	0	0	2	0	5	1	0	0	2	.000	0	0-0	0	8.79	10.80
9 ML YEARS		436	61	2	66	725.0	3095	762	349	323	72	22	16	18	229	24	499	24	0	43	38	.531	2	2-12	58	4.10	4.01

Tyler Duffey

Pitches: R **Bats:** R **Pos:** RP-56   **Ht:** 6'3" **Wt:** 220 **Born:** 12/27/1990 **Age:** 27

Year Team	Lg	G	GS	CG	GF	IP	BFP	H	R	ER	HR	SH	SF	HB	TBB	IBB	SO	WP	Bk	W	L	Pct	Sh	Sv-Op	Hld	ERC	ERA
			HOW MUCH HE PITCHED							**WHAT HE GAVE UP**												**THE RESULTS**				
2015 Min	AL	10	10	0	0	58.0	242	56	20	20	4	3	0	0	20	0	53	1	0	5	1	.833	0	0-0	0	3.51	3.10
2016 Min	AL	26	26	0	0	133.0	596	167	103	95	25	2	2	6	32	1	114	9	1	9	12	.429	0	0-0	0	5.66	6.43
2017 Min	AL	56	0	0	7	71.0	310	79	41	39	9	1	3	1	18	5	67	4	0	2	3	.400	0	1-3	12	4.17	4.94
3 ML YEARS		92	36	0	7	262.0	1148	302	164	154	38	6	5	7	70	8	234	14	1	16	16	.500	0	1-3	12	4.76	5.29

Danny Duffy

Pitches: L **Bats:** L **Pos:** SP-24   **Ht:** 6'3" **Wt:** 205 **Born:** 12/21/1988 **Age:** 29

Year Team	Lg	G	GS	CG	GF	IP	BFP	H	R	ER	HR	SH	SF	HB	TBB	IBB	SO	WP	Bk	W	L	Pct	Sh	Sv-Op	Hld	ERC	ERA
			HOW MUCH HE PITCHED							**WHAT HE GAVE UP**												**THE RESULTS**				
2011 KC	AL	20	20	0	0	105.1	474	119	66	66	15	2	2	5	51	1	87	4	1	4	8	.333	0	0-0	0	5.76	5.64
2012 KC	AL	6	6	0	0	27.2	121	26	13	12	2	0	0	0	18	1	28	0	1	2	2	.500	0	0-0	0	4.58	3.90
2013 KC	AL	5	5	0	0	24.1	104	19	5	5	0	0	0	1	14	0	22	2	0	2	0	1.000	0	0-0	0	3.02	1.85
2014 KC	AL	31	25	0	1	149.1	606	113	52	42	12	3	4	5	53	2	113	5	0	9	12	.429	0	0-0	1	2.62	2.53
2015 KC	AL	30	24	0	1	136.2	588	137	64	62	15	3	5	9	53	0	102	11	0	7	8	.467	0	1-1	2	4.44	4.08
2016 KC	AL	42	26	1	5	179.2	731	163	71	70	27	4	2	7	42	0	188	4	0	12	3	.800	0	0-0	1	3.44	3.51
2017 KC	AL	24	24	0	0	146.1	609	143	67	62	18	6	2	4	41	0	130	2	2	9	10	.474	0	0-0	0	3.55	3.81
Postseason		9	0	0	1	10.2	44	10	6	6	2	1	1	0	4	0	14	0	0	2	0	1.000	0	0-0	0	4.35	5.06
7 ML YEARS		158	130	1	7	769.1	3233	720	338	319	84	18	15	31	272	4	670	28	4	45	43	.511	0	1-1	4	3.80	3.73

Matt Duffy

Bats: R Throws: R Pos: IF

Ht: 6'2" Wt: 170 Born: 1/15/1991 Age: 27

Year	Team	Lg	G	AB	H	2B	3B	HR	(Hm	Rd)	TB	R	RBI	RC	TBB	IBB	SO	HBP	SH	SF	SB	CS	GDP	Avg	OBP	Slg	OPS
2014	SF	NL	34	60	16	2	0	0	(0	0)	18	5	8	8	1	0	14	2	1	0	0	1	1	.267	.302	.300	.602
2015	SF	NL	149	573	169	28	6	12	(7	5)	245	77	77	84	30	0	96	5	2	2	12	0	22	.295	.334	.428	.762
2016	2 Tms		91	333	86	14	2	5	(1	4)	119	41	28	30	23	0	53	4	2	4	8	5	13	.258	.310	.357	.668
16	SF	NL	70	257	65	11	2	4	(1	3)	92	32	21	23	20	0	40	4	2	3	8	4	9	.253	.313	.358	.671
16	TB	AL	21	76	21	3	0	1	(0	1)	27	9	7	7	3	0	13	0	0	1	0	1	4	.276	.300	.355	.655
	Postseason		8	6	1	0	0	0	(0	0)	1	2	0	0	0	0	2	0	1	0	0	0	0	.167	.167	.167	.333
	3 ML YEARS		274	966	271	44	8	17	(8	9)	382	123	113	122	54	0	163	11	5	6	20	6	36	.281	.324	.395	.719

Zach Duke

Pitches: L Bats: L Pos: RP-27

Ht: 6'2" Wt: 210 Born: 4/19/1983 Age: 35

Year	Team	Lg	G	GS	CG	GF	IP	BFP	H	R	ER	HR	SH	SF	HB	TBB	IBB	SO	WP	Bk	W	L	Pct	Sh	Sv-Op	Hld	ERC	ERA
2017 Memp*		AAA	6	0	0	1	6.0	21	2	0	0	0	0	0	1	0	6	0	0	0	0	-	0	0--	-	0.45	0.00
2005	Pit	NL	14	14	0	0	84.2	341	79	20	17	3	3	1	2	23	2	58	1	0	8	2	.800	0	0-0	0	2.96	1.81
2006	Pit	NL	34	34	2	0	215.1	935	255	116	107	17	13	4	7	68	6	117	8	1	10	15	.400	1	0-0	0	4.82	4.47
2007	Pit	NL	20	19	0	0	107.1	482	161	74	66	14	2	4	3	25	2	41	0	1	3	8	.273	0	0-0	0	6.96	5.53
2008	Pit	NL	31	31	1	0	185.0	829	230	111	99	19	14	4	7	47	1	87	2	2	5	14	.263	1	0-0	0	4.99	4.82
2009	Pit	NL	32	32	3	0	213.0	891	231	101	96	23	18	10	3	49	0	106	2	1	11	16	.407	1	0-0	0	4.05	4.06
2010	Pit	NL	29	29	0	0	159.0	730	212	115	101	25	9	6	4	51	2	96	4	3	8	15	.348	0	0-0	0	6.22	5.72
2011	Ari	NL	21	9	0	5	76.2	338	101	42	42	6	3	3	1	19	0	32	1	0	3	4	.429	0	1-1	0	5.27	4.93
2012	Was	NL	8	0	0	3	13.2	56	11	2	2	0	0	0	0	4	0	10	0	0	1	0	1.000	0	0-0	1	2.00	1.32
2013	2 Tms	NL	26	1	0	3	31.1	142	39	23	21	3	2	2	1	10	3	18	2	0	1	2	.333	0	0-0	1	5.04	6.03
2014	Mil	NL	74	0	0	13	58.2	238	49	19	16	3	0	4	0	17	1	74	3	0	5	1	.833	0	0-4	12	2.46	2.45
2015	CWS	AL	71	0	0	14	60.2	255	47	26	23	9	2	1	3	32	4	66	0	0	3	6	.333	0	1-3	26	3.82	3.41
2016	2 Tms		81	0	0	13	61.0	258	48	16	16	2	3	1	4	29	3	68	4	0	2	1	.667	0	2-5	26	2.93	2.36
2017	StL	NL	27	0	0	1	18.1	74	13	8	8	3	0	0	2	6	2	12	2	0	1	1	.500	0	0-0	6	2.95	3.93
13	Was	NL	12	1	0	1	20.2	101	31	22	20	2	2	2	1	8	3	11	1	0	1	1	.500	0	0-0	0	6.83	8.71
13	Cin	NL	14	0	0	2	10.2	41	8	1	1	1	0	0	0	2	0	7	1	0	0	1	.000	0	0-0	1	2.01	0.84
16	CWS	AL	53	0	0	9	37.2	159	31	11	11	2	2	1	2	16	3	42	2	0	2	0	1.000	0	1-4	20	2.97	2.63
16	StL	NL	28	0	0	4	23.1	99	17	5	5	0	1	0	2	13	0	26	2	0	0	1	.000	0	1-1	6	2.85	1.93
	13 ML YEARS		468	169	6	52	1284.2	5569	1476	673	614	127	69	36	37	380	26	785	29	8	61	85	.418	3	4-13	71	4.63	4.30

Ryan Dull

Pitches: R Bats: R Pos: RP-49

Ht: 5'9" Wt: 175 Born: 10/2/1989 Age: 28

Year	Team	Lg	G	GS	CG	GF	IP	BFP	H	R	ER	HR	SH	SF	HB	TBB	IBB	SO	WP	Bk	W	L	Pct	Sh	Sv-Op	Hld	ERC	ERA
2015	Oak	AL	13	0	0	3	17.0	66	12	8	8	4	0	1	0	6	1	16	0	0	1	2	.333	0	1-2	2	3.19	4.24
2016	Oak	AL	70	0	0	9	74.1	290	50	23	20	10	0	5	1	15	4	73	6	0	5	5	.500	0	3-6	15	1.84	2.42
2017	Oak	AL	49	0	0	4	42.0	177	37	30	24	7	0	1	3	16	1	45	6	0	2	2	.500	0	0-2	20	4.08	5.14
	3 ML YEARS		132	0	0	16	133.1	533	99	61	52	21	0	7	4	37	6	134	12	0	8	9	.471	0	4-10	37	2.66	3.51

Mike Dunn

Pitches: L Bats: L Pos: RP-68

Ht: 6'0" Wt: 215 Born: 5/23/1985 Age: 33

Year	Team	Lg	G	GS	CG	GF	IP	BFP	H	R	ER	HR	SH	SF	HB	TBB	IBB	SO	WP	Bk	W	L	Pct	Sh	Sv-Op	Hld	ERC	ERA
2009	NYY	AL	4	0	0	3	4.0	20	3	3	3	1	0	0	0	5	0	5	1	0	0	0	-	0	0-0	0	7.17	6.75
2010	Atl	NL	25	0	0	5	19.0	88	15	4	4	1	0	0	0	17	2	27	2	0	2	0	1.000	0	0-0	1	4.19	1.89
2011	Fla	NL	72	0	0	11	63.0	267	51	28	24	9	4	2	2	31	2	68	3	0	5	6	.455	0	0-4	15	3.77	3.43
2012	Mia	NL	60	0	0	8	44.0	208	49	31	24	3	2	4	0	29	8	47	2	0	0	3	.000	0	1-6	18	5.10	4.91
2013	Mia	NL	75	0	0	15	67.2	282	53	21	20	5	1	3	0	28	4	72	2	0	3	4	.429	0	2-5	18	2.68	2.66
2014	Mia	NL	75	0	0	15	57.0	245	47	25	20	4	4	1	4	22	1	67	2	0	10	6	.625	0	1-4	22	3.03	3.16
2015	Mia	NL	72	0	0	9	54.0	235	46	27	27	6	0	1	2	29	1	65	2	0	2	5	.286	0	0-3	23	3.96	4.50
2016	Mia	NL	51	0	0	5	42.1	176	43	16	16	5	1	2	3	11	0	38	2	0	6	1	.857	0	0-4	8	4.13	3.40
2017	Col	NL	68	0	0	10	50.1	220	43	25	25	8	0	3	0	28	0	57	4	0	5	1	.833	0	0-1	19	4.24	4.47
	Postseason		3	0	0	1	1.1	6	2	0	0	0	0	0	0	0	0	2	0	0	0	0	-	0	0-1	0	4.47	0.00
	9 ML YEARS		502	0	0	81	401.1	1741	350	180	163	42	12	16	11	200	18	446	20	0	33	26	.559	0	4-27	124	3.79	3.66

Adam Duvall

Bats: R Throws: R Pos: LF-151;PH-6;1B-3;DH-2

Ht: 6'1" Wt: 215 Born: 9/4/1988 Age: 29

Year	Team	Lg	G	AB	H	2B	3B	HR	(Hm	Rd)	TB	R	RBI	RC	TBB	IBB	SO	HBP	SH	SF	SB	CS	GDP	Avg	OBP	Slg	OPS
2014	SF	NL	28	73	14	2	0	3	(2	1)	25	8	5	4	3	0	20	1	0	0	0	0	0	.192	.234	.342	.576
2015	Cin	NL	27	64	14	2	0	5	(3	2)	31	6	9	9	6	1	26	2	0	0	0	0	0	.219	.306	.484	.790
2016	Cin	NL	150	552	133	31	6	33	(16	17)	275	85	103	80	41	1	164	6	0	8	6	5	7	.241	.297	.498	.795
2017	Cin	NL	157	587	146	37	3	31	(12	19)	282	78	99	75	39	1	170	10	0	11	5	3	11	.249	.301	.480	.782
	4 ML YEARS		362	1276	307	72	9	72	(33	39)	613	177	216	168	89	3	380	19	0	19	11	8	18	.241	.296	.480	.776

Jarrod Dyson

Bats: L Throws: R Pos: CF-96;LF-12;PH-4;PR-3;DH-1 juh-ROD Ht: 5'10" Wt: 165 Born: 8/15/1984 Age: 33

Year	Team	Lg	G	AB	H	2B	3B	HR	(Hm	Rd)	TB	R	RBI	RC	TBB	IBB	SO	HBP	SH	SF	SB	CS	GDP	Avg	OBP	Slg	OPS
2010	KC	AL	18	57	12	4	2	0	(1	0)	23	11	5	9	6	0	16	0	2	0	9	1	2	.211	.286	.404	.689
2011	KC	AL	26	44	9	1	0	0	(0	0)	10	8	3	7	7	0	14	0	1	1	11	1	0	.205	.308	.227	.535
2012	KC	AL	102	292	76	8	5	0	(0	0)	94	52	9	36	30	1	56	1	1	1	30	5	5	.260	.328	.322	.650
2013	KC	AL	87	213	55	9	4	2	(2	0)	78	30	17	28	21	1	45	1	3	1	34	6	4	.258	.326	.366	.692
2014	KC	AL	120	260	70	4	4	1	(1	0)	85	33	24	32	22	0	52	0	6	2	36	7	5	.269	.324	.327	.651
2015	KC	AL	90	200	50	8	6	2	(2	0)	76	31	18	25	14	0	37	4	6	1	26	3	3	.250	.311	.380	.691
2016	KC	AL	107	299	83	14	8	1	(1	0)	116	46	25	45	26	2	39	3	8	1	30	7	3	.278	.340	.388	.728
2017	Sea	AL	111	346	87	13	3	5	(2	3)	121	56	30	40	28	2	55	10	4	3	28	7	3	.251	.324	.350	.674
	Postseason		19	20	2	0	0	0	(0	0)	2	3	0	0	2	0	6	0	1	0	4	2	1	.100	.182	.100	.282
	8 ML YEARS		661	1711	442	61	32	12	(9	3)	603	267	131	222	154	6	314	19	34	11	204	37	26	.258	.325	.352	.677

Sam Dyson

Pitches: R Bats: R Pos: RP-55 Ht: 6'1" Wt: 205 Born: 5/7/1988 Age: 30

Year	Team	Lg	G	GS	CG	GF	IP	BFP	H	R	ER	HR	SH	SF	HB	TBB	IBB	SO	WP	Bk	W	L	Pct	Sh	Sv-Op	Hld	ERC	ERA
2012	Tor	AL	2	0	0	0	0.2	8	4	3	3	0	0	0	0	2	0	1	0	0	0	0	-	0	0-0	0	56.02	40.50
2013	Mia	NL	5	1	0	1	11.0	54	16	12	11	2	1	1	1	5	1	5	0	0	0	2	.000	0	0-0	0	7.96	9.00
2014	Mia	NL	31	0	0	12	42.0	181	41	14	10	1	2	0	3	15	4	33	1	0	3	1	.750	0	0-1	0	3.36	2.14
2015	2 Tms		75	0	0	16	75.1	309	65	26	22	4	4	1	4	21	1	71	8	0	5	4	.556	0	2-4	21	2.77	2.63
2016	Tex	AL	73	0	0	53	70.1	285	63	19	19	5	1	0	3	23	0	55	3	0	3	2	.600	0	38-43	10	3.32	2.43
2017	2 Tms		55	0	0	34	54.2	260	67	41	37	8	1	0	3	30	7	34	2	1	4	10	.286	0	14-21	4	6.34	6.09
15	Mia	NL	44	0	0	10	44.0	190	41	21	18	3	3	1	3	17	1	41	6	0	3	3	.500	0	0-2	9	3.63	3.68
15	Tex	AL	31	0	0	6	31.1	119	24	5	4	1	1	0	1	4	0	30	2	0	2	1	.667	0	2-2	12	1.68	1.15
17	Tex	AL	17	0	0	8	16.2	91	31	23	20	6	0	0	0	12	3	7	1	0	1	6	.143	0	0-4	3	13.30	10.80
17	SF	NL	38	0	0	26	38.0	169	36	18	17	2	1	0	3	18	4	27	1	1	3	4	.429	0	14-17	1	3.80	4.03
	Postseason		5	0	0	2	4.2	21	6	1	1	1	0	0	0	1	1	3	0	0	0	0	-	0	1-2	0	5.32	1.93
	6 ML YEARS		241	1	0	116	254.0	1097	256	115	102	20	9	2	14	96	13	199	14	1	15	19	.441	0	54-69	35	4.04	3.61

Adam Eaton

Bats: L Throws: L Pos: CF-20;LF-5;RF-2;PH-1 Ht: 5'8" Wt: 185 Born: 12/6/1988 Age: 29

Year	Team	Lg	G	AB	H	2B	3B	HR	(Hm	Rd)	TB	R	RBI	RC	TBB	IBB	SO	HBP	SH	SF	SB	CS	GDP	Avg	OBP	Slg	OPS
2012	Ari	NL	22	85	22	3	2	2	(1	1)	35	19	5	13	14	0	15	3	1	0	2	3	0	.259	.382	.412	.794
2013	Ari	NL	66	250	63	10	4	3	(2	1)	90	40	22	27	17	0	44	6	3	1	5	2	4	.252	.314	.360	.674
2014	CWS	AL	123	486	146	26	10	1	(1	0)	195	76	35	77	43	0	83	5	2	2	15	9	4	.300	.362	.401	.763
2015	CWS	AL	153	610	175	28	9	14	(6	8)	263	98	56	96	58	2	131	14	5	2	18	8	5	.287	.361	.431	.792
2016	CWS	AL	157	619	176	29	9	14	(7	7)	265	91	59	92	63	2	115	14	7	3	14	5	6	.284	.362	.428	.790
2017	Was	NL	23	91	27	7	1	2	(1	1)	42	24	13	19	14	0	18	1	0	1	3	1	5	.297	.393	.462	.854
	6 ML YEARS		544	2141	609	103	35	36	(18	18)	890	348	190	324	209	4	406	43	18	9	57	28	19	.284	.358	.416	.774

Josh Edgin

Pitches: L Bats: R Pos: RP-46 EDGE-inn Ht: 6'1" Wt: 245 Born: 12/17/1986 Age: 31

Year	Team	Lg	G	GS	CG	GF	IP	BFP	H	R	ER	HR	SH	SF	HB	TBB	IBB	SO	WP	Bk	W	L	Pct	Sh	Sv-Op	Hld	ERC	ERA
2012	NYM	NL	34	0	0	6	25.2	107	19	14	13	5	2	0	2	10	0	30	0	0	1	2	.333	0	0-2	5	3.52	4.56
2013	NYM	NL	34	0	0	5	28.2	122	26	12	12	2	1	0	2	12	3	20	0	0	1	1	.500	0	1-2	3	3.57	3.77
2014	NYM	NL	47	0	0	5	27.1	104	19	6	4	2	0	1	0	6	0	28	2	0	1	0	1.000	0	0-1	5	1.77	1.32
2016	NYM	NL	16	0	0	4	10.1	45	10	6	6	1	0	2	0	6	0	11	1	0	1	0	1.000	0	0-0	0	4.70	5.23
2017	NYM	NL	46	0	0	9	37.0	166	39	16	15	3	0	0	5	18	1	27	1	1	0	1	.000	0	1-1	4	5.18	3.65
	5 ML YEARS		177	0	0	29	129.0	544	113	54	50	13	3	3	9	52	4	116	4	1	4	4	.500	0	2-6	17	3.68	3.49

Carl Edwards Jr.

Pitches: R Bats: R Pos: RP-73 Ht: 6'3" Wt: 170 Born: 9/3/1991 Age: 26

Year	Team	Lg	G	GS	CG	GF	IP	BFP	H	R	ER	HR	SH	SF	HB	TBB	IBB	SO	WP	Bk	W	L	Pct	Sh	Sv-Op	Hld	ERC	ERA
2015	ChC	NL	5	0	0	3	4.2	19	3	3	2	0	0	0	0	3	0	4	0	0	0	0	-	0	0-0	0	2.50	3.86
2016	ChC	NL	36	0	0	10	36.0	138	15	15	15	4	0	2	0	14	1	52	5	0	0	1	.000	0	2-3	6	1.33	3.75
2017	ChC	NL	73	0	0	8	66.1	262	29	22	22	6	1	1	4	38	2	94	4	0	5	4	.556	0	0-4	25	1.99	2.98
	Postseason		8	0	0	0	6.1	26	5	2	2	0	1	0	0	4	0	4	1	0	0	1	.000	0	0-0	4	3.29	2.84
	3 ML YEARS		114	0	0	21	107.0	419	47	40	39	10	1	3	4	55	3	150	9	0	5	5	.500	0	2-7	31	1.74	3.28

Zach Eflin

Pitches: R Bats: R Pos: SP-11 Ht: 6'6" Wt: 215 Born: 4/8/1994 Age: 24

Year	Team	Lg	G	GS	CG	GF	IP	BFP	H	R	ER	HR	SH	SF	HB	TBB	IBB	SO	WP	Bk	W	L	Pct	Sh	Sv-Op	Hld	ERC	ERA
2013	FtWyn	A	22	22	0	0	118.2	502	110	53	36	7	2	5	4	31	2	86	7	0	7	6	.538	0	0--	-	2.91	2.73
2014	Lk Els	A+	24	24	0	0	128.0	536	138	56	54	9	4	6	4	31	0	93	3	0	10	7	.588	0	0--	-	3.88	3.80
2015	Rdng	AA	23	23	0	0	131.2	541	136	63	54	12	6	1	4	23	2	68	3	0	8	6	.571	0	0--	-	3.46	3.69
2016	LV	AAA	11	11	0	0	68.1	263	49	24	22	2	0	3	3	11	0	55	4	0	5	2	.714	0	0--	-	1.60	2.90

Year Team	Lg	G	GS	CG	GF	IP	BFP	H	R	ER	HR	SH	SF	HB	TBB	IBB	SO	WP	Bk	W	L	Pct	Sh	Sv-Op	Hld	ERC	ERA
2017 LV	AAA	8	7	0	1	43.1	190	48	22	22	3	1	4	4	15	0	38	3	0	1	4	.200	0	0--	-	4.68	4.57
2016 Phi	NL	11	11	2	0	63.1	272	67	42	39	12	1	4	1	17	1	31	1	0	3	5	.375	1	0-0	0	4.49	5.54
2017 Phi	NL	11	11	0	0	64.1	280	79	45	44	16	2	5	5	12	0	35	2	0	1	5	.167	0	0-0	0	6.00	6.16
2 ML YEARS		22	22	2	0	127.2	552	146	87	83	28	3	9	6	29	1	66	3	0	4	10	.286	1	0-0	0	5.23	5.85

Brett Eibner

Bats: R **Throws:** R **Pos:** LF-6;CF-5;PH-5;RF-3;PR-1   eye-b-nur   **Ht:** 6'4" **Wt:** 215 **Born:** 12/2/1988 **Age:** 29

Year Team	Lg	G	AB	H	2B	3B	HR	(Hm	Rd)	TB	R	RBI	RC	TBB	IBB	SO	HBP	SH	SF	SB	CS	GDP	Avg	OBP	Slg	OPS
2013 NWArk	AA	114	441	107	17	9	19	(-	-)	199	74	41	69	53	0	149	6	1	3	7	3	6	.243	.330	.451	.781
2014 Omha	AAA	74	274	66	13	2	7	(-	-)	104	42	27	35	30	0	78	2	2	3	5	2	7	.241	.317	.380	.697
2014 Wilmg	A+	13	41	9	3	0	1	(-	-)	15	5	3	6	10	0	16	0	0	0	3	2	0	.220	.373	.366	.738
2015 Omha	AAA	103	389	118	23	1	19	(-	-)	200	65	81	74	38	3	79	1	0	2	10	0	9	.303	.364	.514	.878
2016 Omha	AAA	50	184	53	7	1	11	(-	-)	95	37	32	38	30	2	48	1	1	3	5	1	5	.288	.385	.516	.902
2017 OkCity	AAA	37	117	27	4	1	4	(-	-)	45	18	14	13	9	0	34	1	0	1	0	1	4	.231	.289	.385	.674
2016 2 Tms	AL	70	187	36	10	1	6	(4	2)	66	21	22	14	19	1	50	0	1	1	0	2	3	.193	.266	.353	.619
2017 LAD	NL	17	33	6	0	0	2	(1	1)	12	3	6	4	2	0	17	1	0	0	0	0	1	.182	.250	.364	.614
16 KC	AL	26	78	18	6	0	3	(2	1)	33	11	10	7	6	1	23	0	1	0	0	0	1	.231	.286	.423	.709
16 Oak	AL	44	109	18	4	1	3	(2	1)	33	10	12	7	13	0	27	0	0	1	0	2	2	.165	.252	.303	.555
2 ML YEARS		87	220	42	10	1	8	(5	3)	78	24	28	18	21	1	67	1	1	1	0	2	3	.191	.263	.355	.618

Jerad Eickhoff

Pitches: R **Bats:** R **Pos:** SP-24   EYE-koff   **Ht:** 6'4" **Wt:** 245 **Born:** 7/2/1990 **Age:** 27

Year Team	Lg	G	GS	CG	GF	IP	BFP	H	R	ER	HR	SH	SF	HB	TBB	IBB	SO	WP	Bk	W	L	Pct	Sh	Sv-Op	Hld	ERC	ERA
2015 Phi	NL	8	8	0	0	51.0	203	40	16	15	5	0	1	0	13	0	49	1	0	3	3	.500	0	0-0	0	2.40	2.65
2016 Phi	NL	33	33	0	0	197.1	811	187	88	80	30	6	10	8	42	2	167	6	2	11	14	.440	0	0-0	0	3.56	3.65
2017 Phi	NL	24	24	0	0	128.0	576	142	74	67	16	3	9	5	53	4	118	6	1	4	8	.333	0	0-0	0	5.00	4.71
3 ML YEARS		65	65	0	0	376.1	1590	369	178	162	51	9	20	13	108	6	334	13	3	18	25	.419	0	0-0	0	3.87	3.87

Roenis Elias

Pitches: L **Bats:** L **Pos:** RP-1   roh-EN-ees ehl-LEE-us   **Ht:** 6'1" **Wt:** 205 **Born:** 8/1/1988 **Age:** 29

Year Team	Lg	G	GS	CG	GF	IP	BFP	H	R	ER	HR	SH	SF	HB	TBB	IBB	SO	WP	Bk	W	L	Pct	Sh	Sv-Op	Hld	ERC	ERA
2017 Pwtckt*	AAA	7	7	0	0	34.0	156	43	25	25	9	0	2	4	9	0	25	1	2	1	4	.200	0	0--	-	6.78	6.62
2014 Sea	AL	29	29	1	0	163.2	693	151	77	70	16	4	4	11	64	3	143	6	4	10	12	.455	1	0-0	0	3.89	3.85
2015 Sea	AL	22	20	0	0	115.1	490	106	57	53	15	1	4	9	44	1	97	1	1	5	8	.385	0	0-0	1	4.10	4.14
2016 Bos	AL	3	1	0	2	7.2	41	15	11	11	2	0	0	0	5	1	3	0	0	0	1	.000	0	0-0	0	13.11	12.91
2017 Bos	AL	1	0	0	1	0.1	2	0	0	0	0	0	0	0	1	0	1	0	0	0	0	-	0	0-0	0	7.00	0.00
4 ML YEARS		55	50	1	3	287.0	1226	272	145	134	33	5	8	20	114	5	244	7	5	15	21	.417	1	0-0	1	4.18	4.20

Brian Ellington

Pitches: R **Bats:** R **Pos:** RP-42   **Ht:** 6'3" **Wt:** 215 **Born:** 8/4/1990 **Age:** 27

Year Team	Lg	G	GS	CG	GF	IP	BFP	H	R	ER	HR	SH	SF	HB	TBB	IBB	SO	WP	Bk	W	L	Pct	Sh	Sv-Op	Hld	ERC	ERA
2017 NewOr*	AAA	20	0	0	8	23.2	94	11	7	6	3	1	0	1	11	0	36	2	0	1	0	1.000	0	5--	-	1.89	2.28
2015 Mia	NL	23	0	0	9	25.0	105	17	10	8	1	0	2	2	13	2	18	1	0	2	1	.667	0	0-0	2	2.59	2.88
2016 Mia	NL	32	0	0	7	33.0	142	27	10	9	2	1	1	2	16	2	32	3	1	4	2	.667	0	0-0	3	3.24	2.45
2017 Mia	NL	42	0	0	12	44.2	219	48	39	36	7	0	0	6	35	0	48	4	0	1	1	.500	0	0-1	11	7.11	7.25
3 ML YEARS		97	0	0	28	102.2	466	92	59	53	10	1	3	10	64	4	98	8	1	7	4	.636	0	0-1	11	4.64	4.65

A.J. Ellis

Bats: R **Throws:** R **Pos:** C-39;PH-12   **Ht:** 6'2" **Wt:** 225 **Born:** 4/9/1981 **Age:** 37

Year Team	Lg	G	AB	H	2B	3B	HR	(Hm	Rd)	TB	R	RBI	RC	TBB	IBB	SO	HBP	SH	SF	SB	CS	GDP	Avg	OBP	Slg	OPS
2008 LAD	NL	4	3	0	0	0	0	(0	0)	0	1	0	0	0	0	2	0	0	0	0	0	0	.000	.000	.000	.000
2009 LAD	NL	8	10	1	0	0	0	(0	0)	1	0	1	0	0	0	1	0	0	0	0	0	0	.100	.100	.100	.200
2010 LAD	NL	44	108	30	5	0	0	(0	0)	35	6	16	16	14	1	18	1	4	1	0	0	5	.278	.363	.324	.687
2011 LAD	NL	31	85	23	1	1	2	(0	2)	32	8	11	11	14	0	16	3	1	0	0	1	2	.271	.392	.376	.769
2012 LAD	NL	133	423	114	20	1	13	(6	7)	175	44	52	61	65	11	107	7	4	0	0	0	17	.270	.373	.414	.786
2013 LAD	NL	115	390	93	17	1	10	(2	8)	142	43	52	43	45	1	78	3	4	6	0	2	11	.238	.318	.364	.682
2014 LAD	NL	93	283	54	9	0	3	(0	3)	72	21	25	22	53	5	57	4	3	4	0	0	15	.191	.323	.254	.577
2015 LAD	NL	63	181	43	9	0	7	(3	4)	73	24	25	25	32	1	38	1	0	0	0	0	4	.238	.355	.403	.758
2016 2 Tms	NL	64	171	37	8	0	2	(1	1)	51	11	22	19	19	2	31	2	3	1	2	1	5	.216	.301	.298	.599
2017 Mia	NL	51	143	30	5	0	6	(2	4)	53	17	14	13	12	0	29	6	2	0	0	0	6	.210	.298	.371	.669
16 LAD	NL	53	139	27	5	0	1	(0	1)	35	8	13	10	16	2	24	2	3	1	1	1	5	.194	.285	.252	.537
16 Phi	NL	11	32	10	3	0	1	(1	0)	16	3	9	9	3	0	7	0	0	0	1	0	0	.313	.371	.500	.871
Postseason		17	52	19	5	1	2	(2	0)	32	7	5	11	7	1	9	1	1	0	0	0	0	.365	.450	.615	1.065
10 ML YEARS		606	1797	425	74	3	43	(14	29)	634	175	214	210	254	21	377	27	26	16	2	4	65	.237	.337	.353	.690

Jacoby Ellsbury

Bats: L **Throws:** L **Pos:** CF-97;PH-10;DH-8;PR-7   **Ht:** 6'1" **Wt:** 195 **Born:** 9/11/1983 **Age:** 34

Year	Team	Lg	G	AB	H	2B	3B	HR	(Hm	Rd)	TB	R	RBI	RC	TBB	IBB	SO	HBP	SH	SF	SB	CS	GDP	Avg	OBP	Slg	OPS
2007	Bos	AL	33	116	41	7	1	3	(3	0)	59	20	18	26	8	0	15	1	0	2	9	0	2	.353	.394	.509	.902
2008	Bos	AL	145	554	155	22	7	9	(4	5)	218	98	47	71	41	2	80	7	4	3	50	11	10	.280	.336	.394	.729
2009	Bos	AL	153	624	188	27	10	8	(4	4)	259	94	60	97	49	3	74	6	6	6	70	12	13	.301	.355	.415	.770
2010	Bos	AL	18	78	15	4	0	0	(0	0)	19	10	5	4	4	0	9	1	0	0	7	1	0	.192	.241	.244	.485
2011	Bos	AL	158	660	212	46	5	32	(15	17)	364	119	105	134	52	1	98	9	3	5	39	15	3	.321	.376	.552	.928
2012	Bos	AL	74	303	82	18	0	4	(3	1)	112	43	26	37	19	0	43	0	0	1	14	3	5	.271	.313	.370	.682
2013	Bos	AL	134	577	172	31	8	9	(4	5)	246	92	53	90	47	3	92	5	1	2	52	4	12	.298	.355	.426	.781
2014	NYY	AL	149	575	156	27	5	16	(7	9)	241	71	70	84	49	5	93	3	0	7	39	5	9	.271	.328	.419	.747
2015	NYY	AL	111	452	116	15	2	7	(3	4)	156	66	33	51	35	1	86	7	1	3	21	9	6	.257	.318	.345	.663
2016	NYY	AL	148	551	145	24	5	9	(4	5)	206	71	56	77	54	1	84	2	4	3	20	8	11	.263	.330	.374	.703
2017	NYY	AL	112	356	94	20	4	7	(4	3)	143	65	39	52	41	3	63	5	2	0	22	3	7	.264	.348	.402	.750
Postseason			39	134	40	11	2	0	(0	0)	55	26	17	25	13	2	24	0	0	1	11	2	4	.299	.358	.410	.769
11 ML YEARS			1235	4846	1376	241	47	104	(51	53)	2023	749	512	723	399	19	737	46	21	32	343	71	83	.284	.342	.417	.760

Edwin Encarnacion

Bats: R **Throws:** R **Pos:** DH-132;1B-23;PH-2   **Ht:** 6'1" **Wt:** 230 **Born:** 1/7/1983 **Age:** 35

Year	Team	Lg	G	AB	H	2B	3B	HR	(Hm	Rd)	TB	R	RBI	RC	TBB	IBB	SO	HBP	SH	SF	SB	CS	GDP	Avg	OBP	Slg	OPS
2005	Cin	NL	69	211	49	16	0	9	(3	6)	92	25	31	24	20	2	60	3	0	0	3	0	8	.232	.308	.436	.744
2006	Cin	NL	117	406	112	33	1	15	(7	8)	192	60	72	66	41	3	78	13	0	3	6	3	9	.276	.359	.473	.831
2007	Cin	NL	139	502	145	25	1	16	(10	6)	220	66	76	86	39	4	86	14	0	1	8	1	5	.289	.356	.438	.794
2008	Cin	NL	146	506	127	29	1	26	(15	11)	236	75	68	72	61	1	102	10	0	5	1	0	13	.251	.340	.466	.807
2009	2 Tms		85	293	66	11	2	13	(5	8)	120	35	39	37	37	0	67	5	0	3	2	1	5	.225	.320	.410	.729
2010	Tor	AL	96	332	81	16	0	21	(7	14)	160	47	51	41	29	1	60	2	0	4	1	0	9	.244	.305	.482	.787
2011	Tor	AL	134	481	131	36	0	17	(14	3)	218	70	55	67	43	2	77	3	0	3	8	2	17	.272	.334	.453	.787
2012	Tor	AL	151	542	152	24	0	42	(23	19)	302	93	110	124	84	12	94	11	0	7	13	3	6	.280	.384	.557	.941
2013	Tor	AL	142	530	144	29	1	36	(12	24)	283	90	104	102	82	7	62	4	0	5	7	1	20	.272	.370	.534	.904
2014	Tor	AL	128	477	128	27	2	34	(19	15)	261	75	96	86	62	6	82	2	0	1	2	0	18	.268	.354	.547	.901
2015	Tor	AL	146	528	146	31	0	39	(18	21)	294	94	111	110	77	5	98	9	0	10	3	2	14	.277	.372	.557	.929
2016	Tor	AL	160	601	158	34	0	42	(20	22)	318	99	127	104	87	3	138	5	0	8	2	0	22	.263	.357	.529	.886
2017	Cle	AL	157	554	143	20	1	38	(15	23)	279	96	107	102	104	5	133	5	0	5	2	0	18	.258	.377	.504	.881
09	Cin	NL	43	139	29	6	1	5	(3	2)	52	10	16	19	24	0	38	2	0	0	1	1	3	.209	.333	.374	.707
09	Tor	AL	42	154	37	5	1	8	(2	6)	68	25	23	18	13	0	29	3	0	3	1	0	2	.240	.306	.442	.748
Postseason			20	75	21	3	0	4	(3	1)	36	10	14	14	11	5	13	0	0	0	0	0	2	.280	.372	.480	.852
13 ML YEARS			1670	5963	1582	331	9	348	(168	180)	2975	925	1049	1021	766	51	1137	86	0	55	58	13	164	.265	.354	.499	.853

Adam Engel

Bats: R **Throws:** R **Pos:** CF-95;LF-1;PH-1;PR-1   **Ht:** 6'2" **Wt:** 210 **Born:** 12/9/1991 **Age:** 26

Year	Team	Lg	G	AB	H	2B	3B	HR	(Hm	Rd)	TB	R	RBI	RC	TBB	IBB	SO	HBP	SH	SF	SB	CS	GDP	Avg	OBP	Slg	OPS
2013	Gr Falls	R+	56	239	72	12	3	3	(-	-)	99	44	30	42	21	0	34	10	2	2	31	8	4	.301	.379	.414	.793
2014	3 Tms	Low	103	428	113	17	10	7	(-	-)	171	71	38	62	38	1	113	9	2	2	39	12	6	.264	.335	.400	.735
2015	WinSa	A+	136	529	133	23	9	7	(-	-)	195	90	43	78	62	0	132	6	8	3	64	11	5	.251	.335	.369	.704
2016	Brham	AA	74	306	78	18	9	4	(-	-)	126	56	25	50	39	0	70	7	5	0	31	9	3	.255	.352	.412	.764
2016	WinSa	A+	14	55	18	6	1	0	(-	-)	26	15	5	12	7	0	11	1	1	0	6	0	0	.327	.413	.473	.885
2016	Charltt	AAA	41	149	36	6	2	3	(-	-)	55	19	16	16	10	0	50	2	0	0	8	5	1	.242	.298	.369	.667
2017	Charltt	AAA	46	165	36	12	2	8	(-	-)	76	20	19	24	19	1	51	4	3	1	4	3	0	.218	.312	.461	.773
2017	CWS	AL	97	301	50	11	3	6	(4	2)	85	34	21	16	19	0	117	8	8	0	8	1	1	.166	.235	.282	.517

Dietrich Enns

Pitches: L **Bats:** L **Pos:** SP-1; RP-1   **Ht:** 6'1" **Wt:** 210 **Born:** 5/16/1991 **Age:** 27

Year	Team	Lg	G	GS	CG	GF	IP	BFP	H	R	ER	HR	SH	SF	HB	TBB	IBB	SO	WP	Bk	W	L	Pct	Sh	Sv-Op	Hld	ERC	ERA
2013	2 Tms	Low	28	8	0	8	82.2	343	59	39	27	4	3	3	5	35	0	112	1	0	4	6	.400	0	1--	-	2.52	2.94
2014	Tampa	A+	13	1	0	1	25.1	99	16	4	4	1	1	0	1	10	0	26	1	0	3	2	.600	0	0--	-	2.01	1.42
2015	2 Tms	Low	13	12	0	1	58.2	232	33	12	4	0	2	3	1	20	0	55	4	0	2	1	.667	0	0--	-	1.30	0.61
2016	Trntn	AA	12	12	1	0	70.0	283	55	15	15	3	2	1	1	30	0	74	0	0	7	2	.778	0	0--	-	2.80	1.93
2016	S-WB	AAA	14	10	0	2	65.0	255	47	13	11	3	1	0	2	26	0	50	1	0	7	2	.778	0	1--	-	2.51	1.52
2017	S-WB	AAA	7	7	0	0	39.1	157	30	11	10	1	0	0	0	10	0	37	0	0	1	1	.500	0	0--	-	2.05	2.29
2017	Min	AL	2	1	0	0	4.0	21	7	4	3	2	0	0	0	1	0	2	0	0	0	0	-	0	0-0	0	10.81	6.75

Nathan Eovaldi

Pitches: R **Bats:** R **Pos:** P   eh-VOLL-dee   **Ht:** 6'2" **Wt:** 225 **Born:** 2/13/1990 **Age:** 28

Year	Team	Lg	G	GS	CG	GF	IP	BFP	H	R	ER	HR	SH	SF	HB	TBB	IBB	SO	WP	Bk	W	L	Pct	Sh	Sv-Op	Hld	ERC	ERA
2011	LAD	NL	10	6	0	1	34.2	146	28	14	14	2	2	0	2	20	0	23	0	0	1	2	.333	0	0-0	1	3.75	3.63
2012	2 Tms	NL	22	22	0	0	119.1	526	133	59	57	10	1	6	3	47	3	78	1	0	4	13	.235	0	0-0	0	4.67	4.30
2013	Mia	NL	18	18	0	0	106.1	451	100	44	40	7	6	1	1	40	3	78	3	0	4	6	.400	0	0-0	0	3.41	3.39
2014	Mia	NL	33	33	0	0	199.2	854	223	107	97	14	9	5	7	43	5	142	6	0	6	14	.300	0	0-0	0	3.89	4.37
2015	NYY	AL	27	27	0	0	154.1	673	175	72	72	10	3	3	3	49	0	121	8	0	14	3	.824	0	0-0	0	4.34	4.20
2016	NYY	AL	24	21	0	2	124.2	525	123	66	66	23	1	1	1	40	2	97	5	0	9	8	.529	0	0-0	0	4.30	4.76
12	LAD	NL	10	10	0	0	56.1	241	63	27	26	5	0	3	0	20	2	34	1	0	1	6	.143	0	0-0	0	4.54	4.15
12	Mia	NL	12	12	0	0	63.0	285	70	32	31	5	1	3	1	27	1	44	0	0	3	7	.300	0	0-0	0	4.79	4.43
6 ML YEARS			134	127	0	3	739.0	3175	782	362	346	66	22	16	17	239	13	539	23	0	38	46	.452	0	0-0	1	4.10	4.21

Phillip Ervin

Bats: R Throws: R Pos: PH-10;CF-9;LF-5;RF-5;PR-2

Ht: 5'10" Wt: 207 Born: 7/15/1992 Age: 25

Year	Team	Lg	G	AB	H	2B	3B	HR	(Hm	Rd)	TB	R	RBI	RC	TBB	IBB	SO	HBP	SH	SF	SB	CS	GDP	Avg	OBP	Slg	OPS
2013	2 Tms	Low	46	172	57	11	1	9	(-	-)	97	34	35	42	25	0	34	3	0	2	14	1	2	.331	.425	.564	.989
2014	Dayton	A	132	498	118	34	7	7	(-	-)	187	68	68	65	46	1	110	7	0	10	30	5	10	.237	.305	.376	.680
2015	Dytona	A+	109	405	98	18	0	12	(-	-)	152	68	63	60	53	2	83	9	1	7	30	7	4	.242	.338	.375	.713
2015	Pnscla	AA	17	51	12	3	0	2	(-	-)	21	7	8	9	13	0	15	2	0	0	4	3	2	.235	.409	.412	.821
2016	Pnscla	AA	123	419	100	22	3	13	(-	-)	167	71	45	70	65	0	88	18	0	3	36	10	4	.239	.362	.399	.761
2017	Lsvlle	AAA	99	363	93	20	2	7	(-	-)	138	46	40	49	37	0	83	2	5	0	23	6	13	.256	.328	.380	.709
2017	Cin	NL	28	58	15	2	0	3	(1	2)	26	8	10	10	4	0	15	1	1	0	4	1	1	.259	.317	.448	.766

Jake Esch

Pitches: R Bats: R Pos: RP-1

esh

Ht: 6'3" Wt: 205 Born: 3/27/1990 Age: 28

Year	Team	Lg	G	GS	CG	GF	IP	BFP	H	R	ER	HR	SH	SF	HB	TBB	IBB	SO	WP	Bk	W	L	Pct	Sh	Sv-Op	Hld	ERC	ERA
2013	Jupiter	A+	23	19	0	0	94.0	418	99	57	49	5	1	6	7	38	0	57	3	0	2	10	.167	0	0- -	-	4.32	4.69
2014	Jupiter	A+	25	24	1	0	135.1	580	147	73	61	7	4	4	5	34	0	105	5	0	6	6	.500	0	0- -	-	3.77	4.06
2015	Jaxnvl	AA	15	15	0	0	85.1	351	69	34	33	5	3	4	2	33	1	68	1	0	6	5	.545	0	0- -	-	2.83	3.48
2015	NewOr	AAA	6	6	0	0	30.0	137	41	20	18	3	1	4	2	9	1	20	0	0	1	3	.250	0	0- -	-	6.13	5.40
2016	Jaxnvl	AA	22	22	0	0	118.1	500	117	53	53	8	8	6	5	37	0	82	2	1	10	9	.526	0	0- -	-	3.64	4.03
2017	SnAnt	AA	6	4	1	1	34.2	153	37	17	11	2	1	2	1	16	1	19	1	0	0	3	.000	0	0- -	-	4.50	2.86
2017	Lk Els	A+	7	7	1	0	42.1	189	56	32	27	5	1	2	2	8	0	31	4	0	1	4	.200	0	0- -	-	5.41	5.74
2016	Mia	NL	3	3	0	0	13.0	59	17	8	8	4	0	0	1	6	1	10	0	0	0	1	.000	0	0-0	0	8.49	5.54
2017	SD	NL	1	0	0	0	0.0	2	0	0	0	0	0	0	0	2	0	0	0	0	0	0	-	0	0-0	0		
	2 ML YEARS		4	3	0	0	13.0	61	17	8	8	4	0	0	1	8	1	10	0	0	0	1	.000	0	0-0	0	9.25	5.54

Alcides Escobar

Bats: R Throws: R Pos: SS-162

al-SEE-dess

Ht: 6'1" Wt: 185 Born: 12/16/1986 Age: 31

Year	Team	Lg	G	AB	H	2B	3B	HR	(Hm	Rd)	TB	R	RBI	RC	TBB	IBB	SO	HBP	SH	SF	SB	CS	GDP	Avg	OBP	Slg	OPS
2008	Mil	NL	9	4	2	0	0	0	(0	0)	2	2	0	0	0	0	1	0	0	0	0	0	0	.500	.500	.500	1.000
2009	Mil	NL	38	125	38	3	1	1	(0	1)	46	20	11	16	4	0	18	2	2	1	4	2	0	.304	.333	.368	.701
2010	Mil	NL	145	506	119	14	10	4	(3	1)	165	57	41	51	36	7	70	3	4	3	10	4	8	.235	.288	.326	.614
2011	KC	AL	158	548	139	21	8	4	(0	4)	188	69	46	46	25	1	73	4	18	3	26	9	10	.254	.290	.343	.633
2012	KC	AL	155	605	177	30	7	5	(5	0)	236	68	52	72	27	2	100	8	8	0	35	5	14	.293	.331	.390	.721
2013	KC	AL	158	607	142	20	4	4	(1	3)	182	57	52	51	19	1	84	3	9	4	22	0	12	.234	.259	.300	.559
2014	KC	AL	162	579	165	34	5	3	(2	1)	218	74	50	68	23	1	83	6	8	4	31	6	12	.285	.317	.377	.694
2015	KC	AL	148	612	157	20	5	3	(0	3)	196	76	47	60	26	1	75	6	8	11	17	5	10	.257	.293	.320	.614
2016	KC	AL	162	637	166	24	6	7	(5	2)	223	57	55	66	27	2	96	3	10	5	17	4	16	.261	.292	.350	.642
2017	KC	AL	162	599	150	36	5	6	(4	2)	214	71	54	58	15	1	102	4	7	5	4	7	14	.250	.272	.357	.629
	Postseason		31	135	42	9	3	2	(1	1)	63	21	14	24	1	0	21	3	6	2	2	1	2	.311	.326	.467	.793
	10 ML YEARS		1297	4822	1255	202	51	37	(18	19)	1670	551	408	488	202	16	702	41	77	29	166	42	96	.260	.294	.346	.640

Eduardo Escobar

Bats: B Throws: R Pos: 3B-79;DH-20;SS-16;PH-15;2B-9;LF-2;C-1

Ht: 5'10" Wt: 185 Born: 1/5/1989 Age: 29

Year	Team	Lg	G	AB	H	2B	3B	HR	(Hm	Rd)	TB	R	RBI	RC	TBB	IBB	SO	HBP	SH	SF	SB	CS	GDP	Avg	OBP	Slg	OPS
2011	CWS	AL	9	7	2	0	0	0	(0	0)	2	0	0	1	0	0	1	0	0	0	0	0	0	.286	.286	.286	.571
2012	2 Tms	AL	50	131	28	4	1	0	(0	0)	34	18	9	12	11	0	31	1	2	1	3	0	0	.214	.278	.260	.537
2013	Min	AL	66	165	39	5	2	3	(2	1)	57	23	10	14	11	0	34	0	2	1	0	2	0	.236	.282	.345	.628
2014	Min	AL	133	433	119	35	2	6	(2	4)	176	52	37	53	24	1	93	2	4	2	1	1	6	.275	.315	.406	.721
2015	Min	AL	127	409	107	31	4	12	(2	10)	182	48	58	55	28	1	86	2	2	5	2	3	7	.262	.309	.445	.754
2016	Min	AL	105	352	83	14	2	6	(3	3)	119	32	37	38	21	1	72	1	2	1	1	3	7	.236	.280	.338	.618
2017	Min	AL	129	457	116	16	5	21	(12	9)	205	62	73	72	33	3	98	5	1	3	5	1	5	.254	.309	.449	.758
	12 CWS	AL	36	87	18	4	1	0	(0	0)	24	14	3	7	9	0	23	0	1	0	2	0	0	.207	.281	.276	.557
	12 Min	AL	14	44	10	0	0	0	(0	0)	10	4	6	5	2	0	8	1	1	1	1	0	0	.227	.271	.227	.498
	7 ML YEARS		619	1954	494	105	16	48	(21	27)	775	235	224	245	128	6	415	11	13	13	12	10	25	.253	.301	.397	.697

Yunel Escobar

Bats: R Throws: R Pos: 3B-87;DH-1;PH-1

you-NELL

Ht: 6'2" Wt: 215 Born: 11/2/1982 Age: 35

Year	Team	Lg	G	AB	H	2B	3B	HR	(Hm	Rd)	TB	R	RBI	RC	TBB	IBB	SO	HBP	SH	SF	SB	CS	GDP	Avg	OBP	Slg	OPS
2007	Atl	NL	94	319	104	25	0	5	(3	2)	144	54	28	52	27	1	44	5	2	2	5	3	5	.326	.385	.451	.837
2008	Atl	NL	136	514	148	24	2	10	(5	5)	206	71	60	70	59	4	62	5	7	2	5	2	24	.288	.366	.401	.766
2009	Atl	NL	141	528	158	26	2	14	(7	7)	230	89	76	90	57	3	62	10	7	2	5	4	21	.299	.377	.436	.812
2010	2 Tms		135	497	127	19	0	4	(2	2)	158	60	35	53	56	1	57	5	9	0	6	2	18	.256	.337	.318	.655
2011	Tor	AL	133	513	149	24	3	11	(8	3)	212	77	48	84	61	1	70	6	5	5	3	3	14	.290	.369	.413	.782
2012	Tor	AL	145	558	141	22	1	9	(6	3)	192	58	51	51	35	1	70	4	7	4	5	1	21	.253	.300	.344	.644
2013	TB	AL	153	508	130	27	2	9	(5	4)	186	61	56	60	57	2	73	3	6	4	4	4	19	.256	.332	.366	.698
2014	TB	AL	137	476	123	18	0	7	(2	5)	162	33	39	49	43	3	60	4	4	2	1	1	15	.258	.324	.340	.664
2015	Was	NL	139	535	168	25	1	9	(5	4)	222	75	56	78	45	0	70	8	1	2	2	2	24	.314	.375	.415	.790
2016	LAA	AL	132	517	157	28	1	5	(4	1)	202	68	39	74	40	0	67	3	3	4	0	3	21	.304	.355	.391	.745
2017	LAA	AL	89	350	96	20	1	7	(4	3)	139	43	31	44	29	0	51	2	0	0	1	4	15	.274	.333	.397	.730
	10 Atl	NL	75	261	62	12	0	0	(0	0)	74	28	19	25	37	1	31	1	2	0	5	1	9	.238	.334	.284	.618
	10 Tor	AL	60	236	65	7	0	4	(2	2)	84	32	16	28	19	0	26	4	7	0	1	1	9	.275	.340	.356	.696
	Postseason		5	19	8	2	0	0	(0	0)	10	3	2	4	0	0	1	0	0	0	0	0	1	.421	.421	.526	.947
	11 ML YEARS		1434	5315	1501	258	12	90	(51	39)	2053	689	519	705	509	16	686	55	51	27	34	32	198	.282	.350	.386	.736

Paolo Espino

Pitches: R **Bats:** R **Pos:** RP-10; SP-2   **Ht:** 5'10" **Wt:** 215 **Born:** 1/10/1987 **Age:** 31

Year	Team	Lg	G	GS	CG	GF	IP	BFP	H	R	ER	HR	SH	SF	HB	TBB	IBB	SO	WP	Bk	W	L	Pct	Sh	Sv-Op	Hld	ERC	ERA
2013	Akron	AA	15	13	0	0	79.0	355	90	52	47	10	1	4	5	27	0	73	1	1	2	5	.286	0	0--	-	5.03	5.35
2013	Clmbs	AAA	17	8	0	2	62.0	267	66	30	27	6	1	1	3	17	2	68	0	1	4	6	.400	0	0--	-	4.04	3.92
2014	Hrsbrg	AA	24	16	0	3	113.0	467	98	52	50	12	1	4	11	23	0	112	1	0	6	5	.545	0	0--	-	2.99	3.98
2015	Hrsbrg	AA	8	7	1	0	38.0	155	35	18	18	3	0	1	0	11	0	32	1	0	0	3	.000	0	0--	-	3.14	4.26
2015	Syrcse	AAA	20	19	0	0	117.2	475	116	47	43	13	4	2	4	19	0	88	1	0	8	6	.571	0	0--	-	3.34	3.21
2016	Syrcse	AAA	26	24	1	1	152.2	631	146	60	56	13	2	5	6	29	0	133	4	0	8	11	.421	0	0--	-	3.07	3.30
2017	ColSpr	AAA	16	14	0	0	75.2	320	86	40	38	12	2	1	1	14	1	73	1	0	4	2	.667	0	0--	-	4.44	4.52
2017	2 Tms		12	2	0	7	24.0	109	23	17	16	7	1	0	3	10	0	20	0	0	0	0	-	0	0-0	1	5.64	6.00
17	Mil	NL	6	2	0	3	17.2	82	17	13	12	5	1	0	3	8	0	13	0	0	0	0	-	0	0-0	0	5.94	6.11
17	Tex	AL	6	0	0	4	6.1	27	6	4	4	2	0	0	0	2	0	7	0	0	0	0	-	0	0-0	1	4.79	5.68

Danny Espinosa

Bats: B **Throws:** R **Pos:** 2B-78;PH-9;3B-4;SS-4;PR-4;1B-2;DH-1   **Ht:** 6'0" **Wt:** 205 **Born:** 4/25/1987 **Age:** 31

Year	Team	Lg	G	AB	H	2B	3B	HR	(Hm	Rd)	TB	R	RBI	RC	TBB	IBB	SO	HBP	SH	SF	SB	CS	GDP	Avg	OBP	Slg	OPS
2010	Was	NL	28	103	22	4	1	6	(4	2)	46	16	15	15	9	1	30	0	0	0	0	2	0	.214	.277	.447	.723
2011	Was	NL	158	573	135	29	5	21	(11	10)	237	72	66	83	57	4	166	19	5	4	17	6	6	.236	.323	.414	.737
2012	Was	NL	160	594	147	37	2	17	(7	10)	239	82	56	69	46	4	189	13	3	2	20	6	11	.247	.315	.402	.717
2013	Was	NL	44	158	25	9	0	3	(2	1)	43	11	12	8	4	0	47	3	1	1	1	0	1	.158	.193	.272	.465
2014	Was	NL	114	333	73	14	3	8	(5	3)	117	31	27	26	18	5	122	12	0	1	8	1	5	.219	.283	.351	.634
2015	Was	NL	118	367	88	21	1	13	(6	7)	150	59	37	40	33	5	106	6	3	3	5	2	6	.240	.311	.409	.719
2016	Was	NL	157	516	108	15	0	24	(12	12)	195	66	72	64	54	12	174	20	7	4	9	2	4	.209	.306	.378	.684
2017	3 Tms	AL	93	266	46	10	0	6	(5	1)	74	30	31	18	21	1	109	5	1	2	4	5	2	.173	.245	.278	.523
17	LAA	AL	77	228	37	8	0	6	(5	1)	63	27	29	16	19	1	91	4	1	2	3	5	2	.162	.237	.276	.513
17	Sea	AL	8	16	3	2	0	0	(0	0)	5	2	2	2	1	0	7	0	0	0	1	0	0	.188	.235	.313	.548
17	TB	AL	8	22	6	0	0	0	(0	0)	6	1	0	0	1	0	11	1	0	0	0	0	0	.273	.333	.273	.606
	Postseason		12	33	3	0	0	0	(0	0)	3	3	1	1	3	0	16	3	2	0	0	0	0	.091	.231	.091	.322
8 ML YEARS			872	2910	644	139	12	98	(52	46)	1101	367	316	323	242	32	943	78	20	17	64	24	35	.221	.297	.378	.675

Carlos Estevez

Pitches: R **Bats:** R **Pos:** RP-35   **Ht:** 6'4" **Wt:** 210 **Born:** 12/28/1992 **Age:** 25

Year	Team	Lg	G	GS	CG	GF	IP	BFP	H	R	ER	HR	SH	SF	HB	TBB	IBB	SO	WP	Bk	W	L	Pct	Sh	Sv-Op	Hld	ERC	ERA
2013	2 Tms	Low	24	0	0	4	39.1	163	34	19	16	4	3	1	1	15	0	36	5	0	6	1	.857	0	0--	-	3.42	3.66
2014	Ashvll	A	33	0	0	5	53.1	226	62	34	28	4	1	2	1	11	0	50	7	0	1	3	.250	0	0--	-	4.18	4.73
2015	Mdest	A+	14	0	0	10	19.2	72	12	3	3	0	0	0	0	5	0	25	0	0	5	0	1.000	0	5--	-	1.31	1.37
2015	NwBrit	AA	34	0	0	26	36.0	157	39	19	18	2	2	3	1	9	0	43	2	0	0	3	.000	0	13--	-	3.66	4.50
2016	Albq	AAA	5	0	0	2	5.2	26	6	2	2	0	0	0	0	3	0	4	0	0	1	0	1.000	0	0--	-	4.05	3.18
2017	Albq	AAA	33	0	0	19	33.2	130	23	6	5	2	0	0	1	10	0	34	1	0	1	4	.200	0	4--	-	2.01	1.34
2016	Col	NL	63	0	0	26	55.0	246	50	32	32	6	1	4	5	28	4	59	3	0	3	7	.300	0	11-18	11	4.23	5.24
2017	Col	NL	35	0	0	9	32.1	149	39	21	20	3	1	0	1	14	2	31	1	1	5	0	1.000	0	0-0	6	5.31	5.57
2 ML YEARS			98	0	0	35	87.1	395	89	53	52	9	2	4	6	42	6	90	4	1	8	7	.533	0	11-18	17	4.62	5.36

Marco Estrada

Pitches: R **Bats:** R **Pos:** SP-33   **Ht:** 6'0" **Wt:** 180 **Born:** 7/5/1983 **Age:** 34

Year	Team	Lg	G	GS	CG	GF	IP	BFP	H	R	ER	HR	SH	SF	HB	TBB	IBB	SO	WP	Bk	W	L	Pct	Sh	Sv-Op	Hld	ERC	ERA
2008	Was	NL	11	0	0	3	12.2	63	17	13	11	4	0	0	2	5	1	10	0	0	0	0	-	0	0-1	3	8.13	7.82
2009	Was	NL	4	1	0	1	7.1	33	6	6	5	1	1	0	0	4	0	9	1	0	0	1	.000	0	0-0	0	3.67	6.14
2010	Mil	NL	7	1	0	0	11.1	58	14	13	12	3	1	0	1	6	0	13	2	0	0	0	-	0	0-0	0	7.17	9.53
2011	Mil	NL	43	7	0	12	92.2	381	83	45	42	11	7	1	2	29	2	88	4	2	4	8	.333	0	0-3	4	3.39	4.08
2012	Mil	NL	29	23	0	0	138.1	562	129	62	56	18	7	3	0	29	0	143	4	1	5	7	.417	0	0-0	1	3.18	3.64
2013	Mil	NL	21	21	0	0	128.0	512	109	56	55	19	3	2	2	29	0	118	3	0	7	4	.636	0	0-0	0	3.01	3.87
2014	Mil	NL	39	18	0	3	150.2	624	137	77	73	29	4	4	3	44	0	127	2	1	7	6	.538	0	0-0	0	3.85	4.36
2015	Tor	AL	34	28	0	3	181.0	725	134	67	63	24	2	3	5	55	2	131	2	0	13	8	.619	0	0-0	0	2.64	3.13
2016	Tor	AL	29	29	0	0	176.0	723	132	73	68	23	0	3	4	65	1	165	5	0	9	9	.500	0	0-0	0	2.88	3.48
2017	Tor	AL	33	33	0	0	186.0	806	186	104	103	31	0	6	2	71	0	176	1	0	10	9	.526	0	0-0	0	4.48	4.98
	Postseason		10	6	1	2	47.2	180	36	15	14	5	2	0	0	4	0	43	1	0	3	3	.500	0	0-0	0	1.73	2.64
10 ML YEARS			250	161	0	22	1084.0	4487	947	516	488	163	25	22	21	337	6	980	24	4	55	52	.514	0	0-4	8	3.43	4.05

Andre Ethier

Bats: L **Throws:** L **Pos:** PH-14;LF-8   EE-thee-er   **Ht:** 6'2" **Wt:** 210 **Born:** 4/10/1982 **Age:** 36

Year	Team	Lg	G	AB	H	2B	3B	HR	(Hm	Rd)	TB	R	RBI	RC	TBB	IBB	SO	HBP	SH	SF	SB	CS	GDP	Avg	OBP	Slg	OPS
2006	LAD	NL	126	396	122	20	7	11	(9	2)	189	50	55	62	34	2	77	5	0	6	5	5	11	.308	.365	.477	.842
2007	LAD	NL	153	447	127	32	2	13	(8	5)	202	50	64	65	46	12	68	4	0	8	0	4	10	.284	.350	.452	.802
2008	LAD	NL	141	525	160	38	5	20	(10	10)	268	90	77	99	59	0	88	4	1	7	6	3	6	.305	.375	.510	.885
2009	LAD	NL	160	596	162	42	3	31	(22	9)	303	92	106	94	72	10	116	13	0	4	6	4	19	.272	.361	.508	.869
2010	LAD	NL	139	517	151	33	1	23	(14	9)	255	71	82	89	59	11	102	3	0	6	2	1	11	.292	.364	.493	.857
2011	LAD	NL	135	487	142	30	0	11	(8	3)	205	67	62	73	58	9	103	3	0	3	0	1	8	.292	.368	.421	.789
2012	LAD	NL	149	556	158	36	1	20	(14	6)	256	79	89	89	62	6	124	9	0	3	2	2	13	.284	.351	.460	.812
2013	LAD	NL	142	482	131	33	2	12	(6	6)	204	54	52	62	61	11	95	7	0	3	4	3	9	.272	.360	.423	.783
2014	LAD	NL	130	341	85	17	6	4	(4	0)	126	29	42	42	31	7	74	6	1	1	2	2	5	.249	.322	.370	.691
2015	LAD	NL	142	395	116	20	7	14	(9	5)	192	54	53	59	43	2	75	4	0	3	2	3	11	.294	.366	.486	.852

Year	Team	Lg	G	AB	H	2B	3B	HR	(Hm	Rd)	TB	R	RBI	RC	TBB	IBB	SO	HBP	SH	SF	SB	CS	GDP	Avg	OBP	Slg	OPS
2016	LAD	NL	16	24	5	1	0	1	(1	0)	9	2	2	1	2	1	6	0	0	0	0	0	1	.208	.269	.375	.644
2017	LAD	NL	22	34	8	1	0	2	(1	1)	15	3	3	4	4	1	10	0	0	0	0	0	0	.235	.316	.441	.757
Postseason			43	113	27	6	1	4	(1	3)	47	17	9	12	16	0	31	1	0	0	0	1		.239	.338	.416	.754
12 ML YEARS			1455	4800	1367	303	34	162	(106	56)	2224	641	687	739	519	68	938	58	2	44	29	28	104	.285	.359	.463	.822

Phillip Evans

Bats: R **Throws:** R **Pos:** PH-13;3B-6;2B-2 **Ht:** 5'10" **Wt:** 223 **Born:** 9/10/1992 **Age:** 25

Year	Team	Lg	G	AB	H	2B	3B	HR	(Hm	Rd)	TB	R	RBI	RC	TBB	IBB	SO	HBP	SH	SF	SB	CS	GDP	Avg	OBP	Slg	OPS
2013	Savann	A	106	350	71	13	1	2	(-	-)	92	35	25	25	30	0	60	3	1	5	4	2	14	.203	.268	.263	.531
2014	2 Tms	Low	112	392	98	16	0	4	(-	-)	126	34	39	43	39	0	60	2	1	6	0	1	15	.250	.317	.321	.638
2015	Stluci	A+	77	252	59	14	3	0	(-	-)	79	19	32	25	24	0	44	1	0	3	2	2	7	.234	.300	.313	.613
2016	Bnghtn	AA	96	361	121	30	3	8	(-	-)	175	50	39	64	19	0	60	4	1	1	1	1	5	.335	.374	.485	.859
2017	LsVgs	AAA	127	466	130	26	3	11	(-	-)	195	58	56	68	42	0	79	2	0	0	2	3	19	.279	.341	.418	.760
2017	NYM	NL	19	33	10	2	0	0	(0	0)	12	4	1	5	4	0	8	1	0	0	0	0	0	.303	.395	.364	.758

Jeurys Familia

Pitches: R **Bats:** R **Pos:** RP-26 jer-ISS fa-MEAL-ya **Ht:** 6'3" **Wt:** 240 **Born:** 10/10/1989 **Age:** 28

Year	Team	Lg	G	GS	CG	GF	IP	BFP	H	R	ER	HR	SH	SF	HB	TBB	IBB	SO	WP	Bk	W	L	Pct	Sh	Sv-Op	Hld	ERC	ERA
2017	2 Tms*	Low	5	0	0	0	5.0	18	2	0	0	0	0	0	0	2	0	6	0	0	0	0	-	0	0- -		1.01	0.00
2012	NYM	NL	8	1	0	4	12.1	52	10	8	8	0	0	0	0	9	0	10	0	0	0	0	-	0	0-0	0	3.76	5.84
2013	NYM	NL	9	0	0	3	10.2	52	12	5	5	2	2	0	0	9	1	8	3	0	0	0	-	0	1-1	0	7.20	4.22
2014	NYM	NL	76	0	0	16	77.1	322	59	26	19	3	4	2	2	32	5	73	9	0	2	5	.286	0	5-10	23	2.45	2.21
2015	NYM	NL	76	0	0	65	78.0	308	59	16	16	6	1	1	2	19	1	86	4	0	2	2	.500	0	43-48	1	2.19	1.85
2016	NYM	NL	78	0	0	67	77.2	321	63	25	22	1	2	1	1	31	6	84	3	0	3	4	.429	0	51-56	0	2.44	2.55
2017	NYM	NL	26	0	0	15	24.2	111	21	14	12	1	2	2	1	15	3	25	1	0	2	2	.500	0	6-7	2	3.48	4.38
Postseason			13	0	0	10	15.2	57	7	5	4	2	0	0	0	3	0	10	0	0	0	1	.000	0	5-8	1	1.09	2.30
6 ML YEARS			273	1	0	170	280.2	1166	224	94	82	13	11	6	6	115	16	286	20	0	9	13	.409	0	106-122	26	2.67	2.63

Jake Faria

Pitches: R **Bats:** R **Pos:** SP-14; RP-2 fuh-REE-ah **Ht:** 6'4" **Wt:** 235 **Born:** 7/30/1993 **Age:** 24

Year	Team	Lg	G	GS	CG	GF	IP	BFP	H	R	ER	HR	SH	SF	HB	TBB	IBB	SO	WP	Bk	W	L	Pct	Sh	Sv-Op	Hld	ERC	ERA
2013	Prnctn	R+	12	12	0	0	62.1	248	53	21	14	2	1	3	2	9	0	71	5	0	3	3	.500	0	0- -		2.06	2.02
2014	BG	A	23	23	1	0	119.2	498	113	60	46	9	4	4	3	32	0	107	9	0	7	9	.438	1	0- -		3.19	3.46
2015	Charltt	A+	12	10	0	0	74.1	284	51	13	11	1	2	4	0	22	0	63	3	0	10	1	.909	0	0- -		1.67	1.33
2015	Mont	AA	13	13	0	0	75.1	301	52	25	21	5	1	1	1	30	0	96	2	0	7	3	.700	0	0- -		2.33	2.51
2016	Mont	AA	14	14	0	0	83.1	344	64	39	39	5	3	0	1	36	0	93	5	0	1	6	.143	0	0- -		2.75	4.21
2016	Drhm	AAA	13	13	0	0	67.2	276	46	31	28	7	0	1	1	32	0	64	1	0	4	4	.500	0	0- -		2.75	3.72
2017	Drhm	AAA	11	11	0	0	58.2	242	44	23	20	7	0	2	1	22	0	84	4	0	6	1	.857	0	0- -		2.80	3.07
2017	TB	AL	16	14	0	1	86.2	357	71	35	33	11	1	4	5	31	0	84	6	0	5	4	.556	0	0-0	0	3.37	3.43

Buck Farmer

Pitches: R **Bats:** L **Pos:** SP-11 **Ht:** 6'4" **Wt:** 225 **Born:** 2/20/1991 **Age:** 27

Year	Team	Lg	G	GS	CG	GF	IP	BFP	H	R	ER	HR	SH	SF	HB	TBB	IBB	SO	WP	Bk	W	L	Pct	Sh	Sv-Op	Hld	ERC	ERA
2017	Toledo*	AAA	21	21	0	0	123.2	519	133	58	54	9	0	2	2	31	1	114	2	0	6	4	.600	0	0- -		3.83	3.93
2014	Det	AL	4	2	0	1	9.1	46	12	12	12	2	0	0	2	5	0	11	0	0	1	0	1.000	0	0-0	0	8.29	11.57
2015	Det	AL	14	5	0	0	40.1	186	53	35	33	10	1	1	3	17	2	24	1	0	0	4	.000	0	0-0	0	7.65	7.36
2016	Det	AL	14	1	0	7	29.1	131	25	15	15	4	1	1	2	20	1	27	2	0	0	1	.000	0	0-0	0	4.71	4.60
2017	Det	AL	11	11	0	0	48.0	219	55	38	36	9	0	2	4	20	0	49	1	0	5	5	.500	0	0-0	0	5.99	6.75
4 ML YEARS			43	19	0	8	127.0	582	145	100	96	25	2	4	10	62	3	111	4	0	5	11	.313	0	0-0	0	6.35	6.80

Kyle Farmer

Bats: R **Throws:** R **Pos:** PH-13;3B-4;C-3;1B-1 **Ht:** 6'0" **Wt:** 214 **Born:** 8/17/1990 **Age:** 27

Year	Team	Lg	G	AB	H	2B	3B	HR	(Hm	Rd)	TB	R	RBI	RC	TBB	IBB	SO	HBP	SH	SF	SB	CS	GDP	Avg	OBP	Slg	OPS
2013	Ogden	R+	41	167	58	19	0	4	(-	-)	89	37	36	34	7	0	21	6	0	4	1	1	3	.347	.386	.533	.919
2014	2 Tms	Low	93	359	102	21	5	2	(-	-)	139	33	50	49	25	0	52	6	2	3	11	3	17	.284	.338	.387	.726
2015	Rcuca	A+	44	163	55	14	6	1	(-	-)	84	33	27	33	12	0	25	5	0	2	5	2	6	.337	.396	.515	.911
2015	Tulsa	AA	76	283	77	26	1	2	(-	-)	111	25	39	35	14	3	55	4	0	4	0	1	11	.272	.311	.392	.704
2016	Tulsa	AA	74	266	68	18	2	5	(-	-)	105	31	31	36	25	0	44	3	0	3	2	0	14	.256	.323	.395	.718
2017	Tulsa	AA	33	124	42	7	0	3	(-	-)	58	21	18	24	16	1	13	0	0	1	1	0	6	.339	.411	.468	.879
2017	OkCity	AAA	59	223	68	16	1	7	(-	-)	107	32	38	36	13	0	36	4	0	0	0	4	9	.305	.354	.480	.834
2017	LAD	NL	20	20	6	1	0	0	(0	0)	7	1	2	1	0	0	3	0	0	0	0	0	2	.300	.300	.350	.650

Danny Farquhar

Pitches: R **Bats:** R **Pos:** RP-52 FAHR-kwahr **Ht:** 5'9" **Wt:** 185 **Born:** 2/17/1987 **Age:** 31

			HOW MUCH HE PITCHED						WHAT HE GAVE UP										THE RESULTS						
Year	Team	Lg	G	GS	CG	GF	IP	BFP	H	R	ER	HR	SH	SF	HB	TBB	IBB	SO	WP	Bk	W	L	Pct	Sh	Sv-Op	Hld	ERC	ERA
2017	Charllt*	AAA	8	0	0	6	9.0	34	6	3	3	2	0	0	0	2	0	12	0	0	0	0	-	0	1--	-	2.43	3.00
2011	Tor	AL	3	0	0	2	2.0	11	4	4	3	0	1	0	0	2	0	1	0	0	0	0	-	0	0-0	0	13.16	13.50
2013	Sea	AL	46	0	0	27	55.2	228	44	29	26	2	1	2	0	22	4	79	2	1	0	3	.000	0	16-20	5	2.44	4.20
2014	Sea	AL	66	0	0	22	71.0	290	58	23	21	5	1	1	4	22	1	81	6	2	3	1	.750	0	1-3	13	2.78	2.66
2015	Sea	AL	43	0	0	10	51.0	219	53	33	29	9	1	1	1	17	2	48	1	1	1	8	.111	0	1-3	4	4.60	5.12
2016	TB	AL	35	0	0	11	35.1	158	33	14	12	8	2	0	4	15	1	46	1	0	1	0	1.000	0	0-1	7	5.01	3.06
2017	2 Tms	AL	52	0	0	20	49.1	215	39	23	23	3	3	5	4	28	4	45	4	0	4	2	.667	0	0-2	13	3.45	4.20
17	TB	AL	37	0	0	17	35.0	154	28	16	16	2	2	4	4	22	4	33	4	0	2	2	.500	0	0-1	9	3.81	4.11
17	CWS	AL	15	0	0	3	14.1	61	11	7	7	1	1	1	0	6	0	12	0	0	2	0	1.000	0	0-1	4	2.61	4.40
6 ML YEARS			245	0	0	92	264.1	1121	231	126	114	27	8	10	13	106	12	300	14	4	9	14	.391	0	18-29	43	3.52	3.88

Luke Farrell

Pitches: R **Bats:** L **Pos:** RP-9; SP-1 **Ht:** 6'6" **Wt:** 210 **Born:** 6/7/1991 **Age:** 27

			HOW MUCH HE PITCHED						WHAT HE GAVE UP										THE RESULTS						
Year	Team	Lg	G	GS	CG	GF	IP	BFP	H	R	ER	HR	SH	SF	HB	TBB	IBB	SO	WP	Bk	W	L	Pct	Sh	Sv-Op	Hld	ERC	ERA
2013	Idaho	R+	10	10	0	0	43.1	192	52	32	32	5	3	1	5	15	0	45	5	0	1	3	.250	0	0--	-	5.79	6.65
2014	Lxngtn	A	23	19	0	2	108.0	485	117	76	63	13	2	5	2	47	0	102	14	0	2	12	.143	0	1--	-	4.86	5.25
2015	Wilmg	A+	7	3	0	3	29.2	121	27	12	10	0	2	2	3	6	0	41	5	2	2	0	1.000	0	2--	-	2.62	3.03
2015	NWArk	AA	19	16	0	1	93.1	393	89	38	32	7	3	3	4	29	0	65	4	1	5	3	.625	0	0--	-	3.48	3.09
2016	Omha	AAA	19	14	0	2	91.0	390	85	44	38	12	3	3	2	40	0	78	5	0	6	3	.667	0	0--	-	4.20	3.76
2017	Omha	AAA	17	16	0	0	97.1	406	89	48	44	13	4	4	2	33	0	94	1	0	7	4	.636	0	0--	-	3.70	4.07
2017	2 Tms		10	1	0	3	13.0	61	12	8	8	2	0	0	0	10	0	9	0	0	0	0	-	0	0-0	1	5.40	5.54
17	KC	AL	1	1	0	0	2.2	18	7	5	5	1	0	0	0	3	0	2	0	0	0	0	-	0	0-0	0	21.83	16.88
17	Cin	NL	9	0	0	3	10.1	43	5	3	3	1	0	0	0	7	0	7	0	0	0	0	-	0	0-0	1	2.34	2.61

Taylor Featherston

Bats: R **Throws:** R **Pos:** 2B-11;SS-3;PH-3;1B-2;3B-2 **Ht:** 6'1" **Wt:** 185 **Born:** 10/8/1989 **Age:** 28

			BATTING																	RUNNING			AVERAGES			
Year	Team	Lg	G	AB	H	2B	3B	HR	(Hm	Rd)	TB	R	RBI	RC	TBB	IBB	SO	HBP	SH	SF	SB	CS	GDP	Avg	OBP	Slg	OPS
2017	LV*	AAA	46	137	37	8	0	3	(-	-)	54	22	20	23	21	0	34	2	0	2	6	0	2	.270	.370	.394	.765
2017	Drhm*	AAA	31	120	24	5	0	4	(-	-)	41	12	15	10	7	0	58	1	0	1	2	0	1	.200	.248	.342	.590
2015	LAA	AL	101	154	25	5	1	2	(0	2)	38	23	9	7	7	0	46	3	4	1	4	2	3	.162	.212	.247	.459
2016	Phi	NL	19	26	3	1	0	0	(0	0)	4	2	1	0	2	0	11	0	0	0	2	0	0	.115	.179	.154	.332
2017	TB	AL	17	39	7	1	0	2	(1	1)	14	6	6	3	5	0	15	1	0	2	1	0	1	.179	.277	.359	.636
3 ML YEARS			137	219	35	7	1	4	(1	3)	56	31	16	10	14	0	72	4	4	3	7	2	4	.160	.221	.256	.477

Erick Fedde

Pitches: R **Bats:** R **Pos:** SP-3 fed-ee **Ht:** 6'4" **Wt:** 180 **Born:** 2/25/1993 **Age:** 25

			HOW MUCH HE PITCHED						WHAT HE GAVE UP										THE RESULTS						
Year	Team	Lg	G	GS	CG	GF	IP	BFP	H	R	ER	HR	SH	SF	HB	TBB	IBB	SO	WP	Bk	W	L	Pct	Sh	Sv-Op	Hld	ERC	ERA
2015	2 Tms	Low	14	14	0	0	64.0	272	62	30	24	2	0	1	4	16	0	59	3	0	5	3	.625	0	0--	-	3.06	3.38
2016	Ptomc	A+	18	17	0	0	91.2	372	85	35	29	7	0	1	4	19	0	95	3	0	6	4	.600	0	0--	-	3.00	2.85
2016	Hrsbrg	AA	5	5	1	0	29.1	129	33	13	13	1	0	2	1	10	0	28	0	0	2	1	.667	0	0--	-	4.20	3.99
2017	Hrsbrg	AA	17	7	0	2	56.1	228	45	21	19	4	0	0	1	18	1	54	4	0	3	3	.500	0	0--	-	2.58	3.04
2017	Syrcse	AAA	12	6	0	0	34.0	142	37	18	18	3	1	1	1	5	0	25	1	0	1	2	.333	0	0--	-	3.61	4.76
2017	Was	NL	3	3	0	0	15.1	76	25	16	16	5	2	0	1	8	2	15	0	0	0	1	.000	0	0-0	0	11.01	9.39

Tim Federowicz

Bats: R **Throws:** R **Pos:** PH-7;C-6;1B-1 fed-er-oh-vich **Ht:** 5'10" **Wt:** 215 **Born:** 8/5/1987 **Age:** 30

			BATTING																	RUNNING			AVERAGES			
Year	Team	Lg	G	AB	H	2B	3B	HR	(Hm	Rd)	TB	R	RBI	RC	TBB	IBB	SO	HBP	SH	SF	SB	CS	GDP	Avg	OBP	Slg	OPS
2017	Scrmto*	AAA	77	283	85	19	0	9	(-	-)	131	34	43	49	30	1	65	0	0	1	3	0	6	.300	.366	.463	.829
2011	LAD	NL	7	13	2	0	0	0	(0	0)	2	0	1	1	2	0	4	1	0	0	0	0	0	.154	.313	.154	.466
2012	LAD	NL	3	3	1	0	0	0	(0	0)	1	0	0	1	1	0	2	0	0	0	0	0	0	.333	.500	.333	.833
2013	LAD	NL	56	160	37	8	0	4	(1	3)	57	12	16	9	10	5	56	0	2	1	0	0	5	.231	.275	.356	.631
2014	LAD	NL	23	71	8	3	0	1	(0	1)	14	2	5	0	3	0	18	1	2	1	0	0	3	.113	.158	.197	.355
2016	ChC	NL	17	31	6	2	0	0	(0	0)	8	3	3	2	1	0	12	0	0	1	0	0	1	.194	.212	.258	.470
2017	SF	NL	13	13	3	0	0	2	(1	1)	9	3	3	3	1	0	4	0	0	0	0	0	1	.231	.286	.692	.978
6 ML YEARS			119	291	57	13	0	7	(2	5)	91	20	28	16	18	5	96	2	4	3	0	0	10	.196	.245	.313	.558

Scott Feldman

Pitches: R **Bats:** L **Pos:** SP-21 **Ht:** 6'6" **Wt:** 225 **Born:** 2/7/1983 **Age:** 35

			HOW MUCH HE PITCHED						WHAT HE GAVE UP										THE RESULTS						
Year	Team	Lg	G	GS	CG	GF	IP	BFP	H	R	ER	HR	SH	SF	HB	TBB	IBB	SO	WP	Bk	W	L	Pct	Sh	Sv-Op	Hld	ERC	ERA
2005	Tex	AL	8	0	0	3	9.1	37	9	1	1	0	0	0	0	2	1	4	0	0	0	1	.000	0	0-0	-	2.48	0.96
2006	Tex	AL	36	0	0	5	41.1	175	42	19	18	4	2	1	4	10	0	30	0	0	0	2	.000	0	0-1	7	3.94	3.92
2007	Tex	AL	29	0	0	10	39.0	192	44	26	25	3	0	2	3	32	5	19	2	2	1	2	.333	0	0-0	0	6.40	5.77
2008	Tex	AL	28	25	0	2	151.1	651	161	103	89	22	1	9	10	56	2	74	4	2	6	8	.429	0	0-0	0	5.03	5.29
2009	Tex	AL	34	31	0	0	189.2	791	178	87	86	18	1	3	6	65	0	113	5	2	17	8	.680	0	0-0	0	3.74	4.08
2010	Tex	AL	29	22	0	2	141.1	641	181	98	86	18	5	8	5	45	2	75	11	0	7	11	.389	0	0-0	0	5.71	5.48
2011	Tex	AL	11	2	0	5	32.0	129	25	14	14	3	0	1	2	10	0	22	2	0	2	1	.667	0	0-0	0	2.83	3.94
2012	Tex	AL	29	21	0	5	123.2	536	139	79	70	14	0	5	1	32	2	96	2	1	6	11	.353	0	0-0	0	4.27	5.09

Year	Team	Lg	G	GS	CG	GF	IP	BFP	H	R	ER	HR	SH	SF	HB	TBB	IBB	SO	WP	Bk	W	L	Pct	Sh	Sv-Op	Hld	ERC	ERA
2013	2 Tms		30	30	2	0	181.2	758	159	87	78	19	7	7	9	56	1	132	7	1	12	12	.500	1	0-0	0	3.24	3.86
2014	Hou	AL	29	29	2	0	180.1	765	185	86	75	16	2	7	11	50	5	107	6	1	8	12	.400	1	0-0	0	3.89	3.74
2015	Hou	AL	18	18	0	0	108.1	451	115	49	47	13	1	5	0	27	1	61	8	0	5	5	.500	0	0-0	0	4.01	3.90
2016	2 Tms	AL	40	5	0	13	77.0	338	87	42	34	10	5	3	3	19	3	56	0	0	7	4	.636	0	0-1	0	4.42	3.97
2017	Cin	NL	21	21	1	0	111.1	472	116	62	59	21	6	1	6	35	2	93	3	0	7	7	.500	1	0-0	0	4.89	4.77
13	ChC	NL	15	15	1	0	91.0	376	79	42	35	10	6	4	3	25	0	67	4	0	7	6	.538	0	0-0	0	3.05	3.46
13	Bal	AL	15	15	1	0	90.2	382	80	45	43	9	1	3	6	31	1	65	3	1	5	6	.455	1	0-0	0	3.44	4.27
16	Hou	AL	26	5	0	9	62.0	265	64	27	20	8	4	3	3	13	3	42	0	0	5	3	.625	0	0-1	0	3.75	2.90
16	Tor	AL	14	0	0	4	15.0	73	23	15	14	2	1	0	0	6	0	14	0	0	2	1	.667	0	0-0	0	7.53	8.40
	Postseason		9	0	0	1	13.2	56	8	5	5	0	2	0	2	6	2	11	0	0	1	0	1.000	0	0-1	0	1.75	3.29
	13 ML YEARS		342	204	5	45	1386.1	5936	1441	753	682	161	30	52	63	439	24	882	50	9	78	84	.481	3	0-2	8	4.26	4.43

Michael Feliz

Pitches: R **Bats:** R **Pos:** RP-46   **Ht:** 6'4" **Wt:** 230 **Born:** 6/28/1993 **Age:** 25

Year	Team	Lg	G	GS	CG	GF	IP	BFP	H	R	ER	HR	SH	SF	HB	TBB	IBB	SO	WP	Bk	W	L	Pct	Sh	Sv-Op	Hld	ERC	ERA
2015	Hou	AL	5	0	0	5	8.0	38	9	7	7	2	0	0	1	4	0	7	0	1	0	0	-	0	0-0	0	6.79	7.88
2016	Hou	AL	47	0	0	17	65.0	270	55	33	32	10	0	2	0	22	0	95	6	0	8	1	.889	0	0-3	5	3.32	4.43
2017	Hou	AL	46	0	0	13	48.0	218	53	31	30	8	0	4	0	22	1	70	7	0	4	2	.667	0	0-2	2	5.28	5.63
	3 ML YEARS		98	0	0	35	121.0	526	117	71	69	20	0	6	1	48	1	172	13	1	12	3	.800	0	0-5	7	4.29	5.13

Neftali Feliz

neff-TAH-lee

Pitches: R **Bats:** R **Pos:** RP-49   **Ht:** 6'3" **Wt:** 235 **Born:** 5/2/1988 **Age:** 30

Year	Team	Lg	G	GS	CG	GF	IP	BFP	H	R	ER	HR	SH	SF	HB	TBB	IBB	SO	WP	Bk	W	L	Pct	Sh	Sv-Op	Hld	ERC	ERA
2009	Tex	AL	20	0	0	3	31.0	117	13	6	6	2	1	0	3	8	0	39	0	0	1	0	1.000	0	2-3	9	1.14	1.74
2010	Tex	AL	70	0	0	59	69.1	269	43	21	21	5	1	0	5	18	1	71	5	0	4	3	.571	0	40-43	3	1.75	2.73
2011	Tex	AL	64	0	0	56	62.1	252	42	22	19	4	3	2	0	30	1	54	2	1	2	3	.400	0	32-38	3	2.45	2.74
2012	Tex	AL	8	7	1	0	42.2	175	28	15	15	5	0	0	2	23	0	37	0	0	3	1	.750	0	0-0	0	3.11	3.16
2013	Tex	AL	6	0	0	2	4.2	21	5	0	0	0	0	0	0	2	0	4	0	0	0	0	-	0	0-0	0	4.78	0.00
2014	Tex	AL	30	0	0	22	31.2	122	20	7	7	5	1	1	0	11	0	21	1	0	2	1	.667	0	13-14	0	2.38	1.99
2015	2 Tms	AL	48	0	0	24	48.0	212	57	34	34	5	1	1	1	18	6	39	4	0	3	4	.429	0	10-17	2	5.03	6.38
2016	Pit	NL	62	0	0	6	53.2	218	40	21	21	10	2	1	1	21	1	61	3	0	4	2	.667	0	2-4	29	3.30	3.52
2017	2 Tms		49	0	0	31	46.0	196	40	33	28	9	0	1	1	23	2	37	1	0	2	5	.286	0	8-9	2	4.49	5.48
15	Tex	AL	18	0	0	12	19.2	91	24	10	10	2	0	0	0	9	3	16	2	0	1	2	.333	0	6-9	0	5.26	4.58
15	Det	AL	30	0	0	12	28.1	121	33	24	24	3	1	1	1	9	3	23	2	0	2	2	.500	0	4-8	2	4.87	7.62
17	Mil	NL	29	0	0	21	27.0	115	23	22	18	8	0	1	0	15	2	21	0	0	1	5	.167	0	8-9	0	5.22	6.00
17	KC	AL	20	0	0	10	19.0	81	17	11	10	1	0	0	1	8	0	16	1	0	1	0	1.000	0	0-0	2	3.46	4.74
	Postseason		18	0	0	15	18.2	76	8	4	4	1	1	0	1	13	1	23	1	0	0	0	-	0	7-8	0	2.04	1.93
	9 ML YEARS		357	7	1	203	389.1	1582	288	159	151	45	9	6	14	154	11	363	16	1	21	19	.525	0	107-128	45	2.90	3.49

Jeff Ferrell

Pitches: R **Bats:** R **Pos:** RP-11   **Ht:** 6'4" **Wt:** 205 **Born:** 11/23/1990 **Age:** 27

Year	Team	Lg	G	GS	CG	GF	IP	BFP	H	R	ER	HR	SH	SF	HB	TBB	IBB	SO	WP	Bk	W	L	Pct	Sh	Sv-Op	Hld	ERC	ERA
2013	Lkland	A+	25	19	0	3	119.1	500	121	61	53	15	2	2	3	36	0	77	5	0	6	6	.500	0	0--	-	4.11	4.00
2014	Erie	AA	25	25	0	0	138.0	612	174	85	85	17	3	4	4	38	0	92	1	0	10	9	.526	0	0--	-	5.41	5.54
2015	Erie	AA	17	1	0	15	27.0	105	21	5	5	4	1	0	1	4	0	35	0	0	0	0	-	0	12--	-	2.41	1.67
2015	Toledo	AAA	11	0	0	10	11.1	46	8	6	6	3	0	0	0	5	1	10	0	0	0	1	.000	0	4--	-	3.59	4.76
2016	Toledo	AAA	6	0	0	2	7.1	39	16	6	6	1	1	0	0	2	0	13	1	0	2	1	.667	0	0--	-	11.58	7.36
2017	Erie	AA	9	0	0	6	9.2	34	4	1	1	1	0	0	0	1	0	10	1	0	1	0	1.000	0	1--	-	0.77	0.93
2017	Toledo	AAA	41	0	0	10	46.2	192	39	14	13	1	2	0	1	14	2	51	2	0	2	1	.667	0	2--	-	2.33	2.51
2015	Det	AL	9	0	0	2	11.1	50	12	8	8	3	0	1	0	4	0	6	0	0	0	0	-	0	0-0	0	5.28	6.35
2017	Det	AL	11	0	0	4	9.1	49	17	7	7	2	0	1	0	5	1	6	0	0	0	0	-	0	0-0	0	10.75	6.75
	2 ML YEARS		20	0	0	6	20.2	99	29	15	15	5	0	2	0	9	1	12	0	0	0	0	-	0	0-0	0	7.65	6.53

Josh Fields

Pitches: R **Bats:** R **Pos:** RP-57   **Ht:** 6'0" **Wt:** 195 **Born:** 8/19/1985 **Age:** 32

Year	Team	Lg	G	GS	CG	GF	IP	BFP	H	R	ER	HR	SH	SF	HB	TBB	IBB	SO	WP	Bk	W	L	Pct	Sh	Sv-Op	Hld	ERC	ERA
2013	Hou	AL	41	0	0	16	38.0	160	31	21	21	8	1	0	0	18	4	40	0	0	1	3	.250	0	5-6	6	3.94	4.97
2014	Hou	AL	54	0	0	16	54.2	231	50	29	27	2	0	5	2	17	3	70	0	0	4	6	.400	0	4-8	8	2.87	4.45
2015	Hou	AL	54	0	0	19	50.2	209	39	20	20	2	2	1	1	19	3	67	1	0	4	1	.800	0	0-2	5	2.35	3.55
2016	2 Tms		37	0	0	12	35.0	158	43	22	18	4	0	1	1	11	2	42	0	0	1	0	1.000	0	0-0	2	5.12	4.63
2017	LAD	NL	57	0	0	13	57.0	223	40	19	18	10	0	1	1	15	1	60	1	1	5	0	1.000	0	2-5	15	2.51	2.84
16	Hou	AL	15	0	0	7	15.2	71	23	14	12	2	0	1	0	3	0	20	0	0	0	0	-	0	0-0	0	6.23	6.89
16	LAD	NL	22	0	0	5	19.1	87	20	8	6	2	0	0	1	8	2	22	0	0	1	0	1.000	0	0-0	2	4.27	2.79
	Postseason		6	0	0	1	4.0	17	2	2	2	1	0	0	0	3	0	8	0	0	0	0	-	0	0-1	0	3.65	4.50
	5 ML YEARS		243	0	0	76	235.1	981	203	111	104	26	3	8	5	80	13	279	2	1	15	10	.600	0	11-21	36	3.15	3.98

Casey Fien

Pitches: R **Bats:** R **Pos:** RP-10
FEEN
Ht: 6'2" **Wt:** 210 **Born:** 10/21/1983 **Age:** 34

Year	Team	Lg	G	GS	CG	GF	IP	BFP	H	R	ER	HR	SH	SF	HB	TBB	IBB	SO	WP	Bk	W	L	Pct	Sh	Sv-Op	Hld	ERC	ERA
2017	Tacom*	AAA	5	0	0	2	5.1	25	7	2	2	0	0	0	0	0	0	3	1	0	0	1	.000	0	1--	-	3.13	3.38
2017	LV*	AAA	14	0	0	1	16.0	65	15	9	9	3	2	1	0	3	1	13	1	1	0	1	.000	0	0--	-	3.37	5.06
2009	Det	AL	9	0	0	5	11.1	53	13	11	10	2	0	2	0	6	0	9	0	0	0	1	.000	0	0-0	0	5.92	7.94
2010	Det	AL	2	0	0	2	2.2	12	4	3	3	2	1	0	0	0	0	0	0	0	0	0	-	0	0-0	0	9.96	10.13
2012	Min	AL	35	0	0	7	35.0	141	25	9	8	3	1	2	1	9	4	32	0	0	2	1	.667	0	0-0	6	1.90	2.06
2013	Min	AL	73	0	0	20	62.0	244	51	28	27	9	3	2	0	12	3	73	2	0	5	2	.714	0	0-2	17	2.59	3.92
2014	Min	AL	73	0	0	15	63.1	260	64	29	28	7	2	4	0	10	0	51	2	0	5	6	.455	0	1-5	26	3.25	3.98
2015	Min	AL	62	0	0	6	63.1	257	61	26	25	6	2	3	0	8	0	41	0	0	4	6	.400	0	0-4	18	2.77	3.55
2016	2 Tms		39	0	0	7	39.1	169	45	24	24	11	0	0	0	10	3	35	1	0	1	1	.500	0	0-1	6	5.84	5.49
2017	2 Tms		10	0	0	4	12.0	62	23	17	17	5	1	0	0	6	2	10	0	0	0	1	.000	0	0-0	0	13.52	12.75
16	Min	AL	14	0	0	2	13.2	63	21	12	12	5	0	0	0	3	0	12	1	0	1	0	1.000	0	0-0	1	8.81	7.90
16	LAD	NL	25	0	0	5	25.2	106	24	12	12	8	1	0	0	7	3	23	0	0	0	1	.000	0	0-1	5	4.42	4.21
17	Sea	AL	6	0	0	2	6.0	29	9	10	10	3	0	0	0	4	0	6	0	0	0	0	-	0	0-0	0	12.63	15.00
17	Phi	NL	4	0	0	2	6.0	33	14	7	7	2	1	0	0	2	2	4	0	0	0	1	.000	0	0-0	0	14.37	10.50
8 ML YEARS			303	0	0	66	289.0	1198	286	147	142	47	11	13	1	61	12	251	5	0	17	18	.486	0	1-12	73	3.62	4.42

Mike Fiers

Pitches: R **Bats:** R **Pos:** SP-28; RP-1
FIRES
Ht: 6'2" **Wt:** 200 **Born:** 6/15/1985 **Age:** 33

Year	Team	Lg	G	GS	CG	GF	IP	BFP	H	R	ER	HR	SH	SF	HB	TBB	IBB	SO	WP	Bk	W	L	Pct	Sh	Sv-Op	Hld	ERC	ERA
2011	Mil	NL	2	0	0	2	2.0	10	2	0	0	0	0	0	0	3	0	2	0	0	0	0	-	0	0-0	0	8.25	0.00
2012	Mil	NL	23	22	0	1	127.2	539	125	56	53	12	4	4	2	36	0	135	4	0	9	10	.474	0	0-0	0	3.50	3.74
2013	Mil	NL	11	3	0	4	22.1	103	28	20	18	8	1	2	0	6	0	15	1	0	1	4	.200	0	0-0	0	6.65	7.25
2014	Mil	NL	14	10	0	1	71.2	274	46	19	17	7	2	1	0	17	1	76	1	0	6	5	.545	0	0-0	0	1.68	2.13
2015	2 Tms		31	30	1	0	180.1	761	162	83	74	24	3	8	6	64	5	180	8	0	7	10	.412	1	0-0	0	3.64	3.69
2016	Hou	AL	31	30	0	0	168.2	724	187	89	84	26	3	5	7	42	0	134	17	0	11	8	.579	0	0-0	0	4.66	4.48
2017	Hou	AL	29	28	0	0	153.1	671	157	95	89	32	3	1	13	62	0	146	11	1	8	10	.444	0	0-0	0	5.44	5.22
15	Mil	NL	21	21	0	0	118.0	509	117	57	51	14	3	6	5	43	5	121	6	0	5	9	.357	0	0-0	0	4.11	3.89
15	Hou	NL	10	9	1	0	62.1	252	45	26	23	10	0	2	1	21	0	59	2	0	2	1	.667	0	0-0	0	2.78	3.32
Postseason			1	0	0	0	1.0	4	1	1	1	0	1	1	0	0	0	0	0	0	0	0	-	0	0-0	0	1.95	9.00
7 ML YEARS			141	123	1	8	726.0	3082	707	362	335	109	16	21	28	230	6	688	42	1	42	47	.472	1	0-0	0	4.09	4.15

Brandon Finnegan

Pitches: L **Bats:** L **Pos:** SP-4
Ht: 5'11" **Wt:** 212 **Born:** 4/14/1993 **Age:** 25

Year	Team	Lg	G	GS	CG	GF	IP	BFP	H	R	ER	HR	SH	SF	HB	TBB	IBB	SO	WP	Bk	W	L	Pct	Sh	Sv-Op	Hld	ERC	ERA
2014	KC	AL	7	0	0	1	7.0	28	6	1	1	0	0	0	0	1	0	10	0	0	0	1	.000	0	0-0	1	1.77	1.29
2015	2 Tms		20	4	0	3	48.0	197	37	19	19	8	3	1	1	21	0	45	0	0	5	2	.714	0	0-1	0	3.55	3.56
2016	Cin	NL	31	31	1	0	172.0	734	150	86	76	29	5	5	4	84	2	145	6	2	10	11	.476	0	0-0	0	4.30	3.98
2017	Cin	NL	4	4	0	0	13.0	59	9	6	6	1	0	0	0	13	0	16	1	0	1	1	.500	0	0-0	0	4.55	4.15
15	KC	AL	14	0	0	3	24.1	99	16	8	8	3	1	1	1	13	0	21	0	0	3	0	1.000	0	0-1	0	3.14	2.96
15	Cin	NL	6	4	0	0	23.2	98	21	11	11	5	2	0	0	8	0	24	0	0	2	2	.500	0	0-0	0	3.96	4.18
Postseason			7	0	0	0	6.0	31	9	7	7	0	3	0	0	5	1	4	0	0	1	1	.500	0	0-1	1	7.77	10.50
4 ML YEARS			62	39	1	4	240.0	1018	202	112	102	38	8	6	5	119	2	216	7	2	16	15	.516	0	0-1	1	4.08	3.83

Derek Fisher

Bats: L **Throws:** R **Pos:** LF-38;RF-12;PH-5;PR-5;CF-3;DH-2
Ht: 6'3" **Wt:** 205 **Born:** 8/21/1993 **Age:** 24

Year	Team	Lg	G	AB	H	2B	3B	HR	(Hm	Rd)	TB	R	RBI	RC	TBB	IBB	SO	HBP	SH	SF	SB	CS	GDP	Avg	OBP	Slg	OPS
2014	2 Tms	Low	42	155	48	5	3	2	(-	-)	65	31	18	27	17	1	35	3	0	1	17	4	2	.310	.386	.419	.806
2015	2 Tms	Low	123	495	136	21	8	22	(-	-)	239	106	87	92	66	1	132	5	0	3	31	7	3	.275	.364	.483	.847
2016	CpChr	AA	102	371	91	13	4	16	(-	-)	160	54	59	66	74	7	128	2	0	1	23	7	4	.245	.373	.431	.804
2016	Fresno	AAA	27	107	31	8	0	5	(-	-)	54	17	17	19	9	0	26	1	0	1	5	0	2	.290	.347	.505	.852
2017	Fresno	AAA	84	343	109	26	1	21	(-	-)	200	63	66	74	35	1	74	3	1	2	16	10	11	.318	.384	.583	.967
2017	Hou	AL	53	146	31	4	1	5	(3	2)	52	21	17	18	17	1	54	3	0	0	3	3	1	.212	.307	.356	.663

Doug Fister

Pitches: R **Bats:** L **Pos:** SP-15; RP-3
Ht: 6'8" **Wt:** 210 **Born:** 2/4/1984 **Age:** 34

Year	Team	Lg	G	GS	CG	GF	IP	BFP	H	R	ER	HR	SH	SF	HB	TBB	IBB	SO	WP	Bk	W	L	Pct	Sh	Sv-Op	Hld	ERC	ERA
2009	Sea	AL	11	10	0	0	61.0	256	63	29	28	11	0	0	2	15	0	36	1	0	3	4	.429	0	0-0	0	4.36	4.13
2010	Sea	AL	28	28	0	0	171.0	720	187	85	78	13	2	4	6	32	2	93	8	3	6	14	.300	0	0-0	0	3.73	4.11
2011	2 Tms	AL	32	31	3	0	216.1	875	193	76	68	11	4	9	12	37	2	146	3	1	11	13	.458	0	0-0	0	2.53	2.83
2012	Det	AL	26	26	2	0	161.2	673	156	73	62	15	3	0	7	37	1	137	1	0	10	10	.500	1	0-0	0	3.33	3.45
2013	Det	AL	33	32	1	0	208.2	881	229	91	85	14	2	5	16	44	2	159	7	0	14	9	.609	0	0-0	0	4.00	3.67
2014	Was	NL	25	25	1	0	164.0	662	153	52	44	18	6	2	7	24	0	98	5	0	16	6	.727	1	0-0	0	2.98	2.41
2015	Was	NL	25	15	0	0	103.0	449	120	56	48	14	7	5	6	23	1	63	1	0	5	7	.417	0	1-1	0	4.79	4.19
2016	Hou	AL	32	32	0	0	180.1	779	195	98	93	24	0	3	7	62	1	115	10	0	12	13	.480	0	0-0	0	4.76	4.64
2017	Bos	AL	18	15	1	0	90.1	392	87	55	49	9	3	5	3	38	3	83	2	1	5	9	.357	0	0-0	0	4.01	4.88
11	Sea	AL	21	21	3	0	146.0	602	139	57	54	7	3	7	9	32	2	89	3	1	3	12	.200	0	0-0	0	3.02	3.33
11	Det	AL	11	10	0	0	70.1	273	54	19	14	4	1	2	3	5	0	57	0	0	8	1	.889	0	0-0	0	1.63	1.79
Postseason			9	8	0	0	55.1	232	54	16	16	2	2	0	3	16	0	40	1	1	4	2	.667	0	0-0	0	3.32	2.60
9 ML YEARS			230	214	8	6	1356.1	5687	1383	615	555	129	27	33	66	313	14	930	38	5	82	85	.491	2	1-1	0	3.68	3.68

Jack Flaherty

Pitches: R **Bats:** R **Pos:** SP-5; RP-1   **Ht:** 6'4" **Wt:** 205 **Born:** 10/15/1995 **Age:** 22

			HOW MUCH HE PITCHED						WHAT HE GAVE UP												THE RESULTS							
Year	Team	Lg	G	GS	CG	GF	IP	BFP	H	R	ER	HR	SH	SF	HB	TBB	IBB	SO	WP	Bk	W	L	Pct	Sh	Sv-Op	Hld	ERC	ERA
2014	Cards	R	8	6	0	0	22.2	94	18	9	4	1	0	0	3	4	1	28	2	0	1	1	.500	0	0--	-	2.18	1.59
2015	Peoria	A	18	18	0	0	95.0	410	92	38	30	2	2	2	7	31	0	97	10	1	9	3	.750	0	0--	-	3.31	2.84
2016	PlmBh	A+	24	23	0	0	134.0	564	129	63	53	8	6	3	2	45	0	126	11	0	5	9	.357	0	0--	-	3.42	3.56
2017	Sprgfld	AA	10	10	0	0	63.1	242	47	10	10	2	1	1	0	11	0	62	1	0	7	2	.778	0	0--	-	1.62	1.42
2017	Memp	AAA	15	15	0	0	85.1	339	73	26	26	10	1	0	0	24	2	85	4	0	7	2	.778	0	0--	-	3.01	2.74
2017	StL	NL	6	5	0	0	21.1	94	23	15	15	4	0	2	1	10	1	20	0	0	0	2	.000	0	0-0	0	5.71	6.33

Ryan Flaherty

Bats: L **Throws:** R **Pos:** 2B-12;3B-5;SS-5;PH-2;PR-2;LF-1;RF-1   **Ht:** 6'3" **Wt:** 220 **Born:** 7/27/1986 **Age:** 31

					BATTING																	RUNNING			AVERAGES			
Year	Team	Lg	G	AB	H	2B	3B	HR	(Hm	Rd)	TB	R	RBI	RC	TBB	IBB	SO	HBP	SH	SF	SB	CS	GDP	Avg	OBP	Slg	OPS
2017	Bowie*	AA	12	38	15	3	0	2	(-	-)	24	18	6	12	10	0	3	1	0	0	0	0	2	.395	.531	.632	1.162
2012	Bal	AL	77	153	33	2	1	6	(3	3)	55	15	19	15	6	0	43	3	3	1	1	0	3	.216	.258	.359	.617
2013	Bal	AL	85	246	55	11	0	10	(6	4)	96	28	27	27	19	3	62	5	1	0	2	0	2	.224	.293	.390	.683
2014	Bal	AL	102	281	62	15	1	7	(7	0)	100	33	32	34	22	2	68	5	3	1	1	0	3	.221	.288	.356	.644
2015	Bal	AL	91	267	54	8	3	9	(2	7)	95	34	31	24	26	2	81	4	2	2	0	0	8	.202	.281	.356	.637
2016	Bal	AL	74	157	34	7	0	3	(3	0)	50	16	15	18	17	1	48	0	1	1	2	0	1	.217	.291	.318	.610
2017	Bal	AL	23	38	8	1	0	0	(0	0)	9	5	4	5	4	0	10	1	0	0	0	0	0	.211	.302	.237	.539
	Postseason		11	32	9	0	0	2	(0	2)	15	5	5	4	4	0	9	0	0	0	0	0	0	.281	.361	.469	.830
	6 ML YEARS		452	1142	246	44	5	35	(21	14)	405	131	128	123	94	8	312	18	10	5	6	0	17	.215	.284	.355	.639

Chris Flexen

Pitches: R **Bats:** R **Pos:** SP-9; RP-5   **Ht:** 6'3" **Wt:** 250 **Born:** 7/1/1994 **Age:** 23

					HOW MUCH HE PITCHED						WHAT HE GAVE UP												THE RESULTS						
Year	Team	Lg	G	GS	CG	GF	IP	BFP	H	R	ER	HR	SH	SF	HB	TBB	IBB	SO	WP	Bk	W	L	Pct	Sh	Sv-Op	Hld	ERC	ERA
2013	Kngspt	R+	11	11	2	0	69.0	271	53	18	16	6	0	0	6	12	0	62	3	0	8	1	.889	2	0--	-	2.31	2.09
2014	Savann	A	13	13	0	0	69.0	318	75	41	37	5	1	4	4	37	0	46	5	0	3	5	.375	0	0--	-	5.10	4.83
2015	3 Tms	Low	12	9	0	0	52.0	214	45	17	14	0	1	2	1	16	0	51	1	0	4	2	.667	0	0--	-	2.44	2.42
2016	Stluci	A+	25	25	1	0	134.0	572	125	62	53	6	6	7	6	51	0	95	5	0	10	9	.526	1	0--	-	3.42	3.56
2017	Bnghtn	AA	7	7	2	0	48.2	179	28	10	9	4	2	0	0	7	0	50	1	0	6	1	.857	1	0--	-	1.22	1.66
2017	NYM	NL	14	9	0	1	48.0	233	62	44	42	11	1	2	2	35	0	36	1	0	3	6	.333	0	0-0	0	8.75	7.88

Ramon Flores

Bats: L **Throws:** L **Pos:** RF-3   **Ht:** 5'10" **Wt:** 190 **Born:** 3/26/1992 **Age:** 26

					BATTING																	RUNNING			AVERAGES			
Year	Team	Lg	G	AB	H	2B	3B	HR	(Hm	Rd)	TB	R	RBI	RC	TBB	IBB	SO	HBP	SH	SF	SB	CS	GDP	Avg	OBP	Slg	OPS
2017	Salt Lk*	AAA	115	413	129	21	5	10	(-	-)	190	65	71	83	68	0	70	2	6	4	12	2	11	.312	.409	.460	.869
2015	NYY	AL	12	32	7	1	0	0	(0	0)	8	3	0	1	0	0	4	0	1	0	0	0	0	.219	.219	.250	.469
2016	Mil	NL	104	249	51	8	0	2	(1	1)	65	18	19	14	31	3	58	2	3	4	3	0	11	.205	.294	.261	.555
2017	LAA	AL	3	8	1	0	0	0	(0	0)	1	0	1	0	0	0	1	0	0	1	0	0	0	.125	.111	.125	.236
	3 ML YEARS		119	289	59	9	0	2	(1	1)	74	21	20	15	31	3	63	2	4	5	3	0	11	.204	.281	.256	.537

Wilmer Flores

Bats: R **Throws:** R **Pos:** 3B-55;1B-29;PH-21;2B-12;DH-1   **Ht:** 6'3" **Wt:** 205 **Born:** 8/6/1991 **Age:** 26

					BATTING																	RUNNING			AVERAGES			
Year	Team	Lg	G	AB	H	2B	3B	HR	(Hm	Rd)	TB	R	RBI	RC	TBB	IBB	SO	HBP	SH	SF	SB	CS	GDP	Avg	OBP	Slg	OPS
2013	NYM	NL	27	95	20	5	0	1	(0	0)	28	8	13	7	5	0	23	0	0	1	0	0	1	.211	.248	.295	.542
2014	NYM	NL	78	259	65	13	1	6	(4	2)	98	28	29	25	12	2	31	1	1	1	1	0	6	.251	.286	.378	.664
2015	NYM	NL	137	483	127	22	0	16	(8	8)	197	55	59	58	19	2	63	4	2	2	0	1	12	.263	.295	.408	.703
2016	NYM	NL	103	307	82	14	0	16	(12	4)	144	38	49	39	23	0	48	2	0	3	1	1	9	.267	.319	.469	.788
2017	NYM	NL	110	336	91	17	1	18	(9	9)	164	42	52	39	17	1	54	3	0	6	1	1	14	.271	.307	.488	.795
	Postseason		13	41	8	2	1	0	(0	0)	12	4	0	5	5	2	9	1	1	0	1	0	1	.195	.298	.293	.591
	5 ML YEARS		455	1480	385	71	2	57	(33	24)	631	171	202	168	76	5	219	10	3	13	3	3	42	.260	.298	.426	.725

Pedro Florimon

floh-ree-MOHN

Bats: B **Throws:** R **Pos:** CF-8;SS-2;RF-2;2B-1;3B-1;LF-1;PH-1   **Ht:** 6'2" **Wt:** 185 **Born:** 12/10/1986 **Age:** 31

					BATTING																	RUNNING			AVERAGES			
Year	Team	Lg	G	AB	H	2B	3B	HR	(Hm	Rd)	TB	R	RBI	RC	TBB	IBB	SO	HBP	SH	SF	SB	CS	GDP	Avg	OBP	Slg	OPS
2017	LV*	AAA	90	310	82	13	1	10	(-	-)	127	32	33	46	34	1	94	6	1	2	4	3	9	.265	.347	.410	.756
2011	Bal	AL	4	8	1	1	0	0	(0	0)	2	1	2	1	1	0	6	0	1	0	0	0	0	.125	.250	.250	.472
2012	Min	AL	43	137	30	5	2	1	(1	0)	42	16	10	8	10	0	30	0	3	0	3	1	0	.219	.272	.307	.579
2013	Min	AL	134	403	89	17	0	9	(3	6)	133	44	44	38	33	1	115	2	5	3	15	6	7	.221	.281	.330	.611
2014	Min	AL	33	76	7	1	1	0	(0	0)	10	7	1	0	8	0	22	0	2	0	6	0	2	.092	.179	.132	.310
2015	Pit	NL	24	23	2	0	1	0	(0	0)	4	5	1	0	2	0	12	0	1	0	1	0	0	.087	.160	.174	.334
2016	Pit	NL	18	24	5	1	1	0	(0	0)	8	4	4	1	1	0	12	0	0	0	0	1	0	.208	.240	.333	.573
2017	Phi	NL	15	46	16	4	1	0	(0	0)	22	6	6	8	3	0	16	0	0	0	1	0	0	.348	.388	.478	.866
	7 ML YEARS		271	717	150	29	6	10	(4	6)	221	83	68	56	58	1	213	2	11	3	25	8	13	.209	.269	.308	.577

Dylan Floro

Pitches: R Bats: L Pos: RP-3   Ht: 6'2" Wt: 175 Born: 12/27/1990 Age: 27

			HOW MUCH HE PITCHED						WHAT HE GAVE UP											THE RESULTS							
Year	Team	Lg	G	GS	CG	GF	IP	BFP	H	R	ER	HR	SH	SF	HB	TBB	IBB	SO	WP	Bk	W	L	Pct	Sh	Sv-Op	Hld	ERC	ERA
2013	2 Tms	Low	23	23	2	0	137.1	536	123	39	27	4	4	1	2	21	0	99	11	0	11	2	.846	1	0- -	-	2.30	1.77
2014	Mont	AA	28	28	3	0	178.2	746	209	80	69	4	3	3	3	24	0	112	11	2	11	13	.458	2	0- -	-	3.56	3.48
2015	Drham	AAA	25	22	1	1	132.2	571	160	78	74	10	5	6	0	21	0	81	3	1	9	12	.429	0	0- -	-	4.06	5.02
2016	Drham	AAA	32	0	0	13	50.0	207	53	21	16	6	0	0	1	9	0	40	1	0	1	2	.333	0	7- -	-	3.79	2.88
2017	Iowa	AAA	25	2	0	8	48.2	208	54	28	21	9	2	1	1	8	0	26	0	0	3	2	.600	0	1- -	-	4.33	3.88
2017	OkCity	AAA	8	0	0	5	11.1	53	18	8	7	0	1	0	0	3	0	12	1	0	0	1	.000	0	1- -	-	6.29	5.56
2016	TB	AL	12	0	0	4	15.0	72	23	8	7	0	0	1	0	5	1	14	2	0	0	1	.000	0	0-0	0	5.96	4.20
2017	ChC	NL	3	0	0	2	9.2	45	15	7	7	2	0	0	1	2	0	6	0	0	0	0	-	0	0-0	0	8.12	6.52
	2 ML YEARS		15	0	0	6	24.2	117	38	15	14	2	0	1	1	7	1	20	2	0	0	1	.000	0	0-0	0	6.79	5.11

Tyler Flowers

Bats: R Throws: R Pos: C-85;PH-13;DH-1   Ht: 6'4" Wt: 260 Born: 1/24/1986 Age: 32

								BATTING													RUNNING			AVERAGES			
Year	Team	Lg	G	AB	H	2B	3B	HR	(Hm	Rd)	TB	R	RBI	RC	TBB	IBB	SO	HBP	SH	SF	SB	CS	GDP	Avg	OBP	Slg	OPS
2009	CWS	AL	10	16	3	1	0	0	(0	0)	4	3	0	2	3	0	8	1	0	0	0	0	1	.188	.350	.250	.600
2010	CWS	AL	8	11	1	0	0	0	(0	0)	1	2	0	1	4	0	5	0	0	0	0	0	0	.091	.333	.091	.424
2011	CWS	AL	38	110	23	5	1	5	(3	2)	45	13	16	13	14	0	38	3	0	2	0	1	2	.209	.310	.409	.719
2012	CWS	AL	52	136	29	6	0	7	(5	2)	56	19	13	13	12	0	56	4	1	0	2	1	2	.213	.296	.412	.708
2013	CWS	AL	84	256	50	11	0	10	(7	3)	91	24	24	14	14	1	94	4	0	1	0	1	9	.195	.247	.355	.603
2014	CWS	AL	127	407	98	16	1	15	(7	8)	161	42	50	43	25	0	159	8	1	1	0	1	10	.241	.297	.396	.693
2015	CWS	AL	112	331	79	12	0	9	(3	6)	118	21	39	36	21	0	104	6	2	1	0	1	8	.239	.295	.356	.652
2016	Atl	NL	83	281	76	18	0	8	(5	3)	118	27	41	46	29	1	91	11	0	4	0	0	3	.270	.357	.420	.777
2017	Atl	NL	99	317	89	16	0	12	(6	6)	141	41	49	50	31	1	82	20	0	2	0	1	6	.281	.378	.445	.823
	9 ML YEARS		613	1865	448	85	2	66	(36	30)	735	192	232	218	153	3	637	57	4	11	2	6	41	.240	.315	.394	.710

Brian Flynn

Pitches: L Bats: L Pos: RP-1   Ht: 6'7" Wt: 250 Born: 4/19/1990 Age: 28

			HOW MUCH HE PITCHED						WHAT HE GAVE UP											THE RESULTS							
Year	Team	Lg	G	GS	CG	GF	IP	BFP	H	R	ER	HR	SH	SF	HB	TBB	IBB	SO	WP	Bk	W	L	Pct	Sh	Sv-Op	Hld	ERC	ERA
2017	Omha*	AAA	22	4	0	4	50.0	230	68	36	30	10	1	1	1	12	2	50	6	0	5	3	.625	0	0- -	-	6.19	5.40
2013	Mia	NL	4	4	0	0	18.0	88	27	17	17	4	2	0	0	13	0	15	3	0	0	2	.000	0	0-0	0	10.17	8.50
2014	Mia	NL	2	1	0	0	7.0	35	12	7	7	0	0	0	0	3	0	6	1	0	0	1	.000	0	0-0	0	7.75	9.00
2016	KC	AL	36	1	0	11	55.1	221	38	19	16	5	4	1	1	23	0	44	8	0	1	2	.333	0	0-0	2	2.55	2.60
2017	KC	AL	1	0	0	0	2.1	8	3	1	1	0	0	0	0	0	0	0	0	0	0	0	-	0	0-0	0	4.29	3.86
	4 ML YEARS		43	6	0	11	82.2	352	80	44	41	9	6	1	1	39	0	65	12	0	1	5	.167	0	0-0	2	4.40	4.46

Mike Foltynewicz

Pitches: R Bats: R Pos: SP-28; RP-1   fohl-tuh-neh-vich   Ht: 6'4" Wt: 220 Born: 10/7/1991 Age: 26

			HOW MUCH HE PITCHED						WHAT HE GAVE UP											THE RESULTS							
Year	Team	Lg	G	GS	CG	GF	IP	BFP	H	R	ER	HR	SH	SF	HB	TBB	IBB	SO	WP	Bk	W	L	Pct	Sh	Sv-Op	Hld	ERC	ERA
2014	Hou	AL	16	0	0	9	18.2	84	23	11	11	3	0	0	0	7	0	14	3	0	0	1	.000	0	0-0	1	5.80	5.30
2015	Atl	NL	18	15	0	0	86.2	399	112	63	55	17	2	6	4	29	0	77	3	1	4	6	.400	0	0-0	1	6.43	5.71
2016	Atl	NL	22	22	0	0	123.1	525	125	61	59	18	5	4	6	35	2	111	13	1	9	5	.643	0	0-0	0	4.18	4.31
2017	Atl	NL	29	28	0	0	154.0	692	169	86	82	20	11	2	10	59	2	143	4	0	10	13	.435	0	0-0	0	4.97	4.79
	4 ML YEARS		85	65	0	10	382.2	1700	429	221	207	58	18	12	20	130	4	345	23	2	23	25	.479	0	0-0	2	5.07	4.87

Wilmer Font

Pitches: R Bats: R Pos: RP-3   FAHNT   Ht: 6'4" Wt: 265 Born: 5/24/1990 Age: 28

			HOW MUCH HE PITCHED						WHAT HE GAVE UP											THE RESULTS							
Year	Team	Lg	G	GS	CG	GF	IP	BFP	H	R	ER	HR	SH	SF	HB	TBB	IBB	SO	WP	Bk	W	L	Pct	Sh	Sv-Op	Hld	ERC	ERA
2017	OkCity*	AAA	25	25	0	0	134.1	554	114	52	51	11	2	1	3	35	0	178	2	3	10	8	.556	0	0- -	-	2.67	3.42
2012	Tex	AL	3	0	0	0	2.0	10	0	2	2	0	0	0	0	4	0	1	1	0	0	0	-	0	0-0	0	3.47	9.00
2013	Tex	AL	2	0	0	2	1.1	7	1	0	0	0	0	0	0	2	0	0	0	0	0	0	-	0	0-0	0	5.91	0.00
2017	LAD	NL	3	0	0	2	3.2	22	7	7	7	2	0	0	0	4	0	3	0	0	0	0	-	0	0-0	0	17.78	17.18
	3 ML YEARS		8	0	0	4	7.0	39	8	9	9	2	0	0	0	10	0	4	1	0	0	0	-	0	0-0	0	10.96	11.57

Nolan Fontana

Bats: L Throws: R Pos: 2B-9;PR-3;DH-1;PH-1   Ht: 5'11" Wt: 195 Born: 6/6/1991 Age: 27

								BATTING													RUNNING			AVERAGES			
Year	Team	Lg	G	AB	H	2B	3B	HR	(Hm	Rd)	TB	R	RBI	RC	TBB	IBB	SO	HBP	SH	SF	SB	CS	GDP	Avg	OBP	Slg	OPS
2013	Lancst	A+	104	386	100	18	6	8	(-	-)	154	88	60	75	102	1	100	3	5	3	16	5	6	.259	.415	.399	.814
2014	CpChr	AA	66	229	60	21	1	1	(-	-)	86	33	26	41	61	0	76	2	11	2	5	8	0	.262	.418	.376	.794
2015	Fresno	AAA	117	361	87	21	6	3	(-	-)	129	56	40	53	74	0	99	3	12	6	6	11	1	.241	.369	.357	.727
2016	Fresno	AAA	106	359	70	15	0	3	(-	-)	94	35	27	25	32	0	108	5	7	4	4	3	2	.195	.268	.262	.529
2016	CpChr	AA	10	36	10	4	0	0	(-	-)	14	4	4	6	8	2	5	0	0	0	1	0	1	.278	.409	.389	.798
2017	Salt Lk	AAA	105	361	98	27	4	10	(-	-)	163	82	51	72	75	2	97	3	8	6	14	2	3	.271	.396	.452	.847
2017	LAA	AL	12	20	1	0	0	1	(0	1)	4	1	1	0	3	0	8	0	0	0	1	1	1	.050	.174	.200	.374

Logan Forsythe

Bats: R **Throws:** R **Pos:** 2B-80;3B-42;PH-13;LF-3;SS-2;1B-1   **Ht:** 6'1" **Wt:** 205 **Born:** 1/14/1987 **Age:** 31

									BATTING										RUNNING			AVERAGES			
Year	Team	Lg	G	AB	H	2B	3B	HR	(Hm | Rd)	TB	R	RBI	RC	TBB	IBB	SO	HBP	SH	SF	SB	CS	GDP	Avg	OBP	Slg	OPS
2011	SD	NL	62	150	32	9	1	0	(0 | 0)	43	12	12	15	12	3	33	3	2	2	3	1	3	.213	.281	.287	.568
2012	SD	NL	91	315	86	13	3	6	(5 | 1)	123	45	26	37	28	0	57	6	0	1	8	2	6	.273	.343	.390	.733
2013	SD	NL	75	220	47	6	1	6	(2 | 4)	73	22	19	16	19	2	54	2	1	1	6	1	6	.214	.281	.332	.613
2014	TB	AL	110	301	67	12	1	6	(2 | 4)	99	32	26	26	25	0	71	4	2	4	2	0	9	.223	.287	.329	.616
2015	TB	AL	153	540	152	33	2	17	(8 | 9)	240	69	68	73	55	2	111	14	0	6	9	4	12	.281	.359	.444	.804
2016	TB	AL	127	511	135	24	4	20	(12 | 8)	227	76	52	74	46	0	127	8	0	2	6	6	8	.264	.333	.444	.778
2017	LAD	NL	119	361	81	19	0	6	(4 | 2)	118	56	36	45	69	1	109	4	0	5	3	2	12	.224	.351	.327	.678
	7 ML YEARS		737	2398	600	116	12	61	(33 | 28)	923	312	239	286	254	8	562	41	5	21	37	16	55	.250	.330	.385	.715

Dexter Fowler

Bats: B **Throws:** R **Pos:** CF-109;PH-8;DH-1   **Ht:** 6'5" **Wt:** 195 **Born:** 3/22/1986 **Age:** 32

									BATTING										RUNNING			AVERAGES			
Year	Team	Lg	G	AB	H	2B	3B	HR	(Hm | Rd)	TB	R	RBI	RC	TBB	IBB	SO	HBP	SH	SF	SB	CS	GDP	Avg	OBP	Slg	OPS
2008	Col	NL	13	26	4	0	0	0	(0 | 0)	4	3	0	0	0	0	5	1	0	0	0	1	0	.154	.185	.154	.339
2009	Col	NL	135	433	115	29	10	4	(2 | 2)	176	73	34	68	67	1	116	1	14	3	27	10	4	.266	.363	.406	.770
2010	Col	NL	132	439	114	20	14	6	(5 | 1)	180	73	36	68	57	0	104	2	7	0	13	8	5	.260	.347	.410	.757
2011	Col	NL	125	481	128	35	15	5	(3 | 2)	208	84	45	79	68	3	130	6	7	1	12	9	6	.266	.363	.432	.796
2012	Col	NL	143	454	136	18	11	13	(10 | 3)	215	72	53	81	68	1	128	0	6	2	12	5	5	.300	.389	.474	.863
2013	Col	NL	119	415	109	18	3	12	(7 | 5)	169	71	42	62	65	1	105	6	4	2	19	9	5	.263	.369	.407	.776
2014	Hou	AL	116	434	120	21	4	8	(5 | 3)	173	61	35	65	66	2	108	3	1	1	11	4	6	.276	.375	.399	.774
2015	ChC	NL	156	596	149	29	8	17	(11 | 6)	245	102	46	77	84	1	154	5	2	3	20	7	5	.250	.346	.411	.757
2016	ChC	NL	125	456	126	25	7	13	(4 | 9)	204	84	48	83	79	0	124	11	1	4	13	4	3	.276	.393	.447	.840
2017	StL	NL	118	420	111	22	9	18	(11 | 7)	205	68	64	74	63	6	101	4	0	4	7	3	10	.264	.363	.488	.851
	Postseason		30	122	31	7	0	5	(3 | 2)	53	18	11	14	5	0	26	1	2	2	2	1	1	.254	.285	.434	.719
	10 ML YEARS		1182	4154	1112	217	81	96	(58 | 38)	1779	691	403	657	617	15	1075	39	42	20	134	60	49	.268	.366	.428	.794

Dustin Fowler

Bats: L **Throws:** L **Pos:** RF-1   **Ht:** 6'0" **Wt:** 195 **Born:** 12/29/1994 **Age:** 23

									BATTING										RUNNING			AVERAGES			
Year	Team	Lg	G	AB	H	2B	3B	HR	(Hm | Rd)	TB	R	RBI	RC	TBB	IBB	SO	HBP	SH	SF	SB	CS	GDP	Avg	OBP	Slg	OPS
2013	Yanks1	R	30	112	27	8	4	0	(- | -)	43	8	9	12	4	1	23	1	0	0	3	1	1	.241	.274	.384	.657
2014	CtnSC	A	66	257	66	13	6	9	(- | -)	118	33	41	34	13	0	53	0	1	1	3	2	1	.257	.292	.459	.751
2015	2 Teams	Low	123	487	145	20	6	5	(- | -)	192	64	70	65	26	3	90	2	0	3	30	13	2	.298	.334	.394	.728
2016	Trntn	AA	132	541	152	30	15	12	(- | -)	248	67	88	79	22	0	86	4	2	5	25	11	6	.281	.311	.458	.770
2017	S-WB	AAA	70	297	87	19	8	13	(- | -)	161	49	43	52	15	1	63	1	0	0	13	5	2	.293	.329	.542	.871
2017	NYY	AL	1	0	0	0	0	0	(0 | 0)	0	0	0	0	0	0	0	0	0	0	0	0	0	-	-	-	-

Maikel Franco

Bats: R **Throws:** R **Pos:** 3B-144;PH-7;1B-2;DH-2   MY-kell   **Ht:** 6'1" **Wt:** 215 **Born:** 8/26/1992 **Age:** 25

									BATTING										RUNNING			AVERAGES			
Year	Team	Lg	G	AB	H	2B	3B	HR	(Hm | Rd)	TB	R	RBI	RC	TBB	IBB	SO	HBP	SH	SF	SB	CS	GDP	Avg	OBP	Slg	OPS
2014	Phi	NL	16	56	10	2	0	0	(0 | 0)	12	5	5	1	1	0	13	0	0	1	0	0	1	.179	.190	.214	.404
2015	Phi	NL	80	304	85	22	1	14	(7 | 7)	151	45	50	48	26	2	52	4	0	1	1	0	8	.280	.343	.497	.840
2016	Phi	NL	152	581	148	23	1	25	(10 | 15)	248	67	88	74	40	7	106	5	0	4	1	1	13	.255	.306	.427	.733
2017	Phi	NL	154	575	132	29	1	24	(14 | 10)	235	66	76	53	41	3	95	2	0	5	0	0	21	.230	.281	.409	.690
	4 ML YEARS		402	1516	375	76	3	63	(31 | 32)	646	183	219	176	108	12	266	11	0	11	2	1	43	.247	.300	.426	.726

Nick Franklin

Bats: B **Throws:** R **Pos:** PH-40;LF-19;2B-9;RF-2;SS-1   **Ht:** 6'1" **Wt:** 190 **Born:** 3/2/1991 **Age:** 27

									BATTING										RUNNING			AVERAGES			
Year	Team	Lg	G	AB	H	2B	3B	HR	(Hm | Rd)	TB	R	RBI	RC	TBB	IBB	SO	HBP	SH	SF	SB	CS	GDP	Avg	OBP	Slg	OPS
2013	Sea	AL	102	369	83	20	1	12	(4 | 8)	141	38	45	48	42	1	113	0	0	1	6	1	2	.225	.303	.382	.686
2014	2 Tms	AL	28	81	13	2	1	1	(1 | 0)	20	7	6	6	6	0	32	1	0	2	2	0	2	.160	.222	.247	.469
2015	TB	AL	44	101	16	4	1	3	(2 | 1)	31	11	7	4	7	0	37	0	1	0	1	0	2	.158	.213	.307	.520
2016	TB	AL	60	174	47	10	1	6	(4 | 2)	77	18	26	25	12	1	42	3	2	0	6	1	1	.270	.328	.443	.771
2017	2 Tms	AL	66	106	19	3	1	2	(2 | 0)	30	9	12	11	10	0	22	3	0	0	2	0	1	.179	.269	.283	.552
14	Sea	AL	17	47	6	0	1	0	(0 | 0)	8	3	2	1	3	0	21	1	0	1	1	0	0	.128	.192	.170	.363
14	TB	AL	11	34	7	2	0	1	(1 | 0)	12	4	4	5	3	0	11	0	0	1	1	0	2	.206	.263	.353	.616
17	Mil	NL	53	82	16	2	1	2	(2 | 0)	26	7	10	8	5	0	19	2	0	0	2	0	1	.195	.258	.317	.576
17	LAA	AL	13	24	3	1	0	0	(0 | 0)	4	2	2	3	5	0	3	1	0	0	0	0	0	.125	.300	.167	.467
	5 ML YEARS		300	831	178	39	5	24	(13 | 11)	299	83	96	94	77	2	246	7	3	3	17	2	8	.214	.285	.360	.645

Seth Frankoff

Pitches: R **Bats:** R **Pos:** RP-1   **Ht:** 6'5" **Wt:** 210 **Born:** 8/27/1988 **Age:** 29

			HOW MUCH HE PITCHED						WHAT HE GAVE UP										THE RESULTS						
Year	Team	Lg	G	GS	CG	GF	IP	BFP	H	R	ER	HR	SH	SF	HB	TBB	IBB	SO	WP	Bk	W	L	Pct	Sh	Sv-Op	Hld	ERC	ERA
2013	Stcktn	A+	48	0	0	12	74.1	306	57	32	23	6	4	0	5	23	1	93	11	0	2	0	1.000	0	4- -	-	2.58	2.78
2014	Mdlnd	AA	27	0	0	23	33.2	141	29	10	9	3	4	1	0	11	2	47	0	0	2	2	.500	0	15- -	-	2.83	2.41
2014	Scrmto	AAA	22	0	0	8	30.2	132	30	16	15	3	0	3	1	10	0	22	2	0	1	1	.500	0	1- -	-	3.72	4.40
2015	Mdlnd	AA	38	0	0	16	50.0	207	48	21	18	5	0	3	0	14	0	50	4	0	0	1	.000	0	8- -	-	3.41	3.24

Year	Team	Lg	G	GS	CG	GF	IP	BFP	H	R	ER	HR	SH	SF	HB	TBB	IBB	SO	WP	Bk	W	L	Pct	Sh	Sv-Op	Hld	ERC	ERA
2015	Nashv	AAA	9	0	0	2	10.2	46	6	7	7	2	1	0	1	9	0	7	1	0	0	1	.000	0	0--	-	4.48	5.91
2016	Tulsa	AA	21	9	0	3	60.2	265	73	36	28	2	1	2	1	15	0	58	9	0	3	4	.429	0	0--	-	4.19	4.15
2017	Iowa	AAA	24	21	0	0	116.2	493	102	61	57	18	4	6	8	47	0	119	10	1	2	8	.200	0	0--	-	4.08	4.40
2017	ChC	NL	1	0	0	0	2.0	9	4	2	2	1	0	0	0	0	0	2	0	0	0	1	.000	0	0-0	0	13.26	9.00

Adam Frazier

Bats: L **Throws:** R **Pos:** LF-52;2B-42;PH-24;RF-15;CF-4;3B-1;SS-1;DH-1;PR-1   **Ht:** 5'9" **Wt:** 185 **Born:** 12/14/1991 **Age:** 26

Year	Team	Lg	G	AB	H	2B	3B	HR	(Hm	Rd)	TB	R	RBI	RC	TBB	IBB	SO	HBP	SH	SF	SB	CS	GDP	Avg	OBP	Slg	OPS
2013	Jmstwn	A-	58	224	72	7	1	0	(-	-)	81	34	27	34	25	1	31	6	0	3	5	8	2	.321	.399	.362	.761
2014	Bradtn	A+	121	492	124	21	2	1	(-	-)	152	62	42	49	37	0	61	3	6	2	14	8	5	.252	.307	.309	.616
2015	Altna	AA	103	377	122	21	4	2	(-	-)	157	59	30	62	34	0	42	3	9	0	11	7	4	.324	.384	.416	.801
2016	Indy	AAA	68	261	87	16	4	0	(-	-)	111	34	22	44	29	0	27	2	5	2	17	15	2	.333	.401	.425	.827
2016	Pit	NL	66	146	44	8	1	2	(2	0)	60	21	11	23	12	0	26	1	0	1	4	1	0	.301	.356	.411	.767
2017	Pit	NL	121	406	112	20	6	6	(2	4)	162	55	53	61	36	2	57	8	1	3	9	5	9	.276	.344	.399	.743
	2 ML YEARS		187	552	156	28	7	8	(4	4)	222	76	64	84	48	2	83	9	1	4	13	6	9	.283	.347	.402	.750

Clint Frazier

Bats: R **Throws:** R **Pos:** LF-30;RF-7;DH-2;PH-2;PR-1   **Ht:** 6'1" **Wt:** 190 **Born:** 9/6/1994 **Age:** 23

Year	Team	Lg	G	AB	H	2B	3B	HR	(Hm	Rd)	TB	R	RBI	RC	TBB	IBB	SO	HBP	SH	SF	SB	CS	GDP	Avg	OBP	Slg	OPS
2013	Indns	R	44	172	51	11	5	5	(-	-)	87	32	28	32	17	0	61	3	0	4	3	2	1	.297	.362	.506	.868
2014	Lk Cty	A	120	474	126	18	6	13	(-	-)	195	70	50	72	56	1	161	7	1	4	12	6	6	.266	.349	.411	.761
2015	Lynbrg	A+	133	501	143	36	3	16	(-	-)	233	88	72	92	68	2	125	9	5	5	15	7	4	.285	.377	.465	.842
2016	Akron	AA	89	341	94	25	1	13	(-	-)	160	56	48	60	41	0	86	3	3	3	13	4	7	.276	.356	.469	.825
2016	S-WB	AAA	25	101	23	2	3	3	(-	-)	40	17	7	11	7	0	30	0	0	0	0	0	1	.228	.278	.396	.674
2017	S-WB	AAA	74	273	70	19	2	12	(-	-)	129	46	42	48	37	2	69	3	0	7	9	2	4	.256	.344	.473	.816
2017	NYY	AL	39	134	31	9	4	4	(3	1)	60	16	17	17	7	0	43	0	0	1	1	0	2	.231	.268	.448	.715

Todd Frazier

Bats: R **Throws:** R **Pos:** 3B-133;DH-12;1B-4;PH-3   **Ht:** 6'3" **Wt:** 220 **Born:** 2/12/1986 **Age:** 32

Year	Team	Lg	G	AB	H	2B	3B	HR	(Hm	Rd)	TB	R	RBI	RC	TBB	IBB	SO	HBP	SH	SF	SB	CS	GDP	Avg	OBP	Slg	OPS
2011	Cin	NL	41	112	26	5	0	6	(2	4)	49	17	15	13	7	0	27	2	0	0	1	0	2	.232	.289	.438	.727
2012	Cin	NL	128	422	115	26	6	19	(10	9)	210	55	67	59	36	1	103	3	0	4	3	2	9	.273	.331	.498	.829
2013	Cin	NL	150	531	124	29	3	19	(12	7)	216	63	73	67	50	1	125	14	2	3	6	5	14	.234	.314	.407	.721
2014	Cin	NL	157	597	163	22	1	29	(20	9)	274	88	80	84	52	2	139	7	0	4	20	8	9	.273	.336	.459	.795
2015	Cin	NL	157	**619**	158	43	1	35	(19	16)	308	82	89	73	44	3	137	7	1	7	13	8	19	.255	.309	.498	.806
2016	CWS	AL	158	590	133	21	0	40	(16	24)	274	89	98	71	64	1	163	4	1	7	15	5	11	.225	.302	.464	.767
2017	2 Tms	AL	147	474	101	19	1	27	(9	18)	203	74	76	69	83	2	125	14	0	5	4	3	10	.213	.344	.428	.772
17	CWS	AL	81	280	58	15	0	16	(5	11)	121	41	44	39	48	1	71	4	0	3	4	3	4	.207	.328	.432	.761
17	NYY	AL	66	194	43	4	1	11	(4	7)	82	33	32	30	35	1	54	10	0	2	0	0	6	.222	.365	.423	.788
	Postseason		5	10	2	1	0	0	(0	0)	3	0	1	0	1	0	3	0	0	0	0	0	0	.200	.273	.300	.573
	7 ML YEARS		938	3345	820	165	12	175	(88	87)	1534	468	498	436	336	10	819	51	4	30	62	31	74	.245	.321	.459	.779

Kyle Freeland

Pitches: L **Bats:** L **Pos:** SP-28; RP-5   **Ht:** 6'3" **Wt:** 170 **Born:** 5/14/1993 **Age:** 25

Year	Team	Lg	G	GS	CG	GF	IP	BFP	H	R	ER	HR	SH	SF	HB	TBB	IBB	SO	WP	Bk	W	L	Pct	Sh	Sv-Op	Hld	ERC	ERA
2014	2 Tms	Low	10	10	0	0	39.0	148	30	8	5	1	0	0	1	6	0	33	1	0	3	0	1.000	0	0--	-	1.74	1.15
2015	2 Tms	Low	9	9	0	0	46.2	196	50	22	21	5	1	4	2	10	0	28	2	0	3	2	.600	0	0--	-	4.00	4.05
2016	Hrtfrd	AA	14	14	0	0	88.1	367	84	43	38	9	3	6	1	25	0	51	3	0	5	7	.417	0	0--	-	3.42	3.87
2016	Albq	AAA	12	12	0	0	73.2	308	81	36	32	7	2	1	1	19	0	57	1	0	6	3	.667	0	0--	-	4.20	3.91
2017	Col	NL	33	28	0	0	156.0	688	169	78	71	17	**14**	7	8	63	4	107	1	2	11	11	.500	0	0-0	0	4.83	4.10

Freddie Freeman

Bats: L **Throws:** R **Pos:** 1B-105;3B-16;PH-1   **Ht:** 6'5" **Wt:** 220 **Born:** 9/12/1989 **Age:** 28

Year	Team	Lg	G	AB	H	2B	3B	HR	(Hm	Rd)	TB	R	RBI	RC	TBB	IBB	SO	HBP	SH	SF	SB	CS	GDP	Avg	OBP	Slg	OPS
2010	Atl	NL	20	24	4	1	0	1	(0	1)	8	3	1	0	0	0	8	0	0	0	0	0	1	.167	.167	.333	.500
2011	Atl	NL	157	571	161	32	0	21	(9	12)	256	67	76	79	53	3	142	6	0	5	4	4	15	.282	.346	.448	.795
2012	Atl	NL	147	540	140	33	2	23	(12	11)	246	91	94	82	64	4	129	7	0	**9**	2	0	10	.259	.340	.456	.796
2013	Atl	NL	147	551	176	27	2	23	(16	7)	276	89	109	124	66	10	121	7	0	5	1	0	11	.319	.396	.501	.897
2014	Atl	NL	**162**	607	175	43	4	18	(7	11)	280	93	78	101	90	4	145	8	0	3	3	4	18	.288	.386	.461	.847
2015	Atl	NL	118	416	115	27	0	18	(5	13)	196	62	66	77	56	4	98	7	0	2	3	1	6	.276	.370	.471	.841
2016	Atl	NL	158	589	178	43	6	34	(15	19)	335	102	91	119	89	18	171	10	0	5	6	1	12	.302	.400	.569	.968
2017	Atl	NL	117	440	135	35	2	28	(11	17)	258	84	71	93	65	14	95	7	0	2	8	5	9	.307	.403	.586	.989
	Postseason		5	20	8	2	0	0	(0	0)	10	4	0	2	2	0	5	0	0	0	0	0	0	.400	.455	.500	.955
	8 ML YEARS		1026	3738	1084	241	16	166	(75	91)	1855	591	586	675	483	57	909	52	0	31	27	15	82	.290	.376	.496	.872

Mike Freeman

Bats: L Throws: R Pos: PH-14;SS-10;2B-6;PR-4;1B-3;3B-3;DH-1   Ht: 6'0" Wt: 190 Born: 8/4/1987 Age: 30

Year	Team	Lg	G	AB	H	2B	3B	HR	(Hm	Rd)	TB	R	RBI	RC	TBB	IBB	SO	HBP	SH	SF	SB	CS	GDP	Avg	OBP	Slg	OPS
2013	Mobile	AA	131	454	112	20	0	1	(-	-)	135	60	40	56	65	1	84	6	6	5	29	10	8	.247	.345	.297	.643
2014	Mobile	AA	52	196	42	7	3	5	(-	-)	70	27	16	22	20	0	41	2	2	1	7	1	2	.214	.292	.357	.649
2014	Reno	AAA	71	218	67	11	7	1	(-	-)	95	37	25	37	21	0	25	0	0	2	6	0	6	.307	.365	.436	.801
2015	Reno	AAA	113	398	126	23	5	3	(-	-)	168	79	41	66	34	2	51	1	1	1	10	0	6	.317	.371	.422	.793
2016	Reno	AAA	88	341	108	17	6	1	(-	-)	140	56	24	58	38	1	75	2	2	1	11	1	1	.317	.387	.411	.798
2016	Tacom	AAA	26	105	32	6	0	3	(-	-)	47	15	15	18	13	1	19	0	0	1	1	0	2	.305	.378	.448	.826
2017	Tacom	AAA	16	60	21	3	1	1	(-	-)	29	12	9	12	7	1	10	0	0	0	2	0	1	.350	.418	.483	.901
2017	OkCity	AAA	41	121	37	4	2	0	(-	-)	45	17	16	19	13	0	31	3	1	1	5	0	4	.306	.384	.372	.756
2017	Iowa	AAA	23	77	21	3	0	2	(-	-)	30	10	6	11	7	1	19	2	1	1	3	0	0	.273	.345	.390	.734
2016	2 Tms		21	22	5	1	0	0	(0	0)	6	1	1	1	2	0	7	0	0	0	0	0	2	.227	.292	.273	.564
2017	3 Tms		35	60	6	2	0	1	(1	0)	11	6	1	2	6	1	19	0	0	0	0	0	1	.100	.182	.183	.365
16	Ari	NL	8	9	0	0	0	0	(0	0)	0	0	0	0	2	0	5	0	0	0	0	0	1	.000	.182	.000	.182
16	Sea	AL	13	13	5	1	0	0	(0	0)	6	1	1	1	0	0	2	0	0	0	0	0	1	.385	.385	.462	.846
17	Sea	AL	16	30	2	0	0	1	(1	0)	5	3	1	0	4	1	9	0	0	0	0	0	0	.067	.176	.167	.343
17	LAD	NL	4	5	0	0	0	0	(0	0)	0	0	0	0	0	0	2	0	0	0	0	0	0	.000	.000	.000	.000
17	ChC	NL	15	25	4	2	0	0	(0	0)	6	3	0	2	2	0	8	0	0	0	0	0	1	.160	.222	.240	.462
	2 ML YEARS		56	82	11	3	0	1	(1	0)	17	7	2	3	8	1	26	0	0	0	0	0	3	.134	.211	.207	.418

Sam Freeman

Pitches: L Bats: R Pos: RP-58   Ht: 5'11" Wt: 180 Born: 6/24/1987 Age: 31

Year	Team	Lg	G	GS	CG	GF	IP	BFP	H	R	ER	HR	SH	SF	HB	TBB	IBB	SO	WP	Bk	W	L	Pct	Sh	Sv-Op	Hld	ERC	ERA
2017	Gwnntt*	AAA	9	0	0	4	10.1	40	5	2	1	1	0	0	0	6	0	8	0	0	3	1	.750	0	1--	-	2.17	0.87
2012	StL	NL	24	0	0	7	20.0	86	17	13	12	2	1	0	1	10	0	18	0	0	0	2	.000	0	0-0	2	3.84	5.40
2013	StL	NL	13	0	0	2	12.1	50	8	3	3	0	1	0	0	5	0	8	2	0	1	0	1.000	0	0-0	1	1.67	2.19
2014	StL	NL	44	0	0	9	38.0	169	34	13	11	2	1	1	4	19	0	35	3	0	2	0	1.000	0	0-0	11	3.89	2.61
2015	Tex	AL	54	0	0	10	38.1	171	31	13	13	4	0	1	3	25	0	40	0	0	0	0	-	0	0-0	12	4.31	3.05
2016	Mil	NL	7	0	0	4	7.2	44	13	11	11	2	0	2	0	9	0	8	1	0	0	0	-	0	0-0	0	13.79	12.91
2017	Atl	NL	58	0	0	5	60.0	254	48	19	17	3	1	1	3	27	2	59	2	0	2	0	1.000	0	0-3	12	2.97	2.55
	Postseason		1	0	0	0	0.2	2	0	0	0	0	0	0	0	2	0	0	0	0	0	0	-	0	0-0	0	-	-
	6 ML YEARS		200	0	0	37	176.1	774	151	72	67	13	4	5	11	95	2	168	8	0	5	2	.714	0	0-3	38	3.82	3.42

David Freese

Bats: R Throws: R Pos: 3B-116;PH-11;1B-3;DH-3   FREEZE   Ht: 6'2" Wt: 220 Born: 4/28/1983 Age: 35

Year	Team	Lg	G	AB	H	2B	3B	HR	(Hm	Rd)	TB	R	RBI	RC	TBB	IBB	SO	HBP	SH	SF	SB	CS	GDP	Avg	OBP	Slg	OPS
2009	StL	NL	17	31	10	2	0	1	(0	1)	15	3	7	4	2	0	7	0	0	1	0	0	1	.323	.353	.484	.837
2010	StL	NL	70	240	71	12	1	4	(3	1)	97	28	36	36	21	0	59	4	4	1	1	1	7	.296	.361	.404	.765
2011	StL	NL	97	333	99	16	1	10	(6	4)	147	41	55	50	24	0	75	4	0	2	1	0	18	.297	.350	.441	.791
2012	StL	NL	144	501	147	25	1	20	(8	12)	234	70	79	79	57	2	122	7	0	2	3	3	19	.293	.372	.467	.839
2013	StL	NL	138	462	121	26	1	9	(4	5)	176	53	60	48	47	1	106	9	0	3	1	2	26	.262	.340	.381	.721
2014	LAA	AL	134	462	120	25	1	10	(6	4)	177	53	55	55	38	0	124	6	0	5	1	3	16	.260	.321	.383	.704
2015	LAA	AL	121	424	109	27	0	14	(9	5)	178	53	56	60	31	0	107	12	0	3	1	1	12	.257	.323	.420	.743
2016	Pit	NL	141	437	118	23	0	13	(5	8)	180	63	55	61	45	2	142	10	0	0	0	0	15	.270	.352	.412	.764
2017	Pit	NL	130	426	112	16	0	10	(7	3)	158	44	52	63	58	5	116	15	0	4	0	1	21	.263	.368	.371	.739
	Postseason		51	174	49	15	1	8	(4	4)	90	21	30	31	19	2	47	2	0	1	0	1	8	.282	.357	.517	.874
	9 ML YEARS		992	3316	907	172	5	91	(48	43)	1362	408	455	456	323	10	858	67	4	21	8	11	118	.274	.348	.411	.759

David Freitas

Bats: R Throws: R Pos: C-6   FRAY-dus   Ht: 6'3" Wt: 225 Born: 3/18/1989 Age: 29

Year	Team	Lg	G	AB	H	2B	3B	HR	(Hm	Rd)	TB	R	RBI	RC	TBB	IBB	SO	HBP	SH	SF	SB	CS	GDP	Avg	OBP	Slg	OPS
2013	Scrmto	AAA	29	97	26	8	0	1	(-	-)	37	13	9	14	11	0	14	2	0	0	0	0	5	.268	.355	.381	.736
2013	Mdlnd	AA	61	224	48	6	0	9	(-	-)	81	34	21	24	20	0	39	2	0	0	0	0	9	.214	.285	.362	.646
2014	Bowie	AA	53	168	42	11	0	5	(-	-)	68	22	25	23	19	0	24	1	1	1	0	0	7	.250	.328	.405	.733
2015	Bowie	AA	71	248	60	12	0	8	(-	-)	96	28	33	31	17	0	37	6	1	4	1	0	7	.242	.302	.387	.689
2016	Tenn	AA	66	248	71	20	1	4	(-	-)	105	37	38	37	21	0	47	1	0	0	0	0	11	.286	.344	.423	.768
2016	Iowa	AA	25	84	27	7	0	2	(-	-)	40	7	15	15	7	0	20	0	1	3	3	0	2	.321	.362	.476	.838
2017	Gwnntt	AAA	72	236	62	13	0	3	(-	-)	84	28	21	31	25	0	35	4	0	4	0	0	10	.263	.338	.356	.694
2017	Atl	NL	6	17	4	2	0	0	(0	0)	6	2	2	1	0	0	4	0	0	0	0	0	1	.235	.235	.353	.588

Max Fried

Pitches: L Bats: L Pos: RP-5; SP-4   Ht: 6'4" Wt: 200 Born: 1/18/1994 Age: 24

Year	Team	Lg	G	GS	CG	GF	IP	BFP	H	R	ER	HR	SH	SF	HB	TBB	IBB	SO	WP	Bk	W	L	Pct	Sh	Sv-Op	Hld	ERC	ERA
2013	FtWyn	A	23	23	0	0	118.2	500	107	54	46	7	4	3	8	56	1	100	10	3	6	7	.462	0	0--	-	3.90	3.49
2014	2 Tms	Low	5	5	0	0	10.2	50	15	6	6	1	0	0	0	5	0	10	0	0	1	0	1.000	0	0--	-	6.86	5.06
2016	Rome	A	21	20	0	0	103.0	425	87	52	45	10	2	3	4	47	0	112	11	3	8	7	.533	0	0--	-	3.70	3.93
2017	Missi	AA	19	19	0	0	86.2	385	88	61	57	8	4	3	7	43	2	85	6	2	2	11	.154	0	0--	-	4.83	5.92
2017	Atl	NL	9	4	0	4	26.0	121	30	15	11	3	0	0	4	12	1	22	0	0	1	1	.500	0	0-0	-	5.92	3.81

Christian Friedrich

Pitches: L Bats: R Pos: P

FREE-drick

Ht: 6'4" Wt: 222 Born: 7/8/1987 Age: 30

Year	Team	Lg	G	GS	CG	GF	IP	BFP	H	R	ER	HR	SH	SF	HB	TBB	IBB	SO	WP	Bk	W	L	Pct	Sh	Sv-Op	Hld	ERC	ERA
2012	Col	NL	16	16	0	0	84.2	377	102	61	58	14	6	2	2	30	0	74	8	0	5	8	.385	0	0-0	0	5.71	6.17
2014	Col	NL	16	3	0	3	24.1	110	25	21	16	3	1	2	2	10	1	27	5	0	0	4	.000	0	0-0	3	4.59	5.92
2015	Col	NL	68	0	0	13	58.1	270	75	37	34	5	4	6	1	25	2	45	3	0	0	4	.000	0	0-0	9	5.76	5.25
2016	SD	NL	24	23	0	0	129.1	567	131	74	69	13	3	5	2	52	2	100	7	0	5	12	.294	0	0-0	0	4.14	4.80
4 ML YEARS			124	42	0	16	296.2	1324	333	193	177	35	14	15	7	117	5	246	23	0	10	28	.263	0	0-0	12	4.93	5.37

Ernesto Frieri

Pitches: R Bats: R Pos: RP-6

free-AIR-ee

Ht: 6'0" Wt: 205 Born: 7/19/1985 Age: 32

Year	Team	Lg	G	GS	CG	GF	IP	BFP	H	R	ER	HR	SH	SF	HB	TBB	IBB	SO	WP	Bk	W	L	Pct	Sh	Sv-Op	Hld	ERC	ERA
2017 S-WB*	AAA		17	0	0	14	21.0	84	13	8	7	3	0	0	0	9	0	24	0	0	2	0	1.000	0	7- -	-	2.46	3.00
2017 RdRck*	AAA		7	0	0	2	6.1	27	5	1	1	0	2	0	0	3	0	10	0	0	0	1	.000	0	0- -	-	2.50	1.42
2017 Tacom*	AAA		7	0	0	0	12.0	54	9	7	7	1	1	1	0	9	0	18	0	0	1	2	.333	0	0- -	-	3.82	5.25
2009 SD	NL		2	0	0	2	2.0	7	0	0	0	0	0	0	0	1	0	2	0	0	0	0	-	0	0-0	0	0.27	0.00
2010 SD	NL		33	0	0	12	31.2	128	18	7	6	2	0	0	0	17	3	41	2	0	1	1	.500	0	0-0	7	1.99	1.71
2011 SD	NL		59	0	0	19	63.0	276	35	21	19	3	1	1	9	34	5	76	1	1	1	2	.333	0	0-0	4	3.60	2.71
2012 2 Tms			67	0	0	51	66.0	269	35	20	17	9	1	1	7	30	0	98	1	0	5	2	.714	0	23-26	7	2.43	2.32
2013 LAA	AL		67	0	0	51	68.2	292	55	29	29	11	2	2	3	30	1	98	1	0	2	4	.333	0	37-41	2	3.64	3.80
2014 2 Tms			48	0	0	30	41.2	184	47	34	34	11	0	0	2	14	2	48	0	0	1	4	.200	0	11-14	3	5.89	7.34
2015 TB	AL		22	0	0	6	23.1	100	20	12	12	6	0	2	1	11	0	19	1	0	1	0	1.000	0	2-3	0	4.84	4.63
2017 Tex	AL		6	0	0	2	7.0	31	6	4	4	0	1	0	0	6	2	5	0	0	0	1	.000	0	0-0	2	3.89	5.14
12 SD	NL		11	0	0	5	11.2	50	9	5	3	2	0	0	2	4	0	18	0	0	1	0	1.000	0	0-0	1	3.67	2.31
12 LAA	AL		56	0	0	46	54.1	219	26	15	14	7	1	1	5	26	0	80	1	0	4	2	.667	0	23-26	6	2.18	2.32
14 LAA	AL		34	0	0	22	31.0	133	33	22	22	8	0	0	1	9	1	38	0	0	0	3	.000	0	11-14	3	5.21	6.39
14 Pit	NL		14	0	0	8	10.2	51	14	12	12	3	0	0	1	5	1	10	0	0	1	1	.500	0	0-0	0	7.97	10.13
8 ML YEARS			304	0	0	173	303.1	1287	232	127	121	42	5	6	22	143	13	387	6	1	11	14	.440	0	73-84	25	3.53	3.59

Jace Fry

Pitches: L Bats: L Pos: RP-11

Ht: 6'1" Wt: 190 Born: 7/9/1993 Age: 24

Year	Team	Lg	G	GS	CG	GF	IP	BFP	H	R	ER	HR	SH	SF	HB	TBB	IBB	SO	WP	Bk	W	L	Pct	Sh	Sv-Op	Hld	ERC	ERA
2014 Gr Falls	R+		7	0	0	1	9.1	38	7	3	3	0	1	0	0	3	0	10	0	0	1	0	1.000	0	0- -	-	1.85	2.89
2015 WinSa	A+		10	10	0	0	52.0	231	60	26	21	1	1	4	0	17	0	39	3	0	1	8	.111	0	0- -	-	4.00	3.63
2017 Brham	AA		33	0	0	19	45.1	192	36	14	14	1	0	1	1	24	2	52	8	0	2	1	.667	0	3- -	-	2.94	2.78
2017 CWS	AL		11	0	0	3	6.2	36	12	8	8	1	0	0	0	5	1	3	3	0	0	0	-	0	0-0	0	10.97	10.80

Eric Fryer

Bats: R Throws: R Pos: C-26;PH-13;PR-1

Ht: 6'2" Wt: 215 Born: 8/26/1985 Age: 32

Year	Team	Lg	G	AB	H	2B	3B	HR	(Hm	Rd)	TB	R	RBI	RC	TBB	IBB	SO	HBP	SH	SF	SB	CS	GDP	Avg	OBP	Slg	OPS
2011 Pit	NL		10	26	7	0	0	0	(0	0)	7	5	0	2	3	1	7	0	0	0	1	1	0	.269	.345	.269	.614
2012 Pit	NL		6	4	1	0	0	0	(0	0)	1	0	0	1	1	0	1	0	0	0	0	0	0	.250	.400	.250	.650
2013 Min	AL		6	13	5	1	0	1	(1	0)	9	2	4	5	3	0	3	0	0	0	0	0	1	.385	.500	.692	1.192
2014 Min	AL		28	75	16	4	0	1	(0	1)	23	11	5	6	5	0	15	1	0	0	1	0	0	.213	.272	.307	.578
2015 Min	AL		15	22	5	2	0	0	(0	0)	7	2	2	3	5	0	11	0	0	0	0	0	0	.227	.370	.318	.689
2016 2 Tms	NL		60	116	31	4	1	0	(0	0)	37	19	13	13	13	0	25	0	2	2	0	3	1	.267	.336	.319	.655
2017 StL	NL		34	71	11	3	0	0	(0	0)	14	7	3	3	11	0	18	1	0	0	0	0	3	.155	.277	.197	.474
16 StL	NL		24	38	14	2	0	0	(0	0)	16	7	5	5	3	0	7	0	0	0	0	1	0	.368	.415	.421	.836
16 Pit	NL		36	78	17	2	1	0	(0	0)	21	12	8	8	10	0	18	0	2	2	0	2	1	.218	.300	.269	.569
7 ML YEARS			159	327	76	14	1	2	(1	1)	98	46	27	33	41	1	80	2	2	2	2	4	5	.232	.320	.300	.620

Rey Fuentes

Bats: L Throws: L Pos: CF-41;PH-20;LF-9;RF-4;PR-4

foo-WHEN-tayz

Ht: 6'0" Wt: 160 Born: 2/12/1991 Age: 27

Year	Team	Lg	G	AB	H	2B	3B	HR	(Hm	Rd)	TB	R	RBI	RC	TBB	IBB	SO	HBP	SH	SF	SB	CS	GDP	Avg	OBP	Slg	OPS
2017 Reno*	AAA		45	175	60	11	3	0	(-	-)	77	30	14	32	12	1	30	2	0	3	13	1	2	.343	.386	.440	.825
2013 SD	NL		23	33	5	0	0	0	(0	0)	5	4	1	1	3	0	16	0	0	0	3	0	0	.152	.222	.152	.374
2016 KC	AL		13	41	13	1	0	0	(0	0)	14	2	5	5	3	0	8	0	0	0	0	2	0	.317	.364	.341	.705
2017 Ari	NL		64	136	32	1	2	3	(1	2)	46	19	9	11	8	0	35	0	1	0	4	1	0	.235	.278	.338	.616
3 ML YEARS			100	210	50	2	2	3	(1	2)	65	25	15	17	14	0	59	0	1	0	7	3	0	.238	.286	.310	.595

Carson Fulmer

Pitches: R Bats: R Pos: SP-5; RP-2

Ht: 6'0" Wt: 195 Born: 12/13/1993 Age: 24

Year	Team	Lg	G	GS	CG	GF	IP	BFP	H	R	ER	HR	SH	SF	HB	TBB	IBB	SO	WP	Bk	W	L	Pct	Sh	Sv-Op	Hld	ERC	ERA
2015 2 Tms	Low		9	9	0	0	23.0	93	17	5	5	2	1	0	2	9	0	26	3	0	0	0	-	0	0- -	-	2.98	1.96
2016 Brham	AA		17	17	0	0	87.0	393	82	51	46	7	4	4	3	51	0	90	7	1	4	9	.308	0	0- -	-	4.41	4.76
2017 Charllt	AAA		25	25	0	0	126.0	570	132	89	81	18	2	4	7	65	0	96	9	3	7	9	.438	0	0- -	-	5.36	5.79
2016 CWS	AL		8	0	0	4	11.2	53	12	11	11	2	0	0	2	7	0	10	2	0	0	2	.000	0	0-1	0	6.57	8.49
2017 CWS	AL		7	5	0	0	23.1	101	16	10	10	4	1	0	2	13	0	19	0	2	3	1	.750	0	0-0	0	3.71	3.86
2 ML YEARS			15	5	0	4	35.0	154	28	21	21	6	1	0	4	20	0	29	2	2	3	3	.500	0	0-1	0	4.60	5.40

Michael Fulmer

Pitches: R **Bats:** R **Pos:** SP-25   **Ht:** 6'3" **Wt:** 210 **Born:** 3/15/1993 **Age:** 25

Year Team	Lg	G	GS	CG	GF	IP	BFP	H	R	ER	HR	SH	SF	HB	TBB	IBB	SO	WP	Bk	W	L	Pct	Sh	Sv-Op	Hld	ERC	ERA
2013 2 Tms	Low	9	9	0	0	46.0	193	33	17	17	1	1	3	5	19	0	42	1	0	3	3	.500	0	0--	-	2.49	3.33
2014 Stluci	A+	19	19	0	0	95.0	435	112	52	42	7	3	1	8	31	0	86	6	0	6	10	.375	0	0--	-	4.83	3.98
2015 Bnghtn	AA	15	15	0	0	86.0	349	73	25	18	3	4	0	1	23	0	83	3	1	6	2	.750	0	0--	-	2.42	1.88
2015 Erie	AA	6	6	0	0	31.2	124	27	10	10	4	0	0	0	7	0	33	2	0	4	1	.800	0	0--	-	2.86	2.84
2016 Det	AL	26	26	1	0	159.0	647	136	57	54	16	4	2	9	42	1	132	1	1	11	7	.611	1	0-0	0	3.02	3.06
2017 Det	AL	25	25	1	0	164.2	676	150	80	70	13	3	8	8	40	2	114	3	1	10	12	.455	0	0-0	0	3.04	3.83
2 ML YEARS		51	51	2	0	323.2	1323	286	137	124	29	7	10	17	82	3	246	4	2	21	19	.525	1	0-0	0	3.03	3.45

Rocky Gale

Bats: R **Throws:** R **Pos:** C-3   **Ht:** 6'1" **Wt:** 185 **Born:** 2/22/1988 **Age:** 30

Year Team	Lg	G	AB	H	2B	3B	HR	(Hm	Rd)	TB	R	RBI	RC	TBB	IBB	SO	HBP	SH	SF	SB	CS	GDP	Avg	OBP	Slg	OPS
2013 SnAnt	AA	62	207	51	5	0	1	(-	-)	59	15	22	16	10	0	19	2	3	2	0	4	8	.246	.285	.285	.570
2014 ElPaso	AAA	77	228	69	12	0	0	(-	-)	81	21	35	27	10	1	33	0	2	3	1	0	4	.303	.328	.355	.683
2015 ElPaso	AAA	102	322	99	16	4	1	(-	-)	126	34	39	45	17	2	59	5	4	3	1	1	10	.307	.349	.391	.740
2016 SnAnt	AA	63	210	46	8	1	2	(-	-)	62	21	20	23	29	1	38	4	2	2	1	0	6	.219	.322	.295	.618
2016 ElPaso	AAA	44	144	40	2	0	3	(-	-)	51	16	14	17	5	1	19	5	2	3	0	0	7	.278	.318	.354	.673
2017 ElPaso	AAA	103	342	95	20	2	2	(-	-)	125	43	37	43	24	1	55	4	2	5	0	0	10	.278	.328	.365	.693
2015 SD	NL	11	10	1	0	0	0	(0	0)	1	0	0	0	0	0	1	0	0	0	0	0	1	.100	.100	.100	.200
2017 SD	NL	3	10	1	0	0	1	(1	0)	4	1	2	1	0	0	2	0	0	0	0	0	0	.100	.100	.400	.500
2 ML YEARS		14	20	2	0	0	1	(1	0)	5	1	2	1	0	0	3	0	0	0	0	0	1	.100	.100	.250	.350

Cam Gallagher

Bats: R **Throws:** R **Pos:** C-13;PH-1;PR-1   **Ht:** 6'3" **Wt:** 230 **Born:** 12/6/1992 **Age:** 25

Year Team	Lg	G	AB	H	2B	3B	HR	(Hm	Rd)	TB	R	RBI	RC	TBB	IBB	SO	HBP	SH	SF	SB	CS	GDP	Avg	OBP	Slg	OPS
2013 Lxngtn	A	66	222	47	15	0	2	(-	-)	68	19	18	22	24	0	28	6	1	3	0	0	6	.212	.302	.306	.608
2014 Wilmg	A+	96	312	71	18	0	5	(-	-)	104	24	34	35	37	0	38	1	5	6	1	0	8	.228	.306	.333	.640
2015 Wilmg	A+	77	253	62	15	0	5	(-	-)	92	24	23	32	28	2	34	2	5	2	0	0	11	.245	.323	.364	.686
2016 NWArk	AA	91	301	78	16	1	4	(-	-)	108	23	24	41	37	1	52	5	0	2	2	2	10	.259	.348	.359	.707
2017 Omha	AAA	73	260	76	13	0	5	(-	-)	104	26	37	35	18	2	33	0	2	2	0	1	12	.292	.336	.400	.736
2017 KC	AL	13	24	6	1	0	1	(0	1)	10	2	5	4	3	0	4	0	0	0	0	0	1	.250	.333	.417	.750

Yovani Gallardo

guy-YARR-doe

Pitches: R **Bats:** R **Pos:** SP-22; RP-6   **Ht:** 6'2" **Wt:** 205 **Born:** 2/27/1986 **Age:** 32

Year Team	Lg	G	GS	CG	GF	IP	BFP	H	R	ER	HR	SH	SF	HB	TBB	IBB	SO	WP	Bk	W	L	Pct	Sh	Sv-Op	Hld	ERC	ERA
2007 Mil	NL	20	17	0	1	110.1	466	103	48	45	8	4	3	2	37	2	101	3	0	9	5	.643	0	0-0	0	3.30	3.67
2008 Mil	NL	4	4	0	0	24.0	97	22	5	5	3	2	1	0	8	0	20	0	0	0	0	-	0	0-0	0	3.66	1.88
2009 Mil	NL	30	30	1	0	185.2	793	150	78	77	21	5	3	5	94	5	204	9	0	13	12	.520	0	0-0	0	3.57	3.73
2010 Mil	NL	31	31	2	0	185.0	803	178	89	79	12	11	4	3	75	5	200	7	1	14	7	.667	2	0-0	0	3.61	3.84
2011 Mil	NL	33	33	1	0	207.1	865	193	92	81	27	10	7	1	59	1	207	12	0	17	10	.630	1	0-0	0	3.43	3.52
2012 Mil	NL	33	33	0	0	204.0	860	185	86	83	26	11	6	0	81	3	204	5	0	16	9	.640	0	0-0	0	3.72	3.66
2013 Mil	NL	31	31	0	0	180.2	773	180	92	84	18	8	7	3	66	1	144	5	0	12	10	.545	0	0-0	0	3.98	4.18
2014 Mil	NL	32	32	0	0	192.1	817	195	86	75	21	8	3	4	54	2	146	8	0	8	11	.421	0	0-0	0	3.79	3.51
2015 Tex	AL	33	33	0	0	184.1	793	193	76	70	15	1	3	6	68	0	121	10	0	13	11	.542	0	0-0	0	4.13	3.42
2016 Bal	AL	23	23	0	0	118.0	526	126	74	71	16	1	6	1	61	2	85	6	0	6	8	.429	0	0-0	0	5.26	5.42
2017 Sea	AL	28	22	0	4	130.2	578	138	84	83	24	4	3	2	60	3	94	7	0	5	10	.333	0	1-1	0	5.30	5.72
Postseason		6	5	0	0	31.0	129	26	11	8	2	1	0	0	14	3	21	4	0	2	2	.500	0	0-0	0	3.05	2.32
11 ML YEARS		298	289	4	5	1722.1	7371	1663	810	753	191	65	46	22	663	24	1526	72	1	113	93	.549	3	1-1	0	3.92	3.93

Giovanny Gallegos

GUY-yay-gohs

Pitches: R **Bats:** R **Pos:** RP-16   **Ht:** 6'2" **Wt:** 210 **Born:** 8/14/1991 **Age:** 26

Year Team	Lg	G	GS	CG	GF	IP	BFP	H	R	ER	HR	SH	SF	HB	TBB	IBB	SO	WP	Bk	W	L	Pct	Sh	Sv-Op	Hld	ERC	ERA
2013 Stnlld	A-	16	16	0	0	65.1	276	71	32	31	9	0	2	5	14	0	43	3	1	2	8	.200	0	0--	-	4.47	4.27
2014 CtnSC	A	29	6	0	6	88.2	391	108	56	45	8	1	5	3	19	1	91	6	0	5	5	.500	0	1--	-	4.57	4.57
2015 Tampa	A+	30	0	0	17	53.1	201	32	11	8	2	3	1	2	7	0	54	2	1	3	1	.750	0	5--	-	1.18	1.35
2016 Trntn	AA	17	0	0	10	33.0	124	20	6	5	1	0	0	0	7	0	53	1	0	2	1	.667	0	2--	-	1.28	1.36
2016 S-WB	AAA	25	0	0	7	45.0	170	28	7	7	4	0	2	1	10	1	53	4	1	5	1	.833	0	2--	-	1.61	1.40
2017 S-WB	AAA	28	0	0	14	43.1	169	28	12	10	4	1	0	1	11	0	69	5	0	4	2	.667	0	5--	-	1.79	2.08
2017 NYY	AL	16	0	0	7	20.1	88	21	12	11	3	1	0	1	5	1	22	1	1	0	1	.000	0	0-1	0	3.76	4.87

Joey Gallo

Bats: L **Throws:** R **Pos:** 3B-72;1B-59;LF-18;PR-5;PH-3;DH-1   **Ht:** 6'5" **Wt:** 235 **Born:** 11/19/1993 **Age:** 24

Year Team	Lg	G	AB	H	2B	3B	HR	(Hm	Rd)	TB	R	RBI	RC	TBB	IBB	SO	HBP	SH	SF	SB	CS	GDP	Avg	OBP	Slg	OPS
2015 Tex	AL	36	108	22	3	1	6	(4	2)	45	16	14	13	15	3	57	0	0	0	3	0	0	.204	.301	.417	.717
2016 Tex	AL	17	25	1	0	0	1	(1	0)	4	2	1	0	5	0	19	0	0	0	1	0	0	.040	.200	.160	.360
2017 Tex	AL	145	449	94	18	3	41	(22	19)	241	85	80	84	75	1	196	8	0	0	7	2	3	.209	.333	.537	.869
3 ML YEARS		198	582	117	21	4	48	(27	21)	290	103	95	97	95	4	272	8	0	0	11	2	3	.201	.321	.498	.819

Freddy Galvis

Bats: B **Throws:** R **Pos:** SS-155;PH-6;LF-1;CF-1   GAL-viss   **Ht:** 5'10" **Wt:** 185 **Born:** 11/14/1989 **Age:** 28

Year	Team	Lg	G	AB	H	2B	3B	HR	(Hm	Rd)	TB	R	RBI	RC	TBB	IBB	SO	HBP	SH	SF	SB	CS	GDP	Avg	OBP	Slg	OPS
2012	Phi	NL	58	190	43	15	1	3	(3	0)	69	14	24	14	7	0	29	0	3	0	0	0	6	.226	.254	.363	.617
2013	Phi	NL	70	205	48	5	4	6	(4	2)	79	13	19	20	13	2	45	1	3	0	1	0	5	.234	.283	.385	.668
2014	Phi	NL	43	119	21	3	1	4	(2	2)	38	14	12	9	8	0	30	0	0	1	1	0	0	.176	.227	.319	.546
2015	Phi	NL	151	559	147	14	5	7	(6	1)	192	62	50	64	30	1	103	3	7	4	10	1	11	.263	.302	.343	.645
2016	Phi	NL	158	584	141	26	3	20	(11	9)	233	61	67	59	25	6	136	3	8	4	17	6	16	.241	.274	.399	.673
2017	Phi	NL	162	608	155	29	6	12	(10	2)	232	71	61	77	45	2	111	4	2	4	14	5	12	.255	.309	.382	.690
	6 ML YEARS		642	2265	555	92	20	52	(36	16)	843	236	233	243	128	11	454	11	23	13	43	12	50	.245	.287	.372	.659

Ben Gamel

Bats: L **Throws:** L **Pos:** LF-85;RF-50;PH-5;1B-1   **Ht:** 5'11" **Wt:** 185 **Born:** 5/17/1992 **Age:** 26

Year	Team	Lg	G	AB	H	2B	3B	HR	(Hm	Rd)	TB	R	RBI	RC	TBB	IBB	SO	HBP	SH	SF	SB	CS	GDP	Avg	OBP	Slg	OPS
2013	Tampa	A+	96	364	99	28	4	3	(-	-)	144	50	49	57	48	2	77	1	3	7	21	5	7	.272	.352	.396	.748
2013	Trntn	AA	16	67	16	4	0	1	(-	-)	23	5	5	6	4	0	18	0	1	0	1	0	0	.239	.282	.343	.625
2014	Trntn	AA	131	544	142	31	3	2	(-	-)	185	58	51	60	36	0	88	2	1	3	13	5	10	.261	.308	.340	.648
2015	S-WB	AAA	129	500	150	28	14	10	(-	-)	236	77	64	86	46	5	108	1	1	3	13	5	9	.300	.358	.472	.830
2016	S-WB	AAA	116	483	149	26	5	6	(-	-)	203	80	51	77	43	3	94	2	1	4	19	8	7	.308	.365	.420	.785
2017	Tacom	AAA	19	60	18	1	1	1	(-	-)	24	6	8	11	12	0	11	2	0	1	1	1	2	.300	.427	.400	.827
2016	2 Tms	AL	33	48	9	2	0	1	(0	1)	14	9	5	4	6	0	16	0	3	0	0	0	1	.188	.278	.292	.569
2017	Sea	AL	134	509	140	27	5	11	(5	6)	210	68	59	68	36	1	122	1	1	3	4	1	8	.275	.322	.413	.735
16	NYY	AL	6	8	1	0	0	0	(0	0)	1	1	0	0	1	0	1	0	1	0	0	0	1	.125	.222	.125	.347
16	Sea	AL	27	40	8	2	0	1	(0	1)	13	8	5	4	5	0	15	0	2	0	0	0	0	.200	.289	.325	.614
	2 ML YEARS		167	557	149	29	5	12	(5	7)	224	77	64	72	42	1	138	1	4	3	4	1	9	.268	.318	.402	.721

John Gant

Pitches: R **Bats:** R **Pos:** RP-5; SP-2   **Ht:** 6'3" **Wt:** 200 **Born:** 8/6/1992 **Age:** 25

Year	Team	Lg	G	GS	CG	GF	IP	BFP	H	R	ER	HR	SH	SF	HB	TBB	IBB	SO	WP	Bk	W	L	Pct	Sh	Sv-Op	Hld	ERC	ERA
2013	Bklyn	A-	13	13	1	0	71.2	293	53	30	23	1	7	5	5	28	0	81	3	2	6	4	.600	1	0--	-	2.39	2.89
2014	Savann	A	21	21	2	0	123.0	510	107	47	35	5	1	2	3	40	0	114	7	1	11	5	.688	2	0--	-	2.79	2.56
2015	Bnghtn	AA	11	11	0	0	59.1	265	67	38	29	2	3	3	1	26	0	43	2	1	4	5	.444	0	0--	-	4.54	4.40
2015	Stluci	A+	6	6	0	0	40.1	162	27	9	8	4	0	1	1	10	0	48	0	0	2	0	1.000	0	0--	-	1.85	1.79
2015	Missi	AA	7	7	0	0	40.2	157	28	11	9	1	3	1	0	14	0	43	2	1	4	0	1.000	0	0--	-	1.90	1.99
2016	Gwnntt	AAA	12	10	0	1	56.0	245	58	29	26	5	1	1	0	22	0	57	7	0	3	3	.500	0	0--	-	4.13	4.18
2017	Memp	AAA	18	18	0	0	103.1	434	109	47	44	10	4	0	4	25	1	99	2	1	6	5	.545	0	0--	-	3.92	3.83
2016	Atl	NL	20	7	0	6	50.0	222	54	32	27	7	3	2	2	21	3	49	4	0	1	4	.200	0	0-0	0	4.97	4.86
2017	StL	NL	7	2	0	1	17.1	76	17	9	9	4	0	1	1	10	1	11	0	0	0	1	.000	0	0-0	0	6.01	4.67
	2 ML YEARS		27	9	0	7	67.1	298	71	41	36	11	3	3	3	31	4	60	4	0	1	5	.167	0	0-0	0	5.23	4.81

Adonis Garcia

Bats: R **Throws:** R **Pos:** 3B-39;PH-12;LF-1   ah-DOH-niss   **Ht:** 5'9" **Wt:** 205 **Born:** 4/12/1985 **Age:** 33

Year	Team	Lg	G	AB	H	2B	3B	HR	(Hm	Rd)	TB	R	RBI	RC	TBB	IBB	SO	HBP	SH	SF	SB	CS	GDP	Avg	OBP	Slg	OPS
2015	Atl	NL	58	191	53	12	0	10	(8	2)	95	20	26	16	5	0	35	0	0	0	0	0	9	.277	.293	.497	.790
2016	Atl	NL	134	532	145	29	0	14	(5	9)	216	65	65	60	24	4	93	6	0	0	3	2	18	.273	.311	.406	.717
2017	Atl	NL	52	173	41	4	0	5	(2	3)	60	19	19	15	7	0	23	2	0	1	4	0	9	.237	.273	.347	.620
	3 ML YEARS		244	896	239	45	0	29	(15	14)	371	104	110	91	36	4	151	8	0	3	7	2	36	.267	.300	.414	.714

Avisail Garcia

Bats: R **Throws:** R **Pos:** RF-132;DH-4;PH-1   ah-vee-SAH-eel   **Ht:** 6'4" **Wt:** 240 **Born:** 6/12/1991 **Age:** 27

Year	Team	Lg	G	AB	H	2B	3B	HR	(Hm	Rd)	TB	R	RBI	RC	TBB	IBB	SO	HBP	SH	SF	SB	CS	GDP	Avg	OBP	Slg	OPS
2012	Det	AL	23	47	15	0	0	0	(0	0)	15	7	3	5	3	1	10	1	0	0	0	2	1	.319	.373	.319	.692
2013	2 Tms	AL	72	244	69	7	3	7	(3	4)	103	31	31	30	9	0	59	1	0	2	3	3	8	.283	.309	.422	.731
2014	CWS	AL	46	172	42	8	0	7	(2	5)	71	19	29	20	14	1	44	2	0	2	4	1	5	.244	.305	.413	.718
2015	CWS	AL	148	553	142	17	2	13	(8	5)	202	66	59	58	36	3	141	8	0	4	7	7	13	.257	.309	.365	.675
2016	CWS	AL	120	413	101	18	2	12	(5	7)	159	59	51	56	34	0	115	4	0	2	4	4	9	.245	.307	.385	.692
2017	CWS	AL	136	518	171	27	5	18	(9	9)	262	75	80	96	33	5	111	9	0	1	5	3	14	.330	.380	.506	.885
13	Det	AL	30	83	20	3	1	2	(1	1)	31	12	10	7	4	0	21	0	0	1	0	1	3	.241	.273	.373	.646
13	CWS	AL	42	161	49	4	2	5	(2	3)	72	19	21	23	5	0	38	1	0	1	3	2	5	.304	.327	.447	.775
	Postseason		12	23	6	1	0	0	(0	0)	7	0	4	4	2	0	5	0	0	0	1	0	0	.261	.320	.304	.624
	6 ML YEARS		545	1947	540	77	12	57	(27	30)	812	257	253	265	129	10	480	25	0	11	23	20	50	.277	.329	.417	.746

Greg Garcia

Bats: L **Throws:** R **Pos:** PH-63;3B-41;2B-34;SS-12   **Ht:** 6'0" **Wt:** 190 **Born:** 8/8/1989 **Age:** 28

Year	Team	Lg	G	AB	H	2B	3B	HR	(Hm	Rd)	TB	R	RBI	RC	TBB	IBB	SO	HBP	SH	SF	SB	CS	GDP	Avg	OBP	Slg	OPS
2014	StL	NL	14	14	2	1	0	0	(0	0)	3	2	1	1	1	0	6	3	0	0	0	0	0	.143	.333	.214	.548
2015	StL	NL	49	75	18	5	0	2	(1	1)	29	7	4	7	10	1	12	1	1	0	0	0	2	.240	.337	.387	.724

(Batting — Jaime Garcia)

Year	Team	Lg	G	AB	H	2B	3B	HR	(Hm	Rd)	TB	R	RBI	RC	TBB	IBB	SO	HBP	SH	SF	SB	CS	GDP	Avg	OBP	Slg	OPS
2016	StL	NL	99	214	59	11	0	3	(0	3)	79	33	17	31	38	4	50	4	0	1	1	1	3	.276	.393	.369	.762
2017	StL	NL	133	241	61	9	2	2	(1	1)	80	27	20	30	37	0	64	6	5	1	2	1	6	.253	.365	.332	.697
	Postseason		3	3	0	0	0	0	(0	0)	0	0	0	0	0	0	1	0	0	0	0	0	0	.000	.000	.000	.000
	4 ML YEARS		295	544	140	26	2	7	(2	5)	191	69	42	69	86	5	132	14	6	2	3	2	11	.257	.372	.351	.723

Jaime Garcia

Pitches: L **Bats:** L **Pos:** SP-27

HY-may

Ht: 6'2" **Wt:** 215 **Born:** 7/8/1986 **Age:** 31

Year	Team	Lg	G	GS	CG	GF	IP	BFP	H	R	ER	HR	SH	SF	HB	TBB	IBB	SO	WP	Bk	W	L	Pct	Sh	Sv-Op	Hld	ERC	ERA
2008	StL	NL	10	1	0	4	16.0	69	14	10	10	4	0	0	1	8	0	8	3	0	1	1	.500	0	0-0	3	5.15	5.63
2010	StL	NL	28	28	1	0	163.1	695	151	64	49	9	3	3	3	64	4	132	4	1	13	8	.619	1	0-0	0	3.34	2.70
2011	StL	NL	32	32	2	0	194.2	826	207	100	77	15	10	5	2	50	2	156	12	1	13	7	.650	2	0-0	0	3.73	3.56
2012	StL	NL	20	20	0	0	121.2	515	136	58	53	7	8	7	0	30	1	98	12	1	7	7	.500	0	0-0	0	3.86	3.92
2013	StL	NL	9	9	0	0	55.1	234	57	26	22	6	2	0	0	15	0	43	3	0	5	2	.714	0	0-0	0	3.78	3.58
2014	StL	NL	7	7	0	0	43.2	177	39	20	20	6	0	0	3	7	0	39	1	0	3	1	.750	0	0-0	0	3.08	4.12
2015	StL	NL	20	20	0	0	129.2	510	106	37	35	6	3	3	3	30	0	97	4	0	10	6	.625	0	0-0	0	2.31	2.43
2016	StL	NL	32	30	1	0	171.2	741	179	94	89	26	7	2	7	57	3	150	8	0	10	13	.435	1	0-0	0	4.56	4.67
2017	3 Tms		27	27	0	0	157.0	673	157	86	77	18	2	4	1	64	5	129	8	3	5	10	.333	0	0-0	0	4.22	4.41
17	Atl	NL	18	18	0	0	113.0	474	108	58	54	12	2	1	1	41	4	85	5	3	4	7	.364	0	0-0	0	3.76	4.30
17	Min	AL	1	1	0	0	6.2	29	8	3	3	0	0	0	0	3	0	7	0	0	1	0	1.000	0	0-0	0	4.88	4.05
17	NYY	AL	8	8	0	0	37.1	170	41	25	20	6	0	3	0	20	1	37	3	0	0	3	.000	0	0-0	0	5.59	4.82
	Postseason		7	7	0	0	29.2	132	33	18	13	4	3	0	1	12	2	26	1	0	0	3	.000	0	0-0	0	5.02	3.94
	9 ML YEARS		185	174	4	4	1053.0	4440	1046	495	432	97	35	24	20	325	15	852	55	6	67	55	.549	4	0-0	3	3.70	3.69

Jarlin Garcia

Pitches: L **Bats:** L **Pos:** RP-68

har-LEEN

Ht: 6'3" **Wt:** 215 **Born:** 1/18/1993 **Age:** 25

Year	Team	Lg	G	GS	CG	GF	IP	BFP	H	R	ER	HR	SH	SF	HB	TBB	IBB	SO	WP	Bk	W	L	Pct	Sh	Sv-Op	Hld	ERC	ERA
2013	Batvia	A-	15	15	0	0	69.2	284	58	31	24	7	1	1	2	18	0	74	4	2	2	3	.400	0	0--	-	2.74	3.10
2014	Grnsbr	A	25	25	0	0	133.1	569	152	78	65	13	8	3	5	21	1	111	8	0	10	5	.667	0	0--	-	3.99	4.39
2015	Jupiter	A+	18	18	1	0	97.0	402	96	40	33	4	1	3	2	23	0	69	4	1	3	5	.375	1	0--	-	3.10	3.06
2015	Jaxnvl	AA	7	7	0	0	36.2	161	38	24	20	4	4	1	0	17	0	35	2	0	1	3	.250	0	0--	-	4.62	4.91
2016	Jaxnvl	AA	9	9	0	0	39.2	168	38	22	20	4	2	3	2	11	0	27	2	0	1	3	.250	0	0--	-	3.54	4.54
2016	2 Tms	Low	8	3	0	0	11.0	40	5	1	1	0	0	0	0	1	0	11	1	0	0	0	-	0	0--	-	0.79	0.82
2017	Mia	NL	68	0	0	14	53.1	225	47	29	28	6	2	2	4	17	0	42	5	0	1	2	.333	0	0-1	15	3.46	4.73

Leury Garcia

lay-OOH-ree

Bats: B **Throws:** R **Pos:** CF-51;LF-24;RF-6;PH-5;2B-3;PR-3;SS-2

Ht: 5'8" **Wt:** 170 **Born:** 3/18/1991 **Age:** 27

Year	Team	Lg	G	AB	H	2B	3B	HR	(Hm	Rd)	TB	R	RBI	RC	TBB	IBB	SO	HBP	SH	SF	SB	CS	GDP	Avg	OBP	Slg	OPS
2013	2 Tms	AL	45	101	20	1	1	0	(0	0)	23	10	2	4	7	0	34	0	2	1	7	2	0	.198	.248	.228	.475
2014	CWS	AL	74	145	24	3	0	1	(0	1)	30	13	6	0	5	1	48	0	4	1	11	1	6	.166	.192	.207	.399
2015	CWS	AL	18	14	3	0	0	0	(0	0)	3	0	1	2	1	0	7	0	0	0	1	0	0	.214	.267	.214	.481
2016	CWS	AL	18	48	11	1	1	1	(1	0)	17	6	5	5	1	0	13	1	0	0	2	1	0	.229	.260	.354	.614
2017	CWS	AL	87	300	81	15	2	9	(5	4)	127	41	33	39	13	0	69	8	3	2	8	5	4	.270	.316	.423	.739
13	Tex	AL	25	52	10	0	1	0	(0	0)	12	8	1	2	3	0	16	0	2	0	1	0	0	.192	.236	.231	.467
13	CWS	AL	20	49	10	1	0	0	(0	0)	11	2	1	2	4	0	18	0	0	1	6	2	0	.204	.259	.224	.484
	5 ML YEARS		242	608	139	20	4	11	(6	5)	200	70	47	50	27	1	171	9	9	4	29	9	10	.229	.270	.329	.599

Luis Garcia

Pitches: R **Bats:** R **Pos:** RP-66

Ht: 6'3" **Wt:** 230 **Born:** 1/30/1987 **Age:** 31

Year	Team	Lg	G	GS	CG	GF	IP	BFP	H	R	ER	HR	SH	SF	HB	TBB	IBB	SO	WP	Bk	W	L	Pct	Sh	Sv-Op	Hld	ERC	ERA
2013	Phi	NL	24	0	0	6	31.1	138	27	15	13	3	0	0	1	23	0	23	3	0	1	1	.500	0	0-0	1	4.85	3.73
2014	Phi	NL	13	0	0	5	14.0	69	14	12	10	2	1	0	0	13	0	12	4	0	1	0	1.000	0	0-0	0	6.43	6.43
2015	Phi	NL	72	0	0	14	66.2	304	72	28	26	4	3	2	0	37	8	63	6	1	4	6	.400	0	2-4	16	4.59	3.51
2016	Phi	NL	17	0	0	7	15.1	76	21	11	11	2	0	1	1	8	1	14	2	0	1	1	.500	0	0-1	1	7.04	6.46
2017	Phi	NL	66	0	0	16	71.1	295	61	22	21	3	1	2	0	26	5	60	9	0	2	5	.286	0	2-7	14	2.69	2.65
	5 ML YEARS		192	0	0	48	198.2	882	195	88	81	14	5	5	2	107	14	172	24	1	9	13	.409	0	4-12	32	4.21	3.67

Onelki Garcia

Pitches: L **Bats:** L **Pos:** SP-1; RP-1

OH-nel-key

Ht: 6'3" **Wt:** 225 **Born:** 8/2/1989 **Age:** 28

Year	Team	Lg	G	GS	CG	GF	IP	BFP	H	R	ER	HR	SH	SF	HB	TBB	IBB	SO	WP	Bk	W	L	Pct	Sh	Sv-Op	Hld	ERC	ERA
2013	Chatt	AA	25	6	0	6	52.1	227	41	19	16	3	1	1	2	32	0	53	6	4	2	3	.400	0	1--	-	3.54	2.75
2013	Albq	AAA	10	0	0	1	9.2	37	5	4	4	0	0	0	1	3	0	14	1	0	0	1	.000	0	0--	-	1.33	3.72
2015	Brham	AA	13	0	0	4	17.2	81	19	13	10	0	0	0	1	7	0	24	3	0	0	1	1.000	0	0--	-	3.80	5.09
2015	Charllt	AAA	25	0	0	11	38.1	182	45	23	20	3	0	2	1	22	0	48	2	3	0	1	.000	0	3--	-	5.62	4.70
2017	Omha	AAA	20	10	0	3	75.0	337	84	51	42	6	3	2	2	32	2	63	5	0	7	3	.700	0	0--	-	4.75	5.04
2013	LAD	NL	3	0	0	1	1.1	9	1	2	2	1	0	0	0	4	0	1	0	0	0	0	-	0	0-0	0	21.19	13.50
2017	KC	AL	2	1	0	0	6.0	32	12	9	9	2	0	0	0	5	0	2	0	0	0	1	.000	0	0-0	0	16.25	13.50
	2 ML YEARS		5	1	0	1	7.1	41	13	11	11	3	0	0	0	9	0	3	0	0	0	1	.000	0	0-0	0	17.15	13.50

Willy Garcia

Bats: R **Throws:** R **Pos:** RF-17;LF-13;CF-11;PR-4;PH-3;DH-2   **Ht:** 6'2" **Wt:** 215 **Born:** 9/4/1992 **Age:** 25

Year	Team	Lg	G	AB	H	2B	3B	HR	(Hm	Rd)	TB	R	RBI	RC	TBB	IBB	SO	HBP	SH	SF	SB	CS	GDP	Avg	OBP	Slg	OPS
2013	Bradtn	A+	118	449	115	21	6	16	(-	-)	196	51	60	58	23	1	154	2	3	3	13	6	5	.256	.294	.437	.730
2014	Altna	AA	126	439	119	27	5	18	(-	-)	210	59	63	66	24	2	145	3	4	4	8	4	13	.271	.311	.478	.789
2015	Altna	AA	53	204	64	7	2	5	(-	-)	90	26	28	32	11	2	47	3	3	3	3	2	9	.314	.353	.441	.794
2015	Indy	AAA	71	276	68	11	4	10	(-	-)	117	36	38	32	12	0	76	3	0	0	1	4	4	.246	.285	.424	.709
2016	Indy	AAA	129	462	113	30	4	6	(-	-)	169	53	43	48	31	1	131	2	1	3	5	9	21	.245	.293	.366	.659
2017	Charltt	AAA	31	112	32	6	0	5	(-	-)	53	20	20	22	18	0	38	3	0	1	1	0	1	.286	.396	.473	.869
2017	CWS	AL	44	105	25	5	3	2	(1	1)	42	15	12	11	11	0	31	0	1	2	0	0	2	.238	.305	.400	.705

Nick Gardewine

Pitches: R **Bats:** R **Pos:** RP-12   GAR-duh-wine   **Ht:** 6'1" **Wt:** 179 **Born:** 8/15/1993 **Age:** 24

Year	Team	Lg	G	GS	CG	GF	IP	BFP	H	R	ER	HR	SH	SF	HB	TBB	IBB	SO	WP	Bk	W	L	Pct	Sh	Sv-Op	Hld	ERC	ERA
2013	Rngrs	R	14	6	0	3	47.2	198	34	21	17	2	1	0	1	20	0	37	6	1	3	3	.500	0	1--	-	2.30	3.21
2014	Spkane	A-	15	15	0	0	71.0	298	62	38	36	6	1	2	7	23	0	60	1	1	6	3	.667	0	0--	-	3.38	4.56
2015	Hkry	A	22	17	0	2	96.0	412	111	52	46	11	3	2	5	23	1	80	10	0	6	8	.429	0	1--	-	4.69	4.31
2016	Hi Dsrt	A+	29	0	0	16	54.2	212	39	15	15	5	0	1	0	14	1	60	0	0	5	1	.833	0	7--	-	2.04	2.47
2017	Frisco	AA	33	0	0	26	36.2	154	35	10	9	2	0	1	2	12	0	53	0	1	1	2	.333	0	6--	-	3.49	2.21
2017	Tex	AL	12	0	0	1	8.0	40	10	8	5	1	0	0	0	7	0	3	1	0	0	0	-	0	0-0	0	7.82	5.63

Brett Gardner

Bats: L **Throws:** L **Pos:** LF-122;CF-22;PH-9;DH-7;PR-2   **Ht:** 5'11" **Wt:** 195 **Born:** 8/24/1983 **Age:** 34

Year	Team	Lg	G	AB	H	2B	3B	HR	(Hm	Rd)	TB	R	RBI	RC	TBB	IBB	SO	HBP	SH	SF	SB	CS	GDP	Avg	OBP	Slg	OPS
2008	NYY	AL	42	127	29	5	2	0	(0	0)	38	18	16	17	8	0	30	2	3	1	13	1	0	.228	.283	.299	.582
2009	NYY	AL	108	248	67	6	6	3	(1	2)	94	48	23	38	26	0	40	3	6	1	26	5	3	.270	.345	.379	.724
2010	NYY	AL	150	477	132	20	7	5	(5	0)	181	97	47	77	79	1	101	5	5	3	47	9	6	.277	.383	.379	.762
2011	NYY	AL	159	510	132	19	8	7	(4	3)	188	87	36	77	60	1	93	8	8	2	49	13	5	.259	.345	.369	.713
2012	NYY	AL	16	31	10	2	0	0	(0	0)	12	7	3	7	5	0	7	0	1	0	2	2	0	.323	.417	.387	.804
2013	NYY	AL	145	539	147	33	10	8	(6	2)	224	81	52	88	52	1	127	8	7	3	24	8	8	.273	.344	.416	.759
2014	NYY	AL	148	555	142	25	8	17	(8	9)	234	87	58	81	56	0	134	6	13	6	21	5	3	.256	.327	.422	.749
2015	NYY	AL	151	571	148	26	3	16	(12	4)	228	94	66	90	68	1	135	6	3	3	20	5	8	.259	.343	.399	.742
2016	NYY	AL	148	547	143	26	7	7	(5	2)	198	80	41	77	70	0	106	8	4	5	16	4	6	.261	.351	.362	.713
2017	NYY	AL	151	594	157	26	4	21	(11	10)	254	96	63	95	72	2	122	8	5	3	23	5	4	.264	.350	.428	.778
	Postseason		34	69	14	1	0	0	(0	0)	15	8	7	5	4	0	20	0	2	1	5	2	0	.203	.243	.217	.461
	10 ML YEARS		1218	4199	1107	184	54	84	(52	32)	1651	695	405	647	496	6	895	54	60	27	241	57	43	.264	.347	.393	.740

Dustin Garneau

Bats: R **Throws:** R **Pos:** C-40;PH-3;PR-1   GARR-noh   **Ht:** 6'0" **Wt:** 200 **Born:** 8/13/1987 **Age:** 30

Year	Team	Lg	G	AB	H	2B	3B	HR	(Hm	Rd)	TB	R	RBI	RC	TBB	IBB	SO	HBP	SH	SF	SB	CS	GDP	Avg	OBP	Slg	OPS
2017	Albq*	AAA	36	128	36	9	2	10	(-	-)	79	24	26	27	13	0	22	1	0	2	0	1	4	.281	.347	.617	.964
2015	Col	NL	22	70	11	3	0	2	(0	2)	20	6	8	5	6	2	14	0	0	0	0	0	2	.157	.224	.286	.509
2016	Col	NL	24	68	16	6	0	1	(0	1)	25	7	6	6	6	0	22	0	0	1	0	0	1	.235	.293	.368	.661
2017	2 Tms		41	112	21	8	0	2	(1	1)	35	10	9	6	12	0	36	1	1	0	0	0	3	.188	.272	.313	.585
17	Col	NL	22	68	14	7	0	1	(1	0)	24	5	6	4	4	0	24	1	1	0	0	0	1	.206	.260	.353	.613
17	Oak	AL	19	44	7	1	0	1	(0	1)	11	5	3	2	8	0	12	0	0	0	0	0	2	.159	.288	.250	.538
	3 ML YEARS		87	250	48	17	0	5	(1	4)	80	23	23	17	24	2	72	1	1	1	0	0	6	.192	.264	.320	.584

Amir Garrett

Pitches: L **Bats:** R **Pos:** SP-14; RP-2   **Ht:** 6'5" **Wt:** 228 **Born:** 5/3/1992 **Age:** 26

Year	Team	Lg	G	GS	CG	GF	IP	BFP	H	R	ER	HR	SH	SF	HB	TBB	IBB	SO	WP	Bk	W	L	Pct	Sh	Sv-Op	Hld	ERC	ERA
2013	2 Tms	Low	13	13	0	0	57.2	256	62	38	33	4	1	2	3	26	0	32	10	1	2	4	.333	0	0--	-	4.72	5.15
2014	Dayton	A	27	27	2	0	133.1	561	115	65	54	11	4	5	3	51	0	127	8	2	7	8	.467	2	0--	-	3.21	3.65
2015	Dytona	A+	26	26	1	0	140.1	575	117	50	38	4	4	3	4	55	0	133	9	1	9	7	.563	1	0--	-	2.85	2.44
2016	Pnscla	AA	13	12	0	0	77.0	311	51	20	15	0	2	1	3	28	1	78	7	0	5	3	.625	0	0--	-	1.71	1.75
2016	Lsvlle	AAA	12	11	0	0	67.2	274	48	30	26	6	2	2	1	31	2	54	2	0	2	5	.286	0	0--	-	2.74	3.46
2017	Lsvlle	AAA	14	14	1	0	67.2	302	79	50	43	7	4	4	2	24	0	61	5	1	2	4	.333	1	0--	-	4.98	5.72
2017	Cin	NL	16	14	0	0	70.2	321	74	60	58	23	1	3	2	40	2	63	1	0	3	8	.273	0	0-0	1	6.86	7.39

Ryan Garton

Pitches: R **Bats:** R **Pos:** RP-20   **Ht:** 5'10" **Wt:** 190 **Born:** 12/5/1989 **Age:** 28

Year	Team	Lg	G	GS	CG	GF	IP	BFP	H	R	ER	HR	SH	SF	HB	TBB	IBB	SO	WP	Bk	W	L	Pct	Sh	Sv-Op	Hld	ERC	ERA
2013	BG	A	40	0	0	30	70.0	300	54	19	19	3	5	1	5	34	6	62	4	0	4	3	.571	0	8--	-	2.87	2.44
2014	Charltt	A+	40	0	0	25	67.0	281	61	29	23	3	1	1	1	28	0	44	5	0	6	2	.750	0	4--	-	3.39	3.09
2015	Mont	AA	41	0	0	8	61.0	259	44	22	20	2	1	1	2	32	1	70	3	0	6	1	.857	0	0--	-	2.66	2.95
2016	Drham	AAA	22	0	0	5	32.0	138	31	14	11	1	2	2	1	10	0	39	2	0	4	0	1.000	0	2--	-	3.14	3.09
2017	Drham	AAA	24	1	0	11	33.0	128	18	6	6	2	0	1	0	16	0	46	1	0	2	0	1.000	0	4--	-	1.90	1.64
2017	Tacom	AAA	7	0	0	2	12.0	58	11	11	8	0	0	0	2	8	0	15	2	1	0	2	.000	0	0--	-	4.30	6.00
2016	TB	AL	37	0	0	14	39.1	171	44	20	19	5	1	0	0	11	2	33	2	0	1	2	.333	0	1-1	2	4.33	4.35

Year	Team	Lg	G	GS	CG	GF	IP	BFP	H	R	ER	HR	SH	SF	HB	TBB	IBB	SO	WP	Bk	W	L	Pct	Sh	Sv-Op	Hld	ERC	ERA
2017	2 Tms	AL	20	0	0	6	22.0	90	18	12	12	4	1	1	0	6	0	16	2	0	0	1	.000	0	0-1	1	3.07	4.91
17	TB	AL	7	0	0	3	10.1	48	13	10	10	3	1	0	0	5	0	9	2	0	0	0	.000	0	0-1	0	7.49	8.71
17	Sea	AL	13	0	0	3	11.2	42	5	2	2	1	0	1	0	1	0	7	0	0	0	0	-	0	0-0	1	0.71	1.54
	2 ML YEARS		57	0	0	20	61.1	261	62	32	31	9	2	1	0	17	2	49	4	0	1	3	.250	0	1-2	3	3.87	4.55

Mitch Garver

Bats: R **Throws:** R **Pos:** C-13;DH-5;PH-5;1B-3;LF-2 **Ht:** 6'1" **Wt:** 220 **Born:** 1/15/1991 **Age:** 27

Year	Team	Lg	G	AB	H	2B	3B	HR	(Hm	Rd)	TB	R	RBI	RC	TBB	IBB	SO	HBP	SH	SF	SB	CS	GDP	Avg	OBP	Slg	OPS
2013	Elizab	R+	56	202	49	15	2	2	(-	-)	74	16	30	24	19	1	31	2	1	1	0	0	4	.243	.313	.366	.679
2014	Crpds	A	120	430	128	29	1	16	(-	-)	207	65	79	85	61	1	65	12	0	1	7	5	7	.298	.399	.481	.880
2015	FtMyrs	A+	127	433	106	24	1	4	(-	-)	144	46	58	59	69	1	82	10	0	8	5	3	14	.245	.356	.333	.688
2016	Chatt	AA	95	358	92	25	0	11	(-	-)	150	44	66	52	43	1	86	1	0	5	1	3	8	.257	.334	.419	.753
2016	Roch	AAA	22	76	25	5	0	1	(-	-)	33	6	8	12	7	0	21	0	0	1	0	0	3	.329	.381	.434	.815
2017	Roch	AAA	88	320	93	29	0	17	(-	-)	173	56	45	67	50	0	85	1	0	1	2	0	11	.291	.387	.541	.928
2017	Min	AL	23	46	9	1	3	0	(0	0)	16	5	3	5	6	0	15	0	0	0	0	0	1	.196	.288	.348	.636

Matt Garza

Pitches: R **Bats:** R **Pos:** SP-22; RP-2 **Ht:** 6'4" **Wt:** 220 **Born:** 11/26/1983 **Age:** 34

Year	Team	Lg	G	GS	CG	GF	IP	BFP	H	R	ER	HR	SH	SF	HB	TBB	IBB	SO	WP	Bk	W	L	Pct	Sh	Sv-Op	Hld	ERC	ERA
2006	Min	AL	10	9	0	0	50.0	232	62	33	32	6	0	3	0	23	0	38	1	0	3	6	.333	0	0-0	0	5.82	5.76
2007	Min	AL	16	15	0	1	83.0	367	96	44	34	8	1	4	4	32	4	67	4	0	5	7	.417	0	0-0	0	5.08	3.69
2008	TB	AL	30	30	3	0	184.2	772	170	83	76	19	3	9	6	59	2	128	3	2	11	9	.550	2	0-0	0	3.47	3.70
2009	TB	AL	32	32	0	0	203.0	861	177	93	89	25	2	8	11	79	0	189	3	0	8	12	.400	0	0-0	0	3.69	3.95
2010	TB	AL	33	32	3	1	204.2	855	193	94	89	28	1	6	7	63	2	150	12	2	15	10	.600	1	1-1	0	3.80	3.91
2011	ChC	NL	31	31	2	0	198.0	839	186	90	73	14	11	2	3	63	5	197	6	0	10	10	.500	0	0-0	0	3.21	3.32
2012	ChC	NL	18	18	0	0	103.2	424	90	48	45	15	5	1	4	32	0	96	1	0	5	7	.417	0	0-0	0	3.50	3.91
2013	2 Tms		24	24	1	0	155.1	652	150	73	66	20	8	3	5	42	3	136	6	0	10	6	.625	0	0-0	0	3.66	3.82
2014	Mil	NL	27	27	1	0	163.1	680	143	77	66	12	9	4	4	50	2	126	3	1	8	8	.500	1	0-0	0	2.92	3.64
2015	Mil	NL	26	25	0	1	148.2	666	176	102	93	23	7	2	2	57	3	104	7	0	6	14	.300	0	0-0	0	5.51	5.63
2016	Mil	NL	19	19	0	1	101.2	461	117	67	51	11	4	4	3	36	2	70	3	0	6	8	.429	0	0-0	0	4.78	4.51
2017	Mil	NL	24	22	0	0	114.2	504	121	72	63	17	7	3	1	45	4	79	4	0	6	9	.400	0	0-0	0	4.65	4.94
13	ChC	NL	11	11	0	0	71.0	293	61	26	25	8	2	1	4	20	2	62	2	0	6	1	.857	0	0-0	0	3.12	3.17
13	Tex	AL	13	13	1	0	84.1	359	89	47	41	12	6	2	1	22	1	74	4	0	4	5	.444	0	0-0	0	4.14	4.38
	Postseason		5	5	0	0	31.0	131	26	13	12	5	0	1	1	14	0	29	2	0	2	1	.667	0	0-0	0	3.95	3.48
	12 ML YEARS		290	284	10	4	1710.2	7313	1681	876	777	198	58	49	50	581	27	1380	53	5	93	106	.467	4	1-1	0	3.93	4.09

Evan Gattis

Bats: R **Throws:** R **Pos:** C-49;DH-29;PH-7;1B-1 GAT-iss **Ht:** 6'4" **Wt:** 270 **Born:** 8/18/1986 **Age:** 31

Year	Team	Lg	G	AB	H	2B	3B	HR	(Hm	Rd)	TB	R	RBI	RC	TBB	IBB	SO	HBP	SH	SF	SB	CS	GDP	Avg	OBP	Slg	OPS
2013	Atl	NL	105	354	86	21	0	21	(8	13)	170	44	65	43	21	4	81	4	0	3	0	0	10	.243	.291	.480	.771
2014	Atl	NL	108	369	97	17	1	22	(12	10)	182	41	52	45	22	3	97	8	0	2	0	0	9	.263	.317	.493	.810
2015	Hou	AL	153	566	139	20	11	27	(15	12)	262	66	88	73	30	3	119	3	0	5	0	1	13	.246	.285	.463	.748
2016	Hou	AL	128	447	112	19	0	32	(19	13)	227	58	72	64	43	6	127	4	0	5	2	1	12	.251	.319	.508	.826
2017	Hou	AL	84	300	79	22	0	12	(4	8)	137	41	55	44	18	0	50	4	0	3	0	1	10	.263	.311	.457	.767
	Postseason		10	37	9	0	0	0	(0	0)	9	4	2	3	2	0	9	0	0	0	0	0	1	.243	.282	.243	.525
	5 ML YEARS		578	2036	513	99	12	114	(58	56)	978	250	332	269	134	16	474	23	0	18	2	3	54	.252	.303	.480	.783

Kevin Gausman

Pitches: R **Bats:** L **Pos:** SP-34 GAHZ-man **Ht:** 6'3" **Wt:** 190 **Born:** 1/6/1991 **Age:** 27

Year	Team	Lg	G	GS	CG	GF	IP	BFP	H	R	ER	HR	SH	SF	HB	TBB	IBB	SO	WP	Bk	W	L	Pct	Sh	Sv-Op	Hld	ERC	ERA
2013	Bal	AL	20	5	0	3	47.2	201	51	30	30	8	2	1	0	13	2	49	4	0	3	5	.375	0	0-2	2	4.41	5.66
2014	Bal	AL	20	20	1	0	113.1	476	111	48	45	7	3	7	1	38	0	88	9	0	7	7	.500	0	0-0	0	3.52	3.57
2015	Bal	AL	25	17	0	1	112.1	470	109	56	53	17	2	3	2	29	1	103	7	0	4	7	.364	0	0-0	1	3.74	4.25
2016	Bal	AL	30	30	0	0	179.2	757	183	76	72	28	4	3	5	47	1	174	6	0	9	12	.429	0	0-0	0	4.13	3.61
2017	Bal	AL	34	34	0	0	186.2	816	208	99	97	29	1	3	5	71	0	179	8	1	11	12	.478	0	0-0	0	5.24	4.68
	Postseason		3	0	0	1	8.0	27	4	1	1	1	0	0	0	1	0	7	0	0	0	0	-	0	0-0	0	1.05	1.13
	5 ML YEARS		129	106	1	4	639.2	2720	662	309	297	89	12	17	13	198	4	593	36	1	34	43	.442	0	0-2	3	4.28	4.18

Sam Gaviglio

Pitches: R **Bats:** R **Pos:** SP-13; RP-3 gah-VEE-leo **Ht:** 6'2" **Wt:** 195 **Born:** 5/22/1990 **Age:** 28

Year	Team	Lg	G	GS	CG	GF	IP	BFP	H	R	ER	HR	SH	SF	HB	TBB	IBB	SO	WP	Bk	W	L	Pct	Sh	Sv-Op	Hld	ERC	ERA
2013	2 Tms	Low	9	8	0	0	47.2	187	33	13	12	2	3	2	1	13	0	39	1	0	4	1	.800	0	0- -	-	1.79	2.27
2014	Sprgfld	AA	25	24	0	0	136.2	604	153	79	65	8	9	2	9	46	2	126	12	3	5	12	.294	0	0- -	-	4.43	4.28
2015	Tacom	AAA	21	17	0	1	101.2	442	102	64	58	16	2	3	4	36	0	79	4	0	8	7	.533	0	0- -	-	4.43	5.13
2016	Jacksn	AA	18	17	0	0	102.0	423	104	51	47	7	3	1	1	22	0	73	3	0	5	5	.500	0	0- -	-	3.31	4.15
2016	Tacom	AAA	10	9	1	0	63.0	259	59	29	26	7	0	1	1	14	0	50	2	0	3	2	.600	1	0- -	-	3.17	3.71
2017	Tacom	AAA	13	13	1	0	72.0	301	72	35	31	5	2	4	5	12	0	57	1	0	3	6	.333	0	0- -	-	3.22	3.88
2017	2 Tms	AL	16	13	0	1	74.1	313	76	41	36	16	1	2	3	26	1	49	1	2	4	5	.444	0	0-0	0	5.11	4.36
17	Sea	AL	12	11	0	1	62.1	259	63	37	32	15	1	2	2	21	1	40	1	2	3	5	.375	0	0-0	0	5.16	4.62
17	KC	AL	4	2	0	0	12.0	54	13	4	4	1	0	0	1	5	0	9	0	0	1	0	1.000	0	0-0	0	4.80	3.00

Cory Gearrin

Pitches: R **Bats:** R **Pos:** RP-68
GARE-inn
Ht: 6'3" **Wt:** 200 **Born:** 4/14/1986 **Age:** 32

Year	Team	Lg	G	GS	CG	GF	IP	BFP	H	R	ER	HR	SH	SF	HB	TBB	IBB	SO	WP	Bk	W	L	Pct	Sh	Sv-Op	Hld	ERC	ERA
2011	Atl	NL	18	0	0	4	18.1	85	17	16	16	0	0	1	2	12	4	25	1	0	1	1	.500	0	0-1	3	3.84	7.85
2012	Atl	NL	22	0	0	7	20.0	80	17	4	4	1	0	0	2	5	0	20	2	0	0	1	.000	0	0-1	4	2.86	1.80
2013	Atl	NL	37	0	0	12	31.0	133	30	13	13	2	1	0	4	16	2	23	3	0	2	1	.667	0	1-3	1	4.73	3.77
2015	SF	NL	7	0	0	0	3.2	13	1	2	2	0	0	0	0	1	0	5	0	0	0	0	-	0	0-0	3	0.47	4.91
2016	SF	NL	56	0	0	10	48.1	197	42	24	23	4	0	2	3	14	2	45	1	0	3	2	.600	0	3-7	15	2.89	4.28
2017	SF	NL	68	0	0	21	68.0	285	50	16	15	4	1	2	7	35	4	64	3	0	4	3	.571	0	0-0	8	3.15	1.99
	6 ML YEARS		208	0	0	54	189.1	793	157	75	73	11	2	5	16	83	12	182	10	0	10	8	.556	0	4-12	34	3.29	3.47

Dillon Gee

Pitches: R **Bats:** R **Pos:** RP-14; SP-4
JEE
Ht: 6'1" **Wt:** 205 **Born:** 4/28/1986 **Age:** 32

Year	Team	Lg	G	GS	CG	GF	IP	BFP	H	R	ER	HR	SH	SF	HB	TBB	IBB	SO	WP	Bk	W	L	Pct	Sh	Sv-Op	Hld	ERC	ERA
2017	RdRck*	AAA	9	9	0	0	51.0	219	53	25	22	7	0	2	1	13	0	43	1	1	3	4	.429	0	0--	-	3.72	3.88
2017	Roch*	AAA	5	5	0	0	27.0	106	24	6	6	1	0	0	3	3	0	20	0	0	3	1	.750	0	0--	-	2.52	2.00
2010	NYM	NL	5	5	0	0	33.0	136	25	10	8	2	3	0	0	15	2	17	0	0	2	2	.500	0	0-0	0	2.66	2.18
2011	NYM	NL	30	27	1	1	160.2	706	150	85	79	18	10	5	14	71	4	114	6	1	13	6	.684	0	0-0	0	4.23	4.43
2012	NYM	NL	17	17	0	0	109.2	463	108	56	50	12	2	3	6	29	0	97	0	1	6	7	.462	0	0-0	0	3.74	4.10
2013	NYM	NL	32	32	2	0	199.0	841	208	84	80	24	9	3	7	47	0	142	4	0	12	11	.522	0	0-0	0	3.97	3.62
2014	NYM	NL	22	22	0	0	137.1	570	128	61	61	18	7	3	5	43	0	94	3	1	7	8	.467	0	0-0	0	3.77	4.00
2015	NYM	NL	8	7	0	0	39.2	183	55	29	26	5	2	2	1	11	3	25	0	0	0	3	.000	0	0-0	0	5.98	5.90
2016	KC	AL	33	14	0	3	125.0	551	146	67	65	24	3	3	6	37	3	89	1	1	8	9	.471	0	0-0	0	5.47	4.68
2017	2 Tms	AL	18	4	0	4	49.1	212	54	24	19	8	0	2	4	15	0	41	0	0	3	2	.600	0	1-1	0	5.13	3.47
17	Tex	AL	4	1	0	2	13.0	61	17	10	6	4	0	0	2	6	0	10	0	0	0	0	-	0	0-0	0	8.87	4.15
17	Min	AL	14	3	0	2	36.1	151	37	14	13	4	0	2	2	9	0	31	0	0	3	2	.600	0	1-1	0	3.95	3.22
	8 ML YEARS		165	128	3	8	853.2	3662	874	416	388	111	36	21	43	268	12	619	14	4	51	48	.515	0	1-1	0	4.27	4.09

Scooter Gennett

Bats: L **Throws:** R **Pos:** 2B-99;PH-23;3B-10;LF-9;RF-6;DH-3
jen-ETT
Ht: 5'10" **Wt:** 185 **Born:** 5/1/1990 **Age:** 28

Year	Team	Lg	G	AB	H	2B	3B	HR	(Hm	Rd)	TB	R	RBI	RC	TBB	IBB	SO	HBP	SH	SF	SB	CS	GDP	Avg	OBP	Slg	OPS
2013	Mil	NL	69	213	69	11	2	6	(0	6)	102	29	21	35	10	0	42	1	5	1	2	1	0	.324	.356	.479	.834
2014	Mil	NL	137	440	127	31	3	9	(6	3)	191	55	54	59	22	5	67	0	8	4	6	3	11	.289	.320	.434	.754
2015	Mil	NL	114	375	99	18	4	6	(5	1)	143	42	29	36	12	5	68	4	0	0	1	3	11	.264	.294	.381	.675
2016	Mil	NL	136	498	131	30	1	14	(8	6)	205	58	56	61	38	1	114	2	1	2	8	1	11	.263	.317	.412	.728
2017	Cin	NL	141	461	136	22	3	27	(16	11)	245	80	97	81	30	1	114	4	0	2	3	2	15	.295	.342	.531	.874
	5 ML YEARS		597	1987	562	112	13	62	(35	27)	886	264	257	272	112	12	405	11	14	9	20	10	48	.283	.323	.446	.769

Craig Gentry

Bats: R **Throws:** R **Pos:** RF-31;LF-30;PR-16;CF-9;PH-7;DH-1
JEN-tree
Ht: 6'2" **Wt:** 190 **Born:** 11/29/1983 **Age:** 34

Year	Team	Lg	G	AB	H	2B	3B	HR	(Hm	Rd)	TB	R	RBI	RC	TBB	IBB	SO	HBP	SH	SF	SB	CS	GDP	Avg	OBP	Slg	OPS
2017	Norfolk*	AAA	37	148	36	6	2	1	(-	-)	49	16	16	15	11	0	36	3	0	0	6	3	2	.243	.309	.331	.640
2009	Tex	AL	11	17	2	1	0	0	(0	0)	3	4	1	1	2	0	5	0	0	0	0	0	0	.118	.211	.176	.387
2010	Tex	AL	20	33	7	0	0	0	(0	0)	7	4	3	1	1	0	11	0	0	1	1	0	1	.212	.229	.212	.441
2011	Tex	AL	64	133	36	5	1	1	(1	0)	46	26	13	21	10	1	27	6	3	1	18	0	2	.271	.347	.346	.693
2012	Tex	AL	122	240	73	12	3	1	(0	1)	94	31	26	33	14	1	41	10	5	0	13	7	4	.304	.367	.392	.759
2013	Tex	AL	106	246	69	12	4	2	(2	0)	95	39	22	42	29	2	46	8	3	1	24	3	5	.280	.373	.386	.759
2014	Oak	AL	94	232	59	6	1	0	(0	0)	67	38	12	27	17	2	44	5	2	0	20	2	2	.254	.319	.289	.608
2015	Oak	AL	26	50	6	0	2	0	(0	0)	10	6	3	2	4	0	15	1	0	1	1	1	0	.120	.196	.200	.396
2016	LAA	AL	14	34	5	1	0	0	(0	0)	6	2	2	1	3	0	6	1	1	0	0	0	2	.147	.237	.176	.413
2017	Bal	AL	77	101	26	5	1	2	(1	1)	39	17	11	14	11	0	24	1	3	1	5	4	1	.257	.333	.386	.719
	Postseason		14	17	5	0	0	0	(0	0)	5	2	1	3	1	0	4	1	1	0	2	1	0	.294	.368	.294	.663
	9 ML YEARS		534	1086	283	42	12	6	(4	2)	367	167	93	142	91	6	219	32	17	5	82	17	17	.261	.334	.338	.672

Domingo German

Pitches: R **Bats:** R **Pos:** RP-7
hair-MAHN
Ht: 6'2" **Wt:** 175 **Born:** 8/4/1992 **Age:** 25

Year	Team	Lg	G	GS	CG	GF	IP	BFP	H	R	ER	HR	SH	SF	HB	TBB	IBB	SO	WP	Bk	W	L	Pct	Sh	Sv-Op	Hld	ERC	ERA
2013	2 Tms	Low	13	13	0	0	67.0	263	48	18	12	1	1	1	6	10	0	61	2	1	5	3	.625	0	0--	-	1.59	1.61
2014	Grnsbr	A	25	25	0	0	123.1	504	116	43	34	6	1	1	11	25	0	113	9	1	9	3	.750	0	0--	-	3.06	2.48
2016	2 Tms	Low	10	10	0	0	49.2	198	41	21	17	3	1	1	3	11	0	38	6	1	1	3	.250	0	0--	-	2.51	3.08
2017	Trntn	AA	6	6	1	0	33.0	142	32	13	11	4	1	0	2	10	0	38	2	0	1	4	.200	0	0--	-	3.85	3.00
2017	S-WB	AAA	14	13	0	0	76.1	311	59	26	24	5	1	1	6	22	0	81	4	0	7	2	.778	0	0--	-	2.53	2.83
2017	NYY	AL	7	0	0	5	14.1	62	11	6	5	1	1	1	0	9	0	18	3	0	0	1	.000	0	0-0	0	3.44	3.14

Johnny Giavotella

gee-uh-vo-TELL-uh

Bats: R **Throws:** R **Pos:** 2B-5;PH-3 **Ht:** 5'8" **Wt:** 185 **Born:** 7/10/1987 **Age:** 30

Year Team	Lg	G	AB	H	2B	3B	HR	(Hm	Rd)	TB	R	RBI	RC	TBB	IBB	SO	HBP	SH	SF	SB	CS	GDP	Avg	OBP	Slg	OPS
2017 Norfolk*	AAA	83	333	102	22	4	5	(-	-)	147	43	45	56	34	0	41	3	1	8	4	3	13	.306	.368	.441	.809
2011 KC	AL	46	178	44	9	4	2	(2	0)	67	20	21	15	6	0	32	1	0	2	5	2	4	.247	.273	.376	.649
2012 KC	AL	53	181	43	7	1	1	(1	0)	55	21	15	14	8	0	35	0	0	0	3	0	4	.238	.270	.304	.574
2013 KC	AL	14	41	9	3	0	0	(0	0)	12	4	4	5	5	0	4	2	0	0	0	0	0	.220	.333	.293	.626
2014 KC	AL	12	37	8	1	0	0	(0	1)	12	8	5	2	1	0	5	2	0	1	0	1	1	.216	.268	.324	.593
2015 LAA	AL	129	453	123	25	5	4	(3	1)	170	51	49	63	32	0	59	2	9	6	2	1	7	.272	.318	.375	.694
2016 LAA	AL	99	346	90	20	1	6	(3	3)	130	44	31	31	13	0	39	1	4	3	4	3	11	.260	.287	.376	.662
2017 Bal	AL	7	10	1	0	0	0	(0	0)	1	0	0	0	0	0	4	0	0	0	1	0	0	.100	.100	.100	.200
7 ML YEARS		360	1246	318	65	11	14	(9	5)	447	148	125	130	65	0	178	8	13	12	15	7	27	.255	.294	.359	.653

Kyle Gibson

Pitches: R **Bats:** R **Pos:** SP-29 **Ht:** 6'6" **Wt:** 215 **Born:** 10/23/1987 **Age:** 30

Year Team	Lg	G	GS	CG	GF	IP	BFP	H	R	ER	HR	SH	SF	HB	TBB	IBB	SO	WP	Bk	W	L	Pct	Sh	Sv-Op	Hld	ERC	ERA
2013 Min	AL	10	10	0	0	51.0	238	69	38	37	7	0	2	5	20	0	29	4	0	2	4	.333	0	0-0	0	6.98	6.53
2014 Min	AL	31	31	0	0	179.1	757	178	91	89	12	4	3	2	57	0	107	11	0	13	12	.520	0	0-0	0	3.54	4.47
2015 Min	AL	32	32	1	0	194.2	821	186	88	83	18	6	6	7	65	6	145	7	0	11	11	.500	0	0-0	0	3.63	3.84
2016 Min	AL	25	25	1	0	147.1	653	175	89	83	20	3	4	4	55	3	104	9	0	6	11	.353	0	0-0	0	5.47	5.07
2017 Min	AL	29	29	0	0	158.0	693	182	93	89	24	1	2	6	60	0	121	4	0	12	10	.545	0	0-0	0	5.53	5.07
5 ML YEARS		127	127	2	0	730.1	3162	790	399	381	81	14	17	24	257	9	506	35	0	44	48	.478	0	0-0	0	4.58	4.70

Ken Giles

Pitches: R **Bats:** R **Pos:** RP-63 **Ht:** 6'2" **Wt:** 205 **Born:** 9/20/1990 **Age:** 27

Year Team	Lg	G	GS	CG	GF	IP	BFP	H	R	ER	HR	SH	SF	HB	TBB	IBB	SO	WP	Bk	W	L	Pct	Sh	Sv-Op	Hld	ERC	ERA
2014 Phi	NL	44	0	0	11	45.2	166	25	7	6	1	2	1	0	11	1	64	1	0	3	1	.750	0	1-1	13	1.15	1.18
2015 Phi	NL	69	0	0	28	70.0	298	59	23	14	2	1	2	1	25	2	87	1	0	6	3	.667	0	15-20	12	2.53	1.80
2016 Hou	AL	69	0	0	24	65.2	286	60	32	30	8	2	1	2	25	1	102	14	0	2	5	.286	0	15-20	18	3.66	4.11
2017 Hou	AL	63	0	0	55	62.2	247	44	16	16	4	1	2	1	21	0	83	3	0	1	3	.250	0	34-38	2	2.17	2.30
4 ML YEARS		245	0	0	118	244.0	997	188	78	66	15	6	6	4	82	4	336	19	0	12	12	.500	0	65-79	45	2.41	2.43

Conor Gillaspie

guh-LESS-pee

Bats: L **Throws:** R **Pos:** PH-26;3B-20;1B-4 **Ht:** 6'1" **Wt:** 195 **Born:** 7/18/1987 **Age:** 30

Year Team	Lg	G	AB	H	2B	3B	HR	(Hm	Rd)	TB	R	RBI	RC	TBB	IBB	SO	HBP	SH	SF	SB	CS	GDP	Avg	OBP	Slg	OPS
2017 Scrmto*	AAA	29	90	28	7	0	0	(-	-)	35	13	4	11	3	0	8	0	0	0	3	2	4	.311	.333	.389	.722
2008 SF	NL	8	5	1	0	0	0	(0	0)	1	1	0	1	2	0	0	0	0	0	0	0	0	.200	.429	.200	.629
2011 SF	NL	15	19	5	0	0	1	(1	0)	8	2	2	4	2	0	1	0	0	0	0	0	0	.263	.333	.421	.754
2012 SF	NL	6	20	3	1	0	0	(0	0)	4	2	2	0	0	0	2	0	0	0	0	0	0	.150	.150	.200	.350
2013 CWS	AL	134	408	100	14	3	13	(8	5)	159	46	40	46	37	4	79	1	0	6	0	1	7	.245	.305	.390	.695
2014 CWS	AL	130	464	131	31	5	7	(3	4)	193	50	57	68	36	4	78	3	0	3	0	4	5	.282	.336	.416	.752
2015 2 Tms	AL	75	237	54	15	2	4	(3	1)	85	14	24	20	13	2	47	1	0	2	0	1	2	.228	.269	.359	.627
2016 SF	NL	101	191	50	8	4	6	(3	3)	84	24	25	23	12	3	28	1	0	1	1	2	3	.262	.307	.440	.747
2017 SF	NL	44	80	13	4	0	2	(1	1)	23	8	8	3	5	0	10	1	0	1	0	0	3	.163	.218	.288	.506
15 CWS	AL	58	173	41	11	1	3	(2	1)	63	10	15	14	9	1	34	1	0	2	0	1	2	.237	.276	.364	.640
15 LAA	AL	17	64	13	4	1	1	(1	0)	22	4	9	6	4	1	13	0	0	0	0	0	0	.203	.250	.344	.594
Postseason		5	19	8	0	1	1	(0	1)	13	3	6	5	0	0	5	0	0	0	0	0	1	.421	.421	.684	1.105
8 ML YEARS		513	1424	357	73	14	33	(19	14)	557	147	158	165	107	13	245	7	0	13	1	8	20	.251	.304	.391	.695

Sean Gilmartin

Pitches: L **Bats:** L **Pos:** RP-2 **Ht:** 6'2" **Wt:** 206 **Born:** 5/8/1990 **Age:** 28

Year Team	Lg	G	GS	CG	GF	IP	BFP	H	R	ER	HR	SH	SF	HB	TBB	IBB	SO	WP	Bk	W	L	Pct	Sh	Sv-Op	Hld	ERC	ERA
2017 LsVgs*	AAA	8	8	0	0	37.0	176	52	30	29	6	2	1	2	14	0	31	1	0	2	2	.500	0	0- -	-	7.12	7.05
2017 Memp*	AAA	8	1	0	4	12.2	55	15	8	8	2	0	0	0	2	0	8	0	0	0	1	.000	0	1- -	-	4.44	5.68
2017 Cards*	R	5	5	0	0	5.2	20	3	3	3	0	0	0	0	1	0	7	1	0	0	0	-	0	0- -	-	0.60	4.76
2015 NYM	NL	50	1	0	13	57.1	235	50	17	17	2	2	1	2	18	5	54	1	0	3	2	.600	0	0-1	2	2.67	2.67
2016 NYM	NL	14	1	0	3	17.2	79	21	14	14	4	1	0	1	7	1	11	0	0	0	1	.000	0	0-0	1	6.39	7.13
2017 NYM	NL	2	0	0	1	3.1	19	8	5	5	2	1	1	0	1	0	4	1	0	0	0	-	0	0-0	0	17.83	13.50
Postseason		1	0	0	1	0.2	2	0	0	0	0	0	0	0	0	0	0	0	0	0	0	-	0	0-0	-	0.00	0.00
3 ML YEARS		66	2	0	17	78.1	333	79	36	36	8	4	2	3	26	6	69	2	0	3	3	.500	0	0-1	3	3.94	4.14

Chris Gimenez

JIMM-inn-ezz

Bats: R **Throws:** R **Pos:** C-59;1B-7;PH-6;LF-5;3B-1;DH-1;PR-1 **Ht:** 6'2" **Wt:** 230 **Born:** 12/27/1982 **Age:** 35

Year Team	Lg	G	AB	H	2B	3B	HR	(Hm	Rd)	TB	R	RBI	RC	TBB	IBB	SO	HBP	SH	SF	SB	CS	GDP	Avg	OBP	Slg	OPS
2009 Cle	AL	45	111	16	2	0	3	(0	3)	27	12	7	3	17	0	36	0	1	1	1	1	3	.144	.256	.243	.499
2010 Cle	AL	28	58	11	5	0	1	(1	0)	19	6	8	5	8	0	22	0	1	0	0	0	1	.190	.288	.328	.615
2011 Sea	AL	24	59	12	1	0	1	(0	1)	16	6	6	5	9	0	13	0	0	1	0	1	1	.203	.314	.271	.585
2012 TB	AL	42	100	26	4	0	1	(0	1)	33	10	9	10	8	0	24	1	0	1	0	0	4	.260	.315	.330	.645
2013 TB	AL	4	3	1	1	0	0	(0	0)	2	1	0	1	1	0	1	0	0	0	0	0	0	.333	.500	.667	1.167
2014 2 Tms	AL	42	116	28	10	0	0	(0	0)	38	13	11	12	12	1	29	0	0	0	0	1	3	.241	.313	.328	.640

			BATTING																					RUNNING			AVERAGES			
Year	Team	Lg	G	AB	H	2B	3B	HR	(Hm	Rd)	TB	R	RBI	RC	TBB	IBB	SO	HBP	SH	SF	SB	CS	GDP	Avg	OBP	Slg	OPS
2015	Tex	AL	36	98	25	6	1	5	(3	2)	48	19	14	15	10	0	19	1	4	0	2	0	2	.255	.330	.490	.820
2016	Cle	AL	68	139	30	4	0	4	(1	3)	46	17	11	8	10	0	41	1	4	1	0	0	8	.216	.272	.331	.602
2017	Min	AL	77	186	41	9	0	7	(5	2)	71	28	16	24	33	0	60	4	2	0	1	0	3	.220	.350	.382	.731
14	Tex	AL	34	107	28	10	0	0	(0	0)	38	13	11	12	11	1	26	0	0	0	0	1	3	.262	.331	.355	.686
14	Cle	AL	8	9	0	0	0	0	(0	0)	0	0	0	0	1	0	3	0	0	0	0	0	0	.000	.100	.000	.100
	Postseason		2	8	2	0	0	0	(0	0)	2	1	0	0	0	0	1	0	1	0	0	0	0	.250	.250	.250	.500
	9 ML YEARS		366	870	190	42	1	22	(10	12)	300	111	82	82	109	1	245	6	13	3	4	3	26	.218	.309	.345	.654

Lucas Giolito

Pitches: R Bats: R Pos: SP-7

jee-oh-LEE-toh

Ht: 6'6" Wt: 255 Born: 7/14/1994 Age: 23

			HOW MUCH HE PITCHED						WHAT HE GAVE UP											THE RESULTS							
Year	Team	Lg	G	GS	CG	GF	IP	BFP	H	R	ER	HR	SH	SF	HB	TBB	IBB	SO	WP	Bk	W	L	Pct	Sh	Sv-Op	Hld	ERC	ERA
2013	2 Tms	Low	11	11	0	0	36.2	147	28	9	8	1	0	2	2	14	0	39	5	0	2	1	.667	0	0--	-	2.58	1.96
2014	Hgrstn	A	20	20	0	0	98.0	386	70	28	24	7	0	1	1	28	0	110	1	0	10	2	.833	0	0--	-	2.07	2.20
2015	Ptomc	A+	13	11	0	0	69.2	292	65	24	21	1	2	1	3	20	0	86	7	1	3	5	.375	0	0--	-	2.86	2.71
2015	Hrsbrg	AA	8	8	0	0	47.1	202	48	21	20	2	1	0	3	17	0	45	2	0	4	2	.667	0	0--	-	3.90	3.80
2016	Hrsbrg	AA	14	14	0	0	71.0	313	67	37	25	2	3	1	4	34	0	72	3	0	5	3	.625	0	0--	-	3.73	3.17
2016	Syrcse	AAA	7	7	0	0	37.1	149	31	11	9	3	0	0	1	10	0	40	1	0	1	2	.333	0	0--	-	2.71	2.17
2017	Charllt	AAA	24	24	2	0	128.2	551	122	66	64	17	2	4	4	59	0	134	9	0	6	10	.375	2	0--	-	4.44	4.48
2016	Was	NL	6	4	0	1	21.1	101	26	16	16	7	0	0	1	12	0	11	1	0	0	1	.000	0	0-0	0	8.14	6.75
2017	CWS	AL	7	7	0	0	45.1	179	31	14	12	8	1	0	3	12	0	34	2	0	3	3	.500	0	0-0	0	2.63	2.38
	2 ML YEARS		13	11	0	1	66.2	280	57	32	28	15	1	0	4	24	0	45	3	1	3	4	.429	0	0-0	0	4.19	3.78

Mychal Givens

Pitches: R Bats: R Pos: RP-69

michael

Ht: 6'0" Wt: 210 Born: 5/13/1990 Age: 28

			HOW MUCH HE PITCHED						WHAT HE GAVE UP											THE RESULTS							
Year	Team	Lg	G	GS	CG	GF	IP	BFP	H	R	ER	HR	SH	SF	HB	TBB	IBB	SO	WP	Bk	W	L	Pct	Sh	Sv-Op	Hld	ERC	ERA
2015	Bal	AL	22	0	0	5	30.0	117	20	7	6	1	1	1	1	6	0	38	0	0	2	0	1.000	0	0-0	4	1.49	1.80
2016	Bal	AL	66	0	0	8	74.2	313	59	28	26	6	2	1	6	36	2	96	3	0	8	2	.800	0	0-1	13	3.44	3.13
2017	Bal	AL	69	0	0	8	78.2	315	57	24	24	10	0	0	5	25	1	88	2	0	8	1	.889	0	0-5	21	2.74	2.75
	Postseason		1	0	0	0	2.1	6	0	0	0	0	0	0	0	0	0	3	0	0	0	0	-	0	0-0	0	0.00	0.00
	3 ML YEARS		157	0	0	21	183.1	745	136	59	56	17	3	2	12	67	3	222	5	0	18	3	.857	0	0-6	38	2.78	2.75

Tyler Glasnow

Pitches: R Bats: L Pos: SP-13; RP-2

Ht: 6'8" Wt: 220 Born: 8/23/1993 Age: 24

			HOW MUCH HE PITCHED						WHAT HE GAVE UP											THE RESULTS							
Year	Team	Lg	G	GS	CG	GF	IP	BFP	H	R	ER	HR	SH	SF	HB	TBB	IBB	SO	WP	Bk	W	L	Pct	Sh	Sv-Op	Hld	ERC	ERA
2013	WV	A	24	24	0	0	111.1	452	54	35	27	9	2	1	9	61	0	164	11	1	9	3	.750	0	0--	-	2.13	2.18
2014	Bradtn	A+	23	23	0	0	124.1	493	74	29	24	3	3	5	3	57	0	157	5	2	12	5	.706	0	0--	-	1.87	1.74
2015	Altna	AA	12	12	0	0	63.0	248	41	22	17	2	1	3	0	19	0	82	4	0	5	3	.625	0	0--	-	1.59	2.43
2015	Indy	AAA	8	8	0	0	41.0	174	33	16	10	1	1	0	1	22	0	48	2	0	2	1	.667	0	0--	-	3.13	2.20
2016	Indy	AAA	20	20	0	0	110.2	438	65	23	23	4	2	2	0	62	0	133	6	0	8	3	.727	0	0--	-	2.20	1.87
2017	Indy	AAA	15	15	0	0	93.1	364	57	21	20	6	5	2	1	32	0	140	9	0	9	2	.818	0	0--	-	1.75	1.93
2016	Pit	NL	7	4	0	0	23.1	105	22	13	11	2	1	0	3	13	0	24	2	1	0	2	.000	0	0-0	0	4.80	4.24
2017	Pit	NL	15	13	0	0	62.0	305	81	61	53	13	4	1	2	44	2	56	3	0	2	7	.222	0	0-0	1	8.32	7.69
	2 ML YEARS		22	17	0	0	85.1	410	103	74	64	15	5	1	5	57	2	80	5	1	2	9	.182	0	0-0	1	7.30	6.75

Koda Glover

Pitches: R Bats: R Pos: RP-23

Ht: 6'5" Wt: 225 Born: 4/13/1993 Age: 25

			HOW MUCH HE PITCHED						WHAT HE GAVE UP											THE RESULTS							
Year	Team	Lg	G	GS	CG	GF	IP	BFP	H	R	ER	HR	SH	SF	HB	TBB	IBB	SO	WP	Bk	W	L	Pct	Sh	Sv-Op	Hld	ERC	ERA
2015	2 Tms	Low	19	0	0	15	30.0	117	22	8	6	2	2	2	1	2	0	38	0	0	1	1	.500	0	5--	-	1.50	1.80
2016	Ptomc	A+	7	0	0	5	9.2	36	3	0	0	0	0	0	0	4	0	15	0	0	0	0	-	0	2--	-	0.76	0.00
2016	Hrsbrg	AA	17	0	0	12	22.1	93	20	9	8	1	2	0	0	7	0	29	0	0	2	0	1.000	0	4--	-	2.80	3.22
2016	Syrcse	AAA	16	0	0	8	24.0	88	16	6	6	2	2	0	1	3	0	22	0	0	1	1	.500	0	2--	-	1.60	2.25
2016	Was	NL	19	0	0	4	19.2	83	15	12	11	3	0	0	1	7	1	16	1	0	2	0	1.000	0	0-2	2	2.99	5.03
2017	Was	NL	23	0	0	12	19.1	80	20	11	11	1	0	1	0	4	0	17	1	0	0	1	.000	0	8-10	5	3.21	5.12
	2 ML YEARS		42	0	0	16	39.0	163	35	23	22	4	0	1	1	11	1	33	2	0	2	1	.667	0	8-12	7	3.10	5.08

Zack Godley

Pitches: R Bats: R Pos: SP-25; RP-1

Ht: 6'3" Wt: 240 Born: 4/21/1990 Age: 28

			HOW MUCH HE PITCHED						WHAT HE GAVE UP											THE RESULTS							
Year	Team	Lg	G	GS	CG	GF	IP	BFP	H	R	ER	HR	SH	SF	HB	TBB	IBB	SO	WP	Bk	W	L	Pct	Sh	Sv-Op	Hld	ERC	ERA
2017	Reno*	AAA	5	3	0	0	28.0	110	14	11	8	0	0	1	1	17	0	29	1	0	2	1	.667	0	0--	-	1.84	2.57
2015	Ari	NL	9	6	0	1	36.2	150	29	13	13	4	1	1	3	17	1	34	2	0	5	1	.833	0	0-0	0	3.67	3.19
2016	Ari	NL	27	9	0	1	74.2	335	86	54	53	13	7	1	4	25	4	60	5	0	5	4	.556	0	0-1	0	5.31	6.39
2017	Ari	NL	26	25	0	1	155.0	627	124	61	58	15	6	2	5	53	2	165	13	0	8	9	.471	0	0-0	0	2.92	3.37
	3 ML YEARS		62	40	0	3	266.1	1112	239	128	124	32	14	4	12	95	7	259	20	0	18	14	.563	0	0-1	0	3.66	4.19

Erik Goeddel

Pitches: R Bats: R Pos: RP-33 — guh-DELL — Ht: 6'3" Wt: 191 Born: 12/20/1988 Age: 29

Year Team	Lg	G	GS	CG	GF	IP	BFP	H	R	ER	HR	SH	SF	HB	TBB	IBB	SO	WP	Bk	W	L	Pct	Sh	Sv-Op	Hld	ERC	ERA
2017 LsVgs*	AAA	25	0	0	6	29.2	134	35	23	22	7	2	2	0	12	2	25	2	1	2	4	.333	0	0- -	-	6.02	6.67
2014 NYM	NL	6	0	0	5	6.2	26	3	2	2	0	0	0	0	4	1	6	1	0	0	0	—	0	0-0	-	1.37	2.70
2015 NYM	NL	35	0	0	9	33.1	132	24	9	9	1	0	3	2	9	2	34	2	0	1	1	.500	0	0-0	2	1.89	2.43
2016 NYM	NL	36	0	0	10	35.2	157	33	20	18	5	0	1	1	14	1	36	5	0	2	2	.500	0	0-1	2	3.83	4.54
2017 NYM	NL	33	0	0	14	29.0	122	28	17	17	8	1	1	0	11	0	33	2	0	0	1	.000	0	0-0	1	5.09	5.28
Postseason		1	0	0	0	0.0	4	4	3	3	1	0	0	0	0	0	0	0	0	0	0	—	0	0-0	0	—	—
4 ML YEARS		110	0	0	38	104.2	437	88	48	46	14	1	5	3	38	4	109	10	0	3	4	.429	0	0-1	5	3.33	3.96

David Goforth

Pitches: R Bats: R Pos: RP-1 — Ht: 5'10" Wt: 205 Born: 10/11/1988 Age: 29

Year Team	Lg	G	GS	CG	GF	IP	BFP	H	R	ER	HR	SH	SF	HB	TBB	IBB	SO	WP	Bk	W	L	Pct	Sh	Sv-Op	Hld	ERC	ERA
2017 ColSpr*	AAA	48	0	0	25	54.1	246	57	25	24	7	5	1	4	26	2	38	4	0	3	4	.429	0	5- -	-	5.09	3.98
2015 Mil	NL	20	0	0	9	24.2	111	32	13	11	4	2	2	0	8	2	24	2	0	1	0	1.000	0	0-0	0	5.87	4.01
2016 Mil	NL	10	0	0	7	10.2	55	18	14	13	3	0	0	0	4	1	9	1	0	0	0	—	0	0-0	0	9.27	10.97
2017 Mil	NL	1	0	0	1	1.0	4	0	0	0	0	0	0	0	1	0	0	0	0	0	0	—	0	0-0	0	0.95	0.00
3 ML YEARS		31	0	0	17	36.1	170	50	27	24	7	2	2	0	13	3	33	3	0	1	0	1.000	0	0-0	0	6.65	5.94

Luiz Gohara

Pitches: L Bats: L Pos: SP-5 — Ht: 6'3" Wt: 210 Born: 7/31/1996 Age: 21

Year Team	Lg	G	GS	CG	GF	IP	BFP	H	R	ER	HR	SH	SF	HB	TBB	IBB	SO	WP	Bk	W	L	Pct	Sh	Sv-Op	Hld	ERC	ERA
2013 Pulski	R+	6	6	0	0	21.2	98	22	14	10	1	1	0	2	9	0	27	3	0	1	2	.333	0	0- -	-	4.08	4.15
2014 2 Tms	Low	13	13	0	0	49.2	238	57	47	37	6	3	0	5	26	0	53	11	0	1	7	.125	0	0- -	-	5.85	6.70
2015 2 Tms	Low	16	16	0	0	63.1	299	77	47	39	4	3	0	4	38	0	67	8	1	3	8	.273	0	0- -	-	6.19	5.54
2016 2 Tms	Low	13	13	0	0	69.2	279	57	17	14	2	1	0	0	23	1	81	5	0	7	2	.778	0	0- -	-	2.44	1.81
2017 Florida	A+	7	7	0	0	36.1	146	33	8	8	0	0	0	0	10	0	39	3	0	3	1	.750	0	0- -	-	2.54	1.98
2017 Missi	AA	12	11	0	0	52.0	217	42	17	15	2	1	2	3	18	1	60	4	0	2	1	.667	0	0- -	-	2.61	2.60
2017 Gwnntt	AAA	7	7	0	0	35.1	154	31	16	13	4	1	1	1	16	0	48	1	0	2	2	.500	0	0- -	-	3.72	3.31
2017 Atl	NL	5	5	0	0	29.1	123	32	17	16	2	2	0	0	8	0	31	1	0	1	3	.250	0	0-0	0	3.94	4.91

Ryan Goins

Bats: L Throws: R Pos: SS-87;2B-56;PH-11;3B-8;PR-4;DH-1 — GO-inns — Ht: 5'10" Wt: 180 Born: 2/13/1988 Age: 30

Year Team	Lg	G	AB	H	2B	3B	HR	(Hm	Rd)	TB	R	RBI	RC	TBB	IBB	SO	HBP	SH	SF	SB	CS	GDP	Avg	OBP	Slg	OPS
2013 Tor	AL	34	119	30	5	0	2	(2	0)	41	11	8	11	2	0	28	0	0	0	0	0	1	.252	.264	.345	.609
2014 Tor	AL	67	181	34	6	3	1	(1	0)	49	14	15	7	5	0	42	0	6	1	0	1	4	.188	.209	.271	.479
2015 Tor	AL	128	376	94	16	4	5	(4	1)	133	52	45	48	39	0	83	1	7	5	2	1	12	.250	.318	.354	.672
2016 Tor	AL	77	183	34	9	2	3	(1	2)	56	13	12	9	9	0	48	1	3	0	1	1	6	.186	.228	.306	.534
2017 Tor	AL	143	418	99	21	1	9	(3	6)	149	37	62	53	31	0	96	0	5	5	3	2	14	.237	.286	.356	.643
Postseason		14	41	6	1	0	1	(1	0)	10	5	5	3	2	0	14	0	3	0	0	0	2	.146	.186	.244	.430
5 ML YEARS		449	1277	291	57	10	20	(11	9)	428	127	142	128	86	0	297	2	21	11	6	5	37	.228	.275	.335	.611

Brad Goldberg

Pitches: R Bats: R Pos: RP-11 — Ht: 6'4" Wt: 220 Born: 2/21/1990 Age: 28

Year Team	Lg	G	GS	CG	GF	IP	BFP	H	R	ER	HR	SH	SF	HB	TBB	IBB	SO	WP	Bk	W	L	Pct	Sh	Sv-Op	Hld	ERC	ERA
2013 3 Tms	Low	16	0	0	7	35.0	130	17	8	6	1	1	0	1	9	0	49	4	0	3	0	1.000	0	3- -	-	1.08	1.54
2014 WinSa	A+	35	7	0	9	75.2	363	90	59	44	2	2	8	7	46	0	62	10	0	4	4	.500	0	2- -	-	5.77	5.23
2015 WinSa	A+	39	0	0	25	57.2	246	57	25	19	4	5	4	2	25	0	58	1	0	1	4	.200	0	11- -	-	4.16	2.97
2016 Charltt	AAA	43	0	0	30	50.2	214	42	18	16	3	2	2	2	23	1	44	4	0	3	5	.375	0	10- -	-	3.20	2.84
2017 Charltt	AAA	30	0	0	16	40.1	179	40	19	15	2	1	4	0	22	0	47	4	1	3	2	.600	0	5- -	-	4.22	3.35
2017 CWS	AL	11	0	0	4	12.0	62	14	11	11	2	0	0	0	14	0	3	1	0	0	0	—	0	0-0	0	10.14	8.25

Paul Goldschmidt

Bats: R Throws: R Pos: 1B-151;DH-2;PH-2 — Ht: 6'3" Wt: 225 Born: 9/10/1987 Age: 30

Year Team	Lg	G	AB	H	2B	3B	HR	(Hm	Rd)	TB	R	RBI	RC	TBB	IBB	SO	HBP	SH	SF	SB	CS	GDP	Avg	OBP	Slg	OPS
2011 Ari	NL	48	156	39	9	1	8	(2	6)	74	28	26	26	20	0	53	5	0	1	4	0	4	.250	.333	.474	.808
2012 Ari	NL	145	514	147	43	1	20	(10	10)	252	82	82	86	60	4	130	4	0	9	18	3	9	.286	.359	.490	.850
2013 Ari	NL	160	602	182	36	3	36	(17	19)	332	103	125	131	99	19	145	3	0	5	15	7	25	.302	.401	.551	.952
2014 Ari	NL	109	406	122	39	1	19	(10	9)	220	75	69	83	64	10	110	2	0	3	9	3	10	.300	.396	.542	.938
2015 Ari	NL	159	567	182	38	2	33	(13	20)	323	103	110	135	118	29	151	2	0	7	21	5	16	.321	.435	.570	1.005
2016 Ari	NL	158	579	172	33	3	24	(13	11)	283	106	95	113	110	15	150	7	0	8	32	5	14	.297	.411	.489	.899
2017 Ari	NL	155	558	166	34	3	36	(20	16)	314	117	120	131	94	15	147	8	0	4	18	5	14	.297	.404	.563	.966
Postseason		4	16	7	0	0	2	(1	1)	13	4	6	5	2	0	5	1	0	0	1	0	0	.438	.526	.813	1.339
7 ML YEARS		934	3382	1010	232	14	176	(87	89)	1798	614	627	705	565	92	886	26	0	37	117	28	92	.299	.399	.532	.931

Yan Gomes

YAHN GOHMS

Bats: R **Throws:** R **Pos:** C-103;PH-3 **Ht:** 6'2" **Wt:** 215 **Born:** 7/19/1987 **Age:** 30

Year	Team	Lg	G	AB	H	2B	3B	HR	(Hm	Rd)	TB	R	RBI	RC	TBB	IBB	SO	HBP	SH	SF	SB	CS	GDP	Avg	OBP	Slg	OPS
2012	Tor	AL	43	98	20	4	0	4	(3	1)	36	9	13	11	6	0	32	3	1	3	0	0	3	.204	.264	.367	.631
2013	Cle	AL	88	293	86	18	2	11	(6	5)	141	45	38	42	18	0	67	7	0	4	2	0	12	.294	.345	.481	.826
2014	Cle	AL	135	485	135	25	3	21	(9	12)	229	61	74	65	24	3	120	3	0	6	0	0	13	.278	.313	.472	.785
2015	Cle	AL	95	363	84	22	0	12	(5	7)	142	38	45	25	13	1	104	7	0	6	0	0	11	.231	.267	.391	.659
2016	Cle	AL	74	251	42	11	1	9	(4	5)	82	22	34	18	9	0	69	2	0	2	0	0	7	.167	.201	.327	.527
2017	Cle	AL	105	341	79	15	0	14	(5	9)	136	43	56	41	31	0	99	8	1	2	0	0	9	.232	.309	.399	.708
	Postseason		5	8	2	1	0	0	(0	0)	3	0	0	0	0	0	2	0	0	0	0	0	1	.250	.250	.375	.625
	6 ML YEARS		540	1831	446	95	6	71	(32	39)	766	218	260	202	101	4	491	30	2	23	2	0	55	.244	.291	.418	.709

Carlos Gomez

Bats: R **Throws:** R **Pos:** CF-102;PH-4;DH-1 **Ht:** 6'3" **Wt:** 220 **Born:** 12/4/1985 **Age:** 32

Year	Team	Lg	G	AB	H	2B	3B	HR	(Hm	Rd)	TB	R	RBI	RC	TBB	IBB	SO	HBP	SH	SF	SB	CS	GDP	Avg	OBP	Slg	OPS
2007	NYM	NL	58	125	29	3	0	2	(1	1)	38	14	12	11	8	2	27	3	0	3	12	3	0	.232	.288	.304	.592
2008	Min	AL	153	577	149	24	7	7	(3	4)	208	79	59	66	25	0	142	7	3	2	33	11	7	.258	.296	.360	.657
2009	Min	AL	137	315	72	15	5	3	(1	2)	106	51	28	33	22	0	72	4	7	1	14	7	1	.229	.287	.337	.623
2010	Mil	NL	97	291	72	11	3	5	(3	2)	104	38	24	28	17	1	72	4	6	0	18	3	10	.247	.298	.357	.655
2011	Mil	NL	94	231	52	11	3	8	(4	4)	93	37	24	25	15	0	64	2	8	2	16	2	2	.225	.276	.403	.679
2012	Mil	NL	137	415	108	19	4	19	(11	8)	192	72	51	59	20	1	98	8	6	3	37	6	6	.260	.305	.463	.768
2013	Mil	NL	147	536	152	27	10	24	(15	9)	271	80	73	81	37	2	146	10	1	6	40	7	11	.284	.338	.506	.843
2014	Mil	NL	148	574	163	34	4	23	(13	10)	274	95	73	98	47	0	141	19	1	3	34	12	11	.284	.356	.477	.833
2015	2 Tms		115	435	111	29	1	12	(6	6)	178	61	56	63	31	1	101	7	3	1	17	9	5	.255	.314	.409	.724
2016	2 Tms	AL	118	411	95	22	1	13	(8	5)	158	45	53	54	34	2	136	5	3	0	18	5	11	.231	.298	.384	.682
2017	Tex	AL	105	368	94	23	1	17	(12	5)	170	51	51	55	31	0	127	**19**	3	5	13	5	3	.255	.340	.462	.802
15	Mil	NL	74	286	75	20	1	8	(6	2)	121	42	43	45	23	0	70	5	0	0	7	6	4	.262	.328	.423	.751
15	Hou	AL	41	149	36	9	0	4	(0	4)	57	19	13	18	8	1	31	2	3	1	10	3	1	.242	.288	.383	.670
16	Hou	AL	85	295	62	16	1	5	(2	3)	95	27	29	29	21	2	100	4	3	0	13	2	11	.210	.272	.322	.594
16	Tex	AL	33	116	33	6	0	8	(6	2)	63	18	24	25	13	0	36	1	0	0	5	3	0	.284	.362	.543	.905
	Postseason		18	46	11	0	0	3	(1	2)	20	7	6	6	2	0	13	2	2	0	3	1	0	.239	.300	.435	.735
	11 ML YEARS		1309	4278	1097	218	39	133	(77	56)	1792	623	504	573	287	9	1126	88	41	26	252	70	67	.256	.315	.419	.733

Jeanmar Gomez

JENN-marr

Pitches: R **Bats:** R **Pos:** RP-18 **Ht:** 6'3" **Wt:** 215 **Born:** 2/10/1988 **Age:** 30

Year	Team	Lg	G	GS	CG	GF	IP	BFP	H	R	ER	HR	SH	SF	HB	TBB	IBB	SO	WP	Bk	W	L	Pct	Sh	Sv-Op	Hld	ERC	ERA
2017	ColSpr*	AAA	7	0	0	2	8.1	30	7	2	2	1	1	0	0	1	0	7	0	0	0	0	-	0	0- -	-	2.56	2.16
2017	Tacom*	AAA	5	0	0	5	5.2	23	3	1	1	1	0	0	0	2	0	4	0	0	1	0	1.000	0	1- -	-	1.83	1.59
2010	Cle	AL	11	11	0	0	57.2	265	73	36	30	7	0	3	2	22	3	34	1	0	4	5	.444	0	0-0	0	5.75	4.68
2011	Cle	AL	11	10	0	0	58.1	259	73	31	29	6	0	2	1	15	1	31	2	0	5	3	.625	0	0-0	0	4.99	4.47
2012	Cle	AL	20	17	0	1	90.2	395	95	66	60	15	2	7	4	34	5	47	2	0	5	8	.385	0	0-0	0	4.83	5.96
2013	Pit	NL	34	8	0	6	80.2	333	65	35	30	6	4	6	3	28	3	53	6	0	3	0	1.000	0	0-0	3	2.75	3.35
2014	Pit	NL	44	0	0	20	62.0	270	70	24	22	6	3	2	2	23	7	38	2	0	2	2	.500	0	1-1	2	4.70	3.19
2015	Phi	NL	65	0	0	21	74.2	319	82	28	25	4	1	4	2	17	4	50	3	0	2	3	.400	0	0-3	5	3.63	3.01
2016	Phi	NL	70	0	0	59	68.2	297	78	38	37	6	0	3	2	22	2	47	3	0	3	5	.375	0	37-43	1	4.58	4.85
2017	Phi	NL	18	0	0	12	22.1	100	31	19	18	7	2	0	2	7	2	21	1	0	3	2	.600	0	2-3	0	8.41	7.25
	Postseason		1	0	0	0	4.0	17	3	2	0	0	1	0	0	2	0	0	0	0	0	0	-	0	0-0	0	2.40	0.00
	8 ML YEARS		273	46	0	119	515.0	2238	567	277	251	57	12	27	18	168	27	321	20	0	27	28	.491	0	40-50	13	4.51	4.39

Miguel Gomez

Bats: B **Throws:** R **Pos:** PH-17;2B-6 **Ht:** 5'10" **Wt:** 185 **Born:** 12/17/1992 **Age:** 25

Year	Team	Lg	G	AB	H	2B	3B	HR	(Hm	Rd)	TB	R	RBI	RC	TBB	IBB	SO	HBP	SH	SF	SB	CS	GDP	Avg	OBP	Slg	OPS
2015	SlKzr	A-	66	276	88	14	1	6	(-	-)	122	30	52	40	5	0	24	1	0	2	0	1	7	.319	.331	.442	.773
2016	2 Tms	Low	109	439	145	26	3	17	(-	-)	228	66	67	84	20	2	53	4	1	3	4	2	10	.330	.363	.519	.882
2017	Rchmd	AA	78	308	94	19	2	8	(-	-)	141	43	38	46	12	0	36	0	1	1	0	0	15	.305	.330	.458	.788
2017	SF	NL	22	33	8	2	0	0	(0	0)	10	3	2	2	0	0	6	0	0	1	0	0	1	.242	.235	.303	.538

Roberto Gomez

Pitches: R **Bats:** B **Pos:** RP-4 **Ht:** 6'5" **Wt:** 180 **Born:** 8/3/1989 **Age:** 28

Year	Team	Lg	G	GS	CG	GF	IP	BFP	H	R	ER	HR	SH	SF	HB	TBB	IBB	SO	WP	Bk	W	L	Pct	Sh	Sv-Op	Hld	ERC	ERA
2013	Charltt	A+	21	19	1	0	111.1	477	115	66	58	7	2	9	7	39	0	65	8	0	5	8	.385	1	0- -	-	4.11	4.69
2014	2 Tms	Low	10	10	0	0	47.2	214	57	29	26	3	3	1	1	21	0	28	2	0	1	4	.200	0	0- -	-	5.25	4.91
2014	Mont	AA	8	8	0	0	37.2	167	51	28	25	2	1	2	4	6	0	21	7	0	2	4	.333	0	0- -	-	5.33	5.97
2017	Scrmto	AAA	38	13	0	8	97.1	425	100	52	44	8	4	2	3	38	2	89	5	1	3	9	.250	0	0- -	-	4.14	4.07
2017	SF	NL	4	0	0	2	5.1	26	9	5	5	0	0	0	0	1	0	6	0	0	0	0	-	0	0-0	0	6.33	8.44

Marco Gonzales

Pitches: L Bats: L Pos: SP-8; RP-3   Ht: 6'1" Wt: 195 Born: 2/16/1992 Age: 26

			HOW MUCH HE PITCHED						WHAT HE GAVE UP												THE RESULTS						
Year	Team	Lg	G	GS	CG	GF	IP	BFP	H	R	ER	HR	SH	SF	HB	TBB	IBB	SO	WP	Bk	W	L	Pct	Sh	Sv-Op	Hld	ERC	ERA
2017	Memp*	AAA	11	11	0	0	68.1	272	54	25	22	6	2	3	4	17	0	57	0	0	6	4	.600	0	0- -	-	2.59	2.90
2014	StL	NL	10	5	0	0	34.2	156	32	16	16	4	0	1	1	21	1	31	0	0	4	2	.667	0	0-0	1	4.59	4.15
2015	StL	NL	1	1	0	0	2.2	16	7	4	4	1	0	1	0	1	0	1	0	0	0	0	-	0	0-0	0	17.70	13.50
2017	2 Tms		11	8	0	1	40.0	185	59	27	27	8	0	1	1	11	0	32	2	0	1	1	.500	0	0-0	0	7.40	6.08
17	StL	NL	1	1	0	0	3.1	16	6	5	5	3	0	0	0	0	0	2	0	0	0	0	-	0	0-0	0	13.65	13.50
17	Sea	AL	10	7	0	1	36.2	169	53	22	22	5	0	1	1	11	0	30	2	0	1	1	.500	0	0-0	0	6.82	5.40
	Postseason		6	0	0	0	6.0	24	4	3	3	0	1	0	0	2	0	4	0	0	2	1	.667	0	0-1	0	1.57	4.50
3 ML YEARS			22	14	0	1	77.1	357	98	47	47	13	0	3	2	33	1	64	2	0	5	3	.625	0	0-0	1	6.39	5.47

Adrian Gonzalez

Bats: L Throws: L Pos: 1B-60;PH-14   Ht: 6'2" Wt: 215 Born: 5/8/1982 Age: 36

			BATTING																			RUNNING			AVERAGES			
Year	Team	Lg	G	AB	H	2B	3B	HR	(Hm	Rd)	TB	R	RBI	RC	TBB	IBB	SO	HBP	SH	SF	SB	CS	GDP	Avg	OBP	Slg	OPS
2004	Tex	AL	16	42	10	3	0	1	(1	0)	16	7	7	7	2	0	6	0	0	0	0	0	0	.238	.273	.381	.654
2005	Tex	AL	43	150	34	7	1	6	(3	3)	61	17	17	13	10	2	37	0	0	2	0	0	3	.227	.272	.407	.678
2006	SD	NL	156	570	173	38	1	24	(10	14)	285	83	82	82	52	9	113	3	1	5	0	1	24	.304	.362	.500	.862
2007	SD	NL	161	646	182	46	3	30	(10	20)	324	101	100	108	65	9	140	3	0	6	0	0	6	.282	.347	.502	.849
2008	SD	NL	162	616	172	32	1	36	(14	22)	314	103	119	107	74	18	142	7	0	3	0	0	24	.279	.361	.510	.871
2009	SD	NL	160	552	153	27	2	40	(12	28)	304	90	99	109	119	22	109	5	1	4	1	1	20	.277	.407	.551	.958
2010	SD	NL	160	591	176	33	0	31	(11	20)	302	87	101	122	93	35	114	2	2	4	0	0	15	.298	.393	.511	.904
2011	Bos	AL	159	630	213	45	3	27	(10	17)	345	108	117	121	74	20	119	6	0	5	1	0	28	.338	.410	.548	.957
2012	2 Tms		159	629	188	47	1	18	(9	9)	291	75	108	113	42	5	110	5	0	8	2	0	10	.299	.344	.463	.806
2013	LAD	NL	157	583	171	32	0	22	(11	11)	269	69	100	89	47	6	98	1	0	10	1	0	12	.293	.342	.461	.803
2014	LAD	NL	159	591	163	41	0	27	(13	14)	285	83	116	95	56	9	112	2	0	11	1	1	13	.276	.335	.482	.817
2015	LAD	NL	156	571	157	33	0	28	(17	11)	274	76	90	84	62	10	107	6	0	3	0	1	21	.275	.350	.480	.830
2016	LAD	NL	156	568	162	31	0	18	(6	12)	247	69	90	85	55	9	117	4	0	6	0	2	16	.285	.349	.435	.784
2017	LAD	NL	71	231	56	17	0	3	(2	1)	82	14	30	22	16	1	43	0	0	4	0	1	7	.242	.287	.355	.642
12	Bos	AL	123	484	145	37	0	15	(8	7)	227	63	86	89	31	4	81	5	0	7	0	0	9	.300	.343	.469	.812
12	LAD	NL	36	145	43	10	1	3	(1	2)	64	12	22	24	11	1	29	0	0	1	2	0	1	.297	.344	.441	.785
	Postseason		34	128	34	3	0	7	(4	3)	58	17	21	13	12	1	29	0	0	0	1	0	3	.266	.329	.453	.782
14 ML YEARS			1875	6970	2010	432	12	311	(129	182)	3399	982	1176	1157	767	155	1367	44	4	71	6	7	202	.288	.359	.488	.847

Carlos Gonzalez

Bats: L Throws: L Pos: RF-125;PH-9;DH-3   Ht: 6'1" Wt: 220 Born: 10/17/1985 Age: 32

			BATTING																			RUNNING			AVERAGES			
Year	Team	Lg	G	AB	H	2B	3B	HR	(Hm	Rd)	TB	R	RBI	RC	TBB	IBB	SO	HBP	SH	SF	SB	CS	GDP	Avg	OBP	Slg	OPS
2008	Oak	AL	85	302	73	22	1	4	(3	1)	109	31	26	30	13	1	81	0	1	0	4	1	7	.242	.273	.361	.634
2009	Col	NL	89	278	79	14	7	13	(7	6)	146	53	29	42	28	3	70	3	5	3	16	4	3	.284	.353	.525	.878
2010	Col	NL	145	587	197	34	9	34	(26	8)	351	111	117	116	40	8	135	2	0	7	26	8	9	.336	.376	.598	.974
2011	Col	NL	127	481	142	27	3	26	(16	10)	253	92	92	95	48	8	105	7	0	6	20	5	11	.295	.363	.526	.889
2012	Col	NL	135	518	157	31	5	22	(13	9)	264	89	85	88	56	11	115	2	0	3	20	5	11	.303	.371	.510	.881
2013	Col	NL	110	391	118	23	6	26	(12	14)	231	72	70	69	41	2	118	1	0	3	21	3	7	.302	.367	.591	.958
2014	Col	NL	70	260	62	15	1	11	(5	6)	112	35	38	32	19	2	70	1	0	1	3	0	7	.238	.292	.431	.723
2015	Col	NL	153	554	150	25	2	40	(24	16)	299	87	97	94	46	6	133	1	1	6	2	0	11	.271	.325	.540	.864
2016	Col	NL	150	584	174	42	2	25	(18	7)	295	87	100	99	46	6	129	1	0	2	2	2	10	.298	.350	.505	.855
2017	Col	NL	136	470	123	34	0	14	(8	6)	199	72	57	58	56	3	119	2	0	6	3	0	9	.262	.339	.423	.762
	Postseason		4	17	10	2	0	1	(1	0)	15	5	1	5	2	0	1	0	0	0	2	1	0	.588	.632	.882	1.514
10 ML YEARS			1200	4425	1275	267	36	215	(132	83)	2259	729	711	725	393	50	1075	20	7	36	117	28	85	.288	.346	.511	.857

Erik Gonzalez

Bats: R Throws: R Pos: 2B-36;SS-11;3B-8;PR-8;PH-2;LF-1;DH-1   Ht: 6'3" Wt: 195 Born: 8/31/1991 Age: 26

			BATTING																			RUNNING			AVERAGES			
Year	Team	Lg	G	AB	H	2B	3B	HR	(Hm	Rd)	TB	R	RBI	RC	TBB	IBB	SO	HBP	SH	SF	SB	CS	GDP	Avg	OBP	Slg	OPS
2013	2 Tms	Low	132	508	129	32	12	9	(-	-)	212	75	76	63	29	0	109	1	3	5	11	6	13	.254	.293	.417	.710
2014	Carlina	A+	74	308	89	14	7	3	(-	-)	126	44	46	44	23	1	65	0	3	2	15	6	12	.289	.336	.409	.745
2014	Akron	AA	31	129	46	6	3	1	(-	-)	61	21	16	24	7	0	23	0	0	0	6	1	2	.357	.390	.473	.863
2015	Akron	AA	72	311	88	18	4	6	(-	-)	132	38	46	41	11	0	56	1	1	3	10	5	12	.283	.307	.424	.731
2015	Clmbs	AAA	65	238	53	6	3	3	(-	-)	74	32	23	21	15	0	47	3	5	0	8	2	7	.223	.277	.311	.588
2016	Clmbs	AAA	104	429	127	31	1	11	(-	-)	193	62	53	62	19	2	88	3	7	2	12	10	8	.296	.329	.450	.779
2017	Clmbs	AAA	40	160	41	4	3	6	(-	-)	69	21	13	20	7	0	53	0	2	1	5	1	0	.256	.286	.431	.717
2016	Cle	AL	21	16	5	0	0	0	(0	0)	5	2	0	1	1	0	8	0	0	0	0	1	0	.313	.353	.313	.665
2017	Cle	AL	60	110	28	6	0	4	(1	3)	46	18	11	9	3	0	37	0	1	1	1	2	1	.255	.272	.418	.690
2 ML YEARS			81	126	33	6	0	4	(1	3)	51	20	11	10	4	0	45	0	1	1	1	3	1	.262	.282	.405	.687

Gio Gonzalez

Pitches: L Bats: R Pos: SP-32   Ht: 6'0" Wt: 205 Born: 9/19/1985 Age: 32
JEE-oh

			HOW MUCH HE PITCHED						WHAT HE GAVE UP												THE RESULTS						
Year	Team	Lg	G	GS	CG	GF	IP	BFP	H	R	ER	HR	SH	SF	HB	TBB	IBB	SO	WP	Bk	W	L	Pct	Sh	Sv-Op	Hld	ERC	ERA
2008	Oak	AL	10	7	0	3	34.0	163	32	34	29	9	2	1	3	25	1	34	1	0	1	4	.200	0	0-0	0	6.54	7.68
2009	Oak	AL	20	17	0	0	98.2	455	113	68	63	14	2	3	1	56	2	109	2	0	6	7	.462	0	0-0	0	5.96	5.75
2010	Oak	AL	33	33	1	0	200.2	851	171	75	72	15	5	2	4	92	1	171	4	1	15	9	.625	0	0-0	0	3.39	3.23
2011	Oak	AL	32	32	0	0	202.0	864	175	81	70	17	3	2	8	91	1	197	6	1	16	12	.571	0	0-0	0	3.56	3.12
2012	Was	NL	32	32	2	0	199.1	822	149	69	64	9	9	7	5	76	3	207	10	1	21	8	.724	1	0-0	0	2.37	2.89
2013	Was	NL	32	32	1	0	195.2	819	169	79	73	17	7	1	2	76	1	192	4	1	11	8	.579	2	0-0	0	3.23	3.36

Year	Team	Lg	G	GS	CG	GF	IP	BFP	H	R	ER	HR	SH	SF	HB	TBB	IBB	SO	WP	Bk	W	L	Pct	Sh	Sv-Op	Hld	ERC	ERA
2014	Was	NL	27	27	0	0	158.2	653	134	66	63	10	7	4	3	56	0	162	2	0	10	10	.500	0	0-0	0	2.91	3.57
2015	Was	NL	31	31	0	0	175.2	758	181	79	74	8	3	9	4	69	3	169	4	0	11	8	.579	0	0-0	0	3.92	3.79
2016	Was	NL	32	32	0	0	177.1	765	179	98	90	19	8	5	9	59	2	171	7	0	11	11	.500	0	0-0	0	4.08	4.57
2017	Was	NL	32	32	0	0	201.0	827	158	69	66	21	7	3	7	79	5	188	7	0	15	9	.625	0	0-0	0	3.05	2.96
Postseason			4	4	0	0	18.1	81	14	10	8	1	0	1	0	13	0	15	2	0	0	0	-	0	0-0	0	3.59	3.93
10 ML YEARS			281	275	4	3	1643.0	6977	1461	718	664	139	53	37	46	679	19	1600	47	4	117	86	.576	2	0-0	0	3.50	3.64

Marwin Gonzalez

MARR-win

Bats: B Throws: R Pos: LF-47;SS-38;1B-31;2B-22;3B-19;PH-8;RF-2;PR-2

Ht: 6'1" Wt: 205 Born: 3/14/1989 Age: 29

Year	Team	Lg	G	AB	H	2B	3B	HR	(Hm	Rd)	TB	R	RBI	RC	TBB	IBB	SO	HBP	SH	SF	SB	CS	GDP	Avg	OBP	Slg	OPS
2012	Hou	NL	80	205	48	13	0	2	(1	1)	67	21	12	12	13	0	29	0	1	0	3	3	9	.234	.280	.327	.607
2013	Hou	AL	72	204	45	8	0	4	(2	2)	65	22	14	10	9	0	37	0	8	1	6	2	5	.221	.252	.319	.571
2014	Hou	AL	103	285	79	15	1	6	(3	3)	114	33	23	26	17	0	58	4	4	0	2	4	6	.277	.327	.400	.727
2015	Hou	AL	120	344	96	18	1	12	(6	6)	152	44	34	39	16	0	74	3	7	0	4	5	9	.279	.317	.442	.759
2016	Hou	AL	141	484	123	26	3	13	(8	5)	194	55	51	47	22	1	118	5	6	1	12	6	16	.254	.293	.401	.694
2017	Hou	AL	134	455	138	34	0	23	(15	8)	241	67	90	93	49	4	99	6	3	2	8	3	8	.303	.377	.530	.907
Postseason			4	3	0	0	0	0	(0	0)	0	0	0	0	0	0	2	0	0	0	0	0	0	.000	.000	.000	.000
6 ML YEARS			650	1977	529	114	5	60	(35	25)	833	242	224	227	126	5	415	18	29	4	35	23	53	.268	.317	.421	.738

Miguel Gonzalez

Pitches: R Bats: R Pos: SP-27

Ht: 6'1" Wt: 170 Born: 5/27/1984 Age: 34

Year	Team	Lg	G	GS	CG	GF	IP	BFP	H	R	ER	HR	SH	SF	HB	TBB	IBB	SO	WP	Bk	W	L	Pct	Sh	Sv-Op	Hld	ERC	ERA
2012	Bal	AL	18	15	0	0	105.1	434	92	38	38	13	1	2	5	35	2	77	3	2	9	4	.692	0	0-0	0	3.49	3.25
2013	Bal	AL	30	28	0	1	171.1	712	157	81	72	24	3	6	3	53	3	120	4	0	11	8	.579	0	0-0	0	3.58	3.78
2014	Bal	AL	27	26	1	0	159.0	671	155	61	57	25	0	3	8	51	1	111	4	1	10	9	.526	1	0-0	0	4.25	3.23
2015	Bal	AL	26	26	0	0	144.2	622	151	81	79	24	2	2	8	51	2	109	4	0	9	12	.429	0	0-0	0	4.88	4.91
2016	CWS	AL	24	23	0	0	135.0	566	132	61	56	11	1	5	6	35	1	95	3	0	5	8	.385	0	0-0	0	3.45	3.73
2017	2 Tms	AL	27	27	0	0	156.0	684	167	88	80	22	2	5	6	55	2	100	1	0	8	13	.381	0	0-0	0	4.70	4.62
17	CWS	AL	22	22	0	0	133.2	588	145	72	64	16	2	4	4	47	2	85	1	0	7	10	.412	0	0-0	0	4.57	4.31
17	Tex	AL	5	5	0	0	22.1	96	22	16	16	6	0	1	2	8	0	15	0	0	1	3	.250	0	0-0	0	5.46	6.45
Postseason			2	2	0	0	12.2	52	9	3	2	0	1	0	2	4	1	12	1	0	0	1	.000	0	0-0	0	2.07	1.42
6 ML YEARS			152	145	1	1	871.1	3689	854	410	382	119	9	23	36	280	11	612	19	3	52	54	.491	1	0-0	0	4.08	3.95

Niko Goodrum

Bats: B Throws: R Pos: 2B-8;PH-3;PR-2;RF-1;DH-1

Ht: 6'3" Wt: 198 Born: 2/28/1992 Age: 26

Year	Team	Lg	G	AB	H	2B	3B	HR	(Hm	Rd)	TB	R	RBI	RC	TBB	IBB	SO	HBP	SH	SF	SB	CS	GDP	Avg	OBP	Slg	OPS
2013	Crpds	A	103	385	100	22	4	4	(-	-)	142	62	45	59	60	1	105	4	4	2	20	4	10	.260	.364	.369	.732
2014	FtMyrs	A+	122	438	109	19	5	3	(-	-)	147	63	49	60	58	0	99	2	2	4	35	4	7	.249	.337	.336	.672
2015	FtMyrs	A+	53	205	45	11	1	4	(-	-)	70	24	19	25	32	4	59	2	0	1	11	5	3	.220	.329	.341	.671
2015	Chatt	AA	61	209	51	6	5	5	(-	-)	82	33	19	31	28	0	51	0	0	1	18	4	4	.244	.332	.392	.724
2016	Chatt	AA	49	182	50	10	2	6	(-	-)	82	25	27	31	22	2	53	2	0	1	8	2	4	.275	.357	.451	.808
2017	Roch	AAA	127	461	122	25	5	13	(-	-)	196	71	66	61	30	0	119	2	1	5	11	7	6	.265	.309	.425	.734
2017	Min	AL	11	17	1	0	0	0	(0	0)	1	1	0	0	1	0	10	0	0	0	0	0	0	.059	.111	.059	.170

Brian Goodwin

Bats: L Throws: R Pos: CF-34;LF-31;RF-11;PH-9;PR-2

Ht: 6'0" Wt: 205 Born: 11/2/1990 Age: 27

Year	Team	Lg	G	AB	H	2B	3B	HR	(Hm	Rd)	TB	R	RBI	RC	TBB	IBB	SO	HBP	SH	SF	SB	CS	GDP	Avg	OBP	Slg	OPS
2013	Hrsbrg	AA	122	457	115	19	11	10	(-	-)	186	82	40	70	66	0	121	8	1	1	19	11	4	.252	.355	.407	.762
2014	Syrcse	AAA	81	275	60	10	4	4	(-	-)	90	31	32	34	50	0	95	1	3	0	6	4	6	.218	.340	.327	.668
2015	Hrsbrg	AA	114	429	97	17	4	8	(-	-)	146	58	46	44	38	2	93	2	0	3	15	7	7	.226	.290	.340	.631
2016	Hrsbrg	AA	119	436	121	25	1	14	(-	-)	190	51	67	70	46	1	106	3	2	5	15	3	7	.278	.347	.436	.783
2017	Syrcse	AAA	25	90	23	4	0	2	(-	-)	33	9	11	11	10	0	29	0	2	1	2	1	0	.256	.327	.367	.693
2016	Was	NL	22	42	12	4	1	0	(0	0)	18	1	5	6	2	0	14	0	0	0	0	0	1	.286	.318	.429	.747
2017	Was	NL	74	251	63	21	1	13	(9	4)	125	41	30	31	23	2	69	1	0	3	6	0	3	.251	.313	.498	.811
2 ML YEARS			96	293	75	25	2	13	(9	4)	143	42	35	37	25	2	83	1	0	3	6	0	4	.256	.314	.488	.802

Nick Goody

Pitches: R Bats: R Pos: RP-56

Ht: 5'11" Wt: 195 Born: 7/6/1991 Age: 26

Year	Team	Lg	G	GS	CG	GF	IP	BFP	H	R	ER	HR	SH	SF	HB	TBB	IBB	SO	WP	Bk	W	L	Pct	Sh	Sv-Op	Hld	ERC	ERA
2015	NYY	AL	7	0	0	5	5.2	26	6	3	3	0	0	1	0	3	0	3	0	0	0	0	-	0	0-0	0	4.90	4.76
2016	NYY	AL	27	0	0	10	29.0	128	30	15	15	7	1	1	1	12	1	34	0	0	0	0	-	0	0-0	0	5.42	4.66
2017	Cle	AL	56	0	0	14	54.2	221	39	20	17	7	1	0	3	20	2	72	4	0	1	2	.333	0	0-0	6	2.78	2.80
3 ML YEARS			90	0	0	29	89.1	375	75	38	35	14	2	1	5	35	3	109	4	0	1	2	.333	0	0-0	6	3.73	3.53

Alex Gordon

Bats: L **Throws:** R **Pos:** LF-140;CF-15;PH-2;RF-1   **Ht:** 6'1" **Wt:** 220 **Born:** 2/10/1984 **Age:** 34

								BATTING												RUNNING			AVERAGES			
Year Team	Lg	G	AB	H	2B	3B	HR	(Hm Rd)	TB	R	RBI	RC	TBB	IBB	SO	HBP	SH	SF	SB	CS	GDP	Avg	OBP	Slg	OPS
2007 KC	AL	151	543	134	36	4	15	(8 7)	223	60	60	69	41	4	137	13	1	2	14	4	12	.247	.314	.411	.725
2008 KC	AL	134	493	128	35	1	16	(9 7)	213	72	59	71	66	5	120	6	1	5	9	2	8	.260	.351	.432	.783
2009 KC	AL	49	164	38	6	0	6	(2 4)	62	28	22	16	21	0	43	2	1	1	5	0	5	.232	.324	.378	.703
2010 KC	AL	74	242	52	10	0	8	(5 3)	86	34	20	23	34	1	62	2	2	1	1	5	9	.215	.315	.355	.671
2011 KC	AL	151	611	185	45	4	23	(12 11)	307	101	87	103	67	2	139	7	0	3	17	8	9	.303	.376	.502	.879
2012 KC	AL	161	642	189	51	5	14	(6 8)	292	93	72	94	73	3	140	3	0	3	10	5	14	.294	.368	.455	.822
2013 KC	AL	156	633	168	27	6	20	(10 10)	267	90	81	90	52	7	141	9	0	6	11	3	4	.265	.327	.422	.749
2014 KC	AL	156	563	150	34	1	19	(11 8)	243	87	74	95	65	5	126	11	0	4	12	3	11	.266	.351	.432	.783
2015 KC	AL	104	354	96	18	0	13	(4 9)	153	40	48	60	49	7	92	14	0	5	2	5	2	.271	.377	.432	.809
2016 KC	AL	128	445	98	16	2	17	(8 9)	169	62	40	48	52	3	148	8	0	1	8	1	9	.220	.312	.380	.692
2017 KC	AL	148	476	99	20	2	9	(3 6)	150	52	45	45	45	3	126	14	2	4	7	4	7	.208	.293	.315	.608
Postseason		31	108	24	10	0	3	(1 2)	43	17	17	13	14	2	30	4	0	0	4	0	3	.222	.333	.398	.731
11 ML YEARS		1412	5166	1337	298	25	160	(78 82)	2165	719	608	714	565	40	1274	89	7	35	96	40	90	.259	.340	.419	.759

Dee Gordon

Bats: L **Throws:** R **Pos:** 2B-153;PH-7;SS-3   **Ht:** 5'11" **Wt:** 170 **Born:** 4/22/1988 **Age:** 30

								BATTING												RUNNING			AVERAGES			
Year Team	Lg	G	AB	H	2B	3B	HR	(Hm Rd)	TB	R	RBI	RC	TBB	IBB	SO	HBP	SH	SF	SB	CS	GDP	Avg	OBP	Slg	OPS
2011 LAD	NL	56	224	68	9	2	0	(0 0)	81	34	11	25	7	0	27	0	2	0	24	7	1	.304	.325	.362	.686
2012 LAD	NL	87	303	69	9	2	1	(0 1)	85	38	17	22	20	0	62	3	2	2	32	10	5	.228	.280	.281	.561
2013 LAD	NL	38	94	22	1	1	1	(1 0)	28	9	6	9	10	2	21	1	1	0	10	2	0	.234	.314	.298	.612
2014 LAD	NL	148	609	176	24	12	2	(2 0)	230	92	34	76	31	0	107	4	3	3	64	19	3	.289	.326	.378	.704
2015 Mia	NL	145	615	205	24	8	4	(2 2)	257	88	46	94	25	2	91	2	6	5	58	20	6	.333	.359	.418	.776
2016 Mia	NL	79	325	87	7	6	1	(1 0)	109	47	14	33	18	1	55	0	1	1	30	7	4	.268	.305	.335	.641
2017 Mia	NL	158	653	201	20	9	2	(0 2)	245	114	33	81	25	0	93	10	2	4	60	16	7	.308	.341	.375	.716
Postseason		6	17	3	0	0	0	(0 0)	3	0	2	0	2	0	6	0	0	0	1	1	0	.176	.263	.176	.440
7 ML YEARS		711	2823	828	94	40	11	(6 5)	1035	422	161	340	136	5	456	20	17	15	278	81	26	.293	.329	.367	.695

Terrance Gore

Bats: R **Throws:** R **Pos:** PR-8;PH-4;DH-3;LF-2   **Ht:** 5'7" **Wt:** 165 **Born:** 6/8/1991 **Age:** 27

								BATTING												RUNNING			AVERAGES			
Year Team	Lg	G	AB	H	2B	3B	HR	(Hm Rd)	TB	R	RBI	RC	TBB	IBB	SO	HBP	SH	SF	SB	CS	GDP	Avg	OBP	Slg	OPS
2017 NWArk*	AA	19	59	15	1	0	0	(- -)	16	9	1	5	2	0	13	0	1	0	8	0	1	.254	.279	.271	.550
2017 Omha*	AAA	65	166	41	3	3	1	(- -)	53	29	10	20	16	0	38	3	5	2	13	3	1	.247	.321	.319	.640
2014 KC	AL	11	1	0	0	0	0	(0 0)	0	5	0	1	0	0	0	1	0	0	5	0	0	.000	.500	.000	.500
2015 KC	AL	9	3	0	0	0	0	(0 0)	0	1	0	0	0	0	1	0	0	0	3	0	0	.000	.250	.000	.250
2016 KC	AL	17	3	0	0	0	0	(0 0)	0	6	0	0	0	0	1	0	0	0	11	2	0	.000	.000	.000	.000
2017 KC	AL	12	4	0	0	0	0	(0 0)	0	2	0	0	1	0	2	0	0	0	2	2	0	.000	.200	.000	.200
Postseason		8	0	0	0	0	0	(0 0)	0	2	0	0	0	0	0	0	0	0	4	1	0	-	-	-	-
4 ML YEARS		49	11	0	0	0	0	(0 0)	0	14	0	1	1	0	4	2	0	0	21	4	0	.000	.214	.000	.214

Tuffy Gosewisch

GOES-uh-wish

Bats: R **Throws:** R **Pos:** C-10;1B-1   **Ht:** 5'11" **Wt:** 200 **Born:** 8/17/1983 **Age:** 34

								BATTING												RUNNING			AVERAGES			
Year Team	Lg	G	AB	H	2B	3B	HR	(Hm Rd)	TB	R	RBI	RC	TBB	IBB	SO	HBP	SH	SF	SB	CS	GDP	Avg	OBP	Slg	OPS
2017 Tacom*	AAA	85	279	64	22	0	4	(- -)	98	27	33	33	29	0	68	7	2	4	1	0	6	.229	.313	.351	.665
2013 Ari	NL	14	45	8	2	0	0	(0 0)	10	1	3	0	0	0	8	0	1	1	0	0	0	.178	.174	.222	.396
2014 Ari	NL	41	129	29	8	0	1	(0 1)	40	6	7	5	3	0	24	0	0	0	0	0	6	.225	.242	.310	.553
2015 Ari	NL	38	128	27	6	0	1	(1 0)	36	9	13	8	8	0	23	1	0	1	2	1	2	.211	.261	.281	.542
2016 Ari	NL	33	90	14	1	1	3	(1 2)	26	8	7	6	7	0	22	1	1	0	0	0	2	.156	.224	.289	.513
2017 Sea	AL	11	28	2	0	0	0	(0 0)	2	1	0	0	1	0	14	0	2	0	0	0	2	.071	.103	.071	.175
5 ML YEARS		137	420	80	17	1	5	(2 3)	114	25	30	19	19	0	91	2	4	2	2	1	14	.190	.228	.271	.499

Phil Gosselin

GAHSS-eh-lin

Bats: R **Throws:** R **Pos:** PH-19;2B-16;3B-3;SS-3;PR-3;1B-1;DH-1   **Ht:** 6'1" **Wt:** 200 **Born:** 10/3/1988 **Age:** 29

								BATTING												RUNNING			AVERAGES			
Year Team	Lg	G	AB	H	2B	3B	HR	(Hm Rd)	TB	R	RBI	RC	TBB	IBB	SO	HBP	SH	SF	SB	CS	GDP	Avg	OBP	Slg	OPS
2017 Indy*	AAA	63	241	64	10	2	1	(- -)	81	27	26	25	14	0	46	0	1	2	3	2	7	.266	.304	.336	.640
2017 RdRck*	AAA	10	32	7	1	0	0	(- -)	8	3	3	2	2	0	9	0	0	0	0	0	0	.219	.265	.250	.515
2013 Atl	NL	4	6	2	0	0	0	(0 0)	2	2	0	1	1	1	2	0	0	0	0	0	0	.333	.429	.333	.762
2014 Atl	NL	46	128	34	4	0	1	(1 0)	41	17	3	10	5	0	27	2	1	0	2	2	1	.266	.304	.320	.624
2015 2 Tms	NL	44	106	33	9	1	3	(2 1)	53	19	15	22	9	0	16	2	0	1	2	1	2	.311	.373	.500	.873
2016 Ari	NL	122	220	61	12	1	2	(1 1)	81	26	13	24	5	1	46	1	2	2	3	0	0	.277	.324	.368	.692
2017 2 Tms	NL	40	48	7	2	0	0	(0 0)	9	3	2	0	2	0	12	0	0	1	0	1	0	.146	.180	.188	.368
15 Atl	NL	20	40	13	4	0	0	(0 0)	17	2	2	6	2	0	5	0	0	0	2	0	0	.325	.357	.425	.782
15 Atl	NL	24	66	20	5	1	3	(2 1)	36	17	13	16	7	0	11	2	0	1	0	1	2	.303	.382	.545	.927
17 Pit	NL	28	40	6	1	0	0	(0 0)	7	3	2	0	2	0	9	0	0	1	0	1	0	.150	.190	.175	.365
17 Tex	AL	12	8	1	1	0	0	(0 0)	2	0	0	0	0	0	3	0	0	0	0	0	0	.125	.125	.250	.375
5 ML YEARS		256	508	137	27	2	6	(4 2)	186	67	33	57	32	1	103	5	3	3	7	4	4	.270	.318	.366	.684

Daniel Gossett

Pitches: R Bats: R Pos: SP-18

Ht: 6'2" Wt: 185 Born: 11/13/1992 Age: 25

Year	Team	Lg	G	GS	CG	GF	IP	BFP	H	R	ER	HR	SH	SF	HB	TBB	IBB	SO	WP	Bk	W	L	Pct	Sh	Sv-Op	Hld	ERC	ERA
2014	Vrmnt	A-	12	1	0	2	24.0	88	16	6	6	1	0	2	0	1	0	25	0	0	1	0	1.000	0	0- -	-	1.13	2.25
2015	Beloit	A	27	27	2	0	144.2	629	151	92	76	16	5	7	6	52	0	112	10	1	5	13	.278	0	0- -	-	4.41	4.73
2016	Stcktn	A+	9	9	0	0	46.0	193	40	20	17	4	0	1	1	13	0	53	4	1	4	1	.800	0	0- -	-	2.85	3.33
2016	Mdlnd	AA	16	16	0	0	94.0	374	76	37	26	4	4	3	1	25	0	94	13	0	5	5	.500	0	0- -	-	2.29	2.49
2017	Nashv	AAA	14	14	0	0	76.1	321	70	35	31	6	3	0	1	24	1	71	10	0	4	4	.500	0	0- -	-	3.15	3.66
2017	Oak	AL	18	18	0	0	91.1	414	116	67	62	21	2	2	0	31	0	72	10	0	4	11	.267	0	0-0	0	6.38	6.11

Trevor Gott

Pitches: R Bats: R Pos: RP-4

Ht: 6'0" Wt: 185 Born: 8/26/1992 Age: 25

Year	Team	Lg	G	GS	CG	GF	IP	BFP	H	R	ER	HR	SH	SF	HB	TBB	IBB	SO	WP	Bk	W	L	Pct	Sh	Sv-Op	Hld	ERC	ERA
2017	Syrcse*	AAA	30	0	0	13	37.1	164	39	19	16	2	1	1	1	13	1	35	5	0	2	0	1.000	0	4- -	-	3.78	3.86
2015	LAA	AL	48	0	0	7	47.2	202	43	18	16	2	2	3	3	16	3	27	1	0	4	2	.667	0	0-4	14	3.03	3.02
2016	Was	NL	9	0	0	1	6.0	28	6	1	1	0	0	0	1	3	1	6	0	0	0	0	-	0	0-0	1	3.93	1.50
2017	Was	NL	4	0	0	1	3.0	23	11	10	10	1	0	0	0	3	1	3	1	0	1	0	1.000	0	0-0	0	28.38	30.00
	3 ML YEARS		61	0	0	9	56.2	253	60	29	27	3	2	3	4	22	5	36	2	0	5	2	.714	0	0-4	15	4.09	4.29

Matt Grace

Pitches: L Bats: L Pos: RP-39; SP-1

Ht: 6'4" Wt: 215 Born: 12/14/1988 Age: 29

Year	Team	Lg	G	GS	CG	GF	IP	BFP	H	R	ER	HR	SH	SF	HB	TBB	IBB	SO	WP	Bk	W	L	Pct	Sh	Sv-Op	Hld	ERC	ERA
2017	Syrcse*	AAA	13	1	0	2	19.2	87	21	9	8	2	0	0	1	8	0	21	0	0	1	3	.250	0	0- -	-	4.71	3.66
2015	Was	NL	26	0	0	5	17.0	84	26	11	8	0	0	2	1	8	2	14	1	0	2	1	.667	0	0-2	4	6.71	4.24
2016	Was	NL	5	0	0	1	3.0	10	1	0	0	0	0	0	0	0	0	4	0	0	0	0	-	0	0-0	0	0.25	0.00
2017	Was	NL	40	1	0	11	50.0	215	50	25	24	3	3	3	3	18	4	31	2	0	1	0	1.000	0	2-2	4	3.76	4.32
	3 ML YEARS		71	1	0	17	70.0	309	77	36	32	3	3	5	4	26	6	49	3	0	3	1	.750	0	2-4	8	4.19	4.11

Yasmani Grandal

Bats: B Throws: R Pos: C-117;PH-15

yahz-MAH-nee gran-DAHL

Ht: 6'1" Wt: 235 Born: 11/8/1988 Age: 29

Year	Team	Lg	G	AB	H	2B	3B	HR	(Hm	Rd)	TB	R	RBI	RC	TBB	IBB	SO	HBP	SH	SF	SB	CS	GDP	Avg	OBP	Slg	OPS
2012	SD	NL	60	192	57	7	1	8	(3	5)	90	28	36	37	31	1	39	1	0	2	0	0	8	.297	.394	.469	.863
2013	SD	NL	28	88	19	8	0	1	(1	0)	30	13	9	12	18	2	18	1	0	1	0	0	1	.216	.352	.341	.693
2014	SD	NL	128	377	85	19	1	15	(7	8)	151	47	49	45	58	1	115	2	0	6	3	0	7	.225	.327	.401	.728
2015	LAD	NL	115	355	83	12	0	16	(8	8)	143	43	47	47	65	1	92	2	1	3	0	1	16	.234	.353	.403	.756
2016	LAD	NL	126	390	89	14	1	27	(20	7)	186	49	72	63	64	1	116	2	0	1	1	3	11	.228	.339	.477	.816
2017	LAD	NL	129	438	108	27	1	22	(13	9)	201	50	58	48	40	0	130	0	1	3	0	1	10	.247	.308	.459	.767
	Postseason		14	38	4	0	0	1	(1	0)	7	1	5	2	8	0	17	0	1	0	0	0	1	.105	.261	.184	.445
	6 ML YEARS		586	1840	441	87	3	89	(52	37)	801	230	271	252	276	6	510	8	2	16	4	5	53	.240	.339	.435	.774

Curtis Granderson

Bats: L Throws: R Pos: CF-65;RF-38;LF-33;PH-24;DH-3;PR-1

Ht: 6'1" Wt: 200 Born: 3/16/1981 Age: 37

Year	Team	Lg	G	AB	H	2B	3B	HR	(Hm	Rd)	TB	R	RBI	RC	TBB	IBB	SO	HBP	SH	SF	SB	CS	GDP	Avg	OBP	Slg	OPS
2004	Det	AL	9	25	6	1	1	0	(0	0)	9	2	0	2	3	0	8	0	0	0	0	0	1	.240	.321	.360	.681
2005	Det	AL	47	162	44	6	3	8	(5	3)	80	18	20	26	10	0	43	0	2	0	1	1	2	.272	.314	.494	.808
2006	Det	AL	159	596	155	31	9	19	(7	12)	261	90	68	89	66	0	174	4	7	6	8	5	4	.260	.335	.438	.773
2007	Det	AL	158	612	185	38	23	23	(10	13)	338	122	74	106	52	3	141	5	5	2	26	1	3	.302	.361	.552	.913
2008	Det	AL	141	553	155	26	13	22	(11	11)	273	112	66	100	71	1	111	3	1	1	12	4	1	.280	.365	.494	.858
2009	Det	AL	160	631	157	23	8	30	(10	20)	286	91	71	92	72	4	141	2	3	2	20	6	1	.249	.327	.453	.780
2010	NYY	AL	136	466	115	17	7	24	(14	10)	218	76	67	71	53	3	116	2	4	3	12	2	3	.247	.324	.468	.792
2011	NYY	AL	156	583	153	26	10	41	(21	20)	322	136	119	113	85	0	169	12	4	7	25	10	12	.262	.364	.552	.916
2012	NYY	AL	160	596	138	18	4	43	(26	17)	293	102	106	92	75	4	195	5	1	7	10	3	5	.232	.319	.492	.811
2013	NYY	AL	61	214	49	13	2	7	(2	5)	87	31	15	23	27	1	69	1	2	1	8	2	1	.229	.317	.407	.723
2014	NYM	NL	155	564	128	27	2	20	(7	13)	219	73	66	70	79	1	141	6	0	5	8	2	1	.227	.326	.388	.714
2015	NYM	NL	157	580	150	33	2	26	(12	14)	265	98	70	104	91	3	151	7	0	4	11	6	3	.259	.364	.457	.821
2016	NYM	NL	150	545	129	24	5	30	(13	17)	253	88	59	69	74	7	130	9	0	5	4	2	10	.237	.335	.464	.799
2017	2 Trms	NL	147	449	95	24	3	26	(7	19)	203	74	64	64	71	2	123	4	0	3	6	2	5	.212	.323	.452	.775
17	NYM	NL	111	337	77	22	3	19	(6	13)	162	58	52	56	53	2	90	2	0	3	4	2	4	.228	.334	.481	.815
17	LAD	NL	36	112	18	2	0	7	(1	6)	41	16	12	8	18	0	33	2	0	0	2	0	1	.161	.288	.366	.654
	Postseason		51	188	45	8	3	9	(6	3)	86	26	29	35	29	1	45	1	1	3	9	3	2	.239	.339	.457	.797
	14 ML YEARS		1796	6576	1659	307	92	319	(145	174)	3107	1113	865	1021	829	29	1712	60	29	46	151	46	58	.252	.339	.472	.812

Zack Granite

Bats: L Throws: L Pos: CF-24;LF-8;PH-7;PR-4;RF-2;DH-2

Ht: 6'1" Wt: 175 Born: 9/17/1992 Age: 25

Year	Team	Lg	G	AB	H	2B	3B	HR	(Hm	Rd)	TB	R	RBI	RC	TBB	IBB	SO	HBP	SH	SF	SB	CS	GDP	Avg	OBP	Slg	OPS
2013	Elizab	R+	61	242	69	4	5	0	(-	-)	83	39	24	33	29	1	25	2	2	3	14	7	5	.285	.362	.343	.705
2014	2 Trms	Low	25	93	26	2	2	0	(-	-)	32	13	2	9	6	0	12	0	1	1	4	4	0	.280	.320	.344	.664

Year Team	Lg	G	AB	H	2B	3B	HR	(Hm Rd)	TB	R	RBI	RC	TBB	IBB	SO	HBP	SH	SF	SB	CS	GDP	Avg	OBP	Slg	OPS
2015 2 Tms	Low	124	448	119	15	5	1	(- -)	147	76	31	58	53	0	69	6	14	3	28	13	0	.266	.349	.328	.677
2016 Chatt	AA	127	525	155	18	8	4	(- -)	201	86	52	79	42	0	42	3	9	5	55	14	6	.295	.348	.383	.731
2017 Roch	AAA	71	284	96	16	4	5	(- -)	135	46	29	53	24	1	34	1	4	0	15	6	2	.338	.392	.475	.867
2017 Min	AL	40	93	22	2	0	1	(0 1)	27	14	13	11	12	0	9	0	1	1	2	2	6	.237	.321	.290	.611

Juan Graterol

Bats: R Throws: R Pos: C-47;PR-1   Ht: 6'1" Wt: 205 Born: 2/14/1989 Age: 29

Year Team	Lg	G	AB	H	2B	3B	HR	(Hm Rd)	TB	R	RBI	RC	TBB	IBB	SO	HBP	SH	SF	SB	CS	GDP	Avg	OBP	Slg	OPS
2013 NWArk	AA	56	182	52	6	0	3	(- -)	67	17	17	22	6	0	22	2	4	1	3	0	7	.286	.314	.368	.682
2014 NWArk	AA	70	246	69	17	0	4	(- -)	98	17	28	31	9	0	29	3	5	1	0	0	11	.280	.313	.398	.711
2015 S-WB	AAA	20	70	14	1	0	1	(- -)	18	8	9	3	1	0	10	0	0	1	0	0	6	.200	.208	.257	.465
2016 Salt Lk	AAA	68	227	68	10	0	2	(- -)	84	24	23	30	10	0	27	5	2	2	2	1	13	.300	.340	.370	.710
2016 LAA	AL	9	14	4	2	0	0	(0 0)	6	2	3	1	0	0	3	0	1	0	0	0	0	.286	.286	.429	.714
2017 LAA	AL	48	84	17	4	0	0	(0 0)	21	5	10	0	1	0	13	0	0	2	0	0	4	.202	.207	.250	.457
2 ML YEARS		57	98	21	6	0	0	(0 0)	27	7	13	1	1	0	16	0	1	2	0	0	4	.214	.218	.276	.493

Kendall Graveman

Pitches: R Bats: R Pos: SP-19   Ht: 6'2" Wt: 200 Born: 12/21/1990 Age: 27

Year Team	Lg	G	GS	CG	GF	IP	BFP	H	R	ER	HR	SH	SF	HB	TBB	IBB	SO	WP	Bk	W	L	Pct	Sh	Sv-Op	Hld	ERC	ERA
2014 Tor	AL	5	0	0	1	4.2	18	4	2	2	0	0	0	0	0	0	4	1	0	0	0	-	0	0-0	0	1.44	3.86
2015 Oak	AL	21	21	1	0	115.2	502	126	57	52	15	1	2	5	38	0	77	4	0	6	9	.400	0	0-0	0	4.72	4.05
2016 Oak	AL	31	31	2	0	186.0	786	196	87	85	22	2	6	7	47	2	108	2	0	10	11	.476	1	0-0	0	4.08	4.11
2017 Oak	AL	19	19	0	0	105.1	444	114	50	49	12	0	1	4	32	1	70	5	0	6	4	.600	0	0-0	0	4.53	4.19
4 ML YEARS		76	71	3	1	411.2	1750	440	196	188	49	3	9	16	117	3	259	12	0	22	24	.478	1	0-0	0	4.34	4.11

Jon Gray

Pitches: R Bats: R Pos: SP-20   Ht: 6'4" Wt: 235 Born: 11/5/1991 Age: 26

Year Team	Lg	G	GS	CG	GF	IP	BFP	H	R	ER	HR	SH	SF	HB	TBB	IBB	SO	WP	Bk	W	L	Pct	Sh	Sv-Op	Hld	ERC	ERA
2015 Col	NL	9	9	0	0	40.2	185	52	26	25	4	2	4	2	14	2	40	3	0	0	2	.000	0	0-0	0	5.60	5.53
2016 Col	NL	29	29	1	0	168.0	712	153	92	86	18	5	5	12	59	2	185	7	0	10	10	.500	1	0-0	0	3.71	4.61
2017 Col	NL	20	20	0	0	110.1	461	113	47	45	10	2	2	2	30	0	112	3	1	10	4	.714	0	0-0	0	3.76	3.67
3 ML YEARS		58	58	1	0	319.0	1358	318	165	156	32	9	11	16	103	4	337	13	1	20	16	.556	1	0-0	0	3.96	4.40

Sonny Gray

Pitches: R Bats: R Pos: SP-27   Ht: 5'10" Wt: 190 Born: 11/7/1989 Age: 28

Year Team	Lg	G	GS	CG	GF	IP	BFP	H	R	ER	HR	SH	SF	HB	TBB	IBB	SO	WP	Bk	W	L	Pct	Sh	Sv-Op	Hld	ERC	ERA
2013 Oak	AL	12	10	0	0	64.0	261	51	22	19	4	0	3	0	20	0	67	2	1	5	3	.625	0	0-0	0	2.42	2.67
2014 Oak	AL	33	33	2	0	219.0	899	187	84	75	15	**8**	5	7	74	2	183	15	0	14	10	.583	2	0-0	0	2.99	3.08
2015 Oak	AL	31	31	3	0	208.0	831	166	71	63	17	1	4	2	59	0	169	13	0	14	7	.667	2	0-0	0	2.53	2.73
2016 Oak	AL	22	22	0	0	117.0	517	133	80	74	18	0	7	2	42	0	94	15	0	5	11	.313	0	0-0	0	5.16	5.69
2017 2 Tms	AL	27	27	1	0	162.1	678	139	79	64	19	1	2	3	57	1	153	11	0	10	12	.455	0	0-0	0	3.26	3.55
17 Oak	AL	16	16	0	0	97.0	400	84	48	37	8	0	2	1	30	0	94	7	0	6	5	.545	0	0-0	0	2.93	3.43
17 NYY	AL	11	11	1	0	65.1	278	55	31	27	11	1	0	2	27	1	59	4	0	4	7	.364	0	0-0	0	3.77	3.72
Postseason		2	2	0	0	13.0	53	10	3	3	1	1	0	0	6	1	12	0	0	0	1	.000	0	0-0	0	2.87	2.08
5 ML YEARS		125	123	6	0	770.1	3186	676	336	295	73	10	21	14	252	3	666	56	1	48	43	.527	4	0-0	0	3.17	3.45

Chad Green

Pitches: R Bats: L Pos: RP-39; SP-1   Ht: 6'3" Wt: 210 Born: 5/24/1991 Age: 27

Year Team	Lg	G	GS	CG	GF	IP	BFP	H	R	ER	HR	SH	SF	HB	TBB	IBB	SO	WP	Bk	W	L	Pct	Sh	Sv-Op	Hld	ERC	ERA
2013 2 Tms		12	2	0	2	20.1	84	19	8	8	1	0	0	0	6	0	16	0	0	4	0	1.000	0	1--	-	3.00	3.54
2014 Wmich	A	23	23	0	0	130.1	523	121	51	45	8	3	6	3	28	0	125	5	0	6	4	.600	0	0--	-	2.89	3.11
2015 Erie	AA	27	27	1	0	148.2	655	170	84	65	9	7	5	7	43	2	137	5	0	5	14	.263	0	0--	-	4.29	3.93
2016 S-WB	AAA	16	16	0	0	94.2	365	68	21	16	3	1	2	1	21	0	100	2	0	7	6	.538	0	0--	-	1.68	1.52
2017 S-WB	AAA	5	5	0	0	26.2	123	32	15	14	1	0	0	0	11	0	33	0	0	2	1	.667	0	0--	-	4.67	4.73
2016 NYY	AL	12	8	0	4	45.2	198	49	26	24	12	1	1	1	15	0	52	1	0	2	4	.333	0	1-1	0	5.46	4.73
2017 NYY	AL	40	1	0	4	69.0	253	34	14	14	4	2	1	2	17	0	103	3	0	5	0	1.000	0	0-1	9	1.20	1.83
2 ML YEARS		52	9	0	8	114.2	451	83	40	38	16	3	2	3	32	0	155	4	0	7	4	.636	0	1-2	9	2.55	2.98

Grant Green

Bats: R Throws: R Pos: 2B-2   Ht: 6'3" Wt: 180 Born: 9/27/1987 Age: 30

Year Team	Lg	G	AB	H	2B	3B	HR	(Hm Rd)	TB	R	RBI	RC	TBB	IBB	SO	HBP	SH	SF	SB	CS	GDP	Avg	OBP	Slg	OPS
2017 Syrcse*	AAA	40	130	32	5	0	0	(- -)	37	11	2	12	14	0	34	0	0	0	0	2	2	.246	.319	.285	.604
2017 Charllt*	AAA	28	90	19	7	0	1	(- -)	29	9	10	8	10	1	19	0	0	1	0	1	3	.211	.287	.322	.609
2017 NewOr*	AAA	14	46	14	1	0	0	(- -)	15	4	8	5	3	0	9	0	0	1	1	1	1	.304	.340	.326	.666
2013 2 Tms	AL	45	140	35	8	1	1	(1 0)	48	16	17	16	10	0	44	1	0	2	0	0	3	.250	.301	.343	.644
2014 LAA	AL	43	99	27	5	0	1	(1 0)	35	7	11	8	2	0	20	0	0	0	1	4	2	.273	.282	.354	.635
2015 LAA	AL	21	42	8	0	0	1	(0 1)	11	6	3	1	2	1	14	0	0	0	0	1	2	.190	.227	.262	.489

Year	Team	Lg	G	AB	H	2B	3B	HR	(Hm	Rd)	TB	R	RBI	RC	TBB	IBB	SO	HBP	SH	SF	SB	CS	GDP	Avg	OBP	Slg	OPS
				BATTING																	**RUNNING**			**AVERAGES**			
2016	SF	NL	18	46	12	2	0	1	(1	0)	17	7	7	1	3	0	8	0	0	1	0	0	3	.261	.300	.370	.670
2017	Was	NL	2	3	0	0	0	0	(0	0)	0	0	0	0	0	0	2	0	0	0	0	0	0	.000	.000	.000	.000
13	Oak	AL	5	15	0	0	0	0	(0	0)	0	0	1	0	0	0	6	0	0	1	0	0	0	.000	.000	.000	.000
13	LAA	AL	40	125	35	8	1	1	(1	0)	48	16	16	16	10	0	38	1	0	1	0	0	3	.280	.336	.384	.720
5 ML YEARS			129	330	82	15	1	4	(3	1)	111	36	38	26	17	1	88	1	0	5	1	5	11	.248	.283	.336	.620

Shane Greene

Pitches: R **Bats:** R **Pos:** RP-71

Ht: 6'4" **Wt:** 210 **Born:** 11/17/1988 **Age:** 29

Year	Team	Lg	G	GS	CG	GF	IP	BFP	H	R	ER	HR	SH	SF	HB	TBB	IBB	SO	WP	Bk	W	L	Pct	Sh	Sv-Op	Hld	ERC	ERA
				HOW MUCH HE PITCHED						**WHAT HE GAVE UP**												**THE RESULTS**					
2014	NYY	AL	15	14	0	0	78.2	345	81	38	33	8	0	1	6	29	0	81	1	0	5	4	.556	0	0-0	0	4.43	3.78
2015	Det	AL	18	16	0	1	83.2	373	103	67	64	13	2	4	6	27	4	50	1	0	4	8	.333	0	0-0	0	5.83	6.88
2016	Det	AL	50	3	0	4	60.1	256	58	39	39	3	2	2	4	22	1	59	0	0	5	4	.556	0	2-3	16	3.65	5.82
2017	Det	AL	71	0	0	26	67.2	283	50	21	20	6	0	1	4	34	4	73	1	0	4	3	.571	0	9-13	14	3.14	2.66
4 ML YEARS			154	33	0	31	290.1	1257	292	165	156	30	4	8	20	112	9	263	3	0	18	19	.486	0	11-16	30	4.34	4.84

Luke Gregerson

Pitches: R **Bats:** L **Pos:** RP-65

Ht: 6'3" **Wt:** 205 **Born:** 5/14/1984 **Age:** 34

Year	Team	Lg	G	GS	CG	GF	IP	BFP	H	R	ER	HR	SH	SF	HB	TBB	IBB	SO	WP	Bk	W	L	Pct	Sh	Sv-Op	Hld	ERC	ERA
				HOW MUCH HE PITCHED						**WHAT HE GAVE UP**												**THE RESULTS**					
2009	SD	NL	72	0	0	7	75.0	318	62	29	27	3	3	1	3	31	9	93	4	0	2	4	.333	0	1-7	27	2.72	3.24
2010	SD	NL	80	0	0	9	78.1	297	47	30	28	8	1	1	1	18	2	89	0	0	4	7	.364	0	2-7	**40**	1.56	3.22
2011	SD	NL	61	0	0	11	55.2	241	57	23	17	2	5	1	2	19	3	34	2	0	3	3	.500	0	0-4	16	3.55	2.75
2012	SD	NL	77	0	0	15	71.2	294	57	19	19	7	5	0	3	21	3	72	3	0	2	0	1.000	0	9-13	24	2.64	2.39
2013	SD	NL	73	0	0	17	66.1	268	49	24	20	3	4	1	4	18	2	64	1	0	6	8	.429	0	4-9	25	2.07	2.71
2014	Oak	AL	72	0	0	17	72.1	284	58	20	17	6	3	1	1	15	3	59	6	0	5	5	.500	0	3-11	22	2.25	2.12
2015	Hou	AL	64	0	0	53	61.0	239	48	24	21	5	2	0	2	10	2	59	1	0	7	3	.700	0	31-36	0	2.09	3.10
2016	Hou	AL	59	0	0	25	57.2	230	38	23	21	5	0	2	2	18	2	67	6	0	4	3	.571	0	15-21	15	1.99	3.28
2017	Hou	AL	65	0	0	13	61.0	263	62	31	31	13	1	1	0	20	4	70	5	1	2	3	.400	0	1-4	18	4.50	4.57
Postseason			5	0	0	3	4.2	21	3	1	1	1	0	0	1	3	0	8	1	0	0	0	-	0	3-3	1	4.60	1.93
9 ML YEARS			623	0	0	167	599.0	2434	478	223	201	52	24	8	18	170	30	607	28	1	35	36	.493	0	66-112	187	2.52	3.02

Didi Gregorius

Bats: L **Throws:** R **Pos:** SS-135;PH-3;DH-1

dee-dee greh-GORE-ee-us

Ht: 6'3" **Wt:** 205 **Born:** 2/18/1990 **Age:** 28

Year	Team	Lg	G	AB	H	2B	3B	HR	(Hm	Rd)	TB	R	RBI	RC	TBB	IBB	SO	HBP	SH	SF	SB	CS	GDP	Avg	OBP	Slg	OPS
					BATTING																**RUNNING**			**AVERAGES**			
2012	Cin	NL	8	20	6	0	0	0	(0	0)	6	1	2	2	0	0	5	0	1	0	0	0	0	.300	.300	.300	.600
2013	Ari	NL	103	357	90	16	3	7	(3	4)	133	47	28	42	37	5	65	6	2	1	0	2	4	.252	.332	.373	.704
2014	Ari	NL	80	270	61	9	5	6	(3	3)	98	35	27	37	22	3	52	3	2	2	3	0	1	.226	.290	.363	.653
2015	NYY	AL	155	525	139	24	2	9	(6	3)	194	57	56	64	33	0	85	11	3	6	5	3	4	.265	.318	.370	.688
2016	NYY	AL	153	562	155	32	2	20	(11	9)	251	68	70	71	19	2	82	6	5	5	7	1	9	.276	.304	.447	.751
2017	NYY	AL	136	534	153	27	0	25	(12	13)	255	73	87	84	25	1	70	3	0	7	3	1	7	.287	.318	.478	.796
Postseason			1	3	1	0	0	0	(0	0)	1	0	0	0	0	0	0	0	0	0	0	0	0	.333	.333	.333	.667
6 ML YEARS			635	2268	604	108	12	67	(35	32)	937	281	270	300	136	11	359	29	13	21	18	7	25	.266	.313	.413	.727

Zack Greinke

Pitches: R **Bats:** R **Pos:** SP-32

GRAIN-key

Ht: 6'2" **Wt:** 200 **Born:** 10/21/1983 **Age:** 34

Year	Team	Lg	G	GS	CG	GF	IP	BFP	H	R	ER	HR	SH	SF	HB	TBB	IBB	SO	WP	Bk	W	L	Pct	Sh	Sv-Op	Hld	ERC	ERA
				HOW MUCH HE PITCHED						**WHAT HE GAVE UP**												**THE RESULTS**					
2004	KC	AL	24	24	0	0	145.0	599	143	64	64	26	3	2	8	26	3	100	1	1	8	11	.421	0	0-0	0	3.85	3.97
2005	KC	AL	33	33	2	0	183.0	829	233	125	118	23	4	4	13	53	0	114	4	2	5	17	.227	0	0-0	0	5.71	5.80
2006	KC	AL	3	0	0	1	6.1	28	7	3	3	1	0	0	0	3	2	5	0	0	1	0	1.000	0	0-0	0	4.93	4.26
2007	KC	AL	52	14	0	7	122.0	507	122	52	50	12	3	4	3	36	5	106	3	1	7	7	.500	0	1-1	12	3.77	3.69
2008	KC	AL	32	32	1	0	202.1	851	202	87	78	21	2	4	6	56	1	183	8	1	13	10	.565	0	0-0	0	3.68	3.47
2009	KC	AL	33	33	6	0	229.1	915	195	64	55	11	8	3	4	51	0	242	5	0	16	8	.667	3	0-0	0	**2.39**	**2.16**
2010	KC	AL	33	33	3	0	220.0	919	219	114	102	18	6	7	7	55	1	181	4	0	10	14	.417	0	0-0	0	3.48	4.17
2011	Mil	NL	28	28	0	0	171.2	715	161	82	73	19	6	1	4	45	0	201	10	0	16	6	.727	0	0-0	0	3.35	3.83
2012	2 Tms		34	34	0	0	212.1	868	200	84	82	18	7	2	2	54	0	200	8	0	15	5	.750	0	0-0	0	3.17	3.48
2013	LAD	NL	28	28	1	0	177.2	717	152	54	52	13	8	1	7	46	1	148	5	0	15	4	.789	1	0-0	0	2.78	2.63
2014	LAD	NL	32	32	0	0	202.1	821	190	69	61	19	2	4	2	43	3	207	12	0	17	8	.680	0	0-0	0	3.03	2.71
2015	LAD	NL	32	32	1	0	222.2	843	148	43	41	14	6	2	5	40	1	200	7	0	19	3	**.864**	0	0-0	0	1.56	**1.66**
2016	Ari	NL	26	26	1	0	158.2	667	161	80	77	23	7	4	0	41	3	134	1	0	13	7	.650	0	0-0	0	3.86	4.37
2017	Ari	NL	32	32	1	0	202.1	801	172	80	72	25	4	3	0	45	2	215	12	0	17	7	.708	0	0-0	0	2.79	3.20
12	Mil	NL	21	21	0	0	123.0	504	120	49	47	7	3	0	0	28	0	122	4	0	9	3	.750	0	0-0	0	3.02	3.44
12	LAA	AL	13	13	0	0	89.1	364	80	35	35	11	4	2	2	26	0	78	4	0	6	2	.750	0	0-0	0	3.38	3.53
Postseason			9	9	0	0	58.1	232	50	26	23	7	1	1	2	9	0	54	1	0	3	3	.500	0	0-0	0	2.65	3.55
14 ML YEARS			422	381	16	8	2455.2	10080	2305	1001	928	243	71	41	59	594	20	2236	80	5	172	107	.616	5	1-1	12	3.23	3.40

Randal Grichuk

Bats: R Throws: R Pos: LF-58;RF-55;PH-15;CF-5;PR-2   GRICH-ick   Ht: 6'1" Wt: 205 Born: 8/13/1991 Age: 26

Year	Team	Lg	G	AB	H	2B	3B	HR	(Hm	Rd)	TB	R	RBI	RC	TBB	IBB	SO	HBP	SH	SF	SB	CS	GDP	Avg	OBP	Slg	OPS
2017	Memp*	AAA	14	63	17	3	0	6	(-	-)	38	11	9	11	3	1	20	1	0	0	0	0	2	.270	.313	.603	.917
2014	StL	NL	47	110	27	6	1	3	(2	1)	44	11	8	7	5	0	31	0	1	0	0	2	4	.245	.278	.400	.678
2015	StL	NL	103	323	89	23	7	17	(10	7)	177	49	47	47	22	2	110	4	0	1	4	2	6	.276	.329	.548	.877
2016	StL	NL	132	446	107	29	3	24	(12	12)	214	66	68	62	28	0	141	3	0	1	5	4	9	.240	.289	.480	.769
2017	StL	NL	122	412	98	25	3	22	(13	9)	195	53	59	47	26	3	133	2	0	2	6	1	9	.238	.285	.473	.758
Postseason			13	43	8	0	0	3	(1	2)	17	5	4	2	1	0	17	0	0	0	0	0	0	.186	.205	.395	.600
4 ML YEARS			404	1291	321	83	14	66	(37	29)	630	179	182	163	81	5	415	9	1	4	15	9	28	.249	.297	.488	.785

A.J. Griffin

Pitches: R Bats: R Pos: SP-15; RP-3   Ht: 6'5" Wt: 230 Born: 1/28/1988 Age: 30

			HOW MUCH HE PITCHED						WHAT HE GAVE UP											THE RESULTS							
Year	Team	Lg	G	GS	CG	GF	IP	BFP	H	R	ER	HR	SH	SF	HB	TBB	IBB	SO	WP	Bk	W	L	Pct	Sh	Sv-Op	Hld	ERC	ERA
2012	Oak	AL	15	15	0	0	82.1	336	74	29	28	10	0	2	1	19	0	64	0	0	7	1	.875	1	0-0	0	3.06	3.06
2013	Oak	AL	32	32	1	0	200.0	823	171	91	85	36	4	4	4	54	2	171	7	0	14	10	.583	1	0-0	0	3.33	3.83
2016	Tex	AL	23	23	0	0	119.0	509	116	68	67	28	0	3	7	46	1	107	0	1	7	4	.636	0	0-0	0	5.14	5.07
2017	Tex	AL	18	15	1	2	77.1	338	76	52	51	20	0	4	6	28	0	61	2	0	6	6	.500	0	0-0	0	5.23	5.94
Postseason			1	1	0	0	5.0	21	7	2	2	1	1	0	0	0	0	0	1	0	0	0	-	0	0-0	0	5.60	3.60
4 ML YEARS			88	85	2	2	478.2	2006	437	240	231	94	4	13	18	147	3	403	9	1	34	21	.618	2	0-0	0	4.00	4.34

Jason Grilli

Pitches: R Bats: R Pos: RP-46   GRILL-ee   Ht: 6'5" Wt: 235 Born: 11/11/1976 Age: 41

			HOW MUCH HE PITCHED						WHAT HE GAVE UP											THE RESULTS							
Year	Team	Lg	G	GS	CG	GF	IP	BFP	H	R	ER	HR	SH	SF	HB	TBB	IBB	SO	WP	Bk	W	L	Pct	Sh	Sv-Op	Hld	ERC	ERA
2000	Fla	NL	1	1	0	0	6.2	35	11	4	4	0	2	0	2	2	0	3	0	0	1	0	1.000	0	0-0	0	7.84	5.40
2001	Fla	NL	6	5	0	1	26.2	115	30	18	18	6	1	0	2	11	0	17	0	0	2	2	.500	0	0-0	0	6.44	6.08
2004	CWS	AL	8	8	1	0	45.0	203	52	38	37	11	2	1	3	20	0	26	2	0	2	3	.400	0	0-0	0	6.67	7.40
2005	Det	AL	3	2	0	0	16.0	63	14	6	6	1	1	1	0	6	0	5	0	0	1	1	.500	0	0-0	0	3.27	3.38
2006	Det	AL	51	0	0	18	62.0	270	61	31	29	6	2	4	5	25	3	31	5	0	2	3	.400	0	0-0	9	4.23	4.21
2007	Det	AL	57	0	0	13	79.2	352	81	46	42	5	1	5	5	32	1	62	5	0	5	3	.625	0	0-2	11	4.09	4.74
2008	2 Tms		60	0	0	16	75.0	323	67	27	25	2	1	3	2	38	7	69	4	0	3	3	.500	0	1-2	4	3.34	3.00
2009	2 Tms		52	0	0	11	45.2	212	50	27	27	4	2	1	1	27	2	49	2	0	2	3	.400	0	1-1	7	5.25	5.32
2011	Pit	NL	28	0	0	4	32.2	140	24	10	9	2	1	0	4	15	5	37	3	0	1	1	.667	0	1-1	9	2.79	2.48
2012	Pit	NL	64	0	0	11	58.2	244	45	20	19	7	2	1	2	22	4	90	0	1	1	6	.143	0	2-5	32	2.85	2.91
2013	Pit	NL	54	0	0	41	50.0	202	40	15	15	4	1	0	1	13	0	74	1	0	0	2	.000	0	33-35	2	2.44	2.70
2014	2 Tms		62	0	0	22	54.0	235	51	26	24	4	5	3	4	21	2	57	1	0	1	5	.167	0	12-17	12	3.73	4.00
2015	Atl	NL	36	0	0	29	33.2	140	28	13	11	2	0	1	0	10	1	45	2	0	3	4	.429	0	24-26	0	2.43	2.94
2016	2 Tms		67	0	0	14	59.0	251	44	28	27	10	0	3	2	32	1	81	2	0	7	6	.538	0	4-8	23	3.80	4.12
2017	2 Tms		46	0	0	19	40.0	184	46	30	28	12	0	0	1	18	0	48	2	0	2	5	.286	0	1-3	4	6.70	6.30
08	Det	AL	9	0	0	4	13.2	59	12	5	5	1	0	0	1	7	1	10	1	0	0	1	.000	0	0-1	0	3.85	3.29
08	Col	NL	51	0	0	12	61.1	264	55	22	20	1	1	3	1	31	6	59	3	0	3	2	.600	0	1-1	4	3.23	2.93
09	Col	NL	22	0	0	6	19.1	99	29	13	13	2	1	0	0	13	2	22	2	0	0	1	.000	0	1-1	3	8.02	6.05
09	Tex	AL	30	0	0	5	26.1	113	21	14	14	2	1	0	1	14	0	27	0	0	2	2	.500	0	0-0	4	3.44	4.78
14	Pit	NL	22	0	0	16	20.1	93	22	11	11	4	1	0	1	11	1	21	0	0	0	2	.000	0	11-15	1	5.99	4.87
14	LAA	AL	40	0	0	6	33.2	142	29	15	13	0	4	3	3	10	1	36	1	0	1	3	.250	0	1-2	11	2.53	3.48
16	Atl	NL	21	0	0	8	17.0	81	16	11	10	2	0	1	1	13	1	23	1	0	1	2	.333	0	2-4	2	5.33	5.29
16	Tor	AL	46	0	0	6	42.0	170	28	17	17	8	0	2	1	19	0	58	1	0	6	4	.600	0	2-4	21	3.19	3.64
17	Tor	AL	26	0	0	10	20.2	95	24	17	16	9	0	0	0	9	0	23	1	0	2	4	.333	0	1-3	1	7.58	6.97
17	Tex	AL	20	0	0	9	19.1	89	22	13	12	3	0	0	1	9	0	25	1	0	0	1	.000	0	0-0	3	5.72	5.59
Postseason			16	0	0	4	12.0	45	5	0	0	0	0	0	0	4	1	10	0	0	0	0	-	0	1-1	3	0.82	0.00
15 ML YEARS			595	16	1	199	684.2	2969	644	339	321	76	21	23	34	292	26	694	29	0	34	47	.420	0	79-100	113	4.05	4.22

Justin Grimm

Pitches: R Bats: R Pos: RP-50   Ht: 6'3" Wt: 210 Born: 8/16/1988 Age: 29

			HOW MUCH HE PITCHED						WHAT HE GAVE UP											THE RESULTS							
Year	Team	Lg	G	GS	CG	GF	IP	BFP	H	R	ER	HR	SH	SF	HB	TBB	IBB	SO	WP	Bk	W	L	Pct	Sh	Sv-Op	Hld	ERC	ERA
2017	Iowa*	AAA	10	0	0	4	11.2	50	10	5	5	2	1	0	0	5	0	18	0	0	0	1	.000	0	3--	-	3.80	3.86
2012	Tex	AL	5	2	0	3	14.0	65	22	14	14	1	0	2	0	3	0	13	3	0	1	1	.500	0	0-0	0	6.54	9.00
2013	2 Tms		27	17	0	3	98.0	442	120	70	65	15	4	2	2	34	1	76	4	0	7	9	.438	0	0-0	3	5.61	5.97
2014	ChC	NL	73	0	0	19	69.0	292	59	32	29	4	1	3	4	27	2	70	8	0	5	2	.714	0	0-1	11	3.14	3.78
2015	ChC	NL	62	0	0	11	49.2	204	31	18	11	4	0	3	1	26	1	67	8	0	3	5	.375	0	3-6	15	2.48	1.99
2016	ChC	NL	68	0	0	11	52.2	225	47	24	24	5	0	0	1	23	2	65	7	0	2	1	.667	0	0-0	10	3.59	4.10
2017	ChC	NL	50	0	0	13	55.1	232	47	34	34	12	1	1	1	27	0	59	4	1	1	2	.333	0	1-3	4	4.57	5.53
13	Tex	AL	17	17	0	0	89.0	406	116	67	63	15	2	2	1	31	1	68	4	0	7	7	.500	0	0-0	0	6.21	6.37
13	ChC	NL	10	0	0	3	9.0	36	4	3	2	0	2	0	1	3	0	8	0	0	0	2	.000	0	0-0	3	1.12	2.00
Postseason			9	0	0	0	6.1	28	7	6	6	0	0	0	1	1	0	7	1	0	0	0	-	0	0-0	0	3.52	8.53
6 ML YEARS			285	19	0	60	338.2	1460	326	192	177	41	6	11	9	140	6	350	34	1	19	20	.487	0	4-10	43	4.15	4.70

Robbie Grossman

Bats: B Throws: L Pos: DH-62;RF-35;LF-18;PH-13 Ht: 6'0" Wt: 215 Born: 9/16/1989 Age: 28

Year	Team	Lg	G	AB	H	2B	3B	HR	(Hm	Rd)	TB	R	RBI	RC	TBB	IBB	SO	HBP	SH	SF	SB	CS	GDP	Avg	OBP	Slg	OPS
2013	Hou	AL	63	257	69	14	0	4	(3	1)	95	29	21	37	23	0	70	2	5	1	6	7	2	.268	.332	.370	.702
2014	Hou	AL	103	360	84	14	2	6	(2	4)	120	42	37	48	55	1	105	2	3	2	9	3	7	.233	.337	.333	.670
2015	Hou	AL	24	49	7	2	0	1	(1	0)	12	7	5	4	5	0	17	0	0	0	0	0	0	.143	.222	.245	.467
2016	Min	AL	99	332	93	19	1	11	(8	3)	147	49	37	52	55	0	96	2	0	0	2	3	3	.280	.386	.443	.828
2017	Min	AL	119	382	94	22	1	9	(5	4)	145	62	45	58	67	0	79	3	2	2	3	1	6	.246	.361	.380	.741
	5 ML YEARS		408	1380	347	71	4	31	(19	12)	519	189	145	199	205	1	367	9	10	5	20	14	18	.251	.351	.376	.727

Robert Gsellman

Pitches: R Bats: R Pos: SP-22; RP-3 guh-ZELL-man Ht: 6'4" Wt: 205 Born: 7/18/1993 Age: 24

Year	Team	Lg	G	GS	CG	GF	IP	BFP	H	R	ER	HR	SH	SF	HB	TBB	IBB	SO	WP	Bk	W	L	Pct	Sh	Sv-Op	Hld	ERC	ERA
2013	3 Tms	Low	19	19	0	0	108.0	448	99	43	31	5	3	1	7	23	0	83	3	0	6	6	.500	0	0- -	-	2.79	2.58
2014	Savann	A	20	20	4	0	116.0	500	122	42	33	2	6	7	9	34	0	92	6	0	10	6	.625	1	0- -	-	3.67	2.56
2015	Stluci	A+	8	8	0	0	51.0	196	37	10	10	1	0	1	3	11	0	37	2	1	6	0	1.000	0	0- -	-	1.81	1.76
2015	Bnghtn	AA	16	16	0	0	92.1	387	89	47	36	4	5	4	1	26	1	49	6	0	7	7	.500	0	0- -	-	3.06	3.51
2016	Bnghtn	AA	11	11	0	0	66.1	266	57	23	20	2	0	0	6	15	0	48	3	0	3	4	.429	0	0- -	-	2.64	2.71
2016	LsVgs	AAA	9	9	0	0	48.2	215	56	35	31	8	3	0	0	16	0	40	1	0	1	5	.167	0	0- -	-	5.08	5.73
2016	NYM	NL	8	7	0	0	44.2	185	42	12	12	1	4	2	1	15	2	42	1	0	4	2	.667	0	0-0	-	3.05	2.42
2017	NYM	NL	25	22	1	1	119.2	549	138	85	69	17	4	2	8	42	3	82	4	0	8	7	.533	0	0-1	1	5.16	5.19
	2 ML YEARS		33	29	1	1	164.1	734	180	97	81	18	8	4	9	57	5	124	5	0	12	9	.571	0	0-1	1	4.56	4.44

Reymin Guduan

Pitches: L Bats: L Pos: RP-22 ray-meen goo-DWAHN Ht: 6'4" Wt: 205 Born: 3/16/1992 Age: 26

Year	Team	Lg	G	GS	CG	GF	IP	BFP	H	R	ER	SH	SF	HB	TBB	IBB	SO	WP	Bk	W	L	Pct	Sh	Sv-Op	Hld	ERC	ERA
2013	Astros	R	10	2	0	1	20.2	95	19	16	10	3	0	1	10	0	28	2	1	0	1	.000	0	0- -	-	4.70	4.35
2014	Grnvlle	R+	13	9	0	1	44.1	216	53	32	22	2	2	0	27	0	58	8	0	2	5	.286	0	0- -	-	5.63	4.47
2015	2 Tms	Low	19	0	0	10	29.1	122	18	10	7	0	1	1	14	2	40	4	0	3	3	.500	0	4- -	-	1.71	2.15
2015	CpChr	AA	16	0	0	4	16.1	89	20	23	21	3	1	1	19	0	19	5	1	1	3	.250	0	0- -	-	9.17	11.57
2016	CpChr	AA	9	0	0	6	13.0	48	7	1	1	1	0	0	3	0	19	0	0	1	0	1.000	0	2- -	-	1.29	0.69
2016	Fresno	AAA	34	0	0	16	43.0	203	43	25	25	2	0	1	34	2	44	8	0	2	3	.400	0	0- -	-	5.06	5.23
2017	Fresno	AAA	39	0	0	8	46.0	208	61	33	30	4	0	0	14	0	47	6	1	5	7	.417	0	1- -	-	5.61	5.87
2017	Hou	AL	22	0	0	3	16.0	83	24	14	14	1	0	0	12	0	16	3	0	0	0	-	0	0-0	1	8.22	7.88

Deolis Guerra

Pitches: R Bats: R Pos: RP-19 day-OH-lis GAIR-uh Ht: 6'5" Wt: 245 Born: 4/17/1989 Age: 29

Year	Team	Lg	G	GS	CG	GF	IP	BFP	H	R	ER	HR	SH	SF	HB	TBB	IBB	SO	WP	Bk	W	L	Pct	Sh	Sv-Op	Hld	ERC	ERA
2017	Salt Lk*	AAA	31	0	0	15	41.0	155	26	9	9	3	0	0	2	8	0	41	2	0	4	1	.800	0	2- -	-	1.60	1.98
2015	Pit	NL	10	0	0	4	16.2	74	26	12	12	5	0	0	1	3	0	17	2	0	2	0	1.000	0	0-0	0	8.96	6.48
2016	LAA	AL	44	0	0	11	53.1	220	52	23	19	6	1	1	2	7	0	36	2	1	3	0	1.000	0	0-4	5	3.08	3.21
2017	LAA	AL	19	0	0	5	25.0	105	20	13	13	4	0	1	0	12	0	22	2	0	2	2	.500	0	0-1	0	3.70	4.68
	3 ML YEARS		73	0	0	20	95.0	399	98	48	44	15	1	2	3	22	0	75	6	1	7	2	.778	0	0-5	5	4.12	4.17

Javy Guerra

Pitches: R Bats: R Pos: RP-16 GAIR-uh Ht: 6'1" Wt: 225 Born: 10/31/1985 Age: 32

Year	Team	Lg	G	GS	CG	GF	IP	BFP	H	R	ER	HR	SH	SF	HB	TBB	IBB	SO	WP	Bk	W	L	Pct	Sh	Sv-Op	Hld	ERC	ERA
2017	NewOr*	AAA	35	0	0	11	51.2	215	46	29	27	7	2	2	0	21	2	44	3	0	2	4	.333	0	2- -	-	3.73	4.70
2011	LAD	NL	47	0	0	38	46.2	195	37	12	12	2	3	1	3	18	1	38	2	0	2	2	.500	0	21-23	0	2.73	2.31
2012	LAD	NL	45	0	0	17	45.0	196	44	13	13	1	4	2	1	23	5	37	1	0	2	3	.400	0	8-13	4	3.76	2.60
2013	LAD	NL	9	0	0	5	10.2	55	15	9	8	1	0	1	1	6	0	12	0	0	0	0	-	0	0-0	0	7.24	6.75
2014	CWS	AL	42	0	0	10	46.1	198	41	15	15	3	2	4	5	20	5	38	2	0	2	4	.333	0	1-6	7	3.60	2.91
2015	CWS	AL	3	0	0	1	1.2	7	2	0	0	0	0	0	0	1	0	0	0	0	0	0	-	0	0-0	1	5.91	0.00
2016	LAA	AL	7	0	0	1	6.1	30	5	4	4	1	0	0	1	7	1	4	1	0	0	0	-	0	0-0	1	6.80	5.68
2017	Mia	NL	16	0	0	5	21.0	88	23	8	7	2	1	0	0	7	1	12	0	0	1	1	.500	0	0-1	0	4.40	3.00
	7 ML YEARS		169	0	0	76	177.2	769	167	61	59	10	10	8	11	82	13	141	6	0	7	10	.412	0	30-43	12	3.82	2.99

Junior Guerra

Pitches: R Bats: R Pos: SP-14; RP-7 GAIR-uh Ht: 6'0" Wt: 205 Born: 1/16/1985 Age: 33

Year	Team	Lg	G	GS	CG	GF	IP	BFP	H	R	ER	HR	SH	SF	HB	TBB	IBB	SO	WP	Bk	W	L	Pct	Sh	Sv-Op	Hld	ERC	ERA
2017	ColSpr*	AAA	6	6	0	0	30.0	121	27	8	7	0	1	1	0	12	0	20	0	0	2	2	.500	0	0- -	-	3.01	2.10
2015	CWS	AL	3	0	0	3	4.0	18	7	3	3	1	0	0	0	1	1	3	1	0	0	0	-	0	0-0	0	9.70	6.75
2016	Mil	NL	20	20	0	0	121.2	492	94	40	38	10	3	2	3	43	2	100	7	1	9	3	.750	0	0-0	0	2.68	2.81
2017	Mil	NL	21	14	0	2	70.1	314	61	44	40	18	1	1	4	43	0	67	5	0	1	4	.200	0	0-0	0	5.53	5.12
	3 ML YEARS		44	34	0	5	196.0	824	162	87	81	29	4	3	7	87	3	170	13	1	10	7	.588	0	0-0	0	3.76	3.72

Jason Gurka

Pitches: L Bats: L Pos: RP-3
gurr-KAH
Ht: 6'0" Wt: 170 Born: 1/10/1988 Age: 30

		HOW MUCH HE PITCHED						WHAT HE GAVE UP										THE RESULTS						
Year Team	Lg	G	GS	CG	GF	IP	BFP	H	R	ER	HR	SH	SF	HB	TBB	IBB	SO	WP	Bk	W	L	Pct	Sh	Sv-Op	Hld	ERC	ERA
2017 S-WB*	AAA	13	0	0	4	16.2	79	25	14	10	4	0	2	1	2	0	20	0	0	0	0	-	0	0--	-	6.98	5.40
2017 Salt Lk*	AAA	30	0	0	7	34.0	141	29	11	8	1	0	1	5	11	0	36	1	0	3	1	.750	0	1--	-	3.14	2.12
2015 Col	NL	9	0	0	4	7.2	39	16	8	8	1	0	0	0	2	0	7	0	0	0	0	-	0	0-0	0	11.05	9.39
2016 Col	NL	6	0	0	5	9.2	45	16	10	10	1	0	1	0	2	0	7	0	0	0	0	-	0	0-0	0	7.42	9.31
2017 LAA	AL	3	0	0	0	0.2	5	2	0	0	0	0	0	0	1	0	0	0	0	0	0	-	0	0-0	0	22.07	0.00
3 ML YEARS		18	0	0	9	18.0	89	34	18	18	2	0	1	0	5	0	14	0	0	0	0	-	0	0-0	0	9.44	9.00

Yulieski Gurriel

Bats: R Throws: R Pos: 1B-131;3B-7;DH-3;PH-2;2B-1
yoo-lee-ES-kee goo-REE-el
Ht: 6'0" Wt: 190 Born: 6/9/1984 Age: 34

							BATTING														RUNNING			AVERAGES			
Year Team	Lg	G	AB	H	2B	3B	HR	(Hm	Rd)	TB	R	RBI	RC	TBB	IBB	SO	HBP	SH	SF	SB	CS	GDP	Avg	OBP	Slg	OPS
2016 Hou	AL	36	130	34	7	0	3	(1	2)	50	13	15	13	5	0	12	1	0	1	1	1	7	.262	.292	.385	.677
2017 Hou	AL	139	529	158	43	1	18	(8	10)	257	69	75	83	22	1	62	7	0	6	3	2	12	.299	.332	.486	.817
2 ML YEARS		175	659	192	50	1	21	(9	12)	307	82	90	96	27	1	74	8	0	7	4	3	19	.291	.324	.466	.790

Jandel Gustave

Pitches: R Bats: R Pos: RP-6
hahn-DELL goo-STAH-vay
Ht: 6'2" Wt: 210 Born: 10/12/1992 Age: 25

		HOW MUCH HE PITCHED						WHAT HE GAVE UP										THE RESULTS						
Year Team	Lg	G	GS	CG	GF	IP	BFP	H	R	ER	HR	SH	SF	HB	TBB	IBB	SO	WP	Bk	W	L	Pct	Sh	Sv-Op	Hld	ERC	ERA
2013 Grnvlle	R+	10	10	0	0	43.2	193	38	23	13	2	1	3	4	23	0	49	2	0	2	3	.400	0	0--	-	3.77	2.68
2014 QuadC	A	23	14	0	5	79.0	371	94	57	44	3	1	2	13	29	0	82	14	1	5	5	.500	0	2--	-	5.11	5.01
2015 CpChr	AA	46	0	0	38	58.2	248	51	18	14	2	2	2	2	25	1	49	3	1	5	2	.714	0	20--	-	3.13	2.15
2016 Fresno	AAA	47	0	0	20	57.0	247	46	27	24	1	1	5	8	23	1	55	4	2	3	3	.500	0	3--	-	2.92	3.79
2016 Hou	AL	14	0	0	4	15.1	60	13	6	6	2	0	0	0	4	0	16	2	0	1	0	1.000	0	0-0	0	3.04	3.52
2017 Hou	AL	6	0	0	2	5.0	25	5	4	3	0	0	0	0	7	0	2	0	0	0	0	-	0	0-0	0	7.65	5.40
2 ML YEARS		20	0	0	6	20.1	85	18	10	9	2	0	0	0	11	0	18	2	0	1	0	1.000	0	0-0	0	4.14	3.98

Jeremy Guthrie

Pitches: R Bats: R Pos: SP-1
Ht: 6'1" Wt: 205 Born: 4/8/1979 Age: 39

		HOW MUCH HE PITCHED						WHAT HE GAVE UP										THE RESULTS						
Year Team	Lg	G	GS	CG	GF	IP	BFP	H	R	ER	HR	SH	SF	HB	TBB	IBB	SO	WP	Bk	W	L	Pct	Sh	Sv-Op	Hld	ERC	ERA
2004 Cle	AL	6	0	0	2	11.2	49	9	6	6	1	0	0	1	6	0	7	1	0	0	0	-	0	0-0	0	3.58	4.63
2005 Cle	AL	1	0	0	1	6.0	29	9	4	4	2	1	1	0	2	0	3	0	0	0	0	-	0	0-0	0	8.58	6.00
2006 Cle	AL	9	1	0	1	19.1	93	24	15	15	2	0	0	2	15	1	14	3	0	0	0	-	0	0-0	0	7.78	6.98
2007 Bal	AL	32	26	0	3	175.1	723	165	78	72	23	4	6	4	47	2	123	8	1	7	5	.583	0	0-1	0	3.55	3.70
2008 Bal	AL	30	30	1	0	190.2	796	176	82	77	24	2	2	7	58	2	120	3	0	10	12	.455	0	0-0	0	3.59	3.63
2009 Bal	AL	33	33	1	0	200.0	874	224	120	112	35	1	8	9	60	1	110	1	1	10	17	.370	0	0-0	0	5.08	5.04
2010 Bal	AL	32	32	0	0	209.1	872	193	93	89	25	3	9	16	50	1	119	1	1	11	14	.440	0	0-0	0	3.44	3.83
2011 Bal	AL	34	32	2	1	208.0	889	213	113	100	26	5	10	9	66	5	130	0	0	9	17	.346	0	0-0	0	4.21	4.33
2012 2 Tms		33	29	0	0	181.2	788	206	109	96	30	8	6	9	50	2	101	2	2	8	12	.400	0	0-1	0	5.03	4.76
2013 KC	AL	33	33	3	0	211.2	905	236	99	95	30	2	8	8	59	1	111	7	0	15	12	.556	2	0-0	0	4.76	4.04
2014 KC	AL	32	32	1	0	202.2	864	215	100	93	23	2	10	14	49	0	124	3	0	13	11	.542	0	0-0	0	4.18	4.13
2015 KC	AL	30	24	0	4	148.1	664	186	101	98	29	5	6	9	44	1	84	4	0	8	8	.500	0	0-0	0	6.16	5.95
2017 Was	NL	1	1	0	0	2.0	12	6	10	10	0	0	2	0	4	0	0	0	0	0	1	.000	0	0-0	0	100.0	135.0
12 Col	NL	19	15	0	0	90.2	422	122	72	64	21	5	3	7	31	2	45	1	1	3	9	.250	0	0-1	0	7.26	6.35
12 KC	AL	14	14	0	0	91.0	366	84	37	32	9	3	3	2	19	0	56	1	1	5	3	.625	0	0-0	0	3.06	3.16
Postseason		3	3	0	0	13.1	53	11	6	6	0	0	2	1	2	0	5	0	0	1	1	.500	0	0-0	0	1.93	4.05
13 ML YEARS		306	273	8	12	1765.1	7558	1862	930	867	250	33	68	88	510	16	1046	33	5	91	109	.455	2	0-2	0	4.45	4.42

Franklin Gutierrez

Bats: R Throws: R Pos: PH-21;LF-17
Ht: 6'2" Wt: 200 Born: 2/21/1983 Age: 35

							BATTING														RUNNING			AVERAGES			
Year Team	Lg	G	AB	H	2B	3B	HR	(Hm	Rd)	TB	R	RBI	RC	TBB	IBB	SO	HBP	SH	SF	SB	CS	GDP	Avg	OBP	Slg	OPS
2005 Cle	AL	7	1	0	0	0	0	(0	0)	0	2	0	0	1	0	0	0	0	0	0	0	0	.000	.500	.000	.500
2006 Cle	AL	43	136	37	9	0	1	(1	0)	49	21	8	12	3	0	28	0	0	0	0	0	4	.272	.288	.360	.648
2007 Cle	AL	100	271	72	13	2	13	(10	3)	128	41	36	36	21	1	77	1	5	3	8	3	7	.266	.318	.472	.790
2008 Cle	AL	134	399	99	26	2	8	(6	2)	153	54	41	37	27	1	87	8	4	2	9	3	10	.248	.307	.383	.691
2009 Sea	AL	153	565	160	24	1	18	(7	11)	240	85	70	80	46	3	122	8	1	7	16	5	14	.283	.339	.425	.764
2010 Sea	AL	152	568	139	25	3	12	(6	6)	206	61	64	61	50	5	137	1	2	8	25	3	10	.245	.303	.363	.666
2011 Sea	AL	92	322	72	13	0	1	(0	1)	88	26	19	25	16	1	56	1	3	2	13	2	6	.224	.261	.273	.534
2012 Sea	AL	40	150	39	10	1	4	(2	2)	63	18	17	19	9	0	31	2	1	1	3	1	5	.260	.309	.420	.729
2013 Sea	AL	41	145	36	7	0	10	(6	4)	73	18	24	16	5	0	43	0	1	0	3	1	2	.248	.273	.503	.777
2015 Sea	AL	59	171	50	11	0	15	(6	9)	106	27	35	30	14	1	54	3	0	1	0	0	5	.292	.354	.620	.974
2016 Sea	AL	98	248	61	9	0	14	(8	6)	112	33	39	36	29	0	85	3	0	3	1	0	6	.246	.329	.452	.780
2017 LAD	NL	35	56	13	3	0	1	(1	0)	19	8	8	3	7	0	16	0	0	0	0	1	2	.232	.317	.339	.657
Postseason		10	29	6	0	0	1	(0	1)	9	5	4	3	5	0	11	0	0	0	0	0	1	.207	.324	.310	.634
12 ML YEARS		954	3032	778	150	9	97	(53	44)	1237	394	361	355	228	12	736	22	31	22	78	19	71	.257	.311	.408	.719

Brandon Guyer

Bats: R **Throws:** R **Pos:** RF-37;LF-33;PH-10;PR-4 GUY-er **Ht:** 6'2" **Wt:** 200 **Born:** 1/28/1986 **Age:** 32

Year	Team	Lg	G	AB	H	2B	3B	HR	(Hm	Rd)	TB	R	RBI	RC	TBB	IBB	SO	HBP	SH	SF	SB	CS	GDP	Avg	OBP	Slg	OPS
									BATTING												RUNNING			AVERAGES			
2011	TB	AL	15	41	8	1	0	2	(1	1)	15	7	3	2	1	0	9	0	1	0	0	0	1	.195	.214	.366	.580
2012	TB	AL	3	7	1	0	0	1	(0	1)	4	2	1	0	0	0	1	0	0	0	0	0	0	.143	.143	.571	.714
2014	TB	AL	97	259	69	15	1	3	(1	2)	95	37	26	37	16	0	52	11	7	1	6	1	3	.266	.334	.367	.701
2015	TB	AL	128	332	88	21	2	8	(5	3)	137	51	28	51	25	0	61	24	3	1	10	4	5	.265	.359	.413	.771
2016	2 Tms	AL	101	293	78	17	1	9	(7	2)	124	39	32	46	19	1	55	31	1	1	3	2	6	.266	.372	.423	.795
2017	Cle	AL	70	165	39	7	1	2	(0	2)	54	23	20	21	15	0	43	8	2	2	2	0	4	.236	.326	.327	.654
16	TB	AL	63	212	51	12	1	7	(6	1)	86	27	18	29	12	1	42	23	1	1	2	1	3	.241	.347	.406	.752
16	Cle	AL	38	81	27	5	0	2	(1	1)	38	12	14	17	7	0	13	8	0	0	1	1	3	.333	.438	.469	.907
	Postseason		10	18	6	1	0	0	(0	0)	7	6	3	4	4	0	5	2	0	0	0	0	0	.333	.500	.389	.889
	6 ML YEARS		414	1097	283	61	5	25	(14	11)	429	159	110	157	76	1	221	74	14	5	21	7	19	.258	.346	.391	.737

Jedd Gyorko

Bats: R **Throws:** R **Pos:** 3B-109;PH-12;1B-10;2B-5;LF-1;DH-1 JERK-oh **Ht:** 5'10" **Wt:** 215 **Born:** 9/23/1988 **Age:** 29

Year	Team	Lg	G	AB	H	2B	3B	HR	(Hm	Rd)	TB	R	RBI	RC	TBB	IBB	SO	HBP	SH	SF	SB	CS	GDP	Avg	OBP	Slg	OPS
									BATTING												RUNNING			AVERAGES			
2013	SD	NL	125	486	121	26	0	23	(13	10)	216	62	63	48	33	1	123	4	0	2	1	1	14	.249	.301	.444	.745
2014	SD	NL	111	400	84	17	1	10	(7	3)	133	37	51	42	36	1	100	4	0	3	3	2	8	.210	.280	.333	.612
2015	SD	NL	128	421	104	15	0	16	(9	7)	167	34	57	46	27	1	107	5	0	5	0	1	13	.247	.297	.397	.694
2016	StL	NL	128	400	97	9	1	30	(12	18)	198	58	59	54	37	1	96	0	0	1	0	0	11	.243	.306	.495	.801
2017	StL	NL	125	426	116	21	2	20	(9	11)	201	52	67	65	47	1	105	1	0	7	6	2	12	.272	.341	.472	.813
	5 ML YEARS		617	2133	522	88	4	99	(50	49)	915	243	297	255	180	5	531	14	0	18	10	6	58	.245	.305	.429	.734

Josh Hader

Pitches: L **Bats:** L **Pos:** RP-35 **Ht:** 6'3" **Wt:** 185 **Born:** 4/7/1994 **Age:** 24

Year	Team	Lg	G	GS	CG	GF	IP	BFP	H	R	ER	HR	SH	SF	HB	TBB	IBB	SO	WP	Bk	W	L	Pct	Sh	Sv-Op	Hld	ERC	ERA
					HOW MUCH HE PITCHED						WHAT HE GAVE UP												THE RESULTS				
2013	2 Tms	Low	22	22	0	0	107.1	462	81	49	33	4	5	4	10	54	0	95	8	1	5	6	.455	0	0- -	-	3.02	2.77
2014	Lancst	A+	22	15	0	3	103.0	421	76	41	31	9	3	1	10	38	1	112	10	0	9	2	.818	0	2- -	-	2.87	2.71
2014	CpChr	AA	5	4	0	0	20.0	94	16	14	14	2	1	0	3	16	0	24	3	0	1	1	.500	0	0- -	-	5.04	6.30
2015	CpChr	AA	17	10	0	2	65.1	285	60	31	23	5	2	2	4	24	0	69	4	0	3	3	.500	0	1- -	-	3.48	3.17
2015	Biloxi	AA	7	7	0	0	38.2	152	27	13	12	3	3	0	3	11	0	50	5	0	1	4	.200	0	0- -	-	2.29	2.79
2016	Biloxi	AA	11	11	0	0	57.0	223	38	7	6	1	5	0	3	19	0	73	2	0	2	1	.667	0	0- -	-	1.87	0.95
2016	ColSpr	AAA	14	14	0	0	69.0	300	63	42	40	5	2	2	3	36	0	88	2	1	1	7	.125	0	0- -	-	4.07	5.22
2017	ColSpr	AAA	12	12	0	0	52.0	228	49	32	31	14	3	0	0	31	0	51	1	0	3	4	.429	0	0- -	-	5.90	5.37
2017	Mil	NL	35	0	0	2	47.2	188	25	11	11	4	1	1	4	22	1	68	0	0	2	3	.400	0	0-1	12	2.09	2.08

Jesse Hahn

Pitches: R **Bats:** R **Pos:** SP-13; RP-1 **Ht:** 6'4" **Wt:** 215 **Born:** 7/30/1989 **Age:** 28

Year	Team	Lg	G	GS	CG	GF	IP	BFP	H	R	ER	HR	SH	SF	HB	TBB	IBB	SO	WP	Bk	W	L	Pct	Sh	Sv-Op	Hld	ERC	ERA
					HOW MUCH HE PITCHED						WHAT HE GAVE UP												THE RESULTS				
2017	Nashv*	AAA	6	5	0	0	25.0	112	28	14	12	1	0	1	0	14	0	18	4	0	2	0	1.000	0	0- -	-	5.05	4.32
2014	SD	NL	14	12	0	2	73.1	306	57	26	25	4	3	1	4	32	1	70	4	0	7	4	.636	0	0-0	0	2.91	3.07
2015	Oak	AL	16	16	1	0	96.2	406	88	46	36	5	1	2	8	25	1	64	7	0	6	6	.500	1	0-0	0	3.00	3.35
2016	Oak	AL	9	9	0	0	46.1	203	57	32	31	8	1	1	0	19	1	23	2	0	2	4	.333	0	0-0	0	6.22	6.02
2017	Oak	AL	14	13	0	1	69.2	316	78	46	41	4	3	6	3	27	0	55	2	0	3	6	.333	0	0-0	0	4.46	5.30
	4 ML YEARS		53	50	1	3	286.0	1231	280	150	133	21	8	10	15	103	3	212	15	0	18	20	.474	1	0-0	0	3.80	4.19

Justin Haley

Pitches: R **Bats:** R **Pos:** RP-10 **Ht:** 6'5" **Wt:** 230 **Born:** 6/16/1991 **Age:** 27

Year	Team	Lg	G	GS	CG	GF	IP	BFP	H	R	ER	HR	SH	SF	HB	TBB	IBB	SO	WP	Bk	W	L	Pct	Sh	Sv-Op	Hld	ERC	ERA
					HOW MUCH HE PITCHED						WHAT HE GAVE UP												THE RESULTS				
2013	Grnvlle	A	26	24	0	0	124.2	525	97	64	51	10	2	6	0	74	0	124	10	2	7	11	.389	0	0- -	-	3.54	3.68
2014	Salem	A+	19	11	1	4	92.2	372	77	34	29	4	5	2	6	23	0	74	6	0	7	4	.636	1	1- -	-	2.54	2.82
2014	Portlnd	AA	6	6	0	0	37.2	155	30	5	5	2	1	1	2	16	0	33	1	0	3	2	.600	0	0- -	-	3.03	1.19
2015	Portlnd	AA	27	27	0	0	124.0	552	142	80	71	7	1	4	6	50	0	95	15	1	5	16	.238	0	0- -	-	4.83	5.15
2016	Portlnd	AA	12	12	1	0	61.1	245	49	15	15	1	0	0	2	19	0	59	0	1	5	4	.556	1	0- -	-	2.33	2.20
2016	Pwtckt	AAA	15	14	1	1	85.1	338	70	34	34	8	5	1	2	26	1	67	1	0	8	6	.571	1	0- -	-	2.89	3.59
2017	Roch	AAA	5	4	0	0	17.1	69	17	8	7	3	0	0	0	3	0	11	1	0	1	0	1.000	0	0- -	-	3.65	3.63
2017	Pwtckt	AAA	7	7	1	0	44.0	168	35	13	13	7	0	0	1	7	0	35	0	1	1	2	.333	0	0- -	-	2.62	2.66
2017	Min	AL	10	0	0	5	18.0	81	22	12	12	3	0	1	1	6	0	14	0	0	0	0	-	0	1-1	0	5.85	6.00

Cole Hamels

Pitches: L **Bats:** L **Pos:** SP-24 **Ht:** 6'4" **Wt:** 205 **Born:** 12/27/1983 **Age:** 34

Year	Team	Lg	G	GS	CG	GF	IP	BFP	H	R	ER	HR	SH	SF	HB	TBB	IBB	SO	WP	Bk	W	L	Pct	Sh	Sv-Op	Hld	ERC	ERA
					HOW MUCH HE PITCHED						WHAT HE GAVE UP												THE RESULTS				
2006	Phi	NL	23	23	0	0	132.1	558	117	66	60	19	6	8	3	48	4	145	5	0	9	8	.529	0	0-0	0	3.61	4.08
2007	Phi	NL	28	28	2	0	183.1	743	163	72	69	25	5	5	3	43	4	177	5	0	15	5	.750	0	0-0	0	3.12	3.39
2008	Phi	NL	33	33	2	0	227.1	914	193	89	78	28	6	2	1	53	7	196	0	0	14	10	.583	2	0-0	0	2.76	3.09
2009	Phi	NL	32	32	2	0	193.2	814	206	95	93	24	7	5	5	43	4	168	1	0	10	11	.476	2	0-0	0	3.98	4.32
2010	Phi	NL	33	33	1	0	208.2	856	185	74	71	26	7	0	8	61	5	211	3	0	12	11	.522	0	0-0	0	3.36	3.06
2011	Phi	NL	32	31	3	0	216.0	850	169	68	67	19	9	3	5	44	2	194	3	3	14	9	.609	0	0-0	0	2.23	2.79
2012	Phi	NL	31	31	2	0	215.1	867	190	80	73	24	6	4	3	52	3	216	2	0	17	6	.739	2	0-0	0	2.98	3.05

Year	Team	Lg	G	GS	CG	GF	IP	BFP	H	R	ER	HR	SH	SF	HB	TBB	IBB	SO	WP	Bk	W	L	Pct	Sh	Sv-Op	Hld	ERC	ERA
2013	Phi	NL	33	33	1	0	220.0	905	205	94	88	21	11	3	9	50	5	202	4	0	8	14	.364	0	0-0	0	3.15	3.60
2014	Phi	NL	30	30	0	0	204.2	829	176	60	56	14	7	7	8	59	3	198	6	1	9	9	.500	0	0-0	0	2.88	2.46
2015	2 Tms		32	32	2	0	212.1	880	190	88	86	22	6	2	10	62	3	215	9	4	13	8	.619	1	0-0	0	3.28	3.65
2016	Tex	AL	32	32	0	0	200.2	848	185	83	74	24	1	2	8	77	1	200	4	1	15	5	.750	0	0-0	0	3.90	3.32
2017	Tex	AL	24	24	1	0	148.0	614	125	74	69	18	0	2	11	53	1	105	6	0	11	6	.647	0	0-0	0	3.54	4.20
15	Phi	NL	20	20	1	0	128.2	537	113	53	52	12	5	1	6	39	3	137	7	2	6	7	.462	1	0-0	0	3.13	3.64
15	Tex	AL	12	12	1	0	83.2	343	77	35	34	10	1	1	4	23	0	78	2	2	7	1	.875	0	0-0	0	3.54	3.66
	Postseason		16	16	1	0	98.1	401	81	45	38	12	4	2	2	26	2	92	1	0	7	6	.538	1	0-0	0	2.78	3.48
	12 ML YEARS		363	362	16	0	2362.1	9678	2104	943	884	264	71	43	74	645	42	2227	49	11	147	102	.590	7	0-0	0	3.19	3.37

Billy Hamilton

Bats: B **Throws:** R **Pos:** CF-137;PH-3

Ht: 6'0" **Wt:** 160 **Born:** 9/9/1990 **Age:** 27

							BATTING												RUNNING			AVERAGES			
Year	Team	Lg	G	AB	H	2B	3B	HR	(Hm | Rd)	TB	R	RBI	RC	TBB	IBB	SO	HBP	SH	SF	SB	CS	GDP	Avg	OBP	Slg	OPS
2013	Cin	NL	13	19	7	2	0	0	(0 | 0)	9	9	1	5	2	0	4	0	1	0	13	1	0	.368	.429	.474	.902
2014	Cin	NL	152	563	141	25	8	6	(3 | 3)	200	72	48	64	34	0	117	1	9	4	56	23	1	.250	.292	.355	.648
2015	Cin	NL	114	412	93	8	3	4	(2 | 2)	119	56	28	32	28	0	75	1	9	4	57	8	5	.226	.274	.289	.563
2016	Cin	NL	119	411	107	19	3	3	(2 | 1)	141	69	17	46	36	0	93	1	11	1	58	8	5	.260	.321	.343	.664
2017	Cin	NL	139	582	144	17	11	4	(3 | 1)	195	85	38	62	44	0	133	0	5	2	59	13	5	.247	.299	.335	.634
	5 ML YEARS		537	1987	492	71	25	17	(10 | 7)	664	291	132	209	144	0	422	3	35	11	243	53	16	.248	.298	.334	.632

Jason Hammel

Pitches: R **Bats:** R **Pos:** SP-32

Ht: 6'6" **Wt:** 225 **Born:** 9/2/1982 **Age:** 35

					HOW MUCH HE PITCHED					WHAT HE GAVE UP										THE RESULTS							
Year	Team	Lg	G	GS	CG	GF	IP	BFP	H	R	ER	HR	SH	SF	HB	TBB	IBB	SO	WP	Bk	W	L	Pct	Sh	Sv-Op	Hld	ERC	ERA
2006	TB	AL	9	9	0	0	44.0	208	61	38	38	7	0	3	1	21	0	32	3	2	0	6	.000	0	0-0	0	7.40	7.77
2007	TB	AL	24	14	0	2	85.0	384	100	58	58	12	2	0	2	40	1	64	3	0	3	5	.375	0	0-0	0	5.86	6.14
2008	TB	AL	40	5	0	21	78.1	346	83	45	40	11	2	2	2	35	4	44	7	0	4	4	.500	0	2-2	1	4.94	4.60
2009	Col	NL	34	30	1	0	176.2	771	203	94	85	17	10	9	9	42	6	133	4	0	10	8	.556	0	0-0	0	4.37	4.33
2010	Col	NL	30	30	0	0	177.2	770	201	97	95	18	11	6	6	47	1	141	13	2	10	9	.526	0	0-0	0	4.41	4.81
2011	Col	NL	32	27	0	2	170.1	739	175	100	90	21	11	6	6	68	3	94	8	1	7	13	.350	0	1-1	0	4.54	4.76
2012	Bal	AL	20	20	1	0	118.0	493	104	48	45	9	3	1	2	42	2	113	3	0	8	6	.571	1	0-0	0	3.14	3.43
2013	Bal	AL	26	23	0	1	139.1	611	155	81	77	22	2	8	8	48	1	96	1	0	7	8	.467	0	1-1	1	5.19	4.97
2014	2 Tms		30	29	0	1	176.1	715	154	70	68	23	4	4	8	44	2	158	6	0	10	11	.476	0	0-0	0	3.21	3.47
2015	ChC	NL	31	31	0	0	170.2	710	158	79	71	23	4	6	6	40	4	172	10	0	10	7	.588	0	0-0	0	3.32	3.74
2016	ChC	NL	30	30	0	0	166.2	692	148	77	71	25	7	3	9	53	0	144	9	0	15	10	.600	0	0-0	0	3.72	3.83
2017	KC	AL	32	32	0	0	180.1	804	209	109	106	26	0	10	4	49	2	145	7	1	8	13	.381	0	0-0	0	4.85	5.29
14	ChC	NL	17	17	0	0	108.2	429	88	36	36	10	2	3	5	23	2	104	4	0	8	5	.615	0	0-0	0	2.51	2.98
14	Oak	AL	13	12	0	1	67.2	286	66	34	32	13	1	1	3	21	0	54	2	0	2	6	.250	0	0-0	0	4.42	4.26
	Postseason		6	5	0	1	19.1	88	20	15	15	4	0	1	0	14	2	19	0	0	0	2	.000	0	0-0	0	6.73	6.98
	12 ML YEARS		338	280	2	27	1683.1	7243	1751	896	844	214	55	58	68	528	26	1336	74	6	92	100	.479	1	4-4	2	4.29	4.51

Brad Hand

Pitches: L **Bats:** L **Pos:** RP-72

Ht: 6'3" **Wt:** 228 **Born:** 3/20/1990 **Age:** 28

					HOW MUCH HE PITCHED					WHAT HE GAVE UP										THE RESULTS							
Year	Team	Lg	G	GS	CG	GF	IP	BFP	H	R	ER	HR	SH	SF	HB	TBB	IBB	SO	WP	Bk	W	L	Pct	Sh	Sv-Op	Hld	ERC	ERA
2011	Fla	NL	12	12	0	0	60.0	263	53	32	28	10	4	3	1	35	1	38	0	1	1	8	.111	0	0-0	0	4.68	4.20
2012	Mia	NL	1	1	0	0	3.2	23	6	7	7	1	0	0	0	6	1	3	0	0	0	1	.000	0	0-0	0	14.74	17.18
2013	Mia	NL	7	2	0	2	20.2	82	13	7	7	2	0	0	0	8	0	15	1	0	1	1	.500	0	0-0	0	2.10	3.05
2014	Mia	NL	32	16	0	5	111.0	474	112	56	54	10	6	2	2	39	3	67	5	0	3	8	.273	0	1-1	0	3.91	4.38
2015	Mia	NL	38	12	0	7	93.1	408	107	55	55	9	2	5	3	32	1	67	2	0	4	7	.364	0	0-0	2	4.83	5.30
2016	SD	NL	82	0	0	16	89.1	364	63	32	29	8	2	2	1	36	4	111	7	0	4	4	.500	0	1-7	21	2.44	2.92
2017	SD	NL	72	0	0	32	79.1	311	54	20	19	9	1	1	7	20	1	104	4	0	3	4	.429	0	21-26	16	2.30	2.16
	7 ML YEARS		244	43	0	62	457.1	1925	408	209	199	49	18	10	14	176	11	405	19	1	16	33	.327	0	23-34	39	3.57	3.92

Ryan Hanigan

Bats: R **Throws:** R **Pos:** C-30;PH-3

HANN-eh-gann

Ht: 6'0" **Wt:** 225 **Born:** 8/16/1980 **Age:** 37

							BATTING												RUNNING			AVERAGES			
Year	Team	Lg	G	AB	H	2B	3B	HR	(Hm | Rd)	TB	R	RBI	RC	TBB	IBB	SO	HBP	SH	SF	SB	CS	GDP	Avg	OBP	Slg	OPS
2017	Albq*	AAA	17	53	14	3	0	0	(- | -)	17	9	8	8	10	0	16	1	0	5	0	0	0	.264	.362	.321	.683
2007	Cin	NL	5	10	3	1	0	0	(0 | 0)	4	3	2	2	1	1	2	0	0	0	0	0	0	.300	.364	.400	.764
2008	Cin	NL	31	85	23	2	0	2	(1 | 1)	31	9	9	12	10	1	9	3	0	0	0	0	2	.271	.367	.365	.732
2009	Cin	NL	90	251	66	6	1	3	(3 | 0)	83	22	11	25	37	7	31	2	2	1	0	0	9	.263	.361	.331	.692
2010	Cin	NL	70	203	61	11	0	5	(2 | 3)	87	25	40	41	33	4	21	4	1	2	0	0	9	.300	.405	.429	.834
2011	Cin	NL	91	266	71	6	0	6	(4 | 2)	95	27	31	38	35	3	32	2	1	0	0	0	3	.267	.356	.357	.714
2012	Cin	NL	112	317	87	14	0	2	(0 | 2)	107	25	24	40	44	13	37	3	4	3	0	0	14	.274	.365	.338	.703
2013	Cin	NL	75	222	44	8	0	2	(1 | 1)	58	17	21	18	29	9	27	6	2	1	0	1	7	.198	.306	.261	.567
2014	TB	AL	84	225	49	9	0	5	(4 | 1)	73	18	34	27	31	0	39	3	2	2	1	0	6	.218	.318	.324	.642
2015	Bos	AL	54	174	43	8	0	2	(2 | 0)	57	28	16	18	20	0	39	4	1	1	0	0	6	.247	.337	.328	.664
2016	Bos	AL	35	105	18	4	0	1	(0 | 1)	25	9	14	4	7	0	27	1	0	0	0	0	5	.171	.230	.238	.468
2017	Col	NL	33	101	27	2	0	2	(2 | 0)	35	9	12	11	8	2	26	1	1	1	0	0	5	.267	.324	.347	.671
	Postseason		7	22	3	0	0	0	(0 | 0)	3	3	3	3	1	0	3	1	0	0	0	0	1	.136	.174	.136	.310
	11 ML YEARS		680	1959	492	71	1	30	(17 | 13)	655	192	214	236	255	40	290	29	14	11	1	1	55	.251	.344	.334	.679

Mitch Haniger

Bats: R **Throws:** R **Pos:** RF-94;CF-6;LF-2;PH-1   **Ht:** 6'2" **Wt:** 215 **Born:** 12/23/1990 **Age:** 27

Year	Team	Lg	G	AB	H	2B	3B	HR	(Hm	Rd)	TB	R	RBI	RC	TBB	IBB	SO	HBP	SH	SF	SB	CS	GDP	Avg	OBP	Slg	OPS
2013	2 Tms	Low	129	473	125	36	5	11	(-	-)	204	76	68	75	57	1	92	7	0	6	9	2	6	.264	.348	.431	.779
2014	Hntsvl	AA	67	243	62	7	1	10	(-	-)	101	41	34	34	19	1	41	4	2	3	4	0	5	.255	.316	.416	.732
2015	Mobile	AA	55	153	43	10	1	1	(-	-)	58	23	19	21	16	1	32	2	0	3	4	4	2	.281	.351	.379	.730
2015	Visalia	A+	49	202	67	16	3	12	(-	-)	125	40	36	47	17	0	39	2	0	5	8	2	2	.332	.381	.619	.999
2016	Mobile	AA	55	197	57	14	2	5	(-	-)	90	21	30	38	30	0	37	8	0	1	4	3	2	.289	.403	.457	.859
2016	Reno	AAA	74	261	89	20	3	20	(-	-)	175	58	64	73	39	0	62	5	1	6	8	1	6	.341	.428	.670	1.098
2017	Tacom	AAA	11	39	10	2	0	3	(-	-)	21	6	6	8	7	0	5	1	0	1	0	0	0	.256	.375	.538	.913
2016	Ari	NL	34	109	25	2	1	5	(4	1)	44	9	17	16	12	2	27	1	0	1	0	0	3	.229	.309	.404	.713
2017	Sea	AL	96	369	104	25	2	16	(6	10)	181	58	47	55	31	0	93	9	1	0	5	4	9	.282	.352	.491	.843
	2 ML YEARS		130	478	129	27	3	21	(10	11)	225	67	64	71	43	2	120	10	1	1	5	4	12	.270	.342	.471	.813

Jacob Hannemann

Bats: L **Throws:** L **Pos:** CF-7;LF-2;DH-2;PH-2;PR-2   **Ht:** 6'1" **Wt:** 200 **Born:** 4/29/1991 **Age:** 27

Year	Team	Lg	G	AB	H	2B	3B	HR	(Hm	Rd)	TB	R	RBI	RC	TBB	IBB	SO	HBP	SH	SF	SB	CS	GDP	Avg	OBP	Slg	OPS
2013	2 Tms	Low	17	71	19	5	2	1	(-	-)	31	9	7	9	2	0	12	0	1	0	4	1	0	.268	.288	.437	.724
2014	2 Tms	Low	124	487	122	23	5	8	(-	-)	179	74	51	63	42	0	111	5	8	3	37	7	1	.251	.315	.368	.682
2015	MrtlBh	A+	16	61	20	4	0	0	(-	-)	24	12	4	10	6	0	15	0	1	0	7	1	0	.328	.388	.393	.782
2015	Tenn	AA	112	434	101	20	9	6	(-	-)	157	60	41	50	32	0	113	5	10	4	17	1	5	.233	.291	.362	.652
2016	Tenn	AA	74	291	72	14	4	10	(-	-)	124	37	30	44	25	0	55	9	2	0	26	8	3	.247	.326	.426	.752
2017	Tenn	AA	34	122	22	9	1	1	(-	-)	36	17	6	11	14	1	44	4	1	0	6	3	2	.180	.286	.295	.581
2017	Iowa	AAA	80	287	76	23	1	5	(-	-)	116	40	26	42	24	0	69	3	4	4	23	3	6	.265	.324	.404	.728
2017	Sea	AL	11	20	3	0	0	1	(0	1)	6	3	1	0	0	0	4	0	0	0	0	1	0	.150	.150	.300	.450

Alen Hanson

Bats: B **Throws:** R **Pos:** PH-34;2B-28;RF-20;PR-13;CF-11;LF-8;DH-5;3B-2;SS-2   **Ht:** 5'11" **Wt:** 170 **Born:** 10/22/1992 **Age:** 25

Year	Team	Lg	G	AB	H	2B	3B	HR	(Hm	Rd)	TB	R	RBI	RC	TBB	IBB	SO	HBP	SH	SF	SB	CS	GDP	Avg	OBP	Slg	OPS
2013	Bradtn	A+	92	367	103	23	8	9	(-	-)	163	51	48	56	33	1	70	2	2	5	24	14	2	.281	.339	.444	.783
2013	Altna	AA	35	137	35	4	5	1	(-	-)	52	13	10	16	8	0	26	1	3	1	6	2	2	.255	.299	.380	.679
2014	Altna	AA	118	482	135	21	12	11	(-	-)	213	64	58	71	31	0	88	3	8	3	25	11	2	.280	.326	.442	.768
2015	Indy	AAA	117	475	125	17	12	6	(-	-)	184	66	43	62	37	1	91	0	12	5	35	12	9	.263	.313	.387	.701
2016	Indy	AAA	110	432	115	15	7	8	(-	-)	168	58	32	57	32	1	78	2	10	2	36	15	7	.266	.318	.389	.707
2016	Pit	NL	27	31	7	1	0	0	(0	0)	8	5	1	1	2	1	5	0	0	0	2	1	0	.226	.273	.258	.531
2017	2 Tms		106	217	48	9	3	4	(3	1)	75	36	11	14	12	0	52	1	1	3	11	3	5	.221	.262	.346	.607
17	Pit	NL	37	57	11	0	2	0	(0	0)	15	8	1	2	2	0	9	0	0	0	2	1	0	.193	.220	.263	.483
17	CWS	AL	69	160	37	9	1	4	(3	1)	60	28	10	12	10	0	43	1	1	3	9	2	5	.231	.276	.375	.651
	2 ML YEARS		133	248	55	10	3	4	(3	1)	83	41	12	15	14	1	57	1	1	3	13	4	5	.222	.263	.335	.598

Ian Happ

Bats: B **Throws:** R **Pos:** CF-54;2B-44;LF-29;PH-19;RF-14;3B-4;PR-1   **Ht:** 6'0" **Wt:** 205 **Born:** 8/12/1994 **Age:** 23

Year	Team	Lg	G	AB	H	2B	3B	HR	(Hm	Rd)	TB	R	RBI	RC	TBB	IBB	SO	HBP	SH	SF	SB	CS	GDP	Avg	OBP	Slg	OPS
2015	2 Tms	Low	67	251	65	17	4	9	(-	-)	117	50	33	45	40	1	67	0	0	4	10	1	5	.259	.356	.466	.822
2016	MrtlBh	A+	69	240	71	16	3	7	(-	-)	114	37	42	50	48	1	69	1	0	4	10	3	3	.296	.410	.475	.885
2016	Tenn	AA	65	248	65	14	0	8	(-	-)	103	35	32	34	20	0	60	2	0	4	6	2	5	.262	.318	.415	.733
2017	Iowa	AAA	26	104	31	6	0	9	(-	-)	64	21	25	22	11	1	27	0	0	1	2	1	0	.298	.362	.615	.977
2017	ChC	NL	115	364	92	17	3	24	(15	9)	187	62	68	57	39	5	129	4	2	4	8	4	12	.253	.328	.514	.842

J.A. Happ

Pitches: L **Bats:** L **Pos:** SP-25   JAY   **Ht:** 6'5" **Wt:** 205 **Born:** 10/19/1982 **Age:** 35

Year	Team	Lg	G	GS	CG	GF	IP	BFP	H	R	ER	HR	SH	SF	HB	TBB	IBB	SO	WP	Bk	W	L	Pct	Sh	Sv-Op	Hld	ERC	ERA
2007	Phi	NL	1	1	0	0	4.0	21	7	5	5	3	0	0	0	2	0	5	0	0	0	1	.000	0	0-0	0	15.13	11.25
2008	Phi	NL	8	4	0	1	31.2	138	28	13	13	3	2	1	1	14	1	26	1	0	1	0	1.000	0	0-0	1	3.55	3.69
2009	Phi	NL	35	23	3	4	166.0	685	149	55	54	20	7	6	5	56	2	119	2	0	12	4	.750	2	0-0	0	3.57	2.93
2010	2 Tms	NL	16	16	1	0	87.1	374	73	37	33	8	5	4	1	47	1	70	4	0	6	4	.600	1	0-0	0	3.69	3.40
2011	Hou	NL	28	28	0	0	156.1	698	157	103	93	21	12	8	2	83	5	134	3	2	6	15	.286	0	0-0	0	4.86	5.35
2012	2 Tms		28	24	0	3	144.2	627	147	79	77	19	9	4	2	56	1	144	7	0	10	11	.476	0	0-0	1	4.37	4.79
2013	Tor	AL	18	18	0	0	92.2	415	91	53	47	10	1	3	2	45	0	77	5	0	5	7	.417	0	0-0	0	4.36	4.56
2014	Tor	AL	30	26	0	0	158.0	673	160	79	74	22	1	5	2	51	0	133	1	0	11	11	.500	0	0-0	0	4.17	4.22
2015	2 Tms		32	31	0	0	172.0	717	173	71	69	16	2	0	2	45	4	151	6	0	11	8	.579	0	0-0	0	3.56	3.61
2016	Tor	AL	32	32	0	0	195.0	796	168	72	69	22	2	2	6	60	0	163	3	2	20	4	.833	0	0-0	0	3.22	3.18
2017	Tor	AL	25	25	0	0	145.1	626	145	64	57	18	1	4	0	46	1	142	4	0	10	11	.476	0	0-0	0	3.81	3.53
10	Phi	NL	3	3	0	0	15.1	70	13	4	3	1	1	1	0	12	0	9	1	0	1	0	1.000	0	0-0	0	4.40	1.76
10	Hou	NL	13	13	1	0	72.0	304	60	33	30	7	4	3	1	35	1	61	3	0	5	4	.556	1	0-0	0	3.53	3.75
12	Hou	NL	18	18	0	0	104.1	457	112	58	56	17	7	2	1	39	0	98	5	0	7	9	.438	0	0-0	0	4.86	4.83
12	Tor	AL	10	6	0	3	40.1	170	35	21	21	2	2	2	1	17	1	46	2	0	3	2	.600	0	0-0	1	3.16	4.69
15	Sea	AL	21	20	0	0	108.2	468	121	58	56	13	1	0	2	32	3	82	4	0	4	6	.400	0	0-0	0	4.49	4.64
15	Pit	NL	11	11	0	0	63.1	249	52	13	13	3	1	0	0	13	1	69	2	0	7	2	.778	0	0-0	0	2.12	1.85
	Postseason		10	3	0	0	19.1	91	25	8	8	2	0	0	0	10	0	19	1	0	1	1	.500	0	0-0	1	6.32	3.72
	11 ML YEARS		253	228	4	10	1353.0	5770	1298	631	591	162	42	37	23	505	15	1164	36	4	92	76	.548	3	0-0	2	3.93	3.93

Blaine Hardy

Pitches: L Bats: L Pos: RP-35 Ht: 6'2" Wt: 215 Born: 3/14/1987 Age: 31

			HOW MUCH HE PITCHED						WHAT HE GAVE UP										THE RESULTS						
Year	Team	Lg	G	GS	CG	GF	IP	BFP	H	R	ER	HR	SH	SF	HB	TBB	IBB	SO	WP	Bk	W	L	Pct	Sh	Sv-Op	Hld	ERC	ERA
2017	Toledo*	AAA	34	2	0	8	40.2	153	32	14	14	1	0	3	0	5	0	45	3	0	7	3	.700	0	3--	-	1.65	3.10
2014	Det	AL	38	0	0	7	39.0	167	34	12	11	1	1	2	1	20	3	31	1	0	2	1	.667	0	0-1	4	3.28	2.54
2015	Det	AL	70	0	0	11	61.1	265	61	23	21	2	3	4	1	22	2	55	5	0	5	3	.625	0	0-3	13	3.38	3.08
2016	Det	AL	21	0	0	10	25.2	112	25	11	10	2	1	0	0	12	1	20	1	0	1	0	1.000	0	0-0	0	3.95	3.51
2017	Det	AL	35	0	0	9	33.1	156	46	24	22	7	0	4	0	13	1	28	1	0	1	1	1.000	0	0-0	6	7.12	5.94
	4 ML YEARS		164	0	0	37	159.1	700	166	70	64	12	5	10	2	67	7	134	8	0	9	4	.692	0	0-4	23	4.17	3.62

J.J. Hardy

Bats: R Throws: R Pos: SS-71;PH-1;PR-1 Ht: 6'1" Wt: 200 Born: 8/19/1982 Age: 35

			BATTING																		RUNNING			AVERAGES			
Year	Team	Lg	G	AB	H	2B	3B	HR	(Hm	Rd)	TB	R	RBI	RC	TBB	IBB	SO	HBP	SH	SF	SB	CS	GDP	Avg	OBP	Slg	OPS
2005	Mil	NL	124	372	92	22	1	9	(6	3)	143	46	50	49	44	7	48	1	8	2	0	0	10	.247	.327	.384	.711
2006	Mil	NL	35	128	31	5	0	5	(4	1)	51	13	14	13	10	0	23	0	0	1	1	1	4	.242	.295	.398	.693
2007	Mil	NL	151	592	164	30	1	26	(15	11)	274	89	80	84	40	1	73	1	4	1	2	3	13	.277	.323	.463	.786
2008	Mil	NL	146	569	161	31	4	24	(14	10)	272	78	74	78	52	3	98	1	5	2	2	1	18	.283	.343	.478	.821
2009	Mil	NL	115	414	95	16	2	11	(6	5)	148	53	47	32	43	0	85	2	1	5	0	1	14	.229	.302	.357	.659
2010	Min	AL	101	340	91	19	3	6	(1	5)	134	44	38	41	28	1	54	0	3	4	1	1	8	.268	.320	.394	.714
2011	Bal	AL	129	527	142	27	0	30	(15	15)	259	76	80	78	31	3	92	2	2	5	0	0	10	.269	.310	.491	.801
2012	Bal	AL	158	663	158	30	2	22	(15	7)	258	85	68	72	38	4	106	3	7	2	0	0	21	.238	.282	.389	.671
2013	Bal	AL	159	601	158	27	0	25	(11	14)	260	66	76	71	38	3	73	0	3	2	2	1	14	.263	.306	.433	.738
2014	Bal	AL	141	527	142	28	0	9	(4	5)	197	56	52	60	29	1	104	4	3	4	0	0	12	.268	.309	.372	.682
2015	Bal	AL	114	411	90	14	0	8	(4	4)	128	45	37	32	20	0	88	0	2	4	0	0	11	.219	.253	.311	.564
2016	Bal	AL	115	405	109	29	0	9	(4	5)	165	43	48	50	26	1	68	0	1	6	0	0	14	.269	.309	.407	.716
2017	Bal	AL	73	254	55	13	1	4	(2	2)	82	24	24	18	12	0	48	1	1	0	0	1	7	.217	.255	.323	.578
	Postseason		21	80	18	5	0	1	(1	0)	26	6	7	8	6	1	14	0	0	0	0	0	1	.225	.279	.325	.604
	13 ML YEARS		1561	5805	1488	291	14	188	(102	86)	2371	718	688	677	411	24	960	15	40	38	8	9	156	.256	.305	.408	.714

Bryce Harper

Bats: L Throws: R Pos: RF-110;PH-2 Ht: 6'3" Wt: 215 Born: 10/16/1992 Age: 25

			BATTING																		RUNNING			AVERAGES			
Year	Team	Lg	G	AB	H	2B	3B	HR	(Hm	Rd)	TB	R	RBI	RC	TBB	IBB	SO	HBP	SH	SF	SB	CS	GDP	Avg	OBP	Slg	OPS
2012	Was	NL	139	533	144	26	9	22	(10	12)	254	98	59	82	56	0	120	2	3	3	18	6	8	.270	.340	.477	.817
2013	Was	NL	118	424	116	24	3	20	(13	7)	206	71	58	73	61	4	94	5	3	4	11	4	4	.274	.368	.486	.854
2014	Was	NL	100	352	96	10	2	13	(5	8)	149	41	32	43	38	4	104	1	3	1	2	2	6	.273	.344	.423	.768
2015	Was	NL	153	521	172	38	1	42	(23	19)	338	118	99	138	124	15	131	5	0	4	6	4	15	.330	.460	.649	1.109
2016	Was	NL	147	506	123	24	2	24	(12	12)	223	84	86	90	108	20	117	3	0	10	21	10	15	.243	.373	.441	.814
2017	Was	NL	111	420	134	27	1	29	(12	17)	250	95	87	93	68	11	99	1	0	3	4	2	15	.319	.413	.595	1.008
	Postseason		14	57	12	3	1	4	(2	2)	29	10	7	9	8	0	17	1	0	0	3	0	0	.211	.318	.509	.827
	6 ML YEARS		768	2756	785	149	18	150	(75	75)	1420	507	421	519	455	54	665	17	9	25	62	28	59	.285	.386	.515	.902

Lucas Harrell

Pitches: R Bats: B Pos: RP-4 HAH-rell Ht: 6'2" Wt: 205 Born: 6/3/1985 Age: 33

			HOW MUCH HE PITCHED						WHAT HE GAVE UP										THE RESULTS						
Year	Team	Lg	G	GS	CG	GF	IP	BFP	H	R	ER	HR	SH	SF	HB	TBB	IBB	SO	WP	Bk	W	L	Pct	Sh	Sv-Op	Hld	ERC	ERA
2017	Buffalo*	AAA	7	6	0	1	30.1	130	27	7	7	1	0	1	0	13	0	24	3	0	0	1	.000	0	0--	-	3.08	2.08
2010	CWS	AL	8	3	0	3	24.0	119	34	14	13	2	1	0	0	17	1	15	1	0	1	0	1.000	0	0-0	0	7.77	4.88
2011	2 Tms		9	2	0	2	18.0	86	23	12	9	0	1	1	1	8	0	15	1	1	2	2	.000	0	0-0	0	5.16	4.50
2012	Hou	NL	32	32	1	0	193.2	827	185	90	81	13	8	10	1	78	5	140	10	3	11	11	.500	1	0-0	0	3.59	3.76
2013	Hou	AL	36	22	0	8	153.2	707	174	111	100	20	6	5	6	88	5	89	8	0	6	17	.261	0	0-1	0	5.95	5.86
2014	Hou	AL	3	3	0	0	12.1	66	19	14	13	2	0	2	0	9	1	9	1	0	0	3	.000	0	0-0	0	8.91	9.49
2016	2 Tms		9	9	0	0	47.0	208	46	24	22	4	2	2	4	25	0	36	5	0	3	2	.600	0	0-0	0	4.78	4.21
2017	Tor	AL	4	0	0	1	6.1	33	10	5	5	1	0	0	0	4	0	6	1	0	0	0	-	0	0-0	0	9.00	7.11
	11 CWS	AL	3	0	0	2	5.0	26	11	4	4	0	0	0	0	1	0	5	0	0	0	0	-	0	0-0	0	10.11	7.20
	11 Hou	NL	6	2	0	0	13.0	60	12	8	5	0	1	1	1	7	0	10	1	1	2	2	.000	0	0-0	0	3.57	3.46
	16 Atl	NL	5	5	0	0	29.1	124	25	13	11	1	1	1	3	12	0	21	3	0	2	2	.500	0	0-0	0	3.28	3.38
	16 Tex	AL	4	4	0	0	17.2	84	21	11	11	3	1	1	1	13	0	15	2	0	1	0	1.000	0	0-0	0	7.64	5.60
	7 ML YEARS		101	71	1	14	455.0	2046	491	274	243	42	18	20	12	229	12	310	27	4	21	35	.375	1	0-1	0	4.95	4.81

Will Harris

Pitches: R Bats: R Pos: RP-46 Ht: 6'4" Wt: 250 Born: 8/28/1984 Age: 33

			HOW MUCH HE PITCHED						WHAT HE GAVE UP										THE RESULTS						
Year	Team	Lg	G	GS	CG	GF	IP	BFP	H	R	ER	HR	SH	SF	HB	TBB	IBB	SO	WP	Bk	W	L	Pct	Sh	Sv-Op	Hld	ERC	ERA
2012	Col	NL	20	0	0	10	17.2	89	27	16	16	3	2	1	1	6	1	19	4	0	1	1	.500	0	0-0	3	7.39	8.15
2013	Ari	NL	61	0	0	11	52.2	217	50	17	17	3	0	4	2	15	1	53	4	0	4	1	.800	0	0-1	4	3.25	2.91
2014	Ari	NL	29	0	0	8	29.0	120	27	14	14	3	1	1	2	9	2	35	1	0	0	3	.000	0	0-1	3	3.62	4.34
2015	Hou	AL	68	0	0	18	71.0	276	42	18	15	8	2	1	1	22	1	68	2	0	5	5	.500	0	2-6	13	1.79	1.90
2016	Hou	AL	66	0	0	19	64.0	255	52	17	16	3	1	2	1	15	1	69	4	0	1	2	.333	0	12-15	28	2.21	2.25
2017	Hou	AL	46	0	0	5	45.1	177	37	15	15	7	0	0	0	7	0	52	1	0	3	2	.600	0	2-4	20	2.52	2.98
	Postseason		4	0	0	0	3.0	16	8	5	4	0	0	0	0	0	0	2	0	0	0	1	.000	0	0-0	3	12.84	12.00
	6 ML YEARS		290	0	0	71	279.2	1134	235	99	93	27	6	9	7	74	6	296	16	0	14	14	.500	0	16-27	71	2.76	2.99

Josh Harrison

Bats: R **Throws:** R **Pos:** 2B-83;3B-49;LF-8;PH-3;RF-1;PR-1   **Ht:** 5'8" **Wt:** 180 **Born:** 7/8/1987 **Age:** 30

Year	Team	Lg	G	AB	H	2B	3B	HR	(Hm	Rd)	TB	R	RBI	RC	TBB	IBB	SO	HBP	SH	SF	SB	CS	GDP	Avg	OBP	Slg	OPS
2011	Pit	NL	65	195	53	13	2	1	(1	0)	73	21	16	19	3	0	24	0	5	1	4	1	6	.272	.281	.374	.656
2012	Pit	NL	104	249	58	9	5	3	(1	2)	86	34	16	22	10	0	37	7	7	3	7	3	3	.233	.279	.345	.624
2013	Pit	NL	60	88	22	1	2	3	(1	2)	36	10	14	11	2	0	10	3	2	0	2	0	4	.250	.290	.409	.699
2014	Pit	NL	143	520	164	38	7	13	(4	9)	255	77	52	84	22	1	81	4	2	2	18	7	6	.315	.347	.490	.837
2015	Pit	NL	114	418	120	29	1	4	(2	2)	163	57	28	48	19	1	71	7	3	2	10	8	4	.287	.327	.390	.717
2016	Pit	NL	131	487	138	25	7	4	(2	2)	189	57	59	61	18	0	76	5	4	8	19	4	10	.283	.311	.388	.699
2017	Pit	NL	128	486	132	26	2	16	(9	7)	210	66	47	65	28	2	90	23	2	3	12	4	5	.272	.339	.432	.771
	Postseason		4	7	2	0	0	0	(0	0)	2	1	0	0	0	0	2	1	0	0	0	1	0	.286	.375	.286	.661
	7 ML YEARS		745	2443	687	141	26	44	(20	24)	1012	322	232	310	102	4	389	49	25	19	72	27	38	.281	.321	.414	.735

Donnie Hart

Pitches: L **Bats:** L **Pos:** RP-51   **Ht:** 5'11" **Wt:** 180 **Born:** 9/6/1990 **Age:** 27

			HOW MUCH HE PITCHED						WHAT HE GAVE UP										THE RESULTS						
Year	Team	Lg	G	GS	CG	GF	IP	BFP	H	R	ER	HR	SH	SF	HB	TBB	IBB	SO	WP	Bk	W	L	Pct	Sh	Sv-Op	Hld	ERC	ERA
2013	Abrdn	A-	19	0	0	13	24.0	103	24	10	6	0	0	2	3	7	2	26	0	0	3	1	.750	0	5- -	-	3.31	2.25
2014	Dlmrva	A	24	0	0	16	29.1	123	25	13	12	2	1	0	1	11	1	31	3	0	1	3	.250	0	4- -	-	3.04	3.68
2015	2 Tms	Low	46	0	0	31	52.0	211	40	10	8	0	4	0	3	14	2	46	4	0	6	2	.750	0	13- -	-	1.92	1.38
2016	Bowie	AA	40	0	0	11	46.1	185	41	17	14	1	0	0	4	7	1	50	0	0	3	1	.750	0	4- -	-	2.38	2.72
2017	Norfolk	AAA	13	0	0	4	15.1	64	17	4	4	1	1	1	0	2	1	20	0	0	1	0	1.000	0	0- -	-	3.27	2.35
2016	Bal	AL	22	0	0	3	18.1	71	12	1	1	1	2	1	0	6	1	12	0	0	0	0	-	0	0-0	1	1.76	0.49
2017	Bal	AL	51	0	0	12	43.2	190	48	19	18	5	0	1	4	13	0	29	1	1	2	0	1.000	0	0-2	5	4.75	3.71
	Postseason		1	0	0	0	0.1	1	0	0	0	0	0	0	0	0	0	0	0	0	0	0	-	0	0-0	0	0.00	0.00
	2 ML YEARS		73	0	0	15	62.0	261	60	20	19	6	2	2	4	19	1	41	1	1	2	0	1.000	0	0-2	9	3.78	2.76

Matt Harvey

Pitches: R **Bats:** R **Pos:** SP-18; RP-1   **Ht:** 6'4" **Wt:** 215 **Born:** 3/27/1989 **Age:** 29

			HOW MUCH HE PITCHED						WHAT HE GAVE UP										THE RESULTS						
Year	Team	Lg	G	GS	CG	GF	IP	BFP	H	R	ER	HR	SH	SF	HB	TBB	IBB	SO	WP	Bk	W	L	Pct	Sh	Sv-Op	Hld	ERC	ERA
2012	NYM	NL	10	10	0	0	59.1	245	42	19	18	5	3	3	3	26	0	70	3	0	3	5	.375	0	0-0	0	2.75	2.73
2013	NYM	NL	26	26	1	0	178.1	690	135	46	45	7	5	4	4	31	1	191	2	0	9	5	.643	1	0-0	0	1.76	2.27
2015	NYM	NL	29	29	0	0	189.1	755	156	62	57	18	7	2	5	37	2	188	4	0	13	8	.619	0	0-0	0	2.44	2.71
2016	NYM	NL	17	17	0	0	92.2	402	111	55	50	8	5	4	1	25	1	76	4	0	4	10	.286	0	0-0	0	4.65	4.86
2017	NYM	NL	19	18	0	0	92.2	431	110	70	69	21	3	2	6	47	3	67	6	1	5	7	.417	0	0-0	0	6.87	6.70
	Postseason		4	4	0	0	26.2	109	21	10	9	2	0	1	1	8	1	27	0	0	2	0	1.000	0	0-0	0	2.49	3.04
	5 ML YEARS		101	100	1	0	612.1	2523	554	252	239	59	23	15	19	166	7	592	19	1	34	35	.493	1	0-0	0	3.15	3.51

Chris Hatcher

Pitches: R **Bats:** R **Pos:** RP-49   **Ht:** 6'1" **Wt:** 200 **Born:** 1/12/1985 **Age:** 33

			HOW MUCH HE PITCHED						WHAT HE GAVE UP										THE RESULTS						
Year	Team	Lg	G	GS	CG	GF	IP	BFP	H	R	ER	HR	SH	SF	HB	TBB	IBB	SO	WP	Bk	W	L	Pct	Sh	Sv-Op	Hld	ERC	ERA
2011	Fla	NL	11	0	0	4	10.1	48	14	8	8	2	0	3	0	4	1	8	2	0	0	0	-	0	0-0	0	6.69	6.97
2012	Mia	NL	11	0	0	7	14.2	66	17	9	7	3	0	0	1	6	0	10	1	0	0	0	-	0	0-0	0	6.19	4.30
2013	Mia	NL	7	0	0	2	8.2	44	13	13	12	1	0	0	0	4	1	7	0	0	0	1	.000	0	0-0	0	6.92	12.46
2014	Mia	NL	52	0	0	15	56.0	232	55	22	21	4	1	1	0	12	1	60	1	2	0	3	.000	0	0-2	6	3.03	3.38
2015	LAD	NL	49	0	0	12	39.0	166	35	19	16	4	2	1	3	13	2	45	3	0	3	5	.375	0	4-6	13	3.46	3.69
2016	LAD	NL	37	0	0	10	40.2	181	40	26	25	8	1	0	1	21	4	43	4	0	5	4	.556	0	0-1	9	5.07	5.53
2017	2 Tms		49	0	0	17	59.2	257	58	29	28	10	2	2	0	21	2	63	2	1	1	2	.333	0	1-5	11	4.07	4.22
17	LAD	NL	26	0	0	15	36.2	158	37	20	19	7	2	1	0	12	0	43	2	1	0	1	.000	0	0-1	2	4.40	4.66
17	Oak	AL	23	0	0	2	23.0	99	21	9	9	3	0	1	0	9	2	20	0	0	1	1	.500	0	1-4	9	3.56	3.52
	Postseason		4	0	0	1	3.2	12	0	0	0	0	0	0	0	1	0	5	0	0	0	0	-	0	0-0	2	0.09	0.00
	7 ML YEARS		216	0	0	67	229.0	994	232	126	117	32	6	7	5	81	11	236	13	3	9	15	.375	0	5-14	34	4.21	4.60

Mike Hauschild

Pitches: R **Bats:** R **Pos:** RP-4   HOUSE-child   **Ht:** 6'3" **Wt:** 210 **Born:** 1/22/1990 **Age:** 28

			HOW MUCH HE PITCHED						WHAT HE GAVE UP										THE RESULTS						
Year	Team	Lg	G	GS	CG	GF	IP	BFP	H	R	ER	HR	SH	SF	HB	TBB	IBB	SO	WP	Bk	W	L	Pct	Sh	Sv-Op	Hld	ERC	ERA
2013	2 Tms	Low	28	19	0	2	123.1	514	129	58	48	8	3	1	5	30	1	88	4	0	9	4	.692	0	0- -	-	3.69	3.50
2014	Lancst	A+	8	4	0	1	34.2	142	40	17	17	3	1	3	0	9	1	31	3	0	2	1	.667	0	0- -	-	4.50	4.41
2014	CpChr	AA	20	16	0	1	98.2	409	95	53	47	5	8	3	5	25	1	87	2	1	2	9	.182	0	1- -	-	3.19	4.29
2015	CpChr	AA	10	8	0	0	50.2	207	53	19	18	2	0	1	3	8	0	35	0	0	5	1	.833	0	1- -	-	3.30	3.20
2015	Fresno	AAA	15	15	0	0	87.2	373	86	37	34	6	0	2	4	27	0	81	7	0	7	5	.583	0	0- -	-	3.56	3.49
2016	Fresno	AAA	24	24	0	0	139.2	585	138	64	50	7	2	5	5	40	1	119	11	0	9	10	.474	0	0- -	-	3.39	3.22
2017	Fresno	AAA	18	18	0	0	90.1	401	85	46	46	8	1	5	6	53	1	79	8	0	6	2	.750	0	0- -	-	4.70	4.58
2017	Tex	AL	4	0	0	2	8.0	39	14	10	10	5	0	0	1	2	0	7	1	0	0	0	-	0	0-0	0	13.92	11.25

Austin Hays

Bats: R **Throws:** R **Pos:** RF-14;CF-8 · **Ht:** 6'1" **Wt:** 195 **Born:** 7/5/1995 **Age:** 22

Year Team	Lg	G	AB	H	2B	3B	HR	(Hm	Rd)	TB	R	RBI	RC	TBB	IBB	SO	HBP	SH	SF	SB	CS	GDP	Avg	OBP	Slg	OPS
2016 Abrdn	A-	38	140	47	9	2	4	(-	-)	72	14	21	26	11	0	32	1	0	1	4	3	1	.336	.386	.514	.900
2017 Bowie	AA	64	261	86	17	2	16	(-	-)	155	39	54	55	13	0	45	4	2	3	1	1	5	.330	.367	.594	.960
2017 Frdrck	A+	64	262	86	15	3	16	(-	-)	155	42	41	53	12	0	40	4	0	2	4	6	5	.328	.364	.592	.956
2017 Bal	AL	20	60	13	3	0	1	(0	1)	19	4	8	5	2	0	16	0	0	1	0	0	2	.217	.238	.317	.555

Jeremy Hazelbaker

Bats: L **Throws:** R **Pos:** PH-19;LF-11;RF-8;CF-6;PR-6 · **Ht:** 6'3" **Wt:** 190 **Born:** 8/14/1987 **Age:** 30

Year Team	Lg	G	AB	H	2B	3B	HR	(Hm	Rd)	TB	R	RBI	RC	TBB	IBB	SO	HBP	SH	SF	SB	CS	GDP	Avg	OBP	Slg	OPS
2013 Pwtckt	AAA	121	428	110	13	2	11	(-	-)	160	62	54	57	36	3	131	1	10	5	37	7	4	.257	.313	.374	.687
2014 Chatt	AA	87	271	68	9	8	4	(-	-)	105	31	33	36	30	2	70	0	6	0	15	7	5	.251	.326	.387	.713
2014 Albq	AAA	22	90	20	3	2	4	(-	-)	39	12	11	9	2	0	27	0	0	0	6	2	0	.222	.239	.433	.672
2015 Tulsa	AA	14	53	13	2	2	0	(-	-)	19	5	2	6	3	0	11	0	2	0	6	0	0	.245	.286	.358	.644
2015 Sprgfld	AA	40	143	44	13	3	3	(-	-)	72	30	20	30	18	1	33	3	3	1	10	0	3	.308	.394	.503	.897
2015 Memp	AAA	58	207	70	10	7	10	(-	-)	124	38	46	49	23	0	60	2	0	3	8	2	3	.338	.408	.599	1.007
2016 Memp	AAA	13	40	13	3	0	1	(-	-)	19	8	11	8	6	0	12	2	2	0	2	1	0	.325	.438	.475	.913
2017 Reno	AAA	52	190	53	13	5	6	(-	-)	94	31	25	34	19	1	57	0	0	2	11	0	2	.279	.341	.495	.836
2016 StL	NL	114	200	47	7	3	12	(3	9)	96	35	28	29	18	2	64	0	4	2	5	2	1	.235	.295	.480	.775
2017 Ari	NL	41	52	18	2	2	2	(0	2)	30	10	10	16	9	2	20	0	0	0	1	0	0	.346	.443	.577	1.020
2 ML YEARS		155	252	65	9	5	14	(3	11)	126	45	38	45	27	4	84	0	4	2	6	2	1	.258	.327	.500	.827

Chase Headley

Bats: B **Throws:** R **Pos:** 3B-86;1B-45;DH-14;PH-11;2B-1   HEDD-lee · **Ht:** 6'2" **Wt:** 215 **Born:** 5/9/1984 **Age:** 34

Year Team	Lg	G	AB	H	2B	3B	HR	(Hm	Rd)	TB	R	RBI	RC	TBB	IBB	SO	HBP	SH	SF	SB	CS	GDP	Avg	OBP	Slg	OPS
2007 SD	NL	8	18	4	1	0	0	(0	0)	5	1	0	1	2	0	4	1	0	0	0	0	2	.222	.333	.278	.611
2008 SD	NL	91	331	89	19	2	9	(4	5)	139	34	38	42	30	1	104	5	0	2	4	1	5	.269	.337	.420	.757
2009 SD	NL	156	543	142	31	2	12	(7	5)	213	62	64	68	62	3	133	5	0	2	10	2	19	.262	.342	.392	.734
2010 SD	NL	161	610	161	29	3	11	(3	8)	229	77	58	70	56	3	139	3	1	4	17	5	11	.264	.327	.375	.702
2011 SD	NL	113	381	110	28	1	4	(1	3)	152	43	44	61	52	8	92	2	1	3	13	2	6	.289	.374	.399	.773
2012 SD	NL	161	604	173	31	2	31	(13	18)	301	95	115	112	86	2	157	4	0	5	17	6	7	.286	.376	.498	.875
2013 SD	NL	141	520	130	35	2	13	(5	8)	208	59	50	64	67	7	142	11	0	2	8	4	9	.250	.347	.400	.747
2014 2 Tms		135	470	114	20	1	13	(7	6)	175	55	49	54	51	1	122	9	0	1	7	3	17	.243	.328	.372	.700
2015 NYY	AL	156	580	150	29	1	11	(6	5)	214	74	62	71	51	0	135	7	0	4	0	2	17	.259	.324	.369	.693
2016 NYY	AL	140	467	118	18	1	14	(11	3)	180	58	51	64	51	3	118	6	0	5	8	2	7	.253	.331	.385	.716
2017 NYY	AL	147	512	140	30	1	12	(7	5)	208	77	61	72	60	2	132	6	1	7	9	2	10	.273	.352	.406	.758
14 SD	NL	77	279	64	12	1	7	(2	5)	99	27	32	29	22	0	73	5	0	1	4	1	12	.229	.296	.355	.651
14 NYY	AL	58	191	50	8	0	6	(5	1)	76	28	17	25	29	1	49	4	0	0	3	2	5	.262	.371	.398	.768
Postseason		1	2	0	0	0	0	(0	0)	0	0	0	0	1	0	1	0	0	0	0	0	0	.000	.333	.000	.333
11 ML YEARS		1409	5036	1331	271	16	130	(64	66)	2024	635	592	679	568	30	1278	59	3	35	93	29	110	.264	.344	.402	.746

Ryon Healy

Bats: R **Throws:** R **Pos:** DH-78;1B-39;3B-34;PH-3 · **Ht:** 6'5" **Wt:** 225 **Born:** 1/10/1992 **Age:** 26

Year Team	Lg	G	AB	H	2B	3B	HR	(Hm	Rd)	TB	R	RBI	RC	TBB	IBB	SO	HBP	SH	SF	SB	CS	GDP	Avg	OBP	Slg	OPS
2013 2 Tms	Low	47	174	40	10	1	6	(-	-)	70	16	29	18	5	1	28	2	0	3	2	1	6	.230	.255	.402	.658
2014 Stcktn	A+	136	561	160	28	2	16	(-	-)	240	73	83	78	28	1	79	3	0	8	0	0	20	.285	.318	.428	.746
2015 MdInd	AA	124	507	153	31	1	10	(-	-)	216	63	62	74	30	0	82	1	1	4	0	1	21	.302	.339	.426	.765
2016 MdInd	AA	36	145	49	12	3	8	(-	-)	91	27	34	35	18	0	35	0	0	1	1	0	0	.338	.409	.628	1.036
2016 Nashv	AAA	49	192	61	16	1	6	(-	-)	97	33	30	34	13	1	40	2	0	3	0	1	4	.318	.362	.505	.867
2016 Oak	AL	72	269	82	20	0	13	(8	5)	141	36	37	43	12	1	60	1	1	0	0	0	7	.305	.337	.524	.861
2017 Oak	AL	149	576	156	29	0	25	(14	11)	260	66	78	75	23	0	142	4	0	2	0	1	16	.271	.302	.451	.754
2 ML YEARS		221	845	238	49	0	38	(22	16)	401	102	115	118	35	1	202	5	1	2	0	1	23	.282	.313	.475	.788

Andrew Heaney

Pitches: L **Bats:** L **Pos:** SP-5   HEE-nee · **Ht:** 6'2" **Wt:** 195 **Born:** 6/5/1991 **Age:** 27

		HOW MUCH HE PITCHED						WHAT HE GAVE UP										THE RESULTS						
Year Team	Lg	G	GS	CG	GF	IP	BFP	H	R	ER	HR	SH	SF	HB	TBB	IBB	SO	WP	Bk	W	L	Pct	Sh	Sv-Op	Hld	ERC	ERA
2014 Mia	NL	7	5	0	2	29.1	126	32	19	19	6	2	0	3	7	0	20	2	0	0	3	.000	0	0-0	0	5.17	5.83
2015 LAA	AL	18	18	0	0	105.2	438	99	41	41	9	1	3	6	28	1	78	4	0	6	4	.600	0	0-0	0	3.35	3.49
2016 LAA	AL	1	1	0	0	6.0	25	7	4	4	2	0	0	0	0	0	7	0	0	0	1	.000	0	0-0	0	4.78	6.00
2017 LAA	AL	5	5	0	0	21.2	101	27	17	17	12	2	0	0	9	0	27	2	0	1	2	.333	0	0-0	0	8.99	7.06
4 ML YEARS		31	29	0	2	162.2	690	165	81	81	29	5	3	9	44	1	132	8	0	7	10	.412	0	0-0	0	4.41	4.48

Adeiny Hechavarria

Bats: R **Throws:** R **Pos:** SS-96;PH-1;PR-1   a-DAY-nee hetch-a-VA-ree-a · **Ht:** 6'0" **Wt:** 195 **Born:** 4/15/1989 **Age:** 29

Year Team	Lg	G	AB	H	2B	3B	HR	(Hm	Rd)	TB	R	RBI	RC	TBB	IBB	SO	HBP	SH	SF	SB	CS	GDP	Avg	OBP	Slg	OPS
2012 Tor	AL	41	126	32	8	0	2	(1	1)	46	10	15	15	4	0	32	1	5	1	0	0	2	.254	.280	.365	.645
2013 Mia	NL	148	543	123	14	8	3	(1	2)	162	30	42	37	30	1	96	0	4	1	11	10	19	.227	.267	.298	.565
2014 Mia	NL	146	536	148	20	10	1	(0	1)	191	53	34	49	26	5	86	1	4	6	7	5	21	.276	.308	.356	.664
2015 Mia	NL	130	470	132	17	6	5	(3	2)	176	54	48	49	23	4	78	2	0	4	7	2	18	.281	.315	.374	.689

Year Team	Lg	G	AB	H	2B	3B	HR	(Hm	Rd)	TB	R	RBI	RC	TBB	IBB	SO	HBP	SH	SF	SB	CS	GDP	Avg	OBP	Slg	OPS
2016 Mia	NL	155	508	120	17	6	3	(1	2)	158	52	38	33	7	73	1	2	3	1	0	10	.236	.283	.311	.594
2017 2 Tms		97	330	86	14	5	8	(4	4)	134	37	30	36	13	1	67	1	2	2	4	1	7	.261	.289	.406	.695
17 Mia	NL	20	65	18	2	1	1	(0	1)	25	8	6	8	1	0	9	0	1	0	0	0	1	.277	.288	.385	.672
17 TB	AL	77	265	68	12	4	7	(4	3)	109	29	24	28	12	1	58	1	1	2	4	1	6	.257	.289	.411	.701
6 ML YEARS		717	2513	641	90	35	22	(10	12)	867	236	207	226	129	18	432	6	17	17	30	18	77	.255	.291	.345	.636

Austin Hedges

Bats: R Throws: R Pos: C-115;PH-6;DH-1   **Ht: 6'1" Wt: 206 Born: 8/18/1992 Age: 25**

							BATTING										RUNNING			AVERAGES			
Year Team	Lg	G	AB	H	2B	3B	HR	(Hm	Rd)	TB	R	RBI	RC	TBB	IBB	SO	HBP	SH	SF	SB	CS	GDP	Avg	OBP	Slg	OPS
2015 SD	NL	56	137	23	2	0	3	(2	1)	34	13	11	7	8	1	38	1	3	3	0	0	1	.168	.215	.248	.463
2016 SD	NL	8	24	3	1	0	0	(0	0)	4	2	1	0	0	0	7	1	0	1	0	1	0	.125	.154	.167	.321
2017 SD	NL	120	387	83	17	0	18	(9	9)	154	36	55	39	23	3	122	3	1	3	4	1	10	.214	.262	.398	.660
3 ML YEARS		184	548	109	20	0	21	(11	10)	192	51	67	46	31	4	167	5	4	7	4	2	11	.199	.245	.350	.596

Chris Heisey

Bats: R Throws: R Pos: LF-19;PH-18;RF-5;PR-1   HY-zee   **Ht: 6'1" Wt: 220 Born: 12/14/1984 Age: 33**

							BATTING										RUNNING			AVERAGES			
Year Team	Lg	G	AB	H	2B	3B	HR	(Hm	Rd)	TB	R	RBI	RC	TBB	IBB	SO	HBP	SH	SF	SB	CS	GDP	Avg	OBP	Slg	OPS
2010 Cin	NL	97	201	51	10	1	8	(2	6)	87	33	21	22	16	1	57	6	1	2	1	2	3	.254	.324	.433	.757
2011 Cin	NL	120	279	71	9	1	18	(11	7)	136	44	50	40	19	3	78	5	1	4	6	1	1	.254	.309	.487	.797
2012 Cin	NL	120	347	92	16	5	7	(4	3)	139	44	31	42	18	0	81	7	3	0	6	3	8	.265	.315	.401	.715
2013 Cin	NL	87	224	53	11	1	9	(6	3)	93	29	23	26	9	0	51	5	4	2	3	0	4	.237	.279	.415	.694
2014 Cin	NL	119	275	61	15	2	8	(4	4)	104	34	22	22	15	0	64	2	5	2	9	2	3	.222	.265	.378	.643
2015 LAD	NL	33	55	10	2	0	2	(2	0)	18	8	9	10	15	2	17	0	0	2	0	1	1	.182	.347	.327	.674
2016 Was	NL	83	139	30	3	1	9	(4	5)	62	18	17	14	13	0	44	2	0	1	0	1	0	.216	.290	.446	.736
2017 Was	NL	38	74	12	3	1	1	(1	0)	20	8	5	2	5	0	22	0	0	0	0	0	1	.162	.215	.270	.485
Postseason		11	10	1	0	0	1	(1	0)	4	2	3	0	0	0	4	0	0	1	0	0	1	.100	.091	.400	.491
8 ML YEARS		697	1594	380	69	12	62	(34	28)	659	218	178	178	110	6	414	27	14	13	25	10	21	.238	.296	.413	.710

Ben Heller

Pitches: R Bats: R Pos: RP-9   **Ht: 6'3" Wt: 205 Born: 8/5/1991 Age: 26**

		HOW MUCH HE PITCHED						WHAT HE GAVE UP										THE RESULTS						
Year Team	Lg	G	GS	CG	GF	IP	BFP	H	R	ER	HR	SH	SF	HB	TBB	IBB	SO	WP	Bk	W	L	Pct	Sh	Sv-Op	Hld	ERC	ERA
2013 MhVlly	A-	21	1	0	8	37.1	163	37	16	13	0	0	2	1	14	1	39	4	0	1	3	.250	0	2- -	-	3.34	3.13
2014 2 Tms	Low	45	0	0	22	53.0	218	27	16	14	4	1	0	5	29	0	81	6	1	5	1	.833	0	5- -	-	2.24	2.38
2015 Lynbrg	A+	36	0	0	31	34.1	148	30	18	17	0	1	1	2	13	0	43	6	0	0	2	.000	0	12- -	-	2.78	4.46
2015 Akron	AA	5	0	0	0	6.0	26	5	1	1	0	0	0	0	1	0	15	5	0	0	0	-	0	0- -	-	1.60	1.50
2016 Akron	AA	15	0	0	14	16.1	60	3	1	1	1	0	0	2	5	0	23	0	0	1	0	1.000	0	7- -	-	0.67	0.55
2016 Clmbs	AAA	28	0	0	13	25.1	104	20	7	7	1	1	0	4	7	2	25	2	1	2	2	.500	0	5- -	-	2.60	2.49
2016 S-WB	AAA	6	0	0	6	6.1	25	3	1	1	0	1	0	0	2	0	7	0	0	1	0	1.000	0	1- -	-	0.95	1.42
2017 S-WB	AAA	41	0	0	29	56.1	223	34	21	18	6	0	1	3	21	1	82	8	0	5	4	.556	0	6- -	-	2.16	2.88
2016 NYY	AL	10	0	0	4	7.0	40	11	5	5	3	0	0	2	4	1	6	0	0	1	0	1.000	0	0-1	1	11.69	6.43
2017 NYY	AL	9	0	0	4	11.0	43	5	1	1	0	0	1	0	6	0	9	1	0	1	0	1.000	0	0-0	0	1.40	0.82
2 ML YEARS		19	0	0	8	18.0	83	16	6	6	3	0	1	2	10	1	15	1	0	2	0	1.000	0	0-1	1	4.73	3.00

Jeremy Hellickson

Pitches: R Bats: R Pos: SP-30   **Ht: 6'1" Wt: 190 Born: 4/8/1987 Age: 31**

		HOW MUCH HE PITCHED						WHAT HE GAVE UP										THE RESULTS						
Year Team	Lg	G	GS	CG	GF	IP	BFP	H	R	ER	HR	SH	SF	HB	TBB	IBB	SO	WP	Bk	W	L	Pct	Sh	Sv-Op	Hld	ERC	ERA
2010 TB	AL	10	4	0	0	36.1	149	32	14	14	5	0	1	2	8	2	33	2	0	4	0	1.000	0	0-1	0	3.10	3.47
2011 TB	AL	29	29	2	0	189.0	774	146	64	62	21	1	2	4	72	8	117	8	1	13	10	.565	1	0-0	0	2.89	2.95
2012 TB	AL	31	31	0	0	177.0	741	163	68	61	25	4	3	4	59	3	124	5	0	10	11	.476	0	0-0	0	3.73	3.10
2013 TB	AL	32	31	0	1	174.0	737	185	103	100	24	2	5	4	50	0	135	7	2	12	10	.545	0	0-0	0	4.40	5.17
2014 TB	AL	13	13	0	0	63.2	281	71	35	32	8	0	1	2	21	1	54	8	0	1	5	.167	0	0-0	0	4.70	4.52
2015 Ari	NL	27	27	0	0	146.0	636	151	79	75	22	8	6	6	43	3	121	5	0	9	12	.429	0	0-0	0	4.25	4.62
2016 Phi	NL	32	32	1	0	189.0	772	173	86	78	24	4	6	6	45	0	154	6	1	12	10	.545	1	0-0	0	3.31	3.71
2017 2 Tms		30	30	0	0	164.0	695	160	105	99	35	5	7	8	47	2	96	4	1	8	11	.421	0	0-0	0	4.43	5.43
17 Phi	NL	20	20	0	0	112.1	472	111	62	59	22	5	5	6	30	2	65	3	1	6	5	.545	0	0-0	0	4.35	4.73
17 Bal	AL	10	10	0	0	51.2	223	49	43	40	13	0	2	2	17	0	31	1	0	2	6	.250	0	0-0	0	4.60	6.97
Postseason		2	2	0	0	5.0	22	5	3	3	3	0	0	0	3	0	1	0	0	1	0	1.000	0	0-0	0	8.99	5.40
8 ML YEARS		204	197	3	1	1139.0	4785	1081	554	521	164	24	31	36	345	19	834	45	5	69	69	.500	2	0-1	0	3.81	4.12

Heath Hembree

Pitches: R Bats: R Pos: RP-62   HEHM-bree   **Ht: 6'4" Wt: 210 Born: 1/13/1989 Age: 29**

		HOW MUCH HE PITCHED						WHAT HE GAVE UP										THE RESULTS						
Year Team	Lg	G	GS	CG	GF	IP	BFP	H	R	ER	HR	SH	SF	HB	TBB	IBB	SO	WP	Bk	W	L	Pct	Sh	Sv-Op	Hld	ERC	ERA
2013 SF	NL	9	0	0	2	7.2	29	4	0	0	0	0	0	0	2	0	12	0	0	0	0	-	0	0-0	0	1.02	0.00
2014 Bos	AL	6	0	0	3	10.0	43	11	5	5	1	0	0	0	5	2	6	1	0	0	0	-	0	0-0	0	4.94	4.50
2015 Bos	AL	22	0	0	9	25.1	106	25	10	10	5	0	0	0	9	2	15	1	0	2	0	1.000	0	0-0	1	4.46	3.55
2016 Bos	AL	38	0	0	8	51.0	223	51	23	15	6	0	1	0	17	1	47	0	0	4	1	.800	0	0-2	5	3.78	2.65
2017 Bos	AL	62	0	0	8	62.0	271	72	29	25	10	1	2	1	18	0	70	2	0	2	3	.400	0	0-3	14	5.07	3.63
5 ML YEARS		137	0	0	30	156.0	672	163	67	55	22	1	3	1	51	5	150	4	0	8	4	.667	0	0-5	20	4.28	3.17

Kyle Hendricks

Pitches: R Bats: R Pos: SP-24   Ht: 6'3" Wt: 190 Born: 12/7/1989 Age: 28

		HOW MUCH HE PITCHED						WHAT HE GAVE UP										THE RESULTS						
Year	Team	Lg	G	GS	CG	GF	IP	BFP	H	R	ER	HR	SH	SF	HB	TBB	IBB	SO	WP	Bk	W	L	Pct	Sh	Sv-Op	Hld	ERC	ERA
2014	ChC	NL	13	13	0	0	80.1	321	72	24	22	4	4	1	4	15	2	47	0	0	7	2	.778	0	0-0	0	2.61	2.46
2015	ChC	NL	32	32	1	0	180.0	739	166	82	79	17	6	0	8	43	1	167	3	1	8	7	.533	1	0-0	0	3.18	3.95
2016	ChC	NL	31	30	2	0	190.0	745	142	53	45	15	4	3	8	44	3	170	5	0	16	8	.667	1	0-0	0	2.19	2.13
2017	ChC	NL	24	24	0	0	139.2	570	126	49	47	17	6	1	2	40	1	123	0	0	7	5	.583	0	0-0	0	3.34	3.03
	Postseason		7	7	0	0	34.0	135	28	10	9	5	2	1	1	8	0	30	0	0	1	1	.500	0	0-0	0	2.96	2.38
	4 ML YEARS		100	99	3	0	590.0	2375	506	208	193	53	20	5	22	142	7	507	8	1	38	22	.633	2	0-0	0	2.81	2.94

Liam Hendriks

Pitches: R Bats: R Pos: RP-70   Ht: 6'0" Wt: 200 Born: 2/10/1989 Age: 29

		HOW MUCH HE PITCHED						WHAT HE GAVE UP										THE RESULTS						
Year	Team	Lg	G	GS	CG	GF	IP	BFP	H	R	ER	HR	SH	SF	HB	TBB	IBB	SO	WP	Bk	W	L	Pct	Sh	Sv-Op	Hld	ERC	ERA
2011	Min	AL	4	4	0	0	23.1	100	29	16	16	3	0	1	0	6	0	16	1	0	0	2	.000	0	0-0	0	5.26	6.17
2012	Min	AL	16	16	1	0	85.1	381	106	61	53	17	3	1	4	26	3	50	4	0	1	8	.111	0	0-0	0	6.03	5.59
2013	Min	AL	10	8	0	1	47.1	224	67	39	36	10	0	2	3	14	1	34	1	0	1	3	.250	0	0-0	0	7.16	6.85
2014	2 Tms	AL	9	6	0	0	32.2	143	38	21	19	3	0	2	3	7	0	23	1	0	1	2	.333	0	0-0	1	4.56	5.23
2015	Tor	AL	58	0	0	14	64.2	261	59	23	21	3	0	2	1	11	1	71	4	0	5	0	1.000	0	0-2	5	2.51	2.92
2016	Oak	AL	53	0	0	10	64.2	275	69	31	27	6	0	4	1	14	3	71	3	0	0	4	.000	0	0-1	10	3.63	3.76
2017	Oak	AL	70	0	0	13	64.0	273	57	34	30	7	0	1	0	23	0	78	6	0	4	2	.667	0	1-4	16	3.30	4.22
14	Tor	AL	3	3	0	0	13.1	57	12	9	9	3	0	0	2	4	0	8	0	0	1	0	1.000	0	0-0	0	4.58	6.08
14	KC	AL	6	3	0	0	19.1	86	26	12	10	0	0	2	1	3	0	15	1	0	0	2	.000	0	0-0	1	4.52	4.66
	Postseason		3	0	0	1	5.0	18	5	3	3	0	0	1	0	0	0	2	0	0	0	0	-	0	0-0	0	2.23	5.40
	7 ML YEARS		220	34	1	38	382.0	1657	425	225	202	49	3	13	13	101	8	343	20	0	12	21	.364	0	1-7	32	4.45	4.76

Guillermo Heredia

ghee-YAIR-moh

Bats: R Throws: L Pos: CF-63;LF-62;PR-5;PH-4;RF-1;DH-1   Ht: 5'10" Wt: 180 Born: 1/31/1991 Age: 27

					BATTING														RUNNING			AVERAGES			
Year	Team	Lg	G	AB	H	2B	3B	HR	(Hm | Rd)	TB	R	RBI	RC	TBB	IBB	SO	HBP	SH	SF	SB	CS	GDP	Avg	OBP	Slg	OPS
2016	Jacksn	AA	58	205	60	7	2	2	(- | -)	77	39	34	36	36	0	32	9	1	9	2	5	11	.293	.405	.376	.781
2016	Tacom	AAA	35	138	43	6	1	2	(- | -)	57	27	13	23	12	0	15	4	1	2	3	0	6	.312	.378	.413	.791
2016	Sea	AL	45	92	23	3	0	1	(1 | 0)	29	12	12	12	12	0	15	2	1	0	1	1	1	.250	.349	.315	.664
2017	Sea	AL	123	386	96	16	0	6	(4 | 2)	130	43	24	37	27	2	64	11	1	1	1	5	9	.249	.315	.337	.652
	2 ML YEARS		168	478	119	19	0	7	(5 | 2)	159	55	36	49	39	2	79	13	2	1	2	6	10	.249	.322	.333	.655

Ariel Hernandez

Pitches: R Bats: R Pos: RP-19   Ht: 6'4" Wt: 230 Born: 3/2/1992 Age: 26

		HOW MUCH HE PITCHED						WHAT HE GAVE UP										THE RESULTS						
Year	Team	Lg	G	GS	CG	GF	IP	BFP	H	R	ER	HR	SH	SF	HB	TBB	IBB	SO	WP	Bk	W	L	Pct	Sh	Sv-Op	Hld	ERC	ERA
2013	Giants	R	10	0	0	5	7.2	42	4	10	9	0	0	0	4	12	0	10	6	0	0	0	-	0	1- -	-	6.95	10.57
2015	Hlsbro	A-	22	0	0	7	22.1	108	18	15	15	1	0	0	2	21	0	32	11	0	1	1	.500	0	2- -	-	4.86	6.04
2016	2 Tms	Low	43	0	0	13	62.0	258	29	18	15	1	1	3	2	39	0	74	8	1	3	2	.600	0	5- -	-	1.72	2.18
2017	Pnscla	AA	24	0	0	5	33.0	131	18	8	8	0	1	1	1	20	0	39	6	1	2	0	1.000	0	1- -	-	2.03	2.18
2017	Lsvlle	AAA	15	0	0	7	17.0	83	14	10	10	1	2	1	1	19	2	19	5	0	1	2	.333	0	0- -	-	5.55	5.29
2017	Cin	NL	19	0	0	5	24.1	108	14	14	14	6	0	1	0	22	1	29	2	0	0	0	-	0	0-0	0	4.62	5.18

Cesar Hernandez

Bats: B Throws: R Pos: 2B-127;SS-1;PH-1;PR-1   Ht: 5'10" Wt: 160 Born: 5/23/1990 Age: 28

					BATTING														RUNNING			AVERAGES			
Year	Team	Lg	G	AB	H	2B	3B	HR	(Hm | Rd)	TB	R	RBI	RC	TBB	IBB	SO	HBP	SH	SF	SB	CS	GDP	Avg	OBP	Slg	OPS
2013	Phi	NL	34	121	35	5	0	0	(0 | 0)	40	17	10	13	9	0	26	1	0	0	0	3	2	.289	.344	.331	.674
2014	Phi	NL	66	114	27	2	0	1	(1 | 0)	32	13	4	7	9	1	33	0	1	1	1	1	1	.237	.290	.281	.571
2015	Phi	NL	127	405	110	20	4	1	(1 | 0)	141	57	35	52	40	1	86	2	4	1	19	5	6	.272	.339	.348	.687
2016	Phi	NL	155	547	161	14	11	6	(4 | 2)	215	67	39	82	66	4	116	2	5	2	17	13	6	.294	.371	.393	.764
2017	Phi	NL	128	511	150	26	6	9	(6 | 3)	215	85	34	80	61	1	104	4	0	1	15	5	8	.294	.373	.421	.793
	5 ML YEARS		510	1698	483	67	21	17	(12 | 5)	643	239	122	234	185	7	365	9	10	5	52	27	23	.284	.357	.379	.736

David Hernandez

Pitches: R Bats: R Pos: RP-64   Ht: 6'3" Wt: 245 Born: 5/13/1985 Age: 33

		HOW MUCH HE PITCHED						WHAT HE GAVE UP										THE RESULTS						
Year	Team	Lg	G	GS	CG	GF	IP	BFP	H	R	ER	HR	SH	SF	HB	TBB	IBB	SO	WP	Bk	W	L	Pct	Sh	Sv-Op	Hld	ERC	ERA
2017	Gwnntt*	AAA	7	0	0	5	8.0	29	4	2	1	0	0	0	0	2	0	9	0	0	1	0	1.000	0	4- -	-	0.98	1.13
2009	Bal	AL	20	19	0	0	101.1	462	118	62	61	27	2	3	1	46	0	68	3	0	4	10	.286	0	0-0	0	6.55	5.42
2010	Bal	AL	41	8	0	16	79.1	348	72	40	38	9	1	3	4	42	4	72	9	0	8	8	.500	0	2-6	2	4.28	4.31
2011	Ari	NL	74	0	0	28	69.1	291	49	27	26	4	3	2	2	30	1	77	7	1	5	3	.625	0	11-14	23	2.40	3.38
2012	Ari	NL	72	0	0	21	68.1	278	48	21	19	4	0	1	6	22	1	98	4	1	2	3	.400	0	4-10	25	2.10	2.50
2013	Ari	NL	62	0	0	12	62.1	263	50	33	31	10	2	0	4	24	4	66	6	0	5	6	.455	0	2-8	15	3.45	4.48
2015	Ari	NL	40	0	0	7	33.2	144	33	18	16	6	1	0	3	11	0	33	1	0	1	5	.167	0	0-0	7	4.62	4.28
2016	Phi	NL	70	0	0	16	72.2	322	77	34	31	11	1	1	2	32	5	80	6	0	3	4	.429	0	1-3	15	4.95	3.84
2017	2 Tms		64	0	0	15	55.0	214	48	20	19	4	1	2	1	9	0	52	5	0	3	1	.750	0	2-4	18	2.50	3.11
17	LAA	AL	38	0	0	10	36.1	140	29	10	9	0	1	0	1	8	0	37	3	0	1	0	1.000	0	1-2	8	1.96	2.23
17	Phi	NL	26	0	0	5	18.2	74	19	10	10	4	0	2	0	1	0	15	2	0	2	1	.667	0	1-2	10	3.55	4.82
	Postseason		4	0	0	1	5.0	17	2	2	2	1	0	0	0	0	0	5	0	0	0	0	-	0	0-0	0	0.74	3.60
	8 ML YEARS		443	27	0	115	542.0	2322	495	252	241	75	11	12	20	216	15	546	41	2	31	40	.437	0	22-45	105	3.94	4.00

Felix Hernandez

Pitches: R **Bats:** R **Pos:** SP-16

Ht: 6'3" **Wt:** 225 **Born:** 4/8/1986 **Age:** 32

		HOW MUCH HE PITCHED						WHAT HE GAVE UP												THE RESULTS								
Year	Team	Lg	G	GS	CG	GF	IP	BFP	H	R	ER	HR	SH	SF	HB	TBB	IBB	SO	WP	Bk	W	L	Pct	Sh	Sv-Op	Hld	ERC	ERA
2005	Sea	AL	12	12	0	0	84.1	328	61	26	25	5	1	2	2	23	0	77	3	0	4	4	.500	0	0-0	0	2.08	2.67
2006	Sea	AL	31	31	2	0	191.0	816	195	105	96	23	2	3	6	60	2	176	11	0	12	14	.462	1	0-0	0	4.11	4.52
2007	Sea	AL	30	30	1	0	190.1	808	209	88	83	20	6	1	3	53	4	165	7	1	14	7	.667	1	0-0	0	4.27	3.92
2008	Sea	AL	31	31	2	0	200.2	857	198	85	77	17	4	6	8	80	7	175	8	1	9	11	.450	0	0-0	0	4.05	3.45
2009	Sea	AL	34	34	2	0	238.2	977	200	81	66	15	6	11	8	71	0	217	17	1	19	5	.792	1	0-0	0	2.72	2.49
2010	Sea	AL	34	**34**	6	0	249.2	1001	194	80	63	17	6	3	8	70	1	232	14	1	13	12	.520	1	0-0	0	2.39	**2.27**
2011	Sea	AL	33	33	5	0	233.2	964	218	99	90	19	3	7	7	67	0	222	12	1	14	14	.500	0	0-0	0	3.31	3.47
2012	Sea	AL	33	33	5	0	232.0	939	209	84	79	14	2	2	12	56	0	223	13	2	13	9	.591	**5**	0-0	0	2.94	3.06
2013	Sea	AL	31	31	0	0	204.1	823	185	74	69	15	4	6	3	46	1	216	13	0	12	10	.545	0	0-0	0	2.82	3.04
2014	Sea	AL	34	**34**	2	0	236.0	912	170	68	56	16	4	5	5	46	1	248	18	0	15	6	.714	0	0-0	0	**1.81**	**2.14**
2015	Sea	AL	31	31	2	0	201.2	826	180	80	79	15	4	5	3	58	0	191	10	0	18	9	.667	**2**	0-0	0	3.37	3.53
2016	Sea	AL	25	25	0	0	153.1	655	138	76	65	19	3	0	10	65	0	122	6	0	11	8	.579	0	0-0	0	4.07	3.82
2017	Sea	AL	16	16	0	0	86.2	368	86	46	42	17	1	1	6	26	0	78	8	0	6	5	.545	0	0-0	0	4.62	4.36
13 ML YEARS			375	375	25	0	2502.1	10274	2243	992	890	220	46	51	87	721	16	2342	140	7	160	114	.584	11	0-0	0	3.16	3.20

Gorkys Hernandez

Bats: R **Throws:** R **Pos:** LF-57;CF-50;PH-26;RF-20;PR-6   GORE-keez

Ht: 6'1" **Wt:** 190 **Born:** 9/7/1987 **Age:** 30

					BATTING																RUNNING			AVERAGES			
Year	Team	Lg	G	AB	H	2B	3B	HR	(Hm	Rd)	TB	R	RBI	RC	TBB	IBB	SO	HBP	SH	SF	SB	CS	GDP	Avg	OBP	Slg	OPS
2012 2 Tms		NL	70	156	30	2	3	3	(2	1)	47	18	13	15	13	0	42	3	1	0	7	2	2	.192	.267	.301	.569
2015 Pit		NL	8	5	0	0	0	0	(0	0)	0	0	0	0	0	0	0	0	0	0	1	0	0	.000	.000	.000	.000
2016 SF		NL	26	54	14	5	0	2	(1	1)	25	7	4	5	3	0	11	0	0	0	0	1	0	.259	.298	.463	.761
2017 SF		NL	128	310	79	20	1	0	(0	0)	101	40	22	31	31	3	73	3	2	2	12	4	6	.255	.327	.326	.652
12 Pit		NL	25	24	2	0	0	0	(0	0)	2	2	2	0	1	0	5	1	0	0	2	0	1	.083	.154	.083	.237
12 Mia		NL	45	132	28	2	3	3	(2	1)	45	16	11	15	12	0	37	2	1	0	5	2	1	.212	.288	.341	.629
Postseason			3	6	1	0	0	0	(0	0)	1	0	0	0	0	0	2	0	0	0	0	1	0	.167	.167	.167	.333
4 ML YEARS			232	525	123	27	4	5	(3	2)	173	65	39	51	47	3	126	6	3	2	20	7	8	.234	.303	.330	.633

Kike Hernandez

kee-KAY

Bats: R **Throws:** R **Pos:** PH-52;CF-34;LF-28;SS-24;RF-18;3B-14;2B-9;1B-3;DH-1;PR-1

Ht: 5'11" **Wt:** 200 **Born:** 8/24/1991 **Age:** 26

					BATTING																RUNNING			AVERAGES			
Year	Team	Lg	G	AB	H	2B	3B	HR	(Hm	Rd)	TB	R	RBI	RC	TBB	IBB	SO	HBP	SH	SF	SB	CS	GDP	Avg	OBP	Slg	OPS
2014 2 Tms			42	121	30	6	3	3	(1	2)	51	13	14	18	12	0	21	1	0	0	0	0	1	.248	.321	.421	.742
2015 LAD		NL	76	202	62	12	2	7	(2	5)	99	24	22	32	11	0	46	2	1	2	0	2	3	.307	.346	.490	.836
2016 LAD		NL	109	216	41	8	0	7	(5	2)	70	25	18	16	28	1	64	0	0	0	2	0	3	.190	.283	.324	.607
2017 LAD		NL	140	297	64	24	2	11	(7	4)	125	46	37	39	41	2	80	0	1	3	3	0	4	.215	.308	.421	.729
14 Hou		AL	24	81	23	4	2	1	(1	0)	34	10	8	14	8	0	11	0	0	0	0	0	0	.284	.348	.420	.768
14 Mia		NL	18	40	7	2	1	2	(0	2)	17	3	6	4	4	0	10	1	0	0	0	0	1	.175	.267	.425	.692
Postseason			10	21	4	0	0	0	(0	0)	4	3	0	1	5	1	6	0	0	0	1	0	1	.190	.346	.190	.537
4 ML YEARS			367	836	197	50	7	28	(15	13)	345	108	91	105	92	3	211	3	2	5	5	2	11	.236	.312	.413	.725

Marco Hernandez

Bats: L **Throws:** R **Pos:** 3B-9;2B-6;SS-5;PR-2

Ht: 6'0" **Wt:** 200 **Born:** 9/6/1992 **Age:** 25

					BATTING																RUNNING			AVERAGES			
Year	Team	Lg	G	AB	H	2B	3B	HR	(Hm	Rd)	TB	R	RBI	RC	TBB	IBB	SO	HBP	SH	SF	SB	CS	GDP	Avg	OBP	Slg	OPS
2013 Kane		A	111	417	106	17	3	4	(-	-)	141	45	34	42	16	1	72	4	4	2	21	7	8	.254	.287	.338	.625
2014 Dytona		A+	122	441	119	13	7	3	(-	-)	155	61	55	52	30	2	90	2	7	6	22	8	7	.270	.315	.351	.667
2015 Portlnd		AA	68	282	92	21	4	5	(-	-)	136	30	31	46	9	0	49	1	2	0	4	2	5	.326	.349	.482	.832
2015 Pwtckt		AAA	46	181	49	9	2	4	(-	-)	74	27	22	22	8	2	39	0	0	1	1	0	1	.271	.300	.409	.709
2016 Pwtckt		AAA	57	223	69	7	4	5	(-	-)	99	26	29	34	12	0	51	0	1	1	4	2	4	.309	.343	.444	.787
2016 Bos		AL	40	51	15	1	0	1	(0	1)	19	11	5	6	5	0	10	0	0	0	1	0	0	.294	.357	.373	.730
2017 Bos		AL	21	58	16	3	0	0	(0	0)	19	7	2	4	1	0	15	1	0	0	0	1	0	.276	.300	.328	.628
Postseason			2	0	0	0	0	0	(0	0)	0	0	0	0	0	0	0	0	0	0	0	0	0	-	-	-	-
2 ML YEARS			61	109	31	4	0	1	(0	1)	38	18	7	10	6	0	25	1	0	0	1	1	0	.284	.328	.349	.676

Teoscar Hernandez

tay-OH-skar

Bats: R **Throws:** R **Pos:** LF-18;CF-5;RF-3;PH-2

Ht: 6'2" **Wt:** 180 **Born:** 10/15/1992 **Age:** 25

					BATTING																RUNNING			AVERAGES			
Year	Team	Lg	G	AB	H	2B	3B	HR	(Hm	Rd)	TB	R	RBI	RC	TBB	IBB	SO	HBP	SH	SF	SB	CS	GDP	Avg	OBP	Slg	OPS
2013 QuadC		A	123	499	135	25	9	13	(-	-)	217	97	55	74	41	0	135	4	17	4	24	11	8	.271	.328	.435	.763
2014 Lancst		A+	96	391	115	33	8	17	(-	-)	215	72	75	85	49	0	117	5	5	5	31	6	7	.294	.376	.550	.925
2014 CpChr		AA	23	95	27	4	1	4	(-	-)	45	12	10	12	2	0	36	0	1	0	2	3	1	.284	.299	.474	.773
2015 CpChr		AA	121	470	103	12	2	17	(-	-)	170	92	48	51	33	1	126	4	5	2	33	5	11	.219	.275	.362	.637
2016 CpChr		AA	69	279	85	19	0	6	(-	-)	122	53	30	50	32	0	55	5	3	2	29	11	2	.305	.384	.437	.821
2016 Fresno		AAA	38	144	45	9	3	4	(-	-)	72	20	23	26	13	0	25	0	0	3	5	4	3	.313	.365	.500	.865
2017 Fresno		AAA	79	301	84	20	3	12	(-	-)	146	54	44	55	39	2	72	5	0	2	12	7	7	.279	.369	.485	.854
2017 Buffalo		AAA	26	99	22	6	2	6	(-	-)	50	14	22	15	8	0	30	2	0	0	4	1	0	.222	.294	.505	.799
2016 Hou		AL	41	100	23	7	0	4	(1	3)	42	15	11	11	11	1	28	0	0	1	0	2	5	.230	.304	.420	.724
2017 2 Tms		AL	27	88	23	6	0	8	(5	3)	53	16	20	15	6	0	36	0	0	1	0	1	0	.261	.305	.602	.908
17 Hou		AL	1	0	0	0	0	0	(0	0)	0	0	0	0	0	0	0	0	0	0	0	0	0	-	-	-	-
17 Tor		AL	26	88	23	6	0	8	(5	3)	53	16	20	15	6	0	36	0	0	1	0	1	0	.261	.305	.602	.908
2 ML YEARS			68	188	46	13	0	12	(6	6)	95	31	31	26	17	1	64	0	0	2	0	3	5	.245	.304	.505	.810

Kelvin Herrera

Pitches: R Bats: R Pos: RP-64   Ht: 5'10" Wt: 200 Born: 12/31/1989 Age: 28

Year	Team	Lg	G	GS	CG	GF	IP	BFP	H	R	ER	HR	SH	SF	HB	TBB	IBB	SO	WP	Bk	W	L	Pct	Sh	Sv-Op	Hld	ERC	ERA
2011	KC	AL	2	0	0	0	2.0	9	2	3	3	1	1	0	1	0	0	0	0	0	0	1	.000	0	0-0	1	7.30	13.50
2012	KC	AL	76	0	0	10	84.1	344	79	24	22	4	5	0	2	21	6	77	3	1	4	3	.571	0	3-4	19	2.84	2.35
2013	KC	AL	59	0	0	16	58.1	245	48	27	25	9	0	3	2	21	2	74	5	0	5	7	.417	0	2-4	20	3.35	3.86
2014	KC	AL	70	0	0	12	70.0	285	54	12	11	0	4	0	3	26	0	59	1	0	4	3	.571	0	0-1	20	2.31	1.41
2015	KC	AL	72	0	0	8	69.2	286	52	23	21	5	1	5	2	26	1	64	4	0	4	3	.571	0	0-7	21	2.53	2.71
2016	KC	AL	72	0	0	23	72.0	283	57	23	22	6	1	1	3	12	0	86	3	0	2	6	.250	0	12-15	26	2.20	2.75
2017	KC	AL	64	0	0	48	59.1	259	60	33	28	9	1	2	1	20	2	56	2	0	3	3	.500	0	26-31	4	4.17	4.25
	Postseason		22	0	0	0	28.2	115	21	5	4	0	0	1	0	10	0	38	0	0	2	0	1.000	0	0-0	6	1.90	1.26
	7 ML YEARS		415	0	0	117	415.2	1711	352	145	132	34	13	11	14	126	11	416	18	1	22	26	.458	0	43-62	111	2.85	2.86

Odubel Herrera

Bats: L Throws: R Pos: CF-133;PH-7   oh-DOO-bull   Ht: 5'11" Wt: 205 Born: 12/29/1991 Age: 26

Year	Team	Lg	G	AB	H	2B	3B	HR	(Hm	Rd)	TB	R	RBI	RC	TBB	IBB	SO	HBP	SH	SF	SB	CS	GDP	Avg	OBP	Slg	OPS
2015	Phi	NL	147	495	147	30	3	8	(4	4)	207	64	41	66	28	0	129	8	5	1	16	8	6	.297	.344	.418	.762
2016	Phi	NL	159	583	167	21	6	15	(7	8)	245	87	49	93	63	7	134	6	2	2	25	7	6	.286	.361	.420	.781
2017	Phi	NL	138	526	148	42	3	14	(8	6)	238	67	56	63	31	4	126	4	0	2	8	5	13	.281	.325	.452	.778
	3 ML YEARS		444	1604	462	93	12	37	(19	18)	690	218	146	222	122	11	389	18	7	5	49	20	25	.288	.344	.430	.774

Ronald Herrera

Pitches: R Bats: R Pos: RP-2   Ht: 5'11" Wt: 185 Born: 5/3/1995 Age: 23

Year	Team	Lg	G	GS	CG	GF	IP	BFP	H	R	ER	HR	SH	SF	HB	TBB	IBB	SO	WP	Bk	W	L	Pct	Sh	Sv-Op	Hld	ERC	ERA
2013	2 Tms	Low	16	10	0	0	78.1	334	86	42	35	3	1	3	5	13	0	66	3	2	7	4	.636	0	0- -	-	3.50	4.02
2014	2 Tms	Low	26	25	0	0	132.2	566	146	71	58	11	4	8	11	25	0	82	4	2	6	9	.400	0	0- -	-	4.02	3.93
2015	Lk Els	A+	18	17	0	0	102.0	424	100	48	44	6	1	2	5	28	0	69	7	1	5	6	.455	0	0- -	-	3.45	3.88
2015	SnAnt	AA	8	8	1	0	43.2	195	48	25	22	4	0	4	3	14	0	35	1	1	3	1	.750	1	0- -	-	4.45	4.53
2016	Trntn	AA	23	23	0	0	132.0	549	131	61	55	9	0	2	4	35	0	123	4	0	10	7	.588	0	0- -	-	3.45	3.75
2017	Trntn	AA	9	9	0	0	56.0	211	34	10	7	2	1	0	2	12	0	42	1	0	8	0	1.000	0	0- -	-	1.39	1.13
2017	NYY	AL	2	0	0	1	3.0	14	3	2	2	1	0	0	1	1	0	3	0	0	0	1	.000	0	0-0	0	6.85	6.00

Chris Herrmann

Bats: L Throws: R Pos: C-45;PH-37;LF-22;PR-6;1B-5;RF-2   HERR-men   Ht: 6'0" Wt: 200 Born: 11/24/1987 Age: 30

Year	Team	Lg	G	AB	H	2B	3B	HR	(Hm	Rd)	TB	R	RBI	RC	TBB	IBB	SO	HBP	SH	SF	SB	CS	GDP	Avg	OBP	Slg	OPS
2012	Min	AL	7	18	1	0	0	0	(0	0)	1	0	1	0	1	0	5	0	0	0	0	0	0	.056	.105	.056	.161
2013	Min	AL	57	157	32	7	0	4	(1	3)	51	16	18	15	18	0	49	0	3	0	0	1	3	.204	.286	.325	.611
2014	Min	AL	33	75	16	3	0	0	(0	0)	19	8	4	5	4	0	17	0	0	0	1	0	2	.213	.253	.253	.506
2015	Min	AL	45	103	15	5	1	2	(2	0)	28	13	10	8	7	0	37	2	1	0	0	0	1	.146	.214	.272	.486
2016	Ari	NL	56	148	42	5	4	6	(3	3)	73	21	28	31	16	1	44	0	1	1	4	0	2	.284	.352	.493	.845
2017	Ari	NL	106	226	41	7	0	10	(7	3)	78	35	27	26	29	0	67	0	0	1	5	0	1	.181	.273	.345	.619
	6 ML YEARS		304	727	147	27	5	22	(13	9)	250	93	88	85	75	1	219	2	5	2	10	1	9	.202	.278	.344	.622

Chris Heston

Pitches: R Bats: R Pos: RP-2; SP-1   Ht: 6'3" Wt: 195 Born: 4/10/1988 Age: 30

Year	Team	Lg	G	GS	CG	GF	IP	BFP	H	R	ER	HR	SH	SF	HB	TBB	IBB	SO	WP	Bk	W	L	Pct	Sh	Sv-Op	Hld	ERC	ERA
2017	Tacom*	AAA	6	6	1	0	31.2	127	26	12	12	2	0	0	2	11	0	28	0	0	2	1	.667	1	0- -	-	3.04	3.41
2017	Roch*	AAA	8	6	0	0	27.0	143	56	32	30	8	0	3	0	15	0	12	2	0	0	3	.000	0	0- -	-	14.42	10.00
2014	SF	NL	3	1	0	2	5.1	24	6	3	3	0	0	1	0	3	0	4	1	0	0	0	-	0	0-0	0	4.74	5.06
2015	SF	NL	31	31	2	0	177.2	746	169	82	78	16	2	0	13	64	3	141	6	1	12	11	.522	1	0-0	0	3.94	3.95
2016	SF	NL	4	0	0	0	5.0	29	9	6	6	0	0	0	0	6	2	3	3	0	1	1	.500	0	0-0	0	10.88	10.80
2017	2 Tms	AL	3	1	0	0	6.0	38	15	12	11	3	0	0	0	5	0	3	0	0	0	1	.000	0	0-0	0	20.66	16.50
17	Sea	AL	2	1	0	0	5.0	34	14	12	11	3	0	0	0	5	0	3	0	0	0	1	.000	0	0-0	0	25.36	19.80
17	Min	AL	1	0	0	0	1.0	4	1	0	0	0	0	0	0	0	0	0	0	0	0	0	-	0	0-0	0	1.95	0.00
	4 ML YEARS		41	33	2	2	194.0	837	199	103	98	19	3	1	13	78	5	151	9	1	13	13	.500	1	0-0	0	4.53	4.55

Jason Heyward

Bats: L Throws: L Pos: RF-120;CF-13;PH-4   Ht: 6'5" Wt: 240 Born: 8/9/1989 Age: 28

Year	Team	Lg	G	AB	H	2B	3B	HR	(Hm	Rd)	TB	R	RBI	RC	TBB	IBB	SO	HBP	SH	SF	SB	CS	GDP	Avg	OBP	Slg	OPS
2010	Atl	NL	142	520	144	29	5	18	(9	9)	237	83	72	96	91	2	128	10	0	2	11	6	13	.277	.393	.456	.849
2011	Atl	NL	128	396	90	18	2	14	(5	9)	154	50	42	49	51	4	93	4	0	3	9	2	7	.227	.319	.389	.708
2012	Atl	NL	158	587	158	30	6	27	(9	18)	281	93	82	87	58	1	152	2	0	3	21	8	5	.269	.335	.479	.814
2013	Atl	NL	104	382	97	22	1	14	(10	4)	163	67	38	55	48	1	73	8	1	0	2	4	7	.254	.349	.427	.776
2014	Atl	NL	149	573	155	26	3	11	(5	6)	220	74	58	84	67	3	98	6	0	3	20	4	2	.271	.351	.384	.735
2015	StL	NL	154	547	160	33	4	13	(5	8)	240	79	60	78	56	4	90	2	0	3	23	3	13	.293	.359	.439	.797
2016	ChC	NL	142	530	122	27	1	7	(3	4)	172	61	49	53	54	0	93	5	1	2	11	4	12	.230	.306	.325	.631
2017	ChC	NL	126	432	112	15	4	11	(4	7)	168	59	59	60	41	1	67	3	2	2	4	4	8	.259	.326	.389	.715
	Postseason		29	101	16	3	1	2	(0	2)	27	7	7	5	4	1	31	1	0	0	4	0	2	.158	.198	.267	.465
	8 ML YEARS		1103	3967	1038	200	26	115	(50	65)	1635	566	460	562	466	16	794	40	4	18	101	35	67	.262	.344	.412	.756

Aaron Hicks

Bats: B **Throws:** R **Pos:** CF-52;LF-22;RF-14;PH-11 · **Ht:** 6'1" **Wt:** 202 **Born:** 10/2/1989 **Age:** 28

Year	Team	Lg	G	AB	H	2B	3B	HR	(Hm	Rd)	TB	R	RBI	RC	TBB	IBB	SO	HBP	SH	SF	SB	CS	GDP	Avg	OBP	Slg	OPS
2013	Min	AL	81	281	54	11	3	8	(3	5)	95	37	27	25	24	0	84	2	4	2	9	3	0	.192	.259	.338	.597
2014	Min	AL	69	186	40	8	0	1	(0	1)	51	22	18	22	36	0	56	0	2	1	4	3	2	.215	.341	.274	.615
2015	Min	AL	97	352	90	11	3	11	(6	5)	140	48	33	45	34	2	66	2	0	2	13	3	6	.256	.323	.398	.721
2016	NYY	AL	123	327	71	13	1	8	(7	1)	110	32	31	28	30	1	68	0	1	3	3	4	7	.217	.281	.336	.617
2017	NYY	AL	88	301	80	18	0	15	(12	3)	143	54	52	52	51	0	67	3	1	5	10	5	8	.266	.372	.475	.847
	5 ML YEARS		458	1447	335	61	7	43	(28	15)	539	193	161	172	175	3	341	7	8	13	39	18	23	.232	.315	.372	.687

John Hicks

Bats: R **Throws:** R **Pos:** 1B-26;C-18;DH-12;PH-11 · **Ht:** 6'2" **Wt:** 230 **Born:** 8/31/1989 **Age:** 28

Year	Team	Lg	G	AB	H	2B	3B	HR	(Hm	Rd)	TB	R	RBI	RC	TBB	IBB	SO	HBP	SH	SF	SB	CS	GDP	Avg	OBP	Slg	OPS
2017	Toledo*	AAA	52	208	56	10	1	7	(-	-)	89	21	35	25	4	0	54	1	1	4	5	3	7	.269	.281	.428	.709
2015	Sea	AL	17	32	2	1	0	0	(0	0)	3	1	1	0	1	0	18	0	1	0	1	1	0	.063	.091	.094	.185
2016	Det	AL	1	2	1	1	0	0	(0	0)	2	1	0	0	0	0	0	0	0	0	0	0	0	.500	.500	1.000	1.500
2017	Det	AL	60	173	46	12	0	6	(3	3)	76	25	22	25	13	0	51	3	0	1	2	1	5	.266	.326	.439	.766
	3 ML YEARS		78	207	49	14	0	6	(3	3)	81	27	23	25	14	0	69	3	1	1	3	2	5	.237	.293	.391	.685

Kyle Higashioka

Bats: R **Throws:** R **Pos:** C-8;DH-1;PH-1 · hig-ah-shee-oh-kah · **Ht:** 6'1" **Wt:** 200 **Born:** 4/20/1990 **Age:** 28

Year	Team	Lg	G	AB	H	2B	3B	HR	(Hm	Rd)	TB	R	RBI	RC	TBB	IBB	SO	HBP	SH	SF	SB	CS	GDP	Avg	OBP	Slg	OPS
2014	2 Tms	Low	17	49	11	4	0	1	(-	-)	18	8	3	6	7	0	11	0	0	2	0	0	1	.224	.310	.367	.678
2015	Tampa	A+	88	307	78	18	2	5	(-	-)	115	25	36	36	22	0	49	1	0	1	0	0	3	.254	.305	.375	.680
2016	Trntn	AA	63	222	65	15	0	11	(-	-)	113	31	51	41	26	0	42	0	0	8	0	1	7	.293	.355	.509	.864
2016	S-WB	AAA	39	148	37	9	0	10	(-	-)	76	24	30	23	12	2	31	0	0	0	0	1	3	.250	.306	.514	.820
2017	S-WB	AAA	14	53	14	4	0	2	(-	-)	24	5	11	7	4	0	7	0	0	0	0	0	0	.264	.316	.453	.769
2017	NYY	AL	9	18	0	0	0	0	(0	0)	0	2	0	0	2	0	6	0	0	0	0	0	0	.000	.100	.000	.100

Trevor Hildenberger

Pitches: R **Bats:** R **Pos:** RP-37 · **Ht:** 6'2" **Wt:** 211 **Born:** 12/15/1990 **Age:** 27

			HOW MUCH HE PITCHED						WHAT HE GAVE UP											THE RESULTS						
Year	Team	Lg	G	GS	CG	GF	IP	BFP	H	R	ER	HR	SH	SF	HB	TBB	IBB	SO	WP	Bk	W	L	Pct	Sh	Sv-Op	Hld	ERC	ERA
2014	2 Tms	Low	24	0	0	23	29.0	122	27	12	8	1	2	0	1	5	2	32	0	0	1	4	.200	0	10--	-	2.36	2.48
2015	2 Tms	Low	41	0	0	32	64.0	238	39	13	11	0	5	2	2	7	0	80	4	0	3	2	.600	0	17--	-	1.03	1.55
2016	FtMyrs	A+	6	0	0	5	9.1	39	11	2	1	0	0	0	0	0	0	8	0	0	1	1	.500	0	3--	-	2.78	0.96
2016	Chatt	AA	32	0	0	29	38.2	144	21	4	3	2	3	0	1	6	1	45	0	0	2	3	.400	0	16--	-	1.08	0.70
2017	Roch	AAA	21	0	0	10	30.2	126	27	7	7	1	1	1	1	8	1	35	1	0	2	1	.667	0	6--	-	2.55	2.05
2017	Min	AL	37	0	0	8	42.0	170	38	15	15	4	1	1	4	6	2	44	1	0	3	3	.500	0	1-3	12	2.87	3.21

Aaron Hill

Bats: R **Throws:** R **Pos:** PH-18;2B-7;3B-7;LF-6 · **Ht:** 5'11" **Wt:** 200 **Born:** 3/21/1982 **Age:** 36

Year	Team	Lg	G	AB	H	2B	3B	HR	(Hm	Rd)	TB	R	RBI	RC	TBB	IBB	SO	HBP	SH	SF	SB	CS	GDP	Avg	OBP	Slg	OPS
2005	Tor	AL	105	361	99	25	3	3	(3	0)	139	49	40	50	34	0	41	5	3	4	2	1	5	.274	.342	.385	.727
2006	Tor	AL	155	546	159	28	3	6	(4	2)	211	70	50	68	42	5	66	9	4	5	5	2	15	.291	.349	.386	.735
2007	Tor	AL	160	608	177	47	2	17	(8	9)	279	87	78	88	41	1	102	0	3	5	4	3	21	.291	.333	.459	.792
2008	Tor	AL	55	205	54	14	0	2	(1	1)	74	19	20	24	16	0	31	3	4	1	4	2	4	.263	.324	.361	.685
2009	Tor	AL	158	682	195	37	0	36	(21	15)	340	103	108	110	42	1	98	5	1	4	6	2	17	.286	.330	.499	.829
2010	Tor	AL	138	528	108	22	0	26	(15	11)	208	70	68	57	41	2	85	8	1	2	2	2	9	.205	.271	.394	.665
2011	2 Tms		137	520	128	27	3	8	(4	4)	185	61	61	61	35	1	72	7	2	7	21	7	10	.246	.299	.356	.655
2012	Ari	NL	156	609	184	44	6	26	(14	12)	318	93	85	101	52	7	86	4	1	2	14	5	15	.302	.360	.522	.882
2013	Ari	NL	87	327	95	21	1	11	(7	4)	151	45	44	45	29	2	48	5	0	1	1	4	6	.291	.356	.462	.818
2014	Ari	NL	133	501	122	26	3	10	(6	4)	184	45	60	57	28	0	92	6	0	7	4	3	16	.244	.287	.367	.654
2015	Ari	NL	116	313	72	18	0	6	(3	3)	108	32	39	30	31	0	54	1	0	8	7	2	9	.230	.295	.345	.640
2016	2 Tms		125	378	99	14	0	10	(3	7)	143	48	38	47	41	2	59	3	0	4	4	2	6	.262	.336	.378	.714
2017	SF	NL	34	68	9	2	1	1	(0	1)	16	7	7	3	11	0	13	0	0	1	0	0	2	.132	.250	.235	.485
11	Tor	AL	104	396	89	15	1	6	(3	3)	124	38	45	38	23	1	53	4	0	6	16	3	8	.225	.270	.313	.584
11	Ari	NL	33	124	39	12	2	2	(1	1)	61	23	16	23	12	0	19	3	2	1	5	4	2	.315	.386	.492	.878
16	Mil	NL	78	254	72	11	0	8	(3	5)	107	34	29	36	30	0	43	2	0	4	4	2	5	.283	.359	.421	.780
16	Bos	AL	47	124	27	3	0	2	(0	2)	36	14	9	11	11	2	16	1	0	0	0	0	1	.218	.287	.290	.577
	Postseason		6	19	5	0	0	1	(1	0)	8	3	1	2	5	0	4	0	0	0	0	0	1	.263	.417	.421	.838
	13 ML YEARS		1559	5646	1501	325	22	162	(89	73)	2356	736	695	732	443	21	847	55	19	51	74	35	134	.266	.323	.417	.740

Rich Hill

Pitches: L **Bats:** L **Pos:** SP-25 · **Ht:** 6'5" **Wt:** 220 **Born:** 3/11/1980 **Age:** 38

			HOW MUCH HE PITCHED						WHAT HE GAVE UP											THE RESULTS						
Year	Team	Lg	G	GS	CG	GF	IP	BFP	H	R	ER	HR	SH	SF	HB	TBB	IBB	SO	WP	Bk	W	L	Pct	Sh	Sv-Op	Hld	ERC	ERA
2005	ChC	NL	10	4	0	1	23.2	115	25	24	24	3	1	0	1	17	1	21	0	0	0	2	.000	0	0-0	0	5.81	9.13
2006	ChC	NL	17	16	2	1	99.1	417	83	51	46	16	8	3	2	39	1	90	3	0	6	7	.462	1	0-0	0	3.59	4.17
2007	ChC	NL	32	32	0	0	195.0	812	170	89	85	27	9	4	12	63	3	183	1	1	11	8	.579	0	0-0	0	3.56	3.92
2008	ChC	NL	5	5	0	0	19.2	89	13	9	9	2	0	2	1	18	0	15	1	0	1	0	1.000	0	0-0	0	4.38	4.12
2009	Bal	AL	14	13	0	0	57.2	275	68	53	50	7	2	2	1	40	2	46	1	1	3	3	.500	0	0-0	0	6.55	7.80

			HOW MUCH HE PITCHED						WHAT HE GAVE UP												THE RESULTS							
Year	Team	Lg	G	GS	CG	GF	IP	BFP	H	R	ER	HR	SH	SF	HB	TBB	IBB	SO	WP	Bk	W	L	Pct	Sh	Sv-Op	Hld	ERC	ERA
2010	Bos	AL	6	0	0	0	4.0	18	5	0	0	0	0	0	0	1	0	3	1	0	1	0	1.000	0	0-0	1	4.05	0.00
2011	Bos	AL	9	0	0	3	8.0	30	3	0	0	0	0	0	1	3	0	12	1	0	0	0	-	0	0-0	3	1.10	0.00
2012	Bos	AL	25	0	0	3	19.2	83	17	4	4	0	0	0	0	11	1	21	0	0	1	0	1.000	0	0-0	6	3.24	1.83
2013	Cle	AL	63	0	0	3	38.2	182	38	30	27	3	1	2	2	29	6	51	6	1	1	2	.333	0	0-2	13	5.07	6.28
2014	2 Tms	AL	16	0	0	2	5.1	29	7	2	2	0	0	0	1	6	1	9	1	0	0	0	-	0	0-0	1	8.55	3.38
2015	Bos	AL	4	4	1	0	29.0	106	14	5	5	2	0	0	2	5	0	36	0	0	2	1	.667	1	0-0	0	1.13	1.55
2016	2 Tms		20	20	0	0	110.1	439	77	29	26	4	1	2	8	33	0	129	0	0	12	5	.706	0	0-0	0	2.04	2.12
2017	LAD	NL	25	25	1	0	135.2	552	99	51	50	18	4	2	9	49	1	166	2	1	12	8	.600	0	0-0	0	2.96	3.32
	14 LAA	AL	2	0	0	0	0.0	4	1	1	1	0	0	0	0	3	0	1	1	0	0	0	-	0	0-0	0		
	14 NYY	AL	14	0	0	2	5.1	25	6	1	1	0	0	0	1	3	1	9	0	0	0	0	-	0	0-0	1	5.10	1.69
	16 Oak	AL	14	14	0	0	76.0	311	55	22	19	2	0	1	8	28	0	90	0	0	9	3	.750	0	0-0	0	2.44	2.25
	16 LAD	AL	6	6	0	0	34.1	128	22	7	7	2	1	1	0	5	0	39	0	0	3	2	.600	0	0-0	0	1.34	1.83
	Postseason		4	4	0	0	16.0	75	17	8	8	2	0	0	3	8	1	22	0	0	1	2	.333	0	0-0	0	5.63	4.50
	13 ML YEARS		246	119	4	13	746.0	3147	619	347	328	82	26	17	40	314	16	782	16	4	50	36	.581	2	0-2	24	3.47	3.96

Jeff Hoffman

Pitches: R Bats: R Pos: SP-16; RP-7　　　　　　**Ht: 6'5" Wt: 225 Born: 1/8/1993 Age: 25**

			HOW MUCH HE PITCHED						WHAT HE GAVE UP												THE RESULTS							
Year	Team	Lg	G	GS	CG	GF	IP	BFP	H	R	ER	HR	SH	SF	HB	TBB	IBB	SO	WP	Bk	W	L	Pct	Sh	Sv-Op	Hld	ERC	ERA
2015	Dnedin	A+	11	11	0	0	56.0	227	59	20	20	4	1	1	3	15	0	38	6	0	3	3	.500	0	0- -	-	4.11	3.21
2015	NwBrit	AA	7	7	0	0	36.1	143	27	14	13	3	1	1	2	10	1	29	1	0	2	2	.500	0	0- -	-	2.39	3.22
2016	Albq	AAA	22	22	0	0	118.2	512	117	60	53	11	3	9	7	44	0	124	5	0	6	9	.400	0	0- -	-	4.07	4.02
2017	Albq	AAA	10	10	0	0	49.2	219	44	31	26	3	3	2	5	19	0	47	8	0	3	3	.500	0	0- -	-	3.37	4.71
2016	Col	NL	8	6	0	0	31.1	147	37	29	17	7	1	0	0	17	1	22	4	0	0	4	.000	0	0-0	0	6.55	4.88
2017	Col	NL	23	16	0	3	99.1	440	106	66	65	15	3	5	4	40	1	82	2	0	6	5	.545	0	0-0	0	4.97	5.89
	2 ML YEARS		31	22	0	3	130.2	587	143	95	82	22	4	5	4	57	2	104	6	0	6	9	.400	0	0-0	0	5.34	5.65

Bryan Holaday

Bats: R Throws: R Pos: C-11;PH-2;2B-1;DH-1　　　HAHL-ih-daye　　　**Ht: 6'0" Wt: 205 Born: 11/19/1987 Age: 30**

			BATTING																	RUNNING			AVERAGES			
Year	Team	Lg	G	AB	H	2B	3B	HR	(Hm	Rd)	TB	R	RBI	RC	TBB	IBB	SO	HBP	SH	SF	SB	CS	GDP	Avg	OBP	Slg	OPS
2017	Toledo*	AAA	93	309	83	20	0	12	(- | -)	139	31	50	46	22	0	54	6	5	5	0	0	3	9	.269	.325	.450	.774
2012	Det	AL	6	12	3	1	0	0	(0 | 0)	4	3	0	1	0	0	2	0	1	0	0	0	0	0	.250	.250	.333	.583
2013	Det	AL	16	27	8	1	0	1	(1 | 0)	12	8	2	3	2	0	3	1	3	0	0	0	0	0	.296	.367	.444	.811
2014	Det	AL	62	156	36	5	1	0	(0	0)	43	14	15	11	8	0	37	1	2	4	1	1	4	.231	.266	.276	.542
2015	Det	AL	24	64	18	5	0	2	(1	1)	29	3	13	9	1	0	13	0	0	0	0	0	0	.281	.292	.453	.745
2016	2 Tms	AL	44	117	27	7	1	2	(1	1)	42	17	14	14	7	0	28	2	1	2	0	1	1	.231	.281	.359	.640
2017	Det	AL	13	29	7	2	0	0	(0	0)	9	1	2	2	0	0	1	0	0	0	0	0	2	.241	.241	.310	.552
	16 Tex	AL	30	84	20	6	1	2	(1	1)	34	14	13	12	5	0	16	2	1	2	0	1	0	.238	.290	.405	.695
	16 Bos	AL	14	33	7	1	0	0	(0	0)	8	3	1	2	2	0	12	0	0	0	0	0	1	.212	.257	.242	.500
	Postseason		1	2	0	0	0	0	(0	0)	0	0	0	0	0	0	1	0	0	0	0	0	0	.000	.000	.000	.000
	6 ML YEARS		165	405	99	21	2	5	(3	2)	139	46	46	40	18	0	84	4	7	6	1	2	7	.244	.279	.343	.623

Jonathan Holder

Pitches: R Bats: R Pos: RP-37　　　　　　**Ht: 6'2" Wt: 235 Born: 6/9/1993 Age: 25**

			HOW MUCH HE PITCHED						WHAT HE GAVE UP												THE RESULTS							
Year	Team	Lg	G	GS	CG	GF	IP	BFP	H	R	ER	HR	SH	SF	HB	TBB	IBB	SO	WP	Bk	W	L	Pct	Sh	Sv-Op	Hld	ERC	ERA
2014	2 Tms	Low	12	8	0	0	36.1	154	42	21	16	1	1	1	0	13	0	34	3	0	2	3	.400	0	0- -	-	4.45	3.96
2015	2 Tms	Low	22	21	1	1	112.1	457	97	34	29	3	2	2	5	21	0	86	2	0	7	5	.583	0	0- -	-	2.25	2.32
2016	Trntn	AA	28	0	0	21	41.0	155	27	10	10	2	0	1	3	7	0	59	0	0	3	1	.750	0	10- -	-	1.60	2.20
2016	S-WB	AAA	12	0	0	11	20.1	68	7	2	2	1	0	0	0	0	0	35	0	0	2	0	1.000	0	6- -	-	0.35	0.89
2017	S-WB	AAA	12	0	0	4	16.0	70	15	3	3	1	0	1	1	8	0	21	0	0	0	0	-	0	1- -	-	4.11	1.69
2016	NYY	AL	8	0	0	1	8.1	36	8	5	5	1	0	1	0	4	0	5	0	0	0	0	-	0	0-0	0	4.34	5.40
2017	NYY	AL	37	0	0	12	39.1	171	45	17	17	5	1	0	3	8	1	40	2	0	1	1	.500	0	0-2	3	4.54	3.89
	2 ML YEARS		45	0	0	13	47.2	207	53	22	22	6	1	1	3	12	1	45	2	0	1	1	.500	0	0-2	3	4.51	4.15

Derek Holland

Pitches: L Bats: B Pos: SP-26; RP-3　　　　　　**Ht: 6'2" Wt: 215 Born: 10/9/1986 Age: 31**

			HOW MUCH HE PITCHED						WHAT HE GAVE UP												THE RESULTS							
Year	Team	Lg	G	GS	CG	GF	IP	BFP	H	R	ER	HR	SH	SF	HB	TBB	IBB	SO	WP	Bk	W	L	Pct	Sh	Sv-Op	Hld	ERC	ERA
2009	Tex	AL	33	21	1	0	138.1	611	160	98	94	26	2	3	4	47	0	107	3	3	8	13	.381	1	0-1	2	5.52	6.12
2010	Tex	AL	14	10	0	2	57.1	253	55	30	26	6	0	2	4	24	0	54	0	1	3	4	.429	0	0-0	1	4.17	4.08
2011	Tex	AL	32	32	4	0	198.0	843	201	97	87	22	1	3	6	67	1	162	2	1	16	5	.762	4	0-0	0	4.15	3.95
2012	Tex	AL	29	27	0	1	175.1	730	162	100	91	32	5	4	3	52	0	145	1	0	12	7	.632	0	0-0	0	3.86	4.67
2013	Tex	AL	33	33	2	0	213.0	894	210	90	81	20	8	9	3	64	0	189	9	1	10	9	.526	2	0-0	0	3.64	3.42
2014	Tex	AL	6	5	0	0	37.0	145	34	8	6	0	2	1	0	5	1	25	1	0	2	0	1.000	0	0-0	0	2.07	1.46
2015	Tex	AL	10	10	1	0	58.2	245	59	32	32	11	3	1	5	17	2	41	1	0	4	3	.571	1	0-0	0	4.71	4.91
2016	Tex	AL	22	20	0	0	107.1	461	116	62	59	15	1	2	2	35	2	67	2	0	7	9	.438	0	0-0	0	4.61	4.95
2017	CWS	AL	29	26	0	0	135.0	626	156	106	93	31	1	3	8	75	2	104	7	0	7	14	.333	0	0-0	0	6.96	6.20
	Postseason		14	5	0	2	37.2	161	37	23	21	10	0	0	1	16	0	24	2	0	3	1	.750	0	0-0	2	5.47	5.02
	9 ML YEARS		208	184	8	3	1120.0	4808	1153	623	569	163	23	28	35	386	8	894	26	6	69	64	.519	8	0-1	3	4.48	4.57

Greg Holland

Pitches: R **Bats:** R **Pos:** RP-61   **Ht:** 5'10" **Wt:** 205 **Born:** 11/20/1985 **Age:** 32

Year Team	Lg	G	GS	CG	GF	IP	BFP	H	R	ER	HR	SH	SF	HB	TBB	IBB	SO	WP	Bk	W	L	Pct	Sh	Sv-Op	Hld	ERC	ERA
2010 KC	AL	15	0	0	10	18.2	87	23	15	14	3	1	0	0	8	0	23	2	0	0	1	.000	0	0-0	0	5.88	6.75
2011 KC	AL	46	0	0	15	60.0	233	37	13	12	3	1	1	1	19	3	74	7	0	5	1	.833	0	4-6	18	1.60	1.80
2012 KC	AL	67	0	0	36	67.0	289	58	22	22	2	4	3	0	34	7	91	3	1	7	4	.636	0	16-20	9	3.07	2.96
2013 KC	AL	68	0	0	61	67.0	255	40	11	9	3	1	1	0	18	1	103	2	0	2	1	.667	0	47-50	1	1.41	1.21
2014 KC	AL	65	0	0	60	62.1	240	37	13	10	3	1	1	0	20	0	90	9	0	1	3	.250	0	46-48	0	1.54	1.44
2015 KC	AL	48	0	0	40	44.2	193	39	20	19	2	3	1	0	26	1	49	7	0	3	2	.600	0	32-37	5	3.68	3.83
2017 Col	NL	61	0	0	58	57.1	235	40	24	23	7	0	1	1	26	1	70	7	0	3	6	.333	0	**41-45**	1	2.86	3.61
Postseason		11	0	0	10	11.0	43	4	1	1	0	0	0	0	5	1	15	0	0	0	0	-	0	7-7	0	0.86	0.82
7 ML YEARS		370	0	0	280	377.0	1532	274	118	109	23	11	8	2	151	13	500	37	1	21	18	.538	0	186-206	29	2.37	2.60

Header spanning: HOW MUCH HE PITCHED | WHAT HE GAVE UP | THE RESULTS

Matt Holliday

Bats: R **Throws:** R **Pos:** DH-90;1B-8;PH-8   **Ht:** 6'4" **Wt:** 240 **Born:** 1/15/1980 **Age:** 38

Year Team	Lg	G	AB	H	2B	3B	HR	(Hm	Rd)	TB	R	RBI	RC	TBB	IBB	SO	HBP	SH	SF	SB	CS	GDP	Avg	OBP	Slg	OPS
2004 Col	NL	121	400	116	31	3	14	(10	4)	195	65	57	61	31	0	86	6	1	1	3	3	9	.290	.349	.488	.837
2005 Col	NL	125	479	147	24	7	19	(12	7)	242	68	87	88	36	1	79	7	0	4	14	3	11	.307	.361	.505	.866
2006 Col	NL	155	602	196	45	5	34	(22	12)	353	119	114	112	47	3	110	15	0	3	10	5	22	.326	.387	.586	.973
2007 Col	NL	158	636	**216**	50	6	36	(25	11)	**386**	120	**137**	134	63	7	126	10	0	4	11	4	23	**.340**	.405	.607	1.012
2008 Col	NL	139	539	173	38	2	25	(15	10)	290	107	88	104	74	6	104	8	0	2	28	2	9	.321	.409	.538	.947
2009 2 Tms		156	581	182	39	3	24	(16	8)	299	94	109	112	72	8	101	10	0	7	14	7	13	.313	.394	.515	.909
2010 StL	NL	158	596	186	45	1	28	(13	15)	317	95	103	107	69	10	93	8	0	2	9	5	13	.312	.390	.532	.922
2011 StL	NL	124	446	132	36	0	22	(12	10)	234	83	75	81	60	4	93	8	0	2	2	1	21	.296	.388	.525	.912
2012 StL	NL	157	599	177	36	2	27	(13	14)	298	95	102	99	75	3	132	9	0	5	4	4	16	.295	.379	.497	.877
2013 StL	NL	141	520	156	31	1	22	(14	8)	255	103	94	99	69	5	86	9	0	4	6	1	**31**	.300	.389	.490	.879
2014 StL	NL	156	574	156	37	0	20	(13	7)	253	83	90	97	74	4	100	17	0	2	4	1	20	.272	.370	.441	.811
2015 StL	NL	73	229	64	16	1	4	(0	4)	94	24	35	44	39	5	49	6	0	3	2	1	9	.279	.394	.410	.804
2016 StL	NL	110	382	94	20	1	20	(9	11)	176	48	62	51	35	1	71	8	0	1	0	0	9	.246	.322	.461	.782
2017 NYY	AL	105	373	86	18	0	19	(11	8)	161	50	64	54	46	0	114	3	0	5	1	0	14	.231	.316	.432	.748
09 Oak	AL	93	346	99	23	1	11	(7	4)	157	52	54	62	46	3	58	6	0	2	12	3	8	.286	.378	.454	.831
09 StL	NL	63	235	83	16	2	13	(9	4)	142	42	55	50	26	5	43	4	0	5	2	4	5	.353	.419	.604	1.023
Postseason		72	279	69	9	1	13	(5	8)	119	42	37	31	17	0	58	6	0	0	1	1	5	.247	.305	.427	.731
14 ML YEARS		1878	6956	2081	466	32	314	(185	129)	3553	1154	1217	1243	790	57	1344	124	1	45	108	37	220	.299	.378	.511	.889

Header spanning: BATTING | RUNNING | AVERAGES

David Holmberg

Pitches: L **Bats:** R **Pos:** RP-30; SP-7   **Ht:** 6'3" **Wt:** 245 **Born:** 7/19/1991 **Age:** 26

Year Team	Lg	G	GS	CG	GF	IP	BFP	H	R	ER	HR	SH	SF	HB	TBB	IBB	SO	WP	Bk	W	L	Pct	Sh	Sv-Op	Hld	ERC	ERA
2017 Charllt*	AAA	10	4	0	1	32.1	126	26	10	10	4	0	1	0	8	0	24	0	0	3	1	.750	0	0- -	-	2.69	2.78
2013 Ari	NL	1	1	0	0	3.2	20	6	3	3	0	0	1	0	3	0	0	0	0	0	0	-	0	0-0	0	8.70	7.36
2014 Cin	NL	7	5	0	1	30.0	137	27	16	16	8	2	2	6	16	1	18	2	0	2	2	.500	0	0-0	0	6.03	4.80
2015 Cin	NL	6	6	0	0	28.1	136	36	24	24	10	4	2	2	16	0	15	1	0	1	4	.200	0	0-0	0	8.86	7.62
2017 CWS	AL	37	7	0	10	57.2	272	63	37	30	12	0	3	6	34	3	33	3	0	2	4	.333	0	0-1	0	6.56	4.68
4 ML YEARS		51	19	0	11	119.2	565	132	80	73	30	6	8	14	69	4	66	6	0	5	10	.333	0	0-1	0	7.02	5.49

Header spanning: HOW MUCH HE PITCHED | WHAT HE GAVE UP | THE RESULTS

Brock Holt

Bats: L **Throws:** R **Pos:** 2B-31;LF-10;PH-10;3B-9;PR-9;DH-3;1B-2;RF-2   **Ht:** 5'10" **Wt:** 180 **Born:** 6/11/1988 **Age:** 30

Year Team	Lg	G	AB	H	2B	3B	HR	(Hm	Rd)	TB	R	RBI	RC	TBB	IBB	SO	HBP	SH	SF	SB	CS	GDP	Avg	OBP	Slg	OPS
2017 Pwtckt*	AAA	20	70	15	1	0	3	(-	-)	25	9	9	7	6	0	14	1	0	0	0	0	0	.214	.286	.357	.643
2012 Pit	NL	24	65	19	2	1	0	(0	0)	23	6	3	10	4	0	14	0	2	1	0	0	1	.292	.329	.354	.682
2013 Bos	AL	26	59	12	2	0	0	(0	0)	14	9	11	7	7	0	4	0	3	3	1	0	0	.203	.275	.237	.513
2014 Bos	AL	106	449	126	23	5	4	(1	3)	171	68	29	56	33	0	98	2	5	3	12	2	7	.281	.331	.381	.711
2015 Bos	AL	129	454	127	27	6	2	(1	1)	172	56	45	65	46	0	97	3	4	2	8	1	7	.280	.349	.379	.727
2016 Bos	AL	94	290	74	16	0	7	(4	3)	111	45	34	36	27	0	58	3	1	3	4	3	5	.255	.322	.383	.705
2017 Bos	AL	64	140	28	6	0	0	(0	0)	34	20	5	7	12	0	34	3	0	2	2	1	3	.200	.305	.243	.548
Postseason		3	10	4	1	0	1	(0	1)	8	1	1	2	0	0	2	0	0	0	0	0	0	.400	.400	.800	1.200
6 ML YEARS		443	1457	386	76	12	13	(6	7)	525	204	129	186	136	0	305	11	15	14	27	7	23	.265	.329	.360	.690

Header spanning: BATTING | RUNNING | AVERAGES

J.J. Hoover

Pitches: R **Bats:** R **Pos:** RP-52   **Ht:** 6'3" **Wt:** 240 **Born:** 8/13/1987 **Age:** 30

Year Team	Lg	G	GS	CG	GF	IP	BFP	H	R	ER	HR	SH	SF	HB	TBB	IBB	SO	WP	Bk	W	L	Pct	Sh	Sv-Op	Hld	ERC	ERA
2017 Reno*	AAA	9	0	0	2	10.1	41	6	1	1	1	0	0	0	7	0	12	0	0	0	0	-	0	0- -	-	3.05	0.87
2012 Cin	NL	28	0	0	6	30.2	123	17	7	7	2	2	2	0	13	1	31	0	0	1	0	1.000	0	1-2	1	1.64	2.05
2013 Cin	NL	69	0	0	23	66.0	269	47	21	21	6	3	3	2	26	6	67	1	0	5	5	.500	0	3-5	13	2.46	2.86
2014 Cin	NL	54	0	0	22	62.2	275	56	36	34	13	1	5	1	31	3	75	0	0	1	10	.091	0	0-4	4	4.52	4.88
2015 Cin	NL	67	0	0	12	64.1	264	44	24	21	7	5	2	2	31	1	52	3	0	8	2	.800	0	1-7	18	2.87	2.94
2016 Cin	NL	18	0	0	8	18.2	97	29	29	28	9	0	0	1	12	1	15	0	0	1	2	.333	0	1-2	1	12.20	13.50
2017 Ari	NL	52	0	0	8	41.1	197	47	20	18	7	0	0	1	26	1	54	1	0	3	1	.750	0	0-2	10	6.32	3.92
Postseason		3	0	0	0	3.1	10	0	0	0	0	0	0	0	2	0	2	0	0	0	0	-	0	0-0	0	0.45	0.00
6 ML YEARS		288	0	0	79	283.2	1225	240	137	129	44	11	12	7	139	13	294	5	0	19	20	.487	0	6-22	44	3.94	4.09

Header spanning: HOW MUCH HE PITCHED | WHAT HE GAVE UP | THE RESULTS

Rhys Hoskins

Bats: R **Throws:** R **Pos:** LF-30;1B-27   rees   **Ht:** 6'4" **Wt:** 225 **Born:** 3/17/1993 **Age:** 25

								BATTING												RUNNING			AVERAGES			
Year	Team	Lg	G	AB	H	2B	3B	HR	(Hm | Rd)	TB	R	RBI	RC	TBB	IBB	SO	HBP	SH	SF	SB	CS	GDP	Avg	OBP	Slg	OPS
2014	Wmspt	A-	70	245	58	15	0	9	(- | -)	100	30	40	32	21	1	54	6	0	1	3	3	6	.237	.311	.408	.720
2015	2 Tms	Low	135	498	159	36	6	17	(- | -)	258	86	90	101	55	2	99	10	0	4	4	4	11	.319	.395	.518	.913
2016	Rdng	AA	135	498	140	26	1	38	(- | -)	282	95	116	108	71	1	125	11	0	9	8	3	7	.281	.377	.566	.943
2017	LV	AAA	115	401	114	24	4	29	(- | -)	233	78	91	90	64	0	75	5	0	5	4	2	8	.284	.385	.581	.966
2017	Phi	NL	50	170	44	7	0	18	(10 | 8)	105	37	48	45	37	1	46	3	0	2	2	0	2	.259	.396	.618	1.014

Eric Hosmer

Bats: L **Throws:** L **Pos:** 1B-157;DH-5;PH-1   HOZZ-mer   **Ht:** 6'4" **Wt:** 225 **Born:** 10/24/1989 **Age:** 28

								BATTING												RUNNING			AVERAGES			
Year	Team	Lg	G	AB	H	2B	3B	HR	(Hm | Rd)	TB	R	RBI	RC	TBB	IBB	SO	HBP	SH	SF	SB	CS	GDP	Avg	OBP	Slg	OPS
2011	KC	AL	128	523	153	27	3	19	(3 | 16)	243	66	78	71	34	7	82	1	0	5	11	5	13	.293	.334	.465	.799
2012	KC	AL	152	535	124	22	2	14	(8 | 6)	192	65	60	61	56	4	95	2	0	5	16	1	10	.232	.304	.359	.663
2013	KC	AL	159	623	188	34	3	17	(10 | 7)	279	86	79	88	51	4	100	1	1	4	11	4	15	.302	.353	.448	.801
2014	KC	AL	131	503	136	35	1	9	(5 | 4)	200	54	58	62	35	4	93	3	0	6	4	2	12	.270	.318	.398	.716
2015	KC	AL	158	599	178	33	5	18	(10 | 8)	275	98	93	94	61	6	108	3	1	3	7	3	16	.297	.363	.459	.822
2016	KC	AL	158	605	161	24	1	25	(8 | 17)	262	80	104	87	57	5	132	1	0	4	5	3	18	.266	.328	.433	.761
2017	KC	AL	162	603	192	31	1	25	(16 | 9)	300	98	94	116	66	3	104	0	0	2	6	1	20	.318	.385	.498	.882
	Postseason		31	123	34	5	1	3	(1 | 2)	50	18	29	21	12	2	33	0	0	3	1	1	1	.276	.333	.407	.740
	7 ML YEARS		1048	3991	1132	206	16	127	(60 | 67)	1751	547	566	579	360	33	714	11	2	29	60	19	104	.284	.342	.439	.781

T.J. House

Pitches: L **Bats:** R **Pos:** RP-2   **Ht:** 6'1" **Wt:** 205 **Born:** 9/29/1989 **Age:** 28

			HOW MUCH HE PITCHED						WHAT HE GAVE UP											THE RESULTS						
Year	Team	Lg	G	GS	CG	GF	IP	BFP	H	R	ER	HR	SH	SF	HB	TBB	IBB	SO	WP	Bk	W	L	Pct	Sh	Sv-Op	Hld	ERC	ERA
2017	Buffalo*	AAA	24	24	1	0	133.1	605	149	73	64	11	3	4	8	63	1	108	7	1	9	11	.450	1	0- --		5.15	4.32
2014	Cle	AL	19	18	0	1	102.0	429	113	41	38	10	1	1	7	22	1	80	1	0	5	3	.625	0	0-0	0	4.30	3.35
2015	Cle	AL	4	4	0	0	13.0	73	21	19	19	1	0	1	2	12	1	7	0	0	0	4	.000	0	0-0	0	10.45	13.15
2016	Cle	AL	4	0	0	0	2.2	14	6	1	1	0	0	1	1	0	0	2	0	0	0	0	-	0	0-0	0	11.69	3.38
2017	Tor	AL	2	0	0	2	2.0	10	3	1	1	0	0	0	0	1	0	1	0	0	0	0	-	0	0-0	0	6.48	4.50
	4 ML YEARS		29	22	0	3	119.2	526	143	62	59	11	1	3	10	35	2	90	1	0	5	7	.417	0	0-0	0	5.10	4.44

J.P. Howell

Pitches: L **Bats:** L **Pos:** RP-16   **Ht:** 6'0" **Wt:** 180 **Born:** 4/25/1983 **Age:** 35

			HOW MUCH HE PITCHED						WHAT HE GAVE UP											THE RESULTS						
Year	Team	Lg	G	GS	CG	GF	IP	BFP	H	R	ER	HR	SH	SF	HB	TBB	IBB	SO	WP	Bk	W	L	Pct	Sh	Sv-Op	Hld	ERC	ERA
2017	Buffalo*	AAA	8	0	0	2	7.0	34	9	6	5	1	0	0	2	3	0	6	0	0	0	1	.000	0	0- --		7.54	6.43
2005	KC	AL	15	15	0	0	72.2	328	73	55	50	9	3	3	6	39	0	54	7	0	3	5	.375	0	0-0	0	5.18	6.19
2006	TB	AL	8	8	0	0	42.1	187	52	25	24	4	0	2	3	14	0	33	1	0	1	3	.250	0	0-0	0	5.51	5.10
2007	TB	AL	10	10	0	0	51.0	244	69	45	43	8	2	1	3	21	0	49	3	0	1	6	.143	0	0-0	0	6.84	7.59
2008	TB	AL	64	0	0	9	89.1	370	62	29	22	6	6	1	4	39	1	92	5	0	6	1	.857	0	3-5	14	2.51	2.22
2009	TB	AL	69	0	0	41	66.2	278	47	22	21	7	2	1	3	33	3	79	3	1	7	5	.583	0	17-25	4	2.99	2.84
2011	TB	AL	46	0	0	5	30.2	138	30	24	21	5	1	1	2	18	1	26	2	2	2	3	.400	1	1-2	10	5.43	6.16
2012	TB	AL	55	0	0	10	50.1	203	39	17	17	7	2	0	4	22	2	42	1	0	1	0	1.000	0	0-0	3	3.68	3.04
2013	LAD	NL	67	0	0	6	62.0	246	42	15	15	2	1	3	1	23	3	54	3	0	4	1	.800	0	0-0	11	1.92	2.18
2014	LAD	NL	68	0	0	8	49.0	199	31	14	13	2	4	0	1	25	1	48	3	0	3	3	.500	0	0-0	27	2.26	2.39
2015	LAD	NL	65	0	0	18	44.0	190	47	9	7	3	0	1	2	14	1	39	3	1	6	1	.857	0	1-4	9	4.07	1.43
2016	LAD	NL	64	0	0	11	50.2	220	56	23	23	4	1	2	3	15	2	44	3	0	1	1	.500	0	0-0	2	4.30	4.09
2017	Tor	AL	16	0	0	6	11.0	52	13	9	9	2	0	0	0	7	0	6	1	0	1	1	.500	0	0-1	0	6.78	7.36
	Postseason		24	0	0	3	20.1	89	21	7	7	2	1	3	2	7	1	23	2	0	0	3	.000	0	0-1	4	4.34	3.10
	12 ML YEARS		547	33	0	114	619.2	2655	561	287	265	59	22	15	32	270	14	566	35	4	36	30	.545	0	22-37	80	3.84	3.85

Jared Hoying

Bats: L **Throws:** R **Pos:** CF-25;RF-10;PH-3;PR-2;LF-1   **Ht:** 6'3" **Wt:** 205 **Born:** 5/18/1989 **Age:** 29

								BATTING												RUNNING			AVERAGES			
Year	Team	Lg	G	AB	H	2B	3B	HR	(Hm	Rd)	TB	R	RBI	RC	TBB	IBB	SO	HBP	SH	SF	SB	CS	GDP	Avg	OBP	Slg	OPS
2013	Frisco	AA	40	153	37	9	3	5	(-	-)	67	17	24	21	13	0	45	1	0	1	3	1	1	.242	.304	.438	.741
2013	RdRck	AAA	53	188	50	5	5	8	(-	-)	89	31	24	26	6	0	60	1	0	1	4	2	2	.266	.291	.473	.764
2014	RdRck	AAA	135	509	138	33	7	26	(-	-)	263	86	78	87	40	1	140	2	1	3	20	7	5	.271	.325	.517	.842
2015	RdRck	AAA	129	486	104	25	6	23	(-	-)	210	66	60	58	29	3	110	3	1	1	20	6	4	.214	.263	.433	.696
2016	RdRck	AAA	100	390	105	20	6	16	(-	-)	185	62	66	66	37	1	78	4	0	4	18	4	5	.269	.336	.474	.810
2017	RdRck	AAA	95	366	96	24	2	10	(-	-)	154	55	44	52	31	1	80	2	0	0	16	6	5	.262	.323	.421	.744
2016	Tex	AL	39	46	10	2	0	0	(0	0)	12	8	5	3	3	0	8	0	0	0	1	0	0	.217	.265	.261	.526
2017	Tex	AL	36	72	16	3	0	1	(1	0)	22	13	7	6	4	0	23	0	0	1	3	0	0	.222	.260	.306	.565
	Postseason		2	1	0	0	0	0	(0	0)	0	1	0	0	0	0	1	0	0	0	0	0	0	.000	.000	.000	.000
	2 ML YEARS		75	118	26	5	0	1	(1	0)	34	21	12	9	7	0	31	0	0	1	4	0	0	.220	.262	.288	.550

James Hoyt

Pitches: R Bats: R Pos: RP-43　　　　　　　　　　　　　　　　　　　　　　Ht: 6'6" Wt: 230 Born: 9/30/1986 Age: 31

		HOW MUCH HE PITCHED						WHAT HE GAVE UP												THE RESULTS							
Year Team	Lg	G	GS	CG	GF	IP	BFP	H	R	ER	HR	SH	SF	HB	TBB	IBB	SO	WP	Bk	W	L	Pct	Sh	Sv-Op	Hld	ERC	ERA
2013 Lynbrg	A+	17	3	0	1	49.2	213	39	27	27	3	0	4	1	25	0	72	10	0	3	2	.600	0	0- -	-	3.06	4.89
2013 Missi	AA	22	0	0	4	32.2	130	17	9	9	1	0	0	1	13	0	33	5	0	0	1	.000	0	1- -	-	1.44	2.48
2014 Missi	AA	28	0	0	12	31.2	126	19	5	4	1	3	1	0	10	0	43	2	0	2	2	.500	0	6- -	-	1.44	1.14
2014 Gwnntt	AAA	24	0	0	12	28.0	140	38	18	17	4	1	2	2	14	2	34	6	0	1	1	.500	0	1- -	-	6.89	5.46
2015 Fresno	AAA	47	0	0	30	49.0	211	48	23	19	1	0	2	3	11	2	66	5	0	0	1	.000	0	9- -	-	2.83	3.49
2016 Fresno	AAA	49	0	0	44	55.0	212	29	14	10	2	4	1	0	19	2	93	4	0	4	3	.571	0	29- -	-	1.30	1.64
2017 Fresno	AAA	13	0	0	9	14.0	58	10	3	3	1	0	0	1	6	0	18	3	0	2	0	1.000	0	4- -	-	2.74	1.93
2016 Hou	AL	22	0	0	7	22.0	91	16	12	11	5	1	1	1	9	1	28	3	0	1	1	.500	0	0-1	1	3.55	4.50
2017 Hou	AL	43	0	0	7	49.1	211	51	24	24	7	0	0	2	14	0	66	4	0	1	0	1.000	0	0-0	7	4.25	4.38
2 ML YEARS		65	0	0	14	71.1	302	67	36	35	12	1	1	3	23	1	94	7	0	2	1	.667	0	0-1	8	4.03	4.42

Chih-Wei Hu

chee-way

Pitches: R Bats: R Pos: RP-6　　　　　　　　　　　　　　　　　　　　　　Ht: 6'0" Wt: 220 Born: 11/4/1993 Age: 24

		HOW MUCH HE PITCHED						WHAT HE GAVE UP												THE RESULTS							
Year Team	Lg	G	GS	CG	GF	IP	BFP	H	R	ER	HR	SH	SF	HB	TBB	IBB	SO	WP	Bk	W	L	Pct	Sh	Sv-Op	Hld	ERC	ERA
2013 Twins	R	12	5	0	2	36.2	146	28	11	10	0	1	2	0	8	0	39	2	0	2	0	1.000	0	0- -	-	1.62	2.45
2014 2 Tms	Low	13	12	0	1	71.0	274	47	23	17	0	3	0	2	15	0	64	0	1	8	2	.800	0	0- -	-	1.38	2.15
2015 2 Tms	Low	20	19	0	1	103.0	427	102	46	38	6	2	5	3	27	0	93	4	2	5	6	.455	0	1- -	-	3.37	3.32
2016 Mont	AA	24	24	0	0	142.2	581	128	49	42	7	5	5	3	36	1	107	4	1	7	8	.467	0	0- -	-	2.73	2.65
2017 Drham	AAA	31	4	0	5	61.2	249	59	28	21	9	0	2	0	12	0	57	2	0	4	1	.800	0	2- -	-	3.38	3.06
2017 TB	AL	6	0	0	1	10.0	40	5	4	3	2	0	1	0	4	0	9	0	0	1	1	.500	0	0-0	-	2.01	2.70

Daniel Hudson

Pitches: R Bats: R Pos: RP-71　　　　　　　　　　　　　　　　　　　　　　Ht: 6'3" Wt: 225 Born: 3/9/1987 Age: 31

		HOW MUCH HE PITCHED						WHAT HE GAVE UP												THE RESULTS							
Year Team	Lg	G	GS	CG	GF	IP	BFP	H	R	ER	HR	SH	SF	HB	TBB	IBB	SO	WP	Bk	W	L	Pct	Sh	Sv-Op	Hld	ERC	ERA
2009 CWS	AL	6	2	0	1	18.2	82	16	9	7	3	0	1	1	9	0	14	1	0	1	1	.500	0	0-0	0	4.15	3.38
2010 2 Tms		14	14	0	0	95.1	372	68	26	26	8	2	2	4	27	1	84	5	0	8	2	.800	0	0-0	0	2.26	2.45
2011 Ari	NL	33	33	3	0	222.0	921	217	98	86	17	6	6	8	50	1	169	4	1	16	12	.571	0	0-0	0	3.26	3.49
2012 Ari	NL	9	9	0	0	45.1	202	62	37	37	9	2	1	0	12	0	37	2	0	3	2	.600	0	0-0	0	6.56	7.35
2014 Ari	NL	3	0	0	0	2.2	13	4	4	4	0	0	0	0	0	0	2	0	0	0	1	.000	0	0-0	0	4.08	13.50
2015 Ari	NL	64	1	0	13	67.2	290	64	34	29	7	1	3	0	25	2	71	5	0	4	3	.571	0	4-6	20	3.58	3.86
2016 Ari	NL	70	0	0	17	60.1	268	65	40	35	6	0	0	4	22	3	58	5	0	3	2	.600	0	5-7	17	4.51	5.22
2017 Pit	NL	71	0	0	18	61.2	271	57	34	30	7	1	2	5	33	1	66	4	0	2	7	.222	0	0-2	21	4.63	4.38
10 CWS	AL	3	3	0	0	15.2	71	17	11	11	1	1	1	0	11	0	14	2	0	1	1	.500	0	0-0	0	5.69	6.32
10 Ari	AL	11	11	0	0	79.2	301	51	15	15	7	1	1	4	16	1	70	3	0	7	1	.875	0	0-0	0	1.70	1.69
Postseason		1	1	0	0	5.1	24	9	5	5	1	0	0	0	0	0	6	0	0	0	1	.000	0	0-0	0	7.35	8.44
8 ML YEARS		270	59	3	49	573.2	2419	553	282	254	57	12	15	22	178	8	501	26	1	37	30	.552	0	9-15	58	3.66	3.98

Chad Huffman

Bats: R Throws: R Pos: PH-11;RF-1;DH-1　　　　　　　　　　　　　　　　Ht: 6'1" Wt: 215 Born: 4/29/1985 Age: 33

								BATTING													RUNNING			AVERAGES			
Year Team	Lg	G	AB	H	2B	3B	HR	(Hm Rd)	TB	R	RBI	RC	TBB	IBB	SO	HBP	SH	SF	SB	CS	GDP	Avg	OBP	Slg	OPS
2013 Memp	AAA	108	309	87	18	1	13	(- -)	146	49	55	58	47	0	70	4	1	4	2	0	10	.282	.379	.472	.852
2016 Toledo	AAA	122	430	123	33	5	17	(- -)	217	78	70	87	61	0	93	14	0	6	11	5	11	.286	.387	.505	.892
2017 Memp	AAA	59	174	43	13	1	6	(- -)	76	27	25	32	32	1	39	8	0	1	1	0	3	.247	.386	.437	.823
2017 Syrcse	AAA	28	74	15	5	0	1	(- -)	23	6	5	7	7	0	20	3	1	1	0	0	1	.203	.294	.311	.605
2010 NYY	AL	9	18	3	0	0	0	(0 0)	3	1	2	2	2	0	5	1	0	0	0	0	0	.167	.286	.167	.452
2017 StL	NL	12	14	4	0	1	0	(0 0)	6	3	0	2	1	0	6	0	0	0	0	0	0	.286	.333	.429	.762
2 ML YEARS		21	32	7	0	1	0	(0 0)	9	4	2	2	3	0	11	1	0	0	0	0	1	.219	.306	.281	.587

Jared Hughes

Pitches: R Bats: R Pos: RP-67　　　　　　　　　　　　　　　　　　　　　　Ht: 6'7" Wt: 240 Born: 7/4/1985 Age: 32

		HOW MUCH HE PITCHED						WHAT HE GAVE UP												THE RESULTS							
Year Team	Lg	G	GS	CG	GF	IP	BFP	H	R	ER	HR	SH	SF	HB	TBB	IBB	SO	WP	Bk	W	L	Pct	Sh	Sv-Op	Hld	ERC	ERA
2011 Pit	NL	12	0	0	1	11.0	46	9	5	5	1	1	0	0	4	0	10	0	0	0	1	.000	0	0-0	2	2.85	4.09
2012 Pit	NL	66	0	0	20	75.2	316	65	30	24	7	1	0	5	22	4	50	5	0	2	2	.500	0	2-4	11	2.99	2.85
2013 Pit	NL	29	0	0	8	32.0	148	37	17	17	2	2	1	2	16	1	23	2	0	2	3	.400	0	0-0	3	5.27	4.78
2014 Pit	NL	63	0	0	16	64.1	256	51	21	14	4	6	2	6	19	5	36	2	0	7	5	.583	0	0-2	13	2.68	1.96
2015 Pit	NL	76	0	0	11	67.0	284	70	21	17	3	6	4	7	19	2	36	3	0	3	1	.750	0	0-3	21	3.93	2.28
2016 Pit	NL	67	0	0	18	59.1	257	62	24	20	6	4	2	5	22	3	34	5	0	1	1	.500	0	1-3	4	4.55	3.03
2017 Mil	NL	67	0	0	15	59.2	244	49	21	20	4	2	0	6	24	5	48	6	0	5	3	.625	0	1-4	12	3.27	3.02
Postseason		1	0	0	0	1.0	7	3	2	2	0	0	0	0	1	0	1	0	0	0	0	-	0	0-0	0	19.55	18.00
7 ML YEARS		380	0	0	89	369.0	1551	343	139	117	27	22	9	31	126	20	237	23	0	20	16	.556	0	4-16	66	3.57	2.85

Phil Hughes

Pitches: R Bats: R Pos: SP-9; RP-5   Ht: 6'5" Wt: 240 Born: 6/24/1986 Age: 32

Year	Team	Lg	G	GS	CG	GF	IP	BFP	H	R	ER	HR	SH	SF	HB	TBB	IBB	SO	WP	Bk	W	L	Pct	Sh	Sv-Op	Hld	ERC	ERA
2007	NYY	AL	13	13	0	0	72.2	306	64	39	36	8	2	1	2	29	0	58	4	0	5	3	.625	0	0-0	0	3.61	4.46
2008	NYY	AL	8	8	0	0	34.0	157	43	26	25	3	1	3	1	15	0	23	2	0	0	4	.000	0	0-0	0	5.84	6.62
2009	NYY	AL	51	7	0	6	86.0	351	68	31	29	8	0	4	5	28	1	96	4	2	8	3	.727	0	3-6	18	2.86	3.03
2010	NYY	AL	31	29	0	0	176.1	730	162	83	82	25	2	5	0	58	1	146	9	1	18	8	.692	0	0-0	0	3.65	4.19
2011	NYY	AL	17	14	1	1	74.2	334	84	48	48	9	3	3	4	27	2	47	3	0	5	5	.500	1	0-0	0	4.92	5.79
2012	NYY	AL	32	32	1	0	191.1	815	196	101	89	35	1	4	6	46	0	165	3	0	16	13	.552	0	0-0	0	4.21	4.19
2013	NYY	AL	30	29	0	0	145.2	642	170	91	84	24	3	11	5	42	4	121	6	0	4	14	.222	0	0-0	0	5.13	5.19
2014	Min	AL	32	32	1	0	209.2	855	221	88	82	16	3	7	5	16	1	186	1	0	16	10	.615	0	0-0	0	3.05	3.52
2015	Min	AL	27	25	1	1	155.1	651	184	76	76	29	1	3	2	16	0	94	1	0	11	9	.550	0	0-0	0	4.59	4.40
2016	Min	AL	12	11	1	0	59.0	259	76	40	39	11	1	2	0	13	0	34	0	0	1	7	.125	0	0-0	0	5.68	5.95
2017	Min	AL	14	9	0	3	53.2	244	72	38	35	12	1	1	1	13	2	38	0	0	4	3	.571	0	0-0	0	6.32	5.87
	Postseason		18	5	0	2	39.2	176	41	20	20	5	1	0	0	18	3	38	3	0	2	4	.333	0	0-1	2	4.49	4.54
11 ML YEARS			267	209	5	11	1258.1	5344	1340	661	625	180	18	44	31	303	11	1008	33	3	88	79	.527	1	3-6	18	4.18	4.47

Nick Hundley

Bats: R Throws: R Pos: C-82;PH-25;DH-1;PR-1   Ht: 6'1" Wt: 205 Born: 9/8/1983 Age: 34

Year	Team	Lg	G	AB	H	2B	3B	HR	(Hm	Rd)	TB	R	RBI	RC	TBB	IBB	SO	HBP	SH	SF	SB	CS	GDP	Avg	OBP	Slg	OPS
2008	SD	NL	60	198	47	7	1	5	(4	1)	71	21	24	17	11	0	52	2	0	5	0	0	1	.237	.278	.359	.636
2009	SD	NL	78	256	61	15	2	8	(4	4)	104	23	30	33	28	1	76	1	1	3	5	1	2	.238	.313	.406	.719
2010	SD	NL	85	273	68	18	2	8	(7	1)	114	33	43	37	25	0	66	1	2	6	0	5	8	.249	.308	.418	.726
2011	SD	NL	82	281	81	16	5	9	(6	3)	134	34	29	40	22	3	74	4	0	1	1	1	3	.288	.347	.477	.824
2012	SD	NL	58	204	32	7	1	3	(1	2)	50	14	22	6	15	2	56	2	1	3	0	3	4	.157	.219	.245	.464
2013	SD	NL	114	373	87	19	0	13	(6	7)	145	35	44	36	26	5	98	5	1	3	1	0	7	.233	.290	.389	.679
2014	2 Tms		83	218	53	7	0	6	(4	2)	78	18	22	21	10	0	63	0	2	3	1	0	3	.243	.273	.358	.631
2015	Col	NL	103	366	110	21	5	10	(7	3)	171	45	43	44	21	0	76	1	0	1	5	6	8	.301	.339	.467	.807
2016	Col	NL	83	289	75	20	1	10	(4	6)	127	30	48	41	25	3	65	1	1	1	0	0	12	.260	.320	.439	.759
2017	SF	NL	101	287	70	23	0	9	(4	5)	120	27	35	25	12	2	81	0	2	2	0	0	6	.244	.272	.418	.691
14	SD	NL	33	59	16	3	0	1	(1	0)	22	1	3	5	0	0	13	0	0	0	0	0	1	.271	.271	.373	.644
14	Bal	AL	50	159	37	4	0	5	(3	2)	56	17	19	16	10	0	50	0	2	3	1	0	2	.233	.273	.352	.625
	Postseason		5	15	1	0	0	0	(0	0)	1	0	1	0	0	0	5	0	0	0	0	0	0	.067	.067	.067	.133
10 ML YEARS			847	2745	684	153	17	81	(47	34)	1114	280	340	300	195	16	707	17	10	28	13	16	54	.249	.300	.406	.706

Tommy Hunter

Pitches: R Bats: R Pos: RP-61   Ht: 6'3" Wt: 250 Born: 7/3/1986 Age: 31

Year	Team	Lg	G	GS	CG	GF	IP	BFP	H	R	ER	HR	SH	SF	HB	TBB	IBB	SO	WP	Bk	W	L	Pct	Sh	Sv-Op	Hld	ERC	ERA
2008	Tex	AL	3	3	0	0	11.0	63	23	20	20	4	0	0	1	3	0	9	0	0	0	2	.000	0	0-0	0	12.66	16.36
2009	Tex	AL	19	19	1	0	112.0	475	113	55	51	13	2	1	2	33	2	64	6	1	9	6	.600	0	0-0	0	3.86	4.10
2010	Tex	AL	23	22	1	0	128.0	536	126	55	53	21	3	2	3	33	0	68	1	0	13	4	.765	0	0-0	0	3.95	3.73
2011	2 Tms	AL	20	11	0	2	84.2	367	100	50	44	12	2	2	4	15	1	45	0	0	4	4	.500	0	0-1	1	4.65	4.68
2012	Bal	AL	33	20	0	5	133.2	573	161	85	81	32	3	6	4	27	2	77	0	1	7	8	.467	0	0-1	0	5.63	5.45
2013	Bal	AL	68	0	0	20	86.1	336	71	28	27	11	1	0	2	14	1	68	0	0	6	5	.545	0	4-6	21	2.53	2.81
2014	Bal	AL	60	0	0	24	60.2	241	55	22	20	4	1	2	1	12	3	45	2	0	3	2	.600	0	11-17	12	2.65	2.97
2015	2 Tms	AL	58	0	0	17	60.1	249	61	29	28	7	1	3	1	14	2	47	2	0	4	2	.667	0	1-2	7	3.65	4.18
2016	2 Tms	AL	33	0	0	8	34.0	139	35	13	12	1	1	0	2	8	1	23	0	0	2	2	.500	0	0-1	1	3.43	3.18
2017	TB	AL	61	0	0	11	58.2	228	43	18	17	6	0	0	1	14	0	64	2	0	3	5	.375	0	1-1	25	2.21	2.61
11	Tex	AL	8	0	0	2	15.1	62	12	6	5	1	1	1	0	5	0	10	0	0	1	1	.500	0	0-1	0	2.44	2.93
11	Bal	AL	12	11	0	0	69.1	305	88	44	39	11	1	1	4	10	1	35	0	0	3	3	.500	0	0-0	1	5.19	5.06
15	Bal	AL	39	0	0	12	44.2	180	41	19	18	3	1	3	1	11	2	32	2	0	2	2	.500	0	0-1	6	2.92	3.63
15	ChC	NL	19	0	0	5	15.2	69	20	10	10	4	0	0	0	3	0	15	0	0	2	0	1.000	0	1-1	1	5.91	5.74
16	Cle	AL	21	0	0	5	21.2	90	21	10	9	1	1	0	2	5	1	17	0	0	2	2	.500	0	0-1	0	3.22	3.74
16	Bal	AL	12	0	0	3	12.1	49	14	3	3	0	0	0	0	3	0	6	0	0	0	0	-	0	0-0	1	3.82	2.19
	Postseason		7	3	0	2	14.1	65	19	8	7	2	0	2	1	2	0	15	0	1	0	2	.000	0	0-0	0	4.40	4.40
10 ML YEARS			378	75	2	87	769.1	3207	788	375	353	111	14	16	21	173	12	510	13	2	51	40	.560	0	17-29	67	3.93	4.13

Jason Hursh

Pitches: R Bats: R Pos: RP-9   Ht: 6'3" Wt: 200 Born: 10/2/1991 Age: 26

Year	Team	Lg	G	GS	CG	GF	IP	BFP	H	R	ER	HR	SH	SF	HB	TBB	IBB	SO	WP	Bk	W	L	Pct	Sh	Sv-Op	Hld	ERC	ERA
2013	Rome	A	9	9	0	0	27.0	108	20	9	2	1	0	0	1	10	0	15	4	0	1	1	.500	0	0- -	-	2.40	0.67
2014	Missi	AA	27	26	1	0	148.1	615	151	70	59	5	8	2	7	43	0	83	6	0	11	7	.611	1	0- -	-	3.58	3.58
2015	Missi	AA	24	15	0	5	82.1	379	111	52	47	3	2	1	0	32	0	60	2	0	3	6	.333	0	2- -	-	5.59	5.14
2015	Gwnntt	AAA	10	0	0	2	15.0	64	16	9	9	2	0	1	1	5	0	5	0	0	1	0	1.000	0	0- -	-	4.83	5.40
2016	Missi	AA	35	0	0	14	57.0	236	42	16	13	0	4	1	3	23	0	42	6	1	3	2	.600	0	3- -	-	2.24	2.05
2016	Gwnntt	AAA	8	0	0	2	16.0	66	15	3	3	0	0	1	2	8	0	8	0	0	0	0	-	0	0- -	-	4.20	1.69
2017	Gwnntt	AAA	28	0	0	3	37.2	178	53	26	23	3	1	0	1	12	0	41	3	0	3	4	.429	0	0- -	-	5.98	5.50
2017	Missi	AA	10	0	0	8	14.2	55	10	2	2	0	2	0	0	5	0	10	2	2	1	0	-	0	5- -	-	1.78	1.23
2016	Atl	NL	2	0	0	0	1.1	11	4	5	5	0	0	0	0	3	0	1	1	0	0	0	-	0	0-0	0	25.85	33.75
2017	Atl	NL	9	0	0	4	10.2	47	13	6	6	1	0	1	1	4	1	7	1	0	1	0	1.000	0	0-0	0	5.65	5.06
2 ML YEARS			11	0	0	4	12.0	58	17	11	11	1	0	1	1	7	1	8	2	0	1	0	1.000	0	0-0	0	7.64	8.25

Jae-Gyun Hwang

Bats: R Throws: R Pos: 3B-15;1B-3;PH-2   jay-wun   Ht: 6'0" Wt: 215 Born: 7/28/1987 Age: 30

Year	Team	Lg	G	AB	H	2B	3B	HR	(Hm	Rd)	TB	R	RBI	RC	TBB	IBB	SO	HBP	SH	SF	SB	CS	GDP	Avg	OBP	Slg	OPS
2017	Scrmto	AAA	98	351	100	21	4	10	(-	-)	159	44	55	55	27	2	83	1	0	7	7	1	4	.285	.332	.453	.785
2017	SF	NL	18	52	8	1	0	1	(1	0)	12	2	5	3	5	0	15	0	0	0	0	0	1	.154	.228	.231	.459

Chris Iannetta

Bats: R Throws: R Pos: C-78;PH-15;3B-1   eye-ah-NETT-ah   Ht: 6'0" Wt: 230 Born: 4/8/1983 Age: 35

Year	Team	Lg	G	AB	H	2B	3B	HR	(Hm	Rd)	TB	R	RBI	RC	TBB	IBB	SO	HBP	SH	SF	SB	CS	GDP	Avg	OBP	Slg	OPS
2006	Col	NL	21	77	20	4	0	2	(0	2)	30	12	10	9	13	2	17	1	1	1	0	1	1	.260	.370	.390	.759
2007	Col	NL	67	197	43	8	3	4	(1	3)	69	22	27	27	29	3	58	5	1	2	0	0	3	.218	.330	.350	.681
2008	Col	NL	104	333	88	22	2	18	(11	7)	168	50	65	65	56	0	92	14	2	2	0	0	6	.264	.390	.505	.895
2009	Col	NL	93	289	66	15	2	16	(8	8)	133	41	52	47	43	3	75	11	1	6	0	1	4	.228	.344	.460	.804
2010	Col	NL	61	188	37	6	1	9	(7	2)	72	20	27	21	30	2	48	4	0	1	1	0	4	.197	.318	.383	.701
2011	Col	NL	112	345	82	17	1	14	(10	4)	143	51	55	62	70	5	89	5	2	4	6	3	10	.238	.370	.414	.785
2012	LAA	AL	79	221	53	6	1	9	(3	6)	88	27	26	27	29	0	60	2	0	1	1	3	4	.240	.332	.398	.730
2013	LAA	AL	115	325	73	15	0	11	(1	10)	121	40	39	44	68	2	100	2	0	4	0	1	8	.225	.358	.372	.731
2014	LAA	AL	108	306	77	22	0	7	(6	1)	120	41	43	56	54	3	91	8	0	5	3	0	3	.252	.373	.392	.765
2015	LAA	AL	92	272	51	10	0	10	(3	7)	91	28	34	27	41	1	83	1	0	3	0	1	11	.188	.293	.335	.628
2016	Sea	AL	94	295	62	14	0	7	(5	2)	97	23	24	27	38	0	83	2	1	2	0	0	4	.210	.303	.329	.631
2017	Ari	AL	89	272	69	19	0	17	(7	10)	139	38	43	46	37	0	87	6	0	1	0	0	3	.254	.354	.511	.865
	Postseason		3	10	1	0	0	1	(1	0)	4	1	1	0	1	0	2	0	0	0	0	0	0	.100	.182	.400	.582
	12 ML YEARS		1035	3120	721	158	10	124	(62	62)	1271	393	445	458	508	21	883	61	8	32	11	10	61	.231	.347	.407	.754

Jose Iglesias

Bats: R Throws: R Pos: SS-130   ee-GLAY-see-us   Ht: 5'11" Wt: 185 Born: 1/5/1990 Age: 28

Year	Team	Lg	G	AB	H	2B	3B	HR	(Hm	Rd)	TB	R	RBI	RC	TBB	IBB	SO	HBP	SH	SF	SB	CS	GDP	Avg	OBP	Slg	OPS
2011	Bos	AL	10	6	2	0	0	0	(0	0)	2	3	0	0	0	0	2	0	0	0	0	0	0	.333	.333	.333	.667
2012	Bos	AL	25	68	8	2	0	0	(0	1)	13	5	2	0	4	0	16	3	2	0	1	0	2	.118	.200	.191	.391
2013	2 Tms	AL	109	350	106	16	2	3	(1	2)	135	39	29	45	15	0	60	11	4	2	5	2	7	.303	.349	.386	.735
2015	Det	AL	120	416	125	17	3	2	(1	1)	154	44	23	47	25	2	44	6	4	3	11	8	10	.300	.347	.370	.717
2016	Det	AL	137	467	119	26	4	4	(1	3)	157	57	32	47	28	1	50	8	7	3	7	4	12	.255	.306	.336	.643
2017	Det	AL	130	463	118	33	1	6	(4	2)	171	56	54	54	21	0	65	1	3	1	7	4	6	.255	.288	.369	.657
	13 Bos	AL	63	215	71	10	2	1	(0	1)	88	27	19	34	11	0	30	6	0	2	3	1	4	.330	.376	.409	.785
	13 Det	AL	46	135	35	6	0	2	(1	1)	47	12	10	11	4	0	30	5	4	0	2	1	3	.259	.306	.348	.654
	Postseason		11	26	6	0	0	0	(0	0)	6	2	1	0	1	0	5	1	3	0	0	1	1	.231	.286	.231	.516
	6 ML YEARS		531	1770	478	94	6	16	(7	9)	632	204	140	193	93	3	237	29	20	9	31	18	37	.270	.316	.357	.673

Raisel Iglesias

Pitches: R Bats: R Pos: RP-63   rye-SELL ee-GLAY-see-us   Ht: 6'2" Wt: 188 Born: 1/4/1990 Age: 28

Year	Team	Lg	G	GS	CG	GF	IP	BFP	H	R	ER	HR	SH	SF	HB	TBB	IBB	SO	WP	Bk	W	L	Pct	Sh	Sv-Op	Hld	ERC	ERA
2015	Cin	NL	18	16	0	1	95.1	395	81	45	44	11	4	0	7	28	0	104	2	2	3	7	.300	0	0-0	-	3.24	4.15
2016	Cin	NL	37	5	0	15	78.1	325	63	22	22	7	1	2	5	26	1	83	3	1	3	2	.600	0	6-8	7	2.90	2.53
2017	Cin	NL	63	0	0	57	76.0	306	57	22	21	5	1	1	1	27	1	92	1	0	3	3	.500	0	28-30	0	2.43	2.49
	3 ML YEARS		118	21	0	73	249.2	1026	201	89	87	23	6	3	13	81	2	279	6	3	9	12	.429	0	34-38	7	2.88	3.14

Ender Inciarte

Bats: L Throws: L Pos: CF-156;PH-1;PR-1   END-er in-see-ARR-tay   Ht: 5'11" Wt: 190 Born: 10/29/1990 Age: 27

Year	Team	Lg	G	AB	H	2B	3B	HR	(Hm	Rd)	TB	R	RBI	RC	TBB	IBB	SO	HBP	SH	SF	SB	CS	GDP	Avg	OBP	Slg	OPS
2014	Ari	NL	118	418	116	18	2	4	(1	3)	150	54	27	49	25	0	53	0	4	0	19	3	6	.278	.318	.359	.677
2015	Ari	NL	132	524	159	27	5	6	(1	5)	214	73	45	69	26	0	58	4	2	5	21	10	8	.303	.338	.408	.747
2016	Atl	NL	131	522	152	24	7	3	(1	2)	199	85	29	58	45	5	68	4	5	2	16	7	8	.291	.351	.381	.732
2017	Atl	NL	158	662	201	27	5	11	(6	5)	271	93	57	95	49	3	94	0	3	4	22	9	8	.304	.350	.409	.759
	4 ML YEARS		539	2126	628	96	19	24	(9	15)	834	305	158	271	145	8	273	8	14	11	78	29	27	.295	.341	.392	.733

Gregory Infante

Pitches: R Bats: R Pos: RP-52   Ht: 6'2" Wt: 215 Born: 7/10/1987 Age: 30

Year	Team	Lg	G	GS	CG	GF	IP	BFP	H	R	ER	HR	SH	SF	HB	TBB	IBB	SO	WP	Bk	W	L	Pct	Sh	Sv-Op	Hld	ERC	ERA
2013	Chatt	AA	27	0	0	14	37.2	162	33	14	14	2	3	2	0	25	2	36	7	0	1	1	.500	0	0- -	-	4.11	3.35
2014	Nham	AA	36	0	0	33	38.2	157	28	8	8	0	1	2	3	16	0	34	0	0	0	1	.000	0	22- -	-	2.36	1.86
2014	Buffalo	AAA	5	0	0	1	7.2	27	2	2	2	0	0	0	0	2	0	10	0	0	2	1	.667	0	0- -	-	0.44	2.35
2015	Buffalo	AAA	45	0	0	17	48.2	214	43	15	15	3	0	1	0	32	0	41	4	0	1	2	.333	0	7- -	-	4.19	2.77
2015	Nham	AA	6	0	0	4	8.0	44	12	10	5	0	0	0	0	7	0	9	3	0	0	1	.000	0	1- -	-	7.86	5.63
2016	LV	AAA	9	1	0	1	17.0	76	17	11	11	3	0	1	2	12	0	12	0	0	2	1	.667	0	0- -	-	6.82	5.82
2016	Rdng	AA	30	1	0	3	44.2	205	49	25	24	4	6	2	1	23	3	53	5	0	4	2	.667	0	0- -	-	4.91	4.84
2017	Charllt	AAA	12	0	0	9	15.0	58	7	3	3	0	0	1	0	8	1	18	1	1	0	1	.000	0	3- -	-	1.37	1.80
2010	CWS	AL	5	0	0	5	4.2	19	2	0	0	0	0	0	0	4	0	5	0	0	0	0	-	0	0-0	0	2.16	0.00
2017	CWS	AL	52	0	0	18	54.2	227	45	20	19	4	0	5	3	20	4	49	1	0	2	1	.667	0	0-1	5	2.93	3.13
	2 ML YEARS		57	0	0	23	59.1	246	47	20	19	4	0	5	3	24	4	54	1	0	2	1	.667	0	0-1	5	2.87	2.88

Hisashi Iwakuma

Pitches: R Bats: R Pos: SP-6 he-SAH-shee ee-wuh-KOO-muh **Ht: 6'3" Wt: 210 Born: 4/12/1981 Age: 37**

Year Team	Lg	HOW MUCH HE PITCHED						WHAT HE GAVE UP												THE RESULTS							
		G	GS	CG	GF	IP	BFP	H	R	ER	HR	SH	SF	HB	TBB	IBB	SO	WP	Bk	W	L	Pct	Sh	Sv-Op	Hld	ERC	ERA
2012 Sea	AL	30	16	0	6	125.1	519	117	49	44	17	1	1	3	43	3	101	5	0	9	5	.643	0	2-2	0	3.87	3.16
2013 Sea	AL	33	33	0	0	219.2	866	179	69	65	25	3	6	2	42	4	185	10	0	14	6	.700	0	0-0	0	2.43	2.66
2014 Sea	AL	28	28	0	0	179.0	709	167	70	70	20	0	1	2	21	2	154	2	0	15	9	.625	0	0-0	0	2.77	3.52
2015 Sea	AL	20	20	1	0	129.2	516	117	53	51	18	4	3	1	21	1	111	1	0	9	5	.643	1	0-0	0	2.93	3.54
2016 Sea	AL	33	33	0	0	199.0	836	218	95	91	28	6	7	5	46	3	147	4	0	16	12	.571	0	0-0	0	4.37	4.12
2017 Sea	AL	6	6	0	0	31.0	128	27	16	15	7	0	0	2	12	0	16	1	0	0	2	.000	0	0-0	0	4.56	4.35
6 ML YEARS		150	136	1	6	883.2	3574	825	352	336	115	14	18	15	185	13	714	23	0	63	39	.618	1	2-2	0	3.26	3.42

Austin Jackson

Bats: R Throws: R Pos: LF-38;CF-38;RF-18;PH-5 **Ht: 6'1" Wt: 205 Born: 2/1/1987 Age: 31**

Year Team	Lg	BATTING						(Hm	Rd)	TB	R	RBI	RC	TBB	IBB	SO	HBP	SH	SF	RUNNING			AVERAGES			
		G	AB	H	2B	3B	HR													SB	CS	GDP	Avg	OBP	Slg	OPS
2010 Det	AL	151	618	181	34	10	4	(0	4)	247	103	41	84	47	4	170	4	3	3	27	6	5	.293	.345	.400	.745
2011 Det	AL	153	591	147	22	11	10	(5	5)	221	90	45	67	56	3	181	4	14	3	22	5	11	.249	.317	.374	.690
2012 Det	AL	137	543	163	29	10	16	(6	10)	260	103	66	90	67	0	134	2	2	3	12	9	9	.300	.377	.479	.856
2013 Det	AL	129	552	150	30	7	12	(3	9)	230	99	49	73	52	0	129	4	3	3	8	4	12	.272	.337	.417	.754
2014 2 Tms	AL	154	597	153	30	6	4	(2	2)	207	71	47	58	47	0	144	2	1	9	20	6	15	.256	.308	.347	.655
2015 2 Tms		136	491	131	25	3	9	(5	4)	189	56	48	63	29	0	126	3	3	1	17	10	5	.267	.311	.385	.696
2016 CWS	AL	54	181	46	12	2	0	(0	0)	62	24	18	24	17	0	39	1	2	2	2	1	3	.254	.318	.343	.661
2017 Cle	AL	85	280	89	19	3	7	(2	5)	135	46	35	47	33	0	64	1	0	4	3	1	13	.318	.387	.482	.869
14 Det	AL	100	374	102	25	5	4	(2	2)	149	52	33	42	35	0	85	2	1	8	9	4	9	.273	.332	.398	.730
14 Sea	AL	54	223	51	5	1	0	(0	0)	58	19	14	16	12	0	59	0	0	1	11	2	6	.229	.267	.260	.527
15 Sea	AL	107	419	114	18	3	8	(5	3)	162	46	38	52	24	0	107	1	3	1	15	9	4	.272	.312	.387	.699
15 ChC	NL	29	72	17	7	0	1	(0	1)	27	10	10	11	5	0	19	2	0	0	2	1	1	.236	.304	.375	.679
Postseason		40	141	31	7	1	2	(1	1)	46	19	11	15	20	0	58	1	2	0	3	2	2	.220	.321	.326	.647
8 ML YEARS		999	3853	1060	201	52	62	(23	39)	1551	592	349	506	348	7	987	21	28	28	111	42	73	.275	.336	.403	.739

Edwin Jackson

Pitches: R Bats: R Pos: SP-13; RP-3 **Ht: 6'2" Wt: 215 Born: 9/9/1983 Age: 34**

Year Team	Lg	HOW MUCH HE PITCHED						WHAT HE GAVE UP												THE RESULTS							
		G	GS	CG	GF	IP	BFP	H	R	ER	HR	SH	SF	HB	TBB	IBB	SO	WP	Bk	W	L	Pct	Sh	Sv-Op	Hld	ERC	ERA
2017 Norfolk*	AAA	12	1	0	3	20.1	86	20	7	7	1	1	1	2	10	0	17	2	0	0	0	-	0	2--	-	4.63	3.10
2017 Syrcse*	AAA	5	4	0	0	20.1	80	9	1	1	0	0	0	1	10	0	22	0	0	2	0	1.000	0	0--	-	1.35	0.44
2003 LAD	NL	4	3	0	0	22.0	91	17	6	6	2	1	1	1	11	1	19	3	0	2	1	.667	0	0-0	0	3.36	2.45
2004 LAD	NL	8	5	0	1	24.2	113	31	20	20	7	1	0	0	11	1	16	0	0	2	1	.667	0	0-0	0	7.21	7.30
2005 LAD	NL	7	6	0	0	28.2	134	31	22	20	2	0	2	1	17	0	13	2	1	2	2	.500	0	0-0	0	5.13	6.28
2006 TB	AL	23	1	0	7	36.1	174	42	27	22	2	2	2	1	25	0	27	3	1	0	0	-	0	0-0	0	5.86	5.45
2007 TB	AL	32	31	1	0	161.0	755	195	116	103	19	5	6	4	88	3	128	7	1	5	15	.250	1	0-0	0	6.11	5.76
2008 TB	AL	32	31	0	0	183.1	792	199	91	90	23	3	2	2	77	1	108	7	1	14	11	.560	0	0-1	0	4.99	4.42
2009 Det	AL	33	33	1	0	214.0	890	200	93	86	27	4	2	5	70	3	161	6	0	13	9	.591	0	0-0	0	3.72	3.62
2010 2 Tms		32	32	1	0	209.1	902	214	111	104	21	6	4	6	78	4	181	20	0	10	12	.455	1	0-0	0	4.20	4.47
2011 2 Tms		32	31	1	1	199.2	861	225	92	84	16	15	6	2	62	4	148	9	2	12	9	.571	0	0-0	0	4.34	3.79
2012 Was	NL	31	31	1	0	189.2	790	173	90	85	23	9	8	2	58	5	168	3	0	10	11	.476	0	0-0	0	3.36	4.03
2013 ChC	NL	31	31	0	0	175.1	777	197	110	97	16	8	3	5	59	7	135	14	0	8	18	.308	0	0-0	0	4.46	4.98
2014 ChC	NL	28	27	0	0	140.2	633	168	105	99	18	6	4	3	63	3	123	9	0	6	15	.286	0	0-0	0	5.75	6.33
2015 2 Tms	NL	47	0	0	18	55.2	228	44	25	19	4	1	3	1	21	1	40	5	1	4	3	.571	0	1-2	5	2.75	3.07
2016 2 Tms		21	13	0	3	84.0	373	92	56	55	14	2	4	1	41	3	61	6	0	5	7	.417	0	0-0	0	5.55	5.89
2017 2 Tms		16	13	0	0	76.0	339	86	53	44	20	4	3	0	29	2	60	3	0	5	6	.455	0	0-0	0	5.87	5.21
10 Ari	NL	21	21	1	0	134.1	587	141	80	77	13	6	2	5	60	2	104	13	0	6	10	.375	1	0-0	0	4.72	5.16
10 CWS	AL	11	11	0	0	75.0	315	73	31	27	8	0	2	1	18	2	77	7	0	4	2	.667	0	0-0	0	3.32	3.24
11 CWS	AL	19	19	1	0	121.2	522	134	55	53	8	6	4	0	39	2	97	7	1	7	7	.500	1	0-0	0	4.10	3.92
11 StL	NL	13	12	0	1	78.0	339	91	37	31	8	9	2	2	23	2	51	2	1	5	2	.714	0	0-0	0	4.73	3.58
15 ChC	NL	23	0	0	11	31.0	134	30	14	11	0	1	2	1	12	1	23	3	1	2	1	.667	0	0-1	0	3.19	3.19
15 Atl	NL	24	0	0	7	24.2	94	14	11	8	4	0	1	0	9	0	17	2	0	2	2	.500	0	1-1	5	2.16	2.92
16 Mia	NL	8	0	0	3	10.2	47	13	7	7	2	0	0	0	6	1	7	1	0	0	1	.000	0	0-0	0	7.01	5.91
16 SD	NL	13	13	0	0	73.1	326	79	49	48	12	2	4	1	35	2	54	5	0	5	6	.455	0	0-0	0	5.89	5.89
17 Bal	AL	3	0	0	0	5.0	29	11	7	4	2	1	0	0	4	0	2	0	0	0	0	-	0	0-0	0	17.51	7.20
17 Was	NL	13	13	0	0	71.0	310	75	46	40	18	3	3	0	25	2	58	3	0	5	6	.455	0	0-0	0	5.19	5.07
Postseason		9	5	0	2	28.0	124	30	17	17	6	2	0	0	15	1	23	0	0	1	2	.333	0	0-0	1	5.97	5.46
15 ML YEARS		377	288	5	30	1800.1	7852	1914	1017	934	214	67	51	34	710	38	1388	97	7	98	120	.450	3	1-3	5	4.61	4.67

Luke Jackson

Pitches: R Bats: R Pos: RP-43 **Ht: 6'2" Wt: 210 Born: 8/24/1991 Age: 26**

Year Team	Lg	HOW MUCH HE PITCHED						WHAT HE GAVE UP												THE RESULTS							
		G	GS	CG	GF	IP	BFP	H	R	ER	HR	SH	SF	HB	TBB	IBB	SO	WP	Bk	W	L	Pct	Sh	Sv-Op	Hld	ERC	ERA
2017 Gwnntt*	AAA	9	4	0	1	24.1	112	26	17	17	2	0	0	0	16	0	23	2	0	0	3	.000	0	1--	-	5.39	6.29
2015 Tex	AL	7	0	0	4	6.1	27	5	3	3	1	0	0	0	2	0	6	1	0	0	0	-	0	0-0	0	2.81	4.26
2016 Tex	AL	8	0	0	2	11.2	62	22	14	14	4	0	1	0	8	0	3	0	0	0	0	-	0	0-0	0	13.93	10.80
2017 Atl	NL	43	0	0	17	50.2	224	55	26	26	4	1	2	4	19	4	33	4	0	2	0	1.000	0	0-0	0	4.50	4.62
3 ML YEARS		58	0	0	23	68.2	313	82	43	43	9	1	3	4	29	4	42	5	0	2	0	1.000	0	0-0	1	5.69	5.64

Paul Janish

Bats: R Throws: R Pos: SS-14;PR-1   YONN-ish   Ht: 6'2" Wt: 200 Born: 10/12/1982 Age: 35

Year Team	Lg	G	AB	H	2B	3B	HR	(Hm	Rd)	TB	R	RBI	RC	TBB	IBB	SO	HBP	SH	SF	SB	CS	GDP	Avg	OBP	Slg	OPS
2017 Norfolk*	AAA	73	223	57	10	1	3	(-	-)	78	23	28	30	24	0	38	7	2	2	1	0	1	.256	.344	.350	.694
2008 Cin	NL	38	80	15	2	0	1	(1	0)	20	5	6	5	7	0	18	2	0	0	0	0	2	.188	.270	.250	.520
2009 Cin	NL	90	256	54	21	0	1	(1	0)	78	36	16	18	26	1	40	5	5	0	2	0	8	.211	.296	.305	.601
2010 Cin	NL	82	200	52	10	0	5	(0	5)	77	23	25	31	22	2	30	2	3	1	1	3	4	.260	.338	.385	.723
2011 Cin	NL	114	336	72	14	1	0	(0	0)	88	27	23	21	18	1	46	4	3	5	3	2	7	.214	.259	.262	.521
2012 Atl	NL	55	167	31	6	1	0	(0	0)	39	18	9	13	17	0	30	2	0	0	1	0	3	.186	.269	.234	.502
2013 Atl	NL	52	41	7	2	0	0	(0	0)	9	7	2	1	3	0	11	0	0	1	0	0	3	.171	.222	.220	.442
2015 Bal	AL	14	35	10	3	0	0	(0	0)	13	4	3	3	0	0	3	0	0	1	0	0	0	.286	.278	.371	.649
2016 Bal	AL	14	31	6	1	0	0	(0	0)	7	3	0	3	3	0	3	1	0	0	0	0	0	.194	.286	.226	.512
2017 Bal	AL	14	26	2	0	0	0	(0	0)	2	0	3	0	1	0	6	0	1	0	0	0	1	.077	.111	.077	.188
Postseason		2	1	0	0	0	0	(0	0)	0	0	0	0	0	0	0	0	1	0	0	0	0	.000	.000	.000	.000
9 ML YEARS		473	1172	249	59	2	7	(2	5)	333	123	87	95	97	4	187	16	12	8	7	5	26	.212	.280	.284	.564

Jordan Jankowski

Pitches: R Bats: R Pos: RP-3   Ht: 6'1" Wt: 225 Born: 5/17/1989 Age: 29

		HOW MUCH HE PITCHED						WHAT HE GAVE UP												THE RESULTS							
Year Team	Lg	G	GS	CG	GF	IP	BFP	H	R	ER	HR	SH	SF	HB	TBB	IBB	SO	WP	Bk	W	L	Pct	Sh	Sv-Op	Hld	ERC	ERA
2013 2 Tms	Low	37	12	0	12	106.1	424	94	37	36	12	1	1	4	21	0	103	7	0	3	1	.750	0	5- -	-	2.96	3.05
2014 CpChr	AA	30	14	0	7	108.0	433	90	44	43	12	3	4	3	26	0	120	5	0	5	6	.455	0	3- -	-	2.79	3.58
2015 Fresno	AAA	55	0	0	16	62.1	275	55	24	22	0	5	2	1	34	2	77	4	0	8	3	.727	0	5- -	-	3.22	3.18
2016 Fresno	AAA	51	2	0	17	71.2	299	54	32	30	6	1	2	3	31	3	103	9	0	2	3	.400	0	5- -	-	2.85	3.77
2017 Fresno	AAA	37	0	0	23	40.1	185	39	24	23	4	1	5	0	23	2	53	8	0	2	3	.400	0	10- -	-	4.31	5.13
2017 Hou	AL	3	0	0	2	4.1	22	7	6	6	3	0	0	0	2	0	5	0	0	1	0	1.000	0	0-0	0	13.26	12.46

Travis Jankowski

Bats: L Throws: R Pos: LF-19;CF-4;RF-3;PH-3   Ht: 6'2" Wt: 185 Born: 6/15/1991 Age: 27

		BATTING																		RUNNING			AVERAGES			
Year Team	Lg	G	AB	H	2B	3B	HR	(Hm	Rd)	TB	R	RBI	RC	TBB	IBB	SO	HBP	SH	SF	SB	CS	GDP	Avg	OBP	Slg	OPS
2017 ElPaso*	AAA	35	139	37	5	1	0	(-	-)	44	20	11	18	18	0	28	0	0	0	8	1	2	.266	.350	.317	.667
2015 SD	NL	34	90	19	2	2	2	(0	2)	31	9	12	10	4	0	24	0	2	0	2	1	1	.211	.245	.344	.589
2016 SD	NL	131	335	82	13	2	2	(1	1)	105	53	12	34	42	0	100	2	3	0	30	12	5	.245	.332	.313	.646
2017 SD	NL	27	75	14	2	0	0	(0	0)	16	10	1	5	9	0	28	1	2	0	4	0	2	.187	.282	.213	.496
3 ML YEARS		192	500	115	17	4	4	(1	3)	152	72	25	49	55	0	152	3	7	0	36	13	8	.230	.310	.304	.614

Kenley Jansen

Pitches: R Bats: B Pos: RP-65   KEN-lee JANN-sen   Ht: 6'5" Wt: 275 Born: 9/30/1987 Age: 30

		HOW MUCH HE PITCHED						WHAT HE GAVE UP												THE RESULTS							
Year Team	Lg	G	GS	CG	GF	IP	BFP	H	R	ER	HR	SH	SF	HB	TBB	IBB	SO	WP	Bk	W	L	Pct	Sh	Sv-Op	Hld	ERC	ERA
2010 LAD	NL	25	0	0	8	27.0	109	12	2	2	0	1	0	1	15	1	41	1	0	1	0	1.000	0	4-4	4	1.40	0.67
2011 LAD	NL	51	0	0	13	53.2	218	30	17	17	3	0	1	2	26	0	96	0	2	2	1	.667	0	5-6	9	1.96	2.85
2012 LAD	NL	65	0	0	40	65.0	252	33	18	17	6	0	1	3	22	1	99	3	0	5	3	.625	0	25-32	8	1.55	2.35
2013 LAD	NL	75	0	0	45	76.2	292	48	16	16	6	0	0	3	18	1	111	2	0	4	3	.571	0	28-32	16	1.65	1.88
2014 LAD	NL	68	0	0	57	65.1	268	55	20	20	5	1	2	0	19	2	101	2	0	2	3	.400	0	44-49	0	2.60	2.76
2015 LAD	NL	54	0	0	50	52.1	200	33	14	14	6	0	2	2	8	0	80	0	0	2	1	.667	0	36-38	1	1.58	2.41
2016 LAD	NL	71	0	0	63	68.2	251	35	14	14	4	3	1	2	11	2	104	1	0	3	2	.600	0	47-53	0	1.03	1.83
2017 LAD	NL	65	0	0	57	68.1	258	44	11	10	5	0	0	2	7	0	109	2	1	5	0	1.000	0	41-42	1	1.35	1.32
Postseason		17	0	0	15	20.1	83	12	6	6	1	0	0	1	9	2	35	0	0	0	0	-	0	8-8	1	1.82	2.66
8 ML YEARS		474	0	0	333	477.0	1848	290	112	110	35	5	7	15	126	7	741	11	3	24	13	.649	0	230-256	39	1.60	2.08

John Jaso

Bats: L Throws: R Pos: PH-59;RF-46;1B-29;LF-17;PR-1   JAY-soe   Ht: 6'2" Wt: 202 Born: 9/19/1983 Age: 34

		BATTING																		RUNNING			AVERAGES			
Year Team	Lg	G	AB	H	2B	3B	HR	(Hm	Rd)	TB	R	RBI	RC	TBB	IBB	SO	HBP	SH	SF	SB	CS	GDP	Avg	OBP	Slg	OPS
2008 TB	AL	5	10	2	0	0	0	(0	0)	2	2	0	0	0	0	2	0	0	0	0	0	1	.200	.200	.200	.400
2010 TB	AL	109	339	89	18	3	5	(1	4)	128	57	44	57	59	1	39	2	1	3	4	0	8	.263	.372	.378	.750
2011 TB	AL	89	246	55	15	1	5	(3	2)	87	26	27	20	25	0	36	1	1	0	1	2	9	.224	.298	.354	.651
2012 Sea	AL	108	294	81	19	2	10	(6	4)	134	41	50	68	56	1	51	5	1	5	0	5	6	.276	.394	.456	.850
2013 Oak	AL	70	207	56	12	0	3	(0	3)	77	31	21	36	38	0	45	2	1	1	2	1	5	.271	.387	.372	.759
2014 Oak	AL	99	307	81	18	3	9	(5	4)	132	42	40	44	28	1	60	7	0	2	2	0	5	.264	.337	.430	.767
2015 TB	AL	70	185	53	17	0	5	(3	2)	85	23	22	32	28	1	39	1	0	2	1	2	5	.286	.380	.459	.839
2016 Pit	NL	132	380	102	25	3	8	(4	4)	157	45	42	55	45	0	74	5	1	1	0	4	8	.268	.353	.413	.766
2017 Pit	NL	126	256	54	19	0	10	(5	5)	103	28	35	30	40	2	66	5	0	1	1	1	5	.211	.328	.402	.730
Postseason		5	14	3	0	0	0	(0	0)	3	0	1	1	1	0	3	0	0	0	0	0	0	.214	.267	.214	.481
9 ML YEARS		808	2224	573	143	12	55	(27	28)	905	295	281	342	319	6	412	28	5	15	16	10	52	.258	.356	.407	.763

Jon Jay

Bats: L **Throws:** L **Pos:** LF-64;CF-54;PH-46;RF-19;DH-2   **Ht:** 5'11" **Wt:** 195 **Born:** 3/15/1985 **Age:** 33

Year	Team	Lg	G	AB	H	2B	3B	HR	(Hm	Rd)	TB	R	RBI	RC	TBB	IBB	SO	HBP	SH	SF	SB	CS	GDP	Avg	OBP	Slg	OPS
2010	StL	NL	105	287	86	19	2	4	(2	2)	121	47	27	40	24	0	50	3	8	1	2	4	5	.300	.359	.422	.780
2011	StL	NL	159	455	135	24	2	10	(5	5)	193	56	37	56	28	1	81	7	9	4	6	7	11	.297	.344	.424	.768
2012	StL	NL	117	443	135	22	4	4	(3	1)	177	70	40	65	34	3	71	15	9	1	19	7	9	.305	.373	.400	.773
2013	StL	NL	157	548	151	27	2	7	(2	5)	203	75	67	74	52	7	103	14	9	5	10	5	13	.276	.351	.370	.721
2014	StL	NL	140	413	125	16	3	3	(0	3)	156	52	46	57	28	3	78	20	3	4	6	3	17	.303	.372	.378	.750
2015	StL	NL	79	210	44	5	1	1	(0	1)	54	25	10	11	19	5	36	11	3	2	0	2	7	.210	.306	.257	.563
2016	SD	NL	90	347	101	26	1	2	(1	1)	135	49	26	55	19	0	78	6	1	0	2	0	5	.291	.339	.389	.728
2017	ChC	NL	141	379	112	18	3	2	(1	1)	142	65	34	58	37	3	80	12	3	2	6	2	11	.296	.374	.375	.749
	Postseason		58	190	44	4	1	0	(0	0)	50	24	15	20	19	1	30	4	4	2	5	2	4	.232	.312	.263	.575
	8 ML YEARS		988	3082	889	157	18	33	(14	19)	1181	439	287	416	241	22	577	88	45	19	51	30	78	.288	.355	.383	.738

Myles Jaye

Pitches: R **Bats:** B **Pos:** RP-3; SP-2   **Ht:** 6'3" **Wt:** 170 **Born:** 12/28/1991 **Age:** 26

Year	Team	Lg	G	GS	CG	GF	IP	BFP	H	R	ER	HR	SH	SF	HB	TBB	IBB	SO	WP	Bk	W	L	Pct	Sh	Sv-Op	Hld	ERC	ERA
2013	2 Tms	Low	27	27	1	0	159.1	684	158	77	64	10	0	5	9	61	0	126	11	1	13	7	.650	1	0- --	-	3.96	3.62
2014	Brham	AA	24	24	1	0	132.0	583	146	87	78	10	3	10	9	53	0	73	9	1	4	12	.250	0	0- --	-	4.85	5.32
2015	Brham	AA	26	26	0	0	147.2	613	135	64	54	8	3	3	7	47	1	104	9	1	12	9	.571	0	0- --	-	3.20	3.29
2016	Erie	AA	21	21	1	0	122.2	520	127	60	55	11	2	1	3	29	1	104	12	0	4	8	.333	0	0- --	-	3.61	4.04
2016	Toledo	AAA	7	7	0	0	39.0	160	30	18	16	2	1	2	2	12	1	31	1	0	1	4	.200	0	0- --	-	2.34	3.69
2017	Erie	AA	14	14	1	0	71.1	318	77	41	34	8	2	1	6	23	0	73	6	0	1	7	.125	1	0- --	-	4.56	4.29
2017	Toledo	AAA	11	11	0	0	60.1	272	71	31	24	3	4	2	5	23	1	42	3	0	3	6	.333	0	0- --	-	4.96	3.58
2017	Det	AL	5	2	0	0	12.2	71	18	18	17	2	0	2	3	10	0	4	2	0	1	2	.333	0	0-0	0	9.45	12.08

Jeremy Jeffress

Pitches: R **Bats:** R **Pos:** RP-60; SP-1   JEFF-ress   **Ht:** 6'0" **Wt:** 205 **Born:** 9/21/1987 **Age:** 30

Year	Team	Lg	G	GS	CG	GF	IP	BFP	H	R	ER	HR	SH	SF	HB	TBB	IBB	SO	WP	Bk	W	L	Pct	Sh	Sv-Op	Hld	ERC	ERA
2010	Mil	NL	10	0	0	5	10.0	42	8	4	3	0	0	1	0	6	1	8	1	0	1	0	1.000	0	0-0	0	2.96	2.70
2011	KC	AL	14	0	0	6	15.1	67	12	8	8	1	2	0	0	11	0	13	1	0	1	1	.500	0	1-2	0	3.87	4.70
2012	KC	AL	13	0	0	6	13.1	73	19	14	10	0	0	0	0	13	0	13	1	0	0	0	-	0	0-0	0	7.87	6.75
2013	Tor	AL	10	0	0	3	10.1	43	8	1	1	1	0	0	0	5	0	12	0	0	1	0	1.000	0	0-0	0	3.17	0.87
2014	2 Tms		32	0	0	12	32.0	135	35	10	10	1	3	1	2	10	2	29	1	0	1	1	.500	0	0-1	6	4.06	2.81
2015	Mil	NL	72	0	0	8	68.0	285	64	22	20	5	3	0	3	22	5	67	4	2	5	0	1.000	0	0-5	23	3.36	2.65
2016	2 Tms		59	0	0	41	58.0	241	55	17	15	2	2	1	4	18	3	42	3	0	3	2	.600	0	27-28	6	3.26	2.33
2017	2 Tms		61	1	0	12	65.1	295	73	35	34	10	1	2	2	34	4	51	6	0	5	2	.714	0	0-1	8	5.75	4.68
14	Tor	AL	3	0	0	3	3.1	21	8	4	4	0	0	1	2	3	0	4	0	0	0	0	-	0	0-0	0	19.06	10.80
14	Mil	NL	29	0	0	9	28.2	114	27	6	6	1	3	0	0	7	2	25	1	0	1	1	.500	0	0-1	6	2.75	1.88
16	Mil	NL	47	0	0	40	44.2	190	45	13	11	2	2	1	4	11	3	35	0	0	2	2	.500	0	27-28	6	3.38	2.22
16	Tex	AL	12	0	0	1	13.1	51	10	4	4	0	0	0	0	7	0	7	3	0	1	0	1.000	0	0-0	0	2.84	2.70
17	Tex	AL	39	0	0	10	40.2	183	49	25	24	8	0	1	2	19	2	29	3	0	1	2	.333	0	0-0	4	6.63	5.31
17	Mil	NL	22	1	0	2	24.2	112	24	10	10	2	1	0	0	15	2	22	3	0	4	0	1.000	0	0-1	4	4.39	3.65
	Postseason		1	0	0	0	1.0	4	1	1	0	0	0	0	0	1	0	1	0	0	0	0	-	0	0-0	0	6.99	0.00
	8 ML YEARS		271	1	0	93	272.1	1181	274	111	101	20	11	4	11	119	15	235	17	2	17	6	.739	0	28-37	43	4.18	3.34

Dan Jennings

Pitches: L **Bats:** L **Pos:** RP-77   **Ht:** 6'3" **Wt:** 210 **Born:** 4/17/1987 **Age:** 31

Year	Team	Lg	G	GS	CG	GF	IP	BFP	H	R	ER	HR	SH	SF	HB	TBB	IBB	SO	WP	Bk	W	L	Pct	Sh	Sv-Op	Hld	ERC	ERA
2012	Mia	NL	22	0	0	4	19.0	86	18	5	4	2	0	0	2	11	1	8	0	0	1	0	1.000	0	0-0	2	4.85	1.89
2013	Mia	NL	47	0	0	6	40.2	171	39	17	17	1	0	2	0	16	2	38	3	0	2	4	.333	0	0-2	1	3.27	3.76
2014	Mia	NL	47	0	0	12	40.1	182	45	11	6	3	2	3	0	17	1	38	2	0	0	0	.000	0	0-2	3	4.50	1.34
2015	CWS	AL	53	0	0	17	56.1	244	55	28	25	3	4	1	0	24	6	46	4	0	2	3	.400	0	0-0	4	3.52	3.99
2016	CWS	AL	64	0	0	15	60.2	259	57	18	14	1	2	6	3	28	0	46	4	0	3	1	.571	0	1-3	10	3.65	2.08
2017	2 Tms	AL	77	0	0	12	62.2	267	53	27	24	8	0	1	1	31	7	51	3	0	3	1	.750	0	0-2	14	3.68	3.45
17	CWS	AL	48	0	0	8	44.1	185	35	20	17	6	0	1	1	19	4	38	0	0	3	1	.750	0	0-1	7	3.22	3.45
17	TB	AL	29	0	0	4	18.1	82	18	7	7	2	0	0	0	12	3	13	3	0	0	0	-	0	0-1	7	4.83	3.44
	6 ML YEARS		310	0	0	66	279.2	1209	267	106	90	18	8	13	6	127	17	227	16	0	12	13	.480	0	1-9	34	3.78	2.90

A.J. Jimenez

Bats: R **Throws:** R **Pos:** C-5;PH-2;DH-1   **Ht:** 6'0" **Wt:** 195 **Born:** 5/1/1990 **Age:** 28

Year	Team	Lg	G	AB	H	2B	3B	HR	(Hm	Rd)	TB	R	RBI	RC	TBB	IBB	SO	HBP	SH	SF	SB	CS	GDP	Avg	OBP	Slg	OPS
2013	Nham	AA	50	203	56	15	0	3	(-	-)	80	28	29	27	16	0	37	1	0	3	1	2	6	.276	.327	.394	.721
2014	Nham	AA	25	94	21	8	0	1	(-	-)	32	11	13	9	6	0	19	1	0	1	1	0	3	.223	.275	.340	.615
2014	Buffalo	AAA	58	219	57	13	1	2	(-	-)	78	21	24	24	13	0	33	0	0	5	1	1	7	.260	.295	.356	.652
2015	Buffalo	AAA	23	87	19	7	1	0	(-	-)	28	6	9	9	9	0	12	1	0	1	2	0	2	.218	.296	.322	.618
2016	Buffalo	AAA	67	228	55	17	1	4	(-	-)	86	24	28	26	13	0	33	4	0	3	1	1	9	.241	.290	.377	.668
2017	RdRck	AAA	51	196	48	9	0	7	(-	-)	78	18	16	22	7	0	45	2	0	2	1	0	4	.245	.275	.398	.673
2017	Tex	AL	7	12	1	0	0	0	(0	0)	1	0	0	0	0	0	7	0	1	0	0	0	1	.083	.083	.083	.167

Joe Jimenez

Pitches: R Bats: R Pos: RP-24
Ht: 6'3" Wt: 220 Born: 1/17/1995 Age: 23

Year	Team	Lg	G	GS	CG	GF	IP	BFP	H	R	ER	HR	SH	SF	HB	TBB	IBB	SO	WP	Bk	W	L	Pct	Sh	Sv-Op	Hld	ERC	ERA
2013	Tigers	R	8	0	0	3	18.0	68	9	1	1	0	2	2	0	6	0	24	0	0	3	0	1.000	0	1- -	-	1.11	0.50
2014	Conn	A-	23	0	0	16	26.2	110	22	10	8	1	1	0	2	6	0	41	4	0	3	2	.600	0	4- -	-	2.34	2.70
2015	Wmich	A	40	0	0	34	43.0	162	23	8	7	2	0	1	0	11	0	61	2	0	5	1	.833	0	17- -	-	1.21	1.47
2016	Lkland	A+	17	0	0	17	17.1	63	5	0	0	0	0	0	2	5	0	28	0	0	0	0	-	0	10- -	-	0.71	0.00
2016	Erie	AA	21	0	0	19	20.2	80	12	5	5	0	1	1	0	8	1	34	1	0	3	2	.600	0	12- -	-	1.41	2.18
2016	Toledo	AAA	17	0	0	16	15.2	60	9	5	4	1	0	1	0	4	0	16	0	0	0	1	.000	0	8- -	-	1.38	2.30
2017	Toledo	AAA	26	0	0	14	25.0	102	19	4	4	1	0	1	0	12	2	36	0	0	1	1	.500	0	4- -	-	2.64	1.44
2017	Det	AL	24	0	0	6	19.0	99	31	28	26	4	0	1	2	9	0	17	0	0	0	2	.000	0	0-1	0	9.60	12.32

Ubaldo Jimenez

Pitches: R Bats: R Pos: SP-25; RP-6
ooh-BALL-doh
Ht: 6'5" Wt: 210 Born: 1/22/1984 Age: 34

Year	Team	Lg	G	GS	CG	GF	IP	BFP	H	R	ER	HR	SH	SF	HB	TBB	IBB	SO	WP	Bk	W	L	Pct	Sh	Sv-Op	Hld	ERC	ERA
2006	Col	NL	2	1	0	0	7.2	30	5	4	3	1	0	0	0	3	0	3	0	0	0	0	-	0	0-0	0	2.48	3.52
2007	Col	NL	15	15	0	0	82.0	354	70	46	39	10	3	1	6	37	4	68	3	0	4	4	.500	0	0-0	0	3.80	4.28
2008	Col	NL	34	34	1	0	198.2	868	182	97	88	11	7	4	10	103	4	172	16	0	12	12	.500	0	0-0	0	3.92	3.99
2009	Col	NL	33	33	0	0	218.0	914	183	87	84	13	15	6	10	85	6	198	8	3	15	12	.556	0	0-0	0	3.03	3.47
2010	Col	NL	33	33	4	0	221.2	894	164	73	71	10	7	1	9	92	7	214	16	1	19	8	.704	2	0-0	0	2.57	2.88
2011	2 Tms		32	32	2	0	188.1	822	186	111	98	17	2	2	9	78	5	180	8	0	10	13	.435	1	0-0	0	4.13	4.68
2012	Cle	AL	31	31	0	0	176.2	805	190	116	106	25	2	3	8	95	3	143	16	1	9	17	.346	0	0-0	0	5.55	5.40
2013	Cle	AL	32	32	0	0	182.2	777	163	75	67	16	1	11	3	80	0	194	8	0	13	9	.591	0	0-0	0	3.61	3.30
2014	Bal	AL	25	22	0	0	125.1	553	113	68	67	14	3	1	4	77	0	116	4	0	6	9	.400	0	0-0	1	4.62	4.81
2015	Bal	AL	32	32	0	0	184.0	791	182	89	84	20	1	4	11	68	1	168	6	0	12	10	.545	0	0-0	0	4.21	4.11
2016	Bal	AL	29	25	1	2	142.1	638	150	93	86	16	1	1	3	72	1	125	5	1	8	12	.400	0	1-1	0	4.97	5.44
2017	Bal	AL	31	25	0	2	142.2	648	169	109	108	33	1	4	5	58	0	139	3	0	6	11	.353	0	0-0	0	6.32	6.81
11	Col	NL	21	21	2	0	123.0	532	118	68	61	10	2	2	7	51	5	118	6	0	6	9	.400	1	0-0	0	3.94	4.46
11	Cle	AL	11	11	0	0	65.1	290	68	43	37	7	0	0	2	27	0	62	2	0	4	4	.500	0	0-0	0	4.48	5.10
	Postseason		6	5	0	1	28.0	126	29	14	14	4	0	1	1	16	2	24	1	0	0	3	.000	0	0-0	0	5.37	4.50
	12 ML YEARS		329	315	9	4	1870.0	8094	1757	968	901	186	43	38	78	848	31	1720	93	6	114	117	.494	3	1-1	1	4.10	4.34

Brian Johnson

Pitches: L Bats: L Pos: SP-5
Ht: 6'4" Wt: 235 Born: 12/7/1990 Age: 27

Year	Team	Lg	G	GS	CG	GF	IP	BFP	H	R	ER	HR	SH	SF	HB	TBB	IBB	SO	WP	Bk	W	L	Pct	Sh	Sv-Op	Hld	ERC	ERA
2013	3 Tms	Low	19	19	0	0	85.0	350	60	31	24	4	2	0	4	35	0	84	8	1	2	6	.250	0	0- -	-	2.39	2.54
2014	Salem	A+	5	5	0	0	25.2	109	23	13	11	0	1	1	0	7	0	33	3	1	3	1	.750	0	0- -	-	2.30	3.86
2014	Portlnd	AA	20	20	2	0	118.0	452	78	29	23	6	4	4	0	32	0	99	5	0	10	2	.833	0	0- -	-	1.67	1.75
2015	Pwtckt	AAA	18	18	1	0	96.0	390	74	34	27	6	1	2	4	32	0	90	5	0	9	6	.600	1	0- -	-	2.55	2.53
2016	Pwtckt	AAA	15	15	0	0	77.0	329	74	38	35	9	1	4	1	36	0	54	2	1	5	6	.455	0	0- -	-	4.38	4.09
2017	Pwtckt	AAA	17	17	0	0	90.1	375	82	32	31	10	3	2	1	28	0	70	0	0	3	4	.429	0	0- -	-	3.34	3.09
2015	Bos	AL	1	1	0	0	4.1	19	3	4	4	0	0	1	0	4	0	3	0	0	0	1	.000	0	0-0	0	3.72	8.31
2017	Bos	AL	5	5	1	0	27.0	121	32	13	13	5	0	0	0	8	1	21	0	0	2	0	1.000	1	0-0	0	5.16	4.33
	2 ML YEARS		6	6	1	0	31.1	140	35	17	17	5	0	1	0	12	1	24	0	0	2	1	.667	1	0-0	0	4.98	4.88

Jim Johnson

Pitches: R Bats: R Pos: RP-61
Ht: 6'6" Wt: 250 Born: 6/27/1983 Age: 35

Year	Team	Lg	G	GS	CG	GF	IP	BFP	H	R	ER	HR	SH	SF	HB	TBB	IBB	SO	WP	Bk	W	L	Pct	Sh	Sv-Op	Hld	ERC	ERA
2006	Bal	AL	1	1	0	0	3.0	21	9	8	8	1	0	1	1	3	0	0	0	0	0	1	.000	0	0-0	0	26.81	24.00
2007	Bal	AL	1	0	0	1	2.0	11	3	2	2	0	0	1	1	2	0	1	0	0	0	0	-	0	0-0	0	8.58	9.00
2008	Bal	AL	54	0	0	18	68.2	281	54	18	17	0	2	1	3	28	3	38	1	1	2	4	.333	0	1-1	19	2.45	2.23
2009	Bal	AL	64	0	0	29	70.0	300	73	32	32	8	2	2	3	23	3	49	2	1	4	6	.400	0	10-16	14	4.28	4.11
2010	Bal	AL	26	0	0	6	26.1	117	32	11	10	2	3	0	1	5	1	22	4	0	1	1	.500	0	1-6	11	4.26	3.42
2011	Bal	AL	69	0	0	20	91.0	366	80	30	27	5	4	2	2	21	3	58	2	1	6	5	.545	0	9-14	18	2.58	2.67
2012	Bal	AL	71	0	0	63	68.2	269	55	21	19	3	1	0	3	15	1	41	1	0	2	1	.667	0	51-54	0	2.22	2.49
2013	Bal	AL	74	0	0	63	70.1	291	72	26	23	5	2	0	7	18	4	56	2	0	3	8	.273	0	50-59	0	3.89	2.94
2014	2 Tms	AL	54	0	0	21	53.1	263	69	46	42	5	3	2	6	35	6	42	4	0	5	2	.714	0	2-3	2	7.13	7.09
2015	2 Tms	NL	72	0	0	15	66.2	291	77	36	33	5	3	3	5	20	2	50	3	0	2	6	.250	0	10-17	25	4.70	4.46
2016	Atl	NL	65	0	0	36	64.2	266	57	23	22	3	0	1	3	20	0	68	6	0	2	6	.250	0	20-23	8	2.95	3.06
2017	Atl	NL	61	0	0	38	56.2	256	59	39	35	8	0	3	1	25	3	61	3	0	6	3	.667	0	22-31	1	4.63	5.56
14	Oak	AL	38	0	0	18	40.1	200	60	33	32	5	2	2	3	23	3	28	4	0	4	2	.667	0	2-3	2	8.28	7.14
14	Det	AL	16	0	0	3	13.0	63	9	13	10	0	1	0	3	12	3	14	0	0	1	0	1.000	0	0-0	0	3.86	6.92
15	Atl	NL	49	0	0	13	48.0	196	45	14	12	2	3	2	1	14	2	33	2	0	2	3	.400	0	9-13	20	3.02	2.25
15	LAD	NL	23	0	0	2	18.2	95	32	22	21	3	0	1	4	6	0	17	1	0	0	3	.000	0	1-4	5	9.81	10.13
	Postseason		5	0	0	3	5.1	25	8	6	5	2	0	0	0	1	0	4	0	0	0	1	.000	0	2-3	0	8.18	8.44
	12 ML YEARS		612	1	0	310	641.1	2732	640	292	270	45	20	16	35	215	26	486	28	3	33	43	.434	0	176-224	98	3.78	3.79

Micah Johnson

Bats: L **Throws:** R **Pos:** PH-8;PR-8;LF-3　　　　**Ht:** 6'0" **Wt:** 210 **Born:** 12/18/1990 **Age:** 27

Year Team	Lg	G	AB	H	2B	3B	HR	(Hm	Rd)	TB	R	RBI	RC	TBB	IBB	SO	HBP	SH	SF	SB	CS	GDP	Avg	OBP	Slg	OPS
2017 Gwnntt*	AAA	40	135	39	6	3	1	(-	-)	54	19	15	21	18	0	38	1	1	0	6	4	1	.289	.377	.400	.777
2015 CWS	AL	36	100	23	4	0	0	(0	0)	27	10	4	8	9	0	30	2	2	0	3	2	0	.230	.306	.270	.576
2016 LAD	NL	7	6	1	0	0	0	(0	0)	1	1	0	0	0	0	1	0	0	0	0	0	0	.167	.167	.167	.333
2017 Atl	NL	18	10	2	0	0	0	(0	0)	2	2	0	0	0	0	4	0	1	0	1	0	0	.200	.200	.200	.400
3 ML YEARS		61	116	26	4	0	0	(0	0)	30	13	4	8	9	0	35	2	3	0	4	2	0	.224	.291	.259	.550

Pierce Johnson

Pitches: R **Bats:** R **Pos:** RP-1　　　　**Ht:** 6'3" **Wt:** 200 **Born:** 5/10/1991 **Age:** 27

Year Team	Lg	G	GS	CG	GF	IP	BFP	H	R	ER	HR	SH	SF	HB	TBB	IBB	SO	WP	Bk	W	L	Pct	Sh	Sv-Op	Hld	ERC	ERA
2013 2 Tms	Low	23	21	0	1	118.1	492	109	41	36	5	0	2	9	43	0	124	4	1	11	6	.647	0	0- -	-	3.50	2.74
2014 Tenn	AA	18	17	0	0	91.2	373	60	27	26	8	3	2	5	54	0	91	3	0	5	4	.556	0	0- -	-	3.19	2.55
2015 Tenn	AA	16	16	1	0	95.0	383	76	24	22	4	4	2	4	32	0	72	2	0	6	2	.750	0	0- -	-	2.62	2.08
2016 Iowa	AAA	22	11	0	1	63.0	288	60	44	43	8	2	4	5	43	0	75	3	2	4	6	.400	0	0- -	-	5.52	6.14
2017 Iowa	AAA	43	1	0	25	54.1	234	52	26	26	3	0	1	4	27	1	74	4	0	3	2	.600	0	9- -	-	4.27	4.31
2017 ChC	NL	1	0	0	0	1.0	7	2	2	0	0	0	0	0	1	0	2	0	0	0	0	-	0	0-0	0	10.22	0.00

Adam Jones

Bats: R **Throws:** R **Pos:** CF-147　　　　**Ht:** 6'2" **Wt:** 215 **Born:** 8/1/1985 **Age:** 32

Year Team	Lg	G	AB	H	2B	3B	HR	(Hm	Rd)	TB	R	RBI	RC	TBB	IBB	SO	HBP	SH	SF	SB	CS	GDP	Avg	OBP	Slg	OPS
2006 Sea	AL	32	74	16	4	0	1	(0	1)	23	6	8	4	2	0	22	0	0	0	3	1	3	.216	.237	.311	.548
2007 Sea	AL	41	65	16	2	1	2	(1	1)	26	16	4	5	4	0	21	1	1	0	2	1	0	.246	.300	.400	.700
2008 Bal	AL	132	477	129	21	7	9	(4	5)	191	61	57	56	23	0	108	7	2	5	10	3	12	.270	.311	.400	.711
2009 Bal	AL	119	473	131	22	3	19	(11	8)	216	83	70	71	36	3	93	7	0	3	10	4	13	.277	.335	.457	.792
2010 Bal	AL	149	581	165	25	5	19	(9	10)	257	76	69	72	23	1	119	3	0	2	7	7	17	.284	.325	.442	.767
2011 Bal	AL	151	567	159	26	2	25	(19	6)	264	68	83	77	29	2	113	9	1	12	12	4	16	.280	.319	.466	.785
2012 Bal	AL	162	648	186	39	3	32	(15	17)	327	103	82	101	34	0	126	13	0	2	16	7	15	.287	.334	.505	.839
2013 Bal	AL	160	653	186	35	1	33	(17	16)	322	100	108	101	25	4	136	8	0	3	14	3	15	.285	.318	.493	.811
2014 Bal	AL	159	644	181	30	2	29	(14	15)	302	88	96	92	19	1	133	12	0	7	7	1	11	.281	.311	.469	.780
2015 Bal	AL	137	546	147	25	3	27	(17	10)	259	74	82	73	24	3	102	8	0	3	3	1	21	.269	.308	.474	.782
2016 Bal	AL	152	619	164	19	0	29	(14	15)	270	86	83	82	39	2	115	5	1	8	2	0	15	.265	.310	.436	.746
2017 Bal	AL	147	597	170	28	1	26	(17	9)	278	82	73	89	27	1	113	7	1	3	2	1	18	.285	.322	.466	.787
Postseason		14	58	9	0	0	1	(1	0)	12	7	4	3	3	0	16	1	0	1	1	0	1	.155	.206	.207	.413
12 ML YEARS		1541	5944	1650	276	28	251	(138	113)	2735	843	815	823	285	17	1201	90	8	48	88	33	154	.278	.318	.460	.778

JaCoby Jones

Bats: R **Throws:** R **Pos:** CF-51;PH-6;PR-4;RF-1　　　　**Ht:** 6'2" **Wt:** 205 **Born:** 5/10/1992 **Age:** 26

Year Team	Lg	G	AB	H	2B	3B	HR	(Hm	Rd)	TB	R	RBI	RC	TBB	IBB	SO	HBP	SH	SF	SB	CS	GDP	Avg	OBP	Slg	OPS
2013 Jmstwn	A-	15	61	19	2	2	1	(-	-)	28	14	10	10	3	0	14	2	0	1	3	2	1	.311	.358	.459	.817
2014 WV	A	117	445	128	21	3	23	(-	-)	224	72	70	79	33	0	132	12	3	8	17	9	8	.288	.347	.503	.851
2015 Bradtn	A+	93	379	96	18	3	10	(-	-)	150	48	58	50	31	0	113	4	4	5	14	4	7	.253	.313	.396	.708
2015 Erie	AA	37	136	34	7	2	6	(-	-)	63	26	20	24	17	0	52	2	0	5	10	3	4	.250	.331	.463	.794
2016 Erie	AA	20	77	24	6	2	4	(-	-)	46	11	20	17	10	0	23	1	0	1	2	1	0	.312	.393	.597	.991
2016 Toledo	AAA	79	292	71	14	5	3	(-	-)	104	33	23	34	25	1	97	4	0	3	11	4	7	.243	.309	.356	.665
2017 Toledo	AAA	90	351	86	19	2	9	(-	-)	136	57	44	45	33	2	104	3	5	1	12	4	9	.245	.314	.387	.702
2016 Det	AL	13	28	6	3	0	0	(0	0)	9	3	2	2	0	0	12	0	0	0	0	0	1	.214	.214	.321	.536
2017 Det	AL	56	141	24	3	1	3	(2	1)	38	14	13	7	9	0	65	4	0	0	6	2	5	.170	.240	.270	.510
2 ML YEARS		69	169	30	6	1	3	(2	1)	47	17	15	9	9	0	77	4	0	0	6	2	6	.178	.236	.278	.514

Nate Jones

Pitches: R **Bats:** R **Pos:** RP-11　　　　**Ht:** 6'5" **Wt:** 220 **Born:** 1/28/1986 **Age:** 32

Year Team	Lg	G	GS	CG	GF	IP	BFP	H	R	ER	HR	SH	SF	HB	TBB	IBB	SO	WP	Bk	W	L	Pct	Sh	Sv-Op	Hld	ERC	ERA
2012 CWS	AL	65	0	0	11	71.2	301	67	19	19	4	2	4	1	32	3	65	5	0	8	0	1.000	0	0-3	7	3.67	2.39
2013 CWS	AL	70	0	0	17	78.0	315	69	40	36	5	3	6	1	26	1	89	8	1	4	5	.444	0	0-4	16	3.09	4.15
2014 CWS	AL	2	0	0	0	0.0	5	2	4	0	0	0	0	0	3	0	0	0	0	0	0	-	0	0-1	0	-	-
2015 CWS	AL	19	0	0	3	19.0	72	12	7	7	5	2	0	0	6	0	27	0	0	2	2	.500	0	0-1	6	2.87	3.32
2016 CWS	AL	71	0	0	11	70.2	274	48	20	18	7	2	2	3	15	3	80	7	0	5	3	.625	0	3-12	28	1.87	2.29
2017 CWS	AL	11	0	0	1	11.2	49	9	3	3	1	1	0	1	6	1	15	1	0	1	0	1.000	0	0-0	4	3.43	2.31
6 ML YEARS		238	0	0	43	251.0	1016	207	93	87	22	10	12	6	88	8	276	21	1	20	10	.667	0	3-21	61	2.98	3.12

Ryder Jones

Bats: L **Throws:** R **Pos:** 1B-30;3B-18;PH-8;LF-1　　　　**Ht:** 6'3" **Wt:** 215 **Born:** 6/7/1994 **Age:** 24

Year Team	Lg	G	AB	H	2B	3B	HR	(Hm	Rd)	TB	R	RBI	RC	TBB	IBB	SO	HBP	SH	SF	SB	CS	GDP	Avg	OBP	Slg	OPS
2013 Giants	R	37	145	46	9	0	1	(-	-)	58	29	18	24	14	0	38	5	0	1	0	0	3	.317	.394	.400	.794
2014 2 Tms	Low	118	476	107	26	2	10	(-	-)	167	60	67	48	25	0	114	10	3	2	7	1	9	.225	.277	.351	.628

Year	Team	Lg	G	AB	H	2B	3B	HR	Hm	Rd	TB	R	RBI	RC	TBB	IBB	SO	HBP	SH	SF	SB	CS	GDP	Avg	OBP	Slg	OPS
2015	SnJos	A+	105	406	109	29	2	6	-	-	160	49	47	48	16	1	80	5	1		2	2	5	.268	.296	.394	.690
2016	Rchmd	AA	126	474	117	26	0	15	-	-	188	49	67	56	26	0	79	5	3		5	1	9	.247	.290	.397	.687
2017	Scrmto	AAA	64	237	74	19	2	13	-	-	136	44	44	54	29	1	53	5	0	2	7	0	3	.312	.396	.574	.969
2017	SF	NL	53	150	26	5	2	2	(1	1)	41	12	5	9	10	3	52	4	0	0	1	0	3	.173	.244	.273	.517

Felix Jorge

Pitches: R **Bats:** R **Pos:** SP-2 **Ht:** 6'2" **Wt:** 170 **Born:** 1/2/1994 **Age:** 24

Year	Team	Lg	G	GS	CG	GF	IP	BFP	H	R	ER	HR	SH	SF	HB	TBB	IBB	SO	WP	Bk	W	L	Pct	Sh	Sv-Op	Hld	ERC	ERA
2013	Elizab	R+	12	12	0	0	61.0	254	56	26	20	2	2	2	2	18	0	72	5	1	2	2	.500	0	0--	-	2.91	2.95
2014	2 Tms	Low	24	20	2	3	105.0	454	115	60	58	11	4	3	6	34	0	84	9	0	6	7	.462	1	0--	-	4.64	4.97
2015	Crpds	A	23	22	0	0	142.0	561	118	52	44	11	1	0	3	32	0	114	6	2	6	7	.462	0	0--	-	2.52	2.79
2016	FtMyrs	A+	14	14	2	0	93.0	356	76	19	16	3	4	0	4	11	0	77	3	0	9	3	.750	1	0--	-	1.93	1.55
2016	Chatt	AA	11	11	1	0	74.1	300	83	34	34	7	1	0	1	12	0	32	2	0	3	5	.375	0	0--	-	3.98	4.12
2017	Chatt	AA	22	22	0	0	134.2	563	142	57	53	11	3	1	2	37	0	99	4	1	10	3	.769	0	0--	-	3.89	3.54
2017	Min	AL	2	2	0	0	7.2	36	14	9	9	4	0	0	0	2	0	4	0	0	1	0	1.000	0	0-0	0	13.28	10.57

Caleb Joseph

Bats: R **Throws:** R **Pos:** C-79;3B-8;PH-4;PR-3 **Ht:** 6'3" **Wt:** 180 **Born:** 6/18/1986 **Age:** 32

Year	Team	Lg	G	AB	H	2B	3B	HR	Hm	Rd	TB	R	RBI	RC	TBB	IBB	SO	HBP	SH	SF	SB	CS	GDP	Avg	OBP	Slg	OPS
2014	Bal	AL	82	246	51	9	0	9	(4	5)	87	22	28	22	17	0	69	3	6	3	0	1	6	.207	.264	.354	.618
2015	Bal	AL	100	320	75	16	1	11	(5	6)	126	38	49	44	27	2	72	3	3	1	0	0	7	.234	.299	.394	.693
2016	Bal	AL	49	132	23	3	0	1	(0	0)	26	7	0	0	7	0	28	2	0	0	0	0	6	.174	.216	.197	.413
2017	Bal	AL	89	254	65	14	1	8	(3	5)	105	31	28	28	10	0	72	1	1	0	0	0	7	.256	.287	.413	.700
	Postseason		3	9	2	0	0	0	(0	0)	2	0	1	1	0	0	4	0	0	1	0	0	0	.222	.200	.222	.422
	4 ML YEARS		320	952	214	42	2	28	(12	16)	344	98	105	94	61	2	241	7	12	4	0	1	26	.225	.275	.361	.637

Tommy Joseph

Bats: R **Throws:** R **Pos:** 1B-130;PH-11;DH-2 **Ht:** 6'1" **Wt:** 255 **Born:** 7/16/1991 **Age:** 26

Year	Team	Lg	G	AB	H	2B	3B	HR	Hm	Rd	TB	R	RBI	RC	TBB	IBB	SO	HBP	SH	SF	SB	CS	GDP	Avg	OBP	Slg	OPS
2013	LV	AAA	21	67	14	1	0	3	-	-	24	6	14	6	4	0	15	1	0	0	0	1	2	.209	.264	.358	.622
2013	2 Tms	Low	12	45	5	2	0	0	-	-	7	0	1	0	2	0	14	0	0	0	0	0	1	.111	.149	.156	.304
2014	Rdng	AA	21	78	22	4	1	5	-	-	43	8	19	15	5	0	13	3	0	0	0	0	1	.282	.345	.551	.896
2015	LV	AAA	45	166	32	9	0	3	-	-	50	9	18	10	3	0	33	3	2	1	0	0	6	.193	.220	.301	.521
2015	Phillies	R	13	33	16	3	0	3	-	-	28	6	10	13	7	0	0	1	0	0	0	0	1	.485	.585	.848	1.434
2016	LV	AAA	27	95	33	7	0	6	-	-	58	11	17	20	4	0	12	0	0	1	0	1	5	.347	.370	.611	.981
2016	Phi	NL	107	315	81	15	0	21	(10	11)	159	47	47	37	22	0	75	4	0	6	1	1	11	.257	.308	.505	.813
2017	Phi	NL	142	495	119	27	1	22	(12	10)	214	51	69	54	33	1	129	2	0	3	1	0	21	.240	.289	.432	.721
	2 ML YEARS		249	810	200	42	1	43	(22	21)	373	98	116	91	55	1	204	6	0	9	2	1	32	.247	.297	.460	.757

Matt Joyce

Bats: L **Throws:** R **Pos:** RF-115;LF-24;PH-15;DH-2;CF-1;PR-1 **Ht:** 6'2" **Wt:** 205 **Born:** 8/3/1984 **Age:** 33

Year	Team	Lg	G	AB	H	2B	3B	HR	Hm	Rd	TB	R	RBI	RC	TBB	IBB	SO	HBP	SH	SF	SB	CS	GDP	Avg	OBP	Slg	OPS
2008	Det	AL	92	242	61	16	3	12	(6	6)	119	40	33	36	31	0	65	2	0	2	0	2	3	.252	.339	.492	.831
2009	TB	AL	11	32	6	1	0	3	(2	1)	16	3	7	5	3	0	7	1	0	1	1	0	0	.188	.270	.500	.770
2010	TB	AL	77	216	52	15	3	10	(4	6)	103	30	40	41	40	2	55	2	0	3	2	2	2	.241	.360	.477	.837
2011	TB	AL	141	462	128	32	2	19	(11	8)	221	69	75	77	49	9	106	4	0	7	13	1	7	.277	.347	.478	.825
2012	TB	AL	124	399	96	18	3	17	(4	13)	171	55	59	59	55	4	102	6	1	1	4	3	10	.241	.341	.429	.769
2013	TB	AL	140	413	97	22	0	18	(8	10)	173	61	47	51	59	0	87	2	0	7	7	3	8	.235	.328	.419	.747
2014	TB	AL	140	418	106	23	2	9	(2	7)	160	51	52	52	62	4	111	4	0	9	2	5	11	.254	.349	.383	.732
2015	LAA	AL	93	247	43	12	1	5	(4	1)	72	17	21	15	30	1	67	4	0	2	0	3	5	.174	.272	.291	.564
2016	Pit	NL	140	231	56	10	1	13	(10	3)	107	45	42	47	59	4	67	3	0	0	1	1	9	.242	.403	.463	.866
2017	Oak	AL	141	469	114	33	0	25	(11	14)	222	78	68	70	66	0	113	2	0	7	4	1	10	.243	.335	.473	.808
	Postseason		12	32	5	1	0	1	(0	1)	9	1	4	3	1	0	13	0	0	0	1	0	0	.156	.182	.281	.463
	10 ML YEARS		1099	3129	759	182	15	131	(62	69)	1364	449	444	453	454	24	780	30	2	39	34	21	65	.243	.340	.436	.776

Aaron Judge

Bats: R **Throws:** R **Pos:** RF-141;DH-10;PH-3;PR-1 **Ht:** 6'7" **Wt:** 282 **Born:** 4/26/1992 **Age:** 26

Year	Team	Lg	G	AB	H	2B	3B	HR	Hm	Rd	TB	R	RBI	RC	TBB	IBB	SO	HBP	SH	SF	SB	CS	GDP	Avg	OBP	Slg	OPS
2014	2 Tms	Low	131	467	144	24	4	17	-	-	227	80	78	99	89	2	131	3	0	4	1	0	10	.308	.419	.486	.905
2015	Trntn	AA	63	250	71	16	3	12	-	-	129	36	44	46	24	1	70	3	0	3	1	0	9	.284	.350	.516	.866
2015	S-WB	AAA	61	228	51	10	0	8	-	-	85	27	28	28	29	0	74	0	0	3	6	2	6	.224	.308	.373	.680
2016	S-WB	AAA	93	352	95	18	1	19	-	-	172	62	65	66	47	0	98	8	0	3	5	0	7	.270	.366	.489	.854
2016	NYY	AL	27	84	15	2	0	4	(3	1)	29	10	10	6	9	0	42	1	0	1	0	1	2	.179	.263	.345	.608
2017	NYY	AL	155	542	154	24	3	52	(33	19)	340	128	114	131	127	11	208	5	0	4	9	4	15	.284	.422	.627	1.049
	2 ML YEARS		182	626	169	26	3	56	(36	20)	369	138	124	137	136	11	250	6	0	5	9	5	17	.270	.402	.589	.992

Taylor Jungmann

Pitches: R Bats: R Pos: RP-1

YOUNG-man

Ht: 6'6" Wt: 210 Born: 12/18/1989 Age: 28

| | | | HOW MUCH HE PITCHED | | | | | WHAT HE GAVE UP | | | | | | | | | | THE RESULTS | | | | | | |
Year	Team	Lg	G	GS	CG	GF	IP	BFP	H	R	ER	HR	SH	SF	HB	TBB	IBB	SO	WP	Bk	W	L	Pct	Sh	Sv-Op	Hld	ERC	ERA
2017	Biloxi*	AA	9	6	0	1	33.0	145	35	18	16	5	1	1	1	17	0	31	4	1	1	2	.333	0	0- -	-	5.56	4.36
2017	ColSpr*	AAA	17	15	0	0	90.1	372	69	28	26	4	3	3	7	39	2	82	2	0	9	2	.818	0	0- -	-	2.87	2.59
2015	Mil	NL	21	21	1	0	119.1	501	106	55	50	11	2	5	8	47	1	107	8	0	9	8	.529	0	0-0	0	3.69	3.77
2016	Mil	NL	8	6	0	2	26.2	126	30	24	23	4	1	2	3	17	1	18	0	0	0	5	.000	0	0-0	0	6.66	7.76
2017	Mil	NL	1	0	0	0	0.2	6	2	1	1	0	0	0	1	1	0	1	0	0	0	0	-	0	0-0	0	29.63	13.50
	3 ML YEARS		30	27	1	2	146.2	633	138	80	74	15	3	7	12	65	2	126	8	0	9	13	.409	0	0-0	0	4.29	4.54

Jakob Junis

Pitches: R Bats: R Pos: SP-16; RP-4

Ht: 6'2" Wt: 225 Born: 9/16/1992 Age: 25

| | | | HOW MUCH HE PITCHED | | | | | WHAT HE GAVE UP | | | | | | | | | | THE RESULTS | | | | | | |
Year	Team	Lg	G	GS	CG	GF	IP	BFP	H	R	ER	HR	SH	SF	HB	TBB	IBB	SO	WP	Bk	W	L	Pct	Sh	Sv-Op	Hld	ERC	ERA
2013	Idaho	R+	13	13	0	0	59.2	285	85	59	49	13	2	3	5	17	0	55	3	1	2	6	.250	0	0- -	-	7.31	7.39
2014	Lxngtn	A	26	22	0	0	136.0	573	136	74	65	16	1	4	10	38	0	109	6	1	9	8	.529	0	0- -	-	4.07	4.30
2015	Wilmg	A+	26	26	0	0	155.2	625	145	71	63	11	5	8	6	29	0	123	8	1	5	11	.313	0	0- -	-	2.91	3.64
2016	NWArk	AA	21	21	0	0	119.0	486	110	48	43	12	4	1	6	27	0	117	6	1	9	7	.563	0	0- -	-	3.24	3.25
2016	Omha	AAA	6	6	0	0	30.0	133	39	24	24	6	0	0	4	7	0	26	4	0	1	3	.250	0	0- -	-	6.70	7.20
2017	Omha	AAA	12	12	0	0	71.0	288	61	24	23	6	0	2	2	15	0	86	1	0	3	5	.375	0	0- -	-	2.61	2.92
2017	KC	AL	20	16	0	1	98.1	422	101	52	47	15	3	3	9	25	1	80	3	1	9	3	.750	0	0-0	0	4.36	4.30

Tommy Kahnle

Pitches: R Bats: R Pos: RP-69

KAIN-lee

Ht: 6'1" Wt: 235 Born: 8/7/1989 Age: 28

| | | | HOW MUCH HE PITCHED | | | | | WHAT HE GAVE UP | | | | | | | | | | THE RESULTS | | | | | | |
Year	Team	Lg	G	GS	CG	GF	IP	BFP	H	R	ER	HR	SH	SF	HB	TBB	IBB	SO	WP	Bk	W	L	Pct	Sh	Sv-Op	Hld	ERC	ERA
2014	Col	NL	54	0	0	7	68.2	285	51	39	32	7	2	3	1	31	2	63	7	0	2	1	.667	0	0-2	8	2.91	4.19
2015	Col	NL	36	0	0	8	33.1	155	31	22	18	3	1	2	0	28	1	39	3	0	0	1	.000	0	2-3	10	5.31	4.86
2016	CWS	AL	29	0	0	12	27.1	119	21	8	8	2	0	0	0	20	3	25	3	0	0	1	.000	0	1-2	4	3.74	2.63
2017	2 Tms	AL	69	0	0	17	62.2	256	53	20	18	4	1	4	2	17	1	96	5	0	2	4	.333	0	0-6	15	2.63	2.59
17	CWS	AL	37	0	0	10	36.0	141	28	12	10	3	1	2	0	7	1	60	2	0	1	3	.250	0	0-4	7	2.04	2.50
17	NYY	AL	32	0	0	7	26.2	115	25	8	8	1	0	2	2	10	0	36	3	0	1	1	.500	0	0-2	8	3.47	2.70
	4 ML YEARS		188	0	0	44	192.0	815	156	89	76	16	4	9	3	96	7	223	18	0	4	7	.364	0	3-13	37	3.32	3.56

Jung Ho Kang

Bats: R Throws: R Pos: 3B

GAHNG

Ht: 6'0" Wt: 210 Born: 4/5/1987 Age: 31

| | | | BATTING | | | | | | | | | | | | | | | | | RUNNING | | | AVERAGES | | | |
Year	Team	Lg	G	AB	H	2B	3B	HR	(Hm	Rd)	TB	R	RBI	RC	TBB	IBB	SO	HBP	SH	SF	SB	CS	GDP	Avg	OBP	Slg	OPS
2016	Indy	AAA	16	48	7	0	0	2	(-	-)	13	5	7	3	7	0	11	0	0	2	0	1	0	.146	.246	.271	.516
2015	Pit	NL	126	421	121	24	2	15	(5	10)	194	60	58	60	28	0	99	11	0	1	5	4	10	.287	.355	.461	.816
2016	Pit	NL	103	318	81	19	0	21	(10	11)	163	45	62	47	36	1	79	14	0	2	3	1	11	.255	.354	.513	.867
	2 ML YEARS		229	739	202	43	2	36	(15	21)	357	105	120	107	64	1	178	31	0	3	8	5	21	.273	.355	.483	.838

Nathan Karns

Pitches: R Bats: R Pos: SP-8; RP-1

Ht: 6'3" Wt: 225 Born: 11/25/1987 Age: 30

| | | | HOW MUCH HE PITCHED | | | | | WHAT HE GAVE UP | | | | | | | | | | THE RESULTS | | | | | | |
Year	Team	Lg	G	GS	CG	GF	IP	BFP	H	R	ER	HR	SH	SF	HB	TBB	IBB	SO	WP	Bk	W	L	Pct	Sh	Sv-Op	Hld	ERC	ERA
2013	Was	NL	3	3	0	0	12.0	61	17	11	10	5	1	0	1	6	0	11	0	0	0	1	.000	0	0-0	0	9.80	7.50
2014	TB	AL	2	2	0	0	12.0	49	7	6	6	3	0	0	2	4	0	13	0	0	1	1	.500	0	0-0	0	3.12	4.50
2015	TB	AL	27	26	0	0	147.0	621	132	62	60	19	3	4	5	56	1	145	15	0	7	5	.583	0	0-0	0	3.77	3.67
2016	Sea	AL	22	15	0	2	94.1	417	95	55	54	11	0	2	3	45	1	101	5	1	6	2	.750	0	1-1	0	4.65	5.15
2017	KC	AL	9	8	0	0	45.1	188	41	21	21	9	0	0	2	13	1	51	2	0	2	2	.500	0	0-0	0	3.91	4.17
	5 ML YEARS		63	54	0	2	310.2	1336	292	155	151	47	4	6	13	124	3	321	22	1	16	11	.593	0	1-1	0	4.24	4.37

Scott Kazmir

Pitches: L Bats: L Pos: P

KAZ-meer

Ht: 6'0" Wt: 195 Born: 1/24/1984 Age: 34

| | | | HOW MUCH HE PITCHED | | | | | WHAT HE GAVE UP | | | | | | | | | | THE RESULTS | | | | | | |
Year	Team	Lg	G	GS	CG	GF	IP	BFP	H	R	ER	HR	SH	SF	HB	TBB	IBB	SO	WP	Bk	W	L	Pct	Sh	Sv-Op	Hld	ERC	ERA
2004	TB	AL	8	7	0	0	33.1	152	33	22	21	4	0	0	2	21	0	41	3	0	2	3	.400	0	0-0	0	5.36	5.67
2005	TB	AL	32	32	0	0	186.0	818	172	90	78	12	6	9	10	100	3	174	7	1	10	9	.526	0	0-0	0	4.13	3.77
2006	TB	AL	24	24	1	0	144.2	610	132	59	52	15	0	5	2	52	3	163	6	0	10	8	.556	1	0-0	0	3.47	3.24
2007	TB	AL	34	34	0	0	206.2	887	196	91	80	18	6	3	7	89	1	239	10	0	13	9	.591	0	0-0	0	3.97	3.48
2008	TB	AL	27	27	0	0	152.1	641	123	61	59	23	4	5	4	70	2	166	5	0	12	8	.600	0	0-0	0	3.69	3.49
2009	2 Tms	AL	26	26	0	0	147.1	647	149	85	80	16	1	4	6	60	0	117	13	0	10	9	.526	0	0-0	0	4.36	4.89
2010	LAA	AL	28	28	0	0	150.0	682	158	103	99	25	3	6	12	79	2	93	6	0	9	15	.375	0	0-0	0	5.74	5.94
2011	LAA	AL	1	1	0	0	1.2	14	5	5	5	1	0	0	2	4	0	0	1	0	0	0	-	0	0-0	0	35.08	27.00
2013	Cle	AL	29	29	0	0	158.0	672	162	76	71	19	2	1	3	47	1	162	5	1	10	9	.526	0	0-0	0	4.02	4.04
2014	Oak	AL	32	32	2	0	190.1	777	171	81	75	16	5	1	4	50	1	164	9	1	15	9	.625	0	0-0	0	3.00	3.55
2015	2 Tms	AL	31	31	0	0	183.0	763	162	77	63	20	5	6	9	59	0	155	5	2	7	11	.389	0	0-0	0	3.41	3.10
2016	LAD	NL	26	26	0	0	136.1	590	133	71	69	21	2	3	7	52	3	134	5	0	10	6	.625	0	0-0	0	4.41	4.56
09	TB	AL	20	20	0	0	111.0	504	121	77	73	15	1	4	5	50	0	91	10	0	8	7	.533	0	0-0	0	5.18	5.92
09	LAA	AL	6	6	0	0	36.1	143	28	8	7	1	0	0	1	10	0	26	3	0	2	2	.500	0	0-0	0	2.13	1.73

Year	Team	Lg	G	GS	CG	GF	IP	BFP	H	R	ER	HR	SH	SF	HB	TBB	IBB	SO	WP	Bk	W	L	Pct	Sh	Sv-Op	Hld	ERC	ERA
15	Oak	AL	18	18	0	0	109.2	440	84	35	29	7	3	4	3	35	0	101	2	2	5	5	.500	0	0-0	0	2.45	2.38
15	Hou	AL	13	13	0	0	73.1	323	78	42	34	13	2	2	6	24	0	54	3	0	2	6	.250	0	0-0	0	5.01	4.17
	Postseason		9	8	0	0	41.2	197	42	25	24	6	3	2	3	27	0	30	2	0	1	2	.333	0	0-0	0	5.63	5.18
12 ML YEARS			298	297	3	0	1689.2	7253	1596	821	752	190	34	43	68	681	16	1608	74	6	108	96	.529	1	0-0	0	4.02	4.01

Keone Kela

Pitches: R Bats: R Pos: RP-39

KEY-oh-nee KELL-uh

Ht: 6'1" Wt: 215 Born: 4/16/1993 Age: 25

			HOW MUCH HE PITCHED						WHAT HE GAVE UP												THE RESULTS							
Year	Team	Lg	G	GS	CG	GF	IP	BFP	H	R	ER	HR	SH	SF	HB	TBB	IBB	SO	WP	Bk	W	L	Pct	Sh	Sv-Op	Hld	ERC	ERA
2015	Tex	AL	68	0	0	11	60.1	243	52	18	16	4	1	0	0	18	0	68	6	1	7	5	.583	0	1-4	22	2.79	2.39
2016	Tex	AL	35	0	0	2	34.0	150	30	23	23	6	2	1	3	17	0	45	2	1	5	1	.833	0	0-1	15	4.68	6.09
2017	Tex	AL	39	0	0	13	38.2	151	18	12	12	4	0	0	1	17	1	51	1	1	4	1	.800	0	2-3	11	1.64	2.79
	Postseason		4	0	0	1	4.2	16	1	1	1	1	0	0	0	2	0	3	0	0	1	0	1.000	0	0-1	1	1.27	1.93
3 ML YEARS			142	0	0	26	133.0	544	100	53	51	14	3	1	4	52	1	164	9	3	16	7	.696	0	3-8	48	2.87	3.45

Shawn Kelley

Pitches: R Bats: R Pos: RP-33

Ht: 6'2" Wt: 230 Born: 4/26/1984 Age: 34

			HOW MUCH HE PITCHED						WHAT HE GAVE UP												THE RESULTS							
Year	Team	Lg	G	GS	CG	GF	IP	BFP	H	R	ER	HR	SH	SF	HB	TBB	IBB	SO	WP	Bk	W	L	Pct	Sh	Sv-Op	Hld	ERC	ERA
2017	Syrcse*	AAA	8	2	0	0	6.2	30	8	6	6	3	0	0	0	2	0	9	0	0	1	1	.500	0	0- --	-	7.26	8.10
2009	Sea	AL	41	0	0	12	46.0	191	45	23	23	9	2	2	3	9	1	41	2	1	5	4	.556	0	0-4	9	4.02	4.50
2010	Sea	AL	22	0	0	7	25.0	112	26	11	11	5	0	0	1	12	2	26	0	0	3	1	.750	0	0-0	3	5.38	3.96
2011	Sea	AL	10	0	0	2	12.2	47	7	0	0	0	0	0	0	3	1	10	0	0	0	0	-	0	0-0	1	1.01	0.00
2012	Sea	AL	47	0	0	10	44.1	190	43	20	16	5	4	3	0	16	5	45	2	0	2	4	.333	0	0-2	6	3.49	3.25
2013	NYY	AL	57	0	0	13	53.1	227	47	28	26	8	0	2	0	23	2	71	8	0	4	2	.667	0	0-1	11	3.80	4.39
2014	NYY	AL	59	0	0	15	51.2	220	45	26	26	5	3	1	1	20	4	67	3	0	3	6	.333	0	4-7	12	3.20	4.53
2015	SD	NL	53	0	0	14	51.1	205	41	18	14	4	0	4	0	15	4	63	0	0	2	2	.500	0	0-0	7	2.40	2.45
2016	Was	NL	67	0	0	26	58.0	224	41	19	17	9	0	2	0	11	2	80	2	0	3	2	.600	0	7-9	13	2.06	2.64
2017	Was	NL	33	0	0	18	26.0	121	29	21	21	12	0	0	1	11	1	25	2	0	3	2	.600	0	4-6	6	7.40	7.27
	Postseason		2	0	0	0	1.2	6	1	0	0	0	0	0	0	0	0	3	0	0	0	0	-	0	0-0	1	0.75	0.00
9 ML YEARS			389	0	0	117	368.1	1537	324	166	154	57	9	14	6	119	23	428	19	2	25	23	.521	0	15-29	64	3.42	3.76

Carson Kelly

Bats: R Throws: R Pos: C-31;PH-11

Ht: 6'2" Wt: 220 Born: 7/14/1994 Age: 23

			BATTING																	RUNNING			AVERAGES			
Year	Team	Lg	G	AB	H	2B	3B	HR	(Hm	Rd)	TB	R	RBI	RC	TBB	IBB	SO	HBP	SH	SF	SB	CS	GDP	Avg	OBP	Slg	OPS
2013	2 Tms	Low	113	417	107	22	1	6	(-	-)	149	53	45	50	33	1	56	8	7	2	1	0	18	.257	.322	.357	.679
2014	Peoria	A	98	363	90	17	4	6	(-	-)	133	41	49	47	37	1	54	7	4	4	1	0	14	.248	.326	.366	.692
2015	PlmBh	A+	108	389	85	18	1	8	(-	-)	129	30	51	34	22	0	64	3	0	5	0	0	17	.219	.263	.332	.594
2016	Sprgfld	AA	64	216	62	7	0	6	(-	-)	87	29	18	30	14	0	46	3	2	1	0	1	5	.287	.338	.403	.740
2016	Memp	AAA	32	113	33	10	0	0	(-	-)	43	14	14	16	11	0	17	0	1	1	0	0	6	.292	.362	.381	.733
2017	Memp	AAA	68	244	69	13	0	10	(-	-)	112	37	41	43	33	0	40	3	0	0	0	2	11	.283	.375	.459	.834
2016	StL	NL	10	13	2	1	0	0	(0	0)	3	1	1	0	0	0	2	1	0	0	0	0	0	.154	.214	.231	.445
2017	StL	NL	34	69	12	3	0	0	(0	0)	15	5	6	4	5	0	11	1	0	0	0	0	3	.174	.240	.217	.457
2 ML YEARS			44	82	14	4	0	0	(0	0)	18	6	7	4	5	0	13	2	0	0	0	0	3	.171	.236	.220	.455

Joe Kelly

Pitches: R Bats: R Pos: RP-54

Ht: 6'1" Wt: 190 Born: 6/9/1988 Age: 30

			HOW MUCH HE PITCHED						WHAT HE GAVE UP												THE RESULTS							
Year	Team	Lg	G	GS	CG	GF	IP	BFP	H	R	ER	HR	SH	SF	HB	TBB	IBB	SO	WP	Bk	W	L	Pct	Sh	Sv-Op	Hld	ERC	ERA
2012	StL	NL	24	16	0	4	107.0	457	112	50	42	10	4	1	3	36	2	75	4	0	5	7	.417	0	0-0	0	4.17	3.53
2013	StL	NL	37	15	0	8	124.0	532	124	42	37	10	2	2	5	44	4	79	3	0	10	5	.667	0	0-1	2	3.88	2.69
2014	2 Tms		17	17	0	0	96.1	415	88	48	45	8	2	4	7	42	0	66	3	0	6	4	.600	0	0-0	0	3.92	4.20
2015	Bos	AL	25	25	0	0	134.1	587	145	76	72	15	0	5	6	49	0	110	9	0	10	6	.625	0	0-0	0	4.68	4.82
2016	Bos	AL	20	6	0	6	40.0	188	44	23	23	5	0	4	2	24	0	48	0	0	4	0	1.000	0	0-1	2	5.80	5.18
2017	Bos	AL	54	0	0	14	58.0	238	42	19	18	3	0	2	1	27	1	52	4	0	4	1	.800	0	0-4	13	2.61	2.79
14	StL	NL	7	7	0	0	35.0	156	41	19	17	3	1	1	3	10	0	25	3	0	2	2	.500	0	0-0	0	4.82	4.37
14	Bos	AL	10	10	0	0	61.1	259	47	29	28	5	1	3	4	32	0	41	0	0	4	2	.667	0	0-0	0	3.43	4.11
	Postseason		14	4	0	1	33.0	138	26	13	12	2	1	0	1	13	1	27	1	0	0	1	.000	0	0-0	0	2.70	3.27
6 ML YEARS			177	79	0	32	559.2	2417	555	258	237	51	8	18	24	222	7	430	23	0	39	23	.629	0	0-6	17	4.12	3.81

Ty Kelly

Bats: B Throws: R Pos: PH-41;2B-14;LF-9;PR-5;3B-4;RF-3;CF-1

Ht: 6'0" Wt: 180 Born: 7/20/1988 Age: 29

			BATTING																	RUNNING			AVERAGES			
Year	Team	Lg	G	AB	H	2B	3B	HR	(Hm	Rd)	TB	R	RBI	RC	TBB	IBB	SO	HBP	SH	SF	SB	CS	GDP	Avg	OBP	Slg	OPS
2013	Bowie	AA	72	283	80	21	2	1	(-	-)	108	51	47	48	51	0	49	2	1	6	4	2	5	.283	.389	.382	.771
2013	Tacom	AAA	54	197	63	6	1	3	(-	-)	80	34	17	40	51	2	41	0	2	2	3	7	4	.320	.456	.406	.862
2014	Tacom	AAA	134	456	120	19	2	15	(-	-)	188	81	80	79	85	0	96	3	3	2	11	3	7	.263	.381	.412	.793
2015	Memp	AAA	79	227	46	5	4	2	(-	-)	65	23	21	23	38	0	43	1	1	2	3	3	4	.203	.317	.286	.604
2015	Buffalo	AAA	38	144	38	4	0	1	(-	-)	45	16	12	15	14	1	10	1	0	1	0	2	2	.264	.326	.313	.644
2016	LsVgs	AAA	81	271	89	21	1	2	(-	-)	118	45	35	49	38	0	42	1	3	3	5	6	3	.328	.409	.435	.844
2016	NYM	NL	39	58	14	1	1	1	(0	1)	20	9	7	8	11	0	9	0	0	2	0	0	2	.241	.352	.345	.697
2017	2 Tms	NL	70	89	17	7	0	2	(0	2)	30	11	14	12	8	0	25	1	4	3	0	0	0	.191	.257	.337	.595

Year	Team	Lg		BATTING															RUNNING			AVERAGES			
			G	AB	H	2B	3B	HR	(Hm | Rd)	TB	R	RBI	RC	TBB	IBB	SO	HBP	SH	SF	SB	CS	GDP	Avg	OBP	Slg	OPS
17	NYM	NL	1	1	0	0	0	0	(0 | 0)	0	0	0	0	0	0	1	0	0	0	0	0	0	.000	.000	.000	.000
17	Phi	NL	69	88	17	7	0	2	(0 | 2)	30	11	14	12	8	0	24	1	4	3	0	0	0	.193	.260	.341	.601
	Postseason		1	1	1	0	0	0	(0 | 0)	1	0	0	0	0	0	0	0	0	0	0	0	0	1.000	1.000	1.000	2.000
	2 ML YEARS		109	147	31	8	1	3	(0 | 3)	50	20	20	20	19	0	34	1	4	5	0	0	2	.211	.297	.340	.637

Matt Kemp

Bats: R Throws: R Pos: LF-103;PH-8;DH-5

Ht: 6'4" Wt: 210 Born: 9/23/1984 Age: 33

Year	Team	Lg		BATTING															RUNNING			AVERAGES			
			G	AB	H	2B	3B	HR	(Hm	Rd)	TB	R	RBI	RC	TBB	IBB	SO	HBP	SH	SF	SB	CS	GDP	Avg	OBP	Slg	OPS
2006	LAD	NL	52	154	39	7	1	7	(4	3)	69	30	23	20	9	1	53	0	0	3	6	0	1	.253	.289	.448	.737
2007	LAD	NL	98	292	100	12	5	10	(9	1)	152	47	42	49	16	0	66	0	0	3	10	5	6	.342	.373	.521	.894
2008	LAD	NL	155	606	176	38	5	18	(14	4)	278	93	76	86	46	6	153	1	1	3	35	11	11	.290	.340	.459	.799
2009	LAD	NL	159	606	180	25	7	26	(13	13)	297	97	101	100	52	6	139	3	0	6	34	8	14	.297	.352	.490	.842
2010	LAD	NL	162	602	150	25	6	28	(15	13)	271	82	89	74	53	4	170	4	0	9	19	15	14	.249	.310	.450	.760
2011	LAD	NL	161	602	195	33	4	39	(19	20)	353	115	126	129	74	24	159	6	0	7	40	11	16	.324	.399	.586	.986
2012	LAD	NL	106	403	122	22	2	23	(13	10)	217	74	69	75	40	8	104	3	0	3	9	4	10	.303	.367	.538	.906
2013	LAD	NL	73	263	71	15	0	6	(0	6)	104	35	33	27	22	3	76	2	0	3	9	0	11	.270	.328	.395	.723
2014	LAD	NL	150	541	155	38	3	25	(17	8)	274	77	89	79	52	3	145	0	0	6	8	5	21	.287	.346	.506	.852
2015	SD	NL	154	596	158	31	3	23	(13	10)	264	80	100	81	39	0	147	5	0	8	12	2	17	.265	.312	.443	.755
2016	2 Tms	NL	156	623	167	39	0	35	(14	21)	311	89	108	85	36	6	156	1	0	12	1	0	17	.268	.304	.499	.803
2017	Atl	NL	115	438	121	23	1	19	(7	12)	203	47	64	46	27	5	99	0	0	1	0	2	25	.276	.318	.463	.781
16	SD	NL	100	409	107	24	0	23	(8	15)	200	54	69	58	16	3	100	0	0	6	0	0	8	.262	.285	.489	.774
16	Atl	NL	56	214	60	15	0	12	(6	6)	111	35	39	27	20	3	56	1	0	6	1	0	9	.280	.336	.519	.855
	Postseason		20	79	20	3	0	3	(2	1)	32	6	7	2	5	0	28	0	0	1	0	2	3	.253	.298	.405	.703
	12 ML YEARS		1541	5726	1634	308	37	259	(138	121)	2793	866	920	851	466	66	1466	25	1	64	183	63	163	.285	.338	.488	.826

Tony Kemp

Bats: L Throws: R Pos: LF-10;CF-4;PR-4;DH-1;PH-1

Ht: 5'6" Wt: 165 Born: 10/31/1991 Age: 26

Year	Team	Lg		BATTING															RUNNING			AVERAGES			
			G	AB	H	2B	3B	HR	(Hm	Rd)	TB	R	RBI	RC	TBB	IBB	SO	HBP	SH	SF	SB	CS	GDP	Avg	OBP	Slg	OPS
2013	2 Tms	Low	75	275	75	8	3	2	(-	-)	95	46	22	39	40	0	47	3	2	4	21	11	6	.273	.366	.345	.712
2014	Lancst	A+	72	295	99	19	4	4	(-	-)	138	79	37	66	45	2	35	8	5	3	28	7	6	.336	.433	.468	.901
2014	CpChr	AA	59	233	68	11	4	4	(-	-)	99	42	21	40	28	0	32	1	5	2	13	6	5	.292	.381	.425	.806
2015	CpChr	AA	50	193	69	10	1	0	(-	-)	81	36	19	40	35	0	28	1	0	1	15	8	3	.358	.457	.420	.876
2015	Fresno	AAA	71	271	74	9	3	3	(-	-)	98	42	29	37	21	0	37	5	12	2	20	6	6	.273	.334	.362	.696
2016	Fresno	AAA	69	255	78	9	4	2	(-	-)	101	36	24	41	34	0	34	2	8	2	10	8	8	.306	.389	.396	.785
2017	Fresno	AAA	118	504	166	23	9	10	(-	-)	237	95	62	91	35	0	43	3	8	2	24	7	9	.329	.375	.470	.845
2016	Hou	AL	59	120	26	4	3	1	(1	0)	39	15	7	11	14	0	27	0	1	1	2	1	5	.217	.296	.325	.621
2017	Hou	AL	17	37	8	1	0	0	(0	0)	9	6	4	4	1	0	5	1	0	0	1	0	0	.216	.256	.243	.500
	2 ML YEARS		76	157	34	5	3	1	(1	0)	48	21	11	15	15	0	32	1	1	1	3	1	5	.217	.287	.306	.593

Howie Kendrick

Bats: R Throws: R Pos: LF-62;2B-15;PH-15;1B-4;RF-3;DH-1

Ht: 5'11" Wt: 220 Born: 7/12/1983 Age: 34

Year	Team	Lg		BATTING															RUNNING			AVERAGES			
			G	AB	H	2B	3B	HR	(Hm	Rd)	TB	R	RBI	RC	TBB	IBB	SO	HBP	SH	SF	SB	CS	GDP	Avg	OBP	Slg	OPS
2006	LAA	AL	72	267	76	21	1	4	(2	2)	111	25	30	32	9	2	44	4	0	3	6	0	5	.285	.314	.416	.730
2007	LAA	AL	88	338	109	24	2	5	(3	2)	152	55	39	41	9	2	61	4	1	15	5	4	15	.322	.347	.450	.796
2008	LAA	AL	92	340	104	26	2	3	(1	2)	143	43	37	50	12	3	58	4	1	4	11	4	5	.306	.333	.421	.754
2009	LAA	AL	105	374	109	21	3	10	(5	5)	166	61	61	58	20	1	71	4	2	0	11	4	11	.291	.334	.444	.778
2010	LAA	AL	158	616	172	41	4	10	(4	6)	251	67	75	75	28	2	94	5	4	5	14	4	16	.279	.313	.407	.721
2011	LAA	AL	140	537	153	30	6	18	(5	13)	249	86	63	69	33	3	119	10	3	0	14	6	18	.285	.338	.464	.802
2012	LAA	AL	147	550	158	32	3	8	(4	4)	220	57	67	65	29	1	115	4	6	5	14	6	26	.287	.325	.400	.725
2013	LAA	AL	122	478	142	21	4	13	(9	4)	210	55	54	55	23	5	89	6	3	3	6	3	15	.297	.335	.439	.775
2014	LAA	AL	157	617	181	33	5	7	(0	7)	245	85	75	94	48	8	110	4	3	2	14	5	15	.293	.347	.397	.744
2015	LAD	NL	117	464	137	22	2	9	(6	3)	190	64	54	62	27	1	82	2	1	1	6	2	17	.295	.336	.409	.746
2016	LAD	NL	146	487	124	26	2	8	(3	5)	178	65	40	55	50	2	96	3	0	3	10	2	8	.255	.326	.366	.691
2017	2 Tms	NL	91	305	96	16	3	9	(4	5)	145	40	41	47	22	0	68	5	0	2	12	5	8	.315	.368	.475	.844
17	Phi	NL	39	141	48	8	1	2	(0	2)	64	16	16	23	11	0	30	3	0	1	8	3	4	.340	.397	.454	.851
17	Was	NL	52	164	48	8	2	7	(4	3)	81	24	25	24	11	0	38	2	0	1	4	2	4	.293	.343	.494	.837
	Postseason		30	103	22	4	1	2	(1	1)	34	11	6	6	2	1	22	0	2	1	4	0	3	.214	.226	.330	.557
	12 ML YEARS		1435	5373	1561	313	37	104	(46	58)	2260	703	636	711	310	30	1007	55	24	29	123	45	172	.291	.334	.421	.755

Kyle Kendrick

Pitches: R Bats: R Pos: SP-2

Ht: 6'3" Wt: 220 Born: 8/26/1984 Age: 33

Year	Team	Lg		HOW MUCH HE PITCHED					WHAT HE GAVE UP											THE RESULTS						
			G	GS	CG	GF	IP	BFP	H	R	ER	HR	SH	SF	HB	TBB	IBB	SO	WP	Bk	W	L	Pct.	Sh	Sv-Op	Hld	ERC	ERA
2017	Pwtckt*	AAA	18	18	2	0	101.2	428	114	67	64	24	2	0	5	16	0	67	1	0	5	7	.417	1	0- --	-	4.96	5.67
2007	Phi	NL	20	20	0	0	121.0	499	129	53	52	16	4	2	7	25	3	49	0	0	10	4	.714	0	0-0	0	4.23	3.87
2008	Phi	NL	31	30	0	1	155.2	722	194	103	95	23	8	4	14	57	2	68	4	1	11	9	.550	0	0-0	0	6.05	5.49
2009	Phi	NL	9	2	0	2	26.1	112	27	11	10	1	1	2	1	9	0	15	0	1	3	1	.750	0	0-0	0	3.75	3.42
2010	Phi	NL	33	31	1	1	180.2	771	199	103	95	26	9	6	3	49	4	84	1	2	11	10	.524	0	0-0	0	4.51	4.73
2011	Phi	NL	34	15	0	5	114.2	478	110	50	41	14	6	3	7	30	5	59	1	1	8	6	.571	0	0-1	0	3.66	3.22
2012	Phi	NL	37	25	1	2	159.1	674	154	76	69	20	8	4	7	49	4	116	1	0	11	12	.478	1	0-1	2	3.84	3.90
2013	Phi	NL	30	30	2	0	182.0	800	207	104	95	18	11	7	7	47	4	110	3	1	10	13	.435	1	0-0	0	4.33	4.70
2014	Phi	NL	32	32	0	0	199.0	865	214	108	102	25	17	5	11	57	4	121	5	0	10	13	.435	0	0-0	0	4.39	4.61

Year Team	Lg	G	GS	CG	GF	IP	BFP	H	R	ER	HR	SH	SF	HB	TBB	IBB	SO	WP	Bk	W	L	Pct	Sh	Sv-Op	Hld	ERC	ERA
2015 Col	NL	27	27	0	0	142.1	629	172	102	100	33	5	2	7	45	2	80	4	0	7	13	.350	0	0-0	0	6.21	6.32
2017 Bos	AL	2	2	0	0	8.1	45	18	12	12	1	0	0	0	3	0	3	0	0	0	2	.000	0	0-0	0	11.65	12.96
Postseason		1	1	0	0	3.2	18	5	5	5	2	0	0	0	2	1	2	0	0	0	1	.000	0	0-0	0	9.97	12.27
10 ML YEARS		255	214	4	11	1289.1	5595	1424	722	671	177	69	35	64	371	28	705	19	6	81	83	.494	2	0-2	2	4.66	4.68

Ian Kennedy

Pitches: R Bats: R Pos: SP-30

Ht: 6'0" Wt: 200 Born: 12/19/1984 Age: 33

Year Team	Lg	G	GS	CG	GF	IP	BFP	H	R	ER	HR	SH	SF	HB	TBB	IBB	SO	WP	Bk	W	L	Pct	Sh	Sv-Op	Hld	ERC	ERA
2007 NYY	AL	3	3	0	0	19.0	77	13	6	4	1	0	0	0	9	0	15	0	0	1	0	1.000	0	0-0	0	2.42	1.89
2008 NYY	AL	10	9	0	1	39.2	194	50	37	36	5	1	4	1	26	0	27	3	0	0	4	.000	0	0-0	0	6.93	8.17
2009 NYY	AL	1	0	0	0	1.0	6	0	0	0	0	0	0	0	2	0	1	0	0	0	0	-	0	0-0	0	7.00	0.00
2010 Ari	NL	32	32	0	0	194.0	810	163	87	82	26	11	5	10	70	2	168	16	0	9	10	.474	0	0-0	1	3.47	3.80
2011 Ari	NL	33	33	1	0	222.0	900	186	73	71	19	9	9	9	55	0	198	11	1	21	4	.840	1	0-0	0	2.71	2.88
2012 Ari	NL	33	33	1	0	208.1	899	216	101	93	28	13	5	14	55	4	187	5	4	15	12	.556	0	0-0	0	4.18	4.02
2013 2 Tms	NL	31	31	0	0	181.1	794	180	108	99	27	8	5	12	73	1	163	10	1	7	10	.412	0	0-0	0	4.64	4.91
2014 SD	NL	33	33	0	0	201.0	846	189	85	81	16	9	8	4	70	4	207	11	0	13	13	.500	0	0-0	0	3.47	3.63
2015 SD	NL	30	30	0	0	168.1	713	166	95	80	31	8	2	7	52	4	174	5	1	9	15	.375	0	0-0	0	4.37	4.28
2016 KC	AL	33	33	0	0	195.2	818	173	81	80	33	1	5	13	66	1	184	4	0	11	11	.500	0	0-0	0	3.94	3.68
2017 KC	AL	30	30	0	0	154.0	655	143	99	92	34	1	6	5	61	2	131	4	1	5	13	.278	0	0-0	0	4.64	5.38
13 Ari	NL	21	21	0	0	124.0	549	128	79	72	18	8	5	10	48	1	108	9	0	3	8	.273	0	0-0	0	4.82	5.23
13 SD	NL	10	10	0	0	57.1	245	52	29	27	9	0	0	2	25	0	55	1	1	4	2	.667	0	0-0	0	4.26	4.24
Postseason		2	2	0	0	12.2	57	13	6	6	1	0	2	3	3	0	8	1	0	0	1	.000	0	0-0	0	4.25	4.26
11 ML YEARS		269	267	2	1	1584.1	6712	1479	772	718	220	61	49	76	539	18	1455	69	8	91	92	.497	1	0-0	1	3.91	4.08

Max Kepler

Bats: L Throws: L Pos: RF-138;CF-13;PH-9;PR-2;DH-1

Ht: 6'4" Wt: 205 Born: 2/10/1993 Age: 25

Year Team	Lg	G	AB	H	2B	3B	HR	(Hm	Rd)	TB	R	RBI	RC	TBB	IBB	SO	HBP	SH	SF	SB	CS	GDP	Avg	OBP	Slg	OPS
2015 Min	AL	3	7	1	0	0	0	(0	0)	1	0	0	0	0	0	3	0	0	0	0	0	0	.143	.143	.143	.286
2016 Min	AL	113	396	93	20	2	17	(8	9)	168	52	63	52	42	3	93	3	1	5	6	2	2	.235	.309	.424	.734
2017 Min	AL	147	511	124	32	2	19	(9	10)	217	67	69	68	47	2	114	6	1	3	6	1	5	.243	.312	.425	.737
3 ML YEARS		263	914	218	52	4	36	(17	19)	386	119	132	120	89	5	210	9	2	8	12	3	7	.239	.310	.422	.732

Clayton Kershaw

Pitches: L Bats: L Pos: SP-27

Ht: 6'4" Wt: 228 Born: 3/19/1988 Age: 30

Year Team	Lg	G	GS	CG	GF	IP	BFP	H	R	ER	HR	SH	SF	HB	TBB	IBB	SO	WP	Bk	W	L	Pct	Sh	Sv-Op	Hld	ERC	ERA
2008 LAD	NL	22	21	0	0	107.2	470	109	51	51	11	3	4	1	52	3	100	7	0	5	5	.500	0	0-0	1	4.53	4.26
2009 LAD	NL	31	30	0	1	171.0	701	119	55	53	7	11	2	1	91	4	185	11	2	8	8	.500	0	0-0	0	2.60	2.79
2010 LAD	NL	32	32	1	0	204.1	848	160	73	66	13	8	4	7	81	9	212	5	2	13	10	.565	1	0-0	0	2.72	2.91
2011 LAD	NL	33	33	5	0	233.1	912	174	66	59	15	11	2	3	54	2	248	5	1	21	5	.808	2	0-0	0	2.00	2.28
2012 LAD	NL	33	33	2	0	227.2	901	170	70	64	16	18	4	5	63	5	229	6	2	14	9	.609	2	0-0	0	2.20	2.53
2013 LAD	NL	33	33	3	0	236.0	908	164	55	48	11	8	3	3	52	2	232	12	2	16	9	.640	2	0-0	0	1.65	1.83
2014 LAD	NL	27	27	6	0	198.1	749	139	42	39	9	6	1	2	31	0	239	7	2	21	3	.875	2	0-0	0	1.53	1.77
2015 LAD	NL	33	33	4	0	232.2	890	163	62	55	15	4	0	5	42	4	301	9	3	16	7	.696	3	0-0	0	1.67	2.13
2016 LAD	NL	21	21	3	0	149.0	544	97	31	28	8	4	1	2	11	0	172	5	3	12	4	.750	3	0-0	0	1.23	1.69
2017 LAD	NL	27	27	1	0	175.0	679	136	49	45	23	4	3	0	30	0	202	4	2	18	4	.818	0	0-0	0	2.27	2.31
Postseason		18	14	0	1	89.0	368	76	49	45	10	4	4	1	27	2	106	9	0	4	7	.364	0	1-1	1	2.98	4.55
10 ML YEARS		292	290	25	1	1935.0	7602	1431	554	508	128	77	23	29	507	27	2120	71	19	144	64	.692	15	0-0	1	2.08	2.36

Dallas Keuchel

Pitches: L Bats: L Pos: SP-23

KY-kull

Ht: 6'3" Wt: 205 Born: 1/1/1988 Age: 30

Year Team	Lg	G	GS	CG	GF	IP	BFP	H	R	ER	HR	SH	SF	HB	TBB	IBB	SO	WP	Bk	W	L	Pct	Sh	Sv-Op	Hld	ERC	ERA
2012 Hou	NL	16	16	1	0	85.1	377	93	56	50	14	9	3	1	39	1	38	2	0	3	8	.273	0	0-0	0	5.39	5.27
2013 Hou	AL	31	22	0	2	153.2	682	184	96	88	20	2	3	5	52	3	123	7	0	6	10	.375	0	0-0	2	5.33	5.15
2014 Hou	AL	29	29	5	0	200.0	808	187	71	65	11	4	5	7	48	2	146	7	0	12	9	.571	1	0-0	0	3.02	2.93
2015 Hou	AL	33	33	3	0	232.0	911	185	68	64	17	1	3	2	51	0	216	9	0	20	8	.714	2	0-0	0	2.26	2.48
2016 Hou	AL	26	26	1	0	168.0	701	168	88	85	20	2	1	2	48	1	144	9	0	9	12	.429	1	0-0	0	3.84	4.55
2017 Hou	AL	23	23	1	0	145.2	584	116	50	47	15	1	0	2	47	0	125	1	0	14	5	.737	0	0-0	0	2.82	2.90
Postseason		3	2	0	0	14.0	58	10	4	4	2	1	0	0	5	2	14	1	0	2	0	1.000	0	0-0	0	2.39	2.57
6 ML YEARS		158	149	11	2	984.2	4063	933	429	399	97	19	15	19	285	7	792	35	0	64	52	.552	4	0-0	2	3.46	3.65

Kevin Kiermaier

Bats: L Throws: R Pos: CF-97;PH-2

KEER-my-urr

Ht: 6'1" Wt: 215 Born: 4/22/1990 Age: 28

Year Team	Lg	G	AB	H	2B	3B	HR	(Hm	Rd)	TB	R	RBI	RC	TBB	IBB	SO	HBP	SH	SF	SB	CS	GDP	Avg	OBP	Slg	OPS
2013 TB	AL	1	0	0	0	0	0	(0	0)	0	0	0	0	0	0	0	0	0	0	0	0	0	-	-	-	-
2014 TB	AL	108	331	87	16	8	10	(4	6)	149	35	35	37	23	2	71	3	5	3	5	4	3	.263	.315	.450	.765
2015 TB	AL	151	505	133	25	12	10	(5	5)	212	62	40	66	24	0	95	2	2	5	18	5	7	.263	.298	.420	.718
2016 TB	AL	105	366	90	20	2	12	(5	7)	150	55	37	54	40	1	74	7	0	1	21	3	5	.246	.331	.410	.741
2017 TB	AL	98	380	105	15	3	15	(8	7)	171	56	39	53	31	2	99	5	4	1	16	7	3	.276	.338	.450	.788
Postseason		1	0	0	0	0	0	(0	0)	0	0	0	0	0	0	0	0	0	0	0	0	0	-	-	-	-
5 ML YEARS		463	1582	415	76	25	47	(22	25)	682	208	151	210	118	5	339	17	11	6	60	19	18	.262	.319	.431	.750

Hyun Soo Kim

Bats: L Throws: R Pos: LF-55;PH-35;RF-11;DH-2;PR-1 hee-YUHN Ht: 6'2" Wt: 210 Born: 1/12/1988 Age: 30

								BATTING											RUNNING			AVERAGES			
Year Team	Lg	G	AB	H	2B	3B	HR	(Hm Rd)	TB	R	RBI	RC	TBB	IBB	SO	HBP	SH	SF	SB	CS	GDP	Avg	OBP	Slg	OPS
2016 Bal	AL	95	305	92	16	1	6	(2 4)	128	36	22	50	36	0	51	4	0	1	1	3	5	.302	.382	.420	.801
2017 2 Tms		96	212	49	8	1	1	(1 0)	62	20	14	22	22	1	46	2	0	2	0	0	3	.231	.307	.292	.599
17 Bal	AL	56	125	29	4	0	1	(1 0)	36	11	10	12	12	0	27	2	0	2	0	0	2	.232	.305	.288	.593
17 Phi	NL	40	87	20	4	1	0	(0 0)	26	9	4	10	10	1	19	0	0	0	0	0	1	.230	.309	.299	.608
Postseason		1	4	0	0	0	0	(0 0)	0	0	0	0	0	0	0	0	0	0	0	0	0	.000	.000	.000	.000
2 ML YEARS		191	517	141	24	2	7	(3 4)	190	56	36	72	58	1	97	6	0	3	1	3	8	.273	.351	.368	.719

Craig Kimbrel

Pitches: R Bats: R Pos: RP-67 KIM-brull Ht: 6'0" Wt: 210 Born: 5/28/1988 Age: 30

		HOW MUCH HE PITCHED						WHAT HE GAVE UP												THE RESULTS						
Year Team	Lg	G	GS	CG	GF	IP	BFP	H	R	ER	HR	SH	SF	HB	TBB	IBB	SO	WP	Bk	W	L	Pct	Sh	Sv-Op	Hld	ERC	ERA
2010 Atl	NL	21	0	0	7	20.2	88	9	2	1	0	0	0	0	16	1	40	4	0	4	0	1.000	0	1-1	0	1.72	0.44
2011 Atl	NL	79	0	0	64	77.0	306	48	19	18	3	1	2	1	32	1	127	4	0	4	3	.571	0	46-54	0	1.88	2.10
2012 Atl	NL	63	0	0	56	62.2	231	27	7	7	3	0	0	2	14	0	116	5	0	3	1	.750	0	42-45	0	0.93	1.01
2013 Atl	NL	68	0	0	60	67.0	258	39	10	9	4	0	0	3	20	2	98	5	0	3	1	.571	0	50-54	0	1.58	1.21
2014 Atl	NL	63	0	0	54	61.2	244	30	13	11	2	3	0	2	26	0	95	6	0	0	3	.000	0	47-51	0	1.41	1.61
2015 SD	NL	61	0	0	53	59.1	239	40	19	17	6	0	0	1	22	1	87	4	0	4	2	.667	0	39-43	0	2.31	2.58
2016 SD	AL	57	0	0	47	53.0	220	28	22	20	4	1	1	4	30	0	83	6	0	2	6	.250	0	31-33	1	2.32	3.40
2017 Bos	AL	67	0	0	51	69.0	254	33	11	11	6	1	0	4	14	0	126	5	0	5	0	1.000	0	35-39	1	1.21	1.43
Postseason		8	0	0	6	8.0	25	1	2	1	0	0	0	0	3	0	13	0	0	0	1	.000	0	1-1	0	0.38	1.13
8 ML YEARS		479	0	0	392	470.1	1840	254	103	94	28	6	3	17	174	5	772	37	0	26	18	.591	0	291-320	4	1.58	1.80

Ian Kinsler

Bats: R Throws: R Pos: 2B-135;DH-3;PH-1 Ht: 6'0" Wt: 200 Born: 6/22/1982 Age: 36

								BATTING											RUNNING			AVERAGES			
Year Team	Lg	G	AB	H	2B	3B	HR	(Hm Rd)	TB	R	RBI	RC	TBB	IBB	SO	HBP	SH	SF	SB	CS	GDP	Avg	OBP	Slg	OPS
2006 Tex	AL	120	423	121	27	1	14	(10 4)	192	65	55	65	40	1	64	3	1	7	11	4	12	.286	.347	.454	.801
2007 Tex	AL	130	483	127	22	2	20	(12 8)	213	96	61	79	62	2	83	9	8	4	23	2	14	.263	.355	.441	.796
2008 Tex	AL	121	518	165	41	4	18	(4 14)	268	102	71	106	45	1	67	6	7	2	26	2	12	.319	.375	.517	.892
2009 Tex	AL	144	566	143	32	4	31	(20 11)	276	101	86	99	59	0	77	6	3	6	31	5	9	.253	.327	.488	.814
2010 Tex	AL	103	391	112	20	1	9	(4 5)	161	73	45	59	56	2	57	7	2	4	15	5	11	.286	.382	.412	.794
2011 Tex	AL	155	620	158	34	4	32	(16 16)	296	121	77	100	89	2	71	8	4	2	30	4	17	.255	.355	.477	.832
2012 Tex	AL	157	655	168	42	5	19	(14 5)	277	105	72	83	60	0	90	10	1	5	21	9	14	.256	.326	.423	.749
2013 Tex	AL	136	545	151	31	2	13	(5 8)	225	85	72	84	51	0	59	8	3	7	15	11	5	.277	.344	.413	.757
2014 Det	AL	161	684	188	40	4	17	(9 8)	287	100	92	89	29	1	79	5	3	5	15	4	20	.275	.307	.420	.727
2015 Det	AL	154	624	185	35	7	11	(6 5)	267	94	73	81	43	0	80	3	0	5	10	6	13	.296	.342	.428	.770
2016 Det	AL	153	618	178	29	4	28	(13 15)	299	117	83	105	45	0	115	13	0	3	14	6	5	.288	.348	.484	.831
2017 Det	AL	139	551	130	25	3	22	(12 10)	227	90	52	68	55	2	86	7	0	0	14	5	9	.236	.313	.412	.725
Postseason		37	134	39	7	1	4	(1 3)	60	18	20	24	24	1	19	1	1	1	6	5	3	.291	.400	.448	.848
12 ML YEARS		1673	6678	1826	378	41	234	(125 109)	2988	1149	839	1018	634	11	928	85	32	55	225	63	141	.273	.342	.447	.789

Brandon Kintzler

Pitches: R Bats: R Pos: RP-72 Ht: 6'0" Wt: 190 Born: 8/1/1984 Age: 33

		HOW MUCH HE PITCHED						WHAT HE GAVE UP												THE RESULTS						
Year Team	Lg	G	GS	CG	GF	IP	BFP	H	R	ER	HR	SH	SF	HB	TBB	IBB	SO	WP	Bk	W	L	Pct	Sh	Sv-Op	Hld	ERC	ERA
2010 Mil	NL	7	0	0	2	7.1	33	10	6	6	2	1	0	0	4	1	9	1	0	0	0	.000	0	0-0	0	8.67	7.36
2011 Mil	NL	9	0	0	3	14.2	61	14	9	6	3	0	2	0	3	0	15	0	1	1	1	.500	0	0-0	0	3.65	3.68
2012 Mil	NL	14	0	0	1	16.2	72	18	7	7	1	0	0	0	7	1	14	1	0	3	0	1.000	0	0-0	2	4.30	3.78
2013 Mil	NL	71	0	0	11	77.0	305	66	26	23	2	4	2	1	16	2	58	1	0	3	3	.500	0	0-4	26	2.21	2.69
2014 Mil	NL	64	0	0	13	58.1	239	62	22	21	8	4	1	0	16	3	31	1	0	3	3	.500	0	0-3	8	4.28	3.24
2015 Mil	NL	7	0	0	4	7.0	36	12	6	5	1	0	0	0	5	0	7	1	0	0	0	.000	0	0-0	0	10.76	6.43
2016 Min	AL	54	0	0	36	54.1	224	59	22	19	5	0	0	3	8	1	35	0	0	0	2	.000	0	17-20	1	3.68	3.15
2017 2 Tms		72	0	0	45	71.1	288	66	25	24	5	1	2	3	16	2	39	1	0	4	3	.571	0	29-35	10	2.99	3.03
17 Min	AL	45	0	0	41	45.1	182	41	15	14	3	0	2	2	11	1	27	1	0	2	2	.500	0	28-32	0	2.97	2.78
17 Was	NL	27	0	0	4	26.0	106	25	10	10	2	1	0	1	5	1	12	0	0	2	1	.667	0	1-3	10	3.04	3.46
8 ML YEARS		298	0	0	115	306.2	1258	307	123	111	27	10	7	6	75	10	208	6	1	14	14	.500	0	46-62	47	3.50	3.26

Jason Kipnis

Bats: L Throws: R Pos: 2B-75;CF-11;PH-3;DH-2 KIP-niss Ht: 5'11" Wt: 195 Born: 4/3/1987 Age: 31

								BATTING											RUNNING			AVERAGES			
Year Team	Lg	G	AB	H	2B	3B	HR	(Hm Rd)	TB	R	RBI	RC	TBB	IBB	SO	HBP	SH	SF	SB	CS	GDP	Avg	OBP	Slg	OPS
2011 Cle	AL	36	136	37	9	1	7	(3 4)	69	24	19	22	11	0	34	2	0	1	5	0	5	.272	.333	.507	.841
2012 Cle	AL	152	591	152	22	4	14	(5 9)	224	86	76	88	67	2	109	5	3	6	31	7	12	.257	.335	.379	.714
2013 Cle	AL	149	564	160	36	4	17	(7 10)	255	86	84	99	76	3	143	3	5	10	30	7	10	.284	.366	.452	.818
2014 Cle	AL	129	500	120	25	1	6	(3 3)	165	61	41	44	50	2	100	2	1	2	22	3	15	.240	.310	.330	.640
2015 Cle	AL	141	565	171	43	7	9	(4 5)	255	86	52	92	57	6	107	9	4	6	12	8	5	.303	.372	.451	.823
2016 Cle	AL	156	610	168	41	4	23	(13 10)	286	91	82	90	60	0	146	6	5	7	15	3	21	.275	.343	.469	.811
2017 Cle	AL	90	336	78	25	0	12	(5 7)	139	43	35	42	28	0	71	2	2	5	6	2	0	.232	.291	.414	.705
Postseason		16	65	14	3	0	4	(2 2)	29	9	8	8	2	0	16	1	0	0	0	0	0	.215	.250	.446	.696
7 ML YEARS		853	3302	886	201	21	88	(42 46)	1393	477	389	477	349	13	710	29	20	37	121	30	63	.268	.340	.422	.762

Andrew Kittredge

Pitches: R Bats: R Pos: RP-15   Ht: 6'1" Wt: 200 Born: 3/17/1990 Age: 28

Year	Team	Lg	G	GS	CG	GF	IP	BFP	H	R	ER	HR	SH	SF	HB	TBB	IBB	SO	WP	Bk	W	L	Pct	Sh	Sv-Op	Hld	ERC	ERA
2013	Jacksn	AA	17	0	0	10	21.2	117	39	16	15	0	1	1	1	12	2	27	0	0	1	3	.250	0	0--	-	8.62	6.23
2013	Tacom	AAA	10	1	0	6	17.1	83	24	14	14	3	0	1	0	9	0	8	2	0	0	0	-	0	0--	-	7.53	7.27
2013	Hi Dsrt	A+	14	0	0	3	23.0	102	28	17	15	6	0	2	2	3	0	23	1	0	0	2	.000	0	1--	-	5.61	5.87
2014	2 Tms	Low	43	0	0	20	85.2	378	92	47	40	11	1	3	2	25	1	114	8	0	7	1	.875	0	8--	-	4.21	4.20
2015	Tacom	AAA	21	2	0	11	42.1	188	46	25	25	5	1	2	1	18	0	29	3	0	0	1	.000	0	0--	-	4.90	5.31
2015	Jacksn	AA	15	1	0	2	32.2	134	29	12	11	1	1	2	0	11	0	31	0	0	2	1	.667	0	0--	-	2.81	3.03
2016	Jacksn	AA	14	4	0	3	34.0	147	37	17	13	0	1	2	1	10	0	37	2	3	1	1	.500	0	0--	-	3.54	3.44
2016	Tacom	AAA	23	1	0	15	38.0	162	39	18	15	5	0	2	0	9	0	47	0	0	2	2	.500	0	7--	-	3.71	3.55
2017	Drham	AAA	41	2	0	14	68.1	265	49	14	11	2	1	3	0	16	1	78	4	0	6	1	.857	0	2--	-	1.65	1.45
2017	TB	AL	15	0	0	2	15.1	66	13	4	3	2	1	0	0	6	1	14	1	0	0	1	.000	0	0-0	1	3.19	1.76

Patrick Kivlehan

Bats: R Throws: R Pos: PH-58;RF-29;1B-12;LF-11;3B-7;CF-4;PR-2
KIV-leh-hann   Ht: 6'2" Wt: 223 Born: 12/22/1989 Age: 28

Year	Team	Lg	G	AB	H	2B	3B	HR	(Hm	Rd)	TB	R	RBI	RC	TBB	IBB	SO	HBP	SH	SF	SB	CS	GDP	Avg	OBP	Slg	OPS
2013	2 Tms	Low	128	489	148	25	3	16	(-	-)	227	74	90	86	43	1	107	10	0	7	15	6	9	.303	.366	.464	.830
2014	Hi Dsrt	A+	34	142	40	9	2	9	(-	-)	80	24	35	27	12	0	32	0	0	3	2	0	8	.282	.331	.563	.895
2014	Jacksn	AA	104	377	113	23	7	11	(-	-)	183	60	68	70	44	1	78	4	0	5	9	4	7	.300	.374	.485	.860
2015	Tacom	AAA	123	472	121	25	1	22	(-	-)	214	58	73	70	36	1	113	5	0	5	14	3	10	.256	.313	.453	.766
2016	RdRck	AAA	37	141	26	8	0	1	(-	-)	37	17	16	8	11	0	36	2	0	1	2	2	5	.184	.252	.262	.514
2016	Tacom	AAA	43	157	46	8	2	8	(-	-)	82	21	25	26	8	0	49	0	0	0	2	2	5	.293	.327	.522	.850
2016	ElPaso	AAA	20	72	22	2	1	3	(-	-)	35	8	8	12	5	0	23	0	0	0	1	0	1	.306	.351	.486	.837
2016	2 Tms	NL	8	21	4	0	0	1	(1	0)	7	5	2	3	2	0	11	1	0	0	0	0	0	.190	.292	.333	.625
2017	Cin	NL	115	178	37	5	1	9	(4	5)	71	23	26	20	22	1	61	3	0	1	1	2	2	.208	.304	.399	.703
16	SD	NL	5	16	4	0	0	1	(1	0)	7	5	2	3	2	0	9	1	0	0	0	0	0	.250	.368	.438	.806
16	Cin	NL	3	5	0	0	0	0	(0	0)	0	0	0	0	0	0	2	0	0	0	0	0	0	.000	.000	.000	.000
	2 ML YEARS		123	199	41	5	1	10	(5	5)	78	28	28	23	24	1	72	4	0	1	1	2	2	.206	.303	.392	.695

Corey Kluber

Pitches: R Bats: R Pos: SP-29
CLUE-burr   Ht: 6'4" Wt: 215 Born: 4/10/1986 Age: 32

Year	Team	Lg	G	GS	CG	GF	IP	BFP	H	R	ER	HR	SH	SF	HB	TBB	IBB	SO	WP	Bk	W	L	Pct	Sh	Sv-Op	Hld	ERC	ERA
2011	Cle	AL	3	0	0	2	4.1	25	6	4	4	0	0	0	2	3	0	5	1	0	0	0	-	0	0-0	0	8.12	8.31
2012	Cle	AL	12	12	0	0	63.0	281	76	44	36	9	1	0	4	18	0	54	2	0	2	5	.286	0	0-0	0	5.38	5.14
2013	Cle	AL	26	24	0	1	147.1	608	153	67	63	15	4	2	5	33	0	136	1	0	11	5	.688	0	0-0	0	3.83	3.85
2014	Cle	AL	34	34	3	0	235.2	951	207	72	64	14	5	2	6	51	3	269	3	0	18	9	.667	1	0-0	0	2.57	2.44
2015	Cle	AL	32	32	4	0	222.0	886	189	92	86	22	7	4	11	45	3	245	6	1	9	16	.360	0	0-0	0	2.74	3.49
2016	Cle	AL	32	32	3	0	215.0	860	170	82	75	22	6	2	7	57	1	227	5	1	18	9	.667	2	0-0	0	2.62	3.14
2017	Cle	AL	29	29	5	0	203.2	777	141	56	51	21	3	1	5	36	2	265	4	0	18	4	.818	3	0-0	0	1.83	2.25
	Postseason		6	6	0	0	34.1	138	28	7	7	3	0	1	3	8	0	35	0	0	4	1	.800	0	0-0	0	2.76	1.83
	7 ML YEARS		168	163	15	3	1091.0	4388	942	417	379	103	26	11	40	243	9	1201	22	2	76	48	.613	6	0-0	0	2.80	3.13

Andrew Knapp

Bats: B Throws: R Pos: C-53;PH-2;1B-1;DH-1;PR-1   Ht: 6'1" Wt: 195 Born: 11/9/1991 Age: 26

Year	Team	Lg	G	AB	H	2B	3B	HR	(Hm	Rd)	TB	R	RBI	RC	TBB	IBB	SO	HBP	SH	SF	SB	CS	GDP	Avg	OBP	Slg	OPS
2013	Wmspt	A-	62	217	55	20	0	4	(-	-)	87	30	23	30	22	0	57	7	0	1	7	5	3	.253	.340	.401	.741
2014	2 Tms	Low	98	366	95	20	4	6	(-	-)	141	46	32	47	32	0	97	4	0	2	4	3	6	.260	.324	.385	.710
2015	Clrwtr	A+	63	244	64	14	3	2	(-	-)	90	38	28	34	29	1	63	7	0	1	0	1	5	.262	.356	.369	.725
2015	Rdng	AA	55	214	77	21	2	11	(-	-)	135	39	56	53	22	0	43	2	0	3	1	0	4	.360	.419	.631	1.050
2016	LV	AAA	107	403	107	24	1	8	(-	-)	157	55	46	53	37	1	107	2	0	1	2	2	9	.266	.330	.390	.719
2017	Phi	NL	56	171	44	8	1	3	(2	1)	63	26	13	20	31	4	56	0	0	2	1	0	5	.257	.368	.368	.736

Corey Knebel

Pitches: R Bats: R Pos: RP-76
kuh-NAY-bull   Ht: 6'4" Wt: 220 Born: 11/26/1991 Age: 26

Year	Team	Lg	G	GS	CG	GF	IP	BFP	H	R	ER	HR	SH	SF	HB	TBB	IBB	SO	WP	Bk	W	L	Pct	Sh	Sv-Op	Hld	ERC	ERA
2014	Det	AL	8	0	0	4	8.2	39	11	7	6	0	0	0	0	3	0	11	1	0	0	0	-	0	0-0	0	4.65	6.23
2015	Mil	NL	48	0	0	15	50.1	209	44	18	18	8	0	0	2	17	1	58	1	0	0	0	-	0	0-1	3	3.69	3.22
2016	Mil	NL	35	0	0	7	32.2	145	32	20	17	3	0	1	1	16	3	38	1	0	1	4	.200	0	2-4	13	4.18	4.68
2017	Mil	NL	76	0	0	48	76.0	309	48	15	15	6	0	0	2	40	5	126	2	0	1	4	.200	0	39-45	11	2.51	1.78
	4 ML YEARS		167	0	0	74	167.2	702	135	60	56	17	0	1	5	76	9	233	5	0	2	8	.200	0	41-50	27	3.28	3.01

Matt Koch

Pitches: R Bats: L Pos: RP-1
cook   Ht: 6'3" Wt: 215 Born: 11/2/1990 Age: 27

Year	Team	Lg	G	GS	CG	GF	IP	BFP	H	R	ER	HR	SH	SF	HB	TBB	IBB	SO	WP	Bk	W	L	Pct	Sh	Sv-Op	Hld	ERC	ERA
2013	Savann	A	18	15	1	1	82.1	350	100	52	43	7	1	4	2	4	0	68	3	0	6	4	.600	0	0--	-	3.82	4.70
2014	Stluci	A+	22	22	0	0	120.1	529	141	67	62	7	2	2	13	32	0	63	8	3	10	4	.714	0	0--	-	4.69	4.64
2015	Bnghtn	AA	35	8	0	3	88.1	367	95	37	34	5	5	3	4	15	1	55	5	0	4	8	.333	0	0--	-	3.50	3.46
2016	Mobile	AA	14	14	0	0	74.2	319	87	41	38	7	3	5	3	13	0	49	0	0	2	4	.333	0	0--	-	4.24	4.70
2016	Reno	AAA	7	7	0	0	46.2	194	55	18	16	3	1	0	0	6	1	25	1	0	4	2	.667	0	0--	-	3.78	3.09

Year Team	Lg	G	GS	CG	GF	IP	BFP	H	R	ER	HR	SH	SF	HB	TBB	IBB	SO	WP	Bk	W	L	Pct	Sh	Sv-Op	Hld	ERC	ERA
2017 Reno	AAA	10	10	0	0	45.0	216	68	42	42	11	1	2	2	15	2	25	1	0	2	2	.500	0	0--	-	8.19	8.40
2016 Ari	NL	7	2	0	4	18.0	69	9	4	4	1	1	0	2	4	0	10	0	0	1	1	.500	0	1-1	0	1.29	2.00
2017 Ari	NL	1	0	0	0	0.0	3	2	3	3	0	0	0	0	1	0	0	0	0	0	0	-	0	0-0	0	-	-
2 ML YEARS		8	2	0	4	18.0	72	11	7	7	1	1	0	2	5	0	10	0	0	1	1	.500	0	1-1	0	1.77	3.50

Tom Koehler

Pitches: R **Bats:** R **Pos:** RP-14; SP-13   COLE-err   **Ht:** 6'3" **Wt:** 235 **Born:** 6/29/1986 **Age:** 32

Year Team	Lg	G	GS	CG	GF	IP	BFP	H	R	ER	HR	SH	SF	HB	TBB	IBB	SO	WP	Bk	W	L	Pct	Sh	Sv-Op	Hld	ERC	ERA
2017 NewOr*	AAA	7	6	0	1	37.2	159	30	12	7	4	2	0	3	13	1	55	5	0	1	1	.500	0	0--	-	3.01	1.67
2012 Mia	NL	8	1	0	0	13.1	56	15	8	8	4	0	0	0	2	1	13	0	0	0	1	.000	0	0-0	0	4.99	5.40
2013 Mia	NL	29	23	0	2	143.0	601	140	72	70	14	3	2	5	54	2	92	7	0	5	10	.333	0	0-0	0	4.08	4.41
2014 Mia	NL	32	32	0	0	191.1	803	177	84	81	16	6	5	7	71	0	153	4	0	10	10	.500	0	0-0	0	3.63	3.81
2015 Mia	NL	32	31	0	0	187.1	800	180	96	85	22	6	5	6	77	3	137	2	0	11	14	.440	0	0-0	0	4.17	4.08
2016 Mia	NL	33	33	0	0	176.2	774	176	93	85	22	6	5	5	83	7	147	9	0	9	13	.409	0	0-0	0	4.58	4.33
2017 2 Tms		27	13	0	0	72.2	334	83	55	54	16	3	1	7	35	3	62	1	0	1	7	.125	0	0-0	2	6.56	6.69
17 Mia	NL	12	12	0	0	55.2	259	67	50	49	15	3	0	5	29	3	44	1	0	1	5	.167	0	0-0	0	7.56	7.92
17 Tor	AL	15	1	0	0	17.0	75	16	5	5	1	0	1	2	6	0	18	0	0	0	2	.000	0	0-0	2	3.64	2.65
6 ML YEARS		161	133	0	2	784.1	3368	771	408	383	94	24	18	30	322	16	604	23	0	36	55	.396	0	0-0	2	4.33	4.39

Adam Kolarek

Pitches: L **Bats:** L **Pos:** RP-12   **Ht:** 6'3" **Wt:** 205 **Born:** 1/14/1989 **Age:** 29

Year Team	Lg	G	GS	CG	GF	IP	BFP	H	R	ER	HR	SH	SF	HB	TBB	IBB	SO	WP	Bk	W	L	Pct	Sh	Sv-Op	Hld	ERC	ERA
2013 Bnghtn	AA	44	0	0	15	63.0	256	47	15	12	3	0	2	2	22	1	63	3	0	3	3	.500	0	1- -	-	2.32	1.71
2014 Bnghtn	AA	48	0	0	17	56.1	278	77	45	38	2	2	4	6	21	1	43	2	0	1	2	.333	0	2- -	-	5.74	6.07
2015 Bnghtn	AA	51	1	0	15	67.0	288	59	35	33	4	3	0	3	28	3	61	4	0	2	4	.333	0	1- -	-	3.27	4.43
2016 Mont	AA	13	0	0	2	19.0	87	14	13	7	0	0	1	2	12	0	17	2	0	3	2	.600	0	0- -	-	3.02	3.32
2016 Drham	AAA	34	0	0	11	41.1	174	28	15	14	1	2	1	4	23	0	46	2	0	0	2	.000	0	2- -	-	2.80	3.05
2017 Drham	AAA	41	0	0	8	43.2	184	37	9	8	0	1	0	3	16	1	46	3	0	3	4	.429	0	2- -	-	2.66	1.65
2017 TB	AL	12	0	0	5	8.1	40	9	6	6	2	1	0	4	4	2	4	1	0	1	0	1.000	0	0-0	2	7.84	6.48

George Kontos

Pitches: R **Bats:** R **Pos:** RP-65   KAHN-tose   **Ht:** 6'3" **Wt:** 215 **Born:** 6/12/1985 **Age:** 33

Year Team	Lg	G	GS	CG	GF	IP	BFP	H	R	ER	HR	SH	SF	HB	TBB	IBB	SO	WP	Bk	W	L	Pct	Sh	Sv-Op	Hld	ERC	ERA
2011 NYY	AL	7	0	0	4	6.0	24	4	2	2	1	0	0	0	3	0	6	0	0	0	0	-	0	0-0	0	3.20	3.00
2012 SF	NL	44	0	0	9	43.2	177	34	15	12	3	0	2	0	12	0	44	1	0	2	1	.667	0	0-1	5	2.23	2.47
2013 SF	NL	52	0	0	9	55.1	238	60	30	27	7	1	4	2	18	2	47	1	0	2	2	.500	0	0-1	5	4.59	4.39
2014 SF	NL	24	0	0	7	32.1	125	24	10	10	1	0	0	0	11	3	27	1	0	4	0	1.000	0	0-0	1	2.07	2.78
2015 SF	NL	73	0	0	12	73.1	284	57	20	19	9	1	3	0	12	3	44	3	0	4	4	.500	0	0-2	14	2.14	2.33
2016 SF	NL	57	0	0	17	53.1	216	42	19	15	3	1	1	2	20	3	35	1	0	3	2	.600	0	0-2	9	2.68	2.53
2017 2 Tms	NL	65	0	0	16	66.1	278	61	27	25	9	5	1	0	20	2	70	2	0	1	6	.143	0	1-7	11	3.40	3.39
17 SF	NL	50	0	0	12	51.2	223	52	24	22	8	4	1	0	17	2	55	2	0	0	5	.000	0	0-5	5	4.08	3.83
17 Pit	NL	15	0	0	4	14.2	55	9	3	3	1	1	0	0	3	0	15	0	0	1	1	.500	0	1-2	6	1.42	1.84
Postseason		9	0	0	1	7.1	29	7	5	5	2	1	0	0	1	0	3	0	0	0	0	-	0	0-0	1	3.93	6.14
7 ML YEARS		322	0	0	74	330.1	1342	282	123	110	33	8	11	4	96	13	273	9	0	16	15	.516	0	1-13	45	2.89	3.00

Pete Kozma

Bats: R **Throws:** R **Pos:** 3B-14;SS-14;PR-10;2B-5;1B-4;PH-2   KAHZ-muh   **Ht:** 6'0" **Wt:** 190 **Born:** 4/11/1988 **Age:** 30

Year Team	Lg	G	AB	H	2B	3B	HR	(Hm	Rd)	TB	R	RBI	RC	TBB	IBB	SO	HBP	SH	SF	SB	CS	GDP	Avg	OBP	Slg	OPS
2017 RdRck*	AAA	11	40	12	4	0	0	(-	-)	16	8	2	5	2	0	8	0	1	0	1	0	0	.300	.333	.400	.733
2011 StL	NL	16	17	3	1	0	0	(0	0)	4	2	1	2	4	0	4	0	1	0	0	0	0	.176	.333	.235	.569
2012 StL	NL	26	72	24	5	3	2	(0	2)	41	11	14	13	7	1	19	0	1	2	2	0	4	.333	.383	.569	.952
2013 StL	NL	143	410	89	20	0	1	(0	1)	112	44	35	39	34	8	91	0	1	3	3	1	6	.217	.275	.273	.548
2014 StL	NL	14	23	7	3	0	0	(0	0)	10	4	2	3	3	0	4	0	0	0	0	0	0	.304	.385	.435	.819
2015 StL	NL	76	99	15	0	0	0	(0	0)	15	15	2	4	10	2	21	1	1	0	3	1	0	.152	.236	.152	.388
2017 2 Tms	AL	39	45	5	0	0	1	(0	1)	8	6	2	1	3	0	20	2	1	0	0	1	0	.111	.200	.178	.378
17 NYY	AL	11	9	1	0	0	0	(0	0)	1	2	0	0	1	0	2	0	0	0	0	0	0	.111	.200	.111	.311
17 Tex	AL	28	36	4	0	0	1	(0	1)	7	4	2	1	2	0	18	2	1	0	0	1	0	.111	.200	.194	.394
Postseason		29	82	14	3	0	1	(0	1)	20	11	9	13	12	3	24	2	1	0	3	1	1	.171	.292	.244	.536
6 ML YEARS		314	666	143	29	3	4	(0	4)	190	82	54	62	61	11	159	3	5	5	8	3	10	.215	.282	.285	.567

Erik Kratz

Bats: R **Throws:** R **Pos:** C-2;DH-2;PH-2   **Ht:** 6'4" **Wt:** 245 **Born:** 6/15/1980 **Age:** 38

Year Team	Lg	G	AB	H	2B	3B	HR	(Hm	Rd)	TB	R	RBI	RC	TBB	IBB	SO	HBP	SH	SF	SB	CS	GDP	Avg	OBP	Slg	OPS
2017 Clmbs*	AAA	86	282	76	16	1	13	(-	-)	133	38	37	50	32	2	64	8	1	1	5	1	5	.270	.359	.472	.831
2010 Pit	NL	9	34	4	0	0	0	(0	0)	4	2	1	2	2	0	9	0	0	0	0	0	0	.118	.167	.118	.284
2011 Phi	NL	2	6	2	1	0	0	(0	0)	3	0	0	1	0	0	1	0	0	0	0	0	0	.333	.333	.500	.833
2012 Phi	NL	50	141	35	9	0	9	(6	3)	71	14	26	20	11	2	34	2	0	3	0	0	2	.248	.306	.504	.809
2013 Phi	NL	68	197	42	7	0	9	(5	4)	76	21	26	15	18	4	45	1	0	2	0	0	11	.213	.280	.386	.666
2014 2 Tms	AL	47	110	24	4	0	5	(1	4)	43	12	13	7	4	1	22	0	0	0	0	0	0	.218	.243	.391	.634
2015 2 Tms		16	26	5	2	0	0	(0	0)	7	3	3	1	1	0	5	0	0	1	0	0	0	.192	.214	.269	.484

(Batting — continued)

Year Team	Lg	G	AB	H	2B	3B	HR	(Hm Rd)	TB	R	RBI	RC	TBB	IBB	SO	HBP	SH	SF	SB	CS	GDP	Avg	OBP	Slg	OPS
2016 2 Tms		33	85	8	2	0	1	(1 0)	13	3	4	0	1	0	32	0	1	0	0	0	3	.094	.105	.153	.258
2017 NYY	AL	4	2	2	1	0	0	(0 0)	3	0	2	2	0	0	0	0	0	0	0	0	0	1.000	1.000	1.500	2.500
14 Tor	AL	34	81	16	3	0	3	(1 2)	28	8	10	5	3	0	12	0	0	0	0	0	3	.198	.226	.346	.572
14 KC	AL	13	29	8	1	0	2	(0 2)	15	4	3	2	1	1	10	0	0	1	0	0	1	.276	.290	.517	.808
15 KC	AL	4	4	0	0	0	0	(0 0)	0	0	1	0	0	0	2	0	0	1	0	0	0	.000	.000	.000	.000
15 Phi	NL	12	22	5	2	0	0	(0 0)	7	3	2	1	1	0	3	0	0	0	0	0	0	.227	.261	.318	.579
16 Hou	AL	15	29	2	1	0	0	(0 0)	3	0	0	0	1	0	14	0	0	0	0	0	1	.069	.100	.103	.203
16 Pit	NL	18	56	6	1	0	1	(1 0)	10	3	4	0	0	0	18	0	1	0	0	0	0	.107	.107	.179	.286
8 ML YEARS		229	601	122	26	0	24	(13 11)	220	55	75	46	37	7	148	3	1	7	0	0	20	.203	.250	.366	.616

Ian Krol

Pitches: L Bats: L Pos: RP-51
KROHL
Ht: 6'1" Wt: 210 Born: 5/9/1991 Age: 27

Year Team	Lg	G	GS	CG	GF	IP	BFP	H	R	ER	HR	SH	SF	HB	TBB	IBB	SO	WP	Bk	W	L	Pct	Sh	Sv-Op	Hld	ERC	ERA
2013 Was	NL	32	0	0	10	27.1	117	28	12	12	5	2	1	0	8	1	22	2	0	2	1	.667	0	0-1	2	4.24	3.95
2014 Det	AL	45	0	0	5	32.2	154	42	23	18	6	0	1	2	13	4	28	1	0	0	0	-	0	1-4	10	6.35	4.96
2015 Det	AL	33	0	0	6	28.0	129	31	19	18	4	2	0	2	17	1	26	0	0	2	3	.400	0	0-1	1	6.23	5.79
2016 Atl	NL	63	0	0	7	51.0	217	54	19	18	4	1	1	3	13	3	56	5	0	2	0	1.000	0	0-2	10	3.84	3.18
2017 Atl	NL	51	0	0	15	49.0	214	50	34	29	8	0	1	4	21	0	44	2	0	2	2	.500	0	0-0	3	5.19	5.33
5 ML YEARS		224	0	0	43	188.0	831	205	107	95	27	5	4	11	72	9	176	10	1	8	6	.571	0	1-8	26	5.02	4.55

Chad Kuhl

Pitches: R Bats: R Pos: SP-31
cool
Ht: 6'3" Wt: 216 Born: 9/10/1992 Age: 25

Year Team	Lg	G	GS	CG	GF	IP	BFP	H	R	ER	HR	SH	SF	HB	TBB	IBB	SO	WP	Bk	W	L	Pct	Sh	Sv-Op	Hld	ERC	ERA
2013 Jmstwn	A-	13	13	0	0	55.1	222	53	22	13	0	1	2	5	6	0	33	1	0	3	4	.429	0	0--	-	2.50	2.11
2014 Bradtn	A+	28	28	0	0	153.1	626	141	67	59	9	1	7	15	42	0	100	3	0	13	5	.722	0	0--	-	3.36	3.46
2015 Altna	AA	26	26	1	0	152.2	620	134	53	42	10	8	3	4	41	0	101	6	0	11	5	.688	0	0--	-	2.83	2.48
2016 Indy	AAA	16	16	0	0	83.2	339	81	27	22	9	2	2	4	16	0	66	2	0	6	3	.667	0	0--	-	3.40	2.37
2016 Pit	NL	14	14	0	0	70.2	301	73	34	33	7	2	2	4	20	0	53	2	0	5	4	.556	0	0-0	0	4.04	4.20
2017 Pit	NL	31	31	0	0	157.1	680	159	81	76	17	6	4	6	72	7	142	8	1	8	11	.421	0	0-0	0	4.60	4.35
2 ML YEARS		45	45	0	0	228.0	981	232	115	109	24	8	6	10	92	7	195	10	1	13	15	.464	0	0-0	0	4.43	4.30

Tommy La Stella

Bats: L Throws: R Pos: PH-44;2B-21;3B-18;1B-1
Ht: 5'11" Wt: 180 Born: 1/31/1989 Age: 29

Year Team	Lg	G	AB	H	2B	3B	HR	(Hm Rd)	TB	R	RBI	RC	TBB	IBB	SO	HBP	SH	SF	SB	CS	GDP	Avg	OBP	Slg	OPS
2017 Iowa*	AAA	33	110	24	2	0	1	(- -)	29	14	6	8	10	0	22	0	0	1	0	1	1	.218	.281	.264	.545
2014 Atl	NL	93	319	80	16	1	1	(1 0)	101	22	31	36	36	2	40	1	3	1	2	1	8	.251	.328	.317	.644
2015 ChC	NL	33	67	18	6	0	1	(1 0)	27	4	11	10	5	0	7	1	0	1	2	0	1	.269	.324	.403	.727
2016 ChC	NL	74	148	40	12	1	2	(1 1)	60	17	11	20	18	1	27	2	0	0	0	1	2	.270	.357	.405	.763
2017 ChC	NL	73	125	36	8	0	5	(0 5)	59	18	22	24	20	1	18	2	0	2	0	0	3	.288	.389	.472	.861
Postseason		7	11	0	0	0	0	(0 0)	0	0	0	0	0	0	3	0	0	0	0	0	0	.000	.000	.000	.000
4 ML YEARS		273	659	174	42	2	9	(3 6)	247	61	75	90	79	4	92	6	3	4	4	2	14	.264	.346	.375	.721

Jairo Labourt

Pitches: L Bats: L Pos: RP-6
HIGH-roh LA-bort
Ht: 6'4" Wt: 205 Born: 3/7/1994 Age: 24

Year Team	Lg	G	GS	CG	GF	IP	BFP	H	R	ER	HR	SH	SF	HB	TBB	IBB	SO	WP	Bk	W	L	Pct	Sh	Sv-Op	Hld	ERC	ERA
2013 Bluefld	R+	12	8	0	0	51.2	211	39	16	11	3	2	1	3	14	0	45	3	1	2	2	.500	0	0--	-	2.23	1.92
2014 2 Tms	Low	21	18	0	0	85.0	372	62	30	24	1	2	1	11	57	0	93	10	1	5	3	.625	0	0--	-	3.50	2.54
2015 2 Tms	Low	25	25	0	0	116.0	533	128	81	66	9	9	5	4	59	0	104	17	1	3	12	.200	0	0--	-	5.01	5.12
2016 Lkland	A+	30	12	0	9	87.1	407	65	55	51	3	5	2	8	70	0	81	14	1	7	9	.438	0	1--	-	3.92	5.26
2017 Lkland	A+	8	0	0	3	13.2	51	8	2	1	0	0	0	2	3	0	22	0	0	0	0	-	0	0--	-	1.13	0.66
2017 Erie	AA	21	0	0	10	30.2	118	23	10	9	3	3	1	0	7	0	36	2	0	1	1	.500	0	4--	-	2.20	2.64
2017 Toledo	AAA	16	0	0	3	22.0	101	12	6	6	1	0	1	1	23	0	21	2	0	0	0	-	0	0--	-	3.71	2.45
2017 Det	AL	6	0	0	4	6.0	28	4	3	3	0	0	1	0	7	1	4	5	0	0	0	-	0	0-0	0	4.05	4.50

John Lackey

Pitches: R Bats: R Pos: SP-30; RP-1
Ht: 6'6" Wt: 235 Born: 10/23/1978 Age: 39

Year Team	Lg	G	GS	CG	GF	IP	BFP	H	R	ER	HR	SH	SF	HB	TBB	IBB	SO	WP	Bk	W	L	Pct	Sh	Sv-Op	Hld	ERC	ERA
2002 LAA	AL	18	18	1	0	108.1	465	113	52	44	10	0	4	4	33	0	69	7	2	9	4	.692	0	0-0	0	4.03	3.66
2003 LAA	AL	33	33	2	0	204.0	885	223	117	105	31	2	6	10	66	4	151	11	1	10	16	.385	2	0-0	0	4.88	4.63
2004 LAA	AL	33	32	1	0	198.1	855	215	108	103	22	9	4	8	60	4	144	11	1	14	13	.519	1	0-0	0	4.39	4.67
2005 LAA	AL	33	33	1	0	209.0	892	208	85	80	13	1	2	11	71	3	199	18	0	14	5	.737	0	0-0	0	3.76	3.44
2006 LAA	AL	33	33	3	0	217.2	922	203	98	86	14	8	6	9	72	4	190	16	0	13	11	.542	2	0-0	0	3.31	3.56
2007 LAA	AL	33	33	2	0	224.0	929	219	87	75	18	1	1	12	52	2	179	9	1	19	9	.679	2	0-0	0	3.40	3.01
2008 LAA	AL	24	24	1	0	163.1	675	161	71	68	26	5	1	10	40	1	130	5	0	12	5	.706	0	0-0	0	4.10	3.75
2009 LAA	AL	27	27	1	0	176.1	748	177	84	75	17	9	10	4	47	1	139	6	0	11	8	.579	1	0-0	0	3.73	3.83
2010 Bos	AL	33	33	0	0	215.0	930	233	114	105	18	4	5	9	72	2	156	3	0	14	11	.560	0	0-0	0	4.37	4.40
2011 Bos	AL	28	28	0	0	160.0	743	203	119	114	20	2	6	19	56	1	108	11	0	12	12	.500	0	0-0	0	6.11	6.41
2013 Bos	AL	29	29	2	0	189.1	778	179	80	74	26	3	3	6	40	0	161	4	0	10	13	.435	0	0-0	0	3.42	3.52
2014 2 Tms	AL	31	31	1	0	198.0	833	206	94	84	24	6	3	1	47	1	164	4	2	14	10	.583	0	0-0	0	3.81	3.82
2015 StL	NL	33	33	1	0	218.0	896	211	71	67	21	11	4	4	53	5	175	5	3	13	10	.565	0	0-0	0	3.34	2.77

Year Team	Lg	G	GS	CG	GF	IP	BFP	H	R	ER	HR	SH	SF	HB	TBB	IBB	SO	WP	Bk	W	L	Pct	Sh	Sv-Op	Hld	ERC	ERA
						HOW MUCH HE PITCHED					WHAT HE GAVE UP											THE RESULTS					
2016 ChC	NL	29	29	0	0	188.1	748	146	74	70	23	8	9	8	53	1	180	4	0	11	8	.579	0	0-0	0	2.81	3.35
2017 ChC	NL	31	30	0	0	170.2	731	165	93	87	36	8	9	12	53	3	149	11	2	12	12	.500	0	0-0	0	4.53	4.59
14 Bos	AL	21	21	1	0	137.1	572	137	60	55	15	2	3	0	32	0	116	3	1	11	7	.611	0	0-0	0	3.46	3.60
14 StL	NL	10	10	0	0	60.2	261	69	34	29	9	4	0	1	15	1	48	1	1	3	3	.500	0	0-0	0	4.63	4.30
Postseason		26	23	0	0	140.1	584	130	54	51	6	3	5	4	45	6	111	7	0	8	6	.571	0	0-0	1	3.06	3.27
15 ML YEARS		448	446	18	0	2840.1	12030	2862	1347	1237	319	72	72	133	815	32	2294	125	12	188	147	.561	8	0-0	0	3.94	3.92

Juan Lagares

Bats: R **Throws:** R **Pos:** CF-85;PH-11;PR-5   luh-GAR-ess   **Ht:** 6'1" **Wt:** 215 **Born:** 3/17/1989 **Age:** 29

Year Team	Lg	G	AB	H	2B	3B	HR	(Hm	Rd)	TB	R	RBI	RC	TBB	IBB	SO	HBP	SH	SF	SB	CS	GDP	Avg	OBP	Slg	OPS
						BATTING														RUNNING			AVERAGES			
2013 NYM	NL	121	392	95	21	5	4	(1	3)	138	35	34	36	20	4	96	2	5	2	6	3	6	.242	.281	.352	.633
2014 NYM	NL	116	416	117	24	3	4	(2	2)	159	46	47	53	20	1	87	7	3	6	13	4	6	.281	.321	.382	.703
2015 NYM	NL	143	441	114	16	5	6	(2	4)	158	47	41	51	16	2	87	4	1	3	7	3	6	.259	.289	.358	.647
2016 NYM	NL	79	142	34	7	2	3	(2	1)	54	15	9	12	11	1	27	2	4	1	4	2	4	.239	.301	.380	.682
2017 NYM	NL	94	252	63	16	2	3	(1	2)	92	37	15	20	14	0	56	3	2	1	7	3	6	.250	.296	.365	.661
Postseason		13	23	8	2	0	0	(0	0)	10	7	0	3	1	0	3	0	1	0	2	0	1	.348	.375	.435	.810
5 ML YEARS		553	1643	423	84	17	20	(8	12)	601	180	146	172	81	8	353	18	15	13	37	15	28	.257	.297	.366	.663

Ryan LaMarre

Bats: R **Throws:** L **Pos:** CF-3;PH-1   la-MARR   **Ht:** 6'1" **Wt:** 210 **Born:** 11/21/1988 **Age:** 29

Year Team	Lg	G	AB	H	2B	3B	HR	(Hm	Rd)	TB	R	RBI	RC	TBB	IBB	SO	HBP	SH	SF	SB	CS	GDP	Avg	OBP	Slg	OPS
						BATTING														RUNNING			AVERAGES			
2017 Salt Lk*	AAA	10	41	11	1	1	0	(-	-)	14	6	7	6	6	0	11	1	0	0	4	1	1	.268	.375	.341	.716
2017 Nashv*	AAA	41	129	31	2	2	0	(-	-)	37	11	12	11	11	0	47	3	2	1	5	5	4	.240	.313	.287	.599
2015 Cin	NL	21	25	2	0	0	0	(0	0)	2	2	0	0	0	0	9	0	1	0	0	0	1	.080	.080	.080	.160
2016 Bos	AL	6	5	0	0	0	0	(0	0)	0	1	0	0	1	0	2	0	0	0	0	0	1	.000	.167	.000	.167
2017 Oak	AL	3	7	0	0	0	0	(0	0)	0	0	0	0	1	0	3	0	0	0	0	0	0	.000	.125	.000	.125
3 ML YEARS		30	37	2	0	0	0	(0	0)	2	3	0	0	2	0	14	0	1	0	0	0	2	.054	.103	.054	.157

Jake Lamb

Bats: L **Throws:** R **Pos:** 3B-144;PH-5;DH-1   **Ht:** 6'3" **Wt:** 215 **Born:** 10/9/1990 **Age:** 27

Year Team	Lg	G	AB	H	2B	3B	HR	(Hm	Rd)	TB	R	RBI	RC	TBB	IBB	SO	HBP	SH	SF	SB	CS	GDP	Avg	OBP	Slg	OPS
						BATTING														RUNNING			AVERAGES			
2014 Ari	NL	37	126	29	4	1	4	(2	2)	47	15	11	7	6	0	37	0	0	1	1	1	4	.230	.263	.373	.636
2015 Ari	NL	107	350	92	15	5	6	(1	5)	135	38	34	39	36	3	97	1	0	3	3	2	5	.263	.331	.386	.716
2016 Ari	NL	151	523	130	31	9	29	(19	10)	266	81	91	84	64	5	154	3	0	13	6	1	13	.249	.332	.509	.840
2017 Ari	NL	149	536	133	30	4	30	(16	14)	261	89	105	90	87	13	152	7	0	5	6	4	15	.248	.357	.487	.844
4 ML YEARS		444	1535	384	80	19	69	(38	31)	709	223	241	220	193	21	440	11	0	13	16	8	37	.250	.336	.462	.798

Dinelson Lamet

Pitches: R **Bats:** R **Pos:** SP-21   din-EL-son LAH-met   **Ht:** 6'4" **Wt:** 187 **Born:** 7/18/1992 **Age:** 25

Year Team	Lg	G	GS	CG	GF	IP	BFP	H	R	ER	HR	SH	SF	HB	TBB	IBB	SO	WP	Bk	W	L	Pct	Sh	Sv-Op	Hld	ERC	ERA
						HOW MUCH HE PITCHED					WHAT HE GAVE UP											THE RESULTS					
2015 FtWyn	A	26	24	0	0	105.1	441	82	42	35	9	3	1	9	44	0	120	9	6	5	8	.385	0	0- -	-	3.19	2.99
2016 Lk Els	A+	12	12	0	0	65.0	268	56	17	17	4	4	2	4	26	0	54	9	1	7	1	.875	0	0- -	-	3.40	2.35
2016 SnAnt	AA	14	14	0	0	74.1	312	57	32	28	2	2	1	2	31	0	91	8	1	5	7	.417	0	0- -	-	2.48	3.39
2017 ElPaso	AAA	8	8	0	0	39.0	167	32	17	14	2	1	1	1	20	0	50	2	0	3	2	.600	0	0- -	-	3.28	3.23
2017 SD	NL	21	21	0	0	114.1	485	88	63	58	18	1	5	6	54	2	139	9	0	7	8	.467	0	0-0	0	3.64	4.57

Mat Latos

Pitches: R **Bats:** R **Pos:** SP-3   LAY-tos   **Ht:** 6'6" **Wt:** 245 **Born:** 12/9/1987 **Age:** 30

Year Team	Lg	G	GS	CG	GF	IP	BFP	H	R	ER	HR	SH	SF	HB	TBB	IBB	SO	WP	Bk	W	L	Pct	Sh	Sv-Op	Hld	ERC	ERA
						HOW MUCH HE PITCHED					WHAT HE GAVE UP											THE RESULTS					
2017 Buffalo*	AAA	6	5	0	0	26.0	115	27	13	11	3	0	3	1	13	0	24	3	0	1	1	.500	0	0- -	-	5.03	3.81
2009 SD	NL	10	10	0	0	50.2	212	43	29	26	7	3	1	0	23	1	39	0	2	4	5	.444	0	0-0	0	3.72	4.62
2010 SD	NL	31	31	1	0	184.2	748	150	63	60	16	4	1	2	50	3	189	5	1	14	10	.583	1	0-0	0	2.52	2.92
2011 SD	NL	31	31	0	0	194.1	799	168	82	75	16	8	7	1	62	3	185	5	0	9	14	.391	0	0-0	0	2.93	3.47
2012 Cin	NL	33	33	2	0	209.1	858	179	87	81	25	9	3	4	64	9	185	3	1	14	4	.778	0	0-0	0	3.08	3.48
2013 Cin	NL	32	32	1	0	210.2	881	197	82	74	14	12	3	10	58	5	187	8	0	14	7	.667	0	0-0	0	3.16	3.16
2014 Cin	NL	16	16	0	0	102.1	420	92	42	37	9	8	1	2	26	2	74	1	0	5	5	.500	0	0-0	0	2.94	3.25
2015 3 Tms		24	21	0	2	116.1	494	120	67	64	13	6	5	1	32	1	100	10	1	4	10	.286	0	0-0	0	3.84	4.95
2016 2 Tms		17	12	0	1	70.0	309	74	40	38	11	2	5	1	30	1	42	1	0	7	3	.700	0	0-0	0	4.96	4.89
2017 Tor	AL	3	3	0	0	15.0	70	19	11	11	5	0	0	0	8	1	10	1	0	0	1	.000	0	0-0	0	8.54	6.60
15 Mia	NL	16	16	0	0	88.1	372	85	46	44	8	4	3	1	25	0	79	9	0	4	7	.364	0	0-0	0	3.36	4.48
15 LAD	NL	6	5	0	1	24.1	106	31	19	18	3	2	2	0	6	1	18	1	1	0	3	.000	0	0-0	0	5.22	6.66
15 LAA	NL	2	0	0	1	3.2	16	4	2	2	2	0	0	0	1	0	3	0	0	0	0	-	0	0-0	0	7.04	4.91
16 CWS	AL	11	11	0	0	60.1	265	63	33	31	10	2	4	1	25	1	32	1	0	6	2	.750	0	0-0	0	4.89	4.62
16 Was	NL	6	1	0	1	9.2	44	11	7	7	1	0	1	0	5	0	10	0	0	1	1	.500	0	0-0	0	5.37	6.52
Postseason		2	1	0	0	8.1	39	11	7	6	2	0	0	0	2	0	5	0	0	1	0	.000	0	0-0	0	6.03	6.48
9 ML YEARS		197	189	4	3	1153.1	4791	1042	503	466	116	52	26	22	353	26	1011	34	5	71	59	.546	1	0-0	0	3.23	3.64

Ryan Lavarnway

Bats: R Throws: R Pos: C-5;PH-1

luh-VARN-way

Ht: 6'4" Wt: 240 Born: 8/7/1987 Age: 30

Year	Team	Lg	G	AB	H	2B	3B	HR	(Hm	Rd)	TB	R	RBI	RC	TBB	IBB	SO	HBP	SH	SF	SB	CS	GDP	Avg	OBP	Slg	OPS
2017	Nashv*	AAA	83	264	63	9	0	6	(-	-)	90	33	26	31	31	0	65	5	1	3	0	2	13	.239	.327	.341	.668
2011	Bos	AL	17	39	9	2	0	2	(0	2)	17	5	8	4	4	0	10	0	0	0	0	0	1	.231	.302	.436	.738
2012	Bos	AL	46	153	24	8	0	2	(0	2)	38	11	12	4	11	0	41	0	0	2	0	0	4	.157	.211	.248	.459
2013	Bos	AL	25	77	23	7	0	1	(1	0)	33	8	14	11	2	0	17	2	0	1	0	0	3	.299	.329	.429	.758
2014	Bos	AL	9	10	0	0	0	0	(0	0)	0	0	0	0	0	0	3	0	0	0	0	0	0	.000	.000	.000	.000
2015	2 Tms		37	94	18	6	0	2	(0	2)	30	6	6	4	12	1	28	0	0	0	0	0	5	.191	.283	.319	.602
2017	Oak	AL	6	11	3	1	0	0	(0	0)	4	0	2	2	1	0	3	1	0	0	0	0	1	.273	.385	.364	.748
15	Bal	AL	10	28	3	1	0	0	(0	0)	4	1	0	0	4	0	7	0	0	0	0	0	0	.107	.219	.143	.362
15	Atl	NL	27	66	15	5	0	2	(0	2)	26	5	6	4	8	1	21	0	0	0	0	0	4	.227	.311	.394	.705
	6 ML YEARS		140	384	77	24	0	7	(1	6)	122	30	42	25	30	1	102	3	0	3	0	0	15	.201	.262	.318	.580

Derek Law

Pitches: R Bats: R Pos: RP-41

Ht: 6'2" Wt: 210 Born: 9/14/1990 Age: 27

Year	Team	Lg	G	GS	CG	GF	IP	BFP	H	R	ER	HR	SH	SF	HB	TBB	IBB	SO	WP	Bk	W	L	Pct	Sh	Sv-Op	Hld	ERC	ERA
2013	3 Tms	Low	46	0	0	27	66.1	263	51	21	17	2	1	1	2	12	3	102	11	0	5	3	.625	0	14- -	-	1.72	2.31
2014	Rchmd	AA	27	0	0	24	28.0	113	19	8	8	1	0	2	1	14	0	29	1	0	2	0	1.000	0	13- -	-	2.54	2.57
2015	Rchmd	AA	28	0	0	21	25.2	116	31	16	13	1	1	1	0	8	0	33	6	0	0	1	.000	0	13- -	-	4.34	4.56
2017	Scrmto	AAA	25	0	0	20	32.2	137	32	9	9	1	2	1	0	12	1	26	3	0	1	1	.500	0	10- -	-	3.36	2.48
2016	SF	NL	61	0	0	12	55.0	214	44	13	13	3	0	0	0	9	0	50	1	0	4	2	.667	0	1-2	14	1.93	2.13
2017	SF	NL	41	0	0	12	37.1	168	45	21	21	5	2	2	2	14	2	35	5	0	4	1	.800	0	4-6	5	5.60	5.06
	Postseason		3	0	0	0	2.1	11	1	1	1	0	0	0	0	1	0	3	0	0	0	0	-	0	0-0	0	0.88	3.86
	2 ML YEARS		102	0	0	24	92.1	382	89	34	34	8	2	2	2	23	2	85	6	0	8	3	.727	0	5-8	19	3.27	3.31

Casey Lawrence

Pitches: R Bats: R Pos: RP-25; SP-2

Ht: 6'2" Wt: 170 Born: 10/28/1987 Age: 30

Year	Team	Lg	G	GS	CG	GF	IP	BFP	H	R	ER	HR	SH	SF	HB	TBB	IBB	SO	WP	Bk	W	L	Pct	Sh	Sv-Op	Hld	ERC	ERA
2013	Dnedin	A+	16	15	0	0	89.1	376	107	48	44	7	4	3	0	15	0	54	1	1	4	6	.400	0	0- -	-	4.18	4.43
2014	Nham	AA	26	22	1	0	151.1	626	161	72	62	9	4	7	2	29	0	93	1	1	9	9	.500	1	0- -	-	3.44	3.69
2015	Nham	AA	26	26	1	0	161.1	707	208	92	83	9	4	8	2	32	1	91	4	0	12	13	.480	0	0- -	-	4.65	4.52
2016	Buffalo	AAA	15	15	0	0	87.0	370	87	47	37	5	3	5	3	24	0	58	2	0	5	6	.455	0	0- -	-	3.41	3.83
2016	Nham	AA	13	13	0	0	75.0	318	92	42	38	8	4	4	1	13	0	50	0	1	3	6	.333	0	0- -	-	4.65	4.56
2017	Tacom	AAA	11	7	1	0	57.1	227	50	26	26	7	2	2	1	10	0	41	0	0	2	4	.333	1	0- -	-	2.78	4.08
2017	2 Tms	AL	27	2	0	12	55.1	264	77	41	39	11	1	2	1	25	4	52	1	0	2	3	.400	0	0-1	0	7.38	6.34
17	Tor	AL	4	2	0	2	13.1	72	21	14	13	2	1	1	0	11	3	7	1	0	0	3	.000	0	0-0	0	9.29	8.78
17	Sea	AL	23	0	0	10	42.0	192	56	27	26	9	0	1	1	14	1	45	1	0	2	0	1.000	0	0-1	0	6.76	5.57

Tommy Layne

Pitches: L Bats: L Pos: RP-19

Ht: 6'2" Wt: 195 Born: 11/2/1984 Age: 33

Year	Team	Lg	G	GS	CG	GF	IP	BFP	H	R	ER	HR	SH	SF	HB	TBB	IBB	SO	WP	Bk	W	L	Pct	Sh	Sv-Op	Hld	ERC	ERA
2017	S-WB*	AAA	6	0	0	3	6.2	26	4	2	2	1	0	0	0	2	0	4	0	0	0	0	-	0	1- -	-	1.94	2.70
2012	SD	NL	26	0	0	5	16.2	68	9	6	6	0	1	0	3	3	0	25	0	0	2	0	1.000	0	2-3	7	1.20	3.24
2013	SD	NL	14	0	0	2	8.2	39	10	4	2	1	1	0	2	5	0	6	1	0	0	2	.000	0	0-0	0	7.38	2.08
2014	Bos	AL	30	0	0	3	19.0	76	14	4	2	0	0	1	1	8	1	14	2	0	2	1	.667	0	0-1	9	2.32	0.95
2015	Bos	AL	64	0	0	9	47.2	207	41	22	21	3	2	1	2	27	2	45	1	0	2	1	.667	0	1-2	9	3.80	3.97
2016	2 Tms	AL	63	0	0	16	44.2	187	37	18	18	3	2	0	3	21	3	38	2	0	2	1	.667	0	1-3	12	3.41	3.63
2017	NYY	AL	19	0	0	4	13.0	63	16	12	11	1	0	0	1	8	0	9	0	0	0	0	-	0	0-0	2	6.41	7.62
16	Bos	AL	34	0	0	12	28.2	120	27	12	12	1	1	0	1	14	2	25	1	0	0	1	.000	0	0-1	2	3.82	3.77
16	NYY	AL	29	0	0	4	16.0	67	10	6	6	2	1	0	2	7	1	13	1	0	2	0	1.000	0	1-2	10	2.72	3.38
	6 ML YEARS		216	0	0	39	149.2	640	127	66	60	8	6	2	12	72	6	137	6	0	8	5	.615	0	4-9	39	3.51	3.61

Mike Leake

Pitches: R Bats: R Pos: SP-31

LEEK

Ht: 5'10" Wt: 170 Born: 11/12/1987 Age: 30

Year	Team	Lg	G	GS	CG	GF	IP	BFP	H	R	ER	HR	SH	SF	HB	TBB	IBB	SO	WP	Bk	W	L	Pct	Sh	Sv-Op	Hld	ERC	ERA
2010	Cin	NL	24	22	0	0	138.1	604	158	77	65	19	7	3	3	49	2	91	2	0	8	4	.667	0	0-0	0	5.12	4.23
2011	Cin	NL	29	26	0	2	167.2	693	159	74	72	23	3	6	8	38	3	118	2	1	12	9	.571	0	0-0	0	3.53	3.86
2012	Cin	NL	30	30	2	0	179.0	757	201	97	91	26	6	7	3	41	3	116	3	0	8	9	.471	0	0-0	0	4.50	4.58
2013	Cin	NL	31	31	0	0	192.1	801	193	78	72	21	8	5	6	48	4	122	2	0	14	7	.667	0	0-0	0	3.69	3.37
2014	Cin	NL	33	33	0	0	214.1	902	217	93	88	23	7	7	13	50	3	164	4	0	11	13	.458	0	0-0	0	3.77	3.70
2015	2 Tms	NL	30	30	2	0	192.0	778	174	80	79	22	6	3	3	49	5	119	6	2	11	10	.524	1	0-0	0	3.18	3.70
2016	StL	NL	30	30	0	0	176.2	757	203	101	92	20	5	**10**	7	30	1	125	7	0	9	12	.429	0	0-0	0	4.22	4.69
2017	2 Tms		31	31	0	0	186.0	782	201	93	81	20	6	6	9	37	3	130	3	0	10	13	.435	0	0-0	0	3.99	3.92
15	Cin	NL	21	21	1	0	136.2	556	123	55	54	14	6	2	2	34	4	90	3	1	9	5	.643	0	0-0	0	3.01	3.56
15	SF	NL	9	9	1	0	55.1	222	51	25	25	8	0	1	1	15	1	29	3	1	2	5	.286	1	0-0	0	3.61	4.07
17	StL	NL	26	26	0	0	154.0	654	169	83	72	19	6	6	7	35	3	103	2	0	7	12	.368	0	0-0	0	4.29	4.21
17	Sea	AL	5	5	0	0	32.0	128	32	10	9	1	0	0	2	2	0	27	1	0	3	1	.750	0	0-0	0	2.53	2.53
	Postseason		1	1	0	0	4.1	20	6	5	5	2	1	0	0	2	0	1	0	0	0	1	.000	0	0-0	0	10.00	10.38
	8 ML YEARS		238	233	4	2	1446.1	6074	1506	693	640	174	48	47	52	342	24	985	29	3	83	77	.519	1	0-0	0	3.94	3.98

Jack Leathersich

Pitches: L Bats: R Pos: RP-7   Ht: 6'0" Wt: 205 Born: 7/14/1990 Age: 27

			HOW MUCH HE PITCHED						WHAT HE GAVE UP												THE RESULTS						
Year	Team	Lg	G	GS	CG	GF	IP	BFP	H	R	ER	HR	SH	SF	HB	TBB	IBB	SO	WP	Bk	W	L	Pct	Sh	Sv-Op	Hld	ERC	ERA
2013	Bnghtn	AA	24	0	0	12	29.1	124	19	5	5	1	1	1	1	16	1	55	0	1	2	0	1.000	0	3--	-	2.35	1.53
2013	LsVgs	AAA	28	0	0	4	29.0	148	32	33	25	2	0	1	3	29	0	47	4	0	2	0	1.000	0	0--	-	7.30	7.76
2014	Bnghtn	AA	37	0	0	12	46.0	199	38	17	15	1	0	2	4	21	0	79	2	0	3	3	.500	0	1--	-	3.09	2.93
2014	LsVgs	AAA	11	0	0	3	8.1	42	8	6	5	2	0	1	1	7	0	14	0	0	0	0	-	0	0--	-	6.97	5.40
2015	LsVgs	AAA	13	0	0	7	13.1	57	10	8	8	3	0	0	1	7	0	22	1	0	0	0	-	0	0--	-	4.34	5.40
2016	Cubs	R	10	1	0	0	8.0	30	4	1	1	0	0	0	0	3	0	16	1	0	1	0	1.000	0	0--	-	1.21	1.13
2016	Tenn	AA	11	0	0	4	10.1	45	11	4	4	0	1	0	1	4	0	12	0	0	0	0	-	0	0--	-	4.11	3.48
2016	Iowa	AAA	5	0	0	0	5.0	21	0	1	0	0	0	0	0	6	0	6	0	0	0	0	-	0	0--	-	1.30	0.00
2017	Iowa	AAA	41	0	0	12	44.1	189	25	19	14	3	4	2	5	28	2	72	2	0	2	4	.333	0	1--	-	2.72	2.84
2015	NYM	NL	17	0	0	6	11.2	52	12	3	3	0	0	0	1	7	0	14	0	0	0	1	.000	0	0-0	2	4.75	2.31
2017	2 Tms	NL	7	0	0	2	5.0	25	4	2	2	0	0	2	0	6	0	6	1	0	0	0	-	0	0-0	1	5.08	3.60
17	ChC	NL	1	0	0	0	0.2	7	1	2	2	0	0	1	0	4	0	1	0	0	0	0	-	0	0-0	0	31.81	27.00
17	Pit	NL	6	0	0	2	4.1	18	3	0	0	0	0	1	0	2	0	6	0	0	0	0	-	0	0-0	0	2.02	0.00
	2 ML YEARS		24	0	0	8	16.2	77	16	5	5	0	0	2	1	13	0	21	0	0	0	1	.000	0	0-0	3	4.85	2.70

Wade LeBlanc

lah-BLAHNK

Pitches: L Bats: L Pos: RP-50   Ht: 6'3" Wt: 205 Born: 8/7/1984 Age: 33

			HOW MUCH HE PITCHED						WHAT HE GAVE UP												THE RESULTS						
Year	Team	Lg	G	GS	CG	GF	IP	BFP	H	R	ER	HR	SH	SF	HB	TBB	IBB	SO	WP	Bk	W	L	Pct	Sh	Sv-Op	Hld	ERC	ERA
2008	SD	NL	5	4	0	0	21.1	104	29	19	19	7	1	0	0	15	2	14	0	0	1	3	.250	0	0-0	0	9.57	8.02
2009	SD	NL	9	9	0	0	46.1	194	35	19	19	6	3	1	4	19	1	30	0	0	3	1	.750	0	0-0	0	3.28	3.69
2010	SD	NL	26	25	0	0	146.0	625	157	69	69	24	7	2	2	51	5	110	2	0	8	12	.400	0	0-0	0	4.84	4.25
2011	SD	NL	14	14	0	0	79.2	339	84	42	41	7	3	3	1	28	1	51	1	1	5	6	.455	0	0-0	0	4.21	4.63
2012	Mia	NL	25	9	0	1	68.2	284	71	30	28	7	5	1	1	19	1	43	1	0	2	5	.286	0	0-0	0	3.94	3.67
2013	2 Tms		17	7	0	1	55.0	259	72	40	33	7	2	1	3	20	3	33	0	0	1	5	.167	0	0-0	0	5.97	5.40
2014	2 Tms	AL	11	3	0	3	29.2	121	27	13	13	2	0	2	2	7	2	21	1	0	1	1	.500	0	0-0	0	2.96	3.94
2016	2 Tms		19	8	0	7	62.0	252	59	30	26	14	0	2	0	11	0	51	0	0	4	0	1.000	0	2-2	1	3.72	3.77
2017	Pit	NL	50	0	0	18	68.0	283	64	35	34	10	1	1	1	17	1	54	2	0	5	2	.714	0	1-3	4	3.48	4.50
13	Mia	NL	13	7	0	0	48.2	222	63	30	28	6	2	1	2	15	2	31	0	0	1	5	.167	0	0-0	0	5.67	5.18
13	Hou	NL	4	0	0	1	6.1	37	9	10	5	1	0	0	1	5	1	2	0	0	0	0	-	0	0-0	0	8.25	7.11
14	LAA	AL	10	3	0	2	28.2	114	25	11	11	2	0	1	1	6	1	21	1	0	1	1	.500	0	0-0	0	2.63	3.45
14	NYY	AL	1	0	0	1	1.0	7	2	2	2	0	0	1	1	1	1	0	0	0	0	0	-	0	0-0	0	13.81	18.00
16	Sea	AL	11	8	0	3	50.0	208	52	27	25	14	0	0	0	9	0	41	0	0	3	0	1.000	0	1-1	0	4.58	4.50
16	Pit	NL	8	0	0	4	12.0	44	7	3	1	0	0	2	0	2	0	10	0	0	1	0	1.000	0	1-1	1	1.03	0.75
	9 ML YEARS		176	79	0	30	576.2	2461	598	297	282	84	22	13	14	187	16	407	7	1	30	35	.462	0	3-5	6	4.39	4.40

Jose Leclerc

leh-KLURK

Pitches: R Bats: R Pos: RP-47   Ht: 6'0" Wt: 190 Born: 12/19/1993 Age: 24

			HOW MUCH HE PITCHED						WHAT HE GAVE UP												THE RESULTS						
Year	Team	Lg	G	GS	CG	GF	IP	BFP	H	R	ER	HR	SH	SF	HB	TBB	IBB	SO	WP	Bk	W	L	Pct	Sh	Sv-Op	Hld	ERC	ERA
2013	Hkry	A	39	0	0	20	59.0	254	53	26	22	2	4	2	6	21	0	77	3	0	3	4	.429	0	5--	-	3.25	3.36
2014	MrtlBh	A+	42	0	0	37	57.1	243	39	23	21	8	1	1	2	37	1	79	5	1	4	1	.800	0	14--	-	3.69	3.30
2015	Frisco	AA	26	22	0	0	103.0	472	97	66	66	8	1	2	6	73	0	98	13	2	6	8	.429	0	0--	-	5.05	5.77
2016	Frisco	AA	10	2	0	2	23.0	95	17	11	9	1	1	2	1	10	0	28	2	0	0	5	.000	0	1--	-	2.62	3.52
2016	RdRck	AAA	29	0	0	4	43.0	176	23	13	13	3	2	2	0	28	0	50	3	1	2	2	.500	0	1--	-	2.39	2.72
2016	Tex	AL	12	0	0	5	15.0	66	11	4	3	0	0	1	0	13	2	15	1	0	0	0	-	0	0-0	0	3.46	1.80
2017	Tex	AL	47	0	0	15	45.2	200	23	21	20	4	0	0	3	40	1	60	5	0	2	3	.400	0	2-3	10	3.28	3.94
	2 ML YEARS		59	0	0	20	60.2	266	34	25	23	4	0	1	3	53	3	75	6	0	2	3	.400	0	2-3	10	3.33	3.41

Zach Lee

Pitches: R Bats: R Pos: RP-2; SP-1   Ht: 6'4" Wt: 227 Born: 9/13/1991 Age: 26

			HOW MUCH HE PITCHED						WHAT HE GAVE UP												THE RESULTS						
Year	Team	Lg	G	GS	CG	GF	IP	BFP	H	R	ER	HR	SH	SF	HB	TBB	IBB	SO	WP	Bk	W	L	Pct	Sh	Sv-Op	Hld	ERC	ERA
2013	Chatt	AA	28	25	1	0	142.2	583	132	57	51	13	6	3	4	35	1	131	5	0	10	10	.500	1	0--	-	3.15	3.22
2014	Albq	AAA	28	27	0	0	150.2	667	177	105	90	18	7	5	6	54	0	97	5	0	7	13	.350	0	0--	-	5.28	5.38
2015	OkCity	AAA	19	19	1	0	113.1	451	107	40	34	5	7	4	4	19	0	81	2	0	11	6	.647	0	0--	-	2.75	2.70
2016	OkCity	AAA	13	13	0	0	73.2	321	95	47	40	11	3	1	0	15	0	57	3	1	7	5	.583	0	0--	-	5.36	4.89
2016	Tacom	AAA	14	14	0	0	74.1	343	98	64	61	11	4	1	4	24	0	50	6	0	0	9	.000	0	0--	-	6.20	7.39
2017	ElPaso	AAA	16	14	0	0	67.0	323	89	55	53	11	4	5	2	34	0	43	0	0	2	5	.286	0	0--	-	7.05	7.12
2015	LAD	NL	1	1	0	0	4.2	24	11	7	7	1	0	0	0	1	0	3	0	0	0	1	.000	0	0-0	0	14.18	13.50
2017	SD	NL	3	1	0	0	8.0	41	8	5	5	1	0	1	0	8	0	6	0	0	1	0	1.000	0	0-0	0	6.40	5.63
	2 ML YEARS		4	2	0	0	12.2	65	19	12	12	2	0	1	0	9	0	9	0	0	1	1	.500	0	0-0	0	8.97	8.53

Mark Leiter

Pitches: R Bats: R Pos: RP-16; SP-11   Ht: 6'0" Wt: 195 Born: 3/13/1991 Age: 27

			HOW MUCH HE PITCHED						WHAT HE GAVE UP												THE RESULTS						
Year	Team	Lg	G	GS	CG	GF	IP	BFP	H	R	ER	HR	SH	SF	HB	TBB	IBB	SO	WP	Bk	W	L	Pct	Sh	Sv-Op	Hld	ERC	ERA
2013	3 Tms	Low	16	4	0	3	45.0	180	34	7	6	1	1	3	1	13	0	50	3	0	4	0	1.000	0	0--	-	2.01	1.20
2014	2 Tms	Low	27	27	1	0	148.2	641	160	82	72	10	6	5	9	37	0	141	7	0	9	12	.429	1	0--	-	3.89	4.36
2015	Clrwtr	A+	19	13	1	2	95.2	386	79	28	24	4	2	2	6	23	0	83	5	0	6	1	.857	0	1--	-	2.45	2.26
2015	Rdng	AA	8	8	1	0	47.0	204	56	26	25	3	2	3	3	11	1	38	0	0	2	6	.250	0	0--	-	4.51	4.79
2016	Rdng	AA	23	17	0	4	103.2	424	91	45	39	9	4	5	6	30	0	94	7	0	6	3	.667	0	1--	-	3.18	3.39
2017	LV	AAA	7	5	0	0	30.0	124	27	15	14	5	0	1	1	6	0	38	2	0	2	1	.667	0	0--	-	3.25	4.20
2017	Phi	NL	27	11	0	5	90.2	395	90	59	50	18	1	2	7	31	2	84	3	0	3	6	.333	0	0-0	0	4.74	4.96

DJ LeMahieu

Bats: R Throws: R Pos: 2B-153;PH-3   la-MAY-hugh   Ht: 6'4" Wt: 215 Born: 7/13/1988 Age: 29

									BATTING											RUNNING			AVERAGES			
Year	Team	Lg	G	AB	H	2B	3B	HR	(Hm	Rd)	TB	R	RBI	RC	TBB	IBB	SO	HBP	SH	SF	SB	CS	GDP	Avg	OBP	Slg	OPS
2011	ChC	NL	37	60	15	2	0	0	(0	0)	17	3	4	3	1	0	12	0	1	0	0	0	2	.250	.262	.283	.546
2012	Col	NL	81	229	68	12	4	2	(1	1)	94	26	22	28	13	4	42	0	3	2	1	2	8	.297	.332	.410	.742
2013	Col	NL	109	404	113	21	3	2	(1	1)	146	39	28	42	19	2	67	1	7	3	18	7	13	.280	.311	.361	.673
2014	Col	NL	149	494	132	15	5	5	(2	3)	172	59	42	47	33	7	97	2	7	2	10	10	13	.267	.315	.348	.663
2015	Col	NL	150	564	170	21	5	6	(3	3)	219	85	61	75	50	4	107	1	3	2	23	3	20	.301	.358	.388	.746
2016	Col	NL	146	552	192	32	8	11	(7	4)	273	104	66	104	66	2	80	3	8	6	11	7	19	**.348**	.416	.495	.911
2017	Col	NL	155	609	189	28	4	8	(3	5)	249	95	64	87	59	1	90	6	3	5	6	5	24	.310	.374	.409	.783
	7 ML YEARS		827	2912	879	131	29	34	(17	17)	1170	411	287	386	241	20	495	13	32	20	69	34	99	.302	.356	.402	.757

Arcenio Leon

Pitches: R Bats: R Pos: RP-6   ar-SEN-eo   Ht: 6'3" Wt: 222 Born: 9/22/1986 Age: 31

			HOW MUCH HE PITCHED					WHAT HE GAVE UP												THE RESULTS							
Year	Team	Lg	G	GS	CG	GF	IP	BFP	H	R	ER	HR	SH	SF	HB	TBB	IBB	SO	WP	Bk	W	L	Pct	Sh	Sv-Op	Hld	ERC	ERA
2013	Hntsvl	AA	35	10	0	8	71.1	324	60	49	45	8	3	3	4	58	0	41	12	1	2	7	.222	0	0- -	-	5.20	5.68
2014	Hntsvl	AA	24	0	0	7	33.0	130	23	9	8	0	2	0	1	8	0	29	8	0	2	0	1.000	0	3- -	-	1.55	2.18
2014	Nashv	AAA	28	0	0	8	39.1	181	44	27	23	3	2	1	1	19	0	32	11	0	1	3	.250	0	0- -	-	4.92	5.26
2015	Charltt	AAA	9	0	0	1	11.1	59	20	15	15	2	0	0	1	8	1	12	4	0	1	0	1.000	0	1- -	-	11.82	11.91
2017	Toledo	AAA	26	0	0	16	22.1	100	15	14	13	2	1	1	1	13	0	21	3	0	1	2	.333	0	10- -	-	2.89	5.24
2017	Det	AL	6	0	0	3	6.2	31	7	9	9	0	0	1	0	6	1	2	0	0	0	0	-	0	0-0	0	5.45	12.15

Sandy Leon

Bats: B Throws: R Pos: C-84;PH-2   lay-OHN   Ht: 5'10" Wt: 225 Born: 3/13/1989 Age: 29

									BATTING											RUNNING			AVERAGES			
Year	Team	Lg	G	AB	H	2B	3B	HR	(Hm	Rd)	TB	R	RBI	RC	TBB	IBB	SO	HBP	SH	SF	SB	CS	GDP	Avg	OBP	Slg	OPS
2012	Was	NL	12	30	8	2	0	0	(0	0)	10	2	2	2	4	0	11	2	0	0	0	0	1	.267	.389	.333	.722
2013	Was	NL	2	1	0	0	0	0	(0	0)	0	0	0	0	0	0	1	0	0	0	0	0	0	.000	.000	.000	.000
2014	Was	NL	20	64	10	1	0	1	(0	1)	14	7	3	2	6	0	20	0	0	0	0	0	1	.156	.229	.219	.447
2015	Bos	AL	41	114	21	2	0	0	(0	0)	23	8	3	1	7	1	28	1	6	0	0	1	4	.184	.238	.202	.439
2016	Bos	AL	78	252	78	17	2	7	(2	5)	120	36	35	44	23	1	66	2	4	2	0	0	4	.310	.369	.476	.845
2017	Bos	AL	85	271	61	14	0	7	(3	4)	96	32	39	32	25	1	74	1	1	3	0	0	5	.225	.290	.354	.644
	Postseason		3	10	1	0	0	1	(0	1)	4	1	1	0	1	0	5	0	0	0	0	0	0	.100	.182	.400	.582
	6 ML YEARS		238	732	178	36	2	15	(5	10)	263	85	82	81	65	3	200	6	11	5	0	1	15	.243	.308	.359	.667

Dominic Leone

Pitches: R Bats: R Pos: RP-65   LEE-own   Ht: 5'11" Wt: 210 Born: 10/26/1991 Age: 26

			HOW MUCH HE PITCHED					WHAT HE GAVE UP												THE RESULTS							
Year	Team	Lg	G	GS	CG	GF	IP	BFP	H	R	ER	HR	SH	SF	HB	TBB	IBB	SO	WP	Bk	W	L	Pct	Sh	Sv-Op	Hld	ERC	ERA
2014	Sea	AL	57	0	0	3	66.1	272	52	18	16	4	1	3	3	25	3	70	4	0	8	2	.800	0	0-2	7	2.71	2.17
2015	2 Tms		13	0	0	6	15.0	74	19	15	14	2	0	1	1	9	2	9	2	0	0	5	.000	0	0-1	1	6.63	8.40
2016	Ari	NL	25	0	0	8	27.0	131	45	21	19	7	0	3	1	12	1	23	4	0	1	1	.000	0	0-1	0	10.37	6.33
2017	Tor	AL	65	0	0	6	70.1	279	51	22	20	6	0	3	0	23	3	81	8	0	3	0	1.000	0	1-5	11	2.25	2.56
	15 Sea	AL	10	0	0	5	11.1	54	11	9	8	1	0	0	0	9	2	7	2	0	0	4	.000	0	0-0	1	4.93	6.35
	15 Ari	NL	3	0	0	1	3.2	20	8	6	6	1	0	1	1	0	0	2	0	0	0	1	.000	0	0-1	0	12.63	14.73
	4 ML YEARS		160	0	0	23	178.2	756	167	76	69	19	1	10	5	69	9	183	18	0	11	8	.579	0	1-9	19	3.77	3.48

Jon Lester

Pitches: L Bats: L Pos: SP-32   Ht: 6'4" Wt: 240 Born: 1/7/1984 Age: 34

			HOW MUCH HE PITCHED					WHAT HE GAVE UP												THE RESULTS							
Year	Team	Lg	G	GS	CG	GF	IP	BFP	H	R	ER	HR	SH	SF	HB	TBB	IBB	SO	WP	Bk	W	L	Pct	Sh	Sv-Op	Hld	ERC	ERA
2006	Bos	AL	15	15	0	0	81.1	367	91	43	43	7	2	8	5	43	1	60	5	0	7	2	.778	0	0-0	0	5.52	4.76
2007	Bos	AL	12	11	0	0	63.0	275	61	33	32	10	1	5	1	31	0	50	1	0	4	0	1.000	0	0-0	0	4.78	4.57
2008	Bos	AL	33	33	2	0	210.1	874	202	78	75	14	6	3	10	66	1	152	3	1	16	6	.727	2	0-0	0	3.55	3.21
2009	Bos	AL	32	32	2	0	203.1	843	186	80	77	20	2	6	3	64	0	225	6	0	15	8	.652	0	0-0	0	3.35	3.41
2010	Bos	AL	32	32	2	0	208.0	861	167	81	75	14	4	6	10	83	0	225	6	0	19	9	.679	0	0-0	0	3.00	3.25
2011	Bos	AL	31	31	0	0	191.2	799	166	77	74	20	2	2	11	75	0	182	4	0	15	9	.625	0	0-0	0	3.62	3.47
2012	Bos	AL	33	33	3	0	205.1	876	216	117	110	25	5	7	4	68	2	166	6	0	9	14	.391	0	0-0	0	4.36	4.82
2013	Bos	AL	33	33	1	0	213.1	903	209	94	89	19	1	1	7	67	0	177	5	0	15	8	.652	1	0-0	0	3.69	3.75
2014	2 Tms		32	32	1	0	219.2	885	194	76	60	16	6	5	5	48	3	220	3	0	16	11	.593	1	0-0	0	2.70	2.46
2015	ChC	NL	32	32	1	0	205.0	828	183	83	76	16	5	4	7	47	0	207	8	0	11	12	.478	0	0-0	0	2.88	3.34
2016	ChC	NL	32	32	2	0	202.2	795	154	57	55	21	4	4	6	52	0	197	4	0	19	5	**.792**	0	0-0	0	2.47	2.44
2017	ChC	NL	32	32	1	0	180.2	763	179	101	87	26	4	4	4	60	3	180	3	0	13	8	.619	0	0-0	0	4.16	4.33
	14 Bos	AL	21	21	0	0	143.0	580	128	52	40	9	5	2	4	32	0	149	2	0	10	7	.588	0	0-0	0	2.73	2.52
	14 Oak	AL	11	11	1	0	76.2	305	66	24	20	7	1	3	1	16	0	71	1	0	6	4	.600	1	0-0	0	2.65	2.35
	Postseason		22	19	0	2	133.2	532	107	42	39	14	6	1	3	31	0	117	3	0	9	7	.563	0	0-0	0	2.52	2.63
	12 ML YEARS		349	348	15	0	2184.1	9070	2008	920	853	208	42	55	73	704	7	2041	54	1	159	92	.633	4	0-0	0	3.47	3.51

Artie Lewicki

Pitches: R **Bats:** R **Pos:** RP-3; SP-1
luh-WIK-ee
Ht: 6'3" **Wt:** 195 **Born:** 4/8/1992 **Age:** 26

Year	Team	Lg	G	GS	CG	GF	IP	BFP	H	R	ER	HR	SH	SF	HB	TBB	IBB	SO	WP	Bk	W	L	Pct	Sh	Sv-Op	Hld	ERC	ERA
2014	2 Tms	Low	12	1	0	7	27.2	110	21	8	7	2	1	1	0	10	0	26	1	0	2	2	.500	0	2- -	-	2.55	2.28
2015	Wmich	A	15	15	0	0	79.1	344	87	37	31	4	3	3	2	25	0	77	6	2	3	4	.429	0	0- -	-	4.03	3.52
2016	Lkland	A+	5	3	0	0	21.2	92	21	10	8	0	0	1	1	6	0	20	1	0	2	1	.667	0	0- -	-	2.90	3.32
2016	Erie	AA	12	12	0	0	67.1	282	67	35	26	4	2	2	2	13	0	57	1	0	1	7	.125	0	0- -	-	3.05	3.48
2017	Erie	AA	20	20	0	0	110.0	460	107	53	46	5	3	2	3	24	0	90	1	0	9	4	.692	0	0- -	-	2.94	3.76
2017	Toledo	AAA	5	5	0	0	31.0	122	28	7	7	2	1	0	1	7	0	33	0	0	5	0	1.000	0	0- -	-	2.92	2.03
2017	Det	AL	4	1	0	1	10.1	52	19	8	7	1	0	0	0	4	0	6	0	0	0	1	.000	0	0-0	0	9.42	6.10

Adam Liberatore

Pitches: L **Bats:** L **Pos:** RP-4
LEE-ber-ah-toor
Ht: 6'3" **Wt:** 243 **Born:** 5/12/1987 **Age:** 31

Year	Team	Lg	G	GS	CG	GF	IP	BFP	H	R	ER	HR	SH	SF	HB	TBB	IBB	SO	WP	Bk	W	L	Pct	Sh	Sv-Op	Hld	ERC	ERA
2017	OkCity*	AAA	10	0	0	2	11.2	45	9	3	3	0	1	0	1	1	0	10	1	0	0	1	.000	0	0- -	-	1.58	2.31
2015	LAD	NL	39	0	0	5	29.2	122	26	14	14	3	0	1	0	9	4	29	1	0	2	2	.500	0	0-1	10	2.85	4.25
2016	LAD	NL	58	0	0	9	42.2	176	34	16	16	2	0	2	2	17	4	47	1	0	2	2	.500	0	0-2	13	2.70	3.38
2017	LAD	NL	4	0	0	1	3.1	15	3	1	1	0	0	0	0	2	0	5	0	0	0	0	-	0	0-0	1	3.46	2.70
	3 ML YEARS		101	0	0	15	75.2	313	63	31	31	5	0	3	2	28	8	81	2	0	4	4	.500	0	0-3	24	2.79	3.69

Tzu-Wei Lin

Bats: L **Throws:** R **Pos:** 2B-10;3B-9;SS-6;PH-4;DH-1;PR-1
Ht: 5'9" **Wt:** 155 **Born:** 2/15/1994 **Age:** 24

Year	Team	Lg	G	AB	H	2B	3B	HR	(Hm	Rd)	TB	R	RBI	RC	TBB	IBB	SO	HBP	SH	SF	SB	CS	GDP	Avg	OBP	Slg	OPS
2013	Lowell	A-	60	230	52	9	2	1	(-	-)	68	34	20	24	28	0	59	1	1	1	12	4	2	.226	.312	.296	.607
2014	Grnvlle	A	102	402	92	22	1	1	(-	-)	119	55	42	42	54	0	74	0	4	7	10	7	9	.229	.315	.296	.611
2015	Salem	A+	73	281	79	12	3	2	(-	-)	103	37	34	37	22	0	32	0	2	2	15	3	6	.281	.331	.367	.698
2015	Portlnd	AA	46	173	35	5	3	0	(-	-)	46	21	14	13	16	0	27	0	4	1	8	3	4	.202	.268	.266	.534
2016	Portlnd	AA	108	372	83	10	5	2	(-	-)	109	39	27	32	34	0	55	0	4	1	10	7	7	.223	.287	.293	.580
2017	Portlnd	AA	48	159	48	9	3	5	(-	-)	78	31	19	31	20	0	27	1	2	2	8	2	0	.302	.379	.491	.870
2017	Pwtckt	AAA	35	141	32	5	1	2	(-	-)	45	12	9	12	11	0	28	0	2	0	2	4	2	.227	.283	.319	.602
2017	Bos	AL	25	56	15	0	2	0	(0	0)	19	7	2	7	9	0	17	0	1	0	1	1	0	.268	.369	.339	.709

Adam Lind

Bats: L **Throws:** L **Pos:** PH-48;1B-39;LF-25;DH-7
Ht: 6'2" **Wt:** 195 **Born:** 7/17/1983 **Age:** 34

Year	Team	Lg	G	AB	H	2B	3B	HR	(Hm	Rd)	TB	R	RBI	RC	TBB	IBB	SO	HBP	SH	SF	SB	CS	GDP	Avg	OBP	Slg	OPS
2006	Tor	AL	18	60	22	8	0	2	(0	2)	36	8	8	13	5	0	12	0	0	0	0	0	0	.367	.415	.600	1.015
2007	Tor	AL	89	290	69	14	0	11	(10	1)	116	34	46	38	16	0	65	1	2	2	1	2	7	.238	.278	.400	.678
2008	Tor	AL	88	326	92	16	4	9	(2	7)	143	48	40	39	16	3	59	2	1	4	2	0	8	.282	.316	.439	.755
2009	Tor	AL	151	587	179	46	0	35	(14	21)	330	93	114	114	58	7	110	5	0	4	1	1	15	.305	.370	.562	.932
2010	Tor	AL	150	569	135	32	3	23	(16	7)	242	57	72	65	38	3	144	3	0	3	0	0	10	.237	.287	.425	.712
2011	Tor	AL	125	499	125	16	0	26	(12	14)	219	56	87	67	32	4	107	3	0	8	1	1	12	.251	.295	.439	.734
2012	Tor	AL	93	321	82	14	2	11	(6	5)	133	28	45	47	29	1	61	0	0	3	0	0	10	.255	.314	.414	.729
2013	Tor	AL	143	465	134	26	1	23	(14	9)	231	67	67	76	51	5	103	1	0	4	1	0	20	.288	.357	.497	.854
2014	Tor	AL	96	290	93	24	2	6	(5	1)	139	38	40	54	28	3	48	0	0	0	0	0	8	.321	.381	.479	.860
2015	Mil	NL	149	502	139	32	0	20	(10	10)	231	72	87	91	66	11	100	1	0	3	0	0	7	.277	.360	.460	.820
2016	Sea	AL	126	401	96	17	0	20	(15	5)	173	48	58	47	26	3	89	1	0	2	0	1	14	.239	.286	.431	.717
2017	Was	NL	116	267	81	14	0	14	(7	7)	137	39	59	48	28	5	47	0	0	6	1	0	6	.303	.362	.513	.875
	12 ML YEARS		1344	4577	1247	259	12	200	(105	95)	2130	588	723	699	393	45	945	17	3	39	7	5	117	.272	.330	.465	.795

Josh Lindblom

Pitches: R **Bats:** R **Pos:** RP-4
LIN-bloom
Ht: 6'4" **Wt:** 240 **Born:** 6/15/1987 **Age:** 31

Year	Team	Lg	G	GS	CG	GF	IP	BFP	H	R	ER	HR	SH	SF	HB	TBB	IBB	SO	WP	Bk	W	L	Pct	Sh	Sv-Op	Hld	ERC	ERA
2017	Indy*	AAA	17	4	0	3	37.2	158	37	17	17	5	2	1	3	8	0	33	1	0	0	2	.000	0	0- -	-	3.77	4.06
2011	LAD	NL	27	0	0	8	29.2	116	21	9	9	0	2	3	2	10	3	28	3	0	1	0	1.000	0	0-1	3	1.90	2.73
2012	2 Tms	NL	74	0	0	18	71.0	304	61	31	28	13	2	0	4	35	2	70	2	0	3	5	.375	0	1-4	22	4.47	3.55
2013	Tex	AL	8	5	0	2	31.1	137	35	19	19	4	0	0	1	11	2	21	2	0	1	3	.250	0	0-0	0	4.64	5.46
2014	Oak	AL	1	1	0	0	4.2	22	5	2	2	1	0	0	1	2	0	2	0	0	0	0	-	0	0-0	0	6.25	3.86
2017	Pit	NL	4	0	0	1	10.1	51	18	9	9	0	0	0	0	3	0	10	0	0	0	0	-	0	0-0	0	7.25	7.84
	12 LAD	NL	48	0	0	12	47.2	197	42	16	16	9	2	0	3	18	0	43	1	0	2	2	.500	0	0-2	15	4.31	3.02
	12 Phi	NL	26	0	0	6	23.1	107	19	15	12	4	0	0	1	17	2	27	1	0	1	3	.250	0	1-2	7	4.77	4.63
	5 ML YEARS		114	6	0	29	147.0	630	140	70	67	18	4	3	7	61	7	131	7	0	5	8	.385	0	1-5	25	4.18	4.10

Francisco Lindor

Bats: B **Throws:** R **Pos:** SS-158;DH-1
lin-DOHR
Ht: 5'11" **Wt:** 190 **Born:** 11/14/1993 **Age:** 24

Year	Team	Lg	G	AB	H	2B	3B	HR	(Hm	Rd)	TB	R	RBI	RC	TBB	IBB	SO	HBP	SH	SF	SB	CS	GDP	Avg	OBP	Slg	OPS
2015	Cle	AL	99	390	122	22	4	12	(8	4)	188	50	51	64	27	0	69	1	13	7	12	2	12	.313	.353	.482	.835
2016	Cle	AL	158	604	182	30	3	15	(6	9)	263	99	78	87	57	3	88	5	3	15	19	5	18	.301	.358	.435	.794
2017	Cle	AL	159	651	178	44	4	33	(16	17)	329	99	89	107	60	6	93	4	5	3	15	3	11	.273	.337	.505	.842
	Postseason		15	58	18	3	0	2	(2	0)	27	5	6	9	4	0	16	0	0	0	1	3	1	.310	.355	.466	.820
	3 ML YEARS		416	1645	482	96	11	60	(30	30)	780	248	218	258	144	9	250	10	21	25	46	10	41	.293	.349	.474	.823

Francisco Liriano

Pitches: L Bats: L Pos: RP-20; SP-18   Ht: 6'2" Wt: 225 Born: 10/26/1983 Age: 34

Year	Team	Lg	G	GS	CG	GF	IP	BFP	H	R	ER	HR	SH	SF	HB	TBB	IBB	SO	WP	Bk	W	L	Pct	Sh	Sv-Op	Hld	ERC	ERA
2005	Min	AL	6	4	0	2	23.2	93	19	15	15	4	0	0	0	7	0	33	0	0	1	2	.333	0	0-0	0	3.15	5.70
2006	Min	AL	28	16	0	2	121.0	473	89	31	29	9	4	2	1	32	0	144	9	1	12	3	.800	0	1-1	1	2.12	2.16
2008	Min	AL	14	14	0	0	76.0	329	74	40	33	7	2	3	1	32	1	67	3	0	6	4	.600	0	0-0	0	3.97	3.91
2009	Min	AL	29	24	0	0	136.2	609	147	93	88	21	5	6	6	65	0	122	5	1	5	13	.278	0	0-0	0	5.46	5.80
2010	Min	AL	31	31	0	0	191.2	806	184	77	77	9	6	2	10	58	0	201	10	1	14	10	.583	0	0-0	0	3.34	3.62
2011	Min	AL	26	24	1	0	134.1	591	125	81	76	14	0	6	7	75	1	112	9	0	9	10	.474	1	0-0	0	4.58	5.09
2012	2 Tms	AL	34	28	0	2	156.2	693	143	97	93	19	4	8	7	87	5	167	11	1	6	12	.333	0	0-0	1	4.47	5.34
2013	Pit	NL	26	26	2	0	161.0	666	134	54	54	9	3	1	0	63	0	163	7	2	16	8	.667	0	0-0	0	2.86	3.02
2014	Pit	NL	29	29	0	0	162.1	691	130	68	61	13	6	5	4	81	3	175	12	0	7	10	.412	0	0-0	0	3.28	3.38
2015	Pit	NL	31	31	0	0	186.2	773	155	75	70	15	2	1	5	70	1	205	10	1	12	7	.632	0	0-0	0	3.04	3.38
2016	2 Tms		31	29	0	0	163.0	731	157	98	85	26	7	6	9	85	1	168	9	0	8	13	.381	0	0-0	0	4.96	4.69
2017	2 Tms		38	18	0	3	97.0	439	105	66	61	11	2	3	4	53	2	85	5	1	6	7	.462	0	0-0	6	5.43	5.66
12	Min	AL	22	17	0	2	100.0	440	89	63	59	12	2	7	4	55	4	109	6	1	3	10	.231	0	0-0	1	4.27	5.31
12	CWS		12	11	0	0	56.2	253	54	34	34	7	2	1	3	32	1	58	5	0	3	2	.600	0	0-0	0	4.83	5.40
16	Pit	NL	21	21	0	0	113.2	523	115	76	69	19	7	5	7	69	1	116	8	0	6	11	.353	0	0-0	0	5.71	5.46
16	Tor	AL	10	8	0	0	49.1	208	42	22	16	7	0	1	2	16	0	52	1	0	2	2	.500	0	0-0	0	3.34	2.92
17	Tor	AL	18	18	0	0	82.2	375	91	57	54	11	2	3	2	43	1	74	4	1	6	5	.545	0	0-0	0	5.49	5.88
17	Hou	AL	20	0	0	3	14.1	64	14	9	7	0	0	0	2	10	1	11	1	0	0	2	.000	0	0-0	6	5.00	4.40
	Postseason		6	3	0	1	22.2	93	16	11	10	1	0	0	2	8	0	19	2	0	2	0	1.000	0	0-0	0	2.32	3.97
12 ML YEARS			323	274	3	11	1610.0	6894	1462	795	742	157	41	43	54	708	14	1642	90	8	102	99	.507	1	1-1	8	3.83	4.15

Rymer Liriano

Bats: R Throws: R Pos: LF-12;RF-7;DH-2;PR-1   RYE-mur   Ht: 6'0" Wt: 230 Born: 6/20/1991 Age: 27

Year	Team	Lg	G	AB	H	2B	3B	HR	(Hm	Rd)	TB	R	RBI	RC	TBB	IBB	SO	HBP	SH	SF	SB	CS	GDP	Avg	OBP	Slg	OPS
2014	SnAnt	AA	99	371	98	20	2	14	(-	-)	164	55	53	57	35	1	102	6	0	3	17	7	16	.264	.335	.442	.777
2014	ElPaso	AAA	16	62	28	11	1	0	(-	-)	41	14	13	19	8	0	14	1	0	0	3	1	2	.452	.521	.661	1.182
2015	ElPaso	AAA	131	472	138	31	3	14	(-	-)	217	85	64	87	64	1	132	8	1	4	18	8	12	.292	.383	.460	.843
2017	Charllt	AAA	123	449	115	15	3	17	(-	-)	187	67	52	62	42	0	133	4	2	3	7	4	14	.256	.323	.416	.740
2014	SD	NL	38	109	24	2	0	1	(1	0)	29	13	6	5	9	1	39	2	0	1	4	1	6	.220	.289	.266	.555
2017	CWS	AL	21	41	9	2	0	1	(1	0)	14	4	6	4	5	0	14	0	0	0	1	0	0	.220	.304	.341	.646
2 ML YEARS			59	150	33	4	0	2	(2	0)	43	17	12	9	14	1	53	2	0	1	5	1	6	.220	.293	.287	.580

Ben Lively

Pitches: R Bats: R Pos: SP-15   Ht: 6'4" Wt: 190 Born: 3/5/1992 Age: 26

Year	Team	Lg	G	GS	CG	GF	IP	BFP	H	R	ER	HR	SH	SF	HB	TBB	IBB	SO	WP	Bk	W	L	Pct	Sh	Sv-Op	Hld	ERC	ERA
2013	2 Tms	Low	13	13	0	0	41.0	162	23	9	4	0	1	4	1	13	0	56	1	0	0	4	.000	0	0- -	-	1.26	0.88
2014	Bkrsfld	A+	13	13	0	0	79.0	302	57	20	20	6	1	0	1	16	0	95	0	0	10	1	.909	0	0- -	-	1.89	2.28
2014	Pnscla	AA	13	13	0	0	72.0	306	60	32	31	7	2	5	4	36	0	76	2	1	3	6	.333	0	0- -	-	3.79	3.88
2015	Rdng	AA	25	25	1	0	143.2	612	160	69	66	14	7	1	7	45	0	111	2	0	8	7	.533	0	0- -	-	4.69	4.13
2016	Rdng	AA	9	9	0	0	53.0	206	35	11	11	1	1	1	0	15	0	49	0	0	7	0	1.000	0	0- -	-	1.54	1.87
2016	LV	AAA	19	19	1	0	117.2	460	83	45	40	10	4	2	3	27	0	90	0	1	11	5	.688	1	0- -	-	1.96	3.06
2017	LV	AAA	16	16	1	0	97.0	405	91	39	34	3	2	2	4	22	0	82	1	1	7	5	.583	0	0- -	-	2.75	3.15
2017	Phi	NL	15	15	1	0	88.2	372	90	45	42	13	2	3	8	24	1	52	1	1	4	7	.364	0	0-0	0	4.42	4.26

Kyle Lloyd

Pitches: R Bats: R Pos: SP-1   Ht: 6'4" Wt: 220 Born: 10/16/1990 Age: 27

Year	Team	Lg	G	GS	CG	GF	IP	BFP	H	R	ER	HR	SH	SF	HB	TBB	IBB	SO	WP	Bk	W	L	Pct	Sh	Sv-Op	Hld	ERC	ERA
2013	2 Tms	Low	21	0	0	1	50.0	205	44	20	14	5	0	0	0	17	0	55	2	0	4	1	.800	0	0- -	-	3.24	2.52
2014	FtWyn	A	27	21	0	2	119.2	506	114	60	48	8	5	3	2	34	0	155	9	1	6	5	.545	0	0- -	-	3.16	3.61
2015	Lk Els	A+	31	20	0	1	137.1	584	139	85	72	10	4	4	4	41	0	139	8	1	7	11	.389	0	0- -	-	3.67	4.72
2016	SnAnt	AA	30	20	0	3	130.1	539	124	54	48	9	2	4	2	38	1	99	6	0	7	7	.500	0	0- -	-	3.27	3.31
2017	SnAnt	AA	15	15	1	0	89.2	366	78	40	37	2	0	1	1	24	0	89	4	0	7	5	.583	1	0- -	-	2.43	3.71
2017	ElPaso	AAA	12	12	1	0	57.2	266	79	49	45	8	1	2	0	27	0	56	0	0	1	4	.200	0	0- -	-	7.08	7.02
2017	SD	NL	1	1	0	0	4.0	20	6	4	4	1	0	0	0	2	0	2	0	0	0	0	-	0	0-0	0	8.68	9.00

Jose Lobaton

Bats: B Throws: R Pos: C-50;PH-3   LOE-bah-tone   Ht: 6'1" Wt: 205 Born: 10/21/1984 Age: 33

Year	Team	Lg	G	AB	H	2B	3B	HR	(Hm	Rd)	TB	R	RBI	RC	TBB	IBB	SO	HBP	SH	SF	SB	CS	GDP	Avg	OBP	Slg	OPS
2009	SD	NL	7	17	3	0	0	0	(0	0)	3	0	0	0	0	0	5	0	0	0	0	0	1	.176	.176	.176	.353
2011	TB	AL	15	34	4	1	0	0	(0	0)	5	2	0	0	4	0	8	1	0	0	0	0	2	.118	.231	.147	.378
2012	TB	AL	69	167	37	10	0	2	(1	1)	53	16	20	19	24	1	46	2	2	2	0	1	6	.222	.323	.317	.640
2013	TB	AL	100	277	69	15	2	7	(5	2)	109	38	32	32	30	0	65	0	2	2	0	1	5	.249	.320	.394	.714
2014	Was	NL	66	214	50	9	0	2	(2	0)	65	18	12	13	15	1	61	1	0	0	0	0	5	.234	.287	.304	.591
2015	Was	NL	44	136	27	4	0	3	(1	2)	40	11	20	14	15	1	40	1	1	2	0	0	5	.199	.279	.294	.573
2016	Was	NL	39	99	23	3	1	3	(2	1)	37	10	8	9	12	1	18	1	1	1	0	0	4	.232	.319	.374	.692
2017	Was	NL	51	141	24	3	0	4	(1	3)	39	11	11	8	14	1	35	1	1	1	0	0	5	.170	.248	.277	.525
	Postseason		8	16	4	0	0	2	(2	0)	10	2	4	2	0	0	4	0	0	0	0	0	1	.250	.250	.625	.875
8 ML YEARS			391	1085	237	45	3	21	(12	9)	351	106	103	95	114	5	278	7	7	8	0	2	33	.218	.295	.324	.618

221

Tim Locastro

Bats: R **Throws:** R **Pos:** LF-2;PR-2;PH-1   **Ht:** 6'1" **Wt:** 200 **Born:** 7/14/1992 **Age:** 25

Year	Team	Lg	G	AB	H	2B	3B	HR	(Hm	Rd)	TB	R	RBI	RC	TBB	IBB	SO	HBP	SH	SF	SB	CS	GDP	Avg	OBP	Slg	OPS
2013	Bluefld	R+	43	138	39	5	3	1	(-	-)	53	28	13	22	13	0	12	6	4	1	12	2	0	.283	.367	.384	.751
2014	Vancvr	A-	67	256	80	11	0	1	(-	-)	94	49	27	49	12	0	23	32	5	5	32	4	4	.313	.407	.367	.774
2015	2 Tms	Low	111	398	110	19	3	6	(-	-)	153	78	39	66	35	0	55	32	4	4	41	16	1	.276	.377	.384	.762
2016	Rcuca	A+	86	339	98	17	5	5	(-	-)	140	61	39	52	15	0	50	18	2	6	15	4	8	.289	.347	.413	.760
2016	Tulsa	AA	45	191	53	8	1	1	(-	-)	66	27	13	24	8	0	16	7	1	0	9	2	1	.277	.330	.346	.676
2017	Tulsa	AA	96	368	105	21	4	8	(-	-)	158	69	31	63	22	1	56	26	1	2	22	5	2	.285	.366	.429	.795
2017	OkCity	AAA	31	103	40	10	0	2	(-	-)	56	18	9	25	6	0	12	5	0	1	12	2	2	.388	.443	.544	.987
2017	LAD	NL	3	1	0	0	0	0	(0	0)	0	0	0	0	0	0	0	0	0	0	1	0	0	.000	.000	.000	.000

Jeff Locke

Pitches: L **Bats:** L **Pos:** SP-7   LOCK   **Ht:** 6'0" **Wt:** 200 **Born:** 11/20/1987 **Age:** 30

			HOW MUCH HE PITCHED					WHAT HE GAVE UP											THE RESULTS						
Year	Team	Lg	G	GS	CG	GF	IP	BFP	H	R	ER	HR	SH	SF	HB	TBB	IBB	SO	WP	Bk	W	L	Pct	Sh	Sv-Op	Hld	ERC	ERA
2011	Pit	NL	4	4	0	0	16.2	78	21	12	12	3	1	1	1	10	0	5	0	0	0	3	.000	0	0-0	0	7.62	6.48
2012	Pit	NL	8	6	0	1	34.1	148	36	21	21	6	1	0	1	11	0	34	0	0	1	3	.250	0	0-0	0	4.68	5.50
2013	Pit	NL	30	30	0	0	166.1	711	146	69	65	11	8	10	6	84	4	125	8	2	10	7	.588	0	0-0	0	3.72	3.52
2014	Pit	NL	21	21	0	0	131.1	548	127	63	57	16	6	3	4	40	2	89	1	0	7	6	.538	0	0-0	0	3.81	3.91
2015	Pit	NL	30	30	0	0	168.1	736	179	95	84	15	7	8	7	60	4	129	5	0	8	11	.421	0	0-0	0	4.30	4.49
2016	Pit	NL	30	19	1	4	127.1	564	151	81	77	17	8	2	3	44	4	73	7	0	9	8	.529	1	0-0	0	5.25	5.44
2017	Mia	NL	7	7	0	0	32.0	152	42	30	29	4	0	2	0	15	3	26	3	0	0	5	.000	0	0-0	0	6.13	8.16
	7 ML YEARS		130	117	1	5	676.1	2937	702	371	345	72	31	26	22	264	17	481	24	2	35	43	.449	1	0-0	0	4.41	4.59

Boone Logan

Pitches: L **Bats:** R **Pos:** RP-38   **Ht:** 6'5" **Wt:** 215 **Born:** 8/13/1984 **Age:** 33

			HOW MUCH HE PITCHED					WHAT HE GAVE UP											THE RESULTS						
Year	Team	Lg	G	GS	CG	GF	IP	BFP	H	R	ER	HR	SH	SF	HB	TBB	IBB	SO	WP	Bk	W	L	Pct	Sh	Sv-Op	Hld	ERC	ERA
2006	CWS	AL	21	0	0	4	17.1	93	21	18	16	2	1	3	0	15	2	15	1	0	0	0	-	0	1-2	2	7.56	8.31
2007	CWS	AL	68	0	0	13	50.2	226	59	30	28	7	2	6	0	20	3	35	2	0	2	1	.667	0	0-2	11	5.18	4.97
2008	CWS	AL	55	0	0	12	42.1	197	57	31	28	7	2	0	1	14	3	42	1	0	2	3	.400	0	0-1	3	6.24	5.95
2009	Atl	NL	20	0	0	7	17.1	82	21	12	10	1	0	0	1	9	3	10	0	0	1	1	.500	0	0-0	1	5.29	5.19
2010	NYY	AL	51	0	0	8	40.0	169	34	13	13	3	0	1	1	20	3	38	1	0	2	0	1.000	0	0-0	13	3.50	2.93
2011	NYY	AL	64	0	0	6	41.2	185	43	20	16	4	2	1	4	13	3	46	1	0	5	3	.625	0	0-2	10	4.04	3.46
2012	NYY	AL	80	0	0	8	55.1	239	48	23	23	6	1	3	2	28	6	68	3	0	7	2	.778	0	1-4	23	3.78	3.74
2013	NYY	AL	61	0	0	9	39.0	159	33	15	14	7	3	3	0	13	4	50	3	0	5	2	.714	0	0-2	11	3.38	3.23
2014	Col	NL	35	0	0	8	25.0	116	31	20	19	6	2	2	1	11	1	32	3	0	2	3	.400	0	0-4	7	6.84	6.84
2015	Col	NL	60	0	0	12	35.1	168	40	17	17	3	1	2	5	17	1	44	3	0	0	3	.000	0	0-4	23	5.43	4.33
2016	Col	NL	66	0	0	9	46.1	187	27	23	19	4	2	0	2	20	5	57	4	0	2	5	.286	0	1-4	27	1.96	3.69
2017	Cle	AL	38	0	0	4	21.0	91	20	13	11	2	1	0	1	9	0	28	0	0	1	0	1.000	0	0-1	4	4.08	4.71
	Postseason		13	0	0	1	7.2	30	7	2	2	1	0	0	0	1	0	9	0	1	0	0	-	0	0-0	2	2.83	2.35
	12 ML YEARS		619	0	0	100	431.1	1912	434	235	214	52	17	19	21	189	34	465	22	0	29	23	.558	0	3-26	135	4.43	4.47

Steve Lombardozzi

Bats: B **Throws:** R **Pos:** 2B-2   lahm-bar-DOZE-ee   **Ht:** 6'0" **Wt:** 195 **Born:** 9/20/1988 **Age:** 29

Year	Team	Lg	G	AB	H	2B	3B	HR	(Hm	Rd)	TB	R	RBI	RC	TBB	IBB	SO	HBP	SH	SF	SB	CS	GDP	Avg	OBP	Slg	OPS
2017	NewOr*	AAA	103	401	110	17	2	2	(-	-)	137	53	18	50	38	1	60	1	3	2	13	6	5	.274	.337	.342	.679
2011	Was	NL	13	31	6	1	0	0	(0	0)	7	3	1	2	1	0	4	0	0	0	0	0	0	.194	.219	.226	.445
2012	Was	NL	126	384	105	16	3	3	(2	1)	136	40	27	46	19	1	46	6	6	1	5	3	1	.273	.317	.354	.671
2013	Was	NL	118	290	75	15	1	0	(1	1)	98	25	22	24	8	1	34	1	5	3	4	3	6	.259	.278	.338	.616
2014	Bal	AL	20	73	21	1	1	0	(0	0)	24	6	2	6	0	0	14	1	0	0	1	0	1	.288	.297	.329	.626
2015	Pit	NL	12	10	0	0	0	0	(0	0)	0	1	0	1	1	0	4	0	0	0	0	0	0	.000	.091	.000	.091
2017	Mia	NL	2	8	0	0	0	0	(0	0)	0	0	0	0	0	0	2	0	0	0	0	0	0	.000	.000	.000	.000
	Postseason		3	3	1	0	0	0	(0	0)	1	0	0	0	0	0	0	0	0	0	0	0	0	.333	.333	.333	.667
	6 ML YEARS		291	796	207	33	5	5	(3	2)	265	75	52	78	29	2	104	8	11	4	10	6	8	.260	.292	.333	.624

Evan Longoria

Bats: R **Throws:** R **Pos:** 3B-142;DH-14   **Ht:** 6'2" **Wt:** 210 **Born:** 10/7/1985 **Age:** 32

Year	Team	Lg	G	AB	H	2B	3B	HR	(Hm	Rd)	TB	R	RBI	RC	TBB	IBB	SO	HBP	SH	SF	SB	CS	GDP	Avg	OBP	Slg	OPS
2008	TB	AL	122	448	122	31	2	27	(18	9)	238	67	85	72	46	4	122	6	0	8	7	0	8	.272	.343	.531	.874
2009	TB	AL	157	584	164	44	0	33	(16	17)	307	100	113	102	72	11	140	8	0	7	9	0	27	.281	.364	.526	.889
2010	TB	AL	151	574	169	46	5	22	(10	12)	291	96	104	99	72	12	124	5	0	10	15	5	15	.294	.372	.507	.879
2011	TB	AL	133	483	118	26	1	31	(14	17)	239	78	99	91	80	6	93	6	0	5	3	2	11	.244	.355	.495	.850
2012	TB	AL	74	273	79	14	0	17	(8	9)	144	39	55	55	33	6	61	3	0	3	2	3	14	.289	.369	.527	.896
2013	TB	AL	160	614	165	39	3	32	(15	17)	306	91	88	90	70	10	162	10	0	6	1	0	16	.269	.343	.498	.842
2014	TB	AL	162	624	158	26	1	22	(12	10)	252	83	91	83	57	11	133	9	1	9	5	0	15	.253	.320	.404	.724
2015	TB	AL	160	604	163	35	1	21	(10	11)	263	74	73	77	51	8	132	6	0	9	3	1	11	.270	.328	.435	.764
2016	TB	AL	160	633	173	41	4	36	(17	19)	330	81	98	95	42	6	144	3	0	7	0	3	13	.273	.318	.521	.840
2017	TB	AL	156	613	160	36	2	20	(10	10)	260	71	86	81	46	3	109	6	0	12	6	1	18	.261	.313	.424	.737
	Postseason		30	115	22	5	0	9	(4	5)	54	16	21	13	11	0	38	0	0	0	0	0	4	.191	.262	.470	.731
	10 ML YEARS		1435	5450	1471	338	19	261	(130	131)	2630	780	892	845	569	77	1220	55	1	76	51	15	148	.270	.341	.483	.823

Jorge Lopez

Pitches: R Bats: R Pos: RP-1   Ht: 6'3" Wt: 195 Born: 2/10/1993 Age: 25

Year	Team	Lg	G	GS	CG	GF	IP	BFP	H	R	ER	HR	SH	SF	HB	TBB	IBB	SO	WP	Bk	W	L	Pct	Sh	Sv-Op	Hld	ERC	ERA
2013	Wisc	A	25	22	0	3	117.0	513	120	78	68	13	1	1	9	48	0	92	13	0	7	8	.467	0	2- -	-	4.69	5.23
2014	BrvdCt	A+	25	25	1	0	137.1	583	144	80	70	12	2	3	4	46	0	119	8	0	10	10	.500	0	0- -	-	4.20	4.59
2015	Biloxi	AA	24	24	0	0	143.1	572	105	37	36	9	3	1	3	52	0	137	13	0	12	5	.706	0	0- -	-	2.43	2.26
2016	ColSpr	AAA	17	16	0	0	79.1	389	101	66	60	12	3	2	5	55	1	66	11	3	1	7	.125	0	0- -	-	7.66	6.81
2016	Biloxi	AA	8	8	0	0	45.1	193	45	21	20	5	2	1	1	16	0	47	9	0	2	4	.333	0	0- -	-	4.03	3.97
2017	Biloxi	AA	39	13	1	14	103.2	437	92	53	49	7	2	5	5	38	2	105	11	0	8	8	.500	1	7- -	-	3.27	4.25
2015	Mil	NL	2	2	0	0	10.0	46	14	6	6	0	0	0	1	5	0	10	1	0	1	1	.500	0	0-0	0	6.87	5.40
2017	Mil	NL	1	0	0	1	2.0	10	4	1	1	0	0	0	0	1	0	0	0	0	0	0	-	0	0-0	0	10.75	4.50
	2 ML YEARS		3	2	0	1	12.0	56	18	7	7	0	0	0	1	6	0	10	1	0	1	1	.500	0	0-0	0	7.48	5.25

Raffy Lopez

Bats: L Throws: R Pos: C-24;3B-1;PH-1   Ht: 5'9" Wt: 200 Born: 10/2/1987 Age: 30

Year	Team	Lg	G	AB	H	2B	3B	HR	(Hm	Rd)	TB	R	RBI	RC	TBB	IBB	SO	HBP	SH	SF	SB	CS	GDP	Avg	OBP	Slg	OPS
2017	Nham*	AA	14	42	11	1	1	4	(-	-)	26	7	11	9	8	0	15	0	0	0	0	0	1	.262	.380	.619	.999
2017	Buffalo*	AAA	59	198	58	13	1	12	(-	-)	109	31	34	40	21	2	46	3	0	1	0	0	4	.293	.368	.551	.918
2014	ChC	NL	7	11	2	0	0	0	(0	0)	2	0	1	1	2	0	4	0	0	1	0	0	0	.182	.286	.182	.468
2016	Cin	NL	8	7	0	0	0	0	(0	0)	0	0	0	0	0	0	3	0	0	0	0	0	0	.000	.000	.000	.000
2017	Tor	AL	24	54	12	1	0	4	(2	2)	25	9	12	9	7	0	21	0	0	1	0	0	1	.222	.306	.463	.769
	3 ML YEARS		39	72	14	1	0	4	(2	2)	27	9	13	10	9	0	28	0	0	2	0	0	1	.194	.277	.375	.652

Reynaldo Lopez

ray-NAHL-doh

Pitches: R Bats: R Pos: SP-8   Ht: 6'0" Wt: 185 Born: 1/4/1994 Age: 24

Year	Team	Lg	G	GS	CG	GF	IP	BFP	H	R	ER	HR	SH	SF	HB	TBB	IBB	SO	WP	Bk	W	L	Pct	Sh	Sv-Op	Hld	ERC	ERA
2014	2 Tms	Low	16	16	0	0	83.1	312	42	12	10	1	2	0	2	26	0	70	3	1	7	3	.700	0	0- -	-	1.18	1.08
2015	Ptomc	A+	19	19	1	0	99.0	404	93	47	45	5	4	0	3	28	0	94	9	0	6	7	.462	0	0- -	-	3.16	4.09
2016	Hrsbrg	AA	14	14	0	0	76.1	329	69	35	27	7	3	5	3	25	0	100	5	1	3	5	.375	0	0- -	-	3.26	3.18
2016	Syrcse	AAA	5	5	1	0	33.0	129	21	12	12	6	0	1	1	10	1	26	0	0	2	2	.500	1	0- -	-	2.40	3.27
2017	Charllt	AAA	22	22	0	0	121.0	515	101	56	51	16	0	3	3	49	0	131	3	1	6	7	.462	0	0- -	-	3.44	3.79
2016	Was	NL	11	6	0	1	44.0	201	47	27	24	4	3	2	0	22	2	42	5	0	5	3	.625	0	0-0	1	4.60	4.91
2017	CWS	AL	8	8	0	0	47.2	207	49	29	25	7	0	2	1	14	0	30	3	0	3	3	.500	0	0-0	0	4.12	4.72
	Postseason		1	0	0	0	2.0	9	2	1	1	0	0	0	0	1	0	3	0	0	0	0	-	0	0-0	0	3.63	4.50
	2 ML YEARS		19	14	0	1	91.2	408	96	56	49	11	3	4	1	36	2	72	8	0	8	6	.571	0	0-0	1	4.36	4.81

Michael Lorenzen

Pitches: R Bats: R Pos: RP-70   Ht: 6'3" Wt: 217 Born: 1/4/1992 Age: 26

Year	Team	Lg	G	GS	CG	GF	IP	BFP	H	R	ER	HR	SH	SF	HB	TBB	IBB	SO	WP	Bk	W	L	Pct	Sh	Sv-Op	Hld	ERC	ERA
2015	Cin	NL	27	21	0	1	113.1	515	131	70	68	18	2	1	6	57	6	83	4	0	4	9	.308	0	0-0	1	6.09	5.40
2016	Cin	NL	35	0	0	4	50.0	202	41	16	16	5	0	0	6	13	0	48	2	2	2	1	.667	0	0-2	10	3.11	2.88
2017	Cin	NL	70	0	0	14	83.0	361	78	43	41	9	2	1	4	34	5	80	12	1	8	4	.667	0	2-7	18	3.89	4.45
	3 ML YEARS		132	21	0	19	246.1	1078	250	129	125	32	4	2	16	104	11	211	18	3	14	14	.500	0	2-9	29	4.69	4.57

Aaron Loup

LOOP

Pitches: L Bats: L Pos: RP-70   Ht: 5'11" Wt: 210 Born: 12/19/1987 Age: 30

Year	Team	Lg	G	GS	CG	GF	IP	BFP	H	R	ER	HR	SH	SF	HB	TBB	IBB	SO	WP	Bk	W	L	Pct	Sh	Sv-Op	Hld	ERC	ERA
2012	Tor	AL	33	0	0	3	30.2	117	26	10	9	0	2	1	0	2	0	21	1	1	0	2	.000	0	0-1	6	1.59	2.64
2013	Tor	AL	64	0	0	12	69.1	282	66	23	19	5	2	4	7	13	4	53	2	0	4	6	.400	0	2-3	8	3.20	2.47
2014	Tor	AL	71	0	0	15	68.2	283	50	25	24	4	3	3	6	30	5	56	5	0	4	4	.500	0	4-8	13	2.75	3.15
2015	Tor	AL	60	0	0	6	42.1	186	47	24	21	6	2	0	6	7	0	46	0	0	2	5	.286	0	0-4	9	4.54	4.46
2016	Tor	AL	21	0	0	2	14.1	62	15	8	8	2	0	3	3	4	0	15	3	0	0	0	-	0	0-1	1	5.13	5.02
2017	Tor	AL	70	0	0	8	57.2	265	59	27	24	4	5	0	6	29	5	64	3	0	2	3	.400	0	0-0	6	4.56	3.75
	Postseason		4	0	0	0	2.0	7	1	1	1	0	0	0	0	2	0	0	0	0	0	0	-	0	0-0	0	3.75	4.50
	6 ML YEARS		319	0	0	46	283.0	1195	263	117	105	21	14	11	28	85	14	255	14	1	12	20	.375	0	6-17	43	3.45	3.34

Jed Lowrie

LAU-ree

Bats: B Throws: R Pos: 2B-136;DH-14;PH-6;3B-1   Ht: 6'0" Wt: 180 Born: 4/17/1984 Age: 34

Year	Team	Lg	G	AB	H	2B	3B	HR	(Hm	Rd)	TB	R	RBI	RC	TBB	IBB	SO	HBP	SH	SF	SB	CS	GDP	Avg	OBP	Slg	OPS
2008	Bos	AL	81	260	67	25	3	2	(0	2)	104	34	46	35	35	0	68	1	2	8	1	0	8	.258	.339	.400	.739
2009	Bos	AL	32	68	10	2	0	2	(1	1)	18	5	11	5	6	0	20	0	0	2	0	0	0	.147	.211	.265	.475
2010	Bos	AL	55	171	49	14	0	9	(3	6)	90	31	24	32	25	0	25	1	0	1	1	1	2	.287	.381	.526	.907
2011	Bos	AL	88	309	78	14	4	6	(3	3)	118	40	36	33	23	2	60	2	1	6	1	1	6	.252	.303	.382	.685
2012	Hou	NL	97	340	83	18	0	16	(9	7)	149	43	42	45	43	0	65	2	0	2	2	0	3	.244	.331	.438	.769
2013	Oak	AL	154	603	175	45	2	15	(7	8)	269	80	75	88	50	3	91	2	3	4	1	0	17	.290	.344	.446	.791
2014	Oak	AL	136	502	125	29	3	6	(4	2)	178	59	50	52	51	5	79	5	2	6	0	0	14	.249	.321	.355	.676
2015	Hou	AL	69	230	51	14	0	9	(5	4)	92	35	30	29	28	5	43	3	0	2	1	0	3	.222	.312	.400	.712

Year	Team	Lg	G	AB	H	2B	3B	HR	(Hm Rd)	TB	R	RBI	RC	TBB	IBB	SO	HBP	SH	SF	SB	CS	GDP	Avg	OBP	Slg	OPS
2016	Oak	AL	87	338	89	12	1	2	(1 1)	109	30	27	36	26	0	65	1	1	0	0	0	10	.263	.314	.322	.637
2017	Oak	AL	153	567	157	49	3	14	(8 6)	254	86	69	94	73	2	100	2	0	3	0	1	10	.277	.360	.448	.808
	Postseason		22	60	9	2	0	1	(0 1)	14	6	5	4	7	0	16	1	1	1	0	0	1	.150	.246	.233	.480
	10 ML YEARS		952	3388	884	222	16	81	(41 40)	1381	443	410	449	360	17	616	19	8	37	7	3	73	.261	.332	.408	.740

Josh Lucas

Pitches: R **Bats:** R **Pos:** RP-5   **Ht:** 6'6" **Wt:** 185 **Born:** 11/5/1990 **Age:** 27

			HOW MUCH HE PITCHED						WHAT HE GAVE UP										THE RESULTS							
Year	Team	Lg	G	GS	CG	GF	IP	BFP	H	R	ER	HR	SH	SF	HB	TBB	IBB	SO	WP	Bk	W	L	Pct	Sh	Sv-Op	Hld	ERC	ERA
2013	3 Tms	Low	6	5	0	0	27.2	139	49	32	23	2	0	0	3	6	0	15	1	1	0	5	.000	0	0- -	-	8.22	7.48
2014	3 Tms	Low	31	0	0	21	42.0	177	33	15	8	0	2	3	9	10	4	50	3	0	3	3	.500	0	7- -	-	2.29	1.71
2015	PlmBh	A+	41	0	0	27	56.0	218	42	11	8	2	3	2	5	12	2	41	4	1	4	3	.571	0	9- -	-	2.06	1.29
2016	Sprgfld	AA	38	0	0	24	52.2	217	47	20	19	5	1	2	0	12	3	61	4	0	4	2	.667	0	16- -	-	2.68	3.25
2016	Memp	AAA	7	0	0	5	7.2	35	9	9	8	0	0	0	0	4	0	5	0	0	0	0	-	0	0- -	-	4.80	9.39
2017	Memp	AAA	47	0	0	32	60.0	248	58	23	21	3	2	0	3	12	1	68	2	0	8	1	.889	0	17- -	-	2.97	3.15
2017	StL	NL	5	0	0	2	7.1	32	7	3	3	2	0	0	1	4	0	7	1	0	0	0	-	0	0-0	0	6.58	3.68

Jonathan Lucroy

Bats: R **Throws:** R **Pos:** C-110;DH-10;PH-5;1B-1   LOO-croy   **Ht:** 6'0" **Wt:** 200 **Born:** 6/13/1986 **Age:** 32

			BATTING																RUNNING			AVERAGES			
Year	Team	Lg	G	AB	H	2B	3B	HR	(Hm Rd)	TB	R	RBI	RC	TBB	IBB	SO	HBP	SH	SF	SB	CS	GDP	Avg	OBP	Slg	OPS
2010	Mil	NL	75	277	70	9	0	4	(4 0)	91	24	26	23	18	1	44	1	0	1	4	2	9	.253	.300	.329	.628
2011	Mil	NL	136	430	114	16	1	12	(8 4)	168	45	59	50	29	0	99	2	4	3	2	1	7	.265	.313	.391	.703
2012	Mil	NL	96	316	101	17	4	12	(7 5)	162	46	58	61	22	1	44	4	1	3	4	1	12	.320	.368	.513	.881
2013	Mil	NL	147	521	146	25	6	18	(9 9)	237	59	82	78	46	2	69	5	0	8	9	1	16	.280	.340	.455	.795
2014	Mil	NL	153	585	176	53	2	13	(6 7)	272	73	69	90	66	3	71	2	0	2	4	4	13	.301	.373	.465	.837
2015	Mil	NL	103	371	98	20	3	7	(3 4)	145	51	43	46	36	0	64	1	1	6	1	0	18	.264	.326	.391	.717
2016	2 Tms		142	490	143	24	3	24	(15 9)	245	67	81	74	47	5	100	3	0	4	5	0	12	.292	.355	.500	.855
2017	2 Tms		123	423	112	21	3	6	(2 4)	157	45	40	53	46	6	51	8	0	4	1	0	16	.265	.345	.371	.716
16	Mil	NL	95	338	101	17	3	13	(9 4)	163	48	50	46	33	3	70	1	0	4	5	0	12	.299	.359	.482	.841
16	Tex	AL	47	152	42	7	0	11	(6 5)	82	19	31	28	14	2	30	2	0	0	0	0	0	.276	.345	.539	.885
17	Tex	AL	77	281	68	15	0	4	(0 4)	95	27	27	28	19	0	32	4	0	2	1	0	10	.242	.297	.338	.635
17	Col	NL	46	142	44	6	3	2	(2 0)	62	18	13	25	27	6	19	4	0	2	0	0	6	.310	.429	.437	.865
	Postseason		13	44	9	1	0	1	(1 0)	13	4	5	4	0	0	10	0	0	0	0	0	0	.205	.205	.295	.500
	8 ML YEARS		975	3413	960	185	22	96	(54 42)	1477	410	458	475	310	18	542	26	6	31	30	9	107	.281	.343	.433	.776

Seth Lugo

Pitches: R **Bats:** R **Pos:** SP-18; RP-1   **Ht:** 6'4" **Wt:** 225 **Born:** 11/17/1989 **Age:** 28

			HOW MUCH HE PITCHED						WHAT HE GAVE UP										THE RESULTS							
Year	Team	Lg	G	GS	CG	GF	IP	BFP	H	R	ER	HR	SH	SF	HB	TBB	IBB	SO	WP	Bk	W	L	Pct	Sh	Sv-Op	Hld	ERC	ERA
2013	2 Tms	Low	12	12	0	0	66.1	267	56	25	25	7	2	1	2	19	0	66	3	0	4	6	.400	0	0- -	-	2.83	3.39
2014	Stluci	A+	27	4	0	10	105.0	455	100	55	48	12	2	1	4	38	0	114	7	0	8	3	.727	0	3- -	-	3.84	4.11
2015	Bnghtn	AA	19	19	0	0	109.0	466	108	54	46	8	3	3	5	30	1	97	6	0	6	5	.545	0	0- -	-	3.47	3.80
2015	LsVgs	AAA	5	5	0	0	27.0	114	27	13	12	3	0	0	2	5	0	30	2	0	2	2	.500	0	0- -	-	3.56	4.00
2016	LsVgs	AAA	21	14	0	1	73.1	341	103	63	53	10	6	1	1	20	0	62	4	0	3	4	.429	0	0- -	-	6.19	6.50
2016	NYM	NL	17	8	0	2	64.0	260	49	19	19	7	8	4	4	21	3	45	1	1	5	2	.714	0	0-0	0	2.81	2.67
2017	NYM	NL	19	18	0	1	101.1	436	114	57	53	13	2	5	2	25	1	85	2	1	7	5	.583	0	0-0	0	4.43	4.71
	2 ML YEARS		36	26	0	3	165.1	696	163	76	72	20	10	9	6	46	4	130	3	2	12	7	.632	0	0-0	0	3.78	3.92

Jordan Luplow

Bats: R **Throws:** R **Pos:** RF-14;LF-10;PH-5   **Ht:** 6'1" **Wt:** 195 **Born:** 9/26/1993 **Age:** 24

			BATTING																RUNNING			AVERAGES			
Year	Team	Lg	G	AB	H	2B	3B	HR	(Hm Rd)	TB	R	RBI	RC	TBB	IBB	SO	HBP	SH	SF	SB	CS	GDP	Avg	OBP	Slg	OPS
2014	Jmstwn	A-	62	220	61	12	1	6	(- -)	93	31	30	35	27	0	44	3	6	3	10	6	2	.277	.360	.423	.782
2015	WV	A	106	390	103	36	3	12	(- -)	181	74	67	72	59	2	67	6	6	4	11	2	9	.264	.366	.464	.830
2016	Bradtn	A+	104	354	90	23	3	10	(- -)	149	63	54	60	60	4	78	4	1	6	6	2	13	.254	.363	.421	.784
2017	Altna	AA	73	254	73	15	0	16	(- -)	136	45	37	49	29	2	45	4	0	1	1	3	5	.287	.368	.535	.903
2017	Indy	AAA	44	160	52	7	1	7	(- -)	82	29	19	33	16	1	36	5	0	1	4	1	1	.325	.401	.513	.914
2017	Pit	NL	27	78	16	3	1	3	(3 0)	30	6	11	8	6	0	22	2	0	1	0	0	4	.205	.276	.385	.660

Jordan Lyles

Pitches: R **Bats:** R **Pos:** RP-33; SP-5   **Ht:** 6'4" **Wt:** 230 **Born:** 10/19/1990 **Age:** 27

			HOW MUCH HE PITCHED						WHAT HE GAVE UP										THE RESULTS							
Year	Team	Lg	G	GS	CG	GF	IP	BFP	H	R	ER	HR	SH	SF	HB	TBB	IBB	SO	WP	Bk	W	L	Pct	Sh	Sv-Op	Hld	ERC	ERA
2017	ElPaso*	AAA	5	5	0	0	20.0	87	20	11	10	1	0	1	0	8	1	20	1	0	1	1	.500	0	0- -	-	3.83	4.50
2011	Hou	NL	20	15	0	2	94.0	415	107	61	56	14	7	1	5	26	1	67	0	0	2	8	.200	0	0-0	0	4.87	5.36
2012	Hou	NL	25	25	1	0	141.1	628	159	97	80	20	6	4	5	42	4	99	2	0	5	12	.294	1	0-0	0	4.67	5.09
2013	Hou	AL	27	25	0	1	141.2	642	165	98	88	17	0	3	11	49	1	93	5	2	7	9	.438	0	1-1	0	5.20	5.59
2014	Col	NL	22	22	0	0	126.2	546	127	64	61	12	4	3	8	46	1	90	6	0	7	4	.636	0	0-0	0	4.17	4.33
2015	Col	NL	10	10	0	0	49.0	212	54	32	28	5	3	1	1	19	1	30	2	0	3	5	.286	0	0-0	0	4.51	5.14
2016	Col	NL	40	5	0	7	58.2	273	69	46	38	4	1	2	4	28	2	32	5	0	4	5	.444	0	1-4	3	5.32	5.83
2017	2 Tms		38	5	0	12	69.2	324	96	61	60	16	2	1	4	22	1	55	4	0	1	5	.167	0	0-0	2	7.24	7.75
17	Col	NL	33	0	0	12	46.2	211	61	37	36	11	1	1	4	12	1	33	2	0	0	2	.000	0	0-0	2	6.72	6.94
17	SD	NL	5	5	0	0	23.0	113	35	24	24	5	1	0	0	10	0	22	2	0	1	3	.250	0	0-0	0	8.31	9.39
	7 ML YEARS		182	107	1	22	681.0	3040	777	459	411	85	23	15	40	232	11	466	24	2	28	48	.368	1	2-5	6	5.01	5.43

Lance Lynn

Pitches: R Bats: B Pos: SP-33
Ht: 6'5" **Wt:** 280 **Born:** 5/12/1987 **Age:** 31

Year	Team	Lg	G	GS	CG	GF	IP	BFP	H	R	ER	HR	SH	SF	HB	TBB	IBB	SO	WP	Bk	W	L	Pct	Sh	Sv-Op	Hld	ERC	ERA
2011	StL	NL	18	2	0	2	34.2	136	25	12	12	3	1	0	1	11	1	40	1	0	1	1	.500	0	1-2	3	2.37	3.12
2012	StL	NL	35	29	0	2	176.0	744	168	76	74	16	4	3	10	64	3	180	3	0	18	7	.720	0	0-0	1	3.87	3.78
2013	StL	NL	33	33	0	0	201.2	856	189	92	89	14	11	8	11	76	0	198	6	0	15	10	.600	0	0-0	0	3.67	3.97
2014	StL	NL	33	33	2	0	203.2	866	185	72	62	13	6	4	7	72	1	181	7	0	15	10	.600	1	0-0	0	3.24	2.74
2015	StL	NL	31	31	0	0	175.1	751	172	66	59	13	9	2	5	68	5	167	2	0	12	11	.522	0	0-0	0	3.83	3.03
2017	StL	NL	33	33	0	0	186.1	776	151	80	71	27	9	3	10	78	5	153	2	0	11	8	.579	0	0-0	0	3.62	3.43
	Postseason		24	7	0	3	52.0	232	56	30	26	6	2	3	1	26	5	50	0	0	5	4	.556	0	0-0	3	4.98	4.50
	6 ML YEARS		183	161	2	4	977.2	4129	890	398	367	86	40	20	44	369	15	919	21	0	72	47	.605	1	1-2	4	3.59	3.38

Tyler Lyons

Pitches: L Bats: L Pos: RP-50
Ht: 6'4" **Wt:** 210 **Born:** 2/21/1988 **Age:** 30

Year	Team	Lg	G	GS	CG	GF	IP	BFP	H	R	ER	HR	SH	SF	HB	TBB	IBB	SO	WP	Bk	W	L	Pct	Sh	Sv-Op	Hld	ERC	ERA
2013	StL	NL	12	8	0	1	53.0	223	75	29	28	5	1	0	3	16	0	43	0	0	2	4	.333	0	0-0	0	3.46	4.75
2014	StL	NL	11	4	0	1	36.2	155	33	23	18	4	1	1	2	11	2	36	0	0	0	4	.000	0	0-0	0	3.29	4.42
2015	StL	NL	17	8	0	1	60.0	255	59	29	25	12	3	2	1	15	0	60	4	0	3	1	.750	0	0-0	0	4.04	3.75
2016	StL	NL	30	0	0	10	48.0	187	35	18	18	9	1	1	0	14	0	46	2	0	2	0	1.000	0	0-0	4	2.83	3.38
2017	StL	NL	50	0	0	12	54.0	220	39	17	17	3	1	3	7	20	2	68	1	0	4	1	.800	0	3-4	15	2.68	2.83
	5 ML YEARS		120	20	0	25	251.2	1040	215	116	106	33	7	7	13	76	4	253	7	0	11	10	.524	0	3-4	19	3.29	3.79

Andres Machado

Pitches: R Bats: R Pos: RP-2
Ht: 6'0" **Wt:** 175 **Born:** 4/22/1993 **Age:** 25

Year	Team	Lg	G	GS	CG	GF	IP	BFP	H	R	ER	HR	SH	SF	HB	TBB	IBB	SO	WP	Bk	W	L	Pct	Sh	Sv-Op	Hld	ERC	ERA
2013	Burlgtn	R+	12	11	0	0	45.1	228	75	46	42	7	1	3	6	17	0	21	3	0	0	8	.000	0	0--	-	9.15	8.34
2014	Burlgtn	R+	7	0	0	3	17.1	77	12	9	7	2	0	0	0	11	0	15	3	0	1	2	.333	0	0--	-	3.23	3.63
2016	Idaho	R+	13	13	0	0	58.2	260	67	35	26	5	3	2	4	14	0	64	5	1	2	4	.333	0	0--	-	4.31	3.99
2017	Wilmg	A+	21	9	0	8	73.1	319	88	46	41	8	1	1	2	14	2	72	1	1	6	7	.462	0	2--	-	4.47	5.03
2017	Omha	AAA	7	7	0	0	34.2	149	30	17	14	6	0	1	2	17	0	38	0	0	2	2	.500	0	0--	-	4.46	3.63
2017	KC	AL	2	0	0	1	3.2	24	10	9	9	2	0	0	0	3	0	1	0	0	0	0	-	0	0-0	0	23.02	22.09

Dixon Machado

Bats: R Throws: R Pos: SS-32;2B-27;PH-13;3B-5;DH-5;PR-4
Ht: 6'1" **Wt:** 170 **Born:** 2/22/1992 **Age:** 26

Year	Team	Lg	G	AB	H	2B	3B	HR	(Hm	Rd)	TB	R	RBI	RC	TBB	IBB	SO	HBP	SH	SF	SB	CS	GDP	Avg	OBP	Slg	OPS
2015	Det	AL	24	68	16	3	0	0	(0	0)	19	6	5	5	7	0	14	0	3	0	1	0	3	.235	.307	.279	.586
2016	Det	AL	8	10	1	0	0	0	(0	0)	1	1	0	0	3	0	4	0	0	0	0	0	0	.100	.308	.100	.408
2017	Det	AL	73	166	43	5	1	1	(1	0)	53	17	11	11	10	0	32	1	2	2	1	0	6	.259	.302	.319	.621
	3 ML YEARS		105	244	60	8	1	1	(1	0)	73	24	16	16	20	0	50	1	5	2	2	0	9	.246	.303	.299	.603

Manny Machado

Bats: R Throws: R Pos: 3B-156
muh-CHAH-doe
Ht: 6'3" **Wt:** 185 **Born:** 7/6/1992 **Age:** 25

Year	Team	Lg	G	AB	H	2B	3B	HR	(Hm	Rd)	TB	R	RBI	RC	TBB	IBB	SO	HBP	SH	SF	SB	CS	GDP	Avg	OBP	Slg	OPS
2012	Bal	AL	51	191	50	8	3	7	(7	0)	85	24	26	29	9	0	38	0	1	1	2	0	6	.262	.294	.445	.739
2013	Bal	AL	156	667	189	51	3	14	(5	9)	288	88	71	87	29	2	113	2	9	3	6	7	15	.283	.314	.432	.746
2014	Bal	AL	82	327	91	14	0	12	(9	3)	141	38	32	44	20	2	68	3	2	2	2	0	13	.278	.324	.431	.755
2015	Bal	AL	162	633	181	30	1	35	(21	14)	318	102	86	107	70	2	111	4	2	4	20	8	17	.286	.359	.502	.861
2016	Bal	AL	157	640	188	40	1	37	(18	19)	341	105	96	103	48	9	120	3	0	5	0	3	14	.294	.343	.533	.876
2017	Bal	AL	156	630	163	33	1	33	(22	11)	297	81	95	94	50	3	115	1	0	9	9	4	17	.259	.310	.471	.782
	Postseason		7	23	4	1	0	1	(0	1)	8	2	2	1	2	0	6	0	2	0	0	0	1	.174	.240	.348	.588
	6 ML YEARS		764	3088	862	176	9	138	(82	56)	1470	438	406	464	226	16	565	13	14	24	39	22	82	.279	.329	.476	.805

Jean Machi

Pitches: R Bats: R Pos: RP-5
GENE ma-CHEE
Ht: 6'0" **Wt:** 255 **Born:** 2/1/1982 **Age:** 36

Year	Team	Lg	G	GS	CG	GF	IP	BFP	H	R	ER	HR	SH	SF	HB	TBB	IBB	SO	WP	Bk	W	L	Pct	Sh	Sv-Op	Hld	ERC	ERA
2017	Tacom*	AAA	29	3	0	21	36.2	151	39	15	14	2	0	2	2	8	1	29	1	0	2	4	.333	0	10--	-	3.70	3.44
2017	Charltt*	AAA	12	2	0	3	30.0	118	23	12	12	7	0	1	0	10	0	28	0	0	5	0	1.000	0	0--	-	3.50	3.60
2012	SF	NL	8	0	0	5	6.2	28	7	5	5	2	0	0	0	1	0	4	0	0	0	0	-	0	0-0	0	4.56	6.75
2013	SF	NL	51	0	0	9	53.0	211	46	15	14	2	1	1	0	12	3	51	2	0	3	1	.750	0	0-2	11	2.30	2.38
2014	SF	NL	71	0	0	13	66.1	249	45	19	19	5	5	1	1	18	3	51	5	1	7	1	.875	0	2-5	17	1.93	2.58
2015	2 Tms		59	0	0	17	58.0	257	59	35	33	8	2	3	1	22	0	42	3	0	2	0	1.000	0	4-4	4	4.31	5.12
2017	Sea	AL	5	0	0	0	7.2	31	7	2	1	1	0	1	0	4	0	4	0	0	1	0	1.000	0	0-0	0	4.65	1.17
'15 SF		NL	33	0	0	8	35.0	159	38	21	20	3	2	2	1	14	0	22	1	0	1	0	1.000	0	0-0	2	4.43	5.14
'15 Bos		AL	26	0	0	9	23.0	98	21	14	13	5	0	1	0	8	0	20	2	0	1	0	1.000	0	4-4	2	4.09	5.09
	Postseason		7	0	0	0	5.2	28	9	5	5	2	0	0	0	2	0	4	0	0	0	0	-	0	0-1	0	9.46	7.94
	5 ML YEARS		194	0	0	44	191.2	776	164	76	72	18	8	6	2	57	6	152	10	1	13	2	.867	0	6-11	32	2.91	3.38

Austin Maddox

Pitches: R **Bats:** R **Pos:** RP-13   **Ht:** 6'2" **Wt:** 220 **Born:** 5/13/1991 **Age:** 27

Year	Team	Lg	G	GS	CG	GF	IP	BFP	H	R	ER	HR	SH	SF	HB	TBB	IBB	SO	WP	Bk	W	L	Pct	Sh	Sv-Op	Hld	ERC	ERA
2013	Grnvlle	A	33	7	0	12	88.0	404	109	67	55	13	5	3	3	22	0	65	13	0	4	6	.400	0	1- -	-	5.12	5.63
2014	Salem	A+	10	0	0	2	21.2	87	20	14	14	5	0	1	1	3	0	22	2	0	1	1	.500	0	1- -	-	3.66	5.82
2015	Salem	A+	20	0	0	20	26.2	112	24	13	11	2	1	3	2	5	0	22	4	0	1	4	.200	0	10- -	-	2.77	3.71
2016	Salem	A+	13	0	0	11	24.1	108	29	10	9	0	0	0	0	8	1	24	5	0	2	0	1.000	0	5- -	-	4.04	3.33
2016	Portlnd	AA	23	2	0	12	38.2	161	29	21	17	3	2	3	0	16	1	38	2	0	2	3	.400	0	0- -	-	2.57	3.96
2017	Portlnd	AA	10	0	0	6	13.1	52	9	2	2	0	1	1	1	5	0	8	1	1	1	0	1.000	0	2- -	-	2.05	1.35
2017	Pwtckt	AAA	27	0	0	14	36.0	149	22	14	14	2	1	2	0	21	0	38	3	0	2	2	.500	0	6- -	-	2.41	3.50
2017	Bos	AL	13	0	0	5	17.1	67	13	1	1	1	0	0	0	2	0	14	0	0	0	0	-	0	0-0	0	1.58	0.52

Ryan Madson

Pitches: R **Bats:** L **Pos:** RP-60   **Ht:** 6'6" **Wt:** 225 **Born:** 8/28/1980 **Age:** 37

Year	Team	Lg	G	GS	CG	GF	IP	BFP	H	R	ER	HR	SH	SF	HB	TBB	IBB	SO	WP	Bk	W	L	Pct	Sh	Sv-Op	Hld	ERC	ERA
2003	Phi	NL	1	0	0	0	2.0	6	0	0	0	0	0	0	0	0	0	0	0	0	0	0	-	0	0-0	0	0.00	0.00
2004	Phi	NL	52	1	0	14	77.0	312	68	23	20	6	1	1	5	19	4	55	7	0	9	3	.750	0	1-2	7	2.95	2.34
2005	Phi	NL	78	0	0	10	87.0	365	84	44	40	11	5	5	6	25	6	79	6	1	6	5	.545	0	0-7	32	3.83	4.14
2006	Phi	NL	50	17	0	8	134.1	620	176	92	85	20	9	3	10	50	4	99	12	0	11	9	.550	0	2-4	6	6.50	5.69
2007	Phi	NL	38	0	0	9	56.0	237	48	19	19	5	2	2	2	23	4	43	2	2	2	2	.500	0	1-2	7	3.28	3.05
2008	Phi	NL	76	0	0	14	82.2	340	79	29	28	6	3	2	1	23	4	67	2	1	4	2	.667	0	1-3	17	3.20	3.05
2009	Phi	NL	79	0	0	28	77.1	320	73	29	28	7	3	1	3	22	3	78	1	0	5	5	.500	0	10-16	26	3.39	3.26
2010	Phi	NL	55	0	0	21	53.0	217	42	16	15	4	2	0	4	13	3	64	2	0	6	2	.750	0	5-10	15	2.42	2.55
2011	Phi	NL	62	0	0	46	60.2	246	54	16	16	2	6	1	1	16	8	62	0	0	4	2	.667	0	32-34	3	2.45	2.37
2015	KC	AL	68	0	0	12	63.1	248	47	17	15	5	0	3	2	14	1	58	1	0	1	2	.333	0	3-5	20	2.08	2.13
2016	Oak	AL	63	0	0	53	64.2	270	63	27	26	7	2	1	2	20	3	49	4	1	6	7	.462	0	30-37	3	3.74	3.62
2017	2 Tms		60	0	0	10	59.0	219	38	12	12	2	2	1	4	9	2	67	0	0	5	4	.556	0	2-5	25	1.43	1.83
17	Oak	AL	40	0	0	8	39.1	144	25	9	9	2	2	1	2	6	2	39	0	0	2	4	.333	0	1-4	14	1.42	2.06
17	Was	NL	20	0	0	2	19.2	75	13	3	3	0	0	0	2	3	0	28	0	0	3	0	1.000	0	1-1	11	1.43	1.37
	Postseason		42	0	0	11	43.1	185	45	14	14	6	3	2	1	13	2	58	2	0	4	1	.800	0	2-7	9	4.19	2.91
	12 ML YEARS		682	18	0	225	817.0	3400	772	324	304	75	35	20	40	234	42	721	37	5	59	43	.578	0	87-125	161	3.42	3.35

Kenta Maeda

Pitches: R **Bats:** R **Pos:** SP-25; RP-4   mah-AY-duh   **Ht:** 6'1" **Wt:** 175 **Born:** 4/11/1988 **Age:** 30

Year	Team	Lg	G	GS	CG	GF	IP	BFP	H	R	ER	HR	SH	SF	HB	TBB	IBB	SO	WP	Bk	W	L	Pct	Sh	Sv-Op	Hld	ERC	ERA
2013	HiroCrp	IND	26	26	3	0	175.2	690	129	46	41	13	-	-	2	40	1	158	1	0	15	7	.682	1	0- -	-	1.96	2.10
2014	HiroCrp	IND	27	27	1	0	187.0	746	164	61	54	12	-	-	2	41	1	161	4	1	11	9	.550	1	0- -	-	2.59	2.60
2015	HiroCrp	IND	29	29	5	0	206.1	821	168	49	48	5	-	-	6	41	1	175	3	0	15	8	.652	0	0- -	-	1.94	2.09
2016	LAD	NL	32	32	0	0	175.2	716	150	72	68	20	0	3	8	50	6	179	6	0	16	11	.593	0	0-0	0	3.09	3.48
2017	LAD	NL	29	25	0	1	134.1	557	121	68	63	22	6	4	5	34	1	140	4	0	13	6	.684	0	1-1	0	3.48	4.22
	Postseason		3	3	0	0	10.2	53	12	8	8	1	0	0	2	7	0	12	1	0	0	1	.000	0	0-0	0	6.42	6.75
	2 ML YEARS		61	57	0	1	310.0	1273	271	140	131	42	6	7	13	84	7	319	10	0	29	17	.630	0	1-1	0	3.26	3.80

Damien Magnifico

Pitches: R **Bats:** R **Pos:** RP-1   **Ht:** 6'1" **Wt:** 195 **Born:** 5/24/1991 **Age:** 27

Year	Team	Lg	G	GS	CG	GF	IP	BFP	H	R	ER	HR	SH	SF	HB	TBB	IBB	SO	WP	Bk	W	L	Pct	Sh	Sv-Op	Hld	ERC	ERA
2013	2 Tms	Low	21	18	0	2	80.2	357	83	46	41	6	0	3	6	41	2	63	9	0	5	3	.625	0	0- -	-	4.83	4.57
2014	BrvdCt	A+	22	22	2	0	120.1	503	110	61	50	11	3	2	4	43	0	76	12	0	8	6	.571	2	0- -	-	3.55	3.74
2015	Biloxi	AA	42	0	0	33	53.2	221	41	10	7	3	1	2	1	22	0	38	2	0	4	1	.800	0	20- -	-	2.65	1.17
2016	ColSpr	AAA	52	0	0	43	62.0	272	57	32	28	2	4	2	1	33	0	61	16	0	6	7	.462	0	18- -	-	3.69	4.06
2017	Norfolk	AAA	5	0	0	2	6.1	34	13	8	7	0	0	1	0	3	0	5	1	0	1	0	1.000	0	0- -	-	10.27	9.95
2017	Salt Lk	AAA	31	0	0	13	34.1	165	42	28	26	2	0	2	0	24	0	34	3	1	4	2	.667	0	4- -	-	6.28	6.82
2017	Mobile	AA	9	0	0	5	11.1	52	9	4	4	0	0	0	0	9	0	17	4	0	1	0	1.000	0	0- -	-	3.59	3.18
2016	Mil	NL	3	0	0	3	3.0	15	2	2	2	0	0	1	1	3	0	0	2	0	0	0	-	0	0-0	0	4.81	6.00
2017	LAA	AL	1	0	0	0	0.1	3	0	0	0	0	0	0	0	2	0	1	0	0	0	0	-	0	0-0	0	19.60	0.00
	2 ML YEARS		4	0	0	3	3.1	18	2	2	2	0	0	1	1	5	0	1	2	0	0	0	-	0	0-0	0	6.15	5.40

Tyler Mahle

Pitches: R **Bats:** R **Pos:** SP-4   **Ht:** 6'3" **Wt:** 210 **Born:** 9/29/1994 **Age:** 23

Year	Team	Lg	G	GS	CG	GF	IP	BFP	H	R	ER	HR	SH	SF	HB	TBB	IBB	SO	WP	Bk	W	L	Pct	Sh	Sv-Op	Hld	ERC	ERA
2013	Reds	R	12	4	0	0	34.1	144	32	18	9	0	1	0	0	8	0	30	2	0	1	3	.250	0	0- -	-	2.37	2.36
2014	Billings	R+	15	15	0	0	76.2	325	80	43	33	5	1	3	2	15	0	71	5	1	5	4	.556	2	0- -	-	3.33	3.87
2015	Dayton	A	27	26	0	0	152.0	620	145	54	41	7	4	3	11	25	0	135	3	1	13	8	.619	0	0- -	-	2.88	2.43
2016	Dytona	A+	13	13	1	0	79.1	308	58	24	22	6	3	1	5	17	0	76	2	0	8	3	.727	1	0- -	-	2.14	2.50
2016	Pnscla	AA	14	14	0	0	71.1	309	78	45	38	12	3	2	6	20	0	65	2	0	6	3	.667	0	0- -	-	5.00	4.79
2017	Pnscla	AA	14	14	1	0	85.0	323	57	15	15	5	2	2	2	17	1	87	0	0	7	3	.700	1	0- -	-	1.61	1.59
2017	Lsvlle	AAA	10	10	0	0	59.1	241	52	24	18	4	3	0	2	13	0	51	5	0	3	4	.429	0	0- -	-	2.66	2.73
2017	Cin	NL	4	4	0	0	20.0	92	19	6	6	2	0	4	1	11	1	14	1	0	1	2	.333	0	0-0	0	4.27	2.70

Mikie Mahtook

MIKE-ee MAH-took

Bats: R **Throws:** R **Pos:** CF-67;RF-25;LF-19;PH-9;PR-4;DH-2   **Ht:** 6'1" **Wt:** 200 **Born:** 11/30/1989 **Age:** 28

Year	Team	Lg	G	AB	H	2B	3B	HR	(Hm	Rd)	TB	R	RBI	RC	TBB	IBB	SO	HBP	SH	SF	SB	CS	GDP	Avg	OBP	Slg	OPS
2015	TB	AL	41	105	31	5	1	9	(3	6)	65	22	19	22	6	0	31	3	1	0	4	3	0	.295	.351	.619	.970
2016	TB	AL	65	185	36	9	0	3	(1	2)	54	16	11	5	7	0	68	2	1	1	0	1	2	.195	.231	.292	.523
2017	Det	AL	109	348	96	15	6	12	(6	6)	159	50	38	48	23	0	79	6	0	2	6	0	4	.276	.330	.457	.787
	3 ML YEARS		215	638	163	29	7	24	(10	14)	278	88	68	75	36	0	178	11	2	3	10	4	6	.255	.305	.436	.741

Luke Maile

MAY-lee

Bats: R **Throws:** R **Pos:** C-46;PH-1   **Ht:** 6'3" **Wt:** 225 **Born:** 2/6/1991 **Age:** 27

Year	Team	Lg	G	AB	H	2B	3B	HR	(Hm	Rd)	TB	R	RBI	RC	TBB	IBB	SO	HBP	SH	SF	SB	CS	GDP	Avg	OBP	Slg	OPS
2017	Buffalo*	AAA	16	54	9	0	0	0	(-	-)	9	5	1	1	4	0	12	0	0	0	0	0	3	.167	.224	.167	.391
2015	TB	AL	15	35	6	3	0	0	(0	0)	9	2	2	0	0	0	8	0	0	0	0	0	3	.171	.171	.257	.429
2016	TB	AL	42	119	27	7	0	3	(2	1)	43	10	15	11	4	1	36	0	3	0	0	0	2	.227	.252	.361	.613
2017	Tor	AL	46	130	19	5	0	2	(1	1)	30	10	7	2	3	0	35	2	0	1	1	0	2	.146	.176	.231	.407
	3 ML YEARS		103	284	52	15	0	5	(3	2)	82	22	24	13	7	1	79	2	3	1	1	0	7	.183	.207	.289	.496

Martin Maldonado

mar-TEEN

Bats: R **Throws:** R **Pos:** C-137;PH-3;1B-1   **Ht:** 6'0" **Wt:** 230 **Born:** 8/16/1986 **Age:** 31

Year	Team	Lg	G	AB	H	2B	3B	HR	(Hm	Rd)	TB	R	RBI	RC	TBB	IBB	SO	HBP	SH	SF	SB	CS	GDP	Avg	OBP	Slg	OPS
2011	Mil	NL	3	1	0	0	0	0	(0	0)	0	0	0	0	0	0	1	0	0	0	0	0	0	.000	.000	.000	.000
2012	Mil	NL	78	233	62	9	0	8	(6	2)	95	22	30	28	17	0	56	2	4	0	1	1	5	.266	.321	.408	.729
2013	Mil	NL	67	183	31	7	1	4	(1	3)	52	13	22	14	13	1	53	3	3	0	0	0	2	.169	.236	.284	.520
2014	Mil	NL	52	111	26	5	0	4	(2	2)	43	14	16	14	11	1	32	3	1	0	0	0	4	.234	.320	.387	.707
2015	Mil	NL	79	229	48	7	0	4	(4	0)	67	19	22	20	23	3	65	1	1	2	0	1	6	.210	.282	.293	.575
2016	Mil	NL	76	208	42	7	0	8	(6	2)	73	21	21	23	35	9	56	6	3	1	1	0	6	.202	.332	.351	.683
2017	LAA	AL	138	429	95	19	1	14	(5	9)	158	43	38	37	15	1	119	18	8	1	0	2	12	.221	.276	.368	.645
	7 ML YEARS		493	1394	304	54	2	42	(24	18)	488	132	149	136	114	15	382	33	20	4	2	4	35	.218	.292	.350	.642

Sean Manaea

muh-NIE-uh

Pitches: L **Bats:** R **Pos:** SP-29   **Ht:** 6'5" **Wt:** 245 **Born:** 2/1/1992 **Age:** 26

			HOW MUCH HE PITCHED						WHAT HE GAVE UP											THE RESULTS						
Year	Team	Lg	G	GS	CG	GF	IP	BFP	H	R	ER	HR	SH	SF	HB	TBB	IBB	SO	WP	Bk	W	L	Pct	Sh	Sv-Op	Hld	ERC	ERA
2014	Wilmg	A+	25	25	1	0	121.2	514	102	54	42	5	3	4	5	54	0	146	4	0	7	8	.467	1	0- -	-	3.13	3.11
2015	2 Tms	Low	5	5	0	0	24.2	100	24	13	9	1	1	1	2	5	0	28	1	0	1	0	1.000	0	0- -	-	3.19	3.28
2015	Mdlnd	AA	7	7	0	0	42.2	173	34	11	9	3	1	0	1	15	0	51	1	0	6	0	1.000	0	0- -	-	2.75	1.90
2016	Oak	AL	25	24	0	0	144.2	594	135	65	62	20	4	4	4	37	1	124	3	0	7	9	.438	0	0-0	0	3.53	3.86
2017	Oak	AL	29	29	0	0	158.2	692	167	88	77	18	1	2	10	55	1	140	8	0	12	10	.545	0	0-0	0	4.51	4.37
	2 ML YEARS		54	53	0	0	303.1	1286	302	153	139	38	5	6	14	92	2	264	11	0	19	19	.500	0	0-0	0	4.04	4.12

Trey Mancini

Bats: R **Throws:** R **Pos:** LF-88;1B-45;DH-18;PH-6;RF-2   **Ht:** 6'4" **Wt:** 215 **Born:** 3/18/1992 **Age:** 26

Year	Team	Lg	G	AB	H	2B	3B	HR	(Hm	Rd)	TB	R	RBI	RC	TBB	IBB	SO	HBP	SH	SF	SB	CS	GDP	Avg	OBP	Slg	OPS
2013	Abrdn	A-	68	256	84	18	2	3	(-	-)	115	43	35	45	20	2	43	5	0	4	3	1	6	.328	.382	.449	.832
2014	2 Tms	Low	137	543	154	32	3	10	(-	-)	222	67	83	73	28	0	95	9	0	6	1	2	22	.284	.326	.409	.735
2015	Frdrck	A+	52	207	65	14	3	8	(-	-)	109	28	32	36	9	1	35	0	0	1	4	2	7	.314	.341	.527	.868
2015	Bowie	AA	84	326	117	29	3	13	(-	-)	191	60	57	72	22	1	58	1	0	5	2	1	11	.359	.395	.586	.981
2016	Bowie	AA	17	63	19	4	0	7	(-	-)	44	18	14	17	10	0	17	2	0	0	0	0	4	.302	.413	.698	1.112
2016	Norfolk	AAA	125	483	135	22	5	13	(-	-)	206	60	54	74	48	1	123	4	0	1	2	2	13	.280	.349	.427	.775
2016	Bal	AL	5	14	5	1	0	3	(3	0)	15	3	5	5	0	0	4	1	0	0	0	0	0	.357	.400	1.071	1.471
2017	Bal	AL	147	543	159	26	4	24	(11	13)	265	65	78	90	33	1	139	6	0	4	1	0	12	.293	.338	.488	.826
	2 ML YEARS		152	557	164	27	4	27	(14	13)	280	68	83	95	33	1	143	7	0	4	1	0	12	.294	.339	.503	.842

Seth Maness

MAY-ness

Pitches: R **Bats:** R **Pos:** RP-8   **Ht:** 6'0" **Wt:** 190 **Born:** 10/14/1988 **Age:** 29

			HOW MUCH HE PITCHED						WHAT HE GAVE UP											THE RESULTS						
Year	Team	Lg	G	GS	CG	GF	IP	BFP	H	R	ER	HR	SH	SF	HB	TBB	IBB	SO	WP	Bk	W	L	Pct	Sh	Sv-Op	Hld	ERC	ERA
2017	Omha*	AAA	24	0	0	11	47.0	207	63	32	32	7	3	2	1	8	2	35	1	0	2	2	.500	0	2- -	-	5.53	6.13
2013	StL	NL	66	0	0	4	62.0	249	65	17	16	4	4	0	1	13	7	35	2	0	5	2	.714	0	1-3	15	3.41	2.32
2014	StL	NL	73	0	0	17	80.1	317	77	29	26	7	5	4	2	11	3	55	2	1	6	4	.600	0	3-3	11	2.90	2.91
2015	StL	NL	76	0	0	13	63.1	270	77	35	30	7	4	1	1	13	4	46	2	0	4	2	.667	0	3-6	20	4.65	4.26
2016	StL	NL	29	0	0	13	31.2	134	34	14	12	2	1	1	0	8	2	16	2	0	2	2	.500	0	0-0	1	3.56	3.41
2017	KC	AL	8	0	0	1	9.2	45	16	5	4	3	0	1	0	2	0	4	0	0	1	0	1.000	0	0-1	0	9.24	3.72
	Postseason		17	0	0	2	12.1	49	13	3	2	1	1	1	0	1	0	6	0	0	1	0	1.000	0	0-1	1	3.09	1.46
	5 ML YEARS		252	0	0	48	247.0	1015	269	100	88	23	14	7	4	47	16	156	8	1	18	10	.643	0	7-13	47	3.76	3.21

Dillon Maples

Pitches: R **Bats:** R **Pos:** RP-6 **Ht:** 6'2" **Wt:** 225 **Born:** 5/9/1992 **Age:** 26

Year	Team	Lg	G	GS	CG	GF	IP	BFP	H	R	ER	HR	SH	SF	HB	TBB	IBB	SO	WP	Bk	W	L	Pct	Sh	Sv-Op	Hld	ERC	ERA
2013	2 Tms	Low	21	16	0	2	76.2	356	70	53	42	1	2	3	15	50	0	75	14	0	5	4	.556	0	1- -	-	4.65	4.93
2014	2 Tms	Low	10	10	0	0	27.2	151	35	35	28	0	1	0	7	26	0	23	15	0	0	4	.000	0	0- -	-	7.87	9.11
2015	2 Tms	Low	18	0	0	6	35.1	155	35	25	18	2	0	1	6	13	0	27	5	0	1	2	.333	0	1- -	-	4.29	4.58
2016	2 Tms	Low	28	0	0	18	32.0	144	27	17	15	1	0	0	4	17	0	23	7	0	1	3	.250	0	9- -	-	3.60	4.22
2017	MrtlBh	A+	21	0	0	7	31.1	128	21	7	7	2	0	0	1	15	0	44	4	1	4	0	1.000	0	3- -	-	2.54	2.01
2017	Tenn	AA	14	0	0	12	13.2	65	11	5	5	0	0	1	1	11	0	28	2	0	1	1	.500	0	6- -	-	3.87	3.29
2017	Iowa	AAA	17	0	0	8	18.1	81	12	7	4	1	0	1	4	11	0	28	1	0	1	2	.333	0	4- -	-	3.41	1.96
2017	ChC	NL	6	0	0	1	5.1	27	6	6	6	0	0	0	0	6	0	11	1	0	0	0	-	0	0-0	0	6.99	10.13

Manuel Margot

Bats: R **Throws:** R **Pos:** CF-123;PH-4 mar-GOH **Ht:** 5'11" **Wt:** 180 **Born:** 9/28/1994 **Age:** 23

Year	Team	Lg	G	AB	H	2B	3B	HR	(Hm	Rd)	TB	R	RBI	RC	TBB	IBB	SO	HBP	SH	SF	SB	CS	GDP	Avg	OBP	Slg	OPS
2013	Lowell	A-	49	185	50	8	2	1	(-	-)	65	29	21	26	22	1	40	1	5	3	18	8	0	.270	.346	.351	.697
2014	2 Tms	Low	115	420	123	25	5	12	(-	-)	194	65	59	73	39	0	54	3	5	2	42	15	8	.293	.356	.462	.818
2015	Salem	A+	46	181	51	6	5	3	(-	-)	76	35	17	27	11	0	15	1	2	3	20	5	4	.282	.321	.420	.741
2015	Portlnd	AA	64	258	70	21	4	3	(-	-)	108	38	33	37	21	1	36	1	0	2	19	8	4	.271	.326	.419	.745
2016	ElPaso	AAA	124	517	157	21	12	6	(-	-)	220	98	55	81	36	0	64	4	5	4	30	11	5	.304	.351	.426	.777
2016	SD	NL	10	37	9	4	1	0	(0	0)	15	4	3	5	0	0	7	0	0	0	2	0	0	.243	.243	.405	.649
2017	SD	NL	126	487	128	18	7	13	(7	6)	199	53	39	55	35	0	106	2	1	4	17	7	6	.263	.313	.409	.721
	2 ML YEARS		136	524	137	22	8	13	(7	6)	214	57	42	60	35	0	113	2	1	4	19	7	6	.261	.308	.409	.716

Jhan Marinez

Pitches: R **Bats:** R **Pos:** RP-43 **Ht:** 6'1" **Wt:** 200 **Born:** 8/12/1988 **Age:** 29

Year	Team	Lg	G	GS	CG	GF	IP	BFP	H	R	ER	HR	SH	SF	HB	TBB	IBB	SO	WP	Bk	W	L	Pct	Sh	Sv-Op	Hld	ERC	ERA
2010	Fla	NL	4	0	0	2	2.2	14	3	3	2	1	0	0	0	3	0	3	0	0	1	1	.500	0	0-2	0	10.25	6.75
2012	CWS	AL	2	0	0	1	2.2	11	2	0	0	0	1	0	0	2	1	1	0	0	0	0	-	0	0-0	0	2.87	0.00
2016	2 Tms	NL	46	0	0	12	62.1	269	62	25	22	4	2	1	6	21	3	50	4	0	1	0	1.000	0	0-0	5	3.86	3.18
2017	3 Tms		43	0	0	19	58.1	262	64	26	24	6	3	1	7	26	3	45	6	0	0	3	.000	0	0-0	3	5.32	3.70
16	TB	AL	3	0	0	2	3.2	13	2	1	1	1	0	0	0	0	0	3	0	0	0	0	-	0	0-0	0	1.32	2.45
16	Mil	NL	43	0	0	10	58.2	256	60	24	21	3	2	1	6	21	3	47	4	0	1	0	1.000	0	0-0	5	4.02	3.22
17	Mil	NL	15	0	0	3	16.2	81	23	12	10	2	0	1	1	11	2	14	2	0	0	2	.000	0	0-0	3	7.88	5.40
17	Pit	NL	24	0	0	12	34.0	148	34	12	12	4	3	1	4	12	1	26	4	0	0	1	.000	0	0-0	3	4.46	3.18
17	Tex	AL	4	0	0	4	7.2	33	7	2	2	0	0	0	2	3	0	5	0	0	0	0	-	0	0-0	0	3.97	2.35
	4 ML YEARS		95	0	0	34	126.0	556	131	54	48	11	6	2	13	52	7	99	10	0	1	5	.167	0	0-2	8	4.62	3.43

Jake Marisnick

Bats: R **Throws:** R **Pos:** CF-93;PR-9;LF-6;PH-6;RF-3;DH-1 mah-RIZ-nick **Ht:** 6'4" **Wt:** 220 **Born:** 3/30/1991 **Age:** 27

Year	Team	Lg	G	AB	H	2B	3B	HR	(Hm	Rd)	TB	R	RBI	RC	TBB	IBB	SO	HBP	SH	SF	SB	CS	GDP	Avg	OBP	Slg	OPS
2013	Mia	NL	40	109	20	2	1	1	(1	0)	27	6	5	7	6	0	27	1	1	1	3	1	1	.183	.231	.248	.478
2014	2 Tms		65	221	55	8	0	3	(3	0)	72	21	19	19	8	3	67	3	2	3	11	3	2	.249	.281	.326	.607
2015	Hou	AL	133	339	80	15	4	9	(4	5)	130	46	36	40	18	0	105	5	6	4	24	9	2	.236	.281	.383	.665
2016	Hou	AL	118	287	60	18	1	5	(1	4)	95	40	21	23	16	0	83	3	4	1	10	5	4	.209	.257	.383	.588
2017	Hou	AL	106	230	56	10	0	16	(10	6)	114	50	35	31	20	1	90	6	2	1	9	4	5	.243	.319	.496	.815
14	Mia	NL	14	48	8	0	0	0	(0	0)	8	3	0	1	3	1	19	0	0	0	5	0	0	.167	.216	.167	.382
14	Hou	AL	51	173	47	8	0	3	(3	0)	64	18	19	18	5	2	48	3	2	3	6	3	2	.272	.299	.370	.669
	Postseason		4	7	3	1	0	0	(0	0)	4	1	0	2	0	0	2	0	0	0	0	0	0	.429	.429	.571	1.000
	5 ML YEARS		462	1186	271	53	6	34	(19	15)	438	163	116	120	68	4	372	18	15	10	57	22	14	.228	.278	.369	.648

Mike Marjama

Bats: R **Throws:** R **Pos:** C-5;PH-2 MAR-juh-mah **Ht:** 6'2" **Wt:** 205 **Born:** 7/20/1989 **Age:** 28

Year	Team	Lg	G	AB	H	2B	3B	HR	(Hm	Rd)	TB	R	RBI	RC	TBB	IBB	SO	HBP	SH	SF	SB	CS	GDP	Avg	OBP	Slg	OPS
2013	Knapol	A	97	375	104	20	1	6	(-	-)	144	48	46	48	20	0	67	7	1	4	9	5	9	.277	.323	.384	.707
2014	WinSa	A+	70	248	66	16	2	3	(-	-)	95	26	17	27	8	0	33	2	2	2	2	3	6	.266	.292	.383	.675
2015	Charltt	A+	90	334	101	22	4	9	(-	-)	158	46	52	51	11	0	52	3	0	3	3	3	4	.302	.328	.473	.801
2016	Mont	AA	74	278	80	26	1	5	(-	-)	123	38	38	43	19	0	46	5	2	3	2	0	12	.288	.341	.442	.783
2017	Drham	AAA	72	263	72	16	1	9	(-	-)	117	32	51	40	21	0	53	7	0	1	3	3	5	.274	.342	.445	.787
2017	Tacom	AAA	21	78	13	3	1	3	(-	-)	27	5	12	6	7	0	15	1	0	0	0	0	0	.167	.244	.346	.590
2017	Sea	AL	5	9	3	1	0	1	(0	1)	7	1	1	2	0	0	1	0	0	0	0	0	0	.333	.333	.778	1.111

Nick Markakis

Bats: L **Throws:** L **Pos:** RF-156;DH-2;PH-2;PR-1 mar-KAY-kiss **Ht:** 6'1" **Wt:** 215 **Born:** 11/17/1983 **Age:** 34

Year	Team	Lg	G	AB	H	2B	3B	HR	(Hm	Rd)	TB	R	RBI	RC	TBB	IBB	SO	HBP	SH	SF	SB	CS	GDP	Avg	OBP	Slg	OPS
2006	Bal	AL	147	491	143	25	2	16	(9	7)	220	72	62	67	43	3	72	3	3	2	2	0	15	.291	.351	.448	.799
2007	Bal	AL	161	637	191	43	3	23	(15	8)	309	97	112	103	61	5	112	5	1	6	18	6	22	.300	.362	.485	.848
2008	Bal	AL	157	595	182	48	1	20	(11	9)	292	106	87	113	99	7	113	2	0	7	10	7	10	.306	.406	.491	.897
2009	Bal	AL	161	642	188	45	2	18	(8	10)	291	94	101	97	56	0	98	3	0	10	6	2	12	.293	.347	.453	.801
2010	Bal	AL	160	629	187	45	3	12	(8	4)	274	79	60	99	73	9	93	2	0	5	7	2	18	.297	.370	.436	.805

Year	Team	Lg	G	AB	H	2B	3B	HR	(Hm	Rd)	TB	R	RBI	RC	TBB	IBB	SO	HBP	SH	SF	SB	CS	GDP	Avg	OBP	Slg	OPS
2011	Bal	AL	160	641	182	31	1	15	(8	7)	260	72	73	90	62	6	75	7	0	6	12	3	16	.284	.351	.406	.756
2012	Bal	AL	104	420	125	28	3	13	(9	4)	198	59	54	69	42	3	51	4	0	5	1	1	11	.298	.363	.471	.834
2013	Bal	AL	160	634	172	24	0	10	(6	4)	226	89	59	66	55	3	76	3	0	8	1	2	17	.271	.329	.356	.685
2014	Bal	AL	155	642	177	27	1	14	(8	6)	248	81	50	82	62	4	84	4	0	2	4	2	10	.276	.342	.386	.729
2015	Atl	NL	156	612	181	38	1	3	(1	2)	230	73	53	81	70	11	83	3	0	1	2	1	17	.296	.370	.376	.746
2016	Atl	NL	158	599	161	38	0	13	(7	6)	238	67	89	82	71	9	101	5	0	9	0	2	16	.269	.346	.397	.744
2017	Atl	NL	160	593	163	39	1	8	(4	4)	228	76	76	77	68	8	110	6	0	3	0	2	16	.275	.354	.384	.738
Postseason			7	31	8	1	0	1	(1	0)	12	4	3	4	1	0	3	0	0	0	1	0	0	.258	.281	.387	.668
12 ML YEARS			1839	7135	2052	431	18	165	(94	71)	3014	965	876	1026	762	68	1068	47	4	58	63	30	180	.288	.358	.422	.780

Justin Marks

Pitches: L Bats: L Pos: RP-1   Ht: 6'3" Wt: 205 Born: 1/12/1988 Age: 30

Year	Team	Lg	G	GS	CG	GF	IP	BFP	H	R	ER	HR	SH	SF	HB	TBB	IBB	SO	WP	Bk	W	L	Pct	Sh	Sv-Op	Hld	ERC	ERA
2017	Drhm*	AAA	9	1	0	0	15.2	64	10	8	8	1	0	0	0	9	0	15	1	0	4	1	.800	0	0- -	-	2.62	4.60
2017	OkCity*	AAA	31	6	0	9	60.0	271	66	38	35	4	1	4	1	27	1	56	2	0	4	3	.571	0	3- -	-	4.57	5.25
2014	KC	AL	1	0	0	0	2.0	13	4	3	3	0	0	0	0	3	0	2	0	0	0	0	-	0	0-0	0	14.34	13.50
2016	TB	AL	4	0	0	0	9.0	42	7	1	1	1	0	0	0	9	0	6	0	0	0	0	-	0	0-0	5	5.27	1.00
2017	TB	AL	1	0	0	1	1.1	7	2	1	1	1	0	0	0	1	0	1	0	0	0	0	-	0	0-0	0	14.59	6.75
3 ML YEARS			6	0	0	1	12.1	62	13	5	5	2	0	0	0	13	0	9	0	0	0	0	-	0	0-0	0	7.61	3.65

German Marquez

Pitches: R Bats: R Pos: SP-29   hair-MAHN   Ht: 6'1" Wt: 185 Born: 2/22/1995 Age: 23

Year	Team	Lg	G	GS	CG	GF	IP	BFP	H	R	ER	HR	SH	SF	HB	TBB	IBB	SO	WP	Bk	W	L	Pct	Sh	Sv-Op	Hld	ERC	ERA
2013	Prnctn	R+	12	12	0	0	53.1	225	46	27	24	2	2	3	2	20	0	38	2	0	2	5	.286	0	0- -	-	2.94	4.05
2014	BG	A	22	18	0	0	98.0	398	83	43	35	5	1	0	4	29	0	95	5	0	5	7	.417	0	0- -	-	2.74	3.21
2015	Charltt	A+	26	23	0	1	139.0	596	147	68	55	6	4	7	13	29	0	104	7	2	7	13	.350	0	0- -	-	3.60	3.56
2016	Hrtfrd	AA	21	21	0	0	135.2	553	124	53	43	9	5	2	7	33	1	126	5	1	9	6	.600	0	0- -	-	3.03	2.85
2016	Albq	AAA	5	5	0	0	31.0	124	30	15	15	5	0	0	0	6	0	29	0	0	2	0	1.000	0	0- -	-	3.58	4.35
2016	Col	NL	6	3	0	0	20.2	98	28	12	12	2	2	1	3	6	0	15	0	0	1	1	.500	0	0-0	0	6.21	5.23
2017	Col	NL	29	29	0	0	162.0	701	174	82	79	25	5	4	8	49	3	147	6	0	11	7	.611	0	0-0	0	4.67	4.39
2 ML YEARS			35	32	0	0	182.2	799	202	94	91	27	7	5	11	55	3	162	6	0	12	8	.600	0	0-0	0	4.84	4.48

Chris Marrero

Bats: R Throws: R Pos: LF-12;PH-4   Ht: 6'3" Wt: 229 Born: 7/2/1988 Age: 29

Year	Team	Lg	G	AB	H	2B	3B	HR	(Hm	Rd)	TB	R	RBI	RC	TBB	IBB	SO	HBP	SH	SF	SB	CS	GDP	Avg	OBP	Slg	OPS
2017	Scrmto*	AAA	17	58	12	4	0	2	(-	-)	22	7	11	7	6	0	12	2	0	1	0	0	2	.207	.299	.379	.678
2011	Was	NL	31	109	27	5	0	0	(0	0)	32	6	10	7	4	0	27	1	0	3	0	0	1	.248	.274	.294	.567
2013	Was	NL	8	16	2	0	0	0	(0	0)	2	0	1	0	0	0	4	0	0	0	0	0	0	.125	.125	.125	.250
2017	SF	NL	15	38	5	0	0	1	(1	0)	8	2	5	1	2	0	9	0	0	1	0	0	4	.132	.171	.211	.381
3 ML YEARS			54	163	34	5	0	1	(1	0)	42	8	16	8	6	0	40	1	0	4	0	0	5	.209	.236	.258	.493

Deven Marrero

Bats: R Throws: R Pos: 3B-53;2B-11;PR-10;SS-6;1B-1;PH-1   Ht: 6'1" Wt: 195 Born: 8/25/1990 Age: 27

Year	Team	Lg	G	AB	H	2B	3B	HR	(Hm	Rd)	TB	R	RBI	RC	TBB	IBB	SO	HBP	SH	SF	SB	CS	GDP	Avg	OBP	Slg	OPS
2017	Pwtckt*	AAA	50	183	44	13	0	3	(-	-)	66	17	14	16	6	0	52	1	2	2	1	4	3	.240	.266	.361	.626
2015	Bos	AL	25	53	12	0	0	1	(0	1)	15	8	3	4	3	0	19	0	0	0	2	1	0	.226	.268	.283	.551
2016	Bos	AL	13	12	1	0	0	0	(0	0)	1	0	0	0	2	0	5	0	0	0	0	0	0	.083	.214	.083	.298
2017	Bos	AL	71	171	36	9	0	4	(1	3)	57	32	27	18	12	0	61	0	3	2	5	0	8	.211	.259	.333	.593
3 ML YEARS			109	236	49	9	0	5	(1	4)	73	40	30	22	17	0	85	0	3	2	7	1	8	.208	.259	.309	.568

Evan Marshall

Pitches: R Bats: R Pos: RP-6   Ht: 6'2" Wt: 225 Born: 4/18/1990 Age: 28

Year	Team	Lg	G	GS	CG	GF	IP	BFP	H	R	ER	HR	SH	SF	HB	TBB	IBB	SO	WP	Bk	W	L	Pct	Sh	Sv-Op	Hld	ERC	ERA
2017	Tacom*	AAA	13	1	0	1	21.2	97	28	12	10	4	0	0	0	7	0	26	1	0	1	0	1.000	0	1- -	-	6.18	4.15
2014	Ari	NL	57	0	0	11	49.1	210	50	17	15	3	2	1	2	17	3	54	3	0	4	4	.500	0	0-1	19	3.76	2.74
2015	Ari	NL	13	0	0	4	13.1	61	20	9	9	3	0	0	0	5	1	7	1	0	0	2	.000	0	0-2	2	8.27	6.08
2016	Ari	NL	15	0	0	8	15.1	79	28	18	15	2	0	0	1	8	2	9	1	0	0	1	.000	0	0-0	1	10.46	8.80
2017	Sea	AL	6	0	0	2	7.2	38	12	8	8	1	0	0	0	5	1	4	0	0	0	0	-	0	0-0	0	8.94	9.39
4 ML YEARS			91	0	0	25	85.2	388	110	52	47	9	2	1	3	35	7	74	5	0	4	7	.364	0	0-3	22	5.94	4.94

Jefry Marte

Bats: R Throws: R Pos: 1B-28;3B-10;PH-6;LF-3;PR-3;DH-2   marr-TAY   Ht: 6'1" Wt: 220 Born: 6/21/1991 Age: 27

Year	Team	Lg	G	AB	H	2B	3B	HR	(Hm	Rd)	TB	R	RBI	RC	TBB	IBB	SO	HBP	SH	SF	SB	CS	GDP	Avg	OBP	Slg	OPS
2017	Salt Lk*	AAA	45	185	49	10	0	9	(-	-)	86	26	39	30	17	0	32	2	0	1	6	1	7	.265	.332	.465	.797

Year Team	Lg	G	AB	H	2B	3B	HR	(Hm	Rd)	TB	R	RBI	RC	TBB	IBB	SO	HBP	SH	SF	SB	CS	GDP	Avg	OBP	Slg	OPS
2015 Det	AL	33	80	17	4	0	4	(1	3)	33	9	11	6	8	0	22	0	2	0	0	0	5	.213	.284	.413	.697
2016 LAA	AL	88	258	65	14	0	15	(10	5)	124	38	44	31	18	0	59	5	0	3	2	2	8	.252	.310	.481	.790
2017 LAA	AL	45	127	22	5	0	4	(1	3)	39	10	14	7	13	0	34	4	0	1	1	0	2	.173	.269	.307	.576
3 ML YEARS		166	465	104	23	0	23	(12	11)	196	57	69	44	39	0	115	9	2	4	3	2	12	.224	.294	.422	.716

Ketel Marte

Bats: B **Throws:** R **Pos:** SS-64;PH-9;3B-3   kuh-TELL marr-TAY   **Ht:** 6'1" **Wt:** 165 **Born:** 10/12/1993 **Age:** 24

Year Team	Lg	G	AB	H	2B	3B	HR	(Hm	Rd)	TB	R	RBI	RC	TBB	IBB	SO	HBP	SH	SF	SB	CS	GDP	Avg	OBP	Slg	OPS
2017 Reno*	AAA	70	311	105	23	7	6	(-	-)	160	62	41	62	25	1	34	2	0	0	7	2	5	.338	.391	.514	.905
2015 Sea	AL	57	219	62	14	3	2	(1	1)	88	25	17	33	24	0	43	0	2	2	8	4	1	.283	.351	.402	.753
2016 Sea	AL	119	437	113	21	2	1	(1	0)	141	55	33	41	18	0	84	2	3	6	11	5	10	.259	.287	.323	.610
2017 Ari	NL	73	223	58	11	2	5	(1	4)	88	30	18	27	29	3	37	1	0	2	3	1	3	.260	.345	.395	.740
3 ML YEARS		249	879	233	46	7	8	(3	5)	317	110	68	101	71	3	164	3	5	10	22	10	14	.265	.319	.361	.679

Starling Marte

Bats: R **Throws:** R **Pos:** LF-56;CF-25;PH-1;PR-1   marr-TAY   **Ht:** 6'1" **Wt:** 190 **Born:** 10/9/1988 **Age:** 29

Year Team	Lg	G	AB	H	2B	3B	HR	(Hm	Rd)	TB	R	RBI	RC	TBB	IBB	SO	HBP	SH	SF	SB	CS	GDP	Avg	OBP	Slg	OPS
2012 Pit	NL	47	167	43	3	6	5	(3	2)	73	18	17	21	8	0	50	3	2	2	12	5	5	.257	.300	.437	.737
2013 Pit	NL	135	510	143	26	10	12	(5	7)	225	83	35	74	25	2	138	24	6	1	41	15	6	.280	.343	.441	.784
2014 Pit	NL	135	495	144	29	6	13	(5	8)	224	73	56	70	33	0	131	17	0	0	30	11	5	.291	.356	.453	.808
2015 Pit	NL	153	579	166	30	2	19	(10	9)	257	84	81	81	27	3	123	19	3	5	30	10	14	.287	.337	.444	.780
2016 Pit	NL	129	489	152	34	5	9	(2	7)	223	71	46	77	23	5	104	16	1	0	47	12	6	.311	.362	.456	.818
2017 Pit	NL	77	309	85	7	2	7	(5	2)	117	48	31	46	20	0	63	8	0	2	21	4	5	.275	.333	.379	.712
Postseason		8	32	4	1	0	1	(0	1)	8	2	1	1	0	7	1	0	0	1	0	2	.125	.176	.250	.426
6 ML YEARS		676	2549	733	129	31	65	(30	35)	1119	377	266	369	136	10	609	87	12	10	181	57	43	.288	.344	.439	.783

Francis Martes

Pitches: R **Bats:** R **Pos:** RP-28; SP-4   **Ht:** 6'1" **Wt:** 225 **Born:** 11/24/1995 **Age:** 22

		HOW MUCH HE PITCHED						WHAT HE GAVE UP										THE RESULTS						
Year Team	Lg	G	GS	CG	GF	IP	BFP	H	R	ER	HR	SH	SF	HB	TBB	IBB	SO	WP	Bk	W	L	Pct	Sh	Sv-Op	Hld	ERC	ERA
2014 2 Tms	Low	12	9	0	0	44.0	190	34	24	20	0	0	2	4	23	0	45	11	1	3	3	.500	0	0--	-	2.74	4.09
2015 2 Tms	Low	16	13	1	3	87.0	345	64	21	15	2	1	3	3	21	0	82	4	0	7	3	.700	1	2--	-	1.81	1.55
2016 CpChr	AA	25	22	0	0	125.1	524	104	53	46	4	4	1	4	47	0	131	9	1	9	6	.600	0	0--	-	2.72	3.30
2017 Fresno	AAA	8	8	0	0	32.1	163	40	24	19	5	0	1	0	28	0	38	0	0	2	2	.000	0	0--	-	7.87	5.29
2017 Hou	AL	32	4	0	7	54.1	249	51	40	35	7	0	2	8	31	3	69	8	0	5	2	.714	0	0-1	1	5.08	5.80

Cody Martin

Pitches: R **Bats:** R **Pos:** RP-1   **Ht:** 6'3" **Wt:** 230 **Born:** 9/4/1989 **Age:** 28

		HOW MUCH HE PITCHED						WHAT HE GAVE UP										THE RESULTS						
Year Team	Lg	G	GS	CG	GF	IP	BFP	H	R	ER	HR	SH	SF	HB	TBB	IBB	SO	WP	Bk	W	L	Pct	Sh	Sv-Op	Hld	ERC	ERA
2017 Tacom*	AAA	20	7	0	2	56.2	240	59	27	26	7	1	1	5	14	0	67	2	0	0	2	.000	0	1--	-	4.27	4.13
2015 2 Tms		25	2	0	4	30.2	141	40	27	27	8	2	2	2	12	0	27	2	0	2	5	.286	0	0-3	7	7.54	7.92
2016 Sea	AL	9	2	0	3	25.2	107	28	11	11	5	2	1	1	9	0	15	0	0	1	2	.333	0	0-0	0	5.55	3.86
2017 Sea	AL	1	0	0	1	2.0	13	5	4	3	0	0	0	0	2	0	0	0	0	0	0	-	0	0-0	0	15.69	13.50
15 Atl	NL	21	0	0	2	21.2	92	24	13	13	4	2	1	1	7	0	24	1	0	2	3	.400	0	0-3	7	5.37	5.40
15 Oak	AL	4	2	0	2	9.0	49	16	14	14	4	0	1	1	5	0	3	1	0	0	2	.000	0	0-0	0	13.36	14.00
3 ML YEARS		35	4	0	8	58.1	261	73	42	41	13	4	3	3	23	0	42	2	0	3	7	.300	0	0-3	7	6.92	6.33

Kyle Martin

Pitches: R **Bats:** R **Pos:** RP-2   **Ht:** 6'7" **Wt:** 230 **Born:** 1/18/1991 **Age:** 27

		HOW MUCH HE PITCHED						WHAT HE GAVE UP										THE RESULTS						
Year Team	Lg	G	GS	CG	GF	IP	BFP	H	R	ER	HR	SH	SF	HB	TBB	IBB	SO	WP	Bk	W	L	Pct	Sh	Sv-Op	Hld	ERC	ERA
2013 2 Tms	Low	19	0	0	12	36.0	141	19	7	5	0	3	1	4	10	0	30	0	0	4	2	.667	0	3--	-	1.28	1.25
2014 Salem	A+	35	0	0	26	80.2	347	84	41	36	11	4	3	10	16	1	82	13	2	4	5	.444	0	10--	-	4.20	4.02
2015 Portlnd	AA	27	0	0	17	42.0	183	43	22	21	3	0	3	1	16	0	48	6	1	2	1	.667	0	5--	-	4.00	4.50
2016 Pwtckt	AAA	36	0	0	21	66.2	271	58	25	25	5	0	1	6	21	2	78	8	0	3	4	.429	0	6--	-	3.29	3.38
2017 Pwtckt	AAA	33	0	0	15	53.2	241	56	26	26	7	1	3	4	26	3	50	6	0	0	4	.000	0	1--	-	5.11	4.36
2017 Bos	AL	2	0	0	0	2.1	11	2	1	1	1	0	0	0	2	0	1	0	0	0	0	-	0	0-0	0	7.57	3.86

Leonys Martin

Bats: L **Throws:** R **Pos:** CF-20;RF-19;PH-6;LF-4;PR-2   lay-OH-nees mar-TEEN   **Ht:** 6'2" **Wt:** 200 **Born:** 3/6/1988 **Age:** 30

Year Team	Lg	G	AB	H	2B	3B	HR	(Hm	Rd)	TB	R	RBI	RC	TBB	IBB	SO	HBP	SH	SF	SB	CS	GDP	Avg	OBP	Slg	OPS
2017 Tacom*	AAA	88	360	110	24	5	11	(-	-)	177	63	39	63	21	1	89	3	0	3	25	6	3	.306	.346	.492	.838
2011 Tex	AL	8	8	3	1	0	0	(0	0)	4	2	0	1	0	0	1	0	0	0	0	0	0	.375	.375	.500	.875
2012 Tex	AL	24	46	8	5	2	0	(0	0)	17	6	6	4	4	0	12	0	1	1	3	0	2	.174	.235	.370	.605
2013 Tex	AL	147	457	119	21	6	8	(5	3)	176	66	49	58	28	0	104	8	12	3	36	9	6	.260	.313	.385	.698
2014 Tex	AL	155	533	146	13	7	7	(4	3)	194	68	40	64	39	3	114	2	7	2	31	12	4	.274	.325	.364	.689
2015 Tex	AL	95	288	63	12	0	5	(1	4)	90	26	25	22	16	1	69	2	3	1	14	5	5	.219	.264	.313	.576
2016 Sea	AL	143	518	128	17	3	15	(7	8)	196	72	47	64	44	0	149	3	4	7	24	6	10	.247	.306	.378	.684

Year Team	Lg	G	AB	H	2B	3B	HR	(Hm Rd)	TB	R	RBI	RC	TBB	IBB	SO	HBP	SH	SF	SB	CS	GDP	Avg	OBP	Slg	OPS
2017 2 Tms		49	128	22	3	1	3	(2 1)	36	14	9	7	8	1	33	2	0	0	7	4	2	.172	.232	.281	.513
17 Sea	AL	34	115	20	2	1	3	(2 1)	33	12	8	5	5	1	29	2	0	0	6	4	2	.174	.221	.287	.508
17 ChC	NL	15	13	2	1	0	0	(0 0)	3	2	1	2	3	0	4	0	0	0	1	0	0	.154	.313	.231	.543
7 ML YEARS		621	1978	489	72	19	38	(17 21)	713	254	176	220	139	5	482	17	27	14	115	36	29	.247	.300	.360	.661

Russell Martin

Bats: R **Throws:** R **Pos:** C-83;3B-10;PH-3 **Ht:** 5'10" **Wt:** 205 **Born:** 2/15/1983 **Age:** 35

Year Team	Lg	G	AB	H	2B	3B	HR	(Hm Rd)	TB	R	RBI	RC	TBB	IBB	SO	HBP	SH	SF	SB	CS	GDP	Avg	OBP	Slg	OPS
2006 LAD	NL	121	415	117	26	4	10	(8 2)	181	65	65	58	45	8	57	4	1	3	10	5	17	.282	.355	.436	.792
2007 LAD	NL	151	540	158	32	3	19	(8 11)	253	87	87	84	67	1	89	7	0	6	21	9	16	.293	.374	.469	.843
2008 LAD	NL	155	553	155	25	0	13	(6 7)	219	87	69	89	90	8	83	5	0	2	18	6	16	.280	.385	.396	.781
2009 LAD	NL	143	505	126	19	0	7	(3 4)	166	63	53	62	69	9	80	11	2	1	11	6	18	.250	.352	.329	.680
2010 LAD	NL	97	331	82	13	0	5	(2 3)	110	45	26	40	48	7	61	4	1	3	6	2	7	.248	.347	.332	.679
2011 NYY	AL	125	417	99	17	0	18	(8 10)	170	57	65	56	50	1	81	5	1	3	8	2	19	.237	.324	.408	.732
2012 NYY	AL	133	422	89	18	0	21	(13 8)	170	50	53	50	53	0	95	8	2	0	6	1	13	.211	.311	.403	.713
2013 Pit	NL	127	438	99	21	0	15	(6 9)	165	51	55	47	58	2	108	8	1	1	9	5	13	.226	.327	.377	.703
2014 Pit	NL	111	379	110	20	0	11	(8 3)	163	45	67	66	59	5	78	15	2	5	4	4	16	.290	.402	.430	.832
2015 Tor	AL	129	441	106	23	2	23	(13 10)	202	76	77	66	53	1	106	8	0	5	4	5	22	.240	.329	.458	.787
2016 Tor	AL	137	455	105	16	0	20	(8 12)	181	62	74	69	64	1	148	10	1	5	2	1	12	.231	.335	.398	.733
2017 Tor	AL	91	307	68	12	0	13	(8 5)	119	49	35	35	50	0	83	7	1	0	1	2	13	.221	.343	.388	.731
Postseason		57	195	36	8	0	5	(3 2)	59	22	18	15	24	0	52	9	0	2	1	0	5	.185	.300	.303	.603
12 ML YEARS		1520	5203	1314	242	9	175	(86 89)	2099	737	726	722	706	43	1069	92	12	34	100	48	182	.253	.350	.403	.753

Carlos Martinez

Pitches: R **Bats:** R **Pos:** SP-32 **Ht:** 6'0" **Wt:** 190 **Born:** 9/21/1991 **Age:** 26

		HOW MUCH HE PITCHED						WHAT HE GAVE UP											THE RESULTS							
Year Team	Lg	G	GS	CG	GF	IP	BFP	H	R	ER	HR	SH	SF	HB	TBB	IBB	SO	WP	Bk	W	L	Pct	Sh	Sv-Op	Hld	ERC	ERA
2013 StL	NL	21	1	0	5	28.1	124	31	16	16	1	1	1	3	9	1	24	0	0	2	1	.667	0	1-1	3	4.20	5.08
2014 StL	NL	57	7	0	13	89.1	386	90	41	40	4	7	1	4	36	8	84	8	1	2	4	.333	0	1-6	17	3.79	4.03
2015 StL	NL	31	29	0	1	179.2	755	168	65	60	13	9	4	8	63	5	184	8	1	14	7	.667	0	0-0	1	3.51	3.01
2016 StL	NL	31	31	0	0	195.1	809	169	68	66	15	2	2	11	70	1	174	8	0	16	9	.640	0	0-0	0	3.29	3.04
2017 StL	NL	32	32	2	0	205.0	858	179	93	83	27	4	2	8	71	3	217	9	0	12	11	.522	2	0-0	0	3.51	3.64
Postseason		16	0	0	1	16.2	65	10	6	6	0	1	1	1	7	1	13	1	0	0	1	.000	0	0-0	5	1.70	3.24
5 ML YEARS		172	100	2	19	697.2	2932	637	283	265	60	23	10	34	249	18	683	33	2	46	32	.590	2	2-7	21	3.51	3.42

J.D. Martinez

Bats: R **Throws:** R **Pos:** RF-113;DH-5;PH-2 **Ht:** 6'3" **Wt:** 220 **Born:** 8/21/1987 **Age:** 30

Year Team	Lg	G	AB	H	2B	3B	HR	(Hm Rd)	TB	R	RBI	RC	TBB	IBB	SO	HBP	SH	SF	SB	CS	GDP	Avg	OBP	Slg	OPS
2011 Hou	NL	53	208	57	13	0	6	(3 3)	88	29	35	30	13	1	48	2	0	3	0	1	4	.274	.319	.423	.742
2012 Hou	NL	113	395	95	14	3	11	(5 6)	148	34	55	45	40	0	96	1	0	2	0	2	18	.241	.311	.375	.685
2013 Hou	AL	86	296	74	17	0	7	(4 3)	112	24	36	29	10	0	82	0	0	3	2	0	8	.250	.272	.378	.650
2014 Det	AL	123	441	139	30	3	23	(13 10)	244	57	76	75	30	5	126	3	0	6	6	3	8	.315	.358	.553	.912
2015 Det	AL	158	596	168	33	2	38	(20 18)	319	93	102	100	53	7	178	5	0	3	3	2	11	.282	.344	.535	.879
2016 Det	AL	120	460	141	35	2	22	(13 9)	246	69	68	77	49	2	128	3	0	5	1	2	13	.307	.373	.535	.908
2017 2 Tms		119	432	131	26	3	45	(27 18)	298	85	104	92	53	8	128	0	0	4	4	0	23	.303	.376	.690	1.066
17 Det	AL	57	200	61	13	2	16	(11 5)	126	38	39	39	29	5	54	0	0	3	2	0	10	.305	.388	.630	1.018
17 Ari	NL	62	232	70	13	1	29	(16 13)	172	47	65	53	24	3	74	0	0	1	2	0	13	.302	.366	.741	1.107
Postseason		3	12	3	1	0	2	(0 2)	10	2	5	3	0	0	4	0	0	0	0	0	0	.250	.250	.833	1.083
7 ML YEARS		772	2828	805	168	13	152	(85 67)	1455	391	476	448	248	23	786	14	0	26	16	10	85	.285	.342	.514	.857

Jose Martinez

Bats: R **Throws:** R **Pos:** 1B-33;PH-32;LF-24;RF-17;DH-3 **Ht:** 6'6" **Wt:** 215 **Born:** 7/25/1988 **Age:** 29

Year Team	Lg	G	AB	H	2B	3B	HR	(Hm Rd)	TB	R	RBI	RC	TBB	IBB	SO	HBP	SH	SF	SB	CS	GDP	Avg	OBP	Slg	OPS
2013 Missi	AA	124	431	123	19	0	6	(- -)	160	46	39	55	37	1	63	1	4	2	6	9	12	.285	.342	.371	.713
2014 Lynbrg	A+	66	257	82	14	3	4	(- -)	114	32	34	45	26	0	37	0	0	5	5	1	4	.319	.375	.444	.819
2015 Omha	AAA	98	341	131	25	3	10	(- -)	192	57	60	86	48	1	55	3	1	3	8	2	8	.384	.461	.563	1.024
2016 Omha	AAA	37	141	42	10	0	3	(- -)	61	18	18	23	14	0	24	1	0	4	2	0	5	.298	.356	.433	.789
2016 Memp	AAA	87	301	81	18	1	8	(- -)	125	34	42	43	25	3	50	1	1	1	9	1	14	.269	.326	.415	.742
2016 StL	NL	12	16	7	1	0	0	(0 0)	8	4	1	4	2	0	1	0	0	0	0	0	0	.438	.500	.500	1.000
2017 StL	NL	106	272	84	13	1	14	(8 6)	141	47	46	47	32	2	60	0	1	2	4	0	9	.309	.379	.518	.897
2 ML YEARS		118	288	91	14	1	14	(8 6)	149	51	47	51	34	2	61	0	1	2	4	0	9	.316	.386	.517	.903

Michael Martinez

Bats: B **Throws:** R **Pos:** 2B-11;3B-9;CF-2;PH-2;PR-2;SS-1;LF-1 **Ht:** 5'9" **Wt:** 180 **Born:** 9/16/1982 **Age:** 35

Year Team	Lg	G	AB	H	2B	3B	HR	(Hm Rd)	TB	R	RBI	RC	TBB	IBB	SO	HBP	SH	SF	SB	CS	GDP	Avg	OBP	Slg	OPS
2017 Clmbs*	AAA	63	213	59	16	2	0	(- -)	79	29	20	26	13	1	35	0	2	1	4	2	7	.277	.317	.371	.688
2011 Phi	NL	88	209	41	5	2	3	(1 2)	59	25	24	20	18	0	35	0	5	2	3	0	2	.196	.258	.282	.540
2012 Phi	NL	45	115	20	3	0	2	(1 1)	29	10	7	5	5	2	21	0	2	0	0	0	4	.174	.208	.252	.461
2013 Phi	NL	29	40	7	0	0	0	(0 0)	7	5	3	3	0	0	12	0	1	0	1	0	1	.175	.175	.175	.350
2014 Pit	NL	26	39	5	1	0	0	(0 0)	6	2	1	2	4	1	13	0	1	0	0	0	0	.128	.209	.154	.363
2015 Cle	AL	16	30	8	2	0	0	(0 0)	10	7	2	3	1	0	12	0	1	0	0	1	1	.267	.290	.333	.624

Year	Team	Lg	G	AB	H	2B	3B	HR	(Hm	Rd)	TB	R	RBI	RC	TBB	IBB	SO	HBP	SH	SF	SB	CS	GDP	Avg	OBP	Slg	OPS
									BATTING												**RUNNING**			**AVERAGES**			
2016	2 Tms	AL	63	101	24	4	0	1	(0	1)	31	16	4	4	4	0	23	0	1	0	0	2	1	.238	.267	.307	.574
2017	2 Tms	AL	28	37	6	1	0	0	(0	0)	7	2	0	1	5	0	15	0	1	0	0	1	0	.162	.262	.189	.451
16	Cle	AL	59	95	23	4	0	1	(0	1)	30	15	4	4	3	0	21	0	1	0	0	2	1	.242	.265	.316	.581
16	Bos	AL	4	6	1	0	0	0	(0	0)	1	1	0	0	1	0	2	0	0	0	0	0	0	.167	.286	.167	.452
17	Cle	AL	15	11	4	1	0	0	(0	0)	5	1	0	1	2	0	5	0	1	0	0	1	0	.364	.462	.455	.916
17	TB	AL	13	26	2	0	0	0	(0	0)	2	1	0	0	3	0	10	0	0	0	0	0	0	.077	.172	.077	.249
	Postseason		9	4	0	0	0	0	(0	0)	0	2	0	0	0	0	3	0	0	0	0	0	0	.000	.000	.000	.000
	7 ML YEARS		295	571	111	16	2	6	(2	4)	149	67	42	37	37	3	131	0	11	2	4	4	9	.194	.243	.261	.504

Nick Martinez

Pitches: R **Bats:** L **Pos:** SP-18; RP-5   **Ht:** 6'1" **Wt:** 200 **Born:** 8/5/1990 **Age:** 27

Year	Team	Lg	G	GS	CG	GF	IP	BFP	H	R	ER	HR	SH	SF	HB	TBB	IBB	SO	WP	Bk	W	L	Pct	Sh	Sv-Op	Hld	ERC	ERA
				HOW MUCH HE PITCHED							**WHAT HE GAVE UP**												**THE RESULTS**					
2017	RdRck*	AAA	7	6	1	0	37.2	149	27	9	9	3	0	0	3	7	0	23	0	0	4	0	1.000	1	0- -	-	2.00	2.15
2014	Tex	AL	29	24	0	3	140.1	610	150	91	71	18	1	6	3	55	1	77	7	0	5	12	.294	0	0-0	2	4.76	4.55
2015	Tex	AL	24	21	0	1	125.0	558	135	66	55	16	1	5	13	46	2	77	4	0	7	7	.500	0	0-0	0	4.99	3.96
2016	Tex	AL	12	5	0	2	38.2	179	45	24	24	8	0	0	5	19	1	16	0	0	2	3	.400	0	0-0	0	6.86	5.59
2017	Tex	AL	23	18	0	2	111.1	478	124	74	70	26	2	1	2	28	0	67	3	0	3	8	.273	0	0-0	0	5.14	5.66
	4 ML YEARS		88	68	0	8	415.1	1825	454	243	220	68	4	12	23	148	4	237	14	0	17	30	.362	0	0-0	2	5.13	4.77

Victor Martinez

Bats: B **Throws:** R **Pos:** DH-104;PH-3   **Ht:** 6'2" **Wt:** 210 **Born:** 12/23/1978 **Age:** 39

Year	Team	Lg	G	AB	H	2B	3B	HR	(Hm	Rd)	TB	R	RBI	RC	TBB	IBB	SO	HBP	SH	SF	SB	CS	GDP	Avg	OBP	Slg	OPS
									BATTING												**RUNNING**			**AVERAGES**			
2002	Cle	AL	12	32	9	1	0	1	(1	0)	13	2	5	5	3	0	2	0	0	1	0	0	1	.281	.333	.406	.740
2003	Cle	AL	49	159	46	4	0	1	(0	1)	53	15	16	17	13	0	21	1	0	1	1	1	8	.289	.345	.333	.678
2004	Cle	AL	141	520	147	38	1	23	(8	15)	256	77	108	90	60	11	69	5	0	6	0	1	16	.283	.359	.492	.851
2005	Cle	AL	147	547	167	33	0	20	(10	10)	260	73	80	90	63	9	78	5	0	7	0	1	16	.305	.378	.475	.853
2006	Cle	AL	153	572	181	37	0	16	(4	12)	266	82	93	96	71	8	78	3	0	6	0	0	27	.316	.391	.465	.856
2007	Cle	AL	147	562	169	40	0	25	(12	13)	284	78	114	108	62	12	76	10	0	11	0	0	19	.301	.374	.505	.879
2008	Cle	AL	73	266	74	17	0	2	(2	0)	97	30	35	36	24	4	32	1	0	3	0	0	12	.278	.337	.365	.701
2009	2 Tms	AL	155	588	178	33	1	23	(7	16)	282	88	108	101	75	3	74	3	0	6	1	1	17	.303	.381	.480	.861
2010	Bos	AL	127	493	149	32	1	20	(10	10)	243	64	79	79	40	5	52	0	0	5	1	0	17	.302	.351	.493	.844
2011	Det	AL	145	540	178	40	0	12	(5	7)	254	76	103	103	46	6	51	2	0	7	1	0	20	.330	.380	.470	.850
2013	Det	AL	159	605	182	36	0	14	(7	7)	260	68	83	75	54	10	62	1	0	8	0	2	23	.301	.355	.430	.785
2014	Det	AL	151	561	188	33	0	32	(15	17)	317	87	103	115	70	28	42	4	0	6	3	2	17	.335	.409	.565	.974
2015	Det	AL	120	440	108	20	0	11	(6	5)	161	39	64	41	31	8	52	7	0	7	0	0	18	.245	.301	.366	.667
2016	Det	AL	154	553	160	22	0	27	(12	15)	263	65	86	82	50	8	90	4	0	3	0	0	19	.289	.351	.476	.826
2017	Det	AL	107	392	100	16	0	10	(5	5)	146	38	47	42	36	3	63	5	0	2	0	0	15	.255	.324	.372	.697
09	Cle	AL	99	377	107	21	1	15	(6	9)	175	56	67	64	51	3	51	2	0	5	0	0	11	.284	.368	.464	.832
09	Bos	AL	56	211	71	12	0	8	(1	7)	107	32	41	37	24	0	23	1	0	1	1	0	6	.336	.405	.507	.912
	Postseason		39	149	47	8	1	6	(4	2)	75	22	22	25	11	3	23	3	0	0	0	0	1	.315	.374	.503	.878
	15 ML YEARS		1840	6830	2036	402	3	237	(104	133)	3155	882	1124	1075	698	115	842	51	0	79	7	7	245	.298	.364	.462	.826

Jeff Mathis

Bats: R **Throws:** R **Pos:** C-58;PH-2   **Ht:** 6'0" **Wt:** 205 **Born:** 3/31/1983 **Age:** 35

Year	Team	Lg	G	AB	H	2B	3B	HR	(Hm	Rd)	TB	R	RBI	RC	TBB	IBB	SO	HBP	SH	SF	SB	CS	GDP	Avg	OBP	Slg	OPS
									BATTING												**RUNNING**			**AVERAGES**			
2005	LAA	AL	5	3	1	0	0	0	(0	0)	1	1	0	0	0	0	1	0	0	0	0	0	0	.333	.333	.333	.667
2006	LAA	AL	23	55	8	2	0	2	(1	1)	16	9	6	4	7	1	14	0	0	1	0	0	0	.145	.238	.291	.529
2007	LAA	AL	59	171	36	12	0	4	(3	1)	60	24	23	13	15	0	49	2	3	4	0	1	3	.211	.276	.351	.627
2008	LAA	AL	94	283	55	8	0	9	(4	5)	90	35	42	33	30	4	90	3	8	4	2	2	1	.194	.275	.318	.593
2009	LAA	AL	84	237	50	8	0	5	(3	2)	73	26	28	24	22	0	73	4	8	1	2	3	2	.211	.288	.308	.596
2010	LAA	AL	68	205	40	6	1	3	(2	1)	57	19	18	10	6	0	59	1	3	3	3	0	3	.195	.219	.278	.497
2011	LAA	AL	93	247	43	12	0	3	(1	2)	64	18	22	12	15	2	75	2	14	3	1	2	3	.174	.225	.259	.484
2012	Tor	AL	71	211	46	13	0	8	(5	3)	83	25	27	18	9	0	68	1	1	0	2	1	3	.218	.249	.393	.642
2013	Mia	NL	73	232	42	7	1	5	(3	2)	66	14	29	15	21	4	76	1	1	1	0	0	5	.181	.251	.284	.535
2014	Mia	NL	64	175	35	7	0	2	(1	1)	48	12	12	11	15	2	64	0	5	0	0	0	2	.200	.263	.274	.537
2015	Mia	NL	32	93	15	4	1	2	(1	1)	27	9	12	9	3	1	24	0	0	3	0	0	1	.161	.214	.290	.504
2016	Mia	NL	41	126	30	4	1	2	(0	2)	42	12	15	10	4	0	36	1	1	0	0	0	1	.238	.267	.333	.601
2017	Ari	NL	60	186	40	10	2	2	(2	0)	60	13	11	14	14	1	61	2	1	0	1	0	6	.215	.277	.323	.601
	Postseason		10	20	9	5	0	0	(0	0)	14	2	2	3	0	0	5	0	1	0	0	0	0	.450	.450	.700	1.150
	13 ML YEARS		767	2224	441	93	6	47	(26	21)	687	217	245	167	165	15	690	16	50	21	10	8	30	.198	.256	.309	.565

Phil Maton

Pitches: R **Bats:** R **Pos:** RP-46   **Ht:** 6'3" **Wt:** 220 **Born:** 3/25/1993 **Age:** 25

Year	Team	Lg	G	GS	CG	GF	IP	BFP	H	R	ER	HR	SH	SF	HB	TBB	IBB	SO	WP	Bk	W	L	Pct	Sh	Sv-Op	Hld	ERC	ERA
				HOW MUCH HE PITCHED							**WHAT HE GAVE UP**												**THE RESULTS**					
2015	TriCity	A-	23	0	0	16	32.2	126	23	6	5	0	1	0	0	5	0	58	1	0	4	2	.667	0	6- -	-	1.31	1.38
2016	2 Tms	Low	33	0	0	24	45.2	180	31	12	9	2	3	1	0	9	0	66	4	0	4	3	.571	0	10- -	-	1.46	1.77
2016	ElPaso	AAA	5	0	0	2	6.0	21	1	1	1	1	0	0	0	2	0	12	0	0	1	0	1.000	0	1- -	-	0.75	1.50
2017	ElPaso	AAA	23	0	0	22	25.1	104	22	10	8	1	0	2	0	8	0	31	1	0	1	1	.500	0	13- -	-	2.67	2.84
2017	SD	NL	46	0	0	12	43.0	180	41	23	20	10	0	0	1	14	0	46	0	0	3	2	.600	0	1-1	8	4.56	4.19

Steven Matz

Pitches: L Bats: R Pos: SP-13   Ht: 6'2" Wt: 200 Born: 5/29/1991 Age: 27

			HOW MUCH HE PITCHED							WHAT HE GAVE UP										THE RESULTS					
Year	Team	Lg	G	GS	CG	GF	IP	BFP	H	R	ER	HR	SH	SF	HB	TBB	IBB	SO	WP	Bk	W	L	Pct	Sh	Sv-Op	Hld	ERC	ERA
2015	NYM	NL	6	6	0	0	35.2	149	34	9	9	4	1	1	1	10	0	34	0	0	4	0	1.000	0	0-0	0	3.55	2.27
2016	NYM	NL	22	22	0	0	132.1	547	129	53	50	14	8	1	5	31	2	129	3	1	9	8	.529	0	0-0	0	3.49	3.40
2017	NYM	NL	13	13	0	0	66.2	298	83	46	45	12	3	1	3	19	2	48	1	0	2	7	.222	0	0-0	0	5.78	6.08
	Postseason		3	3	0	0	14.2	64	17	6	6	0	0	0	0	4	1	13	0	0	0	1	.000	0	0-0	0	3.60	3.68
	3 ML YEARS		41	41	0	0	234.2	994	246	108	104	30	12	3	9	60	4	211	4	1	15	15	.500	0	0-0	0	4.11	3.99

Joe Mauer

Bats: L Throws: R Pos: 1B-125;DH-13;PH-7   Ht: 6'5" Wt: 225 Born: 4/19/1983 Age: 35

								BATTING														RUNNING			AVERAGES			
Year	Team	Lg	G	AB	H	2B	3B	HR	(Hm	Rd)	TB	R	RBI	RC	TBB	IBB	SO	HBP	SH	SF	SB	CS	GDP	Avg	OBP	Slg	OPS
2004	Min	AL	35	107	33	8	1	6	(4	2)	61	18	17	21	11	0	14	1	0	3	1	0	1	.308	.369	.570	.939
2005	Min	AL	131	489	144	26	2	9	(4	5)	201	61	55	78	61	12	64	1	0	3	13	1	9	.294	.372	.411	.783
2006	Min	AL	140	521	181	36	4	13	(3	10)	264	86	84	103	79	21	54	1	0	7	8	3	24	.347	.429	.507	.936
2007	Min	AL	109	406	119	27	3	7	(2	5)	173	62	60	69	57	10	51	3	2	3	7	1	11	.293	.382	.426	.808
2008	Min	AL	146	536	176	31	4	9	(7	2)	242	98	85	103	84	8	50	1	1	11	1	1	21	.328	.413	.451	.864
2009	Min	AL	138	523	191	30	1	28	(16	12)	307	94	96	123	76	14	63	2	0	5	4	1	13	.365	.444	.587	1.031
2010	Min	AL	137	510	167	43	1	9	(1	8)	239	88	75	91	65	14	53	3	0	6	1	4	19	.327	.402	.469	.871
2011	Min	AL	82	296	85	15	0	3	(0	3)	109	38	30	39	32	7	38	3	0	2	0	0	9	.287	.360	.368	.729
2012	Min	AL	147	545	174	31	4	10	(4	6)	243	81	85	108	90	10	88	2	1	3	8	4	23	.319	.416	.446	.861
2013	Min	AL	113	445	144	35	0	11	(5	6)	212	62	47	74	61	7	89	0	0	2	0	1	7	.324	.404	.476	.880
2014	Min	AL	120	455	126	27	2	4	(3	1)	169	60	55	66	60	12	96	1	0	2	3	0	12	.277	.361	.371	.732
2015	Min	AL	158	592	157	34	2	10	(6	4)	225	69	66	85	67	12	112	1	1	5	2	1	22	.265	.338	.380	.718
2016	Min	AL	134	494	129	22	4	11	(3	8)	192	68	49	75	79	10	93	1	0	2	2	0	11	.261	.363	.389	.752
2017	Min	AL	141	525	160	36	1	7	(5	2)	219	69	71	90	66	3	83	3	0	3	2	1	17	.305	.384	.417	.801
	Postseason		9	35	10	1	0	0	(0	0)	11	1	1	2	4	0	7	0	0	0	0	0	0	.286	.359	.314	.673
	14 ML YEARS		1731	6444	1986	401	29	137	(63	74)	2856	954	875	1125	888	140	948	23	5	57	52	18	199	.308	.391	.443	.834

Brandon Maurer

Pitches: R Bats: R Pos: RP-68   MAUW-er   Ht: 6'5" Wt: 230 Born: 7/3/1990 Age: 27

				HOW MUCH HE PITCHED						WHAT HE GAVE UP										THE RESULTS					
Year	Team	Lg	G	GS	CG	GF	IP	BFP	H	R	ER	HR	SH	SF	HB	TBB	IBB	SO	WP	Bk	W	L	Pct	Sh	Sv-Op	Hld	ERC	ERA
2013	Sea	AL	22	14	0	3	90.0	402	114	66	63	16	1	2	6	27	0	70	9	0	5	8	.385	0	0-0	0	6.20	6.30
2014	Sea	AL	38	7	0	4	69.2	301	74	39	36	6	2	3	0	19	2	55	3	0	1	4	.200	0	0-1	5	3.70	4.65
2015	SD	NL	53	0	0	10	51.0	206	39	19	17	3	1	2	1	15	1	39	1	0	7	4	.636	0	0-1	12	2.23	3.00
2016	SD	NL	71	0	0	36	69.2	300	65	37	35	7	0	1	2	23	5	72	3	0	0	5	.000	0	13-19	15	3.35	4.52
2017	2 Tms		68	0	0	43	59.1	267	73	43	43	8	0	2	1	19	2	59	1	0	3	6	.333	0	22-26	6	5.31	6.52
17	SD	NL	42	0	0	33	39.1	162	39	25	25	4	0	1	1	8	1	38	1	0	1	4	.200	0	20-23	2	3.36	5.72
17	KC	AL	26	0	0	10	20.0	105	34	18	18	4	0	1	0	11	1	21	0	0	2	2	.500	0	2-3	4	9.73	8.10
	5 ML YEARS		252	21	0	96	339.2	1476	365	204	194	40	4	10	10	103	10	295	17	0	16	27	.372	0	35-47	36	4.27	5.14

Bruce Maxwell

Bats: L Throws: R Pos: C-74;PH-11   Ht: 6'1" Wt: 250 Born: 12/20/1990 Age: 27

								BATTING														RUNNING			AVERAGES			
Year	Team	Lg	G	AB	H	2B	3B	HR	(Hm	Rd)	TB	R	RBI	RC	TBB	IBB	SO	HBP	SH	SF	SB	CS	GDP	Avg	OBP	Slg	OPS
2013	2 Tms	Low	104	374	103	22	0	7	(-	-)	146	44	49	54	43	1	63	1	3	4	0	0	9	.275	.348	.390	.739
2014	Stckton	A+	79	289	79	11	1	6	(-	-)	110	33	35	43	41	1	58	2	0	2	0	1	3	.273	.365	.381	.746
2014	Mdlnd	AA	25	85	12	3	0	0	(-	-)	15	8	2	1	9	0	32	0	0	0	0	1	6	.141	.223	.176	.400
2015	Mdlnd	AA	96	338	82	16	0	2	(-	-)	104	32	48	36	39	1	54	1	1	2	0	1	14	.243	.321	.308	.629
2016	Nashv	AAA	60	193	62	12	0	10	(-	-)	104	27	41	40	24	0	38	0	0	2	1	0	5	.321	.393	.539	.932
2017	Nashv	AAA	25	84	24	9	0	2	(-	-)	39	11	14	13	8	0	14	0	0	1	0	0	4	.286	.344	.464	.808
2016	Oak	AL	33	92	26	6	1	1	(1	0)	37	8	14	13	8	0	24	0	0	1	0	0	3	.283	.337	.402	.739
2017	Oak	AL	76	219	52	12	0	3	(0	3)	73	21	22	23	31	0	63	0	1	2	0	0	10	.237	.329	.333	.663
	2 ML YEARS		109	311	78	18	1	4	(1	3)	110	29	36	36	39	0	87	0	1	3	0	0	12	.251	.331	.354	.685

Jacob May

Bats: B Throws: R Pos: CF-10;LF-3;RF-2;PH-1;PR-1   Ht: 5'10" Wt: 180 Born: 1/23/1992 Age: 26

								BATTING														RUNNING			AVERAGES			
Year	Team	Lg	G	AB	H	2B	3B	HR	(Hm	Rd)	TB	R	RBI	RC	TBB	IBB	SO	HBP	SH	SF	SB	CS	GDP	Avg	OBP	Slg	OPS
2013	2 Tms	Low	66	251	76	7	4	8	(-	-)	115	41	35	45	23	0	49	6	3	2	24	6	1	.303	.372	.458	.831
2014	WinSa	A+	109	415	107	11	10	2	(-	-)	164	66	27	60	42	0	71	1	12	2	37	8	5	.258	.326	.395	.721
2015	Brham	AA	98	389	107	15	1	2	(-	-)	130	47	32	46	29	0	73	3	9	2	37	17	6	.275	.329	.334	.663
2016	Charlt	AAA	83	301	80	19	2	1	(-	-)	106	38	24	34	15	0	72	4	1	0	19	8	2	.266	.309	.352	.662
2017	Charlt	AAA	110	415	103	10	5	4	(-	-)	135	54	27	46	30	1	112	5	17	0	31	8	9	.248	.307	.325	.632
2017	CWS	AL	15	36	2	0	0	0	(0	0)	2	2	3	0	3	0	17	1	2	0	0	0	1	.056	.150	.056	.206

Cameron Maybin

Bats: R Throws: R Pos: CF-57;LF-50;RF-10;PH-6;PR-2;DH-1   Ht: 6'3" Wt: 215 Born: 4/4/1987 Age: 31

Year	Team	Lg	G	AB	H	2B	3B	HR	(Hm	Rd)	TB	R	RBI	RC	TBB	IBB	SO	HBP	SH	SF	SB	CS	GDP	Avg	OBP	Slg	OPS
2007	Det	AL	24	49	7	3	0	1	(0	1)	13	8	2	2	3	0	21	1	0	0	5	0	0	.143	.208	.265	.473
2008	Fla	NL	8	32	16	2	0	0	(0	0)	18	9	2	8	3	0	8	0	1	0	4	0	0	.500	.543	.563	1.105
2009	Fla	NL	54	176	44	12	2	4	(1	3)	72	30	13	15	17	1	51	1	4	1	1	3	2	.250	.318	.409	.727
2010	Fla	NL	82	291	68	7	3	8	(5	3)	105	46	28	37	24	1	92	5	1	1	9	2	4	.234	.302	.361	.663
2011	SD	NL	137	516	136	24	8	9	(2	7)	203	82	40	69	44	2	125	2	4	2	40	8	6	.264	.323	.393	.716
2012	SD	NL	147	507	123	20	5	8	(3	5)	177	67	45	52	44	1	110	4	3	3	26	7	12	.243	.306	.349	.656
2013	SD	NL	14	51	8	1	0	1	(0	1)	12	7	5	0	4	1	9	1	1	0	4	1	3	.157	.232	.235	.467
2014	SD	NL	95	251	59	13	4	1	(0	1)	83	24	15	22	19	2	56	1	1	0	4	3	8	.235	.290	.331	.621
2015	Atl	NL	141	505	135	18	2	10	(5	5)	187	65	59	64	45	1	102	1	1	3	23	6	16	.267	.327	.370	.697
2016	Det	AL	94	349	110	14	5	4	(3	1)	146	65	43	60	36	0	69	3	2	1	15	6	8	.315	.383	.418	.801
2017	2 Tms	AL	114	395	90	20	2	10	(3	7)	144	63	35	51	51	1	94	2	1	1	33	8	12	.228	.318	.365	.683
17	LAA	AL	93	336	79	19	1	6	(2	4)	118	57	22	42	48	1	78	2	0	1	29	5	11	.235	.333	.351	.685
17	Hou	AL	21	59	11	1	1	4	(1	3)	26	6	13	9	3	0	16	0	1	0	4	3	1	.186	.226	.441	.666
11 ML YEARS			910	3122	796	134	31	56	(22	34)	1160	466	287	380	290	10	737	21	18	13	164	44	71	.255	.321	.372	.693

Mike Mayers

Pitches: R Bats: R Pos: RP-3   MY-erz   Ht: 6'3" Wt: 200 Born: 12/6/1991 Age: 26

	HOW MUCH HE PITCHED						WHAT HE GAVE UP												THE RESULTS							
Year	Team	Lg	G	GS	CG	GF	IP	BFP	H	R	ER	HR	SH	SF	HB	TBB	IBB	SO	WP	Bk	W	L	Pct	Sh	Sv-Op	Hld	ERC	ERA
2013	2 Tms	Low	14	8	0	0	36.1	149	35	14	12	3	0	0	1	11	1	27	3	1	1	3	.250	0	0--	-	3.55	2.97
2014	PlmBh	A+	12	12	1	0	72.2	306	84	35	30	5	2	3	2	13	0	61	1	0	2	7	.222	0	0--	-	4.03	3.72
2014	Sprgfld	AA	13	13	0	0	76.1	325	81	29	24	2	1	5	4	23	0	52	2	1	6	5	.545	0	0--	-	3.77	2.83
2015	Sprgfld	AA	10	10	1	0	46.2	211	53	39	34	8	1	2	5	21	0	36	7	1	1	4	.200	1	0--	-	6.18	6.56
2016	Sprgfld	AA	9	9	0	0	54.2	224	47	17	14	4	0	1	1	17	0	43	3	1	5	2	.714	0	0--	-	2.90	2.30
2016	Memp	AAA	16	16	1	0	89.1	379	87	44	37	8	1	2	5	31	2	84	2	0	4	8	.333	0	0--	-	3.88	3.73
2017	Memp	AAA	31	15	0	3	109.2	477	117	44	40	12	5	2	4	32	1	97	1	0	5	6	.455	0	0--	-	4.17	3.28
2016	StL	NL	4	1	0	0	5.1	35	16	16	16	3	0	1	1	3	0	2	0	0	1	1	.500	0	0-0	0	25.90	27.00
2017	StL	NL	3	0	0	1	4.2	25	8	8	6	2	0	2	0	4	1	3	0	0	0	0	-	0	0-0	0	13.79	11.57
2 ML YEARS			7	1	0	1	10.0	60	24	24	22	5	0	3	1	7	1	5	0	0	1	1	.500	0	0-0	0	20.05	19.80

Tim Mayza

Pitches: L Bats: L Pos: RP-19   Ht: 6'3" Wt: 220 Born: 1/15/1992 Age: 26

	HOW MUCH HE PITCHED						WHAT HE GAVE UP												THE RESULTS							
Year	Team	Lg	G	GS	CG	GF	IP	BFP	H	R	ER	HR	SH	SF	HB	TBB	IBB	SO	WP	Bk	W	L	Pct	Sh	Sv-Op	Hld	ERC	ERA
2013	2 Tms	Low	13	5	0	1	29.0	139	41	28	25	2	1	1	1	12	1	27	4	0	1	4	.200	0	1--	-	6.36	7.76
2014	2 Tms	Low	16	0	0	3	26.2	131	38	25	20	2	0	2	3	16	0	20	6	0	2	4	.333	0	1--	-	7.95	6.75
2015	Lnsng	A	26	1	0	10	55.2	236	49	21	19	0	1	2	0	27	1	62	6	1	3	2	.600	0	3--	-	3.05	3.07
2016	Dnedin	A+	28	0	0	12	48.2	199	36	16	9	1	3	2	0	15	0	52	1	0	2	0	1.000	0	4--	-	1.86	1.66
2016	Nham	AA	14	0	0	2	15.1	75	16	10	7	0	2	0	0	15	0	13	2	0	1	3	.250	0	0--	-	5.81	4.11
2017	Nham	AA	29	0	0	17	33.1	146	32	18	17	5	1	2	1	15	2	42	1	0	1	1	.500	0	4--	-	4.39	4.59
2017	Buffalo	AAA	11	0	0	3	19.1	81	16	2	2	0	0	1	0	7	0	16	0	0	1	1	.500	0	0--	-	2.32	0.93
2017	Tor	AL	19	0	0	7	17.0	79	24	15	13	3	0	0	1	4	0	27	0	0	1	0	1.000	0	0-0	2	6.27	6.88

Nomar Mazara

Bats: L Throws: L Pos: RF-92;LF-47;DH-13;PH-6   Ht: 6'4" Wt: 215 Born: 4/26/1995 Age: 23

Year	Team	Lg	G	AB	H	2B	3B	HR	(Hm	Rd)	TB	R	RBI	RC	TBB	IBB	SO	HBP	SH	SF	SB	CS	GDP	Avg	OBP	Slg	OPS
2013	Hkry	A	126	453	107	23	2	13	(-	-)	173	48	62	56	44	0	131	6	0	3	1	2	6	.236	.310	.382	.692
2014	Hkry	A	106	398	105	21	2	19	(-	-)	187	68	73	69	57	2	99	3	0	3	4	3	9	.264	.358	.470	.828
2014	Frisco	AA	24	85	26	7	1	3	(-	-)	44	10	16	16	9	0	22	2	0	1	0	0	3	.306	.381	.518	.899
2015	Frisco	AA	111	409	116	22	2	13	(-	-)	181	57	56	69	47	0	92	5	0	9	2	0	10	.284	.357	.443	.800
2015	RdRck	AAA	20	81	29	4	0	1	(-	-)	36	11	13	14	5	1	10	2	0	0	0	0	1	.358	.409	.444	.854
2016	Tex	AL	145	516	137	13	3	20	(7	13)	216	59	64	67	39	1	112	6	0	7	0	2	12	.266	.320	.419	.739
2017	Tex	AL	148	554	140	30	2	20	(11	9)	234	64	101	87	55	6	127	4	0	3	2	2	12	.253	.323	.422	.745
Postseason			2	6	1	0	0	0	(0	0)	1	0	0	0	0	0	3	0	0	0	0	0	0	.167	.167	.167	.333
2 ML YEARS			293	1070	277	43	5	40	(18	22)	450	123	165	154	94	7	239	10	0	10	2	4	24	.259	.322	.421	.742

Cory Mazzoni

Pitches: R Bats: R Pos: RP-6   Ht: 6'1" Wt: 210 Born: 10/19/1989 Age: 28

	HOW MUCH HE PITCHED						WHAT HE GAVE UP												THE RESULTS							
Year	Team	Lg	G	GS	CG	GF	IP	BFP	H	R	ER	HR	SH	SF	HB	TBB	IBB	SO	WP	Bk	W	L	Pct	Sh	Sv-Op	Hld	ERC	ERA
2013	Bnghtn	AA	13	12	0	0	66.0	282	70	43	32	4	4	2	2	19	0	74	2	1	5	3	.625	0	0--	-	3.83	4.36
2014	LsVgs	AAA	9	9	0	0	52.0	220	54	29	27	6	3	1	3	12	0	49	0	0	5	1	.833	0	0--	-	3.97	4.67
2015	ElPaso	AAA	26	0	0	9	34.0	142	25	17	15	0	1	2	0	12	1	46	1	1	1	3	.250	0	5--	-	1.79	3.97
2017	ElPaso	AAA	14	0	0	8	20.1	82	18	2	2	0	0	1	0	3	0	31	1	0	1	0	1.000	0	1--	-	1.91	0.89
2017	Padres	R	7	0	0	1	8.0	30	7	0	0	0	0	1	0	0	0	15	1	0	1	0	1.000	0	0--	-	1.54	0.00
2015	SD	NL	8	0	0	4	8.2	53	23	22	20	2	0	1	0	5	0	8	0	0	0	0	-	0	0-0	0	17.75	20.77
2017	SD	NL	6	0	0	3	8.0	46	17	16	12	5	0	0	1	4	0	4	0	0	0	0	-	0	0-0	0	17.74	13.50
2 ML YEARS			14	0	0	7	16.2	99	40	38	32	7	0	1	1	9	0	12	0	0	0	0	-	0	0-0	0	17.82	17.28

Zach McAllister

Pitches: R **Bats:** R **Pos:** RP-50
Ht: 6'6" **Wt:** 240 **Born:** 12/8/1987 **Age:** 30

Year	Team	Lg	G	GS	CG	GF	IP	BFP	H	R	ER	HR	SH	SF	HB	TBB	IBB	SO	WP	Bk	W	L	Pct	Sh	Sv-Op	Hld	ERC	ERA
2011	Cle	AL	4	4	0	0	17.2	84	26	16	12	1	0	0	0	7	1	14	0	0	1	0	.000	0	0-0	0	6.41	6.11
2012	Cle	AL	22	22	0	0	125.1	543	133	78	59	19	2	5	1	38	0	110	0	2	6	8	.429	0	0-0	0	4.37	4.24
2013	Cle	AL	24	24	0	0	134.1	579	134	65	56	13	0	3	6	49	2	101	7	1	9	9	.500	0	0-0	0	4.06	3.75
2014	Cle	AL	22	15	0	2	86.0	377	96	54	50	7	1	5	0	28	1	74	3	0	4	7	.364	0	0-0	1	4.24	5.23
2015	Cle	AL	61	1	0	9	69.0	299	70	28	23	7	1	1	3	23	4	84	3	0	4	4	.500	0	1-2	12	3.95	3.00
2016	Cle	AL	53	2	0	11	52.1	233	53	21	20	6	1	0	2	23	2	54	3	0	3	2	.600	0	0-1	7	4.43	3.44
2017	Cle	AL	50	0	0	18	62.0	249	53	18	18	8	1	0	1	21	0	66	3	0	2	2	.500	0	0-0	0	3.42	2.61
	Postseason		3	0	0	0	3.0	14	4	3	3	0	0	0	0	1	0	2	0	0	0	0	-	0	0-0	0	4.83	9.00
7 ML YEARS			236	68	0	40	546.2	2364	565	280	238	61	6	14	13	189	10	503	19	3	28	33	.459	0	1-3	22	4.18	3.92

Brian McCann

Bats: L **Throws:** R **Pos:** C-95;DH-2;PH-1
Ht: 6'3" **Wt:** 225 **Born:** 2/20/1984 **Age:** 34

Year	Team	Lg	G	AB	H	2B	3B	HR	(Hm	Rd)	TB	R	RBI	RC	TBB	IBB	SO	HBP	SH	SF	SB	CS	GDP	Avg	OBP	Slg	OPS
2005	Atl	NL	59	180	50	7	0	5	(2	3)	72	20	23	25	18	5	26	1	4	1	1	1	5	.278	.345	.400	.745
2006	Atl	NL	130	442	147	34	0	24	(10	14)	253	61	93	94	41	8	54	3	0	6	2	0	12	.333	.388	.572	.961
2007	Atl	NL	139	504	136	38	0	18	(6	12)	228	51	92	68	35	7	74	5	2	6	0	1	19	.270	.320	.452	.772
2008	Atl	NL	145	509	153	42	1	23	(10	13)	266	68	87	84	57	4	64	4	0	3	5	0	17	.301	.373	.523	.896
2009	Atl	NL	138	488	137	35	1	21	(12	9)	237	63	94	83	49	3	83	5	3	6	4	1	17	.281	.349	.486	.834
2010	Atl	NL	143	479	129	25	0	21	(13	8)	217	63	77	76	74	10	98	9	0	4	5	2	12	.269	.375	.453	.828
2011	Atl	NL	128	466	126	19	0	24	(15	9)	217	51	71	76	57	14	89	2	0	2	3	2	10	.270	.351	.466	.817
2012	Atl	NL	121	439	101	14	0	20	(11	9)	175	44	67	45	44	7	76	1	0	3	0	1	15	.230	.300	.399	.698
2013	Atl	NL	102	356	91	13	0	20	(12	8)	164	43	57	51	39	3	66	5	0	2	0	1	9	.256	.336	.461	.796
2014	NYY	AL	140	495	115	15	1	23	(19	4)	201	57	75	58	32	1	77	7	0	4	0	0	16	.232	.286	.406	.692
2015	NYY	AL	135	465	108	15	1	26	(16	10)	203	68	94	77	52	3	97	11	0	7	0	0	7	.232	.320	.437	.756
2016	NYY	AL	130	429	104	13	0	20	(11	9)	177	56	58	51	54	2	99	7	0	2	1	0	15	.242	.335	.413	.748
2017	Hou	AL	97	349	84	12	1	18	(7	11)	152	47	62	46	38	3	58	7	0	5	1	0	9	.241	.323	.436	.759
	Postseason		13	47	9	1	0	3	(2	1)	19	4	9	5	5	0	16	0	0	1	0	0	0	.191	.264	.404	.668
13 ML YEARS			1607	5601	1481	282	5	263	(144	119)	2562	692	950	834	590	70	961	67	9	51	25	8	163	.264	.339	.457	.796

James McCann

Bats: R **Throws:** R **Pos:** C-103;PH-5;DH-3
Ht: 6'2" **Wt:** 210 **Born:** 6/13/1990 **Age:** 28

Year	Team	Lg	G	AB	H	2B	3B	HR	(Hm	Rd)	TB	R	RBI	RC	TBB	IBB	SO	HBP	SH	SF	SB	CS	GDP	Avg	OBP	Slg	OPS
2014	Det	AL	9	12	3	1	0	0	(0	0)	4	2	0	1	0	0	2	0	0	0	1	0	0	.250	.250	.333	.583
2015	Det	AL	114	401	106	18	5	7	(5	2)	155	32	41	34	16	0	90	3	4	1	0	1	17	.264	.297	.387	.683
2016	Det	AL	105	344	76	9	1	12	(7	5)	123	31	48	30	23	0	109	2	1	3	0	1	12	.221	.272	.358	.629
2017	Det	AL	106	352	89	14	2	13	(8	5)	146	39	49	46	26	0	89	9	1	3	1	0	8	.253	.318	.415	.733
4 ML YEARS			334	1109	274	42	8	32	(20	12)	428	104	138	111	65	0	290	14	6	7	2	2	37	.247	.295	.386	.681

Brandon McCarthy

Pitches: R **Bats:** R **Pos:** SP-16; RP-3
Ht: 6'7" **Wt:** 235 **Born:** 7/7/1983 **Age:** 34

Year	Team	Lg	G	GS	CG	GF	IP	BFP	H	R	ER	HR	SH	SF	HB	TBB	IBB	SO	WP	Bk	W	L	Pct	Sh	Sv-Op	Hld	ERC	ERA
2005	CWS	AL	12	10	0	0	67.0	277	62	30	30	13	1	1	2	17	0	48	1	1	3	2	.600	0	0-0	0	3.83	4.03
2006	CWS	AL	53	2	0	13	84.2	354	77	44	44	17	3	1	0	33	9	69	5	0	4	7	.364	0	0-1	11	4.10	4.68
2007	Tex	AL	23	22	0	0	101.2	459	111	62	55	9	3	5	3	48	0	59	4	1	5	10	.333	0	0-0	0	4.89	4.87
2008	Tex	AL	5	5	0	0	22.0	93	20	11	10	3	0	2	1	8	0	10	0	0	1	1	.500	0	0-0	0	3.87	4.09
2009	Tex	AL	17	17	1	0	97.1	420	96	55	50	13	0	5	3	36	0	65	0	0	7	4	.636	1	0-0	0	4.22	4.62
2011	Oak	AL	25	25	5	0	170.2	690	168	73	63	11	4	9	0	25	1	123	3	0	9	9	.500	1	0-0	0	2.80	3.32
2012	Oak	AL	18	18	0	0	111.0	466	115	44	40	10	5	4	6	24	2	73	0	0	8	6	.571	0	0-0	0	3.67	3.24
2013	Ari	NL	22	22	2	0	135.0	577	161	71	68	13	6	1	5	21	3	76	1	1	5	11	.313	1	0-0	0	4.29	4.53
2014	2 Tms		32	32	1	0	200.0	836	222	100	90	25	3	4	3	33	4	175	4	0	10	15	.400	1	0-0	0	3.98	4.05
2015	LAD	NL	4	4	0	0	23.0	94	24	15	15	9	0	0	0	4	0	19	2	0	3	0	1.000	0	0-0	0	5.39	5.87
2016	LAD	NL	10	9	0	0	40.0	171	29	24	22	2	1	2	2	26	1	44	2	0	2	3	.400	0	0-1	0	3.37	4.95
2017	LAD	NL	19	16	0	0	92.2	384	89	43	41	5	4	3	3	27	0	72	4	0	6	4	.600	0	0-0	0	3.31	3.98
14	Ari	NL	18	18	0	0	109.2	466	131	65	61	15	2	3	2	20	4	93	3	0	3	10	.231	0	0-0	0	4.64	5.01
14	NYY	AL	14	14	1	0	90.1	370	91	35	29	10	1	1	1	13	0	82	1	0	7	5	.583	1	0-0	0	3.23	2.89
12 ML YEARS			240	182	9	13	1145.0	4824	1174	572	528	130	30	37	28	302	20	843	24	3	63	72	.467	4	0-2	11	3.86	4.15

Kevin McCarthy

Pitches: R **Bats:** R **Pos:** RP-33
Ht: 6'3" **Wt:** 200 **Born:** 2/22/1992 **Age:** 26

Year	Team	Lg	G	GS	CG	GF	IP	BFP	H	R	ER	HR	SH	SF	HB	TBB	IBB	SO	WP	Bk	W	L	Pct	Sh	Sv-Op	Hld	ERC	ERA
2013	Burlgtn	R+	10	5	0	1	42.1	172	49	18	16	2	0	0	0	5	0	32	2	0	4	2	.667	0	0- -	-	3.61	3.40
2015	2 Tms	Low	22	0	0	14	45.0	172	34	10	8	2	2	2	0	6	1	31	3	1	4	4	.500	0	6- -	-	1.59	1.60
2015	NWArk	AA	11	0	0	3	17.1	84	24	11	11	1	1	2	0	8	1	9	3	1	1	0	1.000	0	0- -	-	6.00	5.71
2016	NWArk	AA	22	0	0	16	34.2	135	26	12	12	3	1	0	1	8	1	29	4	0	3	2	.600	0	11- -	-	2.19	3.12
2016	Omha	AAA	25	0	0	13	33.1	140	28	15	10	4	1	0	1	16	2	30	1	0	2	4	.333	0	5- -	-	3.73	2.70
2017	Omha	AAA	25	0	0	8	32.0	127	32	12	11	3	0	1	0	9	0	17	0	0	1	1	.500	0	2- -	-	3.81	3.09
2016	KC	AL	10	0	0	1	8.1	41	11	8	6	1	1	0	0	5	0	7	0	0	1	0	1.000	0	0-1	0	6.83	6.48
2017	KC	AL	33	0	0	14	45.0	196	50	23	16	4	1	1	0	13	0	27	1	0	1	0	1.000	0	0-0	1	4.13	3.20
2 ML YEARS			43	0	0	15	53.1	237	61	31	22	5	2	1	0	18	0	34	1	0	2	0	1.000	0	0-1	1	4.53	3.71

Lance McCullers Jr.

Pitches: R Bats: L Pos: SP-22 **Ht:** 6'1" **Wt:** 205 **Born:** 10/2/1993 **Age:** 24

		HOW MUCH HE PITCHED						WHAT HE GAVE UP												THE RESULTS							
Year Team	Lg	G	GS	CG	GF	IP	BFP	H	R	ER	HR	SH	SF	HB	TBB	IBB	SO	WP	Bk	W	L	Pct	Sh	Sv-Op	Hld	ERC	ERA
2015 Hou	AL	22	22	1	0	125.2	520	106	49	45	10	0	3	5	43	2	129	8	1	6	7	.462	0	0-0	0	3.02	3.22
2016 Hou	AL	14	14	0	0	81.0	352	80	29	29	5	0	0	0	45	1	106	9	2	6	5	.545	0	0-0	0	4.42	3.22
2017 Hou	AL	22	22	0	0	118.2	512	114	61	56	8	2	2	11	40	1	132	8	1	7	4	.636	0	0-0	0	3.71	4.25
Postseason		1	1	0	0	6.1	25	2	2	2	1	0	0	2	2	0	7	0	0	0	0	-	0	0-0	0	1.80	2.84
3 ML YEARS		58	58	1	0	325.1	1384	300	139	130	23	2	5	16	128	4	367	25	4	19	16	.543	0	0-0	0	3.61	3.60

Andrew McCutchen

Bats: R Throws: R Pos: CF-139;RF-13;DH-2;PH-2 **Ht:** 5'10" **Wt:** 195 **Born:** 10/10/1986 **Age:** 31

		BATTING													RUNNING			AVERAGES								
Year Team	Lg	G	AB	H	2B	3B	HR	Hm	Rd	TB	R	RBI	RC	TBB	IBB	SO	HBP	SH	SF	SB	CS	GDP	Avg	OBP	Slg	OPS
2009 Pit	NL	108	433	124	26	9	12	(8	4)	204	74	54	78	54	2	83	2	0	4	22	5	3	.286	.365	.471	.836
2010 Pit	NL	154	570	163	35	5	16	(8	8)	256	94	56	86	70	1	89	5	1	7	33	10	6	.286	.365	.449	.814
2011 Pit	NL	158	572	148	34	5	23	(10	13)	261	87	89	102	89	3	126	9	2	6	23	10	9	.259	.364	.456	.820
2012 Pit	NL	157	593	194	29	6	31	(15	16)	328	107	96	125	70	12	132	5	0	5	20	12	9	.327	.400	.553	.953
2013 Pit	NL	157	583	185	38	5	21	(9	12)	296	97	84	105	78	12	101	9	0	4	27	10	13	.317	.404	.508	.911
2014 Pit	NL	146	548	172	38	6	25	(10	15)	297	89	83	109	84	8	115	10	0	6	18	3	9	.314	.410	.542	.952
2015 Pit	NL	157	566	165	36	3	23	(13	10)	276	91	96	120	98	12	133	12	0	9	11	5	9	.292	.401	.488	.889
2016 Pit	NL	153	598	153	26	3	24	(10	14)	257	81	79	98	69	7	143	5	0	3	6	7	15	.256	.336	.430	.766
2017 Pit	NL	156	570	159	30	2	28	(9	19)	277	94	88	98	73	5	116	4	0	3	11	5	10	.279	.363	.486	.849
Postseason		8	28	9	1	0	0	(0	0)	10	3	0	5	6	1	4	0	0	0	0	0	0	.321	.441	.357	.798
9 ML YEARS		1346	5033	1463	292	44	203	(92	111)	2452	814	725	906	685	63	1038	61	3	47	171	67	81	.291	.379	.487	.866

T.J. McFarland

Pitches: L Bats: L Pos: RP-42; SP-1 **Ht:** 6'3" **Wt:** 220 **Born:** 6/8/1989 **Age:** 29

		HOW MUCH HE PITCHED						WHAT HE GAVE UP												THE RESULTS							
Year Team	Lg	G	GS	CG	GF	IP	BFP	H	R	ER	HR	SH	SF	HB	TBB	IBB	SO	WP	Bk	W	L	Pct	Sh	Sv-Op	Hld	ERC	ERA
2017 Reno*	AAA	7	0	0	1	11.0	39	6	0	0	0	0	0	0	4	0	9	0	0	0	0	-	0	1--	-	1.41	0.00
2013 Bal	AL	38	1	0	8	74.2	331	83	37	35	7	2	1	0	28	5	58	2	0	4	1	.800	0	0-0	0	4.40	4.22
2014 Bal	AL	37	1	0	14	58.2	255	70	22	18	2	5	0	4	13	2	34	0	0	4	2	.667	0	0-0	5	4.23	2.76
2015 Bal	AL	30	0	0	7	40.1	188	52	26	22	4	0	0	0	18	5	26	3	0	2	2	.500	0	0-0	3	5.68	4.91
2016 Bal	AL	16	0	0	0	24.2	112	33	19	19	3	0	3	2	10	2	7	1	0	2	2	.500	0	0-3	6	6.74	6.93
2017 Ari	NL	43	1	0	22	54.0	241	65	42	32	4	2	3	2	17	6	29	2	0	4	5	.444	0	0-0	2	4.65	5.33
5 ML YEARS		164	3	0	53	252.1	1127	303	146	126	20	9	7	8	86	20	154	8	0	16	12	.571	0	0-3	10	4.83	4.49

Jake McGee

Pitches: L Bats: L Pos: RP-62 **Ht:** 6'3" **Wt:** 230 **Born:** 8/6/1986 **Age:** 31

		HOW MUCH HE PITCHED						WHAT HE GAVE UP												THE RESULTS							
Year Team	Lg	G	GS	CG	GF	IP	BFP	H	R	ER	HR	SH	SF	HB	TBB	IBB	SO	WP	Bk	W	L	Pct	Sh	Sv-Op	Hld	ERC	ERA
2010 TB	AL	8	0	0	3	5.0	20	2	1	1	0	0	0	0	3	0	6	0	0	0	0	-	0	0-0	0	1.32	1.80
2011 TB	AL	37	0	0	9	28.0	124	30	14	14	5	1	0	0	12	1	27	0	0	5	2	.714	0	0-0	4	5.09	4.50
2012 TB	AL	69	0	0	13	55.1	212	33	13	12	3	0	2	1	11	4	73	3	0	5	2	.714	0	0-2	19	1.26	1.95
2013 TB	AL	71	0	0	6	62.2	260	52	28	28	8	1	3	1	22	5	75	4	0	5	3	.625	0	1-5	27	3.07	4.02
2014 TB	AL	73	0	0	31	71.1	274	48	15	15	2	1	1	2	16	1	90	1	0	5	2	.714	0	19-23	14	1.55	1.89
2015 TB	AL	39	0	0	6	37.1	147	27	11	10	3	0	1	1	8	1	48	1	0	1	2	.333	0	6-10	19	1.92	2.41
2016 Col	NL	57	0	0	25	45.2	205	56	25	24	9	0	0	3	16	1	38	4	0	2	3	.400	0	15-19	4	6.26	4.73
2017 Col	NL	62	0	0	13	57.1	229	47	23	23	4	1	1	0	16	0	58	5	0	0	2	.000	0	3-6	20	2.59	3.61
Postseason		5	0	0	1	3.1	17	3	2	2	0	1	0	1	3	1	3	0	0	0	1	.000	0	0-0	2	5.03	5.40
8 ML YEARS		416	0	0	106	362.2	1471	295	130	127	34	4	8	9	104	13	415	18	0	23	16	.590	0	44-65	107	2.67	3.15

Dustin McGowan

Pitches: R Bats: R Pos: RP-63 **Ht:** 6'3" **Wt:** 235 **Born:** 3/24/1982 **Age:** 36

		HOW MUCH HE PITCHED						WHAT HE GAVE UP												THE RESULTS							
Year Team	Lg	G	GS	CG	GF	IP	BFP	H	R	ER	HR	SH	SF	HB	TBB	IBB	SO	WP	Bk	W	L	Pct	Sh	Sv-Op	Hld	ERC	ERA
2005 Tor	AL	13	7	0	2	45.1	205	49	34	32	7	0	4	7	17	0	34	7	0	1	3	.250	0	0-0	1	5.47	6.35
2006 Tor	AL	16	3	0	3	27.1	143	35	27	22	2	0	1	2	25	2	22	3	1	1	2	.333	0	0-1	1	7.72	7.24
2007 Tor	AL	27	27	2	0	169.2	705	146	80	77	14	0	6	2	61	3	144	13	0	12	10	.545	1	0-0	0	3.07	4.08
2008 Tor	AL	19	19	1	0	111.1	474	115	60	54	9	2	8	5	38	1	85	5	0	6	7	.462	0	0-0	0	4.13	4.37
2011 Tor	AL	5	4	0	0	21.0	96	20	15	15	4	0	1	1	13	0	20	3	0	0	2	.000	0	0-0	0	5.50	6.43
2013 Tor	AL	25	0	0	8	25.2	114	19	11	7	2	0	0	2	12	1	26	3	0	0	0	-	0	0-1	6	2.83	2.45
2014 Tor	AL	53	0	0	9	82.0	354	80	41	38	13	0	2	3	33	1	61	2	0	5	3	.625	0	1-5	10	4.50	4.17
2015 Phi	NL	14	1	0	3	23.1	118	29	21	18	7	0	0	0	20	1	21	1	0	1	2	.333	0	0-0	0	9.07	6.94
2016 Mia	NL	55	0	0	24	67.0	279	49	26	21	7	0	2	2	33	7	63	4	0	1	3	.250	0	1-2	3	2.98	2.82
2017 Mia	NL	63	0	0	13	77.2	330	77	42	41	13	4	3	2	27	5	64	5	0	3	2	.600	0	0-3	4	4.32	4.75
10 ML YEARS		290	69	3	62	650.1	2818	619	357	325	78	6	27	26	279	21	540	46	1	35	34	.507	1	2-12	24	4.16	4.50

Kevin McGowan

Pitches: R Bats: R Pos: RP-8 Ht: 6'5" Wt: 233 Born: 10/18/1991 Age: 26

Year	Team	Lg	G	GS	CG	GF	IP	BFP	H	R	ER	HR	SH	SF	HB	TBB	IBB	SO	WP	Bk	W	L	Pct	Sh	Sv-Op	Hld	ERC	ERA
2013	Bklyn	A-	14	1	0	6	30.2	132	33	20	18	2	0	4	8	8	0	27	1	0	0	2	.000	0	3- -	-	4.29	5.28
2014	2 Tms	Low	21	20	1	1	117.2	498	99	54	47	5	4	3	6	46	0	74	7	0	7	7	.500	1	0- -	-	2.96	3.59
2015	Stluci	A+	24	23	0	1	132.0	568	139	77	66	4	6	3	5	49	0	72	8	0	6	10	.375	0	0- -	-	3.89	4.50
2016	Stluci	A+	15	2	0	2	33.0	119	20	4	3	1	0	1	0	4	0	33	2	0	1	0	1.000	0	2- -	-	1.11	0.82
2016	Bnghtn	AA	26	2	0	2	49.2	214	48	20	18	2	5	4	2	17	0	48	3	0	4	1	.800	0	0- -	-	3.36	3.26
2017	LsVgs	AAA	47	1	0	20	65.0	287	63	35	30	4	1	1	1	25	1	57	4	1	6	5	.545	0	4- -	-	3.90	4.15
2017	NYM	NL	8	0	0	1	8.2	40	8	5	5	2	0	0	6	6	0	8	0	0	0	0	-	0	0-0	0	5.68	5.19

Kyle McGrath

Pitches: L Bats: L Pos: RP-17 Ht: 6'2" Wt: 185 Born: 7/31/1992 Age: 25

Year	Team	Lg	G	GS	CG	GF	IP	BFP	H	R	ER	HR	SH	SF	HB	TBB	IBB	SO	WP	Bk	W	L	Pct	Sh	Sv-Op	Hld	ERC	ERA
2014	Padres	R	13	0	0	7	22.2	81	8	3	2	0	0	1	1	6	0	22	1	0	1	1	.500	0	2- -	-	0.71	0.79
2015	FtWyn	A	41	0	0	20	68.2	266	56	15	13	3	0	0	2	8	1	79	1	0	3	0	1.000	0	3- -	-	1.88	1.70
2016	Lk Els	A+	11	0	0	4	17.1	60	8	1	0	0	0	0	1	1	0	26	1	0	1	0	1.000	0	0- -	-	0.65	0.00
2016	SnAnt	AA	33	0	0	9	48.2	181	32	8	7	4	1	0	2	8	0	50	1	1	1	2	.333	0	1- -	-	1.65	1.29
2017	SnAnt	AA	20	0	0	5	23.2	94	16	10	7	2	1	0	1	4	0	27	0	0	1	1	.500	0	0- -	-	1.63	2.66
2017	ElPaso	AAA	5	0	0	2	6.0	22	3	1	1	1	0	0	1	0	0	5	0	0	0	0	-	0	0- -	-	1.30	1.50
2017	SD	NL	17	0	0	8	19.0	75	14	6	6	2	0	2	0	6	1	16	1	0	0	0	-	0	0-0	0	2.39	2.84

Deck McGuire

Pitches: R Bats: R Pos: RP-4; SP-2 Ht: 6'6" Wt: 220 Born: 6/23/1989 Age: 29

Year	Team	Lg	G	GS	CG	GF	IP	BFP	H	R	ER	HR	SH	SF	HB	TBB	IBB	SO	WP	Bk	W	L	Pct	Sh	Sv-Op	Hld	ERC	ERA
2013	Nham	AA	27	26	1	0	157.1	673	148	90	85	12	4	7	4	59	1	143	7	0	9	10	.474	0	0- -	-	3.55	4.86
2014	Nham	AA	10	10	0	0	60.1	257	58	28	20	3	3	1	3	17	0	47	3	0	3	4	.429	0	0- -	-	3.21	2.98
2014	Buffalo	AAA	10	10	0	0	55.0	241	57	37	34	12	2	0	1	23	0	38	1	0	3	5	.375	0	0- -	-	5.29	5.56
2014	Scrmto	AAA	7	6	0	0	34.2	164	49	32	31	5	1	3	0	16	1	16	1	0	2	4	.333	0	0- -	-	7.19	8.05
2015	Tulsa	AA	18	9	0	2	71.0	281	58	28	28	5	2	0	0	19	3	66	4	1	4	2	.667	0	1- -	-	2.43	3.55
2015	OkCity	AAA	12	9	0	2	65.2	270	70	30	28	6	3	2	3	17	1	53	2	0	5	4	.556	0	0- -	-	4.17	3.84
2016	Memp	AAA	26	26	1	0	134.0	569	134	79	76	22	4	1	5	50	4	111	6	1	7	11	.389	1	0- -	-	4.62	5.10
2017	Pnscla	AA	28	27	1	0	168.0	670	125	58	52	13	4	4	4	57	0	170	5	2	9	9	.500	0	0- -	-	2.50	2.79
2017	Cin	NL	6	2	0	2	13.2	56	10	6	4	1	0	0	1	2	0	11	0	0	1	1	.500	0	0-0	0	1.78	2.63

Collin McHugh

Pitches: R Bats: R Pos: SP-12 mick-HYOO Ht: 6'2" Wt: 190 Born: 6/19/1987 Age: 31

Year	Team	Lg	G	GS	CG	GF	IP	BFP	H	R	ER	HR	SH	SF	HB	TBB	IBB	SO	WP	Bk	W	L	Pct	Sh	Sv-Op	Hld	ERC	ERA
2012	NYM	NL	8	4	0	1	21.1	99	27	21	18	5	2	1	2	8	2	17	0	0	0	4	.000	0	0-0	0	6.83	7.59
2013	2 Tms	NL	7	5	0	2	26.0	125	45	29	29	6	2	2	0	5	0	11	0	0	0	4	.429	0	0-0	0	8.82	10.04
2014	Hou	AL	25	25	0	0	154.2	619	117	53	47	13	6	4	6	41	1	157	6	0	11	9	.550	0	0-0	0	2.34	2.73
2015	Hou	AL	32	32	0	0	203.2	859	207	89	88	19	5	4	9	53	2	171	5	0	19	7	.731	0	0-0	0	3.75	3.89
2016	Hou	AL	33	33	1	0	184.2	796	206	92	89	25	1	5	5	54	1	177	9	0	13	10	.565	0	0-0	0	4.69	4.34
2017	Hou	AL	12	12	0	0	63.1	271	62	27	25	7	0	0	5	20	0	62	4	0	5	2	.714	0	0-0	0	4.02	3.55
13	NYM	NL	3	1	0	2	7.0	34	12	8	8	2	0	1	0	3	0	3	0	0	0	1	.000	0	0-0	0	10.77	10.29
13	Col	NL	4	4	0	0	19.0	91	33	21	21	4	2	1	0	2	0	8	0	0	0	3	.000	0	0-0	0	8.14	9.95
	Postseason		2	2	0	0	10.0	40	9	5	5	2	0	0	1	2	0	2	0	0	1	1	.500	0	0-0	0	3.93	4.50
	6 ML YEARS		117	111	1	3	653.2	2769	664	311	296	75	16	16	27	181	6	595	24	0	48	36	.571	0	0-0	0	3.94	4.08

Ryan McMahon

Bats: L Throws: R Pos: 1B-7;PH-7;2B-4;3B-3;PR-2 Ht: 6'2" Wt: 185 Born: 12/14/1994 Age: 23

Year	Team	Lg	G	AB	H	2B	3B	HR	(Hm	Rd)	TB	R	RBI	RC	TBB	IBB	SO	HBP	SH	SF	SB	CS	GDP	Avg	OBP	Slg	OPS
2013	GdJunc	R+	59	218	70	18	3	11	(-	-)	127	42	52	48	28	0	59	2	2	1	4	6	1	.321	.402	.583	.984
2014	Ashvll	A	126	482	136	46	3	18	(-	-)	242	93	102	88	54	1	143	7	2	7	8	5	11	.282	.358	.502	.860
2015	Mdest	A+	132	496	149	43	6	18	(-	-)	258	85	75	92	49	1	153	9	0	2	6	13	5	.300	.372	.520	.892
2016	Hrtfrd	AA	133	466	113	27	5	12	(-	-)	186	49	75	64	55	1	161	5	2	6	11	6	11	.242	.325	.399	.724
2017	Hrtfrd	AA	49	181	59	16	2	6	(-	-)	97	28	32	39	20	2	39	1	0	3	7	0	3	.326	.390	.536	.926
2017	Albq	AAA	70	289	108	23	2	14	(-	-)	177	46	56	68	21	3	53	0	0	4	4	3	8	.374	.411	.612	1.023
2017	Col	NL	17	19	3	1	0	0	(0	0)	4	2	1	1	5	0	5	0	0	0	0	0	1	.158	.333	.211	.544

Adalberto Mejia

Pitches: L Bats: R Pos: SP-21 ah-dahl-BAIR-toe meh-HEE-yah Ht: 6'3" Wt: 195 Born: 6/20/1993 Age: 25

Year	Team	Lg	G	GS	CG	GF	IP	BFP	H	R	ER	HR	SH	SF	HB	TBB	IBB	SO	WP	Bk	W	L	Pct	Sh	Sv-Op	Hld	ERC	ERA
2013	SnJos	A+	16	16	0	0	87.0	355	75	34	32	11	2	0	1	23	0	89	5	0	7	4	.636	0	0- -	-	3.02	3.31
2014	Rchmd	AA	22	21	0	0	108.0	459	119	62	56	9	1	6	0	31	0	82	2	0	7	9	.438	0	0- -	-	4.13	4.67
2015	Rchmd	AA	12	9	0	0	51.1	210	38	14	14	2	5	0	1	18	0	38	2	0	5	2	.714	0	0- -	-	2.20	2.45
2016	Rchmd	AA	11	11	0	0	65.0	254	48	16	14	4	1	0	1	16	0	58	3	1	3	2	.600	0	0- -	-	2.02	1.94
2016	Scrmto	AAA	7	7	0	0	40.2	172	42	19	19	5	1	0	0	11	0	43	0	1	4	1	.800	0	0- -	-	3.89	4.20

Year Team	Lg	G	GS	CG	GF	IP	BFP	H	R	ER	HR	SH	SF	HB	TBB	IBB	SO	WP	Bk	W	L	Pct	Sh	Sv-Op	Hld	ERC	ERA
						HOW MUCH HE PITCHED					WHAT HE GAVE UP											THE RESULTS					
2017 Roch	AAA	6	6	0	0	28.2	114	26	9	9	1	0	0	0	6	0	22	1	0	1	1	.500	0	0--	-	2.51	2.83
2016 Min	AL	1	0	0	0	2.1	13	5	2	2	0	0	1	0	1	0	0	0	0	0	0	-	0	0-0	0	10.38	7.71
2017 Min	AL	21	21	0	0	98.0	443	110	52	49	13	0	3	5	44	4	85	2	2	4	7	.364	0	0-0	0	5.37	4.50
2 ML YEARS		22	21	0	0	100.1	456	115	54	51	13	0	4	5	45	4	85	2	2	4	7	.364	0	0-0	0	5.48	4.57

Alex Mejia

Bats: R Throws: R Pos: 3B-13;2B-7;SS-7;PH-4;PR-3;1B-1   meh-HEE-yah   Ht: 6'1" Wt: 200 Born: 1/18/1991 Age: 27

Year Team	Lg	G	AB	H	2B	3B	HR	(Hm	Rd)	TB	R	RBI	RC	TBB	IBB	SO	HBP	SH	SF	SB	CS	GDP	Avg	OBP	Slg	OPS
								BATTING												RUNNING			AVERAGES			
2013 2 Tms	Low	121	448	104	23	2	1	(-	-)	134	52	37	38	22	0	68	6	14	5	8	4	14	.232	.274	.299	.574
2014 PlmBh	A+	71	275	78	13	1	1	(-	-)	96	30	29	30	9	1	41	1	7	2	4	2	9	.284	.307	.349	.656
2014 Sprgfld	AA	49	163	44	3	1	3	(-	-)	58	13	21	20	13	1	20	2	2	3	2	2	4	.270	.326	.356	.682
2015 Sprgfld	AA	34	115	31	5	1	2	(-	-)	44	12	12	16	11	1	19	2	3	1	1	1	3	.270	.341	.383	.724
2015 Memp	AAA	59	167	46	7	1	3	(-	-)	64	26	17	23	15	1	25	1	2	2	3	0	6	.275	.335	.383	.718
2016 Memp	AAA	34	99	27	7	2	0	(-	-)	38	9	10	12	4	0	12	2	3	0	1	0	3	.273	.314	.384	.698
2016 Sprgfld	AA	44	170	37	7	0	1	(-	-)	47	14	14	13	13	0	26	1	1	2	1	1	9	.218	.274	.276	.551
2017 Sprgfld	AA	63	227	57	17	0	3	(-	-)	83	24	24	26	16	1	36	3	2	3	1	1	7	.251	.305	.366	.671
2017 Memp	AAA	55	206	69	15	0	4	(-	-)	96	25	33	36	14	0	30	2	1	1	1	1	4	.335	.381	.466	.847
2017 StL	NL	29	46	5	0	0	1	(1	0)	8	6	3	6	2	0	13	0	1	0	0	0	2	.109	.146	.174	.320

Francisco Mejia

Bats: B Throws: R Pos: PH-8;DH-5;C-3;PR-1   meh-HEE-yah   Ht: 5'10" Wt: 180 Born: 10/27/1995 Age: 22

Year Team	Lg	G	AB	H	2B	3B	HR	(Hm	Rd)	TB	R	RBI	RC	TBB	IBB	SO	HBP	SH	SF	SB	CS	GDP	Avg	OBP	Slg	OPS
								BATTING												RUNNING			AVERAGES			
2013 Indns	R	30	105	32	9	1	4	(-	-)	55	16	24	19	5	0	18	2	1	0	3	1	1	.305	.348	.524	.872
2014 MhVlly	A-	66	248	70	17	4	2	(-	-)	101	32	36	34	18	1	47	5	0	3	2	4	4	.282	.339	.407	.747
2015 Lk Cty	A	109	391	95	13	0	9	(-	-)	135	45	53	48	38	1	78	10	5	2	4	1	7	.243	.324	.345	.670
2016 2 Tms	Low	102	407	139	29	4	11	(-	-)	209	63	80	75	28	3	63	2	1	5	2	2	11	.342	.382	.514	.896
2017 Akron	AA	92	347	103	21	2	14	(-	-)	170	52	52	60	24	1	53	5	1	6	7	2	7	.297	.346	.490	.835
2017 Cle	AL	11	13	2	0	0	0	(0	0)	2	1	1	0	1	1	3	0	0	0	0	0	0	.154	.214	.154	.368

Mark Melancon

Pitches: R Bats: R Pos: RP-32   muh-LANN-sun   Ht: 6'2" Wt: 210 Born: 3/28/1985 Age: 33

Year Team	Lg	G	GS	CG	GF	IP	BFP	H	R	ER	HR	SH	SF	HB	TBB	IBB	SO	WP	Bk	W	L	Pct	Sh	Sv-Op	Hld	ERC	ERA
						HOW MUCH HE PITCHED					WHAT HE GAVE UP											THE RESULTS					
2009 NYY	AL	13	0	0	4	16.1	74	13	8	7	0	0	0	4	10	0	10	3	0	0	1	.000	0	0-1	0	3.94	3.86
2010 2 Tms		22	0	0	4	21.1	90	19	13	10	2	0	1	1	8	0	22	2	0	2	0	1.000	0	0-1	8	3.53	4.22
2011 Hou	NL	71	0	0	47	74.1	309	65	28	23	5	2	0	2	26	6	66	1	0	8	4	.667	0	20-25	3	2.98	2.78
2012 Bos	AL	41	0	0	17	45.0	194	45	31	31	8	1	2	3	12	1	41	2	0	2	0	.000	0	1-2	4	4.24	6.20
2013 Pit	NL	72	0	0	24	71.0	279	60	15	11	1	0	1	1	8	0	70	6	0	3	2	.600	0	16-21	26	1.78	1.39
2014 Pit	NL	72	0	0	48	71.0	277	51	15	15	2	1	1	3	11	1	71	3	0	3	5	.375	0	33-37	14	1.54	1.90
2015 Pit	NL	78	0	0	63	76.2	293	57	22	19	4	1	1	2	14	2	62	3	0	3	2	.600	0	51-53	1	1.82	2.23
2016 2 Tms	NL	75	0	0	67	71.1	270	52	16	13	3	0	2	1	12	0	65	4	0	2	2	.500	0	47-51	0	1.66	1.64
2017 SF	NL	32	0	0	18	30.0	130	37	16	15	3	0	0	1	6	0	29	2	0	1	2	.333	0	11-16	5	4.78	4.50
10 NYY	AL	2	0	0	0	4.0	19	7	5	4	1	0	1	0	0	0	3	0	0	0	0	-	0	0-0	0	7.95	9.00
10 Hou	NL	20	0	0	2	17.1	71	12	8	6	1	0	0	1	8	0	19	2	0	2	0	1.000	0	0-1	8	2.65	3.12
16 Pit	NL	45	0	0	39	41.2	163	31	10	7	2	0	2	1	9	0	38	1	0	1	1	.500	0	30-33	0	1.89	1.51
16 Was	NL	30	0	0	28	29.2	107	21	6	6	1	0	0	0	3	0	27	3	0	1	1	.500	0	17-18	0	1.41	1.82
Postseason		10	0	0	7	10.0	40	9	4	4	2	0	0	0	3	2	8	0	0	1	0	1.000	0	1-2	0	3.62	3.60
9 ML YEARS		476	0	0	292	477.0	1916	399	164	144	28	5	8	18	107	10	436	26	0	22	20	.524	0	179-207	59	2.42	2.72

Keury Mella

Pitches: R Bats: R Pos: RP-2   KAY-yur-ee MAY-ah   Ht: 6'2" Wt: 200 Born: 8/2/1993 Age: 24

Year Team	Lg	G	GS	CG	GF	IP	BFP	H	R	ER	HR	SH	SF	HB	TBB	IBB	SO	WP	Bk	W	L	Pct	Sh	Sv-Op	Hld	ERC	ERA
						HOW MUCH HE PITCHED					WHAT HE GAVE UP											THE RESULTS					
2013 Giants	R	10	9	0	0	36.0	148	34	12	9	0	1	0	1	11	0	41	4	0	3	2	.600	0	0--	-	2.91	2.25
2014 2 Tms	Low	18	18	1	0	85.1	367	85	41	33	1	4	3	9	19	0	83	11	0	4	4	.500	0	0--	-	3.11	3.48
2015 2 Tms	Low	20	20	0	0	103.0	437	77	45	37	7	4	4	10	41	1	106	9	1	8	4	.667	0	0--	-	2.80	3.23
2016 Dytona	A+	25	24	0	0	131.2	587	150	67	57	7	4	4	9	56	0	95	5	2	8	9	.471	0	0--	-	4.97	3.90
2017 Pnscla	AA	27	26	1	1	134.0	576	135	73	64	14	5	2	6	43	0	109	9	0	4	10	.286	1	1--	-	4.00	4.30
2017 Cin	NL	2	0	0	1	4.0	19	5	3	3	1	0	0	0	2	1	1	0	0	0	0	-	0	0-0	0	6.56	6.75

Tim Melville

Pitches: R Bats: R Pos: RP-2; SP-1   Ht: 6'4" Wt: 225 Born: 10/9/1989 Age: 28

Year Team	Lg	G	GS	CG	GF	IP	BFP	H	R	ER	HR	SH	SF	HB	TBB	IBB	SO	WP	Bk	W	L	Pct	Sh	Sv-Op	Hld	ERC	ERA
						HOW MUCH HE PITCHED					WHAT HE GAVE UP											THE RESULTS					
2014 NWArk	AA	26	26	0	0	129.1	593	144	92	79	14	8	5	2	68	0	105	7	0	2	11	.154	0	0--	-	5.32	5.50
2015 Toledo	AAA	27	27	1	0	151.2	655	141	89	78	14	7	8	7	68	1	102	4	1	7	10	.412	0	0--	-	4.00	4.63
2016 Lsvlle	AAA	6	0	0	0	8.1	41	10	7	4	1	0	0	6	5	0	7	1	0	1	1	.500	0	0--	-	5.92	4.32
2017 Roch	AAA	11	10	1	0	66.2	272	48	21	20	5	1	2	5	23	0	64	2	0	4	3	.571	0	0--	-	2.51	2.70
2016 Cin	NL	3	2	0	0	9.0	54	16	12	11	5	2	0	1	9	0	8	1	0	0	1	.000	0	0-0	0	16.62	11.00
2017 2 Tms		3	1	0	1	5.2	30	7	8	7	1	0	0	1	6	0	7	0	0	0	1	.000	0	0-0	0	9.95	11.12
17 Min	AL	1	1	0	0	3.1	18	4	5	5	1	0	0	1	3	0	4	0	0	0	0	-	0	0-0	0	10.42	13.50
17 SD	NL	2	0	0	1	2.1	12	3	3	2	0	0	0	0	3	0	3	0	0	0	0	-	0	0-0	0	9.14	7.71
2 ML YEARS		6	3	0	1	14.2	84	23	20	18	6	2	0	2	15	0	15	1	0	0	2	.000	0	0-0	0	14.01	11.05

Yohander Mendez

Pitches: L Bats: L Pos: RP-7   yo-HAHN-dair   Ht: 6'5" Wt: 200 Born: 1/17/1995 Age: 23

Year	Team	Lg	G	GS	CG	GF	IP	BFP	H	R	ER	HR	SH	SF	HB	TBB	IBB	SO	WP	Bk	W	L	Pct	Sh	Sv-Op	Hld	ERC	ERA
2013	Spkane	A-	8	8	0	0	33.1	151	31	18	14	4	0	2	3	17	0	23	1	0	1	2	.333	0	0--	-	4.51	3.78
2014	2 Tms	Low	10	9	0	0	36.2	143	34	13	11	4	0	2	0	4	0	35	5	2	3	1	.750	0	0--	-	2.70	2.70
2015	Hkry	A	21	8	0	6	66.1	269	57	20	18	2	3	1	2	15	0	74	6	1	3	3	.500	0	3--	-	2.35	2.44
2016	Hi Dsrt	A+	7	7	0	0	33.0	130	21	9	9	2	0	0	0	11	0	45	1	0	4	1	.800	0	0--	-	1.76	2.45
2016	Frisco	AA	10	10	0	0	46.2	191	39	18	16	2	1	1	4	14	0	46	5	0	4	1	.800	0	0--	-	2.81	3.09
2016	RdRck	AAA	7	4	0	1	31.1	119	12	2	2	0	1	0	1	16	0	22	2	0	4	1	.800	0	0--	-	1.20	0.57
2017	Frisco	AA	24	24	1	0	137.2	556	114	60	58	23	2	2	10	43	0	124	2	2	7	8	.467	1	0--	-	3.63	3.79
2016	Tex	AL	2	0	0	0	3.0	17	5	6	6	0	0	0	0	2	0	0	0	0	0	0	-	0	0-0	0	7.72	18.00
2017	Tex	AL	7	0	0	0	12.1	52	13	9	7	3	0	0	1	3	0	7	0	0	0	1	.000	0	0-0	1	5.19	5.11
	2 ML YEARS		9	0	0	0	15.1	69	18	15	13	3	0	0	1	5	0	7	0	0	0	1	.000	0	0-0	1	5.73	7.63

Daniel Mengden

Pitches: R Bats: R Pos: SP-7   MENG-den   Ht: 6'2" Wt: 190 Born: 2/19/1993 Age: 25

Year	Team	Lg	G	GS	CG	GF	IP	BFP	H	R	ER	HR	SH	SF	HB	TBB	IBB	SO	WP	Bk	W	L	Pct	Sh	Sv-Op	Hld	ERC	ERA
2014	2 Tms	Low	6	1	0	2	11.0	44	9	4	4	0	0	0	1	1	0	17	1	0	0	0	-	0	0--	-	1.73	3.27
2015	3 Tms	Low	26	22	0	3	130.2	554	128	60	54	11	5	3	6	36	0	125	12	2	10	4	.714	0	1--	-	3.53	3.72
2016	Nashv	AAA	13	13	0	0	75.1	294	54	15	14	4	2	2	3	17	1	67	1	0	8	2	.800	0	0--	-	1.87	1.67
2017	Nashv	AAA	9	9	0	0	41.0	180	40	20	19	5	1	1	3	18	0	40	1	1	2	4	.333	0	0--	-	4.55	4.17
2016	Oak	AL	14	14	0	0	72.0	332	83	54	52	9	2	1	4	33	0	71	5	0	2	9	.182	0	0-0	0	5.56	6.50
2017	Oak	AL	7	7	1	0	43.0	169	36	16	15	6	1	2	0	9	0	29	2	0	3	2	.600	1	0-0	0	2.78	3.14
	2 ML YEARS		21	21	1	0	115.0	501	119	70	67	15	3	3	4	42	0	100	7	0	5	11	.313	1	0-0	0	4.47	5.24

Jordy Mercer

Bats: R Throws: R Pos: SS-144;PH-1   Ht: 6'3" Wt: 210 Born: 8/27/1986 Age: 31

Year	Team	Lg	G	AB	H	2B	3B	HR	(Hm	Rd)	TB	R	RBI	RC	TBB	IBB	SO	HBP	SH	SF	SB	CS	GDP	Avg	OBP	Slg	OPS
2012	Pit	NL	42	62	13	5	1	1	(1	0)	23	7	5	6	4	0	14	1	0	1	0	1	0	.210	.265	.371	.636
2013	Pit	NL	103	333	95	22	2	8	(1	7)	145	33	27	46	22	6	62	4	5	1	3	2	7	.285	.336	.435	.772
2014	Pit	NL	149	506	129	27	2	12	(3	9)	196	56	55	45	35	12	89	4	5	5	4	1	14	.255	.305	.387	.693
2015	Pit	NL	116	394	96	21	0	3	(0	3)	126	34	34	34	27	7	73	2	4	3	3	2	7	.244	.293	.320	.613
2016	Pit	NL	149	519	133	22	3	11	(4	7)	194	66	59	58	51	8	83	5	7	2	1	1	11	.256	.328	.374	.701
2017	Pit	NL	145	502	128	24	5	14	(5	9)	204	52	58	60	51	13	88	3	0	2	0	4	16	.255	.326	.406	.733
	Postseason		7	14	2	0	0	0	(0	0)	2	0	0	0	1	1	5	0	0	0	0	0	0	.143	.200	.143	.343
	6 ML YEARS		704	2316	594	121	13	49	(14	35)	888	248	238	249	190	46	409	19	21	14	11	11	55	.256	.316	.383	.700

Whit Merrifield

Bats: R Throws: R Pos: 2B-132;RF-10;LF-7;PR-2;1B-1;3B-1   Ht: 6'0" Wt: 195 Born: 1/24/1989 Age: 29

Year	Team	Lg	G	AB	H	2B	3B	HR	(Hm	Rd)	TB	R	RBI	RC	TBB	IBB	SO	HBP	SH	SF	SB	CS	GDP	Avg	OBP	Slg	OPS
2013	NWArk	AA	94	322	87	20	5	3	(-	-)	126	31	43	42	22	0	57	2	5	2	17	7	14	.270	.319	.391	.710
2014	NWArk	AA	44	162	45	13	1	5	(-	-)	75	22	20	28	22	0	27	1	4	1	5	4	3	.278	.366	.463	.829
2014	Omha	AAA	76	321	109	28	3	3	(-	-)	152	57	29	56	17	1	52	2	2	3	11	7	6	.340	.373	.474	.847
2015	Omha	AAA	135	544	144	29	5	5	(-	-)	198	83	39	68	39	4	66	4	4	3	32	9	13	.265	.317	.364	.681
2016	Omha	AAA	69	274	73	19	0	8	(-	-)	116	46	29	42	22	1	55	2	2	4	20	2	4	.266	.321	.423	.745
2016	KC	AL	81	311	88	22	3	2	(2	0)	122	44	29	38	19	1	72	0	1	1	8	3	1	.283	.323	.392	.716
2017	KC	AL	145	587	169	32	6	19	(13	6)	270	80	78	88	29	0	88	6	1	7	34	8	13	.288	.324	.460	.784
	2 ML YEARS		226	898	257	54	9	21	(15	6)	392	124	107	126	48	1	160	6	2	8	42	11	14	.286	.324	.437	.760

Ryan Merritt

Pitches: L Bats: L Pos: SP-4; RP-1   Ht: 6'0" Wt: 180 Born: 2/21/1992 Age: 26

Year	Team	Lg	G	GS	CG	GF	IP	BFP	H	R	ER	HR	SH	SF	HB	TBB	IBB	SO	WP	Bk	W	L	Pct	Sh	Sv-Op	Hld	ERC	ERA
2013	2 Tms	Low	26	25	0	0	135.1	560	149	67	53	11	2	4	6	19	0	97	8	6	6	9	.400	0	0--	-	3.72	3.52
2014	Carlina	A+	25	25	2	0	160.1	631	128	56	46	12	3	5	5	25	0	127	0	3	13	3	.813	0	0--	-	2.10	2.58
2015	Akron	AA	22	22	2	0	141.0	572	145	63	55	8	7	2	8	16	1	89	3	1	10	7	.588	2	0--	-	3.11	3.51
2015	Clmbs	AAA	5	5	0	0	30.0	132	38	14	14	1	2	0	1	6	0	16	0	1	2	0	1.000	0	0--	-	4.43	4.20
2016	Clmbs	AAA	24	24	2	0	143.1	596	156	67	59	15	5	3	6	23	0	92	2	0	11	8	.579	1	0--	-	3.87	3.70
2017	Clmbs	AAA	19	18	1	0	116.0	473	116	40	39	19	2	0	5	25	0	85	0	0	10	5	.667	0	0--	-	4.06	3.03
2016	Cle	AL	4	1	0	1	11.0	37	6	2	2	0	1	0	0	0	0	6	0	0	1	0	1.000	0	0-0	0	0.67	1.64
2017	Cle	AL	5	4	0	1	20.2	89	26	6	4	0	0	1	0	4	0	7	0	0	2	0	1.000	0	0-0	0	4.03	1.74
	Postseason		1	1	0	0	4.1	14	2	0	0	0	0	0	0	0	0	3	0	0	0	0	-	0	0-0	0	0.50	0.00
	2 ML YEARS		9	5	0	2	31.2	126	32	8	6	0	1	1	0	4	0	13	0	0	3	0	1.000	0	0-0	0	2.52	1.71

Devin Mesoraco

Bats: R Throws: R Pos: C-40;PH-15;DH-2   mezz-er-OCK-oh   Ht: 6'1" Wt: 229 Born: 6/19/1988 Age: 30

Year	Team	Lg	G	AB	H	2B	3B	HR	(Hm	Rd)	TB	R	RBI	RC	TBB	IBB	SO	HBP	SH	SF	SB	CS	GDP	Avg	OBP	Slg	OPS
2017	Pnscla*	AA	13	47	8	1	0	1	(-	-)	12	4	3	3	6	0	10	2	0	0	0	0	0	.170	.291	.255	.546
2011	Cin	NL	18	50	9	3	0	2	(2	0)	18	5	6	5	3	1	10	0	0	0	0	0	1	.180	.226	.360	.586
2012	Cin	NL	54	165	35	8	0	5	(4	1)	58	17	14	10	17	4	33	1	0	1	1	1	2	.212	.288	.352	.640
2013	Cin	NL	103	323	77	13	0	9	(5	4)	117	31	42	30	24	4	61	0	0	5	0	2	9	.238	.287	.362	.649

Year	Team	Lg	G	AB	H	2B	3B	HR	(Hm	Rd)	TB	R	RBI	RC	TBB	IBB	SO	HBP	SH	SF	SB	CS	GDP	Avg	OBP	Slg	OPS
2014	Cin	NL	114	384	105	25	0	25	(14	11)	205	54	80	76	41	4	103	12	0	3	1	3	5	.273	.359	.534	.893
2015	Cin	NL	23	45	8	1	1	0	(0	0)	11	2	2	3	5	0	9	1	0	0	1	0	0	.178	.275	.244	.519
2016	Cin	NL	16	50	7	1	0	0	(0	0)	8	2	1	0	5	0	10	0	0	0	0	1	3	.140	.218	.160	.378
2017	Cin	NL	56	141	30	5	1	6	(4	2)	55	17	14	14	18	0	38	5	0	1	1	0	4	.213	.321	.390	.711
	Postseason		1	1	0	0	0	0	(0	0)	0	0	0	0	0	0	0	0	0	0	0	0	0	.000	.000	.000	.000
	7 ML YEARS		384	1158	271	56	2	47	(29	18)	472	128	159	138	113	13	264	19	0	10	4	7	24	.234	.310	.408	.718

Alex Meyer

Pitches: R **Bats:** R **Pos:** SP-13

MY-er

Ht: 6'9" **Wt:** 225 **Born:** 1/3/1990 **Age:** 28

			HOW MUCH HE PITCHED					WHAT HE GAVE UP											THE RESULTS						
Year	Team	Lg	G	GS	CG	GF	IP	BFP	H	R	ER	HR	SH	SF	HB	TBB	IBB	SO	WP	Bk	W	L	Pct	Sh	Sv-Op	Hld	ERC	ERA
2017	Salt Lk*	AAA	5	5	0	0	24.0	109	30	17	16	4	1	0	1	9	0	31	0	0	0	1	.000	0	0--	-	6.17	6.00
2015	Min	AL	2	0	0	0	2.2	15	4	5	5	2	1	0	0	3	0	3	0	0	0	0	-	0	0-0	0	16.82	16.88
2016	2 Tms	AL	7	6	0	0	25.1	117	25	16	16	3	0	2	0	17	0	29	3	0	1	3	.250	0	0-0	0	5.15	5.68
2017	LAA	AL	13	13	0	0	67.1	292	48	30	28	6	1	1	4	42	0	75	5	1	4	5	.444	0	0-0	0	3.49	3.74
16	Min	AL	2	1	0	0	3.2	23	8	5	5	1	0	0	0	4	0	5	2	0	0	1	.000	0	0-0	0	16.88	12.27
16	LAA	AL	5	5	0	0	21.2	94	17	11	11	2	0	2	0	13	0	24	1	0	1	2	.333	0	0-0	0	3.57	4.57
	3 ML YEARS		22	19	0	0	95.1	424	77	51	49	11	2	3	4	62	0	107	8	1	5	8	.385	0	0-0	0	4.21	4.63

Will Middlebrooks

Bats: R **Throws:** R **Pos:** 3B-19;PH-6;PR-3;1B-1

Ht: 6'3" **Wt:** 220 **Born:** 9/9/1988 **Age:** 29

			BATTING																	RUNNING			AVERAGES			
Year	Team	Lg	G	AB	H	2B	3B	HR	(Hm	Rd)	TB	R	RBI	RC	TBB	IBB	SO	HBP	SH	SF	SB	CS	GDP	Avg	OBP	Slg	OPS
2017	RdRck*	AAA	78	306	79	14	0	23	(-	-)	162	51	64	53	31	1	88	2	0	3	0	1	9	.258	.327	.529	.857
2012	Bos	AL	75	267	77	14	0	15	(9	6)	136	34	54	46	13	0	70	3	0	3	4	1	8	.288	.325	.509	.835
2013	Bos	AL	94	348	79	18	0	17	(4	13)	148	41	49	29	20	3	98	2	1	3	3	1	13	.227	.271	.425	.696
2014	Bos	AL	63	215	41	10	0	2	(1	1)	57	14	19	15	15	1	70	4	0	0	1	1	7	.191	.256	.265	.522
2015	SD	NL	83	255	54	7	2	9	(1	8)	92	23	29	20	11	0	60	0	0	4	2	1	4	.212	.241	.361	.602
2016	Mil	NL	10	27	3	0	0	0	(0	0)	3	2	1	1	4	0	13	0	0	0	0	0	0	.111	.226	.111	.337
2017	Tex	AL	22	38	8	2	2	0	(0	0)	14	5	3	3	1	0	14	0	0	0	0	0	0	.211	.231	.368	.599
	Postseason		10	25	4	2	0	0	(0	0)	6	2	1	2	3	1	10	0	0	0	0	0	0	.160	.250	.240	.490
	6 ML YEARS		347	1150	262	51	4	43	(15	28)	450	119	155	114	64	4	325	9	1	10	10	4	32	.228	.272	.391	.663

Keynan Middleton

Pitches: R **Bats:** R **Pos:** RP-64

Ht: 6'2" **Wt:** 185 **Born:** 9/12/1993 **Age:** 24

			HOW MUCH HE PITCHED					WHAT HE GAVE UP											THE RESULTS						
Year	Team	Lg	G	GS	CG	GF	IP	BFP	H	R	ER	HR	SH	SF	HB	TBB	IBB	SO	WP	Bk	W	L	Pct	Sh	Sv-Op	Hld	ERC	ERA
2013	2 Tms	Low	10	1	0	0	29.0	133	32	25	25	4	0	1	2	18	0	20	7	0	1	3	.250	0	0--	-	6.32	7.76
2014	Orem	R+	14	14	0	0	67.0	302	69	58	48	9	0	1	6	30	0	53	7	0	5	4	.556	0	0--	-	5.01	6.45
2015	Burlgtn	A	26	26	0	0	125.2	549	148	78	74	15	5	10	3	47	0	88	8	1	6	11	.353	0	0--	-	5.38	5.30
2016	InldEm	A+	25	0	0	9	36.1	149	22	15	15	7	0	1	0	20	0	56	4	0	1	1	.500	0	0--	-	3.13	3.72
2016	Ark	AA	13	0	0	9	15.0	60	11	2	2	1	0	0	0	4	0	18	0	0	0	0	-	0	6--	-	1.99	1.20
2016	Salt Lk	AAA	8	0	0	4	14.2	62	14	8	8	1	1	1	0	4	0	14	1	0	0	1	.000	0	2--	-	3.06	4.91
2017	Salt Lk	AAA	10	0	0	6	12.2	52	11	5	4	0	0	0	1	4	0	8	0	0	0	0	-	0	2--	-	2.74	2.84
2017	LAA	AL	64	0	0	17	58.1	246	60	25	25	11	0	2	0	18	0	63	2	0	6	1	.857	0	3-5	10	4.47	3.86

Wade Miley

Pitches: L **Bats:** L **Pos:** SP-32

MY-lee

Ht: 6'0" **Wt:** 220 **Born:** 11/13/1986 **Age:** 31

			HOW MUCH HE PITCHED					WHAT HE GAVE UP											THE RESULTS						
Year	Team	Lg	G	GS	CG	GF	IP	BFP	H	R	ER	HR	SH	SF	HB	TBB	IBB	SO	WP	Bk	W	L	Pct	Sh	Sv-Op	Hld	ERC	ERA
2011	Ari	NL	8	7	0	0	40.0	180	48	20	20	6	3	1	0	18	0	25	1	0	4	2	.667	0	0-0	0	5.90	4.50
2012	Ari	NL	32	29	0	0	194.2	807	193	79	72	14	8	3	2	37	0	144	6	1	16	11	.593	0	0-0	0	3.05	3.33
2013	Ari	NL	33	33	0	0	202.2	847	201	88	80	21	6	2	4	66	4	147	13	0	10	10	.500	0	0-0	0	3.88	3.55
2014	Ari	NL	33	33	0	0	201.1	866	207	103	97	23	8	9	4	75	3	183	9	0	8	12	.400	0	0-0	0	4.31	4.34
2015	Bos	AL	32	32	1	0	193.2	831	201	98	96	17	3	2	4	64	0	147	10	1	11	11	.500	0	0-0	0	4.01	4.46
2016	2 Tms	AL	30	30	1	0	166.0	711	187	100	99	25	2	5	6	49	1	137	8	2	9	13	.409	1	0-0	0	4.98	5.37
2017	Bal	AL	32	32	0	0	157.1	728	179	104	98	25	1	6	4	93	1	142	1	0	8	15	.348	0	0-0	0	6.27	5.61
16	Sea	AL	19	19	1	0	112.0	469	117	66	62	18	2	3	3	34	1	82	5	2	7	8	.467	1	0-0	0	4.58	4.98
16	Bal	AL	11	11	0	0	54.0	242	70	34	37	7	0	2	3	15	0	55	3	0	2	5	.286	0	0-0	0	5.83	6.17
	7 ML YEARS		200	196	2	0	1155.2	4970	1216	592	562	131	31	28	24	402	9	925	48	4	66	74	.471	1	0-0	0	4.36	4.38

Andrew Miller

Pitches: L **Bats:** L **Pos:** RP-57

Ht: 6'7" **Wt:** 205 **Born:** 5/21/1985 **Age:** 33

			HOW MUCH HE PITCHED					WHAT HE GAVE UP											THE RESULTS						
Year	Team	Lg	G	GS	CG	GF	IP	BFP	H	R	ER	HR	SH	SF	HB	TBB	IBB	SO	WP	Bk	W	L	Pct	Sh	Sv-Op	Hld	ERC	ERA
2006	Det	AL	8	0	0	3	10.1	51	8	9	7	0	0	0	2	10	0	6	1	0	0	1	.000	0	0-0	1	4.79	6.10
2007	Det	AL	13	13	0	0	64.0	309	73	43	40	8	3	1	0	39	0	56	4	1	5	5	.500	0	0-0	0	6.31	5.63
2008	Fla	NL	29	20	0	1	107.1	492	120	78	70	7	10	7	4	56	4	89	4	0	6	10	.375	0	0-0	2	5.04	5.87
2009	Fla	NL	20	14	0	1	80.0	366	85	52	43	7	6	4	2	43	1	59	10	0	3	5	.375	0	0-0	1	4.90	4.84
2010	Fla	NL	9	7	0	1	32.2	171	51	34	31	6	5	2	1	26	2	28	5	0	1	5	.167	0	0-0	0	10.20	8.54
2011	Bos	AL	17	12	0	2	65.0	310	77	43	40	6	8	6	5	41	0	50	2	1	6	3	.667	0	0-0	0	6.48	5.54
2012	Bos	AL	53	0	0	4	40.1	169	28	15	15	3	0	3	2	20	1	51	1	0	3	2	.600	0	0-0	13	2.76	3.35
2013	Bos	AL	37	0	0	11	30.2	135	25	12	9	3	1	0	2	17	0	48	2	0	1	2	.333	0	0-1	6	3.83	2.64
2014	2 Tms	AL	73	0	0	15	62.1	242	33	16	14	3	2	2	5	17	2	103	3	0	5	5	.500	0	1-2	22	1.36	2.02
2015	NYY	AL	60	0	0	53	61.2	246	33	16	14	6	1	2	5	20	1	100	2	0	3	2	.600	0	36-38	0	1.61	2.04

Year	Team	Lg	HOW MUCH HE PITCHED						WHAT HE GAVE UP												THE RESULTS							
			G	GS	CG	GF	IP	BFP	H	R	ER	HR	SH	SF	HB	TBB	IBB	SO	WP	Bk	W	L	Pct	Sh	Sv-Op	Hld	ERC	ERA
2016 2 Tms		AL	70	0	0	23	74.1	275	42	13	12	8	1	1	2	9	0	123	1	0	10	1	.909	0	12-14	25	1.27	1.45
2017 Cle		AL	57	0	0	6	62.2	244	31	11	10	3	2	1	5	21	0	95	1	0	4	3	.571	0	2-4	27	1.42	1.44
14 Bos		AL	50	0	0	12	42.1	170	25	13	11	2	2	2	4	13	2	69	2	0	3	5	.375	0	0-0	13	1.62	2.34
14 Bal		AL	23	0	0	3	20.0	72	8	3	3	1	0	0	1	4	0	34	1	0	2	0	1.000	0	1-2	9	0.86	1.35
16 NYY		AL	44	0	0	16	45.1	172	28	8	7	5	1	1	2	7	0	77	0	0	6	1	.857	0	9-11	16	1.55	1.39
16 Cle		AL	26	0	0	7	29.0	103	14	5	5	3	0	0	0	2	0	46	1	0	4	0	1.000	0	3-3	9	0.87	1.55
Postseason			16	0	0	2	27.2	100	13	3	3	2	0	1	1	6	0	40	0	0	2	0	1.000	0	1-1	7	1.14	0.98
12 ML YEARS			446	66	0	120	691.1	3010	606	342	305	61	37	28	40	319	11	808	36	2	47	44	.516	0	51-59	97	3.70	3.97

Brad Miller

Bats: L **Throws:** R **Pos:** 2B-98;PH-13;DH-10   **Ht:** 6'2" **Wt:** 215 **Born:** 10/18/1989 **Age:** 28

Year	Team	Lg	BATTING																			RUNNING			AVERAGES			
			G	AB	H	2B	3B	HR	(Hm	Rd)	TB	R	RBI	RC	TBB	IBB	SO	HBP	SH	SF	SB	CS	GDP	Avg	OBP	Slg	OPS
2013 Sea		AL	76	306	81	11	6	8	(3	5)	128	41	36	41	24	0	52	1	2	2	5	3	2	.265	.318	.418	.737
2014 Sea		AL	123	367	81	15	4	10	(4	6)	134	47	36	41	34	2	95	2	3	3	4	2	2	.221	.288	.365	.653
2015 Sea		AL	144	438	113	22	4	11	(6	5)	176	44	46	58	47	0	101	2	4	6	13	4	7	.258	.329	.402	.730
2016 TB		AL	152	548	133	29	6	30	(22	8)	264	73	81	74	47	4	149	3	0	3	6	4	5	.243	.304	.482	.786
2017 TB		AL	110	338	68	13	3	9	(6	3)	114	43	40	37	63	4	110	2	0	4	5	3	5	.201	.327	.337	.664
5 ML YEARS			605	1997	476	90	23	68	(41	27)	816	248	239	251	215	6	507	10	9	18	33	16	21	.238	.313	.409	.722

Shelby Miller

Pitches: R **Bats:** R **Pos:** SP-4   **Ht:** 6'3" **Wt:** 225 **Born:** 10/10/1990 **Age:** 27

Year	Team	Lg	HOW MUCH HE PITCHED						WHAT HE GAVE UP														THE RESULTS							
			G	GS	CG	GF	IP	BFP	H	R	ER	HR	SH	SF	HB	TBB	IBB	SO	WP	Bk	W	L	Pct	Sh	Sv-Op	Hld	ERC	ERA
2012 StL		NL	6	1	0	1	13.2	54	9	2	2	0	0	0	1	4	0	16	0	0	1	0	1.000	0	0-0	1	1.65	1.32
2013 StL		NL	31	31	1	0	173.1	722	152	65	59	20	7	3	5	57	0	169	2	0	15	9	.625	1	0-0	0	3.34	3.06
2014 StL		NL	32	31	1	0	183.0	764	160	78	76	22	7	4	2	73	4	127	4	0	10	9	.526	1	0-0	0	3.56	3.74
2015 Atl		NL	33	33	2	0	205.1	860	183	82	69	13	8	4	6	73	8	171	5	2	6	17	.261	2	0-0	0	3.12	3.02
2016 Ari		NL	20	20	1	0	101.0	460	127	72	69	14	3	3	2	42	3	70	3	0	3	12	.200	1	0-0	0	6.03	6.15
2017 Ari		NL	4	4	0	0	22.0	99	20	10	10	1	0	0	0	12	1	20	1	1	2	2	.500	0	0-0	0	3.53	4.09
Postseason			5	2	0	0	13.2	61	16	8	8	1	1	1	1	6	0	12	0	0	0	0	-	0	0-0	0	5.46	5.27
6 ML YEARS			126	120	5	1	698.1	2959	651	309	285	70	25	14	16	261	16	573	15	3	37	49	.430	5	0-0	1	3.66	3.67

Hoby Milner

Pitches: L **Bats:** L **Pos:** RP-37   **Ht:** 6'2" **Wt:** 165 **Born:** 1/13/1991 **Age:** 27

Year	Team	Lg	HOW MUCH HE PITCHED						WHAT HE GAVE UP													THE RESULTS							
			G	GS	CG	GF	IP	BFP	H	R	ER	HR	SH	SF	HB	TBB	IBB	SO	WP	Bk	W	L	Pct	Sh	Sv-Op	Hld	ERC	ERA
2013 Clrwtr		A+	26	25	1	0	143.1	595	147	62	61	11	2	4	6	39	0	108	6	0	12	7	.632	0	0--	-	3.82	3.83
2014 Rdng		AA	25	25	1	0	143.1	616	146	72	67	25	5	8	1	56	0	86	0	0	10	6	.625	1	0--	-	4.74	4.21
2015 Rdng		AA	29	2	0	8	61.0	252	61	26	25	6	1	5	1	17	0	40	4	0	2	1	.667	0	0--	-	3.74	3.69
2016 LV		AAA	11	0	0	4	16.0	67	16	8	8	2	0	2	0	3	0	22	0	0	0	1	.000	0	1--	-	3.34	4.50
2016 Rdng		AA	38	0	0	18	49.0	204	41	12	10	3	0	4	4	12	2	54	2	0	5	3	.625	0	5--	-	2.57	1.84
2017 LV		AAA	22	0	0	9	27.2	108	24	8	8	1	0	0	2	4	1	27	1	0	1	2	.333	0	0--	-	2.34	2.60
2017 Phi		NL	37	0	0	5	31.1	139	30	7	7	2	2	1	4	16	3	22	0	0	0	0	-	0	0-1	7	4.39	2.01

Tommy Milone

Pitches: L **Bats:** L **Pos:** RP-9; SP-8   mah-LONE   **Ht:** 6'0" **Wt:** 220 **Born:** 2/16/1987 **Age:** 31

Year	Team	Lg	HOW MUCH HE PITCHED						WHAT HE GAVE UP													THE RESULTS							
			G	GS	CG	GF	IP	BFP	H	R	ER	HR	SH	SF	HB	TBB	IBB	SO	WP	Bk	W	L	Pct	Sh	Sv-Op	Hld	ERC	ERA
2011 Was		NL	5	5	0	0	26.0	110	28	11	11	2	3	2	2	4	0	15	0	0	1	0	1.000	0	0-0	0	3.55	3.81
2012 Oak		AL	31	31	1	0	190.0	791	207	90	79	24	3	3	4	36	2	137	2	0	13	10	.565	0	0-0	0	4.04	3.74
2013 Oak		AL	28	26	1	0	156.1	667	160	83	72	25	0	6	2	39	2	126	1	0	12	9	.571	0	0-0	0	3.98	4.14
2014 2 Tms			22	21	0	1	118.0	519	128	63	55	16	1	2	5	37	2	75	0	0	6	4	.600	0	0-0	0	4.55	4.19
2015 Min		AL	24	23	0	1	128.2	543	128	64	56	17	6	7	1	36	1	91	3	0	9	5	.643	0	1-1	0	3.79	3.92
2016 Min		AL	19	12	0	3	69.1	311	84	53	44	15	4	3	1	22	3	49	3	1	3	5	.375	0	0-0	1	5.77	5.71
2017 2 Tms		NL	17	8	0	2	48.1	221	65	43	41	15	2	0	0	14	3	38	0	0	1	3	.250	0	1-1	0	7.12	7.63
14 Oak		AL	16	16	0	0	96.1	405	91	42	38	12	1	2	4	26	2	61	0	0	6	3	.667	0	0-0	0	3.53	3.55
14 Min		AL	6	5	0	1	21.2	114	37	21	17	4	0	0	1	11	0	14	0	0	0	1	.000	0	0-0	0	9.76	7.06
17 Mil		NL	6	3	0	1	21.0	93	29	15	15	6	0	0	0	2	0	16	0	0	1	0	1.000	0	1-1	0	6.32	6.43
17 NYM		NL	11	5	0	1	27.1	128	36	28	26	9	2	0	0	12	3	22	0	0	0	3	.000	0	0-0	0	7.74	8.56
Postseason			1	1	0	0	6.0	25	5	1	1	0	0	0	1	1	0	6	1	0	0	0	-	0	0-0	0	2.26	1.50
7 ML YEARS			146	126	2	7	736.2	3162	800	407	358	114	19	23	15	188	15	531	9	1	45	36	.556	0	2-2	1	4.39	4.37

Juan Minaya

Pitches: R **Bats:** R **Pos:** RP-40   **Ht:** 6'4" **Wt:** 210 **Born:** 9/18/1990 **Age:** 27

Year	Team	Lg	HOW MUCH HE PITCHED						WHAT HE GAVE UP													THE RESULTS							
			G	GS	CG	GF	IP	BFP	H	R	ER	HR	SH	SF	HB	TBB	IBB	SO	WP	Bk	W	L	Pct	Sh	Sv-Op	Hld	ERC	ERA
2013 QuadC		A	24	5	0	15	54.2	255	63	34	29	5	3	4	4	23	1	57	3	0	3	6	.333	0	8--	-	5.08	4.77
2014 Lancst		A+	29	1	0	10	45.0	198	43	25	22	6	1	1	0	22	1	53	5	1	2	3	.400	0	1--	-	4.33	4.40
2014 CpChr		AA	6	0	0	0	8.2	38	9	3	3	1	0	0	0	4	0	11	1	0	0	0	-	0	0--	-	4.68	3.12
2015 CpChr		AA	29	0	0	10	44.1	190	43	16	16	2	1	2	5	16	1	48	9	0	1	0	1.000	0	1--	-	3.82	3.25
2015 Fresno		AAA	6	0	0	0	10.1	39	6	1	1	0	1	0	1	5	0	11	1	0	0	0	-	0	0--	-	2.14	0.87
2016 Fresno		AAA	17	0	0	8	25.1	109	25	15	11	1	2	2	1	10	1	19	0	0	1	3	.250	0	0--	-	3.66	3.91
2016 Charllt		AAA	17	0	0	5	26.2	114	23	11	10	2	1	0	1	10	2	28	0	0	4	3	.571	0	1--	-	3.03	3.38

Year Team	Lg	G	GS	CG	GF	IP	BFP	H	R	ER	HR	SH	SF	HB	TBB	IBB	SO	WP	Bk	W	L	Pct	Sh	Sv-Op	Hld	ERC	ERA
		HOW MUCH HE PITCHED						**WHAT HE GAVE UP**												**THE RESULTS**							
2017 Charllt	AAA	13	0	0	4	19.0	79	17	3	3	0	0	1	1	5	0	15	0	0	1	0	1.000	0	0- -	-	2.52	1.42
2016 CWS	AL	11	0	0	3	10.1	47	10	6	5	0	0	0	2	5	0	6	0	0	1	0	1.000	0	0-0		4.19	4.35
2017 CWS	AL	40	0	0	20	43.2	184	38	22	22	7	0	1	4	20	0	51	2	1	3	2	.600	0	9-10	2	4.51	4.53
2 ML YEARS		51	0	0	23	54.0	231	48	28	27	7	0	1	6	25	0	57	2	1	4	2	.667	0	9-10	2	4.46	4.50

Mike Minor

Pitches: L **Bats:** R **Pos:** RP-65 **Ht:** 6'4" **Wt:** 210 **Born:** 12/26/1987 **Age:** 30

Year Team	Lg	G	GS	CG	GF	IP	BFP	H	R	ER	HR	SH	SF	HB	TBB	IBB	SO	WP	Bk	W	L	Pct	Sh	Sv-Op	Hld	ERC	ERA
		HOW MUCH HE PITCHED						**WHAT HE GAVE UP**												**THE RESULTS**							
2010 Atl	NL	9	8	0	1	40.2	185	53	28	27	6	1	3	1	11	0	43	0	0	3	2	.600	0	0-0	0	5.71	5.98
2011 Atl	NL	15	15	0	0	82.2	361	93	39	38	7	3	1	1	30	5	77	2	0	5	3	.625	0	0-0	0	4.51	4.14
2012 Atl	NL	30	30	0	0	179.1	728	151	88	82	26	8	8	5	56	7	145	3	0	11	10	.524	0	0-0	0	3.28	4.12
2013 Atl	NL	32	32	1	0	204.2	820	177	79	73	22	5	6	1	46	2	181	5	0	13	9	.591	0	0-0	0	2.76	3.21
2014 Atl	NL	25	25	0	0	145.1	637	165	77	77	21	6	2	6	44	2	120	5	0	6	12	.333	0	0-0	0	4.93	4.77
2017 KC	AL	65	0	0	13	77.2	307	57	23	22	5	3	1	1	22	3	88	5	0	6	6	.500	0	6-9	17	2.07	2.55
Postseason		1	1	0	0	6.1	26	8	1	1	0	1	0	0	1	0	5	0	0	1	0	1.000	0	0-0	0	4.11	1.42
6 ML YEARS		176	110	1	14	730.1	3038	696	334	319	87	26	21	15	209	19	654	20	0	44	42	.512	0	6-9	17	3.56	3.93

A.J. Minter

Pitches: L **Bats:** L **Pos:** RP-16 **Ht:** 6'0" **Wt:** 205 **Born:** 9/2/1993 **Age:** 24

Year Team	Lg	G	GS	CG	GF	IP	BFP	H	R	ER	HR	SH	SF	HB	TBB	IBB	SO	WP	Bk	W	L	Pct	Sh	Sv-Op	Hld	ERC	ERA
		HOW MUCH HE PITCHED						**WHAT HE GAVE UP**												**THE RESULTS**							
2016 2 Tms	Low	13	0	0	4	16.0	58	5	0	0	0	0	1	0	5	0	16	1	0	0	0	-	0	2- -	-	0.61	0.00
2016 Missi	AA	18	0	0	1	18.2	76	13	5	5	0	0	1	0	6	0	31	3	0	1	0	1.000	0	0- -	-	1.62	2.41
2017 2 Tms	Low	6	0	0	0	6.0	21	4	1	1	1	0	0	0	0	0	10	0	0	0	0	-	0	0- -	-	1.48	1.50
2017 Gwnntt	AAA	17	0	0	3	15.1	71	15	11	8	1	1	2	0	10	0	17	1	0	1	2	.333	0	0- -	-	4.56	4.70
2017 Atl	NL	16	0	0	3	15.0	60	13	5	5	1	0	0	0	2	0	26	0	0	0	1	.000	0	0-0	5	2.15	3.00

Ariel Miranda

Pitches: L **Bats:** L **Pos:** SP-29; RP-2 **Ht:** 6'2" **Wt:** 190 **Born:** 1/10/1989 **Age:** 29

Year Team	Lg	G	GS	CG	GF	IP	BFP	H	R	ER	HR	SH	SF	HB	TBB	IBB	SO	WP	Bk	W	L	Pct	Sh	Sv-Op	Hld	ERC	ERA
		HOW MUCH HE PITCHED						**WHAT HE GAVE UP**												**THE RESULTS**							
2015 2 Tms	Low	6	6	0	0	25.0	100	17	10	10	2	1	0	1	8	0	30	0	1	1	1	.500	0	0- -	-	2.15	3.60
2015 Bowie	AA	8	8	0	0	45.0	193	40	23	18	1	2	5	2	18	0	41	3	0	5	2	.714	0	0- -	-	3.07	3.60
2016 Norfolk	AAA	19	19	0	0	100.2	420	95	47	44	11	3	3	2	31	0	87	1	0	4	7	.364	0	0- -	-	3.57	3.93
2016 2 Tms	AL	12	10	0	1	58.0	232	47	28	25	12	0	2	0	18	0	44	2	0	5	2	.714	0	0-0	0	3.44	3.88
2017 Sea	AL	31	29	1	1	160.0	678	140	93	91	37	2	8	5	63	1	137	8	0	8	7	.533	0	0-0	0	4.35	5.12
16 Bal	AL	1	0	0	0	2.0	11	4	3	3	0	0	0	0	0	0	4	0	0	0	0	-	0	0-0	0	6.75	13.50
16 Sea	AL	11	10	0	1	56.0	221	43	25	22	12	0	2	0	18	0	40	2	0	5	2	.714	0	0-0	0	3.32	3.54
2 ML YEARS		43	39	1	2	218.0	910	187	121	116	49	2	10	5	81	1	181	10	0	13	9	.591	0	0-0	0	4.10	4.79

Bryan Mitchell

Pitches: R **Bats:** L **Pos:** RP-19; SP-1 **Ht:** 6'3" **Wt:** 210 **Born:** 4/19/1991 **Age:** 27

Year Team	Lg	G	GS	CG	GF	IP	BFP	H	R	ER	HR	SH	SF	HB	TBB	IBB	SO	WP	Bk	W	L	Pct	Sh	Sv-Op	Hld	ERC	ERA
		HOW MUCH HE PITCHED						**WHAT HE GAVE UP**												**THE RESULTS**							
2017 S-WB*	AAA	14	13	0	0	63.2	260	59	26	23	1	0	2	2	13	0	66	6	0	3	3	.500	0	0- -	-	2.53	3.25
2014 NYY	AL	3	1	0	1	11.0	44	10	3	3	0	0	0	2	3	0	7	0	0	0	1	.000	0	0-0	0	3.34	2.45
2015 NYY	AL	20	2	0	8	29.2	143	37	24	21	4	0	0	2	16	1	29	6	0	0	2	.000	0	1-1	1	6.51	6.37
2016 NYY	AL	5	5	0	0	25.0	107	26	13	9	1	1	0	0	12	0	11	0	0	1	2	.333	0	0-0	0	4.32	3.24
2017 NYY	AL	20	1	0	8	32.2	153	42	24	21	2	0	0	1	13	1	17	2	0	1	1	.500	0	1-1	0	5.40	5.79
4 ML YEARS		48	9	0	17	98.1	447	115	64	54	7	1	0	5	44	2	64	8	0	2	6	.250	0	2-2	1	5.21	4.94

Yadier Molina

Bats: R **Throws:** R **Pos:** C-133;PH-3;1B-1 YAH-dee-air **Ht:** 5'11" **Wt:** 205 **Born:** 7/13/1982 **Age:** 35

Year Team	Lg	G	AB	H	2B	3B	HR	(Hm	Rd)	TB	R	RBI	RC	TBB	IBB	SO	HBP	SH	SF	SB	CS	GDP	Avg	OBP	Slg	OPS
						BATTING														**RUNNING**			**AVERAGES**			
2004 StL	NL	51	135	36	6	0	2	(1	1)	48	12	15	15	13	3	20	0	2	1	0	1	4	.267	.329	.356	.684
2005 StL	NL	114	385	97	15	1	8	(6	2)	138	36	49	46	23	3	30	2	8	3	2	3	10	.252	.295	.358	.654
2006 StL	NL	129	417	90	26	0	6	(2	4)	134	29	49	35	26	2	41	8	2	1	1	2	15	.216	.274	.321	.595
2007 StL	NL	111	353	97	15	0	6	(4	2)	130	30	40	38	34	5	43	3	2	4	1	1	18	.275	.340	.368	.708
2008 StL	NL	124	444	135	18	0	7	(2	5)	174	37	56	57	32	4	29	1	3	5	0	2	21	.304	.349	.392	.740
2009 StL	NL	140	481	141	23	1	6	(5	1)	184	45	54	60	50	2	39	6	4	6	9	3	27	.293	.366	.383	.749
2010 StL	NL	136	465	122	19	0	6	(1	5)	159	34	62	55	42	6	51	7	2	5	8	4	19	.262	.329	.342	.671
2011 StL	NL	139	475	145	32	1	14	(5	9)	221	55	65	64	33	4	44	1	5	4	4	5	21	.305	.349	.465	.814
2012 StL	NL	138	505	159	28	0	22	(9	13)	253	65	76	91	45	4	55	5	3	5	12	3	10	.315	.373	.501	.874
2013 StL	NL	136	505	161	44	0	12	(5	7)	241	68	80	84	30	4	55	3	0	3	3	2	14	.319	.359	.477	.836
2014 StL	NL	110	404	114	21	0	7	(3	4)	156	40	38	47	28	4	55	6	1	6	1	1	14	.282	.333	.386	.719
2015 StL	NL	136	488	132	23	2	4	(3	1)	171	34	61	48	32	4	59	0	1	9	3	1	16	.270	.310	.350	.660
2016 StL	NL	147	534	164	38	1	8	(4	4)	228	56	58	74	39	1	63	6	0	2	3	2	22	.307	.360	.427	.787
2017 StL	NL	136	501	137	27	1	18	(7	11)	220	60	82	67	28	4	74	4	1	9	9	4	14	.273	.312	.439	.751
Postseason		89	315	90	17	0	3	(2	1)	116	25	31	32	25	5	38	1	1	1	1	1	11	.286	.339	.368	.707
14 ML YEARS		1747	6092	1730	335	7	126	(57	69)	2457	601	785	785	455	49	658	52	42	59	56	34	225	.284	.336	.403	.739

Sam Moll

Pitches: L Bats: L Pos: RP-11

Ht: 5'10" Wt: 185 Born: 1/3/1992 Age: 26

Year	Team	Lg	HOW MUCH HE PITCHED						WHAT HE GAVE UP											THE RESULTS					
			G	GS	CG	GF	IP	BFP	H	R	ER	HR	SH	SF	HB	TBB	IBB	SO	WP	Bk	W	L	Pct	Sh	Sv-Op	Hld	ERC	ERA
2013	TriCity	A-	10	6	0	0	30.0	120	20	9	6	0	0	0	0	10	0	29	5	0	3	1	.750	0	0- --		1.57	1.80
2014	TriCity	A-	9	0	0	1	13.0	59	17	6	6	1	0	2	1	4	0	7	0	1	0	1	.000	0	0- --		5.70	4.15
2015	Mdest	A+	25	0	0	9	53.2	210	40	20	18	7	1	1	2	12	0	57	3	0	0	1	.000	0	2- --		2.44	3.02
2015	NwBrit	AA	13	0	0	1	14.2	54	7	2	2	0	0	0	0	4	0	17	0	0	0	0	-	0	0- --		0.94	1.23
2016	Albq	AAA	42	0	0	8	47.1	209	55	30	26	5	1	2	1	19	1	39	3	1	3	5	.375	0	2- --		5.19	4.94
2017	Albq	AAA	44	0	0	16	47.1	215	56	27	22	4	1	1	2	18	0	39	4	0	3	2	.600	0	0- --		5.05	4.18
2017	Nashv	AAA	6	0	0	0	7.0	28	5	0	0	0	0	0	1	1	0	8	0	0	0	0	-	0	0- --		1.62	0.00
2017	Oak	AL	11	0	0	1	6.2	35	13	8	8	2	0	0	0	3	0	7	0	0	0	0	-	0	0-0	3	12.45	10.80

Yoan Moncada

Bats: B Throws: R Pos: 2B-54

yo-AHN

Ht: 6'2" Wt: 205 Born: 5/27/1995 Age: 23

Year	Team	Lg	BATTING													RUNNING			AVERAGES			
			G	AB	H	2B	3B	HR	(Hm | Rd)	TB	R	RBI	RC	TBB	IBB	SO	HBP	SH	SF	SB	CS	GDP	Avg	OBP	Slg	OPS
2015	Grnville	A	81	306	85	19	3	8	(- | -)	134	61	38	62	42	1	83	10	2	3	49	3	3	.278	.380	.438	.817
2016	Salem	A+	61	228	70	25	3	4	(- | -)	113	57	34	55	45	3	60	5	3	3	36	8	4	.307	.427	.496	.923
2016	Portlnd	AA	45	177	49	6	3	11	(- | -)	94	37	28	36	27	1	64	2	1	0	9	4	2	.277	.379	.531	.910
2017	Charllt	AAA	80	309	87	9	3	12	(- | -)	138	57	36	55	49	3	102	0	0	3	17	8	4	.282	.377	.447	.823
2016	Bos	AL	8	19	4	1	0	0	(0 | 0)	5	3	1	0	1	0	12	0	0	0	0	0	0	.211	.250	.263	.513
2017	CWS	AL	54	199	46	8	2	8	(4 | 4)	82	31	22	27	29	0	74	3	0	0	3	2	0	.231	.338	.412	.750
	2 ML YEARS		62	218	50	9	2	8	(4 | 4)	87	34	23	27	30	0	86	3	0	0	3	2	0	.229	.331	.399	.730

Carlos Moncrief

Bats: L Throws: R Pos: PH-21;RF-10;LF-1

Ht: 6'0" Wt: 220 Born: 11/3/1988 Age: 29

Year	Team	Lg	BATTING													RUNNING			AVERAGES			
			G	AB	H	2B	3B	HR	(Hm | Rd)	TB	R	RBI	RC	TBB	IBB	SO	HBP	SH	SF	SB	CS	GDP	Avg	OBP	Slg	OPS
2013	Akron	AA	129	489	139	26	7	17	(- | -)	230	77	75	84	55	3	98	1	1	6	15	7	13	.284	.354	.470	.824
2014	Clmbs	AAA	132	480	130	33	4	12	(- | -)	207	64	63	70	38	5	130	4	6	2	8	3	9	.271	.328	.431	.759
2015	Clmbs	AAA	57	166	31	3	0	7	(- | -)	55	21	24	21	32	1	59	2	1	2	5	0	1	.187	.322	.331	.653
2015	Akron	AA	56	199	52	9	3	4	(- | -)	79	29	27	31	34	1	28	0	2	1	6	4	5	.261	.368	.397	.765
2016	Rchmd	AA	72	176	46	11	0	5	(- | -)	72	27	22	30	28	1	38	3	2	0	6	0	2	.261	.372	.409	.781
2017	Scrmto	AAA	71	171	49	17	0	2	(- | -)	72	17	18	26	17	1	45	0	1	1	4	2	3	.287	.349	.421	.770
2017	SF	NL	28	38	8	1	0	0	(0 | 0)	9	4	5	3	3	0	15	0	0	2	0	0	0	.211	.256	.237	.493

Raul Mondesi

Bats: B Throws: R Pos: 2B-14;SS-9;PR-4;PH-2

Ht: 6'1" Wt: 185 Born: 7/27/1995 Age: 22

Year	Team	Lg	BATTING													RUNNING			AVERAGES			
			G	AB	H	2B	3B	HR	(Hm | Rd)	TB	R	RBI	RC	TBB	IBB	SO	HBP	SH	SF	SB	CS	GDP	Avg	OBP	Slg	OPS
2013	Lxngtn	A	125	482	126	13	7	7	(- | -)	174	61	47	57	34	1	118	2	15	3	24	10	5	.261	.311	.361	.672
2014	Wilmg	A+	110	435	92	14	12	8	(- | -)	154	54	33	41	24	0	122	3	8	2	17	4	7	.211	.256	.354	.610
2015	NWArk	AA	81	304	74	11	5	6	(- | -)	113	36	33	34	17	0	88	0	12	5	19	6	5	.243	.279	.372	.651
2016	NWArk	AA	29	116	31	5	1	5	(- | -)	53	20	17	21	13	1	30	0	1	1	17	1	0	.267	.338	.457	.795
2016	Omha	AAA	14	56	17	2	4	1	(- | -)	30	9	9	10	2	0	19	0	3	0	5	0	0	.304	.328	.536	.863
2017	Omha	AAA	85	321	98	20	8	13	(- | -)	173	52	52	61	18	2	86	2	10	6	21	3	5	.305	.340	.539	.879
2016	KC	AL	47	135	25	1	3	2	(0 | 2)	38	16	13	9	6	0	48	2	6	0	9	1	1	.185	.231	.281	.512
2017	KC	AL	25	53	9	1	0	1	(1 | 0)	13	4	3	0	3	0	22	0	4	0	5	2	2	.170	.214	.245	.460
	Postseason		1	1	0	0	0	0	(0 | 0)	0	0	0	0	0	0	1	0	0	0	0	0	0	.000	.000	.000	.000
	2 ML YEARS		72	188	34	2	3	3	(1 | 2)	51	20	16	9	9	0	70	2	10	0	14	3	3	.181	.226	.271	.497

Frankie Montas

Pitches: R Bats: R Pos: RP-23

MOHN-tahs

Ht: 6'2" Wt: 255 Born: 3/21/1993 Age: 25

Year	Team	Lg	HOW MUCH HE PITCHED						WHAT HE GAVE UP											THE RESULTS					
			G	GS	CG	GF	IP	BFP	H	R	ER	HR	SH	SF	HB	TBB	IBB	SO	WP	Bk	W	L	Pct	Sh	Sv-Op	Hld	ERC	ERA
2013	2 Tms	Low	24	23	1	1	111.0	495	114	75	67	11	5	3	3	50	0	127	17	1	5	11	.313	0	0- --	-	4.47	5.43
2014	2 Tms	Low	14	14	1	0	76.0	296	51	19	13	3	1	2	2	21	0	79	3	2	5	0	1.000	0	0- --	-	1.72	1.54
2015	Brham	AA	23	23	1	0	112.0	465	89	49	37	3	4	5	1	48	0	108	4	1	5	5	.500	1	0- --	-	2.64	2.97
2017	Nashv	AAA	9	8	0	0	29.1	119	25	17	17	4	0	0	0	7	0	37	1	0	0	2	.000	0	0- --	-	2.87	5.22
2015	CWS	AL	7	2	0	2	15.0	66	14	8	8	1	0	0	0	9	1	20	0	0	0	2	.000	0	0-0	0	4.16	4.80
2017	Oak	AL	23	0	0	5	32.0	152	39	25	25	10	0	0	3	20	0	36	1	0	1	1	.500	0	0-0	1	8.72	7.03
	2 ML YEARS		30	2	0	7	47.0	218	53	33	33	11	0	0	3	29	1	56	1	0	1	3	.250	0	0-0	1	7.16	6.32

Miguel Montero

Bats: L Throws: R Pos: C-56;PH-20;DH-3;1B-1

Ht: 5'11" Wt: 210 Born: 7/9/1983 Age: 34

Year	Team	Lg	BATTING													RUNNING			AVERAGES			
			G	AB	H	2B	3B	HR	(Hm | Rd)	TB	R	RBI	RC	TBB	IBB	SO	HBP	SH	SF	SB	CS	GDP	Avg	OBP	Slg	OPS
2006	Ari	NL	6	16	4	1	0	0	(0 | 0)	5	0	3	2	1	0	3	0	0	0	0	0	0	.250	.294	.313	.607
2007	Ari	NL	84	214	48	7	0	10	(7 | 3)	85	30	37	19	20	2	35	3	1	6	0	0	7	.224	.292	.397	.689
2008	Ari	NL	70	184	47	16	1	5	(1 | 4)	80	24	18	21	19	3	49	2	1	1	0	0	1	.255	.330	.435	.765
2009	Ari	NL	128	425	125	30	0	16	(5 | 11)	203	61	59	65	38	5	78	3	4	2	1	2	6	.294	.355	.478	.832
2010	Ari	NL	85	297	79	20	2	9	(0 | 9)	130	36	43	38	29	3	71	2	0	3	0	1	10	.266	.332	.438	.770
2011	Ari	NL	140	493	139	36	1	18	(8 | 10)	231	65	86	84	47	10	97	8	1	4	1	1	14	.282	.351	.469	.820
2012	Ari	NL	141	486	139	25	2	15	(4 | 11)	213	65	88	92	73	6	130	12	0	2	0	0	15	.286	.391	.438	.829
2013	Ari	NL	116	413	95	14	0	11	(8 | 3)	142	44	42	42	51	4	110	5	0	6	0	0	18	.230	.318	.344	.662

243

Year Team	Lg	G	AB	H	2B	3B	HR	(Hm Rd)	TB	R	RBI	RC	TBB	IBB	SO	HBP	SH	SF	SB	CS	GDP	Avg	OBP	Slg	OPS
2014 Ari	NL	136	489	119	23	0	13	(5 8)	181	40	72	63	56	11	97	9	0	6	0	4	12	.243	.329	.370	.699
2015 ChC	NL	113	347	86	11	0	15	(8 7)	142	36	53	52	49	5	103	4	0	3	1	1	9	.248	.345	.409	.754
2016 ChC	NL	86	241	52	8	1	8	(2 6)	86	33	33	31	38	5	58	3	0	2	1	0	8	.216	.327	.357	.684
2017 2 Tms		76	185	40	6	0	6	(4 2)	64	24	16	18	23	1	47	3	0	2	1	0	6	.216	.310	.346	.656
17 ChC	NL	44	98	28	3	0	4	(3 1)	43	12	8	14	11	1	24	2	0	1	1	0	3	.286	.366	.439	.805
17 Tor	AL	32	87	12	3	0	2	(1 1)	21	12	8	4	12	0	23	1	0	1	0	0	3	.138	.248	.241	.489
Postseason		26	60	12	2	0	1	(1 0)	17	6	8	5	7	2	19	0	0	0	0	0	0	.200	.284	.283	.567
12 ML YEARS		1181	3790	973	197	7	126	(52 74)	1562	458	550	527	444	55	878	54	5	37	5	9	106	.257	.340	.412	.752

Rafael Montero

Pitches: R **Bats:** R **Pos:** SP-18; RP-16 **Ht:** 6'0" **Wt:** 185 **Born:** 10/17/1990 **Age:** 27

Year Team	Lg	G	GS	CG	GF	IP	BFP	H	R	ER	HR	SH	SF	HB	TBB	IBB	SO	WP	Bk	W	L	Pct	Sh	Sv-Op	Hld	ERC	ERA
2017 LsVgs*	AAA	5	5	0	0	29.0	115	18	9	8	3	1	2	0	12	0	37	0	0	0	2	.000	0	0- -	-	2.21	2.48
2014 NYM	NL	10	8	0	1	44.1	194	44	21	20	8	0	0	0	23	0	42	0	0	1	3	.250	0	0-0	0	5.16	4.06
2015 NYM	NL	5	1	0	1	10.0	46	9	6	5	0	1	0	0	5	3	13	0	0	1	0	.000	0	0-0	0	2.50	4.50
2016 NYM	NL	9	3	0	1	19.0	93	23	17	17	4	0	0	0	16	1	20	2	0	0	1	.000	0	0-0	0	8.15	8.05
2017 NYM	NL	34	18	0	4	119.0	550	141	75	73	12	9	8	5	67	5	114	6	1	5	11	.313	0	0-0	0	6.01	5.52
4 ML YEARS		58	30	0	7	192.1	883	217	119	115	24	10	8	5	111	9	189	8	1	6	16	.273	0	0-0	1	5.81	5.38

Jordan Montgomery

Pitches: L **Bats:** L **Pos:** SP-29 **Ht:** 6'6" **Wt:** 225 **Born:** 12/27/1992 **Age:** 25

Year Team	Lg	G	GS	CG	GF	IP	BFP	H	R	ER	HR	SH	SF	HB	TBB	IBB	SO	WP	Bk	W	L	Pct	Sh	Sv-Op	Hld	ERC	ERA
2014 2 Tms	Low	10	7	0	0	19.0	79	16	10	8	0	0	0	0	6	0	20	2	0	1	1	.500	0	0- -	-	2.24	3.79
2015 2 Tms	Low	25	24	1	1	134.1	547	118	51	44	5	5	5	1	36	0	132	15	1	10	8	.556	0	0- -	-	2.57	2.95
2016 Trntn	AA	19	19	1	0	102.1	438	94	35	29	5	2	5	2	36	0	97	9	0	9	4	.692	1	0- -	-	3.11	2.55
2016 S-WB	AAA	6	6	0	0	37.0	144	28	4	4	0	3	0	0	9	0	37	1	0	5	1	.833	0	0- -	-	1.71	0.97
2017 NYY	AL	29	29	0	0	155.1	649	140	72	67	21	2	3	1	51	0	144	7	1	9	7	.563	0	0-0	0	3.50	3.88

Mike Montgomery

Pitches: L **Bats:** L **Pos:** RP-30; SP-14 **Ht:** 6'5" **Wt:** 215 **Born:** 7/1/1989 **Age:** 28

Year Team	Lg	G	GS	CG	GF	IP	BFP	H	R	ER	HR	SH	SF	HB	TBB	IBB	SO	WP	Bk	W	L	Pct	Sh	Sv-Op	Hld	ERC	ERA
2015 Sea	AL	16	16	2	0	90.0	395	92	49	46	11	0	0	4	37	1	64	10	0	4	6	.400	2	0-0	0	4.56	4.60
2016 2 Tms		49	7	0	18	100.0	414	79	33	28	8	3	2	10	38	2	92	10	0	4	5	.444	0	0-0	5	3.13	2.52
2017 ChC	NL	44	14	0	11	130.2	540	103	52	49	10	5	2	8	55	4	100	7	0	7	8	.467	0	3-3	3	3.09	3.38
16 Sea	AL	32	2	0	13	61.2	250	49	18	16	3	2	1	6	18	2	54	5	0	3	4	.429	0	0-0	3	2.61	2.34
16 ChC	NL	17	5	0	5	38.1	164	30	15	12	5	1	1	4	20	0	38	5	0	1	1	.500	0	0-0	2	4.01	2.82
Postseason		11	0	0	3	14.1	63	14	5	5	0	1	1	0	7	0	11	1	0	1	1	.500	0	1-1	2	3.53	3.14
3 ML YEARS		109	37	2	29	320.2	1349	274	134	123	29	8	4	22	130	7	256	27	0	15	19	.441	2	3-3	6	3.50	3.45

Andrew Moore

Pitches: R **Bats:** R **Pos:** SP-9; RP-2 **Ht:** 6'0" **Wt:** 185 **Born:** 6/2/1994 **Age:** 24

Year Team	Lg	G	GS	CG	GF	IP	BFP	H	R	ER	HR	SH	SF	HB	TBB	IBB	SO	WP	Bk	W	L	Pct	Sh	Sv-Op	Hld	ERC	ERA
2015 Everett	A-	14	8	0	0	39.0	151	37	12	9	2	0	0	1	2	0	43	1	0	1	1	.500	0	0- -	-	2.37	2.08
2016 Bkrsfld	A+	9	9	0	0	54.2	210	36	14	10	2	3	3	0	13	0	47	1	1	3	1	.750	0	0- -	-	1.51	1.65
2016 Jacksn	AA	19	19	1	0	108.1	436	112	41	38	9	4	4	1	18	0	86	0	0	9	3	.750	1	0- -	-	3.38	3.16
2017 Ark	AA	6	5	0	0	34.2	138	28	8	8	4	1	0	0	9	0	33	2	0	1	2	.333	0	0- -	-	2.65	2.08
2017 Tacom	AAA	15	14	0	0	75.0	306	68	30	29	9	2	1	2	13	0	66	1	0	3	4	.429	0	0- -	-	2.90	3.48
2017 Sea	AL	11	9	0	1	59.0	243	60	36	35	14	0	4	1	8	0	31	0	0	1	5	.167	0	0-1	0	4.04	5.34

Matt Moore

Pitches: L **Bats:** L **Pos:** SP-31; RP-1 **Ht:** 6'3" **Wt:** 210 **Born:** 6/18/1989 **Age:** 29

Year Team	Lg	G	GS	CG	GF	IP	BFP	H	R	ER	HR	SH	SF	HB	TBB	IBB	SO	WP	Bk	W	L	Pct	Sh	Sv-Op	Hld	ERC	ERA
2011 TB	AL	3	1	0	0	9.1	40	9	3	3	1	0	0	0	3	0	15	2	0	1	0	1.000	0	0-0	1	3.54	2.89
2012 TB	AL	31	31	0	0	177.1	759	158	85	75	18	3	4	7	81	5	175	8	1	11	11	.500	0	0-0	0	3.83	3.81
2013 TB	AL	27	27	1	0	150.1	642	119	58	55	14	5	6	4	76	1	143	17	1	17	4	.810	1	0-0	0	3.36	3.29
2014 TB	AL	2	2	0	0	10.0	44	10	3	3	1	0	0	0	5	0	6	0	0	0	2	.000	0	0-0	0	4.48	2.70
2015 TB	AL	12	12	0	0	63.0	278	74	40	38	9	0	3	4	23	1	46	6	0	3	4	.429	0	0-0	0	5.63	5.43
2016 2 Tms		33	33	0	0	198.1	838	184	93	90	25	4	4	6	72	1	178	6	1	13	12	.520	0	0-0	0	3.83	4.08
2017 SF	NL	32	31	0	1	174.1	790	200	116	107	27	6	4	7	67	3	148	10	0	6	15	.286	0	0-0	0	5.33	5.52
16 TB	AL	21	21	0	0	130.0	549	125	62	59	20	3	2	5	40	0	109	3	1	7	7	.500	0	0-0	0	4.02	4.08
16 SF	NL	12	12	0	0	68.1	289	59	31	31	5	1	2	1	32	1	69	3	0	6	5	.545	0	0-0	0	3.47	4.08
Postseason		5	3	0	0	24.1	97	14	11	9	2	0	1	2	8	1	25	2	0	1	1	.500	0	0-0	0	1.78	3.33
7 ML YEARS		140	137	1	1	782.2	3391	754	398	371	95	18	21	28	327	11	711	49	3	51	48	.515	1	0-0	1	4.20	4.27

Tyler Moore

Bats: R **Throws:** R **Pos:** PH-55;1B-45;LF-7;RF-6;PR-2 **Ht:** 6'2" **Wt:** 220 **Born:** 1/30/1987 **Age:** 31

Year	Team	Lg	G	AB	H	2B	3B	HR	(Hm	Rd)	TB	R	RBI	RC	TBB	IBB	SO	HBP	SH	SF	SB	CS	GDP	Avg	OBP	Slg	OPS
2017	NewOr*	AAA	13	39	9	2	0	1	(-	-)	14	3	7	5	7	0	11	0	0	0	0	0	0	.231	.348	.359	.707
2012	Was	NL	75	156	41	9	0	10	(3	7)	80	20	29	26	14	0	46	1	0	0	3	0	3	.263	.327	.513	.840
2013	Was	NL	63	167	37	9	0	4	(2	2)	58	16	21	17	8	1	58	1	1	1	0	0	1	.222	.260	.347	.607
2014	Was	NL	42	91	21	2	0	4	(1	3)	35	8	14	10	7	0	29	2	0	0	0	0	0	.231	.300	.385	.685
2015	Was	NL	97	187	38	12	0	6	(3	3)	68	14	27	19	11	2	45	1	0	1	0	0	2	.203	.250	.364	.614
2017	Mia	NL	104	187	43	14	0	6	(3	3)	75	17	30	19	10	0	56	1	1	4	0	0	7	.230	.267	.401	.668
	Postseason		1	1	1	0	0	0	(0	0)	1	0	2	1	0	0	0	0	0	0	0	0	0	1.000	1.000	1.000	2.000
	5 ML YEARS		381	788	180	46	0	30	(12	18)	316	75	121	91	50	3	234	6	2	6	3	0	15	.228	.278	.401	.679

Kendrys Morales

Bats: B **Throws:** R **Pos:** DH-129;1B-12;PH-9 KEN-dreez **Ht:** 6'1" **Wt:** 225 **Born:** 6/20/1983 **Age:** 35

Year	Team	Lg	G	AB	H	2B	3B	HR	(Hm	Rd)	TB	R	RBI	RC	TBB	IBB	SO	HBP	SH	SF	SB	CS	GDP	Avg	OBP	Slg	OPS
2006	LAA	AL	57	197	46	10	1	5	(1	4)	73	21	22	19	17	1	28	0	0	1	1	1	11	.234	.293	.371	.664
2007	LAA	AL	43	119	35	10	4	2	(2	2)	57	12	15	15	6	2	21	1	0	0	0	1	5	.294	.333	.479	.812
2008	LAA	AL	27	61	13	2	0	3	(0	3)	24	7	8	3	4	0	7	1	0	0	0	1	3	.213	.273	.393	.666
2009	LAA	AL	152	566	173	43	2	34	(21	13)	322	86	108	105	46	10	117	2	0	8	3	7	15	.306	.355	.569	.924
2010	LAA	AL	51	193	56	5	0	11	(7	4)	94	29	39	34	12	3	31	5	0	1	0	1	5	.290	.346	.487	.833
2012	LAA	AL	134	484	132	26	1	22	(10	12)	226	61	73	68	31	1	116	4	0	3	0	1	11	.273	.320	.467	.787
2013	Sea	AL	156	602	167	34	0	23	(12	11)	270	64	80	85	49	6	114	5	0	1	0	0	21	.277	.336	.449	.785
2014	2 Tms	AL	98	367	80	20	0	8	(4	4)	124	28	42	29	27	3	68	3	0	4	0	0	12	.218	.274	.338	.612
2015	KC	AL	158	569	165	41	2	22	(10	12)	276	81	106	98	58	4	103	8	0	4	0	0	24	.290	.362	.485	.847
2016	KC	AL	154	558	147	24	0	30	(12	18)	261	65	93	86	48	2	120	7	0	5	0	0	24	.263	.327	.468	.795
2017	Tor	AL	150	557	139	25	2	28	(13	15)	248	67	85	71	43	2	132	5	0	3	0	0	22	.250	.308	.445	.753
14	Min	AL	39	154	36	11	0	1	(0	1)	50	12	18	11	6	1	27	0	0	2	0	0	4	.234	.259	.325	.584
14	Sea	AL	59	213	44	9	0	7	(4	3)	74	16	24	18	21	2	41	3	0	2	0	0	8	.207	.285	.347	.632
	Postseason		32	98	22	1	0	6	(4	2)	41	8	17	12	6	0	20	1	0	2	0	0	1	.224	.271	.418	.689
	11 ML YEARS		1180	4273	1153	240	6	190	(92	98)	1975	521	671	613	341	34	857	41	0	30	4	12	149	.270	.328	.462	.790

Colin Moran

Bats: L **Throws:** R **Pos:** 1B-4;3B-3;PH-2;SS-1 **Ht:** 6'4" **Wt:** 204 **Born:** 10/1/1992 **Age:** 25

Year	Team	Lg	G	AB	H	2B	3B	HR	(Hm	Rd)	TB	R	RBI	RC	TBB	IBB	SO	HBP	SH	SF	SB	CS	GDP	Avg	OBP	Slg	OPS
2013	Grnsbr	A	42	154	46	8	1	4	(-	-)	68	19	23	25	15	0	25	1	0	5	1	0	2	.299	.354	.442	.796
2014	Jupiter	A+	89	361	106	21	0	5	(-	-)	142	34	33	50	28	1	53	0	0	3	1	2	10	.294	.342	.393	.735
2014	CpChr	AA	28	112	34	6	0	2	(-	-)	46	12	22	16	9	2	23	0	0	2	0	1	2	.304	.350	.411	.760
2015	CpChr	AA	96	366	112	25	2	9	(-	-)	168	47	67	66	43	1	79	4	0	4	1	0	11	.306	.381	.459	.840
2016	Fresno	AAA	117	459	119	18	1	10	(-	-)	169	50	69	58	47	1	124	2	0	3	3	2	10	.259	.329	.368	.697
2017	Fresno	AAA	79	302	93	15	1	18	(-	-)	164	53	63	59	31	3	55	2	0	3	0	3	7	.308	.373	.543	.916
2016	Hou	AL	9	23	3	1	0	0	(0	0)	4	1	2	0	1	0	8	1	0	0	0	0	4	.130	.200	.174	.374
2017	Hou	AL	7	11	4	0	1	1	(0	1)	9	3	3	4	1	0	1	0	0	0	0	0	0	.364	.417	.818	1.235
	2 ML YEARS		16	34	7	1	1	1	(0	1)	13	4	5	4	2	0	9	1	0	0	0	0	4	.206	.270	.382	.653

Mitch Moreland

Bats: L **Throws:** L **Pos:** 1B-138;PH-14;DH-9 **Ht:** 6'2" **Wt:** 230 **Born:** 9/6/1985 **Age:** 32

Year	Team	Lg	G	AB	H	2B	3B	HR	(Hm	Rd)	TB	R	RBI	RC	TBB	IBB	SO	HBP	SH	SF	SB	CS	GDP	Avg	OBP	Slg	OPS
2010	Tex	AL	47	145	37	4	0	9	(3	6)	68	20	25	27	25	5	36	1	0	2	3	1	3	.255	.364	.469	.833
2011	Tex	AL	134	464	120	22	1	16	(7	9)	192	60	51	56	39	6	92	4	2	3	2	2	9	.259	.320	.414	.733
2012	Tex	AL	114	327	90	18	0	15	(10	5)	153	41	50	46	23	5	71	1	2	4	1	1	8	.275	.321	.468	.789
2013	Tex	AL	147	462	107	24	1	23	(10	13)	202	60	60	55	45	1	117	3	0	8	0	0	11	.232	.299	.437	.736
2014	Tex	AL	52	167	41	9	1	2	(1	1)	58	18	23	20	12	0	43	1	2	2	0	0	7	.246	.297	.347	.644
2015	Tex	AL	132	471	131	27	0	23	(9	14)	227	51	85	74	32	2	112	7	0	5	1	0	9	.278	.330	.482	.812
2016	Tex	AL	147	460	107	21	0	22	(13	9)	194	49	60	56	35	5	118	8	0	0	1	0	8	.233	.298	.422	.720
2017	Bos	AL	149	508	125	34	4	22	(10	12)	225	73	79	69	57	6	120	6	0	5	0	1	14	.246	.326	.443	.769
	Postseason		33	97	21	6	0	3	(3	0)	36	8	13	14	9	1	22	1	1	0	0	0	3	.216	.290	.371	.661
	8 ML YEARS		922	3004	758	159	3	132	(63	69)	1319	372	433	403	268	30	709	31	6	29	8	5	69	.252	.317	.439	.756

Diego Moreno

Pitches: R **Bats:** R **Pos:** RP-5 **Ht:** 6'1" **Wt:** 180 **Born:** 7/21/1987 **Age:** 30

Year	Team	Lg	G	GS	CG	GF	IP	BFP	H	R	ER	HR	SH	SF	HB	TBB	IBB	SO	WP	Bk	W	L	Pct	Sh	Sv-Op	Hld	ERC	ERA
2013	Tampa	A+	18	0	0	8	27.2	122	26	16	15	2	0	1	3	10	0	25	5	0	2	4	.333	0	0- -	-	3.73	4.88
2013	Trntn	AA	6	0	0	6	9.1	36	4	1	1	0	0	1	2	2	0	12	3	0	1	0	1.000	0	0- -	-	1.08	0.96
2014	Trntn	AA	8	0	0	8	11.1	41	5	1	1	0	0	1	0	2	0	13	0	0	1	0	1.000	0	0- -	-	0.68	0.79
2014	S-WB	AAA	30	1	0	9	46.1	214	62	25	25	2	3	2	0	15	1	42	1	0	2	3	.400	0	2- -	-	5.17	4.86
2015	S-WB	AAA	26	4	0	8	53.2	207	39	14	13	1	1	4	0	16	0	42	0	0	3	0	1.000	0	1- -	-	1.89	2.18
2016	S-WB	AAA	28	2	0	9	49.0	218	55	32	28	5	0	2	1	17	0	52	1	1	6	1	.857	0	1- -	-	4.59	5.14
2017	Drham	AAA	11	0	0	8	16.1	60	9	2	2	0	0	0	0	3	0	17	1	0	0	0	-	0	5- -	-	0.97	1.10
2017	Clmbs	AAA	9	0	0	2	12.1	45	8	1	1	1	0	0	0	2	0	10	0	0	1	0	1.000	0	0- -	-	1.52	0.73
2015	NYY	AL	4	0	0	1	10.1	45	9	6	6	1	0	2	3	3	0	8	1	0	1	0	1.000	0	0-0	0	3.58	5.23
2017	TB	AL	5	0	0	3	5.2	26	6	4	3	1	0	0	1	2	0	6	0	0	0	1	.000	0	0-0	0	5.39	4.76
	2 ML YEARS		9	0	0	4	16.0	71	15	10	9	2	0	3	5	5	0	14	1	0	1	1	.500	0	0-0	0	4.20	5.06

Adam Morgan

Pitches: L Bats: L Pos: RP-37   Ht: 6'1" Wt: 200 Born: 2/27/1990 Age: 28

Year Team	Lg	G	GS	CG	GF	IP	BFP	H	R	ER	HR	SH	SF	HB	TBB	IBB	SO	WP	Bk	W	L	Pct	Sh	Sv-Op	Hld	ERC	ERA
2017 LV*	AAA	12	0	0	3	17.1	74	19	9	9	1	0	2	1	5	0	14	0	1	0	1	.000	0	0--	-	4.18	4.67
2015 Phi	NL	15	15	0	0	84.1	352	88	45	42	14	1	3	4	17	0	49	2	1	5	7	.417	0	0-0	0	4.21	4.48
2016 Phi	NL	23	21	0	1	113.1	507	141	81	76	23	3	4	4	29	3	95	2	0	2	11	.154	0	0-0	0	5.72	6.04
2017 Phi	NL	37	0	0	6	54.2	229	51	25	25	10	0	0	0	18	2	63	1	0	3	3	.500	0	0-1	6	3.92	4.12
3 ML YEARS		75	36	0	7	252.1	1088	280	151	143	47	4	7	8	64	5	207	5	1	10	21	.323	0	0-1	6	4.81	5.10

Mike Morin

Pitches: R Bats: R Pos: RP-16   Ht: 6'4" Wt: 220 Born: 5/3/1991 Age: 27

MORE-in

Year Team	Lg	G	GS	CG	GF	IP	BFP	H	R	ER	HR	SH	SF	HB	TBB	IBB	SO	WP	Bk	W	L	Pct	Sh	Sv-Op	Hld	ERC	ERA
2017 Salt Lk*	AAA	22	1	0	4	39.1	154	34	14	14	5	0	2	2	7	0	25	0	0	0	1	.000	0	1--	-	2.97	3.20
2014 LAA	AL	60	0	0	10	59.0	246	51	22	19	3	2	4	3	19	6	54	3	0	4	4	.500	0	0-2	9	2.76	2.90
2015 LAA	AL	47	0	0	10	35.1	151	36	28	25	3	2	2	2	9	2	41	0	0	4	2	.667	0	1-1	5	3.61	6.37
2016 LAA	AL	60	0	0	8	55.2	227	52	31	27	6	2	1	1	15	1	49	1	1	2	2	.500	0	0-1	12	3.37	4.37
2017 2 Tms	AL	16	0	0	8	20.0	93	29	16	16	3	1	2	1	5	1	16	0	0	0	0	-	0	0-0	0	6.64	7.20
17 LAA	AL	10	0	0	3	14.1	65	21	11	11	3	1	1	1	2	1	10	0	0	0	0	-	0	0-0	0	6.84	6.91
17 KC	AL	6	0	0	5	5.2	28	8	5	5	0	0	1	0	3	0	6	0	0	0	0	-	0	0-0	0	6.06	7.94
Postseason		1	0	0	0	1.0	6	3	2	2	1	0	1	0	0	0	1	1	0	0	0	-	0	0-0	0	25.51	18.00
4 ML YEARS		183	0	0	36	170.0	717	168	97	87	15	7	9	7	48	10	160	4	1	10	8	.556	0	1-4	26	3.55	4.61

Max Moroff

Bats: B Throws: R Pos: 2B-28;SS-16;PH-9;3B-6;PR-5   Ht: 5'10" Wt: 185 Born: 5/13/1993 Age: 25

Year Team	Lg	G	AB	H	2B	3B	HR	(Hm	Rd)	TB	R	RBI	RC	TBB	IBB	SO	HBP	SH	SF	SB	CS	GDP	Avg	OBP	Slg	OPS
2013 WV	A	115	429	100	18	3	8	(-	-)	148	75	48	53	65	0	102	2	7	3	8	8	7	.233	.335	.345	.680
2014 Bradtn	A+	130	467	114	30	6	1	(-	-)	159	57	50	54	54	0	129	3	7	3	21	15	4	.244	.324	.340	.665
2015 Altna	AA	136	523	153	28	6	7	(-	-)	214	79	51	84	70	3	111	1	13	5	17	13	8	.293	.374	.409	.783
2016 Indy	AAA	133	421	97	18	4	8	(-	-)	147	61	45	61	90	1	129	2	5	2	9	7	6	.230	.367	.349	.716
2017 Indy	AAA	51	185	47	10	0	13	(-	-)	96	31	37	39	41	2	59	1	0	1	5	2	1	.254	.390	.519	.909
2016 Pit	NL	2	2	0	0	0	0	(0	0)	0	0	0	0	0	0	2	0	0	0	0	0	0	.000	.000	.000	.000
2017 Pit	NL	56	120	24	4	1	3	(3	0)	39	19	21	15	16	0	43	2	1	1	0	1	0	.200	.302	.325	.627
2 ML YEARS		58	122	24	4	1	3	(3	0)	39	19	21	15	16	0	45	2	1	1	0	1	0	.197	.298	.320	.618

Reyes Moronta

Pitches: R Bats: R Pos: RP-7   Ht: 6'0" Wt: 175 Born: 1/6/1993 Age: 25

Year Team	Lg	G	GS	CG	GF	IP	BFP	H	R	ER	HR	SH	SF	HB	TBB	IBB	SO	WP	Bk	W	L	Pct	Sh	Sv-Op	Hld	ERC	ERA
2013 SlKzr	A-	6	6	0	0	21.2	98	24	15	12	2	1	1	2	8	0	22	1	1	2	2	.500	0	0--	-	4.81	4.98
2014 Giants	R	20	0	0	9	19.1	87	16	12	10	1	2	0	2	11	0	30	1	1	0	1	.000	0	5--	-	3.72	4.66
2015 Augsta	A	42	0	0	31	48.2	226	56	32	31	1	2	1	1	23	1	64	8	0	1	7	.125	0	12--	-	4.54	5.73
2016 SnJos	A+	60	0	0	30	59.0	243	43	20	17	7	1	1	1	20	0	93	6	0	0	3	.000	0	14--	-	2.53	2.59
2017 Rchmd	AA	19	0	0	12	18.0	81	15	9	8	1	0	0	0	12	0	26	2	0	0	1	.000	0	5--	-	3.76	4.00
2017 Scrmto	AAA	13	0	0	2	17.0	70	13	4	4	1	0	0	0	8	0	17	0	0	3	0	1.000	0	0--	-	2.85	2.12
2017 SF	NL	7	0	0	1	6.2	29	6	2	2	1	0	0	0	3	1	11	0	0	0	0	-	0	0-1	0	3.74	2.70

Akeel Morris

Pitches: R Bats: R Pos: RP-8   Ht: 6'1" Wt: 195 Born: 11/14/1992 Age: 25

ah-KEEL

Year Team	Lg	G	GS	CG	GF	IP	BFP	H	R	ER	HR	SH	SF	HB	TBB	IBB	SO	WP	Bk	W	L	Pct	Sh	Sv-Op	Hld	ERC	ERA
2013 Bklyn	A-	14	3	0	7	45.0	183	29	7	5	1	1	0	1	23	0	60	1	0	4	1	.800	0	1--	-	2.24	1.00
2014 Savann	A	41	0	0	28	57.0	211	19	5	4	1	4	0	1	22	0	89	5	1	4	1	.800	0	16--	-	0.86	0.63
2015 Stluci	A+	24	0	0	20	32.0	120	11	6	6	1	1	2	0	14	0	46	2	1	0	1	.000	0	13--	-	0.99	1.69
2015 Bnghtn	AA	23	0	0	9	29.1	117	17	8	8	1	0	1	0	15	1	35	2	3	0	1	.000	0	0--	-	1.90	2.45
2016 Bnghtn	AA	22	0	0	16	25.1	109	19	13	13	4	1	0	0	16	0	36	0	0	2	2	.500	0	6--	-	4.00	4.62
2016 Missi	AA	25	0	0	4	35.2	152	27	9	9	0	1	1	0	21	1	50	6	0	3	1	.750	0	0--	-	2.74	2.27
2017 Missi	AA	6	0	0	5	7.2	27	2	0	0	0	0	0	0	2	0	9	0	0	0	0	-	0	4--	-	0.44	0.00
2017 Gwnntt	AAA	30	0	0	2	46.2	204	38	18	16	3	1	0	1	23	0	53	4	0	1	3	.250	0	1--	-	3.15	3.09
2015 NYM	NL	1	0	0	0	0.2	8	3	5	5	1	0	0	0	3	0	0	1	0	0	0	-	0	0-0	0	75.11	67.50
2017 Atl	NL	8	0	0	6	7.1	32	6	1	1	0	0	0	0	4	0	9	0	0	0	0	-	0	0-0	0	2.87	1.23
2 ML YEARS		9	0	0	6	8.0	40	9	6	6	1	0	0	0	7	0	9	0	0	0	0	-	0	0-0	0	6.83	6.75

Bryan Morris

Pitches: R Bats: L Pos: RP-20   Ht: 6'3" Wt: 220 Born: 3/28/1987 Age: 31

Year Team	Lg	G	GS	CG	GF	IP	BFP	H	R	ER	HR	SH	SF	HB	TBB	IBB	SO	WP	Bk	W	L	Pct	Sh	Sv-Op	Hld	ERC	ERA
2012 Pit	NL	5	0	0	2	5.0	20	2	2	1	0	0	1	0	2	0	6	1	0	0	0	-	0	0-0	0	1.32	1.80
2013 Pit	NL	55	0	0	21	65.0	270	57	25	25	8	0	5	2	28	5	37	6	0	5	7	.417	0	0-0	0	3.78	3.46
2014 2 Tms	NL	60	0	0	10	64.1	272	58	17	13	6	7	3	4	24	6	50	8	1	8	1	.889	0	0-7	17	3.50	1.82
2015 Mia	NL	67	0	0	18	63.0	277	67	26	22	3	4	0	3	26	0	47	2	0	5	4	.556	0	0-2	18	4.31	3.14
2016 Mia	NL	24	0	0	4	17.2	74	15	7	6	4	0	0	1	10	1	13	0	0	0	0	-	0	1-3	6	5.19	3.06
2017 SF	NL	20	0	0	4	21.0	94	24	16	15	1	3	1	0	11	2	15	1	0	2	0	1.000	0	0-0	0	4.91	6.43

Year Team	Lg	G	GS	CG	GF	IP	BFP	H	R	ER	HR	SH	SF	HB	TBB	IBB	SO	WP	Bk	W	L	Pct	Sh	Sv-Op	Hld	ERC	ERA
		HOW MUCH HE PITCHED						**WHAT HE GAVE UP**												**THE RESULTS**							
14 Pit	NL	21	0	0	7	23.2	103	25	11	10	4	2	2	2	12	3	14	3	1	4	0	1.000	0	0-3	4	5.75	3.80
14 Mia	NL	39	0	0	3	40.2	169	33	6	3	2	5	1	2	12	3	36	5	0	4	1	.800	0	0-4	13	2.39	0.66
Postseason		1	0	0	1	1.0	4	1	0	0	0	0	0	0	0	0	1	0	0	0	0	-	0	0-0	0	1.95	0.00
6 ML YEARS		231	0	0	59	236.0	1007	223	93	82	22	14	10	11	101	14	168	18	1	20	12	.625	0	1-12	49	3.98	3.13

Logan Morrison

Bats: L **Throws:** L **Pos:** 1B-126;DH-17;PH-12

Ht: 6'3" **Wt:** 245 **Born:** 8/25/1987 **Age:** 30

Year Team	Lg	G	AB	H	2B	3B	HR	(Hm	Rd)	TB	R	RBI	RC	TBB	IBB	SO	HBP	SH	SF	SB	CS	GDP	Avg	OBP	Slg	OPS
					BATTING																**RUNNING**		**AVERAGES**			
2010 Fla	NL	62	244	69	20	7	2	(1	1)	109	43	18	41	41	0	51	2	0	0	0	1	4	.283	.390	.447	.837
2011 Fla	NL	123	462	114	25	4	23	(12	11)	216	54	72	55	54	3	99	5	0	4	2	1	9	.247	.330	.468	.797
2012 Mia	NL	93	296	68	15	1	11	(4	7)	118	30	36	27	31	2	58	4	0	3	1	0	9	.230	.308	.399	.707
2013 Mia	NL	85	293	71	13	4	6	(1	5)	110	32	36	37	38	5	56	2	0	0	0	0	10	.242	.333	.375	.709
2014 Sea	AL	99	336	88	20	0	11	(7	4)	141	41	38	46	24	1	59	3	0	2	5	2	9	.262	.315	.420	.735
2015 Sea	AL	146	457	103	15	3	17	(7	10)	175	47	54	53	47	5	81	4	1	2	8	4	7	.225	.302	.383	.685
2016 TB	AL	107	353	84	18	1	14	(6	8)	146	45	43	50	37	1	89	6	0	2	4	2	4	.238	.319	.414	.733
2017 TB	AL	149	512	126	22	1	38	(11	27)	264	75	85	77	81	8	149	5	0	3	2	0	12	.246	.353	.516	.868
8 ML YEARS		864	2953	723	148	21	122	(49	73)	1279	367	382	386	353	25	642	31	1	16	22	10	64	.245	.330	.433	.763

Brandon Morrow

Pitches: R **Bats:** R **Pos:** RP-45

Ht: 6'3" **Wt:** 205 **Born:** 7/26/1984 **Age:** 33

Year Team	Lg	G	GS	CG	GF	IP	BFP	H	R	ER	HR	SH	SF	HB	TBB	IBB	SO	WP	Bk	W	L	Pct	Sh	Sv-Op	Hld	ERC	ERA
		HOW MUCH HE PITCHED						**WHAT HE GAVE UP**												**THE RESULTS**							
2017 OkCity*	AAA	20	0	0	15	20.0	92	25	18	16	5	1	0	1	5	0	22	4	0	0	5	.000	0	6- -		6.04	7.20
2007 Sea	AL	60	0	0	18	63.1	289	56	29	29	3	4	4	1	50	5	66	4	0	3	4	.429	0	0-2	18	4.47	4.12
2008 Sea	AL	45	5	0	24	64.2	265	40	26	24	10	1	0	0	34	1	75	5	0	3	4	.429	0	10-12	3	2.84	3.34
2009 Sea	AL	26	10	0	9	69.2	313	66	38	34	10	1	2	0	44	1	63	3	0	2	4	.333	0	6-8	1	4.99	4.39
2010 Tor	AL	26	26	1	0	146.1	629	136	76	73	11	2	4	9	66	0	178	8	0	10	7	.588	1	0-0	0	3.99	4.49
2011 Tor	AL	30	30	0	0	179.1	777	162	103	94	21	4	9	12	69	1	203	12	1	11	11	.500	0	0-0	0	3.79	4.72
2012 Tor	AL	21	21	3	0	124.2	504	98	45	41	12	1	3	2	41	0	108	3	0	10	7	.588	3	0-0	0	2.73	2.96
2013 Tor	AL	10	10	0	0	54.1	242	63	39	34	12	0	3	1	18	1	42	1	0	2	3	.400	0	0-0	0	5.60	5.63
2014 Tor	AL	13	6	0	2	33.1	148	37	21	21	2	1	0	0	18	0	30	1	1	1	3	.250	0	0-0	1	5.09	5.67
2015 SD	NL	5	5	0	0	33.0	126	29	10	10	3	1	1	0	7	0	23	0	0	2	0	1.000	0	0-0	0	2.84	2.73
2016 SD	NL	18	0	0	2	16.0	68	19	4	4	2	2	1	0	3	1	23	0	0	1	0	1.000	0	0-1	2	4.40	1.69
2017 LAD	NL	45	0	0	10	43.2	170	31	10	10	0	0	0	1	9	1	50	2	0	6	0	1.000	0	2-3	10	1.48	2.06
11 ML YEARS		299	113	4	65	828.1	3531	737	401	373	86	17	27	26	359	11	846	39	2	51	43	.543	4	18-26	35	3.73	4.05

Michael Morse

Bats: R **Throws:** R **Pos:** PH-16;1B-10;LF-1

Ht: 6'5" **Wt:** 245 **Born:** 3/22/1982 **Age:** 36

Year Team	Lg	G	AB	H	2B	3B	HR	(Hm	Rd)	TB	R	RBI	RC	TBB	IBB	SO	HBP	SH	SF	SB	CS	GDP	Avg	OBP	Slg	OPS
					BATTING																**RUNNING**		**AVERAGES**			
2005 Sea	AL	72	230	64	10	1	3	(3	0)	85	27	23	28	18	0	50	8	0	2	3	1	9	.278	.349	.370	.718
2006 Sea	AL	21	43	16	5	0	0	(0	0)	21	5	11	9	3	0	7	0	0	2	1	0	9	.372	.396	.488	.884
2007 Sea	AL	9	18	8	2	0	0	(0	0)	10	1	3	6	1	0	4	1	0	0	0	0	0	.444	.500	.556	1.056
2008 Sea	AL	5	9	2	1	0	0	(0	0)	3	0	0	1	1	0	4	1	0	0	0	0	0	.222	.364	.333	.697
2009 Was	NL	32	52	13	3	0	3	(3	0)	25	4	10	8	3	0	16	0	0	0	0	0	1	.250	.291	.481	.772
2010 Was	NL	98	266	77	12	2	15	(6	9)	138	36	41	42	22	1	64	4	0	1	0	1	6	.289	.352	.519	.870
2011 Was	NL	146	522	158	36	0	31	(11	20)	287	73	95	96	36	5	126	13	0	4	2	3	9	.303	.360	.550	.910
2012 Was	NL	102	406	118	17	1	18	(7	11)	191	53	62	57	16	0	97	4	0	4	0	1	14	.291	.321	.470	.791
2013 2 Tms	AL	88	312	67	13	0	13	(5	8)	119	34	27	24	21	1	87	3	0	1	0	0	12	.215	.270	.381	.651
2014 SF	NL	131	438	122	32	3	16	(6	10)	208	48	61	55	31	0	121	9	0	4	0	0	19	.279	.336	.475	.811
2015 2 Tms	NL	98	229	53	7	1	5	(1	4)	77	14	19	20	23	0	76	4	0	0	0	0	10	.231	.313	.336	.649
2016 Pit	NL	6	8	0	0	0	0	(0	0)	0	0	0	0	0	0	2	0	0	0	0	0	0	.000	.000	.000	.000
2017 SF	NL	24	36	7	1	0	1	(0	1)	11	1	3	1	3	0	14	0	0	1	0	0	1	.194	.250	.306	.556
13 Sea	AL	76	283	64	13	0	13	(5	8)	116	31	27	24	20	1	80	3	0	1	0	0	10	.226	.283	.410	.693
13 Bal	AL	12	29	3	0	0	0	(0	0)	3	3	0	0	1	0	7	0	0	0	0	0	2	.103	.133	.103	.237
15 Mia	NL	53	160	34	4	0	4	(0	4)	50	8	12	9	12	0	55	2	0	0	0	0	6	.213	.276	.313	.588
15 Pit	NL	45	69	19	3	1	1	(1	0)	27	6	7	11	11	0	21	2	0	0	0	0	4	.275	.390	.391	.782
Postseason		16	40	12	1	0	2	(2	0)	19	5	7	5	1	0	9	0	0	1	0	0	1	.300	.310	.475	.785
13 ML YEARS		832	2569	705	139	8	105	(43	62)	1175	296	355	347	178	7	668	47	0	19	6	6	83	.274	.331	.457	.788

Charlie Morton

Pitches: R **Bats:** R **Pos:** SP-25

Ht: 6'5" **Wt:** 235 **Born:** 11/12/1983 **Age:** 34

Year Team	Lg	G	GS	CG	GF	IP	BFP	H	R	ER	HR	SH	SF	HB	TBB	IBB	SO	WP	Bk	W	L	Pct	Sh	Sv-Op	Hld	ERC	ERA
		HOW MUCH HE PITCHED						**WHAT HE GAVE UP**												**THE RESULTS**							
2008 Atl	NL	16	15	0	0	74.2	345	80	56	51	9	5	4	2	41	2	48	2	0	4	8	.333	0	0-0	0	5.21	6.15
2009 Pit	NL	18	18	1	0	97.0	416	102	49	49	7	1	1	5	40	0	62	4	0	5	9	.357	1	0-0	0	4.56	4.55
2010 Pit	NL	17	17	0	0	79.2	382	112	79	67	15	6	6	7	26	3	59	5	1	2	12	.143	0	0-0	0	7.10	7.57
2011 Pit	NL	29	29	2	0	171.2	769	186	82	73	6	12	6	13	77	5	110	9	1	10	10	.500	1	0-0	0	4.52	3.83
2012 Pit	NL	9	9	0	0	50.1	223	62	30	26	5	5	2	2	11	1	25	1	0	2	6	.250	0	0-0	0	4.74	4.65
2013 Pit	NL	20	20	0	0	116.0	493	113	51	42	6	6	2	16	36	1	85	5	0	7	4	.636	0	0-0	0	3.84	3.26
2014 Pit	NL	26	26	0	0	157.1	666	143	76	65	9	7	5	19	57	2	126	8	0	6	12	.333	0	0-0	0	3.64	3.72
2015 Pit	NL	23	23	0	0	129.0	563	137	77	69	13	4	0	12	41	6	96	2	1	9	9	.500	0	0-0	0	4.41	4.81
2016 Phi	NL	4	4	0	0	17.1	71	15	8	8	1	1	0	0	8	0	19	1	1	1	1	.500	0	0-0	0	3.42	4.15
2017 Hou	AL	25	25	0	0	146.2	617	125	65	59	14	2	2	13	50	1	163	4	0	14	7	.667	0	0-0	0	3.34	3.62
Postseason		1	1	0	0	5.2	24	3	2	2	1	1	0	0	4	0	4	0	0	1	0	1.000	0	0-0	0	3.16	3.18
10 ML YEARS		187	186	3	0	1039.2	4545	1075	573	509	85	49	28	89	387	21	793	44	4	60	78	.435	2	0-0	0	4.35	4.41

Brandon Moss

Bats: L Throws: R Pos: DH-89;1B-14;PH-12;LF-5;RF-2   Ht: 6'1" Wt: 210 Born: 9/16/1983 Age: 34

								BATTING													RUNNING			AVERAGES			
Year	Team	Lg	G	AB	H	2B	3B	HR	(Hm	Rd)	TB	R	RBI	RC	TBB	IBB	SO	HBP	SH	SF	SB	CS	GDP	Avg	OBP	Slg	OPS
2007	Bos	AL	15	25	7	2	1	0	(0	0)	11	6	1	3	4	0	6	0	0	0	0	0	1	.280	.379	.440	.819
2008	2 Tms		79	236	58	15	3	8	(4	4)	103	19	34	30	21	1	70	1	0	5	1	2	2	.246	.304	.436	.741
2009	Pit	NL	133	385	91	20	4	7	(4	3)	140	47	41	37	34	3	84	4	0	1	1	5	7	.236	.304	.364	.668
2010	Pit	NL	17	26	4	1	0	0	(0	0)	5	2	2	2	1	0	6	0	0	0	0	0	1	.154	.185	.192	.377
2011	Phi	NL	5	6	0	0	0	0	(0	0)	0	0	0	0	0	0	2	0	0	0	0	0	0	.000	.000	.000	.000
2012	Oak	AL	84	265	77	18	0	21	(9	12)	158	48	52	50	26	2	90	3	0	2	1	1	5	.291	.358	.596	.954
2013	Oak	AL	145	446	114	23	3	30	(10	20)	233	73	87	79	50	3	140	6	0	3	4	2	6	.256	.337	.522	.859
2014	Oak	AL	147	500	117	23	2	25	(12	13)	219	70	81	78	67	7	153	10	0	3	1	0	6	.234	.334	.438	.772
2015	2 Tms		145	469	106	24	2	19	(4	15)	191	47	58	43	49	4	148	5	0	3	0	1	12	.226	.304	.407	.711
2016	StL	NL	128	413	93	19	2	28	(13	15)	200	66	67	57	39	3	141	7	0	5	1	0	8	.225	.300	.484	.784
2017	KC	AL	118	362	75	14	0	22	(15	7)	155	41	50	37	37	0	128	0	0	2	2	0	7	.207	.279	.428	.707
08	Bos	AL	34	78	23	5	1	2	(1	1)	36	7	11	11	6	0	25	0	0	2	1	1	0	.295	.337	.462	.799
08	Pit	NL	45	158	35	10	2	6	(3	3)	67	12	23	19	15	1	45	1	0	3	0	1	2	.222	.288	.424	.712
15	Cle	AL	94	337	73	17	1	15	(2	13)	137	36	50	32	32	2	106	3	0	3	0	0	9	.217	.288	.407	.695
15	StL	NL	51	132	33	7	1	4	(2	2)	54	11	8	11	17	2	42	2	0	0	0	1	3	.250	.344	.409	.753
	Postseason		14	41	7	0	0	3	(0	3)	16	4	7	5	6	1	24	2	0	0	0	0	0	.171	.306	.390	.696
	11 ML YEARS		1016	3133	742	159	17	160	(71	89)	1415	419	473	416	328	23	968	36	0	24	11	11	54	.237	.314	.452	.766

Jason Motte

Pitches: R Bats: R Pos: RP-46   Ht: 6'0" Wt: 205 Born: 6/22/1982 Age: 36

					HOW MUCH HE PITCHED				WHAT HE GAVE UP											THE RESULTS						
Year	Team	Lg	G	GS	CG	GF	IP	BFP	H	R	ER	HR	SH	SF	HB	TBB	IBB	SO	WP	Bk	W	L	Pct	Sh	Sv-Op	Hld	ERC	ERA
2017	Gwnntt*	AAA	7	0	0	5	7.1	27	5	1	1	0	0	0	0	1	0	7	1	0	1	0	1.000	0	2- -		1.26	1.23
2008	StL	NL	12	0	0	4	11.0	40	5	2	1	0	1	0	0	3	0	16	0	0	0	0	-	0	1-1	4	0.89	0.82
2009	StL	NL	69	0	0	14	56.2	244	57	32	30	10	0	3	2	23	1	54	2	1	4	4	.500	0	0-3	15	4.86	4.76
2010	StL	NL	56	0	0	13	52.1	208	41	13	13	5	1	3	0	18	3	54	1	0	4	2	.667	0	2-3	12	2.68	2.24
2011	StL	NL	78	0	0	27	68.0	268	49	22	17	2	1	3	5	16	2	63	1	0	5	2	.714	0	9-13	18	1.87	2.25
2012	StL	NL	67	0	0	58	72.0	279	49	23	22	9	2	1	2	17	1	86	0	0	4	5	.444	0	42-49	0	2.08	2.75
2014	StL	NL	29	0	0	10	25.0	110	29	14	13	7	0	2	0	9	0	17	1	0	1	0	1.000	0	0-0	1	6.22	4.68
2015	ChC	NL	57	0	0	18	48.1	206	48	21	21	4	3	2	2	11	5	34	2	0	8	1	.889	0	6-7	9	3.18	3.91
2016	Col	NL	30	0	0	8	23.2	109	28	15	13	6	0	1	2	8	1	24	0	0	1	0	1.000	0	0-0	6	6.20	4.94
2017	Atl	NL	46	0	0	10	40.2	166	28	16	16	6	0	2	3	20	1	27	1	0	1	0	1.000	0	0-3	1	3.40	3.54
	Postseason		19	0	0	16	21.2	79	12	6	5	2	0	0	0	2	0	10	0	0	1	1	.500	0	8-8	0	1.07	2.08
	9 ML YEARS		444	0	0	162	397.2	1630	334	158	146	49	8	17	16	125	14	375	8	1	27	15	.643	0	60-79	70	3.16	3.30

Taylor Motter

Bats: R Throws: R Pos: SS-39;2B-18;1B-15;LF-15;PH-7;PR-7;3B-6;RF-5;DH-1   Ht: 6'1" Wt: 195 Born: 9/18/1989 Age: 28

									BATTING												RUNNING			AVERAGES			
Year	Team	Lg	G	AB	H	2B	3B	HR	(Hm	Rd)	TB	R	RBI	RC	TBB	IBB	SO	HBP	SH	SF	SB	CS	GDP	Avg	OBP	Slg	OPS
2013	2 Tms	Low	71	221	65	16	2	3	(-	-)	94	27	21	36	24	0	30	1	5	1	20	8	5	.294	.364	.425	.790
2014	Mont	AA	119	452	125	19	3	16	(-	-)	198	60	61	68	34	1	71	5	6	9	15	7	20	.277	.328	.438	.766
2015	Drham	AAA	127	486	142	43	1	14	(-	-)	229	74	72	89	57	1	95	5	1	9	26	8	11	.292	.366	.471	.837
2016	Drham	AAA	88	350	80	17	0	13	(-	-)	136	44	46	44	33	1	65	2	0	2	20	4	9	.229	.297	.389	.686
2017	Tacom	AAA	25	100	35	6	1	7	(-	-)	64	24	18	26	14	0	12	1	0	2	6	3	4	.350	.427	.640	1.067
2016	TB	AL	34	80	15	3	0	2	(0	2)	24	11	9	7	11	0	19	1	0	1	0	1	1	.188	.290	.300	.590
2017	Sea	AL	92	258	51	12	0	7	(5	2)	84	29	26	21	21	0	62	0	0	1	12	1	9	.198	.257	.326	.583
	2 ML YEARS		126	338	66	15	0	9	(5	4)	108	40	35	28	32	0	81	1	0	2	12	2	10	.195	.265	.320	.585

Mike Moustakas

Bats: L Throws: R Pos: 3B-127;DH-17;PH-4   moo-STOCK-us   Ht: 6'0" Wt: 215 Born: 9/11/1988 Age: 29

									BATTING												RUNNING			AVERAGES			
Year	Team	Lg	G	AB	H	2B	3B	HR	(Hm	Rd)	TB	R	RBI	RC	TBB	IBB	SO	HBP	SH	SF	SB	CS	GDP	Avg	OBP	Slg	OPS
2011	KC	AL	89	338	89	18	1	5	(3	2)	124	26	30	31	22	0	51	1	2	2	2	0	5	.263	.309	.367	.675
2012	KC	AL	149	563	136	34	1	20	(10	10)	232	69	73	64	39	4	124	7	0	5	5	2	4	.242	.296	.412	.708
2013	KC	AL	136	472	110	26	0	12	(5	7)	172	42	42	35	32	1	83	5	1	4	2	4	13	.233	.287	.364	.651
2014	KC	AL	140	457	97	21	1	15	(5	10)	165	45	54	44	35	1	74	3	1	4	1	0	12	.212	.271	.361	.632
2015	KC	AL	147	549	156	34	1	22	(9	13)	258	73	82	85	43	1	76	13	4	5	1	2	14	.284	.348	.470	.817
2016	KC	AL	27	104	25	6	0	7	(4	3)	52	12	13	10	9	0	13	0	0	1	0	1	5	.240	.301	.500	.801
2017	KC	AL	148	555	151	24	0	38	(14	24)	289	75	85	77	34	7	94	3	0	6	0	0	18	.272	.314	.521	.835
	Postseason		31	117	26	3	0	6	(3	3)	47	14	15	12	5	0	17	1	1	1	0	0	2	.222	.258	.402	.660
	7 ML YEARS		836	3038	764	163	4	119	(50	69)	1292	342	379	346	214	14	515	32	8	26	11	9	71	.251	.305	.425	.730

Gabriel Moya

Pitches: L Bats: L Pos: RP-7   Ht: 6'0" Wt: 175 Born: 1/9/1995 Age: 23

					HOW MUCH HE PITCHED				WHAT HE GAVE UP											THE RESULTS						
Year	Team	Lg	G	GS	CG	GF	IP	BFP	H	R	ER	HR	SH	SF	HB	TBB	IBB	SO	WP	Bk	W	L	Pct	Sh	Sv-Op	Hld	ERC	ERA
2014	Msoula	R+	15	12	0	0	63.0	287	83	47	42	8	0	1	5	19	0	68	8	3	5	4	.556	0	0- -	-	6.13	6.00
2015	Msoula	R+	25	0	0	6	23.1	92	15	6	5	2	2	1	0	8	0	36	0	1	2	1	.667	0	0- -	-	1.96	1.93
2016	2 Tms	Low	52	0	0	16	63.2	243	38	14	11	2	0	2	1	17	0	82	5	1	6	1	.857	0	5- -	-	1.40	1.55
2017	Jacksn	AA	34	0	0	26	43.2	163	22	5	4	1	1	0	1	12	0	68	2	1	4	1	.800	0	17- -	-	1.14	0.82
2017	Chatt	AA	13	0	0	12	14.2	56	8	1	1	1	1	1	0	3	0	19	0	0	2	0	1.000	0	7- -	-	1.18	0.61
2017	Min	AL	7	0	0	5	6.1	26	5	3	3	2	0	0	0	2	0	5	0	1	0	0	-	0	1-1	0	3.87	4.26

Peter Moylan

Pitches: R Bats: R Pos: RP-79 Ht: 6'2" Wt: 225 Born: 12/2/1978 Age: 39

Year	Team	Lg	G	GS	CG	GF	IP	BFP	H	R	ER	HR	SH	SF	HB	TBB	IBB	SO	WP	Bk	W	L	Pct	Sh	Sv-Op	Hld	ERC	ERA
2006	Atl	NL	15	0	0	5	15.0	68	18	8	8	1	1	0	0	5	1	14	0	0	0	0	-	0	0-0	0	4.47	4.80
2007	Atl	NL	80	0	0	16	90.0	359	65	27	18	6	4	4	7	31	12	63	2	0	5	3	.625	0	1-2	8	2.36	1.80
2008	Atl	NL	7	0	0	2	5.2	25	5	1	1	1	0	0	1	1	0	5	0	0	0	1	.000	0	1-2	4	3.51	1.59
2009	Atl	NL	87	0	0	6	73.0	309	65	29	23	0	4	3	2	35	8	61	1	0	6	2	.750	0	0-5	25	3.06	2.84
2010	Atl	NL	85	0	0	7	63.2	271	53	24	21	5	5	2	2	37	6	52	3	0	6	2	.750	0	1-4	21	3.75	2.97
2011	Atl	NL	13	0	0	0	8.1	38	12	3	3	0	0	0	0	3	0	10	0	0	2	1	.667	0	0-0	2	5.87	3.24
2012	Atl	NL	8	0	0	3	5.0	21	3	3	1	1	1	0	0	2	0	2	1	0	1	0	1.000	0	1-1	1	2.40	1.80
2013	LAD	NL	14	0	0	7	15.1	70	23	11	11	3	0	0	0	7	1	6	0	0	1	0	1.000	0	0-0	1	3.20	6.46
2015	Atl	NL	22	0	0	7	10.1	44	12	5	4	1	0	0	0	8	0	8	0	1	1	0	1.000	0	0-1	3	8.59	3.48
2016	KC	AL	50	0	0	11	44.2	191	42	19	17	4	1	5	2	16	0	34	3	0	2	0	1.000	0	0-0	7	3.67	3.43
2017	KC	AL	79	0	0	7	59.1	243	40	26	23	4	0	1	5	25	3	46	1	0	0	0	-	0	0-1	24	2.48	3.49
	Postseason		4	0	0	0	1.0	6	1	0	0	0	0	0	0	0	0	1	0	0	0	0	-	0	0-1	0	1.26	0.00
	11 ML YEARS		460	0	0	68	390.1	1639	338	156	130	26	16	15	19	162	31	301	11	1	24	9	.727	0	4-16	96	3.27	3.00

Edward Mujica

Pitches: R Bats: R Pos: RP-5 moo-HEE-kah Ht: 6'3" Wt: 220 Born: 5/10/1984 Age: 34

Year	Team	Lg	G	GS	CG	GF	IP	BFP	H	R	ER	HR	SH	SF	HB	TBB	IBB	SO	WP	Bk	W	L	Pct	Sh	Sv-Op	Hld	ERC	ERA
2017	Toledo*	AAA	56	0	0	36	56.0	228	51	17	16	4	1	0	1	9	2	46	0	0	1	1	.500	0	21--	-	2.50	2.57
2006	Cle	AL	10	0	0	2	18.1	78	25	6	6	1	0	2	1	0	0	12	0	0	0	1	.000	0	0-0	0	4.50	2.95
2007	Cle	AL	10	0	0	5	13.0	60	19	12	12	3	0	1	0	2	0	7	0	0	0	0	-	0	0-0	0	6.63	8.31
2008	Cle	AL	33	0	0	13	38.2	168	46	29	29	5	0	4	1	10	3	27	1	0	3	2	.600	0	0-2	1	4.82	6.75
2009	SD	NL	67	4	0	15	93.2	393	101	44	41	14	1	3	0	19	4	76	3	1	3	5	.375	0	2-3	11	4.00	3.94
2010	SD	NL	59	0	0	24	69.2	268	59	29	28	14	1	0	0	6	0	72	1	0	2	1	.667	0	0-1	4	2.68	3.62
2011	Fla	NL	67	0	0	11	76.0	297	64	27	25	7	5	1	2	14	5	63	1	0	9	6	.600	0	0-3	17	2.46	2.96
2012	2 Tms	NL	70	0	0	16	65.1	258	56	24	22	7	1	1	1	12	3	47	1	0	3	0	.000	0	2-8	30	2.58	3.03
2013	StL	NL	65	0	0	49	64.2	255	60	20	20	9	3	1	1	5	1	46	0	1	2	1	.667	0	37-41	5	2.75	2.78
2014	Bos	AL	64	0	0	31	60.0	253	69	28	26	6	2	2	0	14	2	43	1	0	2	4	.333	0	8-9	3	4.28	3.90
2015	2 Tms	AL	49	0	0	13	47.1	194	52	28	25	10	2	1	1	7	2	30	1	3	3	5	.375	0	1-5	4	4.49	4.75
2017	Det	AL	5	0	0	1	6.1	30	11	7	7	4	0	2	0	0	0	7	0	0	0	0	-	0	0-0	1	10.93	9.95
12	Mia	NL	41	0	0	14	39.0	161	36	21	19	6	0	1	1	9	2	26	0	0	3	0	.000	0	2-6	12	3.35	4.38
12	StL	NL	29	0	0	2	26.1	97	20	3	3	1	1	0	0	3	1	21	1	0	0	0	-	0	0-2	18	1.57	1.03
15	Bos	AL	11	0	0	4	13.2	56	15	7	7	3	1	0	1	3	0	8	0	2	1	1	.500	0	0-1	0	5.32	4.61
15	Oak	AL	38	0	0	9	33.2	138	37	21	18	7	1	1	0	4	2	22	1	1	2	4	.333	0	1-4	4	4.17	4.81
	Postseason		11	0	0	3	9.2	39	10	3	3	1	0	1	0	1	0	4	0	0	1	0	1.000	0	0-0	2	3.16	2.79
	11 ML YEARS		499	4	0	180	553.0	2254	562	257	241	80	15	18	7	89	20	430	9	5	24	28	.462	0	50-72	76	3.55	3.92

Daniel Murphy

Bats: L Throws: R Pos: 2B-139;PH-7 Ht: 6'1" Wt: 220 Born: 4/1/1985 Age: 33

Year	Team	Lg	G	AB	H	2B	3B	HR	(Hm	Rd)	TB	R	RBI	RC	TBB	IBB	SO	HBP	SH	SF	SB	CS	GDP	Avg	OBP	Slg	OPS
2008	NYM	NL	49	131	41	9	3	2	(1	1)	62	24	17	26	18	1	28	1	0	1	0	2	4	.313	.397	.473	.871
2009	NYM	NL	155	508	135	38	4	12	(7	5)	217	60	63	60	38	4	69	0	4	6	4	2	13	.266	.313	.427	.741
2011	NYM	NL	109	391	125	28	2	6	(2	4)	175	49	49	57	24	2	42	3	3	2	5	5	14	.320	.362	.448	.809
2012	NYM	NL	156	571	166	40	3	6	(1	5)	230	62	65	78	36	5	82	1	0	4	10	2	12	.291	.332	.403	.735
2013	NYM	NL	161	658	188	38	4	13	(6	7)	273	92	78	86	32	2	95	2	2	5	23	3	13	.286	.319	.415	.733
2014	NYM	NL	143	596	172	37	2	9	(4	5)	240	79	57	78	39	3	86	2	0	5	13	5	15	.289	.332	.403	.734
2015	NYM	NL	130	499	140	38	2	14	(7	7)	224	56	73	71	31	10	38	2	0	6	2	2	15	.281	.322	.449	.770
2016	Was	NL	142	531	184	47	5	25	(10	15)	316	88	104	115	35	10	57	8	0	8	5	3	4	.347	.390	.595	.985
2017	Was	NL	144	534	172	43	3	23	(6	17)	290	94	93	103	52	14	77	4	0	3	2	0	16	.322	.384	.543	.928
	Postseason		19	74	26	2	0	7	(3	4)	49	16	17	19	11	3	14	0	0	1	3	2	1	.351	.430	.662	1.092
	9 ML YEARS		1189	4419	1323	318	28	110	(44	66)	2027	604	599	674	305	51	574	23	7	40	64	24	106	.299	.345	.459	.804

John Ryan Murphy

Bats: R Throws: R Pos: C-5 Ht: 5'11" Wt: 205 Born: 5/13/1991 Age: 27

Year	Team	Lg	G	AB	H	2B	3B	HR	(Hm	Rd)	TB	R	RBI	RC	TBB	IBB	SO	HBP	SH	SF	SB	CS	GDP	Avg	OBP	Slg	OPS
2017	Roch*	AAA	59	194	43	9	0	4	(-	-)	64	21	27	20	22	0	36	0	0	2	0	0	6	.222	.298	.330	.628
2017	Reno*	AAA	19	67	19	0	0	2	(-	-)	25	5	7	9	7	1	7	0	1	0	0	0	1	.284	.351	.373	.724
2013	NYY	AL	16	26	4	1	0	0	(0	0)	5	3	1	0	1	0	9	0	0	0	0	0	0	.154	.185	.192	.377
2014	NYY	AL	32	81	23	4	0	1	(1	0)	30	7	9	10	4	0	22	0	0	0	0	0	0	.284	.318	.370	.688
2015	NYY	AL	67	155	43	9	1	3	(1	2)	63	21	14	17	12	0	43	1	0	3	0	0	4	.277	.327	.406	.734
2016	Min	AL	26	82	12	3	0	1	(1	0)	18	4	3	0	5	0	19	0	2	1	0	0	3	.146	.193	.220	.413
2017	Ari	NL	5	7	1	1	0	0	(0	0)	2	0	1	0	0	0	1	0	0	0	0	0	1	.143	.143	.286	.429
	5 ML YEARS		146	351	83	18	1	5	(3	2)	118	35	28	27	22	0	94	1	3	4	0	0	8	.236	.280	.336	.617

Tom Murphy

Bats: R Throws: R Pos: C-8;PH-5 Ht: 6'1" Wt: 220 Born: 4/3/1991 Age: 27

Year	Team	Lg	G	AB	H	2B	3B	HR	(Hm	Rd)	TB	R	RBI	RC	TBB	IBB	SO	HBP	SH	SF	SB	CS	GDP	Avg	OBP	Slg	OPS
2017	Albq*	AAA	38	141	36	10	1	4	(-	-)	60	22	19	19	9	0	56	3	0	1	0	0	1	.255	.312	.426	.737

Year	Team	Lg	G	AB	H	2B	3B	HR	(Hm	Rd)	TB	R	RBI	RC	TBB	IBB	SO	HBP	SH	SF	SB	CS	GDP	Avg	OBP	Slg	OPS
										BATTING											RUNNING			AVERAGES			
2015	Col	NL	11	35	9	1	0	3	(3	0)	19	5	9	9	4	1	10	0	0	0	0	0	0	.257	.333	.543	.876
2016	Col	NL	21	44	12	2	0	5	(5	0)	29	8	13	10	4	0	19	1	0	0	1	0	2	.273	.347	.659	1.006
2017	Col	NL	12	24	1	1	0	0	(0	0)	2	1	1	0	2	1	9	0	0	0	0	0	0	.042	.115	.083	.199
	3 ML YEARS		44	103	22	4	0	8	(8	0)	50	14	23	19	10	2	38	1	0	0	1	0	2	.214	.289	.485	.775

Joe Musgrove

Pitches: R **Bats:** R **Pos:** RP-23; SP-15   **Ht:** 6'5" **Wt:** 265 **Born:** 12/4/1992 **Age:** 25

Year	Team	Lg	G	GS	CG	GF	IP	BFP	H	R	ER	HR	SH	SF	HB	TBB	IBB	SO	WP	Bk	W	L	Pct	Sh	Sv-Op	Hld	ERC	ERA
					HOW MUCH HE PITCHED						WHAT HE GAVE UP												THE RESULTS				
2013	Astros	R	11	3	0	4	32.2	149	43	22	16	1	0	1	2	4	0	30	3	0	1	3	.250	0	0--	-	4.32	4.41
2014	TriCity	A-	15	13	0	0	77.0	301	64	25	24	4	3	0	2	10	1	67	0	0	7	1	.875	0	0--	-	2.02	2.81
2015	2 Tms	Low	11	7	0	3	55.2	218	50	13	10	2	2	1	3	2	0	66	2	0	8	1	.889	0	0--	-	2.03	1.62
2015	CpChr	AA	8	7	0	1	45.0	174	35	13	11	7	1	0	0	6	0	33	2	0	4	0	1.000	0	1--	-	2.25	2.20
2016	CpChr	AA	6	4	0	1	26.1	102	19	2	1	1	0	0	0	3	0	30	1	0	2	1	.667	0	0--	-	1.40	0.34
2016	Fresno	AAA	10	10	0	0	59.0	237	60	26	25	8	0	0	1	7	0	57	1	0	5	3	.625	0	0--	-	3.42	3.81
2016	Hou	AL	11	10	0	1	62.0	256	59	28	28	9	0	1	3	16	0	55	0	0	4	4	.500	0	0-0	0	3.80	4.06
2017	Hou	AL	38	15	0	5	109.1	462	117	59	58	18	5	2	4	28	1	98	4	0	7	8	.467	0	2-4	5	4.54	4.77
	2 ML YEARS		49	25	0	6	171.1	718	176	87	86	27	5	3	7	44	1	153	4	0	11	12	.478	0	2-4	5	4.27	4.52

Wil Myers

Bats: R **Throws:** R **Pos:** 1B-154;2B-1;DH-1;PH-1   **Ht:** 6'3" **Wt:** 205 **Born:** 12/10/1990 **Age:** 27

Year	Team	Lg	G	AB	H	2B	3B	HR	(Hm	Rd)	TB	R	RBI	RC	TBB	IBB	SO	HBP	SH	SF	SB	CS	GDP	Avg	OBP	Slg	OPS
										BATTING											RUNNING			AVERAGES			
2013	TB	AL	88	335	98	23	0	13	(5	8)	160	50	53	52	33	6	91	1	0	4	5	2	10	.293	.354	.478	.831
2014	TB	AL	87	325	72	14	0	6	(2	4)	104	37	35	32	34	3	90	0	0	2	6	1	10	.222	.294	.320	.614
2015	SD	NL	60	225	57	13	1	8	(3	5)	96	40	29	35	27	0	55	1	0	0	5	2	2	.253	.336	.427	.763
2016	SD	NL	157	599	155	29	4	28	(18	10)	276	99	94	97	68	1	160	4	0	5	28	6	12	.259	.336	.461	.797
2017	SD	NL	155	567	138	29	3	30	(8	22)	263	80	74	80	70	3	180	5	0	7	20	6	15	.243	.328	.464	.792
	Postseason		5	20	2	0	0	0	(0	0)	2	0	0	0	1	0	7	0	0	0	0	0	0	.100	.143	.100	.243
	5 ML YEARS		547	2051	520	108	8	85	(36	49)	899	306	285	296	232	13	576	11	0	18	64	17	49	.254	.330	.438	.768

Mike Napoli

Bats: R **Throws:** R **Pos:** 1B-95;DH-26;PH-7   NAPP-oh-lee   **Ht:** 6'1" **Wt:** 225 **Born:** 10/31/1981 **Age:** 36

Year	Team	Lg	G	AB	H	2B	3B	HR	(Hm	Rd)	TB	R	RBI	RC	TBB	IBB	SO	HBP	SH	SF	SB	CS	GDP	Avg	OBP	Slg	OPS
										BATTING											RUNNING			AVERAGES			
2006	LAA	AL	99	268	61	13	0	16	(10	6)	122	47	42	40	51	0	90	2	3	2	2	3	2	.228	.360	.455	.815
2007	LAA	AL	75	219	54	11	1	10	(5	5)	97	40	34	35	33	2	63	5	1	5	5	2	5	.247	.351	.443	.794
2008	LAA	AL	78	227	62	9	1	20	(10	10)	133	39	49	46	35	5	70	5	1	6	7	3	3	.273	.374	.586	.960
2009	LAA	AL	114	382	104	22	1	20	(10	10)	188	60	56	53	40	1	103	7	0	3	3	3	6	.272	.350	.492	.842
2010	LAA	AL	140	453	108	24	1	26	(13	13)	212	60	68	60	42	2	137	11	0	4	4	2	15	.238	.316	.468	.784
2011	Tex	AL	113	369	118	25	0	30	(13	17)	233	72	75	90	58	2	85	3	0	2	4	2	10	.320	.414	.631	1.046
2012	Tex	AL	108	352	80	9	2	24	(11	13)	165	53	56	54	56	5	125	7	0	2	1	0	9	.227	.343	.469	.812
2013	Bos	AL	139	498	129	38	2	23	(11	12)	240	79	92	79	73	3	187	6	0	1	1	1	15	.259	.360	.482	.842
2014	Bos	AL	119	415	103	20	0	17	(6	11)	174	49	55	54	78	3	133	4	0	3	3	2	11	.248	.370	.419	.789
2015	2 Tms	AL	133	407	91	20	1	18	(13	5)	167	46	50	50	57	3	118	4	0	1	3	3	11	.224	.324	.410	.734
2016	Cle	AL	150	557	133	22	1	34	(22	12)	259	92	101	88	78	2	194	5	0	5	5	1	15	.239	.335	.465	.800
2017	Tex	AL	124	425	82	11	1	29	(15	14)	182	60	66	56	49	3	163	7	0	3	1	2	11	.193	.285	.428	.713
15	Bos	AL	98	329	68	18	1	13	(9	4)	127	37	40	36	45	2	99	3	0	1	3	1	10	.207	.307	.386	.693
15	Tex	AL	35	78	23	2	0	5	(4	1)	40	9	10	14	12	1	19	1	0	0	0	2	1	.295	.396	.513	.908
	Postseason		66	197	45	9	0	8	(1	7)	78	23	30	27	25	2	70	3	0	2	2	1	3	.228	.322	.396	.718
	12 ML YEARS		1392	4572	1125	224	11	267	(139	128)	2172	697	744	705	650	31	1468	69	2	36	39	24	114	.246	.346	.475	.821

Tyler Naquin

Bats: L **Throws:** R **Pos:** CF-11;RF-8;PH-4;PR-3   NAY-kwin   **Ht:** 6'2" **Wt:** 195 **Born:** 4/24/1991 **Age:** 27

Year	Team	Lg	G	AB	H	2B	3B	HR	(Hm	Rd)	TB	R	RBI	RC	TBB	IBB	SO	HBP	SH	SF	SB	CS	GDP	Avg	OBP	Slg	OPS
										BATTING											RUNNING			AVERAGES			
2013	Carlina	A+	108	448	124	27	6	9	(-	-)	190	69	42	67	41	0	112	6	2	1	14	7	8	.277	.345	.424	.769
2013	Akron	AA	18	80	18	3	0	1	(-	-)	24	9	6	5	5	0	22	0	0	1	1	3	0	.225	.271	.300	.571
2014	Akron	AA	76	304	95	12	5	4	(-	-)	129	54	30	51	29	0	71	2	1	5	14	3	4	.313	.371	.424	.795
2015	Akron	AA	34	141	49	12	1	1	(-	-)	66	16	10	29	15	1	24	3	0	1	7	1	3	.348	.419	.468	.887
2015	Clmbs	AAA	50	186	49	13	0	6	(-	-)	80	34	17	30	25	2	49	2	3	2	6	2	3	.263	.353	.430	.784
2016	Clmbs	AAA	17	70	20	3	1	1	(-	-)	28	6	8	10	8	0	15	0	0	1	1	2	1	.286	.354	.400	.754
2017	Clmbs	AAA	80	295	88	14	4	10	(-	-)	140	42	51	51	30	1	71	0	1	4	5	2	4	.298	.359	.475	.833
2016	Cle	AL	116	321	95	18	5	14	(9	5)	165	52	43	53	36	4	112	4	2	2	6	3	4	.296	.372	.514	.886
2017	Cle	AL	19	37	8	2	0	0	(0	0)	10	4	1	2	2	0	9	0	0	1	0	1	1	.216	.250	.270	.520
	Postseason		11	23	4	2	0	0	(0	0)	6	0	2	1	1	1	14	0	1	0	0	0	0	.174	.208	.261	.469
	2 ML YEARS		135	358	103	20	5	14	(9	5)	175	56	44	55	38	4	121	4	2	3	6	4	5	.288	.360	.489	.849

Omar Narvaez

Bats: L Throws: R Pos: C-83;PH-9;1B-1;DH-1   nar-VAH-es   Ht: 5'11" Wt: 215 Born: 2/10/1992 Age: 26

Year	Team	Lg	G	AB	H	2B	3B	HR	(Hm	Rd)	TB	R	RBI	RC	TBB	IBB	SO	HBP	SH	SF	SB	CS	GDP	Avg	OBP	Slg	OPS
2013	HudVal	A-	39	150	40	6	2	0	(-	-)	50	13	13	15	8	0	21	2	1	1	0	2	6	.267	.311	.333	.644
2014	2 Tms	Low	85	267	76	11	0	2	(-	-)	93	25	36	38	36	0	32	3	1	9	3	2	12	.285	.365	.348	.713
2015	WinSa	A+	98	339	93	10	0	1	(-	-)	106	38	27	42	40	1	31	2	1	3	1	0	12	.274	.354	.313	.664
2016	Brham	AA	13	45	10	2	0	0	(-	-)	12	4	5	3	4	0	8	0	0	0	0	0	1	.222	.286	.267	.552
2016	Charllt	AAA	41	143	35	6	0	2	(-	-)	47	14	11	14	9	0	17	1	2	1	0	0	7	.245	.292	.329	.621
2016	CWS	AL	34	101	27	4	0	1	(1	0)	34	13	10	15	14	1	14	0	0	2	0	0	0	.267	.350	.337	.687
2017	CWS	AL	90	253	70	10	0	2	(2	0)	86	23	14	33	38	1	45	1	3	0	0	0	8	.277	.373	.340	.713
	2 ML YEARS		124	354	97	14	0	3	(3	0)	120	36	24	48	52	2	59	1	3	2	0	0	8	.274	.367	.339	.706

Daniel Nava

Bats: B Throws: L Pos: LF-42;PH-33;RF-9;1B-4;DH-1   NAH-vah   Ht: 5'11" Wt: 200 Born: 2/22/1983 Age: 35

Year	Team	Lg	G	AB	H	2B	3B	HR	(Hm	Rd)	TB	R	RBI	RC	TBB	IBB	SO	HBP	SH	SF	SB	CS	GDP	Avg	OBP	Slg	OPS
2010	Bos	AL	60	161	39	14	1	1	(1	0)	58	23	26	26	19	1	46	8	0	0	1	1	5	.242	.351	.360	.711
2012	Bos	AL	88	267	65	21	0	6	(1	5)	104	38	33	33	37	1	63	9	2	2	3	0	5	.243	.352	.390	.742
2013	Bos	AL	134	458	139	29	0	12	(5	7)	204	77	66	79	51	2	93	15	4	8	0	2	10	.303	.385	.445	.831
2014	Bos	AL	113	363	98	21	0	4	(0	4)	131	41	37	49	33	1	81	10	0	2	4	2	5	.270	.346	.361	.706
2015	2 Tms	AL	60	139	27	4	0	1	(1	0)	34	13	10	15	20	0	36	5	1	1	1	0	4	.194	.315	.245	.560
2016	2 Tms	AL	54	130	29	6	0	1	(1	0)	38	11	13	11	10	0	30	5	0	3	0	0	2	.223	.297	.292	.590
2017	Phi		80	183	55	8	1	4	(0	4)	77	21	21	30	26	0	38	3	0	2	1	0	2	.301	.390	.421	.813
15	Bos	AL	29	66	10	2	0	0	(0	0)	12	6	7	5	8	0	17	2	1	1	0	0	3	.152	.260	.182	.442
15	TB	AL	31	73	17	2	0	1	(1	0)	22	7	3	10	12	0	19	3	0	0	1	0	1	.233	.364	.301	.665
16	LAA	AL	45	119	28	5	0	1	(1	0)	36	10	13	11	9	0	26	5	0	3	0	0	2	.235	.309	.303	.611
16	KC	AL	9	11	1	1	0	0	(0	0)	2	1	0	0	1	0	4	0	0	0	0	0	0	.091	.167	.182	.348
	Postseason		9	25	5	1	0	0	(0	0)	6	1	2	2	3	0	9	0	0	0	0	1	1	.200	.286	.240	.526
	7 ML YEARS		589	1701	452	103	2	29	(9	20)	646	224	206	243	196	5	387	55	7	18	10	5	33	.266	.357	.380	.737

Efren Navarro

Bats: L Throws: L Pos: 1B-20;PH-4;DH-1   EFF-ren   Ht: 6'0" Wt: 210 Born: 5/14/1986 Age: 32

Year	Team	Lg	G	AB	H	2B	3B	HR	(Hm	Rd)	TB	R	RBI	RC	TBB	IBB	SO	HBP	SH	SF	SB	CS	GDP	Avg	OBP	Slg	OPS
2017	Toledo*	AAA	131	479	132	23	2	10	(-	-)	189	61	61	75	71	4	101	3	0	4	2	3	12	.276	.370	.395	.764
2011	LAA	AL	8	10	2	1	0	0	(0	0)	3	1	0	0	1	0	1	0	1	0	0	0	1	.200	.273	.300	.573
2013	LAA	AL	4	4	1	0	0	0	(0	0)	1	0	1	1	2	0	1	0	0	0	1	0	0	.250	.500	.250	.750
2014	LAA	AL	64	159	39	10	1	1	(1	0)	54	17	14	19	13	2	27	0	2	0	1	3	0	.245	.302	.340	.642
2015	LAA	AL	54	83	21	4	0	0	(0	0)	25	9	5	5	5	1	16	0	0	0	0	2	5	.253	.295	.301	.597
2017	Det	AL	23	61	14	1	1	2	(2	0)	23	9	2	5	8	1	21	0	0	0	0	1	1	.230	.319	.377	.696
	Postseason		1	1	0	0	0	0	(0	0)	0	0	0	0	0	0	1	0	0	0	0	0	0	.000	.000	.000	.000
	5 ML YEARS		153	317	77	16	2	3	(3	0)	106	36	22	30	29	4	66	0	3	0	2	6	7	.243	.306	.334	.641

Zach Neal

Pitches: R Bats: R Pos: RP-6   Ht: 6'3" Wt: 220 Born: 11/9/1988 Age: 29

			HOW MUCH HE PITCHED					WHAT HE GAVE UP											THE RESULTS							
Year	Team	Lg	G	GS	CG	GF	IP	BFP	H	R	ER	HR	SH	SF	HB	TBB	IBB	SO	WP	Bk	W	L	Pct	Sh	Sv-Op	Hld	ERC	ERA
2013	Mdlnd	AA	28	28	1	0	165.2	696	172	95	80	18	3	5	6	36	1	96	2	2	8	12	.400	1	0--	-	3.77	4.35
2014	Mdlnd	AA	5	5	0	0	31.0	125	25	5	2	0	0	0	3	4	0	25	1	0	3	0	1.000	0	0--	-	1.81	0.58
2014	Scrmto	AAA	20	19	0	0	119.1	500	137	70	54	15	3	2	4	16	0	80	2	0	7	7	.500	0	0--	-	4.20	4.07
2015	Mdlnd	AA	7	7	0	0	36.1	160	43	26	26	7	1	1	1	15	0	22	0	0	3	3	.500	0	0--	-	6.21	6.44
2015	Nashv	AAA	21	20	2	0	131.1	553	151	71	61	10	4	5	5	20	0	78	2	0	7	10	.412	0	0--	-	3.96	4.18
2016	Nashv	AAA	11	11	0	0	61.2	254	62	27	22	5	3	3	1	8	0	32	1	0	7	2	.778	0	0--	-	2.97	3.21
2017	Nashv	AAA	21	16	0	2	99.0	413	115	54	53	9	3	7	6	10	1	43	1	1	4	8	.333	0	0--	-	4.02	4.82
2016	Oak	AL	24	6	0	7	70.0	281	72	35	33	9	0	2	1	6	0	27	2	1	2	4	.333	0	2-3	0	3.28	4.24
2017	Oak	AL	6	0	0	4	14.2	65	19	13	13	5	0	1	0	1	0	10	1	0	0	0	-	0	0-0	0	5.86	7.98
	2 ML YEARS		30	6	0	11	84.2	346	91	48	46	14	0	3	1	7	0	37	3	1	2	4	.333	0	2-3	0	3.71	4.89

Kristopher Negron

Bats: R Throws: R Pos: SS-5;LF-5;PH-3;1B-2;PR-2;2B-1   neh-GRONE   Ht: 6'0" Wt: 190 Born: 2/1/1986 Age: 32

Year	Team	Lg	G	AB	H	2B	3B	HR	(Hm	Rd)	TB	R	RBI	RC	TBB	IBB	SO	HBP	SH	SF	SB	CS	GDP	Avg	OBP	Slg	OPS
2017	Reno*	AAA	120	387	116	17	11	13	(-	-)	194	70	64	73	35	1	88	7	5	3	13	3	8	.300	.366	.501	.867
2012	Cin	NL	4	4	1	0	0	0	(0	0)	1	2	0	1	1	0	2	0	0	0	0	0	0	.250	.400	.250	.650
2014	Cin	NL	49	144	39	10	1	6	(3	3)	69	19	17	23	12	0	40	1	1	0	5	0	2	.271	.331	.479	.810
2015	Cin	NL	43	93	13	2	0	0	(0	0)	15	5	2	2	9	0	23	3	2	0	2	0	2	.140	.238	.161	.399
2017	Ari	NL	14	25	4	1	0	0	(0	0)	5	3	1	1	4	0	7	1	1	0	0	0	1	.160	.300	.200	.500
	4 ML YEARS		110	266	57	13	1	6	(3	3)	90	29	20	27	26	0	72	5	4	0	7	0	5	.214	.296	.338	.635

Jimmy Nelson

Pitches: R **Bats:** R **Pos:** SP-29   **Ht:** 6'6" **Wt:** 250 **Born:** 6/5/1989 **Age:** 29

Year	Team	Lg	G	GS	CG	GF	IP	BFP	H	R	ER	HR	SH	SF	HB	TBB	IBB	SO	WP	Bk	W	L	Pct	Sh	Sv-Op	Hld	ERC	ERA
2013	Mil	NL	4	1	0	0	10.0	37	2	1	1	0	0	1	0	5	0	8	1	0	0	0	-	0	0-0	0	0.64	0.90
2014	Mil	NL	14	12	0	1	69.1	311	82	42	38	6	1	2	8	19	0	57	4	0	2	9	.182	0	0-0	0	4.96	4.93
2015	Mil	NL	30	30	0	0	177.1	752	163	89	81	18	4	7	13	65	4	148	11	1	11	13	.458	0	0-0	0	3.79	4.11
2016	Mil	NL	32	32	0	0	179.1	807	186	108	92	25	7	4	17	86	2	140	8	0	8	16	.333	0	0-0	0	5.29	4.62
2017	Mil	NL	29	29	1	0	175.1	728	171	75	68	16	4	2	9	48	1	199	6	1	12	6	.667	0	0-0	0	3.64	3.49
5 ML YEARS			109	104	1	1	611.1	2635	604	315	280	65	16	16	47	223	7	552	30	2	33	44	.429	0	0-0	0	4.23	4.12

Hector Neris

Pitches: R **Bats:** R **Pos:** RP-74   NAIR-ess   **Ht:** 6'2" **Wt:** 215 **Born:** 6/14/1989 **Age:** 29

Year	Team	Lg	G	GS	CG	GF	IP	BFP	H	R	ER	HR	SH	SF	HB	TBB	IBB	SO	WP	Bk	W	L	Pct	Sh	Sv-Op	Hld	ERC	ERA
2014	Phi	NL	1	0	0	1	1.0	3	0	0	0	0	0	0	0	0	0	1	0	0	1	0	1.000	0	0-0	0	0.00	0.00
2015	Phi	NL	32	0	0	8	40.1	170	38	19	17	8	1	0	4	10	0	41	3	0	2	2	.500	0	0-0	2	4.21	3.79
2016	Phi	NL	79	0	0	13	80.1	328	59	26	23	9	1	2	3	30	3	102	4	1	4	4	.500	0	2-6	28	2.73	2.58
2017	Phi	NL	74	0	0	56	74.2	320	68	26	25	9	1	2	6	26	3	86	2	1	4	5	.444	0	26-29	4	3.74	3.01
4 ML YEARS			186	0	0	78	196.1	821	165	71	65	26	3	4	13	66	6	230	9	2	11	11	.500	0	28-35	34	3.37	2.98

Pat Neshek

Pitches: R **Bats:** B **Pos:** RP-71   NEE-sheck   **Ht:** 6'3" **Wt:** 220 **Born:** 9/4/1980 **Age:** 37

Year	Team	Lg	G	GS	CG	GF	IP	BFP	H	R	ER	HR	SH	SF	HB	TBB	IBB	SO	WP	Bk	W	L	Pct	Sh	Sv-Op	Hld	ERC	ERA
2006	Min	AL	32	0	0	3	37.0	138	23	9	9	6	0	1	0	6	0	53	0	0	4	2	.667	0	0-2	10	1.68	2.19
2007	Min	AL	74	0	0	20	70.1	278	44	25	23	7	4	5	2	27	5	74	2	0	7	2	.778	0	0-3	15	2.12	2.94
2008	Min	AL	15	0	0	3	13.1	56	12	7	7	2	1	1	0	4	1	15	0	0	1	0	1.000	0	0-2	6	3.29	4.73
2010	Min	AL	11	0	0	3	9.0	43	7	5	5	1	0	0	1	8	0	9	0	0	0	1	.000	0	0-1	1	5.13	5.00
2011	SD	NL	25	0	0	13	24.2	112	19	12	11	4	1	0	1	22	1	20	1	0	1	1	.500	0	0-0	0	5.37	4.01
2012	Oak	AL	24	0	0	5	19.2	77	10	3	3	3	0	2	1	6	1	16	1	0	2	1	.667	0	0-2	4	1.66	1.37
2013	Oak	AL	45	0	0	17	40.1	177	40	17	15	6	0	3	0	15	2	29	1	0	2	1	.667	0	0-0	4	4.06	3.35
2014	StL	NL	71	0	0	17	67.1	255	44	14	14	4	2	2	2	9	2	68	1	0	7	2	.778	0	6-10	25	1.38	1.87
2015	Hou	AL	66	0	0	8	54.2	223	49	25	22	8	4	1	2	12	1	51	1	0	3	6	.333	0	1-4	28	3.23	3.62
2016	Hou	AL	60	0	0	9	47.0	185	33	17	16	6	3	1	0	11	7	43	1	0	2	2	.500	0	0-0	18	1.89	3.06
2017	2 Tms		71	0	0	7	62.1	235	48	13	11	3	1	2	0	6	0	69	0	0	5	3	.625	0	1-5	23	1.60	1.59
17 Phi	NL		43	0	0	5	40.1	148	28	5	5	2	1	1	0	5	0	45	0	0	3	2	.600	0	1-3	10	1.45	1.12
17 Col	NL		28	0	0	2	22.0	87	20	8	6	1	0	1	0	1	0	24	0	0	2	1	.667	0	0-2	13	1.94	2.45
Postseason			13	0	0	4	10.1	38	6	3	3	2	0	0	0	0	0	10	0	0	0	2	.000	0	0-1	3	1.20	2.61
11 ML YEARS			494	0	0	105	445.2	1779	329	147	136	50	16	18	9	126	20	447	8	0	33	22	.600	0	8-29	131	2.36	2.75

Dovydas Neverauskas

Pitches: R **Bats:** R **Pos:** RP-24   DOH-vee-das neh-ver-OWS-kus   **Ht:** 6'3" **Wt:** 215 **Born:** 1/14/1993 **Age:** 25

Year	Team	Lg	G	GS	CG	GF	IP	BFP	H	R	ER	HR	SH	SF	HB	TBB	IBB	SO	WP	Bk	W	L	Pct	Sh	Sv-Op	Hld	ERC	ERA
2013	Jmstwn	A-	15	15	0	0	60.2	261	55	33	27	8	2	1	10	22	0	39	11	0	4	4	.500	0	0- -	-	4.33	4.01
2014	WV	A	27	26	1	0	123.2	565	151	86	77	12	4	3	8	55	0	88	16	0	6	12	.333	0	0- -	-	5.87	5.60
2015	3 Tms	Low	31	5	0	15	68.1	292	58	30	24	4	6	2	1	27	0	49	10	1	2	2	.500	0	6- -	-	2.94	3.16
2016	Altna	AA	22	0	0	5	28.0	105	12	10	8	0	1	0	0	11	0	32	4	0	1	0	1.000	0	1- -	-	1.03	2.57
2016	Indy	AAA	25	0	0	12	30.0	132	36	14	12	1	3	0	1	11	4	24	4	0	3	4	.429	0	4- -	-	4.58	3.60
2017	Indy	AAA	40	0	0	24	50.1	213	47	20	16	1	2	4	0	21	0	46	5	0	2	4	.333	0	13- -	-	3.25	2.86
2017	Pit	NL	24	0	0	11	25.1	105	24	11	11	4	1	0	1	8	0	17	2	0	1	1	.500	0	0-1	2	4.09	3.91

Sean Newcomb

Pitches: L **Bats:** L **Pos:** SP-19   **Ht:** 6'5" **Wt:** 255 **Born:** 6/12/1993 **Age:** 25

Year	Team	Lg	G	GS	CG	GF	IP	BFP	H	R	ER	HR	SH	SF	HB	TBB	IBB	SO	WP	Bk	W	L	Pct	Sh	Sv-Op	Hld	ERC	ERA
2014	2 Tms	Low	6	6	0	0	14.1	64	16	10	10	2	1	1	0	6	0	18	3	0	1	0	.000	0	0- -	-	5.08	6.28
2015	2 Tms	Low	20	20	0	0	100.0	424	75	31	25	3	5	3	2	52	0	129	5	0	7	1	.875	0	0- -	-	2.76	2.25
2015	Ark	AA	7	7	0	0	36.0	151	22	12	11	2	1	0	1	24	0	39	1	0	2	2	.500	0	0- -	-	2.82	2.75
2016	Missi	AA	27	27	1	0	140.0	595	113	62	60	4	7	6	7	71	0	152	5	0	8	7	.533	0	0- -	-	3.15	3.86
2017	Gwnntt	AAA	11	11	0	0	57.2	249	45	23	19	3	1	2	1	33	0	74	4	0	3	3	.500	0	0- -	-	3.23	2.97
2017	Atl	NL	19	19	0	0	100.0	456	100	51	48	10	5	3	6	57	6	108	3	0	4	9	.308	0	0-0	0	4.85	4.32

Gift Ngoepe

Bats: R **Throws:** R **Pos:** 2B-20;SS-6;3B-3;PH-1;PR-1   en-GOH-pay   **Ht:** 5'8" **Wt:** 200 **Born:** 1/18/1990 **Age:** 28

Year	Team	Lg	G	AB	H	2B	3B	HR	(Hm	Rd)	TB	R	RBI	RC	TBB	IBB	SO	HBP	SH	SF	SB	CS	GDP	Avg	OBP	Slg	OPS
2013	Altna	AA	72	220	39	10	2	3	(-	-)	62	29	16	19	28	1	82	4	4	3	10	3	2	.177	.278	.282	.560
2013	Bradtn	A+	28	96	28	7	3	0	(-	-)	41	17	6	20	21	1	35	1	5	0	7	1	0	.292	.424	.427	.851
2014	Altna	AA	131	437	104	17	9	9	(-	-)	166	58	52	55	51	0	135	2	7	2	13	8	6	.238	.319	.380	.699
2015	Altna	AA	71	246	64	12	2	3	(-	-)	89	31	25	30	24	1	66	5	5	0	3	6	5	.260	.338	.362	.700
2015	Indy	AAA	21	61	15	4	0	0	(-	-)	19	5	1	5	6	0	15	0	4	0	1	2	2	.246	.313	.311	.625
2016	Indy	AAA	102	332	72	20	1	8	(-	-)	118	40	27	35	31	1	130	3	6	1	5	2	8	.217	.289	.355	.644
2017	Indy	AAA	77	264	58	15	5	6	(-	-)	101	33	27	30	28	0	91	3	1	3	2	4	7	.220	.299	.383	.681
2017	Pit	NL	28	54	12	2	1	0	(0	0)	16	10	6	8	8	0	26	0	1	0	0	0	0	.222	.323	.296	.619

Juan Nicasio

Pitches: R Bats: R Pos: RP-76   nih-KAH-see-oh   Ht: 6'4" Wt: 252 Born: 8/31/1986 Age: 31

Year	Team	Lg	G	GS	CG	GF	IP	BFP	H	R	ER	HR	SH	SF	HB	TBB	IBB	SO	WP	Bk	W	L	Pct	Sh	Sv-Op	Hld	ERC	ERA
2011	Col	NL	13	13	0	0	71.2	299	73	35	33	8	1	0	1	18	3	58	1	0	4	4	.500	0	0-0	0	3.69	4.14
2012	Col	NL	11	11	0	0	58.0	257	72	37	34	7	3	1	1	22	1	54	4	0	2	3	.400	0	0-0	0	5.74	5.28
2013	Col	NL	31	31	0	0	157.2	703	168	97	90	17	6	1	5	64	7	119	6	2	9	9	.500	0	0-0	0	4.52	5.14
2014	Col	NL	33	14	0	7	93.2	409	107	59	56	19	5	2	1	31	1	63	3	1	6	6	.500	0	0-0	1	5.43	5.38
2015	LAD	NL	53	1	0	12	58.1	260	59	25	25	1	3	0	1	32	6	65	2	0	1	3	.250	0	1-3	14	4.00	3.86
2016	Pit	NL	52	12	0	9	118.0	513	117	64	59	15	5	7	7	45	3	138	3	0	10	7	.588	0	0-2	6	4.33	4.50
2017	3 Tms	NL	76	0	0	15	72.1	291	58	22	21	5	1	0	2	20	2	72	1	0	5	5	.500	0	6-10	21	2.46	2.61
17	Pit	NL	65	0	0	8	60.0	243	49	20	19	4	1	0	2	18	2	60	1	0	2	5	.286	0	2-6	21	2.62	2.85
17	Phi	NL	2	0	0	0	1.1	4	0	0	0	0	0	0	0	0	0	1	0	0	1	0	1.000	0	0-0	0	0.00	0.00
17	StL	NL	9	0	0	7	11.0	44	9	2	2	1	0	0	0	2	0	11	0	0	2	0	1.000	0	4-4	0	2.23	1.64
7 ML YEARS			269	82	0	43	629.2	2732	654	339	318	72	24	11	18	232	23	569	20	3	37	37	.500	0	7-15	42	4.33	4.55

Brett Nicholas

Bats: L Throws: R Pos: C-19;PH-3   Ht: 6'2" Wt: 220 Born: 7/18/1988 Age: 29

Year	Team	Lg	G	AB	H	2B	3B	HR	(Hm	Rd)	TB	R	RBI	RC	TBB	IBB	SO	HBP	SH	SF	SB	CS	GDP	Avg	OBP	Slg	OPS
2013	Frisco	AA	136	506	146	25	3	21	(-	-)	240	71	91	89	46	7	123	13	0	10	2	1	8	.289	.357	.474	.831
2014	RdRock	AAA	127	452	124	20	1	10	(-	-)	176	40	58	59	27	2	112	7	1	4	4	1	11	.274	.322	.389	.712
2015	RdRock	AAA	109	403	108	22	0	12	(-	-)	166	49	63	53	27	1	79	2	1	5	2	2	12	.268	.314	.412	.725
2016	RdRock	AAA	101	400	115	27	1	13	(-	-)	183	57	58	65	38	1	88	3	3	3	2	2	15	.288	.351	.458	.809
2017	RdRock	AAA	69	273	85	18	2	7	(-	-)	128	35	38	45	13	1	59	5	1	1	2	1	8	.311	.353	.469	.822
2016	Tex	AL	15	40	11	5	0	2	(1	1)	22	5	4	7	4	0	9	1	0	0	0	0	2	.275	.356	.550	.906
2017	Tex	AL	22	63	15	4	0	2	(2	0)	25	7	11	9	2	0	13	0	0	0	0	0	2	.238	.262	.397	.658
2 ML YEARS			37	103	26	9	0	4	(3	1)	47	12	15	16	6	0	22	1	0	0	0	0	4	.252	.300	.456	.756

Justin Nicolino

Pitches: L Bats: L Pos: RP-12; SP-8   Ht: 6'3" Wt: 195 Born: 11/22/1991 Age: 26

Year	Team	Lg	G	GS	CG	GF	IP	BFP	H	R	ER	HR	SH	SF	HB	TBB	IBB	SO	WP	Bk	W	L	Pct	Sh	Sv-Op	Hld	ERC	ERA
2017	NewOr*	AAA	14	14	0	0	79.0	329	75	34	28	10	3	5	2	24	1	51	0	0	5	5	.500	0	0- -	-	3.71	3.19
2015	Mia	NL	12	12	0	0	74.0	301	72	33	33	8	5	3	3	20	2	23	2	0	5	4	.556	0	0-0	0	3.73	4.01
2016	Mia	NL	18	13	0	0	79.1	346	96	45	44	8	4	6	3	20	1	37	1	0	3	6	.333	0	0-0	0	4.87	4.99
2017	Mia	NL	20	8	0	6	48.0	229	66	33	27	8	3	1	1	20	5	26	0	0	2	3	.400	0	0-0	0	6.72	5.06
3 ML YEARS			50	33	0	6	201.1	876	234	111	104	24	12	10	7	60	8	86	3	0	10	13	.435	0	0-0	0	4.86	4.65

Tomas Nido

Bats: R Throws: R Pos: C-3;PH-2   Ht: 6'0" Wt: 210 Born: 4/12/1994 Age: 24

Year	Team	Lg	G	AB	H	2B	3B	HR	(Hm	Rd)	TB	R	RBI	RC	TBB	IBB	SO	HBP	SH	SF	SB	CS	GDP	Avg	OBP	Slg	OPS
2013	Bklyn	A-	33	119	22	6	0	1	(-	-)	31	3	11	5	4	0	21	1	1	0	0	1	4	.185	.218	.261	.478
2014	Bklyn	A-	58	188	52	6	1	1	(-	-)	63	20	21	21	14	1	41	0	0	1	2	2	4	.277	.325	.335	.660
2015	Savann	A	86	317	82	14	2	6	(-	-)	118	39	40	34	12	1	86	1	1	4	1	1	9	.259	.284	.372	.657
2016	Stluci	A+	90	344	110	23	2	7	(-	-)	158	38	46	56	19	0	42	3	0	4	0	1	9	.320	.357	.459	.816
2017	Bnghtn	AA	102	367	85	19	1	8	(-	-)	130	41	60	39	30	0	63	1	0	6	0	0	27	.232	.287	.354	.641
2017	NYM	NL	5	10	3	1	0	0	(0	0)	4	0	3	2	0	0	2	0	0	0	0	0	0	.300	.300	.400	.700

Kirk Nieuwenhuis

Bats: L Throws: R Pos: PH-8;CF-7;LF-3;PR-1   NEW-enn-hice   Ht: 6'3" Wt: 225 Born: 8/7/1987 Age: 30

Year	Team	Lg	G	AB	H	2B	3B	HR	(Hm	Rd)	TB	R	RBI	RC	TBB	IBB	SO	HBP	SH	SF	SB	CS	GDP	Avg	OBP	Slg	OPS
2017	ColSpr*	AAA	84	205	50	12	0	4	(-	-)	74	32	33	31	38	1	67	1	1	2	5	0	3	.244	.361	.361	.723
2012	NYM	NL	91	282	71	12	1	7	(5	2)	106	40	28	28	25	0	98	2	3	2	4	4	2	.252	.315	.376	.691
2013	NYM	NL	47	95	18	3	1	3	(2	1)	32	10	14	8	12	1	32	0	0	1	2	0	1	.189	.278	.337	.615
2014	NYM	NL	61	112	29	14	1	3	(1	2)	54	16	16	16	16	3	39	0	0	2	4	0	1	.259	.346	.482	.828
2015	2 Tms	NL	74	128	25	11	0	4	(3	1)	48	21	14	10	10	0	49	3	0	0	2	2	2	.195	.270	.375	.645
2016	Mil	NL	125	335	70	18	1	13	(11	2)	129	38	44	40	56	1	133	1	0	0	8	9	5	.209	.324	.385	.709
2017	Mil	NL	16	26	3	1	0	1	(1	0)	7	3	1	1	4	0	15	1	0	0	0	0	0	.115	.258	.269	.527
15	NYM	NL	64	106	22	9	0	4	(3	1)	43	17	13	10	8	0	40	3	0	0	2	1	2	.208	.282	.406	.688
15	LAA	AL	10	22	3	2	0	0	(0	0)	5	4	1	0	2	0	9	0	0	0	0	1	0	.136	.208	.227	.436
Postseason			4	4	0	0	0	0	(0	0)	0	0	0	0	0	0	2	0	0	0	0	0	0	.000	.000	.000	.000
6 ML YEARS			414	978	216	59	4	31	(23	8)	376	128	117	103	123	5	366	7	3	5	20	15	11	.221	.311	.384	.695

Brandon Nimmo

Bats: L Throws: R Pos: LF-32;PH-21;CF-12;RF-8;DH-1   NIH-moe   Ht: 6'3" Wt: 207 Born: 3/27/1993 Age: 25

Year	Team	Lg	G	AB	H	2B	3B	HR	(Hm	Rd)	TB	R	RBI	RC	TBB	IBB	SO	HBP	SH	SF	SB	CS	GDP	Avg	OBP	Slg	OPS
2013	Savann	A	110	395	108	16	6	2	(-	-)	142	62	40	64	71	1	131	11	1	2	10	7	7	.273	.397	.359	.756
2014	Stluci	A+	62	227	73	9	5	4	(-	-)	104	59	25	50	50	1	51	2	0	0	9	3	3	.322	.448	.458	.906
2014	Bnghtn	AA	65	240	57	12	4	6	(-	-)	95	38	26	35	36	0	54	1	2	0	5	1	4	.238	.339	.396	.735
2015	Bnghtn	AA	68	269	75	12	3	2	(-	-)	99	26	16	37	26	2	55	6	0	1	0	2	4	.279	.354	.368	.722
2015	LsVgs	AAA	32	91	24	3	1	3	(-	-)	38	19	8	16	18	1	20	2	0	1	5	4	0	.264	.393	.418	.810
2016	LsVgs	AAA	97	392	138	25	8	11	(-	-)	212	72	61	86	46	1	73	3	2	1	7	8	10	.352	.423	.541	.964

						BATTING															RUNNING			AVERAGES			
Year Team	Lg	G	AB	H	2B	3B	HR	(Hm Rd)	TB	R	RBI	RC	TBB	IBB	SO	HBP	SH	SF	SB	CS	GDP	Avg	OBP	Slg	OPS
2017 LsVgs	AAA	42	163	37	12	1	3	(- -)	60	23	17	24	33	0	49	2	0	0	0	0	1	.227	.364	.368	.732
2016 NYM	NL	32	73	20	1	0	1	(1 0)	24	12	6	9	6	0	20	1	0	0	0	0	0	.274	.338	.329	.666
2017 NYM	NL	69	177	46	11	1	5	(3 2)	74	26	21	26	33	1	60	2	1	2	2	0	3	.260	.379	.418	.797
2 ML YEARS		101	250	66	12	1	6	(4 2)	98	38	27	35	39	1	80	3	1	2	2	0	3	.264	.367	.392	.759

Aaron Nola

Pitches: R **Bats:** R **Pos:** SP-27   NO-luh   **Ht:** 6'2" **Wt:** 195 **Born:** 6/4/1993 **Age:** 25

		HOW MUCH HE PITCHED						WHAT HE GAVE UP										THE RESULTS							
Year Team	Lg	G	GS	CG	GF	IP	BFP	H	R	ER	HR	SH	SF	HB	TBB	IBB	SO	WP	Bk	W	L	Pct	Sh	Sv-Op	Hld	ERC	ERA
2015 Phi	NL	13	13	0	0	77.2	318	74	31	31	11	1	2	1	19	1	68	0	0	6	2	.750	0	0-0	0	3.62	3.59
2016 Phi	NL	20	20	0	0	111.0	483	116	68	59	10	5	4	6	29	3	121	2	0	6	9	.400	0	0-0	0	3.80	4.78
2017 Phi	NL	27	27	0	0	168.0	693	154	67	66	18	2	0	2	49	2	184	1	0	12	11	.522	0	0-0	0	3.30	3.54
3 ML YEARS		60	60	0	0	356.2	1494	344	166	156	39	8	5	10	97	6	373	3	0	24	22	.522	0	0-0	0	3.52	3.94

Ricky Nolasco

Pitches: R **Bats:** R **Pos:** SP-33   **Ht:** 6'2" **Wt:** 235 **Born:** 12/13/1982 **Age:** 35

		HOW MUCH HE PITCHED						WHAT HE GAVE UP										THE RESULTS							
Year Team	Lg	G	GS	CG	GF	IP	BFP	H	R	ER	HR	SH	SF	HB	TBB	IBB	SO	WP	Bk	W	L	Pct	Sh	Sv-Op	Hld	ERC	ERA
2006 Fla	NL	35	22	0	0	140.0	613	157	86	75	20	8	6	10	41	5	99	7	0	11	11	.500	0	0-0	2	4.89	4.82
2007 Fla	NL	5	4	0	0	21.1	99	26	16	13	3	3	5	1	9	2	11	1	0	1	2	.333	0	0-0	0	5.71	5.48
2008 Fla	NL	34	32	1	0	212.1	868	192	88	83	28	6	9	6	42	6	186	1	0	15	8	.652	1	0-0	0	3.03	3.52
2009 Fla	NL	31	31	2	0	185.0	785	188	111	104	23	8	5	2	44	7	195	2	0	13	9	.591	0	0-0	0	3.62	5.06
2010 Fla	NL	26	26	1	0	157.2	665	169	82	79	24	5	5	2	33	1	147	5	0	14	9	.609	0	0-0	0	4.11	4.51
2011 Fla	NL	33	33	2	0	206.0	891	244	117	107	20	11	5	3	44	8	148	6	0	10	12	.455	1	0-0	0	4.34	4.67
2012 Mia	NL	31	31	3	0	191.0	832	214	100	95	18	19	6	8	47	9	125	8	1	12	13	.480	2	0-0	0	4.14	4.48
2013 2 Tms	NL	34	33	0	0	199.1	834	195	90	82	17	10	3	10	46	1	165	5	0	13	11	.542	0	0-0	0	3.38	3.70
2014 Min	AL	27	27	1	0	159.0	695	203	96	95	22	4	5	5	38	1	115	5	0	6	12	.333	0	0-0	0	5.53	5.38
2015 Min	AL	9	8	0	1	37.1	173	50	31	28	3	0	2	1	14	2	35	1	1	5	2	.714	0	0-0	0	5.82	6.75
2016 2 Tms	AL	32	32	1	0	197.2	817	202	104	97	26	3	9	5	44	0	144	7	0	8	14	.364	1	0-0	0	3.87	4.42
2017 LAA	AL	33	33	1	0	181.0	787	205	102	99	35	6	3	1	58	3	143	4	0	6	15	.286	1	0-0	0	5.27	4.92
13 Mia	NL	18	18	0	0	112.1	468	112	50	48	11	7	3	4	25	1	90	4	0	5	8	.385	0	0-0	0	3.49	3.85
13 LAD	NL	16	15	0	0	87.0	366	83	40	34	6	3	0	6	21	0	75	1	0	8	3	.727	0	0-0	0	3.25	3.52
16 Min	AL	21	21	0	0	124.2	527	139	77	71	18	2	9	3	29	0	93	4	0	4	8	.333	0	0-0	0	4.53	5.13
16 LAA	AL	11	11	1	0	73.0	290	63	27	26	8	1	0	2	15	0	51	3	0	4	6	.400	1	0-0	0	2.82	3.21
Postseason		1	1	0	0	4.0	16	3	3	3	1	1	0	0	1	0	4	0	0	0	1	.000	0	0-0	0	3.01	6.75
12 ML YEARS		330	312	12	1	1887.2	8059	2045	1023	957	239	83	63	56	460	45	1513	52	5	114	118	.491	6	0-0	2	4.19	4.56

Bud Norris

Pitches: R **Bats:** R **Pos:** RP-57; SP-3   **Ht:** 6'0" **Wt:** 215 **Born:** 3/2/1985 **Age:** 33

		HOW MUCH HE PITCHED						WHAT HE GAVE UP										THE RESULTS							
Year Team	Lg	G	GS	CG	GF	IP	BFP	H	R	ER	HR	SH	SF	HB	TBB	IBB	SO	WP	Bk	W	L	Pct	Sh	Sv-Op	Hld	ERC	ERA
2009 Hou	NL	11	10	0	0	55.2	249	59	29	28	9	1	3	3	25	1	54	3	0	6	3	.667	0	0-0	0	5.26	4.53
2010 Hou	NL	27	27	0	0	153.2	683	151	94	84	18	6	4	6	77	3	158	5	2	9	10	.474	0	0-0	0	4.61	4.92
2011 Hou	NL	31	31	0	0	186.0	795	177	93	78	24	9	4	5	70	7	176	3	2	6	11	.353	0	0-0	0	3.96	3.77
2012 Hou	NL	29	29	0	0	168.1	733	165	90	87	23	7	2	8	66	2	165	8	0	7	13	.350	0	0-0	0	4.34	4.65
2013 2 Tms	AL	32	30	0	2	176.2	773	196	89	82	17	6	3	5	67	0	147	4	0	10	12	.455	0	0-0	0	4.75	4.18
2014 Bal	AL	28	28	0	0	165.1	687	149	68	67	20	1	4	14	52	2	139	3	0	15	8	.652	0	0-0	0	3.72	3.65
2015 2 Tms		38	11	0	7	83.0	377	100	68	62	15	3	2	4	31	0	71	2	0	3	11	.214	0	0-2	2	5.96	6.72
2016 2 Tms	NL	35	19	0	1	113.0	495	116	67	64	14	3	3	3	49	4	102	7	0	6	10	.375	0	0-0	1	4.59	5.10
2017 LAA	AL	60	3	0	35	62.0	267	56	29	29	8	0	3	2	27	3	74	6	0	2	6	.250	0	19-23	3	3.99	4.21
13 Hou	AL	21	21	0	0	126.0	541	135	62	55	11	4	3	4	43	0	90	3	0	6	9	.400	0	0-0	0	4.34	3.93
13 Bal	AL	11	9	0	2	50.2	232	61	27	27	6	2	0	1	24	0	57	1	0	4	3	.571	0	0-0	0	5.81	4.80
15 Bal	AL	18	11	0	2	66.1	305	84	57	52	14	3	2	3	25	0	50	0	0	2	9	.182	0	0-1	0	6.60	7.06
15 SD	NL	20	0	0	5	16.2	72	16	11	10	1	0	0	1	6	0	21	2	0	1	2	.333	0	0-1	2	3.62	5.40
16 Atl	AL	22	10	0	0	70.1	301	68	34	33	6	3	2	2	28	1	60	3	0	3	7	.300	0	0-0	1	3.89	4.22
16 LAD	NL	13	9	0	1	42.2	194	48	33	31	8	0	1	1	21	3	42	4	0	3	3	.500	0	0-0	0	5.82	6.54
Postseason		2	2	0	0	10.2	46	11	4	4	1	0	0	0	2	0	9	1	0	1	0	1.000	0	0-0	0	3.22	3.38
9 ML YEARS		291	188	0	45	1163.2	5059	1169	627	581	148	36	25	51	464	22	1086	41	4	64	84	.432	0	19-25	6	4.44	4.49

Daniel Norris

Pitches: L **Bats:** L **Pos:** SP-18; RP-4   **Ht:** 6'2" **Wt:** 195 **Born:** 4/25/1993 **Age:** 25

		HOW MUCH HE PITCHED						WHAT HE GAVE UP										THE RESULTS							
Year Team	Lg	G	GS	CG	GF	IP	BFP	H	R	ER	HR	SH	SF	HB	TBB	IBB	SO	WP	Bk	W	L	Pct	Sh	Sv-Op	Hld	ERC	ERA
2017 Toledo*	AAA	6	6	0	0	14.0	80	22	20	19	3	0	2	0	16	0	18	2	0	0	4	.000	0	0- -	-	11.92	12.21
2014 Tor	AL	5	1	0	2	6.2	30	5	4	4	1	0	1	0	5	0	4	0	0	0	0	-	0	0-0	1	4.31	5.40
2015 2 Tms	AL	13	13	0	0	60.0	251	53	31	25	9	1	4	2	19	0	45	3	0	3	2	.600	0	0-0	0	3.55	3.75
2016 Det	AL	14	13	0	1	69.1	302	75	30	26	10	0	3	0	22	0	71	1	0	4	2	.667	0	0-0	0	4.46	3.38
2017 Det	AL	22	18	0	1	101.2	460	120	64	60	12	2	3	3	44	3	86	1	0	5	8	.385	0	0-0	0	5.48	5.31
15 Tor	AL	5	5	0	0	23.1	103	23	11	10	3	1	2	2	12	0	18	2	0	1	1	.500	0	0-0	0	5.10	3.86
15 Det	AL	8	8	0	0	36.2	148	30	20	15	6	0	2	0	7	0	27	1	0	2	1	.667	0	0-0	0	2.64	3.68
4 ML YEARS		54	45	0	4	237.2	1043	253	129	115	32	3	11	5	90	3	206	5	0	12	12	.500	0	0-0	1	4.65	4.35

Derek Norris

Bats: R **Throws:** R **Pos:** C-53   **Ht:** 6'0" **Wt:** 235 **Born:** 2/14/1989 **Age:** 29

							BATTING												RUNNING			AVERAGES			
Year Team	Lg	G	AB	H	2B	3B	HR	(Hm Rd)	TB	R	RBI	RC	TBB	IBB	SO	HBP	SH	SF	SB	CS	GDP	Avg	OBP	Slg	OPS
2012 Oak	AL	60	209	42	8	1	7	(3 4)	73	19	34	27	21	1	66	1	0	1	5	1	6	.201	.276	.349	.625
2013 Oak	AL	98	264	65	16	0	9	(6 3)	108	41	30	40	37	1	71	4	1	2	5	0	5	.246	.345	.409	.754
2014 Oak	AL	127	385	104	19	1	10	(7 3)	155	46	55	66	54	2	86	1	1	1	2	2	12	.270	.361	.403	.763
2015 SD	NL	147	515	129	33	2	14	(9 5)	208	65	62	66	35	1	131	6	0	1	4	1	5	.250	.305	.404	.709
2016 SD	NL	125	415	77	17	0	14	(8 6)	136	50	42	28	36	5	139	4	0	3	9	2	9	.186	.255	.328	.583
2017 TB	AL	53	179	36	5	0	9	(5 4)	68	21	24	16	12	0	48	3	0	4	1	0	5	.201	.258	.380	.637
Postseason		7	18	2	0	0	0	(0 0)	2	1	1	1	0	0	9	0	0	0	0	1	0	.111	.111	.111	.222
6 ML YEARS		610	1967	453	98	4	63	(38 25)	748	242	247	243	195	10	541	19	2	12	26	6	42	.230	.304	.380	.684

Ivan Nova

Pitches: R **Bats:** R **Pos:** SP-31   ee-VAHN   **Ht:** 6'5" **Wt:** 245 **Born:** 1/12/1987 **Age:** 31

		HOW MUCH HE PITCHED						WHAT HE GAVE UP												THE RESULTS							
Year Team	Lg	G	GS	CG	GF	IP	BFP	H	R	ER	HR	SH	SF	HB	TBB	IBB	SO	WP	Bk	W	L	Pct	Sh	Sv-Op	Hld	ERC	ERA
2010 NYY	AL	10	7	0	3	42.0	185	44	22	21	4	1	1	1	17	2	26	2	0	1	2	.333	0	0-1	0	4.31	4.50
2011 NYY	AL	28	27	0	1	165.1	704	163	74	68	13	2	6	6	57	3	98	11	0	16	4	.800	0	0-0	0	3.76	3.70
2012 NYY	AL	28	28	0	0	170.1	748	194	100	95	28	3	6	10	56	3	153	6	2	12	8	.600	0	0-0	0	5.32	5.02
2013 NYY	AL	23	20	3	2	139.1	586	135	49	48	9	2	3	14	44	3	116	3	0	9	6	.600	2	0-0	0	3.77	3.10
2014 NYY	AL	4	4	0	0	20.2	96	32	19	19	6	0	2	2	6	0	12	1	0	2	2	.500	0	0-0	0	9.40	8.27
2015 NYY	AL	17	17	0	0	94.0	413	99	54	53	13	3	2	7	33	0	63	5	0	6	11	.353	0	0-0	0	4.75	5.07
2016 2 Tms		32	26	3	3	162.0	684	175	81	75	23	5	6	9	28	1	127	10	0	12	8	.600	0	1-1	0	4.12	4.17
2017 Pit	NL	31	31	2	0	187.0	785	203	96	86	29	7	3	7	36	2	131	8	0	11	14	.440	1	0-0	0	4.27	4.14
16 NYY	AL	21	15	0	3	97.1	421	107	54	53	19	1	2	6	25	1	75	7	0	7	6	.538	0	1-1	0	4.98	4.90
16 Pit	NL	11	11	3	0	64.2	263	68	27	22	4	4	4	3	3	0	52	3	0	5	2	.714	0	0-0	0	2.93	3.06
Postseason		2	1	0	0	8.1	34	7	4	4	2	0	0	0	4	0	8	0	0	1	1	.500	0	0-0	0	4.66	4.32
8 ML YEARS		173	160	8	9	980.2	4201	1045	495	465	125	23	29	56	277	14	726	46	2	69	55	.556	3	1-2	0	4.41	4.27

Eduardo Nunez

Bats: R **Throws:** R **Pos:** 3B-53;2B-26;LF-19;SS-16;DH-4;RF-2;PH-1   **Ht:** 6'0" **Wt:** 195 **Born:** 6/15/1987 **Age:** 31

							BATTING												RUNNING			AVERAGES			
Year Team	Lg	G	AB	H	2B	3B	HR	(Hm Rd)	TB	R	RBI	RC	TBB	IBB	SO	HBP	SH	SF	SB	CS	GDP	Avg	OBP	Slg	OPS
2010 NYY	AL	30	50	14	1	0	1	(0 1)	18	12	7	8	3	0	2	0	0	0	5	0	4	.280	.321	.360	.681
2011 NYY	AL	112	309	82	18	2	5	(2 3)	119	38	30	42	22	2	37	0	6	1	22	6	6	.265	.313	.385	.698
2012 NYY	AL	38	89	26	4	1	1	(1 0)	35	14	11	15	6	0	12	1	0	4	11	2	1	.292	.330	.393	.723
2013 NYY	AL	90	304	79	17	4	3	(2 1)	113	38	28	31	20	1	51	3	4	5	10	3	3	.260	.307	.372	.679
2014 Min	AL	72	204	51	7	4	4	(4 0)	78	26	24	21	5	0	31	1	3	0	9	3	7	.250	.271	.382	.654
2015 Min	AL	72	188	53	14	1	4	(3 1)	81	23	20	25	12	0	29	1	2	1	8	4	1	.282	.327	.431	.758
2016 2 Tms		141	553	159	24	4	16	(8 8)	239	73	67	74	29	3	88	5	2	6	40	10	8	.288	.325	.432	.758
2017 2 Tms		114	467	146	33	0	12	(5 7)	215	60	58	76	18	0	54	3	1	2	24	7	11	.313	.341	.460	.801
16 Min	AL	91	371	110	15	1	12	(6 6)	163	49	47	54	15	0	58	3	2	5	27	6	6	.296	.325	.439	.764
16 SF	NL	50	182	49	9	3	4	(2 2)	76	24	20	20	14	3	30	2	0	1	13	4	2	.269	.327	.418	.744
17 SF	NL	76	302	93	21	0	4	(1 3)	126	37	31	45	12	0	29	1	1	2	18	5	8	.308	.334	.417	.752
17 Bos	AL	38	165	53	12	0	8	(4 4)	89	23	27	31	6	0	25	2	0	0	6	2	3	.321	.353	.539	.892
Postseason		9	14	3	1	1	1	(0 1)	9	4	1	1	0	0	0	0	0	0	2	0	0	.214	.214	.643	.857
8 ML YEARS		669	2164	610	118	16	46	(25 21)	898	284	245	292	115	6	304	14	18	19	129	35	41	.282	.320	.415	.735

Renato Nunez

Bats: R **Throws:** R **Pos:** LF-3;PH-3;DH-2;3B-1   **Ht:** 6'1" **Wt:** 220 **Born:** 4/4/1994 **Age:** 24

							BATTING												RUNNING			AVERAGES			
Year Team	Lg	G	AB	H	2B	3B	HR	(Hm Rd)	TB	R	RBI	RC	TBB	IBB	SO	HBP	SH	SF	SB	CS	GDP	Avg	OBP	Slg	OPS
2013 Beloit	A	128	508	131	27	0	19	(- -)	215	69	85	66	28	0	136	5	1	3	2	2	18	.258	.301	.423	.725
2014 Stcktn	A+	124	509	142	28	3	29	(- -)	263	75	96	90	34	0	113	13	0	6	2	0	12	.279	.336	.517	.853
2015 Mdlnd	AA	93	381	106	23	0	18	(- -)	183	62	61	62	28	1	66	4	0	3	1	0	4	.278	.332	.480	.812
2016 Nashv	AAA	128	505	115	20	2	23	(- -)	208	61	74	60	31	1	119	7	0	7	2	0	7	.228	.278	.412	.690
2017 Nashv	AAA	126	473	118	27	2	32	(- -)	245	74	78	81	47	1	141	5	0	8	2	1	14	.249	.319	.518	.837
2016 Oak	AL	9	15	2	0	0	0	(0 0)	2	0	1	0	0	0	3	0	0	0	0	0	0	.133	.133	.133	.267
2017 Oak	AL	8	15	3	0	0	1	(0 1)	6	1	3	3	1	0	8	0	0	0	0	0	0	.200	.250	.400	.650
2 ML YEARS		17	30	5	0	0	1	(0 1)	8	1	4	3	1	0	11	0	0	0	0	0	0	.167	.194	.267	.460

Vidal Nuno

Pitches: L **Bats:** L **Pos:** RP-12   vee-DAHL NOON-yoh   **Ht:** 5'11" **Wt:** 210 **Born:** 7/26/1987 **Age:** 30

		HOW MUCH HE PITCHED						WHAT HE GAVE UP												THE RESULTS							
Year Team	Lg	G	GS	CG	GF	IP	BFP	H	R	ER	HR	SH	SF	HB	TBB	IBB	SO	WP	Bk	W	L	Pct	Sh	Sv-Op	Hld	ERC	ERA
2017 Norfolk*	AAA	19	0	0	7	26.2	113	24	12	12	1	0	0	3	7	0	30	0	0	1	3	.250	0	0--	-	2.98	4.05
2013 NYY	AL	5	3	0	2	20.0	82	16	5	5	2	0	0	1	6	0	9	0	0	1	2	.333	0	0-0	0	2.81	2.25
2014 2 Tms		31	28	0	1	161.2	679	157	89	82	25	3	7	6	46	1	129	5	0	2	12	.143	0	0-0	0	3.98	4.56
2015 2 Tms		35	10	0	8	89.0	376	90	38	37	15	1	7	5	22	2	81	3	2	1	5	.167	0	0-0	4	4.20	3.74
2016 Sea	AL	55	1	0	14	58.2	247	67	23	23	11	0	2	2	11	2	51	0	2	1	1	.500	0	0-2	12	4.80	3.53
2017 Bal	AL	12	0	0	5	14.2	77	23	17	17	7	0	0	0	10	2	13	0	0	0	1	.000	0	0-0	0	11.87	10.43
14 NYY	AL	17	14	0	1	78.0	339	86	52	47	15	0	6	2	26	1	60	4	0	2	5	.286	0	0-0	0	5.18	5.42
14 Ari	NL	14	14	0	0	83.2	340	71	37	35	10	3	1	4	20	0	69	1	0	0	7	.000	0	0-0	0	2.96	3.76
15 Ari	NL	3	0	0	1	10.0	33	3	1	1	0	0	0	0	5	1	19	0	1	0	0	.000	0	0-0	0	2.01	1.88
15 Sea	AL	32	10	0	7	74.2	318	80	35	34	14	1	7	5	17	1	62	3	1	1	4	.200	0	0-0	4	4.67	4.10
5 ML YEARS		138	42	0	30	344.0	1461	353	172	164	60	4	16	14	95	7	283	8	4	5	21	.192	0	0-2	16	4.39	4.29

Scott Oberg

Pitches: R Bats: R Pos: RP-66   Ht: 6'2" Wt: 205 Born: 3/13/1990 Age: 28

			HOW MUCH HE PITCHED						WHAT HE GAVE UP											THE RESULTS						
Year Team	Lg	G	GS	CG	GF	IP	BFP	H	R	ER	HR	SH	SF	HB	TBB	IBB	SO	WP	Bk	W	L	Pct	Sh	Sv-Op	Hld	ERC	ERA
2015 Col	NL	64	0	0	11	58.1	259	58	35	33	10	3	1	6	31	2	44	6	1	3	4	.429	0	1-3	15	5.60	5.09
2016 Col	NL	24	0	0	9	26.0	113	26	15	15	3	0	0	1	11	2	20	3	0	1	1	.500	0	1-2	1	4.33	5.19
2017 Col	NL	66	0	0	12	58.1	265	70	35	32	4	1	2	2	24	2	55	3	0	0	1	.000	0	0-1	14	5.11	4.94
3 ML YEARS		154	0	0	32	142.2	637	154	85	80	17	4	3	9	66	6	119	12	1	4	6	.400	0	2-6	30	5.16	5.05

Darren O'Day

Pitches: R Bats: R Pos: RP-64   Ht: 6'4" Wt: 220 Born: 10/22/1982 Age: 35

			HOW MUCH HE PITCHED						WHAT HE GAVE UP											THE RESULTS						
Year Team	Lg	G	GS	CG	GF	IP	BFP	H	R	ER	HR	SH	SF	HB	TBB	IBB	SO	WP	Bk	W	L	Pct	Sh	Sv-Op	Hld	ERC	ERA
2008 LAA	AL	30	0	0	17	43.1	194	49	24	22	2	2	1	4	14	6	29	1	0	0	1	.000	0	0-0	1	4.20	4.57
2009 2 Tms		68	0	0	15	58.2	233	41	14	12	3	1	3	5	18	1	56	1	0	2	1	.667	0	2-2	20	2.20	1.84
2010 Tex	AL	72	0	0	14	62.0	240	43	15	14	5	1	3	5	12	2	45	0	0	6	2	.750	0	0-2	22	1.93	2.03
2011 Tex	AL	16	0	0	7	16.2	74	17	10	10	7	1	1	2	5	0	18	0	0	0	1	.000	0	0-0	3	6.45	5.40
2012 Bal	AL	69	0	0	10	67.0	263	49	17	17	6	3	1	3	14	2	69	0	0	7	1	.875	0	0-2	15	2.06	2.28
2013 Bal	AL	68	0	0	18	62.0	247	47	16	15	7	1	1	5	15	1	59	1	0	5	3	.625	0	2-6	20	2.60	2.18
2014 Bal	AL	68	0	0	18	68.2	271	42	14	13	6	1	2	6	19	4	73	0	0	5	2	.714	0	4-8	25	1.92	1.70
2015 Bal	AL	68	0	0	19	65.1	257	47	13	11	5	0	1	5	14	1	82	0	0	6	2	.750	0	6-11	18	2.09	1.52
2016 Bal	AL	34	0	0	6	31.0	131	25	13	13	6	0	0	1	13	2	38	0	0	3	1	.750	0	3-5	10	3.70	3.77
2017 Bal	AL	64	0	0	16	60.1	240	41	24	23	8	0	1	3	24	2	76	0	1	2	3	.400	0	2-4	17	2.79	3.43
09 NYM	NL	4	0	0	1	3.0	17	5	2	0	0	0	1	1	1	0	2	0	0	0	0	-	0	0-0	1	7.72	0.00
09 Tex	AL	64	0	0	14	55.2	216	36	12	12	3	1	2	4	17	1	54	1	0	2	1	.667	0	2-2	20	1.95	1.94
Postseason		21	0	0	1	16.0	61	11	8	8	4	1	0	1	3	0	16	0	0	0	3	.000	0	0-0	5	2.80	4.50
10 ML YEARS		557	0	0	140	535.0	2150	401	160	150	55	10	14	41	148	21	545	3	1	36	17	.679	0	19-40	151	2.56	2.52

Rougned Odor

Bats: L Throws: R Pos: 2B-158;PH-3;DH-2   ROOG-ned oh-DORE   Ht: 5'11" Wt: 195 Born: 2/3/1994 Age: 24

									BATTING													RUNNING			AVERAGES			
Year Team	Lg	G	AB	H	2B	3B	HR	(Hm	Rd)	TB	R	RBI	RC	TBB	IBB	SO	HBP	SH	SF	SB	CS	GDP	Avg	OBP	Slg	OPS
2014 Tex	AL	114	386	100	14	7	9	(4	5)	155	39	48	46	17	1	71	5	6	3	4	7	7	.259	.297	.402	.698
2015 Tex	AL	120	426	111	21	9	16	(7	9)	198	54	61	62	23	2	79	14	2	5	6	7	3	.261	.316	.465	.781
2016 Tex	AL	150	605	164	33	4	33	(17	16)	304	89	88	77	19	0	135	4	0	4	14	7	6	.271	.296	.502	.798
2017 Tex	AL	162	607	124	21	3	30	(18	12)	241	79	75	61	32	5	162	8	0	4	15	6	13	.204	.252	.397	.649
Postseason		8	28	7	1	0	2	(0	2)	14	9	4	5	3	0	5	2	0	0	0	0	0	.250	.364	.500	.864
4 ML YEARS		546	2024	499	89	23	88	(46	42)	898	261	272	246	91	8	447	31	8	16	39	27	29	.247	.287	.444	.731

Jake Odorizzi

Pitches: R Bats: R Pos: SP-28   oh-duh-RIZZ-ee   Ht: 6'2" Wt: 190 Born: 3/27/1990 Age: 28

			HOW MUCH HE PITCHED						WHAT HE GAVE UP											THE RESULTS						
Year Team	Lg	G	GS	CG	GF	IP	BFP	H	R	ER	HR	SH	SF	HB	TBB	IBB	SO	WP	Bk	W	L	Pct	Sh	Sv-Op	Hld	ERC	ERA
2012 KC	AL	2	2	0	0	7.1	34	8	4	4	1	0	0	0	4	0	4	0	0	0	1	.000	0	0-0	0	5.34	4.91
2013 TB	AL	7	4	0	2	29.2	122	28	13	13	3	0	1	2	8	0	22	1	0	0	1	.000	0	1-1	0	3.62	3.94
2014 TB	AL	31	31	0	0	168.0	719	156	79	77	20	3	8	5	59	0	174	3	0	11	13	.458	0	0-0	0	3.68	4.13
2015 TB	AL	28	28	0	0	169.1	700	149	65	63	18	4	3	3	46	0	150	5	1	9	9	.500	0	0-0	0	3.02	3.35
2016 TB	AL	33	33	0	0	187.2	773	170	80	77	29	3	6	4	54	3	166	3	1	10	6	.625	0	0-0	0	3.56	3.69
2017 TB	AL	28	28	0	0	143.1	604	117	80	66	30	2	7	2	61	1	127	1	0	10	8	.556	0	0-0	0	3.91	4.14
6 ML YEARS		129	126	0	2	705.1	2952	628	321	300	101	12	25	16	232	4	643	13	2	40	38	.513	0	1-1	0	3.55	3.83

Eric O'Flaherty

Pitches: L Bats: L Pos: RP-22   Ht: 6'2" Wt: 210 Born: 2/5/1985 Age: 33

			HOW MUCH HE PITCHED						WHAT HE GAVE UP											THE RESULTS						
Year Team	Lg	G	GS	CG	GF	IP	BFP	H	R	ER	HR	SH	SF	HB	TBB	IBB	SO	WP	Bk	W	L	Pct	Sh	Sv-Op	Hld	ERC	ERA
2006 Sea	AL	15	0	0	5	11.0	57	18	9	5	2	1	0	0	6	3	6	2	0	0	0	-	0	0-0	1	8.63	4.09
2007 Sea	AL	56	0	0	9	52.1	221	45	26	26	1	0	2	5	20	1	36	4	1	7	1	.875	0	0-1	4	3.04	4.47
2008 Sea	AL	7	0	0	1	6.2	42	16	15	15	2	0	1	2	4	2	4	0	0	0	0	.000	0	0-0	2	17.12	20.25
2009 Atl	NL	78	0	0	8	56.1	236	52	23	19	2	1	1	6	18	4	39	2	0	2	1	.667	0	0-2	15	3.26	3.04
2010 Atl	NL	56	0	0	7	44.0	181	37	14	12	2	1	0	1	18	2	36	3	0	3	2	.600	0	0-1	9	2.97	2.45
2011 Atl	NL	78	0	0	5	73.2	301	59	9	8	2	7	2	3	21	8	67	1	0	2	4	.333	0	0-4	32	2.13	0.98
2012 Atl	NL	64	0	0	7	57.1	230	47	14	11	3	3	1	2	19	2	46	1	0	3	0	1.000	0	0-3	28	2.71	1.73
2013 Atl	NL	19	0	0	2	18.0	70	12	5	5	2	0	1	0	5	1	11	0	0	3	0	1.000	0	0-1	12	1.93	2.50
2014 Oak	AL	21	0	0	6	20.0	80	15	5	5	3	1	0	2	4	0	15	3	0	1	0	1.000	0	1-2	3	2.68	2.25
2015 2 Tms		41	0	0	8	30.0	159	47	30	27	2	2	0	2	18	2	21	1	0	1	2	.333	0	0-1	4	7.97	8.10
2016 Atl	NL	39	0	0	8	28.2	136	39	25	22	3	1	0	2	11	2	22	3	0	1	4	.200	0	0-1	6	6.29	6.91
2017 Atl	NL	22	0	0	3	18.1	83	20	16	16	4	1	1	0	9	0	15	1	0	0	0	-	0	0-0	3	5.81	7.85
15 Oak	AL	25	0	0	5	21.1	108	29	17	14	1	2	0	0	13	1	15	0	0	1	2	.333	0	0-1	4	6.26	5.91
15 NYM	NL	16	0	0	3	8.2	51	18	13	13	1	0	0	2	5	1	6	1	0	0	0	-	0	0-0	1	12.63	13.50
Postseason		1	0	0	0	1.0	4	2	0	0	0	0	0	0	0	0	0	0	0	0	0	-	0	0-0	0	9.49	0.00
12 ML YEARS		496	0	0	68	416.1	1796	407	191	171	28	18	9	25	153	27	318	21	1	23	15	.605	0	1-16	116	3.72	3.70

Chris O'Grady

Pitches: L Bats: R Pos: RP-7; SP-6

Ht: 6'4" Wt: 225 Born: 4/17/1990 Age: 28

		HOW MUCH HE PITCHED						WHAT HE GAVE UP											THE RESULTS							
Year Team	Lg	G	GS	CG	GF	IP	BFP	H	R	ER	HR	SH	SF	HB	TBB	IBB	SO	WP	Bk	W	L	Pct	Sh	Sv-Op	Hld	ERC	ERA
2013 2 Tms	Low	24	5	0	3	53.2	212	46	17	13	4	2	2	2	11	0	46	4	0	3	1	.750	0	0- -	-	2.63	2.18
2014 InldEm	A+	45	2	0	11	83.2	346	84	40	31	4	5	2	2	17	1	81	4	0	4	4	.500	0	5- -	-	3.16	3.33
2015 Ark	AA	38	0	0	11	49.0	196	42	20	18	5	2	3	1	10	0	47	1	0	0	5	.000	0	4- -	-	2.68	3.31
2015 Salt Lk	AAA	7	0	0	1	8.2	34	5	3	3	1	0	0	0	4	0	10	0	0	0	0	-	0	0- -	-	2.26	3.12
2016 Salt Lk	AAA	22	2	0	5	34.2	147	41	18	16	3	2	1	0	12	0	24	0	0	2	1	.667	0	0- -	-	5.04	4.15
2016 Ark	AA	15	8	0	2	61.0	248	64	19	19	3	3	2	1	10	0	50	4	0	7	1	.875	0	1- -	-	3.23	2.80
2017 NewOr	AAA	12	9	0	0	54.2	218	44	24	20	7	0	0	2	15	0	54	1	0	3	5	.375	0	0- -	-	2.93	3.29
2017 Mia	NL	13	6	0	1	33.0	145	33	16	16	4	2	1	1	18	1	30	0	1	2	1	.667	0	0-0	2	4.99	4.36

Seung Hwan Oh

Pitches: R Bats: R Pos: RP-62

sing whan

Ht: 5'10" Wt: 205 Born: 7/15/1982 Age: 35

		HOW MUCH HE PITCHED						WHAT HE GAVE UP											THE RESULTS							
Year Team	Lg	G	GS	CG	GF	IP	BFP	H	R	ER	HR	SH	SF	HB	TBB	IBB	SO	WP	Bk	W	L	Pct	Sh	Sv-Op	Hld	ERC	ERA
2016 StL	NL	76	0	0	35	79.2	313	55	20	17	5	2	1	2	18	3	103	3	0	6	3	.667	0	19-23	14	1.69	1.92
2017 StL	NL	62	0	0	38	59.1	264	68	31	27	10	3	4	3	15	9	54	1	0	1	6	.143	0	20-24	7	4.65	4.10
2 ML YEARS		138	0	0	73	139.0	577	123	51	44	15	5	5	5	33	12	157	4	0	7	9	.438	0	39-47	21	2.85	2.85

Mike Ohlman

Bats: R Throws: R Pos: C-6;PH-1

Ht: 6'5" Wt: 240 Born: 12/14/1990 Age: 27

		BATTING																			RUNNING			AVERAGES			
Year Team	Lg	G	AB	H	2B	3B	HR	(Hm	Rd)	TB	R	RBI	RC	TBB	IBB	SO	HBP	SH	SF	SB	CS	GDP	Avg	OBP	Slg	OPS
2013 Frdrck	A+	100	361	113	29	4	13	(-	-)	189	61	53	79	56	2	93	5	0	2	5	0	11	.313	.410	.524	.934
2014 Bowie	AA	113	403	95	25	1	2	(-	-)	128	40	33	43	43	0	86	2	2	4	0	0	10	.236	.310	.318	.627
2015 Sprgfld	AA	103	365	100	17	0	12	(-	-)	153	53	69	57	46	2	76	2	1	2	0	1	10	.274	.357	.419	.776
2016 Memp	AAA	54	168	47	9	2	6	(-	-)	78	34	28	27	15	0	53	0	0	3	1	0	5	.280	.333	.464	.798
2016 Sprgfld	AA	24	83	25	3	0	1	(-	-)	31	9	16	11	10	0	19	0	0	3	0	2	0	.301	.365	.373	.738
2017 Buffalo	AAA	90	282	61	16	0	12	(-	-)	113	35	38	41	48	0	115	2	0	0	4	0	3	.216	.334	.401	.735
2017 Tor	AL	7	13	3	0	0	0	(0	0)	3	1	1	2	0	0	3	0	0	0	0	0	0	.231	.231	.231	.462

Steven Okert

Pitches: L Bats: L Pos: RP-44

Ht: 6'3" Wt: 210 Born: 7/9/1991 Age: 26

		HOW MUCH HE PITCHED						WHAT HE GAVE UP											THE RESULTS							
Year Team	Lg	G	GS	CG	GF	IP	BFP	H	R	ER	HR	SH	SF	HB	TBB	IBB	SO	WP	Bk	W	L	Pct	Sh	Sv-Op	Hld	ERC	ERA
2013 Augsta	A	44	0	0	15	60.2	259	55	27	20	3	7	2	1	24	1	59	2	0	2	2	.500	0	2- -	-	3.21	2.97
2014 SnJos	A+	33	0	0	29	35.1	152	33	6	6	2	2	0	2	11	1	54	0	0	1	2	.333	0	19- -	-	3.18	1.53
2014 Rchmd	AA	24	0	0	11	33.0	131	24	11	10	3	3	1	0	11	1	38	0	1	1	0	1.000	0	5- -	-	2.34	2.73
2015 Scrmto	AAA	52	0	0	11	61.1	270	62	32	26	7	3	2	2	29	1	69	1	0	4	3	.571	0	3- -	-	4.65	3.82
2016 Scrmto	AAA	41	0	0	12	47.1	211	52	27	20	2	2	2	0	11	1	60	2	0	4	3	.571	0	3- -	-	3.33	3.80
2017 Scrmto	AAA	24	0	0	11	25.1	96	15	10	9	4	1	1	2	8	1	21	0	0	3	0	1.000	0	6- -	-	2.36	3.20
2016 SF	NL	16	0	0	3	14.0	58	14	5	5	2	0	0	0	4	1	14	0	0	0	0	-	0	0-1	2	3.87	3.21
2017 SF	NL	44	0	0	3	27.0	118	24	18	17	3	3	2	3	11	2	22	0	0	1	1	.500	0	0-0	11	3.83	5.67
2 ML YEARS		60	0	0	6	41.0	176	38	23	22	5	3	2	3	15	3	36	0	0	1	1	.500	0	0-1	13	3.84	4.83

Matt Olson

Bats: L Throws: R Pos: 1B-43;RF-12;PH-8

Ht: 6'5" Wt: 230 Born: 3/29/1994 Age: 24

		BATTING																			RUNNING			AVERAGES			
Year Team	Lg	G	AB	H	2B	3B	HR	(Hm	Rd)	TB	R	RBI	RC	TBB	IBB	SO	HBP	SH	SF	SB	CS	GDP	Avg	OBP	Slg	OPS
2013 Beloit	A	134	481	108	32	0	23	(-	-)	209	69	93	72	72	2	103	2	0	3	4	3	5	.225	.326	.435	.761
2014 Stcktn	A+	138	512	134	31	1	37	(-	-)	278	111	97	116	117	4	137	5	0	6	2	0	6	.262	.404	.543	.947
2015 Mdlnd	AA	133	466	116	37	0	17	(-	-)	204	82	75	89	105	6	139	6	0	8	5	1	7	.249	.388	.438	.826
2016 Nashv	AAA	131	464	109	34	1	17	(-	-)	196	69	60	70	71	2	132	0	2	3	1	0	9	.235	.335	.422	.757
2017 Nashv	AAA	79	294	80	16	1	23	(-	-)	167	56	60	62	45	0	83	1	0	3	3	0	1	.272	.367	.568	.935
2016 Oak	AL	11	21	2	1	0	0	(0	0)	3	3	0	1	7	0	4	0	0	0	0	0	1	.095	.321	.143	.464
2017 Oak	AL	59	189	49	2	0	24	(12	12)	123	33	45	40	22	1	60	5	0	0	0	0	6	.259	.352	.651	1.003
2 ML YEARS		70	210	51	3	0	24	(12	12)	126	36	45	41	29	1	64	5	0	0	0	0	7	.243	.348	.600	.948

Tyler Olson

Pitches: L Bats: R Pos: RP-30

Ht: 6'3" Wt: 195 Born: 10/2/1989 Age: 28

		HOW MUCH HE PITCHED						WHAT HE GAVE UP											THE RESULTS							
Year Team	Lg	G	GS	CG	GF	IP	BFP	H	R	ER	HR	SH	SF	HB	TBB	IBB	SO	WP	Bk	W	L	Pct	Sh	Sv-Op	Hld	ERC	ERA
2017 Clmbs*	AAA	34	0	0	8	42.0	163	28	16	15	7	0	0	2	13	1	54	1	0	2	0	1.000	0	2- -	-	2.62	3.21
2015 Sea	AL	11	0	0	4	13.1	65	18	8	8	2	2	0	1	10	7	8	0	1	1	1	.500	0	0-0	1	7.64	5.40
2016 NYY	AL	1	0	0	1	2.2	13	3	2	2	0	0	1	0	2	0	0	0	0	0	0	-	0	0-0	0	5.24	6.75
2017 Cle	AL	30	0	0	4	20.0	77	13	0	0	0	1	0	1	6	0	18	0	0	1	0	1.000	0	1-1	8	1.62	0.00
3 ML YEARS		42	0	0	9	36.0	155	34	10	10	2	3	1	2	18	7	26	0	1	2	1	.667	0	1-1	9	3.81	2.50

Paulo Orlando

Bats: R **Throws:** R **Pos:** RF-20;CF-18;PR-3;PH-2   **Ht:** 6'2" **Wt:** 210 **Born:** 11/1/1985 **Age:** 32

Year	Team	Lg	G	AB	H	2B	3B	HR	(Hm	Rd)	TB	R	RBI	RC	TBB	IBB	SO	HBP	SH	SF	SB	CS	GDP	Avg	OBP	Slg	OPS
2017	Omha*	AAA	30	116	34	10	0	2	(-	-)	50	14	19	18	9	0	26	3	0	1	2	2	1	.293	.357	.431	.788
2017	NWArk*	AA	12	41	14	1	0	0	(-	-)	15	4	3	7	6	0	7	0	0	0	0	0	0	.341	.426	.366	.791
2015	KC	AL	86	241	60	14	6	7	(4	3)	107	31	27	30	5	0	53	2	2	1	3	3	0	.249	.269	.444	.713
2016	KC	AL	128	457	138	24	4	5	(3	2)	185	52	43	59	13	1	105	7	3	3	14	3	12	.302	.329	.405	.734
2017	KC	AL	39	86	17	3	0	2	(2	0)	26	9	6	5	1	0	20	2	0	0	1	1	3	.198	.225	.302	.527
	Postseason		12	11	3	0	0	0	(0	0)	3	3	1	1	0	0	2	0	0	1	0	0	0	.273	.250	.273	.523
	3 ML YEARS		253	784	215	41	10	14	(9	5)	318	92	76	94	19	1	178	11	5	4	18	7	15	.274	.300	.406	.705

Danny Ortiz

Bats: L **Throws:** L **Pos:** RF-6;LF-2;CF-1;PH-1   **Ht:** 5'11" **Wt:** 190 **Born:** 1/5/1990 **Age:** 28

Year	Team	Lg	G	AB	H	2B	3B	HR	(Hm	Rd)	TB	R	RBI	RC	TBB	IBB	SO	HBP	SH	SF	SB	CS	GDP	Avg	OBP	Slg	OPS
2013	NwBrit	AA	133	484	125	27	4	12	(-	-)	196	63	60	59	27	1	88	4	2	4	1	4	4	.258	.301	.405	.706
2014	NwBrit	AA	49	182	59	16	2	4	(-	-)	91	22	31	30	4	0	34	1	1	1	3	1	2	.324	.340	.500	.840
2014	Roch	AAA	73	242	62	13	3	8	(-	-)	105	36	33	30	9	0	51	1	0	2	0	0	5	.256	.283	.434	.717
2015	Roch	AAA	131	484	120	31	3	17	(-	-)	208	61	78	64	33	2	105	2	1	6	4	1	4	.248	.295	.430	.725
2016	Indy	AAA	130	436	103	19	4	17	(-	-)	181	41	57	50	25	4	91	1	1	7	6	8	6	.236	.275	.415	.690
2017	Indy	AAA	110	411	111	30	1	15	(-	-)	188	47	63	58	19	5	80	3	2	6	5	2	4	.270	.303	.457	.760
2017	Pit	NL	9	12	1	0	0	0	(0	0)	1	1	0	0	1	0	1	0	0	0	0	0	0	.083	.154	.083	.237

Josh Osich

Pitches: L **Bats:** L **Pos:** RP-54   OH-sitch   **Ht:** 6'2" **Wt:** 230 **Born:** 9/3/1988 **Age:** 29

Year	Team	Lg	G	GS	CG	GF	IP	BFP	H	R	ER	HR	SH	SF	HB	TBB	IBB	SO	WP	Bk	W	L	Pct	Sh	Sv-Op	Hld	ERC	ERA
2017	Scrmto*	AAA	9	0	0	6	9.1	44	12	11	8	0	2	0	0	3	0	8	1	0	1	1	.500	0	2--	-	4.40	7.71
2015	SF	NL	35	0	0	6	28.2	120	24	12	7	4	1	0	0	8	0	27	2	0	2	0	1.000	0	0-2	11	2.88	2.20
2016	SF	NL	59	0	0	9	36.1	160	31	20	19	7	1	0	3	19	1	25	2	0	1	3	.250	0	0-3	18	4.65	4.71
2017	SF	NL	54	0	0	12	43.1	201	48	32	30	7	1	0	1	27	1	43	5	0	3	2	.600	0	0-1	6	6.18	6.23
	3 ML YEARS		148	0	0	27	108.1	481	103	64	56	18	3	1	4	54	2	95	9	0	6	5	.545	0	0-6	35	4.73	4.65

Jose Osuna

Bats: R **Throws:** R **Pos:** PH-53;RF-25;1B-23;LF-14;PR-1   **Ht:** 6'3" **Wt:** 240 **Born:** 12/12/1992 **Age:** 25

Year	Team	Lg	G	AB	H	2B	3B	HR	(Hm	Rd)	TB	R	RBI	RC	TBB	IBB	SO	HBP	SH	SF	SB	CS	GDP	Avg	OBP	Slg	OPS
2013	Bradtn	A+	123	454	111	25	1	8	(-	-)	162	47	48	52	35	1	76	2	4	5	18	6	9	.244	.298	.357	.655
2014	Bradtn	A+	97	365	108	23	3	10	(-	-)	167	47	57	60	28	0	72	4	4	7	4	2	9	.296	.347	.458	.804
2015	Bradtn	A+	44	174	49	12	1	4	(-	-)	75	23	29	26	14	1	33	1	1	3	1	1	4	.282	.333	.431	.764
2015	Altna	AA	85	323	93	20	2	8	(-	-)	141	46	52	47	17	0	61	4	0	5	6	3	15	.288	.327	.437	.763
2016	Altna	AA	70	253	68	18	3	6	(-	-)	110	34	38	38	23	1	44	2	0	5	1	1	5	.269	.329	.435	.763
2016	Indy	AAA	63	220	64	19	1	7	(-	-)	106	27	31	34	13	1	36	1	0	0	2	3	10	.291	.333	.482	.815
2017	Indy	AAA	10	36	9	5	0	0	(-	-)	14	6	1	4	5	1	9	0	0	0	1	1	0	.250	.341	.389	.730
2017	Pit	NL	104	215	50	13	4	7	(3	4)	92	31	30	19	9	0	40	2	0	1	0	0	10	.233	.269	.428	.697

Roberto Osuna

Pitches: R **Bats:** R **Pos:** RP-66   **Ht:** 6'2" **Wt:** 215 **Born:** 2/7/1995 **Age:** 23

Year	Team	Lg	G	GS	CG	GF	IP	BFP	H	R	ER	HR	SH	SF	HB	TBB	IBB	SO	WP	Bk	W	L	Pct	Sh	Sv-Op	Hld	ERC	ERA
2015	Tor	AL	68	0	0	39	69.2	271	48	24	20	7	1	2	1	16	2	75	5	0	1	6	.143	0	20-23	7	1.89	2.58
2016	Tor	AL	72	0	0	61	74.0	288	55	23	22	9	1	3	3	14	4	82	4	1	4	3	.571	0	36-42	0	2.20	2.68
2017	Tor	AL	66	0	0	58	64.0	249	46	26	24	3	1	2	3	9	0	83	4	0	3	4	.429	0	39-49	0	1.61	3.38
	Postseason		14	0	0	12	17.1	59	7	2	2	1	0	0	0	1	0	16	0	0	1	1	.500	0	2-2	0	0.57	1.04
	3 ML YEARS		206	0	0	158	207.2	808	149	70	66	19	3	7	7	39	6	240	13	1	8	13	.381	0	95-114	7	1.90	2.86

Shohei Otani

Pitches: R **Bats:** L **Pos:** SP-5   shoh-hay   **Ht:** 6'3" **Wt:** 189 **Born:** 7/5/1994 **Age:** 23

Year	Team	Lg	G	GS	CG	GF	IP	BFP	H	R	ER	HR	SH	SF	HB	TBB	IBB	SO	WP	Bk	W	L	Pct	Sh	Sv-Op	Hld	ERC	ERA
2013	Hokado	Jap	13	11	0	0	61.2	274	57	30	29	4	-	-	8	33	0	46	2	0	3	0	1.000	0	0--	0	4.53	4.23
2014	Hokado	Jap	24	24	3	0	155.1	639	125	50	45	7	-	-	4	57	0	179	6	1	11	4	.733	2	0--	0	2.67	2.61
2015	Hokado	Jap	22	22	5	0	160.2	621	100	40	40	7	-	-	3	46	0	196	9	0	15	5	.750	3	0--	0	1.58	2.24
2016	Hokado	Jap	21	20	4	0	140.0	548	89	33	29	4	-	-	8	45	0	174	6	0	10	4	.714	1	0--	1	1.75	1.86
2017	Hokado	Jap	5	5	1	0	25.1	105	13	9	9	2	-	-	0	19	0	29	1	0	3	2	.600	1	0--	0	2.74	3.20
	5 JAP YEARS		85	82	13	0	543.0	2187	384	162	152	24	-	-	23	200	0	624	24	1	42	15	.737	7	0--	1	2.26	2.52

Dan Otero

Pitches: R **Bats:** R **Pos:** RP-52   oh-TEHR-oh   **Ht:** 6'3" **Wt:** 205 **Born:** 2/19/1985 **Age:** 33

Year	Team	Lg	G	GS	CG	GF	IP	BFP	H	R	ER	HR	SH	SF	HB	TBB	IBB	SO	WP	Bk	W	L	Pct	Sh	Sv-Op	Hld	ERC	ERA
2012	SF	NL	12	0	0	4	12.1	57	19	11	8	0	0	0	2	2	1	8	1	0	0	0	-	0	0-0	1	6.18	5.84
2013	Oak	AL	33	0	0	8	39.0	159	42	7	6	0	1	0	0	6	1	27	0	0	2	0	1.000	0	0-1	8	2.90	1.38
2014	Oak	AL	72	0	0	14	86.2	349	80	24	22	4	4	3	2	15	7	45	1	0	8	2	.800	0	1-4	12	2.46	2.28
2015	Oak	AL	41	0	0	6	46.2	204	64	35	35	7	1	3	2	6	2	28	1	0	2	4	.333	0	0-1	4	5.70	6.75
2016	Cle	AL	62	0	0	20	70.2	269	54	14	12	2	3	0	0	10	1	57	2	0	5	1	.833	0	1-2	3	1.60	1.53
2017	Cle	AL	52	0	0	14	60.0	242	63	23	19	6	1	1	0	9	4	38	0	0	3	0	1.000	0	0-0	1	3.36	2.85
	Postseason		11	0	0	1	13.2	53	13	4	4	2	1	0	0	1	0	5	0	0	0	1	.000	0	0-0	1	2.91	2.63
6 ML YEARS			272	0	0	66	315.1	1280	322	114	102	19	10	7	6	48	16	203	5	0	20	7	.741	0	2-8	26	3.02	2.91

Adam Ottavino

Pitches: R **Bats:** B **Pos:** RP-63   ott-tah-VEE-no   **Ht:** 6'5" **Wt:** 220 **Born:** 11/22/1985 **Age:** 32

Year	Team	Lg	G	GS	CG	GF	IP	BFP	H	R	ER	HR	SH	SF	HB	TBB	IBB	SO	WP	Bk	W	L	Pct	Sh	Sv-Op	Hld	ERC	ERA
2010	StL	NL	5	3	0	0	22.1	110	37	21	21	5	1	0	0	9	1	12	1	0	0	2	.000	0	0-0	0	9.22	8.46
2012	Col	NL	53	0	0	6	79.0	339	76	42	40	9	3	1	1	34	7	81	8	0	5	1	.833	0	0-2	6	4.01	4.56
2013	Col	NL	51	0	0	5	78.1	335	73	27	23	5	6	4	2	31	5	78	9	1	1	3	.250	0	0-0	8	3.42	2.64
2014	Col	NL	75	0	0	16	65.0	272	67	26	26	6	2	3	4	16	1	70	4	0	1	4	.200	0	1-6	21	3.87	3.60
2015	Col	NL	10	0	0	5	10.1	35	3	0	0	0	0	0	1	2	0	13	0	0	1	0	1.000	0	3-3	6	0.56	0.00
2016	Col	NL	34	0	0	19	27.0	107	18	9	8	0	0	0	2	7	0	35	4	0	1	3	.250	0	7-12	4	2.17	2.67
2017	Col	NL	63	0	0	11	53.1	243	48	30	30	8	0	3	4	39	2	63	8	0	2	3	.400	0	0-2	21	5.51	5.06
7 ML YEARS			291	3	0	62	335.1	1441	322	155	148	36	12	11	14	138	16	352	34	1	11	16	.407	0	11-25	63	4.06	3.97

Dillon Overton

Pitches: L **Bats:** L **Pos:** RP-8; SP-2   **Ht:** 6'2" **Wt:** 175 **Born:** 8/17/1991 **Age:** 26

Year	Team	Lg	G	GS	CG	GF	IP	BFP	H	R	ER	HR	SH	SF	HB	TBB	IBB	SO	WP	Bk	W	L	Pct	Sh	Sv-Op	Hld	ERC	ERA
2014	2 Tms	Low	12	12	0	0	37.0	146	30	12	8	0	2	0	3	4	0	53	0	0	0	3	.000	0	0- -	-	1.75	1.95
2015	Stcktn	A+	14	12	0	2	61.1	247	62	29	26	7	0	2	3	12	0	59	1	0	2	4	.333	0	0- -	-	3.77	3.82
2015	Mdlnd	AA	13	13	0	0	64.2	266	65	22	22	4	1	0	0	15	0	47	1	0	5	2	.714	0	0- -	-	3.24	3.06
2016	Nashv	AAA	21	20	1	0	125.2	530	132	50	46	6	2	2	2	31	0	105	1	1	13	5	.722	0	0- -	-	3.47	3.29
2017	Tacom	AAA	7	6	0	0	27.0	126	34	28	28	9	0	1	0	12	0	22	2	0	1	2	.333	0	0- -	-	7.55	9.33
2017	ElPaso	AAA	12	12	0	0	64.0	286	77	41	40	12	4	2	1	17	0	30	2	0	6	4	.600	0	0- -	-	5.30	5.63
2016	Oak	AL	7	5	0	2	24.1	128	48	31	31	12	0	0	2	7	0	17	1	0	1	3	.250	0	0-0	0	13.58	11.47
2017	2 Tms		10	2	0	4	23.0	103	30	19	17	6	0	2	1	4	2	11	3	0	0	1	1.000	0	0-0	0	6.07	6.65
17	Sea	AL	9	1	0	4	18.1	79	21	15	13	4	0	2	0	2	1	8	3	0	0	0	-	0	0-0	0	4.27	6.38
17	SD	NL	1	1	0	0	4.2	24	9	4	4	2	0	0	1	2	1	3	0	0	0	1	.000	0	0-0	0	14.93	7.71
2 ML YEARS			17	7	0	6	47.1	231	78	50	48	18	0	4	2	11	2	28	4	0	1	4	.200	0	0-0	0	9.72	9.13

Chris Owings

Bats: R **Throws:** R **Pos:** SS-54;RF-25;2B-22;PH-6;LF-1   **Ht:** 5'10" **Wt:** 185 **Born:** 8/12/1991 **Age:** 26

Year	Team	Lg	G	AB	H	2B	3B	HR	(Hm	Rd)	TB	R	RBI	RC	TBB	IBB	SO	HBP	SH	SF	SB	CS	GDP	Avg	OBP	Slg	OPS
2013	Ari	NL	20	55	16	5	0	0	(0	0)	21	5	5	7	6	1	10	0	0	0	2	0	0	.291	.361	.382	.742
2014	Ari	NL	91	310	81	15	6	6	(1	5)	126	34	26	38	16	0	67	2	2	2	8	1	4	.261	.300	.406	.706
2015	Ari	NL	147	515	117	27	5	4	(3	1)	166	59	43	41	26	3	144	1	7	3	16	4	9	.227	.264	.322	.587
2016	Ari	NL	119	437	121	24	11	5	(5	0)	182	52	49	60	20	4	87	5	2	2	21	2	8	.277	.315	.416	.731
2017	Ari	NL	97	362	97	25	1	12	(8	4)	160	41	51	48	17	0	87	1	2	4	12	2	3	.268	.299	.442	.741
5 ML YEARS			474	1679	432	96	23	27	(17	10)	655	191	174	194	85	8	395	9	13	11	59	9	24	.257	.295	.390	.685

Marcell Ozuna

Bats: R **Throws:** R **Pos:** LF-152;PH-4;CF-3;DH-2;RF-1   oh-ZUNE-uh   **Ht:** 6'1" **Wt:** 225 **Born:** 11/12/1990 **Age:** 27

Year	Team	Lg	G	AB	H	2B	3B	HR	(Hm	Rd)	TB	R	RBI	RC	TBB	IBB	SO	HBP	SH	SF	SB	CS	GDP	Avg	OBP	Slg	OPS
2013	Mia	NL	70	275	73	17	4	3	(0	3)	107	31	32	35	13	0	57	2	1	0	5	1	6	.265	.303	.389	.693
2014	Mia	NL	153	565	152	26	5	23	(12	11)	257	72	85	74	41	1	164	1	0	5	3	1	12	.269	.317	.455	.772
2015	Mia	NL	123	459	119	27	0	10	(2	8)	176	47	44	48	30	1	110	3	0	2	2	3	10	.259	.308	.383	.691
2016	Mia	NL	148	557	148	23	6	23	(12	11)	252	75	76	69	43	2	115	4	0	4	0	3	11	.266	.321	.452	.773
2017	Mia	NL	159	613	191	30	2	37	(22	15)	336	93	124	117	64	4	144	0	0	2	1	3	18	.312	.376	.548	.924
5 ML YEARS			653	2469	683	123	17	96	(48	48)	1128	318	361	343	191	8	590	10	1	13	11	11	57	.277	.329	.457	.786

Emilio Pagan

Pitches: R **Bats:** L **Pos:** RP-34   **Ht:** 6'3" **Wt:** 210 **Born:** 5/7/1991 **Age:** 27

Year	Team	Lg	G	GS	CG	GF	IP	BFP	H	R	ER	HR	SH	SF	HB	TBB	IBB	SO	WP	Bk	W	L	Pct	Sh	Sv-Op	Hld	ERC	ERA
2013	2 Tms	Low	20	0	0	16	26.1	105	17	4	3	1	1	1	1	6	0	35	2	0	1	1	.500	0	12- -	-	1.49	1.03
2014	Clinton	A	42	0	0	34	56.0	226	43	19	18	4	2	4	4	14	1	62	1	0	2	3	.400	0	16- -	-	2.36	2.89
2015	Bkrsfld	A+	42	0	0	25	78.1	326	63	29	22	5	2	3	5	27	1	88	4	2	3	8	.273	0	8- -	-	2.79	2.53
2016	Jacksn	AA	18	0	0	10	30.2	125	19	4	4	1	1	0	1	11	0	45	3	0	4	1	.800	0	9- -	-	1.66	1.17
2016	Tacom	AAA	23	0	0	3	34.1	145	28	14	14	6	0	1	1	18	0	39	0	0	1	2	.333	0	1- -	-	4.10	3.67
2017	Tacom	AAA	23	0	0	11	31.2	125	19	9	9	0	1	3	2	9	0	36	0	0	2	1	.667	0	5- -	-	1.33	2.56
2017	Sea	AL	34	0	0	9	50.1	196	39	20	18	7	1	2	1	8	0	56	1	0	2	3	.400	0	0-1	8	2.32	3.22

Joe Panik

Bats: L Throws: R Pos: 2B-137;PH-2;PR-1   PAN-ick   Ht: 6'1" Wt: 190 Born: 10/30/1990 Age: 27

Year	Team	Lg	G	AB	H	2B	3B	HR	(Hm	Rd)	TB	R	RBI	RC	TBB	IBB	SO	HBP	SH	SF	SB	CS	GDP	Avg	OBP	Slg	OPS
2014	SF	NL	73	269	82	10	2	1	(0	1)	99	31	18	33	16	0	33	0	1	1	0	0	4	.305	.343	.368	.711
2015	SF	NL	100	382	119	27	2	8	(4	4)	174	59	37	60	38	0	42	5	3	4	3	2	7	.312	.378	.455	.833
2016	SF	NL	127	464	111	21	7	10	(3	7)	176	67	62	56	50	5	47	4	3	5	5	0	14	.239	.315	.379	.695
2017	SF	NL	138	511	147	28	5	10	(0	10)	215	60	53	73	46	4	54	5	3	8	4	1	10	.288	.347	.421	.768
	Postseason		21	86	23	4	2	1	(1	0)	34	10	10	11	7	0	10	0	1	1	0	0	1	.267	.319	.395	.714
	4 ML YEARS		438	1626	459	86	16	29	(7	22)	664	217	170	222	150	9	176	14	10	18	12	3	35	.282	.345	.408	.753

Eduardo Paredes

Pitches: R Bats: R Pos: RP-18   Ht: 6'1" Wt: 170 Born: 3/6/1995 Age: 23

			HOW MUCH HE PITCHED					WHAT HE GAVE UP												THE RESULTS							
Year	Team	Lg	G	GS	CG	GF	IP	BFP	H	R	ER	HR	SH	SF	HB	TBB	IBB	SO	WP	Bk	W	L	Pct	Sh	Sv-Op	Hld	ERC	ERA
2014	Orem	R+	19	0	0	16	20.1	82	8	4	3	0	1	0	3	8	0	31	2	1	2	1	.667	0	7- -	-	1.16	1.33
2015	2 Tms	Low	48	0	0	41	55.1	220	44	17	15	2	1	3	3	10	0	72	1	2	0	2	.000	0	20- -	-	2.02	2.44
2016	InldEm	A+	19	0	0	16	22.0	92	18	9	8	2	0	2	3	6	0	32	1	0	1	2	.333	0	4- -	-	3.05	3.27
2016	Ark	AA	35	0	0	20	48.1	204	46	21	18	6	2	2	0	14	3	43	5	1	0	3	.000	0	8- -	-	3.39	3.35
2017	Mobile	AA	9	0	0	3	12.2	54	11	2	2	0	0	0	1	4	0	17	2	0	0	0	-	0	1- -	-	2.62	1.42
2017	Salt Lk	AAA	25	0	0	8	37.0	156	27	13	12	3	0	3	3	17	0	38	2	0	1	0	1.000	0	2- -	-	3.01	2.92
2017	LAA	AL	18	0	0	6	22.1	92	21	11	11	2	1	1	3	6	1	17	0	0	0	1	.000	0	1-1	1	3.75	4.43

Edward Paredes

Pitches: L Bats: L Pos: RP-10   Ht: 6'0" Wt: 180 Born: 9/30/1986 Age: 31

			HOW MUCH HE PITCHED					WHAT HE GAVE UP												THE RESULTS							
Year	Team	Lg	G	GS	CG	GF	IP	BFP	H	R	ER	HR	SH	SF	HB	TBB	IBB	SO	WP	Bk	W	L	Pct	Sh	Sv-Op	Hld	ERC	ERA
2013	Akron	AA	6	0	0	1	6.2	31	9	6	6	2	0	0		3	0	12	0	0	0	1	.000	0	0- -	-	8.12	8.10
2016	Ark	AA	46	0	0	13	43.2	178	25	12	11	2	1	1	5	21	0	53	7	0	2	2	.500	0	2- -	-	2.24	2.27
2017	Tulsa	AA	24	0	0	6	32.0	140	33	11	10	1	2	0	5	12	1	45	3	1	2	0	.000	0	1- -	-	4.29	2.81
2017	OkCity	AAA	11	0	0	2	12.0	47	4	2	1	0	0	0	0	6	0	21	0	1	2	1	.667	0	0- -	-	1.10	0.75
2017	LAD	NL	10	0	0	1	8.1	31	8	3	3	1	0	0	0	0	0	11	0	0	1	0	1.000	0	0-0	0	2.61	3.24

Blake Parker

Pitches: R Bats: R Pos: RP-71   Ht: 6'3" Wt: 225 Born: 6/19/1985 Age: 33

			HOW MUCH HE PITCHED					WHAT HE GAVE UP												THE RESULTS							
Year	Team	Lg	G	GS	CG	GF	IP	BFP	H	R	ER	HR	SH	SF	HB	TBB	IBB	SO	WP	Bk	W	L	Pct	Sh	Sv-Op	Hld	ERC	ERA
2012	ChC	NL	7	0	0	0	6.0	32	10	7	4	3	0	0	0	5	1	6	0	0	0	0	-	0	0-0	0	14.02	6.00
2013	ChC	NL	49	0	0	18	46.1	195	39	17	14	4	0	1	2	15	1	55	2	0	1	2	.333	0	1-1	7	2.91	2.72
2014	ChC	NL	18	0	0	10	21.0	91	24	13	12	3	0	1	0	4	0	24	1	0	1	1	.500	0	0-0	1	4.24	5.14
2016	2 Tms	AL	17	0	0	5	17.1	79	17	9	9	1	0	0	2	9	1	15	0	0	1	0	1.000	0	1-1	0	4.41	4.67
2017	LAA	AL	71	0	0	17	67.1	254	40	20	19	7	1	4	1	16	0	86	4	0	3	3	.500	0	8-11	15	1.60	2.54
16	Sea	AL	1	0	0	0	1.0	5	1	0	0	0	0	0	0	1	0	6	0	0	0	0	-	0	0-0	0	5.48	0.00
16	NYY	AL	16	0	0	5	16.1	74	16	9	9	1	0	0	2	8	1	15	0	0	0	0	1.000	0	1-1	0	4.35	4.96
	5 ML YEARS		162	0	0	50	158.0	651	130	66	58	18	1	6	5	49	3	186	7	0	6	6	.500	0	10-13	23	2.95	3.30

Jarrett Parker

Bats: L Throws: L Pos: LF-44;PH-6;RF-5;DH-1   Ht: 6'4" Wt: 210 Born: 1/1/1989 Age: 29

Year	Team	Lg	G	AB	H	2B	3B	HR	(Hm	Rd)	TB	R	RBI	RC	TBB	IBB	SO	HBP	SH	SF	SB	CS	GDP	Avg	OBP	Slg	OPS
2017	Scrmto*	AAA	30	112	26	5	0	3	(-	-)	40	22	8	15	21	0	31	0	0	0	1	1	2	.232	.353	.357	.711
2015	SF	NL	21	49	17	2	0	6	(1	5)	37	11	14	12	5	0	21	0	0	0	1	1	1	.347	.407	.755	1.163
2016	SF	NL	63	127	30	3	1	5	(3	2)	50	22	14	17	19	1	44	5	0	0	0	1	3	.236	.358	.394	.751
2017	SF	NL	51	166	41	12	2	4	(2	2)	69	14	23	22	10	2	54	1	0	0	2	1	2	.247	.294	.416	.709
	3 ML YEARS		135	342	88	17	3	15	(6	9)	156	47	51	51	34	3	119	6	0	0	3	3	6	.257	.335	.456	.791

Ian Parmley

Bats: L Throws: L Pos: LF-1;RF-1;PR-1   Ht: 5'11" Wt: 175 Born: 12/19/1989 Age: 28

Year	Team	Lg	G	AB	H	2B	3B	HR	(Hm	Rd)	TB	R	RBI	RC	TBB	IBB	SO	HBP	SH	SF	SB	CS	GDP	Avg	OBP	Slg	OPS
2013	Vancvr	A-	66	257	66	7	0	0	(-	-)	73	31	15	29	23	0	61	3	2	2	23	2	9	.257	.323	.284	.607
2014	2 Tms	Low	56	156	35	5	0	0	(-	-)	40	18	10	18	27	0	24	0	7	1	14	1	1	.224	.337	.256	.593
2015	Dnedin	A+	35	117	20	2	0	0	(-	-)	22	17	6	6	16	0	36	0	2	2	4	1	1	.171	.267	.188	.455
2015	Nham	AA	43	133	37	4	2	1	(-	-)	48	20	16	16	11	0	20	0	2	1	2	2	2	.278	.331	.361	.692
2016	Nham	AA	92	282	83	6	6	2	(-	-)	107	49	26	40	28	0	75	0	10	2	13	7	2	.294	.356	.379	.735
2017	Buffalo	AAA	79	246	64	12	0	1	(-	-)	79	35	22	26	15	0	59	2	3	2	11	2	2	.260	.306	.321	.627
2017	Tor	AL	3	3	0	0	0	0	(0	0)	0	0	0	0	0	0	1	0	1	0	0	0	0	.000	.000	.000	.000

Gerardo Parra

heh-RAHR-doh PAR-uh

Bats: L **Throws:** L **Pos:** LF-82;RF-22;PH-12;1B-6;CF-1;DH-1   **Ht:** 5'11" **Wt:** 210 **Born:** 5/6/1987 **Age:** 31

								BATTING														RUNNING			AVERAGES			
Year	Team	Lg	G	AB	H	2B	3B	HR	(Hm	Rd)	TB	R	RBI	RC	TBB	IBB	SO	HBP	SH	SF	SB	CS	GDP	Avg	OBP	Slg	OPS
2009	Ari	NL	120	455	132	21	8	5	(4	1)	184	59	60	58	25	1	89	1	4	6	5	7	18	.290	.324	.404	.729
2010	Ari	NL	133	364	95	19	6	3	(1	2)	135	31	30	38	23	10	76	2	3	1	1	0	8	.261	.308	.371	.679
2011	Ari	NL	141	445	130	20	8	8	(3	5)	190	55	46	71	43	16	82	3	0	2	15	1	8	.292	.357	.427	.784
2012	Ari	NL	133	385	105	21	2	7	(5	2)	151	58	36	50	33	4	77	4	6	2	15	9	4	.273	.335	.392	.727
2013	Ari	NL	156	601	161	43	4	10	(6	4)	242	79	48	69	48	3	100	3	7	4	10	10	12	.268	.323	.403	.726
2014	2 Tms		150	529	138	22	4	9	(3	6)	195	64	40	46	32	5	100	5	6	2	9	7	10	.261	.308	.369	.677
2015	2 Tms		155	547	159	36	5	14	(8	6)	247	83	51	71	28	3	92	5	4	5	14	4	8	.291	.328	.452	.780
2016	Col	NL	102	368	93	27	3	7	(5	2)	147	45	39	29	9	1	73	1	1	2	6	4	16	.253	.271	.399	.671
2017	Col	NL	115	392	121	24	1	10	(6	4)	177	56	71	56	20	0	67	4	0	9	2	5	13	.309	.341	.452	.793
14	Ari	NL	104	406	105	18	3	6	(2	4)	147	51	30	37	24	3	72	4	4	2	5	5	6	.259	.305	.362	.667
14	Mil	NL	46	123	33	4	1	3	(1	2)	48	13	10	9	8	2	28	1	2	0	4	2	4	.268	.318	.390	.708
15	Mil	NL	100	323	106	24	5	9	(4	5)	167	53	31	47	20	2	57	3	1	4	9	3	7	.328	.369	.517	.886
15	Bal	AL	55	224	53	12	0	5	(4	1)	80	30	20	24	8	1	35	2	3	1	5	1	1	.237	.268	.357	.625
	Postseason		5	18	1	1	0	0	(0	0)	2	1	0	0	1	0	7	0	0	0	0	0	0	.056	.105	.111	.216
	9 ML YEARS		1205	4086	1134	233	41	73	(41	32)	1668	530	421	488	261	43	756	28	31	33	77	47	97	.278	.323	.408	.731

David Paulino

Pitches: R **Bats:** R **Pos:** SP-6   **Ht:** 6'7" **Wt:** 215 **Born:** 2/6/1994 **Age:** 24

			HOW MUCH HE PITCHED						WHAT HE GAVE UP										THE RESULTS						
Year	Team	Lg	G	GS	CG	GF	IP	BFP	H	R	ER	HR	SH	SF	HB	TBB	IBB	SO	WP	Bk	W	L	Pct	Sh	Sv-Op	Hld	ERC	ERA
2015	3 Tms	Low	13	12	0	1	67.1	267	49	23	21	1	0	0	3	19	0	72	4	3	5	3	.625	0	1- -	-	1.91	2.81
2016	CpChr	AA	14	9	0	2	64.0	246	47	16	13	3	1	1	3	11	0	72	2	0	5	2	.714	0	1- -	-	1.80	1.83
2016	Hou	AL	3	1	0	1	7.0	29	6	4	4	0	0	0	1	3	0	2	2	0	1	0	1.000	0	0-0	0	3.40	5.14
2017	Hou	AL	6	6	0	0	29.0	128	36	21	21	8	0	0	0	7	0	34	5	0	1	1	.500	0	0-0	0	6.08	6.52
	2 ML YEARS		9	7	0	1	36.0	157	42	25	25	8	0	0	1	10	0	36	7	0	2	1	.667	0	0-0	0	5.57	6.25

James Paxton

Pitches: L **Bats:** L **Pos:** SP-24   **Ht:** 6'4" **Wt:** 235 **Born:** 11/6/1988 **Age:** 29

			HOW MUCH HE PITCHED						WHAT HE GAVE UP										THE RESULTS						
Year	Team	Lg	G	GS	CG	GF	IP	BFP	H	R	ER	HR	SH	SF	HB	TBB	IBB	SO	WP	Bk	W	L	Pct	Sh	Sv-Op	Hld	ERC	ERA
2013	Sea	AL	4	4	0	0	24.0	94	15	5	4	2	0	0	0	7	2	21	0	0	3	0	1.000	0	0-0	0	1.61	1.50
2014	Sea	AL	13	13	0	0	74.0	303	60	29	25	3	3	1	1	29	2	59	7	0	6	4	.600	0	0-0	0	2.69	3.04
2015	Sea	AL	13	13	0	0	67.0	297	67	34	29	8	0	3	0	29	1	56	5	0	3	4	.429	0	0-0	0	4.22	3.90
2016	Sea	AL	20	20	0	0	121.0	511	134	62	51	9	0	6	1	24	3	117	5	0	6	7	.462	0	0-0	0	3.70	3.79
2017	Sea	AL	24	24	0	0	136.0	552	113	47	45	9	1	5	3	37	1	156	15	1	12	5	.706	0	0-0	0	2.56	2.98
	5 ML YEARS		74	74	0	0	422.0	1757	389	177	154	31	4	15	5	126	9	409	32	1	30	20	.600	0	0-0	0	3.09	3.28

James Pazos

Pitches: L **Bats:** R **Pos:** RP-59

pah-ZOHSS

Ht: 6'2" **Wt:** 235 **Born:** 5/5/1991 **Age:** 27

			HOW MUCH HE PITCHED						WHAT HE GAVE UP										THE RESULTS						
Year	Team	Lg	G	GS	CG	GF	IP	BFP	H	R	ER	HR	SH	SF	HB	TBB	IBB	SO	WP	Bk	W	L	Pct	Sh	Sv-Op	Hld	ERC	ERA
2015	NYY	AL	11	0	0	1	5.0	21	3	0	0	0	1	0	0	3	0	3	1	0	0	0	-	0	0-0	0	2.03	0.00
2016	NYY	AL	7	0	0	1	3.1	17	7	5	5	2	0	0	0	1	0	3	0	0	1	0	1.000	0	0-0	0	16.29	13.50
2017	Sea	AL	59	0	0	7	53.2	240	51	30	23	7	1	4	5	24	0	65	4	1	4	5	.444	0	0-3	10	4.49	3.86
	3 ML YEARS		77	0	0	9	62.0	278	61	35	28	9	2	4	5	28	0	71	5	1	5	5	.500	0	0-3	10	4.77	4.06

Brad Peacock

Pitches: R **Bats:** R **Pos:** SP-21; RP-13   **Ht:** 6'1" **Wt:** 210 **Born:** 2/2/1988 **Age:** 30

			HOW MUCH HE PITCHED						WHAT HE GAVE UP										THE RESULTS						
Year	Team	Lg	G	GS	CG	GF	IP	BFP	H	R	ER	HR	SH	SF	HB	TBB	IBB	SO	WP	Bk	W	L	Pct	Sh	Sv-Op	Hld	ERC	ERA
2011	Was	NL	3	2	0	0	12.0	48	7	1	1	0	0	0	0	6	0	4	1	0	2	0	1.000	0	0-1	0	1.71	0.75
2013	Hou	AL	18	14	0	1	83.1	365	78	51	48	15	1	1	3	37	0	77	4	0	5	6	.455	0	0-0	2	4.54	5.18
2014	Hou	AL	28	24	0	3	131.2	589	136	80	69	20	0	6	4	70	4	119	6	0	4	9	.308	0	0-0	1	5.29	4.72
2015	Hou	AL	1	1	0	0	5.0	22	5	3	3	0	0	1	1	2	0	3	0	0	1	0	1.000	0	0-0	0	4.20	5.40
2016	Hou	AL	10	5	0	3	31.2	127	21	15	13	6	0	0	0	14	0	28	2	0	0	1	.000	0	0-0	1	3.04	3.69
2017	Hou	AL	34	21	0	7	132.0	546	100	46	44	10	1	0	3	57	0	161	6	1	13	2	.867	0	0-0	3	2.83	3.00
	6 ML YEARS		94	67	0	14	395.2	1697	347	196	178	51	2	8	11	186	4	392	19	1	24	19	.558	0	0-1	3	3.96	4.05

Steve Pearce

Bats: R **Throws:** R **Pos:** LF-85;1B-10;PH-9;DH-2   **Ht:** 5'11" **Wt:** 200 **Born:** 4/13/1983 **Age:** 35

								BATTING														RUNNING			AVERAGES			
Year	Team	Lg	G	AB	H	2B	3B	HR	(Hm	Rd)	TB	R	RBI	RC	TBB	IBB	SO	HBP	SH	SF	SB	CS	GDP	Avg	OBP	Slg	OPS
2007	Pit	NL	23	68	20	5	1	0	(0	0)	27	13	6	9	5	0	12	0	0	0	2	1	2	.294	.342	.397	.740
2008	Pit	NL	37	109	27	7	0	4	(0	4)	46	6	15	13	5	0	22	3	0	2	2	0	1	.248	.294	.422	.716
2009	Pit	NL	60	165	34	13	1	4	(3	1)	61	19	16	17	21	0	43	0	0	0	1	0	2	.206	.296	.370	.665
2010	Pit	NL	15	29	8	2	1	0	(0	0)	12	4	5	7	0	0	6	0	0	2	0	0	0	.276	.364	.414	.809
2011	Pit	NL	50	94	19	2	0	1	(1	0)	24	8	10	5	7	0	21	1	1	2	0	0	6	.202	.260	.255	.515
2012	3 Tms		61	159	38	8	1	4	(2	2)	60	16	26	24	20	1	41	3	2	4	1	2	4	.239	.328	.377	.705
2013	Bal	AL	44	119	31	7	0	4	(3	1)	50	14	13	20	15	2	25	4	0	0	1	0	0	.261	.362	.420	.782
2014	Bal	AL	102	338	99	26	0	21	(12	9)	188	51	49	66	40	1	76	4	0	1	5	0	4	.293	.373	.556	.930
2015	Bal	AL	92	294	64	13	1	15	(7	8)	124	42	40	33	23	1	69	7	0	1	1	1	11	.218	.289	.422	.711

Year Team	Lg	G	AB	H	2B	3B	HR	(Hm	Rd)	TB	R	RBI	RC	TBB	IBB	SO	HBP	SH	SF	SB	CS	GDP	Avg	OBP	Slg	OPS
2016 2 Tms	AL	85	264	76	13	1	13	(6	7)	130	35	35	43	34	2	54	3	0	1	0	3	5	.288	.374	.492	.867
2017 Tor	AL	92	313	79	17	1	13	(6	7)	137	38	37	39	27	1	68	5	0	3	0	0	11	.252	.319	.438	.757
12 Bal	AL	28	71	18	4	0	3	(2	1)	31	8	14	12	8	0	17	0	2	2	0	1	1	.254	.321	.437	.758
12 Hou	NL	21	63	16	4	1	0	(0	0)	22	2	8	9	7	1	16	3	0	2	1	1	3	.254	.347	.349	.696
12 NYY	AL	12	25	4	0	0	1	(0	1)	7	6	4	3	5	0	8	0	0	0	0	0	0	.160	.300	.280	.580
16 TB	AL	60	204	63	11	1	10	(4	6)	106	26	29	37	26	2	40	1	0	1	0	3	4	.309	.388	.520	.908
16 Bal	AL	25	60	13	2	0	3	(2	1)	24	9	6	8	8	0	14	2	0	0	0	0	1	.217	.329	.400	.729
Postseason		7	27	4	1	0	0	(0	0)	5	4	1	2	2	0	3	1	0	0	0	0	0	.148	.233	.185	.419
11 ML YEARS		661	1952	495	113	7	79	(40	39)	859	246	252	274	204	8	437	30	3	16	13	7	46	.254	.331	.440	.771

Joc Pederson

Bats: L **Throws:** L **Pos:** CF-92;PH-16;LF-4;PR-1   JOCK   **Ht:** 6'1" **Wt:** 220 **Born:** 4/21/1992 **Age:** 26

Year Team	Lg	G	AB	H	2B	3B	HR	(Hm	Rd)	TB	R	RBI	RC	TBB	IBB	SO	HBP	SH	SF	SB	CS	GDP	Avg	OBP	Slg	OPS
2017 OkCity*	AAA	65	11	11	1	0	3	(-	-)	21	8	9	4	5	0	14	0	0	1	1	0	0	.169	.225	.323	.548
2014 LAD	NL	18	28	4	0	0	0	(0	0)	4	1	0	1	9	0	11	0	1	0	0	0	1	.143	.351	.143	.494
2015 LAD	NL	151	480	101	19	1	26	(13	13)	200	67	54	62	92	6	170	9	2	2	4	7	5	.210	.346	.417	.763
2016 LAD	NL	137	406	100	26	0	25	(13	12)	201	64	68	71	63	4	130	4	1	2	6	2	5	.246	.352	.495	.847
2017 LAD	NL	102	273	58	20	0	11	(8	3)	111	44	35	35	39	1	68	10	0	1	4	3	7	.212	.331	.407	.738
Postseason		16	40	9	2	0	1	(0	1)	14	5	4	4	7	2	15	1	0	0	2	0	1	.225	.354	.350	.704
4 ML YEARS		408	1187	263	65	1	62	(34	28)	516	176	157	169	203	11	379	23	4	5	14	12	18	.222	.345	.435	.780

Dustin Pedroia

Bats: R **Throws:** R **Pos:** 2B-98;DH-7;PH-2   peh-DROY-uh   **Ht:** 5'9" **Wt:** 175 **Born:** 8/17/1983 **Age:** 34

Year Team	Lg	G	AB	H	2B	3B	HR	(Hm	Rd)	TB	R	RBI	RC	TBB	IBB	SO	HBP	SH	SF	SB	CS	GDP	Avg	OBP	Slg	OPS
2006 Bos	AL	31	89	17	4	0	2	(1	1)	27	5	7	3	7	0	7	1	1	0	0	1	1	.191	.258	.303	.561
2007 Bos	AL	139	520	165	39	1	8	(5	3)	230	86	50	79	47	1	42	7	5	2	7	1	8	.317	.380	.442	.823
2008 Bos	AL	157	653	213	54	2	17	(7	10)	322	118	83	107	50	1	52	7	7	9	20	1	17	.326	.376	.493	.869
2009 Bos	AL	154	626	185	48	1	15	(10	5)	280	115	72	104	74	3	45	5	3	6	20	8	19	.296	.371	.447	.819
2010 Bos	AL	75	302	87	24	1	12	(4	8)	149	53	41	52	37	1	38	4	2	6	9	1	7	.288	.367	.493	.860
2011 Bos	AL	159	635	195	37	3	21	(13	8)	301	102	91	114	86	6	85	1	2	7	26	8	12	.307	.387	.474	.861
2012 Bos	AL	141	563	163	39	3	15	(9	6)	253	81	65	84	48	3	60	5	1	6	20	6	9	.290	.347	.449	.797
2013 Bos	AL	160	641	193	42	2	9	(7	2)	266	91	84	99	73	4	75	3	0	7	17	5	24	.301	.372	.415	.787
2014 Bos	AL	135	551	153	33	0	7	(2	5)	207	72	53	65	51	1	75	1	0	6	6	6	14	.278	.337	.376	.712
2015 Bos	AL	93	381	111	19	1	12	(4	8)	168	46	42	55	38	1	51	2	1	3	2	2	5	.291	.356	.441	.797
2016 Bos	AL	154	633	201	36	1	15	(7	8)	284	105	74	100	61	0	73	0	1	3	7	4	24	.318	.376	.449	.825
2017 Bos	AL	105	406	119	19	0	7	(4	3)	159	46	62	65	49	4	48	2	2	4	4	3	11	.293	.369	.392	.760
Postseason		47	190	46	14	0	5	(2	3)	75	32	25	23	21	0	30	2	1	2	3	1	4	.242	.321	.395	.716
12 ML YEARS		1503	6000	1802	394	15	140	(73	67)	2646	920	724	927	621	25	651	38	25	59	138	46	152	.300	.366	.441	.807

Mike Pelfrey

Pitches: R **Bats:** R **Pos:** SP-21; RP-13   PELL-free   **Ht:** 6'7" **Wt:** 240 **Born:** 1/14/1984 **Age:** 34

		HOW MUCH HE PITCHED						WHAT HE GAVE UP									THE RESULTS						
Year Team	Lg	G	GS	CG	GF	IP	BFP	H	R	ER	HR	SH	SF	HB	TBB	IBB	SO	WP	Bk	W	L	Pct	Sh	Sv-Op	Hld	ERC	ERA
2006 NYM	NL	4	4	0	0	21.1	99	25	14	13	1	1	1	3	12	0	13	2	0	2	1	.667	0	0-0	0	6.05	5.48
2007 NYM	NL	15	13	0	0	72.2	342	85	47	45	6	6	3	4	39	1	45	3	0	3	8	.273	0	0-0	0	5.99	5.57
2008 NYM	NL	32	32	2	0	200.2	851	209	86	83	12	11	5	13	64	1	110	2	0	13	11	.542	0	0-0	0	4.04	3.72
2009 NYM	NL	31	31	0	0	184.1	824	213	103	103	18	8	5	7	66	8	107	1	6	10	12	.455	0	0-0	0	4.83	5.03
2010 NYM	NL	34	33	0	1	204.0	870	213	88	83	12	17	4	6	68	5	113	1	1	15	9	.625	0	1-1	0	3.89	3.66
2011 NYM	NL	34	33	2	0	193.2	860	220	111	102	21	10	8	7	65	7	105	2	2	7	13	.350	0	0-0	0	4.70	4.74
2012 NYM	NL	3	3	0	0	19.2	85	24	5	5	0	1	0	4	4	0	13	1	0	0	0	-	0	0-0	0	3.82	2.29
2013 Min	AL	29	29	0	0	152.2	680	184	92	86	13	1	7	6	53	0	101	1	0	5	13	.278	0	0-0	0	5.13	5.19
2014 Min	AL	5	5	0	0	23.2	119	29	23	21	5	2	2	2	18	0	10	1	0	3	0	.000	0	0-0	0	8.18	7.99
2015 Min	AL	30	30	0	0	164.2	714	198	86	78	11	3	3	12	45	1	86	5	0	6	11	.353	0	0-0	0	4.89	4.26
2016 Det	AL	24	22	0	0	119.0	541	160	76	67	15	2	5	6	46	0	56	3	0	4	10	.286	0	0-0	0	6.69	5.07
2017 CWS	AL	34	21	0	4	120.0	546	127	87	79	25	0	3	10	62	4	79	1	0	3	12	.200	0	0-0	0	6.03	5.93
12 ML YEARS		275	256	4	5	1476.1	6531	1687	827	767	139	62	46	81	542	27	838	23	9	68	103	.398	0	1-1	0	4.95	4.68

Felix Pena

Pitches: R **Bats:** R **Pos:** RP-25   **Ht:** 6'2" **Wt:** 185 **Born:** 2/25/1990 **Age:** 28

		HOW MUCH HE PITCHED						WHAT HE GAVE UP									THE RESULTS						
Year Team	Lg	G	GS	CG	GF	IP	BFP	H	R	ER	HR	SH	SF	HB	TBB	IBB	SO	WP	Bk	W	L	Pct	Sh	Sv-Op	Hld	ERC	ERA
2013 Kane	A	21	17	1	1	103.1	440	102	57	45	5	1	7	3	32	0	77	8	0	4	7	.364	0	1- -	-	3.57	3.92
2014 Dytona	A+	19	19	1	0	96.0	408	88	43	34	6	2	1	4	34	0	76	6	0	4	6	.400	0	0- -	-	3.33	3.19
2014 Tenn	AA	6	6	0	0	27.2	126	30	23	23	5	5	0	2	17	0	26	1	0	2	4	.333	0	0- -	-	6.57	7.48
2015 Tenn	AA	25	23	1	1	129.2	539	111	60	54	10	2	3	5	49	1	140	12	5	7	8	.467	0	0- -	-	3.22	3.75
2016 Iowa	AAA	36	0	0	10	63.1	256	46	24	24	4	1	3	2	23	3	81	1	0	3	4	.429	0	3- -	-	2.34	3.41
2017 Iowa	AAA	24	0	0	8	39.0	174	42	24	24	6	3	3	4	14	3	46	1	0	2	1	.667	0	6- -	-	5.01	5.54
2016 ChC	NL	11	0	0	2	9.0	35	5	4	4	1	0	0	0	3	1	13	1	0	0	0	-	0	1-1	2	1.57	4.00
2017 ChC	NL	25	0	0	15	34.1	155	35	21	20	8	0	0	2	18	1	37	3	0	1	0	1.000	0	0-0	1	5.88	5.24
2 ML YEARS		36	0	0	17	43.1	190	40	25	24	9	0	0	2	21	2	50	4	0	1	0	1.000	0	1-1	3	4.84	4.98

Francisco Pena

Bats: R **Throws:** R **Pos:** C-5;PH-1　　　　　　　　**Ht:** 6'2" **Wt:** 230 **Born:** 10/12/1989 **Age:** 28

Year	Team	Lg	G	AB	H	2B	3B	HR	(Hm	Rd)	TB	R	RBI	RC	TBB	IBB	SO	HBP	SH	SF	SB	CS	GDP	Avg	OBP	Slg	OPS
2017	Norfolk*	AAA	51	180	50	13	0	6	(-	-)	81	15	18	25	8	0	31	0	0	0	1	0	2	.278	.309	.450	.759
2014	KC	AL	1	0	0	0	0	0	(0	0)	0	0	0	0	0	0	0	0	0	0	0	0	0	-	-	-	-
2015	KC	AL	8	7	1	0	0	0	(0	0)	1	0	0	0	0	0	3	0	0	1	0	0	1	.143	.143	.143	.286
2016	Bal	AL	14	40	8	0	0	1	(1	0)	11	5	3	4	2	0	14	0	1	0	0	0	2	.200	.238	.275	.513
2017	Bal	AL	5	10	5	0	0	2	(0	2)	11	3	2	2	0	0	3	0	0	0	0	0	0	.500	.500	1.100	1.600
	4 ML YEARS		28	57	14	0	0	3	(1	2)	23	8	5	6	2	0	20	0	1	0	0	0	3	.246	.271	.404	.675

Hunter Pence

Bats: R **Throws:** R **Pos:** RF-125;PH-11;DH-1　　　　　　**Ht:** 6'4" **Wt:** 220 **Born:** 4/13/1983 **Age:** 35

Year	Team	Lg	G	AB	H	2B	3B	HR	(Hm	Rd)	TB	R	RBI	RC	TBB	IBB	SO	HBP	SH	SF	SB	CS	GDP	Avg	OBP	Slg	OPS
2007	Hou	NL	108	456	147	30	9	17	(7	10)	246	57	69	77	26	0	95	1	0	1	11	5	10	.322	.360	.539	.899
2008	Hou	NL	157	595	160	34	4	25	(14	11)	277	78	83	82	40	2	124	4	0	3	11	10	14	.269	.318	.466	.783
2009	Hou	NL	159	585	165	26	5	25	(14	11)	276	76	72	80	58	1	109	1	0	3	14	11	25	.282	.346	.472	.818
2010	Hou	NL	156	614	173	29	5	25	(14	11)	283	93	91	89	41	2	105	0	0	3	18	9	11	.282	.325	.461	.786
2011	2 Tms	NL	154	606	190	38	5	22	(5	17)	304	84	97	102	56	3	124	1	0	5	8	2	15	.314	.370	.502	.871
2012	2 Tms	NL	160	617	156	26	4	24	(9	15)	262	87	104	81	56	2	145	7	1	7	5	2	15	.253	.319	.425	.743
2013	SF	NL	162	629	178	35	5	27	(10	17)	304	91	99	91	52	3	115	3	0	3	22	3	17	.283	.339	.483	.822
2014	SF	NL	162	650	180	29	10	20	(5	15)	289	106	74	96	52	3	130	3	0	3	13	6	13	.277	.332	.445	.777
2015	SF	NL	52	207	57	13	1	9	(3	6)	99	30	40	28	16	0	48	0	0	0	4	1	8	.275	.327	.478	.806
2016	SF	NL	106	395	114	23	1	13	(6	7)	178	58	57	65	43	1	95	1	0	3	1	1	10	.289	.357	.451	.808
2017	SF	NL	134	493	128	13	5	13	(4	9)	190	55	67	68	40	1	102	2	0	4	2	3	8	.260	.315	.385	.701
11	Hou	NL	100	399	123	26	3	11	(4	7)	188	49	62	63	30	1	86	1	0	2	7	1	7	.308	.356	.471	.828
11	Phi	NL	54	207	67	12	2	11	(1	10)	116	35	35	39	26	2	38	0	0	3	1	1	8	.324	.394	.560	.954
12	Phi	NL	101	398	108	15	2	17	(7	10)	178	59	59	50	37	1	85	3	0	2	4	2	14	.271	.336	.447	.784
12	SF	NL	59	219	48	11	2	7	(2	5)	84	28	45	31	19	1	60	4	1	5	1	0	1	.219	.287	.384	.671
	Postseason		43	169	43	8	0	2	(0	2)	57	23	16	14	12	1	33	0	0	1	4	3	3	.254	.302	.337	.639
	11 ML YEARS		1510	5847	1648	296	52	220	(91	129)	2708	815	853	859	480	18	1192	23	1	35	109	53	146	.282	.337	.463	.800

Cliff Pennington

Bats: B **Throws:** R **Pos:** 2B-47;3B-18;SS-18;PH-13;PR-7;DH-1　　　**Ht:** 5'11" **Wt:** 195 **Born:** 6/15/1984 **Age:** 34

Year	Team	Lg	G	AB	H	2B	3B	HR	(Hm	Rd)	TB	R	RBI	RC	TBB	IBB	SO	HBP	SH	SF	SB	CS	GDP	Avg	OBP	Slg	OPS
2008	Oak	AL	36	99	24	5	0	0	(0	0)	29	14	9	12	13	0	18	2	2	1	4	1	1	.242	.339	.293	.632
2009	Oak	AL	60	208	58	11	3	4	(3	1)	87	27	21	29	19	0	46	1	1	0	7	5	5	.279	.342	.418	.760
2010	Oak	AL	156	508	127	26	8	6	(2	4)	187	64	46	66	50	0	96	3	12	3	29	5	7	.250	.319	.368	.687
2011	Oak	AL	148	515	136	26	2	8	(3	5)	190	57	58	73	42	1	104	1	8	4	14	9	5	.264	.319	.369	.687
2012	Oak	AL	125	418	90	18	2	6	(0	6)	130	50	28	37	35	0	90	2	5	2	15	6	1	.215	.278	.311	.589
2013	Ari	NL	96	269	65	13	1	1	(1	0)	83	25	18	23	26	5	54	1	2	1	2	0	7	.242	.310	.309	.618
2014	Ari	NL	68	177	45	5	3	2	(1	1)	62	21	10	19	20	0	36	3	1	0	6	1	1	.254	.340	.350	.690
2015	2 Tms		105	210	44	6	0	3	(1	2)	59	24	21	18	27	2	49	1	7	4	3	0	6	.210	.298	.281	.578
2016	LAA	AL	74	172	36	4	2	3	(2	1)	53	18	10	11	13	0	55	0	3	0	1	0	4	.209	.265	.308	.573
2017	LAA	AL	87	194	49	6	0	3	(2	1)	64	23	21	22	16	0	58	1	1	5	3	1	2	.253	.306	.330	.635
15	Ari	NL	72	135	32	3	0	1	(1	0)	38	15	10	10	16	2	29	0	4	2	3	0	4	.237	.314	.281	.595
15	Tor	AL	33	75	12	3	0	2	(0	2)	21	9	11	8	11	0	20	1	3	2	0	0	2	.160	.270	.280	.550
	Postseason		9	15	4	0	0	0	(0	0)	4	1	1	2	4	0	4	0	0	0	0	0	0	.267	.421	.267	.688
	10 ML YEARS		955	2770	674	120	21	36	(15	21)	944	323	242	310	261	8	606	15	42	20	84	28	39	.243	.310	.341	.651

David Peralta

Bats: L **Throws:** L **Pos:** RF-78;LF-50;PH-14;DH-2　　pah-RALL-tah　　**Ht:** 6'1" **Wt:** 210 **Born:** 8/14/1987 **Age:** 30

Year	Team	Lg	G	AB	H	2B	3B	HR	(Hm	Rd)	TB	R	RBI	RC	TBB	IBB	SO	HBP	SH	SF	SB	CS	GDP	Avg	OBP	Slg	OPS
2014	Ari	NL	88	329	94	12	9	8	(5	3)	148	40	36	38	16	0	60	1	1	1	6	3	9	.286	.320	.450	.770
2015	Ari	NL	149	462	144	26	10	17	(8	9)	241	61	78	83	44	2	107	4	0	7	9	4	7	.312	.371	.522	.893
2016	Ari	NL	48	171	43	9	5	4	(3	1)	74	23	15	15	8	1	42	3	0	1	2	0	3	.251	.295	.433	.728
2017	Ari	NL	140	525	154	31	3	14	(8	6)	233	82	57	77	43	1	94	6	0	3	8	4	7	.293	.352	.444	.796
	4 ML YEARS		425	1487	435	78	27	43	(24	19)	696	206	186	213	111	4	303	14	1	12	25	11	26	.293	.345	.468	.813

Jhonny Peralta

Bats: R **Throws:** R **Pos:** 3B-15;PH-7　　pah-RALL-tah　　**Ht:** 6'2" **Wt:** 225 **Born:** 5/28/1982 **Age:** 36

Year	Team	Lg	G	AB	H	2B	3B	HR	(Hm	Rd)	TB	R	RBI	RC	TBB	IBB	SO	HBP	SH	SF	SB	CS	GDP	Avg	OBP	Slg	OPS
2017	Pwtckt*	AAA	10	40	8	1	0	2	(-	-)	15	4	5	2	0	0	11	0	0	1	0	0	0	.200	.195	.375	.570
2003	Cle	AL	77	242	55	10	1	4	(3	1)	79	24	21	24	20	0	65	4	2	2	1	3	5	.227	.295	.326	.621
2004	Cle	AL	8	25	6	1	0	0	(0	0)	7	2	2	2	3	0	6	0	0	0	0	1	0	.240	.321	.280	.601
2005	Cle	AL	141	504	147	35	4	24	(14	10)	262	82	78	87	58	3	128	3	1	4	0	2	12	.292	.366	.520	.885
2006	Cle	AL	149	569	146	28	3	13	(7	6)	219	84	68	66	56	0	152	1	3	3	0	1	19	.257	.323	.385	.708
2007	Cle	AL	152	574	155	27	1	21	(16	5)	247	87	72	85	61	2	146	4	1	7	4	4	12	.270	.341	.430	.771
2008	Cle	AL	154	605	167	42	4	23	(11	12)	286	104	89	84	48	2	126	4	2	5	3	1	26	.276	.331	.473	.804
2009	Cle	AL	151	582	148	35	1	11	(2	9)	218	57	83	63	51	0	134	4	2	6	0	2	20	.254	.316	.375	.690
2010	2 Tms	AL	148	551	137	30	2	15	(4	11)	216	60	81	71	53	2	103	1	0	10	1	0	11	.249	.316	.392	.703
2011	Det	AL	146	525	157	25	3	21	(13	8)	251	68	86	77	40	2	95	2	0	9	0	2	17	.299	.345	.478	.824
2012	Det	AL	150	531	127	32	3	13	(6	7)	204	58	63	53	49	3	105	2	1	2	1	2	20	.239	.305	.384	.689
2013	Det	AL	107	409	124	30	0	11	(7	4)	187	50	55	62	35	2	98	1	1	2	3	3	9	.303	.358	.457	.815

Year Team	Lg	G	AB	H	2B	3B	HR	(Hm	Rd)	TB	R	RBI	RC	TBB	IBB	SO	HBP	SH	SF	SB	CS	GDP	Avg	OBP	Slg	OPS
2014 StL	NL	157	560	147	38	0	21	(8	13)	248	61	75	74	58	2	112	6	0	4	3	2	19	.263	.336	.443	.779
2015 StL	NL	155	579	159	26	1	17	(9	8)	238	64	71	65	50	6	111	5	0	6	1	4	23	.275	.334	.411	.745
2016 StL	NL	82	289	75	17	1	8	(4	4)	118	37	29	31	20	0	56	1	0	3	0	0	5	.260	.307	.408	.715
2017 StL	NL	21	54	11	0	0	0	(0	0)	11	3	0	1	4	0	13	0	0	0	0	0	0	.204	.259	.204	.462
10 Cle	AL	91	334	82	23	2	7	(3	4)	130	37	43	41	32	1	69	1	0	6	1	0	7	.246	.308	.389	.698
10 Det	AL	57	217	55	7	0	8	(1	7)	86	23	38	30	21	1	34	0	0	4	0	0	4	.253	.314	.396	.710
Postseason		58	211	54	15	0	8	(5	3)	93	18	26	25	15	0	45	1	1	1	2	0	9	.256	.307	.441	.748
15 ML YEARS		1798	6599	1761	376	24	202	(104	98)	2791	841	873	845	606	24	1450	38	13	63	17	27	200	.267	.329	.423	.752

Wandy Peralta

Pitches: L Bats: L Pos: RP-69   Ht: 6'0" Wt: 220 Born: 7/27/1991 Age: 26

Year Team	Lg	G	GS	CG	GF	IP	BFP	H	R	ER	HR	SH	SF	HB	TBB	IBB	SO	WP	Bk	W	L	Pct	Sh	Sv-Op	Hld	ERC	ERA
2013 Dayton	A	44	4	0	12	85.1	383	91	45	36	9	5	3	2	41	1	79	14	4	2	7	.222	0	1--	-	4.87	3.80
2014 Bkrsfld	A+	28	28	0	0	142.0	631	164	92	76	19	4	4	3	55	0	93	13	2	7	12	.368	0	0--	-	5.28	4.82
2015 Pnscla	AA	29	20	0	2	116.2	524	129	74	66	7	5	4	7	60	0	80	8	1	7	7	.500	0	0--	-	5.17	5.09
2016 Pnscla	AA	13	0	0	3	17.2	73	17	6	6	1	0	2	0	3	0	20	2	0	0	1	.000	0	0--	-	2.67	3.06
2016 Lsvlle	AAA	37	2	0	15	58.0	234	44	18	15	2	4	1	2	23	0	38	2	0	4	1	.800	0	3--	-	2.55	2.33
2016 Cin	NL	10	0	0	3	7.1	39	11	7	7	1	0	0	1	7	0	5	0	0	0	0	-	0	0-0	2	10.93	8.59
2017 Cin	NL	69	0	0	10	64.2	263	53	28	27	8	2	3	1	24	1	57	4	0	3	4	.429	0	0-2	16	3.24	3.76
2 ML YEARS		79	0	0	13	72.0	302	64	35	34	9	2	3	2	31	1	62	4	0	3	4	.429	0	0-2	18	3.91	4.25

Wily Peralta

Pitches: R Bats: R Pos: RP-11; SP-8   pah-RALL-tah   Ht: 6'1" Wt: 255 Born: 5/8/1989 Age: 29

Year Team	Lg	G	GS	CG	GF	IP	BFP	H	R	ER	HR	SH	SF	HB	TBB	IBB	SO	WP	Bk	W	L	Pct	Sh	Sv-Op	Hld	ERC	ERA
2017 ColSpr*	AAA	13	0	0	0	16.0	71	13	12	6	0	0	0	0	10	0	10	4	0	1	0	1.000	0	1--	-	3.11	3.38
2012 Mil	NL	6	5	0	1	29.0	113	24	8	8	0	3	0	0	11	0	23	1	0	2	1	.667	0	0-0	-	2.61	2.48
2013 Mil	NL	32	32	2	0	183.1	802	187	107	89	19	11	3	7	73	3	129	12	0	11	15	.423	1	0-0	-	4.32	4.37
2014 Mil	NL	32	32	0	0	198.2	838	198	88	78	23	9	3	7	61	0	154	7	0	17	11	.607	0	0-0	-	3.98	3.53
2015 Mil	NL	20	20	0	0	108.2	478	130	60	57	14	4	3	4	37	2	60	5	1	5	10	.333	0	0-0	-	5.40	4.72
2016 Mil	NL	23	23	0	0	127.2	554	152	73	69	19	6	4	3	43	1	93	0	0	7	11	.389	0	0-0	-	5.52	4.86
2017 Mil	NL	19	8	0	4	57.1	269	73	51	50	10	1	3	1	32	2	52	5	0	5	4	.556	0	0-0	-	7.07	7.85
6 ML YEARS		132	120	2	5	704.2	3054	764	387	351	85	34	16	22	257	8	511	30	1	47	52	.475	1	0-0	-	4.73	4.48

Jose Peraza

Bats: R Throws: R Pos: 2B-77;SS-55;PH-12;CF-2;PR-2   per-AH-zuh   Ht: 6'0" Wt: 196 Born: 4/30/1994 Age: 24

Year Team	Lg	G	AB	H	2B	3B	HR	(Hm	Rd)	TB	R	RBI	RC	TBB	IBB	SO	HBP	SH	SF	SB	CS	GDP	Avg	OBP	Slg	OPS
2015 LAD	NL	7	22	4	1	1	0	(0	0)	7	3	1	2	2	1	2	0	1	0	3	0	0	.182	.250	.318	.568
2016 Cin	NL	72	241	78	8	2	3	(1	2)	99	25	25	32	7	0	33	5	0	3	21	10	3	.324	.352	.411	.762
2017 Cin	NL	143	487	126	9	4	5	(3	2)	158	50	37	43	20	1	70	7	3	1	23	8	7	.259	.297	.324	.622
3 ML YEARS		222	750	208	18	7	8	(4	4)	264	78	63	77	29	2	105	12	4	4	47	18	10	.277	.313	.352	.665

Luis Perdomo

Pitches: R Bats: R Pos: SP-29   Ht: 6'2" Wt: 185 Born: 5/9/1993 Age: 25

Year Team	Lg	G	GS	CG	GF	IP	BFP	H	R	ER	HR	SH	SF	HB	TBB	IBB	SO	WP	Bk	W	L	Pct	Sh	Sv-Op	Hld	ERC	ERA
2013 Jhscty	R+	12	10	0	0	41.2	207	59	44	25	4	0	2	4	14	0	29	6	0	1	6	.143	0	0--	-	6.33	5.40
2014 3 Tms	Low	14	13	0	1	72.0	317	77	47	34	5	3	2	4	22	0	57	5	1	4	6	.400	0	0--	-	4.02	4.25
2015 2 Tms	Low	23	22	1	0	126.2	542	134	68	56	8	6	3	5	37	0	118	10	1	6	12	.333	0	0--	-	3.89	3.98
2016 SD	NL	35	20	1	8	146.2	662	187	99	93	23	0	4	7	46	7	105	10	0	9	10	.474	0	0-0	0	5.91	5.71
2017 SD	NL	29	29	0	0	163.2	716	182	97	85	17	3	2	8	65	3	118	11	2	8	11	.421	0	0-0	0	5.00	4.67
2 ML YEARS		64	49	1	8	310.1	1378	369	196	178	40	3	6	15	111	10	223	21	2	17	21	.447	0	0-0	0	5.43	5.16

Carlos Perez

Bats: R Throws: R Pos: C-10;PH-2;DH-1   Ht: 6'0" Wt: 210 Born: 10/27/1990 Age: 27

Year Team	Lg	G	AB	H	2B	3B	HR	(Hm	Rd)	TB	R	RBI	RC	TBB	IBB	SO	HBP	SH	SF	SB	CS	GDP	Avg	OBP	Slg	OPS
2017 Salt Lk*	AAA	68	261	92	18	3	5	(-	-)	131	40	40	56	32	0	38	3	0	4	4	1	5	.352	.423	.502	.925
2015 LAA	AL	86	260	65	13	0	4	(4	0)	90	20	21	26	19	0	49	0	2	2	2	0	7	.250	.299	.346	.645
2016 LAA	AL	87	268	56	16	0	6	(2	3)	87	25	31	22	12	0	49	1	8	2	1	0	6	.209	.244	.325	.568
2017 LAA	AL	11	20	2	0	0	1	(0	1)	5	1	3	2	1	0	6	0	0	0	0	0	0	.100	.143	.250	.393
3 ML YEARS		184	548	123	29	0	10	(6	4)	182	46	55	50	32	0	104	1	10	4	3	0	13	.224	.267	.332	.599

Hernan Perez

air-NAHN

Bats: R **Throws:** R **Pos:** LF-53;3B-31;RF-30;CF-18;2B-17;PH-16;SS-7;PR-3;1B-2   **Ht:** 6'1" **Wt:** 215 **Born:** 3/26/1991 **Age:** 27

Year	Team	Lg	G	AB	H	2B	3B	HR	(Hm	Rd)	TB	R	RBI	RC	TBB	IBB	SO	HBP	SH	SF	SB	CS	GDP	Avg	OBP	Slg	OPS
2012	Det	AL	2	2	1	0	0	0	(0	0)	1	1	0	0	0	0	0	0	0	0	0	0	0	.500	.500	.500	1.000
2013	Det	AL	34	66	13	0	1	0	(0	0)	15	13	5	4	2	0	15	0	2	1	1	0	2	.197	.217	.227	.445
2014	Det	AL	8	5	1	0	0	0	(0	0)	1	1	0	0	1	0	1	0	0	0	0	0	0	.200	.333	.200	.533
2015	2 Tms		112	263	64	15	2	1	(0	1)	86	14	21	23	5	1	59	0	3	1	5	1	6	.243	.257	.327	.584
2016	Mil	NL	123	404	110	18	3	13	(7	6)	173	50	56	56	18	0	94	1	3	4	34	7	6	.272	.302	.428	.730
2017	Mil	NL	136	432	112	19	3	14	(7	7)	179	47	51	49	20	1	79	0	2	4	13	4	8	.259	.289	.414	.704
15	Det	AL	22	33	2	0	0	0	(0	0)	2	1	0	0	1	0	11	0	0	0	1	0	2	.061	.088	.061	.149
15	Mil	NL	90	230	62	15	2	1	(0	1)	84	13	21	23	4	1	48	0	3	1	4	1	4	.270	.281	.365	.646
	Postseason		4	2	0	0	0	0	(0	0)	0	1	0	0	0	0	0	0	0	0	0	0	1	.000	.000	.000	.000
	6 ML YEARS		415	1172	301	52	9	28	(14	14)	455	126	133	132	46	2	248	1	10	10	53	12	22	.257	.283	.388	.671

Martin Perez

mar-TEEN

Pitches: L **Bats:** L **Pos:** SP-32   **Ht:** 6'0" **Wt:** 200 **Born:** 4/4/1991 **Age:** 27

Year	Team	Lg	G	GS	CG	GF	IP	BFP	H	R	ER	HR	SH	SF	HB	TBB	IBB	SO	WP	Bk	W	L	Pct	Sh	Sv-Op	Hld	ERC	ERA
2012	Tex	AL	12	6	0	2	38.0	177	47	26	23	3	1	1	2	15	1	25	5	2	1	4	.200	0	0-0	0	5.33	5.45
2013	Tex	AL	20	20	1	0	124.1	529	129	55	50	15	2	3	3	37	0	84	9	2	10	6	.625	0	0-0	0	4.14	3.62
2014	Tex	AL	8	8	2	0	51.1	207	50	25	25	3	1	0	1	19	1	35	1	0	4	3	.571	2	0-0	0	3.82	4.38
2015	Tex	AL	14	14	0	0	78.2	339	88	45	39	3	0	3	2	24	1	48	1	0	3	6	.333	0	0-0	0	4.04	4.46
2016	Tex	AL	33	33	0	0	198.2	855	205	110	97	18	9	8	4	76	0	103	3	2	10	11	.476	0	0-0	0	4.24	4.39
2017	Tex	AL	32	32	0	0	185.0	811	221	108	99	23	4	3	6	63	3	115	4	0	13	12	.520	0	0-0	0	5.35	4.82
	Postseason		1	1	0	0	5.0	21	6	4	4	0	1	0	0	3	1	2	0	0	0	1	.000	0	0-0	0	5.47	7.20
	6 ML YEARS		119	113	3	2	676.0	2918	740	369	333	65	17	18	18	234	6	410	23	6	41	42	.494	2	0-0	0	4.52	4.43

Oliver Perez

Pitches: L **Bats:** L **Pos:** RP-50   **Ht:** 6'3" **Wt:** 225 **Born:** 8/15/1981 **Age:** 36

Year	Team	Lg	G	GS	CG	GF	IP	BFP	H	R	ER	HR	SH	SF	HB	TBB	IBB	SO	WP	Bk	W	L	Pct	Sh	Sv-Op	Hld	ERC	ERA
2002	SD	NL	16	15	0	0	90.0	387	71	37	35	13	5	3	5	48	1	94	3	0	4	5	.444	0	0-0	0	3.93	3.50
2003	2 Tms	NL	24	24	0	0	126.2	579	129	80	77	22	5	2	4	77	3	141	7	1	4	10	.286	0	0-0	0	5.66	5.47
2004	Pit	NL	30	30	2	0	196.0	805	145	71	65	22	9	5	9	81	2	239	2	1	12	10	.545	1	0-0	0	2.99	2.98
2005	Pit	NL	20	20	0	0	103.0	471	102	68	67	23	5	4	6	70	1	97	3	0	7	5	.583	0	0-0	0	6.44	5.85
2006	2 Tms	NL	22	22	1	0	112.2	529	129	90	82	20	5	10	6	68	0	102	5	1	3	13	.188	1	0-0	0	6.62	6.55
2007	NYM	NL	29	29	0	0	177.0	765	153	90	70	22	4	7	7	79	1	174	6	0	15	10	.600	0	0-0	0	3.76	3.56
2008	NYM	NL	34	34	0	0	194.0	847	167	100	91	24	9	7	11	105	4	180	9	1	10	7	.588	0	0-0	0	4.21	4.22
2009	NYM	NL	14	14	0	0	66.0	324	69	51	50	12	5	4	4	58	2	62	2	0	3	4	.429	0	0-0	0	7.16	6.82
2010	NYM	NL	17	7	0	4	46.1	234	54	37	35	9	1	3	4	43	2	37	4	0	0	5	.000	0	0-0	0	8.27	6.80
2012	Sea	AL	33	0	0	6	29.2	123	27	7	7	1	1	1	0	10	2	24	2	0	1	3	.250	0	0-2	5	2.82	2.12
2013	Sea	AL	61	0	0	22	53.0	229	50	23	22	6	1	0	1	26	3	74	1	0	3	3	.500	0	2-3	8	4.23	3.74
2014	Ari	NL	68	0	0	11	58.2	256	50	25	19	5	4	0	7	24	2	76	3	3	3	4	.429	0	0-1	15	3.53	2.91
2015	2 Tms		70	0	0	15	41.0	183	39	24	19	4	1	0	4	15	2	51	3	0	2	4	.333	0	0-3	10	3.81	4.17
2016	Was	NL	64	0	0	7	40.0	182	38	22	22	4	1	1	7	20	3	46	5	0	2	3	.400	0	0-1	15	4.72	4.95
2017	Was	NL	50	0	0	8	33.0	143	32	17	17	4	0	1	4	12	2	39	1	1	0	0	-	0	1-1	12	4.32	4.64
03	SD	NL	19	19	0	0	103.2	473	103	65	62	20	4	2	3	65	2	117	6	1	4	7	.364	0	0-0	0	5.74	5.38
03	Pit	NL	5	5	0	0	23.0	106	26	15	15	2	1	0	1	12	1	24	1	0	0	3	.000	0	0-0	0	5.29	5.87
06	Pit	NL	15	15	0	0	76.0	364	88	64	56	13	5	8	3	51	0	61	4	1	2	10	.167	0	0-0	0	6.85	6.63
06	NYM	NL	7	7	1	0	36.2	165	41	26	26	7	0	2	3	17	0	41	1	0	1	3	.250	1	0-0	0	6.16	6.38
15	Ari	NL	48	0	0	11	29.0	128	25	12	10	2	1	0	4	11	1	37	2	0	2	1	.667	0	0-3	7	3.38	3.10
15	Hou	AL	22	0	0	4	12.0	55	14	12	9	2	0	0	0	4	1	14	1	0	0	3	.000	0	0-0	0	4.89	6.75
	Postseason		8	2	0	0	15.1	67	16	7	7	3	3	0	2	5	1	10	0	0	1	0	1.000	0	0-0	3	5.19	4.11
	15 ML YEARS		552	195	3	73	1367.0	6057	1255	742	678	191	56	48	79	735	31	1436	56	8	69	86	.445	2	3-11	65	4.63	4.46

Roberto Perez

Bats: R **Throws:** R **Pos:** C-71;DH-2;PH-2   **Ht:** 5'11" **Wt:** 220 **Born:** 12/23/1988 **Age:** 29

Year	Team	Lg	G	AB	H	2B	3B	HR	(Hm	Rd)	TB	R	RBI	RC	TBB	IBB	SO	HBP	SH	SF	SB	CS	GDP	Avg	OBP	Slg	OPS
2014	Cle	AL	29	85	23	5	0	1	(1	0)	31	10	4	8	5	0	26	0	5	0	0	0	2	.271	.311	.365	.676
2015	Cle	AL	70	184	42	9	1	7	(4	3)	74	30	21	24	33	1	64	2	5	2	0	0	9	.228	.348	.402	.751
2016	Cle	AL	61	153	28	6	1	3	(1	2)	45	14	17	17	23	0	44	0	5	3	0	0	4	.183	.285	.294	.579
2017	Cle	AL	73	217	45	12	0	8	(6	2)	81	22	38	26	26	0	71	0	4	1	0	1	4	.207	.291	.373	.664
	Postseason		15	43	8	1	0	3	(3	0)	18	5	7	5	7	0	15	0	2	0	0	0	1	.186	.300	.419	.719
	4 ML YEARS		233	639	138	32	2	19	(12	7)	231	76	80	75	87	1	205	2	19	6	0	1	19	.216	.309	.362	.671

Salvador Perez

Bats: R **Throws:** R **Pos:** C-115;DH-13;PH-2   **Ht:** 6'3" **Wt:** 240 **Born:** 5/10/1990 **Age:** 28

Year	Team	Lg	G	AB	H	2B	3B	HR	(Hm	Rd)	TB	R	RBI	RC	TBB	IBB	SO	HBP	SH	SF	SB	CS	GDP	Avg	OBP	Slg	OPS
2011	KC	AL	39	148	49	8	2	3	(1	2)	70	20	21	26	7	0	20	1	0	2	0	0	5	.331	.361	.473	.834
2012	KC	AL	76	289	87	16	0	11	(3	8)	136	38	39	36	12	3	27	1	0	3	0	0	14	.301	.328	.471	.798
2013	KC	AL	138	496	145	25	3	13	(6	7)	215	48	79	77	21	2	63	4	0	5	0	0	13	.292	.323	.433	.757
2014	KC	AL	150	578	150	28	2	17	(8	9)	233	57	70	55	22	2	85	3	0	3	1	0	22	.260	.289	.403	.692
2015	KC	AL	142	531	138	25	0	21	(9	12)	226	52	70	60	13	4	82	4	0	5	1	0	23	.260	.280	.426	.706

Year	Team	Lg	G	AB	H	2B	3B	HR	(Hm	Rd)	TB	R	RBI	RC	TBB	IBB	SO	HBP	SH	SF	SB	CS	GDP	Avg	OBP	Slg	OPS
2016	KC	AL	139	514	127	28	2	22	(11	11)	225	57	64	61	22	3	119	8	0	2	0	0	12	.247	.288	.438	.725
2017	KC	AL	129	471	126	24	1	27	(6	21)	233	57	80	65	17	3	95	5	0	5	1	0	23	.268	.297	.495	.792
	Postseason		31	116	27	4	0	5	(3	2)	46	14	14	10	5	0	19	3	0	0	0	0	3	.233	.282	.397	.679
	7 ML YEARS		813	3027	822	154	10	114	(44	70)	1338	329	423	380	114	17	491	26	0	25	3	0	112	.272	.301	.442	.743

Cam Perkins

Bats: R **Throws:** R **Pos:** PH-19;LF-15;RF-12;CF-4;1B-1;PR-1 **Ht:** 6'5" **Wt:** 195 **Born:** 9/27/1990 **Age:** 27

Year	Team	Lg	G	AB	H	2B	3B	HR	(Hm	Rd)	TB	R	RBI	RC	TBB	IBB	SO	HBP	SH	SF	SB	CS	GDP	Avg	OBP	Slg	OPS
2013	2 Tms	Low	105	394	118	31	5	7	(-	-)	180	55	54	63	26	0	57	7	2	3	4	5	16	.299	.351	.457	.808
2014	Rdng	AA	52	196	67	19	1	3	(-	-)	97	25	34	39	20	1	30	2	4	0	5	3	4	.342	.408	.495	.903
2014	LV	AAA	74	255	55	9	3	2	(-	-)	76	17	17	18	13	1	49	2	2	0	3	3	6	.216	.259	.298	.557
2015	Rdng	AA	100	377	95	25	1	11	(-	-)	155	51	51	51	25	1	53	7	4	5	7	1	11	.252	.307	.411	.718
2016	LV	AAA	117	408	119	20	4	8	(-	-)	171	47	47	58	21	0	59	2	1	1	11	3	14	.292	.329	.419	.748
2017	LV	AAA	76	257	74	18	1	7	(-	-)	115	37	27	44	30	2	47	6	1	1	3	2	3	.288	.374	.447	.822
2017	Phi	NL	42	88	16	5	0	1	(1	0)	24	9	8	7	5	0	23	0	0	1	0	0	1	.182	.237	.273	.510

Glen Perkins

Pitches: L **Bats:** L **Pos:** RP-8 **Ht:** 6'0" **Wt:** 205 **Born:** 3/2/1983 **Age:** 35

Year	Team	Lg	G	GS	CG	GF	IP	BFP	H	R	ER	HR	SH	SF	HB	TBB	IBB	SO	WP	Bk	W	L	Pct	Sh	Sv-Op	Hld	ERC	ERA
2017	2 Tms*	Low	5	3	0	0	4.2	21	5	3	3	1	0	0	0	2	0	7	0	0	0	0	-	0	0- --	-	5.32	5.79
2006	Min	AL	4	0	0	1	5.2	20	3	1	1	0	0	0	0	0	0	6	0	0	0	0	-	0	0-0	1	0.60	1.59
2007	Min	AL	19	0	0	3	28.2	115	23	10	10	2	1	1	2	12	0	20	2	0	0	0	-	0	0-0	3	3.32	3.14
2008	Min	AL	26	26	0	0	151.0	661	183	81	74	25	7	4	3	39	0	74	2	1	12	4	.750	0	0-0	0	5.30	4.41
2009	Min	AL	18	17	0	1	96.1	423	120	64	63	13	1	3	1	23	0	45	2	1	6	7	.462	0	0-0	0	5.14	5.89
2010	Min	AL	13	1	0	5	21.2	98	29	16	14	3	1	2	4	5	1	14	0	0	1	1	.500	0	0-0	0	6.56	5.82
2011	Min	AL	65	0	0	17	61.2	253	55	19	17	2	5	1	1	21	5	65	3	0	4	4	.500	0	2-5	17	2.81	2.48
2012	Min	AL	70	0	0	43	70.1	281	57	25	20	8	3	2	3	16	3	78	3	0	3	1	.750	0	16-20	11	2.63	2.56
2013	Min	AL	61	0	0	53	62.2	240	43	16	16	5	2	1	3	15	0	77	0	0	2	0	1.000	0	36-40	0	2.01	2.30
2014	Min	AL	63	0	0	56	61.2	260	62	29	25	7	2	5	2	11	2	66	3	0	4	3	.571	0	34-41	0	3.33	3.65
2015	Min	AL	60	0	0	45	57.0	238	58	21	21	9	1	0	0	10	2	54	4	0	3	5	.375	0	32-35	3	3.56	3.32
2016	Min	AL	2	0	0	1	2.0	12	5	2	2	0	0	1	0	1	0	3	2	0	0	0	-	0	0-1	0	13.27	9.00
2017	Min	AL	8	0	0	3	5.2	34	8	6	6	0	0	1	3	5	0	2	0	0	0	0	-	0	0-0	0	9.47	9.53
	Postseason		1	0	0	0	0.1	5	2	0	0	0	0	0	0	0	0	0	0	0	0	0	-	0	0-0	0	39.65	0.00
	12 ML YEARS		409	44	0	228	624.1	2635	646	290	269	74	23	21	22	158	13	504	21	2	35	25	.583	0	120-142	35	3.94	3.88

Dillon Peters

Pitches: L **Bats:** L **Pos:** SP-6 **Ht:** 5'9" **Wt:** 195 **Born:** 8/31/1992 **Age:** 25

Year	Team	Lg	G	GS	CG	GF	IP	BFP	H	R	ER	HR	SH	SF	HB	TBB	IBB	SO	WP	Bk	W	L	Pct	Sh	Sv-Op	Hld	ERC	ERA
2015	2 Tms	Low	11	11	0	0	45.0	199	50	29	18	2	3	2	1	13	0	40	1	1	1	4	.200	0	0- --	-	3.85	3.60
2016	Jupiter	A+	20	20	0	0	106.0	432	102	32	29	2	1	3	9	16	0	89	3	0	11	6	.647	0	0- --	-	2.76	2.46
2017	Jaxnvl	AA	9	9	0	0	45.2	179	33	11	10	1	0	0	3	11	0	40	6	0	6	2	.750	0	0- --	-	1.88	1.97
2017	Mia	NL	6	6	0	0	31.1	139	32	18	18	3	0	0	2	19	1	27	3	0	1	2	.333	0	0-0	0	5.38	5.17

Jace Peterson

JAYCE

Bats: L **Throws:** R **Pos:** LF-25;PH-25;2B-15;3B-15;1B-7;SS-4;RF-2;PR-1 **Ht:** 6'0" **Wt:** 215 **Born:** 5/9/1990 **Age:** 28

Year	Team	Lg	G	AB	H	2B	3B	HR	(Hm	Rd)	TB	R	RBI	RC	TBB	IBB	SO	HBP	SH	SF	SB	CS	GDP	Avg	OBP	Slg	OPS
2017	Gwnntt*	AAA	34	128	33	5	1	2	(-	-)	46	20	26	20	25	1	26	0	0	2	6	1	3	.258	.374	.359	.734
2014	SD	NL	27	53	6	0	0	0	(0	0)	6	3	0	0	2	1	18	1	2	0	2	0	1	.113	.161	.113	.274
2015	Atl	NL	152	528	126	23	5	6	(1	5)	177	55	52	56	56	4	120	3	7	3	12	10	5	.239	.314	.335	.649
2016	Atl	NL	115	350	89	16	1	7	(3	4)	128	45	29	42	52	1	69	1	2	3	5	5	9	.254	.350	.366	.715
2017	Atl	NL	89	186	40	9	2	2	(2	0)	59	15	17	20	27	3	48	1	1	0	3	0	4	.215	.318	.317	.635
	4 ML YEARS		383	1117	261	48	8	15	(6	9)	370	118	98	118	137	10	255	6	12	6	22	15	19	.234	.319	.331	.650

Shane Peterson

Bats: L **Throws:** L **Pos:** LF-15;PH-8;RF-5;DH-3;PR-1 **Ht:** 6'0" **Wt:** 225 **Born:** 2/11/1988 **Age:** 30

Year	Team	Lg	G	AB	H	2B	3B	HR	(Hm	Rd)	TB	R	RBI	RC	TBB	IBB	SO	HBP	SH	SF	SB	CS	GDP	Avg	OBP	Slg	OPS
2017	Drhm*	AAA	76	280	80	19	3	12	(-	-)	141	39	40	46	11	0	63	2	2	4	10	0	2	.286	.313	.504	.817
2013	Oak	AL	2	7	1	0	0	0	(0	0)	1	1	1	0	1	0	3	0	0	0	0	0	0	.143	.250	.143	.393
2015	Mil	NL	93	201	52	7	3	2	(0	2)	71	22	16	20	20	1	55	0	3	1	0	1	3	.259	.324	.353	.678
2017	TB	AL	30	79	20	5	0	2	(1	1)	31	9	11	11	5	0	21	2	0	1	2	0	2	.253	.310	.392	.703
	3 ML YEARS		125	287	73	12	3	4	(1	3)	103	32	28	31	26	1	79	2	3	2	2	1	5	.254	.319	.359	.677

Yusmeiro Petit

yooz-MAIR-oh peh-TEET

Pitches: R Bats: R Pos: RP-59; SP-1

Ht: 6'1" Wt: 255 Born: 11/22/1984 Age: 33

Year	Team	Lg	G	GS	CG	GF	IP	BFP	H	R	ER	HR	SH	SF	HB	TBB	IBB	SO	WP	Bk	W	L	Pct	Sh	Sv-Op	Hld	ERC	ERA
2006	Fla	NL	15	1	0	5	26.1	129	46	28	28	7	1	1	0	9	1	20	0	0	1	1	.500	0	0-0	0	10.07	9.57
2007	Ari	NL	14	10	0	2	57.0	243	58	30	29	12	1	1	0	18	1	40	0	1	3	4	.429	0	0-0	0	4.56	4.58
2008	Ari	NL	19	8	0	6	56.1	229	45	29	27	12	4	2	1	14	2	42	3	1	3	5	.375	0	0-0	0	3.08	4.31
2009	Ari	NL	23	17	0	2	89.2	407	102	62	58	19	3	0	0	34	1	74	3	0	3	10	.231	0	0-0	0	5.44	5.82
2012	SF	NL	1	1	0	0	4.2	22	7	2	2	0	1	0	0	4	0	1	1	0	0	0	-	0	0-0	0	9.14	3.86
2013	SF	NL	8	7	1	0	48.0	196	46	19	19	4	2	0	0	11	1	47	0	0	4	1	.800	1	0-0	0	3.08	3.56
2014	SF	NL	39	12	1	14	117.0	461	97	51	48	12	0	3	1	22	5	133	0	0	5	5	.500	0	0-0	0	2.40	3.69
2015	SF	NL	42	1	0	15	76.0	316	75	32	31	11	1	6	1	15	2	59	3	0	1	1	.500	0	1-1	0	3.48	3.67
2016	Was	NL	36	1	0	16	62.0	265	67	33	31	12	3	1	0	15	3	49	3	1	3	5	.375	0	1-2	1	4.42	4.50
2017	LAA	AL	60	1	0	10	91.1	354	69	32	28	9	1	1	1	18	4	101	0	0	5	2	.714	0	4-5	14	2.07	2.76
	Postseason		4	0	0	0	12.2	47	7	2	2	0	0	0	0	4	1	13	1	0	3	0	1.000	0	0-0	0	1.18	1.42
	10 ML YEARS		257	59	2	70	628.1	2622	612	318	301	98	17	15	4	160	20	566	13	3	28	34	.452	1	6-8	15	3.69	4.31

Jake Petricka

puh-TRICH-kuh

Pitches: R Bats: R Pos: RP-27

Ht: 6'5" Wt: 220 Born: 6/5/1988 Age: 30

Year	Team	Lg	G	GS	CG	GF	IP	BFP	H	R	ER	HR	SH	SF	HB	TBB	IBB	SO	WP	Bk	W	L	Pct	Sh	Sv-Op	Hld	ERC	ERA
2017	Charltt*	AAA	5	0	0	0	7.0	28	6	2	2	0	0	1	0	2	0	4	0	0	0	0	-	0	0--	-	2.31	2.57
2013	CWS	AL	16	0	0	3	19.1	85	20	7	7	0	1	1	1	10	1	10	4	0	1	1	.500	0	0-1	0	4.18	3.26
2014	CWS	AL	67	0	0	33	73.0	307	67	24	24	3	3	4	2	33	4	55	2	0	1	6	.143	0	14-18	10	3.52	2.96
2015	CWS	AL	62	0	0	18	52.0	220	56	21	21	2	3	1	1	18	4	33	2	0	4	3	.571	0	2-3	12	3.91	3.63
2016	CWS	AL	9	0	0	1	8.0	39	8	5	4	1	1	0	0	8	0	7	3	0	0	0	-	0	0-0	1	6.76	4.50
2017	CWS	AL	27	0	0	7	25.2	122	39	21	20	6	0	1	1	6	0	26	3	0	1	1	.500	0	0-1	3	7.66	7.01
	5 ML YEARS		181	0	0	62	178.0	773	190	78	76	12	8	7	5	75	9	131	14	0	7	11	.389	0	16-23	26	4.41	3.84

Tommy Pham

FAM

Bats: R Throws: R Pos: LF-86;CF-37;PH-10;RF-1;PR-1

Ht: 6'1" Wt: 210 Born: 3/8/1988 Age: 30

Year	Team	Lg	G	AB	H	2B	3B	HR	(Hm	Rd)	TB	R	RBI	RC	TBB	IBB	SO	HBP	SH	SF	SB	CS	GDP	Avg	OBP	Slg	OPS
2017	Memp*	AAA	25	92	26	8	0	4	(-	-)	46	17	19	17	13	0	21	0	1	0	6	3	1	.283	.371	.500	.871
2014	StL	NL	6	2	0	0	0	0	(0	0)	0	0	0	0	0	0	2	0	0	0	0	0	0	.000	.000	.000	.000
2015	StL	NL	52	153	41	7	5	5	(1	4)	73	28	18	26	19	1	41	0	0	1	2	0	1	.268	.347	.477	.824
2016	StL	NL	78	159	36	7	0	9	(3	6)	70	26	17	21	20	1	71	3	1	0	2	2	3	.226	.324	.440	.764
2017	StL	NL	128	444	136	22	2	23	(6	17)	231	95	73	93	71	0	117	10	2	3	25	7	18	.306	.411	.520	.931
	Postseason		3	5	1	0	0	1	(1	0)	4	1	2	0	0	0	2	0	0	0	0	0	0	.200	.200	.800	1.000
	4 ML YEARS		264	758	213	36	7	37	(10	27)	374	149	108	140	110	2	231	13	3	4	29	9	22	.281	.380	.493	.873

Josh Phegley

FEG-lee

Bats: R Throws: R Pos: C-56;PH-4;PR-1

Ht: 5'10" Wt: 230 Born: 2/12/1988 Age: 30

Year	Team	Lg	G	AB	H	2B	3B	HR	(Hm	Rd)	TB	R	RBI	RC	TBB	IBB	SO	HBP	SH	SF	SB	CS	GDP	Avg	OBP	Slg	OPS
2013	CWS	AL	65	204	42	7	0	4	(2	2)	61	14	22	12	5	0	41	0	2	2	2	0	6	.206	.223	.299	.522
2014	CWS	AL	11	37	8	2	0	3	(3	0)	19	4	7	2	0	0	11	0	0	1	0	0	0	.216	.211	.514	.724
2015	Oak	AL	73	225	56	16	1	9	(6	3)	101	27	34	32	14	0	51	3	0	1	0	0	5	.249	.300	.449	.749
2016	Oak	AL	26	78	20	6	0	1	(1	0)	29	11	10	8	5	0	13	2	0	1	0	0	4	.256	.314	.372	.686
2017	Oak	AL	57	149	30	11	0	3	(0	3)	50	14	10	11	9	0	26	2	0	1	0	1	4	.201	.255	.336	.590
	5 ML YEARS		232	693	156	42	1	20	(12	8)	260	70	83	65	33	0	142	7	2	6	2	1	19	.225	.265	.375	.640

David Phelps

Pitches: R Bats: R Pos: RP-54

Ht: 6'2" Wt: 200 Born: 10/9/1986 Age: 31

Year	Team	Lg	G	GS	CG	GF	IP	BFP	H	R	ER	HR	SH	SF	HB	TBB	IBB	SO	WP	Bk	W	L	Pct	Sh	Sv-Op	Hld	ERC	ERA
2012	NYY	AL	33	11	0	5	99.2	414	81	38	37	14	4	3	6	38	2	96	2	2	4	4	.500	0	0-0	2	3.48	3.34
2013	NYY	AL	22	12	0	3	86.2	376	88	50	48	13	1	2	5	35	1	79	2	0	6	5	.545	0	0-1	1	4.38	4.98
2014	NYY	AL	32	17	1	5	113.0	497	115	62	55	13	4	3	7	46	2	92	2	1	5	5	.500	0	1-1	5	4.52	4.38
2015	Mia	NL	23	19	0	1	112.0	482	119	59	56	11	2	5	4	33	0	77	2	0	4	8	.333	0	0-0	0	4.13	4.50
2016	Mia	NL	64	5	0	6	86.2	352	61	23	22	6	1	2	2	38	6	114	0	1	7	6	.538	0	4-10	25	2.47	2.28
2017	2 Tms		54	0	0	5	55.2	238	51	23	21	5	2	2	1	26	3	62	0	0	4	5	.444	0	0-8	21	3.82	3.40
17	Mia	NL	44	0	0	4	47.0	197	42	20	18	5	2	1	0	21	3	51	0	0	2	4	.333	0	0-6	18	3.68	3.45
17	Sea	AL	10	0	0	1	8.2	41	9	3	3	0	0	1	1	5	0	11	0	0	2	1	.667	0	0-2	3	4.54	3.12
	Postseason		3	0	0	1	3.1	19	7	4	3	0	0	0	0	1	0	2	0	0	0	2	.000	0	0-0	0	8.97	8.10
	6 ML YEARS		228	64	1	25	553.2	2359	515	255	239	57	14	17	25	216	14	520	8	4	30	33	.476	0	5-20	54	3.82	3.89

Brandon Phillips

Bats: R Throws: R Pos: 2B-112;3B-25;PH-7;DH-1

Ht: 6'0" Wt: 211 Born: 6/28/1981 Age: 37

Year	Team	Lg	G	AB	H	2B	3B	HR	(Hm	Rd)	TB	R	RBI	RC	TBB	IBB	SO	HBP	SH	SF	SB	CS	GDP	Avg	OBP	Slg	OPS
2002	Cle	AL	11	31	8	3	1	0	(0	0)	13	5	4	5	3	0	6	1	1	0	0	0	0	.258	.343	.419	.762
2003	Cle	AL	112	370	77	18	1	6	(3	3)	115	36	33	22	14	0	77	3	5	1	4	5	12	.208	.242	.311	.553
2004	Cle	AL	6	22	4	2	0	0	(0	0)	6	1	1	0	2	0	5	0	0	0	0	2	1	.182	.250	.273	.523
2005	Cle	AL	6	9	0	0	0	0	(0	0)	0	1	0	0	0	0	4	0	0	0	0	0	0	.000	.000	.000	.000
2006	Cin	NL	149	536	148	28	1	17	(9	8)	229	65	75	74	35	3	88	6	4	6	25	2	19	.276	.324	.427	.751

Year	Team	Lg	G	AB	H	2B	3B	HR	(Hm	Rd)	TB	R	RBI	RC	TBB	IBB	SO	HBP	SH	SF	SB	CS	GDP	Avg	OBP	Slg	OPS
2007	Cin	NL	158	650	187	26	6	30	(17	13)	315	107	94	88	33	4	109	12	2	5	32	8	26	.288	.331	.485	.816
2008	Cin	NL	141	559	146	24	7	21	(13	8)	247	80	78	74	39	6	93	5	0	6	23	10	13	.261	.312	.442	.754
2009	Cin	NL	153	584	161	30	5	20	(10	10)	261	78	98	80	44	3	75	6	2	8	25	9	21	.276	.329	.447	.776
2010	Cin	NL	155	626	172	33	5	18	(10	8)	269	100	59	77	46	1	83	8	6	1	16	12	14	.275	.332	.430	.762
2011	Cin	NL	150	610	183	38	2	18	(14	4)	279	94	82	92	44	3	85	9	5	6	14	9	15	.300	.353	.457	.810
2012	Cin	NL	147	580	163	30	1	18	(15	3)	249	86	77	78	28	2	79	8	3	4	15	2	19	.281	.321	.429	.750
2013	Cin	NL	151	606	158	24	2	18	(7	11)	240	80	103	82	39	6	98	8	4	9	5	3	19	.261	.310	.396	.706
2014	Cin	NL	121	462	123	25	0	8	(3	5)	172	44	51	53	23	1	74	6	2	6	2	3	13	.266	.306	.372	.678
2015	Cin	NL	148	588	173	19	2	12	(9	3)	232	69	70	78	27	1	68	4	1	3	23	3	13	.294	.328	.395	.723
2016	Cin	NL	141	550	160	34	1	11	(6	5)	229	74	64	65	18	3	68	8	2	6	14	8	17	.291	.320	.416	.736
2017	2 Tms		144	572	163	34	1	13	(8	5)	238	81	60	62	21	1	73	8	2	1	11	8	21	.285	.319	.416	.735
17	Atl	NL	120	470	137	27	1	11	(8	3)	199	68	52	53	19	1	57	8	1	1	10	8	19	.291	.329	.423	.753
17	LAA	AL	24	102	26	7	0	2	(0	2)	39	13	8	9	2	0	16	0	1	0	1	0	0	.255	.269	.382	.652
	Postseason		9	40	13	4	0	2	(0	2)	23	3	8	10	0	0	5	0	0	1	1	0	0	.325	.317	.575	.892
	16 ML YEARS		1893	7355	2026	368	35	210	(124	86)	3094	1001	949	930	416	34	1085	92	39	62	209	84	223	.275	.320	.421	.740

Brett Phillips

Bats: L **Throws:** R **Pos:** CF-26;RF-9;PH-7;LF-4;PR-1   **Ht:** 6'0" **Wt:** 185 **Born:** 5/30/1994 **Age:** 24

Year	Team	Lg	G	AB	H	2B	3B	HR	(Hm	Rd)	TB	R	RBI	RC	TBB	IBB	SO	HBP	SH	SF	SB	CS	GDP	Avg	OBP	Slg	OPS
2013	2 Tms	Low	41	124	30	9	1	0	(-	-)	41	13	12	16	20	1	31	1	0	0	5	4	2	.242	.347	.331	.678
2014	2 Tms	Low	130	493	153	29	14	17	(-	-)	261	87	68	97	50	0	96	6	14	8	23	14	3	.310	.375	.529	.905
2015	Lancst	A+	66	291	93	19	7	15	(-	-)	171	68	53	61	22	0	64	6	3	0	8	6	3	.320	.379	.588	.967
2015	CpChr	AA	31	134	43	8	4	1	(-	-)	62	22	18	23	8	0	26	3	0	0	7	2	2	.321	.372	.463	.835
2015	Biloxi	AA	23	80	20	7	3	0	(-	-)	33	14	6	13	14	0	30	1	1	2	2	1	1	.250	.361	.413	.773
2016	Biloxi	AA	124	441	101	14	6	16	(-	-)	175	60	62	62	67	2	154	2	5	2	12	7	4	.229	.332	.397	.729
2017	ColSpr	AAA	105	383	117	23	10	19	(-	-)	217	79	78	82	45	3	129	1	0	3	9	1	6	.305	.377	.567	.944
2017	Mil	NL	37	87	24	3	0	4	(2	2)	39	9	12	14	9	2	34	1	1	0	5	0	0	.276	.351	.448	.799

Tyler Pill

Pitches: R **Bats:** L **Pos:** RP-4; SP-3   **Ht:** 6'1" **Wt:** 199 **Born:** 5/29/1990 **Age:** 28

Year	Team	Lg	G	GS	CG	GF	IP	BFP	H	R	ER	HR	SH	SF	HB	TBB	IBB	SO	WP	Bk	W	L	Pct	Sh	Sv-Op	Hld	ERC	ERA
2014	Bnghtn	AA	22	21	0	0	124.2	509	115	55	53	11	4	6	3	29	0	120	7	1	9	5	.643	0	0- -	-	3.05	3.83
2015	LsVgs	AAA	18	17	0	0	83.1	380	111	70	69	14	3	5	2	30	0	55	5	0	2	7	.222	0	0- -	-	6.60	7.45
2015	Bnghtn	AA	6	6	0	0	34.2	145	25	10	8	1	0	1	2	17	0	19	1	0	6	0	1.000	0	0- -	-	2.67	2.08
2016	Bnghtn	AA	22	22	3	0	138.2	572	138	67	62	8	3	3	4	34	1	110	6	0	9	10	.474	0	0- -	-	3.32	4.02
2016	LsVgs	AAA	5	5	0	0	27.1	125	41	18	17	5	2	2	1	6	0	22	1	0	1	1	.500	0	0- -	-	7.27	5.60
2017	LsVgs	AAA	13	13	0	0	80.1	342	83	38	31	8	4	1	4	22	1	50	1	0	4	3	.571	0	0- -	-	3.95	3.47
2017	NYM	NL	7	3	0	1	22.0	99	22	16	13	3	3	2	2	10	2	16	0	0	0	3	.000	0	0-0	0	4.71	5.32

Kevin Pillar

Bats: R **Throws:** R **Pos:** CF-153;PH-2   pih-LAHR   **Ht:** 6'0" **Wt:** 205 **Born:** 1/4/1989 **Age:** 29

Year	Team	Lg	G	AB	H	2B	3B	HR	(Hm	Rd)	TB	R	RBI	RC	TBB	IBB	SO	HBP	SH	SF	SB	CS	GDP	Avg	OBP	Slg	OPS
2013	Tor	AL	36	102	21	4	0	3	(1	2)	34	11	13	9	4	0	29	2	2	0	1	0	0	.206	.250	.333	.583
2014	Tor	AL	53	116	31	9	0	2	(2	0)	46	19	7	8	4	0	28	1	0	1	1	2	3	.267	.295	.397	.692
2015	Tor	AL	159	586	163	31	2	12	(6	6)	234	76	56	73	28	1	85	5	4	5	25	4	9	.278	.314	.399	.713
2016	Tor	AL	146	548	146	35	2	7	(3	4)	206	59	53	66	24	0	90	6	3	3	14	6	12	.266	.303	.376	.679
2017	Tor	AL	154	587	150	37	1	16	(6	10)	237	72	42	58	33	0	95	6	3	3	15	6	13	.256	.300	.404	.704
	Postseason		20	74	15	6	0	2	(0	2)	27	7	8	8	5	1	14	0	0	1	3	1	1	.203	.250	.365	.615
	5 ML YEARS		548	1939	511	116	5	40	(18	22)	757	237	171	214	93	1	327	20	12	12	55	19	37	.264	.302	.390	.693

Manny Pina

Bats: R **Throws:** R **Pos:** C-102;PH-10   **Ht:** 6'0" **Wt:** 215 **Born:** 6/5/1987 **Age:** 31

Year	Team	Lg	G	AB	H	2B	3B	HR	(Hm	Rd)	TB	R	RBI	RC	TBB	IBB	SO	HBP	SH	SF	SB	CS	GDP	Avg	OBP	Slg	OPS
2011	KC	AL	4	14	3	2	0	0	(0	0)	5	2	0	1	1	0	2	0	0	0	0	0	1	.214	.267	.357	.624
2012	KC	AL	1	2	0	0	0	0	(0	0)	0	0	0	0	0	0	0	0	0	0	0	0	0	.000	.000	.000	.000
2016	Mil	NL	33	71	18	4	0	2	(1	1)	28	4	12	8	10	0	15	0	0	0	0	1	2	.254	.346	.394	.740
2017	Mil	NL	107	330	92	21	0	9	(6	3)	140	45	43	46	20	0	79	5	1	3	2	0	8	.279	.327	.424	.751
	4 ML YEARS		145	417	113	27	0	11	(7	4)	173	51	55	55	31	0	96	5	1	3	2	1	11	.271	.327	.415	.742

Chad Pinder

Bats: R **Throws:** R **Pos:** RF-35;SS-22;2B-16;PH-10;CF-7;DH-7;LF-2;PR-2   **Ht:** 6'2" **Wt:** 195 **Born:** 3/29/1992 **Age:** 26

Year	Team	Lg	G	AB	H	2B	3B	HR	(Hm	Rd)	TB	R	RBI	RC	TBB	IBB	SO	HBP	SH	SF	SB	CS	GDP	Avg	OBP	Slg	OPS
2013	Vrmnt	A-	42	140	28	4	0	3	(-	-)	41	14	8	13	12	0	41	6	0	3	1	0	5	.200	.286	.293	.579
2014	Stcktn	A+	94	403	116	32	5	13	(-	-)	197	61	55	65	22	0	99	8	1	2	12	9	16	.288	.336	.489	.824
2015	Mdlnd	AA	117	477	151	32	2	15	(-	-)	232	71	86	83	28	3	103	8	4	5	7	5	15	.317	.361	.486	.847
2016	Nashv	AAA	107	426	110	23	3	14	(-	-)	181	72	51	58	25	0	108	9	1	4	5	1	8	.258	.310	.425	.735
2017	Nashv	AAA	17	64	17	2	1	1	(-	-)	24	12	7	8	6	0	23	1	0	0	1	2	1	.266	.338	.375	.713
2016	Oak	AL	22	51	12	4	0	1	(0	1)	19	4	4	5	3	0	14	0	0	1	0	0	1	.235	.273	.373	.645
2017	Oak	AL	87	282	67	15	1	15	(10	5)	129	36	42	37	18	0	92	5	0	3	2	1	7	.238	.292	.457	.750
	2 ML YEARS		109	333	79	19	1	16	(10	6)	148	40	46	42	21	0	106	5	0	4	2	1	8	.237	.289	.444	.734

Michael Pineda

Pitches: R Bats: R Pos: SP-17

pah-NAY-dah

Ht: 6'7" Wt: 260 Born: 1/18/1989 Age: 29

Year	Team	Lg	G	GS	CG	GF	IP	BFP	H	R	ER	HR	SH	SF	HB	TBB	IBB	SO	WP	Bk	W	L	Pct	Sh	Sv-Op	Hld	ERC	ERA
2011	Sea	AL	28	28	0	0	171.0	696	133	76	71	18	4	3	5	55	1	173	9	0	9	10	.474	0	0-0	0	2.73	3.74
2014	NYY	AL	13	13	0	0	76.1	290	56	18	16	5	2	1	0	7	0	59	3	1	5	5	.500	0	0-0	0	1.51	1.89
2015	NYY	AL	27	27	1	0	160.2	668	176	83	78	21	4	6	3	21	0	156	4	0	12	10	.545	0	0-0	0	3.82	4.37
2016	NYY	AL	32	32	0	0	175.2	756	184	98	94	27	0	3	6	53	1	207	7	0	6	12	.333	0	0-0	0	4.45	4.82
2017	NYY	AL	17	17	0	0	96.1	410	103	55	47	20	0	4	2	21	0	92	5	1	8	4	.667	0	0-0	0	4.52	4.39
	5 ML YEARS		117	117	1	0	680.0	2820	652	330	306	91	10	17	16	157	2	687	28	2	40	41	.494	0	0-0	0	3.49	4.05

Ricardo Pinto

Pitches: R Bats: R Pos: RP-25

Ht: 6'0" Wt: 165 Born: 1/20/1994 Age: 24

Year	Team	Lg	G	GS	CG	GF	IP	BFP	H	R	ER	HR	SH	SF	HB	TBB	IBB	SO	WP	Bk	W	L	Pct	Sh	Sv-Op	Hld	ERC	ERA
2014	Wmspt	A-	9	9	0	0	47.0	196	36	17	11	4	0	2	2	15	0	48	2	0	1	5	.167	0	0--	-	2.52	2.11
2015	2 Tms	Low	24	24	0	0	145.1	583	129	55	48	10	6	7	4	37	0	105	8	3	15	4	.789	0	0--	-	2.90	2.97
2016	Rdng	AA	27	25	0	1	156.0	665	150	84	71	20	10	4	8	51	2	101	7	1	7	6	.538	0	0--	-	3.94	4.10
2017	LV	AAA	19	8	0	5	60.2	253	61	35	26	4	0	3	0	18	0	46	6	1	5	3	.625	0	1--	-	3.52	3.86
2017	Phi	NL	25	0	0	6	29.2	147	39	28	26	7	3	2	1	17	1	25	1	1	1	2	.333	0	0-2	2	7.70	7.89

Jose Pirela

Bats: R Throws: R Pos: LF-68;2B-7;1B-5;RF-4;DH-3;PH-2;PR-2;3B-1

Ht: 6'0" Wt: 220 Born: 11/21/1989 Age: 28

Year	Team	Lg	G	AB	H	2B	3B	HR	(Hm	Rd)	TB	R	RBI	RC	TBB	IBB	SO	HBP	SH	SF	SB	CS	GDP	Avg	OBP	Slg	OPS
2017	ElPaso*	AAA	48	181	60	10	3	13	(-	-)	115	37	42	42	15	0	26	2	2	1	8	3	4	.331	.387	.635	1.022
2014	NYY	AL	7	24	8	1	2	0	(0	0)	13	6	3	4	1	0	4	0	0	0	0	0	1	.333	.360	.542	.902
2015	NYY	AL	37	74	17	3	0	1	(1	0)	23	7	5	3	2	0	16	0	1	1	1	0	4	.230	.247	.311	.558
2016	SD	NL	15	39	6	2	0	0	(0	0)	8	2	0	0	1	0	9	0	1	0	0	1	0	.154	.175	.205	.380
2017	SD	NL	83	312	90	25	4	10	(5	5)	153	43	40	50	27	0	71	2	1	2	4	3	8	.288	.347	.490	.837
	4 ML YEARS		142	449	121	31	6	11	(6	5)	197	58	48	57	31	0	100	2	3	3	5	4	13	.269	.318	.439	.756

Stephen Piscotty

Bats: R Throws: R Pos: RF-99;PH-10

Ht: 6'3" Wt: 210 Born: 1/14/1991 Age: 27

Year	Team	Lg	G	AB	H	2B	3B	HR	(Hm	Rd)	TB	R	RBI	RC	TBB	IBB	SO	HBP	SH	SF	SB	CS	GDP	Avg	OBP	Slg	OPS
2015	StL	NL	63	233	71	15	4	7	(4	3)	115	29	39	41	20	2	56	1	0	2	2	1	7	.305	.359	.494	.853
2016	StL	NL	153	582	159	35	3	22	(13	9)	266	86	85	97	51	0	133	12	1	2	7	5	14	.273	.343	.457	.800
2017	StL	NL	107	341	80	16	1	9	(1	8)	125	40	39	43	52	2	87	5	0	3	3	6	11	.235	.342	.367	.708
	Postseason		4	16	6	1	0	3	(1	2)	16	5	6	8	2	0	8	0	0	0	0	0	0	.375	.444	1.000	1.444
	3 ML YEARS		323	1156	310	66	8	38	(18	20)	506	155	163	181	123	4	276	18	1	7	12	12	32	.268	.346	.438	.784

Nick Pivetta

Pitches: R Bats: R Pos: SP-26

Ht: 6'5" Wt: 220 Born: 2/14/1993 Age: 25

Year	Team	Lg	G	GS	CG	GF	IP	BFP	H	R	ER	HR	SH	SF	HB	TBB	IBB	SO	WP	Bk	W	L	Pct	Sh	Sv-Op	Hld	ERC	ERA
2013	2 Tms	Low	9	8	0	0	34.0	143	30	12	11	1	0	2	1	13	0	25	3	1	1	1	.500	0	0--	-	3.01	2.91
2014	Hgrstn	A	26	25	0	0	132.1	569	142	66	62	15	6	5	6	39	0	98	9	1	13	8	.619	0	0--	-	4.37	4.22
2015	Ptomc	A+	15	14	0	1	86.1	348	70	29	22	4	1	5	2	29	0	72	4	0	7	4	.636	0	0--	-	2.63	2.29
2015	Rdng	AA	7	7	0	0	28.1	133	32	24	23	4	1	3	2	19	0	25	4	0	2	2	.500	0	0--	-	6.90	7.31
2016	Rdng	AA	22	22	1	0	124.0	514	108	50	47	10	5	3	6	41	0	111	5	0	11	6	.647	1	0--	-	3.19	3.41
2016	LV	AAA	5	5	0	0	24.2	101	20	7	7	2	2	1	2	10	0	27	1	0	1	2	.333	0	0--	-	3.36	2.55
2017	LV	AAA	5	5	1	0	32.0	123	25	6	5	1	0	0	1	2	0	37	0	2	5	0	1.000	1	0--	-	1.54	1.41
2017	Phi	NL	26	26	0	0	133.0	584	144	91	89	25	4	7	4	57	0	140	11	2	8	10	.444	0	0-0	0	5.52	6.02

Kevin Plawecki

Bats: R Throws: R Pos: C-29;PH-4;1B-2;PR-1

plah-WEH-kee

Ht: 6'2" Wt: 210 Born: 2/26/1991 Age: 27

Year	Team	Lg	G	AB	H	2B	3B	HR	(Hm	Rd)	TB	R	RBI	RC	TBB	IBB	SO	HBP	SH	SF	SB	CS	GDP	Avg	OBP	Slg	OPS
2017	LsVgs*	AAA	64	247	81	17	1	9	(-	-)	127	37	45	48	16	0	38	6	0	6	0	0	10	.328	.375	.514	.889
2015	NYM	NL	73	233	51	9	0	3	(1	2)	69	18	21	22	17	4	60	4	1	3	0	0	4	.219	.280	.296	.576
2016	NYM	NL	48	132	26	6	0	1	(0	1)	35	6	11	11	17	2	33	2	0	0	0	0	1	.197	.298	.265	.563
2017	NYM	NL	37	100	26	5	0	3	(3	0)	40	11	13	15	14	2	17	3	0	1	1	0	2	.260	.364	.400	.764
	3 ML YEARS		158	465	103	20	0	7	(4	3)	144	35	45	48	48	8	110	9	1	4	1	0	7	.222	.304	.310	.614

Trevor Plouffe

Bats: R Throws: R Pos: 3B-64;DH-15;PH-14;1B-11;2B-3;PR-1 PLOOF

Ht: 6'2" Wt: 215 Born: 6/15/1986 Age: 32

Year	Team	Lg	G	AB	H	2B	3B	HR	(Hm	Rd)	TB	R	RBI	RC	TBB	IBB	SO	HBP	SH	SF	SB	CS	GDP	Avg	OBP	Slg	OPS
2010	Min	AL	22	41	6	1	0	2	(1	1)	13	7	6	2	0	0	14	0	2	1	0	0	0	.146	.143	.317	.460
2011	Min	AL	81	286	68	18	1	8	(3	5)	112	47	31	31	25	0	71	4	2	3	3	3	6	.238	.305	.392	.697
2012	Min	AL	119	422	99	19	1	24	(15	9)	192	56	55	48	37	0	92	4	0	2	1	3	9	.235	.301	.455	.756
2013	Min	AL	129	477	121	22	1	14	(8	6)	187	44	52	49	34	1	112	6	1	4	2	1	11	.254	.309	.392	.701
2014	Min	AL	136	520	134	40	2	14	(8	6)	220	69	80	74	53	2	109	4	0	5	2	1	12	.258	.328	.423	.751
2015	Min	AL	152	573	140	35	4	22	(13	9)	249	74	86	79	50	0	124	4	1	4	2	1	28	.244	.307	.435	.742

Year Team	Lg	G	AB	H	2B	3B	HR	(Hm	Rd)	TB	R	RBI	RC	TBB	IBB	SO	HBP	SH	SF	SB	CS	GDP	Avg	OBP	Slg	OPS
2016 Min	AL	84	319	83	13	1	12	(7	5)	134	35	47	38	19	0	60	2	1	3	1	0	11	.260	.303	.420	.723
2017 2 Tms	AL	100	283	56	7	0	9	(7	2)	90	31	19	13	28	2	88	1	0	1	1	2	12	.198	.272	.318	.590
17 Oak	AL	58	182	39	5	0	7	(6	1)	65	22	14	10	16	1	58	0	0	1	1	1	10	.214	.276	.357	.634
17 TB	AL	42	101	17	2	0	2	(1	1)	25	9	5	3	12	1	30	1	0	0	0	1	2	.168	.263	.248	.511
8 ML YEARS		823	2921	707	155	10	105	(62	43)	1197	363	376	334	246	5	670	25	7	23	12	11	89	.242	.304	.410	.714

Gregory Polanco

Bats: L Throws: L Pos: RF-68;LF-25;PH-10;CF-6;DH-2 puh-LAHN-ko Ht: 6'5" Wt: 235 Born: 9/14/1991 Age: 26

Year Team	Lg	G	AB	H	2B	3B	HR	(Hm	Rd)	TB	R	RBI	RC	TBB	IBB	SO	HBP	SH	SF	SB	CS	GDP	Avg	OBP	Slg	OPS
2014 Pit	NL	89	277	65	9	0	7	(5	2)	95	50	33	32	30	1	59	0	2	2	14	5	1	.235	.307	.343	.650
2015 Pit	NL	153	593	152	35	6	9	(6	3)	226	83	52	73	55	6	121	1	1	2	27	10	5	.256	.320	.381	.701
2016 Pit	NL	144	527	136	34	4	22	(9	13)	244	79	86	73	53	6	119	0	1	6	17	6	13	.258	.323	.463	.786
2017 Pit	NL	108	379	95	20	0	11	(7	4)	148	39	35	39	27	4	60	3	0	1	8	1	5	.251	.305	.391	.695
Postseason		1	4	0	0	0	0	(0	0)	0	0	0	0	0	0	2	0	0	0	0	0	0	.000	.000	.000	.000
4 ML YEARS		494	1776	448	98	10	49	(27	22)	713	251	206	217	165	17	359	4	4	11	66	22	24	.252	.315	.401	.717

Jorge Polanco

Bats: B Throws: R Pos: SS-130;DH-2;PH-2 puh-LAHN-ko Ht: 5'11" Wt: 200 Born: 7/5/1993 Age: 24

Year Team	Lg	G	AB	H	2B	3B	HR	(Hm	Rd)	TB	R	RBI	RC	TBB	IBB	SO	HBP	SH	SF	SB	CS	GDP	Avg	OBP	Slg	OPS
2014 Min	AL	5	6	2	1	1	0	(0	0)	5	2	3	4	2	0	2	0	0	0	0	0	0	.333	.500	.833	1.333
2015 Min	AL	4	10	3	0	0	0	(0	0)	3	1	1	3	2	0	1	0	0	0	1	0	0	.300	.417	.300	.717
2016 Min	AL	69	245	69	15	4	4	(1	3)	104	24	27	36	17	0	46	3	2	3	4	3	3	.282	.332	.424	.757
2017 Min	AL	133	488	125	30	3	13	(4	9)	200	60	74	68	41	1	78	2	7	6	13	5	7	.256	.313	.410	.723
4 ML YEARS		211	749	199	46	8	17	(5	12)	312	87	105	111	62	1	127	5	9	9	18	8	10	.266	.322	.417	.739

A.J. Pollock

Bats: R Throws: R Pos: CF-109;PH-9;DH-1 Ht: 6'1" Wt: 195 Born: 12/5/1987 Age: 30

Year Team	Lg	G	AB	H	2B	3B	HR	(Hm	Rd)	TB	R	RBI	RC	TBB	IBB	SO	HBP	SH	SF	SB	CS	GDP	Avg	OBP	Slg	OPS
2012 Ari	NL	31	81	20	4	1	2	(2	0)	32	8	8	9	9	1	11	0	1	2	1	2	2	.247	.315	.395	.710
2013 Ari	NL	137	443	119	28	5	8	(3	5)	181	64	38	58	33	1	82	2	3	1	12	3	5	.269	.322	.409	.730
2014 Ari	NL	75	265	80	19	6	7	(7	0)	132	41	24	43	19	0	46	2	1	0	14	3	4	.302	.353	.498	.851
2015 Ari	NL	157	609	192	39	6	20	(9	11)	303	111	76	106	53	0	89	2	0	9	39	7	19	.315	.367	.498	.865
2016 Ari	NL	12	41	10	0	0	2	(2	0)	16	9	4	5	5	0	8	0	0	0	4	0	1	.244	.326	.390	.716
2017 Ari	NL	112	425	113	33	6	14	(9	5)	200	73	49	66	35	1	71	6	0	0	20	6	8	.266	.330	.471	.801
6 ML YEARS		524	1864	534	123	24	53	(30	23)	864	306	199	287	154	3	307	12	5	12	90	21	39	.286	.343	.464	.806

Drew Pomeranz

Pitches: L Bats: R Pos: SP-32 POMM-er-anze Ht: 6'6" Wt: 240 Born: 11/22/1988 Age: 29

Year Team	Lg	G	GS	CG	GF	IP	BFP	H	R	ER	HR	SH	SF	HB	TBB	IBB	SO	WP	Bk	W	L	Pct	Sh	Sv-Op	Hld	ERC	ERA
2011 Col	NL	4	4	0	0	18.1	77	19	11	11	0	1	0	1	5	0	13	1	0	2	1	.667	0	0-0	0	3.36	5.40
2012 Col	NL	22	22	0	0	96.2	434	97	57	53	14	8	4	4	46	2	83	8	1	2	9	.182	0	0-0	0	4.78	4.93
2013 Col	NL	8	4	0	0	21.2	105	25	15	15	4	1	1	1	19	1	19	0	0	0	4	.000	0	0-0	0	8.04	6.23
2014 Oak	AL	20	10	0	0	69.0	278	51	22	18	7	1	0	1	26	0	64	0	0	5	4	.556	0	0-0	0	2.70	2.35
2015 Oak	AL	53	9	0	9	86.0	357	71	44	35	8	4	5	3	31	1	82	2	0	5	6	.455	0	3-6	12	3.05	3.66
2016 2 Tms		31	30	0	1	170.2	703	137	65	63	22	3	3	1	65	3	186	10	0	11	12	.478	0	0-0	0	3.13	3.32
2017 Bos	AL	32	32	0	0	173.2	740	166	69	64	19	2	6	4	69	0	174	6	0	17	6	.739	0	0-0	0	4.00	3.32
16 SD	NL	17	17	0	0	102.0	411	67	30	28	8	2	3	1	41	2	115	7	0	8	7	.533	0	0-0	0	2.17	2.47
16 Bos	AL	14	13	0	1	68.2	292	70	35	35	14	1	0	0	24	1	71	3	0	3	5	.375	0	0-0	0	4.73	4.59
Postseason		2	0	0	0	3.2	17	4	2	2	1	0	0	0	2	1	7	0	0	0	-	-	0	0-0	0	5.91	4.91
7 ML YEARS		170	111	0	14	636.0	2694	566	283	259	74	20	19	15	261	7	621	27	1	42	42	.500	0	3-6	12	3.70	3.67

Rick Porcello

Pitches: R Bats: R Pos: SP-33 pore-SELL-oh Ht: 6'5" Wt: 205 Born: 12/27/1988 Age: 29

Year Team	Lg	G	GS	CG	GF	IP	BFP	H	R	ER	HR	SH	SF	HB	TBB	IBB	SO	WP	Bk	W	L	Pct	Sh	Sv-Op	Hld	ERC	ERA
2009 Det	AL	31	31	0	0	170.2	720	176	81	75	23	4	2	3	52	0	89	6	1	14	9	.609	0	0-0	0	4.24	3.96
2010 Det	AL	27	27	0	0	162.2	700	188	96	89	18	1	2	7	38	2	84	11	3	10	12	.455	0	0-0	0	4.56	4.92
2011 Det	AL	31	31	0	0	182.0	784	210	103	96	18	5	5	8	46	1	104	12	0	14	9	.609	0	0-0	0	4.57	4.75
2012 Det	AL	31	31	0	0	176.1	783	226	101	90	16	2	3	6	44	3	107	6	0	10	12	.455	0	0-0	0	5.16	4.59
2013 Det	AL	32	29	1	1	177.0	736	185	87	85	18	4	3	4	42	6	142	6	1	13	8	.619	0	0-0	0	3.79	4.32
2014 Det	AL	32	31	3	1	204.2	840	211	89	78	18	3	4	4	41	4	129	0	0	15	13	.536	3	0-0	0	3.50	3.43
2015 Bos	AL	28	28	0	1	172.0	737	196	103	94	25	2	5	10	38	0	149	12	1	9	15	.375	0	0-0	0	4.76	4.92
2016 Bos	AL	33	33	3	0	223.0	890	193	85	78	23	2	3	13	32	0	189	3	0	22	4	.846	0	0-0	0	2.64	3.15
2017 Bos	AL	33	33	2	0	203.1	885	236	125	105	38	1	6	6	48	1	181	5	0	11	17	.393	0	0-0	0	5.04	4.65
Postseason		9	3	0	4	20.2	90	24	15	13	3	0	1	3	2	2	19	1	0	0	3	.000	0	0-0	0	4.47	5.66
9 ML YEARS		278	274	9	2	1671.2	7075	1821	870	790	197	24	33	60	381	15	1174	61	6	118	99	.544	3	0-0	0	4.18	4.25

Buster Posey

Bats: R **Throws:** R **Pos:** C-99;1B-38;DH-7;PH-7

Ht: 6'1" **Wt:** 215 **Born:** 3/27/1987 **Age:** 31

								BATTING												RUNNING			AVERAGES			
Year	Team	Lg	G	AB	H	2B	3B	HR	(Hm | Rd)	TB	R	RBI	RC	TBB	IBB	SO	HBP	SH	SF	SB	CS	GDP	Avg	OBP	Slg	OPS
2009	SF	NL	7	17	2	0	0	0	(0 | 0)	2	1	0	0	0	0	4	0	0	0	0	0	0	.118	.118	.118	.235
2010	SF	NL	108	406	124	23	2	18	(6 | 12)	205	58	67	70	30	5	55	4	0	3	0	2	12	.305	.357	.505	.862
2011	SF	NL	45	162	46	5	0	4	(1 | 3)	63	17	21	26	18	3	30	4	0	1	3	0	4	.284	.368	.389	.756
2012	SF	NL	148	530	178	39	1	24	(7 | 17)	291	78	103	111	69	7	96	2	0	9	1	1	19	.336	.408	.549	.957
2013	SF	NL	148	520	153	34	1	15	(8 | 7)	234	61	72	77	60	8	70	8	0	7	2	1	15	.294	.371	.450	.821
2014	SF	NL	147	547	170	28	2	22	(11 | 11)	268	72	89	94	47	5	69	3	0	8	0	1	16	.311	.364	.490	.854
2015	SF	NL	150	557	177	28	0	19	(6 | 13)	262	74	95	96	56	10	52	3	0	7	2	0	17	.318	.379	.470	.849
2016	SF	NL	146	539	155	33	2	14	(7 | 7)	234	82	80	82	64	7	68	3	0	8	6	1	18	.288	.362	.434	.796
2017	SF	NL	140	494	158	34	0	12	(3 | 9)	228	62	67	84	61	13	66	8	0	5	6	1	17	.320	.400	.462	.861
	Postseason		53	206	51	4	0	4	(1 | 3)	67	17	23	21	23	5	41	1	0	2	1	1	4	.248	.323	.325	.649
	9 ML YEARS		1039	3772	1163	224	8	128	(49 | 79)	1787	505	594	640	405	58	510	35	0	48	20	7	118	.308	.376	.474	.850

Brooks Pounders

Pitches: R **Bats:** R **Pos:** RP-11

Ht: 6'5" **Wt:** 265 **Born:** 9/26/1990 **Age:** 27

			HOW MUCH HE PITCHED					WHAT HE GAVE UP										THE RESULTS						
Year	Team	Lg	G	GS	CG	GF	IP	BFP	H	R	ER	HR	SH	SF	HB	TBB	IBB	SO	WP	Bk	W	L	Pct	Sh	Sv-Op	Hld	ERC	ERA
2013	NWArk	AA	27	19	1	1	116.0	493	107	63	58	12	1	6	11	42	0	100	3	0	5	7	.417	1	1- -	-	3.93	4.50
2014	2 Tms	Low	9	8	0	0	30.1	130	29	18	15	0	2	0	1	12	0	37	2	0	0	2	.000	0	0- -	-	3.24	4.45
2015	3 Tms	Low	7	7	0	0	19.0	79	18	10	7	1	1	0	3	4	0	19	0	0	0	1	.000	0	0- -	-	3.41	3.32
2015	NWArk	AA	8	8	0	0	49.1	198	39	16	12	3	1	0	3	19	0	32	1	1	3	4	.429	0	0- -	-	2.99	2.19
2016	Omha	AAA	31	7	0	7	80.1	342	67	29	28	5	2	1	5	37	3	90	4	1	5	3	.625	0	0- -	-	3.33	3.14
2017	Salt Lk	AAA	38	2	0	20	51.1	211	42	18	15	6	1	0	1	15	0	49	3	0	2	2	.500	0	6- -	-	2.84	2.63
2016	KC	AL	13	0	0	6	12.2	58	19	13	13	6	0	1	0	3	0	13	0	1	2	1	.667	0	0-0	1	9.56	9.24
2017	LAA	AL	11	0	0	10	10.1	54	17	12	12	4	1	0	1	5	1	12	0	1	1	0	1.000	0	0-0	0	11.15	10.45
	2 ML YEARS		24	0	0	16	23.0	112	36	25	25	10	1	1	1	8	1	25	0	2	3	1	.750	0	0-0	1	10.31	9.78

Max Povse

Pitches: R **Bats:** R **Pos:** RP-3

poh-zee

Ht: 6'8" **Wt:** 185 **Born:** 8/23/1993 **Age:** 24

			HOW MUCH HE PITCHED					WHAT HE GAVE UP										THE RESULTS						
Year	Team	Lg	G	GS	CG	GF	IP	BFP	H	R	ER	HR	SH	SF	HB	TBB	IBB	SO	WP	Bk	W	L	Pct	Sh	Sv-Op	Hld	ERC	ERA
2014	Danvle	R+	12	11	0	0	47.1	195	42	19	18	1	1	2	2	11	0	37	2	0	4	2	.667	0	0- -	-	2.48	3.42
2015	2 Tms	Low	17	17	0	0	78.0	329	74	43	36	2	2	1	6	23	1	60	3	3	5	5	.500	0	0- -	-	3.17	4.15
2016	Carlina	A+	15	15	0	0	87.1	364	89	44	36	5	1	4	2	17	0	91	3	4	5	5	.500	0	0- -	-	3.18	3.71
2016	Missi	AA	11	11	0	0	70.2	283	61	25	23	4	4	2	6	12	1	48	6	0	4	1	.800	0	0- -	-	2.55	2.93
2017	Tacom	AAA	13	5	0	1	31.2	145	41	28	26	3	0	1	2	12	0	29	0	0	1	4	.200	0	0- -	-	6.01	7.39
2017	Ark	AA	9	8	0	0	39.0	163	34	17	15	1	0	2	2	14	0	32	0	0	3	2	.600	0	0- -	-	2.94	3.46
2017	Sea	AL	3	0	0	2	3.2	21	9	5	3	1	0	0	0	1	0	2	0	0	0	0	-	0	0-0	0	14.70	7.36

Boog Powell

Bats: L **Throws:** L **Pos:** CF-28;PH-11;DH-9;LF-8;PR-6;RF-1

Ht: 5'10" **Wt:** 185 **Born:** 1/14/1993 **Age:** 25

								BATTING												RUNNING			AVERAGES			
Year	Team	Lg	G	AB	H	2B	3B	HR	(Hm	Rd)	TB	R	RBI	RC	TBB	IBB	SO	HBP	SH	SF	SB	CS	GDP	Avg	OBP	Slg	OPS
2013	Vrmnt	A-	59	212	60	7	3	0	(-	-)	73	30	14	29	26	2	34	1	6	0	14	6	2	.283	.364	.344	.708
2014	2 Tms	Low	83	315	108	10	5	3	(-	-)	137	54	28	64	61	0	53	2	1	1	16	15	3	.343	.451	.435	.886
2015	Mont	AA	61	238	78	6	6	1	(-	-)	99	44	22	42	29	0	38	4	2	1	11	8	2	.328	.408	.416	.824
2015	Drham	AAA	56	206	53	10	3	2	(-	-)	75	22	18	29	32	0	41	2	4	2	7	6	3	.257	.360	.364	.724
2016	Tacom	AAA	64	248	67	9	2	3	(-	-)	89	39	27	30	22	0	42	0	4	3	10	6	5	.270	.326	.359	.685
2017	Tacom	AAA	58	206	70	9	2	6	(-	-)	101	46	33	43	28	0	27	1	1	3	11	5	10	.340	.416	.490	.906
2017	2 Tms	AL	52	117	33	5	0	3	(2	1)	47	24	12	16	15	0	30	0	1	2	0	1	2	.282	.358	.402	.760
17	Sea	AL	23	36	7	0	0	0	(0	0)	7	6	2	3	6	0	9	0	1	0	0	0	1	.194	.310	.194	.504
17	Oak	AL	29	81	26	5	0	3	(2	1)	40	18	10	13	9	0	21	0	0	2	0	1	1	.321	.380	.494	.874

Martin Prado

Bats: R **Throws:** R **Pos:** 3B-34;PH-2;DH-1

mar-TEEN PRAH-doe

Ht: 6'0" **Wt:** 215 **Born:** 10/27/1983 **Age:** 34

								BATTING												RUNNING			AVERAGES			
Year	Team	Lg	G	AB	H	2B	3B	HR	(Hm	Rd)	TB	R	RBI	RC	TBB	IBB	SO	HBP	SH	SF	SB	CS	GDP	Avg	OBP	Slg	OPS
2006	Atl	NL	24	42	11	1	1	1	(1	0)	17	3	9	9	5	0	7	0	2	0	0	0	2	.262	.340	.405	.745
2007	Atl	NL	28	59	17	3	0	0	(0	0)	20	5	2	6	3	0	6	0	0	0	0	0	0	.288	.323	.339	.662
2008	Atl	NL	78	228	73	18	4	2	(1	1)	105	36	33	39	21	0	29	1	2	2	3	1	3	.320	.377	.461	.838
2009	Atl	NL	128	450	138	38	0	11	(4	7)	209	64	49	57	36	1	59	2	11	4	1	3	17	.307	.358	.464	.822
2010	Atl	NL	140	599	184	40	3	15	(4	11)	275	100	66	86	40	2	86	3	3	6	5	3	13	.307	.350	.459	.809
2011	Atl	NL	129	551	143	26	2	13	(9	4)	212	66	57	57	34	1	52	1	1	3	4	8	16	.260	.302	.385	.687
2012	Atl	NL	156	617	186	42	6	10	(4	6)	270	81	70	96	58	2	69	2	4	9	17	4	19	.301	.359	.438	.796
2013	Ari	NL	155	609	172	36	2	14	(7	7)	254	70	82	72	47	2	53	2	0	6	3	5	29	.282	.333	.417	.750
2014	2 Tms	NL	143	536	151	26	4	12	(7	5)	221	62	58	66	26	0	80	7	0	4	3	1	20	.282	.321	.412	.733
2015	Mia	NL	129	500	144	22	2	9	(6	3)	197	52	63	70	37	4	68	5	1	8	1	0	9	.288	.338	.394	.732
2016	Mia	NL	153	600	183	37	3	8	(6	2)	250	70	75	89	49	4	69	4	0	5	2	2	24	.305	.359	.417	.775
2017	Mia	NL	37	140	35	9	0	2	(0	2)	50	13	12	8	6	0	22	0	0	1	0	0	4	.250	.279	.357	.636
14	Ari	NL	106	403	109	17	4	5	(3	2)	149	44	42	43	23	0	57	6	0	4	2	1	17	.270	.317	.370	.686
14	NYY	AL	37	133	42	9	0	7	(4	3)	72	18	16	23	3	0	23	1	0	0	1	0	3	.316	.336	.541	.877
	Postseason		2	5	1	0	0	0	(0	0)	1	0	0	0	0	0	1	0	0	0	0	0	0	.200	.200	.200	.400
	12 ML YEARS		1300	4931	1437	298	27	97	(50	47)	2080	622	576	655	362	16	600	27	24	48	39	27	156	.291	.340	.422	.762

Alex Presley

Bats: L **Throws:** L **Pos:** RF-36;CF-19;LF-13;PH-7;DH-5

Ht: 5'10" **Wt:** 195 **Born:** 7/25/1985 **Age:** 32

								BATTING											RUNNING			AVERAGES			
Year Team	Lg	G	AB	H	2B	3B	HR	(Hm Rd)	TB	R	RBI	RC	TBB	IBB	SO	HBP	SH	SF	SB	CS	GDP	Avg	OBP	Slg	OPS
2017 Toledo*	AAA	43	167	36	6	1	2	(- -)	50	26	9	14	12	0	36	4	2	0	4	2	2	.216	.284	.299	.584
2010 Pit	NL	19	23	6	1	0	0	(0 0)	7	2	0	1	1	0	8	0	1	0	1	1	0	.261	.292	.304	.596
2011 Pit	NL	52	215	64	12	6	4	(1 3)	100	27	20	35	13	1	40	1	1	1	9	3	1	.298	.339	.465	.804
2012 Pit	NL	104	346	82	14	7	10	(2 8)	140	46	25	31	18	0	72	2	4	0	9	7	5	.237	.279	.405	.683
2013 2 Tms		57	185	51	5	2	3	(2 1)	69	17	15	17	9	0	39	1	0	0	1	4	3	.276	.313	.373	.686
2014 Hou	AL	89	254	62	6	1	6	(4 2)	88	22	19	29	13	0	44	1	1	2	5	1	3	.244	.281	.346	.628
2015 Hou	AL	8	12	3	0	0	0	(0 0)	3	1	1	2	1	0	5	0	0	0	0	0	0	.250	.308	.250	.558
2016 2 Tms		50	121	24	2	0	3	(1 2)	35	12	11	12	11	1	25	1	0	1	0	2	2	.198	.269	.289	.558
2017 Det	AL	71	245	77	10	3	3	(2 1)	102	30	20	36	15	0	49	0	3	0	5	0	5	.314	.354	.416	.770
13 Pit	NL	29	72	19	1	1	2	(2 0)	28	8	4	5	1	0	18	0	0	0	0	1	1	.264	.274	.389	.663
13 Min	AL	28	113	32	4	1	1	(0 1)	41	9	11	12	8	0	21	1	0	0	1	3	2	.283	.336	.363	.699
16 Mil	NL	47	116	23	2	0	3	(1 2)	34	12	11	12	11	1	25	1	0	1	0	2	2	.198	.271	.293	.564
16 Det	AL	3	5	1	0	0	0	(0 0)	1	0	0	0	0	0	0	0	0	0	0	0	0	.200	.200	.200	.400
8 ML YEARS		450	1401	369	50	19	29	(12 17)	544	157	111	163	81	2	282	6	10	4	30	18	19	.263	.306	.388	.694

Ryan Pressly

Pitches: R **Bats:** R **Pos:** RP-57

Ht: 6'3" **Wt:** 210 **Born:** 12/15/1988 **Age:** 29

		HOW MUCH HE PITCHED						WHAT HE GAVE UP												THE RESULTS						
Year Team	Lg	G	GS	CG	GF	IP	BFP	H	R	ER	HR	SH	SF	HB	TBB	IBB	SO	WP	Bk	W	L	Pct	Sh	Sv-Op	Hld	ERC	ERA
2017 Roch*	AAA	7	0	0	6	10.0	40	5	1	1	0	2	0	0	5	0	15	0	0	2	0	1.000	0	4- --	1	1.41	0.90
2013 Min	AL	49	0	0	18	76.2	315	71	37	33	5	2	3	0	27	1	49	7	0	3	3	.500	0	0-0	1	3.31	3.87
2014 Min	AL	25	0	0	5	28.1	122	30	10	9	3	2	3	1	8	2	14	1	0	2	0	1.000	0	0-1	2	3.98	2.86
2015 Min	AL	27	0	0	6	27.2	119	27	9	9	0	1	1	0	12	1	22	2	0	3	2	.600	0	0-0	4	3.31	2.93
2016 Min	AL	72	0	0	10	75.1	328	79	34	31	8	4	2	2	23	2	67	7	0	6	7	.462	0	1-6	13	4.01	3.70
2017 Min	AL	57	0	0	10	61.1	252	52	34	32	10	2	1	3	19	5	61	5	0	2	3	.400	0	0-1	6	3.41	4.70
5 ML YEARS		230	0	0	49	269.1	1136	259	124	114	26	11	10	6	89	11	213	22	0	16	15	.516	0	1-8	26	3.60	3.81

David Price

Pitches: L **Bats:** L **Pos:** SP-11; RP-5

Ht: 6'5" **Wt:** 215 **Born:** 8/26/1985 **Age:** 32

		HOW MUCH HE PITCHED						WHAT HE GAVE UP												THE RESULTS						
Year Team	Lg	G	GS	CG	GF	IP	BFP	H	R	ER	HR	SH	SF	HB	TBB	IBB	SO	WP	Bk	W	L	Pct	Sh	Sv-Op	Hld	ERC	ERA
2008 TB	AL	5	1	0	0	14.0	57	9	4	3	1	0	1	4	0	12	0	0	0	0	0	-	0	0-0	1	1.86	1.93
2009 TB	AL	23	23	0	0	128.1	557	119	72	63	17	3	2	4	54	0	102	2	0	10	7	.588	0	0-0	0	4.05	4.42
2010 TB	AL	32	31	2	0	208.2	861	170	71	63	15	4	3	5	79	1	188	5	3	19	6	.760	1	0-0	0	2.91	2.72
2011 TB	AL	34	34	0	0	224.1	918	192	93	87	22	4	7	9	63	5	218	2	0	12	13	.480	0	0-0	0	2.97	3.49
2012 TB	AL	31	31	2	0	211.0	836	173	63	60	16	2	3	5	59	2	205	8	1	20	5	.800	1	0-0	0	2.67	2.56
2013 TB	AL	27	27	4	0	186.2	740	178	78	69	16	1	2	3	27	0	151	6	0	10	8	.556	0	0-0	0	2.89	3.33
2014 2 Tms	AL	34	34	3	0	248.1	1009	230	100	90	25	4	5	3	38	1	271	2	0	15	12	.556	0	0-0	0	2.79	3.26
2015 2 Tms	AL	32	32	3	0	220.1	888	190	70	60	17	4	8	3	47	2	225	4	0	18	5	.783	1	0-0	0	2.54	2.45
2016 Bos	AL	35	35	2	0	230.0	951	227	106	102	30	8	7	7	50	1	228	4	0	17	9	.654	0	0-0	0	3.63	3.99
2017 Bos	AL	16	11	0	1	74.2	317	65	30	28	8	0	2	4	24	0	76	2	0	6	3	.667	0	0-0	1	3.25	3.38
14 TB	AL	23	23	2	0	170.2	689	156	68	59	20	3	3	2	23	1	189	2	0	11	8	.579	0	0-0	0	2.79	3.11
14 Det	AL	11	11	1	0	77.2	320	74	32	31	5	1	0	0	15	0	82	0	0	4	4	.500	0	0-0	0	2.77	3.59
15 Det	AL	21	21	3	0	146.0	592	133	50	41	13	4	5	3	29	2	138	3	0	9	4	.692	1	0-0	0	2.83	2.53
15 Tor	AL	11	11	0	0	74.1	296	57	20	19	4	0	3	0	18	0	87	1	0	9	1	.900	0	0-0	0	2.00	2.30
Postseason		15	9	0	5	66.2	281	68	43	41	12	0	1	3	14	0	62	1	0	2	8	.200	0	1-1	0	4.13	5.54
10 ML YEARS		269	259	16	1	1746.1	7134	1553	687	625	167	30	38	46	445	12	1676	35	4	127	68	.651	3	0-0	2	3.00	3.22

Jurickson Profar

JURR-ick-sun PRO-farr

Bats: B **Throws:** R **Pos:** LF-12;SS-4;3B-3;PH-3;1B-2;2B-1

Ht: 6'0" **Wt:** 190 **Born:** 2/20/1993 **Age:** 25

								BATTING											RUNNING			AVERAGES			
Year Team	Lg	G	AB	H	2B	3B	HR	(Hm Rd)	TB	R	RBI	RC	TBB	IBB	SO	HBP	SH	SF	SB	CS	GDP	Avg	OBP	Slg	OPS
2017 RdRck*	AAA	87	327	94	25	0	7	(- -)	140	50	45	58	43	0	33	8	4	1	5	0	9	.287	.383	.428	.811
2012 Tex	AL	9	17	3	2	0	1	(0 1)	8	2	2	1	0	0	4	0	0	0	0	0	1	.176	.176	.471	.647
2013 Tex	AL	85	286	67	11	0	6	(3 3)	96	30	26	30	26	0	63	5	6	1	2	4	1	.234	.308	.336	.644
2016 Tex	AL	90	272	65	6	3	5	(4 1)	92	35	20	30	30	0	61	3	2	0	2	1	7	.239	.321	.338	.660
2017 Tex	AL	22	58	10	2	0	0	(0 0)	12	8	5	5	9	0	14	1	2	0	1	1	0	.172	.294	.207	.501
Postseason		1	1	1	0	0	0	(0 0)	1	0	0	0	0	0	0	0	0	0	0	0	0	1.000	1.000	1.000	2.000
4 ML YEARS		206	633	145	21	3	12	(7 5)	208	75	53	66	65	0	142	9	10	1	5	6	9	.229	.309	.329	.638

Austin Pruitt

Pitches: R **Bats:** R **Pos:** RP-22; SP-8

Ht: 5'10" **Wt:** 180 **Born:** 8/31/1989 **Age:** 28

		HOW MUCH HE PITCHED						WHAT HE GAVE UP												THE RESULTS						
Year Team	Lg	G	GS	CG	GF	IP	BFP	H	R	ER	HR	SH	SF	HB	TBB	IBB	SO	WP	Bk	W	L	Pct	Sh	Sv-Op	Hld	ERC	ERA
2013 2 Tms	Low	14	7	0	4	50.0	189	36	12	8	3	2	2	2	5	0	39	2	0	0	3	.000	0	1- --	-	1.58	1.44
2014 Charltt	A+	26	25	0	1	147.0	601	144	70	61	12	3	2	1	31	0	106	9	1	9	7	.563	0	0- --	-	3.17	3.73
2015 Mont	AA	26	26	2	0	160.0	658	160	60	55	3	3	3	5	38	0	122	7	0	10	7	.588	1	0- --	-	3.09	3.09
2016 Drham	AAA	28	28	2	0	162.2	657	166	73	68	21	2	6	1	27	0	149	6	0	8	11	.421	0	0- --	-	3.56	3.76
2017 Drham	AAA	9	4	0	1	24.2	93	17	9	7	2	0	0	1	2	0	33	0	0	0	1	.000	0	1- --	-	1.50	2.55
2017 TB	AL	30	8	0	7	83.0	371	103	55	49	11	1	0	5	22	2	66	4	0	7	5	.583	0	1-2	1	5.36	5.31

Cesar Puello

Bats: R Throws: R Pos: LF-9;DH-5;PH-5;RF-2;PR-1
PWAY-oh
Ht: 6'2" Wt: 220 Born: 4/1/1991 Age: 27

							BATTING													RUNNING			AVERAGES			
Year	Team	Lg	G	AB	H	2B	3B	HR	(Hm | Rd)	TB	R	RBI	RC	TBB	IBB	SO	HBP	SH	SF	SB	CS	GDP	Avg	OBP	Slg	OPS
2013	Bnghtn	AA	91	331	108	21	2	16	(- | -)	181	63	73	74	28	2	82	16	0	2	24	7	5	.326	.403	.547	.950
2014	LsVgs	AAA	105	318	80	20	2	7	(- | -)	125	59	37	50	30	3	72	21	2	0	13	1	7	.252	.355	.393	.748
2016	S-WB	AAA	78	230	65	13	0	5	(- | -)	93	35	31	46	35	1	56	18	3	3	18	3	9	.283	.413	.404	.817
2017	RdRck	AAA	43	162	40	8	1	6	(- | -)	68	24	27	22	12	1	38	3	0	2	5	1	7	.247	.307	.420	.727
2017	Salt Lk	AAA	44	184	73	18	1	7	(- | -)	114	42	34	47	13	0	44	2	0	2	13	3	4	.397	.440	.620	1.060
2017	2 Tms	AL	17	34	7	0	0	0	(0 | 0)	7	6	3	3	4	0	12	1	0	0	2	0	2	.206	.308	.206	.514
17	LAA	AL	1	4	1	0	0	0	(0 | 0)	1	0	1	1	0	0	1	0	0	0	2	0	0	.250	.250	.250	.500
17	TB	AL	16	30	6	0	0	0	(0 | 0)	6	6	2	2	4	0	11	1	0	0	0	0	2	.200	.314	.200	.514

Yasiel Puig

Bats: R Throws: R Pos: RF-145;PH-12
yah-SEE-el PWEEG
Ht: 6'2" Wt: 240 Born: 12/7/1990 Age: 27

							BATTING													RUNNING			AVERAGES			
Year	Team	Lg	G	AB	H	2B	3B	HR	(Hm | Rd)	TB	R	RBI	RC	TBB	IBB	SO	HBP	SH	SF	SB	CS	GDP	Avg	OBP	Slg	OPS
2013	LAD	NL	104	382	122	21	2	19	(- | -)	204	66	42	62	36	6	97	11	0	3	11	8	6	.319	.391	.534	.925
2014	LAD	NL	148	558	165	37	9	16	(8 | 8)	268	92	69	95	67	3	124	12	2	1	11	7	7	.296	.382	.480	.863
2015	LAD	NL	79	282	72	12	3	11	(6 | 5)	123	30	38	35	26	1	66	2	0	1	3	3	1	.255	.322	.436	.758
2016	LAD	NL	104	334	88	14	2	11	(6 | 5)	139	45	45	46	24	0	74	7	0	3	5	2	10	.263	.323	.416	.740
2017	LAD	NL	152	499	131	24	2	28	(14 | 14)	243	72	74	73	64	8	100	2	0	5	15	6	21	.263	.346	.487	.833
	Postseason		27	76	20	1	2	0	(0 | 0)	25	11	5	6	5	2	28	2	0	0	0	1	3	.263	.325	.329	.654
	5 ML YEARS		587	2055	578	108	18	85	(43 | 42)	977	305	268	311	217	18	461	34	2	13	45	26	45	.281	.357	.475	.833

Albert Pujols

Bats: R Throws: R Pos: DH-143;1B-6;PH-1
POO-holes
Ht: 6'3" Wt: 240 Born: 1/16/1980 Age: 38

							BATTING													RUNNING			AVERAGES			
Year	Team	Lg	G	AB	H	2B	3B	HR	(Hm	Rd)	TB	R	RBI	RC	TBB	IBB	SO	HBP	SH	SF	SB	CS	GDP	Avg	OBP	Slg	OPS
2001	StL	NL	161	590	194	47	4	37	(18	19)	360	112	130	132	69	6	93	9	1	7	1	3	21	.329	.403	.610	1.013
2002	StL	NL	157	590	185	40	2	34	(14	20)	331	118	127	121	72	13	69	9	0	4	2	4	20	.314	.394	.561	.955
2003	StL	NL	157	591	212	51	1	43	(21	22)	394	137	124	160	79	12	65	10	0	5	5	1	13	.359	.439	.667	1.106
2004	StL	NL	154	592	196	51	2	46	(18	28)	389	133	123	143	84	12	52	7	0	9	5	5	21	.331	.415	.657	1.072
2005	StL	NL	161	591	195	38	2	41	(23	18)	360	129	117	139	97	27	65	9	0	3	16	2	19	.330	.430	.609	1.039
2006	StL	NL	143	535	177	33	1	49	(24	25)	359	119	137	146	92	28	50	4	0	3	7	2	20	.331	.431	.671	1.102
2007	StL	NL	158	565	185	38	1	32	(12	20)	321	99	103	118	99	22	58	7	0	8	2	6	27	.327	.429	.568	.997
2008	StL	NL	148	524	187	44	0	37	(19	18)	342	100	116	130	104	34	54	5	0	8	7	3	16	.357	.462	.653	1.114
2009	StL	NL	160	568	186	45	1	47	(22	25)	374	124	135	145	115	44	64	9	0	8	16	4	23	.327	.443	.658	1.101
2010	StL	NL	159	587	183	39	1	42	(17	25)	350	115	118	131	103	38	76	4	0	6	14	4	23	.312	.414	.596	1.011
2011	StL	NL	147	579	173	29	0	37	(16	21)	313	105	99	100	61	15	58	4	0	7	9	1	29	.299	.366	.541	.906
2012	LAA	AL	154	607	173	50	0	30	(14	16)	313	85	105	100	52	16	76	5	0	6	8	1	19	.285	.343	.516	.859
2013	LAA	AL	99	391	101	19	0	17	(8	9)	171	49	64	54	40	8	55	5	0	7	1	1	18	.258	.330	.437	.767
2014	LAA	AL	159	633	172	37	1	28	(13	15)	295	89	105	86	48	11	71	5	0	9	5	1	28	.272	.324	.466	.790
2015	LAA	AL	157	602	147	22	0	40	(20	20)	289	85	95	82	50	10	72	6	0	3	5	3	15	.244	.307	.480	.787
2016	LAA	AL	152	593	159	19	0	31	(18	13)	271	71	119	91	49	6	75	2	0	6	4	0	24	.268	.323	.457	.780
2017	LAA	AL	149	593	143	17	0	23	(13	10)	229	53	101	66	37	5	93	2	0	4	3	0	26	.241	.286	.386	.672
	Postseason		77	279	90	18	1	19	(7	12)	167	55	54	68	49	20	40	5	0	1	1	2	6	.323	.431	.599	1.030
	17 ML YEARS		2575	9731	2968	619	16	614	(290	324)	5461	1723	1918	1944	1251	307	1146	102	1	103	110	41	362	.305	.386	.561	.947

Zach Putnam

Pitches: R Bats: R Pos: RP-7
Ht: 6'2" Wt: 220 Born: 7/3/1987 Age: 30

			HOW MUCH HE PITCHED						WHAT HE GAVE UP										THE RESULTS					
Year	Team	Lg	G	GS	CG	GF	IP	BFP	H	R	ER	HR	SH	SF	HB	TBB	IBB	SO	WP	Bk	W	L	Pct	Sh	Sv-Op	Hld	ERC	ERA
2011	Cle	AL	8	0	0	3	7.1	34	10	5	5	1	0	0	2	0	0	9	1	0	1	1	.500	0	0-1	0	5.82	6.14
2012	Col	NL	2	0	0	0	2.0	9	3	0	0	0	1	0	0	1	0	0	0	0	0	0	-	0	0-0	0	7.26	0.00
2013	ChC	NL	5	0	0	1	3.1	19	9	7	7	1	0	1	0	0	0	4	0	0	0	0	-	0	0-0	0	15.42	18.90
2014	CWS	AL	49	0	0	13	54.2	213	39	14	12	2	1	1	1	20	1	46	5	0	5	3	.625	0	6-7	16	2.21	1.98
2015	CWS	AL	49	0	0	16	48.2	212	42	24	22	7	4	4	4	24	5	64	5	0	3	3	.500	0	0-3	6	4.14	4.07
2016	CWS	AL	25	0	0	6	27.1	114	25	7	7	2	0	2	0	11	1	30	2	0	1	0	1.000	0	0-0	1	3.43	2.30
2017	CWS	AL	7	0	0	0	8.2	28	2	1	1	0	0	0	0	1	0	9	2	0	0	0	-	0	0-0	1	0.23	1.04
	7 ML YEARS		145	0	0	39	152.0	629	130	58	54	13	6	8	7	57	7	162	15	0	10	7	.588	0	6-11	25	3.25	3.20

Kevin Quackenbush

Pitches: R Bats: R Pos: RP-20
Ht: 6'4" Wt: 235 Born: 11/28/1988 Age: 29

			HOW MUCH HE PITCHED						WHAT HE GAVE UP										THE RESULTS					
Year	Team	Lg	G	GS	CG	GF	IP	BFP	H	R	ER	HR	SH	SF	HB	TBB	IBB	SO	WP	Bk	W	L	Pct	Sh	Sv-Op	Hld	ERC	ERA
2017	ElPaso*	AAA	22	0	0	13	27.2	114	28	15	12	4	1	2	1	9	0	24	1	0	4	1	.800	0	4- -	-	4.50	3.90
2014	SD	NL	56	0	0	18	54.1	222	42	15	15	2	1	3	2	18	4	56	1	1	3	3	.500	0	6-7	10	2.25	2.48
2015	SD	NL	57	0	0	19	58.1	243	52	28	26	6	1	4	1	20	3	58	0	1	3	2	.600	0	0-1	2	3.28	4.01
2016	SD	NL	60	0	0	17	59.2	253	55	27	26	8	2	2	0	22	2	42	2	0	7	7	.500	0	2-3	9	3.67	3.92
2017	SD	NL	20	0	0	4	26.1	125	32	23	23	5	0	1	1	16	0	23	3	0	0	2	.000	0	0-0	1	7.14	7.86
	4 ML YEARS		193	0	0	58	198.2	843	181	93	90	21	4	10	4	76	9	179	6	2	13	14	.481	0	8-11	22	3.55	4.08

Chad Qualls

Pitches: R Bats: R Pos: RP-19   **Ht:** 6'4" **Wt:** 235 **Born:** 8/17/1978 **Age:** 39

Year Team	Lg	G	GS	CG	GF	IP	BFP	H	R	ER	HR	SH	SF	HB	TBB	IBB	SO	WP	Bk	W	L	Pct	Sh	Sv-Op	Hld	ERC	ERA
2017 Albq*	AAA	6	0	0	0	5.0	19	5	1	1	0	0	0	0	1	0	5	0	0	0	0	-	0	0--	-	2.93	1.80
2004 Hou	NL	25	0	0	4	33.0	141	34	13	13	3	0	1	4	8	1	24	0	0	4	0	1.000	0	1-2	9	4.02	3.55
2005 Hou	NL	77	0	0	19	79.2	329	73	33	29	7	4	3	6	23	2	60	1	0	6	4	.600	0	0-0	22	3.42	3.28
2006 Hou	NL	81	0	0	13	88.2	356	76	38	37	10	4	4	6	28	6	56	0	0	7	3	.700	0	0-6	23	3.36	3.76
2007 Hou	NL	79	0	0	16	82.2	345	84	29	28	10	6	2	3	25	5	78	2	0	6	5	.545	0	5-10	21	4.07	3.05
2008 Ari	NL	77	0	0	21	73.2	300	61	29	23	4	4	3	3	18	2	71	6	0	4	8	.333	0	9-17	22	2.40	2.81
2009 Ari	NL	51	0	0	44	52.0	217	53	23	21	5	1	0	2	7	2	45	2	0	2	2	.500	0	24-29	15	3.17	3.63
2010 2 Tms		70	0	0	29	59.0	281	85	56	48	7	4	4	2	21	4	49	4	0	3	4	.429	0	12-19	11	6.63	7.32
2011 SD	NL	77	0	0	20	74.1	306	73	30	29	7	7	1	0	20	5	43	4	0	6	8	.429	0	0-5	22	3.38	3.51
2012 3 Tms		60	0	0	15	52.1	231	63	34	31	7	2	2	0	14	4	27	3	0	2	1	.667	0	0-5	14	4.78	5.33
2013 Mia	NL	66	0	0	12	62.0	252	57	18	18	4	4	0	2	19	7	49	1	0	5	2	.714	0	0-2	15	3.09	2.61
2014 Hou	AL	58	0	0	41	51.1	213	54	22	19	5	2	0	2	5	2	43	1	0	1	5	.167	0	19-25	3	3.22	3.33
2015 Hou	AL	60	0	0	17	49.1	202	46	24	24	6	1	4	2	9	1	46	3	0	3	5	.375	0	4-6	10	3.13	4.38
2016 Col	NL	44	0	0	14	32.2	152	43	22	19	5	1	1	0	9	1	22	1	0	2	0	1.000	0	0-1	4	5.54	5.23
2017 Col	NL	19	0	0	9	16.2	72	17	11	10	1	0	1	0	5	0	11	0	0	1	1	.500	0	0-0	1	4.24	5.40
10 Ari	NL	43	0	0	28	38.0	190	61	41	35	5	4	2	1	15	4	34	3	0	1	4	.200	0	12-16	3	7.80	8.29
10 TB	AL	27	0	0	1	21.0	91	24	15	13	2	0	2	1	6	0	15	1	0	2	0	1.000	0	0-3	8	4.64	5.57
12 Phi	NL	35	0	0	6	31.1	140	39	18	16	7	1	0	0	9	3	19	2	0	1	1	.500	0	0-5	12	5.74	4.60
12 NYY	AL	8	0	0	4	7.1	33	10	5	5	0	0	1	0	3	1	2	1	0	1	0	1.000	0	0-0	0	5.38	6.14
12 Pit	NL	17	0	0	5	13.2	58	14	11	10	0	1	1	0	2	0	6	0	0	0	0	-	0	0-0	2	2.48	6.59
Postseason		17	0	0	0	22.2	94	24	13	13	3	1	0	0	7	3	17	0	0	1	1	.500	0	0-2	4	4.20	5.16
14 ML YEARS		844	0	0	274	807.1	3397	819	382	349	83	41	25	32	211	42	624	28	0	52	48	.520	0	74-127	176	3.73	3.89

Jose Quintana

Pitches: L Bats: R Pos: SP-32   KIN-tahn-ah   **Ht:** 6'1" **Wt:** 220 **Born:** 1/24/1989 **Age:** 29

Year Team	Lg	G	GS	CG	GF	IP	BFP	H	R	ER	HR	SH	SF	HB	TBB	IBB	SO	WP	Bk	W	L	Pct	Sh	Sv-Op	Hld	ERC	ERA
2012 CWS	AL	25	22	0	2	136.1	568	142	62	57	14	5	1	3	42	4	81	10	2	6	6	.500	0	0-0	0	4.13	3.76
2013 CWS	AL	33	33	0	0	200.0	832	188	83	78	23	3	6	5	56	2	164	2	1	9	7	.563	0	0-0	0	3.47	3.51
2014 CWS	AL	32	32	0	0	200.1	830	197	87	74	10	4	6	2	52	3	178	7	0	9	11	.450	0	0-0	0	3.15	3.32
2015 CWS	AL	32	32	1	0	206.1	862	218	81	77	16	4	4	8	44	4	177	5	0	9	10	.474	1	0-0	0	3.67	3.36
2016 CWS	AL	32	32	0	0	208.0	837	192	76	74	22	2	2	4	50	1	181	10	1	13	12	.520	0	0-0	0	3.23	3.20
2017 2 Tms		32	32	1	0	188.2	790	170	92	87	23	1	3	10	61	4	207	8	1	11	11	.500	1	0-0	0	3.57	4.15
17 CWS	AL	18	18	0	0	104.1	444	98	55	52	14	1	2	2	40	1	109	7	1	4	8	.333	0	0-0	0	3.97	4.49
17 ChC	NL	14	14	1	0	84.1	346	72	37	35	9	0	1	8	21	3	98	1	0	7	3	.700	1	0-0	0	3.08	3.74
6 ML YEARS		186	183	2	2	1139.2	4719	1107	481	447	108	19	22	32	305	18	988	42	5	57	57	.500	2	0-0	0	3.50	3.53

Ryan Raburn

Bats: R Throws: R Pos: LF-22;PH-8   RAY-burn   **Ht:** 6'0" **Wt:** 185 **Born:** 4/17/1981 **Age:** 37

Year Team	Lg	G	AB	H	2B	3B	HR	(Hm	Rd)	TB	R	RBI	RC	TBB	IBB	SO	HBP	SH	SF	SB	CS	GDP	Avg	OBP	Slg	OPS
2017 Charlt*	AAA	27	83	23	2	1	3	(-	-)	36	11	13	17	20	1	29	1	0	1	1	0	1	.277	.419	.434	.853
2004 Det	AL	12	29	4	1	0	0	(0	0)	5	4	1	1	2	0	15	0	0	0	1	0	0	.138	.194	.172	.366
2007 Det	AL	49	138	42	12	2	4	(2	2)	70	28	27	21	8	1	33	0	0	1	3	0	7	.304	.340	.507	.847
2008 Det	AL	92	182	43	10	1	4	(2	2)	67	26	20	20	16	1	49	0	1	0	3	1	2	.236	.298	.368	.666
2009 Det	AL	113	261	76	11	2	16	(9	7)	139	44	45	42	26	2	60	2	1	1	5	4	6	.291	.359	.533	.891
2010 Det	AL	113	371	104	25	1	15	(5	10)	176	54	62	54	27	0	92	8	1	3	2	2	8	.280	.340	.474	.814
2011 Det	AL	121	387	99	22	2	14	(7	7)	167	53	49	48	21	2	114	3	4	3	1	1	4	.256	.297	.432	.729
2012 Det	AL	66	205	35	14	0	1	(0	1)	52	14	12	8	13	0	53	2	1	1	1	1	4	.171	.226	.254	.480
2013 Cle	AL	87	243	66	18	0	16	(8	8)	132	40	55	47	29	0	67	4	0	1	0	0	4	.272	.357	.543	.901
2014 Cle	AL	74	195	39	7	0	4	(0	4)	58	18	22	11	13	1	51	1	0	3	0	0	8	.200	.250	.297	.547
2015 Cle	AL	82	173	52	16	1	8	(2	6)	94	22	29	30	23	3	44	4	0	1	0	0	6	.301	.393	.543	.936
2016 Col	NL	113	223	49	10	2	9	(5	4)	90	30	30	24	28	0	80	2	0	3	0	0	6	.220	.309	.404	.712
2017 Was	NL	25	65	17	1	2	2	(0	2)	28	7	6	9	4	0	25	0	0	0	1	1	1	.262	.304	.431	.735
Postseason		10	31	9	2	0	2	(1	1)	17	4	5	4	5	0	9	0	0	0	0	0	3	.290	.389	.548	.937
12 ML YEARS		947	2472	626	147	13	93	(40	53)	1078	340	358	315	210	10	683	26	9	17	16	10	58	.253	.316	.436	.752

Carlos Ramirez

Pitches: R Bats: R Pos: RP-12   **Ht:** 6'5" **Wt:** 205 **Born:** 4/24/1991 **Age:** 27

Year Team	Lg	G	GS	CG	GF	IP	BFP	H	R	ER	HR	SH	SF	HB	TBB	IBB	SO	WP	Bk	W	L	Pct	Sh	Sv-Op	Hld	ERC	ERA
2014 Bluefld	R+	17	0	0	6	34.1	156	32	20	10	2	2	0	4	19	0	24	2	1	1	0	1.000	0	0--	-	4.39	2.62
2015 2 Tms	Low	34	0	0	22	39.2	187	48	25	21	2	1	1	0	24	0	37	7	1	2	3	.400	0	8--	-	5.72	4.76
2016 Dnedin	A+	30	0	0	18	41.0	167	32	10	10	2	1	0	0	21	0	41	4	1	3	0	1.000	0	9--	-	3.09	2.20
2017 Nham	AA	18	0	0	7	23.2	90	10	2	0	0	0	1	1	7	0	29	1	0	2	0	1.000	0	3--	-	0.89	0.00
2017 Buffalo	AAA	7	0	0	1	14.0	50	6	0	0	0	0	0	0	3	0	16	0	0	1	0	1.000	0	0--	-	0.73	0.00
2017 Tor	AL	12	0	0	1	16.2	58	6	5	5	2	0	0	1	3	0	14	0	0	0	0	-	0	0-0	3	1.14	2.70

Erasmo Ramirez

Pitches: R Bats: R Pos: SP-19; RP-18

eh-RASS-moh

Ht: 5'10" Wt: 215 Born: 5/2/1990 Age: 28

Year	Team	Lg	G	GS	CG	GF	IP	BFP	H	R	ER	HR	SH	SF	HB	TBB	IBB	SO	WP	Bk	W	L	Pct	Sh	Sv-Op	Hld	ERC	ERA
2012	Sea	AL	16	8	0	2	59.0	238	47	26	22	6	1	5	3	12	1	48	0	0	1	3	.250	0	0-0	0	2.42	3.36
2013	Sea	AL	14	13	0	0	72.1	321	79	44	40	12	0	3	3	26	0	57	0	0	5	3	.625	0	0-0	0	5.04	4.98
2014	Sea	AL	17	14	0	0	75.1	338	82	44	44	13	1	1	6	34	2	60	3	0	1	6	.143	0	0-0	0	5.68	5.26
2015	TB	AL	34	27	0	5	163.1	666	145	73	68	16	1	1	9	40	0	126	3	0	11	6	.647	0	0-0	0	3.11	3.75
2016	TB	AL	64	1	0	13	90.2	378	90	39	38	14	7	2	4	26	5	63	7	0	7	11	.389	0	2-6	15	4.13	3.77
2017	2 Tms	AL	37	19	0	4	131.1	539	123	70	64	22	2	7	2	31	2	109	1	0	5	6	.455	0	1-2	6	3.58	4.39
17	TB	AL	26	8	0	4	69.1	282	66	39	37	10	1	2	1	16	1	55	1	0	4	3	.571	0	1-2	6	3.53	4.80
17	Sea	AL	11	11	0	0	62.0	257	57	31	27	12	1	5	1	15	1	54	0	0	1	3	.250	0	0-0	0	3.62	3.92
6 ML YEARS			182	82	0	24	592.0	2480	566	296	276	83	12	19	27	169	10	463	14	0	30	35	.462	0	3-8	21	3.83	4.20

Hanley Ramirez

Bats: R Throws: R Pos: DH-108;1B-18;PH-7

Ht: 6'2" Wt: 235 Born: 12/23/1983 Age: 34

Year	Team	Lg	G	AB	H	2B	3B	HR	(Hm	Rd)	TB	R	RBI	RC	TBB	IBB	SO	HBP	SH	SF	SB	CS	GDP	Avg	OBP	Slg	OPS
2005	Bos	AL	2	2	0	0	0	0	(0	0)	0	0	0	0	0	0	2	0	0	0	0	0	0	.000	.000	.000	.000
2006	Fla	NL	158	633	185	46	11	17	(9	8)	304	119	59	101	56	0	128	4	5	2	51	15	7	.292	.353	.480	.833
2007	Fla	NL	154	639	212	48	6	29	(15	14)	359	125	81	115	52	3	95	7	4	4	51	14	10	.332	.386	.562	.948
2008	Fla	NL	153	589	177	34	4	33	(17	16)	318	125	67	116	92	9	122	8	0	4	35	12	5	.301	.400	.540	.940
2009	Fla	NL	151	576	197	42	1	24	(17	7)	313	101	106	122	61	14	101	9	1	5	27	8	9	.342	.410	.543	.954
2010	Fla	NL	142	543	163	28	2	21	(12	9)	258	92	76	90	64	12	93	7	0	5	32	10	14	.300	.378	.475	.853
2011	Fla	NL	92	338	82	16	0	10	(5	5)	128	55	45	46	44	3	66	2	1	0	20	10	6	.243	.333	.379	.712
2012	2 Tms	NL	157	604	155	29	4	24	(11	13)	264	79	92	81	54	4	132	6	0	3	21	7	17	.257	.322	.437	.759
2013	LAD	NL	86	304	105	25	2	20	(8	12)	194	62	57	69	27	3	52	3	0	2	10	2	5	.345	.402	.638	1.040
2014	LAD	NL	128	449	127	35	4	13	(8	5)	201	64	71	69	56	2	84	6	0	1	14	5	10	.283	.369	.448	.817
2015	Bos	AL	105	401	100	12	1	19	(8	11)	171	59	53	47	21	2	71	4	0	4	6	3	11	.249	.291	.426	.717
2016	Bos	AL	147	549	157	28	1	30	(19	11)	277	81	111	94	60	5	120	7	0	4	9	3	17	.286	.361	.505	.866
2017	Bos	AL	133	496	120	24	0	23	(10	13)	213	58	62	55	51	8	116	6	0	0	1	3	15	.242	.320	.429	.750
12	Mia	NL	93	353	87	18	2	14	(7	7)	151	49	48	42	37	1	72	3	0	2	14	4	11	.246	.322	.428	.749
12	LAD	NL	64	251	68	11	2	10	(4	6)	113	30	44	39	17	3	60	3	0	1	7	3	6	.271	.324	.450	.774
Postseason			16	57	19	7	1	1	(0	1)	31	7	11	11	6	3	11	2	0	0	2	0	2	.333	.415	.544	.959
13 ML YEARS			1608	6123	1780	367	32	263	(139	124)	3000	1020	880	1005	638	65	1182	69	11	34	277	92	126	.291	.362	.490	.852

JC Ramirez

Pitches: R Bats: R Pos: SP-24; RP-3

Ht: 6'4" Wt: 250 Born: 8/16/1988 Age: 29

Year	Team	Lg	G	GS	CG	GF	IP	BFP	H	R	ER	HR	SH	SF	HB	TBB	IBB	SO	WP	Bk	W	L	Pct	Sh	Sv-Op	Hld	ERC	ERA
2013	Phi	NL	18	0	0	6	24.0	116	30	22	20	6	1	4	0	15	1	16	0	0	0	1	.000	0	0-0	3	7.59	7.50
2015	2 Tms		20	0	0	6	23.2	106	25	14	14	3	0	0	1	11	3	16	1	0	1	2	.333	0	0-3	5	4.79	5.32
2016	2 Tms		70	0	0	16	78.2	335	77	41	38	12	2	7	4	22	2	59	7	0	3	4	.429	0	2-6	13	3.97	4.35
2017	LAA	AL	27	24	0	1	147.1	620	149	72	66	21	3	4	6	49	1	105	5	1	11	10	.524	0	0-1	0	4.42	4.15
15	Ari	NL	12	0	0	4	15.1	63	15	7	7	1	0	0	0	4	2	11	1	0	1	1	.500	0	0-2	2	3.04	4.11
15	Sea	AL	8	0	0	2	8.1	43	10	7	7	2	0	0	1	7	1	5	0	0	0	1	.000	0	0-1	3	8.47	7.56
16	Cin	NL	27	0	0	7	32.1	139	35	24	23	7	1	3	0	9	2	28	3	0	1	3	.250	0	1-4	1	4.74	6.40
16	LAA	AL	43	0	0	9	46.1	196	42	17	15	5	1	4	4	13	0	31	4	0	2	1	.667	0	1-2	12	3.45	2.91
4 ML YEARS			135	24	0	25	273.2	1177	281	149	140	42	6	15	11	97	7	196	13	1	15	17	.469	0	2-10	18	4.58	4.60

Jose Ramirez

Pitches: R Bats: R Pos: RP-68

Ht: 6'1" Wt: 215 Born: 1/21/1990 Age: 28

Year	Team	Lg	G	GS	CG	GF	IP	BFP	H	R	ER	HR	SH	SF	HB	TBB	IBB	SO	WP	Bk	W	L	Pct	Sh	Sv-Op	Hld	ERC	ERA
2014	NYY	AL	8	0	0	5	10.0	49	11	6	6	2	0	0	2	7	0	10	0	0	0	2	.000	0	0-0	0	7.60	5.40
2015	2 Tms	AL	8	0	0	2	7.2	52	15	14	11	0	0	0	3	10	1	5	3	0	1	0	1.000	0	0-0	0	14.28	12.91
2016	Atl	NL	33	0	0	5	32.2	143	26	16	13	2	0	3	4	18	4	33	3	0	2	2	.500	0	0-0	3	3.51	3.58
2017	Atl	NL	68	0	0	7	62.0	258	45	26	22	9	1	2	5	29	1	56	1	0	2	3	.400	0	0-5	27	3.47	3.19
15	NYY	AL	3	0	0	1	3.0	20	6	5	5	0	0	0	1	4	0	2	3	0	0	0	-	0	0-0	0	15.12	15.00
15	Sea	AL	5	0	0	1	4.2	32	9	9	6	0	0	0	2	6	1	3	0	0	1	0	1.000	0	0-0	0	13.76	11.57
4 ML YEARS			117	0	0	19	112.1	502	97	62	52	13	1	5	14	64	6	104	7	0	5	7	.417	0	0-5	30	4.48	4.17

Jose Ramirez

Bats: B Throws: R Pos: 3B-88;2B-71;PH-1

Ht: 5'9" Wt: 165 Born: 9/17/1992 Age: 25

Year	Team	Lg	G	AB	H	2B	3B	HR	(Hm	Rd)	TB	R	RBI	RC	TBB	IBB	SO	HBP	SH	SF	SB	CS	GDP	Avg	OBP	Slg	OPS
2013	Cle	AL	15	12	4	0	1	0	(0	0)	6	5	0	2	2	0	2	0	0	0	1	0	0	.333	.429	.500	.929
2014	Cle	AL	68	237	62	10	2	2	(1	1)	82	27	17	25	13	0	35	1	13	2	10	1	3	.262	.300	.346	.646
2015	Cle	AL	97	315	69	14	3	6	(1	5)	107	50	27	28	32	0	39	1	5	2	10	4	5	.219	.291	.340	.631
2016	Cle	AL	152	565	176	46	3	11	(8	3)	261	84	76	101	44	1	62	4	1	4	22	7	10	.312	.363	.462	.825
2017	Cle	AL	152	585	186	56	6	29	(10	19)	341	107	83	113	52	5	69	3	0	5	17	5	13	.318	.374	.583	.957
Postseason			15	56	15	2	0	1	(0	1)	20	6	3	4	3	1	8	0	0	0	0	1	1	.268	.305	.357	.662
5 ML YEARS			484	1714	497	126	15	48	(20	28)	797	273	203	269	143	6	207	9	19	13	59	18	31	.290	.345	.465	.810

Neil Ramirez

Pitches: R Bats: R Pos: RP-29 Ht: 6'4" Wt: 215 Born: 5/25/1989 Age: 29

		HOW MUCH HE PITCHED						WHAT HE GAVE UP												THE RESULTS							
Year Team	Lg	G	GS	CG	GF	IP	BFP	H	R	ER	HR	SH	SF	HB	TBB	IBB	SO	WP	Bk	W	L	Pct	Sh	Sv-Op	Hld	ERC	ERA
2017 Syrcse*	AAA	14	0	0	9	14.2	74	23	10	10	3	0	1	2	8	1	20	1	0	2	1	.667	0	1--	-	8.94	6.14
2014 ChC	NL	50	0	0	10	43.2	177	29	11	7	2	0	0	2	17	0	53	3	1	3	3	.500	0	3-5	16	2.12	1.44
2015 ChC	NL	19	0	0	4	14.0	60	12	5	5	1	0	2	0	6	0	15	2	0	1	0	1.000	0	0-0	2	3.14	3.21
2016 3 Tms		18	0	0	7	24.0	107	22	16	16	8	0	3	0	18	2	24	5	0	0	0	-	0	0-0	1	6.88	6.00
2017 2 Tms	NL	29	0	0	9	31.1	153	35	30	25	6	0	3	1	21	0	44	3	0	0	1	.000	0	0-1	2	6.51	7.18
16 ChC	NL	8	0	0	4	7.2	35	5	4	4	1	0	2	0	8	2	10	3	0	0	0	-	0	0-0	1	4.41	4.70
16 Mil	NL	2	0	0	0	1.2	7	2	2	2	2	0	0	0	0	0	3	0	0	0	0	-	0	0-0	0	10.43	10.80
16 Min	AL	8	0	0	3	14.2	65	15	10	10	5	0	1	0	10	0	11	2	0	0	0	-	0	0-0	0	7.60	6.14
17 SF		9	0	0	2	10.1	53	15	15	10	2	0	1	1	4	0	18	2	0	0	0	-	0	0-0	1	7.47	8.71
17 NYM	NL	20	0	0	7	21.0	100	20	15	15	4	0	2	0	17	0	26	1	0	0	1	.000	0	0-1	1	6.04	6.43
4 ML YEARS		116	0	0	30	113.0	497	98	62	53	17	0	8	3	62	2	136	13	1	4	4	.500	0	3-6	21	4.31	4.22

Noe Ramirez

Pitches: R Bats: R Pos: RP-12 no-AY Ht: 6'3" Wt: 205 Born: 12/22/1989 Age: 28

		HOW MUCH HE PITCHED						WHAT HE GAVE UP												THE RESULTS							
Year Team	Lg	G	GS	CG	GF	IP	BFP	H	R	ER	HR	SH	SF	HB	TBB	IBB	SO	WP	Bk	W	L	Pct	Sh	Sv-Op	Hld	ERC	ERA
2017 Pwtckt*	AAA	33	0	0	26	48.2	199	40	19	19	7	0	2	3	16	0	57	1	0	3	3	.500	0	5--	-	3.41	3.51
2015 Bos	AL	17	0	0	3	13.0	61	13	12	6	3	0	0	2	7	0	13	1	0	0	1	.000	0	0-0	0	6.15	4.15
2016 Bos	AL	14	0	0	7	13.0	61	16	9	9	4	0	2	2	8	1	15	0	0	0	0	-	0	0-0	0	9.08	6.23
2017 2 Tms	AL	12	0	0	1	13.0	49	6	5	4	2	0	0	0	5	0	14	0	0	0	0	-	0	0-0	0	1.68	2.77
17 Bos	AL	2	0	0	1	4.2	18	3	2	2	2	0	0	0	1	0	4	0	0	0	0	-	0	0-0	0	3.21	3.86
17 LAA	AL	10	0	0	0	8.1	31	3	3	2	0	0	0	0	4	0	10	0	0	0	0	-	0	0-0	0	1.02	2.16
3 ML YEARS		43	0	0	11	39.0	171	35	26	19	9	0	2	4	20	1	42	1	0	0	1	.000	0	0-0	4	5.33	4.38

AJ Ramos

Pitches: R Bats: R Pos: RP-61 Ht: 5'10" Wt: 200 Born: 9/20/1986 Age: 31

		HOW MUCH HE PITCHED						WHAT HE GAVE UP												THE RESULTS							
Year Team	Lg	G	GS	CG	GF	IP	BFP	H	R	ER	HR	SH	SF	HB	TBB	IBB	SO	WP	Bk	W	L	Pct	Sh	Sv-Op	Hld	ERC	ERA
2012 Mia	NL	11	0	0	4	9.1	40	8	4	4	2	0	0	1	4	0	13	0	0	0	0	-	0	0-1	1	4.65	3.86
2013 Mia	NL	68	0	0	18	80.0	338	58	32	28	4	1	3	2	43	3	86	1	0	3	4	.429	0	0-4	11	2.80	3.15
2014 Mia	NL	68	0	0	12	64.0	270	36	16	15	1	3	1	3	43	7	73	7	0	7	0	1.000	0	0-3	20	2.19	2.11
2015 Mia	NL	71	0	0	51	70.1	277	45	18	18	6	1	2	3	26	0	87	2	0	2	4	.333	0	32-38	4	2.21	2.30
2016 Mia	NL	67	0	0	52	64.0	278	52	21	20	1	2	4	4	35	3	73	6	0	1	4	.200	0	40-43	2	3.15	2.81
2017 2 Tms	NL	61	0	0	55	58.2	258	49	27	26	7	1	2	1	34	1	72	7	0	2	4	.333	0	27-30	1	4.06	3.99
17 Mia	NL	40	0	0	38	39.2	171	30	17	16	4	1	0	2	22	1	47	4	0	2	4	.333	0	20-22	1	3.46	3.63
17 NYM	NL	21	0	0	17	19.0	87	19	10	10	3	0	1	0	12	0	25	3	0	0	0	-	0	7-8	1	5.39	4.74
6 ML YEARS		346	0	0	192	346.1	1461	248	118	111	21	8	11	15	185	14	404	23	0	15	16	.484	0	99-119	39	2.89	2.88

Edubray Ramos

Pitches: R Bats: R Pos: RP-59 eh-DOO-bray Ht: 6'0" Wt: 160 Born: 12/19/1992 Age: 25

		HOW MUCH HE PITCHED						WHAT HE GAVE UP												THE RESULTS							
Year Team	Lg	G	GS	CG	GF	IP	BFP	H	R	ER	HR	SH	SF	HB	TBB	IBB	SO	WP	Bk	W	L	Pct	Sh	Sv-Op	Hld	ERC	ERA
2014 2 Tms	Low	19	1	0	12	32.0	124	19	3	3	0	1	0	2	7	1	37	3	0	1	0	1.000	0	6--	-	1.22	0.84
2015 Clrwtr	A+	29	0	0	16	49.1	181	31	9	8	2	0	2	1	6	0	47	4	2	3	4	.429	0	8--	-	1.25	1.46
2015 Rdng	AA	18	0	0	7	20.1	89	17	9	8	0	2	2	2	10	2	18	0	1	1	2	.333	0	0--	-	2.99	3.54
2016 Rdng	AA	11	0	0	10	15.0	56	9	5	4	1	0	1	1	1	0	15	1	0	1	1	.500	0	7--	-	1.20	2.40
2016 LV	AAA	15	0	0	8	23.2	90	15	1	1	0	0	0	1	3	0	26	1	0	1	0	1.000	0	3--	-	1.14	0.38
2017 LV	AAA	10	0	0	5	11.2	46	7	3	2	0	1	0	0	4	1	10	0	0	1	0	1.000	0	1--	-	1.31	1.54
2016 Phi	NL	42	0	0	6	40.0	160	36	18	17	5	1	0	0	11	1	40	1	1	1	3	.250	0	0-2	15	3.28	3.83
2017 Phi	NL	59	0	0	18	57.2	256	57	29	27	4	2	1	0	28	3	75	5	1	2	7	.222	0	0-3	9	3.97	4.21
2 ML YEARS		101	0	0	24	97.2	416	93	47	44	9	3	1	0	39	4	115	6	2	3	10	.231	0	0-5	24	3.69	4.05

Wilson Ramos

Bats: R Throws: R Pos: C-62;PH-3;DH-1 Ht: 6'1" Wt: 260 Born: 8/10/1987 Age: 30

		BATTING																	RUNNING			AVERAGES			
Year Team	Lg	G	AB	H	2B	3B	HR	(Hm Rd)	TB	R	RBI	RC	TBB	IBB	SO	HBP	SH	SF	SB	CS	GDP	Avg	OBP	Slg	OPS
2010 2 Tms		22	79	22	7	0	1	(1 0)	32	5	5	10	2	0	12	1	0	0	0	0	0	.278	.305	.405	.710
2011 Was	NL	113	389	104	22	1	15	(8 7)	173	48	52	43	38	4	76	2	4	2	0	2	19	.267	.334	.445	.779
2012 Was	NL	25	83	22	2	0	3	(1 2)	33	11	10	12	12	2	19	0	0	1	0	0	1	.265	.354	.398	.752
2013 Was	NL	78	287	78	9	0	16	(6 10)	135	29	59	40	15	1	42	0	0	1	0	1	5	.272	.307	.470	.777
2014 Was	NL	88	341	91	12	0	11	(3 8)	136	32	47	35	17	2	57	0	0	3	0	0	17	.267	.299	.399	.698
2015 Was	NL	128	475	109	16	0	15	(10 5)	170	41	68	39	21	2	101	0	0	8	0	0	16	.229	.258	.358	.616
2016 Was	NL	131	482	148	25	0	22	(12 10)	239	58	80	78	35	4	79	2	0	4	0	0	17	.307	.354	.496	.850
2017 TB	AL	64	208	54	6	0	11	(3 8)	93	19	35	27	10	2	36	0	0	3	0	0	11	.260	.290	.447	.737
10 Min	AL	7	27	8	3	0	0	(0 0)	11	2	1	3	0	0	3	1	0	0	0	0	1	.296	.321	.407	.729
10 Was	AL	15	52	14	4	0	1	(1 0)	21	3	4	7	2	0	9	0	0	0	0	0	1	.269	.296	.404	.700
Postseason		4	17	2	0	0	0	(0 0)	2	1	0	0	1	0	6	0	1	0	0	0	1	.118	.167	.118	.284
8 ML YEARS		649	2344	628	99	1	94	(44 50)	1011	243	356	284	150	19	422	5	4	22	0	3	95	.268	.311	.431	.742

Colby Rasmus

Bats: L **Throws:** L **Pos:** LF-23;RF-7;PH-7;DH-5;CF-1   **Ht:** 6'2" **Wt:** 195 **Born:** 8/11/1986 **Age:** 31

Year	Team	Lg	G	AB	H	2B	3B	HR	(Hm	Rd)	TB	R	RBI	RC	TBB	IBB	SO	HBP	SH	SF	SB	CS	GDP	Avg	OBP	Slg	OPS
2009	StL	NL	147	474	119	22	2	16	(7	9)	193	72	52	60	36	3	95	3	5	2	3	1	5	.251	.307	.407	.714
2010	StL	NL	144	464	128	28	3	23	(11	12)	231	85	66	76	63	9	148	1	2	4	12	8	5	.276	.361	.498	.859
2011	2 Tms		129	471	106	24	6	14	(4	10)	184	75	53	50	50	2	116	0	2	3	5	2	10	.225	.298	.391	.688
2012	Tor	AL	151	565	126	21	5	23	(8	15)	226	75	75	74	47	5	149	7	2	4	4	3	7	.223	.289	.400	.689
2013	Tor	AL	118	417	115	26	1	22	(14	8)	209	57	66	76	37	0	135	3	0	1	0	1	4	.276	.338	.501	.840
2014	Tor	AL	104	346	78	21	1	18	(7	11)	155	45	40	38	29	2	124	1	1	0	4	0	1	.225	.287	.448	.735
2015	Hou	AL	137	432	103	23	2	25	(12	13)	205	67	61	67	47	0	154	2	1	3	2	1	5	.238	.314	.475	.789
2016	Hou	AL	107	369	76	10	0	15	(6	9)	131	38	54	46	43	0	121	0	1	4	4	1	5	.206	.286	.355	.641
2017	TB	AL	37	121	34	7	1	9	(6	3)	70	17	23	19	7	2	45	0	0	1	1	0	1	.281	.318	.579	.896
11	StL	NL	94	338	83	14	6	11	(4	7)	142	61	40	43	45	2	77	0	1	2	5	2	8	.246	.332	.420	.753
11	Tor	AL	35	133	23	10	0	3	(0	3)	42	14	13	7	5	0	39	0	1	1	0	0	2	.173	.201	.316	.517
	Postseason		9	26	11	4	0	4	(1	3)	27	5	7	8	9	2	8	0	0	0	1	0	1	.423	.571	1.038	1.610
	9 ML YEARS		1074	3659	885	182	21	165	(75	90)	1604	531	490	506	359	23	1087	17	13	22	35	17	44	.242	.311	.438	.749

Josh Ravin

Pitches: R **Bats:** R **Pos:** RP-14   **Ht:** 6'4" **Wt:** 215 **Born:** 1/21/1988 **Age:** 30

Year	Team	Lg	G	GS	CG	GF	IP	BFP	H	R	ER	HR	SH	SF	HB	TBB	IBB	SO	WP	Bk	W	L	Pct	Sh	Sv-Op	Hld	ERC	ERA
2017	OkCity*	AAA	30	0	0	8	35.1	156	29	20	17	2	1	3	1	19	2	55	4	0	4	0	1.000	0	2- -	-	3.23	4.33
2015	LAD	NL	9	0	0	4	9.1	47	13	7	7	3	0	0	1	4	0	12	1	0	2	1	.667	0	0-0	0	8.54	6.75
2016	LAD	NL	10	0	0	4	9.2	35	2	1	1	1	0	0		4	0	13	2	0	0	0	-	0	0-0	0	0.83	0.93
2017	LAD	NL	14	0	0	3	16.2	71	12	12	12	4	0	0	1	9	1	19	0	0	0	1	.000	0	1-1	1	4.16	6.48
	3 ML YEARS		33	0	0	11	35.2	153	27	20	20	8	0	0	2	17	1	44	3	0	2	2	.500	0	1-1	1	3.98	5.05

Robbie Ray

Pitches: L **Bats:** L **Pos:** SP-28   **Ht:** 6'2" **Wt:** 195 **Born:** 10/1/1991 **Age:** 26

Year	Team	Lg	G	GS	CG	GF	IP	BFP	H	R	ER	HR	SH	SF	HB	TBB	IBB	SO	WP	Bk	W	L	Pct	Sh	Sv-Op	Hld	ERC	ERA
2014	Det	AL	9	6	0	1	28.2	136	43	26	26	5	1	1	0	11	0	19	2	1	1	4	.200	0	0-0	1	7.72	8.16
2015	Ari	NL	23	23	0	0	127.2	545	121	56	50	9	7	6	8	49	3	119	2	0	5	12	.294	0	0-0	0	3.75	3.52
2016	Ari	NL	32	32	0	0	174.1	776	185	105	95	24	3	2	6	71	4	218	8	0	8	15	.348	0	0-0	0	4.78	4.90
2017	Ari	NL	28	28	1	0	162.0	665	116	57	52	23	4	3	5	71	3	218	8	0	15	5	.750	1	0-0	0	3.08	2.89
	4 ML YEARS		92	89	1	1	492.2	2122	465	244	223	61	15	12	19	202	10	574	20	1	29	36	.446	1	0-0	1	4.09	4.07

Colin Rea

ray

Pitches: R **Bats:** R **Pos:** P   **Ht:** 6'5" **Wt:** 225 **Born:** 7/1/1990 **Age:** 27

Year	Team	Lg	G	GS	CG	GF	IP	BFP	H	R	ER	HR	SH	SF	HB	TBB	IBB	SO	WP	Bk	W	L	Pct	Sh	Sv-Op	Hld	ERC	ERA
2013	2 Tms	Low	31	12	0	5	86.0	389	77	45	39	4	3	6	5	61	3	83	10	2	2	6	.250	0	0- -	-	4.48	4.08
2014	Lk Els	A+	28	28	0	0	139.0	597	151	65	60	11	2	0	7	37	0	118	4	2	11	9	.550	0	0- -	-	4.10	3.88
2015	SnAnt	AA	12	12	0	0	75.0	283	50	15	9	1	1	0	1	11	0	60	1	0	3	2	.600	0	0- -	-	1.28	1.08
2015	ElPaso	AAA	6	6	0	0	26.2	120	29	14	12	2	0	0	2	12	1	20	0	0	2	2	.500	0	0- -	-	4.83	4.05
2015	SD	NL	6	6	0	0	31.2	133	29	16	15	2	1	2	1	11	0	26	0	0	2	2	.500	0	0-0	0	3.29	4.26
2016	2 Tms	NL	20	19	0	0	102.2	454	102	63	55	12	4	2	8	44	4	80	0	1	5	5	.500	0	0-0	0	4.50	4.82
16	SD	NL	19	18	0	0	99.1	443	101	63	55	12	3	2	8	44	4	76	0	1	5	5	.500	0	0-0	0	4.73	4.98
16	Mia	NL	1	1	0	0	3.1	11	1	0	0	0	0	0	0	0	0	4	0	0	0	0	-	0	0-0	0	0.21	0.00
	2 ML YEARS		26	25	0	0	134.1	587	131	79	70	14	5	4	9	55	4	106	0	1	7	7	.500	0	0-0	0	4.21	4.69

Raudy Read

ROW-dee

Bats: R **Throws:** R **Pos:** PH-7;C-3   **Ht:** 6'0" **Wt:** 170 **Born:** 10/29/1993 **Age:** 24

Year	Team	Lg	G	AB	H	2B	3B	HR	(Hm	Rd)	TB	R	RBI	RC	TBB	IBB	SO	HBP	SH	SF	SB	CS	GDP	Avg	OBP	Slg	OPS
2013	Nats	R	40	147	37	5	0	2	(-	-)	48	9	17	12	6	0	17	2	1	2	2	6	4	.252	.287	.327	.613
2014	Auburn	A-	57	210	59	20	0	6	(-	-)	97	27	35	31	14	0	37	3	0	2	0	3	4	.281	.332	.462	.794
2015	2 Tms	Low	87	313	79	22	1	5	(-	-)	118	39	41	38	27	0	53	3	1	3	4	3	10	.252	.315	.377	.692
2016	Ptomc	A+	101	386	101	30	1	9	(-	-)	160	54	51	54	31	3	53	6	0	3	6	3	17	.262	.324	.415	.738
2017	Hrsbrg	AA	108	411	109	25	1	17	(-	-)	187	44	61	60	27	0	79	2	0	2	2	0	9	.265	.312	.455	.767
2017	Was	NL	8	11	3	0	0	0	(0	0)	3	1	0	1	0	0	3	0	0	0	0	0	0	.273	.273	.273	.545

J.T. Realmuto

ray-al-MOO-toh

Bats: R **Throws:** R **Pos:** C-126;1B-9;PH-6;DH-2   **Ht:** 6'1" **Wt:** 210 **Born:** 3/18/1991 **Age:** 27

Year	Team	Lg	G	AB	H	2B	3B	HR	(Hm	Rd)	TB	R	RBI	RC	TBB	IBB	SO	HBP	SH	SF	SB	CS	GDP	Avg	OBP	Slg	OPS
2014	Mia	NL	11	29	7	1	1	0	(0	0)	10	4	9	4	1	0	8	0	0	0	0	0	2	.241	.267	.345	.611
2015	Mia	NL	126	441	114	21	7	10	(6	4)	179	49	47	44	19	2	70	2	1	4	8	4	11	.259	.290	.406	.696
2016	Mia	NL	137	509	154	31	0	11	(3	8)	218	60	48	63	28	1	100	5	0	3	12	4	12	.303	.343	.428	.771
2017	Mia	NL	141	532	148	31	5	17	(5	12)	240	68	65	74	36	4	106	8	0	3	8	2	13	.278	.332	.451	.783
	4 ML YEARS		415	1511	423	84	13	38	(14	24)	647	181	169	185	84	7	284	15	1	10	28	10	38	.280	.322	.428	.750

Anthony Recker

Bats: R **Throws:** R **Pos:** C-4;PH-2;PR-1   **Ht:** 6'2" **Wt:** 240 **Born:** 8/29/1983 **Age:** 34

								BATTING												RUNNING			AVERAGES			
Year	Team	Lg	G	AB	H	2B	3B	HR	(Hm | Rd)	TB	R	RBI	RC	TBB	IBB	SO	HBP	SH	SF	SB	CS	GDP	Avg	OBP	Slg	OPS
2017	Gwnntt*	AAA	41	139	31	8	1	4	(- | -)	53	20	10	17	11	0	48	5	0	1	0	0	5	.223	.301	.381	.683
2017	Roch*	AAA	19	70	20	9	0	0	(- | -)	29	9	8	10	4	0	15	2	0	2	0	0	2	.286	.333	.414	.748
2011	Oak	AL	5	17	3	1	0	0	(0 | 0)	4	3	0	0	4	0	7	0	0	0	0	0	0	.176	.333	.235	.569
2012	2 Tms		22	49	7	2	0	1	(0 | 1)	12	4	4	0	6	0	15	2	1	0	0	0	1	.143	.263	.245	.508
2013	NYM	NL	50	135	29	7	0	6	(4 | 2)	54	17	19	13	13	1	49	0	1	2	0	1	2	.215	.280	.400	.680
2014	NYM	NL	58	174	35	9	0	7	(3 | 4)	65	18	27	17	10	0	64	1	2	2	1	1	2	.201	.246	.374	.620
2015	NYM	NL	32	80	10	1	0	2	(0 | 2)	17	6	5	3	11	2	35	1	0	0	1	0	1	.125	.239	.213	.452
2016	Atl	NL	33	90	25	8	0	2	(0 | 2)	39	6	15	19	16	1	22	2	3	1	1	0	0	.278	.394	.433	.828
2017	Atl	NL	6	7	1	0	0	0	(0 | 0)	1	0	0	0	0	0	1	0	0	0	0	0	1	.143	.143	.143	.286
12	Oak	AL	13	31	4	1	0	0	(0 | 0)	5	3	0	0	4	0	13	1	1	0	0	0	0	.129	.250	.161	.411
12	ChC	NL	9	18	3	1	0	1	(0 | 1)	7	1	4	0	2	0	2	1	0	0	0	0	1	.167	.286	.389	.675
	7 ML YEARS		206	552	110	28	0	18	(7 | 11)	192	55	70	52	60	4	193	6	7	5	3	2	6	.199	.283	.348	.630

Josh Reddick

Bats: L **Throws:** R **Pos:** RF-102;LF-48;CF-11;PH-6;PR-2;1B-1;DH-1   **Ht:** 6'2" **Wt:** 195 **Born:** 2/19/1987 **Age:** 31

								BATTING												RUNNING			AVERAGES			
Year	Team	Lg	G	AB	H	2B	3B	HR	(Hm	Rd)	TB	R	RBI	RC	TBB	IBB	SO	HBP	SH	SF	SB	CS	GDP	Avg	OBP	Slg	OPS
2009	Bos	AL	27	59	10	4	0	2	(0	2)	20	5	4	4	2	0	17	1	0	0	0	0	0	.169	.210	.339	.549
2010	Bos	AL	29	62	12	3	1	1	(1	0)	20	5	5	1	1	0	15	0	0	0	0	1	1	.194	.206	.323	.529
2011	Bos	AL	87	254	71	18	3	7	(2	5)	116	41	28	33	19	1	50	1	0	4	1	2	1	.280	.327	.457	.784
2012	Oak	AL	156	611	148	29	5	32	(18	14)	283	85	85	73	55	8	151	2	1	4	11	1	15	.242	.305	.463	.768
2013	Oak	AL	114	385	87	19	2	12	(2	10)	146	54	56	53	46	1	86	2	1	7	9	2	4	.226	.307	.379	.686
2014	Oak	AL	109	363	96	16	7	12	(5	7)	162	53	54	54	28	0	63	1	0	3	1	1	3	.264	.316	.446	.763
2015	Oak	AL	149	526	143	25	4	20	(7	13)	236	67	77	83	49	1	65	0	1	2	10	2	7	.272	.333	.449	.781
2016	2 Tms		115	398	112	17	1	10	(5	5)	161	53	37	54	39	5	56	0	0	1	8	3	8	.281	.345	.405	.749
2017	Hou	AL	134	477	150	34	4	13	(6	7)	231	77	82	88	43	1	72	0	1	12	7	3	9	.314	.363	.484	.847
16	Oak	AL	68	243	72	11	1	8	(3	5)	109	33	28	42	28	5	34	0	0	0	5	0	7	.296	.368	.449	.816
16	LAD	NL	47	155	40	6	0	2	(2	0)	52	20	9	12	11	0	22	0	0	0	3	3	1	.258	.307	.335	.643
	Postseason		21	64	16	1	0	2	(0	2)	23	7	4	5	6	1	17	0	0	0	3	0	1	.250	.314	.359	.672
	9 ML YEARS		920	3135	829	165	27	109	(46	63)	1375	440	428	443	282	17	575	7	4	33	48	14	48	.264	.323	.439	.762

A.J. Reed

Bats: L **Throws:** L **Pos:** 1B-1;DH-1   **Ht:** 6'4" **Wt:** 275 **Born:** 5/10/1993 **Age:** 25

								BATTING												RUNNING			AVERAGES			
Year	Team	Lg	G	AB	H	2B	3B	HR	(Hm	Rd)	TB	R	RBI	RC	TBB	IBB	SO	HBP	SH	SF	SB	CS	GDP	Avg	OBP	Slg	OPS
2014	2 Tms	Low	68	249	72	20	1	12	(-	-)	130	43	54	49	30	1	54	5	0	1	2	0	4	.289	.375	.522	.898
2015	Lancst	A+	82	318	110	16	4	23	(-	-)	203	75	81	88	59	1	73	4	0	4	0	0	9	.346	.449	.638	1.088
2015	CpChr	AAA	53	205	68	14	1	11	(-	-)	117	38	46	47	27	2	49	1	0	4	0	0	5	.332	.405	.571	.976
2016	Fresno	AAA	70	261	76	22	1	15	(-	-)	145	42	50	53	32	1	67	1	0	2	0	0	8	.291	.368	.556	.924
2017	Fresno	AAA	127	476	124	24	0	34	(-	-)	250	89	104	92	72	3	146	3	0	5	0	0	13	.261	.358	.525	.883
2016	Hou	AL	45	122	20	3	0	3	(2	1)	32	11	8	7	18	0	48	0	0	1	0	0	1	.164	.270	.262	.532
2017	Hou	AL	2	6	0	0	0	0	(0	0)	0	0	0	0	0	0	1	0	0	0	0	0	0	.000	.000	.000	.000
	2 ML YEARS		47	128	20	3	0	3	(2	1)	32	11	8	7	18	0	49	0	0	1	0	0	1	.156	.259	.250	.509

Addison Reed

Pitches: R **Bats:** L **Pos:** RP-77   **Ht:** 6'4" **Wt:** 230 **Born:** 12/27/1988 **Age:** 29

			HOW MUCH HE PITCHED						WHAT HE GAVE UP										THE RESULTS						
Year	Team	Lg	G	GS	CG	GF	IP	BFP	H	R	ER	HR	SH	SF	HB	TBB	IBB	SO	WP	Bk	W	L	Pct	Sh	Sv-Op	Hld	ERC	ERA
2011	CWS	AL	6	0	0	2	7.1	33	10	3	3	1	0	0	0	1	0	12	0	1	0	0	-	0	0-0	0	5.24	3.68
2012	CWS	AL	62	0	0	44	55.0	238	57	30	29	6	0	4	2	18	3	54	0	1	3	2	.600	0	29-33	4	4.09	4.75
2013	CWS	AL	68	0	0	59	71.1	295	56	31	30	6	3	6	2	23	2	72	2	0	5	4	.556	0	40-48	0	2.56	3.79
2014	Ari	NL	62	0	0	55	59.1	252	57	31	28	11	1	1	1	15	2	69	3	0	1	7	.125	0	32-38	0	3.76	4.25
2015	2 Tms	NL	55	0	0	14	56.0	241	58	21	21	3	1	0	0	19	6	51	2	0	3	3	.500	0	4-8	14	3.52	3.38
2016	NYM	NL	80	0	0	13	77.2	304	60	18	17	4	3	2	0	13	4	91	0	0	4	2	.667	0	1-5	40	1.72	1.97
2017	2 Tms	NL	77	0	0	32	76.0	306	65	24	24	11	1	2	1	15	3	76	2	0	2	3	.400	0	19-21	15	2.79	2.84
15	Ari	NL	38	0	0	11	40.2	181	47	19	19	2	1	0	0	14	5	34	2	0	2	2	.500	0	3-5	8	4.10	4.20
15	NYM	NL	17	0	0	3	15.1	60	11	2	2	1	0	0	0	5	1	17	0	0	1	1	.500	0	1-3	6	2.10	1.17
17	NYM	NL	48	0	0	31	49.0	200	49	14	14	6	0	2	0	6	1	48	1	0	1	2	.333	0	19-21	4	3.09	2.57
17	Bos	AL	29	0	0	1	27.0	106	16	10	10	5	1	0	1	9	2	28	1	0	1	1	.500	0	0-0	11	2.27	3.33
	Postseason		10	0	0	0	8.0	35	7	6	5	0	1	1	0	3	2	4	0	0	1	0	1.000	0	0-0	2	2.13	5.63
	7 ML YEARS		410	0	0	219	402.2	1669	363	158	152	42	9	15	6	104	20	425	13	1	18	21	.462	0	125-153	73	2.98	3.40

Cody Reed

Pitches: L **Bats:** L **Pos:** RP-11; SP-1   **Ht:** 6'5" **Wt:** 228 **Born:** 4/15/1993 **Age:** 25

			HOW MUCH HE PITCHED						WHAT HE GAVE UP										THE RESULTS						
Year	Team	Lg	G	GS	CG	GF	IP	BFP	H	R	ER	HR	SH	SF	HB	TBB	IBB	SO	WP	Bk	W	L	Pct	Sh	Sv-Op	Hld	ERC	ERA
2013	Idaho	R+	15	6	0	1	29.2	145	31	24	20	0	2	1	4	23	0	25	4	0	0	1	.000	0	0- -		5.48	6.07
2014	Lxngtn	A	19	19	0	0	84.0	387	105	66	51	5	8	3	3	36	0	58	11	1	3	9	.250	0	0- -		5.47	5.46
2015	Wilmg	A+	13	10	1	2	67.1	278	62	19	16	3	1	3	1	18	0	65	3	0	5	5	.500	0	1- --		2.84	2.14
2015	NWArk	AA	5	5	0	0	28.2	120	26	16	11	3	0	2	1	8	0	19	1	0	2	2	.500	0	0- -		3.23	3.45
2015	Pnscla	AA	8	8	0	0	49.2	201	39	14	12	1	5	1	2	16	0	60	1	1	6	2	.750	0	0- -		2.32	2.17
2016	Lsvlle	AAA	13	13	0	0	73.0	301	71	28	25	6	3	1	3	20	0	65	1	0	6	4	.600	0	0- -		3.55	3.08

	HOW MUCH HE PITCHED				WHAT HE GAVE UP												THE RESULTS							
Year Team	Lg	G GS CG GF	IP	BFP	H	R	ER	HR	SH	SF	HB	TBB	IBB	SO	WP	Bk	W	L	Pct	Sh	Sv-Op	Hld	ERC	ERA
2017 Lsvlle	AAA	21 20 0 1	106.1	479	105	49	42	7	5	0	10	61	0	102	13	0	4	9	.308	0	0--	-	4.86	3.55
2016 Cin	NL	10 10 0 0	47.2	230	67	47	39	12	1	1	4	19	2	43	2	2	0	7	.000	0	0-0	0	8.00	7.36
2017 Cin	NL	12 1 0 3	17.2	79	11	11	10	3	0	0	0	19	3	17	2	0	1	1	.500	0	1-1	-	4.97	5.09
2 ML YEARS		22 11 0 3	65.1	309	78	58	49	15	1	1	4	38	5	60	4	2	1	8	.111	0	1-1	0	7.17	6.75

Rob Refsnyder

REF-snide-er

Bats: R Throws: R Pos: 2B-20;PH-12;LF-10;1B-6;DH-6;PR-6;RF-4

Ht: 6'0" Wt: 200 Born: 3/26/1991 Age: 27

							BATTING												RUNNING			AVERAGES			
Year Team	Lg	G	AB	H	2B	3B	HR	(Hm Rd)	TB	R	RBI	RC	TBB	IBB	SO	HBP	SH	SF	SB	CS	GDP	Avg	OBP	Slg	OPS
2017 S-WB*	AAA	38	138	43	11	2	2	(- -)	64	20	12	26	15	1	30	4	0	2	2	1	2	.312	.390	.464	.854
2015 NYY	AL	16	43	13	3	0	2	(1 1)	22	3	5	6	3	1	7	0	0	0	2	0	3	.302	.348	.512	.859
2016 NYY	AL	58	152	38	9	0	0	(0 0)	47	25	12	14	18	2	30	1	0	3	2	1	5	.250	.328	.309	.637
2017 2 Tms	AL	52	88	15	2	1	0	(0 0)	19	8	0	0	8	1	17	1	0	0	4	1	2	.170	.247	.216	.463
17 NYY	AL	20	37	5	1	1	0	(0 0)	8	3	0	0	3	0	8	0	0	0	2	0	0	.135	.200	.216	.416
17 Tor	AL	32	51	10	1	0	0	(0 0)	11	5	0	0	5	1	9	1	0	0	2	1	2	.196	.281	.216	.496
Postseason		1	3	0	0	0	0	(0 0)	0	0	0	0	0	0	0	0	0	0	0	0	0	.000	.000	.000	.000
3 ML YEARS		126	283	66	14	1	2	(1 1)	88	36	17	20	29	4	54	2	0	3	8	2	10	.233	.306	.311	.617

Jack Reinheimer

Bats: R Throws: R Pos: SS-1;PH-1

Ht: 6'1" Wt: 185 Born: 7/19/1992 Age: 25

							BATTING												RUNNING			AVERAGES			
Year Team	Lg	G	AB	H	2B	3B	HR	(Hm Rd)	TB	R	RBI	RC	TBB	IBB	SO	HBP	SH	SF	SB	CS	GDP	Avg	OBP	Slg	OPS
2013 Everett	A-	66	249	67	6	1	2	(- -)	81	39	30	34	32	0	51	4	4	2	18	5	7	.269	.359	.325	.684
2014 2 Tms	Low	130	521	144	22	5	3	(- -)	185	84	58	70	43	0	88	7	5	3	39	11	6	.276	.338	.355	.693
2015 Jacksn	AA	48	202	56	10	1	1	(- -)	71	25	16	25	14	0	39	0	2	1	12	1	7	.277	.323	.351	.674
2015 Mobile	AA	76	283	75	14	2	4	(- -)	105	39	26	40	37	1	54	4	1	3	9	5	3	.265	.355	.371	.726
2016 Reno	AAA	132	500	144	28	7	2	(- -)	192	64	48	71	48	0	93	4	4	4	20	11	4	.288	.353	.384	.737
2017 Reno	AAA	129	482	134	19	2	4	(- -)	169	87	56	61	47	0	86	2	0	6	12	8	9	.278	.341	.351	.691
2017 Ari	NL	2	5	0	0	0	0	(0 0)	0	0	0	0	0	0	3	0	0	0	0	0	0	.000	.000	.000	.000

Zac Reininger

Pitches: R Bats: B Pos: RP-10

Ht: 6'3" Wt: 170 Born: 1/28/1993 Age: 25

	HOW MUCH HE PITCHED				WHAT HE GAVE UP												THE RESULTS							
Year Team	Lg	G GS CG GF	IP	BFP	H	R	ER	HR	SH	SF	HB	TBB	IBB	SO	WP	Bk	W	L	Pct	Sh	Sv-Op	Hld	ERC	ERA
2013 Conn	A-	22 1 0 16	27.0	107	17	6	3	0	0	1	1	6	1	32	2	1	1	2	.333	0	10--	-	1.25	1.00
2014 Wmich	A	33 0 0 26	56.2	230	42	18	16	3	1	2	3	17	1	58	2	0	4	4	.500	0	11--	-	2.22	2.54
2015 Lkland	A+	7 0 0 5	13.1	52	8	0	0	0	1	0	1	5	1	8	0	0	1	0	1.000	0	3--	-	1.60	0.00
2015 Erie	AA	9 0 0 3	12.1	62	19	16	14	3	1	1	0	7	1	9	2	0	0	2	.000	0	0--	-	9.21	10.22
2016 2 Tms	Low	8 0 0 1	11.2	42	4	0	0	0	0	0	0	4	0	13	1	0	0	0	-	0	0--	-	0.78	0.00
2017 Lkland	A+	17 0 0 5	28.0	109	22	12	12	2	1	0	1	6	0	26	4	0	1	1	.500	0	0--	-	2.29	3.86
2017 Erie	AA	16 0 0 3	24.1	90	13	5	4	0	0	4	0	8	1	29	0	0	1	1	.500	0	1--	-	1.19	1.48
2017 Toledo	AAA	9 0 0 1	11.1	43	7	2	2	0	0	0	0	4	0	5	0	0	1	0	1.000	0	1--	-	1.53	1.59
2017 Det	AL	10 0 0 3	9.2	47	15	8	8	3	0	1	0	3	0	5	2	0	0	0	-	0	0-0	0	8.63	7.45

Anthony Rendon

ren-DOAN

Bats: R Throws: R Pos: 3B-145;PH-2

Ht: 6'1" Wt: 210 Born: 6/6/1990 Age: 28

							BATTING												RUNNING			AVERAGES			
Year Team	Lg	G	AB	H	2B	3B	HR	(Hm Rd)	TB	R	RBI	RC	TBB	IBB	SO	HBP	SH	SF	SB	CS	GDP	Avg	OBP	Slg	OPS
2013 Was	NL	98	351	93	23	1	7	(3 4)	139	40	35	43	31	3	69	5	2	5	1	1	7	.265	.329	.396	.726
2014 Was	NL	153	613	176	39	6	21	(10 11)	290	111	83	97	58	2	104	5	2	5	17	3	11	.287	.351	.473	.824
2015 Was	NL	80	311	82	16	0	5	(3 2)	113	43	25	39	36	0	70	4	0	4	1	2	8	.264	.344	.363	.707
2016 Was	NL	156	567	153	38	2	20	(11 9)	255	91	85	95	65	2	117	7	0	8	12	6	5	.270	.348	.450	.797
2017 Was	NL	147	508	153	41	1	25	(14 11)	271	81	100	115	84	6	82	7	0	6	7	2	7	.301	.403	.533	.937
Postseason		9	39	10	0	0	1	(0 1)	13	1	5	5	2	0	8	0	0	0	1	0	0	.256	.293	.333	.626
5 ML YEARS		634	2350	657	157	10	78	(41 37)	1068	366	328	389	274	13	442	28	4	28	38	14	38	.280	.358	.454	.812

Hunter Renfroe

Bats: R Throws: R Pos: RF-120;PH-3;DH-1

Ht: 6'1" Wt: 220 Born: 1/28/1992 Age: 26

							BATTING												RUNNING			AVERAGES			
Year Team	Lg	G	AB	H	2B	3B	HR	(Hm Rd)	TB	R	RBI	RC	TBB	IBB	SO	HBP	SH	SF	SB	CS	GDP	Avg	OBP	Slg	OPS
2013 2 Tms	Low	43	170	46	14	0	6	(- -)	78	26	25	24	9	1	49	1	1	2	0	0	3	.271	.308	.459	.767
2014 Lk Els	A+	69	278	82	21	3	16	(- -)	157	46	52	58	28	3	81	7	0	3	9	3	5	.295	.370	.565	.935
2014 SnAnt	AA	60	224	52	12	0	5	(- -)	79	17	23	25	25	0	53	0	0	2	2	1	6	.232	.307	.353	.659
2015 SnAnt	AA	112	421	109	22	3	14	(- -)	179	50	54	58	33	1	112	3	0	6	4	1	8	.259	.313	.425	.738
2015 ElPaso	AAA	21	90	30	5	2	6	(- -)	57	15	24	19	4	0	20	0	0	1	1	0	3	.333	.358	.633	.991
2016 ElPaso	AAA	133	533	162	34	5	30	(- -)	296	95	104	97	22	3	115	4	0	4	5	2	11	.304	.334	.555	.889
2017 ElPaso	AAA	14	55	28	7	1	4	(- -)	49	18	18	21	6	1	7	0	0	0	1	0	2	.509	.557	.891	1.448
2016 SD	NL	11	35	13	3	0	4	(4 0)	28	8	14	10	1	1	5	0	0	0	0	0	1	.371	.389	.800	1.189
2017 SD	NL	122	445	103	25	1	26	(14 12)	208	51	58	48	27	1	140	6	0	1	3	0	4	.231	.284	.467	.751
2 ML YEARS		133	480	116	28	1	30	(18 12)	236	59	72	58	28	2	145	6	0	1	3	0	5	.242	.291	.492	.783

Ben Revere

Bats: L **Throws:** R **Pos:** LF-78;PH-29;CF-6;DH-3;PR-2   **Ht:** 5'9" **Wt:** 175 **Born:** 5/3/1988 **Age:** 30

					BATTING																	RUNNING			AVERAGES	
Year	Team	Lg	G	AB	H	2B	3B	HR	(Hm | Rd)	TB	R	RBI	RC	TBB	IBB	SO	HBP	SH	SF	SB	CS	GDP	Avg	OBP	Slg	OPS
2010	Min	AL	13	28	5	0	0	0	(0 | 0)	5	1	2	0	2	0	5	0	0	0	0	1	1	.179	.233	.179	.412
2011	Min	AL	117	450	120	9	5	0	(0 | 0)	139	56	30	51	26	1	41	2	3	0	34	9	7	.267	.310	.309	.619
2012	Min	AL	124	511	150	13	6	0	(0 | 0)	175	70	32	62	29	0	54	3	6	4	40	9	8	.294	.333	.342	.675
2013	Phi	NL	88	315	96	9	3	0	(0 | 0)	111	37	17	39	16	1	36	0	5	0	22	8	10	.305	.338	.352	.691
2014	Phi	NL	151	601	184	13	7	2	(1 | 1)	217	71	28	71	13	1	49	4	7	1	49	8	11	.306	.325	.361	.686
2015	2 Tms		152	592	181	22	7	2	(1 | 1)	223	84	45	78	32	0	64	2	5	3	31	7	5	.306	.342	.377	.719
2016	Was	NL	103	350	76	9	7	2	(2 | 0)	105	44	24	29	18	0	34	3	2	2	14	5	12	.217	.260	.300	.560
2017	LAA	AL	109	291	80	13	2	1	(0 | 1)	100	37	20	31	15	0	25	0	0	2	21	6	7	.275	.308	.344	.652
15	Phi	NL	96	366	109	13	6	1	(1 | 0)	137	49	26	45	19	0	36	1	2	0	24	5	4	.298	.334	.374	.709
15	Tor	AL	56	226	72	9	1	1	(0 | 1)	86	35	19	33	13	0	28	1	3	3	7	2	1	.319	.354	.381	.734
	Postseason		11	47	12	1	0	0	(0 | 0)	13	7	1	4	4	0	7	0	0	0	2	0	0	.255	.314	.277	.590
	8 ML YEARS		857	3138	892	88	37	7	(4 | 3)	1075	400	198	361	151	3	308	14	28	12	211	53	61	.284	.319	.343	.661

Alex Reyes

Pitches: R **Bats:** R **Pos:** P   **Ht:** 6'3" **Wt:** 175 **Born:** 8/29/1994 **Age:** 23

			HOW MUCH HE PITCHED						WHAT HE GAVE UP									THE RESULTS						
Year	Team	Lg	G	GS	CG	GF	IP	BFP	H	R	ER	HR	SH	SF	HB	TBB	IBB	SO	WP	Bk	W	L	Pct	Sh	Sv-Op	Hld	ERC	ERA
2013	Jhscty	R+	12	12	0	0	58.1	253	54	26	22	1	2	2	4	28	0	68	8	1	6	4	.600	0	0--	-	3.67	3.39
2014	Peoria	A	21	21	1	0	109.0	465	82	54	44	6	2	2	3	61	0	137	10	3	7	7	.500	0	0--	-	3.12	3.63
2015	2 Tms	Low	14	14	0	0	66.2	271	49	20	16	0	1	0	4	31	0	99	4	2	2	5	.286	0	0--	-	2.55	2.16
2015	Sprgfld	AA	8	8	0	0	34.2	143	21	14	12	1	1	1	1	18	0	52	5	1	3	2	.600	0	0--	-	2.09	3.12
2016	Memp	AAA	14	14	0	0	65.1	291	63	38	36	6	4	1	4	32	0	93	7	1	2	3	.400	0	0--	-	4.37	4.96
2016	StL	NL	12	5	0	3	46.0	189	33	8	8	1	1	1	0	23	1	52	3	1	4	1	.800	0	1-1	1	2.43	1.57

Jose Reyes

Bats: B **Throws:** R **Pos:** SS-80;3B-36;2B-28;PH-11;LF-1;CF-1   **Ht:** 6'0" **Wt:** 195 **Born:** 6/11/1983 **Age:** 35

					BATTING																	RUNNING			AVERAGES	
Year	Team	Lg	G	AB	H	2B	3B	HR	(Hm | Rd)	TB	R	RBI	RC	TBB	IBB	SO	HBP	SH	SF	SB	CS	GDP	Avg	OBP	Slg	OPS
2003	NYM	NL	69	274	84	12	4	5	(1 | 4)	119	47	32	46	13	0	36	1	0	2	13	3	1	.307	.334	.434	.769
2004	NYM	NL	53	220	56	16	2	2	(1 | 1)	82	33	14	25	5	0	31	0	4	0	19	2	1	.255	.271	.373	.644
2005	NYM	NL	161	696	190	24	17	7	(2 | 5)	269	99	58	84	27	0	78	2	4	4	60	15	7	.273	.300	.386	.687
2006	NYM	NL	153	647	194	30	17	19	(9 | 10)	315	122	81	121	53	6	81	1	2	0	64	17	6	.300	.354	.487	.841
2007	NYM	NL	160	681	191	36	12	12	(7 | 5)	287	119	57	99	77	13	78	1	5	1	78	21	6	.280	.354	.421	.775
2008	NYM	NL	159	688	204	37	19	16	(9 | 7)	327	113	68	117	66	8	82	1	5	3	56	15	9	.297	.358	.475	.833
2009	NYM	NL	36	147	41	7	2	2	(1 | 1)	58	18	15	20	18	1	19	0	0	1	11	2	2	.279	.355	.395	.750
2010	NYM	NL	133	563	159	29	10	11	(8 | 3)	241	83	54	76	31	4	63	2	4	3	30	10	8	.282	.321	.428	.749
2011	NYM	NL	126	537	181	31	16	7	(4 | 3)	265	101	44	90	43	9	41	0	2	4	39	7	5	.337	.384	.493	.877
2012	Mia	NL	160	642	184	37	12	11	(4 | 7)	278	86	57	92	63	9	56	0	5	6	40	11	10	.287	.347	.433	.780
2013	Tor	AL	93	382	113	20	0	10	(7 | 3)	163	58	37	61	34	2	47	1	0	2	15	6	6	.296	.353	.427	.780
2014	Tor	AL	143	610	175	33	4	9	(5 | 4)	243	94	51	77	38	1	73	1	2	4	30	2	4	.287	.328	.398	.726
2015	2 Tms		116	481	132	25	2	7	(5 | 2)	182	57	53	63	26	0	62	0	9	3	24	6	6	.274	.310	.378	.688
2016	NYM	NL	60	255	68	13	4	8	(6 | 2)	113	45	24	35	23	1	49	0	0	1	9	2	3	.267	.326	.443	.769
2017	NYM	NL	145	501	123	25	7	15	(6 | 9)	207	75	58	66	50	1	79	2	5	3	24	6	3	.246	.315	.413	.728
15	Tor	AL	69	288	82	17	0	4	(3 | 1)	111	36	34	42	17	0	38	0	4	2	16	2	3	.285	.322	.385	.708
15	Col	NL	47	193	50	8	2	3	(2 | 1)	71	21	19	21	9	0	24	0	5	1	8	4	3	.259	.291	.368	.659
	Postseason		11	48	11	1	1	1	(1 | 0)	17	7	5	6	3	1	5	0	0	0	3	1	0	.229	.275	.354	.629
	15 ML YEARS		1767	7324	2095	375	128	141	(75 | 66)	3149	1150	703	1072	567	55	875	11	49	38	512	125	77	.286	.337	.430	.767

Mark Reynolds

Bats: R **Throws:** R **Pos:** 1B-138;PH-8;DH-3;LF-1   **Ht:** 6'2" **Wt:** 220 **Born:** 8/3/1983 **Age:** 34

					BATTING																	RUNNING			AVERAGES	
Year	Team	Lg	G	AB	H	2B	3B	HR	(Hm | Rd)	TB	R	RBI	RC	TBB	IBB	SO	HBP	SH	SF	SB	CS	GDP	Avg	OBP	Slg	OPS
2007	Ari	NL	111	366	102	20	4	17	(7 | 10)	181	62	62	62	37	4	129	5	1	5	0	1	5	.279	.349	.495	.843
2008	Ari	NL	152	539	129	28	3	28	(13 | 15)	247	87	97	82	64	0	204	1	3	6	11	2	10	.239	.320	.458	.779
2009	Ari	NL	155	578	150	30	1	44	(19 | 25)	314	98	102	94	76	3	223	5	0	3	24	9	8	.260	.349	.543	.892
2010	Ari	NL	145	499	99	17	2	32	(21 | 11)	216	79	85	77	83	7	211	9	0	5	7	4	8	.198	.320	.433	.753
2011	Bal	AL	155	534	118	27	1	37	(17 | 20)	258	84	86	77	75	2	196	7	0	4	6	4	11	.221	.323	.483	.806
2012	Bal	AL	135	457	101	26	0	23	(11 | 12)	196	65	69	68	73	2	159	6	0	2	1	3	19	.221	.335	.429	.763
2013	2 Tms	AL	135	445	98	14	0	21	(9 | 12)	175	55	67	55	51	1	154	5	0	3	3	1	9	.220	.306	.393	.699
2014	Mil	NL	130	378	74	9	0	22	(9 | 13)	149	47	45	41	47	3	122	3	1	4	5	1	8	.196	.287	.394	.681
2015	StL	NL	140	382	88	21	2	13	(4 | 9)	152	35	48	38	44	2	121	4	0	2	2	3	10	.230	.315	.398	.713
2016	Col	NL	118	393	111	24	0	14	(8 | 6)	177	61	53	60	42	1	112	4	0	2	1	2	6	.282	.356	.450	.806
2017	Col	NL	148	520	139	22	1	30	(21 | 9)	253	82	97	88	69	0	175	1	0	3	2	1	12	.267	.352	.487	.839
13	Cle	AL	99	335	72	8	0	15	(8 | 7)	125	40	48	39	43	1	123	3	0	3	3	0	7	.215	.307	.373	.680
13	NYY	AL	36	110	26	6	0	6	(1 | 5)	50	15	19	16	8	0	31	2	0	0	0	1	2	.236	.300	.455	.755
	Postseason		16	52	7	0	0	2	(1 | 1)	13	3	3	2	3	0	20	3	0	0	1	0	1	.135	.224	.250	.474
	11 ML YEARS		1524	5091	1209	238	14	281	(139 | 142)	2318	755	811	742	661	25	1806	52	3	39	62	31	106	.237	.329	.455	.784

Matt Reynolds

Bats: R **Throws:** R **Pos:** 3B-23;PH-21;SS-10;2B-8;LF-7;PR-6;1B-3;RF-1   **Ht:** 6'1" **Wt:** 198 **Born:** 12/3/1990 **Age:** 27

Year	Team	Lg	G	AB	H	2B	3B	HR	(Hm	Rd)	TB	R	RBI	RC	TBB	IBB	SO	HBP	SH	SF	SB	CS	GDP	Avg	OBP	Slg	OPS
2013	Stluci	A+	117	433	98	21	6	5	(-	-)	146	59	49	48	36	1	80	13	1	5	9	2	15	.226	.302	.337	.639
2014	Bnghtn	AA	58	211	75	5	3	1	(-	-)	89	33	21	40	29	0	41	0	0	2	6	3	1	.355	.430	.422	.852
2014	LsVgs	AAA	68	267	89	16	4	5	(-	-)	128	54	40	51	21	1	60	5	2	6	14	4	3	.333	.385	.479	.864
2015	LsVgs	AAA	115	445	119	32	5	6	(-	-)	179	70	65	61	32	0	92	5	1	7	13	4	14	.267	.319	.402	.721
2016	LsVgs	AAA	71	269	71	15	2	2	(-	-)	96	43	24	35	26	0	64	3	1	0	9	2	12	.264	.336	.357	.692
2017	LsVgs	AAA	33	128	41	9	0	4	(-	-)	62	27	14	24	16	0	30	0	0	0	2	2	5	.320	.396	.484	.880
2016	NYM	NL	47	89	20	8	0	3	(2	1)	37	11	13	10	4	0	34	1	2	0	0	1	2	.225	.266	.416	.682
2017	NYM	NL	68	113	26	1	2	1	(1	0)	34	12	5	11	14	1	37	2	1	0	0	1	2	.230	.326	.301	.626
	2 ML YEARS		115	202	46	9	2	4	(3	1)	71	23	18	21	18	1	71	3	3	0	0	2	4	.228	.300	.351	.652

Jacob Rhame

Pitches: R **Bats:** R **Pos:** RP-9   RAYM   **Ht:** 6'1" **Wt:** 215 **Born:** 3/16/1993 **Age:** 25

Year	Team	Lg	G	GS	CG	GF	IP	BFP	H	R	ER	HR	SH	SF	HB	TBB	IBB	SO	WP	Bk	W	L	Pct	Sh	Sv-Op	Hld	ERC	ERA
2013	Ogden	R+	20	0	0	18	19.2	85	19	13	10	2	0	1	1	9	0	21	2	0	1	2	.333	0	8- -	-	4.39	4.58
2014	Gt Lks	A	51	0	0	34	67.0	262	48	16	15	3	1	4	0	14	3	90	5	1	5	4	.556	0	9- -	-	1.60	2.01
2015	Rcuca	A+	5	0	0	5	7.0	23	2	0	0	0	0	0	0	1	0	13	0	0	0	0	-	0	1- -	-	0.35	0.00
2015	Tulsa	AA	39	0	0	7	50.0	201	34	17	17	5	2	2	1	19	1	57	1	0	3	3	.500	0	2- -	-	2.38	3.06
2016	OkCity	AAA	54	0	0	23	63.0	264	53	24	23	5	2	5	0	28	2	70	4	0	1	7	.125	0	7- -	-	3.21	3.29
2017	OkCity	AAA	41	0	0	13	48.0	202	52	24	23	6	1	1	0	10	1	55	3	0	0	2	.000	0	2- -	-	3.92	4.31
2017	NYM	NL	9	0	0	2	9.0	45	12	9	9	2	1	1	0	7	0	7	0	0	1	1	.500	0	0-0	0	8.82	9.00

Clayton Richard

Pitches: L **Bats:** L **Pos:** SP-32   **Ht:** 6'5" **Wt:** 240 **Born:** 9/12/1983 **Age:** 34

Year	Team	Lg	G	GS	CG	GF	IP	BFP	H	R	ER	HR	SH	SF	HB	TBB	IBB	SO	WP	Bk	W	L	Pct	Sh	Sv-Op	Hld	ERC	ERA
2008	CWS	AL	13	8	0	3	47.2	215	61	37	32	5	0	1	0	13	2	29	1	1	2	5	.286	0	0-0	0	5.06	6.04
2009	2 Tms		38	26	1	3	153.0	663	154	81	75	17	8	5	3	71	0	114	7	3	9	5	.643	0	0-0	0	4.60	4.41
2010	SD	NL	33	33	1	0	201.2	861	206	89	84	16	6	2	4	78	6	153	4	2	14	9	.609	1	0-0	0	4.09	3.75
2011	SD	NL	18	18	0	0	99.2	427	104	52	43	8	4	1	2	38	2	53	3	1	5	9	.357	0	0-0	0	4.22	3.88
2012	SD	NL	33	33	1	0	218.2	910	228	110	97	31	3	6	6	42	4	107	4	2	14	14	.500	1	0-0	0	3.87	3.99
2013	SD	NL	12	11	0	1	52.2	239	65	44	41	13	6	1	0	21	1	24	0	0	2	5	.286	0	0-0	0	6.55	7.01
2015	ChC	NL	23	3	0	6	42.1	181	47	18	18	3	0	0	1	7	1	22	4	0	4	2	.667	0	0-0	2	3.56	3.83
2016	2 Tms		36	9	0	9	67.2	306	81	35	25	4	0	3	2	31	3	41	3	0	3	4	.429	0	1-1	5	5.24	3.33
2017	SD	NL	32	32	2	0	197.1	858	240	114	105	24	6	5	8	59	6	151	7	1	8	15	.348	1	0-0	0	5.33	4.79
	09 CWS	AL	26	14	1	3	89.0	387	94	50	46	10	3	4	3	37	0	66	5	2	4	3	.571	0	0-0	0	4.76	4.65
	09 SD	NL	12	12	0	0	64.0	276	60	31	29	7	5	1	0	34	0	48	2	1	5	2	.714	0	0-0	0	4.38	4.08
	16 ChC	NL	25	0	0	9	14.0	72	23	14	10	0	0	2	2	7	3	7	1	0	0	1	.000	0	1-1	1	7.74	6.43
	16 SD	NL	11	9	0	0	53.2	234	58	21	15	4	0	1	0	24	0	34	2	0	3	3	.500	0	0-0	0	4.61	2.52
	Postseason		8	0	0	0	11.0	42	8	1	1	0	0	0	0	4	0	9	0	0	0	0	-	0	0-0	2	2.05	0.82
	9 ML YEARS		238	173	5	16	1080.2	4660	1186	580	520	121	33	24	26	360	25	694	33	10	61	68	.473	3	1-1	3	4.56	4.33

Garrett Richards

Pitches: R **Bats:** R **Pos:** SP-6   **Ht:** 6'3" **Wt:** 210 **Born:** 5/27/1988 **Age:** 30

Year	Team	Lg	G	GS	CG	GF	IP	BFP	H	R	ER	HR	SH	SF	HB	TBB	IBB	SO	WP	Bk	W	L	Pct	Sh	Sv-Op	Hld	ERC	ERA
2011	LAA	AL	7	3	0	2	14.0	62	16	11	9	4	0	0	0	7	0	9	2	0	0	2	.000	0	0-0	0	6.97	5.79
2012	LAA	AL	30	9	0	4	71.0	318	77	46	37	7	2	4	3	34	1	47	2	0	4	3	.571	0	1-3	5	5.04	4.69
2013	LAA	AL	47	17	1	6	145.0	620	151	73	67	12	9	3	1	44	4	101	11	0	7	8	.467	0	1-2	5	3.78	4.16
2014	LAA	AL	26	26	1	0	168.2	678	124	51	49	5	0	3	7	51	1	164	22	1	13	4	.765	1	0-0	0	2.06	2.61
2015	LAA	AL	32	32	1	0	207.1	865	181	94	84	20	6	10	5	76	2	176	17	0	15	12	.556	1	0-0	0	3.32	3.65
2016	LAA	AL	6	6	0	0	34.2	148	31	16	9	2	2	0	1	15	1	34	3	0	1	3	.250	0	0-0	0	3.39	2.34
2017	LAA	AL	6	6	0	0	27.2	108	18	8	7	1	1	0	0	7	0	27	2	0	0	2	.000	0	0-0	0	1.49	2.28
	7 ML YEARS		154	99	3	12	668.1	2799	598	299	262	51	20	20	17	234	9	558	59	1	40	34	.541	2	2-5	10	3.23	3.53

Joey Rickard

Bats: R **Throws:** L **Pos:** RF-53;LF-43;CF-21;PH-15;PR-8   **Ht:** 6'1" **Wt:** 185 **Born:** 5/21/1991 **Age:** 27

Year	Team	Lg	G	AB	H	2B	3B	HR	(Hm	Rd)	TB	R	RBI	RC	TBB	IBB	SO	HBP	SH	SF	SB	CS	GDP	Avg	OBP	Slg	OPS
2013	BG	A	127	452	122	29	5	8	(-	-)	185	79	63	83	78	0	98	16	5	8	30	10	8	.270	.390	.409	.799
2014	Mont	AA	68	206	50	8	0	1	(-	-)	61	33	17	24	28	0	39	4	4	5	9	4	4	.243	.337	.296	.634
2015	Charltt	A+	23	71	19	3	0	0	(-	-)	22	8	12	12	20	0	13	2	0	1	3	2	2	.268	.436	.310	.746
2015	Mont	AA	65	236	76	19	6	2	(-	-)	113	38	32	52	39	0	42	3	1	3	19	4	2	.322	.420	.479	.899
2015	Drham	AAA	29	89	32	6	2	0	(-	-)	42	16	11	19	10	0	20	3	1	1	1	0	0	.360	.437	.472	.909
2017	Norfolk	AAA	13	47	9	1	0	1	(-	-)	13	8	4	5	11	0	9	0	0	0	0	0	1	.191	.345	.277	.621
2016	Bal	AL	85	257	69	13	0	5	(2	3)	97	32	19	32	18	0	54	2	3	2	4	1	3	.268	.319	.377	.696
2017	Bal	AL	111	261	63	15	0	4	(3	1)	90	29	19	20	9	0	63	4	2	1	8	1	6	.241	.276	.345	.621
	2 ML YEARS		196	518	132	28	0	9	(5	4)	187	61	38	52	27	0	117	6	5	3	12	2	9	.255	.298	.361	.659

J.T. Riddle

Bats: L **Throws:** R **Pos:** SS-69;PR-1 **Ht:** 6'1" **Wt:** 180 **Born:** 10/12/1991 **Age:** 26

								BATTING												RUNNING			AVERAGES			
Year	Team	Lg	G	AB	H	2B	3B	HR	(Hm Rd)	TB	R	RBI	RC	TBB	IBB	SO	HBP	SH	SF	SB	CS	GDP	Avg	OBP	Slg	OPS
2013	Batvia	A-	59	222	54	10	0	2	(- -)	70	38	18	22	10	1	28	5	4	3			6	.243	.288	.315	.603
2014	Grnsbr	A	103	435	122	17	4	9	(- -)	174	65	60	59	26	0	55	4	6	6	5	1	6	.280	.323	.400	.723
2015	Jupiter	A+	45	185	50	6	1	0	(- -)	58	30	9	19	11	0	29	0	2	0	7	3	2	.270	.311	.314	.625
2015	Jaxnvl	AA	44	173	50	6	1	5	(- -)	73	26	20	24	8	0	24	2	3	3	0	0	3	.289	.323	.422	.745
2016	Jaxnvl	AA	101	389	109	18	4	3	(- -)	144	49	51	51	33	2	72	0	4	3	5	1	6	.280	.334	.370	.704
2016	NewOr	AAA	15	56	15	2	0	1	(- -)	20	4	2	5	1	0	9	0	0	0	1	0	3	.268	.281	.357	.638
2017	NewOr	AAA	16	63	18	4	1	2	(- -)	30	9	6	9	1	1	8	0	0	0	1	0	0	.286	.297	.476	.773
2017	Mia	NL	70	228	57	13	1	3	(2 1)	81	20	31	24	12	2	50	0	2	5	0	2	6	.250	.282	.355	.637

Yacksel Rios

YAHK-sel

Pitches: R **Bats:** R **Pos:** RP-13 **Ht:** 6'3" **Wt:** 185 **Born:** 6/27/1993 **Age:** 25

			HOW MUCH HE PITCHED						WHAT HE GAVE UP												THE RESULTS							
Year	Team	Lg	G	GS	CG	GF	IP	BFP	H	R	ER	HR	SH	SF	HB	TBB	IBB	SO	WP	Bk	W	L	Pct	Sh	Sv-Op	Hld	ERC	ERA
2013	Wmspt	A-	15	10	0	1	52.2	223	52	24	21	1	0	5	3	19	0	39	1	2	5	3	.625	0	0- -	-	3.57	3.59
2014	Lakwd	A	33	13	0	11	102.0	449	102	51	42	9	3	2	6	40	0	73	9	3	6	2	.750	0	1- -	-	4.14	3.71
2015	Clrwtr	A+	26	10	0	5	88.1	358	69	33	27	4	1	3	8	23	3	71	7	1	6	5	.545	0	1- -	-	2.36	2.75
2016	Rdng	AA	13	1	0	1	17.2	87	20	9	9	0	0	4	1	14	1	21	1	0	1	1	.500	0	0- -	-	5.63	4.58
2016	2 Tms	Low	24	6	0	2	60.2	263	60	44	41	4	2	6	6	24	1	43	10	0	4	3	.571	0	1- -	-	4.16	6.08
2017	Rdng	AA	24	0	0	7	38.0	146	22	12	8	2	1	2	2	10	1	47	7	1	1	2	.333	0	2- -	-	1.47	1.89
2017	LV	AAA	13	1	0	4	18.1	68	10	4	4	3	1	0	0	4	0	17	3	0	0	1	.000	0	1- -	-	1.57	1.96
2017	Phi	NL	13	0	0	7	16.1	73	15	8	8	4	1	0	0	9	1	17	0	0	1	0	1.000	0	0-0	0	5.06	4.41

Rene Rivera

ruh-NAY

Bats: R **Throws:** R **Pos:** C-71;PH-3;1B-1 **Ht:** 5'10" **Wt:** 215 **Born:** 7/31/1983 **Age:** 34

								BATTING												RUNNING			AVERAGES			
Year	Team	Lg	G	AB	H	2B	3B	HR	(Hm Rd)	TB	R	RBI	RC	TBB	IBB	SO	HBP	SH	SF	SB	CS	GDP	Avg	OBP	Slg	OPS
2004	Sea	AL	2	3	0	0	0	0	(0 0)	0	0	0	0	0	0	1	0	0	0	0	0	0	.000	.000	.000	.000
2005	Sea	AL	16	48	19	3	0	1	(0 1)	25	3	6	8	1	0	11	0	1	0	0	0	0	.396	.408	.521	.929
2006	Sea	AL	35	99	15	4	0	2	(1 1)	25	8	4	4	3	0	29	1	3	0	1	0	2	.152	.184	.253	.437
2011	Min	AL	45	104	15	3	0	1	(0 1)	21	9	5	3	8	0	32	1	0	1	0	0	2	.144	.211	.202	.412
2013	SD	NL	23	67	17	3	1	0	(0 0)	22	4	7	6	2	1	16	0	0	2	0	0	1	.254	.268	.328	.596
2014	SD	NL	103	294	74	18	1	11	(1 10)	127	27	44	41	27	3	76	3	3	2	0	0	6	.252	.319	.432	.751
2015	TB	AL	110	298	53	14	0	5	(4 1)	82	16	26	16	11	0	86	3	5	2	0	0	4	.178	.213	.275	.489
2016	NYM	NL	65	185	41	4	0	6	(4 2)	63	12	26	19	16	3	54	3	1	2	0	0	4	.222	.291	.341	.632
2017	2 Tms	NL	74	218	55	9	0	10	(5 5)	94	23	35	29	14	3	70	3	1	1	0	1	4	.252	.305	.431	.736
17	NYM	NL	54	174	40	4	0	8	(3 5)	68	15	23	18	9	3	54	3	0	1	0	1	3	.230	.278	.391	.669
17	ChC	NL	20	44	15	5	0	2	(2 0)	26	8	12	11	5	0	16	0	1	0	0	0	1	.341	.408	.591	.999
	Postseason		1	3	1	0	0	0	(0 0)	1	0	0	0	0	0	0	0	0	0	0	0	0	.333	.333	.333	.667
	9 ML YEARS		473	1316	289	58	2	36	(15 21)	459	102	153	126	82	10	375	14	14	10	1	1	23	.220	.271	.349	.620

T.J. Rivera

Bats: R **Throws:** R **Pos:** 3B-28;1B-20;PH-17;2B-12;LF-3 **Ht:** 6'1" **Wt:** 203 **Born:** 10/27/1988 **Age:** 29

								BATTING												RUNNING			AVERAGES			
Year	Team	Lg	G	AB	H	2B	3B	HR	(Hm Rd)	TB	R	RBI	RC	TBB	IBB	SO	HBP	SH	SF	SB	CS	GDP	Avg	OBP	Slg	OPS
2013	Stluci	A+	125	502	145	23	1	2	(- -)	176	76	51	66	34	1	73	13	7	3	6	2	19	.289	.348	.351	.698
2014	Stluci	A+	61	252	86	16	0	4	(- -)	114	42	47	44	14	1	37	5	0	3	2	1	11	.341	.383	.452	.836
2014	Bnghtn	AA	54	201	72	13	0	1	(- -)	88	28	28	36	11	1	27	4	0	5	1	0	6	.358	.394	.438	.831
2015	Bnghtn	AA	56	220	75	10	0	5	(- -)	100	37	27	37	12	0	22	2	0	0	1	1	11	.341	.380	.455	.835
2015	LsVgs	AAA	54	183	56	17	1	2	(- -)	81	26	21	28	7	0	25	4	2	0	0	0	6	.306	.345	.443	.788
2016	LsVgs	AAA	105	405	143	31	1	11	(- -)	209	67	85	80	23	2	54	7	2	5	3	3	6	.353	.393	.516	.909
2016	NYM	NL	33	105	35	4	1	3	(2 1)	50	10	16	16	3	0	17	1	0	4	0	0	2	.333	.345	.476	.821
2017	NYM	NL	73	214	62	13	5	4	(4 1)	92	27	27	28	9	0	32	5	1	2	1	0	4	.290	.330	.430	.760
	Postseason			4	1	1	0	0	(0 0)	2	0	0	0	0	0	0	0	0	0	0	0	0	.250	.250	.500	.750
	2 ML YEARS		106	319	97	17	2	8	(6 2)	142	37	43	44	12	0	49	6	1	6	1	0	6	.304	.335	.445	.780

Yadiel Rivera

YA-dee-el

Bats: R **Throws:** R **Pos:** 3B-1;PH-1 **Ht:** 6'3" **Wt:** 185 **Born:** 5/2/1992 **Age:** 26

								BATTING												RUNNING			AVERAGES			
Year	Team	Lg	G	AB	H	2B	3B	HR	(Hm Rd)	TB	R	RBI	RC	TBB	IBB	SO	HBP	SH	SF	SB	CS	GDP	Avg	OBP	Slg	OPS
2017	ColSpr*	AAA	107	376	82	15	3	5	(- -)	118	45	43	34	30	2	104	4	3	1	5	2	12	.218	.282	.314	.596
2015	Mil	NL	7	14	1	0	0	0	(0 0)	1	0	0	0	0	0	4	0	1	0	0	0	0	.071	.071	.071	.143
2016	Mil	NL	35	66	14	4	0	0	(0 0)	18	12	3	3	2	0	20	0	3	0	0	0	4	.212	.235	.273	.508
2017	Mil	NL	1	2	0	0	0	0	(0 0)	0	0	0	0	0	0	1	0	0	0	0	0	0	.000	.000	.000	.000
	3 ML YEARS		43	82	15	4	0	0	(0 0)	19	12	3	3	2	0	25	0	4	0	0	0	4	.183	.202	.232	.434

Felipe Rivero

Pitches: L Bats: L Pos: RP-73

Ht: 6'2" Wt: 210 Born: 7/5/1991 Age: 26

			HOW MUCH HE PITCHED						WHAT HE GAVE UP										THE RESULTS						
Year	Team	Lg	G	GS	CG	GF	IP	BFP	H	R	ER	HR	SH	SF	HB	TBB	IBB	SO	WP	Bk	W	L	Pct	Sh	Sv-Op	Hld	ERC	ERA
2015	Was	NL	49	0	0	17	48.1	189	35	15	15	2	0	1	1	11	2	43	2	1	2	1	.667	0	2-3	6	1.74	2.79
2016 2 Tms		NL	75	0	0	11	77.0	327	66	39	35	7	0	2	6	33	3	92	3	0	1	6	.143	0	1-4	26	3.61	4.09
2017	Pit	NL	73	0	0	40	75.1	300	47	19	14	4	0	1	4	20	0	88	2	1	5	3	.625	0	21-23	14	1.61	1.67
16	Was	NL	47	0	0	8	49.2	203	43	26	25	4	0	1	5	15	2	53	1	0	0	3	.000	0	1-2	16	3.26	4.53
16	Pit	NL	28	0	0	3	27.1	124	23	13	10	3	0	1	1	18	1	39	2	0	1	3	.250	0	0-2	10	4.25	3.29
3 ML YEARS			197	0	0	68	200.2	816	148	73	64	13	0	4	11	64	5	223	7	2	8	10	.444	0	24-30	46	2.34	2.87

Anthony Rizzo

Bats: L Throws: L Pos: 1B-157;2B-10;PH-2;3B-1;LF-1

Ht: 6'3" Wt: 240 Born: 8/8/1989 Age: 28

			BATTING																			RUNNING			AVERAGES			
Year	Team	Lg	G	AB	H	2B	3B	HR	(Hm	Rd)	TB	R	RBI	RC	TBB	IBB	SO	HBP	SH	SF	SB	CS	GDP	Avg	OBP	Slg	OPS
2011	SD	NL	49	128	18	8	1	1	(1	0)	31	9	9	7	21	1	46	4	0	0	2	1	2	.141	.281	.242	.523
2012	ChC	NL	87	337	96	15	0	15	(7	8)	156	44	48	57	27	1	62	3	0	1	3	2	7	.285	.342	.463	.805
2013	ChC	NL	160	606	141	40	2	23	(13	10)	254	71	80	74	76	7	127	6	0	2	6	5	12	.233	.323	.419	.742
2014	ChC	NL	140	524	150	28	1	32	(14	18)	276	89	78	99	73	7	116	15	0	4	5	4	8	.286	.386	.527	.913
2015	ChC	NL	160	586	163	38	3	31	(11	20)	300	94	101	115	78	9	105	30	0	7	17	6	9	.278	.387	.512	.899
2016	ChC	NL	155	583	170	43	4	32	(12	20)	317	94	109	119	74	8	108	16	0	3	3	5	13	.292	.385	.544	.928
2017	ChC	NL	157	572	156	32	3	32	(15	17)	290	99	109	116	91	11	90	24	0	4	10	4	21	.273	.392	.507	.899
Postseason			26	97	24	5	0	5	(3	2)	44	15	12	11	10	2	21	3	0	0	2	0	1	.247	.336	.454	.790
7 ML YEARS			908	3336	894	204	14	166	(73	93)	1624	500	534	587	440	44	654	98	0	21	46	27	72	.268	.368	.487	.854

Tanner Roark

Pitches: R Bats: R Pos: SP-30; RP-2

ROW-ark

Ht: 6'2" Wt: 235 Born: 10/5/1986 Age: 31

			HOW MUCH HE PITCHED						WHAT HE GAVE UP										THE RESULTS						
Year	Team	Lg	G	GS	CG	GF	IP	BFP	H	R	ER	HR	SH	SF	HB	TBB	IBB	SO	WP	Bk	W	L	Pct	Sh	Sv-Op	Hld	ERC	ERA
2013	Was	NL	14	5	0	1	53.2	204	38	11	9	1	3	2	0	11	0	40	0	0	7	1	.875	0	0-0	1	1.54	1.51
2014	Was	NL	31	31	1	0	198.2	798	178	64	63	16	5	2	6	39	1	138	0	0	15	10	.600	1	0-0	0	2.76	2.85
2015	Was	NL	40	12	0	8	111.0	467	119	55	54	17	4	4	5	26	3	70	0	0	4	7	.364	0	1-2	4	4.39	4.38
2016	Was	NL	34	33	0	0	210.0	855	173	72	66	17	10	1	13	73	4	172	6	1	16	10	.615	0	0-0	1	3.08	2.83
2017	Was	NL	32	30	0	0	181.1	776	178	105	94	23	3	2	6	64	5	166	3	1	13	11	.542	0	0-0	0	4.06	4.67
Postseason			3	1	0	1	7.0	35	10	3	3	2	0	0	1	3	1	4	0	0	0	1	.000	0	0-0	0	8.56	3.86
5 ML YEARS			151	111	1	9	754.2	3100	686	307	286	74	25	11	30	213	13	586	9	2	55	39	.585	1	1-2	6	3.28	3.41

Daniel Robertson

Bats: R Throws: R Pos: RF-17;LF-10;PH-4;PR-4;CF-2;DH-1

Ht: 5'8" Wt: 205 Born: 9/30/1985 Age: 32

			BATTING																			RUNNING			AVERAGES			
Year	Team	Lg	G	AB	H	2B	3B	HR	(Hm	Rd)	TB	R	RBI	RC	TBB	IBB	SO	HBP	SH	SF	SB	CS	GDP	Avg	OBP	Slg	OPS
2017	Clmbs*	AAA	57	209	67	8	0	1	(-	-)	78	29	16	31	21	1	35	0	1	0	12	6	2	.321	.383	.373	.756
2014	Tex	AL	70	177	48	9	1	0	(0	0)	59	23	21	23	17	0	28	0	2	1	6	4	3	.271	.333	.333	.667
2015	LAA	AL	37	75	21	2	0	0	(0	0)	23	10	7	8	2	1	7	0	3	0	0	0	1	.280	.299	.307	.605
2016	Sea	AL	9	19	5	1	0	0	(0	0)	6	1	1	1	1	0	3	0	1	0	0	1	2	.263	.300	.316	.616
2017	Cle	AL	32	80	18	4	1	1	(1	0)	27	9	7	6	7	1	3	0	1	0	0	1	6	.225	.287	.338	.625
4 ML YEARS			148	351	92	16	2	1	(1	0)	115	43	36	38	27	2	41	0	7	1	6	6	12	.262	.314	.328	.642

Daniel Robertson

Bats: R Throws: R Pos: 2B-41;SS-24;3B-17;DH-2;LF-1;PH-1

Ht: 5'11" Wt: 200 Born: 3/22/1994 Age: 24

			BATTING																			RUNNING			AVERAGES			
Year	Team	Lg	G	AB	H	2B	3B	HR	(Hm	Rd)	TB	R	RBI	RC	TBB	IBB	SO	HBP	SH	SF	SB	CS	GDP	Avg	OBP	Slg	OPS
2013	Beloit	A	101	401	111	21	1	9	(-	-)	161	59	46	57	41	0	79	7	0	2	1	7	10	.277	.353	.401	.754
2014	Stcktn	A+	132	548	170	37	3	15	(-	-)	258	110	60	107	72	1	94	16	1	5	4	4	10	.310	.402	.471	.873
2015	Mont	AA	78	299	82	20	5	4	(-	-)	124	49	41	47	33	0	58	11	0	4	2	3	7	.274	.363	.415	.778
2016	Drham	AAA	118	436	113	21	3	5	(-	-)	155	50	43	62	58	0	100	11	2	4	2	1	9	.259	.358	.356	.713
2017	Drham	AAA	11	43	16	2	0	1	(-	-)	21	7	1	8	3	0	7	1	0	0	0	1	2	.372	.426	.488	.914
2017	TB	AL	75	218	45	7	2	5	(4	1)	71	22	19	23	29	0	73	4	1	2	1	1	5	.206	.308	.326	.634

David Robertson

Pitches: R Bats: R Pos: RP-61

Ht: 5'11" Wt: 195 Born: 4/9/1985 Age: 33

			HOW MUCH HE PITCHED						WHAT HE GAVE UP										THE RESULTS						
Year	Team	Lg	G	GS	CG	GF	IP	BFP	H	R	ER	HR	SH	SF	HB	TBB	IBB	SO	WP	Bk	W	L	Pct	Sh	Sv-Op	Hld	ERC	ERA
2008	NYY	AL	25	0	0	8	30.1	131	29	18	18	3	0	3	0	15	2	36	6	0	4	0	1.000	0	0-0	0	4.12	5.34
2009	NYY	AL	45	0	0	20	43.2	191	36	19	16	4	0	0	1	23	1	63	6	0	2	1	.667	0	1-1	5	3.51	3.30
2010	NYY	AL	64	0	0	10	61.1	273	59	26	26	5	5	3	3	33	6	71	7	2	4	5	.444	0	1-3	14	4.29	3.82
2011	NYY	AL	70	0	0	8	66.2	272	40	9	8	1	1	0	1	35	6	100	6	1	4	0	1.000	0	1-4	34	1.85	1.08
2012	NYY	AL	65	0	0	17	60.2	248	52	19	18	5	0	1	1	19	0	81	1	1	2	7	.222	0	2-5	30	2.95	2.67
2013	NYY	AL	70	0	0	9	66.1	262	51	15	15	5	3	0	2	18	1	77	1	0	5	1	.833	0	3-5	33	2.37	2.04
2014	NYY	AL	63	0	0	55	64.1	259	45	23	22	7	1	0	1	23	2	96	0	0	4	5	.444	0	39-44	0	2.41	3.08
2015	CWS	AL	60	0	0	53	63.1	250	46	27	24	7	0	0	1	13	2	86	4	0	6	5	.545	0	34-41	0	2.00	3.41
2016	CWS	AL	62	0	0	48	62.1	267	53	24	24	6	3	2	1	32	4	75	1	0	5	3	.625	0	37-44	0	3.63	3.47
2017	2 Tms	AL	61	0	0	34	68.1	264	35	14	14	6	0	1	3	23	5	98	7	0	9	2	.818	0	14-16	8	1.50	1.84

Year	Team	Lg	G	GS	CG	GF	IP	BFP	H	R	ER	HR	SH	SF	HB	TBB	IBB	SO	WP	Bk	W	L	Pct	Sh	Sv-Op	Hld	ERC	ERA
17	CWS	AL	31	0	0	28	33.1	132	21	10	10	4	0	0	2	11	3	47	3	0	4	2	.667	0	13-14	0	2.14	2.70
17	NYY	AL	30	0	0	6	35.0	132	14	4	4	2	0	1	1	12	2	51	4	0	5	0	1.000	0	1-2	8	1.05	1.03
	Postseason		19	0	0	7	17.0	73	15	7	7	2	1	0	1	5	3	17	1	0	3	1	1.000	0	0-0	2	2.99	3.71
	10 ML YEARS		585	0	0	262	587.1	2417	446	194	185	49	13	10	14	234	29	783	39	4	45	29	.608	0	132-163	124	2.70	2.83

Drew Robinson

Bats: L **Throws:** R **Pos:** 3B-20;LF-15;2B-7;SS-6;CF-5;DH-3;PH-3;PR-3   **Ht:** 6'1" **Wt:** 200 **Born:** 4/20/1992 **Age:** 26

Year	Team	Lg	G	AB	H	2B	3B	HR	(Hm	Rd)	TB	R	RBI	RC	TBB	IBB	SO	HBP	SH	SF	SB	CS	GDP	Avg	OBP	Slg	OPS
2013	MrtlBh	A+	122	436	112	26	7	8	(-	-)	176	62	70	72	72	2	124	7	5	3	10	2	9	.257	.369	.404	.772
2014	Frisco	AA	96	331	63	15	5	11	(-	-)	121	41	40	34	37	1	125	2	4	1	6	5	1	.190	.273	.366	.639
2015	Frisco	AA	126	432	100	23	5	21	(-	-)	196	78	64	75	83	6	139	4	0	0	14	8	2	.231	.360	.454	.814
2016	RdRck	AAA	125	467	120	24	10	20	(-	-)	224	76	67	82	66	0	148	2	2	2	17	5	2	.257	.350	.480	.830
2017	RdRck	AAA	66	265	71	19	4	11	(-	-)	131	48	40	49	42	1	74	1	0	1	7	4	0	.268	.369	.494	.863
2017	Tex	AL	48	107	24	5	0	6	(3	3)	47	11	13	12	14	0	42	0	0	0	0	2	2	.224	.314	.439	.753

Shane Robinson

Bats: R **Throws:** R **Pos:** RF-8;CF-5;LF-4;PR-4;PH-2;DH-1   **Ht:** 5'9" **Wt:** 170 **Born:** 10/30/1984 **Age:** 33

Year	Team	Lg	G	AB	H	2B	3B	HR	(Hm	Rd)	TB	R	RBI	RC	TBB	IBB	SO	HBP	SH	SF	SB	CS	GDP	Avg	OBP	Slg	OPS
2017	Salt Lk*	AAA	86	348	111	21	5	2	(-	-)	148	64	47	59	28	1	37	3	1	5	15	1	4	.319	.370	.425	.795
2009	StL	NL	11	25	6	1	0	0	(0	0)	7	1	1	1	0	0	2	0	0	1	1	0	1	.240	.231	.280	.511
2011	StL	NL	9	7	0	0	0	0	(0	0)	0	0	0	0	1	0	2	0	0	0	0	0	1	.000	.125	.000	.125
2012	StL	NL	102	166	42	8	0	3	(1	2)	59	20	16	15	14	2	32	0	0	1	1	0	5	.253	.309	.355	.665
2013	StL	NL	99	144	36	2	1	2	(1	1)	46	22	16	18	23	0	17	0	0	4	5	1	2	.250	.345	.319	.664
2014	StL	NL	47	60	9	1	1	0	(0	0)	12	3	4	0	6	0	10	0	0	0	0	1	3	.150	.227	.200	.427
2015	Min	AL	83	180	45	7	3	0	(0	0)	58	28	16	21	12	0	29	1	3	1	6	1	4	.250	.299	.322	.621
2016	LAA	AL	65	98	17	3	0	1	(0	1)	23	16	10	6	10	0	17	1	2	0	3	2	3	.173	.257	.235	.492
2017	LAA	AL	20	31	6	0	0	0	(0	0)	6	7	1	0	3	0	5	0	0	1	2	0	1	.194	.257	.194	.451
	Postseason		18	24	5	1	0	1	(0	1)	9	4	4	0	1	0	4	0	0	0	0	0	1	.208	.240	.375	.615
	8 ML YEARS		436	711	161	22	5	6	(2	4)	211	97	64	61	69	2	114	2	5	8	18	5	20	.226	.294	.297	.590

Hansel Robles

Pitches: R **Bats:** R **Pos:** RP-46   ROH-blace   **Ht:** 5'11" **Wt:** 185 **Born:** 8/13/1990 **Age:** 27

Year	Team	Lg	G	GS	CG	GF	IP	BFP	H	R	ER	HR	SH	SF	HB	TBB	IBB	SO	WP	Bk	W	L	Pct	Sh	Sv-Op	Hld	ERC	ERA
2017	LsVgs*	AAA	18	0	0	11	23.1	112	27	16	15	5	0	2	2	14	0	22	1	0	1	0	.000	0	4- -		7.04	5.79
2015	NYM	NL	57	0	0	7	54.0	217	37	27	22	8	1	1	2	18	1	61	2	1	4	3	.571	0	0-4	12	2.57	3.67
2016	NYM	NL	68	0	0	15	77.2	331	69	32	30	7	1	5	1	36	4	85	3	0	6	4	.600	0	1-3	13	3.62	3.48
2017	NYM	NL	46	0	0	9	56.2	247	47	31	31	10	3	2	5	29	2	60	2	0	7	5	.583	0	0-2	5	4.38	4.92
	Postseason		3	0	0	2	3.0	9	0	0	0	0	0	0	0	0	0	4	0	0	0	0	-	0	0-0	0	0.00	0.00
	3 ML YEARS		171	0	0	31	188.1	795	153	90	83	25	5	8	8	83	7	206	7	1	17	12	.586	0	1-9	30	3.53	3.97

Victor Robles

Bats: R **Throws:** R **Pos:** RF-6;PH-4;CF-3;LF-2   ROH-blace   **Ht:** 6'0" **Wt:** 185 **Born:** 5/19/1997 **Age:** 21

Year	Team	Lg	G	AB	H	2B	3B	HR	(Hm	Rd)	TB	R	RBI	RC	TBB	IBB	SO	HBP	SH	SF	SB	CS	GDP	Avg	OBP	Slg	OPS
2015	2 Tms	Low	61	213	75	11	5	4	(-	-)	108	48	27	52	18	1	33	21	5	4	24	5	0	.352	.445	.507	.952
2016	3 Tms	Low	110	421	118	17	8	9	(-	-)	178	75	42	72	32	0	77	34	14	3	37	14	6	.280	.376	.423	.798
2017	Ptomc	A+	77	291	84	25	7	7	(-	-)	144	49	33	56	25	1	62	17	4	1	16	7	4	.289	.377	.495	.872
2017	Hrsbrg	AA	37	139	45	12	1	3	(-	-)	68	24	14	27	12	0	22	4	3	0	11	3	0	.324	.394	.489	.883
2017	Was	NL	13	24	6	1	2	0	(0	0)	11	2	4	3	0	0	6	2	1	0	0	1	2	.250	.308	.458	.766

Fernando Rodney

Pitches: R **Bats:** R **Pos:** RP-61   **Ht:** 5'11" **Wt:** 230 **Born:** 3/18/1977 **Age:** 41

Year	Team	Lg	G	GS	CG	GF	IP	BFP	H	R	ER	HR	SH	SF	HB	TBB	IBB	SO	WP	Bk	W	L	Pct	Sh	Sv-Op	Hld	ERC	ERA
2002	Det	AL	20	0	0	10	18.0	89	25	15	12	2	2	1	0	10	2	10	0	1	1	3	.250	0	0-4	0	6.77	6.00
2003	Det	AL	27	0	0	11	29.2	143	35	20	20	2	3	3	1	17	1	33	0	1	1	3	.250	0	3-6	3	5.46	6.07
2005	Det	AL	39	0	0	26	44.0	185	39	14	14	5	2	0	2	17	3	42	2	0	2	3	.400	0	9-15	3	3.59	2.86
2006	Det	AL	63	0	0	30	71.2	304	51	36	28	6	2	0	8	34	4	65	3	0	7	4	.636	0	7-11	18	3.01	3.52
2007	Det	AL	48	0	0	12	50.2	223	46	27	24	5	4	2	3	21	0	54	4	0	2	6	.250	0	1-3	12	3.74	4.26
2008	Det	AL	38	0	0	25	40.1	188	34	22	22	3	1	2	3	30	5	49	3	0	0	6	.000	0	13-19	5	4.29	4.91
2009	Det	AL	73	0	0	65	75.2	330	70	38	37	8	4	2	2	41	4	61	5	0	2	5	.286	0	37-38	0	4.31	4.40
2010	LAA	AL	72	0	0	30	68.0	308	70	33	32	4	1	0	5	35	1	53	4	0	4	3	.571	0	14-21	21	4.63	4.24
2011	LAA	AL	39	0	0	15	32.0	150	26	18	16	1	3	0	3	28	0	26	2	0	3	5	.375	0	3-7	10	4.66	4.50
2012	TB	AL	76	0	0	65	74.2	282	43	9	5	2	4	2	3	15	1	76	4	0	2	2	.500	0	48-50	1	1.22	0.60
2013	TB	AL	68	0	0	55	66.2	290	53	27	25	3	1	1	1	36	3	82	4	1	5	4	.556	0	37-45	0	3.02	3.38
2014	Sea	AL	69	0	0	64	66.1	286	61	24	21	3	4	1	3	28	3	76	4	0	1	6	.143	0	48-51	0	3.42	2.85
2015	2 Tms		68	0	0	32	62.2	277	59	36	33	9	1	1	8	29	3	58	6	0	7	5	.583	0	16-23	9	4.76	4.74
2016	2 Tms	NL	67	0	0	41	65.1	283	54	27	25	5	3	1	5	37	3	74	5	1	2	4	.333	0	25-28	8	3.85	3.44
2017	Ari	NL	61	0	0	53	55.1	231	40	29	26	3	2	1	2	26	3	65	7	0	5	4	.556	0	39-45	0	2.60	4.23
	15 Sea	AL	54	0	0	28	50.2	227	51	32	32	8	1	1	5	25	3	43	5	0	5	5	.500	0	16-22	7	5.25	5.68
	15 ChC	NL	14	0	0	4	12.0	50	8	4	1	1	0	0	3	4	0	15	1	0	2	0	1.000	0	0-1	2	2.88	0.75

			HOW MUCH HE PITCHED						WHAT HE GAVE UP												THE RESULTS							
Year	Team	Lg	G	GS	CG	GF	IP	BFP	H	R	ER	HR	SH	SF	HB	TBB	IBB	SO	WP	Bk	W	L	Pct	Sh	Sv-Op	Hld	ERC	ERA
16	SD	NL	28	0	0	24	28.2	109	13	2	1	0	0	0	2	12	0	33	1	1	0	1	.000	0	17-17	0	1.30	0.31
16	Mia	NL	39	0	0	17	36.2	174	41	25	24	5	3	1	3	25	3	41	4	0	2	3	.400	0	8-11	8	6.45	5.89
	Postseason		12	0	0	2	11.2	53	8	8	6	1	3	0	1	10	1	16	1	0	1	0	1.000	0	0-2	3	4.14	4.63
	15 ML YEARS		828	0	0	534	821.0	3569	706	375	340	61	37	17	49	404	36	824	53	3	44	63	.411	0	300-366	89	3.61	3.73

Carlos Rodon

Pitches: L Bats: L Pos: SP-12

roh-DON

Ht: 6'3" Wt: 235 Born: 12/10/1992 Age: 25

			HOW MUCH HE PITCHED						WHAT HE GAVE UP												THE RESULTS							
Year	Team	Lg	G	GS	CG	GF	IP	BFP	H	R	ER	HR	SH	SF	HB	TBB	IBB	SO	WP	Bk	W	L	Pct	Sh	Sv-Op	Hld	ERC	ERA
2015	CWS	AL	26	23	1	1	139.1	607	130	63	58	11	6	5	8	71	0	139	7	0	9	6	.600	0	0-0	0	4.25	3.75
2016	CWS	AL	28	28	0	0	165.0	715	176	82	74	23	4	6	6	54	3	168	11	1	9	10	.474	0	0-0	0	4.57	4.04
2017	CWS	AL	12	12	0	0	69.1	297	64	35	32	12	1	2	3	31	0	76	4	0	2	5	.286	0	0-0	0	4.57	4.15
	3 ML YEARS		66	63	1	1	373.2	1619	370	180	164	46	11	13	17	156	3	383	22	1	20	21	.488	0	0-0	0	4.46	3.95

Eduardo Rodriguez

Pitches: L Bats: L Pos: SP-24; RP-1

Ht: 6'2" Wt: 220 Born: 4/7/1993 Age: 25

			HOW MUCH HE PITCHED						WHAT HE GAVE UP												THE RESULTS							
Year	Team	Lg	G	GS	CG	GF	IP	BFP	H	R	ER	HR	SH	SF	HB	TBB	IBB	SO	WP	Bk	W	L	Pct	Sh	Sv-Op	Hld	ERC	ERA
2015	Bos	AL	21	21	0	0	121.2	522	120	55	52	13	5	4	4	37	1	98	4	1	10	6	.625	0	0-0	0	3.73	3.85
2016	Bos	AL	20	20	0	0	107.0	458	99	58	56	16	1	4	3	40	1	100	0	0	3	7	.300	0	0-0	0	3.96	4.71
2017	Bos	AL	25	24	0	1	137.1	582	126	66	64	19	1	3	5	50	1	150	1	1	6	7	.462	0	0-0	0	3.87	4.19
	3 ML YEARS		66	65	0	1	366.0	1562	345	179	172	48	7	11	12	127	3	348	5	2	19	20	.487	0	0-0	0	3.85	4.23

Francisco Rodriguez

Pitches: R Bats: R Pos: RP-28

Ht: 6'0" Wt: 195 Born: 1/7/1982 Age: 36

			HOW MUCH HE PITCHED						WHAT HE GAVE UP												THE RESULTS							
Year	Team	Lg	G	GS	CG	GF	IP	BFP	H	R	ER	HR	SH	SF	HB	TBB	IBB	SO	WP	Bk	W	L	Pct	Sh	Sv-Op	Hld	ERC	ERA
2002	LAA	AL	5	0	0	4	5.2	21	3	0	0	0	0	0	1	2	1	13	0	0	0	0	-	0	0-0	0	1.52	0.00
2003	LAA	AL	59	0	0	23	86.0	334	50	30	29	12	2	4	2	35	5	95	7	0	8	3	.727	0	2-6	7	2.25	3.03
2004	LAA	AL	69	0	0	29	84.0	335	51	21	17	2	2	1	1	33	1	123	5	0	4	1	.800	0	12-19	27	1.64	1.82
2005	LAA	AL	66	0	0	58	67.1	279	45	20	20	7	1	1	0	32	3	91	8	0	2	5	.286	0	45-50	0	2.52	2.67
2006	LAA	AL	69	0	0	58	73.0	296	52	16	14	6	3	0	1	28	5	98	10	0	2	3	.400	0	47-51	0	2.35	1.73
2007	LAA	AL	64	0	0	56	67.1	285	50	22	21	3	1	4	1	34	0	90	7	1	5	2	.714	0	40-46	0	2.74	2.81
2008	LAA	AL	76	0	0	69	68.1	288	54	21	17	4	1	1	2	34	4	77	6	0	2	3	.400	0	62-69	0	3.06	2.24
2009	NYM	NL	70	0	0	66	68.0	295	51	34	28	7	4	1	1	38	6	73	1	0	3	6	.333	0	35-42	0	3.18	3.71
2010	NYM	NL	53	0	0	46	57.1	236	45	14	14	3	1	1	2	21	4	67	3	1	4	2	.667	0	25-30	0	2.53	2.20
2011	2 Tms	NL	73	0	0	36	71.2	307	67	24	21	4	2	1	2	26	4	79	4	0	6	2	.750	0	23-29	17	3.25	2.64
2012	Mil	NL	78	0	0	13	72.0	305	65	37	35	8	1	3	0	31	1	72	6	0	2	7	.222	0	3-10	32	3.73	4.38
2013	2 Tms		48	0	0	23	46.2	193	42	14	14	7	3	0	1	14	4	54	2	0	3	2	.600	0	10-10	5	3.44	2.70
2014	Mil	NL	69	0	0	66	68.0	268	49	23	23	14	2	0	1	18	1	73	0	0	5	5	.500	0	44-49	0	2.77	3.04
2015	Mil	NL	60	0	0	55	57.0	216	38	15	14	6	1	2	0	11	1	62	3	0	1	3	.250	0	38-40	0	1.69	2.21
2016	Det	AL	61	0	0	55	58.1	230	45	24	21	6	0	3	1	21	1	52	4	0	3	4	.429	0	44-49	0	2.81	3.24
2017	Det	AL	28	0	0	20	25.1	118	31	23	22	9	0	0	1	11	1	23	2	0	2	5	.286	0	7-13	0	7.57	7.82
11	NYM	NL	42	0	0	34	42.2	187	44	15	15	3	2	1	2	16	4	46	2	0	2	2	.500	0	23-26	0	3.94	3.16
11	Mil	NL	31	0	0	2	29.0	120	23	7	6	1	0	0	0	10	0	33	2	0	4	0	1.000	0	0-3	17	2.32	1.86
13	Mil	NL	25	0	0	18	24.2	97	17	3	3	2	2	0	0	9	3	26	0	0	1	1	.500	0	10-10	1	2.10	1.09
13	Bal	AL	23	0	0	5	22.0	96	25	11	11	5	1	0	1	5	1	28	2	0	2	1	.667	0	0-0	4	5.11	4.50
	Postseason		26	0	0	8	36.2	158	32	15	12	5	1	3	1	18	2	49	5	0	5	4	.556	0	3-5	6	3.99	2.95
	16 ML YEARS		948	0	0	677	976.0	4011	738	336	310	98	24	22	17	389	42	1142	68	2	52	53	.495	0	437-513	88	2.77	2.86

Joely Rodriguez

Pitches: L Bats: L Pos: RP-26

joe-EL-ee

Ht: 6'1" Wt: 200 Born: 11/14/1991 Age: 26

			HOW MUCH HE PITCHED						WHAT HE GAVE UP												THE RESULTS							
Year	Team	Lg	G	GS	CG	GF	IP	BFP	H	R	ER	HR	SH	SF	HB	TBB	IBB	SO	WP	Bk	W	L	Pct	Sh	Sv-Op	Hld	ERC	ERA
2013	2 Tms	Low	26	26	0	0	140.0	579	142	60	42	8	2	1	4	39	0	101	10	0	9	8	.529	0	0--	-	3.59	2.70
2014	Altna	AA	30	21	2	4	134.0	574	151	80	72	10	5	2	1	43	1	73	6	1	6	11	.353	0	1--	-	4.40	4.84
2015	LV	AAA	13	13	1	0	68.1	318	89	48	48	3	2	1	1	37	2	33	4	1	2	6	.250	0	0--	-	6.11	6.32
2015	Rdng	AA	19	8	0	3	61.0	266	73	41	40	8	3	1	0	20	0	41	7	1	5	4	.556	0	0--	-	5.23	5.90
2016	Rdng	AA	33	0	0	14	49.0	198	46	18	14	3	4	1	0	16	1	41	5	0	7	0	1.000	0	2--	-	3.30	2.57
2016	Clrwtr	A+	7	0	0	4	8.1	29	3	0	0	0	0	0	0	1	0	10	0	0	0	0	-	0	3--	-	0.44	0.00
2016	LV	AAA	13	0	0	1	19.1	77	16	6	6	0	1	1	0	6	0	18	0	0	0	0	-	0	0--	-	2.26	2.79
2017	RdRck	AAA	22	0	0	5	27.0	129	31	20	19	6	2	1	2	18	0	21	5	1	2	0	1.000	0	0--	-	7.41	6.33
2016	Phi	NL	12	0	0	1	9.2	39	8	3	3	0	0	0	1	4	1	7	0	0	0	0	-	0	0-0	3	2.91	2.79
2017	Phi	NL	26	0	0	4	27.0	134	37	26	19	4	1	0	4	15	3	18	0	1	1	2	.333	0	0-2	3	7.81	6.33
	2 ML YEARS		38	0	0	5	36.2	173	45	29	22	4	1	0	5	19	4	25	0	1	1	2	.333	0	0-2	6	6.41	5.40

Ricardo Rodriguez

Pitches: R Bats: R Pos: RP-16

Ht: 6'2" Wt: 220 Born: 8/31/1992 Age: 25

			HOW MUCH HE PITCHED						WHAT HE GAVE UP												THE RESULTS							
Year	Team	Lg	G	GS	CG	GF	IP	BFP	H	R	ER	HR	SH	SF	HB	TBB	IBB	SO	WP	Bk	W	L	Pct	Sh	Sv-Op	Hld	ERC	ERA
2013	2 Tms	Low	20	0	0	15	27.0	113	27	12	10	2	4	0	1	4	0	39	4	0	0	3	.000	0	8--	-	3.01	3.33
2014	Hkry	A	29	12	0	4	102.2	424	101	45	35	7	5	4	3	28	0	72	5	1	5	5	.500	0	1--	-	3.46	3.07

Year Team	Lg	G	GS	CG	GF	IP	BFP	H	R	ER	HR	SH	SF	HB	TBB	IBB	SO	WP	Bk	W	L	Pct	Sh	Sv-Op	Hld	ERC	ERA
2015 Hkry	A	5	0	0	2	12.0	55	17	6	4	0	1	0	0	2	0	9	1	0	1	0	1.000	0	1- -	-	4.65	3.00
2017 DwnEast	A+	23	0	0	22	32.0	120	15	5	5	0	0	0	1	9	1	44	0	1	3	1	.750	0	12- -	-	0.96	1.41
2017 Frisco	AA	12	0	0	8	15.0	53	9	2	2	1	0	0	1	1	0	17	1	0	2	0	1.000	0	5- -	-	1.27	1.20
2017 Tex	AL	16	0	0	4	13.0	60	17	9	9	3	0	1	1	4	0	11	0	0	0	1	.000	0	1-3		6.83	6.23

Richard Rodriguez

Pitches: R **Bats:** R **Pos:** RP-5   **Ht:** 6'4" **Wt:** 205 **Born:** 3/4/1990 **Age:** 28

Year Team	Lg	G	GS	CG	GF	IP	BFP	H	R	ER	HR	SH	SF	HB	TBB	IBB	SO	WP	Bk	W	L	Pct	Sh	Sv-Op	Hld	ERC	ERA
2013 2 Tms	Low	30	0	0	12	44.1	194	46	23	22	6	1	5	0	13	0	41	3	0	4	1	.800	0	1- -	-	3.97	4.47
2014 Lancst	A+	7	0	0	1	10.1	43	10	6	6	2	0	1	0	2	0	16	0	0	0	0	-	0	0- -	-	3.61	5.23
2014 OkCity	AAA	16	0	0	4	28.1	108	19	11	11	3	2	1	2	6	0	23	0	0	2	0	1.000	0	0- -	-	2.06	3.49
2014 CpChr	AA	11	0	0	5	20.2	85	21	7	7	1	0	0	1	2	0	28	6	0	2	0	1.000	0	0- -	-	2.83	3.05
2015 Fresno	AAA	23	0	0	5	42.0	169	32	14	12	4	0	2	0	10	2	36	3	0	5	0	1.000	0	0- -	-	2.10	2.57
2015 Bowie	AA	10	0	0	5	21.1	79	11	3	3	2	1	0	1	2	0	23	1	0	1	1	.500	0	0- -	-	1.06	1.27
2015 Norfolk	AAA	13	0	0	1	20.1	91	19	12	8	2	1	0	3	10	2	15	4	1	1	3	.250	0	0- -	-	4.46	3.54
2016 Norfolk	AAA	48	2	0	13	81.2	333	65	23	23	5	0	2	5	25	3	81	4	1	6	2	.750	0	2- -	-	2.58	2.53
2017 Norfolk	AAA	42	1	0	24	70.2	285	56	20	19	5	2	3	3	18	1	80	4	0	4	4	.500	0	10- -	-	2.40	2.42
2017 Bal	AL	5	0	0	1	5.2	31	12	9	9	4	0	0	1	3	1	3	0	0	0	0	-	0	0-0	0	19.81	14.29

Sean Rodriguez

Bats: R **Throws:** R **Pos:** 3B-14;2B-12;RF-10;PH-9;LF-7;SS-6;CF-3;1B-2;PR-1   **Ht:** 6'0" **Wt:** 200 **Born:** 4/26/1985 **Age:** 33

Year Team	Lg	G	AB	H	2B	3B	HR	(Hm	Rd)	TB	R	RBI	RC	TBB	IBB	SO	HBP	SH	SF	SB	CS	GDP	Avg	OBP	Slg	OPS
2008 LAA	AL	59	167	34	8	1	3	(2	1)	53	18	10	12	14	0	55	3	2	1	3	1	3	.204	.276	.317	.593
2009 LAA	AL	12	25	5	0	0	2	(0	2)	11	4	4	2	3	0	7	0	1	0	0	0	2	.200	.276	.440	.716
2010 TB	AL	118	343	86	19	2	9	(5	4)	136	53	40	38	21	1	97	8	5	1	13	3	10	.251	.308	.397	.705
2011 TB	AL	131	373	83	20	3	8	(4	4)	133	45	36	41	38	2	87	18	5	2	11	7	8	.223	.323	.357	.679
2012 TB	AL	112	301	64	14	1	6	(3	3)	98	36	32	32	27	1	75	3	8	3	5	0	7	.213	.281	.326	.607
2013 TB	AL	96	195	48	10	1	5	(3	2)	75	21	23	21	17	0	59	5	3	2	1	3	3	.246	.320	.385	.704
2014 TB	AL	96	237	50	13	3	12	(7	5)	105	30	41	29	10	0	66	6	3	3	2	1	3	.211	.258	.443	.701
2015 Pit	NL	139	224	55	12	1	4	(2	2)	81	25	17	17	5	0	63	6	5	0	2	2	9	.246	.281	.362	.642
2016 Pit	NL	140	369	81	16	1	18	(7	11)	153	49	56	53	33	2	102	5	1	3	2	1	6	.270	.349	.510	.859
2017 2 Tms	NL	54	132	22	2	0	5	(2	3)	39	18	8	8	16	1	57	4	1	0	1	0	3	.167	.276	.295	.572
17 Atl	NL	15	37	6	1	0	2	(0	2)	13	6	3	4	8	1	19	1	1	0	1	0	1	.162	.326	.351	.677
17 Pit	NL	39	95	16	1	0	3	(2	1)	26	12	5	4	8	0	38	3	0	0	0	0	2	.168	.255	.274	.528
Postseason		13	28	5	1	0	1	(0	1)	9	6	2	1	2	0	5	0	0	0	0	0	0	.179	.233	.321	.555
10 ML YEARS		957	2297	528	114	13	72	(35	37)	884	299	267	253	184	7	668	58	33	16	40	18	54	.230	.301	.385	.686

Chaz Roe

Pitches: R **Bats:** R **Pos:** RP-12   ROW   **Ht:** 6'5" **Wt:** 190 **Born:** 10/9/1986 **Age:** 31

Year Team	Lg	G	GS	CG	GF	IP	BFP	H	R	ER	HR	SH	SF	HB	TBB	IBB	SO	WP	Bk	W	L	Pct	Sh	Sv-Op	Hld	ERC	ERA
2017 Drhm*	AAA	17	0	0	10	21.0	88	18	8	7	1	0	0	1	5	0	35	5	0	0	3	.000	0	4- -	-	2.47	3.00
2013 Ari	NL	21	0	0	4	22.1	95	18	10	10	3	2	1	0	13	3	24	1	0	1	0	1.000	0	0-2	1	3.78	4.03
2014 NYY	AL	3	0	0	2	2.0	13	3	3	2	0	0	1	0	3	0	4	1	0	0	0	-	0	0-0	0	9.89	9.00
2015 Bal	AL	36	0	0	6	41.1	177	44	19	19	4	1	1	1	17	2	38	0	0	4	2	.667	0	0-1	4	4.62	4.14
2016 2 Tms	NL	30	0	0	11	29.2	124	22	12	12	2	0	2	1	14	1	37	1	0	2	0	1.000	0	0-1	3	2.82	3.64
2017 2 Tms		12	0	0	3	10.2	44	7	5	3	1	0	0	1	5	0	13	1	0	0	0	-	0	0-0	1	2.84	2.53
16 Bal	AL	9	0	0	6	9.2	44	8	4	4	2	0	0	0	7	0	11	1	0	1	0	1.000	0	0-0	0	5.07	3.72
16 Atl	NL	21	0	0	5	20.0	80	14	8	8	0	0	2	1	7	1	26	0	0	1	0	1.000	0	0-1	3	1.86	3.60
17 Atl	NL	3	0	0	0	2.0	13	3	4	2	0	0	1	0	2	0	1	0	0	0	0	-	0	0-0	0	9.89	9.00
17 TB	AL	9	0	0	3	8.2	31	4	1	1	1	0	0	0	3	0	12	1	0	0	0	-	0	0-0	1	1.51	1.04
5 ML YEARS		102	0	0	26	106.0	453	94	49	46	10	3	5	3	52	6	116	4	0	7	2	.778	0	0-4	9	3.82	3.91

Taylor Rogers

Pitches: L **Bats:** L **Pos:** RP-69   **Ht:** 6'3" **Wt:** 170 **Born:** 12/17/1990 **Age:** 27

Year Team	Lg	G	GS	CG	GF	IP	BFP	H	R	ER	HR	SH	SF	HB	TBB	IBB	SO	WP	Bk	W	L	Pct	Sh	Sv-Op	Hld	ERC	ERA
2013 2 Tms	Low	25	24	3	0	140.2	578	133	58	45	6	5	3	9	36	0	93	9	0	11	7	.611	2	0- -	-	3.15	2.88
2014 NwBrit	AA	24	24	1	0	145.0	606	150	63	53	4	1	2	6	37	0	113	4	0	11	6	.647	0	0- -	-	3.42	3.29
2015 Roch	AAA	28	27	2	1	174.0	732	190	83	77	9	7	6	4	44	2	126	4	2	11	12	.478	0	0- -	-	3.81	3.98
2016 Roch	AAA	7	2	0	1	18.0	85	24	15	9	1	1	2	0	6	0	15	0	0	1	0	1.000	0	0- -	-	5.19	4.50
2016 Min	AL	57	0	0	8	61.1	264	63	29	27	7	0	1	5	16	3	64	1	0	3	1	.750	0	0-0	9	3.99	3.96
2017 Min	AL	69	0	0	7	55.2	237	52	20	19	6	2	0	3	21	5	49	1	0	7	3	.700	0	0-4	30	3.76	3.07
2 ML YEARS		126	0	0	15	117.0	501	115	49	46	13	2	1	8	37	8	113	2	0	10	4	.714	0	0-4	39	3.88	3.54

Miguel Rojas

Bats: R **Throws:** R **Pos:** SS-77;3B-15;PH-3;1B-2;2B-2;PR-1   **Ht:** 5'11" **Wt:** 195 **Born:** 2/24/1989 **Age:** 29

Year Team	Lg	G	AB	H	2B	3B	HR	(Hm	Rd)	TB	R	RBI	RC	TBB	IBB	SO	HBP	SH	SF	SB	CS	GDP	Avg	OBP	Slg	OPS
2014 LAD	NL	85	149	27	3	0	1	(0	1)	33	16	9	6	10	1	28	2	1	0	0	0	5	.181	.242	.221	.464
2015 Mia	NL	60	142	40	7	1	1	(1	0)	52	13	17	15	11	1	16	0	2	2	0	1	4	.282	.329	.366	.695

							BATTING													RUNNING			AVERAGES			
Year	Team	Lg	G	AB	H	2B	3B	HR	(Hm | Rd)	TB	R	RBI	RC	TBB	IBB	SO	HBP	SH	SF	SB	CS	GDP	Avg	OBP	Slg	OPS
2016	Mia	NL	123	194	48	12	0	1	(0 | 1)	63	27	14	14	11	2	27	1	6	2	2	1	10	.247	.288	.325	.613
2017	Mia	NL	90	272	79	16	2	1	(1 | 0)	102	37	26	32	27	5	32	4	1	2	2	1	6	.290	.361	.375	.736
	Postseason		1	1	0	0	0	0	(0 | 0)	0	0	0	0	0	0	0	0	0	0	0	0	0	.000	.000	.000	.000
	4 ML YEARS		358	757	194	38	3	4	(2 | 2)	250	93	66	67	59	9	103	7	10	6	4	3	25	.256	.314	.330	.644

Sal Romano

Pitches: R **Bats:** L **Pos:** SP-16
Ht: 6'5" **Wt:** 270 **Born:** 10/12/1993 **Age:** 24

			HOW MUCH HE PITCHED					WHAT HE GAVE UP											THE RESULTS						
Year	Team	Lg	G	GS	CG	GF	IP	BFP	H	R	ER	HR	SH	SF	HB	TBB	IBB	SO	WP	Bk	W	L	Pct	Sh	Sv-Op	Hld	ERC	ERA
2013	Dayton	A	25	25	0	0	120.1	537	134	81	65	10	5	4	10	57	0	89	9	1	7	11	.389	0	0- -	-	5.36	4.86
2014	Dayton	A	28	28	0	0	148.1	642	169	87	68	9	2	3	8	42	0	128	9	1	8	11	.421	0	0- -	-	4.38	4.13
2015	Dytona	A+	19	18	1	0	104.0	434	103	48	40	2	3	2	2	33	0	79	4	1	6	5	.545	0	0- -	-	3.28	3.46
2015	Pnscla	AA	7	7	0	0	23.0	114	35	28	28	4	2	1	0	12	0	9	0	0	0	4	.000	0	0- -	-	8.41	10.96
2016	Pnscla	AA	27	27	0	0	156.0	654	157	71	61	10	6	5	5	34	1	144	7	0	6	11	.353	0	0- -	-	3.26	3.52
2017	Lsvlle	AAA	10	10	1	0	49.1	212	49	26	19	1	3	2	1	17	0	32	5	0	1	4	.200	0	0- -	-	3.32	3.47
2017	Cin	NL	16	16	0	0	87.0	384	91	49	43	9	6	6	4	37	2	73	5	0	5	8	.385	0	0-0	0	4.61	4.45

Enny Romero

Pitches: L **Bats:** R **Pos:** RP-53
ENN-nee
Ht: 6'3" **Wt:** 215 **Born:** 1/24/1991 **Age:** 27

			HOW MUCH HE PITCHED					WHAT HE GAVE UP											THE RESULTS						
Year	Team	Lg	G	GS	CG	GF	IP	BFP	H	R	ER	HR	SH	SF	HB	TBB	IBB	SO	WP	Bk	W	L	Pct	Sh	Sv-Op	Hld	ERC	ERA
2017	Syrcse*	AAA	7	0	0	0	6.1	29	6	5	3	0	1	0	0	1	0	8	0	0	0	1	.000	0	0- -	-	1.93	4.26
2013	TB	AL	1	1	0	0	4.2	18	1	0	0	0	0	0	0	4	0	1	0	0	0	0	-	0	0-0	0	1.35	0.00
2015	TB	AL	23	0	0	7	30.0	140	39	18	17	1	1	1	0	13	0	31	2	0	0	2	.000	0	0-2	3	5.38	5.10
2016	TB	AL	52	0	0	15	45.2	204	42	31	30	7	0	4	0	28	1	50	1	0	2	0	1.000	0	1-2	6	4.79	5.91
2017	Was	NL	53	0	0	12	55.2	245	55	26	22	7	0	2	3	23	2	65	2	2	2	4	.333	0	2-4	10	4.36	3.56
	4 ML YEARS		129	1	0	34	136.0	607	137	75	69	15	1	7	3	68	3	146	5	2	4	6	.400	0	3-8	19	4.60	4.57

Andrew Romine

ROW-mine
Bats: B **Throws:** R **Pos:** 2B-27;CF-24;3B-23;1B-22;LF-18;PR-12;RF-11;SS-10;PH-10;DH-7;C-1 **Ht:** 6'1" **Wt:** 200 **Born:** 12/24/85 **Age:** 32

							BATTING													RUNNING			AVERAGES			
Year	Team	Lg	G	AB	H	2B	3B	HR	(Hm	Rd)	TB	R	RBI	RC	TBB	IBB	SO	HBP	SH	SF	SB	CS	GDP	Avg	OBP	Slg	OPS
2010	LAA	AL	5	11	1	0	0	0	(0	0)	1	0	0	0	0	0	4	0	1	0	0	0	0	.091	.091	.091	.182
2011	LAA	AL	10	16	2	0	0	0	(0	0)	2	2	0	0	1	0	6	0	1	0	1	0	0	.125	.176	.125	.301
2012	LAA	AL	12	17	7	0	0	0	(0	0)	7	2	1	5	3	0	3	0	1	0	1	0	0	.412	.500	.412	.912
2013	LAA	AL	47	108	28	3	0	0	(0	0)	31	9	10	12	7	0	24	1	6	1	1	0	2	.259	.308	.287	.595
2014	Det	AL	94	251	57	6	0	2	(1	1)	69	30	12	17	18	0	60	0	4	0	12	2	5	.227	.279	.275	.554
2015	Det	AL	109	184	47	5	0	2	(0	2)	58	25	15	13	11	1	46	3	4	1	10	5	4	.255	.304	.315	.622
2016	Det	AL	109	174	41	5	2	2	(1	1)	56	21	16	15	13	0	38	4	3	0	8	0	5	.236	.304	.322	.626
2017	Det	AL	124	318	74	17	2	4	(3	1)	107	45	25	27	22	0	67	4	2	2	6	4	7	.233	.289	.336	.625
	Postseason		3	11	2	0	0	0	(0	0)	2	0	0	0	0	0	4	0	0	0	0	0	0	.182	.182	.182	.364
	8 ML YEARS		510	1079	257	36	4	10	(5	5)	331	134	79	89	75	1	248	12	22	4	39	11	23	.238	.294	.307	.601

Austin Romine

Bats: R **Throws:** R **Pos:** C-67;1B-12;PH-9;DH-1
ROW-mine
Ht: 6'1" **Wt:** 220 **Born:** 11/22/1988 **Age:** 29

							BATTING													RUNNING			AVERAGES			
Year	Team	Lg	G	AB	H	2B	3B	HR	(Hm	Rd)	TB	R	RBI	RC	TBB	IBB	SO	HBP	SH	SF	SB	CS	GDP	Avg	OBP	Slg	OPS
2011	NYY	AL	9	19	3	0	0	0	(0	0)	3	2	0	0	1	0	5	0	0	0	0	0	0	.158	.200	.158	.358
2013	NYY	AL	60	135	28	9	0	1	(0	1)	40	15	10	8	8	0	37	1	3	1	1	0	7	.207	.255	.296	.551
2014	NYY	AL	7	13	3	1	0	0	(0	0)	4	2	1	2	0	0	4	0	0	0	0	0	0	.231	.231	.308	.538
2015	NYY	AL	1	2	0	0	0	0	(0	0)	0	0	0	0	0	0	0	0	0	0	0	0	0	.000	.000	.000	.000
2016	NYY	AL	62	165	40	11	0	4	(1	3)	63	17	26	19	7	1	31	0	1	3	1	0	7	.242	.269	.382	.650
2017	NYY	AL	80	229	50	9	1	2	(2	0)	67	19	21	18	16	0	57	2	2	3	0	0	7	.218	.272	.293	.565
	6 ML YEARS		219	563	124	30	1	7	(3	4)	177	55	58	47	32	1	134	3	6	7	2	0	21	.220	.263	.314	.577

Sergio Romo

Pitches: R **Bats:** R **Pos:** RP-55
Ht: 5'11" **Wt:** 185 **Born:** 3/4/1983 **Age:** 35

			HOW MUCH HE PITCHED					WHAT HE GAVE UP											THE RESULTS						
Year	Team	Lg	G	GS	CG	GF	IP	BFP	H	R	ER	HR	SH	SF	HB	TBB	IBB	SO	WP	Bk	W	L	Pct	Sh	Sv-Op	Hld	ERC	ERA
2008	SF	NL	29	0	0	8	34.0	130	16	13	8	3	2	1	3	8	1	33	0	0	3	1	.750	0	0-0	5	1.27	2.12
2009	SF	NL	45	0	0	9	34.0	143	30	15	15	1	2	0	1	11	0	41	2	0	5	2	.714	0	2-2	10	2.76	3.97
2010	SF	NL	68	0	0	13	62.0	247	46	16	15	6	2	2	4	14	2	70	0	0	5	3	.625	0	0-4	21	2.26	2.18
2011	SF	NL	65	0	0	16	48.0	175	29	8	8	2	2	0	0	5	1	70	0	0	3	1	.750	0	1-2	23	1.08	1.50
2012	SF	NL	69	0	0	27	55.1	215	37	11	11	5	2	0	3	10	1	63	2	0	4	2	.667	0	14-15	23	1.72	1.79
2013	SF	NL	65	0	0	52	60.1	250	53	20	17	5	1	1	1	12	3	58	1	0	5	8	.385	0	38-43	0	2.47	2.54
2014	SF	NL	64	0	0	35	58.0	230	43	24	24	9	2	0	4	12	2	59	2	0	6	4	.600	0	23-28	11	2.54	3.72
2015	SF	NL	70	0	0	14	57.1	230	51	20	19	3	2	0	1	10	2	71	4	0	0	5	.000	0	2-4	34	2.37	2.98
2016	SF	NL	40	0	0	13	30.2	117	26	9	9	5	0	0	0	7	1	33	1	0	1	0	1.000	0	4-4	14	3.13	2.64
2017	2 Tms		55	0	0	12	55.2	224	42	23	22	9	0	1	1	19	2	59	2	1	3	1	.750	0	0-1	11	2.97	3.56
17	LAD	NL	30	0	0	8	25.0	108	23	17	17	7	0	0	0	12	1	31	0	1	1	1	.500	0	0-0	7	5.15	6.12
17	TB	AL	25	0	0	4	30.2	116	19	6	5	2	0	1	1	7	1	28	2	0	2	0	1.000	0	0-1	4	1.54	1.47
	Postseason		27	0	0	13	23.1	90	18	8	8	3	0	0	0	3	0	22	1	0	3	1	.750	0	4-7	4	2.06	3.09
	10 ML YEARS		570	0	0	199	495.1	1961	373	159	148	48	15	5	18	108	15	557	14	1	35	27	.565	0	84-103	152	2.20	2.69

Bruce Rondon

Pitches: R Bats: R Pos: RP-21   rohn-DOHN   Ht: 6'3" Wt: 275 Born: 12/9/1990 Age: 27

Year	Team	Lg	G	GS	CG	GF	IP	BFP	H	R	ER	HR	SH	SF	HB	TBB	IBB	SO	WP	Bk	W	L	Pct	Sh	Sv-Op	Hld	ERC	ERA
2017	Toledo*	AAA	38	0	0	14	36.2	167	34	15	11	2	1	0	0	25	1	43	2	0	2	1	.667	0	1- -	-	4.32	2.70
2013	Det	AL	30	0	0	12	28.2	122	28	11	11	2	1	2	0	11	0	30	7	1	1	2	.333	0	1-3	5	3.69	3.45
2015	Det	AL	35	0	0	15	31.0	145	31	22	20	3	3	2	2	19	1	36	2	0	1	0	1.000	0	5-9	3	4.97	5.81
2016	Det	AL	37	0	0	7	36.1	144	23	12	12	5	2	0	3	12	1	45	1	1	5	2	.714	0	0-2	6	2.43	2.97
2017	Det	AL	21	0	0	3	15.2	76	21	19	19	1	0	1	1	10	2	22	1	1	1	3	.250	0	1-2	7	6.92	10.91
	4 ML YEARS		123	0	0	37	111.2	487	103	64	62	11	6	5	6	52	4	133	11	3	8	7	.533	0	7-16	21	4.03	5.00

Hector Rondon

Pitches: R Bats: R Pos: RP-61   rohn-DOHN   Ht: 6'3" Wt: 230 Born: 2/26/1988 Age: 30

Year	Team	Lg	G	GS	CG	GF	IP	BFP	H	R	ER	HR	SH	SF	HB	TBB	IBB	SO	WP	Bk	W	L	Pct	Sh	Sv-Op	Hld	ERC	ERA
2013	ChC	NL	45	0	0	14	54.2	242	52	29	29	6	4	3	3	25	5	44	4	0	2	1	.667	0	0-1	2	4.10	4.77
2014	ChC	NL	64	0	0	44	63.1	255	52	21	17	2	0	1	0	15	0	63	0	0	4	4	.500	0	29-33	1	2.10	2.42
2015	ChC	NL	72	0	0	47	70.0	281	55	19	13	4	3	1	3	15	2	69	5	1	6	4	.600	0	30-34	8	2.12	1.67
2016	ChC	NL	54	0	0	35	51.0	200	42	20	20	8	1	2	2	8	0	58	3	0	2	3	.400	0	18-23	7	2.75	3.53
2017	ChC	NL	61	0	0	14	57.1	237	50	30	27	10	1	0	1	20	0	69	3	0	4	1	.800	0	0-3	10	3.77	4.24
	Postseason		12	0	0	9	11.0	46	13	5	5	2	0	0	0	2	0	9	0	0	1	0	1.000	0	2-2	1	4.92	4.09
	5 ML YEARS		296	0	0	154	296.1	1215	251	119	106	30	9	7	9	83	7	303	15	1	18	13	.581	0	77-94	28	2.88	3.22

Adam Rosales

Bats: R Throws: R Pos: SS-65;3B-15;2B-11;PH-11;1B-6;PR-2;LF-1;DH-1   Ht: 6'2" Wt: 200 Born: 5/20/1983 Age: 35

Year	Team	Lg	G	AB	H	2B	3B	HR	(Hm	Rd)	TB	R	RBI	RC	TBB	IBB	SO	HBP	SH	SF	SB	CS	GDP	Avg	OBP	Slg	OPS
2008	Cin	NL	18	29	6	1	0	0	(0	0)	7	0	2	2	1	0	4	0	0	0	1	0	0	.207	.233	.241	.475
2009	Cin	NL	87	230	49	10	1	4	(2	2)	73	23	19	22	26	0	46	5	2	3	1	2	2	.213	.303	.317	.620
2010	Oak	AL	80	255	69	8	2	7	(1	6)	102	31	31	31	19	0	65	1	2	2	2	2	1	.271	.321	.400	.721
2011	Oak	AL	24	61	6	0	0	2	(0	2)	12	5	8	0	4	0	13	1	0	2	0	0	4	.098	.162	.197	.358
2012	Oak	AL	42	99	22	5	0	2	(1	1)	33	12	8	6	11	1	24	0	0	1	0	0	4	.222	.297	.333	.631
2013	2 Tms	AL	68	147	28	5	0	5	(2	3)	48	15	12	6	10	1	34	4	4	1	0	0	4	.190	.259	.327	.586
2014	Tex	AL	56	164	43	7	0	4	(2	2)	62	20	19	23	13	0	42	3	0	0	4	2	5	.262	.328	.378	.706
2015	Tex	AL	55	114	26	4	0	3	(1	2)	39	14	7	9	10	0	30	1	0	0	4	4	4	.228	.296	.342	.638
2016	SD	NL	105	214	49	12	3	13	(9	4)	106	37	35	34	29	2	88	1	0	4	4	0	2	.229	.319	.495	.814
2017	2 Tms	AL	105	289	65	16	0	7	(3	4)	102	25	36	26	11	1	100	4	4	4	1	2	6	.225	.260	.353	.613
13	Oak	AL	51	136	26	5	0	4	(2	2)	43	11	8	5	10	1	31	4	4	0	0	0	4	.191	.267	.316	.583
13	Tex	AL	17	11	2	0	0	1	(0	1)	5	4	4	1	0	0	3	0	0	1	0	0	0	.182	.167	.455	.621
17	Oak	AL	71	205	48	11	0	4	(2	2)	71	15	27	22	10	0	66	2	3	3	1	1	2	.234	.273	.346	.619
17	Ari	NL	34	84	17	5	0	3	(1	2)	31	10	9	4	1	1	34	2	1	1	0	1	4	.202	.227	.369	.596
	10 ML YEARS		640	1602	363	68	6	47	(21	26)	584	182	177	159	134	5	446	20	12	17	17	12	32	.227	.292	.365	.656

Alberto Rosario

Bats: R Throws: R Pos: PH-3   Ht: 5'10" Wt: 190 Born: 1/10/1987 Age: 31

Year	Team	Lg	G	AB	H	2B	3B	HR	(Hm	Rd)	TB	R	RBI	RC	TBB	IBB	SO	HBP	SH	SF	SB	CS	GDP	Avg	OBP	Slg	OPS
2013	Portlnd	AA	11	36	6	0	0	0	(-	-)	6	3	4	1	3	0	4	1	0	1	0	0	1	.167	.244	.167	.411
2013	Pwtckt	AAA	30	90	21	3	0	2	(-	-)	30	13	6	9	7	0	22	2	3	0	0	0	3	.233	.303	.333	.636
2014	Chatt	AA	25	47	13	1	0	1	(-	-)	17	3	7	5	3	0	15	0	0	0	0	0	1	.277	.320	.362	.682
2015	Sprgfld	AA	44	149	27	8	0	1	(-	-)	38	9	5	8	9	2	20	3	4	0	0	0	2	.181	.242	.255	.497
2016	Memp	AAA	39	114	32	5	0	0	(-	-)	37	8	13	12	6	0	20	2	0	2	0	0	6	.281	.323	.325	.647
2017	Memp	AAA	50	190	47	6	0	0	(-	-)	53	20	23	16	11	0	31	1	1	1	3	0	5	.247	.291	.279	.570
2016	StL	NL	20	38	7	2	0	0	(0	0)	9	3	2	1	2	0	5	0	1	0	0	0	2	.184	.225	.237	.462
2017	StL	NL	3	3	0	0	0	0	(0	0)	0	0	0	0	0	0	1	0	0	0	0	0	1	.000	.000	.000	.000
	2 ML YEARS		23	41	7	2	0	0	(0	0)	9	3	2	1	2	0	6	0	1	0	0	0	3	.171	.209	.220	.429

Amed Rosario

Bats: R Throws: R Pos: SS-45;PH-2;PR-1   Ht: 6'2" Wt: 189 Born: 11/20/1995 Age: 22

Year	Team	Lg	G	AB	H	2B	3B	HR	(Hm	Rd)	TB	R	RBI	RC	TBB	IBB	SO	HBP	SH	SF	SB	CS	GDP	Avg	OBP	Slg	OPS
2013	Kngspt	R+	58	212	51	8	4	3	(-	-)	76	22	23	19	11	0	43	1	0	7	2	6	7	.241	.279	.358	.637
2014	2 Tms	Low	75	296	81	11	6	2	(-	-)	110	41	27	36	18	0	58	3	2	2	7	3	5	.274	.320	.372	.691
2015	Stluci	A+	103	385	99	20	5	0	(-	-)	129	41	25	42	23	0	73	5	3	1	12	4	11	.257	.307	.335	.642
2016	Stluci	A+	66	265	82	10	8	3	(-	-)	117	27	40	43	21	1	36	1	0	3	13	6	7	.309	.359	.442	.800
2016	Bnghtn	AA	54	214	73	14	5	2	(-	-)	103	38	31	41	19	2	51	1	0	3	6	2	8	.341	.392	.481	.874
2017	LsVgs	AAA	94	393	129	19	7	7	(-	-)	183	66	58	69	23	0	67	4	0	5	19	6	13	.328	.367	.466	.833
2017	NYM	NL	46	165	41	4	4	4	(1	3)	65	16	10	14	3	0	49	2	0	0	7	3	3	.248	.271	.394	.665

Eddie Rosario

Bats: L **Throws:** R **Pos:** LF-138;RF-16;CF-10;DH-1 **Ht:** 6'1" **Wt:** 180 **Born:** 9/28/1991 **Age:** 26

Year Team	Lg	G	AB	H	2B	3B	HR	(Hm	Rd)	TB	R	RBI	RC	TBB	IBB	SO	HBP	SH	SF	SB	CS	GDP	Avg	OBP	Slg	OPS
2015 Min	AL	122	453	121	18	**15**	13	(10	3)	208	60	50	58	15	3	118	0	3	3	11	6	5	.267	.289	.459	.748
2016 Min	AL	92	335	90	17	2	10	(4	6)	141	52	32	35	12	2	91	2	2	3	5	2	4	.269	.295	.421	.716
2017 Min	AL	151	542	157	33	2	27	(20	7)	275	79	78	77	35	1	106	0	4	8	9	8	10	.290	.328	.507	.836
3 ML YEARS		365	1330	368	68	19	50	(34	16)	624	191	160	170	62	6	315	2	9	14	25	16	19	.277	.307	.469	.776

Randy Rosario

Pitches: L **Bats:** L **Pos:** RP-2 **Ht:** 6'1" **Wt:** 200 **Born:** 5/18/1994 **Age:** 24

Year Team	Lg	G	GS	CG	GF	IP	BFP	H	R	ER	HR	SH	SF	HB	TBB	IBB	SO	WP	Bk	W	L	Pct	Sh	Sv-Op	Hld	ERC	ERA
2013 Elizab	R+	9	9	0	0	44.2	191	42	16	14	0	3	2	1	18	1	37	3	1	4	3	.571	0	0--	-	3.11	2.82
2015 2 Tms	Low	13	12	0	0	61.2	264	60	31	21	1	4	1	2	20	0	54	10	3	3	6	.333	0	0--	-	3.15	3.06
2016 FtMyrs	A+	21	16	0	1	74.1	407	102	47	35	3	2	2	2	34	0	68	7	0	6	6	.500	0	1--	-	4.01	3.34
2017 Chatt	AA	32	0	0	8	57.1	245	57	29	26	4	0	1	3	23	0	45	4	0	1	0	1.000	0	1--	-	4.12	4.08
2017 Min	AL	2	0	0	1	2.1	15	7	8	8	1	0	0	1	0	0	2	0	0	0	0	-	0	0-0	0	21.70	30.86

Trevor Rosenthal

Pitches: R **Bats:** R **Pos:** RP-50 **Ht:** 6'2" **Wt:** 230 **Born:** 5/29/1990 **Age:** 28

Year Team	Lg	G	GS	CG	GF	IP	BFP	H	R	ER	HR	SH	SF	HB	TBB	IBB	SO	WP	Bk	W	L	Pct	Sh	Sv-Op	Hld	ERC	ERA
2012 StL	NL	19	0	0	7	22.2	89	14	7	7	2	1	0	1	7	0	25	1	0	0	2	.000	0	0-0	3	1.89	2.78
2013 StL	NL	74	0	0	15	75.1	311	63	25	22	4	3	0	6	20	0	108	3	0	2	4	.333	0	3-8	29	2.68	2.63
2014 StL	NL	72	0	0	59	70.1	308	57	25	25	2	2	4	4	42	5	87	1	1	2	6	.250	0	45-**51**	2	3.36	3.20
2015 StL	NL	68	0	0	57	68.2	287	62	16	16	3	1	0	1	25	3	83	7	0	2	4	.333	0	48-51	0	3.04	2.10
2016 StL	NL	45	0	0	27	40.1	197	48	22	20	3	1	0	3	29	0	56	0	0	2	4	.333	0	14-18	15	6.59	4.46
2017 StL	NL	50	0	0	16	47.2	202	37	20	18	3	1	3	2	20	0	76	2	0	3	4	.429	0	11-13	12	2.80	3.40
Postseason		23	0	0	15	26.0	102	15	2	2	0	0	0	1	11	3	42	1	1	1	0	1.000	0	7-9	2	1.41	0.69
6 ML YEARS		328	0	0	181	325.0	1394	281	115	108	17	9	7	17	143	8	435	14	1	11	24	.314	0	121-141	46	3.30	2.99

Joe Ross

Pitches: R **Bats:** R **Pos:** SP-13 **Ht:** 6'4" **Wt:** 225 **Born:** 5/21/1993 **Age:** 25

Year Team	Lg	G	GS	CG	GF	IP	BFP	H	R	ER	HR	SH	SF	HB	TBB	IBB	SO	WP	Bk	W	L	Pct	Sh	Sv-Op	Hld	ERC	ERA
2017 Syrcse*	AAA	5	5	0	0	27.2	122	33	16	15	3	0	2	0	8	1	22	3	0	2	2	.500	0	0--	-	4.70	4.88
2015 Was	NL	16	13	0	1	76.2	314	64	33	31	7	3	1	2	21	0	69	1	0	5	5	.500	0	0-0	0	2.74	3.64
2016 Was	NL	19	19	0	0	105.0	447	108	43	40	9	7	3	6	29	3	93	2	0	7	5	.583	0	0-0	0	3.84	3.43
2017 Was	NL	13	13	0	0	73.2	323	88	44	41	16	5	0	1	20	2	68	2	0	5	3	.625	0	0-0	0	5.54	5.01
Postseason		1	1	0	0	2.2	15	3	4	4	1	0	0	2	2	0	3	0	0	0	0	-	0	0-0	0	12.09	13.50
3 ML YEARS		48	45	0	1	255.1	1084	260	120	112	32	15	4	9	70	5	230	5	0	17	13	.567	0	0-0	0	3.96	3.95

Tyson Ross

Pitches: R **Bats:** R **Pos:** SP-10; RP-2 **Ht:** 6'6" **Wt:** 245 **Born:** 4/22/1987 **Age:** 31

Year Team	Lg	G	GS	CG	GF	IP	BFP	H	R	ER	HR	SH	SF	HB	TBB	IBB	SO	WP	Bk	W	L	Pct	Sh	Sv-Op	Hld	ERC	ERA
2010 Oak	AL	26	2	0	9	39.1	169	39	24	24	4	1	4	0	20	0	32	5	0	1	4	.200	0	1-2	2	4.60	5.49
2011 Oak	AL	9	6	0	1	36.0	145	33	12	11	1	1	0	0	13	1	24	2	0	3	3	.500	0	0-0	0	3.09	2.75
2012 Oak	AL	18	13	0	3	73.1	342	96	56	53	7	3	3	5	37	3	46	2	1	2	11	.154	0	0-0	0	6.68	6.50
2013 SD	NL	35	16	0	8	125.0	504	100	51	44	8	3	5	7	44	4	119	7	0	3	8	.273	0	0-0	3	2.84	3.17
2014 SD	NL	31	31	2	0	195.2	811	165	75	61	13	10	4	9	72	2	195	12	0	13	14	.481	1	0-0	3	3.07	2.81
2015 SD	NL	33	**33**	1	0	196.0	823	172	78	71	9	3	3	8	**84**	3	212	**14**	0	10	12	.455	0	0-0	0	3.33	3.26
2016 SD	NL	1	1	0	0	5.1	27	9	8	7	0	0	0	2	1	0	5	1	0	0	1	.000	0	0-0	0	8.24	11.81
2017 Tex	AL	12	10	0	0	49.0	238	53	46	42	7	0	1	6	37	0	36	4	0	3	3	.500	0	0-0	0	6.88	7.71
8 ML YEARS		165	112	3	21	719.2	3059	667	350	313	49	21	20	37	308	13	669	47	1	35	56	.385	1	1-2	2	3.79	3.91

Robbie Ross Jr.

Pitches: L **Bats:** L **Pos:** RP-8 **Ht:** 5'11" **Wt:** 215 **Born:** 6/24/1989 **Age:** 29

Year Team	Lg	G	GS	CG	GF	IP	BFP	H	R	ER	HR	SH	SF	HB	TBB	IBB	SO	WP	Bk	W	L	Pct	Sh	Sv-Op	Hld	ERC	ERA
2017 Pwtckt*	AAA	6	0	0	4	6.0	22	1	1	1	0	1	1	0	3	0	7	0	0	1	0	1.000	0	0--	-	0.57	1.50
2012 Tex	AL	58	0	0	9	65.0	265	55	21	16	3	1	2	2	23	3	47	1	1	6	0	1.000	0	0-0	9	2.83	2.22
2013 Tex	AL	65	0	0	16	62.1	267	63	21	21	4	0	0	5	19	2	58	2	0	4	2	.667	0	0-1	15	3.79	3.03
2014 Tex	AL	27	12	0	4	78.1	365	103	65	54	9	2	2	7	30	2	51	6	0	3	6	.333	0	0-0	2	6.34	6.20
2015 Bos	AL	54	0	0	18	60.2	259	59	28	26	7	2	2	3	20	2	53	1	0	0	2	.000	0	6-8	12	3.89	3.86
2016 Bos	AL	54	0	0	8	55.1	238	47	21	20	2	0	1	8	23	0	56	7	0	3	2	.600	0	0-0	8	3.42	3.25
2017 Bos	AL	8	0	0	1	9.0	45	12	7	7	0	0	0	3	5	1	9	2	0	0	0	-	0	0-0	1	7.14	7.00
Postseason		1	0	0	0	0.1	1	0	0	0	0	0	0	0	0	0	1	0	0	0	0	-	0	0-0	0	0.00	0.00
6 ML YEARS		266	12	0	56	330.2	1439	339	163	144	25	5	7	28	120	10	274	19	1	16	12	.571	0	6-9	47	4.20	3.92

Zac Rosscup

Pitches: L **Bats:** R **Pos:** RP-10   ROSS-cup   **Ht:** 6'2" **Wt:** 220 **Born:** 6/9/1988 **Age:** 30

			HOW MUCH HE PITCHED						WHAT HE GAVE UP										THE RESULTS						
Year	Team	Lg	G	GS	CG	GF	IP	BFP	H	R	ER	HR	SH	SF	HB	TBB	IBB	SO	WP	Bk	W	L	Pct	Sh	Sv-Op	Hld	ERC	ERA
2017	Iowa*	AAA	17	1	0	3	27.2	111	21	9	8	3	0	0	2	8	0	39	0	0	2	2	.500		0	1--		2.75	2.60
2017	Alba*	AAA	12	0	0	2	12.2	50	8	3	3	1	0	0	0	4	0	15	3	0			-	0	1--		1.76	2.13
2013	ChC	NL	10	0	0	3	6.2	30	3	1	1	1	0	0	0	7	1	7	0	0	0	0	-	0	0-0		3.56	1.35
2014	ChC	NL	18	0	0	5	13.1	66	14	14	14	2	0	0	0	12	1	21	0	0	1	0	1.000	0	0-0	1	6.54	9.45
2015	ChC	NL	33	0	0	6	26.2	118	26	13	13	5	2	0	0	13	0	29	1	0	2	1	.667	0	0-2	6	4.85	4.39
2017	2 Tms	NL	10	0	0	2	7.2	32	9	4	4	2	0	0	0	0	0	10	0	0	0	0	-	0	0-0		4.37	4.70
17	ChC	NL	1	0	0	0	0.2	2	0	0	0	0	0	0	0	0	0	0	0	0	0	0	-	0	0-0		0.00	0.00
17	Col	NL	9	0	0	2	7.0	30	9	4	4	2	0	0	0	0	0	10	0	0	0	0	-	0	0-0	1	5.20	5.14
	4 ML YEARS		71	0	0	16	54.1	246	52	32	32	10	2	0	0	32	2	67	1	0	3	1	.750	0	0-2	8	5.06	5.30

Chris Rowley

Pitches: R **Bats:** R **Pos:** SP-3; RP-3   **Ht:** 6'2" **Wt:** 195 **Born:** 8/14/1990 **Age:** 27

			HOW MUCH HE PITCHED						WHAT HE GAVE UP										THE RESULTS						
Year	Team	Lg	G	GS	CG	GF	IP	BFP	H	R	ER	HR	SH	SF	HB	TBB	IBB	SO	WP	Bk	W	L	Pct	Sh	Sv-Op	Hld	ERC	ERA
2013	B Jays	R	9	5	0	2	32.2	120	19	5	4	1	0	0	0	3	0	39	1	0	4	0	1.000	0	0--		0.96	1.10
2016	Dnedin	A+	31	14	0	12	123.2	514	128	54	48	14	1	4	2	30	1	86	4	0	10	3	.769	0	1--		3.85	3.49
2017	Nham	AA	17	5	0	5	52.0	198	33	10	10	4	0	2	3	9	1	49	1	0	3	2	.600	0	1--		1.56	1.73
2017	Buffalo	AAA	12	8	0	2	64.1	269	60	21	19	2	3	1	5	17	0	46	1	0	3	5	.375	0	0--		3.03	2.66
2017	Tor	AL	6	3	0	2	18.2	89	24	14	14	4	0	0	0	10	0	11	1	1	1	2	.333	0	0-0	0	7.21	6.75

Ryan Rua

Bats: R **Throws:** R **Pos:** LF-37; 1B-23; PH-6; PR-5; RF-1; DH-1   ROO-ah   **Ht:** 6'2" **Wt:** 205 **Born:** 3/11/1990 **Age:** 28

			BATTING																		RUNNING			AVERAGES			
Year	Team	Lg	G	AB	H	2B	3B	HR	(Hm	Rd)	TB	R	RBI	RC	TBB	IBB	SO	HBP	SH	SF	SB	CS	GDP	Avg	OBP	Slg	OPS
2017	RdRck*	AAA	46	177	47	7	2	8	(-	-)	82	27	28	26	10	0	55	1	0	0	3	0	2	.266	.309	.463	.772
2014	Tex	AL	28	105	31	7	0	2	(1	1)	44	11	14	13	2	0	18	2	0	0	1	0	6	.295	.321	.419	.740
2015	Tex	AL	28	83	16	5	0	4	(2	2)	33	10	7	5	3	0	32	0	0	0	1	0	8	.193	.221	.398	.619
2016	Tex	AL	99	240	62	8	1	8	(3	5)	96	40	22	25	21	2	76	6	0	2	9	0	8	.258	.331	.400	.731
2017	Tex	AL	63	129	28	6	0	3	(2	1)	43	17	12	15	14	0	52	0	1	0	2	2	3	.217	.294	.333	.627
	Postseason		1	3	2	0	0	0	(0	0)	2	0	0	1	0	0	1	0	0	0	0	0	0	.667	.667	.667	1.333
	4 ML YEARS		218	557	137	26	1	17	(8	9)	216	78	55	58	40	2	178	8	1	2	12	2	19	.246	.305	.388	.693

Drew Rucinski

Pitches: R **Bats:** R **Pos:** RP-2   ruh-SIN-ski   **Ht:** 6'2" **Wt:** 190 **Born:** 12/30/1988 **Age:** 29

			HOW MUCH HE PITCHED						WHAT HE GAVE UP										THE RESULTS						
Year	Team	Lg	G	GS	CG	GF	IP	BFP	H	R	ER	HR	SH	SF	HB	TBB	IBB	SO	WP	Bk	W	L	Pct	Sh	Sv-Op	Hld	ERC	ERA
2017	Roch*	AAA	37	2	0	12	63.0	246	54	21	18	3	0	1	1	10	0	57	6	0	2	6	.250	0	2--		2.23	2.57
2014	LAA	AL	3	0	0	2	7.1	34	9	4	4	0	0	0	1	2	0	8	0	0	0	0	-	0	0-0	0	4.52	4.91
2015	LAA	AL	4	1	0	2	7.0	35	10	6	6	1	0	0	1	6	0	4	2	0	0	2	.000	0	0-0	0	10.39	7.71
2017	Min	AL	2	0	0	1	4.1	23	10	5	5	2	0	0	0	2	0	5	0	0	0	0	-	0	0-0	0	18.05	10.38
	3 ML YEARS		9	1	0	5	18.2	92	29	15	15	3	0	0	2	10	0	17	2	0	0	2	.000	0	0-0	0	9.42	7.23

Justin Ruggiano

Bats: R **Throws:** R **Pos:** RF-12; LF-5; PH-3; CF-2   roo-jee-AH-no   **Ht:** 6'1" **Wt:** 210 **Born:** 4/12/1982 **Age:** 36

			BATTING																		RUNNING			AVERAGES			
Year	Team	Lg	G	AB	H	2B	3B	HR	(Hm	Rd)	TB	R	RBI	RC	TBB	IBB	SO	HBP	SH	SF	SB	CS	GDP	Avg	OBP	Slg	OPS
2017	Scrmto*	AAA	45	157	44	13	0	6	(-	-)	75	23	21	24	9	0	33	2	0	1	1	2	6	.280	.325	.478	.803
2007	TB	AL	7	14	3	0	0	0	(0	0)	3	2	3	1	1	0	5	0	0	0	0	0	0	.214	.267	.214	.481
2008	TB	AL	45	76	15	4	0	2	(0	2)	25	9	7	4	4	0	27	1	0	0	2	0	2	.197	.247	.329	.576
2011	TB	AL	46	105	26	4	0	4	(3	1)	42	11	13	16	4	0	26	0	0	1	1	1	2	.248	.273	.400	.673
2012	Mia	NL	91	288	90	23	1	13	(4	9)	154	38	36	46	29	0	84	0	1	1	14	8	6	.313	.374	.535	.909
2013	Mia	NL	128	424	94	18	1	18	(3	15)	168	49	50	42	41	1	114	5	1	0	15	8	9	.222	.298	.396	.694
2014	ChC	NL	81	224	63	13	1	6	(2	4)	96	29	28	32	18	0	70	3	1	4	2	4	5	.281	.337	.429	.766
2015	2 Tms		57	125	31	8	1	6	(1	5)	59	20	15	20	14	0	41	2	0	0	5	2	1	.248	.333	.472	.805
2016	2 Tms		9	24	8	1	0	2	(0	2)	15	4	7	5	2	0	10	0	0	0	0	1	1	.333	.385	.625	1.010
2017	SF	NL	19	60	13	1	0	2	(1	1)	20	2	4	1	1	0	17	1	0	1	1	1	1	.217	.238	.333	.571
15	Sea	AL	36	70	15	4	0	2	(1	1)	25	8	3	9	11	0	27	0	0	0	3	2	0	.214	.321	.357	.678
15	LAD	NL	21	55	16	4	1	4	(0	4)	34	12	12	11	3	0	14	2	0	0	2	0	1	.291	.350	.618	.968
16	Tex	AL	1	4	1	1	0	0	(0	0)	2	0	1	1	0	0	1	0	0	0	0	0	0	.250	.250	.500	.750
16	NYM	NL	8	20	7	0	0	2	(0	2)	13	4	6	4	2	0	9	0	0	0	0	1	1	.350	.409	.650	1.059
	Postseason		3	4	0	0	0	0	(0	0)	0	0	0	0	0	0	3	0	0	0	0	0	0	.000	.000	.000	.000
	9 ML YEARS		483	1340	343	72	4	53	(16	37)	582	164	163	167	114	1	394	12	4	7	40	25	23	.256	.318	.434	.753

Carlos Ruiz

Bats: R **Throws:** R **Pos:** C-47; PH-5; 1B-1; DH-1   **Ht:** 5'10" **Wt:** 215 **Born:** 1/22/1979 **Age:** 39

			BATTING																		RUNNING			AVERAGES			
Year	Team	Lg	G	AB	H	2B	3B	HR	(Hm	Rd)	TB	R	RBI	RC	TBB	IBB	SO	HBP	SH	SF	SB	CS	GDP	Avg	OBP	Slg	OPS
2006	Phi	NL	27	69	18	1	1	3	(2	1)	30	5	10	10	5	2	8	1	2	1	0	0	3	.261	.316	.435	.751
2007	Phi	NL	115	374	97	29	2	6	(4	2)	148	42	54	49	42	10	49	5	5	3	6	1	17	.259	.340	.396	.735
2008	Phi	NL	117	320	70	14	0	4	(2	2)	96	47	31	28	44	6	38	4	4	1	1	2	14	.219	.320	.300	.620
2009	Phi	NL	107	322	82	26	1	9	(5	4)	137	32	43	49	47	8	39	4	4	2	3	2	8	.255	.355	.425	.780
2010	Phi	NL	121	371	112	28	1	8	(3	5)	166	43	53	62	55	13	54	6	0	1	0	1	8	.302	.400	.447	.847

Year Team	Lg	G	AB	H	2B	3B	HR	(Hm	Rd)	TB	R	RBI	RC	TBB	IBB	SO	HBP	SH	SF	SB	CS	GDP	Avg	OBP	Slg	OPS
								BATTING												RUNNING			AVERAGES			
2011 Phi	NL	132	410	116	23	0	6	(1	5)	157	49	40	59	48	10	48	10	3	1	1	0	7	.283	.371	.383	.754
2012 Phi	NL	114	372	121	32	0	16	(8	8)	201	56	68	75	29	6	50	16	0	4	4	0	6	.325	.394	.540	.935
2013 Phi	NL	92	310	83	16	0	5	(4	1)	114	30	37	34	18	3	39	7	4	2	1	0	11	.268	.320	.368	.688
2014 Phi	NL	110	381	96	25	1	6	(2	4)	141	43	31	50	46	1	60	12	1	5	4	2	11	.252	.347	.370	.717
2015 Phi	NL	86	284	60	13	1	2	(1	1)	81	23	22	19	28	2	43	4	3	1	1	1	13	.211	.290	.285	.575
2016 2 Tms	NL	62	201	53	8	0	3	(1	2)	70	21	15	25	27	1	33	5	0	0	3	1	4	.264	.365	.348	.713
2017 Sea	AL	54	125	27	8	0	3	(2	1)	44	14	11	13	14	0	38	4	1	1	1	0	4	.216	.313	.352	.665
16 Phi	NL	48	165	43	6	0	3	(1	2)	58	18	12	21	24	1	28	4	0	0	3	1	3	.261	.368	.352	.719
16 LAD	NL	14	36	10	2	0	0	(0	0)	12	3	3	4	3	0	5	1	0	0	0	0	1	.278	.350	.333	.683
Postseason		53	153	39	9	1	5	(4	1)	65	21	19	27	25	3	18	5	1	0	3	0	2	.255	.377	.425	.802
12 ML YEARS		1137	3539	935	223	7	71	(35	36)	1385	405	415	473	403	62	499	78	27	22	25	10	106	.264	.350	.391	.742

Jose Ruiz

Pitches: R Bats: R Pos: RP-1

Ht: 6'1" Wt: 190 Born: 10/21/1994 Age: 23

Year Team	Lg	G	GS	CG	GF	IP	BFP	H	R	ER	HR	SH	SF	HB	TBB	IBB	SO	WP	Bk	W	L	Pct	Sh	Sv-Op	Hld	ERC	ERA
		HOW MUCH HE PITCHED						WHAT HE GAVE UP												THE RESULTS							
2016 3 Tms	Low	11	0	0	8	12.1	43	3	0	0	0	1	0	0	5	0	14	1	0	2	0	1.000	0	2- -	-	0.63	0.00
2017 Lk Els	A+	44	0	0	11	49.2	224	57	34	33	7	0	1	2	25	0	45	6	0	1	2	.333	0	2- -	-	5.96	5.98
2017 SD	NL	1	0	0	1	1.0	4	0	0	0	0	0	0	0	1	0	1	0	0	0	0	-	0	0-0	0	0.95	0.00

Rio Ruiz

Bats: L Throws: R Pos: 3B-41;PH-11;1B-2

Ht: 6'1" Wt: 230 Born: 5/22/1994 Age: 24

Year Team	Lg	G	AB	H	2B	3B	HR	(Hm	Rd)	TB	R	RBI	RC	TBB	IBB	SO	HBP	SH	SF	SB	CS	GDP	Avg	OBP	Slg	OPS
								BATTING												RUNNING			AVERAGES			
2013 QuadC	A	114	416	108	33	1	12	(-	-)	179	46	63	64	50	0	92	0	1	5	12	3	9	.260	.335	.430	.766
2014 Lancst	A+	131	516	151	37	2	11	(-	-)	225	76	77	92	82	2	91	0	0	4	4	4	14	.293	.387	.436	.823
2015 Missi	AA	127	420	98	21	1	5	(-	-)	136	48	46	50	63	1	94	1	3	2	2	2	16	.233	.333	.324	.657
2016 Gwnntt	AAA	133	465	126	24	3	10	(-	-)	186	52	62	69	61	3	116	2	0	5	1	4	10	.271	.355	.400	.755
2017 Gwnntt	AAA	103	388	96	25	2	16	(-	-)	173	48	56	57	42	1	110	1	0	1	1	2	16	.247	.322	.446	.768
2016 Atl	NL	5	7	2	0	1	0	(0	0)	4	1	2	2	0	0	2	0	0	0	1	0	0	.286	.286	.571	.857
2017 Atl	NL	53	150	29	5	0	4	(2	2)	46	22	19	15	19	1	41	1	0	3	1	0	4	.193	.283	.307	.590
2 ML YEARS		58	157	31	5	1	4	(2	2)	50	23	21	17	19	1	43	1	0	3	2	0	4	.197	.283	.318	.602

Dan Runzler

Pitches: L Bats: L Pos: RP-8

Ht: 6'4" Wt: 210 Born: 3/30/1985 Age: 33

Year Team	Lg	G	GS	CG	GF	IP	BFP	H	R	ER	HR	SH	SF	HB	TBB	IBB	SO	WP	Bk	W	L	Pct	Sh	Sv-Op	Hld	ERC	ERA
		HOW MUCH HE PITCHED						WHAT HE GAVE UP												THE RESULTS							
2017 Indy*	AAA	40	0	0	16	41.1	181	43	15	14	3	1	0	2	22	3	36	1	0	1	4	.200	0	7- -	-	4.85	3.05
2009 SF	NL	11	0	0	0	8.2	38	6	1	1	1	0	0	1	5	0	11	0	0	0	0	-	0	0-0	2	3.54	1.04
2010 SF	NL	41	0	0	7	32.2	144	29	12	11	1	4	0	1	20	3	37	2	0	3	0	1.000	0	0-0	5	3.74	3.03
2011 SF	NL	31	1	0	9	27.1	120	29	21	19	0	0	1	0	16	1	25	1	0	1	2	.333	0	0-0	3	4.48	6.26
2012 SF	NL	6	0	0	0	3.2	15	1	0	0	0	0	0	1	3	1	5	1	0	0	0	-	0	0-0	0	1.73	0.00
2017 Pit	NL	8	0	0	0	4.0	20	7	4	2	2	0	0	0	2	0	4	0	0	0	0	-	0	0-0	0	13.44	4.50
5 ML YEARS		97	1	0	16	76.1	337	72	38	33	4	4	2	3	46	5	82	4	0	4	2	.667	0	0-0	10	4.30	3.89

Cameron Rupp

Bats: R Throws: R Pos: C-88;PH-1

Ht: 6'2" Wt: 260 Born: 9/28/1988 Age: 29

Year Team	Lg	G	AB	H	2B	3B	HR	(Hm	Rd)	TB	R	RBI	RC	TBB	IBB	SO	HBP	SH	SF	SB	CS	GDP	Avg	OBP	Slg	OPS
								BATTING												RUNNING			AVERAGES			
2013 Phi	NL	4	13	4	1	0	0	(0	0)	5	1	2	2	1	0	4	0	0	0	0	0	0	.308	.357	.385	.742
2014 Phi	NL	18	60	11	4	0	0	(0	0)	15	4	6	3	4	0	20	0	0	0	0	0	5	.183	.234	.250	.484
2015 Phi	NL	81	270	63	9	1	9	(4	5)	101	24	28	29	24	5	71	3	0	2	0	1	8	.233	.301	.374	.675
2016 Phi	NL	105	389	98	26	1	16	(8	8)	174	36	54	53	24	0	114	5	0	1	1	0	11	.252	.303	.447	.750
2017 Phi	NL	88	295	64	17	0	14	(10	4)	123	35	34	34	34	3	114	1	0	1	1	0	5	.217	.299	.417	.716
5 ML YEARS		296	1027	240	57	2	39	(22	17)	418	100	124	121	87	8	323	9	0	4	2	1	29	.234	.298	.407	.705

Chris Rusin

Pitches: L Bats: L Pos: RP-60

RUSS-inn

Ht: 6'2" Wt: 195 Born: 10/22/1986 Age: 31

Year Team	Lg	G	GS	CG	GF	IP	BFP	H	R	ER	HR	SH	SF	HB	TBB	IBB	SO	WP	Bk	W	L	Pct	Sh	Sv-Op	Hld	ERC	ERA
		HOW MUCH HE PITCHED						WHAT HE GAVE UP												THE RESULTS							
2012 ChC	NL	7	7	0	0	29.2	135	38	22	21	4	0	0	3	11	0	21	0	0	2	3	.400	0	0-0	0	6.46	6.37
2013 ChC	NL	13	13	0	0	66.1	282	66	30	29	8	1	1	3	24	3	36	1	0	2	6	.250	0	0-0	0	4.21	3.93
2014 ChC	NL	4	0	0	2	12.2	58	16	10	10	1	1	0	0	5	1	8	1	0	0	0	-	0	0-0	0	5.24	7.11
2015 Col	NL	24	22	2	0	131.2	594	170	88	78	19	2	0	3	41	5	86	2	2	6	10	.375	1	0-0	0	5.80	5.33
2016 Col	NL	29	7	0	0	84.1	350	82	36	35	5	7	0	2	23	2	69	4	0	3	5	.375	0	0-1	3	3.30	3.74
2017 Col	NL	60	0	0	7	85.0	340	75	31	25	9	2	3	3	19	1	71	0	0	5	1	.833	0	2-3	12	2.99	2.65
6 ML YEARS		137	49	2	10	409.2	1759	447	217	198	46	13	4	15	123	12	291	12	2	18	25	.419	1	2-4	15	4.42	4.35

Addison Russell

Bats: R **Throws:** R **Pos:** SS-101;PH-13 **Ht:** 6'0" **Wt:** 200 **Born:** 1/23/1994 **Age:** 24

							BATTING														RUNNING			AVERAGES			
Year	Team	Lg	G	AB	H	2B	3B	HR	(Hm	Rd)	TB	R	RBI	RC	TBB	IBB	SO	HBP	SH	SF	SB	CS	GDP	Avg	OBP	Slg	OPS
2015	ChC	NL	142	475	115	29	1	13	(8	5)	185	60	54	53	42	2	149	3	1	2	4	3	8	.242	.307	.389	.696
2016	ChC	NL	151	525	125	25	3	21	(11	10)	219	67	95	73	55	6	135	12	0	6	5	1	11	.238	.321	.417	.738
2017	ChC	NL	110	352	84	21	3	12	(5	7)	147	52	43	40	29	5	91	4	0	0	2	1	5	.239	.304	.418	.722
	Postseason		21	76	16	2	1	3	(0	3)	29	7	14	10	2	1	16	1	1	1	1	0	1	.211	.238	.382	.619
	3 ML YEARS		403	1352	324	75	7	46	(24	22)	551	179	192	166	126	13	375	19	1	8	11	5	24	.240	.312	.408	.719

Josh Rutledge

Bats: R **Throws:** R **Pos:** 3B-20;2B-16;1B-5;PH-3 **Ht:** 6'1" **Wt:** 190 **Born:** 4/21/1989 **Age:** 29

							BATTING														RUNNING			AVERAGES			
Year	Team	Lg	G	AB	H	2B	3B	HR	(Hm	Rd)	TB	R	RBI	RC	TBB	IBB	SO	HBP	SH	SF	SB	CS	GDP	Avg	OBP	Slg	OPS
2012	Col	NL	73	277	76	20	5	8	(5	3)	130	37	37	37	9	0	54	4	0	1	7	0	8	.274	.306	.469	.775
2013	Col	NL	88	285	67	6	1	7	(5	2)	96	45	19	28	22	1	62	2	4	1	12	0	2	.235	.294	.337	.630
2014	Col	NL	105	309	83	16	7	4	(1	3)	125	44	33	42	20	0	83	6	5	2	2	3	6	.269	.323	.405	.728
2015	Bos	AL	39	74	21	1	0	1	(1	0)	25	11	10	11	5	1	26	2	1	3	0	0	0	.284	.333	.338	.671
2016	Bos	AL	28	49	13	6	0	0	(0	0)	19	9	3	5	6	0	19	0	1	0	2	0	3	.265	.345	.388	.733
2017	Bos	AL	37	107	24	2	1	0	(0	0)	28	10	9	9	9	0	31	2	0	0	1	0	1	.224	.297	.262	.558
	6 ML YEARS		370	1101	284	51	14	20	(12	8)	423	156	111	132	71	2	275	16	11	7	24	3	20	.258	.310	.384	.695

Kyle Ryan

Pitches: L **Bats:** L **Pos:** RP-8 **Ht:** 6'5" **Wt:** 215 **Born:** 9/25/1991 **Age:** 26

			HOW MUCH HE PITCHED						WHAT HE GAVE UP											THE RESULTS							
Year	Team	Lg	G	GS	CG	GF	IP	BFP	H	R	ER	HR	SH	SF	HB	TBB	IBB	SO	WP	Bk	W	L	Pct	Sh	Sv-Op	Hld	ERC	ERA
2017	Toledo*	AAA	48	0	0	8	45.1	212	55	26	25	5	2	0	3	27	2	39	8	0	3	1	.750	0	0--	-	6.55	4.96
2014	Det	AL	6	1	0	1	10.1	41	10	3	3	0	0	0	0	2	0	4	0	1	2	0	1.000	0	0-0	0	2.57	2.61
2015	Det	AL	16	6	0	3	56.1	237	60	29	28	9	2	1	1	20	0	30	1	0	2	4	.333	0	0-0	1	4.94	4.47
2016	Det	AL	56	0	0	14	55.2	226	48	21	19	2	2	1	3	15	5	35	1	0	4	2	.667	0	0-1	4	2.55	3.07
2017	Det	AL	8	0	0	0	5.2	29	9	5	5	0	0	1	0	7	1	1	0	0	0	0	-	0	0-1	4	11.19	7.94
	4 ML YEARS		86	7	0	18	128.0	533	127	58	55	11	4	3	4	44	6	70	2	1	8	6	.571	0	0-2	8	3.88	3.87

Hyun-Jin Ryu

Pitches: L **Bats:** R **Pos:** SP-24; RP-1 he-YUN-jin ree-YOO **Ht:** 6'3" **Wt:** 250 **Born:** 3/25/1987 **Age:** 31

			HOW MUCH HE PITCHED						WHAT HE GAVE UP											THE RESULTS							
Year	Team	Lg	G	GS	CG	GF	IP	BFP	H	R	ER	HR	SH	SF	HB	TBB	IBB	SO	WP	Bk	W	L	Pct	Sh	Sv-Op	Hld	ERC	ERA
2013	LAD	NL	30	30	2	0	192.0	783	182	67	64	15	7	3	1	49	4	154	5	0	14	8	.636	1	0-0	0	3.13	3.00
2014	LAD	NL	26	26	0	0	152.0	631	152	60	57	8	6	2	3	29	2	139	2	0	14	7	.667	0	0-0	0	3.00	3.38
2016	LAD	NL	1	1	0	0	4.2	24	8	6	6	1	0	0	0	2	1	4	0	0	0	1	.000	0	0-0	0	9.03	11.57
2017	LAD	NL	25	24	0	1	126.2	541	128	58	53	22	4	1	4	45	3	116	4	1	5	9	.357	0	1-1	0	4.61	3.77
	Postseason		3	3	0	0	16.0	63	14	5	5	1	0	0	0	3	0	9	0	0	1	0	1.000	0	0-0	0	2.44	2.81
	4 ML YEARS		82	81	2	1	475.1	1979	470	191	180	46	17	6	8	125	10	413	11	1	33	25	.569	1	1-1	0	3.51	3.41

Marc Rzepczynski

Pitches: L **Bats:** L **Pos:** RP-64 zepp-CHINN-ski **Ht:** 6'2" **Wt:** 220 **Born:** 8/29/1985 **Age:** 32

			HOW MUCH HE PITCHED						WHAT HE GAVE UP											THE RESULTS							
Year	Team	Lg	G	GS	CG	GF	IP	BFP	H	R	ER	HR	SH	SF	HB	TBB	IBB	SO	WP	Bk	W	L	Pct	Sh	Sv-Op	Hld	ERC	ERA
2009	Tor	AL	11	11	0	0	61.1	261	51	27	25	7	2	1	1	30	0	60	4	1	2	4	.333	0	0-0	0	3.65	3.67
2010	Tor	AL	14	12	0	0	63.2	287	72	37	35	8	1	2	5	30	1	57	4	1	4	4	.500	0	0-0	2	5.71	4.95
2011	2 Tms		71	0	0	7	62.0	256	50	27	23	3	2	0	4	26	1	61	6	0	2	6	.250	0	0-4	18	3.04	3.34
2012	StL	NL	70	0	0	14	46.2	196	46	22	22	7	0	0	0	17	2	33	3	0	1	3	.250	0	0-5	18	4.21	4.24
2013	2 Tms		38	0	0	10	30.2	129	27	13	11	2	1	1	4	10	3	29	0	0	0	0	-	0	0-0	6	3.28	3.23
2014	Cle	AL	73	0	0	8	46.0	196	42	19	14	1	1	2	3	19	3	46	2	0	0	3	.000	0	1-2	13	3.27	2.74
2015	2 Tms		72	0	0	7	35.0	158	40	29	22	3	2	3	2	14	4	41	2	0	2	4	.333	0	0-4	16	4.94	5.66
2016	2 Tms		70	0	0	15	47.2	215	46	17	14	1	1	1	4	29	8	46	5	0	1	0	1.000	0	0-1	11	4.15	2.64
2017	Sea	AL	64	0	0	6	31.1	137	29	16	14	2	0	0	1	20	5	25	3	0	2	2	.500	0	1-3	20	4.29	4.02
11	Tor	AL	43	0	0	6	39.1	158	28	16	13	2	1	0	3	15	0	33	5	0	2	3	.400	0	0-3	10	2.52	2.97
11	StL	AL	28	0	0	1	22.2	98	22	11	10	1	1	0	1	11	1	28	1	0	0	3	.000	0	0-1	8	4.01	3.97
13	StL	NL	11	0	0	4	10.1	50	16	9	9	1	0	1	1	4	1	9	0	0	0	0	-	0	0-0	0	7.69	7.84
13	Cle	AL	27	0	0	6	20.1	79	11	4	2	1	1	0	3	6	2	20	0	0	0	0	-	0	0-0	6	1.57	0.89
15	Cle	AL	45	0	0	6	20.1	94	23	15	10	1	1	0	1	10	3	24	1	0	2	3	.400	0	0-2	12	4.66	4.43
15	SD	NL	27	0	0	1	14.2	64	17	14	12	2	1	2	2	4	1	17	1	0	0	1	.000	0	0-2	4	5.32	7.36
16	Oak	AL	56	0	0	15	36.0	169	38	14	12	1	0	0	2	24	6	37	5	0	1	0	1.000	0	0-1	6	4.75	3.00
16	NL	NL	14	0	0	0	11.2	46	8	3	2	0	1	1	2	5	2	9	0	0	0	0	-	0	0-0	5	2.39	1.54
	Postseason		21	0	0	1	12.2	54	10	6	6	0	0	0	1	6	0	16	1	0	1	1	.500	0	0-1	7	2.82	4.26
	9 ML YEARS		483	23	0	67	424.1	1835	403	207	180	34	10	9	25	195	27	398	29	2	14	26	.350	0	2-19	104	4.06	3.82

CC Sabathia

Pitches: L **Bats:** L **Pos:** SP-27 **Ht:** 6'6" **Wt:** 300 **Born:** 7/21/1980 **Age:** 37

			HOW MUCH HE PITCHED						WHAT HE GAVE UP											THE RESULTS							
Year	Team	Lg	G	GS	CG	GF	IP	BFP	H	R	ER	HR	SH	SF	HB	TBB	IBB	SO	WP	Bk	W	L	Pct	Sh	Sv-Op	Hld	ERC	ERA
2001	Cle	AL	33	33	0	0	180.1	763	149	93	88	19	3	5	7	95	1	171	7	3	17	5	.773	0	0-0	0	3.86	4.39
2002	Cle	AL	33	33	2	0	210.0	891	198	109	102	17	5	10	4	88	2	149	6	3	13	11	.542	0	0-0	0	3.74	4.37
2003	Cle	AL	30	30	2	0	197.2	832	190	85	79	19	10	4	6	66	3	141	4	2	13	9	.591	1	0-0	0	3.70	3.60
2004	Cle	AL	30	30	1	0	188.0	787	176	90	86	20	3	6	7	72	3	139	1	1	11	10	.524	1	0-0	0	3.91	4.12

Year	Team	Lg	G	GS	CG	GF	IP	BFP	H	R	ER	HR	SH	SF	HB	TBB	IBB	SO	WP	Bk	W	L	Pct	Sh	Sv-Op	Hld	ERC	ERA
			HOW MUCH HE PITCHED						**WHAT HE GAVE UP**												**THE RESULTS**							
2005	Cle	AL	31	31	1	0	196.2	823	185	92	88	19	6	3	7	62	1	161	7	0	15	10	.600	0	0-0	0	3.55	4.03
2006	Cle	AL	28	28	**6**	0	192.2	802	182	83	69	17	8	5	7	44	3	172	3	0	12	11	.522	**2**	0-0	0	3.13	3.22
2007	Cle	AL	34	**34**	4	0	**241.0**	975	238	94	86	20	6	6	8	37	1	209	1	0	19	7	.731	1	0-0	0	3.12	3.21
2008	2 Tms		35	35	10	0	253.0	1023	223	85	76	19	9	6	7	59	1	251	2	2	17	10	.630	5	0-0	0	2.78	2.70
2009	NYY	AL	34	34	2	0	230.0	938	197	96	86	18	4	9	9	67	7	197	5	0	**19**	8	.704	1	0-0	0	2.89	3.37
2010	NYY	AL	34	**34**	2	0	237.2	970	209	92	84	20	5	8	7	74	6	197	8	1	**21**	7	.750	0	0-0	0	3.11	3.18
2011	NYY	AL	33	33	3	0	237.1	**985**	230	87	79	17	8	7	7	61	4	230	2	1	19	8	.704	1	0-0	0	3.27	3.00
2012	NYY	AL	28	28	2	0	200.0	833	184	89	75	22	4	3	8	44	2	197	4	1	15	6	.714	0	0-0	0	3.10	3.38
2013	NYY	AL	32	32	2	0	211.0	908	224	**122**	**112**	28	8	8	4	65	5	175	7	1	14	13	.519	0	0-0	0	4.32	4.78
2014	NYY	AL	8	8	0	0	46.0	209	58	31	27	10	1	1	4	10	0	48	2	0	3	4	.429	0	0-0	0	5.98	5.28
2015	NYY	AL	29	29	1	0	167.1	726	188	92	88	28	5	6	6	50	3	137	5	1	6	10	.375	0	0-0	0	5.01	4.73
2016	NYY	AL	30	30	0	0	179.2	768	172	83	78	22	5	2	9	65	1	152	2	1	9	12	.429	0	0-0	0	4.04	3.91
2017	NYY	AL	27	27	0	0	148.2	623	139	64	61	21	2	0	5	50	1	120	5	0	14	5	.737	0	0-0	0	3.90	3.69
08	Cle	AL	18	18	3	0	122.1	507	117	54	52	13	3	3	3	34	1	123	1	2	6	8	.429	2	0-0	0	3.52	3.83
08	Mil	NL	17	17	7	0	130.2	516	106	31	24	6	6	3	4	25	0	128	1	0	11	2	.846	3	0-0	0	2.13	1.65
	Postseason		19	18	1	0	107.1	478	116	57	54	14	5	0	5	51	8	101	4	1	9	5	.643	0	0-0	0	5.19	4.53
17 ML YEARS			509	509	38	0	3317.0	13856	3142	1487	1364	336	92	89	109	1009	44	2846	71	17	237	146	.619	12	0-0	0	3.55	3.70

Tyler Saladino

Bats: R Throws: R Pos: 2B-26;3B-22;DH-14;SS-13;PH-4;1B-3;PR-3   Ht: 6'0" Wt: 200 Born: 7/20/1989 Age: 28

Year	Team	Lg	G	AB	H	2B	3B	HR	(Hm	Rd)	TB	R	RBI	RC	TBB	IBB	SO	HBP	SH	SF	SB	CS	GDP	Avg	OBP	Slg	OPS
			BATTING																		**RUNNING**			**AVERAGES**			
2015	CWS	AL	68	236	53	6	4	4	(4	0)	79	33	20	19	12	0	51	2	3	1	8	2	9	.225	.267	.335	.602
2016	CWS	AL	93	298	84	14	0	8	(5	3)	122	33	38	38	13	0	62	3	2	3	11	5	11	.282	.315	.409	.725
2017	CWS	AL	79	253	45	9	2	0	(0	0)	58	23	10	13	23	0	67	3	2	0	5	4	5	.178	.254	.229	.484
3 ML YEARS			240	787	182	29	6	12	(9	3)	259	89	68	70	48	0	180	8	7	4	24	11	25	.231	.281	.329	.610

Fernando Salas

Pitches: R Bats: R Pos: RP-61   SAH-lahss   Ht: 6'2" Wt: 200 Born: 5/30/1985 Age: 33

Year	Team	Lg	G	GS	CG	GF	IP	BFP	H	R	ER	HR	SH	SF	HB	TBB	IBB	SO	WP	Bk	W	L	Pct	Sh	Sv-Op	Hld	ERC	ERA
			HOW MUCH HE PITCHED						**WHAT HE GAVE UP**												**THE RESULTS**							
2010	StL	NL	27	0	0	11	30.2	133	28	13	12	4	1	1	0	15	2	29	2	0	0	0	-	0	0-1	1	4.03	3.52
2011	StL	NL	68	0	0	46	75.0	295	50	20	19	7	3	0	2	21	3	75	2	0	5	6	.455	0	24-30	4	1.94	2.28
2012	StL	NL	65	0	0	23	58.2	256	56	28	28	5	5	0	1	27	5	60	4	0	1	4	.200	0	0-3	7	3.85	4.30
2013	StL	NL	27	0	0	14	28.0	118	27	15	14	3	1	4	1	6	1	22	2	0	0	3	.000	0	0-2	2	3.22	4.50
2014	LAA	AL	57	0	0	11	58.2	239	50	22	22	5	4	1	1	14	4	61	1	1	5	0	1.000	0	0-1	8	2.54	3.38
2015	LAA	AL	72	0	0	13	63.2	269	61	34	30	8	5	4	3	12	5	74	3	0	5	2	.714	0	0-2	17	3.17	4.24
2016	2 Tms		75	0	0	24	73.2	293	63	32	32	12	0	2	0	19	1	64	1	0	3	7	.300	0	6-11	20	3.19	3.91
2017	2 Tms		61	0	0	11	58.2	263	67	39	34	7	5	7	0	22	6	56	4	0	2	2	.500	0	0-1	12	4.68	5.22
16	LAA	AL	58	0	0	22	56.1	231	52	28	28	9	0	2	0	19	1	45	0	0	3	6	.333	0	6-11	13	3.87	4.47
16	NYM	NL	17	0	0	2	17.1	62	11	4	4	3	0	0	0	0	0	19	1	0	0	1	.000	0	0-0	7	1.36	2.08
17	NYM	NL	48	0	0	7	45.0	214	60	35	30	7	4	3	0	20	6	47	4	0	1	2	.333	0	0-1	11	6.32	6.00
17	LAA	AL	13	0	0	4	13.2	49	7	4	4	0	1	4	0	2	0	9	0	0	1	0	1.000	0	0-0	1	0.81	2.63
	Postseason		18	0	0	3	20.1	83	16	10	8	2	0	0	0	4	1	18	1	1	0	1	.000	0	0-0	4	2.05	3.54
8 ML YEARS			452	0	0	153	447.0	1866	402	203	191	51	24	19	8	136	27	441	19	1	21	24	.467	0	30-51	73	3.21	3.85

Danny Salazar

Pitches: R Bats: R Pos: SP-19; RP-4   SAL-uh-zarr   Ht: 6'0" Wt: 195 Born: 1/11/1990 Age: 28

Year	Team	Lg	G	GS	CG	GF	IP	BFP	H	R	ER	HR	SH	SF	HB	TBB	IBB	SO	WP	Bk	W	L	Pct	Sh	Sv-Op	Hld	ERC	ERA
			HOW MUCH HE PITCHED						**WHAT HE GAVE UP**												**THE RESULTS**							
2013	Cle	AL	10	10	0	0	52.0	211	44	18	18	7	1	0	0	15	0	65	3	0	2	3	.400	0	0-0	0	3.05	3.12
2014	Cle	AL	20	20	1	0	110.0	474	117	57	52	13	1	5	3	35	4	120	3	0	6	8	.429	1	0-0	0	4.30	4.25
2015	Cle	AL	30	30	0	0	185.0	757	156	79	71	23	3	4	7	53	1	195	3	2	14	10	.583	0	0-0	0	3.10	3.45
2016	Cle	AL	25	25	0	0	137.1	584	121	61	59	16	0	4	2	63	3	161	9	3	11	6	.647	0	0-0	0	3.80	3.87
2017	Cle	AL	23	19	0	3	103.0	439	94	51	49	14	1	3	3	44	0	145	6	0	5	6	.455	0	0-0	0	4.09	4.28
	Postseason		3	1	0	0	7.0	30	5	3	3	1	0	0	0	4	1	8	1	0	0	1	.000	0	0-0	0	3.18	3.86
5 ML YEARS			108	104	1	3	587.1	2465	532	266	249	73	6	16	15	210	8	686	24	5	38	33	.535	1	0-0	0	3.65	3.82

Chris Sale

Pitches: L Bats: L Pos: SP-32   SAIL   Ht: 6'6" Wt: 180 Born: 3/30/1989 Age: 29

Year	Team	Lg	G	GS	CG	GF	IP	BFP	H	R	ER	HR	SH	SF	HB	TBB	IBB	SO	WP	Bk	W	L	Pct	Sh	Sv-Op	Hld	ERC	ERA
			HOW MUCH HE PITCHED						**WHAT HE GAVE UP**												**THE RESULTS**							
2010	CWS	AL	21	0	0	8	23.1	92	15	5	5	2	1	0	0	10	0	32	1	0	2	1	.667	0	4-4	2	2.30	1.93
2011	CWS	AL	58	0	0	17	71.0	288	52	22	22	6	3	0	2	27	3	79	2	0	2	2	.500	0	8-10	16	2.55	2.79
2012	CWS	AL	30	29	1	0	192.0	772	167	66	65	19	1	3	6	51	5	192	6	0	17	8	.680	0	0-1	0	3.00	3.05
2013	CWS	AL	30	30	4	0	214.1	866	184	81	73	23	2	4	14	46	2	226	8	1	11	14	.440	1	0-0	0	2.92	3.07
2014	CWS	AL	26	26	2	0	174.0	685	129	48	42	13	2	3	11	39	2	208	3	0	12	4	.750	0	0-0	0	2.18	2.17
2015	CWS	AL	31	31	1	0	208.2	854	185	88	79	23	2	3	**13**	42	2	**274**	7	0	13	11	.542	0	0-0	0	3.00	3.41
2016	CWS	AL	32	32	6	0	226.2	907	190	88	84	27	5	3	**17**	45	2	233	2	0	17	10	.630	1	0-0	0	2.88	3.34
2017	Bos	AL	32	32	1	0	214.1	851	165	73	69	24	2	4	8	43	0	**308**	3	0	17	8	.680	0	0-0	0	2.33	2.90
8 ML YEARS			260	180	15	25	1324.1	5315	1087	471	439	137	18	20	71	303	14	1552	32	1	91	58	.611	2	12-15	18	2.71	2.98

Jarrod Saltalamacchia

Bats: B **Throws:** R **Pos:** C-7;PR-2;DH-1;PH-1   salt-ah-luh-MOCK-ee-ah   **Ht:** 6'4" **Wt:** 235 **Born:** 5/2/1985 **Age:** 33

Year	Team	Lg	G	AB	H	2B	3B	HR	(Hm	Rd)	TB	R	RBI	RC	TBB	IBB	SO	HBP	SH	SF	SB	CS	GDP	Avg	OBP	Slg	OPS
2017	Buffalo*	AAA	33	111	18	6	0	1	(-	-)	27	8	5	7	17	0	51	0	0	1	0	0	0	.162	.271	.243	.515
2007	2 Tms		93	308	82	13	1	11	(6	5)	130	39	33	32	19	1	75	1	0	1	0	0	8	.266	.310	.422	.732
2008	Tex	AL	61	198	50	13	0	3	(2	1)	72	27	26	29	31	1	74	0	0	1	0	2	1	.253	.352	.364	.716
2009	Tex	AL	84	283	66	12	0	9	(6	3)	105	34	34	30	22	1	97	1	3	1	0	2	3	.233	.290	.371	.661
2010	2 Tms	AL	12	24	4	3	0	0	(0	0)	7	2	2	3	6	0	5	0	0	0	0	0	0	.167	.333	.292	.625
2011	Bos	AL	103	358	84	23	3	16	(6	10)	161	52	56	43	24	1	119	3	0	1	1	0	7	.235	.288	.450	.737
2012	Bos	AL	121	405	90	17	1	25	(12	13)	184	55	59	49	38	0	139	1	0	4	0	1	5	.222	.288	.454	.742
2013	Bos	AL	121	425	116	40	0	14	(9	5)	198	68	65	60	43	3	139	0	0	2	4	1	7	.273	.338	.466	.804
2014	Mia	NL	114	373	82	20	0	11	(5	6)	135	43	44	34	55	4	143	2	0	5	0	1	11	.220	.320	.362	.681
2015	2 Tms	NL	79	200	45	15	0	9	(7	2)	87	26	24	21	23	0	69	2	1	1	0	0	5	.225	.310	.435	.745
2016	Det	AL	92	246	42	5	1	12	(5	7)	85	30	38	26	41	1	104	0	0	5	0	0	1	.171	.284	.346	.630
2017	Tor	AL	10	25	1	0	0	0	(0	0)	1	1	0	0	3	0	16	0	0	0	0	0	0	.040	.077	.040	.117
07	Atl	NL	47	141	40	6	0	4	(4	0)	58	11	12	13	10	1	28	1	0	1	0	0	4	.284	.333	.411	.745
07	Tex	AL	46	167	42	7	1	7	(2	5)	72	28	21	19	9	0	47	0	0	0	0	0	4	.251	.290	.431	.721
10	Tex	AL	2	5	1	0	0	0	(0	0)	1	0	1	1	0	0	1	0	0	0	0	0	0	.200	.200	.200	.400
10	Bos	AL	10	19	3	3	0	0	(0	0)	6	2	1	2	6	0	4	0	0	0	0	0	0	.158	.360	.316	.676
15	Mia	NL	9	29	2	1	0	1	(1	0)	6	3	1	0	4	0	12	0	0	0	0	0	2	.069	.182	.207	.389
15	Ari	NL	70	171	43	14	0	8	(6	2)	81	23	23	21	19	0	57	2	1	1	0	0	3	.251	.332	.474	.805
	Postseason		10	32	6	1	0	0	(0	0)	7	1	5	2	3	0	19	0	0	0	0	0	0	.188	.257	.219	.476
	11 ML YEARS		890	2845	662	161	6	110	(58	52)	1165	377	381	327	303	12	980	10	4	21	5	7	48	.233	.307	.409	.716

Jeff Samardzija

Pitches: R **Bats:** R **Pos:** SP-32   suh-MAHR-jah   **Ht:** 6'5" **Wt:** 225 **Born:** 1/23/1985 **Age:** 33

Year	Team	Lg	G	GS	CG	GF	IP	BFP	H	R	ER	HR	SH	SF	HB	TBB	IBB	SO	WP	Bk	W	L	Pct	Sh	Sv-Op	Hld	ERC	ERA
2008	ChC	NL	26	0	0	4	27.2	124	24	12	7	0	1	1	1	15	2	25	2	0	1	0	1.000	0	1-4	3	3.08	2.28
2009	ChC	NL	20	2	0	7	34.2	161	46	29	29	7	4	1	1	15	1	21	2	0	1	3	.250	0	0-0	1	7.13	7.53
2010	ChC	NL	7	3	0	0	19.1	100	21	22	18	4	0	0	2	20	1	9	1	0	2	2	.500	0	0-0	0	8.45	8.38
2011	ChC	NL	75	0	0	18	88.0	380	64	35	29	5	3	2	5	50	3	87	8	0	8	4	.667	0	0-2	13	3.05	2.97
2012	ChC	NL	28	28	1	0	174.2	723	157	79	74	20	5	4	4	56	2	180	10	0	9	13	.409	0	0-0	0	3.41	3.81
2013	ChC	NL	33	33	2	0	213.2	914	210	109	103	25	4	2	8	78	3	214	11	0	8	13	.381	1	0-0	0	4.11	4.34
2014	2 Tms		33	33	2	0	219.2	879	191	86	73	20	3	7	10	43	3	202	10	0	7	13	.350	0	0-0	0	2.74	2.99
2015	CWS	AL	32	32	2	0	214.0	910	**228**	**122**	**118**	**29**	4	9	12	49	0	163	5	0	11	13	.458	**2**	0-0	0	4.24	4.96
2016	SF	NL	32	32	1	0	203.1	829	190	88	86	24	6	4	1	54	4	167	2	0	12	11	.522	0	0-0	0	3.36	3.81
2017	SF	NL	32	32	1	0	**207.2**	847	204	107	102	30	4	4	6	32	1	205	2	0	9	**15**	.375	0	0-0	0	3.43	4.42
14	ChC	NL	17	17	0	0	108.0	449	99	44	34	7	3	4	6	31	3	103	6	0	2	7	.222	0	0-0	0	3.14	2.83
14	Oak	AL	16	16	2	0	111.2	430	92	42	39	13	0	3	4	12	0	99	4	0	5	6	.455	0	0-0	0	2.34	3.14
	Postseason		2	1	0	0	3.0	17	8	5	5	0	0	0	0	1	0	1	0	0	0	1	.000	0	0-0	0	14.52	15.00
	10 ML YEARS		318	195	9	31	1402.2	5867	1335	689	639	164	34	34	50	412	20	1273	53	0	68	87	.439	4	1-6	16	3.64	4.10

Aaron Sanchez

Pitches: R **Bats:** R **Pos:** SP-8   **Ht:** 6'4" **Wt:** 215 **Born:** 7/1/1992 **Age:** 25

Year	Team	Lg	G	GS	CG	GF	IP	BFP	H	R	ER	HR	SH	SF	HB	TBB	IBB	SO	WP	Bk	W	L	Pct	Sh	Sv-Op	Hld	ERC	ERA
2014	Tor	AL	24	0	0	6	33.0	121	14	5	4	1	2	0	1	9	0	27	1	0	2	2	.500	0	3-3	1	0.96	1.09
2015	Tor	AL	41	11	0	4	92.1	380	74	35	33	9	2	1	3	44	2	61	8	0	7	6	.538	0	0-1	10	3.47	3.22
2016	Tor	AL	30	30	0	0	192.0	790	161	69	64	15	1	2	5	63	0	161	5	0	15	2	**.882**	0	0-0	0	2.90	**3.00**
2017	Tor	AL	8	8	0	0	36.0	167	42	24	17	6	0	0	1	20	0	24	1	0	1	3	.250	0	0-0	0	6.36	4.25
	Postseason		11	2	0	1	19.0	77	12	8	7	2	2	0	0	8	0	16	1	0	2	0	1.000	0	0-0	0	2.24	3.32
	4 ML YEARS		103	49	0	10	353.1	1458	291	133	118	31	5	3	10	136	2	273	15	0	25	13	.658	0	3-4	17	3.12	3.01

Adrian Sanchez

Bats: R **Throws:** R **Pos:** PH-11;2B-10;SS-8;3B-7;PR-2   **Ht:** 6'0" **Wt:** 160 **Born:** 8/16/1990 **Age:** 27

Year	Team	Lg	G	AB	H	2B	3B	HR	(Hm	Rd)	TB	R	RBI	RC	TBB	IBB	SO	HBP	SH	SF	SB	CS	GDP	Avg	OBP	Slg	OPS
2013	Ptomc	A+	120	428	103	14	4	1	(-	-)	128	43	42	36	17	1	61	6	10	2	8	4	11	.241	.278	.299	.577
2014	Ptomc	A+	29	96	26	3	1	0	(-	-)	31	6	9	10	5	0	14	2	0	3	4	1	2	.271	.311	.323	.634
2014	Hrsbrg	AA	89	269	60	6	0	3	(-	-)	75	34	29	23	23	0	42	3	1	2	7	3	10	.223	.290	.279	.568
2015	Hrsbrg	AA	59	179	44	11	1	1	(-	-)	60	21	15	17	11	1	22	0	3	1	3	2	13	.246	.288	.335	.623
2015	2 Tms	Low	23	29	2	18	5	0	2	(-	-)	39	13	7	14	5	2	6	0	1	0	6	2	3	.398	.500	.898
2016	Hrsbrg	AA	97	299	76	17	3	0	(-	-)	99	24	25	31	14	0	42	5	4	3	6	1	13	.254	.296	.331	.627
2016	Syrcse	AAA	14	51	11	1	0	0	(-	-)	12	4	3	2	1	0	7	0	0	0	1	0	1	.216	.231	.235	.466
2017	Syrcse	AAA	72	258	63	15	1	4	(-	-)	92	37	18	29	19	0	47	1	2	3	4	1	2	.244	.295	.357	.652
2017	Was	NL	34	71	19	7	0	0	(0	0)	26	6	11	9	1	0	25	1	2	0	1	0	2	.268	.288	.366	.654

Angel Sanchez

Pitches: R **Bats:** R **Pos:** RP-8   **Ht:** 6'1" **Wt:** 190 **Born:** 11/28/1989 **Age:** 28

Year	Team	Lg	G	GS	CG	GF	IP	BFP	H	R	ER	HR	SH	SF	HB	TBB	IBB	SO	WP	Bk	W	L	Pct	Sh	Sv-Op	Hld	ERC	ERA
2013	3 Tms	Low	26	25	1	0	131.1	580	133	73	60	11	2	4	3	51	0	124	12	2	6	10	.375	0	0--	-	3.98	4.11
2014	Jaxnvl	AA	12	12	0	0	52.1	246	69	44	40	2	3	2	3	18	1	30	6	1	0	8	.000	0	0--	-	5.30	6.88
2014	Altna	AA	6	5	0	0	33.1	145	40	18	16	5	2	1	0	10	0	21	2	0	0	2	.000	0	0--	-	5.26	4.32

Year	Team	Lg	G	GS	CG	GF	IP	BFP	H	R	ER	HR	SH	SF	HB	TBB	IBB	SO	WP	Bk	W	L	Pct	Sh	Sv-Op	Hld	ERC	ERA
2015	Altna	AA	13	13	0	0	77.1	318	72	27	24	4	3	1	2	19	0	49	5	0	8	1	.889	0	0--	-	2.91	2.79
2015	Indy	AAA	10	10	0	0	60.0	246	49	18	17	6	0	1	3	15	0	50	4	1	5	1	.833	0	0--	-	2.69	2.55
2017	Indy	AAA	39	0	0	11	55.1	229	51	23	23	4	0	2	1	15	2	65	5	2	3	5	.375	0	1--	-	2.99	3.74
2017	Pit	NL	8	0	0	2	12.1	54	16	12	12	5	0	1	0	1	0	10	2	0	1	0	1.000	0	0-0	0	6.48	8.76

Anibal Sanchez

Pitches: R **Bats:** R **Pos:** SP-17; RP-11   ah-NEE-bahl   **Ht:** 6'0" **Wt:** 205 **Born:** 2/27/1984 **Age:** 34

			HOW MUCH HE PITCHED						WHAT HE GAVE UP												THE RESULTS							
Year	Team	Lg	G	GS	CG	GF	IP	BFP	H	R	ER	HR	SH	SF	HB	TBB	IBB	SO	WP	Bk	W	L	Pct	Sh	Sv-Op	Hld	ERC	ERA
2006	Fla	NL	18	17	2	0	114.1	469	90	39	36	9	3	1	4	46	1	72	4	1	10	3	.769	1	0-0	0	2.96	2.83
2007	Fla	NL	6	6	0	0	30.0	151	43	17	16	3	2	2	2	19	1	14	3	0	2	1	.667	0	0-0	0	7.90	4.80
2008	Fla	NL	10	10	0	0	51.2	241	54	35	32	7	4	2	6	27	2	50	1	0	2	5	.286	0	0-0	0	5.40	5.57
2009	Fla	NL	16	16	0	0	86.0	383	84	39	37	10	2	2	1	46	5	71	0	1	4	8	.333	0	0-0	0	4.51	3.87
2010	Fla	NL	32	32	1	0	195.0	841	192	89	77	10	13	3	7	70	5	157	7	0	13	12	.520	1	0-0	0	3.56	3.55
2011	Fla	NL	32	32	3	0	196.1	830	187	85	80	20	12	1	5	64	8	202	4	5	8	9	.471	2	0-0	0	3.57	3.67
2012	2 Tms		31	31	1	0	195.2	820	200	95	84	20	5	7	5	48	3	167	7	1	9	13	.409	1	0-0	0	3.70	3.86
2013	Det	AL	29	29	1	0	182.0	746	156	56	52	9	4	4	2	54	1	202	7	0	14	8	.636	1	0-0	0	2.63	2.57
2014	Det	AL	22	21	0	0	126.0	514	108	55	48	4	3	4	3	30	1	102	5	0	8	5	.615	0	0-0	0	2.35	3.43
2015	Det	AL	25	25	1	0	157.0	660	152	89	87	29	4	5	1	49	1	138	5	3	10	10	.500	1	0-0	0	4.14	4.99
2016	Det	AL	35	26	0	3	153.1	668	171	108	100	30	4	6	5	53	1	135	7	2	7	13	.350	0	0-0	0	5.40	5.87
2017	Det	AL	28	17	0	6	105.1	482	139	81	75	26	2	3	4	29	1	104	5	1	3	7	.300	0	0-0	0	6.66	6.41
12	Mia	NL	19	19	0	0	121.0	504	119	59	53	12	4	5	2	33	2	110	4	1	5	7	.417	0	0-0	0	3.55	3.94
12	Det	AL	12	12	1	0	74.2	316	81	36	31	8	1	2	3	15	1	57	3	0	4	6	.400	1	0-0	0	3.95	3.74
	Postseason		7	6	0	0	38.2	161	31	14	12	5	0	1	0	14	1	43	4	0	2	4	.333	0	0-0	1	2.96	2.79
12 ML YEARS			284	262	9	9	1592.2	6805	1576	788	724	177	59	37	45	535	30	1414	55	14	90	94	.489	7	0-0	0	3.92	4.09

Gary Sanchez

Bats: R **Throws:** R **Pos:** C-104;DH-18;PH-3;1B-2   **Ht:** 6'2" **Wt:** 230 **Born:** 12/2/1992 **Age:** 25

			BATTING																RUNNING			AVERAGES			
Year	Team	Lg	G	AB	H	2B	3B	HR	(Hm | Rd)	TB	R	RBI	RC	TBB	IBB	SO	HBP	SH	SF	SB	CS	GDP	Avg	OBP	Slg	OPS
2015	NYY	AL	2	2	0	0	0	0	(0 | 0)	0	0	0	0	0	0	1	0	0	0	0	0	0	.000	.000	.000
2016	NYY	AL	53	201	60	12	0	20	(10 | 10)	132	34	42	40	24	2	57	2	0	2	1	0	5	.299	.376	.657	1.032
2017	NYY	AL	122	471	131	20	0	33	(15 | 18)	250	79	90	81	40	1	120	10	0	4	2	1	9	.278	.345	.531	.876
3 ML YEARS			177	674	191	32	0	53	(25 | 28)	382	113	132	121	64	3	178	12	0	6	3	1	14	.283	.353	.567	.920

Hector Sanchez

Bats: B **Throws:** R **Pos:** PH-49;C-25;1B-6;DH-2   **Ht:** 6'0" **Wt:** 235 **Born:** 11/17/1989 **Age:** 28

			BATTING																RUNNING			AVERAGES			
Year	Team	Lg	G	AB	H	2B	3B	HR	(Hm | Rd)	TB	R	RBI	RC	TBB	IBB	SO	HBP	SH	SF	SB	CS	GDP	Avg	OBP	Slg	OPS
2011	SF	NL	13	31	8	2	0	0	(0 | 0)	10	0	1	2	3	0	6	0	0	0	0	0	1	.258	.324	.323	.646
2012	SF	NL	74	218	61	15	0	3	(1 | 2)	85	22	34	22	5	0	52	1	0	3	0	0	8	.280	.295	.390	.685
2013	SF	NL	63	129	32	4	0	3	(0 | 3)	45	8	19	14	7	0	29	3	0	1	0	0	1	.248	.300	.349	.649
2014	SF	NL	66	163	32	8	0	3	(1 | 2)	49	8	28	12	8	1	55	2	0	4	0	1	2	.196	.237	.301	.538
2015	SF	NL	28	56	10	4	0	1	(0 | 1)	17	5	5	3	2	0	14	0	1	0	0	0	1	.179	.207	.304	.510
2016	2 Tms		28	49	13	1	0	3	(0 | 3)	23	3	8	6	4	0	10	1	0	0	0	0	0	.265	.333	.469	.803
2017	SD	NL	75	137	30	4	0	8	(5 | 3)	58	14	25	15	5	1	41	0	0	1	0	0	4	.219	.245	.423	.668
16	CWS	AL	2	7	1	0	0	0	(0 | 0)	1	0	1	0	1	0	2	0	0	0	0	0	0	.143	.250	.143	.393
16	SD	NL	26	42	12	1	0	3	(0 | 3)	22	3	7	6	3	0	8	1	0	0	0	0	0	.286	.348	.524	.872
	Postseason		4	11	1	0	0	0	(0 | 0)	1	1	0	1	2	0	7	0	0	0	0	0	0	.091	.231	.091	.322
7 ML YEARS			347	783	186	38	0	21	(7 | 14)	287	60	120	74	34	2	207	7	1	9	0	1	17	.238	.273	.367	.639

Tony Sanchez

Bats: R **Throws:** R **Pos:** PH-1   **Ht:** 5'11" **Wt:** 220 **Born:** 5/20/1988 **Age:** 30

			BATTING																RUNNING			AVERAGES			
Year	Team	Lg	G	AB	H	2B	3B	HR	(Hm | Rd)	TB	R	RBI	RC	TBB	IBB	SO	HBP	SH	SF	SB	CS	GDP	Avg	OBP	Slg	OPS
2017	Salt Lk*	AAA	70	243	66	13	0	4	(- | -)	91	33	40	34	29	0	61	4	5	3	1	3	6	.272	.355	.374	.729
2013	Pit	NL	22	60	14	4	0	2	(1 | 1)	24	9	5	4	3	0	14	2	0	1	0	0	2	.233	.288	.400	.688
2014	Pit	NL	26	75	20	1	0	2	(0 | 2)	27	3	13	9	3	0	28	1	0	1	0	0	0	.267	.300	.360	.660
2015	Pit	NL	3	8	3	0	0	0	(0 | 0)	3	2	0	1	1	0	3	0	0	0	0	0	0	.375	.444	.375	.819
2017	Atl	NL	1	1	0	0	0	0	(0 | 0)	0	0	0	0	0	0	1	0	0	0	0	0	0	.000	.000	.000	.000
4 ML YEARS			52	144	37	5	0	4	(1 | 3)	54	14	18	14	7	0	46	3	0	2	0	0	2	.257	.301	.375	.676

Yolmer Sanchez

Bats: B **Throws:** R **Pos:** 2B-78;3B-52;PH-10;DH-7;SS-4;PR-4;RF-1   **Ht:** 5'11" **Wt:** 185 **Born:** 6/29/1992 **Age:** 26

			BATTING																RUNNING			AVERAGES			
Year	Team	Lg	G	AB	H	2B	3B	HR	(Hm | Rd)	TB	R	RBI	RC	TBB	IBB	SO	HBP	SH	SF	SB	CS	GDP	Avg	OBP	Slg	OPS
2014	CWS	AL	28	100	25	5	0	0	(0 | 0)	30	6	5	5	3	0	25	0	0	1	1	1	1	.250	.269	.300	.569
2015	CWS	AL	120	389	87	23	1	5	(2 | 3)	127	40	31	30	19	0	81	5	6	1	2	2	9	.224	.268	.326	.595
2016	CWS	AL	53	154	32	9	1	4	(2 | 2)	55	15	21	14	5	0	42	1	2	1	0	1	1	.208	.236	.357	.593
2017	CWS	AL	141	484	129	19	8	12	(8 | 4)	200	63	59	68	35	2	111	4	7	4	8	9	10	.267	.319	.413	.732
4 ML YEARS			342	1127	273	56	10	21	(12 | 9)	412	124	116	117	62	2	259	10	15	7	11	13	21	.242	.286	.366	.652

Pablo Sandoval

Bats: B **Throws:** R **Pos:** 3B-67;1B-9;PH-7;DH-2;2B-1   **Ht:** 5'11" **Wt:** 255 **Born:** 8/11/1986 **Age:** 31

Year Team	Lg	G	AB	H	2B	3B	HR	(Hm	Rd)	TB	R	RBI	RC	TBB	IBB	SO	HBP	SH	SF	SB	CS	GDP	Avg	OBP	Slg	OPS
2017 Pwtckt*	AAA	20	77	17	3	0	1	(-	-)	23	7	4	5	4	0	16	0	0	0	0	0	1	.221	.259	.299	.558
2008 SF	NL	41	145	50	10	1	3	(1	2)	71	24	24	24	4	1	14	1	0	4	0	0	6	.345	.357	.490	.847
2009 SF	NL	153	572	189	44	5	25	(13	12)	318	79	90	113	52	13	83	4	0	5	5	5	10	.330	.387	.556	.943
2010 SF	NL	152	563	151	34	3	13	(9	4)	230	61	63	55	47	12	81	1	0	5	3	2	26	.268	.323	.409	.732
2011 SF	NL	117	426	134	26	3	23	(7	16)	235	55	70	72	32	9	63	0	1	7	2	4	12	.315	.357	.552	.909
2012 SF	NL	108	396	112	25	2	12	(7	5)	177	59	63	60	38	4	59	1	0	7	1	1	13	.283	.342	.447	.789
2013 SF	NL	141	525	146	27	2	14	(6	8)	219	52	79	78	47	5	79	6	0	6	0	0	19	.278	.341	.417	.758
2014 SF	NL	157	588	164	26	3	16	(9	7)	244	68	73	78	39	6	85	4	0	7	0	0	16	.279	.324	.415	.739
2015 Bos	AL	126	470	115	25	1	10	(4	6)	172	43	47	46	25	1	73	7	1	2	0	0	14	.245	.292	.366	.658
2016 Bos	AL	3	6	0	0	0	0	(0	0)	0	0	0	0	1	0	4	0	0	0	0	0	0	.000	.143	.000	.143
2017 2 Tms		79	259	57	11	0	9	(4	5)	95	27	32	20	16	0	53	1	0	3	0	1	11	.220	.265	.367	.632
17 Bos	AL	32	99	21	2	0	4	(2	2)	35	10	12	9	8	0	24	0	0	1	0	1	4	.212	.269	.354	.622
17 SF	NL	47	160	36	9	0	5	(2	3)	60	17	20	11	8	0	29	1	0	2	0	0	7	.225	.263	.375	.638
Postseason		39	154	53	13	0	6	(3	3)	84	21	20	27	10	3	22	2	0	1	0	0	7	.344	.389	.545	.935
10 ML YEARS		1077	3950	1118	228	20	125	(60	65)	1761	468	541	546	301	51	594	25	2	46	11	13	127	.283	.334	.446	.780

Miguel Sano

Bats: R **Throws:** R **Pos:** 3B-82;DH-25;1B-9;PH-4   sah-NO   **Ht:** 6'4" **Wt:** 260 **Born:** 5/11/1993 **Age:** 25

Year Team	Lg	G	AB	H	2B	3B	HR	(Hm	Rd)	TB	R	RBI	RC	TBB	IBB	SO	HBP	SH	SF	SB	CS	GDP	Avg	OBP	Slg	OPS
2015 Min	AL	80	279	75	17	1	18	(10	8)	148	46	52	62	53	1	119	1	0	2	1	1	4	.269	.385	.530	.916
2016 Min	AL	116	437	103	22	1	25	(11	14)	202	57	66	62	54	1	178	1	0	3	1	0	8	.236	.319	.462	.781
2017 Min	AL	114	424	112	15	2	28	(12	16)	215	75	77	71	54	5	173	4	0	1	0	0	12	.264	.352	.507	.859
3 ML YEARS		310	1140	290	54	4	71	(33	38)	565	178	195	195	161	7	470	6	0	6	2	1	24	.254	.348	.496	.844

Carlos Santana

Bats: B **Throws:** R **Pos:** 1B-140;RF-7;DH-7;PH-1   **Ht:** 5'11" **Wt:** 210 **Born:** 4/8/1986 **Age:** 32

Year Team	Lg	G	AB	H	2B	3B	HR	(Hm	Rd)	TB	R	RBI	RC	TBB	IBB	SO	HBP	SH	SF	SB	CS	GDP	Avg	OBP	Slg	OPS
2010 Cle	AL	46	150	39	13	0	6	(2	4)	70	23	22	25	37	2	29	1	0	4	3	0	3	.260	.401	.467	.868
2011 Cle	AL	155	552	132	35	2	27	(14	13)	252	84	79	81	97	7	133	2	0	7	5	3	15	.239	.351	.457	.808
2012 Cle	AL	143	507	128	27	2	18	(7	11)	213	72	76	77	91	4	101	3	0	8	3	5	21	.252	.365	.420	.785
2013 Cle	AL	154	541	145	39	1	20	(12	8)	246	75	74	93	93	6	110	4	0	4	3	1	7	.268	.377	.455	.832
2014 Cle	AL	152	541	125	25	0	27	(13	14)	231	68	85	88	113	5	124	3	0	3	5	2	13	.231	.365	.427	.792
2015 Cle	AL	154	550	127	29	2	19	(6	13)	217	72	85	80	108	8	122	3	0	5	11	3	20	.231	.357	.395	.752
2016 Cle	AL	158	582	151	31	3	34	(20	14)	290	89	87	104	99	9	99	2	0	5	5	2	18	.259	.366	.498	.865
2017 Cle	AL	154	571	148	37	3	23	(11	12)	260	90	79	89	88	6	94	6	0	2	5	1	11	.259	.363	.455	.818
Postseason		16	56	12	2	0	3	(1	2)	23	6	4	5	8	0	12	1	0	0	0	0	0	.214	.323	.411	.734
8 ML YEARS		1116	3994	995	236	13	174	(85	89)	1779	573	587	637	726	38	812	24	0	38	40	17	108	.249	.365	.445	.810

Danny Santana

Bats: B **Throws:** R **Pos:** LF-38;PH-34;RF-9;2B-8;3B-5;CF-3;PR-3;DH-2   **Ht:** 5'11" **Wt:** 185 **Born:** 11/7/1990 **Age:** 27

Year Team	Lg	G	AB	H	2B	3B	HR	(Hm	Rd)	TB	R	RBI	RC	TBB	IBB	SO	HBP	SH	SF	SB	CS	GDP	Avg	OBP	Slg	OPS
2014 Min	AL	101	405	129	27	7	7	(3	4)	191	70	40	72	19	0	98	3	2	1	20	4	3	.319	.353	.472	.824
2015 Min	AL	91	261	56	10	5	0	(0	0)	76	30	21	16	6	1	68	3	7	0	8	4	7	.215	.241	.291	.532
2016 Min	AL	75	233	56	10	2	2	(0	2)	76	29	14	18	12	0	55	1	1	1	12	9	1	.240	.279	.326	.606
2017 2 Tms		82	168	34	10	2	4	(3	1)	60	19	23	17	8	1	41	1	1	0	7	0	3	.202	.243	.357	.600
17 Min	AL	13	25	5	1	0	1	(1	0)	9	3	1	0	1	0	8	0	0	0	1	0	1	.200	.231	.360	.591
17 Atl	NL	69	143	29	9	2	3	(2	1)	51	16	22	17	7	1	33	1	1	0	6	0	2	.203	.245	.357	.602
4 ML YEARS		349	1067	275	57	16	13	(6	7)	403	148	98	123	45	2	262	8	11	2	47	17	14	.258	.292	.378	.670

Domingo Santana

Bats: R **Throws:** R **Pos:** RF-144;PH-8   **Ht:** 6'5" **Wt:** 220 **Born:** 8/5/1992 **Age:** 25

Year Team	Lg	G	AB	H	2B	3B	HR	(Hm	Rd)	TB	R	RBI	RC	TBB	IBB	SO	HBP	SH	SF	SB	CS	GDP	Avg	OBP	Slg	OPS
2014 Hou	AL	6	17	0	0	0	0	(0	0)	0	1	0	0	1	0	14	0	0	0	0	0	0	.000	.056	.000	.056
2015 2 Tms		52	160	38	7	0	8	(3	5)	69	20	26	28	20	0	63	5	0	2	4	1	2	.238	.337	.431	.768
2016 Mil	NL	77	246	63	14	0	11	(3	8)	110	34	32	36	32	0	91	2	0	1	2	3	7	.256	.345	.447	.792
2017 Mil	NL	151	525	146	29	0	30	(19	11)	265	88	85	98	73	2	178	6	0	3	15	4	12	.278	.371	.505	.875
15 Hou	AL	14	39	10	2	0	2	(0	2)	18	6	8	8	2	0	17	1	0	0	2	1	1	.256	.310	.462	.771
15 Mil	NL	38	121	28	5	0	6	(3	3)	51	14	18	20	18	0	46	4	0	2	2	0	1	.231	.345	.421	.766
4 ML YEARS		286	948	247	50	0	49	(25	24)	444	143	143	162	126	2	346	13	0	6	21	8	21	.261	.353	.468	.822

Edgar Santana

Pitches: R **Bats:** R **Pos:** RP-19   **Ht:** 6'2" **Wt:** 180 **Born:** 10/16/1991 **Age:** 26

Year Team	Lg	G	GS	CG	GF	IP	BFP	H	R	ER	HR	SH	SF	HB	TBB	IBB	SO	WP	Bk	W	L	Pct	Sh	Sv-Op	Hld	ERC	ERA
2015 2 Tms	Low	22	0	0	11	42.1	176	37	15	15	4	1	2	3	9	0	48	9	1	1	0	1.000	0	4--	-	2.86	3.19
2016 Bradtn	A+	9	0	0	5	22.1	83	13	2	2	0	2	0	2	2	0	20	0	0	2	0	1.000	0	0--	-	1.04	0.81

Year	Team	Lg	G	GS	CG	GF	IP	BFP	H	R	ER	HR	SH	SF	HB	TBB	IBB	SO	WP	Bk	W	L	Pct	Sh	Sv-Op	Hld	ERC	ERA
2016	Altna	AA	21	0	0	8	41.1	162	32	13	13	4	1	0	2	11	0	39	4	1	2	1	.667	0	2--	-	2.63	2.83
2016	Indy	AAA	13	0	0	8	16.0	74	22	9	9	1	0	0	0	6	1	12	2	0	0	0	-	0	1--	-	5.79	5.06
2017	Indy	AAA	44	0	0	26	58.0	241	62	19	18	4	3	3	2	12	0	54	5	0	1	3	.250	0	8--	-	3.69	2.79
2017	Pit	NL	19	0	0	2	18.0	81	16	8	7	2	1	0	1	12	1	20	0	0	0	0	-	0	0-0	2	4.72	3.50

Ervin Santana

Pitches: R **Bats:** R **Pos:** SP-33

Ht: 6'2" **Wt:** 175 **Born:** 12/12/1982 **Age:** 35

			HOW MUCH HE PITCHED						WHAT HE GAVE UP												THE RESULTS							
Year	Team	Lg	G	GS	CG	GF	IP	BFP	H	R	ER	HR	SH	SF	HB	TBB	IBB	SO	WP	Bk	W	L	Pct	Sh	Sv-Op	Hld	ERC	ERA
2005	LAA	AL	23	23	1	0	133.2	583	139	73	69	17	1	4	8	47	2	99	4	0	12	8	.600	1	0-0	0	4.51	4.65
2006	LAA	AL	33	33	0	0	204.2	846	181	106	97	21	4	10	11	70	2	141	10	2	16	8	.667	0	0-0	0	3.51	4.28
2007	LAA	AL	28	26	0	1	150.0	675	174	103	96	26	3	2	8	58	3	126	7	0	7	14	.333	0	0-0	0	5.69	5.76
2008	LAA	AL	32	32	2	0	219.0	897	198	89	85	23	3	5	8	47	2	214	5	1	16	7	.696	1	0-0	0	3.00	3.49
2009	LAA	AL	24	23	2	0	139.2	614	159	83	78	24	2	1	10	47	4	107	4	0	8	8	.500	2	0-0	1	5.47	5.03
2010	LAA	AL	33	33	4	0	222.2	954	221	104	97	27	8	8	12	73	2	169	11	1	17	10	.630	1	0-0	0	4.10	3.92
2011	LAA	AL	33	33	4	0	228.2	949	207	95	86	26	4	7	8	72	4	178	10	1	11	12	.478	1	0-0	0	3.45	3.38
2012	LAA	AL	30	30	1	0	178.0	764	165	109	102	**39**	2	2	9	61	2	133	4	0	9	13	.409	1	0-0	0	4.38	5.16
2013	KC	AL	32	32	0	0	211.0	859	190	85	76	26	2	3	6	51	3	161	6	0	9	10	.474	0	0-0	0	3.19	3.24
2014	Atl	NL	31	31	0	0	196.0	817	193	90	86	16	12	**12**	4	63	4	179	9	0	14	10	.583	0	0-0	0	3.68	3.95
2015	Min	AL	17	17	0	0	108.0	457	104	50	48	12	4	2	4	36	2	82	3	0	7	5	.583	0	0-0	0	3.82	4.00
2016	Min	AL	30	30	2	0	181.1	748	168	78	68	19	1	5	4	53	2	149	11	3	7	11	.389	1	0-0	0	3.39	3.38
2017	Min	AL	33	33	**5**	0	211.1	864	177	85	77	31	4	4	8	61	2	167	12	1	16	8	.667	**3**	0-0	0	3.21	3.28
	Postseason		8	2	0	3	22.2	101	21	17	14	4	1	1	3	9	1	14	0	0	2	2	.500	0	0-0	0	4.55	5.56
	13 ML YEARS		379	376	21	1	2383.1	10027	2276	1150	1065	307	50	65	100	739	34	1905	96	9	149	124	.546	11	0-0	1	3.83	4.02

Anthony Santander

Bats: B **Throws:** R **Pos:** RF-8;LF-4;PH-4

Ht: 6'2" **Wt:** 190 **Born:** 10/19/1994 **Age:** 23

			BATTING													RUNNING			AVERAGES			
Year	Team	Lg	G	AB	H	2B	3B	HR	(Hm Rd)	TB	R	RBI	RC	TBB	IBB	SO	HBP	SH	SF	SB	CS	GDP	Avg	OBP	Slg	OPS
2013	Lk Cty	A	61	219	53	13	0	5	(- -)	81	27	31	25	13	0	43	6	0	0	6	3	4	.242	.303	.370	.672
2014	Lk Cty	A	43	163	30	9	1	1	(- -)	44	16	10	11	17	0	49	0	0	1	2	0	0	.184	.260	.270	.530
2015	2 Tms	Low	72	279	82	22	0	13	(- -)	143	52	51	51	22	2	61	6	0	4	4	2	10	.294	.354	.513	.866
2016	Lynbrg	A+	128	500	145	42	0	20	(- -)	247	90	95	93	54	1	118	12	1	7	10	5	6	.290	.368	.494	.862
2017	Bowie	AA	15	50	19	5	0	5	(- -)	39	13	14	16	7	1	9	1	0	1	0	0	0	.380	.458	.780	1.238
2017	Bal	AL	13	30	8	3	0	0	(0 0)	11	1	2	2	0	0	8	0	0	1	0	0	0	.267	.258	.367	.625

Hector Santiago

Pitches: L **Bats:** R **Pos:** SP-14; RP-1

Ht: 6'0" **Wt:** 215 **Born:** 12/16/1987 **Age:** 30

			HOW MUCH HE PITCHED						WHAT HE GAVE UP												THE RESULTS							
Year	Team	Lg	G	GS	CG	GF	IP	BFP	H	R	ER	HR	SH	SF	HB	TBB	IBB	SO	WP	Bk	W	L	Pct	Sh	Sv-Op	Hld	ERC	ERA
2017	Roch*	AAA	7	7	0	0	23.2	110	21	16	14	4	0	2	1	17	0	25	1	0	1	2	.333	0	0--	-	5.28	5.32
2011	CWS	AL	2	0	0	1	5.1	18	1	0	0	0	0	0	0	1	1	2	1	0	0	0	-	0	0-0	0	0.16	0.00
2012	CWS	AL	42	4	0	19	70.1	306	54	26	26	10	2	1	7	40	1	79	5	2	4	1	.800	0	4-6	4	4.11	3.33
2013	CWS	AL	34	23	0	4	149.0	656	137	69	59	17	3	3	15	72	2	137	2	0	4	9	.308	0	0-0	0	4.43	3.56
2014	LAA	AL	30	24	0	2	127.1	544	120	63	53	15	1	3	5	53	3	108	5	1	6	9	.400	0	0-0	1	4.02	3.75
2015	LAA	AL	33	32	0	0	180.2	776	156	80	72	**29**	4	4	10	71	5	162	1	3	9	9	.500	0	0-0	0	3.82	3.59
2016	2 Tms	AL	33	33	0	0	182.0	785	169	100	95	33	5	6	5	**79**	4	144	3	1	13	10	.565	0	0-0	0	4.48	4.70
2017	Min	AL	15	14	0	1	70.1	311	70	44	44	15	0	1	5	31	0	51	0	1	4	8	.333	0	0-0	0	5.33	5.63
	16 LAA	AL	22	22	0	0	120.2	515	104	61	57	20	3	4	4	57	0	107	2	1	10	4	.714	0	0-0	0	4.20	4.25
	16 Min	AL	11	11	0	0	61.1	270	65	39	38	13	2	2	1	22	0	37	1	0	3	6	.333	0	0-0	0	5.05	5.58
	Postseason		1	0	0	0	1.1	7	1	2	2	1	0	0	0	2	0	0	0	0	0	0	-	0	0-0	0	12.98	13.50
	7 ML YEARS		189	130	0	27	785.0	3396	707	382	349	119	15	18	45	347	12	683	17	8	40	46	.465	0	4-6	5	4.24	4.00

Luis Santos

Pitches: R **Bats:** R **Pos:** RP-10

Ht: 6'0" **Wt:** 185 **Born:** 2/11/1991 **Age:** 27

			HOW MUCH HE PITCHED						WHAT HE GAVE UP												THE RESULTS							
Year	Team	Lg	G	GS	CG	GF	IP	BFP	H	R	ER	HR	SH	SF	HB	TBB	IBB	SO	WP	Bk	W	L	Pct	Sh	Sv-Op	Hld	ERC	ERA
2013	2 Tms	Low	10	10	1	0	59.1	230	42	14	13	0	2	0	2	14	0	47	5	0	7	1	.875	1	0--	-	1.60	1.97
2014	2 Tms	Low	25	17	1	3	118.0	476	101	53	49	9	6	2	6	23	2	86	9	2	8	5	.615	0	0--	-	2.56	3.74
2015	Dnedin	A+	21	16	0	2	93.0	390	91	49	47	12	5	1	1	22	0	86	2	1	6	6	.500	0	0--	-	3.51	4.55
2016	Dnedin	A+	9	7	0	1	45.0	188	41	23	17	3	0	1	0	15	0	42	1	0	4	1	.800	0	0--	-	3.11	3.40
2016	Nham	AA	17	15	0	0	82.0	350	87	42	39	8	1	0	3	22	0	75	2	0	5	3	.625	0	0--	-	4.03	4.28
2017	Buffalo	AAA	24	21	0	1	108.1	451	91	52	49	13	0	3	3	44	0	98	2	0	3	12	.200	0	0--	-	3.50	4.07
2017	Tor	AL	10	0	0	4	16.2	68	15	5	5	4	0	0	0	4	0	16	1	0	0	1	.000	0	1-1	1	3.78	2.70

Luis Sardinas

Bats: B **Throws:** R **Pos:** PH-17;2B-7;SS-5;3B-4   sar-DEEN-yas   **Ht:** 6'1" **Wt:** 180 **Born:** 5/16/1993 **Age:** 25

			BATTING													RUNNING			AVERAGES			
Year	Team	Lg	G	AB	H	2B	3B	HR	(Hm Rd)	TB	R	RBI	RC	TBB	IBB	SO	HBP	SH	SF	SB	CS	GDP	Avg	OBP	Slg	OPS
2017	Norfolk*	AAA	83	310	99	10	3	5	(- -)	130	34	30	45	12	0	39	2	6	1	6	4	11	.319	.348	.419	.767
2014	Tex	AL	43	115	30	6	0	0	(0 0)	36	12	8	9	5	0	21	2	3	0	5	1	5	.261	.303	.313	.616
2015	Mil	NL	36	97	19	0	1	0	(0 0)	21	8	4	5	6	1	25	0	1	1	0	0	3	.196	.240	.216	.457
2016	2 Tms		66	180	44	6	1	4	(1 3)	64	25	18	22	12	3	48	1	4	0	4	2	3	.244	.295	.356	.651

Year Team	Lg	G	AB	H	2B	3B	HR	(Hm	Rd)	TB	R	RBI	RC	TBB	IBB	SO	HBP	SH	SF	SB	CS	GDP	Avg	OBP	Slg	OPS
2017 SD	NL	29	49	8	0	0	0	(0	0)	8	3	1	2	4	0	11	0	0	1	1	0	1	.163	.226	.163	.390
16 Sea	AL	32	72	13	0	0	2	(1	1)	19	12	5	1	1	0	25	1	3	0	1	1	1	.181	.203	.264	.467
16 SD	NL	34	108	31	6	1	2	(0	2)	45	13	13	21	11	3	23	0	1	0	3	1	0	.287	.353	.417	.770
4 ML YEARS		174	441	101	12	2	4	(1	3)	129	48	31	38	27	4	105	3	8	1	10	3	12	.229	.278	.293	.570

Michael Saunders

Bats: L **Throws:** R **Pos:** RF-54;PH-17;LF-4;DH-2   **Ht:** 6'4" **Wt:** 225 **Born:** 11/19/1986 **Age:** 31

Year Team	Lg	G	AB	H	2B	3B	HR	(Hm	Rd)	TB	R	RBI	RC	TBB	IBB	SO	HBP	SH	SF	SB	CS	GDP	Avg	OBP	Slg	OPS
2017 Buffalo*	AAA	35	146	40	11	1	2	(-	-)	59	22	12	19	9	0	30	1	0	0	1	0	3	.274	.321	.404	.725
2009 Sea	AL	46	122	27	1	3	0	(0	0)	34	13	4	8	6	0	40	0	1	0	4	1	1	.221	.258	.279	.537
2010 Sea	AL	100	289	61	11	2	10	(5	5)	106	29	33	31	35	0	84	0	2	1	6	3	1	.211	.295	.367	.662
2011 Sea	AL	58	161	24	5	0	2	(1	1)	35	16	8	2	12	1	56	0	5	1	6	2	1	.149	.207	.217	.424
2012 Sea	AL	139	507	125	31	3	19	(8	11)	219	71	57	67	43	0	132	1	1	1	21	4	6	.247	.306	.432	.738
2013 Sea	AL	132	406	96	23	3	12	(5	7)	161	59	46	49	54	4	118	1	1	6	13	5	6	.236	.323	.397	.720
2014 Sea	AL	78	231	63	11	3	8	(4	4)	104	38	34	37	26	1	59	0	2	4	4	5	2	.273	.341	.450	.791
2015 Tor	AL	9	31	6	0	0	0	(0	0)	6	2	3	3	5	0	10	0	0	0	0	0	1	.194	.306	.194	.499
2016 Tor	AL	140	490	124	32	3	24	(10	14)	234	70	57	66	59	2	157	5	1	3	1	2	14	.253	.338	.478	.815
2017 2 Tms		73	218	44	9	2	6	(4	2)	75	26	21	17	15	2	55	1	0	0	0	1	2	.202	.256	.344	.600
17 Phi	NL	61	200	41	9	2	6	(4	2)	72	25	20	15	13	2	51	1	0	0	0	1	2	.205	.257	.360	.617
17 Tor	AL	12	18	3	0	0	0	(0	0)	3	1	1	2	2	0	4	0	0	0	0	0	0	.167	.250	.167	.417
Postseason		8	21	8	1	0	1	(1	0)	12	2	1	2	1	0	10	0	0	0	0	0	0	.381	.409	.571	.981
9 ML YEARS		775	2455	570	123	19	81	(37	44)	974	324	263	280	255	10	711	8	13	16	55	23	34	.232	.305	.397	.701

Warwick Saupold

Pitches: R **Bats:** R **Pos:** RP-45   SOW-pold   **Ht:** 6'1" **Wt:** 195 **Born:** 1/16/1990 **Age:** 28

			HOW MUCH HE PITCHED					WHAT HE GAVE UP											THE RESULTS						
Year Team	Lg	G	GS	CG	GF	IP	BFP	H	R	ER	HR	SH	SF	HB	TBB	IBB	SO	WP	Bk	W	L	Pct	Sh	Sv-Op	Hld	ERC	ERA
2013 Erie	AA	22	22	1	0	129.0	547	124	54	47	12	4	2	8	51	0	82	6	0	7	6	.538	0	0- -	-	4.13	3.28
2014 Erie	AA	27	27	2	0	140.0	608	141	92	78	16	3	2	7	65	0	125	16	1	8	11	.421	0	0- -	-	4.78	5.01
2015 Erie	AA	23	15	0	6	103.1	436	102	49	46	5	3	6	3	36	0	71	11	0	5	6	.455	0	1- -	-	3.61	4.01
2015 Toledo	AAA	6	3	0	1	20.1	77	14	10	10	1	0	1	1	6	0	23	0	0	1	2	.333	0	0- -	-	2.10	4.43
2016 Toledo	AAA	18	11	1	1	74.1	297	64	20	19	3	1	0	2	22	1	50	3	0	7	2	.778	0	0- -	-	2.73	2.30
2017 Toledo	AAA	7	7	0	0	40.1	170	38	13	13	2	0	3	1	17	0	33	0	0	2	0	1.000	0	0- -	-	3.66	2.90
2016 Det	AL	6	0	0	2	9.2	49	17	8	8	0	0	2	1	3	0	10	0	0	1	1	.500	0	0-0	-	7.91	7.45
2017 Det	AL	45	0	0	10	62.2	280	64	36	34	9	1	2	6	31	5	44	4	0	3	2	.600	0	0-0	2	5.21	4.88
2 ML YEARS		51	0	0	12	72.1	329	81	44	42	9	1	4	7	34	5	54	4	0	4	3	.571	0	0-0	2	5.56	5.23

Rob Scahill

Pitches: R **Bats:** L **Pos:** RP-18   SKAY-hill   **Ht:** 6'2" **Wt:** 220 **Born:** 2/15/1987 **Age:** 31

			HOW MUCH HE PITCHED					WHAT HE GAVE UP											THE RESULTS						
Year Team	Lg	G	GS	CG	GF	IP	BFP	H	R	ER	HR	SH	SF	HB	TBB	IBB	SO	WP	Bk	W	L	Pct	Sh	Sv-Op	Hld	ERC	ERA
2017 ColSpr*	AAA	27	0	0	24	25.2	103	24	5	4	1	0	0	2	4	0	19	2	0	0	1	.000	0	10- -	-	2.77	1.40
2012 Col	NL	6	0	0	3	8.2	33	7	1	1	0	0	0	0	3	0	4	0	0	0	0	-	0	0-0	0	2.43	1.04
2013 Col	NL	23	0	0	6	33.1	149	40	19	19	5	3	0	4	9	1	20	1	0	1	0	1.000	0	0-0	1	5.55	5.13
2014 Col	NL	12	0	0	3	15.0	72	17	8	8	3	0	2	1	9	2	11	0	0	1	0	1.000	0	0-1	0	6.37	4.80
2015 Pit	NL	28	0	0	13	30.2	142	33	15	9	3	1	1	1	16	5	24	1	0	2	4	.333	0	0-0	1	4.70	2.64
2016 2 Tms	NL	31	0	0	12	34.2	147	34	14	13	2	0	1	4	9	0	27	1	0	0	0	-	0	0-0	2	3.60	3.38
2017 Mil	NL	18	0	0	6	22.1	97	21	14	11	3	0	2	3	10	4	10	2	0	1	3	.250	0	0-0	0	4.50	4.43
16 Pit	NL	15	0	0	5	16.1	71	18	9	8	1	0	1	2	6	0	13	1	0	0	0	-	0	0-0	1	4.89	4.41
16 Mil	NL	16	0	0	7	18.1	76	16	5	5	1	0	0	2	3	0	14	0	0	0	0	-	0	0-0	1	2.58	2.45
6 ML YEARS		118	0	0	43	144.2	640	152	71	61	16	4	6	13	56	12	96	5	0	5	7	.417	0	0-1	4	4.61	3.79

Scott Schebler

Bats: L **Throws:** R **Pos:** RF-120;CF-15;PH-9;PR-1   SHEB-ler   **Ht:** 6'0" **Wt:** 228 **Born:** 10/6/1990 **Age:** 27

Year Team	Lg	G	AB	H	2B	3B	HR	(Hm	Rd)	TB	R	RBI	RC	TBB	IBB	SO	HBP	SH	SF	SB	CS	GDP	Avg	OBP	Slg	OPS
2015 LAD	NL	19	36	9	0	0	3	(1	2)	18	6	4	4	3	1	13	1	0	0	2	1	0	.250	.325	.500	.825
2016 Cin	NL	82	257	68	12	2	9	(5	4)	111	36	40	36	19	2	59	6	0	0	2	4	5	.265	.330	.432	.762
2017 Cin	NL	141	473	110	25	2	30	(13	17)	229	63	67	58	39	5	125	14	0	5	5	3	7	.233	.307	.484	.791
3 ML YEARS		242	766	187	37	4	42	(19	23)	358	105	111	98	61	8	197	21	0	5	9	8	12	.244	.315	.467	.783

Tanner Scheppers

Pitches: R **Bats:** R **Pos:** RP-5   **Ht:** 6'4" **Wt:** 200 **Born:** 1/17/1987 **Age:** 31

			HOW MUCH HE PITCHED					WHAT HE GAVE UP											THE RESULTS						
Year Team	Lg	G	GS	CG	GF	IP	BFP	H	R	ER	HR	SH	SF	HB	TBB	IBB	SO	WP	Bk	W	L	Pct	Sh	Sv-Op	Hld	ERC	ERA
2017 RdRck*	AAA	31	1	0	9	48.1	218	56	28	26	9	1	0	4	14	0	39	4	0	1	3	.250	0	3- -	-	5.42	4.84
2012 Tex	AL	39	0	0	13	32.1	152	47	18	16	6	3	1	2	9	3	30	4	0	1	1	.500	0	1-1	4	7.05	4.45
2013 Tex	AL	76	0	0	11	76.2	302	58	21	16	6	0	0	7	24	4	59	4	0	6	2	.750	0	1-3	27	2.71	1.88
2014 Tex	AL	8	4	0	0	23.0	111	31	24	23	6	0	1	3	10	0	17	2	0	0	0	-	0	0-0	1	8.21	9.00
2015 Tex	AL	42	0	0	7	38.1	176	37	25	24	6	0	3	2	23	3	32	1	0	4	1	.800	0	0-3	12	5.09	5.63
2016 Tex	AL	10	0	0	5	8.2	35	6	4	4	0	0	0	0	3	1	5	2	0	1	1	.500	0	1-1	2	1.57	4.15
2017 Tex	AL	5	0	0	1	4.0	21	5	3	3	0	0	0	1	3	0	5	0	0	0	1	.000	0	0-0	1	6.99	6.75
6 ML YEARS		180	4	0	37	183.0	797	184	95	86	24	3	5	15	72	11	148	13	0	12	7	.632	0	3-8	47	4.57	4.23

Max Scherzer

Pitches: R Bats: R Pos: SP-31

SHERR-zer

Ht: 6'3" Wt: 210 Born: 7/27/1984 Age: 33

Year	Team	Lg	G	GS	CG	GF	IP	BFP	H	R	ER	HR	SH	SF	HB	TBB	IBB	SO	WP	Bk	W	L	Pct	Sh	Sv-Op	Hld	ERC	ERA
2008	Ari	NL	16	7	0	2	56.0	237	48	24	19	5	4	2	5	21	1	66	2	0	0	4	.000	0	0-0	0	3.45	3.05
2009	Ari	NL	30	30	0	0	170.1	741	166	94	78	20	5	6	10	63	1	174	5	1	9	11	.450	0	0-0	0	4.12	4.12
2010	Det	AL	31	31	0	0	195.2	800	174	84	76	20	5	5	7	70	1	184	8	0	12	11	.522	0	0-0	0	3.56	3.50
2011	Det	AL	33	33	0	0	195.0	833	207	101	96	29	3	7	7	56	1	174	12	0	15	9	.625	0	0-0	0	4.48	4.43
2012	Det	AL	32	32	0	0	187.2	787	179	82	78	23	5	1	5	60	2	231	2	1	16	7	.696	0	0-0	0	3.77	3.74
2013	Det	AL	32	32	0	0	214.1	836	152	73	69	18	2	8	4	56	0	240	6	1	**21**	3	**.875**	0	0-0	0	**2.07**	2.90
2014	Det	AL	33	33	1	0	220.1	904	196	80	77	18	4	8	6	63	1	252	10	1	**18**	5	.783	1	0-0	0	3.04	3.15
2015	Was	NL	33	**33**	**4**	0	228.2	**899**	176	74	71	27	11	2	5	34	2	276	10	1	14	12	.538	**3**	0-0	0	2.11	2.79
2016	Was	NL	34	**34**	1	0	**228.1**	902	165	77	75	**31**	7	3	6	56	2	**284**	2	1	**20**	7	.741	0	0-0	0	2.35	2.96
2017	Was	NL	31	31	**2**	0	200.2	780	126	62	56	22	4	1	11	55	2	**268**	4	0	16	6	.727	0	0-0	0	**1.98**	2.51
	Postseason		14	12	0	0	74.2	305	56	32	31	8	2	0	5	27	1	92	4	0	4	4	.500	0	0-0	1	2.90	3.74
	10 ML YEARS		305	296	8	2	1897.0	7719	1589	751	695	213	50	43	66	534	13	2149	61	6	141	75	.653	4	0-0	0	2.97	3.30

Ryan Schimpf

Bats: L Throws: R Pos: 3B-50;PH-3;DH-1

Ht: 5'9" Wt: 180 Born: 4/11/1988 Age: 30

Year	Team	Lg	G	AB	H	2B	3B	HR	(Hm	Rd)	TB	R	RBI	RC	TBB	IBB	SO	HBP	SH	SF	SB	CS	GDP	Avg	OBP	Slg	OPS
2013	Nham	AA	126	442	93	21	3	23	(-	-)	189	67	65	68	79	1	138	1	0	5	3	3	6	.210	.338	.428	.766
2014	Nham	AA	50	185	50	16	1	15	(-	-)	113	35	37	42	28	4	56	3	0	3	3	0	1	.270	.370	.611	.981
2014	Buffalo	AAA	67	212	40	7	1	9	(-	-)	76	29	21	23	24	1	59	7	1	2	0	1	2	.189	.290	.358	.648
2015	Nham	AA	76	258	70	20	0	20	(-	-)	150	43	56	57	42	1	54	4	0	3	2	1	2	.271	.378	.581	.959
2015	Buffalo	AAA	31	110	22	6	0	3	(-	-)	37	12	7	9	11	1	23	0	0	1	0	2	1	.200	.270	.336	.607
2016	ElPaso	AAA	51	166	59	17	0	15	(-	-)	121	36	48	47	20	1	33	3	0	1	0	1	1	.355	.432	.729	1.160
2017	ElPaso	AAA	69	242	49	7	1	19	(-	-)	115	44	44	37	36	1	105	3	0	2	0	0	0	.202	.311	.475	.786
2016	SD	NL	89	276	60	17	5	20	(7	13)	147	48	51	61	42	3	105	9	0	3	1	1	3	.217	.336	.533	.869
2017	SD	NL	53	165	26	2	0	14	(5	9)	70	24	25	21	27	0	70	3	0	2	0	0	0	.158	.284	.424	.709
	2 ML YEARS		142	441	86	19	5	34	(12	22)	217	72	76	82	69	3	175	12	0	5	1	1	3	.195	.317	.492	.809

Jonathan Schoop

Bats: R Throws: R Pos: 2B-159;SS-5

SCOPE

Ht: 6'1" Wt: 225 Born: 10/16/1991 Age: 26

Year	Team	Lg	G	AB	H	2B	3B	HR	(Hm	Rd)	TB	R	RBI	RC	TBB	IBB	SO	HBP	SH	SF	SB	CS	GDP	Avg	OBP	Slg	OPS
2013	Bal	AL	5	14	4	0	0	1	(1	0)	7	5	1	1	1	0	2	0	0	0	0	0	2	.286	.333	.500	.833
2014	Bal	AL	137	455	95	18	0	16	(5	11)	161	48	45	32	13	0	122	8	5	0	2	0	12	.209	.244	.354	.598
2015	Bal	AL	86	305	85	17	0	15	(9	6)	147	34	39	40	9	0	79	4	1	2	2	0	9	.279	.306	.482	.788
2016	Bal	AL	**162**	615	164	38	1	25	(13	12)	279	82	82	72	21	0	137	8	0	3	1	2	16	.267	.298	.454	.752
2017	Bal	AL	160	622	182	35	0	32	(18	14)	313	92	105	100	35	0	142	11	0	7	1	0	20	.293	.338	.503	.841
	Postseason		8	25	4	1	0	0	(0	0)	5	3	2	2	3	0	5	0	0	0	2	0	0	.160	.250	.200	.450
	5 ML YEARS		550	2011	530	108	1	89	(46	43)	907	261	272	245	79	0	482	31	6	12	6	2	59	.264	.300	.451	.751

A.J. Schugel

Pitches: R Bats: R Pos: RP-32

SHOO-gul

Ht: 6'0" Wt: 200 Born: 6/27/1989 Age: 29

Year	Team	Lg	G	GS	CG	GF	IP	BFP	H	R	ER	HR	SH	SF	HB	TBB	IBB	SO	WP	Bk	W	L	Pct	Sh	Sv-Op	Hld	ERC	ERA
2017	Indy*	AAA	26	0	0	7	36.2	156	37	18	17	4	1	2	2	13	2	36	4	0	3	1	.750	0	0--	-	4.22	4.17
2015	Ari	NL	5	0	0	2	9.0	51	17	13	5	2	0	0	0	5	2	5	0	0	0	0	-	0	0-0	0	10.46	5.00
2016	Pit	NL	36	0	0	11	52.0	204	41	22	21	4	0	0	1	13	0	46	2	0	2	2	.500	0	1-2	3	2.40	3.63
2017	Pit	NL	32	0	0	4	32.0	136	31	8	7	3	1	1	0	14	2	27	2	0	4	0	1.000	0	0-1	4	3.97	1.97
	3 ML YEARS		73	0	0	17	93.0	391	89	43	33	9	1	1	1	32	4	78	4	0	6	2	.750	0	1-3	7	3.60	3.19

Kyle Schwarber

Bats: L Throws: R Pos: LF-110;PH-15;DH-8;C-4;1B-1

SHWAR-burr

Ht: 6'0" Wt: 235 Born: 3/5/1993 Age: 25

Year	Team	Lg	G	AB	H	2B	3B	HR	(Hm	Rd)	TB	R	RBI	RC	TBB	IBB	SO	HBP	SH	SF	SB	CS	GDP	Avg	OBP	Slg	OPS
2017	Iowa*	AAA	11	35	12	1	0	4	(-	-)	25	9	9	11	8	1	12	1	0	0	0	0	1	.343	.477	.714	1.192
2015	ChC	NL	69	232	57	6	1	16	(7	9)	113	52	43	39	36	1	77	4	0	1	3	3	4	.246	.355	.487	.842
2016	ChC	NL	2	4	0	0	0	0	(0	0)	0	0	0	0	1	0	2	0	0	0	0	0	0	.000	.200	.000	.200
2017	ChC	NL	129	422	89	16	1	30	(18	12)	197	67	59	55	59	1	150	5	0	0	1	1	6	.211	.315	.467	.782
	Postseason		14	44	16	1	0	5	(3	2)	32	8	10	10	7	0	12	0	0	0	0	0	1	.364	.451	.727	1.178
	3 ML YEARS		200	658	146	22	2	46	(25	21)	310	119	102	94	96	2	229	9	0	1	4	4	10	.222	.329	.471	.800

Robby Scott

Pitches: L Bats: B Pos: RP-57

Ht: 6'3" Wt: 220 Born: 8/29/1989 Age: 28

Year	Team	Lg	G	GS	CG	GF	IP	BFP	H	R	ER	HR	SH	SF	HB	TBB	IBB	SO	WP	Bk	W	L	Pct	Sh	Sv-Op	Hld	ERC	ERA
2013	Salem	A+	31	0	0	15	67.2	278	51	27	21	6	3	5	2	30	2	44	5	0	4	4	.500	0	2--	-	2.95	2.79
2014	PortInd	AA	35	1	0	16	59.2	242	55	17	13	3	3	3	3	15	0	51	5	1	8	2	.800	0	3--	-	2.81	1.96
2015	Pwtckt	AAA	13	1	0	1	31.2	150	47	31	27	5	1	2	0	9	0	27	0	0	1	1	.500	0	1--	-	6.84	7.67
2015	PortInd	AA	25	2	0	10	43.2	179	32	14	10	3	0	3	1	13	0	41	3	1	1	1	.500	0	0--	-	2.14	2.06
2016	Pwtckt	AAA	32	6	0	7	78.0	300	57	22	22	9	0	0	4	14	0	73	3	0	4	3	.571	0	0--	-	2.20	2.54

Year Team	Lg	G	GS	CG	GF	IP	BFP	H	R	ER	HR	SH	SF	HB	TBB	IBB	SO	WP	Bk	W	L	Pct	Sh	Sv-Op	Hld	ERC	ERA
																										HOW MUCH HE PITCHED / WHAT HE GAVE UP / THE RESULTS	

Year Team	Lg	G	GS	CG	GF	IP	BFP	H	R	ER	HR	SH	SF	HB	TBB	IBB	SO	WP	Bk	W	L	Pct	Sh	Sv-Op	Hld	ERC	ERA
2017 Pwtckt	AAA	7	0	0	2	7.1	29	3	0	0	1	0	0	0	5	0	5	1	0	0	0	-	0	0--	-	1.56	0.00
2016 Bos	AL	7	0	0	1	6.0	25	6	0	0	0	0	0	0	2	0	5	1	0	1	0	1.000	0	0-0	1	3.19	0.00
2017 Bos	AL	57	0	0	12	35.2	141	22	16	15	7	0	2	3	13	1	31	3	0	2	1	.667	0	0-2	12	2.85	3.79
2 ML YEARS		64	0	0	13	41.2	166	28	16	15	7	1	2	3	15	1	36	4	0	3	1	.750	0	0-2	13	2.91	3.24

Tanner Scott

Pitches: L Bats: R Pos: RP-2

Ht: 6'2" Wt: 220 Born: 7/22/1994 Age: 23

Year Team	Lg	G	GS	CG	GF	IP	BFP	H	R	ER	HR	SH	SF	HB	TBB	IBB	SO	WP	Bk	W	L	Pct	Sh	Sv-Op	Hld	ERC	ERA
2014 Orioles	R	10	8	0	0	23.0	113	21	22	16	0	1	0	3	20	0	23	2	0	1	5	.167	0	0--	-	4.98	6.26
2015 2 Tms	Low	18	3	0	2	44.1	183	35	21	18	0	3	2	3	22	0	60	4	0	4	3	.571	0	2--	-	3.14	3.83
2016 Frdrck	A+	29	0	0	14	42.1	210	22	33	24	1	0	1	2	42	0	63	5	0	4	2	.667	0	5--	-	2.46	4.47
2016 Bowie	AA	14	0	0	7	16.0	76	18	11	10	0	1	0	1	15	0	18	0	0	1	2	.333	0	0--	-	6.75	5.63
2017 Bowie	AA	24	24	0	0	69.0	290	45	17	17	2	0	2	2	46	0	87	6	0	0	2	.000	0	0--	-	2.87	2.22
2017 Bal	AL	2	0	0	1	1.2	9	2	2	2	0	0	0	0	2	0	2	0	0	0	0	-	0	0-0	0	7.49	10.80

Evan Scribner

Pitches: R Bats: R Pos: RP-8

SKRIBB-nurr

Ht: 6'3" Wt: 190 Born: 7/19/1985 Age: 32

Year Team	Lg	G	GS	CG	GF	IP	BFP	H	R	ER	HR	SH	SF	HB	TBB	IBB	SO	WP	Bk	W	L	Pct	Sh	Sv-Op	Hld	ERC	ERA
2011 SD	NL	10	0	0	5	14.0	64	18	11	11	1	0	0	0	4	0	10	0	0	0	0	-	0	0-0	0	4.92	7.07
2012 Oak	AL	30	0	0	13	35.1	148	30	11	10	2	0	0	0	12	0	30	1	0	2	0	1.000	0	1-1	1	2.70	2.55
2013 Oak	AL	18	0	0	12	26.2	114	26	13	13	3	0	0	0	7	0	19	2	0	0	0	-	0	0-0	4	3.38	4.39
2014 Oak	AL	13	0	0	6	11.2	47	11	6	6	4	0	0	1	0	0	11	0	0	1	0	1.000	0	0-0	0	3.89	4.63
2015 Oak	AL	54	0	0	14	60.0	238	58	31	29	14	0	1	2	4	0	64	2	0	2	2	.500	0	0-4	8	3.57	4.35
2016 Sea	AL	12	0	0	6	14.0	49	5	0	0	0	1	0	1	2	1	15	0	0	0	0	-	0	0-0	3	0.53	0.00
2017 Sea	AL	8	0	0	4	7.1	34	13	9	9	3	1	0	0	0	0	6	0	0	0	2	.000	0	0-0	0	9.69	11.05
Postseason		1	0	0	1	2.0	6	0	0	0	0	0	0	0	0	0	3	0	0	0	0	-	0	0-0	0	0.00	0.00
7 ML YEARS		145	0	0	54	169.0	694	161	81	78	27	2	1	4	29	1	155	5	0	5	4	.556	0	1-5	12	3.37	4.15

Troy Scribner

Pitches: R Bats: R Pos: RP-6; SP-4

SKRIBB-nurr

Ht: 6'3" Wt: 190 Born: 7/2/1991 Age: 26

Year Team	Lg	G	GS	CG	GF	IP	BFP	H	R	ER	HR	SH	SF	HB	TBB	IBB	SO	WP	Bk	W	L	Pct	Sh	Sv-Op	Hld	ERC	ERA
2013 3 Tms	Low	16	4	0	3	53.0	208	37	18	15	3	0	1	1	14	1	78	2	1	4	4	.500	0	0--	-	1.84	2.55
2014 2 Tms	Low	15	13	1	1	75.0	307	58	23	17	5	2	0	2	24	0	95	7	0	8	3	.727	0	1--	-	2.45	2.04
2015 Lancst	A+	29	13	0	5	100.0	444	94	69	61	14	0	7	2	57	0	111	10	1	2	6	.250	0	1--	-	4.78	5.49
2016 Ark	AA	16	16	0	0	85.2	348	64	36	33	8	2	1	4	34	0	82	1	0	8	3	.727	0	0--	-	2.75	3.47
2016 Salt Lk	AAA	8	7	2	1	46.1	190	34	18	17	4	1	2	0	22	0	35	1	0	2	1	.667	1	0--	-	2.88	3.30
2017 Salt Lk	AAA	20	19	0	0	103.1	443	100	52	50	13	0	4	5	38	0	103	1	1	11	4	.733	0	0--	-	4.15	4.35
2017 LAA	AL	10	4	0	3	23.2	99	17	14	11	7	0	0	2	10	0	18	0	0	2	1	.667	0	0-0	1	4.21	4.18

Corey Seager

Bats: L Throws: R Pos: SS-138;PH-9;DH-1

SEE-gurr

Ht: 6'4" Wt: 220 Born: 4/27/1994 Age: 24

Year Team	Lg	G	AB	H	2B	3B	HR	(Hm	Rd)	TB	R	RBI	RC	TBB	IBB	SO	HBP	SH	SF	SB	CS	GDP	Avg	OBP	Slg	OPS
2015 LAD	NL	27	98	33	8	1	4	(3	1)	55	17	17	19	14	1	19	1	0	0	2	0	2	.337	.425	.561	.986
2016 LAD	NL	157	627	193	40	5	26	(18	8)	321	105	72	110	54	5	133	4	0	2	3	3	12	.308	.365	.512	.877
2017 LAD	NL	145	539	159	33	0	22	(12	10)	258	85	77	104	67	5	131	4	0	3	4	2	14	.295	.375	.479	.854
Postseason		16	60	12	2	0	2	(0	2)	20	5	4	1	3	0	21	1	0	0	0	0	2	.200	.250	.333	.583
3 ML YEARS		329	1264	385	81	6	52	(33	19)	634	207	166	233	135	11	283	9	0	5	9	5	28	.305	.374	.502	.876

Kyle Seager

Bats: L Throws: R Pos: 3B-154;PH-1

SEE-gurr

Ht: 6'0" Wt: 210 Born: 11/3/1987 Age: 30

Year Team	Lg	G	AB	H	2B	3B	HR	(Hm	Rd)	TB	R	RBI	RC	TBB	IBB	SO	HBP	SH	SF	SB	CS	GDP	Avg	OBP	Slg	OPS
2011 Sea	AL	53	182	47	13	1	3	(0	3)	69	22	13	16	13	0	36	2	2	2	3	1	4	.258	.312	.379	.691
2012 Sea	AL	155	594	154	35	1	20	(5	15)	251	62	86	88	46	1	110	5	2	4	13	5	9	.259	.316	.423	.738
2013 Sea	AL	160	615	160	32	2	22	(8	14)	262	79	69	90	68	1	122	7	0	5	9	3	8	.260	.338	.426	.764
2014 Sea	AL	159	590	158	27	4	25	(16	9)	268	71	96	96	52	3	118	8	1	3	7	5	12	.268	.334	.454	.788
2015 Sea	AL	161	623	166	37	0	26	(7	19)	281	85	74	75	54	6	98	5	0	4	6	6	17	.266	.328	.451	.779
2016 Sea	AL	158	597	166	36	3	30	(11	19)	298	89	99	110	69	10	108	8	0	2	3	1	18	.278	.359	.499	.859
2017 Sea	AL	154	578	144	33	1	27	(12	15)	260	72	88	84	58	6	110	8	0	6	2	1	6	.249	.323	.450	.773
7 ML YEARS		1000	3779	995	213	11	153	(59	94)	1689	480	525	559	360	27	702	43	5	26	43	22	74	.263	.332	.447	.779

Rob Segedin

Bats: R Throws: R Pos: 1B-6;3B-5;PH-3;LF-1

Ht: 6'2" Wt: 220 Born: 11/10/1988 Age: 29

Year Team	Lg	G	AB	H	2B	3B	HR	(Hm	Rd)	TB	R	RBI	RC	TBB	IBB	SO	HBP	SH	SF	SB	CS	GDP	Avg	OBP	Slg	OPS
2013 Trntn	AA	18	71	24	10	0	3	(-	-)	43	16	17	16	6	0	18	2	0	3	0	0	1	.338	.390	.606	.996
2014 Trntn	AA	92	325	92	21	1	8	(-	-)	139	46	49	61	52	1	60	13	0	4	1	0	12	.283	.398	.428	.826
2014 S-WB	AAA	21	77	11	2	0	1	(-	-)	16	7	11	2	4	0	14	1	0	3	0	0	6	.143	.188	.208	.396
2015 S-WB	AAA	46	162	45	8	1	4	(-	-)	67	24	15	24	15	0	34	3	1	0	2	0	5	.278	.350	.414	.764

Year	Team	Lg	G	AB	H	2B	3B	HR	(Hm	Rd)	TB	R	RBI	RC	TBB	IBB	SO	HBP	SH	SF	SB	CS	GDP	Avg	OBP	Slg	OPS
									BATTING												**RUNNING**			**AVERAGES**			
2015	Trnton	AA	25	89	27	4	0	3	(-	-)	40	8	19	15	11	0	17	1	0	2	1	1		.303	.379	.449	.828
2016	OkCity	AAA	103	373	119	23	9	21	(-	-)	223	71	69	84	40	0	81	7	0	4	3	4	13	.319	.392	.598	.989
2017	OkCity	AAA	25	97	31	7	0	4	(-	-)	50	13	15	16	4	0	16	0	0	0	0	1	5	.320	.347	.515	.862
2016	LAD	NL	40	73	17	2	1	2	(1	1)	27	9	12	8	6	0	22	2	0	2	0	0	1	.233	.301	.370	.671
2017	LAD	NL	13	20	4	2	0	0	(0	0)	6	3	1	1	0	0	7	0	0	0	0	0	0	.200	.200	.300	.500
2 ML YEARS			53	93	21	4	1	2	(1	1)	33	12	13	9	6	0	29	2	0	2	0	0	1	.226	.282	.355	.636

Jean Segura

Bats: R **Throws:** R **Pos:** SS-124;PH-1   GENE seg-ER-uh   **Ht:** 5'10" **Wt:** 205 **Born:** 3/17/1990 **Age:** 28

Year	Team	Lg	G	AB	H	2B	3B	HR	(Hm	Rd)	TB	R	RBI	RC	TBB	IBB	SO	HBP	SH	SF	SB	CS	GDP	Avg	OBP	Slg	OPS
									BATTING												**RUNNING**			**AVERAGES**			
2012	2 Tms		45	151	39	4	3	0	(0	0)	49	19	14	16	13	3	23	0	1	1	7	1		.258	.315	.325	.640
2013	Mil	NL	146	588	173	20	10	12	(7	5)	249	74	49	72	25	1	84	6	2	2	44	13	17	.294	.329	.423	.752
2014	Mil	NL	146	513	126	14	6	5	(3	2)	167	61	31	45	28	5	70	4	10	2	20	9	13	.246	.289	.326	.614
2015	Mil	NL	142	560	144	16	5	6	(4	2)	188	57	50	57	13	2	93	6	3	2	25	6	14	.257	.281	.336	.616
2016	Ari	NL	153	637	203	41	7	20	(12	8)	318	102	64	107	39	1	101	12	4	2	33	10	6	.319	.368	.499	.867
2017	Sea	AL	125	524	157	30	2	11	(7	4)	224	80	45	71	34	3	83	6	0	1	22	8	14	.300	.349	.427	.776
12	LAA	AL	1	3	0	0	0	0	(0	0)	0	0	0	0	0	0	2	0	0	0	0	0		.000	.000	.000	.000
12	Mil	NL	44	148	39	4	3	0	(0	0)	49	19	14	16	13	3	21	0	1	1	7	1	1	.264	.321	.331	.652
6 ML YEARS			757	2973	842	125	33	54	(33	21)	1195	393	253	368	152	15	454	34	20	10	151	47	65	.283	.324	.402	.726

Steve Selsky

Bats: R **Throws:** R **Pos:** PH-3;3B-2;DH-2;PR-2;CF-1   **Ht:** 6'0" **Wt:** 213 **Born:** 7/20/1989 **Age:** 28

Year	Team	Lg	G	AB	H	2B	3B	HR	(Hm	Rd)	TB	R	RBI	RC	TBB	IBB	SO	HBP	SH	SF	SB	CS	GDP	Avg	OBP	Slg	OPS
									BATTING												**RUNNING**			**AVERAGES**			
2013	Pnscla	AA	32	83	15	2	0	0	(-	-)	17	7	12	5	10	1	20	2	3	1	0	0		.181	.281	.205	.486
2013	Bkrsfld	A+	91	340	101	19	5	13	(-	-)	169	54	68	67	37	0	79	15	0	2	9	4	7	.297	.388	.497	.885
2014	Pnscla	AA	64	166	50	8	0	1	(-	-)	61	23	21	28	29	2	42	5	0	5	2	4	6	.301	.410	.367	.777
2014	Lsvlle	AAA	55	121	29	7	1	1	(-	-)	41	15	11	16	21	0	47	2	0	1	0	0	1	.240	.359	.339	.697
2015	Lsvlle	AAA	51	180	57	10	2	2	(-	-)	77	23	29	31	19	1	44	2	0	1	3	1	5	.317	.386	.428	.814
2016	Lsvlle	AAA	85	296	83	24	1	9	(-	-)	136	40	37	51	29	0	74	11	0	3	2	1	9	.280	.363	.459	.822
2017	Pwtckt	AAA	79	297	64	10	0	11	(-	-)	107	30	39	29	18	0	97	5	0	2	1	1	5	.215	.270	.360	.630
2016	Cin	NL	24	51	16	2	0	2	(1	1)	24	9	7	8	2	0	22	0	1	0	1	0	1	.314	.340	.471	.810
2017	Bos	AL	8	9	1	1	0	0	(0	0)	2	0	0	0	0	0	5	0	0	0	0	0	0	.111	.111	.222	.333
2 ML YEARS			32	60	17	3	0	2	(1	1)	26	9	7	8	2	0	27	0	1	0	1	0	1	.283	.306	.433	.740

Marcus Semien

Bats: R **Throws:** R **Pos:** SS-85   SIM-ee-inn   **Ht:** 6'0" **Wt:** 195 **Born:** 9/17/1990 **Age:** 27

Year	Team	Lg	G	AB	H	2B	3B	HR	(Hm	Rd)	TB	R	RBI	RC	TBB	IBB	SO	HBP	SH	SF	SB	CS	GDP	Avg	OBP	Slg	OPS
									BATTING												**RUNNING**			**AVERAGES**			
2013	CWS	AL	21	69	18	4	0	2	(2	0)	28	7	7	7	1	0	22	0	0	1	2	2	1	.261	.268	.406	.673
2014	CWS	AL	64	231	54	10	2	6	(4	2)	86	30	28	31	21	0	70	1	2	0	3	0	6	.234	.300	.372	.673
2015	Oak	AL	155	556	143	23	7	15	(5	10)	225	65	45	57	42	1	132	1	1	1	11	5	16	.257	.310	.405	.715
2016	Oak	AL	159	568	135	27	2	27	(10	17)	247	72	75	77	51	1	139	0	1	1	10	2	12	.238	.300	.435	.735
2017	Oak	AL	85	342	85	19	1	10	(5	5)	136	53	40	48	38	0	85	2	1	3	12	1	3	.249	.325	.398	.722
5 ML YEARS			484	1766	435	83	12	60	(26	34)	722	227	195	220	153	2	448	4	5	6	38	10	38	.246	.307	.409	.716

Antonio Senzatela

Pitches: R **Bats:** R **Pos:** SP-20; RP-16   **Ht:** 6'1" **Wt:** 180 **Born:** 1/21/1995 **Age:** 23

Year	Team	Lg	G	GS	CG	GF	IP	BFP	H	R	ER	HR	SH	SF	HB	TBB	IBB	SO	WP	Bk	W	L	Pct	Sh	Sv-Op	Hld	ERC	ERA
					HOW MUCH HE PITCHED						**WHAT HE GAVE UP**											**THE RESULTS**					
2013	TriCity	A-	8	8	0	0	42.1	189	48	23	18	1	1	2	3	13	0	20	3	0	2	4	.333	0	0- -	-	4.12	3.83
2014	Ashvll	A	26	26	0	0	144.1	602	134	61	50	11	3	6	5	36	0	89	6	2	15	2	.882	0	0- -	-	3.06	3.12
2015	Mdest	A+	26	26	1	0	154.0	623	131	53	43	10	5	6	8	33	0	143	8	0	9	9	.500	0	0- -	-	2.57	2.51
2016	Hrtfrd	AA	7	7	0	0	34.2	137	27	8	7	1	2	0	2	9	0	27	1	0	4	1	.800	0	0- -	-	2.23	1.82
2017	Col	NL	36	20	0	3	134.2	564	128	72	70	18	4	5	4	47	1	102	1	2	10	5	.667	0	0-0	1	4.00	4.68

Luis Severino

Pitches: R **Bats:** R **Pos:** SP-31   **Ht:** 6'2" **Wt:** 215 **Born:** 2/20/1994 **Age:** 24

Year	Team	Lg	G	GS	CG	GF	IP	BFP	H	R	ER	HR	SH	SF	HB	TBB	IBB	SO	WP	Bk	W	L	Pct	Sh	Sv-Op	Hld	ERC	ERA
					HOW MUCH HE PITCHED						**WHAT HE GAVE UP**											**THE RESULTS**					
2015	NYY	AL	11	11	0	0	62.1	255	53	21	20	9	0	0	2	22	0	56	2	1	5	3	.625	0	0-0	0	3.57	2.89
2016	NYY	AL	22	11	0	3	71.0	312	78	48	46	11	0	0	3	25	1	66	3	0	3	8	.273	0	0-0	1	5.00	5.83
2017	NYY	AL	31	31	0	0	193.1	783	150	73	64	21	3	2	6	51	0	230	6	0	14	6	.700	0	0-0	0	2.53	2.98
3 ML YEARS			64	53	0	3	326.2	1350	281	142	130	41	3	2	11	98	1	352	11	1	22	17	.564	0	0-0	1	3.22	3.58

Pedro Severino

Bats: R **Throws:** R **Pos:** C-10;PH-6;PR-2;DH-1   **Ht:** 6'0" **Wt:** 215 **Born:** 7/20/1993 **Age:** 24

Year	Team	Lg	G	AB	H	2B	3B	HR	(Hm	Rd)	TB	R	RBI	RC	TBB	IBB	SO	HBP	SH	SF	SB	CS	GDP	Avg	OBP	Slg	OPS
2017	Syrcse*	AAA	59	211	51	4	0	5	(-	-)	70	17	29	20	15	0	43	0	0	1	1	1	7	.242	.291	.332	.623
2015	Was	NL	2	4	1	1	0	0	(0	0)	2	1	0	0	0	0	1	0	0	0	0	0	0	.250	.250	.500	.750
2016	Was	NL	16	28	9	2	0	2	(1	1)	17	6	4	5	5	0	3	1	0	0	0	0	0	.321	.441	.607	1.048
2017	Was	NL	17	29	5	1	0	0	(0	0)	6	0	3	2	2	1	10	0	0	0	0	0	0	.172	.226	.207	.433
	Postseason		4	10	1	1	0	0	(0	0)	2	1	0	0	0	0	3	0	0	0	0	0	0	.100	.100	.200	.300
	3 ML YEARS		35	61	15	4	0	2	(1	1)	25	7	7	7	7	1	14	1	0	0	0	0	0	.246	.333	.410	.743

Paul Sewald

Pitches: R **Bats:** R **Pos:** RP-57   **Ht:** 6'3" **Wt:** 207 **Born:** 5/26/1990 **Age:** 28

Year	Team	Lg	G	GS	CG	GF	IP	BFP	H	R	ER	HR	SH	SF	HB	TBB	IBB	SO	WP	Bk	W	L	Pct	Sh	Sv-Op	Hld	ERC	ERA
2013	Savann	A	35	0	0	17	56.0	223	48	11	11	0	3	0	3	7	1	67	0	0	3	2	.600	0	8-	-	1.89	1.77
2014	Stluci	A+	40	0	0	28	52.0	211	38	11	10	1	3	1	2	16	1	62	1	0	4	1	.800	0	11-	-	1.94	1.73
2015	Bnghtn	AA	44	0	0	34	51.1	195	34	12	10	3	2	2	0	10	1	56	2	0	3	0	1.000	0	24-	-	1.49	1.75
2016	LsVgs	AAA	56	0	0	40	65.2	278	58	31	24	9	4	1	1	21	2	80	6	0	5	3	.625	0	19-	-	3.30	3.29
2017	LsVgs	AAA	8	0	0	8	8.2	36	7	2	2	1	0	0	0	2	1	12	0	0	1	0	1.000	0	4-	-	2.25	2.08
2017	NYM	NL	57	0	0	12	65.1	275	58	36	33	8	3	3	3	21	2	69	3	1	0	6	.000	0	0-3	13	3.41	4.55

Kevin Shackelford

Pitches: R **Bats:** R **Pos:** RP-26   **Ht:** 6'5" **Wt:** 210 **Born:** 4/7/1989 **Age:** 29

Year	Team	Lg	G	GS	CG	GF	IP	BFP	H	R	ER	HR	SH	SF	HB	TBB	IBB	SO	WP	Bk	W	L	Pct	Sh	Sv-Op	Hld	ERC	ERA
2013	BrvdCt	A+	24	0	0	9	32.0	134	39	18	18	3	0	0	0	4	0	23	0	0	1	3	.250	0	2-	-	4.24	5.06
2013	Hntsvl	AA	20	0	0	12	29.1	119	23	6	4	1	3	2	1	7	2	25	2	1	1	1	.500	0	6-	-	1.96	1.23
2014	Hntsvl	AA	40	0	0	17	50.0	225	60	33	27	3	2	2	2	17	1	25	6	0	2	4	.333	0	1-	-	4.78	4.86
2014	BrvdCt	A+	12	0	0	7	20.1	77	19	2	2	0	0	0	2	4	0	16	1	0	0	0	-	0	5-	-	2.54	0.89
2015	Pnscla	AA	35	0	0	16	38.2	175	45	19	16	1	1	1	3	17	1	25	5	0	2	4	.333	0	3-	-	4.92	3.72
2016	Pnscla	AA	10	0	0	3	13.0	53	11	4	2	1	1	0	0	4	1	11	1	0	1	0	1.000	0	0-	-	2.66	1.38
2016	Lsvlle	AAA	25	0	0	20	31.1	132	25	8	8	1	0	0	0	13	2	20	3	1	1	2	.333	0	8-	-	2.72	2.30
2017	Lsvlle	AAA	35	0	0	27	47.0	193	33	11	8	2	2	4	0	18	2	61	0	0	3	1	.750	0	12-	-	2.17	1.53
2017	Cin	NL	26	0	0	0	30.2	135	30	16	16	6	0	1	3	13	0	38	1	0	0	0	-	0	0-1	3	5.15	4.70

Bryan Shaw

Pitches: R **Bats:** B **Pos:** RP-79   **Ht:** 6'1" **Wt:** 220 **Born:** 11/8/1987 **Age:** 30

Year	Team	Lg	G	GS	CG	GF	IP	BFP	H	R	ER	HR	SH	SF	HB	TBB	IBB	SO	WP	Bk	W	L	Pct	Sh	Sv-Op	Hld	ERC	ERA
2011	Ari	NL	33	0	0	8	28.1	122	30	9	8	2	0	0	4	8	1	24	1	0	1	0	1.000	0	0-0	9	4.31	2.54
2012	Ari	NL	64	0	0	19	59.1	252	60	29	23	4	4	2	2	24	3	41	4	1	1	6	.143	0	2-4	10	4.08	3.49
2013	Cle	AL	70	0	0	11	75.0	316	60	31	27	4	4	2	4	28	2	73	5	0	7	3	.700	0	1-5	12	2.71	3.24
2014	Cle	AL	80	0	0	16	76.1	313	61	26	22	6	5	2	2	22	4	64	4	1	5	5	.500	0	2-9	24	2.45	2.59
2015	Cle	AL	74	0	0	19	64.0	265	59	24	21	8	1	1	1	19	1	54	3	0	3	3	.500	0	2-6	23	3.47	2.95
2016	Cle	AL	75	0	0	9	66.2	275	56	26	24	8	2	1	1	28	3	69	2	0	2	5	.286	0	1-4	25	3.47	3.24
2017	Cle	AL	79	0	0	16	76.2	312	71	36	30	5	1	1	2	22	3	73	3	0	4	6	.400	0	3-6	26	3.01	3.52
	Postseason		16	0	0	2	16.0	69	15	7	5	1	0	1	0	6	3	17	1	0	2	1	.667	0	0-0	5	3.01	2.81
	7 ML YEARS		475	0	0	98	446.1	1855	397	181	155	37	17	8	14	151	17	398	22	2	23	28	.451	0	11-34	129	3.21	3.13

Travis Shaw

Bats: L **Throws:** R **Pos:** 3B-143;1B-1;DH-1;PH-1   **Ht:** 6'4" **Wt:** 230 **Born:** 4/16/1990 **Age:** 28

Year	Team	Lg	G	AB	H	2B	3B	HR	(Hm	Rd)	TB	R	RBI	RC	TBB	IBB	SO	HBP	SH	SF	SB	CS	GDP	Avg	OBP	Slg	OPS
2015	Bos	AL	65	226	61	10	0	13	(8	5)	110	31	36	35	18	1	57	2	0	2	0	1	1	.270	.327	.487	.813
2016	Bos	AL	145	480	116	34	2	16	(7	9)	202	63	71	64	43	4	133	3	0	4	5	1	10	.242	.306	.421	.726
2017	Mil	NL	144	538	147	34	1	31	(13	18)	276	84	101	93	60	6	138	4	1	3	10	0	20	.273	.349	.513	.862
	Postseason		1	2	1	0	0	0	(0	0)	1	0	0	0	0	0	0	0	0	0	0	0	0	.500	.500	.500	1.000
	3 ML YEARS		354	1244	324	78	3	60	(28	32)	588	178	208	192	121	11	328	9	1	9	15	2	31	.260	.328	.473	.801

Jimmie Sherfy

Pitches: R **Bats:** R **Pos:** RP-11   **Ht:** 6'0" **Wt:** 175 **Born:** 12/27/1991 **Age:** 26

Year	Team	Lg	G	GS	CG	GF	IP	BFP	H	R	ER	HR	SH	SF	HB	TBB	IBB	SO	WP	Bk	W	L	Pct	Sh	Sv-Op	Hld	ERC	ERA
2013	2 Tms	Low	18	0	0	15	17.1	72	13	2	2	0	0	1	2	4	0	29	1	0	1	1	.500	0	7-	-	1.89	1.04
2014	Visalia	A+	11	0	0	9	11.0	44	6	5	4	2	0	0	1	5	0	23	2	1	2	0	1.000	0	6-	-	2.78	3.27
2014	Mobile	AA	37	0	0	12	38.0	166	34	21	21	4	2	1	4	18	0	45	0	0	3	1	.750	0	1-	-	4.24	4.97
2015	Mobile	AA	44	0	0	13	49.2	224	50	37	36	3	3	1	3	28	1	50	7	1	1	6	.143	0	2-	-	4.68	6.52
2016	Visalia	A+	12	0	0	11	12.1	46	5	0	0	1	0	0	0	6	0	21	1	0	0	0	-	0	8-	-	1.17	0.00
2016	Mobile	AA	16	0	0	14	19.2	73	6	1	1	1	1	0	2	5	0	31	1	0	2	0	1.000	0	10-	-	0.80	0.00
2016	Reno	AAA	24	0	0	22	23.1	97	20	16	16	5	2	1	0	11	1	27	3	1	1	4	.200	0	12-	-	4.86	6.17
2017	Reno	AAA	44	0	0	33	49.0	191	37	17	17	6	1	2	3	10	0	61	0	1	2	1	.667	0	20-	-	2.48	3.12
2017	Ari	NL	11	0	0	2	10.2	37	5	0	0	0	0	0	0	2	0	9	0	0	2	0	1.000	0	1-1	2	0.80	0.00

Ryan Sherriff

Pitches: L Bats: L Pos: RP-13
Ht: 6'1" Wt: 185 Born: 5/25/1990 Age: 28

Year	Team	Lg	G	GS	CG	GF	IP	BFP	H	R	ER	HR	SH	SF	HB	TBB	IBB	SO	WP	Bk	W	L	Pct	Sh	Sv-Op	Hld	ERC	ERA
2013	PlmBh	A+	13	13	1	0	78.0	309	67	25	20	3	3	2	1	13	0	41	2	1	4	4	.500	1	0- -	-	2.16	2.31
2013	Sprgfld	AA	5	5	0	0	27.0	120	34	10	10	0	2	1	1	9	1	18	2	0	2	1	.667	0	0- -	-	4.70	3.33
2014	Sprgfld	AA	40	3	0	8	64.2	265	63	21	19	3	4	4	1	19	3	48	3	0	2	7	.222	0	2- -	-	3.24	2.64
2015	Sprgfld	AA	27	0	0	8	34.1	147	36	13	12	4	1	0	0	12	1	31	1	0	1	1	.500	0	0- -	-	4.25	3.15
2016	Memp	AAA	49	0	0	7	66.2	288	66	27	21	4	5	2	0	23	1	55	0	1	7	1	.875	0	3- -	-	3.44	2.84
2017	Memp	AAA	48	0	0	23	53.2	212	40	22	19	2	4	1	1	13	2	47	3	0	5	1	.833	0	6- -	-	1.84	3.19
2017	StL	NL	13	0	0	2	14.1	60	13	5	5	2	0	0	1	4	0	15	0	0	2	1	.667	0	0-0	1	3.62	3.14

James Shields

Pitches: R Bats: R Pos: SP-21
Ht: 6'3" Wt: 215 Born: 12/20/1981 Age: 36

Year	Team	Lg	G	GS	CG	GF	IP	BFP	H	R	ER	HR	SH	SF	HB	TBB	IBB	SO	WP	Bk	W	L	Pct	Sh	Sv-Op	Hld	ERC	ERA
2006	TB	AL	21	21	1	0	124.2	540	141	69	67	18	4	3	5	38	5	104	9	0	6	8	.429	0	0-0	0	4.92	4.84
2007	TB	AL	31	31	1	0	215.0	874	202	98	92	28	4	5	10	36	0	184	9	0	12	8	.600	0	0-0	0	3.24	3.85
2008	TB	AL	33	33	3	0	215.0	877	208	94	85	24	6	0	12	40	0	160	6	0	14	8	.636	2	0-0	0	3.41	3.56
2009	TB	AL	33	33	0	0	219.2	930	239	113	101	29	6	3	1	52	1	167	3	1	11	12	.478	0	0-0	0	4.16	4.14
2010	TB	AL	34	33	0	0	203.1	899	246	128	117	34	5	2	5	51	2	187	13	2	13	15	.464	0	0-0	0	5.21	5.18
2011	TB	AL	33	33	11	0	249.1	975	195	83	78	26	5	3	5	65	1	225	4	0	16	12	.571	4	0-0	0	2.58	2.82
2012	TB	AL	33	33	3	0	227.2	944	208	103	89	25	3	2	11	58	2	223	7	1	15	10	.600	2	0-0	0	3.28	3.52
2013	KC	AL	34	34	2	0	228.2	946	215	82	80	20	6	7	8	68	0	196	11	2	13	9	.591	0	0-0	0	3.45	3.15
2014	KC	AL	34	34	1	0	227.0	939	224	95	81	23	3	7	11	44	0	180	12	2	14	8	.636	1	0-0	0	3.41	3.21
2015	SD	NL	33	33	0	0	202.1	860	189	93	88	33	6	1	9	81	5	216	7	1	13	7	.650	0	0-0	0	4.34	3.91
2016	2 Tms		33	33	1	0	181.2	822	208	122	118	40	2	5	8	82	3	135	10	0	6	19	.240	0	0-0	0	6.24	5.85
2017	CWS	AL	21	21	0	0	117.0	516	116	72	68	27	1	0	3	53	3	103	5	0	5	7	.417	0	0-0	0	5.21	5.23
16	SD	NL	11	11	0	0	67.1	284	69	33	32	9	1	1	1	27	2	57	3	0	2	7	.222	0	0-0	0	4.63	4.28
16	CWS	AL	22	22	1	0	114.1	538	139	89	86	31	1	4	7	55	1	78	7	0	4	12	.250	0	0-0	0	7.24	6.77
	Postseason		11	11	0	0	59.1	269	76	37	36	8	1	1	6	15	0	45	6	0	3	6	.333	0	0-0	0	5.80	5.46
12 ML YEARS			373	372	23	0	2411.1	10122	2391	1152	1064	327	51	38	88	668	22	2080	96	9	138	123	.529	9	0-0	0	3.94	3.97

Braden Shipley

Pitches: R Bats: R Pos: RP-7; SP-3
Ht: 6'1" Wt: 190 Born: 2/22/1992 Age: 26

Year	Team	Lg	G	GS	CG	GF	IP	BFP	H	R	ER	HR	SH	SF	HB	TBB	IBB	SO	WP	Bk	W	L	Pct	Sh	Sv-Op	Hld	ERC	ERA
2013	2 Tms	Low	12	12	0	0	39.2	175	44	24	22	3	1	2	2	14	0	40	3	1	0	3	.000	0	0- -	-	4.53	4.99
2014	2 Tms	Low	18	18	0	0	106.0	441	103	54	46	8	3	1	9	32	0	109	9	0	6	6	.500	0	0- -	-	3.81	3.91
2015	Mobile	AA	28	27	1	0	156.2	663	146	68	61	7	6	5	5	56	0	118	5	0	9	11	.450	0	0- -	-	3.28	3.50
2016	Reno	AAA	19	19	1	0	119.1	498	131	53	49	7	4	5	0	22	0	77	1	0	8	5	.615	0	0- -	-	3.51	3.70
2017	Reno	AAA	19	19	1	0	105.0	473	129	68	66	18	0	4	3	42	0	69	3	1	7	6	.538	0	0- -	-	6.16	5.66
2016	Ari	NL	13	11	0	0	70.0	306	80	43	41	14	2	2	1	28	1	43	1	0	4	5	.444	0	0-0	0	5.82	5.27
2017	Ari	NL	10	3	0	2	25.0	122	31	18	16	5	0	2	1	15	1	18	1	0	0	1	.000	0	0-0	0	7.10	5.76
2 ML YEARS			23	14	0	2	95.0	428	111	61	57	19	2	4	2	43	2	61	2	0	4	6	.400	0	0-0	0	6.16	5.40

Matt Shoemaker

Pitches: R Bats: R Pos: SP-14
SHOO-may-kerr
Ht: 6'2" Wt: 225 Born: 9/27/1986 Age: 31

Year	Team	Lg	G	GS	CG	GF	IP	BFP	H	R	ER	HR	SH	SF	HB	TBB	IBB	SO	WP	Bk	W	L	Pct	Sh	Sv-Op	Hld	ERC	ERA
2013	LAA	AL	1	1	0	0	5.0	19	2	0	0	0	0	0	0	2	0	5	1	0	0	0	-	0	0-0	0	0.95	0.00
2014	LAA	AL	27	20	0	5	136.0	543	122	49	46	14	3	5	4	24	0	124	5	0	16	4	.800	0	0-0	0	2.84	3.04
2015	LAA	AL	25	24	0	0	135.1	569	135	70	67	24	4	4	4	35	2	116	3	0	7	10	.412	0	0-0	0	4.12	4.46
2016	LAA	AL	27	27	1	0	160.0	668	166	71	69	18	2	5	7	30	1	143	2	0	9	13	.409	1	0-0	0	3.71	3.88
2017	LAA	AL	14	14	0	0	77.2	326	73	41	39	15	1	1	4	28	0	69	2	1	6	3	.667	0	0-0	0	4.52	4.52
	Postseason		1	1	0	0	6.0	23	5	1	1	0	0	0	0	0	0	6	0	0	0	0	-	0	0-0	0	1.37	1.50
5 ML YEARS			94	86	1	6	514.0	2125	498	231	221	71	10	15	19	119	3	457	13	1	38	30	.559	1	0-0	0	3.66	3.87

Chasen Shreve

Pitches: L Bats: L Pos: RP-44
CHAY-sen shreev
Ht: 6'4" Wt: 195 Born: 7/12/1990 Age: 27

Year	Team	Lg	G	GS	CG	GF	IP	BFP	H	R	ER	HR	SH	SF	HB	TBB	IBB	SO	WP	Bk	W	L	Pct	Sh	Sv-Op	Hld	ERC	ERA
2017	S-WB*	AAA	9	0	0	3	11.1	43	7	2	2	0	0	0	0	3	0	19	0	0	1	0	1.000	0	1- -	-	1.32	1.59
2014	Atl	NL	15	0	0	4	12.1	50	10	1	1	0	1	0	0	3	0	15	1	0	0	0	-	0	0-0	2	1.88	0.73
2015	NYY	AL	59	0	0	13	58.1	251	49	21	20	10	2	0	1	33	2	64	4	0	6	2	.750	0	0-1	15	4.39	3.09
2016	NYY	AL	37	0	0	11	33.0	142	29	19	19	8	1	0	3	13	0	33	0	0	2	1	.667	0	1-1	1	4.70	5.18
2017	NYY	AL	44	0	0	15	45.1	198	35	20	19	8	0	2	0	25	3	58	4	0	4	1	.800	0	0-1	1	3.71	3.77
4 ML YEARS			155	0	0	43	149.0	641	123	61	59	26	4	2	4	74	5	170	9	0	12	4	.750	0	1-3	14	4.02	3.56

Kevin Siegrist

Pitches: L Bats: L Pos: RP-46   SEE-grist   Ht: 6'5" Wt: 230 Born: 7/20/1989 Age: 28

			HOW MUCH HE PITCHED						WHAT HE GAVE UP										THE RESULTS							
Year Team	Lg	G	GS	CG	GF	IP	BFP	H	R	ER	HR	SH	SF	HB	TBB	IBB	SO	WP	Bk	W	L	Pct	Sh	Sv-Op	Hld	ERC	ERA
2013 StL	NL	45	0	0	15	39.2	152	17	2	2	1	0	0	1	18	1	50	0	0	3	1	.750	0	0-0	11	1.27	0.45
2014 StL	NL	37	0	0	5	30.1	140	32	23	23	5	1	1	2	16	0	37	1	0	1	4	.200	0	0-2	16	5.59	6.82
2015 StL	NL	81	0	0	13	74.2	312	53	20	18	4	3	4	3	34	2	90	0	0	7	1	.875	0	6-10	28	2.52	2.17
2016 StL	NL	67	0	0	11	61.2	248	42	20	19	10	0	3	1	26	2	66	5	0	6	3	.667	0	3-8	17	2.91	2.77
2017 2 Tms	NL	46	0	0	7	39.1	172	39	21	21	5	0	1	1	22	2	43	3	0	1	1	.500	0	1-1	9	5.01	4.81
17 StL	NL	39	0	0	7	34.1	151	35	19	19	4	0	1	1	20	2	36	2	0	1	1	.500	0	1-1	6	5.22	4.98
17 Phi	NL	7	0	0	0	5.0	21	4	2	2	1	0	0	0	2	0	7	1	0	0	0	-	0	0-0	3	3.57	3.60
Postseason		12	0	0	1	9.0	39	10	6	5	4	0	1	0	1	0	8	2	0	0	1	.000	0	0-0	2	5.50	5.00
5 ML YEARS		276	0	0	51	245.2	1024	183	86	83	25	4	9	8	116	7	286	9	0	18	10	.643	0	10-21	81	3.08	3.04

Magneuris Sierra

Bats: L Throws: L Pos: RF-8;CF-7;PH-4;LF-3;PR-3   mag-NAIR-is   Ht: 5'11" Wt: 160 Born: 4/7/1996 Age: 22

								BATTING												RUNNING			AVERAGES			
Year Team	Lg	G	AB	H	2B	3B	HR	(Hm	Rd)	TB	R	RBI	RC	TBB	IBB	SO	HBP	SH	SF	SB	CS	GDP	Avg	OBP	Slg	OPS
2014 Cards	R	52	202	78	12	3	2	(-	-)	102	42	30	44	16	2	30	2	2	1	13	3	2	.386	.434	.505	.939
2015 2 Tms	Low	104	394	102	9	3	4	(-	-)	129	57	22	42	26	0	94	1	5	3	19	7	2	.259	.304	.327	.632
2016 Peoria	A	122	524	161	29	4	3	(-	-)	207	78	60	71	22	0	97	3	7	6	31	17	5	.307	.335	.395	.730
2017 PlmBh	A+	20	81	22	3	4	0	(-	-)	33	16	9	10	7	0	15	1	0	0	3	5	2	.272	.337	.407	.744
2017 Sprgfld	AA	81	326	88	18	3	1	(-	-)	115	32	35	39	20	0	59	2	2	3	17	5	1	.270	.313	.353	.666
2017 StL	NL	22	60	19	0	0	0	(0	0)	19	10	5	10	4	0	14	0	0	0	2	2	0	.317	.359	.317	.676

Andrelton Simmons

Bats: R Throws: R Pos: SS-158   ANN-drel-ton   Ht: 6'2" Wt: 200 Born: 9/4/1989 Age: 28

								BATTING												RUNNING			AVERAGES			
Year Team	Lg	G	AB	H	2B	3B	HR	(Hm	Rd)	TB	R	RBI	RC	TBB	IBB	SO	HBP	SH	SF	SB	CS	GDP	Avg	OBP	Slg	OPS
2012 Atl	NL	49	166	48	8	2	3	(3	0)	69	17	19	23	12	1	21	1	0	3	1	0	5	.289	.335	.416	.751
2013 Atl	NL	157	606	150	27	6	17	(5	12)	240	76	59	60	40	1	55	3	5	4	6	5	16	.248	.296	.396	.692
2014 Atl	NL	146	540	132	18	4	7	(3	4)	179	44	46	41	32	4	60	1	3	4	4	5	25	.244	.286	.331	.617
2015 Atl	NL	147	535	142	23	2	4	(2	2)	181	60	44	48	39	6	48	6	1	2	5	3	16	.265	.321	.338	.660
2016 LAA	AL	124	448	126	22	2	4	(4	0)	164	48	44	52	28	0	38	2	1	4	10	1	16	.281	.324	.366	.690
2017 LAA	AL	158	589	164	38	2	14	(10	4)	248	77	69	91	47	0	67	3	0	8	19	6	20	.278	.331	.421	.752
Postseason		5	16	4	1	0	0	(0	0)	5	0	2	1	2	0	3	0	1	0	0	0	1	.250	.333	.313	.646
6 ML YEARS		781	2884	762	136	18	49	(27	22)	1081	322	281	315	198	12	289	15	9	23	45	20	101	.264	.313	.375	.687

Shae Simmons

Pitches: R Bats: R Pos: RP-9   SHAY   Ht: 5'11" Wt: 190 Born: 9/3/1990 Age: 27

			HOW MUCH HE PITCHED						WHAT HE GAVE UP										THE RESULTS							
Year Team	Lg	G	GS	CG	GF	IP	BFP	H	R	ER	HR	SH	SF	HB	TBB	IBB	SO	WP	Bk	W	L	Pct	Sh	Sv-Op	Hld	ERC	ERA
2017 Tacom*	AAA	9	0	0	0	7.1	32	5	4	3	1	0	0	0	6	0	6	1	0	0	0	-	0	0- -		4.24	3.68
2014 Atl	NL	26	0	0	6	21.2	89	15	8	7	1	1	1	0	11	1	23	1	0	1	2	.333	0	1-1	9	2.45	2.91
2016 Atl	NL	7	0	0	2	6.2	25	6	1	1	0	0	0	0	0	0	3	0	0	0	0	-	0	0-0	0	1.63	1.35
2017 Sea	AL	9	0	0	3	7.2	30	4	6	6	1	0	2	0	4	0	8	1	0	0	2	.000	0	0-0	0	2.30	7.04
3 ML YEARS		42	0	0	11	36.0	144	25	15	14	2	1	3	0	15	1	34	2	0	1	4	.200	0	1-1	9	2.26	3.50

Lucas Sims

Pitches: R Bats: R Pos: SP-10; RP-4   Ht: 6'2" Wt: 220 Born: 5/10/1994 Age: 24

			HOW MUCH HE PITCHED						WHAT HE GAVE UP										THE RESULTS							
Year Team	Lg	G	GS	CG	GF	IP	BFP	H	R	ER	HR	SH	SF	HB	TBB	IBB	SO	WP	Bk	W	L	Pct	Sh	Sv-Op	Hld	ERC	ERA
2013 Rome	A	28	18	1	2	116.2	481	83	44	34	3	3	7	15	46	0	134	14	0	12	4	.750	0	0- -	-	2.54	2.62
2014 Lynbrg	A+	28	28	0	0	156.1	676	146	81	73	12	3	9	17	57	0	107	15	1	8	11	.421	0	0- -	-	3.82	4.20
2015 2 Tms	Low	11	11	1	0	45.0	205	46	34	28	2	2	2	5	25	0	44	8	2	3	4	.429	0	0- -	-	4.86	5.60
2015 Missi	AA	9	9	0	0	47.2	199	29	18	17	1	2	3	4	29	0	56	2	0	4	2	.667	0	0- -	-	2.58	3.21
2016 Missi	AA	17	17	0	0	91.0	391	64	34	27	3	4	6	11	55	1	101	5	1	5	5	.500	0	0- -	-	3.23	2.67
2016 Gwnntt	AAA	11	10	0	0	50.0	241	56	44	42	12	1	1	2	37	0	58	9	0	2	6	.250	0	0- -	-	7.51	7.56
2017 Gwnntt	AAA	20	19	0	0	115.1	469	95	49	48	19	0	2	6	36	1	132	5	1	7	4	.636	0	0- -	-	3.44	3.75
2017 Atl	NL	14	10	0	1	57.2	255	64	37	36	9	5	1	4	23	2	44	0	0	3	6	.333	0	0-0	1	5.43	5.62

Tony Sipp

Pitches: L Bats: L Pos: RP-46   Ht: 6'0" Wt: 190 Born: 7/12/1983 Age: 34

			HOW MUCH HE PITCHED						WHAT HE GAVE UP										THE RESULTS							
Year Team	Lg	G	GS	CG	GF	IP	BFP	H	R	ER	HR	SH	SF	HB	TBB	IBB	SO	WP	Bk	W	L	Pct	Sh	Sv-Op	Hld	ERC	ERA
2009 Cle	AL	46	0	0	8	40.0	168	27	16	13	5	3	1	0	25	2	48	3	0	2	0	1.000	0	0-0	9	3.29	2.93
2010 Cle	AL	70	0	0	16	63.0	266	48	30	29	12	3	2	2	39	3	69	4	0	2	2	.500	0	1-3	15	4.42	4.14
2011 Cle	AL	69	0	0	17	62.1	251	45	22	21	10	1	2	0	24	3	57	2	1	6	3	.667	0	0-1	24	2.87	3.03
2012 Cle	AL	63	0	0	7	55.0	233	47	29	27	9	2	1	1	23	4	51	3	0	1	3	.333	0	1-2	12	3.80	4.42
2013 Ari	NL	56	0	0	11	37.2	175	35	22	20	6	3	1	3	22	3	42	3	1	3	2	.600	0	0-2	3	4.90	4.78
2014 Hou	AL	56	0	0	13	50.2	199	28	19	19	5	2	2	0	17	2	63	3	0	4	3	.571	0	4-6	11	1.57	3.38
2015 Hou	AL	60	0	0	12	54.1	216	41	13	12	5	2	1	1	15	1	62	4	0	3	4	.429	0	0-3	13	2.34	1.99
2016 Hou	AL	60	0	0	13	43.2	195	52	26	24	12	0	1	1	18	0	40	0	0	1	2	.333	0	1-2	12	6.80	4.95
2017 Hou	AL	46	0	0	12	37.1	165	36	25	24	8	1	1	1	16	1	39	1	0	0	1	.000	0	0-0	4	4.72	5.79
Postseason		6	0	0	0	5.1	20	1	1	0	0	0	0	0	2	0	5	0	0	0	1	.000	0	0-1	3	0.42	0.00
9 ML YEARS		526	0	0	109	444.0	1867	359	202	189	72	17	10	9	199	16	471	23	2	22	19	.537	0	7-19	103	3.65	3.83

Chance Sisco

Bats: L **Throws:** R **Pos:** C-10;PH-3   **Ht:** 6'2" **Wt:** 195 **Born:** 2/24/1995 **Age:** 23

Year	Team	Lg	G	AB	H	2B	3B	HR	(Hm	Rd)	TB	R	RBI	RC	TBB	IBB	SO	HBP	SH	SF	SB	CS	GDP	Avg	OBP	Slg	OPS
2013	2 Tms	Low	33	102	37	4	1	1	(-	-)	46	16	11	22	18	0	23	1	0	1	1	1	2	.363	.468	.451	.919
2014	Dlmrva	A	114	426	145	27	2	5	(-	-)	191	56	63	79	42	3	79	7	0	3	1	2	8	.340	.406	.448	.854
2015	Frdrck	A+	75	263	81	12	3	4	(-	-)	111	30	26	46	33	0	41	2	0	2	8	1	4	.308	.387	.422	.809
2015	Bowie	AA	20	74	19	4	0	2	(-	-)	29	9	8	10	9	0	14	0	1	0	0	1	3	.257	.337	.392	.729
2016	Bowie	AA	112	410	131	28	1	4	(-	-)	173	53	44	75	59	2	83	4	1	5	2	2	9	.320	.406	.422	.828
2017	Norfolk	AAA	97	344	92	23	0	7	(-	-)	136	47	47	48	32	0	99	8	0	4	2	2	9	.267	.340	.395	.736
2017	Bal	AL	10	18	6	2	0	2	(1	1)	14	3	4	6	3	0	7	1	0	0	0	0	0	.333	.455	.778	1.232

Tyler Skaggs

Pitches: L **Bats:** L **Pos:** SP-16   **Ht:** 6'4" **Wt:** 215 **Born:** 7/13/1991 **Age:** 26

			HOW MUCH HE PITCHED					WHAT HE GAVE UP											THE RESULTS						
Year	Team	Lg	G	GS	CG	GF	IP	BFP	H	R	ER	HR	SH	SF	HB	TBB	IBB	SO	WP	Bk	W	L	Pct	Sh	Sv-Op	Hld	ERC	ERA
2012	Ari	NL	6	6	0	0	29.1	133	30	20	19	6	1	0	2	13	0	21	1	0	1	3	.250	0	0-0	0	5.31	5.83
2013	Ari	NL	7	7	0	0	38.2	170	38	23	22	7	0	2	2	15	2	36	2	0	2	3	.400	0	0-0	0	4.56	5.12
2014	LAA	AL	18	18	0	0	113.0	464	107	59	54	9	2	5	4	30	1	86	7	0	5	5	.500	0	0-0	0	3.31	4.30
2016	LAA	AL	10	10	0	0	49.2	219	51	23	23	5	0	3	2	23	0	50	0	0	3	4	.429	0	0-0	0	4.67	4.17
2017	LAA	AL	16	16	0	0	85.0	365	90	46	43	13	0	2	6	28	0	76	5	2	2	6	.250	0	0-0	0	4.88	4.55
	5 ML YEARS		57	57	0	0	315.2	1351	316	171	161	40	3	12	16	109	3	269	15	2	13	21	.382	0	0-0	0	4.27	4.59

Eric Skoglund

Pitches: L **Bats:** L **Pos:** SP-5; RP-2   **Ht:** 6'7" **Wt:** 200 **Born:** 10/26/1992 **Age:** 25

			HOW MUCH HE PITCHED					WHAT HE GAVE UP											THE RESULTS						
Year	Team	Lg	G	GS	CG	GF	IP	BFP	H	R	ER	HR	SH	SF	HB	TBB	IBB	SO	WP	Bk	W	L	Pct	Sh	Sv-Op	Hld	ERC	ERA
2014	Idaho	R+	9	8	0	0	23.0	106	30	17	13	2	1	0	1	9	0	25	2	0	0	2	.000	0	0--	-	5.94	5.09
2015	Wilmg	A+	15	15	1	0	84.1	341	83	36	33	2	2	5	4	11	1	66	2	0	6	3	.667	0	0--	-	2.67	3.52
2016	NWArk	AA	27	27	0	0	156.1	636	135	63	60	19	3	5	4	38	1	134	3	2	7	10	.412	0	0--	-	2.97	3.45
2017	Omha	AAA	19	19	1	0	100.2	438	110	57	46	14	1	3	3	29	1	102	5	1	4	5	.444	0	0--	-	4.51	4.11
2017	KC	AL	7	5	0	1	18.0	93	30	20	19	2	0	1	0	12	0	14	0	0	1	2	.333	0	0-0	0	9.63	9.50

Dan Slania

Pitches: R **Bats:** R **Pos:** RP-1   SLAY-nee-ah   **Ht:** 6'5" **Wt:** 275 **Born:** 5/24/1992 **Age:** 26

			HOW MUCH HE PITCHED					WHAT HE GAVE UP											THE RESULTS						
Year	Team	Lg	G	GS	CG	GF	IP	BFP	H	R	ER	HR	SH	SF	HB	TBB	IBB	SO	WP	Bk	W	L	Pct	Sh	Sv-Op	Hld	ERC	ERA
2013	SlKzr	A-	12	0	0	9	13.2	58	13	7	6	1	0	1	1	3	0	14	0	0	1	1	.500	0	3--	-	3.15	3.95
2014	Augsta	A	43	0	0	21	58.2	249	56	31	26	5	3	3	1	21	1	46	7	0	2	5	.286	0	12--	-	3.60	3.99
2014	Rchmd	AA	10	0	0	3	11.1	47	10	2	1	0	1	0	0	3	0	3	1	0	0	0	-	0	0--	-	2.26	0.79
2015	SnJos	A+	59	0	0	42	71.1	299	70	35	28	7	3	3	1	15	1	90	6	0	4	5	.444	0	16--	-	3.20	3.53
2016	Rchmd	AA	27	10	0	5	82.2	332	68	30	23	6	4	0	1	22	2	79	3	0	7	6	.538	0	0--	-	2.49	2.50
2016	SnJos	A+	5	4	0	0	24.0	108	27	17	14	3	0	2	2	9	0	18	3	0	2	2	.500	0	0--	-	5.20	5.25
2017	Rchmd	AA	13	13	1	0	80.1	338	81	35	32	5	4	2	0	28	0	55	9	0	5	3	.625	1	0--	-	3.72	3.59
2017	Scrmto	AAA	12	12	0	0	61.0	281	78	54	53	14	2	5	3	31	0	57	3	0	0	8	.000	0	0--	-	7.69	7.82
2017	SF	NL	1	0	0	1	1.0	3	0	0	0	0	0	0	0	0	0	0	0	0	0	0	-	0	0-0	0	0.00	0.00

Austin Slater

Bats: R **Throws:** R **Pos:** LF-30;RF-3;PH-2;3B-1;CF-1   **Ht:** 6'2" **Wt:** 215 **Born:** 12/13/1992 **Age:** 25

Year	Team	Lg	G	AB	H	2B	3B	HR	(Hm	Rd)	TB	R	RBI	RC	TBB	IBB	SO	HBP	SH	SF	SB	CS	GDP	Avg	OBP	Slg	OPS
2014	2 Tms	Low	31	127	44	6	1	2	(-	-)	58	23	25	24	10	1	19	4	0	0	7	1	5	.346	.411	.457	.868
2015	SnJos	A+	60	250	73	15	1	3	(-	-)	99	25	34	32	10	0	44	2	0	3	4	3	12	.292	.321	.396	.717
2015	Rchmd	AA	54	199	59	11	1	0	(-	-)	72	21	13	26	14	0	48	3	1	1	1	1	5	.296	.350	.362	.712
2016	Rchmd	AA	41	145	46	8	1	5	(-	-)	71	20	25	31	24	0	36	1	0	2	6	1	4	.317	.413	.490	.902
2016	Scrmto	AAA	68	245	72	12	0	13	(-	-)	123	36	42	45	33	1	53	0	0	0	2	6	1	.294	.378	.502	.880
2017	Scrmto	AAA	50	184	59	12	0	5	(-	-)	86	28	27	32	15	0	39	3	2	2	4	3	5	.321	.377	.467	.845
2017	SF	NL	34	117	33	3	1	3	(0	3)	47	15	16	17	8	0	29	2	0	0	0	0	3	.282	.339	.402	.740

Aaron Slegers

Pitches: R **Bats:** R **Pos:** SP-3; RP-1   **Ht:** 6'10" **Wt:** 245 **Born:** 9/4/1992 **Age:** 25

			HOW MUCH HE PITCHED					WHAT HE GAVE UP											THE RESULTS						
Year	Team	Lg	G	GS	CG	GF	IP	BFP	H	R	ER	HR	SH	SF	HB	TBB	IBB	SO	WP	Bk	W	L	Pct	Sh	Sv-Op	Hld	ERC	ERA
2013	Elizab	R+	9	0	0	4	19.0	68	16	2	1	0	0	0	1	2	0	18	0	0	0	0	-	0	3--	-	2.03	0.47
2014	2 Tms	Low	23	23	1	0	132.0	548	132	73	64	9	3	4	6	24	0	102	11	1	9	8	.529	0	0--	-	3.30	4.36
2015	FtMyrs	A+	19	19	3	0	119.1	483	103	48	38	4	1	1	7	21	0	80	7	0	8	6	.571	1	0--	-	2.31	2.87
2015	Chatt	AA	6	6	0	0	36.2	162	40	22	20	3	2	4	2	12	0	24	2	0	1	4	.200	0	0--	-	4.34	4.91
2016	Chatt	AA	25	25	0	0	145.1	600	137	61	55	11	4	7	12	46	0	104	5	0	10	7	.588	0	0--	-	3.71	3.41
2017	Roch	AAA	24	24	1	0	148.1	619	154	59	56	11	3	6	2	29	0	119	6	2	15	4	.789	1	0--	-	3.36	3.40
2017	Min	AL	4	3	0	0	15.1	63	12	12	11	3	0	0	0	6	0	9	0	0	0	1	.000	0	0-0	0	3.48	6.46

Caleb Smith

Pitches: L **Bats:** R **Pos:** RP-7; SP-2
Ht: 6'2" **Wt:** 205 **Born:** 7/28/1991 **Age:** 26

		HOW MUCH HE PITCHED						WHAT HE GAVE UP												THE RESULTS							
Year Team	Lg	G	GS	CG	GF	IP	BFP	H	R	ER	HR	SH	SF	HB	TBB	IBB	SO	WP	Bk	W	L	Pct	Sh	Sv-Op	Hld	ERC	ERA
2013 StnIld	A-	13	9	0	0	47.2	190	33	15	10	0	1	3	2	15	0	52	2	1	1	2	.333	0	0--	-	1.74	1.89
2014 2 Tms	Low	27	27	0	0	117.1	487	99	55	48	6	1	0	4	46	0	116	2	1	10	9	.526	0	0--	-	3.04	3.68
2015 Trntn	AA	25	24	1	0	130.2	553	118	53	49	7	5	2	7	51	0	92	5	1	10	7	.588	0	0--	-	3.42	3.38
2016 Trntn	AA	27	7	0	5	63.2	279	66	34	28	4	2	3	5	20	0	70	1	0	3	5	.375	0	3--	-	3.94	3.96
2017 S-WB	AAA	18	17	1	0	98.0	394	75	34	26	7	1	3	4	28	0	97	2	0	9	1	.900	1	0--	-	2.40	2.39
2017 NYY	AL	9	2	0	6	18.2	86	21	16	16	4	0	1	0	10	1	18	1	0	0	1	.000	0	0-0	0	6.09	7.71

Carson Smith

Pitches: R **Bats:** R **Pos:** RP-8
Ht: 6'6" **Wt:** 215 **Born:** 10/19/1989 **Age:** 28

		HOW MUCH HE PITCHED						WHAT HE GAVE UP												THE RESULTS							
Year Team	Lg	G	GS	CG	GF	IP	BFP	H	R	ER	HR	SH	SF	HB	TBB	IBB	SO	WP	Bk	W	L	Pct	Sh	Sv-Op	Hld	ERC	ERA
2017 Pwtckt*	AAA	10	0	0	1	8.2	35	10	5	4	0	0	0	0	3	0	6	0	1	1	1	.500	0	0--	-	4.40	4.15
2014 Sea	AL	9	0	0	1	8.1	29	2	0	0	0	0	0	0	3	0	10	0	0	1	0	1.000	0	0-0	0	0.55	0.00
2015 Sea	AL	70	0	0	24	70.0	284	49	19	18	2	3	0	7	22	4	92	6	0	2	5	.286	0	13-18	22	2.04	2.31
2016 Bos	AL	3	0	0	0	2.2	11	2	1	0	0	0	0	0	1	0	2	0	0	0	0	-	0	0-0	0	2.01	0.00
2017 Bos	AL	8	0	0	1	6.2	27	7	1	1	0	0	0	0	2	0	7	0	0	0	0	-	0	1-1	0	3.46	1.35
4 ML YEARS		90	0	0	26	87.2	351	60	21	19	2	3	0	7	28	4	111	6	0	3	5	.375	0	14-19	25	1.92	1.95

Chris Smith

Pitches: R **Bats:** R **Pos:** SP-9; RP-5
Ht: 6'0" **Wt:** 190 **Born:** 4/9/1981 **Age:** 37

		HOW MUCH HE PITCHED						WHAT HE GAVE UP												THE RESULTS							
Year Team	Lg	G	GS	CG	GF	IP	BFP	H	R	ER	HR	SH	SF	HB	TBB	IBB	SO	WP	Bk	W	L	Pct	Sh	Sv-Op	Hld	ERC	ERA
2017 Nashv*	AAA	15	12	0	3	74.0	309	76	27	26	5	0	1	1	20	0	64	1	0	4	3	.571	0	0--	-	3.60	3.16
2008 Bos	AL	12	0	0	3	18.1	78	18	16	16	6	1	1	0	7	0	13	0	0	1	0	1.000	0	0-0	0	5.53	7.85
2009 Mil	NL	35	0	0	12	46.0	200	41	21	21	11	1	0	3	19	0	35	1	0	0	0	-	0	0-1	0	4.68	4.11
2010 Mil	NL	3	0	0	1	3.1	14	4	2	2	0	0	0	0	1	0	4	0	0	0	0	-	0	0-0	0	4.29	5.40
2016 Oak	AL	13	0	0	8	24.2	100	14	9	8	2	0	2	0	13	0	29	0	0	0	0	-	0	0-0	0	2.18	2.92
2017 Oak	AL	14	9	0	3	55.2	250	60	45	42	16	0	3	1	22	1	31	3	0	0	4	.000	0	0-0	0	5.80	6.79
5 ML YEARS		77	9	0	27	148.0	642	137	93	89	35	2	6	4	62	1	112	4	0	1	4	.200	0	0-1	0	4.73	5.41

Chris Smith

Pitches: R **Bats:** R **Pos:** RP-4
Ht: 6'2" **Wt:** 205 **Born:** 8/19/1988 **Age:** 29

		HOW MUCH HE PITCHED						WHAT HE GAVE UP												THE RESULTS							
Year Team	Lg	G	GS	CG	GF	IP	BFP	H	R	ER	HR	SH	SF	HB	TBB	IBB	SO	WP	Bk	W	L	Pct	Sh	Sv-Op	Hld	ERC	ERA
2014 2 Tms	Low	32	0	0	10	51.1	207	45	21	17	5	0	0	0	14	0	49	5	0	1	2	.333	0	1--	-	2.95	2.98
2015 2 Tms	Low	22	0	0	11	36.1	131	18	3	3	1	1	0	0	5	0	41	1	0	3	1	.750	0	0--	-	0.83	0.74
2015 Trntn	AA	7	0	0	0	13.1	54	11	9	9	0	0	1	1	3	0	12	0	0	1	1	.500	0	0--	-	2.16	6.08
2016 Nham	AA	43	0	0	27	57.0	239	44	20	12	2	2	3	1	21	0	76	5	0	1	2	.333	0	15--	-	2.33	1.89
2017 Buffalo	AAA	29	0	0	21	34.1	144	36	17	17	6	3	2	1	6	1	24	2	0	2	3	.400	0	9--	-	4.00	4.46
2017 Tor	AL	4	0	0	3	5.0	23	7	3	3	1	0	0	0	1	0	1	0	0	0	0	-	0	0-0	0	6.22	5.40

Dominic Smith

Bats: L **Throws:** L **Pos:** 1B-46;PH-4
Ht: 6'0" **Wt:** 239 **Born:** 6/15/1995 **Age:** 23

		BATTING																		RUNNING			AVERAGES			
Year Team	Lg	G	AB	H	2B	3B	HR	(Hm	Rd)	TB	R	RBI	RC	TBB	IBB	SO	HBP	SH	SF	SB	CS	GDP	Avg	OBP	Slg	OPS
2013 2 Tms	Low	51	173	52	13	1	3	(-	-)	76	25	26	31	26	6	37	4	0	3	2	4	4	.301	.398	.439	.837
2014 Savann	A	126	461	125	26	1	1	(-	-)	156	52	44	58	51	2	77	2	1	3	5	4	18	.271	.344	.338	.683
2015 Stluci	A+	118	456	139	33	0	6	(-	-)	190	58	79	69	35	5	75	2	0	4	2	1	19	.305	.354	.417	.771
2016 Bnghtn	AA	130	484	146	29	2	14	(-	-)	221	64	91	84	50	1	74	3	0	5	2	1	13	.302	.367	.457	.824
2017 LsVgs	AAA	114	457	151	34	2	16	(-	-)	237	77	76	89	39	3	87	3	0	1	1	1	14	.330	.386	.519	.905
2017 NYM	NL	49	167	33	6	0	9	(4	5)	66	17	26	19	14	0	49	1	0	1	0	0	5	.198	.262	.395	.658

Joe Smith

Pitches: R **Bats:** R **Pos:** RP-59
Ht: 6'2" **Wt:** 205 **Born:** 3/22/1984 **Age:** 34

		HOW MUCH HE PITCHED						WHAT HE GAVE UP												THE RESULTS							
Year Team	Lg	G	GS	CG	GF	IP	BFP	H	R	ER	HR	SH	SF	HB	TBB	IBB	SO	WP	Bk	W	L	Pct	Sh	Sv-Op	Hld	ERC	ERA
2007 NYM	NL	54	0	0	14	44.1	205	48	18	17	3	2	0	7	21	4	45	2	0	3	2	.600	0	0-0	10	5.04	3.45
2008 NYM	NL	82	0	0	12	63.1	271	51	28	25	4	4	0	4	31	4	52	1	0	6	3	.667	0	0-3	18	3.23	3.55
2009 Cle	AL	37	0	0	5	34.0	142	30	16	13	4	1	1	0	13	0	30	2	0	0	0	-	0	0-1	10	3.49	3.44
2010 Cle	AL	53	0	0	7	40.0	170	30	18	17	4	1	0	4	24	2	32	0	1	2	2	.500	0	0-1	17	3.53	3.83
2011 Cle	AL	71	0	0	13	67.0	267	52	16	15	1	2	2	2	21	1	45	2	0	3	3	.500	0	0-3	16	2.19	2.01
2012 Cle	AL	72	0	0	12	67.0	278	53	27	22	4	1	1	2	25	4	53	1	1	7	4	.636	0	0-3	21	2.60	2.96
2013 Cle	AL	70	0	0	20	63.0	259	54	17	16	5	3	0	3	23	2	54	3	0	6	2	.750	0	3-8	25	3.23	2.29
2014 LAA	AL	76	0	0	26	74.2	285	45	16	15	4	3	0	6	15	3	68	4	0	7	2	.778	0	15-19	32	1.47	1.81
2015 LAA	AL	70	0	0	13	65.1	271	64	26	26	4	2	1	2	19	4	57	1	0	5	5	.500	0	6-9	7	4.19	3.46
2016 2 Tms		54	0	0	19	52.0	217	47	20	20	1	1	1	6	18	3	40	0	1	2	5	.286	0	6-9	14	2.40	3.33
2017 2 Tms	AL	59	0	0	3	54.0	214	46	20	20	4	1	1	5	10	1	71	0	0	3	0	1.000	0	1-2	21	2.40	2.51
16 LAA	AL	38	0	0	16	37.2	160	36	16	16	4	1	1	5	13	3	25	0	1	1	4	.200	0	6-9	6	4.15	3.82
16 ChC	NL	16	0	0	3	14.1	57	11	4	4	4	0	0	1	5	0	15	0	0	1	1	.500	0	0-0	4	4.20	2.51

Year	Team	Lg	HOW MUCH HE PITCHED						WHAT HE GAVE UP												WHAT HE GAVE UP	THE RESULTS							
			G	GS	CG	GF	IP	BFP	H	R	ER	HR	SH	SF	HB	TBB	IBB	SO	WP	Bk	W	L	Pct	Sh	Sv-Op	Hld	ERC	ERA
17	Tor	AL	38	0	0	1	35.2	144	30	13	13	3	1	1	1	10	1	51	0	0	3	0	1.000	0	0-1	13	2.78	3.28
17	Cle	AL	21	0	0	2	18.1	70	16	7	7	1	0	0	0	6	0	20	0	0	0	0	-	0	1-1	8	1.72	3.44
	Postseason		3	0	0	1	2.2	10	1	0	0	0	0	0	0	0	0	3	0	0	0	0	-	0	0-0	0	0.28	0.00
	11 ML YEARS		698	0	0	144	624.2	2579	520	222	206	45	21	7	34	220	28	547	16	3	44	28	.611	0	30-58	195	2.97	2.97

Josh Smith

Pitches: R Bats: R Pos: RP-26

Ht: 6'2" Wt: 220 Born: 8/7/1987 Age: 30

Year	Team	Lg	HOW MUCH HE PITCHED						WHAT HE GAVE UP												THE RESULTS							
			G	GS	CG	GF	IP	BFP	H	R	ER	HR	SH	SF	HB	TBB	IBB	SO	WP	Bk	W	L	Pct	Sh	Sv-Op	Hld	ERC	ERA
2017	Nashv*	AAA	19	2	0	8	41.1	167	33	17	17	4	3	0	3	11	1	44	2	0	4	1	.800	0	1--	-	2.74	3.70
2015	Cin	NL	9	7	0	0	32.2	161	42	27	25	5	0	2	5	21	3	30	0	0	0	4	.000	0	0-0	0	7.82	6.89
2016	Cin	NL	32	2	0	8	59.2	260	57	32	31	11	1	1	1	26	1	48	1	0	3	3	.500	0	0-0	1	4.56	4.68
2017	Oak	AL	26	0	0	15	35.0	151	35	20	19	3	0	1	0	15	1	25	1	0	2	1	.667	0	0-0	1	4.06	4.89
	3 ML YEARS		67	9	0	23	127.1	572	134	79	75	19	1	4	6	62	5	103	2	0	5	8	.385	0	0-0	2	5.22	5.30

Kevan Smith

Bats: R Throws: R Pos: C-79;PH-12;DH-4

Ht: 6'4" Wt: 230 Born: 6/28/1988 Age: 30

Year	Team	Lg	BATTING																		RUNNING			AVERAGES			
			G	AB	H	2B	3B	HR	(Hm	Rd)	TB	R	RBI	RC	TBB	IBB	SO	HBP	SH	SF	SB	CS	GDP	Avg	OBP	Slg	OPS
2013	WinSa	A+	101	384	110	26	3	12	(-	-)	178	66	73	69	38	0	66	15	2	3	4	1	13	.286	.370	.464	.834
2014	Brham	AA	106	389	113	21	3	10	(-	-)	170	45	49	67	46	5	68	9	2	3	1	1	13	.290	.376	.437	.813
2015	Charllt	AAA	97	319	83	13	2	6	(-	-)	118	41	36	41	29	0	66	5	5	2	0	1	13	.260	.330	.370	.699
2016	Charllt	AAA	49	183	40	9	0	8	(-	-)	73	18	24	22	16	0	36	3	2	1	0	0	12	.219	.291	.399	.690
2017	Charllt	AAA	14	53	20	6	0	0	(-	-)	26	10	15	11	6	0	9	1	0	2	0	0	5	.377	.435	.491	.926
2016	CWS	AL	7	16	2	0	0	0	(0	0)	2	2	0	0	0	0	6	0	0	0	0	0	0	.125	.125	.125	.250
2017	CWS	AL	87	276	78	17	0	4	(4	0)	107	23	30	29	9	0	46	3	2	3	0	0	9	.283	.309	.388	.697
	2 ML YEARS		94	292	80	17	0	4	(4	0)	109	25	30	29	9	0	52	3	2	3	0	0	10	.274	.300	.373	.673

Mallex Smith

Bats: L Throws: R Pos: CF-51;LF-24;RF-9;PH-9;PR-3;DH-1

Ht: 5'10" Wt: 180 Born: 5/6/1993 Age: 25

Year	Team	Lg	BATTING																		RUNNING			AVERAGES			
			G	AB	H	2B	3B	HR	(Hm	Rd)	TB	R	RBI	RC	TBB	IBB	SO	HBP	SH	SF	SB	CS	GDP	Avg	OBP	Slg	OPS
2013	FtWyn	A	110	424	111	17	2	4	(-	-)	84	81	29	65	59	0	84	12	11	1	64	16	4	.262	.367	.340	.707
2014	2 Tms	Low	120	477	148	29	7	5	(-	-)	206	99	31	94	69	0	103	6	10	2	88	26	2	.310	.403	.432	.834
2015	Missi	AA	57	206	70	5	2	2	(-	-)	85	35	22	40	27	2	41	2	3	2	23	6	2	.340	.418	.413	.830
2015	Gwnntt	AAA	69	278	78	12	6	0	(-	-)	102	49	13	40	24	0	44	1	3	1	34	7	1	.281	.339	.367	.706
2017	Drham	AAA	45	186	49	7	4	3	(-	-)	73	26	10	25	17	1	45	0	2	0	21	8	3	.263	.325	.392	.718
2016	Atl	NL	72	189	45	7	4	3	(0	3)	69	28	22	26	20	0	48	2	3	1	16	8	3	.238	.316	.365	.681
2017	TB	AL	81	256	69	8	4	2	(2	0)	91	33	12	30	23	0	62	0	2	1	16	5	2	.270	.329	.355	.684
	2 ML YEARS		153	445	114	15	8	5	(2	3)	160	61	34	56	43	0	110	2	5	2	32	13	5	.256	.323	.360	.683

Seth Smith

Bats: L Throws: L Pos: RF-80;PH-18;LF-12;DH-7

Ht: 6'3" Wt: 210 Born: 9/30/1982 Age: 35

Year	Team	Lg	BATTING																		RUNNING			AVERAGES			
			G	AB	H	2B	3B	HR	(Hm	Rd)	TB	R	RBI	RC	TBB	IBB	SO	HBP	SH	SF	SB	CS	GDP	Avg	OBP	Slg	OPS
2007	Col	NL	7	8	5	0	1	0	(0	0)	7	4	0	3	0	0	1	0	0	0	0	0	0	.625	.625	.875	1.500
2008	Col	NL	67	108	28	7	0	4	(2	2)	47	13	15	18	15	0	23	0	0	0	1	0	0	.259	.350	.435	.785
2009	Col	NL	133	335	98	20	4	15	(8	7)	171	61	55	63	46	3	67	2	1	3	4	1	5	.293	.378	.510	.889
2010	Col	NL	133	358	88	19	5	17	(12	5)	168	55	52	51	35	1	67	2	0	3	2	1	5	.246	.314	.469	.783
2011	Col	NL	147	476	135	32	9	15	(9	6)	230	67	59	73	46	7	93	4	0	7	10	2	9	.284	.347	.483	.830
2012	Oak	AL	125	383	92	23	2	14	(6	8)	161	55	52	52	50	7	98	5	0	3	2	2	9	.240	.333	.420	.754
2013	Oak	AL	117	368	93	27	0	8	(3	5)	144	49	40	46	39	4	94	3	0	0	0	0	10	.253	.329	.391	.721
2014	SD	NL	136	443	118	31	5	12	(8	4)	195	55	48	68	69	3	87	4	0	4	1	1	9	.266	.367	.440	.807
2015	Sea	AL	136	395	98	31	5	12	(7	5)	175	54	42	54	47	4	99	4	1	5	0	0	15	.248	.330	.443	.773
2016	Sea	AL	137	378	94	15	0	16	(12	4)	157	46	63	62	62	1	89	8	0	4	0	0	11	.249	.342	.415	.758
2017	Bal	AL	111	330	85	19	0	13	(9	4)	143	50	32	43	36	3	79	6	0	1	2	0	7	.258	.340	.433	.774
	Postseason		18	42	11	2	0	2	(1	1)	19	6	7	7	5	2	13	1	0	0	0	0	0	.262	.354	.452	.807
	11 ML YEARS		1249	3582	934	224	31	126	(76	50)	1598	525	458	533	431	33	797	38	2	30	22	7	75	.261	.344	.446	.790

Tyler Smith

Bats: R Throws: R Pos: SS-6;2B-3;PH-2;PR-1

Ht: 6'0" Wt: 195 Born: 7/1/1991 Age: 26

Year	Team	Lg	BATTING																		RUNNING			AVERAGES			
			G	AB	H	2B	3B	HR	(Hm	Rd)	TB	R	RBI	RC	TBB	IBB	SO	HBP	SH	SF	SB	CS	GDP	Avg	OBP	Slg	OPS
2013	Pulski	R+	52	200	64	16	3	2	(-	-)	92	33	34	38	18	0	32	9	2	4	12	5	0	.320	.394	.460	.854
2014	Hi Dsrt	A+	108	423	121	19	7	9	(-	-)	181	81	44	72	57	1	81	7	3	2	11	7	11	.286	.378	.428	.806
2014	Jacksn	AA	20	70	19	3	1	1	(-	-)	27	12	4	12	16	0	13	1	0	0	1	1	1	.271	.414	.386	.800
2015	Jacksn	AA	121	443	120	24	2	3	(-	-)	157	40	32	63	61	0	85	3	11	2	10	4	13	.271	.361	.354	.716
2016	Tacom	AAA	114	392	105	20	0	5	(-	-)	140	42	37	45	20	2	68	4	2	2	6	2	10	.268	.309	.357	.666
2017	Tacom	AAA	84	285	68	13	0	6	(-	-)	99	34	28	34	37	0	65	3	3	2	5	5	14	.239	.330	.347	.678
2017	RdRck	AAA	13	48	9	2	0	0	(-	-)	11	5	1	2	3	0	11	2	0	0	1	0	3	.188	.264	.229	.493
2017	Sea	AL	10	16	3	1	0	0	(0	0)	4	2	1	1	1	0	8	1	0	1	0	0	0	.188	.263	.250	.513

Dwight Smith Jr.

Bats: L Throws: R Pos: LF-9;PH-2;CF-1;RF-1;PR-1   Ht: 5'11" Wt: 195 Born: 10/26/1992 Age: 25

								BATTING											RUNNING			AVERAGES			
Year	Team	Lg	G	AB	H	2B	3B	HR	(Hm | Rd)	TB	R	RBI	RC	TBB	IBB	SO	HBP	SH	SF	SB	CS	GDP	Avg	OBP	Slg	OPS
2013	Lnsng	A	109	423	120	17	3	7	(- | -)	164	57	46	67	52	0	82	3	0	1	25	5	4	.284	.365	.388	.753
2014	Dnedin	A+	121	472	134	28	8	12	(- | -)	214	83	64	82	58	1	69	1	1	1	15	4	11	.284	.363	.453	.816
2015	Nham	AA	117	460	122	26	2	7	(- | -)	173	74	44	61	47	0	64	2	1	2	4	3	10	.265	.335	.376	.711
2016	Nham	AA	126	471	125	24	5	15	(- | -)	204	56	74	70	45	1	91	5	0	6	12	7	15	.265	.332	.433	.765
2017	Buffalo	AAA	108	395	108	21	1	8	(- | -)	155	56	46	57	47	2	71	2	1	4	8	8	9	.273	.350	.392	.743
2017	Tor	AL	12	27	10	2	0	0	(0 | 0)	12	2	1	4	1	0	10	1	0	0	1	0	0	.370	.414	.444	.858

Justin Smoak

Bats: B Throws: L Pos: 1B-151;PH-8;DH-2   SMOKE   Ht: 6'4" Wt: 220 Born: 12/5/1986 Age: 31

								BATTING											RUNNING			AVERAGES			
Year	Team	Lg	G	AB	H	2B	3B	HR	(Hm | Rd)	TB	R	RBI	RC	TBB	IBB	SO	HBP	SH	SF	SB	CS	GDP	Avg	OBP	Slg	OPS
2010	2 Tms	AL	100	348	76	14	0	13	(4 | 9)	129	40	48	42	46	4	91	0	0	3	1	0	9	.218	.307	.371	.678
2011	Sea	AL	123	427	100	24	0	15	(10 | 5)	169	38	55	55	55	4	105	3	0	4	0	0	10	.234	.323	.396	.719
2012	Sea	AL	132	483	105	14	0	19	(4 | 15)	176	49	51	50	49	2	111	1	0	2	1	0	12	.217	.290	.364	.654
2013	Sea	AL	131	454	108	19	0	20	(9 | 11)	187	53	50	60	64	1	119	2	0	1	0	0	11	.238	.334	.412	.746
2014	Sea	AL	80	248	50	13	0	7	(4 | 3)	84	28	30	23	24	0	66	2	0	2	0	1	8	.202	.275	.339	.614
2015	Tor	AL	132	296	67	16	1	18	(8 | 10)	139	44	59	49	29	0	86	2	0	1	0	0	10	.226	.299	.470	.768
2016	Tor	AL	126	299	65	10	0	14	(10 | 4)	117	33	34	33	40	1	112	2	0	0	1	0	7	.217	.314	.391	.705
2017	Tor	AL	158	560	151	29	1	38	(19 | 19)	296	85	90	100	73	3	128	2	0	2	0	1	17	.270	.355	.529	.883
10	Tex	AL	70	235	49	10	0	8	(4 | 4)	83	29	34	30	38	4	57	0	0	2	1	0	6	.209	.316	.353	.670
10	Sea	AL	30	113	27	4	0	5	(0 | 5)	46	11	14	12	8	0	34	0	0	1	0	0	3	.239	.287	.407	.694
	Postseason		11	10	0	0	0	0	(0 | 0)	0	0	0	0	0	0	5	0	0	0	0	0	0	.000	.000	.000	.000
	8 ML YEARS		982	3115	722	139	2	144	(68 | 76)	1297	370	417	412	380	15	818	14	0	15	3	2	84	.232	.317	.416	.733

Josh Smoker

Pitches: L Bats: L Pos: RP-54   Ht: 6'2" Wt: 246 Born: 11/26/1988 Age: 29

			HOW MUCH HE PITCHED						WHAT HE GAVE UP											THE RESULTS						
Year	Team	Lg	G	GS	CG	GF	IP	BFP	H	R	ER	HR	SH	SF	HB	TBB	IBB	SO	WP	Bk	W	L	Pct	Sh	Sv-Op	Hld	ERC	ERA
2015	2 Tms	Low	20	0	0	12	28.0	117	23	11	10	1	1	0	0	8	1	34	2	0	2	0	1.000	0	6--	-	2.17	3.21
2015	Bnghtn	AA	21	0	0	7	21.0	89	16	8	7	0	2	1	0	11	0	26	1	1	1	0	1.000	0	0--	-	2.56	3.00
2016	LsVgs	AAA	52	0	0	11	57.0	253	66	32	26	5	2	3	0	18	1	81	7	0	3	2	.600	0	3--	-	4.44	4.11
2016	NYM	NL	20	0	0	4	15.1	65	16	10	8	4	0	0	1	4	1	25	0	0	3	0	1.000	0	0-0	7	5.11	4.70
2017	NYM	NL	54	0	0	7	56.1	267	64	34	32	10	2	3	3	32	7	68	2	0	1	2	.333	0	0-0	2	6.05	5.11
	2 ML YEARS		74	0	0	11	71.2	332	80	44	40	14	2	3	4	36	8	93	2	0	4	2	.667	0	0-0	9	5.86	5.02

Jake Smolinski

Bats: R Throws: R Pos: CF-9;PH-4;PR-3;DH-2;LF-1;RF-1 smoh-LYNN-skee   Ht: 5'11" Wt: 205 Born: 2/9/1989 Age: 29

								BATTING											RUNNING			AVERAGES			
Year	Team	Lg	G	AB	H	2B	3B	HR	(Hm	Rd)	TB	R	RBI	RC	TBB	IBB	SO	HBP	SH	SF	SB	CS	GDP	Avg	OBP	Slg	OPS
2014	Tex	AL	24	86	30	5	0	3	(1	2)	44	12	12	15	3	0	24	3	0	0	0	0	1	.349	.391	.512	.903
2015	2 Tms	AL	76	166	32	7	2	6	(2	4)	61	24	26	17	19	0	39	3	0	4	1	1	3	.193	.281	.367	.649
2016	Oak	AL	99	290	69	6	2	7	(4	3)	100	28	27	28	19	0	44	7	1	2	1	2	11	.238	.299	.345	.644
2017	Oak	AL	16	27	7	1	0	0	(0	0)	8	1	0	2	1	0	6	1	0	0	0	0	0	.259	.310	.296	.607
15	Tex	AL	35	60	8	1	0	1	(0	1)	12	12	6	4	11	0	20	1	0	2	1	0	1	.133	.270	.200	.470
15	Oak	AL	41	106	24	6	2	5	(2	3)	49	12	20	13	8	0	19	2	0	2	0	1	2	.226	.288	.462	.750
	4 ML YEARS		215	569	138	19	4	16	(7	9)	213	65	65	62	42	0	113	14	1	6	2	3	15	.243	.307	.374	.682

Drew Smyly

Pitches: L Bats: L Pos: P   SMY-lee   Ht: 6'3" Wt: 190 Born: 6/13/1989 Age: 29

			HOW MUCH HE PITCHED						WHAT HE GAVE UP											THE RESULTS						
Year	Team	Lg	G	GS	CG	GF	IP	BFP	H	R	ER	HR	SH	SF	HB	TBB	IBB	SO	WP	Bk	W	L	Pct	Sh	Sv-Op	Hld	ERC	ERA
2012	Det	AL	23	18	0	0	99.1	416	93	49	44	12	2	3	2	33	1	94	3	0	4	3	.571	0	0-0	1	3.68	3.99
2013	Det	AL	63	0	0	9	76.0	303	62	20	20	4	0	1	2	17	1	81	5	0	6	0	1.000	0	2-6	21	2.21	2.37
2014	2 Tms	AL	28	25	1	0	153.0	618	136	57	55	18	1	3	1	42	2	133	8	0	9	10	.474	1	0-0	1	3.17	3.24
2015	TB	AL	12	12	0	0	66.2	275	58	24	23	11	1	1	2	20	0	77	2	0	5	2	.714	0	0-0	0	3.45	3.11
2016	TB	AL	30	30	0	0	175.1	738	174	103	95	32	5	11	2	49	2	167	10	0	7	12	.368	0	0-0	0	4.13	4.88
14	Det	AL	21	18	0	0	105.1	445	111	48	46	14	0	3	1	31	1	89	4	0	6	9	.400	1	0-0	1	4.26	3.93
14	TB	AL	7	7	1	0	47.2	173	25	9	9	4	1	0	0	11	1	44	4	0	3	1	.750	0	0-0	0	1.28	1.70
	Postseason		10	0	0	1	7.0	30	3	3	2	0	0	0	0	6	1	7	0	0	1	0	1.000	0	0-0	2	1.81	2.57
	5 ML YEARS		156	85	1	9	570.1	2350	523	253	237	77	9	19	7	161	6	552	28	0	31	27	.534	1	2-6	23	3.44	3.74

Blake Snell

Pitches: L Bats: L Pos: SP-24   Ht: 6'4" Wt: 200 Born: 12/4/1992 Age: 25

			HOW MUCH HE PITCHED						WHAT HE GAVE UP											THE RESULTS						
Year	Team	Lg	G	GS	CG	GF	IP	BFP	H	R	ER	HR	SH	SF	HB	TBB	IBB	SO	WP	Bk	W	L	Pct	Sh	Sv-Op	Hld	ERC	ERA
2013	BG	A	23	23	0	0	99.0	447	90	55	47	8	5	0	2	73	0	106	13	1	4	9	.308	0	0--	-	4.88	4.27
2014	2 Tms	Low	24	24	1	0	115.1	491	95	50	41	2	3	3	5	56	0	119	13	1	8	8	.500	1	0--	-	3.04	3.20
2015	Mont	AA	12	12	0	0	68.2	268	45	13	12	5	1	1	1	29	0	79	5	0	6	2	.750	0	0--	-	2.35	1.57
2015	Drham	AAA	9	9	0	0	44.1	171	29	11	9	2	2	0	1	13	0	57	5	0	6	2	.750	0	0--	-	1.74	1.83
2016	Drham	AAA	12	12	0	0	63.0	270	56	23	21	4	0	1	1	28	0	90	6	0	3	5	.375	0	0--	-	3.50	3.00

HOW MUCH HE PITCHED								WHAT HE GAVE UP												THE RESULTS							
Year Team	Lg	G	GS	CG	GF	IP	BFP	H	R	ER	HR	SH	SF	HB	TBB	IBB	SO	WP	Bk	W	L	Pct	Sh	Sv-Op	Hld	ERC	ERA
2017 Drham	AAA	7	7	0	0	44.0	187	43	13	13	5	0	2	0	15	0	61	4	0	5	0	1.000	0	0--	-	3.79	2.66
2016 TB	AL	19	19	0	0	89.0	401	93	44	35	5	2	2	0	51	0	98	6	1	6	8	.429	0	0-0	-	4.69	3.54
2017 TB	AL	24	24	0	0	129.1	547	113	65	58	15	4	1	0	59	1	119	8	0	5	7	.417	0	0-0	0	3.71	4.04
2 ML YEARS		43	43	0	0	218.1	948	206	109	93	20	6	3	0	110	1	217	14	1	11	15	.423	0	0-0	0	4.11	3.83

Miguel Socolovich

Pitches: R Bats: R Pos: RP-15

Ht: 6'1" Wt: 205 Born: 7/24/1986 Age: 31

HOW MUCH HE PITCHED								WHAT HE GAVE UP												THE RESULTS							
Year Team	Lg	G	GS	CG	GF	IP	BFP	H	R	ER	HR	SH	SF	HB	TBB	IBB	SO	WP	Bk	W	L	Pct	Sh	Sv-Op	Hld	ERC	ERA
2017 Memp*	AAA	30	1	0	12	39.0	154	35	19	18	4	2	1	1	9	1	29	1	0	2	1	.667	0	1--	-	3.07	4.15
2012 2 Tms		12	0	0	2	16.1	72	15	11	11	3	0	0	0	9	0	12	0	1	0	0		0	0-1	1	4.79	6.06
2015 StL	NL	28	0	0	11	29.2	125	25	7	6	1	2	0	0	10	1	27	1	0	4	1	.800	0	0-0	1	2.45	1.82
2016 StL	NL	15	0	0	6	18.0	64	5	4	4	2	0	1	0	5	0	16	0	0	1	0	1.000	0	0-0	0	0.78	2.00
2017 StL	NL	15	0	0	1	18.2	87	27	20	18	4	0	1	2	4	0	14	0	0	0	1	.000	0	1-1	0	7.36	8.68
12 Bal	AL	6	0	0	1	10.1	47	11	8	8	2	0	0	0	6	0	6	0	1	0	0	-	0	0-1	0	5.91	6.97
12 ChC	NL	6	0	0	1	6.0	25	4	3	3	1	0	0	0	3	0	6	0	0	0	0	-	0	0-0	1	3.05	4.50
4 ML YEARS		70	0	0	26	82.2	348	72	42	39	10	2	2	2	28	1	69	1	1	5	2	.714	0	1-2	2	3.30	4.25

Eric Sogard

Bats: L Throws: R Pos: 2B-60;SS-26;PH-24;3B-7;LF-1

SO-guard

Ht: 5'9" Wt: 180 Born: 5/22/1986 Age: 32

BATTING																		RUNNING			AVERAGES			
Year Team	Lg	G	AB	H	2B	3B	HR	(Hm | Rd)	TB	R	RBI	RC	TBB	IBB	SO	HBP	SH	SF	SB	CS	GDP	Avg	OBP	Slg	OPS
2017 ColSpr*	AAA	24	91	30	8	0	3	(- | -)	47	30	17	21	15	0	12	0	0	1	5	0	0	.330	.421	.516	.937
2010 Oak	AL	4	7	3	0	0	0	(0 | 0)	3	0	0	1	2	0	1	0	0	0	0	1	0	.429	.556	.429	.984
2011 Oak	AL	27	70	14	3	0	2	(0 | 2)	23	7	4	3	4	0	13	0	0	0	0	0	2	.200	.243	.329	.572
2012 Oak	AL	37	102	17	3	1	2	(0 | 2)	28	8	7	7	5	0	17	0	1	0	2	0	1	.167	.206	.275	.480
2013 Oak	AL	130	368	98	24	3	2	(0 | 2)	134	45	35	43	27	2	51	5	6	4	10	5	4	.266	.322	.364	.686
2014 Oak	AL	117	291	65	10	0	1	(1 | 0)	78	38	22	27	31	0	37	1	4	2	11	4	6	.223	.298	.268	.567
2015 Oak	AL	120	372	92	12	3	1	(1 | 0)	113	40	37	36	23	1	50	2	3	1	6	1	9	.247	.294	.304	.598
2017 Mil	NL	94	249	68	15	1	3	(2 | 1)	94	37	18	37	45	2	37	4	1	0	3	3	7	.273	.393	.378	.770
Postseason		5	13	1	0	0	0	(0 | 0)	1	0	0	0	1	0	3	0	0	0	0	0	0	.077	.143	.077	.220
7 ML YEARS		529	1459	357	67	8	11	(4 | 7)	473	175	123	154	137	5	206	12	15	7	32	14	29	.245	.313	.324	.638

Yangervis Solarte

yahn-HAIR-vees so-LAHR-tay

Bats: B Throws: R Pos: 2B-79;SS-28;3B-22;1B-8;PH-4;DH-2

Ht: 5'11" Wt: 205 Born: 7/7/1987 Age: 30

BATTING																		RUNNING			AVERAGES			
Year Team	Lg	G	AB	H	2B	3B	HR	(Hm	Rd)	TB	R	RBI	RC	TBB	IBB	SO	HBP	SH	SF	SB	CS	GDP	Avg	OBP	Slg	OPS
2014 2 Tms		131	469	122	19	1	10	(5	5)	173	56	48	59	53	1	58	4	3	6	0	1	13	.260	.336	.369	.705
2015 SD	NL	152	526	142	33	4	14	(5	9)	225	63	63	74	34	0	56	6	2	3	1	0	15	.270	.320	.428	.748
2016 SD	NL	109	405	116	26	1	15	(4	11)	189	55	71	68	30	1	63	4	0	3	1	1	7	.286	.341	.467	.808
2017 SD	NL	128	466	119	21	0	18	(8	10)	194	49	64	59	37	4	61	5	0	4	3	0	18	.255	.314	.416	.731
14 NYY	AL	75	252	64	14	0	6	(3	3)	96	26	31	33	30	0	34	3	1	3	0	0	8	.254	.337	.381	.718
14 SD	NL	56	217	58	5	1	4	(2	2)	77	30	17	26	23	1	24	1	2	3	0	1	5	.267	.336	.355	.691
4 ML YEARS		520	1866	499	99	6	57	(22	35)	781	223	246	260	154	6	238	20	5	16	5	2	53	.267	.327	.419	.746

Jorge Soler

HOR-hay so-LAIR

Bats: R Throws: R Pos: RF-15;DH-11;LF-7;PH-5

Ht: 6'4" Wt: 215 Born: 2/25/1992 Age: 26

BATTING																		RUNNING			AVERAGES			
Year Team	Lg	G	AB	H	2B	3B	HR	(Hm	Rd)	TB	R	RBI	RC	TBB	IBB	SO	HBP	SH	SF	SB	CS	GDP	Avg	OBP	Slg	OPS
2017 Omha*	AAA	74	273	73	9	0	24	(-	-)	154	49	59	60	50	0	82	4	0	0	1	0	7	.267	.388	.564	.952
2014 ChC	NL	24	89	26	8	1	5	(1	4)	51	11	20	15	6	0	24	0	0	2	1	0	3	.292	.330	.573	.903
2015 ChC	NL	101	366	96	18	1	10	(7	3)	146	39	47	43	32	5	121	3	0	3	3	1	9	.262	.324	.399	.723
2016 ChC	NL	86	227	54	9	0	12	(6	6)	99	37	31	31	31	0	66	3	0	3	0	0	5	.238	.333	.436	.769
2017 KC	AL	35	97	14	5	0	2	(2	0)	25	7	6	5	12	1	36	1	0	0	0	0	5	.144	.245	.258	.503
Postseason		15	32	11	3	1	3	(2	1)	25	6	5	9	9	0	9	0	0	0	0	0	1	.344	.488	.781	1.269
4 ML YEARS		246	779	190	40	2	29	(16	13)	321	94	104	94	81	6	247	7	0	8	4	1	22	.244	.318	.412	.730

Sammy Solis

SOH-lees

Pitches: L Bats: R Pos: RP-30

Ht: 6'5" Wt: 250 Born: 8/10/1988 Age: 29

HOW MUCH HE PITCHED								WHAT HE GAVE UP												THE RESULTS							
Year Team	Lg	G	GS	CG	GF	IP	BFP	H	R	ER	HR	SH	SF	HB	TBB	IBB	SO	WP	Bk	W	L	Pct	Sh	Sv-Op	Hld	ERC	ERA
2017 Syrcse*	AAA	13	1	0	2	12.2	56	13	9	9	5	1	1	0	6	0	8	1	0	1	3	.250	0	0--	-	6.70	6.39
2015 Was	NL	18	0	0	6	21.1	94	25	11	8	2	1	2	1	4	2	17	0	0	1	1	.500	0	0-0	1	4.08	3.38
2016 Was	NL	37	0	0	10	41.0	172	31	12	11	1	3	0	1	21	2	47	2	0	2	4	.333	0	0-1	9	2.70	2.41
2017 Was	NL	30	0	0	7	26.0	112	22	17	17	4	0	0	0	13	0	28	3	0	1	0	1.000	0	1-1	6	3.94	5.88
Postseason		5	0	0	1	4.2	19	3	1	1	0	0	0	0	2	1	2	0	0	1	0	1.000	0	0-0	1	1.49	1.93
3 ML YEARS		85	0	0	23	88.1	378	78	40	36	7	4	2	2	38	4	92	5	0	4	5	.444	0	1-2	16	3.40	3.67

Joakim Soria

Pitches: R **Bats:** R **Pos:** RP-59
wah-KEEM SORE-ee-uh
Ht: 6'3" **Wt:** 200 **Born:** 5/18/1984 **Age:** 34

Year	Team	Lg	G	GS	CG	GF	IP	BFP	H	R	ER	HR	SH	SF	HB	TBB	IBB	SO	WP	Bk	W	L	Pct	Sh	Sv-Op	Hld	ERC	ERA
2007	KC	AL	62	0	0	38	69.0	270	46	20	19	3	1	3	1	19	3	75	2	0	2	3	.400	0	17-21	9	1.63	2.48
2008	KC	AL	63	0	0	57	67.1	260	39	13	12	5	2	2	6	19	1	66	1	1	2	3	.400	0	42-45	1	1.72	1.60
2009	KC	AL	47	0	0	41	53.0	222	44	14	13	5	1	2	2	16	1	69	3	0	3	2	.600	0	30-33	0	2.80	2.21
2010	KC	AL	66	0	0	56	65.2	270	53	13	13	4	3	4	2	16	1	71	3	1	1	2	.333	0	43-46	0	2.27	1.78
2011	KC	AL	60	0	0	47	60.1	256	60	29	27	7	3	2	2	17	0	60	1	0	5	5	.500	0	28-35	0	3.80	4.03
2013	Tex	AL	26	0	0	9	23.2	101	18	10	10	2	1	0	1	14	2	28	2	0	1	0	1.000	0	0-0	6	3.45	3.80
2014	2 Tms	AL	48	0	0	37	44.1	182	38	19	16	2	1	2	2	6	2	48	1	0	2	4	.333	0	18-20	1	2.04	3.25
2015	2 Tms	AL	72	0	0	40	67.2	272	55	20	19	8	1	1	2	19	1	64	5	0	3	1	.750	0	24-30	11	2.87	2.53
2016	KC	AL	70	0	0	18	66.2	293	70	31	30	10	4	2	2	27	0	68	2	3	5	8	.385	0	1-8	20	4.86	4.05
2017	KC	AL	59	0	0	10	56.0	232	49	24	23	1	0	1	1	20	2	64	4	0	4	3	.571	0	1-8	20	2.73	3.70
14	Tex	AL	35	0	0	32	33.1	133	25	12	10	0	1	1	1	4	1	42	0	0	1	3	.250	0	17-19	0	1.38	2.70
14	Det	AL	13	0	0	5	11.0	49	13	7	6	2	0	1	1	2	1	6	1	0	1	1	.500	0	1-1	1	4.92	4.91
15	Det	AL	43	0	0	35	41.0	165	32	13	13	8	1	0	2	11	1	36	0	0	3	1	.750	0	23-26	0	3.15	2.85
15	Pit	NL	29	0	0	5	26.2	107	23	7	6	0	0	1	0	8	0	28	5	0	0	0	-	0	1-4	11	2.39	2.03
Postseason			3	0	0	1	2.0	13	4	5	5	0	0	0	0	3	1	3	0	0	0	1	.000	0	0-1	0	12.98	22.50
10 ML YEARS			573	0	0	353	573.2	2358	472	193	182	47	17	19	21	173	13	613	24	5	28	31	.475	0	204-246	67	2.73	2.86

Geovany Soto

Bats: R **Throws:** R **Pos:** C-13;PH-1
Ht: 6'1" **Wt:** 225 **Born:** 1/20/1983 **Age:** 35

Year	Team	Lg	G	AB	H	2B	3B	HR	(Hm	Rd)	TB	R	RBI	RC	TBB	IBB	SO	HBP	SH	SF	SB	CS	GDP	Avg	OBP	Slg	OPS
2005	ChC	NL	1	1	0	0	0	0	(0	0)	0	0	0	0	0	0	0	0	0	0	0	0	0	.000	.000	.000	.000
2006	ChC	NL	11	25	5	1	0	0	(0	0)	6	1	2	0	0	0	5	1	0	0	0	0	0	.200	.231	.240	.471
2007	ChC	NL	18	54	21	6	0	3	(2	1)	36	12	8	13	5	0	14	0	0	1	0	0	1	.389	.433	.667	1.100
2008	ChC	NL	141	494	141	35	2	23	(11	12)	249	66	86	81	62	6	121	2	0	5	0	1	11	.285	.364	.504	.868
2009	ChC	NL	102	331	72	19	1	11	(6	5)	126	27	47	34	50	3	77	3	0	5	1	0	19	.218	.321	.381	.702
2010	ChC	NL	105	322	90	19	0	17	(12	5)	160	47	53	59	62	4	83	0	0	3	0	1	5	.280	.393	.497	.890
2011	ChC	NL	125	421	96	26	0	17	(7	10)	173	46	54	43	45	3	124	6	0	2	0	0	12	.228	.310	.411	.721
2012	2 Tms		99	324	64	12	1	11	(3	8)	111	45	39	30	30	1	76	3	2	2	1	0	12	.198	.270	.343	.613
2013	Tex	AL	54	163	40	9	0	9	(7	2)	76	20	22	23	20	0	60	0	1	0	1	2	6	.245	.328	.466	.794
2014	2 Tms	AL	24	80	20	6	0	1	(1	0)	29	8	11	6	6	0	19	0	1	0	0	0	6	.250	.302	.363	.665
2015	CWS	AL	78	187	41	8	0	9	(6	3)	76	20	21	19	21	0	63	1	1	0	0	1	1	.219	.301	.406	.708
2016	LAA	AL	26	78	21	5	0	4	(0	4)	38	11	9	12	6	0	21	0	0	0	0	0	2	.269	.321	.487	.809
2017	CWS	AL	13	42	8	0	0	3	(3	0)	17	5	9	5	4	0	10	1	0	1	0	0	2	.190	.271	.405	.676
12	ChC	NL	52	176	35	6	1	6	(2	4)	61	26	14	15	19	1	35	2	0	0	0	0	6	.199	.284	.347	.631
12	Tex		47	148	29	6	0	5	(1	4)	50	19	25	15	11	0	41	1	2	2	1	0	6	.196	.253	.338	.591
14	Tex	AL	10	38	9	2	0	1	(1	0)	14	5	3	1	0	0	11	0	0	0	0	0	3	.237	.237	.368	.605
14	Oak	AL	14	42	11	4	0	0	(0	0)	15	3	8	5	6	0	8	0	1	0	0	0	3	.262	.354	.357	.711
Postseason			7	20	3	1	0	1	(0	1)	7	1	2	1	3	0	6	0	0	0	0	0	0	.150	.261	.350	.611
13 ML YEARS			797	2522	619	146	4	108	(58	50)	1097	308	361	325	311	17	673	17	7	19	3	5	73	.245	.330	.435	.765

Steven Souza Jr.

Bats: R **Throws:** R **Pos:** RF-138;DH-6;CF-3;PH-3
SOO-zuh
Ht: 6'4" **Wt:** 225 **Born:** 4/24/1989 **Age:** 29

Year	Team	Lg	G	AB	H	2B	3B	HR	(Hm	Rd)	TB	R	RBI	RC	TBB	IBB	SO	HBP	SH	SF	SB	CS	GDP	Avg	OBP	Slg	OPS
2014	Was	NL	21	23	3	0	0	2	(1	1)	9	2	2	1	3	0	7	0	0	0	0	0	1	.130	.231	.391	.622
2015	TB	AL	110	373	84	15	1	16	(6	10)	149	59	40	40	46	0	144	5	1	1	12	6	7	.225	.318	.399	.717
2016	TB	AL	120	430	106	17	1	17	(7	10)	176	58	49	53	31	0	159	5	0	2	7	6	5	.247	.303	.409	.713
2017	TB	AL	148	523	125	21	2	30	(14	16)	240	78	78	85	84	2	179	7	2	1	16	4	9	.239	.351	.459	.810
4 ML YEARS			399	1349	318	53	4	65	(28	37)	574	197	169	179	164	2	489	17	3	4	35	16	22	.236	.325	.426	.751

Denard Span

Bats: L **Throws:** L **Pos:** CF-123;PH-12
Ht: 6'0" **Wt:** 210 **Born:** 2/27/1984 **Age:** 34

Year	Team	Lg	G	AB	H	2B	3B	HR	(Hm	Rd)	TB	R	RBI	RC	TBB	IBB	SO	HBP	SH	SF	SB	CS	GDP	Avg	OBP	Slg	OPS
2008	Min	AL	93	347	102	16	7	6	(2	4)	150	70	47	68	50	3	60	4	8	2	18	7	3	.294	.387	.432	.819
2009	Min	AL	145	578	180	16	10	8	(5	3)	240	97	68	100	70	3	89	10	12	6	23	10	7	.311	.392	.415	.807
2010	Min	AL	153	629	166	24	10	3	(0	3)	219	85	58	85	60	0	74	4	10	2	26	4	12	.264	.331	.348	.679
2011	Min	AL	70	284	75	11	5	2	(1	1)	102	37	16	32	27	0	36	0	0	0	6	1	3	.264	.328	.359	.687
2012	Min	AL	128	516	146	38	4	4	(2	2)	204	71	41	69	47	0	62	0	4	1	17	6	10	.283	.342	.395	.738
2013	Was	NL	153	610	170	28	11	4	(2	2)	232	75	47	74	42	0	77	2	7	1	20	6	11	.279	.327	.380	.707
2014	Was	NL	147	610	184	39	8	5	(1	4)	254	94	37	94	50	1	65	2	3	3	31	7	6	.302	.355	.416	.771
2015	Was	NL	61	246	74	17	0	5	(0	5)	106	38	22	45	25	0	26	1	1	2	11	0	5	.301	.365	.431	.796
2016	SF	NL	143	572	152	23	5	11	(5	6)	218	70	53	70	53	2	79	4	6	2	12	7	8	.266	.331	.381	.712
2017	SF	NL	129	497	135	31	5	12	(6	6)	212	73	43	71	40	0	69	3	1	1	12	7	11	.272	.329	.427	.756
Postseason			14	66	17	3	1	0	(0	0)	22	4	2	2	2	0	9	0	0	0	2	2	2	.258	.279	.333	.613
10 ML YEARS			1222	4889	1384	243	65	60	(24	36)	1937	710	432	708	464	9	637	30	52	20	176	55	76	.283	.348	.396	.744

Cory Spangenberg

Bats: L Throws: R Pos: 3B-96;LF-32;PH-9;2B-7

SPAN-jen-burg

Ht: 6'0" Wt: 195 Born: 3/16/1991 Age: 27

Year Team	Lg	G	AB	H	2B	3B	HR	(Hm	Rd)	TB	R	RBI	RC	TBB	IBB	SO	HBP	SH	SF	SB	CS	GDP	Avg	OBP	Slg	OPS
2017 ElPaso*	AAA	17	66	23	3	1	1	(-	-)	31	8	7	12	4	0	8	2	0	0	3	2	2	.348	.403	.470	.872
2014 SD	NL	20	62	18	2	1	2	(1	1)	28	7	9	9	2	0	14	0	1	0	4	2	1	.290	.313	.452	.764
2015 SD	NL	108	303	82	17	5	4	(3	1)	121	38	21	40	28	1	75	2	8	3	9	4	4	.271	.333	.399	.733
2016 SD	NL	14	48	11	1	1	1	(1	0)	17	6	8	7	4	0	13	1	0	0	1	0	0	.229	.302	.354	.656
2017 SD	NL	129	444	117	18	2	13	(6	7)	178	57	46	58	34	1	128	5	2	1	11	3	2	.264	.322	.401	.723
4 ML YEARS		271	857	228	38	9	20	(10	10)	344	108	84	114	68	2	230	8	11	4	25	9	7	.266	.324	.401	.726

Glenn Sparkman

Pitches: R Bats: B Pos: RP-2

Ht: 6'2" Wt: 210 Born: 5/11/1992 Age: 26

Year Team	Lg	G	GS	CG	GF	IP	BFP	H	R	ER	HR	SH	SF	HB	TBB	IBB	SO	WP	Bk	W	L	Pct	Sh	Sv-Op	Hld	ERC	ERA
2013 Idaho	R+	20	0	0	13	36.2	144	25	8	7	1	0	4	1	10	1	47	1	1	1	0	1.000	0	2- -	-	1.66	1.72
2014 Wilmg	A+	29	18	0	3	121.0	471	94	28	21	2	3	2	0	25	0	117	4	4	8	3	.727	0	1- -	-	1.77	1.56
2016 3 Tms	Low	12	12	0	0	42.2	181	49	28	26	4	1	1	3	5	0	45	3	2	2	5	.286	0	0- -	-	4.02	5.48
2017 Tor	AL	2	0	0	1	1.0	12	9	7	7	0	0	0	0	1	0	1	0	0	0	0	-	0	0-0	0	79.03	63.00

George Springer

Bats: R Throws: R Pos: CF-84;RF-78;DH-7;PH-2

Ht: 6'3" Wt: 215 Born: 9/19/1989 Age: 28

Year Team	Lg	G	AB	H	2B	3B	HR	(Hm	Rd)	TB	R	RBI	RC	TBB	IBB	SO	HBP	SH	SF	SB	CS	GDP	Avg	OBP	Slg	OPS
2014 Hou	AL	78	295	68	8	1	20	(5	15)	138	45	51	45	39	4	114	9	0	2	5	2	4	.231	.336	.468	.804
2015 Hou	AL	102	388	107	19	2	16	(9	7)	178	59	41	60	50	0	109	8	2	3	16	4	4	.276	.367	.459	.826
2016 Hou	AL	162	644	168	29	5	29	(13	16)	294	116	82	100	88	2	178	11	0	1	9	10	12	.261	.359	.457	.815
2017 Hou	AL	140	548	155	29	0	34	(16	18)	286	112	85	99	64	1	111	11	0	4	5	7	11	.283	.367	.522	.889
Postseason		6	23	5	2	0	1	(0	1)	10	5	3	3	3	0	11	0	0	0	0	0	0	.217	.308	.435	.742
4 ML YEARS		482	1875	498	85	8	99	(43	56)	896	332	259	304	241	7	512	39	2	10	35	23	31	.266	.359	.478	.837

Jacob Stallings

Bats: R Throws: R Pos: C-5

Ht: 6'5" Wt: 220 Born: 12/22/1989 Age: 28

Year Team	Lg	G	AB	H	2B	3B	HR	(Hm	Rd)	TB	R	RBI	RC	TBB	IBB	SO	HBP	SH	SF	SB	CS	GDP	Avg	OBP	Slg	OPS
2013 Bradtn	A+	78	251	55	16	2	6	(-	-)	93	36	23	37	45	0	62	7	2	1	1	1	12	.219	.352	.371	.722
2014 Bradtn	A+	68	212	51	11	0	4	(-	-)	74	22	30	26	28	0	52	2	5	2	1	2	1	.241	.332	.349	.681
2015 Altna	AA	75	265	73	14	1	3	(-	-)	98	25	32	33	15	0	65	3	1	8	4	1	7	.275	.313	.370	.683
2016 Indy	AAA	80	257	55	17	0	6	(-	-)	90	23	28	22	11	1	66	2	5	0	0	1	2	.214	.252	.350	.602
2017 Indy	AAA	62	216	65	16	0	4	(-	-)	93	35	38	34	17	1	30	4	3	3	1	2	5	.301	.358	.431	.789
2016 Pit	NL	5	15	6	1	0	0	(0	0)	7	0	2	3	0	0	4	0	0	0	1	0	0	.400	.400	.467	.867
2017 Pit	NL	5	14	5	2	0	0	(0	0)	7	3	3	3	2	1	2	0	0	0	0	0	0	.357	.438	.500	.938
2 ML YEARS		10	29	11	3	0	0	(0	0)	14	3	5	6	2	1	6	0	0	0	1	0	0	.379	.419	.483	.902

Craig Stammen

Pitches: R Bats: R Pos: RP-60

STAMM-enn

Ht: 6'4" Wt: 230 Born: 3/9/1984 Age: 34

Year Team	Lg	G	GS	CG	GF	IP	BFP	H	R	ER	HR	SH	SF	HB	TBB	IBB	SO	WP	Bk	W	L	Pct	Sh	Sv-Op	Hld	ERC	ERA
2009 Was	NL	19	19	1	0	105.2	448	112	67	60	14	4	3	3	24	1	48	7	0	4	7	.364	0	0-0	0	4.03	5.11
2010 Was	NL	35	19	0	3	128.0	562	151	78	73	13	5	6	1	41	4	85	3	0	4	4	.500	0	0-0	1	4.79	5.13
2011 Was	NL	7	0	0	2	10.1	38	3	1	1	0	0	0	0	4	0	12	1	0	1	1	.500	0	0-0	1	0.67	0.87
2012 Was	NL	59	0	0	15	88.1	370	70	27	23	7	5	1	2	36	4	87	3	0	6	1	.857	0	1-2	10	2.84	2.34
2013 Was	NL	55	0	0	14	81.2	339	78	30	25	4	8	4	2	27	3	79	2	1	7	6	.538	0	0-1	7	3.32	2.76
2014 Was	NL	49	0	0	15	72.2	304	78	34	31	5	3	1	3	14	2	56	1	1	4	5	.444	0	0-0	7	3.61	3.84
2015 Was	NL	5	0	0	0	4.0	17	2	0	0	0	0	1	0	3	1	3	0	0	0	0	-	0	0-0	2	1.66	0.00
2017 SD	NL	60	0	0	9	80.1	329	68	29	28	12	2	0	2	28	3	74	2	0	2	3	.400	0	0-2	11	3.46	3.14
Postseason		6	0	0	0	7.0	34	8	4	4	1	1	1	3	2	0	5	0	0	0	0	-	0	0-0	1	6.41	5.14
8 ML YEARS		289	38	1	58	571.0	2407	562	266	241	55	27	16	13	177	18	444	19	2	28	27	.509	0	1-5	39	3.67	3.80

Ryne Stanek

Pitches: R Bats: R Pos: RP-21

Ht: 6'4" Wt: 215 Born: 7/26/1991 Age: 26

Year Team	Lg	G	GS	CG	GF	IP	BFP	H	R	ER	HR	SH	SF	HB	TBB	IBB	SO	WP	Bk	W	L	Pct	Sh	Sv-Op	Hld	ERC	ERA
2014 3 Tms	Low	13	13	0	0	58.2	244	60	31	26	2	4	0	1	18	0	50	3	0	4	5	.444	0	0- -	-	3.54	3.99
2015 Charltt	A+	9	9	0	0	50.2	191	33	13	10	2	1	0	0	15	0	38	2	0	4	2	.667	0	0- -	-	1.68	1.78
2015 Mont	AA	16	8	0	2	61.2	261	52	30	28	7	3	1	1	31	0	41	4	0	4	3	.571	0	1- -	-	3.81	4.09
2016 Mont	AA	18	11	0	3	78.1	323	64	36	33	6	2	2	2	35	0	91	1	0	2	6	.250	0	2- -	-	3.28	3.79
2016 Drham	AAA	16	0	0	2	24.1	107	22	17	16	3	1	0	1	13	0	22	4	0	2	4	.333	0	1- -	-	4.59	5.92
2017 Drham	AAA	37	0	0	22	44.2	174	26	6	6	0	1	0	1	16	0	60	2	0	3	0	1.000	0	8- -	-	1.44	1.21
2017 TB	AL	21	0	0	4	20.0	95	26	14	13	6	0	1	0	12	2	29	4	0	0	0	-	0	0-1	4	8.31	5.85

Giancarlo Stanton

Bats: R **Throws:** R **Pos:** RF-149;PH-5;DH-4

john-CAHR-loh

Ht: 6'6" **Wt:** 245 **Born:** 11/8/1989 **Age:** 28

Year	Team	Lg	G	AB	H	2B	3B	HR	(Hm	Rd)	TB	R	RBI	RC	TBB	IBB	SO	HBP	SH	SF	SB	CS	GDP	Avg	OBP	Slg	OPS
2010	Fla	NL	100	359	93	21	1	22	(7	15)	182	45	59	56	34	6	123	2	0	1	5	2	7	.259	.326	.507	.833
2011	Fla	NL	150	516	135	30	5	34	(16	18)	277	79	87	81	70	6	166	9	0	6	5	5	11	.262	.356	.537	.893
2012	Mia	NL	123	449	130	30	1	37	(16	21)	273	75	86	79	46	9	143	5	0	1	6	2	5	.290	.361	.608	.969
2013	Mia	NL	116	425	106	26	0	24	(15	9)	204	62	62	66	74	5	140	4	0	1	1	0	10	.249	.365	.480	.845
2014	Mia	NL	145	539	155	31	1	37	(24	13)	299	89	105	109	94	24	170	3	0	2	13	1	16	.288	.395	.555	.950
2015	Mia	NL	74	279	74	12	1	27	(13	14)	169	47	67	54	34	6	95	2	0	3	4	2	5	.265	.346	.606	.952
2016	Mia	NL	119	413	99	20	1	27	(13	14)	202	56	74	56	50	5	140	4	0	2	0	0	6	.240	.326	.489	.815
2017	Mia	NL	159	597	168	32	0	59	(31	28)	377	123	132	117	85	13	163	7	0	3	2	2	13	.281	.376	.631	1.007
	8 ML YEARS		986	3577	960	202	10	267	(135	132)	1983	576	672	618	487	74	1140	36	0	19	36	14	73	.268	.360	.554	.914

Brock Stassi

Bats: L **Throws:** L **Pos:** PH-28;1B-21;LF-3

STASS-ee

Ht: 6'2" **Wt:** 190 **Born:** 8/7/1989 **Age:** 28

Year	Team	Lg	G	AB	H	2B	3B	HR	(Hm	Rd)	TB	R	RBI	RC	TBB	IBB	SO	HBP	SH	SF	SB	CS	GDP	Avg	OBP	Slg	OPS
2013	Clrwtr	A+	89	288	85	11	5	3	(-	-)	115	32	32	42	23	0	43	1	2	2	8	1	6	.295	.347	.399	.746
2014	Rdng	AA	124	440	102	12	3	8	(-	-)	144	49	44	46	39	1	49	6	2	2	3	1	6	.232	.302	.327	.629
2015	Rdng	AA	133	466	140	32	1	15	(-	-)	219	76	90	91	77	4	64	1	0	10	3	2	10	.300	.394	.470	.863
2016	LV	AAA	117	375	100	26	1	12	(-	-)	164	49	58	64	60	1	76	3	0	4	1	2	7	.267	.369	.437	.806
2017	LV	AAA	50	173	43	4	0	4	(-	-)	59	18	22	20	18	0	42	2	0	3	0	0	5	.249	.321	.341	.662
2017	Phi	NL	51	78	13	2	1	2	(1	1)	23	6	7	7	12	0	22	0	0	0	0	0	3	.167	.278	.295	.573

Max Stassi

Bats: R **Throws:** R **Pos:** C-11;PH-3;DH-2;1B-1

STASS-ee

Ht: 5'10" **Wt:** 200 **Born:** 3/15/1991 **Age:** 27

Year	Team	Lg	G	AB	H	2B	3B	HR	(Hm	Rd)	TB	R	RBI	RC	TBB	IBB	SO	HBP	SH	SF	SB	CS	GDP	Avg	OBP	Slg	OPS
2017	Fresno*	AAA	73	241	64	14	0	12	(-	-)	114	54	33	45	38	0	67	8	0	0	1	1	5	.266	.383	.473	.856
2013	Hou	AL	3	7	2	0	0	0	(0	0)	2	0	1	0	0	0	2	1	0	0	0	0	1	.286	.375	.286	.661
2014	Hou	AL	7	20	7	2	0	0	(0	0)	9	2	4	4	0	0	6	0	0	0	0	0	0	.350	.350	.450	.800
2015	Hou	AL	11	15	6	0	0	1	(1	0)	9	4	2	3	1	0	5	0	1	0	0	0	1	.400	.438	.600	1.038
2016	Hou	AL	9	13	1	0	0	0	(0	0)	1	1	0	0	0	0	5	0	0	0	0	0	0	.077	.077	.077	.154
2017	Hou	AL	14	24	4	1	0	2	(1	1)	11	5	4	3	6	0	4	0	0	1	0	0	2	.167	.323	.458	.781
	5 ML YEARS		44	79	20	3	0	3	(2	1)	32	12	11	10	7	0	22	1	1	1	0	0	4	.253	.318	.405	.723

Drew Steckenrider

Pitches: R **Bats:** R **Pos:** RP-37

Ht: 6'5" **Wt:** 215 **Born:** 1/10/1991 **Age:** 27

			HOW MUCH HE PITCHED						WHAT HE GAVE UP										THE RESULTS						
Year	Team	Lg	G	GS	CG	GF	IP	BFP	H	R	ER	HR	SH	SF	HB	TBB	IBB	SO	WP	Bk	W	L	Pct	Sh	Sv-Op	Hld	ERC	ERA
2013	Grnsbr	A	5	4	0	1	19.2	85	15	14	10	2	0	0	2	10	0	28	0	0	1	1	.500	0	0- -	-	3.56	4.58
2015	2 Tms	Low	25	13	1	5	96.0	416	97	36	32	4	3	1	2	42	0	78	6	0	5	6	.455	0	1- -	-	3.98	3.00
2016	Jupiter	A+	6	0	0	4	10.0	33	2	0	0	0	0	0	0	2	0	17	0	0	0	0	-	0	1- -	-	0.27	0.00
2016	Jaxnvl	AA	24	0	0	14	30.1	111	12	5	5	0	0	0	1	10	0	39	0	0	1	0	1.000	0	6- -	-	0.90	1.48
2016	NewOr	AAA	10	0	0	7	11.2	53	11	9	7	1	0	0	0	7	0	15	1	0	0	1	.000	0	7- -	-	4.33	5.40
2017	NewOr	AAA	26	0	0	11	33.1	125	18	6	6	3	0	0	1	8	0	44	3	0	0	1	.000	0	5- -	-	1.42	1.62
2017	Mia	NL	37	0	0	7	34.2	151	30	13	9	4	0	1	0	18	1	54	1	0	1	1	.500	0	1-1	10	3.80	2.34

Jackson Stephens

Pitches: R **Bats:** R **Pos:** SP-4; RP-3

Ht: 6'2" **Wt:** 220 **Born:** 5/11/1994 **Age:** 24

			HOW MUCH HE PITCHED						WHAT HE GAVE UP										THE RESULTS						
Year	Team	Lg	G	GS	CG	GF	IP	BFP	H	R	ER	HR	SH	SF	HB	TBB	IBB	SO	WP	Bk	W	L	Pct	Sh	Sv-Op	Hld	ERC	ERA
2013	Dayton	A	14	6	0	5	64.2	284	79	39	33	6	8	1	4	18	0	55	1	1	3	7	.300	0	1- -	-	5.14	4.59
2014	Dayton	A	14	14	0	0	67.0	294	70	40	36	8	1	5	7	22	0	54	3	1	2	7	.222	0	0- -	-	4.60	4.84
2015	Dytona	A+	26	26	0	0	145.1	616	157	56	48	11	4	5	9	30	0	97	5	1	12	7	.632	0	0- -	-	3.86	2.97
2016	Pnscla	AA	27	26	1	0	151.1	638	148	63	56	7	4	4	7	41	0	131	4	0	8	11	.421	1	0- -	-	3.26	3.33
2017	Lsvlle	AAA	26	25	1	0	139.0	616	156	85	76	16	3	4	3	51	0	110	5	0	7	10	.412	1	0- -	-	4.82	4.92
2017	Cin	NL	7	4	0	1	25.0	101	19	13	13	6	0	0	1	9	0	21	1	0	2	1	.667	0	0-0	-	3.73	4.68

Robert Stephenson

Pitches: R **Bats:** R **Pos:** RP-14; SP-11

Ht: 6'2" **Wt:** 200 **Born:** 2/24/1993 **Age:** 25

			HOW MUCH HE PITCHED						WHAT HE GAVE UP										THE RESULTS						
Year	Team	Lg	G	GS	CG	GF	IP	BFP	H	R	ER	HR	SH	SF	HB	TBB	IBB	SO	WP	Bk	W	L	Pct	Sh	Sv-Op	Hld	ERC	ERA
2013	2 Tms	Low	18	18	0	0	97.2	390	75	39	29	8	3	1	3	22	0	118	11	2	7	5	.583	0	0- -	-	2.21	2.67
2014	Pnscla	AA	27	26	0	0	136.2	601	114	81	72	18	3	9	5	74	0	140	9	0	7	10	.412	0	0- -	-	4.00	4.74
2015	Pnscla	AA	14	14	1	0	78.1	325	53	36	32	8	5	4	4	43	0	89	5	0	4	7	.364	0	0- -	-	3.15	3.68
2015	Lsvlle	AAA	11	11	0	0	55.2	242	55	25	25	2	3	2	2	27	0	51	5	0	4	4	.500	0	0- -	-	3.61	4.04
2016	Lsvlle	AAA	24	24	1	0	136.2	591	115	72	67	17	6	5	3	71	0	120	5	0	8	9	.471	0	0- -	-	3.89	4.41
2017	Lsvlle	AAA	8	7	0	0	40.1	161	27	17	17	8	2	1	0	13	0	45	2	0	1	2	.333	0	0- -	-	2.60	3.79
2016	Cin	NL	8	8	0	0	37.0	170	41	26	25	9	0	0	4	19	1	31	2	1	2	3	.400	0	0-0	-	6.78	6.08
2017	Cin	NL	25	11	0	6	84.2	383	81	52	44	12	5	6	2	53	3	86	5	2	5	6	.455	-	1-1	-	5.06	4.68
	2 ML YEARS		33	19	0	6	121.2	553	122	78	69	21	5	6	6	72	4	117	7	3	7	9	.438	0	1-1	0	5.57	5.10

Andrew Stevenson

Bats: L **Throws:** L **Pos:** RF-14;PH-12;LF-9;CF-5;PR-3

Ht: 6'0" **Wt:** 185 **Born:** 6/1/1994 **Age:** 24

Year	Team	Lg	G	AB	H	2B	3B	HR	(Hm	Rd)	TB	R	RBI	RC	TBB	IBB	SO	HBP	SH	SF	SB	CS	GDP	Avg	OBP	Slg	OPS
2015	3 Tms	Low	55	214	66	4	4	1	(-	-)	81	40	25	32	16	0	30	4	2	3	23	7	1	.308	.363	.379	.741
2016	Ptomc	A+	68	273	83	12	8	1	(-	-)	114	37	18	44	24	1	44	0	2	1	27	9	2	.304	.359	.418	.777
2016	Hrsbrg	AA	65	256	63	11	2	2	(-	-)	84	38	16	27	20	0	51	1	2	1	12	5	7	.246	.302	.328	.630
2017	Hrsbrg	AA	20	80	28	5	1	0	(-	-)	35	14	12	14	11	1	19	0	0	0	1	3	0	.350	.429	.438	.866
2017	Syrcse	AAA	79	309	78	7	4	2	(-	-)	99	38	26	31	19	0	72	1	2	0	10	1	5	.252	.298	.320	.618
2017	Was	NL	37	57	9	2	0	0	(0	0)	11	5	1	1	7	0	20	0	2	0	1	0	0	.158	.250	.193	.443

Brock Stewart

Pitches: R **Bats:** L **Pos:** RP-13; SP-4

Ht: 6'3" **Wt:** 210 **Born:** 10/3/1991 **Age:** 26

Year	Team	Lg	G	GS	CG	GF	IP	BFP	H	R	ER	HR	SH	SF	HB	TBB	IBB	SO	WP	Bk	W	L	Pct	Sh	Sv-Op	Hld	ERC	ERA
2014	Ogden	R+	17	1	0	7	34.1	159	36	20	13	1	1	0	2	17	0	45	10	0	3	2	.600	0	3--	-	4.27	3.41
2015	2 Tms	Low	25	19	0	0	101.0	437	113	52	50	10	2	2	5	24	0	103	7	1	4	6	.400	0	0--	-	4.27	4.46
2016	Tulsa	AA	10	10	1	0	59.1	227	41	12	9	0	2	3	2	11	0	65	1	0	3	4	.429	0	0--	-	1.44	1.37
2016	OkCity	AAA	9	9	0	0	50.2	197	41	14	14	4	1	1	0	6	0	54	0	0	4	0	1.000	0	0--	-	1.94	2.49
2017	OkCity	AAA	5	5	0	0	17.1	72	19	6	6	2	0	0	1	3	0	25	0	0	1	0	.000	0	0--	-	4.14	3.12
2016	LAD	NL	7	5	0	0	28.0	126	33	18	18	7	1	0	0	12	1	25	0	0	2	2	.500	0	0-0	-	6.34	5.79
2017	LAD	NL	17	4	0	8	34.1	147	28	18	13	4	2	1	1	19	2	29	0	0	0	0	-	0	1-1	1	3.82	3.41
	2 ML YEARS		24	9	0	8	62.1	273	61	36	31	11	3	1	1	31	3	54	0	0	2	2	.500	0	1-1	1	4.91	4.48

Chris Stewart

Bats: R **Throws:** R **Pos:** C-48;PH-3

Ht: 6'4" **Wt:** 200 **Born:** 2/19/1982 **Age:** 36

Year	Team	Lg	G	AB	H	2B	3B	HR	(Hm	Rd)	TB	R	RBI	RC	TBB	IBB	SO	HBP	SH	SF	SB	CS	GDP	Avg	OBP	Slg	OPS
2006	CWS	AL	6	8	0	0	0	0	(0	0)	0	0	0	0	0	0	2	0	0	0	0	0	0	.000	.000	.000	.000
2007	Tex	AL	17	37	9	2	0	0	(0	0)	11	4	3	3	3	0	6	0	3	0	0	0	2	.243	.300	.297	.597
2008	NYY	AL	1	3	0	0	0	0	(0	0)	0	0	0	0	0	0	1	0	0	0	0	0	0	.000	.000	.000	.000
2010	SD	NL	2	0	0	0	0	0	(0	0)	0	0	0	0	0	0	0	0	0	0	0	0	0	-	-	-	-
2011	SF	NL	67	136	33	8	0	3	(1	2)	50	20	10	10	16	4	18	2	3	0	0	0	2	.204	.283	.309	.592
2012	NYY	AL	55	141	34	8	0	1	(1	0)	45	15	13	10	10	0	21	1	3	2	2	0	1	.241	.292	.319	.611
2013	NYY	AL	109	294	62	6	0	4	(3	1)	80	28	25	24	30	0	49	6	6	4	4	0	8	.211	.293	.272	.566
2014	Pit	NL	49	136	40	5	0	0	(0	0)	45	9	10	15	12	2	27	3	2	1	0	1	2	.294	.362	.331	.693
2015	Pit	NL	58	159	46	8	0	0	(0	0)	54	9	15	17	6	0	29	2	3	2	0	0	3	.289	.320	.340	.659
2016	Pit	NL	34	98	21	4	0	1	(0	1)	28	10	7	7	12	2	15	3	0	0	0	0	3	.214	.319	.286	.604
2017	Pit	NL	51	131	24	1	2	0	(0	0)	29	8	4	6	9	1	22	1	3	0	0	0	3	.183	.241	.221	.463
	Postseason		1	0	0	0	0	0	(0	0)	0	0	0	0	0	0	0	0	0	0	0	0	0	-	-	-	-
	11 ML YEARS		449	1169	269	42	2	9	(5	4)	342	103	87	92	98	9	190	18	23	9	6	1	23	.230	.298	.293	.590

Drew Storen

Pitches: R **Bats:** B **Pos:** RP-58

STORE-inn

Ht: 6'1" **Wt:** 195 **Born:** 8/11/1987 **Age:** 30

Year	Team	Lg	G	GS	CG	GF	IP	BFP	H	R	ER	HR	SH	SF	HB	TBB	IBB	SO	WP	Bk	W	L	Pct	Sh	Sv-Op	Hld	ERC	ERA
2010	Was	NL	54	0	0	22	55.1	232	48	24	22	3	6	2	3	22	3	52	3	0	4	4	.500	0	5-7	10	3.19	3.58
2011	Was	NL	73	0	0	52	75.1	303	57	24	23	8	1	1	2	20	4	74	2	0	6	3	.667	0	43-48	3	2.35	2.75
2012	Was	NL	37	0	0	17	30.1	116	22	8	8	0	0	2	1	8	0	24	1	0	3	1	.750	0	4-5	10	1.79	2.37
2013	Was	NL	68	0	0	20	61.2	267	65	34	31	7	3	1	1	19	2	58	2	0	4	2	.667	0	3-8	24	4.08	4.52
2014	Was	NL	65	0	0	18	56.1	224	44	8	7	2	3	2	3	11	3	46	4	0	2	1	.667	0	11-14	20	1.93	1.12
2015	Was	NL	58	0	0	35	55.0	228	45	23	21	4	1	1	5	16	2	67	2	0	2	2	.500	0	29-34	5	2.79	3.44
2016	2 Tms	AL	57	0	0	14	51.2	228	56	30	30	7	1	0	7	13	1	48	0	1	4	3	.571	0	3-4	10	4.68	5.23
2017	Cin	NL	58	0	0	9	54.2	246	57	32	27	7	0	3	10	23	5	48	1	0	4	2	.667	0	1-3	6	5.25	4.45
16	Tor	AL	38	0	0	13	33.1	156	43	23	23	6	1	0	6	10	1	32	0	1	1	3	.250	0	3-4	6	6.70	6.21
16	Sea	AL	19	0	0	1	18.1	72	13	7	7	1	0	0	1	3	0	16	0	0	3	0	1.000	0	0-0	2	1.67	3.44
	Postseason		6	0	0	5	5.1	25	7	5	5	0	0	1	0	3	0	7	0	0	1	1	.500	0	1-3	0	5.85	8.44
	8 ML YEARS		470	0	0	187	440.1	1844	394	183	169	38	15	12	32	132	20	417	15	1	29	18	.617	0	99-123	88	3.23	3.45

Trevor Story

Bats: R **Throws:** R **Pos:** SS-142;PH-6;PR-1

Ht: 6'1" **Wt:** 210 **Born:** 11/15/1992 **Age:** 25

Year	Team	Lg	G	AB	H	2B	3B	HR	(Hm	Rd)	TB	R	RBI	RC	TBB	IBB	SO	HBP	SH	SF	SB	CS	GDP	Avg	OBP	Slg	OPS
2013	Mdest	A+	130	497	116	34	5	12	(-	-)	196	71	65	66	45	0	183	7	4	1	23	1	2	.233	.305	.394	.700
2014	2 Tms	Low	52	191	63	18	7	5	(-	-)	110	40	28	48	32	1	62	3	0	0	20	4	3	.330	.434	.576	1.010
2014	Tulsa	AA	56	205	41	8	1	9	(-	-)	78	29	20	25	28	0	82	2	2	0	3	1	1	.200	.302	.380	.683
2015	NwBrit	AA	69	256	72	20	6	10	(-	-)	134	46	40	53	35	2	73	5	0	4	15	2	0	.281	.373	.523	.897
2015	Albq	AAA	61	256	71	20	4	10	(-	-)	129	37	40	42	16	1	68	2	0	1	7	1	1	.277	.324	.504	.828
2016	Col	NL	97	372	101	21	4	27	(16	11)	211	67	72	67	35	2	130	5	2	5	8	5	5	.272	.341	.567	.909
2017	Col	NL	145	503	120	32	3	24	(13	11)	230	68	82	66	49	4	**191**	2	0	1	7	2	12	.239	.308	.457	.765
	2 ML YEARS		242	875	221	53	7	51	(29	22)	441	135	154	133	84	6	321	7	2	2	15	7	17	.253	.322	.504	.826

Matt Strahm

Pitches: L Bats: R Pos: RP-21; SP-3

Ht: 6'3" Wt: 185 Born: 11/12/1991 Age: 26

		HOW MUCH HE PITCHED							WHAT HE GAVE UP												THE RESULTS						
Year	Team	Lg	G	GS	CG	GF	IP	BFP	H	R	ER	HR	SH	SF	HB	TBB	IBB	SO	WP	Bk	W	L	Pct	Sh	Sv-Op	Hld	ERC	ERA
2014	Idaho	R+	10	1	0	3	19.1	79	10	6	5	1	1	0	1	10	0	27	1	0	1	0	1.000	0	1--	-	1.89	2.33
2015	2 Tms	Low	29	11	0	9	94.0	375	60	32	27	8	3	1	7	31	0	121	5	0	3	7	.300	0	5--	-	2.14	2.59
2016	NWArk	AA	22	18	0	0	102.1	425	102	47	39	14	1	2	6	23	0	107	1	1	3	8	.273	0	0--	-	3.90	3.43
2016	KC	AL	21	0	0	1	22.0	88	13	4	3	0	0	1	1	11	1	30	1	0	2	2	.500	0	0-0	6	1.84	1.23
2017	KC	AL	24	3	0	3	34.2	154	30	22	21	6	2	0	3	22	2	37	3	0	2	5	.286	0	0-0	5	5.10	5.45
	2 ML YEARS		45	3	0	4	56.2	242	43	26	24	6	2	1	4	33	3	67	4	0	4	7	.364	0	0-0	11	3.73	3.81

Dan Straily
STRAY-lee

Pitches: R Bats: R Pos: SP-33

Ht: 6'2" Wt: 220 Born: 12/1/1988 Age: 29

		HOW MUCH HE PITCHED							WHAT HE GAVE UP												THE RESULTS						
Year	Team	Lg	G	GS	CG	GF	IP	BFP	H	R	ER	HR	SH	SF	HB	TBB	IBB	SO	WP	Bk	W	L	Pct	Sh	Sv-Op	Hld	ERC	ERA
2012	Oak	AL	7	7	0	0	39.1	172	36	19	17	11	1	1	2	16	1	32	0	0	2	1	.667	0	0-0	0	4.94	3.89
2013	Oak	AL	27	27	0	0	152.1	640	132	74	67	16	4	5	7	57	0	124	7	0	10	8	.556	0	0-0	0	3.46	3.96
2014	2 Tms		14	8	0	0	52.0	231	53	41	39	10	0	1	2	24	1	47	2	0	1	3	.250	0	0-0	0	5.22	6.75
2015	Hou	AL	4	3	0	0	16.2	76	16	11	10	2	0	0	1	8	0	14	1	0	0	1	.000	0	0-0	0	4.38	5.40
2016	Cin	NL	34	31	0	0	191.1	792	154	80	80	31	6	3	11	73	4	162	3	1	14	8	.636	0	0-0	0	3.58	3.76
2017	Mia	NL	33	33	0	0	181.2	769	176	90	86	31	10	7	5	60	4	170	2	0	10	9	.526	0	0-0	0	4.20	4.26
14	Oak	AL	7	7	0	0	38.1	159	33	21	21	9	0	1	1	15	1	34	2	0	1	2	.333	0	0-0	0	4.31	4.93
14	ChC	NL	7	1	0	0	13.2	72	20	20	18	1	0	0	1	9	0	13	0	0	0	1	.000	0	-	0	7.78	11.85
	Postseason		1	1	0	0	6.0	22	4	3	3	1	0	0	1	0	0	8	0	0	0	0	-	0	0-0	0	1.99	4.50
	6 ML YEARS		119	109	0	0	633.1	2680	567	315	299	101	21	17	28	238	10	549	15	1	37	30	.552	0	0-0	0	3.96	4.25

Stephen Strasburg
STRAHS-berg

Pitches: R Bats: R Pos: SP-28

Ht: 6'4" Wt: 235 Born: 7/20/1988 Age: 29

		HOW MUCH HE PITCHED							WHAT HE GAVE UP												THE RESULTS						
Year	Team	Lg	G	GS	CG	GF	IP	BFP	H	R	ER	HR	SH	SF	HB	TBB	IBB	SO	WP	Bk	W	L	Pct	Sh	Sv-Op	Hld	ERC	ERA
2010	Was	NL	12	12	0	0	68.0	274	56	25	22	7	2	2	0	17	0	92	2	0	5	3	.625	0	0-0	0	2.41	2.91
2011	Was	NL	5	5	0	0	24.0	88	15	5	4	0	1	1	0	2	0	24	0	0	1	1	.500	0	0-0	0	0.97	1.50
2012	Was	NL	28	28	0	0	159.1	653	136	62	56	15	6	4	4	48	1	197	5	0	15	6	.714	0	0-0	0	2.97	3.16
2013	Was	NL	30	30	1	0	183.0	731	136	71	61	16	5	1	12	56	1	191	7	3	8	9	.471	1	0-0	0	2.58	3.00
2014	Was	NL	34	34	0	0	215.0	868	198	86	75	23	9	4	5	43	4	242	7	0	14	11	.560	0	0-0	0	3.02	3.14
2015	Was	NL	23	23	0	0	127.1	523	115	56	49	14	5	1	3	26	0	155	4	0	11	7	.611	0	0-0	0	2.92	3.46
2016	Was	NL	24	24	0	0	147.2	598	119	59	59	15	5	1	2	44	1	183	2	0	15	4	.789	0	0-0	0	2.72	3.60
2017	Was	NL	28	28	1	0	175.1	701	131	55	49	13	2	4	7	47	5	204	3	0	15	4	.789	1	0-0	0	2.22	2.52
	Postseason		1	1	0	0	5.0	25	8	2	1	0	1	0	1	1	0	2	0	0	0	1	.000	0	0-0	0	6.68	1.80
	8 ML YEARS		184	184	2	0	1099.2	4436	906	419	375	101	35	18	33	283	12	1288	30	3	84	45	.651	2	0-0	0	2.66	3.07

Chris Stratton

Pitches: R Bats: R Pos: SP-10; RP-3

Ht: 6'3" Wt: 190 Born: 8/22/1990 Age: 27

		HOW MUCH HE PITCHED							WHAT HE GAVE UP												THE RESULTS						
Year	Team	Lg	G	GS	CG	GF	IP	BFP	H	R	ER	HR	SH	SF	HB	TBB	IBB	SO	WP	Bk	W	L	Pct	Sh	Sv-Op	Hld	ERC	ERA
2013	Augsta	A	22	22	1	0	132.0	554	128	48	48	5	4	4	3	47	1	123	6	0	9	3	.750	0	0--	-	3.44	3.27
2014	SnJos	A+	19	18	0	0	99.0	427	103	61	56	13	3	4	2	36	0	102	5	0	7	8	.467	0	0--	-	4.49	5.09
2014	Rchmd	AA	5	5	0	0	23.0	107	29	10	9	2	1	2	0	12	0	18	2	0	1	1	.500	0	0--	-	6.04	3.52
2015	Rchmd	AA	9	9	0	0	50.0	212	40	26	23	3	2	1	1	22	1	39	2	0	1	5	.167	0	0--	-	2.88	4.14
2015	Scrmto	AAA	17	17	1	0	98.0	415	88	46	42	6	4	3	5	40	0	72	4	0	4	5	.444	0	0--	-	3.51	3.86
2016	Scrmto	AAA	21	20	1	0	125.2	526	120	57	54	6	7	3	4	39	1	103	6	0	12	6	.667	0	0--	-	3.26	3.87
2017	Scrmto	AAA	15	15	0	0	79.1	352	94	49	45	10	2	2	2	22	0	71	4	0	4	5	.444	0	0--	-	4.87	5.11
2016	SF	NL	7	0	0	7	10.0	43	11	4	4	1	0	0	0	5	0	6	0	0	1	0	1.000	0	0-0	0	5.31	3.60
2017	SF	NL	13	10	0	1	58.2	256	59	25	24	5	2	3	1	28	0	51	2	0	4	4	.500	0	1-2	0	4.42	3.68
	2 ML YEARS		20	10	0	8	68.2	299	70	29	28	6	2	3	1	33	0	57	2	0	5	4	.556	0	1-2	0	4.54	3.67

Huston Street

Pitches: R Bats: R Pos: RP-4

Ht: 6'0" Wt: 205 Born: 8/2/1983 Age: 34

		HOW MUCH HE PITCHED							WHAT HE GAVE UP												THE RESULTS						
Year	Team	Lg	G	GS	CG	GF	IP	BFP	H	R	ER	HR	SH	SF	HB	TBB	IBB	SO	WP	Bk	W	L	Pct	Sh	Sv-Op	Hld	ERC	ERA
2017	Salt Lk*	AAA	5	0	0	0	5.0	18	3	2	2	0	0	0	0	1	0	4	0	0	0	0	-	0	0--	-	1.17	3.60
2005	Oak	AL	67	0	0	47	78.1	306	53	17	15	3	3	2	2	26	4	72	1	0	5	1	.833	0	23-27	0	1.87	1.72
2006	Oak	AL	69	0	0	55	70.2	290	64	28	26	4	3	3	2	13	3	67	4	0	4	4	.500	0	37-48	1	2.49	3.31
2007	Oak	AL	48	0	0	35	50.0	199	35	20	16	5	2	1	0	12	3	63	0	0	5	2	.714	0	16-21	5	1.84	2.88
2008	Oak	AL	63	0	0	37	70.0	287	58	29	29	6	3	3	1	27	6	69	2	0	7	5	.583	0	18-25	6	2.98	3.73
2009	Col	NL	64	0	0	52	61.2	240	43	22	21	7	3	2	0	13	4	70	0	0	4	1	.800	0	35-37	2	1.83	3.06
2010	Col	NL	44	0	0	39	47.1	187	39	21	19	5	0	1	2	11	4	45	2	1	4	4	.500	0	20-25	0	2.66	3.61
2011	Col	NL	62	0	0	47	58.1	239	62	28	25	10	3	1	1	9	1	55	0	0	1	4	.200	0	29-33	0	4.03	3.86
2012	SD	NL	40	0	0	36	39.0	144	17	8	8	2	1	0	1	11	1	47	1	0	2	1	.667	0	23-24	0	0.99	1.85
2013	SD	NL	58	0	0	52	56.2	222	44	17	17	12	0	0	0	14	1	46	4	0	2	5	.286	0	33-35	0	3.00	2.70
2014	2 Tms		61	0	0	51	59.1	229	42	9	9	4	4	0	2	14	3	57	0	0	2	2	.500	0	41-44	0	1.77	1.37
2015	LAA	AL	62	0	0	51	62.1	255	52	22	22	7	2	3	0	20	5	57	6	0	3	3	.500	0	40-45	0	2.85	3.18
2016	LAA	AL	26	0	0	21	22.1	105	31	16	16	5	0	1	0	12	2	14	0	0	3	2	.600	0	9-12	0	8.09	6.45
2017	LAA	AL	4	0	0	2	4.0	15	2	0	0	0	0	0	0	1	0	3	0	0	0	0	-	0	0-0	0	0.94	0.00
14	SD	NL	33	0	0	28	33.0	121	18	4	4	3	0	0	0	7	0	34	0	0	1	0	1.000	0	24-25	0	1.33	1.09
14	LAA	AL	28	0	0	23	26.1	108	24	5	5	1	1	0	0	7	3	23	0	0	1	2	.333	0	17-19	0	2.53	1.71
	Postseason		10	0	0	7	12.0	54	14	9	9	2	1	1	0	6	1	8	0	0	0	3	.000	0	3-4	0	5.92	6.75
	13 ML YEARS		668	0	0	525	680.0	2718	542	237	223	70	21	19	8	183	37	665	20	1	42	34	.553	0	324-376	18	2.52	2.95

Hunter Strickland

Pitches: R Bats: R Pos: RP-68   Ht: 6'4" Wt: 220 Born: 9/24/1988 Age: 29

		HOW MUCH HE PITCHED						WHAT HE GAVE UP										THE RESULTS						
Year	Team	Lg	G	GS	CG	GF	IP	BFP	H	R	ER	HR	SH	SF	HB	TBB	IBB	SO	WP	Bk	W	L	Pct	Sh	Sv-Op	Hld	ERC	ERA
2014	SF	NL	9	0	0	5	7.0	25	5	0	0	0	0	0	0	0	0	9	0	0	1	0	1.000	0	1-1	1	1.08	0.00
2015	SF	NL	55	0	0	11	51.1	191	34	14	14	4	0	0	2	10	1	50	1	0	3	3	.500	0	0-2	20	1.72	2.45
2016	SF	NL	72	0	0	14	61.0	250	50	21	21	4	0	3	2	19	3	57	3	0	3	3	.500	0	3-8	18	2.61	3.10
2017	SF	NL	68	0	0	17	61.1	268	59	20	18	4	1	3	2	29	4	58	3	1	4	3	.571	0	1-3	21	3.91	2.64
	Postseason		11	0	0	5	11.0	43	10	7	7	6	0	0	0	3	0	11	1	0	1	0	1.000	0	1-2	1	6.24	5.73
	4 ML YEARS		204	0	0	47	180.2	734	148	55	53	12	1	6	6	58	8	174	7	1	11	9	.550	0	5-14	60	2.69	2.64

Ross Stripling

Pitches: R Bats: R Pos: RP-47; SP-2   Ht: 6'3" Wt: 210 Born: 11/23/1989 Age: 28

		HOW MUCH HE PITCHED						WHAT HE GAVE UP										THE RESULTS						
Year	Team	Lg	G	GS	CG	GF	IP	BFP	H	R	ER	HR	SH	SF	HB	TBB	IBB	SO	WP	Bk	W	L	Pct	Sh	Sv-Op	Hld	ERC	ERA
2013	Rcuca	A+	6	6	0	0	33.2	134	24	11	11	1	1	1	0	11	0	34	2	0	2	0	1.000	0	0--	-	1.91	2.94
2013	Chatt	AA	21	16	0	1	94.0	387	91	33	29	4	4	2	0	19	1	83	4	0	6	4	.600	0	1--	-	2.75	2.78
2015	Tulsa	AA	13	13	1	0	67.1	273	61	29	29	7	1	1	0	19	0	55	4	0	3	6	.333	0	0--	-	3.20	3.88
2016	OkCity	AAA	5	4	0	0	16.2	71	20	7	7	2	1	1	0	2	0	17	1	0	0	2	.000	0	0--	-	4.18	3.78
2016	LAD	NL	22	14	0	4	100.0	419	96	46	44	10	3	1	1	30	3	74	6	0	5	9	.357	0	0-0	0	3.46	3.96
2017	LAD	NL	49	2	0	12	74.1	304	69	31	31	10	2	3	0	19	4	74	2	0	3	5	.375	0	2-5	4	3.29	3.75
	Postseason		5	0	0	3	4.1	19	6	5	4	0	0	1	0	1	0	2	0	0	0	0	-	0	0-0	0	5.00	8.31
	2 ML YEARS		71	16	0	16	174.1	723	165	77	75	20	5	4	1	49	7	148	8	0	8	14	.364	0	2-5	4	3.39	3.87

Marcus Stroman

Pitches: R Bats: R Pos: SP-33   Ht: 5'8" Wt: 180 Born: 5/1/1991 Age: 27

		HOW MUCH HE PITCHED						WHAT HE GAVE UP										THE RESULTS						
Year	Team	Lg	G	GS	CG	GF	IP	BFP	H	R	ER	HR	SH	SF	HB	TBB	IBB	SO	WP	Bk	W	L	Pct	Sh	Sv-Op	Hld	ERC	ERA
2014	Tor	AL	26	20	1	1	130.2	534	125	56	53	7	0	2	3	28	1	111	9	1	11	6	.647	1	1-1	0	2.93	3.65
2015	Tor	AL	4	4	0	0	27.0	103	20	5	5	2	0	0	1	6	0	18	2	1	4	0	1.000	0	0-0	0	2.16	1.67
2016	Tor	AL	32	32	0	0	204.0	855	209	104	99	21	2	2	4	54	0	166	9	1	9	10	.474	0	0-0	0	3.81	4.37
2017	Tor	AL	33	33	2	0	201.0	834	201	82	69	21	0	4	6	62	1	164	3	1	13	9	.591	0	0-0	0	3.97	3.09
	Postseason		5	5	0	0	30.2	128	29	16	15	4	0	1	0	7	0	21	2	0	1	1	.500	0	0-0	0	3.24	4.40
	4 ML YEARS		95	89	3	1	562.2	2326	555	247	226	51	2	8	14	150	2	459	23	4	37	25	.597	1	1-1	0	3.57	3.61

Pedro Strop

Pitches: R Bats: R Pos: RP-69   Ht: 6'1" Wt: 220 Born: 6/13/1985 Age: 33
STROPE

		HOW MUCH HE PITCHED						WHAT HE GAVE UP										THE RESULTS						
Year	Team	Lg	G	GS	CG	GF	IP	BFP	H	R	ER	HR	SH	SF	HB	TBB	IBB	SO	WP	Bk	W	L	Pct	Sh	Sv-Op	Hld	ERC	ERA
2009	Tex	AL	7	0	0	3	7.0	30	6	6	6	0	0	0	0	4	0	9	0	0	0	0	-	0	0-0	0	3.27	7.71
2010	Tex	AL	15	0	0	5	10.2	60	17	12	12	2	1	0	1	11	0	11	5	1	0	0	-	0	0-0	1	11.92	10.13
2011	2 Tms	AL	23	0	0	6	22.0	90	15	5	5	0	2	1	1	10	0	21	2	2	2	1	.667	0	0-2	4	2.15	2.05
2012	Bal	AL	70	0	0	17	66.1	283	52	18	18	2	1	1	4	37	2	58	5	0	5	2	.714	0	3-10	24	3.22	2.44
2013	2 Tms		66	0	0	22	57.1	254	45	30	29	5	7	0	6	26	2	66	8	1	2	5	.286	0	1-4	17	3.21	4.55
2014	ChC	NL	65	0	0	13	61.0	244	40	19	15	2	0	1	6	25	3	71	6	1	2	4	.333	0	2-6	21	2.12	2.21
2015	ChC	NL	76	0	0	12	68.0	270	39	24	22	5	1	3	4	29	6	81	6	0	2	6	.250	0	3-5	28	1.94	2.91
2016	ChC	NL	54	0	0	8	47.1	187	27	16	15	4	0	2	4	15	1	60	7	0	2	2	.500	0	0-4	21	1.78	2.85
2017	ChC	NL	69	0	0	8	60.1	250	45	22	19	4	2	1	3	26	1	65	7	1	5	4	.556	0	0-4	21	2.78	2.83
11	Tex	AL	11	0	0	4	9.2	44	7	4	4	0	1	1	1	7	0	9	2	2	0	1	.000	0	0-1	0	3.34	3.72
11	Bal	AL	12	0	0	2	12.1	46	8	1	1	0	1	0	0	3	0	12	0	0	2	0	1.000	0	0-1	4	1.39	0.73
13	Bal	AL	29	0	0	15	22.1	111	23	19	18	4	4	0	2	15	2	24	5	1	0	3	.000	0	0-3	3	5.81	7.25
13	ChC	NL	37	0	0	7	35.0	143	22	11	11	1	3	0	4	11	0	42	3	0	2	2	.500	0	1-1	14	1.80	2.83
	Postseason		16	0	0	2	13.0	50	7	3	3	1	1	0	3	4	0	11	1	0	1	0	1.000	0	0-0	2	2.19	2.08
	9 ML YEARS		445	0	0	94	400.0	1668	286	152	141	24	14	9	27	183	15	442	46	6	20	24	.455	0	9-35	137	2.70	3.17

Drew Stubbs

Bats: R Throws: R Pos: CF-10;PR-1   Ht: 6'4" Wt: 205 Born: 10/4/1984 Age: 33

			BATTING																			RUNNING			AVERAGES			
Year	Team	Lg	G	AB	H	2B	3B	HR	(Hm	Rd)	TB	R	RBI	RC	TBB	IBB	SO	HBP	SH	SF	SB	CS	GDP	Avg	OBP	Slg	OPS
2017	Scrmto*	AAA	10	39	10	1	0	2	(-	-)	17	6	7	6	6	1	16	0	0	1	1	0	1	.256	.348	.436	.784
2017	RdRck*	AAA	75	273	81	16	2	7	(-	-)	122	46	35	51	46	0	88	3	0	0	9	6	2	.297	.404	.447	.851
2009	Cin	NL	42	180	48	5	1	8	(7	1)	79	27	17	22	15	0	49	0	1	0	10	4	1	.267	.323	.439	.762
2010	Cin	NL	150	514	131	19	6	22	(13	9)	228	91	77	74	55	2	168	5	3	6	30	6	6	.255	.329	.444	.773
2011	Cin	NL	158	604	147	22	3	15	(9	6)	220	92	44	66	63	1	205	7	6	1	40	10	2	.243	.321	.364	.686
2012	Cin	NL	136	493	105	13	2	14	(6	8)	164	75	40	45	42	0	166	2	6	1	30	7	2	.213	.277	.333	.610
2013	Cle	AL	146	430	100	21	2	10	(6	4)	155	59	45	50	44	1	141	2	2	3	17	2	3	.233	.305	.360	.665
2014	Col	NL	132	388	112	22	4	15	(12	3)	187	67	43	58	30	1	136	2	0	3	20	3	4	.289	.339	.482	.821
2015	2 Tms		78	123	24	4	2	5	(4	1)	47	20	10	13	14	1	60	1	2	1	5	1	1	.195	.283	.382	.665
2016	3 Tms		59	80	18	0	0	3	(2	1)	27	13	7	10	12	0	38	1	0	1	9	1	1	.225	.330	.338	.667
2017	SF	NL	10	22	2	0	0	0	(0	0)	2	0	0	0	2	0	9	0	0	0	0	0	0	.091	.167	.091	.258
15	Col	NL	51	102	22	3	2	5	(4	1)	44	14	10	12	9	1	50	1	2	0	2	1	1	.216	.286	.431	.717
15	Tex	AL	27	21	2	1	0	0	(0	0)	3	6	0	1	5	0	10	0	0	1	3	0	0	.095	.296	.143	.412
16	Atl	NL	20	38	9	0	0	1	(1	0)	12	6	3	4	4	0	20	0	0	1	4	0	1	.237	.310	.316	.625
16	Tex	AL	19	20	6	0	0	2	(1	1)	12	6	3	3	4	0	7	0	0	0	4	0	0	.300	.400	.600	1.000
16	Bal	AL	20	22	3	0	0	0	(0	0)	3	1	1	3	4	0	11	1	0	0	1	1	0	.136	.296	.136	.433
	Postseason		12	29	5	1	1	0	(0	0)	8	4	1	1	2	0	8	0	0	0	0	0	0	.172	.226	.276	.502
	9 ML YEARS		911	2834	687	106	20	92	(57	35)	1109	444	283	338	277	6	972	19	22	15	161	34	20	.242	.313	.391	.704

Daniel Stumpf

Pitches: L Bats: L Pos: RP-55   Ht: 6'2" Wt: 200 Born: 1/4/1991 Age: 27

		HOW MUCH HE PITCHED						WHAT HE GAVE UP												THE RESULTS						
Year Team	Lg	G	GS	CG	GF	IP	BFP	H	R	ER	HR	SH	SF	HB	TBB	IBB	SO	WP	Bk	W	L	Pct	Sh	Sv-Op	Hld	ERC	ERA
2013 Lxngtn	A	25	25	4	0	137.2	554	103	58	47	10	1	4	7	50	0	117	6	0	10	10	.500	1	0- -	-	2.68	3.07
2014 Wilmg	A+	32	8	0	16	74.0	316	82	34	31	1	1	2	1	19	0	79	5	0	3	8	.273	0	2- -	-	3.57	3.77
2015 NWArk	AA	42	1	0	15	70.2	296	55	31	28	6	2	2	2	31	0	76	6	0	5	4	.556	0	3- -	-	3.02	3.57
2016 NWArk	AA	14	0	0	6	21.1	85	14	5	5	0	4	0	2	4	0	26	1	0	2	0	1.000	0	1- -	-	1.41	2.11
2017 Toledo	AAA	24	0	0	4	21.1	84	19	8	8	3	3	0	0	5	2	26	0	0	1	2	.333	0	0- -	-	3.08	3.38
2016 Phi	NL	7	0	0	3	5.0	25	9	6	6	1	1	0	0	2	0	2	1	0	0	0	-	0	0-0	1	10.22	10.80
2017 Det	AL	55	0	0	13	37.2	160	37	16	16	5	0	4	2	15	1	33	2	1	0	1	.000	0	0-2	9	4.48	3.82
2 ML YEARS		62	0	0	16	42.2	185	46	22	22	6	1	4	2	17	1	35	3	1	0	1	.000	0	0-2	10	5.08	4.64

Albert Suarez

Pitches: R Bats: R Pos: RP-18   SWAH-rez   Ht: 6'3" Wt: 235 Born: 10/8/1989 Age: 28

		HOW MUCH HE PITCHED						WHAT HE GAVE UP												THE RESULTS						
Year Team	Lg	G	GS	CG	GF	IP	BFP	H	R	ER	HR	SH	SF	HB	TBB	IBB	SO	WP	Bk	W	L	Pct	Sh	Sv-Op	Hld	ERC	ERA
2014 Mont	AA	11	11	0	0	56.0	249	67	34	27	4	3	3	2	19	2	32	1	0	3	6	.333	0	0- -	-	4.85	4.34
2015 Ark	AA	27	24	1	0	163.0	652	142	64	54	14	2	1	1	40	0	121	4	0	11	9	.550	0	0- -	-	2.78	2.98
2016 Scrmto	AAA	9	7	0	0	45.2	195	46	26	22	3	5	4	2	14	0	39	1	0	4	3	.571	0	0- -	-	3.68	4.34
2017 2 Tms	Low	5	5	0	0	10.2	44	9	8	7	2	0	0	0	3	0	6	0	0	0	1	.000	0	0- -	-	3.26	5.91
2016 SF	NL	22	12	0	2	84.0	355	84	42	40	11	4	3	4	26	5	54	1	0	3	5	.375	0	0-0	1	4.07	4.29
2017 SF	NL	18	0	0	1	31.2	135	28	18	18	4	0	1	1	11	2	34	1	0	0	3	.000	0	1-3	0	3.37	5.12
2 ML YEARS		40	12	0	10	115.2	490	112	60	58	15	4	4	5	37	7	88	2	0	3	8	.273	0	1-3	1	3.87	4.51

Eugenio Suarez

Bats: R Throws: R Pos: 3B-153;PH-4;SS-1   ay-yoo-HAY-nee-oh SWAH-rez   Ht: 5'11" Wt: 213 Born: 7/18/1991 Age: 26

		BATTING																RUNNING			AVERAGES			
Year Team	Lg	G	AB	H	2B	3B	HR	(Hm Rd)	TB	R	RBI	RC	TBB	IBB	SO	HBP	SH	SF	SB	CS	GDP	Avg	OBP	Slg	OPS
2014 Det	AL	85	244	59	9	1	4	(2 2)	82	33	23	30	22	1	67	5	5	1	3	2	3	.242	.316	.336	.652
2015 Cin	NL	97	372	104	19	2	13	(4 9)	166	42	48	49	17	0	94	3	4	2	4	1	7	.280	.315	.446	.761
2016 Cin	NL	159	565	140	25	2	21	(10 11)	232	78	70	77	51	0	155	8	0	3	11	5	10	.248	.317	.411	.728
2017 Cin	NL	156	534	139	25	2	26	(21 5)	246	87	82	81	84	1	147	9	0	5	4	5	16	.260	.367	.461	.828
Postseason		1	1	0	0	0	0	(0 0)	0	0	0	0	0	0	0	0	0	0	0	0	0	.000	.000	.000	.000
4 ML YEARS		497	1715	442	78	7	64	(37 27)	726	240	223	237	174	2	463	25	9	11	22	13	36	.258	.333	.423	.756

Jesus Sucre

Bats: R Throws: R Pos: C-61;PH-2   SUE-cray   Ht: 6'0" Wt: 200 Born: 4/30/1988 Age: 30

		BATTING																RUNNING			AVERAGES			
Year Team	Lg	G	AB	H	2B	3B	HR	(Hm Rd)	TB	R	RBI	RC	TBB	IBB	SO	HBP	SH	SF	SB	CS	GDP	Avg	OBP	Slg	OPS
2013 Sea	AL	8	26	5	0	0	0	(0 0)	5	1	3	1	2	0	1	0	0	1	0	0	2	.192	.241	.192	.434
2014 Sea	AL	21	61	13	2	0	0	(0 0)	15	4	5	6	2	0	17	0	3	0	0	0	0	.213	.213	.246	.459
2015 Sea	AL	52	127	20	6	0	1	(1 0)	29	9	7	1	6	0	21	0	9	0	0	0	6	.157	.195	.228	.424
2016 Sea	AL	9	25	12	2	0	1	(0 1)	17	4	5	9	2	0	5	2	0	0	0	0	1	.480	.552	.680	1.232
2017 TB	AL	63	176	45	6	0	7	(3 4)	72	20	29	21	7	0	35	3	2	4	2	0	6	.256	.289	.409	.699
5 ML YEARS		153	415	95	16	0	9	(4 5)	138	38	49	38	17	0	79	5	14	5	2	0	15	.229	.265	.333	.597

Andrew Susac

Bats: R Throws: R Pos: PH-6;C-2   SOO-sack   Ht: 6'1" Wt: 215 Born: 3/22/1990 Age: 28

		BATTING																RUNNING			AVERAGES			
Year Team	Lg	G	AB	H	2B	3B	HR	(Hm Rd)	TB	R	RBI	RC	TBB	IBB	SO	HBP	SH	SF	SB	CS	GDP	Avg	OBP	Slg	OPS
2017 ColSpr*	AAA	51	171	35	10	0	8	(- -)	69	22	35	23	26	1	53	1	0	4	0	0	1	.205	.307	.404	.710
2014 SF	NL	35	84	24	8	0	3	(1 2)	41	13	19	16	7	0	28	0	0	0	0	0	0	.273	.326	.466	.792
2015 SF	NL	52	133	29	7	2	3	(2 1)	49	14	14	13	14	0	43	1	0	0	0	0	2	.218	.297	.368	.666
2016 Mil	NL	9	17	4	1	0	1	(0 1)	8	3	2	2	2	0	5	0	0	0	0	0	0	.235	.316	.471	.786
2017 Mil	NL	8	12	1	0	0	0	(0 0)	1	0	0	0	0	0	6	0	0	0	0	0	0	.083	.083	.083	.167
Postseason		4	4	1	0	0	0	(0 0)	1	0	0	1	0	0	1	0	0	0	0	0	0	.250	.250	.250	.500
4 ML YEARS		104	250	58	16	2	7	(3 4)	99	30	35	31	23	0	82	1	0	0	0	0	2	.232	.299	.396	.695

Brent Suter

Pitches: L Bats: L Pos: SP-14; RP-8   SOO-ter   Ht: 6'5" Wt: 195 Born: 8/29/1989 Age: 28

		HOW MUCH HE PITCHED						WHAT HE GAVE UP												THE RESULTS						
Year Team	Lg	G	GS	CG	GF	IP	BFP	H	R	ER	HR	SH	SF	HB	TBB	IBB	SO	WP	Bk	W	L	Pct	Sh	Sv-Op	Hld	ERC	ERA
2013 2 Tms	Low	24	23	1	1	139.0	584	139	61	53	11	4	2	3	41	0	113	1	0	7	10	.412	0	0- -	-	3.64	3.43
2014 Hntsvl	AA	28	27	1	0	152.1	630	144	72	67	14	5	0	7	53	1	118	6	0	10	10	.500	0	0- -	-	3.80	3.96
2015 Biloxi	AA	20	11	0	0	83.0	337	71	20	18	2	6	2	5	33	1	64	0	0	5	3	.625	0	0- -	-	3.12	1.95
2015 ColSpr	AAA	6	6	0	0	35.1	141	35	15	13	4	2	3	0	6	0	19	1	0	3	1	.750	0	0- -	-	3.31	3.31
2016 ColSpr	AAA	26	15	0	2	110.2	453	129	45	43	5	5	3	3	14	0	75	0	0	6	6	.500	0	2- -	-	3.79	3.50
2017 ColSpr	AAA	10	8	0	0	36.2	154	42	18	18	5	2	0	0	8	0	38	1	0	3	1	.750	0	0- -	-	4.51	4.42
2016 Mil	NL	14	2	0	4	21.2	91	25	8	8	3	1	0	1	5	0	15	1	0	2	2	.500	0	0-0	2	4.90	3.32
2017 Mil	NL	22	14	0	1	81.2	341	83	33	31	8	1	1	2	22	2	64	1	0	3	2	.600	0	0-0	2	3.75	3.42
2 ML YEARS		36	16	0	5	103.1	432	108	41	39	11	2	1	3	27	2	79	2	0	5	4	.556	0	0-0	2	3.98	3.40

Ichiro Suzuki

EE-chee-row soo-ZOO-kee

Bats: L Throws: R Pos: PH-109;RF-16;CF-10;LF-9;DH-1;PR-1   **Ht: 5'11" Wt: 175 Born: 10/22/1973 Age: 44**

Year	Team	Lg	G	AB	H	2B	3B	HR	(Hm	Rd)	TB	R	RBI	RC	TBB	IBB	SO	HBP	SH	SF	SB	CS	GDP	Avg	OBP	Slg	OPS
2001	Sea	AL	157	692	242	34	8	8	(5	3)	316	127	69	124	30	10	53	8	4	4	56	14	3	.350	.381	.457	.838
2002	Sea	AL	157	647	208	27	8	8	(4	4)	275	111	51	110	68	27	62	5	3	5	31	15	8	.321	.388	.425	.813
2003	Sea	AL	159	679	212	29	8	13	(8	5)	296	111	62	107	36	7	69	6	3	1	34	8	3	.312	.352	.436	.788
2004	Sea	AL	161	704	262	24	5	8	(4	4)	320	101	60	125	49	19	63	4	2	3	36	11	6	.372	.414	.455	.869
2005	Sea	AL	162	679	206	21	12	15	(8	7)	296	111	68	109	48	23	66	4	2	6	33	8	5	.303	.350	.436	.786
2006	Sea	AL	161	695	224	20	9	9	(6	3)	289	110	49	107	49	16	71	5	1	2	45	2	2	.322	.370	.416	.786
2007	Sea	AL	161	678	238	22	7	6	(3	3)	292	111	68	128	49	13	77	3	4	2	37	8	7	.351	.396	.431	.827
2008	Sea	AL	162	686	213	20	7	6	(3	3)	265	103	42	100	51	12	65	5	3	4	43	4	8	.310	.361	.386	.747
2009	Sea	AL	146	639	225	31	4	11	(6	5)	297	88	46	111	32	15	71	4	2	1	26	9	1	.352	.386	.465	.851
2010	Sea	AL	162	680	214	30	3	6	(1	5)	268	74	43	96	45	13	86	3	3	1	42	9	3	.315	.359	.394	.754
2011	Sea	AL	161	677	184	22	3	5	(4	1)	227	80	47	80	39	13	69	0	1	4	40	7	11	.272	.310	.335	.645
2012	2 Tms		162	629	178	28	6	9	(6	3)	245	77	55	63	22	5	61	2	5	5	29	7	12	.283	.307	.390	.696
2013	NYY	AL	150	520	136	15	3	7	(5	2)	178	57	35	56	26	4	63	1	6	2	20	4	6	.262	.297	.342	.639
2014	NYY	AL	143	359	102	13	2	1	(1	0)	122	42	22	39	21	1	68	1	2	2	15	3	3	.284	.324	.340	.664
2015	Mia	NL	153	398	91	5	6	1	(1	0)	111	45	21	30	31	1	51	0	5	4	11	5	8	.229	.282	.279	.561
2016	Mia	NL	143	327	95	15	5	1	(1	0)	123	48	22	44	30	1	42	3	3	2	10	2	4	.291	.354	.376	.730
2017	Mia	NL	136	196	50	6	0	3	(0	3)	65	19	20	25	17	1	35	1	1	0	1	1	2	.255	.318	.332	.649
	12 Sea	AL	95	402	105	15	5	4	(1	3)	142	49	28	33	17	4	40	0	4	4	15	2	10	.261	.288	.353	.642
	12 NYY	AL	67	227	73	13	1	5	(5	0)	103	28	27	30	5	1	21	2	1	1	14	5	2	.322	.340	.454	.794
	Postseason		19	78	27	4	0	1	(1	0)	34	10	8	11	7	2	9	0	1	0	4	3	0	.346	.400	.436	.836
	17 ML YEARS		2636	9885	3080	362	96	117	(66	51)	3985	1415	780	1454	643	181	1072	55	50	48	509	117	92	.312	.355	.403	.759

Kurt Suzuki

Bats: R Throws: R Pos: C-77;PH-7   **Ht: 5'11" Wt: 205 Born: 10/4/1983 Age: 34**

Year	Team	Lg	G	AB	H	2B	3B	HR	(Hm	Rd)	TB	R	RBI	RC	TBB	IBB	SO	HBP	SH	SF	SB	CS	GDP	Avg	OBP	Slg	OPS
2007	Oak	AL	68	213	53	13	0	7	(4	3)	87	27	39	33	24	0	39	3	3	5	0	0	4	.249	.327	.408	.735
2008	Oak	AL	148	530	148	25	1	7	(5	2)	196	54	42	66	44	2	69	11	2	1	2	3	20	.279	.346	.370	.716
2009	Oak	AL	147	570	156	37	1	15	(8	7)	240	74	88	77	28	0	59	8	1	7	8	2	14	.274	.313	.421	.734
2010	Oak	AL	131	495	120	18	2	13	(8	5)	181	55	71	54	33	3	49	12	0	4	3	2	22	.242	.303	.366	.669
2011	Oak	AL	134	460	109	26	0	14	(8	6)	177	54	44	42	38	1	64	7	3	7	2	2	14	.237	.301	.385	.686
2012	2 Tms		118	408	96	20	0	6	(3	3)	134	36	43	39	20	3	73	5	4	5	2	0	5	.235	.276	.328	.605
2013	2 Tms		94	285	66	13	1	5	(2	3)	96	25	32	34	22	6	35	3	2	4	2	0	2	.232	.290	.337	.627
2014	Min	AL	131	452	130	34	0	3	(1	2)	173	37	61	65	34	0	46	9	1	7	0	1	9	.288	.345	.383	.727
2015	Min	AL	131	433	104	17	0	5	(3	2)	136	36	50	46	29	4	59	7	6	4	0	0	14	.240	.296	.314	.610
2016	Min	AL	106	345	89	24	1	8	(4	4)	139	34	49	45	18	0	48	5	1	4	0	0	9	.258	.301	.403	.704
2017	Atl	NL	81	276	78	13	0	19	(8	11)	148	38	50	49	17	2	39	13	1	2	0	0	5	.283	.351	.536	.887
	12 Oak	AL	75	262	57	15	0	1	(1	0)	75	19	18	16	9	0	53	3	2	1	0	0	3	.218	.250	.286	.536
	12 Was	NL	43	146	39	5	0	5	(2	3)	59	17	25	23	11	3	20	2	2	3	1	0	2	.267	.321	.404	.725
	13 Was	AL	79	252	56	11	1	3	(0	3)	78	19	25	26	20	6	32	3	2	4	2	0	2	.222	.283	.310	.593
	13 Oak	AL	15	33	10	2	0	2	(2	0)	18	6	7	8	2	0	3	0	0	0	0	0	0	.303	.343	.545	.888
	Postseason		5	17	4	0	0	0	(0	0)	4	0	2	2	2	0	4	0	0	0	0	0	0	.235	.316	.235	.551
	11 ML YEARS		1289	4467	1149	240	6	102	(54	48)	1707	470	569	550	307	21	580	83	24	50	19	10	118	.257	.314	.382	.696

Dansby Swanson

Bats: R Throws: R Pos: SS-142;PR-3;PH-2   **Ht: 6'1" Wt: 190 Born: 2/11/1994 Age: 24**

Year	Team	Lg	G	AB	H	2B	3B	HR	(Hm	Rd)	TB	R	RBI	RC	TBB	IBB	SO	HBP	SH	SF	SB	CS	GDP	Avg	OBP	Slg	OPS
2015	Hlsbro	A-	22	83	24	7	3	1	(-	-)	40	19	11	16	14	2	14	1	0	1	0	0	0	.289	.394	.482	.876
2016	Carlina	A+	21	78	26	12	0	1	(-	-)	41	14	10	19	15	2	13	0	0	0	7	1	1	.333	.441	.526	.967
2016	Missi	AA	84	333	87	13	5	8	(-	-)	134	54	45	49	35	2	71	7	0	2	7	2	6	.261	.342	.402	.745
2017	Gwnntt	AAA	11	38	9	1	0	1	(-	-)	13	5	5	5	6	0	9	1	0	0	1	0	1	.237	.356	.342	.698
2016	Atl	NL	38	129	39	7	1	3	(1	2)	57	20	17	17	13	5	34	0	1	2	3	0	2	.302	.361	.442	.803
2017	Atl	NL	144	488	113	23	2	6	(2	4)	158	59	51	55	59	10	120	0	4	4	3	3	7	.232	.312	.324	.636
	2 ML YEARS		182	617	152	30	3	9	(3	6)	215	79	68	72	72	15	154	0	5	6	6	3	9	.246	.322	.348	.671

Anthony Swarzak

SWORE-zack

Pitches: R Bats: R Pos: RP-70   **Ht: 6'4" Wt: 215 Born: 9/10/1985 Age: 32**

Year	Team	Lg	G	GS	CG	GF	IP	BFP	H	R	ER	HR	SH	SF	HB	TBB	IBB	SO	WP	Bk	W	L	Pct	Sh	Sv-Op	Hld	ERC	ERA
2009	Min	AL	12	12	0	0	59.0	268	76	43	41	12	1	1	2	20	0	34	0	0	3	7	.300	0	0-0	0	6.50	6.25
2011	Min	AL	27	11	0	2	102.0	441	111	53	49	9	2	3	6	26	1	55	3	1	4	7	.364	0	0-0	0	4.11	4.32
2012	Min	AL	44	5	0	9	96.2	413	106	57	54	15	3	6	0	31	8	62	3	0	3	6	.333	0	0-1	1	4.63	5.03
2013	Min	AL	48	0	0	8	96.0	387	89	33	31	7	2	5	1	22	1	69	1	0	3	2	.600	0	0-2	3	2.94	2.91
2014	Min	AL	50	4	0	11	86.0	378	100	48	44	5	1	2	0	28	5	47	0	2	3	2	.600	0	0-1	3	4.29	4.60
2015	Cle	AL	10	0	0	0	13.1	61	18	9	8	5	1	0	0	4	1	13	0	0	0	0		0	0-0	0	5.34	3.38
2016	NYY	AL	26	0	0	6	31.0	124	28	19	19	10	0	1	1	7	0	31	1	0	1	2	.333	0	0-1	1	4.51	5.52
2017	2 Tms		70	0	0	6	77.1	303	58	21	20	6	1	3	2	22	2	91	2	0	6	4	.600	0	2-5	27	2.29	2.33
	17 CWS	AL	41	0	0	5	48.1	186	37	12	12	2	0	2	2	13	2	52	2	0	4	3	.571	0	1-3	10	2.06	2.23
	17 Mil	NL	29	0	0	1	29.0	117	21	9	8	4	1	1	2	9	2	39	0	0	2	1	.667	0	1-2	17	2.69	2.48
	8 ML YEARS		287	32	0	45	561.1	2375	586	283	263	65	10	21	12	160	20	402	10	3	23	30	.434	0	2-10	35	4.04	4.22

Blake Swihart

Bats: B Throws: R Pos: C-4;PR-4;DH-1;PH-1 — SWY-hart — Ht: 6'1" Wt: 200 Born: 4/3/1992 Age: 26

							BATTING													RUNNING			AVERAGES			
Year	Team	Lg	G	AB	H	2B	3B	HR	(Hm | Rd)	TB	R	RBI	RC	TBB	IBB	SO	HBP	SH	SF	SB	CS	GDP	Avg	OBP	Slg	OPS
2017	Pwtckt*	AAA	53	195	37	6	1	4	(- | -)	57	22	23	13	13	0	54	2	1	1	1	0	8	.190	.246	.292	.539
2015	Bos	AL	84	288	79	17	1	5	(2 | 3)	113	47	31	34	18	0	77	1	2	0	4	2	8	.274	.319	.392	.712
2016	Bos	AL	19	62	16	0	3	0	(0 | 0)	22	9	5	8	11	0	17	0	0	1	0	1	0	.258	.365	.355	.720
2017	Bos	AL	6	5	1	0	0	0	(0 | 0)	1	1	0	1	2	0	3	0	0	0	0	0	0	.200	.429	.200	.629
	3 ML YEARS		109	355	96	17	4	5	(2 | 3)	136	57	36	43	31	0	97	1	2	1	4	3	8	.270	.330	.383	.713

Noah Syndergaard

Pitches: R Bats: L Pos: SP-7 — sin-DER-gard — Ht: 6'6" Wt: 240 Born: 8/29/1992 Age: 25

			HOW MUCH HE PITCHED					WHAT HE GAVE UP											THE RESULTS						
Year	Team	Lg	G	GS	CG	GF	IP	BFP	H	R	ER	HR	SH	SF	HB	TBB	IBB	SO	WP	Bk	W	L	Pct	Sh	Sv-Op	Hld	ERC	ERA
2015	NYM	NL	24	24	0	0	150.0	603	126	60	54	19	5	3	3	31	2	166	6	0	9	7	.563	0	0-0	0	2.70	3.24
2016	NYM	NL	31	30	0	0	183.2	744	168	61	53	11	3	4	2	43	2	218	10	1	14	9	.609	0	0-0	1	2.79	2.60
2017	NYM	NL	7	7	0	0	30.1	124	29	14	10	0	1	1	1	3	1	34	3	0	1	2	.333	0	0-0	0	2.13	2.97
	Postseason		5	4	0	0	26.0	103	17	7	7	0	1	0	0	11	1	36	1	0	2	1	.667	0	0-0	1	1.75	2.42
	3 ML YEARS		62	61	0	0	364.0	1471	323	135	117	30	9	8	6	77	5	418	19	1	24	18	.571	0	0-0	2	2.70	2.89

Matt Szczur

Bats: R Throws: R Pos: PH-52;LF-49;CF-21;RF-18;PR-2 — SEE-zur — Ht: 6'0" Wt: 200 Born: 7/20/1989 Age: 28

							BATTING													RUNNING			AVERAGES			
Year	Team	Lg	G	AB	H	2B	3B	HR	(Hm	Rd)	TB	R	RBI	RC	TBB	IBB	SO	HBP	SH	SF	SB	CS	GDP	Avg	OBP	Slg	OPS
2014	ChC	NL	33	62	14	2	0	1	(1	1)	22	6	5	7	4	0	11	0	0	0	0	0	1	.226	.273	.355	.628
2015	ChC	NL	47	72	16	5	0	1	(1	0)	24	5	8	6	6	0	15	0	1	1	2	0	1	.222	.278	.333	.612
2016	ChC	NL	107	185	48	9	1	5	(4	1)	74	30	24	20	13	2	39	1	1	0	2	4	2	.259	.312	.400	.712
2017	2 Tms	NL	119	195	44	12	2	3	(2	1)	69	28	18	27	34	4	44	4	3	1	0	2	2	.226	.350	.354	.704
17	ChC	NL	15	19	4	1	0	0	(0	0)	5	2	3	3	2	0	4	0	1	1	0	0	0	.211	.273	.263	.536
17	SD	NL	104	176	40	11	2	3	(2	1)	64	26	15	24	32	0	40	4	2	0	0	2	2	.227	.358	.364	.722
	4 ML YEARS		306	514	122	28	3	11	(8	3)	189	69	55	60	57	2	109	5	5	2	4	6	6	.237	.318	.368	.686

Travis Taijeron

Bats: R Throws: R Pos: RF-15;PH-11 — TIE-rohn — Ht: 6'2" Wt: 224 Born: 1/20/1989 Age: 29

							BATTING													RUNNING			AVERAGES			
Year	Team	Lg	G	AB	H	2B	3B	HR	(Hm	Rd)	TB	R	RBI	RC	TBB	IBB	SO	HBP	SH	SF	SB	CS	GDP	Avg	OBP	Slg	OPS
2013	Stluci	A+	55	188	57	20	1	9	(-	-)	106	33	27	42	23	0	54	8	0	3	1	1	2	.303	.396	.564	.960
2013	Bnghtn	AA	65	232	57	18	0	14	(-	-)	117	33	42	38	24	0	77	3	0	2	0	0	1	.246	.322	.504	.826
2014	Bnghtn	AA	101	330	82	30	0	15	(-	-)	157	57	64	57	48	0	107	8	0	1	1	3	7	.248	.357	.476	.832
2015	LsVgs	AAA	127	394	108	22	3	25	(-	-)	211	67	71	85	65	2	147	15	0	4	2	2	6	.274	.393	.536	.929
2016	LsVgs	AAA	129	459	126	42	5	19	(-	-)	235	86	88	89	67	0	166	8	0	7	1	3	6	.275	.372	.512	.884
2017	LsVgs	AAA	125	448	122	32	3	25	(-	-)	235	75	78	92	70	0	146	12	0	3	2	1	14	.272	.383	.525	.907
2017	NYM	NL	26	52	9	2	0	1	(1	0)	14	3	3	5	5	0	24	2	0	0	0	0	1	.173	.271	.269	.540

Jameson Taillon

Pitches: R Bats: R Pos: SP-25 — TIE-yohn — Ht: 6'5" Wt: 225 Born: 11/18/1991 Age: 26

			HOW MUCH HE PITCHED					WHAT HE GAVE UP											THE RESULTS						
Year	Team	Lg	G	GS	CG	GF	IP	BFP	H	R	ER	HR	SH	SF	HB	TBB	IBB	SO	WP	Bk	W	L	Pct	Sh	Sv-Op	Hld	ERC	ERA
2013	Altna	AA	20	19	0	0	110.1	478	112	54	45	8	0	2	5	36	0	106	6	0	4	7	.364	0	0- -	-	3.82	3.67
2013	Indy	AAA	6	6	0	0	37.0	162	31	16	16	1	2	1	4	16	3	37	3	0	1	3	.250	0	0- -	-	3.01	3.89
2016	Indy	AAA	10	10	0	0	61.2	236	44	14	14	2	2	3	1	6	0	61	1	0	4	2	.667	0	0- -	-	1.37	2.04
2016	Pit	NL	18	18	0	0	104.0	418	99	40	39	13	4	1	3	17	1	85	1	2	5	4	.556	0	0-0	0	3.21	3.38
2017	Pit	NL	25	25	0	0	133.2	587	152	69	66	11	8	4	4	46	3	125	7	0	8	7	.533	0	0-0	0	4.61	4.44
	2 ML YEARS		43	43	0	0	237.2	1005	251	109	105	24	12	5	7	63	4	210	8	2	13	11	.542	0	0-0	0	3.99	3.98

Masahiro Tanaka

Pitches: R Bats: R Pos: SP-30 — mah-sah-HEE-roh tuh-NAH-kah — Ht: 6'3" Wt: 215 Born: 11/1/1988 Age: 29

			HOW MUCH HE PITCHED					WHAT HE GAVE UP											THE RESULTS						
Year	Team	Lg	G	GS	CG	GF	IP	BFP	H	R	ER	HR	SH	SF	HB	TBB	IBB	SO	WP	Bk	W	L	Pct	Sh	Sv-Op	Hld	ERC	ERA
2014	NYY	AL	20	20	3	0	136.1	542	123	47	42	15	2	3	4	21	0	141	4	0	13	5	.722	1	0-0	0	2.83	2.77
2015	NYY	AL	24	24	1	0	154.0	609	126	66	60	25	1	8	1	27	0	139	4	0	12	7	.632	0	0-0	0	2.65	3.51
2016	NYY	AL	31	31	0	0	199.2	805	179	75	68	22	4	3	3	36	0	165	7	0	14	4	.778	0	0-0	0	2.80	3.07
2017	NYY	AL	30	30	1	0	178.1	752	180	100	94	35	1	2	7	41	1	194	7	0	13	12	.520	1	0-0	0	4.23	4.74
	Postseason		1	1	0	0	5.0	21	4	2	2	2	0	0	0	3	0	3	0	0	0	1	.000	0	0-0	0	6.06	3.60
	4 ML YEARS		105	105	5	0	668.1	2708	608	288	264	97	8	16	15	125	1	639	22	0	52	28	.650	2	0-0	0	3.14	3.56

Raimel Tapia

Bats: L Throws: L Pos: PH-28;RF-22;LF-18;CF-6;PR-4;DH-1 — rye-MELL — Ht: 6'2" Wt: 160 Born: 2/4/1994 Age: 24

							BATTING													RUNNING			AVERAGES			
Year	Team	Lg	G	AB	H	2B	3B	HR	(Hm	Rd)	TB	R	RBI	RC	TBB	IBB	SO	HBP	SH	SF	SB	CS	GDP	Avg	OBP	Slg	OPS
2013	GdJunc	R+	66	258	92	20	6	7	(-	-)	145	53	47	54	15	2	31	5	5	3	10	9	4	.357	.399	.562	.961
2014	Ashvll	A	122	481	157	32	1	9	(-	-)	218	93	72	85	35	2	90	11	8	4	33	16	5	.326	.382	.453	.836
2015	Mdest	A+	131	544	166	34	9	12	(-	-)	254	74	71	87	24	3	105	5	7	13	26	10	6	.305	.333	.467	.800
2016	Hrtfrd	AA	104	424	137	20	5	8	(-	-)	191	79	34	68	25	2	49	3	2	3	17	14	7	.323	.363	.450	.813
2016	Albq	AAA	24	104	36	5	5	0	(-	-)	51	14	14	18	2	0	12	1	0	3	6	3	2	.346	.355	.490	.845

Year	Team	Lg	G	AB	H	2B	3B	HR	(Hm	Rd)	TB	R	RBI	RC	TBB	IBB	SO	HBP	SH	SF	SB	CS	GDP	Avg	OBP	Slg	OPS
2017	Albq	AAA	58	263	97	20	8	2	(-	-)	139	45	30	54	13	1	42	0	0	1	12	2	1	.369	.397	.529	.926
2016	Col	NL	22	38	10	0	0	0	(0	0)	10	4	3	5	2	0	11	0	0	1	3	0	0	.263	.293	.263	.556
2017	Col	NL	70	160	46	12	2	2	(1	1)	68	27	16	20	8	1	36	2	1	0	5	2	3	.288	.329	.425	.754
2 ML YEARS			92	198	56	12	2	2	(1	1)	78	31	19	25	10	1	47	2	1	1	8	2	3	.283	.322	.394	.716

Mike Tauchman

Bats: L Throws: L Pos: PH-19;PR-6;LF-3;CF-3;RF-3 **Ht:** 6'2" **Wt:** 200 **Born:** 12/3/1990 **Age:** 27

Year	Team	Lg	G	AB	H	2B	3B	HR	(Hm	Rd)	TB	R	RBI	RC	TBB	IBB	SO	HBP	SH	SF	SB	CS	GDP	Avg	OBP	Slg	OPS
2013	TriCity	A-	64	236	70	13	3	0	(-	-)	89	38	23	39	33	1	55	3	1	1	20	7	4	.297	.388	.377	.765
2014	2 Tms	Low	60	222	65	12	4	4	(-	-)	97	38	22	40	33	1	43	1	0	2	15	3	4	.293	.384	.437	.821
2015	NwBrit	AA	131	507	149	23	6	3	(-	-)	193	62	43	72	47	2	69	2	5	2	25	13	8	.294	.355	.381	.736
2016	Albq	AAA	129	475	136	24	7	1	(-	-)	177	72	51	64	40	2	77	2	6	4	23	10	6	.286	.342	.373	.714
2017	Albq	AAA	110	420	139	30	8	16	(-	-)	233	82	80	90	40	3	73	4	1	10	16	7	8	.331	.386	.555	.941
2017	Col	NL	31	27	6	0	1	0	(0	0)	8	2	2	2	5	0	10	0	0	0	1	2	1	.222	.344	.296	.640

Ben Taylor

Pitches: R Bats: R Pos: RP-14 **Ht:** 6'3" **Wt:** 225 **Born:** 11/12/1992 **Age:** 25

			HOW MUCH HE PITCHED						WHAT HE GAVE UP										THE RESULTS						
Year	Team	Lg	G	GS	CG	GF	IP	BFP	H	R	ER	HR	SH	SF	HB	TBB	IBB	SO	WP	Bk	W	L	Pct	Sh	Sv-Op	Hld	ERC	ERA
2015	2 Tms	Low	14	10	0	0	55.0	231	51	25	19	2	2	2	2	17	0	54	3	0	0	2	.000	0	0- -	-	3.03	3.11
2016	Salem	A+	15	3	0	5	45.0	179	35	14	13	0	1	1	3	10	0	56	4	0	0	2	.000	0	3- -	-	1.93	2.60
2016	Portlnd	AA	21	0	0	14	34.0	139	28	13	13	4	0	0	1	12	0	42	1	0	1	0	1.000	0	5- -	-	3.21	3.44
2017	Pwtckt	AAA	12	0	0	5	13.1	51	7	4	4	2	1	0	0	5	0	12	0	0	0	0	-	0	2- -	-	1.90	2.70
2017	Bos	AL	14	0	0	3	17.1	80	20	10	10	3	0	0	0	9	0	18	1	0	0	1	.000	0	1-1	1	5.97	5.19

Chris Taylor

Bats: R Throws: R Pos: CF-49;LF-48;2B-22;SS-14;PH-13;3B-8 **Ht:** 6'1" **Wt:** 195 **Born:** 8/29/1990 **Age:** 27

Year	Team	Lg	G	AB	H	2B	3B	HR	(Hm	Rd)	TB	R	RBI	RC	TBB	IBB	SO	HBP	SH	SF	SB	CS	GDP	Avg	OBP	Slg	OPS
2017	OkCity*	AAA	10	43	10	2	2	1	(-	-)	19	8	5	6	5	0	5	1	0	0	1	2	3	.233	.327	.442	.768
2014	Sea	AL	47	136	39	8	0	0	(0	0)	47	16	9	18	11	0	39	2	1	1	5	2	3	.287	.347	.346	.692
2015	Sea	AL	37	94	16	3	1	0	(0	0)	21	9	1	1	6	0	31	0	2	0	3	2	0	.170	.220	.223	.443
2016	2 Tms		36	61	13	2	2	1	(0	1)	22	8	7	5	4	1	15	0	0	0	0	0	3	.213	.262	.361	.622
2017	LAD	NL	140	514	148	34	5	21	(7	14)	255	85	72	88	50	0	142	3	0	1	17	4	2	.288	.354	.496	.850
16	Sea	AL	2	3	1	0	0	0	(0	0)	1	0	0	0	0	0	2	0	0	0	0	0	0	.333	.333	.333	.667
16	LAD	NL	34	58	12	2	2	1	(0	1)	21	8	7	5	4	1	13	0	0	0	0	0	3	.207	.258	.362	.620
4 ML YEARS			260	805	216	47	8	22	(7	15)	345	118	89	112	71	1	227	5	3	2	25	8	8	.268	.331	.429	.759

Michael A. Taylor

Bats: R Throws: R Pos: CF-111;PH-6;RF-2;PR-1 **Ht:** 6'3" **Wt:** 210 **Born:** 3/26/1991 **Age:** 27

Year	Team	Lg	G	AB	H	2B	3B	HR	(Hm	Rd)	TB	R	RBI	RC	TBB	IBB	SO	HBP	SH	SF	SB	CS	GDP	Avg	OBP	Slg	OPS
2014	Was	NL	17	39	8	3	0	1	(Hm	Rd)	14	5	5	3	3	0	17	1	0	0	2	1	1	.205	.279	.359	.638
2015	Was	NL	138	472	108	15	2	14	(6	8)	169	49	63	60	35	9	158	1	1	2	16	3	5	.229	.282	.358	.640
2016	Was	NL	76	221	51	11	0	7	(1	6)	83	28	16	20	14	0	77	1	0	1	14	3	2	.231	.278	.376	.654
2017	Was	NL	118	399	108	23	3	19	(11	8)	194	55	53	57	29	3	137	1	1	2	17	7	3	.271	.320	.486	.806
Postseason			3	2	0	0	0	0	(0	0)	0	0	0	0	0	0	2	0	0	0	0	0	0	.000	.000	.000	.000
4 ML YEARS			349	1131	275	52	5	41	(18	23)	460	137	137	140	81	12	389	4	2	5	47	15	11	.243	.295	.407	.702

Junichi Tazawa

Pitches: R Bats: R Pos: RP-55 joo-NEE-chee tah-ZAH-wah **Ht:** 5'11" **Wt:** 200 **Born:** 6/6/1986 **Age:** 32

			HOW MUCH HE PITCHED						WHAT HE GAVE UP										THE RESULTS						
Year	Team	Lg	G	GS	CG	GF	IP	BFP	H	R	ER	HR	SH	SF	HB	TBB	IBB	SO	WP	Bk	W	L	Pct	Sh	Sv-Op	Hld	ERC	ERA
2009	Bos	AL	6	4	0	1	25.1	130	43	23	21	4	0	3	3	9	0	13	0	0	2	3	.400	0	0-0	0	9.14	7.46
2011	Bos	AL	3	0	0	2	3.0	13	3	2	2	1	0	0	0	1	0	4	0	0	0	0	-	0	0-0	0	5.31	6.00
2012	Bos	AL	37	0	0	13	44.0	172	37	7	7	1	1	1	2	5	0	45	0	0	1	1	.500	0	1-1	5	1.94	1.43
2013	Bos	AL	71	0	0	10	68.1	284	70	25	24	9	2	5	1	12	1	72	3	1	5	4	.556	0	0-8	25	3.55	3.16
2014	Bos	AL	71	0	0	14	63.0	261	58	23	20	5	1	1	0	17	1	64	5	0	4	3	.571	0	0-5	16	2.97	2.86
2015	Bos	AL	61	0	0	13	58.2	247	65	28	27	5	0	1	1	13	1	56	9	1	2	7	.222	0	3-10	16	3.96	4.14
2016	Bos	AL	53	0	0	5	49.2	208	47	23	23	9	0	1	1	14	1	54	4	0	3	2	.600	0	0-2	16	3.89	4.17
2017	Mia	NL	55	0	0	8	55.1	238	55	35	35	8	2	1	2	22	4	38	2	0	3	5	.375	0	0-3	9	4.42	5.69
Postseason			13	0	0	0	7.1	26	6	1	1	0	0	0	0	1	0	6	1	0	1	0	1.000	0	0-0	6	1.84	1.23
8 ML YEARS			357	4	0	64	367.1	1553	378	166	159	42	6	13	10	93	8	346	23	2	20	25	.444	0	4-29	87	3.83	3.90

Julio Teheran

Pitches: R Bats: R Pos: SP-32 tay-RAHN **Ht:** 6'2" **Wt:** 205 **Born:** 1/27/1991 **Age:** 27

			HOW MUCH HE PITCHED						WHAT HE GAVE UP										THE RESULTS						
Year	Team	Lg	G	GS	CG	GF	IP	BFP	H	R	ER	HR	SH	SF	HB	TBB	IBB	SO	WP	Bk	W	L	Pct	Sh	Sv-Op	Hld	ERC	ERA
2011	Atl	NL	5	5	0	0	19.2	87	21	11	11	4	2	1	0	8	0	10	1	0	1	1	.500	0	0-0	0	5.19	5.03
2012	Atl	NL	2	1	0	0	6.1	24	5	4	4	0	0	0	0	1	0	5	0	0	0	0	-	0	0-0	0	1.64	5.68
2013	Atl	NL	30	30	0	0	185.2	774	173	69	66	22	8	5	13	45	4	170	2	0	14	8	.636	0	0-0	0	3.45	3.20
2014	Atl	NL	33	33	4	0	221.0	884	188	82	71	22	13	4	4	51	4	186	1	1	14	13	.519	2	0-0	0	2.71	2.89

Year	Team	Lg	G	GS	CG	GF	IP	BFP	H	R	ER	HR	SH	SF	HB	TBB	IBB	SO	WP	Bk	W	L	Pct	Sh	Sv-Op	Hld	ERC	ERA
2015	Atl	NL	33	33	0	0	200.2	843	189	99	90	27	10	3	9	73	3	171	2	0	11	8	.579	0	0-0	0	4.07	4.04
2016	Atl	NL	30	30	1	0	188.0	758	157	70	67	22	4	1	9	41	2	167	7	1	7	10	.412	1	0-0	0	2.79	3.21
2017	Atl	NL	32	32	0	0	188.1	812	186	103	94	31	7	3	7	72	3	151	6	0	11	13	.458	0	0-0	0	4.52	4.49
	Postseason		1	1	0	0	2.2	17	8	6	6	1	0	1	0	1	0	5	1	0	0	1	.000	0	0-0	0	20.77	20.25
	7 ML YEARS		165	162	5	0	1009.2	4182	919	438	403	128	44	17	42	291	16	860	19	2	58	53	.523	3	0-0	0	3.49	3.59

Ruben Tejada

Bats: R Throws: R Pos: SS-36;3B-6;2B-4;PH-1   Ht: 5'11" Wt: 200 Born: 10/27/1989 Age: 28

Year	Team	Lg	G	AB	H	2B	3B	HR	(Hm	Rd)	TB	R	RBI	RC	TBB	IBB	SO	HBP	SH	SF	SB	CS	GDP	Avg	OBP	Slg	OPS
2017	S-WB*	AAA	37	130	35	7	0	6	(-	-)	60	22	21	21	15	0	17	1	0	2	0	2	4	.269	.345	.462	.806
2017	Norfolk*	AAA	13	45	14	3	0	0	(-	-)	17	9	2	7	4	0	4	2	0	0	0	0	1	.311	.392	.378	.770
2010	NYM	NL	78	216	46	12	0	1	(0	1)	61	28	15	16	22	3	38	8	6	3	2	2	2	.213	.305	.282	.588
2011	NYM	NL	96	328	93	15	1	0	(0	0)	110	31	36	41	35	3	50	6	4	3	5	1	6	.284	.360	.335	.696
2012	NYM	NL	114	464	134	26	0	1	(0	1)	163	53	25	49	27	0	73	5	3	2	4	4	9	.289	.333	.351	.685
2013	NYM	NL	57	208	42	12	0	0	(0	0)	54	20	10	15	15	0	24	1	3	0	2	1	3	.202	.259	.260	.519
2014	NYM	NL	119	355	84	11	0	5	(1	4)	110	30	34	42	50	11	73	8	4	2	1	2	8	.237	.342	.310	.652
2015	NYM	NL	116	360	94	23	0	3	(2	1)	126	36	28	42	38	5	70	5	2	2	2	1	6	.261	.338	.350	.688
2016	2 Tms	NL	36	66	11	5	0	0	(0	0)	16	9	5	2	7	0	13	1	1	3	0	0	1	.167	.247	.242	.489
2017	Bal	AL	41	113	26	6	0	0	(0	0)	32	17	5	5	8	0	15	2	1	0	0	0	6	.230	.293	.283	.576
16	StL	NL	23	34	6	2	0	0	(0	0)	8	6	3	0	2	0	8	1	0	3	0	0	1	.176	.225	.235	.460
16	SF	NL	13	32	5	3	0	0	(0	0)	8	3	2	2	5	0	5	0	1	0	0	0	0	.156	.270	.250	.520
	Postseason		2	5	0	0	0	0	(0	0)	0	1	0	0	1	0	5	0	0	0	0	0	0	.000	.167	.000	.167
	8 ML YEARS		657	2110	530	110	1	10	(3	7)	672	224	158	212	202	22	356	36	24	15	16	11	41	.251	.325	.318	.643

Tomas Telis

Bats: B Throws: R Pos: 1B-28;PH-21;C-6   TOH-mahs tay-LEES   Ht: 5'8" Wt: 220 Born: 6/18/1991 Age: 27

Year	Team	Lg	G	AB	H	2B	3B	HR	(Hm	Rd)	TB	R	RBI	RC	TBB	IBB	SO	HBP	SH	SF	SB	CS	GDP	Avg	OBP	Slg	OPS
2017	NewOr*	AAA	73	280	78	14	2	5	(-	-)	111	39	34	38	18	0	29	3	2	3	5	0	7	.279	.326	.396	.722
2014	Tex	AL	18	68	17	2	0	0	(0	0)	19	7	8	7	1	0	10	1	1	0	0	0	0	.250	.271	.279	.551
2015	2 Tms		23	38	6	0	0	0	(0	0)	6	2	2	1	1	1	4	2	0	0	0	0	2	.158	.220	.158	.377
2016	Mia	NL	10	13	4	0	0	1	(0	1)	7	1	4	3	0	0	2	0	0	0	0	0	0	.308	.308	.538	.846
2017	Mia	NL	48	104	25	5	3	0	(0	0)	36	13	9	8	3	0	10	3	0	1	0	0	1	.240	.279	.346	.625
15	Tex	AL	6	11	2	0	0	0	(0	0)	2	1	2	1	0	0	1	1	0	0	0	0	0	.182	.250	.182	.432
15	Mia	NL	17	27	4	0	0	0	(0	0)	4	1	0	1	1	1	3	1	0	0	0	0	2	.148	.207	.148	.355
	4 ML YEARS		99	223	52	7	3	1	(0	1)	68	23	23	19	5	1	26	6	1	1	0	0	5	.233	.268	.305	.573

Ryan Tepera

Pitches: R Bats: R Pos: RP-73   tuh-PAIR-uh   Ht: 6'2" Wt: 195 Born: 11/3/1987 Age: 30

Year	Team	Lg	G	GS	CG	GF	IP	BFP	H	R	ER	HR	SH	SF	HB	TBB	IBB	SO	WP	Bk	W	L	Pct	Sh	Sv-Op	Hld	ERC	ERA
2015	Tor	AL	32	0	0	12	33.0	128	23	14	12	8	0	0	3	6	0	22	2	0	0	2	.000	0	1-1	0	2.87	3.27
2016	Tor	AL	20	0	0	13	18.1	85	17	8	6	1	1	4	0	8	1	18	3	0	1	0	1.000	0	0-0	0	3.81	2.95
2017	Tor	AL	73	0	0	12	77.2	319	57	35	31	7	1	1	8	31	4	81	5	0	7	1	.875	0	2-4	17	2.94	3.59
	Postseason		2	0	0	1	2.1	14	5	4	4	0	0	3	0	2	0	1	0	0	0	0	-	0	0-0	0	12.37	15.43
	3 ML YEARS		125	0	0	37	129.0	532	97	57	49	16	2	1	14	45	5	121	10	0	7	4	.636	0	3-5	17	3.07	3.42

Nick Tepesch

Pitches: R Bats: R Pos: SP-4   TEPP-esh   Ht: 6'4" Wt: 240 Born: 10/12/1988 Age: 29

Year	Team	Lg	G	GS	CG	GF	IP	BFP	H	R	ER	HR	SH	SF	HB	TBB	IBB	SO	WP	Bk	W	L	Pct	Sh	Sv-Op	Hld	ERC	ERA
2017	Roch*	AAA	6	5	0	0	29.0	131	36	24	18	6	1	1	1	9	1	27	0	0	1	3	.250	0	0- --	-	5.97	5.59
2013	Tex	AL	19	17	0	1	93.0	407	100	53	50	12	1	4	7	27	3	76	0	0	4	6	.400	0	0-0	0	4.49	4.84
2014	Tex	AL	23	22	0	1	126.0	537	128	66	61	15	3	4	7	44	2	56	1	0	5	11	.313	0	0-0	0	4.37	4.36
2016	LAD	NL	1	1	0	0	4.0	19	7	5	5	1	0	0	0	0	0	3	0	0	0	1	.000	0	0-0	0	7.95	11.25
2017	2 Tms	AL	4	4	0	0	15.2	80	22	15	9	6	1	0	3	9	1	9	0	0	1	2	.333	0	0-0	0	10.52	5.17
17	Min	AL	1	1	0	0	1.2	13	5	7	1	1	0	0	0	2	0	2	0	0	1	0	1.000	0	0-0	0	26.04	5.40
17	Tor	AL	3	3	0	0	14.0	67	17	8	8	5	1	0	3	7	1	7	0	0	1	1	.500	0	0-0	0	8.83	5.14
	4 ML YEARS		47	44	0	2	238.2	1043	257	139	125	34	5	8	17	80	6	144	1	0	10	20	.333	0	0-0	0	4.83	4.71

Eric Thames

Bats: L Throws: R Pos: 1B-108;LF-25;PH-13;RF-5;DH-2   thayms   Ht: 6'0" Wt: 210 Born: 11/10/1986 Age: 31

Year	Team	Lg	G	AB	H	2B	3B	HR	(Hm	Rd)	TB	R	RBI	RC	TBB	IBB	SO	HBP	SH	SF	SB	CS	GDP	Avg	OBP	Slg	OPS
2011	Tor	AL	95	362	95	24	5	12	(10	2)	165	58	37	42	23	0	88	5	1	3	2	1	7	.262	.313	.456	.769
2012	2 Tms	AL	86	271	63	12	3	9	(6	3)	108	27	25	25	15	0	87	1	1	2	1	1	7	.232	.273	.399	.672
2017	Mil	NL	138	469	116	26	4	31	(20	11)	243	83	63	77	75	5	163	7	0	0	4	2	6	.247	.359	.518	.877
12	Tor	AL	46	148	36	7	1	3	(1	2)	54	17	11	13	9	0	40	1	0	2	0	1	7	.243	.288	.365	.652
12	Sea	AL	40	123	27	5	2	6	(5	1)	54	10	14	12	6	0	47	0	1	0	1	0	0	.220	.256	.439	.695
	3 ML YEARS		319	1102	274	62	12	52	(36	16)	516	168	125	144	113	5	338	13	2	5	7	4	20	.249	.324	.468	.793

Jesen Therrien

Pitches: R Bats: R Pos: RP-15

TAIR-en

Ht: 6'2" Wt: 200 Born: 3/18/1993 Age: 25

Year	Team	Lg	G	GS	CG	GF	IP	BFP	H	R	ER	HR	SH	SF	HB	TBB	IBB	SO	WP	Bk	W	L	Pct	Sh	Sv-Op	Hld	ERC	ERA
2013	Phillies	R	11	6	0	1	38.0	177	42	32	23	4	2	1	7	15	0	26	1	0	2	3	.400	0	0- -		5.35	5.45
2014	2 Tms	Low	35	1	0	9	71.0	321	72	47	44	4	4	3	5	30	0	54	6	0	4	1	.800	0	3- -		4.08	5.58
2015	2 Tms	Low	39	0	0	15	63.0	255	50	14	10	1	5	0	4	17	4	54	10	1	5	0	1.000	0	5- -		2.14	1.43
2016	2 Tms	Low	28	0	0	15	38.2	166	25	16	9	3	1	2	1	22	1	54	3	0	2	2	.500	0	4- -		2.64	2.09
2016	Rdng	AA	11	0	0	3	17.0	72	20	7	7	2	0	0	0	5	0	22	1	0	1	1	.500	0	0- -		4.96	3.71
2017	Rdng	AA	21	0	0	13	28.2	99	14	5	4	1	2	0	0	3	0	39	0	0	2	1	.667	0	7- -		0.80	1.26
2017	LV	AAA	18	0	0	7	28.2	117	25	7	5	2	1	0	0	6	0	26	1	0	0	0	-	0	2- -		2.45	1.57
2017	Phi	NL	15	0	0	1	18.1	86	24	17	17	5	0	0	1	7	0	10	0	0	0	0	-	0	0-1	0	7.39	8.35

Jake Thompson

Pitches: R Bats: R Pos: SP-8; RP-3

Ht: 6'4" Wt: 225 Born: 1/31/1994 Age: 24

Year	Team	Lg	G	GS	CG	GF	IP	BFP	H	R	ER	HR	SH	SF	HB	TBB	IBB	SO	WP	Bk	W	L	Pct	Sh	Sv-Op	Hld	ERC	ERA
2013	Wmich	A	17	16	0	0	83.1	370	79	36	29	4	2	0	11	32	0	91	4	0	3	3	.500	0	0- -	-	3.79	3.13
2014	Lkland	A+	16	16	0	0	83.0	342	75	31	29	3	1	1	7	25	0	79	4	1	6	4	.600	0	0- -	-	3.14	3.14
2014	Frisco	AA	7	6	0	0	35.2	148	28	13	13	3	0	1	1	18	0	44	1	0	3	1	.750	0	0- -	-	3.39	3.28
2015	Frisco	AA	17	17	1	0	87.2	386	94	51	46	7	3	0	7	30	0	78	5	0	6	6	.500	0	0- -	-	4.42	4.72
2015	Rdng	AA	7	7	0	0	45.0	166	33	9	9	3	1	1	0	12	0	34	2	0	5	1	.833	0	0- -	-	2.20	1.80
2016	LV	AAA	21	21	0	0	129.2	517	105	44	36	10	4	3	6	37	1	87	5	0	11	5	.688	0	0- -	-	2.72	2.50
2017	LV	AAA	22	22	0	0	118.1	527	136	83	69	12	8	3	5	47	1	90	9	0	5	14	.263	0	0- -	-	5.04	5.25
2016	Phi	NL	10	10	0	0	53.2	237	53	34	34	10	2	3	4	28	1	32	4	0	3	6	.333	0	0-0	0	5.51	5.70
2017	Phi	NL	11	8	0	1	46.1	210	50	27	20	9	0	2	5	22	0	35	1	0	3	2	.600	0	0-0	0	6.06	3.88
	2 ML YEARS		21	18	0	1	100.0	447	103	61	54	19	2	5	9	50	1	67	5	0	6	8	.429	0	0-0	0	5.77	4.86

Trayce Thompson

Bats: R Throws: R Pos: CF-9;RF-8;LF-7;PH-7;PR-2

Ht: 6'3" Wt: 217 Born: 3/15/1991 Age: 27

Year	Team	Lg	G	AB	H	2B	3B	HR	(Hm	Rd)	TB	R	RBI	RC	TBB	IBB	SO	HBP	SH	SF	SB	CS	GDP	Avg	OBP	Slg	OPS
2017	OkCity*	AAA	95	339	72	12	6	9	(-	-)	123	44	33	32	26	1	93	1	1	2	3	5	6	.212	.269	.363	.632
2015	CWS	AL	44	122	36	8	3	5	(3	2)	65	17	16	20	13	0	26	0	0	0	1	0	3	.295	.363	.533	.896
2016	LAD	NL	80	236	53	11	0	13	(9	4)	103	31	32	26	26	0	66	0	0	0	5	1	3	.225	.302	.436	.738
2017	LAD	NL	27	49	6	2	1	1	(0	1)	13	6	2	1	6	1	23	0	0	0	0	0	0	.122	.218	.265	.483
	3 ML YEARS		151	407	95	21	4	19	(12	7)	181	54	50	47	45	1	115	0	0	0	6	1	6	.233	.310	.445	.754

Tyler Thornburg

Pitches: R Bats: R Pos: P

Ht: 5'11" Wt: 190 Born: 9/29/1988 Age: 29

Year	Team	Lg	G	GS	CG	GF	IP	BFP	H	R	ER	HR	SH	SF	HB	TBB	IBB	SO	WP	Bk	W	L	Pct	Sh	Sv-Op	Hld	ERC	ERA
2012	Mil	NL	8	3	0	3	22.0	95	24	11	11	8	1	0	1	7	0	20	1	0	0	0	-	0	0-0	0	6.44	4.50
2013	Mil	NL	18	7	0	4	66.2	270	53	17	15	1	4	1	3	26	2	48	2	1	3	1	.750	0	0-0	0	2.59	2.03
2014	Mil	NL	27	0	0	4	29.2	131	24	14	14	1	1	1	0	21	0	28	4	0	3	1	.750	0	0-0	5	3.71	4.25
2015	Mil	NL	24	0	0	9	34.1	151	31	22	14	7	0	2	3	12	1	34	3	1	0	2	.000	0	0-0	1	4.20	3.67
2016	Mil	NL	67	0	0	23	67.0	263	38	19	16	6	0	1	2	25	1	90	4	0	8	5	.615	0	13-21	26	1.82	2.15
	5 ML YEARS		144	10	0	43	219.2	910	170	83	70	23	6	5	9	91	4	220	14	2	14	9	.609	0	13-21	26	3.08	2.87

Chris Tillman

Pitches: R Bats: R Pos: SP-19; RP-5

Ht: 6'5" Wt: 200 Born: 4/15/1988 Age: 30

Year	Team	Lg	G	GS	CG	GF	IP	BFP	H	R	ER	HR	SH	SF	HB	TBB	IBB	SO	WP	Bk	W	L	Pct	Sh	Sv-Op	Hld	ERC	ERA
2009	Bal	AL	12	12	0	0	65.0	285	77	40	39	15	0	0	2	24	1	39	4	0	2	5	.286	0	0-0	0	6.28	5.40
2010	Bal	AL	11	11	0	0	53.2	236	51	37	35	9	1	3	1	31	1	31	2	0	2	5	.286	0	0-0	0	5.12	5.87
2011	Bal	AL	13	13	0	0	62.0	287	77	41	38	5	1	1	4	25	0	46	1	1	3	5	.375	0	0-0	0	5.58	5.52
2012	Bal	AL	15	15	0	0	86.0	347	66	38	28	12	1	2	1	24	0	66	5	0	9	3	.750	0	0-0	0	2.65	2.93
2013	Bal	AL	33	33	1	0	206.1	845	184	87	85	33	4	6	3	68	2	179	6	1	16	7	.696	0	0-0	0	3.72	3.71
2014	Bal	AL	34	34	1	0	207.1	871	189	83	77	21	1	5	4	66	1	150	8	0	13	6	.684	1	0-0	0	3.33	3.34
2015	Bal	AL	31	31	0	0	173.0	741	176	97	96	20	3	8	5	64	1	120	4	0	11	11	.500	0	0-0	0	4.32	4.99
2016	Bal	AL	30	30	0	0	172.0	715	155	73	72	19	2	4	7	66	1	140	9	0	16	6	.727	0	0-0	0	3.78	3.77
2017	Bal	AL	24	19	0	1	93.0	444	125	86	81	24	1	2	4	51	0	63	11	0	1	7	.125	0	0-0	0	8.43	7.84
	Postseason		3	3	0	0	13.2	60	15	9	9	4	0	0	0	4	0	13	0	0	1	0	1.000	0	0-0	0	5.44	5.93
	9 ML YEARS		203	198	2	1	1118.1	4771	1100	582	551	158	14	31	31	419	7	834	50	2	73	55	.570	1	0-0	0	4.31	4.43

Andrew Toles

Bats: L Throws: R Pos: LF-21;CF-10;PH-10

Ht: 5'9" Wt: 192 Born: 5/24/1992 Age: 26

Year	Team	Lg	G	AB	H	2B	3B	HR	(Hm	Rd)	TB	R	RBI	RC	TBB	IBB	SO	HBP	SH	SF	SB	CS	GDP	Avg	OBP	Slg	OPS
2013	BG	A	121	519	169	35	16	2	(-	-)	242	79	57	91	22	1	105	7	1	3	62	17	6	.326	.359	.466	.826
2014	2 Tms	Low	52	223	59	10	2	1	(-	-)	76	32	15	25	12	0	37	2	3	3	24	10	7	.265	.304	.341	.645
2016	Rcuca	A+	22	92	34	8	2	0	(-	-)	46	22	9	19	6	0	13	1	1	0	9	3	1	.370	.414	.500	.914
2016	Tulsa	AA	43	175	55	14	3	5	(-	-)	90	27	22	33	12	0	30	2	0	1	13	3	2	.314	.363	.514	.877
2016	OkCity	AAA	17	56	18	5	0	2	(-	-)	29	6	7	8	2	0	8	0	0	1	1	5		.321	.339	.518	.857

Year	Team	Lg	G	AB	H	2B	3B	HR	(Hm	Rd)	TB	R	RBI	RC	TBB	IBB	SO	HBP	SH	SF	SB	CS	GDP	Avg	OBP	Slg	OPS
2016	LAD	NL	48	105	33	9	1	3	(1	2)	53	19	16	21	8	2	25	1	0	1	1	1	1	.314	.365	.505	.870
2017	LAD	NL	31	96	26	3	0	5	(3	2)	44	17	15	13	5	0	16	1	0	0	0	1	3	.271	.314	.458	.772
	Postseason		11	22	8	2	0	0	(0	0)	10	6	2	4	1	0	3	2	0	1	0	0	1	.364	.423	.455	.878
	2 ML YEARS		79	201	59	12	1	8	(4	4)	97	36	31	34	13	2	41	2	0	1	1	2	4	.294	.341	.483	.824

Ashur Tolliver

Pitches: L **Bats:** L **Pos:** RP-3

Ht: 6'0" **Wt:** 170 **Born:** 1/24/1988 **Age:** 30

Year	Team	Lg	G	GS	CG	GF	IP	BFP	H	R	ER	HR	SH	SF	HB	TBB	IBB	SO	WP	Bk	W	L	Pct	Sh	Sv-Op	Hld	ERC	ERA
2013	2 Tms	Low	19	1	0	7	48.1	196	42	16	16	4	1	1	4	14	0	42	4	0	1	0	1.000	0	1- -	-	2.96	2.98
2014	Bowie	AA	18	1	0	7	22.2	97	27	9	8	1	0	0	0	5	0	25	0	0	3	1	.750	0	0- -	-	4.08	3.18
2014	Frdrck	A+	9	0	0	6	14.1	61	14	4	4	1	0	1	0	2	0	15	0	0	1	0	1.000	0	2- -	-	2.60	2.51
2015	Bowie	AA	39	2	0	9	58.2	249	51	19	19	2	1	2	0	29	0	61	4	1	1	2	.333	0	1- -	-	3.29	2.91
2016	Bowie	AA	18	0	0	6	26.0	103	22	9	7	4	2	0	0	8	0	25	0	0	1	1	.500	0	2- -	-	3.35	2.42
2016	Norfolk	AAA	11	0	0	3	12.2	54	11	2	2	0	0	0	1	6	0	16	0	0	0	0	-	0	0- -	-	3.28	1.42
2017	Fresno	AAA	31	0	0	5	35.1	178	39	28	28	2	1	6	3	33	1	28	6	0	2	0	1.000	0	0- -	-	6.74	7.13
2017	Ark	AA	5	0	0	1	8.0	33	7	3	3	0	0	1	1	2	0	7	1	0	1	0	1.000	0	0- -	-	2.68	3.38
2016	Bal	AL	5	0	0	2	4.2	22	5	4	3	1	0	0	0	3	0	5	0	0	1	0	1.000	0	0-0	0	6.25	5.79
2017	Hou	AL	3	0	0	0	5.0	22	4	2	2	0	0	0	1	4	0	5	1	0	0	0	-	0	0-0	0	4.79	3.60
	2 ML YEARS		8	0	0	2	9.2	44	9	6	5	1	0	0	1	7	0	10	1	0	1	0	1.000	0	0-0	0	5.55	4.66

Yasmany Tomas

Bats: R **Throws:** R **Pos:** LF-42;PH-5

yahz-MAH-nee toh-MAHS

Ht: 6'2" **Wt:** 250 **Born:** 11/14/1990 **Age:** 27

Year	Team	Lg	G	AB	H	2B	3B	HR	(Hm	Rd)	TB	R	RBI	RC	TBB	IBB	SO	HBP	SH	SF	SB	CS	GDP	Avg	OBP	Slg	OPS
2015	Ari	NL	118	406	111	19	3	9	(4	5)	163	40	48	32	17	0	110	2	0	1	5	2	16	.273	.305	.401	.707
2016	Ari	NL	140	530	144	30	1	31	(16	15)	269	72	83	71	31	4	136	1	0	1	2	4	18	.272	.313	.508	.820
2017	Ari	NL	47	166	40	11	1	8	(6	2)	77	19	32	25	13	0	50	0	0	1	0	0	2	.241	.294	.464	.758
	3 ML YEARS		305	1102	295	60	5	48	(26	22)	509	131	163	128	61	4	296	3	0	3	7	6	36	.268	.307	.462	.769

Josh Tomlin

Pitches: R **Bats:** R **Pos:** SP-26

Ht: 6'1" **Wt:** 190 **Born:** 10/19/1984 **Age:** 33

Year	Team	Lg	G	GS	CG	GF	IP	BFP	H	R	ER	HR	SH	SF	HB	TBB	IBB	SO	WP	Bk	W	L	Pct	Sh	Sv-Op	Hld	ERC	ERA
2010	Cle	AL	12	12	1	0	73.0	301	72	38	37	10	3	3	3	19	3	43	1	0	6	4	.600	0	0-0	0	3.89	4.56
2011	Cle	AL	26	26	0	0	165.1	662	157	80	78	24	1	3	3	21	2	89	3	0	12	7	.632	0	0-0	0	3.11	4.25
2012	Cle	AL	21	16	0	0	103.1	452	126	74	73	18	2	3	3	25	3	56	4	0	5	8	.385	0	0-0	0	5.34	6.36
2013	Cle	AL	1	0	0	0	2.0	9	2	0	0	0	0	0	0	0	0	0	0	0	0	0	-	0	0-0	0	1.68	0.00
2014	Cle	AL	25	16	1	6	104.0	446	120	66	55	18	1	3	1	14	3	94	6	0	6	9	.400	1	0-0	0	4.28	4.76
2015	Cle	AL	10	10	2	0	65.2	251	47	22	22	13	0	0	2	8	0	57	1	0	7	2	.778	0	0-0	0	2.24	3.02
2016	Cle	AL	30	29	0	1	174.0	725	187	97	85	36	4	4	3	20	2	118	4	0	13	9	.591	0	0-0	0	4.06	4.40
2017	Cle	AL	26	26	1	0	141.0	585	166	80	78	23	0	3	4	14	0	109	1	0	10	9	.526	0	0-0	0	4.49	4.98
	Postseason		4	4	0	0	17.2	72	15	9	9	1	0	0	0	5	0	11	0	0	2	1	.667	0	0-0	0	2.55	4.58
	8 ML YEARS		151	135	5	7	828.1	3431	877	457	428	142	11	19	19	121	13	566	20	0	59	48	.551	1	0-0	0	3.94	4.65

Kelby Tomlinson

Bats: R **Throws:** R **Pos:** PH-51;3B-24;2B-20;SS-11;LF-9;PR-4

Ht: 6'3" **Wt:** 180 **Born:** 6/16/1990 **Age:** 28

Year	Team	Lg	G	AB	H	2B	3B	HR	(Hm	Rd)	TB	R	RBI	RC	TBB	IBB	SO	HBP	SH	SF	SB	CS	GDP	Avg	OBP	Slg	OPS
2017	Scrmto*	AAA	26	108	32	6	0	0	(-	-)	38	17	8	16	13	0	12	1	0	0	9	2	0	.296	.377	.352	.729
2015	SF	NL	54	178	54	6	3	2	(2	0)	72	23	20	22	14	0	40	1	0	0	5	4	3	.303	.358	.404	.762
2016	SF	NL	52	106	31	4	0	0	(0	0)	35	13	6	18	12	1	18	1	1	0	5	1	1	.292	.370	.330	.700
2017	SF	NL	104	194	50	4	2	1	(1	0)	61	32	11	19	23	2	46	0	2	3	9	1	8	.258	.332	.314	.646
	Postseason		3	6	0	0	0	0	(0	0)	0	0	0	0	0	0	3	0	0	0	0	0	0	.000	.000	.000	.000
	3 ML YEARS		210	478	135	14	5	3	(3	0)	168	68	37	59	49	3	104	2	3	3	19	6	12	.282	.350	.351	.701

Michael Tonkin

Pitches: R **Bats:** R **Pos:** RP-16

TAHN-kin

Ht: 6'7" **Wt:** 220 **Born:** 11/19/1989 **Age:** 28

Year	Team	Lg	G	GS	CG	GF	IP	BFP	H	R	ER	HR	SH	SF	HB	TBB	IBB	SO	WP	Bk	W	L	Pct	Sh	Sv-Op	Hld	ERC	ERA
2017	Roch*	AAA	31	0	0	22	41.2	169	31	8	8	1	1	0	4	13	0	61	0	0	4	2	.667	0	5- -	-	2.30	1.73
2013	Min	AL	9	0	0	6	11.1	47	9	6	1	0	0	0	0	3	0	10	1	0	0	0	-	0	0-0	0	1.82	0.79
2014	Min	AL	25	0	0	8	19.0	87	23	13	10	2	2	1	2	6	0	16	1	0	0	0	-	0	0-0	4	5.36	4.74
2015	Min	AL	26	0	0	10	23.1	99	21	9	9	4	0	1	1	9	2	19	1	0	0	0	-	0	0-0	1	3.99	3.47
2016	Min	AL	65	0	0	23	71.2	315	80	46	40	13	2	0	3	24	0	80	5	0	3	2	.600	0	0-2	2	5.25	5.02
2017	Min	AL	16	0	0	8	21.0	97	22	15	12	6	0	1	1	12	0	24	2	0	0	1	.000	0	0-0	0	6.63	5.14
	5 ML YEARS		141	0	0	55	146.1	645	155	89	72	25	4	3	7	54	2	149	10	0	3	3	.500	0	0-2	11	4.94	4.43

Luis Torrens

Bats: R **Throws:** R **Pos:** C-51;PH-7 **Ht:** 6'0" **Wt:** 175 **Born:** 5/2/1996 **Age:** 22

Year	Team	Lg	G	AB	H	2B	3B	HR	(Hm	Rd)	TB	R	RBI	RC	TBB	IBB	SO	HBP	SH	SF	SB	CS	GDP	Avg	OBP	Slg	OPS
2013	Yanks2	R	47	174	42	7	0	1	(-	-)	52	17	14	21	27	1	40	2	0	1	2	0	8	.241	.348	.299	.647
2014	3 Tms	Low	62	227	58	14	3	3	(-	-)	87	32	22	28	20	0	50	6	0	1	1	2	6	.256	.331	.383	.714
2016	2 Tms	Low	52	184	46	10	0	2	(-	-)	62	15	15	23	26	0	33	3	0	1	2	2	9	.250	.350	.337	.687
2017	SD	NL	56	123	20	3	1	0	(0	0)	25	7	7	4	12	3	30	1	3	0	0	0	4	.163	.243	.203	.446

Carlos Torres

Pitches: R **Bats:** R **Pos:** RP-67 **Ht:** 6'1" **Wt:** 180 **Born:** 10/22/1982 **Age:** 35

Year	Team	Lg	G	GS	CG	GF	IP	BFP	H	R	ER	HR	SH	SF	HB	TBB	IBB	SO	WP	Bk	W	L	Pct	Sh	Sv-Op	Hld	ERC	ERA
2009	CWS	AL	8	5	0	2	28.1	130	30	20	19	5	3	3	2	17	2	22	0	0	1	2	.333	0	0-0	0	6.05	6.04
2010	CWS	AL	5	1	0	1	13.2	71	23	13	13	2	0	1	0	9	1	13	0	0	0	1	.000	0	0-0	0	9.84	8.56
2012	Col	NL	31	0	0	9	53.0	231	49	31	31	2	6	4	4	26	1	42	6	0	5	3	.625	0	0-0	1	3.85	5.26
2013	NYM	NL	33	9	0	6	86.1	352	79	34	33	15	4	1	4	17	1	75	4	1	4	6	.400	0	0-0	3	3.47	3.44
2014	NYM	NL	73	1	0	20	97.0	405	89	35	33	11	2	1	2	38	4	96	6	0	8	6	.571	0	2-5	12	3.77	3.06
2015	NYM	NL	59	0	0	19	57.2	243	61	32	30	5	1	3	0	18	6	48	5	0	5	6	.455	0	0-1	11	3.86	4.68
2016	Mil	NL	72	0	0	12	82.1	339	65	26	25	8	3	2	4	30	3	78	1	1	3	3	.500	0	2-5	20	2.94	2.73
2017	Mil	NL	67	0	0	16	72.2	322	78	37	34	10	2	4	3	33	1	56	4	0	4	4	.500	0	1-4	13	5.19	4.21
	8 ML YEARS		348	16	0	85	491.0	2093	474	228	218	58	21	19	19	188	19	430	26	2	30	31	.492	0	5-15	60	4.07	4.00

Jose Torres

Pitches: L **Bats:** L **Pos:** RP-62 **Ht:** 6'2" **Wt:** 175 **Born:** 9/24/1993 **Age:** 24

Year	Team	Lg	G	GS	CG	GF	IP	BFP	H	R	ER	HR	SH	SF	HB	TBB	IBB	SO	WP	Bk	W	L	Pct	Sh	Sv-Op	Hld	ERC	ERA
2013	Vrmnt	A-	9	5	0	2	30.2	136	28	15	9	2	0	0	1	12	0	21	4	0	3	2	.600	0	0--	-	3.28	2.64
2014	Vrmnt	A-	5	1	0	4	61.2	264	62	37	30	4	1	6	3	22	0	47	6	0	0	6	.000	0	2--	-	3.91	4.38
2015	2 Tms	Low	47	0	0	23	77.1	313	55	24	22	4	10	4	4	24	2	84	3	0	4	5	.444	0	8--	-	2.09	2.56
2016	Lk Els	A+	20	0	0	7	25.1	105	21	11	10	2	0	1	0	10	0	25	2	0	0	2	.000	0	1--	-	3.00	3.55
2016	SnAnt	AA	25	0	0	9	36.1	136	20	5	5	1	2	1	0	12	1	36	1	1	1	2	.333	0	2--	-	1.35	1.24
2016	SD	NL	4	0	0	1	3.0	14	3	0	0	0	0	0	0	2	0	3	1	0	0	0	.---	0	0-0	1	4.23	0.00
2017	SD	NL	62	0	0	16	68.1	284	63	34	32	13	3	3	4	16	0	63	2	3	7	4	.636	0	1-2	3	3.80	4.21
	2 ML YEARS		66	0	0	17	71.1	298	66	34	32	13	3	3	4	18	0	66	3	3	7	4	.636	0	1-2	4	3.83	4.04

Ramon Torres

Bats: B **Throws:** R **Pos:** 2B-20;3B-12;SS-3;PR-2 **Ht:** 5'11" **Wt:** 170 **Born:** 1/22/1993 **Age:** 25

Year	Team	Lg	G	AB	H	2B	3B	HR	(Hm	Rd)	TB	R	RBI	RC	TBB	IBB	SO	HBP	SH	SF	SB	CS	GDP	Avg	OBP	Slg	OPS
2013	2 Tms	Low	68	249	64	14	2	3	(-	-)	91	28	25	25	13	0	29	1	8	2	6	8	3	.257	.294	.365	.660
2014	2 Tms	Low	117	425	121	20	5	5	(-	-)	166	60	34	58	26	0	56	3	21	2	20	7	2	.285	.329	.391	.720
2015	Wilmg	A+	71	288	74	10	3	1	(-	-)	93	29	18	27	11	0	32	1	8	0	14	7	6	.257	.287	.323	.610
2015	NWArk	AA	51	189	52	10	1	4	(-	-)	76	23	13	24	17	0	23	1	7	0	4	8	2	.275	.338	.402	.740
2016	NWArk	AA	41	164	44	5	1	1	(-	-)	54	20	8	20	18	0	18	0	2	1	9	4	2	.268	.339	.329	.668
2016	Omha	AAA	73	297	77	12	1	2	(-	-)	97	35	21	30	15	0	61	0	3	0	12	3	4	.259	.295	.327	.621
2017	Omha	AAA	75	295	86	10	1	6	(-	-)	116	43	41	40	15	0	32	1	3	3	17	4	5	.292	.325	.393	.718
2017	KC	AL	33	74	18	3	0	0	(0	0)	21	9	4	7	4	0	12	1	0	0	1	0	1	.243	.291	.284	.575

Ronald Torreyes

tore-RAY-ess

Bats: R **Throws:** R **Pos:** 2B-54;SS-36;3B-26;PH-7;PR-5;RF-1;DH-1 **Ht:** 5'8" **Wt:** 151 **Born:** 9/2/1992 **Age:** 25

Year	Team	Lg	G	AB	H	2B	3B	HR	(Hm	Rd)	TB	R	RBI	RC	TBB	IBB	SO	HBP	SH	SF	SB	CS	GDP	Avg	OBP	Slg	OPS
2015	LAD	NL	8	6	2	1	0	0	(0	0)	3	1	1	2	1	0	1	0	1	0	0	0	0	.333	.429	.500	.929
2016	NYY	AL	72	155	40	7	4	1	(0	1)	58	20	12	19	10	0	20	1	1	1	2	1	4	.258	.305	.374	.680
2017	NYY	AL	108	315	92	15	1	3	(2	1)	118	35	36	37	11	0	43	1	5	4	2	0	9	.292	.314	.375	.689
	3 ML YEARS		188	476	134	23	5	4	(2	2)	179	56	49	58	22	0	64	2	7	5	4	1	13	.282	.313	.376	.689

Devon Travis

Bats: R **Throws:** R **Pos:** 2B-50;PH-1;PR-1 DEV-in **Ht:** 5'9" **Wt:** 190 **Born:** 2/21/1991 **Age:** 27

Year	Team	Lg	G	AB	H	2B	3B	HR	(Hm	Rd)	TB	R	RBI	RC	TBB	IBB	SO	HBP	SH	SF	SB	CS	GDP	Avg	OBP	Slg	OPS
2015	Tor	AL	62	217	66	18	0	8	(4	4)	108	38	35	40	18	0	43	2	0	1	3	1	4	.304	.361	.498	.859
2016	Tor	AL	101	410	123	28	1	11	(2	9)	186	54	50	61	20	0	87	0	1	1	4	1	6	.300	.332	.454	.785
2017	Tor	AL	50	185	48	18	0	5	(2	3)	81	22	24	25	7	0	38	2	1	2	4	2	5	.259	.291	.438	.729
	Postseason		3	12	1	0	0	0	(0	0)	1	2	0	0	0	0	1	0	0	0	0	0	4	.083	.083	.083	.167
	3 ML YEARS		213	812	237	64	1	24	(8	16)	375	114	109	126	45	0	168	4	2	4	11	4	15	.292	.331	.462	.792

Sam Travis

Bats: R Throws: R Pos: 1B-21;PH-10;DH-4;PR-1   Ht: 6'0" Wt: 205 Born: 8/27/1993 Age: 24

							BATTING														RUNNING			AVERAGES			
Year	Team	Lg	G	AB	H	2B	3B	HR	(Hm	Rd)	TB	R	RBI	RC	TBB	IBB	SO	HBP	SH	SF	SB	CS	GDP	Avg	OBP	Slg	OPS
2014	2 Tms	Low	67	272	86	16	2	7	(-	-)	127	40	44	44	11	1	32	4	1	1	5	2	7	.316	.351	.467	.818
2015	Salem	A+	66	246	77	15	4	5	(-	-)	115	35	40	44	26	1	43	2	0	4	10	6	7	.313	.378	.467	.845
2015	Portlnd	AA	65	243	73	17	2	4	(-	-)	106	35	38	42	33	0	34	2	0	3	9	6	9	.300	.384	.436	.821
2016	Pwtckt	AAA	47	173	47	10	0	6	(-	-)	75	26	29	25	15	0	40	1	0	1	1	0	3	.272	.332	.434	.765
2017	Pwtckt	AAA	82	304	82	14	0	6	(-	-)	114	40	24	43	37	0	57	1	0	0	6	2	6	.270	.351	.375	.726
2017	Bos	AL	33	76	20	6	0	0	(0	0)	26	13	1	5	6	0	23	1	0	0	1	0	2	.263	.325	.342	.667

Blake Treinen

Pitches: R Bats: R Pos: RP-72   TRY-nen   Ht: 6'5" Wt: 225 Born: 6/30/1988 Age: 30

			HOW MUCH HE PITCHED					WHAT HE GAVE UP											THE RESULTS						
Year	Team	Lg	G	GS	CG	GF	IP	BFP	H	R	ER	HR	SH	SF	HB	TBB	IBB	SO	WP	Bk	W	L	Pct	Sh	Sv-Op	Hld	ERC	ERA
2014	Was	NL	15	7	0	6	50.2	214	57	17	14	1	0	0	3	13	1	30	1	0	2	3	.400	0	0-0	0	3.86	2.49
2015	Was	NL	60	0	0	17	67.2	280	62	32	29	4	1	1	2	32	6	65	4	0	2	5	.286	0	0-3	10	3.76	3.86
2016	Was	NL	73	0	0	17	67.0	263	51	19	17	5	2	2	0	31	6	63	1	0	4	1	.800	0	1-3	22	2.92	2.28
2017	2 Tms		72	0	0	35	75.2	325	80	35	33	6	0	3	5	25	3	74	4	0	3	6	.333	0	16-21	15	4.24	3.93
17	Was	NL	37	0	0	11	37.2	169	48	24	24	3	0	3	3	13	1	32	1	0	0	2	.000	0	3-5	5	5.71	5.73
17	Oak	AL	35	0	0	24	38.0	156	32	11	9	3	0	0	2	12	2	42	3	0	3	4	.429	0	13-16	5	2.92	2.13
	Postseason		3	0	0	0	2.2	12	3	2	2	0	0	0	1	0	0	5	0	0	1	1	.500	0	0-0	0	3.84	6.75
	4 ML YEARS		220	7	0	75	261.0	1082	250	103	93	16	3	6	9	101	16	232	10	0	11	15	.423	0	17-27	42	3.70	3.21

Andrew Triggs

Pitches: R Bats: R Pos: SP-12   Ht: 6'4" Wt: 220 Born: 3/16/1989 Age: 29

			HOW MUCH HE PITCHED					WHAT HE GAVE UP											THE RESULTS						
Year	Team	Lg	G	GS	CG	GF	IP	BFP	H	R	ER	HR	SH	SF	HB	TBB	IBB	SO	WP	Bk	W	L	Pct	Sh	Sv-Op	Hld	ERC	ERA
2013	Wilmg	A+	39	0	0	37	60.1	259	58	29	17	1	3	4	7	12	1	63	6	2	5	3	.625	0	9- -	-	2.87	2.54
2014	NWArk	AA	43	1	0	32	61.1	260	55	28	20	4	2	3	5	16	1	38	2	0	4	3	.571	0	19- -	-	2.97	2.93
2015	Bowie	AA	43	0	0	30	61.0	235	42	9	7	0	2	1	7	11	1	70	6	0	0	2	.000	0	17- -	-	1.59	1.03
2016	Nashv	AAA	16	0	0	9	18.1	81	16	7	6	0	0	1	4	5	1	21	0	0	2	1	.667	0	2- -	-	2.83	2.95
2016	Oak	AL	24	6	0	7	56.1	238	56	30	27	5	1	1	3	13	1	55	2	0	1	1	.500	0	0-0	0	3.46	4.31
2017	Oak	AL	12	12	0	0	65.1	283	68	42	31	9	1	3	4	19	0	50	5	0	5	6	.455	0	0-0	0	4.35	4.27
	2 ML YEARS		36	18	0	7	121.2	521	124	72	58	14	2	4	7	32	1	105	7	0	6	7	.462	0	0-0	0	3.93	4.29

Mike Trout

Bats: R Throws: R Pos: CF-108;DH-6   Ht: 6'2" Wt: 235 Born: 8/7/1991 Age: 26

							BATTING														RUNNING			AVERAGES			
Year	Team	Lg	G	AB	H	2B	3B	HR	(Hm	Rd)	TB	R	RBI	RC	TBB	IBB	SO	HBP	SH	SF	SB	CS	GDP	Avg	OBP	Slg	OPS
2011	LAA	AL	40	123	27	6	0	5	(1	4)	48	20	16	14	9	0	30	2	0	1	4	0	2	.220	.281	.390	.672
2012	LAA	AL	139	559	182	27	8	30	(16	14)	315	129	83	127	67	4	139	6	0	7	49	5	7	.326	.399	.564	.963
2013	LAA	AL	157	589	190	39	9	27	(13	14)	328	109	97	141	110	10	136	9	0	8	33	7	8	.323	.432	.557	.988
2014	LAA	AL	157	602	173	39	9	36	(19	17)	338	115	111	131	83	6	184	10	0	10	16	2	6	.287	.377	.561	.939
2015	LAA	AL	159	575	172	32	6	41	(20	21)	339	104	90	131	92	14	158	10	0	5	11	7	11	.299	.402	.590	.991
2016	LAA	AL	159	549	173	32	5	29	(14	15)	302	123	100	137	116	12	137	11	0	5	30	7	5	.315	.441	.550	.991
2017	LAA	AL	114	402	123	25	3	33	(20	13)	253	92	72	110	94	15	90	7	0	4	22	4	8	.306	.442	.629	1.071
	Postseason		3	12	1	0	0	1	(0	1)	4	1	1	0	3	0	2	0	0	0	0	1	0	.083	.267	.333	.600
	7 ML YEARS		925	3399	1040	200	40	201	(103	98)	1923	692	569	791	571	61	874	55	0	40	165	32	47	.306	.410	.566	.976

Mark Trumbo

Bats: R Throws: R Pos: DH-111;RF-31;PH-3;1B-2;3B-2   Ht: 6'4" Wt: 225 Born: 1/16/1986 Age: 32

							BATTING														RUNNING			AVERAGES			
Year	Team	Lg	G	AB	H	2B	3B	HR	(Hm	Rd)	TB	R	RBI	RC	TBB	IBB	SO	HBP	SH	SF	SB	CS	GDP	Avg	OBP	Slg	OPS
2010	LAA	AL	8	15	1	0	0	0	(0	0)	1	2	2	0	1	0	8	0	0	0	0	0	0	.067	.125	.067	.192
2011	LAA	AL	149	539	137	31	1	29	(14	15)	257	65	87	69	25	6	120	5	0	4	9	4	17	.254	.291	.477	.768
2012	LAA	AL	144	544	146	19	3	32	(12	20)	267	66	95	80	36	3	153	4	0	2	4	5	12	.268	.317	.491	.808
2013	LAA	AL	159	620	145	30	2	34	(19	15)	281	85	100	74	54	6	184	0	0	4	5	2	18	.234	.294	.453	.747
2014	Ari	NL	88	328	77	15	4	14	(7	7)	136	37	61	44	28	3	89	1	0	5	2	3	8	.235	.293	.415	.707
2015	2 Tms		142	508	133	23	3	22	(12	10)	228	62	64	58	36	1	132	0	0	1	0	0	12	.262	.310	.449	.759
2016	Bal	AL	159	613	157	27	1	47	(25	22)	327	94	108	102	51	1	170	3	0	0	2	0	14	.256	.316	.533	.850
2017	Bal	AL	146	559	131	22	0	23	(14	9)	222	79	65	57	42	0	149	1	0	1	1	0	13	.234	.289	.397	.686
15	Ari	NL	46	174	45	10	3	9	(4	5)	88	23	23	21	10	0	39	0	0	0	0	0	4	.259	.299	.506	.805
15	Sea	AL	96	334	88	13	0	13	(8	5)	140	39	41	37	26	1	93	0	0	1	0	0	8	.263	.316	.419	.735
	Postseason		1	4	1	0	0	1	(0	1)	4	1	2	2	0	0	1	0	0	0	0	0	0	.250	.250	1.000	1.250
	8 ML YEARS		995	3726	927	167	11	201	(103	98)	1719	490	582	484	273	20	1005	14	0	17	23	14	94	.249	.301	.461	.763

Jen-Ho Tseng

Pitches: R Bats: L Pos: SP-1; RP-1   seng   Ht: 6'1" Wt: 195 Born: 10/3/1994 Age: 23

			HOW MUCH HE PITCHED					WHAT HE GAVE UP											THE RESULTS						
Year	Team	Lg	G	GS	CG	GF	IP	BFP	H	R	ER	HR	SH	SF	HB	TBB	IBB	SO	WP	Bk	W	L	Pct	Sh	Sv-Op	Hld	ERC	ERA
2014	Kane	A	19	17	1	0	105.0	400	76	29	28	7	6	2	4	15	0	85	2	1	6	1	.857	0	0- -	-	1.73	2.40
2015	MrtlBh	A+	22	22	0	0	119.0	495	115	48	47	5	3	5	8	30	0	87	4	0	7	7	.500	0	0- -	-	3.23	3.55

Year	Team	Lg	G	GS	CG	GF	IP	BFP	H	R	ER	HR	SH	SF	HB	TBB	IBB	SO	WP	Bk	W	L	Pct	Sh	Sv-Op	Hld	ERC	ERA
2016	Tenn	AA	22	22	0	0	113.1	502	138	67	54	12	7	11	4	32	0	69	4	1	6	8	.429	0	0- -	-	5.04	4.29
2017	Tenn	AA	15	15	0	0	90.1	376	79	38	30	7	3	3	6	24	0	83	5	1	7	3	.700	0	0- -	-	2.97	2.99
2017	Iowa	AAA	9	9	0	0	55.0	221	48	15	11	5	2	1	0	14	1	39	1	0	6	1	.857	0	0- -	-	2.80	1.80
2017	ChC	NL	2	1	0	1	6.0	26	5	5	5	2	0	1	1	2	0	8	0	0	1	0	1.000	0	0-0	0	5.05	7.50

Sam Tuivailala

Pitches: R **Bats:** R **Pos:** RP-37   TOO-ee-vah-la-la   **Ht:** 6'3" **Wt:** 225 **Born:** 10/19/1992 **Age:** 25

			HOW MUCH HE PITCHED						WHAT HE GAVE UP												THE RESULTS							
Year	Team	Lg	G	GS	CG	GF	IP	BFP	H	R	ER	HR	SH	SF	HB	TBB	IBB	SO	WP	Bk	W	L	Pct	Sh	Sv-Op	Hld	ERC	ERA
2017	Memp*	AAA	18	0	0	15	21.1	79	13	3	3	2	0	2	0	3	0	21	0	0	1	0	1.000	0	6- -	-	1.60	1.27
2014	StL	NL	2	0	0	0	1.0	10	5	4	4	2	0	0	0	2	0	1	0	0	0	0	-	0	0-0	0	72.46	36.00
2015	StL	NL	14	0	0	5	14.2	65	13	5	5	2	0	0	0	8	1	20	3	0	0	1	.000	0	0-0	2	4.06	3.07
2016	StL	NL	12	0	0	4	9.0	47	12	6	6	0	0	0	2	6	0	7	1	0	0	0	-	0	0-0	0	7.05	6.00
2017	StL	NL	37	0	0	19	42.1	171	35	12	12	4	1	0	2	11	3	34	2	0	3	3	.500	0	0-0	1	2.69	2.55
4 ML YEARS			65	0	0	28	67.0	293	65	27	27	8	1	0	4	27	4	62	6	0	3	4	.429	0	0-0	3	4.16	3.63

Troy Tulowitzki

Bats: R **Throws:** R **Pos:** SS-64;PH-2   too-luh-WIT-skee   **Ht:** 6'3" **Wt:** 205 **Born:** 10/10/1984 **Age:** 33

			BATTING																		RUNNING			AVERAGES			
Year	Team	Lg	G	AB	H	2B	3B	HR	(Hm	Rd)	TB	R	RBI	RC	TBB	IBB	SO	HBP	SH	SF	SB	CS	GDP	Avg	OBP	Slg	OPS
2006	Col	NL	25	96	23	2	0	1	(0	1)	28	15	6	10	10	3	25	1	1	0	3	0	1	.240	.318	.292	.609
2007	Col	NL	155	609	177	33	5	24	(15	9)	292	104	99	95	57	3	130	9	5	2	7	6	14	.291	.359	.479	.838
2008	Col	NL	101	377	99	24	2	8	(4	4)	151	48	46	42	38	5	56	2	2	2	1	6	16	.263	.332	.401	.732
2009	Col	NL	151	543	161	25	9	32	(17	15)	300	101	92	96	73	4	112	3	0	9	20	11	20	.297	.377	.552	.930
2010	Col	NL	122	470	148	32	3	27	(15	12)	267	89	95	88	48	4	78	5	1	5	11	2	17	.315	.381	.568	.949
2011	Col	NL	143	537	162	36	2	30	(17	13)	292	81	105	101	59	12	79	4	1	5	9	3	16	.302	.372	.544	.916
2012	Col	NL	47	181	52	8	2	8	(3	5)	88	33	27	27	19	1	19	2	0	1	2	2	7	.287	.360	.486	.846
2013	Col	NL	126	446	139	27	0	25	(14	11)	241	72	82	80	57	5	85	4	0	5	1	0	9	.312	.391	.540	.931
2014	Col	NL	91	315	107	18	1	21	(14	7)	190	71	52	70	50	4	57	5	0	5	1	1	4	.340	.432	.603	1.035
2015	2 Tms		128	486	136	27	4	17	(11	6)	214	77	70	69	38	5	114	6	0	4	1	0	17	.280	.337	.440	.777
2016	Tor	AL	131	492	125	21	0	24	(13	11)	218	54	79	71	43	1	101	5	0	4	1	0	14	.254	.318	.443	.761
2017	Tor	AL	66	241	60	10	0	7	(5	2)	91	16	26	21	17	1	40	1	0	1	0	1	10	.249	.300	.378	.678
15	Col	NL	87	323	97	19	0	12	(7	5)	152	46	53	53	24	4	72	1	0	3	0	0	13	.300	.348	.471	.818
15	Tor	AL	41	163	39	8	4	5	(4	1)	62	31	17	16	14	1	42	5	0	1	1	0	4	.239	.317	.380	.697
Postseason			35	136	29	7	1	4	(1	3)	50	11	22	15	8	0	35	1	0	1	0	1	4	.213	.260	.368	.628
12 ML YEARS			1286	4793	1389	263	24	224	(128	96)	2372	761	779	770	509	48	896	47	10	43	57	32	145	.290	.361	.495	.856

Nik Turley

Pitches: L **Bats:** L **Pos:** RP-7; SP-3   **Ht:** 6'4" **Wt:** 195 **Born:** 9/11/1989 **Age:** 28

			HOW MUCH HE PITCHED						WHAT HE GAVE UP												THE RESULTS							
Year	Team	Lg	G	GS	CG	GF	IP	BFP	H	R	ER	HR	SH	SF	HB	TBB	IBB	SO	WP	Bk	W	L	Pct	Sh	Sv-Op	Hld	ERC	ERA
2013	Trntn	AA	27	26	0	1	139.0	609	119	69	60	11	0	3	16	73	0	137	9	6	11	8	.579	0	0- -	-	4.08	3.88
2014	S-WB	AAA	13	13	0	0	60.1	282	55	36	31	8	3	3	9	43	0	44	7	0	5	3	.625	0	0- -	-	5.67	4.62
2015	Scrmto	AAA	19	19	0	0	102.2	440	93	64	52	15	4	4	1	48	0	85	13	0	7	8	.467	0	0- -	-	4.19	4.56
2016	Portlnd	AA	20	2	0	7	35.2	161	26	20	17	3	2	0	2	28	0	48	9	1	1	2	.333	0	2- -	-	4.11	4.29
2017	Chatt	AA	5	3	1	1	24.1	86	6	1	1	0	1	0	1	7	0	45	0	0	0	1	.000	0	0- -	-	0.50	0.37
2017	Roch	AAA	18	10	0	2	67.2	273	58	24	20	4	1	2	2	22	0	79	4	0	5	4	.556	0	0- -	-	2.96	2.66
2017	Min	AL	10	3	0	3	17.2	89	30	22	22	5	1	2	2	8	1	13	2	0	0	2	.000	0	0-0	0	11.06	11.21

Jacob Turner

Pitches: R **Bats:** R **Pos:** RP-16; SP-2   **Ht:** 6'5" **Wt:** 215 **Born:** 5/21/1991 **Age:** 27

			HOW MUCH HE PITCHED						WHAT HE GAVE UP												THE RESULTS							
Year	Team	Lg	G	GS	CG	GF	IP	BFP	H	R	ER	HR	SH	SF	HB	TBB	IBB	SO	WP	Bk	W	L	Pct	Sh	Sv-Op	Hld	ERC	ERA
2017	Syrcse*	AAA	14	14	0	0	65.2	293	72	38	38	5	0	3	4	33	0	53	3	1	2	6	.250	0	0- -	-	5.22	5.21
2011	Det	AL	3	3	0	0	12.2	60	17	13	12	3	0	1	1	4	0	8	0	0	0	1	.000	0	0-0	0	7.03	8.53
2012	2 Tms		10	10	0	0	55.0	231	50	32	27	9	1	2	0	16	3	36	5	0	2	5	.286	0	0-0	0	3.42	4.42
2013	Mia	NL	20	20	1	0	118.0	514	116	55	49	11	8	5	4	54	5	77	11	0	3	8	.273	0	0-0	0	4.25	3.74
2014	2 Tms	NL	28	18	0	4	113.0	501	148	81	77	12	6	4	1	33	2	71	6	1	6	11	.353	0	0-0	0	5.59	6.13
2016	CWS	AL	18	2	0	8	24.2	122	33	27	18	5	0	2	2	16	1	18	2	0	1	2	.333	0	0-0	2	8.38	6.57
2017	Was	NL	18	2	0	6	39.0	170	43	23	22	8	1	0	1	15	1	23	3	0	2	3	.400	0	0-3	1	5.52	5.08
12	Det	AL	3	3	0	0	12.1	61	17	11	11	4	0	1	0	7	1	7	1	0	1	1	.500	0	0-0	0	8.66	8.03
12	Mia	NL	7	7	0	0	42.2	170	33	21	16	5	1	1	0	9	2	29	4	0	1	4	.200	0	0-0	0	2.20	3.38
14	Mia	NL	20	12	0	4	78.1	352	106	54	52	8	2	3	1	23	1	54	3	1	4	7	.364	0	0-0	0	5.84	5.97
14	ChC	NL	8	6	0	0	34.2	149	42	27	25	4	4	1	0	10	1	17	3	0	2	4	.333	0	0-0	0	5.03	6.49
6 ML YEARS			97	55	1	18	362.1	1598	407	231	205	48	16	14	9	138	12	233	27	1	14	30	.318	0	0-3	4	5.02	5.09

Justin Turner

Bats: R **Throws:** R **Pos:** 3B-121;PH-6;DH-5   **Ht:** 5'11" **Wt:** 205 **Born:** 11/23/1984 **Age:** 33

			BATTING																		RUNNING			AVERAGES			
Year	Team	Lg	G	AB	H	2B	3B	HR	(Hm	Rd)	TB	R	RBI	RC	TBB	IBB	SO	HBP	SH	SF	SB	CS	GDP	Avg	OBP	Slg	OPS
2009	Bal	AL	12	18	3	0	0	0	(0	0)	3	2	3	1	4	0	3	0	0	0	0	0	1	.167	.318	.167	.485
2010	2 Tms		9	17	1	1	0	0	(0	0)	2	1	0	0	1	0	3	0	0	0	0	0	0	.059	.111	.118	.229
2011	NYM	NL	117	435	113	30	0	4	(3	1)	155	49	51	59	39	2	59	10	2	1	7	2	9	.260	.334	.356	.690
2012	NYM	NL	94	171	46	13	1	2	(2	0)	67	20	19	19	9	0	24	4	0	1	1	1	9	.269	.319	.392	.711
2013	NYM	NL	86	200	56	13	1	2	(0	2)	77	12	16	17	11	1	34	1	1	1	0	1	6	.280	.319	.385	.704

Year Team	Lg	G	AB	H	2B	3B	HR	(Hm	Rd)	TB	R	RBI	RC	TBB	IBB	SO	HBP	SH	SF	SB	CS	GDP	Avg	OBP	Slg	OPS
2014 LAD	NL	109	288	98	21	1	7	(5	2)	142	46	43	55	28	1	58	4	0	2	6	1	6	.340	.404	.493	.897
2015 LAD	NL	126	385	113	26	1	16	(8	8)	189	55	60	65	36	1	71	13	1	4	5	2	10	.294	.370	.491	.861
2016 LAD	NL	151	556	153	34	3	27	(11	16)	274	79	90	96	48	1	107	10	0	8	4	1	16	.275	.339	.493	.832
2017 LAD	NL	130	457	147	32	0	21	(10	11)	242	72	71	95	59	5	56	19	1	7	7	1	12	.322	.415	.530	.945
10 Bal	AL	5	9	0	0	0	0	(0	0)	0	0	0	0	0	0	3	0	0	0	0	0	0	.000	.000	.000	.000
10 NYM	NL	4	8	1	1	0	0	(0	0)	2	1	0	0	1	0	0	0	0	0	0	0	0	.125	.222	.250	.472
Postseason		18	56	20	6	1	2	(1	1)	34	8	12	17	8	1	9	4	0	0	2	0	0	.357	.471	.607	1.078
9 ML YEARS		834	2527	730	170	7	79	(39	40)	1151	336	353	407	235	11	415	61	5	24	30	9	69	.289	.360	.455	.816

Stuart Turner

Bats: R **Throws:** R **Pos:** C-28;PH-11   **Ht:** 6'2" **Wt:** 220 **Born:** 12/27/1991 **Age:** 26

Year Team	Lg	G	AB	H	2B	3B	HR	(Hm	Rd)	TB	R	RBI	RC	TBB	IBB	SO	HBP	SH	SF	SB	CS	GDP	Avg	OBP	Slg	OPS
2013 Elizab	R	34	121	32	5	0	3	(-	-)	46	15	19	17	12	0	22	4	1	4	0	1	1	.264	.340	.380	.721
2014 FtMyrs	A+	93	325	81	16	2	7	(-	-)	122	49	40	43	31	0	61	5	1	2	7	0	7	.249	.322	.375	.698
2015 Chatt	AA	98	327	73	13	1	4	(-	-)	100	40	37	36	45	0	69	4	0	3	5	2	3	.223	.322	.306	.628
2016 Chatt	AA	97	322	77	22	0	6	(-	-)	117	40	41	41	35	0	72	7	1	5	5	3	12	.239	.322	.363	.686
2017 Lsvlle	AAA	15	59	14	0	0	0	(-	-)	14	2	3	4	3	0	14	2	0	0	0	1	1	.237	.297	.237	.534
2017 Cin	NL	37	82	11	3	0	2	(2	0)	20	4	7	2	5	0	22	0	1	0	0	0	5	.134	.182	.244	.426

Trea Turner

Bats: R **Throws:** R **Pos:** SS-95;PH-1;PR-1   TRAY   **Ht:** 6'1" **Wt:** 185 **Born:** 6/30/1993 **Age:** 25

Year Team	Lg	G	AB	H	2B	3B	HR	(Hm	Rd)	TB	R	RBI	RC	TBB	IBB	SO	HBP	SH	SF	SB	CS	GDP	Avg	OBP	Slg	OPS
2015 Was	NL	27	40	9	1	0	1	(0	1)	13	5	1	2	4	0	12	0	0	0	2	2	0	.225	.295	.325	.620
2016 Was	NL	73	307	105	14	8	13	(7	6)	174	53	40	62	14	0	59	1	0	2	33	6	1	.342	.370	.567	.937
2017 Was	NL	98	412	117	24	6	11	(6	5)	186	75	45	67	30	0	80	4	0	1	46	8	4	.284	.338	.451	.789
Postseason		5	22	7	0	0	0	(0	0)	7	5	1	3	1	0	11	0	0	1	2	0	0	.318	.333	.318	.652
3 ML YEARS		198	759	231	39	14	25	(13	12)	373	133	86	131	48	0	151	5	0	3	81	16	5	.304	.348	.491	.840

Koji Uehara

Pitches: R **Bats:** R **Pos:** RP-49   KOH-jee ooh-ih-HAR-uh   **Ht:** 6'2" **Wt:** 195 **Born:** 4/3/1975 **Age:** 43

		HOW MUCH HE PITCHED						WHAT HE GAVE UP											THE RESULTS							
Year Team	Lg	G	GS	CG	GF	IP	BFP	H	R	ER	HR	SH	SF	HB	TBB	IBB	SO	WP	Bk	W	L	Pct	Sh	Sv-Op	Hld	ERC	ERA
2009 Bal	AL	12	12	0	0	66.2	279	71	33	30	7	1	3	0	12	1	48	0	0	2	4	.333	0	0-0	0	3.56	4.05
2010 Bal	AL	43	0	0	22	44.0	174	37	15	14	5	1	0	0	5	0	55	1	0	1	2	.333	0	13-15	6	2.22	2.86
2011 2 Tms	AL	65	0	0	22	65.0	243	38	17	17	11	1	1	0	9	1	85	0	0	2	3	.400	0	0-1	22	1.48	2.35
2012 Tex	AL	37	0	0	13	36.0	130	20	7	7	4	1	1	0	3	0	43	1	0	0	0	-	0	1-1	7	1.12	1.75
2013 Bos	AL	73	0	0	40	74.1	265	33	10	9	5	1	1	1	9	2	101	1	0	4	1	.800	0	21-24	13	0.79	1.09
2014 Bos	AL	64	0	0	50	64.1	249	51	18	18	10	3	1	1	8	0	80	1	0	6	5	.545	0	26-31	1	2.35	2.52
2015 Bos	AL	43	0	0	38	40.1	160	28	14	10	3	1	1	0	9	1	47	4	0	2	4	.333	0	25-27	0	1.67	2.23
2016 Bos	AL	50	0	0	12	47.0	184	34	18	18	8	1	0	2	11	1	63	1	0	2	3	.400	0	7-9	18	2.58	3.45
2017 ChC	AL	49	0	0	10	43.0	178	38	21	19	7	1	1	0	12	3	50	0	0	3	4	.429	0	2-5	14	3.24	3.98
11 Bal	AL	43	0	0	19	47.0	174	25	9	9	6	1	1	0	8	1	62	0	0	1	1	.500	0	0-1	13	1.27	1.72
11 Tex	AL	22	0	0	3	18.0	69	13	8	8	5	0	0	0	1	0	23	0	0	1	2	.333	0	0-0	9	2.21	4.00
Postseason		19	0	0	14	18.0	66	13	6	6	4	0	0	0	2	0	21	0	0	1	1	.500	0	7-7	0	2.33	3.00
9 ML YEARS		436	12	0	207	480.2	1862	350	153	142	60	11	9	4	78	9	572	9	0	22	26	.458	0	95-113	81	1.95	2.66

Justin Upton

Bats: R **Throws:** R **Pos:** LF-151;PH-1   **Ht:** 6'2" **Wt:** 205 **Born:** 8/25/1987 **Age:** 30

Year Team	Lg	G	AB	H	2B	3B	HR	(Hm	Rd)	TB	R	RBI	RC	TBB	IBB	SO	HBP	SH	SF	SB	CS	GDP	Avg	OBP	Slg	OPS
2007 Ari	NL	43	140	31	8	3	2	(2	0)	51	17	11	13	11	4	37	1	0	0	2	0	3	.221	.283	.364	.647
2008 Ari	NL	108	356	89	19	6	15	(12	3)	165	52	42	47	54	6	121	4	0	3	1	4	3	.250	.353	.463	.816
2009 Ari	NL	138	526	158	30	4	26	(14	12)	280	84	86	94	55	3	137	2	1	4	20	5	10	.300	.366	.532	.899
2010 Ari	NL	133	495	135	27	3	17	(8	9)	219	73	69	73	64	5	152	4	1	7	18	8	20	.273	.356	.442	.799
2011 Ari	NL	159	592	171	39	5	31	(20	11)	313	105	88	103	59	9	126	19	0	4	21	9	8	.289	.369	.529	.898
2012 Ari	NL	150	554	155	24	4	17	(11	6)	238	107	67	82	63	5	121	5	0	6	18	8	7	.280	.355	.430	.785
2013 Atl	NL	149	558	147	27	2	27	(13	14)	259	94	70	84	75	4	161	5	1	4	8	1	12	.263	.354	.464	.818
2014 Atl	NL	154	566	153	34	2	29	(18	11)	278	77	102	84	60	1	171	6	0	8	8	4	10	.270	.342	.491	.833
2015 SD	NL	150	542	136	26	3	26	(15	11)	246	85	81	85	68	5	159	4	0	5	19	5	10	.251	.336	.454	.790
2016 Det	AL	153	570	140	28	2	31	(14	17)	265	81	87	77	50	3	179	4	0	2	9	4	15	.246	.310	.465	.775
2017 2 Tms	AL	152	557	152	44	0	35	(17	18)	301	100	109	109	74	3	180	3	0	1	14	5	9	.273	.361	.540	.901
17 Det	AL	125	459	128	37	0	28	(13	15)	249	81	94	98	57	2	147	3	0	1	10	5	6	.279	.362	.542	.904
17 LAA	AL	27	98	24	7	0	7	(4	3)	52	19	15	11	17	1	33	0	0	0	4	0	3	.245	.357	.531	.887
Postseason		15	48	11	2	1	2	(0	2)	21	7	4	7	10	0	13	2	0	0	1	0	0	.229	.383	.438	.821
11 ML YEARS		1489	5456	1467	306	37	256	(144	112)	2615	875	812	851	633	48	1544	57	3	44	138	53	107	.269	.348	.479	.828

Jose Urena

Pitches: R Bats: R Pos: SP-28; RP-6   oo-RAY-nuh   Ht: 6'2" Wt: 200 Born: 9/12/1991 Age: 26

Year	Team	Lg	G	GS	CG	GF	IP	BFP	H	R	ER	HR	SH	SF	HB	TBB	IBB	SO	WP	Bk	W	L	Pct	Sh	Sv-Op	Hld	ERC	ERA
2015	Mia	NL	20	9	0	4	61.2	274	73	37	36	5	3	5	3	25	2	28	2	1	1	5	.167	0	0-1	0	5.27	5.25
2016	Mia	NL	28	12	0	4	83.2	373	91	59	57	11	3	4	6	29	6	58	0	0	4	9	.308	0	1-3	1	4.70	6.13
2017	Mia	NL	34	28	0	2	169.2	724	152	77	72	26	5	3	14	64	4	113	5	1	14	7	.667	0	0-0	0	4.07	3.82
	3 ML YEARS		82	49	0	10	315.0	1371	316	173	165	42	11	12	23	118	12	199	7	2	19	21	.475	0	1-4	1	4.47	4.71

Richard Urena

Bats: B Throws: R Pos: SS-20;2B-1;PR-1   oo-RAY-nuh   Ht: 6'0" Wt: 185 Born: 2/26/1996 Age: 22

Year	Team	Lg	G	AB	H	2B	3B	HR	(Hm	Rd)	TB	R	RBI	RC	TBB	IBB	SO	HBP	SH	SF	SB	CS	GDP	Avg	OBP	Slg	OPS
2014	2 Tms	Low	62	250	77	17	3	2	(-	-)	106	38	25	38	19	0	56	0	2	2	6	4	2	.308	.354	.424	.778
2015	2 Tms	Low	121	508	133	16	5	16	(-	-)	207	71	66	59	16	0	110	2	4	6	8	6	10	.262	.284	.407	.691
2016	Dnedin	A+	97	394	120	18	5	8	(-	-)	176	52	41	62	25	2	64	4	6	2	9	6	15	.305	.351	.447	.797
2016	Nham	AA	30	124	33	6	5	0	(-	-)	49	14	18	13	4	0	19	0	1	3	0	2	2	.266	.282	.395	.678
2017	Nham	AA	129	510	126	36	3	5	(-	-)	183	44	60	54	30	2	100	1	3	7	0	1	8	.247	.286	.359	.645
2017	Tor	AL	21	68	14	4	0	1	(1	0)	21	6	4	5	6	0	28	0	1	0	1	0	0	.206	.270	.309	.579

Julio Urias

Pitches: L Bats: L Pos: SP-5   oo-ree-AHS   Ht: 6'0" Wt: 215 Born: 8/12/1996 Age: 21

Year	Team	Lg	G	GS	CG	GF	IP	BFP	H	R	ER	HR	SH	SF	HB	TBB	IBB	SO	WP	Bk	W	L	Pct	Sh	Sv-Op	Hld	ERC	ERA
2013	Gt Lks	A	18	18	0	0	54.1	211	44	15	15	5	0	0	1	16	0	67	2	0	2	0	1.000	0	0- -	-	2.83	2.48
2014	Rcuca	A+	25	20	0	1	87.2	356	60	25	23	4	0	2	7	37	0	109	5	1	2	2	.500	0	0- -	-	2.48	2.36
2015	Tulsa	AA	13	13	0	0	68.1	268	54	24	21	4	3	0	1	15	0	74	1	1	3	4	.429	0	0- -	-	2.16	2.77
2016	OkCity	AAA	11	7	0	1	45.0	168	31	7	7	2	3	1	1	8	0	49	0	1	5	1	.833	0	0- -	-	1.59	1.40
2017	OkCity	AAA	6	6	0	0	31.1	123	20	9	9	1	0	0	0	15	0	32	4	0	3	0	1.000	0	0- -	-	2.15	2.59
2016	LAD	NL	18	15	0	1	77.0	336	81	32	29	5	4	1	4	31	0	84	3	0	5	2	.714	0	0-0	0	4.37	3.39
2017	LAD	NL	5	5	0	0	23.1	102	23	15	14	1	2	0	1	14	1	11	1	1	0	2	.000	0	0-0	0	4.61	5.40
	Postseason		2	1	0	0	5.2	25	5	4	4	1	0	0	0	4	0	5	0	0	1	1	.500	0	0-0	0	5.31	6.35
	2 ML YEARS		23	20	0	1	100.1	438	104	47	43	6	6	1	5	45	1	95	4	1	5	4	.556	0	0-0	0	4.43	3.86

Giovanny Urshela

Bats: R Throws: R Pos: 3B-60;2B-5;SS-5;PR-5;1B-2   URR-sha-lah   Ht: 6'0" Wt: 215 Born: 10/11/1991 Age: 26

Year	Team	Lg	G	AB	H	2B	3B	HR	(Hm	Rd)	TB	R	RBI	RC	TBB	IBB	SO	HBP	SH	SF	SB	CS	GDP	Avg	OBP	Slg	OPS
2013	Akron	AA	116	445	120	23	2	8	(-	-)	171	42	43	50	14	0	48	1	4	2	1	1	17	.270	.292	.384	.676
2014	Akron	AA	24	90	27	9	0	5	(-	-)	51	15	19	17	6	1	16	1	0	1	1	1	2	.300	.347	.567	.914
2014	Clmbs	AAA	105	396	109	27	6	13	(-	-)	187	63	65	62	30	1	52	3	1	1	0	2	11	.275	.330	.472	.802
2015	Clmbs	AAA	22	81	22	5	1	3	(-	-)	38	12	9	11	3	0	12	0	0	0	0	0	4	.272	.298	.469	.767
2016	Clmbs	AAA	117	468	128	24	1	8	(-	-)	178	54	57	53	15	0	58	1	1	6	0	0	11	.274	.294	.380	.674
2017	Clmbs	AAA	76	297	79	12	1	6	(-	-)	111	34	34	37	20	1	45	5	1	2	0	0	8	.266	.321	.374	.695
2015	Cle	AL	81	267	60	8	1	6	(3	3)	88	25	21	19	18	0	58	2	1	0	0	1	9	.225	.279	.330	.608
2017	Cle	AL	67	156	35	7	0	1	(0	1)	45	14	15	10	8	0	22	0	1	0	0	0	6	.224	.262	.288	.551
	2 ML YEARS		148	423	95	15	1	7	(3	4)	133	39	36	29	26	0	80	2	2	0	0	1	15	.225	.273	.314	.587

Chase Utley

Bats: L Throws: R Pos: 2B-80;PH-44;1B-17;DH-3   UTT-lee   Ht: 6'1" Wt: 195 Born: 12/17/1978 Age: 39

Year	Team	Lg	G	AB	H	2B	3B	HR	(Hm	Rd)	TB	R	RBI	RC	TBB	IBB	SO	HBP	SH	SF	SB	CS	GDP	Avg	OBP	Slg	OPS
2003	Phi	NL	43	134	32	10	1	2	(1	1)	50	13	21	19	11	0	22	6	0	1	2	0	3	.239	.322	.373	.696
2004	Phi	NL	94	267	71	11	2	13	(8	5)	125	36	57	37	15	1	40	2	1	2	4	1	6	.266	.308	.468	.776
2005	Phi	NL	147	543	158	39	6	28	(12	16)	293	93	105	102	69	5	109	9	0	7	16	3	10	.291	.376	.540	.915
2006	Phi	NL	160	658	203	40	4	32	(16	16)	347	131	102	122	63	1	132	14	0	4	15	4	9	.309	.379	.527	.906
2007	Phi	NL	132	530	176	48	5	22	(14	8)	300	104	103	111	50	1	89	25	1	7	9	1	7	.332	.410	.566	.976
2008	Phi	NL	159	607	177	41	4	33	(20	13)	325	113	104	113	64	14	104	27	1	8	14	2	9	.292	.380	.535	.915
2009	Phi	NL	156	571	161	28	4	31	(16	15)	290	112	93	115	88	3	110	24	0	4	23	0	5	.282	.397	.508	.905
2010	Phi	NL	115	425	117	20	2	16	(10	6)	189	75	65	83	63	3	63	18	0	5	13	2	4	.275	.387	.445	.832
2011	Phi	NL	103	398	103	21	6	11	(8	3)	169	54	44	57	39	4	47	14	1	2	14	0	3	.259	.344	.425	.769
2012	Phi	NL	83	301	77	15	2	11	(8	3)	129	48	45	49	43	7	43	12	0	6	11	1	4	.256	.365	.429	.793
2013	Phi	NL	131	476	135	26	6	18	(8	10)	226	73	69	78	45	4	79	5	0	5	8	3	12	.284	.348	.475	.823
2014	Phi	NL	155	589	159	36	6	11	(6	5)	240	74	78	86	53	12	85	13	0	9	10	1	8	.270	.339	.407	.746
2015	2 Tms	NL	107	373	79	21	2	8	(3	5)	128	37	39	30	32	4	64	10	0	8	4	0	7	.212	.286	.343	.629
2016	LAD	NL	138	512	129	26	3	14	(4	10)	203	79	52	72	40	1	115	11	1	1	2	2	0	.252	.319	.396	.716
2017	LAD	NL	127	309	73	20	4	8	(4	4)	125	43	34	39	32	0	57	9	1	2	6	1	3	.236	.324	.405	.728
15	Phi	NL	73	249	54	12	1	5	(1	4)	83	23	30	19	22	4	35	4	0	7	3	0	6	.217	.284	.333	.617
15	LAD	NL	34	124	25	9	1	3	(2	1)	45	14	9	11	10	0	29	6	0	1	1	0	1	.202	.291	.363	.654
	Postseason		59	195	47	7	1	10	(5	5)	86	40	27	37	37	3	47	6	0	1	11	2	3	.241	.377	.441	.818
	15 ML YEARS		1850	6693	1850	401	57	258	(138	120)	3139	1085	1011	1113	707	60	1159	199	6	71	151	21	90	.276	.359	.469	.828

Pat Valaika

vuh-LAKE-uh

Bats: R **Throws:** R **Pos:** PH-66;SS-22;3B-19;2B-8;1B-5;LF-5;DH-2   **Ht:** 5'11" **Wt:** 200 **Born:** 9/9/1992 **Age:** 25

								BATTING											RUNNING			AVERAGES			
Year	Team	Lg	G	AB	H	2B	3B	HR	(Hm | Rd)	TB	R	RBI	RC	TBB	IBB	SO	HBP	SH	SF	SB	CS	GDP	Avg	OBP	Slg	OPS
2013	TriCity	A-	42	146	35	15	2	1	(- | -)	57	27	18	21	23	0	33	2	4	3	5	3	4	.240	.345	.390	.735
2014	2 Tms	Low	120	458	137	26	6	12	(- | -)	211	71	70	74	33	2	127	2	8	5	19	8	5	.299	.345	.461	.806
2015	NwBrit	AA	124	468	110	25	5	8	(- | -)	169	57	57	49	30	1	117	2	6	6	19	8	5	.235	.281	.361	.642
2016	Hrtfrd	AA	108	431	116	33	3	13	(- | -)	194	66	67	60	28	0	95	2	9	4	8	9	8	.269	.314	.450	.764
2016	Albq	AAA	28	110	23	8	1	1	(- | -)	36	8	13	8	2	0	28	1	0	2	2	0	0	.209	.226	.327	.553
2017	Albq	AAA	11	45	12	2	1	1	(- | -)	19	6	11	6	4	0	11	0	1	0	0	0	0	.267	.327	.422	.749
2016	Col	NL	13	19	5	1	0	1	(0 | 1)	9	3	2	5	0	0	8	0	0	0	0	0	0	.263	.263	.474	.737
2017	Col	NL	110	182	47	11	0	13	(9 | 4)	97	28	40	31	7	0	53	0	5	1	0	0	1	.258	.284	.533	.817
	2 ML YEARS		123	201	52	12	0	14	(9 | 5)	106	31	42	32	7	0	61	0	5	1	0	0	1	.259	.282	.527	.810

Luis Valbuena

val-BWAY-nah

Bats: L **Throws:** R **Pos:** 3B-59;1B-48;PH-19;DH-3   **Ht:** 5'10" **Wt:** 215 **Born:** 11/30/1985 **Age:** 32

								BATTING											RUNNING			AVERAGES			
Year	Team	Lg	G	AB	H	2B	3B	HR	(Hm	Rd)	TB	R	RBI	RC	TBB	IBB	SO	HBP	SH	SF	SB	CS	GDP	Avg	OBP	Slg	OPS
2008	Sea	AL	18	49	12	5	0	0	(0	0)	17	6	1	5	4	0	11	1	0	0	0	0	0	.245	.315	.347	.662
2009	Cle	AL	103	368	92	25	3	10	(2	8)	153	52	31	35	26	0	83	0	2	2	2	3	8	.250	.298	.416	.714
2010	Cle	AL	91	275	53	12	0	2	(1	1)	71	22	24	21	28	1	61	3	2	2	1	2	5	.193	.273	.258	.531
2011	Cle	AL	17	43	9	0	0	1	(0	1)	12	4	1	2	1	0	9	0	0	1	1	0	0	.209	.227	.279	.506
2012	ChC	NL	90	265	58	20	0	4	(2	2)	90	26	28	27	36	1	55	0	0	2	0	2	6	.219	.310	.340	.650
2013	ChC	NL	108	331	72	15	1	12	(4	8)	125	34	37	43	53	4	63	4	1	2	1	4	4	.218	.331	.378	.708
2014	ChC	NL	149	478	119	33	4	16	(7	9)	208	68	51	65	65	4	113	2	1	1	1	2	8	.249	.341	.435	.776
2015	Hou	AL	132	434	97	18	0	25	(15	10)	190	62	56	51	50	1	106	6	0	3	1	0	13	.224	.310	.438	.748
2016	Hou	AL	90	292	76	11	1	13	(9	4)	134	38	40	47	44	2	81	1	3	2	1	1	5	.260	.357	.459	.816
2017	LAA	AL	117	347	69	15	0	22	(10	12)	150	42	65	48	48	1	106	1	0	5	0	2	6	.199	.294	.432	.727
	Postseason		6	17	3	0	0	1	(0	1)	6	2	2	2	4	0	8	0	0	0	0	0	0	.176	.333	.353	.686
	10 ML YEARS		915	2882	657	160	9	105	(50	55)	1150	354	334	344	355	14	688	18	9	19	8	16	55	.228	.315	.399	.714

Cesar Valdez

Pitches: R **Bats:** R **Pos:** RP-7; SP-4   **Ht:** 6'2" **Wt:** 200 **Born:** 3/17/1985 **Age:** 33

			HOW MUCH HE PITCHED						WHAT HE GAVE UP										THE RESULTS						
Year	Team	Lg	G	GS	CG	GF	IP	BFP	H	R	ER	HR	SH	SF	HB	TBB	IBB	SO	WP	Bk	W	L	Pct	Sh	Sv-Op	Hld	ERC	ERA
2016	Fresno	AAA	30	18	1	2	138.1	556	143	49	48	7	4	3	1	6	13	1	114	0	1	12	1	.923	1	0- -	-	3.03	3.12
2017	Buffalo	AAA	11	10	1	0	61.1	250	56	25	22	3	1	3	3	12	0	44	2	1	3	3	.500	0	0- -	-	2.70	3.23
2010	Ari	NL	9	2	0	3	20.0	97	29	19	17	2	0	0	1	10	2	13	3	0	1	2	.333	0	0-0	0	7.29	7.65
2017	2 Tms	AL	11	4	0	5	30.2	140	41	29	26	7	0	0	1	11	1	21	1	1	1	1	.500	0	0-0	0	7.11	7.63
17	Oak	AL	4	1	0	2	9.1	44	14	10	10	4	0	0	0	4	0	5	0	0	0	0	-	0	0-0	0	10.35	9.64
17	Tor	AL	7	3	0	3	21.1	96	27	19	16	3	0	0	1	7	1	16	1	1	1	1	.500	0	0-0	0	5.81	6.75
	2 ML YEARS		20	6	0	8	50.2	237	70	48	43	9	0	0	2	21	3	34	4	1	2	3	.400	0	0-0	0	7.20	7.64

Jose Valdez

Pitches: R **Bats:** R **Pos:** RP-14   **Ht:** 6'1" **Wt:** 200 **Born:** 3/1/1990 **Age:** 28

			HOW MUCH HE PITCHED						WHAT HE GAVE UP										THE RESULTS						
Year	Team	Lg	G	GS	CG	GF	IP	BFP	H	R	ER	HR	SH	SF	HB	TBB	IBB	SO	WP	Bk	W	L	Pct	Sh	Sv-Op	Hld	ERC	ERA
2017	Salt Lk*	AAA	10	0	0	3	12.0	52	10	8	8	0	1	0	0	5	0	15	2	0	1	1	.500	0	1- -	-	2.46	6.00
2017	ElPaso*	AAA	23	0	0	10	28.2	130	34	16	16	2	1	0	0	11	0	30	8	0	2	3	.400	0	0- -	-	4.77	5.02
2015	Det	AL	7	0	0	3	9.0	39	10	4	4	2	0	0	0	4	0	4	2	0	1	0	1.000	0	0-1	0	6.01	4.00
2016	LAA	AL	25	0	0	4	23.1	100	17	11	11	4	0	0	0	16	0	22	2	1	2	3	.400	0	0-1	5	4.24	4.24
2017	2 Tms		14	0	0	4	18.0	80	21	18	17	8	0	1	2	5	0	17	1	0	0	0	-	0	0-0	0	7.65	8.50
17	LAA	AL	1	0	0	0	1.0	5	1	2	2	1	0	0	0	1	0	1	0	0	0	0	-	0	0-0	0	14.27	18.00
17	SD	NL	13	0	0	4	17.0	75	20	16	15	7	0	1	2	4	0	16	1	0	0	0	-	0	0-0	0	7.30	7.94
	3 ML YEARS		46	0	0	11	50.1	219	48	33	32	14	0	1	2	25	0	43	5	1	2	4	.333	0	0-2	5	5.74	5.72

Danny Valencia

Bats: R **Throws:** R **Pos:** 1B-118;RF-10;PH-10;3B-1;PR-1 vuh-LENN-see-yah   **Ht:** 6'2" **Wt:** 210 **Born:** 9/19/1984 **Age:** 33

								BATTING											RUNNING			AVERAGES			
Year	Team	Lg	G	AB	H	2B	3B	HR	(Hm	Rd)	TB	R	RBI	RC	TBB	IBB	SO	HBP	SH	SF	SB	CS	GDP	Avg	OBP	Slg	OPS
2010	Min	AL	85	299	93	18	1	7	(4	3)	134	30	40	50	20	0	46	0	0	3	2	0	11	.311	.351	.448	.799
2011	Min	AL	154	564	139	28	2	15	(9	6)	216	63	72	57	40	2	102	0	0	4	2	6	15	.246	.294	.383	.677
2012	2 Tms	AL	44	154	29	6	1	3	(3	0)	46	14	21	7	3	0	38	0	0	4	0	1	6	.188	.199	.299	.497
2013	Bal	AL	52	161	49	14	1	8	(4	4)	89	20	23	25	8	0	33	0	0	1	0	2	5	.304	.335	.553	.888
2014	2 Tms	AL	86	264	68	16	1	4	(1	3)	98	30	30	25	14	0	62	2	0	4	1	1	8	.258	.296	.371	.667
2015	2 Tms	AL	105	345	100	23	1	18	(7	11)	179	59	66	57	29	3	80	1	1	2	2	2	13	.290	.345	.519	.864
2016	Oak	AL	130	471	135	22	1	17	(6	11)	210	72	51	69	41	1	115	3	0	2	1	1	11	.287	.346	.446	.792
2017	Sea	AL	130	450	115	19	3	15	(5	10)	185	54	66	62	40	0	122	2	0	8	2	2	15	.256	.314	.411	.725
12	Min	AL	34	126	25	6	1	2	(2	0)	39	13	17	7	3	0	32	0	0	3	0	1	5	.198	.212	.310	.522
12	Bos	AL	10	28	4	0	0	1	(1	0)	7	1	4	0	0	0	6	0	0	1	0	0	1	.143	.138	.250	.388
14	KC	AL	36	110	31	5	0	2	(0	2)	42	8	11	8	7	0	27	1	0	1	0	0	4	.282	.328	.382	.710
14	Tor	AL	50	154	37	11	1	2	(1	1)	56	12	19	17	7	0	35	1	0	3	1	1	4	.240	.273	.364	.636
15	Tor	AL	58	162	48	13	0	7	(4	3)	82	26	29	26	9	0	40	0	1	0	1	1	4	.296	.331	.506	.838
15	Oak	AL	47	183	52	10	1	11	(3	8)	97	33	37	31	20	3	40	1	0	2	1	1	9	.284	.356	.530	.886
	Postseason		3	9	2	1	0	0	(0	0)	3	1	2	1	1	0	3	0	0	1	0	0	0	.222	.273	.333	.606
	8 ML YEARS		786	2708	728	146	11	87	(37	50)	1157	332	369	352	195	6	598	8	1	28	10	15	85	.269	.317	.427	.744

Breyvic Valera

Bats: B **Throws:** R **Pos:** 2B-3;PH-3 **Ht:** 5'11" **Wt:** 160 **Born:** 1/8/1992 **Age:** 26

Year	Team	Lg	G	AB	H	2B	3B	HR	(Hm	Rd)	TB	R	RBI	RC	TBB	IBB	SO	HBP	SH	SF	SB	CS	GDP	Avg	OBP	Slg	OPS
2013	Peoria	A	128	515	159	18	6	0	(-	-)	189	71	48	71	40	0	30	1	4	2	13	7	10	.309	.358	.367	.725
2014	PlmBh	A+	73	294	98	8	4	0	(-	-)	114	35	37	45	25	0	13	1	1	2	13	10	6	.333	.385	.388	.773
2014	Sprgfld	AA	59	227	65	8	2	0	(-	-)	77	31	20	25	15	0	22	0	4	1	4	5	4	.286	.329	.339	.668
2015	Sprgfld	AA	105	360	85	9	2	3	(-	-)	107	37	31	34	34	0	27	1	2	4	2	4	13	.236	.301	.297	.598
2015	PlmBh	A+	14	51	18	3	1	0	(-	-)	23	9	7	10	11	0	2	0	0	0	0	3	1	.353	.468	.451	.919
2016	Sprgfld	AA	52	178	46	5	1	0	(-	-)	53	16	12	16	9	0	18	0	2	3	3	1	4	.258	.289	.298	.587
2016	Memp	AAA	73	217	74	14	1	0	(-	-)	90	32	31	41	31	1	22	1	3	5	8	4	2	.341	.417	.415	.832
2017	Memp	AAA	117	424	133	22	6	8	(-	-)	191	68	41	70	38	1	34	1	3	4	11	11	7	.314	.368	.450	.819
2017	StL	NL	5	10	1	0	0	0	(0	0)	1	0	0	0	1	0	0	0	0	0	0	0	0	.100	.182	.100	.282

Scott Van Slyke

Bats: R **Throws:** R **Pos:** PH-18;LF-11;1B-9;CF-1;RF-1 **Ht:** 6'4" **Wt:** 215 **Born:** 7/24/1986 **Age:** 31

Year	Team	Lg	G	AB	H	2B	3B	HR	(Hm	Rd)	TB	R	RBI	RC	TBB	IBB	SO	HBP	SH	SF	SB	CS	GDP	Avg	OBP	Slg	OPS
2017	OkCity*	AAA	55	182	44	12	0	5	(-	-)	71	30	20	25	19	0	54	6	0	1	1	1	3	.242	.332	.390	.722
2017	Lsvlle*	AAA	15	48	7	3	0	1	(-	-)	13	5	3	4	7	0	12	1	0	1	2	0	1	.146	.263	.271	.534
2012	LAD	NL	27	54	9	2	0	2	(1	1)	17	4	7	4	2	0	14	0	1	0	1	0	2	.167	.196	.315	.511
2013	LAD	NL	53	129	31	8	0	7	(4	3)	60	13	19	15	20	0	37	1	0	2	1	1	3	.240	.342	.465	.807
2014	LAD	NL	98	212	63	13	1	11	(2	9)	111	32	29	34	28	0	71	4	0	2	4	2	3	.297	.386	.524	.910
2015	LAD	NL	96	222	53	14	0	6	(4	2)	85	19	30	26	23	2	62	4	1	3	3	1	5	.239	.317	.383	.700
2016	LAD	NL	52	102	23	6	0	1	(0	1)	32	10	7	5	5	1	24	5	0	1	1	2	3	.225	.292	.314	.606
2017	LAD	NL	29	41	5	1	0	2	(1	1)	12	6	3	2	7	1	15	0	0	0	1	0	0	.122	.250	.293	.543
	Postseason		3	1	0	0	0	0	(0	0)	0	0	0	0	0	0	0	0	0	0	0	0	0	.000	.000	.000	.000
	6 ML YEARS		355	760	184	44	1	29	(12	17)	317	84	95	86	85	4	223	14	2	8	11	6	20	.242	.326	.417	.744

Ildemaro Vargas

Bats: B **Throws:** R **Pos:** PH-7;2B-3;3B-2;PR-2 **Ht:** 6'0" **Wt:** 170 **Born:** 7/16/1991 **Age:** 26

Year	Team	Lg	G	AB	H	2B	3B	HR	(Hm	Rd)	TB	R	RBI	RC	TBB	IBB	SO	HBP	SH	SF	SB	CS	GDP	Avg	OBP	Slg	OPS
2013	Peoria	A	115	419	104	15	3	1	(-	-)	128	54	39	41	31	1	49	3	13	1	8	4	19	.248	.304	.305	.609
2014	PlmBh	A+	112	431	104	17	1	1	(-	-)	126	46	40	34	16	0	51	4	20	6	1	4	16	.241	.271	.292	.564
2015	Kane	A	86	336	108	18	3	5	(-	-)	147	62	39	59	35	1	16	3	5	5	9	6	8	.321	.385	.438	.823
2016	Mobile	AA	83	323	89	15	2	4	(-	-)	120	41	19	42	24	1	24	0	3	1	8	0	4	.276	.325	.372	.696
2016	Reno	AAA	49	198	70	13	0	2	(-	-)	89	35	18	40	20	0	13	2	4	0	13	1	6	.354	.418	.449	.868
2017	Reno	AAA	113	487	152	35	4	10	(-	-)	225	87	65	82	30	0	40	7	3	8	8	3	9	.312	.355	.462	.817
2017	Ari	NL	12	13	4	1	0	0	(0	0)	5	4	4	2	0	0	3	0	0	0	0	0	1	.308	.308	.385	.692

Jason Vargas

Pitches: L **Bats:** L **Pos:** SP-32 **Ht:** 6'0" **Wt:** 215 **Born:** 2/2/1983 **Age:** 35

			HOW MUCH HE PITCHED					WHAT HE GAVE UP										THE RESULTS							
Year	Team	Lg	G	GS	CG	GF	IP	BFP	H	R	ER	HR	SH	SF	HB	TBB	IBB	SO	WP	Bk	W	L	Pct	Sh	Sv-Op	Hld	ERC	ERA
2005	Fla	NL	17	13	1	0	73.2	325	71	34	33	4	4	1	4	31	4	59	0	0	5	5	.500	0	0-0	0	3.68	4.03
2006	Fla	NL	12	5	0	3	43.0	213	50	39	35	9	4	4	4	30	3	25	2	0	1	2	.333	0	0-0	0	7.30	7.33
2007	NYM	NL	2	2	0	0	10.1	51	17	14	14	4	0	0	0	2	1	4	1	1	0	1	.000	0	0-0	0	8.95	12.19
2009	Sea	AL	23	14	0	4	91.2	385	98	53	50	16	3	6	3	24	1	54	1	0	3	6	.333	0	0-0	0	4.64	4.91
2010	Sea	AL	31	31	0	0	192.2	811	187	86	81	18	4	7	1	54	3	116	1	4	9	12	.429	0	0-0	0	3.37	3.78
2011	Sea	AL	32	32	4	0	201.0	857	205	105	95	22	3	4	4	59	4	131	3	1	10	13	.435	3	0-0	0	3.86	4.25
2012	Sea	AL	33	33	2	0	217.1	887	201	94	93	35	3	6	3	55	1	141	5	0	14	11	.560	2	0-0	0	3.57	3.85
2013	LAA	AL	24	24	3	0	150.0	644	162	68	67	17	3	3	5	46	2	109	1	1	9	8	.529	2	0-0	0	4.40	4.02
2014	KC	AL	30	30	1	0	187.0	790	197	82	77	19	3	1	6	41	4	128	1	1	11	10	.524	1	0-0	0	3.76	3.71
2015	KC	AL	9	9	0	0	43.0	183	46	20	19	5	0	0	1	12	0	27	0	0	5	2	.714	0	0-0	0	4.22	3.98
2016	KC	AL	3	3	0	0	12.0	47	8	3	3	1	0	0	0	3	0	11	0	0	0	0	-	0	0-0	0	1.73	2.25
2017	KC	AL	32	32	1	0	179.2	756	181	84	83	27	2	6	5	58	2	134	6	1	18	11	.621	1	0-0	0	4.33	4.16
	Postseason		3	3	0	0	15.1	61	11	6	6	3	0	0	0	6	0	11	1	0	1	0	1.000	0	0-0	0	3.20	3.52
	12 ML YEARS		248	228	12	7	1401.1	5949	1423	682	650	177	29	38	36	415	25	939	20	9	85	81	.512	7	0-0	0	4.01	4.17

Kennys Vargas

Bats: B **Throws:** R **Pos:** 1B-40;DH-30;PH-12 KEN-ee **Ht:** 6'5" **Wt:** 290 **Born:** 8/1/1990 **Age:** 27

Year	Team	Lg	G	AB	H	2B	3B	HR	(Hm	Rd)	TB	R	RBI	RC	TBB	IBB	SO	HBP	SH	SF	SB	CS	GDP	Avg	OBP	Slg	OPS
2017	Roch*	AAA	51	178	45	8	1	9	(-	-)	82	26	28	31	31	1	53	0	0	2	0	0	5	.253	.360	.461	.821
2014	Min	AL	53	215	59	10	1	9	(8	1)	98	26	38	27	12	2	63	3	0	4	0	0	5	.274	.316	.456	.772
2015	Min	AL	58	175	42	4	0	5	(5	0)	61	18	17	13	9	0	54	0	0	0	0	0	7	.240	.277	.349	.626
2016	Min	AL	47	152	35	11	0	10	(4	6)	76	27	20	21	24	1	57	0	0	1	0	0	2	.230	.333	.500	.833
2017	Min	AL	78	241	61	13	0	11	(5	6)	107	33	41	31	20	1	77	2	0	1	0	0	10	.253	.314	.444	.758
	4 ML YEARS		236	783	197	38	1	35	(22	13)	342	104	116	92	65	4	251	5	0	6	0	0	24	.252	.311	.437	.748

Christian Vazquez

Bats: R Throws: R Pos: C-95;3B-2;DH-2;PH-1;PR-1   VAZ-kehz   Ht: 5'9" Wt: 195 Born: 8/21/1990 Age: 27

								BATTING														RUNNING			AVERAGES			
Year	Team	Lg	G	AB	H	2B	3B	HR	(Hm	Rd)	TB	R	RBI	RC	TBB	IBB	SO	HBP	SH	SF	SB	CS	GDP	Avg	OBP	Slg	OPS
2014	Bos	AL	55	175	42	9	0	1	(1	0)	54	15	20	19	19	1	33	0	3	4	0	0	4	.240	.308	.309	.617
2016	Bos	AL	57	172	39	9	1	1	(1	0)	53	21	12	11	10	1	39	2	0	0	0	0	3	.227	.277	.308	.585
2017	Bos	AL	99	324	94	18	2	5	(4	1)	131	43	32	41	17	0	64	3	0	1	7	2	14	.290	.330	.404	.735
	3 ML YEARS		211	671	175	36	3	7	(6	1)	238	79	64	71	46	2	136	5	3	5	7	2	21	.261	.311	.355	.666

Vince Velasquez

Pitches: R Bats: R Pos: SP-15   Ht: 6'3" Wt: 205 Born: 6/7/1992 Age: 26

			HOW MUCH HE PITCHED						WHAT HE GAVE UP										THE RESULTS						
Year	Team	Lg	G	GS	CG	GF	IP	BFP	H	R	ER	HR	SH	SF	HB	TBB	IBB	SO	WP	Bk	W	L	Pct	Sh	Sv-Op	Hld	ERC	ERA
2015	Hou	AL	19	7	0	5	55.2	231	50	28	27	5	0	0	2	21	0	58	3	0	1	1	.500	0	0-0	0	3.58	4.37
2016	Phi	NL	24	24	1	0	131.0	551	129	64	60	21	9	5	1	45	1	152	3	0	8	6	.571	1	0-0	0	4.25	4.12
2017	Phi	NL	15	15	0	0	72.0	315	74	44	41	15	2	2	3	34	1	68	2	1	2	7	.222	0	0-0	0	5.58	5.13
	3 ML YEARS		58	46	1	5	258.2	1097	253	136	128	41	11	7	6	100	2	278	8	1	11	14	.440	1	0-0	0	4.46	4.45

Hector Velazquez

Pitches: R Bats: R Pos: RP-5; SP-3   Ht: 6'0" Wt: 180 Born: 11/26/1988 Age: 29

			HOW MUCH HE PITCHED						WHAT HE GAVE UP										THE RESULTS						
Year	Team	Lg	G	GS	CG	GF	IP	BFP	H	R	ER	HR	SH	SF	HB	TBB	IBB	SO	WP	Bk	W	L	Pct	Sh	Sv-Op	Hld	ERC	ERA
2017	Pwtckt	AAA	19	19	0	0	102.0	395	78	27	25	7	1	1	2	24	0	79	0	0	8	4	.667	0	0- -	-	2.20	2.21
2017	Bos	AL	8	3	0	4	24.2	96	21	8	8	4	0	0	0	7	0	19	0	0	3	1	.750	0	0-0	0	3.39	2.92

Alex Verdugo

Bats: L Throws: L Pos: PH-7;CF-6;LF-3;RF-3   Ht: 6'0" Wt: 205 Born: 5/15/1996 Age: 22

								BATTING														RUNNING			AVERAGES			
Year	Team	Lg	G	AB	H	2B	3B	HR	(Hm	Rd)	TB	R	RBI	RC	TBB	IBB	SO	HBP	SH	SF	SB	CS	GDP	Avg	OBP	Slg	OPS
2014	2 Tms	Low	54	190	67	15	3	0	(-	-)	97	31	41	43	20	0	18	4	0	2	11	0	4	.353	.421	.511	.932
2015	2 Tms	Low	124	512	159	32	4	9	(-	-)	226	70	61	77	21	2	65	3	1	3	14	5	14	.311	.340	.441	.781
2016	Tulsa	AA	126	477	130	23	1	13	(-	-)	194	58	63	67	44	5	67	4	0	4	2	6	12	.273	.336	.407	.743
2017	OkCity	AAA	117	433	136	27	4	6	(-	-)	189	67	62	78	52	1	50	4	1	5	9	3	8	.314	.389	.436	.825
2017	LAD	NL	15	23	4	0	0	1	(1	0)	7	1	1	0	2	0	4	0	0	0	0	1	1	.174	.240	.304	.544

Drew VerHagen

Pitches: R Bats: R Pos: RP-22; SP-2   verr-HAY-gen   Ht: 6'6" Wt: 230 Born: 10/22/1990 Age: 27

			HOW MUCH HE PITCHED						WHAT HE GAVE UP										THE RESULTS						
Year	Team	Lg	G	GS	CG	GF	IP	BFP	H	R	ER	HR	SH	SF	HB	TBB	IBB	SO	WP	Bk	W	L	Pct	Sh	Sv-Op	Hld	ERC	ERA
2017	Toledo*	AAA	19	19	0	0	97.1	430	108	59	53	7	2	5	4	43	1	69	2	0	7	7	.500	0	0- -	-	4.89	4.90
2014	Det	AL	1	1	0	0	5.0	20	5	3	3	0	0	0	0	3	0	4	0	0	0	1	.000	0	0-0	0	4.67	5.40
2015	Det	AL	20	0	0	2	26.1	106	18	6	6	1	1	0	1	14	2	13	1	0	2	0	1.000	0	0-1	3	2.61	2.05
2016	Det	AL	19	0	0	4	19.0	90	28	15	15	3	0	1	0	7	1	10	1	0	1	0	1.000	0	0-0	2	7.50	7.11
2017	Det	AL	24	2	0	4	34.1	145	42	22	22	10	0	1	0	9	1	25	4	0	0	3	.000	0	0-1	5	6.43	5.77
	4 ML YEARS		64	3	0	10	84.2	361	93	46	46	14	1	2	2	33	4	52	6	0	3	4	.429	0	0-2	10	5.30	4.89

Justin Verlander

Pitches: R Bats: R Pos: SP-33   Ht: 6'5" Wt: 225 Born: 2/20/1983 Age: 35

			HOW MUCH HE PITCHED						WHAT HE GAVE UP										THE RESULTS						
Year	Team	Lg	G	GS	CG	GF	IP	BFP	H	R	ER	HR	SH	SF	HB	TBB	IBB	SO	WP	Bk	W	L	Pct	Sh	Sv-Op	Hld	ERC	ERA
2005	Det	AL	2	2	0	0	11.1	54	15	9	9	1	0	0	1	5	0	7	1	0	0	2	.000	0	0-0	0	6.41	7.15
2006	Det	AL	30	30	1	0	186.0	776	187	78	75	21	2	4	6	60	1	124	5	1	17	9	.654	1	0-0	0	4.12	3.63
2007	Det	AL	32	32	1	0	201.2	866	181	88	82	20	3	1	19	67	3	183	17	2	18	6	.750	1	0-0	0	3.53	3.66
2008	Det	AL	33	33	1	0	201.0	880	195	119	108	18	4	6	14	87	8	163	6	3	11	17	.393	0	0-0	0	4.17	4.84
2009	Det	AL	35	35	3	0	240.0	982	219	99	92	20	6	4	6	63	5	269	8	4	19	9	.679	1	0-0	0	3.06	3.45
2010	Det	AL	33	33	4	0	224.1	925	190	89	84	14	6	8	6	71	0	219	11	2	18	9	.667	0	0-0	0	2.79	3.37
2011	Det	AL	34	34	4	0	251.0	969	174	73	67	24	2	3	3	57	0	250	7	2	24	5	.828	2	0-0	0	1.92	2.40
2012	Det	AL	33	33	6	0	238.1	956	192	81	70	19	4	3	5	60	2	239	2	1	17	8	.680	1	0-0	0	2.45	2.64
2013	Det	AL	34	34	0	0	218.1	925	212	94	84	19	2	6	4	75	1	217	3	1	13	12	.520	0	0-0	0	3.68	3.46
2014	Det	AL	32	32	0	0	206.0	893	223	114	104	18	6	5	5	65	1	159	5	1	15	12	.556	0	0-0	0	4.19	4.54
2015	Det	AL	20	20	1	0	133.1	535	113	56	50	13	1	6	3	32	1	113	2	0	5	8	.385	1	0-0	0	2.75	3.38
2016	Det	AL	34	34	2	0	227.2	903	171	81	77	30	4	7	8	57	1	254	6	0	16	9	.640	0	0-0	0	2.54	3.04
2017	2 Tms	AL	33	33	0	0	206.0	849	170	80	77	27	1	4	4	72	4	219	5	0	15	8	.652	0	0-0	0	3.19	3.36
17	Det	AL	28	28	0	0	172.0	729	153	76	73	23	1	4	3	67	4	176	5	0	10	8	.556	0	0-0	0	3.67	3.82
17	Hou	AL	5	5	0	0	34.0	120	17	4	4	4	0	0	1	5	0	43	0	0	5	0	1.000	0	0-0	0	1.22	1.06
	Postseason		16	16	1	0	98.1	401	77	40	37	13	1	1	1	30	0	112	6	1	7	5	.583	1	0-0	0	2.77	3.39
	13 ML YEARS		385	385	23	0	2545.0	10513	2242	1061	979	244	41	57	84	771	27	2416	78	17	188	114	.623	7	0-0	0	3.15	3.46

Logan Verrett

Pitches: R Bats: R Pos: RP-4
vuh-RETT
Ht: 6'2" Wt: 190 Born: 6/19/1990 Age: 28

Year Team	Lg	G	GS	CG	GF	IP	BFP	H	R	ER	HR	SH	SF	HB	TBB	IBB	SO	WP	Bk	W	L	Pct	Sh	Sv-Op	Hld	ERC	ERA
2017 Norfolk*	AAA	40	2	0	20	60.0	261	56	40	34	9	2	2	4	22	3	49	2	0	2	6	.250	0	5--	-	4.03	5.10
2015 2 Tms		18	4	0	4	47.2	190	34	20	19	6	2	3	2	15	4	39	1	0	1	2	.333	0	1-2	0	2.48	3.59
2016 NYM	NL	35	12	0	10	91.2	406	100	55	53	16	3	3	4	43	3	66	4	1	3	8	.273	0	0-0	0	5.68	5.20
2017 Bal	AL	4	0	0	2	10.2	47	11	6	5	3	2	0	2	3	1	9	0	0	2	0	1.000	0	0-0	0	5.72	4.22
15 Tex	AL	4	0	0	1	9.0	42	11	7	6	1	0	2	0	4	1	3	1	0	0	1	.000	0	0-0	0	5.30	6.00
15 NYM	NL	14	4	0	3	38.2	148	23	13	13	5	2	1	2	11	3	36	0	0	1	1	.500	0	1-2	0	1.90	3.03
3 ML YEARS		57	16	0	16	150.0	643	145	81	77	25	7	6	8	61	8	114	5	1	6	10	.375	0	1-2	0	4.58	4.62

Thyago Vieira

Pitches: R Bats: R Pos: RP-1
Ht: 6'2" Wt: 210 Born: 7/1/1993 Age: 24

Year Team	Lg	G	GS	CG	GF	IP	BFP	H	R	ER	HR	SH	SF	HB	TBB	IBB	SO	WP	Bk	W	L	Pct	Sh	Sv-Op	Hld	ERC	ERA
2013 Everett	A-	14	13	0	0	68.0	303	60	30	29	2	3	4	16	34	0	51	8	1	4	5	.444	0	0--	-	4.24	3.84
2014 Clinton	A	13	0	0	9	20.1	88	16	12	12	1	2	1	2	14	0	23	4	0	1	1	.500	0	1--	-	4.15	5.31
2015 Clinton	A	22	0	0	9	31.0	152	35	32	24	2	1	5	4	20	0	22	9	0	1	4	.200	0	0--	-	5.91	6.97
2016 Bkrsfld	A+	34	0	0	26	44.1	189	37	19	14	1	2	0	2	18	0	53	9	0	0	1	1.000	0	8--	-	2.81	2.84
2017 Ark	AA	29	0	0	22	36.1	152	30	18	15	1	1	0	2	15	0	35	4	1	2	3	.400	0	2--	-	2.92	3.72
2017 Tacom	AAA	12	0	0	7	17.2	77	18	9	9	1	0	0	1	7	0	11	8	1	0	1	.000	0	2--	-	4.09	4.58
2017 Sea	AL	1	0	0	1	1.0	3	0	0	0	0	0	0	0	0	0	1	0	0	0	0	-	0	0-0	0	0.00	0.00

Christian Villanueva

Bats: R Throws: R Pos: 3B-9;PH-4
Ht: 5'11" Wt: 210 Born: 6/19/1991 Age: 27

Year Team	Lg	G	AB	H	2B	3B	HR	(Hm	Rd)	TB	R	RBI	RC	TBB	IBB	SO	HBP	SH	SF	SB	CS	GDP	Avg	OBP	Slg	OPS
2013 Tenn	AA	133	490	128	41	2	19	(-	-)	230	60	72	73	34	1	117	9	3	6	5	7	10	.261	.317	.469	.787
2014 Iowa	AAA	64	223	47	18	0	6	(-	-)	83	22	26	24	21	2	64	2	1	1	2	1	7	.211	.283	.372	.656
2014 Tenn	AA	62	234	58	20	0	4	(-	-)	90	31	32	29	19	2	42	3	1	2	0	1	6	.248	.310	.385	.695
2015 Iowa	AAA	123	455	118	23	2	18	(-	-)	199	56	88	65	35	1	80	5	4	9	2	3	16	.259	.313	.437	.751
2017 ElPaso	AAA	109	398	118	28	2	20	(-	-)	210	69	86	78	43	0	83	6	1	6	4	2	13	.296	.369	.528	.896
2017 SD	NL	12	32	11	1	0	4	(3	1)	24	5	7	8	0	0	10	0	0	0	0	0	0	.344	.344	.750	1.094

Jonathan Villar

Bats: B Throws: R Pos: 2B-98;PH-27;CF-6;PR-2;DH-1
vee-YARR
Ht: 6'1" Wt: 215 Born: 5/2/1991 Age: 27

Year Team	Lg	G	AB	H	2B	3B	HR	(Hm	Rd)	TB	R	RBI	RC	TBB	IBB	SO	HBP	SH	SF	SB	CS	GDP	Avg	OBP	Slg	OPS
2013 Hou	AL	58	210	51	9	2	1	(0	1)	67	26	8	22	24	1	71	0	7	0	18	8	5	.243	.321	.319	.640
2014 Hou	AL	87	263	55	13	2	7	(3	4)	93	31	27	24	19	1	80	2	4	1	17	4	4	.209	.267	.354	.620
2015 Hou	AL	53	116	33	7	1	2	(0	2)	48	18	11	15	10	0	29	0	1	1	7	2	3	.284	.339	.414	.752
2016 Mil	NL	156	589	168	38	3	19	(6	13)	269	92	63	102	79	4	174	2	5	4	62	18	7	.285	.369	.457	.826
2017 Mil	NL	122	403	97	18	1	11	(7	4)	150	49	40	45	30	1	132	0	2	1	23	8	4	.241	.293	.372	.665
Postseason		1	0	0	0	0	0	(0	0)	0	1	0	0	0	0	0	0	0	0	1	0	0	-	-	-	-
5 ML YEARS		476	1581	404	85	9	40	(16	24)	627	216	149	208	162	7	486	4	19	7	127	40	23	.256	.325	.397	.722

Zach Vincej

Bats: R Throws: R Pos: PH-5;SS-3;2B-1
VIN-see
Ht: 6'0" Wt: 190 Born: 5/1/1991 Age: 27

Year Team	Lg	G	AB	H	2B	3B	HR	(Hm	Rd)	TB	R	RBI	RC	TBB	IBB	SO	HBP	SH	SF	SB	CS	GDP	Avg	OBP	Slg	OPS
2013 Dayton	A	104	377	99	17	5	3	(-	-)	135	51	31	48	36	0	72	6	2	4	13	7	9	.263	.333	.358	.691
2014 Bkrsfld	A+	115	428	116	23	1	1	(-	-)	144	72	40	52	44	0	73	3	4	2	11	8	12	.271	.342	.336	.678
2015 Pnscla	AA	90	286	69	10	0	5	(-	-)	94	39	22	36	44	1	48	4	2	3	7	4	4	.241	.347	.329	.676
2016 Pnscla	AA	121	399	112	24	3	3	(-	-)	151	45	47	51	25	0	85	6	4	4	7	6	9	.281	.329	.378	.708
2017 Lsvlle	AAA	110	378	102	21	4	3	(-	-)	140	36	38	47	28	1	49	4	8	2	4	3	13	.270	.325	.370	.696
2017 Cin	NL	9	9	1	0	0	0	(0	0)	1	2	0	1	1	0	5	2	0	0	0	0	0	.111	.333	.111	.444

Nick Vincent

Pitches: R Bats: R Pos: RP-69
Ht: 6'0" Wt: 185 Born: 7/12/1986 Age: 31

Year Team	Lg	G	GS	CG	GF	IP	BFP	H	R	ER	HR	SH	SF	HB	TBB	IBB	SO	WP	Bk	W	L	Pct	Sh	Sv-Op	Hld	ERC	ERA
2012 SD	NL	27	0	0	3	26.1	105	19	5	5	2	1	0	1	7	0	28	1	0	2	0	1.000	0	0-1	5	2.13	1.71
2013 SD	NL	45	0	0	5	46.1	180	33	11	11	4	1	4	0	11	0	49	0	0	6	3	.667	0	1-1	10	1.67	2.14
2014 SD	NL	63	0	0	7	55.0	215	44	22	22	5	3	0	2	11	1	62	1	0	1	2	.333	0	0-2	20	2.39	3.60
2015 SD	NL	26	0	0	8	23.0	100	25	8	6	0	0	1	0	10	1	22	0	0	0	1	.000	0	0-2	0	3.95	2.35
2016 Sea	AL	60	0	0	15	60.1	247	53	26	25	11	1	1	1	15	5	65	0	0	4	4	.500	0	3-9	17	3.28	3.73
2017 Sea	AL	69	0	0	7	64.2	262	62	23	23	3	4	4	0	13	5	50	0	0	3	3	.500	0	0-2	29	2.67	3.20
6 ML YEARS		290	0	0	47	275.2	1109	236	95	92	22	13	6	6	67	15	276	2	0	16	13	.552	0	4-17	81	2.62	3.00

Arodys Vizcaino

Pitches: R Bats: R Pos: RP-62
ah-ROH-dis vees-kai-EE-no
Ht: 6'0" Wt: 230 Born: 11/13/1990 Age: 27

		HOW MUCH HE PITCHED						WHAT HE GAVE UP												THE RESULTS							
Year Team	Lg	G	GS	CG	GF	IP	BFP	H	R	ER	HR	SH	SF	HB	TBB	IBB	SO	WP	Bk	W	L	Pct	Sh	Sv-Op	Hld	ERC	ERA
2011 Atl	NL	17	0	0	2	17.1	77	16	9	9	1	0	0	1	9	1	17	5	0	1	1	.500	0	0-2	5	3.89	4.67
2014 ChC	NL	5	0	0	5	5.0	22	5	3	3	1	0	1	0	3	0	4	0	0	0	0	-	0	0-0	0	5.79	5.40
2015 Atl	NL	36	0	0	25	33.2	139	27	7	6	1	2	0	0	13	2	37	7	0	1	0	.750	0	9-10	3	2.42	1.60
2016 Atl	NL	43	0	0	24	38.2	182	37	25	19	3	1	0	1	26	3	50	3	1	1	4	.200	0	10-14	4	4.52	4.42
2017 Atl	NL	62	0	0	28	57.1	235	42	19	18	7	0	1	2	21	1	64	6	0	5	3	.625	0	14-17	17	2.75	2.83
5 ML YEARS		163	0	0	84	152.0	655	127	63	55	13	3	1	4	72	7	172	21	1	10	9	.526	0	33-43	25	3.33	3.26

Dan Vogelbach

Bats: L Throws: R Pos: PH-8;1B-7;DH-2
voh-GULL-bock
Ht: 6'0" Wt: 250 Born: 12/17/1992 Age: 25

								BATTING													RUNNING			AVERAGES			
Year Team	Lg	G	AB	H	2B	3B	HR	(Hm	Rd)	TB	R	RBI	RC	TBB	IBB	SO	HBP	SH	SF	SB	CS	GDP	Avg	OBP	Slg	OPS
2013 2 Tms	Low	131	483	137	23	0	19	(-	-)	217	68	76	85	73	3	89	2	0	8	5	4	11	.284	.375	.449	.824
2014 Dytona	A+	132	482	129	28	1	16	(-	-)	207	71	76	78	66	1	91	5	0	7	4	4	15	.268	.357	.429	.787
2015 Tenn	AA	76	254	69	16	1	7	(-	-)	108	41	39	48	57	1	61	0	0	2	1	1	12	.272	.403	.425	.828
2016 Iowa	AAA	89	305	97	18	2	16	(-	-)	167	53	64	71	55	5	67	3	0	2	0	0	9	.318	.425	.548	.972
2016 Tacom	AAA	44	154	37	7	0	7	(-	-)	65	26	32	30	42	2	34	1	0	1	0	0	7	.240	.404	.422	.826
2017 Tacom	AAA	125	459	133	25	0	17	(-	-)	209	65	84	86	76	2	98	1	0	5	3	1	16	.290	.388	.455	.844
2016 Sea	AL	8	12	1	0	0	0	(0	0)	1	0	0	0	1	0	6	0	0	0	0	0	0	.083	.154	.083	.237
2017 Sea	AL	16	28	6	1	0	0	(0	0)	7	0	2	2	3	0	9	0	0	0	0	0	2	.214	.290	.250	.540
2 ML YEARS		24	40	7	1	0	0	(0	0)	8	0	2	2	4	0	15	0	0	0	0	0	2	.175	.250	.200	.450

Stephen Vogt

Bats: L Throws: R Pos: C-81;PH-20;DH-7;LF-1
VOTE
Ht: 6'0" Wt: 225 Born: 11/1/1984 Age: 33

								BATTING													RUNNING			AVERAGES			
Year Team	Lg	G	AB	H	2B	3B	HR	(Hm	Rd)	TB	R	RBI	RC	TBB	IBB	SO	HBP	SH	SF	SB	CS	GDP	Avg	OBP	Slg	OPS
2012 TB	AL	18	25	0	0	0	0	(-	-)	0	0	0	0	2	0	2	0	0	0	0	0	0	.000	.074	.000	.074
2013 Oak	AL	47	135	34	6	1	4	(3	1)	54	18	16	15	9	1	28	0	2	2	0	1	2	.252	.295	.400	.695
2014 Oak	AL	84	269	75	10	2	9	(4	5)	116	26	35	38	16	2	39	1	0	1	1	0	2	.279	.321	.431	.752
2015 Oak	AL	136	445	116	21	3	18	(5	13)	197	58	71	75	56	6	97	2	0	8	0	2	9	.261	.341	.443	.783
2016 Oak	AL	137	490	123	30	2	14	(4	10)	199	54	56	51	35	3	83	4	0	3	0	0	6	.251	.305	.406	.711
2017 2 Tms		99	279	65	15	1	12	(6	6)	118	25	40	33	21	1	56	0	1	2	0	1	1	.233	.285	.423	.708
17 Oak	AL	54	157	34	8	1	4	(1	3)	56	12	20	19	16	1	31	0	0	1	0	0	1	.217	.287	.357	.644
17 Mil	NL	45	122	31	7	0	8	(5	3)	62	13	20	14	5	0	25	0	1	1	0	0	1	.254	.281	.508	.789
Postseason		6	19	3	0	1	0	(0	0)	5	2	1	1	2	0	8	0	0	0	0	0	0	.158	.238	.263	.501
6 ML YEARS		521	1643	413	82	9	57	(22	35)	684	181	218	212	139	13	305	7	3	16	1	4	21	.251	.310	.416	.726

Luke Voit

Bats: R Throws: R Pos: PH-37;1B-31;DH-1
Ht: 6'3" Wt: 225 Born: 2/13/1991 Age: 27

								BATTING													RUNNING			AVERAGES			
Year Team	Lg	G	AB	H	2B	3B	HR	(Hm	Rd)	TB	R	RBI	RC	TBB	IBB	SO	HBP	SH	SF	SB	CS	GDP	Avg	OBP	Slg	OPS
2013 StCol	A-	46	149	36	7	0	2	(-	-)	49	14	16	20	21	1	29	6	0	1	1	0	6	.242	.356	.329	.685
2014 PlmBh	A+	93	351	97	21	5	9	(-	-)	155	57	51	54	32	0	79	4	1	2	1	1	8	.276	.342	.442	.783
2015 PlmBh	A+	130	462	126	18	5	11	(-	-)	187	52	77	73	63	2	104	5	0	9	2	0	14	.273	.360	.405	.765
2016 Sprgfld	AA	134	482	143	20	5	19	(-	-)	230	70	74	87	52	1	83	8	0	4	1	2	16	.297	.372	.477	.849
2017 Memp	AAA	74	269	88	23	1	13	(-	-)	152	35	50	60	29	1	53	8	0	1	1	1	3	.327	.407	.565	.972
2017 StL	NL	62	114	28	9	0	4	(4	0)	49	18	18	12	7	0	31	3	0	0	0	0	4	.246	.306	.430	.736

Edinson Volquez

Pitches: R Bats: R Pos: SP-17
VOHL-kezz
Ht: 6'0" Wt: 220 Born: 7/3/1983 Age: 34

		HOW MUCH HE PITCHED						WHAT HE GAVE UP												THE RESULTS							
Year Team	Lg	G	GS	CG	GF	IP	BFP	H	R	ER	HR	SH	SF	HB	TBB	IBB	SO	WP	Bk	W	L	Pct	Sh	Sv-Op	Hld	ERC	ERA
2005 Tex	AL	6	3	0	0	12.2	75	25	22	20	3	0	1	2	10	0	11	0	0	0	4	.000	0	0-0	0	14.15	14.21
2006 Tex	AL	8	8	0	0	33.1	164	52	28	27	7	0	1	1	17	0	15	0	0	1	6	.143	0	0-0	0	9.27	7.29
2007 Tex	AL	6	6	0	0	34.0	149	34	18	17	4	0	2	2	15	0	29	0	0	2	1	.667	0	0-0	0	4.63	4.50
2008 Cin	NL	33	32	0	1	196.0	838	167	82	70	14	6	5	14	93	5	206	10	1	17	6	.739	0	0-0	0	3.61	3.21
2009 Cin	NL	9	9	0	0	49.2	218	34	25	24	6	2	1	5	32	0	47	2	1	4	2	.667	0	0-0	0	3.77	4.35
2010 Cin	NL	12	12	0	0	62.2	275	59	30	30	6	3	1	3	35	0	67	5	0	4	3	.571	0	0-0	0	4.60	4.31
2011 Cin	NL	20	20	0	0	108.2	489	106	72	69	19	5	6	4	65	3	104	5	2	5	7	.417	0	0-0	0	5.42	5.71
2012 SD	NL	32	32	1	0	182.2	802	160	88	84	14	5	4	9	105	6	174	9	1	11	11	.500	1	0-0	0	4.04	4.14
2013 2 Tms	NL	33	32	0	0	170.1	777	193	114	108	14	5	4	11	77	2	142	16	0	9	12	.429	0	0-0	0	5.11	5.71
2014 Pit	NL	32	31	1	0	192.2	809	166	75	65	17	13	6	14	71	6	140	15	0	13	7	.650	0	0-0	0	3.37	3.04
2015 KC	AL	34	33	1	0	200.1	850	190	80	79	16	5	7	8	72	1	155	3	0	13	9	.591	0	0-0	0	3.66	3.55
2016 KC	AL	34	34	0	0	189.1	853	217	124	113	23	6	6	7	76	1	139	5	1	10	11	.476	0	0-0	0	5.20	5.37
2017 Mia	NL	17	17	1	0	92.1	397	78	46	43	8	5	5	3	53	3	81	4	0	4	8	.333	1	0-0	0	3.93	4.19
13 SD	NL	27	27	0	0	142.1	659	168	100	95	14	7	3	3	69	2	116	11	0	9	10	.474	0	0-0	0	5.45	6.01
13 LAD	NL	6	5	0	0	28.0	118	25	14	13	5	2	1	0	8	0	26	5	0	0	2	.000	0	0-0	0	3.45	4.18
Postseason		7	7	0	0	35.1	154	27	22	21	4	1	3	2	23	2	26	0	0	1	4	.200	0	0-0	0	3.98	5.35
13 ML YEARS		276	269	4	1	1524.2	6696	1481	813	749	156	59	49	75	721	27	1310	74	6	93	87	.517	2	0-0	0	4.39	4.42

Chris Volstad

Pitches: R **Bats:** R **Pos:** RP-4; SP-2
VOHL-stadd
Ht: 6'8" **Wt:** 235 **Born:** 9/23/1986 **Age:** 31

Year Team	Lg	G	GS	CG	GF	IP	BFP	H	R	ER	HR	SH	SF	HB	TBB	IBB	SO	WP	Bk	W	L	Pct	Sh	Sv-Op	Hld	ERC	ERA
2017 Charllt*	AAA	27	18	2	3	118.0	518	161	82	73	12	2	4	4	23	0	71	6	0	3	10	.231	0	1--	-	5.65	5.57
2008 Fla	NL	15	14	0	0	84.1	365	76	30	27	3	6	1	5	36	4	52	0	0	6	4	.600	0	0-0	0	3.30	2.88
2009 Fla	NL	29	29	1	0	159.0	682	169	100	92	29	8	3	3	59	3	107	8	0	9	13	.409	1	0-0	0	5.05	5.21
2010 Fla	NL	30	30	2	0	175.0	758	187	94	89	17	8	7	8	60	5	102	8	1	12	9	.571	1	0-0	0	4.38	4.58
2011 Fla	NL	29	29	0	0	165.2	719	187	96	90	23	12	10	1	49	6	117	2	1	5	13	.278	0	0-0	0	4.63	4.89
2012 ChC	NL	21	21	0	0	111.1	507	137	81	78	16	5	8	3	43	4	61	2	1	3	12	.200	0	0-0	0	5.73	6.31
2013 Col	NL	6	0	0	1	8.1	47	19	10	10	1	0	0	2	1	0	3	0	0	0	0	-	0	0-0	0	12.25	10.80
2015 Pit	NL	1	0	0	0	2.0	7	2	0	0	0	0	0	2	0	0	0	0	0	0	0	-	0	0-0	1	2.31	0.00
2017 CWS	AL	6	2	0	2	19.1	76	16	11	10	4	0	1	1	5	0	10	0	0	1	2	.333	0	0-0	0	3.62	4.66
8 ML YEARS		137	125	3	3	725.0	3161	793	422	396	93	39	30	23	253	22	452	20	3	36	53	.404	2	0-0	1	4.71	4.92

Joey Votto

Bats: L **Throws:** R **Pos:** 1B-162
VAH-toe
Ht: 6'2" **Wt:** 220 **Born:** 9/10/1983 **Age:** 34

Year Team	Lg	G	AB	H	2B	3B	HR	Hm	Rd	TB	R	RBI	RC	TBB	IBB	SO	HBP	SH	SF	SB	CS	GDP	Avg	OBP	Slg	OPS
2007 Cin	NL	24	84	27	7	0	4	4	0	46	11	17	17	5	1	15	0	0	0	1	0	0	.321	.360	.548	.907
2008 Cin	NL	151	526	156	32	3	24	14	10	266	69	84	91	59	9	102	2	0	2	7	5	7	.297	.368	.506	.874
2009 Cin	NL	131	469	151	38	1	25	14	11	266	82	84	99	70	10	106	4	0	1	4	1	8	.322	.414	.567	.981
2010 Cin	NL	150	547	177	36	2	37	18	19	328	106	113	132	91	8	125	7	0	3	16	5	11	.324	.424	.600	1.024
2011 Cin	NL	161	599	185	40	3	29	13	16	318	101	103	131	110	15	129	4	0	6	8	6	20	.309	.416	.531	.947
2012 Cin	NL	111	374	126	44	0	14	10	4	212	59	56	97	94	18	85	5	0	6	5	3	15	.337	.474	.567	1.041
2013 Cin	NL	162	581	177	30	3	24	11	13	285	101	73	121	135	19	138	4	0	6	6	3	15	.305	.435	.491	.926
2014 Cin	NL	62	220	56	16	0	6	6	0	90	32	23	36	47	2	49	3	0	2	1	1	5	.255	.390	.409	.799
2015 Cin	NL	158	545	171	33	2	29	14	15	295	95	80	135	143	15	135	5	0	2	11	3	11	.314	.459	.541	1.000
2016 Cin	NL	158	556	181	34	2	29	16	13	306	101	97	130	108	15	120	5	0	8	8	1	16	.326	.434	.550	.985
2017 Cin	NL	162	559	179	34	1	36	20	16	323	106	100	130	134	20	83	8	0	6	5	1	16	.320	.454	.578	1.032
Postseason		9	32	8	0	0	0	0	0	8	3	1	3	4	0	9	0	0	1	0	0	1	.250	.324	.250	.574
11 ML YEARS		1430	5060	1586	344	17	257	140	117	2735	863	830	1128	996	132	1087	47	0	38	72	29	117	.313	.428	.541	.969

Michael Wacha

Pitches: R **Bats:** R **Pos:** SP-30
WOCK-uh
Ht: 6'6" **Wt:** 215 **Born:** 7/1/1991 **Age:** 26

Year Team	Lg	G	GS	CG	GF	IP	BFP	H	R	ER	HR	SH	SF	HB	TBB	IBB	SO	WP	Bk	W	L	Pct	Sh	Sv-Op	Hld	ERC	ERA
2013 StL	NL	15	9	0	2	64.2	260	52	20	20	5	1	3	0	19	0	65	3	0	4	1	.800	0	0-1	0	2.52	2.78
2014 StL	NL	19	19	0	0	107.0	447	95	41	38	6	1	2	5	33	0	94	2	0	5	6	.455	0	0-0	0	3.00	3.20
2015 StL	NL	30	30	0	0	181.1	762	162	74	68	19	8	3	6	58	4	153	4	1	17	7	.708	0	0-0	0	3.28	3.38
2016 StL	NL	27	24	0	1	138.0	606	159	86	78	15	4	5	1	45	6	114	6	0	7	7	.500	0	0-0	0	4.66	5.09
2017 StL	NL	30	30	1	0	165.2	701	170	82	76	17	3	4	3	55	3	158	5	0	12	9	.571	1	0-0	0	4.07	4.13
Postseason		7	6	0	1	35.1	144	24	16	16	7	0	0	1	16	4	38	0	0	4	3	.571	0	0-0	0	3.15	4.08
5 ML YEARS		121	112	1	3	656.2	2776	638	303	280	62	17	17	15	210	13	584	20	1	45	30	.600	1	0-1	0	3.63	3.84

Tyler Wade

Bats: L **Throws:** R **Pos:** 2B-15;SS-7;LF-5;PH-4;PR-3;RF-2;DH-1
Ht: 6'1" **Wt:** 185 **Born:** 11/23/1994 **Age:** 23

Year Team	Lg	G	AB	H	2B	3B	HR	Hm	Rd	TB	R	RBI	RC	TBB	IBB	SO	HBP	SH	SF	SB	CS	GDP	Avg	OBP	Slg	OPS
2013 2 Tms	Low	50	175	51	10	0	0	-	-	61	37	13	29	34	0	46	2	2	0	11	1	4	.291	.412	.349	.761
2014 CtnSC	A	129	507	138	24	6	1	-	-	177	77	51	67	57	1	118	6	2	4	22	13	7	.272	.350	.349	.699
2015 Tampa	A+	98	368	103	11	5	2	-	-	130	51	28	50	39	0	65	2	5	4	31	15	4	.280	.349	.353	.702
2015 Trntn	AA	29	113	23	4	0	1	-	-	30	6	3	5	2	0	24	1	1	0	2	1	1	.204	.224	.265	.490
2016 Trntn	AA	133	505	131	16	7	5	-	-	176	90	27	70	66	0	103	7	4	1	27	8	2	.259	.352	.349	.701
2017 S-WB	AAA	85	339	105	22	4	7	-	-	156	68	31	64	38	0	75	4	1	4	26	5	3	.310	.382	.460	.842
2017 NYY	AL	30	58	9	4	0	0	0	0	13	7	2	1	5	0	19	0	0	0	1	1	2	.155	.222	.224	.446

Bobby Wahl

Pitches: R **Bats:** R **Pos:** RP-7
Ht: 6'2" **Wt:** 210 **Born:** 3/21/1992 **Age:** 26

Year Team	Lg	G	GS	CG	GF	IP	BFP	H	R	ER	HR	SH	SF	HB	TBB	IBB	SO	WP	Bk	W	L	Pct	Sh	Sv-Op	Hld	ERC	ERA
2013 2 Tms	Low	10	5	0	2	21.2	94	20	11	10	3	0	1	0	8	0	28	3	0	0	0	-	0	2--	-	3.67	4.15
2014 2 Tms	Low	29	7	0	13	53.0	245	54	36	29	7	1	2	3	25	0	62	4	0	0	4	.000	0	4--	-	4.73	4.92
2015 Mdlnd	AA	24	0	0	12	32.1	143	36	17	15	2	2	0	0	14	1	36	5	0	2	0	1.000	0	4--	-	4.54	4.18
2016 Mdlnd	AA	33	0	0	18	40.2	159	26	11	10	3	3	0	1	17	1	48	3	0	0	1	.000	0	10--	-	2.25	2.21
2016 Nashv	AAA	9	0	0	7	9.2	41	7	3	3	0	0	0	0	6	1	14	2	0	1	0	1.000	0	4--	-	2.57	2.79
2017 Nashv	AAA	11	0	0	5	13.0	58	13	8	6	3	0	0	0	5	0	22	1	0	1	1	.500	0	3--	-	4.74	4.15
2017 Oak	AL	7	0	0	1	7.2	36	8	4	4	0	0	0	1	4	0	8	2	0	0	0	-	0	0-0	0	4.41	4.70

Adam Wainwright

Pitches: R **Bats:** R **Pos:** SP-23; RP-1
Ht: 6'7" **Wt:** 235 **Born:** 8/30/1981 **Age:** 36

			HOW MUCH HE PITCHED						WHAT HE GAVE UP											THE RESULTS						
Year	Team	Lg	G	GS	CG	GF	IP	BFP	H	R	ER	HR	SH	SF	HB	TBB	IBB	SO	WP	Bk	W	L	Pct	Sh	Sv-Op	Hld	ERC	ERA
2005	StL	NL	2	0	0	1	2.0	9	2	3	3	1	0	0	0	1	0	0	0	0	0	0	-	0	3-5	17	7.30	13.50
2006	StL	NL	61	0	0	10	75.0	309	64	26	26	6	4	1	4	22	2	72	3	0	2	1	.667	0	3-5	17	2.92	3.12
2007	StL	NL	32	32	1	0	202.0	882	212	93	83	13	9	5	9	70	4	136	6	0	14	12	.538	0	0-0	0	4.01	3.70
2008	StL	NL	20	20	1	0	132.0	544	122	51	47	12	6	4	3	34	1	91	3	0	11	3	.786	0	0-0	0	3.14	3.20
2009	StL	NL	34	34	1	0	233.0	970	216	75	68	17	10	5	3	66	1	212	7	0	19	8	.704	0	0-0	0	3.08	2.63
2010	StL	NL	33	33	5	0	230.1	910	186	68	62	15	13	6	4	56	2	213	2	0	20	11	.645	2	0-0	0	2.36	2.42
2012	StL	NL	32	32	3	0	198.2	831	196	96	87	15	9	6	6	52	3	184	5	2	14	13	.519	2	0-0	0	3.41	3.94
2013	StL	NL	34	34	5	0	241.2	956	223	83	79	15	13	2	6	35	2	219	5	0	19	9	.679	2	0-0	0	2.60	2.94
2014	StL	NL	32	32	5	0	227.0	898	184	64	60	10	8	3	7	50	5	179	4	1	20	9	.690	3	0-0	0	2.20	2.38
2015	StL	NL	7	4	0	2	28.0	111	25	7	5	0	2	0	0	4	0	20	0	0	2	1	.667	0	0-0	0	1.97	1.61
2016	StL	NL	33	33	1	0	198.2	847	220	108	102	25	9	5	5	59	4	161	1	0	13	9	.591	1	0-0	0	4.50	4.62
2017	StL	NL	24	23	0	0	123.1	546	140	73	70	14	5	1	5	45	4	96	2	0	12	5	.706	0	0-0	0	4.93	5.11
	Postseason		24	12	1	9	89.0	361	82	33	30	9	2	2	2	15	0	96	3	0	4	4	.500	0	4-5	0	2.85	3.03
	12 ML YEARS		344	277	22	13	1891.2	7813	1790	747	692	140	87	42	52	494	28	1583	38	3	146	81	.643	10	3-5	17	3.18	3.29

Christian Walker

Bats: R **Throws:** R **Pos:** PH-10; 1B-1; DH-1
Ht: 6'0" **Wt:** 220 **Born:** 3/28/1991 **Age:** 27

			BATTING																		RUNNING			AVERAGES			
Year	Team	Lg	G	AB	H	2B	3B	HR	(Hm	Rd)	TB	R	RBI	RC	TBB	IBB	SO	HBP	SH	SF	SB	CS	GDP	Avg	OBP	Slg	OPS
2017	Reno*	AAA	133	514	159	34	9	32	(-	-)	307	104	114	116	61	3	104	6	0	10	5	2	12	.309	.382	.597	.980
2014	Bal	AL	6	18	3	1	0	1	(1	0)	7	1	1	1	1	0	9	0	0	0	0	0	0	.167	.211	.389	.599
2015	Bal	AL	7	9	1	0	0	0	(0	0)	1	0	0	1	3	0	4	0	0	0	0	0	0	.111	.333	.111	.444
2017	Ari	NL	11	12	3	1	0	2	(2	0)	10	2	2	2	1	0	5	2	0	0	0	0	0	.250	.400	.833	1.233
	3 ML YEARS		24	39	7	2	0	3	(3	0)	18	3	3	3	5	0	18	2	0	0	0	0	0	.179	.304	.462	.766

Neil Walker

Bats: B **Throws:** R **Pos:** 2B-95; 1B-17; PH-8; 3B-4
Ht: 6'3" **Wt:** 210 **Born:** 9/10/1985 **Age:** 32

			BATTING																		RUNNING			AVERAGES			
Year	Team	Lg	G	AB	H	2B	3B	HR	(Hm	Rd)	TB	R	RBI	RC	TBB	IBB	SO	HBP	SH	SF	SB	CS	GDP	Avg	OBP	Slg	OPS
2009	Pit	NL	17	36	7	1	0	0	(0	0)	8	5	0	2	4	0	11	0	0	0	1	0	1	.194	.275	.222	.497
2010	Pit	NL	110	426	126	29	3	12	(5	7)	197	57	66	66	34	1	83	3	2	4	2	3	4	.296	.349	.462	.811
2011	Pit	NL	159	596	163	36	4	12	(4	8)	243	76	83	77	54	5	112	4	0	8	9	6	15	.273	.334	.408	.742
2012	Pit	NL	129	472	132	27	4	14	(7	7)	201	62	69	72	47	1	104	2	1	8	7	5	11	.280	.342	.426	.768
2013	Pit	NL	133	478	120	24	4	16	(8	8)	200	62	53	62	50	4	85	15	5	3	1	2	14	.251	.339	.418	.757
2014	Pit	NL	137	512	139	25	3	23	(10	13)	239	74	76	72	45	2	88	11	1	2	2	2	12	.271	.342	.467	.809
2015	Pit	NL	151	543	146	32	3	16	(8	8)	232	69	71	73	44	5	110	8	0	8	4	1	9	.269	.328	.427	.756
2016	NYM	NL	113	412	116	9	1	23	(10	13)	196	57	55	66	42	3	84	1	0	3	3	1	11	.282	.347	.476	.823
2017	2 Tms	NL	111	385	102	21	2	14	(7	7)	169	59	49	66	55	2	77	5	1	2	0	2	9	.265	.362	.439	.801
17	NYM	NL	73	265	70	13	2	10	(4	6)	117	40	36	46	27	1	47	4	1	2	0	1	4	.264	.339	.442	.780
17	Mil	NL	38	120	32	8	0	4	(3	1)	52	19	13	20	28	1	30	1	0	0	0	1	5	.267	.409	.433	.843
	Postseason		8	31	2	1	0	0	(0	0)	3	1	1	1	2	0	9	0	0	0	0	0	0	.065	.121	.097	.218
	9 ML YEARS		1060	3860	1051	204	20	130	(59	71)	1685	521	522	556	375	23	754	49	10	38	29	22	86	.272	.341	.437	.778

Taijuan Walker

TIE-wahn

Pitches: R **Bats:** R **Pos:** SP-28
Ht: 6'4" **Wt:** 235 **Born:** 8/13/1992 **Age:** 25

			HOW MUCH HE PITCHED						WHAT HE GAVE UP											THE RESULTS						
Year	Team	Lg	G	GS	CG	GF	IP	BFP	H	R	ER	HR	SH	SF	HB	TBB	IBB	SO	WP	Bk	W	L	Pct	Sh	Sv-Op	Hld	ERC	ERA
2013	Sea	AL	3	3	0	0	15.0	60	11	7	6	0	2	0	2	4	0	12	0	0	1	0	1.000	0	0-0	0	1.63	3.60
2014	Sea	AL	8	5	1	2	38.0	160	31	12	11	2	0	3	3	18	1	34	2	1	2	3	.400	0	0-0	0	3.34	2.61
2015	Sea	AL	29	29	1	0	169.2	706	163	92	86	25	4	5	9	40	1	157	4	1	11	8	.579	0	0-0	0	3.74	4.56
2016	Sea	AL	25	25	1	0	134.1	573	129	75	63	27	3	3	8	37	2	119	4	1	8	11	.421	1	0-0	0	4.20	4.22
2017	Ari	NL	28	28	0	0	157.1	684	148	76	61	17	5	8	9	61	7	146	7	1	9	9	.500	0	0-0	0	3.85	3.49
	5 ML YEARS		93	90	3	2	514.1	2183	482	262	227	71	12	18	29	160	11	468	17	4	31	31	.500	1	0-0	0	3.80	3.97

Chad Wallach

Bats: R **Throws:** R **Pos:** C-3; PH-3; 1B-1
Ht: 6'3" **Wt:** 230 **Born:** 11/4/1991 **Age:** 26

			BATTING																		RUNNING			AVERAGES			
Year	Team	Lg	G	AB	H	2B	3B	HR	(Hm	Rd)	TB	R	RBI	RC	TBB	IBB	SO	HBP	SH	SF	SB	CS	GDP	Avg	OBP	Slg	OPS
2013	Batvia	A-	43	146	33	6	0	0	(-	-)	39	19	13	12	11	0	27	4	0	2	0	0	9	.226	.294	.267	.562
2014	2 Tms	Low	97	335	108	22	1	7	(-	-)	153	54	57	71	62	2	46	5	2	4	3	0	14	.322	.431	.457	.888
2015	Dytona	A+	106	370	91	28	1	3	(-	-)	130	41	32	45	39	0	77	7	1	3	2	3	5	.246	.327	.351	.678
2016	Pnscla	AA	69	200	48	10	0	8	(-	-)	82	27	30	32	37	2	46	2	3	1	0	1	2	.240	.363	.410	.773
2017	Lsvlle	AAA	64	226	51	12	0	9	(-	-)	90	28	18	26	13	0	62	4	0	0	1	0	5	.226	.280	.398	.678
2017	Cin	NL	6	11	1	0	0	0	(0	0)	1	0	0	0	0	0	5	0	0	0	0	0	0	.091	.091	.091	.182

Wei-Chung Wang

Pitches: L Bats: L Pos: RP-8
way-CHUNG WONG
Ht: 6'2" Wt: 185 Born: 4/25/1992 Age: 26

Year Team	Lg	HOW MUCH HE PITCHED						WHAT HE GAVE UP												THE RESULTS							
		G	GS	CG	GF	IP	BFP	H	R	ER	HR	SH	SF	HB	TBB	IBB	SO	WP	Bk	W	L	Pct	Sh	Sv-Op	Hld	ERC	ERA
2013 Pirates	R	12	11	0	1	47.1	185	37	18	17	2	1	2	1	4	0	42	3	0	1	3	.250	0	0--	-	1.59	3.23
2014 3 Tms	Low	7	6	0	0	26.1	103	21	8	7	0	1	1	0	4	0	22	1	0	1	2	.333	0	0--	-	1.60	2.39
2015 BrvdCt	A+	25	25	3	0	139.2	594	146	69	55	9	2	4	2	39	0	91	5	1	10	6	.625	0	0--	-	3.66	3.54
2016 Biloxi	AA	19	19	0	0	107.1	438	102	45	42	7	6	3	1	33	0	91	3	1	6	5	.545	0	0--	-	3.35	3.52
2016 ColSpr	AAA	5	5	0	0	26.0	110	32	16	14	2	0	1	0	2	0	23	0	0	1	3	.250	0	0--	-	3.91	4.85
2017 ColSpr	AAA	47	0	0	12	57.0	236	57	17	13	6	1	1	0	12	0	48	2	0	6	2	.750	0	1--	-	3.37	2.05
2014 Mil	NL	14	0	0	10	17.1	92	30	23	21	6	0	0	1	8	1	13	1	0	0	0	-	0	0-0	0	11.03	10.90
2017 Mil	NL	8	0	0	1	1.1	9	5	2	2	1	0	0	0	0	0	2	0	0	0	0	-	0	0-0	0	29.54	13.50
2 ML YEARS		22	0	0	11	18.2	101	35	25	23	7	0	0	1	8	1	15	1	0	0	0	-	0	0-0	0	12.18	11.09

Adam Warren

Pitches: R Bats: R Pos: RP-46
Ht: 6'1" Wt: 224 Born: 8/25/1987 Age: 30

Year Team	Lg	HOW MUCH HE PITCHED						WHAT HE GAVE UP												THE RESULTS							
		G	GS	CG	GF	IP	BFP	H	R	ER	HR	SH	SF	HB	TBB	IBB	SO	WP	Bk	W	L	Pct	Sh	Sv-Op	Hld	ERC	ERA
2012 NYY	AL	1	1	0	0	2.1	17	8	6	6	2	0	0	0	2	0	1	0	0	0	0	-	0	0-0	0	33.34	23.14
2013 NYY	AL	34	2	0	17	77.0	331	80	29	29	10	0	0	2	30	2	64	3	0	3	2	.600	0	1-1	1	4.60	3.39
2014 NYY	AL	69	0	0	11	78.2	324	63	27	26	4	5	4	3	24	1	76	4	0	3	6	.333	0	3-6	23	2.45	2.97
2015 NYY	AL	43	17	0	5	131.1	534	114	51	48	10	2	2	7	39	1	104	7	0	7	7	.500	0	1-1	3	3.07	3.29
2016 2 Tms		58	1	0	7	65.1	277	59	37	34	11	3	2	1	29	6	52	3	0	7	4	.636	0	0-3	12	4.14	4.68
2017 NYY	AL	46	0	0	7	57.1	223	35	19	15	4	0	5	1	15	2	54	5	0	3	2	.600	0	1-4	11	1.53	2.35
16 ChC	NL	29	1	0	4	35.0	152	31	24	23	7	2	1	0	19	4	27	0	0	3	2	.600	0	0-1	6	4.53	5.91
16 NYY	NL	29	0	0	3	30.1	125	28	13	11	4	1	1	1	10	2	25	3	0	4	2	.667	0	0-2	6	3.71	3.26
6 ML YEARS		251	21	0	47	412.0	1706	359	169	158	41	10	13	14	139	12	351	22	0	23	21	.523	0	6-15	50	3.24	3.45

David Washington

Bats: L Throws: L Pos: RF-2;DH-1;PH-1
Ht: 6'5" Wt: 260 Born: 11/20/1990 Age: 27

Year Team	Lg	BATTING																			RUNNING			AVERAGES			
		G	AB	H	2B	3B	HR	(Hm	Rd)	TB	R	RBI	RC	TBB	IBB	SO	HBP	SH	SF	SB	CS	GDP	Avg	OBP	Slg	OPS
2013 2 Tms	Low	75	270	71	19	0	10	(-	-)	120	35	51	48	46	9	78	5	0	4			7	.263	.375	.444	.820
2014 2 Tms	Low	92	327	76	17	2	16	(-	-)	145	45	53	46	36	2	109	3	0	4	2	2	7	.232	.311	.443	.754
2015 Sprgfld	AA	97	340	93	17	1	16	(-	-)	160	39	45	54	34	1	121	1	0	4	4	4	7	.274	.338	.471	.808
2015 PlmBh	A+	23	78	11	5	1	0	(-	-)	18	8	8	4	10	0	29	1	0	3	0	0	1	.141	.239	.231	.470
2016 Sprgfld	AA	22	76	21	4	1	5	(-	-)	42	15	15	16	16	0	27	0	0	3	0	0	1	.276	.402	.553	.955
2016 Memp	AAA	105	345	88	17	1	25	(-	-)	182	52	62	64	51	1	142	1	0	4	4	5	7	.255	.349	.528	.877
2017 Norfolk	AAA	103	368	97	23	1	18	(-	-)	176	49	42	56	27	0	137	1	0	1	7	3	5	.264	.315	.478	.793
2017 Bal	AL	3	6	0	0	0	0	(0	0)	0	0	0	0	0	0	5	0	0	0	0	0	0	.000	.000	.000	.000

Tony Watson

Pitches: L Bats: L Pos: RP-71
Ht: 6'4" Wt: 220 Born: 5/30/1985 Age: 33

Year Team	Lg	HOW MUCH HE PITCHED						WHAT HE GAVE UP												THE RESULTS							
		G	GS	CG	GF	IP	BFP	H	R	ER	HR	SH	SF	HB	TBB	IBB	SO	WP	Bk	W	L	Pct	Sh	Sv-Op	Hld	ERC	ERA
2011 Pit	NL	43	0	0	6	41.0	174	34	18	18	6	2	1	1	20	4	37	0	0	2	2	.500	0	0-1	10	3.75	3.95
2012 Pit	NL	68	0	0	10	53.1	215	37	21	20	5	2	2	1	23	1	53	1	0	5	2	.714	0	0-2	16	2.62	3.38
2013 Pit	NL	67	0	0	14	71.2	280	51	19	19	5	3	1	6	12	1	54	2	0	3	1	.750	0	2-4	22	1.88	2.39
2014 Pit	NL	78	0	0	3	77.1	305	64	16	14	5	5	3	6	15	0	81	0	0	10	2	.833	0	2-9	34	2.54	1.63
2015 Pit	NL	77	0	0	4	75.1	293	55	17	16	3	1	3	4	17	1	62	1	0	4	1	.800	0	1-3	41	1.92	1.91
2016 Pit	NL	70	0	0	27	67.2	272	52	26	23	10	4	3	3	20	1	58	0	0	2	5	.286	0	15-20	23	2.92	3.06
2017 2 Tms	NL	71	0	0	23	66.2	291	72	26	25	9	5	2	5	20	7	53	0	0	7	4	.636	0	10-18	14	4.50	3.38
17 Pit	NL	47	0	0	22	46.2	209	57	20	19	7	3	2	3	14	4	35	0	0	5	3	.625	0	10-17	6	5.45	3.66
17 LAD	NL	24	0	0	1	20.0	82	15	6	6	2	2	0	2	6	3	18	0	0	2	1	.667	0	0-1	8	2.52	2.70
Postseason		5	0	0	0	5.0	21	4	1	1	1	0	0	1	1	0	2	0	0	0	0	-	0	0-0	1	3.57	1.80
7 ML YEARS		474	0	0	87	453.0	1830	365	143	135	43	22	15	26	127	15	398	4	0	33	17	.660	0	30-57	160	2.76	2.68

Jered Weaver

Pitches: R Bats: R Pos: SP-9
Ht: 6'7" Wt: 210 Born: 10/4/1982 Age: 35

Year Team	Lg	HOW MUCH HE PITCHED						WHAT HE GAVE UP												THE RESULTS							
		G	GS	CG	GF	IP	BFP	H	R	ER	HR	SH	SF	HB	TBB	IBB	SO	WP	Bk	W	L	Pct	Sh	Sv-Op	Hld	ERC	ERA
2006 LAA	AL	19	19	0	0	123.0	490	94	36	35	15	2	2	3	33	1	105	2	0	11	2	.846	0	0-0	-	2.57	2.56
2007 LAA	AL	28	28	0	0	161.0	695	178	77	70	17	5	5	2	45	3	115	4	0	13	7	.650	0	0-0	-	4.24	3.91
2008 LAA	AL	30	30	0	0	176.2	745	173	88	85	20	1	4	6	54	3	115	4	0	11	10	.524	0	0-0	-	3.80	4.33
2009 LAA	AL	33	33	4	0	211.0	882	196	91	88	26	6	8	4	66	3	174	3	0	16	8	.667	2	0-0	-	3.56	3.75
2010 LAA	AL	34	34	0	0	224.1	905	187	83	75	23	2	5	0	54	0	233	7	1	13	12	.520	0	0-0	-	2.59	3.01
2011 LAA	AL	33	33	4	0	235.2	926	182	65	63	20	5	5	3	56	0	198	8	0	18	8	.692	2	0-0	-	2.27	2.41
2012 LAA	AL	30	30	3	0	188.2	739	147	63	59	20	0	4	4	45	0	142	2	0	20	5	.800	2	0-0	-	2.48	2.81
2013 LAA	AL	24	24	0	0	154.1	634	139	58	56	17	1	3	7	37	0	117	2	0	11	8	.579	0	0-0	-	3.17	3.27
2014 LAA	AL	34	34	1	0	213.1	888	193	87	85	27	4	4	6	65	1	169	3	0	18	9	.667	1	0-0	-	3.46	3.59
2015 LAA	AL	26	26	1	0	159.0	669	163	84	82	24	5	2	12	33	3	90	2	0	7	12	.368	1	0-0	-	4.09	4.64
2016 LAA	AL	31	31	1	0	178.0	767	209	106	100	37	1	6	4	51	2	103	1	2	12	12	.500	1	0-0	-	5.59	5.06
2017 SD	NL	9	9	0	0	42.1	191	51	41	35	16	1	1	4	12	0	23	0	0	0	5	.000	0	0-0	-	7.27	7.44
Postseason		7	4	0	2	27.2	107	15	8	8	5	0	1	0	12	0	28	0	0	2	1	.667	0	0-0	1	2.37	2.60
12 ML YEARS		331	331	14	0	2067.1	8531	1912	879	833	262	34	49	55	551	17	1621	37	3	150	98	.605	8	0-0	0	3.43	3.63

Luke Weaver

Pitches: R Bats: R Pos: SP-10; RP-3

Ht: 6'2" Wt: 170 Born: 8/21/1993 Age: 24

		HOW MUCH HE PITCHED						WHAT HE GAVE UP										THE RESULTS							
Year Team	Lg	G	GS	CG	GF	IP	BFP	H	R	ER	HR	SH	SF	HB	TBB	IBB	SO	WP	Bk	W	L	Pct	Sh	Sv-Op	Hld	ERC	ERA
2014 2 Tms	Low	6	6	0	0	9.1	46	15	8	8	1	0	0	1	4	0	12	0	1	0	1	.000	0	0- -	-	8.66	7.71
2015 PlmBh	A+	19	19	0	0	105.1	426	98	34	19	2	5	6	0	19	0	88	8	1	8	5	.615	0	0- -	-	2.37	1.62
2016 Sprgfld	AA	12	12	0	0	77.0	308	62	23	12	4	0	1	2	10	0	88	5	0	6	3	.667	0	0- -	-	1.85	1.40
2017 Memp	AAA	15	15	0	0	77.2	305	63	24	22	3	1	0	1	19	1	76	6	0	10	2	.833	0	0- -	-	2.23	2.55
2016 StL	NL	9	8	0	0	36.1	167	46	29	23	7	2	3	2	12	0	45	1	0	1	4	.200	0	0-0	0	6.23	5.70
2017 StL	NL	13	10	0	0	60.1	252	59	27	26	7	1	1	1	17	1	72	0	0	7	2	.778	0	0-0	0	3.66	3.88
2 ML YEARS		22	18	0	0	96.2	419	105	56	49	14	3	4	3	29	1	117	1	0	8	6	.571	0	0-0	0	4.58	4.56

Tyler Webb

Pitches: L Bats: R Pos: RP-9

Ht: 6'5" Wt: 230 Born: 7/20/1990 Age: 27

		HOW MUCH HE PITCHED						WHAT HE GAVE UP										THE RESULTS							
Year Team	Lg	G	GS	CG	GF	IP	BFP	H	R	ER	HR	SH	SF	HB	TBB	IBB	SO	WP	Bk	W	L	Pct	Sh	Sv-Op	Hld	ERC	ERA
2013 2 Tms	Low	20	0	0	9	35.1	137	24	14	13	4	0	1	1	8	0	48	0	0	3	1	.750	0	3- -	-	1.99	3.31
2014 Tampa	A+	8	0	0	7	13.0	48	7	4	4	0	0	0	1	1	0	17	1	0	0	0	-	0	4- -	-	0.87	2.77
2014 Trntn	AA	23	0	0	9	35.2	159	35	16	16	2	4	1	3	14	2	51	4	0	1	6	.143	0	7- -	-	3.76	4.04
2014 S-WB	AAA	17	0	0	4	20.0	85	17	10	9	3	0	1	0	7	0	26	2	0	2	0	1.000	0	1- -	-	3.28	4.05
2015 S-WB	AAA	25	0	0	7	38.0	167	40	18	12	4	3	0	0	11	0	41	1	0	2	3	.400	0	2- -	-	3.82	2.84
2016 S-WB	AAA	36	5	0	9	72.2	303	67	31	29	5	3	4	0	23	0	82	3	1	4	3	.571	0	1- -	-	2.93	3.24
2017 S-WB	AAA	21	0	0	6	33.1	138	33	12	12	3	0	0	2	3	0	47	1	0	3	1	.750	0	1- -	-	6.93	6.48
2017 ColSpr	AAA	17	0	0	5	16.2	75	21	12	12	4	2	2	0	7	0	17	1	0	1	2	.333	0	0- -	-	6.93	5.63
2017 2 Tms		9	0	0	3	8.0	36	9	5	5	2	0	0	0	5	1	8	0	0	0	0	-	0	0-1	0	3.11	4.50
17 NYY	AL	7	0	0	2	6.0	23	3	3	3	1	0	0	0	4	0	5	0	0	0	0	-	0	0-0	0	3.11	4.50
17 Mil	NL	2	0	0	1	2.0	13	6	2	2	1	0	0	0	1	1	3	0	0	0	0	-	0	0-1	0	21.60	9.00

Ryan Weber

Pitches: R Bats: R Pos: SP-1

Ht: 6'1" Wt: 180 Born: 8/12/1990 Age: 27

		HOW MUCH HE PITCHED						WHAT HE GAVE UP										THE RESULTS							
Year Team	Lg	G	GS	CG	GF	IP	BFP	H	R	ER	HR	SH	SF	HB	TBB	IBB	SO	WP	Bk	W	L	Pct	Sh	Sv-Op	Hld	ERC	ERA
2017 Tacom*	AAA	6	5	0	0	31.2	117	20	3	3	1	0	1	1	4	0	19	0	0	2	0	1.000	0	0- -	-	1.26	0.85
2015 Atl	NL	5	5	0	0	28.1	109	25	15	15	3	0	0	2	6	0	19	0	0	0	3	.000	0	0-0	0	3.26	4.76
2016 Atl	NL	16	2	0	6	36.1	157	46	22	22	7	1	0	2	5	2	23	1	0	1	1	.500	0	0-1	0	5.40	5.45
2017 Sea	AL	1	1	0	0	3.2	14	3	1	1	0	0	0	0	0	0	0	0	0	0	0	-	0	0-0	0	1.32	2.45
3 ML YEARS		22	8	0	6	68.1	280	74	38	38	10	1	0	4	11	2	42	1	0	1	4	.200	0	0-1	0	4.23	5.00

Rickie Weeks Jr.

Bats: R Throws: R Pos: DH-17;1B-12;PH-11

Ht: 6'0" Wt: 210 Born: 9/13/1982 Age: 35

		BATTING																		RUNNING			AVERAGES			
Year Team	Lg	G	AB	H	2B	3B	HR	(Hm	Rd)	TB	R	RBI	RC	TBB	IBB	SO	HBP	SH	SF	SB	CS	GDP	Avg	OBP	Slg	OPS
2003 Mil	NL	7	12	2	1	0	0	(0	0)	3	1	0	1	1	0	6	1	0	0	0	0	0	.167	.286	.250	.536
2005 Mil	NL	96	360	86	13	2	13	(8	5)	142	56	42	49	40	2	96	11	2	1	15	2	11	.239	.333	.394	.727
2006 Mil	NL	95	359	100	15	3	8	(6	2)	145	73	34	53	30	1	92	19	2	3	19	5	6	.279	.363	.404	.766
2007 Mil	NL	118	409	96	21	6	16	(5	11)	177	87	36	65	78	5	116	14	3	2	25	2	3	.235	.374	.433	.807
2008 Mil	NL	129	475	111	22	7	14	(3	11)	189	89	46	67	66	0	115	14	1	4	19	5	5	.234	.342	.398	.740
2009 Mil	NL	37	147	40	5	2	9	(7	2)	76	28	24	27	12	0	39	3	0	0	2	1	1	.272	.340	.517	.857
2010 Mil	NL	160	651	175	32	4	29	(16	13)	302	112	83	110	76	0	184	25	0	2	11	4	5	.269	.366	.464	.830
2011 Mil	NL	118	453	122	26	2	20	(10	10)	212	77	49	68	50	3	107	8	1	3	9	2	6	.269	.350	.468	.818
2012 Mil	NL	157	588	135	29	4	21	(10	11)	235	85	63	77	74	2	169	13	0	2	16	3	9	.230	.328	.400	.728
2013 Mil	NL	104	350	73	20	1	10	(6	4)	125	40	24	28	40	0	105	9	0	0	3	4	7	.209	.306	.357	.663
2014 Mil	NL	121	252	69	19	1	8	(4	4)	114	36	29	38	25	0	73	8	0	1	3	4	7	.274	.357	.452	.809
2015 Sea	AL	37	84	14	1	0	2	(0	2)	21	7	9	7	9	0	25	2	0	0	0	0	3	.167	.263	.250	.513
2016 Ari	NL	108	180	43	9	1	9	(6	3)	81	29	27	26	20	0	54	4	0	1	5	0	8	.239	.327	.450	.777
2017 TB	AL	37	97	21	6	0	2	(1	1)	33	13	8	10	12	0	49	3	0	0	1	0	0	.216	.321	.340	.662
Postseason		14	45	6	1	1	2	(2	0)	15	5	4	2	2	0	8	2	0	0	0	0	3	.133	.204	.333	.537
14 ML YEARS		1324	4417	1087	219	33	161	(82	79)	1855	733	474	625	533	13	1230	134	9	19	132	32	77	.246	.344	.420	.764

Joey Wendle

Bats: L Throws: R Pos: 2B-5;PH-4

Ht: 6'1" Wt: 190 Born: 4/26/1990 Age: 28

		BATTING																		RUNNING			AVERAGES			
Year Team	Lg	G	AB	H	2B	3B	HR	(Hm	Rd)	TB	R	RBI	RC	TBB	IBB	SO	HBP	SH	SF	SB	CS	GDP	Avg	OBP	Slg	OPS
2013 Carlina	A+	107	413	122	32	5	16	(-	-)	212	73	64	82	44	1	79	10	1	6	15	2	10	.295	.372	.513	.885
2014 Akron	AA	87	336	85	20	5	8	(-	-)	139	46	50	45	26	1	56	4	0	4	4	2	4	.253	.311	.414	.725
2015 Nashv	AAA	137	577	167	42	8	10	(-	-)	255	80	57	85	22	1	114	9	5	5	12	2	9	.289	.323	.442	.765
2016 Nashv	AAA	125	491	137	31	9	12	(-	-)	222	81	64	74	26	2	112	7	1	1	14	4	10	.279	.324	.452	.776
2017 Nashv	AAA	118	478	136	29	8	8	(-	-)	205	67	54	69	19	1	82	12	0	1	13	4	6	.285	.327	.429	.756
2016 Oak	AL	28	96	25	1	0	1	(0	1)	29	11	11	10	6	0	16	0	0	2	2	0	3	.260	.298	.302	.600
2017 Oak	AL	8	13	4	1	0	1	(0	1)	8	3	5	4	1	1	3	0	0	0	0	0	0	.308	.357	.615	.973
2 ML YEARS		36	109	29	2	0	2	(0	2)	37	14	16	14	7	1	19	0	0	2	2	0	3	.266	.305	.339	.645

Jayson Werth

Bats: R **Throws:** R **Pos:** LF-51;RF-16;DH-2;PH-1

Ht: 6'5" **Wt:** 235 **Born:** 5/20/1979 **Age:** 39

BATTING / RUNNING / AVERAGES

Year	Team	Lg	G	AB	H	2B	3B	HR	(Hm	Rd)	TB	R	RBI	RC	TBB	IBB	SO	HBP	SH	SF	SB	CS	GDP	Avg	OBP	Slg	OPS
2002	Tor	AL	15	46	12	2	1	0	(0	0)	16	4	6	5	6	0	11	0	0	1	1	0	4	.261	.340	.348	.687
2003	Tor	AL	26	48	10	4	0	2	(0	2)	20	7	10	6	3	0	22	0	0	1	1	0	4	.208	.255	.417	.672
2004	LAD	NL	89	290	76	11	3	16	(11	5)	141	56	47	47	30	0	85	4	1	1	4	1	1	.262	.338	.486	.825
2005	LAD	NL	102	337	79	22	2	7	(1	6)	126	46	43	44	48	2	114	6	1	3	11	2	10	.234	.338	.374	.711
2007	Phi	NL	94	255	76	11	3	8	(1	7)	117	43	49	57	44	1	73	2	2	1	7	1	0	.298	.404	.459	.863
2008	Phi	NL	134	418	114	16	3	24	(11	13)	208	73	67	74	57	1	119	4	0	3	20	1	2	.273	.363	.498	.861
2009	Phi	NL	159	571	153	26	1	36	(21	15)	289	98	99	107	91	8	156	8	0	6	20	3	11	.268	.373	.506	.879
2010	Phi	NL	156	554	164	46	2	27	(18	9)	295	106	85	91	82	6	147	7	0	9	13	3	11	.296	.388	.532	.921
2011	Was	NL	150	561	130	26	1	20	(10	10)	218	69	58	74	74	5	160	10	0	4	19	3	10	.232	.330	.389	.718
2012	Was	NL	81	300	90	21	3	5	(4	1)	132	42	31	48	42	2	57	1	0	1	8	2	3	.300	.387	.440	.827
2013	Was	NL	129	462	147	24	0	25	(13	12)	246	84	82	94	60	3	101	5	0	5	10	1	9	.318	.398	.532	.931
2014	Was	NL	147	534	156	37	1	16	(5	11)	243	85	82	104	83	3	113	9	0	3	9	1	9	.292	.394	.455	.849
2015	Was	NL	88	331	73	16	1	12	(6	6)	127	51	42	38	38	0	84	3	0	6	0	1	8	.221	.302	.384	.685
2016	Was	NL	143	565	128	28	0	21	(9	12)	219	84	69	68	71	0	139	4	0	6	5	1	17	.244	.335	.417	.752
2017	Was	NL	70	252	57	10	1	10	(6	4)	99	35	29	31	35	1	69	1	0	1	4	3	4	.226	.322	.393	.715
	Postseason		58	209	54	12	2	15	(10	5)	115	37	30	34	37	4	72	2	0	1	6	0	3	.258	.373	.550	.924
	15 ML YEARS		1583	5484	1465	300	22	229	(116	113)	2496	883	799	888	764	32	1450	64	4	50	132	23	99	.267	.360	.455	.816

Rob Whalen

Pitches: R **Bats:** R **Pos:** SP-1; RP-1

Ht: 6'2" **Wt:** 220 **Born:** 1/31/1994 **Age:** 24

HOW MUCH HE PITCHED / WHAT HE GAVE UP / THE RESULTS

Year	Team	Lg	G	GS	CG	GF	IP	BFP	H	R	ER	HR	SH	SF	HB	TBB	IBB	SO	WP	Bk	W	L	Pct	Sh	Sv-Op	Hld	ERC	ERA
2013	Kngspt	R+	12	12	0	0	72.1	296	50	26	15	1	2	2	7	17	0	76	4	0	3	2	.600	0	0--	-	1.67	1.87
2014	2 Tms	Low	14	12	0	1	69.2	282	48	19	15	2	1	1	5	21	1	63	8	0	9	2	.818	0	0--	-	1.90	1.94
2015	2 Tms	Low	18	17	0	1	96.2	409	83	45	36	6	0	2	8	38	0	68	11	0	5	7	.417	0	0--	-	3.35	3.35
2016	Missi	AA	18	18	0	0	101.1	423	87	35	28	4	6	1	4	37	0	94	2	0	7	5	.583	0	0--	-	2.93	2.49
2017	Tacom	AAA	10	10	1	0	53.1	239	61	44	39	9	1	1	3	20	0	43	5	0	0	7	.000	0	0--	-	5.55	6.58
2016	Atl	NL	5	5	0	0	24.2	110	20	20	18	4	2	1	3	12	0	25	1	0	1	2	.333	0	0-0	0	4.14	6.57
2017	Sea	AL	2	1	0	1	7.1	31	7	5	5	1	0	0	2	2	0	2	0	0	0	1	.000	0	0-0	0	4.88	6.14
	2 ML YEARS		7	6	0	1	32.0	141	27	25	23	5	2	1	5	14	0	27	1	0	1	3	.250	0	0-0	0	4.30	6.47

Jason Wheeler

Pitches: L **Bats:** L **Pos:** RP-2

Ht: 6'6" **Wt:** 255 **Born:** 10/27/1990 **Age:** 27

HOW MUCH HE PITCHED / WHAT HE GAVE UP / THE RESULTS

Year	Team	Lg	G	GS	CG	GF	IP	BFP	H	R	ER	HR	SH	SF	HB	TBB	IBB	SO	WP	Bk	W	L	Pct	Sh	Sv-Op	Hld	ERC	ERA
2013	FtMyrs	A+	26	26	0	0	143.1	630	156	72	59	16	6	5	10	58	0	91	5	0	9	4	.692	0	0--	-	5.05	3.70
2014	FtMyrs	A+	13	13	1	0	79.0	328	77	31	22	2	3	1	1	19	0	57	2	0	6	5	.545	1	0--	-	2.88	2.51
2014	NwBrit	AA	12	12	1	0	74.1	305	69	23	23	9	0	0	4	16	0	55	1	1	5	4	.556	0	0--	-	3.34	2.78
2015	Roch	AAA	15	15	1	0	78.0	355	104	69	57	11	2	3	5	24	1	40	2	0	1	7	.125	0	0--	-	6.30	6.58
2015	Chatt	AA	10	10	0	0	59.2	249	58	28	26	7	0	0	3	16	0	50	2	0	4	3	.571	0	0--	-	3.76	3.92
2016	Roch	AAA	24	24	1	0	145.1	607	137	60	57	13	3	5	3	37	0	113	5	0	11	6	.647	0	0--	-	3.18	3.53
2017	Roch	AAA	8	7	0	0	44.0	184	47	25	22	5	1	0	0	10	0	37	1	0	4	1	.800	0	0--	-	3.90	4.50
2017	Norfolk	AAA	13	6	0	2	41.0	172	37	15	14	5	4	1	2	11	1	33	0	0	1	2	.333	0	1--	-	3.29	3.07
2017	Min	AL	2	0	0	1	3.0	18	6	5	3	1	0	0	0	4	0	0	0	0	0	0	-	0	0-0	0	18.41	9.00

Zack Wheeler

Pitches: R **Bats:** L **Pos:** SP-17

Ht: 6'4" **Wt:** 195 **Born:** 5/30/1990 **Age:** 28

HOW MUCH HE PITCHED / WHAT HE GAVE UP / THE RESULTS

Year	Team	Lg	G	GS	CG	GF	IP	BFP	H	R	ER	HR	SH	SF	HB	TBB	IBB	SO	WP	Bk	W	L	Pct	Sh	Sv-Op	Hld	ERC	ERA
2013	NYM	NL	17	17	0	0	100.0	431	90	42	38	10	3	7	4	46	2	84	6	0	7	5	.583	0	0-0	0	3.88	3.42
2014	NYM	NL	32	32	1	0	185.1	794	167	84	73	14	5	3	11	79	3	187	9	0	11	11	.500	1	0-0	0	3.68	3.54
2017	NYM	NL	17	17	0	0	86.1	386	97	53	50	15	0	1	3	40	1	81	1	0	3	7	.300	0	0-0	0	5.81	5.21
	3 ML YEARS		66	66	1	0	371.2	1611	354	179	161	39	8	11	18	165	6	352	16	0	21	23	.477	1	0-0	0	4.20	3.90

Tyler White

Bats: R **Throws:** R **Pos:** 1B-19;2B-4;PH-4;LF-2

Ht: 5'11" **Wt:** 225 **Born:** 10/29/1990 **Age:** 27

BATTING / RUNNING / AVERAGES

Year	Team	Lg	G	AB	H	2B	3B	HR	(Hm	Rd)	TB	R	RBI	RC	TBB	IBB	SO	HBP	SH	SF	SB	CS	GDP	Avg	OBP	Slg	OPS
2013	3 Tms	Low	64	239	77	14	0	6	(-	-)	109	40	52	46	27	1	24	9	0	3	3	2	3	.322	.406	.456	.863
2014	2 Tms	Low	114	389	113	33	2	15	(-	-)	195	69	64	83	63	1	67	19	0	5	0	1	8	.290	.410	.501	.911
2015	CpChr	AA	59	190	54	6	0	7	(-	-)	81	33	40	37	42	1	35	2	0	2	1	0	7	.284	.415	.426	.842
2015	Fresno	AAA	57	213	77	19	1	7	(-	-)	119	37	59	55	42	1	38	2	0	2	0	1	5	.362	.467	.559	1.026
2016	Fresno	AAA	44	174	42	4	1	13	(-	-)	87	28	29	27	16	0	30	0	0	0	1	1	6	.241	.305	.500	.805
2017	Fresno	AAA	111	436	131	22	1	25	(-	-)	230	84	89	86	47	0	101	6	1	7	7	3	9	.300	.371	.500	.898
2016	Hou	AL	86	249	54	16	0	8	(2	6)	94	24	28	25	23	1	65	2	0	2	1	0	6	.217	.286	.378	.664
2017	Hou	AL	22	61	17	6	0	3	(3	0)	32	7	10	10	4	0	16	1	0	1	0	1	0	.279	.328	.525	.853
	2 ML YEARS		108	310	71	22	0	11	(5	6)	126	31	38	35	27	1	81	3	0	3	1	1	6	.229	.294	.406	.701

Chase Whitley

Pitches: R Bats: R Pos: RP-41   Ht: 6'4" Wt: 220 Born: 6/14/1989 Age: 29

Year	Team	Lg	G	GS	CG	GF	IP	BFP	H	R	ER	HR	SH	SF	HB	TBB	IBB	SO	WP	Bk	W	L	Pct	Sh	Sv-Op	Hld	ERC	ERA
2017	Drham*	AAA	5	2	0	1	9.0	41	13	13	13	6	0	0	0	4	0	8	0	0	0	3	.000	0	0- -	-	12.47	13.00
2014	NYY	AL	24	12	0	3	75.2	330	94	44	44	10	1	2	4	18	0	60	2	0	4	3	.571	0	0-0	0	5.37	5.23
2015	NYY	AL	4	4	0	0	19.1	84	20	9	9	3	0	0	2	5	0	16	2	0	1	2	.333	0	0-0	0	4.47	4.19
2016	TB	AL	5	1	0	0	14.1	61	13	7	4	2	0	0	0	3	0	15	0	0	0	0	-	0	0-0	3	2.91	2.51
2017	TB	AL	41	0	0	12	57.1	238	48	29	26	4	1	2	3	16	2	43	2	0	2	1	.667	0	2-3	5	2.66	4.08
	4 ML YEARS		74	17	0	15	166.2	713	175	89	83	19	2	4	9	42	2	134	6	0	7	6	.538	0	2-3	8	4.05	4.48

Matt Wieters

Bats: B Throws: R Pos: C-118;PH-8   WEE-ters   Ht: 6'5" Wt: 230 Born: 5/21/1986 Age: 32

Year	Team	Lg	G	AB	H	2B	3B	HR	(Hm	Rd)	TB	R	RBI	RC	TBB	IBB	SO	HBP	SH	SF	SB	CS	GDP	Avg	OBP	Slg	OPS
2009	Bal	AL	96	354	102	15	1	9	(5	4)	146	35	43	43	28	2	86	1	0	2	0	0	11	.288	.340	.412	.753
2010	Bal	AL	130	446	111	22	1	11	(3	8)	168	37	55	47	47	7	94	2	0	7	0	1	13	.249	.319	.377	.695
2011	Bal	AL	139	500	131	28	0	22	(13	9)	225	72	68	76	48	3	84	2	0	1	1	0	16	.262	.328	.450	.778
2012	Bal	AL	144	526	131	27	1	23	(11	12)	229	67	83	73	60	4	112	4	0	3	0	0	17	.249	.329	.435	.764
2013	Bal	AL	148	523	123	29	0	22	(13	9)	218	59	79	65	43	5	104	0	1	12	2	0	7	.235	.287	.417	.704
2014	Bal	AL	26	104	32	5	0	5	(2	3)	52	13	18	17	6	0	19	0	0	2	0	1	1	.308	.339	.500	.839
2015	Bal	AL	75	258	69	14	1	8	(3	5)	109	24	25	33	21	0	67	0	0	3	0	0	4	.267	.319	.422	.742
2016	Bal	AL	124	423	103	17	1	17	(10	7)	173	48	66	56	32	1	85	5	1	3	1	0	10	.243	.302	.409	.711
2017	Was	NL	123	422	95	20	0	10	(5	5)	145	43	52	41	38	4	94	1	0	4	1	0	14	.225	.288	.344	.632
	Postseason		7	28	3	1	0	0	(0	0)	4	2	0	0	2	0	6	0	0	0	0	0	0	.107	.167	.143	.310
	9 ML YEARS		1005	3556	897	177	5	127	(65	62)	1465	398	489	451	323	26	745	15	2	37	8	2	93	.252	.314	.412	.726

Tom Wilhelmsen

Pitches: R Bats: R Pos: RP-27   will-HELM-senn   Ht: 6'6" Wt: 220 Born: 12/16/1983 Age: 34

Year	Team	Lg	G	GS	CG	GF	IP	BFP	H	R	ER	HR	SH	SF	HB	TBB	IBB	SO	WP	Bk	W	L	Pct	Sh	Sv-Op	Hld	ERC	ERA
2017	ColSpr*	AAA	16	0	0	6	13.0	73	27	21	19	3	1	1	2	7	0	11	4	0	0	1	.000	0	0- -	-	13.96	13.15
2011	Sea	AL	25	0	0	10	32.2	136	25	13	12	2	0	2	2	13	0	30	6	1	0	1	.000	0	0-0	3	2.78	3.31
2012	Sea	AL	73	0	0	48	79.1	326	59	24	22	5	1	2	2	29	3	87	3	0	4	3	.571	0	29-34	7	2.38	2.50
2013	Sea	AL	59	0	0	40	59.0	251	45	28	27	2	3	3	1	33	5	45	6	0	0	3	.000	0	24-29	2	2.87	4.12
2014	Sea	AL	57	2	0	18	79.1	317	47	22	20	6	1	3	2	36	6	72	4	0	3	2	.600	0	1-3	8	2.03	2.27
2015	Sea	AL	53	0	0	20	62.0	267	56	24	22	3	4	3	2	29	3	60	2	0	2	2	.500	0	13-15	7	3.49	3.19
2016	2 Tms	AL	50	0	0	5	46.1	209	60	35	35	11	0	1	2	19	0	28	0	0	2	4	.333	0	1-4	12	7.39	6.80
2017	Ari	AL	27	0	0	10	26.1	113	25	13	13	4	0	1	1	12	0	17	7	0	1	1	.500	0	0-0	3	4.61	4.44
16	Tex	AL	21	0	0	3	21.1	109	38	25	25	7	0	1	2	9	0	11	0	0	2	3	.400	0	0-2	3	11.90	10.55
16	Sea	AL	29	0	0	2	25.0	100	22	10	10	4	0	0	0	10	0	17	0	0	0	1	.000	0	1-2	9	4.04	3.60
	7 ML YEARS		344	2	0	151	385.0	1619	317	159	151	33	9	15	12	171	17	339	28	1	14	15	.483	0	68-85	42	3.25	3.53

Adam Wilk

Pitches: L Bats: L Pos: SP-2; RP-2   Ht: 6'2" Wt: 180 Born: 12/9/1987 Age: 30

Year	Team	Lg	G	GS	CG	GF	IP	BFP	H	R	ER	HR	SH	SF	HB	TBB	IBB	SO	WP	Bk	W	L	Pct	Sh	Sv-Op	Hld	ERC	ERA
2017	LsVgs*	AAA	6	6	0	0	32.0	140	40	22	21	5	1	1	2	5	0	29	1	0	2	3	.400	0	0- -	-	5.18	5.91
2011	Det	AL	5	0	0	1	13.1	57	14	10	8	3	0	0	0	3	0	10	0	0	0	0	-	0	0-0	0	4.40	5.40
2012	Det	AL	3	3	0	0	11.0	55	21	11	10	4	0	1	0	3	0	7	0	0	0	3	.000	0	0-0	0	11.90	8.18
2015	LAA	AL	1	0	0	1	2.0	10	2	1	1	1	0	0	1	1	0	2	0	0	0	0	-	0	0-0	0	12.61	4.50
2017	2 Tms		4	2	0	0	14.0	74	24	15	14	6	2	0	0	9	1	8	2	0	0	2	.000	0	0-0	0	12.61	9.00
17	NYM	NL	1	1	0	0	3.2	20	8	6	5	3	1	0	0	1	0	2	0	0	0	1	.000	0	0-0	0	18.02	12.27
17	Min	AL	3	1	0	0	10.1	54	16	9	9	3	1	0	0	8	1	6	2	0	0	1	.000	0	0-0	0	10.71	7.84
	4 ML YEARS		13	5	0	2	40.1	196	61	37	33	14	2	1	1	16	1	27	2	0	0	5	.000	0	0-0	0	9.32	7.36

Aaron Wilkerson

Pitches: R Bats: R Pos: SP-2; RP-1   Ht: 6'3" Wt: 190 Born: 5/24/1989 Age: 29

Year	Team	Lg	G	GS	CG	GF	IP	BFP	H	R	ER	HR	SH	SF	HB	TBB	IBB	SO	WP	Bk	W	L	Pct	Sh	Sv-Op	Hld	ERC	ERA
2014	Lowell	A-	8	8	0	0	50.0	192	32	11	9	3	3	1	2	11	1	54	2	0	5	1	.833	0	0- -	-	1.58	1.62
2015	2 Tms	Low	22	13	0	3	96.0	381	79	38	35	4	3	2	1	26	0	102	1	0	7	2	.778	0	0- -	-	2.26	3.28
2015	Portlnd	AA	7	7	0	0	40.2	160	28	13	12	0	0	0	1	13	0	35	0	0	4	1	.800	0	0- -	-	1.71	2.66
2016	Portlnd	AA	8	8	0	0	44.1	174	28	10	9	2	0	0	0	14	0	48	0	0	2	1	.667	0	0- -	-	1.62	1.83
2016	Pwtckt	AAA	9	8	0	1	48.0	200	41	18	13	5	0	1	4	11	0	54	0	1	4	2	.667	0	0- -	-	2.93	2.44
2016	ColSpr	AAA	11	11	0	0	54.2	248	67	41	39	5	3	4	3	16	0	57	1	0	2	6	.250	0	0- -	-	5.02	6.42
2017	Biloxi	AA	24	24	2	0	142.1	562	117	54	50	12	3	8	2	36	2	143	3	0	11	4	.733	2	0- -	-	2.58	3.16
2017	Mil	NL	3	2	0	1	10.1	37	6	4	4	1	0	0	0	1	0	7	0	0	1	0	1.000	0	0-0	0	1.20	3.48

Mason Williams

Bats: L **Throws:** R **Pos:** CF-5;RF-1

Ht: 6'1" **Wt:** 185 **Born:** 8/21/1991 **Age:** 26

						BATTING														RUNNING			AVERAGES			
Year Team	Lg	G	AB	H	2B	3B	HR	(Hm	Rd)	TB	R	RBI	RC	TBB	IBB	SO	HBP	SH	SF	SB	CS	GDP	Avg	OBP	Slg	OPS
2017 S-WB*	AAA	106	399	105	10	3	2	(-	1)	127	44	30	43	28	1	66	1	3	6	19	5	11	.263	.309	.318	.627
2015 NYY	AL	8	21	6	3	0	1	(0	1)	12	3	3	4	1	0	3	0	0	0	0	0	0	.286	.318	.571	.890
2016 NYY	AL	12	27	8	1	0	0	(0	0)	9	4	2	3	1	0	12	0	1	0	0	0	0	.296	.321	.333	.655
2017 NYY	AL	5	16	4	0	0	0	(0	0)	4	3	1	1	1	0	2	0	0	0	2	0	0	.250	.294	.250	.544
3 ML YEARS		25	64	18	4	0	1	(0	1)	25	10	6	8	3	0	17	0	1	0	2	0	0	.281	.313	.391	.704

Nick Williams

Bats: L **Throws:** L **Pos:** RF-58;CF-16;LF-12;PH-3;DH-1

Ht: 6'3" **Wt:** 195 **Born:** 9/8/1993 **Age:** 24

						BATTING														RUNNING			AVERAGES			
Year Team	Lg	G	AB	H	2B	3B	HR	(Hm	Rd)	TB	R	RBI	RC	TBB	IBB	SO	HBP	SH	SF	SB	CS	GDP	Avg	OBP	Slg	OPS
2013 Hkry	A	95	376	110	19	12	17	(-	-)	204	70	60	67	15	0	110	11	0	2	8	5	7	.293	.337	.543	.879
2014 2 Tms	Low	97	390	114	28	5	13	(-	-)	191	64	70	63	20	1	119	11	0	1	5	7	8	.292	.344	.490	.833
2014 Frisco	AA	15	62	14	2	1	0	(-	-)	18	4	4	4	2	1	21	0	0	0	1	1	1	.226	.250	.290	.540
2015 Frisco	AA	97	378	113	21	4	13	(-	-)	181	56	45	64	32	0	77	3	1	1	10	8	6	.299	.357	.479	.836
2015 Rdng	AA	22	97	31	5	2	4	(-	-)	52	21	10	17	3	0	20	0	0	0	3	0	0	.320	.340	.536	.876
2016 LV	AAA	125	497	128	33	6	13	(-	-)	212	78	64	61	19	1	136	4	1	6	6	4	12	.258	.287	.427	.714
2017 LV	AAA	78	282	79	16	2	15	(-	-)	144	43	44	46	16	1	90	5	1	2	5	4	7	.280	.328	.511	.839
2017 Phi	NL	83	313	90	14	4	12	(6	6)	148	45	55	47	20	0	97	6	0	4	1	2	8	.288	.338	.473	.811

Taylor Williams

Pitches: R **Bats:** B **Pos:** RP-5

Ht: 5'11" **Wt:** 195 **Born:** 7/21/1991 **Age:** 26

		HOW MUCH HE PITCHED						WHAT HE GAVE UP										THE RESULTS						
Year Team	Lg	G	GS	CG	GF	IP	BFP	H	R	ER	HR	SH	SF	HB	TBB	IBB	SO	WP	Bk	W	L	Pct	Sh	Sv-Op	Hld	ERC	ERA
2013 Helena	R+	12	6	0	0	42.1	183	42	22	20	5	0	1	2	17	0	42	9	0	3	1	.750	0	4--	-	4.38	4.25
2014 2 Tms	Low	27	17	2	8	132.1	533	107	48	40	8	7	2	7	28	0	137	10	1	9	3	.750	0	0--	-	2.31	2.72
2017 Biloxi	AA	22	14	0	0	46.2	199	42	22	16	2	2	2	1	21	1	57	7	0	0	2	.000	0	0--	-	3.38	3.09
2017 Mil	NL	5	0	0	5	4.2	20	4	1	1	0	0	0	0	2	0	4	0	0	0	0	-	0	0-0	0	2.67	1.93

Trevor Williams

Pitches: R **Bats:** R **Pos:** SP-25; RP-6

Ht: 6'3" **Wt:** 230 **Born:** 4/25/1992 **Age:** 26

		HOW MUCH HE PITCHED						WHAT HE GAVE UP										THE RESULTS						
Year Team	Lg	G	GS	CG	GF	IP	BFP	H	R	ER	HR	SH	SF	HB	TBB	IBB	SO	WP	Bk	W	L	Pct	Sh	Sv-Op	Hld	ERC	ERA
2013 3 Tms	Low	12	12	0	0	34.0	145	31	15	9	0	0	1	1	8	0	24	0	0	0	2	.000	0	0--	-	2.34	2.38
2014 Jupiter	A+	23	23	0	0	129.0	537	138	49	40	5	4	6	0	29	0	90	4	0	8	6	.571	0	0--	-	3.40	2.79
2015 Jaxnvl	AA	22	21	0	0	117.0	500	126	53	52	9	3	1	1	36	0	88	3	0	7	8	.467	0	0--	-	4.04	4.00
2016 Indy	AAA	20	19	0	0	110.1	459	103	43	31	5	7	4	4	30	2	74	2	1	9	6	.600	0	0--	-	2.97	2.53
2016 Pit	NL	7	1	0	1	12.2	61	19	13	11	4	0	0	0	5	0	11	0	0	1	1	.500	0	0-1	0	8.89	7.82
2017 Pit	NL	31	25	0	0	150.1	642	145	73	68	14	8	4	9	52	4	117	2	0	7	9	.438	0	0-0	0	3.82	4.07
2 ML YEARS		38	26	0	2	163.0	703	164	86	79	18	8	4	9	57	4	128	2	0	8	10	.444	0	0-1	0	4.17	4.36

Mac Williamson

Bats: R **Throws:** R **Pos:** RF-12;LF-9;PH-7;PR-1

Ht: 6'4" **Wt:** 240 **Born:** 7/15/1990 **Age:** 27

						BATTING														RUNNING			AVERAGES			
Year Team	Lg	G	AB	H	2B	3B	HR	(Hm	Rd)	TB	R	RBI	RC	TBB	IBB	SO	HBP	SH	SF	SB	CS	GDP	Avg	OBP	Slg	OPS
2017 Scrmto*	AAA	94	351	86	21	0	14	(-	-)	149	54	50	46	25	0	100	4	0	2	4	1	9	.245	.301	.425	.726
2015 SF	NL	10	32	7	0	1	0	(0	0)	9	2	1	1	0	0	8	1	0	1	0	0	1	.219	.235	.281	.517
2016 SF	NL	54	112	25	3	0	6	(1	5)	46	14	15	11	13	0	35	2	0	0	1	1	4	.223	.315	.411	.726
2017 SF	NL	28	68	16	2	0	3	(0	3)	27	8	6	5	5	1	25	0	0	0	1	1	2	.235	.288	.397	.685
3 ML YEARS		92	212	48	5	1	9	(1	8)	82	24	22	17	18	1	68	3	0	1	2	2	7	.226	.295	.387	.682

Alex Wilson

Pitches: R **Bats:** R **Pos:** RP-66

Ht: 6'0" **Wt:** 215 **Born:** 11/3/1986 **Age:** 31

		HOW MUCH HE PITCHED						WHAT HE GAVE UP										THE RESULTS						
Year Team	Lg	G	GS	CG	GF	IP	BFP	H	R	ER	HR	SH	SF	HB	TBB	IBB	SO	WP	Bk	W	L	Pct	Sh	Sv-Op	Hld	ERC	ERA
2013 Bos	AL	26	0	0	9	27.2	127	34	16	16	0	0	1	1	14	1	22	1	0	1	1	.500	0	0-0	1	5.19	4.88
2014 Bos	AL	18	0	0	3	28.1	109	20	8	6	3	0	1	2	5	0	19	1	0	1	0	1.000	0	0-1	1	2.08	1.91
2015 Det	AL	59	1	0	16	70.0	273	61	19	17	5	2	2	2	11	1	38	2	0	3	3	.500	0	2-4	7	2.47	2.19
2016 Det	AL	62	0	0	8	73.0	297	68	26	24	5	0	5	1	21	5	49	2	0	4	0	1.000	0	0-4	14	3.09	2.96
2017 Det	AL	66	0	0	11	60.0	260	67	34	30	7	0	2	3	15	5	42	4	0	2	5	.286	0	2-7	17	4.31	4.50
5 ML YEARS		231	1	0	45	259.0	1066	250	103	92	20	2	11	9	66	12	170	10	0	11	9	.550	0	4-16	39	3.29	3.20

Justin Wilson

Pitches: L **Bats:** L **Pos:** RP-65

Ht: 6'2" **Wt:** 205 **Born:** 8/18/1987 **Age:** 30

		HOW MUCH HE PITCHED						WHAT HE GAVE UP										THE RESULTS						
Year Team	Lg	G	GS	CG	GF	IP	BFP	H	R	ER	HR	SH	SF	HB	TBB	IBB	SO	WP	Bk	W	L	Pct	Sh	Sv-Op	Hld	ERC	ERA
2012 Pit	NL	8	0	0	3	4.2	26	10	1	1	0	1	0	0	3	0	7	1	0	0	0	-	0	0-0	0	11.83	1.93
2013 Pit	NL	58	0	0	8	73.2	295	50	17	17	4	3	1	3	28	1	59	6	0	6	1	.857	0	0-3	14	2.20	2.08
2014 Pit	NL	70	0	0	15	60.0	256	49	30	28	4	0	0	3	30	5	61	4	0	3	4	.429	0	0-3	16	3.29	4.20
2015 NYY	AL	74	0	0	9	61.0	244	49	21	21	3	2	0	2	20	0	66	4	0	5	0	1.000	0	0-2	29	2.63	3.10
2016 Det	AL	66	0	0	10	58.2	251	61	29	27	6	1	0	1	17	2	65	4	0	4	5	.444	0	1-6	25	3.87	4.14
2017 2 Tms		65	0	0	30	58.0	248	40	23	22	5	0	1	1	35	1	80	4	0	4	4	.500	0	13-16	9	3.08	3.41

Year Team	Lg	G	GS	CG	GF	IP	BFP	H	R	ER	HR	SH	SF	HB	TBB	IBB	SO	WP	Bk	W	L	Pct	Sh	Sv-Op	Hld	ERC	ERA
17 Det	AL	42	0	0	26	40.1	157	22	12	12	5	0	1	0	16	0	55	3	0	3	4	.429	0	13-15	8	1.91	2.68
17 ChC	NL	23	0	0	4	17.2	91	18	11	10	0	0	0	1	19	1	25	1	0	1	0	1.000	0	0-1	1	5.98	5.09
Postseason		4	0	0	0	4.1	18	3	1	1	0	0	0	0	3	0	4	1	0	0	0	-	0	0-0	0	2.92	2.08
6 ML YEARS		341	0	0	69	316.0	1320	259	121	116	22	7	2	10	133	9	338	22	0	22	14	.611	0	14-30	93	3.07	3.30

Tyler Wilson

Pitches: R **Bats:** R **Pos:** RP-8; SP-1 **Ht:** 6'2" **Wt:** 185 **Born:** 9/25/1989 **Age:** 28

Year Team	Lg	G	GS	CG	GF	IP	BFP	H	R	ER	HR	SH	SF	HB	TBB	IBB	SO	WP	Bk	W	L	Pct	Sh	Sv-Op	Hld	ERC	ERA
2017 Norfolk*	AAA	20	20	0	0	114.0	498	128	64	60	10	1	2	7	35	0	68	7	1	7	8	.467	0	0- --		4.59	4.74
2015 Bal	AL	9	5	0	2	36.0	149	39	14	14	1	0	2	1	11	1	13	0	0	2	2	.500	0	0-0	-	3.90	3.50
2016 Bal	AL	24	13	0	5	94.0	414	110	57	55	15	1	3	4	24	1	55	2	0	4	6	.400	0	0-0	0	5.01	5.27
2017 Bal	AL	9	1	0	3	15.1	70	22	14	12	3	0	1	1	4	1	9	1	1	2	2	.500	0	0-0	1	7.17	7.04
3 ML YEARS		42	19	0	10	145.1	633	171	85	81	19	1	6	6	39	3	77	3	1	8	10	.444	0	0-0	1	4.95	5.02

Alex Wimmers

Pitches: R **Bats:** L **Pos:** RP-6 **Ht:** 6'2" **Wt:** 215 **Born:** 11/1/1988 **Age:** 29

Year Team	Lg	G	GS	CG	GF	IP	BFP	H	R	ER	HR	SH	SF	HB	TBB	IBB	SO	WP	Bk	W	L	Pct	Sh	Sv-Op	Hld	ERC	ERA
2013 Twins	R	6	6	0	0	15.0	78	25	15	12	1	0	1	2	5	0	18	2	0	0	1	.000	0	0- --	-	7.88	7.20
2014 FtMyrs	A+	18	7	0	2	62.1	282	71	44	28	2	1	3	3	25	0	70	3	2	3	3	.500	0	0- --	-	4.50	4.04
2014 NwBrit	AA	13	1	0	2	21.2	89	19	9	9	0	0	0	0	6	0	27	1	0	1	0	1.000	0	1- --	-	3.16	3.74
2015 Chatt	AA	30	18	0	6	115.1	489	117	58	58	7	4	8	1	43	0	100	5	0	8	4	.667	0	0- --	-	3.87	4.53
2016 Chatt	AA	6	0	0	1	7.0	30	10	5	5	0	0	0	0	1	0	6	0	0	0	1	.000	0	0- --	-	4.97	6.43
2016 Roch	AAA	39	0	0	20	49.2	214	42	22	20	2	1	1	2	24	1	50	6	0	2	1	.667	0	11- --	-	3.23	3.62
2017 Roch	AAA	34	0	0	22	47.1	182	33	17	17	5	2	4	0	11	1	48	2	0	7	3	.700	0	7- --	-	1.95	3.23
2016 Min	AL	16	0	0	7	17.1	72	14	8	8	2	0	2	0	11	1	14	0	0	1	3	.250	0	0-1	4	4.15	4.15
2017 Min	AL	6	0	0	1	7.1	38	8	4	4	2	0	0	0	8	0	7	0	0	0	0	-	0	0-0	0	8.90	4.91
2 ML YEARS		22	0	0	3	24.2	110	22	12	12	4	0	2	0	19	1	21	0	0	1	3	.250	0	0-1	4	5.48	4.38

Jesse Winker

Bats: L **Throws:** L **Pos:** RF-25;PH-19;LF-2;DH-2 **Ht:** 6'3" **Wt:** 215 **Born:** 8/17/1993 **Age:** 24

Year Team	Lg	G	AB	H	2B	3B	HR	(Hm	Rd)	TB	R	RBI	RC	TBB	IBB	SO	HBP	SH	SF	SB	CS	GDP	Avg	OBP	Slg	OPS
2013 Dayton	A	112	417	117	18	5	16	(-	-)	193	73	76	77	63	2	75	4	0	2	6	1	10	.281	.379	.463	.841
2014 Bkrsfld	A+	53	205	65	15	0	13	(-	-)	119	42	49	51	40	0	46	1	0	3	5	1	4	.317	.426	.580	1.006
2014 Pnscla	AA	21	77	16	5	0	2	(-	-)	27	15	8	9	14	0	22	0	0	1	0	0	3	.208	.326	.351	.677
2015 Pnscla	AA	123	443	125	24	2	13	(-	-)	192	69	55	80	74	4	84	6	0	3	8	4	10	.282	.390	.433	.823
2016 Lsvlle	AAA	106	380	115	22	0	3	(-	-)	146	39	45	64	59	6	59	4	0	5	0	0	10	.303	.397	.384	.782
2017 Lsvlle	AAA	85	299	94	22	0	2	(-	-)	122	33	41	51	38	3	46	5	0	5	2	4	9	.314	.395	.408	.803
2017 Cin	NL	47	121	36	7	0	7	(2	5)	64	21	15	18	15	0	24	0	1	0	1	1	2	.298	.375	.529	.904

Dan Winkler

Pitches: R **Bats:** R **Pos:** RP-16 **Ht:** 6'3" **Wt:** 205 **Born:** 2/2/1990 **Age:** 28

Year Team	Lg	G	GS	CG	GF	IP	BFP	H	R	ER	HR	SH	SF	HB	TBB	IBB	SO	WP	Bk	W	L	Pct	Sh	Sv-Op	Hld	ERC	ERA
2017 Gwnntt*	AAA	10	0	0	2	10.0	44	14	7	7	2	0	1	0	1	0	12	0	0	1	0	1.000	0	0- --	-	5.91	6.30
2015 Atl	NL	2	0	0	0	1.2	8	2	2	2	2	0	0	0	1	0	2	0	0	0	0	-	0	0-0	0	14.99	10.80
2016 Atl	NL	3	0	0	0	2.1	8	0	0	0	0	0	0	0	1	0	4	0	0	0	0	-	0	0-0	0	0.20	0.00
2017 Atl	NL	16	0	0	1	14.1	53	7	4	4	1	1	0	0	6	0	18	0	0	1	1	.500	0	0-0	4	1.57	2.51
3 ML YEARS		21	0	0	1	18.1	69	9	6	6	3	1	0	0	8	0	24	0	0	1	1	.500	0	0-0	4	2.08	2.95

Matt Wisler

Pitches: R **Bats:** R **Pos:** RP-19; SP-1 WISS-lurr **Ht:** 6'3" **Wt:** 205 **Born:** 9/12/1992 **Age:** 25

Year Team	Lg	G	GS	CG	GF	IP	BFP	H	R	ER	HR	SH	SF	HB	TBB	IBB	SO	WP	Bk	W	L	Pct	Sh	Sv-Op	Hld	ERC	ERA
2017 Gwnntt*	AAA	18	14	1	1	93.2	395	101	44	37	7	0	6	1	20	0	64	10	1	7	5	.583	1	0- --	-	3.64	3.56
2015 Atl	NL	20	19	0	0	109.0	478	119	59	59	16	4	5	4	40	4	72	2	3	8	8	.500	0	0-0	-	4.91	4.71
2016 Atl	NL	27	26	0	1	156.2	671	159	90	87	26	2	3	4	49	3	115	5	1	7	13	.350	0	1-1	-	4.32	5.00
2017 Atl	NL	20	1	0	8	32.1	153	43	31	30	5	2	3	2	13	0	22	0	0	0	1	.000	0	0-0	-	6.68	8.35
3 ML YEARS		67	46	0	9	298.0	1302	321	180	174	47	8	11	10	102	7	209	7	4	15	22	.405	0	1-1	-	4.79	5.26

Nick Wittgren

Pitches: R **Bats:** R **Pos:** RP-38 **Ht:** 6'2" **Wt:** 210 **Born:** 5/29/1991 **Age:** 27

Year Team	Lg	G	GS	CG	GF	IP	BFP	H	R	ER	HR	SH	SF	HB	TBB	IBB	SO	WP	Bk	W	L	Pct	Sh	Sv-Op	Hld	ERC	ERA
2013 Jupiter	A+	48	0	0	38	54.1	214	42	7	5	1	3	2	0	10	1	59	0	0	2	1	.667	0	25- --	-	1.76	0.83
2014 Jaxnvl	AA	52	0	0	42	66.0	280	73	31	26	6	2	2	2	14	4	56	2	1	5	5	.500	0	20- --	-	3.90	3.55
2015 NewOr	AAA	51	0	0	39	62.1	251	58	22	21	6	5	0	1	8	0	64	1	0	1	6	.143	0	19- --	-	2.70	3.03
2016 NewOr	AAA	10	0	0	8	12.2	46	6	2	2	1	0	0	0	4	0	11	1	0	1	0	1.000	0	2- --	-	1.32	1.42

Year Team	Lg	G	GS	CG	GF	IP	BFP	H	R	ER	HR	SH	SF	HB	TBB	IBB	SO	WP	Bk	W	L	Pct	Sh	Sv-Op	Hld	ERC	ERA
		HOW MUCH HE PITCHED						**WHAT HE GAVE UP**												**THE RESULTS**							
2017 NewOr	AAA	5	0	0	5	5.0	19	3	0	0	0	0	0	0	0	0	6	0	0	0	0	-	0	0--	-	0.71	0.00
2016 Mia	NL	48	0	0	9	51.2	213	50	18	18	6	3	2	1	10	2	42	1	0	4	3	.571	0	0-2	6	3.21	3.14
2017 Mia	NL	38	0	0	3	42.1	182	46	22	22	5	0	3	0	13	1	43	2	0	3	1	.750	0	0-0	5	4.29	4.68
2 ML YEARS		86	0	0	12	94.0	395	96	40	40	11	3	5	1	23	3	85	3	0	7	4	.636	0	0-2	11	3.68	3.83

Asher Wojciechowski

Pitches: R **Bats:** R **Pos:** RP-17; SP-8

wo-jah-HOW-ski

Ht: 6'4" **Wt:** 235 **Born:** 12/21/1988 **Age:** 29

Year Team	Lg	G	GS	CG	GF	IP	BFP	H	R	ER	HR	SH	SF	HB	TBB	IBB	SO	WP	Bk	W	L	Pct	Sh	Sv-Op	Hld	ERC	ERA
		HOW MUCH HE PITCHED						**WHAT HE GAVE UP**												**THE RESULTS**							
2013 CpChr	AA	6	3	0	3	26.0	98	17	6	6	1	0	1	0	7	1	27	0	0	2	1	.667	0	1--	-	1.58	2.08
2013 OkCity	AAA	22	21	2	0	134.0	554	116	56	53	10	1	2	1	44	1	104	4	0	9	7	.563	1	0--	-	2.93	3.56
2014 OkCity	AAA	15	14	0	1	76.0	330	89	46	40	10	1	0	4	21	1	59	4	0	4	4	.500	0	0--	-	5.06	4.74
2015 Fresno	AAA	20	20	1	0	115.1	511	129	68	63	13	6	5	6	41	0	87	11	0	8	4	.667	0	0--	-	4.87	4.92
2016 Fresno	AAA	5	5	0	0	25.1	122	29	21	15	1	0	2	3	13	0	22	0	0	2	2	.500	0	0--	-	5.18	5.33
2016 NewOr	AAA	13	10	0	0	49.2	231	61	31	29	10	2	2	3	24	0	32	2	1	2	3	.400	0	0--	-	6.87	5.26
2017 Lsvlle	AAA	8	5	0	0	30.2	126	24	8	7	2	1	0	1	8	0	35	1	0	2	0	1.000	0	0--	-	2.26	2.05
2015 Hou	AL	5	3	0	2	16.1	79	23	13	13	2	0	2	0	7	0	16	1	0	0	1	.000	0	0-0	0	6.66	7.16
2017 Cin	NL	25	8	0	2	62.1	279	71	48	45	14	5	2	5	19	1	64	1	0	4	3	.571	0	0-0	2	5.65	6.50
2 ML YEARS		30	11	0	4	78.2	358	94	61	58	16	5	4	5	26	1	80	2	0	4	4	.500	0	0-0	2	5.87	6.64

Tony Wolters

Bats: L **Throws:** R **Pos:** C-77;PH-9;2B-4;3B-1;PR-1

WAHL-ters

Ht: 5'10" **Wt:** 200 **Born:** 6/9/1992 **Age:** 26

Year Team	Lg	G	AB	H	2B	3B	HR	(Hm	Rd)	TB	R	RBI	RC	TBB	IBB	SO	HBP	SH	SF	SB	CS	GDP	Avg	OBP	Slg	OPS
		BATTING																		**RUNNING**			**AVERAGES**			
2013 Carlina	A+	80	289	80	13	0	3	(-	-)	102	36	33	41	41	0	58	3	4	4	3	6	4	.277	.369	.353	.722
2014 Akron	AA	94	341	85	15	2	1	(-	-)	107	36	34	37	35	1	74	3	2	6	3	2	10	.249	.319	.314	.633
2015 Akron	AA	65	239	50	7	2	2	(-	-)	67	23	17	20	21	0	63	7	2	2	3	2	5	.209	.290	.280	.570
2017 Albq	AAA	14	54	14	5	1	2	(-	-)	27	9	8	8	3	0	15	1	0	0	1	0	1	.259	.310	.500	.810
2016 Col	NL	71	205	53	15	2	3	(2	1)	81	27	30	30	21	2	53	0	4	0	4	1	1	.259	.327	.395	.723
2017 Col	NL	83	229	55	8	1	0	(0	0)	65	30	16	25	33	9	55	2	2	0	0	1	9	.240	.341	.284	.625
2 ML YEARS		154	434	108	23	3	3	(2	1)	146	57	46	55	54	11	108	2	6	0	4	2	10	.249	.335	.336	.671

Kolten Wong

Bats: L **Throws:** R **Pos:** 2B-106;PH-3;PR-2

COLT-enn

Ht: 5'9" **Wt:** 185 **Born:** 10/10/1990 **Age:** 27

Year Team	Lg	G	AB	H	2B	3B	HR	(Hm	Rd)	TB	R	RBI	RC	TBB	IBB	SO	HBP	SH	SF	SB	CS	GDP	Avg	OBP	Slg	OPS
		BATTING																		**RUNNING**			**AVERAGES**			
2013 StL	NL	32	59	9	1	0	0	(0	0)	10	6	0	0	3	0	12	0	0	0	3	0	2	.153	.194	.169	.363
2014 StL	NL	113	402	100	14	3	12	(10	2)	156	52	42	41	21	3	71	4	5	1	20	4	12	.249	.292	.388	.680
2015 StL	NL	150	557	146	28	4	11	(5	6)	215	71	61	67	36	2	95	15	0	5	15	8	10	.262	.321	.386	.707
2016 StL	NL	121	313	75	7	7	5	(3	2)	111	39	23	36	34	2	52	9	0	5	7	0	3	.240	.327	.355	.682
2017 StL	NL	108	354	101	27	3	4	(3	1)	146	55	42	56	41	11	60	12	1	3	8	2	4	.285	.376	.412	.788
Postseason		19	49	10	4	1	4	(3	1)	28	5	7	5	1	1	11	0	0	0	2	0	2	.204	.220	.571	.791
5 ML YEARS		524	1685	431	77	17	32	(21	11)	638	223	168	200	135	18	290	40	6	14	53	14	31	.256	.323	.379	.702

Alex Wood

Pitches: L **Bats:** R **Pos:** SP-25; RP-2

Ht: 6'4" **Wt:** 215 **Born:** 1/12/1991 **Age:** 27

Year Team	Lg	G	GS	CG	GF	IP	BFP	H	R	ER	HR	SH	SF	HB	TBB	IBB	SO	WP	Bk	W	L	Pct	Sh	Sv-Op	Hld	ERC	ERA
		HOW MUCH HE PITCHED						**WHAT HE GAVE UP**												**THE RESULTS**							
2013 Atl	NL	31	11	0	9	77.2	327	76	29	27	3	6	4	1	27	1	77	4	2	3	3	.500	0	0-0	1	3.40	3.13
2014 Atl	NL	35	24	1	2	171.2	694	151	58	53	16	7	3	6	45	1	170	5	0	11	11	.500	0	0-0	2	3.04	2.78
2015 2 Tms	NL	32	32	0	0	189.2	801	198	86	81	15	15	3	4	59	4	139	6	1	12	12	.500	0	0-0	0	3.94	3.84
2016 LAD	NL	14	10	0	0	60.1	255	56	30	25	5	0	2	3	20	0	66	4	0	1	4	.200	0	0-0	0	3.49	3.73
2017 LAD	NL	27	25	0	0	152.1	614	123	50	46	15	4	0	6	38	6	151	2	0	16	3	.842	0	0-0	1	2.58	2.72
15 Atl	NL	20	20	0	0	119.1	509	132	50	47	8	11	1	2	36	2	90	5	0	7	6	.538	0	0-0	0	4.15	3.54
15 LAD	NL	12	12	0	0	70.1	292	66	36	34	7	4	2	2	23	2	49	1	1	5	6	.455	0	0-0	0	3.58	4.35
Postseason		4	0	0	1	7.1	35	9	8	4	2	0	0	1	2	1	6	1	0	0	0	-	0	0-0	0	6.20	4.91
5 ML YEARS		139	102	1	11	651.2	2691	604	253	232	54	32	12	20	189	12	603	21	3	43	33	.566	0	0-0	4	3.27	3.20

Blake Wood

Pitches: R **Bats:** R **Pos:** RP-72

Ht: 6'5" **Wt:** 233 **Born:** 8/8/1985 **Age:** 32

Year Team	Lg	G	GS	CG	GF	IP	BFP	H	R	ER	HR	SH	SF	HB	TBB	IBB	SO	WP	Bk	W	L	Pct	Sh	Sv-Op	Hld	ERC	ERA
		HOW MUCH HE PITCHED						**WHAT HE GAVE UP**												**THE RESULTS**							
2010 KC	AL	51	0	0	13	49.2	220	54	29	28	6	2	6	1	22	5	31	3	0	1	3	.250	0	0-4	15	4.83	5.07
2011 KC	AL	55	0	0	20	69.2	303	66	30	29	5	5	3	3	32	7	62	2	0	5	3	.625	0	1-3	5	3.82	3.75
2013 Cle	AL	2	0	0	1	1.1	8	1	0	0	0	0	0	0	3	0	1	0	0	0	0	-	0	0-0	0	8.88	0.00
2014 Cle	AL	7	0	0	3	6.1	30	4	5	5	0	0	0	1	7	2	7	0	0	0	1	.000	0	0-0	0	3.89	7.11
2016 Cin	NL	70	0	0	21	76.2	330	72	38	34	9	1	2	2	38	3	81	8	0	6	5	.545	0	1-6	15	4.35	3.99
2017 2 Tms		72	0	0	19	74.1	332	84	49	45	8	0	4	1	33	2	84	7	2	3	4	.429	0	0-1	3	5.09	5.45
17 Cin	NL	55	0	0	17	57.1	259	64	40	36	5	0	4	1	29	1	62	6	2	1	4	.200	0	0-1	3	5.13	5.65
17 LAA	AL	17	0	0	2	17.0	73	20	9	9	3	0	0	0	4	1	22	1	0	2	0	1.000	0	0-0	0	4.90	4.76
6 ML YEARS		257	0	0	77	278.0	1223	281	151	141	28	8	15	8	135	19	266	20	2	15	16	.484	0	2-14	38	4.51	4.56

Hunter Wood

Pitches: R **Bats:** R **Pos:** RP-1 **Ht:** 6'1" **Wt:** 165 **Born:** 8/12/1993 **Age:** 24

		HOW MUCH HE PITCHED						WHAT HE GAVE UP												THE RESULTS							
Year Team	Lg	G	GS	CG	GF	IP	BFP	H	R	ER	HR	SH	SF	HB	TBB	IBB	SO	WP	Bk	W	L	Pct	Sh	Sv-Op	Hld	ERC	ERA
2013 Prnctn	R+	16	6	0	6	45.0	186	38	20	19	5	1	2	2	11	0	59	2	1	3	3	.500	0	2--	-	2.84	3.80
2014 2 Tms	Low	19	19	0	0	88.1	375	75	37	33	7	3	2	10	28	0	78	5	0	4	4	.500	0	0--	-	3.19	3.36
2015 2 Tms	Low	29	10	0	11	106.1	410	68	28	26	4	3	5	3	25	1	113	8	1	2	7	.222	0	4--	-	1.50	2.20
2016 Charltt	A+	11	9	0	0	63.2	248	34	15	12	2	2	2	1	24	0	56	3	1	3	3	.500	0	0--	-	1.43	1.70
2016 Mont	AA	10	9	0	0	49.1	199	36	21	18	5	0	3	1	20	0	49	4	0	6	2	.750	0	0--	-	2.79	3.28
2017 Mont	AA	12	12	0	0	70.0	292	68	38	37	7	1	2	2	24	0	68	1	0	4	4	.500	0	0--	-	3.89	4.76
2017 Drham	AAA	19	6	0	1	53.1	230	54	28	26	8	0	0	1	20	0	47	3	0	3	1	.750	0	0--	-	4.48	4.39
2017 TB	AL	1	0	0	1	0.1	1	0	0	0	0	0	0	0	0	0	0	0	0	0	0	-	0	0-0	0	0.00	0.00

Travis Wood

Pitches: L **Bats:** R **Pos:** RP-25; SP-14 **Ht:** 5'11" **Wt:** 175 **Born:** 2/6/1987 **Age:** 31

		HOW MUCH HE PITCHED						WHAT HE GAVE UP												THE RESULTS							
Year Team	Lg	G	GS	CG	GF	IP	BFP	H	R	ER	HR	SH	SF	HB	TBB	IBB	SO	WP	Bk	W	L	Pct	Sh	Sv-Op	Hld	ERC	ERA
2010 Cin	NL	17	17	0	0	102.2	419	85	45	40	9	3	3	4	26	1	86	0	1	5	4	.556	0	0-0	0	2.64	3.51
2011 Cin	NL	22	18	0	2	106.0	463	118	57	57	10	9	7	4	40	5	76	2	0	6	6	.500	0	0-0	0	4.73	4.84
2012 ChC	NL	26	26	0	0	156.0	649	133	80	74	25	9	4	8	54	3	119	2	1	6	13	.316	0	0-0	0	3.65	4.27
2013 ChC	NL	32	32	0	0	200.0	821	163	73	69	18	7	4	7	66	2	144	6	0	9	12	.429	0	0-0	0	2.90	3.11
2014 ChC	NL	31	31	0	0	173.2	781	190	110	97	20	8	4	7	76	1	146	2	0	8	13	.381	0	0-0	0	5.00	5.03
2015 ChC	NL	54	9	0	12	100.2	419	86	48	43	11	1	2	1	39	5	118	2	0	5	4	.556	0	4-4	3	3.27	3.84
2016 ChC	NL	77	0	0	16	61.0	252	45	24	20	8	1	0	1	24	2	47	0	0	4	0	1.000	0	0-1	12	2.83	2.95
2017 2 Tms		39	14	0	10	94.0	436	118	77	71	19	4	5	2	45	0	65	1	0	4	7	.364	0	0-1	1	6.85	6.80
17 KC	AL	28	3	0	10	41.2	195	56	33	32	4	0	4	1	20	0	29	1	0	1	3	.250	0	0-1	1	6.61	6.91
17 SD	NL	11	11	0	0	52.1	241	62	44	39	15	4	1	1	25	0	36	0	0	3	4	.429	0	0-0	0	7.00	6.71
Postseason		16	0	0	1	17.1	68	12	6	6	1	0	1	0	4	1	22	0	0	2	0	1.000	0	0-0	3	1.61	3.12
8 ML YEARS		298	147	0	40	994.0	4240	938	514	471	120	42	29	35	370	19	801	15	2	47	59	.443	0	4-6	16	3.91	4.26

Brandon Woodruff

Pitches: R **Bats:** L **Pos:** SP-8 **Ht:** 6'4" **Wt:** 215 **Born:** 2/10/1993 **Age:** 25

		HOW MUCH HE PITCHED						WHAT HE GAVE UP												THE RESULTS							
Year Team	Lg	G	GS	CG	GF	IP	BFP	H	R	ER	HR	SH	SF	HB	TBB	IBB	SO	WP	Bk	W	L	Pct	Sh	Sv-Op	Hld	ERC	ERA
2014 Helena	R+	14	8	0	2	46.2	208	48	35	17	2	2	3	3	16	0	37	8	0	1	2	.333	0	0--	-	3.74	3.28
2015 BrvdCt	A+	21	19	0	2	109.2	457	112	48	42	2	2	4	3	33	0	71	5	0	4	7	.364	0	0--	-	3.43	3.45
2016 BrvdCt	A+	8	8	0	0	44.1	176	33	12	9	2	1	1	3	10	0	49	3	0	4	1	.800	0	0--	-	2.04	1.83
2016 Biloxi	AA	20	20	1	0	113.2	457	88	39	38	4	2	2	4	30	0	124	6	0	10	8	.556	0	0--	-	2.13	3.01
2017 ColSpr	AAA	16	16	0	0	75.1	325	78	44	36	8	0	2	5	25	1	70	4	1	6	5	.545	0	0--	-	4.32	4.30
2017 Mil	NL	8	8	0	0	43.0	184	43	23	23	5	1	0	3	14	1	32	0	0	2	3	.400	0	0-0	0	4.16	4.81

Brandon Workman

Pitches: R **Bats:** R **Pos:** RP-33 **Ht:** 6'5" **Wt:** 235 **Born:** 8/13/1988 **Age:** 29

		HOW MUCH HE PITCHED						WHAT HE GAVE UP												THE RESULTS							
Year Team	Lg	G	GS	CG	GF	IP	BFP	H	R	ER	HR	SH	SF	HB	TBB	IBB	SO	WP	Bk	W	L	Pct	Sh	Sv-Op	Hld	ERC	ERA
2017 Pwtckt*	AAA	18	0	0	8	29.0	113	16	6	5	1	0	1	0	13	0	35	2	0	4	1	.800	0	2--	-	1.65	1.55
2013 Bos	AL	20	3	0	5	41.2	180	44	23	23	5	2	1	0	15	1	47	1	0	6	3	.667	0	0-1	1	4.34	4.97
2014 Bos	AL	19	15	0	2	87.0	378	88	57	50	11	3	3	1	36	0	70	2	0	1	10	.091	0	0-0	1	4.43	5.17
2017 Bos	AL	33	0	0	8	39.2	162	37	17	14	7	2	1	1	11	2	37	1	0	1	1	.500	0	0-1	4	3.83	3.18
Postseason		7	0	0	0	8.2	35	7	1	0	0	1	0	0	3	1	4	0	0	0	1	.000	0	0-0	0	2.09	0.00
3 ML YEARS		72	18	0	15	168.1	720	169	97	87	23	7	5	2	62	3	154	4	0	8	14	.364	0	0-2	6	4.27	4.65

Vance Worley

Pitches: R **Bats:** R **Pos:** SP-12; RP-12 **Ht:** 6'2" **Wt:** 250 **Born:** 9/25/1987 **Age:** 30

		HOW MUCH HE PITCHED						WHAT HE GAVE UP												THE RESULTS							
Year Team	Lg	G	GS	CG	GF	IP	BFP	H	R	ER	HR	SH	SF	HB	TBB	IBB	SO	WP	Bk	W	L	Pct	Sh	Sv-Op	Hld	ERC	ERA
2017 NewOr*	AAA	8	8	1	0	44.2	191	53	26	22	4	2	2	2	11	0	22	0	0	2	5	.286	0	0--	-	4.75	4.43
2010 Phi	NL	5	2	0	2	13.0	51	8	2	2	1	2	0	0	4	0	12	1	0	1	1	.500	0	0-0	0	1.66	1.38
2011 Phi	NL	25	21	1	0	131.2	553	116	47	44	10	9	5	3	46	2	119	2	1	11	3	.786	0	0-0	2	3.12	3.01
2012 Phi	NL	23	23	0	0	133.0	590	154	69	62	12	11	3	6	47	4	107	1	0	6	9	.400	0	0-0	0	4.87	4.20
2013 Min	AL	10	10	0	0	48.2	234	82	43	39	9	0	1	3	15	1	25	1	0	1	5	.167	0	0-0	0	9.17	7.21
2014 Pit	NL	18	17	1	0	110.2	458	112	43	35	9	0	3	6	22	1	79	4	0	8	4	.667	1	0-0	0	3.35	2.85
2015 Pit	NL	23	8	0	6	71.2	310	81	36	32	6	3	2	2	21	3	49	3	0	4	6	.400	0	0-1	1	4.34	4.02
2016 Bal	AL	35	4	0	13	86.2	365	84	37	34	11	0	3	3	35	0	56	3	0	2	2	.500	0	1-1	3	4.37	3.53
2017 Mia	NL	24	12	0	8	71.2	333	99	56	55	9	2	3	6	30	5	50	1	0	2	6	.250	0	1-1	1	7.07	6.91
Postseason		2	0	0	0	1.1	8	3	1	1	0	0	0	0	1	0	0	0	0	0	0	-	0	0-0	1	12.64	6.75
8 ML YEARS		163	97	2	29	667.0	2894	736	333	303	67	33	21	26	220	16	497	16	1	35	36	.493	1	2-3	2	4.54	4.09

Daniel Wright

Pitches: R **Bats:** R **Pos:** RP-3; SP-2 **Ht:** 6'2" **Wt:** 205 **Born:** 4/3/1991 **Age:** 27

		HOW MUCH HE PITCHED						WHAT HE GAVE UP												THE RESULTS							
Year Team	Lg	G	GS	CG	GF	IP	BFP	H	R	ER	HR	SH	SF	HB	TBB	IBB	SO	WP	Bk	W	L	Pct	Sh	Sv-Op	Hld	ERC	ERA
2013 Billings	R+	14	0	0	0	42.2	192	57	30	28	4	0	3	2	5	0	43	7	1	3	3	.500	0	0--	-	4.88	5.91
2014 2 Tms	Low	28	25	0	0	152.1	619	141	67	60	20	3	4	11	22	0	141	11	1	14	7	.667	0	0--	-	3.17	3.54
2015 Pnscla	AA	27	27	0	0	155.0	649	154	83	78	6	7	4	7	47	0	130	3	0	10	11	.476	0	0--	-	3.48	4.53
2016 Pnscla	AA	8	2	0	0	20.0	73	10	1	1	0	0	0	0	4	0	22	0	1	2	0	1.000	0	0--	-	0.87	0.45

Year Team	Lg	G	GS	CG	GF	IP	BFP	H	R	ER	HR	SH	SF	HB	TBB	IBB	SO	WP	Bk	W	L	Pct	Sh	Sv-Op	Hld	ERC	ERA
2016 Lsvlle	AAA	17	12	2	2	83.2	387	109	66	57	10	4	7	4	25	1	65	2	0	6	5	.545	0	0--	-	5.65	6.13
2017 Salt Lk	AAA	19	18	0	0	92.2	429	112	83	72	17	2	5	8	35	0	61	9	0	6	10	.375	0	0--	-	6.13	6.99
2016 2 Tms		9	7	0	0	39.2	179	57	32	27	7	2	2	5	8	0	21	2	0	1	5	.167	0	0-0	0	7.25	6.13
2017 LAA	AL	5	2	0	3	19.2	85	21	12	10	1	1	0	2	8	0	11	1	0	0	1	.000	0	0-0	0	4.70	4.58
16 Cin	NL	4	2	0	0	13.0	64	25	16	11	2	1	1	0	2	0	6	1	0	0	2	.000	0	0-0	0	9.35	7.62
16 LAA	AL	5	5	0	0	26.2	115	32	16	16	5	1	1	5	6	0	15	1	0	1	3	.250	0	0-0	0	6.27	5.40
2 ML YEARS		14	9	0	3	59.1	264	78	44	37	8	3	2	7	16	0	32	3	0	1	6	.143	0	0-0	0	6.38	5.61

David Wright

Bats: R Throws: R Pos: 3B

Ht: 6'0" Wt: 205 Born: 12/20/1982 Age: 35

Year Team	Lg	G	AB	H	2B	3B	HR	(Hm Rd)	TB	R	RBI	RC	TBB	IBB	SO	HBP	SH	SF	SB	CS	GDP	Avg	OBP	Slg	OPS
2004 NYM	NL	69	263	77	17	1	14	(8 6)	138	41	40	42	14	0	40	3	0	3	6	0	7	.293	.332	.525	.857
2005 NYM	NL	160	575	176	42	1	27	(12 15)	301	99	102	105	72	2	113	7	0	3	17	7	16	.306	.388	.523	.912
2006 NYM	NL	154	582	181	40	5	26	(13 13)	309	96	116	119	66	13	113	5	0	8	20	5	15	.311	.381	.531	.912
2007 NYM	NL	160	604	196	42	1	30	(16 14)	330	113	107	127	94	6	115	6	0	7	34	5	14	.325	.416	.546	.963
2008 NYM	NL	160	626	189	42	2	33	(21 12)	334	115	124	116	94	5	118	4	0	11	15	5	15	.302	.390	.534	.924
2009 NYM	NL	144	535	164	39	3	10	(5 5)	239	88	72	86	74	8	140	3	0	6	27	9	16	.307	.390	.447	.837
2010 NYM	NL	157	587	166	36	3	29	(12 17)	295	87	103	97	69	9	161	2	0	12	19	11	12	.283	.354	.503	.856
2011 NYM	NL	102	389	99	23	1	14	(5 9)	166	60	61	58	52	4	97	3	0	3	13	2	5	.254	.345	.427	.771
2012 NYM	NL	156	581	178	41	2	21	(12 9)	286	91	93	105	81	16	112	3	0	5	15	10	15	.306	.391	.492	.883
2013 NYM	NL	112	430	132	23	6	18	(6 12)	221	63	58	78	55	5	79	5	0	5	17	3	11	.307	.390	.514	.904
2014 NYM	NL	134	535	144	30	1	8	(6 2)	200	54	63	60	42	5	113	4	0	5	8	5	22	.269	.324	.374	.698
2015 NYM	NL	38	152	44	7	0	5	(1 4)	66	24	17	25	22	0	36	0	0	0	2	1	4	.289	.379	.434	.814
2016 NYM	NL	37	137	31	8	0	7	(2 5)	60	18	14	19	26	0	55	0	0	0	3	2	0	.226	.350	.438	.788
Postseason		24	91	18	5	0	2	(1 1)	29	10	13	11	15	2	28	0	0	0	1	1	2	.198	.311	.319	.630
13 ML YEARS		1583	5996	1777	390	26	242	(119 123)	2945	949	970	1037	761	73	1292	45	0	65	196	65	152	.296	.376	.491	.867

Mike Wright

Pitches: R Bats: R Pos: RP-13

Ht: 6'6" Wt: 215 Born: 1/3/1990 Age: 28

Year Team	Lg	G	GS	CG	GF	IP	BFP	H	R	ER	HR	SH	SF	HB	TBB	IBB	SO	WP	Bk	W	L	Pct	Sh	Sv-Op	Hld	ERC	ERA
2017 Norfolk*	AAA	16	16	1	0	83.0	356	81	41	34	6	1	2	4	26	0	71	1	0	4	6	.400	0	0--	-	3.56	3.69
2015 Bal	AL	12	9	0	0	44.2	204	52	30	30	9	0	2	5	18	3	26	2	0	3	5	.375	0	0-0	0	6.20	6.04
2016 Bal	AL	18	12	0	5	74.2	328	81	53	48	12	1	5	9	26	0	50	2	0	3	4	.429	0	0-0	0	5.38	5.79
2017 Bal	AL	13	0	0	4	25.0	109	26	16	16	5	0	1	3	7	0	28	1	0	0	0	-	0	0-0	0	5.01	5.76
3 ML YEARS		43	21	0	9	144.1	641	159	99	94	26	1	8	17	51	3	104	5	0	6	9	.400	0	0-0	0	5.57	5.86

Steven Wright

Pitches: R Bats: R Pos: SP-5

Ht: 6'2" Wt: 215 Born: 8/30/1984 Age: 33

Year Team	Lg	G	GS	CG	GF	IP	BFP	H	R	ER	HR	SH	SF	HB	TBB	IBB	SO	WP	Bk	W	L	Pct	Sh	Sv-Op	Hld	ERC	ERA
2013 Bos	AL	4	1	0	2	13.1	59	12	8	8	0	0	0	1	9	0	10	2	0	2	0	1.000	0	0-0	0	4.22	5.40
2014 Bos	AL	6	1	0	3	21.0	86	21	8	6	2	0	0	4	4	0	22	1	0	0	1	.000	0	0-0	0	3.25	2.57
2015 Bos	AL	16	9	0	3	72.2	310	67	38	33	12	1	1	1	27	0	52	2	0	5	4	.556	0	0-0	0	3.99	4.09
2016 Bos	AL	24	24	4	0	156.2	656	138	74	58	12	2	2	8	57	1	127	10	0	13	6	.684	1	0-0	0	3.34	3.33
2017 Bos	AL	5	5	0	0	24.0	114	40	24	22	9	0	1	2	5	1	13	1	0	1	3	.250	0	0-0	0	10.27	8.25
5 ML YEARS		55	40	4	8	287.2	1225	278	152	127	35	3	4	12	102	2	224	16	0	21	14	.600	1	0-0	0	4.03	3.97

Jimmy Yacabonis

Pitches: R Bats: R Pos: RP-14

Ht: 6'3" Wt: 205 Born: 3/21/1992 Age: 26

Year Team	Lg	G	GS	CG	GF	IP	BFP	H	R	ER	HR	SH	SF	HB	TBB	IBB	SO	WP	Bk	W	L	Pct	Sh	Sv-Op	Hld	ERC	ERA
2013 Abrdn	A-	18	0	0	12	29.2	119	15	5	5	0	3	0	1	14	1	28	1	1	3	1	.750	0	4--	-	1.41	1.52
2014 2 Tms	Low	38	0	0	26	53.2	247	43	30	30	2	1	4	6	43	1	54	15	1	1	5	.167	0	14--	-	4.42	5.03
2015 Frdrck	A+	43	0	0	9	62.2	293	74	41	28	3	3	2	5	33	2	66	12	0	3	3	.500	0	2--	-	5.49	4.02
2016 Frdrck	A+	16	0	0	10	20.1	83	17	9	9	2	1	1	0	6	0	21	1	0	0	2	.000	0	5--	-	2.78	3.98
2016 Bowie	AA	34	0	0	21	44.1	184	34	13	10	2	3	2	4	14	1	46	5	0	2	2	.500	0	6--	-	2.45	2.03
2017 Norfolk	AAA	41	0	0	27	61.1	241	30	9	9	0	2	1	2	28	1	48	5	0	4	0	1.000	0	11--	-	1.36	1.32
2017 Bal	AL	14	0	0	7	20.2	90	18	10	10	2	0	3	0	14	1	8	1	0	0	0	1.000	0	0-0	0	4.44	4.35

Kirby Yates

Pitches: R Bats: L Pos: RP-62

Ht: 5'10" Wt: 210 Born: 3/25/1987 Age: 31

Year Team	Lg	G	GS	CG	GF	IP	BFP	H	R	ER	HR	SH	SF	HB	TBB	IBB	SO	WP	Bk	W	L	Pct	Sh	Sv-Op	Hld	ERC	ERA
2017 Salt Lk*	AAA	6	0	0	1	7.0	33	8	2	2	0	0	0	1	3	0	14	0	0	0	0	-	0	1--	-	4.66	2.57
2014 TB	AL	37	0	0	12	36.0	156	33	16	15	4	0	1	3	15	3	42	2	0	0	2	.000	0	1-2	0	3.94	3.75
2015 TB	AL	20	0	0	10	20.1	92	23	18	18	10	0	1	0	7	0	21	0	0	1	0	1.000	0	0-0	0	7.58	7.97
2016 NYY	AL	41	0	0	11	41.1	184	41	24	24	5	1	1	4	19	1	50	1	0	2	1	.667	0	0-2	2	4.77	5.23
2017 2 Tms		62	0	0	12	56.2	231	44	28	25	12	0	1	2	19	2	88	1	0	4	5	.444	0	1-4	20	3.42	3.97
17 LAA	AL	1	0	0	0	1.0	5	2	2	2	0	0	0	0	0	0	1	0	0	0	0	-	0	0-0	0	25.07	18.00
17 SD	NL	61	0	0	12	55.2	226	42	26	23	10	0	1	2	19	2	87	1	0	4	5	.444	0	1-4	20	3.13	3.72
4 ML YEARS		160	0	0	45	154.1	663	141	86	82	31	1	3	10	60	6	201	3	1	7	8	.467	0	2-8	22	4.43	4.78

Christian Yelich

Bats: L Throws: R Pos: CF-155;PH-1   YELL-itch   Ht: 6'3" Wt: 195 Born: 12/5/1991 Age: 26

Year	Team	Lg	G	AB	H	2B	3B	HR	(Hm	Rd)	TB	R	RBI	RC	TBB	IBB	SO	HBP	SH	SF	SB	CS	GDP	Avg	OBP	Slg	OPS
2013	Mia	NL	62	240	69	12	1	4	(0	4)	95	34	16	35	31	1	66	1	0	1	10	0	4	.288	.370	.396	.766
2014	Mia	NL	144	582	165	30	6	9	(2	7)	234	94	54	87	70	3	137	3	3	2	21	7	9	.284	.362	.402	.764
2015	Mia	NL	126	476	143	30	2	7	(1	6)	198	63	44	64	47	2	101	2	0	0	16	5	13	.300	.366	.416	.782
2016	Mia	NL	155	578	172	38	3	21	(8	13)	279	78	98	89	72	4	138	4	0	5	9	4	20	.298	.376	.483	.859
2017	Mia	NL	156	602	170	36	2	18	(7	11)	264	100	81	99	80	4	137	6	0	6	16	2	13	.282	.369	.439	.807
5 ML YEARS			643	2478	719	146	14	59	(18	41)	1070	369	293	374	300	14	579	16	3	14	72	18	59	.290	.369	.432	.800

Gabriel Ynoa

Pitches: R Bats: R Pos: RP-5; SP-4   ee-NOH-uh   Ht: 6'2" Wt: 205 Born: 5/26/1993 Age: 25

Year	Team	Lg	G	GS	CG	GF	IP	BFP	H	R	ER	HR	SH	SF	HB	TBB	IBB	SO	WP	Bk	W	L	Pct	Sh	Sv-Op	Hld	ERC	ERA
2013	Savann	A	22	22	1	0	135.2	542	123	45	41	9	3	6	1	16	0	106	2	0	15	4	.789	0	0- -	- -	2.33	2.72
2014	Stluci	A+	14	14	0	0	82.0	352	95	40	36	7	4	4	1	13	0	64	0	0	8	2	.800	0	0- -	- -	3.89	3.95
2014	Bnghtn	AA	11	11	2	0	66.1	280	74	32	31	9	1	1	3	12	1	42	2	0	3	2	.600	1	0- -	- -	4.29	4.21
2015	Bnghtn	AA	25	24	2	0	152.1	638	157	70	66	14	6	2	6	31	1	82	3	1	9	9	.500	1	0- -	- -	3.57	3.90
2016	LsVgs	AAA	25	25	0	0	154.1	656	170	77	68	15	8	6	6	40	2	78	2	1	12	5	.706	0	0- -	- -	4.28	3.97
2017	Norfolk	AAA	21	21	0	0	106.1	472	129	69	62	8	2	6	5	24	0	72	11	0	6	9	.400	0	0- -	- -	4.54	5.25
2016	NYM	NL	10	3	0	2	18.1	88	26	13	13	0	0	2	1	7	0	17	0	0	1	0	1.000	0	0-0	0	5.80	6.38
2017	Bal	AL	9	4	0	2	34.2	147	39	17	16	5	1	2	1	8	0	26	0	0	2	3	.400	0	0-0	0	4.60	4.15
2 ML YEARS			19	7	0	4	53.0	235	65	30	29	5	1	4	2	15	0	43	0	0	3	3	.500	0	0-0	0	5.03	4.92

Michael Ynoa

Pitches: R Bats: R Pos: RP-22   ee-NOH-uh   Ht: 6'7" Wt: 210 Born: 9/24/1991 Age: 26

Year	Team	Lg	G	GS	CG	GF	IP	BFP	H	R	ER	HR	SH	SF	HB	TBB	IBB	SO	WP	Bk	W	L	Pct	Sh	Sv-Op	Hld	ERC	ERA
2013	2 Tms	Low	22	21	0	1	75.2	333	68	39	31	5	0	1	9	35	0	68	7	1	3	3	.500	0	1- -	- -	3.95	3.69
2014	Stcktn	A+	25	0	0	6	45.2	201	42	28	28	5	2	3	5	21	2	64	7	0	4	2	.667	0	0- -	- -	4.28	5.52
2015	WinSa	A+	28	0	0	16	38.0	169	37	14	11	2	0	1	7	16	0	40	4	0	0	2	.000	0	6- -	- -	4.41	2.61
2016	Charltt	AAA	18	0	0	6	23.2	108	25	12	12	2	2	1	3	12	2	20	3	0	1	3	.250	0	4- -	- -	5.09	4.56
2017	Charltt	AAA	8	0	0	3	8.1	36	7	5	5	2	0	0	1	6	0	10	1	0	1	0	1.000	0	1- -	- -	6.42	5.40
2016	CWS	AL	23	0	0	7	30.0	135	20	11	10	0	1	2	5	17	2	30	4	0	1	0	1.000	0	0-0	1	2.57	3.00
2017	CWS	AL	22	0	0	10	29.0	141	28	22	19	4	0	0	5	22	0	23	3	0	1	0	1.000	0	0-0	0	6.24	5.90
2 ML YEARS			45	0	0	17	59.0	276	48	33	29	4	1	2	10	39	2	53	7	0	2	0	1.000	0	0-0	1	4.25	4.42

Chris Young

Pitches: R Bats: R Pos: RP-12; SP-2   Ht: 6'10" Wt: 255 Born: 5/25/1979 Age: 39

Year	Team	Lg	G	GS	CG	GF	IP	BFP	H	R	ER	HR	SH	SF	HB	TBB	IBB	SO	WP	Bk	W	L	Pct	Sh	Sv-Op	Hld	ERC	ERA
2004	Tex	AL	7	7	0	0	36.1	158	36	21	19	7	1	0	2	10	0	27	1	0	3	2	.600	0	0-0	0	4.26	4.71
2005	Tex	AL	31	31	0	0	164.2	700	162	84	78	19	2	4	7	45	2	137	3	0	12	7	.632	0	0-0	0	3.71	4.26
2006	SD	NL	31	31	0	0	179.1	735	134	72	69	28	8	3	6	69	4	164	6	1	11	5	.688	0	0-0	0	3.12	3.46
2007	SD	NL	30	30	0	0	173.0	705	118	66	60	10	3	6	7	72	0	167	7	4	9	8	.529	0	0-0	0	2.35	3.12
2008	SD	NL	18	18	1	0	102.1	434	84	46	45	13	4	1	1	48	4	93	3	1	7	6	.538	0	0-0	0	3.50	3.96
2009	SD	NL	14	14	0	0	76.0	336	70	47	44	12	4	5	2	40	3	50	1	0	4	6	.400	0	0-0	0	4.55	5.21
2010	SD	NL	4	4	0	0	20.0	82	10	2	2	1	1	0	0	11	0	15	1	0	2	0	1.000	0	0-0	0	1.72	0.90
2011	NYM	NL	4	4	0	0	24.0	95	12	5	5	3	1	0	1	11	0	22	0	0	1	0	1.000	0	0-0	0	2.04	1.88
2012	NYM	NL	20	20	0	0	115.0	493	119	58	53	16	9	4	2	36	5	80	3	0	4	9	.308	0	0-0	0	4.19	4.15
2014	Sea	AL	30	29	0	0	165.0	688	143	70	67	26	4	9	4	60	3	108	5	1	12	9	.571	0	0-1	0	3.63	3.65
2015	KC	AL	34	18	0	3	123.1	500	91	44	42	16	4	2	0	43	0	83	5	0	11	6	.647	0	0-0	0	2.66	3.06
2016	KC	AL	34	13	0	2	88.2	406	104	63	61	28	4	0	8	43	1	94	3	0	3	9	.250	0	1-1	1	7.16	6.19
2017	KC	AL	14	2	0	5	30.0	148	47	27	25	7	0	0	1	14	2	22	1	0	0	0	—	0	0-0	0	9.10	7.50
Postseason			5	3	0	1	22.1	84	12	5	5	2	1	1	0	8	1	27	1	0	2	0	1.000	0	0-0	0	1.60	2.01
13 ML YEARS			271	221	1	15	1297.2	5480	1130	605	570	186	41	38	33	502	24	1062	39	7	79	67	.541	0	1-2	3	3.66	3.95

Chris Young

Bats: R Throws: R Pos: LF-39;DH-25;PH-20;RF-8;PR-3   Ht: 6'2" Wt: 200 Born: 9/5/1983 Age: 34

Year	Team	Lg	G	AB	H	2B	3B	HR	(Hm	Rd)	TB	R	RBI	RC	TBB	IBB	SO	HBP	SH	SF	SB	CS	GDP	Avg	OBP	Slg	OPS
2006	Ari	NL	30	70	17	4	0	2	(1	1)	27	10	10	11	6	0	12	1	0	1	2	1	0	.243	.308	.386	.693
2007	Ari	NL	148	569	135	29	3	32	(14	18)	266	85	68	68	43	1	141	6	1	5	27	6	5	.237	.295	.467	.763
2008	Ari	NL	160	625	155	42	7	22	(9	13)	277	85	85	84	62	2	165	1	6	5	14	5	10	.248	.315	.443	.758
2009	Ari	NL	134	433	92	28	4	15	(7	8)	173	54	42	47	59	2	133	4	3	2	11	4	3	.212	.311	.400	.711
2010	Ari	NL	156	584	150	33	0	27	(20	7)	264	94	91	86	74	0	145	2	1	3	28	7	10	.257	.341	.452	.793
2011	Ari	NL	156	567	134	38	3	20	(14	6)	238	89	71	84	80	4	139	4	1	7	22	9	3	.236	.331	.420	.751
2012	Ari	NL	101	325	75	24	0	14	(5	9)	141	36	41	46	36	0	79	2	0	0	8	3	4	.231	.311	.434	.745
2013	Oak	AL	107	335	67	18	3	12	(4	8)	127	46	40	32	36	3	93	2	0	2	10	3	7	.200	.280	.379	.659
2014	2 Tms		111	325	72	20	0	11	(8	3)	125	40	38	37	32	2	70	5	1	3	8	3	3	.222	.299	.385	.683
2015	NYY	AL	140	318	80	20	1	14	(6	8)	144	53	42	46	30	2	73	3	3	6	3	1	6	.252	.320	.453	.773
2016	Bos	AL	76	203	56	18	0	9	(2	7)	101	29	24	28	21	0	50	3	0	4	2	0	4	.276	.352	.498	.850
2017	Bos	AL	90	243	57	12	2	7	(4	3)	94	30	25	28	30	0	55	2	0	1	3	2	4	.235	.322	.387	.709
14 NYM		NL	88	254	52	12	0	8	(6	2)	88	31	28	25	25	2	54	4	1	3	7	3	3	.205	.283	.346	.630
14 NYY		AL	23	71	20	8	0	3	(2	1)	37	9	10	12	7	0	16	1	0	0	1	0	0	.282	.354	.521	.876
Postseason			14	46	14	2	0	5	(3	2)	31	9	9	12	11	0	19	1	0	0	3	2	0	.304	.448	.674	1.122
12 ML YEARS			1409	4597	1090	286	23	185	(94	91)	1977	651	577	597	509	16	1155	35	16	31	140	46	59	.237	.316	.430	.746

Eric Young Jr.

Bats: B **Throws:** R **Pos:** LF-22;CF-15;PR-10;PH-5;DH-3;RF-2   **Ht:** 5'10" **Wt:** 195 **Born:** 5/25/1985 **Age:** 33

Year	Team	Lg	G	AB	H	2B	3B	HR	(Hm	Rd)	TB	R	RBI	RC	TBB	IBB	SO	HBP	SH	SF	SB	CS	GDP	Avg	OBP	Slg	OPS
2017	Salt Lk*	AAA	83	341	104	15	5	8	(-	-)	153	67	52	60	33	0	56	6	4	1	20	7	12	.305	.375	.449	.824
2009	Col	NL	30	57	14	1	0	1	(1	0)	18	7	1	2	4	0	12	0	0	0	4	4	1	.246	.295	.316	.611
2010	Col	NL	51	172	42	5	1	0	(0	0)	49	26	8	16	17	0	32	1	0	0	17	6	2	.244	.312	.285	.597
2011	Col	NL	77	198	49	4	3	0	(0	0)	59	34	10	27	26	0	38	3	1	1	27	4	1	.247	.342	.298	.640
2012	Col	NL	98	174	55	7	2	4	(2	2)	78	36	15	29	13	0	31	4	5	0	14	2	1	.316	.377	.448	.825
2013	2 Tms	NL	148	539	134	27	7	2	(1	1)	181	70	32	58	46	1	100	2	10	1	46	11	6	.249	.310	.336	.645
2014	NYM	NL	100	280	64	10	5	1	(0	1)	87	48	17	30	24	1	60	5	5	2	30	6	2	.229	.299	.311	.610
2015	2 Tms	NL	53	85	13	4	2	0	(0	0)	21	16	5	6	6	1	18	1	2	0	6	2	1	.153	.217	.247	.464
2016	NYY	AL	6	1	0	0	0	0	(0	0)	0	2	0	0	0	0	0	0	0	0	1	0	0	.000	.000	.000	.000
2017	LAA	AL	47	110	29	5	0	4	(3	1)	46	24	16	23	5	0	31	7	3	0	12	3	0	.264	.336	.418	.754
13	Col	NL	57	165	40	9	3	1	(0	1)	58	22	6	14	11	0	33	0	4	0	8	4	1	.242	.290	.352	.641
13	NYM	NL	91	374	94	18	4	1	(1	0)	123	48	26	44	35	1	67	2	6	1	38	7	5	.251	.318	.329	.647
15	Atl	NL	35	77	13	4	2	0	(0	0)	21	7	5	6	6	1	17	0	2	0	3	0	1	.169	.229	.273	.502
15	NYM	NL	18	8	0	0	0	0	(0	0)	0	9	0	0	0	0	1	1	0	0	3	2	0	.000	.111	.000	.111
	Postseason		2	1	0	0	0	0	(0	0)	0	0	0	0	0	0	0	0	0	0	0	0	0	.000	.000	.000	.000
	9 ML YEARS		610	1616	400	63	20	12	(7	5)	539	263	104	191	141	3	322	22	26	4	157	38	14	.248	.316	.334	.649

Mark Zagunis

Bats: R **Throws:** R **Pos:** RF-4;PH-3   **Ht:** 6'0" **Wt:** 205 **Born:** 2/5/1993 **Age:** 25

Year	Team	Lg	G	AB	H	2B	3B	HR	(Hm	Rd)	TB	R	RBI	RC	TBB	IBB	SO	HBP	SH	SF	SB	CS	GDP	Avg	OBP	Slg	OPS
2014	3 Tms	Low	57	212	61	16	3	2	(-	-)	89	44	32	43	42	2	42	7	0	1	16	2	7	.288	.420	.420	.840
2015	MrtlBh	A+	115	413	112	24	5	8	(-	-)	170	78	54	76	80	1	86	16	0	3	12	10	7	.271	.406	.412	.818
2016	Tenn	AA	51	179	54	11	3	4	(-	-)	81	30	24	34	30	0	36	2	0	0	1	2	9	.302	.408	.453	.860
2016	Iowa	AAA	50	179	49	12	4	6	(-	-)	87	31	25	34	22	0	42	5	0	5	4	0	5	.274	.360	.486	.846
2017	Iowa	AAA	97	330	88	21	1	13	(-	-)	150	59	55	65	70	0	93	7	0	1	4	3	8	.267	.404	.455	.859
2017	ChC	NL	7	14	0	0	0	0	(0	0)	0	1	0	6	4	0	6	0	0	0	2	0	0	.000	.222	.000	.222

Rob Zastryzny

Pitches: L **Bats:** R **Pos:** RP-4   za-STRIZ-nee   **Ht:** 6'3" **Wt:** 205 **Born:** 3/26/1992 **Age:** 26

Year	Team	Lg	G	GS	CG	GF	IP	BFP	H	R	ER	HR	SH	SF	HB	TBB	IBB	SO	WP	Bk	W	L	Pct	Sh	Sv-Op	Hld	ERC	ERA
2013	2 Tms	Low	11	7	0	0	24.0	101	24	6	6	0	0	2	8	0	22	1	0	1	0	1.000	0	0--	-	3.53	2.25
2014	Dytona	A+	23	23	0	0	110.0	479	121	58	57	10	5	0	7	33	0	110	8	0	4	6	.400	0	0--	-	4.44	4.66
2015	Tenn	AA	14	14	0	0	60.2	282	77	47	42	9	3	3	0	28	0	48	1	0	2	5	.286	0	0--	-	6.27	6.23
2016	Tenn	AA	9	9	0	0	54.2	225	50	29	26	6	0	0	1	20	0	42	3	1	3	2	.600	0	0--	-	3.71	4.28
2016	Iowa	AAA	15	14	0	1	81.0	339	67	42	39	7	10	3	2	31	1	77	6	0	7	3	.700	0	0--	-	3.04	4.33
2017	Iowa	AAA	14	7	0	1	47.0	202	50	32	31	7	1	2	0	14	0	40	2	0	2	3	.400	0	1--	-	4.34	5.94
2016	ChC	NL	8	1	0	1	16.0	66	12	3	2	0	0	2	1	5	0	17	0	0	1	0	1.000	0	0-0	0	2.01	1.13
2017	ChC	NL	4	0	0	0	13.0	62	19	13	12	2	0	0	1	7	0	11	0	0	0	0	-	0	0-0	0	8.66	8.31
	2 ML YEARS		12	1	0	1	29.0	128	31	16	14	2	0	2	2	12	0	28	0	0	1	0	1.000	0	0-0	0	4.61	4.34

Brad Ziegler

Pitches: R **Bats:** R **Pos:** RP-53   ZIGG-lerr   **Ht:** 6'4" **Wt:** 220 **Born:** 10/10/1979 **Age:** 38

Year	Team	Lg	G	GS	CG	GF	IP	BFP	H	R	ER	HR	SH	SF	HB	TBB	IBB	SO	WP	Bk	W	L	Pct	Sh	Sv-Op	Hld	ERC	ERA
2008	Oak	AL	47	0	0	21	59.2	229	47	8	7	2	4	3	1	22	3	30	0	0	3	0	1.000	0	11-13	9	2.60	1.06
2009	Oak	AL	69	0	0	23	73.1	313	82	27	25	2	1	3	1	28	4	54	0	0	2	4	.333	0	7-10	4	4.25	3.07
2010	Oak	AL	64	0	0	12	60.2	257	54	24	22	4	1	1	3	28	9	41	0	1	3	7	.300	0	0-4	18	3.48	3.26
2011	2 Tms		66	0	0	16	58.1	239	53	21	14	0	1	2	1	19	3	44	1	0	3	2	.600	0	1-2	10	2.68	2.16
2012	Ari	NL	77	0	0	15	68.2	263	54	21	19	2	2	2	1	21	2	42	1	0	6	1	.857	0	0-2	17	2.33	2.49
2013	Ari	NL	78	0	0	33	73.0	297	61	20	18	3	2	2	3	22	6	44	0	0	8	1	.889	0	13-15	11	2.51	2.22
2014	Ari	NL	68	0	0	11	67.0	281	60	29	26	5	2	4	3	24	6	54	0	0	5	3	.625	0	1-9	29	3.22	3.49
2015	Ari	NL	66	0	0	46	68.0	263	48	17	14	3	1	0	1	17	3	36	2	0	0	3	.000	0	30-32	4	1.74	1.85
2016	2 Tms		69	0	0	42	68.0	289	67	21	17	2	2	1	3	26	7	58	1	0	4	7	.364	0	22-28	8	3.49	2.25
2017	Mia	NL	53	0	0	21	47.0	211	57	29	25	1	3	0	6	16	6	26	1	0	1	4	.200	0	10-15	7	4.82	4.79
11	Oak	AL	43	0	0	12	37.2	160	38	14	10	0	1	1	1	13	3	29	1	0	3	2	.600	0	1-2	6	3.21	2.39
11	Ari	NL	23	0	0	4	20.2	79	15	7	4	0	0	1	0	6	0	15	0	0	0	0	-	0	0-0	4	1.77	1.74
16	Ari	NL	36	0	0	30	38.1	165	41	13	12	1	1	1	2	15	5	27	0	0	2	3	.400	0	18-20	1	3.98	2.82
16	Bos	AL	33	0	0	12	29.2	124	26	8	5	1	1	0	1	11	2	31	1	0	2	4	.333	0	4-8	8	2.89	1.52
	Postseason		3	0	0	0	1.0	11	4	4	4	0	0	1	0	3	1	1	0	0	0	0	-	0	0-0	0	31.44	36.00
	10 ML YEARS		657	0	0	240	643.2	2642	583	217	187	24	19	18	23	223	49	429	6	1	35	32	.522	0	95-130	127	3.04	2.61

Bradley Zimmer

Bats: L **Throws:** R **Pos:** CF-97;PH-13;PR-3   **Ht:** 6'5" **Wt:** 220 **Born:** 11/27/1992 **Age:** 25

Year	Team	Lg	G	AB	H	2B	3B	HR	(Hm	Rd)	TB	R	RBI	RC	TBB	IBB	SO	HBP	SH	SF	SB	CS	GDP	Avg	OBP	Slg	OPS
2014	2 Tms	Low	48	179	54	12	2	6	(-	-)	88	36	32	36	21	0	33	9	0	1	12	4	2	.302	.400	.492	.892
2015	Lynbrg	A+	78	286	88	17	3	10	(-	-)	141	60	39	60	37	1	77	10	0	2	32	5	4	.308	.403	.493	.896
2015	Akron	AA	49	187	41	9	1	6	(-	-)	70	24	24	25	18	0	54	8	0	1	12	2	4	.219	.303	.374	.687
2016	Akron	AA	93	340	86	20	6	14	(-	-)	160	58	53	63	56	1	115	8	3	0	33	13	8	.253	.371	.471	.842
2016	Clmbs	AAA	37	128	31	5	0	1	(-	-)	39	18	9	15	21	0	56	0	1	0	5	1	1	.242	.349	.305	.654
2017	Clmbs	AAA	33	126	37	11	2	5	(-	-)	67	22	14	25	14	1	43	2	1	1	9	3	0	.294	.371	.532	.902
2017	Cle	AL	101	299	72	15	2	8	(5	3)	115	41	39	37	26	1	99	4	0	3	18	1	5	.241	.307	.385	.692

Ryan Zimmerman

Bats: R Throws: R Pos: 1B-143;PH-4;DH-1

Ht: 6'3" Wt: 225 Born: 9/28/1984 Age: 33

Year Team	Lg	G	AB	H	2B	3B	HR	(Hm Rd)	TB	R	RBI	RC	TBB	IBB	SO	HBP	SH	SF	SB	CS	GDP	Avg	OBP	Slg	OPS
2005 Was	NL	20	58	23	10	0	0	(0 0)	33	6	6	9	3	0	12	0	0		0	0	1	.397	.419	.569	.988
2006 Was	NL	157	614	176	47	3	20	(10 10)	289	84	110	101	61	7	120	2	1	4	11	8	15	.287	.351	.471	.822
2007 Was	NL	**162**	653	174	43	5	24	(11 13)	289	99	91	83	61	3	125	3	0	5	4	1	26	.266	.330	.458	.788
2008 Was	NL	106	428	121	24	1	14	(7 7)	189	51	51	48	31	1	71	3	0	4	1	1	12	.283	.333	.442	.774
2009 Was	NL	157	610	178	37	3	33	(17 16)	320	110	106	96	72	9	119	2	0	9	2	0	**22**	.292	.364	.525	.888
2010 Was	NL	142	525	161	32	0	25	(9 16)	268	85	85	97	69	6	98	4	0	5	4	1	16	.307	.388	.510	.899
2011 Was	NL	101	395	114	21	2	12	(7 5)	175	52	49	58	41	4	73	1	0	3	3	1	14	.289	.355	.443	.798
2012 Was	NL	145	578	163	36	1	25	(16 9)	276	93	95	84	57	8	116	2	0	4	5	2	**20**	.275	.344	.478	.824
2013 Was	NL	147	568	156	26	2	26	(7 19)	264	84	79	83	60	2	133	2	0	3	6	0	16	.280	.344	.465	.809
2014 Was	NL	61	214	60	19	1	5	(1 4)	96	26	38	32	22	0	37	0	0	4	1	0	6	.280	.342	.449	.790
2015 Was	NL	95	346	86	25	1	16	(9 7)	161	43	73	49	33	0	79	1	0	10	1	0	13	.249	.308	.465	.773
2016 Was	NL	115	427	93	18	1	15	(9 6)	158	60	46	36	29	1	104	5	0	6	1	1	12	.218	.272	.370	.642
2017 Was	NL	144	524	159	33	0	36	(19 17)	300	90	108	94	44	1	126	3	0	5	1	0	16	.303	.358	.573	.930
Postseason		14	42	15	3	0	2	(1 1)	24	4	6	8	3	0	9	0	0	1	0	0	0	.357	.391	.571	.963
13 ML YEARS		1552	5940	1664	371	20	251	(122 129)	2828	883	937	870	583	42	1213	28	1	63	42	15	189	.280	.344	.476	.820

Jordan Zimmermann

Pitches: R Bats: R Pos: SP-29

Ht: 6'2" Wt: 225 Born: 5/23/1986 Age: 32

Year Team	Lg	G	GS	CG	GF	IP	BFP	H	R	ER	HR	SH	SF	HB	TBB	IBB	SO	WP	Bk	W	L	Pct	Sh	Sv-Op	Hld	ERC	ERA
2009 Was	NL	16	16	0	0	91.1	391	95	51	47	10	5	3	4	29	0	92	0	0	3	5	.375	0	0-0	0	4.25	4.63
2010 Was	NL	7	7	0	0	31.0	135	31	20	17	8	1	1	2	10	1	27	0	0	1	2	.333	0	0-0	0	5.02	4.94
2011 Was	NL	26	26	1	0	161.1	662	154	62	57	12	8	2	7	31	2	124	3	1	8	11	.421	0	0-0	0	3.02	3.18
2012 Was	NL	32	32	0	0	195.2	805	186	69	64	18	8	4	6	43	2	153	3	0	12	8	.600	0	0-0	0	3.22	2.94
2013 Was	NL	32	32	4	0	213.1	865	192	81	77	19	9	4	7	40	0	161	3	0	**19**	9	.679	2	0-0	0	2.79	3.25
2014 Was	NL	32	32	3	0	199.2	800	185	67	59	13	5	3	6	29	0	182	4	0	14	5	.737	2	0-0	0	2.64	2.66
2015 Was	NL	33	**33**	0	0	201.2	831	204	89	82	24	8	2	8	39	3	164	2	1	13	10	.565	0	0-0	0	3.63	3.66
2016 Det	AL	19	18	0	1	105.1	450	118	63	57	14	1	5	2	26	0	66	3	0	9	7	.563	0	0-0	0	4.48	4.87
2017 Det	AL	29	29	0	0	160.0	713	204	111	**108**	29	3	8	7	44	2	103	3	0	8	13	.381	0	0-0	0	6.00	6.08
Postseason		3	2	0	0	12.2	47	10	6	6	1	1	0	0	1	0	11	0	0	0	1	.000	0	0-0	0	1.80	4.26
9 ML YEARS		226	225	8	1	1359.1	5652	1369	613	568	147	48	32	51	291	10	1072	21	2	87	70	.554	4	0-0	0	3.60	3.76

Ben Zobrist

Bats: B Throws: R Pos: 2B-81;LF-36;RF-32;PH-20;1B-5;SS-5   ZOH-brist

Ht: 6'3" Wt: 210 Born: 5/26/1981 Age: 37

Year Team	Lg	G	AB	H	2B	3B	HR	(Hm Rd)	TB	R	RBI	RC	TBB	IBB	SO	HBP	SH	SF	SB	CS	GDP	Avg	OBP	Slg	OPS
2006 TB	AL	52	183	41	6	2	2	(2 0)	57	10	18	13	10	1	26	0	2	3	2	3	2	.224	.260	.311	.572
2007 TB	AL	31	97	15	2	0	1	(0 1)	20	8	9	3	3	0	21	1	2	2	2	0	1	.155	.184	.206	.391
2008 TB	AL	62	198	50	10	2	12	(4 8)	100	32	30	31	25	1	37	2	0	2	3	0	4	.253	.339	.505	.844
2009 TB	AL	152	501	149	28	7	27	(18 9)	272	91	91	109	91	4	104	2	1	4	17	6	7	.297	.405	.543	.948
2010 TB	AL	151	541	129	28	2	10	(3 7)	191	77	75	84	92	1	107	3	7	**12**	24	3	10	.238	.346	.353	.699
2011 TB	AL	156	588	158	46	6	20	(9 11)	276	99	91	100	77	1	128	2	2	5	19	6	9	.269	.353	.469	.822
2012 TB	AL	157	560	151	39	7	20	(8 12)	264	88	74	102	97	7	103	3	2	6	14	9	13	.270	.377	.471	.848
2013 TB	AL	157	612	168	36	3	12	(7 5)	246	77	71	85	72	4	91	7	1	6	11	3	18	.275	.354	.402	.756
2014 TB	AL	146	570	155	34	3	10	(4 6)	225	83	52	75	75	4	84	1	2	6	10	5	8	.272	.354	.395	.749
2015 2 Tms	AL	126	467	129	36	3	13	(5 8)	210	76	56	72	62	3	56	1	0	5	3	4	8	.276	.359	.450	.809
2016 ChC	NL	147	523	142	31	3	18	(5 13)	233	94	76	81	96	6	82	4	4	4	6	4	17	.272	.386	.446	.831
2017 ChC	NL	128	435	101	20	3	12	(5 7)	163	58	50	50	54	2	71	2	2	3	2	2	13	.232	.318	.375	.693
15 Oak	AL	67	235	63	20	2	6	(2 4)	105	39	33	38	33	2	26	0	0	3	1	1	5	.268	.354	.447	.801
15 KC	AL	59	232	66	16	1	7	(3 4)	105	37	23	34	29	1	30	1	0	2	2	3	3	.284	.364	.453	.816
Postseason		54	196	50	15	1	4	(2 2)	79	31	14	20	20	2	31	1	1	2	1	0	3	.255	.324	.403	.727
12 ML YEARS		1465	5275	1388	316	41	157	(70 87)	2257	793	693	802	754	34	910	28	25	58	113	45	110	.263	.355	.428	.783

Mike Zunino

Bats: R Throws: R Pos: C-120;PH-4;DH-2;PR-1   zoo-NEE-no

Ht: 6'2" Wt: 220 Born: 3/25/1991 Age: 27

Year Team	Lg	G	AB	H	2B	3B	HR	(Hm Rd)	TB	R	RBI	RC	TBB	IBB	SO	HBP	SH	SF	SB	CS	GDP	Avg	OBP	Slg	OPS
2017 Tacom*	AAA	12	41	12	2	0	5	(- -)	29	7	11	9	4	0	5	0	0	1	0	0	1	.293	.356	.707	1.063
2013 Sea	AL	52	173	37	5	0	5	(3 2)	57	22	14	13	16	0	49	3	0	1	1	0	5	.214	.290	.329	.620
2014 Sea	AL	131	438	87	20	2	22	(10 12)	177	51	60	39	17	1	158	**17**	0	4	0	3	13	.199	.254	.404	.658
2015 Sea	AL	112	350	61	11	0	11	(6 5)	105	28	28	14	21	0	132	6	5	2	0	1	6	.174	.230	.300	.530
2016 Sea	AL	55	164	34	7	0	12	(9 3)	77	16	31	28	21	0	65	6	0	1	0	0	0	.207	.318	.470	.787
2017 Sea	AL	124	387	97	25	0	25	(14 11)	197	52	64	55	39	0	160	8	0	1	1	0	2	.251	.331	.509	.840
5 ML YEARS		474	1512	316	68	2	75	(42 33)	613	169	197	149	114	1	564	39	8	9	2	4	32	.209	.280	.405	.686

Tony Zych

Pitches: R Bats: R Pos: RP-45   zick

Ht: 6'3" Wt: 190 Born: 8/7/1990 Age: 27

Year Team	Lg	G	GS	CG	GF	IP	BFP	H	R	ER	HR	SH	SF	HB	TBB	IBB	SO	WP	Bk	W	L	Pct	Sh	Sv-Op	Hld	ERC	ERA
2015 Sea	AL	13	0	0	4	18.1	76	17	6	5	1	0	0	0	3	0	24	1	0	0	0	-	0	0-0	1	2.88	2.45
2016 Sea	AL	12	0	0	3	13.2	60	10	6	5	0	0	1	1	10	2	21	0	0	1	0	1.000	0	0-0	1	3.18	3.29
2017 Sea	AL	45	0	0	7	40.2	173	30	12	12	2	1	2	5	21	3	35	1	1	6	3	.667	0	1-2	12	3.11	2.66
3 ML YEARS		70	1	0	14	72.2	309	57	24	22	3	1	3	8	34	5	80	2	1	7	3	.700	0	1-2	14	3.08	2.72

Fielding Statistics

Alex Vigderman

Stop me if you've heard this before: Andrelton Simmons is the top defensive player in baseball. After an injury-shortened 2016 campaign, the Angels shortstop heads the Defensive Runs Saved leaderboard for the third time in his career, and leads his position for the fourth time in five years. He barely edged out last year's leader, Red Sox right fielder Mookie Betts, 32 to 31.

Simmons' 2017 campaign underscores his excellence across all dimensions of shortstop play. He trailed only Betts in Range and Positioning Runs Saved, but he was also the only player to save at least three runs on both double play execution and making good plays while avoiding misplays. On the other side of the coin is Giants center fielder Denard Span. He not only cost his team the most runs of any player this season (27), but he was the only player to cost his team four runs each with his arm and with misplays.

The following tables display defensive information for both regulars and backups at all of the eight non-pitcher positions. They include traditional statistics such as putouts, assists, errors, and fielding percentage, as well as Bases Saved and Runs Saved information. The section on the far right of each table gives the number of Runs Saved due to different components of overall Defensive Runs Saved, with the last column showing the total runs that the player saved or cost his team at that position.

The components of Defensive Runs Saved differ for different positions, with Good Fielding Plays / Defensive Misplays + Errors (GFP/DME) Runs Saved applying across the board. All non-catchers have Range and Positioning Runs Saved, while catchers have Stolen Base Runs Saved. In the third Runs Saved column, all infielders have a GDP component, with Bunt Runs Saved included for first and third basemen. In that space, outfielders have Outfield Arm Runs Saved (Throws), while catchers have Strike Zone Runs Saved (SZ). Catchers also have an "Other" column which includes the combination of Bunt Runs Saved and Adjusted Earned Runs Saved.

First Basemen - Regulars

Player	Tm	G	GS	Inn	PO	A	E	DP	Pct.	Bases Saved	R/P	Runs Saved GFP/DME	Bunts/GDP	Total
Belt, Brandon	SF	98	89	826	771	64	2	74	.998	+16	11	0	0	11
Votto, Joey	Cin	162	162	1392	1227	165	4	109	.997	+14	10	2	-1	11
Moreland, Mitch	Bos	138	126	1170	938	67	5	95	.995	+11	8	1	1	10
Goldschmidt, Paul	Ari	151	150	1292	1254	103	4	116	.997	+7	5	3	2	10
Santana, Carlos	Cle	140	139	1226	1055	95	5	129	.996	+6	4	3	3	10
Rizzo, Anthony	ChC	157	155	1341	1222	150	3	112	.998	+11	8	1	0	9
Mauer, Joe	Min	125	118	1041	947	63	2	90	.998	+6	5	3	-1	7
Bell, Josh	Pit	147	139	1186	1139	86	10	116	.992	+8	6	0	0	6
Cron, C.J.	LAA	98	92	816	745	61	4	63	.995	+3	3	0	0	3
Valencia, Danny	Sea	118	111	984	897	64	11	98	.989	0	0	0	2	2
Morrison, Logan	TB	126	119	1078	1015	59	8	91	.993	+8	6	-1	-4	1
Carpenter, Matt	StL	120	110	949	895	74	7	103	.993	+3	2	-1	0	1
Smoak, Justin	Tor	151	145	1301	1244	66	2	127	.998	+3	2	1	-2	1
Napoli, Mike	Tex	95	90	782	748	44	7	92	.991	+2	1	1	-1	1
Myers, Wil	SD	154	153	1333	1295	72	8	147	.994	-1	-1	1	1	1
Abreu, Jose	CWS	139	138	1197	1135	78	8	130	.993	-1	0	-1	1	0
Duda, Lucas	TOT	93	90	792	693	46	4	52	.995	-4	-3	1	1	-1
Bour, Justin	Mia	102	100	862	757	51	1	84	.999	-6	-4	1	1	-2
Freeman, Freddie	Atl	105	100	877	829	56	4	72	.996	-10	-7	2	3	-2
Reynolds, Mark	Col	138	132	1173	1218	62	6	131	.995	-13	-9	3	2	-4
Davis, Chris	Bal	125	124	1093	1015	80	7	122	.994	-2	-2	-3	0	-5
Gurriel, Yulieski	Hou	131	130	1109	991	90	8	116	.993	-3	-3	-2	0	-5
Thames, Eric	Mil	108	103	857	805	71	6	79	.993	-5	-4	-2	1	-5
Hosmer, Eric	KC	157	155	1338	1235	75	4	124	.997	-9	-7	1	-1	-7
Cabrera, Miguel	Det	115	115	938	761	63	1	90	.999	-5	-4	-2	-2	-8
Zimmerman, Ryan	Was	143	131	1162	1005	49	12	100	.989	-8	-6	0	-2	-8
Alonso, Yonder	TOT	135	121	1070	964	63	10	96	.990	-10	-7	-2	0	-9
Joseph, Tommy	Phi	130	125	1048	948	58	8	99	.992	-16	-11	0	1	-10

Second Basemen - Regulars

Player	Tm	G	GS	Inn	PO	A	E	DP	Pct.	Range	Bases Saved	R/P	Runs Saved GFP/DME	GDP	Total
LeMahieu, DJ	Col	153	151	1302	251	470	8	106	.989	4.98	+7	5	2	1	8
Kinsler, Ian	Det	135	134	1137	263	327	10	95	.983	4.67	+16	12	-3	-3	6
Merrifield, Whit	KC	132	131	1143	232	341	11	93	.981	4.51	+6	4	1	0	5
Drury, Brandon	Ari	114	109	947	154	276	10	61	.977	4.09	+6	4	2	-1	5
Odor, Rougned	Tex	158	157	1366	321	429	19	129	.975	4.94	+6	4	-1	0	3
Altuve, Jose	Hou	149	148	1283	201	351	10	86	.982	3.87	+3	3	-1	1	3
Gordon, Dee	Mia	153	146	1293	266	390	12	96	.982	4.56	+1	1	2	0	3
Schoop, Jonathan	Bal	159	158	1385	329	446	15	132	.981	5.04	0	0	0	2	2
Villar, Jonathan	Mil	98	84	769	155	237	15	56	.963	4.59	+3	2	-2	1	1
Cano, Robinson	Sea	150	148	1287	254	339	10	97	.983	4.15	-5	-4	-1	5	0
Wong, Kolten	StL	106	99	880	191	276	10	78	.979	4.78	-1	-1	2	-2	-1
Lowrie, Jed	Oak	136	132	1161	199	344	5	98	.991	4.21	-1	-1	0	-1	-2
Pedroia, Dustin	Bos	98	97	835	156	208	2	59	.995	3.92	-2	-2	1	-1	-2
Hernandez, Cesar	Phi	127	124	1096	224	337	11	79	.981	4.61	-2	-2	1	-1	-2
Dozier, Brian	Min	152	151	1311	264	405	5	109	.993	4.59	-4	-4	1	-1	-4
Miller, Brad	TB	98	87	790	133	213	11	58	.969	3.94	-5	-4	-1	1	-4
Walker, Neil	TOT	95	90	770	141	200	6	51	.983	3.99	-8	-6	1	0	-5
Castro, Starlin	NYY	109	108	936	175	226	11	46	.973	3.86	-4	-3	-1	-2	-6
Phillips, Brandon	TOT	112	111	946	163	278	7	66	.984	4.20	-8	-6	-1	0	-7
Gennett, Scooter	Cin	99	87	769	156	203	7	40	.981	4.20	-7	-5	-1	-2	-8
Panik, Joe	SF	137	131	1191	249	332	9	86	.985	4.39	-17	-13	3	-1	-11
Murphy, Daniel	Was	139	136	1196	218	353	9	86	.984	4.30	-15	-12	-2	-1	-15

Third Basemen - Regulars

Player	Tm	G	GS	Inn	PO	A	E	DP	Pct.	Range	Bases Saved	R/P	Runs Saved GFP/DME	Bunts/GDP	Total
Arenado, Nolan	Col	157	156	1343	103	311	9	39	.979	2.77	+22	17	3	0	20
Gyorko, Jedd	StL	109	102	900	53	212	9	27	.967	2.65	+21	16	-1	1	16
Longoria, Evan	TB	142	142	1240	96	267	12	33	.968	2.63	+12	9	-1	3	11
Frazier, Todd	TOT	133	128	1108	71	240	13	39	.960	2.53	+12	9	-1	2	10
Freese, David	Pit	116	114	978	66	222	12	29	.960	2.65	+11	8	-1	1	8
Rendon, Anthony	Was	145	143	1268	83	244	7	28	.979	2.32	+8	6	0	1	7
Machado, Manny	Bal	156	156	1370	114	297	14	37	.967	2.70	+8	6	1	-1	6
Turner, Justin	LAD	121	119	1000	69	184	8	16	.969	2.28	+7	5	1	0	6

Player	Tm	G	GS	Inn	PO	A	E	DP	Pct.	Range	Bases Saved	Runs Saved R/P	GFP/ DME	Bunts/ GDP	Total
Suarez, Eugenio	Cin	153	149	1302	103	267	9	30	.976	2.56	+5	4	1	0	5
Donaldson, Josh	Tor	105	103	921	64	195	14	13	.949	2.53	+5	3	1	-1	3
Shaw, Travis	Mil	143	142	1221	90	255	9	32	.975	2.54	+4	3	0	0	3
Bryant, Kris	ChC	144	139	1213	72	260	18	23	.949	2.46	+1	1	0	0	1
Seager, Kyle	Sea	154	153	1353	130	311	14	46	.969	2.93	-8	-6	1	3	-2
Bregman, Alex	Hou	132	127	1093	86	241	10	28	.970	2.69	-5	-4	1	0	-3
Dietrich, Derek	Mia	103	93	817	55	144	9	19	.957	2.19	-8	-6	0	2	-4
Franco, Maikel	Phi	144	143	1251	103	215	15	23	.955	2.29	-9	-7	1	2	-4
Headley, Chase	NYY	86	85	751	56	175	13	17	.947	2.77	-10	-7	1	-1	-7
Moustakas, Mike	KC	127	127	1093	74	226	12	17	.962	2.47	-11	-8	-1	1	-8
Escobar, Yunel	LAA	87	87	755	54	126	12	12	.938	2.14	-9	-7	-1	-1	-9
Lamb, Jake	Ari	144	143	1264	84	241	14	20	.959	2.31	-14	-10	-2	-1	-13
Spangenberg, Cory	SD	96	86	766	47	173	13	20	.944	2.58	-13	-10	-2	-2	-14
Castellanos, Nicholas	Det	129	128	1098	77	202	19	21	.936	2.29	-14	-11	-1	-2	-14

Shortstops - Regulars

Player	Tm	G	GS	Inn	PO	A	E	DP	Pct.	Range	Bases Saved	Runs Saved R/P	GFP/ DME	GDP	Total
Simmons, Andrelton	LAA	158	158	1370	235	436	14	99	.980	4.41	+35	26	3	3	32
Russell, Addison	ChC	101	91	808	113	258	12	49	.969	4.13	+22	16	-1	0	15
Story, Trevor	Col	142	133	1185	191	408	11	101	.982	4.55	+8	6	3	2	11
Seager, Corey	LAD	138	134	1162	185	324	11	77	.979	3.94	+14	11	-3	2	10
Crawford, Brandon	SF	138	135	1201	221	374	11	85	.982	4.46	+10	8	1	0	9
Arcia, Orlando	Mil	152	137	1240	253	415	20	103	.971	4.85	+5	4	-2	4	6
Hechavarria, Adeiny	TOT	96	91	813	119	239	4	46	.989	3.96	+8	6	-1	0	5
Lindor, Francisco	Cle	158	158	1377	210	391	10	111	.984	3.93	+2	2	0	3	5
Iglesias, Jose	Det	130	128	1116	199	332	7	83	.987	4.28	+7	5	1	-2	4
Correa, Carlos	Hou	108	108	946	127	282	9	62	.978	3.89	-2	-1	2	3	4
Andrus, Elvis	Tex	157	157	1365	245	493	17	107	.977	4.86	+5	3	0	0	3
Cozart, Zack	Cin	112	112	968	146	288	11	65	.975	4.04	+1	1	0	1	2
Gregorius, Didi	NYY	135	132	1175	144	360	9	47	.982	3.86	+6	4	0	-3	1
Beckham, Tim	TOT	119	118	1047	140	317	18	66	.962	3.93	+4	2	0	-3	-1
Polanco, Jorge	Min	130	127	1120	154	335	18	70	.964	3.93	0	0	1	-2	-1
Mercer, Jordy	Pit	144	143	1242	176	359	10	88	.982	3.88	-6	-4	1	2	-1
Turner, Trea	Was	95	95	847	134	234	8	57	.979	3.91	-4	-3	1	-1	-3
Segura, Jean	Sea	124	124	1084	136	298	17	61	.962	3.60	-6	-4	-1	2	-3
Aybar, Erick	SD	99	93	793	117	273	9	63	.977	4.43	-5	-4	-1	1	-4
Escobar, Alcides	KC	162	162	1404	202	468	15	97	.978	4.29	-5	-4	1	-1	-4
Galvis, Freddy	Phi	155	155	1359	226	404	7	94	.989	4.17	-6	-5	0	0	-5
Swanson, Dansby	Atl	142	135	1202	196	358	20	84	.965	4.15	-10	-8	-1	2	-7
Anderson, Tim	CWS	145	145	1264	197	363	28	85	.952	3.99	-7	-5	-3	0	-8
Bogaerts, Xander	Bos	146	142	1310	199	336	17	75	.969	3.67	-11	-9	0	-2	-11

Left Fielders - Regulars

Player	Tm	G	GS	Inn	PO	A	E	DP	Pct.	Range	Bases Saved	Runs Saved R/P	GFP/ DME	Throws	Total
Gardner, Brett	NYY	122	116	1024	205	10	0	1	1.000	1.89	+20	11	3	3	17
Ozuna, Marcell	Mia	152	151	1335	305	10	5	0	.984	2.12	+20	8	1	2	11
Gordon, Alex	KC	140	135	1179	259	8	2	0	.993	2.04	+11	5	3	1	9
Benintendi, Andrew	Bos	123	116	1078	189	11	5	1	.976	1.67	+1	1	4	4	9
Upton, Justin	TOT	151	151	1288	318	9	8	0	.976	2.29	+21	11	0	-3	8
Duvall, Adam	Cin	151	147	1277	267	15	6	1	.979	1.99	-4	-1	2	7	8
Dickerson, Corey	TB	93	87	753	182	4	1	2	.995	2.22	+1	1	-1	-1	-1
Braun, Ryan	Mil	95	95	798	146	7	2	0	.987	1.72	+2	0	-1	-4	-5
Rosario, Eddie	Min	138	126	1108	225	5	4	1	.983	1.87	-11	-6	-2	2	-6
Schwarber, Kyle	ChC	110	101	821	141	7	5	1	.967	1.62	-12	-6	-2	-1	-9
Cabrera, Melky	TOT	104	103	878	172	9	2	0	.989	1.86	-27	-13	2	1	-10
Davis, Khris	Oak	116	115	993	212	2	1	1	.995	1.94	+1	0	-3	-10	-13
Kemp, Matt	Atl	103	102	852	148	3	1	2	.993	1.60	-24	-13	-1	-3	-17

Center Fielders - Regulars

Player	Tm	G	GS	Inn	PO	A	E	DP	Pct.	Range	Bases Saved	Runs Saved R/P	GFP/ DME	Throws	Total
Buxton, Byron	Min	137	131	1143	389	6	5	1	.988	3.11	+45	24	0	0	24
Kiermaier, Kevin	TB	97	95	830	242	5	6	1	.976	2.68	+39	19	2	1	22
Pillar, Kevin	Tor	153	148	1343	316	8	1	0	.997	2.17	+20	10	2	3	15

Player	Tm	G	GS	Inn	PO	A	E	DP	Pct.	Range	Bases Saved	R/P	GFP/DME	Throws	Total
Dyson, Jarrod	Sea	96	87	772	221	10	2	5	.991	2.69	+9	5	1	4	10
Bradley Jr., Jackie	Bos	132	131	1204	300	6	4	1	.987	2.29	+5	3	7	0	10
Hamilton, Billy	Cin	137	135	1175	301	13	3	4	.991	2.40	-5	0	3	6	9
Margot, Manuel	SD	123	121	1050	273	6	3	0	.989	2.39	+14	8	-2	2	8
Pollock, A.J.	Ari	109	99	873	213	6	1	2	.995	2.26	+16	7	2	-1	8
Taylor, Michael A.	Was	111	106	940	258	8	4	1	.985	2.55	-1	1	2	5	8
Cain, Lorenzo	KC	151	151	1275	430	6	7	3	.984	3.08	+23	11	0	-6	5
Inciarte, Ender	Atl	156	154	1360	410	7	3	0	.993	2.76	+10	7	-2	0	5
Herrera, Odubel	Phi	133	128	1144	323	6	2	3	.994	2.59	+1	3	-1	2	4
Engel, Adam	CWS	95	91	799	253	5	2	2	.992	2.91	-1	1	0	-2	-1
Ellsbury, Jacoby	NYY	97	90	807	193	1	3	0	.985	2.16	+12	5	-2	-6	-3
Gomez, Carlos	Tex	102	100	862	229	5	4	1	.983	2.44	-6	-4	0	0	-4
Blackmon, Charlie	Col	158	158	1366	339	4	4	3	.988	2.26	+10	4	-2	-7	-5
Yelich, Christian	Mia	155	155	1369	370	1	1	0	.997	2.44	+10	2	-2	-6	-6
Trout, Mike	LAA	108	108	948	253	5	1	0	.996	2.45	-15	-9	2	1	-6
Broxton, Keon	Mil	139	113	1029	231	5	7	0	.971	2.06	-13	-6	0	-1	-7
Jones, Adam	Bal	147	147	1267	331	5	5	1	.985	2.39	-18	-11	3	-4	-12
McCutchen, Andrew	Pit	139	139	1188	270	8	4	2	.986	2.11	-32	-15	0	-1	-16
Fowler, Dexter	StL	109	108	933	222	5	1	1	.996	2.19	-37	-18	0	0	-18
Span, Denard	SF	123	116	1039	276	1	2	0	.993	2.40	-40	-19	-4	-4	-27

Right Fielders - Regulars

Player	Tm	G	GS	Inn	PO	A	E	DP	Pct.	Range	Bases Saved	R/P	GFP/DME	Throws	Total
Betts, Mookie	Bos	153	153	1389	366	8	5	1	.987	2.42	+46	27	4	0	31
Heyward, Jason	ChC	120	104	919	207	5	2	5	.991	2.08	+30	14	2	2	18
Puig, Yasiel	LAD	145	135	1202	259	4	1	0	.996	1.97	+27	13	2	3	18
Stanton, Giancarlo	Mia	149	149	1312	320	9	4	1	.988	2.26	+15	7	2	1	10
Judge, Aaron	NYY	141	141	1239	265	5	5	2	.982	1.96	+12	6	1	2	9
Piscotty, Stephen	StL	99	92	817	162	5	2	0	.988	1.84	+17	8	0	0	8
Haniger, Mitch	Sea	94	91	789	203	5	5	1	.977	2.37	+6	3	1	4	8
Souza Jr., Steven	TB	138	136	1197	240	5	5	1	.980	1.84	+5	5	0	2	7
Bruce, Jay	TOT	133	131	1140	251	5	4	0	.985	2.02	+12	5	-1	2	6
Reddick, Josh	Hou	102	95	770	141	5	3	0	.980	1.71	+6	3	0	2	5
Harper, Bryce	Was	110	109	938	173	8	2	2	.989	1.74	-3	0	1	3	4
Kepler, Max	Min	138	120	1086	264	7	2	3	.993	2.25	+5	3	0	0	3
Calhoun, Kole	LAA	154	153	1338	312	10	4	1	.988	2.17	-2	-2	0	4	2
Renfroe, Hunter	SD	120	117	1015	204	9	9	1	.959	1.89	+4	1	1	-1	1
Garcia, Avisail	CWS	132	131	1120	263	13	9	3	.968	2.22	-3	-1	0	2	1
Schebler, Scott	Cin	120	115	987	188	7	5	2	.975	1.78	-10	-4	1	3	0
Pence, Hunter	SF	125	120	1047	256	5	1	0	.996	2.24	-2	0	-1	-2	-3
Gonzalez, Carlos	Col	125	123	1064	201	3	3	1	.986	1.73	-2	-2	0	-1	-3
Mazara, Nomar	Tex	92	86	758	155	6	3	0	.982	1.91	-12	-6	1	2	-3
Markakis, Nick	Atl	156	153	1354	286	6	1	1	.997	1.94	-14	-6	0	2	-4
Martinez, J.D.	TOT	113	112	946	197	3	4	2	.980	1.90	+2	2	-3	-4	-5
Santana, Domingo	Mil	144	138	1211	224	4	5	1	.979	1.69	-2	-3	-3	1	-5
Joyce, Matt	Oak	115	103	907	205	4	7	2	.968	2.07	-3	-1	-1	-6	-8
Bautista, Jose	Tor	143	140	1243	274	10	5	2	.983	2.06	-20	-10	-1	3	-8

Catchers - Regulars

Player	Tm	G	GS	Inn	PO	A	E	DP	PB	Pct.	SB Att	CS	Pit CS	CS Pct	Cat ERA	Stk Sav	GFP/DME	SB	SZ	Other	Total
Maldonado, Martin	LAA	137	131	1146	1046	65	2	2	8	.998	68	22	7	.32	4.17	97	3	3	12	4	22
Hedges, Austin	SD	115	109	933	921	56	10	9	3	.990	60	15	11	.25	4.59	112	4	1	13	2	20
Grandal, Yasmani	LAD	117	113	999	1089	54	6	4	16	.995	59	15	6	.25	3.22	99	0	4	12	1	17
Leon, Sandy	Bos	84	77	699	767	42	6	2	7	.993	47	16	2	.34	3.44	69	0	3	8	4	15
Pina, Manny	Mil	102	83	760	721	52	6	7	4	.992	57	19	2	.33	3.80	12	2	6	1	5	14
Vazquez, Christian	Bos	95	85	771	794	47	8	2	11	.991	48	19	2	.40	4.05	123	-1	3	15	-5	12
Barnhart, Tucker	Cin	110	105	926	863	89	1	9	4	.999	69	28	4	.41	4.74	-80	3	7	-10	11	11
Flowers, Tyler	Atl	85	85	745	643	46	5	4	9	.993	67	12	4	.18	4.88	166	-3	-3	20	-3	11
Castro, Jason	Min	108	104	900	707	34	3	5	5	.996	55	13	2	.24	4.18	22	-1	0	3	8	10
Joseph, Caleb	Bal	79	69	622	569	27	3	0	2	.995	54	9	1	.17	4.23	21	4	-4	2	8	10
Molina, Yadier	StL	133	133	1126	1082	55	7	13	6	.994	66	23	1	.35	4.02	33	1	3	4	-1	7
Suzuki, Kurt	Atl	77	71	641	553	42	3	2	10	.995	54	12	1	.22	4.49	-3	2	1	0	1	4
Zunino, Mike	Sea	120	116	994	894	56	7	5	10	.993	68	14	3	.21	4.35	23	-4	1	3	4	4
Martin, Russell	Tor	83	78	684	646	41	3	3	3	.996	60	12	0	.20	4.48	25	1	1	3	-2	3
Chirinos, Robinson	Tex	85	80	691	559	24	6	2	4	.990	54	8	7	.15	4.62	-19	4	-1	-2	1	2
Posey, Buster	SF	99	96	826	724	52	4	2	1	.995	51	15	7	.29	4.53	23	-1	2	3	-2	2

Player	Tm	G	GS	Inn	PO	A	E	DP	PB	Pct.	SB Att	CS	Pit CS	CS Pct	Cat ERA	Stk Sav	Runs Saved GFP/DME	SB	SZ	Other	Total
Sanchez, Gary	NYY	104	99	881	935	60	13	4	16	.987	56	19	4	.34	3.45	7	-5	3	1	2	1
Iannetta, Chris	Ari	78	70	633	617	36	6	1	5	.991	31	6	2	.19	4.03	29	0	0	3	-2	1
Perez, Salvador	KC	115	113	942	784	46	5	3	3	.994	69	15	5	.22	4.29	-50	3	-1	-6	4	0
d'Arnaud, Travis	NYM	93	88	771	759	44	4	10	2	.995	64	9	2	.14	4.80	-9	2	-4	-1	2	-1
Contreras, Willson	ChC	108	91	821	782	86	13	7	7	.985	81	20	3	.25	3.91	-68	-1	6	-8	2	-1
Gomes, Yan	Cle	103	96	856	938	60	9	5	4	.991	55	22	2	.40	3.36	-17	2	3	-2	-4	-1
Wieters, Matt	Was	118	113	1004	1023	43	8	5	5	.993	75	18	1	.24	3.62	-37	-2	0	-4	3	-3
Avila, Alex	TOT	78	70	614	533	33	3	6	5	.995	50	12	5	.24	4.60	-57	3	-1	-7	1	-4
Hundley, Nick	SF	82	65	608	510	30	7	3	5	.987	49	13	2	.27	4.50	-36	-1	-1	-4	1	-5
Realmuto, J.T.	Mia	126	125	1096	929	87	6	11	9	.994	74	21	4	.28	4.96	-29	1	3	-3	-6	-5
Smith, Kevan	CWS	79	70	623	572	27	2	2	5	.997	63	7	1	.11	4.84	5	-1	-5	1	-1	-6
McCann, James	Det	103	97	836	745	34	2	7	10	.997	75	18	6	.24	5.70	-19	0	0	-2	-4	-6
Narvaez, Omar	CWS	83	75	648	513	36	6	2	6	.989	65	13	3	.20	4.97	-33	-2	0	-4	0	-6
Cervelli, Francisco	Pit	78	75	645	500	47	5	6	7	.991	53	9	2	.17	4.28	-23	-1	-2	-3	0	-6
McCann, Brian	Hou	95	94	827	905	48	5	4	6	.995	61	7	1	.11	4.36	32	-2	-4	4	-6	-8
Castillo, Welington	Bal	88	86	753	647	42	4	9	5	.994	45	20	4	.44	5.62	-46	2	5	-6	-10	-9
Rupp, Cameron	Phi	88	83	749	688	50	8	4	11	.989	59	14	4	.24	4.44	-88	0	0	-10	0	-10
Lucroy, Jonathan	TOT	110	108	948	758	63	4	5	6	.995	71	16	4	.23	4.46	-91	-3	2	-11	-3	-15

All Other Fielders

Player	Tm	Pos	G	GS	Inn	PO	A	E	DP	Pct.	Rng	BSv	RS
Adames, C	Col	1B	1	0	1	2	0	0	0	1.000	-	0	0
	Col	2B	1	0	1	0	0	0	0	-	.00	-1	-1
	Col	SS	1	1	7	1	1	0	0	1.000	2.57	+1	0
Adams, L	Atl	LF	27	5	85	27	0	1	0	.964	2.86	-1	-1
	Atl	CF	11	6	63	12	1	1	0	.929	1.87	-3	-1
	Atl	RF	7	2	24	9	0	0	0	1.000	3.33	+2	0
Adams, M	TOT	1B	62	58	515	499	32	5	43	.991	-	+3	1
	TOT	LF	19	18	129	25	0	0	0	.926	1.74	-9	-5
Adduci, J	Det	RF	26	22	194	50	2	0	0	1.000	2.41	0	3
Adrianza, E	Min	1B	4	1	12	13	1	0	1	1.000	-	0	0
	Min	2B	9	3	37	9	6	1	0	.938	3.65	+1	0
	Min	3B	9	6	56	4	21	0	1	1.000	3.99	+2	1
	Min	SS	29	23	212	26	74	2	13	.980	4.24	+3	1
	Min	LF	17	9	93	28	1	0	0	1.000	2.82	+1	1
Aguilar, J	Mil	1B	77	52	505	455	44	6	65	.988	-	+4	2
	Mil	3B	1	0	1	0	0	0	0	-	.00	0	0
Ahmed, N	Ari	SS	48	41	382	44	140	5	29	.974	4.34	+3	3
Albies, O	Atl	2B	57	57	497	91	139	3	33	.987	4.16	+1	1
Alcantara, A	Cin	2B	10	6	55	9	17	3	2	.897	4.25	0	0
	Cin	3B	4	0	9	0	2	0	1	1.000	1.93	0	0
	Cin	SS	6	1	21	2	9	0	1	1.000	4.64	+1	0
	Cin	LF	3	0	5	1	0	0	0	1.000	1.80	0	0
	Cin	CF	7	3	38	14	1	0	0	1.000	3.55	+3	2
	Cin	RF	7	1	23	8	0	0	0	1.000	3.18	-1	0
Alfaro, J	Phi	1B	2	1	9	8	2	0	1	1.000	-	0	0
Alford, A	Tor	LF	3	2	17	2	0	0	0	1.000	1.06	0	2
	Tor	RF	2	0	3	2	0	0	0	1.000	6.00	0	0
Allen, G	Cle	LF	5	0	14	3	0	0	0	1.000	1.93	0	0
	Cle	CF	21	5	95	23	0	0	0	1.000	2.18	-3	0
Almonte, A	Cle	LF	20	10	105	23	1	0	0	1.000	2.05	+1	0
	Cle	CF	8	8	55	15	0	0	0	1.000	2.45	+2	1
	Cle	RF	32	28	249	32	1	1	0	.971	1.19	-3	-2
Almora Jr., A	ChC	LF	1	0	0	0	0	0	0	-	.00	0	0
	ChC	CF	104	65	643	161	4	1	0	.994	2.31	-4	-1
	ChC	RF	1	0	1	0	0	0	0	-	.00	-1	-1
Altherr, A	Phi	LF	52	42	387	94	2	2	1	.980	2.23	+3	0
	Phi	CF	19	12	101	36	2	1	1	.974	3.38	-6	-3
	Phi	RF	50	38	349	81	3	0	2	1.000	2.17	-1	-1
Alvarez, P	Bal	1B	2	1	9	11	1	0	2	1.000	-	+1	0
Amarista, A	Col	2B	19	8	89	18	29	0	6	1.000	4.75	0	0
	Col	3B	1	1	6	0	1	1	0	.500	1.59	-1	-1
	Col	SS	18	11	106	7	30	4	6	.902	3.13	-2	-2
	Col	LF	5	2	20	2	0	0	0	1.000	.92	-1	-2
	Col	CF	9	1	25	3	0	0	0	1.000	1.07	-1	-1
	Col	RF	9	2	23	1	0	0	0	1.000	.39	-2	-2
Anderson, B	Mia	3B	25	21	198	20	31	3	2	.944	2.32	-3	-3
Andujar, M	NYY	3B	3	0	9	1	1	0	0	1.000	2.00	0	0
Aoki, N	TOT	LF	64	55	452	75	7	0	1	1.000	1.63	-6	6
	TOT	CF	2	1	10	3	0	0	0	1.000	2.70	0	0
	TOT	RF	47	31	303	55	0	1	0	.982	1.63	-10	-6
Arroyo, C	SF	2B	2	2	18	4	7	0	2	1.000	5.50	+2	2
	SF	3B	22	21	194	14	43	2	5	.966	2.64	-1	0
	SF	SS	10	9	83	12	19	1	3	.969	3.38	0	0
Asche, C	CWS	1B	2	2	17	19	0	0	1	1.000	-	0	0
	CWS	3B	1	0	1	1	0	0	0	1.000	9.00	0	0
	CWS	LF	1	0	3	0	0	0	0	-	.00	0	0
Asuaje, C	SD	1B	1	0	0	0	0	0	0	-	-	0	0
	SD	2B	84	78	681	143	218	3	68	.992	4.77	-5	-3
Austin, T	NYY	1B	8	5	45	49	1	0	1	1.000	-	0	-1
	NYY	RF	7	1	21	2	0	0	0	1.000	.86	0	0
Avila, A	TOT	1B	19	11	110	79	3	0	11	1.000	-	0	0
Aviles, M	Mia	1B	2	0	3	2	0	0	0	1.000	-	0	0
	Mia	2B	6	4	35	6	19	0	5	1.000	6.43	0	0
	Mia	3B	6	4	37	0	7	0	0	1.000	1.72	0	0
	Mia	SS	15	12	103	14	35	0	8	1.000	4.28	-2	0
	Mia	RF	1	0	2	0	0	0	0	-	.00	0	0
Bader, H	StL	LF	7	2	29	7	0	0	0	1.000	2.17	+1	1
	StL	CF	20	17	152	42	1	2	0	.956	2.55	+3	2
	StL	RF	3	1	8	0	0	0	0	-	.00	0	0
Baez, J	ChC	1B	4	0	1	1	0	0	1	1.000	-	0	0
	ChC	2B	80	56	504	105	132	4	33	.983	4.23	+11	5
	ChC	3B	8	4	43	8	11	0	2	1.000	3.98	-1	-1
	ChC	SS	73	67	573	91	165	11	39	.959	4.02	+3	1
	ChC	RF	1	0	2	0	0	0	0	-	.00	0	0
Barnes, A	LAD	2B	21	4	77	12	17	1	4	.967	3.40	+2	1
	LAD	3B	1	0	0	0	0	0	0	-	.00	0	0
Barney, D	Tor	2B	73	58	512	87	166	2	40	.992	4.45	-3	-3
	Tor	3B	44	32	295	14	74	4	8	.957	2.69	-2	-3
	Tor	SS	12	5	54	12	13	2	4	.926	4.17	+3	1
	Tor	LF	4	1	13	1	0	0	0	1.000	.69	-2	-1
Barreto, F	Oak	2B	10	7	68	12	21	1	2	.971	4.37	-1	-2
	Oak	SS	11	9	89	16	33	3	10	.942	4.96	-4	-3
Bautista, J	Tor	1B	1	0	1	2	0	0	0	1.000	-	0	0
	Tor	3B	8	4	38	4	10	0	2	1.000	3.32	0	0
Bautista, R	Was	LF	1	0	2	0	0	0	0	-	.00	0	0
	Was	CF	1	0	1	0	0	0	0	-	.00	0	0
	Was	RF	11	4	51	11	0	0	0	1.000	1.94	+4	1
Beckham, G	Sea	2B	5	0	10	5	5	0	4	1.000	9.00	0	0
	Sea	3B	1	1	9	2	3	0	1	1.000	5.00	0	0
	Sea	SS	4	2	19	2	3	0	0	1.000	2.33	0	0
Beckham, T	TOT	2B	17	17	141	28	32	2	11	.968	3.83	+1	1
	TOT	3B	1	0	1	1	0	0	0	1.000	9.00	0	-1
Bellinger, C	LAD	1B	93	83	749	656	36	4	62	.994	-	+4	2
	LAD	LF	39	37	313	53	1	1	0	.982	1.55	+9	2
	LAD	CF	4	3	27	9	1	0	0	1.000	3.33	0	1
	LAD	RF	5	3	26	7	0	0	0	1.000	2.45	+3	2
Belt, B	SF	LF	15	10	79	19	0	2	0	.905	2.16	+1	-1
	SF	RF	1	0	2	1	0	0	0	1.000	4.50	0	0
Beltran, C	Hou	LF	13	11	86	11	0	0	0	1.000	1.15	-3	-1
	Hou	RF	1	1	6	0	0	0	0	-	.00	0	0
Beltre, A	Tex	3B	65	65	552	50	135	5	13	.974	3.01	+8	6
Benintendi, A	Bos	LF	30	27	241	68	0	0	0	1.000	2.54	-3	-2
Berry, Q	Mil	LF	2	0	4	2	0	0	0	1.000	4.50	0	0
	Mil	CF	1	0	1	0	0	0	0	1.000	9.00	0	0
Bethancourt, C	SD	2B	1	0	0	0	0	0	0	-	.00	0	0
Bird, G	NYY	1B	46	40	361	302	12	0	20	1.000	-	-1	-1
Blanco, A	Phi	1B	11	0	24	17	2	0	3	1.000	-	0	0
	Phi	2B	15	13	114	12	32	2	3	.957	3.47	+1	1
	Phi	3B	16	7	71	4	11	0	0	1.000	1.89	+2	1
	Phi	SS	4	0	10	5	1	0	1	1.000	5.59	0	0
Blanco, G	Ari	LF	44	18	212	37	0	0	0	1.000	1.57	+4	1
	Ari	CF	35	32	258	54	0	2	0	.964	1.89	-6	-4
	Ari	RF	6	2	24	6	0	1	0	.857	2.25	+3	0
Blash, J	SD	LF	18	17	130	21	0	3	0	.875	1.45	-6	-4
	SD	RF	33	29	264	54	5	2	1	.967	2.01	+6	2
Bonifacio, E	Atl	LF	8	1	22	7	0	0	0	1.000	2.91	0	0
	Atl	CF	1	0	1	0	0	0	0	1.000	9.00	0	0
	Atl	RF	2	1	11	3	0	0	0	1.000	2.45	0	0
Bonifacio, J	KC	LF	9	6	57	12	0	0	0	1.000	1.89	+1	0
	KC	CF	1	1	8	1	0	0	0	1.000	1.13	0	0
	KC	RF	92	82	743	160	4	4	1	.976	1.99	+5	-3
Bostick, C	Pit	2B	3	3	26	8	7	0	0	1.000	5.19	0	0
	Pit	LF	3	1	13	4	0	0	0	1.000	2.77	0	0
Bourjos, P	TB	1B	41	21	207	41	2	0	0	1.000	1.87	0	1
	TB	CF	37	18	193	52	1	0	0	1.000	2.47	+2	1
	TB	RF	14	7	76	26	0	0	0	1.000	3.08	+8	4
Brantley, M	Cle	LF	87	86	731	135	8	1	1	.993	1.76	-2	4
Bregman, A	Hou	2B	4	0	9	0	5	0	2	1.000	5.00	0	0
	Hou	SS	30	21	215	31	58	4	14	.957	3.73	0	-2
Brinson, L	Mil	LF	8	5	51	6	0	0	0	1.000	1.07	+2	1
	Mil	CF	8	7	61	18	0	0	0	1.000	2.64	+1	0
Bruce, J	TOT	1B	12	10	91	77	6	2	7	.976		0	0
Brugman, J	Oak	LF	4	3	26	6	0	0	0	1.000	2.08	-2	0
	Oak	CF	40	37	316	77	1	2	1	.975	2.22	-13	-9
	Oak	RF	1	0	6	2	0	0	0	1.000	3.00	0	0
Bryant, K	ChC	1B	2	1	10	12	3	0	0	1.000	-	+1	1
	ChC	LF	2	2	15	0	0	0	0	-	-	-1	0
	ChC	CF	2	0	5	2	0	0	0	1.000	3.00	0	0
	ChC	RF	7	6	44	16	0	0	0	1.000	3.27	+2	0
Burns, B	KC	CF	4	0	9	2	0	0	0	1.000	2.00	-1	-1
	KC	RF	1	0	1	0	0	0	0	-	.00	0	0
Butera, D	KC	1B	4	0	10	13	1	0	1	1.000	-	-1	0
Cabrera, A	NYM	2B	32	32	274	60	85	0	23	1.000	4.76	-5	-6
	NYM	3B	44	40	350	19	62	6	6	.931	2.08	-2	1

All Other Fielders

Player	Tm	Pos	G	GS	Inn	PO	A	E	DP	Pct.	Rng	BSv	RS
	NYM	SS	45	44	387	49	124	11	31	.940	4.03	-11	-8
Cabrera, M	TOT		46	43	349	65	3	0		1.000	1.76	-17	-10
Calhoun, W	Tex	LF	11	8	74	11	1	1	0	.923	1.46	-2	-1
Calixte, O	SF	3B	5	2	17	1	1	0	0	1.000	1.06	-1	-1
	SF	SS	4	0	9	5	2	0	0	1.000	7.00	0	0
	SF	LF	9	7	59	11	0	2	0	.846	1.67	0	0
	SF	CF	2	1	9	1	0	0	0	1.000	1.00	-1	-1
	SF	RF	3	1	10	3	0	0	0	1.000	2.61	0	0
Camargo, J	Atl	2B	9	6	57	9	14	0	5	1.000	3.63	+1	0
	Atl	3B	43	30	286	30	61	3	7	.968	2.86	0	0
	Atl	SS	27	23	205	16	64	1	10	.988	3.51	-2	0
	Atl	LF	1	0	1	0	0	0	0	-	.00	0	0
Candelario, J	TOT	1B	1	1	6	1	0	1	0	1.000	-	0	0
	TOT	3B	36	32	288	23	56	5	4	.940	2.47	-7	-7
Canha, M	Oak	1B	3	0	7	6	2	0	0	1.000	-	-1	0
	Oak	LF	20	12	124	29	0	1	0	.967	2.10	+3	-1
	Oak	CF	19	16	124	33	0	1	0	.971	2.40	-1	-2
	Oak	RF	22	16	134	39	1	3	0	.930	2.68	-2	-2
Caratini, V	ChC	1B	8	3	41	33	2	0	3	1.000	-	0	0
	ChC	LF	1	0	1	0	0	0	0	-	.00	0	0
	ChC	CF	1	0	0	0	0	0	0	-	.00	0	0
Cardullo, S	Col	LF	6	5	41	9	0	0	0	1.000	1.96	+2	1
	Col	RF	2	1	14	4	0	0	0	1.000	2.57	0	0
Carpenter, M	StL	2B	13	13	103	15	32	4	9	.922	4.11	+1	1
	StL	3B	16	16	111	5	26	2	5	.939	2.51	-1	0
Carrera, E	Tor	LF	91	50	495	95	3	2	0	.980	1.78	-9	-8
	Tor	CF	10	8	77	19	0	2	0	.905	2.23	-5	-3
	Tor	RF	27	13	131	26	2	0	0	1.000	1.93	-6	-3
Carter, C	NYY	1B	56	48	433	391	22	4	31	.990	-	-2	-2
	NYY	RF	2	0	3	0	0	0	0	-	.00	0	0
Castellanos, N	Det	RF	21	20	173	26	0	1	0	.963	1.35	-11	-7
Cecchini, G	NYM	2B	20	18	156	33	33	0	10	1.000	3.82	-3	-3
Ceciliani, D	Tor	LF	1	0	4	2	0	0	0	1.000	4.50	0	0
	Tor	CF	1	1	2	0	0	0	0	-	.00	0	0
Cespedes, Y	NYM	LF	74	74	631	137	6	6	1	.960	2.04	-1	2
Chapman, M	Oak	3B	84	83	727	72	203	13	34	.955	3.40	+22	19
Chisenhall, L	Cle	1B	7	0	13	14	1	0	4	1.000	-	-1	-1
	Cle	LF	11	8	60	13	0	0	0	1.000	1.95	-2	-1
	Cle	CF	19	19	164	40	0	0	0	1.000	2.19	-1	0
	Cle	RF	45	33	312	49	2	0	1	1.000	1.47	-2	-1
Choi, J	NYY	1B	6	4	40	35	1	1	3	.973	-	0	0
Choo, S	Tex	RF	77	75	648	151	7	4	0	.975	2.20	-11	-6
Coghlan, C	Tor	2B	3	3	23	2	10	0	1	1.000	4.70	-1	-1
	Tor	3B	13	13	111	6	22	4	3	.875	2.26	-1	-1
	Tor	LF	8	6	55	7	0	0	0	1.000	1.15	-4	-2
Coleman, D	SD	SS	27	19	175	28	67	4	16	.960	4.89	+4	3
Collins, T	Det	LF	4	1	18	6	0	0	0	1.000	3.06	+1	1
	Det	CF	26	23	200	66	1	1	0	.985	3.02	+12	4
	Det	RF	17	15	129	23	2	1	0	.962	1.75	-6	-2
Colon, C	TOT	2B	10	8	71	14	27	0	8	1.000	5.20	+1	2
	TOT	3B	10	8	64	5	10	0	2	1.000	2.12	+1	1
Conforto, M	NYM	LF	52	45	416	91	3	2	1	.979	2.04	-2	1
	NYM	CF	43	39	329	67	2	1	1	.986	1.89	-8	-4
	NYM	RF	11	8	74	17	0	0	0	1.000	2.06	+3	1
Contreras, W	ChC	1B	5	1	20	17	3	0	4	1.000	-	+1	1
	ChC	3B	1	0	2	0	1	0	0	1.000	4.50	0	0
	ChC	LF	4	3	26	3	0	1	0	.750	1.04	0	0
	ChC	RF	2	0	6	0	0	0	0	-	.00	0	0
Cooper, G	NYY	1B	13	13	103	101	5	0	8	1.000	-	-1	0
Cordero, F	SD	LF	1	1	4	0	0	0	0	-	.00	0	0
	SD	CF	25	22	192	43	2	2	1	.957	2.11	+2	1
Cordoba, A	SD	2B	1	0	3	0	0	0	0	-	.00	0	0
	SD	3B	3	0	9	0	1	1	0	.500	.96	-1	0
	SD	SS	28	15	159	26	38	4	13	.941	3.62	-4	-3
	SD	LF	43	24	237	43	1	0	0	1.000	1.67	+3	2
	SD	CF	7	2	25	5	0	0	0	1.000	1.80	-1	0
	SD	RF	3	1	13	1	0	0	0	1.000	.69	0	0
Cowart, K	LAA	2B	30	26	225	35	76	2	21	.982	4.43	-2	0
	LAA	3B	24	2	57	3	9	0	1	1.000	1.88	-2	-1
Crawford, J	Phi	2B	4	4	32	4	9	0	1	1.000	3.62	+1	1
	Phi	3B	13	11	101	14	29	0	6	1.000	3.83	+8	6
	Phi	SS	6	6	55	8	20	0	5	1.000	4.58		-1
Cruz, N	Sea	RF	5	5	28	7	0	0	0	1.000	2.25	-3	-1
Culberson, C	LAD	2B	2	1	10	2	3	0	0	1.000	4.50	+1	0
	LAD	3B	1	0	1	0	0	0	0	-	.00	0	0
	LAD	SS	11	1	34	6	16	1	5	.957	5.82	+2	2
Cuthbert, C	KC	1B	6	2	26	19	1	1	2	.952	-	-1	-1
	KC	2B	3	1	13	4	1	0	1	1.000	3.55	-1	0
	KC	3B	44	29	281	21	65	5	6	.945	2.75	-2	-1
d'Arnaud, C	TOT	1B	1	0	1	0	0	0	0	-	-	0	0
	TOT	2B	4	1	15	3	7	1	3	.909	6.00	-1	-1
	TOT	3B	3	2	13	1	3	0	1	1.000	2.77	0	0
	TOT	SS	10	8	73	17	16	2	6	.943	4.09	-1	-1
	TOT	LF	4	1	13	3	0	0	0	1.000	2.08	0	0
	TOT	RF	1	0	2	1	0	0	0	1.000	5.40	0	0
d'Arnaud, T	NYM	2B	1	0	3	1	0	0	0	1.000	2.70	0	0
	NYM	3B	1	1	6	0	0	0	0	-	.00	0	0
Davidson, M	CWS	1B	19	18	154	140	7	4	11	.974	-	+2	1
	CWS	3B	34	32	289	14	49	3	7	.955	1.96	-4	-4
Davis, C	Bal	3B	2	1	10	0	0	0	0	-	.00	-2	-1
Davis, J	Hou	1B	2	0	3	0	0	0	0	-	-	0	0
	Hou	3B	22	14	149	11	38	0	4	1.000	2.97	-3	-3
Davis, R	TOT	LF	25	13	125	17	0	1	0	.944	1.23	-1	0
	TOT	CF	68	65	602	156	5	2	2	.988	2.41	-7	0
	TOT	RF	7	3	36	5	0	0	0	1.000	1.25	0	-1
Davis, T	ChC	1B	2	0	9	9	0	0	0	1.000	-	0	0
	ChC	3B	2	1	14	0	2	0	0	1.000	1.29	0	0
De Aza, A	Was	LF	13	7	72	13	2	0	1	1.000	1.87	+3	4
	Was	CF	1	1	7	2	0	0	0	1.000	2.57	0	0
	Was	RF	14	6	61	12	0	2	0	.857	1.77	-1	-1
Decker, J	Oak	LF	1	1	9	1	0	0	0	1.000	1.00	0	0
	Oak	CF	12	11	94	27	1	2	0	.933	2.69	-3	-4
	Oak	RF	4	3	29	5	1	0	1	1.000	1.86	0	1
DeJong, P	StL	2B	20	19	158	30	53	3	15	.965	4.73	-1	-1
	StL	SS	68	85	747	111	233	9	56	.975	4.14	+1	1
Delmonico, N	CWS	1B	4	3	28	29	1	0	4	1.000	-	+1	0
	CWS	LF	27	25	221	66	1	1	0	.985	2.72	-1	-1
den Dekker, M	Det	LF	1	1	9	6	0	0	0	1.000	6.00	+1	1
	Det	RF	2	0	5	0	0	0	0	-	.00	0	0
Descalso, D	Ari	1B	19	8	90	84	6	0	6	1.000	-	+1	1
	Ari	2B	45	37	335	75	109	7	36	.963	4.94	-2	-1
	Ari	3B	15	6	75	4	11	2	1	.882	1.81	-2	-1
	Ari	SS	1	0	2	0	0	0	0	-	.00	0	0
	Ari	LF	36	32	249	25	0	2	0	.926	.90	-2	-3
DeShields, D	Tex	LF	60	57	478	99	6	1	2	.991	1.98	+9	5
	Tex	CF	51	42	383	109	3	1	1	.991	2.63	+8	2
Desmond, I	Col	1B	27	22	191	200	5	1	12	.995	-	-3	-1
	Col	SS	1	1	5	1	3	0	0	1.000	6.75	0	0
	Col	LF	66	64	557	101	2	3	0	.972	1.66	-1	-4
	Col	CF	1	1	9	3	0	0	0	1.000	5.00	+1	1
Devers, R	Bos	3B	56	56	508	28	107	14	12	.906	2.39	+2	-1
Diaz, A	StL	2B	1	0	2	2	2	0	1	1.000	18.00	0	0
	StL	3B	4	3	23	2	3	0	1	1.000	1.96	+1	1
	StL	SS	68	66	589	81	148	6	41	.974	3.50	-12	-10
	StL	LF	3	0	9	2	0	0	0	1.000	2.00	0	0
Diaz, Y	Cle	3B	40	37	282	19	50	2	8	.972	2.20	-1	0
	Cle	LF	3	3	20	2	0	1	0	.667	.90	-2	-1
Dickson, O	LAD	LF	5	1	12	3	0	0	0	1.000	2.25	+1	0
Dietrich, D	Mia	1B	10	4	49	40	1	0	3	1.000	-	+1	1
	Mia	2B	10	6	63	13	21	0	5	1.000	4.86	-3	-2
	Mia	LF	5	2	19	3	0	0	0	1.000	1.40	-3	-1
Difo, W	Was	2B	25	13	138	22	35	1	6	.983	3.73	-2	-3
	Was	3B	6	6	52	0	8	0	2	1.000	1.39	0	0
	Was	SS	57	52	473	76	165	6	24	.976	4.58	+19	14
	Was	LF	2	1	7	0	0	0	0	-	.00	0	0
	Was	CF	1	1	6	3	0	0	0	1.000	4.50	0	0
	Was	RF	3	2	17	7	0	0	0	1.000	3.71	-1	0
Donaldson, J	Tor	SS	4	2	18	4	2	0	0	1.000	3.00	-1	0
Drew, S	Was	2B	2	2	17	3	7	0	1	1.000	5.29	+1	0
	Was	3B	11	7	69	7	7	0	1	1.000	1.83	0	0
	Was	SS	13	11	92	11	25	1	2	.973	3.53	0	-1
Drury, B	Ari	3B	1	1	7	1	3	1	0	.800	5.14	0	-1
Duvall, A	Cin	1B	3	0	7	9	0	0	0	1.000	-	0	0
Dyson, J	Sea	LF	12	12	108	15	1	1	1	.941	1.34	+3	5

All Other Fielders

Player	Tm	Pos	G	GS	Inn	PO	A	E	DP	Pct.	Rng	BSv	RS
Eaton, A	Was	LF	5	2	24	11	0	0	0	1.000	4.13	+1	1
	Was	CF	20	19	168	35	2	0	0	1.000	1.99	-13	-6
	Was	RF	2	1	9	4	0	0	0	1.000	4.00	0	0
Eibner, B	LAD	LF	6	1	25	3	0	0	0	1.000	1.09	0	0
	LAD	CF	5	4	30	5	0	0	0	1.000	1.50	-3	-1
	LAD	RF	3	2	15	3	0	0	0	1.000	1.80	0	0
Encarnacion, E	Cle	1B	23	23	198	152	10	1	16	.994	-	-3	-2
Engel, A	CWS	LF	1	0	1	0	0	0	0	-	.00	0	0
Ervin, P	Cin	LF	5	1	17	5	0	0	0	1.000	2.65	0	0
	Cin	CF	9	7	63	21	0	1	0	.955	3.00	-1	-2
	Cin	RF	5	3	29	10	0	1	0	.909	3.10	0	0
Escobar, E	Min	2B	9	7	63	10	20	0	5	1.000	4.29	-2	-1
	Min	3B	79	77	680	31	127	6	15	.963	2.09	-5	-5
	Min	SS	16	12	104	14	31	0	12	1.000	3.89	-3	-2
	Min	LF	2	0	5	0	0	0	0	-	.00	0	0
Espinosa, D	TOT	1B	2	1	11	8	0	1	1	.889	-	0	0
	TOT	2B	78	71	643	124	175	4	39	.987	4.19	-3	-1
	TOT	3B	4	1	16	3	4	0	0	1.000	3.94	0	0
	TOT	SS	4	1	14	0	6	1	0	.857	3.86	0	0
Ethier, A	LAD	LF	8	8	58	7	0	1	0	.875	1.09	0	-1
Evans, P	NYM	2B	2	2	17	3	10	0	1	1.000	6.75	0	0
	NYM	3B	6	4	39	5	5	0	0	1.000	2.31	+1	0
Farmer, K	LAD	1B	1	1	8	10	1	0	1	1.000	-	-1	0
	LAD	3B	4	0	7	0	0	0	0	-	.00	-1	0
Featherston, T	TB	1B	2	0	6	3	1	0	0	1.000	-	+1	1
	TB	2B	11	8	78	10	23	2	3	.943	3.81	-1	-1
	TB	3B	2	1	12	0	1	0	0	1.000	.75	-1	-1
	TB	SS	3	1	10	1	1	0	0	1.000	1.80	0	0
Federowicz, T	SF	1B	1	0	1	0	0	0	0	-	-	0	0
Fisher, D	Hou	LF	38	30	267	52	2	0	0	1.000	1.82	+4	2
	Hou	CF	3	2	18	5	0	0	0	1.000	2.50	-1	0
	Hou	RF	12	7	75	19	0	1	0	.950	2.28	+2	1
Flaherty, R	Bal	2B	12	2	33	6	12	0	2	1.000	4.91	+1	1
	Bal	3B	5	2	19	1	1	1	0	.667	.95	-2	-2
	Bal	SS	5	3	29	7	5	0	0	1.000	3.72	-1	-1
	Bal	LF	1	1	8	4	1	0	0	1.000	5.63	-2	-1
	Bal	RF	1	1	8	4	0	0	0	1.000	4.50	+1	1
Flores, R	LAA	RF	3	3	24	6	0	0	0	1.000	2.25	-1	0
Flores, W	NYM	1B	29	20	178	158	6	0	16	1.000	-	-2	-3
	NYM	2B	12	10	91	19	22	1	6	.976	4.05	-1	-1
	NYM	3B	55	49	426	23	81	8	8	.929	2.20	-8	-8
Florimon, P	Phi	2B	1	1	9	2	3	0	0	1.000	5.00	0	0
	Phi	3B	1	0	4	0	0	0	0	-	.00	0	0
	Phi	SS	2	1	13	1	5	0	0	1.000	4.15	+1	0
	Phi	LF	1	1	9	4	1	0	0	1.000	5.00	+1	2
	Phi	CF	8	8	60	13	0	0	0	1.000	1.95	-1	1
	Phi	RF	2	1	10	1	0	0	0	1.000	.90	0	0
Fontana, N	LAA	2B	9	5	49	4	15	0	4	1.000	3.49	0	0
Forsythe, L	LAD	1B	1	1	7	7	1	0	0	1.000	-	-1	0
	LAD	2B	80	68	588	106	157	3	35	.989	4.03	+6	5
	LAD	3B	42	31	302	17	60	3	3	.963	2.30	+5	4
	LAD	SS	2	1	2	0	1	0	0	1.000	3.86	0	0
	LAD	LF	3	0	6	1	0	0	0	1.000	1.50	+1	0
Fowler, D	NYY	RF	1	1	1	0	0	0	0	-	.00	0	0
Franco, M	Phi	1B	2	2	17	14	1	0	2	1.000	-	0	0
Franklin, N	TOT	2B	9	7	77	19	27	0	7	1.000	5.38	+3	2
	TOT	SS	1	0	1	0	0	0	0	-	.00	0	0
	TOT	LF	19	11	90	13	3	1	1	.941	1.59	-4	1
	TOT	RF	2	2	11	2	0	0	0	1.000	1.64	0	0
Frazier, A	Pit	2B	42	35	306	69	85	8	21	.951	4.53	+1	0
	Pit	3B	1	1	8	0	4	0	0	1.000	4.50	+1	1
	Pit	SS	1	1	7	2	2	1	0	.800	5.14	-1	-1
	Pit	LF	52	44	400	92	3	1	0	.990	2.14	+12	6
	Pit	CF	4	1	16	3	0	0	0	1.000	1.69	+1	1
	Pit	RF	15	10	95	19	0	0	0	1.000	1.80	-3	-2
Frazier, C	NYY	LF	30	27	236	36	0	1	0	.973	1.37	-6	-4
	NYY	RF	7	6	53	14	0	1	0	.933	2.38	0	0
Frazier, T	TOT	1B	4	1	17	8	1	1	1	.900	-	-1	-2
Freeman, F	Atl	3B	16	16	136	13	21	1	1	.971	2.25	+4	3
Freeman, M	TOT	1B	3	2	18	18	4	0	4	1.000	-	-1	-1
	TOT	2B	6	2	24	4	3	1	2	.875	2.63	0	0
	TOT	3B	3	2	20	1	3	0	0	1.000	1.80	-1	-1
	TOT	SS	10	4	55	10	20	2	4	.938	4.94	+1	1
Freese, D	Pit	1B	3	2	15	13	1	0	3	1.000	-	-1	-1
Fuentes, R	Ari	LF	9	2	31	4	0	0	0	1.000	1.15	0	0
	Ari	CF	41	27	273	58	1	2	0	.967	1.95	+7	3
	Ari	RF	4	0	5	0	0	0	0	-	.00	0	0
Gallo, J	Tex	1B	59	52	458	458	17	2	48	.996	-	-3	-1
	Tex	3B	72	66	586	47	126	13	18	.930	2.66	-1	-4
	Tex	LF	18	17	146	34	2	1	1	.973	2.22	0	2
Galvis, F	Phi	LF	1	0	2	0	0	0	0	-	.00	0	0
	Phi	CF	1	1	9	5	0	0	0	1.000	5.00	0	0
Gamel, B	Sea	1B	1	0	1	1	0	0	0	1.000	-	0	0
	Sea	LF	85	82	712	130	6	4	2	.971	1.72	-6	-6
	Sea	RF	50	45	422	108	1	1	1	.991	2.33	-2	-2
Garcia, A	Atl	3B	39	39	341	21	66	5	6	.946	2.30	-4	-1
	Atl	LF	1	1	9	0	0	0	0	-	.00	0	0
Garcia, G	StL	2B	34	21	218	60	73	3	20	.978	5.50	+3	0
	StL	3B	41	23	240	14	52	2	3	.971	2.47	-3	-4
	StL	SS	12	8	79	9	21	1	7	.968	3.42	-1	1
Garcia, L	CWS	2B	3	2	13	2	6	0	0	1.000	5.54	+2	1
	CWS	SS	2	2	19	1	5	1	1	.857	2.84	+1	1
	CWS	LF	24	21	185	39	1	1	0	.976	1.94	-10	-6
	CWS	CF	51	47	406	120	7	2	0	.984	2.82	+1	3
	CWS	RF	6	6	48	13	1	0	0	1.000	2.64	+1	2
Garcia, W	CWS	LF	13	8	73	17	0	0	0	1.000	2.10	-4	-2
	CWS	CF	11	9	85	25	0	2	0	.926	2.66	-5	-3
	CWS	RF	17	12	109	25	0	0	0	1.000	2.06	+1	1
Gardner, B	NYY	CF	22	18	165	36	2	0	1	1.000	2.08	0	3
Garver, M	Min	1B	3	3	24	18	2	1	2	.952	-	0	0
	Min	LF	2	1	6	2	0	0	0	1.000	3.00	0	0
Gattis, E	Hou	1B	1	0	1	2	0	0	0	1.000	-	0	0
Gennett, S	Cin	3B	10	8	71	4	13	2	1	.895	2.15	-2	-1
	Cin	LF	9	6	55	13	0	0	0	1.000	2.13	+2	1
	Cin	RF	6	4	41	11	0	0	0	1.000	2.40	-1	0
Gentry, C	Bal	LF	30	11	132	30	1	1	1	.969	2.11	0	1
	Bal	CF	9	2	32	8	0	0	0	1.000	2.25	-1	-1
	Bal	RF	31	12	147	30	1	2	0	.939	1.90	+4	2
Giavotella, J	Bal	2B	5	2	19	2	3	0	0	1.000	2.37	-1	-2
Gillaspie, C	SF	1B	4	1	12	7	1	0	0	1.000	-	0	0
	SF	3B	20	12	130	11	20	0	3	1.000	2.15	-2	-2
Gimenez, C	Min	1B	7	2	24	18	1	0	1	1.000	-	0	0
	Min	3B	1	0	1	0	1	0	0	1.000	9.00	0	0
	Min	LF	5	1	15	6	0	0	0	1.000	3.60	-1	0
Goins, R	Tor	2B	56	42	383	70	111	3	23	.984	4.25	+5	3
	Tor	3B	8	1	22	0	4	0	1	1.000	1.64	0	0
	Tor	SS	87	75	670	104	212	4	49	.988	4.24	-9	-5
Gomez, M	SF	2B	6	5	37	7	7	0	1	1.000	3.41	+2	2
Gonzalez, A	LAD	1B	60	57	501	414	31	2	41	.996	-	0	-2
Gonzalez, E	Cle	2B	36	18	201	38	53	0	16	1.000	4.07	+3	3
	Cle	3B	8	3	32	1	7	0	2	1.000	2.27	+1	0
	Cle	SS	11	3	42	3	11	2	4	.875	3.02	0	0
	Cle	LF	1	1	7	1	0	0	0	1.000	1.29	0	0
Gonzalez, M	Hou	1B	31	20	194	151	14	2	16	.988	-	0	-1
	Hou	2B	22	14	137	24	45	1	17	.986	4.54	-2	0
	Hou	3B	19	15	139	12	29	3	2	.932	2.66	0	0
	Hou	SS	38	33	281	39	88	2	23	.984	4.06	-3	-3
	Hou	LF	47	38	331	48	2	0	0	1.000	1.36	-5	0
	Hou	RF	2	0	4	0	0	0	0	-	.00	0	0
Goodrum, N	Min	2B	8	1	24	4	3	0	1	1.000	2.63	0	0
	Min	RF	1	1	6	3	0	0	0	1.000	4.50	+1	1
Goodwin, B	Was	LF	31	22	197	41	1	1	0	.977	1.92	+1	0
	Was	CF	34	31	276	61	2	1	1	.984	2.06	-9	-6
	Was	RF	11	6	68	16	2	0	1	1.000	2.38	-3	-1
Gordon, A	KC	CF	15	4	61	15	0	0	0	1.000	2.21	+3	3
	KC	RF	1	1	9	2	0	0	0	1.000	2.00	-1	0
Gordon, D	Mia	SS	3	2	16	1	7	0	1	1.000	4.41	0	0
Gore, T	KC	LF	2	0	4	2	0	0	0	1.000	4.50	-1	-1
Gosewisch, T	Sea	1B	1	0	1	0	0	0	0	-	-	0	0
Gosselin, P	TOT	1B	1	0	2	3	0	0	0	1.000	-	0	0
	TOT	2B	16	7	65	17	15	2	5	.941	4.45	-1	-2
	TOT	3B	3	0	7	0	1	0	0	1.000	1.35	-1	-1
	TOT	SS	3	0	7	0	4	0	0	1.000	5.14	-1	0
Granderson, C	TOT	LF	33	27	234	37	0	0	0	1.000	1.42	+1	-3

All Other Fielders

Player	Tm	Pos	G	GS	Inn	PO	A	E	DP	Pct.	Rng	BSv	RS
	TOT	CF	65	58	473	112	1	2	0	.983	2.15	-10	-6
	TOT	RF	38	30	273	60	2	0	0	1.000	2.04	+10	6
Granite, Z	Min	LF	8	4	34	13	0	0	0	1.000	3.44	-1	0
	Min	CF	24	18	174	56	1	1	0	.983	2.95	+8	4
	Min	RF	2	0	5	2	0	0	0	1.000	3.60	-1	0
Green, G	Was	2B	2	1	10	1	2	0	1	1.000	2.70	-1	-1
Grichuk, R	StL	LF	58	48	440	76	1	2	1	.975	1.57	+5	3
	StL	CF	5	2	29	7	0	0	0	1.000	2.17	+1	1
	StL	RF	55	50	446	110	3	1	0	.991	2.28	+5	2
Grossman, R	Min	LF	18	17	133	29	0	2	0	.935	1.96	+4	0
	Min	RF	35	28	224	54	1	2	0	.965	2.21	-8	-3
Gurriel, Y	Hou	2B	1	0	7	1	2	0	1	1.000	3.86	0	0
	Hou	3B	7	4	49	6	10	1	1	.941	2.94	0	0
Gutierrez, F	LAD	LF	17	14	87	13	0	0	0	1.000	1.34	+1	-1
Guyer, B	Cle	LF	33	18	181	30	0	0	0	1.000	1.49	-3	-3
	Cle	RF	37	27	228	43	2	2	1	.957	1.77	+5	4
Gyorko, J	StL	1B	10	3	40	33	6	1	2	.975	-	0	0
	StL	2B	5	5	42	5	15	0	3	1.000	4.32	+1	1
	StL	LF	1	0	2	2	0	0	0	1.000	9.00	0	0
Haniger, M	Sea	LF	2	1	8	1	0	0	0	1.000	1.13	-1	0
	Sea	CF	6	3	28	9	1	2	0	.833	3.21	0	-1
Hannemann, J	Sea	LF	2	0	3	0	0	0	0	-	.00	0	0
	Sea	CF	7	4	41	16	0	1	0	.941	3.48	+1	-1
Hanson, A	TOT	2B	28	20	180	33	67	1	14	.990	5.00	+2	1
	TOT	3B	2	0	4	0	2	0	0	1.000	4.50	0	0
	TOT	SS	2	0	8	3	2	0	2	1.000	5.63	-1	0
	TOT	LF	8	5	53	7	0	2	0	.778	1.19	-1	-2
	TOT	CF	11	6	52	18	2	2	1	.909	3.46	+1	2
	TOT	RF	20	12	120	24	0	1	0	.960	1.80	-7	-4
Happ, I	ChC	2B	44	28	260	39	79	2	13	.983	4.08	+1	0
	ChC	3B	4	1	17	3	5	0	2	1.000	4.24	0	0
	ChC	LF	29	11	113	14	1	0	0	1.000	1.19	-3	-2
	ChC	CF	54	41	347	77	3	2	0	.976	2.08	+1	3
	ChC	RF	14	8	73	9	0	0	0	1.000	1.11	0	-1
Hardy, J	Bal	SS	71	70	613	86	200	5	48	.983	4.20	+2	0
Harrison, J	Pit	2B	83	79	653	147	212	7	52	.981	4.95	+4	6
	Pit	3B	49	37	342	39	75	4	12	.966	3.00	+1	2
	Pit	LF	8	6	57	13	0	0	0	1.000	2.06	0	0
	Pit	RF	1	0	1	0	0	0	0	-	.00	0	0
Hays, A	Bal	LF	8	7	55	11	0	0	0	1.000	1.80	0	0
	Bal	RF	14	9	89	17	0	3	0	.850	1.71	-2	-2
Hazelbaker, J	Ari	LF	11	1	31	8	0	0	0	1.000	2.30	+4	1
	Ari	CF	6	4	37	3	0	0	0	1.000	.73	0	-1
	Ari	RF	8	2	39	6	1	0	1	1.000	2.17	+3	2
Headley, C	NYY	1B	45	37	328	285	19	1	16	.997	-	0	0
	NYY	2B	1	0	1	0	0	0	0	-	.00	0	0
Healy, R	Oak	1B	39	38	307	269	27	2	24	.993	-	+1	1
	Oak	3B	34	31	260	9	57	11	2	.857	2.28	-3	-2
Heisey, C	Was	LF	19	9	108	29	0	0	0	1.000	2.42	+1	1
	Was	RF	5	3	26	4	1	0	0	1.000	1.75	+1	0
Heredia, G	Sea	LF	62	50	464	108	3	0	0	1.000	2.15	-3	4
	Sea	CF	63	53	465	157	2	2	1	.988	3.08	-2	-1
	Sea	RF	1	1	8	5	1	0	0	1.000	6.75	+3	3
Hernandez, C	Phi	SS	1	0	4	0	2	0	0	1.000	4.50	+1	1
Hernandez, G	SF	LF	57	31	325	60	1	0	0	1.000	1.69	+8	-1
	SF	CF	50	39	331	104	1	1	0	.991	2.85	-3	-3
	SF	RF	20	8	87	20	2	1	0	.957	2.27	0	0
Hernandez, K	LAD	1B	3	2	20	16	0	0	1	1.000	-	0	0
	LAD	2B	9	2	30	7	9	1	2	.941	4.80	-1	0
	LAD	3B	14	8	77	6	15	1	1	.955	2.44	-1	0
	LAD	SS	24	16	150	21	50	3	5	.959	4.26	+6	4
	LAD	LF	28	12	123	25	2	0	1	1.000	1.98	+6	6
	LAD	CF	34	16	164	39	3	1	3	.977	2.31	-6	-1
	LAD	RF	18	15	119	15	0	0	0	1.000	1.13	-3	-2
Hernandez, M	Bos	2B	6	4	39	5	12	0	0	1.000	3.92	0	1
	Bos	3B	9	9	72	4	16	5	1	.800	2.50	0	0
	Bos	SS	5	5	40	5	10	1	5	.938	3.38	+2	1
Hernandez, T	TOT	LF	18	16	146	21	1	1	0	.957	1.36	-3	-1
	TOT	CF	5	4	36	13	0	0	0	1.000	3.25	0	0
	TOT	RF	3	2	22	5	0	0	0	1.000	2.01	0	0
Herrmann, C	Ari	1B	5	1	17	14	1	1	1	.938	-	-1	0
	Ari	LF	22	17	149	27	1	0	0	1.000	1.69	-3	-4

Player	Tm	Pos	G	GS	Inn	PO	A	E	DP	Pct.	Rng	BSv	RS
	Ari	RF	2	1	9	0	0	0	0	-	.00	0	0
Heyward, J	ChC	CF	13	12	89	23	1	0	0	1.000	2.42	0	0
Hicks, A	NYY	LF	22	16	147	24	2	1	1	.963	1.59	+3	3
	NYY	CF	52	50	441	115	1	1	0	.991	2.37	+18	12
	NYY	RF	14	10	102	13	0	0	0	1.000	1.15	0	0
Hicks, J	Det	1B	26	19	181	164	12	2	20	.989	-	-2	-2
Hill, A	SF	2B	7	7	57	5	16	0	4	1.000	3.30	-3	-2
	SF	3B	7	6	54	3	11	2	0	.875	2.33	-3	-2
	SF	LF	6	2	22	3	0	0	0	1.000	1.21	-2	-1
Holaday, B	Det	2B	1	0	0	0	0	0	0	-	.00	0	0
Holliday, M	NYY	1B	8	7	54	46	6	2	4	.963	-	0	-1
Holt, B	Bos	1B	2	1	10	9	0	1	0	.900	-	-1	0
	Bos	2B	31	17	188	40	51	2	9	.978	4.35	+3	2
	Bos	3B	9	8	77	5	12	1	4	.944	1.99	-1	0
	Bos	LF	10	8	70	13	1	0	0	1.000	1.80	+2	2
	Bos	RF	2	1	11	3	1	0	0	1.000	3.27	-1	1
Hoskins, R	Phi	1B	27	21	203	185	18	3	17	.985	-	+2	0
	Phi	LF	30	29	237	44	2	1	0	.979	1.74	-5	-1
Hoying, J	Tex	LF	1	0	1	0	0	0	0	-	.00	0	0
	Tex	CF	25	16	155	39	0	1	0	.975	2.26	+3	1
	Tex	RF	10	1	26	7	0	0	0	1.000	2.42	-1	-1
Huffman, C	StL	RF	1	1	8	2	0	0	0	1.000	2.25	-1	1
Hwang, J	SF	1B	3	2	17	17	1	1	3	.947	-	0	-1
	SF	3B	15	13	105	11	22	0	1	1.000	2.83	+3	3
Iannetta, C	Ari	3B	1	0	1	0	0	0	0	-	.00	0	0
Jackson, A	Cle	LF	38	29	255	44	1	0	1	1.000	1.59	+2	-1
	Cle	CF	38	38	284	60	2	1	0	.984	1.97	-4	1
	Cle	RF	18	12	114	20	1	1	0	.955	1.66	-5	-2
Janish, P	Bal	SS	14	9	78	14	26	1	13	.976	4.62	-6	-3
Jankowski, T	SD	LF	19	17	144	28	0	0	0	1.000	1.75	+2	1
	SD	CF	4	3	23	7	0	0	0	1.000	2.74	+1	1
	SD	RF	3	2	17	5	0	0	0	1.000	2.60	+1	0
Jaso, J	Pit	1B	29	7	107	110	3	0	11	1.000	-	+1	1
	Pit	LF	17	12	107	18	1	1	0	.950	1.60	+2	1
	Pit	RF	46	34	311	65	0	1	0	.985	1.88	-11	-8
Jay, J	ChC	LF	64	32	326	48	3	0	0	1.000	1.41	-8	0
	ChC	CF	54	43	340	75	0	0	0	1.000	1.98	-1	-4
	ChC	RF	19	11	110	15	0	0	0	1.000	1.23	+1	0
Johnson, M	Atl	LF	3	1	9	2	0	0	0	1.000	2.00	0	0
Jones, J	Det	CF	51	42	363	132	0	1	0	.992	3.28	+15	5
	Det	RF	1	1	0	0	0	0	0	-	.00	0	0
Jones, R	SF	1B	30	27	235	207	15	3	14	.987	-	-1	-1
	SF	3B	18	13	119	5	26	1	2	.969	2.34	-2	0
	SF	LF	1	1	8	0	0	0	0	1.000	-	-1	0
Joseph, C	Bal	3B	8	0	9	1	1	0	0	1.000	2.00	-1	-1
Joyce, M	Oak	LF	24	18	157	42	1	0	0	1.000	2.46	0	2
	Oak	CF	1	1	8	2	0	0	0	1.000	2.16	0	0
Kelly, T	TOT	2B	14	10	95	15	23	0	5	1.000	3.60	-1	-1
	TOT	3B	4	1	13	1	1	0	0	1.000	1.35	0	0
	TOT	LF	9	3	36	4	0	0	0	1.000	.99	-1	0
	TOT	CF	1	0	0	0	0	0	0	-	.00	0	0
	TOT	RF	3	0	6	1	1	0	1	1.000	3.18	-2	-1
Kemp, T	Hou	LF	10	8	68	10	0	0	0	1.000	1.32	+1	1
	Hou	CF	4	2	22	4	0	0	0	1.000	1.64	+2	1
Kendrick, H	TOT	1B	4	1	25	10	0	0	1	1.000	-	0	0
	TOT	2B	15	15	129	27	38	2	10	.970	4.53	+2	1
	TOT	LF	62	54	459	95	0	1	0	.990	1.86	+1	-4
	TOT	RF	3	3	22	5	0	0	0	1.000	2.05	0	0
Kepler, M	Min	CF	13	8	69	26	0	0	0	1.000	3.39	+3	2
Kim, H	TOT	CF	55	43	357	77	3	0	1	1.000	2.02	-6	-5
	TOT	RF	11	7	66	12	2	0	2	1.000	1.92	-1	-1
Kipnis, J	Cle	2B	75	74	621	107	171	7	41	.975	4.03	-3	-2
	Cle	CF	11	11	71	14	0	0	0	1.000	1.77	-6	-3
Kivlehan, P	Cin	1B	12	0	30	35	2	0	3	1.000	-	0	0
	Cin	3B	7	5	48	5	15	0	0	1.000	3.78	+4	3
	Cin	LF	11	6	59	9	0	0	0	1.000	1.38	+1	0
	Cin	CF	4	2	20	3	0	0	0	1.000	1.35	-1	0
	Cin	RF	29	15	148	30	2	2	1	.941	1.95	-5	-3
Knapp, A	Phi	1B	1	0	2	0	0	0	0	-	-	0	0
Kozma, P	TOT	1B	4	0	5	8	0	1	1	.889	-	0	0
	TOT	2B	5	2	22	6	8	0	4	1.000	5.73	+1	0
	TOT	3B	14	6	63	6	12	1	1	.947	2.57	-2	-2

All Other Fielders

Player	Tm	Pos	G	GS	Inn	PO	A	E	DP	Pct.	Rng	BSv	RS
	TOT	SS	14	4	51	5	13	1	6	.947	3.18	-3	-2
La Stella, T	ChC	1B	1	0	0	0	0	0	0	-	-	0	0
	ChC	2B	21	13	133	27	26	1	13	.981	3.58	-8	-6
	ChC	3B	18	10	92	9	14	0	0	1.000	2.24	-4	-2
Lagares, J	NYM	CF	85	58	567	162	7	3	1	.983	2.68	+8	15
LaMarre, R	Oak	CF	3	2	18	3	0	0	0	1.000	1.50	+1	1
Lin, T	Bos	2B	10	3	44	4	12	0	3	1.000	3.27	+1	1
	Bos	3B	9	6	57	1	10	1	2	.917	1.74	0	1
	Bos	SS	6	6	55	2	16	0	2	1.000	2.95	0	0
Lind, A	Was	1B	39	30	270	226	23	5	25	.980	-	-3	-2
	Was	LF	25	25	197	45	1	0	0	1.000	2.10	-1	-3
Liriano, R	CWS	LF	12	10	86	20	1	0	0	1.000	2.20	+5	2
	CWS	RF	7	0	14	4	0	0	0	1.000	2.57	+1	0
Locastro, T	LAD	LF	2	0	3	1	0	0	0	1.000	3.00	0	0
Lombardozzi, S	Mia	2B	2	2	15	6	4	0	1	1.000	5.87	0	0
Lopez, R	Tor	3B	1	0	1	0	0	0	0	-	.00	0	0
Lowrie, J	Oak	3B	1	0	3	0	1	0	0	1.000	3.00	+1	1
Lucroy, J	TOT	1B	1	0	3	4	0	0	1	1.000	-	0	0
Luplow, J	Pit	LF	10	7	68	21	0	0	0	1.000	2.78	+3	1
	Pit	RF	14	13	113	19	1	1	0	.952	1.59	-4	-3
Machado, D	Det	2B	27	11	118	23	51	2	12	.974	5.63	-2	-3
	Det	3B	5	4	33	5	6	0	1	1.000	3.00	0	0
	Det	SS	32	25	230	51	55	2	11	.981	4.15	-2	-3
Mahtook, M	Det	LF	19	11	113	29	0	0	0	1.000	2.30	-4	-5
	Det	CF	67	60	530	166	2	2	1	.988	2.85	+1	-5
	Det	RF	25	15	145	29	1	0	0	1.000	1.86	-2	-3
Maldonado, M	LAA	1B	1	0	1	0	0	0	0	-	-	-1	-1
Mancini, T	Bal	1B	45	35	324	285	16	3	33	.990	-	-6	-4
	Bal	LF	88	85	729	152	5	3	2	.981	1.94	-6	-1
	Bal	RF	2	2	13	4	0	0	0	1.000	2.77	0	0
Marisnick, J	Hou	LF	6	3	37	4	1	1	0	.833	1.22	-1	2
	Hou	CF	93	63	592	127	2	1	0	.992	1.96	-4	0
	Hou	RF	3	0	7	0	0	0	0	-	.00	0	0
Marrero, C	SF	LF	12	9	73	14	0	0	0	1.000	1.73	+3	0
Marrero, D	Bos	1B	1	0	3	0	0	0	0	-	-	0	0
	Bos	2B	16	6	60	17	17	0	7	1.000	5.10	0	0
	Bos	3B	53	39	364	26	75	3	10	.971	2.50	+6	5
	Bos	SS	6	4	44	4	9	0	2	1.000	2.66	0	0
Marte, J	LAA	1B	28	24	211	172	12	2	21	.989	-	-1	-1
	LAA	3B	10	9	65	3	16	0	1	1.000	2.64	+1	1
	LAA	LF	3	1	14	3	0	0	0	1.000	1.93	-4	-2
Marte, K	Ari	3B	3	2	11	1	0	0	0	1.000	.79	0	0
	Ari	SS	64	57	508	68	166	9	43	.963	4.15	+7	4
Marte, S	Pit	LF	56	56	476	100	6	0	0	1.000	2.00	+9	9
	Pit	CF	25	19	189	57	2	1	0	.983	2.80	-4	-1
Martin, L	TOT	LF	4	0	7	0	0	0	0	-	.00	0	0
	TOT	CF	20	16	155	46	0	1	0	.979	2.67	+7	5
	TOT	RF	19	14	138	37	1	0	1	1.000	2.48	+3	3
Martin, R	Tor	3B	10	9	77	5	16	0	1	1.000	2.45	0	0
Martinez, J	StL	1B	33	29	259	232	16	2	28	.992	-	0	-1
	StL	LF	24	20	180	26	0	1	0	.963	1.30	-8	-4
	StL	RF	17	10	100	28	0	0	0	1.000	2.52	-3	-2
Martinez, M	TOT	2B	11	7	71	16	26	2	6	.955	5.32	0	1
	TOT	3B	9	0	20	0	3	0	0	1.000	1.35	+1	1
	TOT	SS	1	0	2	0	1	0	0	1.000	4.50	0	0
	TOT	LF	1	0	1	1	0	0	0	1.000	9.00	0	0
	TOT	CF	2	0	9	2	0	0	0	1.000	2.08	-1	0
May, J	CWS	LF	3	1	12	2	0	0	0	1.000	1.50	-1	0
	CWS	CF	10	9	80	19	0	0	0	1.000	2.14	-3	-1
	CWS	RF	2	1	12	3	0	0	0	1.000	2.25	0	0
Maybin, C	TOT	LF	50	47	411	93	3	2	0	.980	2.10	+7	3
	TOT	CF	57	50	451	129	3	0	0	1.000	2.64	+7	1
	TOT	RF	10	5	52	10	0	1	0	1.000	1.90	-3	-2
Mazara, N	Tex	LF	47	43	374	77	2	3	0	.963	1.90	-6	-3
McCutchen, A	Pit	RF	13	13	115	20	1	0	0	1.000	1.64	-1	2
McMahon, R	Col	1B	7	3	33	36	3	0	0	1.000	-	0	0
	Col	2B	4	0	5	1	2	0	1	1.000	5.40	0	0
	Col	3B	3	0	4	0	1	0	0	1.000	2.08	+1	0
Mejia, A	StL	1B	1	0	1	1	0	0	0	1.000	-	0	0
	StL	2B	7	3	30	2	8	0	2	1.000	3.00	+2	1
	StL	3B	13	4	62	4	15	1	4	.950	2.76	+2	2
	StL	SS	7	3	35	6	12	0	6	1.000	4.63	-2	-1
Merrifield, W	KC	1B	1	0	2	3	0	0	0	1.000	-	0	0
	KC	3B	1	0	1	0	1	0	0	1.000	9.00	0	0
	KC	LF	7	4	43	10	1	0	0	1.000	2.30	+1	2
	KC	RF	10	8	70	13	0	1	0	.929	1.67	-3	-2
Middlebrooks, W	Tex	1B	1	1	9	7	0	0	2	1.000	-	0	0
	Tex	3B	19	6	84	9	25	2	2	.944	3.64	+2	1
Mitchell, B	NYY	1B	1	0	1	1	0	1	0	.500	-	0	0
Molina, Y	StL	1B	1	0	2	4	0	0	0	1.000	-	0	0
Moncada, Y	CWS	2B	54	54	467	61	169	8	29	.966	4.43	+11	6
Moncrief, C	SF	LF	1	0	1	0	0	0	0	-	.00	0	0
	SF	RF	10	6	54	11	1	0	0	1.000	2.00	0	-1
Mondesi, R	KC	2B	14	13	122	24	30	0	12	1.000	3.97	+2	0
	KC	SS	9	0	25	7	9	1	1	.941	5.68	-1	-3
Montero, M	TOT	1B	1	0	2	2	0	0	0	1.000	-	0	0
Moore, T	Mia	1B	45	32	285	270	21	0	30	1.000	-	0	0
	Mia	LF	7	3	29	3	0	0	0	1.000	.92	+1	0
	Mia	RF	6	1	17	0	0	0	0	-	.00	0	0
Morales, K	Tor	1B	12	12	104	104	3	1	6	.991	-	0	1
Moran, C	Hou	1B	4	0	10	9	0	1	2	.900	-	0	0
	Hou	3B	3	2	17	0	0	0	0	-	.00	-1	0
	Hou	SS	1	0	2	1	0	0	0	1.000	4.50	0	0
Moroff, M	Pit	2B	28	13	156	34	45	0	16	1.000	4.56	+4	4
	Pit	3B	6	3	32	2	8	0	3	1.000	2.84	+1	1
	Pit	SS	16	10	108	13	42	0	4	1.000	4.58	+1	0
Morse, M	SF	1B	10	7	44	38	2	0	2	1.000	-	-1	-2
	SF	LF	1	0	3	1	0	0	0	1.000	3.00	-1	-1
Moss, B	KC	1B	14	5	62	62	2	0	9	1.000	-	-1	0
	KC	LF	5	3	29	3	0	0	0	1.000	.93	0	-2
	KC	RF	2	1	14	2	0	0	0	1.000	1.29	+1	0
Motter, T	Sea	1B	15	8	77	69	1	1	9	.986	-	0	0
	Sea	2B	18	11	110	19	27	1	4	.979	3.78	+1	0
	Sea	3B	6	4	40	2	4	0	1	1.000	1.35	0	0
	Sea	SS	39	31	287	42	76	2	18	.983	3.70	-3	0
	Sea	LF	15	13	102	24	2	0	0	1.000	2.30	0	-1
	Sea	RF	5	1	14	3	0	0	0	1.000	1.93	-2	-1
Myers, W	SD	2B	1	0	0	0	0	0	0	-	-	0	0
Naquin, T	Cle	CF	11	7	58	9	0	0	0	1.000	1.39	+3	3
	Cle	RF	8	2	30	6	0	0	0	1.000	1.80	-3	-1
Narvaez, O	CWS	1B	1	0	5	5	0	1	0	.833	-	0	0
Nava, D	Phi	1B	4	1	15	13	1	0	0	1.000	-	0	0
	Phi	LF	42	32	293	66	3	0	1	1.000	2.12	+1	3
	Phi	RF	9	5	41	13	0	1	0	.929	2.88	0	0
Navarro, E	Det	1B	20	14	138	114	8	0	12	1.000	-	+2	2
Negron, K	Ari	1B	2	1	8	7	1	0	1	1.000	-	0	0
	Ari	2B	1	0	1	0	0	0	0	-	.00	0	0
	Ari	SS	5	3	32	3	14	1	5	.944	4.78	0	0
	Ari	LF	5	2	21	3	0	0	0	1.000	1.29	0	0
Ngoepe, G	Pit	2B	20	10	110	27	37	0	9	1.000	5.22	+1	1
	Pit	3B	3	1	15	0	1	0	0	1.000	.61	-1	-1
	Pit	SS	6	2	26	6	6	0	1	1.000	4.15	0	-1
Nieuwenhuis, K	Mil	LF	3	1	12	2	0	0	0	1.000	1.54	0	0
	Mil	CF	7	4	45	8	0	0	0	1.000	1.60	0	0
Nimmo, B	NYM	LF	32	29	259	77	0	0	0	1.000	2.67	+6	1
	NYM	CF	12	8	75	18	2	0	0	1.000	2.39	-1	-3
	NYM	RF	8	6	57	13	0	0	0	.929	2.05	0	0
Nunez, E	TOT	2B	26	25	214	39	54	2	15	.979	3.92	-5	-4
	TOT	3B	53	51	448	28	106	9	9	.937	2.69	-2	0
	TOT	SS	16	15	123	16	27	2	1	.956	3.15	-4	-5
	TOT	LF	19	17	153	40	1	0	0	1.000	2.42	-7	-4
	TOT	RF	2	1	11	0	0	0	0	-	.00	0	0
Nunez, R	Oak	3B	1	0	2	0	1	0	0	1.000	4.50	0	0
	Oak	LF	3	1	9	1	0	0	0	1.000	1.00	-1	0
Olson, M	Oak	1B	43	38	350	352	26	2	41	.995	-	+3	4
	Oak	RF	12	10	91	21	3	0	1	1.000	2.37	-2	3
Orlando, P	KC	CF	18	6	85	20	0	0	0	1.000	2.13	+4	1
	KC	RF	20	14	135	29	1	0	0	1.000	2.00	+2	0
Ortiz, D	Pit	2B	1	1	2	1	1	0	0	1.000	.84	0	0
	Pit	CF	1	1	7	1	0	1	0	.500	1.29	0	0
	Pit	RF	6	0	13	2	0	0	0	1.000	2.08	0	0
Osuna, J	Pit	1B	23	14	127	116	4	1	12	.992	-	+1	-1
	Pit	LF	14	9	88	12	4	0	0	1.000	1.64	-5	-1
	Pit	RF	25	19	159	36	0	2	0	.947	2.04	-12	-9

All Other Fielders

Player	Tm	Pos	G	GS	Inn	PO	A	E	DP	Pct.	Rng	BSv	RS
Owings, C	Ari	2B	22	15	139	26	42	1	8	.986	4.41	+1	0
	Ari	SS	54	51	434	43	140	11	18	.943	3.80	-4	-5
	Ari	LF	1	0	1	1	0	0	0	1.000	6.75	0	0
	Ari	RF	25	23	201	37	3	2	0	.952	1.79	+3	2
Ozuna, M	Mia	CF	3	2	18	7	0	0	0	1.000	3.50	0	-1
	Mia	RF	1	0	1	2	0	0	0	1.000	13.50	0	0
Parker, J	SF	LF	44	42	350	69	4	2	1	.973	1.88	+2	4
	SF	RF	5	2	23	7	0	0	0	1.000	2.74	+4	2
Parmley, I	Tor	LF	1	0	1	0	0	0	0	-	.00	0	0
	Tor	RF	1	1	9	3	0	0	0	1.000	3.12	0	0
Parra, G	Col	1B	6	4	29	34	0	0	4	1.000	-	+1	0
	Col	LF	82	74	654	124	8	2	1	.985	1.82	+6	4
	Col	CF	1	1	9	1	0	0	0	1.000	1.00	-1	-1
	Col	RF	22	19	169	30	1	0	0	1.000	1.65	+2	2
Pearce, S	Tor	1B	10	5	55	60	2	0	4	1.000	-	+1	1
	Tor	LF	85	77	637	132	2	2	0	.985	1.89	-5	-6
Pederson, J	LAD	1B	4	2	21	2	0	0	0	1.000	.86	0	0
	LAD	CF	92	72	656	133	1	1	0	.993	1.84	-19	-12
Pennington, C	LAA	2B	47	35	310	41	86	3	23	.977	3.69	-1	-1
	LAA	3B	18	11	108	8	19	0	0	1.000	2.25	-1	-1
	LAA	SS	18	4	71	7	21	1	5	.966	3.55	0	1
Peralta, D	Ari	LF	50	48	404	72	5	2	1	.975	1.72	+6	3
	Ari	RF	78	74	665	174	2	2	0	.989	2.38	+15	3
Peralta, J	StL	3B	15	14	114	11	21	2	1	.941	2.53	+2	1
Peraza, J	Cin	2B	77	69	603	122	184	3	50	.990	4.57	0	1
	Cin	SS	55	48	422	47	125	5	19	.972	3.67	-4	-6
	Cin	CF	2	2	16	3	0	0	0	1.000	1.69	-2	-1
Perez, H	Mil	1B	2	0	3	1	1	0	0	1.000	-	0	0
	Mil	2B	17	16	116	24	32	1	10	1.000	4.34	+4	2
	Mil	3B	31	16	175	13	48	4	6	.938	3.13	0	0
	Mil	SS	7	5	45	11	12	1	4	.958	4.63	+1	0
	Mil	LF	53	34	337	69	3	1	0	.986	1.92	+9	7
	Mil	CF	18	10	94	19	0	1	0	.950	1.83	0	-2
	Mil	RF	30	17	166	25	2	1	0	.964	1.47	+3	2
Perkins, C	Phi	1B	1	0	2	0	0	0	0	-	-	0	0
	Phi	LF	15	9	88	23	0	0	0	1.000	2.35	-1	-1
	Phi	CF	4	1	15	4	0	0	0	1.000	2.40	-1	0
	Phi	RF	12	6	61	10	0	0	0	1.000	1.47	-4	-3
Peterson, J	Atl	1B	7	5	55	56	3	0	6	1.000	-	-2	-1
	Atl	2B	15	10	106	23	35	2	7	.967	4.92	-4	-3
	Atl	3B	15	6	67	5	11	1	0	.941	2.16	+1	1
	Atl	SS	4	4	34	4	9	1	0	.929	3.44	-2	-1
	Atl	LF	25	18	152	38	0	1	0	.974	2.25	+1	-3
	Atl	RF	2	2	16	5	0	0	0	1.000	2.81	-2	-1
Peterson, S	TB	LF	15	14	119	28	0	0	0	1.000	2.12	0	0
	TB	RF	5	5	40	9	1	0	0	1.000	2.25	0	1
Pham, T	StL	LF	86	85	736	143	6	1	0	.993	1.82	+4	10
	StL	CF	37	30	281	75	2	0	1	1.000	2.46	+2	1
	StL	RF	1	1	9	2	0	0	0	1.000	2.00	+1	0
Phillips, B	TOT	3B	25	25	218	5	40	0	3	1.000	1.86	-1	-1
Phillips, B	Mil	1B	0	0	6	0	0	0	0	-	.00	0	0
	Mil	CF	26	22	177	47	4	1	1	.981	2.59	+6	7
	Mil	RF	9	2	30	6	0	0	0	1.000	1.80	+1	1
Pinder, C	Oak	2B	16	13	117	25	34	1	7	.983	4.54	+1	2
	Oak	SS	22	18	156	29	51	4	9	.952	4.62	-2	-2
	Oak	LF	2	2	15	3	0	0	0	1.000	1.80	+1	0
	Oak	CF	7	4	41	10	0	0	0	1.000	2.20	-3	-2
	Oak	RF	35	28	242	64	1	1	0	.985	2.42	+6	2
Pirela, J	SD	1B	5	3	30	29	0	1	6	.967	-	-1	-1
	SD	2B	7	4	39	2	9	0	1	1.000	2.54	0	0
	SD	3B	1	1	6	0	2	0	0	1.000	3.00	0	0
	SD	LF	68	64	537	117	5	3	2	.976	2.05	+4	3
	SD	RF	4	4	33	3	0	0	0	1.000	.82	+2	1
Plawecki, K	NYM	1B	2	2	17	15	1	0	0	1.000	-	0	0
Plouffe, T	TOT	1B	11	8	76	70	8	1	11	.987	-	+2	1
	TOT	2B	3	1	16	0	2	0	0	1.000	1.13	0	0
	TOT	3B	64	56	505	48	102	8	10	.949	2.67	+1	1
Polanco, G	Pit	LF	25	25	207	32	0	1	0	.970	1.39	0	-2
	Pit	CF	6	2	32	13	0	0	0	1.000	3.66	-2	-1
	Pit	RF	68	68	584	116	5	1	3	.992	1.91	+7	4
Posey, B	SF	1B	38	30	259	223	25	2	19	.992	-	+1	1
Powell, B	TOT	LF	8	4	44	14	0	0	0	1.000	2.86	+3	1
	TOT	CF	28	22	197	62	2	1	0	.985	2.92	0	2
	TOT	RF	1	0	1	0	0	0	0	-	.00	0	0
Prado, M	Mia	3B	34	33	280	22	63	2	6	.977	2.73	+4	3
Presley, A	Det	LF	13	10	95	14	1	0	0	1.000	1.42	-2	-1
	Det	CF	19	17	149	38	0	1	0	.974	2.30	-3	-3
	Det	RF	36	29	260	55	0	0	0	1.000	1.91	-9	-7
Profar, J	Tex	1B	2	0	4	1	0	0	0	1.000	-	0	0
	Tex	2B	1	0	2	1	3	0	1	1.000	18.00	0	0
	Tex	3B	3	2	19	0	6	0	0	1.000	2.84	+1	1
	Tex	SS	4	4	35	3	14	0	3	1.000	4.37	0	0
	Tex	LF	12	12	100	20	1	0	1	1.000	1.88	+1	1
Puello, C	TOT	LF	9	8	63	13	1	0	0	1.000	2.00	+1	2
	TOT	RF	2	2	19	3	0	0	0	1.000	3.00	0	0
Pujols, A	LAA	1B	6	6	50	38	3	3	6	.932	-	0	-1
Raburn, R	Was	LF	22	14	126	15	2	0	0	1.000	1.22	-1	1
Ramirez, H	Bos	1B	18	17	146	119	6	0	12	1.000	-	0	-1
Ramirez, J	Cle	2B	71	65	577	118	170	6	55	.980	4.49	+4	5
	Cle	3B	88	86	737	61	146	6	23	.972	2.53	+1	0
Rasmus, C	TB	LF	23	19	169	40	4	0	1	1.000	2.34	+2	4
	TB	CF	1	0	1	1	0	0	0	1.000	9.00	0	0
	TB	RF	7	7	67	13	0	0	0	1.000	1.75	-1	0
Realmuto, J	Mia	1B	9	8	72	79	0	0	7	1.000	-	+2	2
Reddick, J	Hou	1B	1	0	1	2	0	0	0	1.000	-	0	0
	Hou	LF	48	20	231	42	1	1	0	.977	1.67	+2	0
	Hou	RF	11	6	69	12	0	1	0	.923	1.57	-3	-1
Reed, A	Hou	1B	1	0	3	3	1	0	0	1.000	-	0	0
Refsnyder, R	TOT	1B	6	4	31	23	0	0	2	1.000	-	-1	0
	TOT	2B	20	12	119	26	43	3	8	.958	5.22	+3	1
	TOT	LF	10	2	30	1	0	0	0	1.000	.30	0	0
	TOT	RF	4	2	24	8	0	1	0	.889	2.96	+2	1
Reinheimer, J	Ari	SS	1	1	9	0	2	0	1	1.000	2.00	0	0
Revere, B	LAA	LF	78	65	595	140	4	2	1	.986	2.18	+1	-7
	LAA	CF	6	1	20	8	1	1	0	.900	4.05	+1	1
Reyes, J	NYM	2B	28	23	207	39	54	0	14	1.000	4.04	-6	-5
	NYM	3B	36	31	279	18	59	5	4	.939	2.48	-5	-5
	NYM	SS	80	71	630	75	182	3	34	.988	3.67	-18	-15
	NYM	LF	1	1	5	0	0	0	0	-	.00	-2	-1
	NYM	CF	1	0	1	0	0	0	0	-	.00	0	0
Reynolds, M	Col	LF	1	0	0	0	0	0	0	-	.00	0	0
Reynolds, M	NYM	1B	3	1	9	6	0	0	0	1.000	-	0	0
	NYM	2B	8	3	29	2	10	0	1	1.000	3.77	+1	1
	NYM	3B	23	10	110	6	21	0	2	1.000	2.21	+1	-1
	NYM	SS	10	4	43	6	15	1	2	.955	4.40	-3	-2
	NYM	LF	7	4	35	7	0	0	0	1.000	1.78	-1	-1
	NYM	RF	1	1	6	1	0	0	0	1.000	1.50	0	0
Rickard, J	Bal	LF	43	22	226	41	1	0	0	1.000	1.68	+4	2
	Bal	CF	21	6	87	28	0	2	0	.933	2.90	+3	0
	Bal	RF	53	29	291	66	4	0	2	1.000	2.16	+14	8
Riddle, J	Mia	SS	69	61	561	81	177	8	33	.970	4.14	+9	7
Rivera, R	TOT	1B	1	0	5	2	1	0	0	1.000	-	0	0
Rivera, T	NYM	1B	20	17	151	128	12	1	16	.993	-	0	0
	NYM	2B	12	8	76	18	18	0	2	1.000	4.28	0	0
	NYM	3B	28	25	207	17	45	5	5	.925	2.70	-6	-4
	NYM	LF	3	1	9	1	0	0	0	1.000	.96	+1	0
Rivera, Y	Mil	3B	1	0	3	0	0	0	0	-	.00	0	0
Rizzo, A	ChC	2B	10	4		0	2	0	1	1.000	4.15	-1	-1
	ChC	3B	1	0	1	0	0	0	0	-	.00	0	0
	ChC	LF	1	0	0	0	0	0	0	-	.00	0	0
Robertson, D	Cle	LF	10	7	68	14	1	0	1	1.000	1.99	+1	2
	Cle	CF	2	1	7	3	0	0	0	1.000	3.86	-2	-1
	Cle	RF	17	13	115	15	2	1	0	.944	1.33	+1	3
Robertson, D	TB	2B	41	38	319	47	86	1	20	.993	3.75	+2	0
	TB	3B	17	10	96	10	24	1	6	.971	3.19	+1	0
	TB	SS	24	18	160	26	48	3	6	.961	4.16	+1	2
	TB	LF	1	0	1	0	0	0	0	-	.00	0	0
Robinson, D	Tex	2B	7	3	36	9	17	0	3	1.000	6.50	+1	1
	Tex	3B	20	17	127	13	23	2	3	.947	2.54	+1	1
	Tex	SS	6	0	9	3	2	0	0	1.000	5.00	+2	1
	Tex	LF	15	8	82	14	0	2	0	.875	1.53	-1	-2
	Tex	CF	4	4	34	12	1	0	0	1.000	3.44	-2	0
Robinson, S	LAA	LF	4	4	24	4	0	0	0	1.000	1.50	-1	-3
	LAA	CF	5	3	29	12	0	0	0	1.000	3.72	+4	2

All Other Fielders

Player	Tm	Pos	G	GS	Inn	PO	A	E	DP	Pct.	Rng	BSv	RS
	LAA	RF	8	2	35	12	0	0	0	1.000	3.06	+4	2
Robles, V	Was	LF	2	0	2	0	0	0	0	-	.00	0	0
	Was	CF	3	2	19	4	0	0	0	1.000	1.88	-1	-1
	Was	RF	6	3	32	10	1	0	1	1.000	3.09	+3	2
Rodriguez, S	TOT	1B	2	0	3	2	0	0	0	1.000	-	0	0
	TOT	2B	12	7	72	9	26	2	7	.946	4.40	0	1
	TOT	3B	14	9	93	5	31	2	1	.947	3.50	0	-1
	TOT	SS	6	6	50	8	14	2	3	.917	3.96	+1	1
	TOT	LF	7	5	50	9	1	0	0	1.000	1.81	+1	1
	TOT	CF	3	0	8	2	0	0	0	1.000	2.25	+1	0
	TOT	RF	10	6	52	13	0	0	0	1.000	2.26	-2	0
Rojas, M	Mia	1B	2	0	3	4	0	0	1	1.000	-	0	0
	Mia	2B	2	2	15	4	3	0	0	1.000	4.20	0	0
	Mia	3B	15	3	47	2	9	0	0	1.000	2.11	+1	1
	Mia	SS	77	70	613	118	192	10	57	.969	4.55	-1	3
Romine, A	Det	1B	22	4	65	56	4	0	3	1.000	-	0	0
	Det	2B	27	17	164	29	50	1	11	.988	4.33	-6	-6
	Det	3B	23	5	66	5	16	1	3	.955	2.86	-1	-1
	Det	SS	10	9	74	11	21	0	7	1.000	3.89	-3	-2
	Det	LF	18	15	127	43	1	0	0	1.000	3.13	+2	2
	Det	CF	24	20	179	50	0	1	0	.980	2.51	+1	-1
	Det	RF	11	9	76	16	0	0	0	1.000	1.89	+2	1
Romine, A	NYY	1B	12	4	54	46	9	0	5	1.000	-	+1	1
Rosales, A	TOT	1B	6	1	25	17	2	0	3	1.000	-	+1	1
	TOT	2B	11	8	71	16	17	1	8	.971	4.18	-2	-1
	TOT	3B	11	5	95	9	18	1	2	.964	2.56	+4	4
	TOT	SS	65	59	514	80	173	9	42	.966	4.43	-8	-6
	TOT	LF	1	1	5	0	0	0	0	-	.00	-1	-1
Rosario, A	NYM	SS	45	43	375	59	107	6	22	.965	3.99	+2	1
Rosario, E	Min	CF	10	5	50	18	0	0	0	1.000	3.24	-8	-3
	Min	RF	16	11	99	22	0	0	0	1.000	2.00	-1	-1
Rua, R	Tex	1B	23	19	173	153	13	1	18	.994	-	+1	2
	Tex	LF	37	17	179	45	1	0	0	1.000	2.31	+3	2
	Tex	RF	1	0	3	0	0	0	0	-	.00	0	0
Ruggiano, J	SF	LF	5	4	33	6	0	0	0	1.000	1.64	0	0
	SF	CF	2	0	5	2	0	0	0	1.000	3.60	-1	0
	SF	RF	12	10	99	19	1	0	0	1.000	1.82	-4	-4
Ruiz, C	Sea	1B	1	0	1	0	0	0	0	-	-	0	0
Ruiz, R	Atl	1B	2	1	7	11	0	1	4	.917	-	0	0
	Atl	3B	41	40	337	28	77	3	8	.972	2.80	-	0
Rutledge, J	Bos	1B	5	1	14	11	0	0	0	1.000	-	0	0
	Bos	2B	16	10	101	17	28	1	5	.978	4.01	0	0
	Bos	3B	20	15	139	18	28	3	1	.939	2.99	-4	-3
Saladino, T	CWS	1B	3	1	13	10	0	0	0	1.000	-	0	0
	CWS	2B	26	26	218	49	84	1	21	.993	5.50	+3	4
	CWS	3B	22	18	168	18	51	3	7	.958	3.69	+1	1
	CWS	SS	13	12	108	19	32	0	7	1.000	4.26	-1	-1
Sanchez, A	Was	2B	10	5	51	13	14	0	1	1.000	4.73	-2	0
	Was	3B	7	6	58	1	13	0	3	1.000	2.17	+1	1
	Was	SS	8	4	35	10	18	1	4	.966	7.20	+2	1
Sanchez, G	NYY	1B	2	0	3	7	0	0	1	1.000	-	0	0
Sanchez, H	SD	1B	6	2	25	21	2	1	2	.958	-	0	0
Sanchez, Y	CWS	2B	78	69	620	132	184	6	53	.981	4.59	+8	8
	CWS	3B	52	45	393	43	87	3	11	.977	2.97	+9	8
	CWS	SS	4	3	31	6	10	0	3	1.000	4.65	-1	-1
	CWS	RF	1	0	2	1	0	0	0	1.000	4.50	0	0
Sandoval, P	TOT	1B	9	6	59	55	1	0	8	1.000	-	0	-1
	TOT	2B	1	0	1	0	0	0	0	-	.00	0	0
	TOT	3B	67	62	519	33	93	8	6	.940	2.19	-7	-6
Sano, M	Min	1B	9	8	65	68	4	2	7	.973	-	0	-1
	Min	3B	82	79	698	64	138	7	12	.967	2.61	-4	-5
Santana, C	Cle	RF	7	7	53	9	1	0	1	1.000	1.70	-4	-2
Santana, D	TOT	2B	8	1	24	5	5	0	2	1.000	3.80	-1	0
	TOT	3B	5	3	26	1	2	0	0	1.000	1.09	-1	-1
	TOT	LF	38	20	212	59	3	1	0	.984	2.63	+5	4
	TOT	CF	3	2	18	3	0	1	0	.750	1.50	-1	-2
	TOT	RF	9	5	46	12	0	0	0	1.000	2.36	-1	0
Santander, A	Bal	LF	4	0	6	0	0	0	0	-	.00	0	0
	Bal	RF	8	6	53	16	0	0	0	1.000	2.72	+3	1
Sardinas, L	SD	2B	7	1	23	7	6	0	1	1.000	5.09	0	0
	SD	3B	4	2	21	1	6	0	0	1.000	3.00	0	0
	SD	SS	5	3	32	8	15	2	5	.920	6.54	0	0
Saunders, M	TOT	LF	4	2	16	4	1	0	1	1.000	2.87	-1	0
	TOT	RF	54	50	435	93	4	1	0	.990	2.01	-5	-1
Schebler, S	Cin	CF	15	13	118	37	0	0	0	1.000	2.83	+1	0
Schimpf, R	SD	3B	50	46	398	21	113	7	8	.950	3.03	-3	-2
Schoop, J	Bal	SS	5	2	19	1	14	0	3	1.000	7.11	0	0
Schwarber, K	ChC	1B	1	0	0	0	0	0	0	-	-	0	0
Segedin, R	LAD	1B	6	3	30	26	0	0	3	1.000	-	-1	0
	LAD	3B	5	1	15	1	1	0	0	1.000	1.20	0	0
	LAD	LF	1	0	0	0	0	0	0	-	.00	0	0
Selsky, S	Bos	3B	2	0	4	0	1	0	0	1.000	2.45	-1	0
	Bos	CF	1	1	7	2	0	0	0	1.000	2.57	+2	1
Semien, M	Oak	SS	85	85	747	125	241	9	45	.976	4.41	-8	-9
Shaw, T	Mil	1B	1	0	5	3	0	0	1	1.000	-	0	0
Sierra, M	StL	LF	3	2	19	5	0	0	0	1.000	2.37	+1	1
	StL	CF	7	5	55	7	0	0	0	1.000	1.15	+1	0
	StL	RF	8	7	63	18	0	3	0	.857	2.56	+3	0
Slater, A	SF	3B	1	0	2	0	1	0	0	1.000	3.86	0	0
	SF	LF	30	29	244	52	2	1	0	.982	1.99	0	-1
	SF	CF	3	3	0	3	0	0	0	1.000	8.10	0	0
	SF	RF	3	3	26	5	0	0	0	1.000	1.73	0	0
Smith, D	NYM	1B	46	44	378	327	26	2	32	.994	-	-5	-7
Smith, M	TB	LF	24	14	141	30	1	0	0	1.000	1.98	+4	2
	TB	CF	51	47	406	101	0	3	0	.971	2.24	+16	3
	TB	RF	9	7	62	11	1	0	0	1.000	1.74	0	0
Smith, S	Bal	LF	12	10	75	13	1	0	0	1.000	1.68	-1	-1
	Bal	RF	80	72	588	127	3	0	0	1.000	1.99	-7	-6
Smith, T	Sea	2B	3	0	5	2	2	0	0	1.000	7.20	0	0
	Sea	SS	6	4	40	5	17	0	4	1.000	4.95	+3	2
Smith Jr., D	Tor	LF	9	5	54	2	0	0	0	1.000	.34	-2	-2
	Tor	CF	1	1	5	1	0	0	0	1.000	1.80	+1	1
	Tor	RF	1	0	1	0	0	0	0	-	.00	0	0
Smolinski, J	Oak	LF	1	0	2	0	0	0	0	-	.00	-1	-1
	Oak	CF	9	7	61	21	0	0	0	1.000	3.10	+2	1
	Oak	RF	3	3	31	0	0	0	0	1.000	3.00	0	0
Sogard, E	Mil	2B	60	37	365	66	97	2	28	.988	4.02	+2	5
	Mil	3B	7	2	29	2	4	1	0	.857	1.88	0	0
	Mil	SS	26	20	160	29	54	0	9	1.000	4.68	+3	2
	Mil	LF	1	1	8	1	0	0	0	1.000	1.13	0	0
Solarte, Y	SD	1B	8	4	41	47	2	0	8	1.000	-	-1	0
	SD	2B	79	74	629	93	187	3	53	.989	4.01	-5	-2
	SD	3B	22	18	157	16	38	3	5	.947	3.10	+2	0
	SD	SS	28	24	199	32	55	4	18	.956	3.93	0	1
Soler, J	KC	LF	7	3	35	10	1	0	0	1.000	2.83	-1	-1
	KC	RF	15	13	117	26	0	0	0	1.000	2.00	-5	-3
Souza Jr., S	TB	CF	3	2	15	2	0	1	0	.667	1.20	0	0
Spangenberg, C	SD	2B	7	4	42	12	13	0	3	1.000	5.36	0	0
	SD	LF	32	25	206	32	1	0	1	1.000	1.44	-2	-1
Springer, G	Hou	CF	84	79	644	151	2	1	2	.994	2.14	+6	5
	Hou	RF	78	50	477	92	3	0	0	1.000	1.79	-14	-7
Stassi, B	Phi	1B	21	12	119	109	10	0	8	1.000	-	+2	1
	Phi	LF	3	2	14	1	0	0	0	1.000	.64	-1	0
Stassi, M	Hou	1B	1	0	4	3	0	0	0	1.000	-	0	0
Stevenson, A	Was	LF	9	1	24	2	0	0	0	1.000	.75	+1	1
	Was	CF	5	2	30	12	0	0	0	1.000	3.60	0	0
	Was	RF	14	9	91	24	0	0	0	1.000	2.37	+1	1
Stubbs, D	StL	CF	10	6	64	15	0	0	0	1.000	2.11	-1	-1
Suarez, E	Cin	SS	1	0	3	0	2	0	0	1.000	5.40	0	0
Suzuki, I	Mia	LF	9	6	59	19	1	0	0	1.000	3.05	0	0
	Mia	CF	10	5	56	16	0	0	0	1.000	2.57	-2	-2
	Mia	RF	11	10	110	29	0	0	0	1.000	2.37	+2	0
Szczur, M	TOT	LF	49	14	180	41	0	0	0	1.000	2.05	+4	0
	TOT	CF	21	14	142	36	2	1	1	.974	2.41	-3	-1
	TOT	RF	18	11	109	27	0	0	0	1.000	2.24	+1	0
Taijeron, T	NYM	RF	15	13	105	15	0	0	0	1.000	1.29	-3	-3
Tapia, R	Col	LF	18	14	133	26	0	2	0	.929	1.76	+2	-2
	Col	CF	6	1	20	5	0	0	0	1.000	2.25	-2	-1
	Col	RF	22	16	157	29	0	1	0	.967	1.66	-3	-5
Tauchman, M	Col	LF	3	1	15	2	0	1	0	.667	1.17	-2	-1
	Col	CF	3	0	8	1	0	0	0	1.000	1.13	0	0
	Col	RF	3	1	11	0	0	0	0	-	.00	0	0
Taylor, C	LAD	2B	22	19	167	33	52	5	16	.944	4.59	+2	2
	LAD	3B	8	3	38	5	5	1	0	.909	2.35	-1	-1

All Other Fielders

Player	Tm	Pos	G	GS	Inn	PO	A	E	DP	Pct.	Rng	BSv	RS
	LAD	SS	14	10	96	11	37	3	8	.941	4.48	+1	0
	LAD	LF	48	46	406	91	4	1	0	.990	2.11	+6	5
	LAD	CF	49	47	395	85	3	1	0	.989	2.01	0	0
Taylor, M	Was	RF	2	0	3	1	0	0	0	1.000	3.00	0	0
Tejada, R	Bal	2B	4	0	4	2	0	0	0	1.000	4.50	0	0
	Bal	3B	6	3	31	2	8	0	0	1.000	2.90	+1	1
	Bal	SS	36	29	262	37	77	2	18	.983	3.92	-2	0
Telis, T	Mia	1B	28	18	167	162	12	2	17	.989	-	-1	-1
Thames, E	Mil	LF	25	15	142	25	0	1	0	.962	1.58	-6	-4
	Mil	RF	5	3	28	5	0	0	0	1.000	1.63	-1	0
Thompson, T	LAD	LF	7	3	31	3	0	2	0	.600	.88	-1	-1
	LAD	CF	9	8	57	13	0	0	0	1.000	2.06	+1	1
	LAD	RF	8	1	25	5	0	0	0	1.000	1.80	+1	1
Toles, A	LAD	LF	21	13	126	24	0	1	0	.960	1.71	+2	1
	LAD	CF	10	6	64	18	0	0	0	1.000	2.52	+2	1
Tomas, Y	Ari	LF	42	42	342	44	0	0	0	1.000	1.16	-4	-6
Tomlinson, K	SF	2B	20	17	149	30	39	3	9	.958	4.18	-2	-1
	SF	3B	24	11	125	6	29	1	2	.972	2.52	0	1
	SF	SS	11	8	69	5	18	1	4	.958	2.99	-1	0
	SF	LF	9	2	33	11	0	0	0	1.000	3.00	0	0
Torres, R	KC	2B	20	11	110	19	32	0	5	1.000	4.17	0	-1
	KC	3B	12	6	63	4	13	0	1	1.000	2.44	0	0
	KC	SS	3	0	8	1	6	0	1	1.000	7.88	+1	1
Torreyes, R	NYY	2B	54	43	405	90	105	2	19	.990	4.34	+3	0
	NYY	3B	26	16	149	9	39	1	3	.980	2.90	-3	-2
	NYY	SS	36	26	221	28	62	1	12	.989	3.67	0	-2
	NYY	RF	1	0	1	1	0	0	0	1.000	9.00	0	0
Travis, D	LAD	2B	50	46	424	93	117	4	34	.981	4.45	+1	3
Travis, S	Bos	1B	21	17	140	114	4	1	10	.992	-	-1	-1
Trumbo, M	Bal	1B	2	2	15	8	2	1	3	.909	-	0	0
	Bal	3B	2	0	2	0	0	0	0	-	.00	0	0
	Bal	RF	31	31	249	46	3	1	0	.980	1.77	-7	-5
Tulowitzki, T	Tor	SS	64	64	562	68	188	8	41	.970	4.10	0	0
Urena, R	Tor	2B	1	1	12	3	4	0	1	1.000	5.40	+1	1
	Tor	SS	20	16	161	34	42	2	12	.974	4.26	-5	-4
Urshela, G	Cle	1B	2	0	2	2	0	0	1	1.000	-	0	0
	Cle	2B	5	3	24	2	8	1	2	.909	3.80	-1	-1
	Cle	3B	60	36	378	28	66	4	7	.959	2.24	-2	0
	Cle	SS	5	1	20	2	8	0	2	1.000	4.50	+1	1
Utley, C	LAD	1B	17	10	88	83	4	1	7	.989	-	-1	-1
	LAD	2B	80	68	574	94	131	5	33	.978	3.53	+1	1
Valaika, P	Col	1B	5	1	11	10	2	0	4	1.000	-	0	0
	Col	2B	8	3	33	10	8	1	2	.947	4.96	+1	0
	Col	3B	19	5	83	10	15	1	3	.962	2.70	0	0
	Col	SS	22	16	134	13	47	1	10	.984	4.04	-2	-2
	Col	LF	5	2	16	4	0	0	0	1.000	2.25	-3	-2
Valbuena, L	LAA	1B	48	40	363	316	24	0	33	1.000	-	0	-1
	LAA	3B	59	53	455	33	92	7	8	.947	2.47	-5	-2
Valencia, D	Sea	3B	1	1	7	1	2	0	1	1.000	3.86	-1	0
	Sea	RF	10	5	51	14	1	0	0	1.000	2.65	-2	-1
Valera, B	StL	2B	3	2	18	2	3	0	1	1.000	2.50	-1	-1
Van Slyke, S	LAD	1B	9	5	41	29	5	1	7	.971	-	0	1
	LAD	LF	11	2	38	5	0	0	0	1.000	1.18	-1	0
	LAD	CF	1	0	1	1	0	0	0	1.000	9.00	0	0
	LAD	RF	1	0	2	0	0	0	0	-	.00	0	0
Vargas, I	Ari	2B	3	0	7	1	3	0	2	1.000	5.14	0	0
	Ari	3B	2	0	9	0	1	1	0	.500	1.00	0	0
Vargas, K	Min	1B	40	30	270	241	18	2	29	.992	-	+6	3
Vazquez, C	Bos	3B	2	0	2	0	0	0	0	-	.00	0	0
Verdugo, A	LAD	LF	3	0	7	1	0	0	0	1.000	1.29	0	0
	LAD	CF	6	4	33	2	0	0	0	1.000	.55	-3	-1
	LAD	RF	3	0	4	1	0	0	0	1.000	2.25	0	0
Villanueva, C	SD	3B	9	7	62	4	11	0	2	1.000	2.18	+2	0
Villar, J	Mil	CF	6	6	39	2	1	1	0	.750	.69	-5	-2
Vincej, Z	Cin	2B	1	0	3	1	1	0	0	1.000	6.00	0	0
	Cin	SS	1	1	15	2	4	0	0	1.000	3.60	0	0
Vogelbach, D	Sea	1B	7	5	44	31	5	1	2	.973	-	-3	-2
Vogt, S	TOT	LF	1	0	2	2	0	0	0	1.000	9.00	0	0
Voit, L	StL	1B	31	18	186	154	15	0	15	1.000	-	+3	2
Wade, T	NYY	2B	15	11	98	21	17	1	6	.974	3.49	+1	0
	NYY	SS	7	1	20	3	3	0	0	1.000	2.70	0	0
	NYY	LF	5	1	16	1	0	1	0	.500	.56	-2	-1

Player	Tm	Pos	G	GS	Inn	PO	A	E	DP	Pct.	Rng	BSv	RS
	NYY	RF	2	1	10	2	0	1	0	.667	1.80	0	0
Walker, C	Ari	1B	1	1	9	11	0	1	2	.917	-	-1	-1
Walker, N	TOT	1B	17	8	86	77	6	1	7	.988	-	0	-1
	TOT	3B	4	4	34	3	5	0	0	1.000	2.10	+1	0
Wallach, C	Cin	1B	1	0	1	0	0	0	0	-	-	0	0
Washington, D	Bal	RF	2	0	3	0	0	0	0	-	.00	0	0
Weeks Jr., R	TB	1B	12	12	90	70	4	0	8	1.000	-	+2	1
Wendle, J	Oak	2B	5	3	26	6	7	0	3	1.000	4.50	0	0
Werth, J	Was	LF	51	51	423	92	1	1	0	.989	1.98	0	-3
	Was	RF	16	16	129	24	0	3	0	.889	1.67	+1	-2
White, T	Hou	1B	19	12	121	110	4	3	11	.974	-	-3	-2
	Hou	2B	4	0	10	1	2	0	0	1.000	2.70	0	0
	Hou	3B	2	1	11	2	0	0	0	1.000	1.64	-2	-1
Williams, M	NYY	CF	5	4	36	7	0	0	0	1.000	1.75	-6	-3
	NYY	RF	1	1	4	0	0	0	0	-	.00	0	0
Williams, N	Phi	LF	12	10	89	12	1	0	0	1.000	1.31	-5	0
	Phi	CF	16	12	111	25	0	0	0	1.000	2.02	-6	-4
	Phi	RF	58	56	485	73	3	0	1	1.000	1.41	-18	-9
Williamson, M	SF	LF	9	8	69	12	1	1	0	.929	1.70	-1	0
	SF	RF	12	11	92	24	0	1	0	.960	2.35	-2	-2
Winker, J	Cin	LF	2	2	17	1	0	0	0	1.000	.53	-1	0
	Cin	RF	25	24	202	40	2	1	0	.977	1.87	-8	-4
Wolters, T	Col	2B	4	0	8	2	5	0	1	1.000	7.88	+1	1
	Col	3B	1	0	1	0	0	0	0	-	.00	0	0
Young, C	Bos	LF	39	34	298	47	0	0	1	1.000	1.42	-8	-6
	Bos	RF	8	7	65	18	1	0	1	1.000	2.63	+3	2
Young Jr., E	LAA	LF	22	20	177	40	1	0	0	1.000	2.08	+2	1
	LAA	CF	15	10	94	27	0	0	0	1.000	2.59	-1	0
	LAA	RF	2	0	3	1	0	0	0	1.000	3.00	0	0
Zagunis, M	ChC	RF	4	4	32	5	0	0	0	1.000	1.41	+2	1
Zimmer, B	Cle	CF	97	73	698	168	8	0	1	1.000	2.27	-2	4
Zobrist, B	ChC	1B	5	0	3	5	0	0	3	1.000	-	0	0
	ChC	2B	81	65	542	99	147	3	35	.988	4.09	+1	5
	ChC	SS	5	0	11	2	2	0	1	1.000	3.27	0	0
	ChC	LF	36	13	132	33	0	0	0	1.000	2.26	+6	2
	ChC	RF	32	27	228	49	0	0	0	1.000	1.93	-5	-6

All Other Catchers

Player	Tm	G	GS	Inn	PO	A	E	DP	PB	Pct.	SB Att	CS	Pit CS	CS Pct	Cat ERA	Stk Sav	GFP/ DME	SB	SZ	Other	Total
Alfaro, Jorge	Phi	28	28	243	220	12	2	3	3	.991	17	4	0	.24	4.51	-27	-1	-1	-3	0	-5
Bandy, Jett	Mil	50	44	399	362	26	2	3	5	.995	41	7	0	.17	4.87	5	0	-3	1	-3	-5
Barnes, Austin	LAD	55	49	438	497	16	3	4	3	.994	29	5	2	.17	3.74	54	1	0	6	-3	4
Brantly, Rob	CWS	6	5	42	23	1	0	0	0	1.000	5	1	0	.20	6.86	0	0	0	0	0	0
Butera, Drew	KC	74	43	432	397	18	2	2	7	.995	31	4	5	.13	5.48	-55	0	-1	-7	-3	-11
Caratini, Victor	ChC	12	7	76	76	10	2	1	0	.977	8	2	0	.25	2.38	-3	0	0	0	0	0
Casali, Curt	TB	8	2	28	42	5	0	0	0	1.000	3	1	0	.33	2.57	4	0	0	1	0	1
Centeno, Juan	Hou	22	15	141	151	8	2	1	6	.988	12	1	0	.08	3.52	-17	-1	-1	-2	0	-4
Davis, Taylor	ChC	1	1	3	6	0	0	0	0	1.000	2	0	0	.00	15.00	0	0	0	0	0	0
Diaz, Elias	Pit	55	44	407	356	37	4	4	3	.990	27	8	0	.30	4.24	-55	1	2	-7	1	-3
Ellis, A.J.	Mia	39	36	329	267	26	0	2	3	1.000	14	4	1	.29	4.43	-40	1	0	-5	1	-3
Escobar, Eduardo	Min	1	0	1	0	0	0	0	0	-	0	0	0	-	0.00	0	0	0	0	0	0
Farmer, Kyle	LAD	3	0	7	5	0	0	0	0	1.000	0	0	0	-	3.86	0	0	0	0	0	0
Federowicz, Tim	SF	6	1	17	17	2	0	0	0	1.000	1	0	0	.00	3.12	-1	0	0	0	0	0
Freitas, David	Atl	6	5	42	48	3	0	0	0	1.000	1	0	1	.00	3.86	2	0	0	0	0	0
Fryer, Eric	StL	26	15	163	141	5	0	1	1	1.000	7	2	1	.29	4.04	14	0	0	2	0	2
Gale, Rocky	SD	3	3	23	18	0	1	0	0	.947	5	0	0	.00	7.43	1	0	0	0	0	0
Gallagher, Cam	KC	13	6	64	51	1	0	0	1	1.000	6	0	1	.00	3.94	-2	0	-1	0	0	-1
Garneau, Dustin	TOT	40	33	297	236	18	1	2	8	.996	14	5	1	.36	3.76	-29	0	2	-4	2	0
Garver, Mitch	Min	13	4	51	54	3	1	0	1	.983	4	1	0	.25	6.39	-3	0	0	0	0	0
Gattis, Evan	Hou	49	47	414	473	14	9	2	4	.982	39	4	0	.10	3.87	23	-2	-1	3	2	2
Gimenez, Chris	Min	59	54	476	418	26	1	5	10	.998	42	12	1	.29	5.22	-3	-2	1	0	-1	-2
Gosewisch, Tuffy	Sea	10	8	76	75	1	0	1	0	1.000	4	1	0	.25	4.62	-1	0	-1	0	0	-1
Graterol, Juan	LAA	47	26	245	233	22	1	1	0	.996	29	9	1	.31	4.19	5	4	0	1	0	5
Hanigan, Ryan	Col	30	29	257	239	14	1	1	2	.996	11	1	2	.09	4.03	-46	2	-1	-5	1	-3
Herrmann, Chris	Ari	45	35	318	320	23	1	1	3	.997	30	5	5	.17	3.20	-21	2	-2	-2	1	-1
Hicks, John	Det	18	12	115	119	9	3	1	1	.977	6	2	0	.33	5.54	7	0	0	1	0	1
Higashioka, Kyle	NYY	8	5	48	55	2	0	0	1	1.000	2	0	0	.00	3.56	3	0	0	0	0	0
Holaday, Bryan	Det	11	7	63	44	1	0	0	1	1.000	2	0	0	.00	3.71	-6	-1	-1	-1	0	-3
Jimenez, A.J.	Tex	5	1	20	16	1	0	0	0	1.000	0	0	0	-	4.05	0	0	0	0	0	0
Kelly, Carson	StL	31	14	162	150	8	1	0	0	.994	8	2	3	.25	3.94	4	1	0	0	0	1
Knapp, Andrew	Phi	53	51	448	408	22	4	4	3	.991	38	5	3	.13	4.80	-30	-2	-2	-4	0	-8
Kratz, Erik	NYY	2	0	2	2	0	0	0	0	1.000	0	0	0	-	13.50	0	0	0	0	0	0
Lavarnway, Ryan	Oak	5	4	35	31	1	1	0	0	.970	2	1	0	.50	3.34	-1	-1	0	0	0	-1
Lobaton, Jose	Was	50	43	376	386	20	6	5	3	.985	39	6	2	.15	4.48	-7	0	-2	-1	-2	-5
Lopez, Raffy	Tor	24	17	158	138	5	3	1	0	.979	17	1	0	.06	4.49	-1	1	-1	0	0	0
Maile, Luke	Tor	46	36	339	343	15	4	0	4	.989	26	9	0	.35	3.50	13	1	2	2	3	8
Marjama, Mike	Sea	5	2	20	21	1	0	0	0	1.000	1	1	0	1.00	4.05	-2	0	1	0	0	1
Mathis, Jeff	Ari	58	56	475	489	44	3	6	4	.994	29	10	4	.34	3.53	38	1	1	5	-1	6
Maxwell, Bruce	Oak	74	62	563	454	31	0	8	3	1.000	60	16	1	.27	4.86	-20	-2	-1	-2	-2	-7
Mejia, Francisco	Cle	3	0	4	4	0	0	0	0	1.000	0	0	0	-	2.25	0	0	0	0	0	0
Mesoraco, Devin	Cin	40	37	305	260	22	2	6	4	.993	32	6	1	.19	6.19	-28	0	-1	-3	-2	-6
Montero, Miguel	TOT	56	50	412	397	24	6	3	1	.986	61	3	2	.05	4.74	26	0	-6	-3	-2	-5
Murphy, John Ryan	Ari	5	1	16	19	1	0	0	0	1.000	0	0	0	-	3.38	1	0	0	0	0	0
Murphy, Tom	Col	8	6	54	46	4	0	1	2	1.000	6	1	0	.17	7.00	-5	0	-1	-1	1	-1
Nicholas, Brett	Tex	19	16	145	106	7	0	2	0	1.000	10	0	0	.00	4.97	-23	0	-1	-3	0	-4
Nido, Tomas	NYM	3	2	19	18	0	0	0	0	1.000	0	0	0	.00	9.47	2	0	0	0	0	0
Norris, Derek	TB	53	52	454	414	19	6	2	6	.986	39	6	2	.15	3.93	23	-2	-1	3	1	1
Ohlman, Mike	Tor	6	3	35	29	2	2	0	0	.939	2	0	0	.00	7.01	-2	1	0	0	0	1
Pena, Francisco	Bal	5	3	26	16	1	1	0	0	.944	2	0	0	.00	3.46	1	0	0	0	0	0
Perez, Carlos	LAA	10	5	49	44	7	2	1	2	.962	9	4	0	.44	4.93	2	-1	1	0	0	0
Perez, Roberto	Cle	71	66	581	664	33	2	6	5	.997	28	11	2	.39	3.22	67	2	1	8	3	14
Phegley, Josh	Oak	56	45	395	356	25	6	2	8	.984	34	10	3	.29	4.24	10	0	1	1	1	3
Plawecki, Kevin	NYM	29	24	223	191	11	0	1	2	1.000	30	5	1	.17	5.00	-30	1	-1	-4	0	-4
Ramos, Wilson	TB	62	57	500	469	38	4	1	5	.992	34	5	1	.15	3.78	13	-4	-2	1	0	-5
Read, Raudy	Was	3	1	11	12	1	0	0	1	1.000	1	0	0	.00	4.91	-1	0	0	0	0	0
Recker, Anthony	Atl	4	1	13	12	0	1	0	1	.923	1	0	0	.00	9.69	0	0	0	0	0	0
Rivera, Rene	TOT	71	59	537	568	35	1	3	5	.998	38	12	3	.32	4.94	-1	-3	3	0	-3	-3
Romine, Andrew	Det	1	0	0	0	0	0	0	0	-	0	0	0	-	27.00	0	0	0	0	0	0
Romine, Austin	NYY	67	58	518	525	42	1	1	4	.998	28	2	1	.07	4.22	23	0	-3	3	-3	-3
Ruiz, Carlos	Sea	47	40	350	282	19	1	2	5	.997	28	5	2	.18	4.75	-46	0	0	-6	0	-6
Saltalamacchia,J	Tor	7	6	52	52	0	0	0	0	1.000	9	0	0	.00	5.02	2	0	-1	0	0	-1
Sanchez, Hector	SD	25	19	164	144	4	2	3	2	.987	15	3	0	.20	4.73	-16	-3	0	-2	0	-5
Schwarber, Kyle	ChC	4	0	7	9	0	0	0	0	1.000	0	0	0	-	3.86	1	0	0	0	0	0
Severino, Pedro	Was	10	5	56	65	4	1	1	1	.986	5	2	0	.40	4.34	1	-1	1	0	0	0
Sisco, Chance	Bal	10	4	40	37	1	0	0	1	1.000	5	0	0	.00	5.40	-2	0	-1	0	0	-1
Soto, Geovany	CWS	13	12	109	91	7	0	0	0	1.000	9	1	0	.11	2.48	-7	0	-1	-1	1	-1
Stallings, Jacob	Pit	5	3	33	26	1	1	0	1	.964	6	1	0	.17	5.40	-6	0	0	-1	0	-1
Stassi, Max	Hou	11	6	64	70	1	1	0	1	.986	3	1	0	.33	3.92	5	0	0	1	0	1
Stewart, Chris	Pit	48	40	355	379	26	6	1	4	.985	35	8	0	.23	4.01	20	0	2	0	0	2
Sucre, Jesus	TB	61	51	463	435	21	0	3	4	1.000	26	7	0	.27	4.35	26	0	2	3	-3	2
Susac, Andrew	Mil	2	2	13	7	0	0	0	0	1.000	0	0	0	-	6.92	1	0	0	0	0	0
Swihart, Blake	Bos	4	0	12	16	1	0	0	1	1.000	1	0	0	.00	0.75	1	0	0	0	0	0
Telis, Tomas	Mia	6	1	18	21	0	1	0	0	.955	4	0	0	.00	3.00	-2	0	-1	0	0	-1
Torrens, Luis	SD	51	31	311	260	15	2	1	3	.993	16	2	3	.13	4.81	-43	-1	-1	-5	-1	-8
Turner, Stuart	Cin	28	18	177	165	10	2	1	5	.989	13	2	1	.15	5.84	-16	-2	0	-2	-1	-5
Vogt, Stephen	TOT	81	69	585	558	18	9	1	3	.985	69	3	8	.04	4.31	27	1	-10	3	0	-6
Wallach, Chad	Cin	3	2	21	20	1	1	0	0	.955	1	0	0	.00	3.43	-1	0	0	0	0	0
Wolters, Tony	Col	77	66	586	528	43	2	5	7	.997	35	13	0	.37	5.07	-17	1	4	-2	-4	-1

Runs Saved Multi-Year Summary

Brian Reiff

Everybody knows that Andrelton Simmons is a good fielder. You don't need numbers to tell you that—you can just see it when you watch him play. However, we have the numbers, and the story they tell is quite remarkable.

Defensive Runs Saved estimates the number of runs a player saves or costs his team relative to the average player at his position. Simmons played his first game in 2012, the first year of the data in the following section. That year and each year since, he's saved his team at least 18 runs, something no one else can claim. His 163 runs saved since 2012 are 46 more than second-place Jason Heyward and 59 more than the next-best infielder, Nolan Arenado. They're also the most a player has saved over any six-year stretch since we started measuring DRS in 2003.

Of course, this section contains more than just incredible Andrelton Simmons facts. Defensive metrics are still relatively new, and so this section helps to put them into context. As you'll see, the best players will generally save their teams upwards of 15 to 20 runs a season, while the worst will cost their teams a similar number.

Some players are consistently good every season, like Simmons, Heyward, and Arenado. Others, like Matt Kemp and Jose Reyes, are the opposite. There are also players who are improving, like Yasiel Puig, who's increased his runs saved total each of the past three seasons and was among the best at his position in 2017. Going in the other direction, you'll see a player like Jonathan Lucroy, who saved double-digit runs each season between 2012 and 2014 but has cost his teams 10 runs since then.

A player must have over 2,500 innings played over the past six seasons or 700 innings in the most recent season at his primary position in order to qualify for this list. A secondary position is listed if the player has played at a second position over 1,000 innings over six seasons (or 200 innings in the most recent season).

Defensive Runs Saved By Season

Player	YOB	Pos 1	Pos 2	12	13	14	15	16	17
Abreu, Jose	1987	1B				-10	1	-5	0
Adams, Matt	1988	1B		1	-2	8	5	1	-4
Alonso, Yonder	1987	1B		2	6	9	9	-5	-9
Altuve, Jose	1990	2B		-18	-3	-7	3	-2	3
Alvarez, Pedro	1987	3B		-5	3	-5	-13	-4	0
Anderson, Tim	1993	SS						6	-8
Andrus, Elvis	1988	SS		8	11	-14	-1	-3	3
Aoki, Nori	1982	RF	LF	3	10	-7	-1	-4	0
Arcia, Orlando	1994	SS						-1	6
Arenado, Nolan	1991	3B			30	16	18	20	20
Avila, Alex	1987	C		5	-2	3	-7	-1	-4
Aybar, Erick	1984	SS		3	-7	-3	-3	-6	-4
Barney, Darwin	1985	2B	3B	29	11	10	-1	9	-6
Barnhart, Tucker	1991	C				2	-3	-3	11
Bautista, Jose	1980	RF		6	6	-2	-3	-8	-8
Beckham, Gordon	1986	2B		-6	-3	0	6	-11	0
Beckham, Tim	1990	SS			0		-5	3	-1
Bell, Josh	1992	1B						-8	6
Belt, Brandon	1988	1B		4	4	3	6	10	10
Beltran, Carlos	1977	RF		5	-7	-5	-14	-6	-1
Beltre, Adrian	1979	3B		13	-5	9	18	15	6
Benintendi, Andrew	1994	LF	CF					-1	7
Betts, Mookie	1992	RF	CF			4	10	32	31
Blackmon, Charlie	1986	CF		5	-6	2	-7	-2	-5
Bogaerts, Xander	1992	SS			-1	-16	-1	-10	-11
Bour, Justin	1988	1B				0	-7	0	-2
Bradley Jr., Jackie	1990	CF			-3	15	8	11	10
Brantley, Michael	1987	LF	CF	0	4	-1	-2	1	4
Braun, Ryan	1983	LF	RF	6	3	-8	-1	6	-5
Bregman, Alex	1994	3B	SS					4	-5
Broxton, Keon	1990	CF					0	9	-7
Bruce, Jay	1987	RF		-1	16	-7	5	-11	6
Bryant, Kris	1992	3B					4	10	2
Buxton, Byron	1993	CF					4	3	24
Cabrera, Asdrubal	1985	SS	2B	-5	-16	-17	-8	-7	-13
Cabrera, Melky	1984	LF	RF	1	-4	-5	-2	-5	-20
Cabrera, Miguel	1983	1B	3B	-4	-18	-2	4	-6	-8
Cain, Lorenzo	1986	CF		5	23	22	18	11	5
Calhoun, Kole	1987	RF		1	-7	1	6	2	2
Cano, Robinson	1982	2B		15	6	0	-9	11	0
Carpenter, Matt	1985	3B	1B	-5	0	-2	-10	-5	2
Carter, Chris	1986	1B		-5	-9	0	-6	-5	-2
Castellanos, Nicholas	1992	3B			-1	-30	-9	-11	-21
Castillo, Welington	1987	C		-4	3	-8	-9	2	-9
Castro, Jason	1987	C		-8	-5	2	11	4	10
Castro, Starlin	1990	SS	2B	3	-8	-7	-2	-8	-6
Cervelli, Francisco	1986	C		0	1	1	8	6	-6
Cespedes, Yoenis	1985	LF	CF	-6	-1	10	11	-3	2
Chirinos, Robinson	1984	C			0	1	0	-1	2
Choo, Shin-Soo	1982	RF	CF	-10	-18	-12	-11	-4	-6
Contreras, Willson	1992	C						-1	0
Correa, Carlos	1994	SS					0	-3	4
Cozart, Zack	1985	SS		12	4	19	7	8	2
Crawford, Brandon	1987	SS		12	2	8	20	20	9
Cron, C.J.	1990	1B				-5	-5	3	3
Cruz, Nelson	1980	RF		-12	-3	4	-8	-3	-1
d'Arnaud, Travis	1989	C			1	-8	0	-4	-1
Davis, Chris	1986	1B		-4	-7	8	1	6	-6
Davis, Khris	1987	LF			-2	4	-6	-1	-13
Davis, Rajai	1980	LF	CF	3	4	-10	3	-8	-1
Desmond, Ian	1985	SS	LF	-6	-3	1	1	-4	-4
Dickerson, Corey	1989	LF			0	-2	-7	2	-1
Dietrich, Derek	1989	3B	2B		-6	-9	-9	0	-6
Donaldson, Josh	1985	3B		3	12	20	11	2	3
Dozier, Brian	1987	2B		1	9	0	-5	3	-4
Drury, Brandon	1992	2B					0	-13	4
Duda, Lucas	1986	1B		-15	-12	5	4	0	-1
Duvall, Adam	1988	LF				2	-1	16	8
Dyson, Jarrod	1984	CF		4	6	13	11	19	15
Eaton, Adam	1988	CF	RF	1	-2	11	-14	20	-5
Ellis, A.J.	1981	C		-6	-4	-6	-7	-3	-3
Ellsbury, Jacoby	1983	CF		2	13	-3	1	8	-3
Encarnacion, Edwin	1983	1B		-4	-7	-6	0	0	-2
Escobar, Alcides	1986	SS		-2	4	-4	-1	-6	-4
Escobar, Yunel	1982	SS	3B	14	4	-23	-11	-11	-9
Espinosa, Danny	1987	2B	SS	7	3	0	5	8	-1
Flowers, Tyler	1986	C		9	1	11	14	2	11
Forsythe, Logan	1987	2B	3B	-10	-2	3	6	1	9
Fowler, Dexter	1986	CF		-12	-4	-20	-12	1	-18
Franco, Maikel	1992	3B				1	-8	-6	-4
Frazier, Todd	1986	3B		-1	5	8	6	-2	8
Freeman, Freddie	1989	1B		3	7	-7	3	9	1
Freese, David	1983	3B		2	-14	-9	-2	5	7
Galvis, Freddy	1989	SS		9	-4	-4	-7	5	-5
Gamel, Ben	1992	LF	RF					-3	-8
Garcia, Avisail	1991	RF		-1	-4	-8	-11	1	1
Gardner, Brett	1983	LF	CF	1	5	4	1	12	20
Gennett, Scooter	1990	2B			2	-5	3	-4	-8
Gillaspie, Conor	1987	3B		-3	-5	-12	-10	5	-2
Goldschmidt, Paul	1987	1B		1	13	1	18	4	10
Gomes, Yan	1987	C		1	21	8	-1	0	-1
Gomez, Carlos	1985	CF		2	32	0	6	-6	-4
Gonzalez, Adrian	1982	1B		14	11	11	10	3	-2
Gonzalez, Carlos	1985	RF	LF	-13	11	-5	5	4	-3
Gordon, Alex	1984	LF		24	17	26	7	4	12
Gordon, Dee	1988	2B		-14	-3	-5	13	1	3
Grandal, Yasmani	1988	C		15	4	-5	5	14	17
Granderson, Curtis	1981	RF	LF	-7	3	-5	11	3	-3
Gregorius, Didi	1990	SS		1	-1	2	5	-9	1
Gurriel, Yulieski	1984	1B						0	-5
Gyorko, Jedd	1988	2B	3B		-4	-9	-6	5	17
Hamilton, Billy	1990	CF			1	14	8	15	9
Hanigan, Ryan	1980	C		23	2	4	2	-3	-3
Haniger, Mitch	1990	RF						1	7
Hardy, J.J.	1982	SS		18	8	10	4	6	0
Harper, Bryce	1992	RF	LF	14	4	0	9	-3	4
Headley, Chase	1984	3B	1B	-3	5	13	-7	-7	-7
Hechavarria, Adeiny	1989	SS		-1	-3	-3	9	9	5
Hedges, Austin	1992	C					6	-1	20
Hernandez, Cesar	1990	2B			-4	-6	-7	4	-1
Herrera, Odubel	1991	CF					10	6	4
Heyward, Jason	1989	RF		17	14	26	24	18	18
Hicks, Aaron	1989	CF			2	-3	1	4	15
Hill, Aaron	1982	2B	3B	-2	-9	-10	3	-3	-5
Holliday, Matt	1980	LF		-6	-13	-1	-4	-1	
Hosmer, Eric	1989	1B		-6	3	3	0	-6	-7
Hundley, Nick	1983	C		-4	-12	-3	-11	-16	-5
Iannetta, Chris	1983	C		-6	-22	-14	7	-10	1
Iglesias, Jose	1990	SS		7	-1		-3	3	4
Inciarte, Ender	1990	CF				20	29	15	5
Jackson, Austin	1987	CF	LF	6	4	-1	-1	-5	-2
Jay, Jon	1985	CF	LF	1	-10	6	3	-5	-4
Jones, Adam	1985	CF		-13	-1	3	4	-10	-12
Joseph, Tommy	1991	1B						-6	-10
Joyce, Matt	1984	RF	LF	4	3	1	-3	-2	
Judge, Aaron	1992	RF						-1	9
Kemp, Matt	1984	RF	LF	-10	-5	-22	-15	-18	-17
Kendrick, Howie	1983	2B	LF	2	-3	7	-12	-5	-3
Kepler, Max	1993	RF					0	6	5
Kiermaier, Kevin	1990	CF			0	14	42	25	22
Kinsler, Ian	1982	2B		1	11	20	19	12	6
Kipnis, Jason	1987	2B		3	-1	-11	1	4	-5
Lagares, Juan	1989	CF			28	26	2	8	15
Lamb, Jake	1990	3B				0	7	-8	-13
LeMahieu, DJ	1988	2B		8	11	17	3	3	8
Lind, Adam	1983	1B		1	-7	-3	5	-2	-5
Lindor, Francisco	1993	SS					10	17	5
Lobaton, Jose	1984	C		-1	-2	6	0	-2	
Longoria, Evan	1985	3B		1	12	-5	-1	-9	11
Lowrie, Jed	1984	SS	2B	-3	-21	-10	-3	-8	-1
Lucroy, Jonathan	1986	C		16	11	24	2	3	-15
Machado, Manny	1992	3B		7	35	6	13	16	6

Player	YOB	Position 1	Position 2	DRS 12	13	14	15	16	17
Maldonado, Martin	1986	C		12	10	5	9	7	21
Margot, Manuel	1994	CF						4	8
Markakis, Nick	1983	RF		-7	-7	0	-6	10	-4
Marte, Starling	1988	LF		5	20	5	24	17	8
Martin, Leonys	1988	CF		0	14	16	15	-2	8
Martin, Russell	1983	C		4	21	19	5	6	3
Martinez, J.D.	1987	RF	LF	-2	-9	0	4	-22	-5
Mathis, Jeff	1983	C		7	10	8	1	8	6
Mauer, Joe	1983	1B	C	-6	8	4	0	6	7
Maybin, Cameron	1987	CF	LF	7	-5	2	-16	-11	2
Mazara, Nomar	1995	RF	LF					-5	-6
McCann, Brian	1984	C		13	6	6	-4	-5	-8
McCann, James	1990	C				-1	-6	9	-6
McCutchen, Andrew	1986	CF		-6	5	-13	-8	-28	-14
Mercer, Jordy	1986	SS		3	-2	9	0	-9	-1
Merrifield, Whit	1989	2B						6	5
Mesoraco, Devin	1988	C		-2	-5	-5	-1	0	-6
Middlebrooks, Will	1988	3B		-3	-7	-5	-7	2	1
Miller, Brad	1989	SS	2B		-3	-5	-20	-17	-4
Molina, Yadier	1982	C		29	30	7	9	2	7
Montero, Miguel	1983	C		9	-2	10	7	-2	-5
Moreland, Mitch	1985	1B		0	1	1	2	7	10
Morrison, Logan	1987	1B		-2	-4	2	-7	-4	1
Moustakas, Mike	1988	3B		14	-3	-2	4	1	-8
Murphy, Daniel	1985	2B		-10	-15	-11	-5	-11	-15
Myers, Wil	1990	1B	RF		-1	-8	-6	7	1
Napoli, Mike	1981	1B		-12	10	8	1	-4	1
Norris, Derek	1989	C		6	-1	-3	3	15	1
Odor, Rougned	1994	2B				-11	-7	-9	3
Ozuna, Marcell	1990	CF	LF		4	9	-3	-5	10
Panik, Joe	1990	2B				-1	2	3	-11
Parra, Gerardo	1987	RF	LF	9	37	0	-10	-11	5
Pederson, Joc	1992	CF				0	-3	1	-12
Pedroia, Dustin	1983	2B		11	15	17	-3	12	-2
Pence, Hunter	1983	RF		-6	-8	-1	0	-3	-3
Peralta, Jhonny	1982	SS		-1	0	17	-7	-8	1
Perez, Salvador	1990	C		7	11	7	1	3	0
Pham, Tommy	1988	LF	CF			0	3	-4	11
Phillips, Brandon	1981	2B	3B	11	1	6	4	-7	-8
Pillar, Kevin	1989	CF			4	3	22	21	15
Pina, Manny	1987	C		0				-1	14
Piscotty, Stephen	1991	RF					-5	3	8
Plouffe, Trevor	1986	3B		-8	0	6	3	-4	2
Polanco, Gregory	1991	RF	LF			-2	12	2	1
Polanco, Jorge	1993	SS				1	0	-8	-1
Pollock, A.J.	1987	CF		1	12	8	14	3	8
Posey, Buster	1987	C	1B	15	16	10	21	24	3
Prado, Martin	1983	3B	LF	18	2	9	10	3	3
Puig, Yasiel	1990	RF			8	-1	2	7	18
Pujols, Albert	1980	1B		9	1	6	4	-4	-1
Ramirez, Jose	1992	3B	2B		1	6	5	-1	5
Ramos, Wilson	1987	C		-2	10	2	10	-1	-5
Rasmus, Colby	1986	CF	LF	7	12	-6	2	20	4
Realmuto, J.T.	1991	C				0	1	-13	-3
Reddick, Josh	1987	RF	LF	15	13	10	1	6	4
Rendon, Anthony	1990	3B	2B		-11	16	-1	8	7
Renfroe, Hunter	1992	RF						-1	1
Revere, Ben	1988	CF	LF	10	-3	-16	-1	2	-6
Reyes, Jose	1983	SS	2B	-16	-4	-16	-8	-8	-26
Reynolds, Mark	1983	1B		-9	-11	6	-2	4	-4
Rivera, Rene	1983	C			9	15	-6	6	-3
Rizzo, Anthony	1989	1B		4	16	6	10	11	8
Rosario, Eddie	1991	LF					11	2	-10
Ruiz, Carlos	1979	C		4	0	1	-12	4	-6
Rupp, Cameron	1988	C			0	-1	6	-10	-10
Russell, Addison	1994	SS					19	19	15
Saltalamacchia, J	1985	C		5	-5	-21	-5	-9	-1
Sanchez, Gary	1992	C						3	1
Sandoval, Pablo	1986	3B		-4	-5	4	-11	-1	-7
Santana, Carlos	1986	1B	C	-14	-19	-10	-5	1	8
Santana, Domingo	1992	RF				-1	-4	-10	-5
Schebler, Scott	1990	RF						2	2
Schoop, Jonathan	1991	2B			-1	11	-3	-1	2

Player	YOB	Position 1	Position 2	DRS 12	13	14	15	16	17
Schwarber, Kyle	1993	LF					-6	0	-9
Seager, Corey	1994	SS						2	10
Seager, Kyle	1987	3B		-4	-8	10	1	15	-2
Segura, Jean	1990	SS	2B	0	3	2	-3	0	-3
Semien, Marcus	1990	SS			5	-4	5	-6	-9
Shaw, Travis	1990	3B					-1	14	3
Simmons, Andrelton	1989	SS		19	41	28	25	18	32
Smoak, Justin	1986	1B		0	-8	-4	4	-5	1
Sogard, Eric	1986	2B		3	4	3	6		7
Solarte, Yangervis	1987	3B	2B		-7	-1	-2	1	
Souza Jr., Steven	1989	RF				0	-4	2	7
Span, Denard	1984	CF		19	3	-2	-10	-7	-27
Spangenberg, Cory	1991	3B	LF			-1	3	2	-15
Springer, George	1989	RF	CF			-2	6	6	-2
Stanton, Giancarlo	1989	RF		9	-6	6	9	4	10
Stewart, Chris	1982	C		11	10	3	4	-5	2
Story, Trevor	1992	SS						4	11
Stubbs, Drew	1984	CF		1	-7	0	2	-7	-1
Suarez, Eugenio	1991	3B	SS			-4	-12	1	5
Suzuki, Ichiro	1973	RF		5	10	1	6	6	-1
Suzuki, Kurt	1983	C		-11	-8	-17	-9	-12	4
Swanson, Dansby	1994	SS						0	-7
Taylor, Michael A.	1991	CF				-1	5	-2	8
Tejada, Ruben	1989	SS		0	-6	3	-18	1	1
Thames, Eric	1986	1B		-6					-9
Trout, Mike	1991	CF		19	-11	-12	5	6	-6
Tulowitzki, Troy	1984	SS		-6	6	7	5	10	0
Turner, Justin	1984	3B		-3	0	6	5	7	6
Turner, Trea	1993	SS					2	0	-3
Upton, Justin	1987	LF	RF	1	-8	-3	8	0	8
Utley, Chase	1978	2B		9	-4	3	0	-3	1
Valbuena, Luis	1985	3B	1B	4	6	-11	1		-3
Valencia, Danny	1984	1B	3B	-1	0	-2	-6	-18	1
Vazquez, Christian	1990	C				14		5	12
Villar, Jonathan	1991	2B	SS		-5	-2	1	0	-1
Vogt, Stephen	1984	C		0	0	0	-4	-10	-6
Votto, Joey	1983	1B		9	6	5	6	-14	11
Walker, Neil	1985	2B		-4	9	-2	-2	0	-6
Weeks Jr., Rickie	1982	2B		-30	-15	-17	-2	-7	1
Werth, Jayson	1979	RF	LF	-11	0	-4	-11	-8	-5
Wieters, Matt	1986	C		13	-10	-4	-7	-3	-3
Wong, Kolten	1990	2B			0	9	5	4	-1
Yelich, Christian	1991	LF	CF		1	11	8	6	-6
Zimmerman, Ryan	1984	1B	3B	-1	-1	-4	-1	-2	-8
Zobrist, Ben	1981	2B	RF	5	9	6	-12	-3	1
Zunino, Mike	1991	C			0	8	8	8	4

Baserunning

Alex Vigderman

The top of the baserunning leaderboard is perhaps the least suspenseful of any in baseball. A player's speed is one of the easiest skills to spot when watching a game, because you can tell a guy is fast even if he doesn't get on base or make a play in the field. Correspondingly, we can get a pretty good sense of which players are the most valuable baserunners from just the "eye test."

To that point, it isn't surprising that Byron Buxton tops the list of most valuable baserunners this season (+55 bases), because his speed jumps off the screen on offense and defense. He added at least 27 bases each from stolen bases and extra bases taken, making him the most balanced of the leaders. He also managed to ground into a double play just once all season. Buxton gets extra credit for this achievement in my book because he has so many fewer opportunities to make hay with his speed than his competitors. With a low on-base percentage and a tendency to hit in the bottom half of the order, the fact that he outran guys like Dee Gordon and Mookie Betts (who fare better in both of those respects) is all the more impressive.

In Betts' case, he comes in a close second with +54 bases, and like Buxton he made it to the top of the list without getting to even 30 stolen bases. The Red Sox right fielder easily paced the league with a 60 percent first-to-third advancement rate. Gordon finished next behind Betts with +51 bases, and he is the first player on the leaderboard to get the vast majority of his value from stolen bases. His +28 stolen base gain trailed only Billy Hamilton and Trea Turner, and he scored 42 percent of the time he reached base, trailing only Rajai Davis among players with at least 100 times on base.

I would be remiss not to further acknowledge Billy Hamilton, who missed out on a three-peat in this category. His late-season thumb injury prevented him from topping the list, but he still finished fourth this season with +44 bases. In contrast to Buxton, Hamilton's baserunning value comes mostly from stolen bases, as he led MLB with +33 stolen bases gained.

One of this year's most-improved baserunners was Cameron Maybin, who showed how team context can affect baserunning results. Maybin moved from the

Tigers to the Angels in the offseason, joining a team managed by the typically-aggressive Mike Scioscia that led the league in stolen base attempts in 2017. As a result, he nearly doubled his stolen base attempts and gained +14 bases in that category alone compared to 2016.

On the other end of that spectrum is Matt Kemp, who fell from slightly above average to the second-worst baserunner in the league and has clearly lost the athleticism that made him an MVP candidate and nearly a 40-40 player in 2011. He more than doubled the rate at which he grounded into double plays and also suffered a dramatic downturn in Bases Taken, the number of times a player moves up a base on a wild pitch, passed ball, balk, sacrifice fly, or defensive indifference.

The only baserunner worse than Kemp this year was Joey Votto, whose excellence at the plate provides him the most opportunities in the league to showcase his poor baserunning. To go with his league-leading number of times on base, Votto was second-worst in the league in overall advancement rate, taking an extra base in just 9 of 83 opportunities (11 percent) compared to a league average of 40 percent.

Net Gain is a statistic that measures baserunning production that includes all baserunning advancements on both hits and outs (BR Gain) and stolen bases (SB Gain). It estimates the number of bases a player gained or lost for his team due to his baserunning. BR Gain is the sum of extra baserunning advances a player made over the league average, minus a penalty for the number of BR Outs he made above the league average. SB Gain estimates how many bases each runner gained or lost his team based on his successful and unsuccessful stolen base attempts.

2017 Baserunning

Player	1st to 3rd		2nd to Home		1st to Home		Bases Taken	Out Adv	Doubled Off	BR Outs	GDP	GDP Opps	BR Gain	SB Gain	Net Gain
	Moved	Chances	Moved	Chances	Moved	Chances									
Abreu,Jose	6	27	12	17	6	12	22	5	2	7	21	138	-9	+3	-6
Adams,Lane	3	7	2	5	1	2	1	2	0	2	3	31	-6	+10	+4
Adams,Matt	1	18	6	11	2	2	7	1	1	2	5	61	-3	0	-3
Adrianza,Ehire	2	6	12	15	2	7	0	1	0	1	0	34	+1	+6	+7
Aguilar,Jesus	3	13	4	7	0	3	6	1	0	1	8	58	-3	0	-3
Ahmed,Nick	7	7	2	5	1	1	2	0	0	0	6	21	+2	-5	-3
Albies,Ozzie	3	11	8	11	1	4	8	0	0	0	3	35	+7	+6	+13
Almonte,Abraham	3	8	6	8	3	5	10	1	0	1	2	39	+10	0	+10
Almora Jr.,Albert	7	13	3	9	1	7	7	3	0	3	8	67	-7	+1	-6
Alonso,Yonder	8	30	4	16	2	12	13	3	1	4	9	90	-11	+2	-9
Altherr,Aaron	10	19	8	12	6	7	7	4	0	4	12	90	-2	-3	-5
Altuve,Jose	24	59	16	26	6	8	24	5	0	5	19	151	+11	+20	+31
Amarista,Alexi	1	9	3	4	2	2	5	2	0	2	5	34	-3	+1	-2
Anderson,Tim	9	24	10	18	2	4	17	3	1	4	13	105	+1	+13	+14
Andrus,Elvis	13	26	23	24	10	16	26	3	1	5	18	147	+21	+5	+26
Aoki,Nori	7	19	6	13	4	8	10	3	3	6	12	59	-16	+6	-10
Arcia,Orlando	6	21	6	10	8	8	15	3	1	4	10	91	+3	0	+3
Arenado,Nolan	13	33	16	19	2	4	18	2	1	3	21	157	+8	-1	+7
Asuaje,Carlos	5	15	4	7	1	3	7	4	1	5	6	63	-10	-2	-12
Avila,Alex	3	15	2	4	0	4	11	2	2	4	10	80	-9	-2	-11
Aybar,Erick	6	12	7	16	2	5	12	2	1	3	5	71	+3	+3	+6
Baez,Javier	7	18	11	15	5	6	18	1	0	1	10	109	+19	+4	+23
Bandy,Jett	1	8	1	4	0	1	5	0	0	0	5	37	0	+1	+1
Barnes,Austin	3	10	4	7	4	7	13	3	1	4	6	47	-1	+2	+1
Barney,Darwin	5	15	5	7	1	3	11	1	1	2	13	65	-3	+3	0
Barnhart,Tucker	1	12	6	15	1	2	7	4	1	5	12	95	-18	+4	-14
Bautista,Jose	13	41	9	15	1	4	13	4	2	6	16	125	-11	0	-11
Beckham,Tim	9	24	13	15	3	8	17	3	4	7	10	89	-3	-4	-7
Bell,Josh	3	30	10	20	3	11	9	5	1	6	15	120	-25	-6	-31
Bellinger,Cody	5	20	8	13	4	10	15	2	0	3	5	111	+8	+4	+12
Belt,Brandon	6	27	13	20	0	1	15	7	0	7	5	82	-7	-1	-8
Beltran,Carlos	2	14	8	16	0	8	13	2	0	2	9	90	-2	0	-2
Beltre,Adrian	1	10	2	4	1	11	11	4	1	5	7	70	-13	+1	-12
Benintendi,Andrew	8	26	9	16	8	14	23	6	3	10	16	132	-12	+10	-2
Betts,Mookie	18	30	21	26	6	10	27	2	1	3	9	125	+34	+20	+54
Blackmon,Charlie	12	53	21	30	6	9	28	3	4	7	4	77	+7	-6	+1
Blanco,Gregor	5	13	7	7	7	8	5	0	0	0	2	40	+13	+13	+26
Blash,Jabari	5	8	2	5	1	2	5	1	0	1	5	39	+2	-3	-1
Bogaerts,Xander	15	39	18	21	7	11	22	4	2	6	17	135	+8	+13	+21
Bonifacio,Jorge	6	15	5	9	2	3	14	2	0	2	8	83	+8	-1	+7
Bour,Justin	3	22	3	13	3	7	5	3	0	3	10	84	-16	+1	-15
Bourjos,Peter	6	18	6	10	0	1	5	0	0	0	2	38	+6	-3	+3
Bradley Jr.,Jackie	10	27	6	6	5	6	13	1	2	3	8	130	+13	+2	+15
Brantley,Michael	4	18	6	6	1	3	15	0	0	0	8	71	+12	+9	+21
Braun,Ryan	4	15	6	8	0	5	16	1	0	1	15	103	+5	+4	+9
Bregman,Alex	10	35	18	23	3	5	21	2	3	5	15	111	+3	+7	+10
Broxton,Keon	9	25	8	10	1	5	11	4	0	4	3	70	+3	+7	+10
Bruce,Jay	5	28	6	16	5	10	13	2	2	4	11	117	-7	-1	-8
Brugman,Jaycob	1	9	2	3	0	1	5	1	0	1	1	33	+1	-3	-2
Bryant,Kris	13	26	18	28	9	13	24	2	0	2	8	129	+28	-3	+25
Butera,Drew	2	9	4	5	2	5	3	0	0	0	0	33	+6	0	+6
Buxton,Byron	11	20	13	16	5	5	15	0	1	1	1	86	+28	+27	+55
Cabrera,Asdrubal	4	34	4	10	0	6	15	6	0	6	19	112	-24	-1	-25
Cabrera,Melky	8	37	7	11	7	14	17	6	2	8	19	138	-17	-3	-20
Cabrera,Miguel	4	32	5	12	0	8	9	5	0	5	15	112	-23	-2	-25
Cain,Lorenzo	12	36	14	24	8	11	30	3	3	6	20	113	+3	+22	+25
Calhoun,Kole	14	35	12	17	3	9	14	6	2	8	10	101	-9	+3	-6
Camargo,Johan	3	11	6	6	1	2	6	2	0	2	5	45	0	0	0
Candelario,Jeimer	0	9	2	2	0	1	3	0	0	0	3	22	-1	0	-1
Cano,Robinson	8	32	9	18	1	10	13	1	1	3	18	148	-9	+1	-8
Carpenter,Matt	11	45	9	18	1	9	19	4	2	6	5	97	-5	0	-5
Carrera,Ezequiel	6	20	2	6	2	3	14	0	0	0	4	50	+12	+8	+20
Carter,Chris	1	6	2	4	0	0	4	2	0	2	5	41	-5	0	-5

367

2017 Baserunning

Player	1st to 3rd Moved	Chances	2nd to Home Moved	Chances	1st to Home Moved	Chances	Bases Taken	Out Adv	Doubled Off	BR Outs	GDP	GDP Opps	BR Gain	SB Gain	Net Gain
Castellanos,Nick	11	25	6	12	3	11	20	3	4	7	12	114	-4	-6	-10
Castillo,Welington	3	21	3	8	2	6	6	5	1	6	10	75	-22	0	-22
Castro,Jason	7	31	7	14	2	5	9	2	2	4	10	86	-10	0	-10
Castro,Starlin	7	24	12	18	4	6	15	1	0	1	9	71	+10	+2	+12
Cervelli,Francisco	5	21	8	11	2	3	2	1	0	1	7	59	-3	-4	-7
Cespedes,Yoenis	7	12	4	8	2	5	14	2	2	4	7	76	+3	-2	+1
Chapman,Matt	11	16	4	4	0	2	11	1	0	1	2	67	+18	-6	+12
Chirinos,Robinson	2	18	3	8	1	2	13	2	1	3	5	54	-2	+1	-1
Chisenhall,Lonnie	7	16	1	5	4	7	10	2	0	2	6	58	+4	-2	+2
Choo,Shin-Soo	6	37	10	19	1	10	24	3	1	4	18	126	-6	+6	0
Conforto,Michael	7	19	6	9	5	10	15	0	2	2	3	63	+12	+2	+14
Contreras,Willson	7	21	4	9	1	3	7	8	0	8	13	79	-26	-3	-29
Cordoba,Allen	2	11	4	4	1	1	3	3	0	3	2	30	-5	-2	-7
Correa,Carlos	10	26	10	21	7	12	13	5	1	6	12	103	-8	0	-8
Cozart,Zack	11	29	8	15	2	8	10	3	1	4	5	72	-3	+3	0
Crawford,Brandon	6	23	6	19	3	6	20	1	1	2	18	136	+1	-7	-6
Cron,C.J.	2	18	5	8	0	3	6	1	0	1	5	79	0	-1	-1
Cruz,Nelson	8	43	8	16	1	8	14	2	0	2	15	140	-5	-1	-6
d'Arnaud,Travis	3	19	10	13	1	2	4	1	0	1	12	65	-6	0	-6
Davidson,Matt	1	15	4	10	1	2	6	4	1	5	12	95	-18	-2	-20
Davis,Chris	5	21	4	9	1	4	12	2	0	2	7	103	+4	-1	+3
Davis,Khris	5	27	11	18	1	7	14	1	3	4	20	129	-13	+4	-9
Davis,Rajai	3	9	8	10	5	7	16	2	0	2	12	61	+6	+15	+21
DeJong,Paul	4	22	3	9	3	6	7	4	2	6	8	111	-14	+1	-13
Delmonico,Nick	2	19	4	7	1	3	5	0	0	0	5	34	-2	+2	0
Descalso,Daniel	2	20	7	8	3	8	3	0	0	0	6	62	-1	+4	+3
DeShields,Delino	11	24	16	18	7	8	21	3	3	6	2	70	+18	+13	+31
Desmond,Ian	7	20	12	15	4	7	13	0	1	1	13	74	+8	+7	+15
Devers,Rafael	6	12	3	9	2	4	11	2	0	2	5	29	+2	+1	+3
Diaz,Aledmys	4	11	4	6	2	4	7	2	0	2	9	53	-3	+2	-1
Diaz,Elias	4	5	2	7	1	2	5	2	0	2	8	41	-5	+1	-4
Diaz,Yandy	0	14	3	6	1	2	8	2	0	2	5	41	-5	+2	-3
Dickerson,Corey	11	35	6	14	4	10	27	3	1	4	11	106	+9	-2	+7
Dietrich,Derek	1	18	9	10	5	5	10	2	0	2	4	85	+7	-2	+5
Difo,Wilmer	11	19	6	9	3	7	10	0	1	1	7	53	+9	+8	+17
Donaldson,Josh	6	18	6	9	5	7	11	1	1	2	5	81	+8	-2	+6
Dozier,Brian	13	37	9	14	5	8	12	5	0	5	11	107	-3	+2	-1
Drury,Brandon	6	13	4	14	3	7	13	2	1	3	9	88	-1	-1	-2
Duda,Lucas	0	18	5	9	1	6	7	4	2	6	9	98	-19	0	-19
Duvall,Adam	4	26	13	21	3	8	10	3	0	3	11	173	+1	-1	0
Dyson,Jarrod	7	17	11	17	5	5	15	1	2	3	3	59	+12	+14	+26
Ellsbury,Jacoby	5	25	14	24	1	4	17	2	0	2	7	89	+7	+16	+23
Encarnacion,Edwin	4	34	4	10	1	15	16	3	0	3	18	121	-16	+2	-14
Engel,Adam	6	10	6	11	1	3	4	1	0	1	1	61	+7	+6	+13
Escobar,Alcides	8	28	15	19	6	7	21	0	1	1	14	125	+20	-10	+10
Escobar,Eduardo	9	21	8	13	3	6	16	4	0	4	5	95	+10	+3	+13
Escobar,Yunel	3	14	7	10	1	4	11	2	0	2	15	63	-7	-7	-14
Espinosa,Danny	6	12	6	11	2	2	2	2	0	2	2	48	+1	-6	-5
Fisher,Derek	1	9	2	3	0	2	5	1	0	1	1	23	0	-3	-3
Flores,Wilmer	4	17	5	9	2	7	8	1	1	2	14	61	-10	-1	-11
Flowers,Tyler	7	16	5	7	3	8	5	0	0	0	6	61	+5	-2	+3
Forsythe,Logan	7	24	7	15	8	10	14	0	0	0	12	74	+8	-1	+7
Fowler,Dexter	9	17	10	12	1	3	19	4	3	7	10	83	0	+1	+1
Franco,Maikel	5	27	6	18	4	11	14	0	0	0	21	125	-5	0	-5
Frazier,Adam	9	21	8	16	3	6	17	1	0	1	9	58	+9	-1	+8
Frazier,Todd	10	33	5	11	2	7	15	3	2	5	10	107	-5	-2	-7
Freeman,Freddie	8	24	15	19	5	10	9	2	0	2	9	108	+7	-2	+5
Freese,David	8	39	2	10	4	6	6	2	2	4	10	88	-16	-2	-18
Gallo,Joey	6	19	7	9	2	7	18	2	0	2	3	99	+18	+3	+21
Galvis,Freddy	11	32	12	17	2	6	26	6	3	9	12	140	+1	+4	+5
Gamel,Ben	14	28	8	13	2	5	18	2	2	4	8	92	+10	+2	+12
Garcia,Adonis	1	8	4	5	4	5	4	2	1	3	9	36	-10	+4	-6
Garcia,Avisail	12	30	11	18	5	7	20	2	1	3	14	105	+9	-1	+8
Garcia,Greg	3	11	6	7	3	4	5	2	0	2	6	58	0	0	0

2017 Baserunning

Player	1st to 3rd		2nd to Home		1st to Home		Bases Taken	Out Adv	Doubled Off	BR Outs	GDP	GDP Opps	BR Gain	SB Gain	Net Gain
	Moved	Chances	Moved	Chances	Moved	Chances									
Garcia,Leury	4	13	7	10	0	0	10	1	0	1	4	55	+8	-2	+6
Gardner,Brett	15	31	9	17	5	11	25	2	3	5	4	91	+16	+13	+29
Gattis,Evan	1	11	7	10	2	6	7	1	0	1	10	64	-3	-2	-5
Gennett,Scooter	7	27	5	15	3	6	22	3	2	5	15	111	-4	-1	-5
Gentry,Craig	2	4	4	4	1	1	6	1	0	1	1	17	+6	-3	+3
Gimenez,Chris	0	9	3	7	0	2	8	0	0	0	3	37	+3	+1	+4
Goins,Ryan	4	15	3	7	1	1	12	1	2	3	14	77	-7	-1	-8
Goldschmidt,Paul	12	27	11	18	6	11	21	1	0	1	14	138	+19	+8	+27
Gomes,Yan	5	16	5	7	4	7	7	1	1	2	9	78	0	0	0
Gomez,Carlos	3	9	7	10	1	1	12	3	1	4	3	62	+3	+3	+6
Gonzalez,Adrian	1	11	2	8	0	0	7	1	0	1	7	44	-5	-2	-7
Gonzalez,Carlos	8	25	9	15	3	9	16	3	0	3	9	105	+5	+3	+8
Gonzalez,Marwin	5	27	6	9	6	12	17	6	2	8	8	99	-10	+2	-8
Goodwin,Brian	1	11	2	9	1	2	14	2	1	3	3	41	-1	+6	+5
Gordon,Alex	7	31	9	15	6	8	12	2	0	2	7	95	+6	-1	+5
Gordon,Dee	16	33	16	20	7	12	25	3	0	3	7	75	+23	+28	+51
Grandal,Yasmani	3	15	3	8	2	8	8	3	1	5	10	87	-15	-2	-17
Granderson,Curtis	4	23	6	15	3	7	14	0	1	1	5	86	+6	+2	+8
Gregorius,Didi	6	29	10	14	4	7	21	3	0	3	7	123	+15	+1	+16
Grichuk,Randal	6	12	3	9	1	5	11	2	0	2	6	94	+3	+4	+7
Grossman,Robbie	9	32	11	17	3	9	15	3	0	3	6	92	+6	+1	+7
Gurriel,Yulieski	6	28	6	19	5	9	22	1	1	2	12	111	+5	-1	+4
Guyer,Brandon	1	14	6	9	1	4	1	1	0	1	4	53	-5	+2	-3
Gyorko,Jedd	4	25	6	13	3	7	11	3	1	4	12	87	-12	+2	-10
Hamilton,Billy	10	22	12	19	3	7	18	3	0	3	5	64	+11	+33	+44
Haniger,Mitch	7	18	9	17	1	7	14	3	0	3	9	93	+2	-3	-1
Hanson,Alen	3	9	7	9	3	5	10	0	1	1	5	42	+8	+5	+13
Hardy,J.J.	5	15	3	6	0	1	9	2	0	2	7	47	-1	-2	-3
Harper,Bryce	12	32	8	18	10	17	15	4	0	4	15	114	-1	-2	-1
Harrison,Josh	13	32	12	14	3	8	7	0	2	3	5	87	+5	+4	+9
Headley,Chase	10	33	8	14	3	9	24	6	1	8	10	123	-2	+5	+3
Healy,Ryon	6	27	9	12	3	4	8	3	0	3	16	104	-8	-2	-10
Hechavarria,Adeiny	2	16	9	11	0	2	11	0	0	0	7	64	+8	+2	+10
Hedges,Austin	4	12	4	11	1	2	10	2	0	3	10	78	-5	+2	-3
Heredia,Guillermo	6	22	7	13	4	4	13	3	0	3	9	74	+1	-9	-8
Hernandez,Cesar	6	31	13	19	10	16	11	4	0	4	8	71	-5	+5	0
Hernandez,Gorkys	7	13	11	14	4	4	7	2	2	4	6	49	0	+4	+4
Hernandez,Kike	5	10	6	7	2	2	7	0	1	1	4	63	+10	+3	+13
Herrera,Odubel	4	18	8	19	3	7	20	4	1	5	13	117	-4	-2	-6
Herrmann,Chris	3	14	5	7	0	2	11	0	1	1	1	47	+10	+5	+15
Heyward,Jason	5	31	8	13	3	3	15	1	1	2	8	82	+4	-4	0
Hicks,Aaron	6	17	7	8	2	5	19	0	4	4	8	84	+8	0	+8
Hicks,John	4	12	2	5	3	4	5	0	0	0	5	44	+4	0	+4
Holliday,Matt	2	20	3	9	0	3	7	1	0	1	14	84	-11	+1	-10
Holt,Brock	3	14	5	7	0	2	7	3	0	3	3	23	-5	0	-5
Hoskins,Rhys	3	12	1	2	2	4	5	0	0	0	2	46	+6	+2	+8
Hosmer,Eric	11	48	13	19	8	11	21	2	2	4	20	139	+1	+4	+5
Hundley,Nick	7	13	4	8	0	2	5	3	0	3	6	60	-4	0	-4
Iannetta,Chris	1	7	5	9	2	8	6	2	1	3	3	54	-5	0	-5
Iglesias,Jose	6	19	8	15	8	10	14	3	0	3	6	82	+8	-1	+7
Inciarte,Ender	12	36	18	21	8	16	20	5	0	5	8	71	+7	+4	+11
Jackson,Austin	5	18	6	8	5	9	12	0	0	0	13	61	+5	+1	+6
Jaso,John	7	15	5	9	0	2	9	0	2	2	5	58	+4	-1	+3
Jay,Jon	7	26	11	15	4	6	26	1	1	2	11	70	+16	+2	+18
Jones,Adam	6	23	11	19	5	7	20	2	0	2	18	111	+5	0	+5
Joseph,Caleb	0	9	3	8	1	2	8	0	0	0	7	46	0	0	0
Joseph,Tommy	1	15	4	12	3	6	5	1	1	2	21	102	-20	+1	-19
Joyce,Matt	7	25	7	14	6	12	15	3	0	3	10	97	+2	+2	+4
Judge,Aaron	12	32	16	24	4	15	25	2	3	5	15	142	+7	+1	+8
Kemp,Matt	7	26	5	6	0	3	3	4	1	5	25	94	-30	-4	-34
Kendrick,Howie	5	18	9	15	0	3	8	1	1	2	8	56	-4	+2	-2
Kepler,Max	5	23	8	15	3	4	19	1	1	2	5	94	+13	+4	+17
Kiermaier,Kevin	8	24	12	14	2	4	17	0	1	1	3	79	+21	+2	+23

2017 Baserunning

	1st to 3rd		2nd to Home		1st to Home		Bases Taken	Out Adv	Doubled Off	BR Outs	GDP	GDP Opps	BR Gain	SB Gain	Net Gain
Player	Moved	Chances	Moved	Chances	Moved	Chances									
Kim,Hyun Soo	2	9	2	6	3	5	4	0	0	0	3	44	+3	0	+3
Kinsler,Ian	7	21	19	24	2	6	14	4	2	6	9	67	-5	+4	-1
Kipnis,Jason	6	14	7	9	1	5	8	0	0	0	0	56	+14	+2	+16
Kivlehan,Patrick	2	10	1	4	1	2	8	0	0	0	2	36	+6	-3	+3
Knapp,Andrew	4	13	4	9	1	2	8	1	1	2	5	37	-2	+1	-1
La Stella,Tommy	4	14	2	6	1	1	4	0	1	1	3	36	0	0	0
Lagares,Juan	5	12	7	10	5	6	7	1	0	1	6	52	+7	+1	+8
Lamb,Jake	7	27	14	20	4	10	12	2	1	3	15	127	-2	-2	-4
LeMahieu,DJ	12	39	12	21	10	20	24	3	0	3	24	139	+2	-4	-2
Leon,Sandy	2	10	2	8	0	3	8	4	1	5	5	55	-13	0	-13
Lind,Adam	3	13	1	3	2	5	7	0	1	1	6	55	0	+1	+1
Lindor,Francisco	14	27	12	24	6	11	25	2	0	3	11	104	+16	+9	+25
Longoria,Evan	9	23	8	14	3	7	12	1	1	3	18	145	-2	+4	+2
Lowrie,Jed	1	25	8	20	4	14	22	1	1	2	10	109	0	-2	-2
Lucroy,Jonathan	1	14	6	9	3	6	11	2	1	3	16	79	-12	+1	-11
Machado,Dixon	1	13	1	3	1	4	5	1	0	1	6	38	-6	+1	-5
Machado,Manny	8	35	11	22	5	5	20	7	0	7	17	146	-8	+1	-7
Mahtook,Mikie	3	13	5	10	6	9	11	2	1	3	4	73	+3	+6	+9
Maldonado,Martin	3	21	5	9	3	6	7	1	0	1	12	76	-6	-4	-10
Mancini,Trey	8	24	12	17	3	9	17	1	1	2	12	107	+8	+1	+9
Margot,Manuel	10	27	5	9	0	2	12	4	0	4	6	65	-2	+3	+1
Marisnick,Jake	2	6	6	11	3	3	13	1	1	2	5	43	+6	+1	+7
Markakis,Nick	10	37	15	22	3	6	11	1	0	1	16	126	+2	-4	-2
Marrero,Deven	1	9	10	14	1	3	3	0	0	0	8	40	-2	+5	+3
Marte,Ketel	1	5	4	5	3	7	6	0	1	1	3	42	+3	+1	+4
Marte,Starling	8	20	9	11	1	2	10	2	1	3	5	45	+3	+13	+16
Martin,Russell	5	16	8	13	1	6	13	1	0	1	13	78	+2	-3	-1
Martinez,J.D.	5	17	9	15	3	8	9	2	0	2	23	102	-13	+4	-9
Martinez,Jose	6	20	6	11	2	4	8	2	0	2	9	66	-2	+4	+2
Martinez,Victor	1	20	2	10	0	6	13	1	0	1	15	94	-9	0	-9
Mathis,Jeff	0	2	3	4	0	1	3	1	0	1	6	45	-3	+1	-2
Mauer,Joe	8	43	10	22	4	16	19	1	1	2	17	115	-7	0	-7
Maxwell,Bruce	2	10	0	6	0	5	4	0	0	0	10	47	-9	0	-9
Maybin,Cameron	5	13	11	16	4	6	17	0	0	0	12	75	+14	+17	+31
Mazara,Nomar	8	28	7	11	3	8	11	4	0	4	12	124	-4	-2	-6
McCann,Brian	2	25	4	7	0	7	10	3	1	4	9	86	-13	+1	-12
McCann,James	4	22	7	11	1	1	5	2	0	2	8	82	-4	+1	-3
McCutchen,Andrew	11	41	10	22	6	12	16	2	0	2	10	122	+5	+1	+6
Mercer,Jordy	5	23	9	16	1	3	14	2	0	2	16	111	-3	-8	-11
Merrifield,Whit	6	24	9	16	6	9	24	2	3	5	13	98	+2	+18	+20
Mesoraco,Devin	2	5	0	4	1	2	2	0	0	0	4	33	-1	+1	0
Miller,Brad	2	23	8	13	0	4	17	1	0	1	5	83	+9	-1	+8
Molina,Yadier	2	25	6	11	0	11	14	0	0	0	14	101	-3	+1	-2
Moncada,Yoan	5	14	4	7	0	3	8	0	0	0	0	39	+10	-1	+9
Montero,Miguel	1	8	3	4	2	8	6	0	0	0	6	36	0	+1	+1
Moore,Tyler	3	11	2	5	0	0	2	0	0	0	7	41	-3	0	-3
Morales,Kendrys	4	28	4	16	4	11	6	4	1	5	22	123	-32	0	-32
Moreland,Mitch	6	27	10	15	1	8	15	3	1	4	14	108	-7	-2	-9
Morrison,Logan	6	25	5	11	2	4	13	0	1	1	12	113	+4	+2	+6
Moss,Brandon	3	13	1	6	1	6	8	0	0	0	7	84	+3	+2	+5
Motter,Taylor	2	8	4	8	0	3	6	0	1	1	9	73	-2	+10	+8
Moustakas,Mike	1	21	5	12	0	12	16	3	0	3	18	112	-15	0	-15
Murphy,Daniel	11	34	11	18	5	11	12	3	0	4	16	127	-5	+2	-3
Myers,Wil	9	27	11	18	5	11	17	3	0	4	15	126	+1	+8	+9
Napoli,Mike	6	16	5	9	0	7	15	2	0	2	11	81	+2	-3	-1
Narvaez,Omar	1	20	5	8	1	4	6	0	1	1	8	47	-8	0	-8
Nava,Daniel	4	12	3	5	0	2	7	4	0	4	2	39	-5	+1	-4
Nimmo,Brandon	2	7	5	7	1	2	5	1	0	1	3	45	+3	+2	+5
Norris,Derek	0	6	3	5	1	1	3	2	0	2	5	31	-7	+1	-6
Nunez,Eduardo	6	20	6	12	2	4	15	3	0	4	11	95	-2	+10	+8
Odor,Rougned	4	11	8	12	5	7	14	2	0	2	13	110	+7	+3	+10
Olson,Matt	2	6	0	0	0	1	7	3	0	3	6	51	-4	0	-4
Osuna,Jose	3	11	6	9	3	5	4	1	0	1	10	48	-4	0	-4
Owings,Chris	9	19	4	7	1	3	10	3	0	3	3	65	+5	+8	+13

2017 Baserunning

Player	1st to 3rd Moved	Chances	2nd to Home Moved	Chances	1st to Home Moved	Chances	Bases Taken	Out Adv	Doubled Off	BR Outs	GDP	GDP Opps	BR Gain	SB Gain	Net Gain
Ozuna,Marcell	12	37	4	15	4	12	16	4	2	6	18	143	-15	-5	-20
Panik,Joe	10	31	9	14	3	11	26	4	1	5	10	87	+6	+2	+8
Parker,Jarrett	6	10	0	0	0	0	5	0	1	1	2	41	+6	0	+6
Parra,Gerardo	6	13	8	12	4	9	14	3	0	3	13	88	+1	-8	-7
Pearce,Steve	2	11	4	9	2	5	6	3	0	3	11	74	-11	0	-11
Pederson,Joc	5	11	5	12	1	2	10	1	1	2	7	60	+1	-2	-1
Pedroia,Dustin	3	31	6	11	0	12	12	5	0	5	11	89	-20	-2	-22
Pence,Hunter	6	27	11	14	4	9	18	0	1	2	8	117	+14	-4	+10
Pennington,Cliff	3	20	2	4	2	3	6	0	0	0	2	35	+4	+1	+5
Peralta,David	8	29	13	18	2	9	25	2	1	3	7	92	+14	0	+14
Peraza,Jose	9	20	11	18	4	6	14	1	0	1	7	76	+13	+7	+20
Perez,Hernan	6	25	5	6	4	7	12	1	0	1	8	88	+9	+5	+14
Perez,Roberto	0	11	1	4	0	6	1	0	0	0	4	53	-6	-2	-8
Perez,Salvador	5	13	8	13	1	3	6	0	0	0	23	131	-5	+1	-4
Peterson,Jace	2	9	5	5	0	1	5	0	0	0	4	43	+5	+3	+8
Pham,Tommy	15	30	10	16	8	11	17	2	0	2	18	121	+11	+11	+22
Phillips,Brandon	10	26	18	21	1	7	18	3	3	6	21	125	-6	-5	-11
Pillar,Kevin	9	28	9	15	3	8	15	2	1	3	13	117	+2	+3	+5
Pina,Manny	3	14	5	13	0	1	8	1	0	1	8	62	-3	+2	-1
Pinder,Chad	3	10	4	7	4	12	7	4	1	5	7	58	-12	0	-12
Pirela,Jose	7	13	8	13	4	5	13	2	1	3	8	64	+6	-2	+4
Piscotty,Stephen	9	25	9	12	0	1	9	4	1	6	11	76	-12	-9	-21
Plouffe,Trevor	2	10	2	4	2	4	13	2	0	2	12	59	-1	-3	-4
Polanco,Gregory	4	14	5	8	2	2	6	3	1	4	5	70	-5	+6	+1
Polanco,Jorge	3	21	10	15	2	8	15	2	1	3	7	117	+4	+3	+7
Pollock,A.J.	6	18	9	12	3	6	13	2	0	2	8	96	+9	+8	+17
Posey,Buster	9	31	10	21	3	9	21	2	0	2	17	105	+1	+4	+5
Powell,Boog	5	9	1	4	2	4	6	0	0	0	2	29	+7	-2	+5
Presley,Alex	8	23	4	9	1	3	7	3	0	3	5	49	-4	+5	+1
Puig,Yasiel	5	21	5	12	2	4	12	6	1	7	21	109	-26	+3	-23
Pujols,Albert	5	27	5	11	1	5	13	4	1	5	26	136	-22	+3	-19
Ramirez,Hanley	9	25	5	12	2	6	18	6	2	8	15	95	-16	-5	-21
Ramirez,Jose	6	27	13	19	7	10	24	7	1	9	13	137	-4	+7	+3
Ramos,Wilson	2	10	3	5	1	4	4	1	0	1	11	44	-8	0	-8
Realmuto,J.T.	14	30	6	15	3	8	18	1	3	4	13	123	+4	+4	+8
Reddick,Josh	10	25	7	14	3	6	15	1	2	3	9	113	+6	+1	+7
Rendon,Anthony	12	40	10	13	5	8	18	3	1	4	7	106	+9	+3	+12
Renfroe,Hunter	4	17	1	5	2	5	5	1	1	2	4	90	-1	+3	+2
Revere,Ben	7	14	5	6	1	3	18	0	0	0	7	52	+18	+9	+27
Reyes,Jose	3	21	11	16	3	6	16	3	0	3	3	101	+10	+12	+22
Reynolds,Mark	4	39	13	22	2	8	19	2	1	3	12	113	-3	0	-3
Reynolds,Matt	4	6	0	1	1	3	5	1	0	1	2	19	+2	-2	0
Rickard,Joey	5	16	5	7	2	4	9	0	1	1	6	60	+6	+6	+12
Riddle,J.T.	1	8	5	9	0	2	4	1	0	1	6	54	-3	-4	-7
Rivera,Rene	0	7	1	6	0	5	3	0	0	0	4	37	-5	-2	-7
Rivera,T.J.	1	13	4	7	1	3	4	0	0	0	4	44	0	+1	+1
Rizzo,Anthony	8	35	16	22	1	7	17	4	3	7	21	178	-12	+2	-10
Robertson,Daniel	4	11	4	5	0	3	5	2	1	3	5	47	-5	-1	-6
Rojas,Miguel	6	14	6	11	4	6	6	2	0	2	6	52	0	0	0
Romine,Andrew	5	25	13	17	1	1	9	2	1	4	7	53	-6	-2	-8
Romine,Austin	5	17	2	5	0	3	6	0	0	0	7	51	+1	0	+1
Rosales,Adam	4	13	3	7	0	2	3	0	1	1	6	65	-3	-3	-6
Rosario,Eddie	11	21	11	17	4	7	18	3	1	4	10	112	+11	-7	+4
Rupp,Cameron	2	14	2	3	0	5	6	3	2	5	6	49	-15	+1	-14
Russell,Addison	4	14	7	11	2	4	8	0	0	0	5	73	+9	0	+9
Saladino,Tyler	4	20	4	7	3	5	6	0	0	0	5	43	+3	-3	0
Sanchez,Gary	3	23	8	15	1	5	15	5	1	7	9	126	-11	0	-11
Sanchez,Yolmer	5	25	8	12	4	5	18	3	1	4	10	91	+2	-10	-8
Sandoval,Pablo	1	8	2	6	1	3	4	0	1	1	11	54	-9	-2	-11
Sano,Miguel	9	22	10	20	4	12	9	5	0	5	12	105	-10	0	-10
Santana,Carlos	7	41	14	23	3	6	18	3	0	4	11	132	0	+3	+3
Santana,Domingo	12	27	8	15	8	10	20	5	1	6	12	103	+3	+7	+10
Saunders,Michael	2	8	7	7	2	2	7	0	0	0	2	49	+13	-2	+11
Schebler,Scott	5	26	4	8	3	6	13	1	0	1	7	103	+8	-1	+7

2017 Baserunning

Player	1st to 3rd Moved	Chances	2nd to Home Moved	Chances	1st to Home Moved	Chances	Bases Taken	Out Adv	Doubled Off	BR Outs	GDP	GDP Opps	BR Gain	SB Gain	Net Gain
Schoop,Jonathan	10	29	11	17	6	9	20	5	0	5	20	140	0	+1	+1
Schwarber,Kyle	7	20	3	6	2	6	8	1	2	3	6	74	-2	-1	-3
Seager,Corey	7	32	9	18	9	16	29	0	1	1	14	119	+18	0	+18
Seager,Kyle	9	30	11	19	3	8	18	3	3	6	6	129	+3	0	+3
Segura,Jean	8	27	14	18	2	5	24	2	5	8	14	71	-8	+6	-2
Semien,Marcus	4	12	10	17	4	6	16	1	0	1	3	69	+16	+10	+26
Shaw,Travis	4	28	9	16	1	8	27	5	1	6	20	110	-10	+10	0
Simmons,Andrelton	8	18	11	12	2	10	20	2	0	2	20	130	+7	+7	+14
Smith,Kevan	2	17	4	8	0	3	3	1	0	1	9	52	-10	0	-10
Smith,Mallex	9	16	2	6	2	3	13	3	0	3	2	51	+9	+6	+15
Smith,Seth	3	25	3	10	1	3	8	1	0	1	7	54	-6	+2	-4
Smoak,Justin	5	25	7	16	3	13	10	1	0	1	17	133	-7	-2	-9
Sogard,Eric	2	11	6	12	2	6	11	1	1	2	7	34	-4	-3	-7
Solarte,Yangervis	7	16	2	9	2	5	14	1	1	2	18	86	-5	+3	-2
Souza Jr.,Steven	12	38	6	14	4	8	20	1	0	1	9	118	+15	+8	+23
Span,Denard	5	28	10	24	4	8	27	4	1	5	11	66	-3	-2	-5
Spangenberg,Cory	9	25	7	12	5	7	13	3	1	4	2	86	+9	+5	+14
Springer,George	13	42	10	24	7	13	24	4	4	8	11	77	-9	-9	-18
Stanton,Giancarlo	4	32	13	26	2	11	19	5	0	5	13	130	-10	-2	-12
Story,Trevor	13	27	7	10	4	4	13	1	2	3	12	101	+8	+3	+11
Suarez,Eugenio	8	38	10	17	4	7	18	3	2	5	16	121	-7	-6	-13
Sucre,Jesus	1	8	4	5	0	0	2	0	0	0	6	36	-2	+2	0
Suzuki,Ichiro	1	14	4	4	1	2	2	1	0	1	2	40	-2	-1	-3
Suzuki,Kurt	4	18	3	7	0	2	5	0	0	0	5	56	+1	0	+1
Swanson,Dansby	11	32	20	27	2	2	5	3	3	6	7	106	-6	-3	-9
Szczur,Matt	5	14	6	8	1	1	10	2	0	2	2	47	+8	-4	+4
Tapia,Raimel	4	10	3	5	2	2	10	0	2	2	3	29	+5	+1	+6
Taylor,Chris	11	30	3	12	5	6	27	2	2	4	2	81	+18	+9	+27
Taylor,Michael	6	14	12	17	0	1	0	0	0	0	3	80	+6	+3	+9
Thames,Eric	1	18	3	9	7	13	8	2	0	2	6	88	-4	0	-4
Tomas,Yasmany	1	7	3	5	1	2	1	0	0	0	2	32	0	0	0
Tomlinson,Kelby	5	13	8	11	1	3	7	0	1	1	8	41	+1	+7	+8
Torreyes,Ronald	6	17	9	12	1	4	8	4	1	5	9	69	-9	+2	-7
Travis,Devon	3	9	2	4	0	1	9	0	0	0	5	35	+6	0	+6
Trout,Mike	13	28	11	17	8	10	19	2	3	5	8	94	+11	+14	+25
Trumbo,Mark	11	34	13	20	5	12	13	2	1	3	13	94	-1	+1	0
Tulowitzki,Troy	3	9	0	4	0	2	5	1	2	3	10	60	-12	-2	-14
Turner,Justin	9	30	7	11	5	14	15	2	0	2	12	133	+6	+5	+11
Turner,Trea	3	21	10	19	3	5	15	1	1	2	4	59	+4	+30	+34
Upton,Justin	10	29	19	24	3	5	14	3	1	4	9	125	+9	+4	+13
Urshela,Giovanny	1	6	2	2	0	2	3	1	0	1	6	33	-4	0	-4
Utley,Chase	6	16	7	14	1	3	9	2	2	4	3	53	-3	+4	+1
Valbuena,Luis	2	14	0	6	0	3	7	0	0	1	6	72	-3	-4	-7
Valencia,Danny	5	24	6	10	1	6	15	2	0	2	16	97	-4	-2	-6
Vargas,Kennys	5	18	4	8	2	2	6	1	1	2	10	54	-6	0	-6
Vazquez,Christian	7	19	7	11	1	3	10	2	1	3	14	73	-6	+3	-3
Villar,Jonathan	3	16	5	8	5	7	11	0	2	2	4	58	+5	+7	+12
Vogt,Stephen	3	12	2	8	0	3	5	3	0	3	2	55	-6	-2	-8
Votto,Joey	4	49	4	22	1	12	13	5	2	7	16	158	-37	+3	-34
Walker,Neil	5	16	7	12	3	13	14	1	1	2	9	84	+2	-4	-2
Werth,Jayson	4	15	5	6	2	5	2	2	0	2	4	49	-4	-2	-6
Wieters,Matt	3	17	1	11	1	10	5	4	0	4	14	99	-24	+1	-23
Williams,Nick	4	17	1	4	5	7	8	4	0	4	8	81	-6	-3	-9
Wolters,Tony	4	11	2	5	2	5	7	1	0	1	9	41	-3	-2	-5
Wong,Kolten	12	24	8	11	1	4	12	3	2	5	4	80	+4	+4	+8
Yelich,Christian	16	43	15	17	6	12	23	1	1	2	13	153	+24	+12	+36
Young,Chris	2	7	3	7	3	4	9	1	0	1	4	54	+6	-1	+5
Young Jr.,Eric	3	7	3	6	1	2	2	0	1	1	0	23	+1	+6	+7
Zimmer,Bradley	8	16	5	10	1	4	19	1	0	1	5	71	+18	+16	+34
Zimmerman,Ryan	9	30	16	21	6	9	7	3	0	3	16	117	-3	+1	-2
Zobrist,Ben	8	19	3	10	3	8	11	1	1	2	13	91	-3	-2	-5
Zunino,Mike	2	25	4	14	0	0	10	1	1	2	8	86	-7	+1	-6

Career Baserunning

Players with 1000 Career Games
(Data goes back to 2002)

Player	1st to 3rd		2nd to Home		1st to Home		Bases Taken	Out Adv	Doubled Off	BR Outs	GDP	GDP Opps	BR Gain	SB Gain	Net Gain
	Moved	Chances	Moved	Chances	Moved	Chances									
Andrus, Elvis	163	314	143	185	59	89	227	27	21	49	132	1037	+148	+80	+228
Aybar, Erick	114	241	133	185	35	60	205	42	20	64	107	1047	+62	+31	+93
Bautista, Jose	116	333	114	182	56	107	168	35	22	57	168	1319	-31	+8	-23
Beltran, Carlos	148	463	169	276	64	129	244	25	15	42	165	1793	+120	+158	+278
Beltre, Adrian	145	465	160	268	64	148	244	46	6	52	236	1926	+13	+24	+37
Braun, Ryan	98	301	123	178	54	91	181	30	13	43	151	1304	+47	+85	+132
Bruce, Jay	64	249	82	152	33	68	127	26	8	34	90	1141	+17	-12	+5
Cabrera, Asdrubal	89	285	110	172	36	83	182	49	8	61	138	1142	-33	+22	-11
Cabrera, Melky	105	355	115	194	51	109	206	40	16	58	158	1297	-20	+26	+6
Cabrera, Miguel	136	616	178	327	48	149	251	49	14	65	294	1954	-159	-4	-163
Cano, Robinson	117	411	182	291	44	105	231	41	23	65	252	1812	-63	-25	-88
Castro, Starlin	55	225	86	127	31	65	117	22	10	32	130	863	-44	-9	-53
Choo, Shin-Soo	89	332	124	193	40	87	202	26	18	44	84	943	+56	+28	+84
Cruz, Nelson	52	270	78	135	14	68	137	28	12	40	110	1062	-56	+13	-43
Davis, Chris	50	237	75	135	26	63	99	18	8	28	51	851	+8	-5	+3
Davis, Rajai	69	166	90	131	43	54	169	13	7	20	77	729	+135	+194	+329
Desmond, Ian	79	205	85	136	33	50	152	18	9	28	103	893	+68	+64	+132
Drew, Stephen	59	227	78	144	22	71	128	32	11	44	50	840	-9	+3	-6
Ellsbury, Jacoby	80	272	122	210	27	61	193	28	7	36	83	878	+63	+201	+264
Encarnacion, Edwin	82	321	100	163	37	106	144	28	9	37	164	1354	-39	+32	-7
Escobar, Alcides	85	239	119	173	43	63	145	15	13	28	96	880	+78	+82	+160
Escobar, Yunel	110	365	128	183	34	88	153	37	19	57	198	1057	-119	-30	-149
Ethier, Andre	67	340	125	181	35	74	112	20	9	30	104	1132	+2	-27	-25
Fowler, Dexter	146	248	103	156	33	55	181	39	26	66	49	670	+69	+14	+83
Freeman, Freddie	51	218	87	138	21	69	120	17	5	22	82	914	+25	-3	+22
Gardner, Brett	97	240	98	154	38	64	187	18	16	34	43	761	+137	+127	+264
Gomez, Carlos	65	173	108	142	26	39	110	35	23	58	67	802	-25	+112	+87
Gonzalez, Adrian	70	411	96	233	43	139	171	36	16	53	202	1602	-168	-8	-176
Gonzalez, Carlos	57	196	107	164	45	80	147	21	6	27	85	947	+75	+61	+136
Gordon, Alex	96	326	128	196	44	81	162	17	9	26	90	999	+90	+16	+106
Granderson, Curtis	117	385	127	228	70	116	198	19	18	37	58	1230	+141	+59	+200
Hardy, J.J.	74	287	94	171	30	88	142	21	9	31	156	1165	-35	-10	-45
Headley, Chase	68	297	103	186	29	69	174	29	10	42	110	1081	-5	+35	+30
Heyward, Jason	86	246	103	150	41	63	129	21	7	28	67	858	+84	+31	+115
Hill, Aaron	81	304	108	170	37	79	160	19	8	28	134	1215	+44	+4	+48
Holliday, Matt	144	447	185	281	64	124	203	44	14	58	220	1678	-12	+34	+22
Hosmer, Eric	57	238	98	149	39	62	116	21	8	31	104	831	-9	+22	+13
Iannetta, Chris	33	172	46	100	16	48	89	14	6	20	61	696	-14	-9	-23
Jones, Adam	92	287	105	160	60	93	169	20	10	31	154	1225	+57	+22	+79
Joyce, Matt	57	179	73	109	27	51	95	13	8	21	65	722	+41	-8	+33
Kemp, Matt	109	307	132	191	41	73	153	43	23	67	163	1320	-55	+57	+2
Kendrick, Howie	124	295	119	194	48	88	169	28	17	47	172	1081	-10	+33	+23
Kinsler, Ian	147	349	195	268	58	108	241	27	22	49	141	1178	+131	+99	+230
Lind, Adam	65	213	60	127	26	76	97	22	7	31	117	962	-55	-3	-58
Longoria, Evan	73	275	109	174	31	78	149	16	12	29	148	1239	+8	+21	+29
Markakis, Nick	118	494	164	267	47	124	198	25	8	34	180	1415	-6	+3	-3
Martin, Russell	84	328	118	191	41	83	158	28	14	43	182	1177	-61	+4	-57
Martinez, Victor	59	436	102	234	23	138	188	37	8	46	245	1625	-205	-7	-212
Mauer, Joe	129	426	153	239	57	132	235	17	13	32	199	1481	+70	+16	+86
McCann, Brian	48	319	45	142	16	101	111	32	11	44	163	1327	-183	+9	-174
McCutchen, Andrew	89	335	126	190	45	87	137	16	10	26	81	1007	+59	+37	+96
Molina, Yadier	60	336	79	181	18	79	141	28	10	40	225	1298	-182	-12	-194
Montero, Miguel	37	226	65	120	28	73	99	27	9	36	106	801	-92	-13	-105
Morales, Kendrys	57	249	53	100	14	70	103	28	4	33	149	864	-115	-20	-135
Moss, Brandon	37	157	43	90	22	53	86	11	2	13	54	708	+31	-11	+20
Murphy, Daniel	79	238	85	126	44	77	125	21	8	30	106	936	+30	+16	+46
Napoli, Mike	78	277	92	148	24	77	130	31	7	39	114	1057	-22	-9	-31
Parra, Gerardo	58	189	101	144	26	52	133	36	6	43	97	799	-12	-17	-29
Pedroia, Dustin	92	367	136	216	51	145	191	45	15	62	152	1244	-75	+46	-29
Pence, Hunter	104	336	116	177	69	98	190	20	13	35	146	1239	+78	+3	+81
Peralta, Jhonny	66	356	115	221	35	115	166	38	17	55	200	1492	-147	-37	-184

Career Baserunning
Players with 1000 Career Games
(Data goes back to 2002)

Player	1st to 3rd Moved	1st to 3rd Chances	2nd to Home Moved	2nd to Home Chances	1st to Home Moved	1st to Home Chances	Bases Taken	Out Adv	Doubled Off	BR Outs	GDP	GDP Opps	BR Gain	SB Gain	Net Gain
Phillips, Brandon	142	361	152	218	48	86	249	53	20	75	223	1484	-14	+41	+27
Posey, Buster	46	227	68	137	28	77	136	13	4	17	118	843	-12	+6	-6
Prado, Martin	110	299	111	172	35	85	169	30	13	43	156	994	-12	-15	-27
Pujols, Albert	180	559	207	301	58	153	275	73	19	95	341	2393	-121	+33	-88
Ramirez, Hanley	111	336	151	233	50	90	194	56	16	74	126	1197	-29	+93	+64
Rasmus, Colby	70	175	76	105	31	46	94	12	14	26	44	785	+79	+1	+80
Reyes, Jose	130	377	187	278	49	86	288	62	20	82	77	1073	+91	+262	+353
Reynolds, Mark	57	250	83	149	24	81	143	19	12	31	106	738	-66	+5	-61
Ruiz, Carlos	45	172	73	119	14	44	89	16	14	32	106	738	-66	+5	-61
Sandoval, Pablo	40	230	63	116	15	56	118	24	7	31	127	884	-73	-15	-88
Santana, Carlos	62	253	79	139	28	82	121	27	7	35	108	908	-47	+6	-41
Seager, Kyle	66	179	56	105	17	41	116	25	7	33	74	770	+8	-1	+7
Smith, Seth	60	221	73	127	38	59	104	21	7	30	75	716	-1	+8	+7
Span, Denard	99	280	126	211	39	73	225	26	22	49	76	699	+68	+66	+134
Suzuki, Ichiro	169	649	225	356	73	145	323	35	18	54	89	1481	+169	+247	+416
Suzuki, Kurt	62	239	81	157	25	60	102	15	2	18	118	960	-11	-1	-12
Tulowitzki, Troy	101	310	107	177	25	67	165	34	17	52	145	1231	-36	-7	-43
Upton, Justin	106	305	130	188	57	94	147	19	16	35	107	1231	+83	+32	+115
Utley, Chase	170	389	161	225	61	103	216	33	18	51	90	1471	+190	+109	+299
Votto, Joey	95	392	108	201	33	117	163	43	20	64	117	1215	-104	+14	-90
Walker, Neil	63	213	70	113	31	71	110	12	11	23	86	790	+18	-15	+3
Weeks Jr., Rickie	87	251	121	170	41	74	151	34	25	59	77	777	-4	+68	+64
Werth, Jayson	109	351	117	183	43	85	169	26	5	32	99	1172	+86	+86	+172
Wieters, Matt	25	181	44	107	10	52	63	15	2	17	93	701	-86	+4	-82
Wright, David	109	348	123	188	53	121	182	33	17	53	152	1425	+7	+66	+73
Young, Chris	48	190	91	140	46	69	124	20	11	31	59	942	+64	+48	+112
Zimmerman, Ryan	97	319	132	200	53	107	169	25	6	31	189	1402	+27	+12	+39
Zobrist, Ben	114	304	103	176	48	99	199	20	11	31	110	1143	+110	+23	+133

2002-2017 MLB Averages

1st to 3rd	2nd to Home	1st to Home
28%	59%	44%

2017 Team Baserunning

Team	1st to 3rd Moved	1st to 3rd Chances	2nd to Home Moved	2nd to Home Chances	1st to Home Moved	1st to Home Chances	Bases Taken	Out Adv	Doubled Off	BR Outs	GDP	GDP Opps	BR Gain	SB Gain	Net Gain
Arizona D-Backs	81	254	106	165	42	95	151	18	7	25	106	1129	+63	+43	+106
Cleveland Indians	78	302	99	166	41	103	192	27	2	32	125	1199	+41	+42	+83
Minnesota Twins	93	311	124	202	39	92	167	28	8	36	105	1185	+43	+39	+82
Tampa Bay Rays	90	308	93	148	21	57	174	19	11	31	115	1166	+52	+20	+72
New York Yankees	87	308	111	187	29	85	210	34	16	52	119	1283	+16	+46	+62
Los Angeles Angels	83	271	97	151	29	73	168	25	8	34	141	1095	+9	+48	+57
Texas Rangers	67	233	103	147	38	90	196	36	12	49	110	1101	+29	+25	+54
Los Angeles Dodgers	75	261	74	149	46	94	187	23	12	37	119	1137	+25	+21	+46
Colorado Rockies	91	308	117	177	49	94	192	20	12	32	143	1170	+55	-9	+46
Milwaukee Brewers	60	256	73	136	38	82	161	27	6	33	115	1042	-3	+46	+43
Kansas City Royals	69	285	93	155	46	85	169	17	10	27	159	1169	+10	+29	+39
San Diego Padres	82	239	72	133	29	56	138	28	7	37	98	1047	+14	+23	+37
Washington Nationals	89	292	104	182	44	97	133	26	9	36	116	1123	-13	+48	+35
Boston Red Sox	98	306	115	182	37	91	199	41	13	56	141	1211	-14	+44	+30
Chicago Cubs	90	284	101	173	37	82	174	28	10	38	131	1221	+22	0	+22
San Francisco Giants	87	290	106	187	31	73	185	26	10	37	136	1124	+14	+8	+22
Miami Marlins	85	309	100	175	37	82	145	27	10	37	119	1164	-12	+31	+19
Cincinnati Reds	71	292	81	176	28	70	146	27	8	35	115	1184	-30	+42	+12
Oakland Athletics	62	236	75	143	33	98	171	25	7	33	129	1128	-2	+13	+11
Atlanta Braves	85	303	141	190	34	75	119	23	9	32	136	1141	-8	+15	+7
Seattle Mariners	83	306	99	181	23	71	177	22	17	41	131	1181	-16	+19	+3
Chicago White Sox	76	296	93	152	34	69	165	28	12	40	124	1101	-6	+9	+3
Baltimore Orioles	75	294	91	166	37	79	168	31	6	37	138	1131	-16	+6	-10
St Louis Cardinals	93	300	92	154	34	86	164	33	14	48	139	1221	-29	+19	-10
Houston Astros	95	333	110	203	47	99	202	37	17	54	139	1164	-28	+14	-14
New York Mets	60	259	86	150	32	88	150	26	13	39	118	1125	-31	+12	-19
Pittsburgh Pirates	94	309	99	180	34	72	126	24	9	34	120	1100	-22	-5	-27
Toronto Blue Jays	72	260	63	130	28	74	150	21	12	33	153	1155	-41	+5	-36
Philadelphia Phillies	68	276	88	165	41	86	150	38	13	51	128	1177	-65	+9	-56
Detroit Tigers	68	294	101	169	33	85	146	33	11	45	127	1138	-58	-3	-61
MLB Totals	2407	8575	2907	4974	1071	2483	4975	818	311	1151	3795	34512			

Stolen Base Attempt Times

Lindsay Zeck

Billy Hamilton, for the third season in a row, finished with not the fastest, but the second-fastest average stolen base time of all players with at least six attempts. After losing to Rico Noel in 2015 and Terrance Gore in 2016, this season he finished 0.03 seconds slower than Mallex Smith of the Tampa Bay Rays. In his sophomore campaign, Smith finished with an average stolen base time of 3.44 seconds, 0.10 seconds faster than his eighth-place finish his rookie season. In third place this season was rookie Bradley Zimmer of the Indians. He finished with an average time just 0.04 seconds slower than Hamilton. Both Zimmer and Smith are likely to give Hamilton a speedy run for his money for seasons to come. Not only did Hamilton finish with the second-fastest average stolen base attempt time, but he also—for the fourth season in a row—finished second in MLB in number of stolen bases with 59 in 2017. Dee Gordon swiped 60 bags, beating him out for the third time in the last four seasons.

While the three players with the greatest number of stolen bases in 2017—Dee Gordon, Billy Hamilton, and Trea Turner—and the two players who finished with the highest stolen base success rates of qualified players—Byron Buxton and Bradley Zimmer—all finished within the top 11 of stolen base attempt times, speed isn't everything. Cameron Maybin stole 33 bases for the Astros and Angels, the fifth most in the league, with an average stolen base time of 3.67 seconds—tied for 53rd overall. Additionally, six players who finished in the bottom quarter of average stolen base times of players with at least six timed attempts—Jean Segura, Andrew Benintendi, Paul Goldschmidt, Yasiel Puig, Domingo Santana, and Gregor Blanco—all stole at least 15 bags.

Hamilton led the Reds to the fastest average time of all teams at 3.60 seconds, while the Blue Jays finished with the slowest average time of 3.79 seconds. Their fastest players were Ezequiel Carrera and Kevin Pillar, ranked tied for 31st and 38th overall, respectively, averaging a combined 3.62 seconds in their timed attempts. Their teammates, in 15 combined timed attempts, finished with an average time of 3.96 seconds!

Stolen Base Times 2B Only

Runner	Timed Attempts	Average
Mallex Smith	14	3.44
Billy Hamilton	44	3.47
Bradley Zimmer	15	3.51
Byron Buxton	21	3.52
Eric Young Jr.	10	3.52
Jarrod Dyson	23	3.54
Keon Broxton	19	3.54
Trea Turner	28	3.54
Lorenzo Cain	14	3.55
Michael Taylor	15	3.55
Dee Gordon	55	3.55
Jake Marisnick	9	3.56
Starling Marte	18	3.56
Jose Altuve	25	3.57
Rajai Davis	18	3.57
Brett Gardner	20	3.58
Kevin Kiermaier	16	3.58
Delino DeShields	21	3.59
Carlos Gomez	13	3.59
Mookie Betts	17	3.59
Jose Peraza	18	3.60
Tim Anderson	9	3.60
Whit Merrifield	22	3.60
Ben Revere	16	3.60
Eduardo Nunez	16	3.60
Xander Bogaerts	7	3.60
Josh Harrison	8	3.60
Justin Upton	10	3.61
Trevor Story	6	3.61
Jose Ramirez	13	3.61
Rougned Odor	16	3.62
Wilmer Difo	11	3.62
Leury Garcia	9	3.62
Ian Kinsler	13	3.62
Jose Reyes	15	3.62
Ezequiel Carrera	7	3.62
Jonathan Villar	13	3.62
A.J. Pollock	9	3.63
Juan Lagares	7	3.63
Jacoby Ellsbury	16	3.63
Kevin Pillar	8	3.63
Taylor Motter	8	3.64
Tommy Pham	17	3.64
Wil Myers	12	3.64
Mike Trout	14	3.64
Charlie Blackmon	18	3.65
JaCoby Jones	6	3.65
Amed Rosario	8	3.65
Shin-Soo Choo	6	3.66
Andrew McCutchen	7	3.66
Lane Adams	7	3.66
Jose Iglesias	7	3.66
Aaron Altherr	7	3.67
Cameron Maybin	25	3.67
Joey Rickard	6	3.67
Alen Hanson	8	3.67
Anthony Rendon	6	3.68
Christian Yelich	10	3.68
Leonys Martin	6	3.69
Andrelton Simmons	9	3.69
Cesar Hernandez	15	3.69
Ian Desmond	14	3.69
Jorge Polanco	10	3.69
Nori Aoki	8	3.70
Francisco Lindor	13	3.71
Cory Spangenberg	8	3.71
George Springer	6	3.71
Alex Bregman	15	3.71
Chris Taylor	11	3.71
Michael Brantley	6	3.71
Jason Kipnis	6	3.71

Runner	Timed Attempts	Average
Brian Dozier	15	3.71
Elvis Andrus	18	3.71
Eddie Rosario	7	3.72
Ender Inciarte	20	3.72
Ryan Braun	7	3.72
Manuel Margot	9	3.72
Adam Frazier	7	3.72
Kris Bryant	7	3.72
Marcus Semien	8	3.72
Andrew Benintendi	17	3.73
Ian Happ	9	3.73
Jason Heyward	7	3.73
Denard Span	10	3.73
Jean Segura	21	3.73
Scott Schebler	6	3.73
Yolmer Sanchez	10	3.73
Paul Goldschmidt	9	3.74
Howie Kendrick	10	3.74
Ozzie Albies	6	3.74
Aaron Judge	7	3.74
Orlando Arcia	8	3.74
Yasiel Puig	7	3.75
Andrew Romine	6	3.75
Randal Grichuk	6	3.77
Domingo Santana	9	3.77
Freddie Freeman	7	3.79
Tim Beckham	9	3.79
Freddy Galvis	11	3.82
Gregor Blanco	9	3.82
Adam Duvall	6	3.83
Gorkys Hernandez	10	3.85
Chase Headley	9	3.85
Aaron Hicks	8	3.85
Erick Aybar	8	3.87
Brandon Phillips	9	3.93

Relief Pitching

Lindsay Zeck

The Colorado Rockies' offseason acquisition of Greg Holland had a significant impact on their bullpen. Coming off Tommy John surgery, the former Royals' closer tied for the most saves in the National League, saving 41 games out of his 45 opportunities. After the Rockies' bullpen saved only 57 percent of its opportunities in 2016—tied for the second worst in the baseball—it saved 77 percent in 2017 with Holland as its primary closer. This was second only to the Cleveland Indians' bullpen (79 percent) which finished with the only sub-3.00 ERA in all of baseball.

Alex Colome of the Rays led MLB in saves in 2017, saving 47 of 53 opportunities. The player who tied with Holland with 41 saves was Kenley Jansen of the Dodgers, who had the lowest ERA of all qualified relievers. His 41 saves came out of 42 opportunities, giving him the highest save percentage (98 percent) of all closers. Jansen entered the game with the tying runner on base four separate times and prevented the runner from scoring to save the game in all four of these high-pressure situations, classified as Tough Saves in the data.

The worst closers of the season were likely Jim Johnson of the Atlanta Braves and Roberto Osuna of the Blue Jays. Of all pitchers with at least 25 save opportunities, Johnson finished with the lowest save percentage (71 percent), saving only 22 of his 31 opportunities. His nine blown saves were the second most in baseball behind only Osuna, who had 10 blown saves in 49 opportunities. Half of Osuna's blown saves came in "easy" situations—games in which he pitched one inning or less, and the first batter he faced did not represent at least the tying run. Out of 29 "easy" save opportunities, he only saved 83 percent of them, the lowest success rate in the league.

In addition to information about saves and relief results, this section also includes details about usage and inherited runners. Here, we can see that the Angels' set-up man, Yusmeiro Petit, was the only pitcher who inherited at least 20 runners this season and didn't allow a single one to score. Jorge de La Rosa, in his transition from a Rockies' starter to a left-handed specialist in the bullpen for the Diamondbacks, wasn't far behind, allowing only 1 of his 33 inherited runners to score. In contrast, Zach McAllister of the Indians allowed 11 of 20 inherited runners to score (55 percent) despite only having 18 earned runs against his name. This was the highest percentage allowed of any pitcher who inherited at least 20 runners. The following tables include information on the performance of the most used relievers from each major league team. To qualify, a reliever must have had at least 10 appearances during the 2017 season.

Arizona Diamondbacks

Pitcher	Pos	T	Rel G	Early Entry	Cons Days	Long	Lev Ind	#	Scrd	Pct	Easy	Reg	Tough	Clean	BS Win	BS	Holds	Sv/Hld Pct	Opp OPS	Rel ERA
Rodney, Fernando	CL	R	61	0	18	6	1.9	7	1	.14	23 - 27	16 - 18	0 - 0	47	1	6	0	.87	.582	4.23
Bradley, Archie	SU	R	63	4	14	14	1.4	36	8	.22	0 - 0	1 - 4	0 - 3	46	0	6	25	.81	.567	1.73
Hernandez, David	SU	R	26	5	6	0	1.2	16	4	.25	1 - 1	0 - 0	0 - 1	20	0	1	10	.92	.749	4.82
Chafin, Andrew	LT	L	71	11	21	2	1.0	49	15	.31	0 - 0	0 - 0	0 - 0	47	0	0	17	1.00	.699	3.51
de la Rosa, Jorge	LT	L	66	18	14	3	1.0	33	1	.03	0 - 0	0 - 1	0 - 0	44	0	1	17	.94	.718	4.21
McFarland, T.J.	LT	L	42	11	9	12	0.8	16	4	.25	0 - 0	0 - 0	0 - 0	23	0	0	2	1.00	.722	4.19
Delgado, Randall	LM	R	21	8	2	15	0.7	6	1	.17	0 - 0	1 - 2	0 - 0	12	0	1	2	.75	.670	4.30
Hoover, J.J.	UR	R	52	16	12	6	1.0	31	11	.35	0 - 0	0 - 2	0 - 0	32	0	2	10	.83	.846	3.92
Barrett, Jake	UR	R	28	6	7	6	0.8	11	4	.36	0 - 0	0 - 0	0 - 1	17	1	1	2	.67	.847	5.00
Wilhelmsen, Tom	UR	R	27	6	5	4	0.6	15	5	.33	0 - 0	0 - 0	0 - 0	14	0	0	3	1.00	.761	4.44
Bracho, Silvino	UR	R	21	7	4	3	0.3	11	1	.09	0 - 0	0 - 0	0 - 0	14	0	0	0		.725	5.66
Sherfy, Jimmie	UR	R	11	1	2	1	1.0	2	0	.00	0 - 0	1 - 1	0 - 0	11	0	0	2	1.00	.418	0.00

Atlanta Braves

Pitcher	Pos	T	Rel G	Early Entry	Cons Days	Long	Lev Ind	#	Scrd	Pct	Easy	Reg	Tough	Clean	BS Win	BS	Holds	Sv/Hld Pct	Opp OPS	Rel ERA
Johnson, Jim	CL	R	61	1	20	8	1.8	3	0	.00	19 - 21	3 - 10	0 - 0	40	1	9	1	.72	.737	5.56
Ramirez, Jose	SU	R	68	2	15	5	1.4	16	4	.25	0 - 2	0 - 2	0 - 1	50	1	5	27	.84	.678	3.19
Vizcaino, Arodys	SU	R	62	0	15	0	1.6	12	4	.33	7 - 8	6 - 7	1 - 2	50	0	3	17	.91	.627	2.83
Minter, A.J.	SU	L	16	4	0	1	1.0	4	0	.00	0 - 0	0 - 0	0 - 1	12	0	0	5	1.00	.595	3.00
Freeman, Sam	LT	L	58	12	12	8	0.7	19	10	.53	0 - 0	0 - 2	0 - 1	38	0	3	12	.80	.592	2.55
Krol, Ian	LT	L	51	12	4	12	0.6	32	9	.28	0 - 0	0 - 0	0 - 0	27	0	0	3	1.00	.803	5.33
Brothers, Rex	LT	L	27	2	4	3	0.7	17	6	.35	0 - 0	0 - 0	0 - 0	14	0	0	2	1.00	.767	7.23
O'Flaherty, Eric	LT	L	22	4	8	2	0.7	10	3	.30	0 - 0	0 - 0	0 - 0	14	0	0	3	1.00	.909	7.85
Wisler, Matt	LM	R	19	7	2	8	0.2	6	3	.50	0 - 0	0 - 0	0 - 0	8	0	0	0		.978	8.89
Motte, Jason	UR	R	46	11	11	1	0.7	24	9	.38	0 - 0	0 - 1	0 - 2	32	0	3	5	.63	.690	3.54
Jackson, Luke	UR	R	43	16	6	9	0.3	33	14	.42	0 - 0	0 - 0	0 - 0	28	0	0	1	1.00	.759	4.62
Winkler, Daniel	UR	R	16	5	1	2	1.0	16	6	.38	0 - 0	0 - 0	0 - 0	12	0	0	4	1.00	.511	2.51
Collmenter, Josh	UR	R	11	4	0	7	0.5	0	0	.00	0 - 0	0 - 0	0 - 0	5	0	0	0		1.117	9.00

Baltimore Orioles

Pitcher	Pos	T	Rel G	Early Entry	Cons Days	Long	Lev Ind	#	Scrd	Pct	Easy	Reg	Tough	Clean	BS Win	BS	Holds	Sv/Hld Pct	Opp OPS	Rel ERA
Brach, Brad	CL	R	67	0	16	11	1.6	11	3	.27	13 - 15	4 - 7	1 - 2	50	1	6	9	.82	.620	3.18
Britton, Zach	CL	L	38	0	8	2	1.6	16	1	.06	7 - 8	6 - 6	2 - 3	30	0	2	0	.88	.690	2.89
Givens, Mychal	SU	R	69	21	13	18	1.6	47	17	.36	0 - 0	0 - 2	0 - 3	47	1	5	21	.81	.617	2.75
O'Day, Darren	SU	R	64	10	14	5	1.2	26	5	.19	0 - 0	2 - 3	0 - 1	46	0	2	17	.90	.609	3.43
Bleier, Richard	LT	L	57	25	15	10	0.6	45	10	.22	0 - 0	0 - 0	0 - 0	39	0	0	3	1.00	.671	1.99
Hart, Donnie	LT	L	51	8	10	5	0.7	29	7	.24	0 - 0	0 - 1	0 - 1	34	0	2	5	.71	.755	3.71
Nuno, Vidal	LT	L	12	4	3	4	0.3	9	3	.33	0 - 0	0 - 0	0 - 0	4	0	0	0		1.205	10.43
Castro, Miguel	LM	R	38	19	6	19	0.8	31	11	.35	0 - 0	0 - 0	0 - 0	19	0	0	1	1.00	.657	3.29
Asher, Alec	LM	R	18	9	2	10	0.8	11	5	.45	0 - 0	0 - 0	0 - 0	11	0	0	0		.778	3.56
Yacabonis, Jimmy	UR	R	14	5	0	7	0.4	9	4	.44	0 - 0	0 - 0	0 - 0	8	0	0	0		.725	4.35
Wright, Mike	UR	R	13	6	1	8	0.3	7	4	.57	0 - 0	0 - 0	0 - 0	5	0	0	0		.830	5.76

Boston Red Sox

Pitcher	Pos	T	Usage					Inherited Runners			Saves			Relief Results						
			Rel G	Early Entry	Cons Days	Long	Lev Ind	#	Scrd	Pct	Easy	Reg	Tough	Clean	BS Win	BS	Holds	Sv/Hld Pct	Opp OPS	Rel ERA
Kimbrel, Craig	CL	R	67	0	19	7	1.6	13	1	.08	24 - 24	11 - 14	0 - 1	57	2	4	1	.90	.444	1.43
Barnes, Matt	SU	R	70	5	11	7	1.2	18	3	.17	0 - 1	1 - 2	0 - 0	49	0	2	21	.92	.655	3.88
Kelly, Joe	SU	R	54	8	7	11	1.1	27	11	.41	0 - 0	0 - 1	0 - 3	38	0	4	13	.76	.573	2.79
Reed, Addison	SU	R	29	1	8	1	1.5	17	5	.29	0 - 0	0 - 0	0 - 0	22	0	0	11	1.00	.606	3.33
Scott, Robby	LT	L	57	6	15	2	1.1	50	11	.22	0 - 0	0 - 0	0 - 2	39	0	2	12	.86	.660	3.79
Abad, Fernando	LT	L	48	17	6	5	0.7	28	8	.29	0 - 0	1 - 2	0 - 0	29	0	1	2	.75	.672	3.30
Hembree, Heath	UR	R	62	19	10	14	1.1	46	22	.48	0 - 0	0 - 2	0 - 1	35	0	3	14	.82	.803	3.63
Workman, Brandon	UR	R	33	10	7	7	0.8	7	0	.00	0 - 0	0 - 1	0 - 0	20	1	1	4	.80	.782	3.18
Boyer, Blaine	UR	R	32	9	6	11	0.7	13	3	.23	0 - 0	0 - 0	0 - 1	24	0	1	2	.67	.808	4.35
Taylor, Ben	UR	R	14	6	2	6	0.7	6	3	.50	0 - 0	1 - 1	0 - 0	6	0	0	1	1.00	.841	5.19
Maddox, Austin	UR	R	13	4	1	5	0.5	8	0	.00	0 - 0	0 - 0	0 - 0	12	0	0	0		.485	0.52

Chicago Cubs

Pitcher	Pos	T	Usage					Inherited Runners			Saves			Relief Results						
			Rel G	Early Entry	Cons Days	Long	Lev Ind	#	Scrd	Pct	Easy	Reg	Tough	Clean	BS Win	BS	Holds	Sv/Hld Pct	Opp OPS	Rel ERA
Davis, Wade	CL	R	59	0	14	7	1.8	5	2	.40	18 - 18	14 - 15	0 - 0	49	0	1	0	.97	.600	2.30
Edwards Jr., Carl	SU	R	73	12	12	6	1.4	35	9	.26	0 - 0	0 - 2	0 - 2	58	0	4	25	.86	.503	2.98
Strop, Pedro	SU	R	69	10	9	5	1.2	40	13	.33	0 - 0	0 - 2	0 - 2	50	0	4	21	.84	.619	2.83
Uehara, Koji	SU	R	49	0	6	1	1.2	10	5	.50	1 - 2	1 - 2	0 - 1	31	1	3	14	.84	.679	3.98
Duensing, Brian	LT	L	68	23	18	12	0.7	33	5	.15	0 - 0	0 - 1	0 - 0	49	0	1	13	.93	.673	2.74
Wilson, Justin	LT	L	23	5	3	2	0.8	7	3	.43	0 - 0	0 - 0	0 - 1	12	0	1	1	.50	.756	5.09
Grimm, Justin	LM	R	50	17	7	12	0.6	26	11	.42	0 - 0	1 - 2	0 - 1	30	0	2	4	.71	.760	5.53
Montgomery, Mike	LM	L	30	13	0	19	1.0	10	1	.10	0 - 0	3 - 3	0 - 0	17	0	0	1	1.00	.622	2.49
Rondon, Hector	UR	R	61	10	11	7	0.8	23	10	.43	0 - 2	0 - 0	0 - 1	42	0	3	10	.77	.724	4.24
Pena, Felix	UR	R	25	4	4	11	0.2	5	4	.80	0 - 0	0 - 0	0 - 0	11	0	0	1	1.00	.866	5.24

Chicago White Sox

Pitcher	Pos	T	Usage					Inherited Runners			Saves			Relief Results						
			Rel G	Early Entry	Cons Days	Long	Lev Ind	#	Scrd	Pct	Easy	Reg	Tough	Clean	BS Win	BS	Holds	Sv/Hld Pct	Opp OPS	Rel ERA
Robertson, David	CL	R	31	0	6	5	1.8	9	4	.44	7 - 7	6 - 7	0 - 0	23	1	1	0	.93	.577	2.70
Swarzak, Anthony	SU	R	41	20	11	7	1.4	35	9	.26	0 - 0	0 - 1	1 - 2	30	0	2	10	.85	.555	2.23
Kahnle, Tommy	SU	R	37	0	7	0	1.4	9	1	.11	0 - 0	0 - 3	0 - 1	27	1	4	7	.64	.571	2.50
Bummer, Aaron	LT	L	30	4	10	1	1.3	17	2	.12	0 - 0	0 - 0	0 - 1	20	0	1	7	.88	.692	4.50
Holmberg, David	LT	L	30	9	8	6	0.4	17	9	.53	0 - 0	0 - 1	0 - 0	17	0	1	0	.00	.888	4.03
Fry, Jace	LT	L	11	2	1	0	0.2	3	0	.00	0 - 0	0 - 0	0 - 0	7	0	0	0		1.085	10.80
Beck, Chris	LM	R	57	28	11	16	0.4	38	15	.39	0 - 0	0 - 0	0 - 1	25	0	1	3	.75	.926	6.40
Jennings, Dan	LM	L	48	18	13	13	0.8	35	7	.20	0 - 0	0 - 1	0 - 0	32	0	1	7	.88	.642	3.45
Ynoa, Michael	LM	R	22	8	0	13	0.2	12	5	.42	0 - 0	0 - 0	0 - 0	9	0	0	0		.846	5.90
Pelfrey, Mike	LM	R	13	8	1	8	0.3	9	4	.44	0 - 0	0 - 0	0 - 0	7	0	0	0		.755	5.49
Infante, Gregory	UR	R	52	13	13	11	0.7	37	11	.30	0 - 0	0 - 0	0 - 1	32	1	1	5	.83	.646	3.13
Minaya, Juan	UR	R	40	11	10	9	1.1	24	5	.21	4 - 4	5 - 6	0 - 0	24	0	1	2	.92	.765	4.53
Petricka, Jake	UR	R	27	5	5	5	0.8	22	6	.27	0 - 0	0 - 1	0 - 0	16	0	1	3	.75	.947	7.01
Farquhar, Danny	UR	R	15	1	3	1	1.3	8	1	.13	0 - 1	0 - 0	0 - 0	10	0	1	4	.80	.604	4.40
Clippard, Tyler	UR	R	11	0	3	3	1.6	4	2	.50	2 - 2	0 - 0	0 - 0	7	0	0	0	1.00	.585	1.80
Goldberg, Brad	UR	R	11	1	0	4	0.3	3	1	.33	0 - 0	0 - 0	0 - 0	3	0	0	0		1.006	8.25
Jones, Nate	UR	R	11	0	2	2	1.4	3	1	.33	0 - 0	0 - 0	0 - 0	8	0	0	4	1.00	.675	2.31
Alburquerque, Al	UR	R	10	1	3	0	0.9	5	4	.80	0 - 0	0 - 0	0 - 0	7	0	0	2	1.00	.358	1.13

Cincinnati Reds

Pitcher	Pos	T	Rel G	Early Entry	Cons Days	Long	Lev Ind	#	Scrd	Pct	Easy	Reg	Tough	Clean	BS Win	BS	Holds	Sv/Hld Pct	Opp OPS	Rel ERA
Iglesias, Raisel	CL	R	63	1	12	17	1.4	18	4	.22	11 - 12	15 - 16	2 - 2	49	0	2	0	.93	.576	2.49
Lorenzen, Michael	SU	R	70	14	10	14	1.2	29	10	.34	2 - 2	0 - 5	0 - 0	45	2	5	18	.80	.695	4.45
Peralta, Wandy	LT	L	69	14	14	4	0.9	26	9	.35	0 - 0	0 - 2	0 - 0	52	0	2	16	.89	.681	3.76
Cingrani, Tony	LT	L	25	5	2	1	0.6	10	3	.30	0 - 0	0 - 1	0 - 0	14	0	1	4	.80	.965	5.40
Reed, Cody	LT	L	11	6	0	5	0.5	2	0	.00	0 - 0	0 - 0	1 - 1	8	0	0	0	1.00	.588	1.72
Wood, Blake	LM	R	55	19	9	14	0.5	23	10	.43	0 - 0	0 - 1	0 - 0	33	0	1	3	.75	.772	5.65
Brice, Austin	LM	R	22	10	2	8	0.5	9	2	.22	0 - 0	0 - 0	0 - 0	12	0	0	1	1.00	.756	4.96
Hernandez, Ariel	LM	R	19	10	2	8	0.3	9	3	.33	0 - 0	0 - 0	0 - 0	12	0	0	0		.745	5.18
Wojciechowski, Asher	LM	R	17	9	0	8	0.6	3	0	.00	0 - 0	0 - 0	0 - 0	11	0	0	2	1.00	.668	4.00
Stephenson, Robert	LM	R	14	8	1	10	0.5	7	3	.43	0 - 0	1 - 1	0 - 0	5	0	0	0	1.00	.976	7.43
Storen, Drew	UR	R	58	12	8	4	0.8	10	5	.50	1 - 1	0 - 2	0 - 0	40	1	2	6	.78	.790	4.45
Shackelford, Kevin	UR	R	26	10	2	5	0.8	6	2	.33	0 - 0	0 - 1	0 - 0	17	0	1	3	.75	.764	4.70
Adleman, Tim	UR	R	10	5	1	5	0.9	5	0	.00	0 - 0	0 - 0	0 - 0	3	0	0	2	1.00	.880	5.82

Cleveland Indians

Pitcher	Pos	T	Rel G	Early Entry	Cons Days	Long	Lev Ind	#	Scrd	Pct	Easy	Reg	Tough	Clean	BS Win	BS	Holds	Sv/Hld Pct	Opp OPS	Rel ERA
Allen, Cody	CL	R	69	0	18	4	2.0	14	2	.14				51	1	4	4	.89	.649	2.94
Shaw, Bryan	SU	R	79	14	23	8	1.2	33	9	.27	2 - 4	0 - 1	1 - 1	52	0	3	26	.91	.653	3.52
Miller, Andrew	SU	L	57	7	15	13	1.6	29	6	.21	2 - 2	0 - 1	0 - 1	47	0	2	27	.94	.440	1.44
Olson, Tyler	SU	L	30	8	10	2	1.0	17	2	.12	1 - 1	0 - 0	0 - 0	29	0	0	8	1.00	.481	0.00
Smith, Joe	SU	R	21	5	3	0	1.0	14	1	.07	0 - 0	0 - 0	1 - 1	17	0	0	8	1.00	.557	3.44
Logan, Boone	LT	L	39	18	11	0	0.6	19	4	.21	0 - 0	0 - 0	0 - 1	27	0	1	4	.80	.683	4.71
Goody, Nick	UR	R	56	24	6	5	0.7	28	8	.29	0 - 0	0 - 0	0 - 0	37	0	0	6	1.00	.632	2.80
Otero, Dan	UR	R	52	17	8	9	0.5	26	9	.35	0 - 0	0 - 0	0 - 0	35	0	0	1	1.00	.693	2.85
McAllister, Zach	UR	R	50	15	5	12	0.4	20	11	.55	0 - 0	0 - 0	0 - 0	32	0	0	2	1.00	.670	2.61
Armstrong, Shawn	UR	R	21	3	5	5	0.1	7	4	.57	0 - 0	0 - 0	0 - 0	14	0	0	0		.737	4.38

Colorado Rockies

Pitcher	Pos	T	Rel G	Early Entry	Cons Days	Long	Lev Ind	#	Scrd	Pct	Easy	Reg	Tough	Clean	BS Win	BS	Holds	Sv/Hld Pct	Opp OPS	Rel ERA
Holland, Greg	CL	R	61	0	14	3	2.1	12	3	.25	28 - 28	13 - 17	0 - 0	44	1	4	1	.91	.623	3.61
Ottavino, Adam	SU	R	63	2	11	5	1.1	25	9	.36	0 - 0	0 - 1	0 - 1	43	0	2	21	.91	.786	5.06
McGee, Jake	SU	L	62	2	13	5	1.3	28	8	.29	1 - 1	1 - 2	1 - 3	44	0	3	20	.88	.624	3.61
Neshek, Pat	SU	R	28	0	7	0	1.5	10	1	.10	0 - 0	0 - 2	0 - 0	20	0	2	13	.87	.594	2.45
Dunn, Mike	LT	L	68	10	16	4	0.9	36	9	.25	0 - 0	0 - 1	0 - 0	50	0	1	19	.95	.730	4.47
Rusin, Chris	LM	L	60	28	6	15	1.0	33	6	.18	0 - 0	2 - 2	0 - 1	37	0	1	12	.93	.645	2.65
Lyles, Jordan	LM	R	33	14	2	14	0.6	17	8	.47	0 - 0	0 - 0	0 - 0	16	0	0	2	1.00	.921	6.94
Senzatela, Antonio	LM	R	16	9	1	7	0.5	6	1	.17	0 - 0	0 - 0	0 - 0	10	0	0	1	1.00	.472	3.04
Oberg, Scott	UR	R	66	23	15	5	0.8	38	6	.16	0 - 0	0 - 0	0 - 1	41	0	1	14	.93	.800	4.94
Estevez, Carlos	UR	R	35	11	10	5	0.6	16	1	.06	0 - 0	0 - 0	0 - 0	26	0	0	6	1.00	.778	5.57
Qualls, Chad	UR	R	19	3	4	0	0.6	6	1	.17	0 - 0	0 - 0	0 - 0	11	0	0	1	1.00	.780	5.40

Detroit Tigers

Pitcher	Pos	T	Rel G	Early Entry	Cons Days	Long	Lev Ind	#	Scrd	Pct	Easy	Reg	Tough	Clean	BS Win	BS	Holds	Sv/Hld Pct	Opp OPS	Rel ERA
Wilson, Justin	CL	L	42	0	6	7	1.6	12	1	.08	8 - 8	3 - 5	2 - 2	33	0	2	8	.91	.563	2.68
Greene, Shane	SU	R	71	12	17	5	1.4	47	9	.19	3 - 3	5 - 6	1 - 4	51	1	4	14	.85	.631	2.66
Wilson, Alex	SU	R	66	4	14	5	1.1	32	13	.41	0 - 0	2 - 5	0 - 2	40	1	5	17	.79	.764	4.50
Rondon, Bruce	SU	R	21	0	4	1	1.2	2	0	.00	1 - 2	0 - 0	0 - 0	14	0	1	7	.89	.890	10.91
Stumpf, Daniel	LT	L	55	12	23	3	0.7	39	12	.31	0 - 0	0 - 1	0 - 1	37	0	2	9	.82	.762	3.82
Hardy, Blaine	LT	L	35	12	7	9	0.7	26	8	.31	0 - 0	0 - 0	0 - 0	16	0	0	6	1.00	.925	5.94
Saupold, Warwick	LM	R	45	22	5	18	0.5	32	12	.38	0 - 0	0 - 0	0 - 0	23	0	0	2	1.00	.779	4.88
Bell, Chad	LM	L	24	16	3	12	0.3	15	5	.33	0 - 0	0 - 0	0 - 0	12	0	0	1	1.00	.842	6.13
Rodriguez, Francisco	UR	R	28	0	3	3	1.6	10	6	.60	6 - 6	1 - 6	0 - 1	14	2	6	0	.54	1.006	7.82
Jimenez, Joe	UR	R	24	3	3	2	0.4	17	7	.41	0 - 0	0 - 1	0 - 1	9	0	1	0	.00	.999	12.32
VerHagen, Drew	UR	R	22	8	6	4	0.7	12	4	.33	0 - 0	0 - 0	0 - 1	11	0	1	5	.83	.918	4.91
Sanchez, Anibal	UR	R	11	5	0	7	0.2	3	2	.67	0 - 0	0 - 0	0 - 0	4	0	0	0		1.107	9.00
Ferrell, Jeff	UR	R	11	5	2	1	0.2	7	4	.57	0 - 0	0 - 0	0 - 0	6	0	0	0		1.054	6.75
Reininger, Zac	UR	R	10	2	1	3	0.1	11	6	.55	0 - 0	0 - 0	0 - 0	4	0	0	0		.988	7.45

Houston Astros

Pitcher	Pos	T	Rel G	Early Entry	Cons Days	Long	Lev Ind	#	Scrd	Pct	Easy	Reg	Tough	Clean	BS Win	BS	Holds	Sv/Hld Pct	Opp OPS	Rel ERA
Giles, Ken	CL	R	63	0	13	5	1.4	18	7	.39	22 - 22	11 - 14	1 - 2	50	1	4	2	.90	.566	2.30
Devenski, Chris	SU	R	62	16	9	16	1.6	41	9	.22	1 - 1	2 - 5	1 - 4	42	0	6	24	.82	.588	2.68
Harris, Will	SU	R	46	10	7	3	1.4	23	10	.43	1 - 1	1 - 1	0 - 2	34	0	2	20	.92	.613	2.98
Musgrove, Joe	SU	R	23	7	2	6	1.0	11	3	.27	0 - 0	1 - 3	1 - 1	18	1	2	5	.78	.565	1.44
Liriano, Francisco	SU	L	20	6	1	1	1.0	13	5	.38	0 - 0	0 - 0	0 - 0	11	0	0	6	1.00	.772	4.40
Sipp, Tony	LT	L	46	11	9	5	0.4	15	7	.47	0 - 0	0 - 0	0 - 0	29	0	0	4	1.00	.830	5.79
Guduan, Reymin	LT	L	22	6	6	3	0.3	13	2	.15	0 - 0	0 - 0	0 - 0	13	0	0	1	1.00	.899	7.88
Feliz, Michael	LM	R	46	21	6	9	0.7	27	14	.52	0 - 0	0 - 0	0 - 2	27	0	2	2	.50	.854	5.63
Hoyt, James	LM	R	43	19	8	9	0.7	29	14	.48	0 - 0	0 - 0	0 - 0	23	0	0	7	1.00	.748	4.38
Martes, Francis	LM	R	28	10	0	13	0.7	15	3	.20	0 - 1	0 - 0	0 - 0	12	0	1	1	.50	.778	6.63
Gregerson, Luke	UR	R	65	2	15	2	0.9	10	5	.50	0 - 1	1 - 3	0 - 0	47	1	3	18	.86	.790	4.57
Clippard, Tyler	UR	R	16	3	3	2	1.0	6	3	.50	1 - 1	1 - 2	0 - 0	9	0	1	1	.75	.740	6.43
Peacock, Brad	UR	R	13	3	3	4	0.5	3	1	.33	0 - 0	0 - 0	0 - 0	9	0	0	0		.483	1.77

Kansas City Royals

Pitcher	Pos	T	Rel G	Early Entry	Cons Days	Long	Lev Ind	#	Scrd	Pct	Easy	Reg	Tough	Clean	BS Win	BS	Holds	Sv/Hld Pct	Opp OPS	Rel ERA
Herrera, Kelvin	CL	R	64	0	18	4	1.6	6	1	.17	18 - 19	8 - 12	0 - 0	44	0	5	4	.86	.786	4.25
Moylan, Peter	SU	R	79	21	30	5	1.1	64	15	.23	0 - 0	0 - 0	0 - 1	59	0	1	24	.96	.576	3.49
Minor, Mike	SU	L	65	19	14	15	1.4	34	14	.41	1 - 1	5 - 6	0 - 2	44	0	3	17	.88	.585	2.55
Soria, Joakim	SU	R	59	0	15	5	1.6	7	3	.43	1 - 2	0 - 5	0 - 1	44	1	7	20	.75	.592	3.70
Buchter, Ryan	LT	L	29	7	9	3	0.7	14	3	.21	0 - 0	0 - 0	0 - 0	22	0	0	5	1.00	.561	2.67
Wood, Travis	LT	L	25	6	2	9	0.5	15	5	.33	0 - 0	0 - 1	0 - 0	12	0	1	1	.50	.851	6.28
Alexander, Scott	LM	L	58	30	11	15	1.2	53	12	.23	0 - 0	1 - 1	3 - 5	35	1	2	9	.87	.645	2.48
Strahm, Matt	LM	L	21	9	0	5	1.3	16	7	.44	0 - 0	0 - 0	0 - 0	11	0	0	5	1.00	.727	4.30
McCarthy, Kevin	UR	R	33	11	6	13	0.3	6	2	.33	0 - 0	0 - 0	0 - 0	21	0	0	1	1.00	.704	3.20
Maurer, Brandon	UR	R	26	2	5	3	1.0	8	2	.25	1 - 2	1 - 1	0 - 0	15	1	1	4	.86	1.074	8.10
Feliz, Neftali	UR	R	20	1	5	3	0.5	1	1	1.00	0 - 0	0 - 0	0 - 0	14	0	0	2	1.00	.696	4.74
Young, Chris	UR	R	12	6	0	7	0.4	5	4	.80	0 - 0	0 - 0	0 - 0	4	0	0	0		.912	6.17
Alburquerque, Al	UR	R	11	1	2	1	0.4	0	0	.00	0 - 0	0 - 0	0 - 0	8	0	0	1	1.00	.504	3.60

Los Angeles Angels

Pitcher	Pos	T	Usage					Inherited Runners			Saves			Relief Results						
			Rel G	Early Entry	Cons Days	Long	Lev Ind	#	Scrd	Pct	Easy	Reg	Tough	Clean	BS Win	BS	Holds	Sv/Hld Pct	Opp OPS	Rel ERA
Norris, Bud	CL	R	57	3	18	7	1.7	16	5	.31	7 - 8	10 - 12	2 - 3	41	1	4	3	.85	.720	4.70
Parker, Blake	SU	R	71	19	11	5	1.1	37	8	.22	3 - 5	3 - 4	2 - 2	55	1	3	15	.88	.527	2.54
Petit, Yusmeiro	SU	R	59	24	7	17	1.0	20	0	.00	2 - 3	2 - 2	0 - 0	41	0	1	14	.95	.579	2.89
Bedrosian, Cam	SU	R	48	6	5	6	1.4	11	5	.45	2 - 3	4 - 7	0 - 1	31	1	5	10	.76	.705	4.43
Alvarez, Jose	LT	L	64	23	16	2	0.8	35	6	.17	1 - 1	0 - 1	0 - 1	49	0	2	13	.88	.733	3.88
Paredes, Eduardo	LM	R	18	9	3	7	0.9	5	1	.20	0 - 0	1 - 1	0 - 0	12	0	0	1	1.00	.725	4.43
Wood, Blake	LM	R	17	11	3	5	0.8	8	4	.50	0 - 0	0 - 0	0 - 0	10	0	0	0		.793	4.76
Chavez, Jesse	LM	R	17	9	1	7	0.8	8	3	.38	0 - 1	0 - 0	0 - 0	9	0	1	1	.50	.798	5.84
Middleton, Keynan	UR	R	64	14	14	5	1.1	29	10	.34	2 - 2	0 - 0	1 - 3	43	0	2	10	.87	.791	3.86
Hernandez, David	UR	R	38	1	5	1	0.8	10	3	.30	1 - 2	0 - 0	0 - 0	31	0	1	8	.90	.535	2.23
Guerra, Deolis	UR	R	19	5	0	7	0.7	5	1	.20	0 - 0	0 - 1	0 - 0	11	0	1	0	.00	.729	4.68
Salas, Fernando	UR	R	13	1	3	0	0.6	5	1	.20	0 - 0	0 - 0	0 - 0	8	0	0	1	1.00	.449	2.63
Pounders, Brooks	UR	R	11	0	1	2	0.3	4	2	.50	0 - 0	0 - 0	0 - 0	7	0	0	0		1.157	10.45
Ramirez, Noe	UR	R	10	6	2	0	1.0	12	2	.17	0 - 0	0 - 0	0 - 0	7	0	0	0		.374	2.16
Morin, Mike	UR	R	10	5	1	5	0.4	8	3	.38	0 - 0	0 - 0	0 - 0	4	0	0	0		.958	6.91

Los Angeles Dodgers

Pitcher	Pos	T	Usage					Inherited Runners			Saves			Relief Results						
			Rel G	Early Entry	Cons Days	Long	Lev Ind	#	Scrd	Pct	Easy	Reg	Tough	Clean	BS Win	BS	Holds	Sv/Hld Pct	Opp OPS	Rel ERA
Jansen, Kenley	CL	R	65	0	15	6	1.7	20	4	.20	21 - 21	16 - 17	4 - 4	55	0	1	1	.98	.476	1.32
Baez, Pedro	SU	R	66	13	16	11	1.3	20	2	.10	0 - 0	0 - 3	0 - 0	50	0	3	23	.88	.728	2.95
Watson, Tony	SU	L	24	6	5	1	1.4	12	3	.25	0 - 0	0 - 0	0 - 1	18	0	1	8	.89	.607	2.70
Avilan, Luis	LT	L	61	16	17	3	0.9	22	4	.18	0 - 0	0 - 0	0 - 2	48	0	2	13	.87	.703	2.93
Dayton, Grant	LT	L	29	11	8	1	0.7	11	1	.09	0 - 0	0 - 1	0 - 0	21	0	1	4	.80	.749	4.94
Cingrani, Tony	LT	L	22	4	4	3	0.7	7	2	.29	0 - 0	0 - 0	0 - 0	17	0	0	5	1.00	.562	2.79
Paredes, Edward	LT	L	10	5	2	0	0.7	7	2	.29	0 - 0	0 - 0	0 - 0	8	0	0	0		.613	3.24
Stripling, Ross	LM	R	47	22	5	21	0.9	16	5	.31	0 - 1	2 - 4	0 - 0	26	0	3	4	.67	.715	4.02
Hatcher, Chris	LM	R	26	5	3	13	0.5	7	0	.00	0 - 0	0 - 1	0 - 0	15	0	1	2	.67	.769	4.66
Fields, Josh	UR	R	57	20	11	1	0.9	23	10	.43	1 - 1	1 - 3	0 - 1	42	1	3	15	.85	.630	2.84
Morrow, Brandon	UR	R	45	7	7	1	1.1	9	2	.22	2 - 2	0 - 1	0 - 0	37	0	1	10	.92	.454	2.06
Romo, Sergio	UR	R	30	9	8	3	0.7	13	5	.38	0 - 0	0 - 0	0 - 0	19	0	0	7	1.00	.845	6.12
Ravin, Josh	UR	R	14	4	2	4	0.6	10	5	.50	0 - 0	1 - 1	0 - 0	6	0	0	1	1.00	.818	6.48
Stewart, Brock	UR	R	13	2	1	6	0.3	1	0	.00	0 - 0	1 - 1	0 - 0	10	0	0	1	1.00	.574	2.18

Miami Marlins

Pitcher	Pos	T	Usage					Inherited Runners			Saves			Relief Results						
			Rel G	Early Entry	Cons Days	Long	Lev Ind	#	Scrd	Pct	Easy	Reg	Tough	Clean	BS Win	BS	Holds	Sv/Hld Pct	Opp OPS	Rel ERA
Ziegler, Brad	CL	R	53	13	15	2	1.4	24	7	.29	6 - 6	3 - 6	1 - 3	35	0	5	7	.77	.756	4.79
Ramos, A.J.	CL	R	40	0	8	5	1.5	7	1	.14	12 - 12	7 - 9	1 - 1	29	0	2	0	.91	.646	3.63
Barraclough, Kyle	SU	R	66	5	11	4	1.5	9	5	.56	0 - 1	1 - 4	0 - 0	48	1	4	22	.85	.638	3.00
Phelps, David	SU	R	44	4	12	7	1.3	7	3	.43	0 - 2	0 - 3	0 - 1	33	1	6	18	.75	.699	3.45
Steckenrider, Drew	SU	R	37	7	8	7	1.3	21	11	.52	0 - 0	1 - 1	0 - 0	24	0	0	10	1.00	.674	2.34
Garcia, Jarlin	LT	L	68	26	18	2	1.0	42	8	.19	0 - 0	0 - 0	0 - 1	48	0	1	15	.94	.695	4.73
Nicolino, Justin	LT	L	12	4	0	5	0.4	10	5	.50	0 - 0	0 - 0	0 - 0	4	0	0	0		.882	4.70
McGowan, Dustin	LM	R	63	31	12	16	0.7	38	17	.45	0 - 0	0 - 1	0 - 2	35	1	3	3	.50	.781	4.75
Tazawa, Junichi	UR	R	55	13	10	13	1.2	16	0	.00	0 - 0	0 - 3	0 - 0	34	0	3	9	.75	.766	5.69
Ellington, Brian	UR	R	42	11	12	14	0.6	4	3	.75	0 - 0	0 - 1	0 - 0	25	0	1	6	.86	.873	7.25
Wittgren, Nick	UR	R	38	13	8	9	0.6	15	6	.40	0 - 0	0 - 0	0 - 0	18	0	0	5	1.00	.800	4.68
Guerra, Javy	UR	R	16	6	1	4	0.8	11	7	.64	0 - 0	0 - 0	0 - 1	7	0	1	0	.00	.757	3.00
Worley, Vance	UR	R	12	4	1	6	0.4	5	3	.60	0 - 0	1 - 1	0 - 0	5	0	0	0	1.00	.955	5.59
Despaigne, Odrisamer	UR	R	10	4	2	3	0.6	5	3	.60	1 - 1	0 - 0	0 - 0	6	0	0	1	1.00	.771	3.86

Milwaukee Brewers

Pitcher	Pos	T	Rel G	Early Entry	Cons Days	Long	Lev Ind	#	Scrd	Pct	Easy	Reg	Tough	Clean	Win	BS	Holds	Sv/Hld Pct	Opp OPS	Rel ERA
					Usage				**Inherited Runners**			**Saves**				**Relief Results**				
Knebel, Corey	CL	R	76	0	26	11	2.1	17	4	.24	19 - 19	20 - 24	0 - 2	63	0	6	11	.89	.568	1.78
Barnes, Jacob	SU	R	73	10	19	8	1.4	17	5	.29	1 - 3	1 - 2	0 - 2	51	1	5	24	.84	.664	4.00
Hader, Josh	SU	L	35	17	2	12	1.2	12	3	.25	0 - 0	0 - 1	0 - 0	26	0	1	12	.92	.554	2.08
Swarzak, Anthony	SU	R	29	0	10	1	1.7	9	4	.44	1 - 1	0 - 1	0 - 0	20	0	1	17	.95	.660	2.48
Drake, Oliver	LM	R	61	22	16	5	0.7	30	5	.17	1 - 1	0 - 1	0 - 2	43	0	3	5	.67	.791	4.44
Jeffress, Jeremy	LM	R	21	14	4	5	0.9	10	5	.50	0 - 0	0 - 1	0 - 0	14	0	1	4	.80	.695	3.18
Scahill, Rob	LM	R	18	10	1	5	0.9	19	6	.32	0 - 0	0 - 0	0 - 0	8	0	0	0		.777	4.43
Hughes, Jared	UR	R	67	19	20	2	1.0	33	7	.21	1 - 1	0 - 2	0 - 1	51	1	3	12	.81	.723	3.02
Torres, Carlos	UR	R	67	23	10	15	0.9	33	7	.21	1 - 2	0 - 2	0 - 0	44	0	3	13	.82	.785	4.21
Feliz, Neftali	UR	R	29	0	8	4	1.3	6	0	.00	5 - 5	3 - 3	0 - 1	16	0	1	0	.89	.866	6.00
Marinez, Jhan	UR	R	15	7	5	6	0.7	8	4	.50	0 - 0	0 - 0	0 - 0	7	0	0	3	1.00	.983	5.40
Peralta, Wily	UR	R	11	4	0	9	0.7	2	0	.00	0 - 0	0 - 0	0 - 0	3	0	0	0		1.059	11.94

Minnesota Twins

Pitcher	Pos	T	Rel G	Early Entry	Cons Days	Long	Lev Ind	#	Scrd	Pct	Easy	Reg	Tough	Clean	Win	BS	Holds	Sv/Hld Pct	Opp OPS	Rel ERA
					Usage				**Inherited Runners**			**Saves**				**Relief Results**				
Kintzler, Brandon	CL	R	45	0	12	4	1.7	8	3	.38	19 - 21	7 - 8	2 - 3	33	1	4	0	.88	.626	2.78
Rogers, Taylor	SU	L	69	4	19	2	1.4	35	5	.14	0 - 0	0 - 3	0 - 1	55	0	4	30	.88	.693	3.07
Belisle, Matt	SU	R	62	6	13	4	1.2	26	4	.15	6 - 6	3 - 8	0 - 0	45	0	5	17	.84	.662	4.03
Hildenberger, Trevor	SU	R	37	8	12	7	1.0	25	5	.20	0 - 0	1 - 2	0 - 1	25	1	2	12	.87	.664	3.21
Duffey, Tyler	LM	R	56	27	7	18	1.0	37	17	.46	0 - 0	1 - 2	0 - 1	30	0	2	12	.87	.721	4.94
Boshers, Buddy	LM	L	38	20	5	6	0.5	31	11	.35	0 - 0	0 - 0	0 - 0	18	0	0	3	1.00	.801	4.89
Breslow, Craig	LM	L	30	12	6	4	0.4	22	7	.32	0 - 0	0 - 1	0 - 0	18	0	1	0	.00	.850	5.23
Gee, Dillon	LM	R	11	10	0	8	0.7	8	1	.13	0 - 0	1 - 1	0 - 0	8	0	0	0	1.00	.627	1.14
Pressly, Ryan	UR	R	57	20	8	6	0.8	38	11	.29	0 - 0	0 - 0	0 - 1	35	0	1	6	.86	.697	4.70
Busenitz, Alan	UR	R	28	10	4	6	0.8	23	5	.22	0 - 0	0 - 0	0 - 1	18	0	1	2	.67	.611	1.99
Tonkin, Michael	UR	R	16	6	1	8	0.2	10	1	.10	0 - 0	0 - 0	0 - 0	6	0	0	0		.903	5.14
Haley, Justin	UR	R	10	4	0	4	0.6	7	2	.29	0 - 0	1 - 1	0 - 0	4	0	0	0	1.00	.879	6.00

New York Mets

Pitcher	Pos	T	Rel G	Early Entry	Cons Days	Long	Lev Ind	#	Scrd	Pct	Easy	Reg	Tough	Clean	Win	BS	Holds	Sv/Hld Pct	Opp OPS	Rel ERA
					Usage				**Inherited Runners**			**Saves**				**Relief Results**				
Reed, Addison	CL	R	48	0	19	2	1.8	16	8	.50	10 - 10	7 - 8	2 - 3	34	0	2	4	.92	.681	2.57
Blevins, Jerry	SU	L	75	2	20	1	1.3	50	14	.28	0 - 1	0 - 1	1 - 6	56	2	7	19	.74	.652	2.94
Smoker, Josh	LM	L	54	27	12	13	0.7	38	11	.29	0 - 0	0 - 0	0 - 0	32	0	0	7	1.00	.858	5.11
Salas, Fernando	LM	R	48	13	12	9	0.9	33	8	.24	0 - 1	0 - 0	0 - 0	24	0	1	11	.92	.862	6.00
Edgin, Josh	LM	L	46	19	14	7	0.7	40	10	.25	0 - 0	0 - 0	1 - 1	30	0	0	4	1.00	.772	3.65
Robles, Hansel	LM	R	46	17	9	14	0.9	36	18	.50	0 - 0	0 - 2	0 - 0	26	0	2	5	.71	.750	4.92
Bradford, Chase	LM	R	28	14	6	5	0.5	18	4	.22	0 - 0	0 - 0	0 - 0	20	0	0	3	1.00	.657	3.74
Sewald, Paul	UR	R	57	17	10	10	0.9	30	11	.37	0 - 1	0 - 2	0 - 0	37	0	3	13	.81	.706	4.55
Goeddel, Erik	UR	R	33	9	6	5	0.5	22	3	.14	0 - 0	0 - 0	0 - 0	20	0	0	1	1.00	.873	5.28
Familia, Jeurys	UR	R	26	1	8	4	1.3	6	1	.17	4 - 4	1 - 2	1 - 1	18	0	1	2	.89	.636	4.38
Ramos, A.J.	UR	R	21	0	3	5	1.6	9	1	.11	4 - 5	1 - 1	2 - 2	14	0	1	1	.89	.789	4.74
Ramirez, Neil	UR	R	20	3	2	8	0.2	16	4	.25	0 - 0	0 - 0	0 - 1	10	0	1	1	.50	.790	6.43
Montero, Rafael	UR	R	16	6	3	7	0.7	4	0	.00	0 - 0	0 - 0	0 - 0	6	0	0	0		.910	7.33

New York Yankees

Pitcher	Pos	T	Usage					Inherited Runners			Saves			Relief Results						
			Rel G	Early Entry	Cons Days	Long	Lev Ind	#	Scrd	Pct	Easy	Reg	Tough	Clean	BS Win	BS	Holds	Sv/Hld Pct	Opp OPS	Rel ERA
Chapman, Aroldis	CL	L	52	2	9	7	1.9	15	4	.27	15 - 16	6 - 8	1 - 2	36	0	4	1	.85	.584	3.22
Betances, Dellin	SU	R	66	1	17	5	1.6	17	4	.24	6 - 6	3 - 5	1 - 2	51	0	3	19	.91	.538	2.87
Warren, Adam	SU	R	46	15	8	13	1.1	29	5	.17	0 - 0	1 - 4	0 - 0	32	1	3	11	.80	.491	2.35
Clippard, Tyler	SU	R	40	3	12	5	1.4	20	6	.30	1 - 1	0 - 2	0 - 3	26	1	5	8	.64	.735	4.95
Kahnle, Tommy	SU	R	32	9	6	2	1.1	19	8	.42	0 - 0	0 - 1	0 - 1	21	1	2	8	.80	.648	2.70
Robertson, David	SU	R	30	4	10	4	1.2	9	2	.22	1 - 1	0 - 1	0 - 0	26	0	1	8	.90	.399	1.03
Shreve, Chasen	LT	L	44	12	6	12	0.9	28	6	.21	0 - 0	0 - 0	0 - 1	27	0	1	1	.50	.712	3.77
Layne, Tommy	LT	L	19	6	2	2	0.3	9	0	.00	0 - 0	0 - 0	0 - 0	12	0	0	2	1.00	.841	7.62
Green, Chad	LM	R	39	23	1	21	0.8	31	4	.13	0 - 0	0 - 1	0 - 0	29	0	1	9	.90	.440	1.61
Mitchell, Bryan	LM	R	19	6	1	7	0.4	5	3	.60	0 - 0	1 - 1	0 - 0	9	0	0	0	1.00	.793	6.51
Holder, Jonathan	UR	R	37	10	4	6	0.8	15	9	.60	0 - 0	0 - 1	0 - 1	23	0	2	3	.60	.770	3.89
Gallegos, Giovanny	UR	R	16	5	0	7	0.5	10	5	.50	0 - 0	0 - 1	0 - 0	6	0	1	0	.00	.740	4.87

Oakland Athletics

Pitcher	Pos	T	Usage					Inherited Runners			Saves			Relief Results						
			Rel G	Early Entry	Cons Days	Long	Lev Ind	#	Scrd	Pct	Easy	Reg	Tough	Clean	BS Win	BS	Holds	Sv/Hld Pct	Opp OPS	Rel ERA
Casilla, Santiago	CL	R	63	2	12	4	1.5	6	4	.67	12 - 13	4 - 10	0 - 0	42	1	7	4	.74	.757	4.27
Treinen, Blake	CL	R	35	2	13	3	1.9	18	8	.44	6 - 6	6 - 4	3 - 6	25	0	3	5	.86	.633	2.13
Dull, Ryan	SU	R	49	14	13	3	1.2	24	6	.25	0 - 1	0 - 0	0 - 1	31	0	2	20	.91	.724	5.14
Madson, Ryan	SU	R	40	2	11	2	1.2	13	2	.15	0 - 0	0 - 1	1 - 3	33	1	3	14	.83	.496	2.06
Doolittle, Sean	SU	L	23	2	5	1	1.2	5	2	.40	2 - 2	1 - 1	0 - 1	18	0	1	8	.92	.467	3.38
Hatcher, Chris	SU	R	23	1	8	1	1.5	7	3	.43	1 - 2	0 - 1	0 - 1	16	0	3	9	.77	.685	3.52
Coulombe, Daniel	LT	L	72	16	18	6	0.7	49	15	.31	0 - 0	0 - 0	0 - 1	50	0	1	13	.93	.714	3.48
Moll, Sam	LT	L	11	5	5	2	0.5	5	1	.20	0 - 0	0 - 0	0 - 0	3	0	0	3	1.00	1.176	10.80
Castro, Simon	LM	R	26	15	4	9	0.7	13	2	.15	0 - 0	0 - 1	0 - 0	11	0	1	0	.00	.762	4.38
Montas, Frankie	LM	R	23	10	0	10	0.5	11	4	.36	0 - 0	0 - 0	0 - 0	9	0	0	1	1.00	.974	7.03
Hendriks, Liam	UR	R	70	22	16	10	1.1	37	8	.22	0 - 0	0 - 1	1 - 3	48	0	3	16	.85	.663	4.22
Smith, Josh	UR	R	26	4	5	11	0.4	8	3	.38	0 - 0	0 - 0	0 - 0	15	0	0	1	1.00	.805	4.89
Axford, John	UR	R	22	5	5	6	0.5	6	1	.17	0 - 0	0 - 1	0 - 0	10	0	1	1	.50	.886	6.43
Brady, Michael	UR	R	16	4	1	7	0.2	4	2	.50	0 - 0	0 - 0	0 - 0	6	0	0	0		.883	5.68

Philadelphia Phillies

Pitcher	Pos	T	Usage					Inherited Runners			Saves			Relief Results						
			Rel G	Early Entry	Cons Days	Long	Lev Ind	#	Scrd	Pct	Easy	Reg	Tough	Clean	BS Win	BS	Holds	Sv/Hld Pct	Opp OPS	Rel ERA
Neris, Hector	CL	R	74	0	22	5	1.7	7	0	.00	16 - 17	9 - 11	1 - 1	55	0	3	4	.91	.689	3.01
Garcia, Luis	SU	R	66	12	23	6	1.2	20	6	.30	1 - 1	1 - 5	0 - 1	51	1	5	14	.76	.593	2.65
Benoit, Joaquin	SU	R	44	3	13	1	1.1	4	0	.00	1 - 1	1 - 4	0 - 0	34	0	3	13	.83	.648	4.07
Neshek, Pat	SU	R	43	2	11	2	1.2	10	2	.20	0 - 1	0 - 1	1 - 1	39	0	2	10	.85	.501	1.12
Morgan, Adam	LT	L	37	10	4	15	0.6	11	4	.36	0 - 0	0 - 0	0 - 1	23	0	1	6	.86	.737	4.12
Milner, Hoby	LT	L	37	10	8	2	0.6	18	4	.22	0 - 0	0 - 0	0 - 1	31	0	1	7	.88	.736	2.01
Rodriguez, Joely	LM	L	26	10	6	8	1.0	18	12	.67	0 - 0	0 - 1	0 - 1	13	0	2	3	.60	.930	6.33
Pinto, Ricardo	LM	R	25	11	3	9	0.6	7	1	.14	0 - 0	0 - 2	0 - 0	16	0	2	2	.50	.951	7.89
Leiter, Mark	LM	R	16	7	1	9	0.5	5	3	.60	0 - 0	0 - 0	0 - 0	7	0	0	0		.670	4.50
Ramos, Edubray	UR	R	59	15	15	11	1.0	18	5	.28	0 - 0	0 - 2	0 - 1	39	0	3	9	.75	.699	4.21
Gomez, Jeanmar	UR	R	18	4	1	7	1.3	5	0	.00	1 - 2	0 - 0	1 - 1	7	1	1	0	.67	1.037	7.25
Therrien, Jesen	UR	R	15	8	3	4	0.3	9	3	.33	0 - 1	0 - 0	0 - 0	8	0	1	0	.00	.923	8.35
Rios, Yacksel	UR	R	13	5	1	4	0.3	4	2	.50	0 - 0	0 - 0	0 - 0	9	0	0	0		.825	4.41
Arano, Victor	UR	R	10	3	3	3	0.9	2	0	.00	0 - 0	0 - 1	0 - 0	8	0	0	2	1.00	.475	1.69

Pittsburgh Pirates

			Usage					Inherited Runners			Saves			Relief Results						
Pitcher	Pos	T	Rel G	Early Entry	Cons Days	Long	Lev Ind	#	Scrd	Pct	Easy	Reg	Tough	Clean	BS Win	BS	Holds	Sv/Hld Pct	Opp OPS	Rel ERA
Rivero, Felipe	CL	L	73	1	20	5	1.5	23	4	.17	13 - 13	5 - 7	3 - 3	59	0	2	14	.95	.473	1.67
Watson, Tony	CL	L	47	2	11	3	2.0	16	9	.56	6 - 9	4 - 5	0 - 3	32	1	7	6	.70	.824	3.66
Hudson, Daniel	SU	R	71	13	20	6	1.1	28	7	.25	0 - 0	0 - 0	0 - 2	45	0	2	21	.91	.761	4.38
Nicasio, Juan	SU	R	65	8	20	3	1.3	20	5	.25	2 - 2	0 - 2	0 - 2	54	0	4	21	.85	.617	2.85
Kontos, George	SU	R	15	0	4	1	1.0	6	0	.00	1 - 1	0 - 1	0 - 0	12	0	1	6	.88	.516	1.84
LeBlanc, Wade	LM	L	50	23	5	16	0.5	16	2	.13	0 - 0	1 - 2	0 - 1	31	0	2	4	.71	.717	4.50
Marinez, Jhan	LM	R	24	8	3	9	0.4	12	7	.58	0 - 0	0 - 0	0 - 0	12	0	0	0		.782	3.18
Barbato, Johnny	LM	R	24	8	5	8	0.4	7	1	.14	0 - 0	0 - 0	0 - 0	16	0	0	0		.755	4.08
Santana, Edgar	LM	R	19	9	3	1	0.7	6	0	.00	0 - 0	0 - 0	0 - 0	13	0	0	2	1.00	.780	3.50
Schugel, A.J.	UR	R	32	12	7	2	0.7	29	14	.48	0 - 0	0 - 0	0 - 1	19	0	1	4	.80	.725	1.97
Neverauskas, Dovydas	UR	R	24	2	8	4	0.7	4	0	.00	0 - 0	0 - 1	0 - 0	17	0	1	2	.67	.749	3.91

San Diego Padres

			Usage					Inherited Runners			Saves			Relief Results						
Pitcher	Pos	T	Rel G	Early Entry	Cons Days	Long	Lev Ind	#	Scrd	Pct	Easy	Reg	Tough	Clean	BS Win	BS	Holds	Sv/Hld Pct	Opp OPS	Rel ERA
Hand, Brad	CL	L	72	0	17	6	1.7	35	8	.23	14 - 15	6 - 6	1 - 5	56	2	5	16	.88	.580	2.16
Maurer, Brandon	CL	R	42	0	10	0	1.6	9	4	.44	12 - 13	8 - 9	0 - 1	30	0	3	2	.88	.691	5.72
Buchter, Ryan	SU	L	42	5	10	4	1.2	12	5	.42	1 - 1	0 - 1	0 - 1	28	0	2	15	.89	.696	3.05
Torres, Jose	LT	L	62	19	13	13	0.8	25	7	.28	1 - 1	0 - 1	0 - 0	39	0	1	3	.80	.753	4.21
Baumann, Buddy	LT	L	23	6	8	1	0.8	18	4	.22	0 - 0	0 - 0	0 - 1	16	0	1	4	.80	.695	2.55
McGrath, Kyle	LT	L	17	4	0	4	0.5	10	6	.60	0 - 0	0 - 0	0 - 0	10	0	0	0		.595	2.84
Yates, Kirby	LM	R	61	9	16	5	0.9	16	1	.06	1 - 2	0 - 2	0 - 0	44	0	3	20	.88	.666	3.72
Stammen, Craig	LM	R	60	30	9	18	0.9	55	14	.25	0 - 0	0 - 0	0 - 2	41	0	2	11	.85	.684	3.14
Diaz, Miguel	LM	R	28	13	3	8	0.2	11	6	.55	0 - 0	0 - 0	0 - 0	10	0	0	0		.934	7.94
Quackenbush, Kevin	LM	R	20	12	4	11	0.5	6	2	.33	0 - 0	0 - 0	0 - 0	12	0	0	1	1.00	.869	7.86
Maton, Phil	UR	R	46	11	6	3	0.9	22	10	.45	1 - 1	0 - 0	0 - 0	28	0	0	8	1.00	.778	4.19
Valdez, Jose	UR	R	13	6	3	4	0.3	8	4	.50	0 - 0	0 - 0	0 - 0	6	0	0	0		1.067	7.94
Capps, Carter	UR	R	11	1	1	1	0.2	2	0	.00	0 - 0	0 - 0	0 - 0	6	0	0	1	1.00	.699	6.57

San Francisco Giants

			Usage					Inherited Runners			Saves			Relief Results						
Pitcher	Pos	T	Rel G	Early Entry	Cons Days	Long	Lev Ind	#	Scrd	Pct	Easy	Reg	Tough	Clean	BS Win	BS	Holds	Sv/Hld Pct	Opp OPS	Rel ERA
Dyson, Sam	CL	R	38	0	10	3	2.2	3	0	.00	8 - 9	6 - 8	0 - 0	30	0	3	1	.83	.700	4.03
Melancon, Mark	CL	R	32	0	7	1	1.8	1	0	.00	7 - 10	4 - 6	0 - 0	24	1	5	5	.76	.794	4.50
Strickland, Hunter	SU	R	68	1	19	4	1.5	27	12	.44	1 - 1	0 - 2	0 - 0	49	0	2	21	.92	.702	2.64
Osich, Josh	LT	L	54	6	11	7	0.5	30	6	.20	0 - 0	0 - 1	0 - 0	35	0	1	6	.86	.839	6.23
Okert, Steven	LT	L	44	5	12	3	1.2	25	6	.24	0 - 0	0 - 0	0 - 0	31	0	0	11	1.00	.755	5.67
Kontos, George	LM	R	50	11	9	8	1.0	33	15	.45	0 - 0	0 - 1	0 - 4	28	0	5	5	.50	.758	3.83
Suarez, Albert	LM	R	18	9	2	11	0.6	7	1	.14	0 - 0	1 - 3	0 - 0	9	0	2	0	.33	.698	5.12
Gearrin, Cory	UR	R	68	19	11	11	0.9	41	20	.49	0 - 0	0 - 0	0 - 0	49	0	0	8	1.00	.645	1.99
Law, Derek	UR	R	41	4	7	4	1.2	15	6	.40	2 - 2	2 - 4	0 - 0	26	1	2	5	.82	.840	5.06
Crick, Kyle	UR	R	30	6	4	9	0.4	21	3	.14	0 - 0	0 - 0	0 - 0	19	0	0	1	1.00	.596	3.06
Morris, Bryan	UR	R	20	7	1	2	0.8	10	4	.40	0 - 0	0 - 0	0 - 0	14	0	0	1	1.00	.790	6.43
Blach, Ty	UR	L	10	4	0	3	0.9	3	0	.00	0 - 0	0 - 0	0 - 0	8	0	0	0		.610	4.50

Seattle Mariners

Pitcher	Pos	T	Rel G	Early Entry	Cons Days	Long	Lev Ind	#	Scrd	Pct	Easy	Reg	Tough	Clean	BS Win	BS	Holds	Sv/Hld Pct	Opp OPS	Rel ERA
			Usage					Inherited Runners			Saves			Relief Results						
Diaz, Edwin	CL	R	66	0	21	7	2.0	18	6	.33	15 - 16	16 - 18	3 - 5	48	0	5	2	.88	.619	3.27
Vincent, Nick	SU	R	69	5	15	1	1.5	32	7	.22	0 - 0	0 - 0	0 - 2	53	0	2	29	.94	.643	3.20
Rzepczynski, Marc	SU	L	64	10	14	1	1.5	52	8	.15	0 - 0	0 - 1	1 - 2	50	0	2	20	.91	.707	4.02
Zych, Tony	SU	R	45	12	10	6	1.4	31	8	.26	0 - 0	0 - 1	1 - 1	28	0	1	12	.93	.617	2.66
Cishek, Steve	SU	R	23	5	6	0	1.2	13	4	.31	1 - 1	0 - 1	0 - 2	16	0	3	6	.70	.601	3.15
Pazos, James	LT	L	59	24	10	8	1.0	32	16	.50	0 - 0	0 - 1	0 - 2	35	0	3	10	.77	.723	3.86
Pagan, Emilio	LM	R	34	13	4	10	0.8	16	4	.25	0 - 0	0 - 1	0 - 0	22	0	1	8	.89	.610	3.22
Lawrence, Casey	LM	R	23	12	1	11	0.3	8	3	.38	0 - 1	0 - 0	0 - 0	10	0	1	0	.00	.875	5.57
Altavilla, Dan	UR	R	41	9	8	8	0.7	24	7	.29	0 - 2	0 - 1	0 - 1	23	0	4	2	.33	.765	4.24
Garton, Ryan	UR	R	13	6	3	1	0.5	7	1	.14	0 - 0	0 - 0	0 - 0	10	0	0	1	1.00	.368	1.54
Phelps, David	UR	R	10	1	1	1	1.9	4	3	.75	0 - 0	0 - 1	0 - 1	6	1	2	3	.60	.660	3.12

St Louis Cardinals

Pitcher	Pos	T	Rel G	Early Entry	Cons Days	Long	Lev Ind	#	Scrd	Pct	Easy	Reg	Tough	Clean	BS Win	BS	Holds	Sv/Hld Pct	Opp OPS	Rel ERA
			Usage					Inherited Runners			Saves			Relief Results						
Oh, Seung Hwan	CL	R	62	1	17	6	1.9	17	8	.47	13 - 13	5 - 7	2 - 4	38	1	4	7	.87	.794	4.10
Bowman, Matt	SU	R	75	16	16	4	1.3	51	15	.29	1 - 1	0 - 1	1 - 3	51	0	3	23	.89	.659	3.99
Rosenthal, Trevor	SU	R	50	0	8	7	2.0	6	1	.17	5 - 6	4 - 5	2 - 2	36	0	2	12	.92	.572	3.40
Cecil, Brett	LT	L	73	17	19	4	1.1	32	13	.41	1 - 3	0 - 3	0 - 1	49	0	6	13	.70	.714	3.88
Lyons, Tyler	LT	L	50	10	12	10	0.9	17	5	.29	1 - 1	2 - 2	0 - 1	36	0	1	15	.95	.608	2.83
Siegrist, Kevin	LT	L	39	3	8	2	0.9	12	5	.42	1 - 1	0 - 0	0 - 0	27	0	0	6	1.00	.813	4.98
Duke, Zach	LT	L	27	7	5	0	0.9	28	5	.18	0 - 0	0 - 0	0 - 0	19	0	0	6	1.00	.647	3.93
Sherriff, Ryan	LT	L	13	6	1	2	1.0	9	2	.22	0 - 0	0 - 0	0 - 0	10	0	0	1	1.00	.682	3.14
Brebbia, John	UR	R	50	15	11	5	0.7	22	10	.45	0 - 0	0 - 0	0 - 1	34	0	1	5	.83	.640	2.44
Tuivailala, Samuel	UR	R	37	5	4	5	0.7	0	0	.00	0 - 0	0 - 0	0 - 0	26	0	0	1	1.00	.626	2.55
Broxton, Jonathan	UR	R	20	2	3	1	0.8	7	3	.43	0 - 0	0 - 0	0 - 0	13	0	0	1	1.00	.969	6.89
Socolovich, Miguel	UR	R	15	2	2	4	0.5	6	3	.50	0 - 0	1 - 1	0 - 0	4	0	0	0	1.00	1.004	8.68

Tampa Bay Rays

Pitcher	Pos	T	Rel G	Early Entry	Cons Days	Long	Lev Ind	#	Scrd	Pct	Easy	Reg	Tough	Clean	BS Win	BS	Holds	Sv/Hld Pct	Opp OPS	Rel ERA
			Usage					Inherited Runners			Saves			Relief Results						
Colome, Alex	CL	R	65	0	15	7	2.4	19	2	.11	32 - 34	11 - 14	4 - 5	46	1	6	1	.89	.636	3.24
Hunter, Tommy	SU	R	61	7	13	4	1.2	25	6	.24	1 - 1	0 - 0	0 - 0	45	0	0	25	1.00	.588	2.61
Cishek, Steve	SU	R	26	6	9	1	1.3	11	1	.09	0 - 0	0 - 0	0 - 0	24	0	0	9	1.00	.399	1.09
Ramirez, Erasmo	SU	R	18	9	2	8	1.3	8	1	.13	1 - 2	0 - 0	0 - 0	12	0	1	6	.88	.543	3.23
Alvarado, Jose	LT	L	35	10	6	1	1.0	18	4	.22	0 - 0	0 - 0	0 - 0	24	0	0	7	1.00	.570	3.64
Jennings, Dan	LT	L	29	8	7	1	0.9	21	6	.29	0 - 0	0 - 1	0 - 0	22	0	1	7	.88	.723	3.44
Kolarek, Adam	LT	L	12	2	2	0	0.5	8	2	.25	0 - 0	0 - 0	0 - 0	6	0	0	2	1.00	.984	6.48
Farquhar, Danny	LM	R	37	5	10	7	1.0	20	7	.35	0 - 1	0 - 0	0 - 0	25	0	1	9	.90	.659	4.11
Pruitt, Austin	LM	R	22	10	0	13	0.7	8	4	.50	0 - 1	1 - 1	0 - 0	6	0	1	1	.67	.875	6.53
Whitley, Chase	UR	R	41	14	6	8	0.6	27	5	.19	1 - 1	1 - 2	0 - 0	24	0	1	5	.88	.630	4.08
Diaz, Jumbo	UR	R	31	8	5	3	1.3	20	7	.35	0 - 0	0 - 0	0 - 3	17	0	3	6	.67	.806	5.70
Boxberger, Brad	UR	R	30	6	3	2	1.3	11	2	.18	0 - 1	0 - 0	0 - 1	22	0	2	5	.71	.665	3.38
Romo, Sergio	UR	R	25	8	4	3	1.0	13	5	.38	0 - 0	0 - 0	0 - 1	19	0	1	4	.80	.494	1.47
Stanek, Ryne	UR	R	21	2	2	5	0.8	11	5	.45	0 - 0	0 - 1	0 - 0	10	0	1	4	.80	.985	5.85
Kittredge, Andrew	UR	R	15	7	2	1	1.0	4	0	.00	0 - 0	0 - 0	0 - 0	12	0	0	1	1.00	.665	1.76

Texas Rangers

Pitcher	Pos	T	Rel G	Early Entry	Cons Days	Long	Lev Ind	#	Scrd	Pct	Easy	Reg	Tough	Clean	BS Win	BS	Holds	Sv/Hld Pct	Opp OPS	Rel ERA
Claudio, Alex	SU	L	69	4	19	14	1.3	44	13	.30	6-6	2-2	3-7	48	1	4	7	.82	.575	2.29
Bush, Matt	SU	R	57	2	11	8	1.4	13	3	.23	5-6	4-7	1-2	38	0	5	10	.80	.750	3.78
Kela, Keone	SU	R	39	1	8	4	1.2	12	3	.25	2-2	0-1	0-0	32	0	1	11	.93	.479	2.79
Diekman, Jake	SU	L	11	0	2	0	1.4	8	5	.63	0-0	1-1	0-0	8	0	0	5	1.00	.523	2.53
Barnette, Tony	LM	R	50	23	6	13	0.9	43	22	.51	1-1	1-2	0-3	24	0	4	4	.60	.809	5.49
Jeffress, Jeremy	LM	R	39	13	8	9	0.7	28	10	.36	0-0	0-0	0-0	21	0	0	4	1.00	.898	5.31
Alvarez, Dario	LM	L	20	6	2	5	1.0	24	13	.54	0-0	0-0	0-0	10	0	0	3	1.00	.799	2.76
Bibens-Dirkx, Austin	LM	R	18	12	0	10	0.4	20	9	.45	0-0	0-0	0-0	6	0	0	0		.787	4.63
Leclerc, Jose	UR	R	47	7	6	7	1.0	22	7	.32	0-0	2-3	0-0	32	0	1	10	.92	.585	3.94
Grilli, Jason	UR	R	20	0	2	2	0.8	0	0	.00	0-0	0-0	0-0	12	0	0	3	1.00	.841	5.59
Dyson, Sam	UR	R	17	1	1	0	1.7	2	2	1.00	0-2	0-1	0-1	9	0	4	3	.43	1.156	10.80
Rodriguez, Ricardo	UR	R	16	4	3	0	1.0	10	6	.60	1-2	0-0	0-1	10	0	2	1	.50	.904	6.23
Gardewine, Nick	UR	R	12	3	1	0	0.4	8	1	.13	0-0	0-0	0-0	7	0	0	0		.849	5.63

Toronto Blue Jays

Pitcher	Pos	T	Rel G	Early Entry	Cons Days	Long	Lev Ind	#	Scrd	Pct	Easy	Reg	Tough	Clean	BS Win	BS	Holds	Sv/Hld Pct	Opp OPS	Rel ERA
Osuna, Roberto	CL	R	66	0	16	3	2.1	12	2	.17	24-29	13-18	2-2	51	1	10	0	.80	.507	3.38
Smith, Joe	SU	R	38	2	9	0	1.5	11	4	.36	0-1	0-0	0-0	27	1	1	13	.93	.623	3.28
Biagini, Joe	SU	R	26	8	4	4	1.7	18	3	.17	0-1	0-1	1-1	17	0	2	9	.83	.649	4.26
Loup, Aaron	LT	L	70	25	11	12	0.9	41	9	.22	0-0	0-0	0-0	48	0	0	6	1.00	.722	3.75
Beliveau, Jeff	LT	L	19	4	4	5	0.4	11	4	.36	0-0	0-0	0-0	10	0	0	2	1.00	.898	7.47
Mayza, Tim	LT	L	19	4	3	2	0.4	5	3	.60	0-0	0-0	0-0	10	0	0	2	1.00	.874	6.88
Howell, J.P.	LT	L	16	3	2	1	0.5	13	7	.54	0-0	0-0	0-1	8	0	1	0	.00	.940	7.36
Dermody, Matt	LM	L	23	10	4	6	0.7	16	4	.25	0-0	0-0	0-0	13	0	0	1	1.00	.822	4.43
Tepera, Ryan	UR	R	73	9	16	10	1.4	34	8	.24	1-1	1-2	0-1	50	1	2	17	.90	.633	3.59
Leone, Dominic	UR	R	65	25	13	9	1.0	54	12	.22	0-0	1-3	0-2	42	1	4	11	.75	.625	2.56
Barnes, Danny	UR	R	60	20	8	10	1.2	37	5	.14	0-0	0-3	0-1	40	1	4	11	.73	.646	3.55
Grilli, Jason	UR	R	26	1	3	3	1.2	7	3	.43	1-1	0-1	0-1	16	0	2	1	.50	1.010	6.97
Koehler, Tom	UR	R	14	1	1	0	1.1	1	1	1.00	0-0	0-0	0-0	11	0	0	2	1.00	.711	3.00
Campos, Leonel	UR	R	13	4	1	2	0.2	10	4	.40	0-0	0-0	0-0	9	0	0	0		.765	2.63
Ramirez, Carlos	UR	R	12	5	1	2	0.9	5	0	.00	0-0	0-0	0-0	10	0	0	3	1.00	.487	2.70
Santos, Luis	UR	R	10	5	1	5	0.8	5	4	.80	0-0	1-1	0-0	4	0	0	1	1.00	.779	2.70

Washington Nationals

Pitcher	Pos	T	Rel G	Early Entry	Cons Days	Long	Lev Ind	#	Scrd	Pct	Easy	Reg	Tough	Clean	BS Win	BS	Holds	Sv/Hld Pct	Opp OPS	Rel ERA
Doolittle, Sean	CL	L	30	0	6	1	1.9	1	0	.00	12-13	8-8	1-1	23	1	1	1	.96	.551	2.40
Kintzler, Brandon	SU	R	27	0	6	0	1.8	6	3	.50	0-1	1-2	0-0	22	0	2	10	.85	.659	3.46
Glover, Koda	SU	R	23	0	6	1	1.8	12	2	.17	5-6	2-2	1-2	16	0	2	5	.87	.647	5.12
Madson, Ryan	SU	R	20	0	3	0	1.5	0	0	.00	1-1	0-0	0-0	18	0	0	11	1.00	.483	1.37
Romero, Enny	LT	L	53	6	13	15	1.0	15	3	.20	1-2	1-2	0-0	34	0	2	10	.86	.736	3.56
Perez, Oliver	LT	L	50	11	6	4	0.8	35	5	.14	0-0	1-1	0-0	38	0	0	12	1.00	.772	4.64
Grace, Matt	LT	L	39	10	6	9	0.7	13	2	.15	2-2	0-0	0-0	21	0	0	4	1.00	.726	4.73
Solis, Sammy	LT	L	30	6	4	2	0.9	14	2	.14	1-1	0-0	0-0	18	0	0	6	1.00	.706	5.88
Albers, Matt	UR	R	63	6	16	8	0.9	41	15	.37	1-1	1-3	0-1	48	1	3	14	.84	.520	1.62
Blanton, Joe	UR	R	51	12	9	7	0.6	22	4	.18	0-0	0-0	0-0	32	0	0	7	1.00	.882	5.68
Treinen, Blake	UR	R	37	8	8	5	1.1	18	8	.44	3-4	0-0	0-1	19	0	2	5	.80	.832	5.73
Kelley, Shawn	UR	R	33	1	6	2	1.3	11	3	.27	1-3	2-2	1-1	21	0	2	2	.75	.963	7.27
Turner, Jacob	UR	R	16	7	2	6	1.0	7	3	.43	0-0	0-1	0-2	8	1	3	1	.25	.901	5.20

Pitchers Hitting, Fielding & Holding Runners, and Hitters Pitching

Lindsay Zeck

In 2017, despite being injured for over half of the season, Madison Bumgarner didn't disappoint when he came up to the plate. He hit three more home runs in 2017, giving him 17 for his career and placing him 16th on the all-time leaderboard for most career home runs by a pitcher, right behind Cy Young. While Bumgarner's power-hitting performance has come to be expected, the best hitting pitcher this season may have been rookie pitcher, Tyler Glasnow of the Pirates. Glasnow led all pitchers with at least 20 plate appearances in OPS, with a line of .294/.455/.294. Another good performance came from fellow Pennsylvania rookie, Ben Lively of the Phillies. Lively finished the season with the fourth highest OPS (.692) and—in only 26 at bats—hit two home runs and batted in eight runs. The only two pitchers to finish with more RBIs were Cardinals' teammates Adam Wainwright and Carlos Martinez, with 11 in 42 and 62 at-bats, respectively.

This section not only gives offensive statistics for pitchers, but the last column in the tables also gives their Defensive Runs Saved (RS). The best defensive pitchers this season were Dallas Keuchel and Tyler Chatwood, who each saved nine runs for the Astros and Rockies, respectively. Keuchel's outstanding defense comes as no surprise, as he has finished first in Defensive Runs Saved for three of the past four seasons. He has saved 39 runs in that time, 14 more than any other pitcher. Chatwood, however, is a surprise. Prior to this season, he had saved a combined four runs in 97 games. In 2017, he had three Good Fielding Plays with no Defensive Misplays or Errors. Runners stole just five bases against him successfully and were caught five times—four times by the catcher and once by Chatwood himself. He also picked off two runners. Chatwood saved runs in all four components used for calculating Defensive Runs Saved for pitchers—1. Range and Positioning, 2. Stolen Bases, 3. Bunts, and 4. Good Fielding Plays and Defensive Misplays plus Errors.

The final table in the section shows the pitching statistics for hitters who pitched, both for this season and for their careers. The most notable pitching performances by a batter in 2017 were:

- Chris Gimenez - appeared in six (!) games for the Twins and didn't walk a single hitter
- Daniel Descalso - pitched a perfect inning on two separate occasions for the Diamondbacks
- J.D. Davis - struck out three in 1.2 scoreless innings for the Astros

Pitchers Hitting, Fielding and Holding Runners

Pitcher	T	2017 Hitting Avg	AB	H	HR	RBI	SH	Career Hitting Avg	AB	H	2B	3B	HR	RBI	BB	SO	SH	Inn	PO	A	E	DP	Pct	SBA	CS	PCS	PPO	CS%	RS
Abad, Fernando, Bos	L	-	0	0	0	0	0	.111	9	1	0	0	0	0	0	5	0	43.2	0	6	0	1	1.000	6	1	0	0	.17	1
Adams, Austin, Was	R	-	0	0	0	0	0	-	0	0	0	0	0	0	0	0	0	5.0	1	0	0	0	1.000	0	0	0	0	-	0
Adleman, Tim, Cin	R	.103	29	3	0	2	3	.140	50	7	3	0	0	5	0	21	5	122.1	15	12	0	1	1.000	8	2	0	2	.25	1
Albers, Andrew, Sea	L	1.000	1	1	0	1	2	1.000	1	1	0	0	0	1	0	0	2	41.0	1	5	0	0	1.000	0	0	0	0	-	1
Albers, Matt, Was	R	-	0	0	0	0	0	.086	35	3	1	0	0	0	0	21	3	61.0	1	5	0	0	1.000	4	1	0	0	.25	-1
Alburquerque, Al, KC-CWS	R	-	0	0	0	0	0	-	0	0	0	0	0	0	0	0	0	18.0	2	7	0	0	1.000	0	0	0	0	-	1
Alcantara, Raul, Oak	R	-	0	0	0	0	0	-	0	0	0	0	0	0	0	0	0	24.0	0	1	1	0	.500	0	0	0	0	-	0
Alcantara, Sandy, StL	R	-	0	0	0	0	0	-	0	0	0	0	0	0	0	0	0	8.1	0	2	1	2	.667	0	0	0	0	-	0
Alcantara, Victor, Det	R	-	0	0	0	0	0	-	0	0	0	0	0	0	0	0	0	7.1	0	1	0	0	1.000	0	0	0	0	-	0
Alexander, Scott, KC	L	.000	3	0	0	0	0	.000	3	0	0	0	0	0	0	1	0	69.0	6	7	2	0	.867	3	0	0	0	.00	1
Allen, Cody, Cle	R	-	0	0	0	0	0	-	0	0	0	0	0	0	0	0	0	67.1	1	7	0	0	1.000	7	1	0	0	.14	-1
Almonte, Miguel, KC	R	-	0	0	0	0	0	-	0	0	0	0	0	0	0	0	0	2.0	0	0	0	0	-	1	0	0	0	.00	0
Altavilla, Dan, Sea	R	-	0	0	0	0	0	-	0	0	0	0	0	0	0	0	0	46.2	4	3	0	0	1.000	5	0	0	0	.00	-1
Alvarado, Jose, TB	L	-	0	0	0	0	0	-	0	0	0	0	0	0	0	0	0	29.2	2	3	0	0	1.000	2	0	0	0	.00	-1
Alvarez, Dario, Tex	L	-	0	0	0	0	0	-	0	0	0	0	0	0	0	0	0	16.1	0	1	0	0	1.000	2	0	0	0	.00	0
Alvarez, Henderson, Phi	R	.000	6	0	0	0	0	.220	100	22	4	0	1	9	1	36	12	14.2	1	5	0	0	1.000	0	0	0	0	-	2
Alvarez, Jose, LAA	L	-	0	0	0	0	0	.000	2	0	0	0	0	0	1	0	0	48.2	4	8	0	2	1.000	1	0	0	0	.00	2
Anderson, Brett, ChC-Tor	L	.143	7	1	0	1	0	.093	75	7	3	0	0	5	6	46	10	55.1	2	13	1	0	.938	7	1	1	0	.14	-1
Anderson, Chase, Mil	R	.135	52	7	0	3	3	.095	179	17	1	0	0	7	2	93	22	141.1	9	16	1	0	.962	15	4	0	2	.27	2
Anderson, Drew, Phi	R	-	0	0	0	0	0	-	0	0	0	0	0	0	0	0	0	2.1	0	0	0	0	-	2	0	0	0	.00	0
Anderson, Tyler, Col	L	.038	26	1	0	0	6	.082	61	5	0	0	1	3	5	28	9	86.0	2	17	2	2	.905	7	1	0	2	.14	1
Andriese, Matt, TB	R	-	0	0	0	0	0	.000	2	0	0	0	0	0	0	0	0	86.0	6	5	0	0	1.000	7	2	0	0	.29	-1
Aquino, Jayson, Bal	L	.000	2	0	0	0	0	.000	2	0	0	0	0	0	0	2	0	13.1	0	0	1	0	.000	1	0	0	0	.00	0
Arano, Victor, Phi	R	-	0	0	0	0	0	-	0	0	0	0	0	0	0	0	0	10.2	0	1	0	0	1.000	1	0	0	0	.00	0
Archer, Chris, TB	R	.250	8	2	0	1	0	.071	28	2	0	0	0	1	1	13	0	201.0	8	6	1	0	.933	8	2	0	0	.25	-3
Armstrong, Shawn, Cle	R	-	0	0	0	0	0	-	0	0	0	0	0	0	0	0	0	24.2	1	2	0	0	1.000	1	0	0	0	.00	0
Arrieta, Jake, ChC	R	.131	61	8	1	5	2	.175	269	47	5	4	5	20	10	135	17	168.1	15	26	2	2	.953	23	4	0	1	.17	-2
Arroyo, Bronson, Cin	R	.154	26	4	0	0	3	.129	629	81	16	0	6	29	14	276	85	71.0	6	6	0	0	1.000	3	2	0	0	.67	1
Asher, Alec, Bal	R	.000	1	0	0	0	0	.167	18	3	1	0	0	2	0	9	0	60.0	3	6	0	2	1.000	5	0	0	0	.00	-3
Astin, Barrett, Cin	R	.000	1	0	0	0	0	.000	1	0	0	0	0	0	0	1	0	8.0	2	2	0	0	1.000	1	1	0	1	1.00	1
Avilan, Luis, LAD	L	.000	2	0	0	0	0	.167	6	1	0	0	0	0	0	1	2	46.0	2	3	1	1	.833	6	3	1	0	.50	-1
Axford, John, Oak	R	-	0	0	0	0	0	.000	1	0	0	0	0	0	0	1	0	21.0	1	4	0	0	1.000	2	0	0	0	.00	0
Baez, Pedro, LAD	R	.000	1	0	0	1	0	.000	2	0	0	0	0	0	1	1	1	64.0	2	4	0	0	1.000	3	1	0	0	.33	0
Bailey, Andrew, LAA	R	-	0	0	0	0	0	-	0	0	0	0	0	0	0	0	0	4.0	0	0	0	0	-	0	0	0	0	-	0
Bailey, Homer, Cin	R	.250	28	7	0	0	7	.164	342	56	8	0	0	17	10	131	48	91.0	7	12	1	0	.950	11	3	1	1	.27	0
Banda, Anthony, Ari	L	.000	5	0	0	0	1	.000	5	0	0	0	0	0	0	3	1	25.2	0	3	0	0	1.000	0	0	0	0	-	0
Barbato, Johnny, Pit	R	.000	1	0	0	0	0	.000	1	0	0	0	0	0	0	0	0	28.2	2	4	0	0	1.000	0	0	0	0	-	1
Barnes, Danny, Tor	R	-	0	0	0	0	0	-	0	0	0	0	0	0	0	0	0	66.0	3	3	0	0	1.000	9	1	0	0	.11	-1
Barnes, Jacob, Mil	R	-	0	0	0	0	0	-	0	0	0	0	0	0	1	0	0	72.0	7	10	3	1	.850	5	1	1	0	.20	-1
Barnes, Matt, Bos	R	-	0	0	0	0	0	-	0	0	0	0	0	0	0	0	0	69.2	4	7	0	0	1.000	7	3	0	0	.43	0
Barnette, Tony, Tex	R	-	0	0	0	0	0	-	0	0	0	0	0	0	0	0	0	57.1	6	3	0	0	1.000	2	1	0	0	.50	1
Barraclough, Kyle, Mia	R	.000	1	0	0	0	0	.000	2	0	0	0	0	0	0	2	0	66.0	4	6	0	0	1.000	6	1	0	1	.17	-1
Barrett, Jake, Ari	R	-	0	0	0	0	0	-	0	0	0	0	0	0	0	0	0	27.0	2	0	1	0	.667	1	0	0	0	.00	-1
Bass, Anthony, Tex	R	-	0	0	0	0	0	.105	38	4	0	1	0	6	0	17	1	5.2	0	0	0	0	-	0	0	0	0	-	0
Bastardo, Antonio, Pit	L	-	0	0	0	0	0	.000	8	0	0	0	0	0	2	5	1	9.2	0	0	0	0	-	3	0	0	0	.00	-1
Bauer, Trevor, Cle	R	.000	3	0	0	0	0	.048	21	1	0	0	0	1	1	11	2	176.1	9	10	1	3	.950	10	6	1	0	.60	0
Baumann, Buddy, SD	L	-	0	0	0	0	0	-	0	0	0	0	0	0	0	0	0	17.2	1	1	0	0	1.000	2	1	1	0	.50	0
Beato, Pedro, Phi	R	-	0	0	0	0	0	-	0	0	0	0	0	0	0	0	0	0.2	0	0	0	0	-	0	0	0	0	-	0
Beck, Chris, CWS	R	-	0	0	0	0	0	-	0	0	0	0	0	0	0	0	0	64.2	5	8	1	0	.929	7	2	1	0	.29	1
Bedrosian, Cam, LAA	R	-	0	0	0	0	0	-	0	0	0	0	0	0	0	0	0	44.2	0	1	0	0	1.000	5	2	0	0	.40	0
Belisle, Matt, Min	R	-	0	0	0	0	0	.079	89	7	3	0	0	3	3	49	18	60.1	5	8	0	0	1.000	5	1	0	0	.20	1
Beliveau, Jeff, Tor	L	-	0	0	0	0	0	-	0	0	0	0	0	0	0	0	0	15.2	0	2	0	0	1.000	0	0	0	0	-	0
Bell, Chad, Det	L	-	0	0	0	0	0	-	0	0	0	0	0	0	0	0	0	62.1	1	9	0	1	1.000	7	2	0	0	.29	-1
Benoit, Joaquin, Phi-Pit	R	-	0	0	0	0	0	.000	9	0	0	0	0	0	0	4	0	50.1	1	5	0	0	1.000	3	1	0	0	.33	-1
Bergman, Christian, Sea	R	.000	1	0	0	0	0	.114	35	4	0	0	0	1	1	10	3	54.0	3	7	0	0	1.000	3	1	0	0	.33	0
Berrios, Jose, Min	R	.200	5	1	0	0	0	.333	6	2	0	0	0	0	0	2	0	145.2	8	13	1	2	.955	9	3	0	0	.33	-1
Betances, Dellin, NYY	R	-	0	0	0	0	0	-	0	0	0	0	0	0	0	0	0	59.2	5	4	0	0	1.000	11	3	0	0	.27	-1
Bethancourt, C., SD	R	.143	7	1	0	0	0	.222	469	104	20	0	8	46	18	119	0	3.2	0	0	0	0	-	1	0	0	0	.00	0
Bettis, Chad, Col	R	.091	11	1	0	1	3	.049	103	5	0	0	0	4	9	45	11	46.1	2	11	0	1	1.000	2	2	1	0	1.00	1
Biagini, Joe, Tor	R	.000	2	0	0	1	1	.000	2	0	0	0	0	0	1	0	0	119.2	8	13	2	0	.913	20	1	0	0	.05	-5
Bibens-Dirkx, Austin, Tex	R	.000	3	0	0	0	0	.000	3	0	0	0	0	0	0	3	0	69.1	6	8	0	1	1.000	3	0	0	0	.00	0
Blach, Ty, SF	L	.227	44	10	1	7	4	.250	48	12	2	0	1	7	4	21	4	163.2	21	21	2	2	.955	6	2	0	0	.33	2
Blackburn, Paul, Oak	R	.000	3	0	0	0	0	.000	3	0	0	0	0	0	0	2	0	58.2	1	8	0	0	1.000	4	3	1	0	.75	2
Blair, Aaron, Atl	R	1.000	1	1	0	0	0	.091	22	2	0	0	0	0	1	9	2	3.0	0	1	0	0	1.000	2	0	0	0	.00	0
Blanton, Joe, Was	R	-	0	0	0	0	0	.106	216	23	0	0	0	6	9	92	31	44.1	3	3	0	0	1.000	9	1	0	0	.11	-3
Blazek, Michael, Mil	R	.000	2	0	0	0	0	.167	6	1	1	0	0	1	0	3	0	8.2	0	1	0	0	1.000	0	0	0	0	-	-1
Bleier, Richard, Bal	L	-	0	0	0	0	0	-	0	0	0	0	0	0	0	0	0	63.1	5	16	1	2	.955	6	1	1	0	.17	3
Blevins, Jerry, NYM	L	-	0	0	0	0	0	.000	2	0	0	0	0	0	0	1	0	49.0	0	5	1	0	.833	2	1	0	0	.50	-1
Bolsinger, Mike, Tor	R	-	0	0	0	0	0	.045	66	3	1	0	0	1	0	37	3	41.1	0	1	0	0	1.000	5	0	0	0	.00	-3

Pitchers Hitting, Fielding and Holding Runners

Pitcher	T	2017 Hitting						Career Hitting										2017 Fielding and Holding Runners											
		Avg	AB	H	HR	RBI	SH	Avg	AB	H	2B	3B	HR	RBI	BB	SO	SH	Inn	PO	A	E	DP	Pct	SBA	CS	PCS	PPO	CS%	RS
Bonilla, Lisalverto, Cin	R	.167	6	1	0	0	0	.167	6	1	0	0	0	0	1	3	0	36.2	4	2	0	0	1.000	5	1	0	0	.20	-1
Boshers, Buddy, Min	L	-	0	0	0	0	0	-	0	0	0	0	0	0	0	0	0	35.0	0	4	0	0	1.000	6	2	0	0	.33	-1
Bowman, Matt, StL	R	-	0	0	0	0	1	.000	1	0	0	0	0	0	0	1	2	58.2	5	14	1	0	.950	3	1	0	0	.33	2
Boxberger, Brad, TB	R	-	0	0	0	0	0	.000	3	0	0	0	0	0	0	1	1	29.1	5	5	0	0	1.000	3	0	0	0	.00	0
Boyd, Matt, Det	L	.333	3	1	0	0	0	.333	3	1	0	0	0	0	0	0	0	135.0	3	15	2	0	.900	10	6	3	0	.60	0
Boyer, Blaine, Bos	R	-	0	0	0	0	0	.000	9	0	0	0	0	0	0	6	1	41.1	1	0	0	0	1.000	1	1	0	0	1.00	-3
Brach, Brad, Bal	R	-	0	0	0	0	0	.000	1	0	0	0	0	0	0	0	1	68.0	7	8	0	2	1.000	2	2	0	0	1.00	2
Bracho, Silvino, Ari	R	-	0	0	0	0	0	.000	1	0	0	0	0	0	0	1	0	20.2	2	3	0	0	1.000	1	0	0	0	.00	1
Bradford, Chasen, NYM	R	.000	1	0	0	0	0	.000	1	0	0	0	0	0	0	1	0	33.2	1	5	0	0	1.000	2	1	0	0	.50	-1
Bradley, Archie, Ari	R	.250	4	1	0	1	0	.098	61	6	0	0	0	5	0	37	4	73.0	3	9	1	1	.923	5	1	1	0	.20	0
Brady, Michael, Oak	R	-	0	0	0	0	0	-	0	0	0	0	0	0	0	0	0	31.2	0	3	0	1	1.000	1	1	0	0	1.00	0
Brault, Steven, Pit	L	.231	13	3	0	2	0	.238	21	5	1	0	0	2	0	0	1	34.2	3	10	0	1	1.000	2	0	0	0	.00	1
Brebbia, John, StL	R	.000	1	0	0	0	0	.000	1	0	0	0	0	0	0	0	0	51.2	1	5	0	0	1.000	4	0	0	0	.00	-1
Breslow, Craig, Min-Cle	L	-	0	0	0	0	0	.000	4	0	0	0	0	0	0	2	0	35.1	0	2	0	0	1.000	3	1	0	0	.33	1
Brice, Austin, Cin	R	.000	4	0	0	0	0	.000	4	0	0	0	0	0	0	2	0	32.2	4	1	0	0	1.000	5	1	0	0	.20	1
Bridwell, Parker, LAA	R	-	0	0	0	0	0	-	0	0	0	0	0	0	0	0	0	121.0	9	5	2	0	.875	2	2	0	1	1.00	1
Britton, Zach, Bal	L	-	0	0	0	0	0	.625	8	5	1	0	1	2	0	1	0	37.1	3	6	1	0	.900	4	1	1	0	.25	1
Brothers, Rex, Atl	L	-	0	0	0	0	0	.000	4	0	0	0	0	0	0	4	1	23.2	0	3	0	1	1.000	0	0	0	0	-	0
Broxton, Jonathan, StL	R	-	0	0	0	0	0	.000	5	0	0	0	0	0	2	2	1	15.2	0	3	0	0	1.000	2	1	0	0	.50	0
Buchanan, Jake, Cin	R	.500	2	1	0	1	0	.250	4	1	0	0	0	1	1	2	0	14.1	0	3	1	0	.750	0	0	0	0	-	0
Buchholz, Clay, Phi	R	.000	2	0	0	0	0	.133	15	2	0	0	0	0	1	7	1	7.1	0	0	0	0	-	0	0	0	0	-	0
Buchter, Ryan, SD-KC	L	-	0	0	0	0	0	-	0	0	0	0	0	0	0	0	0	65.1	2	4	0	0	1.000	4	2	2	0	.50	2
Buehler, Walker, LAD	R	-	0	0	0	0	0	-	0	0	0	0	0	0	0	0	0	9.1	2	1	1	0	1.000	1	0	0	0	.00	0
Bumgarner, Madison, SF	L	.206	34	7	3	5	0	.185	487	90	16	0	17	54	30	195	36	111.0	2	10	0	1	1.000	8	3	2	0	.38	2
Bummer, Aaron, CWS	L	-	0	0	0	0	0	-	0	0	0	0	0	0	0	0	0	22.0	1	6	1	1	.875	2	1	1	0	.50	1
Bundy, Dylan, Bal	R	-	0	0	0	0	0	.000	3	0	0	0	0	0	0	2	0	169.2	5	12	1	3	.944	9	4	0	0	.44	1
Busenitz, Alan, Min	R	-	0	0	0	0	0	-	0	0	0	0	0	0	0	0	0	31.2	0	2	1	0	.667	2	1	0	0	.50	0
Bush, Matt, Tex	R	-	0	0	0	0	0	-	0	0	0	0	0	0	0	0	0	52.1	6	4	1	0	.909	10	1	0	0	.10	-1
Butler, Eddie, ChC	R	.067	15	1	0	0	3	.051	59	3	0	0	0	0	1	24	8	54.2	7	10	0	1	1.000	4	0	0	3	.00	1
Cahill, Trevor, SD-KC	R	.286	14	4	0	2	3	.117	179	21	3	1	0	12	5	62	20	84.0	3	20	0	3	1.000	19	2	0	0	.11	-2
Cain, Matt, SF	R	.156	32	5	0	2	2	.121	611	74	13	1	7	34	21	308	73	124.1	12	18	1	3	.968	19	4	1	0	.21	-1
Callahan, Jamie, NYM	R	-	0	0	0	0	0	-	0	0	0	0	0	0	0	0	0	6.2	1	1	0	0	1.000	0	0	0	0	-	-1
Campos, Leonel, Tor	R	-	0	0	0	0	0	-	0	0	0	0	0	0	0	0	0	13.2	1	0	0	0	1.000	1	0	0	0	.00	0
Capps, Carter, SD	R	-	0	0	0	0	0	.500	2	1	0	0	0	0	0	1	0	12.1	0	1	0	0	1.000	3	1	0	0	.33	0
Carle, Shane, Col	R	-	0	0	0	0	0	-	0	0	0	0	0	0	0	0	0	4.0	0	0	0	0	-	0	0	0	0	-	0
Carrasco, Carlos, Cle	R	.000	4	0	0	0	0	.083	12	1	0	0	0	0	1	6	4	200.0	4	17	0	1	1.000	13	8	0	0	.62	3
Cashner, Andrew, Tex	R	.200	5	1	0	1	1	.162	197	32	2	1	1	8	7	83	18	166.2	5	20	0	1	1.000	12	4	0	1	.33	2
Casilla, Santiago, Oak	R	-	0	0	0	0	0	.250	4	1	0	0	0	1	1	1	0	59.0	4	5	1	2	.900	10	0	0	0	.00	-4
Castillo, Fabio, LAD	R	-	0	0	0	0	0	-	0	0	0	0	0	0	0	0	0	1.1	0	0	0	0	-	0	0	0	0	-	0
Castillo, Luis, Cin	R	.069	29	2	0	1	3	.069	29	2	0	0	0	1	1	11	3	89.1	8	18	0	0	1.000	1	0	0	0	.00	0
Castro, Miguel, Bal	R	-	0	0	0	0	0	-	0	0	0	0	0	0	0	0	0	66.1	2	10	0	1	1.000	7	3	0	0	.43	2
Castro, Simon, Oak	R	-	0	0	0	0	0	-	0	0	0	0	0	0	0	0	0	37.0	0	2	1	0	.667	8	1	0	0	.13	-1
Cecil, Brett, StL	L	.000	1	0	0	0	0	.000	7	0	0	0	0	0	0	6	0	67.1	1	15	1	0	.941	7	2	1	0	.29	2
Cedeno, Xavier, TB	L	-	0	0	0	0	0	.000	1	0	0	0	0	0	0	1	0	3.0	0	2	1	0	.667	0	0	0	0	-	0
Cervenka, Hunter, Mia	L	-	0	0	0	0	0	-	0	0	0	0	0	0	0	0	0	4.2	0	1	0	0	1.000	0	0	0	0	-	0
Cessa, Luis, NYY	R	-	0	0	0	0	0	-	0	0	0	0	0	0	0	0	0	36.0	4	5	0	0	1.000	4	2	0	0	.50	1
Chacin, Alejandro, Cin	R	-	0	0	0	0	0	-	0	0	0	0	0	0	0	0	0	6.0	0	0	0	0	-	0	0	0	0	-	0
Chacin, Jhoulys, SD	R	.222	54	12	0	4	7	.193	275	53	7	0	1	20	7	59	21	180.1	1	34	1	5	.972	8	3	0	1	.38	7
Chafin, Andrew, Ari	L	-	0	0	0	0	0	.200	5	1	0	0	0	1	0	2	0	51.1	6	5	0	0	1.000	2	1	1	0	.50	-2
Chapman, Aroldis, NYY	L	-	0	0	0	0	0	.000	2	0	0	0	0	0	0	1	0	50.1	1	3	0	0	1.000	12	2	2	0	.17	-2
Chatwood, Tyler, Col	R	.154	39	6	0	2	7	.217	161	35	3	1	0	14	6	39	21	147.2	6	37	0	3	1.000	10	5	1	2	.50	9
Chavez, Jesse, LAA	R	.000	5	0	0	0	1	.063	16	1	0	0	0	0	0	15	4	138.0	4	11	0	1	1.000	11	6	1	1	.55	1
Chen, Wei-Yin, Mia	L	.125	8	1	0	0	0	.017	58	1	0	0	0	0	0	24	6	33.0	3	8	0	0	1.000	0	0	0	0	-	2
Cingrani, Tony, Cin-LAD	L	-	0	0	0	0	0	.192	52	10	1	0	0	2	1	16	8	42.2	1	5	0	0	1.000	3	1	0	0	.33	1
Cishek, Steve, Sea-TB	R	-	0	0	0	0	0	.000	1	0	0	0	0	0	0	0	0	44.2	2	5	3	1	.700	0	0	0	0	-	-3
Claiborne, Preston, Tex	R	-	0	0	0	0	0	-	0	0	0	0	0	0	0	0	0	2.0	0	0	0	0	-	0	0	0	0	-	0
Claudio, Alex, Tex	L	-	0	0	0	0	0	-	0	0	0	0	0	0	0	0	0	82.2	2	14	0	3	1.000	0	0	0	0	-	2
Clevinger, Mike, Cle	R	.000	2	0	0	0	1	.000	4	0	0	0	0	0	0	1	1	121.2	5	15	2	1	.909	14	10	2	1	.71	2
Clippard, T., NYY-CWS-Hou	R	-	0	0	0	0	0	.200	15	3	1	0	0	0	0	6	3	60.1	1	5	2	0	.750	11	1	0	0	.09	-1
Cloyd, Tyler, Sea	R	-	0	0	0	0	0	.103	29	3	1	0	0	1	5	7	2	1.0	0	0	0	0	-	0	0	0	0	-	0
Cobb, Alex, TB	R	.000	6	0	0	0	0	.059	17	1	1	0	0	1	0	6	0	179.1	15	26	3	1	.932	18	4	1	4	.22	6
Cole, A.J., Was	R	.143	14	2	0	0	0	.087	23	2	0	0	0	0	2	9	1	52.0	3	5	0	0	1.000	6	1	0	0	.17	-2
Cole, Gerrit, Pit	R	.164	55	9	1	3	12	.174	235	41	2	0	3	15	6	99	28	203.0	16	30	2	5	.958	19	2	0	1	.11	2
Cole, Taylor, Tor	R	-	0	0	0	0	0	-	0	0	0	0	0	0	0	0	0	1.0	0	0	0	0	-	0	0	0	0	-	-1
Collmenter, Josh, Atl	R	-	0	0	0	0	0	.123	154	19	2	0	0	6	9	56	14	17.0	1	5	0	0	1.000	1	0	0	0	.00	1
Colome, Alex, TB	R	-	0	0	0	0	0	.000	2	0	0	0	0	0	0	1	0	66.2	5	10	0	0	1.000	1	0	0	0	.00	1
Colon, Bartolo, Atl-Min	R	.000	19	0	0	0	1	.085	295	25	4	0	1	11	1	163	22	143.0	8	24	2	3	.941	8	2	0	1	.25	-1
Conley, Adam, Mia	L	.125	24	3	0	0	6	.145	83	12	0	0	0	4	3	44	14	102.2	2	11	0	0	1.000	0	0	0	0	-	-1
Corbin, Patrick, Ari	L	.125	56	7	0	0	8	.160	231	37	7	3	0	14	13	93	23	189.2	12	34	0	1	1.000	11	5	3	0	.45	5
Cosart, Jarred, SD	R	.000	4	0	0	0	2	.121	58	7	0	0	0	1	0	22	8	24.0	0	5	0	0	1.000	3	1	0	0	.33	0

Pitchers Hitting, Fielding and Holding Runners

Pitcher	T	2017 Hitting						Career Hitting										2017 Fielding and Holding Runners											
		Avg	AB	H	HR	RBI	SH	Avg	AB	H	2B	3B	HR	RBI	BB	SO	SH	Inn	PO	A	E	DP	Pct	SBA	CS	PCS	PPO	CS%	RS
Cotton, Jharel, Oak	R	.000	2	0	0	0	0	.000	2	0	0	0	0	0	0	1	0	129.0	8	10	0	1	1.000	13	6	1	0	.46	-1
Coulombe, Daniel, Oak	L	-	0	0	0	0	0	.000	1	0	0	0	0	0	0	1	0	51.2	5	6	1	0	.917	6	4	1	0	.67	1
Covey, Dylan, CWS	R	.000	1	0	0	0	0	.000	1	0	0	0	0	0	0	1	0	70.0	4	7	0	1	1.000	11	1	0	0	.09	0
Crichton, Stefan, Bal	R	-	0	0	0	0	0	-	0	0	0	0	0	0	0	0	0	12.1	1	0	0	0	1.000	1	1	0	0	1.00	0
Crick, Kyle, SF	R	-	0	0	0	0	0	-	0	0	0	0	0	0	0	0	0	32.1	5	4	1	0	.900	2	1	0	1	.50	1
Crockett, Kyle, Cle	L	-	0	0	0	0	0	-	0	0	0	0	0	0	0	0	0	1.2	0	0	0	0	-	0	0	0	0	-	0
Cueto, Johnny, SF	R	.087	46	4	0	3	4	.106	500	53	1	0	0	18	14	163	84	147.1	7	15	0	3	1.000	7	2	1	2	.29	1
Cuevas, William, Det	R	-	0	0	0	0	0	-	0	0	0	0	0	0	0	0	0	0.1	0	0	0	0	-	0	0	0	0	-	0
Curtis, Zac, Sea-Phi	L	-	0	0	0	0	0	-	0	0	0	0	0	0	0	0	0	8.1	0	2	0	0	1.000	0	0	0	0	-	0
Curtiss, John, Min	R	-	0	0	0	0	0	-	0	0	0	0	0	0	0	0	0	8.2	1	2	0	0	1.000	2	0	0	0	.00	0
Danish, Tyler, CWS	R	-	0	0	0	0	0	-	0	0	0	0	0	0	0	0	0	5.0	0	0	0	0	-	0	0	0	0	-	0
Darvish, Yu, Tex-LAD	R	.059	17	1	0	0	2	.129	31	4	1	0	1	1	1	20	2	186.2	8	18	1	3	.963	22	2	1	1	.09	-2
Davies, Zach, Mil	R	.125	48	6	0	3	14	.105	114	12	2	0	4	8	40	22	191.1	12	36	0	2	1.000	10	3	1	2	.30	6
Davis, Rookie, Cin	R	.167	6	1	0	0	1	.167	6	1	1	0	0	0	0	5	1	24.0	6	1	1	0	.875	5	0	0	0	.00	0
Davis, Wade, ChC	R	-	0	0	0	0	0	.250	8	2	0	0	0	0	0	4	3	58.2	2	8	0	0	1.000	4	0	0	0	.00	1
Dayton, Grant, LAD	L	-	0	0	0	0	0	.000	1	0	0	0	0	0	0	1	0	23.2	1	0	0	0	1.000	0	0	0	0	-	0
De Jong, Chase, Sea	R	-	0	0	0	0	0	-	0	0	0	0	0	0	0	0	0	28.1	2	2	0	0	1.000	5	2	0	0	.40	1
de la Rosa, Jorge, Ari	L	-	0	0	0	0	2	.127	378	48	4	0	0	27	6	160	31	51.1	5	6	0	0	1.000	5	0	0	0	.00	0
de la Rosa, Rubby, Ari	R	-	0	0	0	0	0	.106	94	10	0	0	0	3	1	29	8	7.2	0	1	0	0	1.000	0	0	0	0	-	0
De Leon, Jose, TB	R	-	0	0	0	0	0	.000	4	0	0	0	0	0	0	0	0	2.2	1	0	0	0	1.000	2	0	0	0	.00	-1
deGrom, Jacob, NYM	R	.211	71	15	1	4	4	.193	218	42	5	0	1	12	9	63	19	201.1	6	25	1	1	.969	21	3	2	0	.14	-2
Delgado, Randall, Ari	R	.000	8	0	0	0	1	.161	87	14	0	0	0	2	1	36	12	62.2	7	8	0	0	1.000	8	2	0	1	.25	-1
Dermody, Matt, Tor	L	-	0	0	0	0	0	-	0	0	0	0	0	0	0	0	0	22.1	3	0	0	0	1.000	3	0	0	0	.00	-1
Despaigne, O., Mia	R	.105	19	2	0	1	1	.055	73	4	1	0	0	1	2	26	7	58.1	6	9	0	0	1.000	2	0	0	0	.00	0
Devenski, Chris, Hou	R	.000	1	0	0	0	0	.000	1	0	0	0	0	0	0	1	0	80.2	9	9	0	2	1.000	14	2	0	1	.14	-2
Diaz, Dayan, Hou	R	-	0	0	0	0	0	-	0	0	0	0	0	0	0	0	0	13.0	1	2	0	0	1.000	5	0	0	0	.00	-1
Diaz, Edwin, Sea	R	.000	1	0	0	0	0	.000	2	0	0	0	0	0	0	1	0	66.0	2	4	1	0	.857	14	2	0	0	.14	-3
Diaz, Jairo, Col	R	-	0	0	0	0	0	-	0	0	0	0	0	0	0	0	0	5.0	1	1	0	2	1.000	2	0	0	0	.00	0
Diaz, Jumbo, TB	R	-	0	0	0	0	0	.000	1	0	0	0	0	0	0	0	0	30.0	1	3	0	0	1.000	3	0	0	0	.00	0
Diaz, Miguel, SD	R	.000	3	0	0	0	1	.000	3	0	0	0	0	0	0	0	1	41.2	3	5	1	0	.889	3	2	0	0	.67	0
Dickey, R.A., Atl	R	.148	61	9	0	5	7	.169	267	45	3	0	0	16	4	49	34	190.0	15	44	2	1	.967	9	5	1	3	.56	7
Diekman, Jake, Tex	L	-	0	0	0	0	0	-	0	0	0	0	0	0	0	0	0	10.2	0	0	0	0	-	0	0	0	0	-	0
Doolittle, Sean, Oak-Was	L	-	0	0	0	0	0	.000	1	0	0	0	0	0	0	0	0	51.1	1	2	0	0	1.000	3	0	0	0	.00	0
Drake, Oliver, Bal-Mil	R	-	0	0	0	0	0	.000	1	0	0	0	0	0	0	1	0	56.0	10	5	0	0	1.000	2	1	0	0	.50	-2
Duensing, Brian, ChC	L	.000	4	0	0	0	0	.000	11	0	0	0	0	0	0	7	0	62.1	11	6	0	1	1.000	5	1	0	0	.20	0
Duffey, Tyler, Min	R	-	0	0	0	0	0	.000	1	0	0	0	0	0	0	1	1	71.0	3	11	1	0	.933	2	0	0	0	.00	-1
Duffy, Danny, KC	L	.500	2	1	0	0	0	.125	16	2	0	0	0	1	0	7	2	146.1	5	12	0	1	1.000	3	1	1	2	.33	-1
Duke, Zach, StL	L	-	0	0	0	0	0	.180	317	57	7	0	2	23	12	117	43	18.1	3	2	0	0	1.000	2	1	1	0	.50	-1
Dull, Ryan, Oak	R	-	0	0	0	0	0	-	0	0	0	0	0	0	0	0	0	42.0	2	3	0	0	1.000	6	3	0	0	.50	1
Dunn, Mike, Col	L	-	0	0	0	0	0	.200	5	1	0	0	0	0	0	1	0	50.1	0	2	0	0	1.000	4	1	0	0	.25	0
Dyson, Sam, Tex-SF	R	-	0	0	0	0	0	.000	2	0	0	0	0	0	0	0	0	54.2	2	8	0	0	1.000	13	4	0	0	.31	-3
Edgin, Josh, NYM	L	-	0	0	0	0	0	.000	1	0	0	0	0	0	0	1	0	37.0	1	4	0	2	1.000	1	1	0	0	1.00	0
Edwards Jr., Carl, ChC	R	.000	1	0	0	0	0	.000	3	0	0	0	0	0	0	0	0	66.1	6	9	0	0	1.000	5	0	0	0	.00	1
Eflin, Zach, Phi	R	.143	21	3	0	2	1	.205	44	9	2	0	0	2	0	21	1	64.1	5	13	1	1	.947	2	1	0	1	.50	1
Eickhoff, Jerad, Phi	R	.161	31	5	0	0	3	.142	106	15	4	0	0	7	1	32	5	128.0	6	18	1	3	.960	19	4	3	0	.21	-2
Elias, Roenis, Bos	L	-	0	0	0	0	0	.000	4	0	0	0	0	0	0	1	0	0.1	0	0	0	0	-	0	0	0	0	-	0
Ellington, Brian, Mia	R	.000	1	0	0	0	0	.000	2	0	0	0	0	0	0	1	0	44.2	3	2	0	0	1.000	4	2	0	0	.50	0
Enns, Dietrich, Min	L	.500	2	1	0	0	0	.500	2	1	0	0	0	0	0	1	0	4.0	0	1	0	0	.000	0	0	0	0	-	-1
Esch, Jake, SD	R	-	0	0	0	0	0	.200	5	1	0	0	0	0	0	2	0	0.0	0	0	0	0	-	0	0	0	0	-	0
Espino, Paolo, Mil-Tex	R	.250	4	1	0	0	1	.250	4	1	0	0	0	0	0	1	1	24.0	1	2	0	0	1.000	0	0	0	0	-	0
Estevez, Carlos, Col	R	-	0	0	0	0	0	-	0	0	0	0	0	0	0	0	0	32.1	0	2	0	0	1.000	0	0	0	0	-	0
Estrada, Marco, Tor	R	.000	4	0	0	0	0	.142	134	19	4	0	0	7	7	63	20	186.0	5	17	1	0	.957	12	4	0	0	.33	0
Familia, Jeurys, NYM	R	.000	1	0	0	0	0	.400	5	2	0	0	0	1	0	2	0	24.2	1	4	1	0	.833	9	1	0	0	.11	-1
Faria, Jake, TB	R	-	0	0	0	0	0	-	0	0	0	0	0	0	0	0	0	86.2	4	8	0	0	1.000	7	4	1	0	.57	2
Farmer, Buck, Det	R	-	0	0	0	0	0	.250	4	1	0	0	0	0	0	3	0	48.0	0	3	0	0	1.000	2	1	0	1	.50	0
Farquhar, D., TB-CWS	R	-	0	0	0	0	0	-	0	0	0	0	0	0	0	0	0	49.1	1	7	1	0	.889	2	0	0	0	.00	0
Farrell, Luke, KC-Cin	R	-	0	0	0	0	0	-	0	0	0	0	0	0	0	0	0	13.0	1	0	0	0	1.000	0	0	0	0	-	-1
Fedde, Erick, Was	R	.000	4	0	0	0	1	.000	4	0	0	0	0	0	0	3	1	15.1	0	2	0	0	1.000	2	0	0	0	.00	0
Feldman, Scott, Cin	R	.029	34	1	0	0	4	.116	95	11	3	0	1	9	0	41	9	111.1	19	14	0	0	1.000	18	5	0	0	.28	-1
Feliz, Michael, Hou	R	.000	1	0	0	0	0	.000	1	0	0	0	0	0	0	1	0	48.0	0	2	1	0	.667	2	0	0	0	.00	-1
Feliz, Neftali, Mil-KC	R	-	0	0	0	0	0	.000	2	0	0	0	0	0	0	1	0	46.0	5	5	1	2	.909	2	0	0	0	.00	1
Ferrell, Jeff, Det	R	-	0	0	0	0	0	-	0	0	0	0	0	0	0	0	0	9.1	1	1	0	0	1.000	2	0	0	0	.00	0
Fields, Josh, LAD	R	-	0	0	0	0	0	.000	1	0	0	0	0	0	0	1	0	57.0	4	3	0	0	1.000	3	3	0	0	1.00	1
Fien, Casey, Sea-Phi	R	-	0	0	0	0	0	-	0	0	0	0	0	0	0	0	0	12.0	1	3	0	1	1.000	2	1	1	0	.50	1
Fiers, Mike, Hou	R	.000	1	0	0	0	0	.081	86	7	0	0	0	2	0	45	18	153.1	16	6	2	1	.917	20	2	0	1	.10	-2
Finnegan, Brandon, Cin	L	.000	5	0	0	0	1	.097	62	6	2	0	0	2	3	21	8	13.0	2	0	0	0	1.000	1	0	0	0	.00	0
Fister, Doug, Bos	R	.000	2	0	0	0	0	.152	105	16	3	0	4	3	42	20	90.1	8	10	1	0	.947	1	1	0	0	1.00	2
Flaherty, Jack, StL	R	.000	6	0	0	0	0	.000	6	0	0	0	0	0	0	2	0	21.1	1	3	0	0	1.000	1	1	0	0	1.00	1
Flexen, Chris, NYM	R	.154	13	2	0	0	1	.154	13	2	1	0	0	0	0	7	1	48.0	3	9	0	1	1.000	5	1	0	0	.20	2
Floro, Dylan, ChC	R	.000	4	0	0	0	0	.000	4	0	0	0	0	0	0	2	0	9.2	1	1	0	0	1.000	0	0	0	0	-	-1

Pitchers Hitting, Fielding and Holding Runners

Pitcher	T	2017 Hitting Avg	AB	H	HR	RBI	SH	Career Hitting Avg	AB	H	2B	3B	HR	RBI	BB	SO	SH	2017 Fielding and Holding Runners Inn	PO	A	E	DP	Pct	SBA	CS	PCS	PPO	CS%	RS
Flynn, Brian, KC	L	-	0	0	0	0	0	.286	7	2	0	0	0	0	0	2	1	2.1	0	0	0	0	-	0	0	0	0	-	0
Foltynewicz, Mike, Atl	R	.048	42	2	0	0	7	.085	106	9	2	0	0	4	1	65	13	154.0	5	15	1	1	.952	10	3	0	0	.30	-2
Font, Wilmer, LAD	R	-	0	0	0	0	0	-	0	0	0	0	0	0	0	0	0	3.2	0	0	0	0	-	0	0	0	0	-	0
Frankoff, Seth, ChC	R	-	0	0	0	0	0	-	0	0	0	0	0	0	0	0	0	2.0	0	0	0	0	-	0	0	0	0	-	0
Freeland, Kyle, Col	L	.154	52	8	1	2	3	.154	52	8	1	0	1	2	1	30	3	156.0	3	32	3	2	.921	11	3	1	1	.27	1
Freeman, Sam, Atl	L	.000	2	0	0	0	0	.000	2	0	0	0	0	0	0	1	0	60.0	2	6	0	1	1.000	2	0	0	0	.00	1
Fried, Max, Atl	L	.000	7	0	0	0	1	.000	7	0	0	0	0	0	1	3	1	26.0	0	6	1	0	.857	1	1	1	0	1.00	0
Frieri, Ernesto, Tex	R	-	0	0	0	0	0	.000	1	0	0	0	0	0	0	1	0	7.0	0	0	0	0	-	1	1	0	0	1.00	1
Fry, Jace, CWS	R	-	0	0	0	0	0	-	0	0	0	0	0	0	0	0	0	6.2	0	0	0	0	-	0	0	0	0	-	0
Fulmer, Carson, CWS	R	-	0	0	0	0	0	-	0	0	0	0	0	0	0	0	0	23.1	0	1	0	0	1.000	0	0	0	0	-	0
Fulmer, Michael, Det	R	.000	5	0	0	0	0	.000	7	0	0	0	0	0	0	4	0	164.2	9	10	1	0	.950	5	1	0	0	.20	-2
Gallardo, Yovani, Sea	R	.500	2	1	0	0	0	.202	426	86	21	0	12	42	13	149	36	130.2	8	17	0	2	1.000	5	0	0	0	.00	1
Gallegos, Giovanny, NYY	R	-	0	0	0	0	0	-	0	0	0	0	0	0	0	0	0	20.1	0	1	0	0	1.000	0	0	0	0	-	0
Gant, John, StL	R	.000	3	0	0	0	0	.000	10	0	0	0	0	0	0	1	3	17.1	1	4	0	0	1.000	1	1	1	0	1.00	1
Garcia, Jai., Atl-Min-NYY	L	.152	33	5	1	7	3	.148	305	45	3	1	3	23	12	99	27	157.0	4	28	2	2	.941	26	5	1	0	.19	0
Garcia, Jarlin, Mia	L	-	0	0	0	0	0	-	0	0	0	0	0	0	0	0	0	53.1	1	7	0	0	1.000	3	2	1	0	.67	1
Garcia, Luis, Phi	R	-	0	0	0	0	0	.000	2	0	0	0	0	0	0	1	1	71.1	2	10	0	0	1.000	5	0	0	0	.00	-3
Garcia, Onelki, KC	L	-	0	0	0	0	0	-	0	0	0	0	0	0	0	0	0	6.0	0	1	0	0	1.000	0	0	0	0	-	-1
Gardewine, Nick, Tex	R	-	0	0	0	0	0	-	0	0	0	0	0	0	0	0	0	8.0	1	0	0	0	1.000	2	0	0	0	.00	0
Garrett, Amir, Cin	L	.053	19	1	0	1	4	.053	19	1	1	0	0	1	0	6	4	70.2	4	11	2	0	.882	8	4	1	0	.50	1
Garton, Ryan, TB-Sea	R	-	0	0	0	0	0	-	0	0	0	0	0	0	0	0	0	22.0	2	4	0	1	1.000	1	0	0	0	.00	1
Garza, Matt, Mil	R	.086	35	3	0	1	1	.080	274	22	3	0	4	6	155	31		114.2	7	7	2	0	.875	12	1	0	0	.08	-3
Gausman, Kevin, Bal	R	.000	2	0	0	0	0	.000	8	0	0	0	0	1	6	0		186.2	10	16	1	2	.963	12	3	0	0	.25	-4
Gaviglio, Sam, Sea-KC	R	.200	5	1	0	0	0	.200	5	1	0	0	0	0	0	2	0	74.1	7	4	1	1	.917	12	3	1	0	.25	-2
Gearrin, Cory, SF	R	.000	2	0	0	0	0	.333	3	1	0	0	0	0	0	2	0	68.0	7	7	0	0	1.000	7	3	0	0	.43	0
Gee, Dillon, Tex-Min	R	-	0	0	0	0	0	.108	194	21	3	1	0	11	9	89	28	49.1	1	7	0	1	1.000	2	2	0	0	1.00	1
German, Domingo, NYY	R	-	0	0	0	0	0	-	0	0	0	0	0	0	0	0	0	14.1	2	0	1	0	.667	0	0	0	0	-	0
Gibson, Kyle, Min	R	-	0	0	0	0	0	.125	16	2	0	0	0	1	9	0		158.0	19	23	0	4	1.000	6	5	1	1	.83	5
Giles, Ken, Hou	R	-	0	0	0	0	0	-	0	0	0	0	0	0	0	0	0	62.2	3	6	1	0	.900	4	0	0	0	.00	-1
Gilmartin, Sean, NYM	L	1.000	1	1	0	1	0	.429	7	3	1	0	0	1	0	3	0	3.1	0	0	0	0	-	0	0	0	0	-	-1
Giolito, Lucas, CWS	R	-	0	0	0	0	0	.250	4	1	0	0	0	0	0	1	2	45.1	2	3	1	0	.833	6	4	0	0	.67	1
Givens, Mychal, Bal	R	-	0	0	0	0	0	.000	2	0	0	0	0	0	0	1	0	78.2	3	21	0	1	1.000	7	1	0	0	.14	3
Glasnow, Tyler, Pit	R	.294	17	5	0	3	1	.250	24	6	0	0	3	4	11	1		62.0	4	7	1	0	.917	23	8	0	0	.35	-4
Glover, Koda, Was	R	-	0	0	0	0	0	-	0	0	0	0	0	0	0	0	0	19.1	1	7	0	0	1.000	2	0	0	0	.00	1
Godley, Zack, Ari	R	.048	42	2	0	2	9	.072	69	5	0	0	2	2	41	11		155.0	10	20	3	2	.909	1	0	0	2	.00	0
Goeddel, Erik, NYM	R	-	0	0	0	0	0	.000	1	0	0	0	0	0	0	0	0	29.0	3	2	0	0	1.000	3	1	0	0	.33	0
Goforth, David, Mil	R	-	0	0	0	0	0	.000	3	0	0	0	0	0	0	3	1	1.0	0	0	0	0	-	0	0	0	0	-	0
Gohara, Luiz, Atl	L	.000	9	0	0	0	1	.000	9	0	0	0	0	0	0	7	1	29.1	1	8	1	0	.900	3	1	1	0	.33	0
Goldberg, Brad, CWS	R	-	0	0	0	0	0	-	0	0	0	0	0	0	0	0	0	12.0	0	2	0	0	1.000	0	0	0	0	-	0
Gomez, Jeanmar, Phi	R	-	0	0	0	0	0	.158	19	3	0	0	0	0	0	11	1	22.1	0	6	0	1	1.000	0	0	0	1	-	1
Gomez, Roberto, SF	R	-	0	0	0	0	0	-	0	0	0	0	0	0	0	0	0	5.1	0	1	0	0	-	0	0	0	0	-	0
Gonzales, M., StL-Sea	L	.500	2	1	0	0	1	.333	12	4	2	0	0	0	3	3	0	40.0	1	3	1	0	.800	3	1	0	1	.33	-1
Gonzalez, Gio, Was	L	.091	66	6	0	5	5	.096	334	32	6	0	3	16	7	142	45	201.0	6	23	0	1	1.000	19	5	0	0	.26	1
Gonzalez, M., CWS-Tex	R	.000	6	0	0	0	1	.000	16	0	0	0	0	1	6	2		156.0	7	13	0	2	1.000	10	2	0	0	.20	0
Goody, Nick, Cle	R	-	0	0	0	0	0	-	0	0	0	0	0	0	0	0	0	54.2	0	4	1	1	.800	1	0	0	0	.00	0
Gossett, Daniel, Oak	R	.200	5	1	0	0	2	.200	5	1	0	0	0	0	0	4	2	91.1	8	12	0	0	1.000	4	2	0	1	.50	4
Gott, Trevor, Was	R	-	0	0	0	0	0	-	0	0	0	0	0	0	0	0	0	3.0	0	0	0	0	-	0	0	0	0	-	-1
Grace, Matt, Was	L	.000	5	0	0	0	0	.000	5	0	0	0	0	0	0	4	0	50.0	1	8	1	1	.900	7	1	0	0	.14	-5
Graveman, Kendall, Oak	R	.000	1	0	0	0	0	.000	5	0	0	0	0	0	0	4	1	105.1	12	15	2	4	.931	8	1	0	1	.13	0
Gray, Jon, Col	R	.079	38	3	1	3	4	.104	96	10	2	0	1	7	5	63	10	110.1	6	9	1	0	.938	11	2	0	2	.18	-1
Gray, Sonny, Oak-NYY	R	.000	0	0	0	0	0	.100	10	1	0	0	0	0	6	1		162.1	16	21	3	1	.925	14	3	0	0	.21	0
Green, Chad, NYY	R	-	0	0	0	0	0	.000	4	0	0	0	0	0	0	4	0	69.0	1	3	0	0	1.000	7	2	0	0	.29	0
Greene, Shane, Det	R	-	0	0	0	0	0	.000	7	0	0	0	0	0	0	5	0	67.2	1	4	2	1	.714	2	1	0	0	.50	-2
Gregerson, Luke, Hou	R	-	0	0	0	0	0	.000	2	0	0	0	0	0	0	0	0	61.0	5	12	0	1	1.000	11	0	0	0	.00	1
Greinke, Zack, Ari	R	.210	62	13	0	4	5	.217	405	88	21	0	6	21	21	85	39	202.1	26	30	0	5	1.000	14	9	2	0	.64	4
Griffin, A.J., Tex	R	.000	5	0	0	0	0	.000	11	0	0	0	0	0	2	10	0	77.1	1	5	0	0	1.000	3	1	0	1	.33	0
Grilli, Jason, Tor-Tex	R	-	0	0	0	0	0	.200	15	3	0	0	1	3	0	3	3	40.0	1	4	0	1	1.000	4	1	0	0	.25	0
Grimm, Justin, ChC	R	.000	3	0	0	0	0	.000	7	0	0	0	0	0	0	4	0	55.1	5	5	0	0	1.000	9	1	0	0	.11	0
Gsellman, Robert, NYM	R	.147	34	5	0	4	3	.122	49	6	0	0	0	4	6	23	5	119.2	8	18	4	2	.867	10	3	0	0	.30	1
Guduan, Reymin, Hou	L	-	0	0	0	0	0	-	0	0	0	0	0	0	0	0	0	16.0	0	0	0	0	-	1	0	0	0	.00	-1
Guerra, Deolis, LAA	R	-	0	0	0	0	0	.000	1	0	0	0	0	0	0	0	0	25.0	2	1	0	0	1.000	2	1	0	0	.50	0
Guerra, Javy, Mia	R	.000	1	0	0	0	0	.000	1	0	0	0	0	0	1	1	0	21.0	1	1	0	0	1.000	0	0	0	0	-	-1
Guerra, Junior, Mil	R	.000	16	0	0	0	5	.157	51	8	2	0	0	0	0	17	13	70.1	4	6	2	1	.833	2	1	0	3	.50	-1
Gurka, Jason, LAA	L	-	0	0	0	0	0	-	0	0	0	0	0	0	0	0	0	0.2	0	0	0	0	-	0	0	0	0	-	0
Gustave, Jandel, Hou	R	-	0	0	0	0	0	-	0	0	0	0	0	0	0	0	0	5.0	0	1	0	0	1.000	0	0	0	0	-	0
Guthrie, Jeremy, Was	R	-	0	0	0	0	0	.100	60	6	2	0	0	1	1	27	6	0.2	0	0	0	0	-	1	0	0	0	.00	0
Hader, Josh, Mil	L	.000	4	0	0	0	0	.000	4	0	0	0	0	0	0	2	0	47.2	2	3	0	1	1.000	2	1	0	0	.50	0
Hahn, Jesse, Oak	R	-	0	0	0	0	0	.077	26	2	0	0	0	1	0	15	2	69.2	3	12	2	0	.882	5	1	1	0	.20	0
Haley, Justin, Min	R	-	0	0	0	0	0	-	0	0	0	0	0	0	0	0	0	18.0	1	1	0	0	1.000	1	0	0	0	.00	0
Hamels, Cole, Tex	L	.000	3	0	0	1	0	.172	621	107	15	2	1	29	17	259	62	148.0	10	15	3	1	.893	14	6	4	0	.43	2

396

Pitchers Hitting, Fielding and Holding Runners

Pitcher	T	2017 Hitting						Career Hitting										2017 Fielding and Holding Runners											
		Avg	AB	H	HR	RBI	SH	Avg	AB	H	2B	3B	HR	RBI	BB	SO	SH	Inn	PO	A	E	DP	Pct	SBA	CS	PCS	PPO	CS%	RS
Hammel, Jason, KC	R	.000	8	0	0	0	1	.152	341	52	8	0	1	21	7	132	38	180.1	4	11	0	0	1.000	23	3	0	0	.13	-5
Hand, Brad, SD	L	.000	1	0	0	0	0	.070	71	5	0	0	0	4	0	22	15	79.1	1	5	0	0	1.000	3	0	0	0	.00	1
Happ, J.A., Tor	L	.000	2	0	0	0	0	.096	188	18	2	0	1	6	9	83	30	145.1	4	16	2	0	.909	10	2	0	0	.20	-3
Hardy, Blaine, Det	L	-	0	0	0	0	0	.000	1	0	0	0	0	0	0	0	0	33.1	1	3	0	0	1.000	2	1	1	0	.50	0
Harrell, Lucas, Tor	R	-	0	0	0	0	0	.135	74	10	0	0	0	1	3	39	3	6.1	1	0	0	0	-	0	0	0	0	-	0
Harris, Will, Hou	R	-	0	0	0	0	0	.000	1	0	0	0	0	0	0	1	0	45.1	7	6	0	0	1.000	3	1	0	0	.33	1
Hart, Donnie, Bal	L	-	0	0	0	0	0	.000	1	0	0	0	0	0	0	1	0	43.2	3	6	0	0	1.000	2	0	0	0	.00	0
Harvey, Matt, NYM	R	.059	34	2	0	1	1	.117	197	23	7	0	1	13	2	86	13	92.2	5	12	1	1	.944	5	1	0	0	.20	-1
Hatcher, Chris, LAD-Oak	R	-	0	0	0	0	0	.083	12	1	0	0	0	1	2	6	0	59.2	0	6	0	0	1.000	1	0	0	0	.00	0
Hauschild, Mike, Tex	R	-	0	0	0	0	0	-	0	0	0	0	0	0	0	0	0	8.0	1	0	0	0	1.000	0	0	0	0	-	0
Heaney, Andrew, LAA	L	-	0	0	0	0	0	.077	13	1	0	0	0	0	0	5	2	21.2	3	5	0	0	1.000	1	1	1	0	1.00	0
Heller, Ben, NYY	R	-	0	0	0	0	0	-	0	0	0	0	0	0	0	0	0	11.0	1	1	0	0	1.000	1	0	0	0	.00	0
Hellickson, J., Phi-Bal	R	.091	33	3	0	2	3	.164	134	22	2	1	0	13	9	50	15	164.0	10	26	0	3	1.000	11	4	1	2	.36	6
Hembree, Heath, Bos	R	-	0	0	0	0	0	-	0	0	0	0	0	0	0	0	0	62.0	2	5	1	0	.875	10	2	0	0	.20	-1
Hendricks, Kyle, ChC	R	.100	50	5	0	5	1	.099	192	19	2	0	0	9	5	92	15	139.2	17	29	1	3	.979	17	4	1	6	.24	2
Hendriks, Liam, Oak	R	-	0	0	0	0	0	.000	2	0	0	0	0	0	1	1	0	64.0	5	7	1	0	.923	13	1	1	1	.08	-3
Hernandez, Ariel, Cin	R	.000	2	0	0	0	0	.000	2	0	0	0	0	0	0	1	0	24.1	0	2	0	0	1.000	6	0	0	0	.00	-1
Hernandez, D., LAA-Ari	R	-	0	0	0	0	0	.250	4	1	0	0	0	0	0	1	0	55.0	5	3	0	0	1.000	7	3	1	0	.43	-3
Hernandez, Felix, Sea	R	-	0	0	0	0	0	.093	43	4	1	0	1	7	2	20	7	86.2	4	7	1	1	.917	3	1	0	0	.33	-2
Herrera, Kelvin, KC	R	-	0	0	0	0	0	-	0	0	0	0	0	0	0	0	0	59.1	2	10	0	0	1.000	5	0	0	0	.00	0
Herrera, Ronald, NYY	R	-	0	0	0	0	0	-	0	0	0	0	0	0	0	0	0	3.0	1	1	0	0	1.000	1	0	0	0	.00	0
Heston, Chris, Sea-Min	R	-	0	0	0	0	0	.192	52	10	2	0	0	3	0	19	7	6.0	1	0	0	0	1.000	1	0	0	0	.00	0
Hildenberger, Trevor, Min	R	-	0	0	0	0	0	-	0	0	0	0	0	0	0	0	0	42.0	2	5	0	1	1.000	5	0	0	0	.00	-1
Hill, Rich, LAD	L	.111	45	5	0	4	1	.111	171	19	4	0	0	10	2	77	7	135.2	2	10	1	0	.923	18	6	4	0	.33	-2
Hoffman, Jeff, Col	R	.091	33	3	0	1	3	.073	41	3	1	0	0	1	0	19	4	99.1	5	11	0	0	1.000	2	0	0	0	.00	-1
Holder, Jonathan, NYY	R	-	0	0	0	0	0	-	0	0	0	0	0	0	0	0	0	39.1	2	2	0	0	1.000	1	0	0	0	.00	-1
Holland, Derek, CWS	L	1.000	1	1	0	0	0	.133	15	2	0	0	0	0	2	7	2	135.0	5	16	3	1	.875	11	2	1	3	.18	-1
Holland, Greg, Col	R	-	0	0	0	0	0	-	0	0	0	0	0	0	0	0	0	57.1	7	3	1	0	.909	5	1	0	0	.20	-2
Holmberg, David, CWS	L	-	0	0	0	0	0	.071	14	1	0	0	0	0	2	8	3	57.2	4	5	1	0	.900	3	1	0	0	.33	-1
Hoover, J.J., Ari	R	-	0	0	0	0	0	-	0	0	0	0	0	0	1	0	0	41.1	1	3	1	0	.800	2	1	1	0	.50	-1
House, T.J., Tor	L	-	0	0	0	0	0	.000	2	0	0	0	0	0	0	2	0	2.0	0	0	0	0	-	0	0	0	0	-	0
Howell, J.P., Tor	L	-	0	0	0	0	0	.154	13	2	0	0	0	1	0	7	0	11.0	1	1	0	0	1.000	0	0	0	0	-	1
Hoyt, James, Hou	R	.000	1	0	0	0	0	.000	1	0	0	0	0	0	0	1	0	49.1	1	1	0	1	1.000	4	0	0	0	-	-2
Hu, Chih-Wei, TB	R	-	0	0	0	0	0	-	0	0	0	0	0	0	0	0	0	10.0	0	1	0	0	1.000	1	0	0	0	.00	0
Hudson, Daniel, Pit	R	-	0	0	0	0	0	.226	106	24	5	0	1	21	5	35	14	61.2	4	10	1	2	.933	8	3	0	0	.38	3
Hughes, Jared, Mil	R	-	0	0	0	0	0	.000	6	0	0	0	0	0	0	5	1	59.2	5	17	2	1	.917	17	5	1	0	.29	2
Hughes, Phil, Min	R	-	0	0	0	0	0	.000	17	0	0	0	0	0	0	8	2	53.2	2	3	0	0	1.000	6	3	0	0	.50	1
Hunter, Tommy, TB	R	-	0	0	0	0	0	.000	3	0	0	0	0	0	0	2	0	58.2	2	2	2	0	.667	5	1	1	0	.20	0
Hursh, Jason, Atl	R	-	0	0	0	0	0	-	0	0	0	0	0	0	0	0	0	10.2	1	1	0	0	1.000	-	0	0	0	-	-1
Iglesias, Raisel, Cin	R	1.000	1	1	0	0	0	.095	42	4	1	1	0	1	0	15	1	76.0	10	9	1	2	.950	6	3	0	0	.50	1
Infante, Gregory, CWS	R	-	0	0	0	0	0	-	0	0	0	0	0	0	0	0	0	54.2	3	3	0	0	1.000	8	0	0	0	.00	-2
Iwakuma, Hisashi, Sea	R	-	0	0	0	0	0	.000	11	0	0	0	0	0	1	8	3	31.0	1	2	0	1	1.000	3	2	0	0	.67	0
Jackson, Edwin, Bal-Was	R	.095	21	2	0	0	0	.168	292	49	4	0	2	13	14	126	23	76.0	1	7	2	0	.800	10	2	0	0	.20	-5
Jackson, Luke, Atl	R	.000	2	0	0	0	1	.000	2	0	0	0	0	0	0	0	1	50.2	4	4	0	1	1.000	5	0	0	1	.00	-1
Jankowski, Jordan, Hou	R	-	0	0	0	0	0	-	0	0	0	0	0	0	0	0	0	4.1	0	2	0	0	1.000	0	0	0	0	-	0
Jansen, Kenley, LAD	R	.500	4	2	0	1	0	.429	7	3	1	0	1	1	1	1	0	68.1	4	1	0	0	1.000	11	0	0	0	.00	-3
Jaye, Myles, Det	R	-	0	0	0	0	0	-	0	0	0	0	0	0	0	0	0	12.2	4	2	0	0	1.000	0	0	0	0	-	0
Jeffress, Jeremy, Tex-Mil	R	.000	2	0	0	0	0	.000	2	0	0	0	0	0	0	2	0	65.1	4	12	0	1	1.000	2	0	0	1	.00	0
Jennings, Dan, CWS-TB	L	-	0	0	0	0	0	.000	1	0	0	0	0	0	0	0	0	62.2	2	9	0	0	1.000	4	1	0	0	.25	2
Jimenez, Joe, Det	R	-	0	0	0	0	0	-	0	0	0	0	0	0	0	0	0	19.0	1	1	0	0	1.000	2	1	0	0	.50	-1
Jimenez, Ubaldo, Bal	R	.200	5	1	0	0	0	.117	291	34	0	0	0	11	17	102	33	142.2	8	11	1	0	.950	22	4	1	0	.18	-4
Johnson, Brian, Bos	L	.000	2	0	0	0	0	.000	2	0	0	0	0	0	0	0	0	27.0	1	4	0	0	1.000	1	0	0	0	.00	0
Johnson, Jim, Atl	R	-	0	0	0	0	0	.000	2	0	0	0	0	0	0	2	0	56.2	0	9	0	0	1.000	3	0	0	0	.00	0
Johnson, Pierce, ChC	R	-	0	0	0	0	0	-	0	0	0	0	0	0	0	0	0	1.0	0	0	0	0	-	0	0	0	0	-	0
Jones, Nate, CWS	R	-	0	0	0	0	0	-	0	0	0	0	0	0	0	0	0	11.2	0	2	0	0	1.000	-	0	0	0	-	1
Jorge, Felix, Min	R	-	0	0	0	0	0	-	0	0	0	0	0	0	0	0	0	7.2	0	2	0	0	1.000	1	0	0	0	-	1
Jungmann, Taylor, Mil	R	-	0	0	0	0	0	.244	45	11	2	0	0	0	1	16	6	0.2	0	0	0	0	-	-	0	0	0	-	0
Junis, Jakob, KC	R	.000	3	0	0	0	0	.000	3	0	0	0	0	0	0	3	0	98.1	5	5	1	0	.909	6	4	0	0	.67	1
Kahnle, T., CWS-NYY	R	-	0	0	0	0	0	.000	3	0	0	0	0	0	0	1	1	62.2	3	1	0	0	1.000	2	0	0	0	.00	-2
Karns, Nathan, KC	R	-	0	0	0	0	0	.125	8	1	0	0	1	1	0	4	3	45.1	0	8	1	0	.889	7	1	0	0	.14	0
Kela, Keone, Tex	R	-	0	0	0	0	0	-	0	0	0	0	0	0	0	0	0	38.2	0	1	0	0	1.000	4	1	0	0	.25	0
Kelley, Shawn, Was	R	-	0	0	0	0	0	.000	0	0	0	0	0	0	0	0	0	26.0	0	3	0	1	.000	2	0	0	0	.00	-2
Kelly, Joe, Bos	R	-	0	0	0	0	0	.172	87	15	4	0	0	5	0	25	8	58.0	3	3	1	0	.857	2	1	1	0	.50	2
Kendrick, Kyle, Bos	R	.000	1	0	0	0	1	.139	374	52	9	1	1	9	18	158	45	8.1	0	2	0	0	1.000	2	0	0	0	.00	-1
Kennedy, Ian, KC	R	.333	3	1	0	0	0	.129	319	41	11	1	1	18	33	154	42	154.0	5	8	3	0	.813	9	5	1	0	.56	1
Kershaw, Clayton, LAD	L	.184	49	9	0	2	6	.157	567	89	8	1	1	29	25	173	89	175.0	4	19	1	0	.957	5	2	1	1	.40	-2
Keuchel, Dallas, Hou	L	.000	3	0	0	0	0	.086	35	3	0	0	0	1	2	20	6	145.2	7	34	5	3	.891	5	2	1	0	.40	9
Kimbrel, Craig, Bos	R	-	0	0	0	0	0	.000	1	0	0	0	0	0	0	1	0	69.0	6	6	0	1	1.000	10	6	0	1	.60	4
Kintzler, B., Min-Was	R	-	0	0	0	0	0	.000	2	0	0	0	0	0	0	1	0	71.1	5	14	0	2	1.000	6	2	0	0	.33	2
Kittredge, Andrew, TB	R	-	0	0	0	0	0	-	0	0	0	0	0	0	0	0	0	15.1	1	1	0	0	1.000	0	0	0	0	-	-1

Pitchers Hitting, Fielding and Holding Runners

Pitcher	T	2017 Hitting Avg	AB	H	HR	RBI	SH	Career Hitting Avg	AB	H	2B	3B	HR	RBI	BB	SO	SH	2017 Fielding and Holding Runners Inn	PO	A	E	DP	Pct	SBA	CS	PCS	PPO	CS%	RS
Kluber, Corey, Cle	R	.500	2	1	0	0	0	.158	19	3	1	0	0	0	1	9	3	203.2	15	15	1	0	.968	15	2	5	0	.13	-1
Knebel, Corey, Mil	R	-	0	0	0	0	0	-	0	0	0	0	0	0	0	0	0	76.0	2	3	1	0	.833	15	0	0	0	.13	-2
Koch, Matt, Ari	R	-	0	0	0	0	0	.000	3	0	0	0	0	0	1	3	2	0.0	0	0	0	0	-	0	0	0	0	-	0
Koehler, Tom, Mia-Tor	R	.048	21	1	0	0	0	.085	212	18	1	0	0	5	4	116	26	72.2	2	2	2	0	.667	8	3	0	0	.38	-2
Kolarek, Adam, TB	L	-	0	0	0	0	0	-	0	0	0	0	0	0	0	0	0	8.1	0	2	0	0	1.000	1	1	0	0	1.00	0
Kontos, George, SF-Pit	R	.000	2	0	0	0	0	.000	7	0	0	0	0	0	0	4	3	66.1	5	9	1	0	.933	6	0	0	0	.00	-1
Krol, Ian, Atl	L	.000	1	0	0	0	0	.000	3	0	0	0	0	0	0	0	0	49.0	2	8	2	1	.833	7	1	1	0	.14	1
Kuhl, Chad, Pit	R	.104	48	5	0	3	3	.099	71	7	2	0	0	3	2	25	5	157.1	10	19	0	2	1.000	12	3	0	1	.25	1
Labourt, Jairo, Det	L	-	0	0	0	0	0	-	0	0	0	0	0	0	0	0	0	6.0	0	2	0	0	1.000	0	0	0	0	-	0
Lackey, John, ChC	R	.132	53	7	0	1	5	.110	236	26	7	0	0	8	9	97	20	170.2	27	15	0	1	1.000	15	2	0	0	.13	-1
Lamet, Dinelson, SD	R	.086	35	3	0	0	3	.086	35	3	0	0	0	0	0	22	3	114.1	2	10	1	0	.923	10	3	0	0	.30	-1
Latos, Mat, Tor	R	.000	3	0	0	0	0	.131	327	43	6	0	4	15	6	148	43	15.0	3	1	0	1	1.000	2	1	0	0	.50	0
Law, Derek, SF	R	-	0	0	0	0	0	.000	1	0	0	0	0	0	0	0	0	37.1	2	3	0	0	1.000	3	1	0	0	.33	-1
Lawrence, C., Tor-Sea	R	.000	2	0	0	0	1	.000	2	0	0	0	0	0	0	1	1	55.1	3	3	0	1	1.000	9	0	0	0	.00	-1
Layne, Tommy, NYY	L	-	0	0	0	0	0	-	0	0	0	0	0	0	0	0	0	13.0	1	2	0	0	1.000	1	0	0	0	.00	0
Leake, Mike, StL-Sea	R	.170	47	8	0	4	5	.200	460	92	18	1	6	31	15	181	44	186.0	17	30	0	1	1.000	9	3	0	2	.33	8
Leathersich, J., ChC-Pit	L	-	0	0	0	0	0	-	0	0	0	0	0	0	0	0	0	5.0	0	0	0	0	-	2	0	0	0	.00	0
LeBlanc, Wade, Pit	L	.200	5	1	0	1	0	.248	117	29	1	0	3	3	29	15	68.0	4	9	0	0	1.000	1	0	0	0	.00	1
Leclerc, Jose, Tex	R	-	0	0	0	0	0	-	0	0	0	0	0	0	0	0	0	45.2	3	4	0	2	1.000	5	1	1	0	.20	0
Lee, Zach, SD	R	.000	3	0	0	0	0	.000	5	0	0	0	0	0	0	0	0	8.0	0	1	0	0	1.000	0	0	0	0	-	0
Leiter, Mark, Phi	R	.080	25	2	0	0	0	.080	25	2	0	0	0	0	0	12	1	90.2	10	8	0	0	1.000	12	2	0	0	.17	-2
Leon, Arcenio, Det	R	-	0	0	0	0	0	-	0	0	0	0	0	0	0	0	0	6.2	1	0	0	0	1.000	1	1	0	0	1.00	-1
Leone, Dominic, Tor	R	-	0	0	0	0	0	-	0	0	0	0	0	0	0	0	0	70.1	1	6	0	0	1.000	5	0	0	0	.00	0
Lester, Jon, ChC	L	.148	54	8	1	6	6	.085	211	18	6	0	1	13	14	96	27	180.2	14	23	0	1	1.000	31	12	3	1	.39	-1
Lewicki, Artie, Det	R	-	0	0	0	0	0	-	0	0	0	0	0	0	0	0	0	10.1	0	0	0	0	-	1	0	0	0	.00	-1
Liberatore, Adam, LAD	L	-	0	0	0	0	0	.000	2	0	0	0	0	0	0	2	0	3.1	0	0	0	0	-	0	0	0	0	-	0
Lindblom, Josh, Pit	R	.000	2	0	0	0	0	.000	3	0	0	0	0	0	0	2	0	21.0	1	0	0	0	1.000	1	1	1	0	1.00	0
Liriano, F., Tor-Hou	L	-	0	0	0	0	0	.153	216	33	3	0	2	15	8	85	14	97.0	2	9	0	1	1.000	12	3	0	0	.25	1
Lively, Ben, Phi	R	.231	26	6	2	8	0	.231	26	6	0	0	2	8	0	9	0	88.2	9	10	2	2	.905	5	2	1	0	.40	0
Lloyd, Kyle, SD	R	.000	1	0	0	0	0	.000	1	0	0	0	0	0	0	0	0	4.0	0	1	0	0	1.000	1	0	0	0	.00	0
Locke, Jeff, Mia	L	.000	10	0	0	0	0	.092	195	18	1	0	0	2	8	104	21	32.0	0	2	0	0	1.000	5	0	0	0	.00	-1
Logan, Boone, Cle	L	-	0	0	0	0	0	-	0	0	0	0	0	0	0	0	1	21.0	1	0	0	0	1.000	0	0	0	0	-	-2
Lopez, Jorge, Mil	R	-	0	0	0	0	0	.000	2	0	0	0	0	0	0	2	1	2.0	0	0	0	0	-	0	0	0	0	-	0
Lopez, Reynaldo, CWS	R	-	0	0	0	0	0	.083	12	1	0	0	0	0	0	7	2	47.2	1	2	0	0	1.000	1	1	0	0	1.00	0
Lorenzen, Michael, Cin	R	.167	12	2	1	1	0	.226	53	12	0	1	2	8	0	20	4	83.0	13	8	0	2	1.000	4	1	0	0	.25	0
Loup, Aaron, Tor	L	-	0	0	0	0	0	.000	2	0	0	0	0	0	0	0	0	57.2	1	8	2	1	.818	5	1	0	0	.20	0
Lucas, Josh, StL	R	-	0	0	0	0	0	-	0	0	0	0	0	0	0	0	0	7.1	1	1	0	0	1.000	2	1	0	0	.50	0
Lugo, Seth, NYM	R	.138	29	4	1	2	5	.156	45	7	3	0	1	3	1	12	5	101.1	8	7	0	1	1.000	7	2	0	0	.29	-1
Lyles, Jordan, Col-SD	R	.231	13	3	0	3	0	.134	157	21	4	0	2	10	7	74	11	69.2	2	6	0	2	1.000	3	0	0	0	.00	0
Lynn, Lance, StL	R	.074	54	4	0	0	0	.085	272	23	5	0	0	5	12	152	35	186.1	9	17	2	2	.929	11	7	0	0	.64	-1
Lyons, Tyler, StL	L	.000	1	0	0	0	0	.125	40	5	0	0	1	5	5	16	3	54.0	2	3	1	0	.833	4	1	0	0	.25	-1
Machado, Andres, KC	R	-	0	0	0	0	0	-	0	0	0	0	0	0	0	0	0	3.2	0	0	0	0	-	0	0	0	0	-	-1
Machi, Jean, Sea	R	.000	1	0	0	0	0	.000	6	0	0	0	0	0	0	4	1	7.2	0	0	1	0	.000	1	0	0	0	.00	0
Maddox, Austin, Bos	R	-	0	0	0	0	0	-	0	0	0	0	0	0	0	0	0	17.1	1	1	0	0	1.000	1	0	0	0	.00	0
Madson, Ryan, Oak-Was	R	-	0	0	0	0	0	.122	49	6	1	0	0	2	2	21	7	59.0	1	3	0	0	1.000	10	2	0	1	.20	-2
Maeda, Kenta, LAD	R	.128	39	5	0	4	5	.125	96	12	2	0	1	8	1	19	13	134.1	11	15	3	3	.897	6	2	0	0	.33	2
Magnifico, Damien, LAA	R	-	0	0	0	0	0	-	0	0	0	0	0	0	0	0	0	0.1	0	0	0	0	-	0	0	0	0	-	0
Mahle, Tyler, Cin	R	.143	7	1	0	0	0	.143	7	1	0	0	0	0	0	2	0	20.0	0	7	0	0	1.000	0	0	0	0	-	0
Manaea, Sean, Oak	L	.000	3	0	0	0	1	.000	5	0	0	0	0	0	1	3	1	158.2	5	14	1	0	.950	14	5	4	0	.36	1
Maness, Seth, KC	R	-	0	0	0	0	0	.214	14	3	0	0	0	0	6	0	0	9.2	0	1	0	1	1.000	2	1	0	0	.50	0
Maples, Dillon, ChC	R	-	0	0	0	0	0	-	0	0	0	0	0	0	0	0	0	5.1	0	0	0	0	-	1	1	0	0	1.00	0
Marinez, J., Mil-Pit-Tex	R	.167	6	1	0	0	0	.111	9	1	0	0	0	0	0	5	0	58.1	4	6	0	2	1.000	0	0	0	0	-	0
Marks, Justin, TB	L	-	0	0	0	0	0	-	0	0	0	0	0	0	0	0	0	1.1	0	0	0	0	-	0	0	0	0	-	0
Marquez, German, Col	R	.178	45	8	0	5	8	.157	51	8	2	0	0	5	0	21	10	162.0	6	17	2	2	.920	11	5	1	0	.45	0
Marshall, Evan, Sea	R	-	0	0	0	0	0	-	0	0	0	0	0	0	0	0	0	7.2	0	0	0	0	-	0	0	0	0	-	-1
Martes, Francis, Hou	R	-	0	0	0	0	0	-	0	0	0	0	0	0	0	0	0	54.1	4	4	0	0	1.000	0	0	0	0	-	-1
Martin, Cody, Sea	R	-	0	0	0	0	0	-	0	0	0	0	0	0	0	0	1	2.0	0	0	0	0	-	2	0	0	0	.00	0
Martin, Kyle, Bos	R	-	0	0	0	0	0	-	0	0	0	0	0	0	0	0	0	2.1	0	0	0	0	-	0	0	0	0	-	0
Martinez, Carlos, StL	R	.177	62	11	0	11	5	.188	191	36	6	0	0	19	2	60	15	205.0	12	12	4	0	.857	8	4	0	0	.50	-3
Martinez, Nick, Tex	R	.000	1	0	0	0	0	.000	10	0	0	0	0	0	1	5	0	111.1	10	9	2	0	.905	8	1	0	1	.13	-1
Maton, Phil, SD	R	-	0	0	0	0	0	-	0	0	0	0	0	0	0	0	0	43.0	3	4	0	1	1.000	2	1	0	1	.50	1
Matz, Steven, NYM	L	.143	21	3	0	1	3	.169	71	12	2	1	0	8	4	19	7	66.2	1	13	1	1	.933	9	0	0	0	.00	-3
Maurer, Brandon, SD-KC	R	-	0	0	0	0	0	.000	4	0	0	0	0	0	0	0	0	59.1	3	5	0	0	1.000	2	0	0	0	.00	-1
Mayers, Mike, StL	R	-	0	0	0	0	0	-	0	0	0	0	0	0	0	0	0	4.2	1	0	0	0	1.000	0	0	0	0	-	0
Mayza, Tim, Tor	L	-	0	0	0	0	0	-	0	0	0	0	0	0	0	0	0	17.0	0	1	0	0	1.000	3	1	0	0	.33	0
Mazzoni, Cory, SD	R	-	0	0	0	0	0	-	0	0	0	0	0	0	0	0	0	8.0	0	1	1	0	.500	1	0	0	0	.00	0
McAllister, Zach, Cle	R	-	0	0	0	0	0	.167	6	1	0	0	0	0	0	2	0	62.0	7	6	0	2	1.000	5	2	1	0	.40	0
McCarthy, Brandon, LAD	R	.043	23	1	0	0	2	.051	117	6	0	0	0	5	9	57	10	92.2	3	13	0	1	1.000	13	3	0	0	.23	-1
McCarthy, Kevin, KC	R	-	0	0	0	0	0	-	0	0	0	0	0	0	0	0	0	45.0	6	7	0	1	1.000	1	0	0	0	.00	1
McCullers Jr., Lance, Hou	R	.000	3	0	0	0	0	.125	8	1	0	0	0	0	0	1	0	118.2	13	15	3	2	.903	6	2	0	0	.33	1

Pitchers Hitting, Fielding and Holding Runners

Pitcher	T	2017 Hitting						Career Hitting										2017 Fielding and Holding Runners											
		Avg	AB	H	HR	RBI	SH	Avg	AB	H	2B	3B	HR	RBI	BB	SO	SH	Inn	PO	A	E	DP	Pct	SBA	CS	PCS	PPO	CS%	RS
McFarland, T.J., Ari	L	.200	5	1	0	0	0	.200	5	1	0	0	0	0	0	3	1	54.0	5	13	0	3	1.000	2	0	0	0	.00	-1
McGee, Jake, Col	L	-	0	0	0	0	0	-	0	0	0	0	0	0	0	0	0	57.1	1	3	0	0	1.000	2	1	1	0	.50	-1
McGowan, Dustin, Mia	R	.000	6	0	0	0	1	.074	27	2	0	0	0	0	0	19	2	77.2	1	12	1	0	.929	4	1	0	0	.25	1
McGowan, Kevin, NYM	R	-	0	0	0	0	0	-	0	0	0	0	0	0	0	0	0	8.2	0	0	0	0	-	0	0	0	0	-	0
McGrath, Kyle, SD	L	-	0	0	0	0	0	-	0	0	0	0	0	0	0	0	0	19.0	0	2	0	0	1.000	4	2	1	0	.50	1
McGuire, Deck, Cin	R	.000	3	0	0	1	0	.000	3	0	0	0	0	1	0	1	0	13.2	1	3	1	0	.800	0	0	0	0	-	0
McHugh, Collin, Hou	R	.000	2	0	0	0	0	.071	28	2	0	0	0	0	0	12	3	63.1	3	5	1	3	.889	4	0	0	0	.00	0
Mejia, Adalberto, Min	L	-	0	0	0	0	0	-	0	0	0	0	0	0	0	0	0	98.0	2	6	4	0	.667	5	2	0	0	.40	-3
Melancon, Mark, SF	R	-	0	0	0	0	0	-	0	0	0	0	0	1	0	0	0	30.0	2	9	0	1	1.000	1	0	0	0	.00	0
Mella, Keury, Cin	R	-	0	0	0	0	0	-	0	0	0	0	0	0	0	0	0	4.0	0	1	0	0	1.000	0	0	0	0	-	0
Melville, Tim, Min-SD	R	-	0	0	0	0	0	.000	2	0	0	0	0	0	0	2	0	5.2	1	0	0	0	1.000	0	0	0	0	-	0
Mendez, Yohander, Tex	L	-	0	0	0	0	0	-	0	0	0	0	0	0	0	0	0	12.1	2	1	0	1	1.000	2	0	0	0	.00	0
Mengden, Daniel, Oak	R	.500	2	1	0	0	1	.125	8	1	0	0	0	0	1	3	1	43.0	3	7	0	1	1.000	2	2	1	0	1.00	2
Merritt, Ryan, Cle	L	-	0	0	0	0	0	-	0	0	0	0	0	0	0	0	0	20.2	1	2	0	0	1.000	2	0	0	0	.00	1
Meyer, Alex, LAA	R	.500	2	1	0	0	0	.500	2	1	0	0	0	0	0	1	0	67.1	1	7	0	0	1.000	9	2	1	0	.22	1
Middleton, Keynan, LAA	R	-	0	0	0	0	0	-	0	0	0	0	0	0	0	0	0	58.1	2	4	0	0	1.000	1	1	0	0	1.00	0
Miley, Wade, Bal	L	.250	4	1	0	0	0	.151	212	32	5	0	1	12	8	55	27	157.1	3	21	2	2	.923	9	4	2	2	.44	4
Miller, Andrew, Cle	L	.000	1	0	0	0	0	.055	73	4	0	0	0	3	0	37	4	62.2	4	1	0	0	1.000	1	0	0	0	.00	0
Miller, Shelby, Ari	R	.000	6	0	0	0	0	.111	198	22	10	1	1	6	9	107	34	22.0	1	2	0	0	1.000	1	0	0	0	.00	-1
Milner, Hoby, Phi	L	.000	2	0	0	0	0	.000	2	0	0	0	0	0	0	2	0	31.1	3	8	0	1	1.000	1	1	0	0	.00	0
Milone, Tommy, Mil-NYM	L	.111	9	1	0	1	1	.194	36	7	0	0	1	7	2	10	5	48.1	3	9	0	0	1.000	5	1	1	0	.20	2
Minaya, Juan, CWS	R	-	0	0	0	0	0	-	0	0	0	0	0	0	0	0	0	43.2	5	2	0	0	1.000	10	2	0	0	.20	-1
Minor, Mike, KC	L	-	0	0	0	0	0	.121	198	24	5	0	2	10	9	89	15	77.2	1	9	0	1	1.000	5	1	1	0	.20	0
Minter, A.J., Atl	L	-	0	0	0	0	0	-	0	0	0	0	0	0	0	0	0	15.0	1	0	0	0	1.000	0	0	0	0	-	-1
Miranda, Ariel, Sea	L	.000	6	0	0	0	0	.000	6	0	0	0	0	0	0	3	0	160.0	3	10	3	0	.813	3	2	0	0	.67	1
Mitchell, Bryan, NYY	R	-	0	0	0	0	0	.000	1	0	0	0	0	0	0	1	0	32.2	1	5	3	0	.667	1	0	0	0	.00	-1
Moll, Sam, Oak	L	-	0	0	0	0	0	-	0	0	0	0	0	0	0	0	0	6.2	0	1	0	0	1.000	0	0	0	0	-	1
Montas, Frankie, Oak	R	-	0	0	0	0	0	-	0	0	0	0	0	0	0	0	0	32.0	1	1	0	0	1.000	2	0	0	0	.00	0
Montero, Rafael, NYM	R	.080	25	2	0	1	3	.047	43	2	0	0	0	1	0	19	5	119.0	4	13	0	1	1.000	16	2	0	2	.13	-7
Montgomery, J., NYY	L	.000	3	0	0	0	0	.000	3	0	0	0	0	0	2	2	0	155.1	2	6	1	0	.889	3	1	0	0	.33	-2
Montgomery, Mike, ChC	L	.185	27	5	1	3	3	.146	41	6	1	0	1	4	0	17	3	130.2	5	23	0	3	1.000	9	3	1	0	.33	-2
Moore, Andrew, Sea	R	-	0	0	0	0	0	-	0	0	0	0	0	0	0	0	0	59.0	4	6	0	0	1.000	3	1	1	0	.33	0
Moore, Matt, SF	L	.128	47	6	0	4	4	.106	85	9	0	0	0	5	2	34	10	174.1	3	23	3	0	.897	12	4	2	0	.33	0
Moreno, Diego, TB	R	-	0	0	0	0	0	-	0	0	0	0	0	0	0	0	0	5.2	0	1	0	1	1.000	1	0	0	0	.00	0
Morgan, Adam, Phi	L	.500	2	1	0	0	0	.100	60	6	2	0	0	2	2	24	4	54.2	1	6	0	1	1.000	7	0	0	0	.00	-2
Morin, Mike, LAA-KC	R	-	0	0	0	0	0	-	0	0	0	0	0	0	0	0	0	20.0	0	0	0	0	-	0	0	0	0	-	-1
Moronta, Reyes, SF	R	-	0	0	0	0	0	-	0	0	0	0	0	0	0	0	0	6.2	0	0	0	0	-	0	0	0	0	-	0
Morris, Akeel, Atl	R	-	0	0	0	0	0	-	0	0	0	0	0	0	0	0	0	7.1	0	0	0	0	-	0	0	0	0	-	0
Morris, Bryan, SF	R	-	0	0	0	0	0	.143	7	1	0	0	0	0	0	4	0	21.0	1	2	1	0	.750	2	2	0	1	1.00	0
Morrow, Brandon, LAD	R	-	0	0	0	0	0	.000	23	0	0	0	0	0	1	14	0	43.2	3	2	0	0	1.000	5	1	0	0	.20	-1
Morton, Charlie, Hou	R	.000	3	0	0	0	0	.074	258	19	4	0	0	6	3	132	37	146.2	10	9	4	1	.826	5	1	0	2	.20	-4
Motte, Jason, Atl	R	-	0	0	0	0	0	.000	4	0	0	0	0	0	0	4	0	40.2	7	13	0	3	1.000	7	0	0	0	.00	2
Moya, Gabriel, Min	L	-	0	0	0	0	0	-	0	0	0	0	0	0	0	0	0	6.1	1	0	0	0	1.000	0	0	0	0	-	0
Moylan, Peter, KC	R	-	0	0	0	0	0	.000	7	0	0	0	0	0	1	6	0	59.1	3	16	1	0	.950	3	1	1	1	.33	2
Mujica, Edward, Det	R	-	0	0	0	0	0	.182	11	2	0	0	0	0	0	4	2	6.1	0	0	0	0	-	0	0	0	0	-	0
Musgrove, Joe, Hou	R	.000	5	0	0	0	0	.000	5	0	0	0	0	0	0	1	1	109.1	15	21	1	2	.973	4	2	0	0	.50	5
Neal, Zach, Oak	R	-	0	0	0	0	0	.000	2	0	0	0	0	0	0	0	0	14.2	1	0	0	0	1.000	2	0	0	0	.00	0
Nelson, Jimmy, Mil	R	.105	57	6	0	2	2	.103	185	19	2	0	0	7	4	110	13	175.1	11	15	2	0	.929	22	4	1	1	.18	-3
Neris, Hector, Phi	R	-	0	0	0	0	0	.000	1	0	0	0	0	0	0	1	0	74.2	3	9	1	0	.923	5	1	0	0	.20	1
Neshek, Pat, Phi-Col	R	-	0	0	0	0	0	-	0	0	0	0	0	0	0	0	0	62.1	4	7	0	1	1.000	4	1	1	0	.25	0
Neverauskas, D., Pit	R	-	0	0	0	0	0	-	0	0	0	0	0	0	0	0	0	25.1	3	3	0	1	1.000	2	1	0	0	.50	1
Newcomb, Sean, Atl	L	.037	27	1	0	0	6	.037	27	1	0	0	0	0	2	17	6	100.0	2	14	1	0	.941	3	1	0	0	.33	0
Nicasio, Juan, Pit-Phi-StL	R	.000	1	0	0	0	0	.124	121	15	2	0	0	9	6	69	15	72.1	4	8	1	0	.923	5	2	0	0	.40	1
Nicolino, Justin, Mia	L	.000	11	0	0	0	2	.052	58	3	0	0	0	1	21	5	48.0	7	9	2	1	.889	2	0	0	0	.00	-1
Nola, Aaron, Phi	R	.083	48	4	0	1	2	.069	101	7	1	0	0	8	58	5	168.0	9	21	0	1	1.000	23	2	0	0	.09	-1
Nolasco, Ricky, LAA	R	.000	5	0	0	0	0	.134	382	51	12	0	1	26	25	179	62	181.0	11	10	2	0	.913	11	7	0	1	.64	0
Norris, Bud, LAA	R	-	0	0	0	0	0	.157	204	32	5	1	0	12	7	66	38	62.0	3	3	2	0	.750	8	2	0	0	.25	0
Norris, Daniel, Det	L	-	0	0	0	0	0	.250	4	1	0	0	1	2	2	1	0	101.2	3	14	0	0	1.000	22	7	5	0	.32	0
Nova, Ivan, Pit	R	.020	51	1	0	0	9	.055	91	5	0	0	0	6	2	62	14	187.0	18	34	1	1	.981	13	3	1	0	.23	5
Nuno, Vidal, Bal	L	.000	1	0	0	0	0	.077	26	2	0	0	0	1	0	8	6	14.2	1	1	0	0	1.000	1	0	0	0	.00	-1
Oberg, Scott, Col	R	-	0	0	0	0	0	-	0	0	0	0	0	0	0	0	0	58.1	2	7	0	0	1.000	1	0	0	0	.00	2
O'Day, Darren, Bal	R	-	0	0	0	0	0	.000	6	0	0	0	0	0	0	0	0	60.1	3	10	1	0	.929	6	3	0	0	.50	2
Odorizzi, Jake, TB	R	.333	3	1	0	1	1	.133	15	2	0	0	3	1	6	2	143.1	7	10	2	0	.895	11	4	0	0	.36	0
O'Flaherty, Eric, Atl	L	-	0	0	0	0	0	.000	2	0	0	0	0	0	2	0	18.1	1	3	0	0	1.000	1	0	0	0	.00	0
O'Grady, Chris, Mia	L	.000	8	0	0	0	1	.000	8	0	0	0	0	0	0	5	1	33.0	2	5	0	0	1.000	2	1	1	0	.50	0
Oh, Seung Hwan, StL	R	-	0	0	0	0	0	.000	2	0	0	0	0	0	0	2	0	59.1	2	6	0	0	1.000	0	0	0	0	-	0
Okert, Steven, SF	L	.000	1	0	0	0	0	.000	2	0	0	0	0	0	0	2	0	27.0	0	2	0	0	1.000	1	1	0	0	1.00	0
Olson, Tyler, Cle	L	-	0	0	0	0	0	-	0	0	0	0	0	0	0	0	0	20.0	0	3	0	0	1.000	0	0	0	0	-	1
Osich, Josh, SF	L	-	0	0	0	0	0	.000	1	0	0	0	0	0	0	1	2	43.1	2	3	0	0	1.000	0	0	0	0	-	-1
Osuna, Roberto, Tor	R	-	0	0	0	0	0	-	0	0	0	0	0	0	0	0	0	64.0	1	8	0	1	1.000	6	0	0	0	.00	0

Pitchers Hitting, Fielding and Holding Runners

Pitcher	T	2017 Hitting						Career Hitting										2017 Fielding and Holding Runners											
		Avg	AB	H	HR	RBI	SH	Avg	AB	H	2B	3B	HR	RBI	BB	SO	SH	Inn	PO	A	E	DP	Pct	SBA	CS	PCS	PPO	CS%	RS
Otero, Dan, Cle	R	-	0	0	0	0	0	.000	1	0	0	0	0	0	0	1	0	60.0	4	11	1	0	.938	3	1	0	0	.33	2
Ottavino, Adam, Col	R		0	0	0	0	0	.083	24	2	0	0	0	1	17	3	53.1	5	6	2	0	.846	12	2	0	0	.17	-1
Overton, Dillon, Sea-SD	L	.000	1	0	0	0	0	.000	1	0	0	0	0	0	0	1	0	23.0	0	2	0	0	1.000	2	1	0	1	.50	1
Pagan, Emilio, Sea	R	.000	2	0	0	0	0	.000	2	0	0	0	0	0	0	1	0	50.1	0	1	0	0	1.000	2	0	0	0	.00	-1
Paredes, Eduardo, LAA	R	-	0	0	0	0	0	-	0	0	0	0	0	0	0	0	0	22.1	2	6	0	0	1.000	1	1	0	0	1.00	0
Paredes, Edward, LAD	L	-	0	0	0	0	0	-	0	0	0	0	0	0	0	0	0	8.1	0	0	0	0	-	1	0	0	0	.00	0
Parker, Blake, LAA	R	-	0	0	0	0	0	-	0	0	0	0	0	0	0	0	0	67.1	2	2	0	0	1.000	8	2	0	0	.25	-2
Paulino, David, Hou	R	-	0	0	0	0	0	-	0	0	0	0	0	0	0	0	0	29.0	1	1	0	0	1.000	2	0	0	0	.00	-1
Paxton, James, Sea	L	-	0	0	0	0	0	.000	7	0	0	0	0	0	2	7	1	136.0	4	6	0	0	1.000	7	3	1	0	.43	0
Pazos, James, Sea	L	-	0	0	0	0	0	-	0	0	0	0	0	0	0	0	0	53.2	4	6	0	1	1.000	9	1	0	0	.11	-3
Peacock, Brad, Hou	R	.286	7	2	0	2	0	.125	16	2	1	0	0	2	1	10	1	132.0	6	21	1	1	.964	12	2	0	1	.17	2
Pelfrey, Mike, CWS	R	-	0	0	0	0	0	.104	268	28	5	0	0	13	13	72	24	120.0	6	13	0	0	1.000	29	3	0	0	.10	-3
Pena, Felix, ChC	R	.000	3	0	0	0	0	.000	3	0	0	0	0	0	1	1	0	34.1	2	5	0	0	1.000	4	0	0	1	.00	0
Peralta, Wandy, Cin	L	-	0	0	0	0	0	-	0	0	0	0	0	0	0	0	0	64.2	5	10	0	1	1.000	2	1	0	0	.50	1
Peralta, Wily, Mil	R	.231	13	3	0	1	1	.100	200	20	4	0	1	11	7	83	23	57.1	2	1	0	0	1.000	7	5	0	0	.71	0
Perdomo, Luis, SD	R	.109	46	5	0	3	6	.119	84	10	2	4	0	4	2	35	9	163.2	11	22	1	2	.971	12	4	1	0	.33	-3
Perez, Martin, Tex	L	.000	6	0	0	0	0	.059	17	1	0	0	0	0	0	14	2	185.0	6	19	2	1	.926	6	5	1	0	.83	1
Perez, Oliver, Was	L	-	0	0	0	0	0	.163	344	56	2	0	0	15	14	116	39	33.0	0	4	0	0	1.000	4	1	0	0	.25	0
Perkins, Glen, Min	L	-	0	0	0	0	0	.000	4	0	0	0	0	0	0	4	3	5.2	2	0	0	0	1.000	0	0	0	0	-	0
Peters, Dillon, Mia	L	.000	9	0	0	0	2	.000	9	0	0	0	0	0	0	8	2	31.1	1	9	0	0	1.000	1	1	0	0	1.00	0
Petit, Yusmeiro, LAA	R	-	0	0	0	0	0	.051	118	6	0	0	0	3	3	49	7	91.1	6	4	1	0	.909	7	2	0	0	.29	-1
Petricka, Jake, CWS	R	-	0	0	0	0	0	-	0	0	0	0	0	0	0	0	0	25.2	1	3	0	1	1.000	3	0	0	0	.00	0
Phelps, David, Mia-Sea	R	.000	1	0	0	0	0	.115	52	6	0	0	0	1	0	23	8	55.2	5	3	0	0	1.000	3	1	0	0	.33	0
Pill, Tyler, NYM	R	.000	5	0	0	0	0	.000	5	0	0	0	0	0	0	1	0	22.0	2	6	0	0	1.000	1	0	0	0	.00	1
Pineda, Michael, NYY	R	.333	3	1	0	0	0	.182	11	2	0	0	0	0	0	6	1	96.1	6	14	1	2	.952	9	3	1	0	.33	2
Pinto, Ricardo, Phi	R	.000	1	0	0	0	0	.000	1	0	0	0	0	0	0	1	0	29.2	0	2	1	0	.667	2	1	0	1	.50	0
Pivetta, Nick, Phi	R	.068	44	3	0	0	4	.068	44	3	0	0	0	0	0	21	4	133.0	3	8	1	0	.917	13	5	0	2	.38	-3
Pomeranz, Drew, Bos	L	.000	1	0	0	0	0	.171	70	12	2	0	2	5	1	41	9	173.2	2	15	3	4	.850	10	4	0	0	.40	-2
Porcello, Rick, Bos	R	.000	4	0	0	0	0	.156	32	5	0	0	0	2	0	14	3	203.1	10	17	3	2	.900	19	4	0	0	.21	-1
Pounders, Brooks, LAA	R	-	0	0	0	0	0	-	0	0	0	0	0	0	0	0	0	10.1	0	0	0	0	-	2	0	0	0	.00	0
Povse, Max, Sea	R	-	0	0	0	0	0	-	0	0	0	0	0	0	0	0	0	3.2	0	0	0	0	-	0	0	0	0	-	0
Pressly, Ryan, Min	R	-	0	0	0	0	0	-	0	0	0	0	0	0	0	0	0	61.1	5	5	0	0	1.000	4	0	0	0	.00	-3
Price, David, Bos	L	1.000	1	1	0	0	0	.063	48	3	0	0	0	0	3	24	0	74.2	6	6	1	0	.923	4	1	0	0	.50	1
Pruitt, Austin, TB	R	-	0	0	0	0	0	-	0	0	0	0	0	0	0	0	0	83.0	6	6	1	1	.923	8	0	0	1	.00	-4
Putnam, Zach, CWS	R	-	0	0	0	0	0	-	0	0	0	0	0	0	0	0	0	8.2	0	0	0	0	-	0	0	0	0	-	0
Quackenbush, Kevin, SD	R	.000	1	0	0	0	0	.000	1	0	0	0	0	0	0	1	0	26.1	1	4	0	0	1.000	1	0	0	0	.00	0
Qualls, Chad, Col	R	-	0	0	0	0	0	.000	6	0	0	0	0	0	0	5	0	16.2	0	2	0	0	1.000	1	0	0	0	.00	0
Quintana, J., CWS-ChC	L	.080	25	2	0	4	6	.041	49	2	0	0	0	4	2	31	9	188.2	6	23	1	2	.967	16	6	1	2	.38	1
Ramirez, Carlos, Tor	R	-	0	0	0	0	0	-	0	0	0	0	0	0	0	0	0	16.2	0	0	0	0	-	1	0	0	0	.00	0
Ramirez, E., TB-Sea	R	.667	3	2	0	1	0	.182	11	2	0	0	0	1	0	5	1	131.1	6	12	1	2	.947	7	2	0	0	.29	-1
Ramirez, JC, LAA	R	.000	3	0	0	0	0	.000	4	0	0	0	0	0	0	1	0	147.1	10	12	2	2	.917	19	5	1	0	.26	-2
Ramirez, Jose, Atl	R	-	0	0	0	0	0	-	0	0	0	0	0	0	0	0	0	62.0	2	6	0	1	1.000	9	1	0	0	.11	-1
Ramirez, Neil, SF-NYM	R	.000	1	0	0	0	0	.000	1	0	0	0	0	0	0	1	0	31.1	4	3	0	0	1.000	2	1	1	0	.50	0
Ramirez, Noe, Bos-LAA	R	-	0	0	0	0	0	-	0	0	0	0	0	0	0	0	0	13.0	0	0	1	0	.000	0	0	0	0	-	-1
Ramos, A.J., Mia-NYM	R	-	0	0	0	0	0	-	0	0	0	0	0	0	0	0	0	58.2	3	5	1	0	.889	1	0	0	0	.00	-1
Ramos, Edubray, Phi	R	.000	1	0	0	0	0	.000	1	0	0	0	0	0	1	1	0	57.2	1	4	2	0	.714	4	2	0	0	.50	0
Ravin, Josh, LAD	R	.000	1	0	0	0	1	.000	1	0	0	0	0	0	0	0	1	16.2	1	3	0	0	1.000	1	0	0	0	.00	0
Ray, Robbie, Ari	L	.245	53	13	0	2	5	.194	139	27	5	0	1	4	4	63	16	162.0	0	11	1	1	.917	16	8	3	0	.50	-1
Reed, Addison, NYM-Bos	R	-	0	0	0	0	0	.000	2	0	0	0	0	0	0	0	0	76.0	4	3	0	0	1.000	1	1	0	0	1.00	0
Reed, Cody, Cin	L	.000	2	0	0	0	0	.000	13	0	0	0	0	0	1	8	2	17.2	1	3	0	0	1.000	0	0	0	0	-	0
Reininger, Zac, Det	R	-	0	0	0	0	0	-	0	0	0	0	0	0	0	0	0	9.2	1	1	0	1	1.000	0	0	0	0	-	0
Rhame, Jacob, NYM	R	-	0	0	0	0	0	-	0	0	0	0	0	0	0	0	0	9.0	0	3	0	0	1.000	0	0	0	0	-	1
Richard, Clayton, SD	L	.123	57	7	1	4	8	.117	283	33	9	0	2	25	6	134	34	197.1	7	36	0	3	1.000	14	10	7	1	.71	2
Richards, Garrett, LAA	R	-	0	0	0	0	0	.000	13	0	0	0	0	0	0	5	0	27.2	4	4	0	0	1.000	0	0	0	0	-	-1
Rios, Yacksel, Phi	R	.000	1	0	0	0	0	.000	1	0	0	0	0	0	0	1	0	16.1	0	0	0	0	-	0	0	0	0	-	0
Rivero, Felipe, Pit	L	-	0	0	0	0	0	.000	1	0	0	0	0	0	0	1	0	75.1	5	13	1	0	.947	5	1	0	0	.20	1
Roark, Tanner, Was	R	.091	55	5	0	0	7	.133	218	29	5	0	0	4	7	82	27	181.1	11	19	1	4	.968	13	5	0	1	.38	0
Robertson, D., CWS-NYY	R	-	0	0	0	0	0	-	0	0	0	0	0	0	0	0	0	68.1	6	3	1	0	.900	1	0	0	0	.00	-1
Robles, Hansel, NYM	R	-	0	0	0	0	1	.000	3	0	0	0	0	0	0	2	1	56.2	3	2	0	0	1.000	5	2	0	0	.40	0
Rodney, Fernando, Ari	R	-	0	0	0	0	0	.000	1	0	0	0	0	0	0	0	0	55.1	0	1	0	0	1.000	7	2	0	0	.29	-1
Rodon, Carlos, CWS	L	.333	6	2	0	2	1	.200	10	2	1	0	0	2	0	5	3	69.1	2	7	0	0	1.000	14	2	0	1	.14	0
Rodriguez, Eduardo, Bos	L	.000	7	0	0	0	0	.000	11	0	0	0	0	0	0	6	1	137.1	5	11	1	1	.941	5	3	0	0	.60	-1
Rodriguez, F., Det	R	-	0	0	0	0	0	.500	2	1	0	0	0	0	0	1	0	25.1	2	1	0	0	1.000	4	1	1	0	.25	0
Rodriguez, Joely, Phi	L	-	0	0	0	0	0	-	0	0	0	0	0	0	0	0	0	27.0	2	6	1	0	.889	0	0	0	0	-	-1
Rodriguez, Ricardo, Tex	R	-	0	0	0	0	0	-	0	0	0	0	0	0	0	0	0	13.0	0	1	0	0	1.000	1	0	0	0	.00	0
Rodriguez, Richard, Bal	R	-	0	0	0	0	0	-	0	0	0	0	0	0	0	0	0	5.2	1	0	0	0	1.000	0	0	0	0	-	0
Roe, Chaz, Atl-TB	R	-	0	0	0	0	0	.000	1	0	0	0	0	0	0	1	0	10.2	0	0	0	0	-	1	0	0	0	-	-1
Rogers, Taylor, Min	L	-	0	0	0	0	0	-	0	0	0	0	0	0	0	0	0	55.2	1	5	0	0	1.000	5	1	1	0	.20	0
Romano, Sal, Cin	R	.042	24	1	0	0	5	.042	24	1	1	0	0	0	1	15	5	87.0	12	13	1	0	.962	6	4	2	0	.67	1
Romero, Enny, Was	L	.000	1	0	0	0	0	.000	1	0	0	0	0	0	0	1	0	55.2	0	2	0	0	1.000	12	2	1	0	.17	-1

Pitchers Hitting, Fielding and Holding Runners

Pitcher	T	2017 Hitting						Career Hitting										2017 Fielding and Holding Runners											
		Avg	AB	H	HR	RBI	SH	Avg	AB	H	2B	3B	HR	RBI	BB	SO	SH	Inn	PO	A	E	DP	Pct	SBA	CS	PCS	PPO	CS%	RS
Romo, Sergio, LAD-TB	R	-	0	0	0	0	0	.000	6	0	0	0	0	0	0	4	0	55.2	1	5	0	0	1.000	6	1	0	0	.17	0
Rondon, Bruce, Det	R	-	0	0	0	0	0	-	0	0	0	0	0	0	0	0	0	15.2	2	0	0	0	1.000	3	1	0	0	.33	0
Rondon, Hector, ChC	R	.500	2	1	0	0	0	.333	3	1	0	0	0	0	0	1	0	57.1	5	4	0	1	1.000	7	1	0	0	.14	-2
Rosario, Randy, Min	L	-	0	0	0	0	0	-	0	0	0	0	0	0	0	0	0	2.1	0	0	0	-		0	0	0	0	-	0
Rosenthal, Trevor, StL	R	-	0	0	0	0	0	.000	4	0	0	0	0	0	0	4	0	47.2	1	3	0	0	1.000	2	1	0	0	.50	0
Ross, Joe, Was	R	.182	33	6	0	1	3	.188	101	19	4	0	0	2	4	42	5	73.2	1	8	0	0	1.000	2	0	0	0	.00	0
Ross, Tyson, Tex	R	-	0	0	0	0	0	.201	149	30	2	1	1	9	5	62	13	49.0	4	9	1	0	.929	10	1	0	1	.00	0
Ross Jr., Robbie, Bos	L	-	0	0	0	0	0	.000	3	0	0	0	0	0	1	1	0	9.0	0	1	0	1	1.000	0	0	0	0	-	0
Rosscup, Zac, ChC-Col	L	-	0	0	0	0	0	-	0	0	0	0	0	0	0	0	0	7.2	2	0	0	-		0	0	0	0	-	0
Rowley, Chris, Tor	R	-	0	0	0	0	0	-	0	0	0	0	0	0	0	0	0	18.2	0	1	0	0	1.000	1	0	0	0	.00	0
Rucinski, Drew, Min	R	-	0	0	0	0	0	-	0	0	0	0	0	0	0	0	0	4.1	0	1	0	0	1.000	0	0	0	0	-	0
Ruiz, Jose, SD	R	-	0	0	0	0	0	-	0	0	0	0	0	0	0	0	0	1.0	0	0	0	-		0	0	0	0	-	0
Runzler, Dan, Pit	L	-	0	0	0	0	0	.000	1	0	0	0	0	0	1	1	0	4.0	0	0	0	-		0	0	0	0	-	-1
Rusin, Chris, Col	L	.333	9	3	0	0	1	.186	118	22	0	2	1	9	0	25	8	85.0	2	15	0	3	1.000	5	3	2	0	.60	1
Ryan, Kyle, Det	L	-	0	0	0	0	0	-	0	0	0	0	0	0	0	0	0	5.2	0	0	0	-		1	0	0	0	.00	0
Ryu, Hyun-Jin, LAD	L	.133	30	4	0	0	4	.169	136	23	6	1	0	7	6	58	18	126.2	3	13	1	2	.941	3	1	0	0	.33	-1
Rzepczynski, Marc, Sea	L	-	0	0	0	0	0	.000	1	0	0	0	0	0	0	1	0	31.1	2	4	1	0	.857	4	1	0	0	.25	-2
Sabathia, CC, NYY	L	.000	3	0	0	0	0	.212	118	25	3	0	3	15	2	34	4	148.2	2	19	1	0	.955	9	5	0	0	.56	0
Salas, F., NYM-LAA	R	.500	2	1	0	0	0	.167	6	1	0	0	0	0	0	3	0	58.2	2	7	0	0	1.000	8	3	0	0	.38	0
Salazar, Danny, Cle	R	-	0	0	0	0	0	.000	14	0	0	0	0	0	0	12	0	103.0	3	5	1	0	.889	4	3	0	0	.75	1
Sale, Chris, Bos	L	.333	3	1	0	0	0	.130	23	3	1	0	0	0	0	11	1	214.1	8	22	0	3	1.000	12	2	0	0	.17	2
Samardzija, Jeff, SF	R	.094	64	6	1	2	3	.128	290	37	12	0	3	21	7	118	26	207.2	12	32	1	1	.978	13	7	2	1	.54	5
Sanchez, Aaron, Tor	R	-	0	0	0	0	0	.000	9	0	0	0	0	0	1	5	0	36.0	3	4	1	0	.875	6	1	0	0	.17	-2
Sanchez, Angel, Pit	R	.000	1	0	0	0	0	.000	1	0	0	0	0	0	0	0	0	12.1	1	2	0	0	1.000	0	0	0	0	-	0
Sanchez, Anibal, Det	R	.000	2	0	0	0	0	.087	253	22	1	1	0	7	16	120	31	105.1	4	6	3	0	.769	19	6	0	0	.32	-6
Santana, Edgar, Pit	R	-	0	0	0	0	0	-	0	0	0	0	0	0	0	0	0	18.0	1	1	0	0	1.000	1	0	0	0	.00	-1
Santana, Ervin, Min	R	.200	10	2	0	5	0	.126	103	13	3	0	0	8	2	49	10	211.1	19	16	2	0	.946	13	2	0	0	.15	-1
Santiago, Hector, Min	L	-	0	0	0	0	0	.188	16	3	0	0	0	0	6	6	3	70.1	5	6	0	0	1.000	10	2	0	0	.20	0
Santos, Luis, Tor	R	-	0	0	0	0	0	-	0	0	0	0	0	0	0	0	0	16.2	0	1	0	0	1.000	1	0	0	0	.00	-1
Saupold, Warwick, Det	R	-	0	0	0	0	0	-	0	0	0	0	0	0	0	0	0	62.2	7	13	0	2	1.000	9	3	1	1	.33	2
Scahill, Rob, Mil	R	.000	1	0	0	0	0	.000	5	0	0	0	0	0	1	2	1	22.1	1	2	0	0	1.000	2	0	0	0	.00	0
Scheppers, Tanner, Tex	R	-	0	0	0	0	0	-	0	0	0	0	0	0	0	0	0	4.0	1	0	0	0	1.000	1	0	0	0	.00	0
Scherzer, Max, Was	R	.161	62	10	1	5	6	.182	280	51	4	0	1	21	12	92	35	200.2	9	9	1	1	.947	10	3	0	0	.30	-1
Schugel, A.J., Pit	R	.000	1	0	0	0	0	.000	3	0	0	0	0	0	1	1	1	32.0	2	2	0	0	1.000	1	1	0	1	1.00	0
Scott, Robby, Bos	L	-	0	0	0	0	0	-	0	0	0	0	0	0	0	0	0	35.2	1	4	0	0	1.000	1	1	1	1	1.00	1
Scott, Tanner, Bal	L	-	0	0	0	0	0	-	0	0	0	0	0	0	0	0	0	1.2	0	0	0	-		0	0	0	0	-	0
Scribner, Evan, Sea	R	-	0	0	0	0	0	-	0	0	0	0	0	0	0	0	0	7.1	0	2	0	0	1.000	1	0	0	0	.00	0
Scribner, Troy, LAA	R	-	0	0	0	0	0	-	0	0	0	0	0	0	0	0	0	23.2	0	2	0	0	1.000	0	0	0	0	-	1
Senzatela, Antonio, Col	R	.125	32	4	0	5	7	.125	32	4	1	0	0	5	0	20	7	134.2	9	24	1	2	.971	5	1	0	0	.20	2
Severino, Luis, NYY	R	.200	5	1	0	0	0	.143	7	1	0	0	0	0	0	1	0	193.1	7	27	2	2	.944	6	2	1	0	.33	4
Sewald, Paul, NYM	R	.000	2	0	0	0	0	.000	2	0	0	0	0	0	0	1	0	65.1	2	6	1	0	.889	0	0	0	0	-	1
Shackelford, Kevin, Cin	R	.333	3	1	0	0	0	.333	3	1	0	0	0	0	0	1	0	30.2	5	2	0	1	1.000	0	0	0	0	-	0
Shaw, Bryan, Cle	R	-	0	0	0	0	0	-	0	0	0	0	0	0	0	0	0	76.2	5	9	2	1	.875	3	0	0	0	.00	-3
Sherfy, Jimmie, Ari	R	-	0	0	0	0	0	-	0	0	0	0	0	0	0	0	0	10.2	1	0	0	0	1.000	2	1	0	0	.50	0
Sherriff, Ryan, StL	L	-	0	0	0	0	0	-	0	0	0	0	0	0	0	0	0	14.1	2	2	0	0	1.000	1	0	0	0	.00	0
Shields, James, CWS	R	-	0	0	0	0	0	.169	136	23	3	0	0	6	3	53	8	117.0	5	12	0	0	1.000	9	0	0	1	.00	-1
Shipley, Braden, Ari	R	.000	6	0	0	0	0	.094	32	3	1	0	0	2	0	12	1	25.0	0	0	0	-		2	0	0	0	.00	-1
Shoemaker, Matt, LAA	R	.000	2	0	0	0	0	.000	6	0	0	0	0	0	1	3	1	77.2	2	8	1	1	.909	7	3	1	1	.43	1
Shreve, Chasen, NYY	L	.000	2	0	0	0	0	.000	2	0	0	0	0	0	0	1	0	45.1	1	4	0	0	1.000	0	0	0	0	-	0
Siegrist, Kevin, StL-Phi	L	-	0	0	0	0	0	.000	1	0	0	0	0	0	0	1	0	39.1	1	7	0	2	1.000	4	2	1	1	.50	0
Simmons, Shae, Sea	R	-	0	0	0	0	0	-	0	0	0	0	0	0	0	0	0	7.2	0	0	1	0	.000	0	0	0	0	-	0
Sims, Luke, Atl	R	.067	15	1	0	0	3	.067	15	1	0	0	0	0	0	8	3	57.2	3	5	2	0	.800	8	5	0	1	.63	1
Sipp, Tony, Hou	L	.000	1	0	0	0	0	.000	1	0	0	0	0	0	0	0	0	37.1	4	7	0	0	1.000	6	0	0	1	.00	-1
Skaggs, Tyler, LAA	L	.000	1	0	0	0	0	.095	21	2	0	0	0	1	0	12	5	85.0	1	2	0	0	1.000	10	1	1	0	.10	-4
Skoglund, Eric, KC	L	-	0	0	0	0	0	-	0	0	0	0	0	0	0	0	0	18.0	1	2	0	0	1.000	1	1	1	0	1.00	0
Slania, Dan, SF	R	-	0	0	0	0	0	-	0	0	0	0	0	0	0	0	0	1.0	0	0	0	-		0	0	0	0	-	0
Slegers, Aaron, Min	R	-	0	0	0	0	0	-	0	0	0	0	0	0	0	0	0	15.1	0	1	0	0	1.000	2	1	0	0	.50	0
Smith, Caleb, NYY	L	-	0	0	0	0	0	-	0	0	0	0	0	0	0	0	0	18.2	0	1	0	0	1.000	0	0	0	0	-	0
Smith, Carson, Bos	R	-	0	0	0	0	0	-	0	0	0	0	0	0	0	0	0	6.2	0	1	0	0	1.000	1	0	0	1	1.00	0
Smith, Chris, Tor	R	-	0	0	0	0	0	-	0	0	0	0	0	0	0	0	0	5.0	0	2	0	0	1.000	0	0	0	0	-	1
Smith, Chris, Oak	R	.000	1	0	0	0	0	.000	3	0	0	0	0	0	1	1	0	55.2	4	6	1	0	.909	4	2	0	0	.50	0
Smith, Joe, Tor-Cle	R	-	0	0	0	0	0	.000	2	0	0	0	0	0	0	2	0	54.0	3	12	0	2	1.000	4	1	0	0	.25	2
Smith, Josh, Oak	R	-	0	0	0	0	0	.200	20	4	1	1	0	0	0	8	1	35.0	2	2	0	0	1.000	3	1	0	0	.33	0
Smoker, Josh, NYM	L	.000	4	0	0	0	0	.000	4	0	0	0	0	0	0	3	0	56.1	2	4	0	0	1.000	8	2	1	0	.25	-2
Snell, Blake, TB	L	.000	5	0	0	0	1	.000	7	0	0	0	0	0	2	2	1	129.1	6	13	0	1	1.000	7	2	0	0	.29	3
Socolovich, Miguel, StL	R	.000	1	0	0	0	0	.000	2	0	0	0	0	0	0	0	0	18.2	0	3	0	0	1.000	0	0	0	0	-	0
Solis, Sammy, Was	L	-	0	0	0	0	0	.200	5	1	0	0	0	0	0	1	0	26.0	1	6	0	1	1.000	0	0	0	0	-	0
Soria, Joakim, KC	R	-	0	0	0	0	0	-	0	0	0	0	0	0	0	0	0	56.0	11	6	0	3	1.000	0	0	0	0	-	-1
Sparkman, Glenn, Tor	R	-	0	0	0	0	0	-	0	0	0	0	0	0	0	0	0	1.0	0	0	0	-		2	0	0	0	.00	-1
Stammen, Craig, SD	R	.500	6	3	0	0	0	.221	95	21	8	0	0	10	6	37	10	80.1	2	15	1	1	.944	6	1	0	0	.17	-1

Pitchers Hitting, Fielding and Holding Runners

Pitcher	T	2017 Hitting Avg	AB	H	HR	RBI	SH	Career Hitting Avg	AB	H	2B	3B	HR	RBI	BB	SO	SH	2017 Fielding Inn	PO	A	E	DP	Pct	SBA	CS	PCS	PPO	CS%	RS
Stanek, Ryne, TB	R	-	0	0	0	0	0	-	0	0	0	0	0	0	0	0	0	20.0	1	1	0	0	1.000	5	1	0	0	.20	0
Steckenrider, Drew, Mia	R	-	0	0	0	0	0	-	0	0	0	0	0	0	0	0	0	34.2	1	2	0	1	1.000	3	1	0	0	.33	0
Stephens, Jackson, Cin	R	.333	6	2	0	2	0	.333	6	2	0	0	0	2	0	2	0	25.0	7	1	0	0	1.000	4	2	0	0	.50	-1
Stephenson, Robert, Cin	R	.043	23	1	0	0	2	.030	33	1	0	0	0	0	0	20	5	84.2	4	5	3	0	.750	9	5	0	0	.56	-2
Stewart, Brock, LAD	R	.250	4	1	0	1	1	.143	14	2	0	0	0	1	0	9	1	34.1	0	3	0	1	1.000	1	0	0	0	.00	0
Storen, Drew, Cin	R	.000	1	0	0	0	0	.333	3	1	0	0	0	0	0	1	0	54.2	2	5	0	1	1.000	4	2	0	0	.50	0
Strahm, Matt, KC	L	-	0	0	0	0	0	-	0	0	0	0	0	0	0	0	0	34.2	1	2	0	1	1.000	1	1	0	0	1.00	-1
Straily, Dan, Mia	R	.073	55	4	0	1	8	.045	110	5	1	0	0	2	5	76	19	181.2	13	19	2	0	.941	16	6	1	1	.38	-2
Strasburg, Stephen, Was	R	.130	54	7	2	3	4	.152	322	49	8	0	3	18	18	114	42	175.1	13	10	1	0	.958	11	4	1	0	.36	0
Stratton, Chris, SF	R	.143	14	2	0	0	2	.133	15	2	0	0	0	0	0	3	2	58.2	5	8	1	0	.929	4	1	0	0	.25	0
Street, Huston, LAA	R	-	0	0	0	0	0	.000	2	0	0	0	0	0	0	0	0	4.0	0	2	0	0	1.000	0	0	0	0	-	0
Strickland, Hunter, SF	R	-	0	0	0	0	0	.000	1	0	0	0	0	0	0	1	0	61.1	3	5	0	0	1.000	6	2	0	0	.33	1
Stripling, Ross, LAD	R	.000	9	0	0	0	0	.061	33	2	0	0	0	1	2	16	1	74.1	5	11	1	0	.941	4	1	0	0	.25	1
Stroman, Marcus, Tor	R	.286	7	2	1	1	0	.167	12	2	1	0	1	1	0	4	1	201.0	9	37	1	6	.979	15	5	0	1	.33	5
Strop, Pedro, ChC	R	.000	1	0	0	0	0	.000	2	0	0	0	0	0	0	0	0	60.1	11	9	2	2	.909	3	1	0	0	.33	1
Stumpf, Daniel, Det	L	-	0	0	0	0	0	-	0	0	0	0	0	0	0	0	0	37.2	4	2	1	1	.857	2	0	0	0	.00	0
Suarez, Albert, SF	R	.000	2	0	0	0	0	.174	23	4	2	0	0	2	0	11	3	31.2	5	3	0	0	1.000	2	0	0	0	.00	-1
Suter, Brent, Mil	L	.167	18	3	0	1	2	.150	20	3	0	0	0	1	0	9	2	81.2	7	19	2	3	.929	3	1	1	2	.33	4
Swarzak, A., CWS-Mil	R	-	0	0	0	0	0	.000	5	0	0	0	0	0	0	4	0	77.1	1	3	0	0	1.000	5	1	0	0	.20	1
Syndergaard, Noah, NYM	R	.222	9	2	0	0	1	.200	110	22	4	0	4	10	11	65	9	30.1	1	5	0	0	1.000	4	2	0	0	.50	1
Taillon, Jameson, Pit	R	.158	38	6	0	0	5	.129	70	9	0	0	0	2	0	32	9	133.2	7	17	0	1	1.000	15	0	0	0	.00	-4
Tanaka, Masahiro, NYY	R	.000	2	0	0	0	0	.050	20	1	0	0	0	0	1	11	1	178.1	8	22	0	1	1.000	7	3	1	1	.43	2
Taylor, Ben, Bos	R	-	0	0	0	0	0	-	0	0	0	0	0	0	0	0	0	17.1	0	0	0	0	-	0	0	0	0	-	0
Tazawa, Junichi, Mia	R	.000	1	0	0	0	0	.000	1	0	0	0	0	0	0	0	0	55.1	2	2	0	0	1.000	4	0	0	0	.00	-2
Teheran, Julio, Atl	R	.140	57	8	0	6	12	.150	287	43	5	0	0	18	8	80	51	188.1	10	40	3	6	.943	32	6	1	3	.19	5
Tepera, Ryan, Tor	R	.000	1	0	0	0	0	.000	1	0	0	0	0	0	0	1	0	77.2	1	11	1	0	.923	13	2	0	0	.15	0
Tepesch, Nick, Min-Tor	R	.000	2	0	0	0	0	.125	8	1	0	0	0	0	0	4	0	15.2	1	5	0	1	1.000	1	0	0	0	.00	2
Therrien, Jesen, Phi	R	.000	2	0	0	0	0	.000	2	0	0	0	0	0	0	2	0	18.1	2	3	0	0	1.000	2	0	0	0	-	0
Thompson, Jake, Phi	R	.167	12	2	0	0	1	.154	26	4	2	0	0	0	1	10	4	46.1	5	1	0	0	1.000	2	0	0	0	.00	-1
Tillman, Chris, Bal	R	-	0	0	0	0	0	.000	14	0	0	0	0	0	0	7	4	93.0	6	4	1	0	.909	4	2	0	0	.50	-2
Tolliver, Ashur, Hou	L	-	0	0	0	0	0	-	0	0	0	0	0	0	0	0	0	5.0	0	2	0	0	1.000	0	0	0	0	-	0
Tomlin, Josh, Cle	R	.143	7	1	0	0	0	.368	19	7	1	0	0	1	0	8	1	141.0	9	12	1	1	.955	2	1	0	0	.50	-1
Tonkin, Michael, Min	R	-	0	0	0	0	0	.000	2	0	0	0	0	0	0	1	0	21.0	0	0	0	0	-	1	1	0	0	1.00	-1
Torres, Carlos, Mil	R	-	0	0	0	0	0	.118	34	4	0	0	0	2	2	19	6	72.2	8	10	2	1	.900	9	2	0	1	.22	0
Torres, Jose, SD	L	1.000	1	1	0	0	0	1.000	1	1	0	0	0	0	0	0	0	68.1	2	9	1	0	.917	5	0	0	0	.00	-2
Treinen, Blake, Was-Oak	R	-	0	0	0	0	0	.071	14	1	0	0	0	0	1	9	4	75.2	4	10	1	0	.933	4	1	0	0	.25	-3
Triggs, Andrew, Oak	R	-	0	0	0	0	0	.000	2	0	0	0	0	0	0	2	0	65.1	2	4	1	0	.857	19	4	0	0	.21	-4
Tseng, Jen-Ho, ChC	R	.000	1	0	0	1	0	.000	1	0	0	0	0	1	0	0	0	6.0	0	0	0	0	-	3	1	0	0	.33	0
Tuivailala, Samuel, StL	R	-	0	0	0	0	0	-	0	0	0	0	0	0	0	0	0	42.1	3	6	0	0	1.000	2	0	0	0	.00	0
Turley, Nik, Min	L	.000	2	0	0	0	0	.000	2	0	0	0	0	0	0	0	0	17.2	0	2	0	0	1.000	2	0	0	0	.00	0
Turner, Jacob, Was	R	.000	5	0	0	0	2	.091	77	7	2	1	0	0	2	38	12	39.0	2	3	0	0	1.000	4	1	1	0	.25	-2
Uehara, Koji, ChC	R	-	0	0	0	0	0	.000	2	0	0	0	0	0	1	1	0	43.0	0	5	0	0	1.000	1	1	0	0	1.00	1
Urena, Jose, Mia	R	.104	48	5	0	2	8	.115	78	9	1	0	0	2	1	48	12	169.2	9	21	1	2	.968	7	2	1	0	.29	-2
Urias, Julio, LAD	L	.167	6	1	0	0	1	.143	28	4	0	0	0	2	0	13	5	23.1	1	0	3	0	.250	3	2	0	0	.67	0
Valdez, Cesar, Oak-Tor	R	-	0	0	0	0	0	.000	4	0	0	0	0	0	0	3	0	30.2	1	5	0	0	1.000	3	3	0	0	1.00	0
Valdez, Jose, LAA-SD	R	-	0	0	0	0	0	-	0	0	0	0	0	0	0	0	0	18.0	1	1	1	0	.667	0	0	0	0	-	0
Vargas, Jason, KC	L	.250	4	1	0	0	0	.262	65	17	3	0	0	4	3	17	2	179.2	9	23	0	2	1.000	19	6	4	0	.32	3
Velasquez, Vince, Phi	R	.250	24	6	0	1	0	.219	64	14	1	0	0	1	2	20	3	72.0	2	8	1	0	.909	5	4	1	0	.80	2
Velazquez, Hector, Bos	R	.000	1	0	0	0	0	.000	1	0	0	0	0	0	0	0	0	24.2	2	2	0	0	1.000	2	2	0	0	1.00	1
VerHagen, Drew, Det	R	-	0	0	0	0	0	-	0	0	0	0	0	0	0	0	0	34.1	0	4	0	0	1.000	3	1	0	1	.33	-1
Verlander, J., Det-Hou	R	.167	6	1	0	1	0	.093	43	4	0	0	0	1	0	21	10	206.0	10	13	1	1	.958	10	1	0	1	.10	0
Verrett, Logan, Bal	R	-	0	0	0	0	0	.038	26	1	1	0	0	0	0	14	4	10.2	0	2	0	0	1.000	1	0	0	0	.00	-1
Vieira, Thyago, Sea	R	-	0	0	0	0	0	-	0	0	0	0	0	0	0	0	0	1.0	1	0	0	0	1.000	0	0	0	0	-	0
Vincent, Nick, Sea	R	-	0	0	0	0	0	.000	2	0	0	0	0	0	0	2	0	64.2	2	8	0	0	1.000	2	1	1	0	.50	0
Vizcaino, Arodys, Atl	R	-	0	0	0	0	0	-	0	0	0	0	0	0	0	0	0	57.1	1	4	2	0	.714	1	0	0	0	.00	-2
Volquez, Edinson, Mia	R	.192	26	5	0	1	2	.091	308	28	2	0	1	9	8	156	45	92.1	3	14	0	0	1.000	17	5	0	0	.29	-1
Volstad, Chris, CWS	R	-	0	0	0	0	0	.139	201	28	6	0	0	7	2	94	28	19.1	1	2	0	0	1.000	1	0	0	1	.00	0
Wacha, Michael, StL	R	.043	46	2	0	3	7	.080	187	15	1	0	0	12	8	92	20	165.2	13	20	0	2	1.000	17	3	0	0	.18	0
Wahl, Bobby, Oak	R	-	0	0	0	0	0	-	0	0	0	0	0	0	0	0	0	7.2	1	0	0	0	1.000	1	0	0	0	.00	0
Wainwright, Adam, StL	R	.262	42	11	2	11	7	.204	624	127	34	2	10	68	22	198	53	123.1	19	18	0	4	1.000	3	1	0	0	.33	3
Walker, Taijuan, Ari	R	.231	52	12	1	5	1	.213	61	13	2	0	1	6	1	24	2	157.1	10	21	4	1	.886	16	1	0	3	.06	-2
Wang, Wei-Chung, Mil	L	-	0	0	0	0	0	-	0	0	0	0	0	0	0	0	0	1.1	0	1	0	0	1.000	0	0	0	0	-	0
Warren, Adam, NYY	R	-	0	0	0	0	0	.000	6	0	0	0	0	0	0	4	1	57.1	1	10	0	0	1.000	4	1	0	0	.25	2
Watson, Tony, Pit-LAD	L	.000	1	0	0	0	0	.143	7	1	0	0	0	0	0	6	3	66.2	2	14	0	1	1.000	4	1	0	0	.25	2
Weaver, Jered, SD	R	.000	10	0	0	0	0	.073	55	4	0	0	0	1	2	25	0	42.1	0	6	0	0	1.000	5	0	0	1	.00	1
Weaver, Luke, StL	R	.158	19	3	0	1	3	.250	32	8	0	0	0	1	1	13	0	60.1	11	11	1	1	.957	3	3	1	1	1.00	4
Webb, Tyler, NYY-Mil	L	-	0	0	0	0	0	-	0	0	0	0	0	0	0	0	0	8.0	0	0	0	0	-	0	0	0	0	-	0
Weber, Ryan, Sea	R	-	0	0	0	0	0	.000	16	0	0	0	0	0	0	11	0	3.2	1	1	0	0	1.000	0	0	0	0	-	0
Whalen, Rob, Sea	R	-	0	0	0	0	0	.200	10	2	0	0	0	0	0	3	1	7.1	0	0	0	0	-	2	0	0	0	.00	0
Wheeler, Jason, Min	L	-	0	0	0	0	0	-	0	0	0	0	0	0	0	0	0	3.0	0	0	0	0	-	0	0	0	0	-	-1

Pitchers Hitting, Fielding and Holding Runners

Pitcher	T	2017 Hitting						Career Hitting										2017 Fielding and Holding Runners											
		Avg	AB	H	HR	RBI	SH	Avg	AB	H	2B	3B	HR	RBI	BB	SO	SH	Inn	PO	A	E	DP	Pct	SBA	CS	PCS	PPO	CS%	RS
Wheeler, Zack, NYM	R	.074	27	2	0	0	1	.093	107	10	3	0	0	5	3	49	16	86.1	8	10	1	1	.947	10	2	0	0	.20	-1
Whitley, Chase, TB	R	-	0	0	0	0	0	.200	5	1	0	0	0	0	0	0	0	57.1	4	4	0	0	1.000	3	0	0	0	.00	0
Wilhelmsen, Tom, Ari	R	.000	1	0	0	0	0	.000	1	0	0	0	0	0	0	1	0	26.1	3	4	1	0	.875	2	0	0	1	.00	0
Wilk, Adam, NYM-Min	L	.000	1	0	0	0	0	.000	2	0	0	0	0	0	0	1	0	14.0	5	2	0	0	1.000	3	1	1	0	.33	0
Wilkerson, Aaron, Mil	R	.000	4	0	0	0	0	.000	4	0	0	0	0	0	0	1	0	10.1	1	0	0	0	1.000	0	0	0	0	-	0
Williams, Taylor, Mil	R	-	0	0	0	0	0	-	0	0	0	0	0	0	0	0	0	4.2	1	0	0	0	1.000	0	0	0	0	-	0
Williams, Trevor, Pit	R	.049	41	2	0	0	4	.048	42	2	0	0	0	1	4	18	4	150.1	7	26	2	1	.943	10	3	0	1	.30	-2
Wilson, Alex, Det	R	-	0	0	0	0	0	-	0	0	0	0	0	0	0	0	0	60.0	5	5	2	0	.833	1	0	0	0	.00	1
Wilson, Justin, Det-ChC	L	-	0	0	0	0	0	.000	6	0	0	0	0	0	0	6	1	58.0	2	4	0	0	1.000	5	0	0	0	.00	-1
Wilson, Tyler, Bal	R	-	0	0	0	0	0	.000	2	0	0	0	0	0	0	1	0	15.1	0	2	0	0	1.000	5	2	0	0	.40	-1
Wimmers, Alex, Min	R	-	0	0	0	0	0	-	0	0	0	0	0	0	0	0	0	7.1	1	0	0	0	1.000	1	0	0	0	.00	0
Winkler, Dan, Atl	R	-	0	0	0	0	0	-	0	0	0	0	0	0	0	0	0	14.1	0	2	0	0	1.000	0	0	0	0	-	0
Wisler, Matt, Atl	R	.000	2	0	0	0	1	.143	77	11	0	0	0	3	3	27	11	32.1	2	5	0	0	1.000	1	0	0	0	.00	0
Wittgren, Nick, Mia	R	.000	4	0	0	0	0	.000	4	0	0	0	0	0	0	1	0	42.1	3	5	0	0	1.000	2	2	1	0	1.00	2
Wojciechowski, A., Cin	R	.071	14	1	0	0	0	.071	14	1	0	0	0	0	0	11	0	62.1	6	2	1	0	.889	4	1	0	0	.25	0
Wood, Alex, LAD	L	.058	52	3	0	4	4	.103	185	19	2	0	0	12	9	115	20	152.1	3	22	4	1	.862	4	2	2	1	.50	3
Wood, Blake, Cin-LAA	R	.000	1	0	0	0	0	.000	4	0	0	0	0	0	0	4	0	74.1	9	7	0	0	1.000	9	4	1	0	.44	0
Wood, Hunter, TB	R	-	0	0	0	0	0	-	0	0	0	0	0	0	0	0	0	0.1	0	0	0	0	-	0	0	0	0	-	0
Wood, Travis, KC-SD	L	.222	18	4	2	6	0	.185	298	55	8	1	11	37	7	115	20	94.0	4	11	1	1	.938	5	3	2	0	.60	0
Woodruff, Brandon, Mil	R	.200	10	2	0	0	1	.200	10	2	0	0	0	0	1	2	1	43.0	4	9	0	0	1.000	6	2	0	1	.33	1
Workman, Brandon, Bos	R	-	0	0	0	0	0	.000	3	0	0	0	0	0	0	3	1	39.2	1	3	0	0	1.000	3	3	1	0	1.00	1
Worley, Vance, Mia	R	.182	22	4	0	3	5	.140	157	22	4	0	0	10	2	61	20	71.2	4	12	0	1	1.000	5	2	0	0	.40	0
Wright, Daniel, LAA	R	-	0	0	0	0	0	.000	5	0	0	0	0	0	0	2	1	19.2	1	2	0	0	1.000	3	2	1	1	.67	1
Wright, Mike, Bal	R	-	0	0	0	0	0	.500	2	1	0	0	0	0	0	1	1	25.0	2	3	0	0	1.000	1	0	0	0	.00	0
Wright, Steven, Bos	R	-	0	0	0	0	0	.000	5	0	0	0	0	0	0	3	1	24.0	2	0	1	0	.667	1	1	0	0	1.00	-1
Yacabonis, Jimmy, Bal	R	.000	2	0	0	1	0	.000	2	0	0	0	0	1	0	1	0	20.2	3	2	0	1	1.000	0	0	0	0	-	-1
Yates, Kirby, LAA-SD	R	-	0	0	0	0	0	-	0	0	0	0	0	0	0	0	0	56.2	0	2	0	0	1.000	9	0	0	0	.00	-3
Ynoa, Gabriel, Bal	R	.000	1	0	0	0	0	.000	4	0	0	0	0	0	0	0	0	34.2	6	6	0	3	1.000	1	1	0	0	1.00	1
Ynoa, Michael, CWS	R	-	0	0	0	0	0	-	0	0	0	0	0	0	0	0	0	29.0	0	3	0	0	1.000	4	2	0	1	.50	1
Young, Chris, KC	R	-	0	0	0	0	0	.150	207	31	6	1	1	17	10	82	27	30.0	0	0	0		-	11	3	0	0	.27	-2
Zastryzny, Rob, ChC	L	.333	3	1	0	0	0	.167	6	1	0	0	0	0	0	2	0	13.0	0	4	0	2	1.000	0	0	0	0	-	1
Ziegler, Brad, Mia	R	-	0	0	0	0	0	.143	7	1	0	0	0	0	0	3	0	47.0	5	11	0	1	1.000	2	0	0	0	.00	0
Zimmermann, J., Det	R	.167	6	1	0	0	0	.170	330	56	6	0	1	15	10	100	44	160.0	7	6	1	0	.929	13	3	0	0	.23	-3
Zych, Tony, Sea	R	-	0	0	0	0	0	-	0	0	0	0	0	0	0	0	0	40.2	1	3	0	0	1.000	3	0	0	0	.00	0

Hitters Pitching

Player	2017 Pitching											Career Pitching										
	G	W	L	Sv	IP	H	R	ER	BB	SO	ERA	G	W	L	Sv	IP	H	R	ER	BB	SO	ERA
Amarista, Alexi, Col	-	-	-	-	-	-	-	-	-	-		2	0	0	0	0.2	0	0	0	0	0	0.00
Aoki, Nori, Hou-Tor-NYM	1	-	-	-	1.0	1	3	3	2	-	27.00	1	0	0	0	1.0	1	3	3	2	0	27.00
Aybar, Erick, SD	2	-	-	-	1.1	-	-	-	1	-	0.00	2	0	0	0	1.1	0	0	0	1	0	0.00
Barney, Darwin, Tor	-	-	-	-	-	-	-	-	-	-		1	0	1	0	1.0	1	1	1	0	1	9.00
Blanco, Andres, Phi	1	-	-	-	0.1	1	1	1	-	-	27.00	1	0	0	0	0.1	1	1	1	0	0	27.00
Brantly, Rob, CWS	1	-	-	-	1.0	1	1	1	-	-	9.00	1	0	0	0	1.0	1	1	1	0	0	9.00
Butera, Drew, KC	-	-	-	-	-	-	-	-	-	-		5	0	0	0	4.0	3	2	2	1	4	4.50
Davis, Chris, Bal	-	-	-	-	-	-	-	-	-	-		1	1	0	0	2.0	2	0	0	1	2	0.00
Davis, J.D., Hou	2	-	-	-	1.2	1	-	-	1	3	0.00	2	0	0	0	1.2	1	0	0	1	3	0.00
Decker, Jaff, Oak	-	-	-	-	-	-	-	-	-	-		1	0	0	0	1.0	2	0	0	0	0	0.00
Descalso, Daniel, Ari	2	-	-	-	2.0	-	-	-	-	-	0.00	3	0	0	0	2.1	0	0	0	0	0	0.00
Escobar, Eduardo, Min	-	-	-	-	-	-	-	-	-	-		1	0	0	0	1.0	1	0	0	0	0	0.00
Flaherty, Ryan, Bal	-	-	-	-	-	-	-	-	-	-		1	0	0	0	1.0	3	2	2	0	0	18.00
Franklin, Nick, Mil-LAA	-	-	-	-	-	-	-	-	-	-		1	0	0	0	1.0	3	2	2	0	0	18.00
Freeman, M., Sea-LAD-ChC	1	-	-	-	1.0	3	1	1	-	-	9.00	1	0	0	0	1.0	3	1	1	0	0	9.00
Garcia, Leury, CWS	-	-	-	-	-	-	-	-	-	-		2	0	1	0	2.0	2	2	2	2	1	9.00
Gennett, Scooter, Cin	1	-	-	-	1.0	2	2	2	1	-	18.00	1	0	0	0	1.0	2	2	2	1	0	18.00
Gentry, Craig, Bal	-	-	-	-	-	-	-	-	-	-		1	0	0	0	1.0	3	2	2	1	0	18.00
Gimenez, Chris, Min	6	-	-	-	5.0	7	4	4	-	-	7.20	9	0	0	0	9.0	11	8	8	0	1	8.00
Goins, Ryan, Tor	-	-	-	-	-	-	-	-	-	-		1	0	0	0	1.0	2	0	0	1	0	0.00
Harrison, Josh, Pit	-	-	-	-	-	-	-	-	-	-		1	0	0	0	0.1	0	0	0	0	0	0.00
Holaday, Bryan, Det	-	-	-	-	-	-	-	-	-	-		1	0	0	0	1.1	0	0	0	0	0	0.00
Hoying, Jared, Tex	-	-	-	-	-	-	-	-	-	-		1	0	0	0	1.0	1	1	1	0	0	9.00
Janish, Paul, Bal	-	-	-	-	-	-	-	-	-	-		2	0	0	0	2.0	9	11	11	2	3	49.50
Jay, Jon, ChC	1	-	-	-	1.0	1	-	-	-	-	0.00	1	0	0	0	1.0	1	0	0	0	0	0.00
Kratz, Erik, NYY	-	-	-	-	-	-	-	-	-	-		2	0	0	0	2.0	5	2	1	0	1	4.50
LaMarre, Ryan, Oak	-	-	-	-	-	-	-	-	-	-		1	0	0	0	1.0	2	0	0	0	0	0.00
Maldonado, Martin, LAA	-	-	-	-	-	-	-	-	-	-		1	0	0	0	1.0	1	0	0	0	0	0.00
Martin, Leonys, Sea-ChC	1	-	-	-	0.2	3	2	2	-	-	27.00	1	0	0	0	0.2	3	2	2	0	0	27.00
Martinez, Michael, Cle-TB	1	-	-	-	1.0	1	-	-	-	-	0.00	1	0	0	0	1.0	1	0	0	0	0	0.00
Mathis, Jeff, Ari	-	-	-	-	-	-	-	-	-	-		2	0	0	0	2.0	4	2	2	1	0	9.00
Montero, Miguel, ChC-Tor	1	-	-	-	1.0	-	-	-	2	-	0.00	2	0	0	0	2.1	4	1	1	2	0	3.86
Moore, Tyler, Mia	-	-	-	-	-	-	-	-	-	-		1	0	0	0	0.2	0	0	0	0	0	0.00
Moreland, Mitch, Bos	1	-	-	-	1.0	2	-	-	-	1	0.00	2	0	0	0	2.0	2	0	0	0	1	0.00
Motter, Taylor, Sea	-	-	-	-	-	-	-	-	-	-		1	0	0	0	0.1	1	0	0	0	0	0.00
Nicholas, Brett, Tex	1	-	-	-	1.0	5	4	4	-	-	36.00	1	0	0	0	1.0	5	4	4	0	0	36.00
Perez, Hernan, Mil	1	-	-	-	1.0	1	-	-	1	-	0.00	1	0	0	0	1.0	1	0	0	1	0	0.00
Phegley, Josh, Oak	-	-	-	-	-	-	-	-	-	-		1	0	0	0	0.2	0	0	0	0	1	0.00
Plawecki, Kevin, NYM	2	-	-	-	3.0	5	4	4	-	-	12.00	2	0	0	0	3.0	5	4	4	0	0	12.00
Raburn, Ryan, Was	-	-	-	-	-	-	-	-	-	-		2	0	0	0	1.2	1	2	0	1	1	0.00
Recker, Anthony, Atl	-	-	-	-	-	-	-	-	-	-		1	0	0	0	1.0	1	2	2	1	0	18.00
Robinson, Shane, LAA	-	-	-	-	-	-	-	-	-	-		1	0	0	0	1.0	0	0	0	1	1	0.00
Romine, Andrew, Det	2	-	-	-	1.0	1	-	-	1	-	0.00	4	0	0	0	2.2	5	3	3	3	1	10.13
Rosales, Adam, Oak-Ari	-	-	-	-	-	-	-	-	-	-		2	0	0	0	2.0	2	3	2	1	1	9.00
Ruiz, Carlos, Sea	1	-	-	-	1.0	2	1	1	2	1	9.00	1	0	0	0	1.0	2	1	1	2	1	9.00
Sardinas, Luis, SD	1	-	-	-	1.0	1	-	-	-	-	0.00	2	0	0	0	2.0	1	0	0	0	0	0.00
Sucre, Jesus, TB	1	-	-	-	1.0	2	3	3	2	-	27.00	3	0	0	0	3.0	8	6	6	2	0	18.00
Suzuki, Ichiro, Mia	-	-	-	-	-	-	-	-	-	-		1	0	0	0	1.0	2	1	1	0	0	9.00
Tejada, Ruben, Bal	-	-	-	-	-	-	-	-	-	-		1	0	0	0	1.0	2	2	2	0	0	18.00
White, Tyler, Hou	1	-	-	-	1.0	2	2	2	-	-	18.00	2	0	0	0	2.0	3	3	3	0	0	13.50

Hitter Analysis

Bill James

The pages which follow have a very simple goal.   That goal is to describe each major league hitter, not in terms of his output, but in terms of HOW he goes about his work.   We ask seven basic questions about each hitter:

1) How many plate appearances did he have?—the only one of these questions, by the way, which is the same as an "output" category, but you have to establish context,

2) How many pitches did he see?

3) How many of those did he take, and how many did he swing at?

4) Of those that he took, how many were called balls, and how many were called strikes?

5) When he swung, how often did he swing and miss, and how often did he make contact?

6) When he made contact, how often was the ball foul, and how often was it fair?

7) Of the fair balls, how many were ground balls, how many fly balls, and how many line drives?

We're sorting through the thousands of pitches, winnowing down to the few hundred outcomes, thus getting to the question "How does he go about his work?"   These are really important questions about how each hitter does his work, and they are not questions which have standard answers.   Matt Carpenter, for example, took 854 more pitches than he swung at, while Brett Gardner and Mookie Betts took almost 800 more than they swung at.   On the other hand, Corey Dickerson swung at 435 more pitches than he took, and Adam Jones swung at almost 400 more.   Those are very different approaches to an at bat.

When he swung at a pitch, Jonathan Lucroy missed only 10% of the time, whereas Evan Longoria swung and missed 20% of the time, Nelson Cruz swung and missed 30% of the time, and Joey Gallo swung and missed more than 40% of the time.   These are very different results.

When they did hit the ball, about half of the hitters usually hit the ball fair; a little less than half of them usually hit the ball foul.   Mookie Betts, for example, hit the ball fair 250 times more than he hit it foul—well, 249 times—whereas Corey Dickerson hit almost 200 more foul balls than fair balls.   These are very different outcomes.

We use the answers to these simple questions to characterize each hitter as patient, aggressive, very patient, very aggressive, medium, and as a Ground Ball or Fly Ball hitter; for some reason we are using the term "air ball", which is something you usually chant at an opposing team basketball player who throws up a shot that misses everything.   Anyway, it is *descriptive* information, rather than *evaluative* information.   We're describing the hitter for you.   You can get something out of it, if you spend a little time with the data.   Thanks.

Hitter Analysis

Hitter	PA	PS	T	Sw	St	B	S/M	F	In P	P/PA	Group	GB	LD	FB	Hits
Abreu, Jose	675	2560	1326	1234	423	903	263	465	506	3.79	Aggressive	229	92	184	Medium
Adams, Lane	122	475	242	233	75	167	82	77	74	3.89	Neutral	32	16	25	Medium
Adams, Matt*	367	1436	661	775	187	474	221	299	255	3.91	Neutral	99	47	109	Air
Adrianza, Ehire#	186	718	402	316	135	267	33	139	144	3.86	Neutral	57	28	55	Air
Aguilar, Jesus	311	1319	706	613	244	462	197	228	188	4.24	Very Patient	77	40	71	Air
Ahmed, Nick	178	625	298	327	108	190	88	111	128	3.51	Very Aggressive	61	26	41	Ground
Albies, Ozzie#	244	912	437	475	104	333	99	192	184	3.74	Aggressive	74	34	73	Air
Alcantara, Arismendy#	108	415	202	213	80	122	70	75	68	3.84	Aggressive	39	8	19	Ground
Alfaro, Jorge	114	391	149	242	44	105	85	83	74	3.43	Very Aggressive	39	12	23	Ground
Almonte, Abraham#	195	769	404	365	107	297	89	148	128	3.94	Neutral	65	28	34	Ground
Almora Jr., Albert*	323	1113	534	579	186	348	138	190	251	3.45	Very Aggressive	121	51	73	Ground
Alonso, Yonder	521	2077	1098	979	258	840	246	400	333	3.99	Patient	113	76	144	Air
Altherr, Aaron	412	1593	885	708	290	595	203	236	269	3.87	Neutral	116	52	101	Medium
Altuve, Jose	662	2308	1204	1104	372	832	173	420	511	3.49	Very Aggressive	236	102	164	Ground
Amarista, Alexi*	176	698	341	357	120	221	68	158	131	3.97	Neutral	60	31	39	Ground
Anderson, Tim	606	2117	952	1165	327	625	334	403	428	3.49	Very Aggressive	222	81	118	Ground
Andrus, Elvis	689	2547	1341	1206	459	882	224	435	547	3.70	Very Aggressive	265	109	172	Ground
Aoki, Nori*	374	1460	786	674	263	523	89	287	298	3.90	Neutral	170	51	75	Ground
Arcia, Orlando	548	1984	908	1076	264	644	265	400	411	3.62	Very Aggressive	210	81	116	Ground
Arenado, Nolan	680	2627	1361	1266	370	991	280	478	507	3.86	Neutral	172	107	227	Air
Arroyo, Christian	135	533	255	278	81	174	51	133	94	3.95	Neutral	57	17	20	Ground
Asuaje, Carlos*	343	1327	712	615	220	492	119	259	237	3.87	Neutral	93	55	82	Medium
Avila, Alex*	376	1610	1017	593	321	696	210	190	193	4.28	Very Patient	74	53	65	Air
Aybar, Erick#	370	1361	710	651	233	477	104	266	281	3.68	Very Aggressive	141	54	78	Ground
Baez, Javier	508	1845	803	1042	227	576	368	341	333	3.63	Very Aggressive	158	52	117	Ground
Bandy, Jett	188	731	355	376	117	238	89	169	118	3.89	Neutral	46	30	42	Air
Barnes, Austin	262	1068	679	389	237	442	54	160	175	4.08	Patient	79	45	51	Ground
Barney, Darwin	362	1332	663	669	243	420	112	279	278	3.68	Very Aggressive	126	56	88	Ground
Barnhart, Tucker#	423	1542	804	738	225	579	131	297	310	3.65	Very Aggressive	139	79	84	Ground
Bautista, Jose	686	2977	1756	1221	547	1209	336	461	424	4.34	Very Patient	160	70	194	Air
Beckham, Tim	575	2313	1142	1171	347	795	352	451	368	4.02	Patient	177	79	107	Ground
Bell, Josh#	620	2551	1441	1110	409	1032	233	441	436	4.11	Very Patient	223	77	136	Ground
Bellinger, Cody*	548	2205	1220	985	328	892	306	342	337	4.02	Patient	116	58	155	Air
Belt, Brandon*	451	1858	1005	853	216	789	202	372	279	4.12	Very Patient	81	64	128	Air
Beltran, Carlos#	509	1928	1005	923	332	673	179	373	371	3.79	Aggressive	160	61	150	Air
Beltre, Adrian	389	1578	841	737	250	591	131	312	294	4.06	Patient	127	58	109	Medium
Benintendi, Andrew*	658	2533	1415	1118	449	966	204	444	470	3.85	Neutral	187	100	179	Air
Betts, Mookie	712	2804	1795	1009	663	1132	150	305	554	3.94	Neutral	224	93	237	Air
Bird, Gregory*	170	725	414	311	118	296	92	112	107	4.26	Very Patient	32	19	55	Air
Blackmon, Charlie*	725	2884	1547	1337	498	1049	239	583	515	3.98	Patient	208	114	189	Air
Blanco, Andres#	144	552	258	295	75	183	81	116	98	3.84	Aggressive	49	15	33	Ground
Blanco, Gregor*	256	1105	662	443	220	442	86	191	166	4.32	Very Patient	68	35	56	Medium
Blash, Jabari	195	808	445	363	112	333	145	119	99	4.14	Very Patient	37	22	40	Air
Bogaerts, Xander	635	2544	1478	1066	599	879	213	396	457	4.01	Patient	223	94	139	Ground
Bonifacio, Jorge	422	1683	797	886	185	612	265	354	267	3.99	Patient	105	69	93	Air
Bour, Justin*	429	1744	963	781	300	663	211	284	286	4.07	Patient	124	66	96	Medium
Bourjos, Peter	203	814	415	399	118	297	113	149	137	4.01	Patient	65	21	48	Ground
Bradley Jr., Jackie*	541	2033	1076	957	328	748	268	329	360	3.76	Aggressive	176	66	117	Ground
Brantley, Michael*	375	1391	776	615	256	520	75	248	292	3.71	Very Aggressive	144	65	83	Ground
Braun, Ryan	425	1550	745	805	223	522	170	327	308	3.65	Very Aggressive	151	58	98	Ground
Bregman, Alex	626	2302	1272	1030	403	869	159	404	467	3.68	Very Aggressive	179	101	186	Air
Broxton, Keon	463	1915	1033	882	317	716	347	294	241	4.14	Very Patient	107	48	82	Medium
Bruce, Jay*	617	2432	1223	1209	312	911	321	469	419	3.94	Neutral	136	87	195	Air
Brugman, Jaycob*	162	658	372	286	117	255	67	113	106	4.06	Patient	49	27	28	Ground
Bryant, Kris	665	2652	1448	1204	365	1083	279	498	427	3.99	Patient	161	85	181	Air
Butera, Drew	177	720	391	329	125	266	67	139	123	4.07	Patient	37	30	55	Air
Buxton, Byron	511	1991	1003	988	322	681	289	380	319	3.90	Neutral	115	69	113	Air
Cabrera, Asdrubal#	540	2062	1093	969	300	793	177	390	402	3.82	Aggressive	173	81	144	Medium
Cabrera, Melky#	666	2421	1302	1119	438	864	133	432	554	3.64	Very Aggressive	270	122	160	Ground
Cabrera, Miguel	529	2045	1016	1029	277	739	231	436	362	3.87	Neutral	144	99	119	Medium
Cain, Lorenzo	645	2515	1276	1239	377	899	230	523	486	3.90	Neutral	216	110	160	Medium
Calhoun, Kole*	654	2522	1314	1208	348	966	294	473	441	3.86	Neutral	193	93	154	Medium
Camargo, Johan#	256	953	472	481	151	321	105	183	193	3.72	Aggressive	91	41	59	Ground
Candelario, Jeimer#	142	529	291	238	98	193	67	74	97	3.73	Aggressive	44	18	35	Medium
Canha, Mark	187	822	411	411	140	271	103	190	118	4.40	Very Patient	39	24	55	Air
Cano, Robinson*	648	2315	1111	1204	288	823	206	488	510	3.57	Very Aggressive	255	99	156	Ground
Carpenter, Matt*	622	2764	1809	955	626	1183	175	401	379	4.44	Very Patient	100	83	189	Air
Carrera, Ezequiel*	325	1329	803	526	268	535	118	191	217	4.09	Patient	98	46	59	Ground
Carter, Chris	208	890	465	425	123	342	166	149	110	4.28	Very Patient	33	22	55	Air
Castellanos, Nicholas	665	2605	1271	1334	365	906	347	510	477	3.92	Neutral	178	117	182	Air
Castillo, Wellington	365	1445	819	626	304	515	150	230	246	3.96	Neutral	97	60	89	Air
Castro, Jason*	407	1645	908	737	263	645	210	277	250	4.04	Patient	104	61	83	Medium

407

Hitter Analysis

Hitter	PA	PS	T	Sw	St	B	S/M	F	In P	P/PA	Group	GB	LD	FB	Hits
Castro, Starlin	473	1839	921	918	284	637	207	358	353	3.89	Neutral	183	71	99	Ground
Cervelli, Francisco	304	1212	711	501	234	477	116	184	201	3.99	Patient	104	41	54	Ground
Cespedes, Yoenis	321	1317	673	644	210	463	128	284	232	4.10	Patient	80	37	115	Air
Chapman, Matt	326	1344	768	576	273	495	162	214	200	4.12	Very Patient	67	32	101	Air
Chirinos, Robinson	309	1274	717	557	199	518	169	202	186	4.12	Very Patient	74	25	85	Air
Chisenhall, Lonnie*	270	1071	527	544	140	387	117	240	187	3.97	Neutral	71	29	84	Air
Choo, Shin-Soo*	636	2545	1474	1071	461	1013	238	415	418	4.00	Patient	201	103	108	Ground
Collins, Tyler*	169	697	382	315	119	263	96	123	96	4.12	Very Patient	34	20	41	Air
Conforto, Michael*	440	1828	1045	783	323	722	220	301	262	4.15	Very Patient	99	64	99	Air
Contreras, Willson	428	1606	835	771	250	585	223	266	282	3.75	Aggressive	147	48	81	Ground
Cordoba, Allen	227	861	478	383	179	299	104	129	150	3.79	Aggressive	77	21	47	Ground
Correa, Carlos	481	1895	1095	800	352	743	169	297	334	3.94	Neutral	160	68	106	Ground
Cowart, Kaleb#	117	443	231	212	69	162	61	75	76	3.79	Aggressive	34	14	25	Medium
Cozart, Zack	507	2125	1257	868	433	824	129	375	364	4.19	Very Patient	139	71	154	Air
Crawford, Brandon*	570	2172	1055	1117	260	795	298	405	414	3.81	Aggressive	191	80	142	Medium
Cron, C.J.	373	1405	669	736	217	452	191	297	246	3.77	Aggressive	80	56	110	Air
Cruz, Nelson	645	2474	1307	1167	337	970	348	396	423	3.84	Aggressive	171	75	177	Air
Cuthbert, Cheslor	153	572	274	298	84	190	82	111	105	3.74	Aggressive	44	24	37	Medium
d'Arnaud, Travis	376	1364	652	712	193	459	160	260	292	3.63	Very Aggressive	123	49	120	Air
Davidson, Matt	443	1855	957	898	313	644	313	331	254	4.19	Very Patient	92	44	118	Air
Davis, Chris*	524	2118	1210	908	410	800	309	334	265	4.04	Patient	97	62	105	Air
Davis, Khris	652	2591	1367	1224	335	1032	395	451	378	3.97	Patient	145	73	160	Air
Davis, Rajai	366	1333	658	675	205	453	161	259	255	3.64	Very Aggressive	117	47	88	Medium
DeJong, Paul	443	1757	851	906	248	603	240	372	294	3.97	Neutral	99	69	126	Air
Delmonico, Nick*	166	679	367	312	84	283	70	132	110	4.09	Patient	43	24	40	Air
Descalso, Daniel*	398	1580	939	641	295	644	146	238	257	3.97	Patient	100	46	111	Air
DeShields, Delino	440	1814	1085	729	405	680	163	282	284	4.12	Very Patient	114	51	88	Medium
Desmond, Ian	373	1373	719	654	235	484	172	224	258	3.68	Very Aggressive	160	42	53	Ground
Devers, Rafael*	240	892	437	455	145	292	113	177	165	3.72	Aggressive	80	25	58	Ground
Diaz, Aledmys	301	1070	504	566	159	345	119	201	246	3.55	Very Aggressive	110	40	91	Medium
Diaz, Elias	200	756	366	390	105	261	70	169	151	3.78	Aggressive	79	27	45	Ground
Diaz, Yandy	179	719	439	280	138	301	49	109	122	4.02	Patient	72	27	23	Ground
Dickerson, Corey*	629	2493	1029	1464	254	775	400	625	438	3.96	Neutral	183	98	157	Medium
Dietrich, Derek*	464	1834	981	853	323	658	162	379	312	3.95	Neutral	114	71	127	Air
Difo, Wilmer#	365	1344	631	713	185	446	176	271	266	3.68	Very Aggressive	129	62	63	Ground
Donaldson, Josh	496	2099	1214	885	340	874	235	344	306	4.23	Very Patient	125	51	129	Air
Dozier, Brian	705	2828	1648	1180	539	1109	277	425	478	4.01	Patient	182	90	202	Air
Drew, Stephen*	106	440	263	177	82	181	37	63	77	4.15	Very Patient	26	16	35	Air
Drury, Brandon	480	1847	1009	838	364	645	187	307	344	3.85	Aggressive	168	75	101	Ground
Duda, Lucas*	491	2024	1211	813	402	809	213	310	290	4.12	Very Patient	88	61	141	Air
Duvall, Adam	647	2484	1288	1196	441	847	301	467	428	3.84	Aggressive	142	78	208	Air
Dyson, Jarrod*	390	1412	783	629	276	507	91	241	297	3.62	Very Aggressive	130	53	94	Ground
Eaton, Adam*	107	443	253	190	74	179	37	79	74	4.14	Very Patient	39	11	23	Ground
Ellis, A.J.	163	641	371	270	135	236	49	105	116	3.93	Neutral	55	15	41	Ground
Ellsbury, Jacoby*	409	1563	888	675	272	616	115	260	295	3.82	Aggressive	133	67	90	Ground
Encarnacion, Edwin	669	2870	1637	1233	450	1187	299	507	426	4.29	Very Patient	158	90	178	Air
Engel, Adam	336	1320	681	639	236	445	208	239	192	3.93	Neutral	73	24	80	Air
Escobar, Alcides	629	2233	1029	1204	322	707	245	451	508	3.55	Very Aggressive	202	108	185	Air
Escobar, Eduardo#	499	2006	954	1052	290	664	219	470	363	4.02	Patient	122	76	164	Air
Escobar, Yunel	381	1357	720	637	204	516	119	219	299	3.56	Very Aggressive	174	53	72	Ground
Espinosa, Danny#	295	1104	518	586	137	381	233	193	160	3.74	Aggressive	64	21	66	Air
Fisher, Derek*	166	668	403	265	129	274	80	93	92	4.02	Patient	49	22	19	Ground
Flores, Wilmer	362	1469	709	760	210	499	119	353	288	4.06	Patient	103	53	132	Air
Flowers, Tyler	370	1436	748	688	208	540	161	290	237	3.88	Neutral	100	58	79	Medium
Forsythe, Logan	439	1921	1297	624	492	805	135	232	257	4.38	Very Patient	113	59	85	Medium
Fowler, Dexter#	491	1972	1121	851	312	809	183	345	323	4.02	Patient	127	72	123	Air
Franco, Maikel	623	2334	1160	1174	305	855	250	439	485	3.75	Aggressive	220	87	178	Medium
Franklin, Nick#	119	476	277	199	77	200	46	69	84	4.00	Patient	39	19	25	Ground
Frazier, Adam*	454	1756	949	807	330	619	101	353	353	3.87	Neutral	168	89	94	Ground
Frazier, Clint	142	565	288	277	79	209	77	108	92	3.98	Patient	35	16	41	Air
Frazier, Todd	576	2493	1488	1005	453	1035	243	408	354	4.33	Very Patient	121	65	168	Air
Freeman, Freddie*	514	1929	909	1020	159	750	242	431	347	3.75	Aggressive	121	85	141	Air
Freese, David	503	2076	1176	900	373	803	202	384	314	4.13	Very Patient	179	64	71	Ground
Fuentes, Rey*	145	584	292	292	90	202	79	111	102	4.03	Patient	46	22	31	Ground
Gallo, Joey*	532	2242	1186	1056	261	925	444	359	253	4.21	Very Patient	70	45	136	Air
Galvis, Freddy#	663	2641	1349	1292	441	908	210	579	503	3.98	Patient	180	118	192	Air
Gamel, Ben*	550	2188	1208	980	419	789	196	393	391	3.98	Patient	175	85	130	Medium
Garcia, Adonis	183	707	334	373	97	237	71	151	151	3.86	Neutral	82	24	44	Air
Garcia, Avisail	561	1995	819	1176	162	657	332	436	408	3.56	Very Aggressive	213	83	112	Ground
Garcia, Greg*	290	1210	727	483	236	491	94	206	183	4.17	Very Patient	84	53	38	Ground
Garcia, Leury#	326	1111	492	619	152	340	135	248	236	3.41	Very Aggressive	126	47	55	Ground
Garcia, Willy	119	479	269	210	87	182	64	69	77	4.03	Patient	38	12	26	Ground
Gardner, Brett*	682	2890	1839	1051	675	1164	160	411	480	4.24	Very Patient	209	105	156	Medium
Garneau, Dustin	126	516	243	273	62	181	82	114	77	4.10	Patient	23	18	35	Air
Gattis, Evan	325	1118	568	550	173	395	114	183	253	3.44	Very Aggressive	93	53	107	Air

Hitter Analysis

Hitter	PA	PS	T	Sw	St	B	S/M	F	In P	P/PA	Group	GB	LD	FB	Hits
Gennett, Scooter*	497	1932	981	951	304	677	202	400	349	3.89	Neutral	143	73	130	Air
Gentry, Craig	117	450	246	204	72	174	43	80	81	3.85	Aggressive	38	16	20	Ground
Gimenez, Chris	225	943	546	397	169	377	106	163	128	4.19	Very Patient	46	32	46	Air
Goins, Ryan*	459	1707	941	766	344	597	158	276	332	3.72	Aggressive	162	48	112	Ground
Goldschmidt, Paul	665	2762	1631	1131	545	1086	291	424	415	4.15	Very Patient	192	78	145	Medium
Gomes, Yan	383	1460	694	766	206	488	207	314	245	3.81	Aggressive	98	42	101	Air
Gomez, Carlos	426	1595	698	897	173	525	264	384	249	3.74	Aggressive	95	50	98	Air
Gonzalez, Adrian*	252	895	444	451	125	319	106	152	192	3.55	Very Aggressive	79	42	71	Air
Gonzalez, Carlos*	534	1941	970	971	234	736	296	318	357	3.63	Very Aggressive	173	70	113	Ground
Gonzalez, Erik	115	456	205	251	68	137	86	90	75	3.97	Neutral	42	15	16	Ground
Gonzalez, Marwin#	515	2114	1218	896	411	807	173	362	361	4.10	Patient	154	70	127	Medium
Goodwin, Brian*	278	1143	670	473	224	446	115	173	185	4.11	Very Patient	70	35	79	Air
Gordon, Alex*	541	2200	1157	1043	327	830	233	454	356	4.07	Patient	150	86	116	Medium
Gordon, Dee*	695	2397	1098	1299	399	699	175	557	566	3.45	Very Aggressive	308	122	105	Ground
Grandal, Yasmani#	482	1916	1019	897	312	707	242	343	312	3.98	Patient	135	51	124	Air
Granderson, Curtis*	527	2382	1469	913	509	960	169	415	329	4.52	Very Patient	107	61	160	Air
Granite, Zack*	107	431	266	165	92	174	9	70	86	4.03	Patient	43	18	23	Ground
Gregorius, Didi*	570	2069	860	1209	182	678	245	492	471	3.63	Very Aggressive	170	94	206	Air
Grichuk, Randal	442	1692	825	867	265	560	240	346	281	3.83	Aggressive	101	60	120	Air
Grossman, Robbie#	456	1822	1121	701	355	766	114	280	307	4.00	Patient	123	75	104	Medium
Gurriel, Yulieski	564	1933	1000	933	326	674	161	299	473	3.43	Very Aggressive	218	88	166	Medium
Guyer, Brandon	192	762	433	329	130	303	76	127	126	3.97	Neutral	48	31	44	Air
Gyorko, Jedd	481	1907	991	916	260	731	223	365	328	3.96	Neutral	133	66	129	Air
Hamilton, Billy#	633	2518	1349	1169	447	902	219	494	456	3.98	Patient	198	102	132	Ground
Hanigan, Ryan	112	406	226	180	83	143	36	67	77	3.63	Very Aggressive	47	12	17	Ground
Haniger, Mitch	410	1599	926	673	324	602	145	251	277	3.90	Neutral	121	53	101	Medium
Hanson, Alen#	234	855	418	437	126	292	107	161	169	3.65	Very Aggressive	83	26	55	Ground
Happ, Ian#	413	1618	819	799	209	610	265	293	241	3.92	Neutral	96	48	95	Air
Hardy, J.J.	268	1035	626	409	276	350	73	129	207	3.86	Neutral	93	36	76	Medium
Harper, Bryce*	492	1967	1000	967	224	776	248	395	324	4.00	Patient	130	71	121	Air
Harrison, Josh	542	2029	953	1076	274	679	221	454	401	3.74	Aggressive	143	89	160	Air
Headley, Chase#	586	2331	1296	1035	405	891	257	391	387	3.98	Patient	166	95	121	Medium
Healy, Ryon	605	2279	1195	1084	432	763	278	370	436	3.77	Aggressive	186	83	166	Air
Hechavarria, Adeiny	348	1170	492	678	147	345	155	256	267	3.36	Very Aggressive	127	51	83	Ground
Hedges, Austin	417	1536	720	816	225	495	250	297	269	3.68	Very Aggressive	97	47	121	Air
Heredia, Guillermo	426	1585	875	710	301	574	101	285	324	3.72	Aggressive	148	55	109	Medium
Hernandez, Cesar#	577	2316	1364	952	456	908	189	355	408	4.01	Patient	208	89	97	Ground
Hernandez, Gorkys	348	1416	740	676	210	530	163	272	241	4.07	Patient	109	50	72	Ground
Hernandez, Kike	342	1393	739	654	219	520	160	273	221	4.07	Patient	91	41	87	Air
Herrera, Odubel*	563	2180	1017	1163	298	719	295	466	402	3.87	Neutral	174	84	137	Medium
Herrmann, Chris*	256	1091	616	475	184	432	126	189	160	4.26	Very Patient	70	28	61	Medium
Heyward, Jason*	481	1729	925	804	266	659	128	306	369	3.59	Very Aggressive	174	73	120	Ground
Hicks, Aaron#	361	1483	899	584	281	618	149	195	240	4.11	Very Patient	104	37	95	Air
Hicks, John	190	727	303	424	73	230	136	165	123	3.83	Aggressive	62	24	36	Ground
Holliday, Matt	427	1733	964	769	307	657	215	290	264	4.06	Patient	126	39	99	Medium
Holt, Brock*	164	716	445	271	166	279	39	124	108	4.37	Very Patient	64	18	25	Ground
Hoskins, Rhys	212	985	608	377	193	415	74	177	126	4.65	Very Patient	39	30	57	Air
Hosmer, Eric*	671	2573	1362	1211	374	988	249	461	501	3.83	Aggressive	278	111	111	Ground
Hundley, Nick	303	1134	535	599	153	382	157	232	210	3.74	Aggressive	88	40	80	Air
Iannetta, Chris	316	1369	761	608	215	546	160	262	186	4.33	Very Patient	69	38	79	Air
Iglesias, Jose	489	1819	966	853	414	552	127	324	402	3.72	Aggressive	200	92	105	Ground
Inciarte, Ender*	718	2539	1190	1349	368	822	186	589	574	3.54	Very Aggressive	260	132	161	Ground
Jackson, Austin	318	1365	788	577	260	528	122	235	220	4.29	Very Patient	105	46	68	Ground
Jaso, John*	302	1298	708	590	196	512	141	258	191	4.30	Very Patient	64	37	90	Air
Jay, Jon*	433	1705	822	883	264	558	172	407	304	3.94	Neutral	138	85	70	Ground
Jones, Adam	635	2285	952	1333	223	729	301	544	488	3.60	Very Aggressive	217	101	166	Medium
Jones, JaCoby	154	593	305	288	107	198	108	104	76	3.85	Neutral	38	14	23	Ground
Jones, Ryder*	164	586	281	305	105	176	94	113	98	3.57	Very Aggressive	37	14	46	Air
Joseph, Caleb	266	1029	521	508	184	337	128	197	183	3.87	Neutral	84	44	54	Ground
Joseph, Tommy	533	2026	1021	1005	324	697	260	376	369	3.80	Aggressive	154	71	144	Air
Joyce, Matt*	544	2266	1307	959	379	928	232	364	363	4.17	Very Patient	137	70	155	Air
Judge, Aaron	678	2989	1761	1228	469	1292	412	478	338	4.41	Very Patient	118	74	146	Air
Kelly, Ty#	105	432	266	166	107	159	36	59	71	4.11	Very Patient	28	14	25	Air
Kemp, Matt	467	1676	756	920	191	565	262	317	340	3.59	Very Aggressive	165	79	96	Ground
Kendrick, Howie	334	1310	681	629	231	450	131	259	239	3.92	Neutral	137	52	48	Ground
Kepler, Max*	568	2128	1207	921	416	791	201	319	401	3.75	Aggressive	170	70	157	Air
Kiermaier, Kevin*	421	1666	857	809	242	615	205	318	286	3.96	Neutral	139	51	90	Ground
Kim, Hyun Soo*	239	986	570	416	176	394	74	173	168	4.13	Very Patient	78	40	48	Ground
Kinsler, Ian	613	2417	1343	1074	456	887	156	453	465	3.94	Neutral	153	96	216	Air
Kipnis, Jason*	373	1448	779	669	265	514	137	260	272	3.88	Neutral	98	53	119	Air
Kivlehan, Patrick	204	799	430	369	127	303	120	131	118	3.92	Neutral	52	21	45	Medium
Knapp, Andrew#	204	817	472	345	134	338	91	137	117	4.00	Patient	69	20	28	Ground
La Stella, Tommy*	151	633	351	282	108	243	37	134	109	4.19	Very Patient	47	25	37	Medium
Lagares, Juan	272	1033	545	488	200	345	103	186	199	3.80	Aggressive	97	39	55	Ground
Lamb, Jake*	635	2558	1539	1019	492	1047	230	400	389	4.03	Patient	160	80	149	Air

Hitter Analysis

Hitter	PA	PS	T	Sw	St	B	S/M	F	In P	P/PA	Group	GB	LD	FB	Hits
LeMahieu, DJ	682	2676	1562	1114	567	995	128	459	527	3.92	Neutral	290	129	103	Ground
Leon, Sandy#	301	1241	678	563	222	456	113	249	201	4.12	Very Patient	72	50	75	Air
Lind, Adam*	301	1173	644	529	236	408	89	214	226	3.90	Neutral	104	40	82	Medium
Lindor, Francisco#	723	2727	1435	1292	444	991	188	538	566	3.77	Aggressive	218	102	236	Air
Lobaton, Jose#	158	627	323	304	86	237	75	121	108	3.97	Neutral	54	18	34	Ground
Longoria, Evan	677	2492	1251	1241	385	866	248	477	516	3.68	Very Aggressive	224	102	190	Medium
Lowrie, Jed#	645	2584	1339	1245	321	1018	212	563	470	4.01	Patient	138	127	204	Air
Lucroy, Jonathan	481	1868	1088	780	418	670	81	323	376	3.88	Neutral	201	70	105	Ground
Machado, Dixon	181	677	401	276	147	254	57	81	138	3.74	Aggressive	77	25	33	Ground
Machado, Manny	690	2548	1299	1249	350	949	261	464	524	3.69	Very Aggressive	219	82	219	Air
Mahtook, Mikie	379	1561	887	674	316	571	132	271	271	4.12	Very Patient	125	55	90	Ground
Maile, Luke	136	506	262	244	97	145	53	95	96	3.72	Aggressive	48	9	38	Medium
Maldonado, Martin	471	1777	896	881	313	583	231	331	319	3.77	Aggressive	147	45	111	Medium
Mancini, Trey	586	2280	1120	1160	311	809	321	431	408	3.89	Neutral	208	79	121	Ground
Margot, Manuel	529	2026	1100	926	394	706	187	353	386	3.83	Aggressive	154	88	138	Air
Marisnick, Jake	259	1069	528	541	149	379	190	208	143	4.13	Very Patient	50	21	65	Air
Markakis, Nick*	670	2717	1612	1105	574	1038	157	462	486	4.06	Patient	236	108	142	Ground
Marrero, Deven	188	803	423	380	142	281	103	162	115	4.27	Very Patient	57	25	26	Ground
Marte, Jefry	145	543	305	238	96	209	64	80	94	3.74	Aggressive	44	18	32	Ground
Marte, Ketel#	255	947	501	446	160	341	71	187	188	3.71	Very Aggressive	83	38	63	Medium
Marte, Starling	339	1318	655	663	218	437	143	272	248	3.89	Neutral	117	50	71	Ground
Martin, Leonys*	138	521	254	267	71	183	71	101	95	3.78	Aggressive	41	13	35	Medium
Martin, Russell	365	1492	893	599	282	611	137	237	225	4.09	Patient	108	53	63	Ground
Martinez, J.D.	489	1911	929	982	226	703	294	380	308	3.91	Neutral	118	57	133	Air
Martinez, Jose	307	1242	726	516	253	473	103	198	215	4.05	Patient	90	57	67	Medium
Martinez, Victor#	435	1656	882	774	260	622	121	322	331	3.81	Aggressive	139	78	113	Medium
Mathis, Jeff	203	748	357	391	121	236	125	140	126	3.68	Very Aggressive	52	29	44	Medium
Mauer, Joe*	597	2601	1649	952	625	1024	115	392	445	4.36	Very Patient	227	110	104	Ground
Maxwell, Bruce*	253	1132	662	470	217	445	93	218	159	4.47	Very Patient	75	32	51	Ground
Maybin, Cameron	450	1838	1149	689	405	744	156	230	303	4.08	Patient	172	43	83	Ground
Mazara, Nomar*	616	2445	1318	1127	394	924	281	416	430	3.97	Neutral	200	83	147	Medium
McCann, Brian*	399	1582	899	683	280	619	109	278	296	3.96	Neutral	122	50	122	Air
McCann, James	391	1466	728	738	237	491	170	301	267	3.75	Aggressive	100	75	91	Air
McCutchen, Andrew	650	2621	1445	1176	415	1030	237	482	457	4.03	Patient	186	100	171	Air
Mercer, Jordy	558	2187	1270	917	457	813	138	363	416	3.92	Neutral	200	86	128	Ground
Merrifield, Whit	630	2370	1167	1203	391	776	195	501	507	3.76	Aggressive	188	109	202	Air
Mesoraco, Devin	165	671	346	325	106	240	82	139	104	4.07	Patient	43	20	41	Air
Miller, Brad*	407	1650	895	755	226	669	221	302	232	4.05	Patient	109	38	83	Medium
Molina, Yadier	543	1998	945	1053	291	654	186	430	437	3.68	Very Aggressive	184	89	163	Medium
Moncada, Yoan#	231	971	554	417	172	382	127	165	125	4.20	Very Patient	57	24	44	Medium
Montero, Miguel*	213	858	457	401	148	309	88	173	140	4.03	Patient	59	22	59	Air
Moore, Tyler	203	771	378	393	108	270	110	147	136	3.80	Aggressive	49	19	67	Air
Morales, Kendrys#	608	2332	1176	1156	327	849	321	407	428	3.84	Aggressive	207	79	142	Ground
Moreland, Mitch*	576	2267	1215	1052	350	865	261	398	393	3.94	Neutral	170	80	142	Medium
Moroff, Max#	140	612	352	260	117	235	79	102	79	4.37	Very Patient	29	15	33	Air
Morrison, Logan*	601	2356	1272	1084	337	935	296	422	366	3.92	Neutral	122	75	169	Air
Moss, Brandon*	401	1648	852	796	232	620	270	290	236	4.11	Very Patient	78	53	105	Air
Motter, Taylor	280	1115	617	498	216	401	99	202	197	3.98	Patient	82	40	74	Air
Moustakas, Mike*	598	2240	992	1248	255	737	244	537	467	3.75	Aggressive	162	91	213	Air
Murphy, Daniel*	593	2174	1150	1024	347	803	130	434	460	3.67	Very Aggressive	154	127	179	Air
Myers, Wil	649	2669	1489	1180	451	1038	295	491	394	4.11	Very Patient	147	77	168	Air
Napoli, Mike	485	2132	1211	921	389	822	309	346	265	4.40	Very Patient	88	39	138	Air
Narvaez, Omar*	295	1201	679	522	194	485	71	240	211	4.07	Patient	90	57	59	Ground
Nava, Daniel#	214	859	504	355	175	329	61	147	147	4.01	Patient	64	41	42	Ground
Nimmo, Brandon*	215	946	597	349	196	401	82	147	120	4.40	Very Patient	51	29	39	Medium
Norris, Derek	198	751	380	371	113	267	98	138	135	3.79	Aggressive	37	34	64	Air
Nunez, Eduardo	491	1721	806	915	268	538	143	356	416	3.51	Very Aggressive	220	72	120	Ground
Odor, Rougned*	651	2405	1132	1273	320	812	321	503	449	3.69	Very Aggressive	184	72	187	Air
Olson, Matt*	216	914	503	411	135	368	126	156	129	4.23	Very Patient	48	20	88	Air
Osuna, Jose	227	841	416	425	138	278	85	164	176	3.70	Very Aggressive	93	32	51	Ground
Owings, Chris	386	1369	601	768	178	423	168	319	281	3.55	Very Aggressive	117	60	98	Medium
Ozuna, Marcell	679	2560	1290	1270	356	934	333	466	471	3.77	Aggressive	222	91	158	Ground
Panik, Joe*	573	2182	1238	944	406	832	99	377	468	3.81	Aggressive	203	101	157	Medium
Parker, Jarrett*	177	738	405	333	125	280	89	132	112	4.17	Very Patient	58	15	39	Ground
Parra, Gerardo*	425	1536	737	799	234	503	144	321	334	3.61	Very Aggressive	153	75	99	Ground
Pearce, Steve	348	1372	721	651	206	515	138	265	248	3.94	Neutral	101	53	94	Air
Pederson, Joc*	323	1361	767	594	215	552	136	252	206	4.21	Very Patient	96	39	71	Medium
Pedroia, Dustin	463	1843	1079	764	369	710	82	318	364	3.98	Patient	176	81	104	Ground
Pence, Hunter	539	2136	1178	958	359	819	247	316	395	3.96	Neutral	226	53	116	Ground
Pennington, Cliff#	217	888	487	401	163	324	95	164	142	4.09	Patient	56	27	56	Air
Peralta, David*	577	2144	1102	1042	320	782	212	396	434	3.72	Aggressive	239	80	115	Ground
Peraza, Jose	518	1856	896	960	313	583	144	350	421	3.58	Very Aggressive	194	89	129	Ground
Perez, Hernan	458	1567	742	825	270	472	176	290	359	3.42	Very Aggressive	170	64	118	Ground
Perez, Roberto	248	1096	660	436	214	446	107	178	151	4.42	Very Patient	73	25	47	Ground
Perez, Salvador	499	1737	716	1021	194	522	206	433	381	3.48	Very Aggressive	127	75	179	Air

Hitter Analysis

Hitter	PA	PS	T	Sw	St	B	S/M	F	In P	P/PA	Group	GB	LD	FB	Hits
Peterson, Jace*	215	870	531	339	176	355	90	110	139	4.05	Patient	79	17	41	Ground
Pham, Tommy	530	2120	1316	804	422	894	166	306	332	4.00	Patient	170	73	86	Ground
Phegley, Josh	161	559	277	282	102	175	61	97	124	3.47	Very Aggressive	44	21	59	Air
Phillips, Brandon	604	2108	922	1186	277	645	229	455	502	3.49	Very Aggressive	247	111	141	Ground
Pillar, Kevin	632	2220	1062	1158	380	682	184	476	498	3.51	Very Aggressive	213	101	180	Medium
Pina, Manny	359	1425	706	719	214	492	157	307	255	3.97	Neutral	88	59	107	Air
Pinder, Chad	309	1172	565	607	165	400	176	237	193	3.79	Aggressive	79	37	77	Air
Pirela, Jose	344	1306	694	612	228	466	152	216	244	3.80	Aggressive	114	51	76	Ground
Piscotty, Stephen	401	1617	856	761	256	600	180	324	257	4.03	Patient	126	45	85	Ground
Plawecki, Kevin	118	479	254	225	70	184	48	93	84	4.06	Patient	41	20	23	Ground
Plouffe, Trevor	313	1255	692	563	241	451	133	234	196	4.01	Patient	92	46	64	Ground
Polanco, Gregory*	411	1544	769	775	219	550	141	313	320	3.76	Aggressive	135	65	120	Air
Polanco, Jorge#	544	2065	1158	907	415	743	126	358	423	3.80	Aggressive	155	79	175	Air
Pollock, A.J.	466	1739	1002	737	365	637	127	256	354	3.73	Aggressive	157	82	113	Ground
Posey, Buster	568	2073	1156	917	340	816	142	342	433	3.65	Very Aggressive	189	101	143	Medium
Powell, Boog*	135	567	347	220	128	219	47	83	90	4.20	Very Patient	40	16	31	Medium
Prado, Martin	147	625	392	233	172	220	33	81	119	4.25	Very Patient	58	24	37	Ground
Presley, Alex*	264	1063	560	503	192	368	84	219	199	4.03	Patient	89	61	46	Ground
Puig, Yasiel	570	2119	1136	983	311	825	235	344	404	3.72	Aggressive	195	65	144	Ground
Pujols, Albert	636	2486	1314	1172	447	867	230	438	504	3.91	Neutral	219	93	192	Medium
Ramirez, Hanley	553	2084	1083	1001	307	776	246	375	380	3.77	Aggressive	159	80	141	Medium
Ramirez, Jose#	645	2576	1459	1117	455	1004	147	449	521	3.99	Patient	202	111	206	Air
Ramos, Wilson	224	718	316	402	96	220	84	140	175	3.21	Very Aggressive	91	31	53	Ground
Rasmus, Colby*	129	478	216	262	58	158	97	88	77	3.71	Very Aggressive	23	20	32	Air
Realmuto, J.T.	579	2171	1123	1048	382	741	192	427	429	3.75	Aggressive	205	77	147	Ground
Reddick, Josh*	540	2037	1138	899	374	764	134	340	418	3.77	Aggressive	139	100	175	Air
Rendon, Anthony	605	2645	1575	1070	496	1079	143	495	432	4.37	Very Patient	147	81	204	Air
Renfroe, Hunter	479	1856	964	892	310	654	284	302	306	3.87	Neutral	116	51	139	Air
Revere, Ben*	308	1122	631	491	242	389	44	179	268	3.64	Very Aggressive	149	68	50	Ground
Reyes, Jose#	561	2074	1137	937	403	734	159	348	430	3.70	Very Aggressive	157	83	182	Air
Reynolds, Mark	593	2470	1369	1101	397	972	366	387	348	4.17	Very Patient	146	75	126	Medium
Reynolds, Matt	130	535	319	216	106	213	55	84	77	4.12	Very Patient	41	9	25	Ground
Rickard, Joey	277	1084	579	505	237	342	116	188	201	3.91	Neutral	68	51	73	Air
Riddle, J.T.*	247	898	426	472	135	291	100	187	185	3.64	Very Aggressive	96	33	51	Ground
Rivera, Rene	237	875	391	484	125	266	152	182	150	3.69	Very Aggressive	53	37	58	Air
Rivera, T.J.	231	780	369	411	117	252	83	143	185	3.38	Very Aggressive	65	46	73	Air
Rizzo, Anthony	691	2723	1457	1266	425	1032	219	561	486	3.94	Neutral	196	97	189	Air
Robertson, Daniel	254	1051	615	436	228	387	103	185	148	4.14	Very Patient	67	26	53	Medium
Robinson, Drew*	121	545	292	253	88	204	74	114	65	4.50	Very Patient	30	12	23	Medium
Rodriguez, Sean	153	593	296	297	88	208	113	108	76	3.88	Neutral	29	16	29	Air
Rojas, Miguel	306	1121	571	550	191	380	73	234	243	3.66	Very Aggressive	114	60	63	Ground
Romine, Andrew#	348	1332	621	711	175	446	160	296	255	3.83	Aggressive	118	66	68	Ground
Romine, Austin	252	951	483	468	153	330	122	169	177	3.77	Aggressive	78	44	52	Ground
Rosales, Adam	312	1219	632	587	213	419	199	191	197	3.91	Neutral	67	42	80	Air
Rosario, Amed	170	642	286	356	114	172	122	118	116	3.78	Aggressive	59	23	34	Ground
Rosario, Eddie*	589	2155	963	1192	251	712	270	474	448	3.66	Very Aggressive	187	89	165	Medium
Rua, Ryan	144	563	304	259	104	200	95	86	78	3.91	Neutral	33	21	23	Ground
Ruiz, Carlos	145	629	398	231	146	252	46	96	89	4.34	Very Patient	39	19	30	Medium
Ruiz, Rio*	173	683	348	335	91	257	88	135	112	3.95	Neutral	63	15	34	Ground
Rupp, Cameron	331	1370	746	624	238	508	213	229	182	4.14	Very Patient	88	29	65	Ground
Russell, Addison	385	1485	740	745	222	518	201	283	261	3.86	Neutral	105	60	96	Air
Rutledge, Josh	118	459	261	198	123	138	47	75	76	3.89	Neutral	45	14	17	Ground
Saladino, Tyler	281	1153	663	490	228	435	113	189	188	4.10	Patient	84	31	68	Medium
Sanchez, Gary	525	2031	1059	972	327	732	261	356	355	3.87	Neutral	150	75	130	Medium
Sanchez, Hector#	143	560	267	293	75	192	86	110	97	3.92	Neutral	34	21	42	Air
Sanchez, Yolmer#	534	2004	996	1008	350	646	226	398	384	3.75	Aggressive	167	81	127	Medium
Sandoval, Pablo#	279	1097	464	633	104	360	143	281	209	3.93	Neutral	99	34	76	Medium
Sano, Miguel	483	1974	1015	959	250	765	370	337	252	4.09	Patient	98	52	102	Air
Santana, Carlos#	667	2648	1590	1058	467	1123	197	382	479	3.97	Patient	194	95	187	Air
Santana, Danny#	178	625	274	351	78	196	93	130	128	3.51	Very Aggressive	65	18	37	Ground
Santana, Domingo	607	2491	1338	1153	390	948	355	448	350	4.10	Patient	157	96	97	Ground
Saunders, Michael*	234	985	513	472	142	371	106	203	163	4.21	Very Patient	73	27	63	Medium
Schebler, Scott*	531	1886	893	993	207	686	276	364	353	3.55	Very Aggressive	160	57	134	Medium
Schimpf, Ryan*	197	846	520	326	180	340	82	147	97	4.29	Very Patient	19	16	62	Air
Schoop, Jonathan	675	2544	1210	1334	316	894	359	488	487	3.77	Aggressive	204	102	181	Air
Schwarber, Kyle*	486	2110	1170	940	341	829	267	401	272	4.34	Very Patient	103	41	125	Air
Seager, Corey*	613	2240	1117	1123	252	865	286	426	411	3.65	Very Aggressive	173	102	136	Medium
Seager, Kyle*	650	2565	1464	1101	471	993	225	402	474	3.95	Neutral	147	80	242	Air
Segura, Jean	566	2186	1107	1079	371	736	166	470	442	3.86	Neutral	239	85	116	Ground
Semien, Marcus	386	1592	879	713	266	613	172	280	261	4.12	Very Patient	97	53	109	Air
Shaw, Travis*	606	2396	1310	1086	384	926	218	464	404	3.95	Neutral	171	80	151	Air
Simmons, Andrelton	647	2295	1232	1063	404	828	135	398	530	3.55	Very Aggressive	261	100	166	Ground
Slater, Austin	127	466	247	219	84	163	57	74	88	3.67	Very Aggressive	54	12	22	Ground
Smith, Dominic*	183	742	380	362	114	266	101	142	119	4.05	Patient	60	19	40	Ground
Smith, Kevan	294	1043	468	575	154	314	114	225	235	3.55	Very Aggressive	132	45	54	Ground

Hitter Analysis

Hitter	PA	PS	T	Sw	St	B	S/M	F	In P	P/PA	Group	GB	LD	FB	Hits
Smith, Mallex*	282	1080	542	538	162	380	150	191	197	3.83	Aggressive	89	39	49	Ground
Smith, Seth*	373	1580	933	647	338	595	129	266	252	4.24	Very Patient	109	58	85	Medium
Smoak, Justin#	637	2591	1477	1114	427	1050	245	435	434	4.07	Patient	149	92	193	Air
Sogard, Eric*	299	1228	786	442	294	492	43	186	213	4.11	Patient	80	59	67	Medium
Solarte, Yangervis#	512	1773	860	913	251	609	137	367	409	3.46	Very Aggressive	170	67	172	Air
Soler, Jorge	110	439	262	177	84	178	61	55	61	3.99	Patient	23	11	27	Air
Souza Jr., Steven	617	2490	1392	1098	378	1014	342	409	347	4.04	Patient	152	72	117	Medium
Span, Denard*	542	2032	1135	897	405	730	101	366	430	3.75	Aggressive	190	90	142	Medium
Spangenberg, Cory*	486	1794	905	889	275	630	232	338	319	3.69	Very Aggressive	149	69	84	Ground
Springer, George	629	2550	1410	1140	379	1031	248	449	441	4.05	Patient	213	79	149	Ground
Stanton, Giancarlo	692	2736	1562	1174	424	1138	358	379	437	3.95	Neutral	195	70	172	Medium
Stewart, Chris	144	567	333	234	133	200	35	87	112	3.94	Neutral	44	28	35	Medium
Story, Trevor	555	2284	1184	1100	356	828	331	456	313	4.12	Very Patient	104	57	148	Air
Suarez, Eugenio	632	2687	1555	1132	487	1068	265	475	392	4.25	Very Patient	152	94	145	Air
Sucre, Jesus	192	720	375	345	121	254	81	117	147	3.75	Aggressive	57	32	56	Air
Suzuki, Ichiro*	215	866	468	398	172	296	69	167	162	4.03	Patient	91	30	39	Ground
Suzuki, Kurt	309	1105	521	584	152	369	90	254	240	3.58	Very Aggressive	83	44	111	Air
Swanson, Dansby	551	2188	1214	974	403	811	223	379	372	3.97	Aggressive	176	86	109	Ground
Szczur, Matt	237	933	521	412	162	359	82	175	155	3.94	Neutral	58	28	64	Air
Tapia, Raimel*	171	613	254	359	67	187	74	160	125	3.58	Very Aggressive	52	35	36	Ground
Taylor, Chris	568	2268	1227	1041	385	842	256	412	373	3.99	Patient	154	84	133	Medium
Taylor, Michael	432	1630	822	808	255	567	257	286	265	3.77	Aggressive	111	53	95	Medium
Tejada, Ruben	124	450	228	222	70	158	32	91	99	3.63	Very Aggressive	39	21	38	Air
Telis, Tomas#	111	421	239	182	90	149	18	69	95	3.79	Aggressive	48	23	24	Ground
Thames, Eric*	551	2342	1330	1012	390	940	309	397	306	4.25	Very Patient	117	62	126	Air
Toles, Andrew*	102	382	183	199	41	142	35	84	80	3.75	Aggressive	42	14	23	Ground
Tomas, Yasmany	180	662	314	348	90	224	107	124	117	3.68	Very Aggressive	55	24	38	Ground
Tomlinson, Kelby	222	845	465	380	166	299	63	164	153	3.81	Aggressive	72	36	35	Ground
Torrens, Luis	139	535	272	263	87	185	61	106	96	3.85	Aggressive	55	15	23	Ground
Torreyes, Ronald	336	1075	438	637	143	295	98	258	281	3.20	Very Aggressive	143	47	83	Ground
Travis, Devon	197	747	393	354	136	257	65	140	149	3.79	Aggressive	55	39	54	Air
Trout, Mike	507	2127	1325	802	411	914	137	349	316	4.20	Very Patient	116	58	142	Air
Trumbo, Mark	603	2309	1164	1145	355	809	329	405	411	3.83	Aggressive	178	66	167	Air
Tulowitzki, Troy	260	966	526	440	198	328	75	163	202	3.72	Aggressive	106	29	67	Ground
Turner, Justin	543	2030	1141	889	328	813	135	345	409	3.74	Aggressive	128	85	195	Air
Turner, Trea	447	1694	947	747	312	635	162	252	333	3.79	Aggressive	171	49	111	Ground
Upton, Justin	635	2695	1499	1196	455	1044	352	466	378	4.24	Very Patient	139	74	165	Air
Urshela, Giovanny	165	592	272	320	89	183	53	132	135	3.59	Very Aggressive	61	31	42	Ground
Utley, Chase*	353	1353	835	518	306	529	71	192	255	3.83	Aggressive	110	47	97	Medium
Valaika, Pat	195	686	303	383	100	203	117	131	135	3.52	Very Aggressive	42	21	64	Air
Valbuena, Luis*	401	1702	949	753	284	665	209	298	246	4.24	Very Patient	94	35	116	Air
Valencia, Danny	500	2000	1142	858	403	739	244	278	336	4.00	Patient	161	71	104	Ground
Vargas, Kennys#	264	1121	612	509	201	411	147	197	165	4.25	Very Patient	80	32	53	Ground
Vazquez, Christian	345	1357	754	603	306	448	102	240	261	3.93	Neutral	123	65	73	Ground
Villar, Jonathan#	436	1765	908	857	278	630	252	331	274	4.05	Patient	152	55	58	Ground
Vogt, Stephen*	303	1237	685	552	241	444	94	232	226	4.08	Patient	85	42	98	Air
Voit, Luke	124	466	224	242	56	168	66	93	83	3.76	Aggressive	40	15	28	Ground
Votto, Joey*	707	2733	1590	1143	407	1183	165	496	482	3.87	Neutral	188	111	183	Air
Walker, Neil#	448	1708	994	714	324	670	142	261	311	3.81	Aggressive	112	68	129	Air
Weeks Jr., Rickie	112	482	271	211	78	193	96	67	48	4.30	Very Patient	19	9	19	Air
Werth, Jayson	289	1302	800	502	300	500	107	211	184	4.51	Very Patient	73	33	78	Air
Wieters, Matt#	465	1774	903	871	257	646	174	365	332	3.82	Aggressive	141	70	121	Medium
Williams, Nick*	343	1217	498	719	126	372	233	266	220	3.55	Very Aggressive	109	51	60	Ground
Winker, Jesse*	137	499	286	213	100	186	36	79	98	3.64	Very Aggressive	51	16	30	Ground
Wolters, Tony*	266	1035	581	454	187	394	89	189	176	3.89	Neutral	94	37	41	Ground
Wong, Kolten*	411	1504	808	696	243	565	129	269	298	3.66	Very Aggressive	139	58	92	Ground
Yelich, Christian*	695	2883	1658	1225	508	1150	263	490	471	4.15	Very Patient	260	91	118	Ground
Young, Chris	276	1110	674	436	226	448	85	162	189	4.02	Patient	67	36	86	Air
Young Jr., Eric#	125	434	211	223	63	148	61	80	82	3.47	Very Aggressive	45	11	21	Ground
Zimmer, Bradley*	332	1304	689	615	192	497	188	224	203	3.93	Neutral	92	39	61	Ground
Zimmerman, Ryan	576	2222	1237	985	415	822	230	352	403	3.86	Neutral	187	80	136	Ground
Zobrist, Ben#	496	1939	1169	770	421	748	105	296	369	3.91	Neutral	187	57	122	Ground
Zunino, Mike	435	1800	909	891	247	662	329	334	228	4.14	Very Patient	73	51	104	Air

For some players Swings and Misses, Fouls, and Balls in Play do not add up to overall Swings. This is because of the rare occasions when a swing results in a Catcher Interference.

Switch Hitter

* Bats Left

Lords of the Flies

Brian Reiff

Generally, when you hit a fly ball 400 feet, you can expect some pretty good results. The data backs that up: more than 85 percent of those balls went for home runs this year, while just a shade under 8 percent resulted in an out. Hit it shorter than that, and you weren't quite so lucky—fly balls hit between 320 and 359 feet resulted in an out nearly 90 percent of the time.

With 103 long outs, Kyle Seager was Lord of the (Long) Flies. What exactly does that mean? Well, he hit 27 home runs, so there was clearly some power there. Among balls that he hit between 380 and 399 feet, 9 of the 13 resulted in an out. That might indicate he was a little unlucky. However, he hit the ball between 320 and 359 feet more often than he hit it further than that, so it's not a surprise that his long fly balls stayed in the park more often than not.

On the other hand, Giancarlo Stanton was Lord of the Big Flies. He had just 42 long outs compared to his 59 home runs. He was one of just four players with at least 30 home runs to hit more home runs than long outs (the others being Aaron Judge, J.D. Martinez, and Josh Donaldson). He hit 36 balls at least 400 feet, all of which resulted in home runs, and only 26 balls between 320 and 359 feet.

In this section, you'll find how often a ball that was hit a certain distance resulted in an out or a home run. The 330 under Long Fly Outs is the number of fly ball outs the player hit between 320 and 339 feet. The 350 column indicates the ball traveled between 340 and 359 feet. And so forth. The same goes for the Home Run Distances. The Long column indicates the ball traveled at least 300 feet, and the HR column excludes inside-the-park home runs, which is why those totals might occasionally not match what you see elsewhere.

Long Outs and Home Runs

Player	Long Out Distances						Home Run Distances					
	330	350	370	390	400+	Long	330	350	370	390	400+	HR
Stanton, Giancarlo	15	7	4	2	0	42	0	4	5	14	36	59
Judge, Aaron	11	10	8	5	2	49	2	1	5	15	29	52
Martinez, J.D.	12	9	5	4	1	44	0	2	4	10	29	45
Davis, Khris	17	13	16	6	0	66	0	2	5	9	27	43
Gallo, Joey	10	7	9	3	2	40	1	2	3	4	30	40
Cruz, Nelson	20	14	12	9	0	66	0	1	5	7	26	39
Bellinger, Cody	17	15	11	5	1	59	1	1	6	15	16	39
Morrison, Logan	12	16	5	5	1	55	0	1	7	9	21	38
Smoak, Justin	20	19	10	9	0	68	0	2	6	9	21	38
Moustakas, Mike	14	15	9	11	1	71	0	3	9	12	14	38
Encarnacion, Edwin	20	10	12	9	1	66	3	6	6	12	11	38
Ozuna, Marcell	14	7	6	4	1	48	0	3	1	12	21	37
Arenado, Nolan	25	19	14	7	1	88	0	0	5	11	21	37
Zimmerman, Ryan	13	15	9	2	1	50	0	2	6	7	21	36
Votto, Joey	17	28	7	7	0	90	1	2	5	8	20	36
Goldschmidt, Paul	12	12	16	8	1	62	0	1	3	13	19	36
Bruce, Jay	20	20	21	3	2	85	0	1	6	12	17	36
Blackmon, Charlie	14	20	14	9	6	77	0	1	6	6	22	35
Upton, Justin	13	13	4	8	2	55	1	4	5	7	18	35
Springer, George	22	13	8	3	1	58	1	5	4	8	15	34
Trout, Mike	10	9	9	2	0	41	0	1	3	6	23	33
Sanchez, Gary	7	11	6	4	0	37	0	2	5	5	21	33
Donaldson, Josh	9	2	2	8	0	32	0	3	4	6	20	33
Abreu, Jose	18	20	13	6	1	72	0	4	4	8	17	33
Machado, Manny	27	26	11	7	1	96	1	2	7	6	17	33
Lindor, Francisco	29	22	11	5	2	89	1	2	6	13	11	33
Dozier, Brian	22	21	9	8	0	77	0	5	6	12	10	33
Rizzo, Anthony	26	17	5	4	0	67	0	4	1	8	19	32
Schoop, Jonathan	12	13	10	5	2	52	1	2	7	7	15	32
Duvall, Adam	21	10	11	5	0	67	1	1	5	7	17	31
Thames, Eric	19	11	9	1	0	53	0	4	5	10	12	31
Shaw, Travis	17	15	8	5	0	60	0	3	6	11	11	31
Lamb, Jake	11	11	13	5	0	55	1	2	3	3	21	30
Reynolds, Mark	11	11	9	3	1	42	0	0	4	7	19	30
Schebler, Scott	7	11	6	8	0	36	0	1	7	5	17	30
Myers, Wil	17	14	18	7	1	75	0	2	3	9	16	30
Schwarber, Kyle	10	5	3	4	1	33	0	2	8	6	14	30
Duda, Lucas	19	8	10	2	0	48	0	3	7	7	13	30
Santana, Domingo	8	10	10	3	0	43	1	4	5	7	13	30
Odor, Rougned	15	16	15	0	3	63	1	2	10	6	10	30
Harper, Bryce	15	9	7	3	0	45	0	2	0	7	20	29
Souza Jr., Steven	8	10	7	4	1	38	1	5	3	3	17	29
Bryant, Kris	16	18	4	4	1	63	0	1	9	6	13	29
Napoli, Mike	13	7	5	6	0	40	1	1	6	9	12	29
Ramirez, Jose	25	16	11	5	0	76	0	4	6	11	8	29
Morales, Kendrys	17	14	9	6	2	63	0	2	1	4	20	28
Puig, Yasiel	10	9	12	5	0	46	0	0	6	5	17	28
Freeman, Freddie	16	15	10	5	1	59	0	1	3	8	16	28
Sano, Miguel	13	12	3	1	0	36	0	1	5	8	14	28
Alonso, Yonder	8	14	5	5	0	52	0	2	5	9	12	28
McCutchen, Andrew	17	9	11	7	2	63	1	5	4	9	9	28
Perez, Salvador	17	20	8	8	1	71	0	1	4	6	16	27
Dickerson, Corey	18	8	8	5	0	57	2	2	3	4	16	27
Conforto, Michael	5	11	4	3	1	33	2	2	4	6	13	27
Seager, Kyle	29	27	14	9	0	103	0	3	8	4	12	27
Frazier, Todd	12	12	10	8	0	55	0	3	8	6	9	27
Rosario, Eddie	24	14	10	8	0	74	0	3	7	9	8	27
Gennett, Scooter	10	6	10	2	0	41	3	5	4	10	5	27
Davidson, Matt	8	8	7	5	0	36	0	3	1	5	17	26
Bell, Josh	10	12	5	2	0	42	0	1	6	4	15	26
Renfroe, Hunter	8	12	7	4	0	42	0	2	6	3	15	26
Davis, Chris	12	13	5	2	1	41	0	1	8	3	14	26
Suarez, Eugenio	13	9	14	1	0	54	0	3	5	7	11	26
Granderson, Curtis	15	14	15	7	0	66	1	2	5	9	9	26
Jones, Adam	10	15	5	7	1	55	0	6	3	8	9	26
Healy, Ryon	17	16	11	2	2	63	0	0	1	8	16	25
Rendon, Anthony	17	13	15	2	0	60	0	1	2	7	15	25
Zunino, Mike	3	7	4	4	0	21	0	1	3	6	15	25
Bour, Justin	5	8	8	2	0	34	1	2	4	4	14	25
Castellanos, Nick	22	20	11	13	4	89	0	1	6	6	12	25
Hosmer, Eric	11	11	1	4	1	42	0	1	5	8	11	25
DeJong, Paul	6	7	5	6	1	31	0	1	7	6	11	25
Joyce, Matt	23	10	9	7	0	65	1	2	5	7	10	25

Long Outs and Home Runs

Player	Long Out Distances						Home Run Distances					
	330	350	370	390	400+	Long	330	350	370	390	400+	HR
Gregorius, Didi	20	9	7	2	0	60	1	6	7	8	3	25
Story, Trevor	17	12	9	6	6	60	0	1	2	5	16	24
Altuve, Jose	13	10	7	7	1	56	2	3	2	4	12	24
Betts, Mookie	20	20	18	9	2	84	3	0	3	7	11	24
Correa, Carlos	7	12	11	2	0	50	0	4	2	8	10	24
Mancini, Trey	17	10	10	5	0	48	1	4	3	6	10	24
Cozart, Zack	15	13	6	2	0	53	1	2	6	8	7	24
Franco, Maikel	17	13	10	3	1	64	0	3	8	7	6	24
Happ, Ian	10	9	4	1	0	28	0	1	12	6	5	24
Grichuk, Randal	9	14	6	8	2	45	0	0	1	5	17	23
Pujols, Albert	12	20	15	7	1	70	0	2	3	4	14	23
Ramirez, Hanley	10	12	8	7	1	53	0	3	3	3	14	23
Carpenter, Matt	20	22	21	10	0	98	0	2	2	7	12	23
Pham, Tommy	9	8	3	3	1	33	1	1	4	5	12	23
Trumbo, Mark	16	8	5	5	1	56	0	0	5	7	11	23
Bautista, Jose	17	23	10	8	0	66	1	0	3	7	11	23
Baez, Javier	5	5	4	9	1	34	0	2	5	5	11	23
Cano, Robinson	19	22	15	6	0	81	1	0	8	4	10	23
Gonzalez, Marwin	5	6	5	6	1	34	2	4	5	4	8	23
Murphy, Daniel	15	16	14	8	0	72	0	2	5	9	7	23
Santana, Carlos	18	9	6	9	2	60	2	3	4	7	7	23
Seager, Corey	15	8	16	6	1	61	0		2	5	15	22
Choo, Shin-Soo	17	14	8	3	0	57	0	2	4	2	14	22
Joseph, Tommy	14	14	6	3	0	49	0	1	6	4	11	22
Beckham, Tim	8	12	5	2	0	42	2	0	3	7	10	22
Moss, Brandon	6	9	7	4	1	34	1	3	3	5	10	22
Moreland, Mitch	13	12	10	4	0	54	0	1	7	5	9	22
Grandal, Yasmani	9	13	9	3	0	45	0	3	3	8	8	22
Valbuena, Luis	8	10	4	7	0	41	0	1	8	6	7	22
Kinsler, Ian	28	15	16	8	0	91	0	3	3	13	3	22
Contreras, Willson	4	5	4	2	1	24	0	0	4	4	13	21
Turner, Justin	23	19	17	11	0	92	0	3	2	6	10	21
Escobar, Eduardo	18	17	9	5	0	70	0	0	1	11	9	21
Gardner, Brett	16	15	12	4	0	64	1	5	2	7	6	21
Andrus, Elvis	14	15	9	4	0	65	0	0	3	3	14	20
Mazara, Nomar	15	16	6	4	0	57	0	2	1	5	12	20
Broxton, Keon	7	11	5	3	0	36	0	0	3	7	10	20
Taylor, Chris	12	12	7	4	1	51	0	1	2	7	10	20
Benintendi, Andrew	17	19	6	5	0	72	0	2	3	6	9	20
Longoria, Evan	20	16	14	4	1	72	0	2	3	6	9	20
Gyorko, Jedd	10	8	7	3	1	42	1	2	5	2	9	20
Adams, Matt	11	6	4	5	1	32	1	2	1	9	7	20
Castillo, Welington	10	10	8	2	0	38	3	0	4	7	6	20
Holliday, Matt	7	8	3	1	0	23	0	2	3	3	11	19
Calhoun, Kole	20	13	10	6	0	68	0	2	3	4	10	19
Kepler, Max	9	10	7	3	0	49	0	3	3	4	9	19
Kemp, Matt	16	8	4	2	0	38	0	1	3	7	8	19
Altherr, Aaron	9	7	3	0	0	32	0	4	3	4	8	19
Merrifield, Whit	31	27	10	2	0	96	0	0	3	9	7	19
Bregman, Alex	16	14	11	4	5	65	1	5	2	4	7	19
Suzuki, Kurt	10	7	7	2	0	36	0	2	5	10	2	19
Yelich, Christian	10	10	5	5	1	51	1	1	2	3	11	18
Garcia, Avisail	17	7	8	0	0	42	0	1	4	3	10	18
Belt, Brandon	9	8	11	8	1	49	1	1	4	2	10	18
Taylor, Michael	6	9	6	3	0	33	1	3	2	5	7	18
Flores, Wilmer	14	14	9	4	0	60	0	1	6	4	7	18
Solarte, Yangervis	21	15	5	8	1	67	0	1	7	4	6	18
Hedges, Austin	12	9	6	6	0	46	0	3	7	2	6	18
Fowler, Dexter	14	9	15	3	1	54	0	1	5	7	5	18
Gurriel, Yulieski	17	17	9	8	0	65	2	2	4	5	5	18
McCann, Brian	9	8	3	7	1	43	3	1	4	5	5	18
Molina, Yadier	16	23	18	9	0	83	0	1	2	11	4	18
Beltre, Adrian	15	7	8	2	0	39	0	2	2	2	11	17
Iannetta, Chris	6	5	2	2	1	22	0	1	1	5	10	17
Anderson, Tim	8	9	3	4	0	41	0	1	2	4	10	17
Braun, Ryan	5	7	7	6	2	34	0	0	5	2	10	17
Gomez, Carlos	9	7	5	4	1	32	0	1	4	2	10	17
Bradley Jr., Jackie	12	6	6	2	5	46	0	0	2	6	9	17
Chirinos, Robinson	6	3	6	1	0	23	1	0	3	5	8	17
Cespedes, Yoenis	13	15	8	4	0	51	0	0	2	8	7	17
Bonifacio, Jorge	13	3	4	6	0	38	0	3	1	7	6	17
Cabrera, Melky	14	11	10	8	0	62	0	2	6	5	4	17
Aguilar, Jesus	2	9	8	1	2	27	0	1	0	5	10	16
Cron, C.J.	12	10	8	4	1	44	0	1	2	4	9	16
d'Arnaud, Travis	12	9	11	1	1	46	0	2	2	4	8	16
Castro, Starlin	9	5	4	1	0	30	0	1	2	6	7	16

Long Outs and Home Runs

Player	Long Out Distances						Home Run Distances					
	330	350	370	390	400+	Long	330	350	370	390	400+	HR
Pillar, Kevin	18	12	9	5	1	63	0	2	3	4	7	16
Cabrera, Miguel	14	11	9	9	4	57	0	2	6	2	6	16
Realmuto, J.T.	11	17	7	5	0	58	0	0	5	6	5	16
Haniger, Mitch	13	11	6	2	0	42	0	4	2	6	4	16
Harrison, Josh	19	17	11	3	0	65	1	5	3	4	3	16
Pinder, Chad	6	6	6	2	0	30	0	1	1	3	10	15
Kiermaier, Kevin	9	7	3	1	1	28	0	0	3	2	10	15
Cain, Lorenzo	20	16	9	2	0	69	0	1	1	4	8	15
Valencia, Danny	8	7	7	1	0	38	1	1	4	3	6	15
Buxton, Byron	15	7	6	3	0	41	0	1	3	6	5	15
Hicks, Aaron	12	9	8	1	1	35	3	4	1	4	3	15
Reyes, Jose	16	15	12	0	0	58	0	1	5	8	1	15
Chapman, Matt	4	7	4	6	0	31	1	0	2	1	10	14
Pollock, A.J.	11	11	7	5	0	53	0	0	1	4	9	14
Gonzalez, Carlos	4	15	10	3	1	45	1	1	1	2	9	14
Arcia, Orlando	17	13	8	1	0	55	0	2	2	2	8	14
Walker, Neil	15	8	9	8	2	52	0	2	2	2	8	14
Martinez, Jose	5	3	6	4	0	25	0	1	3	3	7	14
Herrera, Odubel	11	10	5	4	0	44	1	1	4	1	7	14
Mercer, Jordy	20	14	9	3	0	62	1	1	2	4	6	14
Crawford, Brandon	13	20	11	6	0	61	0	3	1	4	6	14
Simmons, Andrelton	20	21	10	3	0	71	0	1	4	3	6	14
Perez, Hernan	9	10	6	4	0	39	0	0	1	8	5	14
Lowrie, Jed	19	20	11	7	0	82	0	0	3	6	5	14
Lind, Adam	12	11	8	2	0	40	0	2	1	6	5	14
Avila, Alex	5	11	8	3	0	33	0	1	4	4	5	14
Gomes, Yan	6	6	8	3	0	27	1	1	4	3	5	14
Maldonado, Martin	8	9	9	2	0	36	0	1	3	6	4	14
Cabrera, Asdrubal	14	9	13	6	1	65	0	1	0	10	3	14
Beltran, Carlos	14	17	11	6	0	62	1	2	4	4	3	14
Spangenberg, Cory	11	7	5	1	1	35	0	0	2	2	9	13
Martin, Russell	6	3	5	2	0	21	1	0	2	2	8	13
McCann, James	11	11	7	2	1	37	1	0	4	0	8	13
Margot, Manuel	13	12	9	2	0	49	0	1	2	3	7	13
Drury, Brandon	11	5	8	1	0	37	0	0	1	6	6	13
Smith, Seth	10	5	7	2	0	32	1	0	4	2	6	13
Pence, Hunter	18	14	7	7	0	64	0	3	2	2	6	13
Goodwin, Brian	6	10	3	2	1	25	0	2	2	4	5	13
Peralta, David	11	13	6	5	2	57	1	1	3	3	5	13
Polanco, Jorge	13	20	6	4	0	63	0	3	2	3	5	13
Dietrich, Derek	8	10	4	6	2	43	0	3	3	2	5	13
Phillips, Brandon	17	15	4	0	0	48	0	0	5	4	4	13
Pearce, Steve	13	7	7	1	0	36	0	3	4	3	3	13
Reddick, Josh	15	15	9	8	0	67	2	2	4	2	3	13
Mahtook, Mikie	10	11	7	3	0	42	0	1	1	2	8	12
Gattis, Evan	12	7	5	0	1	37	0	1	1	3	7	12
Owings, Chris	10	11	8	3	0	42	0	0	2	5	5	12
Vogt, Stephen	13	11	7	1	1	38	0	1	1	4	5	12
Headley, Chase	12	13	4	2	0	51	0	1	4	2	5	12
Russell, Addison	11	10	3	1	0	33	0	1	4	2	5	12
Posey, Buster	18	16	16	6	1	72	1	0	4	2	5	12
Zobrist, Ben	10	17	3	6	0	48	0	1	2	5	4	12
Sanchez, Yolmer	18	10	5	4	0	52	0	0	4	4	4	12
Kipnis, Jason	13	12	6	4	2	46	0	1	3	4	4	12
Chisenhall, Lonnie	8	6	7	2	0	25	0	1	4	3	4	12
Flowers, Tyler	9	5	4	2	0	30	0	2	2	5	3	12
Galvis, Freddy	20	18	11	9	0	78	0	2	6	2	2	12
Nunez, Eduardo	8	8	3	4	0	35	2	3	2	5	0	12
Hernandez, Kike	9	8	4	4	0	34	0	1	1	3	6	11
Pederson, Joc	6	5	5	3	1	28	0	0	2	4	5	11
Polanco, Gregory	9	13	7	4	0	44	0	0	3	3	5	11
Villar, Jonathan	5	6	5	2	0	22	0	1	2	3	5	11
Segura, Jean	18	10	5	3	0	55	0	3	1	1	5	11
Turner, Trea	14	11	5	2	0	47	0	1	2	4	4	11
Williams, Nick	7	5	2	2	1	26	1	1	2	3	4	11
Heyward, Jason	5	8	8	4	1	39	0	0	5	2	4	11
Span, Denard	14	15	5	4	0	47	2	0	4	1	4	11
Gamel, Ben	16	11	6	3	0	55	0	2	2	4	3	11
Inciarte, Ender	18	10	10	4	0	62	1	2	3	3	2	11
Pirela, Jose	7	8	5	4	0	33	0	1	1	0	8	10
Jaso, John	5	14	4	5	0	33	0	1	2	0	7	10
Wieters, Matt	16	15	5	2	0	57	0	0	1	3	6	10
Werth, Jayson	4	6	7	5	0	29	0	0	1	5	4	10
Parra, Gerardo	16	16	4	5	1	54	0	0	1	5	4	10
Bogaerts, Xander	17	7	5	0	1	48	1	0	3	2	4	10
Freese, David	10	7	7	4	0	38	1	1	3	1	4	10

Long Outs and Home Runs

Player	Long Out Distances						Home Run Distances					
	330	350	370	390	400+	Long	330	350	370	390	400+	HR
Castro, Jason	5	8	8	3	0	36	0	1	3	3	3	10
Martinez, Victor	14	12	12	8	0	63	0	2	3	2	3	10
Panik, Joe	12	15	10	3	1	65	1	1	1	5	2	10
Maybin, Cameron	15	3	1	4	1	36	1	0	1	7	1	10
Semien, Marcus	11	11	8	2	0	46	1	1	2	5	1	10
Miller, Brad	9	8	4	2	1	40	1	0	0	2	6	9
Piscotty, Stephen	9	12	8	6	0	38	0	0	2	1	6	9
Kendrick, Howie	5	4	0	2	0	16	0	0	0	4	5	9
Brantley, Michael	9	8	3	1	0	35	0	0	0	4	5	9
Goins, Ryan	12	8	4	2	1	41	1	1	0	2	5	9
Descalso, Daniel	11	13	9	6	3	50	0	0	3	1	5	9
Gordon, Alex	6	11	9	5	1	48	1	1	2	0	5	9
Plouffe, Trevor	9	7	0	2	0	26	0	0	3	3	3	9
Pina, Manny	7	13	9	3	1	40	0	1	2	3	3	9
Sandoval, Pablo	11	6	5	3	1	32	0	0	3	4	2	9
Grossman, Robbie	14	9	8	0	0	44	0	0	3	4	2	9
Hernandez, Cesar	19	10	6	3	0	51	0	2	2	3	2	9
Hundley, Nick	5	5	6	1	1	23	0	2	1	3	2	9
Garcia, Leury	9	3	2	1	0	20	0	1	5	2	1	9
Zimmer, Bradley	2	1	4	2	0	18	0	0	1	3	4	8
Utley, Chase	14	10	12	3	0	52	0	0	2	2	4	8
Markakis, Nick	16	13	5	2	1	61	0	0	2	4	2	8
Almora Jr., Albert	9	5	3	1	0	27	0	1	1	4	2	8
Hechavarria, Adeiny	6	4	3	2	0	27	0	1	2	3	2	8
LeMahieu, DJ	14	7	4	5	2	49	1	0	3	2	2	8
Escobar, Yunel	10	11	7	4	0	40	0	0	0	2	5	7
Barnhart, Tucker	9	13	6	3	0	48	0	0	1	1	5	7
Marte, Starling	8	6	8	2	0	31	0	0	1	1	5	7
Mauer, Joe	17	11	6	2	0	62	0	0	2	2	3	7
Aybar, Erick	11	6	5	5	0	37	0	1	1	2	3	7
Diaz, Aledmys	6	8	4	2	0	25	0	0	4	0	3	7
Motter, Taylor	13	4	3	1	0	32	0	2	1	2	2	7
Carrera, Ezequiel	5	10	3	2	0	23	0	1	2	3	1	7
Rosales, Adam	4	5	3	0	0	26	0	1	2	3	1	7
Jackson, Austin	3	8	4	3	1	26	0	2	3	1	1	7
Young, Chris	5	4	3	2	0	20	0	2	2	1	1	7
Leon, Sandy	4	9	1	0	0	20	0	1	2	4	0	7
Pedroia, Dustin	16	11	4	2	0	39	0	0	4	3	0	7
Ellsbury, Jacoby	11	6	3	1	0	32	1	1	3	2	0	7
Lucroy, Jonathan	13	6	4	3	1	41	0	0	0	2	4	6
Swanson, Dansby	17	13	8	0	0	53	0	1	0	1	4	6
Albies, Ozzie	8	9	7	1	1	31	0	0	0	4	2	6
Forsythe, Logan	20	12	8	5	0	55	0	0	1	3	2	6
Barney, Darwin	11	6	2	0	0	29	0	1	3	0	2	6
Escobar, Alcides	13	17	12	4	2	74	0	1	2	2	1	6
Heredia, Guillermo	7	5	4	3	0	35	0	2	1	2	1	6
Iglesias, Jose	13	5	6	0	0	33	1	1	1	2	1	6
Engel, Adam	6	6	2	3	0	26	0	2	2	1	1	6
Difo, Wilmer	6	3	6	0	0	26	0	0	0	1	4	5
Frazier, Adam	4	8	7	3	0	40	0	0	1	1	3	5
Peraza, Jose	12	9	6	2	0	36	0	1	0	1	3	5
DeShields, Delino	12	7	5	0	0	36	0	0	1	2	2	5
Vazquez, Christian	6	5	5	1	0	27	1	1	0	1	2	5
Marte, Ketel	4	3	5	4	1	28	0	2	2	0	1	5
Rivera, T.J.	15	5	4	3	0	34	0	1	2	2	0	5
Dyson, Jarrod	9	5	4	3	0	30	0	1	2	2	0	5
Davis, Rajai	10	9	5	1	0	33	0	1	2	2	0	5
Aoki, Nori	10	5	3	1	0	27	1	1	1	2	0	5
Wong, Kolten	8	8	5	2	0	38	0	0	0	1	3	4
Camargo, Johan	6	6	1	1	0	18	0	0	1	1	2	4
Asuaje, Carlos	9	12	3	4	1	40	0	1	0	1	2	4
Romine, Andrew	8	8	5	2	0	32	0	0	2	0	2	4
Hardy, J.J.	6	15	4	2	0	36	0	1	0	2	1	4
Hamilton, Billy	13	7	1	1	0	34	0	0	3	1	0	4
Rickard, Joey	9	8	3	2	0	27	0	1	2	1	0	4
Sogard, Eric	10	7	0	2	0	29	0	0	1	0	2	3
Gonzalez, Adrian	8	10	8	2	0	39	0	0	2	0	1	3
Torreyes, Ronald	8	6	4	1	0	28	0	2	0	0	1	3
Presley, Alex	6	4	4	0	0	20	1	0	1	1	0	3
Gordon, Dee	11	3	7	3	0	39	0	0	1	0	1	2
Narvaez, Omar	7	3	1	1	0	17	0	1	1	0	0	2
Jay, Jon	12	8	3	4	0	39	0	1	1	0	0	2
Revere, Ben	7	5	3	2	0	30	0	0	1	0	0	1
Rojas, Miguel	2	6	4	1	0	18	0	0	1	0	0	1
Hernandez, Gorkys	4	7	7	2	0	29	0	0	0	0	0	0

Pitcher Analysis

Lindsay Zeck

The Chicago Cubs won their division for the second year in a row, becoming the first World Series Champions to win their division the next season since the Philadelphia Phillies did so in 2009. They weren't quite as dominant this season as they were in 2016, however, and this is evident when examining their starting pitching performance. In 2016, the Cubs' starters posted the lowest ERA (2.96), WHIP (1.07), and batting average against (.210) in the league. In 2017, the Cubs' starters finished with an ERA of 4.05, a WHIP of 1.27, and a batting average against of .244. Their starting rotation clearly saw a dip in performance in 2017, but it was the runner-up for the 2016 NL Cy Young Award, Jon Lester, who saw the greatest decline.

Of all pitchers who started at least 20 games in both 2016 and 2017, Lester had the third-highest increase in ERA—2.44 in 2016 to 4.33 in 2017—and seventh-highest increase in WHIP—1.02 in 2016 to 1.32 in 2017. In looking at the details of his performance this season, we find that he threw 62 percent of his pitches for strikes, down from 64 percent in 2016, but still achieved a very respectable strikeout percentage of 23.6. His percentages of line drives, groundballs, and fly balls were all close to his 2016 numbers. The percentage of batters that he walked, however, did jump from 6.5 to 7.9.

While Lester did see some waning in his control this season, the components of his pitching do not indicate a pitcher who deserves an ERA nearly double that of the previous season. Something to take note of, however, is that Jon Lester had the 14th-highest Batting Average allowed on Balls in Play (BABIP) in 2017 among qualified pitchers (.310), while he had the 8th-lowest in 2016 (.256). This was an increase of over 50 points. Now, while such a substantial change could signal a shift in luck for the Cubs' ace or a change in the quality of batted balls against him, the fielding behind him likely also played a role. The Cubs finished with the record for the most Defensive Runs Saved ever in a season in 2016 with 107, while finishing with a respectable, but much lower, 37 runs saved in 2017. With such an exceptional defense behind him in 2016, it makes sense that Lester would have allowed fewer hits, and in turn fewer runs. In fact, the Cubs starters as a whole went from a BABIP of .252 in 2016 to .287 in 2017.

Pitcher Analysis
Pitchers with 50+ Batters Faced in 2017

Pitcher	BF	Pitches	K	BB	GB	LD	FB	Str%	S/Str	1-0	0-1	Full	2 Strike	3 Ball
Abad, Fernando	182	769	37	14	58	25	46	61%	12%	77	87	39	93	52
Adleman, Tim	531	2088	108	51	123	68	167	63%	18%	210	266	78	267	106
Albers, Andrew	178	723	37	10	43	34	51	71%	12%	52	115	16	107	24
Albers, Matt	233	966	63	17	74	27	44	63%	15%	87	126	37	136	52
Alburquerque, Al	71	263	14	8	27	10	12	65%	20%	28	33	9	31	16
Alcantara, Raul	108	444	12	12	39	15	26	59%	14%	46	49	24	53	31
Alexander, Scott	283	1059	59	28	144	30	21	63%	22%	111	136	38	138	57
Allen, Cody	282	1165	92	21	55	33	76	63%	24%	116	150	36	172	53
Altavilla, Dan	203	768	52	20	47	22	61	62%	22%	91	88	28	101	42
Alvarado, Jose	123	463	29	9	44	13	25	64%	18%	42	65	16	62	29
Alvarez, Dario	82	321	17	14	21	6	22	57%	25%	40	33	15	45	21
Alvarez, Henderson	67	261	6	11	23	10	17	60%	8%	30	32	6	28	17
Alvarez, Jose	203	760	45	12	56	35	53	66%	17%	75	93	33	107	45
Anderson, Brett	251	900	38	21	93	54	42	63%	14%	107	111	29	102	45
Anderson, Chase	569	2254	133	41	148	68	162	64%	17%	222	290	85	305	119
Anderson, Tyler	362	1404	81	26	107	56	82	66%	18%	125	190	43	195	63
Andriese, Matt	374	1441	76	28	118	53	92	65%	18%	144	191	46	188	63
Aquino, Jayson	62	237	13	6	19	5	19	62%	18%	18	34	7	32	12
Archer, Chris	852	3406	249	60	224	117	192	64%	21%	320	449	109	484	158
Armstrong, Shawn	108	430	20	10	30	13	34	65%	17%	42	55	15	54	18
Arrieta, Jake	707	2743	163	55	215	98	164	63%	14%	293	344	95	371	146
Arroyo, Bronson	322	1159	45	19	76	53	121	66%	12%	128	152	33	136	48
Asher, Alec	265	1069	47	23	72	35	78	61%	15%	124	124	40	135	60
Avilan, Luis	194	829	52	22	63	29	25	60%	25%	88	94	41	116	55
Axford, John	109	473	21	17	34	17	17	61%	12%	44	59	21	65	32
Baez, Pedro	280	1174	64	29	64	41	80	65%	25%	118	140	46	169	63
Bailey, Homer	420	1575	67	42	132	80	84	62%	16%	163	203	50	189	84
Banda, Anthony	115	418	25	10	27	17	30	63%	18%	39	58	15	56	21
Barbato, Johnny	130	478	23	18	33	20	34	64%	18%	54	59	14	68	24
Barnes, Danny	265	1063	62	24	57	28	92	63%	19%	100	133	36	141	57
Barnes, Jacob	304	1228	80	33	98	36	50	63%	25%	117	151	43	180	69
Barnes, Matt	287	1204	83	28	85	40	49	61%	21%	123	144	48	163	66
Barnette, Tony	252	1035	57	22	70	38	62	64%	21%	96	127	40	147	56
Barraclough, Kyle	286	1159	76	38	71	38	56	59%	21%	126	137	52	159	81
Barrett, Jake	121	471	26	15	30	16	34	59%	20%	53	55	22	59	33
Bastardo, Antonio	52	227	8	9	6	8	21	56%	14%	25	22	8	27	15
Bauer, Trevor	749	3148	196	60	224	104	155	61%	16%	325	365	133	437	188
Baumann, Buddy	72	297	21	7	14	3	24	65%	25%	30	36	13	44	18
Beck, Chris	294	1152	42	34	86	45	82	61%	13%	127	138	45	142	74
Bedrosian, Cam	190	765	53	17	51	20	48	64%	21%	74	98	25	112	38
Belisle, Matt	247	937	54	22	68	35	64	69%	16%	77	151	30	133	48
Beliveau, Jeff	70	296	17	6	18	7	20	64%	14%	30	37	11	40	15
Bell, Chad	293	1187	57	31	91	42	69	61%	15%	121	137	59	155	76
Benoit, Joaquin	213	861	46	22	47	24	70	65%	21%	77	108	33	116	47
Bergman, Christian	230	800	33	15	66	38	71	66%	12%	76	116	17	99	31
Berrios, Jose	616	2388	139	48	160	86	164	63%	16%	252	305	75	312	118
Betances, Dellin	261	1106	100	44	51	14	40	59%	22%	125	121	42	172	71
Bettis, Chad	200	736	30	11	74	29	50	64%	15%	80	99	20	90	32
Biagini, Joe	517	1936	97	42	206	65	99	64%	13%	187	267	57	251	86
Bibens-Dirkx, Austin	299	1171	38	20	95	51	92	59%	15%	117	157	42	133	66
Blach, Ty	692	2519	73	43	261	120	178	64%	10%	263	348	79	291	123
Blackburn, Paul	238	937	22	16	111	37	49	59%	10%	124	87	48	104	62
Blanton, Joe	195	765	39	13	47	31	63	65%	21%	72	103	31	105	39
Bleier, Richard	265	914	26	13	150	25	43	69%	14%	105	122	16	109	29
Blevins, Jerry	217	914	69	24	48	24	45	62%	21%	94	114	34	134	54
Bolsinger, Mike	196	756	39	27	62	20	45	62%	13%	76	93	23	102	39
Bonilla, Lisalverto	172	652	28	22	49	25	40	61%	20%	66	84	30	82	41
Boshers, Buddy	153	560	28	10	51	23	38	65%	17%	49	84	17	75	23
Bowman, Matt	247	977	46	18	95	29	50	63%	16%	87	132	41	131	49
Boxberger, Brad	121	500	40	11	28	11	28	65%	19%	46	63	19	75	27
Boyd, Matt	605	2356	110	53	164	96	170	64%	16%	242	302	83	306	122
Boyer, Blaine	178	691	33	14	43	37	46	66%	16%	70	86	20	88	34
Brach, Brad	275	1175	70	26	75	33	69	65%	19%	115	130	46	173	66
Bracho, Silvino	87	349	25	7	24	5	26	66%	20%	38	40	13	48	16
Bradford, Chasen	143	507	27	13	57	15	30	66%	19%	49	68	13	68	23
Bradley, Archie	290	1158	79	21	89	43	54	66%	16%	118	151	45	170	59
Brady, Michael	136	447	24	6	33	18	47	69%	16%	47	64	9	58	14
Brault, Steven	162	640	23	14	50	24	46	61%	13%	76	69	22	76	39

Pitcher Analysis
Pitchers with 50+ Batters Faced in 2017

Pitcher	BF	Pitches	K	BB	GB	LD	FB	Str%	S/Str	1-0	0-1	Full	2 Strike	3 Ball
Brebbia, John	209	783	51	11	35	26	78	69%	19%	57	132	22	122	28
Breslow, Craig	159	593	23	14	47	24	47	62%	10%	64	73	18	65	33
Brice, Austin	137	497	26	7	50	17	32	66%	17%	50	70	16	66	25
Bridwell, Parker	492	1759	73	30	145	81	155	64%	15%	180	245	48	216	73
Britton, Zach	161	587	29	18	82	22	9	60%	21%	70	67	19	68	32
Brothers, Rex	105	379	33	14	23	15	21	67%	22%	38	55	8	59	19
Broxton, Jonathan	78	296	16	11	20	13	14	63%	21%	32	37	11	40	17
Buchanan, Jake	77	226	4	7	35	13	13	66%	8%	26	33	7	23	10
Buchter, Ryan	268	1098	65	26	56	23	91	64%	17%	108	131	38	146	58
Bumgarner, Madison	450	1666	101	20	131	58	132	67%	16%	146	241	59	232	75
Bummer, Aaron	91	374	17	15	31	8	18	57%	20%	44	41	13	47	22
Bundy, Dylan	698	2819	152	51	158	96	227	65%	18%	282	348	107	396	143
Busenitz, Alan	121	503	23	9	33	15	40	66%	11%	52	59	20	74	25
Bush, Matt	240	944	58	19	59	31	68	66%	19%	106	109	30	130	46
Butler, Eddie	237	918	30	28	77	39	58	61%	12%	92	120	38	101	62
Cahill, Trevor	381	1523	87	45	135	44	64	60%	19%	152	188	63	197	95
Cain, Matt	568	2083	75	49	183	100	148	63%	8%	207	282	67	248	111
Campos, Leonel	60	226	15	8	14	4	18	63%	32%	29	23	6	31	10
Carrasco, Carlos	798	3058	226	46	231	111	169	66%	21%	295	421	96	438	133
Cashner, Andrew	704	2636	86	64	263	104	174	62%	10%	290	326	98	307	154
Casilla, Santiago	259	1025	57	22	69	37	66	62%	19%	114	116	44	133	56
Castillo, Luis	359	1484	98	32	130	27	64	63%	21%	153	173	50	208	75
Castro, Miguel	274	1033	38	28	100	35	68	62%	16%	115	131	36	117	66
Castro, Simon	153	595	35	14	33	18	50	63%	11%	62	81	21	74	32
Cecil, Brett	277	990	66	16	79	40	66	67%	21%	106	130	31	132	45
Cessa, Luis	160	624	30	17	50	20	40	62%	17%	67	81	24	82	34
Chacin, Jhoulys	765	2937	153	72	254	96	167	63%	13%	314	370	111	392	170
Chafin, Andrew	221	879	61	21	76	29	30	61%	19%	102	101	33	124	50
Chapman, Aroldis	210	874	69	20	57	19	41	68%	21%	78	116	28	137	42
Chatwood, Tyler	631	2461	120	77	244	85	91	58%	18%	294	270	81	296	155
Chavez, Jesse	586	2312	119	45	172	94	153	62%	13%	220	298	104	305	139
Chen, Wei-Yin	132	493	25	19	34	18	41	66%	14%	49	67	14	64	20
Cingrani, Tony	176	727	52	12	45	17	47	65%	22%	68	96	31	107	37
Cishek, Steve	174	729	41	14	64	20	30	63%	17%	62	97	27	104	35
Claudio, Alex	323	1132	56	15	164	41	41	68%	15%	116	167	21	157	40
Clevinger, Mike	502	2105	137	60	118	72	109	60%	21%	186	276	86	288	129
Clippard, Tyler	264	1113	72	31	50	26	78	63%	23%	108	131	52	156	69
Cobb, Alex	742	2849	128	44	267	123	169	64%	11%	303	359	107	369	150
Cole, A.J.	229	937	44	27	66	25	59	62%	17%	87	122	41	124	62
Cole, Gerrit	849	3298	196	55	265	119	195	65%	15%	310	447	121	457	155
Collmenter, Josh	87	327	18	6	20	10	31	65%	17%	34	46	10	42	14
Colome, Alex	281	996	58	23	94	34	65	65%	19%	105	129	25	137	46
Colon, Bartolo	648	2286	89	35	214	99	199	68%	8%	226	331	61	303	89
Conley, Adam	463	1723	72	42	130	61	137	63%	16%	189	212	61	219	97
Corbin, Patrick	826	3084	178	61	290	115	170	64%	18%	304	417	107	407	158
Cosart, Jarred	114	485	15	19	39	16	22	56%	13%	55	53	20	59	37
Cotton, Jharel	566	2173	105	53	146	66	183	63%	16%	229	265	70	285	109
Coulombe, Daniel	219	905	39	22	86	26	41	61%	16%	104	98	45	123	62
Covey, Dylan	309	1159	41	34	112	38	81	59%	11%	136	128	40	120	76
Crichton, Stefan	62	246	8	4	23	12	15	59%	8%	30	25	12	27	17
Crick, Kyle	134	606	28	17	33	14	40	62%	19%	58	67	30	85	40
Cueto, Johnny	648	2533	136	53	173	109	157	64%	17%	228	338	113	339	152
Darvish, Yu	766	3054	209	58	198	109	179	65%	20%	314	382	121	448	162
Davies, Zach	817	3089	124	55	308	139	167	62%	12%	348	374	88	385	149
Davis, Rookie	123	522	20	14	36	17	31	58%	16%	45	68	28	65	35
Davis, Wade	242	1060	79	28	53	28	50	62%	25%	98	118	60	154	68
Dayton, Grant	102	418	20	12	21	9	37	61%	18%	50	42	18	56	24
De Jong, Chase	125	458	13	13	30	21	47	60%	9%	62	53	12	47	25
de la Rosa, Jorge	219	852	45	21	66	24	56	62%	24%	94	104	34	112	56
deGrom, Jacob	827	3168	239	59	234	109	174	67%	21%	293	425	110	468	143
Delgado, Randall	259	1050	60	14	83	41	57	64%	19%	83	148	50	148	59
Dermody, Matt	95	341	15	5	25	12	36	61%	19%	47	32	13	38	19
Despaigne, Odrisamer	254	968	31	24	73	46	75	62%	13%	94	130	34	113	50
Devenski, Chris	316	1270	100	26	72	28	81	66%	27%	108	174	47	187	68
Diaz, Dayan	58	268	20	4	14	11	9	64%	22%	23	30	18	44	19
Diaz, Edwin	278	1130	89	32	59	22	70	64%	26%	121	136	40	166	63
Diaz, Jumbo	136	541	28	15	27	20	41	67%	17%	41	82	19	81	28
Diaz, Miguel	192	774	33	25	52	23	54	60%	14%	100	74	31	103	46
Dickey, R.A.	815	2924	136	67	277	116	197	66%	14%	286	417	93	385	141

Pitcher Analysis
Pitchers with 50+ Batters Faced in 2017

Pitcher	BF	Pitches	K	BB	GB	LD	FB	Str%	S/Str	Counts 1-0	0-1	Full	2 Strike	3 Ball
Doolittle, Sean	197	786	62	10	39	23	62	74%	22%	57	114	9	122	17
Drake, Oliver	251	1049	62	25	78	40	42	63%	19%	91	130	46	145	60
Duensing, Brian	257	1032	61	18	84	31	58	61%	18%	108	128	40	128	55
Duffey, Tyler	310	1126	67	18	109	42	69	67%	17%	106	160	33	148	56
Duffy, Danny	609	2277	130	41	167	84	172	67%	18%	214	331	61	325	90
Duke, Zach	74	276	12	6	27	10	16	66%	18%	25	41	13	36	15
Dull, Ryan	177	733	45	16	43	21	47	64%	20%	59	102	31	111	38
Dunn, Mike	220	878	57	28	44	29	61	58%	18%	106	93	32	106	54
Dyson, Sam	260	927	34	30	119	32	38	63%	13%	118	110	26	105	53
Edgin, Josh	166	614	27	18	54	20	40	62%	16%	59	84	26	73	38
Edwards Jr., Carl	262	1129	94	38	55	24	45	61%	25%	108	135	43	171	69
Eflin, Zach	280	1020	35	12	98	39	85	66%	11%	99	143	27	123	42
Eickhoff, Jerad	576	2133	118	53	147	87	157	62%	15%	246	255	73	275	113
Ellington, Brian	219	930	48	32	46	24	60	58%	22%	99	100	39	116	62
Espino, Paolo	109	438	20	10	28	14	31	60%	13%	47	52	17	55	29
Estevez, Carlos	149	575	31	14	46	29	27	62%	18%	63	69	18	77	29
Estrada, Marco	806	3246	176	71	167	107	277	65%	17%	333	398	113	432	169
Familia, Jeurys	111	411	25	15	41	14	13	59%	18%	60	38	13	51	24
Faria, Jake	357	1445	84	31	90	51	94	62%	20%	162	170	58	203	86
Farmer, Buck	219	900	49	20	47	30	68	62%	18%	80	120	34	118	51
Farquhar, Danny	215	889	45	28	55	18	59	63%	21%	85	110	32	129	50
Farrell, Luke	61	246	9	10	14	5	21	62%	15%	22	32	11	32	15
Fedde, Erick	76	298	15	8	29	8	10	63%	9%	20	44	11	41	16
Feldman, Scott	472	1909	93	35	139	88	98	62%	14%	181	233	73	253	101
Feliz, Michael	218	899	70	22	39	34	53	65%	23%	79	120	32	138	44
Feliz, Neftali	196	847	37	23	43	29	60	62%	19%	72	109	38	112	49
Fields, Josh	223	892	60	15	43	31	71	68%	21%	72	121	30	124	39
Fien, Casey	62	208	10	6	20	11	14	68%	21%	21	28	7	29	11
Fiers, Mike	671	2630	146	62	189	88	164	63%	15%	265	339	83	355	132
Finnegan, Brandon	59	241	16	13	16	6	8	56%	22%	31	21	14	30	20
Fister, Doug	392	1531	83	38	133	54	76	62%	12%	153	197	63	196	95
Flaherty, Jack	94	358	20	10	30	14	19	64%	22%	35	50	12	50	18
Flexen, Chris	233	911	36	35	65	33	59	61%	14%	90	123	36	119	57
Foltynewicz, Mike	692	2770	143	59	184	114	169	62%	16%	257	377	111	363	151
Freeland, Kyle	688	2573	107	63	265	91	136	61%	13%	307	301	102	302	154
Freeman, Sam	254	950	59	27	96	25	43	63%	19%	106	110	29	129	50
Fried, Max	121	422	22	12	54	15	14	59%	15%	61	43	10	51	25
Fulmer, Carson	101	427	19	13	19	11	36	62%	15%	48	41	16	56	25
Fulmer, Michael	676	2479	114	40	250	111	147	64%	15%	255	326	85	306	112
Gallardo, Yovani	578	2291	94	60	182	80	151	60%	14%	241	269	106	270	157
Gallegos, Giovanny	88	363	22	5	21	13	25	70%	21%	28	50	13	57	16
Gant, John	76	290	11	10	29	7	18	60%	17%	30	39	13	36	22
Garcia, Jaime	673	2430	129	64	259	88	126	62%	18%	289	289	77	309	128
Garcia, Jarlin	225	892	42	17	62	32	65	63%	19%	101	106	27	116	43
Garcia, Luis	295	997	60	26	116	37	53	62%	20%	121	122	33	114	58
Garrett, Amir	321	1236	63	40	92	39	81	62%	15%	139	146	50	159	75
Garton, Ryan	90	353	16	6	28	15	24	63%	18%	36	46	18	46	21
Garza, Matt	504	1910	79	45	146	81	138	63%	13%	202	235	73	239	104
Gausman, Kevin	816	3357	179	71	238	123	196	63%	18%	323	428	136	459	190
Gaviglio, Sam	313	1169	49	26	114	42	75	63%	12%	121	157	38	148	61
Gearrin, Cory	285	1069	64	35	85	34	58	62%	19%	109	143	33	145	59
Gee, Dillon	212	801	41	15	61	28	59	66%	17%	76	111	30	113	39
German, Domingo	62	253	18	9	18	7	8	61%	19%	24	35	9	37	15
Gibson, Kyle	693	2610	121	60	255	116	131	62%	17%	282	327	101	317	141
Giles, Ken	247	952	83	21	62	25	54	67%	25%	93	128	28	142	43
Giolito, Lucas	179	704	34	12	58	26	45	64%	17%	69	85	30	91	38
Givens, Mychal	315	1326	88	25	84	34	79	64%	19%	133	155	48	198	70
Glasnow, Tyler	305	1220	56	44	86	41	72	59%	14%	132	140	51	151	80
Glover, Koda	80	317	17	4	26	13	20	66%	17%	35	36	11	43	15
Godley, Zack	627	2436	165	53	215	72	102	62%	22%	245	319	92	328	137
Goeddel, Erik	122	501	33	11	33	12	32	63%	24%	52	57	17	78	22
Gohara, Luiz	123	432	31	8	29	17	36	68%	20%	47	61	9	62	15
Goldberg, Brad	62	262	3	14	21	11	11	53%	15%	31	27	15	26	25
Gomez, Jeanmar	100	363	21	7	34	16	17	62%	17%	44	44	7	40	18
Gonzales, Marco	185	701	32	11	64	32	45	64%	15%	74	93	22	94	33
Gonzalez, Gio	827	3364	188	79	247	103	189	60%	15%	367	372	143	442	209
Gonzalez, Miguel	684	2531	100	55	187	101	228	65%	11%	226	356	91	327	135
Goody, Nick	221	901	72	20	35	29	60	65%	26%	91	107	31	141	44
Gossett, Daniel	414	1581	72	31	132	75	99	63%	15%	181	196	45	196	76

Pitcher	BF	Pitches	K	BB	GB	LD	FB	Str%	S/Str	Counts				
										1-0	0-1	Full	2 Strike	3 Ball
Grace, Matt	215	753	31	18	96	29	32	65%	12%	80	107	22	89	40
Graveman, Kendall	444	1675	70	32	172	64	100	62%	11%	193	206	58	210	91
Gray, Jon	461	1833	112	30	154	71	90	65%	15%	180	246	63	253	88
Gray, Sonny	678	2664	153	57	242	90	126	62%	20%	261	340	105	349	152
Green, Chad	253	1141	103	17	34	35	60	64%	25%	85	152	54	173	65
Greene, Shane	283	1077	73	34	81	31	59	63%	15%	111	138	39	144	62
Gregerson, Luke	263	968	70	20	86	31	55	64%	25%	90	137	38	136	55
Greinke, Zack	801	3163	215	45	249	96	187	64%	20%	301	422	125	452	155
Griffin, A.J.	338	1322	61	28	69	32	141	64%	13%	127	176	32	181	59
Grilli, Jason	184	800	48	18	31	31	54	62%	19%	79	87	43	108	54
Grimm, Justin	232	964	59	27	62	28	54	60%	21%	100	108	43	133	59
Gsellman, Robert	549	2049	82	42	199	87	118	63%	12%	193	296	73	252	109
Guduan, Reymin	83	324	16	12	30	13	12	62%	15%	35	42	13	42	19
Guerra, Deolis	105	424	22	12	26	7	37	60%	25%	42	53	16	55	25
Guerra, Javy	88	320	12	7	37	12	19	70%	8%	28	51	6	47	12
Guerra, Junior	314	1238	67	43	66	45	86	58%	19%	142	140	37	148	71
Hader, Josh	188	779	68	22	31	13	46	65%	27%	78	96	33	121	45
Hahn, Jesse	316	1209	55	27	103	57	66	61%	12%	133	141	42	146	72
Haley, Justin	81	330	14	6	23	22	15	63%	10%	30	42	11	42	14
Hamels, Cole	614	2312	105	53	210	83	149	62%	16%	269	277	85	292	131
Hammel, Jason	804	3029	145	48	227	124	246	65%	15%	299	411	96	413	138
Hand, Brad	311	1201	104	20	82	35	60	64%	21%	130	141	34	177	52
Happ, J.A.	626	2487	142	46	203	84	146	64%	16%	239	320	91	328	130
Hardy, Blaine	156	593	28	13	38	26	51	63%	17%	67	71	17	75	31
Harris, Will	177	670	52	7	56	19	41	64%	21%	72	82	20	93	28
Hart, Donnie	190	709	29	13	76	20	47	62%	17%	83	85	26	83	36
Harvey, Matt	431	1686	67	47	130	70	102	63%	13%	179	200	56	225	93
Hatcher, Chris	257	1009	63	21	55	36	78	64%	21%	95	127	39	144	57
Heaney, Andrew	101	415	27	9	19	14	30	63%	22%	40	51	18	56	25
Hellickson, Jeremy	695	2618	96	47	185	113	232	63%	14%	282	329	85	317	124
Hembree, Heath	271	1113	70	18	70	37	73	65%	22%	105	142	44	160	54
Hendricks, Kyle	570	2276	123	40	198	82	115	64%	14%	208	322	72	308	106
Hendriks, Liam	273	1164	78	23	71	33	67	64%	20%	110	139	56	165	67
Hernandez, Ariel	108	434	29	22	24	8	24	56%	23%	53	42	17	57	31
Hernandez, David	214	799	52	9	65	25	61	67%	20%	88	100	18	114	30
Hernandez, Felix	368	1382	78	26	119	59	76	65%	15%	141	181	42	188	67
Herrera, Kelvin	259	994	56	20	86	33	62	67%	18%	101	133	26	141	40
Hildenberger, Trevor	170	624	44	6	67	20	27	66%	18%	58	93	20	89	27
Hill, Rich	552	2224	166	49	116	54	144	67%	18%	208	300	78	353	112
Hoffman, Jeff	440	1610	82	40	127	55	127	63%	13%	173	208	63	210	88
Holder, Jonathan	171	657	40	8	50	22	47	69%	19%	55	99	19	99	27
Holland, Derek	626	2460	104	75	164	95	176	60%	12%	227	333	105	306	151
Holland, Greg	235	883	70	26	57	18	62	63%	25%	91	121	25	129	46
Holmberg, David	272	1075	33	34	85	34	79	59%	12%	114	131	46	127	74
Hoover, J.J.	197	822	54	26	38	32	46	57%	23%	92	89	40	106	60
Howell, J.P.	52	193	6	7	22	8	8	52%	14%	31	17	9	15	17
Hoyt, James	211	850	66	14	52	30	46	64%	27%	79	116	29	123	41
Hudson, Daniel	271	1101	66	33	71	34	59	61%	20%	117	125	46	144	69
Hughes, Jared	244	910	48	24	102	31	31	60%	20%	99	109	26	105	50
Hughes, Phil	244	907	38	13	58	46	87	66%	11%	77	142	27	112	40
Hunter, Tommy	228	872	64	14	65	31	51	66%	19%	78	119	28	120	39
Iglesias, Raisel	306	1232	92	27	78	47	60	66%	22%	106	166	43	180	58
Infante, Gregory	227	939	49	20	56	35	64	60%	17%	110	92	46	120	62
Iwakuma, Hisashi	128	471	16	12	40	16	42	63%	13%	51	66	17	63	23
Jackson, Edwin	339	1302	60	29	90	40	113	61%	17%	149	144	50	152	80
Jackson, Luke	224	815	33	19	75	32	59	63%	17%	80	110	28	96	47
Jansen, Kenley	258	1012	109	7	53	29	56	74%	25%	70	164	18	180	20
Jaye, Myles	71	268	4	10	26	14	13	57%	7%	39	23	10	27	15
Jeffress, Jeremy	295	1144	51	34	120	35	48	62%	17%	133	126	40	149	63
Jennings, Dan	267	1040	51	31	107	34	38	62%	14%	99	133	37	143	56
Jimenez, Joe	99	407	17	9	24	16	30	63%	20%	38	47	23	60	28
Jimenez, Ubaldo	648	2587	139	58	190	92	159	61%	14%	301	280	104	333	160
Johnson, Brian	121	448	21	8	33	17	42	68%	12%	45	60	11	65	16
Johnson, Jim	256	975	60	25	81	35	51	63%	16%	99	127	24	136	46
Junis, Jakob	422	1525	80	25	122	60	122	64%	15%	159	206	48	197	71
Kahnle, Tommy	256	1017	96	17	57	30	53	67%	26%	96	135	28	160	41
Karns, Nathan	188	749	51	13	60	15	46	63%	20%	78	91	25	109	34
Kela, Keone	151	614	51	17	25	10	47	61%	19%	64	73	19	86	31
Kelley, Shawn	121	513	25	11	22	12	50	68%	21%	33	80	9	71	19

Pitcher Analysis
Pitchers with 50+ Batters Faced in 2017

Pitcher	BF	Pitches	K	BB	GB	LD	FB	Str%	S/Str	1-0	0-1	Full	2 Strike	3 Ball
													Counts	
Kelly, Joe	238	1025	52	27	80	37	41	63%	18%	85	136	50	136	61
Kennedy, Ian	655	2641	131	61	164	74	217	63%	15%	274	310	98	350	144
Kershaw, Clayton	679	2521	202	30	210	83	145	69%	21%	210	380	80	384	91
Keuchel, Dallas	584	2194	125	47	268	62	71	62%	18%	232	280	85	277	120
Kimbrel, Craig	254	1148	126	14	40	21	47	68%	30%	94	153	33	199	46
Kintzler, Brandon	288	1110	39	16	124	42	60	64%	9%	107	149	34	133	52
Kittredge, Andrew	66	245	14	6	20	8	15	67%	19%	22	35	6	32	10
Kluber, Corey	777	2945	265	36	208	103	156	68%	23%	276	412	90	450	113
Knebel, Corey	309	1359	126	40	54	24	63	63%	23%	146	139	62	210	90
Koehler, Tom	334	1282	62	35	90	49	85	60%	15%	149	146	50	175	75
Kontos, George	278	1020	70	20	85	36	61	66%	26%	101	141	30	152	45
Krol, Ian	214	862	44	21	59	32	52	62%	19%	83	113	38	112	57
Kuhl, Chad	680	2687	142	72	189	105	157	62%	16%	280	329	93	346	151
Lackey, John	731	2772	149	53	209	100	198	64%	17%	249	387	109	364	147
Lamet, Dinelson	485	1941	139	54	105	56	122	62%	20%	211	228	63	265	104
Latos, Mat	70	262	10	8	22	7	21	60%	19%	30	30	13	34	15
Law, Derek	168	638	35	14	44	26	45	61%	17%	71	75	25	82	35
Lawrence, Casey	264	973	52	25	86	45	54	62%	19%	95	127	30	124	55
Layne, Tommy	63	245	9	8	21	13	11	60%	11%	28	30	11	30	13
Leake, Mike	782	2779	130	37	322	131	147	66%	13%	282	396	80	351	124
LeBlanc, Wade	283	1068	54	17	95	47	65	64%	16%	113	149	32	138	48
Leclerc, Jose	200	865	60	40	38	10	48	56%	29%	89	93	42	117	64
Leiter, Mark	395	1510	84	31	132	55	83	63%	15%	155	205	48	197	73
Leone, Dominic	279	1082	81	23	70	31	73	64%	24%	119	134	40	156	56
Lester, Jon	763	3131	180	60	235	109	165	62%	18%	320	378	145	426	181
Lewicki, Artie	52	192	6	4	17	7	18	66%	13%	17	28	7	21	10
Lindblom, Josh	51	186	10	3	15	8	15	68%	15%	18	25	6	25	7
Liriano, Francisco	439	1742	85	53	131	59	102	59%	17%	197	192	83	220	119
Lively, Ben	372	1411	52	24	108	50	125	64%	12%	150	186	40	178	70
Locke, Jeff	152	574	26	15	52	22	37	64%	13%	59	77	18	74	29
Logan, Boone	91	363	28	9	26	12	14	64%	29%	39	39	18	49	20
Lopez, Reynaldo	207	767	30	14	49	35	78	64%	14%	82	98	21	91	32
Lorenzen, Michael	361	1366	80	34	130	48	60	62%	18%	167	152	47	169	80
Loup, Aaron	265	1008	64	29	85	32	42	64%	16%	97	130	33	145	52
Lugo, Seth	436	1641	85	25	135	76	108	65%	14%	177	206	51	212	73
Lyles, Jordan	324	1259	55	22	119	46	76	62%	15%	143	154	50	158	68
Lynn, Lance	776	3151	153	78	231	104	190	60%	16%	346	352	147	398	206
Lyons, Tyler	220	902	68	20	52	26	46	65%	17%	83	121	27	144	40
Maddox, Austin	67	267	14	2	13	7	30	68%	21%	27	32	10	37	11
Madson, Ryan	219	855	67	9	75	33	29	66%	21%	89	103	31	128	41
Maeda, Kenta	557	2181	140	34	140	80	147	66%	20%	200	294	72	304	93
Mahle, Tyler	92	369	14	11	32	9	20	61%	12%	35	50	17	53	24
Manaea, Sean	692	2688	140	55	212	99	170	65%	18%	274	344	95	364	139
Marinez, Jhan	262	970	45	26	91	36	53	62%	18%	121	107	37	120	60
Marquez, German	701	2661	147	49	221	106	162	66%	15%	277	349	84	351	128
Martes, Francis	249	1027	69	31	60	31	50	62%	21%	98	127	53	151	68
Martinez, Carlos	858	3132	217	71	283	104	165	65%	17%	349	407	79	427	132
Martinez, Nick	478	1815	67	28	157	80	140	63%	11%	193	237	62	220	92
Maton, Phil	180	730	46	14	53	26	38	65%	21%	70	93	23	112	31
Matz, Steven	298	1170	48	19	105	48	70	64%	12%	120	153	44	158	60
Maurer, Brandon	267	1027	59	19	72	49	66	66%	16%	85	147	40	139	55
Mayza, Tim	79	340	27	4	20	14	14	65%	26%	21	52	13	51	17
McAllister, Zach	249	975	66	21	57	34	68	67%	15%	89	128	35	140	46
McCarthy, Brandon	384	1447	72	27	116	68	92	66%	13%	133	214	49	201	64
McCarthy, Kevin	196	715	27	13	84	29	42	66%	14%	73	93	23	87	31
McCullers Jr., Lance	512	2014	132	40	198	62	63	63%	20%	226	229	69	278	97
McFarland, T.J.	241	829	29	17	126	29	33	63%	11%	109	93	23	86	40
McGee, Jake	229	944	58	16	62	29	62	66%	15%	85	123	36	129	43
McGowan, Dustin	330	1176	64	27	118	44	70	61%	19%	131	140	45	143	71
McGrath, Kyle	75	307	16	6	15	10	28	65%	17%	34	38	10	45	16
McGuire, Deck	56	210	11	2	12	5	25	63%	15%	23	27	10	29	13
McHugh, Collin	271	1080	62	20	59	40	81	63%	20%	100	144	42	150	60
Mejia, Adalberto	443	1752	85	44	120	69	116	63%	17%	190	200	60	227	92
Melancon, Mark	130	502	29	6	49	20	24	64%	16%	57	59	14	64	27
Mendez, Yohander	52	191	7	3	14	8	19	63%	14%	24	20	6	22	8
Mengden, Daniel	169	650	29	9	51	25	54	62%	14%	71	82	17	81	33
Merritt, Ryan	89	320	7	4	42	20	16	66%	9%	22	56	11	40	13
Meyer, Alex	292	1169	75	42	79	38	53	59%	18%	137	133	46	156	79
Middleton, Keynan	246	977	63	18	62	35	68	65%	26%	103	121	36	147	52

Pitcher Analysis
Pitchers with 50+ Batters Faced in 2017

Pitcher	BF	Pitches	K	BB	GB	LD	FB	Str%	S/Str	1-0	0-1	Full	2 Strike	3 Ball
Miley, Wade	728	3054	142	93	242	110	129	58%	15%	335	319	166	377	244
Miller, Andrew	244	987	95	21	47	29	43	68%	25%	89	135	23	159	33
Miller, Shelby	99	386	20	12	29	14	23	60%	17%	44	41	17	49	27
Milner, Hoby	139	542	22	16	43	19	33	61%	17%	54	69	24	71	35
Milone, Tommy	221	866	38	14	59	40	67	64%	13%	73	124	33	105	50
Minaya, Juan	184	809	51	20	38	24	46	60%	20%	80	90	37	112	50
Minor, Mike	307	1192	88	22	81	31	79	66%	19%	104	166	39	169	57
Minter, A.J.	60	248	26	2	12	7	13	70%	27%	22	30	5	42	5
Miranda, Ariel	678	2662	137	63	147	75	242	63%	19%	264	341	103	354	144
Mitchell, Bryan	153	535	17	13	66	31	25	62%	11%	64	68	12	59	24
Montas, Frankie	152	620	36	20	33	22	38	63%	19%	57	77	26	82	38
Montero, Rafael	550	2219	114	67	169	68	114	62%	17%	198	287	103	298	146
Montgomery, Jordan	649	2527	144	51	183	80	187	64%	19%	259	335	76	336	124
Montgomery, Mike	540	2075	100	55	214	62	94	61%	15%	215	254	80	262	127
Moore, Andrew	243	919	31	8	58	45	99	67%	13%	86	131	34	119	44
Moore, Matt	790	2875	148	67	209	113	232	65%	14%	304	379	90	385	135
Morgan, Adam	229	906	63	18	67	30	50	67%	25%	86	121	28	138	42
Morin, Mike	93	344	16	5	33	11	24	68%	20%	27	52	11	49	16
Morris, Bryan	94	320	15	11	31	15	19	61%	21%	36	44	11	37	21
Morrow, Brandon	170	612	50	9	49	26	34	69%	24%	50	88	22	86	29
Morton, Charlie	617	2387	163	50	200	74	112	64%	18%	233	313	81	337	122
Motte, Jason	166	652	27	20	52	17	46	62%	13%	57	83	25	86	37
Moylan, Peter	243	902	46	25	102	27	38	64%	18%	90	125	28	123	43
Musgrove, Joe	462	1760	98	28	146	69	110	68%	18%	167	250	45	243	68
Neal, Zach	65	244	10	1	22	11	21	67%	16%	25	31	9	32	12
Nelson, Jimmy	728	2752	199	48	234	104	127	67%	18%	279	363	73	399	116
Neris, Hector	320	1232	86	26	64	45	87	67%	25%	126	150	46	178	61
Neshek, Pat	235	940	69	6	56	27	71	74%	19%	68	138	23	148	29
Neverauskas, Dovydas	105	422	17	8	33	17	27	62%	12%	41	56	12	53	20
Newcomb, Sean	456	1831	108	57	121	63	92	63%	19%	184	221	75	267	107
Nicasio, Juan	291	1227	72	20	88	42	63	67%	17%	94	167	45	168	55
Nicolino, Justin	229	840	26	20	83	48	47	65%	11%	87	112	28	106	43
Nola, Aaron	693	2665	184	49	227	87	142	66%	14%	247	365	79	383	124
Nolasco, Ricky	787	3091	143	58	230	119	224	61%	19%	314	388	115	397	168
Norris, Bud	267	1103	74	27	73	40	50	62%	21%	122	120	50	153	69
Norris, Daniel	460	1827	86	44	125	71	126	60%	16%	203	210	59	227	102
Nova, Ivan	785	2677	131	36	270	138	183	66%	13%	275	382	67	340	94
Nuno, Vidal	77	305	13	10	22	5	26	62%	13%	28	39	12	38	19
Oberg, Scott	265	992	55	24	104	35	43	65%	20%	82	148	31	136	53
O'Day, Darren	240	1011	76	24	65	20	51	65%	18%	81	134	39	151	53
Odorizzi, Jake	604	2627	127	61	125	90	193	61%	19%	279	281	128	350	164
O'Flaherty, Eric	83	301	15	9	27	10	20	62%	21%	33	44	6	34	16
O'Grady, Chris	145	552	30	18	32	23	39	60%	14%	59	70	24	71	38
Oh, Seung Hwan	264	1030	54	15	54	41	93	70%	20%	89	144	24	158	37
Okert, Steven	118	461	22	11	24	17	38	64%	16%	47	60	13	59	20
Olson, Tyler	77	300	18	6	27	11	13	68%	15%	28	43	9	43	13
Osich, Josh	201	761	43	27	57	27	43	63%	15%	79	98	27	105	45
Osuna, Roberto	249	961	83	9	73	27	52	67%	26%	90	133	30	149	36
Otero, Dan	242	849	38	9	122	47	23	70%	11%	75	125	24	112	33
Ottavino, Adam	243	1052	63	39	51	30	56	56%	17%	128	103	46	133	80
Overton, Dillon	103	374	11	4	35	16	35	67%	14%	34	57	10	46	15
Pagan, Emilio	196	717	56	8	29	27	74	69%	21%	73	99	21	108	27
Paredes, Eduardo	92	356	17	6	30	12	22	65%	14%	36	41	13	47	18
Parker, Blake	254	1068	86	16	70	27	52	65%	22%	102	130	46	166	51
Paulino, David	128	529	34	7	25	16	42	62%	18%	53	68	14	68	25
Paxton, James	552	2268	156	37	158	79	115	65%	20%	197	324	77	325	99
Pazos, James	240	929	65	24	74	32	39	64%	20%	87	126	29	127	44
Peacock, Brad	546	2248	161	57	141	60	122	63%	20%	202	292	91	332	123
Pelfrey, Mike	546	2291	79	62	198	62	134	59%	11%	220	265	110	281	161
Pena, Felix	155	605	37	18	34	14	50	61%	20%	78	61	18	74	32
Peralta, Wandy	263	1017	57	24	97	29	53	63%	25%	115	118	42	142	62
Peralta, Wily	269	1121	52	32	81	40	61	61%	15%	97	147	47	144	67
Perdomo, Luis	716	2558	118	65	320	89	109	62%	15%	276	351	83	303	138
Perez, Martin	811	3097	115	63	293	154	173	62%	12%	330	393	108	368	172
Perez, Oliver	143	604	39	12	29	16	43	66%	17%	49	84	22	89	31
Peters, Dillon	139	519	27	19	57	14	19	60%	17%	58	60	21	69	35
Petit, Yusmeiro	354	1347	101	18	76	42	113	67%	17%	125	184	31	202	48
Petricka, Jake	122	481	26	6	42	23	24	64%	12%	46	66	13	63	21
Phelps, David	238	971	62	26	66	37	43	63%	15%	91	123	43	138	57

Pitcher Analysis
Pitchers with 50+ Batters Faced in 2017

Pitcher	BF	Pitches	K	BB	GB	LD	FB	Str%	S/Str	Counts 1-0	0-1	Full	2 Strike	3 Ball
Pill, Tyler	99	390	16	10	33	17	17	61%	14%	42	41	20	50	25
Pineda, Michael	410	1553	92	21	148	54	89	66%	19%	144	227	47	212	63
Pinto, Ricardo	147	576	25	17	44	21	35	61%	16%	66	63	19	68	33
Pivetta, Nick	584	2439	140	57	165	75	137	63%	15%	239	303	85	338	129
Pomeranz, Drew	740	3080	174	69	209	106	169	62%	16%	294	379	126	413	168
Porcello, Rick	885	3383	181	48	253	135	258	67%	15%	290	491	99	469	132
Pounders, Brooks	54	214	12	5	9	9	17	62%	20%	26	22	7	29	10
Pressly, Ryan	252	890	61	19	84	28	54	66%	19%	101	113	20	120	38
Price, David	317	1253	76	24	85	46	82	65%	20%	101	175	48	171	59
Pruitt, Austin	371	1333	66	22	132	57	88	66%	15%	127	188	44	183	57
Quackenbush, Kevin	125	510	23	16	37	20	26	61%	13%	52	59	21	71	28
Qualls, Chad	72	252	11	5	31	6	17	63%	17%	33	28	8	30	11
Quintana, Jose	790	3176	207	61	226	105	174	62%	14%	257	441	143	418	178
Ramirez, Carlos	58	215	14	3	11	7	22	64%	25%	29	22	8	33	11
Ramirez, Erasmo	539	1998	109	31	170	73	150	66%	16%	205	260	57	255	88
Ramirez, JC	620	2303	105	49	234	83	138	64%	14%	248	310	80	291	111
Ramirez, Jose	258	1031	56	29	76	19	70	64%	19%	107	124	34	140	58
Ramirez, Neil	153	641	44	21	27	17	43	62%	20%	62	84	29	96	39
Ramos, AJ	258	1104	72	34	59	30	58	60%	20%	123	116	54	157	73
Ramos, Edubray	256	1007	75	28	56	40	54	64%	18%	99	131	36	141	55
Ravin, Josh	71	278	19	9	16	7	19	66%	21%	26	35	10	42	15
Ray, Robbie	665	2715	218	71	147	71	147	63%	23%	265	341	108	397	162
Reed, Addison	306	1188	76	15	87	38	88	71%	20%	98	174	35	185	47
Reed, Cody	79	331	17	19	26	6	11	54%	26%	47	27	13	38	31
Richard, Clayton	858	3045	151	59	372	132	124	65%	14%	317	421	70	387	134
Richards, Garrett	108	427	27	7	39	12	21	65%	19%	43	55	14	63	17
Rios, Yacksel	73	277	17	9	16	8	22	61%	19%	41	25	7	35	15
Rivero, Felipe	300	1167	88	20	99	35	53	68%	24%	124	139	32	182	46
Roark, Tanner	776	3216	166	64	256	105	170	63%	17%	319	388	125	431	160
Robertson, David	264	1032	98	23	65	22	51	65%	27%	104	130	38	164	55
Robles, Hansel	247	949	60	29	51	33	66	61%	15%	110	115	34	120	60
Rodney, Fernando	231	978	65	26	70	21	43	61%	21%	94	114	37	133	60
Rodon, Carlos	297	1181	76	31	82	41	63	61%	18%	131	141	41	157	68
Rodriguez, Eduardo	582	2462	150	50	131	83	161	64%	19%	224	301	116	357	148
Rodriguez, Francisco	118	433	23	11	25	16	42	63%	16%	54	50	16	53	20
Rodriguez, Joely	134	499	18	15	55	17	22	62%	15%	47	63	17	60	33
Rodriguez, Ricardo	60	242	11	4	14	13	16	68%	12%	18	40	6	33	9
Rogers, Taylor	237	870	49	21	72	39	49	65%	14%	93	112	30	122	44
Romano, Sal	384	1498	73	37	131	52	77	62%	15%	172	179	44	197	76
Romero, Enny	245	1026	65	23	60	29	65	64%	21%	111	107	40	147	57
Romo, Sergio	224	912	59	19	54	29	62	63%	24%	90	112	39	130	50
Rondon, Bruce	76	328	22	10	17	13	13	63%	20%	38	30	19	50	24
Rondon, Hector	237	999	69	20	70	24	51	65%	19%	86	131	36	139	53
Rosenthal, Trevor	202	883	76	20	42	29	32	66%	25%	84	103	35	147	42
Ross, Joe	323	1204	68	20	84	55	85	66%	16%	114	167	35	159	53
Ross, Tyson	238	968	36	37	73	29	54	56%	13%	127	91	39	108	72
Rowley, Chris	89	309	11	10	26	13	27	62%	22%	39	35	13	40	18
Rusin, Chris	340	1202	71	19	141	41	59	65%	20%	138	157	35	157	51
Ryu, Hyun-Jin	541	2128	116	45	166	84	118	63%	18%	211	274	93	283	118
Rzepczynski, Marc	137	502	25	20	63	14	13	59%	20%	65	50	16	60	33
Sabathia, CC	623	2340	120	50	218	97	122	64%	15%	241	298	100	297	128
Salas, Fernando	263	1038	56	22	85	29	65	67%	20%	101	136	34	154	50
Salazar, Danny	439	1814	145	44	96	62	87	65%	26%	173	227	71	271	95
Sale, Chris	851	3428	308	43	188	99	199	68%	23%	282	480	105	536	134
Samardzija, Jeff	847	3273	205	32	248	132	218	67%	16%	296	467	89	463	119
Sanchez, Aaron	167	613	24	20	58	29	35	59%	11%	68	83	14	65	38
Sanchez, Angel	54	208	10	1	18	8	17	64%	20%	19	28	5	26	9
Sanchez, Anibal	482	1855	104	29	121	84	135	63%	16%	187	246	72	243	98
Santana, Edgar	81	296	20	12	21	12	14	64%	22%	31	41	8	43	18
Santana, Ervin	864	3235	167	61	255	101	263	63%	17%	311	459	116	402	161
Santiago, Hector	311	1236	51	31	67	41	114	62%	13%	138	139	50	160	70
Santos, Luis	68	274	16	4	16	7	25	64%	23%	34	31	7	37	11
Saupold, Warwick	280	1088	44	31	85	40	72	60%	14%	110	135	50	134	70
Scahill, Rob	97	344	10	10	40	14	20	64%	11%	38	42	12	40	20
Scherzer, Max	780	3111	268	55	160	74	204	68%	24%	273	431	97	496	128
Schugel, A.J.	136	496	27	14	49	18	26	63%	13%	43	69	17	64	29
Scott, Robby	141	594	31	13	40	15	39	61%	19%	74	57	26	86	34
Scribner, Troy	99	383	18	10	17	11	41	62%	16%	41	52	10	48	22
Senzatela, Antonio	564	2217	102	47	203	88	114	62%	12%	213	285	88	287	123

Pitcher Analysis
Pitchers with 50+ Batters Faced in 2017

Pitcher	BF	Pitches	K	BB	GB	LD	FB	Str%	S/Str	1-0	0-1	Full	2 Strike	3 Ball
Severino, Luis	783	3082	230	51	248	92	150	67%	20%	273	431	114	456	141
Sewald, Paul	275	1132	69	21	57	39	81	65%	19%	106	148	34	166	53
Shackelford, Kevin	135	517	38	13	47	10	24	66%	25%	56	64	18	72	23
Shaw, Bryan	312	1208	73	22	119	47	47	65%	19%	130	145	43	170	58
Sherriff, Ryan	60	218	15	4	26	4	10	68%	15%	20	30	4	31	8
Shields, James	516	2016	103	53	136	65	155	61%	17%	214	244	77	265	121
Shipley, Braden	122	487	18	15	37	14	36	59%	13%	49	59	25	62	35
Shoemaker, Matt	326	1264	69	28	85	33	103	64%	18%	117	173	45	173	62
Shreve, Chasen	198	851	58	25	43	20	52	60%	25%	80	104	42	118	64
Siegrist, Kevin	172	681	43	22	38	27	41	62%	18%	73	83	27	90	39
Sims, Luke	255	985	44	23	67	40	69	63%	14%	81	143	39	133	58
Sipp, Tony	165	664	39	16	52	14	40	63%	21%	75	77	27	95	36
Skaggs, Tyler	365	1394	76	28	105	54	92	65%	13%	138	182	46	192	68
Skoglund, Eric	93	387	14	12	24	16	26	63%	10%	36	49	13	49	19
Slegers, Aaron	63	231	9	6	22	7	18	61%	15%	30	23	8	30	11
Smith, Caleb	86	341	18	10	16	17	25	62%	22%	37	40	11	44	17
Smith, Chris	250	970	31	22	72	39	84	58%	14%	114	104	44	112	68
Smith, Joe	214	801	71	10	65	28	38	70%	17%	69	111	24	122	29
Smith, Josh	151	586	25	15	51	20	40	63%	12%	68	67	22	69	31
Smoker, Josh	267	1057	68	32	69	36	56	63%	21%	108	132	44	162	65
Snell, Blake	547	2278	119	59	158	66	136	60%	18%	253	251	95	287	148
Socolovich, Miguel	87	325	14	4	22	14	30	67%	16%	30	49	6	45	10
Solis, Sammy	112	439	28	13	33	11	27	60%	15%	49	52	19	60	31
Soria, Joakim	232	993	64	20	80	32	34	63%	22%	97	122	39	141	53
Stammen, Craig	329	1285	74	28	114	38	69	64%	18%	110	178	44	175	64
Stanek, Ryne	95	423	29	12	19	12	23	61%	25%	36	53	19	56	29
Steckenrider, Drew	151	699	54	18	33	16	30	66%	22%	47	95	29	111	37
Stephens, Jackson	101	414	21	9	25	12	32	64%	14%	44	49	13	56	20
Stephenson, Robert	383	1464	86	53	87	50	95	60%	22%	172	161	54	191	93
Stewart, Brock	147	585	29	19	39	18	38	63%	17%	55	79	14	72	29
Storen, Drew	246	909	48	23	82	29	53	66%	14%	90	123	26	126	47
Strahm, Matt	154	647	37	22	33	17	39	61%	17%	60	81	20	84	40
Straily, Dan	769	3085	170	60	178	104	239	65%	20%	291	403	110	446	155
Strasburg, Stephen	701	2742	204	47	204	83	149	67%	20%	249	369	81	407	114
Stratton, Chris	256	1042	51	28	74	49	50	62%	15%	105	129	40	141	60
Strickland, Hunter	268	984	58	19	69	30	79	64%	18%	99	131	24	133	49
Stripling, Ross	304	1179	74	19	102	45	60	65%	18%	104	162	36	154	49
Stroman, Marcus	834	3143	164	62	372	109	118	63%	16%	345	396	106	418	160
Strop, Pedro	250	1019	65	26	90	16	46	60%	26%	114	111	45	142	67
Stumpf, Daniel	160	656	33	15	47	22	41	61%	13%	59	80	24	79	41
Suarez, Albert	135	550	34	11	40	19	29	63%	19%	55	69	22	82	31
Suter, Brent	341	1283	64	22	113	60	77	68%	14%	110	194	30	172	46
Swarzak, Anthony	303	1259	91	22	82	29	76	66%	22%	101	171	41	197	60
Syndergaard, Noah	124	459	34	3	49	16	20	67%	21%	54	57	15	66	19
Taillon, Jameson	587	2322	125	46	190	101	111	64%	14%	217	283	91	311	126
Tanaka, Masahiro	752	2810	194	41	249	92	165	67%	23%	265	394	97	399	127
Taylor, Ben	80	366	18	9	14	13	26	65%	13%	30	42	13	48	17
Tazawa, Junichi	238	962	38	22	62	43	69	63%	14%	85	128	42	125	59
Teheran, Julio	812	3074	151	72	228	115	227	65%	15%	291	432	94	403	147
Tepera, Ryan	319	1275	81	31	82	35	80	62%	22%	117	162	54	176	74
Tepesch, Nick	80	300	9	9	21	10	26	60%	10%	34	38	10	39	17
Therrien, Jesen	86	313	10	7	33	17	18	63%	18%	31	44	7	34	15
Thompson, Jake	210	803	35	22	68	23	56	60%	13%	92	102	26	92	47
Tillman, Chris	444	1795	63	51	128	76	120	57%	13%	232	178	79	193	129
Tomlin, Josh	585	2088	109	14	179	105	168	68%	13%	183	325	57	275	75
Tonkin, Michael	97	397	24	12	21	13	26	62%	21%	38	51	19	56	24
Torres, Carlos	322	1248	56	33	102	45	76	63%	16%	139	144	40	171	63
Torres, Jose	284	1071	63	16	69	36	90	65%	18%	122	132	27	148	39
Treinen, Blake	325	1194	74	25	128	41	50	64%	21%	130	159	41	163	61
Triggs, Andrew	283	1084	50	19	104	37	68	61%	17%	120	130	44	136	59
Tuivailala, Samuel	171	643	34	11	60	24	39	67%	15%	58	93	13	94	26
Turley, Nik	89	323	13	8	28	15	22	59%	12%	45	34	12	35	23
Turner, Jacob	170	631	23	15	56	24	49	62%	10%	74	78	27	73	36
Uehara, Koji	178	676	50	12	28	29	57	70%	24%	48	106	12	108	20
Urena, Jose	724	2882	113	64	224	97	199	61%	14%	295	345	125	351	184
Urias, Julio	102	412	11	14	29	20	23	62%	15%	48	42	17	54	27
Valdez, Cesar	140	500	21	11	46	28	33	64%	18%	55	65	15	60	21
Valdez, Jose	80	294	17	5	18	10	27	64%	18%	36	30	7	37	13
Vargas, Jason	756	2925	134	58	223	107	224	63%	16%	258	421	111	391	153

Pitcher Analysis
Pitchers with 50+ Batters Faced in 2017

Pitcher	BF	Pitches	K	BB	GB	LD	FB	Str%	S/Str	Counts 1-0	0-1	Full	2 Strike	3 Ball
Velasquez, Vince	315	1269	68	34	88	47	72	65%	15%	115	171	41	170	62
Velazquez, Hector	96	382	19	7	30	16	24	67%	13%	38	47	18	51	19
VerHagen, Drew	145	532	25	9	56	17	38	62%	15%	62	69	11	61	25
Verlander, Justin	849	3531	219	72	184	131	235	66%	17%	323	446	127	506	173
Vincent, Nick	262	945	50	13	60	40	92	71%	15%	82	136	24	137	38
Vizcaino, Arodys	235	861	64	21	57	24	67	66%	23%	93	115	20	126	33
Volquez, Edinson	397	1516	81	53	114	54	81	61%	16%	173	180	48	182	94
Volstad, Chris	76	269	10	5	37	7	16	64%	6%	26	43	9	33	13
Wacha, Michael	701	2690	158	55	228	100	147	65%	15%	237	366	91	365	127
Wainwright, Adam	546	2155	96	45	186	98	110	63%	13%	217	271	80	288	116
Walker, Taijuan	684	2743	146	61	225	84	151	63%	15%	280	333	102	372	157
Warren, Adam	223	939	54	15	66	26	59	62%	17%	105	103	42	121	54
Watson, Tony	291	1010	53	20	97	46	60	70%	19%	92	150	21	145	38
Weaver, Jered	191	671	23	12	61	33	56	63%	13%	69	96	21	80	31
Weaver, Luke	252	1046	72	17	79	38	43	66%	15%	102	131	35	154	47
Wheeler, Zack	386	1561	81	40	122	58	77	63%	15%	150	190	64	211	93
Whitley, Chase	238	829	43	16	57	41	76	67%	21%	81	119	24	112	39
Wilhelmsen, Tom	113	453	17	12	41	12	30	58%	11%	67	41	14	50	29
Wilk, Adam	74	302	8	9	21	9	24	60%	15%	33	32	18	37	22
Williams, Trevor	642	2423	117	52	216	93	141	64%	14%	249	306	85	312	121
Wilson, Alex	260	951	42	15	82	45	70	65%	14%	112	104	29	117	40
Wilson, Justin	248	1130	80	35	49	24	58	61%	21%	115	118	48	159	71
Wilson, Tyler	70	265	9	4	21	17	17	61%	15%	33	30	8	30	15
Winkler, Dan	53	234	18	6	10	5	13	63%	19%	17	30	14	34	15
Wisler, Matt	153	557	22	13	36	22	55	63%	15%	64	76	12	71	24
Wittgren, Nick	182	753	43	13	42	30	54	64%	18%	62	103	24	102	35
Wojciechowski, Asher	279	1106	64	19	53	36	93	65%	17%	95	150	32	152	51
Wood, Alex	614	2260	151	38	219	83	111	67%	18%	198	339	67	329	94
Wood, Blake	332	1283	84	33	111	49	53	62%	19%	138	161	48	177	72
Wood, Travis	436	1711	65	45	113	68	136	64%	10%	165	222	63	216	90
Woodruff, Brandon	184	716	32	14	63	25	45	66%	14%	70	96	21	93	34
Workman, Brandon	162	609	37	11	48	21	42	65%	17%	68	72	22	80	30
Worley, Vance	333	1238	50	30	119	57	69	63%	9%	133	159	49	153	80
Wright, Daniel	85	314	11	8	19	19	25	58%	15%	38	36	7	30	17
Wright, Mike	109	417	28	7	31	16	24	65%	17%	38	55	15	62	17
Wright, Steven	114	383	13	5	39	22	33	66%	10%	46	51	10	46	15
Yacabonis, Jimmy	90	337	8	14	33	9	26	59%	10%	39	39	11	40	20
Yates, Kirby	231	965	88	19	35	18	68	67%	27%	85	123	30	147	45
Ynoa, Gabriel	147	540	26	8	42	15	53	64%	16%	62	69	18	76	25
Ynoa, Michael	141	594	23	22	32	18	41	56%	17%	70	64	28	67	46
Young, Chris	148	536	22	14	45	27	39	64%	19%	59	70	18	71	31
Zastryzny, Rob	62	247	11	7	21	9	12	59%	14%	29	27	7	28	12
Ziegler, Brad	211	697	26	16	102	32	25	64%	14%	75	95	22	78	36
Zimmermann, Jordan	713	2644	103	44	183	137	232	66%	13%	230	387	92	352	121
Zych, Tony	173	639	35	21	55	23	33	64%	16%	77	77	20	87	35

Pitchers' Repertoires

Brian Reiff

Are we supposed to give a spoiler alert for something that was revealed just under 400 pages ago? I suppose I should, since this isn't exactly your typical book. We're sure there are many of you who are skipping between pages rather than starting from the beginning. Which, on second thought, makes this exactly like a typical book.

Anyway. Spoiler Alert!!! We're about to reveal who our top-ranked starting pitcher is, which was presented back in the Starting Pitcher Rankings section on page 41. Ben Jedlovec wrote a great lead-in to that section, and you should absolutely read it before coming back here

By our methodology, Corey Kluber is the best starting pitcher in baseball right now. He has been consistently great since he won the AL Cy Young Award in 2014, but his numbers in 2017 were even better than they were then. Part of that success is due to his pitch repertoire—he threw three different pitches at least 24 percent of the time, one of only 10 pitchers with at least 1,000 total pitches to do so.

When hitters came up to bat against Kluber, they would have little idea of which pitch they were going to see. Before this season, he had thrown his fastball on over half his pitches, but that changed this year. He threw fastballs just 42 percent of the time, instead leaning more on his curveball which he threw on a career-high 27 percent of pitches, up from 20 percent last season. He continued to use his cutter as well, throwing it just under a quarter of the time while also mixing in an occasional changeup.

All of that and more is available in this section. Here, you'll find complete information on how often every pitcher threw each type of pitch in his repertoire.

If you've read previous editions of this Handbook, you know that Bill James is a fan of the "Pitch Mix Index", which measures how varied a pitcher's repertoire is. This year, the pitcher who used the deepest pitch mix was Jesse Chavez, who threw five different pitches at least eight percent of the time. Meanwhile, Zach

Britton was on the opposite end of that spectrum, throwing his fastball 95 percent of the time and a slider the other 5 percent.

This section includes a pitcher's average fastball velocity as well. It will surprise absolutely nobody that Aroldis Chapman led all pitchers in 2017 in average fastball velocity (he averaged 100.1 miles per hour). But who was the slowest? As it turns out, the answer is Jon Jay, who averaged 58.8 mph on his "fast" ball. That doesn't really tell you much, though—among pitchers, it was Brad Ziegler, who reached just 83.1 mph on average.

As of last year, this section also includes the dates of any and every Tommy John surgery a pitcher has had. This can be useful for many different avenues of research, including looking at a pitcher's velocity before and after his surgery (which you can do using the data in the next section). There are many other ways to use that data and the other data in this section as well, but I leave that up to you.

Player	Tommy John SX	Fastball Velocity	Fastball	Slider	Change	Cutter	Curve	Splitter	Other
Abad,Fernando	-	91.5	52%	-	22%	-	25%	-	
Adams,Austin	-	94.9	53%	47%	-	-	-	-	
Adleman,Tim	-	90.1	58%	-	20%	6%	15%	-	
Albers,Andrew	Jan `09	87.8	65%	19%	8%	-	8%	-	
Albers,Matt	-	93.3	68%	28%	4%	-	<1%	-	
Alburquerque,Al	Jan `05	93.5	46%	54%	-	-	-	-	
Alcantara,Raul	May `14	95.1	62%	-	19%	17%	2%	-	
Alcantara,Sandy	-	98.3	65%	22%	13%	-	-	-	
Alcantara,Victor	-	92.1	75%	12%	13%	-	-	-	
Alexander,Scott	-	93.2	94%	5%	2%	-	-	-	
Allen,Cody	Jan `08	94.3	55%	-	-	-	45%	-	
Almonte,Miguel	-	95.5	52%	20%	8%	-	20%	-	
Altavilla,Dan	-	96.7	63%	37%	<1%	-	-	-	
Alvarado,Jose	-	98.2	76%	6%	<1%	-	18%	-	
Alvarez,Dario	-	92.1	34%	61%	-	5%	-	-	
Alvarez,Henderson	-	91.4	64%	11%	22%	-	3%	-	
Alvarez,Jose	-	91.1	56%	19%	17%	4%	4%	-	
Anderson,Brett	July `11	90.5	53%	21%	14%	-	12%	-	
Anderson,Chase	-	93.1	53%	-	16%	13%	18%	-	
Anderson,Drew	Apr `15	93.6	49%	26%	14%	-	11%	-	
Anderson,Tyler	-	92.0	48%	-	30%	22%	<1%	-	
Andriese,Matt	-	92.1	44%	-	28%	10%	17%	-	
Aoki,Nori	-	75.2	100%	-	-	-	-	-	
Aquino,Jayson	-	88.9	47%	24%	21%	-	8%	-	
Arano,Victor	-	93.4	44%	52%	3%	-	<1%	-	
Archer,Chris	-	95.5	48%	44%	8%	-	-	-	
Armstrong,Shawn	-	93.2	64%	-	-	22%	14%	-	
Arrieta,Jake	-	92.1	64%	-	8%	14%	14%	-	
Arroyo,Bronson	July `14	84.0	41%	26%	9%	-	24%	-	
Asher,Alec	Jan `06	90.9	47%	-	8%	30%	14%	-	
Astin,Barrett	-	92.0	67%	-	-	20%	-	14%	
Avilan,Luis	-	92.7	42%	-	49%	-	9%	-	
Axford,John	Nov `03	95.0	68%	16%	-	-	16%	-	
Aybar,Erick	-	71.1	92%	-	8%	-	-	-	
Baez,Pedro	-	97.0	73%	17%	11%	-	-	-	
Bailey,Andrew	May `05	90.8	59%	-	-	34%	7%	-	
Bailey,Homer	May `15	93.5	57%	20%	-	-	4%	19%	
Banda,Anthony	-	94.2	63%	-	18%	-	18%	-	
Barbato,Johnny	-	94.1	54%	17%	-	-	22%	7%	
Barnes,Danny	-	92.0	67%	5%	28%	-	-	-	
Barnes,Jacob	-	96.7	55%	<1%	-	44%	-	-	
Barnes,Matt	-	95.2	55%	13%	-	-	31%	-	
Barnette,Tony	-	92.9	31%	-	-	46%	18%	5%	
Barraclough,Kyle	-	94.8	54%	41%	4%	-	-	-	
Barrett,Jake	-	96.1	69%	27%	-	-	-	4%	
Bass,Anthony	-	92.3	63%	16%	-	-	-	21%	
Bastardo,Antonio	-	90.5	68%	26%	6%	-	-	-	
Bauer,Trevor	-	94.0	49%	4%	6%	9%	30%	1%	
Baumann,Buddy	-	89.9	81%	16%	3%	-	-	-	
Beato,Pedro	Apr `04	88.6	80%	-	-	-	10%	10%	
Beck,Chris	-	94.6	57%	26%	-	5%	1%	10%	
Bedrosian,Cam	May `11	93.9	58%	42%	-	-	-	-	
Belisle,Matt	-	90.5	53%	33%	2%	-	12%	-	
Beliveau,Jeff	-	90.0	66%	-	7%	9%	18%	-	
Bell,Chad	Apr `13	93.0	58%	19%	12%	-	11%	-	
Benoit,Joaquin	-	94.8	59%	13%	28%	-	-	-	
Bergman,Christian	-	88.3	49%	28%	11%	-	12%	-	

Player	Tommy John SX	Fastball Velocity	Fastball	Slider	Change	Cutter	Curve	Splitter	Other
Berrios,Jose	-	93.5	61%	-	9%	-	30%	-	
Betances,Dellin	-	98.5	46%	54%	-	-	-	-	
Bethancourt,Christian	-	94.1	88%	9%	3%	-	-	-	
Bettis,Chad	-	90.2	51%	-	27%	7%	15%	-	
Biagini,Joe	Jan `10	93.8	53%	11%	14%	-	22%	-	
Bibens-Dirkx,Austin	-	90.3	42%	7%	16%	29%	6%	-	
Blach,Ty	-	90.1	60%	5%	24%	-	11%	-	
Blackburn,Paul	-	90.2	55%	26%	9%	-	9%	-	
Blair,Aaron	-	91.8	53%	25%	12%	-	9%	-	
Blanco,Andres	-	71.8	100%	-	-	-	-	-	
Blanton,Joe	-	90.2	39%	35%	15%	-	12%	-	
Blazek,Michael	-	92.7	59%	25%	11%	-	5%	-	
Bleier,Richard	-	89.1	61%	4%	7%	28%	-	-	
Blevins,Jerry	-	88.9	46%	-	4%	-	50%	-	
Bolsinger,Mike	-	89.3	48%	16%	4%	-	33%	-	
Bonilla,Lisalverto	Apr `15	92.1	50%	-	27%	-	23%	-	
Boshers,Buddy	-	90.7	49%	-	16%	-	35%	-	
Bowman,Matt	-	91.0	64%	12%	-	-	-	24%	
Boxberger,Brad	-	92.3	65%	12%	23%	-	-	-	
Boyd,Matt	-	92.0	51%	11%	21%	-	18%	-	
Boyer,Blaine	-	94.2	56%	37%	-	-	8%	-	
Brach,Brad	-	95.0	63%	14%	22%	<1%	-	-	
Bracho,Silvino	-	93.6	51%	22%	27%	-	-	-	
Bradford,Chasen	-	90.6	71%	25%	4%	-	-	-	
Bradley,Archie	-	96.4	76%	-	<1%	3%	21%	-	
Brady,Michael	-	91.3	35%	-	12%	47%	6%	-	
Brantly,Rob	-	65.6	100%	-	-	-	-	-	
Brault,Steven	-	91.9	72%	13%	13%	-	2%	-	
Brebbia,John	-	94.2	57%	41%	2%	-	-	-	
Breslow,Craig	-	89.4	62%	-	18%	-	19%	-	
Brice,Austin	-	93.8	62%	24%	1%	-	13%	-	
Bridwell,Parker	-	92.4	44%	21%	10%	26%	-	-	
Britton,Zach	-	96.1	95%	5%	-	-	-	-	
Brothers,Rex	-	95.4	65%	34%	<1%	-	-	-	
Broxton,Jonathan	-	94.2	65%	31%	4%	-	-	-	
Buchanan,Jake	-	88.9	51%	27%	10%	-	12%	-	
Buchholz,Clay	-	90.6	40%	-	15%	25%	20%	-	
Buchter,Ryan	-	92.8	78%	6%	-	9%	7%	-	
Buehler,Walker	Aug `15	98.1	70%	7%	-	-	23%	-	
Bumgarner,Madison	-	91.0	43%	36%	6%	-	16%	-	
Bummer,Aaron	Aug `15	93.2	61%	37%	2%	-	-	-	
Bundy,Dylan	June `13	92.2	54%	22%	14%	-	10%	-	
Busenitz,Alan	-	95.7	70%	-	<1%	-	29%	-	
Bush,Matt	Jan `07	97.5	69%	18%	-	-	13%	-	
Butler,Eddie	-	93.4	66%	8%	10%	-	16%	-	
Cahill,Trevor	-	90.9	47%	8%	22%	<1%	22%	-	
Cain,Matt	-	89.3	52%	8%	13%	4%	23%	-	
Callahan,Jamie	-	95.9	63%	26%	-	-	-	11%	
Campos,Leonel	Oct `11	92.9	50%	47%	4%	-	-	-	
Capps,Carter	Mar `16	92.9	62%	37%	1%	-	-	-	
Carle,Shane	-	93.6	53%	25%	8%	-	14%	-	
Carrasco,Carlos	Sept `11	94.3	48%	20%	17%	-	15%	-	
Cashner,Andrew	-	93.4	65%	12%	14%	-	8%	-	
Casilla,Santiago	-	93.9	63%	11%	5%	-	21%	-	
Castillo,Fabio	-	97.1	50%	40%	10%	-	-	-	
Castillo,Luis	-	97.5	62%	15%	23%	-	-	-	
Castro,Miguel	-	95.6	61%	28%	11%	-	-	-	
Castro,Simon	Jan `14	93.6	73%	26%	<1%	-	-	-	

432

Player	Tommy John SX	Fastball Velocity	Pitch Repertoire						
			Fastball	Slider	Change	Cutter	Curve	Splitter	Other
Cecil,Brett	-	91.5	41%	-	14%	17%	28%	-	Knuckleball <1%
Cedeno,Xavier	-	-	-	-	-	79%	21%	-	
Cervenka,Hunter	-	93.1	32%	39%	-	-	30%	-	
Cessa,Luis	-	95.6	42%	31%	19%	-	8%	-	
Chacin,Alejandro	-	88.5	47%	36%	16%	-	-	-	
Chacin,Jhoulys	-	91.4	54%	35%	6%	<1%	5%	-	
Chafin,Andrew	Jan `10	93.7	61%	38%	<1%	-	-	-	
Chapman,Aroldis	-	100.1	77%	20%	4%	-	-	-	
Chatwood,Tyler	July `14 Jan `06	94.7	64%	-	5%	21%	11%	-	
Chavez,Jesse	-	92.0	33%	16%	14%	28%	8%	-	
Chen,Wei-Yin	Jan `06	90.9	65%	9%	13%	-	13%	-	
Cingrani,Tony	-	94.4	80%	12%	-	-	-	8%	
Cishek,Steve	-	90.3	50%	49%	1%	-	-	-	
Claiborne,Preston	-	91.8	59%	29%	12%	-	-	-	
Claudio,Alex	-	86.7	57%	13%	30%	-	-	-	
Clevinger,Mike	Aug `12	92.5	53%	19%	16%	-	12%	-	
Clippard,Tyler	-	91.1	38%	-	36%	10%	-	16%	
Cloyd,Tyler	May `16	90.3	71%	-	7%	21%	-	-	
Cobb,Alex	May `15	91.7	51%	-	14%	-	34%	-	
Cole,A.J.	-	93.1	55%	23%	7%	-	15%	-	
Cole,Gerrit	-	96.0	60%	17%	11%	-	12%	-	
Cole,Taylor	-	92.8	59%	-	41%	-	-	-	
Collmenter,Josh	-	84.5	55%	-	33%	-	12%	-	
Colome,Alex	-	95.1	33%	-	-	67%	-	-	
Colon,Bartolo	-	87.8	83%	7%	10%	<1%	-	-	
Conley,Adam	-	89.5	64%	16%	18%	-	1%	-	
Corbin,Patrick	Mar `14	92.4	53%	38%	9%	-	-	-	
Cosart,Jarred	-	92.8	68%	9%	9%	-	13%	-	
Cotton,Jharel	-	93.0	47%	-	22%	23%	9%	-	
Coulombe,Daniel	Mar `11	91.0	30%	32%	-	-	37%	-	
Covey,Dylan	-	92.6	60%	17%	-	-	12%	11%	
Crichton,Stefan	-	94.3	67%	33%	-	-	-	-	
Crick,Kyle	-	95.5	75%	20%	5%	-	-	-	
Crockett,Kyle	-	87.9	71%	29%	-	-	-	-	
Cueto,Johnny	-	91.3	51%	7%	19%	20%	3%	-	
Cuevas,William	-	88.7	60%	-	13%	-	27%	-	
Curtis,Zac	-	91.2	56%	22%	22%	-	-	-	
Curtiss,John	Aug `12	95.2	77%	21%	2%	-	-	-	
Danish,Tyler	-	89.7	54%	11%	15%	13%	8%	-	
Darvish,Yu	Mar `15	94.2	52%	25%	2%	15%	6%	<1%	
Davies,Zach	-	89.7	58%	-	14%	13%	15%	-	
Davis,J.D.	-	91.4	94%	-	-	-	6%	-	
Davis,Rookie	-	92.4	63%	20%	5%	-	10%	1%	
Davis,Wade	-	94.3	48%	-	<1%	31%	21%	-	
Dayton,Grant	Aug `17	91.2	84%	-	-	-	16%	-	
De Jong,Chase	-	90.1	59%	14%	12%	-	14%	-	
De La Rosa,Jorge	June `11	93.7	48%	-	34%	13%	5%	-	
De La Rosa,Rubby	Aug `11	97.1	53%	46%	<1%	-	-	-	
De Leon,Jose	-	91.7	60%	16%	16%	-	7%	-	
deGrom,Jacob	Jan `10	95.2	55%	23%	12%	-	10%	-	
Delgado,Randall	-	94.2	57%	14%	28%	-	2%	-	
Dermody,Matt	-	92.1	57%	42%	1%	-	-	-	
Descalso,Daniel	-	78.8	81%	-	-	-	19%	-	
Despaigne,Odrisamer	-	92.3	53%	<1%	12%	29%	4%	-	
Devenski,Chris	-	94.1	40%	22%	38%	-	-	-	
Diaz,Dayan	Jan `09	94.3	60%	24%	17%	-	-	-	
Diaz,Edwin	-	97.3	68%	31%	<1%	-	-	-	

Player	Tommy John SX	Fastball Velocity	Fastball	Slider	Change	Cutter	Curve	Splitter	Other
Diaz,Jairo	Mar '16	97.3	77%	13%	-	-	9%	-	
Diaz,Jumbo	Jan '07	96.9	47%	53%	-	-	-	<1%	
Diaz,Miguel	-	95.9	65%	18%	14%	-	3%	-	
Dickey,R.A.	-	83.4	18%	-	3%	-	<1%	-	Knuckleball 78%
Diekman,Jake	-	94.7	68%	32%	-	-	-	-	
Doolittle,Sean	-	94.7	88%	5%	7%	-	-	-	
Drake,Oliver	-	91.9	51%	<1%	-	-	-	48%	
Duensing,Brian	Mar '04	91.9	49%	24%	13%	-	13%	-	
Duffey,Tyler	-	92.1	60%	-	5%	-	35%	-	
Duffy,Danny	June '12	92.8	47%	29%	23%	-	<1%	-	
Duke,Zach	Oct '16	88.0	57%	13%	4%	20%	6%	-	
Dull,Ryan	-	91.3	50%	41%	10%	-	-	-	
Dunn,Mike	-	92.4	52%	41%	-	-	7%	-	
Dyson,Sam	Nov '10	95.1	64%	4%	15%	17%	-	-	
Edgin,Josh	Mar '15	91.3	44%	20%	2%	34%	-	-	
Edwards Jr.,Carl	-	95.2	70%	-	<1%	-	30%	-	
Eflin,Zach	-	92.7	68%	13%	7%	-	11%	-	
Eickhoff,Jerad	-	90.4	50%	17%	<1%	-	33%	-	
Elias,Roenis	-	92.3	55%	-	27%	-	18%	-	
Ellington,Brian	Sept '07	98.2	76%	15%	9%	-	-	-	
Enns,Dietrich	June '14	89.6	64%	21%	15%	-	-	-	
Esch,Jake	-	90.5	67%	22%	-	-	11%	-	
Espino,Paolo	-	88.6	56%	13%	8%	-	23%	-	
Estevez,Carlos	-	97.1	74%	18%	8%	-	-	-	
Estrada,Marco	-	89.9	54%	-	32%	7%	8%	-	
Familia,Jeurys	-	95.9	82%	16%	-	-	-	2%	
Faria,Jake	-	91.8	54%	24%	18%	-	5%	-	
Farmer,Buck	-	91.7	61%	18%	17%	-	4%	-	
Farquhar,Danny	-	93.1	56%	-	34%	-	11%	-	
Farrell,Luke	-	91.0	57%	26%	-	-	8%	9%	
Fedde,Erick	June '14	92.9	61%	2%	14%	9%	13%	-	
Feldman,Scott	Jan '03	89.5	33%	-	-	36%	27%	4%	
Feliz,Michael	-	96.2	72%	27%	1%	-	-	-	
Feliz,Neftali	Aug '12	96.2	63%	21%	15%	<1%	-	-	
Ferrell,Jeff	-	93.5	61%	-	39%	-	-	-	
Fields,Josh	-	95.4	79%	-	3%	-	18%	-	
Fien,Casey	-	93.5	38%	15%	-	46%	-	-	
Fiers,Mike	-	89.7	48%	5%	18%	9%	19%	-	
Finnegan,Brandon	-	93.0	69%	12%	18%	-	-	-	
Fister,Doug	-	89.8	60%	17%	7%	-	17%	-	
Flaherty,Jack	-	93.2	55%	25%	6%	-	14%	-	
Flexen,Chris	July '14	92.4	60%	23%	10%	-	6%	-	
Floro,Dylan	-	91.3	68%	-	5%	28%	-	-	
Flynn,Brian	-	92.6	66%	34%	-	-	-	-	
Foltynewicz,Mike	-	95.3	61%	21%	6%	-	12%	-	
Font,Wilmer	Oct '10	93.8	68%	21%	-	-	9%	2%	
Frankoff,Seth	-	91.5	54%	-	3%	30%	14%	-	
Freeland,Kyle	-	92.0	64%	4%	7%	25%	-	-	
Freeman,Mike	-	70.1	100%	-	-	-	-	-	
Freeman,Sam	Mar '10	95.1	57%	22%	21%	-	-	-	
Fried,Max	Aug '14	92.4	63%	-	10%	-	27%	-	
Frieri,Ernesto	-	94.2	60%	35%	6%	-	-	-	
Fry,Jace	June '15 June '12	93.6	48%	8%	7%	20%	17%	-	
Fulmer,Carson	-	93.3	52%	-	11%	25%	12%	-	
Fulmer,Michael	-	95.8	59%	21%	19%	-	<1%	-	
Gallardo,Yovani	-	92.2	50%	23%	9%	-	18%	-	
Gallegos,Giovanny	Jan '11	94.1	64%	31%	5%	-	<1%	-	

434

Player	Tommy John SX	Fastball Velocity	Fastball	Slider	Change	Cutter	Curve	Splitter	Other
Gant, John	-	93.0	65%	6%	20%	-	9%	-	
Garcia, Jaime	Sept `08	90.7	61%	14%	18%	-	7%	-	
Garcia, Jarlin	-	94.2	50%	32%	19%	-	-	-	
Garcia, Luis	-	97.2	63%	23%	-	-	-	14%	
Garcia, Onelki	-	93.2	62%	-	20%	-	18%	-	
Gardewine, Nick	-	94.6	74%	-	4%	22%	-	-	
Garrett, Amir	-	91.7	62%	22%	16%	-	-	-	
Garton, Ryan		92.5	54%	-	2%	32%	12%	-	
Garza, Matt		91.9	61%	22%	7%	-	10%	-	
Gausman, Kevin	-	95.0	64%	14%	2%	-	1%	18%	
Gaviglio, Sam	-	88.6	57%	21%	9%	-	13%	-	
Gearrin, Cory	Apr `14	91.7	55%	35%	11%	-	-	-	
Gee, Dillon	-	91.0	47%	22%	15%	-	16%	-	
Gennett, Scooter	-	65.8	100%	-	-	-	-	-	
German, Domingo	Mar `15	96.4	51%	-	21%	-	28%	-	
Gibson, Kyle	Sept `11	92.0	58%	18%	14%	-	10%	-	
Giles, Ken	-	98.1	53%	47%	-	-	-	-	
Gilmartin, Sean	-	89.8	60%	16%	20%	-	4%	-	
Gimenez, Chris	-	70.5	100%	-	-	-	-	-	
Giolito, Lucas	Aug `12	92.1	60%	13%	16%	-	11%	-	
Givens, Mychal	-	95.6	72%	19%	8%	-	-	-	
Glasnow, Tyler	-	94.6	65%	-	12%	-	23%	-	
Glover, Koda	Jan `11	96.5	37%	-	6%	48%	8%	-	
Godley, Zack	-	91.9	33%	-	8%	24%	36%	-	
Goeddel, Erik	Jan `07	92.5	46%	-	-	-	19%	36%	
Goforth, David	-	95.0	53%	24%	-	-	24%	-	
Gohara, Luiz	-	96.3	57%	32%	11%	-	-	-	
Goldberg, Brad	-	96.1	65%	26%	-	-	-	9%	
Gomez, Jeanmar	-	90.6	61%	13%	26%	-	-	-	
Gomez, Roberto	-	95.2	52%	28%	2%	-	19%	-	
Gonzales, Marco	Apr `16	91.5	52%	-	31%	-	17%	-	
Gonzalez, Gio	-	89.9	57%	-	19%	-	25%	-	
Gonzalez, Miguel	Mar `09	91.0	50%	21%	-	-	17%	13%	
Goody, Nick	Apr `13	91.7	52%	48%	-	-	-	-	
Gossett, Daniel	-	91.5	53%	22%	11%	-	14%	-	
Gott, Trevor	-	95.0	67%	-	6%	-	27%	-	
Grace, Matt	-	91.0	72%	24%	4%	-	-	-	
Graveman, Kendall	-	93.4	69%	6%	10%	15%	-	-	
Gray, Jon	-	96.0	57%	28%	1%	-	14%	-	
Gray, Sonny	-	93.0	55%	16%	15%	-	14%	-	
Green, Chad	-	95.8	69%	22%	<1%	8%	-	-	
Greene, Shane	May `08	95.0	56%	28%	-	14%	2%	-	
Gregerson, Luke	-	89.5	52%	46%	1%	-	-	-	
Greinke, Zack	-	91.0	48%	23%	16%	-	13%	-	
Griffin, A.J.	Apr `14	87.3	53%	5%	12%	-	30%	-	
Grilli, Jason	Jan `02	92.7	64%	34%	3%	-	-	-	
Grimm, Justin	-	94.9	56%	2%	-	-	41%	-	
Gsellman, Robert	-	92.7	63%	16%	10%	-	12%	-	
Guduan, Reymin	-	95.1	64%	36%	-	-	-	-	
Guerra, Deolis	-	91.7	39%	16%	38%	2%	5%	-	
Guerra, Javy	Jan `05	92.3	55%	29%	7%	-	9%	-	
Guerra, Junior	-	91.9	65%	16%	-	-	-	19%	
Gurka, Jason	-	91.6	43%	-	-	-	57%	-	
Gustave, Jandel	Jun `17	95.9	56%	44%	-	-	-	-	
Guthrie, Jeremy	-	91.9	64%	15%	15%	-	6%	-	
Hader, Josh	-	94.3	82%	11%	7%	-	-	-	
Hahn, Jesse	Jan `10	93.8	62%	10%	11%	-	18%	-	
Haley, Justin	-	89.9	65%	12%	14%	-	9%	-	

Player	Tommy John SX	Fastball Velocity	Fastball	Slider	Change	Cutter	Curve	Splitter	Other
Hamels,Cole	-	92.0	48%	-	21%	19%	13%	-	
Hammel,Jason	-	92.1	50%	37%	4%	-	9%	-	
Hand,Brad	-	93.5	51%	45%	<1%	-	4%	-	
Happ,J.A.	-	91.8	70%	12%	12%	-	5%	-	
Hardy,Blaine	-	89.9	45%	14%	27%	-	14%	-	
Harrell,Lucas	-	92.0	63%	-	3%	24%	10%	-	
Harris,Will	Jan `09	-	-	-	-	69%	31%	-	
Hart,Donnie	-	87.6	48%	35%	17%	-	-	-	
Harvey,Matt	Oct `13	93.8	59%	22%	11%	-	7%	-	
Hatcher,Chris	-	94.6	51%	25%	21%	1%	1%	-	
Hauschild,Mike	-	92.0	57%	22%	6%	-	-	14%	
Heaney,Andrew	July `16	91.9	61%	16%	22%	-	-	-	
Heller,Ben	-	94.7	51%	33%	16%	-	-	-	
Hellickson,Jeremy	-	90.2	46%	-	29%	12%	13%	-	
Hembree,Heath	-	95.4	53%	38%	-	-	9%	-	
Hendricks,Kyle	-	85.8	64%	-	28%	-	8%	-	
Hendriks,Liam	-	94.7	74%	22%	<1%	-	3%	-	
Hernandez,Ariel	-	98.0	67%	-	6%	-	27%	-	
Hernandez,David	Apr `14	93.7	52%	25%	-	-	23%	-	
Hernandez,Felix	-	90.5	44%	8%	26%	-	21%	-	
Herrera,Kelvin	-	97.5	67%	16%	17%	-	-	-	
Herrera,Ronald	-	91.6	38%	-	38%	18%	7%	-	
Heston,Chris	-	87.0	68%	18%	7%	-	7%	-	
Hildenberger,Trevor	-	88.8	51%	15%	34%	-	-	-	
Hill,Rich	June `11	89.0	54%	4%	<1%	4%	37%	-	
Hoffman,Jeff	May `14	94.4	67%	9%	6%	-	18%	-	
Holder,Jonathan	-	92.7	38%	-	2%	33%	28%	-	
Holland,Derek	-	91.1	55%	14%	9%	-	22%	-	
Holland,Greg	Oct `15	93.5	44%	49%	-	-	6%	<1%	
Holmberg,David	-	87.6	48%	18%	19%	-	14%	-	
Hoover,J.J.	-	92.6	58%	35%	1%	-	6%	-	
House,T.J.	-	88.5	55%	28%	5%	-	13%	-	
Howell,J.P.	-	85.2	63%	-	9%	-	28%	-	
Hoyt,James	-	93.4	40%	50%	-	-	-	10%	
Hu,Chih-Wei	-	93.5	59%	8%	34%	-	-	-	
Hudson,Daniel	June `13 July `12	95.6	60%	26%	14%	-	-	-	
Hughes,Jared	-	93.5	77%	21%	2%	-	-	-	
Hughes,Phil	-	89.7	46%	-	13%	21%	20%	-	
Hunter,Tommy	-	96.3	42%	<1%	-	32%	26%	-	
Hursh,Jason	Aug `11	95.0	71%	17%	-	-	-	12%	
Iglesias,Raisel	-	96.4	57%	30%	13%	-	-	-	
Infante,Gregory	-	95.5	58%	23%	2%	-	17%	-	
Iwakuma,Hisashi	-	85.1	42%	31%	-	3%	7%	17%	
Jackson,Edwin	-	93.5	49%	24%	6%	13%	8%	-	
Jackson,Luke	-	94.7	52%	30%	<1%	-	18%	-	
Jankowski,Jordan	-	91.1	53%	31%	-	-	16%	-	
Jansen,Kenley	-	93.3	92%	8%	-	-	-	-	
Jay,Jon	-	57.3	100%	-	-	-	-	-	
Jaye,Myles	-	89.6	61%	20%	7%	-	12%	-	
Jeffress,Jeremy	-	94.5	66%	-	15%	-	19%	-	
Jennings,Dan	-	91.8	52%	48%	-	-	-	-	
Jimenez,Joe	-	95.3	63%	25%	12%	-	-	-	
Jimenez,Ubaldo	-	90.5	56%	19%	3%	<1%	4%	18%	
Johnson,Brian	-	87.3	56%	11%	5%	-	28%	-	
Johnson,Jim	-	93.4	68%	-	5%	-	27%	-	
Johnson,Pierce	-	92.2	45%	-	-	-	55%	-	
Jones,Nate	July `14	97.2	52%	47%	<1%	-	-	-	

Player	Tommy John SX	Fastball Velocity	Fastball	Slider	Change	Cutter	Curve	Splitter	Other
Jorge,Felix	-	92.4	50%	15%	23%	7%	5%	-	
Jungmann,Taylor	-	91.1	91%	-	-	-	9%	-	
Junis,Jakob	-	91.2	55%	32%	7%	-	6%	-	
Kahnle,Tommy	-	97.9	66%	12%	22%	-	-	-	
Karns,Nathan	-	92.9	49%	-	14%	-	36%	-	
Kela,Keone	-	96.5	58%	-	2%	-	40%	-	
Kelley,Shawn	Sept `10 Jan `03	91.8	59%	41%	-	-	-	-	
Kelly,Joe	-	99.0	64%	15%	2%	-	19%	-	
Kendrick,Kyle	-	91.5	51%	-	14%	35%	-	-	
Kennedy,Ian	-	91.9	62%	-	11%	12%	16%	-	
Kershaw,Clayton	-	92.7	47%	35%	1%	-	17%	-	
Keuchel,Dallas	-	88.7	58%	19%	13%	10%	-	-	
Kimbrel,Craig	-	98.3	69%	-	-	-	31%	-	
Kintzler,Brandon	-	93.4	82%	14%	4%	-	-	-	
Kittredge,Andrew	-	94.5	29%	71%	-	-	-	-	
Kluber,Corey	-	92.6	42%	-	6%	24%	27%	-	
Knebel,Corey	-	97.4	72%	-	-	-	28%	-	
Koch,Matt	-	91.6	56%	-	11%	33%	-	-	
Koehler,Tom	-	92.9	52%	20%	6%	-	21%	-	
Kolarek,Adam	-	88.1	88%	5%	7%	-	-	-	
Kontos,George	July `09	91.0	25%	19%	2%	53%	2%	-	
Krol,Ian	-	93.3	51%	-	1%	39%	9%	-	
Kuhl,Chad		95.5	64%	20%	10%	-	6%	-	
Labourt,Jairo	-	93.0	31%	63%	6%	-	-	-	
Lackey,John	Nov `11	90.9	52%	35%	5%	-	8%	-	
Lamet,Dinelson	-	95.0	55%	40%	5%	-	-	-	
Latos,Mat	-	91.3	60%	29%	8%	-	3%	-	
Law,Derek	June `14	93.7	54%	21%	7%	-	18%	-	
Lawrence,Casey	-	91.2	59%	23%	17%	-	1%	-	
Layne,Tommy	-	88.0	29%	16%	-	36%	4%	15%	
Leake,Mike	-	90.1	46%	14%	11%	22%	7%	-	
Leathersich,Jack	July `15	91.8	83%	-	10%	-	7%	-	
LeBlanc,Wade	-	87.3	36%	6%	27%	26%	5%	-	
Leclerc,Jose	-	95.8	51%	10%	26%	-	6%	7%	
Lee,Zach	-	90.2	62%	28%	5%	-	5%	-	
Leiter,Mark	-	91.0	55%	4%	11%	4%	9%	18%	
Leon,Arcenio	-	95.8	74%	26%	-	-	-	-	
Leone,Dominic	-	94.4	54%	10%	-	36%	-	-	
Lester,Jon	-	91.1	51%	-	9%	28%	13%	-	
Lewicki,Artie	-	92.2	57%	20%	2%	-	21%	-	
Liberatore,Adam	Jan `09	92.4	65%	4%	31%	-	-	-	
Lindblom,Josh	-	90.8	54%	-	7%	22%	9%	8%	
Liriano,Francisco	Nov `06	92.9	50%	33%	17%	-	-	-	
Lively,Ben	-	91.4	61%	13%	6%	-	20%	-	
Lloyd,Kyle	-	85.8	47%	16%	-	-	-	37%	
Locke,Jeff	-	90.5	59%	-	24%	-	17%	-	
Logan,Boone	-	93.9	40%	60%	-	-	-	-	
Lopez,Jorge	-	94.8	74%	-	20%	-	6%	-	
Lopez,Reynaldo	-	94.5	61%	2%	24%	-	13%	-	
Lorenzen,Michael	-	96.4	51%	16%	2%	20%	11%	-	
Loup,Aaron	-	91.9	65%	10%	14%	10%	-	-	
Lucas,Josh	-	92.6	44%	56%	-	-	-	-	
Lugo,Seth	-	91.1	56%	15%	11%	1%	17%	-	
Lyles,Jordan	-	93.8	56%	19%	5%	-	20%	-	
Lynn,Lance	Nov `15	91.8	81%	12%	3%	-	5%	-	
Lyons,Tyler	-	90.0	43%	52%	5%	-	-	-	
Machado,Andres	-	95.8	58%	23%	19%	-	-	-	

Player	Tommy John SX	Fastball Velocity	Pitch Repertoire						
			Fastball	Slider	Change	Cutter	Curve	Splitter	Other
Machi,Jean	-	92.7	53%	11%	-	-	-	36%	
Maddox,Austin	-	95.2	64%	6%	30%	-	-	-	
Madson,Ryan	Apr `12	95.2	66%	-	15%	<1%	19%	-	
Maeda,Kenta	-	91.5	43%	25%	9%	8%	14%	-	
Magnifico,Damien	-	95.2	45%	55%	-	-	-	-	
Mahle,Tyler	-	92.9	66%	25%	7%	-	2%	-	
Manaea,Sean	-	91.6	58%	18%	24%	-	-	-	
Maness,Seth	-	88.0	62%	17%	21%	-	-	-	
Maples,Dillon	-	96.8	43%	52%	-	-	5%	-	
Marinez,Jhan	-	94.8	67%	22%	10%	-	-	-	
Marks,Justin	-	89.5	58%	-	23%	-	19%	-	
Marquez,German	-	95.0	65%	4%	5%	-	25%	-	
Marshall,Evan	-	93.9	66%	-	16%	-	18%	-	
Martes,Francis	-	95.6	55%	-	8%	-	37%	-	
Martin,Cody	-	87.3	40%	24%	10%	-	26%	-	
Martin,Kyle	-	93.1	45%	17%	38%	-	-	-	
Martin,Leonys	-	86.5	88%	12%	-	-	-	-	
Martinez,Carlos	-	95.6	56%	27%	16%	-	<1%	-	
Martinez,Michael	-	79.5	100%	-	-	-	-	-	
Martinez,Nick	-	92.5	55%	-	12%	14%	19%	-	
Maton,Phil	-	93.0	76%	23%	1%	-	-	-	
Matz,Steven	May `10	93.1	59%	4%	13%	-	23%	-	
Maurer,Brandon	-	96.6	56%	29%	14%	-	-	-	
Mayers,Mike	-	94.2	53%	43%	4%	-	-	-	
Mayza,Tim	-	93.9	49%	51%	-	-	-	-	
Mazzoni,Cory	-	93.5	65%	28%	-	-	-	7%	
McAllister,Zach	-	95.3	80%	<1%	-	-	20%	-	
McCarthy,Brandon	Apr `15	93.1	44%	1%	3%	31%	22%	-	
McCarthy,Kevin	-	93.0	61%	19%	20%	-	-	-	
McCullers Jr.,Lance	-	94.2	40%	<1%	12%	-	47%	-	
McFarland,T.J.	-	91.6	73%	14%	12%	-	-	-	
McGee,Jake	July `08	94.9	94%	5%	-	-	2%	-	
McGowan,Dustin	May `04	93.8	59%	34%	7%	-	-	-	
McGowan,Kevin	-	92.6	42%	36%	22%	-	-	-	
McGrath,Kyle	-	86.5	51%	-	42%	-	7%	-	
McGuire,Deck	-	92.7	64%	18%	11%	-	7%	-	
McHugh,Collin	-	90.2	51%	17%	1%	10%	20%	-	
Mejia,Adalberto	-	92.5	56%	14%	18%	-	12%	-	
Melancon,Mark	Oct `06	92.2	6%	-	<1%	69%	25%	-	
Mella,Keury	-	95.9	73%	18%	9%	-	-	-	
Melville,Tim	Oct `12	94.3	63%	19%	4%	-	14%	-	
Mendez,Yohander	-	92.5	61%	23%	15%	-	1%	-	
Mengden,Daniel	-	92.1	56%	-	13%	17%	14%	-	
Merritt,Ryan	-	87.3	30%	-	26%	28%	16%	-	
Meyer,Alex	-	95.7	58%	-	2%	-	40%	-	
Middleton,Keynan	-	96.8	63%	35%	2%	-	-	-	
Miley,Wade	-	91.0	53%	14%	11%	11%	10%	-	
Miller,Andrew	-	94.0	42%	58%	-	-	-	-	
Miller,Shelby	May `17	94.9	58%	-	<1%	25%	16%	-	
Milner,Hoby	-	89.0	66%	23%	11%	-	-	-	
Milone,Tommy	-	88.0	45%	5%	24%	12%	14%	-	
Minaya,Juan	-	94.2	63%	18%	2%	-	17%	-	
Minor,Mike	-	94.4	46%	36%	10%	-	8%	-	
Minter,A.J.	Mar `15	95.9	51%	-	-	49%	-	-	
Miranda,Ariel	-	92.1	58%	5%	16%	-	-	21%	
Mitchell,Bryan	-	96.0	48%	-	<1%	21%	31%	-	
Moll,Sam	-	92.4	58%	34%	8%	-	-	-	
Montas,Frankie	-	97.7	66%	28%	6%	-	-	-	

Player	Tommy John SX	Fastball Velocity	Pitch Repertoire						
			Fastball	Slider	Change	Cutter	Curve	Splitter	Other
Montero,Miguel	-	79.9	96%	-	4%	-	-	-	
Montero,Rafael	-	93.7	55%	25%	20%	-	-	-	
Montgomery,Jordan	-	92.0	42%	13%	19%	-	26%	-	
Montgomery,Mike	-	92.2	53%	-	12%	11%	24%	-	
Moore,Andrew	-	90.8	52%	13%	19%	-	15%	-	
Moore,Matt	Apr `14	92.0	52%	-	16%	15%	18%	-	
Moreland,Mitch	-	90.1	71%	-	-	7%	21%	-	
Moreno,Diego	Apr `12	95.2	43%	15%	39%	-	3%	-	
Morgan,Adam	-	94.4	33%	32%	26%	-	9%	-	
Morin,Mike	-	90.5	38%	28%	34%	-	-	-	
Moronta,Reyes	-	95.7	53%	31%	-	-	16%	-	
Morris,Akeel	-	93.1	55%	10%	34%	-	-	-	
Morris,Bryan	Sept `06	92.9	56%	12%	-	33%	-	-	
Morrow,Brandon	-	97.7	59%	19%	-	22%	-	-	
Morton,Charlie	June `12	95.0	54%	-	6%	11%	28%	-	
Motte,Jason	May `13	93.3	47%	2%	-	51%	-	-	
Moya,Gabriel	-	90.8	46%	14%	40%	-	-	-	
Moylan,Peter	Apr `14 / May `08	90.3	50%	47%	3%	-	-	-	
Mujica,Edward	-	91.7	31%	7%	-	-	-	62%	
Musgrove,Joe	-	92.9	48%	28%	10%	5%	8%	-	
Neal,Zach	-	90.1	61%	20%	14%	-	5%	-	
Nelson,Jimmy	-	93.9	61%	16%	3%	-	20%	-	
Neris,Hector	-	94.7	49%	<1%	-	-	-	51%	
Neshek,Pat	Nov `08	90.3	45%	52%	3%	-	-	-	
Neverauskas,Dovydas	-	97.0	59%	-	<1%	18%	23%	-	
Newcomb,Sean	-	93.7	63%	4%	11%	-	22%	-	
Nicasio,Juan	-	95.4	72%	27%	1%	-	-	-	
Nicholas,Brett	-	60.9	100%	-	-	-	-	-	
Nicolino,Justin	-	90.8	53%	-	20%	10%	17%	-	
Nola,Aaron	-	92.0	54%	-	16%	-	31%	-	
Nolasco,Ricky	-	90.9	48%	27%	-	-	9%	15%	
Norris,Bud	-	94.1	45%	21%	<1%	34%	-	-	
Norris,Daniel	-	93.2	55%	23%	13%	-	10%	-	
Nova,Ivan	Apr `14	92.8	68%	-	10%	-	22%	-	
Nuno,Vidal	-	89.4	33%	8%	7%	43%	8%	-	
O'Day,Darren	-	87.7	54%	46%	-	-	-	-	
O'Flaherty,Eric	May `13	90.4	63%	37%	-	-	-	-	
O'Grady,Chris	-	87.3	41%	-	14%	38%	8%	-	
Oberg,Scott	Jan `11	96.3	57%	35%	9%	-	-	-	
Odorizzi,Jake	-	91.6	49%	11%	23%	12%	6%	-	
Oh,Seung Hwan	Jan `01	92.9	62%	29%	-	-	2%	7%	
Okert,Steven	-	91.9	51%	23%	4%	21%	-	-	
Olson,Tyler	-	89.1	40%	25%	19%	-	17%	-	
Osich,Josh	Jan `10	95.3	55%	-	9%	9%	27%	-	
Osuna,Roberto	July `13	94.6	48%	22%	4%	25%	-	-	
Otero,Dan	Jan `09	90.0	80%	10%	10%	-	-	-	
Ottavino,Adam	May `15	94.4	50%	46%	-	3%	-	-	
Overton,Dillon	July `13	89.2	56%	-	32%	-	12%	-	
Pagan,Emilio	-	93.6	68%	29%	2%	-	-	-	
Paredes,Eduardo	-	93.2	63%	25%	12%	-	-	-	
Paredes,Edward	-	90.6	27%	63%	10%	-	-	-	
Parker,Blake	-	93.5	60%	-	-	-	8%	32%	
Paulino,David	July `13	92.6	46%	22%	15%	-	17%	-	
Paxton,James	-	95.4	65%	-	3%	10%	21%	-	
Pazos,James	-	95.5	74%	26%	-	-	-	-	
Peacock,Brad	-	92.1	51%	38%	4%	-	7%	-	
Pelfrey,Mike	May `12	91.8	59%	11%	-	-	15%	15%	

Player	Tommy John SX	Fastball Velocity	Fastball	Slider	Change	Cutter	Curve	Splitter	Other
Pena,Felix	-	94.3	66%	27%	7%	-	-	-	
Peralta,Wandy	-	96.5	53%	28%	19%	-	-	-	
Peralta,Wily	Jan `07	96.0	59%	35%	3%	-	3%	-	
Perdomo,Luis	-	94.2	63%	32%	6%	-	-	-	
Perez,Hernan	-	71.7	100%	-	-	-	-	-	
Perez,Martin	May `14	93.1	59%	10%	20%	-	11%	-	
Perez,Oliver	-	93.0	57%	43%	-	-	-	-	
Perkins,Glen	-	90.3	67%	33%	-	-	-	-	
Peters,Dillon	July `14	91.4	50%	-	13%	-	37%	-	
Petit,Yusmeiro	-	89.6	48%	15%	17%	-	20%	-	
Petricka,Jake	-	94.2	70%	7%	23%	-	-	-	
Phelps,David	-	94.3	52%	-	<1%	28%	19%	-	
Pill,Tyler	-	89.1	54%	23%	14%	<1%	9%	-	
Pineda,Michael	July `17	93.9	49%	38%	14%	-	-	-	
Pinto,Ricardo	-	95.4	58%	14%	28%	-	-	-	
Pivetta,Nick	-	94.4	66%	15%	4%	-	15%	-	
Plawecki,Kevin	-	78.9	98%	-	2%	-	-	-	
Pomeranz,Drew	-	91.3	55%	-	1%	6%	37%	-	
Porcello,Rick	-	91.1	60%	17%	8%	-	15%	-	
Pounders,Brooks	Sept `13	92.6	53%	41%	3%	-	3%	-	
Povse,Max	-	94.6	71%	-	18%	-	11%	-	
Pressly,Ryan	-	95.8	55%	18%	-	-	27%	-	
Price,David	-	94.3	59%	-	14%	21%	6%	-	
Pruitt,Austin	-	91.6	43%	-	14%	28%	15%	-	
Putnam,Zach	June `17	90.7	40%	-	-	9%	-	51%	
Quackenbush,Kevin	-	90.7	59%	16%	-	-	24%	<1%	
Qualls,Chad	-	91.2	71%	28%	-	-	-	1%	
Quintana,Jose	-	92.1	63%	-	9%	-	28%	-	
Ramirez,Carlos	-	92.1	48%	52%	-	-	-	-	
Ramirez,Erasmo	-	91.6	44%	10%	20%	25%	<1%	-	
Ramirez,JC	-	95.5	51%	33%	-	-	16%	<1%	
Ramirez,Jose	-	97.1	63%	19%	18%	-	-	-	
Ramirez,Neil	-	93.1	49%	32%	<1%	-	19%	-	
Ramirez,Noe	-	89.8	34%	28%	38%	-	-	-	
Ramos,AJ	Apr `08	92.3	37%	43%	17%	-	2%	-	
Ramos,Edubray	-	94.4	42%	57%	<1%	-	-	-	
Ravin,Josh	-	96.2	58%	39%	3%	-	-	-	
Ray,Robbie	-	94.3	59%	18%	<1%	-	22%	-	
Reed,Addison	-	92.3	67%	33%	<1%	-	-	-	
Reed,Cody	-	94.3	51%	37%	12%	-	-	-	
Reininger,Zac	Jan `15	94.8	67%	21%	2%	-	10%	-	
Rhame,Jacob	-	94.9	62%	21%	17%	-	-	-	
Richard,Clayton	-	90.7	69%	19%	11%	1%	-	-	
Richards,Garrett	-	95.8	58%	33%	-	-	8%	-	
Rios,Yacksel	-	94.0	64%	31%	-	-	<1%	4%	
Rivero,Felipe	-	98.5	61%	13%	20%	-	5%	-	
Roark,Tanner	-	92.2	57%	16%	12%	-	15%	-	
Robertson,David	-	91.6	52%	3%	1%	-	43%	-	
Robles,Hansel	-	94.9	66%	25%	9%	-	-	-	
Rodney,Fernando	Apr `04	94.6	60%	2%	39%	-	-	-	
Rodon,Carlos	-	93.1	61%	27%	12%	-	-	-	
Rodriguez,Eduardo	-	93.3	65%	11%	18%	5%	-	-	
Rodriguez,Francisco	-	89.0	56%	-	36%	-	9%	-	
Rodriguez,Joely	-	93.1	65%	35%	-	-	-	-	
Rodriguez,Ricardo	-	95.4	69%	27%	-	-	4%	-	
Rodriguez,Richard	-	93.8	66%	34%	-	-	-	-	
Roe,Chaz	-	92.8	46%	54%	-	-	-	-	
Rogers,Taylor	-	93.2	62%	-	4%	-	34%	-	

Player	Tommy John SX	Fastball Velocity	Fastball	Slider	Change	Cutter	Curve	Splitter	Other
Romano,Sal	-	95.3	63%	-	9%	-	28%	-	
Romero,Enny	-	98.0	77%	8%	4%	11%	-	-	
Romine,Andrew	-	83.3	100%	-	-	-	-	-	
Romo,Sergio	-	86.1	34%	59%	7%	-	-	-	
Rondon,Bruce	Mar `14	96.8	53%	38%	9%	-	-	-	
Rondon,Hector	Aug `10	96.4	62%	36%	3%	-	-	-	
Rosario,Randy	May `14	93.5	67%	33%	-	-	-	-	
Rosenthal,Trevor	Aug `17	98.4	75%	-	12%	13%	-	-	
Ross Jr.,Robbie	-	91.4	44%	33%	-	-	24%	-	
Ross,Joe	July `17	91.4	55%	34%	8%	-	3%	-	
Ross,Tyson	-	91.6	57%	34%	<1%	9%	-	-	
Rosscup,Zac	-	93.2	53%	44%	3%	-	-	-	
Rowley,Chris	-	89.0	56%	21%	23%	-	-	-	
Rucinski,Drew	-	92.5	40%	6%	1%	28%	-	25%	
Ruiz,Carlos	-	80.6	100%	-	-	-	-	-	
Ruiz,Jose	-	95.3	80%	20%	-	-	-	-	
Runzler,Dan	-	94.9	73%	26%	1%	-	-	-	
Rusin,Chris	-	91.4	43%	3%	27%	28%	-	-	
Ryan,Kyle	-	90.5	66%	-	6%	25%	4%	-	
Ryu,Hyun-Jin	Jan `04	90.3	37%	4%	25%	18%	16%	-	
Rzepczynski,Marc	-	92.4	60%	28%	9%	-	3%	-	
Sabathia,CC	-	90.9	24%	31%	15%	30%	-	-	
Salas,Fernando	-	91.1	63%	16%	17%	4%	-	-	
Salazar,Danny	Aug `10	95.1	60%	8%	27%	-	6%	-	
Sale,Chris	-	94.4	49%	33%	18%	-	-	-	
Samardzija,Jeff	-	94.3	47%	22%	-	9%	15%	8%	
Sanchez,Aaron	-	94.9	77%	-	7%	-	17%	-	
Sanchez,Angel	Sept `15	96.1	48%	-	17%	21%	14%	-	
Sanchez,Anibal	Jan `03	90.8	49%	12%	21%	9%	10%	-	
Santana,Edgar	-	95.1	61%	39%	<1%	-	-	-	
Santana,Ervin	-	92.9	53%	36%	11%	-	-	-	
Santiago,Hector	-	90.7	60%	2%	23%	3%	11%	-	
Santos,Luis	-	92.7	53%	27%	17%	-	3%	-	
Sardinas,Luis	-	80.5	69%	-	13%	-	19%	-	
Saupold,Warwick	-	93.0	52%	-	7%	29%	12%	-	
Scahill,Rob	-	93.9	71%	19%	-	-	9%	-	
Scheppers,Tanner	-	94.1	51%	49%	-	-	-	-	
Scherzer,Max	-	94.1	49%	29%	14%	-	8%	-	
Schugel,A.J.	-	91.9	57%	-	38%	-	5%	-	
Scott,Robby	-	88.6	60%	26%	5%	-	9%	-	
Scott,Tanner	-	98.0	70%	30%	-	-	-	-	
Scribner,Evan	-	89.3	54%	21%	-	-	24%	-	
Scribner,Troy	-	87.9	55%	17%	15%	-	13%	-	
Senzatela,Antonio	-	94.3	72%	21%	4%	-	3%	-	
Severino,Luis	-	97.6	51%	35%	13%	-	-	-	
Sewald,Paul	-	91.4	64%	32%	4%	-	-	-	
Shackelford,Kevin	-	95.2	37%	41%	<1%	22%	-	-	
Shaw,Bryan	-	-	-	12%	-	88%	-	-	
Sherfy,Jimmie	-	94.0	47%	-	3%	-	51%	-	
Sherriff,Ryan	-	91.7	70%	30%	-	-	-	-	
Shields,James	-	90.0	38%	-	11%	26%	25%	-	
Shipley,Braden	-	92.7	60%	1%	18%	-	21%	-	
Shoemaker,Matt	-	91.5	49%	19%	-	-	3%	29%	
Shreve,Chasen	-	92.7	49%	8%	-	-	-	43%	
Siegrist,Kevin	-	92.0	63%	3%	18%	-	17%	-	
Simmons,Shae	Feb `15	96.0	56%	17%	-	-	25%	3%	
Sims,Lucas	-	91.8	46%	28%	13%	-	13%	-	
Sipp,Tony	July `07	90.6	49%	40%	10%	-	-	-	

441

Player	Tommy John SX	Fastball Velocity	Fastball	Slider	Change	Cutter	Curve	Splitter	Other
Skaggs,Tyler	Aug `14	91.9	60%	-	9%	-	31%	-	
Skoglund,Eric	-	91.5	64%	16%	2%	-	19%	-	
Slania,Dan	-	92.5	50%	31%	-	-	-	19%	
Slegers,Aaron	-	90.5	65%	23%	12%	-	-	-	
Smith,Caleb	-	94.0	50%	22%	28%	-	-	-	
Smith,Carson	May `16	92.0	49%	46%	4%	-	-	-	
Smith,Chris M.	-	85.5	54%	25%	22%	-	-	-	
Smith,Chris	-	93.6	68%	28%	4%	-	-	-	
Smith,Joe	-	88.9	67%	33%	<1%	-	-	-	
Smith,Josh	Jan `07	91.2	42%	15%	3%	24%	16%	-	
Smoker,Josh	-	94.6	57%	27%	-	-	-	16%	
Snell,Blake	-	94.3	55%	13%	21%	-	10%	-	
Socolovich,Miguel	Jan `05	91.6	43%	20%	37%	-	-	-	
Solis,Sammy	Mar `12	93.9	63%	-	11%	-	26%	-	
Soria,Joakim	Apr `12 Jan `03	92.9	49%	7%	32%	-	12%	-	
Sparkman,Glenn	July `15	94.0	64%	22%	2%	-	13%	-	
Stammen,Craig	-	91.5	63%	27%	2%	-	8%	-	
Stanek,Ryne	-	98.2	67%	18%	2%	-	<1%	12%	
Steckenrider,Drew	May `13	95.3	78%	17%	5%	-	-	-	
Stephens,Jackson	-	93.4	63%	11%	5%	-	20%	-	
Stephenson,Robert	-	93.7	54%	20%	16%	-	10%	-	
Stewart,Brock	-	93.3	62%	12%	26%	-	-	-	
Storen,Drew	Sept `17	90.2	44%	39%	18%	-	-	-	
Strahm,Matt	July `13	93.6	67%	16%	9%	-	8%	-	
Straily,Dan	-	90.3	50%	30%	17%	-	3%	-	
Strasburg,Stephen	Sept `10	95.6	52%	7%	19%	-	22%	-	
Stratton,Chris	-	91.6	62%	11%	8%	-	19%	-	
Street,Huston	-	87.7	49%	44%	7%	-	-	-	
Strickland,Hunter	May `13	95.7	68%	16%	1%	15%	-	-	
Stripling,Ross	Apr `14	92.9	38%	35%	6%	-	20%	-	
Stroman,Marcus	-	93.3	62%	24%	6%	2%	6%	-	
Strop,Pedro	-	96.1	56%	28%	-	15%	-	<1%	
Stumpf,Daniel	-	93.7	60%	33%	7%	-	-	-	
Suarez,Albert	Jan `09	93.5	49%	17%	9%	-	26%	-	
Sucre,Jesus	-	81.8	74%	26%	-	-	-	-	
Suter,Brent	-	85.8	71%	12%	11%	-	6%	-	
Swarzak,Anthony	-	94.7	48%	52%	-	-	-	-	
Syndergaard,Noah	-	98.3	51%	20%	19%	-	10%	-	
Taillon,Jameson	Apr `14	95.3	64%	-	10%	-	26%	-	
Tanaka,Masahiro	-	92.2	28%	31%	-	10%	6%	26%	
Taylor,Ben	-	92.3	66%	25%	9%	-	-	-	
Tazawa,Junichi	Apr `10	92.7	57%	7%	-	-	11%	26%	
Teheran,Julio	-	91.4	65%	19%	7%	-	9%	-	
Tepera,Ryan	-	95.0	59%	1%	<1%	40%	-	-	
Tepesch,Nick	-	88.9	58%	-	3%	20%	19%	-	
Therrien,Jesen	Sept `17	92.6	53%	44%	3%	-	-	-	
Thompson,Jake	-	91.4	51%	19%	17%	9%	3%	-	
Tillman,Chris	-	90.7	50%	4%	15%	22%	8%	-	
Tolliver,Ashur	-	91.4	64%	24%	-	-	-	13%	
Tomlin,Josh	Aug `12	87.7	36%	-	5%	35%	24%	-	
Tonkin,Michael	-	94.0	65%	29%	-	5%	-	-	
Torres,Carlos	-	94.0	18%	1%	-	68%	12%	-	
Torres,Jose	-	94.9	77%	18%	5%	-	-	-	
Treinen,Blake	-	97.2	67%	25%	7%	<1%	-	-	
Triggs,Andrew	Jan `07	88.9	44%	23%	<1%	32%	-	-	
Tseng,Jen-Ho	-	92.0	52%	-	15%	14%	19%	-	
Tuivailala,Sam	-	95.4	62%	19%	-	-	19%	-	

Player	Tommy John SX	Fastball Velocity	Pitch Repertoire						
			Fastball	Slider	Change	Cutter	Curve	Splitter	Other
Turley,Nik	-	93.4	62%	11%	5%	-	22%	-	
Turner,Jacob	-	95.1	66%	12%	8%	-	14%	-	
Uehara,Koji	-	86.9	65%	-	-	2%	-	32%	
Urena,Jose	-	95.5	56%	24%	20%	-	-	-	
Urias,Julio	-	93.1	52%	13%	25%	-	9%	-	
Valdez,Cesar	-	88.1	43%	9%	48%	-	-	-	
Valdez,Jose	-	96.0	53%	45%	2%	-	-	-	
Vargas,Jason	Aug `15	85.6	47%	-	33%	-	20%	-	
Velasquez,Vince	Sept `10	93.9	68%	7%	10%	-	15%	-	
Velazquez,Hector	-	89.6	69%	5%	-	-	6%	20%	
VerHagen,Drew	June `08	94.0	60%	15%	3%	-	21%	-	
Verlander,Justin	-	95.2	58%	22%	4%	<1%	16%	-	
Verrett,Logan	-	91.0	49%	33%	13%	-	5%	-	
Vieira,Thyago	-	98.7	70%	30%	-	-	-	-	
Vincent,Nick	-	89.9	43%	-	5%	52%	<1%	-	
Vizcaino,Arodys	Mar `12	97.8	61%	-	2%	-	36%	-	
Volquez,Edinson	Aug `17 Aug `09	93.1	57%	-	25%	-	18%	-	
Volstad,Chris	-	92.1	62%	6%	14%	-	19%	-	
Wacha,Michael	-	95.1	53%	-	18%	17%	11%	-	
Wahl,Bobby	-	95.0	80%	15%	4%	-	<1%	-	
Wainwright,Adam	Feb `11	89.7	46%	-	3%	24%	27%	-	
Walker,Taijuan	-	93.8	59%	15%	14%	-	13%	-	
Wang,Wei-Chung	Jan `11	94.1	38%	59%	3%	-	-	-	
Warren,Adam	-	93.0	39%	44%	10%	-	7%	-	
Watson,Tony	-	93.6	65%	15%	20%	-	-	-	
Weaver,Jered	-	83.6	50%	14%	17%	-	18%	-	
Weaver,Luke	-	93.2	60%	-	26%	3%	11%	-	
Webb,Tyler	-	91.2	67%	19%	13%	-	-	-	
Weber,Ryan	-	89.5	65%	-	7%	-	27%	-	
Whalen,Rob	-	89.0	65%	13%	4%	-	18%	-	
Wheeler,Jason	-	88.4	59%	21%	20%	-	-	-	
Wheeler,Zack	Mar `15	94.6	62%	20%	5%	-	13%	-	
White,Tyler	-	73.7	100%	-	-	-	-	-	
Whitley,Chase	May `15	90.1	44%	26%	30%	-	<1%	-	
Wilhelmsen,Tom	-	95.3	57%	-	4%	21%	18%	-	
Wilk,Adam	-	88.1	55%	-	19%	13%	13%	-	
Wilkerson,Aaron	Aug `11	89.7	55%	18%	7%	-	20%	-	
Williams,Taylor	Aug `15	95.9	82%	18%	-	-	-	-	
Williams,Trevor	-	92.1	72%	16%	10%	-	2%	-	
Wilson,Alex	July `07	92.8	59%	7%	<1%	34%	-	-	
Wilson,Justin	-	96.0	67%	11%	<1%	22%	-	-	
Wilson,Tyler	-	90.7	72%	21%	7%	-	-	-	
Wimmers,Alex	Aug `12	91.5	48%	6%	37%	-	9%	-	
Winkler,Dan	July `14	93.6	43%	17%	6%	34%	-	-	
Wisler,Matt	-	92.6	56%	37%	2%	-	5%	-	
Wittgren,Nick	-	92.4	73%	-	9%	-	19%	-	
Wojciechowski,Asher	-	92.7	62%	27%	11%	-	-	-	
Wood,Alex	Jan `09	91.8	50%	-	25%	-	24%	-	
Wood,Blake	May `12	96.1	56%	34%	-	-	-	10%	
Wood,Hunter	-	90.0	40%	60%	-	-	-	-	
Wood,Travis	-	88.8	54%	10%	8%	22%	5%	-	
Woodruff,Brandon	-	94.3	60%	27%	13%	-	-	-	
Workman,Brandon	June `15	92.3	51%	-	-	25%	24%	-	
Worley,Vance	-	89.9	57%	-	<1%	36%	7%	-	
Wright,Daniel	-	89.9	48%	15%	20%	-	17%	-	
Wright,Mike	-	93.6	61%	31%	7%	-	<1%	-	
Wright,Steven	-	83.7	11%	-	-	-	2%	-	Knuckleball 87%

Player	Tommy John SX	Fastball Velocity	Pitch Repertoire						
			Fastball	Slider	Change	Cutter	Curve	Splitter	Other
Yacabonis,Jimmy	-	95.4	73%	23%	4%	-	-	-	
Yates,Kirby	Jan `06	94.0	62%	25%	13%	-	-	-	
Ynoa,Gabriel	-	94.3	56%	31%	7%	-	6%	-	
Ynoa,Michael	Aug `10	92.8	54%	25%	5%	-	16%	-	
Young,Chris	-	87.0	43%	57%	-	-	-	-	
Zastryzny,Rob	-	89.9	64%	-	2%	22%	11%	-	
Ziegler,Brad	-	83.1	57%	21%	22%	-	-	-	
Zimmermann,Jordan	Aug `09	92.2	54%	24%	6%	-	16%	-	
Zych,Tony	-	94.4	61%	39%	-	-	-	-	

Average Fastball Velocity by Age

Alex Vigderman

Sports coverage is so ubiquitous now that we have gotten to the point where much of the commentary is just a compilation of different clichés. One of my favorites is used in reference to aging players who have kept up a surprising level of performance in their early-to-mid-thirties. They say, "You know, Father Time is undefeated," meaning that eventually everyone's career succumbs to old age.

Pardon the use of a hitting metaphor for a pitcher, but it looks like Justin Verlander is going down swinging. He was a big part of the Tigers' turnaround in 2006 and was an above-average starter for a few years, but wasn't particularly dominant. And then in 2009 he started developing his secondary pitches, especially the slider, and he became the best pitcher in baseball, dominating through the 2012 season.

From there, Verlander's skills almost immediately deteriorated. After consistently averaging 95-plus miles per hour with his fastball in his heyday, he lost a tick on the pitch in each of the 2012, 2013, and 2014 seasons. With a declining ability to reach back for top-level velocity, he saw his strikeout rate fall and his ERA rise in each of those seasons. That brought up a lot of discussion as to whether he could adjust his approach to make do with reduced velocity, a similar situation to the pitcher who was featured in this section last season, Felix Hernandez.

And then in 2015, at age 32 and in the first season of his new contract, Verlander adjusted. Not only did he stave off further velocity decline, but he also tinkered with his pitch mix. He grew to rely even more on his slider, moving away from his changeup, a pitch that is less effective with a smaller velocity gap between it and the fastball. With that, Verlander was able to get back to the strikeout rate he maintained in his prime. After an abbreviated but encouraging 2015, he finished a close second in Cy Young voting in 2016, signaling that he was very much "back."

One might have thought that he would have ridden this approach into the sunset, but it seems that Verlander has more in the tank than we might have thought. After four seasons sitting 92-93 with his fastball, it appears the old flamethrower has returned, as his velocity has jumped back up to 95. His results weren't quite Cy Young caliber, but he was the Game 1 starter for a 100-win team in the playoffs.

Verlander's uptick in velocity is not exactly an expected occurrence for older pitchers, assuming you exclude cases of starters moving to the bullpen. We are used to pitchers in their thirties going the way of Jake Arrieta and Hisashi Iwakuma, who each lost two miles per hour off their fastball and were less effective pitchers in 2017, with Iwakuma barely pitching due to injury.

Even among pitchers who saw an increase in velocity, Verlander stands alone. There were three other thirty-plus starters whose fastballs were at least two miles per hour faster this season: Doug Fister, Marco Estrada, and Yovani Gallardo. However, outside of a few hot starts from Fister late in the summer, none of them had good seasons, with Estrada in particular enduring a fairly dramatic fall-off from what had been a late career renaissance in his first couple years in Toronto. Their struggles further underscore the impressiveness of Verlander's season, but also illustrate the rarity of success associated with velocity changes in older pitchers.

Of course, velocity changes in younger pitchers are less surprising because they haven't shown a stable baseline yet, but that doesn't make them any less interesting in many cases. On the other end of the age spectrum from Verlander are two young pitchers who went in different directions in 2017, Luis Severino and Joe Ross. Both of these young starters showed promise in their debuts in 2015, with Severino's results perhaps overstating his underlying skills at the time. In 2016 each gave evaluators cause for concern, with Severino seemingly regressing and allowing too much hard contact and Ross showing some durability concerns. Each entered 2017 with intriguing skills but major question marks.

With 2017 in the books, it is clear whose career of the two is in a better position. Severino bumped his fastball velocity up from 96 to 98, improving his strikeout, walk, and home run rates dramatically in the process. Ross lost two ticks, dropping from 93 to 91, more than doubled his home run rate allowed, and only made it halfway through the season before he was shut down and had to undergo Tommy John surgery. Sometimes the outlook for players changes that quickly.

This section contains the average fastball velocity by year, as tracked by Baseball Info Solutions, for each pitcher who has thrown at least 50 innings in at least three of the last four seasons. The listed ages reflect their age as of June 30, 2018.

Average Fastball Velocity by Age

Player	Age	10	11	12	13	14	15	16	17
Osuna, Roberto	23						96	96	95
Severino, Luis	24						95	96	98
McCullers, Lance	24						94	94	94
Nola, Aaron	25						91	90	92
Ross, Joe	25						93	93	91
Norris, Daniel	25					91	92	93	93
Rodriguez, Eduardo	25						94	93	93
Rodon, Carlos	25						93	93	93
Walker, Taijuan	25				95	95	94	94	94
Velasquez, Vince	26						95	94	94
Lorenzen, Michael	26						94	96	96
Foltynewicz, Mike	26					97	95	95	95
Ray, Robbie	26						91	93	94
Martinez, Carlos	26				97	97	95	96	96
Urena, Jose	26						94	95	95
Wacha, Michael	26				93	93	94	93	95
Stroman, Marcus	27					94	92	92	93
Perez, Martin	27			92	93	90	92	93	93
Butler, Eddie	27					93	93	93	93
Boyd, Matt	27						91	91	92
Teheran, Julio	27		93	92	92	90	91	91	91
Bauer, Trevor	27			92	93	94	93	93	94
Wood, Alex	27				92	90	89	91	92
Gausman, Kevin	27				96	95	95	95	95
Duffey, Tyler	27						90	90	92
Graveman, Kendall	27					93	91	93	93
Lyles, Jordan	27		90	92	92	91	92	93	94
Miller, Shelby	27			93	94	93	94	93	95
Giles, Ken	27					97	97	97	98
Cole, Gerrit	27				96	95	96	95	96
Robles, Hansel	27						96	95	95
Martinez, Nick	27					91	90	92	92
Maurer, Brandon	27				93	94	95	95	97
Eickhoff, Jerad	27						91	91	90
Cosart, Jarred	27				94	94	94	92	93
Conley, Adam	28						91	91	90
Ramirez, Erasmo	28			93	92	91	91	91	92
Odorizzi, Jake	28			90	91	90	91	92	92
Hand, Brad	28			90	90	93	92	92	94
Morgan, Adam	28						89	91	94
Delgado, Randall	28		92	92	92	93	93	92	94
Salazar, Danny	28				96	95	95	95	95
Iglesias, Raisel	28						92	93	96
Herrera, Kelvin	28		96	99	98	98	98	97	97
Hendricks, Kyle	28					88	88	88	86
Gray, Sonny	28				93	93	93	93	93
Familia, Jeurys	28			96	95	96	97	96	96
Andriese, Matt	28						91	92	92
Bumgarner, Madison	28	91	92	91	91	92	92	91	91
Hahn, Jesse	28					91	92	94	94
Corbin, Patrick	28			91	92		92	92	92
Montgomery, Mike	28						91	94	92
Ross Jr., Robbie	29			92	93	91	92	94	91
Moore, Matt	29		96	94	92	92	92	93	92
Nelson, Jimmy	29				94	94	93	93	94
Peralta, Wily	29			96	95	96	94	95	96
Sale, Chris	29	96	95	92	93	94	94	93	94
Harvey, Matt	29			95	96		96	94	94
de la Rosa, Rubby	29		96	94	95	94	94	95	97
Hendriks, Liam	29		90	90	91	91	95	94	95
Quintana, Jose	29			90	91	92	92	92	92
Pineda, Michael	29		95			92	93	94	94
Colome, Alex	29				95	94	94	95	95
Reed, Addison	29		95	95	93	92	93	92	92
Porcello, Rick	29	91	90	92	92	90	91	90	91
Duffy, Danny	29		93	95	94	93	94	95	93
Straily, Dan	29			91	90	89	89	89	90
Quackenbush, Kevin	29					91	91	91	91
Pomeranz, Drew	29		90	91	91	91	91	90	91
Allen, Cody	29			95	95	95	95	94	94
Greene, Shane	29					93	92	94	95
Paxton, James	29			95	95	94	97	95	
Tanaka, Masahiro	29				91	92	91	92	
Archer, Chris	29			94	95	95	95	94	95
Strickland, Hunter	29					98	97	97	96
Grimm, Justin	29			92	92	94	95	94	95
Strasburg, Stephen	29	97	96	96	95	95	95	95	96
Treinen, Blake	30					95	96	95	97
deGrom, Jacob	30				93	95	93	95	
Kelly, Joe	30			94	95	95	95	96	99
Kimbrel, Craig	30	95	96	97	97	97	97	97	98
Dyson, Sam	30			92	92	96	96	95	95
Bergman, Christian	30					89	90	89	88
Tillman, Chris	30	90	90	92	92	91	91	92	91
Betances, Dellin	30		93			96	97	98	99
Kershaw, Clayton	30	93	93	93	93	93	94	93	93
Baez, Pedro	30					95	97	97	97
Cahill, Trevor	30	90	89	89	89	90	92	92	91
Chapman, Aroldis	30	100	98	98	98	100	99	100	100
Rondon, Hector	30				94	96	96	96	96
Gomez, Jeanmar	30	91	90	90	91	91	91	91	91
Chacin, Jhoulys	30	91	91	90	90	88	89	91	91
Keuchel, Dallas	30			88	89	90	90	89	89
Britton, Zach	30		92	92	92	95	96	96	96
Santiago, Hector	30		94	93	92	91	90	91	91
Latos, Mat	30	94	93	93	93	91	91	90	91
McAllister, Zach	30		91	92	91	93	95	94	95
Anderson, Chase	30					91	92	91	93
Locke, Jeff	30		90	91	90	90	91	92	91
Leake, Mike	30	89	89	90	90	91	91	91	90
Shaw, Bryan	30		91	90	91	91			
Gibson, Kyle	30			92	91	92	91	92	
Jansen, Kenley	30	94	93	92	92	94	94	93	93
Worley, Vance	30	91	90	90	90	89	89	89	90
Jeffress, Jeremy	30	95	97	95	97	96	95	95	94
Warren, Adam	30			92	93	94	93	93	93
Wilson, Justin	30			94	95	95	95	95	96
Storen, Drew	30	94	95	95	94	93	94	92	90
Nuno, Vidal	30				88	89	89	90	89
McHugh, Collin	31		90	90	92	90	90	90	
Lynn, Lance	31		93	93	92	92		92	
Jennings, Dan	31		90	92	93	92	91	92	
Hellickson, Jeremy	31	91	91	91	91	90	90	90	90
Despaigne, Odrisamer	31					91	91	93	92
Carrasco, Carlos	31	93	92		95	95	95	94	94
Hudson, Daniel	31	93	93	93		95	96	96	96
Milone, Tommy	31		88	88	87	87	88	88	88
Wood, Travis	31	90	90	89	89	88	90	91	89
Diekman, Jake	31			95	96	97	96	95	95
Nova, Ivan	31	93	93	93	93	92	93	93	93
Miley, Wade	31		90	91	91	91	91	90	91
Wilson, Alex	31			92	93	92	92	93	
Rusin, Chris	31		88	88	88	90	90	91	
Holland, Derek	31	92	94	93	94	92	93	92	91
Phelps, David	31		91	90	90	90	94	94	
Roark, Tanner	31		93	91	93	92	92		
Shoemaker, Matt	31		91	91	90	91	92		
Ramos, AJ	31		94	93	91	93	92	92	
Cashner, Andrew	31	96	95	98	95	94	95	94	93
Nicasio, Juan	31		94	93	92	93	95	94	95
Darvish, Yu	31		93	93	92		93	94	
Vincent, Nick	31		90	90	90	90	90	90	
Garcia, Jaime	31	90	90	89	89	91	90	91	91
Hunter, Tommy	31	90	92	92	96	96	96	96	
Cecil, Brett	31	90	88	89	92	93	92	92	92
Koehler, Tom	32			94	93	93	92	92	93
Hughes, Phil	32	93	91	92	92	92	91	90	90
Cishek, Steve	32	93	93	92	92	92	91	91	90
Tazawa, Junichi	32		92	94	94	94	94	93	92
Zimmermann, Jordan	32	92	93	94	94	94	93	92	92
Brach, Brad	32		93	92	92	93	94	94	95
Kluber, Corey	32		92	93	93	93	93	92	93

		Average FB Velocity							
Player	Age	10	11	12	13	14	15	16	17
Hernandez, Felix	32	94	93	92	92	92	92	90	90
Arrieta, Jake	32	93	92	93	94	94	95	94	92
Gallardo, Yovani	32	93	93	92	91	91	90	90	92
Cueto, Johnny	32	93	93	93	92	93	92	91	91
Bastardo, Antonio	32	94	93	92	92	92	93	92	91
Gonzalez, Gio	32	92	92	93	93	92	92	91	90
Davis, Wade	32	92	91	94	92	96	96	95	94
Price, David	32	95	95	96	94	93	94	93	94
Fields, Josh	32				94	94	94	95	95
Chen, Wei-Yin	32			91	91	92	91	91	91
Hughes, Jared	32		93	92	92	92	93	93	93
Fiers, Mike	33		88	88	88	90	89	90	90
Strop, Pedro	33	95	94	97	96	95	95	95	96
Kontos, George	33		91	91	91	91	91	91	91
Salas, Fernando	33	91	91	92	90	91	91	91	91
Watson, Tony	33		91	94	94	94	94	93	94
Dunn, Mike	33	95	94	94	94	95	95	94	92
Miller, Andrew	33	91	93	95	95	94	94	95	94
Robertson, David	33	92	93	92	92	92	92	92	92
Melancon, Mark	33	93	93	93	93	93	92	92	92
Norris, Bud	33	94	93	92	92	93	94	93	94
Otero, Dan	33			90	90	90	90	90	90
Clippard, Tyler	33	92	93	93	92	92	92	91	91
Samardzija, Jeff	33	93	95	95	95	94	94	94	94
Kennedy, Ian	33	89	90	90	90	92	91	92	92
Petit, Yusmeiro	33			88	88	89	88	89	90
Tomlin, Josh	33	89	88	89	90	89	88	88	88
Cain, Matt	33	92	91	91	91	92	91	90	89
Buchholz, Clay	33	94	93	92	92	92	92	92	91
Kintzler, Brandon	33	93	93	93	92	92	91	93	93
Scherzer, Max	33	93	93	94	93	93	94	94	94
Broxton, Jonathan	34	95	94	95	94	93	94	94	94
Gonzalez, Miguel	34			91	91	91	91	91	91
Soria, Joakim	34	92	91		91	90	92	93	93
Gregerson, Luke	34	91	90	89	88	88	89	89	90
Kelley, Shawn	34	93	91	92	92	92	92	92	92
Smith, Joe	34	91	90	89	90	89	88	88	89
Sanchez, Anibal	34	91	92	92	93	92	92	91	91
Fister, Doug	34	88	90	89	89	88	86	87	90
Jimenez, Ubaldo	34	96	93	92	92	91	91	90	91
Pelfrey, Mike	34	92	92	94	92	91	93	93	92
Lester, Jon	34	93	93	93	93	92	92	92	91
Hamels, Cole	34	92	92	91	92	92	93	93	92
Garza, Matt	34	93	94	94	93	93	93	92	92
Morton, Charlie	34	93	91	90	93	91	92	94	95
Liriano, Francisco	34	94	92	93	93	93	92	93	93
Greinke, Zack	34	93	93	92	92	92	92	91	91
Jackson, Edwin	34	94	94	93	93	93	94	92	93
Chavez, Jesse	34	95	93	93	92	91	91	93	92
Estrada, Marco	34	91	91	90	89	89	89	88	90
Volquez, Edinson	34	94	94	94	92	93	94	93	93
Johnson, Jim	35	94	95	94	94	94	94	93	93
Duke, Zach	35	87	87	89	89	90	89	90	88
Axford, John	35	95	96	96	95	95	96	96	95
Romo, Sergio	35	89	89	88	88	88	87	86	86
Verlander, Justin	35	95	95	94	93	92	93	93	95
Feldman, Scott	35	90	92	92	90	89	90	90	89
Nolasco, Ricky	35	91	91	90	90	90	90	90	91
Santana, Ervin	35	92	93	92	92	92	92	93	93
O'Day, Darren	35	86	84	85	86	87	87	86	88
Torres, Carlos	35	90		91	91	92	92	92	94
Happ, J.A.	35	90	90	90	91	93	92	92	92
Weaver, Jered	35	90	89	88	86	86	83	83	84
Hammel, Jason	35	93	93	94	93	92	92	92	92
McGowan, Dustin	36		93		95	94	94	95	94
Rodriguez, Francisco	36	91	90	92	91	91	90	89	89
Shields, James	36	92	91	92	92	92	91	90	90
Wainwright, Adam	36	91		90	91	90	90	90	90
Iwakuma, Hisashi	37			90	90	89	88	88	85
de la Rosa, Jorge	37	93	93	90	91	92	91	90	94
Neshek, Pat	37	86	86	89	89	90	90	89	90
Madson, Ryan	37	94	94				94	94	95
Casilla, Santiago	37	97	94	94	93	94	93	94	94

		Average FB Velocity							
Player	Age	10	11	12	13	14	15	16	17
Sabathia, CC	37	93	94	92	91	89	90	90	91
Ziegler, Brad	38	84	85	86	86	85	84	84	83
Young, Chris	39	85	85	85		85	87	88	87
Lackey, John	39	91	92		92	92	92	92	91
Benoit, Joaquin	40	94	94	94	94	95	94	94	95
Rodney, Fernando	41	96	96	96	96	95	95	94	95
Dickey, R.A.	43	84	84	83	82	82	81	82	83
Colon, Bartolo	45		92	90	90	89	88	88	88

Pinch Hitting

Ben Jedlovec

Pinch hitting is a tough job. Can you imagine showing up for your job every day, not knowing if your boss will have any work for you, but if he does, you'll have about 30 seconds heads-up and no time to get loose or prepare before walking out in front of 40,000 screaming fans and 24 co-workers who are all counting on you, at which point you'll be expected to perform the toughest task in sports—make solid contact with a round ball thrown at 100-mph by some fireballing reliever who, by the way, has only a faint idea of where the ball is going. I'm not sure how I'd get out of bed in the morning if the odds of success in my job were stacked that squarely against me.

The exception to the rule in 2017 is perhaps the most unique player in modern baseball: Ichiro Suzuki. Debatably baseball's all-time hit king (though undoubtedly more likeable as a human being), 43-year-old Ichiro wrote a new and perhaps final chapter of his illustrious career. The fourth man in the Marlins outfield never saw regular time thanks to an unnatural stretch of health from their notoriously injury-prone group of starters. However, Ichiro managed to appear in nearly every Marlins' game last season—136 of them—and appeared as a pinch hitter in an MLB-record 109 of those and performed remarkably well. In early September, it seemed inevitable that he'd catch Jon Vander Wal's record of 28 pinch hits in a season, though a handful of starts and an 0-for-10 pinch hitting slump down the stretch left him just short. Ichiro's remarkable year cannot be denied, however, as a .270 average as a pinch hitter is far better than the Marlins could have hoped from any other pinch hitter available.

You'll see on page 47 that Major League batters combined to hit .255 in 2017 with a .750 OPS. The average pinch hitter batted .223 with a .648 OPS, though the composition of the two samples is not identical. According to The Book, the average hitter loses 10 points of weighted On-Base Average when comparing their starting lineup performance to their pinch hit production.

Despite this evidence, use of pinch hitters has not significantly declined in recent years. In 1973, the year the American League adopted the designated hitter, MLB teams averaged .95 pinch hit plate appearances per team game played. In 1980, that figure rose to 1.08, 1.13 in 1990, 1.01 in 2000, .99 in 2010, and .97 in 2017.

Furthermore, the number of dedicated pinch hitters has remained roughly constant during the same time frame. There were 22 batters with at least 30 pinch hit at-bats in 1973 (across 24 MLB teams), 34 in 1990 (26 teams), and 30 (30 teams) in 2017. In addition to Ichiro, this year saw Jesus Aguilar, Tyler Moore, Pat Valaika, Jose Osuna, and Patrick Kivlehan snag 50 or more pinch hit at-bats.

In the pages that follow, you'll find pinch hitting records for every batter with at least 10 pinch hit plate appearances or pinch total bases in 2017, as well as career totals for every active player with at least 100 career pinch plate appearances.

Pinch Hitting
Pinch Hitters with 10+ PAs or 10+ Total Bases in 2017

Batter	B	AB	H	2B	3B	HR	RBI	TBB	IBB	SO	GDP	Avg	OBP	Slg	OPS
Cristhian Adames	B	9	0	0	0	0	0	1	0	4	0	.000	.100	.000	.100
Lane Adams	R	45	12	2	0	2	12	4	0	16	1	.267	.340	.444	.784
Matt Adams	L	46	13	2	0	2	13	3	1	16	0	.283	.320	.457	.777
Ehire Adrianza	B	13	1	0	0	0	0	1	0	1	0	.077	.143	.077	.220
Jesus Aguilar	R	60	15	3	0	3	10	6	0	21	3	.250	.318	.450	.768
Arismendy Alcantara	B	35	6	2	1	0	2	1	0	11	1	.171	.194	.286	.480
Albert Almora Jr.	R	41	14	3	0	0	10	0	0	6	3	.341	.333	.415	.748
Yonder Alonso	L	10	2	0	0	0	0	3	0	2	0	.200	.385	.200	.585
Alexi Amarista	L	47	9	2	0	1	4	3	0	14	2	.191	.240	.298	.538
Nori Aoki	L	8	1	0	0	0	1	2	0	5	0	.125	.300	.125	.425
Alex Avila	L	19	6	2	0	0	2	3	0	9	1	.316	.409	.421	.830
Mike Aviles	R	10	2	0	0	1	2	0	0	4	0	.200	.333	.500	.833
Erick Aybar	B	11	2	0	0	0	2	1	0	1	0	.182	.250	.182	.432
Jett Bandy	R	8	1	0	0	0	0	1	0	6	0	.125	.300	.125	.425
Austin Barnes	R	31	9	2	0	0	5	2	0	10	0	.290	.353	.355	.708
Darwin Barney	R	16	3	0	0	0	1	2	0	4	0	.188	.278	.188	.465
Tucker Barnhart	B	11	4	2	0	0	3	0	0	2	0	.364	.417	.545	.962
Josh Bell	B	15	3	1	0	1	2	2	0	3	1	.200	.294	.467	.761
Carlos Beltran	B	10	4	0	0	0	1	0	0	1	1	.400	.364	.400	.764
Andres Blanco	B	31	7	3	0	1	4	3	0	6	1	.226	.286	.419	.705
Gregor Blanco	L	13	0	0	0	0	0	3	0	7	0	.000	.188	.000	.188
Jabari Blash	R	10	1	0	0	0	0	1	0	4	0	.100	.250	.100	.350
Emilio Bonifacio	B	26	2	0	1	0	3	0	0	6	0	.077	.074	.154	.228
Chris Bostick	R	11	2	0	0	0	0	2	0	2	0	.182	.308	.182	.490
Peter Bourjos	R	10	3	1	0	0	2	0	0	4	0	.300	.300	.400	.700
Keon Broxton	R	13	5	1	0	1	1	2	0	5	0	.385	.467	.692	1.159
Asdrubal Cabrera	B	13	4	0	0	1	5	2	0	3	3	.308	.438	.538	.976
Johan Camargo	B	14	4	1	0	0	4	0	0	6	0	.286	.286	.357	.643
Victor Caratini	B	12	1	0	0	0	0	1	0	3	0	.083	.267	.083	.350
Ezequiel Carrera	L	14	6	0	0	1	3	2	0	4	0	.429	.529	.643	1.172
Gavin Cecchini	R	12	1	0	0	0	0	0	0	4	0	.083	.083	.083	.167
Lonnie Chisenhall	L	17	4	2	0	2	9	1	1	6	0	.235	.278	.706	.984
Michael Conforto	L	11	4	1	0	0	3	0	0	1	0	.364	.385	.455	.839
Willson Contreras	R	11	1	1	0	0	2	4	1	5	0	.091	.333	.182	.515
Allen Cordoba	R	25	4	0	0	1	1	3	0	6	1	.160	.276	.280	.556
Chase d'Arnaud	R	12	2	0	0	0	0	1	0	6	0	.167	.231	.167	.397
Travis d'Arnaud	R	18	3	0	0	0	1	0	0	2	0	.167	.167	.167	.333
Matt Davidson	R	10	2	1	0	0	0	0	0	4	2	.200	.200	.300	.500
Rajai Davis	R	11	4	2	0	0	1	4	1	0	0	.364	.533	.545	1.079
Daniel Descalso	L	26	6	0	0	2	9	8	0	8	0	.231	.429	.462	.890
Elias Diaz	R	13	2	0	0	0	0	2	0	5	0	.154	.267	.154	.421
Corey Dickerson	L	10	2	1	0	0	0	1	0	3	1	.200	.273	.300	.573
Derek Dietrich	L	17	4	1	0	1	3	0	0	5	0	.235	.316	.471	.786
Wilmer Difo	B	28	5	0	0	0	0	3	0	8	0	.179	.258	.179	.437
Stephen Drew	L	19	6	3	0	0	5	4	0	4	0	.316	.417	.474	.890
Brandon Drury	R	16	6	2	0	0	2	1	0	5	2	.375	.450	.500	.950
Lucas Duda	L	8	1	0	0	0	1	3	0	4	0	.125	.364	.125	.489
A.J. Ellis	R	11	3	0	0	1	3	0	0	3	1	.273	.333	.545	.879
Jacoby Ellsbury	L	6	0	0	0	0	0	4	0	0	0	.000	.400	.000	.400
Phillip Ervin	R	9	1	0	0	0	0	0	0	3	1	.111	.111	.111	.222
Eduardo Escobar	B	9	2	0	0	0	1	5	2	3	0	.222	.533	.222	.756
Andre Ethier	L	11	2	0	0	2	2	1	0	4	0	.182	.250	.727	.977
Phillip Evans	R	12	4	1	0	0	0	0	0	5	0	.333	.333	.417	.750
Kyle Farmer	R	13	5	1	0	0	2	0	0	2	0	.385	.385	.462	.846
Wilmer Flores	R	21	5	1	0	2	5	0	0	4	0	.238	.238	.571	.810
Tyler Flowers	R	10	2	0	0	1	2	3	0	2	1	.200	.385	.500	.885
Logan Forsythe	R	11	1	0	0	0	1	2	0	2	1	.091	.231	.091	.322
Nick Franklin	B	36	8	2	1	0	7	3	0	8	1	.222	.300	.333	.633
Adam Frazier	L	21	8	1	0	0	2	1	0	0	1	.381	.458	.429	.887
Mike Freeman	L	11	0	0	0	0	0	3	1	5	0	.000	.214	.000	.214
David Freese	R	6	2	1	0	0	0	5	1	1	0	.333	.636	.500	1.136
Eric Fryer	R	11	2	1	0	0	0	2	0	4	1	.182	.308	.273	.580
Rey Fuentes	L	18	5	0	2	6	6	2	0	8	0	.278	.350	.611	.961
Adonis Garcia	R	12	3	0	0	1	3	0	0	3	0	.250	.250	.500	.750
Greg Garcia	L	45	10	1	0	0	4	12	0	15	2	.222	.390	.244	.634
Scooter Gennett	L	23	3	0	0	1	5	0	0	7	0	.130	.130	.261	.391
Conor Gillaspie	L	22	5	1	0	2	5	0	0	4	1	.227	.250	.545	.795
Ryan Goins	L	11	3	0	0	0	1	0	0	5	1	.273	.273	.273	.545

Pinch Hitting
Pinch Hitters with 10+ PAs or 10+ Total Bases in 2017

Batter	B	AB	H	2B	3B	HR	RBI	TBB	IBB	SO	GDP	Avg	OBP	Slg	OPS
Miguel Gomez	B	16	2	1	0	0	2	0	0	2	1	.125	.118	.188	.305
Adrian Gonzalez	L	11	4	0	0	0	2	3	0	2	1	.364	.500	.364	.864
Phil Gosselin	R	18	3	0	0	0	1	1	0	4	1	.167	.211	.167	.377
Yasmani Grandal	B	14	3	1	0	0	3	1	0	8	0	.214	.267	.286	.552
Curtis Granderson	L	19	6	2	0	1	3	5	0	5	0	.316	.458	.579	1.037
Randal Grichuk	R	12	2	0	0	0	1	2	0	6	0	.167	.333	.167	.500
Robbie Grossman	B	10	2	1	0	0	1	3	0	3	1	.200	.385	.300	.685
Franklin Gutierrez	R	17	5	1	0	0	3	4	0	5	0	.294	.429	.353	.782
Brandon Guyer	R	9	0	0	0	0	1	0	0	4	0	.000	.100	.000	.100
Jedd Gyorko	R	10	3	1	0	0	4	0	0	3	0	.300	.250	.400	.650
Alen Hanson	B	32	5	0	1	1	2	2	0	12	0	.156	.206	.313	.518
Ian Happ	B	15	3	0	1	1	3	3	0	5	0	.200	.368	.533	.902
Jeremy Hazelbaker	L	16	5	1	0	0	2	3	1	10	0	.313	.421	.375	.796
Chase Headley	B	11	2	0	0	1	2	0	0	2	0	.182	.182	.455	.636
Chris Heisey	R	17	1	0	0	0	0	1	0	6	0	.059	.111	.059	.170
Gorkys Hernandez	R	21	4	0	1	0	0	1	0	7	1	.190	.261	.286	.547
Kike Hernandez	R	46	10	5	0	1	3	6	1	13	1	.217	.308	.391	.699
Chris Herrmann	L	30	2	0	0	0	3	4	0	12	1	.067	.171	.067	.238
Aaron Hicks	B	11	3	0	0	2	2	0	0	1	0	.273	.273	.818	1.091
John Hicks	R	11	3	2	0	0	0	0	0	3	0	.273	.273	.455	.727
Aaron Hill	R	16	4	2	0	0	5	2	0	5	0	.250	.333	.375	.708
Brock Holt	L	9	3	2	0	0	1	1	0	1	0	.333	.400	.556	.956
Chad Huffman	R	10	3	0	1	0	0	1	0	5	0	.300	.364	.500	.864
Nick Hundley	R	22	2	0	0	0	1	1	0	11	0	.091	.125	.091	.216
Chris Iannetta	R	12	3	0	0	1	2	2	0	4	0	.250	.400	.500	.900
John Jaso	L	44	8	1	0	3	10	13	0	12	0	.182	.379	.409	.788
Jon Jay	L	40	13	0	0	1	8	3	0	7	3	.325	.391	.400	.791
Tommy Joseph	R	9	2	0	0	0	0	2	0	2	0	.222	.364	.222	.586
Matt Joyce	L	14	2	1	0	0	0	0	0	6	0	.143	.143	.214	.357
Carson Kelly	R	11	2	0	0	0	1	0	0	0	1	.182	.182	.182	.364
Ty Kelly	B	35	8	5	0	1	7	4	0	9	0	.229	.317	.457	.774
Howie Kendrick	R	14	5	2	0	0	2	1	0	3	2	.357	.400	.500	.900
Hyun Soo Kim	L	35	6	1	0	0	1	0	0	12	1	.171	.171	.200	.371
Patrick Kivlehan	R	51	9	1	1	1	6	6	0	23	1	.176	.263	.294	.557
Tommy La Stella	L	31	9	4	0	0	7	10	0	5	1	.290	.488	.419	.908
Juan Lagares	R	10	2	0	0	0	1	1	0	3	0	.200	.273	.200	.473
Adam Lind	L	45	16	1	0	4	13	3	1	14	0	.356	.396	.644	1.040
Dixon Machado	R	11	4	0	0	0	1	2	0	1	0	.364	.462	.364	.825
Jose Martinez	R	26	12	2	0	2	2	6	2	7	0	.462	.563	.769	1.332
Bruce Maxwell	L	10	1	0	0	0	0	1	0	3	1	.100	.182	.100	.282
Devin Mesoraco	R	13	6	0	0	0	0	2	0	2	1	.462	.533	.462	.995
Brad Miller	L	12	2	1	0	0	2	1	1	8	0	.167	.231	.250	.481
Carlos Moncrief	L	18	3	0	0	0	3	2	0	7	0	.167	.238	.167	.405
Miguel Montero	L	16	3	0	0	0	2	2	0	5	0	.188	.316	.188	.503
Tyler Moore	R	51	14	4	0	1	9	2	0	21	0	.275	.291	.412	.703
Mitch Moreland	L	11	3	0	0	1	6	3	1	3	0	.273	.429	.545	.974
Logan Morrison	L	11	3	0	0	1	2	1	0	3	1	.273	.333	.545	.879
Michael Morse	R	15	4	0	0	1	1	1	0	6	0	.267	.313	.467	.779
Brandon Moss	L	11	1	1	0	0	0	2	0	5	0	.091	.167	.182	.348
Daniel Nava	B	28	9	1	0	0	4	3	0	5	1	.321	.394	.357	.751
Brandon Nimmo	L	16	5	2	0	0	2	4	0	6	0	.313	.450	.438	.888
Jose Osuna	R	50	6	1	0	1	2	1	0	12	6	.120	.154	.200	.354
Gerardo Parra	L	11	2	0	0	0	2	1	0	4	1	.182	.250	.182	.432
Joc Pederson	L	13	1	0	0	0	0	3	0	5	0	.077	.250	.077	.327
Hunter Pence	R	9	3	0	0	1	3	2	0	2	0	.333	.455	.667	1.121
Cliff Pennington	B	12	3	1	0	0	1	0	0	4	1	.250	.231	.333	.564
David Peralta	L	13	7	0	0	0	2	1	0	0	0	.538	.571	.538	1.110
Jose Peraza	R	12	1	1	0	0	2	0	0	1	0	.083	.083	.167	.250
Hernan Perez	R	15	2	1	0	0	1	1	0	2	2	.133	.188	.200	.388
Cam Perkins	R	18	6	2	0	1	2	1	0	4	0	.333	.368	.611	.980
Jace Peterson	L	22	8	2	1	1	2	3	0	3	0	.364	.440	.682	1.122
Tommy Pham	R	9	2	0	0	0	2	1	0	1	0	.222	.300	.222	.522
Chad Pinder	R	10	1	0	0	0	0	0	0	5	0	.100	.100	.100	.200
Stephen Piscotty	R	7	4	1	0	0	2	2	1	2	0	.571	.700	.714	1.414
Trevor Plouffe	R	12	3	0	0	1	2	1	0	2	0	.250	.357	.500	.857
Gregory Polanco	L	10	5	1	0	1	5	0	0	2	0	.500	.500	.900	1.400
Boog Powell	L	9	3	0	0	0	1	1	0	1	0	.333	.400	.333	.733
Yasiel Puig	R	12	0	0	0	0	1	0	0	3	0	.000	.000	.000	.000
Rob Refsnyder	R	8	0	0	0	0	0	4	0	3	1	.000	.333	.000	.333

Pinch Hitting

Pinch Hitters with 10+ PAs or 10+ Total Bases in 2017

Batter	B	AB	H	2B	3B	HR	RBI	TBB	IBB	SO	GDP	Avg	OBP	Slg	OPS
Ben Revere	L	29	10	0	0	0	2	0	0	2	0	.345	.345	.345	.690
Jose Reyes	B	9	2	0	0	0	0	2	0	2	0	.222	.364	.222	.586
Matt Reynolds	R	16	2	0	1	0	0	4	0	6	0	.125	.300	.250	.550
Joey Rickard	R	12	2	1	0	0	1	2	0	2	0	.167	.267	.250	.517
T.J. Rivera	R	15	5	0	0	1	2	2	0	3	0	.333	.412	.533	.945
Andrew Romine	B	8	4	1	0	0	1	1	0	1	0	.500	.600	.625	1.225
Adam Rosales	R	7	3	1	0	2	2	1	1	1	0	.429	.636	.571	1.208
Rio Ruiz	L	11	3	1	0	0	1	0	0	2	0	.273	.273	.364	.636
Addison Russell	R	12	3	1	0	1	2	1	0	4	0	.250	.308	.583	.891
Adrian Sanchez	R	11	1	0	0	0	0	0	0	6	1	.091	.091	.091	.182
Hector Sanchez	B	45	6	0	0	3	9	3	1	16	1	.133	.184	.333	.517
Yolmer Sanchez	B	9	2	0	1	0	0	1	0	2	0	.222	.300	.444	.744
Danny Santana	B	32	7	3	0	1	10	1	0	6	1	.219	.265	.406	.671
Luis Sardinas	B	15	3	0	0	0	1	2	0	5	0	.200	.294	.200	.494
Michael Saunders	L	15	4	2	0	0	1	1	0	4	0	.267	.313	.400	.713
Kyle Schwarber	L	14	2	0	0	1	1	1	0	8	0	.143	.200	.357	.557
Kevan Smith	R	12	2	1	0	1	4	0	0	4	1	.167	.167	.500	.667
Seth Smith	L	14	2	0	0	0	0	3	1	8	0	.143	.294	.143	.437
Eric Sogard	L	16	3	0	0	0	1	7	1	3	2	.188	.435	.188	.622
Denard Span	L	12	3	2	0	0	0	0	0	6	0	.250	.250	.417	.667
Brock Stassi	L	23	3	1	0	0	1	5	0	9	0	.130	.286	.174	.460
Andrew Stevenson	L	11	2	0	0	0	0	1	0	3	0	.182	.250	.182	.432
Ichiro Suzuki	L	100	27	3	0	1	10	7	0	21	0	.270	.324	.330	.654
Matt Szczur	R	45	9	2	0	1	6	6	0	15	0	.200	.288	.311	.600
Travis Taijeron	R	10	1	0	0	0	0	0	0	6	1	.100	.182	.100	.282
Raimel Tapia	L	23	6	2	1	0	5	3	0	6	2	.261	.370	.435	.805
Mike Tauchman	L	16	2	0	0	0	0	3	0	8	1	.125	.263	.125	.388
Chris Taylor	R	13	6	1	0	1	5	0	0	4	0	.462	.462	.769	1.231
Tomas Telis	B	21	6	3	0	0	1	0	0	1	0	.286	.286	.429	.714
Eric Thames	L	12	2	1	0	0	2	1	0	6	0	.167	.231	.250	.481
Andrew Toles	L	9	3	1	0	0	1	1	0	1	1	.333	.400	.444	.844
Kelby Tomlinson	R	44	13	1	1	0	5	3	0	15	2	.295	.320	.364	.684
Stuart Turner	R	11	1	0	0	0	0	0	0	3	0	.091	.091	.091	.182
Chase Utley	L	33	9	3	1	0	3	9	0	7	0	.273	.442	.424	.866
Pat Valaika	R	58	19	8	0	4	16	2	0	24	0	.328	.344	.672	1.017
Luis Valbuena	L	16	3	1	0	0	6	3	0	7	0	.188	.316	.250	.566
Danny Valencia	R	6	2	1	0	0	4	2	0	1	0	.333	.500	.500	1.000
Scott Van Slyke	R	14	2	0	0	1	2	4	0	3	0	.143	.333	.357	.690
Kennys Vargas	B	11	4	0	0	1	4	1	0	4	0	.364	.417	.636	1.053
Jonathan Villar	B	26	6	2	0	0	1	0	0	10	1	.231	.231	.308	.538
Stephen Vogt	L	17	4	1	0	1	3	3	0	6	0	.235	.350	.471	.821
Luke Voit	R	33	10	2	0	1	3	2	0	8	1	.303	.378	.455	.833
Christian Walker	R	9	3	1	0	2	2	0	0	3	0	.333	.400	1.111	1.511
Rickie Weeks Jr.	R	9	1	1	0	0	2	1	0	6	0	.111	.273	.222	.495
Jesse Winker	L	16	6	2	0	2	4	3	0	7	0	.375	.474	.875	1.349
Chris Young	R	14	5	0	0	0	4	3	0	3	0	.357	.526	.357	.883
Bradley Zimmer	L	11	2	1	0	0	1	2	0	7	0	.182	.308	.273	.580
Ben Zobrist	B	18	6	1	0	1	4	2	0	3	0	.333	.400	.556	.956

Career Pinch Hitting
Active Pinch Hitters with 100+ PAs in their careers

Batter	B	AB	H	2B	3B	HR	RBI	TBB	IBB	SO	GDP	Avg	OBP	Slg	OPS
Matt Adams	L	146	46	8	0	9	41	7	2	45	3	.315	.342	.555	.897
Alexi Amarista	L	147	26	6	0	2	11	8	0	37	3	.177	.218	.259	.476
Andres Blanco	B	113	24	11	0	3	13	8	0	24	4	.212	.274	.389	.664
Gregor Blanco	L	148	40	8	2	1	22	14	0	41	1	.270	.331	.372	.703
Emilio Bonifacio	B	121	24	2	2	0	7	8	1	40	1	.198	.252	.248	.500
Chris Coghlan	L	109	25	3	1	4	11	6	0	32	6	.229	.282	.385	.667
Rajai Davis	R	102	19	6	1	0	5	16	2	26	2	.186	.300	.265	.565
Alejandro De Aza	L	112	25	4	0	2	8	14	1	35	0	.223	.308	.313	.620
Daniel Descalso	L	210	44	8	1	5	28	23	0	56	1	.210	.297	.329	.625
Andre Ethier	L	140	40	7	1	6	33	23	3	40	7	.286	.394	.479	.873
Greg Garcia	L	98	28	4	0	2	9	18	0	28	3	.286	.418	.388	.806
Conor Gillaspie	L	112	25	4	2	7	21	12	2	20	2	.223	.302	.482	.784
Phil Gosselin	R	123	30	6	0	1	8	7	1	35	1	.244	.280	.317	.597
Franklin Gutierrez	R	98	22	3	0	2	19	11	0	30	2	.224	.306	.316	.623
Josh Harrison	R	103	17	2	1	3	14	3	0	18	2	.165	.194	.291	.486
Chris Heisey	R	200	48	10	2	14	40	15	1	61	2	.240	.297	.520	.817
Kike Hernandez	R	106	20	7	0	2	7	12	2	35	1	.189	.269	.311	.580
John Jaso	L	162	39	7	0	6	27	36	1	40	5	.241	.380	.395	.775
Jon Jay	L	132	38	3	0	3	18	13	1	31	7	.288	.364	.379	.743
Matt Joyce	L	176	34	9	1	5	31	39	2	58	5	.193	.341	.341	.682
Tommy La Stella	L	81	20	9	0	0	11	17	0	14	2	.247	.390	.358	.748
Adam Lind	L	139	45	7	0	9	35	16	4	45	4	.324	.391	.568	.959
Brian McCann	L	103	19	5	0	3	12	12	4	30	2	.184	.282	.320	.602
Miguel Montero	L	121	23	2	0	4	20	23	3	42	3	.190	.340	.306	.646
Tyler Moore	R	158	27	9	0	4	21	8	1	66	1	.171	.218	.304	.521
Michael Morse	R	114	32	5	2	3	22	14	0	39	2	.281	.357	.439	.795
Brandon Moss	L	143	30	8	1	5	23	16	1	47	5	.210	.305	.385	.689
Daniel Murphy	L	103	25	2	2	4	19	9	2	20	3	.243	.298	.417	.716
Kirk Nieuwenhuis	L	104	23	8	0	1	6	13	1	50	0	.221	.308	.327	.635
Gerardo Parra	L	120	26	5	1	1	11	7	1	29	3	.217	.264	.300	.564
Steve Pearce	R	103	19	5	1	1	9	12	1	34	4	.184	.276	.282	.557
Ryan Raburn	R	167	32	8	1	8	34	28	3	51	4	.192	.320	.395	.715
Shane Robinson	R	113	24	4	1	0	7	19	0	22	2	.212	.323	.265	.589
Sean Rodriguez	R	118	18	2	0	4	14	16	0	53	1	.153	.281	.271	.552
Justin Ruggiano	R	92	23	9	1	2	10	6	0	35	1	.250	.303	.435	.738
Hector Sanchez	B	146	30	5	0	5	27	8	1	48	3	.205	.253	.342	.596
Seth Smith	L	243	70	16	5	9	46	40	4	70	6	.288	.387	.506	.893
Ichiro Suzuki	L	241	63	6	1	2	22	21	2	42	1	.261	.326	.320	.645
Matt Szczur	R	125	26	6	1	1	12	10	0	29	0	.208	.265	.296	.561
Justin Turner	R	157	43	9	0	5	35	12	0	31	8	.274	.322	.427	.749
Chase Utley	L	114	32	7	1	5	26	22	3	33	0	.281	.403	.491	.894
Scott Van Slyke	R	84	22	3	0	4	18	15	2	27	3	.262	.376	.440	.817
Rickie Weeks Jr.	R	166	33	8	1	3	21	24	0	68	6	.199	.323	.313	.636
Chris Young	R	94	26	6	0	3	21	18	1	28	0	.277	.409	.436	.845
Eric Young Jr.	B	150	32	3	1	1	4	18	0	39	2	.213	.306	.267	.573

Manufactured Runs, Productive Outs & Unproductive Outs

Lindsay Zeck

For the third season in a row, the Major League Baseball set a record for the fewest number of manufactured runs since 2002, the first season BIS started tracking them, with 4,122. The teams with the two best records in baseball, the Dodgers and Indians, allowed the fewest manufactured runs—102 and 90, respectively. Six playoff teams finished in the top eight in manufactured runs with the Boston Red Sox manufacturing an MLB-leading 183 runs, 18 more than the second-place team, the Astros with 165. The Red Sox were led by Mookie Betts who contributed to 33 manufactured runs, the second most in baseball, and Xander Bogaerts who finished 10th with 25.

The individual player who contributed to manufacturing the most runs was this season's stolen base leader, Dee Gordon with 42. He had a part in 28 percent of the Marlins 148 total manufactured runs. He also led MLB in 2014 and 2015 and may have also been at the top of the leader board in 2016 if not for his 80-game suspension.

As a team, the Marlins made the most productive outs (285). They were led by Christian Yelich, who led all players with 41. The Marlins also, however, allowed 271 productive outs which was the fourth most after the Mets, Rockies, and Pirates. The Royals were another interesting team in that they had both the fewest productive outs and the most unproductive outs among all teams with 177 and 769, respectively.

In 2016, Evan Longoria finished with the greatest number of unproductive outs (105), and he didn't improve upon this much in 2017 as he finished the season with 95, tied for the third most in baseball. However, this season he also tied for second in productive outs with 39. His 12 sacrifice flies tied with Josh Reddick—who finished tied for sixth in productive outs with 35—for the most in MLB. The player who finished with the most unproductive outs this season was Adam Duvall with 114, over one and a half times his total of 69 in 2016.

Players with the most Manufactured Runs, Productive Outs, & Unproductive Outs

Manufactured Runs		Productive Outs		Unproductive Outs	
Gordon, Dee, Mia	42	Yelich, Christian, Mia	41	Duvall, Adam, Cin	114
Betts, Mookie, Bos	33	Longoria, Evan, TB	39	Judge, Aaron, NYY	96
Hamilton, Billy, Cin	31	Cano, Robinson, Sea	39	Bautista, Jose, Tor	95
DeShields, Delino, Tex	31	Rizzo, Anthony, ChC	37	Longoria, Evan, TB	95
Inciarte, Ender, Atl	29	Mazara, Nomar, Tex	36	Galvis, Freddy, Phi	94
Altuve, Jose, Hou	29	Crawford, Brandon, SF	35	Perez, Salvador, KC	90
Segura, Jean, Sea	27	Panik, Joe, SF	35	Machado, Manny, Bal	88
Phillips, Brandon, Atl-LAA	27	Reddick, Josh, Hou	35	Schoop, Jonathan, Bal	88
Dozier, Brian, Min	26	Choo, Shin-Soo, Tex	34	Odor, Rougned, Tex	87
Bogaerts, Xander, Bos	25	Lamb, Jake, Ari	33	Pujols, Albert, LAA	86
Maybin, Cameron, LAA-Hou	23	Cabrera, Melky, CWS-KC	32	Ramirez, Jose, Cle	85
Springer, George, Hou	23	Altuve, Jose, Hou	31	Stanton, Giancarlo, Mia	85
Andrus, Elvis, Tex	23	Andrus, Elvis, Tex	31	Cain, Lorenzo, KC	84
Merrifield, Whit, KC	23	Rosario, Eddie, Min	31	Sanchez, Gary, NYY	83
Choo, Shin-Soo, Tex	22	LeMahieu, DJ, Col	31	Realmuto, J.T., Mia	82
Blackmon, Charlie, Col	22	Zobrist, Ben, ChC	31	Seager, Corey, LAD	82
Baez, Javier, ChC	22	Gonzalez, Carlos, Col	30	Davis, Khris, Oak	82
Revere, Ben, LAA	21	Franco, Maikel, Phi	30	Franco, Maikel, Phi	82
Buxton, Byron, Min	21	Simmons, Andrelton, LAA	30	Cabrera, Melky, CWS-KC	82
Nunez, Eduardo, SF-Bos	21	Mauer, Joe, Min	30	Polanco, Jorge, Min	81
Yelich, Christian, Mia	21	Markakis, Nick, Atl	30	Seager, Kyle, Sea	81
Turner, Trea, Was	20	Moreland, Mitch, Bos	30	Bruce, Jay, NYM-Cle	81
Gardner, Brett, NYY	20	Polanco, Jorge, Min	29	Story, Trevor, Col	80
Taylor, Chris, LAD	20	Heyward, Jason, ChC	29	McCutchen, Andrew, Pit	80
Pham, Tommy, StL	20	Votto, Joey, Cin	28	Upton, Justin, Det-LAA	80
Dyson, Jarrod, Sea	20	Machado, Manny, Bal	28	Arenado, Nolan, Col	80
Simmons, Andrelton, LAA	20	Santana, Carlos, Cle	27	Abreu, Jose, CWS	80
Jay, Jon, ChC	20	Arenado, Nolan, Col	27	Rizzo, Anthony, ChC	80
Arcia, Orlando, Mil	20	Calhoun, Kole, LAA	27	Headley, Chase, NYY	79
Gamel, Ben, Sea	20	Goins, Ryan, Tor	27	Moustakas, Mike, KC	78
Kinsler, Ian, Det	19	Gregorius, Didi, NYY	27	Healy, Ryon, Oak	78
Bregman, Alex, Hou	19	Polanco, Gregory, Pit	27	Ozuna, Marcell, Mia	78
Judge, Aaron, NYY	19	Pence, Hunter, SF	26	Bregman, Alex, Hou	78
Shaw, Travis, Mil	19	Turner, Justin, LAD	26	Bogaerts, Xander, Bos	77
Hernandez, Cesar, Phi	19	Gardner, Brett, NYY	26	Rosario, Eddie, Min	77
Souza Jr., Steven, TB	19	Schoop, Jonathan, Bal	26	Altuve, Jose, Hou	77
Cain, Lorenzo, KC	19	Wieters, Matt, Was	26	Ramirez, Hanley, Bos	77
LeMahieu, DJ, Col	19	Sanchez, Yolmer, CWS	25	Swanson, Dansby, Atl	76
Swanson, Dansby, Atl	18	Benintendi, Andrew, Bos	25	Pillar, Kevin, Tor	76
Headley, Chase, NYY	18	Maldonado, Martin, LAA	25	Yelich, Christian, Mia	76
Utley, Chase, LAD	18	Peralta, David, Ari	25	DeJong, Paul, StL	76
Rosario, Eddie, Min	18	Hosmer, Eric, KC	25	Cano, Robinson, Sea	76
Bryant, Kris, ChC	18	Pujols, Albert, LAA	25	Bradley Jr., Jackie, Bos	75
Reddick, Josh, Hou	17	Gamel, Ben, Sea	25	Benintendi, Andrew, Bos	75
Pence, Hunter, SF	17	Encarnacion, Edwin, Cle	25	Myers, Wil, SD	75
Upton, Justin, Det-LAA	17	Pedroia, Dustin, Bos	25	Puig, Yasiel, LAD	74
Kiermaier, Kevin, TB	17	Ozuna, Marcell, Mia	24	Castellanos, Nick, Det	74
Belt, Brandon, SF	17	Arcia, Orlando, Mil	24	Andrus, Elvis, Tex	74
Peraza, Jose, Cin	17	McCutchen, Andrew, Pit	24	Reynolds, Mark, Col	74
Benintendi, Andrew, Bos	17	Duvall, Adam, Cin	24	Dozier, Brian, Min	74
Posey, Buster, SF	17	Braun, Ryan, Mil	24	Suarez, Eugenio, Cin	74
Sanchez, Yolmer, CWS	17	Pillar, Kevin, Tor	24	Gordon, Alex, KC	74
Marte, Starling, Pit	17	Realmuto, J.T., Mia	24		
Galvis, Freddy, Phi	17	Abreu, Jose, CWS	24		

Manufactured Runs, Productive Outs, & Unproductive Outs Produced by Team

Team	Manufactured Runs	Productive Outs	Unproductive Outs
Arizona Diamondbacks	130	230	727
Atlanta Braves	151	276	678
Baltimore Orioles	115	194	716
Boston Red Sox	183	230	735
Chicago White Sox	136	219	702
Chicago Cubs	159	268	707
Cincinnati Reds	132	228	729
Cleveland Indians	128	240	733
Colorado Rockies	157	283	674
Detroit Tigers	116	200	720
Houston Astros	165	248	693
Kansas City Royals	127	177	769
Los Angeles Dodgers	128	229	724
Los Angeles Angels	153	249	629
Miami Marlins	148	285	698
Milwaukee Brewers	124	212	662
Minnesota Twins	164	243	754
New York Yankees	155	238	764
New York Mets	106	213	714
Oakland Athletics	103	183	746
Philadelphia Phillies	125	226	746
Pittsburgh Pirates	139	243	654
San Diego Padres	102	213	669
San Francisco Giants	164	267	673
Seattle Mariners	142	210	736
St Louis Cardinals	139	244	728
Tampa Bay Rays	131	212	723
Texas Rangers	155	236	668
Toronto Blue Jays	116	222	708
Washington Nationals	129	231	681

Manufactured Runs, Productive Outs, & Unproductive Outs Allowed by Team

Team	Manufactured Runs	Productive Outs	Unproductive Outs
Arizona Diamondbacks	131	236	616
Atlanta Braves	141	269	730
Baltimore Orioles	135	229	742
Boston Red Sox	130	191	792
Chicago White Sox	130	230	709
Chicago Cubs	151	210	674
Cincinnati Reds	148	247	684
Cleveland Indians	90	162	673
Colorado Rockies	151	277	704
Detroit Tigers	177	244	746
Houston Astros	119	184	719
Kansas City Royals	147	224	731
Los Angeles Dodgers	102	198	668
Los Angeles Angels	112	181	678
Miami Marlins	152	271	724
Milwaukee Brewers	120	237	707
Minnesota Twins	124	240	714
New York Yankees	147	209	693
New York Mets	168	293	730
Oakland Athletics	172	240	706
Philadelphia Phillies	138	258	707
Pittsburgh Pirates	132	273	760
San Diego Padres	146	206	721
San Francisco Giants	132	262	738
Seattle Mariners	130	221	705
St Louis Cardinals	119	242	663
Tampa Bay Rays	160	240	687
Texas Rangers	142	224	706
Toronto Blue Jays	150	236	735
Washington Nationals	126	215	698

Managers Record

Ben Jedlovec

Here, in 2017, we are in the midst of a quiet managerial revolution. There are four primary symptoms of this trend.

1. In-game situational managerial activity is down, way down in most categories, except for pitching changes.
2. Pre-game preparation and subsequent in-game action is at an all-time high.
3. Managerial age has been gradually increasing throughout baseball history but may have finally turned around.
4. Managerial stability has reached an all-time high.

This section is chock-full of evidence of the first symptom. Veteran managers have adapted to modern trends with their second or third (or, in Dusty Baker's case, a fourth) different team. Baker has been a focal point in this section since the early days of the Bill James Handbook. The 2017 season was not his first time leading his league in Long Outings, though his 27 such games is dwarfed by his own notorious 65 long outings with the 2003 Cubs. Having previously led the league in Lineups, Quick Hooks, Stolen Base Attempts, and Pitch Outs with the Padres, Bud Black's successful first season with the Rockies saw him lead the league in just one category: Sacrifice Attempts. Even there, his total of 76 represents fewer sac attempts than he implemented in six of his eight full seasons in San Diego. Hardly a veteran manager, Bryan Price led the league in called pitchouts for the third consecutive year, though his 17 is a far cry from the 28 and 26 of 2015 and 2016, respectively.

Not convinced by anecdotal evidence? BIS has been publishing the Bill James Handbook since 2002. In that time, the usage of pinch hitters has dropped 8 percent (201 per team vs. 184 per team); pinch runners, 38 percent (40 vs. 25); stolen base attempts, 12 percent (131 vs. 115); sacrifices attempted, 39 percent (71 vs. 43); pitchouts, 83 percent (24 vs. 4); and intentional walks, 35 percent (49 vs. 32). Starting pitcher Long Outings, for which we changed the definition in 2002 because they had become so rare under the previous definition, dropped from 28 to 9 in the same time frame, suggesting another definition change is in order. Managers use 23 percent more relievers than they did 16 years ago. (And we wonder why games are so much longer???)

The second point may be most evident in the number of unique and creative lineups utilized throughout the season. Back in 1994, managers averaged 112 unique lineups over the course of the season. That number breached 120 in 2002, and in 2017 we're butting up against 130. They know they can only use one lineup per game, right? Though often not directly the manager's implementation, the dramatic increase in shift usage (see page 79) can also be attributable to the coaching staff's stronger pre-game preparation.

In the 1870s, the typical skipper was a 28-year-old player manager. The average managerial age has been increasing gradually and consistently ever since, breaking 40 around 1915, crossing 50 in 1995, and peaking at 55 in 2011. However, it quickly reversed course as the Mathenys, Greens, Robertses, Servaises, and Ausmuses of the world rolled in to replace the Johnsons, Torres, Coxes, and LaRussas in dugouts across the league.

Finally, managerial posts have been uncharacteristically stable in recent years, especially in 2017. This past season witnessed zero in-season managerial changes; the same 30 men who filled out the lineup card on Opening Day did likewise on October 1. This is extremely rare in baseball history. According to the Lahman database, this has happened just two other times since the end of World War II (2000 and 2006), though in 2006 Buddy Bell missed the last two weeks of the season receiving treatment for a medical issue before returning to helm the Royals in 2007.

We may interpret these trends to be a product of the growth of informed analysis across MLB. Sabermetric analysis has often found tactical plays such as sacrifices, hit-and-runs, and pitchouts to be of minimal value or even harmful to the team's chances of winning. With that in mind, teams have been known to prioritize other skills from managerial candidates, including motivational and leadership traits and a willingness to embrace the abundance of scouting information and statistical analyses available to them in the modern age. While many young managers came of age in the sabermetrics era, many of the veterans you find in this section have remained successful because they have adapted to the changing expectations placed on them. What's that they say about teaching an old dog new tricks?

Brad Ausmus

Year	Team	Lg	G	LUp	PL%	PH	PR	DS	Quick	Slow	LO	RCD	LS	Rel	SBA	SacA	RM	PO	#	Good	NG	Bomb	W	L	Pct
2014	Tigers	AL	162	103	.51	79	43	44	28	55	43	99	1	473	147	32	144	13	34	17	17	5	90	72	.556
2015	Tigers	AL	161	122	.47	83	38	50	33	59	30	131	4	505	134	37	161	7	32	18	14	7	74	87	.460
2016	Tigers	AL	161	111	.48	89	31	50	41	37	18	93	4	476	87	21	95	3	25	12	13	8	86	75	.534
2017	Tigers	AL	162	131	.50	103	30	24	28	52	17	97	6	510	99	16	104	3	42	26	16	8	64	98	.395
	162-Game Average			117	.49	89	36	42	33	51	27	105	4	493	117	27	126	7	33	18	15	6	79	83	.488

Dusty Baker

Year	Team	Lg	G	LUp	PL%	PH	PR	DS	Quick	Slow	LO	RCD	LS	Rel	SBA	SacA	RM	PO	#	Good	NG	Bomb	W	L	Pct
1994	Giants	NL	115	76	.53	177	16	9	29	25	2	86	12	288	154	88		78	40	24	16	8	55	60	.478
1995	Giants	NL	144	97	.41	230	36	13	32	50	8	90	8	381	184	101		77	51	32	19	14	67	77	.465
1996	Giants	NL	162	129	.51	250	17	15	24	58	15	94	8	425	166	103		96	60	37	23	15	68	94	.420
1997	Giants	NL	162	114	.71	212	17	22	46	25	17	132	4	481	170	85		93	57	36	21	12	90	72	.556
1998	Giants	NL	163	130	.62	224	20	12	43	38	8	113	5	433	153	111		41	68	42	26	9	89	74	.546
1999	Giants	NL	162	119	.62	233	16	16	30	51	27	111		450	165	113		40	41	25	16	10	86	76	.531
2000	Giants	NL	162	82	.56	233	26	22	38	50	25	91	3	384	118	86		37	26	17	9	2	97	65	.599
2001	Giants	NL	162	122	.48	261	22	19	40	48	10	114	4	439	99	95		45	49	33	16	6	90	72	.556
2002	Giants	NL	162	118	.43	223	32	38	29	56	53	106	8	417	95	89	42	41	44	28	16	10	95	66	.590
2003	Cubs	NL	162	114	.49	272	25	43	24	58	65	111	3	420	104	93	31	24	36	23	13	4	88	74	.543
2004	Cubs	NL	162	113	.44	254	16	19	37	41	42	129	8	460	94	108	71	62	33	22	11	7	89	73	.549
2005	Cubs	NL	162	121	.59	240	21	29	40	46	36	103	2	457	104	88	107	70	48	27	21	7	79	83	.488
2006	Cubs	NL	162	133	.56	271	9	26	45	39	22	165	2	542	170	108	139	46	44	28	16	11	66	96	.407
2008	Reds	NL	162	119	.58	285	28	27	26	63	39	124	2	507	132	100	101	37	40	28	12	4	74	88	.457
2009	Reds	NL	162	130	.45	252	15	35	30	62	35	115	1	478	136	120	118	23	36	29	7	4	78	84	.481
2010	Reds	NL	162	120	.46	258	19	49	36	41	22	140	0	502	136	91	157	13	32	22	10	9	91	71	.562
2011	Reds	NL	162	142	.42	240	29	42	34	51	20	115	0	501	147	102	226	33	47	26	21	5	79	83	.488
2012	Reds	NL	162	121	.43	201	19	39	33	39	30	78	4	425	114	108	148	19	33	22	11	3	97	65	.599
2013	Reds	NL	162	95	.54	236	20	27	39	40	14	90	3	461	102	110	157	21	28	23	5	3	90	72	.556
2016	Nationals	NL	162	112	.57	220	20	27	35	45	21	119	4	508	160	59	161	3	43	28	15	9	95	67	.586
2017	Nationals	NL	162	124	.59	241	33	26	22	53	27	90	2	487	138	57	113	3	39	29	10	6	97	65	.599
	162-Game Average			118	.52	243	22	27	35	48	26	112	4	459	138	98	121	44	43	28	15	8	85	77	.525

Jeff Banister

Year	Team	Lg	G	LUp	PL%	PH	PR	DS	Quick	Slow	LO	RCD	LS	Rel	SBA	SacA	RM	PO	#	Good	NG	Bomb	W	L	Pct
2015	Rangers	AL	162	127	.57	94	51	46	40	47	11	122	0	498	140	66	158	5	29	19	10	5	88	74	.543
2016	Rangers	AL	162	124	.55	84	58	38	47	44	7	85	1	479	135	26	136	3	16	5	11	8	95	67	.586
2017	Rangers	AL	162	134	.54	66	40	20	39	40	6	71	7	464	157	35	153	0	22	9	13	10	78	84	.481
	162-Game Average			128	.55	81	50	35	42	44	8	93	3	480	144	42	149	3	22	11	11	8	87	75	.537

Bud Black

Year	Team	Lg	G	LUp	PL%	PH	PR	DS	Quick	Slow	LO	RCD	LS	Rel	SBA	SacA	RM	PO	#	Good	NG	Bomb	W	L	Pct
2007	Padres	NL	163	115	.62	279	18	13	63	28	13	122	0	485	79	85	73	56	48	28	20	11	89	74	.546
2008	Padres	NL	162	113	.63	286	25	20	55	36	17	109	0	491	53	75	78	31	61	30	31	17	63	99	.389
2009	Padres	NL	162	137	.64	264	8	34	50	37	8	118	5	527	111	99	84	55	58	42	16	6	75	87	.463
2010	Padres	NL	162	135	.61	285	16	45	55	33	10	132	7	499	174	99	135	31	51	35	16	8	90	72	.556
2011	Padres	NL	162	140	.58	288	20	43	40	36	10	110	2	490	214	69	184	41	56	31	25	13	71	91	.438
2012	Padres	NL	162	132	.74	280	26	35	45	49	11	117	5	529	201	89	162	21	48	34	14	7	76	86	.469
2013	Padres	NL	162	145	.66	271	24	37	35	46	4	102	1	488	152	78	122	12	31	20	11	8	76	86	.469
2014	Padres	NL	162	157	.74	313	23	29	49	33	13	104	1	481	125	74	116	15	32	24	8	4	77	85	.475
2015	Padres	NL	65	50	.54	113	6	6	8	25	3	40	0	199	54	24	46	2	15	11	4	0	32	33	.492
2017	Rockies	NL	162	111	.51	261	19	14	44	36	4	100	2	549	93	76	149	4	20	14	6	3	87	75	.537
	162-Game Average			131	.63	281	20	29	47	38	10	113	2	504	134	82	122	28	45	29	16	8	78	84	.481

Bruce Bochy

Year	Team	Lg	G	LUp	PL%	PH	PR	DS	Quick	Slow	LO	RCD	LS	Rel	SBA	SacA	RM	PO	#	Good	NG	Bomb	W	L	Pct
1995	Padres	NL	144	96	.59	262	30	23	44	41	17	38	3	337	170	68		38	37	19	18	11	70	74	.486
1996	Padres	NL	162	114	.52	289	29	15	51	33	10	67	12	411	164	73		65	47	29	18	12	91	71	.562
1997	Padres	NL	162	111	.60	291	26	9	45	45	3	81	11	426	200	84		58	37	20	17	11	76	86	.469
1998	Padres	NL	162	108	.65	280	62	44	44	45	9	81	12	369	116	84		27	45	31	14	10	98	64	.605
1999	Padres	NL	162	137	.60	298	51	21	44	36	4	68	5	403	241	60		29	48	29	19	13	74	88	.457
2000	Padres	NL	162	134	.52	285	44	14	41	47	14	105	5	443	184	52		27	50	21	29	11	76	86	.469
2001	Padres	NL	162	116	.60	255	54	27	32	47	6	85	10	422	173	43		23	54	31	23	13	79	83	.488
2002	Padres	NL	162	123	.66	259	44	56	39	40	17	106	4	459	115	63	74	14	61	38	23	14	66	96	.407

Year	Team	Lg	G	LUp	PL%	PH	PR	DS	Quick	Slow	LO	RCD	LS	Rel	SBA	SacA	RM	PO	#	Good	NG	Bomb	W	L	Pct
2003	Padres	NL	162	134	.58	339	20	29	34	43	16	100	3	473	115	63	41	6	52	33	19	12	64	98	.395
2004	Padres	NL	162	96	.54	261	28	47	47	32	15	76	3	437	77	75	96	14	39	24	15	10	87	75	.537
2005	Padres	NL	162	128	.58	285	31	49	46	36	23	87	1	456	143	89	111	16	45	33	12	8	82	80	.506
2006	Padres	NL	162	111	.60	264	64	48	43	42	24	111	2	475	154	77	110	21	63	43	20	10	88	74	.543
2007	Giants	NL	162	128	.72	264	50	45	26	50	36	132	2	496	152	86	119	10	41	29	12	3	71	91	.438
2008	Giants	NL	162	134	.68	276	32	39	24	59	42	97	6	478	154	77	155	5	59	40	19	8	72	90	.444
2009	Giants	NL	162	134	.65	231	21	52	42	40	32	84	8	457	106	93	118	5	49	32	17	10	88	74	.543
2010	Giants	NL	162	126	.55	224	45	70	29	37	40	118	12	477	87	102	144	12	58	41	17	8	92	70	.568
2011	Giants	NL	162	138	.62	245	49	42	38	38	44	108	3	480	136	79	175	11	46	36	10	6	86	76	.531
2012	Giants	NL	162	112	.75	220	32	55	22	50	31	136	9	526	157	87	176	15	42	30	12	5	94	68	.580
2013	Giants	NL	162	109	.70	263	19	45	33	52	23	143	4	524	93	78	164	7	64	46	18	4	76	86	.469
2014	Giants	NL	162	131	.66	236	29	64	45	41	19	102	1	475	83	53	147	12	35	25	10	9	88	74	.543
2015	Giants	NL	162	124	.63	230	12	21	45	32	11	137	2	557	129	54	173	8	28	20	8	3	84	78	.519
2016	Giants	NL	162	121	.66	268	7	29	31	42	28	148	4	575	115	54	178	6	30	25	5	4	87	75	.537
2017	Giants	NL	162	136	.61	298	22	12	22	59	20	93	2	502	110	51	135	3	42	29	13	11	64	98	.395
162-Game Average				122	.62	268	35	37	38	43	21	101	5	466	139	72	132	19	47	31	16	9	81	81	.500

Tim Bogar

Year	Team	Lg	G	LUp	PL%	PH	PR	DS	Quick	Slow	LO	RCD	LS	Rel	SBA	SacA	RM	PO	#	Good	NG	Bomb	W	L	Pct
2014	Rangers	AL	22	21	.56	1	5	0	10	3	3	11	0	76	29	6	23	1	9	5	4	3	14	8	.636
162-Game Average				155	.56	7	37	0	74	22	22	81	0	560	214	44	169	7	66	37	29	22	103	59	.636

Kevin Cash

Year	Team	Lg	G	LUp	PL%	PH	PR	DS	Quick	Slow	LO	RCD	LS	Rel	SBA	SacA	RM	PO	#	Good	NG	Bomb	W	L	Pct
2015	Rays	AL	162	137	.62	219	23	38	72	33	10	134	3	530	132	27	173	2	23	17	6	3	80	82	.494
2016	Rays	AL	162	142	.55	103	11	28	42	18		100	8	485	97	24	146	12	25	16	9	4	68	94	.420
2017	Rays	AL	162	126	.57	123	21	24	39	47	16	89	9	511	122	24	143	12	37	25	12	8	80	82	.494
162-Game Average				135	.58	148	18	30	51	44	15	108	7	509	117	25	154	9	28	19	9	5	76	86	.469

Terry Collins

Year	Team	Lg	G	LUp	PL%	PH	PR	DS	Quick	Slow	LO	RCD	LS	Rel	SBA	SacA	RM	PO	#	Good	NG	Bomb	W	L	Pct
1994	Astros	NL	115	74	.54	185	20	13	6	6	0	37	4	268	168	90		37	28	17	11	5	66	49	.574
1995	Astros	NL	144	106	.49	302	38	11	15	7	8	100	8	394	236	97		44	39	27	12	8	76	68	.528
1996	Astros	NL	162	111	.41	257	30	38	13	12	9	70	10	371	243	94		35	42	30	12	4	82	80	.506
1997	Angels	AL	162	117	.70	86	34	22	10	16	15	67	8	400	198	55		60	25	13	12	4	84	78	.519
1998	Angels	AL	162	119	.57	100	64	33	15	11	28	86	11	415	138	69		38	16	6	10	4	85	77	.525
1999	Angels	AL	133	113	.56	93	26	16	10	16	10	68	2	315	93	39		7	10	1	9	3	51	82	.383
2011	Mets	NL	162	121	.68	312	18	28	32	44	23	126	5	514	165	88	151	9	48	35	13	9	77	85	.475
2012	Mets	NL	162	141	.69	329	16	38	39	36	19	113	0	505	117	75	149	8	29	18	11	3	74	88	.457
2013	Mets	NL	162	132	.61	266	12	33	33	42	15	131	4	535	149	67	128	3	38	30	8	3	74	88	.457
2014	Mets	NL	162	135	.55	247	17	26	28	46	23	111	6	489	135	73	119	2	38	23	15	4	79	83	.488
2015	Mets	NL	162	138	.52	255	21	40	47	36	6	119	8	485	76	49	117	1	43	33	10	6	90	72	.556
2016	Mets	NL	162	129	.68	292	17	50	53	33	6	141	4	538	60	55	80	6	39	26	13	9	87	75	.537
2017	Mets	NL	162	149	.66	247	20	32	25	54	8	127	6	568	81	52	97	3	51	27	24	14	70	92	.432
162-Game Average				128	.59	239	27	31	26	29	14	104	6	467	150	73	120	20	36	23	13	6	80	82	.494

Craig Counsell

Year	Team	Lg	G	LUp	PL%	PH	PR	DS	Quick	Slow	LO	RCD	LS	Rel	SBA	SacA	RM	PO	#	Good	NG	Bomb	W	L	Pct
2015	Brewers	NL	137	106	.54	247	14	30	30	47	3	85	1	424	99	56	106	2	30	26	4	3	61	76	.445
2016	Brewers	NL	162	123	.55	284	4	22	40	41	1	115	3	513	237	71	160	0	33	16	17	8	73	89	.451
2017	Brewers	NL	162	123	.53	285	18	44	58	33	5	124	5	550	169	56	159	9	45	30	15	9	86	76	.531
162-Game Average				124	.54	287	13	34	45	43	3	114	3	523	177	64	149	1	38	25	13	7	77	85	.475

John Farrell

Year	Team	Lg	G	LUp	PL%	PH	PR	DS	Quick	Slow	LO	RCD	LS	Rel	SBA	SacA	RM	PO	#	Good	NG	Bomb	W	L	Pct
2011	Blue Jays	AL	162	131	.43	64	48	22	40	41	26	62	3	474	183	40	181	22	28	17	11	5	81	81	.500
2012	Blue Jays	AL	162	131	.50	94	30	16	49	44	7	84	3	495	164	46	211	15	20	11	9	7	73	89	.451
2013	Red Sox	AL	162	126	.68	93	41	20	28	46	34	71	4	450	142	32	147	5	10	5	5	3	97	65	.599
2014	Red Sox	AL	162	145	.55	101	24	17	29	53	28	107	1	493	88	26	124	4	19	11	8	2	71	91	.438
2015	Red Sox	AL	114	96	.56	55	18	20	26	28	6	62	1	326	63	27	105	2	12	6	6	1	50	64	.439

Year	Team	Lg	G	LINEUPS		SUBSTITUTION			PITCHER USAGE						TACTICS				INTENTIONAL BB				RESULTS		
				LUp	PL%	PH	PR	DS	Quick	Slow	LO	RCD	LS	Rel	SBA	SacA	RM	PO	#	Good	NG	Bomb	W	L	Pct
2016	Red Sox	AL	162	118	.53	110	28	11	34	51	26	79	2	463	107	15	169	0	16	8	8	3	93	69	.574
2017	Red Sox	AL	162	137	.54	95	39	17	30	63	33	97	4	515	137	20	131	2	18	13	5	1	93	69	.574
162-Game Average				132	.54	91	34	18	35	49	24	84	3	480	132	31	159	7	18	11	8	3	83	79	.512

Terry Francona

Year	Team	Lg	G	LINEUPS		SUBSTITUTION			PITCHER USAGE						TACTICS				INTENTIONAL BB				RESULTS		
				LUp	PL%	PH	PR	DS	Quick	Slow	LO	RCD	LS	Rel	SBA	SacA	RM	PO	#	Good	NG	Bomb	W	L	Pct
1997	Phillies	NL	162	98	.66	288	19	28	28	54	22	102	9	409	148	91		30	42	23	19	9	68	94	.420
1998	Phillies	NL	162	84	.53	256	20	19	34	57	20	88	7	385	142	85		16	27	10	17	8	75	87	.463
1999	Phillies	NL	162	85	.51	239	13	31	29	41	16	111	7	441	160	81		27	24	14	10	6	77	85	.475
2000	Phillies	NL	162	108	.53	278	17	14	38	43	25	102	5	414	132	89		16	32	22	10	7	65	97	.401
2004	Red Sox	AL	162	141	.65	116	65	58	41	48	32	105	8	437	98	18	91	28	28	22	6	4	98	64	.605
2005	Red Sox	AL	162	104	.67	110	46	37	25	55	30	99	3	442	57	21	79	11	28	18	10	5	95	67	.586
2006	Red Sox	AL	162	116	.59	93	54	49	36	44	13	94	9	454	74	33	98	16	25	11	14	7	86	76	.531
2007	Red Sox	AL	162	109	.60	84	34	23	41	35	32	89	4	451	120	45	90	14	20	14	6	4	96	66	.593
2008	Red Sox	AL	162	131	.59	62	40	40	50	30	20	90	11	466	155	40	87	8	17	10	7	4	95	67	.586
2009	Red Sox	AL	162	113	.58	85	47	28	36	50	30	68	6	463	165	29	68	9	24	15	9	6	95	67	.586
2010	Red Sox	AL	162	143	.62	125	48	34	32	63	49	84	3	443	85	36	125	26	30	17	13	4	89	73	.549
2011	Red Sox	AL	162	123	.67	89	44	11	52	46	27	89	4	444	144	29	163	34	11	6	5	2	90	72	.556
2013	Indians	AL	162	121	.75	78	45	24	47	34	18	122	2	540	153	41	158	5	26	15	11	6	92	70	.568
2014	Indians	AL	162	133	.78	123	16	24	37	37	18	150	7	573	131	58	128	3	51	29	22	13	85	77	.525
2015	Indians	AL	161	127	.75	138	21	13	40	36	23	85	4	476	114	63	87	4	27	20	7	5	81	80	.503
2016	Indians	AL	162	101	.73	114	27	29	47	39	18	103	3	504	165	44	126	2	34	22	12	7	94	67	.584
2017	Indians	AL	162	131	.73	93	43	50	48	31	20	106	4	497	111	35	95	2	15	11	4	3	102	60	.630
162-Game Average				116	.64	140	35	30	39	44	24	99	6	461	127	49	107	15	27	16	11	6	87	75	.537

Ron Gardenhire

Year	Team	Lg	G	LINEUPS		SUBSTITUTION			PITCHER USAGE						TACTICS				INTENTIONAL BB				RESULTS		
				LUp	PL%	PH	PR	DS	Quick	Slow	LO	RCD	LS	Rel	SBA	SacA	RM	PO	#	Good	NG	Bomb	W	L	Pct
2002	Twins	AL	161	111	.69	141	36	42	54	25	10	84	1	435	141	48	44	11	24	16	8	4	94	67	.584
2003	Twins	AL	162	126	.63	144	50	26	49	33	13	85	2	399	138	59	37	14	35	16	19	6	90	72	.556
2004	Twins	AL	162	131	.59	129	45	29	56	21	20	106	4	435	162	66	121	18	27	15	12	7	92	70	.568
2005	Twins	AL	162	135	.58	104	45	26	50	21	5	87	1	396	146	59	138	16	38	28	10	3	83	79	.512
2006	Twins	AL	162	97	.62	93	36	21	60	31	3	82	5	421	143	48	130	11	25	14	11	4	96	66	.593
2007	Twins	AL	162	139	.63	104	42	25	45	30	8	99	4	438	142	45	148	11	33	14	19	9	79	83	.488
2008	Twins	AL	163	103	.64	109	26	12	47	29	5	115	3	485	144	73	143	17	38	25	13	8	88	75	.540
2009	Twins	AL	163	129	.63	83	54	34	43	25	12	115	3	480	117	62	100	21	20	9	11	4	87	76	.534
2010	Twins	AL	162	112	.62	86	55	30	57	28	5	106	1	465	96	47	140	14	19	12	7	4	94	68	.580
2011	Twins	AL	162	150	.58	93	48	21	34	44	17	82	1	457	131	44	170	5	37	21	16	9	63	99	.389
2012	Twins	AL	162	121	.62	64	45	24	42	31	4	82	1	499	172	49	207	10	43	27	16	6	66	96	.407
2013	Twins	AL	162	139	.66	103	42	28	41	43	6	78	1	511	85	37	137	14	31	13	18	6	66	96	.407
2014	Twins	AL	162	132	.64	97	44	23	40	40	2	82	2	491	135	31	149	5	24	11	13	6	70	92	.432
162-Game Average				125	.62	104	44	26	48	31	8	92	2	455	135	51	128	13	30	17	13	6	82	80	.506

John Gibbons

Year	Team	Lg	G	LINEUPS		SUBSTITUTION			PITCHER USAGE						TACTICS				INTENTIONAL BB				RESULTS		
				LUp	PL%	PH	PR	DS	Quick	Slow	LO	RCD	LS	Rel	SBA	SacA	RM	PO	#	Good	NG	Bomb	W	L	Pct
2004	Blue Jays	AL	50	36	.68	42	3	2	16	8	7	22	1	130	34	2	47	21	11	5	6	3	20	30	.400
2005	Blue Jays	AL	162	124	.66	148	11	37	55	18	9	77	12	432	107	28	128	45	29	13	16	9	80	82	.494
2006	Blue Jays	AL	162	120	.53	112	32	40	59	33	17	94	16	482	98	20	127	40	56	32	24	12	87	75	.537
2007	Blue Jays	AL	162	131	.46	139	48	33	45	37	31	75	9	420	79	35	99	37	34	17	17	6	83	79	.512
2008	Blue Jays	AL	74	60	.48	53	15	18	12	20	12	43	0	205	70	23	39	10	26	16	10	6	35	39	.473
2013	Blue Jays	AL	162	136	.63	124	31	24	55	44	14	69	2	487	153	41	160	4	33	17	16	6	74	88	.457
2014	Blue Jays	AL	162	128	.72	202	41	49	45	37	20	73	8	449	99	49	161	6	23	17	6	2	83	79	.512
2015	Blue Jays	AL	162	129	.48	97	41	47	46	37	13	85	6	469	111	45	152	2	20	10	10	3	93	69	.574
2016	Blue Jays	AL	162	141	.44	90	37	54	39	30	6	98	6	487	78	33	109	1	10	6	4	3	89	73	.549
2017	Blue Jays	AL	162	136	.56	126	39	33	41	33	8	100	4	578	77	35	132	4	25	14	11	5	76	86	.469
162-Game Average				130	.56	129	34	38	47	34	16	84	7	472	103	35	132	19	30	17	14	6	82	80	.506

Kirk Gibson

Year	Team	Lg	G	LINEUPS		SUBSTITUTION			PITCHER USAGE						TACTICS				INTENTIONAL BB				RESULTS		
				LUp	PL%	PH	PR	DS	Quick	Slow	LO	RCD	LS	Rel	SBA	SacA	RM	PO	#	Good	NG	Bomb	W	L	Pct
2010	Diamondbacks	NL	83	57	.64	154	7	11	25	21	8	43	1	247	69	28	62	19	19	13	6	2	34	49	.410
2011	Diamondbacks	NL	162	118	.57	253	9	13	33	51	15	116	2	463	188	74	143	12	16	10	6	3	94	68	.580
2012	Diamondbacks	NL	162	140	.56	231	11	9	35	50	16	104	4	461	144	77	120	8	18	11	7	1	81	81	.500

Year	Team	Lg	G	LINEUPS		SUBSTITUTION			PITCHER USAGE						TACTICS				INTENTIONAL BB				RESULTS		
				LUp	PL%	PH	PR	DS	Quick	Slow	LO	RCD	LS	Rel	SBA	SacA	RM	PO	#	Good	NG	Bomb	W	L	Pct
2013	Diamondbacks	NL	162	138	.59	285	22	15	31	44	9	121	0	527	103	67	108	3	42	31	11	5	81	81	.500
2014	Diamondbacks	NL	159	135	.55	247	19	18	43	41	5	92	1	479	117	67	140	13	42	28	14	**10**	63	96	.396
	162-Game Average			131	.57	260	15	15	37	46	12	106	2	484	138	70	128	12	30	21	10	5	79	83	.488

Joe Girardi

Year	Team	Lg	G	LINEUPS		SUBSTITUTION			PITCHER USAGE						TACTICS				INTENTIONAL BB				RESULTS		
				LUp	PL%	PH	PR	DS	Quick	Slow	LO	RCD	LS	Rel	SBA	SacA	RM	PO	#	Good	NG	Bomb	W	L	Pct
2006	Marlins	NL	162	117	.50	250	44	**66**	46	40	28	76	3	438	168	97	108	42	58	37	21	7	78	84	.481
2008	Yankees	AL	162	114	.63	97	37	42	**60**	37	12	88	**10**	475	157	38	**173**	**36**	37	22	15	8	89	73	.549
2009	Yankees	AL	162	106	.73	97	**61**	42	36	45	27	88	**13**	461	139	44	83	33	28	14	14	9	**103**	59	.636
2010	Yankees	AL	162	114	.72	117	44	31	43	39	33	76	3	430	133	47	152	20	37	26	11	6	95	67	.586
2011	Yankees	AL	162	94	.69	72	41	53	51	36	21	88	2	465	193	50	151	26	43	30	13	4	**97**	65	.599
2012	Yankees	AL	162	107	.70	149	33	48	37	53	21	115	7	485	120	47	145	10	32	17	15	6	**95**	67	.586
2013	Yankees	AL	162	141	.59	119	15	29	42	50	23	82	4	428	146	49	131	4	34	20	14	6	85	77	.525
2014	Yankees	AL	162	142	.74	100	27	33	51	28	10	95	7	475	138	44	132	8	23	10	13	9	84	78	.519
2015	Yankees	AL	162	126	.79	118	50	57	48	34	9	80	**10**	497	88	32	92	6	16	8	8	4	87	75	.537
2016	Yankees	AL	162	143	.72	85	32	48	53	44	8	99	7	483	94	35	89	3	15	9	6	4	84	78	.519
2017	Yankees	AL	162	140	.56	112	22	10	49	29	9	79	7	477	112	28	117	3	18	11	7	4	91	71	.562
	162-Game Average			122	.67	120	37	42	47	40	18	88	7	465	135	46	125	17	31	19	12	6	90	72	.556

Fredi Gonzalez

Year	Team	Lg	G	LINEUPS		SUBSTITUTION			PITCHER USAGE						TACTICS				INTENTIONAL BB				RESULTS		
				LUp	PL%	PH	PR	DS	Quick	Slow	LO	RCD	LS	Rel	SBA	SacA	RM	PO	#	Good	NG	Bomb	W	L	Pct
2007	Marlins	NL	162	96	.50	284	29	34	33	**56**	20	119	5	560	139	91	79	22	60	36	24	**16**	71	91	.438
2008	Marlins	NL	161	106	.51	255	38	49	38	39	8	120	3	511	104	61	75	17	66	42	24	14	84	77	.522
2009	Marlins	NL	162	97	.58	281	28	49	48	26	12	116	0	**530**	110	86	88	20	60	38	22	15	87	75	.537
2010	Marlins	NL	70	31	.41	104	12	16	14	13	11	35	1	193	56	33	64	10	18	11	7	5	34	36	.486
2011	Braves	NL	162	119	.60	260	27	29	53	36	21	**144**	0	510	121	95	139	19	**73**	**49**	24	13	89	73	.549
2012	Braves	NL	162	108	.61	268	18	27	50	34	9	115	4	460	133	67	116	20	40	28	12	11	94	68	.580
2013	Braves	NL	162	115	.50	214	**40**	51	50	42	8	124	2	466	95	79	94	11	35	26	9	4	96	66	.593
2014	Braves	NL	162	103	.45	206	**34**	34	27	41	20	**122**	3	472	128	70	106	23	36	24	12	8	79	83	.488
2015	Braves	NL	162	**140**	.61	255	21	31	35	**55**	7	136	0	532	102	80	135	4	**45**	**35**	10	5	67	95	.414
2016	Braves	NL	37	34	.73	58	9	11	9	9	3	33	1	131	26	20	36	0	15	11	4	2	9	28	.243
	162-Game Average			110	.54	252	30	38	41	41	14	125	2	504	117	79	108	17	52	35	17	11	82	80	.506

Andy Green

Year	Team	Lg	G	LINEUPS		SUBSTITUTION			PITCHER USAGE						TACTICS				INTENTIONAL BB				RESULTS		
				LUp	PL%	PH	PR	DS	Quick	Slow	LO	RCD	LS	Rel	SBA	SacA	RM	PO	#	Good	NG	Bomb	W	L	Pct
2016	Padres	NL	162	130	.56	249	29	25	46	53	6	119	4	510	170	48	138	3	44	26	18	9	68	**94**	.420
2017	Padres	NL	162	138	.55	238	10	38	45	43	5	101	3	517	122	63	119	2	28	18	10	4	71	91	.438
	162-Game Average			134	.55	244	20	32	46	48	6	110	3	514	146	56	129	3	36	22	14	7	70	93	.429

Chip Hale

Year	Team	Lg	G	LINEUPS		SUBSTITUTION			PITCHER USAGE						TACTICS				INTENTIONAL BB				RESULTS		
				LUp	PL%	PH	PR	DS	Quick	Slow	LO	RCD	LS	Rel	SBA	SacA	RM	PO	#	Good	NG	Bomb	W	L	Pct
2015	Diamondbacks	NL	162	130	.48	270	14	35	49	35	5	103	**8**	550	**176**	67	146	5	**45**	**35**	10	6	79	83	.488
2016	Diamondbacks	NL	162	139	.45	266	10	30	27	**66**	7	130	**5**	575	168	51	120	0	57	41	16	8	69	93	.426
	162-Game Average			135	.46	268	12	33	38	51	6	117	7	563	172	59	133	3	51	38	13	7	74	88	.457

A.J. Hinch

Year	Team	Lg	G	LINEUPS		SUBSTITUTION			PITCHER USAGE						TACTICS				INTENTIONAL BB				RESULTS		
				LUp	PL%	PH	PR	DS	Quick	Slow	LO	RCD	LS	Rel	SBA	SacA	RM	PO	#	Good	NG	Bomb	W	L	Pct
2009	Diamondbacks	NL	133	115	.63	222	10	13	24	50	24	61	5	392	113	64	41	5	24	12	12	6	58	75	.436
2010	Diamondbacks	NL	79	56	.53	120	7	4	12	40	21	39	1	207	58	19	51	7	19	9	10	9	31	48	.392
2015	Astros	AL	162	**151**	.63	122	40	37	33	41	19	97	0	482	**169**	31	128	6	17	11	6	2	86	76	.531
2016	Astros	AL	162	143	.55	118	35	27	42	35	9	87	1	500	146	38	137	5	19	11	8	6	84	78	.519
2017	Astros	AL	162	144	.56	73	29	39	**57**	35	3	83	8	519	140	21	148	6	17	12	5	3	**101**	61	.623
	162-Game Average			141	.58	152	28	28	39	47	18	85	3	487	145	40	117	7	22	13	10	6	84	78	.519

Clint Hurdle

Year	Team	Lg	G	LINEUPS		SUBSTITUTION			PITCHER USAGE						TACTICS				INTENTIONAL BB				RESULTS		
				LUp	PL%	PH	PR	DS	Quick	Slow	LO	RCD	LS	Rel	SBA	SacA	RM	PO	#	Good	NG	Bomb	W	L	Pct
2002	Rockies	NL	140	100	.52	274	28	41	33	45	17	104	3	437	139	46	50	13	38	22	16	11	67	73	.479
2003	Rockies	NL	162	108	.47	317	17	32	35	40	5	87	4	500	100	82	26	16	51	31	20	13	74	88	.457
2004	Rockies	NL	162	131	.57	289	18	35	36	**63**	20	74	1	473	77	**128**	67	12	**84**	**54**	**30**	12	68	94	.420

				LINEUPS		SUBSTITUTION			PITCHER USAGE						TACTICS				INTENTIONAL BB				RESULTS		
Year	Team	Lg	G	LUp	PL%	PH	PR	DS	Quick	Slow	LO	RCD	LS	Rel	SBA	SacA	RM	PO	#	Good	NG	Bomb	W	L	Pct
2005	Rockies	NL	162	135	.60	273	21	40	42	60	17	89	2	459	97	114	119	22	54	28	26	**15**	67	**95**	.414
2006	Rockies	NL	162	111	.49	259	17	22	34	**52**	17	107	2	499	135	**156**	114	28	81	45	**36**	**23**	76	86	.469
2007	Rockies	NL	163	96	.51	283	32	29	45	37	13	112	1	529	131	**112**	109	26	61	30	**31**	14	**90**	73	.552
2008	Rockies	NL	162	131	.49	253	20	31	40	43	16	85	2	485	**178**	111	116	**43**	49	31	18	6	74	88	.457
2009	Rockies	NL	46	42	.60	73	8	10	11	14	3	31	0	135	45	26	34	3	11	8	3	1	18	28	.391
2011	Pirates	NL	162	134	.60	278	26	63	**58**	27	1	134	3	**549**	160	101	173	20	65	39	**26**	13	72	90	.444
2012	Pirates	NL	162	133	.55	270	26	**60**	50	33	3	74	2	483	125	82	120	17	30	18	12	3	79	83	.488
2013	Pirates	NL	162	127	.51	**289**	24	**61**	**61**	25	7	76	3	465	136	83	**172**	20	26	22	4	2	94	68	.580
2014	Pirates	NL	162	123	.50	**322**	28	38	47	40	7	91	0	452	151	85	**187**	**24**	**43**	26	**17**	7	88	74	.543
2015	Pirates	NL	162	108	.50	269	**48**	**76**	39	40	9	124	1	**500**	143	**81**	173	9	38	31	7	3	98	64	.605
2016	Pirates	NL	162	125	.41	293	**39**	**73**	57	36	1	119	4	525	155	55	154	9	28	15	13	6	78	83	.484
2017	Pirates	NL	162	138	.51	277	23	37	42	39	6	110	8	502	103	59	124	7	32	17	15	7	75	87	.463
	162-Game Average			123	.52	284	27	46	45	42	10	100	3	494	133	93	123	19	49	29	19	10	79	83	.488

Dan Jennings

				LINEUPS		SUBSTITUTION			PITCHER USAGE						TACTICS				INTENTIONAL BB				RESULTS		
Year	Team	Lg	G	LUp	PL%	PH	PR	DS	Quick	Slow	LO	RCD	LS	Rel	SBA	SacA	RM	PO	#	Good	NG	Bomb	W	L	Pct
2015	Marlins	NL	124	98	.53	186	14	23	32	30	4	67	3	379	120	63	97	2	22	12	10	5	55	69	.444
	162-Game Average			128	.53	243	18	30	42	39	5	88	4	495	157	82	127	3	29	16	13	7	72	90	.444

Tom Lawless

				LINEUPS		SUBSTITUTION			PITCHER USAGE						TACTICS				INTENTIONAL BB				RESULTS		
Year	Team	Lg	G	LUp	PL%	PH	PR	DS	Quick	Slow	LO	RCD	LS	Rel	SBA	SacA	RM	PO	#	Good	NG	Bomb	W	L	Pct
2014	Astros	AL	24	23	.64	18	6	9	8	3	5	7	1	67	39	9	35	3	6	2	4	1	11	13	.458
	162-Game Average			155	.64	122	41	61	54	20	34	47	7	452	263	61	236	20	41	14	27	7	74	88	.457

Torey Lovullo

				LINEUPS		SUBSTITUTION			PITCHER USAGE						TACTICS				INTENTIONAL BB				RESULTS		
Year	Team	Lg	G	LUp	PL%	PH	PR	DS	Quick	Slow	LO	RCD	LS	Rel	SBA	SacA	RM	PO	#	Good	NG	Bomb	W	L	Pct
2015	Red Sox	AL	48	40	.58	17	17	4	9	16	10	28	0	149	35	10	32	0	5	3	2	1	28	20	.583
2017	Diamondbacks	NL	162	129	.55	254	28	36	34	45	6	116	2	513	133	50	85	3	45	32	13	6	93	69	.574
	162-Game Average			130	.56	209	35	31	33	47	12	111	2	511	130	46	90	2	39	27	12	5	93	69	.574

Pete Mackanin

				LINEUPS		SUBSTITUTION			PITCHER USAGE						TACTICS				INTENTIONAL BB				RESULTS		
Year	Team	Lg	G	LUp	PL%	PH	PR	DS	Quick	Slow	LO	RCD	LS	Rel	SBA	SacA	RM	PO	#	Good	NG	Bomb	W	L	Pct
2005	Pirates	NL	26	24	.52	54	1	5	11	4	1	22	0	94	19	19	20	2	5	2	3	1	12	14	.462
2007	Reds	NL	80	57	.59	130	10	26	20	22	9	58	3	266	62	44	36	12	18	10	8	3	41	39	.513
2015	Phillies	NL	88	82	.76	143	2	16	25	26	5	58	4	278	70	48	93	9	12	7	5	2	37	51	.420
2016	Phillies	NL	162	144	.64	260	14	46	44	44	4	128	2	505	141	61	138	17	30	19	11	10	71	91	.438
2017	Phillies	NL	162	135	.66	236	11	21	37	44	3	114	2	506	84	40	91	0	39	24	15	4	66	96	.407
	162-Game Average			138	.65	257	12	36	43	44	7	119	3	516	118	66	118	13	33	19	13	6	71	91	.438

Joe Maddon

				LINEUPS		SUBSTITUTION			PITCHER USAGE						TACTICS				INTENTIONAL BB				RESULTS		
Year	Team	Lg	G	LUp	PL%	PH	PR	DS	Quick	Slow	LO	RCD	LS	Rel	SBA	SacA	RM	PO	#	Good	NG	Bomb	W	L	Pct
1996	Angels	AL	22	19	.64	21	5	0	7	6	6	10	3	48	11	20		6	4	3	1	1	8	14	.364
1998	Angels	AL	8	4	.57	2	4	0	1	5	3	5	3	12	2	7		0	1	0	1	0	6	2	.750
1999	Angels	AL	29	19	.58	29	4	1	6	0	4	20	0	85	23	12		7	3	1	2	1	19	10	.655
2006	Devil Rays	AL	162	**145**	.54	81	26	51	41	39	16	79	10	444	186	51	132	48	39	19	20	13	61	**101**	.377
2007	Devil Rays	AL	162	122	.53	80	19	16	31	**56**	19	113	1	483	179	40	118	**50**	31	18	13	4	66	**96**	.407
2008	Rays	AL	162	115	.69	**133**	16	39	48	37	14	112	7	448	192	31	113	26	29	15	14	8	97	65	.599
2009	Rays	AL	162	123	.66	**140**	21	18	28	51	23	**139**	3	510	**255**	29	99	15	22	10	12	7	84	78	.519
2010	Rays	AL	162	129	.67	174	31	18	41	34	26	135	2	491	219	45	166	12	34	**28**	6	3	**96**	66	.593
2011	Rays	AL	162	130	.67	137	16	31	34	46	17	112	6	438	**217**	42	187	4	38	23	15	6	91	71	.562
2012	Rays	AL	162	**151**	.62	156	37	52	43	38	33	123	3	472	178	40	181	7	35	25	10	6	90	72	.556
2013	Rays	AL	163	**147**	.64	193	27	**56**	52	38	16	111	6	485	111	26	117	6	38	21	17	11	92	71	.564
2014	Rays	AL	162	130	.58	171	23	15	44	35	26	110	3	494	90	54	143	2	27	20	7	3	77	85	.475
2015	Cubs	NL	162	119	.60	**288**	22	32	41	31	14	129	2	552	132	48	**180**	3	38	22	16	**10**	97	65	.599
2016	Cubs	NL	162	130	.62	236	19	35	56	29	13	100	3	503	100	54	111	6	24	19	5	3	**103**	58	.640
2017	Cubs	NL	162	143	.65	296	7	**51**	47	30	10	85	3	531	93	54	122	1	29	18	11	7	92	70	.568
	162-Game Average			132	.62	173	22	34	42	38	22	112	4	485	161	45	139	16	32	20	12	7	87	75	.537

Mike Matheny

Year	Team	Lg	G	LUp	PL%	PH	PR	DS	Quick	Slow	LO	RCD	LS	Rel	SBA	SacA	RM	PO	#	Good	NG	Bomb	W	L	Pct
2012	Cardinals	NL	162	122	.62	286	**37**	33	53	37	8	118	5	506	128	95	144	16	28	13	15	7	88	74	.543
2013	Cardinals	NL	162	89	.56	237	30	41	42	49	25	114	**4**	483	67	73	125	6	26	20	6	6	**97**	65	.599
2014	Cardinals	NL	162	119	.56	258	21	35	53	32	17	119	5	485	89	81	155	10	35	20	15	7	90	72	.556
2015	Cardinals	NL	162	135	.52	274	46	41	**51**	29	11	**142**	**8**	515	107	60	168	15	37	29	8	3	**100**	62	.617
2016	Cardinals	NL	162	**146**	.50	284	**39**	42	42	39	8	95	2	481	61	56	107	21	35	19	16	8	86	76	.531
2017	Cardinals	NL	162	144	.45	295	21	30	45	34	5	106	8	546	112	68	125	8	50	33	17	11	83	79	.512
	162-Game Average			126	.54	272	32	37	48	37	12	116	5	503	94	72	137	13	35	22	13	7	91	71	.562

Don Mattingly

Year	Team	Lg	G	LUp	PL%	PH	PR	DS	Quick	Slow	LO	RCD	LS	Rel	SBA	SacA	RM	PO	#	Good	NG	Bomb	W	L	Pct
2011	Dodgers	NL	161	140	.57	233	29	44	45	40	30	86	1	461	166	93	181	13	48	27	21	12	82	79	.509
2012	Dodgers	NL	162	127	.59	247	22	43	51	39	20	118	2	506	67	105	153	8	**62**	38	24	**15**	86	76	.531
2013	Dodgers	NL	162	**145**	.55	210	18	47	40	30	18	118	3	504	106	99	131	10	44	28	16	7	92	70	.568
2014	Dodgers	NL	162	124	.51	237	17	62	49	31	15	107	5	496	**188**	67	168	2	35	20	15	8	94	68	.580
2015	Dodgers	NL	161	136	.70	276	20	45	50	32	11	119	1	508	93	67	136	2	32	18	14	5	91	70	.565
2016	Marlins	NL	161	111	.49	281	28	69	48	35	10	145	1	559	99	63	101	2	**62**	**42**	20	**14**	79	82	.491
2017	Marlins	NL	162	98	.52	271	9	20	43	32	4	120	5	**580**	121	66	125	2	**59**	**39**	20	12	77	85	.475
	162-Game Average			126	.56	251	20	47	47	34	16	116	3	518	132	80	143	6	49	30	19	10	86	76	.531

Lloyd McClendon

Year	Team	Lg	G	LUp	PL%	PH	PR	DS	Quick	Slow	LO	RCD	LS	Rel	SBA	SacA	RM	PO	#	Good	NG	Bomb	W	L	Pct
2001	Pirates	NL	162	131	.51	255	17	32	45	38	2	85	5	410	166	83			74	44	30	19	62	100	.383
2002	Pirates	NL	161	121	.57	261	38	65	**62**	30	3	98	2	458	135	93	73	67	**93**	61	32	**22**	72	89	.447
2003	Pirates	NL	162	114	.57	315	27	59	46	35	27	114	10	457	123	99	55	73	58	34	24	13	75	87	.463
2004	Pirates	NL	161	114	.50	278	13	58	**50**	40	26	133	1	464	103	100	91	61	64	37	27	**16**	55	81	.404
2005	Pirates	NL	136	123	.53	218	8	19	37	34	15	86	5	357	84	62	83	37	60	32	28	16	55	81	.404
2014	Mariners	AL	162	141	.69	93	48	33	**61**	21	11	87	3	497	138	48	187	30	36	21	15	9	87	75	.537
2015	Mariners	AL	162	140	.63	133	52	50	53	31	10	114	5	509	114	49	148	30	41	23	**18**	**10**	76	86	.469
	162-Game Average			129	.56	227	30	46	52	34	14	105	5	462	126	78	109	51	62	37	25	15	73	89	.451

Bob Melvin

Year	Team	Lg	G	LUp	PL%	PH	PR	DS	Quick	Slow	LO	RCD	LS	Rel	SBA	SacA	RM	PO	#	Good	NG	Bomb	W	L	Pct
2003	Mariners	AL	162	111	.59	81	62	33	27	46	43	56	6	366	145	44	37	5	24	14	10	4	93	69	.574
2004	Mariners	AL	162	151	.59	109	**66**	26	26	63	43	82	5	414	152	56	123	24	32	18	14	8	63	99	.389
2005	Diamondbacks	NL	162	120	.68	**310**	26	38	26	56	36	123	**11**	458	93	93	101	30	43	27	16	9	77	85	.475
2006	Diamondbacks	NL	162	114	.72	278	11	35	37	42	15	86	0	461	106	83	61	30	44	28	16	8	76	86	.469
2007	Diamondbacks	NL	162	146	.57	243	11	61	35	42	31	96	2	469	133	74	70	25	38	30	8	4	**90**	72	.556
2008	Diamondbacks	NL	162	134	.57	263	27	30	41	39	16	102	0	444	81	87	79	28	41	27	14	4	82	80	.506
2009	Diamondbacks	NL	29	29	.62	47	6	8	7	4	3	17	0	91	29	17	13	3	3	1	2	2	12	17	.414
2011	Athletics	AL	99	87	.71	83	13	17	24	23	18	59	2	283	103	34	87	23	9	5	4	3	47	52	.475
2012	Athletics	AL	162	132	.71	111	17	18	**63**	29	5	93	2	462	154	41	116	30	34	21	13	6	94	68	.580
2013	Athletics	AL	162	133	.77	166	14	35	48	28	7	84	7	447	102	32	74	8	23	18	5	2	96	66	.593
2014	Athletics	AL	162	137	.77	187	38	44	45	30	11	101	2	441	103	28	91	16	28	20	8	5	88	74	.543
2015	Athletics	AL	162	137	.65	161	24	35	53	36	10	100	**10**	487	107	17	130	20	19	8	11	4	68	**94**	.420
2016	Athletics	AL	162	141	.64	135	28	39	**55**	36	7	96	3	492	73	19	79	5	28	14	**14**	**8**	69	93	.426
2017	Athletics	AL	162	137	.60	**126**	19	32	39	46	5	117	4	525	79	16	85	9	17	12	5	4	75	87	.463
	162-Game Average			134	.66	176	28	35	41	41	20	95	4	457	114	50	90	20	30	19	11	6	81	81	.500

Paul Molitor

Year	Team	Lg	G	LUp	PL%	PH	PR	DS	Quick	Slow	LO	RCD	LS	Rel	SBA	SacA	RM	PO	#	Good	NG	Bomb	W	L	Pct
2015	Twins	AL	162	124	.59	75	34	27	51	27	7	123	4	520	108	44	132	5	34	20	14	8	83	79	.512
2016	Twins	AL	162	148	.61	72	25	18	33	57	4	117	9	**533**	123	47	157	5	26	13	13	**8**	59	103	.364
2017	Twins	AL	162	137	.71	104	22	31	54	32	4	95	8	520	123	46	164	4	37	19	**18**	**11**	85	77	.525
	162-Game Average			136	.64	84	27	25	46	39	5	112	5	524	118	46	151	5	32	17	15	9	76	86	.469

Pat Murphy

Year	Team	Lg	G	LUp	PL%	PH	PR	DS	Quick	Slow	LO	RCD	LS	Rel	SBA	SacA	RM	PO	#	Good	NG	Bomb	W	L	Pct
2015	Padres	NL	96	84	.56	195	12	10	19	39	11	69	2	314	56	46	60	6	19	10	9	4	42	54	.438
	162-Game Average			142	.56	329	20	17	32	66	19	116	3	530	95	78	101	10	32	17	15	7	71	91	.438

Bo Porter

Year	Team	Lg	G	LUp	PL%	PH	PR	DS	Quick	Slow	LO	RCD	LS	Rel	SBA	SacA	RM	PO	#	Good	NG	Bomb	W	L	Pct
2013	Astros	AL	162	138	.60	107	40	26	48	43	14	84	6	448	171	51	155	22	32	19	13	8	51	111	.315
2014	Astros	AL	138	120	.66	69	21	15	28	42	16	74	2	371	120	22	127	18	26	13	13	6	59	79	.428
	162-Game Average			139	.63	95	33	22	41	46	16	85	4	442	157	39	152	22	31	17	14	8	59	103	.364

Bryan Price

Year	Team	Lg	G	LUp	PL%	PH	PR	DS	Quick	Slow	LO	RCD	LS	Rel	SBA	SacA	RM	PO	#	Good	NG	Bomb	W	L	Pct
2014	Reds	NL	162	130	.54	220	21	33	35	37	26	82	3	428	174	87	135	9	33	21	12	5	76	86	.469
2015	Reds	NL	162	118	.57	263	16	26	42	48	15	102	2	521	172	63	144	28	42	29	13	7	64	98	.395
2016	Reds	NL	162	109	.52	230	17	23	37	39	10	67	3	484	190	81	163	26	31	23	8	5	68	94	.420
2017	Reds	NL	162	94	.59	241	13	25	37	42	7	64	13	504	159	68	128	17	37	23	14	7	68	94	.420
	162-Game Average			113	.55	239	17	27	38	42	15	79	5	484	174	75	143	20	36	24	12	6	69	93	.426

Mike Redmond

Year	Team	Lg	G	LUp	PL%	PH	PR	DS	Quick	Slow	LO	RCD	LS	Rel	SBA	SacA	RM	PO	#	Good	NG	Bomb	W	L	Pct
2013	Marlins	NL	162	132	.52		8	9	47	30	4	88	1	471	107	81	124	2	58	42	16	7	62	100	.383
2014	Marlins	NL	162	102	.50	279	9	14	51	37	8	107	4	487	79	81	106	8	35	23	12	7	77	85	.475
2015	Marlins	NL	38	22	.39	65	6	2	11	5	0	18	0	107	37	23	21	0	3	2	1	1	16	22	.421
	162-Game Average			115	.50	261	10	11	49	32	5	95	2	477	100	83	110	4	43	30	13	7	69	93	.426

Rick Renteria

Year	Team	Lg	G	LUp	PL%	PH	PR	DS	Quick	Slow	LO	RCD	LS	Rel	SBA	SacA	RM	PO	#	Good	NG	Bomb	W	L	Pct
2014	Cubs	NL	162	137	.63	275	9	20	50	42	12	103	1	537	105	77	106	5	37	23	14	8	73	89	.451
2017	White Sox	AL	162	150	.57	86	26	9	31	58	6	108	2	520	102	47	133	1	36	19	17	9	67	95	.414
	162-Game Average			144	.60	181	18	15	41	50	9	106	2	529	104	62	120	3	37	21	16	9	70	92	.432

Dave Roberts

Year	Team	Lg	G	LUp	PL%	PH	PR	DS	Quick	Slow	LO	RCD	LS	Rel	SBA	SacA	RM	PO	#	Good	NG	Bomb	W	L	Pct
2015	Padres	NL	1	1	.63	3	0	0	0	1	0	2	0	3	1	1	0	0	1	1	0	0	0	1	.000
2016	Dodgers	NL	162	120	.69	325	11	26	60	26	6	143	5	606	71	45	120	2	51	36	15	10	91	71	.562
2017	Dodgers	NL	162	147	.64	345	10	30	82	22	3	104	18	536	105	45	97	3	33	23	10	6	104	58	.642
	162-Game Average			134	.67	335	10	28	71	24	4	124	11	571	88	45	108	2	42	30	12	8	97	65	.599

Ron Roenicke

Year	Team	Lg	G	LUp	PL%	PH	PR	DS	Quick	Slow	LO	RCD	LS	Rel	SBA	SacA	RM	PO	#	Good	NG	Bomb	W	L	Pct
2011	Brewers	NL	162	105	.45	260	31	36	36	43	31	92	1	434	125	104	141	14	16	9	7	4	96	66	.593
2012	Brewers	NL	162	110	.45	322	20	25	36	50	23	149	1	512	197	91	152	3	20	12	8	2	83	79	.512
2013	Brewers	NL	162	125	.47	275	15	34	39	47	7	96	2	501	192	86	157	6	29	22	7	6	74	88	.457
2014	Brewers	NL	162	115	.44	253	19	37	33	48	12	114	1	478	145	92	127	11	20	16	4	4	82	80	.506
2015	Brewers	NL	25	24	.39	48	4	5	3	9	2	15	0	72	14	18	17	2	6	5	1	1	7	18	.280
	162-Game Average			115	.45	279	21	33	35	47	18	112	1	481	162	94	143	10	22	15	6	4	82	80	.506

Jimmy Rollins

Year	Team	Lg	G	LUp	PL%	PH	PR	DS	Quick	Slow	LO	RCD	LS	Rel	SBA	SacA	RM	PO	#	Good	NG	Bomb	W	L	Pct
2015	Dodgers	NL	1	1	.25	2	2	3	1	0	0	0	0	7	0	0	0	0	0	0	0	0	1	0	1.000
	162-Game Average			162	.25	324	324	486	162	0	0	0	0	1134	0	0	0	0	0	0	0	0	162	0	1.000

Ryne Sandberg

Year	Team	Lg	G	LUp	PL%	PH	PR	DS	Quick	Slow	LO	RCD	LS	Rel	SBA	SacA	RM	PO	#	Good	NG	Bomb	W	L	Pct
2013	Phillies	NL	42	34	.66	66	4	6	6	12	7	18	0	135	14	15	26	0	10	6	4	4	20	22	.476
2014	Phillies	NL	162	105	.70	259	20	31	37	62	30	111	0	461	135	72	140	1	43	31	12	6	73	89	.451
2015	Phillies	NL	74	58	.72	114	7	14	16	22	5	63	2	225	50	36	70	2	25	23	2	0	26	48	.351
	162-Game Average			115	.70	256	18	30	34	56	24	112	1	478	116	72	138	2	45	35	10	6	69	93	.426

Mike Scioscia

Year	Team	Lg	G	LINEUPS LUp	PL%	SUBSTITUTION PH	PR	DS	PITCHER USAGE Quick	Slow	LO	RCD	LS	Rel	TACTICS SBA	SacA	RM	PO	INTENTIONAL BB #	Good	NG	Bomb	RESULTS W	L	Pct
2000	Angels	AL	162	75	.62	110	41	4	56	42	6	95	9	441	145	63		40	44	28	16	7	82	80	.506
2001	Angels	AL	162	130	.62	118	30	8	29	41	5	81	9	384	168	66		50	47	22	25	12	75	87	.463
2002	Angels	AL	162	102	.64	162	57	26	36	33	34	88	8	400	168	62	52	30	24	15	9	5	99	63	.611
2003	Angels	AL	162	130	.64	134	54	40	50	48	11	60	4	375	190	64	79	25	38	26	12	3	77	85	.475
2004	Angels	AL	162	126	.57	94	32	44	37	40	22	61	11	343	189	70	229	33	27	18	9	3	92	70	.568
2005	Angels	AL	162	124	.65	92	37	37	47	37	24	88	9	379	218	58	160	41	24	15	9	4	95	67	.586
2006	Angels	AL	162	114	.63	103	45	38	38	49	21	99	9	380	205	37	166	22	27	18	9	6	89	73	.549
2007	Angels	AL	162	127	.66	103	26	19	39	40	14	94	4	396	194	41	166	44	22	12	10	5	94	68	.580
2008	Angels	AL	162	125	.63	74	30	36	37	48	21	87	1	383	177	39	151	31	32	22	10	6	100	62	.617
2009	Angels	AL	162	123	.69	80	26	37	47	47	33	91	1	434	211	55	137	40	35	22	13	6	97	65	.599
2010	Angels	AL	162	133	.59	96	31	23	41	52	48	76	0	410	156	58	223	28	33	17	16	8	80	82	.494
2011	Angels	AL	162	129	.64	88	14	24	31	37	55	57	1	386	187	69	212	46	34	25	9	5	86	76	.531
2012	Angels	AL	162	121	.55	73	33	47	37	47	31	96	8	444	167	61	236	33	20	11	9	7	89	73	.549
2013	Angels	AL	162	118	.56	88	26	39	31	44	29	130	8	496	116	48	205	33	36	19	17	11	78	84	.481
2014	Angels	AL	162	125	.58	123	46	59	49	39	22	141	0	543	120	35	189	14	41	31	10	5	98	64	.605
2015	Angels	AL	162	125	.53	117	62	73	38	38	12	145	4	518	86	41	168	15	45	34	11	9	85	77	.525
2016	Angels	AL	162	133	.45	98	54	57	47	32	12	99	2	527	107	38	211	14	27	19	8	5	74	88	.457
2017	Angels	AL	162	116	.52	109	38	24	57	26	4	92	8	543	180	23	208	11	25	14	11	7	80	82	.494
	162-Game Average			121	.60	103	38	35	42	41	22	93	5	432	166	52	175	31	32	20	12	6	87	75	.537

Scott Servais

Year	Team	Lg	G	LINEUPS LUp	PL%	SUBSTITUTION PH	PR	DS	PITCHER USAGE Quick	Slow	LO	RCD	LS	Rel	TACTICS SBA	SacA	RM	PO	INTENTIONAL BB #	Good	NG	Bomb	RESULTS W	L	Pct
2016	Mariners	AL	162	114	.72	166	33	43	42	38	8	93	7	476	84	36	79	1	30	16	14	6	86	76	.531
2017	Mariners	AL	162	120	.52	93	29	18	55	32	3	98	7	527	124	26	99	4	28	15	13	7	78	84	.481
	162-Game Average			117	.62	130	31	31	49	35	6	96	7	502	104	31	89	3	29	16	14	7	82	80	.506

Buck Showalter

Year	Team	Lg	G	LINEUPS LUp	PL%	SUBSTITUTION PH	PR	DS	PITCHER USAGE Quick	Slow	LO	RCD	LS	Rel	TACTICS SBA	SacA	RM	PO	INTENTIONAL BB #	Good	NG	Bomb	RESULTS W	L	Pct
1994	Yankees	AL	113	79	.59	95	31	3	24	30	0	38	7	241	95	34		22	24	13	11	4	70	43	.619
1995	Yankees	AL	145	107	.68	124	30	20	29	42	37	57	6	302	80	27		29	21	14	7	1	79	65	.549
1998	Diamondbacks	NL	162	124	.62	252	17	15	34	40	7	43	6	368	111	68		13	32	16	16	9	65	97	.401
1999	Diamondbacks	NL	162	97	.63	220	20	17	37	48	25	74	3	382	176	75		15	48	29	19	8	100	62	.617
2000	Diamondbacks	NL	162	99	.60	250	32	11	46	26	18	74	12	390	141	89		10	53	28	25	16	85	77	.525
2003	Rangers	AL	162	133	.61	88	51	41	35	33	12	89	10	494	90	35	80		45	24	21	14	71	91	.438
2004	Rangers	AL	162	120	.64	86	15	24	53	30	12	82	10	468	105	30	88	5	29	19	10	3	89	73	.549
2005	Rangers	AL	162	98	.59	57	22	11	42	39	17	79	8	454	82	11	103	5	31	10	21	16	79	83	.488
2006	Rangers	AL	162	95	.57	39	34	22	41	27	10	85	4	489	77	30	72	8	18	11	7	5	80	82	.494
2010	Orioles	AL	57	42	.74	20	11	13	23	9	10	24	1	144	38	13	31	1	10	9	1	1	34	23	.596
2011	Orioles	AL	162	117	.53	60	39	27	43	40	14	61	2	478	106	32	133	6	42	31	11	5	69	93	.426
2012	Orioles	AL	162	120	.62	78	28	31	37	42	10	88	0	492	87	46	145	6	36	25	11	5	93	69	.574
2013	Orioles	AL	162	100	.65	90	23	21	31	39	19	84	4	473	108	37	104	4	32	11	21	13	85	77	.525
2014	Orioles	AL	162	120	.49	77	29	51	37	34	17	89	2	479	64	50	101	10	25	16	9	4	96	66	.593
2015	Orioles	AL	162	145	.60	89	21	35	35	41	6	76	8	453	69	26	95	10	27	12	15	8	81	81	.500
2016	Orioles	AL	162	125	.53	74	31	33	36	50	16	68	9	443	32	21	55	10	23	13	10	5	89	73	.549
2017	Orioles	AL	162	115	.44	95	31	40	27	57	21	93	3	492	45	19	40	8	21	15	6	5	75	87	.463
	162-Game Average			115	.59	113	29	26	38	39	16	76	6	442	94	40	92	11	32	19	14	8	84	78	.519

Brian Snitker

Year	Team	Lg	G	LINEUPS LUp	PL%	SUBSTITUTION PH	PR	DS	PITCHER USAGE Quick	Slow	LO	RCD	LS	Rel	TACTICS SBA	SacA	RM	PO	INTENTIONAL BB #	Good	NG	Bomb	RESULTS W	L	Pct
2016	Braves	NL	124	85	.62	214	8	14	31	36	7	96	1	456	83	64	118	7	40	23	17	10	59	65	.476
2017	Braves	NL	162	108	.58	268	38	16	31	52	8	101	1	530	108	76	139	3	39	27	12	9	72	90	.444
	162-Game Average			109	.60	273	26	17	35	50	8	112	1	559	108	79	146	6	45	28	16	11	74	88	.457

Alan Trammell

Year	Team	Lg	G	LINEUPS LUp	PL%	SUBSTITUTION PH	PR	DS	PITCHER USAGE Quick	Slow	LO	RCD	LS	Rel	TACTICS SBA	SacA	RM	PO	INTENTIONAL BB #	Good	NG	Bomb	RESULTS W	L	Pct
2003	Tigers	AL	162	129	.72	138	29	14	48	39	15	73	14	451	161	92	66	28	35	22	13	7	43	119	.265
2004	Tigers	AL	162	131	.65	105	29	19	47	36	26	79	6	432	136	62	99	9	33	16	17	10	72	90	.444
2005	Tigers	AL	162	119	.49	75	26	16	35	39	13	87	2	425	94	56	129	11	33	21	12	7	71	91	.438
2014	Diamondbacks	NL	3	3	.63	6	2	0	1	0	0	1	0	9	2	1	3	0	1	1	0	0	1	2	.333
	162-Game Average			127	.62	107	28	16	43	38	18	80	7	436	130	70	98	16	34	20	14	8	62	100	.383

Robin Ventura

Year	Team	Lg	G	LINEUPS		SUBSTITUTION			PITCHER USAGE						TACTICS				INTENTIONAL BB				RESULTS		
				LUp	PL%	PH	PR	DS	Quick	Slow	LO	RCD	LS	Rel	SBA	SacA	RM	PO	#	Good	NG	Bomb	W	L	Pct
2012	White Sox	AL	162	75	.48	72	64	23	39	44	34	104	4	466	152	42	174	13	29	17	12	7	85	77	.525
2013	White Sox	AL	162	116	.47	76	47	33	24	52	38	133	0	470	147	24	132	15	24	12	12	4	63	99	.389
2014	White Sox	AL	162	115	.55	85	49	44	26	59	29	96	5	453	121	26	150	28	42	25	17	5	73	89	.451
2015	White Sox	AL	162	114	.57	118	29	35	16	66	43	94	3	414	110	39	146	18	34	21	13	8	76	86	.469
2016	White Sox	AL	162	116	.56	53	27	13	29	58	29	128	4	481	113	37	148	10	30	18	12	2	78	84	.481
	162-Game Average			107	.53	81	43	30	27	56	35	111	3	457	129	34	150	17	32	19	13	5	75	87	.463

Ron Washington

Year	Team	Lg	G	LINEUPS		SUBSTITUTION			PITCHER USAGE						TACTICS				INTENTIONAL BB				RESULTS		
				LUp	PL%	PH	PR	DS	Quick	Slow	LO	RCD	LS	Rel	SBA	SacA	RM	PO	#	Good	NG	Bomb	W	L	Pct
2007	Rangers	AL	162	139	.60	89	30	53	47	46	4	78	9	467	113	76	67	13	38	19	19	11	75	87	.463
2008	Rangers	AL	162	129	.64	118	16	14	31	53	11	85	3	458	106	53	74	20	44	19	25	20	79	83	.488
2009	Rangers	AL	162	123	.55	48	11	11	39	47	28	80	9	436	185	44	80	5	14	9	5	3	87	75	.537
2010	Rangers	AL	162	112	.52	86	39	31	46	42	35	110	4	481	171	68	160	10	24	15	9	0	90	72	.556
2011	Rangers	AL	162	106	.48	66	18	23	43	39	40	76	2	417	188	52	182	3	21	12	9	6	96	66	.593
2012	Rangers	AL	162	79	.47	94	25	37	30	48	33	91	0	428	135	46	155	22	15	10	5	5	93	69	.574
2013	Rangers	AL	163	113	.60	142	23	19	48	41	28	105	3	475	195	53	169	11	35	24	11	6	91	72	.558
2014	Rangers	AL	140	109	.54	96	16	16	35	51	11	65	0	400	135	43	155	6	34	25	9	4	53	87	.379
	162-Game Average			116	.55	94	23	26	41	47	24	88	4	453	156	55	132	11	29	17	12	7	84	78	.519

Walt Weiss

Year	Team	Lg	G	LINEUPS		SUBSTITUTION			PITCHER USAGE						TACTICS				INTENTIONAL BB				RESULTS		
				LUp	PL%	PH	PR	DS	Quick	Slow	LO	RCD	LS	Rel	SBA	SacA	RM	PO	#	Good	NG	Bomb	W	L	Pct
2013	Rockies	NL	162	136	.56	260	18	32	50	42	0	96	2	503	144	80	149	15	52	28	24	7	74	88	.457
2014	Rockies	NL	162	134	.51	270	12	26	40	49	2	119	0	547	133	69	140	11	32	16	16	7	66	96	.407
2015	Rockies	NL	162	122	.56	262	9	36	45	47	2	125	1	584	140	58	138	13	42	26	16	6	68	94	.420
2016	Rockies	NL	162	120	.58	255	7	32	32	57	7	120	2	533	105	69	154	3	38	24	14	7	75	87	.463
	162-Game Average			128	.55	262	12	32	42	49	3	115	2	542	131	69	145	11	41	24	18	7	71	91	.438

Matt Williams

Year	Team	Lg	G	LINEUPS		SUBSTITUTION			PITCHER USAGE						TACTICS				INTENTIONAL BB				RESULTS		
				LUp	PL%	PH	PR	DS	Quick	Slow	LO	RCD	LS	Rel	SBA	SacA	RM	PO	#	Good	NG	Bomb	W	L	Pct
2014	Nationals	NL	162	100	.56	248	17	33	62	33	11	67	1	458	124	87	91	3	26	15	11	6	96	66	.593
2015	Nationals	NL	162	121	.48	225	22	17	45	44	15	86	2	468	80	77	79	1	37	17	20	10	83	79	.512
	162-Game Average			111	.52	237	20	25	54	39	13	77	2	463	102	82	85	2	32	16	16	8	90	73	.552

Ned Yost

Year	Team	Lg	G	LINEUPS		SUBSTITUTION			PITCHER USAGE						TACTICS				INTENTIONAL BB				RESULTS		
				LUp	PL%	PH	PR	DS	Quick	Slow	LO	RCD	LS	Rel	SBA	SacA	RM	PO	#	Good	NG	Bomb	W	L	Pct
2003	Brewers	NL	162	97	.44	304	22	39	23	59	18	90	6	460	138	85	40	23	43	28	15	9	68	94	.420
2004	Brewers	NL	161	131	.60	283	25	20	39	41	27	63	2	423	178	79	108	8	27	16	11	8	67	94	.416
2005	Brewers	NL	162	99	.46	259	18	35	26	41	42	71	2	395	113	89	97	50	52	23	29	10	81	81	.500
2006	Brewers	NL	162	106	.48	238	12	14	33	44	18	77	4	427	108	80	82	16	34	14	20	12	75	87	.463
2007	Brewers	NL	162	109	.60	259	11	41	37	42	18	117	7	492	128	74	94	19	37	28	9	9	83	79	.512
2008	Brewers	NL	150	74	.48	217	5	16	37	39	23	69	5	399	141	61	105	31	30	17	13	7	83	67	.553
2010	Royals	AL	127	80	.57	56	25	6	22	39	20	65	0	332	127	40	128	18	25	16	9	5	55	72	.433
2011	Royals	AL	162	87	.58	36	28	16	42	42	21	75	7	420	211	65	203	19	27	15	15	9	71	91	.438
2012	Royals	AL	162	118	.57	60	34	15	48	37	10	108	1	500	170	37	149	25	44	29	15	11	72	90	.444
2013	Royals	AL	162	127	.60	79	48	39	43	44	21	72	2	427	185	48	168	25	21	12	9	5	86	76	.531
2014	Royals	AL	162	101	.52	51	63	46	37	51	26	93	1	451	189	45	159	3	14	7	7	3	89	73	.549
2015	Royals	AL	162	83	.57	40	40	26	51	42	13	90	3	493	138	45	126	5	10	7	3	1	95	67	.586
2016	Royals	AL	162	108	.54	50	38	12	49	44	10	85	2	472	156	55	130	0	8	6	2	2	81	81	.500
2017	Royals	AL	162	86	.53	48	29	25	53	31	2	120	0	538	122	20	110	0	24	14	10	6	80	82	.494
	162-Game Average			103	.54	144	29	26	39	43	20	86	3	455	154	60	124	18	30	18	12	7	79	83	.488

Categories of this record are Games Managed (G), Number of Different Lineups Used (LUp), the percentage of players who had the platoon advantage at the start of the game (PL%), Pinch Hitters Used (PH), Pinch Runners Used (PR), Defensive Substitutes Used (DS), Quick Hooks (Quick), Slow Hooks (Slow), Long Outings by Starting Pitchers (LO), Relievers Used on Consecutive Days (RCD), Long Saves (LS), Relievers Used (Rel), Stolen Base Attempts (SBA), Sacrifice Bunt Attempts (SacA), Runners Moving with the Pitch (RM), Pitchouts ordered (PO), Intentional Walks issued (#), Intentional Walks resulting in a Good Outcome (Good), Intentional Walks resulting Not in a Good Outcome (NG), Intentional Walks Blowing Up on the Manager (Bomb), Wins (W), Losses (L), and Winning Percentage (Pct).

2017 American League Managers

Manager	G	LINEUPS LUp	PL%	SUBSTITUTION PH	PR	DS	PITCHER USAGE Quick	Slow	LO	RCD	LS	Rel	TACTICS SBA	SacA	RM	PO	INTENTIONAL BB #	Good	NG	Bomb	RESULTS W	L	Pct
Buck Showalter, Bal	162	115	.44	95	31	40	27	57	21	93	3	492	45	19	40	8	21	15	6	5	75	87	.463
John Farrell, Bos	162	137	.54	95	39	17	30	**63**	**33**	97	4	515	137	20	131	2	18	13	5	1	93	69	.574
Terry Francona, Cle	162	131	.73	93	**43**	50	48	31	20	106	4	497	102	47	133	1	36	19	17	9	**102**	60	.630
Rick Renteria, CWS	162	**150**	.57	86	26	9	31	58	6	108	2	520	99	16	104	3	**42**	**26**	16	8	67	95	.414
Brad Ausmus, Det	162	131	.50	103	30	24	28	52	17	97	6	510	99	16	104	3	42	26	16	8	64	98	.395
A.J. Hinch, Hou	162	144	.56	73	29	39	**57**	35	3	83	8	519	140	21	148	6	17	12	5	3	**101**	61	.623
Ned Yost, KC	162	86	.53	48	29	25	53	31	2	**120**	0	538	122	20	110	0	24	14	10	6	80	82	.494
Mike Scioscia, LAA	162	116	.52	109	38	24	**57**	26	4	92	8	543	**180**	23	**208**	11	25	14	11	7	80	82	.494
Paul Molitor, Min	162	137	.71	104	22	31	54	32	4	95	8	520	123	46	164	4	37	19	**18**	**11**	85	77	.525
Joe Girardi, NYY	162	140	.56	112	22	10	49	29	9	79	7	477	112	28	117	3	18	11	7	4	91	71	.562
Bob Melvin, Oak	162	137	.60	**126**	19	32	39	46	5	117	4	525	79	16	85	9	17	12	5	4	75	87	.463
Scott Servais, Sea	162	120	.52	93	29	18	55	32	3	98	7	527	124	26	99	4	28	15	13	7	78	84	.481
Kevin Cash, TB	162	126	.57	123	21	24	39	47	16	89	**9**	511	122	24	143	**12**	37	25	12	8	80	82	.494
Jeff Banister, Tex	162	134	.54	66	40	20	39	40	6	71	7	464	157	35	153	0	22	9	13	10	78	84	.481
John Gibbons, Tor	162	136	.56	**126**	39	33	41	33	8	100	4	**578**	77	35	132	4	25	14	11	5	76	86	.469
162-Game Average		129	.56	97	30	26	43	41	10	96	5	516	115	27	124	5	25	15	10	6	82	80	.506

2017 National League Managers

Manager	G	LINEUPS LUp	PL%	SUBSTITUTION PH	PR	DS	PITCHER USAGE Quick	Slow	LO	RCD	LS	Rel	TACTICS SBA	SacA	RM	PO	INTENTIONAL BB #	Good	NG	Bomb	RESULTS W	L	Pct
Torey Lovullo, Ari	162	129	.55	254	28	36	34	45	6	116	2	513	133	50	85	3	45	32	13	6	93	69	.574
Brian Snitker, Atl	162	108	.58	268	**38**	16	31	52	8	101	1	530	108	76	139	3	39	27	12	9	72	90	.444
Joe Maddon, ChC	162	143	.65	296	7	**51**	47	30	10	85	3	531	93	54	122	1	29	18	11	7	92	70	.568
Bryan Price, Cin	162	94	.59	241	13	25	37	42	7	64	13	504	159	68	128	**17**	37	23	14	7	68	94	.420
Bud Black, Col	162	111	.51	261	19	14	44	36	4	100	2	549	93	76	149	4	20	14	6	3	87	75	.537
Dave Roberts, LAD	162	147	.64	**345**	10	30	**82**	22	3	104	**18**	536	105	45	97	3	33	23	10	6	**104**	58	.642
Don Mattingly, Mia	162	98	.52	271	9	20	43	32	4	120	5	**580**	121	66	125	2	**59**	**39**	20	12	77	85	.475
Craig Counsell, Mil	162	123	.53	285	18	44	58	33	5	124	5	550	**169**	56	**159**	0	45	30	15	9	86	76	.531
Terry Collins, NYM	162	**149**	.66	247	20	32	25	54	8	**127**	6	568	81	52	97	3	51	27	**24**	**14**	70	92	.432
Pete Mackanin, Phi	162	135	.66	236	11	21	37	44	3	114	2	506	84	40	91	0	39	24	15	4	66	96	.407
Clint Hurdle, Pit	162	138	.51	277	23	37	42	39	6	110	8	502	103	59	124	7	32	17	15	7	75	87	.463
Andy Green, SD	162	138	.55	238	10	38	45	43	5	101	2	517	122	63	119	2	28	18	10	4	71	91	.438
Bruce Bochy, SF	162	136	.61	298	22	12	22	**59**	20	93	2	502	110	51	135	3	42	29	13	11	64	**98**	.395
Mike Matheny, StL	162	144	.45	295	21	30	45	34	5	106	8	546	112	68	125	8	50	33	17	11	83	79	.512
Dusty Baker, Was	162	124	.59	241	33	26	22	53	**27**	90	2	487	138	57	113	3	39	29	10	6	97	65	.599
162-Game Average		128	.57	270	19	29	41	41	8	104	5	528	115	59	121	4	39	26	14	8	80	82	.494

Ballparks and Park Indices

Alex Vigderman

A park index (sometimes called a park factor) tells you whether a given park is more favorable to pitchers or hitters compared to other MLB parks. The average index is set at 100, meaning that a park with an index of 100 is neutral, and an index of, say, 120 means that the park saw 20 percent more offensive output than average.

We apply park indices to all kinds of statistics, not just overall runs scored, although that tends to be the park index that is discussed most readily. This allows us to dig into the details of a park's effects on the teams that play there. Take Yankee Stadium, for example. While its runs scored park index in 2017 was 102, it actually saw much fewer doubles and triples than the average ballpark (16 and 23 percent, respectively) but 32 percent more home runs than average. That tends to come with the territory of a park with relatively small dimensions, especially down the lines.

Two teams saw notable changes to their parks this season, the Astros and the Braves. The former removed the famous but perilous Tal's Hill from center field, bringing in the center field fence by 26 feet, while the latter christened a new stadium, SunTrust Park. The change in Houston was felt most in the rate of triples, as Minute Maid Park's triples park index plummeted from 135 the previous three years to 66 this year. That sound you hear is a collective sigh of relief from American League center fielders.

As for the Braves, remember that one-year park indices are very hard to trust, which is why we include three-year park indices in this section as well. In the case of SunTrust Park, of course, we only have one year of data, so just take this with a grain of salt. Overall, both it and its predecessor Turner Field played fairly neutral (both at 98). Early returns suggest that SunTrust may be more favorable to left-handed hitters, yielding 16 percent more home runs to lefties than the average ballpark after Turner yielded 21 percent fewer. SunTrust also did not maintain Turner's rather high Errors park index, especially in the infield. From 2014 to 2016, the Braves and their opponents made 55 percent more infield errors in Turner Field than they did at other parks, whereas at Suntrust they made seven percent fewer.

Arizona Diamondbacks - Chase Field
LF: 330   CF: 407   RF:334

| | 2017 Season | | | | | | | 2015-2017 | | | | | | |
| | Home Games | | | Away Games | | | | Home Games | | | Away Games | | | |
	D'Backs	Opp	Total	D'Backs	Opp	Total	Index	D'Backs	Opp	Total	D'Backs	Opp	Total	Index
G	81	81	162	81	81	162		243	243	486	243	243	486	
Avg	.274	.237	.256	.235	.244	.239	107	.271	.263	.267	.249	.252	.251	107
AB	2746	2788	5534	2779	2655	5434	102	8339	8649	16988	8500	8104	16604	102
R	457	346	803	355	313	668	120	1234	1211	2445	1050	1051	2101	116
H	753	661	1414	652	648	1300	109	2263	2277	4540	2115	2045	4160	109
2B	187	152	339	127	124	251	133	492	511	1003	396	420	816	120
3B	23	19	42	16	15	31	133	91	64	155	52	38	90	168
HR	122	93	215	98	78	176	120	304	287	591	260	268	528	109
BB	300	254	554	278	262	540	101	778	821	1599	753	798	1551	101
SO	712	761	1473	744	721	1465	99	2103	2055	4158	2092	1960	4052	100
Foul Outs	49	40	89	49	38	87	100	143	150	293	165	136	301	95
E	54	43	97	54	51	105	92	143	150	293	152	154	306	96
E-Infield	24	15	39	29	15	44	89	56	66	122	71	64	135	90
LHB-Avg	.262	.228	.246	.234	.229	.232	106	.270	.264	.267	.245	.245	.245	109
LHB-HR	40	33	73	35	24	59	118	83	118	201	74	111	185	106
RHB-Avg	.283	.243	.262	.235	.253	.244	107	.272	.263	.268	.251	.257	.254	105
RHB-HR	82	60	142	63	54	117	122	221	169	390	186	157	343	111

Atlanta Braves - SunTrust Park
LF: 335   CF: 400   RF:325

| | 2017 Season | | | | | | | 2014-2016 | | | | | | |
| | Home Games | | | Away Games | | | | Home Games | | | Away Games | | | |
	Braves	Opp	Total	Braves	Opp	Total	Index	Braves	Opp	Total	Braves	Opp	Total	Index
G	81	81	162	81	81	162		242	242	484	243	243	486	
Avg	.264	.265	.265	.261	.261	.261	101	.250	.248	.249	.247	.269	.258	97
AB	2739	2852	5591	2845	2711	5556	101	7998	8365	16363	8404	8079	16483	100
R	346	421	767	386	400	786	98	899	1045	1944	896	1091	1987	98
H	724	755	1479	743	708	1451	102	2002	2075	4077	2079	2170	4249	96
2B	129	187	316	160	139	299	105	365	382	747	421	410	831	91
3B	12	14	26	14	22	36	72	35	38	73	32	64	96	77
HR	77	97	174	88	95	183	94	162	210	372	183	258	441	85
BB	225	279	504	249	305	554	90	743	825	1568	702	744	1446	109
SO	576	636	1212	608	622	1230	98	1841	2001	3842	1875	1675	3550	109
Foul Outs	50	53	103	36	48	84	122	136	171	307	148	155	303	102
E	48	47	95	49	47	96	99	149	163	312	127	115	242	129
E-Infield	16	25	41	26	18	44	93	75	78	153	51	48	99	155
LHB-Avg	.273	.264	.269	.263	.243	.254	106	.254	.263	.259	.271	.270	.271	96
LHB-HR	40	42	82	40	31	71	116	61	98	159	89	112	201	79
RHB-Avg	.255	.265	.261	.259	.275	.267	98	.248	.236	.241	.227	.267	.247	98
RHB-HR	37	55	92	48	64	112	81	101	112	213	94	146	240	90

Baltimore Orioles - Oriole Park at Camden Yards
LF: 333   CF: 410   RF:318

| | 2017 Season | | | | | | | 2015-2017 | | | | | | |
| | Home Games | | | Away Games | | | | Home Games | | | Away Games | | | |
	Orioles	Opp	Total	Orioles	Opp	Total	Index	Orioles	Opp	Total	Orioles	Opp	Total	Index
G	81	81	162	81	81	162		240	240	480	246	246	492	
Avg	.268	.261	.265	.252	.278	.265	100	.265	.257	.261	.246	.266	.255	102
AB	2810	2904	5714	2840	2685	5525	103	8110	8422	16532	8549	8113	16662	102
R	395	407	802	348	434	782	103	1171	1092	2263	1029	1157	2186	106
H	753	759	1512	716	746	1462	103	2151	2164	4315	2101	2155	4256	104
2B	128	141	269	141	152	293	89	367	431	798	413	488	901	89
3B	4	8	12	8	9	17	68	15	26	41	23	32	55	75
HR	135	127	262	97	115	212	119	394	309	703	308	290	598	118
BB	211	297	508	181	282	463	106	662	765	1427	616	842	1458	99
SO	684	616	1300	728	617	1345	93	1883	1868	3751	2184	1846	4030	94
Foul Outs	64	65	129	64	58	122	102	182	170	352	205	182	387	92
E	45	46	91	49	48	97	94	120	131	251	131	115	246	105
E-Infield	15	21	36	19	15	34	106	45	60	105	49	40	89	121
LHB-Avg	.248	.270	.263	.223	.256	.245	107	.253	.260	.257	.235	.259	.249	103
LHB-HR	27	51	78	16	47	63	114	126	121	247	95	120	215	114
RHB-Avg	.273	.256	.265	.259	.292	.272	97	.271	.255	.263	.250	.271	.259	101
RHB-HR	108	76	184	81	68	149	122	268	188	456	213	170	383	121

Boston Red Sox - Fenway Park
LF: 310　　CF: 420　　RF:302

	2017 Season							2015-2017						
	Home Games			Away Games				Home Games			Away Games			
	Red Sox	Opp	Total	Red Sox	Opp	Total	Index	Red Sox	Opp	Total	Red Sox	Opp	Total	Index
G	81	81	162	81	81	162		243	243	486	243	243	486	
Avg	.269	.252	.260	.247	.237	.242	108	.286	.258	.272	.250	.245	.248	110
AB	2795	2933	5728	2874	2714	5588	103	8399	8623	17022	8580	8106	16686	102
R	387	349	736	398	319	717	103	1297	1112	2409	1114	1003	2117	114
H	752	740	1492	709	644	1353	110	2406	2229	4635	2149	1983	4132	112
2B	161	150	311	141	128	269	113	546	447	993	393	381	774	126
3B	10	8	18	9	15	24	73	39	42	81	38	36	74	107
HR	73	91	164	95	104	199	80	255	274	529	282	275	557	93
BB	282	225	507	289	240	529	93	797	686	1483	810	747	1557	93
SO	590	812	1402	634	768	1402	98	1651	2119	3770	1881	2041	3922	94
Foul Outs	64	49	113	68	66	134	82	160	158	318	182	194	376	83
E	67	61	128	40	53	93	138	163	177	340	116	146	262	130
E-Infield	22	22	44	13	24	37	119	65	71	136	48	58	106	128
LHB-Avg	.247	.272	.259	.253	.250	.252	103	.277	.266	.272	.249	.236	.243	112
LHB-HR	32	30	62	46	35	81	71	112	83	195	139	99	238	78
RHB-Avg	.285	.242	.262	.242	.232	.237	111	.293	.254	.273	.252	.250	.251	109
RHB-HR	41	61	102	49	69	118	87	143	191	334	143	176	319	105

Chicago Cubs - Wrigley Field
LF: 355　　CF: 400　　RF:353

	2017 Season							2015-2017						
	Home Games			Away Games				Home Games			Away Games			
	Cubs	Opp	Total	Cubs	Opp	Total	Index	Cubs	Opp	Total	Cubs	Opp	Total	Index
G	81	81	162	81	81	162		243	243	486	243	243	486	
Avg	.264	.241	.252	.247	.235	.241	105	.251	.225	.238	.252	.231	.242	99
AB	2692	2779	5471	2804	2651	5455	100	7961	8263	16224	8529	7952	16481	98
R	436	369	805	386	326	712	113	1151	922	2073	1168	937	2105	98
H	710	670	1380	692	624	1316	105	2002	1862	3864	2150	1833	3983	97
2B	135	140	275	139	110	249	110	384	378	762	455	363	818	95
3B	19	7	26	10	10	20	130	50	34	84	39	35	74	115
HR	116	93	209	107	101	208	100	298	245	543	295	246	541	102
BB	314	295	609	308	259	567	107	946	751	1697	899	705	1604	107
SO	682	728	1410	719	711	1430	98	2036	2222	4258	2222	2089	4311	100
Foul Outs	29	33	62	61	47	108	57	117	106	223	169	140	309	73
E	52	57	109	43	53	96	114	149	135	284	158	153	311	91
E-Infield	17	24	41	17	27	44	93	61	60	121	63	68	131	92
LHB-Avg	.269	.240	.257	.233	.228	.231	112	.247	.227	.238	.252	.227	.241	99
LHB-HR	60	34	94	61	40	101	95	127	89	216	161	93	254	88
RHB-Avg	.257	.242	.248	.262	.240	.250	99	.256	.224	.238	.252	.233	.242	98
RHB-HR	56	59	115	46	61	107	105	171	156	327	134	153	287	114

Chicago White Sox - Guaranteed Rate Field
LF: 330　　CF: 400　　RF:335

	2017 Season							2015-2017						
	Home Games			Away Games				Home Games			Away Games			
	White Sox	Opp	Total	White Sox	Opp	Total	Index	White Sox	Opp	Total	White Sox	Opp	Total	Index
G	81	81	162	81	81	162		243	243	486	243	243	486	
Avg	.251	.243	.247	.261	.266	.263	94	.253	.247	.250	.256	.267	.261	96
AB	2670	2775	5445	2843	2670	5513	99	8063	8421	16484	8533	8106	16639	99
R	366	398	764	340	422	762	100	1001	1065	2066	1013	1171	2184	95
H	670	675	1345	742	709	1451	93	2038	2081	4119	2183	2168	4351	95
2B	126	122	248	130	153	283	89	375	388	763	418	449	867	89
3B	20	11	31	17	21	38	83	52	39	91	45	57	102	90
HR	99	131	230	87	111	198	118	255	317	572	235	272	507	114
BB	214	319	533	187	313	500	108	663	826	1489	597	801	1398	108
SO	697	649	1346	700	544	1244	110	1924	2029	3953	1989	1793	3782	106
Foul Outs	71	76	147	50	49	99	150	193	175	368	163	178	341	109
E	66	69	135	48	42	90	150	165	163	328	145	135	280	117
E-Infield	39	23	62	21	24	45	138	82	62	144	62	62	124	116
LHB-Avg	.256	.221	.236	.261	.269	.265	89	.246	.227	.236	.261	.265	.263	90
LHB-HR	30	54	84	20	48	68	131	79	119	198	66	97	163	122
RHB-Avg	.249	.257	.253	.261	.263	.262	96	.257	.258	.258	.253	.269	.261	99
RHB-HR	69	77	146	67	63	130	111	176	198	374	169	175	344	110

Cincinnati Reds - Great American Ballpark
LF: 328   CF: 404   RF:325

| | 2017 Season | | | | | | | 2015-2017 | | | | | | |
| | Home Games | | | Away Games | | | | Home Games | | | Away Games | | | |
	Reds	Opp	Total	Reds	Opp	Total	Index	Reds	Opp	Total	Reds	Opp	Total	Index
G	81	81	162	81	81	162		243	243	486	243	243	486	
Avg	.254	.249	.252	.253	.278	.265	95	.255	.255	.255	.249	.269	.259	98
AB	2675	2778	5453	2809	2697	5506	99	8120	8508	16628	8422	8072	16494	101
R	402	417	819	351	452	803	102	1111	1224	2335	998	1253	2251	104
H	680	692	1372	710	750	1460	94	2074	2166	4240	2101	2169	4270	99
2B	114	169	283	135	146	281	102	382	456	838	401	437	838	99
3B	22	11	33	16	11	27	123	47	22	69	51	43	94	73
HR	117	127	244	102	121	223	110	293	362	655	257	321	578	112
BB	297	314	611	268	317	585	105	808	897	1705	705	914	1619	104
SO	677	687	1364	652	613	1265	109	1947	2016	3963	1921	1777	3698	106
Foul Outs	55	61	116	53	35	88	133	151	177	328	151	114	265	123
E	32	42	74	49	43	92	80	122	133	255	151	152	303	84
E-Infield	15	19	34	16	21	37	92	51	50	101	66	71	137	74
LHB-Avg	.271	.254	.263	.272	.289	.280	94	.273	.262	.267	.262	.274	.268	100
LHB-HR	55	67	122	54	55	109	119	131	163	294	112	137	249	119
RHB-Avg	.241	.246	.243	.237	.269	.253	96	.243	.249	.246	.241	.265	.253	98
RHB-HR	62	60	122	48	66	114	104	162	199	361	145	184	329	108

Cleveland Indians - Progressive Field
LF: 325   CF: 405   RF:325

| | 2017 Season | | | | | | | 2015-2017 | | | | | | |
| | Home Games | | | Away Games | | | | Home Games | | | Away Games | | | |
	Indians	Opp	Total	Indians	Opp	Total	Index	Indians	Opp	Total	Indians	Opp	Total	Index
G	81	81	162	81	81	162		242	242	484	242	242	484	
Avg	.264	.234	.249	.262	.237	.250	100	.275	.243	.259	.246	.233	.240	108
AB	2677	2747	5424	2834	2631	5465	99	8076	8305	16381	8358	7926	16284	101
R	406	275	681	412	289	701	97	1225	981	2206	1039	899	1938	114
H	707	643	1350	742	624	1366	99	2224	2022	4246	2055	1849	3904	109
2B	165	135	300	168	127	295	102	525	440	965	419	363	782	123
3B	11	5	16	18	7	25	64	29	32	61	58	38	96	63
HR	95	90	185	117	73	190	98	255	280	535	283	230	513	104
BB	311	176	487	293	230	523	94	893	623	1516	775	669	1444	104
SO	562	847	1409	591	767	1358	105	1716	2258	3974	1840	2161	4001	99
Foul Outs	47	46	93	57	55	112	84	155	112	267	185	169	354	75
E	30	50	80	46	37	83	96	113	148	261	131	135	266	98
E-Infield	14	19	33	14	20	34	97	50	56	106	48	61	109	97
LHB-Avg	.280	.253	.268	.251	.250	.251	107	.291	.253	.273	.251	.225	.239	114
LHB-HR	51	47	98	54	32	86	110	138	132	270	144	98	242	110
RHB-Avg	.248	.219	.232	.271	.228	.249	93	.257	.235	.245	.240	.240	.240	102
RHB-HR	44	43	87	63	41	104	87	117	148	265	139	132	271	98

Colorado Rockies - Coors Field
LF: 347   CF: 415   RF:350

| | 2017 Season | | | | | | | 2015-2017 | | | | | | |
| | Home Games | | | Away Games | | | | Home Games | | | Away Games | | | |
	Rockies	Opp	Total	Rockies	Opp	Total	Index	Rockies	Opp	Total	Rockies	Opp	Total	Index
G	81	81	162	81	81	162		243	243	486	243	243	486	
Avg	.298	.273	.286	.248	.255	.251	114	.301	.288	.294	.241	.259	.250	118
AB	2735	2818	5553	2799	2682	5481	101	8377	8642	17019	8343	8024	16367	104
R	488	415	903	336	342	678	133	1445	1375	2820	961	1086	2047	138
H	816	770	1586	694	683	1377	115	2524	2488	5012	2009	2076	4085	123
2B	156	159	315	137	131	268	116	496	539	1035	389	426	815	122
3B	30	31	61	8	19	27	223	97	81	178	37	61	98	175
HR	110	98	208	82	92	174	118	328	297	625	254	257	511	118
BB	278	269	547	241	263	504	107	771	813	1584	630	845	1475	103
SO	641	621	1262	767	649	1416	88	1807	1817	3624	2214	1788	4002	87
Foul Outs	37	42	79	49	53	102	76	107	116	223	166	149	315	68
E	42	45	87	35	46	81	107	148	148	296	134	133	267	111
E-Infield	13	20	33	10	22	32	103	48	62	110	55	58	113	97
LHB-Avg	.322	.274	.297	.243	.244	.244	122	.313	.284	.298	.240	.254	.247	121
LHB-HR	39	40	79	28	38	66	125	129	106	235	109	93	202	117
RHB-Avg	.283	.273	.278	.251	.263	.257	108	.293	.291	.292	.241	.263	.252	116
RHB-HR	71	58	129	54	54	108	113	199	191	390	145	164	309	118

Detroit Tigers - Comerica Park
LF: 345   CF: 420   RF:330

	2017 Season							2015-2017						
	Home Games			Away Games				Home Games			Away Games			
	Tigers	Opp	Total	Tigers	Opp	Total	Index	Tigers	Opp	Total	Tigers	Opp	Total	Index
G	81	81	162	81	81	162		242	242	484	242	242	484	
Avg	.276	.281	.279	.240	.283	.261	107	.275	.264	.269	.256	.276	.266	101
AB	2805	2915	5720	2751	2706	5457	105	8235	8500	16735	8452	8143	16595	101
R	416	462	878	319	432	751	117	1134	1194	2328	1040	1224	2264	103
H	775	820	1595	660	766	1426	112	2262	2245	4507	2164	2249	4413	102
2B	161	146	307	128	144	272	108	429	395	824	401	425	826	99
3B	19	21	40	16	14	30	127	69	81	150	45	56	101	147
HR	109	108	217	78	110	188	110	279	299	578	270	294	564	102
BB	256	261	517	247	277	524	94	727	723	1450	724	766	1490	97
SO	612	584	1196	701	618	1319	87	1781	1793	3574	2094	1741	3835	92
Foul Outs	69	84	153	38	57	95	154	196	237	433	152	171	323	133
E	34	40	74	51	47	98	76	108	135	243	138	121	259	94
E-Infield	13	23	36	17	23	40	90	38	57	95	59	45	104	91
LHB-Avg	.278	.277	.277	.235	.284	.265	104	.247	.259	.255	.243	.271	.261	98
LHB-HR	22	44	66	14	46	60	97	54	129	183	52	116	168	104
RHB-Avg	.276	.284	.280	.241	.282	.259	108	.283	.268	.277	.260	.280	.268	103
RHB-HR	87	64	151	64	64	128	117	225	170	395	218	178	396	101

Houston Astros - Minute Maid Park
LF: 315   CF: 409   RF:326

	2017 Season							2014-2016						
	Home Games			Away Games				Home Games			Away Games			
	Astros	Opp	Total	Astros	Opp	Total	Index	Astros	Opp	Total	Astros	Opp	Total	Index
G	78	78	156	84	84	168		243	243	486	243	243	486	
Avg	.281	.223	.252	.283	.255	.269	94	.245	.244	.245	.247	.261	.254	96
AB	2606	2634	5240	3005	2842	5847	97	8003	8497	16500	8448	8093	16541	100
R	387	306	693	509	394	903	83	1019	946	1965	1063	1096	2159	91
H	732	588	1320	849	726	1575	90	1961	2074	4035	2086	2112	4198	96
2B	163	112	275	183	181	364	84	386	424	810	423	422	845	96
3B	6	10	16	14	13	27	66	40	65	105	34	44	78	135
HR	114	98	212	124	94	218	109	316	216	532	275	252	527	101
BB	227	251	478	282	271	553	96	773	632	1405	762	728	1490	95
SO	485	789	1274	602	804	1406	101	2169	2054	4223	2117	1759	3876	109
Foul Outs	63	47	110	72	39	111	111	137	147	284	191	141	332	86
E	49	51	100	50	57	107	101	130	149	279	138	153	291	96
E-Infield	23	27	50	20	26	46	117	60	51	111	61	59	120	93
LHB-Avg	.272	.219	.243	.274	.247	.260	93	.223	.244	.235	.229	.267	.249	94
LHB-HR	36	41	77	36	40	76	109	117	91	208	98	101	199	104
RHB-Avg	.286	.227	.258	.287	.262	.276	94	.258	.244	.251	.258	.256	.257	98
RHB-HR	78	57	135	88	54	142	109	199	125	324	177	151	328	99

Kansas City Royals - Kauffman Stadium
LF: 330   CF: 410   RF:330

	2017 Season							2015-2017						
	Home Games			Away Games				Home Games			Away Games			
	Royals	Opp	Total	Royals	Opp	Total	Index	Royals	Opp	Total	Royals	Opp	Total	Index
G	81	81	162	81	81	162		243	243	486	243	243	486	
Avg	.262	.260	.261	.257	.271	.264	99	.271	.256	.263	.256	.260	.258	102
AB	2668	2828	5496	2868	2752	5620	98	8106	8502	16608	8557	8112	16669	100
R	339	379	718	363	412	775	93	1092	1063	2155	1009	1081	2090	103
H	699	734	1433	737	746	1483	97	2193	2176	4369	2190	2109	4299	102
2B	135	142	277	125	132	257	110	440	431	871	384	353	737	119
3B	13	22	35	11	18	29	123	61	55	116	38	45	83	140
HR	88	86	174	105	110	215	83	214	245	459	265	312	577	80
BB	197	253	450	193	266	459	100	587	732	1319	568	793	1361	97
SO	531	616	1147	635	600	1235	95	1542	1850	3392	1821	1813	3634	94
Foul Outs	66	61	127	54	70	124	105	174	200	374	177	184	361	104
E	36	35	71	43	50	93	76	115	135	250	146	164	310	81
E-Infield	18	17	35	17	19	36	97	50	51	101	50	66	116	87
LHB-Avg	.257	.272	.264	.259	.272	.265	100	.265	.261	.263	.259	.255	.257	102
LHB-HR	50	35	85	48	39	87	98	115	104	219	131	131	262	85
RHB-Avg	.266	.252	.259	.256	.271	.263	98	.274	.253	.263	.254	.264	.259	102
RHB-HR	38	51	89	57	71	128	72	99	141	240	134	181	315	76

Los Angeles Angels - Angel Stadium of Anaheim
LF: 330   CF: 400   RF:330

| | 2017 Season | | | | | | | 2015-2017 | | | | | | |
| | Home Games | | | Away Games | | | | Home Games | | | Away Games | | | |
	Angels	Opp	Total	Angels	Opp	Total	Index	Angels	Opp	Total	Angels	Opp	Total	Index
G	81	81	162	81	81	162		243	243	486	243	243	486	
Avg	.249	.242	.245	.237	.261	.249	99	.251	.244	.247	.248	.269	.258	96
AB	2668	2801	5469	2747	2659	5406	101	7961	8368	16329	8302	8054	16356	100
R	356	335	691	354	374	728	95	1013	984	1997	1075	1127	2202	91
H	664	678	1342	650	695	1345	100	1999	2041	4040	2056	2167	4223	96
2B	119	122	241	132	143	275	87	358	373	731	415	440	855	86
3B	4	9	13	10	8	18	71	23	22	45	32	34	66	68
HR	97	105	202	89	119	208	96	272	281	553	246	317	563	98
BB	243	203	446	280	267	547	81	693	683	1376	736	751	1487	93
SO	569	670	1239	629	642	1271	96	1614	1963	3577	1725	1706	3431	104
Foul Outs	46	55	101	67	52	119	84	143	183	326	177	176	353	93
E	42	52	94	38	53	91	103	137	147	284	133	141	274	104
E-Infield	17	23	40	15	18	33	121	63	72	135	46	58	104	130
LHB-Avg	.241	.247	.245	.222	.256	.242	101	.235	.247	.242	.233	.264	.251	96
LHB-HR	28	42	70	29	53	82	85	65	109	174	64	125	189	91
RHB-Avg	.252	.238	.246	.243	.266	.253	97	.258	.241	.250	.254	.273	.262	96
RHB-HR	69	63	132	60	66	126	103	207	172	379	182	192	374	102

Los Angeles Dodgers - Dodger Stadium
LF: 330   CF: 395   RF:330

| | 2017 Season | | | | | | | 2015-2017 | | | | | | |
| | Home Games | | | Away Games | | | | Home Games | | | Away Games | | | |
	Dodgers	Opp	Total	Dodgers	Opp	Total	Index	Dodgers	Opp	Total	Dodgers	Opp	Total	Index
G	81	81	162	81	81	162		243	243	486	243	243	486	
Avg	.252	.217	.235	.246	.239	.242	97	.252	.222	.237	.247	.247	.247	96
AB	2633	2723	5356	2775	2657	5432	99	7878	8209	16087	8433	8034	16467	98
R	398	267	665	372	313	685	97	1088	792	1880	1074	1021	2095	90
H	664	592	1256	683	634	1317	95	1984	1825	3809	2085	1984	4069	94
2B	156	111	267	156	118	274	99	424	334	758	423	349	772	101
3B	8	7	15	12	13	25	61	25	21	46	42	45	87	54
HR	115	88	203	106	96	202	102	313	225	538	284	269	553	100
BB	306	213	519	343	229	572	92	809	600	1409	928	701	1629	89
SO	678	787	1465	702	762	1464	101	1919	2299	4218	2040	2156	4196	103
Foul Outs	36	65	101	51	60	111	92	123	159	282	168	158	326	89
E	43	38	81	45	34	79	103	105	139	244	138	103	241	101
E-Infield	15	12	27	19	12	31	87	44	46	90	53	39	92	98
LHB-Avg	.265	.219	.244	.232	.271	.248	98	.255	.221	.240	.245	.263	.252	95
LHB-HR	63	37	100	55	31	86	113	183	81	264	155	85	240	113
RHB-Avg	.241	.217	.227	.259	.222	.239	95	.249	.223	.234	.249	.238	.243	96
RHB-HR	52	51	103	51	65	116	93	130	144	274	129	184	313	90

Miami Marlins - Marlins Park
LF: 344   CF: 407   RF:335

| | 2017 Season | | | | | | | 2016-2017 | | | | | | |
| | Home Games | | | Away Games | | | | Home Games | | | Away Games | | | |
	Marlins	Opp	Total	Marlins	Opp	Total	Index	Marlins	Opp	Total	Marlins	Opp	Total	Index
G	78	78	156	84	84	168		158	158	316	165	165	330	
Avg	.262	.249	.255	.272	.277	.274	93	.256	.243	.249	.273	.271	.272	92
AB	2593	2688	5281	3009	2826	5835	97	5224	5390	10614	5925	5532	11457	97
R	360	345	705	418	477	895	85	662	647	1309	771	857	1628	84
H	679	668	1347	818	782	1600	91	1337	1311	2648	1620	1497	3117	89
2B	103	117	220	168	163	331	73	235	236	471	295	300	595	85
3B	16	19	35	15	18	33	117	32	32	64	41	36	77	90
HR	95	74	169	99	119	218	86	153	139	292	169	206	375	84
BB	250	297	547	236	330	566	107	465	591	1056	468	631	1099	104
SO	586	604	1190	696	598	1294	102	1153	1329	2482	1342	1252	2594	103
Foul Outs	38	50	88	61	58	119	82	87	104	191	106	104	210	98
E	36	52	88	37	44	81	117	76	100	176	83	102	185	99
E-Infield	13	23	36	16	12	28	138	23	41	64	39	42	81	83
LHB-Avg	.262	.251	.256	.285	.278	.281	91	.264	.255	.259	.282	.276	.279	93
LHB-HR	30	30	60	34	46	80	82	52	58	110	58	80	138	86
RHB-Avg	.262	.247	.254	.261	.276	.268	95	.250	.234	.242	.268	.267	.267	91
RHB-HR	65	44	109	65	73	138	88	101	81	182	111	126	237	83

Milwaukee Brewers - Miller Park
LF: 344 CF: 400 RF:345

| | 2017 Season | | | | | | | 2015-2017 | | | | | | |
| | Home Games | | | Away Games | | | | Home Games | | | Away Games | | | |
	Brewers	Opp	Total	Brewers	Opp	Total	Index	Brewers	Opp	Total	Brewers	Opp	Total	Index
G	84	84	168	78	78	156		246	246	492	240	240	480	
Avg	.251	.254	.253	.248	.250	.249	102	.249	.255	.252	.248	.262	.255	99
AB	2799	2922	5721	2668	2557	5225	102	8092	8585	16677	8185	7887	16072	101
R	393	380	773	339	317	656	109	1075	1120	2195	983	1047	2030	105
H	702	743	1445	661	638	1299	103	2011	2193	4204	2029	2070	4099	100
2B	143	158	301	124	118	242	114	417	445	862	373	411	784	106
3B	11	12	23	11	17	28	75	45	42	87	30	56	86	97
HR	120	97	217	104	88	192	103	298	305	603	265	234	499	116
BB	275	304	579	272	249	521	101	800	804	1604	758	798	1556	99
SO	809	716	1525	762	630	1392	100	2215	2014	4229	2198	1767	3965	103
Foul Outs	46	70	116	39	47	86	123	114	170	284	147	144	291	94
E	73	43	116	42	46	88	122	194	134	328	173	138	311	103
E-Infield	30	14	44	21	20	41	100	76	47	123	61	53	114	105
LHB-Avg	.269	.244	.255	.244	.260	.253	101	.266	.258	.262	.244	.261	.253	103
LHB-HR	53	42	95	40	42	82	109	101	143	244	78	102	180	131
RHB-Avg	.240	.262	.251	.250	.240	.246	102	.239	.253	.246	.250	.264	.256	96
RHB-HR	67	55	122	64	46	110	99	197	162	359	187	132	319	108

Minnesota Twins - Target Field
LF: 339 CF: 404 RF:328

| | 2017 Season | | | | | | | 2015-2017 | | | | | | |
| | Home Games | | | Away Games | | | | Home Games | | | Away Games | | | |
	Twins	Opp	Total	Twins	Opp	Total	Index	Twins	Opp	Total	Twins	Opp	Total	Index
G	81	81	162	81	81	162		243	243	486	243	243	486	
Avg	.268	.271	.270	.251	.261	.256	106	.261	.274	.268	.244	.271	.257	104
AB	2754	2904	5658	2803	2683	5486	103	8223	8742	16965	8419	8167	16586	102
R	420	418	838	395	370	765	110	1141	1216	2357	1092	1161	2253	105
H	739	788	1527	704	699	1403	109	2145	2397	4542	2056	2213	4269	106
2B	143	152	295	143	130	273	105	420	477	897	431	426	857	102
3B	23	10	33	8	16	24	133	66	31	97	44	50	94	101
HR	110	122	232	96	102	198	114	293	315	608	269	293	562	106
BB	313	255	568	280	228	508	108	769	678	1447	776	697	1473	96
SO	642	623	1265	700	543	1243	99	1868	1756	3624	2164	1647	3811	93
Foul Outs	67	46	113	70	71	141	78	185	160	345	180	181	361	93
E	44	42	86	34	55	89	97	174	145	319	116	139	255	125
E-Infield	16	16	32	19	25	44	73	67	58	125	51	56	107	117
LHB-Avg	.271	.268	.270	.259	.267	.262	103	.261	.268	.264	.248	.268	.257	103
LHB-HR	59	50	109	48	52	100	109	109	110	219	101	125	226	95
RHB-Avg	.264	.273	.270	.241	.257	.250	108	.261	.279	.271	.241	.273	.257	105
RHB-HR	51	72	123	48	50	98	119	184	205	389	168	168	336	113

New York Mets - Citi Field
LF: 335 CF: 408 RF:330

| | 2017 Season | | | | | | | 2015-2017 | | | | | | |
| | Home Games | | | Away Games | | | | Home Games | | | Away Games | | | |
	Mets	Opp	Total	Mets	Opp	Total	Index	Mets	Opp	Total	Mets	Opp	Total	Index
G	81	81	162	81	81	162		243	243	486	243	243	486	
Avg	.239	.257	.248	.261	.290	.275	90	.237	.243	.240	.256	.271	.263	91
AB	2658	2840	5498	2852	2788	5640	97	7974	8418	16392	8522	8219	16741	98
R	344	394	738	391	469	860	86	996	985	1981	1093	1108	2201	90
H	636	729	1365	743	809	1552	88	1891	2046	3937	2181	2230	4411	89
2B	132	135	267	154	143	297	92	386	364	750	435	407	842	91
3B	8	13	21	20	10	30	72	20	35	55	44	40	84	67
HR	101	96	197	123	124	247	82	298	256	554	321	268	589	96
BB	255	302	557	274	291	565	101	780	727	1507	754	688	1442	107
SO	612	732	1344	679	642	1321	104	1861	2214	4075	2022	1893	3915	106
Foul Outs	73	52	125	57	47	104	123	203	165	368	186	160	346	109
E	49	43	92	43	36	79	116	128	111	239	142	121	263	91
E-Infield	16	22	38	23	12	35	109	45	56	101	62	54	116	87
LHB-Avg	.236	.258	.246	.257	.283	.269	92	.236	.250	.243	.254	.273	.262	93
LHB-HR	65	34	99	72	50	122	84	175	110	285	174	113	287	101
RHB-Avg	.243	.256	.250	.264	.297	.281	89	.238	.237	.237	.258	.270	.264	90
RHB-HR	36	62	98	51	74	125	80	123	146	269	147	155	302	92

New York Yankees - Yankee Stadium
LF: 318   CF: 408   RF:314

	2017 Season							2015-2017						
	Home Games			Away Games				Home Games			Away Games			
	Yankees	Opp	Total	Yankees	Opp	Total	Index	Yankees	Opp	Total	Yankees	Opp	Total	Index
G	81	81	162	81	81	162		243	243	486	243	243	486	
Avg	.265	.217	.241	.258	.240	.249	96	.258	.234	.246	.252	.253	.253	97
AB	2702	2742	5444	2892	2726	5618	97	8098	8417	16515	8521	8119	16640	99
R	451	315	766	407	345	752	102	1195	1013	2208	1107	1047	2154	103
H	716	594	1310	747	654	1401	94	2089	1966	4055	2149	2057	4206	96
2B	120	108	228	146	135	281	84	369	353	722	414	429	843	86
3B	12	3	15	11	9	20	77	26	20	46	36	39	75	62
HR	140	103	243	101	89	190	132	365	327	692	271	261	532	131
BB	313	241	554	303	263	566	101	846	689	1535	799	733	1532	101
SO	681	818	1499	705	742	1447	107	1874	2253	4127	1927	2070	3997	104
Foul Outs	51	52	103	69	49	118	90	156	151	307	169	157	326	95
E	45	69	114	50	63	113	101	131	162	293	142	153	295	99
E-Infield	19	32	51	25	28	53	96	57	73	130	72	75	147	88
LHB-Avg	.257	.205	.233	.265	.240	.254	92	.253	.232	.244	.255	.261	.257	95
LHB-HR	50	37	87	32	29	61	151	191	123	314	135	89	224	142
RHB-Avg	.271	.223	.245	.254	.240	.247	99	.264	.235	.247	.248	.249	.248	99
RHB-HR	90	66	156	69	60	129	123	174	204	378	136	172	308	123

Oakland Athletics - O.co Coliseum
LF: 330   CF: 400   RF:330

	2017 Season							2015-2017						
	Home Games			Away Games				Home Games			Away Games			
	Athletics	Opp	Total	Athletics	Opp	Total	Index	Athletics	Opp	Total	Athletics	Opp	Total	Index
G	81	81	162	81	81	162		243	243	486	243	243	486	97
Avg	.256	.252	.254	.237	.270	.253	100	.250	.250	.250	.246	.268	.257	97
AB	2692	2862	5554	2772	2675	5447	102	8102	8452	16554	8462	8163	16625	100
R	417	404	821	322	422	744	110	1056	1097	2153	1030	1219	2249	96
H	688	722	1410	656	722	1378	102	2022	2114	4136	2079	2191	4270	97
2B	168	150	318	137	150	287	109	437	415	852	415	428	843	102
3B	12	18	30	3	10	13	226	54	32	86	28	35	63	137
HR	129	99	228	105	111	216	104	256	260	516	293	307	600	86
BB	283	266	549	282	236	518	104	711	711	1422	771	729	1500	95
SO	719	652	1371	772	550	1322	102	1748	1829	3577	2007	1740	3747	96
Foul Outs	75	75	150	68	51	119	124	237	251	488	199	152	351	140
E	58	40	98	63	40	103	95	174	132	306	170	134	304	101
E-Infield	28	17	45	27	16	43	105	77	60	137	79	63	142	96
LHB-Avg	.260	.248	.254	.256	.257	.256	99	.247	.246	.247	.250	.260	.255	97
LHB-HR	50	38	88	47	42	89	100	85	105	190	117	121	238	84
RHB-Avg	.253	.255	.254	.225	.279	.251	101	.251	.253	.252	.243	.274	.258	97
RHB-HR	79	61	140	58	69	127	106	171	155	326	176	186	362	87

Philadelphia Phillies - Citizens Bank Park
LF: 329   CF: 401   RF:330

	2017 Season							2015-2017						
	Home Games			Away Games				Home Games			Away Games			
	Phillies	Opp	Total	Phillies	Opp	Total	Index	Phillies	Opp	Total	Phillies	Opp	Total	Index
G	81	81	162	81	81	162		243	243	486	243	243	486	
Avg	.252	.259	.256	.247	.271	.259	99	.243	.262	.253	.249	.279	.263	96
AB	2715	2865	5580	2820	2695	5515	101	8063	8638	16701	8435	8153	16588	101
R	370	392	762	320	390	710	107	987	1148	2135	939	1239	2178	98
H	685	741	1426	697	730	1427	100	1963	2260	4223	2098	2271	4369	97
2B	141	142	283	146	154	300	93	370	434	804	420	470	890	90
3B	19	14	33	17	14	31	105	56	37	93	52	57	109	85
HR	104	127	231	70	94	164	139	254	348	602	211	277	488	123
BB	263	264	527	231	263	494	105	672	741	1413	633	740	1373	102
SO	702	735	1437	715	574	1289	110	2021	2073	4094	2046	1688	3734	109
Foul Outs	58	57	115	53	53	106	107	183	193	376	152	141	293	127
E	33	48	81	49	47	96	84	150	164	314	146	141	287	109
E-Infield	16	22	38	17	20	37	103	75	80	155	50	59	109	142
LHB-Avg	.262	.265	.264	.266	.283	.275	96	.248	.269	.258	.260	.287	.273	95
LHB-HR	36	56	92	25	45	70	136	115	156	271	92	136	228	120
RHB-Avg	.245	.253	.249	.231	.259	.244	102	.239	.256	.248	.238	.271	.255	97
RHB-HR	68	71	139	45	49	94	140	139	192	331	119	141	260	124

Pittsburgh Pirates - PNC Park
LF: 325   CF: 399   RF:320

	2017 Season							2015-2017						
	Home Games			Away Games				Home Games			Away Games			
	Pirates	Opp	Total	Pirates	Opp	Total	Index	Pirates	Opp	Total	Pirates	Opp	Total	Index
G	80	80	160	82	82	164		242	242	484	244	244	488	
Avg	.253	.258	.256	.235	.269	.252	101	.260	.255	.257	.247	.265	.256	101
AB	2667	2838	5505	2791	2717	5508	102	8086	8516	16602	8545	8233	16778	100
R	323	349	672	345	382	727	95	1025	1017	2042	1069	1068	2137	96
H	674	733	1407	657	731	1388	104	2106	2168	4274	2113	2178	4291	100
2B	123	169	292	126	151	277	105	383	470	853	435	429	864	100
3B	16	10	26	20	21	41	63	54	41	95	41	54	95	101
HR	72	80	152	79	102	181	84	214	216	430	230	256	486	89
BB	261	240	501	258	271	529	95	771	736	1507	770	761	1531	99
SO	557	621	1178	656	641	1297	91	1787	1919	3706	2082	1913	3995	94
Foul Outs	42	43	85	36	41	77	110	115	131	246	133	145	278	89
E	49	51	100	50	50	100	103	172	164	336	160	150	310	109
E-Infield	23	18	41	23	21	44	96	74	68	142	78	70	148	97
LHB-Avg	.251	.273	.265	.242	.287	.268	99	.248	.261	.255	.245	.278	.264	97
LHB-HR	24	37	61	24	42	66	90	82	86	168	70	96	166	101
RHB-Avg	.254	.246	.250	.232	.255	.242	103	.266	.250	.259	.248	.256	.252	103
RHB-HR	48	43	91	55	60	115	81	132	130	262	160	160	320	83

San Diego Padres - PETCO Park
LF: 336   CF: 396   RF:322

	2017 Season							2015-2017						
	Home Games			Away Games				Home Games			Away Games			
	Padres	Opp	Total	Padres	Opp	Total	Index	Padres	Opp	Total	Padres	Opp	Total	Index
G	81	81	162	81	81	162		243	243	486	243	243	486	
Avg	.234	.238	.236	.233	.280	.256	92	.241	.245	.243	.234	.268	.251	97
AB	2559	2749	5308	2797	2724	5521	96	7889	8399	16288	8343	8047	16390	99
R	302	341	643	302	475	777	83	973	1069	2042	967	1248	2215	92
H	600	654	1254	651	763	1414	89	1901	2055	3956	1949	2158	4107	96
2B	108	124	232	119	151	270	89	368	396	764	376	422	798	96
3B	17	10	27	14	13	27	104	47	48	95	46	69	115	83
HR	89	93	182	100	133	233	81	246	278	524	268	302	570	93
BB	246	256	502	214	298	512	102	703	771	1474	632	868	1500	99
SO	706	709	1415	793	616	1409	104	2082	2090	4172	2244	1850	4094	103
Foul Outs	70	35	105	68	44	112	98	172	151	323	168	137	305	107
E	60	38	98	53	48	101	97	162	135	297	152	149	301	99
E-Infield	22	12	34	18	16	34	100	60	51	111	66	54	120	93
LHB-Avg	.251	.238	.244	.228	.294	.264	92	.254	.243	.248	.242	.268	.256	97
LHB-HR	30	31	61	32	56	88	76	66	121	187	91	134	225	85
RHB-Avg	.226	.238	.232	.235	.270	.251	92	.233	.246	.239	.229	.268	.247	97
RHB-HR	59	62	121	68	77	145	84	180	157	337	177	168	345	97

San Francisco Giants - AT&T Park
LF: 339   CF: 399   RF:309

	2017 Season							2015-2017						
	Home Games			Away Games				Home Games			Away Games			
	Giants	Opp	Total	Giants	Opp	Total	Index	Giants	Opp	Total	Giants	Opp	Total	Index
G	81	81	162	81	81	162		243	243	486	243	243	486	
Avg	.251	.253	.252	.247	.284	.265	95	.263	.245	.254	.253	.260	.257	99
AB	2742	2905	5647	2809	2745	5554	102	8152	8464	16616	8529	8137	16666	100
R	316	334	650	323	442	765	85	1017	916	1933	1033	1118	2151	90
H	689	736	1425	693	779	1472	97	2144	2077	4221	2161	2116	4277	99
2B	148	146	294	142	151	293	99	427	395	822	431	410	841	98
3B	16	28	44	12	30	42	103	84	74	158	37	77	114	139
HR	48	70	118	80	112	192	60	156	190	346	238	305	543	64
BB	220	246	466	247	250	497	92	755	676	1431	741	690	1431	100
SO	590	636	1226	614	598	1212	99	1669	1896	3565	1801	1812	3613	99
Foul Outs	50	57	107	55	63	118	89	134	174	308	165	170	335	92
E	42	37	79	45	48	93	85	111	124	235	126	137	263	89
E-Infield	21	13	34	20	21	41	83	49	52	101	55	63	118	86
LHB-Avg	.246	.254	.250	.256	.297	.275	91	.264	.248	.257	.257	.272	.264	97
LHB-HR	25	20	45	41	46	87	48	74	67	141	129	130	259	53
RHB-Avg	.256	.253	.254	.240	.276	.258	98	.262	.244	.252	.250	.252	.251	100
RHB-HR	23	50	73	39	66	105	71	82	123	205	109	175	284	74

Seattle Mariners - Safeco Field
LF: 331   CF: 401   RF:326

| | 2017 Season | | | | | | | 2015-2017 | | | | | | |
| | Home Games | | | Away Games | | | | Home Games | | | Away Games | | | |
	Mariners	Opp	Total	Mariners	Opp	Total	Index	Mariners	Opp	Total	Mariners	Opp	Total	Index
G	81	81	162	81	81	162		243	243	486	243	243	486	
Avg	.263	.239	.251	.255	.270	.262	96	.256	.241	.248	.255	.268	.261	95
AB	2693	2799	5492	2858	2703	5561	99	8127	8451	16578	8551	8214	16765	99
R	370	358	728	380	414	794	92	1050	1039	2089	1124	1166	2290	91
H	708	670	1378	728	729	1457	95	2080	2036	4116	2181	2203	4384	94
2B	131	124	255	150	138	288	90	367	393	760	427	427	854	90
3B	10	5	15	7	7	14	108	28	21	49	28	37	65	76
HR	97	113	210	103	124	227	94	303	321	624	318	310	628	100
BB	252	249	501	235	241	476	107	766	698	1464	705	743	1448	102
SO	634	666	1300	633	578	1211	109	1972	2046	4018	1919	1799	3718	109
Foul Outs	44	80	124	51	75	126	100	160	213	373	159	179	338	112
E	45	37	82	58	48	106	77	136	125	261	150	141	291	90
E-Infield	25	13	38	28	12	40	95	75	54	129	70	48	118	109
LHB-Avg	.260	.249	.255	.250	.286	.266	96	.260	.243	.253	.258	.271	.263	96
LHB-HR	35	47	82	42	41	83	104	144	121	265	156	101	257	105
RHB-Avg	.265	.234	.248	.259	.260	.259	96	.251	.240	.245	.252	.267	.260	94
RHB-HR	62	66	128	61	83	144	88	159	200	359	162	209	371	97

St Louis Cardinals - Busch Stadium
LF: 336   CF: 400   RF:335

| | 2017 Season | | | | | | | 2015-2017 | | | | | | |
| | Home Games | | | Away Games | | | | Home Games | | | Away Games | | | |
	Cardinals	Opp	Total	Cardinals	Opp	Total	Index	Cardinals	Opp	Total	Cardinals	Opp	Total	Index
G	81	81	162	81	81	162		243	243	486	243	243	486	
Avg	.259	.248	.253	.254	.258	.256	99	.258	.251	.254	.252	.254	.253	100
AB	2644	2801	5445	2826	2706	5532	98	8011	8483	16494	8491	8094	16585	99
R	359	331	690	402	374	776	89	1029	941	1970	1158	1001	2159	91
H	684	695	1379	718	698	1416	97	2066	2125	4191	2137	2059	4196	100
2B	138	129	267	146	133	279	97	429	378	807	442	402	844	96
3B	14	15	29	14	16	30	98	43	38	81	56	41	97	84
HR	90	84	174	106	99	205	86	254	222	476	304	243	547	88
BB	304	239	543	289	254	543	102	818	675	1493	807	770	1577	95
SO	663	679	1342	685	672	1357	100	1840	1999	3839	2093	1971	4064	95
Foul Outs	43	53	96	39	43	82	119	156	174	330	132	124	256	130
E	47	38	85	47	54	101	84	149	124	273	148	163	311	88
E-Infield	19	17	36	15	26	41	88	69	51	120	61	74	135	89
LHB-Avg	.271	.261	.265	.250	.273	.264	100	.262	.256	.259	.250	.258	.254	102
LHB-HR	24	45	69	22	50	72	95	90	108	198	105	102	207	97
RHB-Avg	.254	.237	.246	.256	.246	.252	98	.256	.246	.251	.253	.251	.252	100
RHB-HR	66	39	105	84	49	133	81	164	114	278	199	141	340	82

Tampa Bay Rays - Tropicana Field Surface: FieldTurf
LF: 315   CF: 404   RF:322

| | 2017 Season | | | | | | | 2015-2017 | | | | | | |
| | Home Games | | | Away Games | | | | Home Games | | | Away Games | | | |
	Rays	Opp	Total	Rays	Opp	Total	Index	Rays	Opp	Total	Rays	Opp	Total	Index
G	78	78	156	84	84	168		243	243	486	243	243	486	
Avg	.245	.232	.239	.244	.250	.247	97	.242	.237	.239	.251	.254	.253	95
AB	2564	2673	5237	2914	2809	5723	99	7957	8342	16299	8487	8087	16574	98
R	339	310	649	355	394	749	93	968	980	1948	1042	1079	2121	92
H	629	621	1250	711	703	1414	95	1922	1977	3899	2134	2056	4190	93
2B	100	119	219	126	151	277	86	368	333	701	424	402	826	86
3B	15	10	25	17	7	24	114	45	22	67	51	23	74	92
HR	103	91	194	125	102	227	93	288	279	567	323	299	622	93
BB	273	230	503	272	273	545	101	713	719	1432	717	752	1469	99
SO	743	701	1444	795	651	1446	109	2198	2171	4369	2132	1893	4025	110
Foul Outs	59	66	125	72	69	141	97	195	227	422	202	195	397	108
E	38	42	80	62	41	103	84	126	119	245	163	126	289	85
E-Infield	17	17	34	27	19	46	80	55	45	100	68	56	124	81
LHB-Avg	.248	.221	.235	.254	.244	.249	94	.242	.231	.236	.256	.242	.249	95
LHB-HR	50	27	77	65	41	106	78	123	107	230	130	105	235	97
RHB-Avg	.243	.240	.241	.236	.254	.245	98	.241	.242	.241	.248	.263	.255	94
RHB-HR	53	64	117	60	61	121	107	165	172	337	193	194	387	90

Texas Rangers - Rangers Ballpark in Arlington
LF: 332   CF: 400   RF:325

| | 2017 Season | | | | | | | 2015-2017 | | | | | | |
| | Home Games | | | Away Games | | | | Home Games | | | Away Games | | | |
	Rangers	Opp	Total	Rangers	Opp	Total	Index	Rangers	Opp	Total	Rangers	Opp	Total	Index
G	81	81	162	81	81	162		243	243	486	243	243	486	
Avg	.265	.266	.265	.224	.256	.240	111	.273	.266	.269	.237	.256	.246	109
AB	2685	2866	5551	2745	2660	5405	103	8133	8573	16706	8333	8057	16390	102
R	449	437	886	350	379	729	122	1278	1215	2493	1037	1091	2128	117
H	711	761	1472	615	682	1297	113	2219	2277	4496	1972	2066	4038	111
2B	134	160	294	121	127	248	115	408	444	852	383	383	766	109
3B	7	10	17	14	3	17	97	42	39	81	34	36	70	114
HR	125	114	239	112	100	212	110	320	309	629	304	277	581	106
BB	304	294	598	240	265	505	115	818	809	1627	665	792	1457	110
SO	696	565	1261	797	542	1339	92	1844	1701	3545	2102	1655	3757	93
Foul Outs	52	67	119	62	60	122	95	150	165	315	194	155	349	89
E	63	55	118	45	45	90	131	176	159	335	148	153	301	111
E-Infield	25	21	46	18	24	42	110	67	69	136	67	75	142	96
LHB-Avg	.255	.263	.259	.205	.247	.224	116	.260	.265	.262	.236	.253	.243	108
LHB-HR	67	41	108	56	39	95	112	175	112	287	161	108	269	107
RHB-Avg	.273	.267	.270	.240	.262	.251	107	.285	.266	.274	.238	.259	.249	110
RHB-HR	58	73	131	56	61	117	108	145	197	342	143	169	312	106

Toronto Blue Jays - Rogers Centre Surface: FieldTurf
LF: 328   CF: 400   RF:328

| | 2017 Season | | | | | | | 2015-2017 | | | | | | |
| | Home Games | | | Away Games | | | | Home Games | | | Away Games | | | |
	Blue Jays	Opp	Total	Blue Jays	Opp	Total	Index	Blue Jays	Opp	Total	Blue Jays	Opp	Total	Index
G	81	81	162	81	81	162		243	243	486	243	243	486	
Avg	.244	.258	.252	.236	.257	.246	102	.261	.245	.253	.244	.254	.249	101
AB	2620	2832	5452	2879	2834	5713	95	7969	8414	16383	8518	8250	16768	98
R	332	386	718	361	398	759	95	1183	1041	2224	1160	1079	2239	99
H	640	732	1372	680	728	1408	97	2077	2060	4137	2081	2093	4174	99
2B	131	169	300	138	141	279	113	461	445	906	392	401	793	117
3B	3	12	15	2	14	16	98	17	43	60	23	37	60	102
HR	105	99	204	117	104	221	97	335	275	610	340	284	624	100
BB	248	267	515	294	282	576	94	863	692	1555	881	715	1596	100
SO	611	685	1296	716	687	1403	97	1779	1934	3713	2061	1869	3930	97
Foul Outs	71	52	123	64	72	136	95	222	180	402	207	202	409	101
E	48	45	93	44	43	87	107	133	128	261	135	146	281	93
E-Infield	18	20	38	21	18	39	97	53	50	103	64	55	119	87
LHB-Avg	.240	.236	.238	.232	.229	.230	103	.244	.242	.243	.236	.239	.238	102
LHB-HR	37	29	66	43	36	79	89	75	121	196	83	113	196	98
RHB-Avg	.247	.272	.260	.239	.275	.256	101	.268	.247	.258	.248	.263	.255	101
RHB-HR	68	70	138	74	68	142	101	260	154	414	257	171	428	101

Washington Nationals - Nationals Park
LF: 336   CF: 402   RF:335

| | 2017 Season | | | | | | | 2015-2017 | | | | | | |
| | Home Games | | | Away Games | | | | Home Games | | | Away Games | | | |
	Nationals	Opp	Total	Nationals	Opp	Total	Index	Nationals	Opp	Total	Nationals	Opp	Total	Index
G	81	81	162	81	81	162		243	243	486	243	243	486	
Avg	.287	.241	.264	.245	.236	.241	110	.266	.238	.252	.250	.244	.247	102
AB	2754	2779	5533	2799	2667	5466	101	8079	8374	16453	8392	7966	16358	101
R	421	345	766	398	327	725	106	1146	961	2107	1139	958	2097	100
H	791	670	1461	686	630	1316	111	2146	1994	4140	2097	1944	4041	102
2B	160	127	287	151	116	267	106	423	367	790	421	367	788	100
3B	12	9	21	19	14	33	63	29	31	60	44	48	92	65
HR	107	99	206	108	90	198	103	300	250	550	295	239	534	102
BB	275	234	509	267	261	528	95	828	637	1465	789	690	1479	98
SO	640	752	1392	687	705	1392	99	1862	2212	4074	2061	2063	4124	98
Foul Outs	55	55	110	62	78	140	78	175	175	350	164	203	367	95
E	40	45	85	46	48	94	90	129	133	262	120	147	267	98
E-Infield	13	20	33	20	12	32	103	55	61	116	45	48	93	125
LHB-Avg	.288	.245	.267	.260	.248	.254	105	.274	.239	.255	.268	.256	.262	98
LHB-HR	41	47	88	54	38	92	90	117	111	228	135	111	246	89
RHB-Avg	.286	.238	.262	.234	.228	.231	113	.260	.237	.249	.239	.235	.237	105
RHB-HR	66	52	118	54	52	106	114	183	139	322	160	128	288	114

2017 American League Ballpark Index Rankings

Home Park	Avg	AB	R	H	2B	3B	HR	BB	SO	FO	E	E-Inf	LHB Avg	LHB HR	RHB Avg	RHB HR
Rangers (Rangers Ballpark in Arlington)	111	103	122	113	115	97	110	115	92	95	131	110	116	112	107	108
Tigers (Comerica Park)	107	105	117	112	108	127	110	94	87	154	76	90	104	97	108	117
Athletics (O.co Coliseum)	100	102	110	102	109	226	104	104	102	124	95	105	99	100	101	106
Twins (Target Field)	106	103	110	109	105	133	114	108	99	78	97	73	103	109	108	119
Red Sox (Fenway Park)	108	103	103	110	113	73	80	93	98	82	138	119	103	71	111	87
Orioles (Oriole Park at Camden Yards)	100	103	103	103	89	68	119	106	93	102	94	106	107	114	97	122
Yankees (Yankee Stadium)	96	97	102	94	84	77	132	101	107	90	101	96	92	151	99	123
White Sox (Guaranteed Rate Field)	94	99	100	93	89	83	118	108	110	150	150	138	89	131	96	111
Indians (Progressive Field)	100	99	97	99	102	64	98	94	105	84	96	97	107	110	93	87
Angels (Angel Stadium of Anaheim)	99	101	95	100	87	71	96	81	96	84	103	121	101	85	97	103
Blue Jays (Rogers Centre)	102	95	95	97	113	98	97	94	97	95	107	97	103	89	101	101
Rays (Tropicana Field)	97	99	93	95	86	114	93	101	109	97	84	80	94	78	98	107
Royals (Kauffman Stadium)	99	98	93	97	110	123	83	100	95	105	76	97	100	98	98	72
Mariners (Safeco Field)	96	99	92	95	90	108	94	107	109	100	77	95	96	104	96	88
Astros (Minute Maid Park)	94	97	83	90	84	66	109	96	101	111	101	117	93	109	94	109

2017 National League Ballpark Index Rankings

Home Park	Avg	AB	R	H	2B	3B	HR	BB	SO	FO	E	E-Inf	LHB Avg	LHB HR	RHB Avg	RHB HR
Rockies (Coors Field)	114	101	133	115	116	223	118	107	88	76	107	103	122	125	108	113
Diamondbacks (Chase Field)	107	102	120	109	133	133	120	101	99	100	92	89	106	118	107	122
Cubs (Wrigley Field)	105	100	113	105	110	130	100	107	98	57	114	93	112	95	99	105
Brewers (Miller Park)	102	102	109	103	114	75	103	101	100	123	122	100	101	109	102	99
Phillies (Citizens Bank Park)	99	101	107	100	93	105	139	105	110	107	84	103	96	136	102	140
Nationals (Nationals Park)	110	101	106	111	106	63	103	95	95	78	90	103	105	90	113	114
Reds (Great American Ballpark)	95	99	102	94	102	123	110	105	109	133	80	92	94	119	96	104
Braves (SunTrust Park)	101	101	98	102	105	72	94	90	98	122	99	93	106	116	98	81
Dodgers (Dodger Stadium)	97	99	97	95	99	61	102	92	101	92	103	87	98	113	95	93
Pirates (PNC Park)	101	102	95	104	105	63	84	95	91	110	103	96	99	90	103	81
Cardinals (Busch Stadium)	99	98	89	97	97	98	86	102	100	119	84	88	100	95	98	81
Mets (Citi Field)	90	97	86	88	92	72	82	101	104	123	116	109	92	84	89	80
Giants (AT&T Park)	95	102	85	97	99	103	60	92	99	89	85	83	91	48	98	71
Marlins (Marlins Park)	93	97	85	91	73	117	86	107	102	82	117	138	91	82	95	88
Padres (PETCO Park)	92	96	83	89	89	104	81	102	104	98	97	100	92	76	92	84

2017 AL Home Runs

Home Park	Index
Yankees	132
Orioles	119
White Sox	118
Twins	114
Tigers	110
Rangers	110
Astros	109
Athletics	104
Indians	98
Blue Jays	97
Angels	96
Mariners	94
Rays	93
Royals	83
Red Sox	80

2017 AL LHB Home Runs

Home Park	Index
Yankees	151
White Sox	131
Orioles	114
Rangers	112
Indians	110
Astros	109
Twins	109
Mariners	104
Athletics	100
Royals	98
Tigers	97
Blue Jays	89
Angels	85
Rays	78
Red Sox	71

2017 AL RHB Home Runs

Home Park	Index
Yankees	123
Orioles	122
Twins	119
Tigers	117
White Sox	111
Astros	109
Rangers	108
Rays	107
Athletics	106
Angels	103
Blue Jays	101
Mariners	88
Indians	87
Red Sox	87
Royals	72

2017 NL Home Runs

Home Park	Index
Phillies	139
Diamondbacks	120
Rockies	118
Reds	110
Brewers	103
Nationals	103
Dodgers	102
Cubs	100
Braves	94
Cardinals	86
Marlins	86
Pirates	84
Mets	82
Padres	81
Giants	60

2017 NL LHB Home Runs

Home Park	Index
Phillies	136
Rockies	125
Reds	119
Diamondbacks	118
Braves	116
Dodgers	113
Brewers	109
Cubs	95
Cardinals	95
Nationals	90
Pirates	90
Mets	84
Marlins	82
Padres	76
Giants	48

2017 NL RHB Home Runs

Home Park	Index
Phillies	140
Diamondbacks	122
Nationals	114
Rockies	113
Cubs	105
Reds	104
Brewers	99
Dodgers	93
Marlins	88
Padres	84
Cardinals	81
Braves	81
Pirates	81
Mets	80
Giants	71

2017 AL Avg	
Home Park	Index
Rangers	111
Red Sox	108
Tigers	107
Twins	106
Blue Jays	102
Athletics	100
Orioles	100
Indians	100
Royals	99
Angels	99
Rays	97
Yankees	96
Mariners	96
White Sox	94
Astros	94

2017 AL LHB Avg	
Home Park	Index
Rangers	116
Orioles	107
Indians	107
Tigers	104
Blue Jays	103
Twins	103
Red Sox	103
Angels	101
Royals	100
Athletics	99
Mariners	96
Rays	94
Astros	93
Yankees	92
White Sox	89

2017 AL RHB Avg	
Home Park	Index
Red Sox	111
Twins	108
Tigers	108
Rangers	107
Blue Jays	101
Athletics	101
Yankees	99
Rays	98
Royals	98
Orioles	97
Angels	97
White Sox	96
Mariners	96
Astros	94
Indians	93

2017 NL Avg	
Home Park	Index
Rockies	114
Nationals	110
Diamondbacks	107
Cubs	105
Brewers	102
Pirates	101
Braves	101
Cardinals	99
Phillies	99
Dodgers	97
Giants	95
Reds	95
Marlins	93
Padres	92
Mets	90

2017 NL LHB Avg	
Home Park	Index
Rockies	122
Cubs	112
Diamondbacks	106
Braves	106
Nationals	105
Brewers	101
Cardinals	100
Pirates	99
Dodgers	98
Phillies	96
Reds	94
Padres	92
Mets	92
Marlins	91
Giants	91

2017 NL RHB Avg	
Home Park	Index
Nationals	113
Rockies	108
Diamondbacks	107
Pirates	103
Brewers	102
Phillies	102
Cubs	99
Giants	98
Cardinals	98
Braves	98
Reds	96
Dodgers	95
Marlins	95
Padres	92
Mets	89

2017 AL Doubles	
Home Park	Index
Rangers	115
Red Sox	113
Blue Jays	113
Royals	110
Athletics	109
Tigers	108
Twins	105
Indians	102
Mariners	90
Orioles	89
White Sox	89
Angels	87
Rays	86
Astros	84
Yankees	84

2017 AL Triples	
Home Park	Index
Athletics	226
Twins	133
Tigers	127
Royals	123
Rays	114
Mariners	108
Blue Jays	98
Rangers	97
White Sox	83
Yankees	77
Red Sox	73
Angels	71
Orioles	68
Astros	66
Indians	64

2017 AL Errors	
Home Park	Index
White Sox	150
Red Sox	138
Rangers	131
Blue Jays	107
Angels	103
Yankees	101
Astros	101
Twins	97
Indians	96
Athletics	95
Orioles	94
Rays	84
Mariners	77
Royals	76
Tigers	76

2017 NL Doubles	
Home Park	Index
Diamondbacks	133
Rockies	116
Brewers	114
Cubs	110
Nationals	106
Pirates	105
Braves	105
Reds	102
Dodgers	99
Giants	99
Cardinals	97
Phillies	93
Mets	92
Padres	89
Marlins	73

2017 NL Triples	
Home Park	Index
Rockies	223
Diamondbacks	133
Cubs	130
Reds	123
Marlins	117
Phillies	105
Padres	104
Giants	103
Cardinals	98
Brewers	75
Mets	72
Braves	72
Pirates	63
Nationals	63
Dodgers	61

2017 NL Errors	
Home Park	Index
Brewers	122
Marlins	117
Mets	116
Cubs	114
Rockies	107
Dodgers	103
Pirates	103
Braves	99
Padres	97
Diamondbacks	92
Nationals	90
Giants	85
Phillies	84
Cardinals	84
Reds	80

2015-2017 American League Ballpark Index Rankings

Home Park	Avg	AB	R	H	2B	3B	HR	BB	SO	FO	E	E-Inf	LHB Avg	LHB HR	RHB Avg	RHB HR
Rangers (Rangers Ballpark in Arlington)	109	102	117	111	109	114	106	110	93	89	111	96	108	107	110	106
Indians (Progressive Field)	108	101	114	109	123	63	104	104	99	75	98	97	114	110	102	98
Red Sox (Fenway Park)	110	102	114	112	126	107	93	93	94	83	130	128	112	78	109	105
Orioles (Oriole Park at Camden Yards)	102	102	106	104	89	75	118	99	94	92	105	121	103	114	101	121
Twins (Target Field)	104	102	105	106	102	101	106	96	93	93	125	117	103	95	105	113
Royals (Kauffman Stadium)	102	100	103	102	119	140	80	97	94	104	81	87	102	85	102	76
Tigers (Comerica Park)	101	101	103	102	99	147	102	97	92	133	94	91	98	104	103	101
Yankees (Yankee Stadium)	97	99	103	96	86	62	131	101	104	95	99	88	95	142	99	123
Blue Jays (Rogers Centre)	101	98	99	99	117	102	100	100	97	101	93	87	102	98	101	101
Athletics (O.co Coliseum)	97	100	96	97	102	137	86	95	96	140	101	96	97	84	97	87
White Sox (Guaranteed Rate Field)	96	99	95	95	89	90	114	108	106	109	117	116	90	122	99	110
Rays (Tropicana Field)	95	98	92	93	86	92	93	99	110	108	85	81	95	97	94	90
Mariners (Safeco Field)	95	99	91	94	90	76	100	102	109	112	90	109	96	105	94	97
Angels (Angel Stadium of Anaheim)	96	100	91	96	86	68	98	93	104	93	104	130	96	91	96	102
Astros (Minute Maid Park)[2]	94	97	83	90	84	66	109	96	101	111	101	117	93	109	94	109

2015-2017 National League Ballpark Index Rankings

Home Park	Avg	AB	R	H	2B	3B	HR	BB	SO	FO	E	E-Inf	LHB Avg	LHB HR	RHB Avg	RHB HR
Rockies (Coors Field)	118	104	138	123	122	175	118	103	87	68	111	97	121	117	116	118
Diamondbacks (Chase Field)	107	102	116	109	120	168	109	101	100	95	96	90	109	106	105	111
Brewers (Miller Park)	99	101	105	100	106	97	116	99	103	94	103	105	103	131	96	108
Reds (Great American Ballpark)	98	101	104	99	99	73	112	104	106	123	84	74	100	119	98	108
Nationals (Nationals Park)	102	101	100	102	100	65	102	98	98	95	98	125	98	89	105	114
Cubs (Wrigley Field)	99	98	98	97	95	115	102	107	100	73	91	92	99	88	98	114
Phillies (Citizens Bank Park)	96	101	98	97	90	85	123	102	109	127	109	142	95	120	97	124
Braves (SunTrust Park)[2]	101	101	98	102	105	72	94	90	98	122	99	93	106	116	98	81
Pirates (PNC Park)	101	100	96	100	100	101	89	99	94	89	109	97	97	101	103	83
Padres (PETCO Park)	97	99	92	96	96	83	93	99	103	107	99	93	97	85	97	97
Cardinals (Busch Stadium)	100	99	91	100	96	84	88	95	95	130	88	89	102	97	100	82
Mets (Citi Field)	91	98	90	89	91	67	96	107	106	109	91	87	93	101	90	92
Giants (AT&T Park)	99	100	90	99	98	139	64	100	99	92	89	86	97	53	100	74
Dodgers (Dodger Stadium)	96	98	90	94	101	54	100	89	103	89	101	98	95	113	96	90
Marlins (Marlins Park)[1]	92	97	84	89	85	90	84	104	103	98	99	83	93	86	91	83

2015-2017 AL Home Runs

Home Park	Index
Yankees	131
Orioles	118
White Sox	114
Astros[2]	109
Rangers	106
Twins	106
Indians	104
Tigers	102
Mariners	100
Blue Jays	100
Angels	98
Red Sox	93
Rays	93
Athletics	86
Royals	80

2015-2017 AL LHB Home Runs

Home Park	Index
Yankees	142
White Sox	122
Orioles	114
Indians	110
Astros[2]	109
Rangers	107
Mariners	105
Tigers	104
Blue Jays	98
Rays	97
Twins	95
Angels	91
Royals	85
Athletics	84
Red Sox	78

2015-2017 AL RHB Home Runs

Home Park	Index
Yankees	123
Orioles	121
Twins	113
White Sox	110
Astros[2]	109
Rangers	106
Red Sox	105
Angels	102
Blue Jays	101
Tigers	101
Indians	98
Mariners	97
Rays	90
Athletics	87
Royals	76

2015-2017 NL Home Runs

Home Park	Index
Phillies	123
Rockies	118
Brewers	116
Reds	112
Diamondbacks	109
Nationals	102
Cubs	102
Dodgers	100
Mets	96
Braves[2]	94
Padres	93
Pirates	89
Cardinals	88
Marlins[1]	84
Giants	64

2015-2017 NL LHB Home Runs

Home Park	Index
Brewers	131
Phillies	120
Reds	119
Rockies	117
Braves[2]	116
Dodgers	113
Diamondbacks	106
Pirates	101
Mets	101
Cardinals	97
Nationals	89
Cubs	88
Marlins[1]	86
Padres	75
Giants	53

2015-2017 NL RHB Home Runs

Home Park	Index
Phillies	124
Rockies	118
Cubs	114
Nationals	114
Diamondbacks	111
Brewers	108
Reds	108
Padres	93
Mets	92
Dodgers	90
Marlins[1]	83
Pirates	83
Cardinals	82
Braves[2]	81
Giants	74

1. 2016-2017 Only

2. 2017 Only

2015-2017 AL Avg	
Home Park	Index
Red Sox	110
Rangers	109
Indians	108
Twins	104
Orioles	102
Royals	102
Blue Jays	101
Tigers	101
Athletics	97
Yankees	97
Angels	96
White Sox	96
Mariners	95
Rays	95
Astros[2]	94

2015-2017 AL LHB Avg	
Home Park	Index
Indians	114
Red Sox	112
Rangers	108
Orioles	103
Twins	103
Royals	102
Blue Jays	102
Tigers	98
Athletics	97
Angels	96
Mariners	96
Rays	95
Yankees	95
Astros[2]	93
White Sox	90

2015-2017 AL RHB Avg	
Home Park	Index
Rangers	110
Red Sox	109
Twins	105
Tigers	103
Indians	102
Royals	102
Orioles	101
Blue Jays	101
Yankees	99
White Sox	99
Athletics	97
Angels	96
Rays	94
Mariners	94
Astros[2]	94

2015-2017 NL Avg	
Home Park	Index
Rockies	118
Diamondbacks	107
Nationals	102
Braves[2]	101
Pirates	101
Cardinals	100
Giants	99
Brewers	99
Cubs	99
Reds	98
Padres	97
Phillies	96
Dodgers	96
Marlins[1]	92
Mets	91

2015-2017 NL LHB Avg	
Home Park	Index
Rockies	121
Diamondbacks	109
Braves[2]	106
Brewers	103
Cardinals	102
Reds	100
Cubs	99
Nationals	98
Giants	97
Pirates	97
Padres	97
Dodgers	95
Phillies	95
Mets	93
Marlins[1]	93

2015-2017 NL RHB Avg	
Home Park	Index
Rockies	116
Diamondbacks	105
Nationals	105
Pirates	103
Giants	100
Cardinals	100
Cubs	98
Braves[2]	98
Reds	98
Phillies	97
Padres	97
Dodgers	96
Brewers	96
Marlins[1]	91
Mets	90

2015-2017 AL Doubles	
Home Park	Index
Red Sox	126
Indians	123
Royals	119
Blue Jays	117
Rangers	109
Twins	102
Athletics	102
Tigers	99
Mariners	90
Orioles	89
White Sox	89
Rays	86
Yankees	86
Angels	86
Astros[2]	84

2015-2017 AL Triples	
Home Park	Index
Tigers	147
Royals	140
Athletics	137
Rangers	114
Red Sox	107
Blue Jays	102
Twins	101
Rays	92
White Sox	90
Mariners	76
Orioles	75
Angels	68
Astros[2]	66
Indians	63
Yankees	62

2015-2017 AL Errors	
Home Park	Index
Red Sox	130
Twins	125
White Sox	117
Rangers	111
Orioles	105
Angels	104
Athletics	101
Astros[2]	101
Yankees	99
Indians	98
Tigers	94
Blue Jays	93
Mariners	90
Rays	85
Royals	81

2015-2017 NL Doubles	
Home Park	Index
Rockies	122
Diamondbacks	120
Brewers	106
Braves[2]	105
Dodgers	101
Pirates	100
Nationals	100
Reds	99
Giants	98
Cardinals	96
Padres	96
Cubs	95
Mets	91
Phillies	90
Marlins[1]	85

2015-2017 NL Triples	
Home Park	Index
Rockies	175
Diamondbacks	168
Giants	139
Cubs	115
Pirates	101
Brewers	97
Marlins[1]	90
Phillies	85
Cardinals	84
Padres	83
Reds	73
Braves[2]	72
Mets	67
Nationals	65
Dodgers	54

2015-2017 NL Errors	
Home Park	Index
Rockies	111
Phillies	109
Pirates	109
Brewers	103
Dodgers	101
Padres	99
Braves[2]	99
Marlins[1]	99
Nationals	98
Diamondbacks	96
Cubs	91
Mets	91
Giants	89
Cardinals	88
Reds	84

1. 2016-2017 Only

2. 2017 Only

2017 Lefty/Righty Statistics

Lindsay Zeck

Of the 375 hitters with at least 40 plate appearances against both left- and right-handed pitchers this season, it was rookie Jose Martinez of the Cardinals who had the most extreme lefty/righty platoon split. He had an outstanding OPS of 1.340 against left-handed pitchers, second only to J.D Martinez (1.356). His OPS against righties, however, was .567 lower. Conversely, the hitter with the most extreme reverse platoon was righty Starling Marte of the Pirates. His OPS was .808 against right-handed pitchers and just half of that, .404, against left-handed pitchers.

Only 15 of the 375 hitters had a difference in OPS of no more than 10 points between left-handed and right-handed pitchers. Two standouts are rookie right-handed hitter Rhys Hoskins of the Phillies and the switch-hitting Jose Ramirez of the Indians. Hoskins finished the season with an OPS above 1.000 against both left- and right- handed pitchers—1.006 and 1.016, respectively. He was the only hitter to accomplish such a feat. Ramirez wasn't too far behind with an OPS of .953 against lefties and .958 against righties.

There were 288 pitchers who faced at least 100 right-handed and 100 left-handed batters. Of these pitchers, the two who had the most extreme reverse platoon splits were Chris Devenski of the Houston Astros and Brett Cecil of the St. Louis Cardinals. Devenski, the right-handed American League All-Star, amazingly finished the 2017 season with the second lowest OPS allowed against left-handed batters, .414. However, his OPS allowed against right-handed batters was .762—.348 higher. This was the fourth biggest OPS difference of any of the 288 pitchers. The biggest difference in OPS came against the left-handed pitcher Cecil. Lefty hitters had an OPS of .936 against him and righties had an OPS of .561, a difference of .375.

Not only did the pitcher with the most extreme reverse platoon splits, Cecil, play for the Cardinals, but the pitcher with the second-most-extreme traditional platoon splits did too. Righty Seung-Hwan Oh had an Opponent OPS of .642 when facing righty batters and 1.006—.364 higher—when facing lefties. He was 1 of only 10 pitchers against whom left-handed batters obtained an OPS above 1.000. The most extreme traditional splits came from the Nationals in right-handed rookie

A.J. Cole. He limited right-handed batters to an Opponent OPS of .601. Against lefties, his OPS increased to .975.

The following tables include platoon splits for all hitters with at least 20 plate appearances and pitchers with at least 20 batters faced in 2017.

Batters vs. Left-Handed and Right-Handed Pitchers

Batter	vs	Avg	AB	H	2B	3B	HR	RBI	BB	SO	OBP	Slg
Abreu,Jose	L	.356	149	53	7	2	10	28	11	31	.402	.631
Bats Right	R	.288	472	136	36	4	23	74	24	88	.339	.528
Adams,Lane	L	.143	28	4	0	0	0	0	5	14	.294	.143
Bats Right	R	.321	81	26	4	1	5	20	5	23	.356	.580
Adams,Matt	L	.180	61	11	3	0	3	12	2	16	.206	.377
Bats Left	R	.295	278	82	19	1	17	53	21	72	.342	.554
Adduci,Jim	L	.300	10	3	0	0	0	0	1	4	.364	.300
Bats Left	R	.233	73	17	6	2	1	10	9	23	.317	.411
Adrianza,Ehire	L	.321	56	18	5	1	1	14	4	8	.355	.500
Bats Both	R	.236	106	25	4	1	1	10	12	17	.309	.321
Aguilar,Jesus	L	.301	103	31	6	1	5	17	11	33	.365	.524
Bats Right	R	.244	176	43	9	1	11	35	14	61	.311	.494
Ahmed,Nick	L	.396	48	19	3	1	2	7	5	10	.453	.625
Bats Right	R	.193	119	23	5	0	4	14	5	29	.232	.336
Albies,Ozzie	L	.327	52	17	2	1	2	8	7	6	.407	.519
Bats Both	R	.273	165	45	7	4	4	20	14	30	.337	.436
Alcantara,Arismendy	L	.079	38	3	1	0	0	3	0	12	.079	.105
Bats Both	R	.224	67	15	2	1	1	4	2	26	.246	.328
Alfaro,Jorge	L	.200	35	7	2	0	0	1	2	13	.243	.257
Bats Right	R	.375	72	27	4	0	5	13	1	20	.416	.639
Allen,Greg	L	.400	10	4	1	0	1	4	2	3	.500	.800
Bats Both	R	.160	25	4	0	0	0	2	0	5	.185	.160
Almonte,Abraham	L	.200	45	9	0	0	1	4	6	13	.294	.267
Bats Both	R	.244	127	31	8	3	2	10	14	33	.322	.402
Almora Jr.,Albert	L	.342	111	38	4	0	4	16	13	17	.411	.486
Bats Right	R	.271	188	51	14	1	4	30	6	36	.291	.420
Alonso,Yonder	L	.181	72	13	2	0	5	10	6	20	.263	.417
Bats Left	R	.282	379	107	20	0	23	57	62	98	.383	.517
Altherr,Aaron	L	.239	109	26	5	0	8	22	14	22	.325	.505
Bats Right	R	.285	263	75	19	5	11	43	18	82	.346	.521
Altuve,Jose	L	.353	139	49	8	0	7	15	14	20	.416	.561
Bats Right	R	.344	451	155	31	4	17	66	44	64	.408	.543
Alvarez,Pedro	L	.667	3	2	0	0	1	1	0	0	.667	1.667
Bats Left	R	.276	29	8	1	0	0	3	2	10	.323	.310
Amarista,Alexi	L	.294	17	5	1	0	0	3	2	3	.368	.353
Bats Left	R	.232	151	35	9	0	3	16	5	35	.256	.351
Anderson,Brian	L	.241	29	7	1	0	0	3	1	10	.267	.276
Bats Right	R	.273	55	15	6	1	0	5	9	18	.369	.418
Anderson,Tim	L	.321	159	51	11	1	4	19	2	37	.333	.478
Bats Right	R	.234	428	100	15	3	13	37	11	125	.256	.374
Andrus,Elvis	L	.294	143	42	9	0	7	21	10	22	.342	.503
Bats Right	R	.298	500	149	35	4	13	67	28	79	.336	.462
Aoki,Nori	L	.218	55	12	1	1	0	6	7	8	.313	.273
Bats Left	R	.288	281	81	19	1	5	29	22	36	.340	.416
Arcia,Orlando	L	.248	117	29	4	0	1	8	12	25	.318	.308
Bats Right	R	.285	389	111	13	2	14	45	24	75	.326	.437
Arenado,Nolan	L	.420	150	63	13	1	16	47	15	17	.473	.840
Bats Right	R	.272	456	124	30	6	21	83	47	89	.341	.502
Arroyo,Christian	L	.235	51	12	1	0	1	5	1	12	.250	.314
Bats Right	R	.162	74	12	4	0	2	9	7	20	.241	.297
Asche,Cody	L	.000	5	0	0	0	0	0	0	1	.000	.000
Bats Left	R	.115	52	6	1	0	1	4	3	20	.193	.192
Asuaje,Carlos	L	.230	74	17	1	0	1	3	6	14	.288	.284
Bats Left	R	.283	233	66	13	1	3	18	22	62	.349	.386
Austin,Tyler	L	.385	13	5	0	0	2	7	2	5	.412	.846
Bats Right	R	.148	27	4	2	0	0	1	2	12	.207	.222
Avila,Alex	L	.216	37	8	0	0	0	7	4	14	.302	.216
Bats Left	R	.270	274	74	13	1	14	42	58	106	.398	.478
Aviles,Mike	L	.258	31	8	0	0	0	1	1	5	.303	.258
Bats Right	R	.218	55	12	2	0	1	7	5	10	.295	.309
Aybar,Erick	L	.244	90	22	3	1	2	9	9	12	.307	.367
Bats Both	R	.230	243	56	12	0	5	13	19	45	.297	.342
Bader,Harrison	L	.400	20	8	2	0	2	4	1	3	.429	.800
Bats Right	R	.185	65	12	1	0	1	6	4	21	.239	.246
Baez,Javier	L	.315	124	39	6	0	9	32	8	34	.353	.581
Bats Right	R	.258	345	89	18	2	14	43	22	110	.304	.443
Bandy,Jett	L	.296	27	8	2	0	2	4	3	7	.387	.593
Bats Right	R	.190	142	27	4	0	4	14	12	44	.268	.303
Barnes,Austin	L	.257	109	28	10	0	6	22	17	20	.372	.514
Bats Right	R	.321	109	35	5	2	2	16	22	23	.444	.459
Barney,Darwin	L	.244	123	30	2	0	1	6	14	29	.324	.285
Bats Right	R	.225	213	48	12	0	5	19	4	35	.243	.352
Barnhart,Tucker	L	.236	72	17	2	0	2	8	8	15	.321	.347
Bats Both	R	.279	298	83	22	2	5	36	34	53	.353	.416
Barreto,Franklin	L	.091	22	2	0	0	0	1	3	16	.200	.091
Bats Right	R	.245	49	12	1	2	2	5	2	17	.275	.469
Bautista,Jose	L	.201	139	28	9	0	3	9	18	43	.298	.331
Bats Right	R	.203	448	91	18	0	20	56	66	127	.310	.377
Bautista,Rafael	L	.250	8	2	0	0	0	0	0	2	.250	.250
Bats Right	R	.118	17	2	0	0	0	0	2	3	.211	.118
Beckham,Tim	L	.257	136	35	4	1	6	20	12	41	.327	.434
Bats Right	R	.285	397	113	14	4	16	42	24	126	.328	.461
Bell,Josh	L	.242	128	31	3	0	8	21	11	22	.305	.453
Bats Both	R	.259	421	109	23	6	18	69	55	95	.342	.470
Bellinger,Cody	L	.271	155	42	6	2	12	42	15	42	.335	.568
Bats Left	R	.265	325	86	20	2	27	55	49	104	.360	.588
Belt,Brandon	L	.223	130	29	9	1	4	15	15	36	.313	.400
Bats Left	R	.250	252	63	18	2	14	36	51	68	.375	.504
Beltran,Carlos	L	.185	119	22	8	0	1	7	6	34	.228	.277
Bats Both	R	.247	348	86	21	0	13	44	27	68	.301	.420
Beltre,Adrian	L	.388	67	26	5	0	4	16	13	8	.482	.642
Bats Right	R	.293	273	80	17	1	13	55	26	44	.356	.505
Benintendi,Andrew	L	.232	112	26	3	0	1	9	18	23	.336	.286
Bats Left	R	.280	461	129	23	1	19	81	52	89	.356	.458
Betts,Mookie	L	.306	124	38	9	1	5	23	23	12	.412	.516
Bats Right	R	.254	504	128	37	1	19	79	54	67	.326	.444
Bird,Gregory	L	.286	28	8	1	0	3	8	3	7	.344	.643
Bats Left	R	.168	119	20	6	0	6	20	16	35	.275	.370
Blackmon,Charlie	L	.333	213	71	9	6	9	26	16	37	.393	.559
Bats Left	R	.329	431	142	26	8	28	78	49	98	.402	.622
Blanco,Andres	L	.195	41	8	2	0	1	2	1	10	.214	.317
Bats Both	R	.191	89	17	2	0	2	11	11	24	.275	.281
Blanco,Gregor	L	.217	60	13	1	0	1	5	2	15	.242	.283
Bats Left	R	.256	164	42	9	3	2	8	29	44	.368	.384
Blash,Jabari	L	.290	69	20	4	0	3	7	9	22	.380	.478
Bats Right	R	.158	95	15	2	0	2	9	19	44	.302	.242
Bogaerts,Xander	L	.294	109	32	6	0	2	10	14	20	.373	.404
Bats Right	R	.268	462	124	26	6	8	52	42	96	.336	.403
Bonifacio,Emilio	L	.000	8	0	0	0	0	0	0	2	.000	.000
Bats Both	R	.167	30	5	1	1	0	3	1	7	.188	.267
Bonifacio,Jorge	L	.246	114	28	6	0	5	14	6	32	.283	.430
Bats Right	R	.259	270	70	9	1	12	26	29	86	.334	.433
Bostick,Chris	L	.250	8	2	0	0	0	0	2	3	.400	.250
Bats Right	R	.316	19	6	2	0	0	1	2	6	.409	.421
Bour,Justin	L	.253	87	22	2	0	6	21	10	29	.327	.483
Bats Left	R	.300	290	87	16	0	19	62	37	66	.378	.552
Bourjos,Peter	L	.260	104	27	6	2	3	8	8	28	.310	.442
Bats Right	R	.179	84	15	3	1	2	7	4	25	.225	.310
Bradley Jr.,Jackie	L	.276	116	32	6	0	3	18	13	27	.361	.405
Bats Left	R	.235	366	86	13	3	14	45	35	97	.311	.402
Brantley,Michael	L	.288	118	34	4	0	2	17	6	16	.323	.373
Bats Left	R	.305	220	67	16	1	7	35	25	34	.375	.482
Brantly,Rob	L	.200	5	1	0	0	0	0	1	3	.333	.200
Bats Left	R	.308	26	8	1	0	2	5	2	11	.400	.577
Braun,Ryan	L	.264	91	24	10	2	3	8	14	10	.355	.516
Bats Right	R	.270	289	78	18	0	14	44	24	66	.330	.478
Bregman,Alex	L	.331	142	47	9	2	7	19	17	21	.404	.570
Bats Right	R	.268	414	111	30	3	12	52	38	76	.334	.442
Brinson,Lewis	L	.200	15	3	0	0	2	3	3	5	.333	.600
Bats Right	R	.063	32	2	0	1	0	0	4	12	.189	.125
Broxton,Keon	L	.225	102	23	3	2	5	11	16	40	.331	.441
Bats Right	R	.218	312	68	12	2	15	38	24	135	.288	.413
Bruce,Jay	L	.222	171	38	7	1	9	24	14	48	.285	.433
Bats Left	R	.268	384	103	22	1	27	77	43	91	.341	.542
Brugman,Jaycob	L	.167	18	3	0	0	0	1	1	5	.211	.167
Bats Left	R	.280	125	35	2	0	3	11	17	33	.364	.368
Bryant,Kris	L	.298	124	37	9	0	6	17	31	24	.439	.516
Bats Right	R	.294	425	125	29	4	23	56	64	104	.400	.544
Butera,Drew	L	.208	48	10	2	0	1	2	5	12	.283	.313
Bats Right	R	.235	115	27	2	1	2	12	7	29	.285	.322
Buxton,Byron	L	.282	131	37	3	2	4	13	17	38	.365	.427
Bats Right	R	.242	331	80	11	4	12	38	21	112	.293	.408
Cabrera,Asdrubal	L	.392	125	49	6	0	3	14	10	17	.434	.512
Bats Both	R	.240	354	85	26	0	11	45	40	66	.323	.407
Cabrera,Melky	L	.285	151	43	6	0	7	24	9	21	.321	.464
Bats Both	R	.286	469	134	24	2	10	61	27	53	.325	.409
Cabrera,Miguel	L	.326	95	31	7	0	3	19	18	26	.434	.495
Bats Right	R	.230	374	86	15	0	13	41	36	84	.300	.374
Cain,Lorenzo	L	.277	130	36	9	1	5	13	14	19	.347	.477
Bats Right	R	.306	454	139	18	4	10	36	40	81	.367	.430
Calhoun,Kole	L	.223	166	37	7	1	5	13	20	36	.320	.367
Bats Left	R	.253	403	102	16	1	14	58	51	98	.339	.402

Batters vs. Left-Handed and Right-Handed Pitchers

Batter	vs	Avg	AB	H	2B	3B	HR	RBI	BB	SO	OBP	Slg
Calhoun,Willie	L	.273	11	3	0	0	0	2	0	2	.333	.273
Bats Left	R	.261	23	6	0	0	1	2	2	5	.320	.391
Calixte,Orlando	L	.154	13	2	1	0	0	3	0	4	.143	.231
Bats Right	R	.139	36	5	0	0	0	3	3	12	.200	.139
Camargo,Johan	L	.403	72	29	10	1	3	9	4	15	.434	.694
Bats Both	R	.254	169	43	11	1	1	18	8	36	.287	.349
Candelario,Jeimer	L	.348	23	8	4	0	0	5	1	6	.400	.522
Bats Both	R	.269	104	28	5	0	3	11	12	24	.350	.404
Canha,Mark	L	.203	74	15	5	1	1	5	2	22	.244	.338
Bats Right	R	.212	99	21	8	0	4	9	5	34	.275	.414
Cano,Robinson	L	.208	178	37	4	0	4	20	11	32	.259	.298
Bats Left	R	.312	414	129	29	0	19	77	38	53	.371	.519
Caratini,Victor	L	.500	12	6	1	0	0	0	1	2	.600	.583
Bats Both	R	.191	47	9	2	0	1	2	3	11	.255	.298
Cardullo,Stephen	L	.190	21	4	0	0	0	2	2	5	.261	.190
Bats Right	R	.000	7	0	0	0	0	1	1	2	.222	.000
Carpenter,Matt	L	.202	109	22	5	1	2	12	22	32	.343	.321
Bats Left	R	.253	388	98	26	1	21	57	87	93	.395	.487
Carrera,Ezequiel	L	.086	35	3	1	0	0	0	6	10	.220	.114
Bats Left	R	.310	252	78	9	1	8	20	24	65	.376	.448
Carter,Chris	L	.179	56	10	2	0	4	7	2	19	.207	.429
Bats Right	R	.211	128	27	3	1	4	19	18	57	.313	.344
Castellanos,Nick	L	.292	137	40	7	1	11	28	9	23	.336	.599
Bats Right	R	.266	477	127	29	9	15	73	32	119	.316	.459
Castillo,Welington	L	.344	93	32	3	0	6	18	4	27	.367	.570
Bats Right	R	.258	248	64	8	0	14	35	18	70	.307	.460
Castro,Jason	L	.263	95	25	5	0	3	17	7	20	.327	.411
Bats Left	R	.234	261	61	17	0	7	30	38	88	.334	.379
Castro,Starlin	L	.321	106	34	9	0	2	7	9	23	.374	.462
Bats Right	R	.294	337	99	9	1	14	56	14	70	.327	.451
Cecchini,Gavin	L	.280	25	7	1	0	1	2	3	6	.379	.440
Bats Right	R	.173	52	9	1	0	0	5	1	13	.189	.192
Centeno,Juan	L	.333	12	4	0	0	0	1	0	2	.333	.333
Bats Left	R	.200	40	8	0	0	2	3	4	10	.273	.350
Cervelli,Francisco	L	.237	59	14	1	1	1	11	8	15	.338	.339
Bats Right	R	.252	206	52	12	1	4	20	24	50	.343	.379
Cespedes,Yoenis	L	.256	78	20	5	1	6	11	8	21	.330	.577
Bats Right	R	.305	213	65	12	1	11	31	18	40	.361	.526
Chapman,Matt	L	.244	82	20	6	0	4	12	10	31	.323	.463
Bats Right	R	.231	208	48	17	2	10	28	22	61	.309	.476
Chirinos,Robinson	L	.366	71	26	3	0	6	14	11	18	.451	.662
Bats Right	R	.214	192	41	10	1	11	24	23	61	.327	.448
Chisenhall,Lonnie	L	.340	47	16	2	0	2	10	9	10	.456	.511
Bats Left	R	.275	189	52	15	1	10	43	16	45	.333	.524
Choo,Shin-Soo	L	.287	122	35	5	0	1	12	20	24	.400	.352
Bats Left	R	.254	422	107	15	1	21	66	57	110	.344	.443
Coghlan,Chris	L	.000	4	0	0	0	0	0	2	1	.429	.000
Bats Left	R	.211	71	15	2	0	1	5	7	21	.288	.282
Coleman,Dusty	L	.077	13	1	0	0	0	0	0	9	.077	.077
Bats Right	R	.264	53	14	3	0	4	9	2	24	.310	.547
Collins,Tyler	L	.100	10	1	1	0	0	0	1	3	.182	.200
Bats Left	R	.200	140	28	3	1	5	14	17	52	.285	.343
Colon,Christian	L	.174	23	4	0	0	0	0	3	4	.269	.174
Bats Right	R	.148	27	4	1	0	0	0	2	6	.207	.185
Conforto,Michael	L	.212	99	21	5	0	6	12	8	41	.284	.444
Bats Left	R	.303	274	83	15	1	21	56	49	72	.417	.595
Contreras,Willson	L	.279	111	31	6	0	7	21	20	24	.394	.523
Bats Right	R	.274	266	73	15	0	14	53	25	74	.339	.489
Cooper,Garrett	L	.368	19	7	2	1	0	1	1	7	.400	.579
Bats Right	R	.292	24	7	3	0	0	5	0	5	.280	.417
Cordero,Franchy	L	.188	16	3	0	0	1	1	1	10	.235	.375
Bats Left	R	.237	76	18	3	3	2	8	5	34	.284	.434
Cordoba,Allen	L	.095	42	4	0	0	1	3	2	15	.133	.167
Bats Right	R	.238	160	38	2	2	3	12	16	39	.319	.331
Correa,Carlos	L	.391	92	36	5	0	5	19	12	12	.457	.609
Bats Right	R	.294	330	97	20	1	19	65	41	80	.372	.533
Cowart,Kaleb	L	.167	18	3	0	0	0	2	1	7	.211	.167
Bats Both	R	.238	84	20	5	1	3	9	9	21	.333	.429
Cozart,Zack	L	.337	98	33	9	1	6	12	14	16	.426	.633
Bats Right	R	.285	340	97	15	6	18	51	48	62	.372	.524
Crawford,Brandon	L	.239	142	34	9	0	3	24	12	26	.295	.366
Bats Left	R	.258	376	97	25	1	11	53	30	87	.309	.418
Crawford,J.P.	L	.087	23	2	1	0	0	0	5	10	.250	.130
Bats Left	R	.277	47	13	3	1	0	6	11	12	.407	.383
Cron,C.J.	L	.233	86	20	3	1	6	17	6	27	.290	.500
Bats Right	R	.253	253	64	11	0	10	39	16	69	.309	.415

Batter	vs	Avg	AB	H	2B	3B	HR	RBI	BB	SO	OBP	Slg
Cruz,Nelson	L	.229	131	30	2	0	8	23	35	35	.407	.427
Bats Right	R	.306	425	130	26	0	31	96	35	105	.364	.586
Cuthbert,Cheslor	L	.216	51	11	3	0	1	4	4	14	.273	.333
Bats Right	R	.239	92	22	4	0	1	14	5	25	.276	.315
d'Arnaud,Chase	L	.120	25	3	0	0	0	0	2	7	.185	.120
Bats Right	R	.242	33	8	2	0	1	3	2	13	.286	.394
d'Arnaud,Travis	L	.302	86	26	8	1	3	19	10	17	.371	.523
Bats Right	R	.225	262	59	11	0	13	38	13	42	.265	.416
Davidson,Matt	L	.250	112	28	6	1	5	15	7	37	.303	.455
Bats Right	R	.209	302	63	10	0	21	53	12	128	.243	.450
Davis,Chris	L	.208	144	30	3	1	4	15	16	65	.293	.326
Bats Left	R	.218	312	68	12	0	22	46	45	130	.317	.468
Davis,J.D.	L	.217	23	5	1	0	3	3	2	8	.308	.652
Bats Right	R	.231	39	9	3	0	1	4	2	12	.262	.385
Davis,Khris	L	.213	122	26	6	1	7	23	24	43	.336	.451
Bats Right	R	.257	444	114	22	0	36	87	49	152	.336	.550
Davis,Rajai	L	.244	119	29	7	1	2	6	11	26	.308	.370
Bats Right	R	.230	217	50	12	1	3	14	16	57	.285	.336
De Aza,Alejandro	L	.154	13	2	0	1	0	4	0	0	.143	.308
Bats Left	R	.204	49	10	2	2	0	5	3	16	.245	.327
Decker,Jaff	L	.375	8	3	0	0	0	0	0	3	.444	.375
Bats Left	R	.167	42	7	1	1	0	1	8	14	.300	.238
DeJong,Paul	L	.288	80	23	5	1	6	14	8	29	.352	.600
Bats Right	R	.285	337	96	21	0	19	51	13	95	.318	.516
Delmonico,Nick	L	.258	31	8	1	0	2	5	7	8	.410	.484
Bats Left	R	.264	110	29	3	0	7	18	16	23	.362	.482
Descalso,Daniel	L	.169	77	13	4	0	2	9	12	22	.289	.299
Bats Left	R	.251	267	67	12	5	8	42	36	67	.344	.423
DeShields,Delino	L	.250	120	30	5	1	4	6	16	42	.343	.408
Bats Right	R	.277	256	71	10	1	2	16	28	67	.348	.348
Desmond,Ian	L	.250	92	23	4	0	2	16	6	23	.304	.359
Bats Right	R	.283	247	70	7	1	5	24	18	64	.335	.381
Devers,Rafael	L	.400	50	20	4	0	2	4	7	17	.474	.600
Bats Left	R	.250	172	43	10	0	8	26	11	40	.295	.448
Diaz,Aledmys	L	.236	55	13	3	0	0	0	6	10	.311	.291
Bats Right	R	.264	231	61	14	0	7	20	7	32	.285	.416
Diaz,Elias	L	.261	46	12	5	0	0	6	1	8	.277	.370
Bats Right	R	.211	142	30	9	0	1	13	10	30	.261	.296
Diaz,Yandy	L	.268	56	15	3	0	0	5	13	12	.406	.321
Bats Right	R	.260	100	26	5	1	0	8	8	23	.318	.330
Dickerson,Corey	L	.308	156	48	12	3	3	13	6	43	.339	.481
Bats Left	R	.273	432	118	21	1	24	49	29	109	.320	.493
Dietrich,Derek	L	.307	75	23	6	1	0	8	6	18	.402	.413
Bats Left	R	.236	331	78	16	4	13	45	30	80	.318	.426
Difo,Wilmer	L	.310	84	26	1	3	3	6	5	17	.348	.500
Bats Both	R	.258	248	64	9	1	2	15	19	57	.310	.327
Donaldson,Josh	L	.271	85	23	4	0	10	21	15	21	.380	.671
Bats Right	R	.270	330	89	17	0	23	57	61	90	.386	.530
Dozier,Brian	L	.331	145	48	11	0	11	25	21	32	.423	.634
Bats Right	R	.250	472	118	19	4	23	68	57	109	.337	.453
Drew,Stephen	L	.400	5	2	0	0	0	2	1	1	.500	.400
Bats Left	R	.244	90	22	7	0	1	15	7	20	.290	.356
Drury,Brandon	L	.271	133	36	13	0	3	12	5	34	.302	.436
Bats Right	R	.266	312	83	24	2	10	51	23	69	.323	.452
Duda,Lucas	L	.188	101	19	7	0	5	14	8	39	.252	.406
Bats Left	R	.227	322	73	21	0	25	50	52	96	.342	.525
Duvall,Adam	L	.279	140	39	11	0	10	25	14	35	.352	.571
Bats Right	R	.239	447	107	26	3	21	74	25	135	.285	.452
Dyson,Jarrod	L	.145	55	8	0	0	0	1	4	6	.230	.145
Bats Left	R	.271	291	79	13	3	5	29	24	49	.342	.388
Eaton,Adam	L	.182	11	2	0	1	0	2	1	3	.231	.364
Bats Left	R	.313	80	25	7	0	2	11	13	15	.415	.475
Eibner,Brett	L	.188	16	3	0	0	2	3	1	9	.235	.563
Bats Right	R	.176	17	3	0	0	0	3	1	8	.263	.176
Ellis,A.J.	L	.154	39	6	2	0	1	1	2	11	.250	.282
Bats Right	R	.231	104	24	3	0	5	13	10	18	.316	.404
Ellsbury,Jacoby	L	.240	104	25	4	0	2	13	8	30	.301	.337
Bats Left	R	.274	252	69	16	4	5	26	33	33	.367	.429
Encarnacion,Edwin	L	.249	173	43	4	1	10	33	42	48	.400	.457
Bats Right	R	.262	381	100	16	0	28	74	62	85	.366	.525
Engel,Adam	L	.217	83	18	3	3	1	10	6	24	.286	.361
Bats Right	R	.147	218	32	8	0	5	11	13	93	.215	.252
Ervin,Phillip	L	.412	17	7	1	0	0	4	2	3	.474	.471
Bats Right	R	.195	41	8	1	0	3	6	2	12	.250	.439
Escobar,Alcides	L	.276	134	37	11	2	1	16	7	22	.310	.410
Bats Right	R	.243	465	113	25	3	5	38	8	80	.260	.342

Batters vs. Left-Handed and Right-Handed Pitchers

Batter	vs	Avg	AB	H	2B	3B	HR	RBI	BB	SO	OBP	Slg
Escobar,Eduardo	L	.255	161	41	4	0	7	24	14	31	.320	.410
Bats Both	R	.253	296	75	12	5	14	49	19	67	.303	.470
Escobar,Yunel	L	.343	102	35	7	0	1	9	8	14	.391	.441
Bats Right	R	.246	248	61	13	1	6	22	21	37	.310	.379
Espinosa,Danny	L	.173	98	17	6	0	1	6	7	35	.234	.265
Bats Both	R	.173	168	29	4	0	5	25	14	74	.251	.286
Ethier,Andre	L	.000	3	0	0	0	0	0	0	0	.000	.000
Bats Left	R	.258	31	8	1	0	2	3	4	10	.343	.484
Evans,Phillip	L	.250	8	2	0	0	0	0	0	3	.250	.250
Bats Right	R	.320	25	8	2	0	0	1	4	5	.433	.400
Farmer,Kyle	L	.250	8	2	0	0	0	0	0	0	.250	.250
Bats Right	R	.333	12	4	1	0	0	2	0	3	.333	.417
Featherston,Taylor	L	.143	14	2	0	0	0	1	4	5	.316	.143
Bats Right	R	.200	25	5	1	0	2	5	1	10	.250	.480
Fisher,Derek	L	.241	29	7	0	1	0	4	4	11	.333	.310
Bats Left	R	.205	117	24	4	0	5	13	13	43	.301	.368
Flaherty,Ryan	L	.125	8	1	0	0	0	0	1	2	.222	.125
Bats Left	R	.233	30	7	1	0	0	4	3	8	.324	.267
Flores,Wilmer	L	.291	103	30	6	0	7	13	2	19	.309	.553
Bats Right	R	.262	233	61	11	1	11	39	15	35	.306	.459
Florimon,Pedro	L	.455	11	5	3	0	0	2	2	3	.538	.727
Bats Both	R	.314	35	11	1	1	0	4	1	13	.333	.400
Flowers,Tyler	L	.283	53	15	3	0	1	7	12	11	.433	.396
Bats Right	R	.280	264	74	13	0	11	42	19	71	.366	.455
Fontana,Nolan	L	.000	2	0	0	0	0	0	1	1	.333	.000
Bats Left	R	.056	18	1	0	0	1	1	2	7	.150	.222
Forsythe,Logan	L	.290	124	36	11	0	3	16	26	37	.418	.452
Bats Right	R	.190	237	45	8	0	3	20	43	72	.315	.262
Fowler,Dexter	L	.252	107	27	8	2	2	12	13	18	.333	.421
Bats Both	R	.268	313	84	14	7	16	52	50	83	.372	.511
Franco,Maikel	L	.209	148	31	5	0	7	18	12	23	.272	.385
Bats Right	R	.237	427	101	24	1	17	58	29	72	.284	.417
Franklin,Nick	L	.000	16	0	0	0	0	0	0	7	.000	.000
Bats Both	R	.211	90	19	3	1	2	12	10	15	.311	.333
Frazier,Adam	L	.304	56	17	1	0	0	10	3	11	.355	.321
Bats Left	R	.271	350	95	19	6	6	43	33	46	.343	.411
Frazier,Clint	L	.257	35	9	2	2	1	2	0	12	.257	.514
Bats Right	R	.222	99	22	7	2	3	15	7	31	.271	.424
Frazier,Todd	L	.207	116	24	2	1	12	30	19	29	.331	.552
Bats Right	R	.215	358	77	17	0	15	46	64	96	.348	.388
Freeman,Freddie	L	.278	126	35	7	0	8	20	12	33	.357	.524
Bats Left	R	.318	314	100	28	2	20	51	53	62	.420	.611
Freeman,Mike	L	.000	8	0	0	0	0	0	2	6	.200	.000
Bats Left	R	.115	52	6	2	0	1	1	4	13	.179	.212
Freese,David	L	.308	107	33	3	0	3	15	20	27	.419	.421
Bats Right	R	.248	319	79	13	0	7	37	38	89	.350	.354
Fryer,Eric	L	.000	10	0	0	0	0	0	3	4	.231	.000
Bats Right	R	.180	61	11	3	0	0	3	8	14	.286	.230
Fuentes,Rey	L	.190	21	4	0	0	0	0	1	7	.227	.190
Bats Left	R	.243	115	28	1	2	3	9	7	28	.287	.365
Gallagher,Cam	L	.500	2	1	0	0	0	0	0	0	.500	.500
Bats Right	R	.227	22	5	1	0	1	5	3	4	.320	.409
Gallo,Joey	L	.226	106	24	6	0	7	17	17	51	.359	.481
Bats Left	R	.204	343	70	12	3	34	63	58	145	.324	.554
Galvis,Freddy	L	.255	192	49	10	1	2	12	8	24	.289	.349
Bats Both	R	.255	416	106	19	5	10	49	37	87	.317	.397
Gamel,Ben	L	.275	120	33	8	2	1	15	4	38	.299	.400
Bats Left	R	.275	389	107	19	3	10	44	32	84	.329	.416
Garcia,Adonis	L	.231	26	6	0	0	2	4	2	3	.310	.462
Bats Right	R	.238	147	35	4	0	3	15	5	20	.266	.327
Garcia,Avisail	L	.424	132	56	8	3	2	20	8	25	.454	.576
Bats Right	R	.298	386	115	19	2	16	60	25	86	.355	.482
Garcia,Greg	L	.086	35	3	0	0	0	0	6	13	.256	.086
Bats Left	R	.282	206	58	9	2	2	20	31	51	.384	.374
Garcia,Leury	L	.302	86	26	4	0	0	10	4	14	.341	.349
Bats Both	R	.257	214	55	11	2	9	23	9	55	.306	.453
Garcia,Willy	L	.250	36	9	1	0	2	3	5	10	.341	.444
Bats Right	R	.232	69	16	4	3	0	9	6	21	.286	.377
Gardner,Brett	L	.209	148	31	4	1	2	12	15	28	.299	.291
Bats Left	R	.283	446	126	22	3	19	51	57	94	.367	.473
Garneau,Dustin	L	.217	60	13	5	0	2	6	6	18	.299	.400
Bats Right	R	.154	52	8	3	0	0	3	6	18	.241	.212
Garver,Mitch	L	.238	21	5	0	2	0	1	3	7	.333	.429
Bats Right	R	.160	25	4	1	1	0	2	3	8	.250	.280
Gattis,Evan	L	.241	87	21	6	0	4	19	5	15	.280	.448
Bats Right	R	.272	213	58	16	0	8	36	13	35	.323	.460

Batter	vs	Avg	AB	H	2B	3B	HR	RBI	BB	SO	OBP	Slg
Gennett,Scooter	L	.248	109	27	5	0	4	20	5	34	.287	.404
Bats Left	R	.310	352	109	17	3	23	77	25	80	.359	.571
Gentry,Craig	L	.271	59	16	3	1	2	7	5	16	.328	.458
Bats Right	R	.238	42	10	2	0	0	4	6	8	.340	.286
Gillaspie,Conor	L	.182	11	2	1	0	0	0	0	2	.250	.273
Bats Left	R	.159	69	11	3	0	2	8	5	8	.213	.290
Gimenez,Chris	L	.208	77	16	4	0	3	7	12	24	.322	.377
Bats Right	R	.229	109	25	5	0	4	9	21	36	.368	.385
Goins,Ryan	L	.246	69	17	4	0	0	5	6	21	.303	.304
Bats Left	R	.235	349	82	17	1	9	57	25	75	.283	.367
Goldschmidt,Paul	L	.311	132	41	5	1	10	30	26	27	.422	.591
Bats Right	R	.293	426	125	29	2	26	90	68	120	.398	.554
Gomes,Yan	L	.245	106	26	4	0	8	24	12	32	.339	.509
Bats Right	R	.226	235	53	11	0	6	32	19	67	.295	.349
Gomez,Carlos	L	.227	88	20	4	0	2	15	4	33	.304	.341
Bats Right	R	.264	280	74	19	1	15	36	27	94	.352	.500
Gomez,Miguel	L	.200	15	3	1	0	0	1	0	4	.188	.267
Bats Both	R	.278	18	5	1	0	0	1	0	2	.278	.333
Gonzalez,Adrian	L	.191	47	9	1	0	0	6	3	9	.240	.213
Bats Left	R	.255	184	47	16	0	3	24	13	34	.299	.391
Gonzalez,Carlos	L	.206	131	27	9	0	2	10	5	42	.241	.321
Bats Left	R	.283	339	96	25	0	12	47	51	77	.373	.463
Gonzalez,Erik	L	.222	36	8	1	0	1	3	2	19	.263	.333
Bats Right	R	.270	74	20	5	0	3	8	1	18	.276	.459
Gonzalez,Marwin	L	.250	120	30	11	0	5	16	11	24	.328	.467
Bats Both	R	.322	335	108	23	0	18	74	38	75	.394	.552
Goodwin,Brian	L	.341	44	15	4	1	2	5	4	17	.388	.614
Bats Left	R	.232	207	48	17	0	11	25	19	52	.297	.473
Gordon,Alex	L	.202	114	23	4	1	0	9	15	24	.348	.254
Bats Left	R	.210	362	76	16	1	9	36	30	102	.274	.334
Gordon,Dee	L	.293	188	55	4	2	0	11	2	25	.313	.335
Bats Left	R	.314	465	146	16	7	2	22	23	68	.352	.391
Gosewisch,Tuffy	L	.077	13	1	0	0	0	0	0	6	.077	.077
Bats Right	R	.067	15	1	0	0	0	0	1	8	.125	.067
Gosselin,Phil	L	.111	18	2	1	0	0	1	2	5	.200	.167
Bats Right	R	.167	30	5	1	0	0	1	0	7	.167	.200
Grandal,Yasmani	L	.233	86	20	4	0	2	7	11	25	.320	.349
Bats Both	R	.250	352	88	23	0	20	51	29	105	.305	.486
Granderson,Curtis	L	.202	104	21	3	1	5	14	11	31	.274	.394
Bats Left	R	.214	345	74	21	2	21	50	60	92	.337	.470
Granite,Zack	L	.353	17	6	0	0	1	6	3	2	.450	.529
Bats Left	R	.211	76	16	2	0	0	7	9	7	.291	.237
Graterol,Juan	L	.148	27	4	1	0	0	4	0	6	.148	.185
Bats Right	R	.228	57	13	3	0	0	6	1	7	.233	.281
Gregorius,Didi	L	.264	144	38	4	0	3	17	6	23	.299	.354
Bats Left	R	.295	390	115	23	0	22	70	19	47	.325	.523
Grichuk,Randal	L	.204	98	20	2	1	5	9	8	29	.264	.398
Bats Right	R	.248	314	78	23	2	17	50	18	104	.292	.497
Grossman,Robbie	L	.238	122	29	7	0	1	9	27	20	.376	.320
Bats Both	R	.250	260	65	15	1	8	36	40	59	.354	.408
Gurriel,Yulieski	L	.252	147	37	10	1	3	18	10	21	.300	.395
Bats Right	R	.317	382	121	33	0	15	57	12	41	.344	.521
Gutierrez,Franklin	L	.195	41	8	3	0	1	3	6	13	.298	.341
Bats Right	R	.333	15	5	0	0	0	5	1	3	.375	.333
Guyer,Brandon	L	.252	111	28	4	1	2	15	10	27	.331	.360
Bats Right	R	.204	54	11	3	0	0	5	5	16	.317	.259
Gyorko,Jedd	L	.327	101	33	4	1	7	17	10	15	.381	.594
Bats Right	R	.255	325	83	17	1	13	50	37	90	.329	.434
Hamilton,Billy	L	.219	169	37	4	3	1	11	5	41	.241	.296
Bats Both	R	.259	413	107	13	8	3	27	39	92	.322	.351
Hanigan,Ryan	L	.467	30	14	2	0	2	9	4	5	.514	.733
Bats Right	R	.183	71	13	0	0	0	3	4	21	.237	.183
Haniger,Mitch	L	.250	92	23	2	2	4	11	5	19	.289	.446
Bats Right	R	.292	277	81	23	0	12	36	26	74	.372	.505
Hannemann,Jacob	L	.000	2	0	0	0	0	0	0	1	.000	.000
Bats Left	R	.167	18	3	0	0	1	1	0	3	.167	.333
Hanson,Alen	L	.265	34	9	3	0	1	1	3	8	.324	.441
Bats Both	R	.213	183	39	6	3	3	10	9	44	.250	.328
Happ,Ian	L	.276	105	29	4	1	5	16	5	32	.313	.476
Bats Both	R	.243	259	63	13	2	19	52	34	97	.334	.529
Hardy,J.J.	L	.195	82	16	2	1	1	7	5	17	.241	.280
Bats Right	R	.227	172	39	11	0	3	17	7	31	.261	.343
Harper,Bryce	L	.311	119	37	7	0	3	13	9	36	.357	.445
Bats Left	R	.322	301	97	20	1	26	74	59	63	.433	.654
Harrison,Josh	L	.286	112	32	2	1	6	11	10	21	.375	.482
Bats Right	R	.267	374	100	24	1	10	36	18	69	.328	.417

Batters vs. Left-Handed and Right-Handed Pitchers

Batter	vs	Avg	AB	H	2B	3B	HR	RBI	BB	SO	OBP	Slg
Hays,Austin	L	.214	14	3	1	0	1	2	0	2	.214	.500
Bats Right	R	.217	46	10	2	0	0	6	2	14	.245	.261
Hazelbaker,Jeremy	L	.364	11	4	1	0	1	5	1	5	.417	.727
Bats Left	R	.341	41	14	1	2	1	5	8	15	.449	.537
Headley,Chase	L	.260	154	40	11	0	4	15	9	34	.299	.409
Bats Both	R	.279	358	100	19	1	8	46	51	98	.373	.405
Healy,Ryon	L	.314	137	43	8	0	7	22	7	30	.347	.526
Bats Right	R	.257	439	113	21	0	18	56	16	112	.289	.428
Hechavarria,Adeiny	L	.256	82	21	3	2	3	7	5	17	.295	.451
Bats Right	R	.262	248	65	11	3	5	23	8	50	.287	.391
Hedges,Austin	L	.214	112	24	5	0	3	10	6	33	.261	.339
Bats Right	R	.215	275	59	12	0	15	45	17	89	.263	.422
Heisey,Chris	L	.238	21	5	2	1	0	1	0	5	.238	.429
Bats Right	R	.132	53	7	1	0	1	4	5	17	.207	.208
Heredia,Guillermo	L	.310	129	40	7	0	3	13	8	21	.360	.434
Bats Right	R	.218	257	56	9	0	3	11	19	43	.294	.288
Hernandez,Cesar	L	.281	153	43	13	4	2	7	16	20	.353	.458
Bats Both	R	.299	358	107	13	2	7	27	45	84	.381	.405
Hernandez,Gorkys	L	.237	135	32	10	0	0	8	12	33	.299	.311
Bats Right	R	.269	175	47	10	1	0	14	19	40	.347	.337
Hernandez,Kike	L	.270	152	41	13	2	10	27	24	33	.367	.579
Bats Right	R	.159	145	23	11	0	1	10	17	47	.244	.255
Hernandez,Marco	L	.313	16	5	0	0	0	1	0	3	.353	.313
Bats Left	R	.262	42	11	3	0	0	1	1	12	.279	.333
Hernandez,Teoscar	L	.192	26	5	1	0	2	5	0	13	.185	.462
Bats Right	R	.290	62	18	5	0	6	15	6	23	.353	.661
Herrera,Odubel	L	.288	153	44	10	3	4	17	5	39	.323	.471
Bats Left	R	.279	373	104	32	0	10	39	26	87	.326	.445
Herrmann,Chris	L	.156	45	7	1	0	2	6	2	12	.191	.311
Bats Left	R	.188	181	34	6	0	8	21	27	55	.292	.354
Heyward,Jason	L	.267	116	31	5	2	1	12	4	26	.292	.371
Bats Left	R	.256	316	81	10	2	10	47	37	41	.338	.396
Hicks,Aaron	L	.312	109	34	7	0	5	19	14	22	.389	.514
Bats Both	R	.240	192	46	11	0	10	33	37	45	.363	.453
Hicks,John	L	.230	61	14	4	0	3	8	5	23	.288	.443
Bats Right	R	.286	112	32	8	0	3	14	8	28	.347	.438
Hill,Aaron	L	.154	26	4	0	0	1	3	6	4	.303	.269
Bats Right	R	.119	42	5	2	1	0	4	5	9	.213	.214
Holaday,Bryan	L	.200	5	1	0	0	0	0	0	1	.200	.200
Bats Right	R	.250	24	6	2	0	0	2	0	0	.250	.333
Holliday,Matt	L	.267	86	23	3	0	5	16	14	28	.366	.477
Bats Right	R	.220	287	63	15	0	14	48	32	86	.301	.418
Holt,Brock	L	.280	25	7	0	0	0	1	4	4	.400	.280
Bats Left	R	.183	115	21	6	0	0	6	15	30	.284	.235
Hoskins,Rhys	L	.171	41	7	0	0	6	16	15	11	.397	.610
Bats Right	R	.287	129	37	7	0	12	32	22	35	.396	.620
Hosmer,Eric	L	.284	194	55	9	1	6	27	13	27	.327	.433
Bats Left	R	.335	409	137	22	0	19	67	53	77	.410	.528
Hoying,Jared	L	.308	13	4	1	0	0	0	1	4	.357	.385
Bats Left	R	.203	59	12	2	0	1	7	3	19	.238	.288
Hundley,Nick	L	.305	95	29	12	0	4	11	6	25	.347	.558
Bats Right	R	.214	192	41	11	0	5	24	6	56	.235	.349
Hwang,Jae-Gyun	L	.250	20	5	0	0	1	4	1	3	.286	.400
Bats Right	R	.094	32	3	1	0	0	1	4	12	.194	.125
Iannetta,Chris	L	.300	80	24	3	0	6	10	13	21	.404	.563
Bats Right	R	.234	192	45	16	0	11	33	24	66	.333	.490
Iglesias,Jose	L	.263	95	25	6	0	1	6	4	8	.293	.358
Bats Right	R	.253	368	93	27	1	5	48	17	57	.287	.372
Inciarte,Ender	L	.291	151	44	3	1	2	14	14	19	.347	.364
Bats Left	R	.307	511	157	24	4	9	43	35	75	.350	.423
Jackson,Austin	L	.352	122	43	11	2	4	15	19	25	.440	.574
Bats Right	R	.291	158	46	8	1	3	20	14	39	.345	.411
Janish,Paul	L	-	0	0	0	0	0	0	0	0	-	-
Bats Right	R	.077	26	2	0	0	0	3	1	6	.111	.077
Jankowski,Travis	L	.125	16	2	0	0	0	0	1	7	.222	.125
Bats Left	R	.203	59	12	2	0	0	1	8	21	.299	.237
Jaso,John	L	.200	30	6	1	0	1	4	4	7	.294	.333
Bats Left	R	.212	226	48	18	0	9	31	36	59	.332	.412
Jay,Jon	L	.318	85	27	2	0	0	8	12	17	.410	.341
Bats Left	R	.289	294	85	16	3	2	26	25	63	.364	.384
Jones,Adam	L	.260	146	38	8	0	5	12	11	30	.321	.418
Bats Right	R	.293	451	132	20	1	21	61	16	83	.322	.481
Jones,JaCoby	L	.158	38	6	1	0	2	6	2	20	.220	.342
Bats Right	R	.175	103	18	2	1	1	7	7	45	.248	.243
Jones,Ryder	L	.161	31	5	0	0	0	0	2	14	.235	.161
Bats Left	R	.176	119	21	5	2	2	5	8	38	.246	.303
Joseph,Caleb	L	.258	62	16	5	0	3	9	3	19	.303	.484
Bats Right	R	.255	192	49	9	1	5	19	7	53	.281	.391
Joseph,Tommy	L	.211	133	28	6	0	7	18	13	37	.279	.414
Bats Right	R	.251	362	91	21	1	15	51	20	92	.293	.439
Joyce,Matt	L	.186	70	13	3	0	1	7	7	18	.266	.271
Bats Left	R	.253	399	101	30	0	24	61	59	95	.346	.509
Judge,Aaron	L	.230	113	26	4	1	8	16	40	48	.439	.496
Bats Right	R	.298	429	128	20	2	44	98	87	160	.417	.662
Kelly,Carson	L	.100	10	1	0	0	0	0	1	3	.182	.100
Bats Right	R	.186	59	11	3	0	0	6	4	8	.250	.237
Kelly,Ty	L	.179	28	5	2	0	0	4	2	10	.242	.250
Bats Both	R	.197	61	12	5	0	2	10	6	15	.265	.377
Kemp,Matt	L	.250	96	24	1	0	3	10	12	16	.330	.354
Bats Right	R	.284	342	97	22	1	16	54	15	83	.314	.494
Kemp,Tony	L	.222	9	2	0	0	0	1	1	1	.300	.222
Bats Left	R	.214	28	6	1	0	0	3	0	4	.241	.250
Kendrick,Howie	L	.322	90	29	5	0	4	11	10	18	.390	.511
Bats Right	R	.312	215	67	11	3	5	30	12	50	.359	.460
Kepler,Max	L	.152	125	19	3	1	2	12	7	40	.213	.240
Bats Left	R	.272	386	105	29	1	17	57	40	74	.343	.484
Kiermaier,Kevin	L	.255	141	36	3	0	4	20	9	41	.321	.362
Bats Left	R	.289	239	69	12	3	11	19	22	58	.349	.502
Kim,Hyun Soo	L	.133	15	2	0	0	0	1	1	7	.188	.133
Bats Left	R	.239	197	47	8	1	1	13	21	39	.315	.305
Kinsler,Ian	L	.278	115	32	6	3	6	15	13	14	.357	.539
Bats Right	R	.225	436	98	19	0	16	37	42	72	.302	.378
Kipnis,Jason	L	.207	116	24	8	0	3	14	11	24	.278	.353
Bats Left	R	.245	220	54	17	0	9	21	17	47	.298	.445
Kivlehan,Patrick	L	.239	71	17	0	0	5	8	9	23	.333	.451
Bats Right	R	.187	107	20	5	1	4	18	13	38	.285	.364
Knapp,Andrew	L	.216	37	8	3	0	0	1	6	12	.326	.297
Bats Both	R	.269	134	36	5	1	3	12	25	44	.379	.388
Kozma,Pete	L	.190	21	4	0	0	1	1	2	6	.261	.333
Bats Right	R	.042	24	1	0	0	0	1	1	14	.148	.042
La Stella,Tommy	L	.385	13	5	0	0	1	2	0	1	.385	.615
Bats Left	R	.277	112	31	8	0	4	20	20	17	.390	.455
Lagares,Juan	L	.218	78	17	6	0	1	6	5	19	.271	.333
Bats Right	R	.264	174	46	10	2	2	9	9	37	.308	.379
Lamb,Jake	L	.144	132	19	4	0	5	19	20	54	.269	.288
Bats Left	R	.282	404	114	26	4	25	86	67	98	.386	.552
LeMahieu,DJ	L	.362	152	55	8	2	5	24	17	15	.421	.539
Bats Right	R	.293	457	134	20	2	3	40	42	75	.358	.365
Leon,Sandy	L	.247	73	18	6	0	2	16	8	15	.321	.411
Bats Both	R	.217	198	43	8	0	5	23	17	59	.279	.333
Lin,Tzu-Wei	L	.333	6	2	0	1	0	0	0	1	.333	.667
Bats Left	R	.260	50	13	0	1	0	2	9	16	.373	.300
Lind,Adam	L	.310	29	9	1	0	0	7	2	6	.344	.345
Bats Left	R	.303	238	72	13	0	14	52	26	41	.364	.534
Lindor,Francisco	L	.305	223	68	17	0	11	22	20	32	.362	.529
Bats Both	R	.257	428	110	27	4	22	67	40	61	.324	.493
Liriano,Rymer	L	.167	6	1	0	0	0	1	1	1	.286	.167
Bats Right	R	.229	35	8	2	0	1	5	4	13	.308	.371
Lobaton,Jose	L	.184	38	7	1	0	0	1	1	6	.205	.211
Bats Both	R	.165	103	17	2	0	4	10	13	29	.263	.301
Longoria,Evan	L	.217	166	36	5	0	7	25	22	39	.304	.373
Bats Right	R	.277	447	124	31	2	13	61	24	70	.317	.443
Lopez,Raffy	L	.091	11	1	0	0	0	2	1	6	.167	.091
Bats Left	R	.256	43	11	1	0	4	10	6	15	.340	.558
Lowrie,Jed	L	.258	132	34	11	1	2	13	19	28	.349	.402
Bats Both	R	.283	435	123	38	2	12	56	54	72	.363	.462
Lucroy,Jonathan	L	.243	107	26	6	0	1	12	12	11	.317	.327
Bats Right	R	.272	316	86	15	3	5	28	34	40	.355	.386
Luplow,Jordan	L	.154	26	4	1	0	2	7	1	8	.241	.423
Bats Right	R	.231	52	12	2	1	1	4	5	14	.293	.365
Machado,Dixon	L	.191	47	9	0	0	0	3	4	8	.245	.191
Bats Right	R	.286	119	34	5	1	1	8	6	24	.325	.370
Machado,Manny	L	.269	156	42	14	0	8	22	11	27	.314	.513
Bats Right	R	.255	474	121	19	1	25	73	39	88	.309	.458
Mahtook,Mikie	L	.263	118	31	7	2	5	16	6	24	.310	.483
Bats Right	R	.283	230	65	8	4	7	22	17	55	.340	.443
Maile,Luke	L	.195	41	8	2	0	0	3	1	12	.233	.244
Bats Right	R	.124	89	11	3	0	2	4	2	23	.151	.225
Maldonado,Martin	L	.228	114	26	5	0	2	11	8	35	.307	.325
Bats Right	R	.219	315	69	14	1	12	27	7	84	.265	.384
Mancini,Trey	L	.293	157	46	5	0	5	17	6	40	.321	.420
Bats Right	R	.293	386	113	21	4	19	61	27	99	.344	.516

Batters vs. Left-Handed and Right-Handed Pitchers

Batter	vs	Avg	AB	H	2B	3B	HR	RBI	BB	SO	OBP	Slg
Margot,Manuel	L	.285	123	35	9	3	3	13	13	24	.353	.480
Bats Right	R	.255	364	93	9	4	10	26	22	82	.298	.385
Marisnick,Jake	L	.266	94	25	7	0	4	8	11	31	.349	.468
Bats Right	R	.228	136	31	3	0	12	27	9	59	.298	.515
Markakis,Nick	L	.265	147	39	10	0	3	24	12	26	.327	.395
Bats Left	R	.278	446	124	29	1	5	52	56	84	.362	.381
Marrero,Chris	L	.167	18	3	0	0	1	4	1	6	.200	.333
Bats Right	R	.100	20	2	0	0	0	1	1	3	.143	.100
Marrero,Deven	L	.291	55	16	5	0	4	13	5	14	.344	.600
Bats Right	R	.172	116	20	4	0	0	14	7	47	.218	.207
Marte,Jefry	L	.185	65	12	2	0	3	7	9	12	.280	.354
Bats Right	R	.161	62	10	3	0	1	7	4	22	.257	.258
Marte,Ketel	L	.242	66	16	3	0	2	5	10	10	.342	.379
Bats Both	R	.268	157	42	8	2	3	13	19	27	.346	.401
Marte,Starling	L	.162	74	12	2	0	0	4		16	.215	.189
Bats Right	R	.311	235	73	5	2	7	29	16	47	.369	.438
Martin,Leonys	L	.238	21	5	1	1	1	4	2	2	.333	.524
Bats Left	R	.159	107	17	2	0	2	5	6	31	.211	.234
Martin,Russell	L	.154	65	10	2	0	2	7	12	22	.304	.277
Bats Right	R	.240	242	58	10	0	11	28	38	61	.354	.417
Martinez,J.D.	L	.376	93	35	10	1	12	29	16	26	.464	.892
Bats Right	R	.283	339	96	16	2	33	75	37	102	.351	.634
Martinez,Jose	L	.407	59	24	5	0	7	15	10	12	.493	.847
Bats Right	R	.282	213	60	8	1	7	31	22	48	.346	.427
Martinez,Michael	L	.125	8	1	0	0	0	0	1	3	.222	.125
Bats Both	R	.172	29	5	1	0	0	0	4	12	.273	.207
Martinez,Victor	L	.255	94	24	3	0	1	14	7	14	.307	.319
Bats Both	R	.255	298	76	13	0	9	33	29	49	.329	.389
Mathis,Jeff	L	.213	47	10	2	1	1	2	7	16	.315	.362
Bats Right	R	.216	139	30	8	1	1	9	7	45	.264	.309
Mauer,Joe	L	.308	130	40	9	0	0	19	12	22	.377	.377
Bats Left	R	.304	395	120	27	1	7	52	54	61	.386	.430
Maxwell,Bruce	L	.188	32	6	0	0	0	0	5	8	.297	.188
Bats Left	R	.246	187	46	12	0	3	22	26	55	.335	.380
May,Jacob	L	.100	10	1	0	0	0	2	1	3	.182	.100
Bats Both	R	.038	26	1	0	0	0	1	2	14	.138	.038
Maybin,Cameron	L	.259	116	30	5	0	1	8	9	25	.312	.328
Bats Right	R	.215	279	60	15	2	9	27	42	69	.321	.380
Mazara,Nomar	L	.228	123	28	6	1	1	13	7	30	.286	.317
Bats Left	R	.260	431	112	24	1	19	88	48	97	.333	.452
McCann,Brian	L	.227	97	22	3	0	5	15	11	13	.324	.412
Bats Left	R	.246	252	62	9	1	13	47	27	45	.323	.444
McCann,James	L	.298	104	31	6	0	7	13	10	16	.371	.558
Bats Right	R	.234	248	58	8	2	6	36	16	73	.296	.355
McCutchen,Andrew	L	.336	125	42	8	2	11	22	22	24	.435	.696
Bats Right	R	.263	445	117	22	0	17	66	51	92	.342	.427
Mejia,Alex	L	.200	15	3	0	0	1	2	0	3	.200	.400
Bats Right	R	.065	31	2	0	0	0	1	2	10	.121	.065
Mercer,Jordy	L	.248	121	30	5	1	4	18	12	22	.319	.405
Bats Right	R	.257	381	98	19	4	10	40	39	66	.329	.407
Merrifield,Whit	L	.273	121	33	6	2	5	12	8	20	.321	.479
Bats Right	R	.292	466	136	26	4	14	66	21	68	.325	.455
Mesoraco,Devin	L	.180	50	9	3	1	1	1	7	13	.305	.340
Bats Right	R	.231	91	21	2	0	5	13	11	25	.330	.418
Middlebrooks,Will	L	.417	12	5	1	2	0	3	1	2	.462	.833
Bats Right	R	.115	26	3	1	0	0	0		12	.115	.154
Miller,Brad	L	.220	82	18	3	2	2	11	9	26	.301	.378
Bats Left	R	.195	256	50	10	1	7	29	54	84	.334	.324
Molina,Yadier	L	.266	109	29	9	0	7	20	5	12	.308	.541
Bats Right	R	.276	392	108	18	1	11	62	23	62	.313	.411
Moncada,Yoan	L	.224	67	15	2	0	2	5	6	23	.297	.343
Bats Both	R	.235	132	31	6	2	6	17	23	51	.357	.447
Moncrief,Carlos	L	.000	3	0	0	0	0	0	1	2	.250	.000
Bats Left	R	.229	35	8	1	0	0	5	2	13	.256	.257
Mondesi,Raul	L	.231	13	3	0	0	0	1	0	7	.231	.231
Bats Both	R	.150	40	6	1	0	1	2	3	15	.209	.250
Montero,Miguel	L	.222	27	6	1	0	0	2	4	4	.323	.259
Bats Left	R	.215	158	34	5	0	6	14	19	43	.308	.361
Moore,Tyler	L	.192	73	14	3	0	1	5	3	24	.221	.274
Bats Right	R	.254	114	29	11	0	5	25	7	32	.296	.482
Morales,Kendrys	L	.362	127	46	6	0	8	30	9	29	.401	.598
Bats Both	R	.216	430	93	19	0	20	55	34	103	.280	.400
Moreland,Mitch	L	.247	73	18	4	0	1	14	10	21	.344	.342
Bats Left	R	.246	435	107	30	0	21	65	47	99	.324	.460
Moroff,Max	L	.219	32	7	3	0	0	10	6	10	.350	.313
Bats Both	R	.193	88	17	1	1	3	11	10	33	.283	.330
Morrison,Logan	L	.233	129	30	6	0	6	16	20	36	.342	.419
Bats Left	R	.251	383	96	16	1	32	69	61	113	.356	.548
Morse,Michael	L	.182	11	2	1	0	0	1	1	6	.250	.273
Bats Right	R	.200	25	5	0	0	1	2	2	8	.250	.320
Moss,Brandon	L	.271	70	19	4	0	3	8	9	28	.354	.457
Bats Left	R	.192	292	56	10	0	19	42	28	100	.261	.421
Motter,Taylor	L	.153	72	11	3	0	0	3	6	15	.215	.194
Bats Right	R	.215	186	40	9	0	7	23	15	47	.274	.376
Moustakas,Mike	L	.270	152	41	3	0	9	20	6	24	.296	.467
Bats Left	R	.273	403	110	21	0	29	65	28	70	.321	.541
Murphy,Daniel	L	.291	127	37	12	0	4	19	8	28	.343	.480
Bats Left	R	.332	407	135	31	3	19	74	44	49	.397	.563
Murphy,Tom	L	.059	17	1	1	0	0	1	2	8	.158	.118
Bats Right	R	.000	7	0	0	0	0	0	0	1	.000	.000
Myers,Wil	L	.234	145	34	9	0	7	12	26	49	.349	.441
Bats Right	R	.246	422	104	20	3	23	62	44	131	.321	.472
Napoli,Mike	L	.196	107	21	3	1	8	17	13	44	.283	.467
Bats Right	R	.192	318	61	8	0	21	49	36	119	.286	.415
Naquin,Tyler	L	.250	4	1	0	0	0	0	0	0	.250	.250
Bats Left	R	.212	33	7	2	0	0	1	2	9	.250	.273
Narvaez,Omar	L	.233	43	10	3	0	0	0	8	13	.365	.302
Bats Left	R	.286	210	60	7	0	2	14	30	32	.375	.348
Nava,Daniel	L	.188	48	9	1	0	1	7	9	15	.310	.271
Bats Both	R	.341	135	46	7	1	3	14	17	23	.423	.474
Navarro,Efren	L	.444	9	4	0	1	1	1	1	2	.500	1.000
Bats Left	R	.192	52	10	1	0	1	1	7	19	.288	.269
Negron,Kristopher	L	.083	12	1	0	0	0	0	3	4	.313	.083
Bats Right	R	.231	13	3	1	0	0	1	1	3	.286	.308
Ngoepe,Gift	L	.091	11	1	0	0	0	0	3	8	.286	.091
Bats Right	R	.256	43	11	2	1	0	6	5	18	.333	.349
Nicholas,Brett	L	.091	11	1	1	0	0	1	1	3	.167	.182
Bats Left	R	.269	52	14	3	0	2	10	1	10	.283	.442
Nieuwenhuis,Kirk	L	-	0	0	0	0	0	0	1	0	1.000	
Bats Left	R	.115	26	3	1	0	1	1	3	15	.233	.269
Nimmo,Brandon	L	.190	42	8	2	0	0	3	10	19	.292	.238
Bats Left	R	.281	135	38	9	1	5	20	27	41	.404	.474
Norris,Derek	L	.190	42	8	0	0	4	9	4	8	.265	.476
Bats Right	R	.204	137	28	5	0	5	15	8	40	.255	.350
Nunez,Eduardo	L	.290	131	38	15	0	1	12	7	14	.324	.427
Bats Right	R	.321	336	108	18	0	11	46	11	40	.348	.473
Odor,Rougned	L	.145	159	23	2	0	5	18	5	42	.200	.252
Bats Left	R	.225	448	101	19	3	25	57	27	120	.270	.449
Olson,Matt	L	.196	46	9	0	0	4	6	5	14	.302	.457
Bats Left	R	.280	143	40	2	0	20	39	17	46	.368	.713
Orlando,Paulo	L	.267	15	4	1	0	0	1	0	3	.313	.333
Bats Right	R	.183	71	13	2	0	2	5	1	17	.205	.296
Osuna,Jose	L	.253	99	25	10	3	1	11	6	14	.295	.444
Bats Right	R	.216	116	25	3	1	6	19	3	26	.246	.414
Owings,Chris	L	.253	87	22	5	1	2	12	4	20	.283	.402
Bats Right	R	.273	275	75	20	0	10	39	13	67	.305	.455
Ozuna,Marcell	L	.305	128	39	4	1	3	15	16	27	.382	.422
Bats Right	R	.313	485	152	26	1	34	109	48	117	.374	.581
Panik,Joe	L	.290	155	45	6	0	1	13	13	21	.349	.348
Bats Left	R	.287	356	102	22	5	9	40	33	33	.347	.452
Parker,Jarrett	L	.250	28	7	1	0	1	4	3	10	.276	.393
Bats Left	R	.246	138	34	11	2	3	19	10	44	.297	.420
Parra,Gerardo	L	.347	98	34	5	0	1	11	4	19	.377	.429
Bats Left	R	.296	294	87	19	1	9	60	16	48	.329	.459
Pearce,Steve	L	.207	87	18	5	0	5	8	7	23	.293	.437
Bats Right	R	.270	226	61	12	1	8	29	20	45	.329	.438
Pederson,Joc	L	.204	49	10	2	0	1	4	6	14	.291	.306
Bats Left	R	.214	224	48	18	0	10	31	33	54	.340	.429
Pedroia,Dustin	L	.344	61	21	5	0	1	13	13	8	.453	.475
Bats Right	R	.284	345	98	14	0	6	49	36	40	.352	.377
Pence,Hunter	L	.286	140	40	5	1	4	20	16	19	.354	.421
Bats Right	R	.249	353	88	8	4	9	47	24	83	.299	.371
Pennington,Cliff	L	.246	61	15	1	0	0	3	1	16	.250	.262
Bats Both	R	.256	133	34	5	0	3	18	15	42	.329	.361
Peralta,David	L	.269	134	36	4	2	2	13	10	22	.338	.373
Bats Left	R	.302	391	118	27	1	12	44	33	72	.357	.468
Peralta,Jhonny	L	.125	24	3	0	0	0		1	8	.160	.125
Bats Right	R	.267	30	8	0	0	0	3		5	.333	.267
Peraza,Jose	L	.282	131	37	2	1	1	10	7	18	.319	.336
Bats Right	R	.250	356	89	7	3	4	27	13	52	.289	.320
Perez,Carlos	L	.000	2	0	0	0	0	0	0	0	.000	.000
Bats Right	R	.111	18	2	0	0	1	3	1	6	.158	.278

Batters vs. Left-Handed and Right-Handed Pitchers

Batter	vs	Avg	AB	H	2B	3B	HR	RBI	BB	SO	OBP	Slg
Perez,Hernan	L	.316	114	36	7	1	2	17	5	20	.342	.447
Bats Right	R	.239	318	76	12	2	12	34	15	59	.271	.403
Perez,Roberto	L	.229	70	16	3	0	5	20	10	22	.321	.486
Bats Right	R	.197	147	29	9	0	3	18	16	49	.276	.320
Perez,Salvador	L	.257	136	35	3	0	10	27	6	28	.288	.500
Bats Right	R	.272	335	91	21	1	17	53	11	67	.301	.493
Perkins,Cam	L	.238	42	10	2	0	1	6	3	8	.292	.357
Bats Right	R	.130	46	6	3	0	0	2	2	15	.184	.196
Peterson,Jace	L	.176	17	3	0	0	1	1	0	6	.176	.353
Bats Left	R	.219	169	37	9	2	1	16	27	42	.330	.314
Peterson,Shane	L	.167	6	1	0	0	0	1	1	2	.286	.167
Bats Left	R	.260	73	19	5	0	2	10	4	19	.313	.411
Pham,Tommy	L	.292	96	28	2	1	7	16	20	24	.412	.552
Bats Right	R	.310	348	108	20	1	16	57	51	93	.411	.511
Phegley,Josh	L	.215	65	14	3	0	2	7	3	11	.246	.354
Bats Right	R	.190	84	16	8	0	1	3	6	15	.261	.321
Phillips,Brandon	L	.297	118	35	3	0	2	11	6	15	.339	.373
Bats Right	R	.282	454	128	31	1	11	49	15	58	.314	.427
Phillips,Brett	L	.111	9	1	0	0	0	0	1	5	.200	.111
Bats Left	R	.295	78	23	3	0	4	12	8	29	.368	.487
Pillar,Kevin	L	.336	143	48	20	0	4	10	10	22	.381	.559
Bats Right	R	.230	444	102	17	1	12	32	23	73	.274	.354
Pina,Manny	L	.287	94	27	8	0	0	14	4	24	.333	.372
Bats Right	R	.275	236	65	13	0	9	29	16	55	.324	.445
Pinder,Chad	L	.247	85	21	5	0	3	7	10	26	.327	.412
Bats Right	R	.234	197	46	10	1	12	35	8	66	.276	.477
Pirela,Jose	L	.305	82	25	9	0	4	8	8	23	.367	.561
Bats Right	R	.283	230	65	16	4	6	32	19	48	.340	.465
Piscotty,Stephen	L	.234	64	15	4	0	1	5	13	16	.380	.344
Bats Right	R	.235	277	65	12	1	8	34	39	71	.332	.372
Plawecki,Kevin	L	.231	26	6	0	0	0	0	6	6	.412	.231
Bats Right	R	.270	74	20	5	0	3	13	8	11	.345	.459
Plouffe,Trevor	L	.257	105	27	2	0	2	5	11	26	.328	.333
Bats Right	R	.163	178	29	5	0	7	14	17	62	.239	.309
Polanco,Gregory	L	.231	91	21	7	0	0	7	5	22	.278	.308
Bats Left	R	.257	288	74	13	0	11	28	22	38	.313	.417
Polanco,Jorge	L	.248	165	41	11	0	4	29	6	26	.277	.388
Bats Both	R	.260	323	84	19	3	9	45	35	52	.330	.421
Pollock,A.J.	L	.277	141	39	10	2	7	20	9	13	.329	.525
Bats Right	R	.261	284	74	23	4	7	29	26	58	.331	.444
Posey,Buster	L	.360	139	50	8	0	7	21	23	19	.451	.568
Bats Right	R	.304	355	108	26	0	5	46	38	47	.379	.420
Powell,Boog	L	.222	9	2	1	0	0	2	4	1	.462	.333
Bats Left	R	.287	108	31	4	0	3	10	11	29	.347	.407
Prado,Martin	L	.290	31	9	2	0	0	3	1	6	.303	.355
Bats Right	R	.239	109	26	7	0	2	9	5	16	.272	.358
Presley,Alex	L	.267	30	8	0	0	0	2	2	8	.313	.267
Bats Left	R	.321	215	69	10	3	3	18	13	41	.360	.437
Profar,Jurickson	L	.200	5	1	1	0	0	2	1	2	.333	.400
Bats Both	R	.170	53	9	1	0	0	3	8	12	.290	.189
Puello,Cesar	L	.150	20	3	0	0	0	0	1	10	.190	.150
Bats Right	R	.286	14	4	0	0	0	3	3	2	.444	.286
Puig,Yasiel	L	.183	120	22	5	0	2	10	24	18	.317	.275
Bats Right	R	.288	379	109	19	2	26	64	40	82	.355	.554
Pujols,Albert	L	.230	139	32	6	0	2	18	12	24	.291	.317
Bats Right	R	.244	454	111	11	0	21	83	25	69	.285	.407
Raburn,Ryan	L	.185	27	5	0	0	0	0	1	8	.214	.185
Bats Right	R	.316	38	12	1	2	2	6	3	17	.366	.605
Ramirez,Hanley	L	.179	106	19	4	0	6	12	17	28	.293	.387
Bats Right	R	.259	390	101	20	0	17	50	34	88	.328	.441
Ramirez,Jose	L	.329	213	70	22	1	10	31	15	25	.371	.582
Bats Both	R	.312	372	116	34	5	19	52	37	44	.375	.583
Ramos,Wilson	L	.310	58	18	3	0	2	13	4	8	.344	.466
Bats Right	R	.240	150	36	3	0	9	22	6	28	.268	.440
Rasmus,Colby	L	.182	11	2	1	0	1	2	0	7	.167	.545
Bats Left	R	.291	110	32	6	1	8	21	7	38	.333	.582
Realmuto,J.T.	L	.283	113	32	6	2	4	14	12	22	.359	.478
Bats Right	R	.277	419	116	25	3	13	51	24	84	.324	.444
Reddick,Josh	L	.315	92	29	3	1	1	19	7	19	.360	.402
Bats Left	R	.314	385	121	31	3	12	63	36	53	.363	.504
Refsnyder,Rob	L	.071	28	2	0	0	0	0	6	5	.257	.071
Bats Right	R	.217	60	13	2	1	0	0	2	12	.242	.283
Rendon,Anthony	L	.337	104	35	9	0	9	25	21	13	.448	.683
Bats Right	R	.292	404	118	32	1	16	75	63	69	.392	.495
Renfroe,Hunter	L	.316	114	36	9	0	11	26	13	23	.392	.684
Bats Right	R	.202	331	67	16	1	15	32	14	117	.244	.393
Revere,Ben	L	.163	49	8	0	0	0	4	1	8	.176	.163
Bats Left	R	.298	242	72	13	2	1	16	14	17	.335	.380
Reyes,Jose	L	.267	120	32	6	2	6	19	12	22	.343	.500
Bats Both	R	.239	381	91	19	5	9	39	38	57	.306	.386
Reynolds,Mark	L	.231	143	33	5	0	7	23	26	53	.347	.413
Bats Right	R	.281	377	106	17	1	23	74	43	122	.355	.515
Reynolds,Matt	L	.233	30	7	1	1	0	3	2	12	.281	.333
Bats Right	R	.229	83	19	0	1	1	2	12	25	.340	.289
Rickard,Joey	L	.279	122	34	9	0	1	4	6	23	.310	.377
Bats Right	R	.209	139	29	6	0	3	15	3	40	.247	.317
Riddle,J.T.	L	.262	61	16	3	0	0	11	1	14	.270	.311
Bats Left	R	.246	167	41	10	1	3	20	11	36	.286	.371
Rivera,Rene	L	.232	56	13	2	0	4	6	3	22	.271	.482
Bats Right	R	.259	162	42	7	0	6	29	11	48	.316	.414
Rivera,T.J.	L	.260	50	13	1	0	2	6	3	13	.296	.400
Bats Right	R	.299	164	49	12	1	3	21	6	19	.341	.439
Rizzo,Anthony	L	.260	150	39	3	2	10	35	18	25	.374	.507
Bats Left	R	.277	422	117	29	1	22	74	73	65	.398	.507
Robertson,Daniel	L	.286	49	14	3	1	0	4	4	1	.340	.388
Bats Right	R	.129	31	4	1	0	1	3	3	2	.206	.258
Robertson,Daniel	L	.185	65	12	2	1	2	7	11	24	.308	.338
Bats Right	R	.216	153	33	5	1	3	12	18	49	.309	.320
Robinson,Drew	L	.333	18	6	1	0	1	3	2	6	.400	.556
Bats Left	R	.202	89	18	4	0	5	10	12	36	.297	.416
Robinson,Shane	L	.238	21	5	0	0	0	0	3	4	.333	.238
Bats Right	R	.100	10	1	0	0	0	1	0	1	.091	.100
Robles,Victor	L	.000	2	0	0	0	0	0	0	0	.000	.000
Bats Right	R	.273	22	6	1	2	0	4	0	6	.333	.500
Rodriguez,Sean	L	.226	53	12	1	0	3	3	10	25	.359	.415
Bats Right	R	.127	79	10	1	0	2	5	6	32	.216	.215
Rojas,Miguel	L	.257	74	19	7	1	0	9	8	8	.333	.378
Bats Right	R	.303	198	60	9	1	1	17	19	24	.371	.374
Romine,Andrew	L	.262	65	17	4	0	1	1	4	17	.304	.369
Bats Both	R	.225	253	57	13	2	3	24	18	50	.285	.328
Romine,Austin	L	.143	56	8	3	1	1	4	5	14	.213	.286
Bats Right	R	.243	173	42	6	0	1	17	11	43	.291	.295
Rosales,Adam	L	.239	113	27	9	0	3	15	7	39	.290	.398
Bats Right	R	.216	176	38	7	0	4	21	4	61	.239	.324
Rosario,Amed	L	.297	37	11	0	1	2	4	1	9	.316	.514
Bats Right	R	.234	128	30	4	3	2	6	2	40	.258	.359
Rosario,Eddie	L	.279	172	48	11	1	2	15	5	35	.293	.390
Bats Left	R	.295	370	109	22	1	25	63	30	71	.344	.562
Rua,Ryan	L	.262	61	16	4	0	1	4	5	22	.318	.377
Bats Right	R	.176	68	12	2	0	2	8	9	30	.273	.294
Ruggiano,Justin	L	.238	21	5	0	0	0	0	1	6	.273	.238
Bats Right	R	.205	39	8	1	0	2	4	0	11	.220	.385
Ruiz,Carlos	L	.172	29	5	2	0	1	2	6	8	.351	.345
Bats Right	R	.229	96	22	6	0	2	9	8	30	.299	.354
Ruiz,Rio	L	.417	12	5	1	0	2	5	1	4	.429	1.000
Bats Left	R	.174	138	24	4	0	2	14	18	37	.270	.246
Rupp,Cameron	L	.267	90	24	7	0	3	7	19	32	.394	.444
Bats Right	R	.195	205	40	10	0	11	27	15	82	.252	.405
Russell,Addison	L	.264	87	23	5	1	3	6	13	25	.373	.448
Bats Right	R	.230	265	61	16	2	9	37	16	66	.279	.408
Rutledge,Josh	L	.222	27	6	2	1	0	3	1	8	.250	.370
Bats Right	R	.225	80	18	0	0	0	6	8	23	.311	.225
Saladino,Tyler	L	.214	84	18	4	0	0	4	9	17	.305	.262
Bats Right	R	.160	169	27	5	2	0	6	14	50	.228	.213
Saltalamacchia,Jarrod	L	.000	10	0	0	0	0	0	0	8	.000	.000
Bats Both	R	.067	15	1	0	0	0	0	1	8	.125	.067
Sanchez,Adrian	L	.294	17	5	1	0	0	2	0	3	.333	.353
Bats Right	R	.259	54	14	6	0	0	9	1	22	.273	.370
Sanchez,Gary	L	.266	109	29	5	0	8	23	14	28	.350	.532
Bats Right	R	.282	362	102	15	0	25	67	26	92	.343	.530
Sanchez,Hector	L	.212	33	7	1	0	2	4	1	11	.235	.424
Bats Both	R	.221	104	23	3	0	6	21	4	30	.248	.423
Sanchez,Yolmer	L	.248	117	29	6	3	1	17	7	31	.283	.376
Bats Both	R	.272	367	100	13	5	11	42	28	80	.330	.425
Sandoval,Pablo	L	.150	60	9	1	0	1	4	2	10	.175	.217
Bats Both	R	.241	199	48	10	0	8	28	14	43	.292	.412
Sano,Miguel	L	.297	101	30	8	1	7	19	15	36	.388	.604
Bats Right	R	.254	323	82	7	1	21	58	39	137	.341	.477
Santana,Carlos	L	.255	220	56	10	0	9	29	33	22	.354	.423
Bats Both	R	.262	351	92	27	3	14	50	55	72	.368	.476
Santana,Danny	L	.103	39	4	2	0	1	2	3	13	.186	.231
Bats Both	R	.233	129	30	8	2	3	21	5	28	.261	.395

Batters vs. Left-Handed and Right-Handed Pitchers

Batter	vs	Avg	AB	H	2B	3B	HR	RBI	BB	SO	OBP	Slg
Santana,Domingo	L	.286	133	38	11	0	6	23	23	40	.389	.504
Bats Right	R	.276	392	108	18	0	24	62	50	138	.364	.505
Santander,Anthony	L	.125	8	1	1	0	0	0	0	3	.125	.250
Bats Both	R	.318	22	7	2	0	0	2	0	5	.304	.409
Sardinas,Luis	L	.238	21	5	0	0	0	1	2	3	.304	.238
Bats Both	R	.107	28	3	0	0	0	0	2	8	.167	.107
Saunders,Michael	L	.193	57	11	1	2	2	8	3	15	.233	.386
Bats Left	R	.205	161	33	8	0	4	13	12	40	.264	.329
Schebler,Scott	L	.276	134	37	11	0	6	18	1	30	.290	.493
Bats Left	R	.215	339	73	14	2	24	49	38	95	.313	.481
Schimpf,Ryan	L	.163	43	7	0	0	4	7	6	17	.275	.442
Bats Left	R	.156	122	19	2	0	10	18	21	53	.288	.418
Schoop,Jonathan	L	.300	150	45	14	0	10	33	14	40	.361	.593
Bats Right	R	.290	472	137	21	0	22	72	21	102	.330	.475
Schwarber,Kyle	L	.171	82	14	3	1	3	8	16	34	.306	.341
Bats Left	R	.221	340	75	13	0	27	51	43	116	.317	.497
Seager,Corey	L	.325	169	55	10	0	8	29	16	43	.389	.527
Bats Left	R	.281	370	104	23	0	14	48	51	88	.369	.457
Seager,Kyle	L	.248	165	41	10	0	8	28	13	34	.311	.455
Bats Left	R	.249	413	103	23	1	19	60	45	76	.328	.448
Segedin,Rob	L	.200	15	3	2	0	0	0	0	5	.200	.333
Bats Right	R	.200	5	1	0	0	0	1	0	2	.200	.200
Segura,Jean	L	.317	123	39	5	0	3	11	14	19	.388	.431
Bats Right	R	.294	401	118	25	2	8	34	20	64	.336	.426
Semien,Marcus	L	.224	98	22	5	0	3	11	11	25	.303	.367
Bats Right	R	.258	244	63	14	1	7	29	27	60	.333	.410
Severino,Pedro	L	.286	7	2	0	0	0	0	0	2	.286	.286
Bats Right	R	.136	22	3	1	0	0	3	2	8	.208	.182
Shaw,Travis	L	.250	140	35	13	1	5	22	11	42	.312	.464
Bats Left	R	.281	398	112	21	0	26	79	49	96	.361	.530
Sierra,Magneuris	L	.462	13	6	0	0	0	2	0	4	.462	.462
Bats Left	R	.277	47	13	0	0	0	3	4	10	.333	.277
Simmons,Andrelton	L	.239	138	33	5	1	3	16	21	19	.335	.355
Bats Right	R	.290	451	131	33	1	11	53	26	48	.329	.441
Slater,Austin	L	.333	36	12	2	1	0	7	2	9	.368	.444
Bats Right	R	.259	81	21	1	0	3	9	6	20	.326	.383
Smith,Dominic	L	.129	31	4	2	0	0	3	5	13	.243	.194
Bats Left	R	.213	136	29	4	0	9	23	9	36	.267	.441
Smith,Kevan	L	.243	111	27	6	0	2	12	2	15	.263	.351
Bats Right	R	.309	165	51	11	0	2	18	7	31	.339	.412
Smith,Mallex	L	.268	41	11	0	1	0	1	1	15	.286	.317
Bats Left	R	.270	215	58	8	3	2	11	22	47	.336	.363
Smith,Seth	L	.250	24	6	3	0	1	4	2	5	.308	.500
Bats Left	R	.258	306	79	16	0	12	28	34	74	.343	.428
Smith Jr.,Dwight	L	.250	8	2	1	0	0	0	1	3	.400	.375
Bats Left	R	.421	19	8	1	0	0	1	0	7	.421	.474
Smoak,Justin	L	.331	124	41	8	0	7	18	18	18	.413	.565
Bats Both	R	.252	436	110	21	1	31	72	55	110	.338	.518
Smolinski,Jake	L	.455	11	5	1	0	0	0	1	1	.538	.545
Bats Right	R	.125	16	2	0	0	0	0	0	5	.125	.125
Sogard,Eric	L	.262	42	11	3	0	1	4	4	11	.340	.405
Bats Left	R	.275	207	57	12	1	2	14	41	26	.402	.372
Solarte,Yangervis	L	.211	128	27	4	0	2	11	10	15	.275	.289
Bats Both	R	.272	338	92	17	0	16	53	27	46	.330	.464
Soler,Jorge	L	.139	36	5	1	0	2	4	5	13	.244	.333
Bats Right	R	.148	61	9	4	0	0	2	7	23	.246	.213
Soto,Geovany	L	.308	13	4	0	0	1	5	1	2	.375	.538
Bats Right	R	.138	29	4	0	0	2	4	3	8	.219	.345
Souza Jr.,Steven	L	.262	141	37	8	1	3	16	27	45	.388	.397
Bats Right	R	.230	382	88	13	1	27	62	57	134	.337	.482
Span,Denard	L	.226	106	24	4	1	0	9	9	17	.293	.283
Bats Left	R	.284	391	111	27	4	12	34	31	52	.339	.465
Spangenberg,Cory	L	.197	122	24	1	0	2	9	5	52	.233	.254
Bats Left	R	.289	322	93	17	2	11	37	29	76	.355	.457
Springer,George	L	.301	133	40	6	0	9	19	24	20	.423	.549
Bats Right	R	.277	415	115	23	0	25	66	40	91	.347	.513
Stanton,Giancarlo	L	.323	127	41	11	0	15	38	28	23	.449	.764
Bats Right	R	.270	470	127	21	0	44	94	57	140	.354	.596
Stassi,Brock	L	.071	14	1	0	0	0	0	1	5	.133	.071
Bats Left	R	.188	64	12	2	1	2	7	11	17	.307	.344
Stassi,Max	L	.167	12	2	1	0	1	2	1	1	.231	.500
Bats Right	R	.167	12	2	0	0	1	2	5	3	.389	.417
Stevenson,Andrew	L	.000	13	0	0	0	0	0	2	7	.133	.000
Bats Left	R	.205	44	9	2	0	0	1	5	13	.286	.250
Stewart,Chris	L	.094	32	3	0	1	0	0	2	4	.147	.156
Bats Right	R	.212	99	21	1	1	0	4	7	18	.271	.242

Batter	vs	Avg	AB	H	2B	3B	HR	RBI	BB	SO	OBP	Slg
Story,Trevor	L	.301	133	40	15	1	10	28	17	50	.380	.654
Bats Right	R	.216	370	80	17	2	14	54	32	141	.281	.386
Stubbs,Drew	L	.091	11	1	0	0	0	0	1	4	.167	.091
Bats Right	R	.091	11	1	0	0	0	0	1	5	.167	.091
Suarez,Eugenio	L	.276	127	35	11	0	6	19	23	37	.392	.504
Bats Right	R	.256	407	104	14	2	20	63	61	110	.359	.447
Sucre,Jesus	L	.231	39	9	0	0	3	9	3	7	.273	.462
Bats Right	R	.263	137	36	6	0	4	20	4	28	.295	.394
Suzuki,Ichiro	L	.340	47	16	3	0	0	5	4	10	.392	.404
Bats Left	R	.228	149	34	3	0	3	15	13	25	.294	.309
Suzuki,Kurt	L	.345	58	20	4	0	7	10	4	6	.415	.776
Bats Right	R	.266	218	58	9	0	12	40	13	33	.333	.472
Swanson,Dansby	L	.263	95	25	6	0	2	12	13	23	.352	.389
Bats Right	R	.224	393	88	17	2	4	39	46	97	.302	.308
Szczur,Matt	L	.200	60	12	2	0	2	5	14	15	.368	.333
Bats Right	R	.237	135	32	10	2	1	13	20	29	.342	.363
Taijeron,Travis	L	.182	22	4	1	0	1	3	3	7	.308	.364
Bats Right	R	.167	30	5	1	0	0	0	2	17	.242	.200
Tapia,Raimel	L	.227	44	10	3	0	1	5	2	13	.277	.364
Bats Left	R	.310	116	36	9	2	1	11	6	23	.350	.448
Tauchman,Mike	L	.400	5	2	0	0	0	1	2	1	.571	.400
Bats Left	R	.182	22	4	0	1	0	1	3	9	.280	.273
Taylor,Chris	L	.297	138	41	12	1	4	9	12	41	.351	.486
Bats Right	R	.285	376	107	22	4	17	63	38	101	.355	.500
Taylor,Michael	L	.308	91	28	4	1	4	13	5	27	.344	.505
Bats Right	R	.260	308	80	19	2	15	40	24	110	.313	.481
Tejada,Ruben	L	.267	30	8	2	0	0	1	1	5	.290	.333
Bats Right	R	.217	83	18	4	0	0	4	7	10	.293	.265
Telis,Tomas	L	.130	23	3	0	1	0	3	1	1	.192	.217
Bats Both	R	.272	81	22	5	2	0	6	2	9	.306	.383
Thames,Eric	L	.182	99	18	3	0	6	11	9	41	.270	.394
Bats Left	R	.265	370	98	23	4	25	52	66	122	.382	.551
Thompson,Trayce	L	.080	25	2	0	1	0	0	3	11	.179	.160
Bats Right	R	.167	24	4	2	0	1	2	3	12	.259	.375
Toles,Andrew	L	.400	5	2	1	0	0	3	0	0	.400	.600
Bats Left	R	.264	91	24	2	0	5	12	5	16	.309	.451
Tomas,Yasmany	L	.185	54	10	3	0	2	5	3	20	.228	.352
Bats Right	R	.268	112	30	8	1	6	27	10	30	.325	.518
Tomlinson,Kelby	L	.270	74	20	1	0	1	5	13	16	.371	.324
Bats Right	R	.250	120	30	3	2	0	6	10	30	.305	.308
Tofrens,Luis	L	.216	37	8	2	1	0	5	2	5	.256	.324
Bats Right	R	.140	86	12	1	0	0	2	10	25	.237	.151
Torres,Ramon	L	.227	22	5	1	0	0	2	1	5	.261	.273
Bats Both	R	.250	52	13	2	0	0	2	3	7	.304	.288
Torreyes,Ronald	L	.338	74	25	3	0	0	4	4	10	.363	.378
Bats Right	R	.278	241	67	12	1	3	32	7	33	.299	.373
Travis,Devon	L	.323	31	10	3	0	2	8	4	7	.400	.613
Bats Right	R	.247	154	38	15	0	3	16	3	31	.267	.403
Travis,Sam	L	.381	42	16	5	0	0	1	5	9	.458	.500
Bats Right	R	.118	34	4	1	0	0	0	1	14	.143	.147
Trout,Mike	L	.280	82	23	2	2	3	11	23	15	.443	.463
Bats Right	R	.313	320	100	23	1	30	61	71	75	.441	.672
Trumbo,Mark	L	.272	147	40	2	0	8	16	9	35	.314	.449
Bats Right	R	.221	412	91	20	0	15	49	33	114	.280	.379
Tulowitzki,Troy	L	.169	65	11	3	0	1	3	4	12	.217	.262
Bats Right	R	.278	176	49	7	0	6	23	13	28	.330	.420
Turner,Justin	L	.380	142	54	13	0	11	30	22	15	.477	.704
Bats Right	R	.295	315	93	19	0	10	41	37	41	.386	.451
Turner,Stuart	L	.125	32	4	0	0	1	2	0	7	.125	.219
Bats Right	R	.140	50	7	3	0	1	5	5	15	.214	.260
Turner,Trea	L	.245	94	23	7	0	0	5	8	17	.311	.319
Bats Right	R	.296	318	94	17	6	11	40	22	63	.346	.491
Upton,Justin	L	.344	125	43	12	0	12	31	16	29	.427	.728
Bats Right	R	.252	432	109	32	0	23	78	58	151	.341	.486
Urena,Richard	L	.250	16	4	0	0	0	1	3	5	.368	.250
Bats Both	R	.192	52	10	4	0	1	3	3	23	.236	.327
Urshela,Giovanny	L	.228	57	13	3	0	0	5	2	10	.254	.281
Bats Right	R	.222	99	22	4	0	1	10	6	12	.267	.293
Utley,Chase	L	.167	24	4	2	0	1	2	2	7	.286	.375
Bats Left	R	.242	285	69	18	4	7	32	30	50	.327	.407
Valaika,Pat	L	.289	76	22	6	0	6	16	5	21	.333	.605
Bats Right	R	.236	106	25	5	0	7	24	2	32	.248	.481
Valbuena,Luis	L	.105	38	4	1	0	1	6	6	10	.213	.211
Bats Left	R	.210	309	65	14	0	21	59	42	96	.305	.460
Valencia,Danny	L	.264	125	33	6	1	5	26	20	31	.356	.448
Bats Right	R	.252	325	82	13	2	10	40	20	91	.296	.397

Batters vs. Left-Handed and Right-Handed Pitchers

Batter	vs	Avg	AB	H	2B	3B	HR	RBI	BB	SO	OBP	Slg
Van Slyke,Scott	L	.138	29	4	1	0	1	2	5	11	.265	.276
Bats Right	R	.083	12	1	0	0	1	1	2	4	.214	.333
Vargas,Kennys	L	.185	65	12	5	0	1	5	10	24	.289	.308
Bats Both	R	.278	176	49	8	0	10	36	10	53	.324	.494
Vazquez,Christian	L	.278	54	15	3	0	2	6	2	8	.304	.444
Bats Right	R	.293	270	79	15	2	3	26	15	56	.336	.396
Verdugo,Alex	L	.200	5	1	0	0	0	0	0	1	.200	.200
Bats Left	R	.167	18	3	0	0	1	1	2	3	.250	.333
Villanueva,Christian	L	.385	13	5	0	0	2	3	0	3	.385	.846
Bats Right	R	.316	19	6	1	0	2	4	0	7	.316	.684
Villar,Jonathan	L	.214	117	25	6	1	2	7	10	40	.273	.333
Bats Both	R	.252	286	72	12	0	9	33	20	92	.301	.388
Vogelbach,Dan	L	.250	4	1	0	0	0	0	0	1	.250	.250
Bats Left	R	.208	24	5	1	0	0	2	3	8	.296	.250
Vogt,Stephen	L	.200	30	6	2	0	0	2	2	2	.242	.267
Bats Left	R	.237	249	59	13	1	12	38	19	54	.290	.442
Voit,Luke	L	.258	31	8	2	0	2	7	0	9	.281	.516
Bats Right	R	.241	83	20	7	0	2	11	7	22	.315	.398
Votto,Joey	L	.292	154	45	10	0	10	28	36	30	.437	.552
Bats Left	R	.331	405	134	24	1	26	72	98	53	.461	.588
Wade,Tyler	L	.091	11	1	0	0	0	0	1	5	.167	.091
Bats Left	R	.170	47	8	4	0	0	2	4	14	.235	.255
Walker,Neil	L	.214	84	18	7	0	0	5	11	19	.313	.298
Bats Both	R	.279	301	84	14	2	14	44	44	58	.376	.478
Weeks Jr.,Rickie	L	.176	51	9	2	0	1	6	11	27	.333	.275
Bats Right	R	.261	46	12	4	0	1	2	1	22	.306	.413
Werth,Jayson	L	.239	46	11	4	0	2	6	9	10	.364	.457
Bats Right	R	.223	206	46	6	1	8	23	26	59	.312	.379
White,Tyler	L	.250	8	2	0	0	2	3	1	0	.333	1.000
Bats Right	R	.283	53	15	6	0	1	7	3	16	.328	.453
Wieters,Matt	L	.244	78	19	2	0	3	13	7	25	.302	.385
Bats Both	R	.221	344	76	18	0	7	39	31	69	.285	.334
Williams,Nick	L	.274	84	23	1	2	2	19	5	27	.333	.405
Bats Left	R	.293	229	67	13	2	10	36	15	70	.340	.498
Williamson,Mac	L	.353	17	6	0	0	1	1	0	6	.353	.529
Bats Right	R	.196	51	10	2	0	2	5	5	19	.268	.353
Winker,Jesse	L	.120	25	3	2	0	0	0	1	4	.154	.200
Bats Left	R	.344	96	33	5	0	7	15	14	20	.427	.615
Wolters,Tony	L	.196	51	10	1	0	0	1	4	17	.281	.216
Bats Left	R	.253	178	45	7	1	0	15	29	38	.357	.303
Wong,Kolten	L	.274	73	20	2	0	1	9	10	16	.360	.342
Bats Left	R	.288	281	81	25	3	3	33	31	44	.380	.431
Yelich,Christian	L	.266	158	42	9	1	3	18	12	33	.329	.392
Bats Left	R	.288	444	128	27	1	15	63	68	104	.382	.455
Young,Chris	L	.200	100	20	3	1	1	5	15	17	.310	.280
Bats Right	R	.259	143	37	9	1	6	20	15	38	.331	.462
Young Jr.,Eric	L	.200	35	7	1	0	1	5	4	10	.282	.314
Bats Both	R	.293	75	22	4	0	3	11	1	21	.361	.467
Zimmer,Bradley	L	.243	74	18	3	0	1	9	4	19	.300	.324
Bats Left	R	.240	225	54	12	2	7	30	22	80	.310	.404
Zimmerman,Ryan	L	.331	127	42	11	0	10	30	13	23	.385	.654
Bats Right	R	.295	397	117	22	0	26	78	31	103	.349	.547
Zobrist,Ben	L	.179	106	19	5	2	1	7	12	17	.261	.292
Bats Both	R	.249	329	82	15	1	11	43	42	54	.336	.401
Zunino,Mike	L	.253	91	23	3	0	8	10	11	35	.333	.549
Bats Right	R	.250	296	74	22	0	17	54	28	125	.330	.497
AL	L	.257	-	-	-	-	-	-	-	-	.328	.419
	R	.255	-	-	-	-	-	-	-	-	.322	.432
NL	L	.253	-	-	-	-	-	-	-	-	.324	.418
	R	.255	-	-	-	-	-	-	-	-	.325	.425
MLB	L	.255	-	-	-	-	-	-	-	-	.326	.419
	R	.255	-	-	-	-	-	-	-	-	.324	.428

Pitchers vs. Left-Handed and Right-Handed Batters

Pitcher	vs	Avg	AB	H	2B	3B	HR	RBI	BB	SO	OBP	Slg
Abad,Fernando	L	.227	66	15	2	0	2	9	5	21	.288	.348
Throws Left	R	.253	99	25	7	0	2	7	9	16	.312	.384
Adams,Austin	L	.222	9	2	1	0	0	1	3	6	.417	.333
Throws Right	R	.200	10	2	0	0	0	2	5	4	.471	.200
Adleman,Tim	L	.269	208	56	13	1	17	40	25	38	.353	.587
Throws Right	R	.261	261	68	21	1	12	33	26	70	.332	.487
Albers,Andrew	L	.316	38	12	3	0	4	13	1	11	.357	.711
Throws Left	R	.246	126	31	4	0	2	6	9	26	.296	.325
Albers,Matt	L	.171	76	13	3	1	2	7	8	19	.267	.316
Throws Right	R	.163	135	22	1	0	4	17	9	44	.224	.259
Alburquerque,Al	L	.095	21	2	0	0	0	0	6	7	.296	.095
Throws Right	R	.190	42	8	2	0	0	5	2	7	.227	.238
Alcantara,Raul	L	.238	42	10	0	0	3	14	9	6	.365	.452
Throws Right	R	.240	50	12	7	0	2	6	3	6	.321	.500
Alcantara,Sandy	L	.333	18	6	1	0	0	3	3	4	.429	.389
Throws Right	R	.200	15	3	0	0	2	3	3	6	.333	.600
Alcantara,Victor	L	.444	18	8	1	0	1	6	2	1	.500	.667
Throws Right	R	.286	14	4	0	0	0	3	2	4	.421	.286
Alexander,Scott	L	.250	72	18	4	0	1	9	9	20	.333	.347
Throws Left	R	.244	180	44	5	1	2	16	19	39	.313	.317
Allen,Cody	L	.209	110	23	3	0	1	7	10	47	.281	.264
Throws Right	R	.230	148	34	5	1	8	18	11	45	.288	.439
Altavilla,Dan	L	.265	68	18	3	0	2	13	4	17	.289	.397
Throws Right	R	.227	110	25	7	0	7	17	16	35	.331	.482
Alvarado,Jose	L	.298	47	14	4	0	0	3	4	9	.353	.383
Throws Left	R	.156	64	10	0	1	1	6	5	20	.214	.234
Alvarez,Dario	L	.250	28	7	1	0	1	9	6	6	.389	.393
Throws Left	R	.324	37	12	2	0	0	9	8	11	.435	.378
Alvarez,Henderson	L	.207	29	6	1	1	1	3	8	2	.378	.414
Throws Right	R	.296	27	8	2	0	1	2	3	4	.367	.481
Alvarez,Jose	L	.245	106	26	6	1	5	17	1	26	.252	.462
Throws Left	R	.286	84	24	2	0	2	7	11	19	.368	.381
Anderson,Brett	L	.436	39	17	6	0	0	5	4	6	.488	.590
Throws Left	R	.298	188	56	17	1	5	33	17	32	.351	.479
Anderson,Chase	L	.212	226	48	9	1	5	19	17	62	.279	.327
Throws Right	R	.226	288	65	18	1	9	27	24	71	.290	.389
Anderson,Tyler	L	.221	86	19	5	1	5	17	4	24	.264	.477
Throws Left	R	.286	241	69	17	1	11	31	22	57	.346	.502
Andriese,Matt	L	.216	148	32	6	0	4	15	13	35	.280	.338
Throws Right	R	.301	193	58	16	0	12	28	15	41	.362	.570
Aquino,Jayson	L	.313	16	5	2	0	1	3	3	6	.421	.625
Throws Left	R	.250	40	10	2	0	3	8	3	7	.302	.525
Arano,Victor	L	.222	9	2	0	1	0	0	3	2	.417	.444
Throws Right	R	.138	29	4	1	0	0	1	1	11	.167	.172
Archer,Chris	L	.263	365	96	17	3	13	43	34	119	.327	.433
Throws Right	R	.232	419	97	20	1	14	46	26	130	.282	.384
Armstrong,Shawn	L	.216	37	8	2	0	1	6	8	5	.370	.351
Throws Right	R	.250	60	15	1	0	4	10	2	15	.274	.467
Arrieta,Jake	L	.268	287	77	21	3	13	38	31	79	.345	.498
Throws Right	R	.209	350	73	12	2	10	34	24	84	.270	.340
Arroyo,Bronson	L	.297	111	33	10	0	13	25	11	19	.360	.739
Throws Right	R	.333	183	61	17	1	10	31	8	26	.365	.601
Asher,Alec	L	.220	109	24	6	1	3	11	13	28	.306	.376
Throws Right	R	.301	123	37	5	0	7	24	10	19	.379	.512
Astin,Barrett	L	.286	14	4	1	1	1	5	3	0	.421	.714
Throws Right	R	.294	17	5	0	0	1	1	4	2	.455	.471
Avilan,Luis	L	.195	82	16	2	1	1	9	10	28	.290	.280
Throws Left	R	.292	89	26	9	1	1	5	12	24	.376	.449
Axford,John	L	.400	35	14	3	0	0	9	2	6	.439	.486
Throws Right	R	.250	52	13	1	0	3	6	15	15	.418	.442
Baez,Pedro	L	.206	102	21	5	2	3	7	13	24	.296	.382
Throws Right	R	.238	147	35	8	2	6	14	16	40	.321	.442
Bailey,Homer	L	.277	177	49	16	0	4	25	27	29	.382	.435
Throws Right	R	.339	186	63	15	0	7	33	15	38	.399	.532
Banda,Anthony	L	.158	38	6	2	0	1	3	3	6	.238	.289
Throws Left	R	.313	64	20	7	3	0	12	7	19	.397	.516
Barbato,Johnny	L	.321	56	18	7	0	1	8	11	5	.441	.500
Throws Right	R	.130	54	7	1	0	3	4	7	18	.242	.315
Barnes,Danny	L	.172	93	16	2	0	2	5	10	27	.260	.258
Throws Right	R	.218	147	32	6	0	9	20	14	35	.286	.442
Barnes,Jacob	L	.235	119	28	9	0	1	11	19	39	.350	.336
Throws Right	R	.199	146	29	5	0	7	20	14	41	.268	.377
Barnes,Matt	L	.261	92	24	3	1	4	9	11	32	.346	.446
Throws Right	R	.204	162	33	7	0	3	15	17	51	.275	.302
Barnette,Tony	L	.319	72	23	6	0	2	20	11	11	.412	.486
Throws Right	R	.273	150	41	11	0	5	32	11	46	.317	.447

Pitcher	vs	Avg	AB	H	2B	3B	HR	RBI	BB	SO	OBP	Slg
Barraclough,Kyle	L	.184	125	23	2	0	3	12	22	40	.309	.272
Throws Right	R	.263	114	30	4	0	2	10	16	36	.351	.351
Barrett,Jake	L	.238	42	10	1	0	3	7	8	11	.353	.476
Throws Right	R	.274	62	17	1	1	4	12	7	15	.343	.516
Bass,Anthony	L	.471	17	8	3	0	1	5	0	0	.444	.824
Throws Right	R	.462	13	6	1	0	0	4	0	1	.462	.538
Bastardo,Antonio	L	.333	12	4	0	0	2	2	4	2	.500	.833
Throws Left	R	.387	31	12	3	0	3	11	5	6	.472	.774
Bauer,Trevor	L	.276	319	88	21	0	16	47	31	83	.346	.492
Throws Right	R	.258	361	93	20	3	9	30	29	113	.313	.404
Baumann,Buddy	L	.148	27	4	1	0	1	4	4	11	.324	.296
Throws Left	R	.200	35	7	1	0	3	4	3	10	.263	.486
Beck,Chris	L	.247	93	23	5	0	7	19	24	16	.403	.527
Throws Right	R	.314	159	50	12	0	9	32	10	26	.362	.560
Bedrosian,Cam	L	.238	80	19	4	2	4	13	6	29	.291	.488
Throws Right	R	.242	91	22	4	0	1	9	11	24	.320	.319
Belisle,Matt	L	.162	74	12	3	1	3	8	7	21	.244	.351
Throws Right	R	.247	146	36	7	0	4	23	15	33	.319	.377
Beliveau,Jeff	L	.269	26	7	1	0	0	2	2	9	.333	.308
Throws Left	R	.294	34	10	3	0	4	13	4	8	.359	.735
Bell,Chad	L	.286	77	22	3	0	3	9	10	23	.375	.442
Throws Left	R	.324	182	59	11	1	9	30	21	34	.400	.544
Benoit,Joaquin	L	.240	100	24	3	2	4	11	11	23	.315	.430
Throws Right	R	.213	89	19	6	0	3	13	11	23	.304	.382
Bergman,Christian	L	.290	93	27	1	0	5	12	7	16	.340	.462
Throws Right	R	.298	114	34	4	1	7	16	8	17	.357	.535
Berrios,Jose	L	.260	246	64	12	1	9	23	34	58	.357	.427
Throws Right	R	.222	302	67	16	1	6	33	14	81	.275	.341
Betances,Dellin	L	.122	98	12	4	0	0	6	13	55	.277	.163
Throws Right	R	.159	107	17	2	0	3	12	31	45	.362	.262
Bethancourt,Christian	L	.375	8	3	0	1	1	7	5	0	.615	1.000
Throws Right	R	.333	9	3	1	0	0	0	3	2	.500	.444
Bettis,Chad	L	.256	86	22	5	2	4	8	5	18	.297	.500
Throws Right	R	.313	96	30	6	0	4	19	6	12	.356	.500
Biagini,Joe	L	.279	201	56	11	2	7	30	16	47	.330	.458
Throws Right	R	.256	270	69	11	2	8	42	26	50	.324	.400
Bibens-Dirkx,Austin	L	.252	119	30	4	1	6	19	12	10	.328	.454
Throws Right	R	.284	155	44	9	0	8	22	8	28	.321	.497
Blach,Ty	L	.250	172	43	8	0	0	19	11	16	.296	.297
Throws Left	R	.295	461	136	28	6	17	63	32	57	.339	.492
Blackburn,Paul	L	.225	102	23	3	0	1	6	11	10	.301	.284
Throws Right	R	.294	119	35	6	0	4	11	5	12	.328	.445
Blanton,Joe	L	.323	65	21	7	1	3	12	6	13	.389	.600
Throws Right	R	.281	114	32	2	1	7	18	7	26	.320	.500
Blazek,Michael	L	.438	16	7	1	0	4	6	0	2	.438	1.250
Throws Right	R	.263	19	5	0	0	2	4	1	5	.300	.579
Bleier,Richard	L	.235	102	24	3	0	4	13	8	12	.296	.382
Throws Left	R	.273	139	38	6	0	2	12	5	14	.306	.360
Blevins,Jerry	L	.197	122	24	1	0	0	8	6	48	.250	.205
Throws Left	R	.288	66	19	5	0	4	11	18	21	.447	.545
Bolsinger,Mike	L	.167	72	12	3	0	2	12	12	22	.291	.292
Throws Right	R	.404	89	36	8	0	7	24	15	17	.482	.730
Bonilla,Lisalverto	L	.348	66	23	5	1	5	20	11	8	.430	.682
Throws Right	R	.244	78	19	4	1	3	10	11	20	.352	.436
Boshers,Buddy	L	.224	58	13	2	1	2	8	2	10	.258	.397
Throws Left	R	.300	80	24	4	0	5	14	8	18	.367	.538
Bowman,Matt	L	.242	95	23	4	1	1	19	7	17	.286	.337
Throws Right	R	.236	123	29	5	1	3	18	11	29	.321	.366
Boxberger,Brad	L	.214	56	12	1	1	1	4	4	17	.262	.321
Throws Right	R	.216	51	11	2	0	3	6	7	23	.322	.431
Boyd,Matt	L	.282	85	24	3	2	0	5	9	17	.347	.365
Throws Left	R	.292	455	133	29	4	18	70	44	93	.355	.492
Boyer,Blaine	L	.367	49	18	3	0	1	3	6	10	.429	.490
Throws Right	R	.286	112	32	5	2	2	15	8	23	.339	.420
Brach,Brad	L	.212	118	25	6	0	1	9	10	30	.271	.288
Throws Right	R	.205	127	26	5	0	6	17	16	40	.290	.386
Bracho,Silvino	L	.258	31	8	1	0	0	1	1	7	.281	.290
Throws Right	R	.204	49	10	1	0	5	9	6	18	.291	.531
Bradford,Chase	L	.273	66	18	3	0	1	10	8	8	.351	.364
Throws Right	R	.190	63	12	4	0	2	7	5	19	.246	.349
Bradley,Archie	L	.223	121	27	7	0	0	6	13	35	.299	.281
Throws Right	R	.193	145	28	2	2	4	14	8	44	.239	.317
Brady,Michael	L	.216	37	8	1	1	3	8	1	6	.231	.541
Throws Right	R	.294	85	25	9	1	4	16	5	18	.365	.565
Brault,Steven	L	.235	34	8	3	0	0	3	4	5	.333	.324
Throws Left	R	.303	109	33	9	0	3	16	10	18	.364	.468

Pitchers vs. Left-Handed and Right-Handed Batters

Pitcher	vs	Avg	AB	H	2B	3B	HR	RBI	BB	SO	OBP	Slg
Brebbia,John	L	.208	77	16	2	1	5	12	5	20	.282	.455
Throws Right	R	.183	115	21	9	0	3	12	6	31	.236	.339
Breslow,Craig	L	.214	42	9	3	0	0	7	5	7	.294	.286
Throws Left	R	.333	96	32	6	1	4	15	9	16	.393	.542
Brice,Austin	L	.191	47	9	1	0	4	7	2	9	.250	.468
Throws Right	R	.308	78	24	3	0	2	10	5	17	.357	.423
Bridwell,Parker	L	.252	214	54	10	1	10	26	20	33	.315	.449
Throws Right	R	.252	242	61	6	0	9	22	10	40	.292	.388
Britton,Zach	L	.250	36	9	3	0	1	5	3	9	.300	.417
Throws Left	R	.286	105	30	2	0	0	8	15	20	.375	.305
Brothers,Rex	L	.216	37	8	0	1	1	6	4	16	.293	.351
Throws Left	R	.273	55	15	5	0	2	11	8	17	.375	.473
Broxton,Jonathan	L	.524	21	11	1	0	1	6	5	5	.615	.714
Throws Right	R	.293	41	12	2	0	1	6	6	11	.367	.415
Buchanan,Jake	L	.400	25	10	3	0	0	2	6	2	.516	.520
Throws Right	R	.359	39	14	2	0	1	10	1	2	.409	.487
Buchholz,Clay	L	.500	20	10	3	0	0	3	2	1	.545	.650
Throws Right	R	.400	15	6	2	0	1	6	1	4	.389	.733
Buchter,Ryan	L	.176	85	15	3	0	4	14	10	28	.265	.353
Throws Left	R	.193	150	29	7	1	6	11	16	37	.282	.373
Buehler,Walker	L	.188	16	3	0	0	0	1	3	7	.316	.188
Throws Right	R	.400	20	8	1	0	2	7	5	5	.520	.750
Bumgarner,Madison	L	.205	73	15	2	0	1	4	4	15	.256	.274
Throws Left	R	.245	351	86	23	2	16	36	16	86	.281	.459
Bummer,Aaron	L	.171	41	7	1	0	2	3	6	8	.277	.341
Throws Left	R	.188	32	6	1	0	2	4	9	9	.372	.406
Bundy,Dylan	L	.261	299	78	19	1	12	38	26	56	.321	.452
Throws Right	R	.222	334	74	15	0	14	36	25	96	.282	.392
Busenitz,Alan	L	.225	40	9	0	0	1	4	2	11	.244	.300
Throws Right	R	.194	67	13	2	1	3	9	7	12	.263	.388
Bush,Matt	L	.284	88	25	5	0	4	14	9	27	.347	.477
Throws Right	R	.250	128	32	3	2	3	13	10	31	.324	.375
Butler,Eddie	L	.217	83	18	4	1	1	6	15	13	.340	.325
Throws Right	R	.262	122	32	9	0	3	15	13	17	.338	.410
Cahill,Trevor	L	.241	145	35	7	1	5	19	26	39	.360	.407
Throws Right	R	.301	186	56	10	1	11	26	19	48	.372	.543
Cain,Matt	L	.312	218	68	12	1	6	36	29	32	.390	.459
Throws Right	R	.308	289	89	13	2	12	39	20	43	.351	.491
Callahan,Jamie	L	.143	14	2	0	0	0	3	1	3	.200	.143
Throws Right	R	.357	14	5	1	1	0	5	0	2	.333	.571
Campos,Leonel	L	.208	24	5	2	0	1	6	1	9	.240	.417
Throws Right	R	.222	27	6	3	0	1	4	7	6	.400	.444
Capps,Carter	L	.350	20	7	1	0	2	4	2	2	.409	.700
Throws Right	R	.192	26	5	0	0	0	2	0	5	.185	.192
Carrasco,Carlos	L	.244	336	82	19	1	14	39	23	101	.295	.432
Throws Right	R	.228	399	91	25	1	7	29	23	125	.281	.348
Cashner,Andrew	L	.243	284	69	7	0	9	33	39	41	.338	.363
Throws Right	R	.256	340	87	18	1	6	22	25	45	.316	.368
Casilla,Santiago	L	.256	90	23	2	1	4	16	15	21	.369	.433
Throws Right	R	.261	134	35	9	0	4	14	7	36	.306	.418
Castillo,Luis	L	.185	146	27	8	2	5	16	14	40	.261	.370
Throws Right	R	.216	171	37	5	0	6	13	18	58	.295	.351
Castro,Miguel	L	.272	92	25	4	0	5	19	15	11	.369	.478
Throws Right	R	.193	145	28	8	0	3	13	13	27	.263	.310
Castro,Simon	L	.180	61	11	2	0	3	7	9	18	.296	.361
Throws Right	R	.280	75	21	6	0	4	14	5	17	.329	.520
Cecil,Brett	L	.343	102	35	11	0	3	21	11	19	.397	.539
Throws Left	R	.208	154	32	7	0	4	15	5	47	.230	.331
Cedeno,Xavier	L	.444	9	4	0	0	1	4	0	0	.444	.778
Throws Left	R	.429	7	3	0	0	2	7	4	0	.636	1.286
Cervenka,Hunter	L	.200	5	1	0	0	0	1	4	2	.545	.200
Throws Left	R	.000	7	0	0	0	0	0	4	4	.417	.000
Cessa,Luis	L	.172	58	10	3	0	1	3	8	10	.273	.276
Throws Right	R	.317	82	26	5	1	6	17	9	20	.404	.622
Chacin,Alejandro	L	.462	13	6	0	0	2	6	2	2	.533	.923
Throws Right	R	.333	15	5	2	0	0	3	2	4	.412	.467
Chacin,Jhoulys	L	.255	321	82	17	2	12	44	46	61	.356	.433
Throws Right	R	.217	346	75	14	0	7	31	26	92	.284	.318
Chafin,Andrew	L	.222	81	18	2	0	1	7	6	23	.281	.284
Throws Left	R	.263	114	30	6	1	4	16	15	38	.354	.439
Chapman,Aroldis	L	.175	57	10	2	0	2	9	4	27	.262	.316
Throws Left	R	.211	128	27	7	0	1	13	16	42	.299	.289
Chatwood,Tyler	L	.270	278	75	13	4	11	38	46	64	.373	.464
Throws Right	R	.230	265	61	13	5	9	34	31	56	.317	.419
Chavez,Jesse	L	.271	251	68	12	1	11	35	17	56	.321	.458
Throws Right	R	.280	286	80	15	2	17	43	28	63	.343	.524

Pitcher	vs	Avg	AB	H	2B	3B	HR	RBI	BB	SO	OBP	Slg
Chen,Wei-Yin	L	.212	33	7	2	0	0	3	2	5	.250	.273
Throws Left	R	.205	88	18	2	2	3	11	7	20	.271	.375
Cingrani,Tony	L	.247	73	18	5	0	6	14	2	25	.276	.562
Throws Left	R	.247	89	22	4	0	4	12	10	27	.323	.427
Cishek,Steve	L	.208	48	10	1	0	2	7	6	11	.309	.354
Throws Right	R	.148	108	16	2	0	1	4	8	30	.218	.194
Claudio,Alex	L	.147	95	14	1	0	1	12	3	23	.178	.189
Throws Left	R	.275	207	57	9	0	4	18	12	33	.317	.377
Clevinger,Mike	L	.257	171	44	13	0	8	21	22	50	.345	.474
Throws Right	R	.180	266	48	12	0	5	21	38	87	.288	.282
Clippard,Tyler	L	.215	93	20	5	0	3	14	13	31	.311	.366
Throws Right	R	.205	132	27	7	1	7	23	18	41	.303	.432
Cobb,Alex	L	.225	284	64	19	0	8	25	29	62	.302	.377
Throws Right	R	.274	405	111	17	1	14	41	15	66	.306	.425
Cole,A.J.	L	.320	103	33	4	1	6	13	17	22	.421	.553
Throws Right	R	.196	92	18	5	0	2	10	10	22	.286	.315
Cole,Gerrit	L	.268	377	101	17	4	18	49	26	92	.317	.477
Throws Right	R	.241	407	98	19	2	13	41	29	104	.295	.393
Collmenter,Josh	L	.250	28	7	2	0	1	5	4	5	.333	.429
Throws Right	R	.440	50	22	3	0	6	13	2	13	.462	.860
Colome,Alex	L	.227	119	27	4	1	3	10	17	30	.324	.353
Throws Right	R	.236	127	30	8	0	1	16	6	28	.273	.323
Colon,Bartolo	L	.313	291	91	26	1	14	44	20	42	.357	.553
Throws Right	R	.324	312	101	24	3	14	60	15	47	.354	.554
Conley,Adam	L	.265	102	27	3	2	6	20	4	16	.312	.510
Throws Left	R	.289	301	87	14	3	13	44	38	56	.376	.485
Corbin,Patrick	L	.220	164	36	5	2	6	20	10	55	.267	.384
Throws Left	R	.292	589	172	42	5	20	71	51	123	.348	.482
Cosart,Jarred	L	.378	37	14	0	0	0	5	9	4	.511	.378
Throws Right	R	.218	55	12	4	1	0	7	10	11	.348	.327
Cotton,Jharel	L	.257	218	56	7	0	14	34	30	44	.347	.482
Throws Right	R	.275	280	77	22	0	14	48	23	61	.333	.504
Coulombe,Daniel	L	.214	103	22	3	1	1	13	11	20	.305	.291
Throws Left	R	.270	89	24	9	1	3	14	11	19	.356	.494
Covey,Dylan	L	.275	131	36	9	0	9	21	14	22	.345	.550
Throws Right	R	.333	141	47	8	1	11	35	20	19	.417	.638
Crichton,Stefan	L	.455	22	10	2	1	0	2	3	2	.500	.636
Throws Right	R	.457	35	16	2	0	2	8	1	6	.472	.686
Crick,Kyle	L	.220	50	11	0	1	0	4	3	4	.264	.260
Throws Right	R	.169	65	11	2	1	2	7	14	24	.325	.323
Cueto,Johnny	L	.286	308	88	23	3	11	36	28	71	.346	.487
Throws Right	R	.268	269	72	12	2	11	33	25	65	.343	.450
Curtis,Zac	L	.000	8	0	0	0	0	0	1	2	.273	.000
Throws Left	R	.273	22	6	2	0	1	4	2	4	.333	.500
Curtiss,John	L	.294	17	5	1	0	2	4	1	5	.333	.706
Throws Right	R	.222	18	4	1	0	0	2	1	5	.300	.278
Danish,Tyler	L	.167	6	1	0	0	0	0	5	3	.545	.167
Throws Right	R	.182	11	2	1	0	0	0	1	3	.250	.273
Darvish,Yu	L	.262	351	92	19	0	16	42	30	104	.325	.453
Throws Right	R	.194	346	67	16	1	11	34	28	105	.259	.341
Davies,Zach	L	.265	358	95	19	4	13	42	36	69	.337	.450
Throws Right	R	.285	383	109	17	3	7	41	19	55	.324	.399
Davis,Rookie	L	.370	46	17	1	0	4	8	9	8	.473	.652
Throws Right	R	.362	58	21	7	0	3	13	5	12	.415	.638
Davis,Wade	L	.156	96	15	4	0	1	6	13	37	.264	.229
Throws Right	R	.211	114	24	4	0	5	9	15	42	.313	.377
Dayton,Grant	L	.171	41	7	1	0	2	5	6	10	.271	.341
Throws Left	R	.267	45	12	3	0	3	9	6	10	.340	.533
De Jong,Chase	L	.309	55	17	3	1	2	9	6	6	.371	.509
Throws Right	R	.255	55	14	2	0	3	10	7	7	.339	.455
De La Rosa,Jorge	L	.194	72	14	4	0	1	4	4	20	.253	.292
Throws Left	R	.267	120	32	5	0	6	14	17	25	.362	.458
De La Rosa,Rubby	L	.286	7	2	0	0	1	1	1	3	.375	.714
Throws Right	R	.217	23	5	1	1	1	4	3	9	.308	.478
deGrom,Jacob	L	.247	368	91	12	3	11	36	33	102	.309	.386
Throws Right	R	.228	390	89	13	0	17	41	26	137	.277	.392
Delgado,Randall	L	.221	104	23	4	1	4	14	4	27	.245	.394
Throws Right	R	.274	135	37	11	1	2	16	10	33	.324	.415
Dermody,Matt	L	.195	41	8	2	0	0	6	1	8	.227	.244
Throws Left	R	.326	46	15	1	0	6	9	4	7	.392	.739
Despaigne,Odrisamer	L	.306	121	37	8	0	2	15	15	15	.384	.421
Throws Right	R	.196	102	20	3	1	1	14	9	16	.272	.275
Devenski,Chris	L	.111	144	16	4	1	4	14	10	61	.178	.236
Throws Right	R	.238	143	34	7	1	7	21	16	39	.314	.448
Diaz,Dayan	L	.278	18	5	1	0	1	5	3	9	.381	.500
Throws Right	R	.333	36	12	5	0	2	7	1	11	.351	.639

Pitchers vs. Left-Handed and Right-Handed Batters

Pitcher	vs	Avg	AB	H	2B	3B	HR	RBI	BB	SO	OBP	Slg
Diaz,Edwin	L	.184	103	19	2	0	5	14	18	44	.306	.350
Throws Right	R	.182	137	25	4	0	5	19	14	45	.269	.321
Diaz,Jairo	L	.500	10	5	0	1	0	3	1	2	.545	.700
Throws Right	R	.500	14	7	2	0	0	3	4	0	.632	.643
Diaz,Jumbo	L	.300	40	12	2	0	3	8	4	11	.364	.575
Throws Right	R	.256	78	20	6	1	1	13	11	17	.341	.397
Diaz,Miguel	L	.338	68	23	1	1	8	23	7	7	.410	.735
Throws Right	R	.228	92	21	6	1	3	11	18	26	.357	.413
Dickey,R.A.	L	.243	329	80	21	3	10	32	26	54	.304	.416
Throws Right	R	.285	397	113	25	2	16	53	41	82	.359	.479
Diekman,Jake	L	.154	13	2	0	0	0	4	3	4	.313	.154
Throws Left	R	.100	20	2	0	0	1	3	7	9	.310	.250
Doolittle,Sean	L	.146	41	6	1	0	0	2	3	14	.200	.171
Throws Left	R	.196	143	28	4	0	5	17	7	48	.230	.329
Drake,Oliver	L	.250	148	37	6	2	3	13	14	39	.315	.378
Throws Right	R	.347	75	26	4	3	3	15	11	23	.430	.600
Duensing,Brian	L	.258	97	25	6	0	2	9	5	25	.301	.381
Throws Left	R	.237	139	33	3	1	4	8	13	36	.307	.360
Duffey,Tyler	L	.243	107	26	3	0	6	18	9	26	.305	.439
Throws Right	R	.294	180	53	7	0	3	30	9	41	.325	.383
Duffy,Danny	L	.167	102	17	2	0	2	5	5	27	.206	.245
Throws Left	R	.278	454	126	23	7	11	54	36	103	.335	.432
Duke,Zach	L	.231	39	9	2	0	1	3	3	6	.302	.359
Throws Left	R	.148	27	4	0	0	2	8	3	6	.258	.370
Dull,Ryan	L	.300	50	15	3	0	2	10	9	15	.417	.480
Throws Right	R	.206	107	22	3	0	5	12	7	30	.265	.374
Dunn,Mike	L	.244	90	22	2	1	4	15	15	30	.349	.422
Throws Left	R	.212	99	21	6	0	4	12	13	27	.298	.394
Dyson,Sam	L	.277	94	26	1	3	5	16	20	9	.414	.511
Throws Right	R	.311	132	41	9	0	3	20	10	25	.364	.447
Edgin,Josh	L	.280	75	21	3	0	2	15	7	17	.372	.400
Throws Left	R	.265	68	18	6	0	1	7	11	10	.375	.397
Edwards Jr.,Carl	L	.119	109	13	2	0	2	8	16	41	.244	.193
Throws Right	R	.148	108	16	1	0	4	15	22	53	.301	.269
Eflin,Zach	L	.306	147	45	7	0	11	31	9	21	.348	.578
Throws Right	R	.312	109	34	7	0	5	12	3	14	.342	.514
Eickhoff,Jerad	L	.314	271	85	23	0	11	41	31	58	.379	.520
Throws Right	R	.243	235	57	12	0	5	25	22	60	.313	.357
Ellington,Brian	L	.259	85	22	8	0	3	17	23	20	.417	.459
Throws Right	R	.280	93	26	6	0	4	14	12	28	.396	.473
Enns,Dietrich	L	.500	4	2	1	0	0	0	0	0	.500	.750
Throws Left	R	.313	16	5	0	0	2	4	1	2	.353	.688
Espino,Paolo	L	.282	39	11	2	0	3	6	9	6	.429	.564
Throws Right	R	.214	56	12	5	0	4	13	1	14	.254	.518
Estevez,Carlos	L	.339	56	19	3	0	0	7	6	9	.403	.393
Throws Right	R	.260	77	20	2	1	3	10	8	22	.337	.429
Estrada,Marco	L	.216	328	71	15	3	15	39	22	78	.268	.418
Throws Right	R	.289	398	115	34	1	16	60	49	98	.364	.500
Familia,Jeurys	L	.282	39	11	1	0	1	7	7	8	.375	.385
Throws Right	R	.192	52	10	2	0	0	8	8	17	.311	.231
Faria,Jake	L	.173	98	17	1	0	2	9	21	24	.314	.245
Throws Right	R	.248	218	54	12	1	9	23	10	60	.294	.436
Farmer,Buck	L	.291	103	30	6	0	5	17	15	23	.380	.495
Throws Right	R	.278	90	25	5	0	4	20	5	26	.337	.467
Farquhar,Danny	L	.185	81	15	0	0	1	14	15	23	.317	.222
Throws Right	R	.255	94	24	6	0	2	11	13	22	.351	.383
Farrell,Luke	L	.250	24	6	1	0	1	4	6	4	.400	.417
Throws Right	R	.222	27	6	1	0	1	3	4	5	.323	.370
Fedde,Erick	L	.297	37	11	1	0	2	6	3	11	.350	.486
Throws Right	R	.500	28	14	1	0	3	7	5	4	.588	.857
Feldman,Scott	L	.286	203	58	11	1	12	36	18	39	.345	.527
Throws Right	R	.262	221	58	9	2	9	24	17	54	.329	.443
Feliz,Michael	L	.280	75	21	11	1	2	16	8	23	.345	.533
Throws Right	R	.274	117	32	6	1	6	26	14	47	.343	.496
Feliz,Neftali	L	.233	73	17	7	0	4	14	11	19	.341	.493
Throws Right	R	.235	98	23	4	1	5	19	12	18	.315	.449
Ferrell,Jeff	L	.267	15	4	0	0	0	2	4	1	.400	.267
Throws Right	R	.464	28	13	3	0	2	8	1	5	.483	.786
Fields,Josh	L	.232	82	19	3	0	6	13	7	20	.292	.488
Throws Right	R	.169	124	21	5	0	4	14	8	40	.224	.306
Fien,Casey	L	.471	17	8	2	0	2	8	4	4	.571	.941
Throws Right	R	.395	38	15	3	0	3	11	2	6	.425	.711
Fiers,Mike	L	.256	289	74	11	2	15	34	37	68	.345	.464
Throws Right	R	.275	302	83	13	1	17	47	25	78	.350	.493
Finnegan,Brandon	L	.167	6	1	0	0	0	0	2	3	.375	.167
Throws Left	R	.200	40	8	2	0	1	5	11	13	.373	.325

Pitcher	vs	Avg	AB	H	2B	3B	HR	RBI	BB	SO	OBP	Slg
Fister,Doug	L	.300	170	51	8	2	6	26	23	40	.386	.476
Throws Right	R	.208	173	36	10	0	3	24	15	43	.271	.318
Flaherty,Jack	L	.341	41	14	2	0	4	9	5	6	.413	.683
Throws Right	R	.225	40	9	0	1	0	4	5	14	.313	.275
Flexen,Chris	L	.286	91	26	6	0	4	15	21	15	.425	.484
Throws Right	R	.353	102	36	6	0	7	21	14	21	.429	.618
Floro,Dylan	L	.273	11	3	1	0	1	2	1	2	.385	.636
Throws Right	R	.387	31	12	2	0	1	7	1	4	.406	.548
Foltynewicz,Mike	L	.308	295	91	20	1	11	39	33	63	.384	.495
Throws Right	R	.248	315	78	17	2	9	41	26	80	.316	.400
Font,Wilmer	L	.286	7	2	2	0	0	1	1	1	.375	.571
Throws Right	R	.455	11	5	1	0	2	6	3	2	.571	1.091
Freeland,Kyle	L	.283	138	39	9	0	4	17	8	42	.320	.435
Throws Left	R	.284	458	130	25	3	13	58	55	65	.366	.437
Freeman,Sam	L	.191	94	18	2	0	1	10	6	27	.262	.245
Throws Left	R	.234	128	30	4	0	2	13	21	32	.340	.313
Fried,Max	L	.258	31	8	2	0	0	0	4	11	.361	.323
Throws Left	R	.297	74	22	3	1	3	13	8	11	.388	.486
Frieri,Ernesto	L	.364	11	4	0	0	0	2	3	0	.500	.364
Throws Right	R	.154	13	2	1	0	0	0	3	5	.313	.231
Fry,Jace	L	.308	13	4	0	1	0	0	4	1	.471	.462
Throws Left	R	.444	18	8	2	0	1	2	1	2	.474	.722
Fulmer,Carson	L	.163	49	8	0	0	3	6	10	12	.317	.347
Throws Right	R	.222	36	8	0	0	1	4	3	7	.300	.306
Fulmer,Michael	L	.264	288	76	13	1	5	35	18	57	.309	.368
Throws Right	R	.225	329	74	10	1	8	36	22	57	.281	.334
Gallardo,Yovani	L	.257	249	64	16	0	10	35	34	48	.345	.442
Throws Right	R	.285	260	74	10	2	14	39	26	46	.352	.500
Gallegos,Giovanny	L	.267	30	8	1	0	2	9	2	14	.313	.500
Throws Right	R	.260	50	13	4	0	1	6	3	8	.296	.400
Gant,John	L	.259	27	7	0	0	3	5	6	5	.394	.593
Throws Right	R	.270	37	10	2	1	1	3	4	6	.349	.459
Garcia,Jaime	L	.252	139	35	8	0	4	13	6	38	.288	.396
Throws Left	R	.263	463	122	35	2	14	55	58	91	.343	.438
Garcia,Jarlin	L	.202	99	20	3	1	3	18	6	23	.259	.343
Throws Left	R	.267	101	27	6	1	3	12	11	19	.348	.436
Garcia,Luis	L	.280	125	35	6	0	2	16	14	20	.353	.376
Throws Right	R	.184	141	26	3	0	1	10	12	40	.245	.227
Garcia,Onelki	L	.500	4	2	1	0	0	1	0	0	.500	.750
Throws Left	R	.435	23	10	1	1	2	10	5	2	.536	.826
Gardewine,Nick	L	.417	12	5	1	0	0	1	2	1	.500	.500
Throws Right	R	.238	21	5	0	0	1	4	5	2	.385	.381
Garrett,Amir	L	.298	57	17	1	0	5	14	7	18	.375	.579
Throws Left	R	.261	218	57	12	1	18	44	33	45	.359	.573
Garton,Ryan	L	.267	30	8	1	0	2	4	4	4	.353	.500
Throws Right	R	.192	52	10	3	0	2	5	2	12	.218	.365
Garza,Matt	L	.270	215	58	14	0	10	32	29	29	.357	.474
Throws Right	R	.270	233	63	11	4	7	30	16	50	.316	.442
Gausman,Kevin	L	.275	305	84	14	1	12	33	41	75	.361	.446
Throws Right	R	.288	431	124	25	1	17	56	30	104	.339	.469
Gaviglio,Sam	L	.258	132	34	11	0	7	16	14	22	.338	.500
Throws Right	R	.282	149	42	7	1	9	21	12	27	.335	.523
Gearrin,Cory	L	.205	83	17	6	0	2	10	19	14	.362	.349
Throws Right	R	.210	157	33	5	2	2	21	16	50	.302	.306
Gee,Dillon	L	.305	82	25	5	0	5	11	11	16	.394	.549
Throws Right	R	.266	109	29	6	1	3	12	4	25	.305	.422
German,Domingo	L	.192	26	5	2	0	0	2	7	8	.353	.269
Throws Right	R	.240	25	6	1	0	1	2	2	10	.296	.400
Gibson,Kyle	L	.301	312	94	18	3	9	41	30	56	.367	.465
Throws Right	R	.282	312	88	14	0	15	43	30	65	.350	.471
Giles,Ken	L	.196	102	20	1	1	3	11	11	37	.270	.314
Throws Right	R	.200	120	24	7	0	1	10	10	46	.267	.283
Giolito,Lucas	L	.200	80	16	1	0	5	8	4	15	.238	.400
Throws Right	R	.181	83	15	3	2	3	4	8	19	.277	.373
Givens,Mychal	L	.184	98	18	2	0	4	13	12	28	.292	.327
Throws Right	R	.209	187	39	8	0	6	23	13	60	.267	.348
Glasnow,Tyler	L	.323	130	42	14	1	7	26	25	30	.439	.608
Throws Right	R	.315	124	39	6	2	6	25	19	26	.403	.540
Glover,Koda	L	.265	34	9	2	0	1	7	2	6	.297	.412
Throws Right	R	.268	41	11	1	0	0	2	2	11	.302	.293
Godley,Zack	L	.219	265	58	19	0	5	21	30	77	.301	.347
Throws Right	R	.223	296	66	14	1	10	34	23	88	.286	.378
Goeddel,Erik	L	.326	43	14	4	0	1	4	7	10	.420	.488
Throws Right	R	.212	66	14	4	0	7	13	4	23	.254	.591
Gohara,Luiz	L	.105	19	2	1	0	0	1	2	6	.190	.158
Throws Left	R	.319	94	30	12	1	2	13	6	25	.360	.532

Pitchers vs. Left-Handed and Right-Handed Batters

Pitcher	vs	Avg	AB	H	2B	3B	HR	RBI	BB	SO	OBP	Slg
Goldberg,Brad	L	.222	27	6	2	0	1	6	8	3	.417	.407
Throws Right	R	.421	19	8	2	0	1	4	6	0	.577	.684
Gomez,Jeanmar	L	.404	47	19	4	0	5	12	4	9	.451	.809
Throws Right	R	.286	42	12	0	0	2	6	3	12	.362	.429
Gomez,Roberto	L	.300	10	3	0	1	0	2	1	4	.364	.500
Throws Right	R	.400	15	6	0	2	0	3	0	2	.400	.667
Gonzales,Marco	L	.326	43	14	0	0	2	5	3	11	.370	.465
Throws Left	R	.349	129	45	6	2	6	17	8	21	.388	.566
Gonzalez,Gio	L	.183	164	30	6	0	2	8	14	41	.251	.256
Throws Left	R	.226	567	128	25	0	19	54	65	147	.310	.370
Gonzalez,Miguel	L	.287	300	86	24	5	11	38	25	49	.347	.510
Throws Right	R	.256	316	81	15	0	11	46	30	51	.322	.408
Goody,Nick	L	.188	64	12	1	0	3	8	5	23	.246	.344
Throws Right	R	.203	133	27	6	1	4	14	15	49	.298	.353
Gossett,Daniel	L	.319	166	53	14	0	6	21	18	24	.386	.512
Throws Right	R	.296	213	63	13	1	15	37	13	48	.333	.577
Gott,Trevor	L	.600	10	6	0	0	1	6	1	2	.636	.900
Throws Right	R	.500	10	5	1	0	0	3	2	1	.583	.600
Grace,Matt	L	.235	81	19	0	0	0	9	9	21	.315	.235
Throws Left	R	.290	107	31	8	1	3	14	9	10	.350	.467
Graveman,Kendall	L	.238	185	44	10	0	6	23	16	35	.302	.389
Throws Right	R	.315	222	70	12	4	6	24	16	35	.368	.486
Gray,Jon	L	.260	246	64	9	4	4	20	21	53	.317	.378
Throws Right	R	.274	179	49	8	1	6	19	9	59	.314	.430
Gray,Sonny	L	.221	281	62	14	1	7	24	28	70	.293	.352
Throws Right	R	.231	334	77	16	1	12	45	29	83	.295	.392
Green,Chad	L	.120	83	10	4	0	2	5	5	44	.170	.241
Throws Right	R	.162	148	24	6	0	2	8	12	59	.233	.243
Greene,Shane	L	.235	98	23	4	1	3	12	19	33	.370	.388
Throws Right	R	.185	146	27	4	0	3	11	15	40	.268	.274
Gregerson,Luke	L	.242	95	23	6	0	6	17	9	24	.308	.495
Throws Right	R	.267	146	39	8	0	7	17	11	46	.316	.466
Greinke,Zack	L	.241	381	92	18	1	10	28	23	107	.284	.373
Throws Right	R	.217	368	80	17	3	15	45	22	108	.260	.402
Griffin,A.J.	L	.242	120	29	6	0	7	17	17	21	.343	.467
Throws Right	R	.261	180	47	14	1	13	32	11	40	.313	.567
Grilli,Jason	L	.259	54	14	4	0	4	7	10	17	.375	.556
Throws Right	R	.288	111	32	9	0	8	17	8	31	.342	.586
Grimm,Justin	L	.238	80	19	1	0	6	13	7	26	.299	.475
Throws Right	R	.230	122	28	4	0	6	26	20	33	.340	.410
Gsellman,Robert	L	.276	232	64	12	2	9	33	24	39	.351	.461
Throws Right	R	.284	261	74	19	2	8	41	18	43	.339	.464
Guduan,Reymin	L	.270	37	10	1	0	1	5	5	8	.357	.378
Throws Left	R	.412	34	14	5	0	0	3	7	8	.512	.559
Guerra,Deolis	L	.234	47	11	3	0	2	5	4	13	.294	.426
Throws Right	R	.200	45	9	4	0	2	8	8	9	.315	.422
Guerra,Javy	L	.297	37	11	1	0	1	8	4	7	.366	.405
Throws Right	R	.279	43	12	3	0	1	7	3	5	.326	.419
Guerra,Junior	L	.235	119	28	4	1	7	13	19	28	.350	.462
Throws Right	R	.226	146	33	4	0	11	24	24	39	.341	.479
Gustave,Jandel	L	.250	8	2	1	0	0	2	3	1	.455	.375
Throws Right	R	.300	10	3	0	0	0	0	4	1	.500	.300
Hader,Josh	L	.140	57	8	1	0	0	5	12	31	.296	.158
Throws Left	R	.165	103	17	7	0	4	5	10	37	.259	.350
Hahn,Jesse	L	.289	121	35	7	3	2	19	18	20	.375	.446
Throws Right	R	.277	155	43	8	0	2	23	9	35	.321	.368
Haley,Justin	L	.360	25	9	0	1	1	5	3	3	.429	.560
Throws Right	R	.271	48	13	1	2	2	8	3	11	.321	.500
Hamels,Cole	L	.161	118	19	4	1	2	13	6	21	.220	.263
Throws Left	R	.247	430	106	24	1	16	51	47	84	.331	.419
Hammel,Jason	L	.281	385	108	24	2	12	44	26	75	.329	.447
Throws Right	R	.287	352	101	11	0	14	49	22	70	.333	.438
Hand,Brad	L	.150	80	12	3	0	4	10	9	34	.253	.338
Throws Left	R	.208	202	42	4	1	5	14	11	70	.265	.312
Happ,J.A.	L	.198	111	22	3	1	3	11	5	23	.229	.324
Throws Left	R	.265	464	123	19	2	15	50	41	119	.323	.412
Hardy,Blaine	L	.269	52	14	3	0	4	11	2	7	.286	.558
Throws Left	R	.368	87	32	6	0	3	18	11	21	.430	.540
Harrell,Lucas	L	.167	6	1	0	0	0	0	1	0	.286	.167
Throws Right	R	.391	23	9	1	0	1	6	3	6	.462	.565
Harris,Will	L	.233	73	17	2	0	2	8	3	19	.263	.342
Throws Right	R	.206	97	20	2	0	5	15	4	33	.238	.381
Hart,Donnie	L	.273	77	21	4	0	2	10	9	18	.371	.403
Throws Left	R	.284	95	27	4	0	3	13	4	11	.317	.421
Harvey,Matt	L	.331	172	57	8	1	12	31	27	28	.426	.599
Throws Right	R	.264	201	53	7	0	9	30	20	39	.341	.433

Pitcher	vs	Avg	AB	H	2B	3B	HR	RBI	BB	SO	OBP	Slg
Hatcher,Chris	L	.213	89	19	3	0	5	13	10	26	.290	.416
Throws Right	R	.273	143	39	8	0	5	14	11	37	.323	.434
Hauschild,Mike	L	.375	8	3	1	0	2	4	1	2	.500	1.250
Throws Right	R	.393	28	11	1	0	3	8	1	5	.414	.750
Heaney,Andrew	L	.294	17	5	2	0	0	2	2	3	.368	.412
Throws Left	R	.301	73	22	0	1	12	15	7	24	.363	.822
Heller,Ben	L	.263	19	5	0	1	0	4	3	4	.364	.368
Throws Right	R	.000	17	0	0	0	0	1	3	5	.143	.000
Hellickson,Jeremy	L	.250	292	73	24	0	17	52	24	44	.312	.507
Throws Right	R	.259	336	87	17	3	18	48	23	52	.311	.488
Hembree,Heath	L	.313	67	21	8	0	0	6	6	25	.370	.433
Throws Right	R	.280	182	51	6	0	10	38	12	45	.325	.478
Hendricks,Kyle	L	.241	241	58	8	0	9	19	27	64	.320	.386
Throws Right	R	.243	280	68	9	0	8	25	13	59	.278	.361
Hendriks,Liam	L	.206	97	20	4	1	3	13	9	32	.274	.361
Throws Right	R	.243	152	37	8	0	4	24	14	46	.305	.375
Hernandez,Ariel	L	.244	41	10	2	0	4	13	11	7	.396	.585
Throws Right	R	.091	44	4	1	0	2	4	11	22	.273	.250
Hernandez,David	L	.200	85	17	3	0	3	12	8	26	.277	.341
Throws Right	R	.267	116	31	5	0	1	10	1	26	.269	.336
Hernandez,Felix	L	.306	144	44	9	0	6	20	13	28	.361	.493
Throws Right	R	.222	189	42	10	0	11	19	13	50	.293	.450
Herrera,Kelvin	L	.282	117	33	6	2	4	18	17	28	.370	.470
Throws Right	R	.229	118	27	6	4	5	13	3	28	.252	.475
Heston,Chris	L	.385	13	5	0	1	1	3	3	1	.500	.769
Throws Right	R	.500	20	10	1	0	2	7	2	2	.545	.850
Hildenberger,Trevor	L	.233	60	14	3	1	1	4	2	11	.270	.367
Throws Right	R	.245	98	24	5	0	3	12	4	33	.292	.388
Hill,Rich	L	.255	98	25	1	1	5	14	19	28	.407	.439
Throws Left	R	.190	390	74	14	1	13	31	30	138	.252	.331
Hoffman,Jeff	L	.232	194	45	11	3	7	29	14	37	.283	.428
Throws Right	R	.314	194	61	16	3	8	30	26	45	.400	.552
Holder,Jonathan	L	.361	36	13	0	0	2	4	4	10	.439	.528
Throws Right	R	.260	123	32	8	1	3	19	4	30	.295	.415
Holland,Derek	L	.237	118	28	4	0	5	15	13	18	.321	.398
Throws Left	R	.305	420	128	27	4	26	79	62	86	.400	.574
Holland,Greg	L	.157	108	17	4	0	2	9	19	43	.283	.250
Throws Right	R	.232	99	23	3	1	5	16	7	27	.287	.434
Holmberg,David	L	.286	77	22	3	2	3	12	6	8	.368	.494
Throws Left	R	.270	152	41	11	0	9	26	28	25	.384	.520
Hoover,J.J.	L	.279	61	17	3	0	1	5	4	16	.333	.377
Throws Right	R	.275	109	30	5	2	6	20	22	38	.397	.523
Howell,J.P.	L	.273	22	6	1	0	1	5	3	1	.360	.455
Throws Left	R	.304	23	7	5	0	1	6	4	5	.407	.652
Hoyt,James	L	.284	95	27	6	1	3	13	7	31	.333	.463
Throws Right	R	.240	100	24	4	0	4	14	7	35	.303	.400
Hu,Chih-Wei	L	.143	14	2	0	0	1	3	3	2	.294	.357
Throws Right	R	.143	21	3	1	0	1	2	1	7	.174	.333
Hudson,Daniel	L	.255	106	27	6	2	3	15	17	28	.365	.434
Throws Right	R	.242	124	30	6	0	4	16	16	38	.340	.387
Hughes,Jared	L	.282	71	20	6	2	3	14	7	10	.363	.549
Throws Right	R	.206	141	29	13	0	1	9	17	38	.309	.319
Hughes,Phil	L	.383	94	36	7	0	7	21	7	17	.426	.681
Throws Right	R	.269	134	36	11	0	5	18	6	21	.303	.463
Hunter,Tommy	L	.170	88	15	3	1	1	6	8	27	.240	.261
Throws Right	R	.224	125	28	5	0	5	16	6	37	.265	.384
Hursh,Jason	L	.222	18	4	0	0	0	1	2	1	.300	.222
Throws Right	R	.391	23	9	2	0	1	3	2	6	.444	.609
Iglesias,Raisel	L	.256	129	33	4	1	2	13	20	35	.360	.349
Throws Right	R	.163	147	24	4	0	3	13	7	57	.200	.252
Infante,Gregory	L	.231	78	18	2	0	2	8	9	18	.307	.333
Throws Right	R	.223	121	27	8	1	2	18	11	31	.295	.355
Iwakuma,Hisashi	L	.340	50	17	6	0	4	8	6	5	.411	.700
Throws Right	R	.156	64	10	1	0	3	5	6	11	.250	.313
Jackson,Edwin	L	.274	146	40	9	0	6	20	14	36	.333	.459
Throws Right	R	.293	157	46	9	1	14	31	15	24	.353	.631
Jackson,Luke	L	.217	83	18	5	0	0	11	11	11	.330	.277
Throws Right	R	.322	115	37	7	1	4	25	8	22	.365	.504
Jankowski,Jordan	L	.385	13	5	1	1	1	3	1	3	.429	.846
Throws Right	R	.286	7	2	0	0	2	4	1	2	.375	1.143
Jansen,Kenley	L	.236	123	29	5	0	4	12	4	45	.266	.374
Throws Right	R	.120	125	15	1	1	1	2	3	64	.147	.168
Jaye,Myles	L	.351	37	13	3	1	2	14	6	2	.447	.649
Throws Right	R	.263	19	5	1	0	0	2	4	2	.417	.316
Jeffress,Jeremy	L	.274	73	20	4	0	3	10	18	11	.419	.452
Throws Right	R	.288	184	53	11	0	7	33	16	40	.348	.462

Pitchers vs. Left-Handed and Right-Handed Batters

Pitcher	vs	Avg	AB	H	2B	3B	HR	RBI	BB	SO	OBP	Slg
Jennings,Dan	L	.213	108	23	1	0	3	12	18	26	.323	.306
Throws Left	R	.240	125	30	3	0	5	15	13	25	.317	.384
Jimenez,Joe	L	.206	34	7	2	0	1	9	4	6	.282	.353
Throws Right	R	.453	53	24	5	0	3	13	5	11	.517	.717
Jimenez,Ubaldo	L	.295	271	80	18	3	20	54	29	70	.366	.605
Throws Right	R	.288	309	89	21	1	13	49	29	69	.352	.489
Johnson,Brian	L	.154	13	2	0	0	0	0	0	3	.154	.154
Throws Left	R	.300	100	30	8	0	5	13	8	18	.352	.530
Johnson,Jim	L	.278	108	30	5	0	5	15	12	34	.350	.463
Throws Right	R	.244	119	29	4	0	3	18	13	27	.316	.353
Jones,Nate	L	.174	23	4	1	0	0	1	4	9	.296	.217
Throws Right	R	.278	18	5	1	0	1	3	2	6	.381	.500
Jorge,Felix	L	.556	9	5	0	0	2	3	0	0	.556	1.222
Throws Right	R	.360	25	9	2	1	2	5	2	4	.407	.760
Junis,Jakob	L	.278	194	54	10	1	7	22	14	38	.335	.448
Throws Right	R	.250	188	47	8	1	8	25	11	42	.309	.431
Kahnle,Tommy	L	.315	92	29	5	0	0	10	7	32	.360	.370
Throws Right	R	.171	140	24	3	1	4	17	10	64	.232	.293
Karns,Nathan	L	.250	68	17	2	1	3	5	12	21	.363	.441
Throws Right	R	.229	105	24	3	1	6	14	1	30	.250	.448
Kela,Keone	L	.170	53	9	2	0	3	7	7	19	.267	.377
Throws Right	R	.113	80	9	0	0	1	3	10	32	.220	.150
Kelley,Shawn	L	.196	46	9	1	0	4	7	7	13	.302	.478
Throws Right	R	.317	63	20	2	0	8	16	4	12	.368	.730
Kelly,Joe	L	.222	72	16	1	0	1	8	20	22	.394	.278
Throws Right	R	.191	136	26	6	0	2	14	7	30	.229	.279
Kendrick,Kyle	L	.538	13	7	2	0	0	4	1	1	.571	.692
Throws Right	R	.379	29	11	2	0	1	5	2	2	.419	.552
Kennedy,Ian	L	.236	275	65	13	2	18	49	34	57	.324	.495
Throws Right	R	.254	307	78	18	1	16	44	27	74	.316	.476
Kershaw,Clayton	L	.248	133	33	3	2	7	12	5	36	.275	.459
Throws Left	R	.203	508	103	17	0	16	36	25	166	.239	.331
Keuchel,Dallas	L	.145	110	16	2	0	3	9	5	36	.190	.245
Throws Left	R	.236	423	100	16	0	12	35	42	89	.307	.359
Kimbrel,Craig	L	.178	107	19	3	0	4	7	8	60	.254	.318
Throws Right	R	.109	128	14	3	0	2	3	6	66	.156	.180
Kintzler,Brandon	L	.195	128	25	3	1	2	8	10	16	.254	.281
Throws Right	R	.297	138	41	5	0	3	19	6	23	.336	.399
Kittredge,Andrew	L	.200	20	4	1	0	1	2	4	6	.333	.400
Throws Right	R	.231	39	9	2	0	1	2	2	8	.268	.359
Kluber,Corey	L	.200	340	68	11	0	10	22	22	115	.255	.321
Throws Right	R	.186	392	73	20	0	11	29	14	150	.218	.321
Knebel,Corey	L	.156	135	21	3	0	2	5	23	61	.288	.222
Throws Right	R	.205	132	27	5	0	4	12	17	65	.295	.333
Koehler,Tom	L	.289	121	35	6	0	9	32	24	24	.427	.562
Throws Right	R	.287	167	48	7	1	7	22	11	38	.337	.467
Kolarek,Adam	L	.364	11	4	0	0	0	1	0	1	.500	.364
Throws Left	R	.250	20	5	2	0	2	6	4	3	.400	.650
Kontos,George	L	.250	88	22	6	0	3	12	14	21	.353	.420
Throws Right	R	.238	164	39	10	0	6	25	6	49	.263	.409
Krol,Ian	L	.291	79	23	2	1	3	17	9	18	.367	.456
Throws Left	R	.248	109	27	7	0	5	19	12	26	.339	.450
Kuhl,Chad	L	.285	284	81	26	4	10	44	41	74	.383	.511
Throws Right	R	.253	308	78	15	1	7	29	31	68	.322	.377
Labourt,Jairo	L	.400	5	2	1	0	0	1	2	1	.571	.600
Throws Left	R	.133	15	2	0	0	0	1	5	3	.333	.133
Lackey,John	L	.276	315	87	16	1	20	46	31	59	.341	.524
Throws Right	R	.230	339	78	14	1	16	42	22	90	.293	.419
Lamet,Dinelson	L	.263	213	56	17	2	10	33	35	61	.365	.502
Throws Right	R	.155	206	32	5	0	8	20	19	78	.241	.296
Latos,Mat	L	.350	20	7	2	0	3	5	3	3	.435	.900
Throws Right	R	.293	41	12	4	0	2	6	5	7	.383	.537
Law,Derek	L	.323	62	20	1	1	4	11	7	11	.403	.565
Throws Right	R	.291	86	25	7	0	1	14	7	24	.340	.407
Lawrence,Casey	L	.392	97	38	3	1	6	23	16	12	.474	.629
Throws Right	R	.283	138	39	6	0	5	18	9	40	.329	.435
Layne,Tommy	L	.304	23	7	2	0	0	5	3	2	.407	.391
Throws Left	R	.290	31	9	1	1	1	4	5	7	.389	.484
Leake,Mike	L	.288	354	102	23	1	10	51	24	49	.342	.444
Throws Right	R	.268	370	99	19	1	10	36	13	81	.295	.405
LeBlanc,Wade	L	.295	88	26	9	0	3	10	4	15	.333	.500
Throws Left	R	.217	175	38	7	1	7	24	13	39	.270	.389
Leclerc,Jose	L	.203	64	13	4	0	2	7	10	16	.329	.359
Throws Right	R	.108	93	10	1	0	2	9	30	44	.331	.183
Lee,Zach	L	.286	14	4	2	0	0	2	2	3	.353	.429
Throws Right	R	.222	18	4	0	0	1	2	6	3	.417	.389

Pitcher	vs	Avg	AB	H	2B	3B	HR	RBI	BB	SO	OBP	Slg
Leiter,Mark	L	.257	167	43	9	1	10	27	13	37	.313	.503
Throws Right	R	.251	187	47	6	1	8	25	18	47	.335	.422
Leon,Arcenio	L	.286	7	2	0	0	0	3	2	0	.400	.286
Throws Right	R	.294	17	5	2	0	0	4	4	2	.429	.412
Leone,Dominic	L	.183	82	15	4	1	3	7	9	28	.261	.366
Throws Right	R	.211	171	36	12	2	3	19	14	53	.267	.357
Lester,Jon	L	.205	161	33	7	0	4	18	5	58	.231	.323
Throws Left	R	.275	530	146	27	3	22	74	55	122	.346	.462
Lewicki,Artie	L	.391	23	9	1	0	1	6	3	3	.462	.565
Throws Right	R	.400	25	10	0	0	0	0	1	3	.423	.400
Lindblom,Josh	L	.364	22	8	1	0	0	3	1	3	.391	.409
Throws Right	R	.385	26	10	2	0	0	6	2	7	.429	.462
Liriano,Francisco	L	.247	93	23	5	1	1	16	5	22	.300	.355
Throws Left	R	.289	284	82	22	2	10	42	48	63	.392	.486
Lively,Ben	L	.286	168	48	10	2	8	21	17	19	.360	.512
Throws Right	R	.251	167	42	17	1	5	23	7	33	.298	.455
Lloyd,Kyle	L	.300	10	3	2	0	0	1	2	1	.417	.500
Throws Right	R	.375	8	3	0	0	1	2	0	1	.375	.750
Locke,Jeff	L	.313	32	10	2	0	2	8	4	4	.378	.563
Throws Left	R	.311	103	32	4	3	2	20	11	22	.374	.466
Logan,Boone	L	.250	48	12	2	0	1	6	7	16	.357	.354
Throws Left	R	.250	32	8	0	0	1	4	2	12	.294	.344
Lopez,Reynaldo	L	.269	93	25	3	0	6	18	7	11	.314	.495
Throws Right	R	.247	97	24	3	3	1	7	7	19	.305	.371
Lorenzen,Michael	L	.246	142	35	7	1	6	28	19	33	.333	.437
Throws Right	R	.242	178	43	5	0	3	16	15	47	.315	.320
Loup,Aaron	L	.280	93	26	5	0	1	9	8	27	.356	.366
Throws Left	R	.250	132	33	5	0	3	16	21	37	.365	.356
Lucas,Josh	L	.333	9	3	0	0	1	3	3	2	.538	.667
Throws Right	R	.222	18	4	0	1	1	3	1	5	.263	.500
Lugo,Seth	L	.293	215	63	12	2	5	24	15	42	.335	.437
Throws Right	R	.273	187	51	10	0	8	25	10	43	.313	.455
Lyles,Jordan	L	.360	136	49	11	0	8	32	12	22	.412	.618
Throws Right	R	.296	159	47	9	2	8	30	10	33	.351	.528
Lynn,Lance	L	.245	326	80	16	2	17	41	53	58	.354	.463
Throws Right	R	.203	350	71	5	5	10	29	25	95	.269	.331
Lyons,Tyler	L	.178	73	13	5	0	1	6	8	22	.286	.288
Throws Left	R	.224	116	26	5	0	2	8	12	46	.311	.319
Machado,Andres	L	.333	9	3	0	1	0	4	1	0	.400	.556
Throws Right	R	.583	12	7	0	0	2	4	2	1	.643	1.083
Machi,Jean	L	.300	10	3	1	0	0	0	2	0	.417	.400
Throws Right	R	.250	16	4	0	0	1	4	2	4	.316	.438
Maddox,Austin	L	.280	25	7	1	0	1	1	0	5	.280	.440
Throws Right	R	.150	40	6	0	0	0	0	2	9	.190	.150
Madson,Ryan	L	.204	98	20	3	0	1	8	3	35	.240	.265
Throws Right	R	.171	105	18	5	0	1	6	6	32	.230	.248
Maeda,Kenta	L	.263	251	66	13	0	12	32	20	49	.322	.458
Throws Right	R	.214	257	55	13	1	10	33	14	91	.258	.389
Mahle,Tyler	L	.286	21	6	3	0	0	5	7	3	.464	.429
Throws Right	R	.241	54	13	1	0	0	1	4	11	.339	.259
Manaea,Sean	L	.227	132	30	5	0	2	17	6	25	.283	.311
Throws Left	R	.279	491	137	30	5	16	61	49	115	.350	.458
Maness,Seth	L	.333	18	6	0	0	2	3	1	3	.368	.667
Throws Right	R	.417	24	10	1	0	1	3	1	1	.423	.583
Maples,Dillon	L	.250	8	2	0	0	0	2	2	5	.400	.250
Throws Right	R	.308	13	4	2	0	0	1	4	6	.471	.462
Marinez,Jhan	L	.280	93	26	8	1	1	11	14	17	.380	.419
Throws Right	R	.288	132	38	11	0	5	23	12	28	.371	.485
Marquez,German	L	.280	314	88	15	5	6	29	27	63	.340	.417
Throws Right	R	.269	320	86	22	2	19	50	22	84	.325	.528
Marshall,Evan	L	.467	15	7	3	0	1	7	3	3	.556	.867
Throws Right	R	.278	18	5	0	0	0	5	2	1	.350	.278
Martes,Francis	L	.253	95	24	4	0	3	11	15	27	.372	.389
Throws Right	R	.239	113	27	6	1	4	18	16	42	.353	.416
Martinez,Carlos	L	.262	374	98	21	2	14	38	44	90	.342	.441
Throws Right	R	.204	398	81	13	2	13	43	27	127	.264	.344
Martinez,Nick	L	.284	194	55	12	2	9	35	19	30	.347	.505
Throws Right	R	.275	251	69	11	0	17	35	9	37	.304	.522
Maton,Phil	L	.300	70	21	3	0	5	13	6	15	.355	.557
Throws Right	R	.211	95	20	1	1	5	14	8	31	.279	.400
Matz,Steven	L	.295	61	18	5	0	0	2	8	9	.386	.377
Throws Left	R	.308	211	65	9	2	12	41	11	39	.347	.540
Maurer,Brandon	L	.271	107	29	10	0	2	13	10	30	.336	.421
Throws Right	R	.319	138	44	7	3	6	29	9	29	.358	.543
Mayers,Mike	L	.500	10	5	2	0	2	6	1	0	.462	1.300
Throws Right	R	.333	9	3	2	0	0	2	3	3	.500	.556

Pitchers vs. Left-Handed and Right-Handed Batters

Pitcher	vs	Avg	AB	H	2B	3B	HR	RBI	BB	SO	OBP	Slg
Mayza,Tim	L	.206	34	7	1	0	0	1	3	12	.270	.235
Throws Left	R	.415	41	17	5	0	3	10	1	15	.429	.756
Mazzoni,Cory	L	.360	25	9	1	0	2	4	3	3	.429	.640
Throws Right	R	.500	16	8	0	0	3	13	1	1	.556	1.063
McAllister,Zach	L	.293	99	29	4	0	5	13	10	23	.358	.485
Throws Right	R	.189	127	24	0	1	3	12	11	43	.259	.276
McCarthy,Brandon	L	.254	185	47	10	1	1	21	11	38	.303	.335
Throws Right	R	.259	162	42	5	1	4	18	16	34	.324	.377
McCarthy,Kevin	L	.314	70	22	2	0	3	9	6	10	.368	.471
Throws Right	R	.252	111	28	5	0	1	13	7	17	.294	.324
McCullers Jr.,Lance	L	.231	199	46	10	0	2	18	13	60	.294	.312
Throws Right	R	.264	258	68	18	2	6	32	27	72	.346	.419
McFarland,T.J.	L	.222	72	16	2	0	1	8	3	16	.256	.292
Throws Left	R	.338	145	49	9	0	3	24	14	13	.398	.462
McGee,Jake	L	.260	77	20	3	0	2	13	5	24	.313	.377
Throws Left	R	.203	133	27	8	1	2	10	11	34	.262	.323
McGowan,Dustin	L	.281	121	34	4	0	4	20	13	17	.346	.413
Throws Right	R	.249	173	43	12	1	9	31	14	47	.311	.486
McGowan,Kevin	L	.222	18	4	1	0	0	1	4	3	.364	.278
Throws Right	R	.250	16	4	1	0	2	6	2	5	.333	.688
McGrath,Kyle	L	.167	24	4	0	0	0	4	3	3	.250	.167
Throws Left	R	.233	43	10	2	0	2	8	3	13	.277	.419
McGuire,Deck	L	.185	27	5	2	0	0	0	2	5	.241	.259
Throws Right	R	.192	26	5	0	0	1	4	0	6	.222	.308
McHugh,Collin	L	.295	112	33	11	0	2	10	10	23	.363	.446
Throws Right	R	.218	133	29	10	0	5	14	10	39	.288	.406
Mejia,Adalberto	L	.275	69	19	2	0	4	10	5	18	.333	.478
Throws Left	R	.283	322	91	26	2	9	36	39	67	.364	.460
Melancon,Mark	L	.246	65	16	3	1	2	8	5	13	.300	.415
Throws Right	R	.362	58	21	5	0	1	8	1	16	.383	.500
Mendez,Yohander	L	.188	16	3	1	0	0	2	1	5	.278	.250
Throws Left	R	.313	32	10	3	0	3	6	2	2	.353	.688
Mengden,Daniel	L	.268	82	22	6	0	3	8	2	18	.282	.451
Throws Right	R	.187	75	14	0	0	3	6	7	11	.253	.307
Merritt,Ryan	L	.455	22	10	3	0	0	1	0	0	.455	.591
Throws Left	R	.258	62	16	2	0	0	5	4	7	.299	.290
Meyer,Alex	L	.228	123	28	7	0	4	13	23	38	.356	.382
Throws Right	R	.165	121	20	6	0	2	10	19	37	.289	.264
Middleton,Keynan	L	.268	97	26	5	0	3	13	8	28	.321	.412
Throws Right	R	.264	129	34	7	1	8	22	10	35	.314	.519
Miley,Wade	L	.230	100	23	3	1	1	10	18	25	.353	.310
Throws Left	R	.298	524	156	27	1	24	86	75	117	.385	.490
Miller,Andrew	L	.164	61	10	0	0	1	3	9	22	.268	.213
Throws Left	R	.136	154	21	4	0	2	11	12	73	.222	.201
Miller,Shelby	L	.280	50	14	5	0	1	6	10	7	.400	.440
Throws Right	R	.162	37	6	2	0	0	2	2	13	.205	.216
Milner,Hoby	L	.159	63	10	2	0	0	6	6	12	.274	.190
Throws Left	R	.377	53	20	5	0	2	5	10	10	.469	.585
Milone,Tommy	L	.212	52	11	1	2	2	9	2	11	.241	.423
Throws Left	R	.353	153	54	10	0	13	29	12	27	.400	.673
Minaya,Juan	L	.194	62	12	1	0	5	9	9	22	.315	.452
Throws Right	R	.268	97	26	6	1	2	13	11	29	.351	.412
Minor,Mike	L	.163	92	15	3	0	0	7	8	36	.228	.196
Throws Left	R	.223	188	42	13	1	5	24	14	52	.281	.383
Minter,A.J.	L	.190	21	4	0	0	0	1	1	10	.227	.190
Throws Left	R	.243	37	9	2	1	1	4	1	16	.263	.432
Miranda,Ariel	L	.241	116	28	6	0	5	15	10	23	.313	.422
Throws Left	R	.231	484	112	21	3	32	70	53	114	.307	.486
Mitchell,Bryan	L	.273	44	12	4	0	1	8	6	7	.360	.432
Throws Right	R	.316	95	30	6	0	1	16	7	10	.369	.411
Moll,Sam	L	.375	24	9	1	1	0	2	2	6	.423	.500
Throws Left	R	.500	8	4	1	0	2	2	1	1	.556	1.375
Montas,Frankie	L	.364	55	20	2	0	7	20	12	11	.485	.782
Throws Right	R	.257	74	19	2	0	3	9	8	25	.345	.405
Montero,Rafael	L	.300	233	70	14	0	5	25	31	49	.383	.425
Throws Right	R	.311	228	71	11	0	7	37	36	65	.404	.452
Montgomery,Jordan	L	.195	87	17	2	0	5	18	8	16	.271	.391
Throws Left	R	.244	505	123	18	3	16	49	43	128	.301	.386
Montgomery,Mike	L	.230	135	31	5	0	3	8	11	24	.297	.333
Throws Left	R	.215	335	72	13	0	7	32	44	76	.315	.316
Moore,Andrew	L	.265	102	27	6	0	8	16	3	12	.280	.559
Throws Right	R	.258	128	33	7	0	6	19	5	19	.287	.453
Moore,Matt	L	.363	171	62	11	4	8	29	18	33	.433	.614
Throws Left	R	.258	535	138	33	5	19	69	49	115	.322	.445
Moreno,Diego	L	.200	10	2	0	0	1	1	1	2	.273	.500
Throws Right	R	.308	13	4	2	0	0	4	1	4	.400	.462
Morgan,Adam	L	.193	88	17	3	1	3	7	6	39	.245	.352
Throws Left	R	.276	123	34	4	1	7	17	12	24	.341	.496
Morin,Mike	L	.432	37	16	2	1	2	13	3	6	.463	.703
Throws Right	R	.277	47	13	3	0	1	5	2	10	.314	.404
Moronta,Reyes	L	.143	7	1	0	0	0	0	2	3	.333	.143
Throws Right	R	.263	19	5	0	0	1	1	1	8	.300	.421
Morris,Akeel	L	.200	15	3	1	0	0	1	1	5	.250	.267
Throws Right	R	.231	13	3	2	0	0	2	3	4	.375	.385
Morris,Bryan	L	.433	30	13	1	1	0	6	7	3	.526	.533
Throws Right	R	.224	49	11	2	0	1	12	4	12	.283	.327
Morrow,Brandon	L	.125	56	7	0	0	0	3	4	19	.183	.125
Throws Right	R	.231	104	24	3	0	0	4	5	31	.273	.260
Morton,Charlie	L	.175	252	44	13	0	6	21	24	94	.263	.298
Throws Right	R	.273	297	81	26	3	8	38	26	69	.343	.461
Motte,Jason	L	.188	48	9	1	0	2	11	8	5	.322	.333
Throws Right	R	.204	93	19	7	0	4	13	12	22	.299	.409
Moya,Gabriel	L	.222	9	2	0	0	1	1	0	3	.222	.556
Throws Left	R	.200	15	3	0	0	1	1	2	2	.294	.400
Moylan,Peter	L	.316	38	12	2	0	2	9	9	7	.460	.526
Throws Right	R	.161	174	28	5	1	2	26	16	39	.244	.236
Mujica,Edward	L	.500	8	4	1	0	1	2	0	1	.500	1.000
Throws Right	R	.350	20	7	2	0	3	7	0	6	.318	.900
Musgrove,Joe	L	.268	194	52	8	3	7	23	12	56	.314	.448
Throws Right	R	.285	228	65	14	0	11	31	16	42	.337	.491
Neal,Zach	L	.258	31	8	1	0	2	7	1	5	.273	.484
Throws Right	R	.344	32	11	1	2	3	7	0	5	.344	.781
Nelson,Jimmy	L	.246	317	78	16	0	10	31	31	107	.319	.391
Throws Right	R	.267	348	93	12	1	6	35	17	92	.311	.359
Neris,Hector	L	.270	148	40	8	0	3	10	14	42	.331	.385
Throws Right	R	.204	137	28	2	1	6	14	12	44	.295	.365
Neshek,Pat	L	.230	87	20	8	0	1	7	4	24	.258	.356
Throws Right	R	.201	139	28	4	0	2	6	2	45	.213	.273
Neverauskas,Dovydas	L	.262	42	11	1	1	1	3	4	7	.326	.405
Throws Right	R	.245	53	13	2	0	3	5	4	10	.310	.453
Newcomb,Sean	L	.261	111	29	4	4	1	10	12	32	.357	.396
Throws Left	R	.259	274	71	17	1	9	36	45	76	.363	.427
Nicasio,Juan	L	.208	120	25	5	1	1	6	6	44	.252	.292
Throws Right	R	.224	147	33	9	0	4	14	14	28	.296	.367
Nicolino,Justin	L	.397	58	23	4	0	2	10	2	5	.417	.569
Throws Left	R	.295	146	43	8	2	6	27	18	21	.373	.500
Nola,Aaron	L	.256	301	77	16	4	8	31	31	76	.325	.415
Throws Right	R	.227	339	77	13	0	10	34	18	108	.270	.354
Nolasco,Ricky	L	.274	354	97	24	0	13	39	32	56	.338	.452
Throws Right	R	.298	362	108	28	1	22	55	26	87	.344	.564
Norris,Bud	L	.188	96	18	3	0	0	4	18	35	.322	.219
Throws Right	R	.270	141	38	3	1	8	26	9	39	.322	.475
Norris,Daniel	L	.287	94	27	6	1	6	19	11	21	.364	.564
Throws Left	R	.297	313	93	21	4	6	40	33	65	.366	.447
Nova,Ivan	L	.309	343	106	21	1	16	44	16	45	.342	.516
Throws Right	R	.249	389	97	19	4	13	46	20	86	.294	.419
Nuno,Vidal	L	.357	28	10	2	0	2	8	5	9	.455	.643
Throws Left	R	.333	39	13	6	0	5	10	5	4	.409	.872
Oberg,Scott	L	.293	92	27	10	0	1	11	12	18	.381	.435
Throws Right	R	.299	144	43	7	2	3	22	12	37	.352	.438
O'Day,Darren	L	.183	82	15	2	0	5	13	12	29	.287	.390
Throws Right	R	.200	130	26	0	1	3	13	12	47	.281	.285
Odorizzi,Jake	L	.210	224	47	10	0	11	25	24	52	.285	.402
Throws Right	R	.228	307	70	11	2	19	50	37	75	.310	.463
O'Flaherty,Eric	L	.189	37	7	2	0	1	6	1	10	.205	.324
Throws Left	R	.371	35	13	6	0	3	11	8	5	.488	.800
O'Grady,Chris	L	.167	48	8	3	0	0	2	6	15	.273	.229
Throws Left	R	.333	75	25	4	2	4	11	12	15	.420	.600
Oh,Seung Hwan	L	.333	99	33	6	0	7	18	8	17	.400	.606
Throws Right	R	.250	140	35	5	1	3	21	7	37	.278	.364
Okert,Steven	L	.263	57	15	3	1	2	11	4	13	.328	.456
Throws Left	R	.214	42	9	4	0	1	6	7	9	.333	.381
Olson,Tyler	L	.162	37	6	2	0	0	2	4	11	.244	.216
Throws Left	R	.219	32	7	0	0	0	0	2	7	.286	.219
Osich,Josh	L	.247	73	18	3	0	4	14	15	23	.375	.452
Throws Left	R	.303	99	30	5	1	3	10	12	20	.384	.465
Osuna,Roberto	L	.204	103	21	2	0	1	11	5	36	.252	.252
Throws Right	R	.191	131	25	5	1	2	14	4	47	.219	.290
Otero,Dan	L	.341	88	30	4	0	3	10	6	13	.383	.489
Throws Right	R	.231	143	33	4	1	3	16	3	25	.245	.336
Ottavino,Adam	L	.209	67	14	2	0	7	13	11	20	.346	.552
Throws Right	R	.262	130	34	5	1	1	11	28	43	.389	.338

Pitchers vs. Left-Handed and Right-Handed Batters

Pitcher	vs	Avg	AB	H	2B	3B	HR	RBI	BB	SO	OBP	Slg
Overton,Dillon	L	.304	23	7	0	0	1	4	0	4	.292	.435
Throws Left	R	.315	73	23	7	0	5	15	4	7	.354	.616
Pagan,Emilio	L	.258	62	16	3	1	4	11	3	19	.292	.532
Throws Right	R	.189	122	23	2	0	3	9	5	37	.223	.279
Paredes,Eduardo	L	.226	31	7	1	0	1	5	4	6	.324	.355
Throws Right	R	.280	50	14	4	0	1	5	2	11	.333	.420
Paredes,Edward	L	.273	22	6	0	0	1	3	0	8	.273	.409
Throws Left	R	.222	9	2	0	0	0	0	0	3	.222	.222
Parker,Blake	L	.168	113	19	3	0	3	12	6	36	.208	.274
Throws Right	R	.176	119	21	6	0	4	13	10	50	.241	.328
Paulino,David	L	.317	60	19	4	0	2	8	4	19	.359	.483
Throws Right	R	.283	60	17	5	0	6	10	3	15	.317	.667
Paxton,James	L	.198	86	17	2	0	0	3	4	22	.242	.221
Throws Left	R	.229	420	96	22	0	9	41	33	134	.285	.345
Pazos,James	L	.218	78	17	1	0	1	10	6	28	.292	.269
Throws Left	R	.266	128	34	7	0	6	24	18	37	.360	.461
Peacock,Brad	L	.249	213	53	10	1	8	30	28	70	.342	.418
Throws Right	R	.173	272	47	12	1	2	10	29	91	.255	.246
Pelfrey,Mike	L	.259	220	57	12	2	15	39	33	38	.367	.536
Throws Right	R	.279	251	70	10	1	10	39	29	41	.362	.446
Pena,Felix	L	.226	62	14	3	0	3	7	14	18	.377	.419
Throws Right	R	.288	73	21	7	0	5	13	4	19	.333	.589
Peralta,Wandy	L	.214	98	21	5	0	2	9	13	25	.313	.327
Throws Left	R	.237	135	32	7	0	6	25	11	32	.289	.422
Peralta,Wily	L	.343	108	37	13	0	5	17	16	25	.429	.602
Throws Right	R	.290	124	36	12	0	5	23	16	27	.366	.508
Perdomo,Luis	L	.305	305	93	23	0	5	34	33	43	.377	.430
Throws Right	R	.267	333	89	16	0	12	46	32	75	.340	.423
Perez,Martin	L	.264	148	39	5	1	2	10	8	35	.314	.351
Throws Left	R	.310	587	182	34	1	21	82	55	80	.370	.479
Perez,Oliver	L	.227	66	15	4	1	1	7	5	20	.301	.364
Throws Left	R	.283	60	17	1	2	3	10	7	19	.371	.517
Perkins,Glen	L	.375	8	3	0	0	0	1	2	1	.545	.375
Throws Left	R	.294	17	5	1	2	0	3	3	1	.435	.588
Peters,Dillon	L	.423	26	11	2	0	0	3	5	3	.531	.500
Throws Left	R	.228	92	21	3	0	3	13	14	24	.336	.359
Petit,Yusmeiro	L	.237	139	33	5	0	3	5	13	32	.307	.338
Throws Right	R	.186	194	36	6	0	6	20	5	69	.205	.309
Petricka,Jake	L	.364	44	16	2	0	2	12	1	9	.383	.545
Throws Right	R	.329	70	23	6	0	4	14	5	17	.373	.586
Phelps,David	L	.278	108	30	5	0	4	16	11	31	.342	.435
Throws Right	R	.212	99	21	2	1	1	8	15	31	.319	.283
Pill,Tyler	L	.303	33	10	4	1	1	6	6	7	.400	.576
Throws Right	R	.245	49	12	1	0	2	9	4	9	.321	.388
Pineda,Michael	L	.253	166	42	6	0	9	23	12	44	.308	.452
Throws Right	R	.281	217	61	8	0	11	24	9	48	.307	.470
Pinto,Ricardo	L	.339	56	19	3	0	4	13	10	10	.426	.607
Throws Right	R	.299	67	20	3	1	3	15	7	15	.373	.507
Pivetta,Nick	L	.253	249	63	11	2	5	35	30	72	.327	.373
Throws Right	R	.308	263	81	16	1	20	49	27	68	.378	.605
Pomeranz,Drew	L	.293	147	43	4	2	3	12	15	47	.373	.408
Throws Left	R	.240	512	123	23	1	16	46	54	127	.309	.383
Porcello,Rick	L	.286	392	112	27	1	21	57	29	88	.336	.520
Throws Right	R	.287	432	124	27	2	17	52	19	93	.321	.477
Pounders,Brooks	L	.400	20	8	1	1	2	7	4	3	.500	.850
Throws Right	R	.333	27	9	2	0	2	6	1	9	.379	.630
Povse,Max	L	.400	10	4	1	0	0	0	0	1	.400	.500
Throws Right	R	.500	10	5	1	0	1	3	1	1	.545	.900
Pressly,Ryan	L	.281	89	25	3	0	4	15	11	22	.366	.449
Throws Right	R	.196	138	27	6	0	6	23	8	39	.248	.370
Price,David	L	.206	63	13	1	0	0	5	4	13	.271	.222
Throws Left	R	.232	224	52	13	0	8	24	20	63	.300	.397
Pruitt,Austin	L	.250	152	38	10	0	4	16	9	31	.309	.395
Throws Right	R	.340	191	65	13	2	7	32	13	35	.385	.539
Putnam,Zach	L	.167	12	2	1	0	0	0	1	4	.231	.250
Throws Right	R	.000	15	0	0	0	0	0	0	5	.000	.000
Quackenbush,Kevin	L	.239	46	11	1	0	2	9	7	7	.340	.391
Throws Right	R	.344	61	21	3	0	3	14	9	16	.431	.541
Qualls,Chad	L	.179	28	5	0	0	2	4	2	3	.233	.393
Throws Right	R	.316	38	12	3	1	1	4	3	8	.366	.526
Quintana,Jose	L	.222	153	34	9	2	1	13	5	44	.258	.327
Throws Left	R	.242	562	136	27	2	22	70	56	163	.318	.415
Ramirez,Carlos	L	.235	17	4	2	0	2	3	0	0	.235	.706
Throws Right	R	.054	37	2	0	0	1	2	3	14	.146	.135
Ramirez,Erasmo	L	.270	196	53	13	0	11	31	17	48	.324	.505
Throws Right	R	.233	301	70	18	0	11	31	14	61	.268	.402

Pitcher	vs	Avg	AB	H	2B	3B	HR	RBI	BB	SO	OBP	Slg
Ramirez,JC	L	.281	267	75	18	1	16	39	27	51	.355	.536
Throws Right	R	.254	291	74	8	0	5	24	22	54	.307	.333
Ramirez,Jose	L	.180	89	16	4	0	3	7	18	28	.321	.326
Throws Right	R	.220	132	29	6	0	6	19	11	28	.297	.402
Ramirez,Neil	L	.212	52	11	0	0	2	11	10	22	.328	.327
Throws Right	R	.316	76	24	5	0	4	20	11	22	.404	.539
Ramirez,Noe	L	.333	9	3	1	0	1	3	1	0	.400	.778
Throws Right	R	.086	35	3	0	0	1	2	4	14	.179	.171
Ramos,A.J.	L	.197	117	23	5	0	4	13	20	39	.314	.342
Throws Right	R	.252	103	26	1	2	3	14	14	33	.350	.388
Ramos,Edubray	L	.299	97	29	2	3	3	16	13	24	.382	.474
Throws Right	R	.219	128	28	5	0	1	7	15	51	.299	.281
Ravin,Josh	L	.167	24	4	0	0	2	8	5	2	.310	.417
Throws Right	R	.216	37	8	1	3	2	7	4	17	.310	.568
Ray,Robbie	L	.216	116	25	2	0	5	9	6	49	.260	.362
Throws Left	R	.195	466	91	16	2	18	42	65	169	.297	.354
Reed,Addison	L	.233	120	28	3	1	5	13	4	29	.262	.400
Throws Right	R	.222	167	37	9	0	6	21	11	47	.268	.383
Reed,Cody	L	.111	18	2	0	0	1	3	4	7	.273	.278
Throws Left	R	.214	42	9	4	0	2	7	15	10	.421	.452
Reininger,Zac	L	.263	19	5	2	0	2	9	3	3	.364	.684
Throws Right	R	.417	24	10	0	0	1	4	0	2	.400	.542
Rhame,Jacob	L	.313	16	5	2	0	1	3	3	6	.400	.625
Throws Right	R	.350	20	7	3	0	1	3	4	1	.458	.650
Richard,Clayton	L	.286	199	57	6	2	1	15	8	62	.324	.352
Throws Left	R	.315	581	183	42	6	23	92	51	89	.372	.527
Richards,Garrett	L	.188	48	9	3	0	1	2	1	13	.204	.313
Throws Right	R	.173	52	9	2	0	0	5	6	14	.259	.212
Rios,Yacksel	L	.258	31	8	1	1	2	4	3	9	.324	.548
Throws Right	R	.219	32	7	1	0	2	6	6	8	.342	.438
Rivero,Felipe	L	.082	85	7	1	0	0	3	5	38	.161	.094
Throws Left	R	.211	190	40	5	0	4	18	15	50	.271	.300
Roark,Tanner	L	.284	352	100	18	2	15	56	41	74	.362	.474
Throws Right	R	.223	349	78	13	2	8	43	23	92	.277	.341
Robertson,David	L	.140	107	15	1	0	3	5	9	50	.207	.234
Throws Right	R	.154	130	20	7	0	3	14	14	48	.250	.277
Robles,Hansel	L	.189	74	14	0	1	4	14	16	21	.333	.378
Throws Right	R	.246	134	33	6	1	6	34	13	39	.331	.440
Rodney,Fernando	L	.233	103	24	3	1	2	13	14	37	.322	.340
Throws Right	R	.165	97	16	3	0	1	13	12	28	.270	.227
Rodon,Carlos	L	.286	63	18	2	0	2	5	5	18	.333	.413
Throws Left	R	.234	197	46	12	0	10	25	26	58	.330	.447
Rodriguez,Eduardo	L	.284	102	29	4	2	3	9	9	30	.357	.451
Throws Left	R	.230	421	97	29	1	16	53	41	120	.300	.418
Rodriguez,Francisco	L	.340	53	18	6	0	6	21	4	13	.386	.792
Throws Right	R	.245	53	13	4	0	3	7	7	10	.344	.491
Rodriguez,Joely	L	.352	54	19	3	0	1	14	8	5	.470	.463
Throws Left	R	.300	60	18	6	0	3	17	7	13	.373	.550
Rodriguez,Ricardo	L	.188	16	3	1	0	1	3	2	3	.263	.438
Throws Right	R	.368	38	14	2	0	2	11	2	8	.415	.579
Rodriguez,Richard	L	.000	7	0	0	0	0	0	2	1	.222	.000
Throws Right	R	.600	20	12	3	0	4	9	1	2	.636	1.350
Roe,Chaz	L	.214	14	3	0	0	1	2	1	4	.313	.429
Throws Right	R	.167	24	4	1	0	0	2	4	9	.286	.208
Rogers,Taylor	L	.173	75	13	1	0	3	7	6	25	.253	.307
Throws Left	R	.287	136	39	7	0	3	10	15	24	.362	.404
Romano,Sal	L	.274	157	43	10	2	4	19	19	37	.354	.439
Throws Right	R	.276	174	48	17	0	5	24	18	36	.345	.460
Romero,Enny	L	.295	78	23	4	0	3	12	8	18	.371	.462
Throws Left	R	.230	139	32	6	1	4	14	15	47	.308	.374
Romo,Sergio	L	.236	55	13	3	0	2	6	7	14	.333	.400
Throws Right	R	.196	148	29	6	0	7	18	12	45	.255	.378
Rondon,Bruce	L	.433	30	13	2	1	1	8	7	7	.553	.667
Throws Right	R	.235	34	8	2	0	0	2	3	15	.289	.294
Rondon,Hector	L	.230	74	17	4	1	4	10	12	23	.337	.473
Throws Right	R	.234	141	33	5	0	6	23	8	46	.280	.397
Rosenthal,Trevor	L	.225	89	20	1	0	1	13	11	35	.308	.270
Throws Right	R	.195	87	17	0	1	2	4	9	41	.278	.287
Ross,Joe	L	.310	155	48	8	1	10	25	10	36	.355	.568
Throws Right	R	.284	141	40	9	0	6	17	10	32	.331	.475
Ross,Tyson	L	.237	97	23	6	0	3	20	18	17	.368	.392
Throws Right	R	.313	96	30	7	0	4	22	19	19	.442	.510
Ross Jr.,Robbie	L	.263	19	5	1	1	0	1	3	7	.364	.421
Throws Left	R	.389	18	7	0	0	0	4	2	2	.522	.389
Rosscup,Zac	L	.000	15	0	0	0	0	1	0	8	.000	.000
Throws Left	R	.563	16	9	1	0	2	6	0	2	.563	1.000

Pitchers vs. Left-Handed and Right-Handed Batters

Pitcher	vs	Avg	AB	H	2B	3B	HR	RBI	BB	SO	OBP	Slg
Rowley,Chris	L	.250	40	10	0	3	4	11	7	6	.362	.700
Throws Right	R	.359	39	14	2	0	0	2	3	5	.405	.410
Rucinski,Drew	L	.500	8	4	2	0	0	1	0	2	.500	.750
Throws Right	R	.462	13	6	0	0	2	5	2	3	.533	.923
Runzler,Dan	L	.333	9	3	1	0	0	2	0	2	.333	.444
Throws Left	R	.444	9	4	1	0	2	2	2	2	.545	1.222
Rusin,Chris	L	.268	123	33	4	1	3	13	7	32	.313	.390
Throws Left	R	.221	190	42	4	0	6	18	12	39	.271	.337
Ryan,Kyle	L	.444	9	4	1	0	0	4	3	1	.538	.556
Throws Left	R	.417	12	5	0	0	0	2	4	0	.563	.417
Ryu,Hyun-Jin	L	.326	129	42	9	0	8	20	10	26	.380	.581
Throws Left	R	.240	358	86	18	2	14	36	35	90	.311	.419
Rzepczynski,Marc	L	.253	75	19	3	0	1	7	6	18	.317	.333
Throws Left	R	.250	40	10	1	0	1	6	14	7	.444	.350
Sabathia,CC	L	.253	99	25	3	0	2	6	10	23	.339	.343
Throws Left	R	.244	467	114	17	3	19	52	40	97	.306	.415
Salas,Fernando	L	.263	80	21	4	0	2	13	11	19	.340	.388
Throws Right	R	.309	149	46	9	0	5	25	11	37	.348	.470
Salazar,Danny	L	.257	179	46	10	0	7	17	24	59	.350	.430
Throws Right	R	.230	209	48	9	0	7	26	20	86	.297	.373
Sale,Chris	L	.203	123	25	1	0	3	9	6	41	.246	.285
Throws Left	R	.209	671	140	33	3	21	62	37	267	.256	.361
Samardzija,Jeff	L	.252	425	107	21	9	19	58	22	115	.294	.478
Throws Right	R	.258	376	97	19	3	11	40	10	90	.279	.412
Sanchez,Aaron	L	.211	57	12	3	0	1	4	11	17	.338	.316
Throws Right	R	.337	89	30	4	0	5	17	9	7	.404	.551
Sanchez,Angel	L	.375	24	9	1	0	4	6	1	6	.400	.917
Throws Right	R	.250	28	7	2	0	1	5	0	4	.241	.429
Sanchez,Anibal	L	.284	222	63	11	1	11	36	14	53	.331	.491
Throws Right	R	.342	222	76	13	0	15	43	15	51	.386	.604
Santana,Edgar	L	.357	28	10	3	0	2	5	7	3	.486	.679
Throws Right	R	.154	39	6	3	0	0	2	5	17	.267	.231
Santana,Ervin	L	.215	363	78	10	2	16	34	21	61	.260	.386
Throws Right	R	.234	423	99	18	3	15	41	40	106	.308	.397
Santiago,Hector	L	.478	46	22	3	0	6	15	10	7	.586	.935
Throws Left	R	.211	228	48	3	0	9	25	21	44	.285	.342
Santos,Luis	L	.207	29	6	3	0	1	1	2	7	.258	.414
Throws Right	R	.257	35	9	2	0	3	8	2	9	.297	.571
Saupold,Warwick	L	.282	85	24	5	0	3	15	13	11	.380	.447
Throws Right	R	.258	155	40	4	0	6	27	18	33	.352	.400
Scahill,Rob	L	.333	39	13	3	0	2	7	5	4	.391	.564
Throws Right	R	.186	43	8	2	0	1	7	5	6	.314	.302
Scheppers,Tanner	L	.375	8	3	1	0	0	1	1	3	.444	.500
Throws Right	R	.222	9	2	1	0	0	0	2	2	.417	.333
Scherzer,Max	L	.215	372	80	18	0	16	30	38	110	.299	.392
Throws Right	R	.136	337	46	12	2	6	23	17	158	.187	.237
Schugel,A.J.	L	.250	44	11	2	1	1	8	9	5	.370	.409
Throws Right	R	.263	76	20	3	0	2	13	5	22	.309	.382
Scott,Robby	L	.121	66	8	1	1	3	8	8	19	.224	.303
Throws Left	R	.246	57	14	2	0	4	13	5	12	.323	.491
Scribner,Evan	L	.385	13	5	2	0	1	1	0	2	.385	.769
Throws Right	R	.400	20	8	1	0	2	6	0	4	.400	.750
Scribner,Troy	L	.184	38	7	1	0	4	6	7	8	.326	.526
Throws Right	R	.204	49	10	2	1	3	6	3	10	.264	.469
Senzatela,Antonio	L	.240	246	59	14	2	10	28	26	46	.310	.435
Throws Right	R	.267	258	69	14	3	8	43	21	56	.329	.438
Severino,Luis	L	.221	326	72	18	0	12	33	26	104	.281	.387
Throws Right	R	.198	394	78	12	0	9	33	25	126	.253	.297
Sewald,Paul	L	.290	93	27	5	0	3	15	14	24	.385	.441
Throws Right	R	.204	152	31	10	1	5	20	7	45	.245	.382
Shackelford,Kevin	L	.275	51	14	0	0	3	5	9	19	.383	.451
Throws Right	R	.239	67	16	2	0	3	9	4	19	.307	.403
Shaw,Bryan	L	.234	107	25	5	1	0	5	8	27	.287	.299
Throws Right	R	.254	181	46	7	1	5	28	14	46	.306	.387
Sherfy,Jimmie	L	.091	11	1	0	0	0	0	1	4	.167	.091
Throws Right	R	.167	24	4	3	0	0	0	1	5	.200	.292
Sherriff,Ryan	L	.080	25	2	0	0	0	1	0	7	.115	.080
Throws Left	R	.367	30	11	2	0	2	5	4	8	.441	.633
Shields,James	L	.279	222	62	8	1	17	35	31	43	.375	.554
Throws Right	R	.228	237	54	14	2	10	32	22	60	.293	.430
Shipley,Braden	L	.250	52	13	4	1	1	9	3	7	.281	.423
Throws Right	R	.353	51	18	5	0	4	10	12	11	.484	.686
Shoemaker,Matt	L	.275	138	38	11	0	6	20	6	26	.306	.486
Throws Right	R	.229	153	35	2	2	9	18	22	43	.339	.444
Shreve,Chasen	L	.164	61	10	3	0	1	7	6	26	.235	.262
Throws Left	R	.227	110	25	8	0	7	16	19	32	.338	.491

Pitcher	vs	Avg	AB	H	2B	3B	HR	RBI	BB	SO	OBP	Slg
Siegrist,Kevin	L	.250	60	15	5	1	2	10	10	19	.361	.467
Throws Left	R	.273	88	24	5	0	3	12	12	24	.360	.432
Simmons,Shae	L	.000	9	0	0	0	0	1	4	3	.286	.000
Throws Right	R	.267	15	4	1	0	1	2	0	5	.250	.533
Sims,Luke	L	.305	95	29	11	1	2	11	15	18	.412	.505
Throws Right	R	.276	127	35	6	1	7	21	8	26	.324	.504
Sipp,Tony	L	.247	73	18	3	2	5	15	5	18	.304	.548
Throws Left	R	.247	73	18	7	0	3	9	11	21	.341	.466
Skaggs,Tyler	L	.267	75	20	5	0	2	8	5	16	.321	.413
Throws Left	R	.276	254	70	14	0	11	32	23	60	.345	.461
Skoglund,Eric	L	.444	9	4	0	0	0	2	1	2	.455	.444
Throws Left	R	.366	71	26	10	0	2	17	11	12	.451	.592
Slegers,Aaron	L	.194	31	6	2	0	2	6	2	6	.242	.452
Throws Right	R	.231	26	6	0	0	1	3	4	3	.333	.346
Smith,Caleb	L	.360	25	9	3	0	0	5	3	6	.414	.480
Throws Left	R	.240	50	12	1	0	4	8	7	12	.333	.500
Smith,Carson	L	.167	6	1	0	0	0	0	0	2	.167	.167
Throws Right	R	.316	19	6	0	0	0	2	2	5	.381	.316
Smith,Chris	L	.286	7	2	2	0	0	0	0	0	.286	.571
Throws Right	R	.333	15	5	1	1	1	3	1	1	.375	.733
Smith,Chris	L	.269	93	25	5	0	2	17	15	11	.367	.387
Throws Right	R	.267	131	35	9	1	14	26	7	20	.305	.672
Smith,Joe	L	.246	69	17	3	0	2	10	8	24	.325	.377
Throws Right	R	.220	132	29	6	0	2	8	2	47	.235	.311
Smith,Josh	L	.281	57	16	7	0	2	9	5	8	.339	.509
Throws Right	R	.244	78	19	9	2	1	14	10	17	.326	.449
Smoker,Josh	L	.281	114	32	11	0	4	23	14	34	.366	.482
Throws Left	R	.283	113	32	5	0	6	18	18	34	.381	.487
Snell,Blake	L	.182	66	12	3	0	0	3	8	18	.267	.227
Throws Left	R	.243	416	101	23	2	15	48	51	101	.325	.416
Socolovich,Miguel	L	.406	32	13	5	0	2	6	2	3	.472	.750
Throws Right	R	.292	48	14	6	0	2	11	2	11	.314	.542
Solis,Sammy	L	.227	44	10	3	0	1	6	3	8	.277	.364
Throws Left	R	.218	55	12	2	0	3	6	10	20	.338	.418
Soria,Joakim	L	.269	93	25	4	1	1	13	6	25	.313	.366
Throws Right	R	.205	117	24	3	0	0	7	14	39	.293	.231
Stammen,Craig	L	.264	129	34	6	0	8	20	8	24	.307	.496
Throws Right	R	.202	168	34	4	0	4	17	20	50	.295	.298
Stanek,Ryne	L	.278	36	10	1	0	0	4	2	13	.308	.306
Throws Right	R	.348	46	16	3	0	6	12	10	16	.464	.804
Steckenrider,Drew	L	.260	50	13	3	0	0	9	9	17	.373	.320
Throws Right	R	.207	82	17	2	0	4	14	9	37	.283	.378
Stephens,Jackson	L	.237	38	9	2	0	3	6	5	8	.341	.526
Throws Right	R	.189	53	10	1	0	3	7	4	13	.246	.377
Stephenson,Robert	L	.250	132	33	6	0	5	22	28	34	.376	.409
Throws Right	R	.259	185	48	16	1	7	27	25	52	.347	.470
Stewart,Brock	L	.236	55	13	1	0	1	5	14	15	.391	.309
Throws Right	R	.217	69	15	2	0	3	7	5	14	.276	.377
Storen,Drew	L	.288	80	23	6	1	2	15	11	19	.396	.463
Throws Right	R	.262	130	34	3	0	5	18	12	29	.347	.400
Strahm,Matt	L	.233	30	7	0	0	1	2	7	12	.395	.333
Throws Left	R	.237	97	23	5	0	5	21	15	25	.351	.443
Straily,Dan	L	.250	352	88	23	4	12	36	38	86	.321	.440
Throws Right	R	.263	335	88	18	1	19	48	22	84	.314	.493
Strasburg,Stephen	L	.193	311	60	15	0	7	20	29	100	.265	.309
Throws Right	R	.215	330	71	16	1	6	30	18	104	.265	.324
Stratton,Chris	L	.295	105	31	7	0	2	8	17	21	.392	.419
Throws Right	R	.239	117	28	4	1	3	12	11	30	.302	.368
Strickland,Hunter	L	.333	90	30	5	1	1	17	16	16	.431	.444
Throws Right	R	.203	143	29	1	3	3	14	13	42	.272	.315
Stripling,Ross	L	.198	121	24	5	0	2	7	11	30	.265	.289
Throws Right	R	.283	159	45	8	0	8	26	8	44	.312	.484
Stroman,Marcus	L	.251	347	87	15	0	4	25	34	71	.321	.329
Throws Right	R	.275	415	114	18	1	17	49	28	93	.324	.446
Strop,Pedro	L	.178	90	16	5	0	0	9	11	28	.265	.233
Throws Right	R	.227	128	29	6	1	4	20	15	37	.322	.383
Stumpf,Daniel	L	.220	59	13	1	0	1	8	8	13	.324	.288
Throws Left	R	.300	80	24	2	2	4	14	7	20	.348	.525
Suarez,Albert	L	.255	51	13	5	1	0	4	5	12	.321	.392
Throws Right	R	.211	71	15	2	0	4	14	6	22	.278	.408
Suter,Brent	L	.192	78	15	4	0	1	5	6	15	.259	.282
Throws Left	R	.287	237	68	7	2	7	26	16	49	.333	.422
Swarzak,Anthony	L	.198	96	19	1	2	1	4	12	26	.294	.281
Throws Right	R	.218	179	39	6	1	5	26	10	65	.259	.346
Syndergaard,Noah	L	.186	59	11	3	1	0	5	2	23	.222	.271
Throws Right	R	.305	59	18	2	0	0	8	1	11	.317	.339

Pitchers vs. Left-Handed and Right-Handed Batters

Pitcher	vs	Avg	AB	H	2B	3B	HR	RBI	BB	SO	OBP	Slg
Taillon,Jameson	L	.313	240	75	19	2	4	29	25	41	.375	.458
Throws Right	R	.270	285	77	19	2	7	34	21	84	.327	.425
Tanaka,Masahiro	L	.252	298	75	11	0	16	37	17	87	.297	.450
Throws Right	R	.261	402	105	31	0	19	53	24	107	.309	.480
Taylor,Ben	L	.240	25	6	2	0	0	1	3	5	.321	.320
Throws Right	R	.304	46	14	1	1	3	10	6	13	.385	.565
Tazawa,Junichi	L	.248	105	26	4	0	4	12	11	16	.319	.400
Throws Right	R	.274	106	29	6	1	4	19	11	22	.350	.462
Teheran,Julio	L	.241	382	92	19	4	17	54	57	77	.342	.445
Throws Right	R	.276	341	94	12	1	14	37	15	74	.313	.440
Tepera,Ryan	L	.194	103	20	4	1	4	13	20	37	.346	.369
Throws Right	R	.211	175	37	8	0	3	19	11	44	.272	.309
Tepesch,Nick	L	.306	36	11	3	0	2	5	3	4	.359	.556
Throws Right	R	.355	31	11	2	0	4	7	6	5	.500	.806
Therrien,Jesen	L	.378	37	14	2	0	2	10	4	5	.439	.595
Throws Right	R	.244	41	10	2	0	3	10	3	5	.311	.512
Thompson,Jake	L	.219	64	14	2	1	1	5	11	10	.338	.328
Throws Right	R	.308	117	36	8	0	8	20	11	25	.383	.581
Tillman,Chris	L	.329	164	54	14	0	7	28	39	22	.458	.543
Throws Right	R	.320	222	71	11	0	17	45	12	41	.363	.599
Tolliver,Ashur	L	.125	8	1	0	0	0	1	1	1	.222	.125
Throws Left	R	.333	9	3	1	0	0	3	3	4	.538	.444
Tomlin,Josh	L	.307	244	75	19	1	9	33	6	44	.321	.504
Throws Right	R	.284	320	91	22	0	14	41	8	65	.309	.484
Tonkin,Michael	L	.333	30	10	3	0	3	6	1	9	.375	.733
Throws Right	R	.226	53	12	2	0	3	7	11	15	.354	.434
Torres,Carlos	L	.261	142	37	8	0	6	23	16	24	.342	.444
Throws Right	R	.297	138	41	2	1	4	19	17	32	.371	.413
Torres,Jose	L	.258	97	25	7	0	3	10	5	20	.291	.423
Throws Left	R	.236	161	38	7	1	10	20	11	43	.298	.478
Treinen,Blake	L	.302	129	39	7	1	5	26	15	37	.387	.488
Throws Right	R	.252	163	41	7	1	1	20	10	37	.297	.325
Triggs,Andrew	L	.215	107	23	2	1	4	18	8	20	.283	.364
Throws Right	R	.302	149	45	6	0	5	22	11	30	.352	.443
Tseng,Jen-Ho	L	.375	8	3	1	0	1	4	2	2	.500	.875
Throws Right	R	.143	14	2	0	0	1	1	0	6	.143	.357
Tuivailala,Samuel	L	.222	54	12	2	0	2	4	8	17	.323	.370
Throws Right	R	.223	103	23	5	0	2	5	3	17	.259	.330
Turley,Nik	L	.385	13	5	1	0	1	4	4	2	.579	.692
Throws Left	R	.397	63	25	9	0	4	15	4	11	.420	.730
Turner,Jacob	L	.219	64	14	4	1	3	10	7	11	.296	.453
Throws Right	R	.326	89	29	4	1	5	14	8	12	.388	.562
Uehara,Koji	L	.250	72	18	3	1	3	7	7	23	.316	.444
Throws Right	R	.217	92	20	1	0	4	10	5	27	.255	.359
Urena,Jose	L	.241	311	75	16	2	12	32	36	39	.331	.421
Throws Right	R	.235	327	77	9	3	14	38	28	74	.309	.410
Urias,Julio	L	.500	20	10	2	1	0	5	7	2	.643	.700
Throws Left	R	.200	65	13	3	0	1	8	7	9	.278	.292
Valdez,Cesar	L	.298	57	17	3	1	1	6	5	8	.355	.439
Throws Right	R	.338	71	24	11	0	6	19	6	13	.397	.746
Valdez,Jose	L	.161	31	5	1	0	2	3	0	8	.188	.387
Throws Right	R	.390	41	16	3	2	6	17	5	9	.458	1.000
Vargas,Jason	L	.311	132	41	6	1	5	20	10	20	.358	.485
Throws Left	R	.253	553	140	27	3	22	62	48	114	.315	.432
Velasquez,Vince	L	.287	129	37	9	1	5	17	21	32	.391	.488
Throws Right	R	.255	145	37	6	0	10	23	13	36	.321	.503
Velazquez,Hector	L	.290	31	9	1	0	2	4	5	8	.389	.516
Throws Right	R	.207	58	12	3	0	2	4	2	11	.233	.362
VerHagen,Drew	L	.317	41	13	3	2	3	10	5	8	.383	.707
Throws Right	R	.309	94	29	4	0	7	13	4	17	.337	.574
Verlander,Justin	L	.221	358	79	17	1	16	40	42	115	.304	.408
Throws Right	R	.222	410	91	12	1	11	29	30	104	.277	.337
Verrett,Logan	L	.267	15	4	1	0	1	1	1	3	.353	.533
Throws Right	R	.280	25	7	1	0	2	5	2	6	.357	.560
Vincent,Nick	L	.281	89	25	5	0	1	9	3	16	.301	.371
Throws Right	R	.243	152	37	9	0	2	18	10	34	.285	.342
Vizcaino,Arodys	L	.217	92	20	3	3	3	8	17	28	.336	.413
Throws Right	R	.185	119	22	2	0	4	10	4	36	.224	.303
Volquez,Edinson	L	.266	173	46	9	2	5	25	34	41	.382	.428
Throws Right	R	.203	158	32	10	0	3	16	19	40	.294	.323
Volstad,Chris	L	.259	27	7	1	0	2	6	5	1	.364	.519
Throws Right	R	.214	42	9	1	0	2	5	0	9	.233	.381
Wacha,Michael	L	.252	286	72	17	1	7	25	34	64	.332	.392
Throws Right	R	.280	350	98	16	2	10	45	21	94	.322	.423
Wahl,Bobby	L	.333	12	4	2	0	0	3	2	2	.429	.500
Throws Right	R	.211	19	4	1	0	0	2	2	6	.318	.263

Pitcher	vs	Avg	AB	H	2B	3B	HR	RBI	BB	SO	OBP	Slg
Wainwright,Adam	L	.289	242	70	13	1	9	30	24	45	.358	.463
Throws Right	R	.282	248	70	14	3	5	32	21	51	.344	.423
Walker,Taijuan	L	.230	287	66	13	3	11	38	35	70	.316	.411
Throws Right	R	.262	313	82	24	2	6	29	26	76	.327	.409
Warren,Adam	L	.208	77	16	3	0	1	4	6	20	.262	.286
Throws Right	R	.152	125	19	3	0	3	14	9	34	.209	.248
Watson,Tony	L	.276	98	27	3	0	2	16	4	20	.324	.367
Throws Left	R	.280	161	45	8	0	7	21	16	33	.348	.460
Weaver,Jered	L	.280	82	23	5	0	5	11	4	11	.330	.524
Throws Right	R	.308	91	28	4	0	11	24	8	12	.373	.714
Weaver,Luke	L	.210	100	21	3	0	2	6	8	31	.275	.300
Throws Right	R	.288	132	38	8	0	5	20	9	41	.331	.462
Webb,Tyler	L	.273	11	3	1	0	1	4	2	4	.385	.636
Throws Left	R	.300	20	6	0	0	1	3	3	4	.391	.450
Whalen,Rob	L	.308	13	4	0	0	1	4	1	0	.357	.538
Throws Right	R	.214	14	3	0	0	0	1	1	2	.353	.214
Wheeler,Zack	L	.275	149	41	4	1	9	24	18	42	.361	.497
Throws Right	R	.290	193	56	11	0	6	22	22	39	.364	.440
Whitley,Chase	L	.227	88	20	5	0	2	13	8	13	.303	.352
Throws Right	R	.219	128	28	10	0	2	13	8	30	.268	.344
Wilhelmsen,Tom	L	.242	33	8	2	1	0	5	5	3	.342	.364
Throws Right	R	.258	66	17	1	0	4	12	7	14	.333	.455
Wilk,Adam	L	.409	22	9	3	0	2	7	3	1	.480	.818
Throws Left	R	.366	41	15	3	0	4	8	6	7	.447	.732
Wilkerson,Aaron	L	.091	11	1	0	1	0	2	0	2	.091	.273
Throws Right	R	.200	25	5	2	0	1	2	1	5	.231	.400
Williams,Taylor	L	.300	10	3	2	0	0	1	1	2	.364	.500
Throws Right	R	.125	8	1	0	0	0	0	1	2	.222	.125
Williams,Trevor	L	.286	283	81	16	1	5	24	22	52	.339	.403
Throws Right	R	.225	285	64	14	1	9	35	30	65	.313	.375
Wilson,Alex	L	.257	109	28	0	2	3	21	8	19	.311	.376
Throws Right	R	.298	131	39	11	1	4	20	7	23	.340	.489
Wilson,Justin	L	.234	64	15	5	0	1	12	10	30	.342	.359
Throws Left	R	.170	147	25	5	2	4	11	25	50	.291	.313
Wilson,Tyler	L	.250	24	6	2	0	2	8	3	6	.321	.583
Throws Right	R	.400	40	16	1	1	1	5	1	3	.429	.550
Wimmers,Alex	L	.308	13	4	0	0	2	4	5	3	.500	.769
Throws Right	R	.235	17	4	0	0	0	3	3	4	.350	.235
Winkler,Daniel	L	.053	19	1	0	0	1	3	1	6	.100	.211
Throws Right	R	.222	27	6	2	0	0	5	5	12	.344	.296
Wisler,Matt	L	.355	62	22	9	1	3	19	9	9	.438	.677
Throws Right	R	.296	71	21	7	1	2	13	4	13	.333	.507
Wittgren,Nick	L	.353	68	24	6	1	1	12	6	15	.400	.515
Throws Right	R	.224	98	22	8	1	4	12	7	28	.271	.449
Wojciechowski,Asher	L	.317	123	39	10	2	7	24	11	30	.377	.602
Throws Right	R	.258	124	32	7	1	7	19	8	34	.319	.500
Wood,Alex	L	.229	157	36	7	0	3	15	9	38	.275	.331
Throws Left	R	.213	409	87	21	0	12	29	29	113	.273	.352
Wood,Blake	L	.350	123	43	6	0	6	36	14	36	.408	.545
Throws Right	R	.240	171	41	8	1	2	17	19	48	.316	.333
Wood,Travis	L	.288	80	23	4	0	3	12	11	15	.370	.450
Throws Left	R	.317	300	95	20	1	16	62	34	50	.385	.550
Woodruff,Brandon	L	.345	84	29	5	0	2	11	7	13	.396	.476
Throws Right	R	.171	82	14	2	0	3	8	7	19	.261	.305
Workman,Brandon	L	.296	54	16	2	1	4	5	1	13	.304	.593
Throws Right	R	.226	93	21	6	1	3	8	10	24	.308	.409
Worley,Vance	L	.333	153	51	17	1	2	25	14	27	.388	.497
Throws Right	R	.345	139	48	9	1	7	27	16	23	.429	.576
Wright,Daniel	L	.278	36	10	1	0	0	5	5	6	.381	.306
Throws Right	R	.289	38	11	1	0	1	4	3	5	.357	.395
Wright,Mike	L	.286	35	10	4	0	3	6	2	10	.316	.657
Throws Right	R	.254	63	16	4	0	2	11	5	18	.338	.413
Wright,Steven	L	.342	38	13	3	0	3	8	2	7	.381	.658
Throws Right	R	.397	68	27	6	1	6	14	3	6	.431	.779
Yacabonis,Jimmy	L	.240	25	6	1	0	0	6	6	4	.364	.280
Throws Right	R	.250	48	12	0	1	2	8	8	4	.351	.417
Yates,Kirby	L	.239	88	21	4	0	7	11	10	36	.316	.523
Throws Right	R	.190	121	23	3	0	5	13	9	52	.256	.339
Ynoa,Gabriel	L	.313	67	21	5	2	4	12	3	9	.342	.627
Throws Right	R	.265	68	18	2	0	1	5	5	17	.315	.338
Ynoa,Michael	L	.255	47	12	2	1	4	12	9	9	.375	.596
Throws Right	R	.239	67	16	6	1	0	8	13	14	.400	.358
Young,Chris	L	.383	60	23	3	0	4	22	10	8	.471	.633
Throws Right	R	.329	73	24	6	0	3	9	4	14	.372	.534
Zastryzny,Rob	L	.286	7	2	0	0	0	1	4	2	.545	.286
Throws Left	R	.362	47	17	4	0	2	12	3	9	.412	.574

Pitchers vs. Left-Handed and Right-Handed Batters

Pitcher	vs	Avg	AB	H	2B	3B	HR	RBI	BB	SO	OBP	Slg
Ziegler,Brad	L	.259	85	22	4	0	0	11	9	9	.357	.306
Throws Right	R	.347	101	35	6	0	1	21	7	17	.400	.436
Zimmermann,Jordan	L	.322	329	106	23	2	15	58	22	57	.362	.541
Throws Right	R	.304	322	98	18	4	14	45	22	46	.356	.516
Zych,Tony	L	.239	46	11	2	0	2	6	7	11	.333	.413
Throws Right	R	.194	98	19	4	0	0	12	14	24	.322	.235
AL	L	.253	-	-	-	-	-	-	-	-	.326	.425
	R	.255	-	-	-	-	-	-	-	-	.320	.428
NL	L	.260	-	-	-	-	-	-	-	-	.337	.430
	R	.253	-	-	-	-	-	-	-	-	.319	.422
MLB	L	.256	-	-	-	-	-	-	-	-	.332	.428
	R	.254	-	-	-	-	-	-	-	-	.319	.425

2017 Leader Boards

Ben Jedlovec

There are two ways that I like to peruse the Leader Boards section, one of my favorites of the Handbook.

First, I will wander through the leader boards aimlessly, stumbling across something interesting at nearly every stop. You could pick one at random and uncover an interesting story that ties in with the rest of the book. Go ahead, close your eyes, flip to a page, and point your finger at a random spot. I'll do it with you. ....aaaannnd there! NL Shortstop Range Factor. Orlando Arcia at the top of the list, by a mile! Interesting. I wouldn't have guessed the youngster would prevail over defensive stalwarts like Addison Russell, Brandon Crawford, and Zack Cozart. In Defensive Runs Saved (Fielding Section, page 347), Arcia checks in squarely above average and even garnered some Fielding Bible Award votes (page 59). Hmm, I wonder how he made so many plays. Oh wait, checking out the Shift Update (page 79), I see that the Brewers actually led MLB in shifts on balls in play in 2017. Now it makes sense. Arcia's Range Factor got a boost from the fact that the Brewers frequently repositioned him to where they thought the ball was going to go, and it worked!

Let's try another one.

After my first stroll through the section, I usually double back and try to extract some insight from a combination of leader boards. Wow, Aaron Judge led 19 different categories in this section, particularly the counting stats where Mike Trout couldn't catch up to him. I won't list them all, but I will point out the Three True Outcomes Triple Crown (Strikeouts, Walks, Home Runs) and his AL-leading OPS on fastballs, curveballs, and changeups. But before you start to think there's no way to get him out, he also sneaks onto the trailer board for worst BPS (Batting average Plus Slugging percentage) on pitches out of the zone.

On the mound, the Corey Kluber versus Chris Sale AL Cy Young debate takes center stage. While Sale struck out substantially more batters (in more innings), Kluber bested Sale in almost every other category, even if the margin is narrow. Kluber edges Sale in ERA, Wins, Opponent Avg/OBP/Slg, Baserunners per 9 IP,

Complete Games, Shutouts, Percent of Pitches in the Strike Zone, and Strikeout-to-Walk Ratio.

Speaking of the AL Cy Young, what happened to Rick Porcello? En route to leading MLB in Losses, he yielded the most runs, hits, doubles, and home runs in the AL in 2017. That's not a good combination. He also threw a league-high 48 percent of pitches in the strike zone, which you can get away with when you're keeping the ball on the ground and getting the best run support in the league, as Porcello did last year. In 2017, however, Porcello did neither.

Not to neglect the National League, the Bill James Leader Boards cite Marlins starters Edinson Volquez and Jeff Locke having the best and worst (respectively) individual starts in baseball last year, perfectly epitomizing Miami's hot and cold season. The Giants starting rotation featured a trio of Tough Loss leaders: Madison Bumgarner, Jeff Samardzija, and Johnny Cueto. In particular, Samardzija's strong season (second in strikeout-to-walk ratio behind only Clayton Kershaw) was masked by poor run support and a terrible Giants defense behind him. If the Giants roll into spring training with a revamped lineup and a couple defensive upgrades, watch how many Wins that rotation will post in 2018.

2017 American League Batting Leaders

Batting Average
(minimum 502 PA)

Altuve, Jose, Hou	.346
Garcia, Avisail, CWS	.330
Hosmer, Eric, KC	.318
Ramirez, Jose, Cle	.318
Reddick, Josh, Hou	.314
Trout, Mike, LAA	.306
Mauer, Joe, Min	.305
Abreu, Jose, CWS	.304
Gonzalez, Marwin, Hou	.303
Cain, Lorenzo, KC	.300

On Base Percentage
(minimum 502 PA)

Trout, Mike, LAA	.442
Judge, Aaron, NYY	.422
Altuve, Jose, Hou	.410
Hosmer, Eric, KC	.385
Mauer, Joe, Min	.384
Garcia, Avisail, CWS	.380
Encarnacion, Edwin, Cle	.377
Gonzalez, Marwin, Hou	.377
Cruz, Nelson, Sea	.375
Ramirez, Jose, Cle	.374

Slugging Average
(minimum 502 PA)

Trout, Mike, LAA	.629
Judge, Aaron, NYY	.627
Ramirez, Jose, Cle	.583
Abreu, Jose, CWS	.552
Cruz, Nelson, Sea	.549
Altuve, Jose, Hou	.547
Upton, Justin, Det-LAA	.540
Gallo, Joey, Tex	.537
Sanchez, Gary, NYY	.531
Gonzalez, Marwin, Hou	.530

Home Runs

Judge, Aaron, NYY	52
Davis, Khris, Oak	43
Gallo, Joey, Tex	41
Cruz, Nelson, Sea	39
Encarnacion, Edwin, Cle	38
Morrison, Logan, TB	38
Moustakas, Mike, KC	38
Smoak, Justin, Tor	38
Upton, Justin, Det-LAA	35
2 tied with	34

Games

Escobar, Alcides, KC	162
Hosmer, Eric, KC	162
Odor, Rougned, Tex	162
Schoop, Jonathan, Bal	160
Lindor, Francisco, Cle	159
Andrus, Elvis, Tex	158
Simmons, Andrelton, LAA	158
Smoak, Justin, Tor	158
3 tied with	157

Plate Appearances

Lindor, Francisco, Cle	723
Betts, Mookie, Bos	712
Dozier, Brian, Min	705
Machado, Manny, Bal	690
Andrus, Elvis, Tex	689
Bautista, Jose, Tor	686
Gardner, Brett, NYY	682
Judge, Aaron, NYY	678
Longoria, Evan, TB	677
2 tied with	675

At Bats

Lindor, Francisco, Cle	651
Andrus, Elvis, Tex	643
Machado, Manny, Bal	630
Betts, Mookie, Bos	628
Schoop, Jonathan, Bal	622
Abreu, Jose, CWS	621
Cabrera, Melky, CWS-KC	620
Dozier, Brian, Min	617
Castellanos, Nick, Det	614
Longoria, Evan, TB	613

Hits

Altuve, Jose, Hou	204
Hosmer, Eric, KC	192
Andrus, Elvis, Tex	191
Abreu, Jose, CWS	189
Ramirez, Jose, Cle	186
Schoop, Jonathan, Bal	182
Lindor, Francisco, Cle	178
Cabrera, Melky, CWS-KC	177
Cain, Lorenzo, KC	175
Garcia, Avisail, CWS	171

Singles

Altuve, Jose, Hou	137
Hosmer, Eric, KC	135
Cabrera, Melky, CWS-KC	128
Cain, Lorenzo, KC	128
Andrus, Elvis, Tex	123
Garcia, Avisail, CWS	121
Mauer, Joe, Min	116
Jones, Adam, Bal	115
Schoop, Jonathan, Bal	115
Segura, Jean, Sea	114

Doubles

Ramirez, Jose, Cle	56
Lowrie, Jed, Oak	49
Betts, Mookie, Bos	46
Andrus, Elvis, Tex	44
Lindor, Francisco, Cle	44
Upton, Justin, Det-LAA	44
Abreu, Jose, CWS	43
Gurriel, Yulieski, Hou	43
Altuve, Jose, Hou	39
Bregman, Alex, Hou	39

Triples

Castellanos, Nick, Det	10
Sanchez, Yolmer, CWS	8
Abreu, Jose, CWS	6
Bogaerts, Xander, Bos	6
Buxton, Byron, Min	6
Mahtook, Mikie, Det	6
Merrifield, Whit, KC	6
Ramirez, Jose, Cle	6
7 tied with	5

Total Bases

Abreu, Jose, CWS	343
Ramirez, Jose, Cle	341
Judge, Aaron, NYY	340
Lindor, Francisco, Cle	329
Altuve, Jose, Hou	323
Schoop, Jonathan, Bal	313
Dozier, Brian, Min	306
Cruz, Nelson, Sea	305
Andrus, Elvis, Tex	303
2 tied with	301

Runs Scored

Judge, Aaron, NYY	128
Altuve, Jose, Hou	112
Springer, George, Hou	112
Ramirez, Jose, Cle	107
Dozier, Brian, Min	106
Betts, Mookie, Bos	101
Andrus, Elvis, Tex	100
Upton, Justin, Det-LAA	100
Lindor, Francisco, Cle	99
Hosmer, Eric, KC	98

RBI

Cruz, Nelson, Sea	119
Judge, Aaron, NYY	114
Davis, Khris, Oak	110
Upton, Justin, Det-LAA	109
Encarnacion, Edwin, Cle	107
Schoop, Jonathan, Bal	105
Abreu, Jose, CWS	102
Betts, Mookie, Bos	102
3 tied with	101

Walks

Judge, Aaron, NYY	127
Encarnacion, Edwin, Cle	104
Trout, Mike, LAA	94
Santana, Carlos, Cle	88
Bautista, Jose, Tor	84
Souza Jr., Steven, TB	84
Frazier, Todd, CWS-NYY	83
Morrison, Logan, TB	81
Dozier, Brian, Min	78
2 tied with	77

Strikeouts

Judge, Aaron, NYY	208
Gallo, Joey, Tex	196
Davis, Chris, Bal	195
Davis, Khris, Oak	195
Upton, Justin, Det-LAA	180
Souza Jr., Steven, TB	179
Sano, Miguel, Min	173
Bautista, Jose, Tor	170
Beckham, Tim, TB-Bal	167
Davidson, Matt, CWS	165

2017 American League Batting Leaders

Intentional Walks	
Trout, Mike, LAA	15
Judge, Aaron, NYY	11
Betts, Mookie, Bos	9
Cano, Robinson, Sea	8
Morrison, Logan, TB	8
Ramirez, Hanley, Bos	8
Benintendi, Andrew, Bos	7
Cruz, Nelson, Sea	7
Moustakas, Mike, KC	7
11 tied with	6

BA Bases Loaded (minimum 10 PA)	
Goins, Ryan, Tor	.714
Machado, Manny, Bal	.583
Gurriel, Yulieski, Hou	.545
Haniger, Mitch, Sea	.545
Mauer, Joe, Min	.545
Pedroia, Dustin, Bos	.545
Gregorius, Didi, NYY	.538
Gonzalez, Marwin, Hou	.533
4 tied with	.500

Sacrifice Hits	
DeShields, Delino, Tex	13
Engel, Adam, CWS	8
Maldonado, Martin, LAA	8
Escobar, Alcides, KC	7
Polanco, Jorge, Min	7
Sanchez, Yolmer, CWS	7
7 tied with	5

Sacrifice Flies	
Longoria, Evan, TB	12
Reddick, Josh, Hou	12
Machado, Manny, Bal	9
Benintendi, Andrew, Bos	8
Rosario, Eddie, Min	8
Simmons, Andrelton, LAA	8
Valencia, Danny, Sea	8
9 tied with	7

BA Close & Late (minimum 50 PA)	
Altuve, Jose, Hou	.441
Perez, Salvador, KC	.423
Martinez, Victor, Det	.367
Revere, Ben, LAA	.356
Andrus, Elvis, Tex	.354
Martin, Russell, Tor	.354
McCann, Brian, Hou	.354
Carrera, Ezequiel, Tor	.340
Beltran, Carlos, Hou	.338
Cain, Lorenzo, KC	.329

Batting Average w/ RISP (minimum 100 PA)	
Jones, Adam, Bal	.361
Gonzalez, Marwin, Hou	.360
Abreu, Jose, CWS	.357
Betts, Mookie, Bos	.355
Benintendi, Andrew, Bos	.351
Reddick, Josh, Hou	.346
Cruz, Nelson, Sea	.340
Mancini, Trey, Bal	.340
Valencia, Danny, Sea	.340
Schoop, Jonathan, Bal	.338

SLG vs. LHP (minimum 125 PA)	
Upton, Justin, Det-LAA	.728
Dozier, Brian, Min	.634
Abreu, Jose, CWS	.631
Castellanos, Nick, Det	.599
Morales, Kendrys, Tor	.598
Schoop, Jonathan, Bal	.593
Ramirez, Jose, Cle	.582
Garcia, Avisail, CWS	.576
Jackson, Austin, Cle	.574
Bregman, Alex, Hou	.570

SLG vs. RHP (minimum 377 PA)	
Trout, Mike, LAA	.672
Judge, Aaron, NYY	.662
Cruz, Nelson, Sea	.586
Ramirez, Jose, Cle	.583
Rosario, Eddie, Min	.562
Gallo, Joey, Tex	.554
Gonzalez, Marwin, Hou	.552
Davis, Khris, Oak	.550
Morrison, Logan, TB	.548
Altuve, Jose, Hou	.543

Leadoff Hitters OBP (minimum 150 PA)	
Choo, Shin-Soo, Tex	.382
Springer, George, Hou	.369
Dozier, Brian, Min	.358
Kiermaier, Kevin, TB	.354
Segura, Jean, Sea	.353
DeShields, Delino, Tex	.350
Gardner, Brett, NYY	.350
Lindor, Francisco, Cle	.346
Joyce, Matt, Oak	.346
Betts, Mookie, Bos	.341

Cleanup Hitters SLG (minimum 150 PA)	
Sano, Miguel, Min	.600
Cruz, Nelson, Sea	.560
Davis, Khris, Oak	.551
Smoak, Justin, Tor	.549
Beltre, Adrian, Tex	.536
Morrison, Logan, TB	.513
Correa, Carlos, Hou	.502
Encarnacion, Edwin, Cle	.497
Jones, Adam, Bal	.495
Hosmer, Eric, KC	.474

BA vs. LHP (minimum 125 PA)	
Garcia, Avisail, CWS	.424
Morales, Kendrys, Tor	.362
Abreu, Jose, CWS	.356
Altuve, Jose, Hou	.353
Jackson, Austin, Cle	.352
Upton, Justin, Det-LAA	.344
Pillar, Kevin, Tor	.336
Dozier, Brian, Min	.331
Bregman, Alex, Hou	.331
Smoak, Justin, Tor	.331

BA vs. RHP (minimum 377 PA)	
Altuve, Jose, Hou	.344
Hosmer, Eric, KC	.335
Gonzalez, Marwin, Hou	.322
Gurriel, Yulieski, Hou	.317
Reddick, Josh, Hou	.314
Trout, Mike, LAA	.313
Ramirez, Jose, Cle	.312
Cano, Robinson, Sea	.312
Cain, Lorenzo, KC	.306
Cruz, Nelson, Sea	.306

Home BA (minimum 251 PA)	
Reddick, Josh, Hou	.344
Garcia, Avisail, CWS	.333
Rosario, Eddie, Min	.332
Ramirez, Jose, Cle	.314
Segura, Jean, Sea	.313
Judge, Aaron, NYY	.312
Trout, Mike, LAA	.312
Cain, Lorenzo, KC	.311
Altuve, Jose, Hou	.311
Hosmer, Eric, KC	.310

Away BA (minimum 251 PA)	
Altuve, Jose, Hou	.381
Garcia, Avisail, CWS	.327
Hosmer, Eric, KC	.326
Gonzalez, Marwin, Hou	.326
Ramirez, Jose, Cle	.322
Gregorius, Didi, NYY	.321
Abreu, Jose, CWS	.313
Gurriel, Yulieski, Hou	.312
Mauer, Joe, Min	.309
Mancini, Trey, Bal	.304

OBP vs. LHP (minimum 125 PA)	
Garcia, Avisail, CWS	.454
Jackson, Austin, Cle	.440
Judge, Aaron, NYY	.439
Upton, Justin, Det-LAA	.427
Springer, George, Hou	.423
Dozier, Brian, Min	.423
Altuve, Jose, Hou	.416
Smoak, Justin, Tor	.413
Betts, Mookie, Bos	.412
Cruz, Nelson, Sea	.407

OBP vs. RHP (minimum 377 PA)	
Trout, Mike, LAA	.441
Judge, Aaron, NYY	.417
Hosmer, Eric, KC	.410
Altuve, Jose, Hou	.408
Gonzalez, Marwin, Hou	.394
Donaldson, Josh, Tor	.386
Mauer, Joe, Min	.386
Alonso, Yonder, Oak-Sea	.383
Ramirez, Jose, Cle	.375
Headley, Chase, NYY	.373

2017 American League Batting Leaders

Stolen Bases

Merrifield, Whit, KC	34
Maybin, C, LAA-Hou	33
Altuve, Jose, Hou	32
Buxton, Byron, Min	29
Davis, Rajai, Oak-Bos	29
DeShields, Delino, Tex	29
Dyson, Jarrod, Sea	28
Betts, Mookie, Bos	26
Cain, Lorenzo, KC	26
Andrus, Elvis, Tex	25

Caught Stealing

Andrus, Elvis, Tex	10
Sanchez, Yolmer, CWS	9
DeShields, Delino, Tex	8
Maybin, C, LAA-Hou	8
Merrifield, Whit, KC	8
Rosario, Eddie, Min	8
Segura, Jean, Sea	8
6 tied with	7

Highest SB Success Pct
(minimum 20 SBA)

Buxton, Byron, Min	96.7
Cain, Lorenzo, KC	92.9
Betts, Mookie, Bos	89.7
Ellsbury, Jacoby, NYY	88.0
Trout, Mike, LAA	84.6
Altuve, Jose, Hou	84.2
Gardner, Brett, NYY	82.1
Merrifield, Whit, KC	81.0
Davis, Rajai, Oak-Bos	80.6
Maybin, C, LAA-Hou	80.5

Lowest SB Success Pct
(minimum 20 SBA)

Dozier, Brian, Min	69.6
Kiermaier, Kevin, TB	69.6
Andrus, Elvis, Tex	71.4
Odor, Rougned, Tex	71.4
Pillar, Kevin, Tor	71.4
Segura, Jean, Sea	73.3
Simmons, Andrelton, LAA	76.0
Smith, Mallex, TB	76.2
Bregman, Alex, Hou	77.3
Ramirez, Jose, Cle	77.3

Steals of Third

Altuve, Jose, Hou	9
DeShields, Delino, Tex	8
Merrifield, Whit, KC	8
Andrus, Elvis, Tex	7
Souza Jr., Steven, TB	7
Anderson, Tim, CWS	5
Betts, Mookie, Bos	5
Cain, Lorenzo, KC	5
Davis, Rajai, Oak-Bos	5
Kiermaier, Kevin, TB	5

Grounded Into DP

Pujols, Albert, LAA	26
Perez, Salvador, KC	23
Morales, Kendrys, Tor	22
Abreu, Jose, CWS	21
Cain, Lorenzo, KC	20
Davis, Khris, Oak	20
Hosmer, Eric, KC	20
Schoop, Jonathan, Bal	20
Simmons, Andrelton, LAA	20
2 tied with	19

Grounded Into DP Pct
(minimum 50 GIDP Ops)

Kipnis, Jason, Cle	0.00
Buxton, Byron, Min	1.16
Engel, Adam, CWS	1.64
DeShields, Delino, Tex	2.86
Chapman, Matt, Oak	2.99
Gallo, Joey, Tex	3.03
Kiermaier, Kevin, TB	3.80
Smith, Mallex, TB	3.92
Semien, Marcus, Oak	4.35
Gardner, Brett, NYY	4.40

Hit By Pitch

Gomez, Carlos, Tex	19
Maldonado, Martin, LAA	18
Abreu, Jose, CWS	15
Frazier, Todd, CWS-NYY	14
Gordon, Alex, KC	14
Cruz, Nelson, Sea	12
Heredia, Guillermo, Sea	11
Schoop, Jonathan, Bal	11
Springer, George, Hou	11
3 tied with	10

Pitches Seen

Judge, Aaron, NYY	2989
Bautista, Jose, Tor	2977
Gardner, Brett, NYY	2890
Encarnacion, Edwin, Cle	2870
Dozier, Brian, Min	2828
Betts, Mookie, Bos	2804
Lindor, Francisco, Cle	2727
Upton, Justin, Det-LAA	2695
Santana, Carlos, Cle	2648
Castellanos, Nick, Det	2605

At Bats Per Home Run
(minimum 502 PA)

Judge, Aaron, NYY	10.4
Gallo, Joey, Tex	11.0
Trout, Mike, LAA	12.2
Davis, Khris, Oak	13.2
Morrison, Logan, TB	13.5
Cruz, Nelson, Sea	14.3
Sanchez, Gary, NYY	14.3
Encarnacion, Edwin, Cle	14.6
Moustakas, Mike, KC	14.6
Smoak, Justin, Tor	14.7

Highest GB/FB Ratio
(minimum 502 PA)

Hosmer, Eric, KC	2.50
Mauer, Joe, Min	2.18
Segura, Jean, Sea	2.06
Garcia, Avisail, CWS	1.90
Anderson, Tim, CWS	1.88
Choo, Shin-Soo, Tex	1.86
Mancini, Trey, Bal	1.72
Cabrera, Melky, CWS-KC	1.69
Beckham, Tim, TB-Bal	1.65
Cano, Robinson, Sea	1.63

Lowest GB/FB Ratio
(minimum 502 PA)

Gallo, Joey, Tex	0.51
Seager, Kyle, Sea	0.61
Lowrie, Jed, Oak	0.68
Kinsler, Ian, Det	0.71
Frazier, Todd, CWS-NYY	0.72
Morrison, Logan, TB	0.72
Moustakas, Mike, KC	0.76
Smoak, Justin, Tor	0.77
Alonso, Yonder, Oak-Sea	0.78
Reddick, Josh, Hou	0.79

Pitches Per Plate App
(minimum 502 PA)

Judge, Aaron, NYY	4.41
Mauer, Joe, Min	4.36
Bautista, Jose, Tor	4.34
Frazier, Todd, CWS-NYY	4.33
Encarnacion, Edwin, Cle	4.29
Upton, Justin, Det-LAA	4.24
Gardner, Brett, NYY	4.24
Gallo, Joey, Tex	4.21
Trout, Mike, LAA	4.20
Joyce, Matt, Oak	4.17

Pct Pitches Taken
(minimum 1500 Pitches)

Betts, Mookie, Bos	64.0
Gardner, Brett, NYY	63.6
Mauer, Joe, Min	63.4
Maybin, C, LAA-Hou	62.5
Trout, Mike, LAA	62.3
Grossman, Robbie, Min	61.5
Santana, Carlos, Cle	60.0
DeShields, Delino, Tex	59.8
Frazier, Todd, CWS-NYY	59.7
Smith, Seth, Bal	59.1

Best BPS on OutZ
(minimum 502 PA)

Altuve, Jose, Hou	.684
Cabrera, Melky, CWS-KC	.677
Upton, Justin, Det-LAA	.639
Garcia, Avisail, CWS	.618
Bregman, Alex, Hou	.607
Gregorius, Didi, NYY	.600
Rosario, Eddie, Min	.599
Dickerson, Corey, TB	.585
Ramirez, Jose, Cle	.581
Santana, Carlos, Cle	.577

Worst BPS on OutZ
(minimum 502 PA)

Joyce, Matt, Oak	.246
Davis, Chris, Bal	.250
Morrison, Logan, TB	.294
Bautista, Jose, Tor	.305
Cruz, Nelson, Sea	.311
Judge, Aaron, NYY	.311
Beckham, Tim, TB-Bal	.312
Souza Jr., Steven, TB	.318
Gordon, Alex, KC	.326
Davis, Khris, Oak	.335

2017 American League Batting Leaders

Best OPS vs Fastballs
(minimum 251 PA)

Judge, Aaron, NYY	1.104
Cruz, Nelson, Sea	1.075
Alonso, Yonder, Oak-Sea	1.063
Gonzalez, Marwin, Hou	1.052
Donaldson, Josh, Tor	1.048
Altuve, Jose, Hou	1.023
Ramirez, Jose, Cle	1.012
Trout, Mike, LAA	.981
Correa, Carlos, Hou	.962
Mancini, Trey, Bal	.954

Best OPS vs Curveballs
(minimum 50 PA)

Judge, Aaron, NYY	1.313
Cabrera, Melky, CWS-KC	1.140
Bregman, Alex, Hou	1.138
Schoop, Jonathan, Bal	1.126
Santana, Carlos, Cle	1.029
Gregorius, Didi, NYY	.974
Sano, Miguel, Min	.958
Correa, Carlos, Hou	.954
Bautista, Jose, Tor	.934
Andrus, Elvis, Tex	.925

Best OPS vs Changeups
(minimum 50 PA)

Judge, Aaron, NYY	1.337
Sanchez, Gary, NYY	1.267
Abreu, Jose, CWS	1.259
Ramirez, Jose, Cle	1.203
Moustakas, Mike, KC	1.185
Schoop, Jonathan, Bal	1.108
Hosmer, Eric, KC	1.068
Cabrera, Miguel, Det	1.049
Upton, Justin, Det-LAA	1.037
Perez, Salvador, KC	1.025

Best OPS vs Sliders
(minimum 32 PA)

Garcia, Leury, CWS	1.132
Encarnacion, Edwin, Cle	1.113
Trout, Mike, LAA	1.104
Hicks, John, Det	1.086
Canha, Mark, Oak	1.068
Polanco, Jorge, Min	1.063
Lindor, Francisco, Cle	1.042
Grossman, Robbie, Min	1.041
Norris, Derek, TB	1.022
Gurriel, Yulieski, Hou	1.017

OPS
(minimum 502 PA)

Trout, Mike, LAA	1.071
Judge, Aaron, NYY	1.049
Altuve, Jose, Hou	.957
Ramirez, Jose, Cle	.957
Cruz, Nelson, Sea	.924
Gonzalez, Marwin, Hou	.907
Abreu, Jose, CWS	.906
Upton, Justin, Det-LAA	.901
Springer, George, Hou	.889
Garcia, Avisail, CWS	.885

OPS First Half
(minimum 260 PA)

Judge, Aaron, NYY	1.139
Springer, George, Hou	.993
Ramirez, Jose, Cle	.988
Correa, Carlos, Hou	.979
Altuve, Jose, Hou	.968
Smoak, Justin, Tor	.936
Alonso, Yonder, Oak-Sea	.934
Morrison, Logan, TB	.931
Sano, Miguel, Min	.906
Dickerson, Corey, TB	.903

OPS Second Half
(minimum 201 PA)

Donaldson, Josh, Tor	.992
Trout, Mike, LAA	.981
Dozier, Brian, Min	.978
Upton, Justin, Det-LAA	.967
Cruz, Nelson, Sea	.960
Abreu, Jose, CWS	.951
Altuve, Jose, Hou	.944
Zunino, Mike, Sea	.943
Judge, Aaron, NYY	.939
Garcia, Avisail, CWS	.933

OPS by Catchers
(minimum 251 PA)

Sanchez, Gary, NYY	.864
Chirinos, Robinson, Tex	.862
Zunino, Mike, Sea	.847
Castillo, Welington, Bal	.825
Perez, Salvador, KC	.802
McCann, Brian, Hou	.750
Narvaez, Omar, CWS	.734
McCann, James, Det	.732
Martin, Russell, Tor	.730
Vazquez, Christian, Bos	.727

OPS by First Basemen
(minimum 251 PA)

Abreu, Jose, CWS	.941
Smoak, Justin, Tor	.887
Hosmer, Eric, KC	.886
Morrison, Logan, TB	.881
Alonso, Yonder, Oak-Sea	.876
Santana, Carlos, Cle	.819
Gurriel, Yulieski, Hou	.808
Mauer, Joe, Min	.797
Moreland, Mitch, Bos	.768
Davis, Chris, Bal	.732

OPS by Second Basemen
(minimum 251 PA)

Ramirez, Jose, Cle	1.020
Altuve, Jose, Hou	.965
Dozier, Brian, Min	.855
Schoop, Jonathan, Bal	.838
Lowrie, Jed, Oak	.825
Cano, Robinson, Sea	.793
Merrifield, Whit, KC	.786
Castro, Starlin, NYY	.781
Pedroia, Dustin, Bos	.779
Sanchez, Yolmer, CWS	.728

OPS by Third Basemen
(minimum 251 PA)

Donaldson, Josh, Tor	.990
Beltre, Adrian, Tex	.979
Sano, Miguel, Min	.947
Ramirez, Jose, Cle	.910
Moustakas, Mike, KC	.858
Gallo, Joey, Tex	.842
Bregman, Alex, Hou	.808
Frazier, Todd, CWS-NYY	.794
Chapman, Matt, Oak	.785
Machado, Manny, Bal	.782

OPS by Shortstops
(minimum 251 PA)

Correa, Carlos, Hou	.951
Lindor, Francisco, Cle	.837
Andrus, Elvis, Tex	.807
Beckham, Tim, TB-Bal	.807
Gregorius, Didi, NYY	.800
Segura, Jean, Sea	.774
Simmons, Andrelton, LAA	.752
Bogaerts, Xander, Bos	.746
Polanco, Jorge, Min	.730
Semien, Marcus, Oak	.722

OPS by Left Fielders
(minimum 251 PA)

Upton, Justin, Det-LAA	.903
Davis, Khris, Oak	.846
Rosario, Eddie, Min	.836
Gardner, Brett, NYY	.796
Brantley, Michael, Cle	.795
Cabrera, Melky, CWS-KC	.791
Pearce, Steve, Tor	.785
Mancini, Trey, Bal	.761
Dickerson, Corey, TB	.745
Benintendi, Andrew, Bos	.744

OPS by Center Fielders
(minimum 251 PA)

Trout, Mike, LAA	1.071
Springer, George, Hou	.897
Mahtook, Mikie, Det	.839
Cain, Lorenzo, KC	.806
Gomez, Carlos, Tex	.801
Kiermaier, Kevin, TB	.789
Jones, Adam, Bal	.787
Ellsbury, Jacoby, NYY	.764
Bradley Jr., Jackie, Bos	.729
Buxton, Byron, Min	.728

OPS by Right Fielders
(minimum 251 PA)

Judge, Aaron, NYY	1.050
Garcia, Avisail, CWS	.878
Haniger, Mitch, Sea	.867
Choo, Shin-Soo, Tex	.860
Mazara, Nomar, Tex	.826
Smith, Seth, Bal	.818
Reddick, Josh, Hou	.810
Joyce, Matt, Oak	.809
Betts, Mookie, Bos	.803
Souza Jr., Steven, TB	.792

OPS by Designated Hitters
(minimum 125 PA)

Cruz, Nelson, Sea	.935
Dickerson, Corey, TB	.934
Davis, Khris, Oak	.926
Encarnacion, Edwin, Cle	.873
Ramirez, Hanley, Bos	.771
Moss, Brandon, KC	.768
Morales, Kendrys, Tor	.765
Davidson, Matt, CWS	.761
Vargas, Kennys, Min	.735
Grossman, Robbie, Min	.734

2017 American League Batting Leaders

OPS Batting Left vs. LHP
(minimum 125 PA)

Gallo, Joey, Tex	.841
Dickerson, Corey, TB	.820
Bradley Jr., Jackie, Bos	.766
Seager, Kyle, Sea	.766
Moustakas, Mike, KC	.763
Morrison, Logan, TB	.761
Hosmer, Eric, KC	.760
Mauer, Joe, Min	.754
Choo, Shin-Soo, Tex	.752
Gamel, Ben, Sea	.699

OPS Batting Left vs. RHP
(minimum 377 PA)

Ramirez, Jose, Cle	.958
Gonzalez, Marwin, Hou	.946
Hosmer, Eric, KC	.938
Rosario, Eddie, Min	.906
Morrison, Logan, TB	.905
Alonso, Yonder, Oak-Sea	.900
Cano, Robinson, Sea	.891
Gallo, Joey, Tex	.878
Reddick, Josh, Hou	.867
Moustakas, Mike, KC	.862

OPS Batting Right vs. LHP
(minimum 125 PA)

Upton, Justin, Det-LAA	1.155
Dozier, Brian, Min	1.057
Abreu, Jose, CWS	1.033
Garcia, Avisail, CWS	1.030
Jackson, Austin, Cle	1.013
Morales, Kendrys, Tor	1.000
Smoak, Justin, Tor	.977
Altuve, Jose, Hou	.977
Bregman, Alex, Hou	.974
Springer, George, Hou	.972

OPS Batting Right vs. RHP
(minimum 377 PA)

Trout, Mike, LAA	1.113
Judge, Aaron, NYY	1.079
Altuve, Jose, Hou	.952
Cruz, Nelson, Sea	.950
Donaldson, Josh, Tor	.917
Encarnacion, Edwin, Cle	.891
Davis, Khris, Oak	.886
Sanchez, Gary, NYY	.874
Abreu, Jose, CWS	.866
Gurriel, Yulieski, Hou	.865

OPS vs. LHP
(minimum 377 PA)

Upton, Justin, Det-LAA	1.155
Dozier, Brian, Min	1.057
Abreu, Jose, CWS	1.033
Garcia, Avisail, CWS	1.030
Jackson, Austin, Cle	1.013
Morales, Kendrys, Tor	1.000
Altuve, Jose, Hou	.977
Smoak, Justin, Tor	.977
Bregman, Alex, Hou	.974
Springer, George, Hou	.972

OPS vs. RHP
(minimum 377 PA)

Trout, Mike, LAA	1.113
Judge, Aaron, NYY	1.079
Ramirez, Jose, Cle	.958
Altuve, Jose, Hou	.952
Cruz, Nelson, Sea	.950
Gonzalez, Marwin, Hou	.946
Hosmer, Eric, KC	.938
Donaldson, Josh, Tor	.917
Rosario, Eddie, Min	.906
Morrison, Logan, TB	.905

RC Per 27 Outs vs. LHP
(minimum 125 PA)

Upton, Justin, Det-LAA	10.1
Betts, Mookie, Bos	9.3
Garcia, Avisail, CWS	9.2
Dozier, Brian, Min	8.8
Morales, Kendrys, Tor	8.0
Bregman, Alex, Hou	7.9
Abreu, Jose, CWS	7.6
Smoak, Justin, Tor	7.6
Springer, George, Hou	7.6
Schoop, Jonathan, Bal	7.5

RC Per 27 Outs vs. RHP
(minimum 377 PA)

Trout, Mike, LAA	10.5
Judge, Aaron, NYY	8.9
Gonzalez, Marwin, Hou	8.8
Hosmer, Eric, KC	8.4
Donaldson, Josh, Tor	8.2
Altuve, Jose, Hou	7.9
Ramirez, Jose, Cle	7.6
Cano, Robinson, Sea	7.3
Cruz, Nelson, Sea	7.2
Reddick, Josh, Hou	6.9

Highest RBI %
(minimum 502 PA)

Trout, Mike, LAA	45.37
Cruz, Nelson, Sea	44.96
Gonzalez, Marwin, Hou	43.19
Upton, Justin, Det-LAA	42.41
Springer, George, Hou	41.71
Judge, Aaron, NYY	41.36
Schoop, Jonathan, Bal	40.52
Abreu, Jose, CWS	40.41
Castellanos, Nick, Det	40.35
Betts, Mookie, Bos	40.30

Lowest RBI %
(minimum 502 PA)

Pillar, Kevin, Tor	21.01
Gordon, Alex, KC	25.07
Anderson, Tim, CWS	26.73
Beltran, Carlos, Hou	26.76
Escobar, Alcides, KC	27.84
Cain, Lorenzo, KC	27.95
Trumbo, Mark, Bal	28.25
Ramirez, Hanley, Bos	28.36
Segura, Jean, Sea	28.43
Buxton, Byron, Min	28.65

Highest Strikeout per PA
(minimum 502 PA)

Davis, Chris, Bal	.372
Gallo, Joey, Tex	.368
Judge, Aaron, NYY	.307
Davis, Khris, Oak	.299
Buxton, Byron, Min	.294
Beckham, Tim, TB-Bal	.290
Souza Jr., Steven, TB	.290
Upton, Justin, Det-LAA	.283
Anderson, Tim, CWS	.267
Odor, Rougned, Tex	.249

Lowest Strikeout per PA
(minimum 502 PA)

Simmons, Andrelton, LAA	.104
Ramirez, Jose, Cle	.107
Gurriel, Yulieski, Hou	.110
Betts, Mookie, Bos	.111
Cabrera, Melky, CWS-KC	.111
Gregorius, Didi, NYY	.123
Altuve, Jose, Hou	.127
Lindor, Francisco, Cle	.129
Cano, Robinson, Sea	.131
Reddick, Josh, Hou	.133

Home Runs At Home

Judge, Aaron, NYY	33
Davis, Khris, Oak	26
Gallo, Joey, Tex	22
Machado, Manny, Bal	22
Rosario, Eddie, Min	20
Trout, Mike, LAA	20
Cruz, Nelson, Sea	19
Smoak, Justin, Tor	19
3 tied with	18

Home Runs Away

Morrison, Logan, TB	27
Moustakas, Mike, KC	24
Encarnacion, Edwin, Cle	23
Perez, Salvador, KC	21
Cruz, Nelson, Sea	20
Donaldson, Josh, Tor	19
Gallo, Joey, Tex	19
Judge, Aaron, NYY	19
Ramirez, Jose, Cle	19
Smoak, Justin, Tor	19

Longest Avg Home Run
(min 10 over the wall)

Morales, Kendrys, Tor	407
Chapman, Matt, Oak	407
Gallo, Joey, Tex	405
Vargas, Kennys, Min	405
Judge, Aaron, NYY	403
Mahtook, Mikie, Det	402
Ramos, Wilson, TB	402
Holliday, Matt, NYY	401
Martinez, J.D., Det	400
Trout, Mike, LAA	400

Shortest Avg Home Run
(min 10 over the wall)

Gregorius, Didi, NYY	362
Hicks, Aaron, NYY	362
Betts, Mookie, Bos	364
Bregman, Alex, Hou	365
Devers, Rafael, Bos	369
Gurriel, Yulieski, Hou	369
Gonzalez, Marwin, Hou	370
Reddick, Josh, Hou	372
Bogaerts, Xander, Bos	373
Souza Jr., Steven, TB	373

2017 American League Batting Leaders

Under Age 26: AB Per HR
(minimum 502 PA)

Judge, Aaron, NYY	10.4
Gallo, Joey, Tex	11.0
Sanchez, Gary, NYY	14.3
Machado, Manny, Bal	19.1
Schoop, Jonathan, Bal	19.4
Lindor, Francisco, Cle	19.7
Ramirez, Jose, Cle	20.2
Odor, Rougned, Tex	20.2
Mancini, Trey, Bal	22.6
Healy, Ryon, Oak	23.0

Under Age 26: OPS
(minimum 502 PA)

Player	OPS
Judge, Aaron, NYY	1.049
Ramirez, Jose, Cle	.957
Sanchez, Gary, NYY	.876
Gallo, Joey, Tex	.869
Lindor, Francisco, Cle	.842
Schoop, Jonathan, Bal	.841
Bregman, Alex, Hou	.827
Mancini, Trey, Bal	.826
Castellanos, Nick, Det	.811
Betts, Mookie, Bos	.803

Under Age 26: RC/27 Outs
(minimum 502 PA)

Judge, Aaron, NYY	8.5
Ramirez, Jose, Cle	7.1
Betts, Mookie, Bos	6.4
Gallo, Joey, Tex	6.2
Sanchez, Gary, NYY	6.1
Mancini, Trey, Bal	6.0
Lindor, Francisco, Cle	5.8
Benintendi, Andrew, Bos	5.7
Schoop, Jonathan, Bal	5.7
Castellanos, Nick, Det	5.5

Longest Home Run

Player	Distance
Judge, Aaron, NYY, 8/16	495
Judge, Aaron, NYY, 6/11	476
Sanchez, Gary, NYY, 8/22	470
Donaldson, Josh, Tor, 5/30	466
Almonte, A, Cle, 7/16	465
Donaldson, Josh, Tor, 8/13	465
Judge, Aaron, NYY, 9/30	464
Morales, K, Tor, 6/14	464
Smoak, Justin, Tor, 7/26	462
Bautista, Jose, Tor, 5/13	461

Swing and Miss %
(minimum 1500 Pitches Seen)

Player	%
Gallo, Joey, Tex	42.6
Sano, Miguel, Min	38.9
Zunino, Mike, Sea	37.4
Davidson, Matt, CWS	35.4
Davis, Chris, Bal	34.5
Moss, Brandon, KC	34.5
Judge, Aaron, NYY	34.0
Napoli, Mike, Tex	33.9
Davis, Khris, Oak	32.8
Souza Jr., Steven, TB	31.6

Highest First Swing %
(minimum 502 PA)

Player	%
Garcia, Avisail, CWS	46.8
Dickerson, Corey, TB	40.0
Altuve, Jose, Hou	38.8
Perez, Salvador, KC	37.7
Gregorius, Didi, NYY	37.4
Jones, Adam, Bal	36.9
Souza Jr., Steven, TB	36.8
Gallo, Joey, Tex	36.1
Castellanos, Nick, Det	36.0
Davis, Khris, Oak	35.8

Lowest First Swing %
(minimum 502 PA)

Player	%
Mauer, Joe, Min	6.6
Gardner, Brett, NYY	10.5
Betts, Mookie, Bos	11.4
Bogaerts, Xander, Bos	11.5
Reddick, Josh, Hou	13.3
Pujols, Albert, LAA	14.9
Ramirez, Jose, Cle	15.0
Gamel, Ben, Sea	15.5
Polanco, Jorge, Min	16.1
Healy, Ryon, Oak	17.3

Home RC Per 27 Outs
(minimum 251 PA)

Trout, Mike, LAA	9.7
Judge, Aaron, NYY	9.6
Upton, Justin, Det-LAA	7.8
Lindor, Francisco, Cle	7.4
Ramirez, Jose, Cle	7.3
Cruz, Nelson, Sea	7.3
Garcia, Avisail, CWS	7.1
Mazara, Nomar, Tex	7.0
Gonzalez, Marwin, Hou	6.9
Hosmer, Eric, KC	6.9

Road RC Per 27 Outs
(minimum 251 PA)

Altuve, Jose, Hou	10.4
Trout, Mike, LAA	10.2
Donaldson, Josh, Tor	9.1
Gonzalez, Marwin, Hou	8.1
Morrison, Logan, TB	7.4
Hosmer, Eric, KC	7.4
Judge, Aaron, NYY	7.3
Benintendi, Andrew, Bos	7.3
Abreu, Jose, CWS	7.2
Cruz, Nelson, Sea	7.1

Lead Changing RBI

Longoria, Evan, TB	39
Cruz, Nelson, Sea	38
Davis, Khris, Oak	37
Pujols, Albert, LAA	36
Schoop, Jonathan, Bal	34
Abreu, Jose, CWS	32
Encarnacion, Edwin, Cle	32
Betts, Mookie, Bos	31
3 tied with	30

2017 National League Batting Leaders

Batting Average (minimum 502 PA)		On Base Percentage (minimum 502 PA)		Slugging Average (minimum 502 PA)		Home Runs	
Blackmon, Charlie, Col	.331	Votto, Joey, Cin	.454	Stanton, Giancarlo, Mia	.631	Stanton, Giancarlo, Mia	59
Murphy, Daniel, Was	.322	Turner, Justin, LAD	.415	Blackmon, Charlie, Col	.601	Bellinger, Cody, LAD	39
Turner, Justin, LAD	.322	Pham, Tommy, StL	.411	Freeman, Freddie, Atl	.586	Arenado, Nolan, Col	37
Votto, Joey, Cin	.320	Bryant, Kris, ChC	.409	Arenado, Nolan, Col	.586	Blackmon, Charlie, Col	37
Posey, Buster, SF	.320	Goldschmidt, Paul, Ari	.404	Bellinger, Cody, LAD	.581	Ozuna, Marcell, Mia	37
Ozuna, Marcell, Mia	.312	Rendon, Anthony, Was	.403	Votto, Joey, Cin	.578	Goldschmidt, Paul, Ari	36
LeMahieu, DJ, Col	.310	Freeman, Freddie, Atl	.403	Zimmerman, Ryan, Was	.573	Votto, Joey, Cin	36
Arenado, Nolan, Col	.309	Posey, Buster, SF	.400	Goldschmidt, Paul, Ari	.563	Zimmerman, Ryan, Was	36
Gordon, Dee, Mia	.308	Blackmon, Charlie, Col	.399	Ozuna, Marcell, Mia	.548	Rizzo, Anthony, ChC	32
Freeman, Freddie, Atl	.307	Rizzo, Anthony, ChC	.392	Cozart, Zack, Cin	.548	3 tied with	31

Games		Plate Appearances		At Bats		Hits	
Galvis, Freddy, Phi	162	Blackmon, Charlie, Col	725	Inciarte, Ender, Atl	662	Blackmon, Charlie, Col	213
Votto, Joey, Cin	162	Inciarte, Ender, Atl	718	Gordon, Dee, Mia	653	Gordon, Dee, Mia	201
Markakis, Nick, Atl	160	Votto, Joey, Cin	707	Blackmon, Charlie, Col	644	Inciarte, Ender, Atl	201
Arenado, Nolan, Col	159	Gordon, Dee, Mia	695	Ozuna, Marcell, Mia	613	Ozuna, Marcell, Mia	191
Bell, Josh, Pit	159	Yelich, Christian, Mia	695	LeMahieu, DJ, Col	609	LeMahieu, DJ, Col	189
Blackmon, Charlie, Col	159	Stanton, Giancarlo, Mia	692	Galvis, Freddy, Phi	608	Arenado, Nolan, Col	187
Ozuna, Marcell, Mia	159	Rizzo, Anthony, ChC	691	Arenado, Nolan, Col	606	Votto, Joey, Cin	179
Stanton, Giancarlo, Mia	159	LeMahieu, DJ, Col	682	Yelich, Christian, Mia	602	Murphy, Daniel, Was	172
Gordon, Dee, Mia	158	Arenado, Nolan, Col	680	Stanton, Giancarlo, Mia	597	Yelich, Christian, Mia	170
Inciarte, Ender, Atl	158	Ozuna, Marcell, Mia	679	Markakis, Nick, Atl	593	Stanton, Giancarlo, Mia	168

Singles		Doubles		Triples		Total Bases	
Gordon, Dee, Mia	170	Arenado, Nolan, Col	43	Blackmon, Charlie, Col	14	Blackmon, Charlie, Col	387
Inciarte, Ender, Atl	158	Murphy, Daniel, Was	43	Hamilton, Billy, Cin	11	Stanton, Giancarlo, Mia	377
LeMahieu, DJ, Col	149	Herrera, Odubel, Phi	42	Fowler, Dexter, StL	9	Arenado, Nolan, Col	355
Blackmon, Charlie, Col	127	Rendon, Anthony, Was	41	Gordon, Dee, Mia	9	Ozuna, Marcell, Mia	336
Ozuna, Marcell, Mia	122	Markakis, Nick, Atl	39	Arenado, Nolan, Col	7	Votto, Joey, Cin	323
Markakis, Nick, Atl	115	Bryant, Kris, ChC	38	Cozart, Zack, Cin	7	Goldschmidt, Paul, Ari	314
Yelich, Christian, Mia	114	Drury, Brandon, Ari	37	Margot, Manuel, SD	7	Zimmerman, Ryan, Was	300
Hamilton, Billy, Cin	112	Duvall, Adam, Cin	37	Reyes, Jose, NYM	7	Bryant, Kris, ChC	295
Posey, Buster, SF	112	Yelich, Christian, Mia	36	6 tied with	6	Murphy, Daniel, Was	290
Hernandez, Cesar, Phi	109	2 tied with	35			Rizzo, Anthony, ChC	290

Runs Scored		RBI		Walks		Strikeouts	
Blackmon, Charlie, Col	137	Stanton, Giancarlo, Mia	132	Votto, Joey, Cin	134	Story, Trevor, Col	191
Stanton, Giancarlo, Mia	123	Arenado, Nolan, Col	130	Carpenter, Matt, StL	109	Myers, Wil, SD	180
Goldschmidt, Paul, Ari	117	Ozuna, Marcell, Mia	124	Bryant, Kris, ChC	95	Santana, Domingo, Mil	178
Gordon, Dee, Mia	114	Goldschmidt, Paul, Ari	120	Goldschmidt, Paul, Ari	94	Broxton, Keon, Mil	175
Bryant, Kris, ChC	111	Rizzo, Anthony, ChC	109	Rizzo, Anthony, ChC	91	Reynolds, Mark, Col	175
Votto, Joey, Cin	106	Zimmerman, Ryan, Was	108	Lamb, Jake, Ari	87	Duvall, Adam, Cin	170
Arenado, Nolan, Col	100	Lamb, Jake, Ari	105	Stanton, Giancarlo, Mia	85	Stanton, Giancarlo, Mia	163
Yelich, Christian, Mia	100	Blackmon, Charlie, Col	104	Rendon, Anthony, Was	84	Thames, Eric, Mil	163
Rizzo, Anthony, ChC	99	Shaw, Travis, Mil	101	Suarez, Eugenio, Cin	84	Lamb, Jake, Ari	152
3 tied with	95	2 tied with	100	Yelich, Christian, Mia	80	Schwarber, Kyle, ChC	150

2017 National League Batting Leaders

Intentional Walks	
Votto, Joey, Cin	20
Baez, Javier, ChC	15
Goldschmidt, Paul, Ari	15
Freeman, Freddie, Atl	14
Murphy, Daniel, Was	14
Bellinger, Cody, LAD	13
Lamb, Jake, Ari	13
Mercer, Jordy, Pit	13
Posey, Buster, SF	13
Stanton, Giancarlo, Mia	13

BA Bases Loaded (minimum 10 PA)	
Murphy, Daniel, Was	.667
Forsythe, Logan, LAD	.625
Contreras, Willson, ChC	.615
Taylor, Chris, LAD	.600
Williams, Nick, Phi	.556
Gyorko, Jedd, StL	.545
Markakis, Nick, Atl	.545
Reynolds, Mark, Col	.545
Suarez, Eugenio, Cin	.538
6 tied with	.500

Sacrifice Hits	
Davies, Zach, Mil	14
Cole, Gerrit, Pit	12
Teheran, Julio, Atl	12
Godley, Zack, Ari	9
Nova, Ivan, Pit	9
Corbin, Patrick, Ari	8
Marquez, German, Col	8
Richard, Clayton, SD	8
Straily, Dan, Mia	8
Urena, Jose, Mia	8

Sacrifice Flies	
Duvall, Adam, Cin	11
Crawford, Brandon, SF	9
Molina, Yadier, StL	9
Parra, Gerardo, Col	9
Panik, Joe, SF	8
Gyorko, Jedd, StL	7
Myers, Wil, SD	7
Turner, Justin, LAD	7
8 tied with	6

BA Close & Late (minimum 50 PA)	
Taylor, Chris, LAD	.368
Turner, Justin, LAD	.365
Phillips, Brandon, Atl	.356
Frazier, Adam, Pit	.355
Cozart, Zack, Cin	.339
Drury, Brandon, Ari	.333
Freeman, Freddie, Atl	.328
Tomlinson, Kelby, SF	.326
Gennett, Scooter, Cin	.324
Harper, Bryce, Was	.320

Batting Average w/ RISP (minimum 100 PA)	
Murphy, Daniel, Was	.409
Arenado, Nolan, Col	.385
Blackmon, Charlie, Col	.383
Rendon, Anthony, Was	.375
Votto, Joey, Cin	.371
Goldschmidt, Paul, Ari	.365
Contreras, Willson, ChC	.363
Seager, Corey, LAD	.361
Ozuna, Marcell, Mia	.356
Gennett, Scooter, Cin	.349

SLG vs. LHP (minimum 125 PA)	
Arenado, Nolan, Col	.840
Stanton, Giancarlo, Mia	.764
Turner, Justin, LAD	.704
McCutchen, Andrew, Pit	.696
Renfroe, Hunter, SD	.684
Rendon, Anthony, Was	.683
Story, Trevor, Col	.654
Zimmerman, Ryan, Was	.654
Goldschmidt, Paul, Ari	.591
Baez, Javier, ChC	.581

SLG vs. RHP (minimum 377 PA)	
Blackmon, Charlie, Col	.622
Stanton, Giancarlo, Mia	.596
Votto, Joey, Cin	.588
Ozuna, Marcell, Mia	.581
Gennett, Scooter, Cin	.571
Murphy, Daniel, Was	.563
Puig, Yasiel, LAD	.554
Goldschmidt, Paul, Ari	.554
Lamb, Jake, Ari	.552
Thames, Eric, Mil	.551

Leadoff Hitters OBP (minimum 150 PA)	
Carpenter, Matt, StL	.418
Blackmon, Charlie, Col	.397
Conforto, Michael, NYM	.388
Hernandez, Cesar, Phi	.371
Taylor, Chris, LAD	.370
Sogard, Eric, Mil	.367
Blanco, Gregor, Ari	.358
Inciarte, Ender, Atl	.351
Pollock, A.J., Ari	.345
Gordon, Dee, Mia	.341

Cleanup Hitters SLG (minimum 150 PA)	
Hoskins, Rhys, Phi	.621
Contreras, Willson, ChC	.608
Goldschmidt, Paul, Ari	.587
Bellinger, Cody, LAD	.570
Stanton, Giancarlo, Mia	.565
Bruce, Jay, NYM	.563
Ozuna, Marcell, Mia	.536
Lamb, Jake, Ari	.533
Zimmerman, Ryan, Was	.529
Shaw, Travis, Mil	.515

BA vs. LHP (minimum 125 PA)	
Arenado, Nolan, Col	.420
Cabrera, Asdrubal, NYM	.392
Turner, Justin, LAD	.380
LeMahieu, DJ, Col	.362
Posey, Buster, SF	.360
Almora Jr., Albert, ChC	.342
Rendon, Anthony, Was	.337
McCutchen, Andrew, Pit	.336
Blackmon, Charlie, Col	.333
Zimmerman, Ryan, Was	.331

BA vs. RHP (minimum 377 PA)	
Murphy, Daniel, Was	.332
Votto, Joey, Cin	.331
Blackmon, Charlie, Col	.329
Gordon, Dee, Mia	.314
Ozuna, Marcell, Mia	.313
Pham, Tommy, StL	.310
Gennett, Scooter, Cin	.310
Inciarte, Ender, Atl	.307
Posey, Buster, SF	.304
Peralta, David, Ari	.302

Home BA (minimum 251 PA)	
Blackmon, Charlie, Col	.391
Zimmerman, Ryan, Was	.345
Posey, Buster, SF	.345
Ozuna, Marcell, Mia	.344
Arenado, Nolan, Col	.336
Gordon, Dee, Mia	.332
Votto, Joey, Cin	.328
LeMahieu, DJ, Col	.327
Cozart, Zack, Cin	.327
Inciarte, Ender, Atl	.326

Away BA (minimum 251 PA)	
Murphy, Daniel, Was	.341
Pham, Tommy, StL	.340
Taylor, Chris, LAD	.336
Bryant, Kris, ChC	.331
Panik, Joe, SF	.320
Turner, Justin, LAD	.319
Realmuto, J.T., Mia	.317
Votto, Joey, Cin	.313
Cabrera, Asdrubal, NYM	.308
Markakis, Nick, Atl	.304

OBP vs. LHP (minimum 125 PA)	
Turner, Justin, LAD	.477
Arenado, Nolan, Col	.473
Posey, Buster, SF	.451
Stanton, Giancarlo, Mia	.449
Rendon, Anthony, Was	.448
Bryant, Kris, ChC	.439
Votto, Joey, Cin	.437
McCutchen, Andrew, Pit	.435
Cabrera, Asdrubal, NYM	.434
Goldschmidt, Paul, Ari	.422

OBP vs. RHP (minimum 377 PA)	
Votto, Joey, Cin	.461
Pham, Tommy, StL	.411
Blackmon, Charlie, Col	.402
Bryant, Kris, ChC	.400
Rizzo, Anthony, ChC	.398
Goldschmidt, Paul, Ari	.398
Murphy, Daniel, Was	.397
Carpenter, Matt, StL	.395
Rendon, Anthony, Was	.392
Lamb, Jake, Ari	.386

2017 National League Batting Leaders

Stolen Bases			Caught Stealing			Highest SB Success Pct			Lowest SB Success Pct	
						(minimum 20 SBA)			(minimum 20 SBA)	
Gordon, Dee, Mia	60		Gordon, Dee, Mia	16		Turner, Trea, Was	85.2		Blackmon, Charlie, Col	58.3
Hamilton, Billy, Cin	59		Hamilton, Billy, Cin	13		Marte, Starling, Pit	84.0		Arcia, Orlando, Mil	66.7
Turner, Trea, Was	46		Blackmon, Charlie, Col	10		Hamilton, Billy, Cin	81.9		Margot, Manuel, SD	70.8
Pham, Tommy, StL	25		Inciarte, Ender, Atl	9		Taylor, Chris, LAD	81.0		Taylor, Michael, Was	70.8
Reyes, Jose, NYM	24		Peraza, Jose, Cin	8		Reyes, Jose, NYM	80.0		Inciarte, Ender, Atl	71.0
Peraza, Jose, Cin	23		Phillips, Brandon, Atl	8		Gordon, Dee, Mia	78.9		Puig, Yasiel, LAD	71.4
Villar, Jonathan, Mil	23		Turner, Trea, Was	8		Goldschmidt, Paul, Ari	78.3		Peraza, Jose, Cin	74.2
Inciarte, Ender, Atl	22		Villar, Jonathan, Mil	8		Nunez, Eduardo, SF	78.3		Villar, Jonathan, Mil	74.2
Broxton, Keon, Mil	21		6 tied with	7		Pham, Tommy, StL	78.1		Broxton, Keon, Mil	75.0
Marte, Starling, Pit	21					2 tied with	76.9		Hernandez, Cesar, Phi	75.0

Steals of Third			Grounded Into DP			Grounded Into DP Pct			Hit By Pitch	
						(minimum 50 GIDP Ops)				
Turner, Trea, Was	14		Kemp, Matt, Atl	25		Spangenberg, Cory, SD	2.33		Rizzo, Anthony, ChC	24
Hamilton, Billy, Cin	12		LeMahieu, DJ, Col	24		Taylor, Chris, LAD	2.47		Harrison, Josh, Pit	23
Shaw, Travis, Mil	8		Arenado, Nolan, Col	21		Reyes, Jose, NYM	2.97		Flowers, Tyler, Atl	20
Pham, Tommy, StL	7		Franco, Maikel, Phi	21		Taylor, Michael, Was	3.75		Turner, Justin, LAD	19
Pollock, A.J., Ari	7		Joseph, Tommy, Phi	21		Broxton, Keon, Mil	4.29		Dietrich, Derek, Mia	18
Villar, Jonathan, Mil	7		Puig, Yasiel, LAD	21		Renfroe, Hunter, SD	4.44		Bryant, Kris, ChC	15
Gordon, Dee, Mia	6		Rizzo, Anthony, ChC	21		Bellinger, Cody, LAD	4.50		Freese, David, Pit	15
Inciarte, Ender, Atl	6		Shaw, Travis, Mil	20		Owings, Chris, Ari	4.62		Schebler, Scott, Cin	14
Margot, Manuel, SD	6		Cabrera, Asdrubal, NYM	19		Dietrich, Derek, Mia	4.71		Suzuki, Kurt, Atl	13
Perez, Hernan, Mil	6		Phillips, Brandon, Atl	19		Conforto, Michael, NYM	4.76		2 tied with	12

Pitches Seen			At Bats Per Home Run			Highest GB/FB Ratio			Lowest GB/FB Ratio	
			(minimum 502 PA)			(minimum 502 PA)			(minimum 502 PA)	
Blackmon, Charlie, Col	2884		Stanton, Giancarlo, Mia	10.1		Gordon, Dee, Mia	2.93		Carpenter, Matt, StL	0.53
Yelich, Christian, Mia	2883		Bellinger, Cody, LAD	12.3		LeMahieu, DJ, Col	2.82		Turner, Justin, LAD	0.66
Carpenter, Matt, StL	2764		Zimmerman, Ryan, Was	14.6		Freese, David, Pit	2.52		Granderson, C, NYM-LAD	0.67
Goldschmidt, Paul, Ari	2762		Thames, Eric, Mil	15.1		Yelich, Christian, Mia	2.20		Duvall, Adam, Cin	0.68
Stanton, Giancarlo, Mia	2736		Goldschmidt, Paul, Ari	15.5		Hernandez, Cesar, Phi	2.14		Story, Trevor, Col	0.70
Votto, Joey, Cin	2733		Votto, Joey, Cin	15.5		Peralta, David, Ari	2.08		Rendon, Anthony, Was	0.72
Rizzo, Anthony, ChC	2723		Freeman, Freddie, Atl	15.7		Pham, Tommy, StL	1.98		Bellinger, Cody, LAD	0.75
Markakis, Nick, Atl	2717		Schebler, Scott, Cin	15.8		Pence, Hunter, SF	1.95		Arenado, Nolan, Col	0.76
Suarez, Eugenio, Cin	2687		Arenado, Nolan, Col	16.4		Arcia, Orlando, Mil	1.81		Freeman, Freddie, Atl	0.86
LeMahieu, DJ, Col	2676		Ozuna, Marcell, Mia	16.6		Markakis, Nick, Atl	1.66		Murphy, Daniel, Was	0.86

Pitches Per Plate App			Pct Pitches Taken			Best BPS on OutZ			Worst BPS on OutZ	
(minimum 502 PA)			(minimum 1500 Pitches)			(minimum 502 PA)			(minimum 502 PA)	
Granderson, C, NYM-LAD	4.52		Forsythe, Logan, LAD	67.5		Turner, Justin, LAD	.657		Reynolds, Mark, Col	.280
Carpenter, Matt, StL	4.44		Carpenter, Matt, StL	65.4		Rendon, Anthony, Was	.638		Freese, David, Pit	.283
Rendon, Anthony, Was	4.37		Pham, Tommy, StL	62.1		Posey, Buster, SF	.620		Rizzo, Anthony, ChC	.311
Suarez, Eugenio, Cin	4.25		Granderson, C, NYM-LAD	61.7		Zimmerman, Ryan, Was	.619		Franco, Maikel, Phi	.316
Thames, Eric, Mil	4.25		Zobrist, Ben, ChC	60.3		Solarte, Yangervis, SD	.615		Lamb, Jake, Ari	.327
Cozart, Zack, Cin	4.19		Lamb, Jake, Ari	60.2		Myers, Wil, SD	.596		Taylor, Chris, LAD	.331
Reynolds, Mark, Col	4.17		Rendon, Anthony, Was	59.5		Bryant, Kris, ChC	.581		Gonzalez, Carlos, Col	.331
Goldschmidt, Paul, Ari	4.15		Descalso, Daniel, Ari	59.4		Yelich, Christian, Mia	.581		Thames, Eric, Mil	.333
Yelich, Christian, Mia	4.15		Markakis, Nick, Atl	59.3		Murphy, Daniel, Was	.554		Votto, Joey, Cin	.340
Freese, David, Pit	4.13		Cozart, Zack, Cin	59.2		Inciarte, Ender, Atl	.552		Galvis, Freddy, Phi	.354

2017 National League Batting Leaders

Best OPS vs Fastballs
(minimum 251 PA)

Goldschmidt, Paul, Ari	1.085
Votto, Joey, Cin	1.075
Harper, Bryce, Was	1.070
Freeman, Freddie, Atl	1.069
Arenado, Nolan, Col	1.039
Cozart, Zack, Cin	1.007
Reynolds, Mark, Col	.987
Stanton, Giancarlo, Mia	.983
Pham, Tommy, StL	.968
Turner, Justin, LAD	.967

Best OPS vs Curveballs
(minimum 50 PA)

McCutchen, Andrew, Pit	1.207
Blackmon, Charlie, Col	1.204
Votto, Joey, Cin	1.118
Ozuna, Marcell, Mia	1.069
Stanton, Giancarlo, Mia	1.003
Freeman, Freddie, Atl	.993
Renfroe, Hunter, SD	.979
LeMahieu, DJ, Col	.978
Turner, Justin, LAD	.944
Schwarber, Kyle, ChC	.934

Best OPS vs Changeups
(minimum 50 PA)

Arenado, Nolan, Col	1.106
Schwarber, Kyle, ChC	1.081
Drury, Brandon, Ari	1.061
Rendon, Anthony, Was	1.051
Goldschmidt, Paul, Ari	1.050
Blackmon, Charlie, Col	1.044
Bryant, Kris, ChC	1.031
Bellinger, Cody, LAD	1.030
Bour, Justin, Mia	.993
Markakis, Nick, Atl	.968

Best OPS vs Sliders
(minimum 32 PA)

Bour, Justin, Mia	1.296
Conforto, Michael, NYM	1.280
Hoskins, Rhys, Phi	1.219
Aguilar, Jesus, Mil	1.164
Panik, Joe, SF	1.132
Kendrick, Howie, Phi-Was	1.109
Dietrich, Derek, Mia	1.106
Martinez, Jose, StL	1.099
Zimmerman, Ryan, Was	1.071
Martinez, J.D., Ari	1.067

OPS
(minimum 502 PA)

Votto, Joey, Cin	1.032
Stanton, Giancarlo, Mia	1.007
Blackmon, Charlie, Col	1.000
Freeman, Freddie, Atl	.989
Goldschmidt, Paul, Ari	.966
Arenado, Nolan, Col	.959
Bryant, Kris, ChC	.946
Turner, Justin, LAD	.945
Rendon, Anthony, Was	.937
2 tied with	.933

OPS First Half
(minimum 260 PA)

Votto, Joey, Cin	1.058
Turner, Justin, LAD	1.056
Harper, Bryce, Was	1.021
Goldschmidt, Paul, Ari	1.005
Zimmerman, Ryan, Was	.969
Murphy, Daniel, Was	.966
Bellinger, Cody, LAD	.961
Rendon, Anthony, Was	.960
Blackmon, Charlie, Col	.950
Conforto, Michael, NYM	.945

OPS Second Half
(minimum 201 PA)

Martinez, J.D., Ari	1.107
Stanton, Giancarlo, Mia	1.095
Blackmon, Charlie, Col	1.064
Arenado, Nolan, Col	1.032
Hoskins, Rhys, Phi	1.014
Votto, Joey, Cin	.996
Bryant, Kris, ChC	.968
Pham, Tommy, StL	.961
Herrera, Odubel, Phi	.928
Cozart, Zack, Cin	.922

OPS by Catchers
(minimum 251 PA)

Suzuki, Kurt, Atl	.902
Contreras, Willson, ChC	.878
Posey, Buster, SF	.863
Iannetta, Chris, Ari	.857
Flowers, Tyler, Atl	.825
Grandal, Yasmani, LAD	.774
d'Arnaud, Travis, NYM	.769
Realmuto, J.T., Mia	.765
Molina, Yadier, StL	.757
Barnhart, Tucker, Cin	.743

OPS by First Basemen
(minimum 251 PA)

Bellinger, Cody, LAD	1.049
Votto, Joey, Cin	1.032
Freeman, Freddie, Atl	1.009
Goldschmidt, Paul, Ari	.959
Zimmerman, Ryan, Was	.915
Thames, Eric, Mil	.912
Bour, Justin, Mia	.908
Rizzo, Anthony, ChC	.904
Duda, Lucas, NYM	.886
Reynolds, Mark, Col	.848

OPS by Second Basemen
(minimum 251 PA)

Murphy, Daniel, Was	.937
Gennett, Scooter, Cin	.904
Wong, Kolten, StL	.794
Hernandez, Cesar, Phi	.788
LeMahieu, DJ, Col	.787
Forsythe, Logan, LAD	.778
Walker, Neil, NYM-Mil	.778
Panik, Joe, SF	.771
Drury, Brandon, Ari	.771
Phillips, Brandon, Atl	.771

OPS by Third Basemen
(minimum 251 PA)

Arenado, Nolan, Col	.964
Bryant, Kris, ChC	.958
Rendon, Anthony, Was	.938
Turner, Justin, LAD	.932
Shaw, Travis, Mil	.867
Lamb, Jake, Ari	.849
Suarez, Eugenio, Cin	.827
Gyorko, Jedd, StL	.826
Spangenberg, Cory, SD	.792
Dietrich, Derek, Mia	.754

OPS by Shortstops
(minimum 251 PA)

Cozart, Zack, Cin	.940
Seager, Corey, LAD	.864
DeJong, Paul, StL	.836
Reyes, Jose, NYM	.794
Turner, Trea, Was	.788
Story, Trevor, Col	.759
Mercer, Jordy, Pit	.734
Arcia, Orlando, Mil	.727
Rojas, Miguel, Mia	.725
Russell, Addison, ChC	.716

OPS by Left Fielders
(minimum 251 PA)

Pham, Tommy, StL	.983
Ozuna, Marcell, Mia	.932
Cespedes, Yoenis, NYM	.894
Braun, Ryan, Mil	.827
Kemp, Matt, Atl	.800
Parra, Gerardo, Col	.799
Duvall, Adam, Cin	.780
Pirela, Jose, SD	.753
Schwarber, Kyle, ChC	.748
Desmond, Ian, Col	.686

OPS by Center Fielders
(minimum 251 PA)

Blackmon, Charlie, Col	1.001
McCutchen, Andrew, Pit	.869
Fowler, Dexter, StL	.829
Taylor, Michael, Was	.811
Yelich, Christian, Mia	.809
Pollock, A.J., Ari	.799
Almora Jr., Albert, ChC	.788
Herrera, Odubel, Phi	.776
Pederson, Joc, LAD	.764
Inciarte, Ender, Atl	.760

OPS by Right Fielders
(minimum 251 PA)

Martinez, J.D., Ari	1.115
Harper, Bryce, Was	1.012
Stanton, Giancarlo, Mia	1.000
Santana, Domingo, Mil	.873
Peralta, David, Ari	.864
Puig, Yasiel, LAD	.852
Bruce, Jay, NYM	.839
Schebler, Scott, Cin	.814
Gonzalez, Carlos, Col	.760
Renfroe, Hunter, SD	.760

OPS by Pitchers
(minimum 50 PA)

Blach, Ty, SF	.596
Ray, Robbie, Ari	.569
Walker, Taijuan, Ari	.553
Greinke, Zack, Ari	.520
deGrom, Jacob, NYM	.519
Chacin, Jhoulys, SD	.500
Lester, Jon, ChC	.463
Kershaw, Clayton, LAD	.449
Perdomo, Luis, SD	.432
Martinez, Carlos, StL	.429

2017 National League Batting Leaders

OPS Batting Left vs. LHP
(minimum 125 PA)

Player		
Votto, Joey, Cin	.988	
Blackmon, Charlie, Col	.956	
Seager, Corey, LAD	.916	
Bellinger, Cody, LAD	.903	
Rizzo, Anthony, ChC	.881	
Freeman, Freddie, Atl	.880	
Murphy, Daniel, Was	.823	
Harper, Bryce, Was	.802	
Herrera, Odubel, Phi	.794	
Schebler, Scott, Cin	.782	

OPS Batting Left vs. RHP
(minimum 377 PA)

Player	
Votto, Joey, Cin	1.048
Blackmon, Charlie, Col	1.023
Murphy, Daniel, Was	.960
Lamb, Jake, Ari	.938
Thames, Eric, Mil	.933
Gennett, Scooter, Cin	.930
Rizzo, Anthony, ChC	.906
Shaw, Travis, Mil	.892
Carpenter, Matt, StL	.883
Yelich, Christian, Mia	.837

OPS Batting Right vs. LHP
(minimum 125 PA)

Player	
Arenado, Nolan, Col	1.313
Stanton, Giancarlo, Mia	1.212
Turner, Justin, LAD	1.181
McCutchen, Andrew, Pit	1.131
Rendon, Anthony, Was	1.131
Renfroe, Hunter, SD	1.077
Zimmerman, Ryan, Was	1.038
Story, Trevor, Col	1.034
Posey, Buster, SF	1.019
Goldschmidt, Paul, Ari	1.013

OPS Batting Right vs. RHP
(minimum 377 PA)

Player	
Ozuna, Marcell, Mia	.955
Goldschmidt, Paul, Ari	.952
Stanton, Giancarlo, Mia	.950
Bryant, Kris, ChC	.943
Pham, Tommy, StL	.922
Puig, Yasiel, LAD	.909
Cozart, Zack, Cin	.896
Zimmerman, Ryan, Was	.895
Rendon, Anthony, Was	.887
Santana, Domingo, Mil	.870

OPS vs. LHP
(minimum 125 PA)

Player	
Arenado, Nolan, Col	1.313
Stanton, Giancarlo, Mia	1.212
Turner, Justin, LAD	1.181
McCutchen, Andrew, Pit	1.131
Rendon, Anthony, Was	1.131
Renfroe, Hunter, SD	1.077
Zimmerman, Ryan, Was	1.038
Story, Trevor, Col	1.034
Posey, Buster, SF	1.019
Goldschmidt, Paul, Ari	1.013

OPS vs. RHP
(minimum 377 PA)

Player	
Votto, Joey, Cin	1.048
Blackmon, Charlie, Col	1.023
Murphy, Daniel, Was	.960
Ozuna, Marcell, Mia	.955
Goldschmidt, Paul, Ari	.952
Stanton, Giancarlo, Mia	.950
Bryant, Kris, ChC	.943
Lamb, Jake, Ari	.938
Thames, Eric, Mil	.933
Gennett, Scooter, Cin	.930

RC Per 27 Outs vs. LHP
(minimum 125 PA)

Player	
Arenado, Nolan, Col	13.1
Rendon, Anthony, Was	11.7
Stanton, Giancarlo, Mia	11.4
Turner, Justin, LAD	11.4
McCutchen, Andrew, Pit	10.6
Goldschmidt, Paul, Ari	10.4
Renfroe, Hunter, SD	8.7
Freese, David, Pit	8.2
Posey, Buster, SF	8.2
LeMahieu, DJ, Col	8.1

RC Per 27 Outs vs. RHP
(minimum 377 PA)

Player	
Blackmon, Charlie, Col	9.6
Votto, Joey, Cin	9.5
Murphy, Daniel, Was	8.0
Goldschmidt, Paul, Ari	7.8
Ozuna, Marcell, Mia	7.5
Rendon, Anthony, Was	7.4
Bryant, Kris, ChC	7.4
Pham, Tommy, StL	7.1
Carpenter, Matt, StL	7.1
Lamb, Jake, Ari	7.0

Highest RBI %
(minimum 502 PA)

Player	
Blackmon, Charlie, Col	47.75
Arenado, Nolan, Col	46.03
Stanton, Giancarlo, Mia	45.05
Votto, Joey, Cin	44.40
Rendon, Anthony, Was	44.37
Goldschmidt, Paul, Ari	43.88
Murphy, Daniel, Was	43.20
Ozuna, Marcell, Mia	42.67
Bellinger, Cody, LAD	40.93
Freeman, Freddie, Atl	40.69

Lowest RBI %
(minimum 502 PA)

Player	
Gordon, Dee, Mia	21.47
Hamilton, Billy, Cin	21.59
Peraza, Jose, Cin	23.70
Hernandez, Cesar, Phi	26.01
Galvis, Freddy, Phi	27.27
Herrera, Odubel, Phi	27.57
Gonzalez, Carlos, Col	27.80
Inciarte, Ender, Atl	27.80
Harrison, Josh, Pit	28.35
Span, Denard, SF	28.82

Highest Strikeout per PA
(minimum 502 PA)

Player	
Story, Trevor, Col	.344
Thames, Eric, Mil	.296
Reynolds, Mark, Col	.295
Santana, Domingo, Mil	.293
Baez, Javier, ChC	.283
Myers, Wil, SD	.277
Bellinger, Cody, LAD	.266
Duvall, Adam, Cin	.263
Taylor, Chris, LAD	.250
Joseph, Tommy, Phi	.242

Lowest Strikeout per PA
(minimum 502 PA)

Player	
Panik, Joe, SF	.094
Turner, Justin, LAD	.103
Posey, Buster, SF	.116
Votto, Joey, Cin	.117
Solarte, Yangervis, SD	.119
Span, Denard, SF	.127
Murphy, Daniel, Was	.130
Rizzo, Anthony, ChC	.130
Inciarte, Ender, Atl	.131
LeMahieu, DJ, Col	.132

Home Runs At Home

Player	
Stanton, Giancarlo, Mia	31
Blackmon, Charlie, Col	24
Ozuna, Marcell, Mia	22
Reynolds, Mark, Col	21
Suarez, Eugenio, Cin	21
Goldschmidt, Paul, Ari	20
Thames, Eric, Mil	20
Votto, Joey, Cin	20
4 tied with	19

Home Runs Away

Player	
Stanton, Giancarlo, Mia	28
Myers, Wil, SD	22
Bellinger, Cody, LAD	20
Duvall, Adam, Cin	19
Granderson, C, NYM-LAD	19
McCutchen, Andrew, Pit	19
Arenado, Nolan, Col	18
Bruce, Jay, NYM	18
Shaw, Travis, Mil	18
7 tied with	17

Longest Avg Home Run
(min 10 over the wall)

Player	
Pollock, A.J., Ari	409
Aguilar, Jesus, Mil	409
Martinez, J.D., Ari	408
Seager, Corey, LAD	407
Stanton, Giancarlo, Mia	407
Spangenberg, Cory, SD	406
Ozuna, Marcell, Mia	404
Reynolds, Mark, Col	404
Lamb, Jake, Ari	403
Renfroe, Hunter, SD	403

Shortest Avg Home Run
(min 10 over the wall)

Player	
Galvis, Freddy, Phi	368
Span, Denard, SF	369
Rupp, Cameron, Phi	372
Inciarte, Ender, Atl	373
Harrison, Josh, Pit	374
Cozart, Zack, Cin	375
Altherr, Aaron, Phi	376
Franco, Maikel, Phi	376
Zobrist, Ben, ChC	376
Gennett, Scooter, Cin	377

2017 National League Batting Leaders

Under Age 26: AB Per HR
(minimum 502 PA)

Bellinger, Cody, LAD	12.3
Santana, Domingo, Mil	17.5
Bryant, Kris, ChC	18.9
Baez, Javier, ChC	20.4
Story, Trevor, Col	21.0
Bell, Josh, Pit	21.1
Franco, Maikel, Phi	24.0
Seager, Corey, LAD	24.5
Yelich, Christian, Mia	33.4
Arcia, Orlando, Mil	33.7

Under Age 26: OPS
(minimum 502 PA)

Bryant, Kris, ChC	.946
Bellinger, Cody, LAD	.933
Santana, Domingo, Mil	.875
Seager, Corey, LAD	.854
Yelich, Christian, Mia	.807
Bell, Josh, Pit	.800
Baez, Javier, ChC	.796
Herrera, Odubel, Phi	.778
Story, Trevor, Col	.765
Arcia, Orlando, Mil	.731

Under Age 26: RC/27 Outs
(minimum 502 PA)

Bryant, Kris, ChC	7.4
Seager, Corey, LAD	7.0
Bellinger, Cody, LAD	6.9
Santana, Domingo, Mil	6.6
Yelich, Christian, Mia	5.8
Bell, Josh, Pit	5.3
Baez, Javier, ChC	5.1
Story, Trevor, Col	4.4
Arcia, Orlando, Mil	4.3
Herrera, Odubel, Phi	4.2

Longest Home Run

Renfroe, Hunter, SD, 6/14	481
Stanton, G, Mia, 5/7	469
Blash, Jabari, SD, 8/29	465
Renfroe, Hunter, SD, 5/24	465
Grichuk, Randal, StL, 6/25	464
Ozuna, Marcell, Mia, 4/8	464
Myers, Wil, SD, 9/9	463
Stanton, G, Mia, 8/12	463
Harper, Bryce, Was, 7/22	462
3 tied with	460

Swing and Miss %
(minimum 1500 Pitches Seen)

Broxton, Keon, Mil	40.2
Baez, Javier, ChC	35.9
Reynolds, Mark, Col	33.6
Happ, Ian, ChC	33.6
Taylor, Michael, Was	32.6
Renfroe, Hunter, SD	32.2
Bellinger, Cody, LAD	31.7
Santana, Domingo, Mil	31.2
Hedges, Austin, SD	31.1
Gonzalez, Carlos, Col	31.0

Highest First Swing %
(minimum 502 PA)

Freeman, Freddie, Atl	42.8
Seager, Corey, LAD	41.3
Schebler, Scott, Cin	39.0
Ozuna, Marcell, Mia	38.8
Franco, Maikel, Phi	38.3
Crawford, Brandon, SF	36.9
Arcia, Orlando, Mil	36.5
Molina, Yadier, StL	35.9
Herrera, Odubel, Phi	35.5
Santana, Domingo, Mil	35.4

Lowest First Swing %
(minimum 502 PA)

Granderson, C, NYM-LAD	10.4
Carpenter, Matt, StL	11.8
Mercer, Jordy, Pit	13.7
Blackmon, Charlie, Col	14.5
Panik, Joe, SF	14.9
LeMahieu, DJ, Col	15.0
Cozart, Zack, Cin	16.0
Lamb, Jake, Ari	17.1
Rendon, Anthony, Was	17.8
Hernandez, Cesar, Phi	18.4

Home RC Per 27 Outs
(minimum 251 PA)

Blackmon, Charlie, Col	12.9
Votto, Joey, Cin	10.4
Goldschmidt, Paul, Ari	9.3
Rizzo, Anthony, ChC	8.9
Rendon, Anthony, Was	8.9
Stanton, Giancarlo, Mia	8.3
Reynolds, Mark, Col	8.2
Seager, Corey, LAD	8.2
Cozart, Zack, Cin	8.2
Ozuna, Marcell, Mia	8.1

Road RC Per 27 Outs
(minimum 251 PA)

Murphy, Daniel, Was	9.1
Pham, Tommy, StL	8.8
Taylor, Chris, LAD	8.7
Bryant, Kris, ChC	8.6
Votto, Joey, Cin	8.0
Goldschmidt, Paul, Ari	7.6
Rendon, Anthony, Was	7.6
Freeman, Freddie, Atl	7.5
Arenado, Nolan, Col	7.2
Shaw, Travis, Mil	7.2

Lead Changing RBI

Stanton, Giancarlo, Mia	46
Votto, Joey, Cin	38
Arenado, Nolan, Col	36
Shaw, Travis, Mil	36
Zimmerman, Ryan, Was	36
Goldschmidt, Paul, Ari	35
Bellinger, Cody, LAD	34
Harper, Bryce, Was	34
Lamb, Jake, Ari	33
Yelich, Christian, Mia	33

2017 American League Pitching Leaders

Earned Run Average
(minimum 162 IP)

Kluber, Corey, Cle	2.25
Sale, Chris, Bos	2.90
Severino, Luis, NYY	2.98
Stroman, Marcus, Tor	3.09
Santana, Ervin, Min	3.28
Carrasco, Carlos, Cle	3.29
Pomeranz, Drew, Bos	3.32
Verlander, Justin, Det-Hou	3.36
Cashner, Andrew, Tex	3.40
Gray, Sonny, Oak-NYY	3.55

Winning Percentage
(minimum 15 Decisions)

Peacock, Brad, Hou	.867
Kluber, Corey, Cle	.818
Carrasco, Carlos, Cle	.750
Pomeranz, Drew, Bos	.739
Keuchel, Dallas, Hou	.737
Sabathia, CC, NYY	.737
Paxton, James, Sea	.706
Severino, Luis, NYY	.700
Sale, Chris, Bos	.680
3 tied with	.667

Opponent Batting Average
(minimum 162 IP)

Kluber, Corey, Cle	.193
Sale, Chris, Bos	.208
Severino, Luis, NYY	.208
Verlander, Justin, Det-Hou	.221
Santana, Ervin, Min	.225
Gray, Sonny, Oak-NYY	.226
Carrasco, Carlos, Cle	.235
Bundy, Dylan, Bal	.240
Fulmer, Michael, Det	.243
Archer, Chris, TB	.246

Baserunners Per 9 IP
(minimum 162 IP)

Kluber, Corey, Cle	8.04
Sale, Chris, Bos	9.07
Severino, Luis, NYY	9.64
Carrasco, Carlos, Cle	10.31
Santana, Ervin, Min	10.48
Verlander, Justin, Det-Hou	10.75
Fulmer, Michael, Det	10.82
Gray, Sonny, Oak-NYY	11.03
Bundy, Dylan, Bal	11.14
Cobb, Alex, TB	11.29

Games

Moylan, Peter, KC	79
Shaw, Bryan, Cle	79
Jennings, Dan, CWS-TB	77
Tepera, Ryan, Tor	73
Coulombe, Daniel, Oak	72
Greene, Shane, Det	71
Parker, Blake, LAA	71
4 tied with	70

Games Started

Archer, Chris, TB	34
Gausman, Kevin, Bal	34
Estrada, Marco, Tor	33
Nolasco, Ricky, LAA	33
Porcello, Rick, Bos	33
Santana, Ervin, Min	33
Stroman, Marcus, Tor	33
Verlander, Justin, Det-Hou	33
7 tied with	32

Complete Games

Kluber, Corey, Cle	5
Santana, Ervin, Min	5
Porcello, Rick, Bos	2
Stroman, Marcus, Tor	2
18 tied with	1

Shutouts

Kluber, Corey, Cle	3
Santana, Ervin, Min	3
Boyd, Matt, Det	1
Bundy, Dylan, Bal	1
Griffin, A.J., Tex	1
Johnson, Brian, Bos	1
Mengden, Daniel, Oak	1
Nolasco, Ricky, LAA	1
Tanaka, Masahiro, NYY	1
Vargas, Jason, KC	1

Wins

Carrasco, Carlos, Cle	18
Kluber, Corey, Cle	18
Vargas, Jason, KC	18
Bauer, Trevor, Cle	17
Pomeranz, Drew, Bos	17
Sale, Chris, Bos	17
Santana, Ervin, Min	16
Verlander, Justin, Det-Hou	15
5 tied with	14

Losses

Porcello, Rick, Bos	17
Miley, Wade, Bal	15
Nolasco, Ricky, LAA	15
Holland, Derek, CWS	14
Biagini, Joe, Tor	13
Gonzalez, M, CWS-Tex	13
Hammel, Jason, KC	13
Kennedy, Ian, KC	13
Zimmermann, Jordan, Det	13
7 tied with	12

No Decisions

Estrada, Marco, Tor	14
Miranda, Ariel, Sea	14
Montgomery, Jordan, NYY	13
Archer, Chris, TB	12
Kennedy, Ian, KC	12
Nolasco, Ricky, LAA	12
Snell, Blake, TB	12
7 tied with	11

Wild Pitches

Archer, Chris, TB	15
Paxton, James, Sea	15
Santana, Ervin, Min	12
Clippard, T, NYY-CWS-Hou	11
Fiers, Mike, Hou	11
Gray, Sonny, Oak-NYY	11
Tillman, Chris, Bal	11
Carrasco, Carlos, Cle	10
Cashner, Andrew, Tex	10
Gossett, Daniel, Oak	10

Strikeouts

Sale, Chris, Bos	308
Kluber, Corey, Cle	265
Archer, Chris, TB	249
Severino, Luis, NYY	230
Carrasco, Carlos, Cle	226
Verlander, Justin, Det-Hou	219
Bauer, Trevor, Cle	196
Tanaka, Masahiro, NYY	194
Porcello, Rick, Bos	181
Gausman, Kevin, Bal	179

Walks Allowed

Miley, Wade, Bal	93
Holland, Derek, CWS	75
Verlander, Justin, Det-Hou	72
Estrada, Marco, Tor	71
Gausman, Kevin, Bal	71
Pomeranz, Drew, Bos	69
Cashner, Andrew, Tex	64
Miranda, Ariel, Sea	63
Perez, Martin, Tex	63
3 tied with	62

Intentional Walks Allowed

Colome, Alex, TB	7
Jennings, Dan, CWS-TB	7
Belisle, Matt, Min	6
10 tied with	5

Hit Batters

Berrios, Jose, Min	13
Fiers, Mike, Hou	13
Morton, Charlie, Hou	13
Betances, Dellin, NYY	11
Hamels, Cole, Tex	11
McCullers, Lance, Hou	11
Carrasco, Carlos, Cle	10
Manaea, Sean, Oak	10
Pelfrey, Mike, CWS	10
3 tied with	9

2017 American League Pitching Leaders

Runs Allowed

Porcello, Rick, Bos	125
Zimmermann, Jordan, Det	111
Hammel, Jason, KC	109
Jimenez, Ubaldo, Bal	109
Perez, Martin, Tex	108
Holland, Derek, CWS	106
Estrada, Marco, Tor	104
Miley, Wade, Bal	104
Nolasco, Ricky, LAA	102
Archer, Chris, TB	101

Hits Allowed

Porcello, Rick, Bos	236
Perez, Martin, Tex	221
Hammel, Jason, KC	209
Gausman, Kevin, Bal	208
Nolasco, Ricky, LAA	205
Zimmermann, Jordan, Det	204
Stroman, Marcus, Tor	201
Archer, Chris, TB	193
Estrada, Marco, Tor	186
Gibson, Kyle, Min	182

Doubles Allowed

Porcello, Rick, Bos	54
Nolasco, Ricky, LAA	52
Estrada, Marco, Tor	49
Carrasco, Carlos, Cle	44
Tanaka, Masahiro, NYY	42
Bauer, Trevor, Cle	41
Tomlin, Josh, Cle	41
Zimmermann, Jordan, Det	41
5 tied with	39

Home Runs Allowed

Porcello, Rick, Bos	38
Miranda, Ariel, Sea	37
Nolasco, Ricky, LAA	35
Tanaka, Masahiro, NYY	35
Kennedy, Ian, KC	34
Jimenez, Ubaldo, Bal	33
Fiers, Mike, Hou	32
Estrada, Marco, Tor	31
Holland, Derek, CWS	31
Santana, Ervin, Min	31

Run Support Per Nine IP
(minimum 162 IP)

Pomeranz, Drew, Bos	6.63
Tanaka, Masahiro, NYY	6.51
Bundy, Dylan, Bal	6.37
Severino, Luis, NYY	6.24
Carrasco, Carlos, Cle	6.21
Stroman, Marcus, Tor	5.87
Perez, Martin, Tex	5.59
Estrada, Marco, Tor	5.56
Fulmer, Michael, Det	5.47
Archer, Chris, TB	5.46

% Pitches In Strike Zone
(minimum 162 IP)

Porcello, Rick, Bos	48.0
Severino, Luis, NYY	47.8
Kluber, Corey, Cle	47.1
Hammel, Jason, KC	46.7
Sale, Chris, Bos	45.7
Carrasco, Carlos, Cle	45.4
Cashner, Andrew, Tex	45.1
Fulmer, Michael, Det	44.6
Bundy, Dylan, Bal	44.4
Cobb, Alex, TB	44.4

Pitches Per Start
(minimum 30 GS)

Sale, Chris, Bos	107.1
Verlander, Justin, Det-Hou	107.0
Porcello, Rick, Bos	102.5
Bauer, Trevor, Cle	101.3
Archer, Chris, TB	100.2
Severino, Luis, NYY	99.4
Gausman, Kevin, Bal	98.7
Estrada, Marco, Tor	98.4
Santana, Ervin, Min	98.0
Perez, Martin, Tex	96.8

Pitches Per Batter
(minimum 162 IP)

Fulmer, Michael, Det	3.67
Tanaka, Masahiro, NYY	3.74
Santana, Ervin, Min	3.74
Cashner, Andrew, Tex	3.74
Hammel, Jason, KC	3.77
Stroman, Marcus, Tor	3.77
Kluber, Corey, Cle	3.79
Perez, Martin, Tex	3.82
Porcello, Rick, Bos	3.82
Carrasco, Carlos, Cle	3.83

Quality Starts

Sale, Chris, Bos	23
Verlander, Justin, Det-Hou	23
Kluber, Corey, Cle	22
Severino, Luis, NYY	21
Archer, Chris, TB	20
Santana, Ervin, Min	20
Stroman, Marcus, Tor	20
Bundy, Dylan, Bal	19
Carrasco, Carlos, Cle	19
Porcello, Rick, Bos	19

Batters Faced

Porcello, Rick, Bos	885
Santana, Ervin, Min	864
Archer, Chris, TB	852
Sale, Chris, Bos	851
Verlander, Justin, Det-Hou	849
Stroman, Marcus, Tor	834
Gausman, Kevin, Bal	816
Perez, Martin, Tex	811
Estrada, Marco, Tor	806
Hammel, Jason, KC	804

Innings Pitched

Sale, Chris, Bos	214.1
Santana, Ervin, Min	211.1
Verlander, Justin, Det-Hou	206.0
Kluber, Corey, Cle	203.2
Porcello, Rick, Bos	203.1
Archer, Chris, TB	201.0
Stroman, Marcus, Tor	201.0
Carrasco, Carlos, Cle	200.0
Severino, Luis, NYY	193.1
Gausman, Kevin, Bal	186.2

Most Pitches in a Game

Bauer, Trevor, Cle	125
Darvish, Yu, Tex	125
Pomeranz, Drew, Bos	123
Boyd, Matt, Det	121
Kluber, Corey, Cle	120
Miley, Wade, Bal	119
Nolasco, Ricky, LAA	119
Stroman, Marcus, Tor	119
Verlander, Justin, Det-Hou	119
Verlander, Justin, Det-Hou	119

Stolen Bases Allowed

Pelfrey, Mike, CWS	26
Hammel, Jason, KC	20
Biagini, Joe, Tor	19
Fiers, Mike, Hou	18
Jimenez, Ubaldo, Bal	18
Darvish, Yu, Tex	16
Kluber, Corey, Cle	15
Norris, Daniel, Det	15
Porcello, Rick, Bos	15
Triggs, Andrew, Oak	15

Caught Stealing Off

Clevinger, Mike, Cle	10
Carrasco, Carlos, Cle	8
Nolasco, Ricky, LAA	7
Norris, Daniel, Det	7
8 tied with	6

Stolen Base Pct Allowed
(minimum 162 IP)

Perez, Martin, Tex	16.7
Nolasco, Ricky, LAA	36.4
Carrasco, Carlos, Cle	38.5
Bauer, Trevor, Cle	40.0
Bundy, Dylan, Bal	55.6
Tanaka, Masahiro, NYY	57.1
Pomeranz, Drew, Bos	60.0
4 tied with	66.7

Pickoffs

Cobb, Alex, TB	5
Norris, Daniel, Det	5
Hamels, Cole, Tex	4
Holland, Derek, CWS	4
Manaea, Sean, Oak	4
Miley, Wade, Bal	4
Vargas, Jason, KC	4
Boyd, Matt, Det	3
Clevinger, Mike, Cle	3
Duffy, Danny, KC	3

2017 American League Pitching Leaders

Strikeouts Per 9 IP
(minimum 162 IP)

Sale, Chris, Bos	12.93
Kluber, Corey, Cle	11.71
Archer, Chris, TB	11.15
Severino, Luis, NYY	10.71
Carrasco, Carlos, Cle	10.17
Bauer, Trevor, Cle	10.00
Tanaka, Masahiro, NYY	9.79
Verlander, Justin, Det-Hou	9.57
Pomeranz, Drew, Bos	9.02
Gausman, Kevin, Bal	8.63

Opp On-Base Percentage
(minimum 162 IP)

Kluber, Corey, Cle	.235
Sale, Chris, Bos	.254
Severino, Luis, NYY	.266
Santana, Ervin, Min	.286
Carrasco, Carlos, Cle	.287
Verlander, Justin, Det-Hou	.290
Gray, Sonny, Oak-NYY	.294
Fulmer, Michael, Det	.294
Bundy, Dylan, Bal	.301
Archer, Chris, TB	.303

Opp Slugging Average
(minimum 162 IP)

Kluber, Corey, Cle	.321
Severino, Luis, NYY	.338
Sale, Chris, Bos	.349
Fulmer, Michael, Det	.350
Cashner, Andrew, Tex	.365
Verlander, Justin, Det-Hou	.370
Gray, Sonny, Oak-NYY	.374
Carrasco, Carlos, Cle	.386
Pomeranz, Drew, Bos	.388
Santana, Ervin, Min	.392

Opponent OPS
(minimum 162 IP)

Kluber, Corey, Cle	.556
Sale, Chris, Bos	.603
Severino, Luis, NYY	.603
Fulmer, Michael, Det	.644
Verlander, Justin, Det-Hou	.660
Gray, Sonny, Oak-NYY	.668
Carrasco, Carlos, Cle	.674
Santana, Ervin, Min	.678
Cashner, Andrew, Tex	.692
Cobb, Alex, TB	.709

Home Runs Per Nine IP
(minimum 162 IP)

Fulmer, Michael, Det	0.71
Cashner, Andrew, Tex	0.81
Kluber, Corey, Cle	0.93
Stroman, Marcus, Tor	0.94
Carrasco, Carlos, Cle	0.95
Severino, Luis, NYY	0.98
Pomeranz, Drew, Bos	0.98
Sale, Chris, Bos	1.01
Gray, Sonny, Oak-NYY	1.05
Cobb, Alex, TB	1.10

Batting Average vs. LHB
(minimum 125 BF)

Devenski, Chris, Hou	.111
Hamels, Cole, Tex	.161
Morton, Charlie, Hou	.175
Tepera, Ryan, Tor	.194
Kluber, Corey, Cle	.200
Sale, Chris, Bos	.203
Odorizzi, Jake, TB	.210
Brach, Brad, Bal	.212
Jennings, Dan, CWS-TB	.213
Santana, Ervin, Min	.215

Batting Average vs. RHB
(minimum 225 BF)

Peacock, Brad, Hou	.173
Clevinger, Mike, Cle	.180
Kluber, Corey, Cle	.186
Severino, Luis, NYY	.198
Darvish, Yu, Tex	.204
Sale, Chris, Bos	.209
Santiago, Hector, Min	.211
Bundy, Dylan, Bal	.222
Berrios, Jose, Min	.222
Verlander, Justin, Det-Hou	.222

Opp BA w/ RISP
(minimum 125 BF)

Cashner, Andrew, Tex	.170
Morton, Charlie, Hou	.190
Santana, Ervin, Min	.199
Verlander, Justin, Det-Hou	.200
Pomeranz, Drew, Bos	.211
Darvish, Yu, Tex	.216
Happ, J.A., Tor	.220
Montgomery, Jordan, NYY	.221
Sabathia, CC, NYY	.225
Hammel, Jason, KC	.226

OBP vs. Leadoff Hitter
(minimum 150 BF)

Kluber, Corey, Cle	.203
Sale, Chris, Bos	.227
Sabathia, CC, NYY	.259
Santana, Ervin, Min	.260
Severino, Luis, NYY	.261
Montgomery, Jordan, NYY	.262
Cobb, Alex, TB	.266
Gray, Sonny, Oak-NYY	.277
Carrasco, Carlos, Cle	.278
Odorizzi, Jake, TB	.278

Strikeouts / Walks Ratio
(minimum 162 IP)

Kluber, Corey, Cle	7.36
Sale, Chris, Bos	7.16
Carrasco, Carlos, Cle	4.91
Tanaka, Masahiro, NYY	4.73
Severino, Luis, NYY	4.51
Archer, Chris, TB	4.15
Porcello, Rick, Bos	3.77
Bauer, Trevor, Cle	3.27
Verlander, Justin, Det-Hou	3.04
Hammel, Jason, KC	3.02

Highest GB/FB Ratio
(minimum 162 IP)

Stroman, Marcus, Tor	3.15
Gray, Sonny, Oak-NYY	1.92
Fulmer, Michael, Det	1.70
Perez, Martin, Tex	1.69
Severino, Luis, NYY	1.65
Cobb, Alex, TB	1.58
Cashner, Andrew, Tex	1.51
Tanaka, Masahiro, NYY	1.51
Bauer, Trevor, Cle	1.45
Carrasco, Carlos, Cle	1.37

Lowest GB/FB Ratio
(minimum 162 IP)

Estrada, Marco, Tor	0.60
Bundy, Dylan, Bal	0.70
Verlander, Justin, Det-Hou	0.78
Hammel, Jason, KC	0.92
Sale, Chris, Bos	0.94
Santana, Ervin, Min	0.97
Porcello, Rick, Bos	0.98
Vargas, Jason, KC	1.00
Nolasco, Ricky, LAA	1.03
Archer, Chris, TB	1.17

Sacrifice Flies Allowed

Hammel, Jason, KC	10
Fulmer, Michael, Det	8
Miranda, Ariel, Sea	8
Zimmermann, Jordan, Det	8
Bundy, Dylan, Bal	7
Odorizzi, Jake, TB	7
Ramirez, Erasmo, TB-Sea	7
12 tied with	6

Sacrifice Hits Allowed

Duffy, Danny, KC	6
Nolasco, Ricky, LAA	6
Loup, Aaron, Tor	5
Musgrove, Joe, Hou	5
7 tied with	4

GIDP Induced

Stroman, Marcus, Tor	34
Perez, Martin, Tex	32
Gibson, Kyle, Min	26
Cashner, Andrew, Tex	23
Keuchel, Dallas, Hou	23
Pomeranz, Drew, Bos	23
Vargas, Jason, KC	22
Gausman, Kevin, Bal	21
Fulmer, Michael, Det	20
3 tied with	19

GIDP Per Nine IP
(minimum 162 IP)

Perez, Martin, Tex	1.56
Stroman, Marcus, Tor	1.52
Cashner, Andrew, Tex	1.24
Pomeranz, Drew, Bos	1.19
Vargas, Jason, KC	1.10
Fulmer, Michael, Det	1.09
Gausman, Kevin, Bal	1.01
Bundy, Dylan, Bal	0.95
Carrasco, Carlos, Cle	0.86
Bauer, Trevor, Cle	0.82

2017 American League Pitching Leaders

Saves			Blown Saves			Save Pct			Save Opportunities		
						(minimum 20 Save Ops)					
Colome, Alex, TB	47		Osuna, Roberto, Tor	10		Kimbrel, Craig, Bos	89.7		Colome, Alex, TB	53	
Osuna, Roberto, Tor	39		Casilla, Santiago, Oak	7		Giles, Ken, Hou	89.5		Osuna, Roberto, Tor	49	
Kimbrel, Craig, Bos	35		Soria, Joakim, KC	7		Colome, Alex, TB	88.7		Diaz, Edwin, Sea	39	
Diaz, Edwin, Sea	34		Brach, Brad, Bal	6		Allen, Cody, Cle	88.2		Kimbrel, Craig, Bos	39	
Giles, Ken, Hou	34		Clippard, T, NYY-CWS-Hou	6		Kintzler, Brandon, Min	87.5		Giles, Ken, Hou	38	
Allen, Cody, Cle	30		Colome, Alex, TB	6		Diaz, Edwin, Sea	87.2		Allen, Cody, Cle	34	
Kintzler, Brandon, Min	28		Devenski, Chris, Hou	6		Chapman, Aroldis, NYY	84.6		Kintzler, Brandon, Min	32	
Herrera, Kelvin, KC	26		Kahnle, T, CWS-NYY	6		Herrera, Kelvin, KC	83.9		Herrera, Kelvin, KC	31	
Chapman, Aroldis, NYY	22		Rodriguez, Francisco, Det	6		Norris, Bud, LAA	82.6		Chapman, Aroldis, NYY	26	
Norris, Bud, LAA	19		7 tied with	5		Osuna, Roberto, Tor	79.6		Brach, Brad, Bal	24	

Easy Saves			Regular Saves			Tough Saves			Holds Adjusted Saves %		
									(minimum 20 Save Ops + Holds)		
Colome, Alex, TB	32		Diaz, Edwin, Sea	16		Colome, Alex, TB	4		Hunter, Tommy, TB	100.0	
Kimbrel, Craig, Bos	24		Osuna, Roberto, Tor	13		Alexander, Scott, KC	3		Moylan, Peter, KC	96.0	
Osuna, Roberto, Tor	24		Colome, Alex, TB	11		Claudio, Alex, Tex	3		Smith, Joe, Tor-Cle	95.7	
Giles, Ken, Hou	22		Giles, Ken, Hou	11		Diaz, Edwin, Sea	3		Miller, Andrew, Cle	93.5	
Kintzler, Brandon, Min	19		Kimbrel, Craig, Bos	11		Treinen, Blake, Oak	3		Vincent, Nick, Sea	93.5	
Allen, Cody, Cle	18		Allen, Cody, Cle	10		7 tied with	2		Barnes, Matt, Bos	91.7	
Herrera, Kelvin, KC	18		Norris, Bud, LAA	10					Harris, Will, Hou	91.7	
Chapman, Aroldis, NYY	15		Herrera, Kelvin, KC	8					Robertson, D, CWS-NYY	91.7	
Diaz, Edwin, Sea	15		Kintzler, Brandon, Min	7					Rzepczynski, Marc, Sea	91.3	
Brach, Brad, Bal	13		3 tied with	6					Wilson, Justin, Det	91.3	

Relief Wins			Relief Losses			Relief Games			Holds		
Robertson, D, CWS-NYY	9		Clippard, T, NYY-CWS-Hou	8		Moylan, Peter, KC	79		Rogers, Taylor, Min	30	
Devenski, Chris, Hou	8		Allen, Cody, Cle	7		Shaw, Bryan, Cle	79		Vincent, Nick, Sea	29	
Givens, Mychal, Bal	8		Barnes, Danny, Tor	7		Jennings, Dan, CWS-TB	77		Miller, Andrew, Cle	27	
Barnes, Matt, Bos	7		Betances, Dellin, NYY	6		Tepera, Ryan, Tor	73		Shaw, Bryan, Cle	26	
Rogers, Taylor, Min	7		Diaz, Edwin, Sea	6		Coulombe, Daniel, Oak	72		Hunter, Tommy, TB	25	
Tepera, Ryan, Tor	7		Dyson, Sam, Tex	6		Greene, Shane, Det	71		Devenski, Chris, Hou	24	
Bedrosian, Cam, LAA	6		Minor, Mike, KC	6		Parker, Blake, LAA	71		Moylan, Peter, KC	24	
Middleton, Keynan, LAA	6		Shaw, Bryan, Cle	6		Barnes, Matt, Bos	70		Barnes, Matt, Bos	21	
Minor, Mike, KC	6		10 tied with	5		Hendriks, Liam, Oak	70		Givens, Mychal, Bal	21	
Zych, Tony, Sea	6					Loup, Aaron, Tor	70		Smith, Joe, Tor-Cle	21	

Relief Innings			Inherited Runners Scrd %			Relief Opp On Base Pct			Relief Opp Slugging Avg		
			(minimum 30 IR)			(minimum 50 IP)			(minimum 50 IP)		
Petit, Yusmeiro, LAA	87.1		Green, Chad, NYY	12.9		Kimbrel, Craig, Bos	.202		Miller, Andrew, Cle	.205	
Devenski, Chris, Hou	80.2		Barnes, Danny, Tor	13.5		Green, Chad, NYY	.207		Betances, Dellin, NYY	.215	
Claudio, Alex, Tex	78.2		Rogers, Taylor, Min	14.3		Parker, Blake, LAA	.225		Green, Chad, NYY	.233	
Givens, Mychal, Bal	78.2		Rzepczynski, Marc, Sea	15.4		Warren, Adam, NYY	.229		Kimbrel, Craig, Bos	.243	
Minor, Mike, KC	77.2		Alvarez, Jose, LAA	17.1		Robertson, D, CWS-NYY	.231		Robertson, D, CWS-NYY	.257	
Tepera, Ryan, Tor	77.2		Greene, Shane, Det	19.1		Osuna, Roberto, Tor	.234		Warren, Adam, NYY	.262	
Shaw, Bryan, Cle	76.2		Hendriks, Liam, Oak	21.6		Miller, Andrew, Cle	.236		Osuna, Roberto, Tor	.274	
Duffey, Tyler, Min	71.0		Parker, Blake, LAA	21.6		Pagan, Emilio, Sea	.246		Kelly, Joe, Bos	.279	
Leone, Dominic, Tor	70.1		Vincent, Nick, Sea	21.9		Devenski, Chris, Hou	.247		Moylan, Peter, KC	.288	
Barnes, Matt, Bos	69.2		2 tied with	22.0		Petit, Yusmeiro, LAA	.251		Soria, Joakim, KC	.290	

2017 American League Pitching Leaders

Relief Opp BA Vs LHB
(minimum 50 AB)

Devenski, Chris, Hou	.111
Scott, Robby, Bos	.121
Betances, Dellin, NYY	.122
Green, Chad, NYY	.123
Robertson, D, CWS-NYY	.140
Claudio, Alex, Tex	.147
Belisle, Matt, Min	.162
Minor, Mike, KC	.163
Miller, Andrew, Cle	.164
Shreve, Chasen, NYY	.164

Relief Opp BA Vs RHB
(minimum 50 AB)

Leclerc, Jose, Tex	.108
Kimbrel, Craig, Bos	.109
Kela, Keone, Tex	.113
Wilson, Justin, Det	.131
Miller, Andrew, Cle	.136
Cishek, Steve, Sea-TB	.148
Warren, Adam, NYY	.152
Robertson, D, CWS-NYY	.154
Green, Chad, NYY	.155
Alvarado, Jose, TB	.156

Relief Opp Batting Average
(minimum 50 IP)

Kimbrel, Craig, Bos	.140
Betances, Dellin, NYY	.141
Green, Chad, NYY	.143
Miller, Andrew, Cle	.144
Robertson, D, CWS-NYY	.148
Parker, Blake, LAA	.172
Warren, Adam, NYY	.173
Devenski, Chris, Hou	.174
Diaz, Edwin, Sea	.183
Moylan, Peter, KC	.189

Relief Earned Run Average
(minimum 50 IP)

Kimbrel, Craig, Bos	1.43
Miller, Andrew, Cle	1.44
Green, Chad, NYY	1.61
Robertson, D, CWS-NYY	1.84
Bleier, Richard, Bal	1.99
Claudio, Alex, Tex	2.29
Giles, Ken, Hou	2.30
Warren, Adam, NYY	2.35
Alexander, Scott, KC	2.48
Parker, Blake, LAA	2.54

Rel OBP 1st Batter Faced
(minimum 40 BF)

Petit, Yusmeiro, LAA	.138
Giles, Ken, Hou	.177
Dull, Ryan, Oak	.184
Moylan, Peter, KC	.190
Miller, Andrew, Cle	.193
Harris, Will, Hou	.196
Parker, Blake, LAA	.200
Smith, Joe, Tor-Cle	.203
Hunter, Tommy, TB	.213
Wilson, Justin, Det	.214

Rel Opp BA w/ Runners On
(minimum 50 IP)

Green, Chad, NYY	.077
Kimbrel, Craig, Bos	.084
Minor, Mike, KC	.153
Betances, Dellin, NYY	.161
Diaz, Edwin, Sea	.162
Miller, Andrew, Cle	.163
Robertson, D, CWS-NYY	.169
Greene, Shane, Det	.179
Warren, Adam, NYY	.182
Devenski, Chris, Hou	.193

Relief Opp BA w/ RISP
(minimum 50 IP)

Kimbrel, Craig, Bos	.063
Green, Chad, NYY	.103
Barnes, Danny, Tor	.118
Betances, Dellin, NYY	.121
Miller, Andrew, Cle	.127
Warren, Adam, NYY	.133
Rogers, Taylor, Min	.152
O'Day, Darren, Bal	.154
Robertson, D, CWS-NYY	.160
Minor, Mike, KC	.162

Fastest Avg Fastball-Relief
(minimum 50 IP)

Chapman, Aroldis, NYY	100.1
Kelly, Joe, Bos	99.0
Betances, Dellin, NYY	98.5
Kimbrel, Craig, Bos	98.3
Giles, Ken, Hou	98.1
Kahnle, T, CWS-NYY	97.9
Bush, Matt, Tex	97.5
Herrera, Kelvin, KC	97.5
Diaz, Edwin, Sea	97.3
Middleton, Keynan, LAA	96.8

Fastest Average Fastball
(minimum 162 IP)

Severino, Luis, NYY	97.6
Fulmer, Michael, Det	95.8
Archer, Chris, TB	95.5
Verlander, Justin, Det-Hou	95.2
Gausman, Kevin, Bal	95.0
Sale, Chris, Bos	94.4
Carrasco, Carlos, Cle	94.3
Bauer, Trevor, Cle	94.0
Cashner, Andrew, Tex	93.4
Stroman, Marcus, Tor	93.3

Slowest Average Fastball
(minimum 162 IP)

Vargas, Jason, KC	85.6
Estrada, Marco, Tor	89.9
Nolasco, Ricky, LAA	90.9
Porcello, Rick, Bos	91.1
Pomeranz, Drew, Bos	91.3
Cobb, Alex, TB	91.7
Hammel, Jason, KC	92.1
Bundy, Dylan, Bal	92.2
Tanaka, Masahiro, NYY	92.2
Kluber, Corey, Cle	92.6

Pitches 100+ Velocity

Chapman, Aroldis, NYY	447
Kelly, Joe, Bos	245
Betances, Dellin, NYY	119
Severino, Luis, NYY	119
Kahnle, T, CWS-NYY	98
Kimbrel, Craig, Bos	67
Diaz, Edwin, Sea	46
Montas, Frankie, Oak	46
Giles, Ken, Hou	43
Stanek, Ryne, TB	42

Pitches 95+ Velocity

Severino, Luis, NYY	1561
Verlander, Justin, Det-Hou	1461
Gausman, Kevin, Bal	1368
Fulmer, Michael, Det	1275
Archer, Chris, TB	1264
Paxton, James, Sea	1121
Ramirez, JC, LAA	931
Sale, Chris, Bos	874
Morton, Charlie, Hou	843
Kimbrel, Craig, Bos	786

Pitches Less Than 80 MPH

Estrada, Marco, Tor	1205
Vargas, Jason, KC	1032
Quintana, Jose, CWS	886
Clippard, T, NYY-CWS-Hou	816
Gonzalez, M, CWS-Tex	744
Cishek, Steve, Sea-TB	704
Bauer, Trevor, Cle	633
Pomeranz, Drew, Bos	621
Porcello, Rick, Bos	596
Cotton, Jharel, Oak	551

Lowest % Fastballs
(minimum 162 IP)

Tanaka, Masahiro, NYY	27.7
Kluber, Corey, Cle	42.5
Vargas, Jason, KC	47.0
Archer, Chris, TB	47.6
Nolasco, Ricky, LAA	48.4
Carrasco, Carlos, Cle	48.4
Sale, Chris, Bos	49.2
Bauer, Trevor, Cle	49.2
Hammel, Jason, KC	50.1
Severino, Luis, NYY	51.4

Highest % Fastballs
(minimum 162 IP)

Cashner, Andrew, Tex	65.3
Gausman, Kevin, Bal	64.4
Stroman, Marcus, Tor	62.1
Porcello, Rick, Bos	59.6
Fulmer, Michael, Det	59.3
Perez, Martin, Tex	58.7
Verlander, Justin, Det-Hou	58.2
Gray, Sonny, Oak-NYY	55.1
Pomeranz, Drew, Bos	55.0
Bundy, Dylan, Bal	53.7

Highest % Curveballs
(minimum 162 IP)

Pomeranz, Drew, Bos	37.0
Cobb, Alex, TB	34.1
Bauer, Trevor, Cle	29.8
Kluber, Corey, Cle	27.4
Vargas, Jason, KC	20.3
Carrasco, Carlos, Cle	16.2
Verlander, Justin, Det-Hou	15.9
Porcello, Rick, Bos	15.5
Gray, Sonny, Oak-NYY	13.9
Perez, Martin, Tex	11.2

2017 American League Pitching Leaders

Highest % Changeups
(minimum 162 IP)

Vargas, Jason, KC	32.7
Estrada, Marco, Tor	31.9
Perez, Martin, Tex	20.5
Fulmer, Michael, Det	18.9
Sale, Chris, Bos	17.9
Carrasco, Carlos, Cle	16.5
Gray, Sonny, Oak-NYY	14.9
Cobb, Alex, TB	14.4
Cashner, Andrew, Tex	14.2
Bundy, Dylan, Bal	13.7

Highest % Sliders
(minimum 162 IP)

Archer, Chris, TB	44.4
Hammel, Jason, KC	36.8
Santana, Ervin, Min	36.5
Severino, Luis, NYY	35.1
Sale, Chris, Bos	32.9
Tanaka, Masahiro, NYY	30.5
Nolasco, Ricky, LAA	27.4
Stroman, Marcus, Tor	23.5
Bundy, Dylan, Bal	22.3
Verlander, Justin, Det-Hou	21.6

Balks

Claudio, Alex, Tex	3
Andriese, Matt, TB	2
Cotton, Jharel, Oak	2
Duffy, Danny, KC	2
Fulmer, Carson, CWS	2
Gaviglio, Sam, Sea-KC	2
Mejia, Adalberto, Min	2
Skaggs, Tyler, LAA	2
55 tied with	1

Strikeout/Hit Ratio
(minimum 50 IP)

Kimbrel, Craig, Bos	3.82
Betances, Dellin, NYY	3.45
Miller, Andrew, Cle	3.06
Green, Chad, NYY	3.03
Robertson, D, CWS-NYY	2.80
Parker, Blake, LAA	2.15
Diaz, Edwin, Sea	2.02
Devenski, Chris, Hou	2.00
Giles, Ken, Hou	1.89
Kluber, Corey, Cle	1.88

Opp OPS vs Fastballs
(minimum 251 BF)

Verlander, Justin, Det-Hou	.555
Peacock, Brad, Hou	.566
Paxton, James, Sea	.575
Sale, Chris, Bos	.584
Keuchel, Dallas, Hou	.618
Fulmer, Michael, Det	.625
Gray, Sonny, Oak-NYY	.635
Alexander, Scott, KC	.637
Kluber, Corey, Cle	.670
Cashner, Andrew, Tex	.674

Opp OPS vs Curveballs
(minimum 100 BF)

Kluber, Corey, Cle	.344
Robertson, D, CWS-NYY	.366
Allen, Cody, Cle	.483
Carrasco, Carlos, Cle	.494
Morton, Charlie, Hou	.501
Montgomery, Jordan, NYY	.587
Cobb, Alex, TB	.589
Meyer, Alex, LAA	.608
Shields, James, CWS	.623
McCullers, Lance, Hou	.629

Opp OPS vs Changeups
(minimum 100 BF)

Carrasco, Carlos, Cle	.359
Severino, Luis, NYY	.423
Salazar, Danny, Cle	.532
Clippard, T, NYY-CWS-Hou	.547
Montgomery, Jordan, NYY	.551
Devenski, Chris, Hou	.569
Vargas, Jason, KC	.577
Sale, Chris, Bos	.582
Duffy, Danny, KC	.612
Rodriguez, Eduardo, Bos	.632

Opp OPS vs Sliders
(minimum 64 BF)

Miller, Andrew, Cle	.366
Cishek, Steve, Sea-TB	.383
Odorizzi, Jake, TB	.407
Minor, Mike, KC	.415
Altavilla, Dan, Sea	.470
Betances, Dellin, NYY	.470
Clevinger, Mike, Cle	.483
Giles, Ken, Hou	.489
Musgrove, Joe, Hou	.520
Faria, Jake, TB	.525

Earned Runs

Jimenez, Ubaldo, Bal	108
Zimmermann, Jordan, Det	108
Hammel, Jason, KC	106
Porcello, Rick, Bos	105
Estrada, Marco, Tor	103
Nolasco, Ricky, LAA	99
Perez, Martin, Tex	99
Miley, Wade, Bal	98
Gausman, Kevin, Bal	97
Tanaka, Masahiro, NYY	94

Hits Per Nine Innings
(minimum 162 IP)

Kluber, Corey, Cle	6.23
Sale, Chris, Bos	6.93
Severino, Luis, NYY	6.98
Verlander, Justin, Det-Hou	7.43
Santana, Ervin, Min	7.54
Gray, Sonny, Oak-NYY	7.71
Carrasco, Carlos, Cle	7.79
Bundy, Dylan, Bal	8.06
Fulmer, Michael, Det	8.20
Cashner, Andrew, Tex	8.42

2017 National League Pitching Leaders

Earned Run Average
(minimum 162 IP)

Kershaw, Clayton, LAD	2.31
Scherzer, Max, Was	2.51
Strasburg, Stephen, Was	2.52
Ray, Robbie, Ari	2.89
Gonzalez, Gio, Was	2.96
Greinke, Zack, Ari	3.20
Lynn, Lance, StL	3.43
Nelson, Jimmy, Mil	3.49
Arrieta, Jake, ChC	3.53
deGrom, Jacob, NYM	3.53

Winning Percentage
(minimum 15 Decisions)

Wood, Alex, LAD	.842
Kershaw, Clayton, LAD	.818
Strasburg, Stephen, Was	.789
Anderson, Chase, Mil	.750
Ray, Robbie, Ari	.750
Scherzer, Max, Was	.727
Greinke, Zack, Ari	.708
Wainwright, Adam, StL	.706
Maeda, Kenta, LAD	.684
3 tied with	.667

Opponent Batting Average
(minimum 162 IP)

Scherzer, Max, Was	.178
Ray, Robbie, Ari	.199
Strasburg, Stephen, Was	.204
Kershaw, Clayton, LAD	.212
Gonzalez, Gio, Was	.216
Lynn, Lance, StL	.223
Greinke, Zack, Ari	.230
Martinez, Carlos, StL	.232
Chacin, Jhoulys, SD	.235
Arrieta, Jake, ChC	.235

Baserunners Per 9 IP
(minimum 162 IP)

Kershaw, Clayton, LAD	8.54
Scherzer, Max, Was	8.61
Strasburg, Stephen, Was	9.50
Greinke, Zack, Ari	9.65
Samardzija, Jeff, SF	10.49
Ray, Robbie, Ari	10.67
deGrom, Jacob, NYM	10.77
Gonzalez, Gio, Was	10.93
Nola, Aaron, Phi	10.98
Martinez, Carlos, StL	11.33

Games

Knebel, Corey, Mil	76
Nicasio, Juan, Pit-Phi-StL	76
Blevins, Jerry, NYM	75
Bowman, Matt, StL	75
Neris, Hector, Phi	74
Barnes, Jacob, Mil	73
Cecil, Brett, StL	73
Edwards Jr., Carl, ChC	73
Rivero, Felipe, Pit	73
Hand, Brad, SD	72

Games Started

Cole, Gerrit, Pit	33
Davies, Zach, Mil	33
Lynn, Lance, StL	33
Straily, Dan, Mia	33
9 tied with	32

Complete Games

Martinez, Carlos, StL	2
Nova, Ivan, Pit	2
Richard, Clayton, SD	2
Scherzer, Max, Was	2
19 tied with	1

Shutouts

Martinez, Carlos, StL	2
11 tied with	1

Wins

Kershaw, Clayton, LAD	18
Davies, Zach, Mil	17
Greinke, Zack, Ari	17
Scherzer, Max, Was	16
Wood, Alex, LAD	16
deGrom, Jacob, NYM	15
Gonzalez, Gio, Was	15
Ray, Robbie, Ari	15
Strasburg, Stephen, Was	15
3 tied with	14

Losses

Chatwood, Tyler, Col	15
Moore, Matt, SF	15
Richard, Clayton, SD	15
Samardzija, Jeff, SF	15
Nova, Ivan, Pit	14
Corbin, Patrick, Ari	13
Foltynewicz, Mike, Atl	13
Teheran, Julio, Atl	13
4 tied with	12

No Decisions

Lynn, Lance, StL	14
Straily, Dan, Mia	14
Eickhoff, Jerad, Phi	12
Hendricks, Kyle, ChC	12
Kuhl, Chad, Pit	12
Dickey, R.A., Atl	11
Lester, Jon, ChC	11
Marquez, German, Col	11
Nelson, Jimmy, Mil	11
Williams, Trevor, Pit	11

Wild Pitches

Arrieta, Jake, ChC	14
Cahill, Trevor, SD	14
Dickey, R.A., Atl	13
Godley, Zack, Ari	13
Chatwood, Tyler, Col	12
Greinke, Zack, Ari	12
Lorenzen, Michael, Cin	12
Lackey, John, ChC	11
Perdomo, Luis, SD	11
Pivetta, Nick, Phi	11

Strikeouts

Scherzer, Max, Was	268
deGrom, Jacob, NYM	239
Ray, Robbie, Ari	218
Martinez, Carlos, StL	217
Greinke, Zack, Ari	215
Samardzija, Jeff, SF	205
Strasburg, Stephen, Was	204
Kershaw, Clayton, LAD	202
Nelson, Jimmy, Mil	199
Cole, Gerrit, Pit	196

Walks Allowed

Gonzalez, Gio, Was	79
Lynn, Lance, StL	78
Chatwood, Tyler, Col	77
Chacin, Jhoulys, SD	72
Kuhl, Chad, Pit	72
Teheran, Julio, Atl	72
Martinez, Carlos, StL	71
Ray, Robbie, Ari	71
3 tied with	67

Intentional Walks Allowed

Oh, Seung Hwan, StL	9
Corbin, Patrick, Ari	8
Kuhl, Chad, Pit	7
Smoker, Josh, NYM	7
Walker, Taijuan, Ari	7
Watson, Tony, Pit-LAD	7
7 tied with	6

Hit Batters

Chacin, Jhoulys, SD	14
Urena, Jose, Mia	14
Lackey, John, ChC	12
Scherzer, Max, Was	11
Arrieta, Jake, ChC	10
Dickey, R.A., Atl	10
Foltynewicz, Mike, Atl	10
Lynn, Lance, StL	10
Storen, Drew, Cin	10
5 tied with	9

2017 National League Pitching Leaders

Runs Allowed			Hits Allowed			Doubles Allowed			Home Runs Allowed	
Moore, Matt, SF	116		Richard, Clayton, SD	240		Richard, Clayton, SD	48		Lackey, John, ChC	36
Richard, Clayton, SD	114		Corbin, Patrick, Ari	208		Corbin, Patrick, Ari	47		Cole, Gerrit, Pit	31
Samardzija, Jeff, SF	107		Davies, Zach, Mil	204		Dickey, R.A., Atl	46		Straily, Dan, Mia	31
Roark, Tanner, Was	105		Samardzija, Jeff, SF	204		Moore, Matt, SF	44		Teheran, Julio, Atl	31
Teheran, Julio, Atl	103		Nova, Ivan, Pit	203		Kuhl, Chad, Pit	41		Samardzija, Jeff, SF	30
Lester, Jon, ChC	101		Moore, Matt, SF	200		Straily, Dan, Mia	41		Adleman, Tim, Cin	29
Dickey, R.A., Atl	99		Cole, Gerrit, Pit	199		Nova, Ivan, Pit	40		Nova, Ivan, Pit	29
Cole, Gerrit, Pit	98		Dickey, R.A., Atl	193		Samardzija, Jeff, SF	40		deGrom, Jacob, NYM	28
Corbin, Patrick, Ari	97		Teheran, Julio, Atl	186		Perdomo, Luis, SD	39		3 tied with	27
Perdomo, Luis, SD	97		Perdomo, Luis, SD	182		Taillon, Jameson, Pit	38			

Run Support Per Nine IP			% Pitches In Strike Zone			Pitches Per Start			Pitches Per Batter	
(minimum 162 IP)			(minimum 162 IP)			(minimum 30 GS)			(minimum 162 IP)	
Scherzer, Max, Was	6.10		Marquez, German, Col	52.0		Gonzalez, Gio, Was	105.1		Nova, Ivan, Pit	3.41
Straily, Dan, Mia	6.04		Strasburg, Stephen, Was	48.9		Roark, Tanner, Was	103.6		Richard, Clayton, SD	3.55
Arrieta, Jake, ChC	6.04		Kershaw, Clayton, LAD	48.1		Samardzija, Jeff, SF	102.3		Perdomo, Luis, SD	3.57
Lester, Jon, ChC	6.03		Wacha, Michael, StL	47.6		deGrom, Jacob, NYM	102.2		Dickey, R.A., Atl	3.59
Ray, Robbie, Ari	6.00		Scherzer, Max, Was	47.3		Scherzer, Max, Was	100.4		Moore, Matt, SF	3.64
Davies, Zach, Mil	5.93		Nelson, Jimmy, Mil	47.2		Cole, Gerrit, Pit	99.9		Blach, Ty, SF	3.64
Urena, Jose, Mia	5.78		Dickey, R.A., Atl	47.1		Greinke, Zack, Ari	98.8		Martinez, Carlos, StL	3.65
deGrom, Jacob, NYM	5.77		Blach, Ty, SF	47.0		Martinez, Carlos, StL	97.9		Kershaw, Clayton, LAD	3.71
Greinke, Zack, Ari	5.60		Martinez, Carlos, StL	46.9		Lester, Jon, ChC	97.8		Corbin, Patrick, Ari	3.73
Marquez, German, Col	5.50		Nola, Aaron, Phi	46.8		Teheran, Julio, Atl	96.1		Nelson, Jimmy, Mil	3.78

Quality Starts			Batters Faced			Innings Pitched			Most Pitches in a Game	
Gonzalez, Gio, Was	22		Martinez, Carlos, StL	858		Samardzija, Jeff, SF	207.2		Richard, Clayton, SD	127
Scherzer, Max, Was	22		Richard, Clayton, SD	858		Martinez, Carlos, StL	205.0		Freeland, Kyle, Col	126
deGrom, Jacob, NYM	21		Cole, Gerrit, Pit	849		Cole, Gerrit, Pit	203.0		Roark, Tanner, Was	125
Cole, Gerrit, Pit	20		Samardzija, Jeff, SF	847		Greinke, Zack, Ari	202.1		Lynn, Lance, StL	123
Kershaw, Clayton, LAD	20		deGrom, Jacob, NYM	827		deGrom, Jacob, NYM	201.1		Richard, Clayton, SD	123
Martinez, Carlos, StL	20		Gonzalez, Gio, Was	827		Gonzalez, Gio, Was	201.0		Ray, Robbie, Ari	122
Samardzija, Jeff, SF	20		Corbin, Patrick, Ari	826		Scherzer, Max, Was	200.2		Dickey, R.A., Atl	121
Strasburg, Stephen, Was	20		Davies, Zach, Mil	817		Richard, Clayton, SD	197.1		Gonzalez, Gio, Was	121
Teheran, Julio, Atl	20		Dickey, R.A., Atl	815		Davies, Zach, Mil	191.1		Scherzer, Max, Was	121
2 tied with	19		Teheran, Julio, Atl	812		Dickey, R.A., Atl	190.0		4 tied with	120

Stolen Bases Allowed			Caught Stealing Off			Stolen Base Pct Allowed			Pickoffs	
						(minimum 162 IP)				
Teheran, Julio, Atl	26		Lester, Jon, ChC	12		Richard, Clayton, SD	28.6		Richard, Clayton, SD	8
Nola, Aaron, Phi	21		Richard, Clayton, SD	10		Greinke, Zack, Ari	35.7		Hendricks, Kyle, ChC	7
Arrieta, Jake, ChC	19		Greinke, Zack, Ari	9		Lynn, Lance, StL	36.4		Dickey, R.A., Atl	4
Lester, Jon, ChC	19		Glasnow, Tyler, Pit	8		Dickey, R.A., Atl	44.4		Hill, Rich, LAD	4
deGrom, Jacob, NYM	18		Ray, Robbie, Ari	8		Samardzija, Jeff, SF	46.2		Lester, Jon, ChC	4
Nelson, Jimmy, Mil	18		Lynn, Lance, StL	7		Martinez, Carlos, StL	50.0		Teheran, Julio, Atl	4
Cole, Gerrit, Pit	17		Samardzija, Jeff, SF	7		Ray, Robbie, Ari	50.0		13 tied with	3
6 tied with	15		Hill, Rich, LAD	6		Corbin, Patrick, Ari	54.5			
			Straily, Dan, Mia	6		Marquez, German, Col	54.5			
			Teheran, Julio, Atl	6		Kershaw, Clayton, LAD	60.0			

2017 National League Pitching Leaders

Strikeouts Per 9 IP
(minimum 162 IP)

Ray, Robbie, Ari	12.11
Scherzer, Max, Was	12.02
deGrom, Jacob, NYM	10.68
Strasburg, Stephen, Was	10.47
Kershaw, Clayton, LAD	10.39
Nelson, Jimmy, Mil	10.21
Nola, Aaron, Phi	9.86
Greinke, Zack, Ari	9.56
Martinez, Carlos, StL	9.53
Lester, Jon, ChC	8.97

Opp On-Base Percentage
(minimum 162 IP)

Kershaw, Clayton, LAD	.246
Scherzer, Max, Was	.247
Strasburg, Stephen, Was	.265
Greinke, Zack, Ari	.272
Samardzija, Jeff, SF	.287
Ray, Robbie, Ari	.290
deGrom, Jacob, NYM	.292
Nola, Aaron, Phi	.297
Gonzalez, Gio, Was	.298
Martinez, Carlos, StL	.302

Opp Slugging Average
(minimum 162 IP)

Strasburg, Stephen, Was	.317
Scherzer, Max, Was	.319
Gonzalez, Gio, Was	.345
Ray, Robbie, Ari	.356
Kershaw, Clayton, LAD	.357
Chacin, Jhoulys, SD	.373
Nelson, Jimmy, Mil	.374
Nola, Aaron, Phi	.383
Greinke, Zack, Ari	.387
deGrom, Jacob, NYM	.389

Opponent OPS
(minimum 162 IP)

Scherzer, Max, Was	.566
Strasburg, Stephen, Was	.581
Kershaw, Clayton, LAD	.604
Gonzalez, Gio, Was	.642
Ray, Robbie, Ari	.646
Greinke, Zack, Ari	.659
Nola, Aaron, Phi	.679
deGrom, Jacob, NYM	.682
Nelson, Jimmy, Mil	.689
Chacin, Jhoulys, SD	.693

Home Runs Per Nine IP
(minimum 162 IP)

Strasburg, Stephen, Was	0.67
Nelson, Jimmy, Mil	0.82
Wacha, Michael, StL	0.92
Blach, Ty, SF	0.93
Perdomo, Luis, SD	0.93
Gonzalez, Gio, Was	0.94
Davies, Zach, Mil	0.94
Chacin, Jhoulys, SD	0.95
Nola, Aaron, Phi	0.96
Scherzer, Max, Was	0.99

Batting Average vs. LHB
(minimum 125 BF)

Edwards Jr., Carl, ChC	.119
Knebel, Corey, Mil	.156
Holland, Greg, Col	.157
Gonzalez, Gio, Was	.183
Barraclough, Kyle, Mia	.184
Castillo, Luis, Cin	.185
Strasburg, Stephen, Was	.193
Ramos, AJ, Mia-NYM	.197
Blevins, Jerry, NYM	.197
Stripling, Ross, LAD	.198

Batting Average vs. RHB
(minimum 225 BF)

Scherzer, Max, Was	.136
Lamet, Dinelson, SD	.155
Hill, Rich, LAD	.190
Ray, Robbie, Ari	.195
Kershaw, Clayton, LAD	.203
Lynn, Lance, StL	.203
Martinez, Carlos, StL	.204
Arrieta, Jake, ChC	.209
Wood, Alex, LAD	.213
Maeda, Kenta, LAD	.214

Opp BA w/ RISP
(minimum 125 BF)

Ray, Robbie, Ari	.171
Gonzalez, Gio, Was	.175
Anderson, Chase, Mil	.180
Montgomery, Mike, ChC	.181
Cueto, Johnny, SF	.193
Walker, Taijuan, Ari	.199
Martinez, Carlos, StL	.205
Scherzer, Max, Was	.205
Williams, Trevor, Pit	.214
Eickhoff, Jerad, Phi	.218

OBP vs. Leadoff Hitter
(minimum 150 BF)

Scherzer, Max, Was	.225
Greinke, Zack, Ari	.249
Kershaw, Clayton, LAD	.258
Ray, Robbie, Ari	.268
Godley, Zack, Ari	.270
Martinez, Carlos, StL	.274
Gonzalez, Gio, Was	.274
Nola, Aaron, Phi	.275
Wacha, Michael, StL	.275
Strasburg, Stephen, Was	.275

Strikeouts / Walks Ratio
(minimum 162 IP)

Kershaw, Clayton, LAD	6.73
Samardzija, Jeff, SF	6.41
Scherzer, Max, Was	4.87
Greinke, Zack, Ari	4.78
Strasburg, Stephen, Was	4.34
Nelson, Jimmy, Mil	4.15
deGrom, Jacob, NYM	4.05
Nola, Aaron, Phi	3.76
Nova, Ivan, Pit	3.64
Cole, Gerrit, Pit	3.56

Highest GB/FB Ratio
(minimum 162 IP)

Richard, Clayton, SD	3.00
Perdomo, Luis, SD	2.94
Davies, Zach, Mil	1.84
Nelson, Jimmy, Mil	1.84
Martinez, Carlos, StL	1.72
Corbin, Patrick, Ari	1.71
Nola, Aaron, Phi	1.60
Wacha, Michael, StL	1.55
Chacin, Jhoulys, SD	1.52
Roark, Tanner, Was	1.51

Lowest GB/FB Ratio
(minimum 162 IP)

Straily, Dan, Mia	0.74
Scherzer, Max, Was	0.78
Moore, Matt, SF	0.90
Ray, Robbie, Ari	1.00
Teheran, Julio, Atl	1.00
Lackey, John, ChC	1.06
Urena, Jose, Mia	1.13
Samardzija, Jeff, SF	1.14
Lynn, Lance, StL	1.22
Gonzalez, Gio, Was	1.31

Sacrifice Flies Allowed

Eickhoff, Jerad, Phi	9
Lackey, John, ChC	9
Montero, Rafael, NYM	8
Walker, Taijuan, Ari	8
Freeland, Kyle, Col	7
Pivetta, Nick, Phi	7
Straily, Dan, Mia	7
5 tied with	6

Sacrifice Hits Allowed

Freeland, Kyle, Col	14
Foltynewicz, Mike, Atl	11
Blach, Ty, SF	10
Straily, Dan, Mia	10
Lynn, Lance, StL	9
Montero, Rafael, NYM	9
Conley, Adam, Mia	8
Taillon, Jameson, Pit	8
Williams, Trevor, Pit	8
7 tied with	7

GIDP Induced

Perdomo, Luis, SD	32
Richard, Clayton, SD	32
Chatwood, Tyler, Col	23
Nova, Ivan, Pit	23
Blach, Ty, SF	22
Davies, Zach, Mil	22
Godley, Zack, Ari	22
Martinez, Carlos, StL	21
Nelson, Jimmy, Mil	21
2 tied with	20

GIDP Per Nine IP
(minimum 162 IP)

Perdomo, Luis, SD	1.76
Richard, Clayton, SD	1.46
Blach, Ty, SF	1.21
Nova, Ivan, Pit	1.11
Nelson, Jimmy, Mil	1.08
Davies, Zach, Mil	1.03
Wacha, Michael, StL	0.98
Lynn, Lance, StL	0.97
Urena, Jose, Mia	0.95
Martinez, Carlos, StL	0.92

2017 National League Pitching Leaders

Saves

Holland, Greg, Col	41
Jansen, Kenley, LAD	41
Knebel, Corey, Mil	39
Rodney, Fernando, Ari	39
Davis, Wade, ChC	32
Iglesias, Raisel, Cin	28
Ramos, AJ, Mia-NYM	27
Neris, Hector, Phi	26
Johnson, Jim, Atl	22
3 tied with	21

Blown Saves

Johnson, Jim, Atl	9
Watson, Tony, Pit-LAD	8
Blevins, Jerry, NYM	7
Bradley, Archie, Ari	6
Cecil, Brett, StL	6
Knebel, Corey, Mil	6
Kontos, George, SF-Pit	6
Phelps, David, Mia	6
Rodney, Fernando, Ari	6
7 tied with	5

Save Pct
(minimum 20 Save Ops)

Jansen, Kenley, LAD	97.6
Davis, Wade, ChC	97.0
Doolittle, Sean, Was	95.5
Iglesias, Raisel, Cin	93.3
Rivero, Felipe, Pit	91.3
Holland, Greg, Col	91.1
Reed, Addison, NYM	90.5
Ramos, AJ, Mia-NYM	90.0
Neris, Hector, Phi	89.7
Maurer, Brandon, SD	87.0

Save Opportunities

Holland, Greg, Col	45
Knebel, Corey, Mil	45
Rodney, Fernando, Ari	45
Jansen, Kenley, LAD	42
Davis, Wade, ChC	33
Johnson, Jim, Atl	31
Iglesias, Raisel, Cin	30
Ramos, AJ, Mia-NYM	30
Neris, Hector, Phi	29
Hand, Brad, SD	26

Easy Saves

Holland, Greg, Col	28
Rodney, Fernando, Ari	23
Jansen, Kenley, LAD	21
Johnson, Jim, Atl	19
Knebel, Corey, Mil	19
Davis, Wade, ChC	18
Neris, Hector, Phi	16
Ramos, AJ, Mia-NYM	16
Hand, Brad, SD	14
2 tied with	13

Regular Saves

Knebel, Corey, Mil	20
Jansen, Kenley, LAD	16
Rodney, Fernando, Ari	16
Iglesias, Raisel, Cin	15
Davis, Wade, ChC	14
Holland, Greg, Col	13
Neris, Hector, Phi	9
Doolittle, Sean, Was	8
Maurer, Brandon, SD	8
Ramos, AJ, Mia-NYM	8

Tough Saves

Jansen, Kenley, LAD	4
Ramos, AJ, Mia-NYM	3
Rivero, Felipe, Pit	3
Iglesias, Raisel, Cin	2
Oh, Seung Hwan, StL	2
Reed, Addison, NYM	2
Rosenthal, Trevor, StL	2
15 tied with	1

Holds Adjusted Saves %
(minimum 20 Save Ops + Holds)

Jansen, Kenley, LAD	97.7
Davis, Wade, ChC	97.0
Doolittle, Sean, Was	95.7
Dunn, Mike, Col	95.0
Rivero, Felipe, Pit	94.6
Iglesias, Raisel, Cin	93.3
Reed, Addison, NYM	92.0
Rosenthal, Trevor, StL	92.0
Strickland, Hunter, SF	91.7
3 tied with	91.3

Relief Wins

Lorenzen, Michael, Cin	8
McGowan, Dustin, Mia	8
Albers, Matt, Was	7
Robles, Hansel, NYM	7
Torres, Jose, SD	7
Watson, Tony, Pit-LAD	7
Barraclough, Kyle, Mia	6
Blevins, Jerry, NYM	6
Johnson, Jim, Atl	6
Morrow, Brandon, LAD	6

Relief Losses

Hudson, Daniel, Pit	7
Ramos, Edubray, Phi	7
Baez, Pedro, LAD	6
Benoit, Joaquin, Phi-Pit	6
Bowman, Matt, StL	6
Holland, Greg, Col	6
Kontos, George, SF-Pit	6
Oh, Seung Hwan, StL	6
Sewald, Paul, NYM	6
9 tied with	5

Relief Games

Knebel, Corey, Mil	76
Nicasio, Juan, Pit-Phi-StL	76
Blevins, Jerry, NYM	75
Bowman, Matt, StL	75
Neris, Hector, Phi	74
Barnes, Jacob, Mil	73
Cecil, Brett, StL	73
Edwards Jr., Carl, ChC	73
Rivero, Felipe, Pit	73
Hand, Brad, SD	72

Holds

Ramirez, Jose, Atl	27
Bradley, Archie, Ari	25
Edwards Jr., Carl, ChC	25
Barnes, Jacob, Mil	24
Baez, Pedro, LAD	23
Bowman, Matt, StL	23
Neshek, Pat, Phi-Col	23
Barraclough, Kyle, Mia	22
5 tied with	21

Relief Innings

Rusin, Chris, Col	85.0
Lorenzen, Michael, Cin	83.0
Stammen, Craig, SD	80.1
Hand, Brad, SD	79.1
McGowan, Dustin, Mia	77.2
Iglesias, Raisel, Cin	76.0
Knebel, Corey, Mil	76.0
Rivero, Felipe, Pit	75.1
Neris, Hector, Phi	74.2
Bradley, Archie, Ari	73.0

Inherited Runners Scrd %
(minimum 30 IR)

de la Rosa, Jorge, Ari	3.0
Perez, Oliver, Was	14.3
Duensing, Brian, ChC	15.2
Oberg, Scott, Col	15.8
Drake, Oliver, Mil	16.7
Rusin, Chris, Col	18.2
Garcia, Jarlin, Mia	19.0
Osich, Josh, SF	20.0
Hughes, Jared, Mil	21.2
Torres, Carlos, Mil	21.2

Relief Opp On Base Pct
(minimum 50 IP)

Jansen, Kenley, LAD	.206
Neshek, Pat, Phi-Col	.231
Rivero, Felipe, Pit	.237
Albers, Matt, Was	.240
Fields, Josh, LAD	.251
Brebbia, John, StL	.255
Hand, Brad, SD	.261
Bradley, Archie, Ari	.266
Edwards Jr., Carl, ChC	.273
Vizcaino, Arodys, Atl	.277

Relief Opp Slugging Avg
(minimum 50 IP)

Edwards Jr., Carl, ChC	.230
Rivero, Felipe, Pit	.236
Jansen, Kenley, LAD	.270
Knebel, Corey, Mil	.277
Albers, Matt, Was	.280
Freeman, Sam, Atl	.284
Rodney, Fernando, Ari	.285
Montgomery, Mike, ChC	.291
Garcia, Luis, Phi	.297
Iglesias, Raisel, Cin	.297

2017 National League Pitching Leaders

Relief Opp BA Vs LHB (minimum 50 AB)	
Rivero, Felipe, Pit	.082
Edwards Jr., Carl, ChC	.119
Morrow, Brandon, LAD	.125
Hader, Josh, Mil	.140
Hand, Brad, SD	.150
Knebel, Corey, Mil	.156
Davis, Wade, ChC	.156
Holland, Greg, Col	.157
Milner, Hoby, Phi	.159
Dyson, Sam, SF	.169

Relief Opp BA Vs RHB (minimum 50 AB)	
Jansen, Kenley, LAD	.120
Barbato, Johnny, Pit	.130
Edwards Jr., Carl, ChC	.148
Albers, Matt, Was	.163
Iglesias, Raisel, Cin	.163
Rodney, Fernando, Ari	.165
Hader, Josh, Mil	.165
Crick, Kyle, SF	.169
Fields, Josh, LAD	.169
Doolittle, Sean, Was	.178

Relief Opp Batting Average (minimum 50 IP)	
Edwards Jr., Carl, ChC	.134
Albers, Matt, Was	.166
Rivero, Felipe, Pit	.171
Jansen, Kenley, LAD	.177
Knebel, Corey, Mil	.180
Davis, Wade, ChC	.186
Hand, Brad, SD	.191
Brebbia, John, StL	.193
Holland, Greg, Col	.193
Fields, Josh, LAD	.194

Relief Earned Run Average (minimum 50 IP)	
Jansen, Kenley, LAD	1.32
Neshek, Pat, Phi-Col	1.59
Albers, Matt, Was	1.62
Rivero, Felipe, Pit	1.67
Bradley, Archie, Ari	1.73
Knebel, Corey, Mil	1.78
Gearrin, Cory, SF	1.99
Hand, Brad, SD	2.16
Davis, Wade, ChC	2.30
Brebbia, John, StL	2.44

Rel OBP 1st Batter Faced (minimum 40 BF)	
Jansen, Kenley, LAD	.169
Iglesias, Raisel, Cin	.190
Benoit, Joaquin, Phi-Pit	.192
Garcia, Jarlin, Mia	.194
LeBlanc, Wade, Pit	.200
Duensing, Brian, ChC	.206
Bradley, Archie, Ari	.210
McGee, Jake, Col	.210
Freeman, Sam, Atl	.211
Rodney, Fernando, Ari	.213

Rel Opp BA w/ Runners On (minimum 50 IP)	
Knebel, Corey, Mil	.121
Neshek, Pat, Phi-Col	.152
Lyons, Tyler, StL	.157
Jansen, Kenley, LAD	.161
Edwards Jr., Carl, ChC	.162
Davis, Wade, ChC	.167
Baez, Pedro, LAD	.170
Hand, Brad, SD	.172
Bradley, Archie, Ari	.174
Vizcaino, Arodys, Atl	.175

Relief Opp BA w/ RISP (minimum 50 IP)	
Neshek, Pat, Phi-Col	.095
Baez, Pedro, LAD	.099
Vizcaino, Arodys, Atl	.103
Montgomery, Mike, ChC	.107
Knebel, Corey, Mil	.132
Jansen, Kenley, LAD	.136
de la Rosa, Jorge, Ari	.140
Lyons, Tyler, StL	.143
Torres, Jose, SD	.152
Hand, Brad, SD	.152

Fastest Avg Fastball-Relief (minimum 50 IP)	
Rivero, Felipe, Pit	98.5
Romero, Enny, Was	98.0
Vizcaino, Arodys, Atl	97.8
Knebel, Corey, Mil	97.4
Garcia, Luis, Phi	97.2
Ramirez, Jose, Atl	97.1
Baez, Pedro, LAD	97.0
Barnes, Jacob, Mil	96.7
Peralta, Wandy, Cin	96.5
Rondon, Hector, ChC	96.4

Fastest Average Fastball (minimum 162 IP)	
Cole, Gerrit, Pit	96.0
Martinez, Carlos, StL	95.6
Strasburg, Stephen, Was	95.6
Urena, Jose, Mia	95.5
deGrom, Jacob, NYM	95.2
Wacha, Michael, StL	95.1
Marquez, German, Col	95.0
Ray, Robbie, Ari	94.3
Samardzija, Jeff, SF	94.3
Perdomo, Luis, SD	94.2

Slowest Average Fastball (minimum 162 IP)	
Dickey, R.A., Atl	83.4
Davies, Zach, Mil	89.7
Gonzalez, Gio, Was	89.9
Blach, Ty, SF	90.1
Straily, Dan, Mia	90.3
Richard, Clayton, SD	90.7
Lackey, John, ChC	90.9
Greinke, Zack, Ari	91.0
Lester, Jon, ChC	91.1
Teheran, Julio, Atl	91.4

Pitches 100+ Velocity	
Rivero, Felipe, Pit	199
Rosenthal, Trevor, StL	158
Romero, Enny, Was	106
Ellington, Brian, Mia	105
Martinez, Carlos, StL	53
Syndergaard, Noah, NYM	38
Iglesias, Raisel, Cin	37
Hernandez, Ariel, Cin	28
Morrow, Brandon, LAD	26
Castillo, Luis, Cin	22

Pitches 95+ Velocity	
Cole, Gerrit, Pit	1680
Urena, Jose, Mia	1277
Kuhl, Chad, Pit	1255
deGrom, Jacob, NYM	1234
Martinez, Carlos, StL	1228
Foltynewicz, Mike, Atl	1153
Taillon, Jameson, Pit	1147
Strasburg, Stephen, Was	1138
Marquez, German, Col	1043
Knebel, Corey, Mil	967

Pitches Less Than 80 MPH	
Dickey, R.A., Atl	1872
Hill, Rich, LAD	929
Quintana, Jose, ChC	886
Gonzalez, Gio, Was	836
Nola, Aaron, Phi	792
Davies, Zach, Mil	693
Eickhoff, Jerad, Phi	693
Hendricks, Kyle, ChC	682
Arroyo, Bronson, Cin	670
Wainwright, Adam, StL	595

Lowest % Fastballs (minimum 162 IP)	
Dickey, R.A., Atl	18.0
Samardzija, Jeff, SF	46.8
Kershaw, Clayton, LAD	47.1
Greinke, Zack, Ari	48.2
Scherzer, Max, Was	48.7
Straily, Dan, Mia	50.5
Lester, Jon, ChC	50.6
Moore, Matt, SF	51.7
Strasburg, Stephen, Was	51.9
Lackey, John, ChC	52.4

Highest % Fastballs (minimum 162 IP)	
Lynn, Lance, StL	81.0
Richard, Clayton, SD	68.7
Nova, Ivan, Pit	68.1
Marquez, German, Col	65.5
Teheran, Julio, Atl	64.5
Arrieta, Jake, ChC	63.9
Perdomo, Luis, SD	62.7
Nelson, Jimmy, Mil	61.3
Cole, Gerrit, Pit	60.1
Blach, Ty, SF	60.0

Highest % Curveballs (minimum 162 IP)	
Nola, Aaron, Phi	30.8
Marquez, German, Col	25.0
Gonzalez, Gio, Was	24.7
Strasburg, Stephen, Was	22.5
Nova, Ivan, Pit	22.2
Ray, Robbie, Ari	21.9
Nelson, Jimmy, Mil	20.1
Moore, Matt, SF	17.8
Kershaw, Clayton, LAD	16.8
Davies, Zach, Mil	15.4

2017 National League Pitching Leaders

Highest % Changeups
(minimum 162 IP)

Blach, Ty, SF	23.8
Urena, Jose, Mia	19.8
Strasburg, Stephen, Was	18.9
Gonzalez, Gio, Was	18.6
Wacha, Michael, StL	18.3
Straily, Dan, Mia	16.8
Martinez, Carlos, StL	16.2
Moore, Matt, SF	15.9
Greinke, Zack, Ari	15.8
Nola, Aaron, Phi	15.6

Highest % Sliders
(minimum 162 IP)

Corbin, Patrick, Ari	38.0
Lackey, John, ChC	35.5
Kershaw, Clayton, LAD	34.9
Chacin, Jhoulys, SD	34.8
Perdomo, Luis, SD	31.5
Straily, Dan, Mia	29.8
Scherzer, Max, Was	28.9
Martinez, Carlos, StL	26.8
Urena, Jose, Mia	23.8
deGrom, Jacob, NYM	22.7

Balks

Garcia, Jaime, Atl	3
Torres, Jose, SD	3
12 tied with	2

Strikeout/Hit Ratio
(minimum 50 IP)

Edwards Jr., Carl, ChC	3.24
Knebel, Corey, Mil	2.63
Jansen, Kenley, LAD	2.48
Scherzer, Max, Was	2.13
Yates, Kirby, SD	2.07
Davis, Wade, ChC	2.03
Hand, Brad, SD	1.93
Ray, Robbie, Ari	1.88
Rivero, Felipe, Pit	1.87
Albers, Matt, Was	1.80

Opp OPS vs Fastballs
(minimum 251 BF)

Montgomery, Mike, ChC	.596
Hill, Rich, LAD	.622
Garcia, Jaime, Atl	.629
Williams, Trevor, Pit	.650
Hendricks, Kyle, ChC	.657
Strasburg, Stephen, Was	.660
Ray, Robbie, Ari	.675
Gonzalez, Gio, Was	.678
deGrom, Jacob, NYM	.679
Scherzer, Max, Was	.682

Opp OPS vs Curveballs
(minimum 100 BF)

Strasburg, Stephen, Was	.462
Blevins, Jerry, NYM	.479
Feldman, Scott, Cin	.492
Anderson, Chase, Mil	.528
Gonzalez, Gio, Was	.533
Kershaw, Clayton, LAD	.540
Godley, Zack, Ari	.549
Nola, Aaron, Phi	.550
Nelson, Jimmy, Mil	.551
Greinke, Zack, Ari	.558

Opp OPS vs Changeups
(minimum 100 BF)

Strasburg, Stephen, Was	.393
Scherzer, Max, Was	.460
Wood, Alex, LAD	.491
Greinke, Zack, Ari	.530
Volquez, Edinson, Mia	.541
Gonzalez, Gio, Was	.622
Ryu, Hyun-Jin, LAD	.656
Nola, Aaron, Phi	.658
Hendricks, Kyle, ChC	.673
Cole, Gerrit, Pit	.695

Opp OPS vs Sliders
(minimum 64 BF)

Scherzer, Max, Was	.409
Neshek, Pat, Phi-Col	.430
Hudson, Daniel, Pit	.449
Iglesias, Raisel, Cin	.482
Hand, Brad, SD	.484
Ramos, Edubray, Phi	.493
Barraclough, Kyle, Mia	.500
Rondon, Hector, ChC	.500
Holland, Greg, Col	.508
Lyons, Tyler, StL	.525

Earned Runs

Moore, Matt, SF	107
Richard, Clayton, SD	105
Samardzija, Jeff, SF	102
Cole, Gerrit, Pit	96
Roark, Tanner, Was	94
Teheran, Julio, Atl	94
Dickey, R.A., Atl	90
Pivetta, Nick, Phi	89
3 tied with	87

Hits Per Nine Innings
(minimum 162 IP)

Scherzer, Max, Was	5.65
Ray, Robbie, Ari	6.44
Strasburg, Stephen, Was	6.72
Kershaw, Clayton, LAD	6.99
Gonzalez, Gio, Was	7.07
Lynn, Lance, StL	7.29
Greinke, Zack, Ari	7.65
Chacin, Jhoulys, SD	7.84
Martinez, Carlos, StL	7.86
Arrieta, Jake, ChC	8.02

2017 American League Fielding Leaders

2B Pivot %
(minimum 98 G)

Miller, Brad, TB	0.808
Cano, Robinson, Sea	0.747
Merrifield, Whit, KC	0.694
Schoop, Jonathan, Bal	0.680
Odor, Rougned, Tex	0.672
Altuve, Jose, Hou	0.671
Lowrie, Jed, Oak	0.651
Dozier, Brian, Min	0.646
Pedroia, Dustin, Bos	0.618
Kinsler, Ian, Det	0.614

SS Pivot %
(minimum 98 G)

Correa, Carlos, Hou	0.698
Simmons, Andrelton, LAA	0.671
Andrus, Elvis, Tex	0.650
Anderson, Tim, CWS	0.613
Lindor, Francisco, Cle	0.603
Bogaerts, Xander, Bos	0.600
Segura, Jean, Sea	0.600
Polanco, Jorge, Min	0.593
Iglesias, Jose, Det	0.581
Escobar, Alcides, KC	0.539

Highest Pct CS by Catchers
(minimum 600 INN or 50 SBA)

Castillo, Welington, Bal	44.4
Gomes, Yan, Cle	40.0
Vazquez, Christian, Bos	39.6
Leon, Sandy, Bos	34.0
Sanchez, Gary, NYY	33.9
Maldonado, Martin, LAA	32.4
Maxwell, Bruce, Oak	26.7
McCann, James, Det	24.0
Castro, Jason, Min	23.6
Perez, Salvador, KC	21.7

Lowest Pct CS by Catchers
(minimum 600 INN or 50 SBA)

Smith, Kevan, CWS	11.1
McCann, Brian, Hou	11.5
Chirinos, Robinson, Tex	14.8
Joseph, Caleb, Bal	16.7
Martin, Russell, Tor	20.0
Narvaez, Omar, CWS	20.0
Zunino, Mike, Sea	20.6
Perez, Salvador, KC	21.7
Castro, Jason, Min	23.6
McCann, James, Det	24.0

2B Double Play %
(minimum 98 G)

Miller, Brad, TB	0.667
Cano, Robinson, Sea	0.636
Odor, Rougned, Tex	0.614
Schoop, Jonathan, Bal	0.600
Lowrie, Jed, Oak	0.588
Altuve, Jose, Hou	0.580
Pedroia, Dustin, Bos	0.576
Merrifield, Whit, KC	0.567
Kinsler, Ian, Det	0.566
Dozier, Brian, Min	0.553

3B Double Play %
(minimum 98 G)

Seager, Kyle, Sea	0.641
Bregman, Alex, Hou	0.520
Longoria, Evan, TB	0.509
Frazier, Todd, CWS-NYY	0.508
Machado, Manny, Bal	0.479
Castellanos, Nick, Det	0.408
Moustakas, Mike, KC	0.400
Donaldson, Josh, Tor	0.289

SS Double Play %
(minimum 98 G)

Simmons, Andrelton, LAA	0.667
Lindor, Francisco, Cle	0.660
Andrus, Elvis, Tex	0.656
Iglesias, Jose, Det	0.609
Correa, Carlos, Hou	0.602
Segura, Jean, Sea	0.596
Escobar, Alcides, KC	0.580
Bogaerts, Xander, Bos	0.560
Anderson, Tim, CWS	0.560
Beckham, Tim, TB-Bal	0.556

Errors

Anderson, Tim, CWS	28
Beckham, Tim, TB-Bal	20
Castellanos, Nick, Det	20
Odor, Rougned, Tex	19
Polanco, Jorge, Min	18
Andrus, Elvis, Tex	17
Bogaerts, Xander, Bos	17
Segura, Jean, Sea	17
Gallo, Joey, Tex	16
2 tied with	15

Fielding Errors

Anderson, Tim, CWS	16
Castellanos, Nick, Det	13
Seager, Kyle, Sea	13
Escobar, Alcides, KC	11
Frazier, Todd, CWS-NYY	10
Odor, Rougned, Tex	10
Polanco, Jorge, Min	10
Segura, Jean, Sea	10
8 tied with	9

Throwing Errors

Anderson, Tim, CWS	12
Beckham, Tim, TB-Bal	12
Bogaerts, Xander, Bos	10
Simmons, Andrelton, LAA	10
Gomes, Yan, Cle	9
Odor, Rougned, Tex	9
Sanchez, Gary, NYY	9
4 tied with	8

Range Factor for 2B
(minimum 98 games)

Schoop, Jonathan, Bal	5.04
Odor, Rougned, Tex	4.94
Kinsler, Ian, Det	4.67
Dozier, Brian, Min	4.59
Merrifield, Whit, KC	4.51
Lowrie, Jed, Oak	4.21
Cano, Robinson, Sea	4.15
Miller, Brad, TB	3.94
Pedroia, Dustin, Bos	3.92
Altuve, Jose, Hou	3.87

Range Factor for 3B
(minimum 98 games)

Seager, Kyle, Sea	2.93
Machado, Manny, Bal	2.70
Bregman, Alex, Hou	2.69
Longoria, Evan, TB	2.63
Donaldson, Josh, Tor	2.53
Frazier, Todd, CWS-NYY	2.53
Moustakas, Mike, KC	2.47
Castellanos, Nick, Det	2.29

Range Factor for SS
(minimum 98 games)

Andrus, Elvis, Tex	4.86
Simmons, Andrelton, LAA	4.41
Escobar, Alcides, KC	4.29
Iglesias, Jose, Det	4.28
Anderson, Tim, CWS	3.99
Beckham, Tim, TB-Bal	3.93
Lindor, Francisco, Cle	3.93
Polanco, Jorge, Min	3.93
Correa, Carlos, Hou	3.89
Gregorius, Didi, NYY	3.86

2017 National League Fielding Leaders

2B Pivot % (minimum 98 G)	
Murphy, Daniel, Was	0.685
Panik, Joe, SF	0.682
Gordon, Dee, Mia	0.662
LeMahieu, DJ, Col	0.617
Drury, Brandon, Ari	0.610
Wong, Kolten, StL	0.600
Hernandez, Cesar, Phi	0.597
Villar, Jonathan, Mil	0.585
Gennett, Scooter, Cin	0.500

SS Pivot % (minimum 98 G)	
Arcia, Orlando, Mil	0.766
Story, Trevor, Col	0.756
Cozart, Zack, Cin	0.680
Mercer, Jordy, Pit	0.667
Seager, Corey, LAD	0.638
Swanson, Dansby, Atl	0.636
Galvis, Freddy, Phi	0.632
Aybar, Erick, SD	0.605
Russell, Addison, ChC	0.604
Crawford, Brandon, SF	0.577

Highest Pct CS by Catchers (minimum 600 INN or 50 SBA)	
Barnhart, Tucker, Cin	40.6
Molina, Yadier, StL	34.8
Pina, Manny, Mil	33.3
Posey, Buster, SF	29.4
Realmuto, J.T., Mia	28.4
Hundley, Nick, SF	26.5
Grandal, Yasmani, LAD	25.4
Hedges, Austin, SD	25.0
Contreras, Willson, ChC	24.7
Wieters, Matt, Was	24.0

Lowest Pct CS by Catchers (minimum 600 INN or 50 SBA)	
d'Arnaud, Travis, NYM	14.1
Cervelli, Francisco, Pit	17.0
Flowers, Tyler, Atl	17.9
Iannetta, Chris, Ari	19.4
Suzuki, Kurt, Atl	22.2
Rupp, Cameron, Phi	23.7
Wieters, Matt, Was	24.0
Contreras, Willson, ChC	24.7
Hedges, Austin, SD	25.0
Grandal, Yasmani, LAD	25.4

2B Double Play % (minimum 98 G)	
LeMahieu, DJ, Col	0.547
Villar, Jonathan, Mil	0.544
Hernandez, Cesar, Phi	0.543
Wong, Kolten, StL	0.532
Murphy, Daniel, Was	0.512
Panik, Joe, SF	0.510
Drury, Brandon, Ari	0.492
Gordon, Dee, Mia	0.487
Gennett, Scooter, Cin	0.386

3B Double Play % (minimum 98 G)	
Dietrich, Derek, Mia	0.548
Gyorko, Jedd, StL	0.510
Suarez, Eugenio, Cin	0.481
Freese, David, Pit	0.466
Arenado, Nolan, Col	0.459
Rendon, Anthony, Was	0.458
Bryant, Kris, ChC	0.377
Shaw, Travis, Mil	0.377
Franco, Maikel, Phi	0.333
Turner, Justin, LAD	0.317

SS Double Play % (minimum 98 G)	
Story, Trevor, Col	0.664
Arcia, Orlando, Mil	0.660
Aybar, Erick, SD	0.637
Cozart, Zack, Cin	0.632
Swanson, Dansby, Atl	0.618
Russell, Addison, ChC	0.608
Crawford, Brandon, SF	0.607
Seager, Corey, LAD	0.605
Mercer, Jordy, Pit	0.604
Galvis, Freddy, Phi	0.585

Errors	
Arcia, Orlando, Mil	20
Swanson, Dansby, Atl	20
Bryant, Kris, ChC	18
Cabrera, Asdrubal, NYM	17
Villar, Jonathan, Mil	16
Baez, Javier, ChC	15
Franco, Maikel, Phi	15
Contreras, Willson, ChC	14
Lamb, Jake, Ari	14
Owings, Chris, Ari	14

Fielding Errors	
Arcia, Orlando, Mil	14
Swanson, Dansby, Atl	13
Cabrera, Asdrubal, NYM	10
Carpenter, Matt, StL	10
Descalso, Daniel, Ari	10
Lamb, Jake, Ari	10
Villar, Jonathan, Mil	10
5 tied with	9

Throwing Errors	
Contreras, Willson, ChC	10
Russell, Addison, ChC	10
Bryant, Kris, ChC	9
Hedges, Austin, SD	9
Baez, Javier, ChC	8
DeJong, Paul, StL	8
Renfroe, Hunter, SD	8
5 tied with	7

Range Factor for 2B (minimum 98 games)	
LeMahieu, DJ, Col	4.98
Wong, Kolten, StL	4.78
Hernandez, Cesar, Phi	4.61
Villar, Jonathan, Mil	4.59
Gordon, Dee, Mia	4.56
Panik, Joe, SF	4.39
Murphy, Daniel, Was	4.30
Gennett, Scooter, Cin	4.20
Drury, Brandon, Ari	4.09

Range Factor for 3B (minimum 98 games)	
Arenado, Nolan, Col	2.77
Freese, David, Pit	2.65
Gyorko, Jedd, StL	2.65
Suarez, Eugenio, Cin	2.56
Shaw, Travis, Mil	2.54
Bryant, Kris, ChC	2.46
Rendon, Anthony, Was	2.32
Lamb, Jake, Ari	2.31
Franco, Maikel, Phi	2.29
Turner, Justin, LAD	2.28

Range Factor for SS (minimum 98 games)	
Arcia, Orlando, Mil	4.85
Story, Trevor, Col	4.55
Crawford, Brandon, SF	4.46
Aybar, Erick, SD	4.43
Galvis, Freddy, Phi	4.17
Swanson, Dansby, Atl	4.15
Russell, Addison, ChC	4.13
Cozart, Zack, Cin	4.04
Seager, Corey, LAD	3.94
Mercer, Jordy, Pit	3.88

2017 Active Career Batting Leaders

Batting Average
(minimum 1000 PA)

Cabrera, Miguel	.317
Altuve, Jose	.316
Votto, Joey	.313
Suzuki, Ichiro	.312
Posey, Buster	.308
Mauer, Joe	.308
Trout, Mike	.306
Pujols, Albert	.305
Blackmon, Charlie	.305
Seager, Corey	.305

On Base Percentage
(minimum 1000 PA)

Votto, Joey	.428
Trout, Mike	.410
Goldschmidt, Paul	.399
Cabrera, Miguel	.395
Mauer, Joe	.391
Bryant, Kris	.388
Harper, Bryce	.386
Pujols, Albert	.386
McCutchen, Andrew	.379
Holliday, Matt	.378

Slugging Average
(minimum 1000 PA)

Trout, Mike	.566
Pujols, Albert	.561
Stanton, Giancarlo	.554
Cabrera, Miguel	.553
Votto, Joey	.541
Braun, Ryan	.540
Arenado, Nolan	.534
Goldschmidt, Paul	.532
Bryant, Kris	.527
Abreu, Jose	.524

Home Runs

Pujols, Albert	614
Beltre, Adrian	462
Cabrera, Miguel	462
Beltran, Carlos	435
Encarnacion, Edwin	348
Bautista, Jose	331
Cruz, Nelson	323
Granderson, Curtis	319
Holliday, Matt	314
Gonzalez, Adrian	311

Games

Beltre, Adrian	2814
Suzuki, Ichiro	2636
Beltran, Carlos	2586
Pujols, Albert	2575
Cabrera, Miguel	2226
Cano, Robinson	1998
Phillips, Brandon	1893
Holliday, Matt	1878
Gonzalez, Adrian	1875
Utley, Chase	1850

At Bats

Beltre, Adrian	10635
Suzuki, Ichiro	9885
Beltran, Carlos	9768
Pujols, Albert	9731
Cabrera, Miguel	8322
Cano, Robinson	7802
Phillips, Brandon	7355
Reyes, Jose	7324
Markakis, Nick	7135
Gonzalez, Adrian	6970

Hits

Suzuki, Ichiro	3080
Beltre, Adrian	3048
Pujols, Albert	2968
Beltran, Carlos	2725
Cabrera, Miguel	2636
Cano, Robinson	2376
Reyes, Jose	2095
Holliday, Matt	2081
Markakis, Nick	2052
Martinez, Victor	2036

Total Bases

Pujols, Albert	5461
Beltre, Adrian	5121
Beltran, Carlos	4751
Cabrera, Miguel	4601
Suzuki, Ichiro	3985
Cano, Robinson	3857
Holliday, Matt	3553
Gonzalez, Adrian	3399
Martinez, Victor	3155
Reyes, Jose	3149

Doubles

Pujols, Albert	619
Beltre, Adrian	613
Beltran, Carlos	565
Cabrera, Miguel	545
Cano, Robinson	512
Holliday, Matt	466
Gonzalez, Adrian	432
Markakis, Nick	431
Martinez, Victor	402
2 tied with	401

Triples

Reyes, Jose	128
Suzuki, Ichiro	96
Granderson, Curtis	92
Fowler, Dexter	81
Beltran, Carlos	78
Span, Denard	65
Drew, Stephen	63
Utley, Chase	57
Gardner, Brett	54
2 tied with	52

Runs Scored

Pujols, Albert	1723
Beltran, Carlos	1582
Beltre, Adrian	1475
Suzuki, Ichiro	1415
Cabrera, Miguel	1371
Holliday, Matt	1154
Reyes, Jose	1150
Kinsler, Ian	1149
Cano, Robinson	1144
Granderson, Curtis	1113

RBI

Pujols, Albert	1918
Beltre, Adrian	1642
Cabrera, Miguel	1613
Beltran, Carlos	1587
Holliday, Matt	1217
Cano, Robinson	1183
Gonzalez, Adrian	1176
Martinez, Victor	1124
Encarnacion, Edwin	1049
Utley, Chase	1011

Walks

Pujols, Albert	1251
Beltran, Carlos	1084
Cabrera, Miguel	1065
Votto, Joey	996
Bautista, Jose	965
Mauer, Joe	888
Granderson, Curtis	829
Beltre, Adrian	814
Holliday, Matt	790
Gonzalez, Adrian	767

Intentional Walks

Pujols, Albert	307
Cabrera, Miguel	226
Suzuki, Ichiro	181
Gonzalez, Adrian	155
Mauer, Joe	140
Votto, Joey	132
Martinez, Victor	115
Beltre, Adrian	110
Cano, Robinson	106
Beltran, Carlos	104

Hit By Pitch

Utley, Chase	199
Weeks Jr., Rickie	134
Holliday, Matt	124
Choo, Shin-Soo	122
Pujols, Albert	102
Rizzo, Anthony	98
Martin, Russell	92
Phillips, Brandon	92
Beltre, Adrian	91
Jones, Adam	90

Strikeouts

Reynolds, Mark	1806
Beltran, Carlos	1795
Granderson, Curtis	1712
Beltre, Adrian	1636
Cabrera, Miguel	1626
Upton, Justin	1544
Davis, Chris	1504
Napoli, Mike	1468
Kemp, Matt	1466
2 tied with	1450

2017 Active Career Batting Leaders

Sacrifice Hits		Sacrifice Flies		Stolen Bases		Seasons Played	
Andrus, Elvis	100	Beltran, Carlos	110	Reyes, Jose	512	Beltran, Carlos	20
Kershaw, Clayton	89	Pujols, Albert	103	Suzuki, Ichiro	509	Beltre, Adrian	20
Arroyo, Bronson	85	Beltre, Adrian	95	Davis, Rajai	394	Colon, Bartolo	20
Cueto, Johnny	84	Martinez, Victor	79	Ellsbury, Jacoby	343	Pujols, Albert	17
Escobar, Alcides	77	Cabrera, Miguel	78	Beltran, Carlos	312	Sabathia, CC	17
Aybar, Erick	75	Longoria, Evan	76	Gordon, Dee	278	Suzuki, Ichiro	17
Cain, Matt	73	Gonzalez, Adrian	71	Ramirez, Hanley	277	Arroyo, Bronson	16
Hamels, Cole	62	Utley, Chase	71	Andrus, Elvis	266	Benoit, Joaquin	16
Nolasco, Ricky	62	Wright, David	65	Gomez, Carlos	252	Phillips, Brandon	16
Gardner, Brett	60	Kemp, Matt	64	Hamilton, Billy	243	Rodriguez, Francisco	16

At Bats Per Home Run (minimum 1000 AB)		Grounded Into DP		Highest SB Success Pct (minimum 100 SBA)		Lowest SB Success Pct (minimum 100 SBA)	
Stanton, Giancarlo	13.4	Pujols, Albert	362	Utley, Chase	87.8	Parra, Gerardo	62.1
Davis, Khris	14.8	Cabrera, Miguel	294	Beltran, Carlos	86.4	Castro, Starlin	64.3
Davis, Chris	15.5	Beltre, Adrian	266	Werth, Jayson	85.2	LeMahieu, DJ	67.0
Carter, Chris	15.6	Cano, Robinson	252	Dyson, Jarrod	84.6	Pence, Hunter	67.3
Pujols, Albert	15.8	Martinez, Victor	245	Trout, Mike	83.8	De Aza, Alejandro	67.4
Sano, Miguel	16.1	Molina, Yadier	225	Cain, Lorenzo	83.6	Martin, Russell	67.6
Cruz, Nelson	16.2	Phillips, Brandon	223	Ellsbury, Jacoby	82.9	Hill, Aaron	67.9
Trout, Mike	16.9	Holliday, Matt	220	Stubbs, Drew	82.6	Aoki, Nori	69.0
Napoli, Mike	17.1	Beltran, Carlos	203	Hamilton, Billy	82.1	Fowler, Dexter	69.1
Encarnacion, Edwin	17.1	Gonzalez, Adrian	202	Suzuki, Ichiro	81.3	Gordon, Alex	70.6

Strikeouts / Walks Ratio (minimum 1000 AB)		At Bats Per GIDP (minimum 1000 AB)		OPS (minimum 1000 PA)		Secondary Average (minimum 1000 PA)	
Pujols, Albert	.916	Blackmon, Charlie	144.3	Trout, Mike	.976	Trout, Mike	.476
Pedroia, Dustin	1.048	Stubbs, Drew	141.7	Votto, Joey	.969	Votto, Joey	.438
Mauer, Joe	1.068	Hamilton, Billy	124.2	Cabrera, Miguel	.948	Goldschmidt, Paul	.435
Votto, Joey	1.091	Young, Eric	115.4	Pujols, Albert	.947	Stanton, Giancarlo	.432
Aoki, Nori	1.103	Bonifacio, Emilio	113.5	Goldschmidt, Paul	.931	Harper, Bryce	.418
Santana, Carlos	1.118	Granderson, Curtis	113.4	Bryant, Kris	.915	Bautista, Jose	.411
Hanigan, Ryan	1.137	Eaton, Adam	112.7	Stanton, Giancarlo	.914	Bryant, Kris	.400
Panik, Joe	1.173	Gordon, Dee	108.6	Braun, Ryan	.905	Pujols, Albert	.396
Martinez, Victor	1.206	Suzuki, Ichiro	107.4	Harper, Bryce	.902	Pederson, Joc	.396
Zobrist, Ben	1.207	Taylor, Michael	102.8	Holliday, Matt	.889	Santana, Carlos	.388

Highest Strikeout per PA (minimum 1000 PA)		Lowest Strikeout per PA (minimum 1000 PA)		Plate Appearances		At Bats Per RBI (minimum 1000 AB)	
Sano, Miguel	.358	Aoki, Nori	.085	Beltre, Adrian	11649	Pujols, Albert	5.1
Zunino, Mike	.335	Revere, Ben	.092	Pujols, Albert	11188	Cabrera, Miguel	5.2
Carter, Chris	.333	Simmons, Andrelton	.092	Beltran, Carlos	11031	Bour, Justin	5.2
Nieuwenhuis, Kirk	.328	Panik, Joe	.097	Suzuki, Ichiro	10681	Stanton, Giancarlo	5.3
Davis, Chris	.320	Pedroia, Dustin	.097	Cabrera, Miguel	9530	Goldschmidt, Paul	5.4
Souza Jr., Steven	.318	Molina, Yadier	.098	Cano, Robinson	8493	Arenado, Nolan	5.5
Taylor, Michael	.318	Suzuki, Ichiro	.100	Markakis, Nick	8006	Correa, Carlos	5.6
Santana, Domingo	.317	Pujols, Albert	.102	Reyes, Jose	7989	Encarnacion, Edwin	5.7
Reynolds, Mark	.309	Altuve, Jose	.107	Phillips, Brandon	7965	Braun, Ryan	5.7
Saltalamacchia, J	.308	2 tied with	.109	Holliday, Matt	7916	Holliday, Matt	5.7

2017 Active Career Pitching Leaders

Earned Run Average (minimum 750 IP)	
Kershaw, Clayton	2.36
Rodriguez, Francisco	2.86
Sale, Chris	2.98
Bumgarner, Madison	3.01
Strasburg, Stephen	3.07
Kluber, Corey	3.13
Hernandez, Felix	3.20
Price, David	3.22
Wainwright, Adam	3.29
Scherzer, Max	3.30

Winning Percentage (minimum 100 Decisions)	
Kershaw, Clayton	.692
Scherzer, Max	.653
Price, David	.651
Strasburg, Stephen	.651
Wainwright, Adam	.643
Lester, Jon	.633
Verlander, Justin	.623
Sabathia, CC	.619
Iwakuma, Hisashi	.618
Greinke, Zack	.616

Opponent Batting Average (minimum 750 IP)	
Kershaw, Clayton	.206
Rodriguez, Francisco	.207
Darvish, Yu	.219
Sale, Chris	.222
Arrieta, Jake	.222
Strasburg, Stephen	.223
Benoit, Joaquin	.223
Scherzer, Max	.226
Rodney, Fernando	.231
Kluber, Corey	.232

Baserunners Per 9 IP (minimum 750 IP)	
Kershaw, Clayton	9.15
Sale, Chris	9.93
Strasburg, Stephen	10.00
Kluber, Corey	10.11
Bumgarner, Madison	10.15
Scherzer, Max	10.39
Iwakuma, Hisashi	10.44
Price, David	10.53
Rodriguez, Francisco	10.55
Hamels, Cole	10.76

Games	
Rodriguez, Francisco	948
Qualls, Chad	844
Rodney, Fernando	828
Benoit, Joaquin	764
Smith, Joe	698
Broxton, Jonathan	694
Madson, Ryan	682
Street, Huston	668
Belisle, Matt	660
Ziegler, Brad	657

Games Started	
Colon, Bartolo	528
Sabathia, CC	509
Lackey, John	446
Verlander, Justin	385
Arroyo, Bronson	383
Greinke, Zack	381
Santana, Ervin	376
Hernandez, Felix	375
Shields, James	372
Hamels, Cole	362

Complete Games	
Sabathia, CC	38
Colon, Bartolo	37
Hernandez, Felix	25
Kershaw, Clayton	25
Shields, James	23
Verlander, Justin	23
Wainwright, Adam	22
Santana, Ervin	21
Lackey, John	18
Cueto, Johnny	17

Shutouts	
Kershaw, Clayton	15
Colon, Bartolo	13
Sabathia, CC	12
Hernandez, Felix	11
Santana, Ervin	11
Wainwright, Adam	10
Shields, James	9
4 tied with	8

Wins	
Colon, Bartolo	240
Sabathia, CC	237
Lackey, John	188
Verlander, Justin	188
Greinke, Zack	172
Hernandez, Felix	160
Lester, Jon	159
Weaver, Jered	150
Santana, Ervin	149
Arroyo, Bronson	148

Losses	
Colon, Bartolo	176
Lackey, John	147
Sabathia, CC	146
Arroyo, Bronson	137
Santana, Ervin	124
Shields, James	123
Jackson, Edwin	120
Cain, Matt	118
Dickey, R.A.	118
Nolasco, Ricky	118

Innings Pitched	
Sabathia, CC	3317.0
Colon, Bartolo	3315.1
Lackey, John	2840.1
Verlander, Justin	2545.0
Hernandez, Felix	2502.1
Greinke, Zack	2455.2
Arroyo, Bronson	2435.2
Shields, James	2411.1
Santana, Ervin	2383.1
Hamels, Cole	2362.1

Batters Faced	
Colon, Bartolo	14027
Sabathia, CC	13856
Lackey, John	12030
Verlander, Justin	10513
Arroyo, Bronson	10338
Hernandez, Felix	10274
Shields, James	10122
Greinke, Zack	10080
Santana, Ervin	10027
Hamels, Cole	9678

Strikeouts	
Sabathia, CC	2846
Colon, Bartolo	2454
Verlander, Justin	2416
Hernandez, Felix	2342
Lackey, John	2294
Greinke, Zack	2236
Hamels, Cole	2227
Scherzer, Max	2149
Kershaw, Clayton	2120
Shields, James	2080

Walks Allowed	
Sabathia, CC	1009
Colon, Bartolo	923
Jimenez, Ubaldo	848
Lackey, John	815
Verlander, Justin	771
Santana, Ervin	739
Perez, Oliver	735
Hernandez, Felix	721
Volquez, Edinson	721
Cain, Matt	712

Hit Batters	
Lackey, John	133
Sabathia, CC	109
Arroyo, Bronson	105
Santana, Ervin	100
Cueto, Johnny	99
Dickey, R.A.	90
Morton, Charlie	89
Guthrie, Jeremy	88
Shields, James	88
Hernandez, Felix	87

Wild Pitches	
Hernandez, Felix	140
Lackey, John	125
Jackson, Edwin	97
Santana, Ervin	96
Shields, James	96
de la Rosa, Jorge	94
Jimenez, Ubaldo	93
Dickey, R.A.	91
Liriano, Francisco	90
Greinke, Zack	80

2017 Active Career Pitching Leaders

Saves	
Rodriguez, Francisco	437
Street, Huston	324
Rodney, Fernando	300
Kimbrel, Craig	291
Jansen, Kenley	230
Chapman, Aroldis	204
Soria, Joakim	204
Holland, Greg	186
Melancon, Mark	179
Johnson, Jim	176

Save Pct (minimum 50 Save Ops)	
Britton, Zach	93.1
Kimbrel, Craig	90.9
Holland, Greg	90.3
Jansen, Kenley	89.8
Davis, Wade	89.8
Chapman, Aroldis	89.1
Allen, Cody	87.1
Frieri, Ernesto	86.9
Familia, Jeurys	86.9
Diaz, Edwin	86.7

Home Runs Allowed	
Colon, Bartolo	407
Arroyo, Bronson	347
Sabathia, CC	336
Shields, James	327
Lackey, John	319
Santana, Ervin	307
Dickey, R.A.	264
Hamels, Cole	264
Weaver, Jered	262
Guthrie, Jeremy	250

Strikeouts Per 9 IP (minimum 750 IP)	
Darvish, Yu	11.04
Sale, Chris	10.55
Strasburg, Stephen	10.54
Rodriguez, Francisco	10.53
Scherzer, Max	10.20
Kluber, Corey	9.91
Kershaw, Clayton	9.86
Archer, Chris	9.72
Perez, Oliver	9.45
Morrow, Brandon	9.19

Opp On-Base Percentage (minimum 750 IP)	
Kershaw, Clayton	.262
Sale, Chris	.276
Strasburg, Stephen	.278
Bumgarner, Madison	.281
Kluber, Corey	.281
Scherzer, Max	.285
Rodriguez, Francisco	.287
Price, David	.288
Iwakuma, Hisashi	.288
Estrada, Marco	.293

Opp Slugging Average (minimum 750 IP)	
Kershaw, Clayton	.307
Rodriguez, Francisco	.341
Rodney, Fernando	.342
Strasburg, Stephen	.346
Sale, Chris	.352
Arrieta, Jake	.355
Gray, Sonny	.356
Hernandez, Felix	.359
Gonzalez, Gio	.361
Darvish, Yu	.361

Hits Per Nine Innings (minimum 750 IP)	
Kershaw, Clayton	6.66
Rodriguez, Francisco	6.81
Darvish, Yu	7.29
Sale, Chris	7.39
Arrieta, Jake	7.40
Strasburg, Stephen	7.41
Benoit, Joaquin	7.44
Scherzer, Max	7.54
Rodney, Fernando	7.74
Kluber, Corey	7.77

Home Runs Per Nine IP (minimum 750 IP)	
Kershaw, Clayton	0.60
Wainwright, Adam	0.67
Rodney, Fernando	0.67
Morton, Charlie	0.74
Gonzalez, Gio	0.76
Cole, Gerrit	0.77
Hernandez, Felix	0.79
Lynn, Lance	0.79
Madson, Ryan	0.83
Strasburg, Stephen	0.83

Strikeouts / Walks Ratio (minimum 750 IP)	
Sale, Chris	5.12
Kluber, Corey	4.94
Tomlin, Josh	4.68
Strasburg, Stephen	4.55
Bumgarner, Madison	4.33
Kershaw, Clayton	4.18
Scherzer, Max	4.02
Iwakuma, Hisashi	3.86
Carrasco, Carlos	3.81
Price, David	3.77

Stolen Base Pct Allowed (minimum 750 IP)	
Cueto, Johnny	42.0
Tillman, Chris	42.0
Miley, Wade	43.6
Fister, Doug	46.5
Lynn, Lance	49.1
Iwakuma, Hisashi	50.0
Tomlin, Josh	50.0
Kershaw, Clayton	51.7
Greinke, Zack	52.0
Duke, Zach	55.1

GIDP Induced	
Colon, Bartolo	306
Sabathia, CC	299
Lackey, John	260
Hernandez, Felix	246
Shields, James	202
Lester, Jon	200
Wainwright, Adam	195
Porcello, Rick	192
Greinke, Zack	191
Arroyo, Bronson	185

GIDP Per Nine IP (minimum 750 IP)	
Keuchel, Dallas	1.16
Richard, Clayton	1.14
Pelfrey, Mike	1.12
Morton, Charlie	1.09
Garcia, Jaime	1.09
Qualls, Chad	1.07
Duke, Zach	1.07
Porcello, Rick	1.03
Buchholz, Clay	1.00
Nova, Ivan	0.97

Complete Game % (minimum 100 GS)	
Kluber, Corey	0.09
Kershaw, Clayton	0.09
Sale, Chris	0.08
Wainwright, Adam	0.08
Sabathia, CC	0.07
Keuchel, Dallas	0.07
Colon, Bartolo	0.07
Hernandez, Felix	0.07
Bumgarner, Madison	0.06
Shields, James	0.06

Quality Start Pct (minimum 100 GS)	
Sale, Chris	73.3
Kershaw, Clayton	73.1
deGrom, Jacob	72.0
Price, David	68.0
Bumgarner, Madison	67.1
Cole, Gerrit	66.9
Hamels, Cole	66.3
Hernandez, Felix	65.9
Gray, Sonny	65.9
2 tied with	65.7

Walks Per 9 IP (minimum 750 IP)	
Tomlin, Josh	1.32
Iwakuma, Hisashi	1.88
Zimmermann, Jordan	1.93
Kluber, Corey	2.01
Hunter, Tommy	2.02
Bumgarner, Madison	2.04
Porcello, Rick	2.05
Sale, Chris	2.06
Fister, Doug	2.08
Leake, Mike	2.13

Games Finished	
Rodriguez, Francisco	677
Rodney, Fernando	534
Street, Huston	525
Kimbrel, Craig	392
Soria, Joakim	353
Jansen, Kenley	333
Chapman, Aroldis	315
Johnson, Jim	310
Broxton, Jonathan	293
Melancon, Mark	292

2017 American League Bill James Leaders

Top Game Scores

Pitcher	Date	Opp	IP	H	R	ER	BB	SO	GS
Bundy, Dylan, Bal	8/29	Sea	9.0	1	0	0	2	12	95
Kluber, Corey, Cle	6/19	Bal	9.0	3	0	0	0	11	92
Santana, Ervin, Min	4/15	CWS	9.0	1	0	0	1	8	92
Mengden, Daniel, Oak	9/15	Phi	9.0	2	0	0	0	7	90
Sale, Chris, Bos	8/8	TB	8.0	2	0	0	1	13	90
Boyd, Matt, Det	9/17	CWS	9.0	1	0	0	1	5	89
Kluber, Corey, Cle	4/21	CWS	9.0	3	0	0	2	9	88
Kluber, Corey, Cle	8/8	Col	9.0	3	1	1	0	11	88
Nolasco, Ricky, LAA	7/1	Sea	9.0	3	0	0	0	7	88
Tanaka, Masahiro, NYY	7/28	TB	8.0	2	1	1	0	14	88
Verlander, Justin, Hou	9/12	LAA	8.0	1	0	0	1	9	88

Worst Game Scores

Pitcher	Date	Opp	IP	H	R	ER	BB	SO	GS
Bergman, C, Sea	5/23	Was	4.0	14	10	10	2	0	-8
Tillman, Chris, Bal	6/10	NYY	1.1	7	9	9	3	1	2
Hahn, Jesse, Oak	6/22	Hou	2.0	6	10	9	3	0	3
Cobb, Alex, TB	6/3	Sea	5.0	14	9	9	2	3	4
Jimenez, Ubaldo, Bal	6/23	TB	2.1	7	9	9	4	1	4
Musgrove, Joe, Hou	6/23	Sea	3.2	12	9	9	1	4	4
Bergman, C, Sea	6/13	Min	2.2	10	9	9	0	3	5
Darvish, Yu, Tex	7/26	Mia	3.2	9	10	10	2	5	6
5 tied with									7

Runs Created

Judge, Aaron, NYY	131
Altuve, Jose, Hou	118
Abreu, Jose, CWS	116
Hosmer, Eric, KC	116
Betts, Mookie, Bos	115
Ramirez, Jose, Cle	113
Cruz, Nelson, Sea	112
Trout, Mike, LAA	110
Upton, Justin, Det-LAA	109
Lindor, Francisco, Cle	107

Runs Created Per 27 Outs

Trout, Mike, LAA	10.0
Judge, Aaron, NYY	8.5
Altuve, Jose, Hou	7.6
Gonzalez, Marwin, Hou	7.5
Ramirez, Jose, Cle	7.1
Cruz, Nelson, Sea	7.1
Hosmer, Eric, KC	7.1
Garcia, Avisail, CWS	7.0
Upton, Justin, Det-LAA	6.9
Abreu, Jose, CWS	6.8

Offensive Winning %

Trout, Mike, LAA	.827
Judge, Aaron, NYY	.757
Altuve, Jose, Hou	.752
Gonzalez, Marwin, Hou	.747
Cruz, Nelson, Sea	.709
Hosmer, Eric, KC	.703
Reddick, Josh, Hou	.702
Ramirez, Jose, Cle	.701
Garcia, Avisail, CWS	.689
Springer, George, Hou	.682

Secondary Average
(minimum 502 PA)

Trout, Mike, LAA	.612
Judge, Aaron, NYY	.594
Gallo, Joey, Tex	.510
Encarnacion, Edwin, Cle	.437
Morrison, Logan, TB	.432
Upton, Justin, Det-LAA	.425
Davis, Khris, Oak	.417
Souza Jr., Steven, TB	.411
Frazier, Todd, CWS-NYY	.399
Alonso, Yonder, Oak-Sea	.390

Isolated Power
(minimum 502 PA)

Judge, Aaron, NYY	.343
Gallo, Joey, Tex	.327
Trout, Mike, LAA	.323
Davis, Khris, Oak	.281
Morrison, Logan, TB	.270
Upton, Justin, Det-LAA	.268
Ramirez, Jose, Cle	.265
Cruz, Nelson, Sea	.261
Smoak, Justin, Tor	.259
Sanchez, Gary, NYY	.253

Power / Speed Number
(minimum 502 PA)

Altuve, Jose, Hou	27.4
Trout, Mike, LAA	26.4
Betts, Mookie, Bos	25.0
Merrifield, Whit, KC	24.4
Andrus, Elvis, Tex	22.2
Gardner, Brett, NYY	22.0
Dozier, Brian, Min	21.8
Ramirez, Jose, Cle	21.4
Souza Jr., Steven, TB	20.9
Lindor, Francisco, Cle	20.6

Speed Scores

Betts, Mookie, Bos	7.55
Trout, Mike, LAA	7.27
Merrifield, Whit, KC	7.22
Anderson, Tim, CWS	7.12
Gardner, Brett, NYY	7.07
Ellsbury, Jacoby, NYY	7.00
Andrus, Elvis, Tex	6.94
Kinsler, Ian, Det	6.91
Cain, Lorenzo, KC	6.86
Semien, Marcus, Oak	6.69

Cheap Wins

Perez, Martin, Tex	6
Zimmermann, Jordan, Det	4
11 tied with	3

Tough Losses

Porcello, Rick, Bos	7
Fulmer, Michael, Det	6
Gray, Sonny, Oak-NYY	6
Chavez, Jesse, LAA	5
Sale, Chris, Bos	5
8 tied with	4

2017 National League Bill James Leaders

Top Game Scores

Pitcher	Date	Opp	IP	H	R	ER	BB	SO	GS
Volquez, Edinson, Mia	6/3	Ari	9.0	0	0	0	2	10	95
Hill, Rich, LAD	8/23	Pit	9.0	1	1	1	0	10	91
Quintana, Jose, ChC	9/24	Mil	9.0	3	0	0	1	10	90
Martinez, Carlos, StL	6/10	Phi	9.0	4	0	0	1	11	89
Ray, Robbie, Ari	5/30	Pit	9.0	4	0	0	0	10	89
Martinez, Carlos, StL	9/4	SD	9.0	3	0	0	3	10	88
Nova, Ivan, Pit	4/29	Mia	9.0	3	0	0	0	7	88
Wacha, Michael, StL	7/18	NYM	9.0	3	0	0	1	8	88
5 tied with									87

Worst Game Scores

Pitcher	Date	Opp	IP	H	R	ER	BB	SO	GS
Locke, Jeff, Mia	7/3	StL	2.2	11	11	11	4	2	-10
Richard, Clayton, SD	7/19	Col	3.2	14	11	10	1	3	-7
Guthrie, Jeremy, Was	4/8	Phi	0.2	6	10	10	4	0	-4
Bailey, Homer, Cin	8/6	StL	3.1	10	10	10	4	3	-1
Blach, Ty, SF	5/6	Cin	3.0	11	10	8	1	0	0
Cain, Matt, SF	5/5	Cin	3.1	10	9	9	6	2	0
Kuhl, Chad, Pit	4/24	ChC	1.2	8	9	9	4	1	0
Nelson, Jimmy, Mil	8/11	Cin	3.2	11	10	9	3	4	2
Garrett, Amir, Cin	4/24	Mil	3.1	8	10	9	4	1	3
Taillon, Jameson, Pit	7/25	SF	3.0	9	10	9	1	1	3

Runs Created

Blackmon, Charlie, Col	151
Votto, Joey, Cin	139
Goldschmidt, Paul, Ari	131
Arenado, Nolan, Col	130
Ozuna, Marcell, Mia	117
Stanton, Giancarlo, Mia	117
Rizzo, Anthony, ChC	116
Rendon, Anthony, Was	115
Bryant, Kris, ChC	113
Seager, Corey, LAD	104

Runs Created Per 27 Outs

Votto, Joey, Cin	9.2
Blackmon, Charlie, Col	8.9
Goldschmidt, Paul, Ari	8.4
Rendon, Anthony, Was	8.3
Freeman, Freddie, Atl	7.7
Arenado, Nolan, Col	7.7
Turner, Justin, LAD	7.7
Bryant, Kris, ChC	7.4
Pham, Tommy, StL	7.3
Cozart, Zack, Cin	7.3

Offensive Winning %

Votto, Joey, Cin	.791
Freeman, Freddie, Atl	.753
Rendon, Anthony, Was	.749
Blackmon, Charlie, Col	.748
Turner, Justin, LAD	.736
Goldschmidt, Paul, Ari	.735
Pham, Tommy, StL	.733
Ozuna, Marcell, Mia	.720
Stanton, Giancarlo, Mia	.718
Cozart, Zack, Cin	.705

Secondary Average
(minimum 502 PA)

Votto, Joey, Cin	.506
Stanton, Giancarlo, Mia	.496
Bellinger, Cody, LAD	.469
Goldschmidt, Paul, Ari	.466
Freeman, Freddie, Atl	.445
Thames, Eric, Mil	.439
Carpenter, Matt, StL	.433
Pham, Tommy, StL	.430
Bryant, Kris, ChC	.428
Lamb, Jake, Ari	.412

Isolated Power
(minimum 502 PA)

Stanton, Giancarlo, Mia	.350
Bellinger, Cody, LAD	.315
Freeman, Freddie, Atl	.280
Arenado, Nolan, Col	.277
Thames, Eric, Mil	.271
Blackmon, Charlie, Col	.270
Zimmerman, Ryan, Was	.269
Goldschmidt, Paul, Ari	.265
Votto, Joey, Cin	.258
Schebler, Scott, Cin	.252

Power / Speed Number
(minimum 502 PA)

Goldschmidt, Paul, Ari	24.0
Myers, Wil, SD	24.0
Pham, Tommy, StL	24.0
Blackmon, Charlie, Col	20.3
Santana, Domingo, Mil	20.0
Puig, Yasiel, LAD	19.5
Taylor, Chris, LAD	18.8
Reyes, Jose, NYM	18.5
Yelich, Christian, Mia	16.9
Bellinger, Cody, LAD	15.9

Speed Scores

Hamilton, Billy, Cin	8.97
Gordon, Dee, Mia	8.84
Blackmon, Charlie, Col	7.75
Villar, Jonathan, Mil	7.43
Inciarte, Ender, Atl	7.25
Fowler, Dexter, StL	7.20
Perez, Hernan, Mil	7.06
Hernandez, Cesar, Phi	6.80
Harrison, Josh, Pit	6.77
Herrera, Odubel, Phi	6.73

Cheap Wins

Davies, Zach, Mil	5
Nova, Ivan, Pit	4
Perdomo, Luis, SD	4
Wainwright, Adam, StL	4
8 tied with	3

Tough Losses

Bumgarner, Madison, SF	6
Castillo, Luis, Cin	5
Foltynewicz, Mike, Atl	5
Samardzija, Jeff, SF	5
Cueto, Johnny, SF	4
Hill, Rich, LAD	4
Martinez, Carlos, StL	4
Nola, Aaron, Phi	4
Nova, Ivan, Pit	4
18 tied with	3

Additional Bill James Leaders

AL Batters Win Shares

Altuve, Jose, Hou	35
Hosmer, Eric, KC	30
Judge, Aaron, NYY	29
Trout, Mike, LAA	29
Ramirez, Jose, Cle	28
Lindor, Francisco, Cle	27
5 tied with	26

NL Batters Win Shares

Blackmon, Charlie, Col	33
Votto, Joey, Cin	33
Seager, Corey, LAD	31
Goldschmidt, Paul, Ari	29
Ozuna, Marcell, Mia	29
Rendon, Anthony, Was	29
Stanton, Giancarlo, Mia	29
Murphy, Daniel, Was	27
Arenado, Nolan, Col	26
Bryant, Kris, ChC	26

AL Pitchers Win Shares

Kluber, Corey, Cle	23
Sale, Chris, Bos	20
Kimbrel, Craig, Bos	19
Carrasco, Carlos, Cle	18
Santana, Ervin, Min	17
Verlander, Justin, Det-Hou	17
Severino, Luis, NYY	16
Stroman, Marcus, Tor	16
Pomeranz, Drew, Bos	15
4 tied with	13

NL Pitchers Win Shares

Scherzer, Max, Was	21
Jansen, Kenley, LAD	19
Kershaw, Clayton, LAD	19
Greinke, Zack, Ari	18
Gonzalez, Gio, Was	17
Knebel, Corey, Mil	17
Ray, Robbie, Ari	17
Rivero, Felipe, Pit	17
Strasburg, Stephen, Was	17
Wood, Alex, LAD	15

Batters Career Win Shares

Pujols, Albert	470
Cabrera, Miguel	388
Beltran, Carlos	369
Beltre, Adrian	364
Suzuki, Ichiro	324
Cano, Robinson	319
Mauer, Joe	290
Utley, Chase	288
Gonzalez, Adrian	282
Votto, Joey	276

Pitchers Career Win Shares

Sabathia, CC	229
Colon, Bartolo	201
Verlander, Justin	194
Hernandez, Felix	187
Greinke, Zack	186
Kershaw, Clayton	176
Lackey, John	170
Hamels, Cole	168
Rodriguez, Francisco	168
Lester, Jon	153

AL Component ERA
(minimum 162 IP)

Kluber, Corey, Cle	1.83
Sale, Chris, Bos	2.33
Severino, Luis, NYY	2.53
Carrasco, Carlos, Cle	2.99
Fulmer, Michael, Det	3.04
Verlander, Justin, Det-Hou	3.19
Santana, Ervin, Min	3.21
Gray, Sonny, Oak-NYY	3.26
Cobb, Alex, TB	3.64
Bundy, Dylan, Bal	3.68

NL Component ERA
(minimum 162 IP)

Scherzer, Max, Was	1.98
Strasburg, Stephen, Was	2.22
Kershaw, Clayton, LAD	2.27
Greinke, Zack, Ari	2.79
Gonzalez, Gio, Was	3.05
Ray, Robbie, Ari	3.08
Nola, Aaron, Phi	3.30
deGrom, Jacob, NYM	3.36
Samardzija, Jeff, SF	3.43
Martinez, Carlos, StL	3.51

AL Highest Avg Game Score
(minimum 30 GS)

Sale, Chris, Bos	64.44
Severino, Luis, NYY	60.35
Carrasco, Carlos, Cle	58.75
Verlander, Justin, Det-Hou	57.85
Santana, Ervin, Min	56.55
Archer, Chris, TB	54.53
Stroman, Marcus, Tor	53.97
Pomeranz, Drew, Bos	53.63
Bauer, Trevor, Cle	52.39
Tanaka, Masahiro, NYY	51.93

AL Lowest Avg Game Score
(minimum 30 GS)

Miley, Wade, Bal	44.84
Perez, Martin, Tex	45.47
Hammel, Jason, KC	46.56
Nolasco, Ricky, LAA	47.27
Kennedy, Ian, KC	47.87
Porcello, Rick, Bos	48.21
Gausman, Kevin, Bal	48.94
Estrada, Marco, Tor	49.55
Vargas, Jason, KC	50.72
Tanaka, Masahiro, NYY	51.93

AL Lowest Offensive Win %

Odor, Rougned, Tex	.288
Gordon, Alex, KC	.302
Escobar, Alcides, KC	.325
Beltran, Carlos, Hou	.333
Pillar, Kevin, Tor	.341
Anderson, Tim, CWS	.352
Trumbo, Mark, Bal	.365
Ramirez, Hanley, Bos	.384
Cabrera, Miguel, Det	.389
Bautista, Jose, Tor	.391

NL Highest Avg Game Score
(minimum 30 GS)

Scherzer, Max, Was	65.58
Greinke, Zack, Ari	58.34
Gonzalez, Gio, Was	58.13
deGrom, Jacob, NYM	57.74
Martinez, Carlos, StL	56.16
Lynn, Lance, StL	54.24
Samardzija, Jeff, SF	53.75
Arrieta, Jake, ChC	53.63
Cole, Gerrit, Pit	53.03
Chacin, Jhoulys, SD	52.94

NL Lowest Avg Game Score
(minimum 30 GS)

Moore, Matt, SF	45.19
Richard, Clayton, SD	46.75
Kuhl, Chad, Pit	49.35
Teheran, Julio, Atl	49.88
Davies, Zach, Mil	49.97
Dickey, R.A., Atl	50.10
Corbin, Patrick, Ari	50.31
Nova, Ivan, Pit	50.39
Roark, Tanner, Was	50.43
Lackey, John, ChC	50.60

NL Lowest Offensive Win %

Peraza, Jose, Cin	.289
Franco, Maikel, Phi	.291
Hamilton, Billy, Cin	.363
Joseph, Tommy, Phi	.369
Gonzalez, Carlos, Col	.405
Swanson, Dansby, Atl	.421
Story, Trevor, Col	.421
Schebler, Scott, Cin	.428
Herrera, Odubel, Phi	.446
Duvall, Adam, Cin	.452

Home Run Robberies

Bill James

The more often you hit the ball into the seats, the more often some inconsiderate punk outfielder, trying to make a name for himself with no regard for anyone else's feelings, will stick his glove over the wall and take it away from you. You probably know that a great many home run records were set in 2017, and that being the case, it is logical that there would also be a record for balls hit over the fence that were NOT home runs because some outfielder wanted to get himself on **Baseball Tonight**. There were in fact a record number of such plays. We here at Baseball Info Solutions have been tracking Home Run Robberies (Home Run Saving Catches) since 2004, and whereas there were only 33 such events in 2014 and only 32 of them in 2009, there were 60 in 2017, seven more than in any previous season. It's a magic number for home runs, 60; I guess you have to be really old now to get the reference, but it used to be a magic number. Now it's a magic number for Non Home Runs.

Altogether there have been 618 of these events in the 14 years that we have been hunched over our screens and freeze-framing videos, or about 44 per season—another magic number for home runs, Henry Aaron's number. With 30 parks that is about one and a half per park per season. Your chance of seeing an outfielder take a home run away from a hitter in any given game is a little less than one in 50, although last year it was a little more than one in 50. The Park where this is most common is Camden Yards; it has happened 64 times at Camden Yards, 46 times at the Big A (Anaheim), and 45 times in the park where the White Sox play. At Camden Yards it has been done 26 times by the left fielders, 36 times by the center fielders, and twice by the right fielders. At Fenway Park it has been done 23 times by right fielders, 3 times by center fielders, but never by a left fielder (Duh), whereas at PNC Park in Pittsburgh it has been done 19 times by left fielders, but never by a center fielder or right fielder. At Yankee Stadium most home run robberies are by Jeffrey Maier.

The career leaders for Home Run Robberies are still Carlos Gomez and Torii Hunter, tied at 12 apiece although neither one has had one since 2014. Adam Jones and Mike Trout, who did take home runs away from deserving hitters in 2017, have 10 each. Adam Jones, Jackie Bradley Jr. and Guillermo Heredia had three each in 2017.

Chris Davis has lost 9 home runs to nuisance outfielders, more than any other player; Adrian Beltre has lost 7, Jay Bruce 6 and Jim Thome 6. Thome had three home runs taken away from him by Torii Hunter, the only player to lose three home runs to one outfielder. Davis, though, has lost 17 RBI to home run-saving catches. No one else has lost more than 10 RBI that way since we started counting. Leonys Martin has lost only 3 home runs to outfielders reaching over the fence where they don't belong, but two of the three were Grand Slams, so he's lost 9 RBI there. He is the only player to have lost two Grand Slams.

This a complete log of the Home Run Saving catches of 2017. Enjoy.

Home Run Robberies

Date	Matchup	Fielder	Pos	Pitcher	Batter	Inn.	Outs	Men On	Score
07/31/2017	Tigers@Yankees	Jim Adduci	9	Michael Fulmer	Todd Frazier	6	0	1__	2-5
05/19/2017	Blue Jays@Orioles	Anthony Alford	7	Aaron Sanchez	J.J. Hardy	6	2	___	3-3
04/04/2017	Cubs@Cardinals	Albert Almora Jr.	8	Koji Uehara	Matt Adams	7	1	___	2-1
05/27/2017	Mariners@Red Sox	Mookie Betts	9	Brian Johnson	Nelson Cruz	4	1	___	0-3
06/07/2017	Red Sox@Yankees	Mookie Betts	9	Rick Porcello	Chris Carter	6	2	___	0-5
05/19/2017	Red Sox@Athletics	Jackie Bradley Jr.	8	Craig Kimbrel	Ryon Healy	9	2	___	2-2
07/16/2017	Yankees@Red Sox	Jackie Bradley Jr.	8	David Price	Aaron Judge	8	1	1__	0-3
09/19/2017	Red Sox@Orioles	Jackie Bradley Jr.	8	Drew Pomeranz	Chris Davis	5	0	___	0-0
08/03/2017	Cardinals@Brewers	Keon Broxton	8	Matt Garza	Jose Martinez	2	1	___	0-0
08/30/2017	Cardinals@Brewers	Keon Broxton	8	Corey Knebel	Randal Grichuk	9	2	1__	5-6
06/13/2017	Cubs@Mets	Jay Bruce	9	Neil Ramirez	Kyle Schwarber	8	0	___	12-1
08/15/2017	Indians@Twins	Byron Buxton	8	Alan Busenitz	Edwin Encarnacion	7	1	___	3-1
05/18/2017	White Sox@Mariners	Melky Cabrera	7	Dylan Covey	Danny Valencia	4	2	___	0-1
07/31/2017	Royals@Orioles	Lorenzo Cain	8	Danny Duffy	Chris Davis	2	0	1__	1-0
09/25/2017	Blue Jays@Red Sox	Ezequiel Carrera	9	Roberto Osuna	Rafael Devers	9	0	___	6-4
05/11/2017	Royals@Rays	Corey Dickerson	7	Jake Odorizzi	Eric Hosmer	1	2	___	0-0
08/08/2017	Astros@White Sox	Adam Engel	8	Derek Holland	Brian McCann	4	0	___	3-6
09/04/2017	Indians@White Sox	Adam Engel	8	James Shields	Austin Jackson	5	1	___	3-0
06/18/2017	Cardinals@Orioles	Dexter Fowler	8	Lance Lynn	Jonathan Schoop	5	1	_3	2-5
08/13/2017	Royals@White Sox	Alex Gordon	8	Neftali Feliz	Nick Delmonico	9	2	_2_	14-6
09/04/2017	Royals@Tigers	Alex Gordon	7	Jakob Junis	Mikie Mahtook	4	2	1_3	5-0
04/16/2017	Rangers@Mariners	Mitch Haniger	9	Marc Rzepczynski	Joey Gallo	8	1	1__	6-6
08/01/2017	Blue Jays@White Sox	Alen Hanson	9	Mike Pelfrey	Jose Bautista	5	0	___	2-2
04/18/2017	Marlins@Mariners	Guillermo Heredia	7	Yovani Gallardo	Marcell Ozuna	1	2	12_	1-0
05/03/2017	Angels@Mariners	Guillermo Heredia	7	Emilio Pagan	Andrelton Simmons	6	0	1_3	2-4
09/20/2017	Rangers@Mariners	Guillermo Heredia	8	Casey Lawrence	Shin-Soo Choo	6	1	123	7-2
09/03/2017	Cardinals@Giants	Gorkys Hernandez	8	Madison Bumgarner	Tommy Pham	1	1	___	0-0
08/03/2017	Phillies@Angels	Odubel Herrera	8	Jerad Eickhoff	Martin Maldonado	4	0	_2_	4-2
07/28/2017	Cubs@Brewers	Jason Heyward	9	Jose Quintana	Ryan Braun	3	0	_2_	0-1
06/14/2017	Yankees@Angels	Aaron Hicks	8	Michael Pineda	Luis Valbuena	1	1	123	4-0
09/26/2017	Rays@Yankees	Aaron Hicks	8	Jordan Montgomery	Wilson Ramos	1	1	123	0-0
06/06/2017	Mets@Rangers	Jared Hoying	8	Dillon Gee	Jay Bruce	3	0	___	3-3
08/01/2017	Indians@Red Sox	Austin Jackson	8	Dan Otero	Hanley Ramirez	5	0	___	7-5
04/16/2017	Padres@Braves	Travis Jankowski	7	Miguel Diaz	Jace Peterson	7	0	_2_	1-4
04/28/2017	Orioles@Yankees	Adam Jones	8	Darren ODay'	Gregory Bird	8	0	___	11-8
06/01/2017	Red Sox@Orioles	Adam Jones	8	Wade Miley	Mookie Betts	1	0	___	0-0
07/29/2017	Orioles@Rangers	Adam Jones	8	Kevin Gausman	Joey Gallo	3	0	___	4-0
06/29/2017	Athletics@Astros	Matt Joyce	9	Daniel Gossett	Josh Reddick	1	1	___	0-0
05/17/2017	Rays@Indians	Kevin Kiermaier	8	Alex Colome	Jason Kipnis	9	2	___	7-4
07/23/2017	Astros@Orioles	Jake Marisnick	8	Lance McCullers	Chris Davis	5	1	_23	3-4
08/01/2017	Reds@Pirates	Starling Marte	7	A.J. Schugel	Jesse Winker	5	2	_3	8-1
09/28/2017	Cubs@Cardinals	Leonys Martin	8	Jen-Ho Tseng	Paul DeJong	11	2	___	2-1
05/02/2017	Angels@Mariners	Cameron Maybin	7	Yusmeiro Petit	Guillermo Heredia	8	2	___	4-3
04/05/2017	Pirates@Red Sox	Andrew McCutchen	9	Jameson Taillon	Mitch Moreland	4	2	1__	0-0
05/27/2017	Angels@Marlins	Marcell Ozuna	7	Vance Worley	Andrelton Simmons	1	1	___	0-0
07/16/2017	Dodgers@Marlins	Marcell Ozuna	7	Nick Wittgren	Kike Hernandez	6	2	___	3-1
05/19/2017	Diamondbacks@Padres	David Peralta	9	Taijuan Walker	Wil Myers	6	1	___	10-0
08/29/2017	Giants@Padres	Jose Pirela	7	Kirby Yates	Pablo Sandoval	8	0	___	2-6
08/23/2017	Diamondbacks@Mets	A.J. Pollock	8	David Hernandez	Travis dArnaud'	8	0	___	2-4
08/08/2017	Dodgers@Diamondbacks	Yasiel Puig	9	Pedro Baez	J.D. Martinez	6	1	___	3-2
08/26/2017	Brewers@Dodgers	Yasiel Puig	9	Brandon Morrow	Domingo Santana	6	2	___	2-0
04/25/2017	Astros@Indians	Josh Reddick	8	Dallas Keuchel	Jason Kipnis	5	0	___	3-1
06/28/2017	Brewers@Reds	Scott Schebler	9	Luis Castillo	Stephen Vogt	2	1	1_3	0-0
08/02/2017	Nationals@Marlins	Giancarlo Stanton	9	Odrisamer Despaigne	Brian Goodwin	9	2	1__	0-7
09/05/2017	Nationals@Marlins	Giancarlo Stanton	9	Odrisamer Despaigne	Daniel Murphy	3	1	___	1-0
08/18/2017	Nationals@Padres	Michael Taylor	8	Matt Grace	Yangervis Solarte	2	0	___	2-0
04/11/2017	Rangers@Angels	Mike Trout	8	Cam Bedrosian	Mike Napoli	10	0	___	5-5
06/16/2017	Rays@Tigers	Justin Upton	7	Daniel Norris	Corey Dickerson	5	2	___	2-6
08/24/2017	Yankees@Tigers	Justin Upton	7	Daniel Stumpf	Aaron Hicks	7	0	1_3	4-6
08/22/2017	Marlins@Phillies	Christian Yelich	8	Jose Urena	Nick Williams	5	2	1__	6-3

Win Shares

Alex Vigderman

Not too shabby for a 5-foot-6 middle infielder. Jose Altuve repeats as the Win Shares leader this season, garnering 35 after leading the league with 36 in 2016. This comes off a three-peat for Mike Trout, so it's quite the era for AL West stars.

With Trout missing several weeks of the season with an injury, Altuve emerged as clearly the most valuable player in the American League by Win Shares, with Eric Hosmer, Trout, and Aaron Judge all between 29 and 30. By comparison, there are three players whose Win Shares lie in between (Joey Votto, Charlie Blackmon, and Corey Seager), which underscores the difficulty of determining the National League MVP this year. Not to mention Giancarlo Stanton, whose 59 home run season gave him 29 Win Shares himself.

One question that comes up around Win Shares is how team context affects a player's value. If a team wins a lot of games, they have more Win Shares to allocate to its players, so you might expect its players to have inflated values compared to similar players on worse teams. While Win Shares do use the team's performance as the basis for computing player value, it turns out the results don't show the bias towards winning teams that you might expect.

A good example of this in 2017 comes with Aaron Judge and Joey Votto. Both had outstanding offensive seasons (an OPS of 1.049 for Judge and 1.032 for Votto) and played representative defense at a corner position. However, Votto played for a last-place team while Judge's team made the playoffs. Even with a larger pie of wins to draw from, Judge actually falls behind Votto in Win Shares. That's because while Cincinnati's pie is smaller, Votto's surrounding cast is inferior enough that he accounts for more of his team's performance than Judge does.

The following tables contain each player's season-by-season Win Shares since 2008. They also include each player's total from before 2008 and career total.

To give a sense of the scale here, a player with around 30 Win Shares is an MVP candidate, more than 20 is a likely All Star, and more than 10 is a solid major league player. Of course, it's a counting statistic, so injuries and platoons can affect a player's total as much as his per-play performance does.

For a full treatment of Win Shares, check out Bill James' book, *Win Shares*.

WIN SHARES BY YEAR

Player	<08	08	09	10	11	12	13	14	15	16	17	Career
Abreu, Jose								29	27	20	24	100
Adams, Matt					1	12	15	3	9	11		51
Aguilar, Jesus									0	1	9	10
Albers, Matt	0	4	2	5	3	6	5	1	6	0	10	42
Albies, Ozzie											8	8
Alexander, Scott									0	1	8	9
Allen, Cody						1	8	14	12	14	11	60
Almora Jr., Albert										5	11	16
Alonso, Yonder				0	4	17	12	6	8	12	17	76
Altherr, Aaron							0	6	3	10		19
Altuve, Jose					2	17	11	30	27	36	35	158
Alvarez, Henderson					4	5	7	14	0		1	31
Alvarez, Pedro			14		3	22	18	11	10	8	1	87
Amarista, Alexi					1	6	10	13	6	2	2	40
Anderson, Brett		8	9	4	3	0	3	8	0	1		36
Anderson, Chase							6	5	6	14		31
Andrus, Elvis			17	20	18	23	15	13	21	26	25	178
Aoki, Nori						15	17	17	12	9	8	78
Archer, Chris						0	10	11	14	8	10	53
Arcia, Orlando										4	18	22
Arenado, Nolan							9	12	26	26	26	99
Arrieta, Jake				5	5	0	3	12	27	16	11	79
Arroyo, Bronson	60	10	13	14	3	13	9	5			0	127
Asche, Cody							4	10	10	2	0	26
Asuaje, Carlos										1	11	12
Avila, Alex			3	7	27	15	6	14	6	2	13	93
Avilan, Luis						4	10	2	3	2	4	25
Aviles, Mike		17	2	10	5	10	8	5	3	1	2	63
Axford, John			1	11	15	7	3	3	7	5	0	52
Aybar, Erick	3	15	20	9	20	16	14	20	13	6	9	145
Baez, Javier								2	1	14	15	32
Bailey, Homer	2	0	5	5	5	12	11	8	0	0	1	49
Barnes, Austin									1	1	13	15
Barney, Darwin				1	14	15	5	6	1	6	5	53
Barnhart, Tucker								1	4	12	14	31
Bastardo, Antonio			0	1	10	3	6	3	6	3	0	32
Bauer, Trevor						0	0	5	8	11	12	36
Bautista, Jose	21	8	6	34	36	13	18	28	25	15	11	215
Beckham, Gordon			12	11	14	13	7	5	3	3	0	68
Beckham, Tim							0		5	5	20	30
Belisle, Matt	12	0	1	11	7	8	5	3	3	5	7	62
Bell, Josh										3	16	19
Bellinger, Cody											23	23
Belt, Brandon					5	17	24	5	20	24	12	107
Beltran, Carlos	209	29	14	8	26	18	22	7	14	18	4	369
Beltre, Adrian	161	13	10	26	16	25	22	27	20	29	15	364
Benintendi, Andrew										4	19	23
Benoit, Joaquin	32	2		9	8	7	14	12	9	6	4	103
Berrios, Jose										0	10	10
Betances, Dellin					0		0	14	14	12	9	49
Betts, Mookie								8	23	29	26	86
Blackmon, Charlie					1	1	7	16	20	22	33	100
Blanco, Gregor		11	0	6		12	13	15	10	3	5	75
Blanton, Joe	36	7	11	4	1	5	0		8	10	1	83
Blevins, Jerry	0	3	1	3	2	7	5	2	2	6	5	36
Bogaerts, Xander							1	7	22	19	16	65
Bonifacio, Emilio	1	2	7	5	20	6	7	11	1	0	0	60
Bonifacio, Jorge											10	10
Bour, Justin								3	12	11	17	43
Bourjos, Peter				3	16	5	4	7	2	5	3	45
Brach, Brad					0	3	1	5	9	12	11	41
Bradley, Archie									0	6	12	18
Bradley Jr., Jackie							1	5	10	19	14	49
Brantley, Michael			3	5	11	18	21	31	21	1	10	121
Braun, Ryan	22	23	36	25	37	28	9	17	20	20	9	246
Bregman, Alex										10	23	33
Breslow, Craig	2	6	6	8	3	6	7	0	3	0	1	42
Bridwell, Parker										0	9	9
Britton, Zach					6	3	1	17	15	19	6	67
Brothers, Rex					4	7	13	1	1		0	26
Broxton, Jonathan	19	10	16	6	0	11	1	9	4	3	0	79
Broxton, Keon									0	7	8	15
Bruce, Jay		7	9	16	22	18	21	10	10	18	21	152

Player	<08	08	09	10	11	12	13	14	15	16	17	Career
Bryant, Kris									30	32	26	88
Buchholz, Clay	3	0	6	18	6	9	12	2	8	5	0	69
Bumgarner, Madison			1	8	12	11	12	16	17	19	8	104
Bundy, Dylan					0					7	11	18
Buxton, Byron									2	5	14	21
Cabrera, Asdrubal	7	12	18	9	25	19	12	15	11	21	17	166
Cabrera, Melky	25	5	14	8	19	25	7	19	16	20	16	174
Cabrera, Miguel	120	20	25	30	38	32	37	28	26	25	7	388
Cahill, Trevor			7	16	9	11	6	0	2	5	3	59
Cain, Lorenzo				6	0	7	12	19	27	13	24	108
Cain, Matt	28	14	20	15	15	16	5	1	0	0	0	114
Calhoun, Kole						0	8	20	21	19	17	85
Cano, Robinson	50	12	18	34	30	34	35	34	21	28	23	319
Carpenter, Matt					0	9	35	27	30	21	20	142
Carrasco, Carlos			0	3	5		0	12	14	12	18	64
Carrera, Ezequiel					5	4	0	1	5	7	8	30
Carter, Chris				0	0	8	13	15	10	11	1	58
Cashner, Andrew				2	1	2	10	9	3	2	13	42
Casilla, Santiago	4	3	0	8	8	9	6	12	9	8	6	73
Castellanos, Nick							0	13	13	15	18	59
Castillo, Welington				1	0	4	10	12	10	14	14	65
Castro, Jason				4		8	18	10	7	9	12	68
Castro, Starlin				12	25	23	7	20	13	15	13	128
Cecil, Brett			3	10	4	1	6	6	6	2	4	42
Cervelli, Francisco		0	3	7	4	0	3	7	17	9	6	56
Cespedes, Yoenis						24	14	18	27	19	10	112
Chacin, Jhoulys			0	10	12	4	15	2	2	5	10	60
Chapman, Aroldis				2	4	21	12	13	13	15	9	89
Chapman, Matt											11	11
Chatwood, Tyler					3	3	11	1		11	8	37
Chen, Wei-Yin						12	7	12	14	2	2	49
Chirinos, Robinson					1		0	11	4	6	10	32
Chisenhall, Lonnie					6	4	7	18	9	14	10	68
Choo, Shin-Soo	5	16	23	27	8	25	31	9	25	5	17	191
Cishek, Steve				1	6	10	14	10	3	11	6	61
Claudio, Alex								1	1	5	12	19
Clevinger, Mike										2	11	13
Clippard, Tyler	1	1	5	9	13	11	10	10	9	7	3	79
Cobb, Alex					3	6	13	13		0	12	47
Coghlan, Chris			21	8	4	1	5	15	16	6	1	77
Cole, Gerrit							8	7	18	6	10	49
Collmenter, Josh					10	5	7	12	6	3	0	43
Colome, Alex							1	2	6	12	12	33
Colon, Bartolo	132	2	3		8	9	17	7	7	13	3	201
Conforto, Michael									8	6	20	34
Contreras, Willson										9	17	26
Corbin, Patrick						4	13		5	5	11	38
Correa, Carlos									18	26	26	70
Cozart, Zack					1	11	12	8	4	12	19	67
Crawford, Brandon					5	13	11	22	20	11	13	105
Cron, C.J.								8	9	14	10	41
Cruz, Nelson	7	7	16	19	16	17	16	22	26	21	24	191
Cueto, Johnny		6	7	12	12	21	5	22	12	19	6	122
d'Arnaud, Travis							1	8	11	3	10	33
Darvish, Yu						14	18	10		8	12	62
Davies, Zach									2	8	13	23
Davis, Chris		8	7	1	4	19	33	12	27	17	8	136
Davis, Khris							6	12	11	15	20	64
Davis, Rajai	5	5	13	14	6	11	6	14	6	13	3	96
Davis, Wade			2	8	6	7	2	15	19	11	12	82
De Aza, Alejandro	1	1	1	9	18	16	11	8	3	1		69
de la Rosa, Jorge	7	5	12	8	4	0	12	11	9	5	4	77
deGrom, Jacob								11	15	11	11	48
DeJong, Paul											13	13
Delgado, Randall					2	3	4	2	6	5	4	26
Descalso, Daniel				1	10	5	11	3	1	8	9	48
DeShields, Delino									16	2	10	28
Desmond, Ian			2	11	16	18	25	19	12	22	7	132
Devenski, Chris										11	10	21
Diaz, Edwin										8	10	18
Dickerson, Corey							4	15	8	9	18	54
Dickey, R.A.	11	3	3	15	11	19	11	11	10	7	8	109
Dietrich, Derek							5	6	6	15	12	44

WIN SHARES BY YEAR

Player	<08	08	09	10	11	12	13	14	15	16	17	Career
Difo, Wilmer									0	2	8	10
Donaldson, Josh			0			8	32	27	32	28	25	152
Doolittle, Sean						5	8	11	2	4	11	41
Dozier, Brian						4	19	19	24	24	26	116
Drew, Stephen	22	21	16	20	10	6	17	4	7	5	3	131
Drury, Brandon									0	9	12	21
Duda, Lucas				0	11	13	8	25	17	3	11	88
Duensing, Brian			6	13	4	2	5	4	3	1	6	44
Duffy, Danny					1	2	3	12	7	15	10	50
Duke, Zach	22	3	12	1	4	2	2	7	5	8	1	67
Dunn, Mike			0	2	5	0	7	6	3	4	5	32
Duvall, Adam								0	2	16	12	30
Dyson, Jarrod				2	2	8	7	9	6	12	8	54
Dyson, Sam						0	0	4	9	14	5	32
Eaton, Adam						2	5	20	24	24	5	80
Edwards Jr., Carl									0	3	8	11
Ellis, A.J.		0	0	4	3	20	16	7	10	6	3	69
Ellsbury, Jacoby	6	16	21	1	34	6	22	22	9	17	10	164
Encarnacion, Edwin	34	14	6	8	11	31	22	19	24	19	18	206
Escobar, Alcides		0	4	12	8	14	10	20	15	13	14	110
Escobar, Eduardo					0	2	2	13	14	7	14	52
Escobar, Yunel	12	13	24	14	20	9	18	10	16	15	7	158
Espinosa, Danny				4	22	18	2	6	10	18	2	82
Estrada, Marco		0	0	4	8	7	5	12	12	7		55
Ethier, Andre	24	23	21	22	18	22	16	10	15	0	1	172
Familia, Jeurys						0	0	9	15	16	2	42
Feldman, Scott	5	4	14	2	2	4	10	9	5	4	4	63
Feliz, Neftali			6	15	12	4	1	6	1	6	2	53
Fiers, Mike					0	8	0	7	9	7	3	34
Fister, Doug			4	7	18	11	14	14	4	6	3	81
Flaherty, Ryan						2	7	9	4	4	1	27
Flores, Wilmer							2	7	16	9	8	42
Flowers, Tyler		0	0	3	3	3	10	7	10	12		48
Forsythe, Logan					3	8	3	4	16	16	10	60
Fowler, Dexter		0	15	13	16	15	13	16	22	22	16	148
Franco, Maikel								1	13	17	6	37
Frazier, Adam										5	13	18
Frazier, Todd					3	13	15	20	13	15	13	92
Freeland, Kyle											11	11
Freeman, Freddie				0	19	18	35	28	22	28	22	172
Freese, David			1	8	13	19	9	12	15	14	15	106
Frieri, Ernesto				0	4	4	11	8	0	1	0	28
Fulmer, Michael										14	10	24
Gallardo, Yovani	9	2	10	11	13	16	8	9	14	3	2	97
Gallo, Joey									2	0	16	18
Galvis, Freddy						3	4	2	15	16	18	58
Gamel, Ben										1	13	14
Garcia, Avisail						1	5	4	10	11	22	53
Garcia, Jaime			1	12	7	6	2	2	12	6	8	56
Garcia, Leury							2	1	1	1	8	13
Garcia, Luis							2	0	4	0	8	14
Gardner, Brett		3	9	17	16	2	22	19	19	17	19	143
Garza, Matt	5	12	12	10	10	5	10	8	0	2	3	77
Gattis, Evan							11	12	11	15	8	57
Gausman, Kevin							1	6	5	12	9	33
Gearrin, Cory					0	2	2		0	4	9	17
Gee, Dillon				3	5	4	10	5	0	6	3	36
Gennett, Scooter							9	14	7	11	17	58
Gentry, Craig			0	0	5	9	11	8	0	0	2	35
Gibson, Kyle							0	8	12	4	7	31
Giles, Ken								7	11	6	12	36
Gillaspie, Conor		0			1	0	9	16	3	4	0	33
Givens, Mychal									4	7	10	21
Godley, Zack									3	1	12	16
Goins, Ryan							2	2	12	3	12	31
Goldschmidt, Paul					6	17	36	20	35	25	29	168
Gomes, Yan						2	14	18	5	4	12	55
Gomez, Carlos	2	13	6	4	7	12	21	27	14	11	11	128
Gomez, Jeanmar					2	3	0	4	4	5	0	25
Gonzalez, Adrian	43	24	34	35	27	24	24	26	22	20	3	282
Gonzalez, Carlos		6	9	25	20	15	15	5	18	18	8	139
Gonzalez, Gio		0	2	15	15	17	11	9	9	6	17	100
Gonzalez, Marwin						2	2	6	8	7	26	51

WIN SHARES BY YEAR

Player	<08	08	09	10	11	12	13	14	15	16	17	Career
Gonzalez, Miguel						10	10	10	5	7	6	48
Gordon, Alex	12	15	2	3	24	20	21	26	16	9	6	154
Gordon, Dee					6	3	2	22	26	7	18	84
Grandal, Yasmani						11	4	12	15	19	12	73
Granderson, Curtis	51	20	20	16	26	21	4	17	29	13	13	230
Gray, Jon									1	9	10	20
Gray, Sonny							5	13	16	0	10	44
Green, Chad										2	9	11
Greene, Shane								4	0	3	9	16
Gregerson, Luke			5	9	4	9	7	8	11	10	3	66
Gregorius, Didi						0	10	9	17	16	18	70
Greinke, Zack	22	15	26	11	10	16	17	15	26	10	18	186
Grichuk, Randal								1	12	13	7	33
Grilli, Jason	10	7	2		4	6	9	2	6	6	1	53
Grossman, Robbie							7	10	0	10	10	37
Gurriel, Yulieski										2	18	20
Guthrie, Jeremy	13	13	7	15	8	7	12	9		0	0	84
Gutierrez, Franklin	7	5	21	14	4	5	3		7	7	0	73
Guyer, Brandon						0	0	8	11	10	3	32
Gyorko, Jedd							12	11	11	12	15	61
Hamels, Cole	23	18	10	16	17	18	13	15	12	16	10	168
Hamilton, Billy							2	15	5	9	10	41
Hammel, Jason	2	3	10	8	5	10	4	9	9	9	5	74
Hand, Brad					1	0	1	3	1	8	14	28
Hanigan, Ryan	1	4	8	13	11	18	5	8	4	2	2	76
Haniger, Mitch										3	12	15
Happ, Ian											12	12
Happ, J.A.	0	2	15	6	1	5	3	7	10	18	10	77
Hardy, J.J.	33	20	6	10	22	20	16	17	5	14	3	166
Harper, Bryce					21	19	9	38	20	22		129
Harris, Will					0	5	1	9	11	5		31
Harrison, Josh					5	4	3	25	12	15	15	79
Harvey, Matt							5	14	14	2	0	35
Headley, Chase	0	8	16	15	16	32	17	15	16	17	14	166
Healy, Ryon										11	12	23
Hechavarria, Adeiny						3	5	13	13	9	9	52
Hedges, Austin									2	0	8	10
Heisey, Chris					4	8	5	3	3	2	0	33
Hellickson, Jeremy				3	15	11	4	1	5	12	5	56
Hendricks, Kyle								7	8	17	11	43
Hernandez, Cesar							3	1	12	24	18	58
Hernandez, David				3	6	10	9	3	1	5	7	44
Hernandez, Felix	30	13	26	23	16	15	16	22	14	8	4	187
Hernandez, Kike								5	9	2	9	25
Herrera, Kelvin					0	10	5	10	8	13	7	53
Herrera, Odubel									16	25	10	51
Heyward, Jason				23	11	22	14	23	21	12	14	140
Hicks, Aaron							4	4	11	4	11	34
Hill, Aaron	43	5	25	12	13	25	12	10	5	9	0	159
Hill, Rich	18	1	0	1	3	0	1	4		12	11	52
Holland, Derek			2	3	14	8	13	4	2	4	0	50
Holland, Greg				0	9	11	18	15	7		12	72
Holliday, Matt	72	21	25	25	21	21	25	26	12	10	7	265
Holt, Brock						3	1	12	14	6	2	38
Hoskins, Rhys											10	10
Hosmer, Eric					13	10	18	14	22	17	30	124
Hudson, Daniel			1	9	16	0	0	4	4	3		37
Hughes, Jared					0	6	1	6	7	4	7	31
Hughes, Phil	4	0	10	11	1	9	2	14	8	0	1	60
Hundley, Nick		3	10	10	12	2	10	6	7	6	5	71
Hunter, Tommy		0	8	10	3	4	10	8	4	3	8	58
Iannetta, Chris	6	17	10	3	16	8	10	17	8	5	10	110
Iglesias, Jose					0	1	13		12	13	11	50
Iglesias, Raisel									4	7	14	25
Inciarte, Ender								10	15	14	22	61
Iwakuma, Hisashi						8	20	11	8	10	1	58
Jackson, Austin				18	14	22	15	11	14	5	10	109
Jackson, Edwin	5	10	17	9	12	9	1	0	4	1	2	70
Jansen, Kenley				6	6	15	16	11	12	17	19	102
Jaso, John		0		16	5	21	9	9	11	5		82
Jay, Jon				8	13	15	17	16	3	12	12	96
Jeffress, Jeremy				1	1	0	1	3	7	10	4	27
Jimenez, Ubaldo	4	11	19	22	6	3	13	3	11	2	0	94

WIN SHARES BY YEAR												
Player	<08	08	09	10	11	12	13	14	15	16	17	Career
Johnson, Jim	0	8	7	3	11	17	11	0	7	10	4	78
Jones, Adam	1	9	13	15	16	26	23	25	15	18	18	179
Jones, Nate						9	4	0	2	10	1	26
Joseph, Caleb								7	12	2	8	29
Joyce, Matt		6	1	10	19	13	11	10	1	11	14	96
Judge, Aaron										0	29	29
Kelley, Shawn			3	2	2	2	4	3	4	8	0	28
Kelly, Joe						5	9	5	6	2	7	34
Kemp, Matt	13	19	26	15	37	21	6	20	18	16	6	197
Kendrick, Howie	15	15	15	19	18	16	13	27	18	11	10	177
Kendrick, Kyle	9	3	2	5	7	8	5	4	2		0	45
Kennedy, Ian	2	0	0	11	20	11	2	9	4	14	3	76
Kepler, Max									0	8	12	20
Kershaw, Clayton		5	12	15	23	19	22	22	21	16	19	174
Keuchel, Dallas						0	3	16	22	6	13	60
Kiermaier, Kevin							0	9	19	13	13	54
Kimbrel, Craig				4	17	18	17	16	11	9	19	111
Kinsler, Ian	29	24	24	13	22	15	20	24	21	29	12	233
Kintzler, Brandon				0	1	2	8	4	0	7	11	33
Kipnis, Jason					6	24	27	10	22	19	9	117
Kluber, Corey				0	1	9	21	14	20	23		88
Knebel, Corey							0	4	2	17		23
Koehler, Tom					0	3	8	7	6	1		25
Kontos, George				0	3	1	3	7	5	6		25
Lackey, John	77	13	12	11	1		10	11	17	11	7	170
Lagares, Juan						7	15	13	2	2		39
Lamb, Jake							1	9	16	17		43
Latos, Mat			1	13	8	16	13	5	3	3	0	62
Leake, Mike				7	9	8	12	10	10	5	8	69
LeMahieu, DJ				0	6	8	9	14	22	20		79
Leon, Sandy					0	0	1	3	12	9		25
Leone, Dominic							7	0	0	8		15
Lester, Jon	9	18	17	17	14	8	12	18	13	18	9	153
Lind, Adam	10	7	21	9	11	9	15	13	20	7	10	132
Lindor, Francisco								14	21	27		62
Liriano, Francisco	16	4	2	14	4	4	12	7	12	6	2	83
Lobaton, Jose			0		1	5	9	5	3	3	1	27
Logan, Boone	3	1	0	4	3	5	5	0	2	6	1	30
Longoria, Evan		19	24	28	25	14	24	21	18	20	18	211
Lowrie, Jed		7	1	8	5	11	23	11	6	8	22	102
Lucroy, Jonathan				4	15	15	19	26	10	22	11	122
Lynn, Lance					2	11	7	16	12		11	59
Machado, Manny						7	20	12	27	28	19	113
Madson, Ryan	24	8	10	8	12			9	8	10		89
Mahtook, Mikie							6	1	8			15
Maldonado, Martin				0	7	3	4	5	7	11		37
Manaea, Sean										7	8	15
Mancini, Trey									1	19		20
Margot, Manuel									1	13		14
Marisnick, Jake						2	5	9	3	6		25
Markakis, Nick	32	23	16	22	19	16	11	20	20	17	14	210
Marquez, German										1	11	12
Marte, Starling					5	20	17	20	17	10		89
Martin, Leonys				0	1	14	14	5	13	1		48
Martin, Russell	36	20	16	9	14	12	16	22	17	15	7	184
Martinez, Carlos						1	4	14	16	12		47
Martinez, J.D.				6	7	3	19	25	17	20		97
Martinez, Jose								1	10	11		11
Martinez, Victor	93	7	21	17	24		11	30	4	15	4	226
Mauer, Joe	79	30	32	27	10	25	23	14	18	14	18	290
Maybin, Cameron	0	3	2	8	17	13	0	5	16	14	10	88
Mazara, Nomar										16	16	32
McAllister, Zach				0	4	7	1	6	4	6		28
McCann, Brian	43	18	20	19	23	12	16	19	21	12	7	210
McCann, James							0	10	9	10		29
McCarthy, Brandon	13	1	5		11	7	3	8	0	0	5	53
McCutchen, Andrew			18	22	28	40	34	33	35	17	22	249
McGee, Jake				0	2	8	5	15	7	4	7	48
McHugh, Collin					0	0	13	13	8	4		38
Melancon, Mark			1	2	10	0	15	15	17	16	3	79
Mercer, Jordy					2	13	10	8	13	12		58
Merrifield, Whit										8	21	29
Mesoraco, Devin					1	3	8	26	0	0	2	40

WIN SHARES BY YEAR												
Player	<08	08	09	10	11	12	13	14	15	16	17	Career
Miley, Wade					2	14	10	7	9	3	4	49
Miller, Andrew	2	0	2	0	2	4	2	9	13	19	11	64
Miller, Brad						10	11	15	15	6		57
Miller, Shelby					2	10	10	11	1	1		35
Milone, Tommy					2	10	6	5	8	1	0	32
Minor, Mike			0	3	7	13	3				11	37
Molina, Yadier	40	15	20	17	18	29	29	19	16	21	19	243
Montero, Miguel	3	4	13	9	29	26	10	15	12	6	3	130
Montgomery, Jordan											9	9
Montgomery, Mike									2	7	10	19
Moore, Matt					1	8	13	1	1	10	1	35
Morales, Kendrys	4	0	23	8		14	17	2	21	15	10	114
Moreland, Mitch			6	8	9	10	3	16	10	12		74
Morrison, Logan			9	11	4	7	11	9	9	16		76
Morrow, Brandon	5	7	4	7	7	10	0	0	2	2	7	51
Morse, Michael	9	0	2	9	25	13	3	13	3	0	0	77
Morton, Charlie		0	4	0	8	0	6	4	2	1	10	35
Moss, Brandon	1	5	5	0	0	13	20	17	7	11	4	83
Motte, Jason		2	2	6	9	14		1	6	1	3	44
Moustakas, Mike					4	14	5	9	21	1	15	69
Mujica, Edward	1	0	4	8	7	10	4	2		0		40
Murphy, Daniel		6	10		14	20	22	21	19	31	27	170
Myers, Wil							14	6	9	19	19	67
Napoli, Mike	18	12	10	12	23	12	16	10	8	14	6	141
Nava, Daniel					5		18	11	2	1	6	48
Nelson, Jimmy						1	0	8	4	13		26
Neris, Hector							0	2	11	11		24
Neshek, Pat	14	1		0	1	3	2	13	4	5	11	54
Nicasio, Juan				4	2	4	3	3	5	10		31
Nola, Aaron									4	3	12	19
Nolasco, Ricky	5	14	6	7	5	8	9	3	0	8	5	70
Norris, Bud		3	3	7	4	8	11	0	4	7		47
Norris, Derek					7	11	16	19	3	3		59
Nova, Ivan				2	11	5	13	0	2	8	8	49
Nunez, Eduardo				2	8	4	6	3	6	15	18	62
O'Day, Darren		2	9	9	0	10	8	10	12	3	6	69
Odor, Rougned								11	16	18	8	53
Odorizzi, Jake					0	1	7	11	11	7		37
O'Flaherty, Eric	4	0	4	5	12	8	3	2	0	0		38
Olson, Matt										0	9	9
Osuna, Roberto									11	15	13	39
Otero, Dan						0	5	9	0	10	5	29
Ottavino, Adam				0		5	7	6	4	5	3	30
Owings, Chris						2	8	6	11	9		36
Ozuna, Marcell							8	19	10	15	29	81
Panik, Joe							10	17	13	15		55
Parker, Blake					0	4	0		1	10		15
Parra, Gerardo			9	6	19	9	15	6	14	2	9	89
Paxton, James							3	5	3	5	11	27
Peacock, Brad					2		2	2	0	1	12	19
Pearce, Steve	2	2	2	1	0	6	4	19	5	9	7	57
Pederson, Joc							0	15	19	7		41
Pedroia, Dustin	20	26	24	12	27	17	25	17	12	21	15	216
Pelfrey, Mike	1	12	4	12	3	2	3	0	7	2	0	46
Pence, Hunter	18	19	17	21	24	18	25	26	7	15	13	203
Pennington, Cliff		3	7	19	18	10	5	4	3	2	4	75
Peralta, David								7	20	2	16	45
Peralta, Jhonny	66	19	10	16	22	12	19	22	20	6	0	212
Peralta, Wily					3	5	12	3	4	0		27
Perez, Hernan					0	1	0	4	11	9		25
Perez, Martin					1	8	2	3	9	9		32
Perez, Roberto							2	7	5	8		22
Perez, Salvador					7	10	23	17	18	18	16	109
Perkins, Glen	3	7	2	0	8	10	13	9	9	0	0	61
Peterson, Jace							1	14	9	3		27
Petit, Yusmeiro	3	3	1		0	2	4	3	2	10		28
Pham, Tommy							0	7	4	21		32
Phelps, David					7	3	4	3	12	4		33
Phillips, Brandon	36	19	19	18	22	19	22	13	17	12	10	207
Pillar, Kevin						1	1	15	15	9		41
Pina, Manny				0	0					2	12	14
Pineda, Michael				10			8	7	6	5		36
Pirela, Jose						1	1	0	13			15

550

Player	<08	08	09	10	11	12	13	14	15	16	17	Career
Piscotty, Stephen									11	22	7	40
Plouffe, Trevor				0	6	8	8	17	18	7	2	66
Polanco, Gregory								8	17	14	6	45
Polanco, Jorge								1	1	8	14	24
Pollock, A.J.						2	14	10	27	1	15	69
Pomeranz, Drew					1	4	0	5	5	12	15	42
Porcello, Rick			13	5	8	7	9	13	5	19	8	87
Posey, Buster			0	20	9	38	24	30	29	24	22	196
Prado, Martin	3	9	12	22	12	23	15	15	17	22	1	151
Presley, Alex				0	8	5	3	6	1	2	6	31
Price, David		1	6	17	13	19	12	16	19	14	7	124
Puig, Yasiel							17	27	9	10	17	80
Pujols, Albert	242	34	39	32	26	25	10	19	18	17	7	469
Qualls, Chad	29	11	8	0	5	1	6	7	3	2	1	73
Quintana, Jose						9	13	12	15	15	10	74
Raburn, Ryan	4	3	9	11	10	1	13	0	6	2	2	61
Ramirez, Erasmo						2	2	0	10	6	6	26
Ramirez, Hanley	52	32	34	22	10	17	23	18	7	17	5	237
Ramirez, JC							0		1	4	8	13
Ramirez, Jose							1	7	4	22	28	62
Ramos, AJ						0	5	8	14	11	6	44
Ramos, Wilson				3	13	3	8	10	11	24	6	78
Rasmus, Colby			13	17	11	15	20	8	15	9	5	113
Ray, Robbie								0	6	7	17	30
Realmuto, J.T.								1	10	19	19	49
Reddick, Josh			0	1	7	16	13	13	17	12	21	100
Reed, Addison					0	7	12	7	4	13	10	53
Rendon, Anthony							12	26	9	22	29	98
Renfroe, Hunter										2	9	11
Revere, Ben				0	9	11	10	16	17	4	5	72
Reyes, Jose	84	28	5	19	26	23	15	19	13	8	15	255
Reynolds, Mark	14	17	20	16	16	12	11	7	7	9	14	143
Richard, Clayton			0	8	10	2	7	0	3	4	5	39
Richards, Garrett					0	1	6	13	14	2	2	38
Rivera, Rene	4				2		2	14	5	6	7	40
Rivero, Felipe									5	4	17	26
Rizzo, Anthony					0	12	14	28	32	29	25	140
Roark, Tanner							7	15	4	17	7	50
Robertson, David		2	3	4	11	7	12	12	13	10	13	87
Rodney, Fernando	18	4	10	6	1	19	11	10	4	7	10	100
Rodriguez, Eduardo									8	4	8	20
Rodriguez, Francisco	73	16	10	11	10	5	7	13	12	11	0	168
Rodriguez, Sean		3	0	9	10	8	4	6	2	13	2	57
Rojas, Miguel								1	4	3	8	16
Romo, Sergio		4	4	8	9	11	9	8	5	4	4	66
Rondon, Hector							2	11	16	7	4	40
Rosales, Adam		0	3	8	0	1	2	5	1	7	5	32
Rosario, Eddie									12	5	14	31
Rosenthal, Trevor						2	7	11	14	1	7	42
Ross, Tyson					0	3	0	5	13	12	0	33
Ruggiano, Justin	0	1			4	11	8	8	5	1	0	38
Ruiz, Carlos	15	6	13	19	18	24	9	15	3	8	3	133
Rupp, Cameron							1	1	7	16	6	31
Rusin, Chris						0	3	0	4	6	11	24
Russell, Addison									13	18	7	38
Ryu, Hyun-Jin							13	9		0	7	29
Sabathia, CC	100	23	18	20	19	14	8	0	5	11	11	229
Salas, Fernando				1	12	2	0	4	4	6	2	31
Salazar, Danny							4	4	14	10	5	37
Sale, Chris				5	11	19	15	17	15	17	20	119
Saltalamacchia,J		5	6	6	0	7	8	15	5	6	0	63
Samardzija, Jeff		3	0	0	7	8	7	11	6	11	8	61
Sanchez, Aaron								6	6	17	1	30
Sanchez, Anibal	11	0	5	11	10	10	17	8	5	1	1	79
Sanchez, Gary									0	11	16	27
Sanchez, Yolmer								1	7	3	14	25
Sandoval, Pablo		6	27	9	23	18	22	21	6	0	2	134
Sano, Miguel									16	11	14	41
Santana, Carlos				7	22	21	26	22	13	19	17	147
Santana, Danny								18	3	1	3	25
Santana, Domingo								0	6	7	21	34
Santana, Ervin	21	19	6	14	14	2	14	9	7	11	17	134
Santiago, Hector					1	7	8	5	11	7	2	41

Player	<08	08	09	10	11	12	13	14	15	16	17	Career
Saunders, Michael		1	6	2	17	10	10	0	12	1		59
Schebler, Scott									1	7	9	17
Scherzer, Max		4	9	13	10	14	20	18	18	20	21	147
Schoop, Jonathan							0	6	9	18	26	59
Schwarber, Kyle									10	0	10	20
Seager, Corey									6	29	31	66
Seager, Kyle					3	24	23	28	17	30	20	145
Segura, Jean						4	21	13	12	23	16	89
Semien, Marcus							2	7	10	21	11	51
Senzatela, Antonio											9	9
Severino, Luis									5	1	16	22
Shaw, Bryan					3	4	7	8	7	7	7	43
Shaw, Travis									7	12	22	41
Shields, James	18	15	11	3	20	12	18	15	9	2	3	126
Shoemaker, Matt							1	11	5	9	4	30
Siegrist, Kevin							6	0	12	7	1	26
Simmons, Andrelton						8	19	13	14	14	24	92
Sipp, Tony			3	4	7	2	1	6	6	0	0	29
Smith, Joe	3	6	2	3	8	6	9	14	8	4	6	69
Smith, Seth	1	3	14	9	13	11	10	20	11	13	7	112
Smoak, Justin				7	10	9	12	4	10	4	23	79
Sogard, Eric					0	1	1	10	7	8	8	35
Solarte, Yangervis								16	18	16	16	66
Soria, Joakim		13	17	12	15	7	2	6	10	5	6	93
Soto, Geovany	3	21	8	15	10	5	8	2	3	3	1	79
Souza Jr., Steven								0	7	10	19	36
Span, Denard		16	21	20	6	15	19	26	12	15	14	164
Spangenberg, Cory								2	10	1	16	29
Springer, George								10	13	23	24	70
Stammen, Craig			3	3	2	9	7	4	1		7	36
Stanton, Giancarlo				13	19	19	15	31	14	12	29	152
Storen, Drew				5	15	5	3	12	9	2	3	54
Story, Trevor										13	13	26
Straily, Dan						2	7	1	0	9	7	26
Strasburg, Stephen				5	2	14	11	13	8	11	17	81
Street, Huston	40	10	15	9	7	9	8	14	12	0	1	125
Stroman, Marcus								9	3	10	16	38
Strop, Pedro			0	0	3	10	5	6	8	5	7	44
Stubbs, Drew			5	18	13	6	10	11	2	2	0	67
Suarez, Eugenio								9	10	16	16	51
Suzuki, Ichiro	191	19	28	23	15	11	10	8	4	10	5	324
Suzuki, Kurt	7	17	17	10	8	10	6	14	8	7	12	116
Swanson, Dansby										4	10	14
Swarzak, Anthony			0		4	2	8	3	0	1	11	29
Syndergaard, Noah									9	18	2	29
Tanaka, Masahiro								12	10	18	8	48
Taylor, Chris								5	1	1	23	30
Taylor, Michael								1	14	4	14	33
Tazawa, Junichi			0		0	6	6	6	4	4	1	27
Teheran, Julio					0	0	12	15	8	13	7	55
Tejada, Ruben				3	11	14	4	15	11	0	1	59
Tepera, Ryan									2	1	8	11
Thames, Eric					7	3					15	25
Tillman, Chris			2	1	1	8	14	13	6	13	0	58
Tomlin, Josh				4	9	0	0	2	6	10	6	37
Torres, Carlos			0	0		3	4	7	2	8	4	28
Travis, Devon									14	6	11	31
Trout, Mike					3	38	40	40	42	35	29	227
Trumbo, Mark				0	14	19	14	8	10	22	5	92
Tulowitzki, Troy	25	9	24	25	25	5	21	16	14	18	4	186
Turner, Justin			0	0	15	4	3	18	18	25	24	107
Turner, Trea									0	17	17	34
Uehara, Koji			4	9	8	5	18	13	9	6	4	76
Upton, Justin	1	8	19	14	26	16	21	21	21	14	22	183
Urena, Jose									0	0	9	9
Utley, Chase	93	30	32	25	18	13	22	24	5	18	8	288
Valbuena, Luis		1	6	4	0	5	9	17	9	12	9	72
Valencia, Danny				12	10	1	5	4	12	16	11	71
Vargas, Jason	5		3	10	8	11	7	10	3	1	12	70
Vazquez, Christian								4		3	11	18
Verlander, Justin	31	8	21	17	27	23	14	8	8	20	17	194
Villar, Jonathan							3	5	4	24	8	44
Vincent, Nick						3	6	4	1	5	6	25

Player	<08	08	09	10	11	12	13	14	15	16	17	Career
Vizcaino, Arodys					1			0	6	2	10	19
Vogt, Stephen						0	4	8	18	9	6	45
Volquez, Edinson	2	16	2	3	0	6	0	11	13	5	3	61
Votto, Joey	3	19	24	33	33	27	30	8	33	33	33	276
Wacha, Michael							4	7	14	2	8	35
Wainwright, Adam	22	11	21	20		9	16	23	3	10	6	141
Walker, Neil			0	16	20	21	20	21	22	19	16	155
Walker, Taijuan							1	3	6	5	11	26
Warren, Adam						0	6	8	9	3	7	33
Watson, Tony					3	5	8	11	12	9	7	55
Weaver, Jered	26	11	17	19	24	16	10	12	5	5	0	145
Weeks Jr., Rickie	33	16	7	29	18	14	4	9	0	4	1	135
Werth, Jayson	35	17	26	22	17	13	26	27	6	13	5	207
Wieters, Matt			9	12	23	23	19	5	7	16	7	121
Wilhelmsen, Tom					3	13	8	8	7	2	2	43
Williams, Nick											8	8
Wilson, Justin						0	8	2	7	5	10	32
Wong, Kolten							1	10	18	9	14	52
Wood, Alex							4	13	8	2	15	42
Wood, Travis				6	3	5	15	3	6	5	1	44
Worley, Vance				2	11	5	0	7	3	6	0	34
Yelich, Christian							8	22	15	21	23	89
Young, Chris	36	5	1	3	3	3		9	11	0	0	71
Young, Chris	16	17	8	19	21	9	7	8	9	5	4	123
Young Jr., Eric			0	2	4	5	11	6	1	0	6	35
Ziegler, Brad		12	7	5	6	8	13	7	13	12	2	85
Zimmer, Bradley											8	8
Zimmerman, Ryan	46	9	21	23	15	22	23	8	10	3	18	198
Zimmermann, Jordan			3	1	11	15	15	16	11	4	3	79
Zobrist, Ben	3	8	27	21	28	27	26	18	17	19	9	203
Zunino, Mike							2	11	5	8	14	40

Instant Replay

Lindsay Zeck

In 2017, there were 1,338 replays with 662 overturned calls. The percent of replays that were overturned decreased slightly from 51 percent last season to 50 this season. The biggest change was that umpires did better on their fair or foul calls in 2017, with only 8 of the 51 replays getting overturned (16 percent), as opposed to 16 of 55 (29 percent) in 2016.

The manager of the Blue Jays, John Gibbons, had only 12 overturned calls out of the 45 that he challenged in 2017, or 27 percent. Not only was his success rate nearly 13 percent lower than the next lowest manager—Dusty Baker of the Nationals, with 13 of 33 of his challenged calls being overturned—but the managers playing against him had a success rate of 62 percent (29 of 47 challenged calls), a difference of 35 percent!

Joe Girardi of the Yankees, on the other hand, had the highest percent of challenges overturned in 2017. Out of his 40 challenged calls, 30 of them were overturned, giving him a 75 percent success rate. The Royals' Ned Yost was the next most successful with 71 percent—25 of 35—of his challenged calls being overturned.

This season's success rates for the three managers mentioned above—Gibbons, Girardi, and Yost—are nothing new. Gibbons has challenged 188 calls for the Blue Jays since Major League Baseball expanded its instant replay rules back in 2014 and only had 68 overturned (36 percent), the lowest success percent of all teams. Conversely, Joe Girardi and Ned Yost have led the Yankees and Royals to the highest challenge success rates during this time frame. Of Girardi's 126 total challenges, 94 have been overturned (75 percent), and of Yost's 143 challenges, 95 have been overturned (66 percent).

2017 Instant Replay Summary

Replay Type	Total Replays	Overturned	Percent
Tag Play	546	256	46.9
Force Play	529	319	60.3
Boundary Call (Over Fence)	101	28	27.7
Hit By Pitch	78	33	42.3
Fair or Foul	51	8	15.7
Trap or Catch	24	15	62.5
Record Keeping	5	2	40.0
Missed Base	4	1	25.0

2017 Challenges

Team	Challenges	Overturned	Pct	Opponent Challenges	Overturned	Pct	Net
Rangers	64	35	54.7	36	19	52.8	16
Rays	60	32	53.3	46	16	34.8	16
Pirates	50	32	64.0	40	17	42.5	15
Yankees	40	30	75.0	33	17	51.5	13
Royals	35	25	71.4	36	17	47.2	8
Twins	28	19	67.9	30	11	36.7	8
Dodgers	37	24	64.9	38	16	42.1	8
Cardinals	49	27	55.1	38	22	57.9	5
Giants	32	19	59.4	32	15	46.9	4
Angels	39	22	56.4	38	19	50.0	3
Reds	39	20	51.3	32	18	56.3	2
Cubs	53	28	52.8	46	27	58.7	1
Brewers	44	18	40.9	43	19	44.2	-1
Astros	38	18	47.4	37	19	51.4	-1
Marlins	36	19	52.8	37	20	54.1	-1
Mets	38	23	60.5	41	24	58.5	-1
Orioles	27	18	66.7	35	19	54.3	-1
Padres	41	18	43.9	38	19	50.0	-1
Phillies	29	18	62.1	36	20	55.6	-2
Diamondbacks	33	18	54.5	47	22	46.8	-4
Braves	47	19	40.4	41	24	58.5	-5
Nationals	33	13	39.4	37	19	51.4	-6
White Sox	36	18	50.0	51	24	47.1	-6
Indians	32	15	46.9	37	22	59.5	-7
Athletics	33	17	51.5	41	25	61.0	-8
Tigers	38	16	42.1	41	24	58.5	-8
Rockies	38	17	44.7	40	25	62.5	-8
Red Sox	42	17	40.5	52	26	50.0	-9
Mariners	35	17	48.6	45	30	66.7	-13
Blue Jays	45	12	26.7	47	29	61.7	-17

Introduction to the 2018 Hitter Projections

Bill James

The Yankees had a rookie last year named Aaron Judge; I think the name is pronounced JUDE-jee. Not sure if you have heard of him. Anyway, we had projected in these pages last year that Mr. Jude-jee would hit .251 with 27 homers. This turned out to be a pretty good projection; we were only off by 25 homers. He didn't hit his 28th homer until the Fourth of July; until then we had a chance to be right. We had projected him for 63 walks. Sure, he finished with 127, but he didn't draw his 64th walk until July 15th. Until then, we were in good shape.

We prefer the term "projection", rather than "prediction". A prediction is that something will happen, something will change. When something happens, when something changes, then we get things wrong.

Well, heck; we're always wrong; it's just a question of margin. We say that a guy is going to hit .277, the chance that he will hit exactly .277 is about 1%. Last year, we only got one player's batting average exactly right, Mitch Moreland. We said Moreland would hit .246, and he did. He's the only one. Usually we get 5 or 6 players exactly right. We're wrong 99% of the time; it's just a matter of the margin. When something actually changes, as in the case of Aaron Judge, then we're wrong by a wide margin. A projection is just taking what has happened in the past and projecting it into the future. As long as nothing changes, we'll be pretty close.

Sometimes. Last year we only hit the player's exact batting average once, but we were within 10 points 23% of the time, and within 20 points 43% of the time. Those aren't great numbers, either, honestly. We guessed the exact number of triples the player would hit 103 times in 432 projections. That's not too hard, though, because 95% of players hit five triples or less, so you can just pick a number between 0 and 5 and you've got a 1-in-6 chance of picking the right one.

Most players will have a year in 2018 that kind of looks like the year they had in 2017. Anthony Rizzo, for example. We projected that he would play 157 games in 2017, which he did, and that he would hit 32 homers, which he did:

Hitter	Label	G	AB	R	H	D	T	HR	RBI	BB	SO	SB	Avg	Slg
Rizzo,Anthony	Actual	157	572	99	156	32	3	32	109	91	90	10	.273	.507
Rizzo,Anthony	Projected	157	595	91	165	41	2	32	103	76	117	6	.277	.514

That's a good projection—our ninth-best of the season—but Anthony Rizzo is easy, because he's the same player every year. It's the third time in four years he has hit 32 homers. The other year he hit 31. If he hits .315 with 11 homers in 2018 we'll be completely wrong in our projection, but as long as he keeps doing what he always does, we'll be OK.

I shouldn't suggest that we are only "right"—only have a good projection—when a player is consistent from year to year. Steve Pearce isn't consistent from year to year; from 2014 to 2016 he hit .293, .218 and .288. We had a good projection for him, though:

Hitter	Label	G	AB	R	H	D	T	HR	RBI	BB	SO	SB	Avg	Slg
Pearce,Steve	Actual	92	313	38	79	17	1	13	37	27	68	0	.252	.438
Pearce,Steve	Projected	104	317	42	82	19	1	14	43	37	70	1	.259	.457

It was a good projection because 1) we guessed about right on his playing time, and 2) when a player bounces up and down between seasons he tends to land in the middle. We guessed that he would land in the middle, and we were more right than wrong. Yasmani Grandal went into last season with a career batting average of .238, but for some reason we thought he would hit .246, which he almost did, which gave us a really good projection for the Yas Man:

Hitter	Label	G	AB	R	H	D	T	HR	RBI	BB	SO	SB	Avg	Slg
Grandal,Yasmani	Actual	129	438	50	108	27	0	22	58	40	130	0	.247	.459
Grandal,Yasmani	Projected	127	382	52	94	19	1	21	63	66	99	1	.246	.466

But I don't mean to give you the impression that we are always as accurate as that; we're not. We "score" the accuracy of a projection by using similarity scores to measure the similarity of the projection and the actual record. These projections below score between 949 and 951—that is, about 950:

Hitter	Label	G	AB	R	H	D	T	HR	RBI	BB	SO	SB	Avg	Slg
Arenado,Nolan	Actual	159	606	100	187	43	7	37	130	62	106	3	.309	.586
Arenado,Nolan	Projected	155	607	99	176	43	4	36	115	51	97	2	.290	.552

Hitter	Label	G	AB	R	H	D	T	HR	RBI	BB	SO	SB	Avg	Slg
Iglesias,Jose	Actual	130	463	56	118	33	1	6	54	21	65	7	.255	.369
Iglesias,Jose	Projected	132	453	54	123	20	1	4	33	27	48	8	.272	.347

Hitter	Label	G	AB	R	H	D	T	HR	RBI	BB	SO	SB	Avg	Slg
Anderson,Tim	Actual	146	587	72	151	26	4	17	56	13	162	15	.257	.402
Anderson,Tim	Projected	154	601	85	166	28	7	11	47	20	146	28	.276	.401

Hitter	Label	G	AB	R	H	D	T	HR	RBI	BB	SO	SB	Avg	Slg
Ramos,Wilson	Actual	64	208	19	54	6	0	11	35	10	36	0	.260	.447
Ramos,Wilson	Projected	85	313	33	85	14	0	12	47	20	56	0	.272	.431

Hitter	Label	G	AB	R	H	D	T	HR	RBI	BB	SO	SB	Avg	Slg
Sanchez,Gary	Actual	122	471	79	131	20	0	33	90	40	120	2	.278	.531
Sanchez,Gary	Projected	122	461	62	127	28	9	25	78	42	94	7	.275	.499

Hitter	Label	G	AB	R	H	D	T	HR	RBI	BB	SO	SB	Avg	Slg
Vargas,Kennys	Actual	78	241	33	61	13	0	11	41	20	77	0	.253	.444
Vargas,Kennys	Projected	112	338	48	85	17	1	17	57	51	91	0	.251	.459

Last year, 19% of our projections were at 950 or better—that is, as good as these projections, or better. These are projections that score at 899 to 901:

Hitter	Label	G	AB	R	H	D	T	HR	RBI	BB	SO	SB	Avg	Slg
Schoop,Jonathan	Actual	160	622	92	182	35	0	32	105	35	142	1	.293	.503
Schoop,Jonathan	Projected	156	588	76	153	32	1	25	76	24	125	2	.260	.446

Hitter	Label	G	AB	R	H	D	T	HR	RBI	BB	SO	SB	Avg	Slg
Frazier,Todd	Actual	147	474	74	101	19	1	27	76	83	125	4	.213	.428
Frazier,Todd	Projected	168	600	84	146	32	1	33	90	56	154	13	.243	.465

Hitter	Label	G	AB	R	H	D	T	HR	RBI	BB	SO	SB	Avg	Slg
Marte,Jefry	Actual	45	127	10	22	5	0	4	14	13	34	1	.173	.307
Marte,Jefry	Projected	61	127	16	31	7	0	5	18	11	25	2	.244	.417

Hitter	Label	G	AB	R	H	D	T	HR	RBI	BB	SO	SB	Avg	Slg
Hosmer,Eric	Actual	162	603	98	192	31	1	25	94	66	104	6	.318	.498
Hosmer,Eric	Projected	156	574	79	158	31	2	20	85	55	114	6	.275	.441

Hitter	Label	G	AB	R	H	D	T	HR	RBI	BB	SO	SB	Avg	Slg
Lobaton,Jose	Actual	51	141	11	24	3	0	4	11	14	35	0	.170	.277
Lobaton,Jose	Projected	55	187	19	45	8	0	4	19	21	43	1	.241	.348

Hitter	Label	G	AB	R	H	D	T	HR	RBI	BB	SO	SB	Avg	Slg
Harper,Bryce	Actual	111	420	95	134	27	1	29	87	68	99	4	.319	.595
Harper,Bryce	Projected	150	537	101	153	30	3	32	87	104	124	17	.285	.531

63% of our projections score at 900 or above, so those are actually below-average projections. We're usually a little closer than that. We had a good year, actually; the 63% of projections scoring at 900 or better was a record for us. We had been at 59% the previous two years. These records go back to 1471, in the reign of King Pierzynski the Third; this was the best we had done. We don't know what that means. It could be just that there hasn't been a lot of turbulence in the data recently, or perhaps we have better policies about who to include a projection for. Maybe it is just luck, and maybe we have actually gotten a little better. Who knows.

We are trying to get better. We're working on it. We have done a bunch of studies, and implemented eleven sets of changes to our projection system, because our studies show that these things should make our future projections more accurate. We have six additions to the system, and five modifications of the previous system. In the past we have projected based on past *results* for each batter. From now on we are also giving some consideration to DIBS, which are Defensive Independent Batting Stats (and, for pitchers, to DIPS, which are things that you dip your potato chips into because the potato chips themselves are not fattening enough.) A player can hit in tough luck for a year, even two years; that is, he can hit a rocket down the third base line which is ordinarily a double, but he just hits it to the wrong man and it turns into an out. In results, this is an out. In DIBS, it may be 20% out and 80% double. It can be shown that DIBS actually predict future batting statistics, in some cases, better than results do, so we have incorporated DIBS into our projections. That's an addition to the system.

We used to project performance based on the player's performance over the previous eight seasons, but our research has shown that it is a little more accurate to use only the last six seasons, so from now on we will use only the last six seasons. That's a modification to the system. We changed the way that we project runs and RBI from the other batting stats. We changed the weighting of stolen bases from past seasons. The system is supposed to work better now than it did in the past. We'll see.

Our worst projection last year was for Greg Bird, but we were almost equally bad in projecting his even bigger teammate:

Hitter	Label	G	AB	R	H	D	T	HR	RBI	BB	SO	SB	Avg	Slg
Judge,Aaron	Actual	155	542	128	154	24	3	52	114	127	208	9	.284	.627
Judge,Aaron	Projected	142	537	77	135	26	2	27	84	63	167	7	.251	.458

Hitter	Label	G	AB	R	H	D	T	HR	RBI	BB	SO	SB	Avg	Slg
Bird,Gregory	Actual	48	147	20	28	7	0	9	28	19	42	0	.190	.422
Bird,Gregory	Projected	146	549	80	146	39	1	29	89	65	124	1	.266	.499

Sure, those are terrible projections, but if you add Bird and Judge together, we weren't actually too bad. Same with Miguel Cabrera and Justin Smoak; individually, the projections were terrible, but if you add them together we weren't actually too bad:

Hitter	Label	G	AB	R	H	D	T	HR	RBI	BB	SO	SB	Avg	Slg
Cabrera,Miguel	Actual	130	469	50	117	22	0	16	60	54	110	0	.249	.399
Cabrera,Miguel	Projected	158	599	96	189	38	1	34	114	83	117	1	.316	.553

Hitter	Label	G	AB	R	H	D	T	HR	RBI	BB	SO	SB	Avg	Slg
Smoak,Justin	Actual	158	560	85	151	29	1	38	90	73	128	0	.270	.529
Smoak,Justin	Projected	129	295	33	65	14	0	12	37	37	91	0	.220	.390

It's just. . .changes. When the underlying realities change, we're wrong. As long as they don't change in unpredictable ways, we're OK. Our best projections last year were for Brian McCann, Mike Aviles, Edwin Encarnacion and Adam Duvall.

Hitter	Label	G	AB	R	H	D	T	HR	RBI	BB	SO	SB	Avg	Slg
McCann,Brian	Actual	97	349	47	84	12	1	18	62	38	58	1	.241	.436
McCann,Brian	Projected	104	367	45	87	13	0	18	58	41	78	1	.237	.420

Hitter	Label	G	AB	R	H	D	T	HR	RBI	BB	SO	SB	Avg	Slg
Aviles,Mike	Actual	37	86	5	20	2	0	1	8	6	15	0	.233	.291
Aviles,Mike	Projected	56	107	12	25	4	0	2	10	5	16	2	.234	.327

Hitter	Label	G	AB	R	H	D	T	HR	RBI	BB	SO	SB	Avg	Slg
Encarnacion,Edwin	Actual	157	554	96	143	20	1	38	107	104	133	2	.258	.504
Encarnacion,Edwin	Projected	155	583	91	149	32	0	38	110	83	123	3	.256	.506

Hitter	Label	G	AB	R	H	D	T	HR	RBI	BB	SO	SB	Avg	Slg
Duvall,Adam	Actual	157	587	78	146	37	3	31	99	39	170	5	.249	.480
Duvall,Adam	Projected	149	547	76	133	30	3	31	92	39	141	5	.243	.479

And if you don't believe those are good projections, here's my suggestion. Find Edwin Encarnacion's wife, and ask her which of those is his real numbers, and which one was the projection. I'm betting she won't know. Thanks for reading.

2018 Hitter Projections

Hitter	Team	Age	G	AB	H	2B	3B	HR	R	RBI	RC	RC27	BB	SO	SB	CS	SB%	Avg	OBP	Slg	OPS
Abreu, Jose	CWS	31	159	629	182	37	3	32	85	105	108	6.2	44	130	2	1	.67	.289	.350	.510	.861
Acuna, Ronald	Atl	20	148	562	155	29	3	29	79	78	87	5.4	40	158	24	14	.63	.276	.328	.493	.821
Adams, Matt	Atl	29	118	314	78	20	1	14	38	51	42	4.7	22	83	0	0	.00	.248	.300	.452	.752
Adrianza, Ehire	Min	28	60	168	41	7	1	2	18	16	17	3.5	15	35	5	2	.71	.244	.314	.333	.647
Aguilar, Jesus	Mil	28	126	344	76	16	1	14	35	51	39	3.7	30	102	0	0	.00	.221	.289	.395	.684
Ahmed, Nick	Ari	28	99	301	69	13	2	7	32	27	29	3.2	18	62	4	3	.57	.229	.277	.355	.633
Albies, Ozzie	Atl	21	151	566	150	28	9	13	81	58	77	4.8	43	127	19	3	.86	.265	.322	.415	.738
Alfaro, Jorge	Phi	25	121	390	86	16	1	11	41	46	34	2.9	16	147	1	1	.50	.221	.266	.351	.617
Allen, Greg	Cle	25	97	341	81	14	2	4	48	29	35	3.5	32	95	14	2	.88	.238	.328	.326	.654
Almonte, Abraham	Cle	29	84	211	53	12	2	4	28	21	26	4.3	21	52	4	1	.80	.251	.322	.384	.706
Almora Jr., Albert	ChC	24	142	508	136	28	3	11	63	61	62	4.3	26	88	4	1	.80	.268	.305	.400	.704
Alonso, Yonder	Sea	31	141	471	123	27	1	17	59	58	69	5.2	57	103	2	1	.67	.261	.343	.431	.774
Altherr, Aaron	Phi	27	127	434	103	24	3	16	57	62	54	4.2	38	124	7	3	.70	.237	.310	.417	.727
Altuve, Jose	Hou	28	158	630	206	41	4	19	96	74	121	7.3	52	82	29	7	.81	.327	.386	.495	.881
Anderson, Brian	Mia	25	151	540	135	24	3	21	74	78	72	4.6	54	153	1	2	.33	.250	.331	.422	.753
Anderson, Tim	CWS	25	146	564	149	24	5	14	72	50	66	4.1	17	157	16	3	.84	.264	.289	.399	.688
Andrus, Elvis	Tex	29	158	599	172	34	4	13	82	71	86	5.2	46	93	22	8	.73	.287	.341	.422	.763
Aoki, Nori	NYM	36	114	363	95	17	2	4	49	28	41	3.9	31	44	8	4	.67	.262	.330	.353	.683
Arcia, Orlando	Mil	23	153	531	128	21	3	14	56	54	58	3.7	38	112	14	6	.70	.241	.294	.371	.665
Arenado, Nolan	Col	27	160	623	188	45	4	39	95	119	127	7.6	55	108	3	3	.50	.302	.362	.575	.937
Arroyo, Christian	SF	23	149	522	138	33	1	11	57	59	63	4.2	31	105	3	2	.60	.264	.314	.395	.709
Asuaje, Carlos	SD	26	142	524	124	23	4	7	58	49	53	3.5	52	113	2	2	.50	.237	.310	.336	.646
Avila, Alex	ChC	31	106	326	72	14	1	11	38	40	42	4.3	61	128	0	0	.00	.221	.345	.371	.717
Aybar, Erick	SD	34	128	423	106	21	2	6	48	36	44	3.5	27	66	9	5	.64	.251	.302	.352	.654
Bader, Harrison	StL	24	142	483	114	18	3	18	63	53	54	3.7	33	161	8	6	.57	.236	.298	.398	.696
Baez, Javier	ChC	25	149	521	130	24	2	26	70	82	69	4.6	32	160	11	4	.73	.250	.301	.453	.754
Bandy, Jett	Mil	28	70	180	41	9	0	6	18	22	19	3.4	12	44	1	1	.50	.228	.294	.378	.672
Barnes, Austin	LAD	28	90	244	63	14	1	7	31	28	35	5	32	47	5	1	.83	.258	.351	.410	.761
Barney, Darwin	Tor	32	100	238	57	11	1	3	26	18	23	3.2	15	42	3	1	.75	.239	.290	.332	.622
Barnhart, Tucker	Cin	27	124	413	105	22	1	7	33	46	49	4.1	43	78	3	1	.75	.254	.329	.363	.692
Bautista, Jose	Tor	37	131	434	98	22	1	22	72	62	63	4.9	72	113	4	2	.67	.226	.342	.433	.776
Beckham, Tim	Bal	28	127	448	115	19	4	15	54	51	57	4.4	32	137	5	3	.63	.257	.311	.417	.728
Bell, Josh	Pit	25	159	525	139	25	4	20	66	78	79	5.3	63	108	2	3	.40	.265	.346	.442	.788
Bellinger, Cody	LAD	22	157	581	148	28	3	45	94	111	110	6.5	78	174	13	3	.81	.255	.346	.546	.892
Belt, Brandon	SF	30	141	518	137	36	5	19	75	73	87	5.9	79	144	3	2	.60	.264	.366	.463	.829
Beltran, Carlos	Hou	41	100	311	75	17	1	11	37	39	38	4.1	24	66	0	0	.00	.241	.300	.408	.708
Beltre, Adrian	Tex	39	138	532	157	29	2	23	75	83	91	6.3	47	75	1	0	1.00	.295	.358	.487	.845
Benintendi, Andrew	Bos	23	151	541	152	32	3	20	79	88	91	6	65	104	17	5	.77	.281	.363	.462	.825
Betts, Mookie	Bos	25	157	644	194	48	5	26	108	101	124	7.1	68	85	25	5	.83	.301	.370	.512	.882
Bird, Greg	NYY	25	154	567	137	36	1	36	79	96	92	5.6	71	151	0	0	.00	.242	.332	.499	.831
Blackmon, Charlie	Col	31	157	625	188	36	8	29	109	82	115	6.7	52	126	14	7	.67	.301	.365	.523	.888
Blanco, Andres	Phi	34	72	119	27	6	0	2	13	10	11	3	9	28	1	1	.50	.227	.292	.328	.620
Blanco, Gregor	Ari	34	102	286	70	13	4	3	44	24	34	4	35	68	12	4	.75	.245	.329	.350	.679
Blash, Jabari	SD	28	54	99	20	4	0	5	13	13	12	3.8	14	41	1	1	.50	.202	.313	.394	.707
Bogaerts, Xander	Bos	25	156	621	172	35	3	14	95	76	87	5	56	125	13	3	.81	.277	.343	.411	.753
Bonifacio, Jorge	KC	25	140	532	138	27	3	26	59	61	79	5.2	45	162	2	1	.67	.259	.322	.468	.790
Bour, Justin	Mia	30	124	409	102	20	0	19	47	71	58	4.9	44	100	1	0	1.00	.249	.324	.438	.761
Bourjos, Peter	TB	31	82	142	31	6	2	3	19	11	13	3	10	40	3	2	.60	.218	.279	.352	.631
Bradley Jr., Jackie	Bos	28	143	513	129	28	4	17	71	65	70	4.7	53	134	7	3	.70	.251	.332	.421	.753
Brantley, Michael	Cle	31	149	589	174	41	2	14	77	84	95	5.9	55	78	16	3	.84	.295	.360	.443	.803
Braun, Ryan	Mil	34	137	516	146	30	3	26	79	81	99	6.3	50	110	14	5	.74	.283	.352	.504	.856
Bregman, Alex	Hou	24	155	565	162	39	5	21	93	81	99	6.3	61	102	14	4	.78	.287	.363	.485	.848
Brinson, Lewis	Mil	24	152	559	127	25	5	20	64	59	63	3.7	42	155	11	4	.73	.227	.288	.397	.685
Broxton, Keon	Mil	28	145	464	97	19	4	18	63	51	52	3.6	50	193	23	7	.77	.209	.292	.384	.675
Bruce, Jay	Cle	31	150	550	145	34	3	32	79	100	93	5.9	54	139	3	1	.75	.264	.332	.511	.843
Bryant, Kris	ChC	26	156	593	169	36	3	37	111	99	122	7.4	90	157	8	4	.67	.285	.393	.543	.936
Butera, Drew	KC	34	77	168	36	7	1	3	17	14	14	2.8	12	44	0	0	.00	.214	.271	.321	.592
Buxton, Byron	Min	24	159	556	138	23	8	21	84	65	76	4.7	44	183	27	2	.93	.248	.309	.432	.741
Cabrera, Asdrubal	NYM	32	148	546	142	33	2	17	70	64	74	4.7	49	106	4	2	.67	.260	.328	.421	.749
Cabrera, Melky	KC	33	148	551	166	33	4	14	70	76	86	5.8	37	69	2	1	.67	.301	.346	.452	.798
Cabrera, Miguel	Det	35	150	578	174	34	1	28	83	98	111	7.2	72	125	0	0	.00	.301	.382	.509	.891
Cain, Lorenzo	KC	32	146	566	163	31	4	13	81	64	85	5.4	46	108	21	4	.84	.288	.348	.426	.774
Calhoun, Kole	LAA	30	148	530	136	27	3	17	74	67	72	4.8	56	124	3	1	.75	.257	.333	.415	.748
Calhoun, Willie	Tex	23	152	561	141	26	3	29	70	83	79	4.9	42	90	2	1	.67	.251	.307	.463	.770
Camargo, Johan	Atl	24	134	476	128	31	4	9	52	52	59	4.4	24	102	1	0	1.00	.269	.307	.408	.714
Candelario, Jeimer	Det	24	145	537	133	37	3	18	62	74	73	4.7	56	144	1	1	.50	.248	.324	.428	.753
Canha, Mark	Oak	29	65	170	40	11	1	6	22	22	21	4.2	14	49	1	0	1.00	.235	.309	.418	.726
Cano, Robinson	Sea	35	158	629	178	35	1	24	87	91	97	5.6	52	98	2	1	.67	.283	.343	.456	.799
Caratini, Victor	ChC	24	133	409	115	26	2	10	50	50	60	5.3	37	87	1	0	1.00	.281	.348	.428	.776
Carpenter, Matt	StL	32	150	553	150	40	4	23	95	74	101	6.5	96	134	2	1	.67	.271	.387	.483	.869
Carrera, Ezequiel	Tor	31	113	253	62	10	2	4	35	20	28	3.7	23	63	7	2	.78	.245	.313	.348	.661
Carter, Chris	Oak	31	94	255	55	12	1	15	34	41	35	4.5	32	100	1	0	1.00	.216	.310	.447	.757
Castellanos, Nick	Det	26	147	550	151	34	5	22	61	80	83	5.4	39	135	3	3	.50	.275	.327	.475	.802
Castillo, Welington	Bal	31	120	435	112	20	0	20	47	62	60	4.8	34	123	1	0	1.00	.257	.319	.441	.760
Castro, Jason	Min	31	119	380	90	22	1	11	47	45	47	4.2	44	121	1	0	1.00	.237	.322	.387	.709
Castro, Starlin	NYY	28	142	535	145	26	2	17	61	64	69	4.6	28	108	3	2	.60	.271	.312	.422	.735
Cecchini, Gavin	NYM	24	148	539	134	25	2	7	57	43	55	3.5	41	94	3	3	.50	.249	.304	.341	.645
Cervelli, Francisco	Pit	32	116	410	107	19	2	6	50	42	51	4.3	53	97	2	2	.50	.261	.358	.361	.719
Cespedes, Yoenis	NYM	32	131	503	133	28	3	26	74	80	78	5.5	41	114	2	1	.67	.264	.326	.487	.813

2018 Hitter Projections

Hitter	Team	Age	G	AB	H	2B	3B	HR	R	RBI	RC	RC27	BB	SO	SB	CS	SB%	Avg	OBP	Slg	OPS
Chapman, Matt	Oak	25	140	491	105	24	3	32	67	72	67	4.5	56	187	3	4	.43	.214	.298	.470	.769
Chirinos, Robinson	Tex	34	103	344	76	17	1	17	47	44	43	4.2	37	102	1	1	.50	.221	.313	.424	.737
Chisenhall, Lonnie	Cle	29	115	449	116	28	2	15	53	67	60	4.7	34	100	4	1	.80	.258	.316	.430	.746
Choo, Shin-Soo	Tex	35	134	506	133	24	2	17	81	62	75	5.2	71	131	8	4	.67	.263	.367	.419	.786
Collins, Tyler	Det	28	63	147	32	6	1	5	15	18	15	3.5	13	46	2	1	.67	.218	.286	.374	.660
Conforto, Michael	NYM	25	147	529	138	32	3	33	84	89	96	6.3	70	148	3	1	.75	.261	.357	.520	.877
Contreras, Willson	ChC	26	117	397	112	24	2	20	52	68	70	6.3	44	94	4	3	.57	.282	.361	.504	.865
Correa, Carlos	Hou	23	155	600	175	39	3	29	94	114	114	7	75	132	8	2	.80	.292	.374	.512	.886
Cowart, Kaleb	LAA	26	125	354	79	17	2	8	39	38	36	3.3	30	99	9	3	.75	.223	.288	.350	.638
Cozart, Zack	Cin	32	131	496	128	26	4	18	71	56	69	4.9	46	91	3	1	.75	.258	.326	.435	.761
Crawford, Brandon	SF	31	153	563	143	33	5	14	65	79	72	4.4	51	125	4	3	.57	.254	.320	.405	.725
Crawford, J.P.	Phi	23	152	559	122	22	5	13	66	52	60	3.6	76	127	5	3	.63	.218	.313	.345	.658
Cron, C.J.	LAA	28	119	396	99	22	1	17	42	62	50	4.4	23	95	1	1	.50	.250	.303	.439	.742
Cruz, Nelson	Sea	37	154	559	145	26	1	34	83	94	91	5.7	59	149	1	1	.50	.259	.339	.492	.831
Cuthbert, Cheslor	KC	25	145	501	120	25	1	13	48	56	54	3.7	37	110	2	1	.67	.240	.294	.371	.666
d'Arnaud, Travis	NYM	29	108	356	88	19	1	14	40	46	46	4.4	28	67	0	0	.00	.247	.307	.424	.732
Davidson, Matt	CWS	27	109	365	69	15	0	16	35	47	32	2.8	27	144	0	0	.00	.189	.253	.362	.614
Davis, Chris	Bal	32	148	496	113	22	1	32	78	79	75	5	68	197	1	1	.50	.228	.328	.470	.798
Davis, J.D.	Hou	25	140	511	126	30	1	23	59	77	69	4.7	45	171	3	2	.60	.247	.313	.444	.757
Davis, Khris	Oak	30	153	561	136	30	2	35	82	95	86	5.3	58	181	3	1	.75	.242	.321	.490	.811
Davis, Rajai	Bos	37	118	345	84	18	3	6	54	29	38	3.7	24	82	23	6	.79	.243	.298	.365	.664
DeJong, Paul	StL	24	149	553	140	30	2	28	66	84	76	4.8	33	175	1	1	.50	.253	.304	.467	.771
Delmonico, Nick	CWS	25	145	547	127	29	2	19	66	65	67	4.1	58	139	4	1	.80	.232	.311	.397	.708
Descalso, Daniel	Ari	31	128	339	81	18	4	10	44	42	44	4.5	42	84	3	1	.75	.239	.328	.404	.732
DeShields, Delino	Tex	25	112	341	81	14	3	5	60	27	39	3.8	41	100	21	6	.78	.238	.325	.340	.665
Desmond, Ian	Col	32	146	540	147	27	3	17	79	74	75	4.9	40	145	17	5	.77	.272	.328	.428	.756
Devers, Rafael	Bos	21	144	571	154	31	3	30	82	85	92	5.7	52	142	3	3	.50	.270	.332	.492	.824
Diaz, Aledmys	StL	27	96	307	77	19	1	9	37	35	37	4.1	20	55	3	2	.60	.251	.303	.407	.710
Diaz, Elias	Pit	27	78	257	61	13	1	3	22	25	24	3.1	14	53	2	1	.67	.237	.279	.331	.610
Diaz, Yandy	Cle	26	49	170	47	7	1	2	21	15	23	4.8	24	38	1	0	1.00	.276	.369	.365	.734
Dickerson, Corey	TB	29	140	494	125	29	4	21	63	57	66	4.6	32	128	3	3	.50	.253	.301	.455	.757
Dietrich, Derek	Mia	28	138	434	107	23	4	14	56	53	55	4.4	37	111	0	0	.00	.247	.337	.415	.751
Difo, Wilmer	Was	26	124	364	92	14	3	4	47	28	39	3.7	26	80	11	2	.85	.253	.306	.341	.647
Donaldson, Josh	Tor	32	146	557	148	31	2	35	96	98	105	6.7	85	132	4	1	.80	.266	.369	.517	.886
Dozier, Brian	Min	31	157	627	159	35	4	31	100	86	97	5.4	71	145	13	5	.72	.254	.337	.470	.808
Drury, Brandon	Ari	25	142	506	133	35	1	15	51	62	65	4.5	31	111	1	1	.50	.263	.312	.425	.737
Duda, Lucas	TB	32	138	488	112	28	0	28	62	72	72	5	67	150	0	0	.00	.230	.333	.459	.792
Duvall, Adam	Cin	29	155	574	137	32	3	31	75	92	77	4.5	39	166	4	2	.67	.239	.296	.467	.763
Dyson, Jarrod	Sea	33	117	330	82	12	5	3	49	25	37	3.8	28	57	22	5	.81	.248	.319	.342	.661
Eaton, Adam	Was	29	143	557	154	28	6	9	87	50	76	4.8	55	108	13	5	.72	.276	.353	.397	.750
Ellis, A.J.	Mia	37	78	214	47	9	0	6	21	24	23	3.5	28	45	1	1	.50	.220	.321	.346	.667
Ellsbury, Jacoby	NYY	34	134	475	124	23	4	9	68	47	61	4.4	44	83	20	5	.80	.261	.329	.383	.712
Encarnacion, Edwin	Cle	35	159	589	155	30	1	39	99	116	111	6.6	93	132	2	0	1.00	.263	.369	.516	.885
Engel, Adam	CWS	26	111	380	72	17	4	9	46	30	31	2.6	31	137	9	3	.75	.189	.265	.326	.591
Escobar, Alcides	KC	31	150	554	145	28	4	6	61	48	58	3.6	21	90	8	3	.73	.262	.294	.359	.653
Escobar, Eduardo	Min	29	122	388	99	21	3	14	46	51	51	4.5	27	84	3	2	.60	.255	.309	.433	.742
Escobar, Yunel	LAA	35	131	504	135	24	1	9	59	46	60	4.2	42	73	1	2	.33	.268	.329	.373	.702
Espinosa, Danny	TB	31	101	270	52	11	1	8	33	27	22	2.6	22	100	3	2	.60	.193	.271	.330	.601
Fisher, Derek	Hou	24	149	547	132	26	3	24	72	77	75	4.6	65	176	14	8	.64	.241	.327	.431	.759
Flores, Wilmer	NYM	26	129	433	114	23	1	19	51	63	59	4.8	24	69	1	1	.50	.263	.307	.453	.759
Flowers, Tyler	Atl	32	102	323	80	15	0	10	33	42	38	4.1	28	97	0	0	.00	.248	.332	.387	.719
Forsythe, Logan	LAD	31	135	463	113	24	2	12	64	47	58	4.3	58	123	4	2	.67	.244	.337	.382	.719
Fowler, Dexter	StL	32	141	530	140	26	7	17	84	57	84	5.5	81	136	10	4	.71	.264	.368	.436	.804
Franco, Maikel	Phi	26	143	538	137	29	2	23	63	78	72	4.7	37	94	1	0	1.00	.255	.306	.444	.750
Frazier, Adam	Pit	26	130	441	127	24	5	5	57	45	61	4.9	40	64	10	6	.63	.288	.355	.399	.754
Frazier, Clint	NYY	23	150	521	119	28	5	20	71	63	65	4.2	50	170	8	2	.80	.228	.301	.417	.717
Frazier, Todd	NYY	32	155	572	137	28	2	32	81	88	84	5	68	148	7	4	.64	.240	.331	.463	.794
Freeman, Freddie	Atl	28	143	538	158	38	3	29	90	90	111	7.5	79	131	7	4	.64	.294	.392	.537	.929
Freese, David	Pit	35	143	491	126	25	1	12	60	63	62	4.4	53	138	0	0	.00	.257	.344	.385	.728
Gallo, Joey	Tex	24	146	502	100	20	3	39	76	87	75	4.8	78	231	6	1	.86	.199	.314	.484	.798
Galvis, Freddy	Phi	28	159	596	149	28	5	13	65	62	67	3.9	38	120	12	4	.75	.250	.298	.379	.677
Gamel, Ben	Sea	26	149	554	142	27	6	10	70	58	66	4.1	43	133	6	2	.75	.256	.312	.381	.693
Garcia, Adonis	Atl	33	87	267	70	14	1	7	30	31	31	4.1	11	45	3	1	.75	.262	.299	.401	.700
Garcia, Avisail	CWS	27	140	521	145	23	3	16	69	70	72	4.9	36	125	5	3	.63	.278	.335	.426	.761
Garcia, Greg	StL	28	119	239	58	11	1	2	28	19	25	3.6	31	60	2	1	.67	.243	.342	.322	.664
Garcia, Leury	CWS	27	80	224	56	8	2	4	26	19	23	3.5	12	56	7	3	.70	.250	.297	.357	.654
Garcia, Willy	CWS	25	102	347	77	16	3	9	39	39	34	3.2	24	121	2	2	.50	.222	.278	.363	.641
Gardner, Brett	NYY	34	143	511	131	23	4	14	78	51	70	4.7	60	111	15	4	.79	.256	.343	.399	.742
Garneau, Dustin	Oak	30	59	153	29	7	0	5	13	15	13	2.7	12	39	0	0	.00	.190	.257	.333	.591
Gattis, Evan	Hou	31	124	460	116	24	2	23	57	74	64	4.8	32	102	1	1	.50	.252	.308	.463	.771
Gennett, Scooter	Cin	28	143	500	130	28	3	17	64	64	65	4.5	30	114	4	2	.67	.260	.306	.430	.736
Gimenez, Chris	Min	35	84	209	45	9	0	5	25	19	20	3.2	24	62	1	1	.50	.215	.302	.330	.632
Goins, Ryan	Tor	30	120	331	77	16	2	5	31	36	31	3.2	23	79	2	2	.50	.233	.285	.338	.623
Goldschmidt, Paul	Ari	30	159	587	172	39	3	34	108	112	128	7.9	102	156	18	5	.78	.293	.403	.543	.946
Gomes, Yan	Cle	30	97	305	70	17	1	11	35	44	34	3.7	20	87	0	0	.00	.230	.288	.400	.688
Gomez, Carlos	Tex	32	124	425	109	24	3	17	59	57	60	4.3	34	131	12	4	.75	.256	.331	.447	.778
Gonzalez, Adrian	LAD	36	131	480	129	29	1	16	55	74	68	5	42	96	0	0	.00	.269	.331	.433	.765
Gonzalez, Carlos	Col	32	141	493	137	31	2	22	75	73	82	6	49	123	3	1	.75	.278	.346	.483	.828
Gonzalez, Marwin	Hou	29	132	413	107	24	1	15	51	54	55	4.6	31	92	6	3	.67	.259	.317	.431	.748
Goodwin, Brian	Was	27	73	198	44	9	1	6	22	21	21	3.6	19	61	4	1	.80	.222	.294	.369	.662
Gordon, Alex	KC	34	130	455	108	23	2	12	58	48	53	4	49	126	5	2	.71	.237	.325	.376	.701

2018 Hitter Projections

Hitter	Team	Age	G	AB	H	2B	3B	HR	R	RBI	RC	RC27	BB	SO	SB	CS	SB%	Avg	OBP	Slg	OPS
Gordon, Dee	Mia	30	152	632	177	21	9	2	93	37	73	4	32	102	48	15	.76	.280	.321	.351	.672
Grandal, Yasmani	LAD	29	133	457	106	23	1	22	56	65	64	4.7	62	133	1	1	.50	.232	.326	.431	.757
Granderson, Curtis	LAD	37	155	556	128	27	3	29	86	68	80	4.9	76	151	6	2	.75	.230	.329	.446	.775
Gregorius, Didi	NYY	28	152	566	150	28	2	20	69	72	74	4.6	33	84	4	1	.80	.265	.312	.428	.740
Grichuk, Randal	StL	26	120	367	87	22	3	20	50	51	49	4.5	22	116	4	2	.67	.237	.286	.477	.763
Grossman, Robbie	Min	28	115	390	99	20	1	9	51	39	52	4.6	58	99	4	3	.57	.254	.353	.379	.733
Gurriel, Yulieski	Hou	34	148	552	153	39	1	17	67	74	75	4.9	24	71	3	2	.60	.277	.316	.444	.759
Guyer, Brandon	Cle	32	99	254	64	14	2	5	37	26	29	4	19	57	2	1	.67	.252	.343	.382	.724
Gyorko, Jedd	StL	29	137	457	116	20	1	21	52	65	64	4.8	42	113	4	2	.67	.254	.319	.440	.759
Hamilton, Billy	Cin	27	126	441	108	15	5	4	64	30	47	3.6	34	99	43	9	.83	.245	.300	.329	.629
Hanigan, Ryan	Col	37	51	120	27	5	0	1	12	12	11	3	14	30	0	0	.00	.225	.316	.292	.608
Haniger, Mitch	Sea	27	150	575	143	30	3	24	72	74	79	4.7	56	147	6	3	.67	.249	.328	.437	.765
Happ, Ian	ChC	23	146	532	130	25	2	32	82	93	80	5.1	53	174	10	4	.71	.244	.319	.479	.798
Hardy, J.J.	Bal	35	104	334	80	16	1	8	36	34	35	3.6	21	64	0	0	.00	.240	.287	.365	.652
Harper, Bryce	Was	25	143	520	148	30	3	32	100	90	110	7.6	93	124	8	4	.67	.285	.396	.538	.935
Harrison, Josh	Pit	30	141	533	146	32	4	12	70	53	68	4.5	27	95	11	5	.69	.274	.326	.417	.742
Hays, Austin	Bal	22	148	549	147	27	3	23	62	87	74	4.8	25	128	1	1	.50	.268	.307	.454	.760
Hazelbaker, Jeremy	Ari	30	91	234	52	10	4	6	30	27	25	3.6	19	84	6	1	.86	.222	.283	.376	.660
Headley, Chase	NYY	34	146	500	126	25	1	14	66	59	64	4.4	56	130	6	2	.75	.252	.336	.390	.726
Healy, Ryon	Oak	26	148	571	153	33	1	23	67	76	78	4.8	29	140	0	0	.00	.268	.307	.450	.757
Hechavarria, Adeiny	TB	29	146	576	142	22	6	7	57	48	56	3.3	31	107	6	3	.67	.247	.287	.342	.629
Hedges, Austin	SD	25	126	406	88	18	1	16	39	56	40	3.3	22	111	3	1	.75	.217	.262	.384	.646
Heredia, Guillermo	Sea	27	133	422	107	17	1	6	54	37	44	3.6	38	72	2	4	.33	.254	.333	.341	.674
Hernandez, Cesar	Phi	28	146	536	145	22	6	6	72	41	67	4.4	57	113	15	7	.68	.271	.344	.368	.711
Hernandez, Gorkys	SF	30	69	126	31	6	1	1	16	10	13	3.5	11	32	3	1	.75	.246	.312	.333	.645
Hernandez, Kike	LAD	26	125	260	58	15	1	8	31	26	29	3.8	27	65	2	1	.67	.223	.299	.381	.679
Hernandez, Teoscar	Tor	25	148	538	129	27	2	21	78	67	66	4.2	45	164	13	6	.68	.240	.303	.414	.718
Herrera, Odubel	Phi	26	153	565	152	30	4	14	73	55	74	4.6	42	134	12	5	.71	.269	.325	.411	.736
Herrmann, Chris	Ari	30	85	196	42	9	1	6	26	22	21	3.5	20	58	4	1	.80	.214	.290	.362	.653
Heyward, Jason	ChC	28	148	526	138	27	3	14	71	62	72	4.8	57	92	8	3	.73	.262	.340	.405	.745
Hicks, Aaron	NYY	28	135	461	111	23	3	16	64	55	62	4.5	59	106	11	5	.69	.241	.330	.408	.737
Holliday, Matt	NYY	38	100	295	72	16	1	13	41	46	42	4.9	36	75	1	0	1.00	.244	.336	.437	.774
Holt, Brock	Bos	30	91	253	65	13	2	3	33	23	29	4	24	55	3	1	.75	.257	.326	.360	.686
Hoskins, Rhys	Phi	25	155	546	137	26	2	43	95	114	102	6.5	78	142	4	1	.80	.251	.353	.542	.895
Hosmer, Eric	KC	28	156	570	161	31	2	20	81	85	89	5.7	58	107	5	2	.71	.282	.350	.449	.799
Hundley, Nick	SF	34	114	390	91	23	1	10	36	45	40	3.5	24	105	1	1	.50	.233	.280	.374	.654
Iannetta, Chris	Ari	35	103	308	67	16	0	12	36	40	38	4.1	45	96	0	0	.00	.218	.325	.386	.711
Iglesias, Jose	Det	28	142	503	132	26	1	6	57	44	53	3.7	28	68	8	5	.62	.262	.309	.354	.663
Inciarte, Ender	Atl	27	152	611	171	27	5	8	85	46	77	4.5	45	96	18	6	.75	.280	.331	.380	.711
Jackson, Austin	Cle	31	94	291	80	18	2	5	42	30	40	4.9	28	71	5	2	.71	.275	.341	.402	.743
Jaso, John	Pit	34	108	255	63	16	1	8	31	33	35	4.8	35	59	1	1	.50	.247	.347	.412	.759
Jay, Jon	ChC	33	112	373	102	18	2	3	54	35	44	4.2	32	78	4	2	.67	.273	.350	.357	.707
Jones, Adam	Bal	32	153	615	167	29	2	27	85	84	86	5	30	121	2	1	.67	.272	.314	.457	.771
Jones, JaCoby	Det	26	145	519	106	22	4	13	63	56	46	2.9	40	201	12	4	.75	.204	.270	.337	.608
Joseph, Caleb	Bal	32	85	231	54	11	1	7	23	27	24	3.5	13	60	0	0	.00	.234	.278	.381	.659
Joseph, Tommy	Phi	26	139	486	118	26	1	24	51	69	63	4.4	31	121	1	1	.50	.243	.294	.449	.742
Joyce, Matt	Oak	33	138	452	106	25	1	19	65	62	64	4.8	69	115	3	2	.60	.235	.341	.420	.761
Judge, Aaron	NYY	26	155	542	133	23	2	44	96	100	106	6.7	96	201	7	3	.70	.245	.365	.542	.907
Kemp, Matt	Atl	33	143	542	149	31	2	24	71	86	83	5.5	39	135	2	1	.67	.275	.326	.472	.798
Kendrick, Howie	Was	34	121	402	113	21	2	8	53	46	54	4.8	30	85	9	4	.69	.281	.337	.403	.740
Kepler, Max	Min	25	156	564	144	32	6	22	74	83	84	5.2	59	124	7	1	.88	.255	.331	.450	.782
Kiermaier, Kevin	TB	28	130	471	121	22	6	14	64	44	62	4.6	38	109	17	5	.77	.257	.320	.418	.739
Kim, Hyun Soo	Phi	30	70	140	35	7	0	2	15	10	16	3.9	16	29	0	0	.00	.250	.335	.343	.678
Kingery, Scott	Phi	24	144	534	136	24	4	19	74	51	68	4.4	33	144	16	3	.84	.255	.307	.421	.728
Kinsler, Ian	Det	36	153	610	168	32	5	21	96	71	90	5.2	49	98	11	5	.69	.275	.330	.448	.785
Kipnis, Jason	Cle	31	146	524	139	34	3	15	72	61	75	5	52	119	10	3	.77	.265	.337	.427	.765
Knapp, Andrew	Phi	26	56	192	46	10	1	4	24	21	22	4	22	60	1	0	1.00	.240	.321	.365	.686
La Stella, Tommy	ChC	29	70	133	35	7	0	2	14	16	14	4.3	15	23	0	0	.00	.263	.342	.361	.703
Lagares, Juan	NYM	29	98	244	61	12	2	3	27	20	25	3.5	13	54	5	2	.71	.250	.296	.352	.649
Lamb, Jake	Ari	27	149	529	138	32	5	29	77	92	93	6.2	73	152	5	3	.63	.261	.356	.505	.861
LeMahieu, DJ	Col	29	156	600	190	31	6	8	89	62	96	6.1	56	97	8	4	.67	.317	.379	.428	.807
Leon, Sandy	Bos	29	88	253	58	13	1	5	27	29	26	3.5	24	66	0	0	.00	.229	.301	.348	.649
Lin, Tzu-Wei	Bos	24	60	150	34	4	2	2	16	10	14	3.1	14	34	3	2	.60	.227	.293	.320	.613
Lind, Adam	Was	34	124	362	97	20	1	15	47	59	55	5.4	36	73	1	0	1.00	.268	.336	.453	.789
Lindor, Francisco	Cle	24	154	609	174	34	5	26	86	82	103	6.1	56	95	15	5	.75	.286	.350	.486	.836
Lobaton, Jose	Was	33	55	119	27	5	0	3	11	12	12	3.4	12	31	0	0	.00	.227	.303	.345	.648
Longoria, Evan	TB	32	157	603	159	33	2	23	74	86	85	5	51	125	4	2	.67	.264	.326	.439	.766
Lowrie, Jed	Oak	34	141	522	138	34	2	12	67	59	71	4.8	57	96	0	0	.00	.264	.340	.406	.746
Lucroy, Jonathan	Col	32	134	485	146	30	3	14	64	69	82	6.3	49	73	2	1	.67	.301	.371	.462	.833
Machado, Dixon	Det	26	73	179	43	8	1	2	19	15	17	3.3	14	34	2	1	.67	.240	.299	.330	.629
Machado, Manny	Bal	25	159	636	176	37	2	35	91	94	106	6	52	118	8	4	.67	.277	.334	.506	.841
Mahtook, Mikie	Det	28	130	421	105	21	4	11	46	45	50	4.1	26	110	6	1	.86	.249	.304	.397	.701
Maldonado, Martin	LAA	31	130	390	81	15	1	12	36	39	35	2.9	28	110	0	0	.00	.208	.281	.344	.625
Mancini, Trey	Bal	26	154	577	157	29	4	26	72	79	87	5.4	41	156	1	0	1.00	.272	.327	.471	.798
Margot, Manuel	SD	23	154	599	162	26	9	15	71	53	81	4.7	42	117	21	7	.75	.270	.321	.419	.740
Marisnick, Jake	Hou	27	111	262	57	12	2	10	37	29	27	3.4	16	87	8	3	.73	.218	.276	.393	.669
Markakis, Nick	Atl	34	155	573	151	33	1	8	70	62	71	4.3	63	100	1	1	.50	.264	.342	.366	.708
Marte, Jefry	LAA	27	42	120	26	6	0	4	13	15	12	3.4	10	29	1	0	1.00	.217	.288	.367	.655
Marte, Ketel	Ari	24	131	472	132	26	4	7	62	42	62	4.7	35	77	9	3	.75	.280	.332	.396	.728
Marte, Starling	Pit	29	143	542	154	29	5	13	78	58	77	5	31	123	29	8	.78	.284	.342	.428	.770
Martin, Leonys	ChC	30	91	257	63	11	2	6	33	23	28	3.7	17	70	10	4	.71	.245	.297	.374	.671

563

2018 Hitter Projections

Hitter	Team	Age	G	AB	H	2B	3B	HR	R	RBI	RC	RC27	BB	SO	SB	CS	SB%	Avg	OBP	Slg	OPS
Martin, Russell	Tor	35	101	338	76	15	0	13	48	46	42	4.1	48	95	1	1	.50	.225	.335	.385	.720
Martinez, J.D.	Ari	30	140	534	146	34	2	37	81	100	99	6.6	52	161	4	2	.67	.273	.341	.552	.894
Martinez, Jose	StL	29	69	148	40	7	0	4	17	17	20	4.8	13	32	2	0	1.00	.270	.329	.399	.728
Martinez, Victor	Det	39	130	468	130	23	0	17	50	64	69	5.3	43	72	0	0	.00	.278	.344	.436	.780
Mathis, Jeff	Ari	35	56	127	26	6	1	2	11	13	10	2.6	9	42	0	0	.00	.205	.263	.315	.578
Mauer, Joe	Min	35	139	487	139	29	2	7	63	58	71	5.3	64	88	2	1	.67	.285	.371	.396	.767
Maxwell, Bruce	Oak	27	77	220	52	12	0	4	20	26	24	3.7	24	56	0	0	.00	.236	.311	.345	.657
Maybin, Cameron	Hou	31	102	364	88	17	3	7	53	36	43	4	39	84	20	6	.77	.242	.319	.363	.681
Mazara, Nomar	Tex	23	151	545	143	28	2	23	62	85	79	5.1	51	123	2	2	.50	.262	.331	.448	.779
McCann, Brian	Hou	34	127	455	106	17	1	21	57	71	57	4.3	47	90	1	0	1.00	.233	.316	.413	.729
McCann, James	Det	28	114	370	90	17	1	11	34	45	41	3.8	23	97	1	0	1.00	.243	.296	.384	.680
McCutchen, Andrew	Pit	31	158	597	169	34	3	26	93	90	106	6.3	81	131	10	5	.67	.283	.375	.481	.856
McMahon, Ryan	Col	23	147	534	140	30	2	18	56	66	70	4.6	39	122	4	4	.50	.262	.312	.427	.739
Meadows, Austin	Pit	23	91	299	73	19	4	8	45	37	38	4.3	24	69	8	2	.80	.244	.305	.415	.719
Mejia, Francisco	Cle	22	126	385	106	19	2	17	50	50	59	5.4	27	78	5	1	.83	.275	.331	.468	.798
Mercer, Jordy	Pit	31	147	514	132	27	3	12	55	56	64	4.3	46	94	1	1	.50	.257	.323	.391	.714
Merrifield, Whit	KC	29	149	538	141	31	3	13	64	54	67	4.3	30	96	22	6	.79	.262	.306	.403	.709
Mesoraco, Devin	Cin	30	75	204	46	9	0	9	21	26	24	4	22	54	1	1	.50	.225	.316	.402	.718
Miller, Brad	TB	28	134	431	100	20	4	15	53	52	55	4.3	53	122	6	3	.67	.232	.319	.401	.720
Molina, Yadier	StL	35	141	521	149	32	1	15	55	71	75	5.2	34	74	6	3	.67	.286	.335	.438	.772
Moncada, Yoan	CWS	23	152	562	125	16	5	21	84	60	68	4	77	216	14	7	.67	.222	.320	.381	.701
Montero, Miguel	Tor	34	85	249	56	10	0	8	27	32	28	3.8	32	65	1	1	.50	.225	.323	.361	.684
Morales, Kendrys	Tor	35	152	564	146	30	1	27	66	86	82	5.1	46	128	0	0	.00	.259	.321	.459	.781
Moran, Colin	Hou	25	129	469	116	20	2	17	48	70	59	4.3	41	128	0	0	.00	.247	.312	.407	.719
Moreland, Mitch	Bos	32	145	541	137	32	0	22	66	79	74	4.8	51	133	1	1	.50	.253	.326	.434	.760
Moroff, Max	Pit	25	94	317	70	13	2	13	42	40	40	4.2	48	110	4	3	.57	.221	.327	.397	.724
Morrison, Logan	TB	30	145	509	122	23	2	27	64	70	75	5	65	133	3	1	.75	.240	.333	.452	.785
Moss, Brandon	KC	34	106	342	77	17	1	19	45	51	46	4.5	36	116	1	0	1.00	.225	.304	.447	.752
Motter, Taylor	Sea	28	80	206	48	11	0	7	24	23	24	3.8	17	45	7	2	.78	.233	.295	.388	.683
Moustakas, Mike	KC	29	146	540	140	30	1	29	65	76	80	5.2	39	92	0	0	.00	.259	.315	.480	.795
Murphy, Daniel	Was	33	149	570	175	41	3	19	83	87	99	6.5	43	77	3	1	.75	.307	.360	.489	.849
Murphy, Tom	Col	27	74	206	41	11	1	7	22	24	18	2.8	12	82	1	1	.50	.199	.250	.364	.614
Myers, Wil	SD	27	156	575	140	30	3	29	84	85	86	5.1	68	171	19	5	.79	.243	.328	.457	.785
Napoli, Mike	Tex	36	113	332	72	13	1	19	47	52	44	4.4	45	121	1	1	.50	.217	.318	.434	.751
Narvaez, Omar	CWS	26	90	293	74	12	0	2	28	20	31	3.7	38	51	0	0	.00	.253	.340	.314	.654
Nava, Daniel	Phi	35	77	165	42	8	0	3	19	18	20	4.1	18	37	1	0	1.00	.255	.342	.358	.700
Nimmo, Brandon	NYM	25	122	332	79	15	3	7	40	30	39	4	43	101	2	1	.67	.238	.331	.364	.695
Nunez, Eduardo	Bos	31	134	508	145	31	3	11	67	62	69	4.9	25	72	24	8	.75	.285	.324	.423	.747
Odor, Rougned	Tex	24	155	566	140	27	5	27	76	78	72	4.4	29	134	12	6	.67	.247	.294	.456	.749
Olson, Matt	Oak	24	150	519	115	26	1	37	71	83	80	5.2	70	173	2	0	1.00	.222	.319	.489	.808
Orlando, Paulo	KC	32	85	252	63	12	2	3	25	23	25	3.4	11	59	4	2	.67	.250	.289	.349	.639
Owings, Chris	Ari	26	105	385	100	22	5	9	45	43	48	4.3	19	92	13	3	.81	.260	.298	.413	.711
Ozuna, Marcell	Mia	27	148	536	149	29	3	27	71	87	89	6	48	126	1	1	.50	.278	.340	.494	.834
Panik, Joe	SF	27	139	514	141	28	5	9	65	55	70	4.8	48	60	4	1	.80	.274	.342	.401	.743
Parker, Jarrett	SF	29	65	143	33	6	1	5	19	17	17	3.9	15	53	1	1	.50	.231	.313	.392	.704
Parra, Gerardo	Col	31	118	382	112	25	3	9	53	45	55	5.3	21	71	3	3	.50	.293	.335	.445	.780
Pearce, Steve	Tor	35	98	289	72	16	1	12	36	36	40	4.8	28	66	0	0	.00	.249	.326	.436	.762
Pederson, Joc	LAD	26	127	374	86	19	1	20	54	48	55	4.9	57	111	6	3	.67	.230	.342	.447	.789
Pedroia, Dustin	Bos	34	129	482	141	29	1	9	65	58	71	5.4	50	62	4	2	.67	.293	.361	.413	.774
Pence, Hunter	SF	35	127	466	119	20	4	14	63	66	59	4.4	40	103	2	1	.67	.255	.317	.406	.723
Pennington, Cliff	LAA	34	65	138	30	5	1	2	15	11	12	2.9	13	39	2	1	.67	.217	.289	.312	.601
Peralta, David	Ari	30	143	532	153	32	7	15	74	66	82	5.6	41	105	7	4	.64	.288	.345	.459	.804
Peraza, Jose	Cin	24	152	540	148	17	5	6	61	44	60	3.9	24	80	25	8	.76	.274	.312	.357	.670
Perez, Hernan	Mil	27	132	422	107	22	3	11	44	46	49	4	19	83	14	3	.82	.254	.287	.398	.685
Perez, Roberto	Cle	29	83	219	45	11	1	5	23	28	22	3.3	29	70	0	0	.00	.205	.301	.333	.635
Perez, Salvador	KC	28	139	523	139	29	1	25	57	77	72	4.9	21	102	1	0	1.00	.266	.301	.468	.769
Peterson, Jace	Atl	28	79	181	42	8	1	3	19	18	20	3.7	24	42	3	1	.75	.232	.325	.337	.662
Pham, Tommy	StL	30	139	494	131	25	4	19	80	69	78	5.5	64	145	18	6	.75	.265	.356	.447	.804
Phegley, Josh	Oak	30	75	214	51	13	1	6	22	25	23	3.7	12	42	0	0	.00	.238	.288	.393	.681
Phillips, Brandon	LAA	37	140	560	154	27	1	12	70	64	67	4.2	24	76	10	5	.67	.275	.313	.391	.704
Phillips, Brett	Mil	24	124	372	78	13	4	13	44	46	40	3.5	38	155	8	1	.89	.210	.286	.371	.657
Pillar, Kevin	Tor	29	146	520	140	33	2	13	62	48	66	4.5	27	86	12	4	.75	.269	.312	.415	.727
Pina, Manny	Mil	31	101	304	73	17	0	7	30	35	32	3.6	20	67	1	0	1.00	.240	.296	.365	.661
Pinder, Chad	Oak	26	126	423	98	22	2	16	50	51	47	3.8	25	136	3	1	.75	.232	.286	.407	.692
Pirela, Jose	SD	28	152	573	145	30	5	15	73	62	71	4.3	41	113	9	4	.69	.253	.307	.412	.719
Piscotty, Stephen	StL	27	126	429	110	27	2	15	54	55	61	4.9	48	102	4	4	.50	.256	.340	.434	.773
Plawecki, Kevin	NYM	27	72	204	49	10	0	5	19	24	22	3.6	15	40	0	0	.00	.240	.305	.363	.668
Plouffe, Trevor	TB	32	94	277	61	14	1	9	32	31	29	3.5	25	73	1	1	.50	.220	.289	.375	.665
Polanco, Gregory	Pit	26	144	519	133	30	3	17	70	65	71	4.7	48	99	15	5	.75	.256	.322	.424	.746
Polanco, Jorge	Min	24	150	551	146	29	5	14	59	71	72	4.6	43	98	13	6	.68	.265	.320	.412	.732
Pollock, A.J.	Ari	30	138	529	150	37	6	19	84	58	86	5.8	44	89	22	6	.79	.284	.344	.473	.817
Posey, Buster	SF	31	144	538	162	34	1	16	72	82	92	6.4	62	73	5	1	.83	.301	.380	.457	.837
Powell, Boog	Oak	25	149	508	138	19	4	9	74	50	65	4.5	52	103	10	7	.59	.272	.342	.378	.720
Prado, Martin	Mia	34	140	533	149	29	2	9	58	60	68	4.6	38	72	1	1	.50	.280	.332	.392	.724
Presley, Alex	Det	32	76	224	55	8	2	3	26	17	22	3.4	15	48	3	2	.60	.246	.299	.339	.638
Profar, Jurickson	Tex	25	143	503	125	26	2	10	61	52	60	4.1	54	87	5	2	.71	.249	.331	.368	.699
Puig, Yasiel	LAD	27	147	519	139	27	3	26	74	75	85	5.7	58	110	12	6	.67	.268	.348	.482	.830
Pujols, Albert	LAA	38	117	382	98	16	0	17	44	61	51	4.7	29	57	2	0	1.00	.257	.312	.432	.744
Ramirez, Hanley	Bos	34	135	448	120	25	1	20	62	69	69	5.4	44	101	3	2	.60	.268	.340	.462	.802
Ramirez, Jose	Cle	25	152	580	169	42	4	21	90	71	99	6.2	50	69	18	6	.75	.291	.351	.486	.837
Ramos, Wilson	TB	30	112	399	103	16	0	17	40	62	51	4.5	24	72	0	0	.00	.258	.302	.426	.728

564

2018 Hitter Projections

Hitter	Team	Age	G	AB	H	2B	3B	HR	R	RBI	RC	RC27	BB	SO	SB	CS	SB%	Avg	OBP	Slg	OPS
Realmuto, J.T.	Mia	27	140	526	142	30	4	15	64	62	72	4.8	35	104	8	2	.80	.270	.323	.428	.751
Reddick, Josh	Hou	31	139	490	148	32	4	14	69	67	84	6.3	46	81	6	2	.75	.302	.363	.469	.833
Reed, A.J.	Hou	25	120	411	90	20	0	23	54	64	54	4.4	50	149	0	0	.00	.219	.307	.436	.742
Rendon, Anthony	Was	28	146	529	151	39	2	22	80	81	97	6.6	71	99	7	2	.78	.285	.377	.491	.869
Renfroe, Hunter	SD	26	141	519	124	28	2	26	62	73	66	4.3	31	152	3	1	.75	.239	.287	.451	.738
Revere, Ben	LAA	30	88	234	65	8	2	1	29	15	26	3.8	11	24	13	4	.76	.278	.313	.342	.655
Reyes, Jose	NYM	35	132	513	130	24	4	12	72	48	63	4.2	44	80	20	5	.80	.253	.314	.386	.700
Reynolds, Mark	Col	34	140	449	109	21	1	23	63	71	66	5	56	148	2	1	.67	.243	.331	.448	.778
Rickard, Joey	Bal	27	70	136	35	7	1	2	17	12	16	4	11	32	3	1	.75	.257	.322	.368	.690
Riddle, J.T.	Mia	26	139	490	128	24	3	8	52	56	54	3.9	27	105	2	2	.50	.261	.301	.371	.673
Rivera, Rene	ChC	34	88	238	54	10	0	8	20	30	24	3.4	16	70	0	0	.00	.227	.284	.370	.654
Rivera, T.J.	NYM	29	82	244	70	13	1	5	28	30	31	4.6	10	40	1	1	.50	.287	.326	.410	.735
Rizzo, Anthony	ChC	28	159	597	167	37	3	32	94	104	113	6.7	84	107	8	4	.67	.280	.387	.513	.899
Robles, Victor	Was	21	145	546	138	37	6	9	80	57	66	4.1	41	117	22	8	.73	.253	.327	.392	.719
Rodriguez, Sean	Pit	33	84	151	33	7	1	5	20	19	16	3.5	13	54	1	1	.50	.219	.293	.377	.671
Rojas, Miguel	Mia	29	117	310	77	14	1	2	35	24	30	3.3	23	42	2	1	.67	.248	.307	.319	.626
Romine, Andrew	Det	32	120	245	60	9	2	3	30	20	24	3.4	18	54	5	2	.71	.245	.305	.335	.639
Romine, Austin	NYY	29	68	159	37	8	0	2	15	17	14	3	10	36	0	0	.00	.233	.282	.321	.603
Rosales, Adam	Ari	35	55	148	31	8	1	4	18	17	14	3	11	51	1	1	.50	.209	.273	.358	.631
Rosario, Amed	NYM	22	154	570	150	22	9	9	67	58	65	4	27	138	18	6	.75	.263	.302	.381	.683
Rosario, Eddie	Min	26	151	546	144	29	5	22	75	71	74	4.7	29	121	8	5	.62	.264	.302	.456	.758
Rua, Ryan	Tex	28	61	107	23	4	0	3	13	11	10	3	8	38	1	0	1.00	.215	.276	.336	.612
Ruiz, Carlos	Sea	39	60	212	49	11	0	4	22	20	22	3.5	22	44	1	0	1.00	.231	.321	.340	.660
Ruiz, Rio	Atl	24	99	313	68	15	1	10	33	37	33	3.5	33	97	1	1	.50	.217	.294	.367	.661
Rupp, Cameron	Phi	29	113	406	85	20	1	16	40	48	43	3.4	36	139	1	0	1.00	.209	.279	.382	.660
Russell, Addison	ChC	24	142	501	121	28	2	19	67	74	64	4.4	46	132	4	2	.67	.242	.314	.419	.733
Saladino, Tyler	CWS	28	76	193	44	7	1	2	21	17	17	2.9	15	47	5	2	.71	.228	.290	.306	.596
Sanchez, Gary	NYY	25	140	549	145	28	0	35	75	95	89	5.7	46	137	3	1	.75	.264	.330	.506	.836
Sanchez, Yolmer	CWS	26	132	449	107	21	3	9	49	46	45	3.4	28	106	7	5	.58	.238	.289	.359	.648
Sandoval, Pablo	SF	31	48	110	26	5	0	3	11	13	12	3.6	8	21	0	0	.00	.236	.294	.364	.658
Sano, Miguel	Min	25	154	572	138	27	2	38	89	100	94	5.6	77	228	1	0	1.00	.241	.335	.495	.830
Santana, Carlos	Cle	32	154	557	141	32	2	24	79	82	91	5.6	96	104	5	2	.71	.253	.367	.447	.814
Santana, Danny	Atl	27	84	205	49	10	2	3	26	18	20	3.3	9	51	8	2	.80	.239	.274	.351	.626
Santana, Domingo	Mil	25	151	533	136	28	1	26	77	82	83	5.4	70	189	11	5	.69	.255	.348	.458	.806
Saunders, Michael	Tor	31	77	194	48	11	1	6	27	21	25	4.4	19	54	1	1	.50	.247	.318	.407	.725
Schebler, Scott	Cin	27	147	519	123	24	5	28	63	67	70	4.6	40	137	5	2	.71	.237	.309	.464	.773
Schimpf, Ryan	SD	30	59	127	23	6	0	7	17	17	14	3.4	16	52	0	0	.00	.181	.283	.394	.676
Schoop, Jonathan	Bal	26	154	589	156	32	1	28	76	85	82	4.9	29	137	1	0	1.00	.265	.309	.465	.775
Schwarber, Kyle	ChC	25	141	506	118	21	1	36	84	81	82	5.5	75	177	2	2	.50	.233	.339	.492	.831
Seager, Corey	LAD	24	156	538	157	36	2	24	82	73	96	6.5	56	122	4	2	.67	.292	.363	.500	.863
Seager, Kyle	Sea	30	159	609	160	36	2	28	79	90	94	5.4	62	116	3	2	.60	.263	.339	.466	.805
Segura, Jean	Sea	28	145	576	157	27	4	11	75	49	71	4.3	33	94	21	7	.75	.273	.320	.391	.710
Semien, Marcus	Oak	27	138	517	125	26	3	17	70	58	66	4.3	53	126	13	3	.81	.242	.315	.402	.717
Senzel, Nick	Cin	23	148	528	141	25	2	24	87	72	80	5.3	54	130	9	7	.56	.267	.335	.458	.793
Shaw, Travis	Mil	28	147	539	145	29	2	26	68	79	87	5.7	56	142	7	1	.88	.269	.342	.475	.817
Simmons, Andrelton	LAA	28	152	568	153	30	2	12	64	59	72	4.4	42	63	14	5	.74	.269	.323	.393	.716
Sisco, Chance	Bal	23	87	311	78	17	0	7	36	36	37	4.1	31	99	1	1	.50	.251	.329	.373	.702
Slater, Austin	SF	25	146	518	141	24	1	14	61	64	69	4.7	46	137	4	4	.50	.272	.337	.403	.741
Smith, Dominic	NYM	23	153	557	143	28	2	18	63	78	71	4.5	45	131	1	1	.50	.257	.316	.411	.727
Smith, Kevan	CWS	30	59	141	35	7	0	2	13	14	14	3.4	8	29	0	0	.00	.248	.298	.340	.638
Smith, Mallex	TB	25	77	193	49	7	3	2	26	13	22	3.8	17	49	13	5	.72	.254	.318	.352	.670
Smith, Seth	Bal	35	137	430	110	24	2	15	63	53	61	5	51	104	1	0	1.00	.256	.343	.426	.768
Smoak, Justin	Tor	31	150	532	134	27	1	31	69	79	86	5.6	66	139	0	0	.00	.252	.338	.481	.819
Sogard, Eric	Mil	32	78	197	50	9	1	3	26	18	24	4.2	24	31	3	1	.75	.254	.341	.355	.696
Solarte, Yangervis	SD	30	140	518	134	27	1	15	58	65	65	4.4	41	72	2	1	.67	.259	.319	.402	.721
Soler, Jorge	KC	26	92	265	60	12	1	13	33	40	36	4.5	34	90	1	0	1.00	.226	.321	.426	.748
Souza Jr., Steven	TB	29	152	547	129	26	1	26	78	73	77	4.7	71	190	13	4	.76	.236	.331	.430	.761
Span, Denard	SF	34	137	537	145	29	5	9	72	44	69	4.5	46	75	12	5	.71	.270	.331	.393	.724
Spangenberg, Cory	SD	27	140	503	130	21	5	11	60	47	60	4.2	37	135	11	4	.73	.258	.316	.386	.701
Springer, George	Hou	28	149	586	159	29	2	32	102	85	102	6.1	75	147	7	4	.64	.271	.365	.491	.856
Stanton, Giancarlo	Mia	28	144	539	144	29	1	46	97	113	113	7.4	78	160	3	1	.75	.267	.366	.581	.947
Stewart, Christin	Det	24	92	316	70	14	1	15	37	45	39	4.1	32	113	1	0	1.00	.222	.299	.415	.714
Story, Trevor	Col	25	145	521	125	30	5	28	72	81	77	5	51	191	8	2	.80	.240	.313	.478	.790
Suarez, Eugenio	Cin	26	148	521	128	25	2	21	71	69	71	4.7	60	141	5	3	.63	.246	.332	.422	.754
Sucre, Jesus	TB	30	74	210	51	8	0	4	18	23	20	3.2	9	42	1	0	1.00	.243	.281	.338	.619
Suzuki, Ichiro	Mia	44	135	200	49	6	2	1	22	13	18	3.2	14	31	3	1	.75	.245	.298	.310	.608
Suzuki, Kurt	Atl	34	91	301	74	16	0	10	30	41	35	4	20	45	0	0	.00	.246	.308	.399	.707
Swanson, Dansby	Atl	24	152	552	137	25	4	10	73	64	65	4.1	64	138	5	2	.71	.248	.330	.362	.692
Szczur, Matt	SD	28	120	201	46	9	1	3	24	16	20	3.3	19	45	2	1	.67	.229	.302	.328	.630
Tapia, Raimel	Col	24	152	567	151	30	8	5	70	49	64	4	25	117	17	4	.81	.266	.301	.374	.675
Taylor, Chris	LAD	27	146	530	140	31	6	14	74	56	75	4.9	52	139	15	5	.75	.264	.334	.425	.759
Taylor, Michael A.	Was	27	108	323	77	15	2	13	40	40	40	4.2	26	113	13	4	.76	.238	.297	.418	.715
Tejada, Ruben	Bal	28	90	270	71	15	0	4	32	23	32	4.1	24	44	0	0	.00	.263	.332	.363	.695
Telis, Tomas	Mia	27	86	242	63	11	2	3	25	23	26	3.8	12	33	2	0	1.00	.260	.301	.360	.660
Thames, Eric	Mil	31	144	507	120	27	4	29	77	63	80	5.3	70	174	4	2	.67	.237	.337	.477	.815
Toles, Andrew	LAD	26	138	508	140	31	5	21	75	70	76	5.3	31	101	6	6	.50	.276	.324	.480	.804
Tomas, Yasmany	Ari	27	135	491	132	28	2	27	59	78	76	5.5	31	136	2	2	.50	.269	.314	.499	.813
Torreyes, Ronald	NYY	25	108	325	84	14	2	3	36	29	32	3.5	16	41	1	1	.50	.258	.299	.342	.641
Travis, Devon	Tor	27	106	411	113	27	2	12	54	52	57	4.9	24	86	7	2	.78	.275	.318	.438	.756
Travis, Sam	Bos	24	66	211	54	11	0	4	27	19	25	4.1	21	50	3	1	.75	.256	.326	.365	.691
Trout, Mike	LAA	26	155	556	169	35	6	38	116	101	141	9.3	108	136	24	5	.83	.304	.426	.594	1.019

2018 Hitter Projections

PLAYER			BATTING												BASERUNNING			AVERAGES			
Hitter	Team	Age	G	AB	H	2B	3B	HR	R	RBI	RC	RC27	BB	SO	SB	CS	SB%	Avg	OBP	Slg	OPS
Trumbo, Mark	Bal	32	148	562	140	25	1	30	76	84	78	4.8	45	154	1	1	.50	.249	.307	.457	.764
Tulowitzki, Troy	Tor	33	124	472	126	25	1	20	58	65	70	5.3	45	94	1	1	.50	.267	.337	.451	.788
Turner, Justin	LAD	33	147	525	158	34	2	22	74	79	97	6.8	55	84	5	1	.83	.301	.383	.499	.882
Turner, Trea	Was	24	151	589	169	31	9	17	92	64	96	5.8	44	132	53	9	.85	.287	.340	.457	.796
Upton, Justin	LAA	30	152	551	135	30	2	29	86	84	83	5.2	65	176	11	4	.73	.245	.329	.465	.794
Utley, Chase	LAD	39	119	345	86	19	3	9	45	38	43	4.3	31	68	4	1	.80	.249	.326	.400	.726
Valaika, Pat	Col	25	94	273	60	13	2	12	29	42	29	3.5	13	83	2	1	.67	.220	.258	.414	.672
Valbuena, Luis	LAA	32	120	371	82	19	1	17	46	50	48	4.3	50	104	1	2	.33	.221	.317	.415	.732
Valencia, Danny	Sea	33	125	405	98	20	1	13	51	53	47	4	32	106	1	1	.50	.242	.301	.393	.693
Vargas, Kennys	Min	27	71	178	40	7	0	9	22	26	23	4.3	21	59	0	0	.00	.225	.310	.416	.726
Vazquez, Christian	Bos	27	112	381	102	22	1	6	47	38	46	4.2	28	79	5	2	.71	.268	.323	.378	.701
Verdugo, Alex	LAD	22	150	522	140	25	2	8	56	57	63	4.3	47	79	5	3	.63	.268	.333	.370	.703
Villar, Jonathan	Mil	27	125	398	95	19	2	10	53	41	47	3.9	39	127	26	8	.76	.239	.308	.372	.680
Vogt, Stephen	Mil	33	128	439	109	24	2	17	50	58	45	4.5	37	88	0	0	.00	.248	.310	.428	.738
Votto, Joey	Cin	34	161	578	176	36	2	31	100	92	134	8.6	130	113	5	2	.71	.304	.438	.535	.972
Walker, Neil	Mil	32	136	501	132	26	2	19	70	66	73	5.2	55	102	1	1	.50	.263	.345	.437	.782
Werth, Jayson	Was	39	128	461	116	24	1	17	68	58	66	4.9	61	122	5	2	.71	.252	.344	.419	.763
Wieters, Matt	Was	32	118	388	94	20	1	12	41	52	46	4.1	34	86	1	0	1.00	.242	.307	.392	.698
Williams, Nick	Phi	24	119	445	107	21	4	17	56	57	51	3.9	23	146	3	3	.50	.240	.287	.420	.707
Winker, Jesse	Cin	24	150	560	151	30	1	11	61	62	75	4.7	67	111	1	1	.50	.270	.353	.386	.739
Wolters, Tony	Col	26	92	304	70	14	2	2	33	27	28	3.1	32	82	1	1	.50	.230	.310	.309	.619
Wong, Kolten	StL	27	136	470	125	24	5	9	63	48	62	4.6	43	82	9	2	.82	.266	.342	.396	.737
Yelich, Christian	Mia	26	155	595	168	37	3	17	89	78	97	5.9	76	138	14	3	.82	.282	.322	.417	.739
Young, Chris	Bos	34	104	264	64	17	1	9	36	31	35	4.5	28	64	3	1	.75	.224	.308	.372	.680
Zimmer, Bradley	Cle	25	131	465	104	22	4	13	61	55	54	3.8	50	181	22	4	.85	.268	.331	.494	.825
Zimmerman, Ryan	Was	33	131	478	128	28	1	26	70	81	77	5.7	42	115	1	0	1.00	.256	.352	.399	.751
Zobrist, Ben	ChC	37	143	511	131	28	3	13	76	59	71	4.8	72	83	1	1	.50	.213	.291	.434	.726
Zunino, Mike	Sea	27	110	343	73	17	1	19	41	52	41	3.9	30	125							

Introduction to the 2018 Pitcher Projections

Bill James

To project whether a pitcher will have a good year or not is, to say the least, a dicey undertaking. If you're a bank robber, it is kind of like predicting what time a cop will come by. If you're a lawyer, it is kind of like predicting who will wind up on your jury. If you're a school teacher, it is kind of like predicting whether you will have two geniuses in your classroom next year, or a bunch of little hooligans. You just never know.

We never know, either. In last year's book we foresaw Chris Sale striking out 259 batters, which is a lot, but it isn't 300. In last year's book we had Clayton Kershaw going 20-4, which turned out to be a pretty good projection, but we had Cory Kluber at just 14-10. They both went 18-4. In last year's book we had Jacob DeGrom striking out 174 batters, which is a good number, but he actually struck out 239. We had Noah Syndergaard striking out 235. We missed by 200. Didn't see that one coming.

Think about stats as details and summaries. Things like strikeouts, walks, hit batsmen and doubles allowed are details. Things like wins, losses, and earned run averages are summaries. Summaries group together large numbers of events—large numbers of details—into one number. WAR is what we could call an ultimate summary stat. It tries to measure EVERYTHING in the wagon load.

The interesting thing that has happened in baseball research over the last 40 years is that the evaluation of *batters* has gone from relying on details toward summaries, while the evaluation of *pitchers* has moved from summaries to details. It used to be that wins, losses and ERA—summary stats—were the be-all and end-all for a pitcher. Not so much anymore.

This change makes projections more realistic. Trying to project next year's summaries based on this year's summaries is an impossible task, and if you do that, whether for pitchers or hitters, you will have huge errors. But trying to project next year's details based on this year's details, that's more realistic. After Rick Porcello went 22-4 in 2016, who would have guessed that he would go 11-17 in 2017? But in the details of what he did. . . well there, actually, we were OK. We had projected him to pitch 220 innings, which was off by 17, and we had projected him to have 158 strikeouts and 37 walks, not actually all that different from his actual totals of 181 and 48. One detail changed everything. We had projected that he would allow 24 homers; he allowed 43.

Somebody will have that kind of a year next year, too. We don't know who it will be. That's our job: to be the guys with egg on our faces. In order for other people to say disparagingly that "the experts all said", somebody has got to volunteer to be the expert, and say things. That's our job, to make the first guess. We're right about some things, too, but you know, don't want to brag. By the way, I hear that this new book, <u>The Man From the Train</u>, is really great. Thanks for reading.

2018 Pitcher Projections

Pitcher	Team	Age	G	GS	IP	H	HR	BB	SO	HB	W	L	Pct	Sv	BR/9	ERA
Abad, Fernando	Bos	32	46	0	39	35	5	14	33	1	2	2	.500	0	11.5	4.08
Adams, Chance	NYY	23	29	29	170	131	18	77	155	4	10	8	.556	0	11.2	3.81
Adleman, Tim	Cin	30	24	24	127	130	20	45	102	5	6	8	.429	0	12.8	4.61
Albers, Andrew	Sea	32	17	11	82	102	10	21	68	2	4	5	.444	0	13.7	4.67
Albers, Matt	Was	35	66	0	64	57	8	19	56	4	4	3	.571	0	11.3	3.93
Alburquerque, Al	CWS	32	40	0	38	34	3	16	37	0	2	2	.500	0	11.8	3.76
Alcantara, Raul	Oak	25	11	6	37	42	5	11	25	2	2	2	.500	0	13.4	4.86
Alexander, Scott	KC	28	68	0	76	74	7	29	61	1	4	4	.500	0	12.3	4.11
Allen, Cody	Cle	29	71	0	70	53	7	25	91	1	5	2	.714	33	10.2	3.07
Altavilla, Dan	Sea	25	37	0	48	39	5	23	56	2	3	2	.600	0	12.0	3.74
Alvarez, Jose	LAA	29	59	0	46	46	5	13	40	1	3	2	.600	0	11.7	3.95
Anderson, Brett	Tor	30	16	16	77	95	8	25	46	1	3	5	.375	0	14.1	5.03
Anderson, Chase	Mil	30	28	28	155	148	24	48	132	6	8	9	.471	0	11.7	4.24
Anderson, Tyler	Col	28	18	18	106	105	12	32	97	3	7	5	.583	0	11.9	4.02
Andriese, Matt	TB	28	20	20	106	109	14	29	95	3	5	6	.455	0	12.0	4.09
Archer, Chris	TB	29	33	33	200	177	23	64	232	5	12	10	.545	0	11.1	3.53
Arrieta, Jake	ChC	32	31	31	182	149	16	58	172	7	12	8	.600	0	10.6	3.54
Asher, Alec	Bal	26	17	17	88	98	15	26	62	4	4	6	.400	0	13.1	4.86
Avilan, Luis	LAD	28	52	0	47	43	3	22	50	2	3	2	.600	0	12.6	3.81
Baez, Pedro	LAD	30	62	0	61	50	8	22	62	2	4	3	.571	0	10.9	3.73
Bailey, Homer	Cin	32	24	24	132	160	19	54	102	10	6	9	.400	0	15.3	5.42
Banda, Anthony	Ari	24	17	17	86	86	9	35	83	2	5	4	.556	0	12.9	4.14
Barnes, Danny	Tor	28	62	0	66	52	7	19	68	1	4	3	.571	0	9.8	3.31
Barnes, Jacob	Mil	28	70	0	75	66	7	32	78	3	4	4	.500	0	12.1	3.85
Barnes, Matt	Bos	28	65	0	64	59	7	27	69	2	4	3	.571	0	12.4	3.90
Barnette, Tony	Tex	34	56	0	64	65	7	22	58	3	3	4	.429	0	12.7	4.22
Barraclough, Kyle	Mia	28	59	0	62	45	3	37	77	2	4	3	.571	8	12.2	3.41
Barrett, Jake	Ari	26	39	0	38	36	4	19	35	1	2	2	.500	0	13.3	4.38
Bauer, Trevor	Cle	27	30	30	193	183	24	71	195	7	12	9	.571	0	12.2	4.00
Baumann, Buddy	SD	30	38	0	31	27	3	12	31	3	2	2	.500	0	12.2	3.84
Beck, Chris	CWS	27	53	0	64	72	8	29	44	3	2	5	.286	0	14.6	5.06
Bedrosian, Cam	LAA	26	47	0	43	36	3	18	52	1	3	2	.600	11	11.5	3.38
Beede, Tyler	SF	25	14	14	74	86	9	32	59	2	3	5	.375	0	14.6	4.93
Belisle, Matt	Min	38	56	0	56	56	5	17	44	2	3	3	.500	23	12.1	4.06
Bell, Chad	Det	29	33	7	78	94	9	34	68	3	3	5	.375	0	15.1	5.02
Benoit, Joaquin	Pit	40	48	0	46	38	5	19	42	1	3	2	.600	0	11.3	3.90
Bergman, Christian	Sea	30	12	3	38	44	6	10	25	1	2	2	.500	0	13.0	4.74
Berrios, Jose	Min	24	32	32	181	161	20	61	177	11	11	9	.550	0	11.6	3.83
Betances, Dellin	NYY	30	66	0	62	35	4	33	99	5	5	2	.714	8	10.6	2.77
Bettis, Chad	Col	29	27	27	151	173	20	48	110	5	8	9	.471	0	13.5	4.77
Biagini, Joe	Tor	28	32	18	110	110	10	37	87	3	6	6	.500	0	12.3	4.08
Bibens-Dirkx, Austin	Tex	33	25	4	62	71	11	19	42	2	3	4	.429	0	13.4	5.09
Blach, Ty	SF	27	27	27	157	172	14	41	84	2	8	9	.471	0	12.3	4.39
Blackburn, Paul	Oak	24	10	10	59	63	5	18	36	1	3	4	.429	0	12.5	4.36
Blanton, Joe	Was	37	50	0	46	46	7	14	42	1	3	2	.600	0	11.9	4.21
Bleier, Richard	Bal	31	66	0	67	77	6	11	32	3	4	4	.500	0	12.2	4.37
Blevins, Jerry	NYM	34	73	0	49	41	4	21	63	3	3	2	.600	0	11.9	3.49
Boshers, Buddy	Min	30	42	0	30	31	3	12	28	1	2	2	.500	0	13.2	4.20
Bowman, Matt	StL	27	74	0	62	66	5	20	46	2	4	3	.571	0	12.8	4.21
Boxberger, Brad	TB	30	40	0	43	33	6	21	55	2	2	2	.500	0	11.7	3.72
Boyd, Matt	Det	27	29	29	163	168	26	56	139	4	8	10	.444	0	12.6	4.50
Boyer, Blaine	Bos	36	32	0	44	48	3	14	28	1	2	2	.500	0	12.9	4.30
Brach, Brad	Bal	32	65	0	69	56	7	26	72	0	4	3	.571	6	10.7	3.52
Bracho, Silvino	Ari	25	36	0	34	30	6	12	41	1	2	2	.500	0	11.4	3.88
Bradford, Chasen	NYM	28	40	0	51	61	4	12	40	1	2	3	.400	0	13.1	4.33
Bradley, Archie	Ari	25	65	0	74	69	6	31	76	3	5	4	.556	0	12.5	3.88
Brady, Michael	Oak	31	20	0	46	51	6	8	39	2	2	3	.400	0	11.9	4.11
Brault, Steven	Pit	26	17	17	95	93	7	41	82	4	5	5	.500	0	13.1	4.14
Brebbia, John	StL	28	64	0	65	62	10	16	64	5	4	3	.571	0	12.4	3.98
Bridwell, Parker	LAA	26	31	31	179	184	27	56	129	6	9	11	.450	0	12.4	4.53
Britton, Zach	Bal	30	59	0	58	47	3	20	55	0	4	2	.667	33	10.4	3.29
Brothers, Rex	Atl	30	36	0	32	25	2	21	43	1	2	2	.500	0	13.2	3.60
Buchholz, Clay	Phi	33	19	19	109	108	13	36	85	5	5	7	.417	0	12.3	4.26
Buchter, Ryan	KC	31	73	0	71	55	7	34	70	3	4	4	.500	0	11.7	3.83
Bumgarner, Madison	SF	28	33	33	210	189	24	44	208	7	13	10	.565	0	10.3	3.51
Bundy, Dylan	Bal	25	32	32	189	183	30	61	172	9	10	11	.476	0	12.0	4.29
Busenitz, Alan	Min	27	43	0	48	50	5	15	43	2	3	3	.500	0	12.6	4.13
Bush, Matt	Tex	32	56	0	55	51	7	17	57	3	3	3	.500	6	11.6	3.82
Butler, Eddie	ChC	27	12	12	71	75	9	28	42	1	4	4	.500	0	13.3	4.76
Cahill, Trevor	KC	30	23	9	70	77	10	36	65	3	3	5	.375	0	14.9	5.08
Carrasco, Carlos	Cle	31	32	32	215	190	24	51	231	8	15	9	.625	0	10.4	3.47
Cashner, Andrew	Tex	31	29	29	181	205	22	70	112	8	8	12	.400	0	14.1	5.12
Casilla, Santiago	Oak	37	62	0	60	59	7	21	56	5	3	4	.429	7	12.8	4.28
Castillo, Luis	Cin	25	30	30	186	162	21	56	191	7	12	9	.571	0	10.9	3.62
Castro, Miguel	Bal	23	44	0	73	76	12	30	46	2	3	5	.375	0	13.3	5.06
Castro, Simon	Oak	30	42	0	63	57	8	26	74	6	3	4	.429	0	12.7	4.07
Cecil, Brett	StL	31	67	0	72	70	7	19	74	1	5	3	.625	0	11.3	3.65
Chacin, Jhoulys	SD	30	31	31	181	168	18	72	148	10	9	12	.429	0	12.4	4.16
Chafin, Andrew	Ari	28	69	0	47	42	4	19	48	1	3	2	.600	0	11.9	3.74

569

2018 Pitcher Projections

Pitcher	Team	Age	G	GS	IP	H	HR	BB	SO	HB	W	L	Pct	Sv	BR/9	ERA
Chapman, Aroldis	NYY	30	52	0	55	38	3	23	79	2	4	2	.667	31	10.3	2.84
Chatwood, Tyler	Col	28	28	28	164	161	21	79	129	5	9	9	.500	0	13.4	4.72
Chavez, Jesse	LAA	34	41	10	104	107	17	33	89	2	5	6	.455	0	12.3	4.46
Chen, Wei-Yin	Mia	32	15	15	84	83	12	19	66	2	5	5	.500	0	11.1	4.06
Cingrani, Tony	LAD	28	54	0	50	43	7	23	52	2	3	3	.500	0	12.2	4.08
Cishek, Steve	TB	32	58	0	55	45	5	20	55	3	3	3	.500	0	11.1	3.63
Claudio, Alex	Tex	26	67	0	81	79	5	16	56	2	5	4	.556	15	10.8	3.74
Clevinger, Mike	Cle	27	30	30	173	148	18	77	181	5	11	8	.579	0	12.0	3.84
Clippard, Tyler	Hou	33	62	0	59	46	9	26	65	2	4	3	.571	0	11.3	3.82
Cobb, Alex	TB	30	31	31	181	192	23	48	130	7	8	12	.400	0	12.3	4.40
Cole, A.J.	Was	26	24	24	135	164	18	53	113	4	7	8	.467	0	14.7	5.07
Cole, Gerrit	Pit	27	31	31	205	202	21	55	193	8	12	11	.522	0	11.6	3.85
Colome, Alex	TB	29	60	0	61	55	5	21	55	3	3	3	.500	44	11.7	3.79
Colon, Bartolo	Min	45	20	20	112	144	18	23	68	2	5	7	.417	0	13.6	5.18
Conley, Adam	Mia	28	28	28	156	166	19	67	117	10	7	10	.412	0	14.0	4.82
Corbin, Patrick	Ari	28	32	32	199	220	30	68	180	5	11	11	.500	0	13.3	4.62
Cosart, Jarred	SD	28	13	13	64	65	6	35	42	2	3	5	.375	0	14.3	4.85
Cotton, Jharel	Oak	26	30	30	169	162	30	59	158	3	9	10	.474	0	11.9	4.29
Coulombe, Daniel	Oak	28	73	0	48	46	3	20	44	2	3	3	.500	0	12.8	3.97
Covey, Dylan	CWS	26	13	13	66	71	16	32	42	2	2	5	.286	0	14.3	5.80
Crick, Kyle	SF	25	39	0	41	41	3	29	40	3	2	3	.400	0	16.0	4.94
Cueto, Johnny	SF	32	30	30	182	177	18	51	159	9	11	10	.524	0	11.7	3.93
Darvish, Yu	LAD	31	31	31	192	151	23	60	225	5	14	7	.667	0	10.1	3.33
Davies, Zach	Mil	25	31	31	196	210	21	58	142	7	10	12	.455	0	12.6	4.36
Davis, Rookie	Cin	25	13	13	66	79	11	24	51	2	3	4	.429	0	14.3	5.11
Davis, Wade	ChC	32	60	0	63	40	3	26	80	3	5	2	.714	33	9.9	2.90
de la Rosa, Jorge	Ari	37	63	0	45	45	7	19	37	2	2	3	.400	0	13.2	4.70
De Leon, Jose	TB	25	16	16	82	74	14	32	95	3	4	5	.444	0	12.0	4.01
deGrom, Jacob	NYM	30	29	29	193	174	21	53	210	3	12	10	.545	0	10.7	3.51
Delgado, Randall	Ari	28	62	0	63	60	7	23	60	1	4	3	.571	0	12.0	3.96
Dermody, Matt	Tor	27	38	0	39	47	7	11	31	2	2	3	.400	0	13.8	5.08
Despaigne, Odrisamer	Mia	31	27	27	148	161	15	57	95	8	7	9	.438	0	13.7	4.77
Devenski, Chris	Hou	27	57	0	71	54	8	20	76	2	5	3	.625	0	9.6	3.30
Diaz, Edwin	Sea	24	63	0	65	53	7	25	86	4	4	3	.571	31	11.4	3.43
Dickey, R.A.	Atl	43	29	29	188	187	23	68	131	10	9	11	.450	0	12.7	4.50
Diekman, Jake	Tex	31	53	0	49	41	4	25	55	2	3	2	.600	0	12.5	3.74
Doolittle, Sean	Was	31	60	0	61	44	7	12	75	0	5	2	.714	27	8.3	2.77
Drake, Oliver	Mil	31	54	0	49	45	4	22	58	0	3	3	.500	0	12.3	3.65
Duensing, Brian	ChC	35	70	0	59	52	6	18	53	2	4	3	.571	0	11.0	3.76
Duffey, Tyler	Min	27	51	0	67	72	8	18	59	2	4	4	.500	7	12.4	4.10
Duffy, Danny	KC	29	29	29	177	170	21	51	158	7	10	10	.500	0	11.6	3.98
Duke, Zach	StL	35	47	0	35	29	3	14	33	2	2	2	.500	0	11.6	3.81
Dull, Ryan	Oak	28	64	0	56	46	7	17	57	2	3	3	.500	0	10.4	3.66
Dunn, Mike	Col	33	67	0	48	46	6	22	50	2	3	3	.500	0	13.1	4.22
Dyson, Sam	SF	30	54	0	53	52	4	22	39	3	3	3	.500	6	13.1	4.26
Edwards Jr., Carl	ChC	26	74	0	68	36	4	39	92	3	5	2	.714	0	10.3	3.02
Eflin, Zach	Phi	24	13	13	73	83	10	18	48	4	3	5	.375	0	12.9	4.68
Eickhoff, Jerad	Phi	27	30	30	171	171	24	56	152	6	8	11	.421	0	12.3	4.24
Ellington, Brian	Mia	27	59	0	66	51	7	41	76	5	4	4	.500	0	13.2	4.05
Estevez, Carlos	Col	25	41	0	39	37	4	16	39	2	2	2	.500	0	12.7	4.05
Estrada, Marco	Tor	34	31	31	190	168	32	68	168	4	10	11	.476	0	11.4	4.14
Familia, Jeurys	NYM	28	72	0	74	60	3	30	77	2	5	4	.556	33	11.2	3.39
Faria, Jake	TB	24	30	30	165	134	19	70	183	5	9	9	.500	0	11.4	3.68
Farmer, Buck	Det	27	15	15	69	83	10	25	62	3	3	5	.375	0	14.5	4.96
Farquhar, Danny	CWS	31	46	0	46	44	6	20	44	2	2	3	.400	0	13.1	4.40
Fedde, Erick	Was	25	17	17	93	107	11	31	82	3	5	5	.500	0	13.6	4.60
Feldman, Scott	Cin	35	20	20	103	107	13	31	78	5	5	6	.455	0	12.5	4.37
Fields, Josh	LAD	32	56	0	58	46	5	17	63	2	4	2	.667	0	10.1	3.22
Fiers, Mike	Hou	33	21	21	114	115	19	38	103	3	6	6	.500	0	12.6	4.54
Finnegan, Brandon	Cin	25	31	31	179	159	28	93	165	4	9	11	.450	0	12.9	4.50
Fister, Doug	Bos	34	23	23	131	141	17	43	95	6	7	8	.467	0	13.1	4.64
Flaherty, Jack	StL	22	16	16	87	81	10	25	85	1	6	4	.600	0	11.1	3.71
Foltynewicz, Mike	Atl	26	31	31	171	179	24	67	159	10	9	10	.474	0	13.5	4.55
Freeland, Kyle	Col	25	30	30	179	197	22	67	123	7	9	10	.474	0	13.6	4.81
Freeman, Sam	Atl	31	64	0	63	59	5	34	58	5	3	4	.429	0	13.7	4.29
Fried, Max	Atl	24	27	27	152	174	19	84	144	14	6	11	.353	0	16.1	5.27
Fulmer, Carson	CWS	24	27	27	169	182	25	94	138	9	6	13	.316	0	15.2	5.22
Fulmer, Michael	Det	25	30	30	163	162	16	43	125	7	9	9	.500	0	11.7	4.05
Gallardo, Yovani	Sea	32	25	19	114	117	16	49	81	2	5	7	.417	0	13.3	4.74
Gant, John	StL	25	12	12	64	71	7	23	58	2	3	4	.429	0	13.5	4.43
Garcia, Jaime	NYY	31	24	24	134	138	20	48	106	3	7	8	.467	0	12.7	4.57
Garcia, Jarlin	Mia	25	64	0	53	54	6	20	41	3	3	3	.500	0	13.1	4.42
Garcia, Luis	Phi	31	69	0	73	72	5	35	64	2	4	5	.444	0	13.4	4.20
Garrett, Amir	Cin	26	23	23	119	121	18	57	105	3	6	7	.462	0	13.7	4.73
Garza, Matt	Mil	34	17	17	86	94	12	32	59	2	4	6	.400	0	13.4	4.81
Gausman, Kevin	Bal	27	32	32	192	200	29	65	181	4	10	11	.476	0	12.6	4.38
Gaviglio, Sam	KC	28	21	21	113	127	14	32	81	5	5	7	.417	0	13.1	4.62
Gearrin, Cory	SF	32	69	0	62	52	4	27	57	5	4	3	.571	0	12.2	3.86
Gee, Dillon	Min	32	28	6	79	90	12	21	58	4	4	5	.444	0	13.1	4.79
Gibson, Kyle	Min	30	29	29	174	194	21	64	132	5	9	11	.450	0	13.6	4.73
Giles, Ken	Hou	27	63	0	68	52	4	24	91	1	5	2	.714	36	10.2	2.92

2018 Pitcher Projections

Pitcher	Team	Age	G	GS	IP	H	HR	BB	SO	HB	W	L	Pct	Sv	BR/9	ERA
Giolito, Lucas	CWS	23	30	30	180	176	25	70	170	8	8	12	.400	0	12.7	4.28
Givens, Mychal	Bal	28	66	0	78	62	7	29	90	6	5	4	.556	0	11.2	3.47
Glasnow, Tyler	Pit	24	27	27	154	130	16	83	187	3	9	8	.529	0	12.6	3.81
Glover, Koda	Was	25	47	0	43	42	4	11	41	1	3	2	.600	0	11.3	3.64
Godley, Zack	Ari	28	30	30	182	165	21	69	178	8	11	9	.550	0	12.0	3.97
Goeddel, Erik	NYM	29	43	0	39	41	6	16	38	1	2	3	.400	0	13.4	4.62
Gohara, Luiz	Atl	21	29	29	163	157	15	63	187	6	10	8	.556	0	12.5	3.78
Gonsalves, Stephen	Min	23	17	17	92	83	10	35	98	4	6	5	.545	0	11.9	3.83
Gonzales, Marco	Sea	26	19	14	75	79	11	24	61	3	4	5	.444	0	12.7	4.50
Gonzalez, Gio	Was	32	32	32	191	182	18	72	176	7	12	9	.571	0	12.3	4.03
Gonzalez, Miguel	Tex	34	28	28	165	192	24	53	108	8	7	11	.389	0	13.8	5.10
Goody, Nick	Cle	26	53	0	50	40	7	18	65	2	4	2	.667	0	10.8	3.43
Gossett, Daniel	Oak	25	29	29	166	180	21	55	141	1	8	10	.444	0	12.8	4.34
Grace, Matt	Was	29	41	0	52	59	3	19	38	2	3	3	.500	0	13.8	4.50
Graveman, Kendall	Oak	27	29	29	168	188	19	49	107	8	8	11	.421	0	13.1	4.69
Gray, Jon	Col	26	31	31	184	183	20	61	190	7	12	9	.571	0	12.3	3.95
Gray, Sonny	NYY	28	28	28	179	157	21	60	162	3	11	9	.550	0	11.1	3.81
Green, Chad	NYY	27	42	0	71	65	6	22	84	2	5	3	.625	0	11.3	3.40
Greene, Shane	Det	29	64	0	66	69	7	27	62	4	3	4	.429	26	13.6	4.50
Gregerson, Luke	Hou	34	61	0	60	51	8	17	64	1	4	2	.667	0	10.4	3.50
Greinke, Zack	Ari	34	31	31	200	184	26	46	192	1	13	9	.591	0	10.4	3.65
Griffin, A.J.	Tex	30	23	17	96	105	26	36	82	7	4	7	.364	0	13.9	5.58
Grilli, Jason	Tex	41	39	0	37	40	7	18	43	1	2	2	.500	0	14.4	4.99
Grimm, Justin	ChC	29	44	0	50	43	7	23	57	1	3	2	.600	0	12.1	3.90
Gsellman, Robert	NYM	24	23	23	125	142	12	42	90	6	6	8	.429	0	13.7	4.58
Guerra, Javy	Mia	32	30	0	42	43	5	21	34	1	2	3	.400	0	13.9	4.71
Guerra, Junior	Mil	33	23	23	126	113	18	60	110	4	6	8	.429	0	12.6	4.39
Hader, Josh	Mil	24	47	0	65	53	8	32	78	3	4	3	.571	0	12.2	3.79
Hahn, Jesse	Oak	28	12	12	63	71	5	27	46	3	3	4	.429	0	14.4	4.79
Hamels, Cole	Tex	34	28	28	181	181	21	63	148	10	9	11	.450	0	12.6	4.38
Hammel, Jason	KC	35	31	31	181	204	28	50	145	9	9	12	.429	0	13.1	4.72
Hand, Brad	SD	28	75	0	81	64	9	26	92	4	5	4	.556	35	10.4	3.38
Happ, J.A.	Tor	35	28	28	173	174	22	54	153	3	10	10	.500	0	12.0	4.12
Hardy, Blaine	Det	31	34	0	37	38	3	12	33	0	2	2	.500	0	12.2	3.94
Harris, Will	Hou	33	58	0	57	46	6	14	60	1	4	2	.667	0	9.6	3.27
Hart, Donnie	Bal	27	55	0	46	49	4	12	39	3	3	3	.500	0	12.5	4.02
Harvey, Matt	NYM	29	20	20	106	116	15	38	83	4	5	7	.417	0	13.4	4.76
Hatcher, Chris	Oak	33	57	0	64	66	9	23	64	1	3	4	.429	0	12.7	4.22
Heaney, Andrew	LAA	27	18	18	96	95	12	28	89	4	5	5	.500	0	11.9	4.02
Hellickson, Jeremy	Bal	31	28	28	159	185	30	44	101	7	7	11	.389	0	13.4	5.24
Hembree, Heath	Bos	29	59	0	59	58	7	19	62	1	4	3	.571	0	11.9	3.86
Hendricks, Kyle	ChC	28	30	30	188	163	17	48	163	6	13	8	.619	0	10.4	3.57
Hendriks, Liam	Oak	29	67	0	61	59	5	15	66	1	4	3	.571	0	11.1	3.44
Hernandez, Ariel	Cin	26	48	0	50	37	5	47	58	1	2	3	.400	0	15.3	4.59
Hernandez, David	Ari	33	68	0	65	61	8	19	64	2	4	3	.571	0	11.4	3.86
Hernandez, Felix	Sea	32	27	27	170	154	21	53	151	9	10	9	.526	0	11.4	3.98
Herrera, Kelvin	KC	28	58	0	55	49	5	17	54	2	3	3	.500	12	11.1	3.63
Hildenberger, Trevor	Min	27	54	0	58	50	4	12	62	3	4	2	.667	0	10.1	3.14
Hill, Rich	LAD	38	23	23	124	91	12	46	143	9	9	5	.643	0	10.6	3.36
Hoffman, Jeff	Col	25	18	18	97	99	13	39	85	5	5	5	.500	0	13.3	4.50
Holder, Jonathan	NYY	25	36	0	38	34	5	11	47	2	2	2	.500	0	11.1	3.52
Holland, Greg	Col	32	59	0	57	44	6	26	67	1	4	2	.667	39	11.2	3.58
Holmberg, David	CWS	26	30	4	45	52	7	18	28	2	1	4	.200	0	14.4	5.30
Honeywell, Brent	TB	23	30	30	166	176	19	48	191	4	9	10	.474	0	12.4	3.85
Hoover, J.J.	Ari	30	56	0	50	51	8	27	56	1	3	3	.500	0	14.2	4.68
Hoyt, James	Hou	31	36	0	42	36	4	14	55	2	3	2	.600	0	11.1	3.23
Hudson, Daniel	Pit	31	67	0	62	62	7	28	62	4	3	4	.429	0	13.6	4.43
Hughes, Jared	Mil	32	69	0	61	57	5	23	43	6	3	4	.429	0	12.7	4.30
Hughes, Phil	Min	32	13	13	63	77	10	11	42	1	3	4	.429	0	12.7	4.72
Hunter, Tommy	TB	31	62	0	65	56	6	15	60	2	4	3	.571	0	10.1	3.48
Iglesias, Raisel	Cin	28	59	0	76	61	8	25	85	3	5	3	.625	25	10.5	3.40
Infante, Gregory	CWS	30	61	0	66	63	5	34	62	3	3	4	.429	0	13.6	4.23
Jackson, Edwin	Was	34	15	15	79	86	12	36	63	2	4	5	.444	0	14.1	5.01
Jackson, Luke	Atl	26	42	0	50	52	5	27	45	2	2	3	.400	0	14.6	4.68
Jansen, Kenley	LAD	30	61	0	67	42	6	10	101	2	6	1	.857	43	7.3	2.20
Jeffress, Jeremy	Mil	30	61	0	60	60	5	26	49	3	3	4	.429	0	13.4	4.35
Jennings, Dan	TB	31	74	0	57	52	4	26	45	1	3	3	.500	0	12.5	4.01
Jimenez, Joe	Det	23	39	0	31	31	3	14	37	1	2	2	.500	0	13.4	3.92
Jimenez, Ubaldo	Bal	34	28	23	126	137	19	56	115	5	6	8	.429	0	14.1	4.89
Johnson, Brian	Bos	27	15	15	81	82	10	32	62	1	4	5	.444	0	12.8	4.39
Johnson, Jim	Atl	35	54	0	48	49	5	19	47	2	3	3	.500	0	13.1	4.13
Jones, Nate	CWS	32	58	0	58	43	8	17	66	3	3	3	.500	15	9.8	3.41
Junis, Jakob	KC	25	28	28	161	172	24	41	153	11	8	9	.471	0	12.5	4.31
Kahnle, Tommy	NYY	28	69	0	61	44	6	26	80	1	4	2	.667	0	10.5	3.14
Karns, Nathan	KC	30	14	14	77	78	11	31	79	3	4	5	.444	0	13.1	4.39
Kela, Keone	Tex	25	56	0	57	40	5	25	75	2	4	2	.667	0	10.6	3.11
Kelley, Shawn	Was	34	46	0	41	39	8	13	47	1	3	2	.600	0	11.6	4.06
Kelly, Joe	Bos	30	55	0	49	60	6	26	56	2	3	3	.500	0	13.0	4.21
Kennedy, Ian	KC	33	30	30	152	155	27	55	132	7	7	10	.412	0	12.8	4.71
Kershaw, Clayton	LAD	30	29	29	188	138	17	30	216	2	15	6	.714	0	8.1	2.72
Keuchel, Dallas	Hou	30	30	30	192	174	18	55	162	3	13	9	.591	0	10.9	3.76

2018 Pitcher Projections

PLAYER			HOW MUCH			WHAT HE WILL GIVE UP					THE RESULTS					
Pitcher	Team	Age	G	GS	IP	H	HR	BB	SO	HB	W	L	Pct	Sv	BR/9	ERA
Kimbrel, Craig	Bos	30	68	0	72	40	6	24	118	4	6	2	.750	37	8.5	2.30
Kintzler, Brandon	Was	33	73	0	74	78	7	17	45	3	4	4	.500	11	11.9	4.27
Kluber, Corey	Cle	32	31	31	235	184	23	50	270	8	18	8	.692	0	9.3	3.03
Knebel, Corey	Mil	26	75	0	79	51	8	37	117	2	6	3	.667	36	10.3	2.94
Koehler, Tom	Tor	32	34	7	61	65	10	26	52	3	3	4	.429	0	13.9	4.94
Kontos, George	Pit	33	59	0	60	55	7	17	52	1	3	3	.500	0	11.0	3.84
Kopech, Michael	CWS	22	25	25	136	110	9	75	168	6	7	8	.467	0	12.6	3.63
Krol, Ian	Atl	27	37	0	40	38	4	17	39	3	2	2	.500	0	13.1	4.17
Kuhl, Chad	Pit	25	29	29	161	165	18	60	135	6	8	9	.471	0	12.9	4.34
Lackey, John	ChC	39	28	28	169	163	25	49	142	8	10	9	.526	0	11.7	4.19
Lamet, Dinelson	SD	25	30	30	168	138	18	80	200	7	9	10	.474	0	12.1	3.72
Lawrence, Casey	Sea	30	36	0	63	78	7	18	45	1	3	4	.429	0	13.9	4.79
Leake, Mike	Sea	30	31	31	191	206	25	41	131	8	10	12	.455	0	12.0	4.36
LeBlanc, Wade	Pit	33	40	0	56	61	6	15	46	1	3	3	.500	0	12.4	4.18
Leclerc, Jose	Tex	24	45	0	44	32	4	32	52	2	2	2	.500	0	13.5	4.03
Leiter, Mark	Phi	27	23	23	127	131	19	39	121	8	6	8	.429	0	12.6	4.32
Leone, Dominic	Tor	26	69	0	70	62	8	26	74	1	4	4	.500	0	11.4	3.73
Lester, Jon	ChC	34	32	32	199	178	21	57	192	6	13	9	.591	0	10.9	3.66
Liriano, Francisco	Hou	34	58	0	51	49	6	25	49	2	3	3	.500	0	13.4	4.41
Lively, Ben	Phi	26	18	18	113	116	12	34	84	6	5	7	.417	0	12.4	4.30
Lopez, Reynaldo	CWS	24	30	30	172	164	28	67	163	4	8	12	.400	0	12.3	4.27
Lorenzen, Michael	Cin	26	71	0	84	79	9	33	75	5	5	5	.500	6	12.5	4.15
Loup, Aaron	Tor	30	68	0	56	57	5	23	60	6	3	3	.500	0	13.8	4.18
Lugo, Seth	NYM	28	21	21	116	131	15	31	97	4	6	7	.462	0	12.9	4.46
Lyles, Jordan	SD	27	25	9	69	76	8	26	53	4	3	5	.375	0	13.8	4.70
Lynn, Lance	StL	31	31	31	182	167	20	73	150	9	10	10	.500	0	12.3	4.20
Lyons, Tyler	StL	30	57	0	60	57	9	16	62	3	4	3	.571	4	11.4	3.93
Madson, Ryan	Was	37	57	0	59	47	4	13	59	3	5	2	.714	4	9.6	3.12
Maeda, Kenta	LAD	30	30	30	164	144	25	45	166	7	11	7	.611	0	10.8	3.79
Mahle, Tyler	Cin	23	29	29	162	160	20	47	145	9	9	9	.500	0	12.0	4.08
Manaea, Sean	Oak	26	30	30	175	176	20	56	158	8	9	10	.474	0	12.3	4.12
Marinez, Jhan	Tex	29	44	0	61	69	6	28	48	5	3	4	.429	0	15.0	5.02
Marquez, German	Col	23	31	31	178	186	26	49	168	9	11	9	.550	0	12.3	4.23
Martes, Francis	Hou	22	42	0	55	55	6	29	63	3	3	3	.500	0	14.2	4.34
Martinez, Carlos	StL	26	31	31	207	183	20	73	208	9	13	10	.565	0	11.5	3.74
Martinez, Nick	Tex	27	24	18	116	130	17	33	71	6	5	8	.385	0	13.1	4.89
Matz, Steven	NYM	27	24	24	134	134	15	36	119	4	7	8	.467	0	11.7	3.97
Maurer, Brandon	KC	27	66	0	55	60	6	17	51	1	3	3	.500	0	12.8	4.17
McAllister, Zach	Cle	30	45	0	53	51	5	18	54	1	3	2	.600	0	11.9	3.80
McCarthy, Brandon	LAD	34	13	7	55	55	6	16	46	2	3	3	.500	0	11.9	4.04
McCarthy, Kevin	KC	26	56	0	70	77	9	25	47	1	3	5	.375	0	13.2	4.70
McCullers Jr., Lance	Hou	24	25	25	134	119	10	52	151	8	9	6	.600	0	12.0	3.64
McFarland, T.J.	Ari	29	45	0	55	63	4	19	32	2	3	3	.500	0	13.7	4.59
McGee, Jake	Col	31	57	0	52	49	5	15	51	2	4	2	.667	0	11.4	3.71
McGowan, Dustin	Mia	36	62	0	75	73	11	34	61	2	4	5	.444	0	13.1	4.68
McGrath, Kyle	SD	25	54	0	60	45	7	15	58	2	4	3	.571	0	9.3	3.35
McHugh, Collin	Hou	31	29	29	168	170	19	50	151	8	10	8	.556	0	12.2	4.08
Mejia, Adalberto	Min	25	30	30	172	180	19	60	147	5	9	10	.474	0	12.8	4.27
Melancon, Mark	SF	33	68	0	66	58	4	13	59	2	4	3	.571	36	10.0	3.31
Mendez, Yohander	Tex	23	29	29	172	162	31	64	150	13	9	10	.474	0	12.5	4.53
Mengden, Daniel	Oak	25	10	10	74	72	8	27	65	3	4	4	.500	0	12.4	4.15
Merritt, Ryan	Cle	26	17	17	92	111	12	19	60	4	5	5	.500	0	13.1	4.70
Meyer, Alex	LAA	28	11	11	56	53	6	31	63	3	3	3	.500	0	14.0	4.34
Middleton, Keynan	LAA	24	71	0	68	64	10	21	69	1	4	4	.500	3	11.4	3.94
Miley, Wade	Bal	31	29	29	150	170	22	67	125	4	7	10	.412	0	14.5	5.07
Miller, Andrew	Cle	33	61	0	65	38	5	18	97	4	6	2	.750	3	8.3	2.37
Miller, Shelby	Ari	27	12	12	61	63	7	23	49	1	3	3	.500	0	12.8	4.36
Milner, Hoby	Phi	27	55	0	46	47	6	15	38	2	2	3	.400	0	12.5	4.31
Milone, Tommy	NYM	31	19	6	47	52	9	12	36	1	2	3	.400	0	12.4	4.70
Minaya, Juan	CWS	27	52	0	52	50	5	22	51	4	2	3	.400	12	13.2	4.15
Minor, Mike	KC	30	64	0	79	75	13	26	82	2	4	4	.500	20	11.7	4.05
Miranda, Ariel	Sea	29	30	30	174	163	33	67	145	5	8	11	.421	0	12.2	4.53
Mitchell, Bryan	NYY	27	19	0	33	37	2	13	27	1	2	2	.500	0	13.9	4.36
Montero, Rafael	NYM	27	19	19	100	105	12	51	95	3	4	7	.364	0	14.3	4.73
Montgomery, Jordan	NYY	25	30	30	168	160	18	57	156	0	10	9	.526	0	11.7	3.90
Montgomery, Mike	ChC	28	27	27	145	128	12	59	115	9	9	7	.563	0	12.2	4.04
Moore, Andrew	Sea	24	30	30	163	167	24	31	125	3	9	9	.500	0	11.1	4.07
Moore, Matt	SF	29	31	31	181	195	25	69	156	7	9	11	.450	0	13.5	4.65
Morgan, Adam	Phi	28	48	0	67	76	11	20	60	2	3	5	.375	0	13.2	4.70
Morrow, Brandon	LAD	33	55	0	53	56	6	15	50	1	3	3	.500	0	12.2	4.08
Morton, Charlie	Hou	34	26	26	160	143	15	56	158	14	10	7	.588	0	12.0	3.86
Motte, Jason	Atl	36	43	0	41	37	6	16	31	2	2	2	.500	0	12.1	4.40
Moylan, Peter	KC	39	40	0	30	27	2	12	22	2	2	2	.500	0	12.3	4.10
Musgrove, Joe	Hou	25	47	7	94	93	15	22	85	3	6	5	.545	0	11.3	4.04
Nelson, Jimmy	Mil	29	17	17	96	91	11	33	94	6	5	6	.455	0	12.2	4.01
Neris, Hector	Phi	29	71	0	75	69	10	29	83	5	4	5	.444	32	12.4	4.08
Neshek, Pat	Col	37	71	0	61	51	6	10	59	1	5	2	.714	0	9.1	3.16
Neverauskas, Dovydas	Pit	25	42	0	43	46	2	19	37	1	2	2	.500	0	13.8	4.19
Newcomb, Sean	Atl	25	30	30	162	153	12	100	179	7	9	9	.500	0	14.4	4.25
Nicasio, Juan	StL	31	71	0	72	69	8	25	72	3	4	4	.500	14	12.1	3.91
Nicolino, Justin	Mia	26	40	10	88	102	11	25	49	2	4	6	.400	0	13.2	4.81

2018 Pitcher Projections

Pitcher	Team	Age	G	GS	IP	H	HR	BB	SO	HB	W	L	Pct	Sv	BR/9	ERA
Nola, Aaron	Phi	25	31	31	194	184	21	52	203	5	11	11	.500	0	11.2	3.65
Nolasco, Ricky	LAA	35	33	33	183	201	31	53	139	4	9	12	.429	0	12.7	4.70
Norris, Bud	LAA	33	62	0	61	58	9	24	60	3	3	4	.429	5	12.5	4.21
Norris, Daniel	Det	25	27	27	157	187	20	74	145	3	7	11	.389	0	15.1	5.05
Nova, Ivan	Pit	31	29	29	169	193	25	36	119	9	8	11	.421	0	12.7	4.69
Oberg, Scott	Col	28	60	0	56	57	5	23	52	3	3	3	.500	0	13.3	4.18
O'Day, Darren	Bal	35	67	0	65	48	8	23	78	4	4	3	.571	0	10.4	3.39
Odorizzi, Jake	TB	28	30	30	162	144	25	57	144	3	8	10	.444	0	11.3	4.08
O'Grady, Chris	Mia	28	13	13	69	73	9	24	61	2	4	4	.500	0	12.9	4.37
Oh, Seung Hwan	StL	35	68	0	63	60	8	16	64	3	4	3	.571	22	11.3	3.79
Olson, Tyler	Cle	28	53	0	37	37	4	12	36	2	2	2	.500	0	12.4	4.03
Osich, Josh	SF	29	53	0	38	38	5	20	34	1	2	2	.500	0	14.0	4.74
Osuna, Roberto	Tor	23	68	0	71	52	7	12	86	3	5	3	.625	37	8.5	2.74
Otero, Dan	Cle	33	55	0	62	65	5	10	41	1	4	3	.571	0	11.0	3.91
Ottavino, Adam	Col	32	60	0	51	43	7	28	58	4	3	3	.500	0	13.2	4.24
Pagan, Emilio	Sea	27	51	0	64	48	7	18	71	2	4	3	.571	0	9.6	3.23
Paredes, Eduardo	LAA	23	31	0	37	33	4	14	35	3	2	2	.500	0	12.2	4.06
Parker, Blake	LAA	33	64	0	65	46	8	19	78	2	5	3	.625	21	9.3	3.11
Paulino, David	Hou	24	16	16	84	80	12	26	90	2	4	5	.556	0	11.6	3.89
Paxton, James	Sea	29	27	27	165	154	15	47	172	2	10	8	.556	0	11.1	3.54
Pazos, James	Sea	27	54	0	48	40	4	24	57	3	3	2	.600	0	12.6	3.74
Peacock, Brad	Hou	30	30	24	150	133	18	65	163	5	10	7	.588	0	12.2	3.91
Pelfrey, Mike	CWS	34	38	15	114	135	16	50	67	9	4	9	.308	0	15.3	5.57
Pena, Felix	LAA	28	33	0	44	42	6	19	48	2	2	2	.500	0	12.9	4.09
Peralta, Wandy	Cin	26	65	0	58	58	5	26	47	2	3	3	.500	0	13.3	4.35
Perdomo, Luis	SD	25	29	29	179	206	24	66	130	9	7	13	.350	0	14.1	5.01
Perez, Martin	Tex	27	32	32	201	238	22	70	122	5	9	13	.409	0	14.0	5.00
Perez, Oliver	Was	36	48	0	31	30	3	13	36	4	2	2	.500	0	13.6	4.21
Perkins, Glen	Min	35	45	0	43	47	6	15	37	3	2	3	.400	0	13.6	4.71
Peters, Dillon	Mia	25	17	17	90	81	7	36	76	5	5	5	.500	0	12.2	4.02
Petit, Yusmeiro	LAA	33	62	0	91	79	13	19	89	1	6	4	.600	0	9.8	3.55
Petricka, Jake	CWS	30	34	0	30	33	3	11	25	1	1	2	.333	0	13.5	4.50
Phelps, David	Sea	31	59	0	60	54	7	25	61	2	3	3	.500	0	12.2	4.01
Pineda, Michael	NYY	29	8	8	48	49	7	11	48	1	3	2	.600	0	11.4	3.88
Pinto, Ricardo	Phi	24	33	0	37	42	5	14	27	1	2	3	.400	0	13.9	4.86
Pivetta, Nick	Phi	25	28	28	144	143	19	55	145	6	7	9	.438	0	12.8	4.22
Pomeranz, Drew	Bos	29	31	31	175	161	21	68	173	3	11	9	.550	0	11.9	3.96
Porcello, Rick	Bos	29	31	31	196	205	27	41	166	8	12	10	.545	0	11.7	4.09
Pressly, Ryan	Min	29	62	0	72	69	8	26	70	2	4	4	.500	0	12.1	3.97
Price, David	Bos	32	28	28	184	180	21	44	181	5	12	9	.571	0	11.2	3.73
Pruitt, Austin	TB	28	30	12	111	124	13	26	97	4	5	7	.417	0	12.5	4.18
Quintana, Jose	ChC	29	31	31	192	176	17	54	190	7	13	8	.619	0	11.1	3.62
Ramirez, Carlos	Tor	27	32	0	44	22	3	12	46	2	3	1	.750	0	7.4	2.70
Ramirez, Erasmo	Sea	28	28	28	158	150	23	41	125	6	9	9	.500	0	11.2	4.09
Ramirez, JC	LAA	29	22	22	143	144	20	49	103	6	7	9	.438	0	12.5	4.50
Ramirez, Jose	Atl	28	64	0	60	53	6	31	57	5	3	4	.429	0	13.4	4.28
Ramos, AJ	NYM	31	65	0	63	49	5	35	74	3	4	3	.571	9	12.4	3.67
Ramos, Edubray	Phi	25	63	0	68	61	5	26	77	1	4	4	.500	0	11.6	3.48
Ray, Robbie	Ari	26	31	31	181	161	23	78	225	6	12	8	.600	0	12.2	3.79
Reed, Addison	Bos	29	79	0	78	76	11	17	75	1	5	4	.556	0	10.8	3.81
Reyes, Alex	StL	23	22	22	116	96	8	58	151	4	8	5	.615	0	12.3	3.47
Richard, Clayton	SD	34	29	29	194	226	21	61	137	8	8	14	.364	0	13.7	4.73
Richards, Garrett	LAA	30	25	25	149	126	11	51	136	4	9	7	.563	0	10.9	3.59
Rivero, Felipe	Pit	26	70	0	72	58	5	24	81	4	5	3	.625	27	10.8	3.28
Roark, Tanner	Was	31	31	31	187	184	22	61	155	8	11	10	.524	0	12.2	4.19
Robertson, David	NYY	33	64	0	65	46	8	23	85	2	5	3	.625	0	9.8	3.15
Robles, Hansel	NYM	27	50	0	58	54	8	27	60	3	3	4	.429	0	13.0	4.34
Rodney, Fernando	Ari	41	64	0	60	52	5	30	64	4	4	3	.571	35	12.9	3.93
Rodon, Carlos	CWS	25	23	23	133	134	16	56	136	6	6	9	.400	0	13.3	4.30
Rodriguez, Eduardo	Bos	25	27	27	161	152	19	55	160	5	10	8	.556	0	11.9	3.90
Rogers, Taylor	Min	27	65	0	50	57	4	16	42	2	3	3	.500	0	13.5	4.41
Romano, Sal	Cin	24	27	27	153	172	14	55	123	5	8	9	.471	0	13.6	4.47
Romero, Enny	Was	27	56	0	61	64	8	27	66	2	3	3	.500	0	13.7	4.43
Romo, Sergio	TB	35	57	0	58	48	9	16	61	1	3	3	.500	0	10.1	3.61
Rondon, Hector	ChC	30	54	0	52	43	6	14	58	1	4	2	.667	0	10.0	3.36
Rosenthal, Trevor	StL	28	55	0	57	47	4	28	81	3	4	3	.571	0	12.3	3.41
Rusin, Chris	Col	31	55	0	72	83	9	19	55	3	4	4	.500	0	13.1	4.63
Ryu, Hyun-Jin	LAD	31	24	24	126	135	18	40	112	4	7	7	.500	0	12.8	4.47
Rzepczynski, Marc	Sea	32	65	0	32	29	2	18	28	2	2	2	.500	0	13.8	4.23
Sabathia, CC	NYY	37	27	27	157	163	25	53	125	7	8	10	.444	0	12.8	4.64
Salas, Fernando	LAA	33	51	0	53	52	8	16	49	1	3	3	.500	0	11.7	4.09
Salazar, Danny	Cle	28	26	26	162	140	22	66	201	6	11	7	.611	0	11.7	3.72
Sale, Chris	Bos	29	31	31	206	168	22	43	259	11	15	8	.652	0	9.7	3.05
Samardzija, Jeff	SF	33	31	31	212	208	25	43	189	7	13	11	.542	0	11.0	3.81
Sanchez, Aaron	Tor	25	29	29	177	168	17	79	139	7	9	10	.474	0	12.9	4.33
Sanchez, Anibal	Det	34	28	22	121	137	22	37	111	3	5	8	.385	0	13.2	4.76
Santana, Ervin	Min	35	33	33	218	213	29	66	169	7	12	12	.500	0	11.8	4.24
Santiago, Hector	Min	30	24	24	125	126	23	58	98	6	6	8	.429	0	13.7	5.08
Santos, Luis	Tor	27	19	0	33	35	6	14	29	1	1	2	.333	0	13.6	4.91
Saupold, Warwick	Det	28	52	0	67	74	7	30	50	3	3	5	.375	0	14.4	4.84
Scherzer, Max	Was	33	33	33	216	164	25	55	267	8	16	8	.667	0	9.5	3.07

573

2018 Pitcher Projections

Pitcher	Team	Age	G	GS	IP	H	HR	BB	SO	HB	W	L	Pct	Sv	BR/9	ERA
Schugel, A.J.	Pit	29	51	0	49	55	4	18	41	2	2	3	.400	0	13.8	4.50
Scott, Robby	Bos	28	50	0	31	28	4	10	27	1	2	2	.500	0	11.3	3.98
Scribner, Troy	LAA	26	17	7	42	37	6	18	39	2	2	2	.500	0	12.2	4.20
Senzatela, Antonio	Col	23	28	28	175	174	21	58	134	6	10	9	.526	0	12.2	4.27
Severino, Luis	NYY	24	29	29	187	162	19	53	208	6	13	8	.619	0	10.6	3.41
Sewald, Paul	NYM	28	59	0	67	59	8	21	72	2	4	3	.571	0	11.0	3.59
Shackelford, Kevin	Cin	29	47	0	54	49	5	23	57	3	3	3	.500	0	12.5	3.88
Shaw, Bryan	Cle	30	80	0	78	69	7	25	73	1	5	3	.625	0	11.0	3.63
Sherfy, Jimmie	Ari	26	41	0	48	38	5	16	55	3	3	2	.600	0	10.7	3.43
Shields, James	CWS	36	24	24	149	160	28	59	125	6	5	11	.313	0	13.6	5.02
Shipley, Braden	Ari	26	11	11	56	64	7	21	38	1	3	3	.500	0	13.8	4.82
Shoemaker, Matt	LAA	31	26	26	155	151	23	41	134	7	8	9	.471	0	11.6	4.14
Shreve, Chasen	NYY	27	41	0	50	38	8	22	61	1	3	2	.600	0	11.0	3.70
Sims, Luke	Atl	24	25	25	134	129	21	65	138	9	7	8	.467	0	13.6	4.60
Skaggs, Tyler	LAA	26	23	23	126	121	14	45	117	6	7	7	.500	0	12.3	4.06
Slegers, Aaron	Min	25	22	22	119	139	13	35	90	5	6	7	.462	0	13.5	4.58
Smith, Carson	Bos	28	62	0	63	56	1	25	66	3	4	3	.571	0	12.0	3.48
Smith, Chris	Oak	37	21	11	75	82	10	27	59	1	3	5	.375	0	13.2	4.62
Smith, Joe	Cle	34	58	0	54	48	5	13	58	3	4	2	.667	0	10.7	3.46
Smoker, Josh	NYM	29	66	0	66	66	8	28	76	2	3	4	.429	0	13.7	4.22
Snell, Blake	TB	25	27	27	156	146	16	72	168	1	8	9	.471	0	12.6	3.94
Solis, Sammy	Was	29	42	0	39	38	4	18	38	1	2	2	.500	0	13.2	4.15
Soria, Joakim	KC	34	44	0	43	40	4	15	45	1	3	2	.600	0	11.7	3.72
Stammen, Craig	SD	34	63	0	77	71	10	24	67	2	4	5	.444	0	11.3	4.02
Steckenrider, Drew	Mia	27	54	0	53	37	6	22	71	1	4	2	.667	0	10.2	3.16
Stephens, Jackson	Cin	24	12	6	42	48	5	16	34	1	2	3	.400	0	13.9	4.72
Stephenson, Robert	Cin	25	29	29	157	141	25	87	152	5	8	9	.471	0	13.4	4.56
Storen, Drew	Cin	30	48	0	46	44	5	16	42	6	2	3	.400	0	12.9	4.21
Strahm, Matt	SD	26	14	14	71	64	11	29	81	5	3	4	.429	0	12.4	4.06
Straily, Dan	Mia	29	31	31	178	169	26	62	160	7	10	10	.500	0	12.0	4.20
Strasburg, Stephen	Was	29	29	29	180	156	18	47	207	3	13	7	.650	0	10.4	3.32
Stratton, Chris	SF	27	17	17	93	101	9	37	77	3	5	6	.455	0	13.6	4.45
Strickland, Hunter	SF	29	67	0	64	56	5	23	61	2	4	3	.571	0	11.4	3.63
Stripling, Ross	LAD	28	54	0	68	66	9	19	61	0	4	3	.571	0	11.3	3.89
Stroman, Marcus	Tor	27	33	33	205	210	21	59	167	6	11	11	.500	0	12.1	4.10
Strop, Pedro	ChC	33	66	0	61	41	4	25	67	4	4	2	.667	0	10.3	3.23
Stumpf, Daniel	Det	27	67	0	45	46	5	17	44	2	2	3	.400	0	13.0	4.30
Suarez, Albert	SF	28	12	12	66	68	7	21	54	2	4	4	.500	0	12.4	4.16
Suter, Brent	Mil	28	27	27	147	162	15	40	116	5	7	9	.438	0	12.7	4.29
Swarzak, Anthony	Mil	32	72	0	79	70	8	22	83	1	5	4	.556	0	10.6	3.44
Syndergaard, Noah	NYM	25	30	30	189	171	16	43	215	4	12	9	.571	0	10.4	3.22
Taillon, Jameson	Pit	26	28	28	153	154	14	41	144	4	9	8	.529	0	11.7	3.80
Tanaka, Masahiro	NYY	29	31	31	188	180	30	40	183	5	11	9	.550	0	10.8	3.84
Tazawa, Junichi	Mia	32	61	0	64	63	9	21	55	2	4	4	.500	0	12.1	4.22
Teheran, Julio	Atl	27	31	31	196	186	28	63	162	7	11	11	.500	0	11.8	4.20
Tepera, Ryan	Tor	30	72	0	75	62	8	30	74	5	4	4	.500	0	11.6	3.86
Thompson, Jake	Phi	24	20	20	101	113	13	43	75	5	4	7	.364	0	14.3	4.95
Tillman, Chris	Bal	30	30	30	173	186	29	73	127	6	8	11	.421	0	13.8	5.07
Tomlin, Josh	Cle	33	27	27	156	176	29	19	116	4	9	9	.500	0	11.5	4.44
Torres, Carlos	Mil	35	65	0	71	71	9	29	58	3	3	5	.375	0	13.1	4.50
Torres, Jose	SD	24	58	0	63	55	9	17	59	3	3	4	.429	0	10.7	3.81
Treinen, Blake	Oak	29	72	0	80	79	6	28	72	3	4	4	.500	26	12.4	3.96
Triggs, Andrew	Oak	29	24	24	138	139	12	37	116	11	7	8	.467	0	12.2	4.02
Tuivailala, Sam	StL	25	45	0	53	48	5	20	53	3	3	3	.500	0	12.1	3.88
Uehara, Koji	ChC	43	47	0	43	35	6	11	50	1	3	2	.600	0	9.8	3.30
Urena, Jose	Mia	26	30	30	176	180	22	63	121	12	9	11	.450	0	13.0	4.61
Vargas, Jason	KC	35	32	32	179	192	28	53	131	5	9	11	.450	0	12.6	4.66
Velasquez, Vince	Phi	26	25	25	138	135	23	56	143	4	6	9	.400	0	12.7	4.44
VerHagen, Drew	Det	27	43	3	62	77	7	27	43	2	2	5	.286	0	15.4	5.30
Verlander, Justin	Hou	35	33	33	224	186	29	69	234	6	15	9	.625	0	10.5	3.58
Vieira, Thyago	Sea	24	58	0	56	55	3	25	48	3	3	3	.500	0	13.3	4.12
Vincent, Nick	Sea	31	65	0	62	59	7	15	55	1	4	3	.571	0	10.9	3.79
Vizcaino, Arodys	Atl	27	60	0	58	48	5	25	65	2	4	3	.571	32	11.6	3.61
Volstad, Chris	CWS	31	11	3	38	50	4	10	21	2	1	3	.250	0	14.7	5.21
Wacha, Michael	StL	26	30	30	171	171	17	56	155	4	10	9	.526	0	12.2	4.00
Wainwright, Adam	StL	36	26	26	149	161	14	46	115	5	8	8	.500	0	12.8	4.32
Walker, Taijuan	Ari	25	29	29	171	164	24	59	157	11	10	9	.526	0	12.3	4.21
Warren, Adam	NYY	30	53	0	62	52	7	20	53	2	4	3	.571	0	10.7	3.75
Watson, Tony	LAD	33	69	0	63	54	7	17	52	4	4	3	.571	0	10.7	3.77
Weaver, Luke	StL	24	29	29	164	154	15	42	177	4	11	7	.611	0	11.0	3.46
Wheeler, Zack	NYM	28	15	15	86	89	11	38	81	4	4	6	.400	0	13.7	4.56
Whitley, Chase	TB	29	34	0	44	43	6	13	35	2	2	3	.400	0	11.9	4.21
Wilkerson, Aaron	Mil	29	27	27	151	147	17	46	146	4	8	8	.500	0	11.7	3.86
Williams, Trevor	Pit	26	29	29	165	179	16	58	126	7	8	10	.444	0	13.3	4.48
Wilson, Alex	Det	31	62	0	55	58	5	15	37	2	3	3	.500	4	12.3	4.27
Wilson, Justin	ChC	30	64	0	55	41	4	27	70	1	4	2	.667	0	11.3	3.27
Wisler, Matt	Atl	25	25	0	36	41	5	11	26	1	2	2	.500	0	13.3	4.75
Wojciechowski, Asher	Cin	29	30	9	73	80	11	26	66	5	4	5	.444	0	13.7	4.75
Wood, Alex	LAD	27	30	30	183	161	18	50	173	6	13	8	.619	0	10.7	3.59
Wood, Blake	LAA	32	76	0	76	81	8	37	79	1	4	5	.444	0	14.1	4.44
Wood, Travis	SD	31	25	25	133	144	19	59	103	3	5	10	.333	0	13.9	4.91

2018 Pitcher Projections

PLAYER			HOW MUCH			WHAT HE WILL GIVE UP					THE RESULTS					
Pitcher	Team	Age	G	GS	IP	H	HR	BB	SO	HB	W	L	Pct	Sv	BR/9	ERA
Woodruff, Brandon	Mil	25	29	29	171	174	16	57	155	10	9	10	.474	0	12.7	4.09
Workman, Brandon	Bos	29	62	0	67	61	10	27	64	1	4	4	.500	0	12.0	4.12
Worley, Vance	Mia	30	27	15	92	105	10	31	60	5	4	6	.400	0	13.8	4.79
Wright, Mike	Bal	28	16	0	33	35	4	11	26	2	2	2	.500	0	13.1	4.50
Wright, Steven	Bos	33	22	22	146	153	19	47	106	6	8	8	.500	0	12.7	4.50
Yacabonis, Jimmy	Bal	26	21	0	31	22	1	16	23	1	2	2	.500	0	11.3	3.81
Yates, Kirby	SD	31	63	0	58	47	9	23	81	4	3	3	.500	0	11.5	3.57
Ynoa, Gabriel	Bal	25	24	24	149	183	18	38	93	6	7	10	.412	0	13.7	4.89
Ziegler, Brad	Mia	38	53	0	50	50	3	17	32	3	3	3	.500	16	12.6	4.26
Zimmermann, Jordan	Det	32	27	27	151	182	22	36	100	6	6	10	.375	0	13.4	4.92
Zych, Tony	Sea	27	56	0	57	54	4	24	57	5	3	3	.500	0	13.1	4.04

The Favorite Toy

Alex Vigderman

The Favorite Toy is a method invented by Bill James to estimate a player's chance to both meet career milestones and to break records. It uses the additional number of seasons a player is likely to play, the performance he needs in each of those seasons to meet said goal, and the rate at which the player has been moving toward the goal.

Adrian Beltre provided one of the few historical milestones this season by becoming the 31st member of the 3,000-hit club. With that, a player has notched his 3,000th hit in each of the last three seasons, as Alex Rodriguez made it to 3,000 in 2015 and Ichiro Suzuki did so in 2016. We are likely to see this trend continue in 2018, as Albert Pujols is just 32 hits shy of the milestone. Even if his decline persists and his playing time is slashed, it is hard to imagine Pujols not being afforded the opportunity to reach the 3,000-hit mark next season.

Pujols' dramatic downturn has reduced his chances at 700 or more homers, but he is still in position to rack up career milestones. He already became the ninth player to hit 600 home runs this June, and his 101 RBI put him within 82 of 2,000 for his career and 379 behind Hank Aaron for the all-time RBI record. The 37 year old would need a few more productive seasons to get there, but a 20 percent chance of doing so is not as unlikely as some might think.

The big riser on the home run lists is Giancarlo Stanton, whose 59-homer season put him on the map in terms of the all-time home run records. Stanton now has a 16 percent chance of breaking the all-time record of 762, and a 12 percent chance of getting all the way to a seemingly-impossible 800 round-trippers.

Aside from Pujols' pursuits, the next player who is likely to reach a major milestone is Miguel Cabrera. His 462 home runs give him a 77 percent chance of making it to 500, and he has a 67 percent chance of notching the 364 hits required to net him 3,000 for his career. His situation mirrors Pujols in that his performance declined dramatically this year and he still has a lot of time left on a large contract. Cabrera hit under .313 for the first time since 2004 and hit fewer than 30 home runs for the third time in four seasons after hitting 30-plus for seven straight years.

It is always interesting to look at the list of most likely no-hitters, because while it can be a who's-who of name brand starters, there are some potential surprises at the top of the list. Chris Sale is no shock as the most likely to throw a no-no, while Robbie Ray's outstanding strikeout ability combined with his penchant for walking a batter makes him even more likely than Cy Young winners Max Scherzer and Corey Kluber to accomplish the feat. Even the mighty Clayton Kershaw falls behind some pitchers who are less prone to allowing contact, a key piece of the no-hitter formula.

3,000 Hits	
% chance to reach milestone	
Suzuki, Ichiro	done
Beltre, Adrian	done
Pujols, Albert	97%
Cabrera, Miguel	67%
Cano, Robinson	57%
Markakis, Nick	28%
Altuve, Jose	25%
Andrus, Elvis	23%
Cabrera, Melky	22%
Beltran, Carlos	21%
Hosmer, Eric	18%
Jones, Adam	17%
Arenado, Nolan	14%
Machado, Manny	14%
Castro, Starlin	12%
Betts, Mookie	12%
McCutchen, Andrew	12%
LeMahieu, DJ	12%
Upton, Justin	12%
Trout, Mike	12%
Bogaerts, Xander	12%
Yelich, Christian	11%
Inciarte, Ender	10%
Longoria, Evan	9%
Segura, Jean	9%
Lindor, Francisco	9%
Mauer, Joe	9%
Ramirez, Jose	8%
Rizzo, Anthony	8%
Freeman, Freddie	7%
Ozuna, Marcell	7%
Votto, Joey	7%
Blackmon, Charlie	6%
Bryant, Kris	6%
Goldschmidt, Paul	6%
Harper, Bryce	6%
Schoop, Jonathan	5%
Pedroia, Dustin	4%
Seager, Corey	4%
Escobar, Alcides	4%
Correa, Carlos	3%
Kemp, Matt	2%
Herrera, Odubel	2%
Odor, Rougned	1%
Castellanos, Nick	< 1%
Murphy, Daniel	< 1%
Phillips, Brandon	< 1%
Seager, Kyle	< 1%

Career Targets

762 Home Runs
% chance to break record

Stanton, Giancarlo	16%
Arenado, Nolan	1%

2,298 RBI
% chance to break record

Pujols, Albert	20%
Arenado, Nolan	8%

2,296 Runs Scored
% chance to break record

Trout, Mike	5%

4,257 Hits
% chance to break record

Altuve, Jose	2%

900 Home Runs
% chance to reach milestone

Stanton, Giancarlo	2%

2,000 RBI
% chance to reach milestone

Pujols, Albert	88%
Cabrera, Miguel	31%
Arenado, Nolan	16%
Stanton, Giancarlo	8%
Rizzo, Anthony	5%
Betts, Mookie	4%
Upton, Justin	3%
Machado, Manny	3%
Goldschmidt, Paul	2%
Hosmer, Eric	< 1%

6,857 Total Bases
% chance to break record

Machado, Manny	3%
Arenado, Nolan	3%

4,000 Hits
% chance to reach milestone

Altuve, Jose	7%

800 Home Runs
% chance to reach milestone

Stanton, Giancarlo	12%

600 Home Runs
% chance to reach milestone

Pujols, Albert	done
Stanton, Giancarlo	29%
Cabrera, Miguel	19%
Arenado, Nolan	15%
Trout, Mike	14%
Encarnacion, Edwin	13%
Bruce, Jay	12%
Machado, Manny	11%
Upton, Justin	11%
Judge, Aaron	10%

793 Doubles
% chance to break record

Ramirez, Jose	9%
Betts, Mookie	9%
Altuve, Jose	5%
Arenado, Nolan	3%
Machado, Manny	< 1%

Most Likely No-Hitter
% chance to reach milestone

Sale, Chris	48%
Ray, Robbie	39%
Scherzer, Max	37%
Kluber, Corey	30%
Salazar, Danny	27%
Severino, Luis	25%
Archer, Chris	24%
deGrom, Jacob	21%
Strasburg, Stephen	20%
Carrasco, Carlos	20%

700 Home Runs
% chance to reach milestone

Pujols, Albert	33%
Stanton, Giancarlo	20%
Arenado, Nolan	7%
Trout, Mike	6%
Machado, Manny	6%
Judge, Aaron	1%

500 Home Runs
% chance to reach milestone

Pujols, Albert	done
Cabrera, Miguel	77%
Beltre, Adrian	67%
Encarnacion, Edwin	54%
Stanton, Giancarlo	42%
Bruce, Jay	34%
Upton, Justin	29%
Davis, Chris	29%
Davis, Khris	23%
Arenado, Nolan	23%

1,000 Stolen Bases
% chance to reach milestone

The 300-Win Candidates

Brian Reiff

For the second year in a row, Max Scherzer is the most likely pitcher to reach 300 wins. He has a 33 percent chance of doing so, which represents quite the turnaround considering he didn't win his 10th game until his age-25 season. Of course, being as good as he is helps (he has a 2.87 ERA since 2013), but the other trait that has propelled Scherzer to the top of the list is his ability to stay on the field. He's made 30 starts each of the past nine years, one of only two pitchers to have done so (Jon Lester, who finds himself tied for fifth on this list, is the other). Heading into his age-33 season, he has made it just under halfway to the historic total, meaning he will likely have to keep this rate up into his forties if he wants to join the exclusive club.

Madison Bumgarner was second on last year's list, but he doesn't appear in this year's edition because of his missed time—to make this list, a pitcher's career wins plus innings pitched from the most recent season must add to at least 300. Still, he's five years younger than Scherzer and only 37 wins behind him, so he may be in an even better position—if the Giants can win over 70 games, that is. Taking Bumgarner's place is Justin Verlander, who won 15 games for the third time in four years and is now at 188 for his career. Despite that, his chances dropped from 17 percent last year to 15 percent this year, meaning that Scherzer is more than twice as likely to reach 300 wins as any other pitcher on this list.

Rounding out the top five are Zack Greinke, Clayton Kershaw, and CC Sabathia. Kershaw is the youngest in that group, as he will be entering his age-30 season in 2018 and already has 144 wins under his belt. While he is undoubtedly among the game's best pitchers, he's only pitched more than 27 games once in the past four seasons, which he'll need to do on a more consistent basis if he wants to improve on the 7 percent chance that he currently has. His former teammate, Greinke, appears one spot ahead of him with a 14 percent chance, despite never having won 20 games in a season. Sabathia, meanwhile, is coming off a 14-win season, which is only four fewer than he had the previous three years combined. His chances of reaching 300 wins have doubled since last year's Handbook, although entering his age-37 season with 237 wins, he's still a longshot to get there.

The only other players on this list under 30 years old are a pair of Red Sox pitchers, Chris Sale and Rick Porcello. Sale's 91 wins are the fewest of any player on this list, but he qualifies because of his MLB-leading 214 innings pitched this year and actually has a better chance than his teammate to reach the mark. There are also a couple of guys over 40 years old—Bartolo Colon and R.A. Dickey—but barring some incredible medical advancements in the near future, neither are capable of making a serious run at this point in their careers. All of the other pitchers in their thirties have between 100 and 200 wins, so picking any one of them is essentially a crapshoot. Based on the numbers, it's more likely than not that one of these pitchers will get there, but figuring out who that will be is more of a challenge.

Pitchers on Course For 300 Wins

Name	2017 Age	R/L	W	L	EWL	Momentum	Chance
Scherzer, Max	32	R	141	75	16.8	.888	33%
Verlander, Justin	34	R	188	114	14.2	.784	15%
Greinke, Zack	33	R	172	107	15.4	.787	14%
Kershaw, Clayton	29	L	144	64	15.5	.773	7%
Sabathia, CC	36	L	237	146	10.4	.632	6%
Sale, Chris	28	L	91	58	17.3	.797	6%
Lester, Jon	33	L	159	92	13.3	.766	6%
Colon, Bartolo	44	R	240	176	8.3	.657	5%
Lackey, John	38	R	188	147	11.1	.745	5%
Porcello, Rick	28	R	118	99	12.7	.757	2%
Santana, Ervin	34	R	149	124	12.5	.699	1%
Gonzalez, Gio	31	L	117	86	13.0	.690	1%
Dickey, R.A.	42	R	120	118	9.7	.699	<1%

EWL: Established Win Level

Baseball Glossary

% Inherited Scored

The percentage of inherited baserunners a relief pitcher allows to score.

% Pitches Taken

The percentage of pitches that a batter does not swing at out of the total number of pitches thrown to him.

1st Batter Average

The Batting Average that a relief pitcher allows to the first batter he faces when he enters a game.

1st Batter OBP

The On-Base Percentage that a relief pitcher allows to the first batter he faces when he enters a game.

1st to 3rd (Baserunning)

"Moved" is the number of times a runner goes from 1st base to 3rd base on a SINGLE. "Chances" are the number of times a runner is on 1st base and a batter is credited with a SINGLE.

1st to Home (Baserunning)

"Moved" is the number of times a runner goes from 1st base to home on a DOUBLE. "Chances" are the number of times a runner is on 1st base and a batter is credited with a DOUBLE.

2nd to Home (Baserunning)

"Moved" is the number of times a runner goes from 2nd base to home on a SINGLE. "Chances" are the number of times a runner is on 2nd base and a batter is credited with a SINGLE.

Active Career Batting Leaders

A list of batting leaders among active (appearing in the most recent season) players. An active player is eligible when he meets the minimum requirements for the following categories:

> 1,000 At Bats—Batting Average, On-Base Percentage, Slugging Average, At Bats Per HR, At Bats Per GDP, At Bats Per RBI, Strikeout to Walk Ratio
> 100 Stolen Base Attempts—Stolen Base Success Percentage

Active Career Pitching Leaders

A list of pitching leaders among active (appearing in the most recent season) players. An active player is eligible when he meets the minimum requirements for the following categories:

> 750 Innings Pitched—Earned Run Average, Opponent Batting Average, all "Per 9 Innings" categories, Strikeout to Walk Ratio
> 250 Games Started—Complete Game Frequency
> 100 Decisions—Win-Loss Percentage

AVG Allowed ScPos

The Batting Average allowed by a pitcher while pitching with runners in scoring position.

AVG Bases Loaded
The Batting Average of a hitter while batting with the bases loaded.

Base Taken
A player is credited with a Base Taken whenever he moves up a base on a Wild Pitch, Passed Ball, Balk, Sacrifice Fly, or Defensive Indifference.

Batters Facing Pitchers (BFP)

Batting Average
Hits divided by at bats.

Blown Save
When a relief pitcher enters a game in a Save Situation (see definition for Save Situation) and allows the other team to score the tying or go-ahead run.

Bomb (Intentional Walk)
An Intentional Walk is counted as a "Bomb" if
1. The next batter, after the IBB, does not ground into a double play, and
2. Multiple runs are scored in the inning, after the intentional walk.

BR Gain (Baserunning)
BR Gain (or Loss if a negative number) is the total of all the types of extra baserunning advances minus the (triple) penalty for all the BR Outs compared with what would be expected based on the MLB averages.

BR Outs (Baserunning)
BR Outs include the sum of Outs Advancing, Doubled Offs, and when a runner is tagged out on the bases when another runner moves up on a Wild Pitch, Passed Ball, or scores on a Sacrifice Fly.

BS Win
A Blown Save Win is a "win" credited to a reliever who has blown a save opportunity.

Career Targets
This method, also called the Favorite Toy, is a way to estimate the probability that a player will achieve a specific career goal. In this example, 3,000 hits will be used. The four components of the formula are:

1. Needed Hits. This is the number of Hits (or any statistic) that a player needs to reach a desired goal.

2. Years Remaining. This is the estimated number of years remaining in the player's career. It is determined using the player's age (on June 30th of the previous year; after a given season ends, use the season when making the calculation). The formula is (42 - age) divided by two. This means a player who is 20 years old will have 11 remaining seasons, a player who is 25 years old will have 8.5 remaining seasons and a player who is 35 years old will have 3.5 remaining seasons. If the player is a catcher, then multiply his remaining seasons by .7. The only stipulation is that years remaining must always be greater than or equal to 1.5.

3. Established Hit Level. The Established Hit Level is a weighted average of the player's hits over the past three seasons. To calculate the Established Hit Level after a given season is complete, add (Hits from two years ago), (Hits from last year multiplied by two), and (Hits from this year multiplied by three), then divide

by six. If the Established Hit Level is less than 75% of the most recent performance, then the Established Hit Level is equal to .75 times the most recent performance.

4. Projected Remaining Hits. This is calculated by multiplying Years Remaining by the Established Hit Level.

The probability of achieving the specified goal is found by dividing Projected Remaining Hits by Needed Hits, then subtracting .5. The maximum that any player has of achieving a goal is .85 raised to the power of (Need Hits / Established Hit Level). This prevents the possibility of a player reaching a goal from being higher than 100 percent, which is impossible.

Catcher's ERA

The ERA for a catcher is equal to the ERA of pitchers pitching while the catcher is playing behind the plate. It is calculated exactly like ERA for pitchers. Take the number of earned runs allowed while the catcher is playing, multiply it by 9 and then divide it by the total number of defensive innings that the catcher was behind the plate.

Cheap Win

A starting pitcher who wins the game with a game score under 50 gets credit for a cheap win.

Clean Outing

A Clean Outing is a game in which the reliever is not charged with a run (earned or otherwise) AND does not allow an inherited runner to score.

Cleanup Slugging Average

The Slugging Average of a batter when he bats in the cleanup spot, or fourth, in the batting order.

Close and Late

A situation in a game that is very similar to a Save Situation. The following requirements are necessary for a Close and Late game:

1. The game is in the seventh inning or later AND
2. The batting team is either leading by one run or tied OR
3. The tying run is on base, at bat, or on deck.

Component ERA (ERC)

A statistic that estimates what a pitcher's ERA should have been, based on his pitching performance. The ERC formula is calculated as follows:

1. Subtract the pitcher's Home Runs Allowed from his Hits Allowed.
2. Multiply Step 1 by 1.255.
3. Multiply his Home Runs Allowed by four.
4. Add Steps 2 and 3 together.
5. Multiply Step 4 by .89.
6. Add his Walks and Hit Batsmen.
7. Multiply Step 6 by .475.
8. Add Steps 5 and 7 together.

This yields the pitcher's total base estimate (PTB), which is:

$$PTB = 0.89 \times (1.255 \times (H - HR) + 4 \times HR) + 0.475 \times (BB + HB)$$

For those pitchers for whom there is intentional walk data, use this formula instead:

$$PTB = 0.89 \times (1.255 \times (H - HR) + 4 \times HR) + 0.56 \times (BB + HB - IBB)$$

9. Add Hits and Walks and Hit Batsmen.
10. Multiply Step 9 by PTB.
11. Divide Step 10 by Batters Facing Pitcher. If BFP data is unavailable, approximate it by multiplying Innings Pitched by 2.9, then adding Step 9.
12. Multiply Step 11 by 9.
13. Divide Step 12 by Innings Pitched.
14. Subtract .56 from Step 13.

This is the pitcher's ERC, which is:

$$\frac{(H + BB + HB) \times PTB}{BFP \times IP} \times 9 - 0.56$$

If the result after Step 13 is less than 2.24, adjust the formula as follows:

$$\frac{(H + BB + HB) \times PTB}{BFP \times IP} \times 9 \times 0.75$$

Consecutive Days
A count of how many times the pitcher was used after having pitched on the previous day or (in a few cases) in an earlier game on the same day.

Defensive Misplay
Any play which is not an error (or a passed ball) on which the fielder surrenders a base advance or the opportunity to make an out when a better play or a different play would have or might have gotten the out or prevented the advancement.

Defensive Runs Saved
Defensive Runs Saved (Runs Saved, for short) is the innovative metric introduced by John Dewan in *The Fielding Bible—Volume II* and modified in *The Fielding Bible—Volume III* and *The Fielding Bible—Volume IV.* The Runs Saved value indicates how many runs a player saved or cost his team in the field compared to the average player at his position. A player of zero Runs Saved is about average; a positive number of runs saved indicates above-average defense, below-average fielders post negative Runs Saved totals. There are eight components of Runs Saved:

Range and Positioning Runs Saved (all positions except Catcher)
Adjusted Earned Runs Saved (Catchers)
Strike Zone Runs Saved (Catchers)
Stolen Base Runs Saved (Catchers, Pitchers)
Bunt Runs Saved (Corner Infielders, Pitchers, Catchers)
Double Play Runs Saved (Infielders)
Outfield Arm Runs Saved (Outfielders)
Good Play/Misplay Runs Saved (All Positions)

Double Play %

Successful Double Plays divided by the number of Double Play opportunities. This statistic includes both the fielder who started the play and the pivot man.

Double Play Opportunity

A fielder is considered to have a double play opportunity when a ground ball is hit with a runner on first base and less than 2 outs and that fielder is involved in the play. This is used to calculate Double Play % and Pivot %.

Doubled Off

A runner is Doubled Off when he is out for failing to get back to his base before he, or the base, is tagged after a ball hit in the air is caught.

Early Entry

A count of the number of times the reliever entered the game in the sixth inning or earlier.

Earned Run Average

The number of earned runs that a pitcher surrenders per nine innings that he pitches. It is calculated by multiplying the total earned runs allowed by nine and dividing by the total number of innings pitched.

Easy Save

This label is used to separate Saves by difficulty level (Easy or Tough). A Save is considered Easy if the relief pitcher enters the game, pitches one inning or less, and the first batter he faces does not at least represent the tying run.

Fielding Percentage

The percentage of plays a player makes in the field without making an error out of the total number of opportunities. It is calculated by adding (Putouts plus Assists) and dividing by (Putouts plus Assists plus Errors).

Games Finished

The relief pitcher who is in the game for each team when the game ends is credited with a Game Finished.

Game Score

To determine the starting pitcher's Game Score:
Start with 50.
Add 1 point for each out recorded by the starting pitcher.
Add 2 points for each inning the pitcher completes after the fourth inning.
Add 1 point for each strikeout.
Subtract 2 points for each hit allowed.
Subtract 4 points for each earned run allowed.
Subtract 2 points for an unearned run.
Subtract 1 point for each walk.

GDP

Grounded into Double Play.

GDP Opportunity

This is a situation where the batter has a chance to ground into a double play. It occurs with at least a runner on first base and less than two outs.

Good Fielding Play

A Good Fielding Play is a play that is made when it is not clear whether or not the play can be made. It is a play that is made when, had the play not been made, no one would have faulted the fielder for not making it.

Ground / Fly Ratio (Grd/Fly, GB/FB)

Calculated for both batters and pitchers. For batters, it is the number of groundballs hit divided by the number of flyballs hit. For pitchers, it is exactly the same but uses the number of groundballs and flyballs allowed. Every fair batted ball is included except for bunts and line drives.

Hold (Hld)

A relief pitcher is given a Hold anytime he enters the game in a Save Situation (see definition for Save Situation), records one out or more, and exits the game without giving up the lead. If the pitcher finishes the game, then he will only earn credit for a Save. He cannot receive credit for both a Hold and a Save.

Holds Adjusted Save Percentage (same as Save/Hold Percentage)

Holds plus Saves divided by Holds plus Saves Opportunities.

Inherited Runner

When a relief pitcher enters the game, any runner who was on base at the time is considered an Inherited Runner.

Isolated Power

Slugging Average minus Batting Average.

K/BB Ratio

Strikeouts divided by Walks.

Leadoff On-Base Percentage

The On-Base Percentage of a batter when he bats leadoff, or first, in the batting order.

Leverage Index

Leverage is the amount of swing in the possible change in win probability, compared to the average swing in all situations. The average swing value, by definition, is indexed to 1.00.

If the score of the game is 12-0 or 14-1 the possible changes in win probability will be very close to negligible. Whether the pitcher gives up a home run or gets a double play ball doesn't really change the outcome of the game. There won't be much swing in either direction for the probability of the win. But in the late innings of a close game, the change in win probability among the various events will have rather wild swings. With a runner on first, two outs, down by one, and in the bottom of the ninth, the game can hinge on one swing of the bat. A home run and an out will both end the game, but with different outcomes for the teams involved. The Leverage Index we use (LI) was developed at the website Tangotiger.net, and compiled at the website FanGraphs.com.

Long Outing

A Long Outing is one in which the starting pitcher throws more than 110 pitches. Prior to 2002, we used 120 pitches as the cutoff in the Manager's Record section.

Long Save

A Long Save is when the pitcher credited with a save pitches more than one inning.

Manufactured Runs

1. A run that scores without a hit, or a run on which the only hit(s) is/are infield hits, is always scored as a Manufactured Run.
2. A run which is driven in by a home run is never scored a Manufactured Run, under any circumstance.
3. A run which is driven in by a double or a triple is scored as a Manufactured Run only if *two* of the four bases result from advancing on one of these four acts: a sacrifice bunt, a stolen base, a hit and run, or a bunt single.
4. Otherwise, a run is considered to be a Manufactured Run if two of the four bases do not result from the runner being forced along by a walk, a hit batsman, or a safe hit reaching the outfield.
5. A forceout or fielder's choice which does not improve the position of the base runners should not be counted as contributing toward a Manufactured Run. Advancing on a forceout or a fielder's choice DOES count toward a manufactured run, if the play is one which improves the position of the baserunners.
6. A base "gained" on a double play does not count as a contribution to a Manufactured Run. A run scored on a double play is a Manufactured Run only if two of the OTHER bases are not attributable to forced advancement.

Net Gain

Net Gain is a statistic that measures baserunning production that includes all baserunning advancements on both hits and outs (BR Gain) and stolen bases (SB Gain).

Not Good Outcome (Intentional Walk)

A Not Good Outcome (NG) for an Intentional Walk occurs when one run scored in the inning after the intentional walk (and the next batter after the intentional walk did not ground into a double play).

Offensive Winning Percentage (OWP)

A player's Offensive Winning Percentage is the winning percentage of a hypothetical team which has an offense consisting of nine of that player, and pitching and defense which is average for the player's league. It is calculated by taking the square of RC/27 (see the definition for Runs Created per 27 Outs), dividing it by the sum of the square of RC/27 and the square of the average runs scored per game in the league.

On-Base Percentage

(Hits plus Walks plus Hit by Pitcher) divided by (At Bats plus Walks plus Hit by Pitcher plus Sacrifice Flies).

$$\frac{H + BB + HBP}{AB + BB + HBP + SF}$$

On-Base Plus Slugging (OPS)
On-Base Percentage plus Slugging Average

$$\frac{H + BB + HBP}{AB + BB + HBP + SF} + \frac{TB}{AB}$$

Opponent Batting Average
Hits Allowed divided by (Batters Faced minus Walks minus Hit Batsmen minus Sacrifice Hits minus Sacrifice Flies minus Catcher's Interference).

$$\frac{H}{BFP - BB - HBP - SH - SF - CI}$$

Out Advancing
A runner is out advancing when he is tagged out attempting to score from 2nd base on a single or from 1st base on a double, attempting to go from 1st base to 3rd base on a single, attempting to advance on an out, or is the batter and is tagged out attempting to take an extra base after reaching safely.

PA*
Used in the denominator for the calculation of On-Base Percentage. It is calculated by subtracting (Sacrifice Hits plus Times Reached Base on Defensive Interference) from Plate Appearances (see definition for Plate Appearances).

Park Index
To calculate the park index for home runs in a given ballpark, we take the total home runs of both the home team and its opponents at the ballpark and compare it to the total home runs of the home team and its opponents in other games. We then divide each of those totals by the at-bats in the equivalent situations, so that if there are more at-bats in either situation the index is not skewed. The result is then multiplied by 100 to yield the familiar form.

The park indices for doubles, triples, walks, strikeouts and home runs by lefties and righties are determined like home runs above—relative to at-bats. Indices of at-bats, runs, hits, errors and infield fielding errors (E-Infield) are calculated relative to games. The three batting average indices are calculated as is, since these are already relative to at-bats.

PCS (Pitchers' Caught Stealing)
The number of runners officially scored as Caught Stealing where the pitcher initiated the play. The normal Caught Stealing is when a runner is out attempting to steal a base but the play was initiated by the catcher. PCS plays are often referred to as pickoffs, but differ when the runner breaks towards the next base as opposed to returning to the base he was currently on. Pickoffs occur when the pitcher throws to a base that a runner is leading from, and the runner is out attempting to return to that base. Pickoffs are not an official statistic.

Pitches per PA
The total number of pitches a hitter sees divided by his total Plate Appearances.

Pivot %

Successful Double Plays turned by pivot man divided by the number of Double Play opportunities with that pivot man involved.

Plate Appearances

At Bats plus Total Walks plus Hit By Pitches plus Sacrifice Hits plus Sacrifice Flies plus Times Reached on Defensive Interference.

Platoon Advantage %

Platoon Advantage % is the percentage of players in the starting lineup who have the platoon advantage (i.e. bats right against a left-handed pitcher or bats left against a right-hander) against the starting pitcher; e.g. if the opposing starting pitcher is right handed and the batting team has six left-handed batters in its lineup, the platoon advantage for that game would be 67%.

Power/Speed Number

A single number that reflects a combination of power and speed. To calculate the Power/Speed Number, multiply Home Runs by Stolen Bases by two, and divide by the sum of Home Runs and Stolen Bases.

$$\frac{2 \times HR \times SB}{HR + SB}$$

PPO (Pitcher Pickoff)

The number of baserunners thrown out when a pitcher throws to a base with a leading baserunner, and the runner is tagged out attempting to return to the base. PPO is not an official statistic and does not count toward Caught Stealing totals.

Productive Out

An out made by the batter which moves at least one baserunner up at least one base. See also Unproductive Out.

Quality Start

A game where the starting pitcher pitches for at least six innings and allows no more than three earned runs.

Quality Start Percentage

Quality Starts divided by Games Started (see the definition for Quality Start).

Quick Hooks

Used in the Manager's Record. For Quick Hooks and Slow Hooks a score is calculated for each game that is the sum of the number of Pitches plus 10 times the number of Runs Allowed. The bottom 25% of scores in the league are considered to be Quick Hooks.

Range and Positioning System

Formerly called the Plus/Minus System, the Range and Positioning System is a method for evaluating defensive plays on batted balls. It is made possible by a game scoring system in which each batted ball is rated for type (line drive, grounder, etc.), velocity within its type (based on hang time for flyballs and time to the infielder or through the infield on groundballs), and location on the field. A player gets credit (a "plus" number) if he makes a play that at least one other player at his position missed during the season and he loses credit (a "minus" number) if he misses a play that at least one player made. The size of the credits are proportional to the percentage of times all players make the play. All plays for each player at his position are summed to get his total Plays Saved for the season. A total of zero would be average and any other number would approximate how many plays more or less the player made than the average player at the position for the number of chances the player had to field batted balls.

Range Factor

The number of Successful Chances (Putouts plus Assists) times nine divided by the number of Defensive Innings Played.

RBI %

The percentage of all potential runs driven in by a certain hitter. Simply put, it's RBIs divided by RBI Opportunities. RBI Opportunities are a weighted total for baserunners available to be driven in by the batter. They are defined like so:

> 1.00 for each runner on third base with less than 2 outs, plus
>
> .70 for each runner on third base with 2 outs, plus
>
> .70 for each runner on second base, plus
>
> .40 for each runner on first base, plus
>
> .10 for each bases-empty plate appearance.

Regular Saves

Any save which does not meet the definition either of an Easy Save or a Tough Save is a "Regular" Save.

Run Support Per 9 IP

The total number of runs scored by a pitcher's team while he is in the game multiplied by nine and divided by total Innings Pitched.

Runs Created

"Runs Created" is an estimate of the number of a team's runs which are created by each individual hitter. Let's assume the Cubs scored 820 runs last year. How many of those were created by Kris Bryant? How many by Anthony Rizzo? How many by Addison Russell?

There are many different formulas for estimating runs created. . .did you want the one that involves swinging a dead cat in the cemetery under a full moon? Yeah, I don't blame you. . .worm-eaten persimmons are so hard to find in the modern world.

This is the one we use now; it is complicated enough. First, there is an "A" Factor in the formula, a "B" Factor, and a "C" factor. The "A" Factor, which represents the number of times the hitter is on base, is Hits, Plus Walks, Plus Hit Batsmen, Minus Caught Stealing, Minus Grounded Into Double Play. The "B" Factor, which represents the hitter's ability to advance other runners, is 1.125 times the player's Singles, plus 1.69 times his Doubles, plus 3.02 times his Triples, plus 3.73 times his Home Runs, plus .29 times his Walks and

Hit Batsmen, not counting intentional walks, plus .492 times Sacrifice Hits, Sacrifice Flies and Stolen Bases, minus .04 times Strikeouts. The "C" Factor, which represents opportunities, is At Bats, Plus Walks, Plus Hit By Pitch, Plus Sacrifice Hits, Plus Sacrifice Flies.

Having made these initial calculations of the A, B and C factors, we then change the "A" factor to "A plus 2.4 times C".

We change the "B" factor to "B plus 3 times C".

We change the "C" factor to "9 times C".

Multiply A times B, divide by the new C ("9 times C"), and subtract .90 times by the original C.

This is our first, temporary estimate of the player's runs created. What we have done here is to ask these questions:

1. How many runs would a team probably score that consisted of eight "ordinary" type of hitters, plus this particular hitter?
2. How many of those runs would be created by the eight ordinary type of hitters?
3. What is the difference and thus, how many runs did our player create?

To estimate this, we have placed our player in the context of eight hitters with a .300 on base percentage (2.4 divided by 8) and a .375 advancement percentage (3 divided by 8). For each trip through the batting order, the eight ordinary-type hitters would produce 9/10 of a run (2.4 times 3, divided by 8). The "9" in the denominator is eight ordinary hitters plus our man. The "-.9" being subtracted at the end is the runs created by the "ordinary" hitters. In essence, we have placed the hitter in a neutral solution, measured the neutral solution without our hitter, measured it with our hitter, and then estimated the contribution of this hitter as being the difference between the two.

We're not quite done. After that, we adjust the player's runs created estimate for his performance in two "run-sensitive" situations. Suppose that a player whose overall batting average is .250, has batted 100 times with runners in scoring position, and has gone 30-for-100. That's five hits better than expected, 30 hits where we would have expected 25. His team will score an extra five runs because he has done that, and so we increase the player's runs created estimate by five runs. If the player has hit poorly with runners in scoring position, we decrease it by the shortfall in the same way.

Suppose that a player has batted 250 times with runners on base, 250 times with the bases empty, and that he has hit 20 home runs overall. We would expect him to have hit 10 with men on base, 10 with the bases empty, right?

Suppose that he didn't. Suppose that he hit 12 with the bases empty, 8 with men on base. His team would score two runs less than expected because he did this, and we would thus penalize him two runs for the shortfall.

This is our second runs created estimate the player's runs created, adjusted for his batting performance in run sensitive situations.

Suppose, however, that we figure the runs created for all of the individuals on a team, and we add them up, and it doesn't match the runs actually scored by the team? What if the formulas say that the team should have scored 800 runs, but they actually scored 820?

Then obviously, the formulas missed. We're trying to measure the runs ACTUALLY created by each hitter as best we can, in the real world, not the theoretical impact of some combination of singles, doubles, triples and walks. If the actual number is different than the estimates, we have to adjust the estimates to fit the facts. In this case—820 runs scored with only 800 runs created— we would multiply each runs created estimate by 820/800, or 1.025. Then we round it off to an integer, and that's the player's estimated runs created.

Let go of that cat, Arthur. Heck, the moon isn't full for three weeks, anyway.

Runs Created per 27 Outs (RC/27)
This statistic estimates the number of runs per game that a team made up of nine of the same player would score. To calculate RC/27, multiply Runs Created by league outs per team game, divide the result by outs made by the player (the sum of at bats plus sacrifice hits plus sacrifice flies plus caught stealing plus grounded into double plays, minus hits). The formula written out is:

$$\frac{\frac{RC \times 3 \times LgIP}{2 \times LgG}}{AB - H + SH + SF + CS + GDP}$$

Runs Saved
See Defensive Runs Saved.

Save Opportunities (Sv-Op)
The sum of Saves and Blown Saves (see Save Situation).

Save/Hold Percentage (same as Holds Adjusted Saves Percentage)
The sum of Saves and Holds, divided by the sum of Saves, Holds, and Blown Saves.
For several years we figured "Save Percentage", which is simply Saves divided by Save Opportunities, and this stat had some currency in the game. But the Save Percentage severely discriminates against middle relievers, who have no real chance to be credited with the Save, since they will be taken out of the game and replaced by the Closer even if they throw 110 miles an hour and strike out everybody they see. Middle relievers typically have Save Percentages of zero, even if they pitch well. The Save/Hold Percentage is a much more realistic evaluation of a pitcher's success in Save situations.

Save Percentage
A pitcher's Saves divided by the total number of Save Situations he faces (see definition for Save Situation).

Save Situation
A relief pitcher is in a Save Situation when he enters the game with his team in the lead, has the opportunity to finish the game, is not the winning pitcher of record at the time, and meets any one of the three following conditions:

1. The pitcher's team is leading by no more than three runs and the pitcher has the chance to pitch for at least one inning,

OR

2. The pitcher enters the game with the potential tying run on base, at bat, or on deck,

OR

3. The pitcher pitches three or more effective innings regardless of the lead. The determination of a save in this situation is made by the official scorer.

It is not possible to have more than one save credited to a single team in a game.

SB Gain (Baserunning)

Stolen Base attempts must be successful greater than about two thirds of the time to have a positive result on the number of runs scored. SB gain is therefore the number of bases stolen minus two times the number of caught stealing (SB Gain = SB - 2CS). For example, a runner steals 30 bases and is caught stealing 7 times. His SB Gain would be 30 - 2 * 7 = +16. Another runner steals 10 bases and is caught stealing 6 times. His SB Gain (actually a loss) would be 10 - 2 * 6 = -2.

SB Success Percentage

Stolen Bases divided by the number of Stolen Base attempts (Stolen Bases plus Caught Stealing).

$$\frac{SB}{SB + CS}$$

Secondary Average

A number meant to reflect everything else except for batting average. A player will have a high Secondary Average if he hits for power, takes walks and steals bases. It is calculated with the following formula:

$$\frac{TB - H + BB + SB}{AB}$$

Similarity Score

A number which reflects the similarity between two different statistical lines, either for a player or for a team. A score of 1,000 means that the statistical lines are identical.

Slow Hooks

Used in the Manager's Record. For Quick Hooks and Slow Hooks a score is calculated for each game that is the sum of the number of Pitches plus 10 times the number of Runs Allowed. The top 25% of scores in the league are considered to be Slow Hooks.

Slugging Average

Total Bases divided by At Bats.

Speed Score

Speed score is an estimate of a player's running speed, based on six indicators of running speed found in his batting and fielding records. Those six indicators are stolen base success rate, the frequency of stolen base attempts, triples, grounding into double plays, runs scored as a percentage of times on base, and defensive position and range.

The full process of estimating Speed Scores is long and complex, and can be found on Bill James Online or by contacting Baseball Info Solutions.

Total Bases (TB)

Hits plus Doubles plus (2 times Triples) plus (3 times Home Runs).

$$H + 2B + (2 \times 3B) + (3 \times HR)$$

Total Bases on Balls (TBB)

Tough Loss

A starting pitcher who loses the game with a game score (see definition for Game Score) over 50 gets credit for a tough loss.

Tough Save

This label is used to separate Saves by difficulty level (Easy or Tough). A Save is considered Tough if the relief pitcher enters the game with the tying run on base.

Unproductive Out

An out made by the batter which is not the third out of an inning, but comes with runners on base which fails to advance any baserunner, or results in a weaker baserunner configuration than before the out. See also Productive Out.

Win Probability

The probability of a team winning the game determined at any time during the game based on the score, inning, outs and base situation.

Win Shares

Win Shares are a system devised by Bill James for valuing a player's overall contribution to his team over a season. This allows us to more effectively compare players across positions, even between pitchers and position players. The use of the word "shares" is important, because they are split up among players based on how many wins a team actually earns. For each win, a team has three Win Shares to allocate among its players. Those shares are then allocated according to how much each player contributed to the team's run scoring and prevention.

Winning Percentage

Wins divided by (Wins plus Losses).

Minor League Abbreviation Key

Abbreviation	Team	Level	League	MLB Affiliate	First Year	Last Year
Abrdn	Aberdeen IronBirds	A-	New York-Penn League	Baltimore Orioles	2013	2017
Akron	Akron Aeros	AA	Eastern League	Cleveland Indians	2013	2013
Akron	Akron RubberDucks	AA	Eastern League	Cleveland Indians	2014	2017
Albq	Albuquerque Isotopes	AAA	Pacific Coast League	Los Angeles Dodgers	2013	2014
Albq	Albuquerque Isotopes	AAA	Pacific Coast League	Colorado Rockies	2015	2017
Altna	Altoona Curve	AA	Eastern League	Pittsburgh Pirates	2013	2017
Amarill	Amarillo Sox	IND	Independent League	Independent	2013	2013
Angels	AZL Angels	R	Arizona League	Los Angeles Angels	2013	2017
Ark	Arkansas Travelers	AA	Texas League	Los Angeles Angels	2013	2016
Ark	Arkansas Travelers	AA	Texas League	Seattle Mariners	2017	2017
As	AZL Athletics	R	Arizona League	Oakland Athletics	2013	2017
Ashvll	Asheville Tourists	A	South Atlantic League	Colorado Rockies	2013	2017
Astros	GCL Astros	R	Gulf Coast League	Houston Astros	2013	2017
Auburn	Auburn Doubledays	A-	New York-Penn League	Washington Nationals	2013	2017
Augsta	Augusta GreenJackets	A	South Atlantic League	San Francisco Giants	2013	2017
B Jays	GCL Blue Jays	R	Gulf Coast League	Toronto Blue Jays	2013	2017
Batvia	Batavia Muckdogs	A-	New York-Penn League	Miami Marlins	2013	2017
Beloit	Beloit Snappers	A	Midwest League	Oakland Athletics	2013	2017
BG	Bowling Green Hot Rods	A	Midwest League	Tampa Bay Rays	2013	2017
Billings	Billings Mustangs	R+	Pioneer League	Cincinnati Reds	2013	2017
Biloxi	Biloxi Shuckers	AA	Southern League	Milwaukee Brewers	2015	2017
Bklyn	Brooklyn Cyclones	A-	New York-Penn League	New York Mets	2013	2017
Bkrsfld	Bakersfield Blaze	A+	California League	Cincinnati Reds	2013	2014
Bkrsfld	Bakersfield Blaze	A+	California League	Seattle Mariners	2015	2016
Bluefld	Bluefield Blue Jays	R+	Appalachian League	Toronto Blue Jays	2013	2017
Bnghtn	Binghamton Mets	AA	Eastern League	New York Mets	2013	2016
Bnghtn	Binghamton Rumble Ponies	AA	Eastern League	New York Mets	2017	2017
Boise	Boise Hawks	A-	Northwest League	Chicago Cubs	2013	2014
Boise	Boise Hawks	A-	Northwest League	Colorado Rockies	2015	2017
Bowie	Bowie Baysox	AA	Eastern League	Baltimore Orioles	2013	2017
Bradtn	Bradenton Marauders	A+	Florida State League	Pittsburgh Pirates	2013	2017
Braves	GCL Braves	R	Gulf Coast League	Atlanta Braves	2013	2017
Brewrs	AZL Brewers	R	Arizona League	Milwaukee Brewers	2013	2017
Brham	Birmingham Barons	AA	Southern League	Chicago White Sox	2013	2017
Brstol	Bristol White Sox	R+	Appalachian League	Chicago White Sox	2013	2013
Brstol	Bristol Pirates	R+	Appalachian League	Pittsburgh Pirates	2014	2017
BrvdCt	Brevard Co. Manatees	A+	Florida State League	Milwaukee Brewers	2013	2016
Buffalo	Buffalo Bisons	AAA	International League	Toronto Blue Jays	2013	2017
BuiesCk	Buies Creek Astros	A+	Carolina League	Houston Astros	2017	2017
Burlgtn	Burlington IA Bees	A	Midwest League	Los Angeles Angels	2013	2017
Burlgtn	Burlington NC Royals	R+	Appalachian League	Kansas City Royals	2013	2017
Cards	GCL Cardinals	R	Gulf Coast League	St Louis Cardinals	2013	2017
Carlina	Carolina Mudcats	A+	Carolina League	Cleveland Indians	2013	2014
Carlina	Carolina Mudcats	A+	Carolina League	Atlanta Braves	2015	2016
Carlina	Carolina Mudcats	A+	Carolina League	Milwaukee Brewers	2017	2017
Charllt	Charlotte NC Knights	AAA	International League	Chicago White Sox	2013	2017
Charltt	Charlotte FL Stone Crabs	A+	Florida State League	Tampa Bay Rays	2013	2017
Chatt	Chattanooga Lookouts	AA	Southern League	Los Angeles Dodgers	2013	2014
Chatt	Chattanooga Lookouts	AA	Southern League	Minnesota Twins	2015	2017
Clinton	Clinton LumberKings	A	Midwest League	Seattle Mariners	2013	2017
Clmbs	Columbus Clippers	AAA	International League	Cleveland Indians	2013	2017
Clrwtr	Clearwater Threshers	A+	Florida State League	Philadelphia Phillies	2013	2017
ColSpr	Colorado Spr. Sky Sox	AAA	Pacific Coast League	Colorado Rockies	2013	2014
ColSpr	Colorado Spr. Sky Sox	AAA	Pacific Coast League	Milwaukee Brewers	2015	2017
Conn	Connecticut Tigers	A-	New York-Penn League	Detroit Tigers	2013	2017
CpChr	Corpus Christi Hooks	AA	Texas League	Houston Astros	2013	2017
Crpds	Cedar Rapids Kernels	A	Midwest League	Minnesota Twins	2013	2017
CtnSC	Charleston RiverDogs	A	South Atlantic League	New York Yankees	2013	2017
Cubs	AZL Cubs	R	Arizona League	Chicago Cubs	2013	2017
Danvle	Danville Braves	R+	Appalachian League	Atlanta Braves	2013	2017
Dayton	Dayton Dragons	A	Midwest League	Cincinnati Reds	2013	2017
Dbcks	AZL D-backs	R	Arizona League	Arizona Diamondbacks	2013	2017

Minor League Abbreviation Key

Abbreviation	Team	Level	League	MLB Affiliate	First Year	Last Year
Ddgrs	AZL Dodgers	R	Arizona League	Los Angeles Dodgers	2013	2017
Dlmrva	Delmarva Shorebirds	A	South Atlantic League	Baltimore Orioles	2013	2017
Dnedin	Dunedin Blue Jays	A+	Florida State League	Toronto Blue Jays	2013	2017
Drham	Durham Bulls	AAA	International League	Tampa Bay Rays	2013	2017
DwnEast	Down East Wood Ducks	A+	Carolina League	Texas Rangers	2017	2017
Dytona	Daytona Cubs	A+	Florida State League	Chicago Cubs	2013	2014
Dytona	Daytona Tortugas	A+	Florida State League	Cincinnati Reds	2015	2017
Elizab	Elizabethton Twins	R+	Appalachian League	Minnesota Twins	2013	2017
ElPaso	El Paso Chihuahuas	AAA	Pacific Coast League	San Diego Padres	2014	2017
Erie	Erie SeaWolves	AA	Eastern League	Detroit Tigers	2013	2017
Eugene	Eugene Emeralds	A-	Northwest League	San Diego Padres	2013	2014
Eugene	Eugene Emeralds	A-	Northwest League	Chicago Cubs	2015	2017
Everett	Everett AquaSox	A-	Northwest League	Seattle Mariners	2013	2017
Florida	Florida Fire Frogs	A+	Florida State League	Atlanta Braves	2017	2017
Frdrck	Frederick Keys	A+	Carolina League	Baltimore Orioles	2013	2017
Fresno	Fresno Grizzlies	AAA	Pacific Coast League	San Francisco Giants	2013	2014
Fresno	Fresno Grizzlies	AAA	Pacific Coast League	Houston Astros	2015	2017
Frisco	Frisco RoughRiders	AA	Texas League	Texas Rangers	2013	2017
FtMyrs	Fort Myers Miracle	A+	Florida State League	Minnesota Twins	2013	2017
FtWyn	Fort Wayne TinCaps	A	Midwest League	San Diego Padres	2013	2017
GdJunc	Grand Junction Rockies	R+	Pioneer League	Colorado Rockies	2013	2017
Giants	AZL Giants	R	Arizona League	San Francisco Giants	2013	2017
Gr Falls	Great Falls Voyagers	R+	Pioneer League	Chicago White Sox	2013	2017
Grnsbr	Greensboro Grasshoppers	A	South Atlantic League	Miami Marlins	2013	2017
Grnvlle	Greeneville Astros	R+	Appalachian League	Houston Astros	2013	2017
Grnvlle	Greenville Drive	A	South Atlantic League	Boston Red Sox	2013	2017
Gt Lks	Great Lakes Loons	A	Midwest League	Los Angeles Dodgers	2013	2017
Gwnntt	Gwinnett Braves	AAA	International League	Atlanta Braves	2013	2017
Helena	Helena Brewers	R+	Pioneer League	Milwaukee Brewers	2013	2017
Hgrstn	Hagerstown Suns	A	South Atlantic League	Washington Nationals	2013	2017
Hi Dsrt	High Desert Mavericks	A+	California League	Seattle Mariners	2013	2014
Hi Dsrt	High Desert Mavericks	A+	California League	Texas Rangers	2015	2016
HiroCrp	Hiroshima Carp	IND	Independent League	Independent	2013	2015
Hkry	Hickory Crawdads	A	South Atlantic League	Texas Rangers	2013	2017
Hlsbro	Hillsboro Hops	A-	Northwest League	Arizona Diamondbacks	2013	2017
Hntsvl	Huntsville Stars	AA	Southern League	Milwaukee Brewers	2013	2014
Hrsbrg	Harrisburg Senators	AA	Eastern League	Washington Nationals	2013	2017
Hrtfrd	Hartford Yard Goats	AA	Eastern League	Colorado Rockies	2016	2017
HudVal	Hudson Valley Renegades	A-	New York-Penn League	Tampa Bay Rays	2013	2017
Idaho	Idaho Falls Chukars	R+	Pioneer League	Kansas City Royals	2013	2017
Indns	AZL Indians	R	Arizona League	Cleveland Indians	2013	2017
Indy	Indianapolis Indians	AAA	International League	Pittsburgh Pirates	2013	2017
InldEm	Inland Empire 66ers	A+	California League	Los Angeles Angels	2013	2017
Iowa	Iowa Cubs	AAA	Pacific Coast League	Chicago Cubs	2013	2017
Jacksn	Jackson Generals	AA	Southern League	Seattle Mariners	2013	2016
Jacksn	Jackson Generals	AA	Southern League	Arizona Diamondbacks	2017	2017
Jaxnvl	Jacksonville Suns	AA	Southern League	Miami Marlins	2013	2016
Jaxnvl	Jacksonville Jumbo Shrimp	AA	Southern League	Miami Marlins	2017	2017
Jhscty	Johnson City Cardinals	R+	Appalachian League	St Louis Cardinals	2013	2017
Jmstwn	Jamestown Jammers	A-	New York-Penn League	Pittsburgh Pirates	2013	2014
Jupiter	Jupiter Hammerheads	A+	Florida State League	Miami Marlins	2013	2017
Kane	Kane County Cougars	A	Midwest League	Chicago Cubs	2013	2014
Kane	Kane County Cougars	A	Midwest League	Arizona Diamondbacks	2015	2017
Knapol	Kannapolis Intimidators	A	South Atlantic League	Chicago White Sox	2013	2017
Kngspt	Kingsport Mets	R+	Appalachian League	New York Mets	2013	2017
Lakwd	Lakewood BlueClaws	A	South Atlantic League	Philadelphia Phillies	2013	2017
Lancst	Lancaster JetHawks	A+	California League	Houston Astros	2013	2016
Lancst	Lancaster JetHawks	A+	California League	Colorado Rockies	2017	2017
Lk Cty	Lake County Captains	A	Midwest League	Cleveland Indians	2013	2017
Lk Els	Lake Elsinore Storm	A+	California League	San Diego Padres	2013	2017
Lkland	Lakeland Flying Tigers	A+	Florida State League	Detroit Tigers	2013	2017
Lnsng	Lansing Lugnuts	A	Midwest League	Toronto Blue Jays	2013	2017
Lowell	Lowell Spinners	A-	New York-Penn League	Boston Red Sox	2013	2017
LsVgs	Las Vegas 51s	AAA	Pacific Coast League	New York Mets	2013	2017

Minor League Abbreviation Key

Abbreviation	Team	Level	League	MLB Affiliate	First Year	Last Year
Lsvlle	Louisville Bats	AAA	International League	Cincinnati Reds	2013	2017
LV	Lehigh Valley IronPigs	AAA	International League	Philadelphia Phillies	2013	2017
Lxngtn	Lexington Legends	A	South Atlantic League	Kansas City Royals	2013	2017
Lynbrg	Lynchburg Hillcats	A+	Carolina League	Atlanta Braves	2013	2014
Lynbrg	Lynchburg Hillcats	A+	Carolina League	Cleveland Indians	2015	2017
Mdest	Modesto Nuts	A+	California League	Colorado Rockies	2013	2016
Mdest	Modesto Nuts	A+	California League	Seattle Mariners	2017	2017
Mdlnd	Midland RockHounds	AA	Texas League	Oakland Athletics	2013	2017
Memp	Memphis Redbirds	AAA	Pacific Coast League	St Louis Cardinals	2013	2017
Mets	GCL Mets	R	Gulf Coast League	New York Mets	2013	2017
MhVlly	Mahoning Valley Scrappers	A-	New York-Penn League	Cleveland Indians	2013	2017
Missi	Mississippi Braves	AA	Southern League	Atlanta Braves	2013	2017
Mobile	Mobile BayBears	AA	Southern League	Arizona Diamondbacks	2013	2016
Mobile	Mobile BayBears	AA	Southern League	Los Angeles Angels	2017	2017
Mont	Montgomery Biscuits	AA	Southern League	Tampa Bay Rays	2013	2017
Mrlns	GCL Marlins	R	Gulf Coast League	Miami Marlins	2013	2017
MrtlBh	Myrtle Beach Pelicans	A+	Carolina League	Texas Rangers	2013	2014
MrtlBh	Myrtle Beach Pelicans	A+	Carolina League	Chicago Cubs	2015	2017
Ms	AZL Mariners	R	Arizona League	Seattle Mariners	2013	2017
Msoula	Missoula Osprey	R+	Pioneer League	Arizona Diamondbacks	2013	2017
Nashv	Nashville Sounds	AAA	Pacific Coast League	Milwaukee Brewers	2013	2014
Nashv	Nashville Sounds	AAA	Pacific Coast League	Oakland Athletics	2015	2017
Nats	GCL Nationals	R	Gulf Coast League	Washington Nationals	2013	2017
NewOr	New Orleans Zephyrs	AAA	Pacific Coast League	Miami Marlins	2013	2016
NewOr	New Orleans Baby Cakes	AAA	Pacific Coast League	Miami Marlins	2017	2017
Nexen	Nexen Heroes	IND	Independent League	Independent	2013	2015
Nham	New Hampshire Fisher Cats	AA	Eastern League	Toronto Blue Jays	2013	2017
Nippon	Hokkaido Nippon Ham Fighters	IND	Independent League	Independent	2013	2015
Norfolk	Norfolk Tides	AAA	International League	Baltimore Orioles	2013	2017
NWArk	NW Arkansas Naturals	AA	Texas League	Kansas City Royals	2013	2017
NwBrit	New Britain Rock Cats	AA	Eastern League	Minnesota Twins	2013	2014
NwBrit	New Britain Rock Cats	AA	Eastern League	Colorado Rockies	2015	2015
Ogden	Ogden Raptors	R+	Pioneer League	Los Angeles Dodgers	2013	2017
OkCity	Oklahoma City RedHawks	AAA	Pacific Coast League	Houston Astros	2013	2014
OkCity	Oklahoma City Dodgers	AAA	Pacific Coast League	Los Angeles Dodgers	2015	2017
Omha	Omaha Storm Chasers	AAA	Pacific Coast League	Kansas City Royals	2013	2017
Orem	Orem Owlz	R+	Pioneer League	Los Angeles Angels	2013	2017
Orioles	GCL Orioles	R	Gulf Coast League	Baltimore Orioles	2013	2017
Padres	AZL Padres	R	Arizona League	San Diego Padres	2013	2017
Peoria	Peoria Chiefs	A	Midwest League	St Louis Cardinals	2013	2017
Phillies	GCL Phillies	R	Gulf Coast League	Philadelphia Phillies	2013	2017
Pirates	GCL Pirates	R	Gulf Coast League	Pittsburgh Pirates	2013	2017
PlmBh	Palm Beach Cardinals	A+	Florida State League	St Louis Cardinals	2013	2017
Pnscla	Pensacola Blue Wahoos	AA	Southern League	Cincinnati Reds	2013	2017
Portlnd	Portland ME Sea Dogs	AA	Eastern League	Boston Red Sox	2013	2017
Prnctn	Princeton Rays	R+	Appalachian League	Tampa Bay Rays	2013	2017
Ptomc	Potomac Nationals	A+	Carolina League	Washington Nationals	2013	2017
Pulski	Pulaski Mariners	R+	Appalachian League	Seattle Mariners	2013	2014
Pulski	Pulaski Yankees	R+	Appalachian League	New York Yankees	2015	2017
Pwtckt	Pawtucket Red Sox	AAA	International League	Boston Red Sox	2013	2017
QuadC	Quad Cities River Bandits	A	Midwest League	Houston Astros	2013	2017
Rays	GCL Rays	R	Gulf Coast League	Tampa Bay Rays	2013	2017
Rchmd	Richmond Flying Squirrels	AA	Eastern League	San Francisco Giants	2013	2017
Rcuca	Rancho Cucamonga Quakes	A+	California League	Los Angeles Dodgers	2013	2017
Rdng	Reading Fightin Phils	AA	Eastern League	Philadelphia Phillies	2013	2017
RdRck	Round Rock Express	AAA	Pacific Coast League	Texas Rangers	2013	2017
Reds	AZL Reds	R	Arizona League	Cincinnati Reds	2013	2017
RedSx	GCL Red Sox	R	Gulf Coast League	Boston Red Sox	2013	2017
Reno	Reno Aces	AAA	Pacific Coast League	Arizona Diamondbacks	2013	2017
Rngrs	AZL Rangers	R	Arizona League	Texas Rangers	2013	2017
Roch	Rochester Red Wings	AAA	International League	Minnesota Twins	2013	2017
Rome	Rome Braves	A	South Atlantic League	Atlanta Braves	2013	2017
Royals	AZL Royals	R	Arizona League	Kansas City Royals	2013	2017
Salem	Salem Red Sox	A+	Carolina League	Boston Red Sox	2013	2017

Minor League Abbreviation Key

Abbreviation	Team	Level	League	MLB Affiliate	First Year	Last Year
Salt Lk	Salt Lake City Bees	AAA	Pacific Coast League	Los Angeles Angels	2013	2017
Savann	Savannah Sand Gnats	A	South Atlantic League	New York Mets	2013	2015
Sbend	South Bend Silver Hawks	A	Midwest League	Arizona Diamondbacks	2013	2014
Sbend	South Bend Cubs	A	Midwest League	Chicago Cubs	2015	2017
Scrmto	Sacramento River Cats	AAA	Pacific Coast League	Oakland Athletics	2013	2014
Scrmto	Sacramento River Cats	AAA	Pacific Coast League	San Francisco Giants	2015	2017
SlKzr	Salem-Keizer Volcanoes	A-	Northwest League	San Francisco Giants	2013	2017
SnAnt	San Antonio Missions	AA	Texas League	San Diego Padres	2013	2017
SnJos	San Jose Giants	A+	California League	San Francisco Giants	2013	2017
Spkane	Spokane Indians	A-	Northwest League	Texas Rangers	2013	2017
Sprgfld	Springfield Cardinals	AA	Texas League	St Louis Cardinals	2013	2017
Stcktn	Stockton Ports	A+	California League	Oakland Athletics	2013	2017
StCol	State College Spikes	A-	New York-Penn League	St Louis Cardinals	2013	2017
Stluci	St. Lucie Mets	A+	Florida State League	New York Mets	2013	2017
Stnlld	Staten Island Yankees	A-	New York-Penn League	New York Yankees	2013	2017
S-WB	Scranton WB RailRiders	AAA	International League	New York Yankees	2013	2017
Syrcse	Syracuse Chiefs	AAA	International League	Washington Nationals	2013	2017
Tacom	Tacoma Rainiers	AAA	Pacific Coast League	Seattle Mariners	2013	2017
Tampa	Tampa Yankees	A+	Florida State League	New York Yankees	2013	2017
Tenn	Tennessee Smokies	AA	Southern League	Chicago Cubs	2013	2017
Tigers	GCL Tigers	R	Gulf Coast League	Detroit Tigers	2013	2015
Toledo	Toledo Mud Hens	AAA	International League	Detroit Tigers	2013	2017
TriCity	Tri-City WA Dust Devils	A-	Northwest League	Colorado Rockies	2013	2014
TriCity	Tri-City WA Dust Devils	A-	Northwest League	San Diego Padres	2015	2017
TriCity	Tri-City NY ValleyCats	A-	New York-Penn League	Houston Astros	2013	2017
Trntn	Trenton Thunder	AA	Eastern League	New York Yankees	2013	2017
Tucsn	Tucson Padres	AAA	Pacific Coast League	San Diego Padres	2013	2013
Tulsa	Tulsa Drillers	AA	Texas League	Colorado Rockies	2013	2014
Tulsa	Tulsa Drillers	AA	Texas League	Los Angeles Dodgers	2015	2017
Twins	GCL Twins	R	Gulf Coast League	Minnesota Twins	2013	2017
Vancvr	Vancouver Canadians	A-	Northwest League	Toronto Blue Jays	2013	2017
Visalia	Visalia Rawhide	A+	California League	Arizona Diamondbacks	2013	2017
Vrmnt	Vermont Lake Monsters	A-	New York-Penn League	Oakland Athletics	2013	2017
Wilmg	Wilmington Blue Rocks	A+	Carolina League	Kansas City Royals	2013	2017
WinSa	Winston-Salem Dash	A+	Carolina League	Chicago White Sox	2013	2017
Wisc	Wisconsin Timber Rattlers	A	Midwest League	Milwaukee Brewers	2013	2017
Wmich	West Michigan Whitecaps	A	Midwest League	Detroit Tigers	2013	2017
Wmspt	Williamsport Crosscutters	A-	New York-Penn League	Philadelphia Phillies	2013	2017
Wsox	AZL White Sox	R	Arizona League	Chicago White Sox	2013	2017
WV	West Virginia Black Bears	A-	New York-Penn League	Pittsburgh Pirates	2015	2017
WV	West Virginia Power	A	South Atlantic League	Pittsburgh Pirates	2013	2017
Yanks1	GCL Yankees	R	Gulf Coast League	New York Yankees	2013	2015
Yanks2	GCL Yankees2	R	Gulf Coast League	New York Yankees	2013	2015

Baseball Info Solutions

It's hard to believe, but Baseball Info Solutions has been around long enough now to be a teenager. Since the beginning, analytics' place in the sport has changed a lot, but BIS has remained true to its objective. The company's mission is to provide the most accurate, in-depth, and timely professional baseball data, including cutting-edge research and analysis, striving to educate major league teams and the public about baseball analytics. BIS is thrilled to work with 25 of the 30 teams in Major League Baseball as a part of that goal.

It all begins with the data collection operation. BIS's staff of operations analysts does excellent work in organizing the ever-expanding crew of highly trained video scouts, and together they record data from every Major League Baseball game and many minor league ones. That data covers everything from basic box score data to pitch locations, types, and velocities to batted ball hang times, defensive shifts, and much more. BIS collects a lot of data that cannot be found any place else, and each game is reviewed multiple times to ensure the utmost accuracy.

The data itself is valuable to many clients, but BIS's research and development department creates analytics and undertakes research projects with the data to help it reach its full potential utility. Their most well-known endeavor is the Defensive Runs Saved statistic, which estimates how many runs fielders save their teams because of a variety of skills such as range, throwing, prevention of stolen bases, pitch framing, and many other factors. Most recently, they worked to synthesize new data available from MLB's StatCast with BIS's own data and research projects.

John Dewan founded Baseball Info Solutions in 2002, having already spent a couple of decades in the industry at the forefront of the sabermetric movement. He got his start in the field as the Executive Director of Project Scoresheet, which was a Bill James-led effort to comprehensively collect baseball data. This led to the incorporation and development of STATS Inc. from a bedroom office to its sale to News Corp in 2000. Without those efforts, many of the statistics and analytics that we all take for granted may not even be available at all.

If you would like to contact Baseball Info Solutions for data inquiries, potential job openings, or additional information, you can reach us at:

Baseball Info Solutions
41 S. 2nd Street
Coplay, PA 18037
610-261-2370
www.baseballinfosolutions.com

Acknowledgments

The Bill James Handbook has successfully been published for another year running thanks to the tremendous efforts put in by everyone involved at every step along the way. As soon as MLB's regular season ended on October 1, we set to work crafting every data table, stat-checking every number, writing every section introduction, and proofreading every word so that this wonderful creation could be in your hands and on your bookshelf by November 1. Many special people dedicated long hours, nights, and weekends to ensure that this was accomplished according to the high standards that we set for ourselves, so we want to be sure to take the time to thank all those involved.

This book would not even be a glint in our eye if not for Bill James. The groundbreaking Baseball Abstracts that he began publishing in 1977 serve as the foundation for the *Handbook*, and Bill's continued dedication to providing people with the best and most interesting baseball data and analysis has provided the inspiration that makes the *Handbook* the indispensable publication that it is. As his article at the outset of this book attests, Bill devoted considerable attention to reconfiguring the Hall of Fame Monitor this year. He was also integral in developing the new Hard Hit Balls section and contributed several other section introductions and guidance on the book overall.

John Dewan and his wife, Sue Dewan, are the primary owners of Baseball Info Solutions. John brings his expertise and editorial wisdom developed over a long and storied history in the sports data industry to the process, providing the final approval on every word that goes into the *Handbook*. Sue serves as the company's Director of Human Resources and provides invaluable guidance to ensure that Baseball Info Solutions is a healthy and successful company.

Ben Jedlovec is the President of Baseball Info Solutions. He facilitates the company's production of the *Handbook*, relying on a few key individuals who play integral roles at great personal inconvenience. Will Creager took on the daunting production responsibilities for the first time and has not missed a beat. Jon Vrecsics has served as Lead Statchecker for several years and is particularly instrumental in assuring the book's accuracy. Brian Reiff, young whippersnapper, was tasked with making countless edits and exhausting formatting changes to the book's many articles.

No *Handbook* would be possible without the technological tools and organization that provide the platform for the production of the book. Director of IT Rob Dougherty does a tremendous job ensuring that the book has a foundation to stand on, all while overseeing a department that needs to keep pace with the myriad needs of our clients during the company's busiest time of year when the *Handbook* overlaps with postseason baseball and the second month of the football season. The rest of the IT Department features Ben Stanczak, Craig Saboe, Will Creager, Brandyn Bechtel, Joe Gownley, and Tricia Wilson. They have all done a fantastic job in keeping the *Handbook* on track while maintaining their other IT responsibilities.

The Operations Department makes up the largest contingent of the company. Promoted to Director of Baseball Operations shortly after the production of last year's *Handbook*, Tim Kwilos has more than impressed in his leadership of the group that deserves the most credit for the breadth and accuracy of the data in this book. The Operations Department is responsible for all of the data collection that we do at Baseball Info Solutions, and for all of the double and triple checking of that data to ensure its accuracy. Thanks to the tireless efforts of the rest of the Operations Department—Jim Swavely, Dan Casey, Todd Radcliffe, Kevin Morrissey, Dan Foehrenbach, James Mehall, Nathan Phares, Jason Paff, Michael Churchward, and Josh Hofer—we can be confident that if any discrepancies exist between our numbers and those found in other sources, then ours are correct.

But this book doesn't just contain raw data—it features advanced metrics and analytics as well, which is where the Research and Development Department struts their stuff. Director of Business Operations, Joe Rosales, is involved in many different facets of the company's work, but the bulk of his efforts are focused in R&D. Along with Lindsay Zeck, Alex Vigderman, Brian Reiff, and interns Matt Petitt and Brittany Haby, the R&D Department is responsible for doing much of the analytical work that goes into efforts like the re-tooling of the hitter and pitcher projection systems, as well as the development and enhancement of other metrics that help add value to the data.

In addition to baseball, we now also have a fully established football operation led by our Director of Football Development, Matt Manocherian. Matt is leading the effort to raise our presence in football similar to what we have done in baseball, and he, along with Dan Foehrenbach, does a great job of keeping the Football

Operations Department running smoothly while so much of the rest of the company is focused on the production of the *Handbook*.

Corey March, our Business Development Associate, is responsible for coordinating the effort of communicating our data, research, and analysis to the public and fostering our relationships with clients.

Office Manager, Carol Olsen, handles a plethora of Human Resources and Administrative duties for the company. She and Jason Trifilo, our Accounting Bookkeeper, play integral roles in keeping the business running, particularly during the intensity of this time of year. It's not just their hard work, but also their warmth and enthusiasm, that help ease the stress of the *Handbook* process for everyone.

We couldn't be more grateful to have such a great team of video scouts. Their dedication and attention to detail provide the foundation of our business. In addition to the growth in the number of video scouts that we employ every year, several of our scouts have grown to become more established members of our staff. Senior Video Scouts include Ted Baarda, Kit Banko, Mark Carlozzi, Jack Cecil, Nathan Cooper, Matt Ducondi, Noah Gatsik, Chris Goudoras, Kyle Hutson, Stefan Lechmanik, Jimmy McDonough, Nick Rabasco, Cole Ratliff, Marc Roche, Justin Stine, John Verros, Dan Wallie, and David Williams. The rest of our video scout team includes Dominic Asta, Mason Bilger, Danny Boessenecker, Jonathan Brens, Jimmy Burns, Evan Butler, Travis Cain, Dillon Cloud, Alexander Cole, Jonathan Corbi, Daniel Crago, Patrick Farrell, Joshua Fellerman, Dakota Fisher, Barnabas Furth, Chris Gabriel, Ken Gaffney, Steve Goldberg, Peter Grupp-Williams, Sean Hamel, John Paul Harris, Samuel Hartley, Kevin Hendricks, Kyle Hermann, Cole Houser, Quinn Ireland, Alec Jacob, Wyatt Jones, Kenny Kirkpatrick, Tyler Klostermann, Eric Lawhorn, Benjamin Lippincott, Brian Nasca, Matthew Noskow, Daniel Palmeri, Peter Panassow, Tim Paul, Kyle Price, David Salway, Hunter Schneider, Miles Semetis, Lance Shelton, Jonathan Simmons, William Sutton, Derek Tarconish, Dominic Theofan, Jesse Tull, Jack Webb, and Harris Yudin.

Our partners at ACTA Publications include President Greg Pierce, Tom Wright, Mary Eggert, Mary Rickey, Abby Pierce, Brian Tobin, Patricia Lynch, Mary Doyle, Hugh Spector, and Isz.

Thank you to our friends in the baseball industry who have helped us over the years. They include Andy Andres, David Appelman, Jim Callis, Dave Cameron, Sean Forman, Peter Gammons, Vince Genarro, Marshall Greenhut, Jason Grey, Eric Karabell, Brian Kenny, Peter Kreutzer, Michael Lehrer, Ben Lindbergh, Gene McCaffrey, Bob Meyerhoff, Mike Murphy, Noel Nash, Rob Neyer, Tomiyasu Onodera, Alex Patton, Mike Phillips, David Pinto, Joe Posnanski, Adam Richman, Hal Richman, Travis Sawchik, Peter Schoenke, Ron Shandler, Joe Sheehan, John Sickels, Mark Simon, Dave Studenmund, Tom Tango, Tom Tippett, Hans Van Slooten, Mark Watson, Rick Wilton, and Don Zminda. We would also like to thank Steve Ruskowski for his assistance in stat-checking, and Ralph Caola for his help clarifying a definition in the glossary.

There are so many other people that we could thank for making this book possible that we don't have the space for in these pages. To all of them, please know that we are eternally grateful for your help in making this book happen.

And finally, thank you to all of our readers. You so wonderfully share our passion for baseball and the statistics that make it such an amazing pastime to follow. That is what inspires us to take on the monumental effort of putting this book together in such a short window of time while still adhering to the high standards of quality that our readers expect every year. We hope that you have enjoyed the product of all that hard work.

NOTES

NOTES

NOTES

NOTES

NOTES

NOTES

NOTES

NOTES